Mergent's
HANDBOOK OF
COMMON STOCKS

Spring 2005

WILEY
Publishers Since 1807

MERGENT

INTRODUCTION

Mergent's Handbook of Common Stocks provides quick and easy access to basic financial and business information on more than 900 stocks that are included in the Russell 1000, S&P 500, S&P 400 and Mergent's Dividend Achievers. The Tab Section provides one-line information on New York Stock Exchange companies.

The price charts, statistics, and analyses are presented in a format that provides the investor with the necessary perspective for acting on investment advice or suggestions. It also affords investors the opportunity to make investment decisions on their own.

Statistics and analyses are revised quarterly. Every effort is made to secure the most current operating results and dividend information available. In the case of year-end results, preliminary results are shown and analyzed as they are received. Full statistical presentations of annual report information are shown in the following edition. The schedule below describes the publication dates and company reporting periods usually covered in each edition.

The Winter Edition (published in January) covers quarterly reports and preliminary annual reports through September 30.

The Spring Edition (published in April) covers quarterly reports and preliminary annual reports through December 31.

The Summer Edition (published in July) covers quarterly reports and preliminary annual reports through March 31.

The Fall Edition (published in October) covers quarterly reports and preliminary annual reports through June 30.

Note: For various reasons, some companies may not report in time to meet our publication deadlines. Company reports received close to press time are shown in the Addenda. The remainder of late reports are published and analyzed in the next edition of the Handbook.

The special section on these opening pages contains a number of features, including a guide on how to use this book, a classification of companies by their major line of business based on their NAIC code, outstanding stock price movements by company, plus long-term charts on popular stock market averages. The Addenda provide the latest developments available just prior to publication but after the company reports have been completed.

TABLE OF CONTENTS

HOW TO USE THIS BOOK

The presentation of historical data and analytical comments provides the answers to four basic questions for each company:

1. What does the company do?
(See G.)
2. How has it done in the past?
(See B, J.)
3. How is it doing now?
(See C, D, H.)
4. How will it fare in the future?
(See I.)

A. CAPSULE STOCK INFORMATION shows where the stock is traded and its symbol, a recent price and price/earnings ratio, plus the yield afforded by the indicated dividend based on a recent price. The indicated dividend is the current annualized dividend based on the most recent price. Some companies are designated as Dividend Achievers. Dividend Achievers have, by *Mergent's* criteria, increased their cash dividend payments for at least ten consecutive years, adjusting for splits. The number of years of consecutive increases is given for each Dividend Achiever.

B. LONG-TERM PRICE CHART illustrates the pattern of monthly stock price movements, fully adjusted for stock dividends and splits. The chart points out the degree of volatility in the price movement of the company's stock and what its long-term trend has been. It also shows how it has performed long-term relative to an initial investment in the S&P 500 Index equal to the price of the company's stock at the beginning of the period shown in the price chart. It indicates areas of price support and resistance, plus other technical points to be considered by the investor. The bars at the base of the long-term price chart indicate the monthly trading volume. Monthly trading volume offers the individual an opportunity to recognize at what periods stock accumulation occurs and what percent of a company's outstanding shares are traded.

PRICE SCORES – Above each company's price/volume chart are its *Mergent's Price Scores*. These are basic measures of the stock's performance. Each stock is measured against the New York Stock Exchange Composite Index.

A score of 100 indicates that the stock did as well as the New York Stock Exchange Composite Index during the time period. A score of less than 100 means that the stock did not do as well; a score of more than 100 means that the stock outperformed the NYSE Composite Index. All stock prices are adjusted for splits and stock dividends. The time periods measured for each company conclude with the date of the recent price shown in the top line of each company's profile.

The *7 YEAR PRICE SCORE* mirrors the common stock's price growth over the previous seven years. The higher the price score, the better the relative performance. It is based on the ratio of the latest 12-month average price to the current seven-year average. This ratio is then indexed against the same ratio for the market as a whole (the New York Stock Exchange Composite Index), which is taken as 100.

The *12 MONTH PRICE SCORE* is a similar measurement but for a shorter period of time. It is based on the ratio of the latest two-month average price to the current 12-month average. As was done for the Long-Term Price Score, this ratio is also indexed to the same ratio for the market as a whole.

C. INTERIM EARNINGS (Per Share) – Figures are reported before effect of extraordinary items, discontinued operations and cumulative effects of accounting changes. Each figure is for the quarterly period indicated. These figures are essentially as reported by the company, although all figures are adjusted for all stock dividends and splits.

A

ILLUSTRATIVE INC.

Exchange	Symbol	Price	52Wk Range	Yield	P/E	Div Acheiver
NYS	ILL	$32.76 (3/31/2005)	38.00-28.87	0.55	18.61	10 Years

*7 Year Price Score 137.72 *NYSE Composite Index=100 *12 Month Price Score 95.27

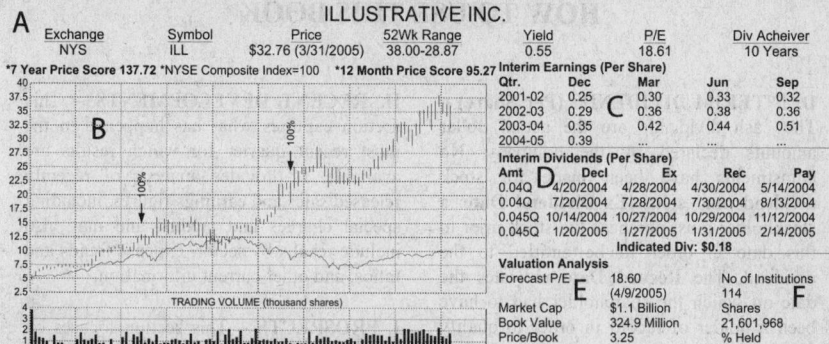

B

Interim Earnings (Per Share)

Qtr.	Dec	Mar	Jun	Sep
2001-02	0.25	0.30	0.33	0.32
2002-03	0.29	0.36	0.38	0.36
2003-04	0.35	0.42	0.44	0.51
2004-05	0.39	...	...	...

C

Interim Dividends (Per Share)

Amt	Decl	Ex	Rec	Pay
0.04Q	4/20/2004	4/28/2004	4/30/2004	5/14/2004
0.04Q	7/20/2004	7/28/2004	7/30/2004	8/13/2004
0.045Q	10/14/2004	10/27/2004	10/29/2004	11/12/2004
0.045Q	1/20/2005	1/27/2005	1/31/2005	2/14/2005

Indicated Div: $0.18

D

Valuation Analysis

Forecast P/E	18.60	No of Institutions
	(4/9/2005)	114
Market Cap	$1.1 Billion	Shares
Book Value	324.9 Million	21,601,968
Price/Book	3.25	% Held
Price/Sales	1.96	67.06

E   F

TRADING VOLUME (thousand shares)

Business Summary: Consumer Accessories (MIC: 4.6 SIC: 995 NAIC: 39995) G

Illustrative is a designer, manufacturer and marketer principally of memorialization products and brand products and services. Memorialization products consist primarily of bronze memorials and memorialization products, caskets and cremation equipment for the cemetery and funeral home industries. Brand products and services include graphics imaging products and services, merchandising solutions and marking products. Co.'s products and operations are comprised of six business segments: Florida Casket, Cremation, Graphics Imaging, Marking Products and Merchandising.

Recent Developments: For the quarter ended Dec 31 2004, net income increased 11.8% to $12,725,000 from net income of $11,383,000 in the year-earlier quarter. Revenues were $148,706,000, up 27.2% from $116,902,000 the year before. Operating income was $20,119,000 versus an income of $19,853,000 in the prior-year quarter, an increase of 1.3%. Total direct expense was $100,287,000 versus $74,279,000 in the prior-year quarter, an increase of 35.0%. Total indirect expense was $28,300,000 versus $22,770,000 in the prior-year quarter, an increase of 24.3%. H

Prospects: Co. is performing well, supported by contributions from recent acquisitions and the favorable impact of foreign currency exchange rates. However, Co. remains concerned with the continued high cost of bronze and steel. While recent cost initiatives and productivity improvements have mitigated some of this impact, the higher costs will be a challenge for the remainder of the fiscal year. Meanwhile, Co. has initiated a restructuring and facility consolidation program within the Merchandising segment and is expected to result in long-term manufacturing and distribution cost savings. For fiscal 2005, Co. expects to achieve diluted earnings per share in the range of $1.80 to $1.85. I

Financial Data J
(US$ in Thousands)

	3 Mos	09/30/2004	09/30/2003	09/30/2002	09/30/2001	09/30/2000	09/30/1999	09/30/1998
Earnings Per Share	1.76	1.72	1.39	1.10	1.01	0.88	0.77	0.67
Cash Flow Per Share	2.63	2.58	1.85	1.80	1.26	1.22	0.83	1.06
Tang Book Value Per Share	2.90	2.81	2.75	0.74	1.29	2.52	1.96	2.41
Dividends Per Share	0.165	0.160	0.110	0.105	0.100	0.095	0.090	0.085
Dividend Payout %	9.40	9.30	7.91	9.55	9.90	10.80	11.69	12.69
Income Statement								
Total Revenue	148,706	508,801	458,865	428,086	283,282	262,365	239,329	211,622
EBITDA	25,936	109,459	91,078	80,484	66,037	59,434	52,753	45,632
Depn & Amortn	4,928	15,628	14,872	13,856	12,932	12,007	10,609	8,033
Income Before Taxes	20,525	91,833	73,354	62,457	51,458	45,938	41,277	37,132
Income Taxes	7,800	35,638	28,461	24,225	19,859	18,015	16,261	14,631
Net Income	12,725	56,195	44,893	35,006	31,599	27,923	25,016	22,502
Average Shares	32,741	32,688	32,314	31,795	31,320	31,703	32,482	33,540
Balance Sheet								
Current Assets	197,367	202,478	166,054	156,020	102,328	94,833	96,891	77,228
Total Assets	536,554	530,542	436,741	422,601	288,952	220,665	225,678	187,206
Current Liabilities	104,558	111,572	76,323	87,186	66,539	46,832	62,291	43,907
Long-Term Obligations	52,723	54,389	57,023	96,487	40,726	13,908	14,144	1,435
Total Liabilities	211,689	218,292	180,513	241,226	145,236	93,810	111,056	82,895
Stockholders' Equity	324,865	312,250	256,228	181,375	143,716	126,856	114,622	104,310
Shares Outstanding	32,211	32,410	32,162	31,167	30,273	31,007	31,319	32,020
Statistical Record								
Return on Assets %	11.79	11.59	10.45	9.84	12.40	12.48	12.12	12.63
Return on Equity %	19.29	19.72	20.52	21.54	23.36	23.06	22.85	21.59
EBITDA Margin %	17.44	21.51	19.85	18.80	23.31	22.65	22.04	21.56
Net Margin %	8.56	11.04	9.78	8.18	11.15	10.64	10.45	10.63
Asset Turnover	1.11	1.05	1.07	1.20	1.11	1.17	1.16	1.19
Current Ratio	1.89	1.81	2.18	1.79	1.54	2.02	1.56	1.76
Debt to Equity	0.16	0.17	0.22	0.53	0.28	0.11	0.12	0.01
Price Range	38.00-28.87	36.08-26.33	28.46-21.71	28.67-21.23	22.30-13.06	15.06-10.06	16.13-12.44	13.94-9.66
P/E Ratio	21.59-16.40	20.98-15.31	20.47-15.62	26.06-19.30	22.08-12.93	17.12-11.43	20.94-16.15	20.80-14.41
Average Yield %	0.50	0.51	0.46	0.43	0.58	0.74	0.63	0.75

Address: Northshore Blvd, Orlando, FL 15212
Telephone: (412) 444-0000
Fax: (412) 444-0001
K

Web Site: www.illustrative.com
Officers: D. M. Jackson - Chmn., Pres., C.E.O.
J. C. Smith - Exec. V.P., Pres.,

Auditors: PricewaterhouseCoopers LLP
Investor Contact: 412-444-0002
Transfer Agents: Computershare
Investor Services LLC, Chicago, IL

HOW TO USE THIS BOOK

D. INTERIM DIVIDENDS (Per Share) – The cash dividends are the actual dollar amounts declared by the company. No adjustments have been made for stock dividends and splits. **Ex-Dividend Date**: a stockholder must purchase the stock prior to this date in order to be entitled to the dividend. The **Record Date** indicates the date on which the shareholder had to have been a holder of record in order to qualify for the dividend. The **Payable Date** indicates the date the company paid or intends to pay the dividend. The cash amount shown in the first column is followed by a letter (example "Q" for quarterly) to indicate the frequency of the dividend. A notation of "Dividend payment suspended" indicates that dividend payments have been suspended within the most recent ten years.

Indicated Dividend This is the annualized amount (fully adjusted for splits) of the latest regular cash dividend. Companies with Dividend Reinvestment Plans are indicated here.

E. VALUATION ANALYSIS is a tool for evaluating a company's stock. Included are: Forecast Price/Earnings, Market Capitalization, Book Value, Price/Book and Price/Sales.

F. INSTITUTIONAL HOLDINGS – indicates the number of investment companies, insurance companies, mutual funds, bank trust and college endowment funds holding the stock and the total number of shares held as last reported.

G. BUSINESS SUMMARY explains what a company does in terms of the products or services it sells, its markets, and the position the company occupies in its industry. For a quick reference, included are the Company's Standard Industrial Classification (SIC), North American Industry Classification (NAIC) and Mergent's Industry Classification (MIC).

H. RECENT DEVELOPMENTS – This section captures what has happened in the most recent quarter for which results are available. It provides analysis of recently released sales and earnings figures, including special charges and credits, and may also include results by sector, expense trends and ratios, and other current information.

I. PROSPECTS – This section focuses on what is anticipated for the immediate future, as well as the outlook for the next few years, based on analysis by Mergent.

J. FINANCIAL DATA (fully adjusted for stock dividends and splits) is provided for at least the past seven fiscal years preceded by the most recent three-, six- and nine-month results if available.

Fiscal Years are the annual financial reporting periods as determined by each company. Annual prices and dividends are displayed based on the Company's fiscal year.

Per Share Data:

The Earnings Per Share figure is based on a trailing 12-month period. Earnings per share, and all per share figures, are adjusted for subsequent stock dividends and splits. Earnings per share reported after 12/15/97 are presented on a diluted basis, as described by Financial Accounting Standards Board Statement 128. Prior to that date, earnings per share are presented on a primary basis.

Cash Flow Per Share represents the annualized cash flow from operating activities (or for quarters, TTM cash flow from operating activities) divided by the average shares outstanding.

Tangible Book Value Per Share is calculated as stockholders equity (the value of common shares, paid-in capital and retained earnings) minus preferred stock and intangibles such as goodwill, patents and excess acquisition costs, divided by shares outstanding. It demonstrates the underlying cash value of each common share if the company were to be liquidated as of that date.

HOW TO USE THIS BOOK

Dividends Per Share is the total of cash payments made per share to shareholders for the trailing 12-month period.

Dividend Payout % is the proportion of earnings available for common stock that is paid to common shareholders in the form of cash dividends. It is significant because it indicates what percentage of earnings is being reinvested in the business for internal growth.

EDITOR'S NOTE: TTM net income is net income for the last 365 days (normally four reported quarters) ended on the quarterly balance sheet date. Where that last 365 days does not exactly equate to the last four reported quarters the net income for any included partial quarter is adjusted on a pro-rata basis.

INCOME STATEMENT, BALANCE SHEET AND STATISTICAL RECORD

Includes pertinent earnings and balance sheet information essential to analyzing a corporation's performance. The comparisons provide the necessary historical perspective to intelligently review the various operating and financial trends. Generic definitions follow.

Income Statement:

Total Revenues consists of all revenues from operations.

EBITDA represents earnings before, interest, taxes, depreciation and amortization, and special items.

Depreciation and Amortization includes all non-cash charges such as depletion and amortization as well as depreciation.

Income Before Taxes is the remaining income *after* deducting all costs, expenses, property charges, interest etc. but *before* deducting income taxes.

Income Taxes includes the amount charged against earnings to provide for current and deferred income taxes.

Net Income consists of all revenues less all expenses (operating and non-operating), and is presented before preference and common dividends.

Average Shares Outstanding is the weighted average number of shares including common equivalent shares outstanding during the year, as reported by the corporation and fully adjusted for all stock dividends and splits. The use of *average shares* minimizes the distortion in *earnings per share* which could result from issuance of a large amount of stock or the company's purchase of a large amount of its own stock during the year.

Balance Sheet:

Current Assets includes the short-term assets expected to be realized or consumed within one year. Normally includes cash and cash equivalents, short term investments, receivables, prepayments and inventories.

Total Assets represents all of the assets of the company, including tangible and intangible, and current and non-current.

Current Liabilities are all of the obligations of the company normally expected to be paid within one year. Includes bank overdrafts, short-term debt, payables and accruals.

Long-Term Obligations are the total long-term debts (due beyond one year) reported by the company, including bonds, capital lease obligations, notes, mortgages, debentures, etc.

Total Liabilities represents all liabilities of the company, whether current or non-current.

Stockholders' Equity is the sum of all capital stock accounts – paid in capital (including additional premium), retained earnings, and all other capital balances.

Shares Outstanding is the number of shares outstanding as of the date of the company's quarterly/annual report, exclusive of treasury stock and adjusted for subsequent stock dividends and splits.

Statistical Record:

Return on Assets % represents the ratio of annualized net income (or for Mos, TTM net income) to average total assets. This ratio represents how effectively assets are being used to produce a profit.

HOW TO USE THIS BOOK

Return on Equity % is the ratio of annualized net income (or for Mos, TTM net income) to average stockholders' equity, expressed as a percentage. This ratio illustrates how effectively the investment of the stockholders is being utilized to earn a profit.

EBITDA Margin % represents earnings before interest, taxes, depreciation and amortization as a percentage of total revenue.

Net Margin % is net income expressed as a percentage of total revenues.

Asset Turnover is annualized total revenue (or for Mos, TTM net income) divided by average total assets. A measure of efficiency for the use of assets.

Current Ratio represents current assets divided by current liabilities. The higher the figure the better the company is able to meet its current liabilities out of its current assets. A key measure of liquidity for industrial companies.

Debt to Equity is the ratio of long-term obligations to stockholders' equity.

Price Ranges are based on each Company's fiscal year. Where actual stock sales did not take place, a range of lowest bid and highest asked prices is shown.

Price/Earnings Ratio is shown as a range. The figures are calculated by dividing the stock's highest price for the year and its lowest price by the year's earnings per share. Growth stocks tend to command higher P/Es than cyclical stocks.

Average Yield % is the ratio of annual dividends to the real average of the prices over the fiscal year.

EDITOR'S NOTE: In order to preserve the historical relationships between prices, earnings and dividends, figures are not restated to reflect subsequent events. Figures are presented in U.S. dollars unless otherwise indicated.

K. ADDITIONAL INFORMATION on each stock includes the officers of the company, investor relations contact, address, telephone number, web site, transfer agents and institutional holdings.

OTHER DEFINITIONS

Factors Pertaining Especially to Real Estate Investment Trusts

Property Income is income from property rental and other associated activities.

Non-Property Income includes interest income and other income not from property activities.

Factors Pertaining Especially to Utilities

Net Property, Plant & Equip is the cost of property, plant and equipment, less its accumulated depreciation.

PPE Turnover represents annualized total revenue (or for Mos, TTM net income) divided by average net property, plant and equipment.

Factors Pertaining Especially to Banks

Interest Income is all interest income, including income from loans and leases, securities and deposits.

Interest Expense is all interest expense, including from loans and leases, securities and deposits.

Net Interest Income is interest income less interest expense. This figure is presented before provision for losses.

Provision for Losses represents the amount charged against earnings to increase the provision made for losses on loans and leases.

Non-Interest Income is any income that is not interest-related. Such income could include trading revenue and gains on the sale of assets.

Non-Interest Expense is all expenses that are not interest-related, including employment costs, office costs, marketing costs, etc.

Net Loans & Leases includes all loans and leases net of provisions for losses. May include commercial, agricultural, real estate, consumer and foreign loans.

Total Deposits are all time and demand deposits entrusted to a bank.

HOW TO USE THIS BOOK

Net Interest Margin % is net interest income before provisions expressed as a percentage of total interest income. A key measure of bank profitability.

Efficiency Ratio % is non-interest expense expressed as a percentage of total revenue.

Loans to Deposits are net loans and leases divided by total deposits. A key measure of bank liquidity.

Factors Pertaining Especially to Insurance Companies

Premium Income is the amount of insurance premiums received from policyholders. This is the primary revenue source for insurance companies.

Benefits and Claims represents the payments made to policyholders under the terms of insurance contracts.

Loss Ratio % is benefits and claims expressed as a percentage of premium income. A key ratio of insurance company profitability.

For the three-month period beginning December 1, 2004 and ending February 28, 2005, the Dow Jones Industrial Average climbed 3.2%, while the broader New York Stock Exchange Composite advanced 4.5%. The Dow and NYSE began the period at 10,428.02 and 7,005.72, respectively. A strong report on consumer confidence helped ease investor worries about sluggish consumer spending, propelling the Dow to its period high of 10,854.54 on December 28, as well as its highest close since the June before the terrorist attacks of September 11, 2001. Meanwhile, the NYSE would wait until February 25 to close at its period high of 7,361.89, following an upwardly revised report on fourth-quarter U.S. gross domestic product, encouraging investors that the economy is on a growth track. Both indices would slump to their period lows on January 24, with the Dow settling at 10,368.61 and the NYSE finishing at 6,984.03. The lows resulted from weakness in the technology and telecommunications sectors, along with a cold snap in the Northeast U.S. that is expected to drive crude oil prices higher. The Dow would close the three-month period at 10,766.23, while the NYSE would finish at 7,321.23.—Richard K. Dee, Jr.

Over the last twelve months, the best performing stock was **AK Steel Holding Corp.**, which is benefiting from increased shipment volumes and higher selling prices.

The second-best price performer was **Valero Energy Corp.** Results are being positively affected by sharply higher profitability from Co.'s refining operations.

Toll Brothers Inc. was the third-best price performer. Results are benefiting from continued strong demand and backlog for Co.'s luxury homes.

The fourth-best performing stock was **Crompton Corp.**, which is benefiting from improved selling prices and the implementation of cost-reduction initiatives.

Boyd Gaming Corp. was the fifth-best price performer. Results are being positively affected by Co.'s aggressive acquisition activity in 2004 as well as strong market conditions in Las Vegas.

The sixth-best performing stock was **Shaw Group Inc.**, which is benefiting from improving conditions in the energy and process industries.

Winn-Dixie Stores, Inc. was the worst performing stock over the last twelve months. Co. filed for reorganization under Chapter 11 of the U.S. Bankruptcy Code to address financial and operational challenges that have been hampering its operating performance.

The second-worst price performer was **Krispy Kreme Doughnuts Inc.** Results were hurt by lower comparable-store sales and higher impairment and store closing costs.

The third-worst performing stock was **Collins & Aikman Corp.**, primarily due to reduced volumes and delays in new program launches scheduled for late 2004.

Unisys Corp. was the fourth-worst price performer. Results were negatively affected by one-time charges and sluggish demand in the technology sector.

Delphi Corp. was the fifth-worst price performer, due to lower global production volumes and commodity pricing pressures.

The sixth-worst price performer was **Maytag Corp.** Results were hampered by lower volume and margins for floor care products, along with increased raw material costs.

SHORT-TERM PRICE SCORES: COMPANY RANKINGS

25 HIGHEST	SHORT-TERM PRICE SCORE♦	LONG-TERM PRICE SCORE♦	PRICE RANGE (52 Wks.)	RECENT PRICE
AK Steel Holding Corp.	149.0	69.5	17.94 - 3.98	11.06
Valero Energy Corp.	145.5	181.5	73.86 - 28.16	73.27
Toll Brothers Inc.	144.5	192.7	90.00 - 36.85	78.85
Crompton Corp.	140.8	67.9	15.65 - 5.36	14.60
Boyd Gaming Corp.	140.2	233.2	57.50 - 21.79	52.15
Shaw Group Inc.	138.3	63.5	23.01 - 9.24	21.80
Diamond Offshore Drilling, Inc.	137.4	92.5	50.89 - 21.55	49.90
Holly Corp.	136.6	211.7	39.17 - 15.93	37.27
Humana Inc.	135.4	129.0	34.86 - 15.55	31.94
TXU Corp.	134.7	115.0	79.97 - 27.74	79.63
Pacificare Health Systems, Inc.	131.7	148.5	64.88 - 29.70	56.92
AES Corp.	131.3	44.7	17.65 - 7.69	16.38
Peabody Energy Corp.	130.8	...	49.89 - 21.63	46.36
Plains Exploration & Production Co.	130.0	...	38.30 - 17.19	34.90
KB HOME	129.9	168.1	126.38 - 61.06	117.46
Lyondell Chemical Co.	129.9	115.2	35.25 - 14.84	27.92
Wesco International, Inc.	129.0	...	36.62 - 14.30	28.00
St. Joe Co. (The)	128.9	158.0	75.65 - 35.75	67.30
United Defense Industries Inc.	128.8	...	73.52 - 31.79	73.42
Rockwell Automation, Inc.	128.6	163.1	62.30 - 31.61	56.64
Ryland Group, Inc.	127.9	206.1	71.81 - 34.69	62.02
Aetna Inc.	127.5	...	76.97 - 38.88	74.95
Crown Holdings Inc.	127.5	66.5	17.07 - 8.13	15.56
Atwood Oceanics, Inc.	127.4	112.3	69.62 - 33.96	66.54
United States Steel Corp.	126.6	146.1	63.12 - 25.78	50.85
25 LOWEST				
Winn-Dixie Stores, Inc.	32.1	20.3	8.20 - 0.61	0.93
Krispy Kreme Doughnuts Inc.	43.7	...	35.01 - 5.36	7.63
Collins & Aikman Corp.	45.5	33.6	6.56 - 0.95	1.23
Unisys Corp.	64.7	52.2	14.75 - 6.67	7.06
Delphi Corp.	67.4	...	10.97 - 4.36	4.48
Maytag Corp.	68.1	49.6	31.95 - 13.31	13.97
Visteon Corp.	69.4	...	12.15 - 5.67	5.71
Airtran Holdings, Inc.	70.7	131.7	15.17 - 7.50	9.05
King Pharmaceuticals, Inc.	73.2	...	17.82 - 8.31	8.31
Six Flags Inc.	73.3	29.2	8.28 - 3.49	4.12
Allied Waste Industries, Inc.	75.1	65.8	13.82 - 6.95	7.31
Commscope, Inc.	75.2	78.1	22.52 - 14.09	14.96
Dana Corp.	76.5	62.5	21.90 - 12.35	12.79
American Axle & Mfg. Holdings	76.8	...	39.86 - 24.11	24.50
Merck & Co., Inc.	76.9	55.8	48.37 - 26.00	32.37
Blockbuster, Inc.	77.3	...	17.50 - 6.78	8.83
Marsh & McLennan Cos., Inc.	77.4	74.1	47.00 - 24.10	30.42
General Motors Corp.	77.9	65.8	49.50 - 28.35	29.39
Forest Laboratories, Inc.	78.2	123.5	75.20 - 36.47	36.95
Gartner, Inc.	78.8	73.4	13.38 - 9.16	9.57
Pfizer Inc.	79.2	71.4	37.62 - 23.86	26.27
DeVRY Inc.	79.2	72.4	32.20 - 14.22	18.92
KEMET Corp.	79.3	57.0	14.94 - 7.58	7.75
Vishay Intertechnology, Inc.	80.0	71.4	22.70 - 11.57	12.43
Solectron Corp.	80.2	26.7	6.56 - 3.39	3.47

♦For definition see page 4a.

The companies comprising the Beer, Wine & Spirits sector have generally outperformed the NYSE Composite Index over the past twelve months. However, within the sector the companies' performances have been influenced by their particular business focus. For instance, companies in the Wine & Spirits sector have been driven by favorable consumption trends, aided by product innovations such as flavored liquors, and strong on-premise marketing to drinkers in the 21-29 age group. Meanwhile, companies in the Beer sector have benefited recently from a decent pricing environment, which has been somewhat offset by expanded global competition and continuing industry consolidation. On Feb 9 2005, Adolph Coors Company merged with Molson Inc. to create Molson Coors Brewing Company.

Anheuser-Busch Companies is the parent holding company of Anheuser-Busch, Inc., a global brewer of beer. Co.'s products are sold under brand names including *Budweiser, Michelob, Busch,* and *Bacardi Silver.* For the year ended Dec 31 2004, net income rose 7.9% to $2.24 billion from $2.08 billion a year earlier. Net sales advanced 5.6% to $14.15 billion from $13.40 billion the previous year. Co.'s results benefited from a favorable pricing environment, with domestic beer revenue per barrel increasing 2.5%. Worldwide Anheuser-Busch beer sales volume for full year 2004 grew 5.3% to 116.8 million barrels. During 2004, Co. introduced *Bacardi Limon, Bacardi Black Cherry, Bacardi Green Apple, BE,* and *Budweiser Select.*

Brown-Forman operates in two business segments: beverages and consumer durables. The beverages segment manufactures, bottles, imports, exports and markets a wide variety of alcoholic beverage brands. Co.'s principal beverage brands include: Jack *Daniel's, Southern Comfort, Finlandia Vodka, Canadian Mist, Korbel champagnes,* and *Fetzer Vineyards, Bolla* and *Bel Arbor* wines. The consumer durables segment sells products

under the *Lenox, Gorham, Dansk and Hartmann* brand names. For the nine months ended Jan 31 2005, net income was $250.6 million compared with $199.9 million in the same period a year earlier. Results for 2005 included a goodwill impairment charge of $37.0 million and a gain of $72.3 million on the sale of an investment in an affiliate. Net sales rose 8.4% to $2.12 billion. Co.'s results were driven primarily by accelerating consumer demand and margin improvement for *Jack Daniel's, Southern Comfort,* and *Finlandia,* and the effect of Co.'s new low-carbohydrate wine brands.

Constellation Brands is a producer, marketer and distributor of premier branded beverage alcohol products in the U.S. and the U.K. Co.'s key products include *Corona Extra, Pacifico, St. Pauli Girl, Black Velvet, Fleischmann's, Mr. Boston, Simi, Estancia, Ravenswood, Blackstone, Banrock Station, Hardys, Nobilo, Alice White, Vendange, Almaden, Arbor Mist, Stowells,* and *Blackthorn.* For the nine months ended Nov 30 2004, net income amounted to $228.8 million compared with $157.6 million in the corresponding year-ago period. Results for 2004 and 2003 included restructuring and related charges of $4.4 million and $27.5 million, respectively. Net sales climbed 14.2% to $3.05 billion from $2.67 billion the previous year, driven by growth from across its branded wine, U.K. wholesale and spirits businesses. On Dec 22 2004, Co. acquired The Robert Mondavi Corporation, a premium wine producer based in Napa, CA.

Looking ahead, competition between and among the companies in the Beer, Wine & Spirits sector is expected to remain intense. To thrive in this challenging environment, companies will need more than ever to capitalize on global growth opportunities, expand product innovation through new products and line extensions, and create effective marketing.

------*Andrew J. Kalinski*

BEER, WINE & SPIRITS

COMPARATIVE STATISTICS

COMPANY	FISCAL DATE	EXCH	SYMBOL	PRICE RANGE (12 MOS.) HIGH	LOW	RECENT PRICE	LATEST: 12 MOS.	EARNINGS PER SHARE 2004	2003	2002	IND. CASH DIV.	BOOK VALUE PER SH.	STKHLDR'S EQUITY ($ MILL)	LONG-TERM DEBT)
Anheuser-Busch Cos., Inc.	12/31/04	NYS	BUD	54.74	27.95	47.00	47.00	2.80	2.51	2.23	0.980	3.40	2668.10	65.32
Boston Beer Co., Inc	12/25/04	NYS	SAM	18.52	27.95	21.38	21.38	0.89	0.72	0.53	nil	5.52	78.37	
Brown-Forman Corp.	4/30/04	NYS	BF A	56.65	44.20	54.59	54.59	...	2.12	1.82	0.980	†10.36	†1085.00	†34.30
Constellation Brands Inc	2/29/04	NYS	STZ	57.35	32.00	52.86	52.86	2.13	2.13	2.26	nil	†22.30	†2377.62	†40.95

BEER, WINE & SPIRITS

FINANCIAL DATA – LATEST ANNUAL RANKINGS

REVENUES ($000,000)

RANK COMPANY	2004 AMT	RANK COMPANY	2004 AMT	RANK COMPANY	2004 AMT
1 Anheuser-Busch Cos. Inc.	14934.20	3 Brown-Forman Corp.	†2213.00	4 Boston Beer Co., Inc	217.21
2 Constellation Brands Inc	†3552.43				

NET INCOME ($000,000)

RANK COMPANY	2004 AMT	RANK COMPANY	2004 AMT	RANK COMPANY	2004 AMT
1 Anheuser-Busch Cos., Inc.	2240.30	3 Constellation Brands Inc	†220.41	4 Boston Beer Co., Inc	12.50
2 Brown-Forman Corp.	†258.00				

OPERATING PROFIT MARGIN (%)

RANK COMPANY	2004 AMT	RANK COMPANY	2004 AMT	RANK COMPANY	2004 AMT
1 Anheuser-Busch Cos., Inc.	22.51	3 Constellation Brands Inc	†13.72	4 Boston Beer Co., Inc	8.97
2 Brown-Forman Corp.	†17.94				

RETURN ON CAPITAL (%)

RANK COMPANY	2004 AMT	RANK COMPANY	2004 AMT	RANK COMPANY	2004 AMT
1 Anheuser-Busch Cos., Inc.	17.06	3 Brown-Forman Corp.	†13.07	4 Constellation Brands Inc	†5.01
2 Boston Beer Co., Inc	15.54				

GROSS PLANT ($000,000)

RANK COMPANY	2004 AMT	RANK COMPANY	2004 AMT	RANK COMPANY	2004 AMT
1 Anheuser-Busch Cos., Inc.	17412.50	3 Brown-Forman Corp.	†1000.00	4 Boston Beer Co., Inc	58.21
2 Constellation Brands Inc	†1449.13				

BEER, WINE & SPIRITS

NET PLANT ($000,000)

RANK	COMPANY	2004 AMT
1	Anheuser-Busch Cos., Inc.	8847.40
2	Constellation Brands Inc	†1097.36
3	Brown-Forman Corp.	†515.00
4	Boston Beer Co., Inc	17.22

RETURN ON NET PLANT (%)

RANK	COMPANY	2004 AMT
1	Boston Beer Co., Inc	72.59
2	Brown-Forman Corp.	†50.10
3	Anheuser-Busch Cos., Inc.	25.32
4	Constellation Brands Inc	†20.09

NET INCOME TO REVENUES (%)

RANK	COMPANY	2004 AMT
1	Anheuser-Busch Cos., Inc.	15.00
2	Brown-Forman Corp.	†11.66
3	Constellation Brands Inc	†6.20
4	Boston Beer Co., Inc	5.76

PE RATIO

RANK	COMPANY	2004 AMT
1	Anheuser-Busch Cos., Inc.	16.79
2	Boston Beer Co., Inc	24.02
3	Constellation Brands Inc	24.82
4	Brown-Forman Corp.	25.75

YIELD (%)

RANK	COMPANY	2004 AMT
1	Anheuser-Busch Cos., Inc.	2.09
2	Brown-Forman Corp.	1.80
3	Boston Beer Co., Inc	...
4	Constellation Brands Inc	...

BEER, WINE & SPIRITS

PRICE SCORE - 12 MONTH

RANK	COMPANY	2004 AMT
1	Constellation Brands Inc	128.21
2	Boston Beer Co., Inc	108.37
3	Brown-Forman Corp.	101.78
4	Anheuser-Busch Cos., Inc.	100.65

Accommodation and Food Services
Accommodation
  Hilton Hotels Corporation
  Host Marriott Corporation
*Marriott International, Inc.
  Park Place Entertainment Corp.
  Viad Corp.
Food Services and Drinking Places
  Brinker International, Inc.
*Darden Restaurants, Inc.
*McDonald's Corporation
  Outback Steakhouse, Inc.
  Ruby Tuesday, Inc.
*Wendy's International, Inc.
*Yum! Brands, Inc.

Administrative & Support and Waste Management & Remediation Services
Administrative and Support Services
*Equifax Inc.
*Manpower Inc.
  Mid Atlantic Medical Services
  MPS Group, Inc.
  Robert Half International, Inc.
*Rollins, Inc.
  ServiceMaster Company (The)
Waste Management and Remediation Services
  Allied Waste Industries, Inc.
*Johnson Controls, Inc.
  Republic Services, Inc.
*Waste Management, Inc.

Arts, Entertainment, and Recreation
  Aztar Corp.
  Boyd Gaming Corp.
  Caesars Entertainment Inc.
*Carnival Corp.
*Cedar Fair, L.P.
*Disney (Walt) Company (The)
  GTECH Holdings Corp.
  Harrah's Entertainment, Inc.
  International Game Technology
  Mandalay Resort Group
  MGM Mirage
  Six Flags, Inc.
  Station Casinos, Inc.

Construction
  ABM Industries Incorporated
*Boston Properties, Inc.
  Centex Corporation
  Dycom Industries, Inc.
  EMCOR Group, Inc.
*Forest City Enterprises, Inc.
*Granite Construction Inc.
  Halliburton Company
  Horton (D.R.) Inc.
  Hovnanian Enterprises, Inc.
  Jacobs Engineering Group Inc.

KB Home
Lennar Corporation
M.D.C. Holdings, Inc.
Martin Marietta Materials, Inc.
*MDU Resources Group, Inc.
Pulte Homes, Inc.
Quanta Services, Inc.
Ryland Group, Inc. (The)
Toll Brothers, Inc.

Educational Services
DeVry Inc.
ITT Educational Services, Inc.

Finance and Insurance
Commercial Banking
*AmSouth Bancorporation
*BancorpSouth, Inc.
*Bank of America Corporation
*Bank of Hawaii Corporation
*Bank of New York Co., Inc.
*BB&T Corporation
*Chittenden Corporation
  City National Corporation
*Colonial Bancgroup Inc.
*Comerica, Inc.
*Commerce Bancorp, Inc.
*Community Bank System, Inc.
  Cullen/Frost Bankers, Inc.
*F.N.B. Corporation
*First Commonwealth Financial
*First Horizon National Corporation
*FleetBoston Financial Corp.
*Hibernia Corporation
*Hudson United Bancorp
*Irwin Financial Corp.
*J.P. Morgan Chase & Co.
*KeyCorp
*M&T Bank Corporation
*Marshall & Ilsley Corporation
  MBNA Corporation
*Mellon Financial Corporation
*North Fork Bancorporation, Inc.
*Old National Bancorp
*PNC Financial Services Group
*Regions Financial Corporation
*State Street Corporation
  Sterling Bancorp
*SunTrust Banks, Inc.
*Synovus Financial Corporation
*TCF Financial Corp.
*U.S. Bancorp
*UnionBanCal Corporation
*Valley National Bancorp
*Wachovia Corporation
*Wells Fargo & Company
*Wilmington Trust Corporation
Direct Health and Medical Insurance Carriers

*AFLAC Incorporated
*Aon Corporation
*CIGNA Corporation
 Conseco, Inc.
 Humana Inc.
 Pacificare Health Systems, Inc.
 Reinsurance Group of America
 UnitedHealth Group Inc.
*UnumProvident Corporation
 WellChoice, Inc.
Direct Life Insurance Carriers
 AmerUs Group Co.
*Jefferson-Pilot Corp.
*Lincoln National Corporation
*Nationwide Financial Services
 Principal Financial Group, Inc.
*Protective Life Corporation
 Prudential Financial, Inc.
 Stancorp Financial Group, Inc.
*Torchmark Corporation
Direct Property and Casualty Insurance Carriers
 Allmerica Financial Corporation
*Allstate Corporation (The)
*American Financial Group, Inc.
 American International Group
 Berkley (W.R.) Corporation
 Berkshire Hathaway Inc.
*Chubb Corporation (The)
 CNA Financial Corporation
 Commerce Group, Inc.
 HCC Insurance Holdings, Inc.
 Horace Mann Educators Corp.
 Leucadia National Corporation
 Loews Corporation
 Markel Corporation
 Mercury General Corporation
 Progressive Corporation (The)
*RLI Corp.
 Transatlantic Holdings, Inc.
*Unitrin, Inc.
 XL Capital Ltd.
 Zenith National Insurance Corp.
Direct Title Insurance Carriers
 Alleghany Corporation
 Fidelity National Financial, Inc.
*First American Corporation (The)
 LandAmerica Financial Group

Insurance Agencies and Brokerages
 Aetna, Inc.
 Anthem, Inc.
 Brown & Brown, Inc.
 ChoicePoint Inc.
 Gallagher (Arthur J.) & Company
*Hartford Financial Services Group
 Hilb, Rogal & Hamilton Company
*Marsh & McLennan Companies

 Metlife, Inc.
Mortgage and Nonmortgage Loan Brokers
*New York Community Bancorp, Inc.
Nondepository Credit Intermediation
*American Express Company
 AmeriCredit Corp.
*Capital One Financial Corp.
*Countrywide Financial Corp.
 Doral Financial Corporation
*Fannie Mae
*Freddie Mac
 General Motors Acceptance Corp.
*Morgan Stanley
*Providian Financial Corp.
 SLM Corporation
 Student Loan Corp. (The)
Real Estate Investment Trusts
 AMB Property Corporation
*Annaly Mortgage Management
 Apartment Investment & Mngmnt
*Archstone-Smith Trust Company
 AvalonBay Communities, Inc.
*BRE Properties, Inc.
 Camden Property Trust
*CBL & Associates Properties
 CenterPoint Properties Trust
*Colonial Properties Trust
*Commercial Net Lease Realty
 Crescent Real Estate Equities
*Developers Diversified Realty
*Duke Realty Corporation
*EastGroup Properties, Inc.
*Equity Office Properties Trust
*Equity Residential Prop. Trust
*Essex Property Trust, Inc.
*Federal Realty Investment Trust
*General Growth Properties, Inc.
*Health Care Property Investors
*Healthcare Realty Trust, Inc.
*Highwoods Properties, Inc.
*Home Properties, Inc.
*Hospitality Properties Trust
*HRPT Properties Trust
*iStar Financial Inc.
*Kimco Realty Corp.
*Lexington Corporate Properties Trust
*Liberty Property Trust
*Macerich Company (The)
*Mack-Cali Realty Corporation
*Mills (The) Corporation
*New Plan Excel Realty Trust
*Pan Pacific Retail Properties
 Plum Creek Timber Company
 Public Storage, Inc.
 Realty Income Corp.
 Reckson Associates Realty Corp.
*Regency Centers Corporation
*Shurgard Storage Centers, Inc.

*Simon Property Group, Inc.
Starwood Hotels & Resorts
*Sun Communities, Inc.
*Thornburg Mortgage, Inc.
*United Dominion Realty Trust
*Universal Health Realty Inc. Trust
*Vornado Realty Trust
*Washington Real Est. Invst Trust
*Weingarten Realty Investors
Reinsurance Carriers
*ACE, Ltd.
Ambac Financial Group, Inc.
MBIA Inc.
MGIC Investment Corporation
Odyssey Re Holdings Corp.
*Old Republic International Corp.
PMI Group, Inc. (The)
Radian Group Inc.
*St. Paul Travelers Companies, Inc. (The)
Savings Institutions
Astoria Financial Corp.
Golden West Financial Corp.
*Sovereign Bancorp, Inc.
*Washington Mutual, Inc.
*Webster Financial Corp.
*Securities, Commodity Contracts, and Other
Financial Investments and Related Activities*
Bear Stearns Companies (The)
Chicago Mercantile Exch. Hldgs.
*Citigroup Inc.
E* Trade Financial Corp
Eaton Vance Corporation
Edwards (A.G.), Inc.
Federated Investors, Inc.
*Franklin Resources, Inc.
Friedman Billings Ramsey Group
Goldman Sachs Group, Inc.
Janus Capital Group, Inc.
Jefferies Group, Inc.
LaBranche & Co., Inc.
Legg Mason, Inc.
*Lehman Brothers Holdings Inc.
*Merrill Lynch & Co., Inc.
Nuveen Investments, Inc.
Raymond James Financial, Inc.
*Schwab (Charles) Corporation
*Waddell & Reed Financial, Inc.
Other Financial Vehicles
BlackRock, Inc.
Triad Hospitals, Inc.
Health Care and Social Assistance
Apria Healthcare Group Inc.
Community Health Systems, Inc.
Coventry Health Care Inc.
DaVita Inc.
HCA Inc.
Health Management Associates
Health Net, Inc.

Kindred Healthcare, Inc.
Laboratory Corp. of America
Manor Care, Inc.
Renal Care Group, Inc.
*Tenet Healthcare Corporation
Universal Health Services, Inc.
Information
*Cable Networks, Program Distribution and
Internet Service Providers*
Fair Isaac Corporation
Univision Communications Inc.
*Information Services and Data Processing
Services*
Affiliated Computer Services
Alliance Data Systems Corp.
Automatic Data Processing, Inc.
Bisys Group, Inc. (The)
Concord EFS, Inc.
DST Systems, Inc.
Dun & Bradstreet Corp. (The)
*Electronic Data Systems Corp.
First Data Corporation
Getty Images, Inc.
Imation Corporation
IMS Health, Inc.
NCR Corporation
*Reynolds and Reynolds Co.
Sabre Holding Corporation
SunGard Data Systems Inc.
Time Warner Inc.
Total System Services, Inc.
*Motion Picture and Sound Recording
Industries*
Liberty Media Corporation
Regal Entertainment Group
Viacom Inc.
Westwood One, Inc.
Publishing Industries
*American Greetings Corporation
Belo Corporation
BMC Software, Inc.
Cadence Design Systems, Inc.
*Computer Associates International
*Dow Jones & Company, Inc.
*Gannett Co., Inc.
Harte-Hanks, Inc.
*Knight Ridder
Lee Enterprises, Inc.
McAfee Inc.
McClatchy Company (The)
*McGraw-Hill Companies, Inc.
*Media General, Inc.
Meredith Corporation
*New York Times Company
Pulitzer, Inc.
*Reader's Digest Association, Inc.
Scripps (E.W.) Company (The)
Sybase, Inc.

Thomson Corp.
*Tribune Company
Washington Post Company
Wiley (John) & Sons Inc.
Radio and Television Broadcasting
Cablevision Systems Corp.
Cox Radio, Inc.
Entercom Communications Corp.
Hearst-Argyle Television, Inc.

Telecommunications
*ALLTEL Corporation
American Tower Corporation
*AT&T Corp.
*BellSouth Corporation
*CenturyTel, Inc.
Certegy, Inc.
Cincinnati Bell Inc.
*Citizens Communications Co.
Crown Castle International Corp.
*Lucent Technologies Inc.
Qwest Communications Internat.
*Sprint Corporation
*Verizon Communications Inc.

Management of Companies & Enterprises
IndyMac Bancorp, Inc.
*National City Corporation
*SBC Communications Inc.
*Temple-Inland Inc.
*Universal Corporation

Manufacturing
Beverage and Tobacco Product Manufacturing
*Altria Group, Inc.
*Anheuser-Busch Companies
*Brown-Forman Corporation
*Coca-Cola Company (The)
*Coca-Cola Enterprises Inc.
Constellation Brands, Inc.
Molson Coors Brewing Company
*Pepsi Bottling Group Inc.
*PepsiAmericas, Inc.
*PepsiCo Inc.
*Reynolds American Inc.
*UST, Inc.
Chemical Manufacturing
*3M Company
*Air Products & Chemicals, Inc.
*Albemarle Corporation
Alberto-Culver Company
*Avon Products, Inc.
Blyth, Inc.
*Cabot Corporation
Charles River Laboratories Int.
*Church & Dwight Company, Inc.
*Clorox Company (The)

*Colgate-Palmolive Company
Cytec Industries, Inc.
Dial Corporation (The)
*Dow Chemical Company
*du Pont (E.I.) de Nemours & Co.
*Eastman Chemical Company
*Eastman Kodak Company
*Ecolab, Inc.
*Estee Lauder Companies, Inc.
*Ferro Corp.
*Fuller (H.B.) Company
Great Lakes Chemical Corp.
*Hercules Inc.
IMC Global, Inc.
*International Flavors & Fragrances
*Lubrizol Corporation
Monsanto Company
*Olin Corporation
*OM Group, Inc.
*PPG Industries, Inc.
*Praxair, Inc.
*Procter & Gamble Company
*Rohm & Haas Company
*RPM International Inc.
Scotts Company (The)
*Sherwin-Williams Company
Smith International, Inc.
*Valspar Corporation (The)

Computer and Electronic Product Manufacturing
Advanced Micro Devices, Inc.
Agilent Technologies, Inc.
*Allegheny Technologies Inc.
*Ametek, Inc.
Analog Devices, Inc.
*Applera Corp. – Applied Biosystems
Avaya Inc.
*AVX Corporation
*Beckman Coulter, Inc.
Commscope, Inc.
*Corning Incorporated
Cypress Semiconductor Corp.
EMC Corporation
*Emerson Electric Co.
Fairchild Semiconductor Int'l.
Gateway Inc.
Global Payments Inc.
Harman International Industries
*Harris Corporation
*Hewlett-Packard Company
*International Business Machines
International Rectifier Corp.
Jabil Circuit, Inc.
KEMET Corporation
L-3 Communications Holdings
Lexmark International, Inc.
LSI Logic Corporation

Maxtor Corporation
*Medtronic, Inc.
MEMC Electronic Materials, Inc.
Mettler-Toledo International Inc.
Micron Technology, Inc.
*Millipore Corporation
*Motorola, Inc.
National Semiconductor Corp.
Plantronics, Inc.
Quantum Corporation
*Raytheon Company
*Rockwell Collins, Inc.
*Scientific-Atlanta Inc.
Solectron Corporation
Storage Technology Corporation
Symbol Technologies, Inc.
*Tektronix, Inc.
Teradyne, Inc.
*Texas Instruments Inc.
Thermo Electron Corporation
*Thomas & Betts Corporation
Unisys Corporation
Vishay Intertechnology, Inc.
VISX, Inc.
Waters Corporation
Western Digital Corporation
Doll, Toy, and Game Manufacturing
*Hasbro, Inc.
Marvel Enterprises, Inc.
*Mattel, Inc.
Electrical Equipment, Appliance, and Component Manufacturing
*Cooper Industries, Ltd.
*Eaton Corporation
Energizer Holdings, Inc.
*General Electric Company
*Hubbell, Inc.
*Maytag Corporation
*Rockwell Automation
*Smith (A.O.) Corporation
*Whirlpool Corporation
Fabricated Metal Product Manufacturing
Alliant Techsystems Inc.
*Ball Corporation
*Crane Co.
Crown Holdings, Inc.
Danaher Corporation
*Fortune Brands, Inc.
*Gillette Company (The)
*Harsco Corporation
*Parker-Hannifin Corp.
Shaw Group Inc. (The)
Simpson Manufacturing Co., Inc.
*Snap-On Incorporated
*Stanley Works
*Timken Company (The)
Food Manufacturing
*Archer Daniels Midland Co.

*Campbell Soup Company
*ConAgra Foods, Inc.
Dean Foods Company
Del Monte Foods Company
*General Mills, Inc.
*Heinz (H.J.) Company
*Hershey Foods Corporation
*Hormel Foods Corporation
*Kellogg Company
Kraft Foods, Inc.
Krispy Kreme Doughnuts, Inc.
*McCormick & Company, Inc.
*Sara Lee Corporation
*Sensient Technologies Corp.
Smithfield Foods, Inc.
*Smucker (J.M.) Company
Tootsie Roll Industries, Inc.
*Tyson Foods, Inc.
*Wrigley (Wm.) Jr. Company
Furniture and Related Product Manufacturing
Furniture Brands International
HNI Corporation
*La-Z-Boy Incorporated
Leggett & Platt, Incorporated
*Masco Corporation
Steelcase Inc.
Machinery Manufacturing
AGCO Corporation
American Standard Companies
*Baker Hughes Inc.
*Black & Decker Corporation
*Briggs & Stratton Corporation
*Brunswick Corporation
*Caterpillar Inc.
Cooper Cameron Corporation
*Cummins Inc.
*Deere & Company
*Diebold, Inc.
*Donaldson Company, Inc.
*Dover Corporation
Flowserve Corporation
FMC Corporation
FMC Technologies, Inc.
*Graco Inc.
Grant Prideco Inc
*ITT Industries Inc.
*Kennametal Inc.
*Manitowoc Company, Inc. (The)
NACCO Industries, Inc.
*Pall Corporation
*Pentair, Inc.
Roper Industries, Inc.
SPX Corporation
Terex Corporation
*Tennant Company
Varian Medical Systems, Inc.
*Xerox Corporation

*York International Corporation

Medical Equipment and Supplies Manufacturing
*Bard (C.R.), Inc.
*Bausch & Lomb, Inc.
*Baxter International Inc.
*Becton, Dickinson and Company
Boston Scientific Corporation
*Guidant Corporation
ResMed Inc.
St. Jude Medical, Inc.
Steris Corporation
Stryker Corporation
*Teleflex Inc.
Zimmer Holdings, Inc.

Nonmetallic Mineral Product Manufacturing
Brink's Company (The)
Florida Rock Industries, Inc.
*Lafarge North America, Inc.
Minerals Technologies Inc.
Owens-Illinois, Inc.
USG Corporation

Paper and Wood Product Manufacturing
*Avery Dennison Corporation
*Bemis Company, Inc.
*Boise Cascade Corporation
*Bowater Inc.
*Georgia-Pacific Corporation
Glatfelter (P.H.) Company
*International Paper Company
*Kimberly-Clark Corporation
Longview Fibre Company
*Louisiana-Pacific Corporation
*MeadWestvaco Corporation
Packaging Corp. of America
*Potlatch Corporation
*Rayonier Inc.
*Sonoco Products Company
St. Joe Company (The)
Tenneco Automotive Inc.

Petroleum and Coal Products Manufacturing
*Amerada Hess Corporation
*Ashland, Inc.
*ChevronTexaco Corp.
*ConocoPhillips
*Exxon Mobil Corporation
Holly Corp.
*Lyondell Chemical Company
Murphy Oil Corporation
Premcor Inc.
*Sunoco, Inc.
Tesoro Petroleum Corporation
Valero Energy Corporation

Pharmaceutical Preparation Manufacturing
*Abbott Laboratories
*Allergan, Inc.

AmerisourceBergen Corporation
Barr Laboratories, Inc.
*Bristol-Myers Squibb Company
Edwards Lifesciences Corp.
Forest Laboratories, Inc.
Genentech, Inc.
*Johnson & Johnson
King Pharmaceuticals, Inc.
*Lilly (Eli) & Company
Medicis Pharmaceutical Corp.
*Merck & Co., Inc.
*Mylan Laboratories Inc.
Par Pharmaceutical Companies, Inc.
*Pfizer Inc.
*Schering-Plough Corporation
Valeant Pharmaceuticals Internat.
Watson Pharmaceuticals, Inc.
*Wyeth

Plastics and Rubber Products Manufacturing
AptarGroup Inc.
*Bandag, Inc.
*Carlisle Companies Incorporated
*Cooper Tire & Rubber Company
*Goodyear Tire & Rubber Co.
*Illinois Tool Works, Incorporated
*Myers Industries, Inc.
*Newell Rubbermaid Inc.
Pactiv Corporation
Sealed Air Corporation
Tupperware Corporation
*West Pharmaceutical Services

Primary Metal Manufacturing
*AK Steel Holding Corporation
*Alcoa, Inc.
*Engelhard Corp.
International Steel Group Inc.
*Nucor Corporation
*Phelps Dodge Corporation
Precision Castparts Corp.
*United States Steel Corporation
*Worthington Industries, Inc.

Printing and Related Support Activities
*Banta Corporation
Deluxe Corporation
*Donnelley (R.R.) & Sons Co.
Quebecor World Inc.

Textiles, Apparel, and Leather Manufacturing
Coach, Inc.
Collins & Aikman Corporation
Jones Apparel Group, Inc.
*Liz Claiborne, Inc.
Mohawk Industries, Inc.
*NIKE, Inc.
Polo Ralph Lauren Corporation
Reebok International, Ltd.
Timberland Co. (The)

*VF Corporation
Transportation Equipment Manufacturing
*ArvinMeritor, Inc.
 Autoliv, Inc.
*Boeing Company (The)
*BorgWarner Inc.
*Clarcor Inc.
*Dana Corporation
*Delphi Corporation
*Federal Signal Corp.
*Ford Motor Company
 General Dynamics Corporation
*General Motors Corporation
*Goodrich Corporation
*Harley-Davidson, Inc.
*Honeywell International Inc.
 *Lockheed Martin Corporation
 Navistar International Corp.
 Northrop Grumman Corporation
*Polaris Industries Inc.
 Sequa Corporation
 Superior Industries International
*Textron Inc.
 Trinity Industries, Inc.
 United Defense Industries Inc
*United Technologies Corp.
*Visteon Corporation
Other Manufacturing
*Brady Corporation
 Callaway Golf Company
*Hillenbrand Industries, Inc.
*Ingersoll-Rand Co. Ltd.
 Tyco International Ltd.
Mining
Activities Support for Mining
 BJ Services Company
 Diamond Offshore Drilling, Inc.
 ENSCO International Inc.
 EOG Resources, Inc.
 Helmerich & Payne, Inc.
*Marathon Oil Corporation
 Peabody Energy Corp.
 Pride International, Inc.
 Rowan Companies, Inc.
 Schlumberger Ltd.
 Transocean, Inc.
 Weatherford International, Ltd.
Mining (except Oil and Gas)
*Arch Coal, Inc.
 CONSOL Energy Inc.
 Freeport-McMoRan Copper & Gold
 Newmont Mining Corporation
*Southern Peru Copper Corp.
*Vulcan Materials Company
Oil and Gas Extraction
*Anadarko Petroleum Corp.
*Apache Corporation
 Atwood Oceanics, Inc.

 Chesapeake Energy Corp.
*Dynegy Inc.
*Enterprise Products Partners L.P.
 Forest Oil Corporation
*Kerr-McGee Corporation
 Newfield Exploration Co.
 Noble Corp.
 Noble Energy, Inc.
*Occidental Petroleum Corp.
 Pioneer Natural Resources Co.
 Plains Exploration & Production Co. L.P.
 Pogo Producing Company
 Unocal Corporation
*XTO Energy, Inc.
Other Services
 ARAMARK Corporation
 Cendant Corporation
 Laidlaw International Inc.
*Regis Corporation
 Service Corporation International
 Weight Watchers International
Professional, Scientific, and Technical Services
 Agere Systems Inc.
 Bearingpoint, Inc.
*Block (H & R), Inc.
 Catalina Marketing Corporation
 Clear Channel Communications
 Computer Sciences Corporation
 Convergys Corporation
 Covance Inc.
 Fluor Corporation
 Gartner Group, Inc.
 Hewitt Associates Inc.
 IDT Corporation
*Interpublic Group of Companies
 Keane, Inc.
 Korn/Ferry International
 Moody's Corporation
*Omnicom Group, Inc.
*PerkinElmer, Inc.
 Quest Diagnostics, Incorporated
 Titan Corporation (The)
 Valassis

Real Estate and Rental and Leasing
Real Estate
 Arden Realty, Inc.
*ProLogis
 Trizec Properties, Inc.

Rental and Leasing Services
 Blockbuster Inc.
 CIT Group Inc.
 Hanover Compressor Co.
 United Rentals, Inc.

Retail Trade

Building Material and Garden Equipment and Supplies Dealers
*Home Depot (The), Inc.
*Lowe's Companies, Inc.
Wesco International, Inc.

Clothing and Clothing Accessories Stores
Abercrombie & Fitch Co.
Aeropostale Inc.
Ann Taylor Stores Corp.
Chico's FAS, Inc.
Claire's Stores, Inc.
*Foot Locker, Inc.
Gap, Inc. (The)
*Limited Brands
Nordstrom, Inc.
Payless ShoeSource Inc.
Talbots (The), Inc.
*Tiffany & Co.
TJX Companies, Inc. (The)

Furniture and Consumer Electronics
Best Buy Co., Inc.
Circuit City Stores, Inc.
Haverty Furniture Companies
*Pier 1 Imports, Inc.
*RadioShack Corporation
Williams-Sonoma, Inc.

General Merchandise Stores
99 Cents Only Stores
Big Lots, Inc.
BJ's Wholesale Club, Inc.
Dillard's, Inc.
Dollar General Corporation
Family Dollar Stores, Inc.
Federated Department Stores
Kohl's Corporation
*May Department Stores Co.
*Neiman Marcus Group, Inc.
Penney (J.C.) Company, Inc.
Saks Incorporated
*Target Corporation
*Wal-Mart Stores, Inc.

Grocery Stores
*Albertson's, Inc.
Kroger Company (The)
*Ruddick Corporation
Safeway Inc.
*Winn-Dixie Stores, Inc.

Health and Personal Care Stores
Caremark Rx, Inc.
*CVS Corporation
*Longs Drug Stores Corporation
Medco Health Solutions, Inc.
*Omnicare, Inc.

*Rite Aid Corporation
*Walgreen Co.

Motor Vehicle and Parts Dealers
Advance Auto Parts, Inc.
Asbury Automotive Group, Inc.
AutoNation, Inc.
AutoZone, Inc.
Carmax Inc.
Group 1 Automotive, Inc.
Sonic Automotive, Inc.
United Auto Group, Inc.

Sporting Goods, Hobby, Book, and Music Stores and other
Barnes & Noble, Inc.
Borders Group, Inc.
*Michaels Stores, Inc.
*Office Depot, Inc.
*Sotheby's Holdings, Inc.
Toys R Us, Inc.

Transportation and Warehousing
AirTran Holdings, Inc.
Alaska Air Group, Inc.
AMR Corporation
*Atmos Energy Corporation
*Burlington Northern Santa Fe
Burlington Resources Inc.
CNF Inc.
Continental Airlines, Inc.
*CSX Corporation
*Delta Air Lines, Inc.
*El Paso Corporation
*FedEx Corporation
*GATX Corporation
Iron Mountain Incorporated
*Norfolk Southern Corporation
*OGE Energy Corp.
Overseas Shipholding Group
Plains All American Pipeline, L.P.
*Ryder System, Inc.
Southwest Airlines Co.
TEPPCO Partners, L.P.
*Tidewater Inc.
*Union Pacific Corp.
United Parcel Service, Inc.
Western Gas Resources, Inc.
Williams Companies, Inc. (The)

Utilities
Utilities - Electric
AES Corporation (The)
Allegheny Energy, Inc.
*ALLETE, INC.
*Alliant Energy Corporation
*Ameren Corporation
*American Electric Power Co.
*Aquila, Inc.
*Black Hills Corporation

Calpine Corporation
*CenterPoint Energy, Inc.
*Cinergy Corporation
*CMS Energy Corporation
*Consolidated Edison, Inc.
*Constellation Energy Group, Inc.
*Dominion Resources, Inc.
*DPL Inc.
*DTE Energy Co.
*Duke Energy Corporation
*Duquesne Light Holdings, Inc.
*Edison International
*Energy East Corporation
*Entergy Corporation
*Exelon Corporation
*FirstEnergy Corporation
*FPL Group, Inc.
*Great Plains Energy Incorporated
*Hawaiian Electric Industries, Inc.
*Idacorp, Inc.
*NiSource, Inc.
*Northeast Utilities
*NSTAR
*Pepco Holdings, Inc.
*PG&E Corporation
*Pinnacle West Capital Corp.
*PNM Resources, Inc.
*PPL Corporation
*Progress Energy, Inc.
*Public Service Enterprise Group
*Puget Energy, Inc.
  Reliant Energy, Inc.
*SCANA Corporation
*Sierra Pacific Resources
*Southern Company (The)
*TECO Energy, Inc.
*TXU Corporation
*Westar Energy, Inc.
*Wisconsin Energy Corporation
*WPS Resources Corporation
*Xcel Energy, Inc.
Utilities - Natural Gas
*AGL Resources Inc.
  Airgas Inc.

*Energen Corporation
*Equitable Resources, Inc.
*KeySpan Corporation
  Kinder Morgan Energy Partner, L.P.
*Kinder Morgan, Inc.
*National Fuel Gas Company
*NICOR Inc.
*Oneok Inc.
*Peoples Energy Corporation
*Piedmont Natural Gas Company
*Questar Corporation
*Sempra Energy
*UGI Corporation
*Vectren Corporation
*WGL Holdings, Inc.
Utilities - Water
*American States Water Co.
*Aqua America, Inc.
*California Water Service Group
Wholesale Trade
Wholesale Trade, Durable Goods
  American Axle & Manufacturing
  Arrow Electronics, Inc.
*Avnet, Inc.
  Ceridian Corporation
  Fisher Scientific International
*Genuine Parts Company
  Grainger (W.W.), Inc.
  Hughes Supply, Inc.
*Ikon Office Solutions, Inc.
  Ingram Micro Inc.
  Lear Corporation
  MSC Industrial Direct Co., Inc.
  National-Oilwell, Inc.
*Owens & Minor, Inc.
*Pitney Bowes Inc.
*Weyerhaeuser Company
Wholesale Trade, Nondurable Goods
  Cardinal Health, Inc.
*Crompton Corporation
*McKesson Corporation
*Supervalu Inc.
*Sysco Corporation

* **Designates companies offering dividend reinvestment plans.**

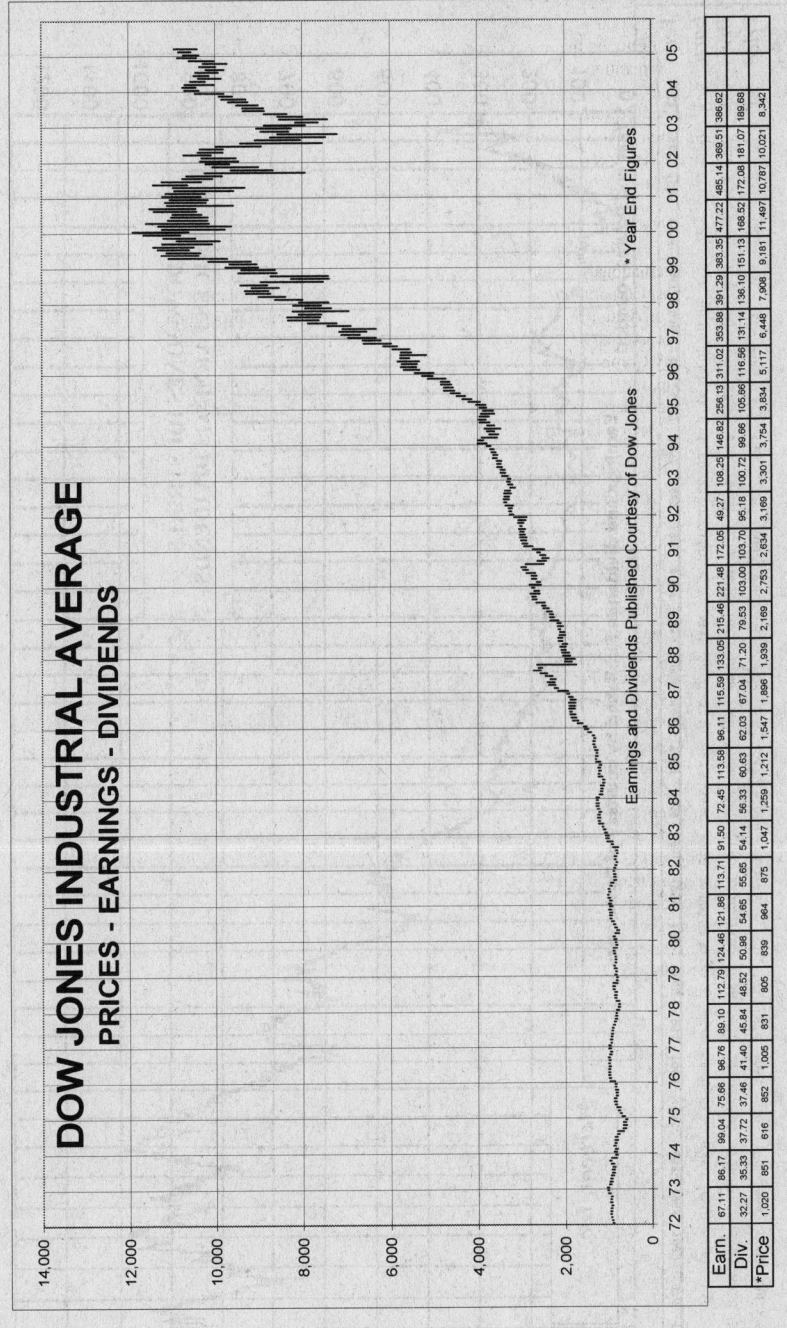

DOW JONES INDUSTRIAL AVERAGE
PRICES - EARNINGS - DIVIDENDS

Earnings and Dividends Published Courtesy of Dow Jones

* Year End Figures

25a

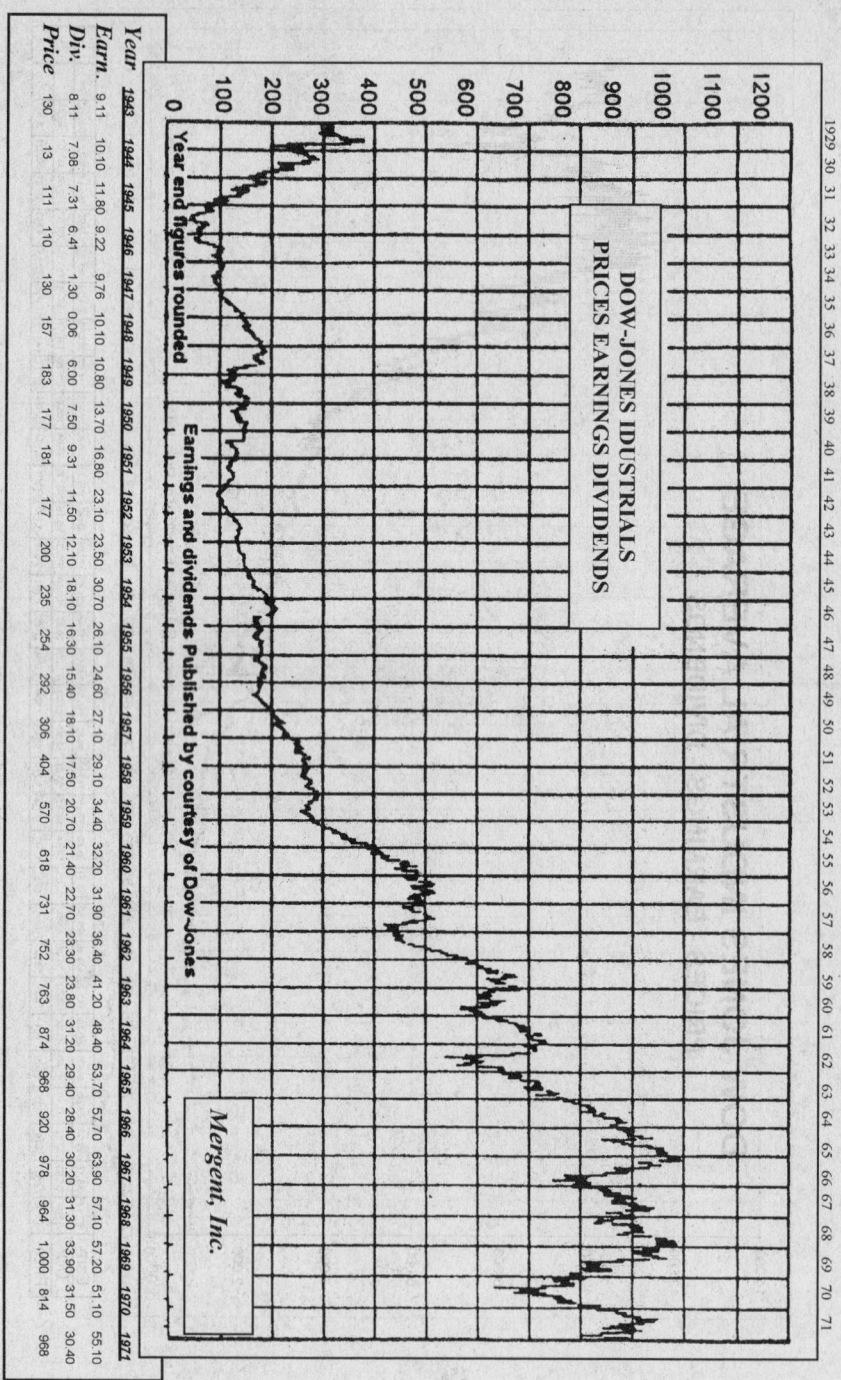

DOW-JONES IDUSTRIALS
PRICES EARNINGS DIVIDENDS

Year end figures rounded

Earnings and dividends Published by courtesy of Dow-Jones

Mergent, Inc.

Year	Earn.	Div.	Price
1943	9.11	8.11	130
1944	10.10	7.08	13
1945	11.80	7.31	111
1946	9.22	6.41	110
1947	9.76	1.30	130
1948	10.10	0.06	157
1949	10.80	6.00	183
1950	13.70	7.50	177
1951	16.80	9.31	181
1952	23.10	11.50	177
1953	23.50	12.10	200
1954	30.70	18.10	235
1955	26.10	16.30	254
1956	24.60	15.40	292
1957	27.10	18.10	306
1958	29.10	17.50	404
1959	34.40	20.70	570
1960	32.20	21.40	618
1961	31.90	22.70	731
1962	36.40	23.30	752
1963	41.20	23.80	763
1964	48.40	31.20	874
1965	53.70	29.40	968
1966	57.70	28.40	920
1967	63.90	30.20	978
1968	57.10	31.30	964
1969	57.20	33.90	1,000
1970	51.10	31.50	814
1971	55.10	30.40	968

26a

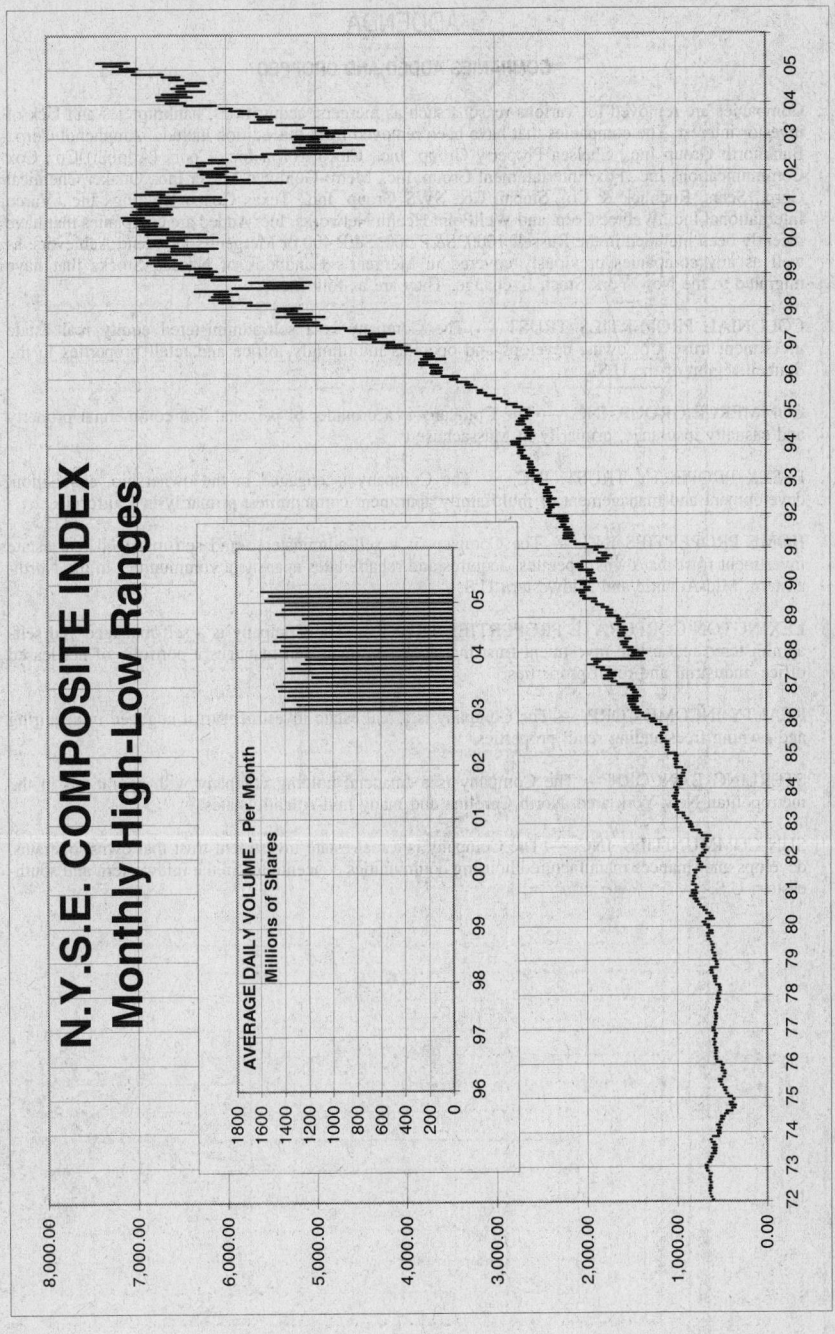

N.Y.S.E. COMPOSITE INDEX
Monthly High-Low Ranges

AVERAGE DAILY VOLUME - Per Month
Millions of Shares

ADDENDA

COMPANIES ADDED AND DROPPED

Companies are removed for various reasons such as mergers, acquisitions, bankruptcies and lack of investor interest. The companies that have been removed from this edition include: Amphenol Corp., Banknorth Group Inc., Chelsea Property Group, Inc., Cleco Corp., Inc., Coors (Adolph) Co., Cox Communications Inc., Fox Entertainment Group, Inc., Metro-Goldwyn-Mayer Inc., Quaker Chemical Corp., Sears, Roebuck & Co., Stepan Co., SWS Group, Inc., Texas Genco Holdings Inc., Varco International Inc., Wabtec Corp. and WellPoint Health Networks, Inc. Added are companies that have recently been included in the Russell 1000, S&P 500, S&P 400 or Mergent's Dividend Achievers, as well as any companies previously covered in Mergent's Handbook of Nasdaq Stocks that have migrated to the New York Stock Exchange. They are as follows:

COLONIAL PROPERTIES TRUST — The Company is a self-administered equity real estate investment trust. Co. owns, develops and operates multifamily, office and retail properties in the Sunbelt region of the U.S.

COMMERCE GROUP, INC. — The Company is a provider of personal and commercial property and casualty insurance, primarily in Massachusetts.

ESSEX PROPERTY TRUST, INC. — The Company is engaged in the ownership, acquisition, development and management of multifamily apartment communities, primarily in California.

HOME PROPERTIES INC. — The Company is a self-administered and self-managed real estate investment trust that owns, operates, acquires and rehabilitates apartment communities in the Northeastern, Mid-Atlantic and Midwestern U.S.

LEXINGTON CORPORATE PROPERTIES TRUST — The Company is a self-managed and self-administered real estate investment trust that acquires, owns and manages a portfolio of net leased office, industrial and retail properties.

REALTY INCOME CORP. — The Company is a real estate investment trust engaged in acquiring and owning freestanding retail properties.

STERLING BANCORP — The Company is a financial holding company with operations in the metropolitan New York area, North Carolina and many mid-Atlantic states.

SUN COMMUNITIES, INC. — The Company is a real estate investment trust that owns, operates, develops and finances manufactured housing communities concentrated in the midwestern and southeastern U.S.

ADDENDA (Continued)

RECENT AND PENDING STOCK DIVIDENDS AND SPLITS

Company	Amount	Ex-Div. Date	Date of Record	Payable Date
Berkley (W.R.) Corp.	50%	4/11/05	3/24/05	4/8/05
Clarcor Inc.	2-for-1	5/2/05	4/15/05	4/29/05
Coach, Inc.	2-for-1	4/5/05	3/21/05	4/4/05
Harris Corp.	100%	3/31/05	3/14/05	3/30/05
KB Home	100%	4/29/05	4/18/05	4/28/05
MGM Mirage	100%	5/19/05	5/4/05	5/18/05
Moody's Corp.	2-for-1	5/19/05	5/4/05	5/18/05
Peabody Energy Corp.	100%	3/31/05	3/16/05	3/30/05
Temple-Inland Inc.	100%	4/4/05	3/1/05	4/1/05
Timberland Co. (The)	2-for-1	5/3/05	4/14/05	5/2/05
Valley National Bancorp	5%	5/4/05	5/6/05	5/20/05

RECENT DIVIDEND CHANGES

Company	–Latest Dividend– Amount	Payable	Company	–Latest Dividend– Amount	Payable
Increased			**Increased**		
Abbott Laboratories	0.28Q	4/13/05	Peoples Energy Corp.	0.55Q	3/18/05
Air Products & Chemicals	0.32Q	3/30/05	Pepsi Bottling Group	0.08Q	6/8/05
AMB Property Corp.	0.44Q	4/1/05	Piedmont Natural Gas Co.	0.23Q	3/22/05
American Greetings Corp.	0.08Q	4/21/05	Quest Diagnostics, Inc.	0.18Q	4/4/05
Autoliv Inc.	0.30Q	5/2/05	Raytheon Co.	0.22Q	3/31/05
AvalonBay Communities	0.71Q	3/30/05	Realty Income Corp.	0.11Q	3/30/05
Blyth, Inc.	0.21S	4/27/05	Rockwell Automation	0.23Q	5/12/05
Cedar Fair, L.P.	0.46Q	4/1/05	Sempra Energy	0.29Q	3/22/05
Chubb Corp.	0.43Q	3/16/05	Sovereign Bancorp, Inc.	0.04Q	4/28/05
Colgate-Palmolive Co.	0.29Q	4/22/05	Sun Communities, Inc.	0.63Q	4/7/05
Deere & Co.	0.31Q	3/29/05	Sunoco, Inc.	0.40Q	5/6/05
Developers Divers. Rlty.	0.54Q	3/17/05	Synovus Financial Corp.	0.18Q	3/22/05
EastGroup Properties, Inc.	0.49Q	3/22/05	Tanger Factory Outlet	0.32Q	4/27/05
Essex Property Trust, Inc.	0.81Q	3/29/05	The Gap, Inc.	0.05Q	4/1/05
First American Corp.	0.18Q	3/29/05	TJX Companies, Inc.	0.06Q	5/10/05
First Data Corp.	0.06Q	3/30/05	United Domin. Rlty. Tr.	0.30Q	4/13/05
Gallagher (Arthur J.) & Co.	0.28Q	3/29/05	Verizon Communications	0.41Q	4/6/05
General Dynamics Corp.	0.40Q	4/5/05	WGL Holdings, Inc.	0.33Q	4/6/05
Hasbro, Inc.	0.09Q	4/28/05	Wrigley (William) Jr. Co.	0.28Q	4/13/05
HCA, Inc.	0.15Q	4/27/05	Zenith Nat. Insurance	0.33Q	4/27/05
Host Marriott Corp.	0.08Q	3/29/05			
Hughes Supply Inc.	0.09Q	4/27/05	**Decreased**		
iStar Financial Inc.	0.73Q	4/13/05	Annaly Mort. Mgmt.	0.45Q	3/30/05
Jefferson-Pilot Corp.	0.42Q	5/18/05	Camden Property Trust	0.22Q	3/29/05
Masco Corp.	0.20Q	4/6/05	Delphi Corp.	0.03Q	3/31/05
MBIA Inc.	0.28Q	3/23/05	Fannie Mae	0.26Q	1/27/05
Mills Corp.	0.63Q	4/20/05	Federal Signal Corp.	0.06Q	3/11/05
MSC Industrial Direct Co.	0.12Q	3/31/05	Forest City Enterprises	0.10Q	5/27/05
Nationwide Fin. Serv.	0.19Q	3/30/05	Franklin Resources, Inc.	0.10Q	3/29/05
Northrop Grumman Corp.	0.26Q	5/26/05			

ADDENDA (Continued)

RECENT AND PENDING NAME CHANGES

Old	New
Anthem, Inc.	WellPoint, Inc.
Networks Associates, Inc.	McAfee Inc.
Reynolds (R.J.) Tobacco Holdings Inc.	Reynolds American Inc.

LATEST DEVELOPMENTS

CHEVRONTEXACO CORP. – On Apr 4 2005, Co. announced that it has entered into an agreement to acquire Unocal Corporation for approximately $18.00 billion, including the assumption of $1.60 billion of debt.

INTERNATIONAL BUSINESS MACHINES CORP. – On Mar 14 2005, Co. announced that it has entered into a definitive agreement to acquire Ascential Software for approximately $1.10 billion in cash. The transaction is expected to close in the second quarter of 2005, subject to shareholder and regulatory approvals.

LIBERTY MEDIA CORP. – On Mar 15 2005, Co. announced that it plans to spin-off to its shareholders a separate company comprised of its ownership interests in Ascent Media Group, Inc. and Discovery Communications, Inc. The transaction, which is expected to be completed during the second quarter of 2005, will create a new publicly-traded company called Discovery Holding Company.

MEDICIS PHARMACEUTICAL CORP. – On Mar 21 2005, Co. entered into a definitive agreement to acquire Inamed Corporation for approximately $2.80 billion. The transaction is expected to be completed by the end of 2005, subject to shareholder and regulatory approvals.

SEARS, ROEBUCK & CO. – On Mar 24 2005, Kmart Holding Corp. completed its acquisition of Co. for approximately $12.30 billion. On Mar 28 2005, the company was renamed Sears Holding Corporation and its common stock began trading on the Nasdaq National Market under the symbol SHLD.

SUNGARD DATA SYSTEMS INC – On Mar 28 2005, Co. announced that it has entered into a definitive agreement to be acquired by a consortium of private equity firms for approximately $10.80 billion and the assumption of about $500.0 million of debt. The acquiring consortium is being led by Silver Lake Partners and includes Bain Capital, The Blackstone Group, Goldman Sachs Capital Partners, Kohlberg Kravis Roberts & Co. L.P., Providence Equity Partners and Texas Pacific Group.

The 2005 Common Dividend Achievers

Companies listed below qualified for the 2005 Edition of Mergent's Dividend Achievers.
Also shown are total numbers of consecutive years of dividend growth.

Company Name	Years of Growth	Company Name	Years of Growth
3M Co.	46	Community Bank System, Inc.	13
Abbott Laboratories	32	ConAgra Foods, Inc.	27
ABM Industries, Inc.	40	Consolidated Edison, Inc.	30
AFLAC Inc.	22	Cullen/Frost Bankers, Inc.	11
Air Products & Chemicals, Inc.	22	Danaher Corp.	11
Albemarle Corp.	10	Diebold, Inc.	51
Alberto-Culver Co.	20	Donnelley (R.R.) & Sons Co.	35
Allstate Corp.	11	Doral Financial Corp.	15
ALLTEL Corp.	44	Dover Corp.	49
Altria Group Inc.	39	Duke Realty Corp.	11
Ambac Financial Group, Inc.	13	EastGroup Properties, Inc.	12
American International Group Inc.	19	Eaton Vance Corp.	23
American States Water Co.	51	Ecolab, Inc.	12
AmSouth Bancorporation	34	Emerson Electric Co.	48
Anheuser-Busch Cos., Inc.	30	Energen Corp.	22
AptarGroup Inc.	11	Essex Property Trust, Inc.	10
Aqua America Inc.	13	Exxon Mobil Corp.	22
Archer Daniels Midland Co.	30	F.N.B. Corp.	20
Atmos Energy Corp.	17	Family Dollar Stores, Inc.	28
Automatic Data Processing Inc.	29	Fannie Mae	19
Avery Dennison Corp.	29	Federal Realty Investment Trust	37
Avon Products, Inc.	14	Fidelity National Financial, Inc.	17
BancorpSouth Inc.	18	First Commonwealth Financial	17
Bandag, Inc.	28	Forest City Enterprises, Inc.	10
Bank of America Corp.	27	Franklin Resources, Inc.	15
Bank of Hawaii Corp.	27	Freddie Mac	14
Banknorth Group Inc.	10	Fuller (H.B.) Company	37
Banta Corporation	26	Gallagher (Arthur J.) & Co.	20
Bard (C.R.), Inc.	33	Gannett Co., Inc.	33
BB&T Corp.	33	General Dynamics Corp.	13
Beckman Coulter, Inc.	13	General Electric Co.	29
Becton, Dickinson and Co.	32	General Growth Properties, Inc.	11
Bemis, Inc.	21	Genuine Parts Co.	48
Black Hills Corporation	33	Golden West Financial Corp.	21
Brady Corp.	20	Grainger (W.W.) Inc.	33
Briggs & Stratton Corp.	13	Granite Construction Inc.	10
Brown & Brown, Inc.	11	Harley-Davidson, Inc.	11
Brown-Forman Corp.	20	Harsco Corp.	10
California Water Service Group	37	Haverty Furniture Cos., Inc.	34
Carlisle Companies Inc.	28	Health Care Property Investors	19
Caterpillar Inc.	11	Healthcare Realty Trust, Inc.	11
CBL & Associates Properties, Inc.	10	Helmerich & Payne, Inc.	28
Cedar Fair, L.P.	17	Hershey Foods Corp.	30
CenturyTel, Inc.	31	Hibernia Corp.	11
ChevronTexaco Corp.	17	Hilb Rogal & Hobbs Co.	18
Chittenden Corp.	12	Hillenbrand Industries, Inc.	34
Chubb Corp.	40	HNI Corp.	16
Citigroup Inc.	18	Holly Corp.	11
City National Corp.	10	Home Depot, Inc.	17
Clarcor Inc.	24	Home Properties Inc.	10
Clorox Co.	28	Hormel Foods Corp.	37
Coca-Cola Co.	42	Hudson United Bancorp	14
Colgate-Palmolive Co.	42	Illinois Tool Works, Inc.	42
Colonial Properties Trust	10	Irwin Financial Corp.	15
Comerica, Inc.	21	Jefferson-Pilot Corp.	37
Commerce Bancorp, Inc.	13	Johnson & Johnson	42
Commerce Group, Inc.	10	Johnson Controls Inc.	29
Commercial Net Lease Realty, Inc.	15	KeyCorp	25

The 2005 Common Dividend Achievers (Cont.)

Company Name	Years of Growth	Company Name	Years of Growth
Kimberly-Clark Corp.	30	Regions Financial Corp.	33
Kimco Realty Corp.	12	RLI Corp.	28
La-Z-Boy Inc.	23	Rohm & Haas Co.	27
Legg Mason, Inc.	21	Roper Industries, Inc.	12
Leggett & Platt, Inc.	33	RPM International Inc.	31
Lexington Corporate Properties Trust	10	Sara Lee Corp.	28
Liberty Property Trust	10	SBC Communications, Inc.	20
Lilly (Eli) & Co.	37	ServiceMaster Co.	34
Lincoln National Corp.	21	Sherwin-Williams Co.	25
Lowe's Cos., Inc.	43	Shurgard Storage Centers, Inc.	10
M & T Bank Corp.	24	SLM Corp.	24
Macerich Co.	10	Smith (A.O.) Corp	12
Marsh & McLennan Cos., Inc.	43	Sonoco Products Co.	21
Marshall & Ilsley Corp.	32	Stanley Works	37
Martin Marietta Materials, Inc.	10	State Street Corp.	24
Masco Corp.	46	Sterling Bancorp	10
May Department Stores Co.	29	Stryker Corp.	12
MBIA Inc.	17	Sun Communities, Inc.	10
MBNA Corp.	13	SunTrust Banks, Inc.	19
McCormick & Co., Inc.	18	Superior Industries International, Inc.	19
McDonald's Corp.	28	Supervalu Inc.	32
McGraw-Hill Cos., Inc.	31	Synovus Financial Corp.	28
MDU Resources Group Inc.	14	Sysco Corp.	28
Media General, Inc.	10	Talbots, Inc.	10
Medtronic, Inc.	27	Tanger Factory Outlet Centers, Inc.	11
Merck & Co., Inc.	21	Target Corp.	33
Mercury General Corp.	18	TCF Financial Corp.	13
Meredith Corp.	11	Teleflex Incorporated	27
Mine Safety Appliances Co.	34	Tennant Co.	32
Myers Industries Inc.	28	TEPPCO Partners, L.P.	12
NACCO Industries Inc.	21	The St Paul Travelers Companies Inc.	18
National City Corp.	12	Tootsie Roll Industries Inc.	41
National Fuel Gas Co.	33	Transatlantic Holdings, Inc.	14
NICOR Inc.	17	UGI Corp.	17
North Fork Bancorporation, Inc.	10	United Dominion Realty Trust, Inc.	19
Nucor Corp.	32	United Technologies Corp.	11
Nuveen Investments Inc.	12	Universal Corp.	34
Old National Bancorp	21	Universal Health Realty Income Trust	17
Old Republic International Corp.	23	Valley National Bancorp	13
Parker-Hannifin Corp.	48	Valspar Corp.	26
Pentair, Inc.	28	Vectren Corp.	29
Peoples Energy Corp.	21	VF Corp.	32
PepsiCo Inc.	33	Vulcan Materials Co.	12
Pfizer Inc.	37	Walgreen Co.	29
Piedmont Natural Gas Co., Inc.	25	Wal-Mart Stores, Inc.	29
Pier 1 Imports Inc.	13	Washington Mutual Inc.	15
Pinnacle West Capital Corp.	11	Washington Real Estate Investment Tr.	43
Pitney Bowes, Inc.	21	Webster Financial Corp.	12
PPG Industries, Inc.	33	Weingarten Realty Investors	16
Praxair, Inc.	12	Wells Fargo & Co.	17
Procter & Gamble Co.	51	West Pharmaceutical Services, Inc.	12
Progress Energy, Inc.	16	WGL Holdings, Inc.	28
Progressive Corp.	35	Wiley (John) & Sons Inc.	11
Prologis	10	Wilmington Trust Corp.	23
Protective Life Corp.	15	Wolverine World Wide, Inc.	11
Questar Corp..	25	WPS Resources Corp.	46
Realty Income Corp.	10	Wrigley (William) Jr. Co.	24
Regency Centers Corp.	10		

j

For more information on these Companies please see the 2005 Spring Dividend Achievers

ABBOTT LABORATORIES

Exchange	Symbol	Price	52Wk Range	Yield	P/E	Div Acheiver
NYS	ABT	$46.62 (3/31/2005)	47.96-37.65	2.36	22.63	32 Years

*7 Year Price Score 88.09 ***NYSE Composite Index=100** ***12 Month Price Score 99.32**

TRADING VOLUME (thousand shares)

Interim Earnings (Per Share)

Qtr.	Mar	Jun	Sep	Dec
2001	(0.14)	0.34	0.40	0.39
2002	0.54	0.38	0.46	0.40
2003	0.51	0.16	0.48	0.60
2004	0.52	0.40	0.51	0.62

Interim Dividends (Per Share)

Amt	Decl	Ex	Rec	Pay
0.26Q	6/11/2004	7/13/2004	7/15/2004	8/15/2004
0.26Q	9/10/2004	10/13/2004	10/15/2004	11/15/2004
0.26Q	12/10/2004	1/12/2005	1/14/2005	2/15/2005
0.275Q	2/18/2005	4/13/2005	4/15/2005	5/15/2005

Indicated Div: $1.10 (Div. Reinv. Plan)

Valuation Analysis

Forecast P/E	18.73	No of Institutions
	(4/7/2005)	1029
Market Cap	$72.7 Billion	Shares
Book Value	14.3 Billion	959,808,128
Price/Book	5.08	% Held
Price/Sales	3.70	61.57

Business Summary: Pharmaceuticals (MIC: 9.1 SIC: 834 NAIC: 25412)

Abbott Laboratories' principal business is the discovery, development, manufacture, and sale of health care products. Co. has five reportable revenue segments. The Pharmaceutical Products segment includes a line of adult and pediatric pharmaceuticals. The Diagnostic Products segment includes diagnostic systems and tests. The Hospital Products segment includes acute care injectable drugs and systems. The Ross Products segment includes a line of pediatric and adult nutritionals. The International segment includes products marketed and manufactured primarily outside of the U.S.

Recent Developments: For the year ended Dec 31 2004, net income increased 17.5% to $3,235,851 thousand from net income of $2,753,233 thousand a year earlier. Revenues were $19,680,016 thousand, up 13.9% from $17,280,333 thousand the year before. Operating income was $3,898,320 thousand versus an income of $2,974,012 thousand in the prior year, an increase of 31.1%. Total direct expense was $8,884,157 thousand versus $7,774,239 thousand in the prior year, an increase of 14.3%. Total indirect expense was $6,897,539 thousand versus $6,532,082 thousand in the prior year, an increase of 5.6%.

Prospects: Co. is continuing to see strong U.S. pharmaceutical sales of HUMIRA®, TriCor®, Omnicef® and Mobic®. In the U.S., Co. estimates that HUMIRA represents approximately 30.0% of new prescriptions within the self-injectable market for rheumatoid arthritis and expects worldwide sales of HUMIRA for 2005 to exceed $1.30 billion. In 2004, Co. submitted numerous new products for regulatory approval, which should provide for strong future growth. Co. expects to see the effects of these approvals and launches throughout 2005 and into 2006. For full-year 2005, Co. expects sales growth of 10.0% to 12.0% and earnings in the range of $2.47 to $2.53 per share, before one-time items and accounting changes.

Financial Data

(US$ in Thousands)	12/31/2004	12/31/2003	12/31/2002	12/31/2001	12/31/2000	12/31/1999	12/31/1998	12/31/1997
Earnings Per Share	2.06	1.75	1.78	0.99	1.78	1.57	1.51	1.34
Cash Flow Per Share	2.75	2.40	2.68	2.30	2.00	1.91	1.79	1.71
Tang Book Value Per Share	2.22	2.90	1.93	1.14	4.54	3.78	2.88	2.54
Dividends Per Share	1.025	0.970	0.915	0.820	0.740	0.660	0.585	0.525
Dividend Payout %	49.76	55.43	51.40	82.83	41.57	42.04	38.74	39.18
Income Statement								
Total Revenue	19,680,016	19,680,561	17,684,663	16,285,246	13,745,916	13,177,625	12,477,845	11,883,462
EBITDA	5,563,387	5,154,531	5,055,978	3,285,925	4,667,059	4,306,659	4,128,960	3,764,502
Depn & Amortn	1,288,700	1,273,991	1,177,345	1,168,018	827,431	828,006	784,243	727,754
Income Before Taxes	4,125,600	3,734,417	3,673,413	1,883,148	3,816,407	3,396,888	3,240,599	2,949,946
Income Taxes	949,764	981,184	879,710	332,758	1,030,430	951,129	907,368	855,484
Net Income	3,235,851	2,753,233	2,793,703	1,550,390	2,785,977	2,445,759	2,333,231	2,094,462
Average Shares	1,570,611	1,571,869	1,573,293	1,565,963	1,565,579	1,557,655	1,545,658	1,561,462
Balance Sheet								
Current Assets	10,734,485	10,290,415	9,121,772	8,419,189	7,376,241	6,419,754	5,553,136	5,038,208
Total Assets	28,767,494	26,715,342	24,259,102	23,296,453	15,283,254	14,471,044	13,216,213	12,061,068
Current Liabilities	6,825,644	7,639,535	7,002,202	7,926,817	4,297,540	4,516,711	4,962,126	5,034,468
Long-Term Obligations	4,787,934	3,452,329	4,273,973	4,335,493	1,076,368	1,336,789	1,339,694	937,983
Total Liabilities	14,441,711	13,643,084	13,594,549	14,236,991	6,712,348	7,043,449	7,502,552	7,062,391
Stockholders' Equity	14,325,783	13,072,258	10,664,553	9,059,432	8,570,906	7,427,595	5,713,661	4,998,677
Shares Outstanding	1,560,023	1,564,517	1,563,068	1,554,530	1,545,934	1,547,019	1,516,063	1,528,188
Statistical Record								
Return on Assets %	11.63	10.80	11.75	8.04	18.68	17.67	18.46	18.07
Return on Equity %	23.56	23.20	28.33	17.59	34.73	37.22	43.56	42.66
EBITDA Margin %	28.27	26.19	28.59	20.18	33.95	32.68	33.09	31.68
Net Margin %	16.44	13.99	15.80	9.52	20.27	18.56	18.70	17.63
Asset Turnover	0.71	0.77	0.74	0.84	0.92	0.95	0.99	1.03
Current Ratio	1.57	1.35	1.30	1.06	1.72	1.42	1.12	1.00
Debt to Equity	0.33	0.26	0.40	0.48	0.13	0.18	0.23	0.19
Price Range	46.99-36.81	44.10-32.16	53.97-29.00	53.10-39.34	52.15-27.71	49.51-31.16	46.53-30.63	32.09-23.56
P/E Ratio	22.81-17.87	25.20-18.38	30.32-16.29	53.64-39.74	29.30-15.57	31.54-19.85	30.82-20.29	23.95-17.58
Average Yield %	2.47	2.51	2.13	1.75	1.90	1.62	1.53	1.82

Address: 100 Abbott Park Road, Abbott Park, IL 60064-6400	**Web Site:** www.abbott.com	**Auditors:** Deloitte & Touche LLP	
Telephone: (847) 937 6100	**Officers:** Miles D. White - Chmn., C.E.O. Richard A. Gonzalez - Pres., C.O.O., Medical Products	**Investor Contact:** 847-937-3923	
Fax: (847) 937 1511		**Transfer Agents:** EquiServe, Providence, RI	

ABERCROMBIE & FITCH CO.

Exchange	Symbol	Price	52Wk Range	Yield	P/E
NYS	ANF	$57.24 (3/31/2005)	57.50-28.00	0.87	26.87

*7 Year Price Score 118.50 *NYSE Composite Index=100 *12 Month Price Score 124.76

TRADING VOLUME (thousand shares)

Interim Earnings (Per Share)

Qtr.	Apr	Jul	Oct	Jan
2001-02	0.20	0.24	0.43	0.78
2002-03	0.23	0.31	0.48	0.93
2003-04	0.26	0.35	0.51	0.95
2004-05	0.31	0.44	0.42	...

Interim Dividends (Per Share)

Amt	Decl	Ex	Rec	Pay
0.125Q	5/20/2004	5/27/2004	6/1/2004	6/22/2004
0.125Q	7/29/2004	8/27/2004	8/31/2004	9/21/2004
0.125Q	10/28/2004	11/26/2004	11/30/2004	12/21/2004
0.125Q	2/15/2005	2/25/2005	3/1/2005	3/22/2005

Indicated Div: $0.50

Valuation Analysis

Forecast P/E	19.59	No of Institutions
	(4/7/2005)	278
Market Cap	$5.2 Billion	Shares
Book Value	791.5 Million	82,948,632
Price/Book	6.55	% Held
Price/Sales	2.73	95.18

Business Summary: Retail - Apparel and Accessory Stores (MIC: 5.8 SIC: 651 NAIC: 48140)

Abercrombie & Fitch is a specialty retailer of casual apparel, personal care products and other accessories for men, women and children. Co. sells merchandise under the Abercrombie & Fitch and Abercrombie trade names through its retail stores, a catalogue, a magazine/catalogue and a web site. Retail activities are also conducted under the Hollister trade name through retail stores and a lifestyle web site. Co. targets its products to men and women approximately 15 to 50 years of age and kids about seven to 14 years of age. As of Jan 31 2004, Co. operated 700 stores, including 171 Abercrombie locations and 172 Hollister stores.

Recent Developments: For the quarter ended Oct 30 2004, net income decreased 20.5% to $40,091 thousand from net income of $50,457 thousand in the year-earlier quarter. Revenues were $520,724 thousand, up 17.0% from $444,979 thousand in the prior-year quarter. Operating income was $62,277 thousand versus an income of $81,450 thousand in the prior-year quarter, a decrease of 23.5%. Total indirect expense was $164,559 thousand versus $102,415 thousand in the prior-year period, an increase of 60.7%.

Prospects: Looking ahead, Co. plans to increase gross square footage by about 9.0% by the end of fiscal 2005 primarily through opening flagship Abercrombie & Fitch stores in New York, NY, Los Angeles, CA and through the addition of about 55 new Hollister stores. In addition, Co. announced it would begin its international expansion with five stores in Canada in 2005, with the development of RUEHL proceeding at a measured pace. Co. added that it has established a European subsidiary and expects to rollout Abercrombie & Fitch stores in Europe for 2006. Assuming net sales growth of about 20.0% in 2005, Co. expects net income per share for 2005 to be in the range of $2.80 to $3.00 per diluted share.

Financial Data

(US$ in Thousands)	9 Mos	6 Mos	3 Mos	01/31/2004	02/01/2003	02/02/2002	02/03/2001	01/29/2000
Earnings Per Share	2.13	2.21	2.12	2.06	1.94	1.65	1.55	1.39
Cash Flow Per Share	3.91	3.59	3.55	2.92	2.99	2.36	1.49	1.50
Tang Book Value Per Share	8.74	9.77	9.37	9.21	7.71	6.02	4.28	3.05
Dividends Per Share	0.375	0.250	0.125	...	...	...	...	...
Dividend Payout %	17.64	11.29	5.89	...	...	...	...	...
Income Statement								
Total Revenue	1,333,999	813,276	411,930	1,707,810	1,595,757	1,364,853	1,237,604	1,042,056
EBITDA	234,131	153,416	66,606	398,238	369,542	312,613	284,383	269,785
Depn & Amortn	55,828	37,388	19,285	66,604	56,925	41,155	30,731	27,721
Income Before Taxes	182,222	118,371	48,306	335,342	316,385	276,522	261,453	249,334
Income Taxes	69,600	45,840	18,630	130,240	121,450	107,850	103,320	99,730
Net Income	112,622	72,531	29,676	205,102	194,935	168,672	158,133	149,604
Average Shares	95,351	97,590	96,872	99,580	100,631	102,524	102,156	107,641
Balance Sheet								
Current Assets	736,398	855,203	737,891	752,655	601,156	405,195	303,562	300,217
Total Assets	1,228,401	1,315,901	1,188,541	1,199,163	994,822	770,546	587,516	458,166
Current Liabilities	376,163	326,817	250,510	280,002	211,470	163,579	154,562	137,866
Total Liabilities	436,938	379,807	300,261	327,906	245,295	175,112	164,816	147,072
Stockholders' Equity	791,463	936,094	888,280	871,257	749,527	595,434	422,700	311,094
Shares Outstanding	90,555	95,773	94,788	94,607	97,268	98,900	98,796	102,000
Statistical Record								
Return on Assets %	17.37	18.23	18.98	18.75	22.15	24.91	29.76	38.60
Return on Equity %	25.73	25.40	25.01	25.38	29.07	33.22	42.40	60.34
EBITDA Margin %	17.55	18.86	16.17	23.32	23.16	22.90	22.98	25.89
Net Margin %	8.44	8.92	7.20	12.01	12.22	12.36	12.78	14.36
Asset Turnover	1.59	1.53	1.61	1.56	1.81	2.02	2.33	2.69
Current Ratio	1.96	2.62	2.95	2.69	2.84	2.48	1.96	2.18
Price Range	39.18-23.49	39.12-23.49	36.10-23.49	33.11-23.49	33.30-15.57	45.98-16.60	30.18-8.19	50.13-20.19
P/E Ratio	18.39-11.03	17.70-10.63	17.03-11.08	16.07-11.40	17.16-8.03	27.87-10.06	19.47-5.28	36.06-14.52
Average Yield %	1.18	0.81	0.43	...	...	...	...	...

Address: 6301 Fitch Path, New Albany, OH 43054	Web Site: www.abercrombie.com	Auditors: PricewaterhouseCoopers LLP
Telephone: (614) 283-6500	Officers: Michael S. Jeffries - Chmn., C.E.O. Robert S. Singer - Pres., C.O.O.	Investor Contact: 614-283-6751

2

ABM INDUSTRIES, INC.

Exchange	Symbol	Price	52Wk Range	Yield	P/E	Div Acheiver
NYS	ABM	$19.23 (3/31/2005)	22.39-16.92	2.18	30.52	40 Years

*7 Year Price Score 106.21 *NYSE Composite Index=100 ***12 Month Price Score 91.38**

TRADING VOLUME (thousand shares)

Interim Earnings (Per Share)

Qtr.	Jan	Apr	Jul	Oct
2001-02	0.16	0.27	0.25	0.24
2002-03	0.09	0.20	0.23	1.29
2003-04	0.14	0.14	0.27	0.06
2004-05	0.16	...	...	...

Interim Dividends (Per Share)

Amt	Decl	Ex	Rec	Pay
0.10Q	6/8/2004	7/8/2004	7/12/2004	8/2/2004
0.10Q	9/8/2004	10/6/2004	10/11/2004	11/1/2004
0.105Q	12/13/2004	1/12/2005	1/14/2005	2/7/2005
0.105Q	3/7/2005	4/6/2005	4/8/2005	5/2/2005
			Indicated Div: $0.42	

Valuation Analysis

Forecast P/E	19.34	No of Institutions
	(4/7/2005)	135
Market Cap	$954.3 Million	Shares
Book Value	457.5 Million	33,560,124
Price/Book	2.09	% Held
Price/Sales	0.38	67.49

Business Summary: Miscellaneous Business Services (MIC: 12.8 SIC: 349 NAIC: 38210)

ABM Industries and its subsidiaries provide janitorial, parking, security, engineering, lighting and mechanical services for commercial, industrial, institutional and retail facilities throughout the United States and in British Columbia, Canada. At Oct 31 2004, Co.'s seven business segments were Janitorial, Parking, Security, Engineering, Lighting, Mechanical, and Facility Services. Co.'s customer base, includes, but is not limited to, commercial office buildings, industrial plants, financial institutions, retail stores, shopping centers, warehouses, airports, health and educational facilities, stadiums and arenas, government buildings, apartment complexes, and theme parks.

Recent Developments: For the quarter ended Jan 31 2005, net income increased 25.1% to $7,924 thousand from net income of $6,335 thousand in the year-earlier quarter. Revenues were $647,363 thousand, up 13.4% from $570,823 thousand the year before. Total indirect expense was $634,347 thousand versus $560,720 thousand in the prior-year quarter, an increase of 13.1%. Comparisons were made with restated prior-year figures.

Prospects: On Dec 22 2004, Co. announced that it has acquired the business of Colin Service Systems, Inc., a facility services company based in New York, for about $13.6 million in cash. Colin Service, with annual revenues exceeding $70.0 million, is a provider of onsite management, commercial office cleaning, specialty snow removal, and engineering services. Co. expects the acquisition of Colin Service will enhance its market position in the Northeast, notably throughout New Jersey, Washington, D.C., and Long Island. Co. stated that it will continue to focus on strategic acquisitions that will expand its market share in major metropolitan areas and strengthen its presence in key customer segments.

Financial Data
(US$ in Thousands)	3 Mos	10/31/2004	10/31/2003	10/31/2002	10/31/2001	10/31/2000	10/31/1999	10/31/1998
Earnings Per Share	0.63	0.61	1.81	0.92	0.65	0.93	0.82	0.72
Cash Flow Per Share	1.32	0.69	1.23	2.26	1.38	0.42	0.80	0.76
Tang Book Value Per Share	3.94	3.95	5.01	4.46	5.08	4.48	3.82	3.12
Dividends Per Share	0.405	0.400	0.380	0.360	0.330	0.310	0.280	0.240
Dividend Payout %	64.44	65.57	20.99	39.13	50.77	33.51	33.94	33.33
Income Statement								
Total Revenue	647,363	2,416,223	2,262,476	2,191,957	1,950,038	1,807,557	1,629,716	1,501,827
EBITDA	17,570	64,029	69,681	84,510	79,273	96,217	87,930	77,101
Depn & Amortn	4,806	17,667	14,829	15,182	26,328	23,524	20,698	19,593
Income Before Taxes	12,764	46,362	54,852	69,328	52,945	72,693	67,232	57,508
Income Taxes	4,840	15,889	18,454	22,600	20,119	28,350	27,565	23,578
Net Income	7,924	30,473	90,458	46,728	32,826	44,343	39,667	33,930
Average Shares	50,402	50,064	50,004	51,015	50,020	47,418	47,496	46,322
Balance Sheet								
Current Assets	504,568	486,088	500,648	437,785	465,541	436,819	367,589	324,308
Total Assets	874,904	842,524	795,983	704,939	683,100	641,985	563,384	501,363
Current Liabilities	269,432	254,428	256,691	227,090	235,999	212,620	183,310	157,824
Long-Term Obligations	...	...	...	...	942	36,811	28,903	33,720
Total Liabilities	417,390	400,363	351,947	318,269	321,923	319,276	280,033	257,429
Stockholders' Equity	457,514	442,161	444,036	386,670	361,177	316,309	276,951	237,534
Shares Outstanding	49,624	48,707	48,367	48,997	48,778	45,998	44,814	43,202
Statistical Record								
Return on Assets %	3.75	3.71	12.05	6.73	4.95	7.34	7.45	7.01
Return on Equity %	6.88	6.86	21.78	12.50	9.69	14.91	15.42	15.59
EBITDA Margin %	2.71	2.65	3.08	3.86	4.07	5.32	5.40	5.13
Net Margin %	1.22	1.26	4.00	2.13	1.68	2.45	2.43	2.26
Asset Turnover	2.99	2.94	3.01	3.16	2.94	2.99	3.06	3.10
Current Ratio	1.87	1.91	1.95	1.93	1.97	2.05	2.01	2.05
Debt to Equity	...	...	...	...	N.M.	0.12	0.10	0.14
Price Range	22.39-16.92	20.87-15.25	16.44-12.72	19.43-13.05	19.10-12.50	13.97-9.69	17.31-11.00	18.41-12.63
P/E Ratio	35.54-26.86	34.21-25.00	9.08-7.03	21.12-14.18	29.38-19.23	15.02-10.42	21.11-13.41	25.56-17.53
Average Yield %	2.13	2.20	2.56	2.23	2.08	2.57	1.94	1.62

Address: 160 Pacific Avenue, Suite 222, San Francisco, CA 94111 Telephone: (415) 733 4000 Fax: (415) 733 5123	Web Site: www.abm.com Officers: Martin H. Mandles - Chmn., Chief Admin. Officer Henrik C. Slipsager - Pres., C.E.O.	Auditors: KPMG LLP Transfer Agents: Mellon Investor Services LLC, San Francisco, CA

ACE, LTD.

Exchange	Symbol	Price	52Wk Range	Yield	P/E
NYS	ACE	$41.27 (3/31/2005)	47.25-33.15	2.04	10.78

*7 Year Price Score 105.48 *NYSE Composite Index=100 *12 Month Price Score 100.11

Interim Earnings (Per Share)

Qtr.	Mar	Jun	Sep	Dec
2001	----------------------(0.74)--------------------			
2002	----------------------0.19--------------------			
2003	0.90	1.32	1.22	1.57
2004	1.53	1.41	(0.05)	0.94

Interim Dividends (Per Share)

Amt	Decl	Ex	Rec	Pay
0.21Q	5/27/2004	6/28/2004	6/30/2004	7/14/2004
0.21Q	8/13/2004	9/28/2004	9/30/2004	10/14/2004
0.21Q	11/18/2004	12/29/2004	12/31/2004	1/14/2005
0.21Q	2/24/2005	3/29/2005	3/31/2005	4/14/2005
		Indicated Div: $0.84		

Valuation Analysis

Forecast P/E	7.07	No of Institutions	
	(4/7/2005)	N/A	
Market Cap	$11.7 Billion	Shares	
Book Value	9.8 Billion	N/A	
Price/Book	1.19	% Held	
Price/Sales	0.95	N/A	

TRADING VOLUME (thousand shares)

Business Summary: Insurance (MIC: 8.2 SIC: 351 NAIC: 24130)

ACE provides a range of insurance and reinsurance products throughout the U.S. and almost 50 other countries. Co. operates through four business segments: Insurance–North American, which includes the operations of ACE USA, ACE Canada and ACE Bermuda; Insurance–Overseas General, which consists of ACE International, Co.'s network of indigenous insurance operations, and the insurance operations of ACE Global Markets; Global Reinsurance, which markets its reinsurance products under ACE Tempest Re and ACE Life Re; and Financial Services, which includes the financial guaranty business of ACE Guaranty and ACE Capital Re International and the financial solutions business in the U.S. and Bermuda.

Recent Developments: For the year ended Dec 31 2004, net income decreased 19.6% to $1,139,089 thousand from net income of $1,417,482 thousand a year earlier. Revenues were $12,332,125 thousand, up 15.1% from $10,717,004 thousand the year before. Net premiums earned were $11,136,474 thousand versus $9,602,383 thousand in the prior year, an increase of 16.0%.

Prospects: Co. is benefiting from property and casualty premium growth, which exceeded 20.0% in 2004, as well as investment income and book value that grew to higher levels. Also, Co. successfully added to its loss reserve position in 2004. Going forward, Co. will look to maintain its strong balance sheet and should be well-positioned to continue its growth in earnings and book value. Separately, Co. announced that it agreed to sell three run-off reinsurance subsidiaries to Randall & Quilter Investment Holdings Limited. Co. expects the sale to close in the first half of 2005.

Financial Data

(US$ in Thousands)	12/31/2004	12/31/2003	12/31/2002	12/31/2001	12/31/2000	12/31/1999	09/30/1998	09/30/1997
Earnings Per Share	3.83	5.01	0.19	(0.74)	2.31	1.85	2.96	2.67
Cash Flow Per Share	17.63	15.61	9.31	5.79	(1.93)	(1.90)	0.36	...
Tang Book Value Per Share	25.38	21.87	13.98	12.83	11.08	7.49	16.39	14.60
Dividends Per Share	0.820	0.740	0.660	0.580	0.500	0.420	0.340	0.267
Dividend Payout %	21.41	14.77	347.37	...	21.65	22.70	11.49	9.98
Income Statement								
Premium Income	11,136,474	9,602,383	6,830,504	5,917,177	4,534,763	2,485,737	894,303	644,838
Total Revenue	12,332,125	10,689,742	7,123,004	6,644,687	5,266,657	3,016,990	1,406,942	1,010,643
Benefits & Claims	172,113	181,077	158,118	401,229	...	...	...	...
Income Before Taxes	1,414,772	1,695,829	(39,139)	(202,418)	636,890	393,647	580,191	...
Income Taxes	275,683	278,347	(115,688)	(78,674)	93,908	28,684	20,040	...
Net Income	1,139,089	1,417,482	76,549	(146,414)	542,982	364,963	560,151	461,354
Average Shares	285,485	275,655	269,870	233,799	227,418	197,626	189,281	...
Balance Sheet								
Total Assets	56,342,436	49,552,793	43,450,937	37,186,764	31,689,526	30,122,888	8,788,753	5,001,546
Total Liabilities	46,506,624	40,717,997	36,751,201	30,769,007	25,958,265	25,672,328	5,074,483	2,382,352
Stockholders' Equity	9,835,812	8,834,796	6,388,686	6,106,707	5,420,211	4,450,560	3,714,270	2,619,194
Shares Outstanding	284,478	279,897	262,679	259,861	232,346	217,460	193,593	165,879
Statistical Record								
Return on Assets %	2.15	3.05	0.19	N.M.	1.75	1.50	8.12	9.64
Return on Equity %	12.17	18.62	1.23	N.M.	10.97	7.14	17.69	18.97
Loss Ratio %	1.55	1.89	2.31	6.78	...	...	...	...
Net Margin %	9.24	13.26	1.07	(2.20)	10.31	12.10	39.81	45.65
Price Range	45.74-33.15	41.42-23.75	44.82-23.32	41.25-20.50	43.56-14.69	34.88-15.50	42.13-26.94	32.17-17.46
P/E Ratio	11.94-8.66	8.27-4.74	235.89-122.74	...	18.86-6.36	18.85-8.38	14.23-9.10	12.05-6.54
Average Yield %	1.98	2.11	1.92	1.61	1.73	1.60	0.99	1.20

Address: 17 Woodbourne Avenue, Hamilton	Web Site: www.acelimited.com	Auditors: PricewaterhouseCoopers LLP
Telephone: (441) 295 5200	Officers: Brian Duperreault - Chmn. Donald Kramer - Vice-Chmn.	Investor Contact: 441 299 9283

4

ADVANCE AUTO PARTS INC

Exchange	Symbol	Price	52Wk Range	Yield	P/E
NYS	AAP	$50.45 (3/31/2005)	52.26-33.15	N/A	20.26

*7 Year Price Score N/A ***NYSE Composite Index=100** ***12 Month Price Score 109.32**

TRADING VOLUME (thousand shares)

Interim Earnings (Per Share)

Qtr.	Apr	Jul	Sep	Dec
2002	0.17	0.22	0.39	0.12
2003	0.07	0.58	0.60	0.41
2004	0.68	0.70	0.68	0.43

Interim Dividends (Per Share)

Amt	Decl	Ex	Rec	Pay
100%	10/29/2003	1/5/2004	12/11/2003	1/2/2004

Valuation Analysis

Forecast P/E	N/A	No of Institutions
Market Cap	$3.7 Billion	Shares
Book Value	762.6 Million	67,526,688
Price/Book	4.86	% Held
Price/Sales	N/A	94.45

Business Summary: Retail - Automotive (MIC: 5.7 SIC: 013 NAIC: 41310)

Advance Auto Parts is a specialty retailer of automotive parts, accessories and maintenance items, primarily in the U.S. Co.'s retail stores operate under the trade names Advance Auto Parts, Advance Discount Auto Parts, Discount Auto Parts in the U.S.. At Jan.1, 2005, Co. operated 2,652 stores within the United States, Peurto Rico, and the Virgin Islands. Co. operated 2,617 stores throughout 39 states. Co.'s stores offer brand name and proprietary automotive replacement parts, accessories and maintenance items for domestic and imported cars and light trucks. In addition, Co. operated 36 stores under the Western Auto trade name, located primarily in Puerto Rico and the Virgin Islands.

Recent Developments: For the year ended Jan 1 2005, income from continuing operations increased 50.1% to $188,027 thousand from income of $125,287 thousand a year earlier. Net income increased 50.5% to $187,988 thousand from net income of $124,935 thousand a year earlier. Revenues were $3,770,297 thousand, up 7.9% from $3,493,696 thousand the year before. Operating income was $328,758 thousand versus an income of $288,234 thousand in the prior year, an increase of 14.1%. Total direct expense was $2,016,926 thousand versus $1,889,178 thousand in the prior year, an increase of 6.8%. Total indirect expense was $1,424,613 thousand versus $1,316,284 thousand in the prior year, an increase of 8.2%.

Prospects: Co. is benefiting from higher sales in the do-it-yourself and do-it-for-me categories, coupled with contributions from new store expansion. Looking ahead, Co. expects earnings per diluted share to be in the range of $0.85 to $0.90 for the first quarter of fiscal 2005, and between $0.82 and $0.88 for the second quarter. Also, Co. is issuing a guidance for earnings per share of $3.00 to $3.10 for fiscal 2005. Additionally, Co. plans to open between 150 and 175 new stores in the coming year, and expects to have more than half of its stores operating with its new 2010 store format by the end of 2005.

Financial Data
(US$ in Thousands)

	01/01/2005	01/03/2004	12/28/2002	12/29/2001	12/30/2000	01/01/2000
Earnings Per Share	2.49	1.67	0.90	0.20	0.34	(0.45)
Cash Flow Per Share	3.58	4.80	3.48	1.81	1.84	...
Tang Book Value Per Share	10.00	8.54	6.55	4.41	2.76	...
Income Statement						
Total Revenue	3,770,297	3,493,696	3,287,883	2,517,639	2,288,022	2,206,945
EBITDA	431,776	347,134	312,112	176,216	173,798	95,408
Depn & Amortn	105,959	105,847	110,702	85,820	79,997	70,526
Income Before Taxes	305,748	203,711	123,191	28,501	27,161	(37,910)
Income Taxes	117,721	78,424	47,799	11,312	10,535	(12,584)
Net Income	187,988	124,935	65,019	11,442	19,559	(25,326)
Average Shares	75,481	74,743	72,376	58,316	57,222	56,538
Balance Sheet						
Current Assets	1,377,427	1,226,454	1,185,472	1,135,848	897,775	...
Total Assets	2,201,962	1,983,071	1,965,225	1,950,615	1,356,360	...
Current Liabilities	961,125	853,945	722,576	693,749	579,192	...
Long-Term Obligations	438,300	422,780	724,832	932,022	576,964	...
Total Liabilities	1,479,647	1,351,827	1,496,869	1,662,044	1,200,089	...
Stockholders' Equity	722,315	631,244	468,356	288,571	156,271	...
Shares Outstanding	72,245	73,884	71,470	65,384	56,578	...
Statistical Record						
Return on Assets %	9.01	6.23	3.33	0.69	...	...
Return on Equity %	27.85	22.36	17.23	5.16	...	...
EBITDA Margin %	11.45	9.94	9.49	7.00	7.60	4.32
Net Margin %	4.99	3.58	1.98	0.45	0.85	N.M.
Asset Turnover	1.81	1.74	1.68	1.53	...	...
Current Ratio	1.43	1.44	1.64	1.64	1.55	...
Debt to Equity	0.61	0.67	1.55	3.23	3.69	...
Price Range	45.91-33.15	41.52-18.79	30.93-20.45	23.52-19.85	...	...
P/E Ratio	18.44-13.31	24.86-11.25	34.37-22.72	117.63-99.25	...	...

Address: 5673 Airport Road, Roanoke, VA 24012	**Web Site:** www.advanceautoparts.com	**Auditors:** Deloitte & Touche LLP
Telephone: (540) 362-4911	**Officers:** Lawrence P. Castellani - Chmn., C.E.O. Jeffrey T. Gray - Exec. V.P., C.F.O.	

ADVANCED MICRO DEVICES, INC.

Exchange	Symbol	Price	52Wk Range	Yield	P/E
NYS	AMD	$16.12 (3/31/2005)	24.85-10.86	N/A	64.48

*7 Year Price Score 90.08 ***NYSE Composite Index=100** ***12 Month Price Score 98.36**

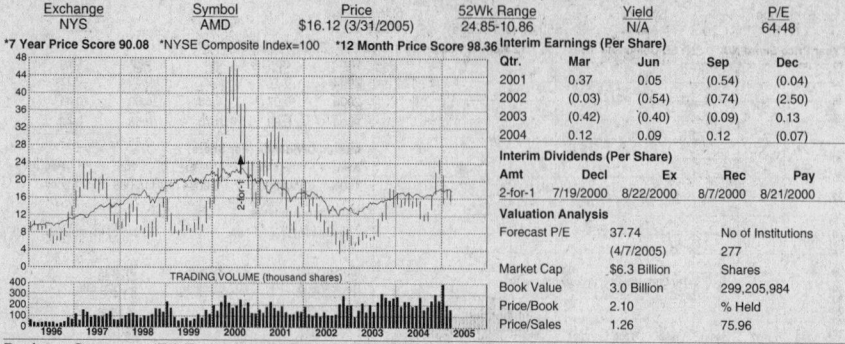

Interim Earnings (Per Share)

Qtr.	Mar	Jun	Sep	Dec
2001	0.37	0.05	(0.54)	(0.04)
2002	(0.03)	(0.54)	(0.74)	(2.50)
2003	(0.42)	(0.40)	(0.09)	0.13
2004	0.12	0.09	0.12	(0.07)

Interim Dividends (Per Share)

Amt	Decl	Ex	Rec	Pay
2-for-1	7/19/2000	8/22/2000	8/7/2000	8/21/2000

Valuation Analysis

Forecast P/E	37.74		No of Institutions
	(4/7/2005)		277
Market Cap	$6.3 Billion		Shares
Book Value	3.0 Billion		299,205,984
Price/Book	2.10		% Held
Price/Sales	1.26		75.96

Business Summary: IT & Technology (MIC: 10.2 SIC: 674 NAIC: 34413)

Advanced Micro Devices designs and manufactures industry-standard digital integrated circuits that are used in many diverse product applications such as desktop and mobile personal computers, workstations, servers, communications equipment and automotive and consumer electronics. Co.'s products include microprocessors, flash memory products and embedded microprocessors for personal connectivity devices. Co.'s products included AMD Opteron, AMD Athlon, AMD Geode and AMD Alchemy processors. Co. has manufacturing facilities located in the U.S., Europe and Asia.

Recent Developments: For the year ended Dec 26 2004, net income was $91,156 thousand versus net loss of $274,490 thousand a year earlier. Revenues were $10,002,870 thousand, up 42.1% from $7,038,336 thousand the year before. Operating income was $221,809 thousand versus a loss of $233,384 thousand in the prior year. Total direct expense was $3,032,585 thousand versus $2,327,063 thousand in the prior year, an increase of 30.3%. Total indirect expense was $1,747,041 thousand versus $1,425,489 thousand in the prior year, an increase of 22.6%.

Prospects: Results are benefiting from a 9.0% sequential increase in Computation Products Group sales. However, Co.'s Memory Group sales were weaker than expected due to an aggressive pricing environment, significantly lower sales in Japan, and a delay in qualifying a new product in the wireless segment. Looking ahead, based on the strong acceptance of AMD64 technology, Co. expects its processor momentum to increase throughout 2005. In the first quarter, Co. expects processor sales to be flat to down slightly. In addition, Co. expects Flash memory sales to be down in the first quarter due to continued imbalance in supply and demand, continued pressure on active server pages and seasonality.

Financial Data

(US$ in Thousands)	12/26/2004	12/28/2003	12/29/2002	12/30/2001	12/31/2000	12/26/1999	12/27/1998	12/28/1997
Earnings Per Share	0.25	(0.79)	(3.81)	(0.18)	2.89	(0.30)	(0.36)	(0.07)
Cash Flow Per Share	3.04	0.85	(0.26)	0.51	3.83	0.89	0.50	1.42
Tang Book Value Per Share	7.68	6.96	7.16	10.64	10.10	6.66	6.89	7.14
Income Statement								
Total Revenue	5,001,435	3,519,168	2,697,029	3,891,754	4,644,187	2,857,604	2,542,141	2,356,375
EBITDA	1,415,561	808,454	(472,475)	547,316	1,831,778	631,937	295,108	309,934
Depn & Amortn	1,224,252	995,663	756,169	622,867	579,070	515,520	467,521	394,465
Income Before Taxes	96,994	(277,467)	(1,264,603)	(93,923)	1,251,899	73,625	(207,429)	(100,832)
Income Taxes	5,838	2,936	44,586	(14,463)	256,868	167,350	(91,878)	(55,155)
Net Income	91,156	(274,490)	(1,303,012)	(60,581)	983,026	(88,936)	(103,960)	(21,090)
Average Shares	371,066	346,934	342,334	332,407	350,000	294,136	287,336	280,906
Balance Sheet								
Current Assets	3,227,997	2,900,278	2,019,678	2,353,109	2,657,689	1,409,878	1,562,027	1,175,267
Total Assets	7,844,210	7,094,345	5,619,181	5,647,242	5,767,735	4,377,698	4,252,968	3,515,271
Current Liabilities	1,846,316	1,452,270	1,372,079	1,313,937	1,224,109	910,652	840,719	726,770
Long-Term Obligations	1,628,268	1,899,674	1,779,837	672,945	1,167,973	1,427,282	1,372,416	662,689
Total Liabilities	4,834,157	4,656,035	3,151,916	2,092,187	2,596,068	2,398,425	2,247,919	1,485,728
Stockholders' Equity	3,010,053	2,438,310	2,467,265	3,555,055	3,171,667	1,979,273	2,005,049	2,029,543
Shares Outstanding	391,738	350,252	344,528	334,192	314,137	297,312	290,954	284,246
Statistical Record								
Return on Assets %	1.22	N.M.	N.M.	N.M.	19.07	N.M.	N.M.	N.M.
Return on Equity %	3.36	N.M.	N.M.	N.M.	37.55	N.M.	N.M.	N.M.
EBITDA Margin %	28.30	22.97	N.M.	14.06	39.44	22.11	11.61	13.15
Net Margin %	1.82	N.M.	N.M.	N.M.	21.17	N.M.	N.M.	N.M.
Asset Turnover	0.67	0.56	0.48	0.68	0.90	0.66	0.66	0.71
Current Ratio	1.75	2.00	1.47	1.79	2.17	1.55	1.86	1.62
Debt to Equity	0.54	0.78	0.72	0.19	0.37	0.72	0.68	0.33
Price Range	24.85-10.86	18.29-4.94	20.00-3.20	34.40-7.93	47.50-13.69	15.94-7.38	16.00-6.50	23.69-8.78
P/E Ratio	99.40-43.44	...	...	...	16.44-4.74	...	...	...

Address: One AMD Place, P.O. Box 3453, Sunnyvale, CA 94088-3453 **Telephone:** (408) 749-4000 **Fax:** (408) 982-6161	Web Site: www.amd.com **Officers:** Hector de J. Ruiz - Chmn., Pres., C.E.O. Robert R. Herb - Exec. V.P., Chief Sales & Mkg. Officer	**Auditors:** ERNST & YOUNG LLP

AEROPOSTALE INC

Exchange	Symbol	Price	52Wk Range	Yield	P/E
NYS	ARO	$32.75 (3/31/2005)	34.15-21.61	N/A	24.62

*7 Year Price Score N/A *NYSE Composite Index=100 *12 Month Price Score 102.63

Interim Earnings (Per Share)

Qtr.	Apr	Jul	Oct	Jan
2002-03	0.01	(0.04)	0.26	0.31
2003-04	0.03	0.05	0.37	0.47
2004-05	0.11	0.19	0.55	...

Interim Dividends (Per Share)

Amt	Decl	Ex	Rec	Pay
50%	3/11/2004	4/27/2004	4/12/2004	4/26/2004

Valuation Analysis

Forecast P/E	N/A	No of Institutions
Market Cap	$1.8 Billion	Shares
Book Value	209.4 Million	53,448,272
Price/Book	8.70	% Held
Price/Sales	2.00	96.01

Business Summary: Retail - Apparel and Accessory Stores (MIC: 5.8 SIC: 621 NAIC: 48120)

Aeropostale is a mall-based specialty retailer of casual apparel and accessories that targets both young women and young men aged 11 to 20. Co. provides its customers with a focused selection of high-quality, active-oriented, fashion basic merchandise. Co. maintains complete control over its proprietary brand by designing and sourcing all of its merchandise. Co.'s products can be purchased only at its stores or at organized sales events at college campuses. Co.'s average store size of approximately 3,500 square feet. As of Jan 31 2004, Co. operated 459 stores in 41 states.

Recent Developments: For the quarter ended Oct 30 2004, net income increased 44.8% to $31,686 thousand from net income of $21,878 thousand in the year-earlier quarter. Revenues were $274,616 thousand, up 24.8% from $220,071 thousand the year before. Operating income was $51,426 thousand versus an income of $35,799 thousand in the prior-year quarter, an increase of 43.7%. Total indirect expense was $46,775 thousand versus $38,123 thousand in the prior-year quarter, an increase of 22.7%.

Prospects: Co. has indicated that it is comfortable with earnings estimates of about $0.15 per diluted share for the first quarter of fiscal 2005. Co. also expects to achieve a high-single digit gain in comparable store sales for the first quarter of fiscal 2005. Separately, Co. anticipates opening an initial group of Jimmy'Z stores in July of 2005. Jimmy'Z is a California lifestyle-oriented brand targeting women and men aged 18-25. In June 2004 Co. acquired the rights to and existing registrations for the JIMMY'Z® brand and trademarks in the U.S. and Canada for clothing and related goods and services. During fiscal 2005, Co. anticipates opening about 14 Jimmy'Z stores in various regions of the U.S.

Financial Data
(US$ in Thousands)

	9 Mos	6 Mos	3 Mos	01/31/2004	02/01/2003	02/02/2002	08/04/2001	07/29/2000
Earnings Per Share	1.33	1.15	1.00	0.93	0.55	0.55	0.19	0.20
Cash Flow Per Share	2.58	1.84	1.75	1.90	1.02	...	0.41	...
Tang Book Value Per Share	3.76	3.42	3.18	3.27	2.42	1.25	0.54	0.11
Income Statement								
Total Revenue	637,122	362,506	167,654	734,868	550,904	284,040	304,767	213,445
EBITDA	90,396	34,830	12,095	96,090	57,740	50,626	21,437	16,577
Depn & Amortn	11,407	7,267	2,093	7,894	5,643	1,809	1,787	551
Income Before Taxes	79,785	28,023	10,261	88,956	52,153	48,525	17,979	15,115
Income Taxes	30,941	10,865	4,000	34,702	20,863	19,888	7,065	5,749
Net Income	48,844	17,158	6,261	54,254	31,290	30,269	11,319	11,368
Average Shares	57,210	57,287	57,700	58,287	56,781	54,000	53,197	52,039
Balance Sheet								
Current Assets	256,983	233,421	192,892	212,447	144,789	89,780	72,695	62,415
Total Assets	382,355	348,343	296,331	307,048	223,032	146,927	121,128	93,539
Current Liabilities	108,912	95,225	64,383	71,568	57,998	51,599	61,885	54,229
Total Liabilities	172,916	156,165	120,104	121,355	95,073	77,120	85,795	69,538
Stockholders' Equity	209,439	192,178	176,227	185,693	127,959	60,190	26,290	16,006
Shares Outstanding	55,669	56,138	55,485	56,794	52,959	48,247	48,247	146,305
Statistical Record								
Return on Assets %	22.08	20.98	22.39	20.53	16.96	22.58	10.38	12.15
Return on Equity %	40.15	39.31	37.88	34.69	33.35	70.00	52.66	71.02
EBITDA Margin %	14.19	9.61	7.21	13.08	10.48	17.82	7.03	7.77
Net Margin %	7.67	4.73	3.73	7.38	5.68	10.66	3.71	5.33
Asset Turnover	2.63	2.70	3.03	2.78	2.99	2.12	2.79	2.28
Current Ratio	2.36	2.45	3.00	2.97	2.50	1.74	1.17	1.15
Price Range	33.75-17.19	30.48-16.70	24.67-11.72	22.69-6.59	18.97-3.57	...	...	...
P/E Ratio	25.38-12.93	26.50-14.52	24.67-11.72	24.40-7.09	34.50-6.48	...	...	...

Address: 1372 Broadway, 8th Floor, New York, NY 10018 **Telephone:** (646) 485-5398	**Web Site:** www.aeropostale.com **Officers:** Julian R. Geiger - Chmn., C.E.O. John S. Mills - Pres., C.O.O.	**Auditors:** Deloitte & Touche LLP

AES CORP.

Exchange	Symbol	Price	52Wk Range	Yield	P/E
NYS	AES	$16.38 (3/31/2005)	17.65-7.69	N/A	28.74

*7 Year Price Score 44.74   *NYSE Composite Index=100   *12 Month Price Score 131.34

TRADING VOLUME (thousand shares)

Interim Earnings (Per Share)

Qtr.	Mar	Jun	Sep	Dec
2001	0.20	0.21	0.01	0.10
2002	(0.58)	(0.22)	(0.58)	(5.13)
2003	0.17	(0.22)	0.12	(0.74)
2004	0.08	0.06	0.21	0.22

Interim Dividends (Per Share)

Amt	Decl	Ex	Rec	Pay
2-for-1	4/18/2000	6/2/2000	5/1/2000	6/1/2000

Valuation Analysis

Forecast P/E	22.92	No of Institutions	
	(4/13/2005)	319	
Market Cap	$10.6 Billion	Shares	
Book Value	1.4 Billion	483,426,176	
Price/Book	7.42	% Held	
Price/Sales	1.18	74.51	

Business Summary: Electricity (MIC: 7.1 SIC: 911 NAIC: 21121)

AES is a global power company that participates primarily in four lines of business. Co.'s large utility business is comprised of three integrated regulated utilities located in the U.S., Brazil and Venezuela. Co.'s contract generation business is made up of multiple power generation facilities under contract around the world. Co.'s competitive supply business consists of generating facilities and retail supply businesses that sell electricity directly to wholesale and retail customers in competitive markets. Co.'s growth distribution business includes distribution facilities in developing countries or regions. At Dec 31 2003, Co.'s facilities had over 38 gigawatts of generating capacity.

Recent Developments: For the year ended Dec 31 2004, income from continuing operations increased 10.2% to $366.0 million compared with $332.0 million, before an accounting change gain of $41.0 million, in the previous year. Earnings excluded income of $20.0 million in 2004 and a loss of $787.0 million in 2003 from discontinued operations. Results for 2004 and 2003 included losses on sale of investments and asset impairment expense of $41.0 million and $201.0 million, respectively. Results for 2003 also included a goodwill impairment charge of $11.0 million. Total revenues advanced 12.7% to $9.49 billion from $8.42 billion a year earlier. Comparisons were made with restated results for the prior year.

Prospects: In 2005, Co. will focus on improving the financial performance of its businesses while looking selectively for attractive growth opportunities. In its generation business, Co. expects further improvements in commercial availability and a continued effort to develop platform extension opportunities at its existing businesses. Co.'s utility businesses will focus on customer service enhancements, tariff and cost management and reducing non-commercial losses. Co. expects to use substantial cash flow to pay down debt and support new growth projects. Meanwhile, Co. has agreed to acquire SeaWest Holdings Inc. a developer and operator of wind farms in the U.S. for about $60.0 million in cash.

Financial Data

(US$ in Thousands)	9 Mos	6 Mos	3 Mos	12/31/2003	12/31/2002	12/31/2001	12/31/2000	12/31/1999
Earnings Per Share	(0.38)	(0.48)	(0.76)	(0.67)	(6.51)	0.51	1.40	0.58
Cash Flow Per Share	2.47	2.27	2.44	2.65	2.68	3.18	1.04	0.51
Tang Book Value Per Share	0.08	N.M.	N.M.	N.M.	...	4.25	4.97	1.77
Income Statement								
Total Revenue	6,943,000	4,520,000	2,257,000	8,415,000	8,632,000	9,327,000	6,691,000	3,253,000
EBITDA	2,490,000	1,599,000	825,000	3,127,000	(95,000)	3,126,000	2,900,000	1,339,000
Depn & Amortn	609,000	399,000	200,000	781,000	837,000	859,000	582,000	278,000
Income Before Taxes	649,000	386,000	201,000	640,000	(2,651,000)	802,000	1,019,000	420,000
Income Taxes	201,000	123,000	64,000	194,000	(27,000)	230,000	252,000	111,000
Net Income	226,000	86,000	48,000	(403,000)	(3,509,000)	273,000	641,000	228,000
Average Shares	651,000	643,000	633,000	597,500	538,900	543,500	473,100	392,500
Balance Sheet								
Current Assets	5,110,000	4,484,000	4,781,000	4,886,000	4,349,000	4,653,000	5,573,000	2,587,000
Total Assets	29,956,000	28,997,000	29,734,000	29,904,000	33,776,000	36,736,000	31,033,000	20,880,000
Current Liabilities	5,688,000	5,236,000	5,949,000	6,487,000	6,511,000	5,041,000	4,882,000	2,570,000
Long-Term Obligations	16,437,000	16,540,000	16,330,000	16,792,000	16,706,000	19,586,000	15,699,000	10,818,000
Total Liabilities	27,300,000	26,657,000	27,492,000	28,454,000	32,321,000	28,689,000	23,612,000	15,777,000
Stockholders' Equity	1,430,000	1,174,000	1,077,000	645,000	(341,000)	5,539,000	4,811,000	2,637,000
Shares Outstanding	648,000	645,000	633,000	626,000	558,000	533,000	481,000	414,000
Statistical Record								
Return on Assets %	N.M.	N.M.	N.M.	N.M.	N.M.	0.81	2.46	1.44
Return on Equity %	N.M.	N.M.	N.M.	N.M.	N.M.	5.28	17.17	10.29
EBITDA Margin %	35.86	35.38	36.55	37.16	N.M.	33.52	43.34	41.16
Net Margin %	3.26	1.90	2.13	N.M.	N.M.	2.93	9.58	7.01
Asset Turnover	0.30	0.28	0.28	0.26	0.24	0.28	0.26	0.21
Current Ratio	0.90	0.86	0.80	0.75	0.67	0.92	1.14	1.01
Debt to Equity	11.49	14.09	15.16	26.03	...	3.54	3.26	4.10
Price Range	10.71-7.42	10.71-5.91	10.71-3.62	9.50-2.72	17.84-0.95	59.70-11.98	70.63-34.81	37.38-16.50
P/E Ratio	...	...	...	...	...	117.06-23.49	50.45-24.87	64.44-28.45

Address: 1001 N. 19th Street, Arlington, VA 22209	Web Site: www.aesc.com	Auditors: Deloitte & Touche LLP
Telephone: (703) 522 1315	Officers: Richard Darman - Chmn. Paul T. Hanrahan - Pres., C.E.O.	Investor Contact: 703-558-4875
Fax: (703) 528 4510		

AETNA INC.

Exchange	Symbol	Price	52Wk Range	Yield	P/E
NYS	AET	$74.95 (3/31/2005)	76.97-38.88	0.03	10.48

*7 Year Price Score N/A   *NYSE Composite Index=100   *12 Month Price Score 127.52

Interim Earnings (Per Share)

Qtr.	Mar	Jun	Sep	Dec
2001	(0.17)	0.04	(0.19)	(0.66)
2002	(9.50)	0.35	0.32	0.35
2003	1.06	0.44	0.68	0.79
2004	1.14	0.90	4.11	1.01

Interim Dividends (Per Share)

Amt	Decl	Ex	Rec	Pay
0.02A	9/27/2002	11/13/2002	11/15/2002	11/29/2002
0.02A	9/26/2003	11/12/2003	11/14/2003	12/1/2003
0.02A	9/24/2004	11/12/2004	11/16/2004	11/30/2004
100%	2/10/2005	3/14/2005	2/25/2005	3/11/2005
		Indicated Div: $0.02		

Valuation Analysis

Forecast P/E	N/A	No of Institutions
Market Cap	$22.0 Billion	Shares
Book Value	9.1 Billion	264,723,392
Price/Book	2.42	% Held
Price/Sales	1.10	89.93

Business Summary: Insurance (MIC: 8.2 SIC: 411 NAIC: 24210)

Aetna is a provider of healthcare, dental, pharmacy, group life, disability and long-term care benefits in the U.S., serving about 13.0 million medical members, 10.9 million dental members, 7.4 million pharmacy members and 12.3 million group insurance members as of Dec 31 2003. Co.'s operations include three business segments. Healthcare consists of health and dental plans offered on both a risk basis and an employer-funded basis. The Group Insurance segment includes group life insurance products offered on a risk basis. Large Case Pensions manages a variety of retirement products primarily for defined benefit and defined contribution plans.

Recent Developments: For the year ended Dec 31 2004, income from continuing operations increased 30.1% to $1,215,100 thousand from income of $933,800 thousand a year earlier. Net income increased 140.4% to $2,245,100 thousand from net income of $933,800 thousand a year earlier. Revenues were $19,904,100 thousand, up 10.7% from $17,976,400 thousand the year before. Net premiums earned were $16,676,700 thousand versus $14,904,000 thousand in the prior year, an increase of 11.9%. Net investment income fell 3.0% to $1,062,500 thousand from $1,095,000 thousand a year ago.

Prospects: Based on Co.'s continued success in the marketplace, combined with its ongoing, rigorous focus on disciplined pricing and cost management, it is increasing its guidance for 2005 operating earnings to $8.75 to $8.90 per share from its prior guidance of $8.40 per share, representing an increase of 20.0% to 22.0% over 2004, and it is increasing its guidance for membership growth to 950,000 to 1.1 million. In addition, Co.'s recently enhanced Aexcel network, which allows members access to quality, cost-effective providers, has seen strong customer acceptance. Co. has expanded Aexcel's availability to nine geographic locations from three, and the number of medical specialties from six to twelve.

Financial Data (US$ in Thousands)	12/31/2004	12/31/2003	12/31/2002	12/31/2001	12/31/2000	12/31/1999	12/31/1998
Earnings Per Share	7.15	2.96	(8.24)	(0.97)	0.45	2.36	...
Cash Flow Per Share	4.73	1.21	1.03	(0.12)	5.39	5.78	...
Tang Book Value Per Share	16.84	12.29	9.38	9.02	8.50	7.24	...
Dividends Per Share	0.020	0.020	0.020	0.020	...	...	...
Dividend Payout %	0.28	0.68	...	...	...	...	...
Income Statement							
Premium Income	16,676,700	14,904,000	16,712,700	21,772,000	23,214,900	18,641,500	13,128,900
Total Revenue	19,904,100	17,976,400	19,878,700	25,190,800	26,818,900	22,109,700	16,589,000
Benefits & Claims	2,191,500	2,090,800	2,245,500	2,458,300	2,153,500	2,231,000	2,296,000
Income Before Taxes	1,898,900	1,441,600	544,800	(378,700)	(39,000)	744,800	842,000
Income Taxes	683,800	507,800	151,600	(87,200)	88,400	345,400	391,600
Net Income	2,245,100	933,800	(2,522,500)	(279,600)	127,100	716,500	846,800
Average Shares	314,000	316,200	305,800	...	...	290,657	...
Balance Sheet							
Total Assets	42,133,700	40,950,200	40,047,500	43,255,100	47,445,700	52,421,900	53,355,200
Total Liabilities	33,052,300	33,026,200	33,067,500	33,364,800	37,318,600	41,718,700	41,650,700
Stockholders' Equity	9,081,400	7,924,000	6,980,000	9,890,300	10,127,100	10,703,200	11,429,500
Shares Outstanding	293,005	305,047	299,932	288,531	285,237	282,967	...
Statistical Record							
Return on Assets %	5.39	2.31	N.M.	N.M.	0.25	1.35	...
Return on Equity %	26.33	12.53	N.M.	N.M.	1.22	6.47	...
Loss Ratio %	13.14	14.03	13.44	11.29	9.28	11.97	17.49
Net Margin %	11.28	5.19	(12.69)	(1.11)	0.47	3.24	5.10
Price Range	63.45-33.00	34.24-20.41	25.88-15.38	20.75-11.62	20.56-16.50	...	...
P/E Ratio	8.87-4.62	11.57-6.90	...	...	45.69-36.67	...	...
Average Yield %	0.04	0.07	0.10	0.13	...	...	...

Address: 151 Farmington Avenue, Hartford, CT 06156 **Telephone:** (860) 273-0123	**Web Site:** www.aetna.com **Officers:** John W. Rowe M.D. - Chmn., C.E.O. Ronald A. Williams - Pres.	**Auditors:** KPMG LLP **Investor Contact:** 860-273-6184

9

AFFILIATED COMPUTER SERVICES, INC.

Exchange	Symbol	Price	52Wk Range	Yield	P/E
NYS	ACS	$53.24 (3/31/2005)	60.76-46.65	N/A	18.68

*7 Year Price Score 124.81 *NYSE Composite Index=100 *12 Month Price Score 90.52

TRADING VOLUME (thousand shares)

Interim Earnings (Per Share)

Qtr.	Sep	Dec	Mar	Jun
2001-02	0.39	0.42	0.46	0.49
2002-03	0.50	0.53	0.57	0.60
2003-04	0.62	1.80	0.72	0.69
2004-05	0.72	0.73	...	...

Interim Dividends (Per Share)

Amt	Decl	Ex	Rec	Pay
100%	1/22/2002	2/25/2002	2/15/2002	2/22/2002

Valuation Analysis

Forecast P/E	14.29	No of Institutions
	(4/13/2005)	399
Market Cap	$6.7 Billion	Shares
Book Value	2.8 Billion	120,688,480
Price/Book	2.39	% Held
Price/Sales	1.63	N/A

Business Summary: IT & Technology (MIC: 10.2 SIC: 374 NAIC: 18210)

Affiliated Computer Services provides business process and information technology outsourcing solutions to commercial and government clients. Co. provides technology-based services with a focus on transaction processing and program management services such as child support payment processing, electronic toll collection, welfare and community services, and traffic violations processing. Co. also designs, develops, implements, and operates large-scale health and human services programs and the information technology solutions that support those programs. Co.'s Government segment includes its relationship with the United States Department of Education.

Recent Developments: For the quarter ended Dec 31 2004, net income decreased 62.0% to $96,145 thousand compared with $253,030 thousand in the corresponding period a year earlier. Results for 2003 included a gain of $284,346 thousand from the sale of a business. Revenues rose 2.9% to $1,027,286 thousand from $997,879 thousand in the equivalent quarter of 2003. The increase in revenues was attributed to internal growth of about 4.0%, and contributions from acquisitions. Operating income $154,924 thousand, down substantially from $402,981 thousand in the comparable period the year before.

Prospects: Co. has reaffirmed its full-year fiscal 2005 revenue guidance of between $4.48 billion and $4.58 billion. Additionally, Co. expects diluted earnings per share to range from $3.10 to $3.17 per share, which has been increased from its previous fiscal year 2005 guidance. Separately, on Aug 26 2004, Co. announced that it has acquired BlueStar Solutions, Inc., in a cash transaction for approximately $73.0 million. BlueStar, with trailing annual revenues of approximately $50.0 million, is an information technology outsourcing provider specializing in applications management of packaged enterprise resource planning and messaging services.

Financial Data

(US$ in Thousands)	6 Mos	3 Mos	06/30/2004	06/30/2003	06/30/2002	06/30/2001	06/30/2000	06/30/1999
Earnings Per Share	2.85	3.91	3.83	2.20	1.76	1.23	1.03	0.83
Cash Flow Per Share	4.38	4.18	3.61	4.12	3.14	1.42	1.56	1.41
Tang Book Value Per Share	3.79	3.10	2.37	1.94	0.11	0.90	6.83	5.78
Income Statement								
Total Revenue	2,073,468	1,046,182	4,106,393	3,787,206	3,062,918	2,063,559	1,962,542	1,642,216
EBITDA	421,212	208,926	1,010,320	651,830	488,569	338,419	304,001	229,854
Depn & Amortn	109,905	54,239	164,100	135,689	97,494	93,617	84,752	66,723
Income Before Taxes	304,483	150,652	829,183	490,947	360,456	221,060	195,270	145,537
Income Taxes	114,181	56,495	299,340	184,105	130,860	86,768	85,958	59,307
Net Income	190,302	94,157	529,843	306,842	229,596	134,292	109,312	86,230
Average Shares	131,933	131,070	139,646	143,430	137,464	116,456	111,612	111,336
Balance Sheet								
Current Assets	982,747	1,030,188	1,044,424	979,498	874,489	809,615	771,874	415,947
Total Assets	3,964,641	3,984,858	3,907,042	3,698,705	3,403,567	1,891,687	1,656,446	1,223,600
Current Liabilities	566,897	594,306	637,570	557,476	485,913	281,052	358,242	221,721
Long-Term Obligations	254,950	366,290	372,439	498,340	708,233	649,313	525,619	349,106
Total Liabilities	1,148,698	1,271,795	1,316,755	1,269,517	1,308,147	1,006,172	945,069	616,179
Stockholders' Equity	2,815,943	2,713,063	2,590,487	2,429,188	2,095,420	885,515	711,377	607,421
Shares Outstanding	126,669	128,542	142,581	133,207	132,024	101,164	99,162	98,490
Statistical Record								
Return on Assets %	9.69	13.79	13.89	8.64	8.67	7.57	7.57	7.94
Return on Equity %	14.06	20.56	21.05	13.56	15.40	16.82	16.53	15.52
EBITDA Margin %	20.31	19.97	24.60	17.21	15.95	16.40	15.49	14.00
Net Margin %	9.18	9.00	12.90	8.10	7.50	6.51	5.57	5.25
Asset Turnover	1.06	1.06	1.08	1.07	1.16	1.16	1.36	1.51
Current Ratio	1.73	1.73	1.64	1.76	1.80	2.88	2.15	1.88
Debt to Equity	0.09	0.14	0.14	0.21	0.34	0.73	0.74	0.57
Price Range	60.76-46.65	57.75-46.11	57.46-43.00	56.17-33.88	56.75-35.48	38.33-16.44	26.28-15.66	25.81-11.53
P/E Ratio	21.32-16.37	14.77-11.79	15.00-11.23	25.53-15.40	32.24-20.16	31.16-13.36	25.52-15.20	31.10-13.89

Address: 2828 North Haskell, Dallas, TX 75204	Web Site: www.acs-inc.com	Auditors: PricewaterhouseCoopers LLP
Telephone: (214) 841-6111	Officers: Darwin Deason - Chmn. Mark A. King - Pres., C.O.O.	Investor Contact: 214-841-8011
Fax: (214) 841-8315		

AFLAC INC.

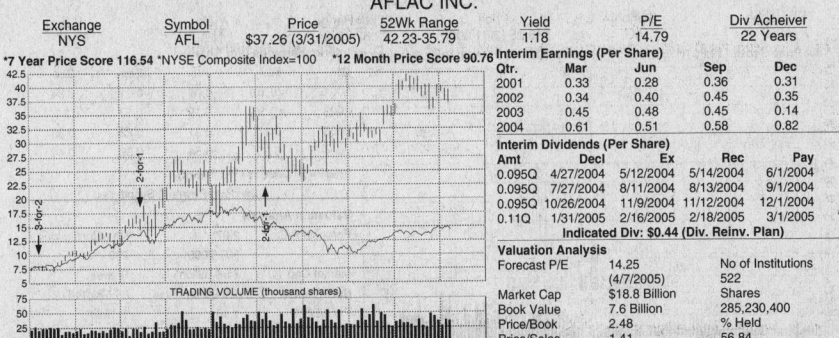

Exchange	Symbol	Price	52Wk Range	Yield	P/E	Div Achiever
NYS	AFL	$37.26 (3/31/2005)	42.23-35.79	1.18	14.79	22 Years

*7 Year Price Score 116.54 *NYSE Composite Index=100 ***12 Month Price Score 90.76**

Interim Earnings (Per Share)

Qtr.	Mar	Jun	Sep	Dec
2001	0.33	0.28	0.36	0.31
2002	0.34	0.40	0.45	0.35
2003	0.45	0.48	0.45	0.14
2004	0.61	0.51	0.58	0.82

Interim Dividends (Per Share)

Amt	Decl	Ex	Rec	Pay
0.095Q	4/27/2004	5/12/2004	5/14/2004	6/1/2004
0.095Q	7/27/2004	8/11/2004	8/13/2004	9/1/2004
0.095Q	10/26/2004	11/9/2004	11/12/2004	12/1/2004
0.11Q	1/31/2005	2/16/2005	2/18/2005	3/1/2005

Indicated Div: $0.44 (Div. Reinv. Plan)

Valuation Analysis

Forecast P/E	14.25	No of Institutions	
	(4/7/2005)	522	
Market Cap	$18.8 Billion	Shares	
Book Value	7.6 Billion	285,230,400	
Price/Book	2.48	% Held	
Price/Sales	1.41	56.84	

Business Summary: Insurance (MIC: 8.2 SIC: 321 NAIC: 24114)

AFLAC is an international insurance organization whose principal subsidiary is American Family Life Assurance Company of Columbus. In addition to life, and health & accident insurance, Co. has pioneered cancer-expense and intensive-care insurance coverage. Co.'s subsidiary Communicorp specializes in printing, advertising, audio-visuals, sales incentives, business meetings and mailings. As of Feb 2 2004, Co. insured more than 40.0 million people worldwide, and offered policies to employees through 288,100 payroll accounts. Also, Co. insures one out of four Japanese households and is the largest life insurer in Japan in terms of individual policies in force.

Recent Developments: For the year ended Dec 31 2004, net income increased 63.4% to $1,299,000 thousand from net income of $795,000 thousand a year earlier. Revenues were $13,281,000 thousand, up 16.0% from $11,447,000 thousand the year before. Net premiums earned were $11,302,000 thousand versus $9,921,000 thousand in the prior year, an increase of 13.9%. Net investment income rose 9.5% to $1,957,000 thousand from $,787,000 thousand a year ago.

Prospects: Co. continues to be encouraged by its actions to generate new sales growth. However, Co. believes new sales in the first quarter of 2005 will be lower, due in part to difficult comparisons in 2004. As a result, Co. estimates that it will be the second quarter at the earliest before it sees improved growth. Accordingly, Co. has targeted a 3.0% to 8.0% increase in new sales for 2005. Also, Co. is confident it can increase operating earnings per diluted share by 15.0% in 2005. Meanwhile, continued expansion of Co.'s product line and sales force, combined with its market position, should enable Co. to produce a 5.0% to 10.0% increase in total new annualized premium sales in yen for 2005.

Financial Data

(US$ in Thousands)	12/31/2004	12/31/2003	12/31/2002	12/31/2001	12/31/2000	12/31/1999	12/31/1998	12/31/1997
Earnings Per Share	2.52	1.52	1.55	1.28	1.26	1.03	0.88	1.04
Cash Flow Per Share	8.82	6.60	5.87	5.43	6.17	5.28	4.68	4.77
Tang Book Value Per Share	15.04	13.03	12.43	10.40	8.87	7.28	7.09	6.44
Dividends Per Share	0.380	0.300	0.230	0.193	0.165	0.145	0.126	0.111
Dividend Payout %	15.08	19.74	14.84	15.04	13.10	14.01	14.35	10.70
Income Statement								
Premium Income	11,302,000	9,921,000	8,595,000	8,061,000	8,239,000	7,264,000	5,943,000	5,873,661
Total Revenue	13,281,000	11,447,000	10,257,000	9,598,000	9,720,000	8,640,000	7,104,000	7,250,702
Benefits & Claims	8,482,000	7,529,000	6,589,000	6,303,000	6,618,000	5,885,000	4,877,000	4,833,077
Income Before Taxes	1,807,000	1,225,000	1,259,000	1,081,000	1,012,000	778,000	551,000	864,820
Income Taxes	508,000	430,000	438,000	394,000	325,000	207,000	64,000	279,797
Net Income	1,299,000	795,000	821,000	687,000	687,000	571,000	487,000	585,023
Average Shares	516,421	522,138	528,326	537,380	544,906	550,846	551,744	563,192
Balance Sheet								
Total Assets	59,326,000	50,964,000	45,058,000	37,860,000	37,232,000	37,041,000	31,183,000	29,454,005
Total Liabilities	51,753,000	44,318,000	38,664,000	32,435,000	32,538,000	33,173,000	27,413,000	26,023,533
Stockholders' Equity	7,573,000	6,646,000	6,394,000	5,425,000	4,694,000	3,868,000	3,770,000	3,430,472
Shares Outstanding	503,608	509,892	514,439	521,615	529,209	531,482	531,368	532,872
Statistical Record								
Return on Assets %	2.35	1.66	1.98	1.83	1.84	1.67	1.61	2.15
Return on Equity %	18.22	12.19	13.89	13.58	16.00	14.95	13.53	21.06
Loss Ratio %	75.05	75.89	76.66	78.19	80.33	81.02	82.06	82.28
Net Margin %	9.78	6.95	8.00	7.16	7.07	6.61	6.86	8.07
Price Range	42.23-34.95	36.67-30.08	33.17-23.12	34.83-23.01	36.53-17.19	27.81-19.88	22.00-11.73	14.19-9.38
P/E Ratio	16.76-13.87	24.13-19.79	21.40-14.92	27.21-17.98	28.99-13.64	27.00-19.30	25.00-13.33	13.64-9.01
Average Yield %	0.96	0.92	0.78	0.67	0.62	0.61	0.77	0.93

Address: 1932 Wynnton Road, Columbus, GA 31999	**Web Site:** www.aflac.com	**Auditors:** KPMG LLP
Telephone: (706) 323-3431	**Officers:** Daniel P. Amos - Chmn., C.E.O. Kriss Cloninger III - Pres., C.F.O., Treas.	**Investor Contact:** 706-596-3264
Fax: (706) 596-3488		**Transfer Agents:** AFLAC Incorporated, Columbus, GA

AGCO CORP.

Exchange	Symbol	Price	52Wk Range	Yield	P/E
NYS	AG	$18.25 (3/31/2005)	22.82-18.04	N/A	10.67

*7 Year Price Score 112.80   *NYSE Composite Index=100   *12 Month Price Score 88.91

Interim Earnings (Per Share)

Qtr.	Mar	Jun	Sep	Dec
2001	(0.10)	0.07	0.01	0.34
2002	(0.36)	0.19	0.13	(1.11)
2003	0.17	0.21	0.22	0.39
2004	0.33	0.54	0.38	0.44

Interim Dividends (Per Share)

Dividend Payment Suspended

Valuation Analysis

Forecast P/E	9.87	No of Institutions
	(4/7/2005)	230
Market Cap	$1.6 Billion	Shares
Book Value	1.4 Billion	85,570,416
Price/Book	1.16	% Held
Price/Sales	0.31	94.76

TRADING VOLUME (thousand shares)

Business Summary: Industrial Machinery and Equipment (MIC: 11.5 SIC: 523 NAIC: 33111)

AGCO manufactures and distributes agricultural equipment and related replacement parts throughout the world. Co. sells a full range of agricultural equipment, including tractors, combines, hay tools, forage equipment and implements. Co. also sells self-propelled sprayers. Co.'s products are marketed under the following brand names: AGCO®, Challenger®, Fendt®, Gleaner®, Hesston®, Massey Ferguson®, New Idea®, RoGator®, Spra-Coupe®, Sunflower®, Terra-Gator®, Valtra® and White™Planters. Co. distributes its products through a combination of approx. 3,900 independent dealers and distributors in more than 140 countries.

Recent Developments: For the year ended Dec 31 2004, net income increased 113.4% to $158,800 thousand from net income of $74,400 thousand a year earlier. Revenues were $5,273,300 thousand, up 50.9% from $3,495,300 thousand the year before. Operating income was $323,500 thousand versus an income of $184,300 thousand in the prior year, an increase of 75.5%. Total direct expense was $4,320,400 thousand versus $2,878,900 thousand in the prior year, an increase of 50.1%. Total indirect expense was $629,400 thousand versus $432,100 thousand in the prior year, an increase of 45.7%.

Prospects: In 2005, Co. expects net sales to grow about 5.0% resulting from currency translation, price realization and higher retail sales in most regions. Also, Co. expects to benefit from improved productivity and other cost reduction initiatives. Co. noted that these benefits are expected to be partially used to fund a 20.0% increase in engineering expense in 2005 in order to accelerate new product introductions, common product platform designs and the expansion of its engine production. However, anticipated market declines from Co.'s profitable South America operations are expected to influence 2005 results. Thus, net income per share for 2005 is expected to remain flat to 5.0% higher versus 2004.

Financial Data

(US$ in Thousands)	12/31/2004	12/31/2003	12/31/2002	12/31/2001	12/31/2000	12/31/1999	12/31/1998	12/31/1997
Earnings Per Share	1.71	0.98	(1.14)	0.33	0.06	(0.20)	0.99	2.71
Cash Flow Per Share	3.08	1.17	0.99	3.30	2.94	3.98	0.19	1.66
Tang Book Value Per Share	5.02	6.48	4.30	5.34	8.45	8.67	10.27	10.36
Dividends Per Share	...	...	...	0.010	0.040	0.040	0.040	0.040
Dividend Payout %	...	...	...	3.03	66.67	...	4.04	1.48
Income Statement								
Total Revenue	5,273,300	3,495,300	2,922,700	2,541,500	2,336,100	2,413,300	2,941,400	3,224,400
EBITDA	401,500	224,200	135,500	143,700	102,400	102,200	221,700	317,700
Depn & Amortn	100,100	65,900	52,300	70,400	69,700	76,800	79,700	72,000
Income Before Taxes	224,400	98,300	25,800	14,700	(13,900)	(32,200)	74,300	245,700
Income Taxes	86,200	41,300	99,800	1,900	(7,600)	(10,200)	27,500	87,500
Net Income	158,800	74,400	(84,400)	22,600	3,500	(11,500)	60,600	168,700
Average Shares	95,600	75,600	74,200	68,500	59,700	58,700	61,200	62,100
Balance Sheet								
Current Assets	2,404,500	1,684,500	1,412,200	1,182,500	1,240,300	1,416,100	1,790,500	1,714,800
Total Assets	4,297,300	2,839,400	2,349,000	2,173,300	2,104,200	2,273,200	2,750,400	2,620,900
Current Liabilities	1,359,000	929,100	785,000	642,800	636,400	682,200	760,600	830,500
Long-Term Obligations	1,151,700	711,100	636,900	617,700	570,200	691,700	924,200	727,400
Total Liabilities	2,874,900	1,933,300	1,631,400	1,373,900	1,314,300	1,444,100	1,768,300	1,629,300
Stockholders' Equity	1,422,400	906,100	717,600	799,400	789,900	829,100	982,100	991,600
Shares Outstanding	90,394	75,409	75,197	72,311	59,589	59,579	59,536	62,972
Statistical Record								
Return on Assets %	4.44	2.87	N.M.	1.06	0.16	N.M.	2.26	7.12
Return on Equity %	13.60	9.16	N.M.	2.84	0.43	N.M.	6.14	19.10
EBITDA Margin %	7.61	6.41	4.64	5.65	4.38	4.23	7.54	9.85
Net Margin %	3.01	2.13	N.M.	0.89	0.15	N.M.	2.06	5.23
Asset Turnover	1.47	1.35	1.29	1.19	1.06	0.96	1.10	1.36
Current Ratio	1.77	1.81	1.80	1.84	1.95	2.08	2.35	2.06
Debt to Equity	0.81	0.78	0.89	0.77	0.72	0.83	0.94	0.73
Price Range	22.82-16.25	22.89-14.41	26.15-14.92	16.85-8.00	14.38-9.69	14.13-6.06	30.56-5.75	35.94-25.31
P/E Ratio	13.35-9.50	23.36-14.70	...	51.06-24.24	239.58-161.46	...	30.87-5.81	13.26-9.34
Average Yield %	...	...	...	0.09	0.35	0.39	0.22	0.13

Address: 4205 River Green Parkway, Duluth, GA 30096 **Telephone:** (770) 813 9200 **Fax:** (770) 813 6070	**Web Site:** www.agcocorp.com **Officers:** Martin Richenhagen - Pres., C.E.O. Andrew H. Beck - Sr. V.P., C.F.O.	**Auditors:** KPMG LLP

AGERE SYSTEMS INC.

Exchange	Symbol	Price	52Wk Range	Yield	P/E
NYS	AGR A	$1.43 (3/31/2005)	3.31-1.02	N/A	N/A

*7 Year Price Score N/A ***NYSE Composite Index=100** ***12 Month Price Score 87.04**

Interim Earnings (Per Share)

Qtr.	Dec	Mar	Jun	Sep
2001-02	(0.23)	(0.13)	(0.20)	(0.54)
2002-03	(0.09)	(0.08)	(0.05)	0.01
2003-04	(0.02)	0.04	0.00	(0.07)
2004-05	(0.04)	...	...	...

Interim Dividends (Per Share)

No Dividends Paid

Valuation Analysis

Forecast P/E	0.00	No of Institutions
	(4/7/2005)	202
Market Cap	$2.5 Billion	Shares
Book Value	365.0 Million	487,852,320
Price/Book	6.79	% Held
Price/Sales	1.38	59.03

TRADING VOLUME (thousand shares)

1996 1997 1998 1999 2000 2001 2002 2003 2004 2005

Business Summary: IT & Technology (MIC: 10.2 SIC: 674 NAIC: 41512)

Agere Systems designs, develops, manufactures, and sells integrated circuit solutions for applications such as high-density storage, mobile wireless communications and enterprise and telecommunications networks. Some of Co.'s solutions include related software and reference designs. Co.'s customers include manufacturers of hard disk drives, mobile phones, high-speed communications systems and personal computers. Co.'s operating segments focus on four target markets: Storage, Mobility, Enterprise and Networking and Telecommunications. Co. has two reportable segments for financial reporting purposes, Consumer Enterprise and Telecommunications.

Recent Developments: For the quarter ended Dec 31 2004, net loss increased 71.8% to $67 million from net loss of $39 million in the year-earlier quarter. Revenues were $410 million, down 20.5% from $516 million the year before. Operating loss was $51 million versus a loss of $25 million in the prior-year quarter, an increase of 104.0%. Total direct expense was $274 million versus $285 million in the prior-year quarter, a decrease of 3.9%. Total indirect expense was $187 million versus $256 million in the prior-year quarter, a decrease of 27.0%.

Prospects: Co. is seeing design win momentum in all areas of the business and is pleased with its continued strength in storage where it increased shipments of read channels and system-on-a-chip applications to key customers targeting personal computer and consumer electronics applications. Overall, Co. believes that it is well positioned for future growth and expects to increase revenues and improve profitability as it moves beyond the second half of fiscal 2005. Separately, on Mar 6 2005, Co. announced that it acquired Modem-Art Ltd., a privately-held developer of advanced processor technology for 3G/UMTS mobile devices. The acquisition is expected to complement Co.'s existing product portfolio.

Financial Data
(US$ in Thousands)

	3 Mos	09/30/2004	09/30/2003	09/30/2002	09/30/2001	09/30/2000	09/30/1999	09/30/1998
Earnings Per Share	(0.07)	(0.05)	(0.20)	(1.11)	(3.46)	(0.07)	0.34	0.29
Cash Flow Per Share	0.10	0.10	(0.07)	(0.40)	...	0.73	0.67	...
Tang Book Value Per Share	0.14	0.17	0.23	0.38	1.30	1.40	...	...
Income Statement								
Total Revenue	410,000	1,912,000	1,839,000	2,177,000	4,080,000	4,708,000	3,714,000	3,101,000
EBITDA	30,000	102,000	43,000	(1,082,000)	(3,525,000)	855,000	913,000	854,000
Depn & Amortn	83,000	217,000	331,000	574,000	900,000	666,000	398,000	320,000
Income Before Taxes	(61,000)	(150,000)	(325,000)	(1,747,000)	(4,507,000)	131,000	477,000	513,000
Income Taxes	6,000	(60,000)	46,000	64,000	105,000	207,000	158,000	210,000
Net Income	(67,000)	(90,000)	(338,000)	(1,811,000)	(4,616,000)	(76,000)	351,000	303,000
Average Shares	1,731,000	1,712,000	1,667,000	1,637,000	1,334,000	1,035,000	1,035,000	1,035,000
Balance Sheet								
Current Assets	1,094,000	1,273,000	1,204,000	1,456,000	4,060,000	1,404,000	1,039,000	...
Total Assets	1,992,000	2,272,000	2,388,000	2,864,000	6,562,000	7,067,000	3,020,000	...
Current Liabilities	658,000	866,000	1,022,000	1,267,000	3,904,000	976,000	820,000	...
Long-Term Obligations	417,000	420,000	451,000	486,000	33,000	46,000	64,000	...
Total Liabilities	1,627,000	1,851,000	1,877,000	2,132,000	4,101,000	1,286,000	1,058,000	...
Stockholders' Equity	365,000	421,000	511,000	732,000	2,461,000	5,781,000	1,962,000	...
Shares Outstanding	1,733,813	1,724,240	1,693,085	1,642,780	1,635,100	1,635,000	...	...
Statistical Record								
EBITDA Margin %	7.32	5.33	2.34	N.M.	N.M.	18.16	24.58	27.54
Net Margin %	N.M.	N.M.	N.M.	N.M.	N.M.	N.M.	9.45	9.77
Asset Turnover	0.84	0.82	0.70	0.46	...	0.93	...	...
Current Ratio	1.66	1.47	1.18	1.15	1.04	1.44	1.27	...
Debt to Equity	1.14	1.00	0.88	0.66	0.01	0.01	0.03	...
Price Range	4.08-1.02	4.08-1.02	3.70-0.57	6.15-1.09	8.91-3.25	...	...	...

Address: 1110 American Parkway N.E., Allentown , PA 18109 Telephone: (610) 712-1000	Web Site: www.agere.com Officers: John A. Young - Chmn. John T. Dickson - Pres., C.E.O.	Auditors: PricewaterhouseCoopers LLP Investor Contact: 610-712-4323

AGILENT TECHNOLOGIES, INC.

Exchange	Symbol	Price	52Wk Range	Yield	P/E
NYS	A	$22.20 (3/31/2005)	32.56-19.68	N/A	28.83

*7 Year Price Score N/A   *NYSE Composite Index=100   *12 Month Price Score 88.98

Interim Earnings (Per Share)

Qtr.	Jan	Apr	Jul	Oct
2001-02	(0.68)	(0.55)	(0.49)	(0.51)
2002-03	(0.78)	(0.31)	(3.28)	0.04
2003-04	0.14	0.21	0.20	0.15
2004-05	0.21	...	...	...

Interim Dividends (Per Share)

No Dividends Paid

Valuation Analysis

Forecast P/E	19.07	No of Institutions
	(4/7/2005)	389
Market Cap	$10.9 Billion	Shares
Book Value	3.8 Billion	335,370,944
Price/Book	2.89	% Held
Price/Sales	1.52	68.28

Business Summary: Instruments and Related Products (MIC: 11.15 SIC: 825 NAIC: 34515)

Agilent Technologies is a global diversified technology company that provides solutions to markets within the communications, electronics, life sciences and chemical analysis industries. Co. has four primary businesses: test and measurement; automated test; semiconductor products; and life sciences and chemical analysis. Co.'s test and measurement, automated test and semiconductor products businesses focus on growth opportunities in the communications and electronics industries, while its life sciences and chemical analysis business focuses on the life sciences industry and in the environmental, chemical, food and petrochemical industries.

Recent Developments: For the quarter ended Jan 31 2005, net income increased 45.1% to $103,000 thousand from net income of $71,000 thousand in the year-earlier quarter. Revenues were $1,658,000 thousand, up 0.9% from $1,643,000 thousand the year before. Operating income was $95,000 thousand versus an income of $79,000 thousand in the prior-year quarter, an increase of 20.3%. Total direct expense was $907,000 thousand versus $904,000 thousand in the prior-year quarter, an increase of 0.3%. Total indirect expense was $656,000 thousand versus $660,000 thousand in the prior-year quarter, a decrease of 0.6%.

Prospects: On Feb 4 2005, Co. completed the sale of its camera module business to Flextronics. Separately, on Feb 3 2005, Co. announced that it has completed its acquisition of Wavics, a Korean-based designer and manufacturer of power amplifier modules for the worldwide mobile handset market. Terms of the transactions were not disclosed. Looking ahead, Co. anticipates relatively flat revenues of between $1.60 billion and $1.70 billion during the second quarter of fiscal 2005, reflecting the absence of $70.0 million of revenues stemming from the divestiture of Co.'s camera module business. In addition, Co. expects second-quarter operating earnings in the range of $0.18 to $0.23 per share.

Financial Data
(US$ in Thousands)

	3 Mos	10/31/2004	10/31/2003	10/31/2002	10/31/2001	10/31/2000	10/31/1999	10/31/1998
Earnings Per Share	0.77	0.71	(4.35)	(2.22)	0.38	1.66	1.35	0.68
Cash Flow Per Share	1.54	1.37	(0.30)	(1.26)	(0.25)	1.86	1.21	1.98
Tang Book Value Per Share	6.74	6.42	5.09	8.44	9.95	10.37	8.90	7.95
Income Statement								
Total Revenue	1,658,000	7,181,000	6,056,000	6,010,000	8,396,000	10,773,000	8,331,000	7,952,000
EBITDA	180,000	732,000	(328,000)	(812,000)	257,000	1,659,000	1,262,000	873,000
Depn & Amortn	63,000	292,000	362,000	735,000	734,000	495,000	475,000	477,000
Income Before Taxes	124,000	440,000	(690,000)	(1,547,000)	(477,000)	1,164,000	787,000	396,000
Income Taxes	21,000	91,000	1,100,000	(525,000)	(71,000)	407,000	275,000	139,000
Net Income	103,000	349,000	(2,058,000)	(1,032,000)	174,000	757,000	512,000	257,000
Average Shares	496,000	490,000	473,000	465,000	458,000	455,000	380,000	380,000
Balance Sheet								
Current Assets	4,649,000	4,577,000	3,889,000	4,880,000	4,799,000	5,655,000	3,538,000	3,075,000
Total Assets	7,150,000	7,056,000	6,297,000	8,203,000	7,986,000	8,425,000	5,444,000	4,987,000
Current Liabilities	1,771,000	1,871,000	1,906,000	2,181,000	2,002,000	2,758,000	1,681,000	1,599,000
Long-Term Obligations	1,150,000	1,150,000	1,150,000	1,150,000	...	...	...	...
Total Liabilities	3,382,000	3,487,000	3,473,000	3,576,000	2,327,000	3,160,000	2,062,000	1,965,000
Stockholders' Equity	3,768,000	3,569,000	2,824,000	4,627,000	5,659,000	5,265,000	3,382,000	3,022,000
Shares Outstanding	491,000	487,000	476,000	467,000	461,000	453,976	380,000	380,000
Statistical Record								
Return on Assets %	5.61	5.21	N.M.	N.M.	2.12	10.89	9.82	5.14
Return on Equity %	11.11	10.89	N.M.	N.M.	3.19	17.46	15.99	8.38
EBITDA Margin %	10.86	10.19	N.M.	N.M.	3.06	15.40	15.15	10.98
Net Margin %	6.21	4.86	N.M.	N.M.	2.07	7.03	6.15	3.23
Asset Turnover	1.06	1.07	0.84	0.74	1.02	1.55	1.60	1.59
Current Ratio	2.63	2.45	2.04	2.24	2.40	2.05	2.10	1.92
Debt to Equity	0.31	0.32	0.41	0.25	...	...	...	...
Price Range	37.49-19.68	37.49-19.68	26.43-11.45	37.31-10.85	67.56-18.86	159.00-38.81	...	...
P/E Ratio	48.69-25.56	52.80-27.72	...	...	177.80-49.63	95.78-23.38	...	...

Address: 395 Page Mill Road, Palo Alto, CA 94306	Web Site: www.agilent.com	Auditors: PricewaterhouseCoopers LLP
Telephone: (650) 752-5000	Officers: William P. Sullivan - Pres., C.E.O. Adrian T. Dillon - Exec. V.P., Fin., Admin., C.F.O.	Investor Contact: 650-752-5329
Fax: (650) 752-5633		

AGL RESOURCES INC.

Exchange	Symbol	Price	52Wk Range	Yield	P/E
NYS	ATG	$34.93 (3/31/2005)	35.86-26.80	3.55	15.32

*7 Year Price Score 115.84 *NYSE Composite Index=100 *12 Month Price Score 104.55

Interim Earnings (Per Share)

Qtr.	Dec	Jun	Sep	Dec
2002	0.89	0.22	0.17	0.55
2003	0.85	0.29	0.34	0.54
2004	1.00	0.33	0.31	0.64

Interim Dividends (Per Share)

Amt	Decl	Ex	Rec	Pay
0.29Q	4/28/2004	5/12/2004	5/14/2004	6/1/2004
0.29Q	7/28/2004	8/11/2004	8/13/2004	9/1/2004
0.29Q	10/27/2004	11/17/2004	11/19/2004	12/1/2004
0.31Q	2/2/2005	2/16/2005	2/18/2005	3/1/2005

Indicated Div: $1.24

Valuation Analysis

Forecast P/E	15.38	No of Institutions
	(4/7/2005)	204
Market Cap	$2.7 Billion	Shares
Book Value	1.4 Billion	48,166,260
Price/Book	1.94	% Held
Price/Sales	1.47	62.59

Business Summary: Gas Utilities (MIC: 7.4 SIC: 924 NAIC: 21210)

AGL Resources is an Atlanta-based energy services holding company. At Dec 31 2003, 1.8 million natural gas customers were served in Atlanta through subsidiaries Atlanta Gas Light Company, Virginia Natural Gas and Chattanooga Gas Company. Houston-based subsidiary Sequent Energy Management provides asset optimization services including the wholesale trading, marketing, gathering and transportation of natural gas. As a member of the SouthStar partnership, Co. markets natural gas to consumers in Georgia under the Georgia Natural Gas brand. AGL Networks, Co.'s telecommunications subsidiary, owns and operates a fiber optic network in Atlanta and Phoenix.

Recent Developments: For the year ended Dec 31 2004, net income increased 19.5% to $153,000 thousand from net income of $128,000 thousand a year earlier. Revenues were $1,832,000 thousand, up 86.4% from $983,000 thousand the year before. Operating income was $332,000 thousand versus an income of $258,000 thousand in the prior year, an increase of 28.7%. Total direct expense was $1,500,000 thousand versus $741,000 thousand in the prior year, an increase of 102.4%. Total indirect expense was $506,000 thousand versus $386,000 thousand in the prior year, an increase of 31.1%.

Prospects: Co.'is benefiting from stronger contributions from its Wholesale Services business and the inclusion of operations resulting from its acquisition of NUI Corporation, which closed on Nov 30 2004. Also, Co.'s results reflect a stronger performance in the Energy Investments segment and lower interest expense, which is partially offsetting higher corporate expenses and income taxes. Due to operational improvements in late 2004 and based on the existing business climate, Co. raised its guidance for 2005 earnings to be in the range of $2.25 to $2.35 per share.

Financial Data

(US$ in Thousands)	12/31/2004	12/31/2003	12/31/2002	12/31/2001	09/30/2001	09/30/2000	09/30/1999	09/30/1998
Earnings Per Share	2.28	2.01	1.82	0.45	1.62	1.29	1.29	1.41
Cash Flow Per Share	4.32	1.94	5.09	(0.32)	1.83	2.74	4.65	3.11
Tang Book Value Per Share	13.40	11.92	9.42	9.24	8.99	11.50	11.44	11.42
Dividends Per Share	1.150	1.110	1.080	1.080	1.080	1.080	1.080	1.080
Dividend Payout %	50.44	55.22	59.34	240.00	66.67	83.72	83.72	76.60
Income Statement								
Total Revenue	1,832,000	983,700	868,900	201,000	1,049,300	607,400	1,068,600	1,338,600
EBITDA	413,000	389,500	336,100	85,500	327,000	244,300	248,300	249,500
Depn & Amortn	99,000	91,400	89,100	23,200	101,300	84,400	81,800	75,700
Income Before Taxes	243,000	222,500	161,000	38,500	138,800	108,300	113,500	119,400
Income Taxes	90,000	86,800	58,000	13,600	49,900	37,200	39,100	38,800
Net Income	153,000	127,900	103,000	24,900	88,900	71,100	74,400	80,600
Average Shares	67,000	63,700	56,600	55,600	54,900	55,200	57,400	57,100
Balance Sheet								
Net PPE	3,178,000	2,352,400	2,194,200	2,085,200	2,058,900	1,637,500	1,598,900	1,534,000
Total Assets	5,640,000	3,977,800	3,742,000	3,454,300	3,368,100	2,019,900	1,969,300	1,981,800
Long-Term Obligations	1,623,000	730,800	767,000	797,000	845,000	590,000	610,000	660,000
Total Liabilities	4,255,000	2,807,200	2,804,700	2,546,200	2,476,800	1,323,700	1,233,500	1,253,400
Stockholders' Equity	1,385,000	945,300	710,100	690,100	671,400	620,900	661,500	654,100
Shares Outstanding	76,953	64,500	56,700	55,600	55,100	54,000	57,800	57,300
Statistical Record								
Return on Assets %	3.17	3.31	2.86	0.73	3.30	3.55	3.77	4.13
Return on Equity %	13.10	15.45	14.71	3.03	13.76	11.06	11.31	12.63
EBITDA Margin %	22.54	39.60	38.68	42.54	31.16	40.22	23.24	18.64
Net Margin %	8.35	13.00	11.85	12.39	8.47	11.71	6.96	6.02
PPE Turnover	0.66	0.43	0.41	0.09	0.57	0.37	0.68	0.88
Asset Turnover	0.38	0.25	0.24	0.06	0.39	0.30	0.54	0.69
Debt to Equity	1.17	0.77	1.08	1.15	1.26	0.95	0.92	1.01
Price Range	33.59-26.80	29.21-22.08	25.00-17.94	23.16-20.00	24.48-19.17	20.31-15.75	23.19-15.94	22.06-18.00
P/E Ratio	14.73-11.75	14.53-10.99	13.74-9.86	51.47-44.44	15.11-11.83	15.75-12.21	17.97-12.35	15.65-12.77
Average Yield %	3.87	4.26	4.74	5.04	4.92	6.15	5.54	5.50

Address: Ten Peachtree Place N.E.,	Web Site: www.aglresources.com	Auditors: Ernst & Young LLP
Atlanta, GA 30309	Officers: Paula G. Rosput - Chmn., Pres., C.E.O.	Investor Contact: 404-584-3801
Telephone: (404) 584 4000	Richard T. O'Brien - Exec. V.P., C.F.O.	

AIR PRODUCTS & CHEMICALS, INC.

Exchange	Symbol	Price	52Wk Range	Yield	P/E	Div Acheiver
NYS	APD	$63.29 (3/31/2005)	65.14-48.02	2.02	22.85	22 Years

*7 Year Price Score 110.20 *NYSE Composite Index=100 *12 Month Price Score 106.41

TRADING VOLUME (thousand shares)

Interim Earnings (Per Share)

Qtr.	Dec	Mar	Jun	Sep
2001-02	0.52	0.57	0.63	0.65
2002-03	0.56	0.51	0.12	0.59
2003-04	0.58	0.62	0.71	0.73
2004-05	0.72	...	...	...

Interim Dividends (Per Share)

Amt	Decl	Ex	Rec	Pay
0.29Q	5/20/2004	6/29/2004	7/1/2004	8/9/2004
0.29Q	9/16/2004	9/29/2004	10/1/2004	11/8/2004
0.29Q	11/18/2004	12/30/2004	1/3/2005	2/14/2005
0.32Q	3/18/2005	3/30/2005	4/1/2005	5/9/2005

Indicated Div: $1.28 (Div. Reinv. Plan)

Valuation Analysis

Forecast P/E	20.18	No of Institutions
	(4/7/2005)	471
Market Cap	$14.4 Billion	Shares
Book Value	4.7 Billion	192,880,080
Price/Book	3.03	% Held
Price/Sales	1.87	84.75

Business Summary: Chemicals (MIC: 11.1 SIC: 813 NAIC: 25120)

Air Products & Chemicals is engaged in the business of industrial gas and related industrial process equipment and is a producer of certain chemicals. The gases business segment recovers and distributes industrial gases such as oxygen, nitrogen, helium, argon, and hydrogen, and a variety of medical and specialty gases, and also includes Co.'s healthcare business. The chemicals business segment produces and markets performance materials and chemical intermediates. The equipment business segment designs and manufactures equipment for cryogenic air separation, gas processing, natural gas liquefaction, and hydrogen purification.

Recent Developments: For the quarter ended Dec 31 2004, net income increased 26.6% to $166,800 thousand from net income of $131,800 thousand in the year-earlier quarter. Revenues were $1,991,000 thousand, up 18.2% from $1,684,900 thousand the year before. Operating income was $238,300 thousand versus an income of $198,800 thousand in the prior-year quarter, an increase of 19.9%. Total direct expense was $1,475,500 thousand versus $1,230,200 thousand in the prior-year quarter, an increase of 19.9%. Total indirect expense was $277,200 thousand versus $255,900 thousand in the prior-year quarter, an increase of 8.3%.

Prospects: Co. recently announced plans to construct an ultra-high purity (UHP) Ammonia plant in Ulsan, Korea to serve the market in Asia. The new plant and transfill station will be operated by Co.'s subsidiary, Korea Industrial Gases. This location is being built to meet growing customer demand, and should reinforce Co.'s market position as a supplier of UHP Ammonia to the global electronics industry. UHP Ammonia is used in the production of thin film transistor liquid crystal displays, integrated circuits and light emitting diodes. Co.'s revenues are benefiting from strong volumes across its Gases and Chemical businesses. For fiscal 2005, Co. expects earnings to range from $2.95 to $3.15 per share.

Financial Data
(US$ in Thousands)

	3 Mos	09/30/2004	09/30/2003	09/30/2002	09/30/2001	09/30/2000	09/30/1999	09/30/1998
Earnings Per Share	2.77	2.64	1.78	2.36	2.12	0.57	2.09	2.48
Cash Flow Per Share	5.45	4.84	4.72	4.90	5.05	5.49	5.13	4.52
Tang Book Value Per Share	16.36	15.45	12.99	13.33	13.67	12.30	11.39	11.08
Dividends Per Share	1.100	1.040	0.880	0.820	0.780	0.740	0.700	0.640
Dividend Payout %	39.67	39.39	49.44	34.75	36.79	129.82	33.49	25.81
Income Statement								
Total Revenue	1,991,000	7,411,400	6,297,300	5,401,200	5,722,700	5,495,500	5,039,800	4,933,800
EBITDA	443,200	1,687,300	1,343,700	1,491,600	1,520,600	908,700	1,373,700	1,492,300
Depn & Amortn	179,400	714,900	654,800	584,800	592,400	593,900	545,600	505,800
Income Before Taxes	236,000	851,400	565,400	784,500	737,000	118,100	669,000	823,700
Income Taxes	64,900	226,600	147,200	240,800	219,000	(13,700)	203,400	276,900
Net Income	166,800	604,100	397,300	525,400	465,600	124,200	450,500	546,800
Average Shares	232,300	228,900	223,600	222,700	219,300	216,200	216,000	220,100
Balance Sheet								
Current Assets	2,611,000	2,416,900	2,067,900	1,909,300	1,684,800	1,805,000	1,782,400	1,641,700
Total Assets	10,653,400	10,040,400	9,431,900	8,495,000	8,084,100	8,270,500	8,235,500	7,489,600
Current Liabilities	1,804,600	1,705,600	1,581,200	1,256,200	1,352,400	1,374,800	1,857,800	1,265,600
Long-Term Obligations	2,241,400	2,113,600	2,168,600	2,041,000	2,027,500	2,615,800	1,961,600	2,274,300
Total Liabilities	5,728,800	5,427,500	5,461,300	4,850,200	4,860,300	5,333,700	5,146,600	4,822,300
Stockholders' Equity	4,740,800	4,444,000	3,782,500	3,460,400	3,105,800	2,821,300	2,961,600	2,667,300
Shares Outstanding	227,311	227,301	227,265	227,219	227,186	229,305	229,304	211,500
Statistical Record								
Return on Assets %	6.24	6.19	4.43	6.34	5.69	1.50	5.73	7.42
Return on Equity %	14.62	14.65	10.97	16.00	15.71	4.28	16.01	20.57
EBITDA Margin %	22.26	22.77	21.34	27.62	26.57	16.54	27.26	30.25
Net Margin %	8.38	8.15	6.31	9.73	8.14	2.26	8.94	11.08
Asset Turnover	0.75	0.76	0.70	0.65	0.70	0.66	0.64	0.67
Current Ratio	1.45	1.42	1.31	1.52	1.25	1.31	0.96	1.30
Debt to Equity	0.47	0.48	0.57	0.59	0.65	0.93	0.66	0.85
Price Range	58.87-47.02	55.00-44.50	48.64-37.49	53.05-36.82	48.00-32.94	39.00-24.19	49.13-27.94	45.13-29.75
P/E Ratio	21.25-16.97	20.83-16.86	27.33-21.06	22.48-15.60	22.64-15.54	68.42-42.43	23.50-13.37	18.20-12.00
Average Yield %	2.11	2.07	2.04	1.77	1.93	2.35	1.88	1.63

Address: 7201 Hamilton Boulevard, Allentown, PA 18195-1501	**Web Site:** www.airproducts.com	**Auditors:** KPMG LLP
Telephone: (610) 481-4911	**Officers:** John P. Jones III - Chmn., Pres., C.E.O. W. Douglas Brown - V.P., Gen. Couns., Sec.	**Investor Contact:** 610-481-5775
Fax: (610) 481-5900		**Transfer Agents:** American Stock Transfer & Trust Company, New York, NY

AIRGAS INC.

Exchange	Symbol	Price	52Wk Range	Yield	P/E
NYS	ARG	$23.89 (3/31/2005)	27.05-20.83	0.75	20.42

*7 Year Price Score 139.64 ***NYSE Composite Index=100** ***12 Month Price Score 96.53**

TRADING VOLUME (thousand shares)

Interim Earnings (Per Share)

Qtr.	Jun	Sep	Dec	Mar
2001-02	0.20	0.21	0.17	0.13
2002-03	0.20	0.27	0.23	0.25
2003-04	0.25	0.26	0.28	0.28
2004-05	0.29	0.30	0.30	...

Interim Dividends (Per Share)

Amt	Decl	Ex	Rec	Pay
0.045Q	5/25/2004	6/14/2004	6/15/2004	6/30/2004
0.045Q	8/4/2004	9/13/2004	9/15/2004	9/30/2004
0.045Q	10/19/2004	12/13/2004	12/15/2004	12/31/2004
0.045Q	1/25/2005	3/11/2005	3/15/2005	3/31/2005

Indicated Div: $0.18

Valuation Analysis

Forecast P/E	15.89	No of Institutions	194
	(4/7/2005)	Shares	55,413,752
Market Cap	$1.8 Billion	% Held	73.53
Book Value	780.8 Million		
Price/Book	2.33		
Price/Sales	0.80		

Business Summary: Gas Utilities (MIC: 7.4 SIC: 923 NAIC: 21210)

Airgas is a U.S. distributor of industrial, medical and specialty gases, welding, safety and related products. Co. also produces dry ice, liquid carbon dioxide, nitrous oxide, process chemicals and specialty gases for distribution throughout the U.S. Co.'s two operating segments are distribution and gas operations. The distribution segment accounts for over 90% of consolidated sales and reflects the distribution of industrial, medical and specialty gases, process chemicals and hardgoods. The gas operations segment produces and distributes certain gas products, principally dry ice, carbon dioxide, nitrous oxide and specialty gases.

Recent Developments: For the quarter ended Dec 31 2004, net income increased 10.0% to $22,973 thousand from net income of $20,891 thousand in the year-earlier quarter. Revenues were $611,540 thousand, up 35.3% from $451,869 thousand the year before. Operating income was $51,022 thousand versus an income of $40,287 thousand in the prior-year quarter, an increase of 26.6%. Total direct expense was $296,103 thousand versus $213,600 thousand in the prior-year quarter, an increase of 38.6%. Total indirect expense was $264,415 thousand versus $197,982 thousand in the prior-year quarter, an increase of 33.6%.

Prospects: Co. is encouraged with its operating performance, supported by ongoing same-store sales growth, the consolidation of National Welders Supply Company, as well as contributions from acquisitions. These results also reflect continued improvement in the manufacturing and other industrial market segments Co. serves. However, Co.'s earnings are softer than expected, largely due to higher fuel costs and cylinder maintenance that increased at a faster pace as volumes continue to grow, as well as some increased product costs. Looking ahead, Co. is planning comprehensive pricing actions to be implemented by the end of fiscal year ending Mar 2005 to help address the issue of higher costs.

Financial Data
(US$ in Thousands)

	9 Mos	6 Mos	3 Mos	03/31/2004	03/31/2003	03/31/2002	03/31/2001	03/31/2000
Earnings Per Share	1.17	1.15	1.11	1.07	0.94	(0.15)	0.42	0.54
Cash Flow Per Share	2.79	3.23	2.97	2.86	2.76	3.66	3.02	1.44
Tang Book Value Per Share	3.23	2.97	2.66	2.29	1.93	1.01	0.35	N.M.
Dividends Per Share	0.175	0.170	0.165	0.160	...	...	...	...
Dividend Payout %	15.00	14.82	14.90	14.95	...	...	...	...
Income Statement								
Total Revenue	1,755,340	1,143,800	544,010	1,895,468	1,786,964	1,636,047	1,628,901	1,542,334
EBITDA	228,814	150,523	73,326	258,019	235,523	198,349	195,902	217,292
Depn & Amortn	80,982	52,726	25,362	87,956	79,844	72,945	86,754	89,308
Income Before Taxes	109,872	73,274	36,109	127,706	109,304	78,391	48,941	70,424
Income Taxes	40,650	27,477	13,541	47,514	41,199	29,806	20,718	31,551
Net Income	67,866	44,893	22,116	80,192	68,105	(10,415)	28,223	38,283
Average Shares	77,400	76,600	76,200	74,700	72,300	69,900	67,200	70,600
Balance Sheet								
Current Assets	417,878	391,048	334,842	326,830	270,582	303,543	333,845	408,790
Total Assets	2,231,669	2,164,815	1,936,015	1,931,079	1,700,243	1,717,057	1,582,725	1,739,331
Current Liabilities	245,684	244,494	228,671	242,469	208,896	221,331	281,590	219,596
Long-Term Obligations	841,461	807,102	662,963	682,698	658,031	764,124	620,664	857,422
Total Liabilities	1,450,900	1,412,048	1,210,271	1,239,178	1,103,310	1,213,971	1,085,876	1,266,824
Stockholders' Equity	780,769	752,767	725,744	691,901	596,933	503,086	496,849	472,507
Shares Outstanding	76,097	76,076	76,031	73,448	72,405	70,315	73,845	72,018
Statistical Record								
Return on Assets %	4.34	4.46	4.57	4.40	3.99	N.M.	1.70	2.22
Return on Equity %	12.34	12.47	12.38	12.41	12.38	N.M.	5.82	8.09
EBITDA Margin %	13.04	13.16	13.48	13.61	13.18	12.12	12.03	14.09
Net Margin %	3.87	3.92	4.07	4.23	3.81	N.M.	1.73	2.48
Asset Turnover	1.10	1.08	1.08	1.04	1.05	0.99	0.98	0.89
Current Ratio	1.70	1.60	1.46	1.35	1.30	1.37	1.19	1.86
Debt to Equity	1.08	1.07	0.91	0.99	1.10	1.52	1.25	1.81
Price Range	27.05-19.85	24.35-18.63	24.35-16.75	24.35-16.75	19.68-11.87	20.61-7.52	9.70-4.63	13.75-6.06
P/E Ratio	23.12-16.97	21.17-15.48	21.94-15.09	22.76-15.65	20.94-12.63	...	23.10-11.01	25.46-11.23
Average Yield %	0.76	0.79	0.81	0.82	...	...	...	...

Address: 259 North Radnor-Chester Road, Radnor, PA 19087-5283 **Telephone:** (610) 687-5253 **Fax:** (610) 687-1052	**Web Site:** www.airgas.com **Officers:** Peter McCausland - Chmn., C.E.O. Glenn M. Fischer - Pres., C.O.O.
	Auditors: KPMG LLP **Investor Contact:** 610-902-6205 **Transfer Agents:** The Bank of New York

AIRTRAN HOLDINGS, INC.

Exchange	Symbol	Price	52Wk Range	Yield	P/E
NYS	AAI	$9.05 (3/31/2005)	15.17-7.50	N/A	64.64

*7 Year Price Score 131.73 ***NYSE Composite Index=100** ***12 Month Price Score 70.73**

Interim Earnings (Per Share)

Qtr.	Mar	Jun	Sep	Dec
2001	0.01	0.18	(0.15)	(0.20)
2002	(0.04)	0.07	0.02	0.11
2003	0.03	0.74	0.24	0.22
2004	0.05	0.18	(0.11)	0.02

Interim Dividends (Per Share)

No Dividends Paid

Valuation Analysis

Forecast P/E	94.20	No of Institutions	
	(4/7/2005)	157	
Market Cap	$783.9 Million	Shares	
Book Value	334.0 Million	65,429,348	
Price/Book	2.35	% Held	
Price/Sales	0.75	75.40	

Business Summary: Aviation (MIC: 1.1 SIC: 512 NAIC: 81111)

AirTran Holdings operates through its wholly-owned subsidiary, Airtran Airways. Co. operates scheduled airline service in short-haul markets principally in the eastern U.S., primarily from its hub in Atlanta, GA. As of Mar 1 2004, Co. operates 75 Boeing 717 aircraft making about 436 scheduled flights per day to 45 airports across the U.S., serving more than 60 communities in 21 states, the District of Columbia and the Bahamas. As of March 2004, Co. served 45 cities from Atlanta, GA and 10 from Baltimore/Washington. Co.'s schedules are designed to provide convenient service and connections for its passengers.

Recent Developments: For the year ended Dec 31 2004, net income decreased 87.8% to $12,255,000 from net income of $100,517,000 a year earlier. Revenues were $20,828,440,00, up 13.4% from $1,836,080,000 the year before. Operating income was $32,844,000 versus an income of $86,318,000 in the prior year, a decrease of 61.9%. Total direct expense was $317,494,000 versus $242,337,000 in the prior year, an increase of 31.0%. Total indirect expense was $691,084,000 versus $589,385,000 in the prior year, an increase of 17.3%.

Prospects: Looking ahead, Co. expects bookings to recover well following the adverse impact of four hurricanes heading into the fourth quarter, which hurt bookings in late 2004. Early indications reflect that bookings are stronger, and that Co. should see a return to healthier load factors. During the fourth quarter, Co. boarded 3.5 million passengers and generated a 22.6% increase in revenue passenger miles on a 23.4% increase in capacity or available seat miles. Separately, Co. recently announced that it would start daily nonstop service to/from Atlanta, GA and Tampa, FL to Indianapolis, IN beginning on Apr 9 2005. In addition, flights between Orlando, FL and Indianapolis, IN will begin June 7 2005.

Financial Data

(US$ in Thousands)	12/31/2004	12/31/2003	12/31/2002	12/31/2001	12/31/2000	12/31/1999	12/31/1998	12/31/1997
Earnings Per Share	0.14	1.21	0.15	(0.04)	0.69	(1.53)	(0.63)	(1.72)
Cash Flow Per Share	0.45	1.77	0.09	1.41	1.05	1.16	(0.09)	(0.28)
Tang Book Value Per Share	3.51	3.23	0.25	N.M.	N.M.	...	0.20	0.57
Income Statement								
Total Revenue	1,041,422	918,040	733,370	665,164	624,094	523,468	439,307	211,456
EBITDA	45,773	122,902	51,048	66,993	107,229	(41,556)	12,607	(69,266)
Depn & Amortn	11,597	10,780	13,988	33,371	26,078	30,432	31,164	32,500
Income Before Taxes	20,023	87,164	9,959	1,140	47,436	(96,655)	(40,738)	(119,438)
Income Taxes	7,768	(13,353)	(786)	3,240	...	2,739	...	(22,775)
Net Income	12,255	100,517	10,745	(2,757)	47,436	(99,394)	(40,738)	(96,663)
Average Shares	89,523	86,607	73,153	67,774	69,175	65,097	64,641	56,068
Balance Sheet								
Total Assets	905,731	808,364	473,450	497,816	546,255	467,014	376,406	433,864
Long-Term Obligations	285,575	241,821	199,713	254,772	365,412	396,119	237,065	241,251
Total Liabilities	557,136	506,151	421,565	464,409	538,395	507,045	320,776	339,417
Stockholders' Equity	334,036	302,213	51,885	33,407	7,860	(40,031)	55,630	94,447
Shares Outstanding	86,617	84,209	71,132	69,528	65,823	65,698	64,898	64,312
Statistical Record								
Return on Assets %	1.43	15.68	2.21	N.M.	9.34	N.M.	N.M.	N.M.
Return on Equity %	3.84	56.77	25.20	N.M.	N.M.	N.M.	N.M.	N.M.
EBITDA Margin %	4.40	13.39	6.96	10.07	17.18	N.M.	2.87	N.M.
Net Margin %	1.18	10.95	1.47	(0.41)	7.60	(18.99)	(9.27)	(45.71)
Asset Turnover	1.21	1.43	1.51	1.27	1.23	1.24	1.08	0.50
Price Range	15.17-9.67	20.76-3.90	7.32-2.64	12.01-3.03	7.25-3.75	6.97-2.63	8.94-2.63	8.38-3.63
P/E Ratio	108.36-69.07	17.16-3.22	48.80-17.60	...	10.51-5.43	...	...	...

Address: 9955 AirTran Boulevard,	Web Site: www.airtran.com	Auditors: ERNST & YOUNG LLP
Orlando, FL 32827	Officers: Joseph B. Leonard - Chmn., C.E.O. Robert	Transfer Agents: American Stock
Telephone: (407) 251-5600	L. Forano - Pres., C.O.O.	Transfer & Trust Co., Brooklyn, NY
Fax: (407) 251-5727		

AK STEEL HOLDING CORP.

Exchange	Symbol	Price	52Wk Range	Yield	P/E
NYS	AKS	$11.06 (3/31/2005)	17.94-3.98	N/A	5.07

*7 Year Price Score 69.54   *NYSE Composite Index=100   ***12 Month Price Score 149.02**

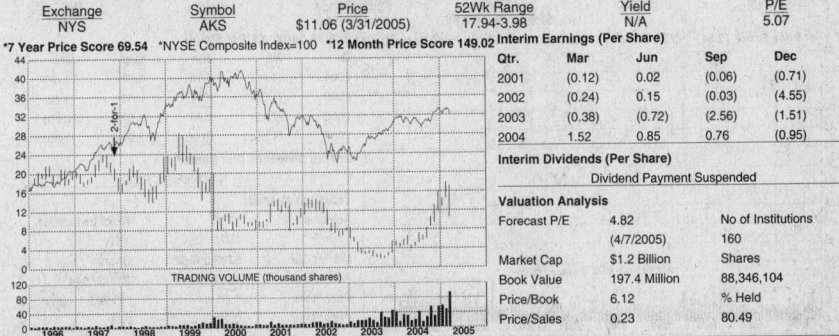

Interim Earnings (Per Share)

Qtr.	Mar	Jun	Sep	Dec
2001	(0.12)	0.02	(0.06)	(0.71)
2002	(0.24)	0.15	0.03	(4.55)
2003	(0.38)	(0.72)	(2.56)	(1.51)
2004	1.52	0.85	0.76	(0.95)

Interim Dividends (Per Share)

Dividend Payment Suspended

Valuation Analysis

Forecast P/E	4.82	No of Institutions	
	(4/7/2005)	160	
Market Cap	$1.2 Billion	Shares	
Book Value	197.4 Million	88,346,104	
Price/Book	6.12	% Held	
Price/Sales	0.23	80.49	

Business Summary: Metal Works (MIC: 11.3 SIC: 312 NAIC: 31111)

AK Steel Holding, through its wholly-owned subsidiary, AK Steel Corporation, is a fully-integrated producer of flat-rolled carbon, stainless and electrical steels and tubular products. As of Dec 31 2004, Co.'s operations consisted of seven steelmaking and finishing plants located in Indiana, Kentucky, Ohio and Pennsylvania. Co.'s operations also included AK Tube LLC, which further finishes flat-rolled carbon and stainless steel at two tube plants located in Ohio and Indiana into welded steel tubing used in the automotive, large truck and construction markets, and European trading companies that buy and sell steel and steel products.

Recent Developments: For the year ended Dec 31 2004, income from continuing operations was $30,500 thousand compared with a loss of $594,400 thousand a year earlier. Net income was $238,400 thousand versus net loss of $560,400 thousand a year earlier. Revenues were $5,217,300 thousand, up 29.1% from $4,041,700 thousand the year before. Operating loss was $79,700 thousand versus a loss of $651,800 thousand in the prior year. Total direct expense was $4,553,600 thousand versus $3,886,900 thousand in the prior year, an increase of 17.2%. Total indirect expense was $743,400 thousand versus $806,600 thousand in the prior year, a decrease of 7.8%.

Prospects: Co.'s results are being influenced by continued strong global demand that has resulted in increased shipment volumes and higher spot market selling prices. Looking ahead, Co. expects to generate substantially higher operating income in 2005 than in 2004, despite facing further price increases for steelmaking raw material inputs. The higher input costs are expected to be more than offset by a combination of higher contract selling prices, higher average spot market selling prices, surcharges, and continued controllable cost reductions and operating efficiencies. Co. stated that it expects to generate 2005 operating profit of approximately $500.0 million on shipments of about 6.3 million tons.

Financial Data

(US$ in Thousands)	12/31/2004	12/31/2003	12/31/2002	12/31/2001	12/31/2000	12/31/1999	12/31/1998	12/31/1997
Earnings Per Share	2.18	(5.17)	(4.67)	(0.87)	1.20	0.56	1.92	2.43
Cash Flow Per Share	2.06	(0.66)	2.88	1.56	3.00	2.43	2.41	8.55
Tang Book Value Per Share	0.92	...	...	3.02	7.42	11.03	10.32	15.75	14.46
Dividends Per Share	...	...	0.500	0.125	0.500	0.500	0.500	0.425
Dividend Payout %	...	...	...	...	41.67	89.29	26.04	17.49
Income Statement								
Total Revenue	5,217,300	4,041,700	4,289,000	3,994,100	4,611,500	4,284,800	2,393,600	2,440,500
EBITDA	135,900	(422,400)	(439,400)	222,600	584,300	482,400	336,100	404,100
Depn & Amortn	219,100	232,800	235,200	236,200	238,100	216,800	103,900	86,300
Income Before Taxes	(193,300)	(773,000)	(802,900)	(146,700)	210,100	141,900	176,200	241,500
Income Taxes	(223,800)	(265,900)	(327,300)	(54,300)	77,700	63,900	61,700	90,600
Net Income	238,400	(560,400)	(502,400)	(92,400)	132,400	65,400	114,500	150,900
Average Shares	109,200	108,500	107,900	107,700	109,600	102,900	59,600	62,000
Balance Sheet								
Current Assets	2,106,800	1,358,000	1,699,700	1,547,800	1,521,800	1,432,500	807,500	1,221,600
Total Assets	5,452,700	5,025,600	5,399,700	5,225,800	5,239,800	5,201,500	3,306,300	3,084,300
Current Liabilities	746,700	778,900	860,300	954,400	890,300	868,000	531,400	563,400
Long-Term Obligations	1,109,700	1,197,800	1,259,900	1,324,500	1,387,600	1,451,000	1,145,000	997,500
Total Liabilities	5,255,300	5,078,400	4,870,400	4,192,500	3,920,500	3,923,700	2,376,800	2,204,700
Stockholders' Equity	197,400	(52,800)	529,300	1,033,300	1,319,300	1,277,800	929,500	879,600
Shares Outstanding	109,151	108,577	107,895	107,713	107,650	110,640	59,022	60,808
Statistical Record								
Return on Assets %	4.54	N.M.	N.M.	N.M.	2.53	1.54	3.58	5.26
Return on Equity %	328.84	N.M.	N.M.	N.M.	10.17	5.93	12.66	18.22
EBITDA Margin %	2.60	N.M.	N.M.	5.57	12.67	11.26	14.04	16.56
Net Margin %	4.57	N.M.	N.M.	N.M.	2.87	1.53	4.78	6.18
Asset Turnover	0.99	0.78	0.81	0.76	0.88	1.01	0.75	0.85
Current Ratio	2.82	1.74	1.98	1.62	1.71	1.65	1.52	2.17
Debt to Equity	5.62	...	2.38	1.28	1.05	1.14	1.23	1.13
Price Range	15.96-3.98	8.43-1.91	14.50-6.49	14.50-7.80	20.06-7.94	28.50-14.31	23.50-13.88	24.00-16.50
P/E Ratio	7.32-1.83	...	...	...	16.72-6.61	50.89-25.56	12.24-7.23	9.88-6.79
Average Yield %	...	...	4.68	1.13	4.83	2.32	2.75	2.11

Address: 703 Curtis Street, Middletown, OH 45043 **Telephone:** (513) 425-5000 **Fax:** (513) 425-5220	**Web Site:** www.aksteel.com **Officers:** Robert H. Jenkins - Chmn. James L. Wainscott - Pres., C.E.O.	**Auditors:** Deloitte & Touche LLP **Investor Contact:** 1-513-425-5392

ALASKA AIR GROUP, INC.

Exchange	Symbol	Price	52Wk Range	Yield	P/E
NYS	ALK	$29.44 (3/31/2005)	33.49-18.88	N/A	N/A

*7 Year Price Score 72.54 *NYSE Composite Index=100 *12 Month Price Score 106.65

Interim Earnings (Per Share)

Qtr.	Mar	Jun	Sep	Dec
2001	(1.25)	0.18	0.95	(1.37)
2002	(1.30)	(0.17)	0.40	(3.42)
2003	(2.12)	1.70	1.52	(0.60)
2004	(1.59)	(0.06)	2.94	(1.86)

Interim Dividends (Per Share)

No Dividends Paid

Valuation Analysis

Forecast P/E	17.91	No of Institutions
	(4/7/2005)	151
Market Cap	$798.6 Million	Shares
Book Value	664.8 Million	28,952,944
Price/Book	1.20	% Held
Price/Sales	0.29	N/A

Business Summary: Aviation (MIC: 1.1 SIC: 512 NAIC: 81111)

Alaska Air Group is the holding company for Alaska Airlines, Inc. and Horizon Air Industries, Inc. As of Dec 31 2003, Alaska Airlines, operated a fleet of 109 aircraft and provided scheduled air transportation to Alaska, Washington, Oregon, California, Arizona, Nevada, Vancouver, Canada and Mexico. The carrier also provides air service between Anchorage, AK and Chicago, IL and between Seattle, WA and five cities on the East Coast including Washington D.C., Boston, MA, Miami, FL, Orlando, FL, and Newark, NJ. Horizon Air provides air service to destinations in Washington, Oregon, Montana, Idaho, California, and Arizona, and Canada through its fleet of 62 aircraft.

Recent Developments: For the year ended Dec 31 2004, net loss was $15,300 thousand versus net income of $13,500 thousand a year earlier. Revenues were $2,723,800 thousand, up 11.4% from $2,444,800 thousand the year before. Operating loss was $79,800 thousand versus a loss of $17,500 thousand in the prior year. Total direct expense was $1,072,500 thousand versus $903,100 thousand in the prior year, an increase of 18.8%. Total indirect expense was $1,729,100 thousand versus $1,554,800 thousand in the prior year, an increase of 11.2%.

Prospects: For full-year 2005, Co. plans to continue pursuing cost savings initiatives that are expected to help it become consistently profitable, and maintain through the pressures of low-cost competition, restructured network airlines and very high fuel prices. Meanwhile, the improvements in Co.'s operating results is showing that it continues to make solid progress with restructuring efforts. Co. is benefiting from its move in early 2004 to simplify fares, coupled with its ongoing focus on customer service, which is contributing to an increase in passenger traffic and loads.

Financial Data
(US$ in Thousands)

	12/31/2004	12/31/2003	12/31/2002	12/31/2001	12/31/2000	12/31/1999	12/31/1998	12/31/1997
Earnings Per Share	(0.57)	0.51	(4.47)	(1.49)	(2.66)	5.06	4.81	3.53
Cash Flow Per Share	12.40	13.33	4.69	10.50	10.00	12.52	13.26	13.88
Tang Book Value Per Share	23.08	23.49	22.76	28.98	30.57	35.85	27.91	22.74
Income Statement								
Total Revenue	2,723,800	2,444,800	2,224,100	2,140,900	2,177,200	2,082,000	1,897,700	1,739,400
EBITDA	210,300	263,900	115,300	161,100	151,300	341,500	313,000	244,700
Depn & Amortn	205,200	202,200	194,700	205,100	170,800	134,900	116,200	103,400
Income Before Taxes	(20,600)	29,000	(101,800)	(57,500)	(15,700)	220,700	204,400	123,600
Income Taxes	(5,300)	15,500	(34,600)	(18,000)	(2,300)	86,500	80,000	51,200
Net Income	(15,300)	13,500	(118,600)	(39,500)	(70,300)	134,200	124,400	72,400
Average Shares	26,859	26,730	26,546	26,499	26,440	26,507	26,367	22,689
Balance Sheet								
Total Assets	3,335,000	3,259,200	2,880,700	2,933,800	2,630,000	2,180,100	1,731,800	1,533,100
Long-Term Obligations	989,600	906,900	856,700	863,300	609,200	337,000	171,500	401,400
Total Liabilities	2,670,200	2,585,000	2,225,000	2,113,500	1,767,700	1,249,400	942,300	1,057,800
Stockholders' Equity	664,800	674,200	655,700	820,300	862,300	930,700	789,500	475,300
Shares Outstanding	27,126	26,761	26,573	26,528	26,457	24,410	26,224	18,283
Statistical Record								
Return on Assets %	N.M.	0.44	N.M.	N.M.	N.M.	6.86	7.62	5.09
Return on Equity %	N.M.	2.03	N.M.	N.M.	N.M.	15.60	19.67	19.36
EBITDA Margin %	7.72	10.79	5.18	7.52	6.95	16.40	16.49	14.07
Net Margin %	(0.56)	0.55	(5.33)	(1.85)	(3.23)	6.45	6.56	4.16
Asset Turnover	0.82	0.80	0.77	0.77	0.90	1.06	1.16	1.22
Price Range	33.49-18.88	31.67-15.66	33.73-14.11	34.00-17.70	36.06-20.75	53.94-33.56	62.50-28.00	40.06-20.88
P/E Ratio	...	62.10-30.71	...	...	...	10.66-6.63	12.99-5.82	11.35-5.91

Address: 19300 Pacific Highway South, Seattle, WA 98188 Telephone: (206) 392 5040	Web Site: www.alaskaair.com Officers: William S. Ayer - Chmn., Pres., C.E.O. Bradley D. Tilden - Exec. V.P., Fin., C.F.O.	Auditors: KPMG LLP Investor Contact: 206-433-3170

ALBEMARLE CORP.

Exchange	Symbol	Price	52Wk Range	Yield	P/E	Div Achiever
NYS	ALB	$36.36 (3/31/2005)	40.32-27.35	1.65	28.19	10 Years

*7 Year Price Score 115.69 *NYSE Composite Index=100 *12 Month Price Score 100.91

Interim Earnings (Per Share)

Qtr.	Mar	Jun	Sep	Dec
2001	0.48	0.32	0.36	0.31
2002	0.38	0.48	0.48	0.39
2003	0.50	0.54	0.23	0.44
2004	0.32	0.49	0.02	0.46

Interim Dividends (Per Share)

Amt	Decl	Ex	Rec	Pay
0.145Q	3/31/2004	6/14/2004	6/15/2004	7/1/2004
0.145Q	6/30/2004	9/13/2004	9/15/2004	10/1/2004
0.15Q	11/17/2004	12/13/2004	12/15/2004	1/1/2005
0.15Q	2/2/2005	3/11/2005	3/15/2005	4/1/2005

Indicated Div: $0.60

Valuation Analysis

Forecast P/E	17.34 (4/7/2005)	No of Institutions 151
Market Cap	$1.5 Billion	Shares 22,410,414
Book Value	711.4 Million	% Held
Price/Book	2.14	48.13
Price/Sales	1.01	

Business Summary: Chemicals (MIC: 11.1 SIC: 821 NAIC: 25211)

Albemarle is a worldwide producer of specialty chemicals. Co.'s operations are managed and reported in two operating segments: Polymer Chemicals and Fine Chemicals. The Polymer Chemicals segment consists of a broad range of chemicals, including flame retardants, catalysts and polymer additives. The Fine Chemicals segment includes a broad range of chemicals, including pharmachemicals, agrichemicals, fine chemistry services and intermediates and performance chemicals. Most of Co.'s products are additives to plastics, polymers and elastomers, cleaning products, personal care products, agricultural compounds, pharmaceuticals, drilling compounds, paper processing chemicals, and biocides.

Recent Developments: For the year ended Dec 31 2004, net income decreased 23.8% to $54,839 thousand from net income of $71,945 thousand a year earlier. Revenues were $1,513,737 thousand, up 36.3% from $1,110,237 thousand the year before. Operating income was $102,081 thousand versus an income of $92,824 thousand in the prior year, an increase of 10.0%. Total direct expense was $1,214,788 thousand versus $871,727 thousand in the prior year, an increase of 39.4%. Total indirect expense was $196,868 thousand versus $145,686 thousand in the prior year, an increase of 35.1%.

Prospects: Co. is hopeful that recent price increases, coupled with good demand across its three operating segments, will lead to margin improvement as 2005 unfolds. Meanwhile, Co. continues to be pleased with the contribution from the refinery catalysts business as integration of that business proceeds. Separately, on Jan 13 2005, Co. announced the opening of a specialty zeolite facility in its Bayport complex, which produces a range of hydrotreating and FCC catalysts and additives. Co. expects the new facility will allow it to expand its capabilities in specialty zeolite production.

Financial Data
(US$ in Thousands)

	12/31/2004	12/31/2003	12/31/2002	12/31/2001	12/31/2000	12/31/1999	12/31/1998	12/31/1997
Earnings Per Share	1.29	1.71	1.73	1.47	2.18	1.87	1.63	1.44
Cash Flow Per Share	4.60	3.64	3.44	3.15	3.37	3.50	2.66	1.79
Tang Book Value Per Share	7.33	12.58	12.82	12.34	11.71	10.23	9.16	9.27
Dividends Per Share	0.585	0.565	0.540	0.520	0.460	0.400	0.370	0.320
Dividend Payout %	45.35	33.04	31.21	35.37	21.10	21.39	22.70	22.22
Income Statement								
Total Revenue	1,513,737	1,110,237	980,215	916,899	917,549	845,925	820,862	829,850
EBITDA	186,462	177,445	189,486	180,342	227,249	212,867	202,297	190,668
Depn & Amortn	97,268	84,014	80,603	77,610	73,750	75,750	75,012	69,044
Income Before Taxes	71,844	88,055	103,813	97,196	147,501	128,738	122,798	120,905
Income Taxes	17,005	13,890	29,068	29,029	45,725	39,909	38,066	40,923
Net Income	54,839	71,945	74,745	68,167	101,776	88,829	84,732	79,982
Average Shares	42,527	42,146	43,137	46,524	46,606	47,513	52,136	55,668
Balance Sheet								
Current Assets	747,410	481,369	413,064	383,661	315,154	332,599	311,530	296,736
Total Assets	2,442,745	1,387,291	1,192,956	1,129,475	981,803	954,094	937,797	888,181
Current Liabilities	373,746	210,071	165,007	303,837	142,116	131,353	107,936	112,560
Long-Term Obligations	899,584	228,389	180,137	12,353	97,681	158,981	192,530	91,414
Total Liabilities	1,731,370	751,070	623,216	536,173	422,896	463,530	486,130	370,845
Stockholders' Equity	711,375	636,221	569,740	593,302	558,907	490,564	451,667	517,336
Shares Outstanding	41,898	41,153	41,692	45,498	45,823	46,199	47,008	53,886
Statistical Record								
Return on Assets %	2.86	5.58	6.44	6.46	10.49	9.39	9.28	9.22
Return on Equity %	8.12	11.93	12.85	11.83	19.34	18.86	17.49	15.64
EBITDA Margin %	12.32	15.98	19.33	19.67	24.77	25.16	24.64	22.98
Net Margin %	3.62	6.48	7.63	7.43	11.09	10.50	10.32	9.64
Asset Turnover	0.79	0.86	0.84	0.87	0.95	0.89	0.90	0.96
Current Ratio	2.00	2.29	2.50	1.26	2.22	2.53	2.89	2.64
Debt to Equity	1.26	0.36	0.32	0.02	0.17	0.32	0.43	0.18
Price Range	40.32-27.35	30.44-22.28	32.89-22.40	25.05-17.35	25.69-14.56	25.19-16.81	26.00-16.63	27.06-17.50
P/E Ratio	31.26-21.20	17.80-13.03	19.01-12.95	17.04-11.80	11.78-6.68	13.47-8.99	15.95-10.20	18.79-12.15
Average Yield %	1.83	2.09	1.92	2.36	2.20	1.96	1.70	1.48

Address: 330 South Fourth Street, P.O. Box 1335, Richmond, VA 23219 **Telephone:** (804) 788-6000 **Fax:** (804) 788-5688	**Web Site:** www.albemarle.com **Officers:** William M. Gottwald - Chmn. Floyd D. Gottwald Jr. - Vice-Chmn.	**Auditors:** PricewaterhouseCoopers LLP **Investor Contact:** 225-388-7320

ALBERTO-CULVER CO.

Exchange	Symbol	Price	52Wk Range	Yield	P/E	Div Acheiver
NYS	ACV	$47.86 (3/31/2005)	55.40-42.05	0.96	23.35	20 Years

*7 Year Price Score 139.93 *NYSE Composite Index=100 *12 Month Price Score 100.47

Interim Earnings (Per Share)

Qtr.	Dec	Mar	Jun	Sep
2001-02	0.33	0.37	0.41	0.44
2002-03	0.40	0.42	0.47	0.51
2003-04	0.02	0.44	0.56	0.52
2004-05	0.53	...	...	...

Interim Dividends (Per Share)

Amt	Decl	Ex	Rec	Pay
50%	1/22/2004	2/23/2004	2/2/2004	2/20/2004
0.10Q	4/22/2004	4/29/2004	5/3/2004	5/20/2004
0.10Q	10/28/2004	11/3/2004	11/5/2004	11/19/2004
0.115Q	1/27/2005	2/3/2005	2/7/2005	2/18/2005

Indicated Div: $0.46

Valuation Analysis

Forecast P/E	19.18 (4/7/2005)	No of Institutions 277
Market Cap	$4.4 Billion	Shares 63,001,912
Book Value	1.4 Billion	% Held 69.11
Price/Book	3.14	
Price/Sales	1.31	

TRADING VOLUME (thousand shares)

Business Summary: Chemicals (MIC: 11.1 SIC: 844 NAIC: 25620)

Alberto-Culver operates two businesses: Global Consumer Products and Beauty Supply Distribution. The Global Consumer Products segment develops, manufactures, and markets beauty, health care, food and household products to the U.S., Canada and internationally. Products include Alberto V05, St. Ives, TRESemme, Motions, Just for Me, Mrs. Dash and Molly McButter. Beauty Supply Distribution, is comprised of two operations: Sally Beauty Supply, a chain of cash-and-carry outlets offering professional beauty supplies to both salon professionals and retail consumers, and Beauty Systems Group, a beauty products distributor offering professional brands to salons and through professional-only stores.

Recent Developments: For the quarter ended Dec 31 2004, net income increased 2738.5% to $49,418 thousand from net income of $1,741 thousand in the year-earlier quarter. Revenues were $847,534 thousand, up 10.8% from $764,751 thousand the year before. Operating income was $77,762 thousand versus an income of $8,058 thousand in the prior-year quarter, an increase of 865.0%. Total direct expense was $421,473 thousand versus $382,718 thousand in the prior-year quarter, an increase of 10.1%. Total indirect expense was $348,299 thousand versus $373,975 thousand in the prior-year quarter, a decrease of 6.9%.

Prospects: Co.'s consumer products group is continuing its strong sales growth, being led by TRESemme, including its recent launch in the U.K., Alberto V05 with its introduction of Nourishing Oasis and St. Ives. Co. anticipates new product launches for its main global brand franchises will be coming both domestically and internationally that should boost sales across the balance of fiscal 2005. In addition, Co. has applied a significant portion of the interest savings from its early debt retirement in 2004 to increasing its advertising and marketing support for its brands and businesses. Separately, Co.'s Beauty Systems group acquired CosmoProf, a full-service professional beauty products distributor.

Financial Data
(US$ in Thousands)

	3 Mos	09/30/2004	09/30/2003	09/30/2002	09/30/2001	09/30/2000	09/30/1999	09/30/1998
Earnings Per Share	2.05	1.54	1.80	1.55	1.27	1.22	1.01	0.91
Cash Flow Per Share	2.70	2.87	2.50	2.69	1.96	1.51	1.06	1.29
Tang Book Value Per Share	8.17	8.24	7.04	5.03	4.60	3.44	3.87	3.84
Dividends Per Share	0.399	0.105	0.405	0.352	0.323	0.290	0.255	0.230
Dividend Payout %	19.50	6.82	22.50	22.79	25.33	23.77	25.33	25.18
Income Statement								
Total Revenue	847,534	3,257,996	2,891,417	2,650,976	2,494,180	2,247,163	1,975,928	1,834,711
EBITDA	91,419	285,212	322,618	281,642	284,181	256,965	216,738	200,639
Depn & Amortn	13,657	51,142	48,827	47,214	95,115	83,475	70,236	59,654
Income Before Taxes	76,028	212,644	251,400	211,792	167,236	154,281	133,783	132,378
Income Taxes	26,610	70,874	89,247	74,127	56,860	51,097	47,493	49,311
Net Income	49,418	141,770	162,153	137,665	110,376	103,184	86,290	83,067
Average Shares	92,450	91,832	89,956	88,821	86,757	84,615	85,743	93,630
Balance Sheet								
Current Assets	1,103,655	1,118,433	1,165,489	984,217	876,949	740,537	645,554	591,565
Total Assets	2,147,667	2,058,780	1,945,609	1,729,491	1,516,501	1,389,819	1,184,534	1,068,184
Current Liabilities	518,230	532,434	465,509	460,447	390,303	340,789	336,401	313,625
Long-Term Obligations	141,368	121,246	320,587	320,181	321,183	340,948	225,173	171,760
Total Liabilities	756,390	745,074	883,480	867,032	780,492	753,338	615,714	534,193
Stockholders' Equity	1,391,277	1,313,706	1,062,129	862,459	736,009	636,481	568,820	533,991
Shares Outstanding	91,165	90,764	88,460	87,268	85,242	83,909	83,588	85,815
Statistical Record								
Return on Assets %	9.06	7.06	8.82	8.48	7.60	7.99	7.66	8.03
Return on Equity %	14.82	11.90	16.85	17.22	16.08	17.07	15.65	16.11
EBITDA Margin %	10.79	8.75	11.16	10.62	11.39	11.44	10.97	10.94
Net Margin %	5.83	4.35	5.61	5.19	4.43	4.59	4.37	4.53
Asset Turnover	1.60	1.62	1.57	1.63	1.72	1.74	1.75	1.77
Current Ratio	2.13	2.10	2.50	2.14	2.25	2.17	1.92	1.89
Debt to Equity	0.10	0.09	0.30	0.37	0.44	0.54	0.40	0.32
Price Range	50.49-39.81	50.49-39.21	39.39-31.45	38.19-25.61	30.28-19.13	21.08-13.04	18.46-14.71	21.71-13.33
P/E Ratio	24.63-19.42	32.79-25.46	21.88-17.47	24.64-16.52	23.84-15.06	17.28-10.69	18.28-14.56	23.86-14.65
Average Yield %	0.22	0.24	1.18	1.09	1.23	1.68	1.51	1.19

Address: 2525 Armitage Avenue, Melrose Park, IL 60160 **Telephone:** (708) 450-3000 **Fax:** (708) 450-3419	**Web Site:** www.alberto.com **Officers:** Carol L. Bernick - Chmn. Bernice E. Lavin - Vice-Chmn., Treas., Sec.	**Auditors:** KPMG LLP **Transfer Agents:** The Corporation Trust Company, Wilmington, DE

ALBERTSON'S, INC.

Exchange	Symbol	Price	52Wk Range	Yield	P/E
NYS	ABS	$20.65 (3/31/2005)	26.88-19.42	3.68	20.25

*7 Year Price Score 62.84   *NYSE Composite Index=100   *12 Month Price Score 85.49

Interim Earnings (Per Share)

Qtr.	Apr	Jul	Oct	Jan
2001-02	0.46	(0.37)	0.43	0.71
2002-03	(0.20)	0.62	0.48	0.32
2003-04	0.47	0.44	0.25	0.35
2004-05	0.10	0.28	0.29	...

Interim Dividends (Per Share)

Amt	Decl	Ex	Rec	Pay
0.19Q	6/10/2004	7/12/2004	7/14/2004	8/10/2004
0.19Q	9/9/2004	10/8/2004	10/13/2004	11/9/2004
0.19Q	12/16/2004	1/10/2005	1/12/2005	2/8/2005
0.19Q	3/24/2005	4/11/2005	4/13/2005	5/10/2005

Indicated Div: $0.76

Valuation Analysis

Forecast P/E	14.81	No of Institutions
	(4/7/2005)	340
Market Cap	$7.6 Billion	Shares
Book Value	5.3 Billion	336,332,576
Price/Book	1.43	% Held
Price/Sales	0.20	91.38

Business Summary: Retail - Food & Beverage (MIC: 5.3 SIC: 411 NAIC: 45110)

Albertson's is one of the largest retail food and drug chains in the United States. As of Jan 29 2004, Co. operated 2,305 stores in 31 states. Co.'s combination food-drug units range between 31,000 sq. ft. and 107,000 sq. ft. and consist of grocery, general merchandise, and meat and produce departments, along with pharmacy, lobby/video, floral, and bakery service departments. Co. also operated 228 fuel centers, which are generally located in the parking lot of stores. Co.'s stores are operated under the Albertson's, Albertson's Express, Albertson's-Osco, Albertson's-Sav-on, Jewel, Jewel-Osco, Acme, Sav-on Drugs, Osco Drug, Max Foods and Super Saver Foods banners.

Recent Developments: For the quarter ended Oct 28 2004, income from continuing operations increased 17.6% to $107,000 thousand from income of $91,000 thousand in the year-earlier quarter. Net income increased 19.6% to $110,000 thousand from net income of $92,000 thousand in the year-earlier quarter. Revenues were $9,995,000 thousand, up 14.7% from $8,715,000 thousand the year before. Operating income was $281,000 thousand versus an income of $254,000 thousand in the prior-year quarter, an increase of 10.6%. Total indirect expense was $2,511,000 thousand versus $2,250,000 thousand in the prior-year quarter, an increase of 11.6%.

Prospects: Co. is not pleased with the performance it turned in during the fourth quarter since it did not achieve its earnings targets. Going forward, Co. will focus on executing better and delivering on its commitments. Separately, in a major cost control program initiated in mid-2001, Co. exceeded its goal of reducing costs by $1.00 billion by the end of fiscal 2005. Through the fourth quarter of 2004, slightly over $1.00 billion in savings had been achieved. Consequently, Co. raised its cost savings target by another $250.0 million over the next two years, establishing a new cost savings target of $1.25 billion to be reached by the end of fiscal 2006.

Financial Data
(US$ in Thousands)

	9 Mos	6 Mos	3 Mos	01/29/2004	01/30/2003	01/31/2002	02/01/2001	02/03/2000
Earnings Per Share	1.02	0.98	1.15	1.51	1.22	1.23	1.83	0.95
Cash Flow Per Share	5.28	4.90	4.27	4.21	5.21	5.17	4.27	3.26
Tang Book Value Per Share	5.77	5.88	10.42	10.46	9.63	10.51	9.85	9.72
Dividends Per Share	0.760	0.760	0.760	0.760	0.760	0.760	0.760	0.720
Dividend Payout %	74.31	77.17	66.37	50.33	62.30	61.79	41.53	75.79
Income Statement								
Total Revenue	28,819,000	18,831,000	8,688,000	35,436,000	35,626,000	37,931,000	36,762,000	37,478,000
EBITDA	1,612,000	1,046,000	439,000	2,266,000	2,749,000	2,331,000	2,660,000	2,164,000
Depn & Amortn	806,000	522,000	246,000	951,000	948,000	1,026,000	1,001,000	912,000
Income Before Taxes	446,000	289,000	90,000	906,000	1,405,000	873,000	1,274,000	899,000
Income Taxes	158,000	108,000	34,000	350,000	540,000	372,000	509,000	472,000
Net Income	249,000	140,000	36,000	556,000	485,000	501,000	765,000	404,000
Average Shares	373,000	371,000	371,000	368,000	399,000	408,000	418,000	423,000
Balance Sheet								
Current Assets	4,596,000	4,233,000	6,090,000	4,419,000	4,268,000	4,609,000	4,300,000	4,582,000
Total Assets	18,712,000	18,115,000	16,977,000	15,394,000	15,211,000	15,967,000	16,078,000	15,701,000
Current Liabilities	4,350,000	4,047,000	3,680,000	3,685,000	3,448,000	3,582,000	3,395,000	4,055,000
Long-Term Obligations	6,902,000	6,563,000	6,417,000	4,804,000	5,257,000	5,336,000	5,942,000	4,992,000
Total Liabilities	13,384,000	12,828,000	11,619,000	10,013,000	10,014,000	10,052,000	10,384,000	9,999,000
Stockholders' Equity	5,328,000	5,287,000	5,358,000	5,381,000	5,197,000	5,915,000	5,694,000	5,702,000
Shares Outstanding	368,000	368,000	368,000	368,000	372,000	407,000	405,000	424,000
Statistical Record								
Return on Assets %	2.24	2.19	2.63	3.64	3.12	3.14	4.83	3.62
Return on Equity %	7.15	6.87	7.99	10.54	8.75	8.65	13.46	9.34
EBITDA Margin %	5.59	5.55	5.05	6.39	7.72	6.15	7.24	5.77
Net Margin %	0.86	0.74	0.41	1.57	1.36	1.32	2.08	1.08
Asset Turnover	2.22	2.19	2.20	2.32	2.29	2.37	2.32	3.36
Current Ratio	1.06	1.05	1.65	1.20	1.24	1.29	1.27	1.13
Debt to Equity	1.30	1.24	1.20	0.89	1.01	0.90	1.04	0.88
Price Range	26.88-19.65	26.88-18.39	25.10-18.07	24.14-17.92	35.17-19.27	36.56-27.40	38.88-20.38	60.50-29.38
P/E Ratio	26.35-19.26	27.43-18.77	21.83-15.71	15.99-11.87	28.83-15.80	29.72-22.28	21.24-11.13	63.68-30.92
Average Yield %	3.26	3.40	3.57	3.74	2.74	2.44	2.72	1.56

Address: 250 Parkcenter Blvd., P.O. Box 20, Boise, ID 83726	**Web Site:** www.albertsons.com	**Auditors:** Deloitte & Touche LLP
Telephone: (208) 395-6200	**Officers:** Lawrence R. Johnston - Chmn., Pres., C.E.O. Felicia D. Thornton - Exec. V.P., C.F.O.	**Investor Contact:** 208-395-6622
Fax: (208) 395-6777		

ALCOA, INC.

Exchange	Symbol	Price	52Wk Range	Yield	P/E
NYS	AA	$30.39 (3/31/2005)	36.50-28.37	1.97	20.40

*7 Year Price Score 91.71   ***NYSE Composite Index=100**   ***12 Month Price Score 90.11**

TRADING VOLUME (thousand shares)

Interim Earnings (Per Share)

Qtr.	Mar	Jun	Sep	Dec
2001	0.46	0.35	0.39	...
2002	0.26	0.27	0.23	(0.26)
2003	0.17	0.26	0.33	0.32
2004	0.41	0.46	0.32	0.30

Interim Dividends (Per Share)

Amt	Decl	Ex	Rec	Pay
0.15Q	4/29/2004	5/6/2004	5/10/2004	5/25/2004
0.15Q	7/9/2004	8/4/2004	8/6/2004	8/25/2004
0.15Q	9/17/2004	11/3/2004	11/5/2004	11/25/2004
0.15Q	1/14/2005	2/2/2005	2/4/2005	2/25/2005

Indicated Div: $0.60

Valuation Analysis

Forecast P/E	14.08	No of Institutions
	(4/7/2005)	631
Market Cap	$26.5 Billion	Shares
Book Value	13.3 Billion	666,814,464
Price/Book	1.99	% Held
Price/Sales	1.13	76.51

Business Summary: Metal Works (MIC: 11.3 SIC: 334 NAIC: 31315)

Alcoa is a producer of primary aluminum, fabricated aluminum and alumina, and is a major participant in all aspects of the industry: technology, mining, refining, smelting, fabricating and recycling. Co. serves customers worldwide in the packaging, consumer, automotive and transportation, aerospace, building and construction, industrial products and distribution markets. In addition, Co. markets consumer brands including Reynolds Wrap® foil and plastic wraps, Alcoa® wheels, and Baco® household wraps. Co.'s other businesses include vinyl siding, closures, precision castings, and vehicle electrical distribution systems.

Recent Developments: For the year ended Dec 31 2004, income from continuing operations increased 32.9% to $1,402,000 thousand from income of $1,055,000 thousand a year earlier. Net income increased 39.7% to $1,310,000 thousand from net income of $938,000 thousand a year earlier. Revenues were $23,478,000 thousand, up 11.3% from $21,092,000 thousand the year before. Total direct expense was $18,623,000 thousand versus $16,754,000 thousand in the prior year, an increase of 11.2%. Total indirect expense was $2,649,000 thousand versus $2,588,000 thousand in the prior year, an increase of 2.4%.

Prospects: In Feb 2005, Co. completed the 250,000 metric ton per year expansion of its alumina refinery in Paranam, Suriname six months ahead of schedule at a total cost of about $65.0 million. Meanwhile, in January 2005, Co. completed the acquisition from RUSAL of two fabricating facilities in Samara and Belaya Kalitva in the Russian Federation for $257.0 million in cash. Separately, to take advantage of higher aluminum prices, Co. is restarting several smelters in North America expected to add 220,000 metric tons of production in 2005. In 2005, Co. plans to invest in a new anode plant in Norway, modernization of a Spanish smelter and improvements at the acquired Russian fabricating facilities.

Financial Data

(US$ in Thousands)	12/31/2004	12/31/2003	12/31/2002	12/31/2000	12/31/1999	12/31/1998	12/31/1997	12/31/1996
Earnings Per Share	1.49	1.08	0.49	1.81	1.41	1.21	1.16	0.73
Cash Flow Per Share	2.52	2.85	2.18	3.49	3.05	3.15	2.74	1.83
Tang Book Value Per Share	6.72	6.30	4.15	6.20	6.71	6.25	6.48	6.39
Dividends Per Share	0.600	0.600	0.600	0.500	0.403	0.344	0.244	0.333
Dividend Payout %	40.27	55.56	122.45	27.62	28.55	28.41	21.10	45.24
Income Statement								
Total Revenue	23,478,000	21,504,000	20,263,000	23,090,000	16,447,000	15,489,400	13,481,700	13,128,400
EBITDA	3,375,000	2,833,000	1,995,000	4,031,000	2,750,000	2,461,000	2,355,300	1,845,900
Depn & Amortn	1,212,000	1,202,000	1,116,000	1,219,000	901,000	856,200	753,600	764,200
Income Before Taxes	2,204,000	1,669,000	925,000	2,812,000	1,849,000	1,604,800	1,601,700	1,081,700
Income Taxes	557,000	404,000	292,000	942,000	553,000	513,500	528,700	360,700
Net Income	1,310,000	938,000	420,000	1,484,000	1,054,000	853,000	805,100	514,900
Average Shares	877,400	856,600	849,800	823,200	747,200	703,234	695,440	697,336
Balance Sheet								
Current Assets	7,493,000	6,740,000	6,313,000	7,578,000	4,800,000	5,025,100	4,416,900	4,281,200
Total Assets	32,609,000	31,711,000	29,810,000	31,691,000	17,066,000	17,462,500	13,070,600	13,449,900
Current Liabilities	6,298,000	5,084,000	4,461,000	7,954,000	3,003,000	3,268,300	2,452,500	2,373,400
Long-Term Obligations	5,346,000	6,692,000	8,365,000	4,987,000	2,657,000	2,877,000	1,457,200	1,689,800
Total Liabilities	17,893,000	18,296,000	18,590,000	18,755,000	9,290,000	9,930,600	7,211,500	7,377,000
Stockholders' Equity	13,300,000	12,075,000	9,927,000	11,422,000	6,318,000	6,055,900	4,419,400	4,462,400
Shares Outstanding	870,980	868,490	844,819	865,517	735,497	733,618	673,104	690,040
Statistical Record								
Return on Assets %	4.06	3.05	1.37	6.07	6.11	5.59	6.07	3.79
Return on Equity %	10.30	8.53	3.93	16.68	17.04	16.29	18.13	11.53
EBITDA Margin %	14.38	13.17	9.85	17.46	16.72	15.89	17.47	14.06
Net Margin %	5.58	4.36	2.07	6.43	6.41	5.51	5.97	3.92
Asset Turnover	0.73	0.70	0.66	0.94	0.95	1.01	1.02	0.97
Current Ratio	1.19	1.33	1.42	0.95	1.60	1.54	1.80	1.80
Debt to Equity	0.40	0.55	0.84	0.44	0.42	0.48	0.33	0.38
Price Range	38.78-28.70	38.91-18.57	45.36-18.03	43.00-23.50	41.50-18.44	20.08-14.83	22.19-15.94	16.56-12.59
P/E Ratio	26.03-19.26	36.03-17.19	92.57-36.80	23.76-12.98	29.43-13.08	16.59-12.25	19.13-13.74	22.69-17.25
Average Yield %	1.82	2.30	1.80	1.57	1.40	1.92	1.31	2.22

Address: 201 Isabella Street, Pittsburgh, PA 15212-5858 **Telephone:** (412) 553-4707 **Fax:** (412) 553-4498	**Web Site:** www.alcoa.com **Officers:** Alain J. P. Belda - Chmn., C.E.O. Richard B. Kelson - Exec. V.P., C.F.O.	**Auditors:** PricewaterhouseCoopers LLP **Investor Contact:** 212-836-2674

ALLEGHANY CORP.

Exchange	Symbol	Price	52Wk Range	Yield	P/E
NYS	Y	$277.00 (3/31/2005)	293.88-242.45	N/A	18.45

*7 Year Price Score 121.44 ***NYSE Composite Index=100** ***12 Month Price Score 94.44**

Interim Earnings (Per Share)

Qtr.	Mar	Jun	Sep	Dec
2001	57.33	(1.19)	(28.21)	0.41
2002	3.28	1.05	2.81	(0.14)
2003	0.99	0.77	9.60	9.47
2004	7.92	6.21	(6.00)	6.88

Interim Dividends (Per Share)

Amt	Decl	Ex	Rec	Pay
2%	3/20/2002	3/27/2002	4/1/2002	4/26/2002
2%	3/19/2003	3/28/2003	4/1/2003	4/25/2003
2%	2/25/2004	3/30/2004	4/1/2004	4/23/2004
2%	3/4/2005	3/30/2005	4/1/2005	4/22/2005

Valuation Analysis

Forecast P/E	N/A	No of Institutions
Market Cap	$2.2 Billion	Shares
Book Value	1.8 Billion	4,676,965
Price/Book	1.24	% Held
Price/Sales	1.75	60.93

Business Summary: Insurance (MIC: 8.2 SIC: 361 NAIC: 24127)

Alleghany is engaged, through its subsidiary, Alleghany Insurance Holdings LLC, and its subsidiaries, RSUI Group, Inc., Capitol Transamerica Corp., Darwin Professional Underwriters, Inc. and Platte River Insurance Co., in the property and casualty and fidelity and surety insurance businesses. Through its subsidiaries, World Minerals Inc., Celite Corp. and Harborlite Corp. and their subsidiaries, Co. is engaged in the industrial minerals business. Co. also conducts a steel fastener importing and distribution business through its subsidiary, Heads & Threads International LLC. Through its subsidiary, Alleghany Properties, Inc., Co. owns and manages properties in California.

Recent Developments: For the year ended Dec 31 2004, income from continuing operations decreased 29.0% to $117,948 thousand from income of $166,188 thousand a year earlier. Net income decreased 27.5% to $117,696 thousand from net income of $162,378 thousand a year earlier. Revenues were $1,240,927 thousand, up 37.1% from $904,956 thousand the year before. Net premiums earned were $805,417 thousand versus $430,914 thousand in the prior year, an increase of 86.9%.

Prospects: Co.'s recent bottom line results included higher operating results from its Alleghany Insurance Holdings LLC unit, which is a holding company for its property and casualty insurance businesses, consisting of RSUI Group, Inc., Capitol Transamerica Corporation and Darwin Professional Underwriters, Inc. Separately, on Dec 31 2004, Co. announced the completion of the sale of its industrial fasteners business Heads & Threads International LLC to an acquisition vehicle formed by a private investor group led by Heads & Threads management and Capital Partners, Inc. of Greenwich, CT. Under the terms of the transaction, Co. received consideration of approximately $54.0 million in cash.

Financial Data
(US$ in Thousands)

	12/31/2004	12/31/2003	12/31/2002	12/31/2001	12/31/2000	12/31/1999	12/31/1998	12/31/1997
Earnings Per Share	15.01	20.88	7.02	28.97	8.44	11.95	11.33	12.49
Cash Flow Per Share	52.31	54.98	5.02	44.51	(14.45)	15.89	16.71	20.09
Tang Book Value Per Share	195.72	170.46	164.29	181.85	152.23	134.53	150.18	185.61
Premium Income	805,417	430,914	125,649	...	365,528	719,846	420,809	376,672
Total Revenue	1,240,927	1,018,233	576,857	924,955	945,208	1,376,163	918,993	796,654
Benefits & Claims	540,598	250,202	100,508	...	392,006	548,459	288,259	261,828
Income Statement								
Income Before Taxes	170,127	240,367	57,404	534,379	(12,144)	161,904	91,016	65,230
Income Taxes	52,179	77,989	2,591	103,816	(46,119)	61,799	27,635	13,830
Net Income	117,696	162,378	54,813	224,230	68,857	100,105	96,106	105,667
Average Shares	7,853	7,779	7,807	7,741	8,156	8,378	8,478	8,454
Balance Sheet								
Total Assets	4,427,725	3,568,040	2,134,382	1,875,005	2,707,616	4,485,025	4,282,444	3,700,376
Total Liabilities	2,671,625	2,005,218	755,040	484,423	1,542,542	3,377,128	3,035,016	2,129,441
Stockholders' Equity	1,756,100	1,562,822	1,379,342	1,390,582	1,165,074	1,107,897	1,247,428	1,570,935
Shares Outstanding	7,829	7,797	7,708	7,646	7,653	8,235	8,306	8,463
Statistical Record								
Return on Assets %	2.94	5.70	2.73	9.79	1.91	2.28	2.41	2.58
Return on Equity %	7.07	11.04	3.96	17.55	6.04	8.50	6.82	7.06
Price Range	293.88-211.73	215.33-147.43	181.40-163.26	206.94-169.03	186.13-146.67	181.37-155.67	215.90-147.26	152.49-107.97
P/E Ratio	19.58-14.11	10.31-7.06	25.84-23.26	7.14-5.83	22.05-17.38	15.18-13.03	19.06-13.00	12.21-8.64

Address: 375 Park Avenue, New York, NY 10152	Web Site: www.alleghanyfunds.com	Auditors: KPMG LLP
Telephone: (212) 752-1356	Officers: F. M. Kirby - Chmn. John J. Burns Jr. - Pres., C.E.O., C.O.O.	
Fax: (212) 759-8149		

ALLEGHENY ENERGY, INC.

Exchange	Symbol	Price	52Wk Range	Yield	P/E
NYS	AYE	$20.66 (3/31/2005)	21.22-13.30	N/A	N/A

*7 Year Price Score 54.55   ***NYSE Composite Index=100**   ***12 Month Price Score 109.64**

TRADING VOLUME (thousand shares)

Interim Earnings (Per Share)

Qtr.	Mar	Jun	Sep	Dec
2001	0.63	1.01	1.32	0.50
2002	0.81	(0.26)	(2.09)	(2.24)
2003	(0.46)	(1.82)	(0.40)	(0.11)
2004	0.25	(0.31)	(2.40)	0.63

Interim Dividends (Per Share)

Dividend Payment Suspended

Valuation Analysis

Forecast P/E	48.38	No of Institutions
	(4/13/2005)	244
Market Cap	$2.8 Billion	Shares
Book Value	1.1 Billion	113,052,416
Price/Book	2.50	% Held
Price/Sales	0.94	82.23

Business Summary: Electricity (MIC: 7.1 SIC: 911 NAIC: 21121)

Allegheny Energy is a utility holding company. Co.'s porfolio of businesses include Allegheny Energy Supply, which owns and operates electric generating facilities, and Allegheny Power, which delivers electric and natural gas service to about 4.0 million people in Pennsylvania, West Virginia, Maryland, Virginia and Ohio. Co. aligns its businesses into two segments: The Generation and Marketing segment comprises Co.'s power generation operations, which are generally unregulated (other than Monongahela's West Virginia jurisdictional generating assets). The Delivery and Services segment comprises Co.'s regulated electric and natural gas transmission and distribution (T&D) operations.

Recent Developments: For the year ended Dec 31 2004, Co. reported income from continuing operations of $129.7 million compared with a loss of $308.9 million, before an accounting change charge of $20.8 million, in the previous year. Earnings excluded losses from discontinued operations of $440.3 million and $25.3 million, respectively. Results for 2004 included a gain on the sale of a power agreement and shares of $94.8 million. Revenues advanced 26.3% to $2.76 billion from $2.18 billion a year earlier. Operating income amounted to $589.2 million versus a loss of $196.4 million the year before.

Prospects: In 2004, Co. earned a profit on its core operations, completed the sale of two non-strategic assets, and made further progress towards its debt reduction goal. Co. continues to pursue a plan to reduce debt and build a more focused company through the sale of non-core assets. Co.'s goal is to reduce debt by $1.50 billion by year-end 2005. Since December 2003, Co. has achieved $1.20 billion of this targeted reduction. Meanwhile, Co.'s performance initiatives launched in 2004 are expected to drive improved profitability in 2005 and beyond. On Dec 31 2004, Co. announced the completed sale of its interest in the Ohio Valley Electric Corporation (OVEC) for total proceeds of $102.0 million in cash.

Financial Data

(US$ in Thousands)	9 Mos	6 Mos	3 Mos	12/31/2003	12/31/2002	12/31/2001	12/31/2000	12/31/1999
Earnings Per Share	(2.57)	(0.57)	(2.06)	(2.80)	(5.04)	3.47	2.14	2.22
Cash Flow Per Share	2.92	3.79	3.14	2.92	2.59	2.78	4.82	5.32
Tang Book Value Per Share	5.35	8.71	9.01	8.72	12.05	16.48	13.80	14.97
Dividends Per Share	...	...	...	...	1.290	1.720	1.720	1.720
Dividend Payout %	...	...	...	...	49.57	80.37	77.48	
Income Statement								
Total Revenue	2,067,624	1,546,834	889,720	2,472,432	2,988,487	10,378,931	4,011,852	2,808,441
EBITDA	592,733	389,566	274,931	194,792	(242,051)	1,024,552	783,625	726,525
Depn & Amortn	222,894	168,482	83,291	291,900	308,552	301,536	247,933	257,456
Income Before Taxes	68,861	(8,762)	60,711	(558,378)	(850,156)	...	...	...
Income Taxes	25,196	(3,723)	25,574	(216,990)	(334,471)	245,067	184,801	164,441
Net Income	(383,020)	(6,178)	33,278	(354,979)	(632,690)	417,775	236,629	258,421
Average Shares	154,217	126,971	152,941	126,848	125,657	120,542	110,436	116,237
Balance Sheet								
Net PPE	6,308,660	7,449,808	7,459,438	7,453,477	6,882,574	6,853,015	5,539,338	5,207,151
Total Assets	9,080,601	9,868,936	10,022,573	10,171,896	10,600,279	11,167,552	7,697,017	6,852,441
Long-Term Obligations	4,849,776	5,307,376	5,319,409	5,159,920	154,998	3,235,730	2,559,510	2,254,463
Total Liabilities	7,870,577	8,280,664	8,397,130	8,568,580	8,572,931	8,353,592	5,882,336	5,083,116
Stockholders' Equity	1,136,024	1,514,272	1,551,443	1,515,859	1,931,507	2,709,969	1,740,681	1,695,325
Shares Outstanding	137,257	127,112	126,969	126,968	126,597	125,276	110,436	110,436
Statistical Record								
Return on Assets %	N.M.	N.M.	N.M.	N.M.	N.M.	4.43	3.24	3.80
Return on Equity %	N.M.	N.M.	N.M.	N.M.	N.M.	18.77	13.74	13.86
EBITDA Margin %	28.67	25.18	30.90	7.88	N.M.	9.87	19.53	25.87
Net Margin %	(18.52)	(0.40)	3.74	(14.36)	(21.17)	4.03	5.90	9.20
PPE Turnover	0.45	0.40	0.36	0.34	0.44	1.68	0.74	0.54
Asset Turnover	0.31	0.29	0.25	0.24	0.27	1.10	0.55	0.41
Debt to Equity	4.27	3.50	3.43	3.40	0.08	1.19	1.47	1.33
Price Range	16.08-9.14	15.41-7.20	13.85-6.21	12.95-4.82	43.53-3.80	54.79-33.25	48.19-24.00	34.94-26.31
P/E Ratio	...	...	...	...	...	15.79-9.58	22.52-11.21	15.74-11.85
Average Yield %	...	...	...	...	5.24	3.93	5.23	5.39

Address: 10435 Downsville Pike, Hagerstown, MD 21740-1766 **Telephone:** (301) 790-3400 **Fax:** (301) 665-2746	**Web Site:** www.alleghenyenergy.com **Officers:** Paul J. Evanson - Chmn., Pres., C.E.O. Jeffrey D. Serkes - Sr. V.P., C.F.O.	**Auditors:** PricewaterhouseCoopers LLP **Investor Contact:** 301-665-2713 **Transfer Agents:** Mellon Investor Services LLC

ALLEGHENY TECHNOLOGIES, INC

Exchange	Symbol	Price	52Wk Range	Yield	P/E
NYS	ATI	$24.11 (3/31/2005)	26.05-9.59	1.00	109.59

*7 Year Price Score 77.04   *NYSE Composite Index=100   *12 Month Price Score 121.59

Interim Earnings (Per Share)

Qtr.	Mar	Jun	Sep	Dec
2001	0.08	0.08	0.10	(0.57)
2002	(0.14)	(0.09)	(0.09)	(0.50)
2003	(0.34)	(0.32)	(0.36)	(2.88)
2004	(0.63)	0.31	0.09	0.40

Interim Dividends (Per Share)

Amt	Decl	Ex	Rec	Pay
0.06Q	6/10/2004	6/17/2004	6/21/2004	6/29/2004
0.06Q	9/2/2004	9/16/2004	9/20/2004	9/28/2004
0.06Q	12/9/2004	12/16/2004	12/20/2004	12/28/2004
0.06Q	2/25/2005	3/17/2005	3/21/2005	3/29/2005

Indicated Div: $0.24

Valuation Analysis

Forecast P/E	11.82	No of Institutions
	(4/7/2005)	196
Market Cap	$2.3 Billion	Shares
Book Value	425.9 Million	65,166,708
Price/Book	5.42	% Held
Price/Sales	0.84	67.96

Business Summary: IT & Technology (MIC: 10.2 SIC: 674 NAIC: 34413)

Allegheny Technologies is a diversified producer of specialty materials including super stainless steel, nickel-based and cobalt-based alloys and superalloys, titanium and titanium alloys, specialty steels, tungsten materials, exotic alloys, which include zirconium, hafnium and niobium, and highly engineered strip and Precision Rolled Strip® products. Also, Co. produces commodity specialty materials, such as stainless steel sheet and plate, silicon electrical and tool steels, and carbon alloy steel impression die forgings and large grey and ductile iron castings. Operations are divided into three segments including Flat-Rolled Products, High Performance Metals, and Engineered Products.

Recent Developments: For the year ended Dec 31 2004, net income was $19,800 thousand versus net loss of $(314,600) thousand a year earlier. Revenues were $2,733,000 thousand, up 41.1% from $1,937,400 thousand the year before. Operating income was $52,000 thousand versus a loss of $247,400 thousand in the prior year. Total direct expense was $2,488,100 thousand versus $1,873,600 thousand in the prior year, an increase of 32.8%. Total indirect expense was $192,900 thousand versus $311,200 thousand in the prior year, a decrease of 38.0%.

Prospects: Co. is optimistic about its growth prospects in the coming year, with much improved end markets, pricing actions and higher raw material surcharges leading to considerable growth in revenues. Co. expects this trend to continue in the near-term, with overall base-prices expected to be higher in 2005 than in 2004 for approximately 95.0% of the shipments in its Flat-Rolled Products and High Performance Metals segments. Co. is also encouraged about the aerospace market's build forecasts, which should lead to increased demand for high performance metal content. Separately, Co. has taken cost cutting measures, which should reduce costs by $100.0 million in fiscal 2005.

Financial Data

(US$ in Thousands)	12/31/2004	12/31/2003	12/31/2002	12/31/2001	12/31/2000	12/31/1999	12/31/1998	12/31/1997
Earnings Per Share	0.22	(3.89)	(0.82)	(0.31)	1.60	3.13	2.44	3.34
Cash Flow Per Share	0.28	1.01	2.53	1.53	1.68	1.08	4.06	2.93
Tang Book Value Per Share	2.30	N.M.	3.15	9.42	10.51	11.02	11.12	9.52
Dividends Per Share	0.240	0.240	0.660	0.800	0.800	...	...	...
Dividend Payout %	109.09	...	...	...	50.00	...	...	...
Income Statement								
Total Revenue	2,733,000	1,937,400	1,907,800	2,128,000	2,460,400	2,296,100	3,923,400	3,745,100
EBITDA	131,400	(177,900)	20,500	91,500	342,900	295,400	519,500	593,300
Depn & Amortn	76,100	74,600	90,000	98,600	99,700	95,300	109,000	98,500
Income Before Taxes	19,800	(280,200)	(103,800)	(36,400)	208,800	174,200	391,200	475,200
Income Taxes	...	33,100	(38,000)	(11,200)	76,300	63,200	150,000	177,600
Net Income	19,800	(314,600)	(65,800)	(25,200)	132,500	300,200	241,200	297,600
Average Shares	90,500	80,800	80,600	80,300	80,300	95,900	99,100	89,200
Balance Sheet								
Current Assets	1,160,200	743,300	812,400	926,100	1,022,800	1,033,500	1,364,500	1,228,700
Total Assets	2,315,700	1,884,900	2,093,200	2,643,200	2,776,200	2,750,600	3,175,500	2,604,500
Current Liabilities	492,800	394,700	342,000	332,700	413,500	540,000	622,300	561,500
Long-Term Obligations	553,300	504,300	509,400	573,000	490,600	200,300	446,800	326,100
Total Liabilities	1,889,800	1,710,200	1,644,400	1,698,500	1,737,000	1,550,400	1,835,600	1,604,800
Stockholders' Equity	425,900	174,700	448,800	944,700	1,039,200	1,200,200	1,339,900	999,700
Shares Outstanding	95,782	80,654	80,634	80,314	80,339	90,368	97,436	87,165
Statistical Record								
Return on Assets %	0.94	N.M.	N.M.	N.M.	4.78	10.13	8.35	11.42
Return on Equity %	6.58	N.M.	N.M.	N.M.	11.80	23.64	20.62	31.81
EBITDA Margin %	4.81	N.M.	1.07	4.30	13.94	12.87	13.24	15.84
Net Margin %	0.72	N.M.	N.M.	N.M.	5.39	13.07	6.15	7.95
Asset Turnover	1.30	0.97	0.81	0.79	0.89	0.77	1.36	1.44
Current Ratio	2.35	1.88	2.38	2.78	2.47	1.91	2.19	2.19
Debt to Equity	1.30	2.89	1.14	0.61	0.47	0.17	0.33	0.33
Price Range	22.93-8.72	13.90-2.45	18.11-5.30	21.07-12.73	26.38-13.00	44.91-20.31	54.91-28.10	61.49-40.45
P/E Ratio	104.23-39.64	...	...	...	16.48-8.13	14.35-6.49	22.50-11.52	18.41-12.11
Average Yield %	1.55	3.78	5.41	4.68	3.97	...	...	...

Address: 1000 Six PPG Place, Pittsburgh, PA 15222-5479	**Web Site:** www.alleghenytechnologies.com	**Auditors:** Ernst & Young LLP
Telephone: (412) 394-2800	**Officers:** Robert P. Bozzone - Chmn. L. Patrick Hassey - Pres., C.E.O.	**Investor Contact:** 412-394-2819
Fax: (412) 394-2805		

ALLERGAN, INC

Exchange	Symbol	Price	52Wk Range	Yield	P/E
NYS	AGN	$69.47 (3/31/2005)	92.06-67.67	0.58	24.63

7 Year Price Score 108.06 *NYSE Composite Index=100 **12 Month Price Score 87.39**

Interim Earnings (Per Share)

Qtr.	Mar	Jun	Sep	Dec
2001	0.39	0.16	0.50	0.63
2002	0.33	0.03	(0.28)	0.49
2003	0.53	(0.83)	0.57	(0.69)
2004	0.61	0.69	0.70	0.83

Interim Dividends (Per Share)

Amt	Decl	Ex	Rec	Pay
0.09Q	4/28/2004	5/10/2004	5/12/2004	6/10/2004
0.09Q	7/28/2004	8/16/2004	8/18/2004	9/16/2004
0.09Q	11/1/2004	11/8/2004	11/10/2004	12/9/2004
0.10Q	2/7/2005	2/10/2005	2/14/2005	3/10/2005

Indicated Div: $0.40

Valuation Analysis

Forecast P/E	N/A	No of Institutions
Market Cap	$9.1 Billion	Shares 118,201,136
Book Value	1.1 Billion	% Held
Price/Book	8.18	88.04
Price/Sales	4.46	

TRADING VOLUME (thousand shares)

Business Summary: Pharmaceuticals (MIC: 9.1 SIC: 834 NAIC: 25412)

Allergan is a global health care company that develops and commercializes specialty pharmaceutical products for the ophthalmic, neurological, dermatological and other specialty markets. Co. target products and technologies related to specific disease areas such as glaucoma, retinal disease, dry eye, psoriasis, acne and movement disorders. Also, Co. develops and markets aesthetic-related pharmaceuticals and over-the-counter products. Co. is also focused on research and development efforts on new therapeutic areas, including gastroenterology, neuropathic pain and various types of cancer.

Recent Developments: For the year ended Dec 31 2004, net income was $377,100 thousand versus net loss of $52,500 thousand a year earlier. Revenues were $2,045,600 thousand, up 16.5% from $1,755,400 thousand the year before. Operating income was $527,400 thousand versus a loss of $23,700 thousand in the prior year. Total direct expense was $386,700 thousand versus $320,300 thousand in the prior year, an increase of 20.7%. Total indirect expense was $1,131,500 thousand versus $1,460,300 thousand in the prior year, a decrease of 22.5%.

Prospects: For the first quarter of 2005, Co. expects total pharmaceutical only sales to range between $490.0 million and $505.0 million, with diluted earnings per share of $0.66 to $0.67. For the second and third quarters of 2005, Co. estimates diluted earnings per share growth between 15.0% and 17.0% compared to the adjusted diluted earnings per share for the second and third quarters of 2004. For the full year of 2005, Co. estimates total pharmaceutical only sales between $2.10 billion and $2.20 billion, with diluted earnings per share for the full year between $3.10 and $3.16.

Financial Data

(US$ in Thousands)	12/31/2004	12/31/2003	12/31/2002	12/31/2001	12/31/2000	12/31/1999	12/31/1998	12/31/1997
Earnings Per Share	2.82	(0.40)	0.57	1.68	1.61	1.39	(0.69)	0.97
Cash Flow Per Share	4.17	3.34	0.37	2.74	2.70	1.92	0.40	1.61
Tang Book Value Per Share	7.81	4.78	5.90	6.48	5.62	3.73	3.98	4.81
Dividends Per Share	0.360	0.360	0.360	0.360	0.320	0.280	0.260	0.260
Dividend Payout %	12.77	...	63.16	21.43	19.88	20.14	...	26.67
Income Statement								
Total Revenue	2,045,600	1,771,400	1,425,300	1,745,500	1,625,500	1,452,400	1,296,100	1,149,000
EBITDA	616,200	39,600	147,400	412,700	386,500	352,200	33,800	236,900
Depn & Amortn	80,100	66,500	56,000	85,500	86,800	82,400	86,800	79,800
Income Before Taxes	532,100	(29,500)	89,800	336,400	303,800	269,000	(57,700)	157,100
Income Taxes	154,000	22,200	25,100	109,100	88,100	80,700	32,800	29,000
Net Income	377,100	(52,500)	75,200	224,900	215,100	188,200	(90,200)	128,300
Average Shares	133,900	130,200	131,100	137,800	133,800	135,200	131,200	131,600
Balance Sheet								
Current Assets	1,376,000	928,200	1,200,200	1,325,300	1,326,300	697,500	661,200	636,400
Total Assets	2,257,000	1,754,900	1,806,600	2,046,200	1,971,000	1,339,100	1,334,400	1,398,900
Current Liabilities	459,600	383,400	403,600	490,000	432,500	419,900	368,500	363,300
Long-Term Obligations	570,100	573,300	526,400	520,600	584,700	208,800	201,100	142,500
Total Liabilities	1,140,800	1,036,300	998,300	1,068,800	1,097,200	704,600	638,400	557,500
Stockholders' Equity	1,116,200	718,600	808,300	977,400	873,800	634,500	696,000	841,400
Shares Outstanding	131,417	130,143	129,498	131,250	131,681	129,819	132,234	130,586
Statistical Record								
Return on Assets %	18.75	N.M.	3.90	11.20	12.96	14.08	N.M.	9.34
Return on Equity %	40.99	N.M.	8.42	24.30	28.44	28.29	N.M.	16.13
EBITDA Margin %	30.12	2.24	10.34	23.64	23.78	24.25	2.61	20.62
Net Margin %	18.43	N.M.	5.28	12.88	13.23	12.96	N.M.	11.17
Asset Turnover	1.02	0.99	0.74	0.87	0.98	1.09	0.95	0.84
Current Ratio	2.99	2.42	2.97	2.70	3.07	1.66	1.79	1.75
Debt to Equity	0.51	0.80	0.65	0.53	0.67	0.33	0.29	0.17
Price Range	92.06-67.67	81.51-56.96	72.30-49.55	89.84-59.25	94.47-43.77	55.27-30.62	31.97-15.26	17.58-12.37
P/E Ratio	32.65-24.00	...	126.84-86.93	53.47-35.27	58.68-27.19	39.77-22.03	...	18.12-12.76
Average Yield %	0.44	0.49	0.60	0.49	0.48	0.61	1.13	1.69

Address: 2525 Dupont Drive, P.O. Box 19534, Irvine, CA 92612-9534 **Telephone:** (714) 246-4500 **Fax:** (714) 246-6987	**Web Site:** www.allergan.com **Officers:** David E.I. Pyott - Chmn., Pres., C.E.O. Herbert W. Boyer Ph.D. - Vice-Chmn.	**Auditors:** KPMG LLP **Investor Contact:** 714-246-4636

ALLETTE INC.

Exchange	Symbol	Price	52Wk Range	Yield	P/E
NYS	ALE	$41.85 (3/31/2005)	43.51-31.06	2.87	11.40

*7 Year Price Score 111.70 ***NYSE Composite Index=100** ***12 Month Price Score 102.75**

TRADING VOLUME (thousand shares)

Interim Earnings (Per Share)

Qtr.	Mar	Jun	Sep	Dec
2001	1.38	1.71	1.41	0.93
2002	1.32	1.41	1.65	0.66
2003	1.62	1.59	1.71	3.60
2004	1.86	1.20	0.45	0.16

Interim Dividends (Per Share)

Amt	Decl	Ex	Rec	Pay
0.30Q	10/22/2004	11/10/2004	11/15/2004	12/1/2004
0.30Q	2/4/2005	2/11/2005	2/15/2005	3/1/2005

Indicated Div: $1.20

Valuation Analysis

Forecast P/E	20.46	No of Institutions
	(4/7/2005)	137
Market Cap	$1.2 Billion	Shares
Book Value	630.5 Million	14,504,392
Price/Book	1.97	% Held
Price/Sales	1.65	48.87

Business Summary: Electricity (MIC: 7.1 SIC: 931 NAIC: 21119)

Allete operates in three business segments: Electric Services, which include electric and gas services, coal mining and telecommunications; Automotive Services, which include a network of vehicle auctions, a finance company, an auto transport company, a vehicle remarketing company, a company that provides field information services and a company that provides Internet-based parts location and insurance adjustment audit services; and Investments, which includes real estate operations, investments in emerging technologies related to the electric utility industry and a securities portfolio.

Recent Developments: For the year ended Dec 31 2004, income from continuing operations increased 31.2% to $39,100 thousand from income of $29,800 thousand a year earlier. Net income decreased 55.8% to $104,400 thousand from net income of $236,400 thousand a year earlier. Revenues were $751,400 thousand, up 8.5% from $692,300 thousand the year before. Total indirect expense was $651,600 thousand versus $596,200 thousand in the prior year, an increase of 9.3%.

Prospects: Net income is benefiting from growth at Co.'s utility business and higher kilowatt hour sales to Minnesota Power's industrial customers. On Jan 4 2005, Co. announced an agreement to assign its power purchase agreement with LSP-Kendall Energy to Constellation Energy Commodities Group. Under the agreement, Co. will pay Constellation Energy $73.0 million in cash to assume the power purchase agreement. The transfer is expected to close in April 2005. Looking ahead to 2005, Co. expects earnings per share from continuing operations growth of 45.0% to 50.0% as a result of continuing strong real estate sales, lower interest expense, and the transfer of the Kendall purchased power agreement.

Financial Data

(US$ in Thousands)	12/31/2004	12/31/2003	12/31/2002	12/31/2001	12/31/2000	12/31/1999	12/31/1998	12/31/1997
Earnings Per Share	3.67	8.52	5.04	5.43	6.33	2.91	4.04	3.71
Cash Flow Per Share	5.94	8.91	16.76	4.10	11.81	7.62	6.86	5.75
Tang Book Value Per Share	21.23	31.47	24.28	23.22	17.19	24.69	25.52	21.96
Dividends Per Share	0.300	3.390	3.300	3.210	3.210	3.210	3.060	3.060
Dividend Payout %	8.17	39.79	65.48	59.12	50.71	110.31	75.84	82.59
Income Statement								
Total Revenue	751,400	1,618,800	1,506,900	1,527,700	1,331,900	1,131,800	1,039,700	953,600
EBITDA	137,400	388,300	335,900	378,100	389,000	262,100	282,400	259,200
Depn & Amortn	49,700	86,700	82,100	101,600	86,700	76,900	75,000	70,800
Income Before Taxes	55,900	235,000	191,600	201,800	233,100	125,700	142,500	124,200
Income Taxes	16,800	91,900	72,600	73,200	84,500	57,700	54,000	46,600
Net Income	104,400	236,400	137,200	138,700	148,600	68,000	88,500	77,600
Average Shares	28,400	27,766	27,233	25,500	23,366	22,800	21,400	20,400
Balance Sheet								
Current Assets	368,100	695,400	658,400	909,900	731,000	564,500	487,500	368,700
Total Assets	1,431,400	3,101,300	3,147,200	3,282,500	2,914,000	2,312,600	2,317,100	2,172,300
Current Liabilities	108,700	526,200	738,200	704,500	707,000	398,300	346,000	325,100
Long-Term Obligations	390,200	747,700	661,300	933,800	952,300	712,800	672,200	685,400
Total Liabilities	800,900	1,641,100	1,839,800	2,063,700	1,938,200	1,400,300	1,425,000	1,414,900
Stockholders' Equity	630,500	1,460,200	1,232,400	1,143,800	900,800	817,300	817,100	682,400
Shares Outstanding	29,700	29,100	28,533	27,966	24,900	24,500	24,133	22,400
Statistical Record								
Return on Assets %	4.59	7.57	4.27	4.48	5.67	2.94	3.94	3.59
Return on Equity %	9.96	17.56	11.55	13.57	17.25	8.32	11.80	11.72
EBITDA Margin %	18.29	23.98	22.29	24.75	29.30	23.16	27.16	27.18
Net Margin %	13.89	14.60	9.10	9.08	11.16	6.01	8.51	8.14
Asset Turnover	0.33	0.52	0.47	0.49	0.51	0.49	0.46	0.44
Current Ratio	3.39	1.32	0.89	1.29	1.03	1.42	1.41	1.13
Debt to Equity	0.62	0.51	0.54	0.82	1.06	0.87	0.82	1.00
Price Range	42.91-31.06	36.71-22.57	36.96-22.99	31.80-24.71	30.37-17.64	26.20-19.35	27.43-22.78	26.16-16.08
P/E Ratio	11.69-8.46	4.31-2.65	7.33-4.56	5.86-4.55	4.80-2.79	9.00-6.65	6.79-5.64	7.05-4.33
Average Yield %	0.81	11.30	10.82	11.39	13.64	14.09	12.36	16.01

Address: 30 West Superior Street, Duluth, MN 55802-2093	**Web Site:** www.allete.com	**Auditors:** PricewaterhouseCoopers LLP
Telephone: (218) 723-3974	**Officers:** David G. Gartzke - Chmn. Donald J. Shippar - Pres., C.E.O.	**Investor Contact:** 218-723-3953
Fax: (218) 720-2502		**Transfer Agents:** Wells Fargo Bank Minnesota, N.A., South St. Paul, MN

ALLIANCE DATA SYSTEMS CORP.

Exchange	Symbol	Price	52Wk Range	Yield	P/E
NYS	ADS	$40.40 (3/31/2005)	48.52-33.07	N/A	33.11

*7 Year Price Score N/A   ***NYSE Composite Index=100**   ***12 Month Price Score 92.22**

Interim Earnings (Per Share)

Qtr.	Mar	Jun	Sep	Dec
2001	(0.10)	(0.04)	0.01	(0.13)
2002	0.06	0.04	0.10	0.14
2003	0.16	0.15	0.23	0.30
2004	0.39	0.33	0.31	0.19

Interim Dividends (Per Share)

No Dividends Paid

Valuation Analysis

Forecast P/E	22.15	No of Institutions
	(4/7/2005)	208
Market Cap	$3.3 Billion	Shares
Book Value	870.5 Million	64,849,004
Price/Book	3.82	% Held
Price/Sales	2.65	78.50

Business Summary: IT & Technology (MIC: 10.2 SIC: 374 NAIC: 18210)

Alliance Data Systems is a provider of transaction services, credit services and marketing services in North America. Co. focuses on facilitating and managing electronic transactions between its clients and their customers through multiple distribution channels including in-store, catalog and the Internet. Co.'s credit and marketing services assists its clients in identifying and acquiring new customers, as well as helping to increase the loyalty and profitability of their existing customers. Co. has a client base in excess of 300 companies, consisting mostly of specialty retailers, petroleum retailers, supermarkets, financial services companies and utilities.

Recent Developments: For the year ended Dec 31 2004, net income increased 52.1% to $102,371 thousand from net income of $67,298 thousand a year earlier. Revenues were $1,257,438 thousand, up 20.2% from $1,046,544 thousand the year before. Operating income was $172,099 thousand versus an income of $130,789 thousand in the prior year, an increase of 31.6%. Total direct expense was $916,201 thousand versus $788,874 thousand in the prior year, an increase of 16.1%. Total indirect expense was $169,138 thousand versus $126,881 thousand in the prior year, an increase of 33.3%.

Prospects: Co.'s results are benefiting from significant client wins over the past two years, as well as client renewals, contract expansions and strong core growth across its business lines. Further, Co. recently achieved a new private label win, Trek Bicycle, as well as contract renewals with J. Crew and New York & Company. In the utility services group, Co. has added Entergy Solutions as well as expanded its contract renewal with Direct Energy. In the loyalty group, Co. has begun the ramp up of Rona, a Canadian home improvement chain, as a national sponsor in its Canadian AIR MILES® Reward Program. Also, Co.'s acquisition of Epsilon Data Management is off to a solid start.

Financial Data

(US$ in Thousands)	12/31/2004	12/31/2003	12/31/2002	12/31/2001	12/31/2000	12/31/1999	12/31/1998
Earnings Per Share	1.22	0.84	0.34	(0.18)	(0.60)	(0.70)	(0.43)
Cash Flow Per Share	4.37	1.61	1.72	2.63	1.83	5.30	...
Tang Book Value Per Share	N.M.	0.93	0.37	0.19	N.M.	N.M.	...
Income Statement							
Total Revenue	1,257,438	1,049,144	871,451	777,351	678,195	583,082	410,913
EBITDA	236,375	200,824	135,106	108,296	95,532	80,255	57,520
Depn & Amortn	65,084	74,561	66,475	74,200	76,144	77,800	52,036
Income Before Taxes	164,319	108,982	47,416	3,995	(19,482)	(40,330)	(22,400)
Income Taxes	61,948	41,684	20,671	11,612	1,841	(6,538)	(4,708)
Net Income	102,371	67,298	26,203	(8,232)	(21,323)	(29,841)	(17,992)
Average Shares	84,040	80,313	76,696	64,555	47,538	47,498	41,729
Balance Sheet							
Current Assets	617,346	582,852	388,940	463,503	523,775	370,618	...
Total Assets	2,239,080	1,868,442	1,453,418	1,477,218	1,420,606	1,301,263	...
Current Liabilities	560,619	490,400	427,430	429,729	491,838	322,787	...
Long-Term Obligations	206,861	189,361	107,918	199,100	274,335	316,911	...
Total Liabilities	1,368,560	1,166,111	910,680	971,490	1,058,215	921,791	...
Stockholders' Equity	870,520	702,331	542,738	505,728	242,991	260,072	...
Shares Outstanding	82,347	79,625	74,938	73,987	47,545	47,529	47,487
Statistical Record							
Return on Assets %	4.97	4.05	1.79	N.M.	N.M.	...	...
Return on Equity %	12.98	10.81	5.00	N.M.	N.M.	...	...
EBITDA Margin %	18.80	19.14	15.50	13.93	14.09	13.76	14.00
Net Margin %	8.14	6.41	3.01	N.M.	N.M.	N.M.	N.M.
Asset Turnover	0.61	0.63	0.59	0.54	0.50	...	...
Current Ratio	1.10	1.19	0.91	1.08	1.06	1.15	...
Debt to Equity	0.24	0.27	0.20	0.39	1.13	1.22	...
Price Range	48.52-26.92	30.51-14.79	25.95-13.85	19.15-11.35	...	...	...
P/E Ratio	39.77-22.07	36.32-17.61	76.32-40.74	...	...	...	...

Address: 17655 Waterview Parkway, Dallas, TX 75252 Telephone: (972) 348-5100	Web Site: www.alliancedatasystems.com Officers: J. Michael Parks - Chmn., C.E.O. Edward J. Heffernan - Exec. V.P., C.F.O.	Auditors: Deloitte & Touche LLP

ALLIANT ENERGY CORP.

Exchange	Symbol	Price	52Wk Range	Yield	P/E
NYS	LNT	$26.78 (3/31/2005)	28.80-23.76	3.92	20.92

*7 Year Price Score 83.99   *NYSE Composite Index=100   *12 Month Price Score 95.12

Interim Earnings (Per Share)

Qtr.	Mar	Jun	Sep	Dec
2001	0.42	0.29	0.78	0.64
2002	0.11	0.07	0.49	0.51
2003	(0.01)	0.35	0.94	0.44
2004	0.31	(0.12)	0.71	0.37

Interim Dividends (Per Share)

Amt	Decl	Ex	Rec	Pay
0.25Q	4/15/2004	4/28/2004	4/30/2004	5/15/2004
0.25Q	7/15/2004	7/28/2004	7/30/2004	8/14/2004
0.263Q	10/11/2004	10/27/2004	10/29/2004	11/15/2004
0.263Q	1/14/2005	1/27/2005	1/31/2005	2/15/2005

Indicated Div: $1.05

Valuation Analysis

Forecast P/E	13.98	No of Institutions
	(4/7/2005)	216
Market Cap	$3.1 Billion	Shares
Book Value	2.8 Billion	60,047,068
Price/Book	1.10	% Held
Price/Sales	1.05	51.68

Business Summary: Electricity (MIC: 7.1 SIC: 931 NAIC: 21121)

Alliant Energy is a diversified holding company for its regulated domestic utilities, Wisconsin Power and Light Co. (WP&L) and Interstate Power and Light Co. (IP&L), and its non-regulated businesses held by Alliant Energy Resources, Inc. At Dec. 31, 2003, Co.'s regulated utility operations supplied electric and gas service to 965,953 and 408,427 (excluding transportation and other) customers, respectively, in selective markets in Iowa, Minnesota, Illinois and Wisconsin. Co.'s non-regulated subsidiaries provide energy products and services to domestic and international markets and provide environmental, engineering and transportation services.

Recent Developments: For the year ended Dec 31 2004, net income decreased 20.7% to $145,500 thousand from net income of $183,500 thousand a year earlier. Revenues were $2,958,700 thousand, up 3.2% from $2,866,800 thousand the year before. Operating income was $419,800 thousand versus an income of $404,900 thousand in the prior year, an increase of 3.7%. Total direct expense was $2,106,000 thousand versus $2,070,200 thousand in the prior year, an increase of 1.7%. Total indirect expense was $432,900 thousand versus $391,700 thousand in the prior year, an increase of 10.5%.

Prospects: Co.'s earnings from its domestic utility business are benefiting from rate increases, a lower effective tax rate and weather-normalized sales growth. Meanwhile, Co. is implementing comprehensive cost-cutting measures and operational efficiency efforts to counter higher operating expenses. Co.'s non-regulated businesses are seeing improved results due to lower interest expense and decreased charges related to debt reduction. In 2005, Co. expects to focus on increasing its returns on invested capital in all of its businesses and to further streamline its portfolio of businesses. On Feb 28 2005, Co. announced it had completed the redemption of $100.0 million of its 7 3/8% due Nov 9 2009.

Financial Data
(US$ in Thousands)

	12/31/2004	12/31/2003	12/31/2002	12/31/2001	12/31/2000	12/31/1999	12/31/1998	12/31/1997
Earnings Per Share	1.28	1.81	1.18	2.14	5.03	2.51	1.26	1.99
Cash Flow Per Share	4.42	4.14	5.99	5.97	5.45	5.40	6.08	4.91
Tang Book Value Per Share	22.13	21.37	19.89	21.39	25.79	27.29	20.69	19.73
Dividends Per Share	1.013	1.000	2.000	2.000	2.000	2.000	2.000	2.000
Dividend Payout %	79.10	55.25	169.49	93.46	39.76	79.68	158.73	100.50
Income Statement								
Total Revenue	2,958,700	3,128,187	2,608,812	2,777,340	2,404,984	2,197,963	2,130,874	919,255
EBITDA	855,800	799,868	645,140	803,979	1,161,260	775,313	608,608	251,547
Depn & Amortn	398,400	378,790	362,184	368,437	366,876	322,017	324,457	115,733
Income Before Taxes	294,600	231,528	112,377	245,070	620,770	317,067	154,788	93,279
Income Taxes	83,800	71,827	36,108	59,840	238,816	120,486	58,113	28,715
Net Income	145,500	183,543	106,881	172,362	398,662	196,581	96,675	61,254
Average Shares	113,701	101,544	90,959	80,636	79,193	78,395	76,912	30,782
Balance Sheet								
Net PPE	4,672,800	4,432,599	3,196,988	3,037,609	3,719,307	3,486,034	3,456,780	1,356,067
Total Assets	8,275,200	7,775,446	7,001,395	6,247,682	6,733,766	6,075,683	4,959,337	1,861,807
Long-Term Obligations	2,299,500	2,123,298	2,637,803	2,457,941	1,910,116	1,512,806	1,556,886	457,520
Total Liabilities	5,470,000	5,160,329	4,960,142	4,215,388	4,582,504	3,806,480	3,239,544	1,194,261
Stockholders' Equity	2,805,200	2,615,117	2,041,253	2,032,294	2,151,262	2,269,203	1,719,793	667,546
Shares Outstanding	115,741	110,962	92,304	89,682	79,010	78,984	77,630	30,789
Statistical Record								
Return on Assets %	1.81	2.48	1.61	2.66	6.21	3.56	2.83	3.26
Return on Equity %	5.35	7.88	5.25	8.24	17.99	9.86	8.10	9.18
EBITDA Margin %	28.92	25.57	24.73	28.95	48.29	35.27	28.56	27.36
Net Margin %	4.92	5.87	4.10	6.21	16.58	8.94	4.54	6.66
PPE Turnover	0.65	0.82	0.84	0.82	0.67	0.63	0.89	0.67
Asset Turnover	0.37	0.42	0.39	0.43	0.37	0.40	0.62	0.49
Debt to Equity	0.82	0.81	1.29	1.21	0.89	0.67	0.91	0.69
Price Range	28.80-23.76	24.94-15.12	30.86-14.39	33.10-27.99	34.63-26.02	32.25-25.88	34.88-28.25	33.81-26.75
P/E Ratio	22.50-18.56	13.78-8.35	26.15-12.19	15.47-13.08	6.88-5.17	12.85-10.31	27.68-22.42	16.99-13.44
Average Yield %	3.91	5.03	8.50	6.59	6.85	7.02	6.34	7.03

Address: 4902 N. Biltmore Lane, Madison, WI 53718-2132	**Web Site:** www.alliantenergy.com	**Auditors:** Deloitte & Touche LLP
Telephone: (608) 458-3311	**Officers:** Erroll B. Davis Jr. - Chmn., C.E.O. William D. Harvey - Pres., C.O.O.	**Investor Contact:** 800-356-5343
Fax: (608) 458-4824		

ALLIANT TECHSYSTEMS INC.

Exchange	Symbol	Price	52Wk Range	Yield	P/E
NYS	ATK	$71.45 (3/31/2005)	73.93-54.40	N/A	18.41

*7 Year Price Score 127.87 *NYSE Composite Index=100 *12 Month Price Score 104.28

Interim Earnings (Per Share)

Qtr.	Jun	Sep	Dec	Mar
2001-02	0.09	0.57	0.61	0.68
2002-03	0.63	0.73	0.93	0.90
2003-04	0.84	0.93	1.06	1.31
2004-05	0.72	0.78	1.25	...

Interim Dividends (Per Share)

Amt	Decl	Ex	Rec	Pay
3-for-2	11/2/2000	11/28/2000	11/10/2000	11/27/2000
3-for-2	8/8/2001	9/10/2001	8/17/2001	9/7/2001
3-for-2	5/9/2002	6/11/2002	5/17/2002	6/10/2002

Valuation Analysis

Forecast P/E	16.07	No of Institutions	
	(4/7/2005)	237	
Market Cap	$2.4 Billion	Shares	
Book Value	670.3 Million	32,909,344	
Price/Book	3.63	% Held	
Price/Sales	0.94	87.05	

Business Summary: Metal Products (MIC: 11.4 SIC: 484 NAIC: 32994)

Alliant Techsystems is an advanced weapon and space systems company. Co.'s Precision Systems segment supplies precision-guided munitions, anti-tank systems, electronic warfare and infantry weapon systems. The Advanced Propulsion and Space Systems segment manufactures boosters, upper stages, and control systems for missile defense systems, orbital insertion motors and specialty ordnance products. The ATK Thiokol segment supplies solid propulsion systems. The Ammunition and Related Products segment supplies ammunition to federal and local law enforcement agencies and commercial markets. ATK Mission Research develops products that address homeland defense and national security requirements.

Recent Developments: For the quarter ended Jan 2 2005, net income increased 14.3% to $47,848 thousand from net income of $41,857 thousand in the year-earlier quarter. Revenues were $684,493 thousand, up 21.4% from $563,817 thousand the year before. Total direct expense was $546,683 thousand versus $440,106 thousand in the prior-year quarter, an increase of 24.2%. Total indirect expense was $55,907 thousand versus $53,260 thousand in the prior-year quarter, an increase of 5.0%.

Prospects: On Feb 2 2005, Co. narrowed its guidance range for fiscal 2005 earnings per share to between $3.95 and $4.00 from $3.90 to $4.00. Co. continues to expect fiscal 2005 sales to exceed $2.75 billion. Looking ahead, Co. expects fiscal 2006 earnings per share of $4.35 to $4.50. This estimate includes an increase in pension expense of about $0.30 per share and costs for moving fuze manufacturing operations of about $0.09 per share. The 2006 earnings per share projections do not include the effect of the adoption of SFAS 123R for the expensing of stock-based compensation. Also, Co. expects fiscal 2006 sales to be in excess of $3.00 billion, reflecting organic sales growth of between 7.0% and 8.0%.

Financial Data
(US$ in Thousands)

	9 Mos	6 Mos	3 Mos	03/31/2004	03/31/2003	03/31/2002	03/31/2001	03/31/2000
Earnings Per Share	3.88	3.75	3.96	4.14	3.16	1.97	2.13	2.16
Cash Flow Per Share	3.84	3.92	3.34	4.66	5.13	4.80	2.40	3.28
Tang Book Value Per Share	N.M.	N.M.	N.M.	N.M.	N.M.	N.M.	2.38	N.M.
Income Statement								
Total Revenue	2,001,938	1,317,445	644,395	2,366,193	2,172,135	1,801,605	1,141,949	1,077,520
EBITDA	260,418	157,401	77,085	346,981	342,677	302,355	181,074	168,395
Depn & Amortn	58,730	37,616	18,746	69,918	67,134	78,673	44,980	47,822
Income Before Taxes	154,309	89,736	43,451	217,796	211,231	140,876	103,394	87,230
Income Taxes	48,741	32,120	15,751	55,041	82,384	53,533	35,473	22,778
Net Income	105,320	57,472	27,574	162,305	124,287	69,327	67,921	73,902
Average Shares	38,242	38,094	38,085	39,176	39,344	35,196	31,848	34,195
Balance Sheet								
Current Assets	852,429	921,251	802,039	805,685	712,316	671,410	332,823	351,050
Total Assets	3,029,742	3,071,600	2,806,139	2,833,329	2,479,264	2,211,292	879,504	905,984
Current Liabilities	421,759	434,459	403,147	428,391	428,053	372,021	291,963	356,593
Long-Term Obligations	1,184,130	1,274,000	1,075,000	1,076,000	820,856	867,638	207,909	277,109
Total Liabilities	2,359,459	2,454,855	2,223,549	2,269,129	2,001,340	1,654,491	681,172	791,037
Stockholders' Equity	670,283	616,745	582,590	564,200	477,924	556,801	198,332	114,947
Shares Outstanding	34,030	37,672	37,622	37,439	38,486	32,406	31,657	30,623
Statistical Record								
Return on Assets %	5.35	5.22	5.89	6.09	5.30	4.49	7.61	8.19
Return on Equity %	23.42	24.82	28.17	31.06	24.02	18.36	43.36	63.08
EBITDA Margin %	13.01	11.95	11.96	14.66	15.78	16.78	15.86	15.63
Net Margin %	5.26	4.36	4.28	6.86	5.72	3.85	5.95	6.86
Asset Turnover	0.93	0.89	0.92	0.89	0.93	1.17	1.28	1.19
Current Ratio	2.02	2.12	1.99	1.88	1.66	1.80	1.14	0.98
Debt to Equity	1.77	2.07	1.85	1.91	1.72	1.56	1.05	2.41
Price Range	67.49-53.89	66.10-48.44	64.06-47.20	60.09-47.20	75.55-43.00	68.00-37.64	39.36-17.44	25.78-15.19
P/E Ratio	17.39-13.89	17.63-12.92	16.18-11.92	14.51-11.40	23.91-13.61	34.52-19.11	18.48-8.19	11.93-7.03

Address: 5050 Lincoln Drive, Edina, MN 55436	Web Site: www.atk.com	Auditors: DELOITTE & TOUCHE LLP
Telephone: (952) 351-3000	Officers: Daniel J. Murphy Jr. - Chmn., Pres., C.E.O. Eric S. Rangen - Exec. V.P., C.F.O.	Investor Contact: 952-351-3056
Fax: (952) 351-3009		

ALLIED WASTE INDUSTRIES, INC.

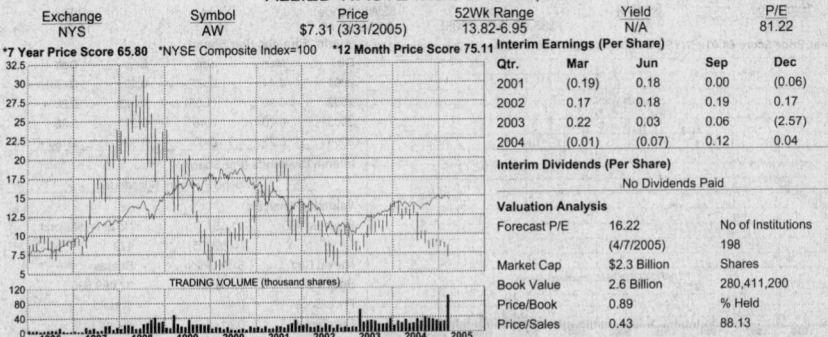

Exchange	Symbol	Price	52Wk Range	Yield	P/E
NYS	AW	$7.31 (3/31/2005)	13.82-6.95	N/A	81.22

*7 Year Price Score 65.80 *NYSE Composite Index=100 *12 Month Price Score 75.11

Interim Earnings (Per Share)

Qtr.	Mar	Jun	Sep	Dec
2001	(0.19)	0.18	0.00	(0.06)
2002	0.17	0.18	0.19	0.17
2003	0.22	0.03	0.06	(2.57)
2004	(0.01)	(0.07)	0.12	0.04

Interim Dividends (Per Share)

No Dividends Paid

Valuation Analysis

Forecast P/E	16.22	No of Institutions
	(4/7/2005)	198
Market Cap	$2.3 Billion	Shares
Book Value	2.6 Billion	280,411,200
Price/Book	0.89	% Held
Price/Sales	0.43	88.13

Business Summary: Sanitation Services (MIC: 7.3 SIC: 953 NAIC: 62219)

Allied Waste Industries is a non-hazardous, solid waste management company. Co. operates as a vertically integrated company that picks up waste from businesses and residences and disposes of that waste in Co.'s own landfills to the extent that it is economically beneficial. Co. provides collection, transfer, recycling and disposal services for approximately 10.0 million residential, commercial and industrial customers. As of Dec 31 2003, Co. served customers through a network of 313 collection companies, 165 transfer stations, 166 active landfills and 57 recycling facilities in 110 major markets within 37 states. Co. operates in the U.S. and Puerto Rico.

Recent Developments: For the year ended Dec 31 2004, income from continuing operations decreased 47.8% to $58,000 thousand from income of $111,200 thousand a year earlier. Net income decreased 61.7% to $49,300 thousand from net income of $128,700 thousand a year earlier. Revenues were $5,362,000 thousand, up 2.2% from $5,247,700 thousand the year before. Operating income was $886,400 thousand versus an income of $1,034,700 thousand in the prior year, a decrease of 14.3%. Total direct expense was $3,374,800 thousand versus $3,190,100 thousand in the prior year, an increase of 5.8%. Total indirect expense was $1,100,800 thousand versus $1,022,900 thousand in the prior year, an increase of 7.6%.

Prospects: Co.'s revenue growth from both higher pricing and increased volume continues to improve and it is making steady progress in the implementation of its Excellence Driven Standards and Best Practices Programs. Looking ahead, Co. is encouraged by its prospects for 2005, during which it intends to establish a platform for further growth and improvement in 2006 and beyond. Co. expects 2005 operating income before depreciation and amortization to range from $1.43 billion to $1.50 billion. Co. intends to increase its reinvestment in the business while maintaining its ability to produce free cash flow for debt reduction.

Financial Data
(US$ in Thousands)

	12/31/2004	12/31/2003	12/31/2002	12/31/2001	12/31/2000	12/31/1999	12/31/1998	12/31/1997
Earnings Per Share	0.09	(2.27)	0.71	(0.07)	0.29	(1.69)	(1.22)	0.00
Cash Flow Per Share	2.06	3.85	5.43	4.77	4.24	2.60	0.93	0.95
Income Statement								
Total Revenue	5,362,000	5,247,700	5,517,306	5,565,260	5,707,485	3,341,071	1,575,612	875,028
EBITDA	686,200	1,501,700	985,810	1,853,241	1,977,580	619,826	239,037	318,938
Depn & Amortn	558,700	600,900	575,099	735,694	718,257	411,249	209,114	136,231
Income Before Taxes	127,500	201,800	410,711	269,966	381,168	(227,255)	(54,478)	90,669
Income Taxes	72,200	88,700	183,614	190,834	237,540	(8,756)	43,773	37,052
Net Income	49,300	128,700	215,111	58,486	124,387	(288,728)	(223,052)	412
Average Shares	319,700	203,800	193,508	194,906	191,122	187,801	182,796	93,444
Balance Sheet								
Current Assets	922,600	1,285,600	1,072,087	1,198,486	1,271,703	2,248,422	499,904	187,459
Total Assets	13,493,900	13,860,900	13,928,922	14,347,093	14,513,634	14,963,101	3,752,592	2,448,660
Current Liabilities	1,756,700	1,567,800	1,449,793	1,433,535	1,599,752	2,629,499	454,873	232,538
Long-Term Obligations	7,429,200	7,984,500	8,718,642	9,237,503	9,635,124	9,240,291	2,118,927	1,356,281
Total Liabilities	10,889,000	11,343,200	11,992,920	12,592,270	12,745,975	13,323,546	2,822,518	1,852,489
Stockholders' Equity	2,604,900	2,517,700	689,098	585,779	697,832	637,996	930,074	596,171
Shares Outstanding	317,500	320,100	196,215	196,236	196,109	184,495	184,495	103,564
Statistical Record								
Return on Assets %	0.36	0.93	1.52	0.41	0.84	N.M.	N.M.	0.02
Return on Equity %	1.92	8.03	33.75	9.11	18.57	N.M.	N.M.	0.09
EBITDA Margin %	12.80	28.62	17.87	33.30	34.65	18.55	15.17	36.45
Net Margin %	0.92	2.45	3.90	1.05	2.18	N.M.	N.M.	0.05
Asset Turnover	0.39	0.38	0.39	0.39	0.39	0.36	0.51	0.37
Current Ratio	0.53	0.82	0.74	0.84	0.79	0.86	1.10	0.81
Debt to Equity	2.85	3.17	12.65	15.77	13.81	14.48	2.28	2.27
Price Range	14.36-8.00	13.99-7.75	14.43-5.80	19.74-9.10	14.56-5.38	23.88-6.69	31.13-17.09	23.94-7.50
P/E Ratio	159.56-88.89	...	20.32-8.17	...	50.22-18.53	...	...	N.M.

Address: 15880 North Greenway-Hayden Loop, Suite 100, Scottsdale, AZ 85260 Telephone: (480) 627-2700 Fax: (480) 423-9424	Web Site: www.alliedwaste.com Officers: Charles H. Cotros - Chmn., C.E.O. Thomas W. Ryan - Vice- Chmn., Exec. V.P.	Auditors: PricewaterhouseCoopers LLP Investor Contact: 480-627-2700

ALLMERICA FINANCIAL CORP.

Exchange	Symbol	Price	52Wk Range	Yield	P/E
NYS	AFC	$35.95 (3/31/2005)	36.50-25.45	N/A	15.36

*7 Year Price Score 64.01 *NYSE Composite Index=100 ***12 Month Price Score 103.69**

Interim Earnings (Per Share)

Qtr.	Mar	Jun	Sep	Dec
2001	0.44	0.25	0.59	(1.33)
2002	0.90	(1.05)	(5.93)	0.28
2003	0.70	0.46	0.21	0.26
2004	0.23	0.60	0.33	1.18

Interim Dividends (Per Share)

Dividend Payment Suspended

Valuation Analysis

Forecast P/E	11.55		No of Institutions
	(4/7/2005)		179
Market Cap	$1.9 Billion		Shares
Book Value	2.3 Billion		37,089,596
Price/Book	0.82		% Held
Price/Sales	0.61		69.49

Business Summary: Insurance (MIC: 8.2 SIC: 331 NAIC: 24126)

Allmerica Financial is a non-insurance holding company. Co.'s operations include The Hanover Insurance Company and Citizens Insurance Company of America, its property and casualty subsidiaries; Allmerica Financial Life Insurance and Annuity Company and First Allmerica Financial Life Insurance Company, its life insurance and annuity subsidiaries; and certain other insurance and non-insurance subsidiaries. Co. is licensed to sell property and casualty insurance in all fifty states in the U.S., as well as the District of Columbia. In 2004, about 38.0% of its net written premium was generated in Michigan and 17.0% was generated in Massachusetts.

Recent Developments: For the year ended Dec 31 2004, net income increased 44.2% to $125,300 thousand from net income of $86,900 thousand a year earlier. Revenues were $3,111,000 thousand, down 4.7% from $3,263,600 thousand the year before. Net premiums earned were $2,288,600 thousand versus $2,282,300 thousand in the prior year, an increase of 0.3%. Net investment income fell 9.0% to $414,500 thousand from $455,700 thousand a year ago.

Prospects: Co.'s results are benefiting from earnings gains from across its core operations. For the fourth quarter ended Dec 31 2004, Property and Casualty segment income was $73.6 million, up from $33.8 million in the fourth quarter of 2003. Co. attributed the increased earnings to favorable loss performance in Personal Lines and Commercial Lines, partially offset by higher expenses. Also, Co.'s Life Companies segment reported segment income of $16.5 million in the fourth quarter of 2004, compared with $5.7 million in 2003, reflecting lower amortization of deferred policy acquisition costs and lower guaranteed minimum death benefit expenses, net of hedge losses.

Financial Data

(US$ in Thousands)	12/31/2004	12/31/2003	12/31/2002	12/31/2001	12/31/2000	12/31/1999	12/31/1998	12/31/1997
Earnings Per Share	2.34	1.63	(5.79)	(0.06)	3.70	5.33	3.33	3.82
Cash Flow Per Share	2.67	(3.29)	0.83	11.34	2.97	0.28	0.63	(3.17)
Tang Book Value Per Share	41.57	39.47	36.69	45.20	45.71	41.33	41.96	39.69
Dividends Per Share	...	...	...	0.250	0.250	0.250	0.200	0.200
Dividend Payout %	...	...	...	...	6.76	4.69	6.01	5.24
Income Statement								
Premium Income	2,288,600	2,282,300	2,320,100	2,254,700	2,068,900	1,950,500	2,305,000	1,980,500
Total Revenue	3,111,000	3,263,600	3,316,600	3,311,800	3,087,900	3,145,200	3,432,500	3,006,400
Benefits & Claims	1,784,000	1,918,700	2,202,000	2,235,500	1,889,300	1,770,700	2,076,500	1,764,000
Income Before Taxes	186,700	79,500	(521,200)	(59,400)	218,600	468,000	279,600	340,000
Income Taxes	4,200	(7,400)	(234,800)	(75,500)	2,700	106,900	49,100	84,700
Net Income	125,300	86,900	(306,100)	(3,100)	199,900	295,800	201,200	209,200
Average Shares	53,700	53,200	52,900	53,100	54,000	55,500	60,300	54,800
Balance Sheet								
Total Assets	23,719,200	25,112,500	26,578,900	30,336,100	31,588,000	30,769,600	27,607,900	22,549,000
Total Liabilities	21,379,700	22,892,300	24,206,700	27,645,000	28,878,900	28,229,400	24,849,300	19,714,800
Stockholders' Equity	2,339,500	2,220,200	2,072,200	2,391,100	2,409,100	2,240,200	2,458,600	2,381,300
Shares Outstanding	53,200	53,000	52,900	52,900	52,700	54,200	58,600	60,000
Statistical Record								
Return on Assets %	0.51	0.34	N.M.	N.M.	0.64	1.01	0.80	1.01
Return on Equity %	5.48	4.05	N.M.	N.M.	8.58	12.59	8.31	10.19
Loss Ratio %	77.95	84.07	94.91	99.15	91.32	90.78	90.09	89.07
Net Margin %	4.03	2.66	(9.23)	(0.09)	6.47	9.40	5.86	6.96
Price Range	38.25-25.45	31.29-9.84	50.33-7.16	67.25-38.17	72.50-35.31	64.44-46.50	72.13-39.25	50.06-32.75
P/E Ratio	16.35-10.88	19.20-6.04	...	...	19.59-9.54	12.09-8.72	21.66-11.79	13.11-8.57
Average Yield %	...	...	...	0.49	0.45	0.45	0.34	0.49

Address: 440 Lincoln Street, Worcester, MA 01653 Telephone: (508) 855 1000 Fax: (508) 853 6332	Web Site: www.allmerica.com Officers: Michael P. Angelini - Chmn. Frederick H. Eppinger Jr. - Pres., C.E.O.	Auditors: PricewaterhouseCoopers LLP Investor Contact: 508-855-2959

ALLSTATE CORP. (THE)

Exchange	Symbol	Price	52Wk Range	Yield	P/E	Div Acheiver
NYS	ALL	$54.06 (3/31/2005)	54.75-43.22	2.37	11.91	11 Years

*7 Year Price Score 109.16 *NYSE Composite Index=100 *12 Month Price Score 101.63

Interim Earnings (Per Share)

Qtr.	Mar	Jun	Sep	Dec
2001	0.68	0.23	0.32	0.37
2002	0.60	0.48	0.35	0.63
2003	0.94	0.84	0.97	1.08
2004	1.34	1.47	0.09	1.64

Interim Dividends (Per Share)

Amt	Decl	Ex	Rec	Pay
0.28Q	5/18/2004	5/26/2004	5/28/2004	7/1/2004
0.28Q	7/13/2004	8/27/2004	8/31/2004	10/1/2004
0.28Q	11/10/2004	11/26/2004	11/30/2004	1/3/2005
0.32Q	2/22/2005	3/9/2005	3/11/2005	4/1/2005

Indicated Div: $1.28 (Div. Reinv. Plan)

Valuation Analysis

Forecast P/E	9.58	No of Institutions
	(4/7/2005)	685
Market Cap	$36.9 Billion	Shares
Book Value	21.8 Billion	464,737,728
Price/Book	1.69	% Held
Price/Sales	1.09	68.42

Business Summary: Insurance (MIC: 8.2 SIC: 331 NAIC: 24126)

Allstate is a holding company for Allstate Insurance. Co.'s business is conducted principally through Allstate Insurance, Allstate Life Insurance and their subsidiaries. Co. is engaged, principally in the U.S. and Canada, in the personal property and casualty insurance business and the life insurance and savings business. As of Dec 31 2003, Co. provided insurance products to more than 16.0 million households through about 12,900 exclusive agents and financial specialists. Co. operates in four business segments: personal property and casualty, life and savings, discontinued lines and coverages, and corporate and other business.

Recent Developments: For the year ended Dec 31 2004, net income increased 17.6% to $3,181 million from net income of $2,705 million a year earlier. Revenues were $33,936 million, up 5.6% from $32,149 million the year before. Net premiums earned were $28,061 million versus $26,981 million in the prior year, an increase of 4.0%. Net investment income rose 6.3% to $5,284 million from $4,972 million a year ago.

Prospects: Co.'s results are benefiting from growth in policies in force (PIF). For example, Allstate brand standard auto and homeowners PIF increased 5.5% and 6.4%, respectively, from Dec 31 2003 levels. Co. noted that both standard auto and homeowners experienced growth in most states. These results excluded the effect from Allstate Canada. Also, Allstate brand standard auto and homeowners new business premiums written grew 5.5% and 4.3%, respectively, for the quarter ended Dec 31 2004. Accordingly, Co.'s annual operating income per diluted share guidance for 2005, assuming the level of average expected catastrophe losses used in pricing for the year, is in the range of $5.40 to $5.80.

Financial Data
(US$ in Thousands)

	12/31/2004	12/31/2003	12/31/2002	12/31/2001	12/31/2000	12/31/1999	12/31/1998	12/31/1997
Earnings Per Share	4.54	3.83	1.60	1.60	2.95	3.38	3.94	3.56
Cash Flow Per Share	7.84	8.09	6.26	3.18	2.32	2.83	3.47	3.85
Tang Book Value Per Share	30.74	27.89	23.52	22.35	22.26	19.51	21.08	18.36
Dividends Per Share	1.120	0.930	0.840	0.760	0.680	0.600	0.540	0.480
Dividend Payout %	24.67	24.28	52.50	47.50	23.05	17.75	13.71	13.50
Income Statement								
Premium Income	28,061,000	26,981,000	25,654,000	24,427,000	24,076,000	21,735,000	20,826,000	20,106,000
Total Revenue	33,936,000	32,149,000	29,579,000	28,865,000	29,134,000	26,959,000	25,879,000	24,949,000
Benefits & Claims	19,461,000	19,283,000	19,427,000	19,203,000	19,585,000	17,257,000	16,016,000	15,751,000
Income Before Taxes	4,586,000	3,571,000	1,540,000	1,285,000	3,047,000	3,907,000	4,745,000	4,434,000
Income Taxes	1,230,000	846,000	65,000	73,000	795,000	1,148,000	1,422,000	1,324,000
Net Income	3,181,000	2,705,000	1,134,000	1,158,000	2,211,000	2,720,000	3,294,000	3,105,000
Average Shares	700,300	706,200	709,900	723,300	748,700	803,800	836,600	874,000
Balance Sheet								
Total Assets	149,725,000	134,142,000	117,426,000	109,175,000	104,808,000	98,119,000	87,691,000	80,918,000
Total Liabilities	127,902,000	113,577,000	99,788,000	91,779,000	86,607,000	80,554,000	69,701,000	64,558,000
Stockholders' Equity	21,823,000	20,565,000	17,438,000	17,196,000	17,451,000	16,601,000	17,240,000	15,610,000
Shares Outstanding	683,000	704,000	702,000	712,000	728,000	787,000	818,000	850,000
Statistical Record								
Return on Assets %	2.24	2.15	1.00	1.08	2.17	2.93	3.91	4.00
Return on Equity %	14.97	14.24	6.55	6.68	12.95	16.08	20.05	21.37
Loss Ratio %	69.35	71.47	75.73	78.61	81.35	79.40	76.90	78.34
Net Margin %	9.37	8.41	3.83	4.01	7.59	10.09	12.73	12.45
Price Range	51.76-42.71	43.03-30.68	41.32-31.56	45.21-31.02	44.00-17.75	40.50-23.50	51.50-37.31	46.88-28.56
P/E Ratio	11.40-9.41	11.23-8.01	25.82-19.72	28.26-19.39	14.92-6.02	11.98-6.95	13.07-9.47	13.17-8.02
Average Yield %	2.39	2.52	2.27	2.01	2.41	1.77	1.22	1.31

Address: 2775 Sanders Road, Northbrook, IL 60062-6127 Telephone: (847) 402-5000 Fax: (847) 402-0169	Web Site: www.allstate.com Officers: Edward M. Liddy - Chmn., Pres., C.E.O. Danny L. Hale - V.P., C.F.O.	Auditors: Deloitte & Touche LLP Investor Contact: 800-416-8803 Transfer Agents: EquiServe Trust Company, N.A., Providence, RI

ALLTEL CORP.

Exchange	Symbol	Price	52Wk Range	Yield	P/E	Div Acheiver
NYS	AT	$54.85 (3/31/2005)	60.56-49.00	2.77	16.18	44 Years

*7 Year Price Score 83.28 ***NYSE Composite Index=100** ***12 Month Price Score 96.84**

TRADING VOLUME (thousand shares)

Interim Earnings (Per Share)

Qtr.	Mar	Jun	Sep	Dec
2001	1.19	0.70	0.71	0.74
2002	0.68	0.69	0.76	0.82
2003	0.90	1.75	0.78	0.82
2004	0.61	0.85	1.05	0.89

Interim Dividends (Per Share)

Amt	Decl	Ex	Rec	Pay
0.37Q	4/22/2004	6/9/2004	6/11/2004	7/3/2004
0.37Q	7/22/2004	9/8/2004	9/10/2004	10/3/2004
0.38Q	10/21/2004	12/8/2004	12/10/2004	1/3/2005
0.38Q	1/20/2005	2/22/2005	2/24/2005	4/3/2005

Indicated Div: $1.52 (Div. Reinv. Plan)

Valuation Analysis

Forecast P/E	16.25	No of Institutions	
	(4/7/2005)	534	
Market Cap	$16.6 Billion	Shares	
Book Value	7.1 Billion	200,265,232	
Price/Book	2.33	% Held	
Price/Sales	2.01	66.21	

Business Summary: Communications (MIC: 10.1 SIC: 813 NAIC: 17310)

ALLTEL is a provider of wireless and wireline local, long-distance, network access and Internet services. Telecommunications products are warehoused and sold by Co.'s distribution subsidiary. A subsidiary also publishes telephone directories for affiliates and other independent telephone companies. In addition, a subsidiary provides billing, customer care and other data processing and outsourcing services to telecommunications companies. As of Dec 31 2003, Co. provided wireless communications service to more than 8.0 million customers in 23 states, and local wireline telephone service to nearly 3.1 million customers primarily located in rural areas in 15 states.

Recent Developments: For the year ended Dec 31 2004, income from continuing operations increased 7.7% to $1,026,700 thousand from income of $953,500 thousand a year earlier. Net income decreased 21.3% to $1,046,200 thousand from net income of $1,330,100 thousand a year earlier. Revenues were $8,246,100 thousand, up 3.3% from $7,979,900 thousand the year before. Operating income was $1,921,600 thousand versus an income of $1,898,000 thousand in the prior year, an increase of 1.2%. Total direct expense was $3,449,700 thousand versus $3,317,100 thousand in the prior year, an increase of 4.0%. Total indirect expense was $2,874,800 thousand versus $2,764,800 thousand in the prior year, an increase of 4.0%.

Prospects: On Jan 10 2005, Co. announced an agreement to acquire Western Wireless Corp. in a transaction valued at $4.40 billion. The deal, if approved by regulators and Western Wireless shareholders, would give Co. the Cellular One brand and make Co. the fifth largest wireless carrier in the U.S. in terms of customers. Co. reported an 11.0% increase to $1.30 billion in wireless revenues for the quarter ended Dec 31 2004, and added 139,000 wireless customers and 26,000 broadband customers. Also, Co. acquired wireless assets of MobileTel in Louisiana and made purchases from U.S. Cellular and TDS Telecom. Going forward, Co. projects earnings per share for full-year 2005 to be between $3.30 and $3.50.

Financial Data

(US$ in Thousands)	12/31/2004	12/31/2003	12/31/2002	12/31/2001	12/31/2000	12/31/1999	12/31/1998	12/31/1997
Earnings Per Share	3.39	4.25	2.96	3.40	6.08	2.47	1.89	2.70
Cash Flow Per Share	8.01	7.94	8.34	6.65	4.75	4.79	4.55	4.29
Tang Book Value Per Share	3.13	2.66	N.M.	6.87	5.92	7.03	5.82	8.67
Dividends Per Share	1.490	1.420	1.370	1.330	1.290	1.235	1.175	1.115
Dividend Payout %	43.95	33.41	46.28	39.12	21.22	50.00	62.17	41.30
Income Statement								
Total Revenue	8,246,100	7,979,900	7,983,400	7,598,900	7,067,000	6,302,271	5,194,008	3,263,563
EBITDA	3,244,200	3,160,400	2,993,500	3,208,400	4,649,900	2,473,199	1,943,137	1,409,644
Depn & Amortn	1,299,700	1,247,700	1,178,600	1,167,700	988,400	862,172	707,129	450,762
Income Before Taxes	1,592,000	1,534,100	1,465,500	1,751,800	3,350,700	1,330,852	972,339	828,701
Income Taxes	565,300	580,600	541,200	704,300	1,385,300	547,218	446,864	320,815
Net Income	1,046,200	1,330,100	924,300	1,067,000	1,928,800	783,634	525,475	507,886
Average Shares	308,400	312,800	312,300	313,500	317,200	316,814	277,276	187,689
Balance Sheet								
Net PPE	7,548,100	7,620,800	7,708,700	6,781,300	6,549,000	5,734,545	4,828,068	3,190,452
Total Assets	16,603,700	16,661,100	16,389,100	12,609,000	12,182,000	10,774,203	9,374,226	5,633,445
Long-Term Obligations	5,352,400	5,581,200	6,145,500	3,861,500	4,611,700	3,750,413	3,491,755	1,874,172
Total Liabilities	9,475,000	9,638,900	10,391,000	7,043,200	7,086,600	6,568,466	6,103,354	3,424,939
Stockholders' Equity	7,128,700	7,022,200	5,998,100	5,565,800	5,095,400	4,205,737	3,270,872	2,208,506
Shares Outstanding	302,267	312,643	311,182	310,529	312,983	314,257	281,198	183,673
Statistical Record								
Return on Assets %	6.27	8.05	6.37	8.61	16.76	7.78	7.00	9.24
Return on Equity %	14.75	20.43	15.99	20.02	41.36	20.96	19.18	23.59
EBITDA Margin %	39.34	39.60	37.50	42.22	65.80	39.24	37.41	43.19
Net Margin %	12.69	16.67	11.58	14.04	27.29	12.43	10.12	15.56
PPE Turnover	1.08	1.04	1.10	1.14	1.15	1.19	1.30	1.05
Asset Turnover	0.49	0.48	0.55	0.61	0.61	0.63	0.69	0.59
Debt to Equity	0.75	0.79	1.02	0.69	0.91	0.89	1.07	0.85
Price Range	60.56-46.58	56.05-41.15	62.58-36.93	68.25-50.49	82.69-48.13	91.38-57.06	61.13-39.25	41.38-30.00
P/E Ratio	17.86-13.74	13.19-9.68	21.14-12.48	20.07-14.85	13.60-7.92	36.99-23.10	32.34-20.77	15.32-11.11
Average Yield %	2.84	3.03	2.76	2.27	2.07	1.74	2.61	3.28

Address: One Allied Drive, Little Rock, AR 72202	Web Site: www.alltel.com	Auditors: PricewaterhouseCoopers LLP
Telephone: (501) 905-8000	Officers: Joe T. Ford - Chmn. Scott T. Ford - Pres., C.E.O.	Investor Contact: 501-905-8991
		Transfer Agents: Wachovia Bank, Charlotte, NC

ALTRIA GROUP INC

Exchange	Symbol	Price	52Wk Range	Yield	P/E	Div Acheiver
NYS	MO	$65.39 (3/31/2005)	67.00-44.95	4.47	14.34	39 Years

*7 Year Price Score 107.94 *NYSE Composite Index=100 *12 Month Price Score 111.21

Interim Earnings (Per Share)

Qtr.	Mar	Jun	Sep	Dec
2001	0.80	1.03	1.06	0.99
2002	1.09	1.21	2.06	0.87
2003	1.07	1.20	1.22	1.02
2004	1.07	1.27	1.29	0.94

Interim Dividends (Per Share)

Amt	Decl	Ex	Rec	Pay
0.68Q	5/26/2004	6/14/2004	6/15/2004	7/9/2004
0.73Q	8/25/2004	9/13/2004	9/15/2004	10/12/2004
0.73Q	12/15/2004	12/22/2004	12/27/2004	1/10/2005
0.73Q	2/23/2005	3/11/2005	3/15/2005	4/11/2005

Indicated Div: $2.92 (Div. Reinv. Plan)

Valuation Analysis

Forecast P/E	12.65	No of Institutions
	(4/7/2005)	896
Market Cap	$134.7 Billion	Shares
Book Value	30.7 Billion	1,445,668,608
Price/Book	4.38	% Held
Price/Sales	1.50	69.90

Business Summary: Tobacco Products (MIC: 4.2 SIC: 111 NAIC: 12221)

Altria Group, through its wholly-owned subsidiaries, Philip Morris USA Inc., Philip Morris International Inc. and its 84.6% majority-owned subsidiary, Kraft Foods Inc., is engaged in the manufacture and sale of various consumer products, including cigarettes, packaged grocery products, snacks, beverages, cheese and convenient meals. Philip Morris USA's major premium brands are Marlboro, Virginia Slims and Parliament. Its principal discount brand is Basic. Philip Morris Capital Corporation, another wholly-owned subsidiary, is primarily engaged in leasing activities.

Recent Developments: For the year ended Dec 31 2004, income from continuing operations increased 3.3% to $9,420,000 thousand from income of $9,121,000 thousand a year earlier. Net income increased 2.3% to $9,416,000 thousand from net income of $9,204,000 thousand a year earlier. Revenues were $89,610,000 thousand, up 10.2% from $81,320,000 thousand the year before. Operating income was $15,180,000 thousand versus an income of $15,759,000 thousand in the prior year, a decrease of 3.7%. Total direct expense was $59,606,000 thousand versus $52,701,000 thousand in the prior year, an increase of 13.1%. Total indirect expense was $14,824,000 thousand versus $12,860,000 thousand in the prior year, an increase of 15.3%.

Prospects: Co. expects fiscal 2005 diluted earnings per share from continuing operations to range from $4.95 to $5.05, including $0.12 per share in charges from the continuing Kraft restructuring and excluding $0.03 per share for discontinued operations. This projection assumes current foreign exchange rates and a base income tax rate of 34.7%. However, it does not include any tax benefits that could arise from the repatriation of funds from its international businesses under provisions of the American Jobs Creation Act, nor does it include any benefit from prior year accrued contributions to the National Tobacco Growers Settlement Trust.

Financial Data
(US$ in Thousands)

	12/31/2004	12/31/2003	12/31/2002	12/31/2001	12/31/2000	12/31/1999	12/31/1998	12/31/1997
Earnings Per Share	4.56	4.52	5.21	3.87	3.75	3.19	2.20	2.58
Cash Flow Per Share	5.31	5.33	5.03	4.08	4.87	4.75	3.34	3.45
Dividends Per Share	2.820	2.640	2.440	2.220	2.020	1.840	1.680	1.600
Dividend Payout %	61.84	58.41	46.83	57.36	53.87	57.68	76.36	62.02
Income Statement								
Total Revenue	89,610,000	81,832,000	80,408,000	89,924,000	80,356,000	78,596,000	74,391,000	72,055,000
EBITDA	16,787,000	17,350,000	20,563,000	18,039,000	16,396,000	15,192,000	11,667,000	13,293,000
Depn & Amortn	1,607,000	1,440,000	1,331,000	2,337,000	1,717,000	1,702,000	1,690,000	1,630,000
Income Before Taxes	14,004,000	14,760,000	18,098,000	14,284,000	13,960,000	12,695,000	9,087,000	10,611,000
Income Taxes	4,540,000	5,151,000	6,424,000	5,407,000	5,450,000	5,020,000	3,715,000	4,301,000
Net Income	9,416,000	9,204,000	11,102,000	8,560,000	8,510,000	7,675,000	5,372,000	6,310,000
Average Shares	2,063,000	2,038,000	2,129,000	2,210,000	2,272,000	2,403,000	2,446,000	2,442,000
Balance Sheet								
Current Assets	25,901,000	21,382,000	17,441,000	17,275,000	17,238,000	20,895,000	20,230,000	17,440,000
Total Assets	101,648,000	96,175,000	87,540,000	84,968,000	79,067,000	61,381,000	59,920,000	55,947,000
Current Liabilities	23,574,000	21,393,000	19,082,000	20,141,000	25,949,000	18,017,000	16,379,000	15,071,000
Long-Term Obligations	18,683,000	21,163,000	21,355,000	19,163,000	20,181,000	12,226,000	12,615,000	12,430,000
Total Liabilities	70,934,000	71,098,000	68,062,000	65,348,000	64,062,000	46,076,000	43,723,000	41,027,000
Stockholders' Equity	30,714,000	25,077,000	19,478,000	19,620,000	15,005,000	15,305,000	16,197,000	14,920,000
Shares Outstanding	2,059,527	2,037,263	2,039,259	2,152,503	2,208,897	2,338,520	2,430,535	2,425,487
Statistical Record								
Return on Assets %	9.49	10.02	12.87	10.44	12.09	12.65	9.27	11.39
Return on Equity %	33.66	41.32	56.79	49.44	56.00	48.73	34.53	43.31
EBITDA Margin %	18.73	21.20	25.57	20.06	20.40	19.33	15.68	18.45
Net Margin %	10.51	11.25	13.81	9.52	10.59	9.77	7.22	8.76
Asset Turnover	0.90	0.89	0.93	1.10	1.14	1.30	1.28	1.30
Current Ratio	1.10	1.00	0.91	0.86	0.66	1.16	1.24	1.16
Debt to Equity	0.61	0.84	1.10	0.98	1.34	0.80	0.78	0.83
Price Range	61.60-44.95	54.92-28.10	57.72-36.17	53.00-40.13	45.25-18.94	55.25-21.50	58.25-35.19	47.50-37.17
P/E Ratio	13.51-9.86	12.15-6.22	11.08-6.94	13.70-10.37	12.07-5.05	17.32-6.74	26.48-15.99	18.41-14.41
Average Yield %	5.40	6.39	5.11	4.70	7.32	5.05	3.79	3.78

Address: 120 Park Avenue, New York, NY 10017	**Web Site:** www.philipmorris.com	**Auditors:** PricewaterhouseCoopers LLP
Telephone: (917) 663-5000	**Officers:** Louis C. Camilleri - Chmn., C.E.O. Nancy J. De Lisi - Sr. V.P., Mergers & Acquisitions	**Investor Contact:** 917-663-3460
		Transfer Agents: First Chicago Trust Company, Jersey City, NJ

AMB PROPERTY CORP.

Exchange	Symbol	Price	52Wk Range	Yield	P/E
NYS	AMB	$37.80 (3/31/2005)	41.08-29.25	4.66	27.19

*7 Year Price Score 116.39 *NYSE Composite Index=100 *12 Month Price Score 97.88

Interim Earnings (Per Share)

Qtr.	Mar	Jun	Sep	Dec
2001	0.50	0.33	0.34	0.30
2002	0.33	0.31	0.30	0.43
2003	0.69	0.19	0.26	0.32
2004	0.19	0.22	0.35	0.66

Interim Dividends (Per Share)

Amt	Decl	Ex	Rec	Pay
0.425Q	5/18/2004	6/30/2004	7/5/2004	7/15/2004
0.425Q	9/23/2004	10/1/2004	10/5/2004	10/15/2004
0.425Q	12/9/2004	12/21/2004	12/23/2004	1/7/2005
0.44Q	3/1/2005	4/1/2005	4/5/2005	4/15/2005

Indicated Div: $1.76

Valuation Analysis

Forecast P/E	14.50 (4/7/2005)	No of Institutions 204
Market Cap	$3.1 Billion	Shares 67,753,824
Book Value	1.7 Billion	% Held
Price/Book	1.88	80.73
Price/Sales	4.73	

Business Summary: Property, Real Estate & Development (MIC: 8.3 SIC: 798 NAIC: 25930)

AMB Property acquires, owns, operates, manages, renovates, expands and develops primarily industrial properties in key distribution markets throughout North America, Europe and Asia. As of Dec 31 2003, Co. owned, managed and had renovation and development projects totaling 101.5 million square feet and 1,057 buildings in 36 markets within seven countries. Co. operates its business through its subsidiary, AMB Property, L.P., a Delaware limited partnership. As of Dec 31 2003, Co. owned an approximate 94.5% general partnership interest in AMB Property. Much of Co.'s portfolio is comprised of strategically located industrial buildings in in-fill submarkets.

Recent Developments: For the year ended Dec 31 2004, income from continuing operations increased 15.6% to $77,840 thousand from income of $67,363 thousand a year earlier. Net income decreased 2.8% to $125,471 thousand from net income of $129,128 thousand a year earlier. Revenues were $665,689 thousand, up 13.5% from $586,629 thousand the year before. Rental income rose 13.9% to $652,794 thousand from $573,292 thousand the year before. Private capital income was down 3.3% to $12,895 thousand from $13,337 thousand a year earlier.

Prospects: Demand fundamentals for industrial real estate continue to show positive momentum. Growth in business inventories is strong and broadly based across the manufacturing, retail and wholesale sectors. This macro activity supports a second consecutive quarter of national industrial real estate absorption in excess of 50.0 million square feet, well above the 10-year average of 33 million square feet per quarter. Co.'s portfolio has gained occupancy consistently over the course of the year with the strongest demand for distribution space coming from markets tied to global trade. Co. believes these occupancy improvements set the stage for rental rate growth in supply-constrained submarkets.

Financial Data
(US$ in Thousands)

	12/31/2004	12/31/2003	12/31/2002	12/31/2001	12/31/2000	12/31/1999	12/31/1998	12/31/1997
Earnings Per Share	1.39	1.47	1.37	1.47	1.35	1.94	1.27	1.38
Cash Flow Per Share	3.57	3.35	3.47	3.43	3.11	2.21	2.06	...
Tang Book Value Per Share	18.83	19.12	19.36	19.76	19.87	20.36	19.43	19.42
Dividends Per Share	1.700	1.660	1.640	1.580	1.480	1.400	1.370	0.134
Dividend Payout %	122.30	112.93	119.71	107.48	109.63	72.16	107.87	9.71
Income Statement								
Property Income	652,794	601,700	588,522	568,066	464,164	439,658	354,658	26,465
Non-Property Income	12,895	13,337	27,321	32,779	13,543	8,525	4,229	29,597
Total Revenue	665,689	615,037	615,843	600,845	477,707	448,183	358,887	56,062
Depn & Amortn	170,780	143,638	139,870	105,742	90,203	64,496	54,734	3,929
Interest Expense	157,852	146,773	147,101	128,985	90,270	88,681	69,670	3,528
Net Income	125,471	134,019	124,237	137,953	121,782	176,103	112,593	18,228
Average Shares	85,368	82,852	84,795	85,214	84,155	86,347	86,235	13,168
Balance Sheet								
Total Assets	6,386,943	5,420,666	4,992,494	4,760,893	4,425,626	3,621,550	3,562,885	2,506,255
Long-Term Obligations	3,257,191	2,574,257	2,235,361	2,135,664	1,836,276	1,270,037	1,368,196	685,652
Total Liabilities	3,519,477	2,761,352	2,417,077	2,274,265	1,983,318	1,359,408	1,472,501	773,073
Stockholders' Equity	1,671,140	1,666,899	1,684,150	1,752,342	1,767,930	1,829,259	1,765,360	1,668,030
Shares Outstanding	83,248	81,792	82,029	83,821	84,138	85,133	85,918	85,875
Statistical Record								
Return on Assets %	2.12	2.57	2.55	3.00	3.02	4.90	3.71	...
Return on Equity %	7.50	8.00	7.23	7.84	6.75	9.80	6.56	...
Net Margin %	18.85	21.79	20.17	22.96	25.49	39.29	31.37	32.51
Price Range	41.08-29.25	33.45-26.00	31.00-24.99	26.64-22.90	26.06-19.25	23.50-18.13	25.81-20.94	25.13-22.75
P/E Ratio	29.55-21.04	22.76-17.69	22.63-18.24	18.12-15.58	19.31-14.26	12.11-9.34	20.32-16.49	18.21-16.49
Average Yield %	4.77	5.75	5.89	6.37	6.50	6.55	5.81	0.57

Address: Pier 1, Bay 1, San Francisco, CA 94111 **Telephone:** (415) 394-9000 **Fax:** (415) 394-9001	Web Site: www.amb.com **Officers:** Hamid R. Moghadam - Chmn., C.E.O. W. Blake Baird - Pres.	**Auditors:** PricewaterhouseCoopers LLP **Investor Contact:** 415-394-9000

AMBAC FINANCIAL GROUP, INC.

Exchange	Symbol	Price	52Wk Range	Yield	P/E	Div Acheiver
NYS	ABK	$74.75 (3/31/2005)	84.42-64.04	0.67	11.45	13 Years

*7 Year Price Score 120.00 *NYSE Composite Index=100 *12 Month Price Score 95.58

Interim Earnings (Per Share)

Qtr.	Mar	Jun	Sep	Dec
2001	0.90	0.99	1.02	1.07
2002	1.07	1.09	1.21	0.59
2003	1.27	1.48	1.45	1.45
2004	1.55	1.63	1.65	1.69

Interim Dividends (Per Share)

Amt	Decl	Ex	Rec	Pay
0.11Q	1/28/2004	2/6/2004	2/10/2004	3/3/2004
0.11Q	5/5/2004	5/13/2004	5/17/2004	6/2/2004
0.125Q	10/20/2004	11/8/2004	11/10/2004	12/1/2004
0.125Q	1/26/2005	2/8/2005	2/10/2005	3/2/2005
		Indicated Div: $0.50		

Valuation Analysis

Forecast P/E	10.92	No of Institutions
	(4/7/2005)	383
Market Cap	$8.1 Billion	Shares
Book Value	5.0 Billion	104,585,152
Price/Book	1.62	% Held
Price/Sales	5.79	96.00

Business Summary: Insurance (MIC: 8.2 SIC: 351 NAIC: 24130)

Ambac Financial Group is a holding company whose subsidiaries provide financial guarantee products and other financial services to clients in both the public and private sectors. Co. provides financial guarantees for public finance and structured finance obligations through its principal operating subsidiary, Ambac Assurance. Through its financial services subsidiaries, Co. provides financial and investment products including investment agreements, interest rate and total return swaps and funding conduits, principally to its clients which include municipalities and their authorities, school districts, health care organizations and asset-backed issuers.

Recent Developments: For the year ended Dec 31 2004, income from continuing operations increased 15.6% to $725,840 thousand from income of $628,099 thousand a year earlier. Net income increased 17.1% to $724,551 thousand from net income of $618,915 thousand a year earlier. Revenues were $1,406,708 thousand, up 10.6% from $1,272,208 thousand the year before. Net premiums earned were $976,865 thousand versus $1,005,557 thousand in the prior year, a decrease of 2.9%. Net investment income fell 76.2% to $1,674 thousand from $7,026 thousand a year ago.

Prospects: Co. is pleased with its overall results and the level of business produced, given the challenging credit spread and competitive business environment. Recent shortfalls in premiums written is indicative of continued weakness in the areas of U.S. public and structured finance, which is more than offsetting growth in Co.'s international businesses. However, Co. remains encouraged about its outlook for the coming year, and believes that the combination of market/product expansion and the creativity and execution capability that Co. brings to those markets, produces a strong outlook for 2005 and beyond.

Financial Data (US$ in Thousands)	12/31/2004	12/31/2003	12/31/2002	12/31/2001	12/31/2000	12/31/1999	12/31/1998	12/31/1997
Earnings Per Share	6.53	5.66	3.97	3.97	3.41	2.87	2.37	2.09
Cash Flow Per Share	8.64	9.42	7.60	6.36	4.57	4.33	3.22	3.09
Tang Book Value Per Share	46.13	39.71	34.20	28.26	24.60	19.23	19.98	17.85
Dividends Per Share	0.470	0.420	0.380	0.340	0.307	0.280	0.253	0.230
Dividend Payout %	7.20	7.42	9.57	8.56	8.99	9.74	10.67	11.02
Income Statement								
Premium Income	716,659	620,317	471,534	378,734	311,276	264,426	113,920	54,289
Total Revenue	1,406,708	1,272,208	971,818	724,920	621,310	533,317	457,036	381,762
Benefits & Claims	69,600	53,400	26,700	20,000	15,000	11,000	6,000	2,854
Income Before Taxes	976,782	849,589	564,190	568,727	482,124	404,658	328,912	285,996
Income Taxes	250,942	221,490	131,596	135,821	115,952	96,741	74,918	62,966
Net Income	724,551	618,915	432,594	432,906	366,172	307,917	253,994	223,030
Average Shares	110,898	109,409	109,066	108,948	107,415	107,049	106,995	106,840
Balance Sheet								
Total Assets	18,585,258	16,747,314	15,355,538	12,267,695	10,120,300	11,345,096	11,212,311	8,249,722
Total Liabilities	13,560,801	12,492,756	11,730,359	9,284,007	7,524,186	9,326,646	9,116,221	6,377,240
Stockholders' Equity	5,024,457	4,254,558	3,625,179	2,983,688	2,596,114	2,018,450	2,096,090	1,872,482
Shares Outstanding	108,915	107,144	105,990	105,584	105,550	104,936	104,913	104,920
Statistical Record								
Return on Assets %	4.09	3.86	3.13	3.87	3.40	2.73	2.61	3.16
Return on Equity %	15.57	15.71	13.09	15.52	15.83	14.97	12.80	12.79
Loss Ratio %	9.71	8.61	5.66	5.28	4.82	4.16	5.27	5.26
Net Margin %	51.51	48.65	44.51	59.72	58.94	57.74	55.57	58.42
Price Range	84.42-64.04	72.19-44.51	69.69-49.90	63.43-45.50	58.31-26.13	40.92-30.08	43.79-27.54	31.54-21.00
P/E Ratio	12.93-9.81	12.75-7.86	17.55-12.57	15.98-11.46	17.10-7.66	14.26-10.48	18.48-11.62	15.09-10.05
Average Yield %	0.63	0.68	0.63	0.61	0.77	0.76	0.69	0.90

Address: One State Street Plaza, New York, NY 10004 Telephone: (212) 668-0340 Fax: (212) 509-9190	Web Site: www.ambac.com Officers: Phillip B. Lassiter - Chmn. Howard C. Pfeffer - Vice-Chmn., Sr. Managing Dir., Public Fin., Investment & Fin. Serv.	Auditors: KPMG LLP Investor Contact: 800-221-1854 Transfer Agents: Citibank, N.A., New York, NY

AMERADA HESS CORP.

Exchange	Symbol	Price	52Wk Range	Yield	P/E
NYS	AHC	$96.21 (3/31/2005)	103.83-62.57	1.25	10.05

*7 Year Price Score 110.75 *NYSE Composite Index=100 *12 Month Price Score 109.05

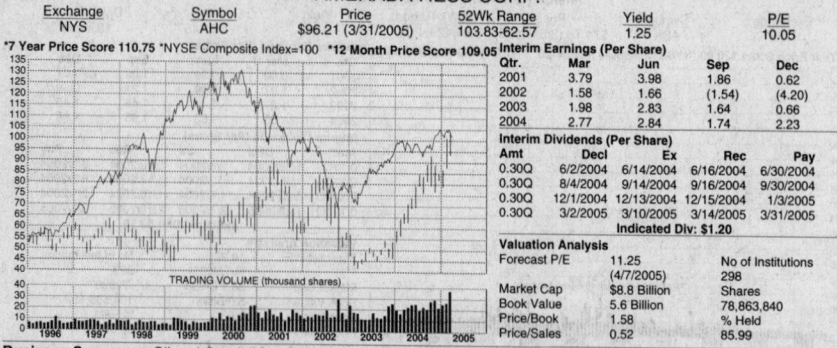

Interim Earnings (Per Share)

Qtr.	Mar	Jun	Sep	Dec
2001	3.79	3.98	1.86	0.62
2002	1.58	1.66	(1.54)	(4.20)
2003	1.98	2.83	1.64	0.66
2004	2.77	2.84	1.74	2.23

Interim Dividends (Per Share)

Amt	Decl	Ex	Rec	Pay
0.30Q	6/2/2004	6/14/2004	6/16/2004	6/30/2004
0.30Q	8/4/2004	9/14/2004	9/16/2004	9/30/2004
0.30Q	12/1/2004	12/13/2004	12/15/2004	1/3/2005
0.30Q	3/2/2005	3/10/2005	3/14/2005	3/31/2005
			Indicated Div: $1.20	

Valuation Analysis

Forecast P/E	11.25	No of Institutions	
	(4/7/2005)	298	
Market Cap	$8.8 Billion	Shares	
Book Value	5.6 Billion		78,863,840
Price/Book	1.58	% Held	
Price/Sales	0.52		85.99

Business Summary: Oil and Gas (MIC: 14.2 SIC: 911 NAIC: 24110)

Amerada Hess and its subsidiaries explore for, produce, purchase, transport and sell crude oil and natural gas. These exploration and production activities take place in the U.S., U.K. Norway, Denmark, Equatorial Guinea, Algeria, Gabon, Indonesia, Thailand, Azerbaijan, Malaysia and other countries. As of Dec 31 2003, Co. owned 50.0% of a refinery joint venture in the U.S. Virgin Islands, and another refining facility, terminals and retail gasoline stations located on the East Coast of the U.S. At Dec 31 2003, Co. had 646.0 million barrels of proved crude oil and natural gas liquids reserves and proved natural gas reserves of 2.33 trillion cubic feet.

Recent Developments: For the year ended Dec 31 2004, income from continuing operations increased 107.7% to $970,000 thousand from income of $467,000 thousand a year earlier. Net income increased 51.9% to $977,000 thousand from net income of $643,000 thousand a year earlier. Revenues were $17,126,000 thousand, up 18.3% from $14,480,000 thousand the year before. Total direct expense was $11,971,000 thousand versus $9,947,000 thousand in the prior year, an increase of 20.3%. Total indirect expense was $3,356,000 thousand versus $3,459,000 thousand in the prior year, a decrease of 3.0%.

Prospects: Co. has recently agreed to secure future natural gas sales from Block A-18 of the Malaysia-Thailand Joint Development Area. Under the agreement, initial natural gas sales will be accelerated to commence during the first quarter of 2005 and will average 200 million cubic feet per day (mmcf/d) for 2005. In the fourth quarter of 2005, natural gas sales are should increase to 390 mmcf/d, when the buyers' gas separation plant is completed. Co.'s net production from the block should exceed 55 mmcf/d in 2005 and 140 mmcf/d in 2006. Separately, following a new oil and gas discovery on Block SB302 offshore Sabah, Malaysia, Co. is planning further exploratory and appraisal drilling in 2005.

Financial Data
(US$ in Thousands)

	12/31/2004	12/31/2003	12/31/2002	12/31/2001	12/31/2000	12/31/1999	12/31/1998	12/31/1997
Earnings Per Share	9.57	7.11	(2.48)	10.25	11.38	4.85	(5.12)	0.08
Cash Flow Per Share	21.22	17.84	22.28	22.26	20.64	8.58	5.79	13.70
Tang Book Value Per Share	50.22	48.39	36.68	44.04	43.76	33.51	29.26	35.16
Dividends Per Share	1.200	1.200	1.200	1.200	0.600	0.600	0.600	0.600
Dividend Payout %	12.54	16.88	...	11.71	5.27	12.37	...	750.00
Income Statement								
Total Revenue	17,126,000	14,480,000	12,093,000	13,613,000	12,277,000	7,461,354	6,617,466	8,340,046
EBITDA	2,528,000	1,834,000	1,269,000	2,405,000	2,386,000	1,350,472	142,880	799,254
Depn & Amortn	970,000	1,053,000	1,320,000	967,000	714,000	648,663	656,991	672,669
Income Before Taxes	1,558,000	781,000	(51,000)	1,438,000	1,672,000	701,809	(514,111)	126,585
Income Taxes	588,000	314,000	167,000	524,000	649,000	264,193	(55,218)	119,085
Net Income	977,000	643,000	(218,000)	914,000	1,023,000	437,616	(458,893)	7,500
Average Shares	102,086	90,342	88,187	88,031	89,878	90,280	89,585	92,163
Balance Sheet								
Current Assets	4,335,000	3,186,000	2,756,000	3,946,000	4,115,000	1,827,570	1,886,706	2,203,632
Total Assets	16,312,000	13,983,000	13,262,000	15,369,000	10,274,000	7,727,712	7,882,983	7,934,619
Current Liabilities	4,697,000	2,669,000	2,553,000	3,718,000	3,538,000	1,578,850	1,796,797	1,739,851
Long-Term Obligations	3,785,000	3,868,000	4,976,000	5,283,000	1,985,000	2,286,660	2,476,145	2,003,033
Total Liabilities	10,715,000	8,643,000	9,013,000	10,462,000	6,391,000	4,689,520	5,239,571	4,718,920
Stockholders' Equity	5,597,000	5,340,000	4,249,000	4,907,000	3,883,000	3,038,192	2,643,412	3,215,699
Shares Outstanding	91,715	89,868	89,193	89,129	88,744	90,676	90,357	91,451
Statistical Record								
Return on Assets %	6.43	4.72	N.M.	7.13	11.33	5.61	N.M.	0.10
Return on Equity %	17.82	13.41	N.M.	20.80	29.48	15.40	N.M.	0.23
EBITDA Margin %	14.76	12.67	10.49	17.67	19.43	18.10	2.16	9.58
Net Margin %	5.70	4.44	N.M.	6.71	8.33	5.87	N.M.	0.09
Asset Turnover	1.13	1.06	0.84	1.06	1.36	0.96	0.84	1.06
Current Ratio	0.92	1.19	1.08	1.06	1.16	1.16	1.05	1.27
Debt to Equity	0.68	0.72	1.17	1.08	0.51	0.75	0.94	0.62
Price Range	92.91-53.17	57.05-41.58	84.21-49.68	89.90-54.15	76.06-48.25	65.94-43.94	60.63-47.38	63.81-47.63

Address: 1185 Avenue of the Americas, New York, NY 10036 **Telephone:** (212) 997-8500 **Fax:** (212) 536-8390	Web Site: www.hess.com Officers: John B. Hess - Chmn., C.E.O. John P. Rielly - Sr. V.P., C.F.O.	Auditors: Ernst & Young LLP Investor Contact: 212-536-8593

AMEREN CORP.

Exchange	Symbol	Price	52Wk Range	Yield		P/E
NYS	AEE	$49.01 (3/31/2005)	51.83-40.78	5.18		17.26

*7 Year Price Score 97.00 ***NYSE Composite Index=100** ***12 Month Price Score 100.05**

Interim Earnings (Per Share)

Qtr.	Mar	Jun	Sep	Dec
2001	0.43	0.69	1.94	0.34
2002	0.42	0.80	1.63	(0.27)
2003	0.63	0.68	1.70	0.23
2004	0.55	0.65	1.20	0.40

Interim Dividends (Per Share)

Amt	Decl	Ex	Rec	Pay
0.635Q	4/27/2004	6/7/2004	6/9/2004	6/30/2004
0.635Q	8/27/2004	9/7/2004	9/9/2004	9/30/2004
0.635Q	10/8/2004	12/6/2004	12/8/2004	12/31/2004
0.635Q	2/11/2005	3/7/2005	3/9/2005	3/31/2005
		Indicated Div: $2.54		

Valuation Analysis

Forecast P/E	16.10	No of Institutions	
	(4/7/2005)	329	
Market Cap	$9.6 Billion	Shares	
Book Value	5.8 Billion	102,619,672	
Price/Book	1.65	% Held	
Price/Sales	1.85	52.68	

Business Summary: Electricity (MIC: 7.1 SIC: 911 NAIC: 21122)

Ameren is a public utility holding company. As of Dec 31 2003, Co. provided energy services to more than 1.7 million electric customers and 515,000 natural gas customers throughout its 52,700 square mile territory in Missouri and Illinois through its regulated subsidiaries, AmerenUE, AmerenCIPS and CILCORP. Co. also operates Ameren Energy Generating Company, a non-regulated electric generating company with a total installed generating capacity of approximately 4,749 megawatts as of Dec 31 2003. Co. has various other subsidiaries responsible for the short and long-term marketing of power, procurement of fuel, management of commodity risks and providing other shared services.

Recent Developments: For the year ended Dec 31 2004, net income increased 1.1% to $530,000 thousand from net income of $524,000 thousand a year earlier. Revenues were $5,160,000 thousand, up 12.0% from $4,608,000 thousand the year before. Operating income was $1,078,000 thousand versus an income of $1,090,000 thousand in the prior year, a decrease of 1.1%. Total direct expense was $3,213,000 thousand versus $2,751,000 thousand in the prior year, an increase of 16.8%. Total indirect expense was $869,000 thousand versus $767,000 thousand in the prior year, an increase of 13.3%.

Prospects: For full-year 2005, Co. expects earnings to range between $2.90 and $3.10 per share, versus earnings of $2.84 per share in fiscal 2004. The expected increase is due to continued solid organic growth in Co.'s service territories, coupled with a return to more normal weather. In addition, Co. expects full-year 2005 earnings to benefit from the Illinois Power acquisition as Co. will realize a full year of Illinois Power's earnings and will eliminate the dilution associated with the pre-funding of the Illinois Power acquisition. However, Co. believes these benefits will be partially offset by higher employee benefit and depreciation expenses in 2005.

Financial Data (US$ in Thousands)	12/31/2004	12/31/2003	12/31/2002	12/31/2001	12/31/2000	12/31/1999	12/31/1998	12/31/1997
Earnings Per Share	2.84	3.25	2.60	3.40	3.33	2.81	2.82	2.44
Cash Flow Per Share	6.04	6.40	5.70	5.37	6.22	6.69	5.85	5.01
Tang Book Value Per Share	24.90	23.20	24.93	24.26	23.30	22.52	22.27	22.00
Dividends Per Share	2.540	2.540	2.540	2.540	2.540	2.540	2.540	...
Dividend Payout %	89.44	78.15	97.69	74.71	76.28	90.39	90.07	...
Income Statement								
Total Revenue	5,160,000	4,593,000	3,841,000	4,505,867	3,855,849	3,523,631	3,318,208	3,326,543
EBITDA	1,691,000	1,646,000	1,566,000	1,631,660	1,588,696	1,418,550	1,460,071	1,433,964
Depn & Amortn	601,000	562,000	469,000	422,458	406,896	376,397	375,343	377,205
Income Before Taxes	812,000	807,000	382,000	475,386	457,094	385,095	386,497	386,536
Income Taxes	282,000	301,000	...	...	...	...	...	...
Net Income	530,000	524,000	382,000	468,545	457,094	385,095	386,497	334,716
Average Shares	186,400	161,100	146,100	137,320	137,215	137,215	137,215	137,215
Balance Sheet								
Net PPE	13,297,000	10,917,000	8,914,000	8,426,562	7,705,672	7,165,185	6,928,039	6,987,085
Total Assets	17,434,000	14,233,000	11,499,000	10,400,575	9,714,430	9,177,615	8,847,439	8,827,547
Long-Term Obligations	5,021,000	4,070,000	3,433,000	2,835,378	2,745,068	2,448,448	2,289,424	2,506,068
Total Liabilities	11,439,000	9,697,000	7,464,000	6,816,618	6,282,562	5,852,718	5,556,122	5,573,382
Stockholders' Equity	5,800,000	4,354,000	3,842,000	3,348,760	3,196,671	3,089,700	3,056,120	3,018,968
Shares Outstanding	195,200	162,900	154,100	138,045	137,215	137,215	137,215	137,215
Statistical Record								
Return on Assets %	3.34	4.07	3.49	4.66	4.83	4.27	4.37	3.77
Return on Equity %	10.41	12.79	10.62	14.32	14.50	12.53	12.72	11.09
EBITDA Margin %	32.77	35.84	40.77	36.21	41.20	40.26	44.00	43.11
Net Margin %	10.27	11.41	9.95	10.40	11.85	10.93	11.65	10.06
PPE Turnover	0.43	0.46	0.44	0.56	0.52	0.50	0.48	0.48
Asset Turnover	0.33	0.36	0.35	0.45	0.41	0.39	0.38	0.37
Debt to Equity	0.87	0.93	0.89	0.85	0.86	0.79	0.75	0.83
Price Range	50.15-40.78	46.49-37.95	45.13-36.55	45.19-37.10	46.81-27.81	42.69-32.38	43.94-36.00	43.38-34.75
P/E Ratio	17.66-14.36	14.30-11.68	17.36-14.06	13.29-10.91	14.06-8.35	15.19-11.52	15.58-12.77	17.78-14.24
Average Yield %	5.53	5.99	6.06	6.19	6.92	6.68	6.35	...

Address: 1901 Chouteau Avenue, St. Louis, MO 63103 **Telephone:** (314) 621-3222 **Fax:** (314) 621-2888	**Web Site:** www.ameren.com **Officers:** Gary L. Rainwater - Chmn., Pres., C.E.O. Warner L. Baxter - Exec. V.P., C.F.O.	**Auditors:** PricewaterhouseCoopers LLP **Investor Contact:** 1-800-255-2237 **Transfer Agents:** Ameren Services Company, St. Louis, MO

AMERICAN AXLE & MANUFACTURING HOLDINGS INC

Exchange	Symbol	Price	52Wk Range	Yield	P/E
NYS	AXL	$24.50 (3/31/2005)	39.86-24.11	2.45	8.22

*7 Year Price Score N/A   *NYSE Composite Index=100   *12 Month Price Score 76.82

Interim Earnings (Per Share)

Qtr.	Mar	Jun	Sep	Dec
2001	0.51	0.72	0.51	0.62
2002	0.75	0.92	0.70	0.99
2003	1.02	0.97	0.71	0.99
2004	0.66	1.02	0.68	0.61

Interim Dividends (Per Share)

Amt	Decl	Ex	Rec	Pay
0.15Q	4/29/2004	6/3/2004	6/7/2004	6/28/2004
0.15Q	8/23/2004	9/2/2004	9/7/2004	9/28/2004
0.15Q	11/19/2004	12/3/2004	12/7/2004	12/28/2004
0.15Q	2/21/2005	3/3/2005	3/7/2005	3/28/2005

Indicated Div: $0.60

Valuation Analysis

Forecast P/E	11.67	No of Institutions	
	(4/7/2005)	148	
Market Cap	$1.2 Billion	Shares	43,089,408
Book Value	955.5 Million	% Held	86.39
Price/Book	1.27		
Price/Sales	0.34		

Business Summary: Automotive (MIC: 15.1 SIC: 714 NAIC: 23120)

American Axle & Manufacturing Holdings is a Tier 1 automotive supplier that manufactures, designs, and validates driveline systems and related powertrain components for light trucks, sport utility vehicles (SUVs) and passenger cars. Co.'s driveline systems include components that transfer power from the transmission and deliver it to the drive wheels. Co.'s driveline and powertrain products include axles, driveshafts, chassis and steering components, driving heads, crankshafts, transmission parts and forged products. Co. supplies the driveline components to GM for its rear-wheel drive light trucks and SUVs manufactured in North America. GM accounted for about 80.0% of 2004 net sales.

Recent Developments: For the year ended Dec 31 2004, net income decreased 19.1% to $159,500 thousand from net income of $197,100 thousand a year earlier. Revenues were $3,599,600 thousand, down 2.3% from $3,682,700 thousand the year before. Operating income was $284,800 thousand versus an income of $346,300 thousand in the prior year, a decrease of 17.8%. Total direct expense was $3,125,100 thousand versus $3,142,400 thousand in the prior year, a decrease of 0.6%. Total indirect expense was $189,700 thousand versus $194,000 thousand in the prior year, a decrease of 2.2%.

Prospects: Results are being hampered by lower sales due to the impact of production cuts scheduled by its customers. Co. is also experiencing narrower margins due to higher steel and other metallic material prices. Going forward, Co. expects near-term results will continue to be challenged by additional production cuts taken by its customers. For the first quarter of 2005, Co. expects production volumes for the major North American light truck programs it supports to be down 18.0% to 20.0%. Co. also anticipates substantial increases in the cost of steel and other purchased metal market commodities. Earnings for the first quarter are expected to be in the range of $0.25 to $0.30 per share.

Financial Data

(US$ in Thousands)	12/31/2004	12/31/2003	12/31/2002	12/31/2001	12/31/2000	12/31/1999	12/31/1998	12/31/1997
Earnings Per Share	2.98	3.70	3.38	2.36	2.60	2.34	0.08	0.43
Cash Flow Per Share	8.76	9.69	7.91	5.16	5.43	7.70	2.51	2.69
Tang Book Value Per Share	16.25	15.05	11.13	8.16	8.51	5.69	1.24	4.54
Dividends Per Share	0.450	...	...	...	...	...	...	...
Dividend Payout %	15.10	...	...	...	...	...	...	...
Income Statement								
Total Revenue	3,599,600	3,682,700	3,480,200	3,107,200	3,069,500	2,953,100	2,040,600	2,147,451
EBITDA	432,400	513,100	470,200	366,900	370,100	327,500	118,700	146,220
Depn & Amortn	171,100	163,100	145,800	126,600	107,900	89,500	68,800	50,177
Income Before Taxes	235,800	303,200	273,800	180,900	203,400	183,400	5,600	94,197
Income Taxes	76,300	106,100	97,700	66,000	74,200	67,800	2,100	38,933
Net Income	159,500	197,100	176,100	114,900	129,200	115,600	3,500	55,264
Average Shares	53,500	53,300	52,100	48,700	49,700	49,500	43,200	126,508
Balance Sheet								
Current Assets	592,600	563,700	566,100	478,000	500,600	509,500	294,000	289,172
Total Assets	2,538,800	2,397,800	2,335,700	2,160,900	1,902,500	1,677,100	1,226,200	1,017,653
Current Liabilities	585,600	554,200	535,200	477,000	510,300	446,700	362,900	385,998
Long-Term Obligations	448,000	449,700	734,100	878,200	817,100	774,900	693,400	507,043
Total Liabilities	1,583,300	1,443,100	1,632,100	1,626,200	1,530,500	1,413,400	1,185,800	980,422
Stockholders' Equity	955,500	954,700	703,600	534,700	372,000	263,700	40,400	37,231
Shares Outstanding	49,700	53,600	49,700	47,100	43,700	46,357	32,456	8,209
Statistical Record								
Return on Assets %	6.44	8.33	7.83	5.66	7.20	7.96	0.31	6.18
Return on Equity %	16.65	23.77	28.44	25.34	40.54	76.03	9.02	38.46
EBITDA Margin %	12.01	13.93	13.51	11.81	12.06	11.09	5.82	6.81
Net Margin %	4.43	5.35	5.06	3.70	4.21	3.91	0.17	2.57
Asset Turnover	1.45	1.56	1.55	1.53	1.71	2.03	1.82	2.40
Current Ratio	1.01	1.02	1.06	1.00	0.98	1.14	0.81	0.75
Debt to Equity	0.47	0.47	1.04	1.64	2.20	2.94	17.16	13.62
Price Range	41.98-26.87	40.53-19.50	36.19-20.26	22.25-7.75	17.00-5.94	16.94-11.69	...	...
P/E Ratio	14.09-9.02	10.95-5.27	10.71-5.99	9.43-3.28	6.54-2.28	7.24-4.99	...	...
Average Yield %	1.31	...	...	...	...	...	...	...

Address: 1840 Holbrook Avenue, Detroit, MI 48212-3488 Telephone: (313) 974-2000	Web Site: www.aam.com Officers: Richard E. Dauch - Chmn., C.E.O. Joel D. Robinson - Vice-Chmn.	Auditors: Deloitte & Touche LLP Investor Contact: 313-974-3074

AMERICAN ELECTRIC POWER COMPANY, INC.

Exchange	Symbol	Price	52Wk Range	Yield	P/E
NYS	AEP	$34.06 (3/31/2005)	35.65-29.01	4.11	12.39

*7 Year Price Score 75.74 ***NYSE Composite Index=100** ***12 Month Price Score 96.53**

TRADING VOLUME (thousand shares)

Interim Earnings (Per Share)

Qtr.	Mar	Jun	Sep	Dec
2001	0.83	0.72	1.31	0.16
2002	0.56	0.19	1.25	(0.50)
2003	1.24	0.44	0.65	(1.99)
2004	0.70	0.25	1.34	0.45

Interim Dividends (Per Share)

Amt	Decl	Ex	Rec	Pay
0.35Q	4/27/2004	5/6/2004	5/10/2004	6/10/2004
0.35Q	7/27/2004	8/6/2004	8/10/2004	9/10/2004
0.35Q	10/26/2004	11/8/2004	11/10/2004	12/10/2004
0.35Q	1/26/2005	2/8/2005	2/10/2005	3/10/2005
			Indicated Div: $1.40	

Valuation Analysis

Forecast P/E	14.51	No of Institutions
	(4/13/2005)	401
Market Cap	$13.5 Billion	Shares
Book Value	8.5 Billion	257,866,080
Price/Book	1.58	% Held
Price/Sales	0.96	65.14

Business Summary: Electricity (MIC: 7.1 SIC: 911 NAIC: 21121)

American Electric Power Company is a public utility holding company. The service area of Co.'s domestic electric utility subsidiaries covers portions of the states of Arkansas, Indiana, Kentucky, Louisiana, Michigan, Ohio, Oklahoma, Tennessee, Texas, Virginia and West Virginia. The electric utility subsidiaries of Co. provide electric service, consisting of generation, transmission and distribution, on an integrated basis to their retail customers. At Dec 31 2003, Co. had more than 5.0 million domestic electric utility customers and owned and operated approximately 42,000 megawatts of generating capacity in the U.S. and the U.K.

Recent Developments: For the year ended Dec 31 2004, Co reported net income of $1.09 billion, up considerably from $110.0 million a year earlier. earlier. The improvement in earnings for 2004 was primarily attributable to gains from asset sales, coupled with the negative impact of charges for impairments for non-core businesses, losses from discontinued operations and changes in accounting practices in the previous year. Revenues were $14.10 billion, down 4.1% from $14.70 billion the year before. Net earnings from Co.'s utility operations were $201.0 million in 2004 compared with $285.0 million the prior year.

Prospects: On Jan 26 2005, Co. announced that it has completed the sale of its controlling interest in Houston Pipe Line Co. (HPL), as well as 30 billion cubic feet of working gas and working capital, to Energy Transfer Partners, LP (ETP) for approximately $1.00 billion. As part of the transaction, Co. will retain a 2.0% ownership interest in the HPL partnership interests and will provide certain transitional administrative services. The sale essentially completes Co.'s divestiture of its natural gas assets in the U.S. Going forward, Co. will focus on growing its core domestic electric utility business. Looking ahead, Co. is targeting full-year 2005 ongoing earnings between $2.30 and $2.50 per share.

Financial Data

(US$ in Thousands)	12/31/2004	12/31/2003	12/31/2002	12/31/2001	12/31/2000	12/31/1999	12/31/1998	12/31/1997
Earnings Per Share	2.75	0.29	(1.57)	3.01	0.83	2.69	2.81	2.70
Cash Flow Per Share	6.54	5.99	5.05	9.17	4.65	4.23	5.40	6.34
Tang Book Value Per Share	21.32	19.74	19.68	20.90	20.72	25.79	25.24	24.62
Dividends Per Share	1.400	1.650	2.400	2.400	2.400	2.400	2.400	2.400
Dividend Payout %	50.91	568.97	...	79.73	289.16	89.22	85.41	88.89
Income Statement								
Total Revenue	14,057,000	14,545,000	14,555,000	61,257,000	13,694,000	6,916,000	6,345,902	5,879,820
EBITDA	3,808,000	2,989,000	2,463,000	3,957,000	2,198,000	1,494,000	...	...
Depn & Amortn	1,361,000	1,337,000	1,443,000	1,413,000	1,299,000	714,000	619,557	608,217
Income Before Taxes	1,699,000	880,000	235,000	1,572,000	899,000	780,000	...	...
Income Taxes	572,000	358,000	214,000	569,000	597,000	260,000	347,831	373,548
Net Income	1,089,000	110,000	(519,000)	971,000	267,000	520,000	536,183	510,961
Average Shares	396,000	385,000	332,000	322,000	322,000	193,000	190,774	189,039
Balance Sheet								
Net PPE	22,801,000	22,029,000	21,684,000	24,543,000	22,393,000	13,055,000	12,571,321	11,632,849
Total Assets	34,663,000	36,744,000	34,741,000	47,281,000	54,548,000	21,488,000	19,483,202	16,615,346
Long-Term Obligations	11,008,000	12,322,000	8,863,000	9,753,000	9,602,000	6,336,000	6,799,641	5,109,463
Total Liabilities	26,087,000	28,809,000	27,532,000	38,896,000	46,333,000	16,318,000	14,595,420	11,871,388
Stockholders' Equity	8,515,000	7,874,000	7,064,000	8,229,000	8,054,000	5,006,000	4,841,780	4,677,234
Shares Outstanding	395,858	395,016	338,835	322,235	322,019	194,103	191,816	189,989
Statistical Record								
Return on Assets %	3.04	0.31	N.M.	1.91	0.70	2.54	2.97	3.14
Return on Equity %	13.25	1.47	N.M.	11.93	4.08	10.56	11.27	11.08
EBITDA Margin %	27.09	20.55	16.92	6.46	16.05	21.60	...	...
Net Margin %	7.75	0.76	(3.57)	1.59	1.95	7.52	8.45	8.69
PPE Turnover	0.63	0.67	0.63	2.61	0.77	0.54	0.52	0.51
Asset Turnover	0.39	0.41	0.35	1.20	0.36	0.34	0.35	0.36
Debt to Equity	1.29	1.56	1.25	1.19	1.19	1.27	1.40	1.09
Price Range	35.23-29.01	31.04-19.94	48.06-17.69	51.11-39.81	48.00-26.06	47.94-30.81	52.94-42.56	52.00-39.63
P/E Ratio	12.81-10.55	107.03-68.76	...	16.98-13.23	57.83-31.40	17.82-11.45	18.84-15.15	19.26-14.68
Average Yield %	4.32	6.12	6.61	5.29	6.75	6.25	5.03	5.49

Address: 1 Riverside Plaza, Columbus, OH 43215-2373 **Telephone:** (614) 716-1000 **Fax:** (614) 223-1823	**Web Site:** www.aep.com **Officers:** Michael G. Morris - Chmn., Pres., C.E.O. Susan Tomasky - Exec. V.P., Policy, Fin., Strategic Planning, C.F.O.	**Auditors:** DELOITTE & TOUCHE LLP **Investor Contact:** 614-716-2840 **Transfer Agents:** EquiServe Trust Company, N.A., Providence, RI

AMERICAN EXPRESS CO.

Exchange	Symbol	Price	52Wk Range	Yield	P/E
NYS	AXP	$51.37 (3/31/2005)	56.92-48.11	0.93	19.17

*7 Year Price Score 103.23 *NYSE Composite Index=100 *12 Month Price Score 96.16

Interim Earnings (Per Share)

Qtr.	Mar	Jun	Sep	Dec
2001	0.40	0.13	0.22	0.22
2002	0.46	0.51	0.52	0.52
2003	0.53	0.59	0.59	0.59
2004	0.61	0.68	0.69	0.70

Interim Dividends (Per Share)

Amt	Decl	Ex	Rec	Pay
0.10Q	5/24/2004	6/30/2004	7/2/2004	8/10/2004
0.12Q	9/27/2004	10/6/2004	10/8/2004	11/10/2004
0.12Q	11/22/2004	1/5/2005	1/7/2005	2/10/2005
0.12Q	3/21/2005	3/30/2005	4/1/2005	5/10/2005

Indicated Div: $0.48

Valuation Analysis

Forecast P/E	16.52 (4/7/2005)	No of Institutions 939
Market Cap	$64.2 Billion	Shares 1,015,617,152
Book Value	16.0 Billion	% Held 81.38
Price/Book	4.01	
Price/Sales	2.20	

TRADING VOLUME (thousand shares)

Business Summary: Credit & Lending (MIC: 8.6 SIC: 159 NAIC: 22298)

American Express is primarily engaged in providing travel-related services, financial advisory services and international banking services worldwide. The Travel Related Services division provides, among other things, global network services, the American Express® Card and other consumer and corporate lending products, and corporate and consumer travel products and services. The Financial Advisors division provides financial planning and advice, a variety of investment products, personal insurance, and retail brokerage services. The American Express Bank provides financial services for corporations, financial institutions and retail customers, including American Express Travelers Cheques.

Recent Developments: For the year ended Dec 31 2004, net income increased 15.3% to $3,445,000 thousand from net income of $2,987,000 thousand a year earlier. Provision for loan losses was $1,963,000 thousand versus $2,071,000 thousand in the prior year, a decrease of 5.2%. Non-interest income rose 12.7% to $29,115,000 thousand, while non-interest expense advanced 16.8% to $18,979,000 thousand.

Prospects: On Feb 1 2005, Co. announced that it plans to spin-off to shareholders its American Express Financial Advisors unit, which generated revenues of approximately $7.00 billion and net income of about $700.0 million in 2004. Under the terms of the transaction, Co.'s shareholders will receive 100.0% of the common shares of American Express Financial Corporation in a tax-free distribution expected to be completed in the third quarter of 2005, subject to regulatory approvals and the receipt of a favorable tax ruling and/or opinion, as well as final board approval. Following the spin-off, Co. plans to raise its return on equity target from between 18.0% and 20.0% to between 28.0% and 30.0%.

Financial Data
(US$ in Thousands)

	12/31/2004	12/31/2003	12/31/2002	12/31/2001	12/31/2000	12/31/1999	12/31/1998	12/31/1997
Earnings Per Share	2.68	2.30	2.01	0.98	2.07	1.81	1.54	1.38
Cash Flow Per Share	7.24	1.98	6.57	4.02	4.77	5.51	3.24	3.71
Tang Book Value Per Share	12.83	11.93	10.62	9.04	8.81	7.53	7.18	6.84
Dividends Per Share	0.320	0.380	0.400	0.320	0.315	0.300	0.225	0.300
Dividend Payout %	11.94	16.52	19.90	32.65	15.22	16.60	14.58	21.69
Income Statement								
Total Revenue	29,115,000	25,866,000	23,807,000	22,582,000	23,675,000	21,278,000	19,132,000	17,760,000
Income Before Taxes	4,951,000	4,247,000	3,727,000	1,596,000	3,908,000	3,438,000	2,925,000	2,750,000
Income Taxes	1,435,000	1,247,000	1,056,000	285,000	1,098,000	963,000	784,000	759,000
Net Income	3,445,000	2,987,000	2,671,000	1,311,000	2,810,000	2,475,000	2,141,000	1,991,000
Average Shares	1,285,000	1,298,000	1,330,000	1,336,000	1,360,000	1,368,000	1,389,000	1,437,000
Balance Sheet								
Total Assets	192,638,000	175,001,000	157,253,000	151,100,000	154,423,000	148,517,000	126,933,000	120,003,000
Total Liabilities	176,618,000	159,678,000	143,392,000	138,563,000	142,239,000	137,922,000	116,735,000	110,429,000
Stockholders' Equity	16,020,000	15,323,000	13,861,000	12,037,000	11,684,000	10,095,000	9,698,000	9,574,000
Shares Outstanding	1,249,000	1,284,000	1,305,000	1,331,000	1,326,000	1,340,700	1,351,500	1,399,200
Statistical Record								
Return on Assets %	1.87	1.80	1.73	0.86	1.85	1.80	1.73	1.74
Return on Equity %	21.92	20.47	20.63	11.05	25.73	25.01	22.22	22.00
Price Range	56.92-47.70	49.01-31.49	44.87-26.60	55.94-25.61	63.00-40.92	55.92-31.98	39.29-23.17	29.85-18.17
P/E Ratio	21.24-17.80	21.31-13.69	22.32-13.23	57.08-26.13	30.43-19.77	30.89-17.67	25.51-15.04	21.63-13.16
Average Yield %	0.62	0.91	1.09	0.83	0.59	0.69	0.71	1.23

Address: World Financial Center, 200 Vesey Street, New York, NY 10285 **Telephone:** (212) 640 2000	**Web Site:** www.americanexpress.com **Officers:** Kenneth I. Chenault - Chmn., C.E.O. Jonathan S. Linen - Vice-Chmn.	**Auditors:** Ernst & Young LLP **Investor Contact:** **Transfer Agents:** Mellon Investor Services LLC, Ridgefield Park, NJ

AMERICAN FINANCIAL GROUP, INC

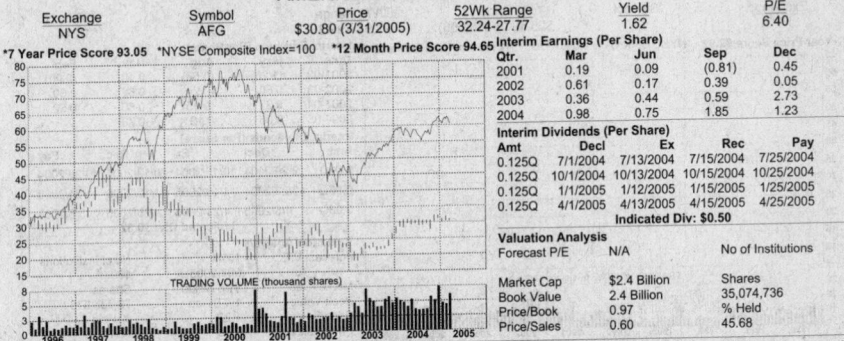

Exchange	Symbol	Price	52Wk Range	Yield	P/E
NYS	AFG	$30.80 (3/31/2005)	32.24-27.77	1.62	6.40

*7 Year Price Score 93.05   *NYSE Composite Index=100   *12 Month Price Score 94.65

Interim Earnings (Per Share)

Qtr.	Mar	Jun	Sep	Dec
2001	0.19	0.09	(0.81)	0.45
2002	0.61	0.17	0.39	0.05
2003	0.36	0.44	0.59	2.73
2004	0.98	0.75	1.85	1.23

Interim Dividends (Per Share)

Amt	Decl	Ex	Rec	Pay
0.125Q	7/1/2004	7/13/2004	7/15/2004	7/25/2004
0.125Q	10/1/2004	10/13/2004	10/15/2004	10/25/2004
0.125Q	1/1/2005	1/12/2005	1/15/2005	1/25/2005
0.125Q	4/1/2005	4/13/2005	4/15/2005	4/25/2005

Indicated Div: $0.50

Valuation Analysis

Forecast P/E	N/A	No of Institutions	
Market Cap	$2.4 Billion	Shares	
Book Value	2.4 Billion	35,074,736	
Price/Book	0.97	% Held	
Price/Sales	0.60	45.68	

Business Summary: Insurance (MIC: 8.2 SIC: 331 NAIC: 24126)

American Financial Group is a holding company that, through its subsidiaries, is engaged primarily in property and casualty insurance and in the sale of retirement annuities, life and supplemental health insurance products. Generally, Co.'s property and casualty insurance interests are in the following areas: insurance, savings and loan, leasing, banking, real estate, communications/ entertainment and food distribution. Co.'s annuity and life operations are conducted through Great American Financial Resources, Inc., a holding company that markets retirement products, primarily fixed and variable annuities, and various forms of life and supplemental health insurance.

Recent Developments: For the year ended Dec 31 2004, net income increased 22.5% to $359,860 thousand from net income of $293,815 thousand a year earlier. Revenues were $3,906,265 thousand, up 16.3% from $3,359,643 thousand the year before. Net premiums earned were $2,461,667 thousand versus $2,241,093 thousand in the prior year, an increase of 9.8%. Investment income rose 3.5% to $800,226 thousand from $773,188 thousand the year before. Net operating earnings were $403,449 thousand, up 15.8% from $348,460 thousand in 2003.

Prospects: Co. expects its Property and Transportation businesses to continue to report solid growth and strong underwriting profits going forward. In Co.'s Specialty Casualty and Specialty Financial groups, it expects slower premium growth year over year with the opportunity for improved underwriting performance in 2005. Co. will continue to focus on adequate pricing of its insurance products as well as managing capital levels in order to generate appropriate underwriting profits and returns within its various business lines. Co. expects continued underwriting profitability in the California workers' compensation business, but anticipates somewhat lower premium growth due to the rate environment.

Financial Data
(US$ in Thousands)

	12/31/2004	12/31/2003	12/31/2002	12/31/2001	12/31/2000	12/31/1999	12/31/1998	12/31/1997
Earnings Per Share	4.81	4.12	1.22	(0.22)	(0.95)	2.35	2.00	0.64
Cash Flow Per Share	13.65	10.72	11.81	10.63	7.47	6.33	6.30	7.14
Tang Book Value Per Share	29.55	26.11	21.37	17.31	18.24	17.25	23.54	22.33
Dividends Per Share	0.500	0.500	0.500	1.000	1.000	1.000	1.000	...
Dividend Payout %	10.40	12.14	40.98	...	...	42.55	50.00	...
Income Statement								
Premium Income	2,461,667	2,241,093	2,708,247	2,874,060	2,725,333	2,334,747	2,869,103	2,945,887
Total Revenue	3,906,265	3,359,643	3,749,568	3,923,632	3,817,327	3,334,482	4,050,034	4,020,723
Benefits & Claims	1,994,631	1,898,830	2,360,936	2,587,733	2,415,639	1,937,722	2,395,101	2,464,527
Income Before Taxes	589,538	301,006	178,019	55,898	109,893	302,061	204,754	319,610
Income Taxes	186,089	(47,454)	17,880	10,078	29,041	98,198	79,584	120,127
Net Income	359,860	293,815	84,640	(14,840)	(56,035)	141,440	124,400	192,250
Average Shares	74,825	70,272	69,203	68,368	59,074	60,210	62,185	60,748
Balance Sheet								
Total Assets	22,559,527	20,197,258	19,504,826	17,401,681	16,415,541	16,054,075	15,845,203	15,755,349
Total Liabilities	19,909,394	17,933,538	17,307,954	15,448,572	14,358,978	14,224,827	13,607,250	13,579,643
Stockholders' Equity	2,430,547	2,076,161	1,725,848	1,498,379	1,548,530	1,339,978	1,716,177	1,662,709
Shares Outstanding	76,634	73,056	69,129	68,491	67,410	58,419	60,928	61,049
Statistical Record								
Return on Assets %	1.68	1.48	0.46	N.M.	N.M.	0.89	0.79	1.25
Return on Equity %	15.93	15.46	5.25	N.M.	N.M.	9.26	7.36	11.95
Loss Ratio %	81.03	84.73	87.18	90.04	88.64	82.99	83.48	83.66
Net Margin %	9.21	8.75	2.26	(0.38)	(1.47)	4.24	3.07	4.78
Price Range	32.24-26.45	26.60-18.25	29.97-19.25	30.30-18.73	28.63-18.50	43.88-25.13	45.31-31.50	48.63-33.13
P/E Ratio	6.70-5.50	6.46-4.43	24.57-15.78	...	...	18.67-10.69	22.66-15.75	75.98-51.76
Average Yield %	1.67	2.25	2.01	4.00	4.22	3.08	2.52	...

Address: One East Fourth Street, Cincinnati, OH 45202
Telephone: (513) 579-2121
Fax: (513) 579-0108

Web Site: www.amfnl.com
Officers: Carl H. Lindner - Chmn., Co-C.E.O. S. Craig Lindner - Co-C.E.O.

Auditors: Ernst & Young LLP
Investor Contact: 513-579-6739

AMERICAN GREETINGS CORP.

Exchange	Symbol	Price	52Wk Range	Yield	P/E
NYS	AM	$25.48 (3/31/2005)	27.91-19.43	1.26	16.44

*7 Year Price Score 92.91 *NYSE Composite Index=100 *12 Month Price Score 95.58

Interim Earnings (Per Share)

Qtr.	May	Aug	Nov	Feb
2001-02	(1.26)	(0.56)	0.10	(0.20)
2002-03	0.60	(0.24)	0.62	0.60
2003-04	0.27	(0.15)	0.60	0.62
2004-05	0.06	0.10	0.78	...

Interim Dividends (Per Share)

Amt	Decl	Ex	Rec	Pay
0.06Q	9/29/2004	10/15/2004	10/19/2004	10/29/2004
0.06Q	12/23/2004	1/10/2005	1/12/2005	1/24/2005
0.08Q	4/5/2005	4/21/2005	4/25/2005	5/5/2005

Indicated Div: $0.32

Valuation Analysis

Forecast P/E	13.44 (4/7/2005)	No of Institutions 189
Market Cap	$1.8 Billion	Shares 79,735,576
Book Value	1.4 Billion	% Held
Price/Book	1.27	79,735,576
Price/Sales	0.90	N/A

Business Summary: Printing (MIC: 13.4 SIC: 771 NAIC: 11191)

American Greetings designs, manufactures and sells everyday and seasonal greeting cards and other social expression products. More than 15,000 designs of greeting cards as well as gift wrap, paper party goods, candles, balloons, stationery and giftware are manufactured and sold in the U.S. by Co., Gibson Greetings, Plus Mark, and Carlton Cards Retail. Co. also manufactures and sells its products in Canada, the U.K, Ireland, Mexico, Australia, New Zealand, and South Africa. AmericanGreetings.com, Inc. (92% owned), markets e-mail greetings, personalized printable greeting cards and other social expression products through Co.'s websites.

Recent Developments: For the quarter ended Nov 30 2004, income from continuing operations decreased 10.5% to $40,344 thousand from income of $45,091 thousand in the year-earlier quarter. Net income increased 35.4% to $62,761 thousand from net income of $46,362 thousand in the year-earlier quarter. Revenues were $586,165 thousand, down 2.9% from $603,754 thousand the year before. Total indirect expense was $238,211 thousand versus $222,926 thousand in the prior-year quarter, an increase of 6.9%.

Prospects: Top-line results are being negatively affected by lower revenues in both the retail segment and Co.'s seasonal gift wrap business. These reductions to sales are being partially offset by incremental revenue from recent acquisitions in the AG Interactive segment and favorable foreign currency exchange rates. Meanwhile, Co. is targeting fiscal 2005 earnings from continuing operation of between $1.02 and $1.07 per share. Looking ahead, the implementation of initiatives focused on reducing supply chain and overhead costs should positively effect results in fiscal 2006. Separately, on Feb 24 2005, Co. announced that it has acquired a European manufacturer of gift-wrap products.

Financial Data
(US$ in Thousands)

	9 Mos	6 Mos	3 Mos	02/29/2004	02/28/2003	02/28/2002	02/28/2001	02/29/2000
Earnings Per Share	1.55	1.37	1.13	1.40	1.63	(1.92)	(1.79)	1.37
Cash Flow Per Share	5.63	5.86	4.27	4.38	1.17	0.57	1.73	2.56
Tang Book Value Per Share	16.48	15.35	15.33	15.39	13.17	11.03	12.87	14.18
Dividends Per Share	0.060	...	...	...	...	0.300	0.720	0.790
Dividend Payout %	3.86	...	...	...	...	...	...	57.66
Income Statement								
Total Revenue	1,411,790	824,929	445,671	2,008,943	1,995,860	2,355,740	2,518,814	2,175,236
EBITDA	122,654	42,736	22,074	320,648	344,743	(33,417)	252,077	239,221
Depn & Amortn	42,425	28,321	15,161	64,069	64,810	84,308	98,057	64,342
Income Before Taxes	80,229	14,415	6,913	170,751	200,838	(196,324)	98,633	140,624
Income Taxes	31,049	5,579	2,675	66,081	79,732	(74,014)	191,306	50,625
Net Income	73,909	11,148	4,238	104,670	121,106	(122,310)	(113,814)	50,625
Average Shares	82,397	69,265	68,846	80,088	78,980	63,615	63,646	65,592
Balance Sheet								
Current Assets	1,279,841	1,113,887	1,015,291	1,176,968	1,234,488	1,066,182	1,205,736	1,100,684
Total Assets	2,467,940	2,314,692	2,263,713	2,484,013	2,584,120	2,614,995	2,712,074	2,517,983
Current Liabilities	470,272	414,660	385,634	422,963	699,397	716,040	1,111,281	582,488
Long-Term Obligations	483,988	483,876	483,783	665,874	726,531	853,113	380,124	442,102
Total Liabilities	1,083,439	1,031,443	992,482	1,216,473	1,506,656	1,712,576	1,664,884	1,265,572
Stockholders' Equity	1,384,501	1,283,249	1,271,231	1,267,540	1,077,464	902,419	1,047,190	1,252,411
Shares Outstanding	68,976	68,514	68,208	67,468	65,899	63,761	63,488	77,802
Statistical Record								
Return on Assets %	4.85	4.45	3.76	4.12	4.66	N.M.	N.M.	3.64
Return on Equity %	9.47	8.81	7.47	8.90	12.23	N.M.	N.M.	6.91
EBITDA Margin %	8.69	5.18	4.95	15.96	17.27	N.M.	10.01	11.00
Net Margin %	5.24	1.35	0.95	5.21	6.07	N.M.	N.M.	4.14
Asset Turnover	0.78	0.84	0.84	0.79	0.77	0.88	0.96	0.88
Current Ratio	2.72	2.69	2.63	2.78	1.77	1.49	1.08	1.89
Debt to Equity	0.35	0.38	0.38	0.53	0.67	0.95	0.36	0.35
Price Range	27.70-19.43	24.12-18.64	23.24-17.11	22.85-12.95	22.97-12.56	15.88-9.95	23.38-8.50	32.06-17.25
P/E Ratio	17.87-12.54	17.61-13.61	20.57-15.14	16.32-9.25	14.09-7.71	...	...	23.40-12.59
Average Yield %	0.26	...	...	...	...	2.35	4.43	3.08

Address: One American Road, Cleveland, OH 44144	**Web Site:** www.americangreetings.com	**Auditors:** ERNST & YOUNG LLP
Telephone: (216) 252-7300	**Officers:** Morry Weiss - Chmn. James C. Spira - Pres., C.O.O.	**Investor Contact:** 216-252-7300
Fax: (216) 255-6777		

AMERICAN INTERNATIONAL GROUP INC

Exchange	Symbol	Price	52Wk Range	Yield	P/E	Div Acheiver
NYS	AIG	$55.41 (3/31/2005)	76.77-54.70	0.90	13.22	19 Years

*7 Year Price Score 86.43 ***NYSE Composite Index=100** ***12 Month Price Score 89.72**

TRADING VOLUME (thousand shares)

Interim Earnings (Per Share)

Qtr.	Mar	Jun	Sep	Dec
2001	0.65	0.69	0.12	0.70
2002	0.75	0.68	0.70	(0.03)
2003	0.74	0.87	0.89	1.03
2004	1.01	1.09	0.95	1.14

Interim Dividends (Per Share)

Amt	Decl	Ex	Rec	Pay
0.075Q	5/19/2004	9/1/2004	9/3/2004	9/17/2004
0.075Q	9/15/2004	12/1/2004	12/3/2004	12/17/2004
0.125Q	1/5/2005	3/2/2005	3/4/2005	3/18/2005
0.125Q	3/16/2005	6/1/2005	6/3/2005	6/17/2005
			Indicated Div: $0.50	

Valuation Analysis

Forecast P/E	11.92	No of Institutions
	(4/13/2005)	1164
Market Cap	$144.3 Billion	Shares
Book Value	78.9 Billion	1,590,554,624
Price/Book	1.83	% Held
Price/Sales	1.52	61.07

Business Summary: Insurance (MIC: 8.2 SIC: 331 NAIC: 24126)

American International Group is a financial services organization, with operations in more than 130 countries and jurisdictions. Co.'s subsidiaries serve commercial, institutional and individual customers. In the U.S., Co.'s subsidiaries underwrite commercial, industrial and life insurance. Co.'s global businesses also include financial services, retirement services and asset management. Co.'s financial services businesses include aircraft leasing, financial products, trading and market making. Co. is engaged in consumer finance through American General Finance, retirement services through AIG SunAmerica and AIG VALIC, and life insurance through AIG American General.

Recent Developments: For the year ended Dec 31 2004, net income advanced 19.1% to $11.05 billion compared with $9.27 billion in the previous year. Results for 2004 included a settlement charge of $53.0 million related to final settlement with the Securities and Exchange Commission with respect to issues arising from certain transactions with Brightpoint, Inc. and The PNC Financial Services Group. Total revenues increased 21.3% to $98.61 billion from $81.30 billion a year earlier. Notably, General Insurance Operations net premiums earned rose 24.3% to $39.46 billion, and Life Insurance & Retirement Services Operations premiums grew 20.9% to $28.40 billion.

Prospects: Co. is taking several steps in response to the regulatory issues that it faced in 2004. Co. is implementing the settlements of the Brightpoint and PNC transactions. In addition, Co. continues to cooperate with state attorneys general and insurance departments in connection with their investigations of certain practices of brokers and insurers. Meanwhile, Co.'s worldwide general insurance operations are performing well with strong cash flow and partnership income. Also, Co.'s U.S. Domestic Brokerage Group is doing well after accounting for the impact of the four hurricanes experienced in 2004.

Financial Data (US$ in Thousands)	9 Mos	6 Mos	3 Mos	12/31/2003	12/31/2002	12/31/2001	12/31/2000	12/31/1999
Earnings Per Share	4.07	4.01	3.79	3.53	2.10	2.02	2.41	2.15
Cash Flow Per Share	13.75	14.28	13.96	13.85	7.15	2.94	2.55	4.44
Tang Book Value Per Share	27.07	25.12	26.49	24.39	20.32	19.94	16.98	14.33
Dividends Per Share	0.270	0.260	0.242	0.224	0.178	0.158	0.141	0.126
Dividend Payout %	6.64	6.48	6.38	6.35	8.48	7.82	5.84	5.87
Income Statement								
Premium Income	50,150,000	32,460,000	16,139,000	54,613,000	44,589,000	38,608,000	31,017,000	27,486,000
Total Revenue	72,857,000	47,446,000	23,637,000	81,303,000	67,482,000	55,459,000	42,440,000	37,751,000
Benefits & Claims	42,709,000	27,275,000	13,734,000	46,886,000	41,927,000	27,222,000	18,565,000	16,738,000
Income Before Taxes	12,638,000	8,680,000	4,291,000	13,908,000	8,142,000	8,139,000	8,349,000	7,512,000
Income Taxes	4,037,000	2,757,000	1,356,000	4,264,000	2,328,000	2,339,000	2,458,000	2,219,000
Net Income	8,030,000	5,518,000	2,656,000	9,274,000	5,519,000	5,363,000	5,636,000	5,055,000
Average Shares	2,628,000	2,631,000	2,633,000	2,628,000	2,634,000	2,650,000	2,343,000	2,350,500
Balance Sheet								
Total Assets	776,420,000	735,982,000	724,154,000	678,346,000	561,229,000	492,982,000	306,577,000	268,238,000
Total Liabilities	697,324,000	662,213,000	647,182,000	606,901,000	499,973,000	438,630,000	265,611,000	234,037,000
Stockholders' Equity	78,903,000	73,577,000	76,779,000	71,253,000	59,103,000	52,150,000	39,619,000	33,306,000
Shares Outstanding	2,604,571	2,605,398	2,608,226	2,608,447	2,609,600	2,615,432	2,332,713	2,323,692
Statistical Record								
Return on Assets %	1.50	1.55	1.51	1.50	1.05	1.34	1.96	2.19
Return on Equity %	14.56	14.85	14.31	14.23	9.92	11.69	15.41	16.73
Loss Ratio %	85.16	84.03	85.10	85.85	94.03	70.51	59.85	60.90
Net Margin %	11.02	11.63	11.24	11.41	8.18	9.67	13.28	13.39
Price Range	76.77-56.59	76.77-55.18	75.12-49.45	66.28-44.47	79.61-51.10	96.88-67.05	103.69-54.29	74.46-51.53
P/E Ratio	18.86-13.90	19.14-13.76	19.82-13.05	18.78-12.60	37.91-24.33	47.96-33.19	43.02-22.53	34.63-23.97
Average Yield %	0.39	0.39	0.39	0.39	0.27	0.19	0.17	0.20

Address: 70 Pine Street, New York, NY 10270	**Web Site:** www.aig.com	**Auditors:** PricewaterhouseCoopers LLP
Telephone: (212) 770 7000	**Officers:** Maurice R. Greenberg - Chmn. Thomas R. Tizzio - Sr. Vice-Chmn., Gen. Insurance	**Investor Contact:** 212-770-6293
Fax: (212) 344 6828		**Transfer Agents:** EquiServe Trust Company, N.A. Providence, RI

AMERICAN STANDARD COS., INC.

Exchange	Symbol	Price	52Wk Range	Yield	P/E
NYS	ASD	$46.48 (3/31/2005)	48.03-34.19	1.29	32.73

*7 Year Price Score 152.09 *NYSE Composite Index=100 *12 Month Price Score 108.20

Interim Earnings (Per Share)

Qtr.	Mar	Jun	Sep	Dec
2001	0.30	0.54	0.41	...
2002	0.26	0.57	0.52	0.33
2003	0.29	0.61	0.55	0.38
2004	0.38	0.73	0.71	(0.39)

Interim Dividends (Per Share)

Amt	Decl	Ex	Rec	Pay
200%	2/5/2004	5/28/2004	5/18/2004	5/27/2004
0.15Q	2/1/2005	2/24/2005	2/28/2005	3/25/2005
		Indicated Div: $0.60		

Valuation Analysis

Forecast P/E	N/A	No of Institutions	
Market Cap	$10.0 Billion	Shares	
Book Value	930.3 Million	167,934,320	
Price/Book	10.74	% Held	
Price/Sales	1.05	78.29	

Business Summary: Purpose Machinery (MIC: 11.13 SIC: 585 NAIC: 33415)

American Standard is a global manufacturer of air conditioning systems and services for commercial and residential buildings; bathroom and kitchen fixtures and fittings in Europe, the U.S. and many countries in Latin America and Asia; and vehicle control systems for medium-sized and heavy trucks, trailers, buses, luxury cars and sports utility vehicles. Co.'s brand names include Trane® and American Standard® for air conditioning systems and services, American Standard®, Ideal Standard®, Standard®, Porcher®, Jado®, Armitage Shanks®, Dolomite®, Meloh®, Venlo®, Venesta®, Sottini® and Borma® for bath and kitchen products, and Wabco® for vehicle control systems.

Recent Developments: For the year ended Dec 31 2004, net income decreased 22.7% to $313,400 thousand from net income of $405,200 thousand a year earlier. Revenues were $9,508,800 thousand, up 11.0% from $8,567,600 thousand the year before. Total direct expense was $6,952,300 thousand versus $6,477,500 thousand in the prior year, an increase of 7.3%. Total indirect expense was $2,028,700 thousand versus $1,370,800 thousand in the prior year, an increase of 48.0%.

Prospects: Going forward, given its large backlog of orders for its commercial air conditioning equipment business and ongoing strength in the rest of its business, Co. appears well-positioned for continued earnings growth in 2005. For 2005, Co. expects sales growth of between 6.0% and 7.0%, with earnings of $2.60 to $2.75 per diluted share, excluding stock-option expenses. In addition, Co. expects to generate more than $890.0 million in net cash provided by operating activities and more than $550.0 million in free cash flow. For the first quarter, sales growth is expected to be between 6.0% and 8.0%, with earnings in the range of $0.44 and $0.47 per diluted share.

Financial Data

(US$ in Thousands)	12/31/2004	12/31/2003	12/31/2002	12/31/2001	12/31/2000	12/31/1999	12/31/1998	12/31/1997
Earnings Per Share	1.42	1.83	1.68	1.35	1.45	0.63	(0.07)	0.42
Cash Flow Per Share	3.55	3.00	2.87	2.31	2.17	2.24	1.92	1.79
Income Statement								
Total Revenue	9,508,800	8,567,600	7,795,400	7,465,300	7,598,370	7,189,500	6,653,881	6,007,509
EBITDA	730,600	911,400	896,500	875,100	917,931	836,729	536,961	587,066
Depn & Amortn	261,900	246,800	212,700	232,300	213,391	202,059	190,048	163,962
Income Before Taxes	362,900	549,200	556,200	476,300	509,433	451,533	165,376	236,788
Income Taxes	49,500	144,000	185,200	181,300	194,201	187,386	131,784	116,928
Net Income	313,400	405,200	371,000	295,000	315,232	138,300	(16,317)	96,223
Average Shares	220,584	221,150	220,924	219,353	216,593	217,999	221,016	228,501
Balance Sheet								
Current Assets	2,889,800	2,490,700	2,014,400	1,896,400	1,878,496	1,725,547	1,591,261	1,393,270
Total Assets	6,841,800	5,878,700	5,143,800	4,831,400	4,744,660	4,685,987	4,156,164	3,764,050
Current Liabilities	2,346,700	2,033,500	1,665,600	1,688,300	1,806,566	2,286,620	2,350,585	1,841,213
Long-Term Obligations	1,429,100	1,626,800	1,918,400	2,142,000	2,375,566	1,886,739	1,527,518	1,550,772
Total Liabilities	5,911,500	5,164,900	4,914,000	4,921,500	5,137,563	5,182,487	4,857,148	4,373,833
Stockholders' Equity	930,300	713,800	229,800	(90,100)	(392,903)	(496,500)	(700,984)	(609,783)
Shares Outstanding	214,947	217,914	217,841	216,215	208,597	212,227	209,775	215,889
Statistical Record								
Return on Assets %	4.91	7.35	7.44	6.16	6.67	3.13	N.M.	2.64
Return on Equity %	38.02	85.88	531.14	...	...	...	...	...
EBITDA Margin %	7.68	10.64	11.50	11.72	12.08	11.64	8.07	9.77
Net Margin %	3.30	4.73	4.76	3.95	4.15	1.92	N.M.	1.60
Asset Turnover	1.49	1.55	1.56	1.56	1.61	1.63	1.68	1.65
Current Ratio	1.23	1.22	1.21	1.12	1.04	0.75	0.68	0.76
Debt to Equity	1.54	2.28	8.35	...	...	...	...	...
Price Range	41.63-33.15	33.84-21.37	26.23-19.50	23.53-15.79	16.44-11.54	16.31-10.48	16.33-7.29	17.13-11.92
P/E Ratio	29.32-23.35	18.49-11.68	15.62-11.61	17.43-11.70	11.34-7.96	25.89-16.63	...	40.77-28.37

Address: One Centennial Avenue, P.O. Box 6820, Piscataway, NJ 08855-6820
Telephone: (732) 980-6000
Fax: (732) 980-6300

Web Site: www.americanstandard.com
Officers: Frederic M. Poses - Chmn., C.E.O. G. Peter D'Aloia - Sr. V.P., C.F.O.

Auditors: ERNST & YOUNG LLP
Transfer Agents: Bank of New York, New York, NY

AMERICAN STATES WATER CO.

Exchange	Symbol	Price	52Wk Range	Yield	P/E	Div Acheiver
NYS	AWR	$25.30 (3/31/2005)	27.55-21.37	3.56	21.44	51 Years

*7 Year Price Score 94.07   ***NYSE Composite Index=100**   ***12 Month Price Score 100.53**

Interim Earnings (Per Share)

Qtr.	Mar	Jun	Sep	Dec
2001	0.20	0.33	0.62	0.18
2002	0.25	0.36	0.50	0.23
2003	0.20	0.19	0.51	(0.12)
2004	0.08	0.44	0.52	0.14

Interim Dividends (Per Share)

Amt	Decl	Ex	Rec	Pay
0.221Q	4/30/2004	5/6/2004	5/10/2004	6/1/2004
0.221Q	7/27/2004	8/5/2004	8/9/2004	9/1/2004
0.225Q	11/2/2004	11/9/2004	11/12/2004	12/1/2004
0.225Q	1/31/2005	2/8/2005	2/10/2005	3/1/2005

Indicated Div: $0.90 (Div. Reinv. Plan)

Valuation Analysis

Forecast P/E	19.19	No of Institutions
	(4/7/2005)	108
Market Cap	$423.8 Million	Shares
Book Value	251.5 Million	5,654,559
Price/Book	1.69	% Held
Price/Sales	1.86	33.72

TRADING VOLUME (thousand shares)

Business Summary: Water Utilities (MIC: 7.2 SIC: 941 NAIC: 21310)

American States Water is a public utility that purchases, produces, distributes, and sells water, and distributes electricity through its primary subsidiary Southern California Water Company (SCW). SCW is organized into one electric customer service area and three water service regions operating within 75 communities in 10 counties in California and provides water service in 21 customer service areas. Through its American States Utility Services subsidiary, Co. performs non-regulated, water related services and operations on a contract basis. Co.'s subsidiary, Chaparral City Water Company, is an Arizona public utility company serving Fountain Hills, AZ and a portion of Scottsdale, AZ.

Recent Developments: For the year ended Dec 31 2004, Co. reported net income of $18,541 thousand compared with $11,892 thousand the year before. Results included income of $998 thousand for 2004 and a loss of $6,177 thousand in 2003 from the refund of water right lease revenues. Total operating revenues increased 7.2% to $228,005 thousand from $212,669 thousand a year earlier. Water revenues rose 7.2% to $200,635 thousand, while electric revenues increased to $25,594 thousand in 2003. Other operating revenues were $1,776 thousand compared with $1,014 thousand the year before. Operating income increased 7.4% to $36,090 thousand from $33,605 thousand in 2003.

Prospects: Operating results should benefit from recently approved rate increases. For instance, on Jan 13 2005, Co. announced that the California Public Utilities Commission approved rate increases for the Region II and Region III customer service areas of its Southern California Water Company (SCW) unit, effective Jan 2005. The rate increases in SCW's Region II will provide for additional annual revenues of approximately $2.8 million and SCW's Region III rate increases will provide for increased annual revenues of $2.5 million. The rate increases should provide Co. with much needed cash flow increases.

Financial Data
(US$ in Thousands)

	12/31/2004	12/31/2003	12/31/2002	12/31/2001	12/31/2000	12/31/1999	12/31/1998	12/31/1997
Earnings Per Share	1.18	0.78	1.34	1.33	1.27	1.19	1.08	1.04
Cash Flow Per Share	3.21	3.08	1.70	2.62	2.18	2.90	2.34	2.14
Tang Book Value Per Share	14.30	13.97	14.05	13.23	12.75	11.82	11.48	11.24
Dividends Per Share	0.888	0.884	0.871	0.867	0.857	0.853	0.840	0.830
Dividend Payout %	75.25	113.33	65.02	65.00	67.28	71.51	77.78	79.81
Income Statement								
Total Revenue	228,005	212,669	209,205	197,514	183,960	173,421	148,060	153,755
Depn & Amortn	20,824	19,792	18,302	17,951	15,339	14,364	12,929	11,387
Income Taxes	7,594	6,070	12,949	15,379	15,127	13,345	10,130	9,830
Net Income	18,541	11,892	20,339	20,447	18,086	16,101	14,623	14,059
Average Shares	15,663	15,227	15,157	15,256	14,116	13,437	13,437	13,435
Balance Sheet								
Net PPE	664,165	602,298	563,311	539,842	509,096	449,595	414,753	383,623
Total Assets	810,277	757,475	701,650	683,764	616,646	533,181	484,671	457,074
Long-Term Obligations	228,902	229,799	231,089	245,692	176,452	167,363	120,809	115,286
Total Liabilities	558,812	544,988	488,371	482,182	422,323	372,735	328,772	304,421
Stockholders' Equity	251,465	212,487	213,279	201,582	194,323	160,446	155,899	152,653
Shares Outstanding	16,752	15,212	15,180	15,119	15,113	13,436	13,437	13,437
Statistical Record								
Return on Assets %	2.36	1.63	2.94	3.14	3.14	3.16	3.11	3.08
Return on Equity %	7.97	5.59	9.81	10.33	10.17	10.18	9.48	6.44
Net Margin %	8.13	5.59	9.72	10.35	9.83	9.28	9.88	9.14
PPE Turnover	0.36	0.36	0.38	0.38	0.38	0.40	0.37	0.40
Asset Turnover	0.29	0.29	0.30	0.30	0.32	0.34	0.31	0.34
Debt to Equity	0.91	1.08	1.08	1.22	0.91	1.04	0.77	0.76
Price Range	26.78-21.37	28.71-21.80	28.85-21.01	25.32-19.35	24.75-17.00	26.50-14.88	19.42-14.50	16.92-13.67
P/E Ratio	22.69-18.11	36.81-27.95	21.53-15.68	19.04-14.55	19.49-13.39	22.27-12.50	17.98-13.43	16.27-13.14
Average Yield %	3.65	3.56	3.54	3.86	4.21	4.20	5.03	5.52

Address: 630 East Foothill Blvd., San Dimas, CA 91773-1212
Telephone: (909) 394-3600
Fax: (909) 394-0711

Web Site: www.aswater.com
Officers: Lloyd E. Ross - Chmn. Floyd E. Wicks - Pres., C.E.O.

Auditors: PricewaterhouseCoopersLLP
Investor Contact: 909-394-3633
Transfer Agents: ChaseMellon Shareholder Services, L.L.C., Ridgefield Park, NJ.

AMERICAN TOWER CORP.

Exchange	Symbol	Price	52Wk Range	Yield	P/E
NYS	AMT	$18.23 (3/31/2005)	19.00-11.35	N/A	N/A

*7 Year Price Score N/A *NYSE Composite Index=100 *12 Month Price Score 106.37

Interim Earnings (Per Share)

Qtr.	Mar	Jun	Sep	Dec
2001	(0.38)	(0.54)	(0.65)	(0.77)
2002	(0.37)	(0.52)	(1.81)	(0.26)
2003	(0.47)	(0.53)	(0.25)	(0.22)
2004	(0.19)	(0.27)	(0.25)	(0.39)

Interim Dividends (Per Share)

No Dividends Paid

Valuation Analysis

Forecast P/E	0.00	No of Institutions	
	(4/13/2005)	226	
Market Cap	$4.1 Billion	Shares	
Book Value	1.6 Billion	234,114,640	
Price/Book	2.55	% Held	
Price/Sales	5.38	N/A	

Business Summary: Communications (MIC: 10.1 SIC: 899 NAIC: 17212)

American Tower is a wireless and broadcast communications company with a portfolio of approximately 15,000 towers in the U.S., Mexico and Brazil, including more than 300 broadcast tower sites. Co.'s primary business is leasing antenna space on multi-tenant communications towers to wireless service providers and radio and television broadcast companies. Co. operates the largest independent portfolio of wireless communications and broadcast towers in North America, based on number of towers and revenue. Co. also offers select tower related services, such as antennae and line installation and site acquisition and zoning services.

Recent Developments: For the year ended Dec 31 2004, Co. reported a loss from continuing operations of $239.2 million compared with a loss of $264.8 million in the previous year. Results for 2004 and 2003 excluded losses from discontinued operations of $8.3 million and $60.5 million, respectively. Results for 2004 and 2003 included impairments, net loss on sales of long-lived assets and restructuring expense of $23.9 million and $31.7 million, respectively. Total revenues increased 11.7% to $706.7 million from $632.5 million a year earlier. Rental and management revenue rose 10.4% to $684.7 million, while network development services grew 73.8% to $22.2 million. Comparisons were made with restated 2003 results.

Prospects: On Mar 8 2005, Co. announced its preliminary outlook for 2005. For full-year 2005, Co. is projecting total revenue of between $740.0 million and $759.0 million, and total segment operating profit of $507.0 million to $517.0 million. Additionally, Co. is projecting a loss from continuing operations for 2005 of between $82.0 million and $66.0 million, and a basic and diluted loss per common share from continuing operations of $0.36 to $0.29. Co. noted that the loss from continuing operations includes a $15.0 million loss from retirement of long-term obligations as a result of its debt repurchases through Mar 8 2005.

Financial Data

(US$ in Thousands)	9 Mos	6 Mos	3 Mos	12/31/2003	12/31/2002	12/31/2001	12/31/2000	12/31/1999
Earnings Per Share	(0.93)	(0.93)	(1.18)	(1.46)	(5.84)	(2.35)	(1.15)	(0.34)
Cash Flow Per Share	1.00	0.94	0.82	0.75	0.54	0.14	(0.15)	0.65
Tang Book Value Per Share	N.M.	0.06	0.16	0.28	N.M.	1.85	2.06	4.76
Income Statement								
Total Revenue	578,339	379,151	186,179	715,144	788,420	1,134,191	735,275	258,081
EBITDA	209,985	156,667	88,608	340,830	193,832	133,907	180,213	95,447
Depn & Amortn	237,754	159,059	77,134	389,060	335,042	459,616	299,017	136,647
Income Before Taxes	(216,461)	(130,181)	(53,044)	(308,628)	(379,403)	(566,881)	(249,946)	(49,141)
Income Taxes	(56,720)	(27,644)	(10,450)	(66,137)	(64,634)	(116,787)	(59,656)	214
Net Income	(159,319)	(103,415)	(42,880)	(303,417)	(1,141,879)	(450,094)	(194,628)	(50,727)
Average Shares	224,839	223,578	220,408	208,098	195,454	191,586	168,715	149,749
Balance Sheet								
Current Assets	245,129	313,670	334,374	411,515	536,253	522,207	471,152	139,407
Total Assets	5,068,434	5,166,270	5,197,910	5,332,488	5,662,203	6,829,723	5,660,679	3,018,866
Current Liabilities	175,871	197,864	254,392	294,778	670,294	342,714	297,786	124,987
Long-Term Obligations	3,211,635	3,260,322	3,216,627	3,283,603	3,194,537	3,549,375	2,457,045	736,086
Total Liabilities	3,434,543	3,504,414	3,500,053	3,602,342	3,906,313	3,946,590	2,767,303	865,130
Stockholders' Equity	1,622,028	1,650,159	1,672,051	1,711,547	1,740,323	2,869,196	2,877,030	2,145,083
Shares Outstanding	226,596	224,142	221,094	219,904	195,683	195,287	180,398	155,670
Statistical Record								
EBITDA Margin %	36.31	41.32	47.59	47.66	24.58	11.81	24.51	36.98
Asset Turnover	0.14	0.14	0.14	0.13	0.13	0.18	0.17	0.11
Current Ratio	1.39	1.59	1.31	1.40	0.80	1.52	1.58	1.12
Debt to Equity	1.98	1.98	1.92	1.92	1.84	1.24	0.85	0.34
Price Range	15.62-9.94	15.38-8.85	12.95-5.51	12.00-3.53	10.22-0.71	41.00-5.98	54.81-29.00	31.94-17.25

Address: 116 Huntington Avenue, Boston, MA 02116	Web Site: www.americantower.com	Auditors: Deloitte & Touche LLP
Telephone: (617) 375-7500	Officers: James D. Taiclet Jr. - Chmn., Pres., C.E.O. J. Michael Gearon Jr. - Vice-Chmn., Pres., American Tower International	Investor Contact: 617-375-7500
Fax: (617) 375-7575		

AMERICREDIT CORP.

Exchange	Symbol	Price	52Wk Range	Yield	P/E
NYS	ACF	$23.44 (3/31/2005)	25.08-15.75	N/A	13.55

*7 Year Price Score 88.55   *NYSE Composite Index=100   *12 Month Price Score 108.24

Interim Earnings (Per Share)

Qtr.	Sep	Dec	Mar	Jun
2001-02	0.88	0.91	1.02	1.06
2002-03	0.81	(0.29)	0.09	(0.15)
2003-04	0.21	0.30	0.40	0.51
2004-05	0.43	0.39	...	...

Interim Dividends (Per Share)

Amt	Decl	Ex	Rec	Pay

Valuation Analysis

Forecast P/E	13.75	No of Institutions	
	(4/13/2005)	210	
Market Cap	$3.6 Billion	Shares	
Book Value	2.1 Billion	155,029,904	
Price/Book	1.67	% Held	
Price/Sales	N/A	N/A	

Business Summary: Credit & Lending (MIC: 8.6 SIC: 141 NAIC: 22291)

AmeriCredit is a consumer finance company specializing in purchasing retail automobile installment sales contracts originated by franchised and select independent dealers in connection with the sale of used and new automobiles. Co. targets consumers who are typically unable to obtain financing from traditional sources. Funding for Co.'s auto lending activities is obtained primarily through the sale of loans in securitization transactions. Co. services its automobile lending portfolio at regional centers using automated loan servicing and collection systems. Co. operated 89 auto lending branch offices in 31 states as of June 30 2004.

Recent Developments: For the second quarter ended Dec 31 2004, net income advanced 36.9% to $64.6 million compared with $47.2 million in the corresponding prior-year quarter. Results included a net charge of 105,000 in 2004 and a net credit of 271,000 in 2003 from restructuring activity. Total revenue increased 22.5% to $344.8 million from $281.5 million a year earlier. Finance charge income climbed 29.6% to $291.7 million, while servicing income fell 15.8% to $40.4 million. Other income rose 49.5% to $12.7 million. Provision for loan losses grew 63.3% to $100.2 million from $61.4 million the year before.

Prospects: Co. is pleased with its operating performance, which is being driven by increased loan volume. Co. stated that it should be well positioned to meet its earnings target for the fiscal year ending on June 30 2005. Co. narrowed its fiscal year 2005 guidance to net income of $240.0 million to $250.0 million and earnings per share of $1.42 to $1.48. The previously outlook was set at net income of $230.0 million to $250.0 million and earnings per share of $1.36 to $1.48. Co.'s new guidance is based on new loan volume of $4.50 billion to $5.00 billion, operating expenses of 2.5% to 3.0% of the managed portfolio, and managed portfolio-level credit losses of 5.5% and 6.5%.

Financial Data (US$ in Thousands)	6 Mos	3 Mos	06/30/2004	06/30/2003	06/30/2002	06/30/2001	06/30/2000	06/30/1999
Earnings Per Share	1.73	1.64	1.42	0.15	3.87	2.60	1.48	1.11
Cash Flow Per Share	5.60	5.51	5.16	16.75	(4.42)	3.42	0.97	0.69
Tang Book Value Per Share	14.07	13.80	13.48	12.02	16.69	12.71	8.85	6.23
Income Statement								
Interest Expense	119,492	57,516	251,963	202,225	135,928	116,024	69,310	38,792
Provision for Losses	198,913	98,716	257,070	307,570	65,161	31,387	16,359	9,629
Non-Interest Income	684,723	339,956	1,215,836	981,281	1,190,232	818,224	509,680	335,456
Non-Interest Expense	353,526	173,223	341,687	437,000	424,131	308,453	233,719	165,345
Income Before Taxes	211,705	109,217	365,116	34,486	565,012	362,360	190,292	121,690
Income Taxes	78,331	40,410	138,133	13,277	217,529	139,508	75,791	46,850
Net Income	133,374	68,807	226,983	21,209	347,483	222,852	114,501	74,840
Average Shares	168,617	159,601	159,630	137,807	89,800	85,852	77,613	67,191
Balance Sheet								
Total Assets	9,409,843	9,510,357	8,824,579	8,108,029	4,224,931	3,384,907	1,862,269	1,063,487
Total Liabilities	7,261,553	7,362,713	6,699,467	6,227,400	2,792,615	2,324,711	1,173,690	663,757
Stockholders' Equity	2,148,290	2,147,644	2,125,112	1,880,629	1,432,316	1,060,196	688,579	399,730
Shares Outstanding	152,667	155,662	157,612	156,450	85,817	83,414	77,772	64,141
Statistical Record								
Return on Assets %	3.19	2.99	2.67	0.34	9.13	8.49	7.81	8.26
Return on Equity %	13.60	12.86	11.30	1.28	27.88	25.49	20.98	21.20
Price Range	24.60-15.75	21.84-10.30	20.25-6.60	26.08-1.64	63.63-14.98	54.88-17.02	21.50-11.06	18.53-7.06
P/E Ratio	14.22-9.10	13.32-6.28	14.26-4.65	173.87-10.93	16.44-3.87	21.11-6.54	14.53-7.47	16.69-6.36

Address: 801 Cherry Street, Suite 3900, Fort Worth, TX 76102 **Telephone:** (817) 302 7000 **Fax:** (817) 336 9519	**Web Site:** www.americredit.com **Officers:** Clifton H. Morris Jr. - Chmn., C.E.O. Daniel E. Berce - Pres.	**Auditors:** PricewaterhouseCoopers LLP **Investor Contact:** 817-302-7009 **Transfer Agents:** ChaseMellon Shareholder Services, Ridgefield Park,

AMERISOURCEBERGEN CORP.

Exchange	Symbol	Price	52Wk Range	Yield	P/E
NYS	ABC	$57.29 (3/31/2005)	63.68-49.91	0.17	15.40

*7 Year Price Score 102.31 *NYSE Composite Index=100 *12 Month Price Score 96.97

Interim Earnings (Per Share)

Qtr.	Dec	Mar	Jun	Sep
2001-02	0.63	0.84	0.82	0.86
2002-03	0.84	1.03	0.99	1.04
2003-04	0.94	1.23	1.09	0.81
2004-05	0.60	...	...	...

Interim Dividends (Per Share)

Amt	Decl	Ex	Rec	Pay
0.025Q	5/7/2004	5/14/2004	5/18/2004	6/7/2004
0.025Q	8/11/2004	8/19/2004	8/23/2004	9/7/2004
0.025Q	11/11/2004	11/18/2004	11/22/2004	12/7/2004
0.025Q	2/7/2005	2/16/2005	2/18/2005	3/7/2005
			Indicated Div: $0.10	

Valuation Analysis

Forecast P/E	18.42	No of Institutions
	(4/7/2005)	306
Market Cap	$6.1 Billion	Shares
Book Value	4.2 Billion	102,606,440
Price/Book	1.44	% Held
Price/Sales	0.11	92.35

TRADING VOLUME (thousand shares)

Business Summary: Pharmaceuticals (MIC: 9.1 SIC: 122 NAIC: 24210)

AmerisourceBergen is engaged in wholesale distribution of pharmaceutical products and furnishes related services to healthcare providers and pharmaceutical manufacturers. Co. distributes a line of brand name and generic pharmaceuticals, over-the-counter healthcare products, and home healthcare supplies and equipment to healthcare providers located throughout the United States, including acute care hospitals and health systems, independent and chain retail pharmacies, mail order facilities, physicians, clinics and other alternate site facilities, and skilled nursing and assisted living centers. Co. operates in two segments: Pharmaceutical Distribution and PharMerica.

Recent Developments: For the quarter ended Dec 31 2004, net income decreased 40.6% to $64,449 thousand from net income of $108,474 thousand in the year-earlier quarter. Revenues were $13,639,042 thousand, up 2.2% from $13,342,171 thousand the year before. Operating income was $137,061 thousand versus an income of $211,398 thousand in the prior-year quarter, a decrease of 35.2%. Total direct expense was $13,178,143 thousand versus $12,817,121 thousand in the prior-year quarter, an increase of 2.8%. Total indirect expense was $323,838 thousand versus $313,652 thousand in the prior-year quarter, an increase of 3.2%.

Prospects: Co. anticipates operating revenue to be essentially flat for the remainder of fiscal 2005, with diluted earnings per share from continuing operations of between $4.00 and $4.10 for fiscal 2005. Co.'s guidance is based on low double-digit growth for the U.S. pharmaceutical market. Meanwhile, Co. remains optimistic about its long-term prospects and sees excellent opportunities as it expands its specialty business, completes its new distribution network, gains new generic opportunities and looks to fully participate in the growth generated by the Medicare Modernization Act in 2006.

Financial Data

(US$ in Thousands)	3 Mos	09/30/2004	09/30/2003	09/30/2002	09/30/2001	09/30/2000	09/30/1999	09/30/1998
Earnings Per Share	3.72	4.06	3.89	3.16	2.10	1.90	1.31	1.04
Cash Flow Per Share	13.23	7.37	3.24	5.11	(0.70)	4.19	0.06	2.63
Tang Book Value Per Share	16.62	17.24	14.42	10.43	6.89	4.81	2.88	1.55
Dividends Per Share	0.100	0.100	0.100	0.100	...	...	...	...
Dividend Payout %	2.69	2.46	2.57	3.16	...	...	...	...
Income Statement								
Total Revenue	13,639,042	53,178,954	49,657,328	45,234,794	16,191,353	11,645,021	9,807,363	8,668,804
EBITDA	160,575	952,849	943,876	773,931	273,224	218,977		
Depn & Amortn	23,471	79,771	73,005	61,150	24,714	17,420	19,844	16,534
Income Before Taxes	115,028	760,373	726,127	572,047	202,833	159,700		
Income Taxes	44,171	291,983	284,898	227,106	77,731	60,686	48,397	32,301
Net Income	64,449	468,390	441,229	344,941	123,796	99,014	67,466	50,519
Average Shares	111,607	117,779	115,954	112,228	62,807	52,020	51,683	48,550
Balance Sheet								
Current Assets	7,947,422	8,295,389	8,858,518	8,349,637	7,512,502	2,320,619	1,920,006	1,418,322
Total Assets	11,310,270	11,654,003	12,040,125	11,213,012	10,291,245	2,458,567	2,060,599	1,552,282
Current Liabilities	5,915,725	6,103,908	6,256,102	6,099,517	5,532,453	1,751,469	1,327,283	1,015,176
Long-Term Obligations	1,123,966	1,157,111	1,722,724	1,756,494	1,597,295	413,217	558,705	453,761
Total Liabilities	7,097,846	7,314,958	8,034,808	7,896,674	7,178,065	2,176,273	1,894,322	1,476,973
Stockholders' Equity	4,212,424	4,339,045	4,005,317	3,316,338	2,838,564	282,294	166,277	75,309
Shares Outstanding	106,085	109,692	112,002	106,581	103,534	58,731	57,812	48,458
Statistical Record								
Return on Assets %	3.66	3.94	3.80	3.21	1.94	4.37	3.73	3.06
Return on Equity %	10.15	11.20	12.05	11.21	7.93	44.03	55.85	112.74
EBITDA Margin %	1.18	1.79	1.90	1.71	1.69	1.88	...	...
Net Margin %	0.47	0.88	0.89	0.76	0.76	0.85	0.69	0.58
Asset Turnover	4.61	4.48	4.27	4.21	2.54	5.14	5.43	5.26
Current Ratio	1.34	1.36	1.42	1.37	1.36	1.32	1.45	1.40
Debt to Equity	0.27	0.27	0.43	0.53	0.56	1.46	3.36	6.03
Price Range	63.68-49.91	65.89-49.91	74.93-46.76	82.26-55.10	70.95-40.69	47.00-11.75	40.53-23.06	38.38-22.72
P/E Ratio	17.12-13.42	16.23-12.29	19.26-12.02	26.03-17.44	33.79-19.38	24.74-6.18	30.94-17.60	36.90-21.84
Average Yield %	0.18	0.17	0.17	0.15	...	...	...	...

Address: 1300 Morris Drive, Suite 100, Chesterbrook, PA 19087-5594 **Telephone:** (610) 727-7000 **Fax:** (610) 647-0141	**Web Site:** www.amerisourcebergen.net **Officers:** James R. Mellor - Chmn. Kurt J. Hilzinger - Pres., C.O.O.	**Auditors:** Ernst & Young LLP **Investor Contact:** 610-727-7118

AMERUS GROUP CO.

Exchange	Symbol	Price	52Wk Range	Yield	P/E
NYS	AMH	$47.25 (3/31/2005)	49.08-36.73	0.85	10.10

*7 Year Price Score 117.25 *NYSE Composite Index=100 *12 Month Price Score 104.78

Interim Earnings (Per Share)

Qtr.	Mar	Jun	Sep	Dec
2001	0.38	0.57	0.51	0.46
2002	0.59	0.10	0.66	0.20
2003	0.91	1.11	1.03	1.02
2004	0.65	1.20	1.05	1.61

Interim Dividends (Per Share)

Amt	Decl	Ex	Rec	Pay
0.40A	11/9/2001	11/15/2001	11/19/2001	12/4/2001
0.40A	11/7/2002	11/14/2002	11/18/2002	12/3/2002
0.40A	11/7/2003	11/25/2003	11/28/2003	12/15/2003
0.40A	11/4/2004	11/23/2004	11/26/2004	12/15/2004

Indicated Div: $0.40

Valuation Analysis

Forecast P/E	10.59 (4/7/2005)	No of Institutions	202
Market Cap	$1.9 Billion	Shares	29,762,190
Book Value	1.6 Billion	% Held	75.46
Price/Book	1.15		
Price/Sales	1.15		

TRADING VOLUME (thousand shares)

Business Summary: Insurance (MIC: 8.2 SIC: 311 NAIC: 24113)

AmerUs Group is a holding company whose subsidiaries are primarily engaged in the business of marketing, underwriting and distributing a broad range of individual life insurance and annuity products to individuals and businesses in all 50 states, the District of Columbia and the U.S. Virgin Islands. Co. has two reportable operating segments. The primary offerings of the protection products segment are interest-sensitive whole life, term life, universal life and equity-indexed life insurance policies. The primary offerings of the accumulation products segment are individual fixed annuities (consisting of traditional fixed annuities and equity-indexed annuities) and funding agreements.

Recent Developments: For the year ended Dec 31 2004, income from continuing operations increased 17.8% to $189,253 thousand from income of $160,628 thousand a year earlier. Net income increased 19.5% to $192,642 thousand from net income of $161,147 thousand a year earlier. Revenues were $1,615,116 thousand, down 3.9% from $1,680,045 thousand the year before. Net premiums earned were $267,666 thousand versus $297,188 thousand in the prior year, a decrease of 9.9%. Net investment income rose 3.5% to $2,074,894 thousand from $2,003,828 thousand a year ago.

Prospects: Going forward, Co. expects its protection products segment to benefit from a shift its sales to higher return products, in particular the equity indexed life products. Co. also expects to continue to realize operating efficiencies from administrative improvements. With respect to its accumulation products segment, Co. anticipates increased product sales from independent marketing organizations but decreased product sales from other distribution channels. Co. also expects to continue the shift of our product mix to higher return products, in particular the equity indexed annuity products. For 2005, Co. expects operating income to be in a range of $4.45 to $4.57 per share, excluding charges.

Financial Data
(US$ in Thousands)

	12/31/2004	12/31/2003	12/31/2002	12/31/2001	12/31/2000	12/31/1999	12/31/1998	12/31/1997
Earnings Per Share	4.68	4.07	1.56	1.95	2.46	2.20	1.86	2.46
Cash Flow Per Share	23.59	10.08	23.02	2.63	21.01	20.92	14.33	9.53
Tang Book Value Per Share	25.95	19.55	15.12	11.00	8.46	9.85	16.13	12.72
Dividends Per Share	0.400	0.400	0.400	0.400	0.500	0.400	0.400	0.300
Dividend Payout %	8.55	9.83	25.64	20.51	20.33	18.18	21.51	12.20
Income Statement								
Premium Income	267,666	297,188	350,812	313,650	88,857	89,521	81,197	48,127
Total Revenue	1,615,116	1,680,045	1,428,396	1,287,454	813,389	734,146	690,616	360,835
Income Before Taxes	228,294	239,238	92,630	118,845	115,316	97,211	88,597	78,381
Income Taxes	39,041	78,610	29,764	39,522	42,516	32,115	28,422	22,022
Net Income	192,642	161,147	62,866	72,907	51,840	66,654	62,829	58,059
Average Shares	41,135	39,618	40,398	37,453	21,035	30,306	33,696	23,572
Balance Sheet								
Total Assets	23,170,869	21,542,242	20,293,665	18,299,152	11,471,522	10,719,353	10,428,810	10,254,008
Total Liabilities	21,547,400	20,132,431	19,030,717	16,991,581	10,439,852	9,771,562	9,361,883	9,240,017
Stockholders' Equity	1,623,469	1,409,811	1,262,948	1,238,517	833,979	733,000	850,198	927,991
Shares Outstanding	39,400	39,194	39,011	41,759	30,011	30,070	25,426	34,735
Statistical Record								
Return on Assets %	0.86	0.77	0.33	0.49	0.47	0.63	0.61	0.79
Return on Equity %	12.67	12.06	5.03	7.04	6.60	8.42	7.07	8.38
Net Margin %	11.93	9.59	4.40	5.66	6.37	9.08	9.10	16.09
Price Range	45.68-34.73	38.00-22.94	39.90-25.87	36.50-27.00	32.38-16.56	28.75-16.81	36.88-14.75	36.88-19.13
P/E Ratio	9.76-7.42	9.34-5.64	25.58-16.58	18.72-13.85	13.16-6.73	13.07-7.64	19.83-7.93	14.99-7.77
Average Yield %	1.00	1.32	1.18	1.24	2.18	1.71	1.38	1.09

Address: 699 Walnut Street, Des Moines, IA 50309-3948
Telephone: (515) 362-3600
Fax: (515) 362-3652

Web Site: www.amerus.com
Officers: Roger K. Brooks - Chmn., C.E.O. Thomas C. Godlasky - Pres., C.O.O.

Auditors: Ernst & Young LLP

AMETEK, INC. (NEW)

Exchange	Symbol	Price	52Wk Range	Yield	P/E
NYS	AME	$40.25 (3/31/2005)	41.14-25.64	0.60	24.69

*7 Year Price Score 161.84 *NYSE Composite Index=100 *12 Month Price Score 113.10

Interim Earnings (Per Share)

Qtr.	Mar	Jun	Sep	Dec
2001	0.28	0.28	0.27	0.17
2002	0.29	0.32	0.32	0.32
2003	0.29	0.33	0.33	0.36
2004	0.36	0.40	0.42	0.45

Interim Dividends (Per Share)

Amt	Decl	Ex	Rec	Pay
0.06Q	5/20/2004	6/14/2004	6/16/2004	6/30/2004
0.06Q	7/23/2004	9/14/2004	9/16/2004	9/30/2004
0.06Q	11/17/2004	12/6/2004	12/8/2004	12/22/2004
0.06Q	1/28/2005	3/15/2005	3/17/2005	3/31/2005

Indicated Div: $0.24

Valuation Analysis

Forecast P/E	N/A	No of Institutions
Market Cap	$2.8 Billion	Shares
Book Value	659.6 Million	53,447,564
Price/Book	4.19	% Held
Price/Sales	2.24	77.40

Business Summary: Electrical (MIC: 11.14 SIC: 621 NAIC: 34513)

Ametek manufactures electronic instruments and electric motors through its operations in North America, Europe, Asia, and South America. Co.'s Electronic Instruments Group builds monitoring, testing, and calibration instruments, and display devices for the process, power, aerospace, and industrial industries. Co.'s Electromechanical Group is a major producer of air-moving electric motors for vacuum cleaners and other floor-care products. This group also produces brushless air-moving motors for aerospace, mass-transit, medical and office product markets, produces specialty metals and offers switches for motive and stationary power systems.

Recent Developments: For the year ended Dec 31 2004, net income increased 28.4% to $112,711 thousand from net income of $87,815 thousand a year earlier. Revenues were $1,232,318 thousand, up 12.9% from $1,091,622 thousand the year before. Operating income was $196,234 thousand versus an income of $156,761 thousand in the prior year, an increase of 25.2%. Total direct expense was $863,827 thousand versus $785,441 thousand in the prior year, an increase of 10.0%. Total indirect expense was $172,257 thousand versus $149,420 thousand in the prior year, an increase of 15.3%.

Prospects: For 2005, Co. expects revenues to be up approximately 10.0% over the prior year, led by solid internal growth in each of its two groups and the full-year benefit of its Taylor Hobson and Hughes-Treitler acquisitions. Earnings are estimated to be approximately $1.85 to $1.95 per diluted share, an increase of 13.0% to 20.0% over 2004, driven by anticipated top-line growth and Co.'s continued focus on operational improvement, including the movement of additional manufacturing to low cost locales. Co.'s first quarter 2005 sales are expected to be up in the low double-digits from the year before, and Co. estimates earnings to be approximately $0.43 to $0.45 per diluted share.

Financial Data
(US$ in Thousands)

	12/31/2004	12/31/2003	12/31/2002	12/31/2001	12/31/2000	12/31/1999	12/31/1998	12/31/1997
Earnings Per Share	1.63	1.30	1.25	0.99	1.05	0.93	0.62	0.75
Cash Flow Per Share	2.37	2.34	1.57	0.85	1.24	2.02	1.20	1.08
Tang Book Value Per Share	N.M.	N.M.	0.38	N.M.	N.M.	N.M.	0.28	1.47
Dividends Per Share	0.240	0.120	0.120	0.120	0.120	0.120	0.120	0.060
Dividend Payout %	14.72	9.23	9.64	12.12	11.37	12.97	19.35	8.05
Income Statement								
Total Revenue	1,232,318	1,091,622	1,040,542	1,019,289	1,024,660	924,797	927,474	847,761
EBITDA	234,031	191,577	181,029	158,725	178,598	158,861	139,386	129,241
Depn & Amortn	39,909	35,473	32,950	46,450	43,257	39,624	38,369	32,866
Income Before Taxes	165,779	130,087	122,898	84,362	106,138	94,461	77,358	78,194
Income Taxes	53,068	42,272	39,200	18,251	37,606	33,693	26,909	27,930
Net Income	112,711	87,815	83,698	66,111	68,532	60,768	41,739	50,413
Average Shares	69,254	67,620	67,254	66,890	65,068	65,850	67,482	67,758
Balance Sheet								
Current Assets	461,940	382,066	350,569	379,347	303,100	256,101	267,840	248,469
Total Assets	1,420,352	1,214,847	1,030,006	1,029,289	858,988	768,150	699,825	555,203
Current Liabilities	272,838	289,231	261,420	336,150	297,655	262,736	233,918	178,729
Long-Term Obligations	400,177	317,674	279,636	303,434	233,616	231,756	226,965	152,293
Total Liabilities	760,770	685,717	609,825	694,231	578,150	551,934	525,776	396,156
Stockholders' Equity	659,582	529,130	420,181	335,058	280,838	216,216	174,049	159,047
Shares Outstanding	68,684	66,982	66,134	65,632	64,890	63,925	64,182	66,000
Statistical Record								
Return on Assets %	8.53	7.82	8.13	7.00	8.40	8.28	6.65	9.22
Return on Equity %	18.91	18.50	22.16	21.47	27.50	31.14	25.06	34.94
EBITDA Margin %	18.99	17.55	17.40	15.57	17.43	17.18	15.03	15.24
Net Margin %	9.15	8.04	8.04	6.49	6.69	6.57	4.50	5.95
Asset Turnover	0.93	0.97	1.01	1.08	1.26	1.26	1.48	1.55
Current Ratio	1.69	1.32	1.34	1.13	1.02	0.97	1.15	1.39
Debt to Equity	0.61	0.60	0.67	0.91	0.83	1.07	1.30	0.96
Price Range	35.86-23.06	24.41-14.85	20.32-13.18	17.00-11.10	13.47-8.00	12.63-8.38	15.50-8.22	13.72-10.94
P/E Ratio	22.00-14.15	18.78-11.42	16.26-10.54	17.17-11.21	12.83-7.62	13.58-9.01	25.00-13.26	18.29-14.58
Average Yield %	0.83	0.60	0.70	0.84	1.17	1.16	0.96	0.50

Address: 37 North Valley Road, Building 4, Paoli, PA 19301	**Web Site:** www.ametek.com	**Auditors:** ERNST & YOUNG LLP
Telephone: (610) 647-2121	**Officers:** Frank S. Hermance - Chmn., C.E.O. John J. Molinelli - Exec. V.P., C.F.O.	**Investor Contact:** 610-647-2121
Fax: (610) 647-0211		

AMR CORP. (DE)

Exchange	Symbol	Price	52Wk Range	Yield	P/E
NYS	AMR	$10.70 (3/31/2005)	13.93-6.49	N/A	N/A

*7 Year Price Score 39.72   *NYSE Composite Index=100   *12 Month Price Score 89.04

Interim Earnings (Per Share)

Qtr.	Mar	Jun	Sep	Dec
2001	(0.28)	(3.29)	(2.68)	(5.17)
2002	(3.71)	(3.19)	(5.93)	(9.74)
2003	(6.68)	(0.47)	0.00	(0.68)
2004	(1.03)	0.03	(1.33)	(2.41)

Interim Dividends (Per Share)

No Dividends Paid

Valuation Analysis

Forecast P/E	0.00	No of Institutions	
	(4/7/2005)	177	
Market Cap	$1.7 Billion	Shares	
Book Value	N/A	167,504,432	
Price/Book	N/A	% Held	
Price/Sales	0.09	N/A	

Business Summary: Aviation (MIC: 1.1 SIC: 512 NAIC: 81111)

AMR is the parent company of American Airlines, Inc., which provides scheduled jet service to approximately 150 destinations throughout North America, the Caribbean, Latin America, Europe and the Pacific as of Dec 31 2003. Co. also provides regional jet service to smaller markets in the U.S., Canada and the Caribbean on American Eagle through its wholly-owned subsidiary, AMR Eagle Holding Corporation. In addition, Co. provides freight and mail services to shippers throughout its system. AMR Investment Services, Inc., a wholly-owned subsidiary, provides investment management activities.

Recent Developments: For the year ended Dec 31 2004, net loss was $761,000 thousand versus net loss of $1,228,000 thousand a year earlier. Revenues were $18,645,000 thousand, up 6.9% from $17,440,000 thousand the year before. Operating loss was $144,000 thousand versus a loss of $844,000 thousand in the prior year. Total direct expense was $9,660,000 thousand versus $8,531,000 thousand in the prior year, an increase of 13.2%. Total indirect expense was $9,129,000 thousand versus $9,753,000 thousand in the prior year, a decrease of 6.4%.

Prospects: Co.'s near-term outlook remains unfavorable, due primarily to continued high fuel prices which translated into $1.10 billion in incremental fuel costs during 2004. In addition, results are being hampered by low fares, reflecting excess industry capacity and continued growth of low-cost carriers. Co. anticipates a loss during the first quarter of 2005. Furthermore, 2005 is expected to be a very difficult year despite Co.'s efforts to reduce its domestic capacity, add additional seats on its MD80, 737, 767 and 777 fleets, and add several new international routes. On Feb 22 2005, Co. announced that it will begin nonstop service from Chicago, IL to Shanghai, China on Apr 2 2006.

Financial Data
(US$ in Thousands)

	12/31/2004	12/31/2003	12/31/2002	12/31/2001	12/31/2000	12/31/1999	12/31/1998	12/31/1997
Earnings Per Share	(4.74)	(7.76)	(22.57)	(11.43)	5.03	6.26	7.52	5.39
Cash Flow Per Share	4.44	3.80	(7.12)	3.32	20.89	14.89	18.91	16.40
Tang Book Value Per Share	...	N.M.	N.M.	17.19	39.67	40.28	35.83	30.43
Income Statement								
Total Revenue	18,645,000	17,440,000	17,299,000	18,963,000	19,703,000	17,730,000	19,205,000	18,570,000
EBITDA	1,256,000	646,000	(1,966,000)	(1,068,000)	2,651,000	2,284,000	3,579,000	3,151,000
Depn & Amortn	1,292,000	1,377,000	1,366,000	1,404,000	1,202,000	1,092,000	1,287,000	1,244,000
Income Before Taxes	(761,000)	(1,308,000)	(3,860,000)	(2,756,000)	1,287,000	1,006,000	2,164,000	1,646,000
Income Taxes	...	(80,000)	(1,337,000)	(994,000)	508,000	350,000	858,000	661,000
Net Income	(761,000)	(1,228,000)	(3,511,000)	(1,762,000)	813,000	985,000	1,314,000	985,000
Average Shares	161,000	158,000	156,000	154,000	162,000	157,000	175,000	182,000
Balance Sheet								
Total Assets	28,773,000	29,330,000	30,267,000	32,841,000	26,213,000	24,374,000	22,303,000	20,915,000
Long-Term Obligations	13,524,000	13,126,000	12,310,000	9,834,000	5,474,000	5,689,000	4,200,000	3,889,000
Total Liabilities	29,354,000	29,284,000	29,310,000	27,468,000	19,037,000	17,516,000	15,605,000	14,699,000
Stockholders' Equity	(581,000)	46,000	957,000	5,373,000	7,176,000	6,858,000	6,698,000	6,216,000
Shares Outstanding	161,155	159,582	156,089	154,484	152,062	148,244	161,351	173,198
Statistical Record								
Return on Assets %	N.M.	N.M.	N.M.	N.M.	3.21	4.22	6.08	4.76
Return on Equity %	...	N.M.	N.M.	N.M.	11.55	14.53	20.35	16.58
EBITDA Margin %	6.74	3.70	N.M.	N.M.	13.45	12.88	18.64	16.97
Net Margin %	(4.08)	(7.04)	(20.30)	(9.29)	4.13	5.56	6.84	5.30
Asset Turnover	0.64	0.59	0.55	0.64	0.78	0.76	0.89	0.90
Price Range	17.38-6.49	14.90-1.41	29.05-3.15	43.75-16.49	39.19-21.09	31.46-22.36	37.79-19.95	27.90-16.67
P/E Ratio	...	...	...	...	7.79-4.19	5.03-3.57	5.02-2.65	5.18-3.09

Address: 4333 Amon Carter Blvd, Ft. Worth, TX 76155 Telephone: (817) 963-1234 Fax: (817) 967-9641	Web Site: www.amrcorp.com Officers: Gerard J. Arpey - Chmn., Pres., C.E.O. Daniel P. Garton - Exec. V.P., Mktg.	Auditors: Ernst & Young LLP Investor Contact: 817-967-2970

AMSOUTH BANCORPORATION

Exchange	Symbol	Price	52Wk Range	Yield	P/E	Div Acheiver
NYS	ASO	$25.95 (3/31/2005)	26.90-21.95	3.85	14.91	34 Years

*7 Year Price Score 97.82   *NYSE Composite Index=100   *12 Month Price Score 94.27

Interim Earnings (Per Share)

Qtr.	Mar	Jun	Sep	Dec
2001	0.34	0.36	0.37	0.39
2002	0.40	0.42	0.43	0.43
2003	0.44	0.44	0.45	0.45
2004	0.45	0.47	0.33	0.49

Interim Dividends (Per Share)

Amt	Decl	Ex	Rec	Pay
0.24Q	4/15/2004	6/15/2004	6/17/2004	7/1/2004
0.24Q	7/15/2004	9/15/2004	9/17/2004	10/1/2004
0.25Q	10/21/2004	12/16/2004	12/20/2004	1/3/2005
0.25Q	1/20/2005	3/16/2005	3/18/2005	4/1/2005

Indicated Div: $1.00 (Div. Reinv. Plan)

Valuation Analysis

Forecast P/E	12.91	No of Institutions
	(4/7/2005)	348
Market Cap	$9.2 Billion	Shares
Book Value	3.6 Billion	146,655,856
Price/Book	2.59	% Held
Price/Sales	2.89	41.53

TRADING VOLUME (thousand shares)

Business Summary: Commercial Banking (MIC: 8.1 SIC: 022 NAIC: 22110)

AmSouth Bancorporation is a regional bank holding company headquartered in Birmingham, AL. As of Dec 31 2003, Co. had assets of $45.60 billion and operated more than 650 branch banking offices and over 1,200 ATMs in the following southeastern states: Alabama, Florida, Tennessee, Mississippi, Georgia, and Louisiana. Co., through its affiliates, provides a full line of traditional and nontraditional financial services including consumer and commercial banking, small business banking, mortgage lending, equipment leasing, annuity and mutual fund sales, and trust and investment management services.

Recent Developments: For the year ended Dec 31 2004, net income decreased 0.4% to $623,498 thousand from net income of $626,121 thousand a year earlier. Net interest income was $1,476,025 thousand, up 4.3% from $1,414,635 thousand the year before. Provision for loan losses was $127,750 thousand versus $173,700 thousand in the prior year, a decrease of 26.5%. Non-interest income rose 20.6% to $1,032,142 thousand, while non-interest expense advanced 20.8% to $1,456,938 thousand.

Prospects: Co. delivered solid performance across all of its lines of business in 2004, and its expects that momentum to carry into 2005. Co. is well-positioned to continue growing loans and deposits as the economy improves. Going forward, Co. expects higher net interest income, supported by a relatively stable net interest margin, improved balance sheet growth with commercial loan growth and higher demand in consumer lending. In addition, Co. anticipates steady growth in non-interest revenues such as service charges, trust, and investment services income. Looking ahead to 2005, Co. expects earnings to range from $2.00 to $2.06 per share.

Financial Data

(US$ in Thousands)	12/31/2004	12/31/2003	12/31/2002	12/31/2001	12/31/2000	12/31/1999	12/31/1998	12/31/1997
Earnings Per Share	1.74	1.77	1.68	1.45	0.86	0.86	1.45	1.21
Cash Flow Per Share	2.72	3.06	3.92	2.40	2.23	0.88	1.13	0.97
Tang Book Value Per Share	10.02	9.18	8.82	8.14	7.53	7.56	8.05	7.64
Dividends Per Share	0.970	0.930	0.890	0.850	0.810	0.707	0.567	0.507
Dividend Payout %	55.75	52.54	52.98	58.62	94.19	82.17	39.17	41.76
Income Statement								
Interest Income	2,165,661	2,086,451	2,254,116	2,634,540	3,070,426	2,932,750	1,462,541	1,377,788
Interest Expense	689,636	671,816	781,476	1,239,656	1,691,323	1,424,804	763,571	701,511
Net Interest Income	1,476,025	1,414,635	1,472,640	1,394,884	1,379,103	1,507,946	698,970	676,277
Provision for Losses	127,750	173,700	213,550	187,100	227,600	165,626	58,134	67,399
Non-Interest Income	1,032,142	855,778	739,361	748,222	669,494	847,557	346,626	266,004
Non-Interest Expense	1,456,938	1,205,577	1,126,622	1,185,394	1,366,435	1,648,506	582,117	526,192
Income Before Taxes	923,479	891,136	871,829	770,612	454,562	541,371	405,345	348,690
Income Taxes	299,981	265,015	262,682	234,266	125,435	200,903	142,633	122,523
Net Income	623,498	626,121	609,147	536,346	329,127	340,468	262,712	226,167
Average Shares	357,952	354,308	362,329	370,948	384,677	396,515	181,921	186,178
Balance Sheet								
Net Loans & Leases	32,434,563	28,955,240	26,969,339	24,760,886	24,236,001	25,903,283	12,693,788	12,058,471
Total Assets	49,548,371	45,615,516	40,571,272	38,600,414	38,935,978	43,406,554	19,901,679	18,622,256
Total Deposits	34,232,779	30,440,353	27,315,624	26,167,017	26,623,304	27,912,443	13,283,804	12,945,197
Total Liabilities	45,979,530	42,385,847	37,455,275	35,645,315	36,122,571	40,447,349	18,474,050	17,237,011
Stockholders' Equity	3,568,841	3,229,669	3,115,997	2,955,099	2,813,407	2,959,205	1,427,629	1,385,245
Shares Outstanding	356,310	351,891	353,424	363,035	373,806	391,374	177,376	181,208
Statistical Record								
Return on Assets %	1.31	1.45	1.54	1.38	0.80	1.08	1.36	1.22
Return on Equity %	18.29	19.73	20.07	18.60	11.37	15.52	18.68	16.26
Net Interest Margin %	68.16	67.80	65.33	52.95	44.92	51.42	47.79	49.08
Efficiency Ratio %	45.56	40.97	37.64	35.04	36.54	43.61	32.18	32.01
Loans to Deposits	0.95	0.95	0.99	0.95	0.91	0.93	0.96	0.93
Price Range	26.90-21.95	24.58-19.09	22.88-18.28	20.15-15.13	19.88-11.88	33.92-18.94	30.42-21.42	25.11-14.07
P/E Ratio	15.46-12.61	13.89-10.79	13.62-10.88	13.90-10.43	23.11-13.81	39.44-22.02	20.98-14.77	20.75-11.63
Average Yield %	3.92	4.28	4.24	4.75	5.08	2.72	2.19	2.77

Address: AMSOUTH CENTER, 1900 Fifth Avenue North, Birmingham, AL 35203	Web Site: www.amsouth.com	Auditors: Ernst & Young LLP
Telephone: (205) 320 7151	Officers: C. Dowd Ritter - Chmn., Pres., C.E.O. Candice W. Bagby - Sr. Exec. V.P., Consumer Banking, Mktg.	Investor Contact: 205-801-0265
Fax: (205) 326 4072		Transfer Agents: The Bank of New York, New York, NY

ANADARKO PETROLEUM CORP

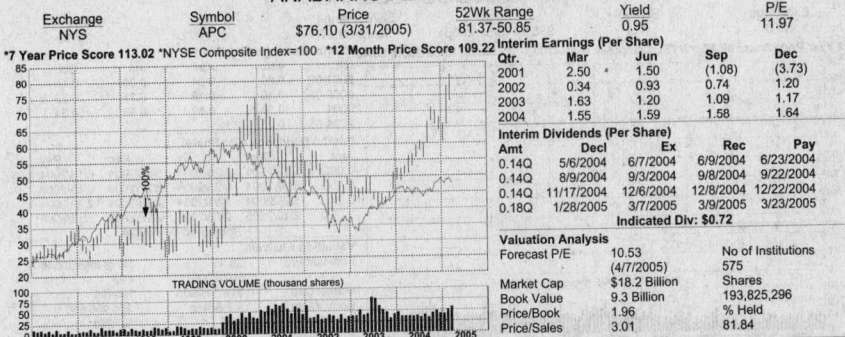

Exchange	Symbol	Price	52Wk Range	Yield	P/E
NYS	APC	$76.10 (3/31/2005)	81.37-50.85	0.95	11.97

*7 Year Price Score 113.02 *NYSE Composite Index=100 ***12 Month Price Score 109.22**

Interim Earnings (Per Share)

Qtr.	Mar	Jun	Sep	Dec
2001	2.50	1.50	(1.08)	(3.73)
2002	0.34	0.93	0.74	1.20
2003	1.63	1.20	1.09	1.17
2004	1.55	1.59	1.58	1.64

Interim Dividends (Per Share)

Amt	Decl	Ex	Rec	Pay
0.14Q	5/6/2004	6/7/2004	6/9/2004	6/23/2004
0.14Q	8/9/2004	9/3/2004	9/8/2004	9/22/2004
0.14Q	11/17/2004	12/6/2004	12/8/2004	12/22/2004
0.18Q	1/28/2005	3/7/2005	3/9/2005	3/23/2005
	Indicated Div: $0.72			

Valuation Analysis

Forecast P/E	10.53 (4/7/2005)	No of Institutions	575
Market Cap	$18.2 Billion	Shares	193,825,296
Book Value	9.3 Billion	% Held	81.84
Price/Book	1.96		
Price/Sales	3.01		

Business Summary: Oil and Gas (MIC: 14.2 SIC: 311 NAIC: 11111)

Anadarko Petroleum is engaged in the exploration, development, production and marketing of natural gas, crude oil, condensate and natural gas liquids (NGLs). Co.'s major areas of operations are located in the U.S., primarily in Texas, Louisiana, the mid-continent region and the western states, Alaska and in the shallow and deep waters of the Gulf of Mexico, as well as in Canada and Algeria. Co. owns and operates gas gathering systems in its core producing areas and engages in the hard minerals business through non-operated joint ventures and royalty arrangements. At Dec 31 2003, proved reserves were: natural gas, 7.72 trillion cubic feet; crude oil, condensate and NGLs, 1.23 billion barrels.

Recent Developments: For the year ended Dec 31 2004, income from continuing operations increased 29.0% to $1,606,000 thousand from income of $1,245,000 thousand a year earlier. Net income increased 24.4% to $1,601,000 thousand from net income of $1,287,000 thousand a year earlier. Revenues were $6,067,000 thousand, up 18.4% from $5,122,000 thousand the year before. Operating income was $2,881,000 thousand versus an income of $2,208,000 thousand in the prior year, an increase of 30.5%. Total direct expense was $932,000 thousand versus $828,000 thousand in the prior year, an increase of 12.6%. Total indirect expense was $2,254,000 thousand versus $2,086,000 thousand in the prior year, an increase of 8.1%.

Prospects: In 2004, Co. completed over $3.00 billion in asset sales and has refocused its efforts into areas where it has a competitive advantage: exploration and unconventional resource exploitation on a global basis. Co. added 335.0 million barrel of oil equivalents in proved reserves in 2004, more than replacing its annual production. Looking ahead to full-year 2005, Co. anticipates total sales of between 159.0 million barrels and 164.0 million barrels of oil equivalent. Capital investment for 2005 is expected to range from $2.70 billion to $3.00 billion. In 2005, Co. is accelerating its drilling of certain proven undeveloped locations to capitalize on the high commodity price environment.

Financial Data

(US$ in Thousands)	12/31/2004	12/31/2003	12/31/2002	12/31/2001	12/31/2000	12/31/1999	12/31/1998	12/31/1997
Earnings Per Share	6.36	5.09	3.21	(0.75)	4.16	0.25	(0.41)	0.89
Cash Flow Per Share	12.79	12.17	8.85	13.28	8.33	2.54	2.00	3.03
Tang Book Value Per Share	32.90	28.33	21.63	19.41	20.80	10.30	8.65	9.17
Dividends Per Share	0.560	0.440	0.325	0.225	0.200	0.200	0.188	0.150
Dividend Payout %	8.81	8.64	10.12	...	4.81	80.00	...	16.85
Income Statement								
Total Revenue	6,067,000	5,122,000	3,860,000	8,369,000	5,686,000	701,104	560,254	673,201
EBITDA	4,276,000	3,524,000	2,544,000	930,000	2,144,000	398,705	198,256	406,445
Depn & Amortn	1,447,000	1,297,000	1,134,000	1,228,000	625,000	219,764	205,644	201,127
Income Before Taxes	2,477,000	1,974,000	1,207,000	(390,000)	1,426,000	104,817	(65,087)	164,359
Income Taxes	871,000	729,000	376,000	(214,000)	602,000	62,238	(22,899)	57,041
Net Income	1,601,000	1,287,000	825,000	(188,000)	796,000	42,579	(42,188)	107,318
Average Shares	252,000	253,000	260,000	250,000	193,000	125,187	120,103	120,254
Balance Sheet								
Current Assets	2,502,000	1,324,000	1,280,000	1,201,000	1,894,000	355,942	229,928	218,994
Total Assets	20,192,000	20,546,000	18,248,000	16,771,000	16,590,000	4,098,363	3,632,990	2,992,465
Current Liabilities	1,993,000	1,715,000	1,861,000	1,801,000	1,676,000	387,171	288,726	252,330
Long-Term Obligations	3,671,000	5,058,000	5,171,000	4,638,000	3,984,000	1,443,322	1,425,392	955,733
Total Liabilities	10,907,000	11,947,000	11,276,000	10,406,000	9,804,000	2,563,809	2,373,534	1,875,685
Stockholders' Equity	9,285,000	8,599,000	6,972,000	6,365,000	6,786,000	1,534,554	1,259,456	1,116,780
Shares Outstanding	239,700	251,400	251,400	248,900	253,303	129,620	122,436	121,772
Statistical Record								
Return on Assets %	7.84	6.64	4.71	N.M.	7.67	1.10	N.M.	3.85
Return on Equity %	17.86	16.53	12.37	N.M.	19.08	3.05	N.M.	10.07
EBITDA Margin %	70.48	68.80	65.91	11.11	37.71	56.87	35.39	60.37
Net Margin %	26.39	25.13	21.37	N.M.	14.00	6.07	N.M.	15.94
Asset Turnover	0.30	0.26	0.22	0.50	0.55	0.18	0.17	0.24
Current Ratio	1.26	0.77	0.69	0.67	1.13	0.92	0.80	0.87
Debt to Equity	0.40	0.59	0.74	0.73	0.59	0.94	1.13	0.86
Price Range	71.05-48.65	51.29-40.49	58.29-38.00	72.99-44.05	74.85-28.44	40.50-26.56	43.19-25.69	38.13-25.44
P/E Ratio	11.17-7.65	10.08-7.95	18.16-11.84	...	17.99-6.84	162.00-106.25	...	42.84-28.58
Average Yield %	0.96	0.98	0.67	0.39	0.40	0.59	0.57	0.47

Address: 1201 Lake Robbins Drive, The Woodlands, TX 77380-1046 **Telephone:** (832) 636-1000 **Fax:** (281) 874-3385	**Web Site:** www.anadarko.com **Officers:** Robert J. Allison Jr. - Chmn. James T. Hackett - Pres., C.E.O.	**Auditors:** KPMG LLP **Investor Contact:** 832-636-3265

ANALOG DEVICES, INC.

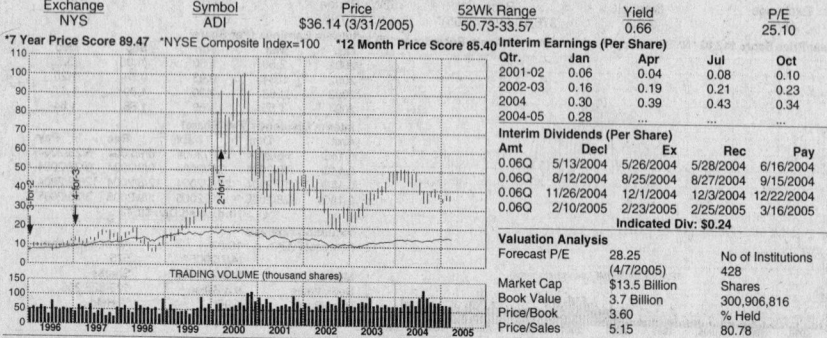

Exchange	Symbol	Price	52Wk Range	Yield	P/E
NYS	ADI	$36.14 (3/31/2005)	50.73-33.57	0.66	25.10

*7 Year Price Score 89.47 *NYSE Composite Index=100 *12 Month Price Score 85.40

Interim Earnings (Per Share)

Qtr.	Jan	Apr	Jul	Oct
2001-02	0.06	0.04	0.08	0.10
2002-03	0.16	0.19	0.21	0.23
2004	0.30	0.39	0.43	0.34
2004-05	0.28	...	...	...

Interim Dividends (Per Share)

Amt	Decl	Ex	Rec	Pay
0.06Q	5/13/2004	5/26/2004	5/28/2004	6/16/2004
0.06Q	8/12/2004	8/25/2004	8/27/2004	9/15/2004
0.06Q	11/26/2004	12/1/2004	12/3/2004	12/22/2004
0.06Q	2/10/2005	2/23/2005	2/25/2005	3/16/2005

Indicated Div: $0.24

Valuation Analysis

Forecast P/E	28.25	No of Institutions
	(4/7/2005)	428
Market Cap	$13.5 Billion	Shares
Book Value	3.7 Billion	300,906,816
Price/Book	3.60	% Held
Price/Sales	5.15	80.78

Business Summary: IT & Technology (MIC: 10.2 SIC: 674 NAIC: 34413)

Analog Devices designs, manufactures and markets analog, mixed-signal and digital signal processing integrated circuits used in signal processing for industrial, communication, computer and consumer applications. Signal processing products are used in high-speed communications, digital entertainment, and other consumer, computer and industrial applications. Co.'s products are used in a wide array of electronic equipment ranging from industrial process control, factory automation systems equipment, defense electronics, base stations, central office equipment, wireless telephones, computers, automobiles, computed tomography scanners, digital cameras and digital video disc players.

Recent Developments: For the quarter ended Jan 29 2005, net income decreased 8.0% to $107,443 thousand from net income of $116,839 thousand in the year-earlier quarter. Revenues were $580,536 thousand, down 4.1% from $605,353 thousand the year before. Operating income was $124,653 thousand versus an income of $145,597 thousand in the prior-year quarter, a decrease of 14.4%. Total direct expense was $245,008 thousand versus $259,888 thousand in the prior-year quarter, a decrease of 5.7%. Total indirect expense was $210,875 thousand versus $199,868 thousand in the prior-year quarter, an increase of 5.5%.

Prospects: With order patterns appearing to improve, Co. expects second quarter fiscal 2005 revenue to increase sequentially by 2.0% to 6.0%. At these current revenue levels, Co. expects gross margin to decline slightly during the second quarter because factory utilization will remain low as Co.'s plan is for inventory to be flat in dollars and down in days compared to the first quarter of fiscal 2005. Actual gross margins are dependent on the mix of business and utilization rates of Co.'s factories, but Co. expects gross margins to remain strong and above 57.0% during this cycle. Also, Co. expects diluted earnings per share to be approximately $0.29 to $0.31 for the second quarter of fiscal 2005.

Financial Data

(US$ in Thousands)	3 Mos	10/30/2004	11/01/2003	11/02/2002	11/03/2001	10/28/2000	10/30/1999	10/31/1998
Earnings Per Share	1.44	1.45	0.78	0.28	0.93	1.59	0.55	0.25
Cash Flow Per Share	1.88	2.08	1.19	0.62	2.31	2.00	1.27	0.70
Tang Book Value Per Share	9.57	9.66	8.42	7.50	7.20	5.90	4.53	3.47
Dividends Per Share	0.220	0.200	...	...	...	...	...	...
Dividend Payout %	15.24	13.79	...	...	...	...	...	...
Income Statement								
Total Revenue	580,536	2,633,800	2,047,268	1,707,508	2,276,915	2,577,547	1,450,379	1,230,571
EBITDA	163,098	849,543	541,154	357,917	647,561	964,793	381,483	272,410
Depn & Amortn	39,013	152,630	168,283	238,002	210,490	156,671	142,598	127,560
Income Before Taxes	138,636	732,736	381,836	140,350	507,244	865,711	257,540	150,459
Income Taxes	31,193	161,998	83,555	35,051	150,867	258,579	60,721	30,971
Net Income	107,443	570,738	298,281	105,299	356,377	607,132	196,819	82,408
Average Shares	388,107	392,854	382,227	381,245	381,962	381,157	362,904	355,750
Balance Sheet								
Current Assets	3,440,492	3,528,611	2,885,716	3,624,225	3,434,919	3,168,014	1,379,110	903,529
Total Assets	4,612,135	4,720,083	4,092,877	4,980,191	4,884,863	4,411,337	2,218,354	1,861,730
Current Liabilities	533,130	567,002	463,477	483,635	527,948	649,897	479,263	320,859
Long-Term Obligations	...	...	...	1,274,487	1,206,038	1,212,960	16,214	340,758
Total Liabilities	877,705	920,511	804,803	2,080,175	2,041,837	2,107,687	602,323	733,341
Stockholders' Equity	3,734,430	3,799,572	3,288,074	2,900,016	2,843,026	2,303,650	1,616,031	1,128,389
Shares Outstanding	372,512	375,840	370,234	363,187	363,250	357,923	349,774	320,620
Statistical Record								
Return on Assets %	12.62	12.99	6.59	2.14	7.54	18.37	9.67	4.56
Return on Equity %	15.69	16.15	9.67	3.68	13.62	31.06	14.38	7.46
EBITDA Margin %	28.09	32.26	26.43	20.96	28.44	37.43	26.30	22.14
Net Margin %	18.51	21.67	14.57	6.17	15.65	23.55	13.57	6.70
Asset Turnover	0.59	0.60	0.45	0.35	0.48	0.78	0.71	0.68
Current Ratio	6.45	6.22	6.23	7.49	6.51	4.87	2.88	2.82
Debt to Equity	...	...	...	0.44	0.42	0.53	0.01	0.30
Price Range	51.39-33.57	51.39-33.57	44.86-23.04	47.95-18.29	65.00-30.99	101.38-27.69	30.22-9.94	19.50-6.63
P/E Ratio	35.69-23.31	35.44-23.15	57.51-29.54	171.25-65.32	69.89-33.32	63.76-17.53	54.94-18.07	78.00-26.50
Average Yield %	0.52	0.45	...	...	...	...	...	...

Address: One Technology Way, P.O. Box 9106, Norwood, MA 02062-9106	**Web Site:** www.analog.com	**Auditors:** ERNST & YOUNG LLP
Telephone: (781) 329-4700	**Officers:** Ray Stata - Chmn. Jerald G. Fishman - Pres., C.E.O.	**Investor Contact:** 1-800-262-5643
Fax: (781) 326-8703		**Transfer Agents:** EquiServe Trust Company, N.A., Providence, RI

ANHEUSER-BUSCH COS., INC.

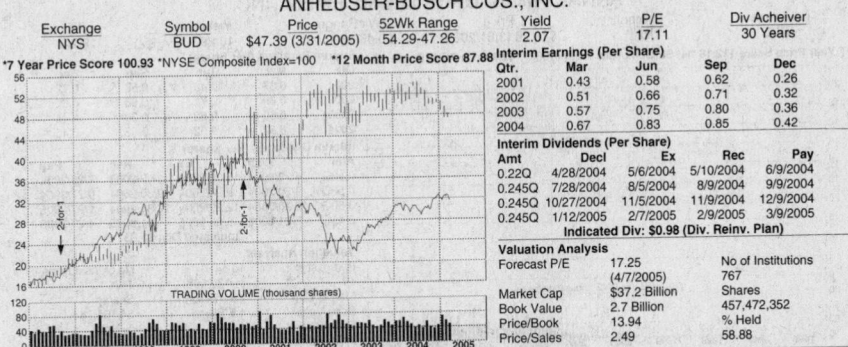

Exchange	Symbol	Price	52Wk Range	Yield	P/E	Div Achiever
NYS	BUD	$47.39 (3/31/2005)	54.29-47.26	2.07	17.11	30 Years

*7 Year Price Score 100.93 *NYSE Composite Index=100   *12 Month Price Score 87.88

Interim Earnings (Per Share)

Qtr.	Mar	Jun	Sep	Dec
2001	0.43	0.58	0.62	0.26
2002	0.51	0.66	0.71	0.32
2003	0.57	0.75	0.80	0.36
2004	0.67	0.83	0.85	0.42

Interim Dividends (Per Share)

Amt	Decl	Ex	Rec	Pay
0.22Q	4/28/2004	5/6/2004	5/10/2004	6/9/2004
0.245Q	7/28/2004	8/5/2004	8/9/2004	9/9/2004
0.245Q	10/27/2004	11/5/2004	11/9/2004	12/9/2004
0.245Q	1/12/2005	2/7/2005	2/9/2005	3/9/2005

Indicated Div: $0.98 (Div. Reinv. Plan)

Valuation Analysis

Forecast P/E	17.25	No of Institutions
	(4/7/2005)	767
Market Cap	$37.2 Billion	Shares
Book Value	2.7 Billion	457,472,352
Price/Book	13.94	% Held
Price/Sales	2.49	58.88

Business Summary: Food (MIC: 4.1 SIC: 082 NAIC: 12120)

Anheuser-Busch Companies is the parent holding company of Anheuser-Busch, Inc., the world's largest brewer of beer. Co.'s beer is sold under brand names including Budweiser, Michelob, Busch, and Natural Light. Worldwide sales of Co.'s beer brands aggregated 111.0 million barrels in 2003. Additionally, theme park operations are conducted through Co.'s subsidiary, Busch Entertainment Corporation, which owned nine theme parks as of Dec 31 2003. Co. also engages in packaging, malt and rice production, international beer, non-beer beverages, real estate development, marketing communications, and transportation services.

Recent Developments: For the year ended Dec 31 2004, net income increased 7.9% to $2,240,300 thousand from net income of $2,075,900 thousand a year earlier. Revenues were $14,934,200 thousand, up 5.6% from $14,146,700 thousand the year before. Operating income was $3,361,000 thousand versus an income of $3,199,300 thousand in the prior year, an increase of 5.1%. Total direct expense was $8,982,500 thousand versus $8,449,100 thousand in the prior year, an increase of 6.3%. Total indirect expense was $2,590,700 thousand versus $2,498,300 thousand in the prior year, an increase of 3.7%.

Prospects: Results are benefiting from significant increases in international volume, which increased 120.5% for the fourth quarter and 64.8% for full year 2004. However, U.S. volume was 22.9 million, a 1.5% drop versus the year-earlier quarter. Moreover, on a yearly basis, Co.'s domestic market share edged down to 49.6% from 49.7% a year earlier. Going froward, Co. anticipates a difficult year for beer segment profit growth, despite the implementation of the second phase of its 2005 pricing initiatives in February 2005. As a result, Co. expects earnings per share growth in the range of 6.0% to 9.0% for 2005, which is below its long-term target of double-digit growth.

Financial Data (US$ in Thousands)	12/31/2004	12/31/2003	12/31/2002	12/31/2001	12/31/2000	12/31/1999	12/31/1998	12/31/1997
Earnings Per Share	2.77	2.48	2.20	1.89	1.69	1.47	1.26	1.17
Cash Flow Per Share	3.67	3.60	3.19	2.65	2.48	2.22	2.26	1.84
Tang Book Value Per Share	1.88	2.74	3.19	4.15	4.11	3.79	3.96	3.62
Dividends Per Share	0.930	0.830	0.750	0.690	0.630	0.580	0.540	0.500
Dividend Payout %	33.57	33.47	34.09	36.51	37.28	39.46	42.69	42.74
Income Statement								
Total Revenue	14,934,200	14,146,700	13,566,400	12,911,500	12,261,800	11,703,700	11,245,800	11,066,200
EBITDA	4,332,400	4,076,900	3,820,600	3,545,300	3,297,200	3,069,900	2,850,700	2,727,400
Depn & Amortn	932,700	877,200	847,300	834,500	803,500	777,000	738,400	683,700
Income Before Taxes	2,999,400	2,824,300	2,623,600	2,377,600	2,179,900	2,007,600	1,852,600	1,832,500
Income Taxes	1,163,000	1,093,300	1,041,500	913,200	828,300	762,900	704,300	703,600
Net Income	2,240,300	2,075,900	1,933,800	1,704,500	1,551,600	1,402,200	1,233,300	1,169,200
Average Shares	808,500	837,000	878,900	901,600	919,700	953,600	975,000	999,400
Balance Sheet								
Current Assets	1,818,400	1,630,300	1,504,700	1,550,400	1,547,900	1,600,600	1,640,400	1,583,900
Total Assets	16,173,400	14,689,500	14,119,500	13,862,000	13,084,500	12,640,400	12,484,300	11,727,100
Current Liabilities	1,969,400	1,857,200	1,787,700	1,732,300	1,675,700	1,987,200	1,730,300	1,500,700
Long-Term Obligations	8,278,600	7,285,400	6,603,200	5,983,900	5,374,500	4,880,600	4,718,600	4,365,600
Total Liabilities	13,505,300	11,977,800	11,067,200	9,800,500	8,955,600	8,718,900	8,268,300	7,685,300
Stockholders' Equity	2,668,100	2,711,700	3,052,300	4,061,500	4,128,900	3,921,500	4,216,000	4,041,800
Shares Outstanding	785,000	813,100	846,600	879,100	903,600	922,200	953,200	974,040
Statistical Record								
Return on Assets %	14.48	14.41	13.82	12.65	12.03	11.16	10.19	10.54
Return on Equity %	83.06	72.03	54.37	41.62	38.44	34.46	29.87	28.97
EBITDA Margin %	29.01	28.82	28.16	27.46	26.89	26.23	25.35	24.65
Net Margin %	15.00	14.67	14.25	13.20	12.65	11.98	10.97	10.57
Asset Turnover	0.97	0.98	0.97	0.96	0.95	0.93	0.93	1.00
Current Ratio	0.92	0.88	0.84	0.89	0.92	0.81	0.95	1.06
Debt to Equity	3.10	2.69	2.16	1.47	1.30	1.24	1.12	1.08
Price Range	54.29-49.45	53.69-45.92	54.97-44.00	46.51-38.50	49.81-27.47	40.81-32.59	34.13-21.72	23.94-19.75
P/E Ratio	19.60-17.85	21.65-18.52	24.99-20.00	24.61-20.37	29.47-16.25	27.76-22.17	27.08-17.24	20.46-16.88
Average Yield %	1.80	1.65	1.49	1.62	1.62	1.59	2.11	2.32

Address: One Busch Place, St. Louis, MO 63118	**Web Site:** www.anheuser-busch.com	**Auditors:** PricewaterhouseCoopers LLP
Telephone: (314) 577-2000	**Officers:** August A. Busch III - Chmn. Patrick T. Stokes - Pres., C.E.O.	**Investor Contact:** 314-577-9629
Fax: (314) 577-2900		**Transfer Agents:** Mellon Investor Services, LLC, Ridgefield Park, NJ

ANNALY MORTGAGE MANAGEMENT INC.

Exchange	Symbol	Price	52Wk Range	Yield	P/E
NYS	NLY	$18.76 (3/31/2005)	20.46-16.11	10.29	9.24

*7 Year Price Score 112.18 *NYSE Composite Index=100 *12 Month Price Score 98.13

Interim Earnings (Per Share)

Qtr.	Mar	Jun	Sep	Dec
2001	0.37	0.48	0.57	0.72
2002	0.69	0.71	0.68	0.60
2003	0.60	0.62	0.30	0.44
2004	0.52	0.52	0.53	0.45

Interim Dividends (Per Share)

Amt	Decl	Ex	Rec	Pay
0.48Q	6/22/2004	6/30/2004	7/2/2004	7/28/2004
0.50Q	9/20/2004	9/28/2004	9/30/2004	10/27/2004
0.50Q	12/20/2004	12/29/2004	12/31/2004	1/27/2005
0.45Q	3/21/2005	3/30/2005	4/1/2005	4/27/2005

Indicated Div: $1.93

Valuation Analysis

Forecast P/E	10.54	No of Institutions
	(4/13/2005)	142
Market Cap	$2.3 Billion	Shares
Book Value	1.7 Billion	34,164,744
Price/Book	1.34	% Held
Price/Sales	4.14	28.17

Business Summary: Property, Real Estate & Development (MIC: 8.3 SIC: 798 NAIC: 25930)

Annaly Mortgage Management owns, manages and finances a portfolio of investment securities, including mortgage pass-through certificates, collateralized mortgage obligations (CMOs), agency callable debentures, and other securities representing interests in or obligations backed by pools of mortgage loans. Co.'s principal business objective is to generate income from the spread between the interest income on its investment securities and the costs of borrowing to finance its acquisition of investment securities. Co. has elected to be taxed as a real estate investment trust (REIT). As a result, substantially all of Co.'s assets consist of qualified REIT real estate assets.

Recent Developments: For the year ended Dec 31 2004, net income increased 38.0% to $248,592,000 from net income of $180,103,000 a year earlier. Interest income was $532,328,000 compared with $337,433,000 in 2003. Interest expense rose 48.4% to $270,116,000 from $182,004,000 the previous year. Net interest income was $262,212,000, up 68.7% from $155,429,000 the year before. Non-interest income plunged to $17,727,000 from $196,336,000, while non-interest expense increased 65.6% to $26,889,000 from $16,233,000 the previous year.

Prospects: The Federal Reserve is directly affecting Co.'s cost of funds by raising the federal funds rate which is driving increases in the 10-year Treasury yield. In the low interest rate environment, these amount to sizeable moves on a percentage basis. Meanwhile, Co. is encouraged by increased contributions from its wholly-owned asset manager Fixed Income Discount Advisory Company (FIDAC), reflecting higher fee income. Looking ahead to 2005, Co. expects nominal interest rates to remain at historically low levels, and in this environment, Co. should generate returns competitive with those of other asset classes.

Financial Data

(US$ in Thousands)	12/31/2004	12/31/2003	12/31/2002	12/31/2001	12/31/2000	12/31/1999	12/31/1998	12/31/1997
Earnings Per Share	2.03	1.94	2.67	2.21	1.15	1.35	1.19	0.78
Cash Flow Per Share	3.52	3.85	3.68	2.41	1.01	1.97	1.48	...
Tang Book Value Per Share	12.24	11.96	12.77	11.15	9.34	7.60	9.95	10.63
Dividends Per Share	1.980	1.950	2.670	1.750	1.150	1.380	1.215	0.400
Dividend Payout %	97.54	100.52	100.00	79.19	100.00	102.22	102.10	51.28
Income Statement								
Interest Income	532,328	337,433	404,165	263,058	109,750	89,812	89,986	24,713
Interest Expense	270,116	182,004	191,758	168,055	92,902	69,846	75,735	19,677
Net Interest Income	262,212	155,429	212,407	95,002	16,849	19,966	14,250	5,036
Non-Interest Income	17,727	40,907	21,063	4,586	2,025	455	3,344	735
Non-Interest Expense	26,889	16,233	13,963	7,311	2,287	2,281	2,106	852
Income Before Taxes	253,050	...	...	...	...	...	...	...
Income Taxes	4,458	...	...	...	...	...	...	...
Net Income	248,592	180,103	219,507	92,278	16,587	18,139	15,489	4,919
Average Shares	118,459	93,031	82,282	41,857	14,377	13,454	13,020	6,300
Balance Sheet								
Total Assets	19,560,299	12,990,286	11,659,084	7,717,314	2,035,029	1,491,322	1,527,352	1,167,740
Total Liabilities	17,859,829	11,841,066	10,579,018	7,049,957	1,899,386	1,388,050	1,401,481	1,032,654
Stockholders' Equity	1,700,470	1,149,220	1,080,066	667,357	135,642	103,272	125,871	135,086
Shares Outstanding	121,263	96,074	84,569	59,826	14,522	13,581	12,648	12,713
Statistical Record								
Return on Assets %	1.52	1.46	...	1.89	0.94	1.20	1.15	...
Return on Equity %	17.40	16.16	...	22.98	13.85	15.83	11.87	...
Net Interest Margin %	49.26	46.06	52.55	36.11	15.35	22.23	15.84	20.38
Efficiency Ratio %	4.89	4.29	3.28	2.73	2.05	2.53	2.26	3.35
Price Range	21.13-16.11	21.10-15.65	21.15-15.56	17.01-8.75	9.50-7.25	11.38-8.06	11.50-6.81	12.81-10.00
P/E Ratio	10.41-7.94	10.88-8.07	7.92-5.83	7.70-3.96	8.26-6.30	8.43-5.97	9.66-5.72	16.43-12.82
Average Yield %	10.84	10.66	14.92	13.78	13.51	14.41	12.97	3.56

Address: 1211 Avenue of the Americas, Suite 2902, New York, NY 10036 **Telephone:** (212) 696-0100 **Fax:** (212) 696-9809	**Web Site:** www.annaly.com **Officers:** Michael A. J. Farrell - Chmn.,Pres., C.E.O. Wellington J. St. Claire - Vice-Chmn., Chief Invest. Officer	**Auditors:** DELOITTE & TOUCHE LLP **Investor Contact:** 888-826-6259

ANN TAYLOR STORES CORP.

Exchange	Symbol	Price	52Wk Range	Yield	P/E
NYS	ANN	$25.59 (3/31/2005)	29.79-20.45	N/A	17.29

*7 Year Price Score 124.14 ***NYSE Composite Index=100** ***12 Month Price Score 88.75**

TRADING VOLUME (thousand shares)

Interim Earnings (Per Share)

Qtr.	Apr	Jul	Oct	Jan
2001-02	0.16	0.10	0.18	0.00
2002-03	0.30	0.26	0.35	0.23
2003-04	0.26	0.30	0.42	0.43
2004-05	0.43	0.41	0.20	...

Interim Dividends (Per Share)

Amt	Decl	Ex	Rec	Pay
50%	4/11/2002	5/21/2002	5/2/2002	5/20/2002
3-for-2	4/30/2004	5/27/2004	5/11/2004	5/26/2004

Valuation Analysis

Forecast P/E	19.99	No of Institutions
	(4/7/2005)	182
Market Cap	$1.8 Billion	Shares
Book Value	944.7 Million	63,733,364
Price/Book	1.91	% Held
Price/Sales	0.99	90.32

Business Summary: Retail - Apparel and Accessory Stores (MIC: 5.8 SIC: 621 NAIC: 48120)

AnnTaylor Stores is a specialty retailer of better quality women's apparel, shoes and accessories sold primarily under the Ann Taylor® and Ann Taylor Loft® brand names. As of Jan 31 2004, Co. operated 648 retail stores in 43 states, the District of Columbia and Puerto Rico, of which 354 were Ann Taylor stores, 268 were Ann Taylor Loft stores and 26 were Ann Taylor Factory stores. Co.'s stores offer a full range of career and casual separates, dresses, tops, weekend wear, shoes and accessories, coordinated as part of a total wardrobing strategy. In addition to its retail stores, Co. sells its products over the Internet through its on-line stores.

Recent Developments: For the quarter ended Oct 30 2004, net income dropped 53.0% to $14.2 million compared with $30.3 million in the corresponding quarter of 2003. Results were negatively affected by higher than anticipated promotional activity and its negative effect on gross margin and earnings. Net sales were $460.4 million, up 16.0% from $396.8 million a year earlier. Gross margin climbed 2.7% to $235.0 million versus $228.8 million a year earlier. Operating income decreased 54.2% to $23.5 million compared with $51.4 million the previous year. Selling, general and administrative expenses grew 19.2% to $211.5 million from $177.4 million in 2003.

Prospects: For the first quarter of fiscal 2005, Co. expects to achieve comparable store sales results in the low single-digit negative to flat range. Also, Co. expects to see continued pressure in its gross margin, specifically at the Ann Taylor division for the same period. This will be partially offset by the anticipated decrease in selling, general and administrative expenses as a percentage of net sales, as marketing as a percentage of net sales at the Ann Taylor division is expected to decline. In the first quarter of 2005, Co. plans to open three new Ann Taylor stores and 13 new Ann Taylor Loft stores. Co. projects earnings per diluted shares for the first quarter in the range of $0.27 to $0.30.

Financial Data (US$ in Thousands)	9 Mos	6 Mos	3 Mos	01/31/2004	02/01/2003	02/02/2002	02/03/2001	01/29/2000
Earnings Per Share	1.48	1.70	1.59	1.42	1.15	0.44	0.78	0.91
Cash Flow Per Share	1.38	2.67	3.22	2.85	2.40	1.21	1.18	1.51
Tang Book Value Per Share	9.34	9.59	8.50	7.99	6.36	4.93	4.26	3.22
Income Statement								
Total Revenue	1,366,245	905,880	433,246	1,587,708	1,380,966	1,299,573	1,232,776	1,084,519
EBITDA	177,400	136,294	69,840	227,158	188,632	116,551	145,446	166,414
Depn & Amortn	50,113	32,543	16,225	55,503	53,618	56,410	47,206	43,264
Income Before Taxes	127,660	103,298	52,946	168,288	131,407	54,662	93,398	115,714
Income Taxes	51,436	41,319	21,178	67,346	51,249	25,557	41,035	50,221
Net Income	76,224	61,979	31,768	100,942	80,158	29,105	52,363	64,531
Average Shares	71,556	74,722	75,098	73,144	72,451	65,490	70,247	71,660
Balance Sheet								
Current Assets	572,320	631,896	651,132	577,368	455,271	325,853	313,809	271,589
Total Assets	1,159,146	1,205,455	1,224,543	1,151,873	1,010,826	882,986	848,115	765,117
Current Liabilities	178,842	185,181	318,775	161,620	151,195	136,614	141,042	120,221
Long-Term Obligations	...	...	...	125,152	121,652	118,280	116,210	114,485
Total Liabilities	214,476	220,673	351,769	321,237	296,408	270,857	274,086	249,495
Stockholders' Equity	944,670	984,782	872,774	830,636	714,418	612,129	574,029	515,622
Shares Outstanding	70,485	72,839	68,960	68,067	67,322	66,098	64,850	64,282
Statistical Record								
Return on Assets %	9.40	10.98	10.29	9.36	8.49	3.37	6.39	8.40
Return on Equity %	12.44	14.33	14.44	13.10	12.12	4.92	9.46	13.65
EBITDA Margin %	12.98	15.05	16.12	14.31	13.66	8.97	11.80	15.34
Net Margin %	5.58	6.84	7.33	6.36	5.80	2.24	4.25	5.95
Asset Turnover	1.58	1.55	1.50	1.47	1.46	1.51	1.50	1.41
Current Ratio	3.20	3.41	2.04	3.57	3.01	2.39	2.22	2.26
Debt to Equity	...	...	...	0.15	0.17	0.19	0.20	0.22
Price Range	31.31-21.76	31.31-18.47	31.31-14.84	27.63-11.77	21.94-12.02	17.22-9.63	19.67-6.78	23.47-9.89
P/E Ratio	21.16-14.70	18.42-10.86	19.69-9.33	19.46-8.29	19.08-10.45	39.14-21.89	25.21-8.69	25.79-10.87

Address: 142 West 57th Street, New York, NY 10019	**Web Site:** www.anntaylor.com	**Auditors:** Deloitte & Touche LLP
Telephone: (212) 541-3300	**Officers:** J. Patrick Spainhour - Chmn., C.E.O. Kay Krill - Pres.	**Investor Contact:** 212-541-3484
Fax: (212) 541-3379		

AON CORP.

Exchange	Symbol	Price	52Wk Range	Yield	P/E
NYS	AOC	$22.84 (3/31/2005)	28.99-19.20	2.63	14.01

*7 Year Price Score 68.53   *NYSE Composite Index=100   *12 Month Price Score 88.52

Interim Earnings (Per Share)

Qtr.	Mar	Jun	Sep	Dec
2001	0.07	0.11	0.26	0.29
2002	0.37	0.00	0.46	0.61
2003	0.48	0.46	0.46	0.67
2004	0.53	0.52	0.36	0.23

Interim Dividends (Per Share)

Amt	Decl	Ex	Rec	Pay
0.15Q	4/16/2004	4/30/2004	5/4/2004	5/17/2004
0.15Q	7/16/2004	7/30/2004	8/3/2004	8/16/2004
0.15Q	10/8/2004	10/29/2004	11/2/2004	11/15/2004
0.15Q	1/21/2005	2/1/2005	2/3/2005	2/16/2005

Indicated Div: $0.60

Valuation Analysis

Forecast P/E	12.70 (4/7/2005)	No of Institutions 284
Market Cap	$7.2 Billion	Shares
Book Value	5.1 Billion	265,304,784
Price/Book	1.42	% Held
Price/Sales	0.71	83.57

TRADING VOLUME (thousand shares)

Business Summary: Insurance (MIC: 8.2 SIC: 321 NAIC: 24114)

Aon is a holding company whose subsidiaries operate in three operating segments. The Risk and Insurance Brokerage Services segment helps clients manage their risks and negotiate and place insurance risk with insurance carriers. The Consulting segment provides advice and services to clients for employee benefits, compensation, management consulting, communications and human resources outsourcing. The Insurance Underwriting segment provides specialty insurance products, including supplemental accident, health and life insurance; credit life, accident and health insurance; extended warranty products, and select property and casualty insurance products and services.

Recent Developments: For the year ended Dec 31 2004, income from continuing operations decreased 14.6% to $577,000 thousand from income of $676,000 thousand a year earlier. Net income decreased 13.1% to $546,000 thousand from net income of $628,000 thousand a year earlier. Revenues were $10,172,000 thousand, up 4.7% from $9,718,000 thousand the year before. Net premiums earned were $2,788,000 thousand versus $2,609,000 thousand in the prior year, an increase of 6.9%.

Prospects: Bottom-line results are being negatively affected by Co.'s decision to terminate contingent commission agreements, which have recently come under scrutiny by the New York attorney general's office. Meanwhile, on Jan 18 2005, Co. announced that it has formed Aon Affinity Latin America in Sao Paulo, Brazil to help serve Co.'s customers in South and Central America. Aon Affinity Latin America will focus initially on the growing market for insurance products in Mexico, Argentina and Colombia. Separately, on Feb 16 2005, Co. announced that it is considering the sale of its U.S.-based wholesale insurance brokerage unit, Swett & Crawford.

Financial Data
(US$ in Thousands)

	12/31/2004	12/31/2003	12/31/2002	12/31/2001	12/31/2000	12/31/1999	12/31/1998	12/31/1997
Earnings Per Share	1.63	1.97	1.64	0.73	1.79	1.33	2.07	1.12
Cash Flow Per Share	3.69	4.13	4.42	2.08	2.83	...	...	...
Tang Book Value Per Share	0.76	N.M.	N.M.	N.M.	N.M.	N.M.	N.M.	N.M.
Dividends Per Share	0.600	0.600	0.825	0.895	0.870	0.813	0.733	0.680
Dividend Payout %	36.81	30.46	50.30	122.60	48.60	61.15	35.37	60.71
Income Statement								
Total Revenue	10,172,000	9,810,000	8,822,000	7,676,000	7,375,000	7,070,000	6,493,000	5,750,600
Benefits & Claims	1,516,000	1,427,000	1,375,000	1,111,000	1,037,000	973,000	896,000	842,300
Income Before Taxes	880,000	1,110,000	793,000	399,000	854,000	635,000	931,000	541,600
Income Taxes	303,000	411,000	293,000	156,000	333,000	243,000	349,000	203,100
Net Income	546,000	628,000	466,000	203,000	474,000	352,000	541,000	298,800
Average Shares	336,600	317,800	283,000	272,000	263,000	262,700	259,350	255,750
Balance Sheet								
Total Assets	28,329,000	27,027,000	25,334,000	22,386,000	22,251,000	21,132,000	19,688,000	18,691,200
Total Liabilities	23,176,000	22,479,000	20,687,000	18,015,000	18,013,000	17,231,000	15,821,000	15,019,100
Stockholders' Equity	5,103,000	4,498,000	3,895,000	3,521,000	3,388,000	3,051,000	3,017,000	2,822,100
Shares Outstanding	316,800	313,600	310,300	247,700	256,100	253,753	256,191	251,956
Statistical Record								
Return on Assets %	1.97	2.40	1.95	0.91	2.18	1.72	2.82	1.84
Return on Equity %	11.34	14.96	12.57	5.88	14.68	11.60	18.53	10.57
Net Margin %	5.37	6.40	5.28	2.64	6.43	4.98	8.33	5.20
Price Range	28.99-19.20	26.46-17.64	39.54-14.60	44.75-31.81	42.75-21.06	46.08-26.94	49.75-34.38	39.08-27.06
P/E Ratio	17.79-11.78	13.43-8.95	24.11-8.90	61.30-43.58	23.88-11.77	34.65-20.25	24.03-16.61	34.90-24.16
Average Yield %	2.35	2.72	3.02	2.50	2.71	2.12	1.76	2.07

Address: 200 E. Randolph Street, Chicago, IL 60601 Telephone: (312) 381-1000	Web Site: www.aon.com Officers: Patrick G. Ryan - Chmn. Gregory C. Case - Pres., C.E.O.	Auditors: Ernst & Young LLP Transfer Agents: EquiServe Trust Company, N.A., Providence, RI

APACHE CORP.

Exchange	Symbol	Price	52Wk Range	Yield	P/E
NYS	APA	$61.23 (3/31/2005)	65.69-38.97	0.52	12.17

*7 Year Price Score 157.28 *NYSE Composite Index=100 *12 Month Price Score 114.03

Interim Earnings (Per Share)

Qtr.	Mar	Jun	Sep	Dec
2001	0.93	0.67	0.52	0.25
2002	0.26	0.48	0.48	0.59
2003	1.05	0.75	0.84	0.80
2004	1.06	1.13	1.31	1.53

Interim Dividends (Per Share)

Amt	Decl	Ex	Rec	Pay
0.06Q	5/26/2004	7/20/2004	7/22/2004	8/23/2004
0.08Q	9/16/2004	10/20/2004	10/22/2004	11/22/2004
0.08Q	12/21/2004	1/19/2005	1/21/2005	2/22/2005
0.08Q	2/14/2005	4/20/2005	4/22/2005	5/23/2005
		Indicated Div: $0.32		

Valuation Analysis

Forecast P/E	10.13	No of Institutions
	(4/13/2005)	659
Market Cap	$20.1 Billion	Shares
Book Value	8.2 Billion	247,010,304
Price/Book	2.44	% Held
Price/Sales	3.76	75.29

Business Summary: Oil and Gas (MIC: 14.2 SIC: 311 NAIC: 11111)

Apache is an independent energy company that explores for, develops and produces natural gas, crude oil and natural gas liquids. In North America, Co.'s exploration and production interests are focused in the Gulf of Mexico, the Gulf Coast, the Permian Basin, the Anadarko Basin and the Western Sedimentary Basin of Canada. Outside of North America, Co. has exploration and production interests offshore Western Australia, offshore and onshore Egypt, offshore The People's Republic of China, offshore the UK in the North Sea and onshore Argentina. As of Dec 31 2003, proved reserves were: oil, natural gas liquids and condensate, 843.9 million barrels; and natural gas 4.88 trillion cubic feet.

Recent Developments: For the year ended Dec 31 2004, net income increased 48.7% to $1,668,754 thousand from net income of $1,121,885 thousand a year earlier. Revenues were $5,332,577 thousand, up 27.3% from $4,190,299 thousand the year before. Total indirect expense was $2,553,009 thousand versus $2,144,302 thousand in the prior year, an increase of 19.1%.

Prospects: Operating results are benefiting from continued high commodity prices and solid production growth, which benefited from a capital investment program of $3.40 billion in 2004. Co. produced an average of 448,000 barrels of oil equivalent (boe) per day in 2004, up from 417,000 boe per day the year before, and added 467 million barrels of oil equivalent in proved reserves through dilling and acquisitions over the 12 months ended Dec 31 2004. Co. noted that its production has increased in 25 of the last 26 years. Looking to 2005, Co. enters the year with record production and a strong portfolio of drilling opportunities across its core areas.

Financial Data (US$ in Thousands)	12/31/2004	12/31/2003	12/31/2002	12/31/2001	12/31/2000	12/31/1999	12/31/1998	12/31/1997
Earnings Per Share	5.03	3.43	1.80	2.37	2.45	0.74	(0.58)	0.71
Cash Flow Per Share	9.88	8.39	4.65	6.72	5.60	2.56	2.08	3.46
Tang Book Value Per Share	24.18	19.25	15.33	13.63	12.07	8.96	7.54	8.02
Dividends Per Share	0.260	0.208	0.190	0.121	0.091	0.121	0.121	0.121
Dividend Payout %	5.17	6.05	10.58	5.12	3.70	16.28	...	16.97
Income Statement								
Total Revenue	5,332,577	4,190,299	2,559,873	2,777,126	2,283,904	1,300,505	875,715	1,176,273
EBITDA	4,004,191	3,112,778	1,833,848	2,071,279	1,896,591	874,537	513,455	718,819
Depn & Amortn	1,224,623	1,075,449	822,045	753,263	586,272	447,698	630,481	387,854
Income Before Taxes	2,663,083	1,922,257	898,970	1,199,254	1,203,681	344,573	(187,563)	258,640
Income Taxes	993,012	827,004	344,641	475,855	483,086	143,718	(58,176)	103,744
Net Income	1,668,754	1,121,885	554,329	723,399	713,056	200,855	(129,387)	154,896
Average Shares	330,477	325,330	304,612	303,246	288,093	250,297	226,532	229,276
Balance Sheet								
Current Assets	1,348,782	899,072	766,781	697,749	630,020	343,068	226,970	348,329
Total Assets	15,502,480	12,416,126	9,459,851	8,933,656	7,481,950	5,502,543	3,996,062	4,138,633
Current Liabilities	1,282,891	820,378	532,235	522,458	553,347	336,778	305,774	343,783
Long-Term Obligations	2,588,390	2,326,966	2,158,815	2,244,357	2,193,258	1,879,650	1,343,258	1,501,380
Total Liabilities	7,298,059	5,883,328	4,535,571	4,515,173	3,727,310	2,833,116	2,194,229	2,409,456
Stockholders' Equity	8,204,421	6,532,798	4,924,280	4,418,483	3,754,640	2,669,427	1,801,833	1,729,177
Shares Outstanding	327,457	324,497	302,506	287,916	285,596	263,331	225,846	215,534
Statistical Record								
Return on Assets %	11.92	10.26	6.03	8.81	10.95	4.23	N.M.	4.09
Return on Equity %	22.58	19.58	11.87	17.70	22.14	8.98	N.M.	9.54
EBITDA Margin %	75.09	74.29	71.64	74.58	83.04	67.25	58.63	61.11
Net Margin %	31.29	26.77	21.65	26.05	31.22	15.44	N.M.	13.17
Asset Turnover	0.38	0.38	0.28	0.34	0.35	0.27	0.22	0.31
Current Ratio	1.05	1.10	1.44	1.34	1.14	1.02	0.74	1.01
Debt to Equity	0.32	0.36	0.44	0.51	0.58	0.70	0.75	0.87
Price Range	54.06-37.23	41.30-26.69	28.42-21.61	30.65-16.77	31.68-14.12	21.48-7.85	16.42-9.15	19.02-13.26
P/E Ratio	10.75-7.40	12.04-7.78	15.79-12.01	12.93-7.08	12.93-5.76	29.03-10.60	...	26.79-18.67
Average Yield %	0.58	0.64	0.74	0.52	0.40	0.82	0.93	0.77

Address: One Post Oak Central, 2000 Post Oak Boulevard, Suite 100, Houston, TX 77056-4400 **Telephone:** (713) 296-6000 **Fax:** (713) 296-6490	**Web Site:** www.apachecorp.com **Officers:** Raymond Plank - Chmn. G. Steven Farris - Pres., C.E.O., C.O.O.	**Auditors:** Ersnt & Young LLP **Investor Contact:** 713-296-6662

APARTMENT INVESTMENT & MANAGEMENT CO.

Exchange	Symbol	Price	52Wk Range	Yield	P/E
NYS	AIV	$37.20 (3/31/2005)	39.21-27.88	6.45	19.79

*7 Year Price Score 74.25   *NYSE Composite Index=100   *12 Month Price Score 101.23

TRADING VOLUME (thousand shares)

Interim Earnings (Per Share)

Qtr.	Mar	Jun	Sep	Dec
2001	(0.07)	0.11	0.02	0.16
2002	0.58	0.26	0.26	(0.20)
2003	0.00	0.39	0.15	0.19
2004	(0.06)	(0.08)	1.48	0.54

Interim Dividends (Per Share)

Amt	Decl	Ex	Rec	Pay
0.60Q	4/30/2004	5/14/2004	5/18/2004	5/28/2004
0.60Q	7/29/2004	8/18/2004	8/20/2004	8/31/2004
0.60Q	10/29/2004	11/17/2004	11/19/2004	11/30/2004
0.60Q	1/28/2005	2/16/2005	2/18/2005	2/28/2005

Indicated Div: $2.40

Valuation Analysis

Forecast P/E	12.94 (4/7/2005)	No of Institutions 224
Market Cap	$3.5 Billion	Shares 84,878,912
Book Value	3.0 Billion	% Held
Price/Book	1.17	89.46
Price/Sales	2.40	

Business Summary: Property, Real Estate & Development (MIC: 8.3 SIC: 798 NAIC: 25930)

Apartment Investment and Management is a self-administered and self-managed real estate investment trust engaged in the ownership, acquisition, redevelopment, and management of apartment properties. As of Dec 31 2003, Co., through its subsidiaries, owned or managed a real estate portfolio of approximately 1,629 apartment properties, including about 287,560 apartment units. Co.'s properties include garden style, mid-rise and high-rise properties and serve approximately one million residents per year. Co.'s properties are located in 47 states, the District of Columbia and Puerto Rico.

Recent Developments: For the year ended Dec 31 2004, income from continuing operations decreased 13.2% to $55,696 thousand from income of $64,148 thousand a year earlier. Net income increased 65.9% to $263,497 thousand from net income of $158,857 thousand a year earlier. Revenues were $1,468,915 thousand, up 5.3% from $1,394,705 thousand the year before. Operating income was $328,758 thousand versus an income of $419,019 thousand in the prior year, a decrease of 21.5%.

Prospects: Co.'s prospects appear positive. Co.'s same-store rental revenue is continuing its recovery and Aimco Capital is continuing to build its business of owning affordable properties and developing them with tax credit equity. Co. has also strengthened its balance sheet, increased its liquidity and lowered its weighted average cost of capital. Co. is looking for further progress in 2005 with a strengthening economy and further refinement and experience with its business plans and objectives. Looking ahead to full-year 2005, Co. expects funds from operations to be in the range of $2.80 to $3.05 per share.

Financial Data

(US$ in Thousands)	12/31/2004	12/31/2003	12/31/2002	12/31/2001	12/31/2000	12/31/1999	12/31/1998	12/31/1997
Earnings Per Share	1.88	0.70	0.87	0.23	0.52	0.38	0.80	1.08
Cash Flow Per Share	3.91	4.63	5.80	6.82	5.91	4.07	3.28	3.04
Tang Book Value Per Share	20.73	21.36	23.66	20.01	23.32	24.27	20.26	19.34
Dividends Per Share	2.400	3.060	3.280	3.120	2.800	2.500	2.250	1.850
Dividend Payout %	127.66	437.14	377.01	1	538.46	657.89	281.25	171.30
Income Statement								
Property Income	1,401,653	1,445,796	1,405,684	1,297,764	1,051,000	533,917	377,139	193,006
Non-Property Income	67,262	70,487	(279,333)	(324,704)	(317,836)	(113,768)	(77,492)	(35,713)
Total Revenue	1,468,915	1,516,283	1,126,351	973,060	733,164	420,149	299,647	157,293
Depn & Amortn	368,844	335,081	292,615	364,378	330,019	137,613	93,370	38,689
Interest Expense	366,617	372,746	339,737	315,860	269,826	140,094	89,424	51,385
Net Income	263,497	158,857	169,046	107,352	99,178	80,959	64,474	28,633
Average Shares	93,118	92,968	86,773	73,648	69,063	63,446	47,624	24,436
Balance Sheet								
Total Assets	10,072,241	10,113,362	10,316,601	8,322,536	7,699,874	5,684,951	4,268,285	2,100,510
Long-Term Obligations	5,973,353	6,084,288	6,233,727	4,760,842	4,031,375	2,375,089	1,242,393	755,431
Total Liabilities	6,580,240	6,756,852	6,687,573	5,104,603	4,694,200	2,878,709	1,881,669	906,913
Stockholders' Equity	3,008,160	2,860,657	3,163,387	2,716,390	2,501,657	2,262,828	1,902,564	1,045,300
Shares Outstanding	94,853	93,887	93,769	74,498	71,337	66,802	48,451	40,601
Statistical Record								
Return on Assets %	2.60	1.56	1.81	1.34	1.48	1.63	2.02	1.96
Return on Equity %	8.96	5.27	5.75	4.11	4.15	3.89	4.37	4.54
Net Margin %	17.94	10.48	15.01	11.03	13.53	19.27	21.52	18.20
Price Range	38.83-27.88	41.98-33.01	51.40-34.64	49.81-41.00	49.94-36.63	44.13-34.69	40.69-30.50	38.00-25.88
P/E Ratio	20.65-14.83	59.97-47.16	59.08-39.82	216.58-178.26	96.03-70.43	116.12-91.28	50.86-38.13	35.19-23.96
Average Yield %	7.22	8.28	7.57	6.90	6.58	6.41	6.12	6.00

Address: 4582 South Ulster Street Parkway, Suite 1100, Denver, CO 80237 **Telephone:** (303) 757-8101 **Fax:** (303) 759-3226	**Web Site:** www.aimco.com **Officers:** Terry Considine - Chmn., C.E.O. Paul J. McAuliffe - Exec. V.P., C.F.O., Investor Relations	**Auditors:** Ernst & Young LLP **Investor Contact:** 303-691-4440 **Transfer Agents:** EquiServe, Providence, Rhode Island

APPLERA CORP.

Exchange	Symbol	Price	52Wk Range	Yield	P/E
NYS	ABI	$19.74 (3/31/2005)	21.75-18.05	0.86	85.83

*7 Year Price Score 50.72   *NYSE Composite Index=100   *12 Month Price Score 95.02

Interim Earnings (Per Share)

Qtr.	Sep	Dec	Mar	Jun
2001-02	0.15	0.23	0.23	(3.03)
2002-03	0.16	0.14	0.19	(0.61)
2003-04	0.16	0.25	0.22	(0.54)
2004-05	0.18	0.37	...	...

Interim Dividends (Per Share)

Amt	Decl	Ex	Rec	Pay
0.043Q	8/19/2004	8/30/2004	9/1/2004	10/1/2004
0.043Q	11/18/2004	11/29/2004	12/1/2004	1/3/2005
0.043Q	1/20/2005	2/25/2005	3/1/2005	4/1/2005
0.043Q	4/4/2005	5/27/2005	6/1/2005	7/1/2005
		Indicated Div: $0.17		

Valuation Analysis

Forecast P/E	N/A	No of Institutions
Market Cap	$5.3 Billion	Shares
Book Value	2.3 Billion	175,250,240
Price/Book	2.32	% Held
Price/Sales	2.93	89.26

TRADING VOLUME (thousand shares)

Business Summary: Instruments and Related Products (MIC: 11.15 SIC: 826 NAIC: 34516)

Applera is a life sciences company comprised of three business segments: the Applied Biosystems group, the Celera Genomics group, and Celera Diagnostics. The Applied Biosystems group serves the life science industry and research community by developing and marketing instrument-based systems, consumables, software, and services. The Celera Genomics group is engaged principally in the discovery and development of targeted therapeutics for cancer, autoimmune, and inflammatory diseases. Celera Diagnostics is a 50/50 joint venture between Applied Biosystems and Celera Genomics. Celera Diagnostics is focused on the discovery, development, and commercialization of diagnostic products.

Recent Developments: For the quarter ended Dec 31 2004, net income increased 28.9% to $54,873 thousand from net income of $42,571 thousand in the year-earlier quarter. Revenues were $477,536 thousand, down 1.6% from $485,335 thousand the year before. Operating income was $64,525 thousand versus an income of $36,334 thousand in the prior-year quarter, an increase of 77.6%. Total direct expense was $224,362 thousand versus $228,778 thousand in the prior-year quarter, a decrease of 1.9%. Total indirect expense was $188,649 thousand versus $220,223 thousand in the prior-year quarter, a decrease of 14.3%.

Prospects: For fiscal 2005, Co.'s Applied Biosystems group expects low-single-digit revenue growth year over year, with real-time PCR/Applied genomics and Mass Spectrometry revenues expected to increase from the year before, while revenues from DNA sequencing, core PCR and DNA synthesis, and other product lines are expected to decline. Meanwhile, Co.'s Celera Genomics group intends to continue advancing its disease association and medical utility studies during fiscal 2005. It also anticipates increased sales of existing products sold through its alliance with Abbott. Celera Diagnostics is also planning the introduction of new products.

Financial Data

(US$ in Thousands)	6 Mos	3 Mos	06/30/2004	06/30/2003	06/30/2002	06/30/2001	06/30/2000	06/30/1999
Earnings Per Share	0.23	0.11	0.09	(0.20)	(2.43)	(2.11)	0.86	0.21
Cash Flow Per Share	0.64	0.67	0.70	0.70	0.77	0.32	0.41	0.28
Tang Book Value Per Share	8.49	8.17	7.97	8.07	7.70	7.78	7.80	3.13
Dividends Per Share	0.170	0.170	0.170	0.170	0.170	0.170	0.170	0.170
Dividend Payout %	74.70	158.46	188.89	...	...	...	19.77	80.95
Income Statement								
Total Revenue	884,697	407,161	1,825,193	1,777,232	1,701,218	1,644,126	1,371,035	1,216,897
EBITDA	132,987	40,789	216,620	205,960	33,643	111,383	180,880	163,279
Depn & Amortn	52,510	25,871	110,000	130,000	105,700	116,134	80,699	48,066
Income Before Taxes	92,554	20,155	129,487	105,577	(28,550)	73,472	136,108	114,299
Income Taxes	21,588	4,062	14,534	(12,903)	12,031	46,238	40,612	4,140
Net Income	70,966	16,093	125,581	102,080	(40,581)	27,234	95,496	175,855
Average Shares	543,000	271,300	280,800	281,886	281,489	281,194	270,741	256,409
Balance Sheet								
Current Assets	2,036,643	1,884,823	1,923,408	2,073,383	2,012,498	2,041,484	2,125,527	994,002
Total Assets	3,075,278	2,910,312	2,972,851	3,257,492	3,075,399	2,887,858	3,083,315	1,519,307
Current Liabilities	583,719	513,040	596,768	630,617	627,239	587,115	646,500	522,652
Long-Term Obligations	...	...	...	17,101	17,983	...	82,100	31,500
Total Liabilities	784,739	709,746	791,802	917,207	850,456	739,547	862,823	697,782
Stockholders' Equity	2,290,539	2,200,566	2,181,049	2,340,285	2,224,943	2,148,311	2,220,492	821,525
Shares Outstanding	269,690	269,298	268,774	285,121	283,793	273,166	267,987	256,730
Statistical Record								
Return on Assets %	4.40	4.13	4.02	3.22	N.M.	0.91	4.14	12.32
Return on Equity %	5.95	5.54	5.54	4.47	N.M.	1.25	6.26	25.38
EBITDA Margin %	15.03	10.02	11.87	11.59	1.98	6.77	13.19	13.42
Net Margin %	8.02	3.95	6.88	5.74	N.M.	1.66	6.97	14.45
Asset Turnover	0.58	0.60	0.58	0.56	0.57	0.55	0.59	0.85
Current Ratio	3.49	3.67	3.22	3.29	3.21	3.48	3.29	1.90
Debt to Equity	...	...	...	0.01	0.01	...	0.04	0.04
Price Range	23.82-18.05	23.82-18.05	23.82-18.24	24.06-14.10	40.17-15.71	128.94-23.00	147.50-26.88	30.06-12.66
P/E Ratio	103.57-78.48	216.55-164.09	264.67-202.67	...	...	...	171.51-31.25	143.15-60.30
Average Yield %	0.84	0.82	0.81	0.93	0.67	0.24	0.30	0.83

Address: 301 Merritt 7, Norwalk, CT 06851-1070
Telephone: (203) 840-2000
Fax: (203) 762-6000

Web Site: www.applera.com
Officers: Tony L. White - Chmn., Pres., C.E.O. Kathy P. Ordoñez - Sr. V.P., Pres., Celera Genomics Group & Celera Diagnostics

Auditors: PricewaterhouseCoopers LLP
Investor Contact: 203-554-2479
Transfer Agents: EquiServe Trust Company, N.A., Providence, RI

APRIA HEALTHCARE GROUP INC.

Exchange	Symbol	Price	52Wk Range	Yield	P/E
NYS	AHG	$32.10 (3/31/2005)	34.00-26.60	N/A	14.14

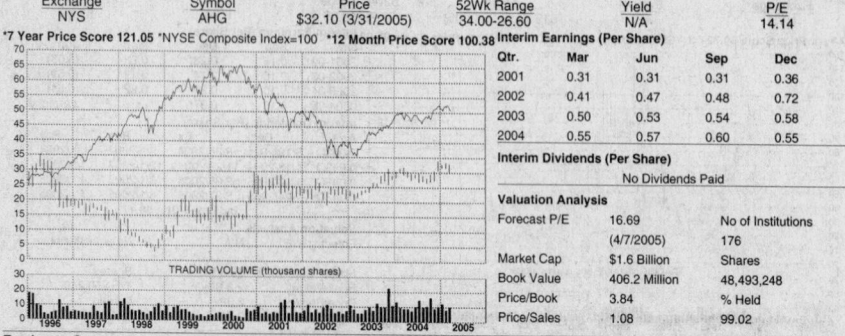

*7 Year Price Score 121.05 *NYSE Composite Index=100 *12 Month Price Score 100.38

Interim Earnings (Per Share)

Qtr.	Mar	Jun	Sep	Dec
2001	0.31	0.31	0.31	0.36
2002	0.41	0.47	0.48	0.72
2003	0.50	0.53	0.54	0.58
2004	0.55	0.57	0.60	0.55

Interim Dividends (Per Share)

No Dividends Paid

Valuation Analysis

Forecast P/E	16.69	No of Institutions
	(4/7/2005)	176
Market Cap	$1.6 Billion	Shares
Book Value	406.2 Million	48,493,248
Price/Book	3.84	% Held
Price/Sales	1.08	99.02

Business Summary: Diagnostic Services (MIC: 9.5 SIC: 082 NAIC: 21610)

Apria Healthcare Group provides a range of home healthcare services through approximately 425 branch locations that serve patients in all 50 states. Co. has three service lines: home respiratory therapy, home infusion therapy and home medical equipment. Home respiratory therapy provides oxygen systems, home ventilators, sleep apnea equipment, nebulizers and respiratory medications and related services. Home infusion therapy provides intravenous administration of anti-infectives, pain management, chemotherapy, nutrients and other medications and related services. Home medical equipment provides patient safety items, ambulatory and in-home equipment, such as wheelchairs and hospital beds.

Recent Developments: For the year ended Dec 31 2004, net income decreased 1.7% to $114,008 thousand from net income of $115,992 thousand a year earlier. Operating income was $201,055 thousand versus an income of $201,599 thousand in the prior year, a decrease of 0.3%. Total direct expense was $407,619 thousand versus $376,743 thousand in the prior year, an increase of 8.2%. Total indirect expense was $842,775 thousand versus $802,603 thousand in the prior year, an increase of 5.0%.

Prospects: Co.'s overall revenue growth rate and earnings are being negatively affected by Medicare respiratory medication reimbursement cuts, which totaled $15.2 million for 2004, and its decision not to renew its contract with Gentiva CareCentrix, Inc. However, Co. is encouraged by recent decrease in sales, distribution and administrative expenses. Looking ahead, Co. will continue to monitor its expenses as it introduces a number of productivity initiatives aimed at lowering its costs. Separately, Co. closed on a $1.6 million acquisition during the fourth quarter of 2004, bringing the total number of acquisitions for the year to 27 for an aggregate consideration of $148.7 million.

Financial Data
(US$ in Thousands)

	12/31/2004	12/31/2003	12/31/2002	12/31/2001	12/31/2000	12/31/1999	12/31/1998	12/31/1997
Earnings Per Share	2.27	2.15	2.08	1.29	1.06	3.81	(4.02)	(5.30)
Cash Flow Per Share	5.58	4.94	4.80	4.47	3.66	1.54	2.59	2.02
Tang Book Value Per Share	N.M.	0.55	1.75	0.81	0.16	N.M.	...	N.M.
Income Statement								
Total Revenue	1,451,449	1,380,945	1,252,196	1,131,915	1,014,201	940,024	933,793	1,180,694
EBITDA	345,799	341,201	297,469	261,633	243,471	216,019	(41,491)	(51,778)
Depn & Amortn	147,474	139,602	118,724	118,406	105,274	100,312	116,531	134,887
Income Before Taxes	178,305	186,573	167,952	117,542	98,141	73,181	(204,938)	(236,058)
Income Taxes	64,297	70,581	52,357	44,097	41,135	(130,954)	3,000	36,550
Net Income	114,008	115,992	115,595	71,917	57,006	204,135	(207,938)	(272,608)
Average Shares	50,180	54,066	55,455	55,778	54,022	53,530	51,732	51,419
Balance Sheet								
Current Assets	348,311	429,335	290,361	239,823	226,470	239,025	229,037	311,573
Total Assets	1,107,664	1,043,435	795,656	695,782	616,603	629,051	496,598	757,170
Current Liabilities	178,335	192,260	183,713	174,750	132,611	159,381	214,108	142,483
Long-Term Obligations	475,957	469,241	247,655	278,234	337,750	394,201	414,147	540,220
Total Liabilities	701,479	677,487	444,347	452,984	470,361	553,582	628,255	682,703
Stockholders' Equity	406,185	365,948	351,309	242,798	146,242	75,469	(131,657)	74,467
Shares Outstanding	48,608	51,107	54,897	54,604	53,067	52,054	51,785	51,569
Statistical Record								
Return on Assets %	10.57	12.61	15.50	10.96	9.13	36.27	N.M.	N.M.
Return on Equity %	29.45	32.34	38.91	36.97	51.28	...	...	N.M.
EBITDA Margin %	23.82	24.71	23.76	23.11	24.01	22.98	N.M.	N.M.
Net Margin %	7.85	8.40	9.23	6.35	5.62	21.72	N.M.	N.M.
Asset Turnover	1.35	1.50	1.68	1.72	1.62	1.67	1.49	1.24
Current Ratio	1.95	2.23	1.58	1.37	1.71	1.50	1.07	2.19
Debt to Equity	1.17	1.28	0.70	1.15	2.31	5.22	...	7.25
Price Range	34.00-26.60	31.32-20.74	28.00-19.00	28.99-20.40	30.00-10.63	21.88-7.44	14.13-3.00	20.25-13.25
P/E Ratio	14.98-11.72	14.57-9.65	13.46-9.13	22.47-15.81	28.30-10.02	5.74-1.95	...	...

Address: 26220 Enterprise Court, Lake Forest, CA 92630 Telephone: (949) 639-2000 Fax: (949) 639-2900	Web Site: www.apria.com Officers: Ralph V. Whitworth - Chmn. Lawrence A. Mastrovich - Pres., C.O.O.	Auditors: DELOITTE & TOUCHE LLP

APTARGROUP INC.

Exchange	Symbol	Price	52Wk Range	Yield	P/E	Div Acheiver
NYS	ATR	$51.98 (3/31/2005)	54.43-37.83	1.15	20.71	11 Years

*7 Year Price Score 121.07 *NYSE Composite Index=100 *12 Month Price Score 102.47

Interim Earnings (Per Share)

Qtr.	Mar	Jun	Sep	Dec
2001	0.50	0.41	0.43	0.26
2002	0.36	0.48	0.49	0.50
2003	0.53	0.58	0.51	0.54
2004	0.57	0.61	0.68	0.65

Interim Dividends (Per Share)

Amt	Decl	Ex	Rec	Pay
0.07Q	4/15/2004	4/28/2004	4/30/2004	5/21/2004
0.15Q	7/16/2004	7/23/2004	7/27/2004	8/17/2004
0.15Q	10/13/2004	10/26/2004	10/28/2004	11/18/2004
0.15Q	1/20/2005	1/31/2005	2/2/2005	2/24/2005

Indicated Div: $0.60

Valuation Analysis

Forecast P/E	19.15	No of Institutions
	(4/7/2005)	185
Market Cap	$2.0 Billion	Shares
Book Value	873.2 Million	31,261,240
Price/Book	2.27	% Held
Price/Sales	1.53	87.44

Business Summary: Plastics (MIC: 11.7 SIC: 089 NAIC: 26199)

AptarGroup is an international company that designs, manufactures and sells consumer product dispensing systems for the personal care, fragrance/cosmetic, pharmaceutical, household and food/beverage markets. Operations are divided into two segments, Dispensing Systems and SeaquistPerfect. The dispensing segment focuses on providing value-added dispensing systems (pumps, closures and aerosol valves), while SeaquistPerfect sells primarily aerosol valves and customer pumps to the personal care, household, and to a lesser degree, the food/beverage markets. Co. has manufacturing facilities located throughout the world, including North America, Europe, Asia and South America.

Recent Developments: For the year ended Dec 31 2004, net income increased 17.1% to $93,287 thousand from net income of $79,679 thousand a year earlier. Revenues were $1,296,608 thousand, up 16.3% from $1,114,689 thousand the year before. Operating income was $140,884 thousand versus an income of $123,946 thousand in the prior year, an increase of 13.7%. Total direct expense was $866,865 thousand versus $732,038 thousand in the prior year, an increase of 18.4%. Total indirect expense was $288,859 thousand versus $258,705 thousand in the prior year, an increase of 11.7%.

Prospects: Co.'s outlook appears decent, reflecting recent top line gains and higher income from both its Dispensing Systems and SeaquistPerfect operating segments. Co. noted that demand for its dispensing systems has been particularly strong from the food, pharmaceutical and fragrance/cosmetic markets. Separately, on Feb 9 2005, Co. announced that it has entered into an agreement to acquire, subject to certain government approvals and other customary closing conditions, EP Spray System SA, a company in Switzerland that manufactures aerosol valves with bag-on-valve technology. The purchase price was equivalent to about $29.0 million. EP Spray's sales for calendar 2004 were approximately $15.0 million.

Financial Data

(US$ in Thousands)	12/31/2004	12/31/2003	12/31/2002	12/31/2001	12/31/2000	12/31/1999	12/31/1998	12/31/1997
Earnings Per Share	2.51	2.16	1.82	1.61	1.78	1.59	1.65	1.27
Cash Flow Per Share	5.05	3.87	4.30	3.60	3.63	3.26	2.36	2.40
Tang Book Value Per Share	18.81	16.76	12.11	9.01	8.55	8.03	10.13	8.38
Dividends Per Share	0.440	0.260	0.240	0.220	0.200	0.180	0.160	0.150
Dividend Payout %	17.53	12.04	13.19	13.66	11.24	11.32	9.70	11.76
Income Statement								
Total Revenue	1,296,608	1,114,689	926,691	891,986	883,481	834,317	713,506	655,390
EBITDA	237,427	210,023	179,111	175,689	186,109	173,524	158,940	132,634
Depn & Amortn	94,493	85,852	72,141	73,584	70,949	68,670	54,446	49,917
Income Before Taxes	137,177	117,270	98,358	88,355	97,922	91,778	99,189	78,596
Income Taxes	43,890	37,591	31,711	29,447	33,256	33,066	38,368	32,067
Net Income	93,287	79,679	66,647	58,844	64,666	58,712	60,821	46,529
Average Shares	37,157	36,901	36,623	36,529	36,369	36,913	36,799	36,518
Balance Sheet								
Current Assets	661,229	602,454	447,196	374,915	407,549	351,234	316,649	256,161
Total Assets	1,374,026	1,264,343	1,047,671	915,327	952,239	863,298	714,673	585,433
Current Liabilities	276,861	283,220	162,688	154,151	203,102	159,905	167,433	125,397
Long-Term Obligations	142,581	125,196	219,182	239,387	252,752	235,649	80,875	70,740
Total Liabilities	500,829	481,292	453,204	446,123	511,699	443,029	299,165	243,378
Stockholders' Equity	873,197	783,051	594,467	469,204	440,540	420,269	415,508	342,055
Shares Outstanding	38,200	37,700	37,200	37,000	36,600	36,500	36,100	36,000
Statistical Record								
Return on Assets %	7.05	6.89	6.79	6.30	7.10	7.44	9.36	8.01
Return on Equity %	11.23	11.57	12.53	12.94	14.98	14.05	16.06	13.73
EBITDA Margin %	18.31	18.84	19.33	19.70	21.07	20.80	22.28	20.24
Net Margin %	7.19	7.15	7.19	6.60	7.32	7.04	8.52	7.10
Asset Turnover	0.98	0.96	0.94	0.96	0.97	1.06	1.10	1.13
Current Ratio	2.39	2.13	2.75	2.43	2.01	2.20	1.89	2.04
Debt to Equity	0.16	0.16	0.37	0.51	0.57	0.56	0.19	0.21
Price Range	54.43-37.38	39.48-26.51	38.70-25.12	36.90-27.38	30.00-19.88	30.81-22.75	32.94-20.25	29.38-16.44
P/E Ratio	21.69-14.89	18.28-12.27	21.26-13.80	22.92-17.00	16.85-11.17	19.38-14.31	19.96-12.27	23.13-12.94
Average Yield %	1.01	0.75	0.75	0.69	0.80	0.66	0.56	0.64

Address: 475 West Terra Cotta Avenue, Suite E, Crystal Lake, IL 60014 **Telephone:** (815) 477-0424 **Fax:** (815) 477-0481	**Web Site:** www.aptargroup.com **Officers:** King Harris - Chmn. Peter Pfeiffer - Vice-Chmn.	**Auditors:** PricewaterhouseCoopers LLP **Transfer Agents:** Mellon Investor Services, LLC, South Hackensack, NJ

AQUA AMERICA INC

Exchange	Symbol	Price	52Wk Range	Yield	P/E	Div Acheiver
NYS	WTR	$24.36 (3/31/2005)	25.63-18.91	2.13	28.66	13 Years

*7 Year Price Score 118.61 *NYSE Composite Index=100 *12 Month Price Score 104.05

Interim Earnings (Per Share)

Qtr.	Mar	Jun	Sep	Dec
2001	0.15	0.18	0.22	0.14
2002	0.14	0.17	0.25	0.22
2003	0.15	0.18	0.26	0.20
2004	0.17	0.19	0.26	0.24

Interim Dividends (Per Share)

Amt	Decl	Ex	Rec	Pay
0.12Q	4/27/2004	5/12/2004	5/14/2004	6/1/2004
0.12Q	8/3/2004	8/12/2004	8/16/2004	9/1/2004
0.13Q	8/3/2004	11/10/2004	11/15/2004	12/1/2004
0.13Q	1/28/2005	2/10/2005	2/14/2005	3/1/2005

Indicated Div: $0.52 (Div. Reinv. Plan)

Valuation Analysis

Forecast P/E	26.11	No of Institutions	
	(4/7/2005)	178	
Market Cap	$2.3 Billion	Shares	
Book Value	748.5 Million	26,666,480	
Price/Book	3.10	% Held	
Price/Sales	5.26	27.93	

Business Summary: Water Utilities (MIC: 7.2 SIC: 941 NAIC: 21310)

Aqua America is a holding company. Through its subsidiaries, Co. is engaged in operating regulated utilities that provide water or wastewater services to approximately 2.5 million people in 14 states. Co.'s largest subsidiary, Aqua Pennsylvania, Inc. provides water or wastewater services to about 1.3 million residents in the suburban areas north and west of the city of Philadelphia and 19 other counties in PA. Co. also provides water and wastewater services through operating and maintenance contracts with municipal authorities and other parties close to its operating companies' service territories. Co. is the largest U.S.-based publicly-traded water utility based on number of people served.

Recent Developments: For the year ended Dec 31 2004, net income increased 13.0% to $80,007 thousand from net income of $70,795 thousand a year earlier. Revenues were $442,039 thousand, up 20.4% from $367,233 thousand the year before. Operating income was $177,234 thousand versus an income of $153,561 thousand in the prior year, an increase of 15.4%. Total indirect expense was $264,805 thousand versus $213,672 thousand in the prior year, an increase of 23.9%.

Prospects: Results are being positively affected by Co.'s aggressive acquisition strategy, as well as its ongoing efforts to increase the operating efficiencies of its new operations. During 2004, Co. completed 29 acquisitions, which added approximately 70,000 new customers. Co.'s acquisition strategy is primarily focused on smaller "tuck-in" acquisitions and growth ventures in and around its existing service territory. On Jan 31 2005, Co. announced that it has acquired the water and wastewater system assets of Bear Brook Village, which serves more than 130 residents and a golf course in Sussex County, NJ.

Financial Data
(US$ in Thousands)

	12/31/2004	12/31/2003	12/31/2002	12/31/2001	12/31/2000	12/31/1999	12/31/1998	12/31/1997
Earnings Per Share	0.85	0.79	0.78	0.70	0.65	0.45	0.53	0.45
Cash Flow Per Share	1.86	1.62	1.42	1.20	1.07	0.93	1.03	0.83
Tang Book Value Per Share	7.64	7.12	5.81	5.53	5.13	4.58	4.28	3.57
Dividends Per Share	0.490	0.486	0.430	0.404	0.376	0.358	0.340	0.319
Dividend Payout %	57.65	61.52	55.41	57.99	58.12	79.55	64.56	70.74
Income Statement								
Total Revenue	442,039	367,233	322,028	307,280	275,538	257,326	150,977	136,171
EBITDA	239,674	212,843	193,970	179,114	161,455	128,516	85,030	73,658
Depn & Amortn	58,864	51,463	44,322	40,168	34,100	31,903	17,630	16,707
Income Before Taxes	132,131	116,718	109,252	99,087	86,995	62,915	48,424	39,061
Income Taxes	52,124	45,923	42,046	38,976	34,105	26,531	19,605	15,873
Net Income	80,007	70,795	67,206	60,111	52,890	36,384	28,819	23,188
Average Shares	94,282	89,244	86,538	85,943	81,767	80,673	54,445	51,314
Balance Sheet								
Net PPE	2,069,812	1,824,291	1,486,703	1,368,115	1,251,427	1,135,364	609,808	534,483
Total Assets	2,340,248	2,069,736	1,717,069	1,560,339	1,414,010	1,280,805	701,450	618,472
Long-Term Obligations	784,461	696,666	582,910	516,520	468,769	413,752	261,826	232,471
Total Liabilities	1,591,780	1,410,706	1,223,972	1,086,506	981,663	911,904	466,691	423,727
Stockholders' Equity	748,468	659,030	493,097	473,833	432,347	368,901	234,759	194,745
Shares Outstanding	95,384	92,589	84,895	85,483	83,868	80,102	54,154	53,712
Statistical Record								
Return on Assets %	3.62	3.74	4.10	4.04	3.91	3.67	4.37	3.86
Return on Equity %	11.34	12.29	13.90	13.27	13.17	12.05	13.42	12.37
EBITDA Margin %	54.22	57.96	60.23	58.29	58.60	49.94	56.32	54.09
Net Margin %	18.10	19.28	20.87	19.56	19.20	14.14	19.09	17.03
PPE Turnover	0.23	0.22	0.23	0.23	0.23	0.29	0.26	0.26
Asset Turnover	0.20	0.19	0.20	0.21	0.20	0.26	0.23	0.23
Debt to Equity	1.05	1.06	1.18	1.09	1.08	1.12	1.12	1.19
Price Range	24.59-18.91	22.25-15.77	19.98-13.02	19.39-12.80	15.88-8.64	15.14-10.30	15.23-9.76	11.30-6.00
P/E Ratio	28.93-22.25	28.16-19.96	25.62-16.70	27.69-18.29	24.43-13.29	33.64-22.90	28.74-18.42	25.12-13.33
Average Yield %	2.30	2.61	2.54	2.51	3.33	3.02	2.88	3.96

Address: 762 W. Lancaster Avenue, Bryn Mawr, PA 19010-3489	Web Site: www.suburbanwater.com	Auditors: PricewaterhouseCoopers LLP
Telephone: (610) 524-8000	Officers: Nicholas DeBenedictis - Chmn., Pres. Roy H. Stahl - Exec. V.P., Sec., Gen. Couns.	Investor Contact: 610-525-1400
Fax: (610) 645-1061		Transfer Agents: BankBoston, N.A., Boston, MA

AQUILA INC (NEW) (DE)

Exchange	Symbol	Price	52Wk Range	Yield	P/E
NYS	ILA	$3.83 (3/31/2005)	4.75-2.34	N/A	N/A

*7 Year Price Score 18.84 ***NYSE Composite Index=100** ***12 Month Price Score 98.38**

Interim Earnings (Per Share)

Qtr.	Mar	Jun	Sep	Dec
2001	0.69	1.21	0.58	(0.08)
2002	0.32	(5.69)	(1.85)	(5.66)
2003	(0.27)	(0.41)	(0.87)	(0.18)
2004	(0.26)	(0.22)	(0.44)	(0.17)

Interim Dividends (Per Share)

Dividend Payment Suspended

Valuation Analysis

Forecast P/E	N/A	No of Institutions	
Market Cap	$925.9 Million	Shares	
Book Value	1.1 Billion	178,879,856	
Price/Book	0.82	% Held	
Price/Sales	0.54	73.99	

Business Summary: Electricity (MIC: 7.1 SIC: 931 NAIC: 21122)

Aquila is an energy service provider that manages its business in two operating segments: Domestic Utilities and Merchant Services. Co.'s Domestic Utilities business serves 446,000 electric distribution customers in Missouri, Kansas and Colorado; and 901,000 natural gas distribution customers in Missouri, Kansas, Colorado, Nebraska, Iowa, Michigan and Minnesota. Co.'s Merchant Services business includes remaining investments in non-regulated merchant power plants, commitments under merchant capacity tolling obligations and long-term gas contracts, and remaining contracts from wholesale energy trading operations.

Recent Developments: For the year ended Dec 31 2004, net loss was $292,500 thousand versus net loss of $336,400 thousand a year earlier. Revenues were $3,422,000 thousand, up 2.2% from $3,348,000 thousand the year before. Total direct expense was $1,214,200 thousand versus $1,124,100 thousand in the prior year, an increase of 8.0%. Total indirect expense was $823,000 thousand versus $937,200 thousand in the prior year, a decrease of 12.2%.

Prospects: Co. reported a narrower fully diluted loss of $1.13 per share for the year ended Dec 31 2004, compared with a loss of $1.73 per fully diluted share in 2003. Co. believes that while it strengthened its credit profile, improved cash flow, increased operational efficiency and completed several rate cases during fiscal 2004, it is not satisfied with the progress it has made on mitigating its utility earnings volatility created by weather and fuel costs. For fiscal 2005, Co. will continue to focus on providing safe and reliable service to its customers and to mitigate earnings volatility factors. Also, Co. is initiating a new repositioning plan to further enhance shareholder value.

Financial Data (US$ in Thousands)	12/31/2004	12/31/2003	12/31/2002	12/31/2001	12/31/2000	12/31/1999	12/31/1998	12/31/1997
Earnings Per Share	(1.13)	(1.73)	(12.83)	2.42	2.21	1.75	1.63	1.51
Cash Flow Per Share	(1.35)	(0.68)	(1.84)	2.00	8.47	5.19	3.46	4.34
Tang Book Value Per Share	4.22	6.39	6.75	22.01	16.94	16.30	15.82	14.49
Dividends Per Share	...	...	0.775	1.200	1.200	1.200	1.200	1.173
Dividend Payout %	...	...	...	49.59	54.30	68.57	73.62	77.87
Income Statement								
Total Revenue	1,711,000	1,674,000	2,377,100	41,272,700	28,974,900	18,621,500	12,563,400	8,926,300
EBITDA	(153,800)	(45,900)	(1,370,400)	977,600	765,000	607,700	501,400	488,700
Depn & Amortn	150,300	173,300	238,000	272,900	225,000	193,700	150,000	129,600
Income Before Taxes	(562,500)	(492,300)	(1,857,900)	481,600	325,000	228,700	218,800	223,800
Income Taxes	(213,300)	(141,700)	(135,100)	202,200	118,200	68,200	86,600	89,700
Net Income	(292,500)	(336,400)	(2,075,100)	279,400	206,800	160,500	132,200	122,100
Average Shares	251,350	194,750	161,720	115,710	93,750	92,110	81,180	81,000
Balance Sheet								
Current Assets	1,548,800	2,718,800	4,074,200	4,807,400	6,868,600	2,272,200	1,765,400	1,614,400
Total Assets	4,777,300	7,719,100	9,259,200	11,948,300	14,115,600	7,538,600	5,991,500	5,113,500
Current Liabilities	854,400	2,261,300	3,596,900	5,677,700	7,484,400	2,344,700	2,092,700	1,809,900
Long-Term Obligations	2,329,900	2,291,200	2,398,000	1,747,900	2,345,900	2,202,300	1,375,800	1,358,600
Total Liabilities	3,646,800	6,359,800	7,651,300	9,146,700	11,866,000	5,663,200	4,445,200	3,849,900
Stockholders' Equity	1,130,500	1,359,300	1,607,900	2,551,600	1,799,600	1,525,400	1,446,300	1,163,600
Shares Outstanding	241,739	195,252	193,775	115,941	100,310	93,605	91,416	80,278
Statistical Record								
Return on Assets %	N.M.	N.M.	N.M.	2.14	1.90	2.37	2.38	2.49
Return on Equity %	N.M.	N.M.	N.M.	12.84	12.41	10.80	10.13	10.52
EBITDA Margin %	N.M.	N.M.	N.M.	2.37	2.64	3.26	3.99	5.47
Net Margin %	N.M.	N.M.	N.M.	0.68	0.71	0.86	1.05	1.37
Asset Turnover	0.27	0.20	0.22	3.17	2.67	2.75	2.26	1.82
Current Ratio	1.81	1.20	1.13	0.85	0.92	0.97	0.84	0.89
Debt to Equity	2.06	1.69	1.49	0.69	1.30	1.44	0.95	1.17
Price Range	4.75-2.34	4.25-1.12	26.70-1.58	37.55-22.48	31.00-15.31	25.56-18.69	26.46-22.63	26.00-16.83
P/E Ratio	...	...	...	15.52-9.29	14.03-6.93	14.61-10.68	16.23-13.88	17.22-11.15
Average Yield %	...	...	6.43	3.94	5.41	5.24	4.91	6.01

Address: 20 West Ninth Street, Kansas City, MO 64105	Web Site: www.aquila.com	Auditors: KPMG LLP
Telephone: (816) 421-6600	Officers: Richard C. Green Jr. - Chmn., Pres., C.E.O.	Investor Contact: 816-421-6600
Fax: (816) 467-3435	Keith G. Stamm - Sr. V.P., C.O.O.	

ARAMARK CORP. (NEW)

Exchange	Symbol	Price	52Wk Range	Yield	P/E
NYS	RMK	$26.28 (3/31/2005)	29.11-21.82	0.84	18.91

*7 Year Price Score N/A   ***NYSE Composite Index=100**   ***12 Month Price Score 95.21**

TRADING VOLUME (thousand shares)

Interim Earnings (Per Share)

Qtr.	Dec	Mar	Jun	Sep
2001-02	0.27	0.31	0.32	0.44
2002-03	0.31	0.19	0.33	0.51
2003-04	0.35	0.24	0.33	0.44
2004-05	0.38	...	...	...

Interim Dividends (Per Share)

Amt	Decl	Ex	Rec	Pay
0.05Q	5/4/2004	5/12/2004	5/14/2004	6/10/2004
0.05Q	8/3/2004	8/11/2004	8/13/2004	9/9/2004
0.055Q	11/2/2004	11/9/2004	11/12/2004	12/9/2004
0.055Q	2/8/2005	2/16/2005	2/18/2005	3/11/2005

Indicated Div: $0.22

Valuation Analysis

Forecast P/E	N/A	No of Institutions
Market Cap	$4.9 Billion	Shares
Book Value	1.2 Billion	116,713,144
Price/Book	4.03	% Held
Price/Sales	0.46	N/A

Business Summary: Hospitality & Tourism (MIC: 5.1 SIC: 812 NAIC: 12331)

Aramark is a provider of a range of outsourced services to business, educational, healthcare and governmental institutions and sports, entertainment and recreational facilities. Co.'s food and support services group operates in the U.S., Canada, U.K., Germany, Spain, Mexico and Korea and, in Japan and Ireland, through its ownership of minority interests in large food service providers. Co.'s uniforms and career apparel services group provides a range of uniform services to its clients across product lines and across the U.S. Co.'s Educational Resources business provides childcare services in the U.S., serving children and their families in 28 states and the District of Columbia.

Recent Developments: For the quarter ended Dec 31 2004, net income increased 7.6% to $72,446 thousand from net income of $67,352 thousand in the year-earlier quarter. Revenues were $2,730,233 thousand, up 11.0% from $2,458,857 thousand the year before. Operating income was $143,964 thousand versus an income of $137,421 thousand in the prior-year quarter, an increase of 4.8%. Total direct expense was $2,474,763 thousand versus $2,221,504 thousand in the prior-year quarter, an increase of 11.4%. Total indirect expense was $111,506 thousand versus $99,932 thousand in the prior-year quarter, an increase of 11.6%.

Prospects: Co. continues to perform well despite the negative impact of the National Hockey League (NHL) lockout, for which Co. provides concessions and facilities management. Areas in which Co. is seeing continued strength include the healthcare and educational businesses in the U.S., uniform and career apparel and international food and support services. Going forward, Co. expects second-quarter earnings of $0.25 to $0.27 a share, on sales of $2.50 billion to $2.70 billion, including the impact of the NHL lockout. Previously, Co. expected a continuation of the lockout to reduce earnings by $0.20 a share for each of the first and second quarters.

Financial Data
(US$ in Thousands)

	3 Mos	10/01/2004	10/03/2003	09/27/2002	09/28/2001	09/29/2000	10/01/1999
Earnings Per Share	1.39	1.36	1.52	1.34	0.97	0.88	0.74
Cash Flow Per Share	3.21	2.75	3.13	3.33	2.90	2.28	...
Dividends Per Share	0.205	0.200	...	...	...	...	...
Dividend Payout %	14.71	14.71	...	...	...	...	...
Income Statement							
Total Revenue	2,730,233	10,192,240	9,447,815	8,769,841	7,788,690	7,262,867	6,742,264
EBITDA	190,344	810,478	803,122	801,267	679,750	640,377	568,869
Depn & Amortn	77,655	272,900	251,100	241,000	240,243	220,794	193,703
Income Before Taxes	112,689	415,216	409,553	423,608	286,215	271,780	239,413
Income Taxes	40,243	152,112	144,185	153,696	109,719	103,820	89,222
Net Income	72,446	263,104	301,092	269,912	176,496	167,960	150,191
Average Shares	188,838	193,454	197,505	200,924	181,327	190,214	202,944
Balance Sheet							
Current Assets	1,343,319	1,340,015	1,226,592	1,098,392	1,020,198	1,098,865	...
Total Assets	4,993,909	4,821,573	4,467,577	4,259,302	3,216,394	3,199,383	...
Current Liabilities	1,250,237	1,454,930	1,415,789	1,303,562	1,084,151	1,066,860	...
Long-Term Obligations	2,052,444	1,843,200	1,711,705	1,835,713	1,635,867	177,660	...
Total Liabilities	3,789,929	3,671,918	3,428,605	3,401,117	2,969,502	1,487,887	...
Stockholders' Equity	1,203,980	1,149,655	1,038,972	858,185	246,892	111,496	...
Shares Outstanding	184,743	182,525	184,245	187,000	167,239	124,450	...
Statistical Record							
Return on Assets %	5.67	5.68	6.79	7.24	5.52	...	...
Return on Equity %	23.35	24.11	31.23	48.98	98.76	...	...
EBITDA Margin %	6.97	7.95	8.50	9.14	8.73	8.82	8.44
Net Margin %	2.65	2.58	3.19	3.08	2.27	2.31	2.23
Asset Turnover	2.21	2.20	2.13	2.35	2.43	...	...
Current Ratio	1.07	0.92	0.87	0.84	0.94	1.03	...
Debt to Equity	1.70	1.60	1.65	2.14	6.63	1.59	...
Price Range	29.11-21.82	29.11-22.68	26.05-18.75	28.05-19.10	...	...	...
P/E Ratio	20.94-15.70	21.40-16.68	17.14-12.34	20.93-14.25	...	...	...
Average Yield %	0.78	0.75	...	...	...	...	...

Address: ARAMARK Tower, 1101 Market Street, Philadelphia, PA 19107 **Telephone:** (215) 238-3000	**Web Site:** www.ARAMARK.com **Officers:** Joseph Neubauer - Chmn., C.E.O. L. Frederick Sutherland - Exec. V.P., C.F.O.	**Auditors:** KPMG LLP **Investor Contact:** 215-238-3361 **Transfer Agents:** Mellon Investor Services LLC, South Hackensack, NJ

ARCH COAL, INC.

Exchange	Symbol	Price	52Wk Range	Yield	P/E
NYS	ACI	$43.01 (3/31/2005)	46.35-28.07	0.74	24.16

*7 Year Price Score 145.63 *NYSE Composite Index=100 *12 Month Price Score 111.91

Interim Earnings (Per Share)

Qtr.	Mar	Jun	Sep	Dec
2001	0.15	0.02	(0.15)	0.18
2002	(0.14)	0.04	0.03	0.02
2003	(0.34)	(0.06)	0.18	0.42
2004	1.14	0.17	0.16	0.30

Interim Dividends (Per Share)

Amt	Decl	Ex	Rec	Pay
0.08Q	4/22/2004	6/2/2004	6/4/2004	6/15/2004
0.08Q	7/23/2004	9/1/2004	9/3/2004	9/15/2004
0.08Q	11/11/2004	12/1/2004	12/3/2004	12/15/2004
0.08Q	2/24/2005	3/2/2005	3/4/2005	3/15/2005
		Indicated Div: $0.32		

Valuation Analysis

Forecast P/E	23.37	No of Institutions
	(4/7/2005)	243
Market Cap	$2.7 Billion	Shares
Book Value	1.1 Billion	59,666,344
Price/Book	2.48	% Held
Price/Sales	1.40	95.13

TRADING VOLUME (thousand shares)

Business Summary: Coal Mining (MIC: 14.4 SIC: 221 NAIC: 12111)

Arch Coal mines, processes and markets compliance and low-sulfur coal from mines located in both the eastern and western U.S. As of Dec 31 2004, Co. had 27 operating mines and controlled about 3.70 billion tons of proven and probable coal reserves. Co. sells substantially all of its coal to producers of electric power, steel producers and industrial facilities. Co. owns a 99.0% equity interest in Arch Western Resources, a joint venture. The operating units of Arch Western are Thunder Basin Coal, which operates mines in Wyoming; Mountain Coal, which operates a mine in Colorado; Canyon Fuel, which operates three mines in Utah; and Arch of Wyoming, which operates two mines in Wyoming.

Recent Developments: For the year ended Dec 31 2004, net income increased 581.4% to $113,706 thousand from net income of $16,686 thousand a year earlier. Revenues were $2,087,575 thousand, up 31.1% from $1,592,237 thousand the year before. Operating income was $178,046 thousand versus an income of $40,371 thousand in the prior year, an increase of 341.0%. Total direct expense was $1,638,284 thousand versus $1,280,608 thousand in the prior year, an increase of 27.9%. Total indirect expense was $260,417 thousand versus $236,868 thousand in the prior year, an increase of 9.9%.

Prospects: Going forward, Co. should benefit from the growing coal market in the U.S. and abroad. For the full year 2005, Co. expects earnings per share between $1.50 and $2.00. This guidance assumes that rail performance will be constrained during the first half of 2005 and that it will improve gradually thereafter. Meanwhile, due to geologic challenges at the Mingo Logan mine in January 2005 as well as rail disruptions, Co. expects first quarter results to be weaker than subsequent quarters. Total sales volume for 2005 is expected to be in the range of 140.0 million to 150.0 million tons, with average realizations on already committed and priced tons increasing by about 10.0%.

Financial Data (US$ in Thousands)	12/31/2004	12/31/2003	12/31/2002	12/31/2001	12/31/2000	12/31/1999	12/31/1998	12/31/1997
Earnings Per Share	1.78	0.19	(0.05)	0.15	(0.33)	(9.02)	0.76	1.00
Cash Flow Per Share	2.62	3.09	3.37	2.99	3.55	7.29	4.74	6.26
Tang Book Value Per Share	16.77	12.81	9.07	9.35	2.91	2.34	10.57	10.75
Dividends Per Share	0.297	0.230	0.230	0.230	0.230	0.460	0.460	0.230
Dividend Payout %	16.71	121.05	...	153.33	...	...	60.53	23.00
Income Statement								
Total Revenue	1,907,168	1,435,488	1,534,139	1,488,728	1,404,621	1,567,382	1,505,635	1,066,873
EBITDA	349,083	102,449	204,029	239,960	275,496	(91,368)	292,154	185,514
Depn & Amortn	179,003	57,822	174,752	177,504	201,512	235,658	204,307	143,632
Income Before Taxes	113,576	(2,870)	(21,562)	2,509	(16,736)	(415,793)	26,401	24,781
Income Taxes	(130)	(23,210)	(19,000)	(4,700)	(4,000)	(65,700)	(5,100)	(5,500)
Net Income	113,706	16,686	(2,562)	7,209	(12,736)	(346,280)	30,013	30,281
Average Shares	63,734	52,885	52,374	48,918	38,164	38,392	39,651	30,408
Balance Sheet								
Current Assets	730,857	513,645	291,713	289,456	277,890	285,952	353,334	243,178
Total Assets	3,256,535	2,387,649	2,182,808	2,203,559	2,232,614	2,332,374	2,918,220	1,656,324
Current Liabilities	375,054	276,638	253,914	239,643	315,446	340,920	333,158	202,274
Long-Term Obligations	1,001,323	700,022	740,242	775,565	1,102,014	1,094,993	1,309,087	248,425
Total Liabilities	2,176,709	1,699,614	1,647,945	1,632,817	2,012,740	2,091,079	2,300,004	1,044,826
Stockholders' Equity	1,079,826	688,035	534,863	570,742	219,874	241,295	618,216	611,498
Shares Outstanding	62,143	53,204	52,434	52,352	38,173	38,164	39,371	39,657
Statistical Record								
Return on Assets %	4.02	0.73	N.M.	0.33	N.M.	N.M.	1.31	2.38
Return on Equity %	12.83	2.73	N.M.	1.82	N.M.	N.M.	4.88	8.16
EBITDA Margin %	18.30	7.14	13.30	16.12	19.61	N.M.	19.40	17.39
Net Margin %	5.96	1.16	N.M.	0.48	N.M.	N.M.	1.99	2.84
Asset Turnover	0.67	0.63	0.70	0.67	0.61	0.60	0.66	0.84
Current Ratio	1.95	1.86	1.15	1.21	0.88	0.84	1.06	1.20
Debt to Equity	0.93	1.02	1.38	1.36	5.01	4.54	2.12	0.41
Price Range	38.23-26.61	31.87-16.35	24.40-14.97	37.67-13.31	14.44-4.81	17.13-8.75	28.88-14.75	30.38-23.75
P/E Ratio	21.48-14.95	167.74-86.05	...	251.13-88.75	...	...	37.99-19.41	30.38-23.75
Average Yield %	0.92	1.04	1.17	1.01	2.66	3.64	2.03	0.84

Address: One CityPlace Drive, Suite 300, St. Louis, MO 63141 **Telephone:** (314) 994-2700 **Fax:** (314) 994-2878	**Web Site:** www.archcoal.com **Officers:** James R. Boyd - Chmn. Steven F. Leer - Pres., C.E.O.	**Auditors:** Ernst & Young LLP **Investor Contact:** 314-994-2717 **Transfer Agents:** American Stock Transfer & Trust Company, New York,

ARCHER DANIELS MIDLAND CO.

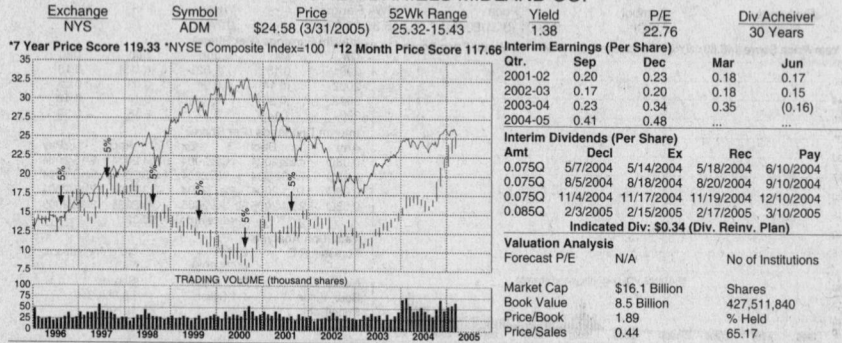

Exchange	Symbol	Price	52Wk Range	Yield	P/E	Div Acheiver
NYS	ADM	$24.58 (3/31/2005)	25.32-15.43	1.38	22.76	30 Years

*7 Year Price Score 119.33 *NYSE Composite Index=100 *12 Month Price Score 117.66

Interim Earnings (Per Share)

Qtr.	Sep	Dec	Mar	Jun
2001-02	0.20	0.23	0.18	0.17
2002-03	0.17	0.20	0.18	0.15
2003-04	0.23	0.34	0.35	(0.16)
2004-05	0.41	0.48	...	...

Interim Dividends (Per Share)

Amt	Decl	Ex	Rec	Pay
0.075Q	5/7/2004	5/14/2004	5/18/2004	6/10/2004
0.075Q	8/5/2004	8/18/2004	8/20/2004	9/10/2004
0.075Q	11/4/2004	11/17/2004	11/19/2004	12/10/2004
0.085Q	2/3/2005	2/15/2005	2/17/2005	3/10/2005

Indicated Div: $0.34 (Div. Reinv. Plan)

Valuation Analysis

Forecast P/E	N/A		No of Institutions
Market Cap	$16.1 Billion	Shares	
Book Value	8.5 Billion		427,511,840
Price/Book	1.89	% Held	
Price/Sales	0.44		65.17

Business Summary: Food (MIC: 4.1 SIC: 075 NAIC: 11225)

Archer-Daniels-Midland is engaged in procuring, transporting, storing, processing and merchandising agricultural commodities and products. Co.'s operations are classified into three business segments. The Oilseeds Processing segment includes processing oilseeds, such as soybeans, cottonseed, sunflower seeds, canola, peanuts, and flaxseed into vegetable oils and meals. The Corn Processing segment includes the production of syrups, starches, dextros and sweeteners used in the food and beverage industry. The Agricultural Services segment buys, stores, cleans and transports agricultural commodities. The Other segment consists of food and feed ingredient businesses and financial activities.

Recent Developments: For the quarter ended Dec 31 2004, net income increased 42.0% to $313,509 thousand from net income of $220,821 thousand in the year-earlier quarter. Revenues were $9,063,526 thousand, down 1.4% from $9,188,504 thousand the year before. Total direct expense was $8,394,818 thousand versus $8,584,210 thousand in the prior-year quarter, a decrease of 2.2%. Total indirect expense was $269,741 thousand versus $265,641 thousand in the prior-year quarter, an increase of 1.5%.

Prospects: On Feb 15 2004, Co. announced that it acquired The Solae Company's global soy isoflavone business, which includes an extensive portfolio of U.S. patents, numerous foreign equivalents, and pending applications. Terms of the transaction were not disclosed. Meanwhile, Co. continues to enjoy favorable earnings growth, despite slightly lower sales. Specifically, Co.'s Oilseeds Processing segment is being hampered by decreased business in its North and South American operations. Also, in Co.'s Corn Processing segment, lower operating profit is largely due to higher net corn and energy costs as compared to last year.

Financial Data

(US$ in Thousands)	6 Mos	3 Mos	06/30/2004	06/30/2003	06/30/2002	06/30/2001	06/30/2000	06/30/1999
Earnings Per Share	1.08	0.94	0.76	0.70	0.78	0.58	0.45	0.39
Cash Flow Per Share	2.84	1.33	0.05	1.67	2.31	1.30	1.21	1.78
Tang Book Value Per Share	12.48	11.56	11.31	10.43	10.39	9.56	9.39	9.13
Dividends Per Share	0.300	0.285	0.270	0.240	0.198	0.188	0.179	0.171
Dividend Payout %	27.88	30.44	35.53	34.29	25.34	32.45	40.05	43.77
Income Statement								
Total Revenue	18,035,937	8,972,411	36,151,394	30,708,033	23,453,561	20,051,421	12,876,817	14,283,335
EBITDA	1,338,995	632,433	1,749,860	1,639,670	1,688,963	1,542,004	1,378,280	1,368,221
Depn & Amortn	337,086	167,447	689,858	648,726	614,070	621,974	647,639	622,181
Income Before Taxes	840,299	385,937	718,011	630,973	718,937	521,899	353,237	419,833
Income Taxes	260,493	119,640	223,301	179,828	207,844	138,615	52,334	138,545
Net Income	579,806	266,297	494,710	451,145	511,093	383,284	300,903	265,964
Average Shares	654,985	652,325	647,698	646,086	656,955	664,507	669,279	685,328
Balance Sheet								
Current Assets	10,083,993	9,854,313	10,338,996	8,421,857	7,363,231	6,150,301	6,162,367	5,789,588
Total Assets	19,375,223	18,893,383	19,368,821	17,182,879	15,416,273	14,339,931	14,423,100	14,029,881
Current Liabilities	5,793,611	6,138,694	6,750,237	5,147,472	4,719,297	3,866,981	4,332,945	3,840,265
Long-Term Obligations	3,695,432	3,690,147	3,739,875	3,872,287	3,111,294	3,351,067	3,277,218	3,191,883
Total Liabilities	10,844,527	10,989,927	11,670,605	10,113,682	8,661,452	8,008,248	8,312,857	7,789,241
Stockholders' Equity	8,530,696	7,903,456	7,698,216	7,069,197	6,754,821	6,331,683	6,110,243	6,240,640
Shares Outstanding	655,953	654,512	650,935	644,855	649,993	662,378	650,682	683,340
Statistical Record								
Return on Assets %	3.57	3.33	2.70	2.77	3.44	2.67	2.11	1.91
Return on Equity %	8.69	8.05	6.68	6.53	7.81	6.16	4.86	4.17
EBITDA Margin %	7.42	7.05	4.84	5.34	7.20	7.69	10.70	9.58
Net Margin %	3.21	2.97	1.37	1.47	2.18	1.91	2.34	1.86
Asset Turnover	1.88	2.03	1.97	1.88	1.58	1.39	0.90	1.03
Current Ratio	1.74	1.61	1.53	1.64	1.56	1.59	1.42	1.51
Debt to Equity	0.43	0.47	0.49	0.55	0.46	0.53	0.54	0.51
Price Range	22.36-14.95	17.59-13.11	17.59-12.08	14.28-10.54	15.60-12.00	15.20-7.92	13.34-8.22	16.25-11.99
P/E Ratio	20.70-13.84	18.71-13.95	23.14-15.89	20.40-15.06	20.00-15.38	26.21-13.65	29.63-18.27	41.66-30.73
Average Yield %	1.73	1.79	1.78	1.98	1.44	1.65	1.66	1.23

Address: 4666 Faries Parkway, Box 1470, Decatur, IL 62525 Telephone: (217) 424-5200 Fax: (217) 424-5381	Web Site: www.admworld.com Officers: G. Allen Andreas - Chmn., C.E.O. Paul B. Mulhollem - Pres., C.O.O.	Auditors: ERNST & YOUNG LLP Investor Contact: 217-424-4647 Transfer Agents: Hickory Point Bank & Trust, fsb, Decatur, IL

ARCHSTONE SMITH TRUST

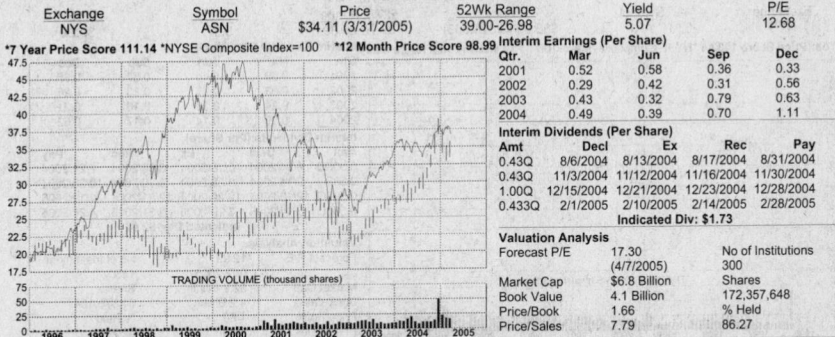

Exchange	Symbol	Price	52Wk Range	Yield	P/E
NYS	ASN	$34.11 (3/31/2005)	39.00-26.98	5.07	12.68

*7 Year Price Score 111.14 *NYSE Composite Index=100 *12 Month Price Score 98.99

Interim Earnings (Per Share)

Qtr.	Mar	Jun	Sep	Dec
2001	0.52	0.58	0.36	0.33
2002	0.29	0.42	0.31	0.56
2003	0.43	0.32	0.79	0.63
2004	0.49	0.39	0.70	1.11

Interim Dividends (Per Share)

Amt	Decl	Ex	Rec	Pay
0.43Q	8/6/2004	8/13/2004	8/17/2004	8/31/2004
0.43Q	11/3/2004	11/12/2004	11/16/2004	11/30/2004
1.00Q	12/15/2004	12/21/2004	12/23/2004	12/28/2004
0.433Q	2/1/2005	2/10/2005	2/14/2005	2/28/2005

Indicated Div: $1.73

Valuation Analysis

Forecast P/E	17.30	No of Institutions
	(4/7/2005)	300
Market Cap	$6.8 Billion	Shares
Book Value	4.1 Billion	172,357,648
Price/Book	1.66	% Held
Price/Sales	7.79	86.27

TRADING VOLUME (thousand shares)

Business Summary: Property, Real Estate & Development (MIC: 8.3 SIC: 798 NAIC: 25930)

Archstone-Smith Trust is a major owner, developer, acquirer and operator of apartments in protected locations in major metropolitan areas across the country. Co. has divisional offices in Arlington, VA, Irvine, CA, and Atlanta, GA. As of Dec 31 2003, 88.5% of Co.'s wholly-owned operations portfolio was concentrated in Washington D.C., Boston, Chicago, California, Southeast Florida, Seattle and New York City. As of Dec 31 2003, Co.'s portfolio consisted of 249 garden-style and high-rise properties, representing a total of 88,183 units, including units under construction.

Recent Developments: For the year ended Dec 31 2004, income from continuing operations increased 46.4% to $155,318 thousand from income of $106,101 thousand a year earlier. Net income increased 25.1% to $542,342 thousand from net income of $433,657 thousand a year earlier. Revenues were $873,329 thousand, up 11.4% from $783,672 thousand the year before. Operating income was $131,797 thousand versus an income of $116,932 thousand in the prior year, an increase of 12.7%.

Prospects: On Mar 1 2005, Co. agreed to acquire 30 apartment communities, representing more than 10,000 units, for $1.40 billion. Co. noted that about 78.0% of the portfolio is concentrated in its core markets, including 40.0% in Southern California, 20.0% located in the Washington, D.C. and an additional 18.0% of the portfolio is located in the San Francisco Bay, CA area, Boston, MA, Chicago, IL and Seattle, WA. The transaction will occur in several stages, a majority of which should close late in the second quarter of 2005. The acquisition is expected to be accretive to earnings by about $0.03 per share on an annual basis and should increase 2005 funds from operations by about $0.015 per share.

Financial Data (US$ in Thousands)	12/31/2004	12/31/2003	12/31/2002	12/31/2001	12/31/2000	12/31/1999	12/31/1998	12/31/1997
Earnings Per Share	2.69	2.18	1.58	1.79	1.78	1.46	1.49	0.65
Cash Flow Per Share	1.88	1.87	2.84	2.37	2.44	2.02	1.87	1.95
Tang Book Value Per Share	20.26	20.52	19.64	17.49	15.23	16.33	16.44	14.04
Dividends Per Share	2.720	1.710	1.700	0.410	1.540	1.480	...	1.300
Dividend Payout %	101.12	78.44	107.59	22.91	86.52	101.37	...	200.00
Income Statement								
Property Income	854,121	881,041	1,070,824	716,168	691,119	637,808	484,539	335,060
Non-Property Income	19,208	19,334	11,467	12,769	32,115	29,064	29,106	20,602
Total Revenue	873,329	900,375	1,082,291	728,937	723,234	666,872	513,645	355,662
Depn & Amortn	227,000	210,427	205,994	135,682	145,571	133,817	96,908	54,541
Interest Expense	175,249	186,832	194,955	141,907	145,173	121,494	83,350	61,153
Net Income	542,342	433,657	315,063	257,878	261,385	228,259	197,960	72,918
Average Shares	199,233	195,640	178,780	137,832	137,730	139,829	125,825	90,230
Balance Sheet								
Total Assets	9,066,044	8,921,695	8,855,068	8,549,915	5,019,697	5,302,437	5,059,898	2,805,686
Long-Term Obligations	4,149,637	3,903,380	4,102,508	3,853,032	2,470,785	2,465,056	2,172,431	1,127,152
Total Liabilities	4,474,768	4,184,592	4,463,421	4,154,388	2,671,188	2,679,628	2,410,114	1,265,250
Stockholders' Equity	4,093,178	4,144,687	3,843,818	3,427,030	2,251,606	2,567,506	2,628,325	1,540,436
Shares Outstanding	199,577	194,762	180,705	174,516	122,838	139,008	143,313	92,634
Statistical Record								
Return on Assets %	6.01	4.88	3.62	3.80	5.05	4.41	5.03	2.87
Return on Equity %	13.13	10.86	8.67	9.08	10.82	8.79	9.50	5.19
Net Margin %	62.10	48.16	29.11	35.38	36.14	34.23	38.54	20.50
Price Range	39.00-26.82	28.12-20.95	28.91-21.75	27.67-23.28	26.44-19.31	23.31-19.00	24.38-18.06	24.94-21.23
P/E Ratio	14.50-9.97	12.90-9.61	18.30-13.77	15.46-13.01	14.85-10.85	15.97-13.01	16.36-12.12	38.37-32.67
Average Yield %	8.90	6.92	6.73	1.62	6.75	7.14	...	5.69

Address: 9200 E. Panorama Circle, Suite 400, Englewood, CO 80112	Web Site: www.archstonecommunities.com	Auditors: KPMG LLP
Telephone: (303) 708-5959	Officers: R. Scott Sellers - Chmn., C.E,O. Charles E. Mueller Jr. - Exec. V.P., C.F.O.	Investor Contact: 800-982-9293
Fax: (303) 708-5999		

ARDEN REALTY, INC.

Exchange	Symbol	Price	52Wk Range	Yield	P/E
NYS	ARI	$33.85 (3/31/2005)	37.72-26.89	5.97	30.22

*7 Year Price Score 108.14 *NYSE Composite Index=100 *12 Month Price Score 98.21

Interim Earnings (Per Share)

Qtr.	Mar	Jun	Sep	Dec
2001	0.38	0.44	0.37	0.35
2002	0.33	0.27	0.23	0.26
2003	0.24	0.30	0.16	0.21
2004	0.29	0.14	0.17	0.52

Interim Dividends (Per Share)

Amt	Decl	Ex	Rec	Pay
0.505Q	6/14/2004	6/28/2004	6/30/2004	7/21/2004
0.505Q	9/14/2004	9/28/2004	9/30/2004	10/20/2004
0.505Q	12/10/2004	12/29/2004	12/31/2004	1/19/2005
0.505Q	3/14/2005	3/29/2005	3/31/2005	4/20/2005
			Indicated Div: $2.02	

Valuation Analysis

Forecast P/E	12.95	No of Institutions	
	(4/7/2005)	145	
Market Cap	$2.2 Billion	Shares	
Book Value	1.2 Billion	61,570,164	
Price/Book	1.88	% Held	
Price/Sales	5.49	92.78	

Business Summary: Property, Real Estate & Development (MIC: 8.3 SIC: 512 NAIC: 31120)

Arden Realty is a self-administered and self-managed real estate investment trust that owns, manages, leases, develops, renovates and acquires commercial properties located in Southern California. Co. performs all property management, construction, accounting, finance and acquisition/disposition activities and a majority of its leasing transactions. As of Dec 31 2003, Co.'s portfolio contained 130 properties comprised of 215 buildings and approximately 18.9 million rentable square feet including one development property with approximately 283,000 rentable square feet under lease-up. As of Dec 31 2003, Co.'s properties were 90.4% occupied.

Recent Developments: For the year ended Dec 31 2004, income from continuing operations decreased 7.5% to $37,049 thousand from income of $40,034 thousand a year earlier. Net income increased 26.1% to $73,775 thousand from net income of $58,509 thousand a year earlier. Revenues were $409,193 thousand, up 3.9% from $393,765 thousand the year before.

Prospects: On Jan 5 2005, Co. announced the purchase of Washington Mutual Tower located at 707 Broadway in downtown San Diego for approximately $48.0 million from the Shidler Group. Also, Co. announced the sale of a portfolio of properties to the Shidler Group for approximately $142.7 million. Co. is pleased with the transactions, which confirms its commitment to its capital recycling program to continually upgrade its portfolio through the purchase of quality assets in highly desirable markets and the sale of non-core assets. Co. believes the 707 Broadway building complements its existing assets in the downtown San Diego submarket and expands its market position.

Financial Data

(US$ in Thousands)	12/31/2004	12/31/2003	12/31/2002	12/31/2001	12/31/2000	12/31/1999	12/31/1998	12/31/1997
Earnings Per Share	1.12	0.92	1.09	1.53	1.52	1.53	1.54	1.41
Cash Flow Per Share	2.82	2.86	3.34	3.21	3.02	2.46	2.45	1.26
Tang Book Value Per Share	18.04	18.79	19.80	20.86	21.29	21.71	22.01	18.80
Dividends Per Share	2.020	2.020	2.020	1.960	1.860	1.780	1.680	1.600
Dividend Payout %	180.36	219.57	185.32	128.10	122.37	116.34	109.09	113.48
Income Statement								
Total Revenue	409,193	413,535	412,054	418,525	384,590	337,853	281,067	133,817
Depn & Amortn	134,143	126,539	116,424	107,325	91,421	72,705	53,763	21,083
Net Income	73,775	58,509	70,175	97,759	96,710	96,626	90,675	39,630
Average Shares	65,740	63,815	64,351	64,014	63,598	63,072	58,814	28,039
Balance Sheet								
Current Assets	33,781	28,089	27,478	78,989	51,758	51,201	40,340	33,973
Total Assets	2,659,997	2,741,433	2,832,409	2,761,443	2,705,597	2,570,458	2,331,919	1,284,004
Current Liabilities	117,207	109,173	108,157	94,093	86,481	78,750	61,830	37,482
Long-Term Obligations	1,326,084	1,349,781	1,402,304	1,251,483	1,177,769	1,029,656	840,477	477,566
Total Liabilities	1,443,291	1,458,954	1,510,461	1,345,576	1,264,250	1,108,406	902,307	515,048
Stockholders' Equity	1,196,292	1,210,285	1,247,377	1,337,206	1,355,171	1,375,758	1,373,390	672,983
Shares Outstanding	66,325	64,425	62,984	64,098	63,646	63,358	62,408	35,797
Statistical Record								
Return on Assets %	2.72	2.10	2.51	3.58	3.66	3.94	5.02	4.32
Return on Equity %	6.11	4.76	5.43	7.26	7.06	7.03	8.86	7.89
Net Margin %	18.03	14.15	17.03	23.36	25.15	28.60	32.26	29.62
Asset Turnover	0.15	0.15	0.15	0.15	0.15	0.14	0.16	0.15
Current Ratio	0.29	0.26	0.25	0.84	0.60	0.65	0.65	0.91
Debt to Equity	1.11	1.12	1.12	0.94	0.87	0.75	0.61	0.71
Price Range	37.72-26.89	30.34-20.62	29.56-21.00	27.89-22.95	27.06-19.56	26.75-17.75	30.88-19.94	32.25-23.75
P/E Ratio	33.68-24.01	32.98-22.41	27.12-19.27	18.23-15.00	17.80-12.87	17.48-11.60	20.05-12.95	22.87-16.84
Average Yield %	6.36	7.82	7.98	7.82	7.90	7.87	6.62	5.72

Address: 11601 Wilshire Blvd., 4th floor, Los Angeles, CA 90025-1740 **Telephone:** (310) 966-2600 **Fax:** (310) 966-2699	**Web Site:** www.ardenrealty.com **Officers:** Richard S. Ziman - Chmn., C.E.O. Victor J. Coleman - Pres., C.O.O.	**Auditors:** Ernst & Young LLP **Investor Contact:** 310-966-2600

ARROW ELECTRONICS, INC.

Exchange	Symbol	Price	52Wk Range	Yield	P/E
NYS	ARW	$25.35 (3/31/2005)	28.46-20.84	N/A	14.49

*7 Year Price Score 90.70   ***NYSE Composite Index=100**   ***12 Month Price Score 98.59**

Interim Earnings (Per Share)

Qtr.	Mar	Jun	Sep	Dec
2001	0.68	0.07	(1.61)	0.07
2002	0.03	(0.06)	(0.11)	0.16
2003	(0.01)	0.07	(0.06)	0.25
2004	0.27	0.55	0.52	0.39

Interim Dividends (Per Share)

No Dividends Paid

Valuation Analysis

Forecast P/E	11.13	No of Institutions	
	(4/7/2005)	196	
Market Cap	$2.9 Billion	Shares	
Book Value	2.2 Billion	109,012,904	
Price/Book	1.34	% Held	
Price/Sales	0.28	93.34	

Business Summary: IT & Technology (MIC: 10.2 SIC: 065 NAIC: 23690)

Arrow Electronics is a global provider of products and services to industrial and commercial users of electronic components and computer products. Co.'s worldwide customer base consists of original equipment manufacturers (OEMs), contract manufacturers, and commercial customers. OEMs include manufacturers of computer and office products, industrial equipment (including machine tools, factory automation, and robotic equipment), telecommunications products, aircraft and aerospace equipment, and scientific and medical devices. Commercial customers are mainly value-added resellers and OEMs of computer systems.

Recent Developments: For the year ended Dec 31 2004, net income increased 707.4% to $207,504 thousand from net income of $25,700 thousand a year earlier. Revenues were $10,646,113 thousand, up 24.8% from $8,528,331 thousand the year before. Operating income was $439,338 thousand versus an income of $184,045 thousand in the prior year, an increase of 138.7%. Total direct expense was $8,922,962 thousand versus $7,107,378 thousand in the prior year, an increase of 25.5%. Total indirect expense was $1,283,813 thousand versus $1,236,908 thousand in the prior year, an increase of 3.8%.

Prospects: Going forward, Co. expects to take restructuring charges of $7.5 million in 2005, reflecting its efforts to optimize use of its mainframe, reduce real estate costs, improve efficiency in its distribution centers, and increase productivity. Co. expects the actions to reduce costs by about $50.0 million annually, with $40.0 million to be realized in 2005. For the first quarter, Co. expects revenues to be in the range of $2.73 billion to $2.83 billion, with earnings per share between $0.52 and $0.56 per share, excluding charges. Separately, in Feb 2005, Co. announced its intention to provide services to contractors to the Federal government, primarily in the defense and aerospace sectors.

Financial Data (US$ in Thousands)	12/31/2004	12/31/2003	12/31/2002	12/31/2001	12/31/2000	12/31/1999	12/31/1998	12/31/1997
Earnings Per Share	1.75	0.25	(6.04)	(0.75)	3.62	1.29	1.50	1.64
Cash Flow Per Share	1.65	2.91	6.69	17.05	(3.47)	(0.35)	0.46	(0.14)
Tang Book Value Per Share	10.49	5.76	4.85	5.43	6.88	6.15	8.01	7.38
Income Statement								
Total Revenue	10,646,113	8,679,313	7,390,154	10,127,604	12,959,250	9,312,625	8,344,659	7,763,945
EBITDA	473,859	256,184	248,920	234,557	880,945	416,189	408,542	422,559
Depn & Amortn	65,675	73,913	78,783	132,157	99,478	78,635	55,101	47,057
Income Before Taxes	304,983	47,284	17,547	(109,294)	610,131	231,205	272,315	308,385
Income Taxes	96,436	21,206	6,166	(34,189)	248,195	101,788	115,018	131,617
Net Income	207,504	25,700	(610,482)	(73,826)	357,931	124,153	145,828	163,656
Average Shares	124,561	100,917	101,068	98,384	98,833	96,045	97,113	99,769
Balance Sheet								
Current Assets	4,027,533	3,769,647	3,333,735	3,471,386	5,764,210	3,157,937	2,860,815	2,630,340
Total Assets	5,509,101	5,332,988	4,667,605	5,358,984	7,604,541	4,483,255	3,839,871	3,537,873
Current Liabilities	1,666,388	1,640,624	1,462,393	1,046,985	2,570,876	1,324,661	1,165,100	1,196,484
Long-Term Obligations	1,465,880	2,016,627	3,614,226	2,441,983	3,027,671	1,533,421	1,040,173	823,099
Total Liabilities	3,314,915	3,827,657	5,239,469	3,592,523	5,690,793	2,932,726	2,352,552	2,177,115
Stockholders' Equity	2,194,186	1,505,331	1,235,249	1,766,461	1,913,748	1,550,529	1,487,319	1,360,758
Shares Outstanding	116,301	101,080	100,447	99,857	98,410	95,945	95,628	96,938
Statistical Record								
Return on Assets %	3.82	0.51	N.M.	N.M.	5.91	2.98	3.95	5.24
Return on Equity %	11.19	1.88	N.M.	N.M.	20.61	8.17	10.24	12.04
EBITDA Margin %	4.45	2.95	3.37	2.32	6.80	4.47	4.90	5.44
Net Margin %	1.95	0.30	N.M.	N.M.	2.76	1.33	1.75	2.11
Asset Turnover	1.96	1.74	1.47	1.56	2.14	2.24	2.26	2.49
Current Ratio	2.42	2.30	2.28	3.32	2.24	2.38	2.46	2.20
Debt to Equity	0.67	1.34	2.93	1.38	1.58	0.99	0.70	0.60
Price Range	28.46-20.84	24.15-11.65	32.61-9.14	32.75-19.11	44.69-20.88	26.69-13.50	35.69-11.94	35.56-26.19
P/E Ratio	16.26-11.91	96.60-46.60	...	...	12.34-5.77	20.69-10.47	23.79-7.96	21.68-15.97

Address: 50 Marcus Drive, Melville, NY 11747
Telephone: (631) 847-2000
Fax: (631) 391-1640

Web Site: www.arrow.com
Officers: Daniel W. Duval - Chmn. William E. Mitchell - Pres., C.E.O.

Auditors: Ernst & Young LLP
Investor Contact: 516-391-1830

ARVINMERITOR, INC.

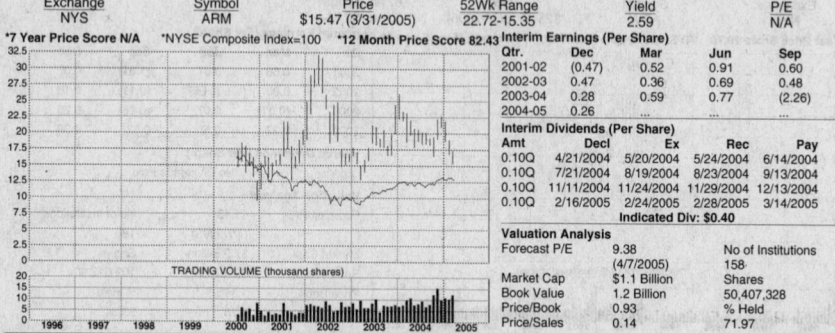

Exchange	Symbol	Price	52Wk Range	Yield	P/E
NYS	ARM	$15.47 (3/31/2005)	22.72-15.35	2.59	N/A

*7 Year Price Score N/A   *NYSE Composite Index=100   *12 Month Price Score 82.43

Interim Earnings (Per Share)

Qtr.	Dec	Mar	Jun	Sep
2001-02	(0.47)	0.52	0.91	0.60
2002-03	0.47	0.36	0.69	0.48
2003-04	0.28	0.59	0.77	(2.26)
2004-05	0.26	...	...	...

Interim Dividends (Per Share)

Amt	Decl	Ex	Rec	Pay
0.10Q	4/21/2004	5/20/2004	5/24/2004	6/14/2004
0.10Q	7/21/2004	8/19/2004	8/23/2004	9/13/2004
0.10Q	11/11/2004	11/24/2004	11/29/2004	12/13/2004
0.10Q	2/16/2005	2/24/2005	2/28/2005	3/14/2005

Indicated Div: $0.40

Valuation Analysis

Forecast P/E	9.38	No of Institutions	
	(4/7/2005)	158	
Market Cap	$1.1 Billion	Shares	
Book Value	1.2 Billion	50,407,328	
Price/Book	0.93	% Held	
Price/Sales	0.14	71.97	

Business Summary: Automotive (MIC: 15.1 SIC: 714 NAIC: 36350)

ArvinMeritor is a global supplier of a broad range of integrated systems, modules and components serving light vehicle, commercial truck, trailer and specialty original equipment manufacturers and certain aftermarkets. Co. serves a range of original equipment manufacturer (OEM) customers worldwide, including truck, light vehicle, trailer producers and specialty vehicle manufacturers, and certain aftermarkets. Co. also provides coil coating applications to the transportation, appliance, construction, heating, ventilation and air conditioning, and doors industries. Operating segments include: Light Vehicle Systems and Commercial Vehicle Systems.

Recent Developments: For the quarter ended Dec 31 2004, income from continuing operations decreased 20.0% to $12 million from income of $15 million in the year-earlier quarter. Net income decreased 5.3% to $18 million from net income of $19 million in the year-earlier quarter. Revenues were $2,090 million, up 8.6% from $1,924 million the year before. Operating income was $36 million versus an income of $42 million in the prior-year quarter, a decrease of 14.3%. Total direct expense was $1,964 million versus $1,775 million in the prior-year quarter, an increase of 10.6%. Total indirect expense was $94 million versus $91 million in the prior-year quarter, an increase of 3.3%.

Prospects: Top-line growth is being driven by increased commercial vehicle systems volumes, favorable foreign currency exchange rates, and the formation of two joint ventures with the Volvo Group, partially offset by the divestitures of certain light vehicle systems businesses. Meanwhile, Co. is targeting sales of about $2.30 billion for the second quarter of fiscal 2005, and earnings per share from continuing operations of between $0.30 and $0.35. Looking ahead, Co. expects fiscal 2005 sales of approximately $8.90 billion, representing growth of about 11.0%, and earnings per share from continuing operations of between $1.60 and $1.80 for the full year.

Financial Data

(US$ in Thousands)	3 Mos	09/30/2004	09/28/2003	09/29/2002	09/30/2001	09/30/2000	09/30/1999	09/30/1998
Earnings Per Share	(0.65)	(0.61)	2.00	1.59	0.53	4.12	3.75	2.84
Cash Flow Per Share	(0.21)	3.22	3.82	2.78	9.15	4.30	5.06	...
Tang Book Value Per Share	3.77	1.60	N.M.	N.M.	N.M.	N.M.	N.M.	...
Dividends Per Share	0.400	0.400	0.400	0.400	0.760	0.220	...	...
Dividend Payout %	...	...	20.00	25.16	143.40	5.34	...	...
Income Statement								
Total Revenue	2,090,000	8,033,000	7,788,000	6,882,000	6,805,000	5,153,000	4,450,000	3,836,000
EBITDA	88,000	362,000	427,000	536,000	416,000	620,000	525,000	397,000
Depn & Amortn	46,000	183,000	214,000	196,000	217,000	162,000	131,000	102,000
Income Before Taxes	14,000	179,000	213,000	235,000	63,000	369,000	333,000	256,000
Income Taxes	4,000	44,000	68,000	75,000	21,000	141,000	129,000	102,000
Net Income	18,000	(42,000)	136,000	107,000	35,000	218,000	194,000	147,000
Average Shares	69,000	68,600	67,900	67,200	66,100	52,900	51,800	51,800
Balance Sheet								
Current Assets	3,034,000	2,986,000	2,239,000	1,976,000	1,755,000	2,189,000	1,332,000	...
Total Assets	5,805,000	5,639,000	5,253,000	4,651,000	4,362,000	4,720,000	2,796,000	...
Current Liabilities	2,199,000	2,273,000	1,878,000	1,743,000	1,672,000	1,725,000	1,124,000	...
Long-Term Obligations	1,516,000	1,487,000	1,541,000	1,435,000	1,313,000	1,537,000	802,000	...
Total Liabilities	4,635,000	4,651,000	4,354,000	3,871,000	3,654,000	3,853,000	2,448,000	...
Stockholders' Equity	1,170,000	988,000	899,000	741,000	651,000	793,000	348,000	...
Shares Outstanding	70,000	69,500	68,500	67,900	65,600	67,900	68,800	...
Statistical Record								
Return on Assets %	N.M.	N.M.	2.75	2.38	0.77	5.79	...	...
Return on Equity %	N.M.	N.M.	16.63	15.42	4.85	38.11	...	...
EBITDA Margin %	4.21	4.51	5.48	7.79	6.11	12.03	11.80	10.35
Net Margin %	0.86	N.M.	1.75	1.55	0.51	4.23	4.36	3.83
Asset Turnover	1.41	1.46	1.58	1.53	1.50	1.37	...	...
Current Ratio	1.38	1.31	1.19	1.13	1.05	1.27	1.19	...
Debt to Equity	1.30	1.51	1.71	1.94	2.02	1.94	2.30	...
Price Range	26.10-16.44	26.10-16.57	21.25-12.77	32.15-14.60	21.75-9.50	18.44-13.81	...	...
P/E Ratio	...	...	10.63-6.38	20.22-9.18	41.04-17.92	4.48-3.35	...	...
Average Yield %	1.96	1.98	2.36	1.74	4.94	1.34	...	...

Address: 2135 West Maple Road, Troy, MI 48084-7186	**Web Site:** www.arvinmeritor.com	**Auditors:** Deloitte & Touche LLP
Telephone: (248) 435-1000	**Officers:** Charles G. McClure - Chmn., Pres., C.E.O.	**Investor Contact:** 248-655-2159
Fax: (248) 435-1393	James Donlon - Sr. V.P., C.F.O.	

ASBURY AUTOMOTIVE GROUP, INC.

Exchange	Symbol	Price	52Wk Range	Yield	P/E
NYS	ABG	$15.40 (3/31/2005)	17.39-12.59	N/A	10.07

*7 Year Price Score N/A   *NYSE Composite Index=100   *12 Month Price Score 100.34

Interim Earnings (Per Share)

Qtr.	Mar	Jun	Sep	Dec
2002	0.17	0.37	0.43	0.16
2003	0.21	0.38	0.50	(0.63)
2004	0.32	0.45	0.37	0.39

Interim Dividends (Per Share)

No Dividends Paid

Valuation Analysis

Forecast P/E	N/A	No of Institutions
Market Cap	$501.7 Million	Shares
Book Value	480.0 Million	4,832,789
Price/Book	1.05	% Held
Price/Sales	0.09	14.82

Business Summary: Retail - Automotive (MIC: 5.7 SIC: 599 NAIC: 41229)

Asbury Automotive Group is a U.S. automotive retailer operating 138 franchises at 96 dealer locations as of Dec 31 2004. Co. offers customers a range of automotive products and services including new and used vehicles and related financing, vehicle maintenance and repair services, replacement parts and warranty, insurance and extended service contracts. Co.'s geographic coverage encompasses 23 different metropolitan markets at 96 locations in 11 states as of Dec 31 2004: Arkansas, California, Florida, Georgia, Mississippi, Missouri, North Carolina, Oregon, South Carolina, Texas and Virginia.

Recent Developments: For the year ended Dec 31 2004, income from continuing operations increased 185.2% to $52,744 thousand from income of $18,491 thousand a year earlier. Net income increased 229.7% to $50,073 thousand from net income of $15,187 thousand a year earlier. Revenues were $5,301,135 thousand, up 15.9% from $4,572,513 thousand the year before. Operating income was $143,167 thousand versus an income of $96,957 thousand in the prior year, an increase of 47.7%. Total direct expense was $8,974,788 thousand versus $7,720,924 thousand in the prior year, an increase of 16.2%. Total indirect expense was $670,574 thousand versus $615,094 thousand in the prior year, an increase of 9.0%.

Prospects: During Jan 2005, Co. reorganized its nine platforms into principally four regions: Florida; West; Mid-Atlantic; and South; with Mississippi and Missouri remaining as stand-alone platforms. As a result, Co. expects to realize annual savings of $4.0 million to $5.0 million by lowering its selling, general and administrative expense ratio, as a percent of gross profit, by approximately 50 to 60 basis points. Separately, Co. remains comfortable with 2005 estimates for earnings per share from continuing operations of between $1.70 and $1.78. This range excludes costs resulting from the regional reorganization as well as the adoption of Statement of Financial Accounting Standard 123(R).

Financial Data
(US$ in Thousands)

	12/31/2004	12/31/2003	12/31/2002	12/31/2001	12/31/2000	12/31/1999
Earnings Per Share	1.53	0.46	1.15	0.80	...	...
Cash Flow Per Share	(0.32)	2.96	2.06	2.84	...	...
Tang Book Value Per Share	0.50	0.91	0.75	N.M.	...	...
Income Statement						
Total Revenue	5,301,135	4,776,505	4,486,038	4,318,292	4,027,790	3,012,134
EBITDA	164,590	119,805	155,702	156,071	140,317	101,292
Depn & Amortn	20,800	20,200	23,928	34,336	25,008	17,429
Income Before Taxes	84,108	41,066	76,604	51,853	42,178	39,199
Income Taxes	31,364	21,268	36,742	5,351	3,511	1,779
Net Income	50,073	15,187	38,085	43,829	28,927	16,148
Average Shares	32,674	32,715	33,073	34,022	...	...
Balance Sheet						
Current Assets	1,143,506	1,012,009	849,783	753,258	775,102	...
Total Assets	1,897,959	1,814,279	1,605,644	1,460,657	1,404,200	...
Current Liabilities	847,510	757,026	692,873	609,997	628,622	...
Long-Term Obligations	495,272	559,128	440,143	492,548	435,879	...
Total Liabilities	1,417,936	1,380,572	1,178,693	1,117,106	1,082,318	...
Stockholders' Equity	480,023	433,707	426,951	343,551	321,882	...
Shares Outstanding	32,577	32,431	33,227	34,000	...	...
Statistical Record						
Return on Assets %	2.69	0.89	2.48	3.06	...	...
Return on Equity %	10.93	3.53	9.89	13.17	...	...
EBITDA Margin %	3.10	2.51	3.47	3.61	3.48	3.36
Net Margin %	0.94	0.32	0.85	1.01	0.72	0.54
Asset Turnover	2.85	2.79	2.93	3.01	...	...
Current Ratio	1.35	1.34	1.23	1.23	1.23	...
Debt to Equity	1.03	1.29	1.03	1.43	1.35	...
Price Range	19.35-12.59	18.99-5.95	22.25-7.30	...	...	...
P/E Ratio	12.65-8.23	41.28-12.93	19.35-6.35	...	...	...

Address: 622 Third Avenue, 37th Floor, New York, NY 10017
Telephone: (212) 885-2500

Web Site: www.asburyauto.com
Officers: Michael J. Durham - Chmn. Kenneth B. Gilman - Pres., C.E.O.

Auditors: Deloitte & Touche LLP
Investor Contact: 212-885-2512
Transfer Agents: EquiServe Trust Company, N.A., Kansas City, MO

ASHLAND, INC.

Exchange	Symbol	Price	52Wk Range	Yield	P/E
NYS	ASH	$67.47 (3/31/2005)	67.78-44.39	1.63	11.08

*7 Year Price Score 117.09 *NYSE Composite Index=100 *12 Month Price Score 109.02

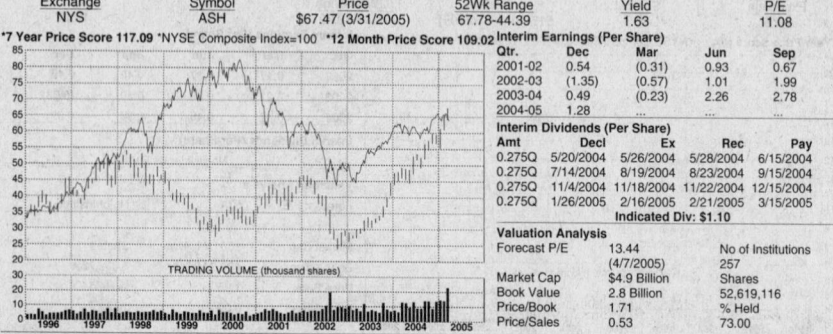

Interim Earnings (Per Share)

Qtr.	Dec	Mar	Jun	Sep
2001-02	0.54	(0.31)	0.93	0.67
2002-03	(1.35)	(0.57)	1.01	1.99
2003-04	0.49	(0.23)	2.26	2.78
2004-05	1.28	...	...	...

Interim Dividends (Per Share)

Amt	Decl	Ex	Rec	Pay
0.275Q	5/20/2004	5/26/2004	5/28/2004	6/15/2004
0.275Q	7/14/2004	8/19/2004	8/23/2004	9/15/2004
0.275Q	11/4/2004	11/18/2004	11/22/2004	12/15/2004
0.275Q	1/26/2005	2/16/2005	2/21/2005	3/15/2005
		Indicated Div: $1.10		

Valuation Analysis

Forecast P/E	13.44	No of Institutions	
	(4/7/2005)	257	
Market Cap	$4.9 Billion	Shares	
Book Value	2.8 Billion	52,619,116	
Price/Book	1.71	% Held	
Price/Sales	0.53	73.00	

Business Summary: Oil and Gas (MIC: 14.2 SIC: 911 NAIC: 24110)

Ashland is an energy company with businesses grouped into five industry segments. APAC performs asphalt and concrete contract construction. Ashland Distribution distributes industrial chemicals and solvents, plastics, composite materials and other ingredients. Ashland Specialty Chemical manufactures and supplies specialty chemical products and services to industries including the automotive, building and construction, foundry, marine, paint, paper, ink, packaging and water treatment industries. Valvoline produces and markets motor oil and automotive chemicals. Refining and Marketing operations are conducted through Marathon Ashland Petroleum, Co.'s joint venture with Marathon Oil.

Recent Developments: For the quarter ended Dec 31 2004, net income increased 176.5% to $94,000 thousand from net income of $34,000 thousand in the year-earlier quarter. Revenues were $2,340,000 thousand, up 17.8% from $1,987,000 thousand the year before. Operating income was $180,000 thousand versus an income of $92,000 thousand in the prior-year quarter, an increase of 95.7%. Total direct expense was $1,849,000 thousand versus $1,611,000 thousand in the prior-year quarter, an increase of 14.8%. Total indirect expense was $311,000 thousand versus $284,000 thousand in the prior-year quarter, an increase of 9.5%.

Prospects: Co. is performing well, helped strong refining and marketing margins. However, high raw material costs are leading to mixed results from its wholly owned subsidiaries. Going forward, Co. will focus on maintaining a low-cost structure and adopting common processes across divisions, which should foster improved performance over time. Separately, Co. and Marathon Oil Corp. have continued their discussions with the IRS under which Co. would transfer its 38.0% interest in Marathon Ashland Petroleum LLC and two wholly-owned businesses to Marathon in a transaction valued at about $3.00 billion. If an agreement is reached, Co. expects the transaction would close in the second quarter of 2005.

Financial Data

(US$ in Thousands)	3 Mos	09/30/2004	09/30/2003	09/30/2002	09/30/2001	09/30/2000	09/30/1999	09/30/1998
Earnings Per Share	6.09	5.31	1.10	1.67	5.93	0.98	3.89	2.63
Cash Flow Per Share	1.21	2.98	3.56	2.72	12.01	6.80	5.27	4.82
Tang Book Value Per Share	31.59	30.46	25.44	24.29	24.61	20.40	27.50	25.39
Dividends Per Share	1.100	1.100	1.100	1.100	1.100	1.100	1.100	1.100
Dividend Payout %	18.05	20.72	100.00	65.87	18.55	112.24	28.28	41.83
Income Statement								
Total Revenue	2,340,000	8,781,000	7,865,000	7,792,000	8,547,000	8,436,000	7,251,000	6,933,000
EBITDA	226,000	849,000	464,000	551,000	1,091,000	901,000	710,000	628,000
Depn & Amortn	46,000	193,000	204,000	220,000	250,000	237,000	228,000	181,000
Income Before Taxes	149,000	548,000	138,000	200,000	681,000	483,000	482,000	317,000
Income Taxes	55,000	150,000	44,000	71,000	275,000	191,000	192,000	114,000
Net Income	94,000	378,000	75,000	117,000	417,000	70,000	290,000	203,000
Average Shares	73,000	71,000	69,000	70,000	70,000	71,000	75,000	77,000
Balance Sheet								
Current Assets	2,097,000	2,302,000	2,085,000	1,925,000	2,213,000	2,131,000	2,059,000	1,828,000
Total Assets	7,563,000	7,502,000	7,006,000	6,725,000	6,945,000	6,771,000	6,424,000	6,082,000
Current Liabilities	1,841,000	1,815,000	1,484,000	1,511,000	1,497,000	1,699,000	1,396,000	1,361,000
Long-Term Obligations	1,087,000	1,109,000	1,512,000	1,606,000	1,786,000	1,899,000	1,627,000	1,507,000
Total Liabilities	4,719,000	4,796,000	4,753,000	4,552,000	4,719,000	4,806,000	4,224,000	3,945,000
Stockholders' Equity	2,844,000	2,706,000	2,253,000	2,173,000	2,226,000	1,965,000	2,200,000	2,137,000
Shares Outstanding	72,084	72,000	68,000	68,000	69,000	70,000	72,000	76,000
Statistical Record								
Return on Assets %	6.11	5.20	1.09	1.71	6.08	1.06	4.64	2.93
Return on Equity %	16.98	15.20	3.39	5.32	19.90	3.35	13.37	9.76
EBITDA Margin %	9.66	9.67	5.90	7.07	12.76	10.68	9.79	9.06
Net Margin %	4.02	4.30	0.95	1.50	4.88	0.83	4.00	2.93
Asset Turnover	1.27	1.21	1.15	1.14	1.25	1.28	1.16	1.00
Current Ratio	1.14	1.27	1.40	1.27	1.48	1.25	1.47	1.34
Debt to Equity	0.38	0.41	0.67	0.74	0.80	0.97	0.74	0.71
Price Range	59.85-43.93	56.60-32.85	34.37-23.78	46.77-26.79	43.85-31.38	37.00-27.47	49.15-31.78	54.17-42.59
P/E Ratio	9.83-7.21	10.66-6.19	31.25-21.62	28.01-16.04	7.39-5.29	37.76-28.03	12.63-8.17	20.60-16.19
Average Yield %	2.15	2.37	3.71	2.75	2.91	3.36	2.67	2.26

Address: 50 E. RiverCenter Boulevard, Covington, KY 41012-0391	Web Site: www.ashland.com	Auditors: ERNST & YOUNG LLP
Telephone: (859) 815-3333	Officers: James J. O'Brien - Chmn., C.E.O. J. Marvin Quin - Sr. V.P., C.F.O.	Investor Contact: 859-815-4095
Fax: (859) 329-5188		

ASTORIA FINANCIAL CORP.

Exchange	Symbol	Price	52Wk Range	Yield	P/E
NYS	AF	$25.30 (3/31/2005)	27.75-22.47	3.16	12.65

*7 Year Price Score 119.45 *NYSE Composite Index=100 *12 Month Price Score 94.59

Interim Earnings (Per Share)

Qtr.	Mar	Jun	Sep	Dec
2001	0.37	0.40	0.40	0.40
2002	0.46	0.49	0.48	0.48
2003	0.46	0.43	0.35	0.43
2004	0.47	0.52	0.53	0.48

Interim Dividends (Per Share)

Amt	Decl	Ex	Rec	Pay
0.167Q	7/21/2004	8/12/2004	8/16/2004	9/1/2004
0.167Q	10/21/2004	11/10/2004	11/15/2004	12/1/2004
0.20Q	1/19/2005	2/11/2005	2/15/2005	3/1/2005
50%	1/19/2005	3/2/2005	2/15/2005	3/1/2005
		Indicated Div: $0.80		

Valuation Analysis

Forecast P/E	10.77	No of Institutions
	(4/13/2005)	209
Market Cap	$2.8 Billion	Shares
Book Value	1.4 Billion	68,900,016
Price/Book	2.04	% Held
Price/Sales	2.48	61.72

Business Summary: Other Depository Banking (MIC: 8.5 SIC: 035 NAIC: 22120)

Astoria Financial, the holding company for Astoria Federal Savings and Loan, with assets of $22.46 billion as of Dec 31 2003, is the second largest thrift institution headquartered in New York and fifth largest in the U.S. Co. invests primarily in mortgage-backed securities, U.S. Government and federal agency securities and other securities. Co.'s primary business is attracting retail deposits from the general public and investing those deposits primarily in one-to-four family mortgage loans, mortgage-backed securities, multi-family mortgage loans and commercial real estate loans.

Recent Developments: For the year ended Dec 31 2004, net income increased 11.5% to $219,537 thousand from net income of $196,846 thousand a year earlier. Net interest income was $470,566 thousand, up 24.0% from $379,538 thousand the year before. Non-interest income fell 33.0% to $80,084 thousand from $119,561 thousand, while non-interest expense advanced 9.2% to $225,011 thousand from $205,877 thousand in the prior year.

Prospects: The slope of the U.S. Treasury yield curve, which has flattened considerably in 2004 and is projected to continue to flatten during 2005, presents a challenge. Nevertheless, Co. should continue to experience solid core business growth. Co. expects deposit growth to remain robust as it launches several new deposit products, specifically a short-term Liquid CD account and a new business money market account, to augment its successful effort in attracting medium term CD accounts. Meanwhile, Co. is encouraged by the strength of the purchase mortgage market and the reduced level of loan prepayments, which should result in continuing strong 1-4 family loan portfolio growth in 2005.

Financial Data
(US$ in Thousands)

	12/31/2004	12/31/2003	12/31/2002	12/31/2001	12/31/2000	12/31/1999	12/31/1998	12/31/1997
Earnings Per Share	2.00	1.66	1.90	1.57	1.44	1.46	0.25	1.01
Cash Flow Per Share	2.56	3.13	1.26	1.64	1.60	2.21	1.98	2.60
Tang Book Value Per Share	10.59	10.11	10.58	9.69	8.50	5.94	7.10	8.13
Dividends Per Share	0.667	0.573	0.513	0.407	0.340	0.320	0.267	0.187
Dividend Payout %	33.33	34.54	27.02	25.96	23.61	21.97	108.11	18.42
Income Statement								
Interest Income	1,045,901	1,057,291	1,266,262	1,438,563	1,517,934	1,495,279	1,224,448	579,401
Interest Expense	575,335	677,753	801,838	969,189	1,010,918	955,331	775,465	364,350
Net Interest Income	470,566	379,538	464,424	469,374	507,016	539,948	448,983	215,051
Provision for Losses	...	...	2,307	4,028	4,014	4,119	15,380	3,061
Non-Interest Income	80,084	119,561	107,407	100,974	69,246	86,696	60,528	22,263
Non-Interest Expense	225,011	205,877	198,029	206,518	200,988	214,691	378,475	115,339
Income Before Taxes	325,639	293,222	371,495	345,190	350,695	399,434	117,510	118,092
Income Taxes	106,102	96,376	123,066	120,036	134,146	163,764	61,825	49,628
Net Income	219,537	196,846	248,429	222,860	216,549	235,670	45,048	68,464
Average Shares	109,806	115,942	127,379	138,261	146,152	157,520	158,658	65,982
Balance Sheet								
Net Loans & Leases	13,180,521	12,603,866	11,975,815	12,084,976	11,344,518	10,212,496	8,739,319	4,304,967
Total Assets	23,415,869	22,457,665	21,697,829	22,667,706	22,336,802	22,696,536	20,587,741	10,528,393
Total Deposits	12,323,257	11,186,594	11,067,196	10,903,693	10,071,687	9,554,534	9,668,286	6,220,918
Total Liabilities	22,046,105	21,061,134	20,143,831	21,000,120	20,698,639	21,374,624	19,125,357	9,628,969
Stockholders' Equity	1,369,764	1,396,531	1,553,998	1,542,586	1,513,163	1,196,912	1,462,384	899,424
Shares Outstanding	110,304	118,005	127,208	136,150	148,930	155,192	163,965	78,594
Statistical Record								
Return on Assets %	0.95	0.89	1.12	0.99	0.96	1.09	0.29	0.77
Return on Equity %	15.83	13.34	16.05	14.59	15.94	17.72	3.81	9.20
Net Interest Margin %	44.99	35.90	36.68	32.63	33.40	36.11	36.67	37.12
Efficiency Ratio %	19.98	17.49	14.42	13.41	12.66	13.57	29.45	19.17
Loans to Deposits	1.07	1.13	1.08	1.11	1.13	1.07	0.90	0.69
Price Range	28.04-22.47	25.48-15.49	23.37-14.57	21.00-16.19	18.15-7.38	17.02-9.50	20.83-10.04	19.38-11.58
P/E Ratio	14.02-11.23	15.35-9.33	12.30-7.67	13.38-10.31	12.60-5.12	11.66-6.51	83.33-40.17	19.18-11.47
Average Yield %	2.68	2.96	2.60	2.21	3.20	2.35	1.59	1.22

Address: One Astoria Federal Plaza,	Web Site: www.astoriafederal.com	Auditors: KPMG LLP
Lake Success, NY 11042-1085	Officers: George L. Engelke Jr. - Chmn., Pres., C.E.O.	Investor Contact: 516-327-7877
Telephone: (516) 327 3000	Monte N. Redman - Exec. V.P., C.F.O.	
Fax: (516) 327 7860		

AT&T CORP

Exchange	Symbol	Price	52Wk Range	Yield	P/E
NYS	T	$18.75 (3/31/2005)	19.85-13.70	5.07	N/A

*7 Year Price Score 36.91   *NYSE Composite Index=100   *12 Month Price Score 104.70

Interim Earnings (Per Share)

Qtr.	Mar	Jun	Sep	Dec
2001	(0.50)	(0.25)	15.65	(1.80)
2002	(1.40)	(17.60)	0.05	(13.39)
2003	0.73	0.68	0.53	0.43
2004	0.38	0.14	(8.99)	0.34

Interim Dividends (Per Share)

Amt	Decl	Ex	Rec	Pay
0.237Q	6/23/2004	6/28/2004	6/30/2004	8/2/2004
0.237Q	9/24/2004	9/28/2004	9/30/2004	11/1/2004
0.237Q	12/20/2004	12/29/2004	12/31/2004	2/1/2005
0.237Q	3/16/2005	3/29/2005	3/31/2005	5/2/2005

Indicated Div: $0.95

Valuation Analysis

Forecast P/E	10.25 (4/7/2005)	No of Institutions 412
Market Cap	$15.0 Billion	Shares 598,912,960
Book Value	7.0 Billion	% Held
Price/Book	2.13	74.83
Price/Sales	0.49	

Business Summary: Communications (MIC: 10.1 SIC: 813 NAIC: 17110)

AT&T is a provider of local, long distance, internet and transaction-based voice and data services. Co.'s primary business segments are AT&T Business Services and AT&T Consumer Services. As of Dec 31 2003, AT&T Business Services offered a variety of global communications services to approximately 3.0 million customers, including large domestic and multinational businesses, small and medium-sized businesses and government agencies. As of Dec 31 2003, AT&T Consumer Services provided domestic and international long distance and transaction based communications services to approximately 35.0 million residential consumers in the United States.

Recent Developments: For the year ended Dec 31 2004, net loss was $6,469 million versus net income of $1,865 million a year earlier. Revenues were $30,537 million, down 11.6% from $34,529 million the year before. Operating loss was $10,088 million versus an income of $3,657 million in the prior year. Total direct expense was $21,296 million versus $23,292 million in the prior year, a decrease of 8.6%. Total indirect expense was $19,329 million versus $7,580 million in the prior year, an increase of 155.0%.

Prospects: Co.'s pending acquisition by SBC Communications Inc. is progressing as planned with the two companies filing for formal approval at the Federal Communications Commission and U.S. Department of Justice on Feb 22 2005. Under the terms of the agreement, Co.'s shareholders will receive 0.77942 shares of SBC common stock for each common share of Co.'s outstanding. Based on SBC's closing stock price on Jan 28 2005, this exchange ratio equals $18.41 per share. The acquisition is subject to approval by Co.'s shareholders and regulatory authorities, and other customary closing conditions. The merger is expected to close in late 2005 or early 2006.

Financial Data

(US$ in Thousands)	12/31/2004	12/31/2003	12/31/2002	12/31/2001	12/31/2000	12/31/1999	12/31/1998	12/31/1997
Earnings Per Share	(8.14)	2.37	(17.08)	12.50	4.40	8.70	11.83	9.47
Cash Flow Per Share	6.91	10.82	14.05	14.48	19.03	18.46	18.92	17.31
Tang Book Value Per Share	2.20	10.93	9.11	N.M.	13.13	47.31	29.21	26.77
Dividends Per Share	0.950	0.850	0.188	0.750	...	1.100	1.100	4.401
Dividend Payout %	...	35.86	...	6.00	...	12.64	9.30	46.48
Income Statement								
Total Revenue	30,537,000	34,529,000	37,827,000	52,550,000	65,981,000	62,391,000	53,223,000	51,319,000
EBITDA	(6,464,000)	8,718,000	9,172,000	11,545,000	16,058,000	15,775,000	13,041,000	11,183,000
Depn & Amortn	3,768,000	4,870,000	4,888,000	9,338,000	10,267,000	7,439,000	4,629,000	3,827,000
Income Before Taxes	(11,035,000)	2,690,000	2,836,000	(1,035,000)	2,608,000	6,685,000	8,307,000	7,193,000
Income Taxes	(4,560,000)	816,000	1,587,000	(791,000)	3,342,000	3,257,000	3,072,000	2,721,000
Net Income	(6,469,000)	1,865,000	(13,082,000)	7,715,000	4,669,000	3,428,000	6,398,000	4,638,000
Average Shares	795,000	789,000	766,000	729,000	709,000	630,400	540,000	489,000
Balance Sheet								
Current Assets	9,387,000	9,848,000	15,903,000	22,528,000	17,087,000	13,884,000	14,118,000	16,179,000
Total Assets	32,804,000	47,988,000	55,272,000	165,282,000	242,223,000	169,406,000	59,550,000	58,635,000
Current Liabilities	9,088,000	8,883,000	12,024,000	25,427,000	50,867,000	28,207,000	15,442,000	16,942,000
Long-Term Obligations	8,779,000	13,066,000	18,812,000	40,527,000	33,092,000	21,591,000	5,556,000	6,826,000
Total Liabilities	25,785,000	34,032,000	42,960,000	105,322,000	129,432,000	81,762,000	34,028,000	35,988,000
Stockholders' Equity	7,019,000	13,956,000	12,312,000	51,680,000	103,198,000	78,927,000	25,522,000	22,647,000
Shares Outstanding	798,570	791,911	783,038	708,481	752,030	639,200	526,200	487,200
Statistical Record								
Return on Assets %	N.M.	3.61	N.M.	3.79	2.26	2.99	10.83	8.12
Return on Equity %	N.M.	14.20	N.M.	9.96	5.11	6.56	26.56	21.60
EBITDA Margin %	N.M.	25.25	24.25	21.97	24.34	25.28	24.50	21.79
Net Margin %	N.M.	5.40	N.M.	14.68	7.08	5.49	12.02	9.04
Asset Turnover	0.75	0.67	0.34	0.26	0.32	0.55	0.90	0.90
Current Ratio	1.03	1.11	1.32	0.89	0.34	0.49	0.91	0.95
Debt to Equity	1.25	0.94	1.53	0.78	0.32	0.27	0.22	0.30
Price Range	21.98-13.70	27.66-13.66	37.21-16.92	41.76-26.82	88.63-24.89	93.07-61.35	77.39-49.10	62.64-30.12
P/E Ratio	...	11.67-5.76	...	3.34-2.15	20.14-5.66	10.70-7.05	6.54-4.15	6.61-3.18
Average Yield %	5.47	4.33	0.72	2.20	...	1.42	1.82	10.91

Address: One AT&T Way, Bedminster, NJ 07921
Telephone: (908) 221-2000

Web Site: www.att.com
Officers: David W. Dorman - Chmn., C.E.O. Thomas W. Horton - Vice-Chmn., C.F.O.

Auditors: PricewaterhouseCoopers LLP
Investor Contact: 908-221-3655

ATMOS ENERGY CORP.

Exchange	Symbol	Price	52Wk Range	Yield	P/E	Div Acheiver
NYS	ATO	$27.00 (3/31/2005)	29.09-23.68	4.59	15.08	17 Years

*7 Year Price Score 93.10 ***NYSE Composite Index=100** ***12 Month Price Score 99.95**

Interim Earnings (Per Share)

Qtr.	Dec	Mar	Jun	Sep
2001-02	0.50	1.01	0.08	(0.14)
2002-03	0.60	1.07	0.00	(0.11)
2003-04	0.57	1.12	0.09	(0.20)
2004-05	0.79	...	...	...

Interim Dividends (Per Share)

Amt	Decl	Ex	Rec	Pay
0.305Q	5/11/2004	5/21/2004	5/25/2004	6/10/2004
0.305Q	8/10/2004	8/23/2004	8/25/2004	9/10/2004
0.31Q	11/9/2004	11/22/2004	11/24/2004	12/10/2004
0.31Q	2/8/2005	2/23/2005	2/25/2005	3/10/2005

Indicated Div: $1.24 (Div. Reinv. Plan)

Valuation Analysis

Forecast P/E	15.77	No of Institutions
	(4/7/2005)	182
Market Cap	$2.1 Billion	Shares
Book Value	1.5 Billion	43,052,140
Price/Book	1.39	% Held
Price/Sales	0.61	54.26

Business Summary: Gas Utilities (MIC: 7.4 SIC: 922 NAIC: 86210)

Atmos Energy is engaged in the natural gas utility business as well as certain non-regulated natural gas businesses. As of Sept. 30, 2004, Co. distributes natural gas through sales and transportation arrangements to about 1,700,000 residential, commercial public authority and industrial customers through its regulated utility operations in 12 states. Co. also transports natural gas through its distribution system. Co. provides natural gas management and marketing services to industrial customers, municipalities and other local gas distribution companies in 18 states. Co. also supplements natural gas used by its customers through natural gas storage fields located in Kentucky and Louisiana.

Recent Developments: For the quarter ended Dec 31 2004, net income increased 101.8% to $59,599 thousand from net income of $29,541 thousand in the year-earlier quarter. Revenues were $1,368,624 thousand, up 79.2% from $763,616 thousand the year before. Operating income was $128,674 thousand versus an income of $63,541 thousand in the prior-year quarter, an increase of 102.5%. Total direct expense was $1,044,172 thousand versus $604,563 thousand in the prior-year quarter, an increase of 72.7%. Total indirect expense was $195,778 thousand versus $95,512 thousand in the prior-year quarter, an increase of 105.0%.

Prospects: Co. remains confident about its full-year 2005 earnings guidance of $1.65 to $1.75 per diluted share, following its solid performance for the first quarter of fiscal 2005. Co. stated these its strong start to the coming year is mainly due to the positives effects stemming from its acquisition of TXU Gas Company in Oct 2004. Separately, on Jan 12 2005, Co. signed a letter of intent with Energy Transfer Partners L.P. to jointly construct, own and operate a 45 mile, 30 inch natural gas pipeline, which is expected to be in operation by Dec 31 2005.

Financial Data
(US$ in Thousands)

	3 Mos	09/30/2004	09/30/2003	09/30/2002	09/30/2001	09/30/2000	09/30/1999	09/30/1998
Earnings Per Share	1.79	1.58	1.54	1.45	1.47	1.14	0.58	1.84
Cash Flow Per Share	4.30	5.00	1.07	7.20	2.18	1.72	2.77	3.07
Tang Book Value Per Share	10.55	14.25	11.35	9.19	12.43	12.28	12.09	12.21
Dividends Per Share	1.225	1.220	1.200	1.180	1.160	1.140	1.100	1.060
Dividend Payout %	68.52	77.22	77.92	81.38	78.91	100.00	189.66	57.61
Income Statement								
Total Revenue	1,368,624	2,920,037	2,799,916	950,849	1,442,275	850,152	690,196	848,208
EBITDA	173,056	301,314	279,225	237,931	206,939	166,980	125,271	...
Depn & Amortn	43,997	98,112	89,194	83,921	70,470	66,920	61,674	53,416
Income Before Taxes	96,517	137,765	126,371	94,836	89,458	56,237	27,299	...
Income Taxes	36,918	51,538	46,910	35,180	33,368	20,319	9,555	31,806
Net Income	59,599	86,227	71,688	59,656	56,090	35,918	17,744	55,265
Average Shares	75,725	54,416	46,496	41,250	38,247	31,594	30,819	30,031
Balance Sheet								
Net PPE	3,223,143	1,722,521	1,515,989	1,300,320	1,335,398	982,346	965,782	917,860
Total Assets	5,406,096	2,869,883	2,518,508	1,980,221	2,036,180	1,348,758	1,230,537	1,141,390
Long-Term Obligations	2,255,173	861,311	863,918	670,463	692,399	363,198	377,483	398,548
Total Liabilities	3,867,018	1,736,424	1,660,991	1,406,986	1,452,316	956,292	852,874	770,232
Stockholders' Equity	1,539,078	1,133,459	857,517	573,235	583,864	392,466	377,663	371,158
Shares Outstanding	79,257	62,799	51,475	41,675	40,791	31,952	31,247	30,398
Statistical Record								
Return on Assets %	2.81	3.19	3.19	2.97	3.31	2.78	1.50	4.96
Return on Equity %	9.56	8.64	10.02	10.31	11.49	9.30	4.74	15.83
EBITDA Margin %	12.64	10.32	9.97	25.02	14.35	19.64	18.15	...
Net Margin %	4.35	2.95	2.56	6.27	3.89	4.22	2.57	6.52
PPE Turnover	1.48	1.80	1.99	0.72	1.24	0.87	0.73	0.96
Asset Turnover	0.85	1.08	1.24	0.47	0.85	0.66	0.58	0.76
Debt to Equity	1.47	0.76	1.01	1.17	1.19	0.93	1.00	1.07
Price Range	27.43-23.68	26.86-23.68	25.45-20.70	24.46-18.37	26.25-19.31	25.00-14.75	32.69-23.06	31.06-24.63
P/E Ratio	15.32-13.23	17.00-14.99	16.53-13.44	16.87-12.67	17.86-13.14	21.93-12.94	56.36-39.76	16.88-13.38
Average Yield %	4.81	4.87	5.21	5.37	5.08	5.85	4.11	3.74

Address: Three Lincoln Centre, Suite 1800, 5430 LBJ Freeway, Dallas, TX 75240	Web Site: www.atmosenergy.com	Auditors: ERNST & YOUNG LLP
Telephone: (972) 934-9227	**Officers:** Robert W. Best - Chmn., Pres., C.E.O. John P. Reddy - Sr. V.P., C.F.O.	
Fax: (972) 855-3075		

ATWOOD OCEANICS, INC.

Exchange	Symbol	Price	52Wk Range	Yield	P/E
NYS	ATW	$66.54 (3/31/2005)	69.62-33.96	N/A	54.10

*7 Year Price Score 112.30 *NYSE Composite Index=100 ***12 Month Price Score 127.42**

Interim Earnings (Per Share)

Qtr.	Dec	Mar	Jun	Sep
2001-02	0.59	0.49	0.44	0.51
2002-03	0.07	0.04	(0.01)	(1.02)
2003-04	(0.14)	0.03	0.40	0.24
2004-05	0.56	...	...	...

Interim Dividends (Per Share)

Amt	Decl	Ex	Rec	Pay

Valuation Analysis

Forecast P/E	42.71	No of Institutions
	(4/12/2005)	138
Market Cap	$1.0 Billion	Shares
Book Value	335.6 Million	12,277,758
Price/Book	3.00	% Held
Price/Sales	5.77	80.94

TRADING VOLUME (thousand shares)

Business Summary: Oil and Gas (MIC: 14.2 SIC: 381 NAIC: 13111)

Atwood Oceanics is engaged in the international offshore drilling and completion of exploratory and developmental oil and gas wells and related support, management and consulting services. Co. is headquartered in Houston, TX. Most of Co.'s drilling units operate outside of U.S. waters, and Co. conducts drilling operations in most of the offshore exploration areas of the world. Co.'s operations revolve around eight offshore mobile drilling units in four regions - Southeast Asia, Australia, the Mediterranean Sea and the U.S. Gulf of Mexico. Co. supports its operations from its Houston headquarters and offices located in Australia, Malaysia, Egypt, Indonesia, Singapore and the United Kingdom.

Recent Developments: For the quarter ended Dec 31 2004, net income was $8,650 thousand versus net loss of $1,904 thousand in the year-earlier quarter. Revenues were $45,426 thousand, up 28.6% from $35,325 thousand the year before. Operating income was $10,126 thousand versus an income of $2,262 thousand in the prior-year quarter, an increase of 347.7%. Total direct expense was $25,203 thousand versus $22,533 thousand in the prior-year quarter, an increase of 11.8%. Total indirect expense was $10,097 thousand versus $10,530 thousand in the prior-year quarter, a decrease of 4.1%.

Prospects: Going forward, Co. is optimistic about the longer-term outlook and fundamentals of the offshore drilling market. Co. has experienced higher bid activity levels for its drilling units for recent contracts and increasing inquiries from its clients for programs commencing in the second half of calendar 2005 and in calendar 2006. However, with the expected downtime for two of its rigs during a portion of the next two quarters in jurisdictions with a higher effective tax rate than the U.S. statutory rate, Co. expects net income for these quarters to be below the first quarter of 2005; however, compared to fiscal 2004, Co. expects full-year 2005 will see increases in both earnings and cash flow.

Financial Data

(US$ in Thousands)	3 Mos	09/30/2004	09/30/2003	09/30/2002	09/30/2001	09/30/2000	09/30/1999	09/30/1998
Earnings Per Share	1.23	0.54	(0.92)	2.02	1.96	1.66	2.01	2.84
Cash Flow Per Share	2.64	1.84	0.99	3.06	4.51	2.83	5.19	3.68
Tang Book Value Per Share	22.21	19.58	19.02	19.94	17.91	15.79	14.06	12.02
Income Statement								
Total Revenue	45,426	163,454	144,765	149,157	147,541	134,514	150,000	151,809
EBITDA	17,011	54,500	34,694	64,752	69,746	69,832	75,149	81,941
Depn & Amortn	6,885	32,896	28,044	24,317	25,686	30,027	24,470	18,023
Income Before Taxes	8,143	12,402	1,636	38,777	41,121	35,898	46,507	60,319
Income Taxes	(507)	4,815	14,438	10,492	13,775	12,750	18,787	20,955
Net Income	8,650	7,587	(12,802)	28,285	27,346	23,148	27,720	39,364
Average Shares	15,422	14,032	13,846	13,994	13,978	13,916	13,791	13,884
Balance Sheet								
Current Assets	82,157	92,966	76,012	71,813	45,721	64,917	50,532	51,587
Total Assets	493,249	498,936	522,674	444,530	353,878	313,251	293,604	281,737
Current Liabilities	54,207	60,053	49,949	24,416	20,664	17,484	19,013	26,723
Long-Term Obligations	81,000	145,000	181,000	115,000	60,000	46,000	54,000	72,000
Total Liabilities	157,675	227,347	259,207	168,397	106,242	95,046	101,375	117,971
Stockholders' Equity	335,574	271,589	263,467	276,133	247,636	218,205	192,229	163,766
Shares Outstanding	15,110	13,873	13,851	13,845	13,823	13,823	13,675	13,625
Statistical Record								
Return on Assets %	3.64	1.48	N.M.	7.09	8.20	7.61	9.64	15.84
Return on Equity %	6.06	2.83	N.M.	10.80	11.74	11.25	15.57	27.48
EBITDA Margin %	37.45	33.34	23.97	43.41	47.27	51.91	50.10	53.98
Net Margin %	19.04	4.64	N.M.	18.96	18.53	17.21	18.48	25.93
Asset Turnover	0.35	0.32	0.30	0.37	0.44	0.44	0.52	0.61
Current Ratio	1.52	1.55	1.52	2.94	2.21	3.71	2.66	1.93
Debt to Equity	0.24	0.53	0.69	0.42	0.24	0.21	0.28	0.44
Price Range	53.75-31.55	48.14-23.53	32.70-23.46	50.32-25.04	49.90-24.20	69.00-28.00	36.50-15.88	61.09-16.31
P/E Ratio	43.70-25.65	89.15-43.57	...	24.91-12.40	25.46-12.35	41.57-16.87	18.16-7.90	21.51-5.74

Address: 15835 Park Ten Place Drive, Houston, TX 77084 Telephone: (281) 749-7800	Web Site: www.atwd.com Officers: John R. Irwin - Pres., C.E.O. James M. Holland - Sr. V.P., C.F.O., Sec.	Auditors: PricewaterhouseCoopers LLP Investor Contact: 713-492-2929 Transfer Agents: Continental Stock Transfer & Trust Company, New York,

AUTOLIV INC.

Exchange	Symbol	Price	52Wk Range	Yield	P/E
NYS	ALV	$47.65 (3/31/2005)	51.80-38.96	2.52	13.77

*7 Year Price Score 128.70 *NYSE Composite Index=100 *12 Month Price Score 104.55

Interim Earnings (Per Share)

Qtr.	Mar	Jun	Sep	Dec
2001	0.21	0.31	(0.30)	0.27
2002	0.40	0.53	0.42	0.49
2003	0.54	0.75	0.54	0.98
2004	0.80	0.94	0.72	1.00

Interim Dividends (Per Share)

Amt	Decl	Ex	Rec	Pay
0.20Q	4/28/2004	8/10/2004	8/12/2004	9/9/2004
0.20Q	8/19/2004	11/8/2004	11/11/2004	12/9/2004
0.25Q	10/25/2004	2/1/2005	2/3/2005	3/3/2005
0.30Q	2/3/2005	5/2/2005	5/4/2005	6/2/2005
		Indicated Div: $1.20		

Valuation Analysis

Forecast P/E	12.70	No of Institutions	
	(4/7/2005)	208	
Market Cap	$4.4 Billion	Shares	
Book Value	2.6 Billion	59,168,976	
Price/Book	1.66	% Held	
Price/Sales	0.71	64.46	

Business Summary: Automotive (MIC: 15.1 SIC: 714 NAIC: 36399)

Autoliv develops and manufactures automotive safety systems for all major automobile manufacturers in the world through its two principal operating subsidiaries. Autoliv AB, Inc. is a Swedish-based developer, manufacturer and supplier to the automotive industry of car occupant restraint systems, including seat belt pretensioners, frontal airbags, side-impact airbags, steering wheels and seat sub-systems. Autoliv ASP, Inc. is an Indiana-based developer and manufacturer of airbag inflators, modules and airbag cushions, seat belts and steering wheels. As of Dec 31 2004, Co. had production facilities in 29 countries.

Recent Developments: For the year ended Dec 31 2004, net income increased 21.6% to $326,300 thousand from net income of $268,400 thousand a year earlier. Revenues were $6,143,900 thousand, up 15.9% from $5,300,800 thousand the year before. Operating income was $513,100 thousand versus an income of $426,800 thousand in the prior year, an increase of 20.2%. Total direct expense was $4,922,700 thousand versus $4,298,100 thousand in the prior year, an increase of 14.5%. Total indirect expense was $696,900 thousand versus $599,700 thousand in the prior year, an increase of 16.2%.

Prospects: Results are benefiting from growth generated by new products, higher market shares for seat belts, expansions in Japan and other Asian markets, as well as a positive vehicle mix and currency effect. Internal cost-reduction initiatives such as plant consolidations, moving production to low-cost countries, consolidation of the supplier base and re-designing of products are also helping to improve bottom-line performance. Looking ahead to 2005, although it expects to continue to improve its market share, Co. does not expect to experience the growth rates seen in 2004. Co. expects light vehicle production in the Triad to decrease by 2.0% in the first quarter and flat for the full year.

Financial Data
(US$ in Thousands)

	12/31/2004	12/31/2003	12/31/2002	12/31/2001	12/31/2000	12/31/1999	12/31/1998	12/31/1997
Earnings Per Share	3.46	2.81	1.84	0.49	1.67	1.95	1.84	(6.70)
Cash Flow Per Share	7.20	5.56	5.19	2.72	2.63	4.26	3.07	3.97
Tang Book Value Per Share	10.08	7.29	3.70	1.94	1.75	3.28	1.92	0.09
Dividends Per Share	0.770	0.540	0.440	0.440	0.440	0.440	0.440	0.220
Dividend Payout %	22.25	19.22	23.91	89.80	26.35	22.56	23.91	...
Income Statement								
Total Revenue	6,143,900	5,300,800	4,443,400	3,991,000	4,116,100	3,812,200	3,488,700	2,739,600
EBITDA	821,000	717,100	583,400	483,600	612,900	626,600	588,500	(280,900)
Depn & Amortn	298,300	278,800	248,500	304,200	269,100	253,400	228,000	162,600
Income Before Taxes	484,500	397,000	286,700	116,800	290,600	329,700	312,500	(477,300)
Income Taxes	149,000	120,200	94,600	59,800	117,200	132,000	123,900	99,100
Net Income	326,300	268,400	180,500	47,900	168,700	199,900	188,300	(579,600)
Average Shares	94,200	95,400	98,000	98,000	...	...	...	...
Balance Sheet								
Current Assets	2,190,800	1,839,400	1,553,800	1,365,600	1,349,000	1,181,500	1,131,800	974,200
Total Assets	5,354,100	4,894,300	4,294,800	4,004,300	4,067,800	3,646,500	3,668,100	3,430,500
Current Liabilities	1,799,300	1,366,900	1,189,800	914,400	1,255,900	1,104,600	1,062,700	999,500
Long-Term Obligations	667,100	846,200	842,700	1,037,100	737,400	470,400	628,600	611,800
Total Liabilities	2,717,700	2,492,300	2,248,100	2,129,000	2,157,700	1,715,500	1,822,100	1,726,500
Stockholders' Equity	2,636,400	2,402,000	2,046,700	1,875,300	1,910,100	1,931,000	1,846,000	1,704,000
Shares Outstanding	92,000	94,900	96,300	97,900	97,800	102,300	102,300	102,200
Statistical Record								
Return on Assets %	6.35	5.84	4.35	1.19	4.36	5.47	5.31	N.M.
Return on Equity %	12.92	12.07	9.20	2.53	8.76	10.59	10.61	N.M.
EBITDA Margin %	13.36	13.53	13.13	12.12	14.89	16.44	16.87	N.M.
Net Margin %	5.31	5.06	4.06	1.20	4.10	5.24	5.40	N.M.
Asset Turnover	1.20	1.15	1.07	0.99	1.06	1.04	0.98	0.51
Current Ratio	1.22	1.35	1.31	1.49	1.07	1.07	1.07	0.97
Debt to Equity	0.25	0.35	0.41	0.55	0.39	0.24	0.34	0.36
Price Range	48.80-37.65	38.24-18.79	25.65-17.20	21.42-13.90	31.44-14.94	41.50-27.81	37.25-25.38	45.13-30.63
P/E Ratio	14.10-10.88	13.61-6.69	13.94-9.35	43.71-28.37	18.82-8.94	21.28-14.26	20.24-13.79	...
Average Yield %	1.82	1.98	2.00	2.46	1.79	1.27	1.38	0.57

Address: 3350 Airport Road, Ogden, UT 84405 Telephone: (801) 629-9800 Fax: (801) 625-4911	Web Site: www.autoliv.com Officers: S. Jay Stewart - Chmn. Lars Westerberg - Pres., C.E.O.	Auditors: Ernst & Young AB Transfer Agents: EquiServe Trust Company N.A., Providence, RI

AUTOMATIC DATA PROCESSING INC.

Exchange	Symbol	Price	52Wk Range	Yield	P/E	Div Acheiver
NYS	ADP	$44.95 (3/31/2005)	46.84-38.88	1.38	27.92	29 Years

*7 Year Price Score 82.04 *NYSE Composite Index=100 *12 Month Price Score 93.95

Interim Earnings (Per Share)

Qtr.	Sep	Dec	Mar	Jun
2001-02	0.31	0.42	0.56	0.46
2002-03	0.34	0.43	0.54	0.36
2003-04	0.32	0.38	0.50	0.35
2004-05	0.35	0.42	...	...

Interim Dividends (Per Share)

Amt	Decl	Ex	Rec	Pay
0.14Q	5/11/2004	6/9/2004	6/11/2004	7/1/2004
0.14Q	8/11/2004	9/8/2004	9/10/2004	10/1/2004
0.155Q	11/9/2004	12/8/2004	12/10/2004	1/1/2005
0.155Q	1/27/2005	3/10/2005	3/14/2005	4/1/2005

Indicated Div: $0.62

Valuation Analysis

Forecast P/E	22.62		No of Institutions
	(4/7/2005)		769
Market Cap	$26.2 Billion		Shares
Book Value	5.7 Billion		419,268,704
Price/Book	4.63		% Held
Price/Sales	3.26		71.90

Business Summary: IT & Technology (MIC: 10.2 SIC: 374 NAIC: 18210)

Automatic Data Processing provides computerized transaction processing, data communication, and information services. Co.'s Employer Services group offers payroll processing, human resource and benefits administration products and services. Co.'s Brokerage Services group provides transaction processing systems, desktop productivity applications and investor communications services to the financial services industry. Co.'s Dealer Services group provides dealer management computer systems to automotive retailers and their manufacturers. Co.'s Claims Services group offers business services to clients in the property and casualty insurance, auto collision repair and auto recycling industries.

Recent Developments: For the quarter ended Dec 31 2004, net income increased 9.4% to $250,103 thousand from net income of $228,580 thousand in the year-earlier quarter. Revenues were $1,993,584 thousand, up 9.1% from $1,827,400 thousand the year before. Revenues for 2004 and 2003 included interest on funds held for Employer Services clients of $91,129 thousand and $82,202 thousand, and PEO revenues of $133,361 thousand and $108,865 thousand, respectively. Total indirect expense was $1,595,964 thousand versus $1,462,260 thousand in the prior-year quarter, an increase of 9.1%.

Prospects: Employer services revenues are benefiting primarily from new business, the number of employees on Co.'s clients' payrolls, strong client retention and an increase in interest earned on client fund balances. Co.'s client retention in the U.S. is improving due to its continued investment and commitment to client service. Separately, brokerage services revenues are growing primarily due to an increase in certain investor communications activity. Meanwhile, dealer services revenues is improving for Co.'s dealer business systems in North America mostly due to growth in its key products and the effect of acquisitions.

Financial Data

(US$ in Thousands)	6 Mos	3 Mos	06/30/2004	06/30/2003	06/30/2002	06/30/2001	06/30/2000	06/30/1999
Earnings Per Share	1.61	1.58	1.56	1.68	1.75	1.44	1.31	1.10
Cash Flow Per Share	2.61	2.55	2.35	2.61	2.48	2.37	1.70	1.39
Tang Book Value Per Share	4.30	4.25	4.23	4.57	5.25	4.97	4.71	3.97
Dividends Per Share	0.575	0.560	0.540	0.475	0.448	0.395	0.339	0.295
Dividend Payout %	35.61	35.54	34.62	28.27	25.57	27.43	25.86	26.82
Income Statement								
Total Revenue	3,848,266	1,854,682	7,754,942	7,147,017	7,004,263	7,017,570	6,287,512	5,540,141
EBITDA	911,159	421,120	1,867,276	1,822,301	1,968,539	1,860,126	1,587,022	1,376,397
Depn & Amortn	215,676	107,942	436,694	274,682	279,077	320,856	284,282	272,807
Income Before Taxes	728,560	330,940	1,494,530	1,645,200	1,786,970	1,525,010	1,289,600	1,084,500
Income Taxes	270,296	122,779	558,960	627,050	686,200	600,290	448,800	387,660
Net Income	458,264	208,161	935,570	1,018,150	1,100,770	924,720	840,800	696,840
Average Shares	591,086	589,952	598,749	605,917	630,579	645,989	646,098	636,892
Balance Sheet								
Current Assets	4,193,873	3,028,533	2,761,589	3,675,501	2,817,257	3,083,460	3,064,452	2,194,257
Total Assets	28,189,379	23,787,478	21,120,559	19,833,671	18,276,522	17,889,090	16,850,816	5,824,820
Current Liabilities	2,600,640	1,659,933	1,768,424	1,998,783	1,411,102	1,336,273	1,296,668	1,286,393
Long-Term Obligations	75,926	76,508	76,200	84,674	90,648	110,227	132,017	145,765
Total Liabilities	22,532,856	18,373,944	15,702,889	14,462,198	13,162,317	13,188,093	12,267,998	1,816,879
Stockholders' Equity	5,656,523	5,413,534	5,417,670	5,371,473	5,114,205	4,700,997	4,582,818	4,007,941
Shares Outstanding	583,096	582,537	587,115	594,839	616,317	623,936	628,746	623,627
Statistical Record								
Return on Assets %	3.66	4.45	4.56	5.34	6.09	5.32	7.40	12.67
Return on Equity %	17.53	17.59	17.30	19.42	22.43	19.92	19.52	18.80
EBITDA Margin %	23.68	22.71	24.08	25.50	28.10	26.51	25.24	24.84
Net Margin %	11.91	11.22	12.06	14.25	15.72	13.18	13.37	12.58
Asset Turnover	0.30	0.37	0.38	0.38	0.39	0.40	0.55	1.01
Current Ratio	1.61	1.82	1.56	1.84	2.00	2.31	2.36	1.71
Debt to Equity	0.01	0.01	0.01	0.02	0.02	0.02	0.03	0.04
Price Range	46.84-38.88	46.84-35.85	46.84-33.86	44.70-27.25	60.27-43.10	68.88-49.56	57.69-38.00	46.19-31.88
P/E Ratio	29.09-24.15	29.65-22.69	30.03-21.71	26.61-16.22	34.44-24.63	47.83-34.42	44.04-29.01	41.99-28.98
Average Yield %	1.34	1.36	1.33	1.30	0.85	0.68	0.71	0.75

Address: One ADP Boulevard, Roseland, NJ 07068-1728 Telephone: (973) 974-5000 Fax: (973) 974-5390	Web Site: www.adp.com Officers: Arthur F. Weinbach - Chmn., C.E.O. Gary C. Butler - Pres., C.O.O.	Auditors: Deloitte & Touche LLP Investor Contact: 973-974-5858 Transfer Agents: Mellon Investor Services, Ridgefield Park, NJ

AUTONATION, INC.

Exchange	Symbol	Price	52Wk Range	Yield	P/E
NYS	AN	$18.94 (3/31/2005)	20.00-15.20	N/A	11.91

*7 Year Price Score 112.94 *NYSE Composite Index=100 *12 Month Price Score 102.73

Interim Earnings (Per Share)

Qtr.	Mar	Jun	Sep	Dec
2001	0.17	0.26	0.24	0.02
2002	0.28	0.32	0.33	0.26
2003	0.63	0.37	0.38	0.28
2004	0.32	0.34	0.34	0.60

Interim Dividends (Per Share)

No Dividends Paid

Valuation Analysis

Forecast P/E	12.76	No of Institutions
	(4/7/2005)	199
Market Cap	$5.0 Billion	Shares
Book Value	4.3 Billion	203,816,672
Price/Book	1.17	% Held
Price/Sales	0.26	76.72

Business Summary: Retail - Automotive (MIC: 5.7 SIC: 599 NAIC: 41229)

AutoNation is a major automotive retailer in the U.S. As of Dec 31 2003, Co. owned and operated 367 new vehicle franchises from 282 stores located in major metropolitan markets in 17 states. Co.'s stores offer a range of automotive products and services, including new vehicles, used vehicles, vehicle maintenance and repair services, vehicle parts, extended service contracts, vehicle protection products and other aftermarket products. Co. also arranges financing for vehicle purchases through third-party finance sources. Approximately 98.0% of the new vehicles sold by Co. in 2003 were manufactured by Ford, General Motors, DaimlerChrysler, Toyota, Nissan, Honda and BMW.

Recent Developments: For the year ended Dec 31 2004, income from continuing operations decreased 23.1% to $396,400 thousand from income of $515,200 thousand a year earlier. Net income decreased 9.5% to $433,600 thousand from net income of $479,200 thousand a year earlier. Revenues were $19,424,700 thousand, up 3.8% from $18,711,400 thousand the year before. Operating income was $766,900 thousand versus an income of $726,400 thousand in the prior year, an increase of 5.6%. Total direct expense was $32,824,000 thousand versus $31,617,600 thousand in the prior year, an increase of 3.8%. Total indirect expense was $2,245,800 thousand versus $2,176,200 thousand in the prior year, an increase of 3.2%.

Prospects: Top line growth is being driven by growth in each of Co.'s business lines, along with continued improvements in Co.'s cost structure to obtain significant cost savings, reducing new and used vehicle inventory levels and the benefit of a streamlined regional management structure. Further, Co.'s streamlined regional management structure is expected to generate approximately $30.0 million in incremental annual cost savings. Looking ahead, Co. anticipates that new vehicle sales will remain stable in the U.S. and continue to be highly competitive. Meanwhile, Co. expects 2005 capital expenditures of approximately $130.0 million, excluding any acquisition-related spending or lease buy-outs.

Financial Data (US$ in Thousands)	12/31/2004	12/31/2003	12/31/2002	12/31/2001	12/31/2000	12/31/1999	12/31/1998	12/31/1997
Earnings Per Share	1.59	1.67	1.19	0.69	0.91	0.66	1.06	1.02
Cash Flow Per Share	1.65	0.94	1.71	1.62	0.78	0.00	(0.81)	(1.48)
Tang Book Value Per Share	4.87	3.91	2.80	2.99	2.65	4.72	11.84	8.05
Income Statement								
Total Revenue	19,424,700	19,381,100	19,478,500	19,989,300	20,609,600	20,111,800	16,118,200	10,305,600
EBITDA	851,500	801,900	802,500	590,300	892,000	109,800	1,586,100	1,317,600
Depn & Amortn	89,700	71,000	69,700	154,800	133,800	123,000	1,051,600	1,003,600
Income Before Taxes	606,600	591,000	618,000	400,800	525,000	(27,500)	522,700	315,400
Income Taxes	210,200	84,900	236,400	-155,800	196,900	4,000	188,100	115,200
Net Income	433,600	479,200	381,600	232,300	329,900	282,900	499,500	439,700
Average Shares	272,500	287,000	321,500	335,200	361,400	429,800	470,900	430,900
Balance Sheet								
Current Assets	3,677,700	3,990,300	3,629,100	3,152,500	4,176,200	4,300,900	8,406,300	6,825,800
Total Assets	8,698,900	8,823,100	8,584,800	8,065,400	8,830,000	9,613,400	13,925,800	10,527,300
Current Liabilities	3,411,200	3,809,500	2,980,700	2,578,100	3,141,300	3,164,500	5,540,400	4,262,600
Long-Term Obligations	797,700	808,500	642,700	647,300	850,400	836,100	2,315,600	2,333,600
Total Liabilities	4,435,800	4,873,400	4,674,600	4,237,500	4,987,500	5,012,200	8,501,600	7,043,000
Stockholders' Equity	4,263,100	3,949,700	3,910,200	3,827,900	3,842,500	4,601,200	5,424,200	3,484,300
Shares Outstanding	264,262	269,713	333,505	321,713	348,085	375,363	458,129	432,705
Statistical Record								
Return on Assets %	4.94	5.51	4.58	2.75	3.57	2.40	4.09	6.15
Return on Equity %	10.53	12.19	9.86	6.06	7.79	5.64	11.21	18.47
EBITDA Margin %	4.38	4.14	4.12	2.95	4.33	0.55	9.84	12.79
Net Margin %	2.23	2.47	1.96	1.16	1.60	1.41	3.10	4.27
Asset Turnover	2.21	2.23	2.34	2.37	2.23	1.71	1.32	1.44
Current Ratio	1.08	1.05	1.22	1.22	1.33	1.36	1.52	1.60
Debt to Equity	0.19	0.20	0.16	0.17	0.22	0.18	0.43	0.67
Price Range	19.21-15.20	19.07-11.67	18.45-9.08	12.69-5.44	9.26-5.00	16.61-7.68	26.44-10.17	38.64-17.96
P/E Ratio	12.08-9.56	11.42-6.99	15.50-7.63	18.39-7.88	10.18-5.49	25.16-11.64	24.94-9.59	37.88-17.61

Address: 110 S.E. 6th Street, Ft. Lauderdale, FL 33301	**Web Site:** www.autonation.com	**Auditors:** KPMG LLP	
Telephone: (954) 769 6000	**Officers:** Michael J. Jackson - Chmn., C.E.O. Michael E. Maroone - Pres., C.O.O.	**Investor Contact:** 954-769-7339	
Fax: (954) 779 3884			

AUTOZONE, INC.

Exchange	Symbol	Price	52Wk Range	Yield	P/E
NYS	AZO	$85.70 (3/31/2005)	99.00-72.25	N/A	12.47

*7 Year Price Score 132.86 *NYSE Composite Index=100 *12 Month Price Score 102.17

TRADING VOLUME (thousand shares)

Interim Earnings (Per Share)

Qtr.	Nov	Jan	Apr	Aug
2001-02	0.76	0.58	0.96	1.71
2002-03	2.08	0.79	1.30	2.22
2003-04	1.35	1.04	1.68	2.50
2004-05	1.52	1.16	...	...

Interim Dividends (Per Share)

No Dividends Paid

Valuation Analysis

Forecast P/E	11.81	No of Institutions	
	(4/7/2005)	312	
Market Cap	$6.8 Billion	Shares	
Book Value	384.7 Million	77,466,384	
Price/Book	17.74	% Held	
Price/Sales	1.20	97.29	

Business Summary: Retail - Automotive (MIC: 5.7 SIC: 013 NAIC: 41310)

AutoZone is a specialty retailer of automotive parts and accessories, with most of its sales to do-it-yourself customers. As of Aug 28 2004, Co. operated 3,420 stores in 48 states and the District of Columbia and 63 stores in Mexico. Each of Co.'s stores carries product line for cars, sport utility vehicles, vans and light trucks, including new and remanufactured automotive hard parts, maintenance items and accessories. Co. also has a commercial sales program in the U.S. that provides commercial credit and delivery of parts and other products to local, regional and national repair garages, dealers and service stations.

Recent Developments: For the quarter ended Feb 12 2005, net income increased 2.7% to $94,093 thousand from net income of $91,654 thousand in the year-earlier quarter. Revenues were $1,204,055 thousand, up 3.9% from $1,159,236 thousand the year before. Operating income was $148,719 thousand versus an income of $168,526 thousand in the prior-year quarter, a decrease of 11.8%. Total direct expense was $621,684 thousand versus $594,925 thousand in the prior-year quarter, an increase of 4.5%. Total indirect expense was $433,652 thousand versus $395,785 thousand in the prior-year quarter, an increase of 9.6%.

Prospects: Co.'s results going forward should benefit from its use of pay-on-scan (POS) arrangements with certain vendors, whereby it does not purchase merchandise supplied by a vendor until that merchandise is sold to its customers. Co. noted that title and certain risks of ownership remain with the vendor until the merchandise is sold to its customers. Upon the sale of the merchandise, Co. recognizes the liability for the goods and pays the vendor. Co. continues to actively negotiate with its vendors to increase the use of POS arrangements. Separately, as part of its plan to open about 200 stores in fiscal year 2005, Co. intends to enter the Puerto Rico marketplace with 10 new stores by fall of 2005.

Financial Data

(US$ in Thousands)	6 Mos	3 Mos	08/28/2004	08/30/2003	08/31/2002	08/25/2001	08/26/2000	08/28/1999
Earnings Per Share	6.87	6.76	6.56	5.34	4.00	1.54	2.00	1.63
Cash Flow Per Share	7.15	7.82	7.53	7.38	6.96	4.08	3.87	2.07
Tang Book Value Per Share	1.03	N.M.	N.M.	0.90	3.87	5.13	5.49	6.83
Income Statement								
Total Revenue	2,490,258	1,286,203	5,637,025	5,457,123	5,325,510	4,818,185	4,482,696	4,116,392
EBITDA	437,567	242,556	1,109,827	1,027,545	889,263	519,024	638,820	561,626
Depn & Amortn	72,535	26,243	111,121	109,748	118,255	131,333	126,800	128,531
Income Before Taxes	319,597	194,523	905,902	833,007	691,148	287,026	435,190	387,783
Income Taxes	102,981	72,000	339,700	315,403	263,000	111,500	167,600	143,000
Net Income	216,616	122,523	566,202	517,604	428,148	175,526	267,590	244,783
Average Shares	80,850	80,748	86,350	96,963	107,111	113,801	133,869	150,257
Balance Sheet								
Current Assets	1,847,054	1,840,244	1,755,757	1,584,994	1,450,128	1,328,511	1,186,780	1,225,084
Total Assets	4,059,437	4,020,050	3,912,565	3,680,466	3,477,791	3,432,512	3,333,218	3,284,767
Current Liabilities	1,645,420	1,869,643	1,818,115	1,675,566	1,533,571	1,266,654	1,034,544	1,000,554
Long-Term Obligations	1,901,500	1,824,775	1,869,250	1,546,845	1,194,517	1,225,402	1,249,937	888,340
Total Liabilities	3,674,706	3,742,662	3,741,172	3,306,708	2,788,664	2,566,299	2,341,039	1,960,966
Stockholders' Equity	384,731	277,388	171,393	373,758	689,127	866,213	992,179	1,323,801
Shares Outstanding	79,620	79,659	79,628	88,708	99,268	109,408	121,510	144,353
Statistical Record								
Return on Assets %	14.70	14.69	14.95	14.50	12.19	5.20	8.11	8.14
Return on Equity %	184.45	151.45	208.29	97.66	54.16	18.94	23.17	18.70
EBITDA Margin %	17.57	18.86	19.69	18.83	16.70	10.77	14.25	13.64
Net Margin %	8.70	9.53	10.04	9.48	8.04	3.64	5.97	5.95
Asset Turnover	1.47	1.46	1.49	1.53	1.52	1.43	1.36	1.37
Current Ratio	1.12	0.98	0.97	0.95	0.95	1.05	1.15	1.22
Debt to Equity	4.94	6.58	10.91	4.14	1.73	1.41	1.26	0.67
Price Range	95.95-72.25	97.76-72.25	103.53-72.25	91.80-58.61	82.95-38.49	48.26-21.13	32.31-21.13	37.06-21.50
P/E Ratio	13.97-10.52	14.46-10.69	15.78-11.01	17.19-10.98	20.74-9.62	31.34-13.72	16.16-10.56	22.74-13.19

Address: 123 South Front Street, Memphis, TN 38103	Web Site: www.autozone.com	Auditors: Ernst & Young LLP
Telephone: (901) 495-6500	Officers: William C. Rhodes III - Pres., C.E.O.	Investor Contact: 901-325-4458
Fax: (901) 495-8300	Michael G. Archbold - Exec. V.P., C.F.O.	

AVALONBAY COMMUNITIES, INC.

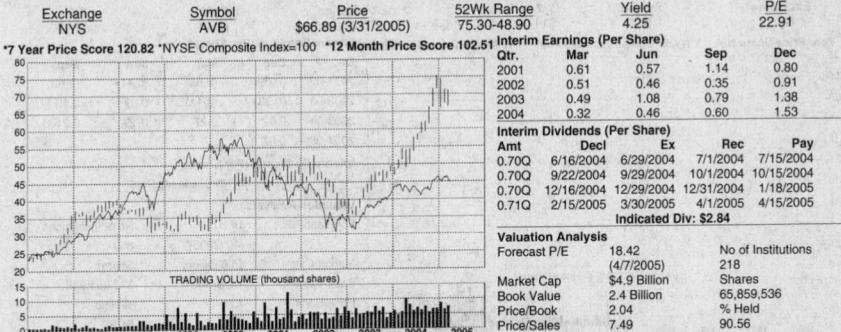

Exchange	Symbol	Price	52Wk Range	Yield	P/E
NYS	AVB	$66.89 (3/31/2005)	75.30-48.90	4.25	22.91

*7 Year Price Score 120.82 *NYSE Composite Index=100 *12 Month Price Score 102.51

Interim Earnings (Per Share)

Qtr.	Mar	Jun	Sep	Dec
2001	0.61	0.57	1.14	0.80
2002	0.51	0.46	0.35	0.91
2003	0.49	1.08	0.79	1.38
2004	0.32	0.46	0.60	1.53

Interim Dividends (Per Share)

Amt	Decl	Ex	Rec	Pay
0.70Q	6/16/2004	6/29/2004	7/1/2004	7/15/2004
0.70Q	9/22/2004	9/29/2004	10/1/2004	10/15/2004
0.70Q	12/16/2004	12/29/2004	12/31/2004	1/18/2005
0.71Q	2/15/2005	3/30/2005	4/1/2005	4/15/2005
		Indicated Div: $2.84		

Valuation Analysis

Forecast P/E	18.42	No of Institutions
	(4/7/2005)	218
Market Cap	$4.9 Billion	Shares
Book Value	2.4 Billion	65,859,536
Price/Book	2.04	% Held
Price/Sales	7.49	90.56

Business Summary: Property, Real Estate & Development (MIC: 8.3 SIC: 798 NAIC: 25930)

AvalonBay Communities is a real estate investment trust company focused on developing, redeveloping, acquiring and managing luxury apartment communities in high barrier-to-entry markets of the United States. These markets include Northern California, Southern California and the Northeast, Mid-Atlantic, Midwest and Pacific Northwest regions of the country. As of Feb 27 2004, Co. owned or held interest in 131 apartment communities containing 38,504 apartment homes in eleven states and the District of Columbia, of which eleven communities were under construction and two were under reconstruction.

Recent Developments: For the year ended Dec 31 2004, income from continuing operations decreased 8.2% to $86,329 thousand from income of $94,041 thousand a year earlier. Net income decreased 19.1% to $219,745 thousand from net income of $271,525 thousand a year earlier. Revenues were $648,454 thousand, up 9.5% from $592,342 thousand the year before.

Prospects: Co. is optimistic regarding its 2005 outlook, due in part to stronger market fundamentals. Thus, Co. expects full-year 2005 earnings per share in the range of $1.93 to $2.13. For the first quarter ended Mar 31 2005, Co. expects earnings per share of between $0.65 and $0.69. Also, Co. expects projected funds from operation (FFO) in the range of $3.51 to $3.71 for the full year 2005, and FFO per share of $0.91 to $0.95 for the first quarter ended Mar 31 2005. The projected FFO ranges for both the full year and first quarter of 2005 include $0.08 to $0.09 related to the potential sale of an investment in a real estate technology company that Co. expects will occur in the first quarter of 2005.

Financial Data

(US$ in Thousands)	12/31/2004	12/31/2003	12/31/2002	12/31/2001	12/31/2000	12/31/1999	12/31/1998	12/31/1997
Earnings Per Share	2.92	3.73	2.23	3.12	2.53	2.00	1.37	1.40
Cash Flow Per Share	3.84	3.50	4.48	4.55	4.43	3.81	3.86	2.89
Tang Book Value Per Share	32.86	32.58	32.18	33.68	36.35	36.04	36.62	30.39
Dividends Per Share	2.800	2.800	2.800	2.560	2.240	2.060	1.530	1.660
Dividend Payout %	95.89	75.07	125.56	82.05	88.54	103.00	111.68	118.57
Income Statement								
Property Income	...	...	630,502	637,379	571,943	503,132	352,017	121,873
Non-Property Income	648,454	609,651	8,464	4,278	1,452	1,412	867	4,161
Total Revenue	648,454	609,651	638,966	641,657	573,395	504,544	352,884	126,034
Depn & Amortn	171,561	161,830	152,487	137,401	126,027	113,723	80,224	27,009
Interest Expense	131,314	134,911	121,380	103,203	83,609	74,699	54,003	...
Net Income	219,745	271,525	173,618	248,997	210,604	172,276	94,434	38,941
Average Shares	73,354	70,203	70,674	69,781	68,140	66,110	50,147	22,472
Balance Sheet								
Total Assets	5,068,281	4,909,582	4,950,835	4,664,289	4,397,225	4,154,662	4,030,204	1,317,650
Long-Term Obligations	2,442,291	2,337,817	2,471,163	2,082,769	1,729,924	1,593,647	1,484,371	487,484
Total Liabilities	2,661,465	2,573,496	2,678,852	2,294,541	1,905,231	1,749,000	1,658,538	515,822
Stockholders' Equity	2,385,291	2,311,334	2,194,540	2,314,555	2,442,493	2,370,285	2,339,453	792,695
Shares Outstanding	72,582	70,937	68,202	68,713	67,191	65,758	63,887	26,078
Statistical Record								
Return on Assets %	4.39	5.51	3.61	5.50	4.91	4.21	3.53	3.84
Return on Equity %	9.33	12.05	7.70	10.47	8.73	7.32	6.03	6.46
Net Margin %	33.89	44.54	27.17	38.81	36.73	34.14	26.76	30.90
Price Range	75.30-46.90	49.55-35.39	52.65-36.72	51.90-42.65	50.25-33.19	37.00-31.06	39.25-30.88	40.31-33.13
P/E Ratio	25.79-16.06	13.28-9.49	23.61-16.47	16.63-13.67	19.86-13.12	18.50-15.53	28.65-22.54	28.79-23.66
Average Yield %	4.83	6.52	6.30	5.43	5.37	6.14	4.30	4.44

Address: 2900 Eisenhower Avenue, Suite 300, Alexandria, VA 22314	Web Site: www.avalonbay.com	Auditors: Ernst & Young LLP
Telephone: (703) 329 6300	**Officers:** Bryce Blair - Chmn., Pres., C.E.O. Thomas J. Sargeant - Exec. V.P., C.F.O., Treas.	
Fax: (408) 984 7060		

AVAYA INC

Exchange	Symbol	Price	52Wk Range	Yield	P/E
NYS	AV	$11.68 (3/31/2005)	17.73-11.41	N/A	17.18

*7 Year Price Score N/A   *NYSE Composite Index=100   *12 Month Price Score 83.56

Interim Earnings (Per Share)

Qtr.	Dec	Mar	Jun	Sep
2001-02	(0.09)	(0.63)	(0.11)	(1.63)
2002-03	(0.33)	(0.11)	0.02	0.18
2003-04	0.02	0.27	0.13	0.21
2004-05	0.07	...	...	...

Interim Dividends (Per Share)

No Dividends Paid

Valuation Analysis

Forecast P/E	14.50	No of Institutions	
	(4/7/2005)	359	
Market Cap	$5.6 Billion	Shares	
Book Value	1.2 Billion	311,951,808	
Price/Book	4.58	% Held	
Price/Sales	1.32	64.99	

Business Summary: Communications (MIC: 10.1 SIC: 661 NAIC: 34210)

Avaya is a provider of communications systems, applications and services for enterprises, including businesses, government agencies and other organizations. Co.'s product offerings include Internet Protocol, or IP, telephony systems; appliances, such as telephone sets; multi-media contact center infrastructure and applications in support of customer relationship management; unified communications applications, which include voice and multi-media messaging; and traditional voice communication systems. Co. supports its customer base with service offerings that help its customers plan, design, implement and manage their communications networks.

Recent Developments: For the quarter ended Dec 31 2004, income from continuing operations increased 10.0% to $33,000 thousand from income of $30,000 thousand in the year-earlier quarter. Net income increased 210.0% to $31,000 thousand from net income of $10,000 thousand in the year-earlier quarter, Revenues were $1,148,000 thousand, up 18.2% from $971,000 thousand the year before. Operating income was $88,000 thousand versus an income of $52,000 thousand in the prior-year quarter, an increase of 69.2%. Total direct expense was $605,000 thousand versus $523,000 thousand in the prior-year quarter, an increase of 15.7%. Total indirect expense was $455,000 thousand versus $396,000 thousand in the prior-year quarter.

Prospects: Co. is experiencing strong revenue growth, primarily reflecting the impact of recent acquisitions and favorable currency rates. For instance, Co. recently completed the acquisition of Tenovis, a major European provider of enterprise communications systems and services. In addition, Co. recently acquired Spectel, an audio and web conferencing for enterprises and service providers, whose products are now being marketed under Avaya Meeting Exchange. Further, during the first quarter, Co. shipped its five millionth Internet protocol telephony line. Also, Co. substantially reduced its debt during the first quarter. Co. believes its strong results position it to meet its goals for the year.

Financial Data

(US$ in Thousands)	3 Mos	09/30/2004	09/30/2003	09/30/2002	09/30/2001	09/30/2000	09/30/1999	09/30/1998
Earnings Per Share	0.68	0.64	(0.23)	(2.44)	(1.33)	(1.39)	1.03	0.17
Cash Flow Per Share	1.04	1.09	0.52	0.60	(0.47)	1.80	1.66	...
Tang Book Value Per Share	N.M.	1.18	0.13	...	0.79	1.99	5.47	...
Income Statement								
Total Revenue	1,148,000	4,069,000	4,338,000	4,956,000	6,793,000	7,680,000	8,268,000	7,754,000
EBITDA	100,000	451,000	300,000	(97,000)	(287,000)	(159,000)	609,000	527,000
Depn & Amortn	56,000	162,000	232,000	273,000	273,000	220,000	212,000	193,000
Income Before Taxes	40,000	242,000	5,000	(401,000)	(570,000)	(448,000)	307,000	240,000
Income Taxes	7,000	(49,000)	93,000	265,000	(218,000)	(73,000)	121,000	197,000
Net Income	31,000	296,000	(88,000)	(666,000)	(352,000)	(375,000)	282,000	43,000
Average Shares	492,000	476,000	378,000	330,000	284,000	269,000	273,000	260,000
Balance Sheet								
Current Assets	2,293,000	2,724,000	2,569,000	2,303,000	2,769,000	3,362,000	3,043,000	3,065,000
Total Assets	5,080,000	4,159,000	4,057,000	3,897,000	4,648,000	5,037,000	4,239,000	4,177,000
Current Liabilities	1,424,000	1,423,000	1,168,000	1,324,000	2,018,000	2,589,000	1,597,000	1,540,000
Long-Term Obligations	251,000	294,000	953,000	933,000	500,000	713,000	...	...
Total Liabilities	3,856,000	3,365,000	3,857,000	3,897,000	3,772,000	4,273,000	2,422,000	2,382,000
Stockholders' Equity	1,224,000	794,000	200,000	...	481,000	764,000	1,817,000	1,795,000
Shares Outstanding	479,450	455,827	418,556	364,195	286,704	282,027	278,292	...
Statistical Record								
Return on Assets %	6.88	7.19	N.M.	N.M.	N.M.	N.M.	6.70	...
Return on Equity %	42.77	59.39	N.M.	N.M.	N.M.	N.M.	15.61	...
EBITDA Margin %	8.71	11.08	6.92	N.M.	N.M.	N.M.	7.37	6.80
Net Margin %	2.70	7.27	N.M.	N.M.	N.M.	N.M.	3.41	0.55
Asset Turnover	0.92	0.99	1.09	1.16	1.40	1.65	1.96	...
Current Ratio	1.61	1.91	2.20	1.74	1.37	1.30	1.91	1.99
Debt to Equity	0.21	0.37	4.76	...	1.04	0.93	...	...
Price Range	18.36-12.05	18.36-10.58	11.05-1.35	13.61-1.15	20.19-9.90	23.38-18.81	...	...
P/E Ratio	27.00-17.72	28.69-16.53	...	...	...	...	...	...

Address: 211 Mount Airy Road, Basking Ridge, NJ 07920
Telephone: (908) 953-6000
Fax: (908) 953-7609

Web Site: www.avaya.com
Officers: Donald K. Peterson - Chmn., C.E.O. Pamela F. Craven - Sr. V.P., Sec., Gen. Couns.

Auditors: PricewaterhouseCoopers LLP
Investor Contact: 908-953-7500
Transfer Agents: Bank of New York, New York, NY

AVERY DENNISON CORP.

Exchange	Symbol	Price	52Wk Range	Yield	P/E	Div Acheiver
NYS	AVY	$61.93 (3/31/2005)	65.78-54.90	2.45	22.28	29 Years

*7 Year Price Score 91.56 *NYSE Composite Index=100 *12 Month Price Score 92.01

Interim Earnings (Per Share)

Qtr.	Mar	Jun	Sep	Dec
2001	0.65	0.61	0.63	0.59
2002	0.66	0.74	0.64	0.56
2003	0.71	0.71	0.67	0.60
2004	0.52	0.68	0.75	0.83

Interim Dividends (Per Share)

Amt	Decl	Ex	Rec	Pay
0.37Q	4/22/2004	5/28/2004	6/2/2004	6/16/2004
0.37Q	7/22/2004	8/30/2004	9/1/2004	9/15/2004
0.38Q	10/28/2004	11/29/2004	12/1/2004	12/15/2004
0.38Q	1/27/2005	2/28/2005	3/2/2005	3/16/2005

Indicated Div: $1.52 (Div. Reinv. Plan)

Valuation Analysis

Forecast P/E	18.55	No of Institutions	
	(4/7/2005)	388	
Market Cap	$6.2 Billion	Shares	
Book Value	1.5 Billion	82,379,224	
Price/Book	4.00	% Held	
Price/Sales	1.16	74.58	

Business Summary: Paper Products (MIC: 11.11 SIC: 672 NAIC: 22222)

Avery Dennison is a worldwide manufacturer of pressure-sensitive adhesives and materials, office products and converted products. A portion of self-adhesive material is converted into labels and other products through embossing, printing, stamping and die-cutting, and some are sold in unconverted form as base materials, tapes and reflective sheeting. Co. also manufactures and sells a variety of office products and other items not involving pressure-sensitive components, such as notebooks, three-ring binders, organization systems, felt-tip markers, glues, fasteners, business forms, tickets, tags, and imprinting equipment.

Recent Developments: For the year ended Jan 1 2005, net income increased 4.4% to $279,700 thousand from net income of $267,900 thousand a year earlier. Revenues were $5,340,900 thousand, up 12.1% from $4,762,600 thousand the year before. Total direct expense was $3,761,400 thousand versus $3,304,600 thousand in the prior year, an increase of 13.8%. Total indirect expense was $1,112,400 thousand versus $1,034,100 thousand in the prior year, an increase of 7.6%.

Prospects: In the first quarter of 2005, Co. expects fully diluted earnings to be in the range of $0.71 to $0.78 per share, with an estimate of annual earnings for 2005 in the range of $3.15 to $3.50 per share, excluding the impact of stock option expenses which it expects to begin reporting in the third quarter of 2005, as well as restructuring charges. Also, Co. expects reported revenue growth in the range of 8.0% to 10.0% in the first quarter and 6.0% to 10.0% for the full year 2005, with an anticipated positive impact from currency translation of 2 to 3 points in the first quarter and 1 to 2 points during the full year.

Financial Data (US$ in Thousands)	01/01/2005	12/27/2003	12/28/2002	12/29/2001	12/30/2000	01/01/2000	01/02/1999	12/27/1997
Earnings Per Share	2.78	2.68	2.59	2.47	2.84	2.13	2.15	1.93
Cash Flow Per Share	5.09	3.38	5.32	3.85	4.18	4.40	4.10	3.58
Tang Book Value Per Share	6.45	4.53	2.53	4.70	3.93	4.18	6.88	6.87
Dividends Per Share	1.490	1.450	1.350	1.230	1.110	0.990	0.870	0.720
Dividend Payout %	53.60	54.10	52.12	49.80	39.08	46.48	40.47	37.31
Income Statement								
Total Revenue	5,340,900	4,762,600	4,206,900	3,803,300	3,893,500	3,768,200	3,459,900	3,345,700
EBITDA	534,400	492,100	501,600	515,800	583,200	480,800	463,900	428,000
Depn & Amortn	161,000	157,200	136,800	156,000	156,900	150,400	127,200	116,800
Income Before Taxes	373,400	334,900	364,800	359,800	426,300	330,400	336,700	311,200
Income Taxes	93,700	92,100	107,600	116,400	142,800	115,000	113,400	106,400
Net Income	279,700	267,900	257,200	243,200	283,500	215,400	223,300	204,800
Average Shares	100,500	100,000	99,400	98,600	99,800	101,300	104,100	106,100
Balance Sheet								
Current Assets	1,542,400	1,440,900	1,215,500	982,500	982,400	956,000	802,000	793,500
Total Assets	4,399,300	4,105,300	3,652,400	2,819,200	2,699,100	2,592,500	2,142,600	2,046,500
Current Liabilities	1,387,300	1,496,000	1,296,100	951,300	800,700	850,400	664,300	629,900
Long-Term Obligations	1,007,200	887,700	837,200	626,700	772,900	617,500	465,900	404,100
Total Liabilities	2,850,600	2,786,600	2,596,000	1,889,800	1,871,000	1,782,600	1,309,300	1,209,300
Stockholders' Equity	1,548,700	1,318,700	1,056,400	929,400	828,100	809,900	833,300	837,200
Shares Outstanding	100,113	99,569	110,467	109,890	110,245	98,800	100,000	102,400
Statistical Record								
Return on Assets %	6.47	6.93	7.97	8.84	10.74	9.12	10.49	10.06
Return on Equity %	19.19	22.62	25.98	27.75	34.71	26.29	26.30	24.61
EBITDA Margin %	10.01	10.33	11.92	13.56	14.98	12.76	13.41	12.79
Net Margin %	5.24	5.63	6.11	6.39	7.28	5.72	6.45	6.12
Asset Turnover	1.24	1.23	1.30	1.38	1.48	1.60	1.63	1.64
Current Ratio	1.11	0.96	0.94	1.03	1.23	1.12	1.21	1.26
Debt to Equity	0.65	0.67	0.79	0.67	0.93	0.76	0.56	0.48
Price Range	65.78-54.90	63.51-47.75	69.49-52.86	60.24-44.39	78.00-43.31	72.88-39.75	60.75-40.88	44.13-33.38
P/E Ratio	23.66-19.75	23.70-17.82	26.83-20.41	24.39-17.97	27.46-15.25	34.21-18.66	28.26-19.01	22.86-17.29
Average Yield %	2.44	2.64	2.19	2.34	1.88	1.71	1.74	1.81

Address: 150 North Orange Grove Boulevard, Pasadena, CA 91103 Telephone: (626) 304-2000 Fax: (626) 792-7312	Web Site: www.averydennison.com Officers: Philip M. Neal - Chmn., C.E.O. Dean A. Scarborough - Pres., C.O.O.	Auditors: PricewaterhouseCoopers LLP Investor Contact: 626-304-2204 Transfer Agents: EquiServe Trust Company, N.A., Providence, RI

AVNET, INC.

Exchange	Symbol	Price	52Wk Range	Yield	P/E
NYS	AVT	$18.42 (3/31/2005)	26.00-15.77	N/A	14.39

*7 Year Price Score 74.41   *NYSE Composite Index=100   *12 Month Price Score 91.27

Interim Earnings (Per Share)

Qtr.	Sep	Dec	Mar	Jun
2001-02	(0.16)	(0.02)	(0.01)	(0.51)
2002-03	...	(0.49)	0.01	0.09
2003-04	(0.09)	0.07	0.22	0.40
2004-05	0.30	0.36		

Interim Dividends (Per Share)

Dividend Payment Suspended

Valuation Analysis

Forecast P/E	11.19	No of Institutions	
	(4/7/2005)	203	
Market Cap	$2.2 Billion	Shares	
Book Value	2.2 Billion	112,151,104	
Price/Book	1.02	% Held	
Price/Sales	0.21	92.98	

Business Summary: Hospitality & Tourism (MIC: 5.1 SIC: 065 NAIC: 23690)

Avnet is an industrial distributor of electronic components, enterprise network and computer equipment and embedded subsystems. Co. distributes electronic components, computer products and software as received from its suppliers or with assembly or other value added. Additionally, Co. provides engineering design, materials management and logistics services, system integration and configuration, and supply chain advisory services. Co. is comprised of two global operating groups: Electronics Marketing and Technology Solutions. Co. markets and sells semiconductors, interconnect, passive and electromechanical devices, mid- to high-end servers, data storage, software and networking solutions.

Recent Developments: For the quarter ended Jan 1 2005, net income increased 387.0% to $43,510 thousand from net income of $8,935 thousand in the year-earlier quarter. Revenues were $2,883,155 thousand, up 12.9% from $2,554,460 thousand the year before. Operating income was $83,978 thousand versus an income of $34,224 thousand in the prior-year quarter, an increase of 145.4%. Total direct expense was $2,509,275 thousand versus $2,225,301 thousand in the prior-year quarter, an increase of 12.8%. Total indirect expense was $289,902 thousand versus $294,935 thousand in the prior-year quarter, a decrease of 1.7%.

Prospects: Co. believes the sequential decline experienced by its Electronics Marketing group for the quarter ended Jan 1 2005 is due primarily to a mid-cycle inventory correction whereby there has been a shortening of lead-times at many suppliers, which has resulted in the targeted reduction of inventory at certain of its customers. Co. stated that it continues to believe this apparent mid-cycle inventory correction is a short-term trend and will recede in the second half of fiscal 2005. Looking forward, Co. expects consolidated sales for its fiscal third quarter ended Mar 31 2005 in the range of $2.67 billion to $2.77 billion, and earnings per share ranging from $0.33 to $0.37.

Financial Data

(US$ in Thousands)	6 Mos	3 Mos	07/03/2004	06/27/2003	06/28/2002	06/29/2001	06/30/2000	07/02/1999
Earnings Per Share	1.28	0.99	0.60	(0.39)	(5.61)	0.13	1.75	2.43
Cash Flow Per Share	1.29	0.01	0.53	5.47	8.26	1.59	(6.05)	0.99
Tang Book Value Per Share	10.54	9.25	8.79	8.16	8.04	8.23	11.83	14.38
Dividends Per Share	...	...	...	...	0.150	0.300	0.300	0.300
Dividend Payout %	...	...	...	...	...	230.77	17.14	12.35
Income Statement								
Total Revenue	5,483,156	2,600,001	10,244,741	9,048,442	8,920,248	12,814,010	9,172,205	6,350,042
EBITDA	188,199	88,433	257,511	114,285	107,649	398,545	414,420	479,662
Depn & Amortn	30,764	15,089	64,540	88,839	103,879	119,398	75,561	52,275
Income Before Taxes	115,310	52,473	98,398	(79,405)	(120,813)	87,252	254,531	375,291
Income Taxes	35,469	16,142	25,501	(33,289)	(36,377)	87,155	109,390	200,834
Net Income	79,841	36,331	72,897	(46,116)	(664,931)	15,402	145,141	174,457
Average Shares	121,426	121,280	121,252	119,456	118,561	118,815	83,124	71,834
Balance Sheet								
Current Assets	3,926,083	3,491,642	3,483,986	3,126,090	3,205,532	3,747,489	3,873,255	2,313,323
Total Assets	5,272,813	4,864,504	4,863,651	4,499,551	4,681,954	5,864,148	5,244,355	2,984,697
Current Liabilities	1,844,495	1,586,800	1,644,993	1,306,050	1,276,836	2,570,065	1,903,774	795,863
Long-Term Obligations	1,192,176	1,202,710	1,196,160	1,278,399	1,565,836	919,493	1,438,610	791,226
Total Liabilities	3,104,219	2,853,676	2,910,225	2,667,029	2,877,444	3,489,558	3,342,384	1,587,089
Stockholders' Equity	2,168,594	2,010,828	1,953,426	1,832,522	1,804,510	2,374,590	1,901,971	1,397,608
Shares Outstanding	120,527	120,486	120,477	119,543	119,423	117,827	88,361	70,382
Statistical Record								
Return on Assets %	3.08	2.56	1.53	N.M.	N.M.	0.28	3.54	6.00
Return on Equity %	7.58	6.25	3.78	N.M.	N.M.	0.72	8.82	12.65
EBITDA Margin %	3.43	3.40	2.51	1.26	1.21	3.11	4.52	7.55
Net Margin %	1.46	1.40	0.71	N.M.	N.M.	0.12	1.58	2.75
Asset Turnover	2.14	2.22	2.15	1.98	1.70	2.31	2.24	2.19
Current Ratio	2.13	2.20	2.12	2.39	2.51	1.46	2.03	2.91
Debt to Equity	0.55	0.60	0.61	0.70	0.87	0.39	0.76	0.57
Price Range	26.35-15.77	26.35-15.77	26.35-12.39	21.99-5.96	29.06-17.59	35.09-17.50	39.31-19.00	30.25-17.28
P/E Ratio	20.59-12.32	26.62-15.93	43.92-20.65	...	...	269.95-134.62	22.46-10.86	12.45-7.11
Average Yield %	...	...	...	...	0.63	1.17	1.06	1.29

Address: 2211 South 47th Street, Phoenix, AZ 85034 Telephone: (480) 643-2000 Fax: (480) 643-7370	Web Site: www.avnet.com Officers: Roy Vallee - Chmn., C.E.O. Raymond Sadowski - Sr. V.P., C.F.O., Asst. Sec.	Auditors: KPMG LLP

AVON PRODUCTS, INC.

Exchange	Symbol	Price	52Wk Range	Yield	P/E	Div Acheiver
NYS	AVP	$42.94 (3/31/2005)	46.14-37.45	1.54	24.26	14 Years

*7 Year Price Score 137.78 ***NYSE Composite Index=100** ***12 Month Price Score 94.23**

Interim Earnings (Per Share)

Qtr.	Mar	Jun	Sep	Dec
2001	0.17	0.28	0.21	0.23
2002	0.20	0.32	0.19	0.40
2003	0.21	0.35	0.28	0.55
2004	0.31	0.49	0.37	0.60

Interim Dividends (Per Share)

Amt	Decl	Ex	Rec	Pay
0.14Q	5/6/2004	5/13/2004	5/17/2004	6/1/2004
0.14Q	8/5/2004	8/16/2004	8/18/2004	9/1/2004
0.14Q	11/4/2004	11/12/2004	11/16/2004	12/1/2004
0.165Q	2/1/2005	2/10/2005	2/14/2005	3/1/2005

Indicated Div: $0.66 (Div. Reinv. Plan)

Valuation Analysis

Forecast P/E	21.73	No of Institutions
	(4/7/2005)	473
Market Cap	$20.2 Billion	Shares
Book Value	950.2 Million	393,030,400
Price/Book	21.31	% Held
Price/Sales	2.61	83.35

Business Summary: Chemicals (MIC: 11.1 SIC: 844 NAIC: 25620)

Avon Products is a global manufacturer and marketer of beauty and related products. Co.'s products fall into three product categories: Beauty, which consists of cosmetics, fragrances and toiletries; Beauty Plus, which consists of fashion jewelry, watches, apparel and accessories; and Beyond Beauty, which consists of home products, gift and decorative products and candles. Sales are made to the consumer principally through approximately 4.4 million independent representatives. As of Apr 3, 2004, Co. had operations in 60 countries and its products were distributed in 72 more for coverage in 132 countries.

Recent Developments: For the year ended Dec 31 2004, net income increased 27.3% to $846,100 thousand from net income of $664,800 thousand a year earlier. Revenues were $7,747,800 thousand, up 13.2% from $6,845,100 thousand the year before. Operating income was $1,229,000 thousand versus an income of $1,042,800 thousand in the prior year, an increase of 17.9%. Total direct expense was $2,911,700 thousand versus $2,611,800 thousand in the prior year, an increase of 11.5%. Total indirect expense was $3,607,100 thousand versus $3,190,500 thousand in the prior year, an increase of 13.1%.

Prospects: For full-year 2005, Co. continues to expect its U.S. operations revenue to decline slightly and operating profit to decrease in the mid-single digits. As the category repositioning gains traction in the U.S. business, Co. remains confident that the U.S. will resume revenue and operating-profit growth in 2006, with revenues expected to increase in the low-to-mid single digits and operating profit projected to grow ahead of revenues. Separately, for the full-year 2005, Co. expects its International operations to show revenue growth in the mid-teens and operating profit is expected to grow over 20.0%, on particular strength in its leading growth markets of Russia, China, Turkey and Brazil.

Financial Data

(US$ in Thousands)	12/31/2004	12/31/2003	12/31/2002	12/31/2001	12/31/2000	12/31/1999	12/31/1998	12/31/1997
Earnings Per Share	1.77	1.39	1.11	0.90	1.00	0.58	0.51	0.64
Cash Flow Per Share	1.86	1.58	1.20	1.59	0.68	0.90	0.62	0.60
Tang Book Value Per Share	2.02	0.79	...	...	...	...	0.54	0.54
Dividends Per Share	0.560	0.420	0.400	0.380	0.370	0.360	0.340	0.315
Dividend Payout %	31.64	30.22	36.04	42.46	37.19	61.54	66.67	49.61
Income Statement								
Total Revenue	7,747,800	6,876,000	6,228,300	5,994,500	5,714,600	5,289,100	5,212,700	5,079,400
EBITDA	1,343,000	1,161,500	1,022,000	846,400	864,300	621,700	546,700	625,800
Depn & Amortn	135,300	133,200	142,900	124,000	97,100	83,000	72,000	72,100
Income Before Taxes	1,187,500	993,500	835,600	665,700	691,000	506,600	455,900	534,900
Income Taxes	330,600	318,900	292,300	230,900	201,700	204,200	190,800	197,900
Net Income	846,100	664,800	534,600	430,000	478,400	302,400	270,000	338,800
Average Shares	477,960	483,140	490,940	492,100	485,900	518,740	531,900	534,000
Balance Sheet								
Current Assets	2,506,400	2,226,100	2,048,200	1,889,100	1,545,700	1,337,800	1,341,400	1,344,000
Total Assets	4,148,100	3,562,300	3,327,500	3,193,100	2,826,400	2,528,600	2,433,500	2,272,900
Current Liabilities	1,525,500	1,587,700	1,975,500	1,461,000	1,359,300	1,712,800	1,329,500	1,355,900
Long-Term Obligations	866,300	877,700	767,000	1,236,300	1,108,200	701,400	201,000	102,200
Total Liabilities	3,197,900	3,191,000	3,455,200	3,267,700	3,042,200	2,934,700	2,148,400	1,987,900
Stockholders' Equity	950,200	371,300	(127,700)	(74,600)	(215,800)	(406,100)	285,100	285,000
Shares Outstanding	471,530	470,596	470,515	473,362	476,324	475,790	525,040	527,256
Statistical Record								
Return on Assets %	21.89	19.30	16.40	14.29	17.82	12.19	11.47	15.07
Return on Equity %	127.70	545.81	...	...	...	...	94.72	128.65
EBITDA Margin %	17.33	16.89	16.41	14.12	15.12	11.75	10.49	12.32
Net Margin %	10.92	9.67	8.58	7.17	8.37	5.72	5.18	6.67
Asset Turnover	2.00	2.00	1.91	1.99	2.13	2.13	2.22	2.26
Current Ratio	1.64	1.40	1.04	1.29	1.14	0.78	1.01	0.99
Debt to Equity	0.91	2.36	...	...	...	...	0.71	0.36
Price Range	46.14-30.86	34.67-24.58	28.48-21.86	24.80-18.39	24.78-12.69	28.09-11.91	23.09-12.69	19.17-12.75
P/E Ratio	26.07-17.44	24.95-17.68	25.66-19.69	27.55-20.43	24.78-12.69	48.44-20.53	45.28-24.88	29.96-19.92
Average Yield %	1.40	1.38	1.58	1.71	1.94	1.69	1.82	1.99

Address: 1345 Avenue of the Americas, New York, NY 10105-0196 **Telephone:** (212) 282-5000 **Fax:** (212) 282-6035	**Web Site:** www.avon.com **Officers:** Andrea Jung - Chmn., C.E.O. Susan J. Kropf - Pres., C.O.O.	**Auditors:** PricewaterhouseCoopers LLP **Investor Contact:** 212-282-5320 **Transfer Agents:** EquiServe Trust Company, N.A. Providence, RI

AVX CORP.

Exchange	Symbol	Price	52Wk Range	Yield	P/E
NYS	AVX	$12.25 (3/31/2005)	17.32-11.17	1.22	51.04

*7 Year Price Score 68.28 ***NYSE Composite Index=100** ***12 Month Price Score 86.78**

Interim Earnings (Per Share)

Qtr.	Jun	Sep	Dec	Mar
2001-02	0.17	(0.16)	(0.04)	(0.01)
2002-03	0.01	0.01	0.00	(0.08)
2003-04	(0.09)	(0.44)	(0.05)	(0.04)
2004-05	0.13	0.11	0.04	...

Interim Dividends (Per Share)

Amt	Decl	Ex	Rec	Pay
0.037Q	5/14/2004	5/19/2004	5/21/2004	6/1/2004
0.037Q	7/21/2004	7/30/2004	8/3/2004	8/13/2004
0.037Q	10/22/2004	11/4/2004	11/8/2004	11/15/2004
0.037Q	2/7/2005	2/16/2005	2/18/2005	2/25/2005

Indicated Div: $0.15

Valuation Analysis

Forecast P/E	34.50	No of Institutions
	(4/7/2005)	104
Market Cap	$2.1 Billion	Shares
Book Value	1.5 Billion	48,469,756
Price/Book	1.45	% Held
Price/Sales	1.64	28.01

Business Summary: Electrical (MIC: 11.14 SIC: 678 NAIC: 34417)

AVX is a worldwide manufacturer and supplier of a line of passive electronic components and related products. Co.'s passive electronic component products include ceramic and tantalum capacitors, film capacitors, varistors and non-linear resistors manufactured in its facilities throughout the world and passive components manufactured by Kyocera Corporation of Japan. Co. also manufactures and sells electronic connectors and distributes and sells certain electronic connectors manufactured by Kyocera. Co.'s customers are multi-national original equipment manufacturers, independent electronic component distributors and contract equipment manufacturers.

Recent Developments: For the quarter ended Dec 31 2004, net income was $7,620 thousand versus net loss of $8,477 thousand in the year-earlier quarter. Revenues were $302,233 thousand, up 1.8% from $296,831 thousand the year before. Operating income was $8,315 thousand versus a loss of $11,752 thousand in the prior-year quarter, a decrease of 170.8%. Total direct expense was $266,894 thousand versus $278,939 thousand in the prior-year quarter, a decrease of 4.3%. Total indirect expense was $27,024 thousand versus $29,644 thousand in the prior-year quarter, a decrease of 8.8%.

Prospects: Results are benefiting from the actions that Co. has taken in 2004 to streamline operations, reduce operating costs and enhance production capabilities. Co. is also seeing an improvement in the markets it serves, some pricing stabilization, improvement in manufacturing capacity utilization and a more normal balance in supply chain inventories. Going forward, near-term results are clouded by the uncertainty in the global economy and end market demand. However, Co. is confident that increases in worldwide demand for electronic devices, cost reductions and improvements in its production processes and opportunities for growth in its advanced product line will enhance its long-term growth.

Financial Data

(US$ in Thousands)	9 Mos	6 Mos	3 Mos	03/31/2004	03/31/2003	03/31/2002	03/31/2001	03/31/2000
Earnings Per Share	0.24	0.15	(0.40)	(0.62)	(0.07)	(0.04)	3.22	0.90
Cash Flow Per Share	0.53	0.48	0.62	0.48	0.70	1.73	3.35	1.02
Tang Book Value Per Share	8.02	7.75	7.69	7.58	7.91	7.99	8.20	5.21
Dividends Per Share	0.150	0.150	0.150	0.150	0.150	0.150	0.140	0.133
Dividend Payout %	62.39	99.64		...	...	...	4.35	14.72
Income Statement								
Total Revenue	977,234	675,001	345,018	1,136,577	1,134,111	1,249,980	2,608,113	1,630,273
EBITDA	129,399	99,842	53,307	(48,978)	93,401	115,232	962,046	324,573
Depn & Amortn	59,707	38,973	19,736	93,797	119,921	138,501	135,860	99,250
Income Before Taxes	77,979	65,903	35,768	(131,671)	(10,438)	(7,006)	841,260	232,126
Income Taxes	28,852	24,396	12,876	(24,065)	2,000	226	273,723	75,194
Net Income	49,127	41,507	22,892	(107,606)	(12,438)	(7,232)	567,537	156,932
Average Shares	173,839	174,009	174,345	173,634	174,325	174,684	176,469	174,976
Balance Sheet								
Current Assets	1,146,372	1,157,020	1,168,991	1,101,979	1,077,957	1,150,868	1,355,286	846,816
Total Assets	1,720,537	1,695,658	1,721,488	1,667,877	1,700,513	1,691,599	1,885,098	1,308,331
Current Liabilities	206,347	223,698	252,372	214,890	185,557	194,677	343,533	282,687
Long-Term Obligations	...	...	...	...	...	...	13,722	18,174
Total Liabilities	261,138	280,785	315,742	281,333	237,357	215,564	380,064	326,310
Stockholders' Equity	1,459,399	1,414,873	1,405,746	1,386,544	1,463,156	1,476,035	1,505,034	982,021
Shares Outstanding	173,127	173,662	173,660	173,648	176,368	176,368	174,702	174,493
Statistical Record								
Return on Assets %	2.55	1.61	N.M.	N.M.	N.M.	N.M.	35.54	13.23
Return on Equity %	3.01	1.92	N.M.	N.M.	N.M.	N.M.	45.64	17.27
EBITDA Margin %	13.24	14.79	15.45	N.M.	8.24	9.22	36.89	19.91
Net Margin %	5.03	6.15	6.64	N.M.	N.M.	N.M.	21.76	9.63
Asset Turnover	0.77	0.77	0.72	0.67	0.67	0.70	1.63	1.37
Current Ratio	5.56	5.17	4.63	5.13	5.81	5.91	3.95	3.00
Debt to Equity	...	...	...	...	...	...	0.01	0.02
Price Range	19.02-11.17	19.02-11.17	19.02-10.03	19.02-9.00	23.50-7.54	24.93-15.10	49.50-15.13	41.31-8.00
P/E Ratio	79.25-46.54	126.80-74.47	...	...	...	...	15.37-4.70	45.90-8.89
Average Yield %	1.05	1.00	1.00	1.08	1.15	0.76	0.52	0.67

Address: 801 17th Avenue South, Myrtle Beach, SC 29577
Telephone: (843) 448-9411
Fax: (843) 448-6091

Web Site: www.avxcorp.com
Officers: Benedict P. Rosen - Chmn. Yasuo Nishiguchi - Vice-Chmn.

Auditors: PricewaterhouseCoopers LLP
Investor Contact: 843-946-0466
Transfer Agents: American Stock Transfer and Trust Company, New York,

AZTAR CORP.

Exchange	Symbol	Price	52Wk Range	Yield	P/E
NYS	AZR	$28.56 (3/31/2005)	35.31-23.51	N/A	37.58

*7 Year Price Score 160.03 *NYSE Composite Index=100 *12 Month Price Score 97.67

Interim Earnings (Per Share)

Qtr.	Mar	Jun	Sep	Dec
2001	0.28	0.40	0.46	0.33
2002	0.35	0.42	0.43	0.32
2003	0.36	0.51	0.46	0.33
2004	0.10	0.25	0.36	0.05

Interim Dividends (Per Share)
No Dividends Paid

Valuation Analysis

Forecast P/E	19.53	No of Institutions
	(4/12/2005)	147
Market Cap	$993.4 Million	Shares
Book Value	566.3 Million	31,989,752
Price/Book	1.75	% Held
Price/Sales	1.22	91.97

Business Summary: Sporting & Recreational (MIC: 13.5 SIC: 999 NAIC: 13290)

Aztar operates in the domestic gaming markets with casino/hotel facilities in Atlantic City, NJ, and in Las Vegas and Laughlin, NV. In addition, Co. operates riverboat casinos in Caruthersville, MO and Evansville, IN. Co.s' Tropicana Casino and Resort in Atlantic City encompasses about 14 acres and 220 yards of ocean beach frontage along the Boardwalk and features 1,625 hotel rooms, and a 137,000 sq. ft. casino. The Tropicana Resort and Casino in Las Vegas is located on an approximate 34-acre site, and has 1,875 hotel rooms and suites and a 62,000 sq. ft. casino. The Ramada Express Hotel and Casino is located on about 31 acres in Laughlin, NV and has 1,500 hotel rooms and a 52,000 sq. ft.

Recent Developments: For the year ended Dec 30 2004, net income decreased 53.3% to $28,475 thousand from net income of $60,930 thousand a year earlier. Revenues were $816,227 thousand, up 0.4% from $813,146 thousand the year before. Operating income was $110,342 thousand versus an income of $125,023 thousand in the prior year, a decrease of 11.7%. Total direct expense was $402,579 thousand versus $401,069 thousand in the prior year, an increase of 0.4%. Total indirect expense was $303,306 thousand versus $287,054 thousand in the prior year, an increase of 5.7%.

Prospects: Co.'s Tropicana Atlantic City expansion opened on a limited basis on Nov 23 2004. The expansion contains a new 502-room hotel tower, a 200,000-square-foot dining, entertainment and retail complex to be known as The Quarter at Tropicana, and a 2,400-space parking garage. Virtually all the dining, entertainment and retail outlets are now open, and Co.'s casino revenues are ramping up. With the traditionally slow months of Dec and Jan behind, Co. is expecting continuing strong increases in casino revenues and earnings before interest, taxes, depreciation and amortization through the spring and summer months of 2005.

Financial Data (US$ in Thousands)	12/30/2004	01/01/2004	01/02/2003	01/03/2002	12/28/2000	12/31/1999	12/31/1998	01/01/1998
Earnings Per Share	0.76	1.66	1.51	1.48	1.23	0.12	0.20	0.08
Cash Flow Per Share	3.06	3.19	3.47	3.64	3.04	1.81	1.92	1.10
Tang Book Value Per Share	15.29	13.70	12.47	12.38	10.92	9.96	10.02	9.82
Income Statement								
Total Revenue	816,227	813,146	834,274	849,463	848,088	800,314	806,136	782,357
EBITDA	160,827	177,455	187,980	180,827	166,377	141,377	133,045	116,990
Depn & Amortn	56,950	52,432	51,958	53,121	55,117	55,744	55,735	54,216
Income Before Taxes	67,672	89,384	95,833	90,083	70,695	34,351	19,876	2,257
Income Taxes	39,197	28,454	36,974	32,074	17,578	12,222	8,368	(2,185)
Net Income	28,475	60,930	58,859	58,009	53,117	6,389	10,162	4,442
Average Shares	36,558	36,563	38,841	38,963	42,577	46,197	46,614	46,687
Balance Sheet								
Current Assets	130,554	129,131	109,272	149,430	107,220	117,627	121,783	118,818
Total Assets	1,511,640	1,347,773	1,210,682	1,060,956	1,011,696	1,049,007	1,077,702	1,091,496
Current Liabilities	144,379	132,056	119,621	106,156	94,119	89,326	100,394	124,729
Long-Term Obligations	731,253	628,603	524,066	458,659	463,011	497,628	487,543	491,932
Total Liabilities	945,349	813,199	695,328	607,115	588,990	621,097	623,601	647,458
Stockholders' Equity	566,291	534,574	515,354	453,841	422,706	427,910	454,101	444,038
Shares Outstanding	34,781	34,270	37,026	36,644	38,696	42,945	45,338	45,199
Statistical Record								
Return on Assets %	2.00	4.78	5.20	5.51	5.18	0.60	0.94	0.40
Return on Equity %	5.19	11.64	12.18	13.02	12.56	1.45	2.27	1.01
EBITDA Margin %	19.70	21.82	22.53	21.29	19.62	17.67	16.50	14.95
Net Margin %	3.49	7.49	7.06	6.83	6.26	0.80	1.26	0.57
Asset Turnover	0.57	0.64	0.74	0.81	0.83	0.75	0.75	0.71
Current Ratio	0.90	0.98	0.91	1.41	1.14	1.32	1.21	0.95
Debt to Equity	1.29	1.18	1.02	1.01	1.10	1.16	1.07	1.11
Price Range	35.31-21.66	23.15-11.52	25.45-11.14	18.80-9.31	16.13-8.81	11.13-4.19	9.38-3.06	8.25-6.13
P/E Ratio	46.46-28.50	13.95-6.94	16.85-7.38	12.70-6.29	13.11-7.16	92.71-34.90	46.88-15.31	103.13-76.56

Address: 2390 E. Camelback Road, Suite 400, Phoenix, AZ 85016-3452
Telephone: (602) 381-4100
Fax: (602) 381-4107

Web Site: www.aztar.com
Officers: Robert M. Haddock - Chmn., Pres., C.E.O. Neil A. Ciarfalia - V.P., C.F.O., Treas.

Auditors: PricewaterhouseCoopers LLP
Investor Contact: 602-381-4111

BAKER HUGHES INC.

Exchange	Symbol	Price	52Wk Range	Yield	P/E
NYS	BHI	$44.49 (3/31/2005)	47.70-33.71	1.03	28.34

*7 Year Price Score 107.04 *NYSE Composite Index=100 *12 Month Price Score 103.37

TRADING VOLUME (thousand shares)

Interim Earnings (Per Share)

Qtr.	Mar	Jun	Sep	Dec
2001	0.21	0.31	0.41	0.38
2002	0.10	0.21	0.19	0.00
2003	0.13	0.24	(0.29)	0.30
2004	0.28	0.35	0.41	0.53

Interim Dividends (Per Share)

Amt	Decl	Ex	Rec	Pay
0.115Q	4/28/2004	5/6/2004	5/10/2004	5/21/2004
0.115Q	7/28/2004	8/5/2004	8/9/2004	8/20/2004
0.115Q	10/27/2004	11/4/2004	11/8/2004	11/19/2004
0.115Q	1/27/2005	2/3/2005	2/7/2005	2/18/2005

Indicated Div: $0.46

Valuation Analysis

Forecast P/E	28.59	No of Institutions
	(4/7/2005)	406
Market Cap	$14.9 Billion	Shares
Book Value	3.7 Billion	309,218,784
Price/Book	4.08	% Held
Price/Sales	2.55	91.43

Business Summary: Oil and Gas (MIC: 14.2 SIC: 533 NAIC: 33132)

Baker Hughes is engaged in the oilfield services industry. Through its six oilfield service operations, Baker Atlas, Baker Oil Tools, Baker Petrolite, Centrilift, Hughes Christensen and INTEQ, Co. is a major supplier of wellbore-related products and technology services and systems to the oil and gas industry on a worldwide basis, including products and services for drilling, formation evaluation, completion and production of oil and natural gas wells. The oilfield segment also includes Co.'s 30.0% interest in WesternGeco, a seismic venture between Co. and Schlumberger.

Recent Developments: For the year ended Dec 31 2004, income from continuing operations increased 196.9% to $528,200 thousand from income of $177,900 thousand a year earlier. Net income increased 310.1% to $528,600 thousand from net income of $128,900 thousand a year earlier. Revenues were $6,103,800 thousand, up 16.2% from $5,252,400 thousand the year before. Operating income was $821,000 thousand versus an income of $560,300 thousand in the prior year, an increase of 46.5%. Total direct expense was $4,367,400 thousand versus $3,820,900 thousand in the prior year, an increase of 14.3%. Total indirect expense was $915,400 thousand versus $871,200 thousand in the prior year, an increase of 5.1%.

Prospects: Strong demand for Co.'s drilling and oilfield services is being driven by sharply higher oil and gas prices. In 2005, results are expected to benefit from continued strong drilling activity in North America, along with increased investment overseas, primarily in Russia, the Caspian Sea region, and the Middle East. Capital expenditures in 2005 are expected to be between $410.0 million and $430.0 million. Looking ahead, Co. is targeting full-year 2005 revenue growth in the range of 9.0% to 11.0%, along with income from continuing operations of between $1.80 and $1.95 per diluted share.

Financial Data

(US$ in Thousands)	9 Mos	6 Mos	3 Mos	12/31/2003	12/31/2002	12/31/2001	12/31/2000	12/31/1999
Earnings Per Share	1.34	0.64	0.53	0.38	0.50	1.30	0.31	0.10
Cash Flow Per Share	2.64	2.42	2.34	1.98	2.01	2.15	1.70	1.65
Tang Book Value Per Share	6.74	6.27	6.06	5.87	6.06	5.69	4.64	4.17
Dividends Per Share	0.460	0.460	0.460	0.460	0.460	0.460	0.460	0.460
Dividend Payout %	34.41	71.52	87.23	121.05	92.00	35.38	148.39	460.00
Income Statement								
Total Revenue	4,424,700	2,886,600	1,398,900	5,292,800	5,020,400	5,382,200	5,233,800	4,546,700
EBITDA	850,900	545,800	261,000	775,000	787,900	1,120,700	1,016,000	1,016,700
Depn & Amortn	269,800	179,900	91,400	349,200	301,600	344,700	611,500	778,400
Income Before Taxes	520,000	321,600	145,500	328,200	380,400	661,800	236,000	84,300
Income Taxes	171,600	110,900	50,200	148,100	156,700	223,100	133,700	32,000
Net Income	349,000	211,100	94,600	128,900	168,900	438,000	102,300	33,300
Average Shares	335,900	334,700	334,100	335,900	337,900	337,400	332,900	329,900
Balance Sheet								
Current Assets	2,599,600	2,541,100	2,601,500	2,523,900	2,555,500	2,697,200	2,486,600	2,329,800
Total Assets	6,307,600	6,269,800	6,340,100	6,302,200	6,400,800	6,676,200	6,452,700	7,039,800
Current Liabilities	1,054,300	1,187,200	1,314,400	1,301,900	1,080,100	1,212,400	987,800	1,000,200
Long-Term Obligations	1,097,300	1,114,300	1,100,200	1,133,000	1,424,300	1,682,400	2,049,600	2,706,000
Total Liabilities	2,648,000	2,778,000	2,924,300	2,951,800	3,003,600	3,348,400	3,406,000	3,968,700
Stockholders' Equity	3,659,600	3,491,800	3,415,800	3,350,400	3,397,200	3,327,800	3,046,700	3,071,100
Shares Outstanding	335,469	333,749	333,096	332,000	335,800	336,000	333,700	329,800
Statistical Record								
Return on Assets %	7.18	3.38	2.82	2.03	2.58	6.67	1.51	0.45
Return on Equity %	12.83	6.18	5.21	3.82	5.02	13.74	3.34	1.06
EBITDA Margin %	19.23	18.91	18.66	14.64	15.69	20.82	19.41	22.36
Net Margin %	7.89	7.31	6.76	2.44	3.36	8.14	1.95	0.73
Asset Turnover	0.94	0.89	0.87	0.83	0.77	0.82	0.77	0.61
Current Ratio	2.47	2.14	1.98	1.94	2.37	2.22	2.52	2.33
Debt to Equity	0.30	0.32	0.32	0.34	0.42	0.51	0.67	0.88
Price Range	44.09-27.10	38.42-27.10	38.42-27.10	35.94-27.10	39.42-22.80	44.99-26.29	42.94-20.25	36.13-16.63
P/E Ratio	32.90-20.22	60.03-42.34	72.49-51.13	94.58-71.32	78.84-45.60	34.61-20.22	138.51-65.32	361.25-166.25
Average Yield %	1.30	1.38	1.43	1.49	1.42	1.27	1.41	1.72

Address: 3900 Essex Lane, Suite 1200, Houston, TX 77027	Web Site: www.bakerhughes.com	Auditors: Deloitte & Touche LLP
Telephone: (713) 439-8600	Officers: Chad C. Deaton - Chmn., C.E.O. James R. Clark - Pres., C.O.O.	Investor Contact: 713-439-8039
Fax: (713) 739-8699		

BALL CORP

Exchange	Symbol	Price	52Wk Range	Yield	P/E
NYS	BLL	$41.48 (3/31/2005)	45.87-30.66	0.96	15.95

*7 Year Price Score 171.34 *NYSE Composite Index=100 *12 Month Price Score 105.26

Interim Earnings (Per Share)

Qtr.	Mar	Jun	Sep	Dec
2001	0.16	(1.48)	0.30	0.07
2002	0.24	0.44	0.44	0.25
2003	0.28	0.65	0.60	0.48
2004	0.41	0.80	0.90	0.50

Interim Dividends (Per Share)

Amt	Decl	Ex	Rec	Pay
2-for-1	7/28/2004	8/24/2004	8/4/2004	8/23/2004
0.10Q	7/28/2004	8/30/2004	9/1/2004	9/15/2004
0.10Q	10/27/2004	11/29/2004	12/1/2004	12/15/2004
0.10Q	1/26/2005	2/25/2005	3/1/2005	3/15/2005

Indicated Div: $0.40

Valuation Analysis

Forecast P/E	14.25	No of Institutions
	(4/7/2005)	283
Market Cap	$4.7 Billion	Shares
Book Value	1.1 Billion	79,937,552
Price/Book	4.30	% Held
Price/Sales	0.86	72.76

Business Summary: Metal Products (MIC: 11.4 SIC: 411 NAIC: 32431)

Ball is a manufacturer of metal and plastic packaging, primarily for beverages and foods, and a supplier of aerospace and other technologies and services to government and commercial customers. Co.'s North American packaging segment is engaged in the manufacture and sale of aluminum, steel and polyethylene terephthalate (PET) containers, primarily for beverages and foods. Co.'s international packaging segment comprises its operations in Europe and Asia. Co.'s aerospace and technologies segment includes defense operations, civil space systems and commercial space operations.

Recent Developments: For the year ended Dec 31 2004, net income increased 28.6% to $295,600 thousand from net income of $229,900 thousand a year earlier. Revenues were $5,440,200 thousand, up 9.3% from $4,977,000 thousand the year before. Operating income was $538,900 thousand versus an income of $460,800 thousand in the prior year, an increase of 16.9%. Total direct expense was $4,433,500 thousand versus $4,080,200 thousand in the prior year, an increase of 8.7%. Total indirect expense was $467,800 thousand versus $436,000 thousand in the prior year, an increase of 7.3%.

Prospects: Co.'s prospects appear constructive. Co. noted that its restructuring initiatives in China are now essentially complete, and it is experiencing growth in demand for beverage cans for the first time in several years. Meanwhile, Co. stated that work is progressing on its new beverage can plant in Belgrade, which is expected to be operational around mid 2005. Co. is also making some significant changes to its beverage can manufacturing plant in Oss, the Netherlands, including converting a line from steel to aluminum. Looking ahead, Co.'s long-term goal remains to increase earnings per diluted share by an average of 10.0% to 15.0% per year over time.

Financial Data (US$ in Thousands)	12/31/2004	12/31/2003	12/31/2002	12/31/2001	12/31/2000	12/31/1999	12/31/1998	12/31/1997
Earnings Per Share	2.60	2.01	1.36	(0.93)	0.54	0.79	0.11	0.44
Cash Flow Per Share	4.82	3.26	4.02	2.92	1.52	2.54	3.18	1.19
Tang Book Value Per Share	N.M.	N.M.	N.M.	1.27	1.71	1.27	0.08	3.14
Dividends Per Share	0.350	0.240	0.180	0.150	0.150	0.150	0.150	0.150
Dividend Payout %	13.46	11.94	13.28	...	28.04	19.05	136.36	34.48
Income Statement								
Total Revenue	5,440,200	4,977,000	3,858,900	3,686,100	3,664,700	3,584,200	2,896,400	2,388,500
EBITDA	754,000	666,300	460,200	127,100	368,200	441,700	260,500	256,900
Depn & Amortn	215,100	205,500	149,200	152,500	159,100	162,900	154,600	117,500
Income Before Taxes	435,200	319,700	235,400	(113,700)	113,900	171,200	27,300	85,900
Income Taxes	139,200	100,100	83,900	(9,700)	42,800	64,900	8,800	32,000
Net Income	295,600	229,900	156,100	(99,200)	68,200	104,200	16,600	58,300
Average Shares	113,790	114,274	115,076	109,760	124,068	129,800	130,368	129,244
Balance Sheet								
Current Assets	1,245,600	923,500	1,224,500	793,500	969,300	895,800	885,600	798,100
Total Assets	4,477,700	4,069,600	4,132,400	2,313,600	2,649,800	2,732,100	2,854,800	2,090,100
Current Liabilities	996,300	861,100	1,068,900	574,700	659,100	670,100	687,600	837,800
Long-Term Obligations	1,537,700	1,579,300	1,854,000	949,100	1,011,600	1,092,700	1,229,800	366,100
Total Liabilities	3,384,700	3,255,600	3,633,900	1,799,800	1,952,500	2,021,500	2,208,100	1,404,200
Stockholders' Equity	1,086,600	807,800	492,900	504,100	682,400	690,900	622,300	634,200
Shares Outstanding	112,691	112,778	113,490	115,634	112,196	119,268	121,819	120,880
Statistical Record								
Return on Assets %	6.90	5.61	4.84	N.M.	2.53	3.73	0.67	3.08
Return on Equity %	31.12	35.35	31.31	N.M.	9.91	15.87	2.64	9.41
EBITDA Margin %	13.86	13.39	11.93	3.45	10.05	12.32	8.99	10.76
Net Margin %	5.43	4.62	4.05	N.M.	1.86	2.91	0.57	2.44
Asset Turnover	1.27	1.21	1.20	1.49	1.36	1.28	1.17	1.26
Current Ratio	1.25	1.07	1.15	1.38	1.47	1.34	1.29	0.95
Debt to Equity	1.42	1.96	3.76	1.88	1.48	1.58	1.98	0.58
Price Range	44.94-28.59	29.79-21.29	26.95-16.32	17.75-9.79	11.81-6.63	14.64-8.95	11.50-7.28	9.73-5.97
P/E Ratio	17.28-11.00	14.82-10.59	19.82-12.00	...	21.87-12.27	18.53-11.33	104.55-66.19	22.12-13.57
Average Yield %	0.97	0.91	0.80	1.16	1.76	1.34	1.59	1.96

Address: 10 Longs Peak Drive, Broomfield, CO 80021 **Telephone:** (303) 469-3131 **Fax:** (303) 460-2127	**Web Site:** www.ball.com **Officers:** R. David Hoover - Chmn., Pres., C.E.O. Leon A. Midgett - Exec. V.P., C.O.O.	**Auditors:** PricewaterhouseCoopers LLP

BANCORPSOUTH INC.

Exchange	Symbol	Price	52Wk Range	Yield	P/E	Div Achiever
NYS	BXS	$20.64 (3/31/2005)	25.22-19.82	3.68	14.43	18 Years

*7 Year Price Score 102.51 *NYSE Composite Index=100   *12 Month Price Score 88.64

Interim Earnings (Per Share)

Qtr.	Mar	Jun	Sep	Dec
2001	0.27	0.28	0.26	0.39
2002	0.36	0.38	0.33	0.32
2003	0.50	0.37	0.43	0.37
2004	0.35	0.40	0.36	0.32

Interim Dividends (Per Share)

Amt	Decl	Ex	Rec	Pay
0.18Q	4/28/2004	6/14/2004	6/15/2004	7/1/2004
0.18Q	7/21/2004	9/13/2004	9/15/2004	10/1/2004
0.19Q	10/27/2004	12/13/2004	12/15/2004	1/3/2005
0.19Q	1/26/2005	3/11/2005	3/15/2005	4/1/2005

Indicated Div: $0.76 (Div. Reinv. Plan)

Valuation Analysis

Forecast P/E	13.41 (4/7/2005)	No of Institutions 106
Market Cap	$1.6 Billion	Shares 15,540,505
Book Value	916.4 Million	% Held
Price/Book	1.76	19.85
Price/Sales	2.36	

Business Summary: Commercial Banking (MIC: 8.1 SIC: 022 NAIC: 22110)

BancorpSouth is a bank holding company headquartered in Tupelo, MS with assets of $10.31 billion and total deposits of $8.60 billion as of Dec 31 2003. Co. operates 246 commercial banking, insurance, trust, broker/dealer and consumer finance locations in Mississippi, Tennessee, Alabama, Arkansas, Texas and Louisiana. Co. and its subsidiaries provide a range of financial services to individuals and small-to-medium size businesses. Co. operates investment services, consumer finance, credit insurance and insurance agency subsidiaries. Co.'s trust department offers a variety of services including personal trust and estate services, and certain employee benefit accounts and plans.

Recent Developments: For the year ended Dec 31 2004, net income decreased 15.6% to $110,620 thousand from net income of $131,134 thousand a year earlier. Net interest income was $333,792 thousand, down 4.9% from $351,106 thousand the year before. Provision for loan losses was $17,485 thousand versus $25,130 thousand in the prior year, a decrease of 30.4%. Non-interest income fell 3.5% to $183,519 thousand, while non-interest expense advanced 6.3% to $342,945 thousand.

Prospects: On Jan 1 2005, Co. announced that it has completed its acquisitions of Premier Bancorp, Inc., of Brentwood, TN and Business Holding Corporation, Inc., of Baton Rouge, LA. The acquisitions should give Co. a banking presence in the Baton Rouge metropolitan market and help expand its market presence in the Nashville suburb of Brentwood. Meanwhile, Co. is experiencing strong loan growth in a number of markets, including South Mississippi, Little Rock, AR, Nashville, TN, Shreveport, LA, and Jackson, TN. However, rising interest rates will likely continue to pressure Co.'s net interest margin during 2005.

Financial Data

(US$ in Thousands)	12/31/2004	12/31/2003	12/31/2002	12/31/2001	12/31/2000	12/31/1999	12/31/1998	12/31/1997
Earnings Per Share	1.43	1.68	1.39	1.19	0.88	1.20	1.01	1.01
Cash Flow Per Share	1.39	3.12	2.10	1.15	1.65	2.12	0.95	0.99
Tang Book Value Per Share	10.34	10.38	10.40	9.92	9.39	8.68	8.48	8.09
Dividends Per Share	0.730	0.660	0.610	0.570	0.530	0.490	0.450	0.395
Dividend Payout %	51.05	39.29	43.88	47.90	60.23	40.83	44.55	38.92
Income Statement								
Interest Income	497,629	526,911	590,418	665,835	674,035	414,187	383,519	307,094
Interest Expense	163,837	175,805	218,892	331,093	346,883	196,686	187,412	144,055
Net Interest Income	333,792	351,106	371,526	334,742	327,152	217,501	196,107	163,039
Provision for Losses	17,485	25,130	29,411	22,259	26,166	14,689	15,014	9,008
Non-Interest Income	183,519	190,086	132,239	128,633	85,578	79,331	53,018	43,667
Non-Interest Expense	342,945	322,594	312,398	295,313	274,227	183,000	152,084	131,988
Income Before Taxes	156,881	193,468	161,956	145,803	112,337	99,143	82,027	65,710
Income Taxes	46,261	62,334	49,938	47,340	37,941	30,190	27,550	20,360
Net Income	110,620	131,134	112,018	98,463	74,396	68,953	54,477	45,350
Average Shares	77,378	78,164	80,481	82,979	84,811	57,524	53,871	44,788
Balance Sheet								
Net Loans & Leases	6,745,025	6,140,955	6,301,510	5,990,050	6,013,585	3,997,975	3,419,083	2,719,150
Total Assets	10,848,193	10,305,035	10,189,247	9,395,429	9,044,034	5,776,926	5,203,741	4,180,143
Total Deposits	9,059,091	8,599,128	8,548,918	7,856,840	7,480,920	4,815,415	4,441,923	3,540,255
Total Liabilities	9,931,765	9,436,129	9,381,424	8,590,026	8,254,458	5,279,526	4,747,384	3,819,721
Stockholders' Equity	916,428	868,906	807,823	805,403	789,576	497,400	456,357	360,422
Shares Outstanding	78,037	77,926	77,680	81,225	84,043	57,304	53,833	44,542
Statistical Record								
Return on Assets %	1.04	1.28	1.14	1.07	1.00	1.26	1.16	1.16
Return on Equity %	12.36	15.64	13.89	12.35	11.53	14.46	13.34	13.42
Net Interest Margin %	67.08	66.63	62.93	50.27	48.54	52.51	51.13	53.09
Efficiency Ratio %	50.35	44.99	43.23	37.17	36.10	37.08	34.84	37.63
Loans to Deposits	0.74	0.71	0.74	0.76	0.80	0.83	0.77	0.77
Price Range	25.22-19.82	24.45-17.72	22.00-16.31	17.00-12.88	17.13-11.88	19.13-15.50	23.75-17.00	23.75-13.25
P/E Ratio	17.64-13.86	14.55-10.55	15.83-11.73	14.29-10.82	19.46-13.49	15.94-12.92	23.51-16.83	23.51-13.12
Average Yield %	3.25	3.12	3.11	3.76	3.61	2.91	2.19	2.47

Address: One Mississippi Plaza, 201 South Spring Street, Tupelo, MS 38804
Telephone: (662) 680 2000
Fax: (601) 680 2570

Web Site: www.bancorpsouth.com
Officers: Aubrey B. Patterson - Chmn., C.E.O. James V. Kelley - Pres., C.O.O.

Auditors: KPMG LLP
Transfer Agents: SunTrust Bank, Atlanta, GA

BANDAG, INC.

Exchange	Symbol	Price	52Wk Range	Yield	P/E	Div Acheiver
NYS	BDG	$46.98 (3/31/2005)	51.05-38.98	2.81	13.86	28 Years

*7 Year Price Score 110.05 ***NYSE Composite Index=100** ***12 Month Price Score 93.17**

Interim Earnings (Per Share)

Qtr.	Mar	Jun	Sep	Dec
2001	0.11	0.46	0.71	0.84
2002	(2.21)	0.57	1.02	0.87
2003	0.12	0.45	1.03	1.50
2004	0.20	0.60	1.02	1.56

Interim Dividends (Per Share)

Amt	Decl	Ex	Rec	Pay
0.325Q	5/11/2004	6/16/2004	6/18/2004	7/19/2004
0.325Q	8/17/2004	9/15/2004	9/17/2004	10/18/2004
0.33Q	11/9/2004	12/16/2004	12/20/2004	1/20/2005
0.33Q	3/15/2005	3/23/2005	3/28/2005	4/20/2005
Indicated Div: $1.32 (Div. Reinv. Plan)				

Valuation Analysis

Forecast P/E	15.13	No of Institutions	
	(4/7/2005)	110	
Market Cap	$913.8 Million	Shares	
Book Value	532.3 Million	5,988,205	
Price/Book	1.72	% Held	
Price/Sales	1.05	65.68	

Business Summary: Rubber Products (MIC: 11.6 SIC: 011 NAIC: 26211)

Bandag is engaged in the manufacture of pre-cured tread rubber, equipment, and supplies primarily for the re-treading of truck and bus tires by a patented cold-bonding reaction process. As of Dec 31 2003, revenues were generated by more than 1,000 franchised dealers in the U.S. and abroad who are licensed to produce and market cold process retreads utilizing the Bandag process. Co. also engages in the sale and maintenance of new and retread tires to principally commercial and industrial customers through its wholly-owned subsidiary, Tire Distribution Systems, Inc. In addition, Co. owns an 87.5% majority interest in Speedco, Inc., a provider of nationwide quick-service truck lubrication.

Recent Developments: For the year ended Dec 31 2004, net income increased 11.1% to $66,880 thousand from net income of $60,200 thousand a year earlier. Revenues were $867,953 thousand, up 5.4% from $823,351 thousand the year before. Operating income was $82,009 thousand versus an income of $81,468 thousand in the prior year, an increase of 0.7%. Total direct expense was $536,116 thousand versus $508,139 thousand in the prior year, an increase of 5.5%. Total indirect expense was $249,828 thousand versus $233,744 thousand in the prior year, an increase of 6.9%.

Prospects: On Jan 20 2005, Co. notified the Securities and Exchange Commission that reported earnings for fiscal years 1997 through 2002 will be restated to correct for an accounting error in 1997 and 1998 related to the acquisition of tire dealerships by TDS. The restatement will have no impact on Co.'s previously reported revenues or cash flows and will not change net earnings for fiscal years 2003 or 2004. Separately, while strong trucking activity in North America is cause for optimism as Co. enters 2005, it continues to take a conservative view of the global economy given continued uncertainties concerning the strength of the U.S. dollar and the volatility of raw material costs.

Financial Data
(US$ in Thousands)

	12/31/2004	12/31/2003	12/31/2002	12/31/2001	12/31/2000	12/31/1999	12/31/1998	12/31/1997
Earnings Per Share	3.39	3.11	0.14	2.12	2.90	2.40	2.63	5.33
Cash Flow Per Share	4.92	4.08	6.65	5.66	4.78	5.18	3.85	3.13
Tang Book Value Per Share	25.55	24.61	21.97	21.22	20.03	18.62	17.84	17.00
Dividends Per Share	1.305	1.285	1.265	1.230	1.190	1.150	1.110	1.025
Dividend Payout %	38.50	41.32	903.57	58.02	41.03	47.92	42.21	19.23
Income Statement								
Total Revenue	867,953	828,186	911,953	982,209	1,013,426	1,027,878	1,079,498	931,702
EBITDA	109,191	113,482	110,708	120,036	158,572	155,581	161,695	243,112
Depn & Amortn	27,182	27,179	32,333	46,155	50,465	53,764	51,410	36,857
Income Before Taxes	84,902	83,900	71,518	66,505	99,375	92,090	99,513	202,916
Income Taxes	17,648	23,700	21,465	22,673	39,042	39,760	40,194	80,922
Net Income	66,880	60,200	2,793	43,832	60,333	52,330	59,319	121,994
Average Shares	19,707	19,369	19,888	20,686	20,778	21,764	22,559	22,908
Balance Sheet								
Current Assets	486,255	466,286	416,082	450,174	427,179	428,118	439,124	598,994
Total Assets	730,727	660,529	617,827	718,572	714,549	722,421	755,729	899,904
Current Liabilities	158,558	148,193	147,861	186,075	132,735	154,053	174,909	306,542
Long-Term Obligations	17,143	22,857	28,571	94,286	100,000	100,000	100,000	100,000
Total Liabilities	198,440	183,452	193,234	229,576	240,392	268,346	288,432	436,490
Stockholders' Equity	532,287	477,077	424,593	488,996	474,157	454,075	467,297	463,414
Shares Outstanding	19,451	19,268	19,151	20,641	20,561	20,770	21,955	22,813
Statistical Record								
Return on Assets %	9.59	9.42	0.42	6.12	8.37	7.08	7.17	16.39
Return on Equity %	13.22	13.35	0.61	9.10	12.96	11.36	12.75	27.91
EBITDA Margin %	12.58	13.70	12.14	12.22	15.65	15.14	14.98	26.09
Net Margin %	7.71	7.27	0.31	4.46	5.95	5.09	5.50	13.09
Asset Turnover	1.24	1.30	1.36	1.37	1.41	1.39	1.30	1.25
Current Ratio	3.07	3.15	2.81	2.42	3.22	2.78	2.51	1.95
Debt to Equity	0.03	0.05	0.07	0.19	0.21	0.22	0.21	0.22
Price Range	51.05-38.98	42.30-28.67	41.16-26.47	46.19-25.34	42.63-22.38	41.25-23.63	59.50-28.38	55.00-45.75
P/E Ratio	15.06-11.50	13.60-9.22	294.00-189.07	21.79-11.95	14.70-7.72	17.19-9.84	22.62-10.79	10.32-8.58
Average Yield %	2.86	3.58	3.63	3.99	4.10	3.62	2.52	2.04

Address: 2905 North Highway 61, Muscatine, IA 52761-5886 **Telephone:** (563) 262-1400 **Fax:** (563) 262-1284	**Web Site:** www.bandag.com **Officers:** Martin G. Carver - Chmn., Pres., C.E.O. Warren W. Heidbreder - V.P., C.F.O., Sec.	**Auditors:** Ernst & Young LLP **Investor Contact:** 319-262-1260 **Transfer Agents:** EquiServe Trust Company, N.A. Providence, RI

BANK OF AMERICA CORP.

Exchange	Symbol	Price	52Wk Range	Yield	P/E	Div Acheiver
NYS	BAC	$44.10 (3/31/2005)	47.44-38.96	4.08	11.95	27 Years

*7 Year Price Score 111.76   ***NYSE Composite Index=100**   ***12 Month Price Score 97.06**

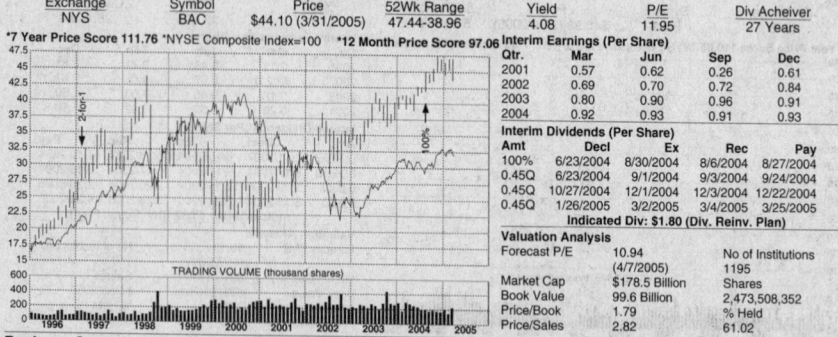

Interim Earnings (Per Share)

Qtr.	Mar	Jun	Sep	Dec
2001	0.57	0.62	0.26	0.61
2002	0.69	0.70	0.72	0.84
2003	0.80	0.90	0.96	0.91
2004	0.92	0.93	0.91	0.93

Interim Dividends (Per Share)

Amt	Decl	Ex	Rec	Pay
100%	6/23/2004	8/30/2004	8/6/2004	8/27/2004
0.45Q	6/23/2004	9/1/2004	9/3/2004	9/24/2004
0.45Q	10/27/2004	12/1/2004	12/3/2004	12/22/2004
0.45Q	1/26/2005	3/2/2005	3/4/2005	3/25/2005

Indicated Div: $1.80 (Div. Reinv. Plan)

Valuation Analysis

Forecast P/E	10.94	No of Institutions	
	(4/7/2005)	1195	
Market Cap	$178.5 Billion	Shares	
Book Value	99.6 Billion	2,473,508,352	
Price/Book	1.79	% Held	
Price/Sales	2.82	61.02	

Business Summary: Commercial Banking (MIC: 8.1 SIC: 021 NAIC: 22110)

Bank of America, with $736.45 billion in total assets as of Dec 31 2003, is a bank holding and financial holding company. Co.'s Consumer and Commercial Banking segment provides banking products and services. Co.'s Asset Management segment offers investment, fiduciary and banking and credit expertise; asset management services; and investment, securities and financial planning services. Co.'s Global Corporate and Investment Banking segment provides capital raising, advisory services, derivatives capabilities, equity and debt sales and trading. Equity Investments includes Principal Investing, which is comprised of investments in privately-held and publicly-traded companies.

Recent Developments: For the year ended Dec 31 2004, net income increased 30.8% to $14,143 million from net income of $10,810 million a year earlier. Net interest income was $28,797 million, up 34.2% from $21,464 million the year before. Provision for loan losses was $2,769 million versus $2,839 million in the prior year, a decrease of 2.5%. Non-interest income rose 22.2% to $20,097 million, while non-interest expense advanced 34.1% to $27,027 million.

Prospects: Co. is continuing with its business model simplification and merger-related cost saving activities. In addition to the impact of the Fleet acquisition, Co.'s net income improvement is being driven by continuing momentum in consumer banking, merger-driven cost savings, lower provision expense and gains on the sale of debt securities. However, despite these signs encouraging signals, Co. will continue to face a number of challenges in the coming year, including a flattening yield curve and continued systems conversions in the northeast territories.

Financial Data

(US$ in Thousands)	12/31/2004	12/31/2003	12/31/2002	12/31/2001	12/31/2000	12/31/1999	12/31/1998	12/31/1997
Earnings Per Share	3.69	3.56	2.96	2.09	2.26	2.24	1.45	2.09
Cash Flow Per Share	(1.05)	8.18	(3.95)	(4.02)	1.59	3.50	3.90	0.19
Tang Book Value Per Share	11.80	11.38	11.88	10.40	9.50	7.83	8.34	7.43
Dividends Per Share	1.700	1.440	1.220	1.140	1.030	0.925	0.795	0.685
Dividend Payout %	46.07	40.39	41.29	54.55	45.58	41.29	54.83	32.85
Income Statement								
Interest Income	43,227,000	31,643,000	32,161,000	38,293,000	43,258,000	37,323,000	38,588,000	16,579,000
Interest Expense	14,430,000	10,179,000	11,238,000	18,003,000	24,816,000	19,086,000	20,290,000	8,681,000
Net Interest Income	28,797,000	21,464,000	20,923,000	20,290,000	18,442,000	18,237,000	18,298,000	7,898,000
Provision for Losses	2,769,000	2,839,000	3,697,000	4,287,000	2,535,000	1,820,000	2,920,000	800,000
Non-Interest Income	20,097,000	16,422,000	13,571,000	14,348,000	14,514,000	14,309,000	13,206,000	5,155,000
Non-Interest Expense	27,027,000	20,127,000	18,436,000	20,709,000	18,633,000	18,511,000	20,536,000	7,457,000
Income Before Taxes	21,221,000	15,861,000	12,991,000	10,117,000	11,788,000	12,215,000	8,048,000	4,796,000
Income Taxes	7,078,000	5,051,000	3,742,000	3,325,000	4,271,000	4,333,000	2,883,000	1,719,000
Net Income	14,143,000	10,810,000	9,249,000	6,792,000	7,517,000	7,882,000	5,165,000	3,077,000
Average Shares	3,823,943	3,030,356	3,130,934	3,251,308	3,329,858	3,520,116	3,551,520	1,475,582
Balance Sheet								
Net Loans & Leases	513,211,000	365,300,000	335,904,000	322,278,000	385,355,000	363,834,000	350,206,000	141,010,000
Total Assets	1,110,457,000	736,445,000	660,458,000	621,764,000	642,191,000	632,574,000	617,679,000	264,562,000
Total Deposits	618,570,000	414,113,000	386,458,000	373,495,000	364,244,000	347,273,000	357,260,000	138,194,000
Total Liabilities	1,010,812,000	688,465,000	610,139,000	573,244,000	594,563,000	588,142,000	571,741,000	243,225,000
Stockholders' Equity	99,645,000	47,980,000	50,319,000	48,520,000	47,628,000	44,432,000	45,938,000	21,337,000
Shares Outstanding	4,046,546	2,882,286	3,001,382	3,118,594	3,227,264	3,354,546	3,448,968	1,424,376
Statistical Record								
Return on Assets %	1.53	1.55	1.44	1.07	1.18	1.26	1.17	1.37
Return on Equity %	19.11	21.99	18.72	14.13	16.29	17.44	15.35	17.56
Net Interest Margin %	66.62	67.83	65.06	52.99	42.63	48.86	47.42	47.64
Efficiency Ratio %	42.68	41.87	40.31	39.34	32.25	35.85	39.65	34.31
Loans to Deposits	0.83	0.88	0.87	0.86	1.06	1.05	0.98	1.02
Price Range	47.44-38.96	41.77-32.81	38.45-27.07	32.50-23.38	30.50-19.00	37.75-24.00	43.97-24.03	35.59-24.34
P/E Ratio	12.86-10.56	11.73-9.22	12.99-9.15	15.55-11.18	13.50-8.41	16.85-10.71	30.32-16.57	17.03-11.65
Average Yield %	3.99	3.82	3.61	3.98	4.23	2.87	2.35	2.25

Address: Bank of America Corporate Center, 100 N. Tryon Street, Charlotte, NC 28255 Telephone: (704) 386-8486 Fax: (704) 388-9278	Web Site: www.bankofamerica.com Officers: Kenneth D. Lewis - Chmn., C.E.O. Marc D. Oken - Exec. V.P., C.F.O.	Auditors: PricewaterhouseCoopers LLP Investor Contact: 704-386-5681 Transfer Agents: Mellon Investor Services LLC, South Hackensack, NJ

BANK OF HAWAII CORP (DE)

Exchange	Symbol	Price	52Wk Range	Yield	P/E	Div Acheiver
NYS	BOH	$45.26 (3/31/2005)	50.95-41.70	2.92	14.69	27 Years

*7 Year Price Score 142.18 *NYSE Composite Index=100 *12 Month Price Score 92.57

Interim Earnings (Per Share)

Qtr.	Mar	Jun	Sep	Dec
2001	0.42	0.32	0.37	0.35
2002	0.41	0.42	0.43	0.44
2003	0.47	0.48	0.61	0.65
2004	0.69	0.79	0.78	0.82

Interim Dividends (Per Share)

Amt	Decl	Ex	Rec	Pay
0.30Q	4/23/2004	5/20/2004	5/24/2004	6/14/2004
0.30Q	7/23/2004	8/26/2004	8/30/2004	9/15/2004
0.33Q	10/22/2004	11/24/2004	11/29/2004	12/14/2004
0.33Q	1/24/2005	2/24/2005	2/28/2005	3/14/2005
		Indicated Div: $1.32 (Div. Reinv. Plan)		

Valuation Analysis

Forecast P/E	N/A	No of Institutions
Market Cap	$2.5 Billion	Shares
Book Value	814.8 Million	36,623,176
Price/Book	3.05	% Held
Price/Sales	3.77	68.50

Business Summary: Commercial Banking (MIC: 8.1 SIC: 022 NAIC: 22110)

Bank of Hawaii, with assets of $9.46 billion as of Dec 31 2003, is a bank holding company. Co. operates in Hawaii, the West Pacific, and American Samoa. The Retail banking segment offers loan, lease and deposit products to consumers and small businesses. The Commercial banking segment provides corporate banking and commercial real estate loans, lease financing, auto dealer financing, deposit and cash management products to mid-to-large sized companies. The Investment Services group includes private banking, trust services, asset management, institutional investment advice and retail brokerage. The Treasury and Other Corporate segment provides corporate asset and liability management.

Recent Developments: For the year ended Dec 31 2004, net income increased 28.2% to $173,339 thousand from net income of $135,195 thousand a year earlier. Net interest income was $390,590 thousand, up 6.7% from $365,942 thousand the year before. Results for 2004 included a recovery of $10,000 thousand for provision for loan losses versus Nil in 2003. Non-interest income rose 3.2% to $205,094 thousand, while non-interest expense declined 6.5% to $334,440 thousand.

Prospects: Co. continues to perform well, supported by further improvement in the credit quality of the loan portfolio and continued strength in the economic environment. Total earning assets were $9.00 billion at Dec 31 2004, up 5.7% from $8.51 billion at Dec 31 2003. Non-performing assets declined 56.3% compared with $31.7 million at the end of 2003. Looking ahead, Hawaii economy remains solid and Co. is optimistic about its outlook. Based on current economic conditions, Co. expects further credit quality improvement and, as a result, the allowance for loan and lease losses may be further reduced. For 2005, Co. expects net income in the range of $174.0 million to $177.0 million.

Financial Data
(US$ in Thousands)

	12/31/2004	12/31/2003	12/31/2002	12/31/2001	12/31/2000	12/31/1999	12/31/1998	12/31/1997
Earnings Per Share	3.08	2.21	1.70	1.46	1.42	1.64	1.32	1.72
Cash Flow Per Share	4.87	5.46	9.13	(3.28)	3.50	1.95	2.48	1.62
Tang Book Value Per Share	13.83	13.38	15.09	16.16	13.93	12.57	12.07	11.47
Dividends Per Share	1.230	0.870	0.730	0.720	0.710	0.680	0.657	0.625
Dividend Payout %	39.94	39.37	42.94	49.32	50.00	41.46	49.81	36.34
Income Statement								
Interest Income	455,014	442,521	516,538	828,262	1,057,493	1,026,519	1,099,786	1,062,576
Interest Expense	64,424	76,579	146,307	368,584	501,262	451,776	523,185	526,278
Net Interest Income	390,590	365,942	370,231	459,678	556,231	574,743	576,601	536,298
Provision for Losses	(10,000)	...	11,616	74,339	142,853	60,915	84,014	30,338
Non-Interest Income	205,094	198,720	199,921	452,619	263,429	265,581	211,751	187,789
Non-Interest Expense	334,440	357,875	370,835	597,616	496,430	553,238	540,279	474,261
Income Before Taxes	271,244	206,787	187,701	239,959	179,990	225,686	163,613	218,000
Income Taxes	97,905	71,592	66,521	122,164	66,329	92,729	56,649	78,512
Net Income	173,339	135,195	121,180	117,795	113,661	132,957	106,964	139,488
Average Shares	56,241	61,085	71,447	80,577	79,813	80,044	81,142	80,946
Balance Sheet								
Net Loans & Leases	5,880,134	5,628,095	5,216,151	5,493,539	9,168,140	9,280,848	9,416,809	9,114,325
Total Assets	9,766,191	9,461,647	9,516,418	10,627,797	14,013,816	14,440,315	15,016,563	14,995,464
Total Deposits	7,564,667	7,332,779	6,920,161	6,673,596	9,080,581	9,394,218	9,576,342	9,621,275
Total Liabilities	8,951,357	8,668,515	8,500,659	9,380,785	12,712,460	13,227,985	13,830,969	13,878,257
Stockholders' Equity	814,834	793,132	1,015,759	1,247,012	1,301,356	1,212,330	1,185,594	1,117,207
Shares Outstanding	54,960	54,928	63,015	73,218	79,612	80,036	80,326	79,685
Statistical Record								
Return on Assets %	1.80	1.42	1.20	0.96	0.80	0.90	0.71	0.96
Return on Equity %	21.50	14.95	10.71	9.24	9.02	11.09	9.29	12.78
Net Interest Margin %	85.84	82.69	71.68	55.50	52.60	55.99	52.43	50.47
Efficiency Ratio %	50.66	55.81	51.76	46.66	37.58	42.82	41.19	37.93
Loans to Deposits	0.78	0.77	0.75	0.82	1.01	0.99	0.98	0.95
Price Range	50.95-41.70	42.72-29.43	30.75-23.88	27.88-16.94	22.94-11.25	24.69-17.38	25.44-14.75	28.00-20.38
P/E Ratio	16.54-13.54	19.33-13.32	18.09-14.05	19.10-11.60	16.15-7.92	15.05-10.59	19.27-11.17	16.28-11.85
Average Yield %	2.68	2.54	2.62	3.13	4.26	3.25	3.03	2.63

Address: 130 Merchant Street, Honolulu, HI 96813 **Telephone:** (808) 538-4727 **Fax:** (808) 521-7602	**Web Site:** www.boh.com **Officers:** Michael E. O'Neill - Chmn., C.E.O. Alton T. Kuioka - Vice-Chair, Commercial Banking	**Auditors:** ERNST & YOUNG LLP **Investor Contact:** 808-537-2037

BANK OF NEW YORK CO., INC.

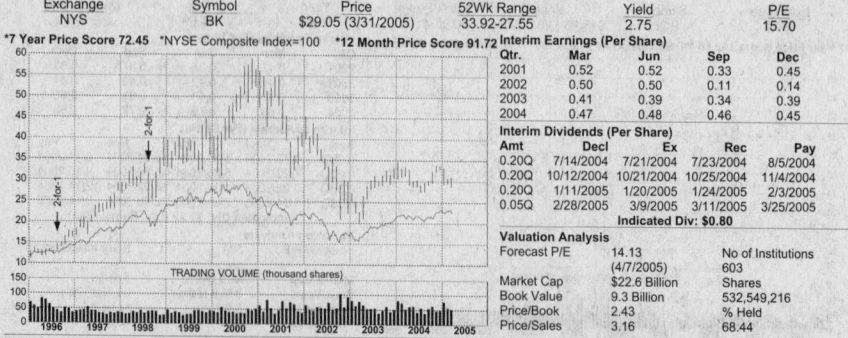

Exchange	Symbol	Price	52Wk Range	Yield	P/E
NYS	BK	$29.05 (3/31/2005)	33.92-27.55	2.75	15.70

*7 Year Price Score 72.45   *NYSE Composite Index=100   *12 Month Price Score 91.72

Interim Earnings (Per Share)

Qtr.	Mar	Jun	Sep	Dec
2001	0.52	0.52	0.33	0.45
2002	0.50	0.50	0.11	0.14
2003	0.41	0.39	0.34	0.39
2004	0.47	0.48	0.46	0.45

Interim Dividends (Per Share)

Amt	Decl	Ex	Rec	Pay
0.20Q	7/14/2004	7/21/2004	7/23/2004	8/5/2004
0.20Q	10/12/2004	10/21/2004	10/25/2004	11/4/2004
0.20Q	1/11/2005	1/20/2005	1/24/2005	2/3/2005
0.05Q	2/28/2005	3/9/2005	3/11/2005	3/25/2005

Indicated Div: $0.80

Valuation Analysis

Forecast P/E	14.13	No of Institutions
	(4/7/2005)	603
Market Cap	$22.6 Billion	Shares
Book Value	9.3 Billion	532,549,216
Price/Book	2.43	% Held
Price/Sales	3.16	68.44

Business Summary: Commercial Banking (MIC: 8.1 SIC: 022 NAIC: 22110)

Bank of New York is a bank holding company with assets of $92.40 billion and total deposits of $56.41 billion as of Dec 31 2003. Co. provides a broad range of banking and other financial services to corporations and individuals worldwide through its basic businesses, including securities servicing and global payment services, corporate banking, asset management and private client services, retail banking and global market services. Co. has operating centers in London, Brussels, Dublin, Singapore and Luxembourg and 28 non-U.S. branch and representative offices in 25 countries and provides securities servicing in over 100 markets.

Recent Developments: For the year ended Dec 31 2004, net income increased 24.5% to $1,440 million from net income of $1,157 million a year earlier. Net interest income was $1,645 million, up 5.1% from $1,154 million the year before. Provision for loan losses was $15 million versus $155 million in the prior year, a decrease of 90.3%. Non-interest income rose 17.1% to $4,691 million, while non-interest expense advanced 11.5% to $4,122 million.

Prospects: Co.'s results are benefiting from gains in securities servicing fees and foreign exchange and other trading revenues. For example, securities servicing fees rose 8.5% sequentially in the fourth quarter ended Dec 31 2004 to $742.0 million, reflecting more active equity markets and the conversion of new business wins. Co. noted that execution and clearing services revenues benefited from a solid rebound in equity market volumes from the weak third quarter. Further, issuer services fees rose due to strong results in depositary receipts, and modest growth in corporate trust. Investor services fees also grew sequentially, reflecting higher global funds services fees driven by new business wins.

Financial Data

(US$ in Thousands)	12/31/2004	12/31/2003	12/31/2002	12/31/2001	12/31/2000	12/31/1999	12/31/1998	12/31/1997
Earnings Per Share	1.85	1.52	1.24	1.81	1.92	2.27	1.53	1.36
Cash Flow Per Share	4.32	5.07	4.38	8.16	(2.95)	(1.31)	2.09	1.09
Tang Book Value Per Share	6.45	5.59	5.66	5.80	8.30	6.95	7.05	6.67
Dividends Per Share	0.790	0.760	0.760	0.720	0.660	0.580	0.540	0.490
Dividend Payout %	42.70	50.00	61.29	39.78	34.38	25.55	35.29	36.16
Income Statement								
Interest Income	2,453,000	2,330,000	2,613,000	3,620,000	4,377,000	3,473,000	3,510,000	3,560,000
Interest Expense	808,000	721,000	948,000	1,939,000	2,507,000	1,772,000	1,859,000	1,705,000
Net Interest Income	1,645,000	1,609,000	1,665,000	1,681,000	1,870,000	1,701,000	1,651,000	1,855,000
Provision for Losses	15,000	155,000	685,000	375,000	105,000	135,000	20,000	280,000
Non-Interest Income	4,691,000	4,006,000	3,143,000	3,540,000	3,109,000	3,493,000	2,283,000	2,137,000
Non-Interest Expense	4,122,000	3,698,000	2,751,000	2,788,000	2,510,000	2,107,000	1,928,000	1,874,000
Income Before Taxes	2,199,000	1,762,000	1,372,000	2,058,000	2,364,000	2,952,000	1,986,000	1,838,000
Income Taxes	759,000	605,000	470,000	715,000	822,000	1,101,000	699,000	669,000
Net Income	1,440,000	1,157,000	902,000	1,343,000	1,429,000	1,739,000	1,192,000	1,104,000
Average Shares	778,000	759,000	728,000	741,000	745,000	765,000	781,000	808,000
Balance Sheet								
Net Loans & Leases	35,190,000	34,615,000	30,508,000	35,131,000	35,645,000	36,952,000	37,750,000	34,486,000
Total Assets	94,529,000	92,397,000	77,564,000	81,025,000	77,114,000	74,756,000	63,503,000	59,961,000
Total Deposits	58,721,000	56,406,000	55,387,000	55,711,000	56,376,000	55,751,000	44,632,000	41,357,000
Total Liabilities	85,239,000	83,969,000	70,880,000	74,708,000	69,462,000	68,113,000	56,755,000	53,959,000
Stockholders' Equity	9,290,000	8,428,000	6,684,000	6,317,000	6,152,000	5,143,000	5,448,000	5,002,000
Shares Outstanding	778,120	775,318	726,456	730,323	741,068	740,214	773,119	750,000
Statistical Record								
Return on Assets %	1.54	1.36	1.14	1.70	1.88	2.52	1.93	1.91
Return on Equity %	16.21	15.31	13.88	21.54	25.23	32.84	22.81	21.80
Net Interest Margin %	67.06	69.06	63.72	46.44	42.72	48.98	47.04	52.11
Efficiency Ratio %	57.70	58.36	47.79	38.94	33.53	30.25	33.28	32.89
Loans to Deposits	0.60	0.61	0.55	0.63	0.63	0.66	0.85	0.83
Price Range	34.71-27.55	33.28-19.98	45.35-20.85	56.25-30.62	59.25-31.00	44.81-32.31	40.25-24.50	29.25-16.56
P/E Ratio	18.76-14.89	21.89-13.14	36.57-16.81	31.08-16.92	30.86-16.15	19.74-14.23	26.31-16.01	21.51-12.18
Average Yield %	2.55	2.72	2.25	1.58	1.42	1.56	1.77	2.21

Address: One Wall Street, 10th Floor, New York, NY 10286
Telephone: (212) 495 1784
Fax: (212) 495 2546

Web Site: www.bankofny.com
Officers: Thomas A. Renyi - Chmn., C.E.O. Alan R. Griffith - Vice-Chmn.

Auditors: ERNST & YOUNG LLP
Investor Contact: 1-800-432-0140

BANTA CORPORATION

Exchange	Symbol	Price	52Wk Range	Yield	P/E	Div Acheiver
NYS	BN	$42.80 (3/31/2005)	47.00-36.84	1.59	16.03	26 Years

*7 Year Price Score 119.64 ***NYSE Composite Index=100** ***12 Month Price Score 96.28**

Interim Earnings (Per Share)
Qtr.	Mar	Jun	Sep	Dec
2001	0.11	0.50	0.75	0.65
2002	0.41	0.52	0.76	0.01
2003	0.44	0.28	0.62	0.47
2004	0.54	0.60	0.76	0.78

Interim Dividends (Per Share)
Amt	Decl	Ex	Rec	Pay
0.17Q	4/27/2004	7/14/2004	7/16/2004	8/2/2004
0.17Q	7/27/2004	10/13/2004	10/15/2004	11/1/2004
0.17Q	12/7/2004	1/19/2005	1/21/2005	2/1/2005
0.17Q	1/25/2005	4/13/2005	4/15/2005	5/2/2005

Indicated Div: $0.68 (Div. Reinv. Plan)

Valuation Analysis
Forecast P/E	14.32	No of Institutions
	(4/7/2005)	183
Market Cap	$1.1 Billion	Shares
Book Value	538.0 Million	21,438,364
Price/Book	1.99	% Held
Price/Sales	0.70	85.28

TRADING VOLUME (thousand shares)

Business Summary: Printing (MIC: 13.4 SIC: 759 NAIC: 23119)

Banta provides a broad range of printing and digital imaging services. Co. operates in three business segments: print, turnkey services, and healthcare. The print segment provides products and services to publishers of educational and general books and special interest magazines. The print segment also supplies direct marketing materials and consumer and business catalogs. The turnkey services segment provides supply-chain management, product assembly, fulfillment and product localization services to technology companies. The healthcare products are primarily engaged in the production of disposable products used in outpatient clinics, dental offices and hospitals.

Recent Developments: For the year ended Jan 1 2005, net income increased 45.9% to $68,005 thousand from net income of $46,614 thousand a year earlier. Revenues were $1,523,252 thousand, up 7.4% from $1,418,497 thousand the year before. Operating income was $109,100 thousand versus an income of $81,614 thousand in the prior year, an increase of 33.7%. Total direct expense was $1,199,394 thousand versus $1,113,113 thousand in the prior year, an increase of 7.8%. Total indirect expense was $214,758 thousand versus $223,770 thousand in the prior year, a decrease of 4.0%.

Prospects: On Feb 14 2005, Co. agreed to sell its single-use healthcare products subsidiary, Banta Healthcare Group, Ltd., to an affiliate of Fidelity Capital Investors, Inc., for $67.0 million in cash. The transaction is expected to close near the end of the first quarter of 2005. Going forward, Co. appears poised to take advantage of growth opportunities in 2005, particularly in educational print, specialty magazines and supply-chain management. For 2005, Co. anticipates revenue will grow between 5.0% to 7.0% from 2004 levels to a range of $1.50 billion to $1.55 billion. Diluted earnings per share are expected to be in the range of $2.80 to $2.95.

Financial Data
(US$ in Thousands)

	01/01/2005	01/03/2004	12/28/2002	12/29/2001	12/30/2000	01/01/2000	01/02/1999	01/03/1998
Earnings Per Share	2.67	1.81	1.71	2.01	2.35	0.59	1.80	1.44
Cash Flow Per Share	3.38	4.26	5.89	7.26	5.05	4.64	4.64	3.81
Tang Book Value Per Share	18.83	17.35	15.46	13.89	12.41	12.31	11.83	11.80
Dividends Per Share	0.680	0.660	0.640	0.610	0.600	0.560	0.510	0.470
Dividend Payout %	25.47	36.46	37.43	30.35	25.53	94.92	28.33	32.64
Income Statement								
Total Revenue	1,523,252	1,418,497	1,366,457	1,457,935	1,537,729	1,278,278	1,335,796	1,202,483
EBITDA	169,462	146,682	161,574	171,295	189,141	115,184	163,777	143,992
Depn & Amortn	59,943	63,848	78,430	75,378	75,744	68,212	66,862	62,107
Income Before Taxes	105,430	74,414	71,801	82,197	96,643	34,610	86,090	70,823
Income Taxes	37,425	27,800	28,002	32,200	37,900	18,600	33,150	27,500
Net Income	68,005	46,614	43,799	49,997	58,743	16,010	52,940	43,323
Average Shares	25,508	25,742	25,565	24,857	24,980	27,177	29,474	30,113
Balance Sheet								
Current Assets	524,241	523,166	460,150	373,616	406,675	355,861	354,620	365,676
Total Assets	905,573	886,023	805,264	788,046	854,524	773,344	769,966	781,216
Current Liabilities	223,606	223,851	185,782	184,750	240,319	245,353	196,491	200,368
Long-Term Obligations	62,333	87,712	111,489	130,981	179,202	113,520	120,628	130,065
Total Liabilities	367,607	372,594	352,151	380,768	483,612	419,569	360,035	367,113
Stockholders' Equity	537,966	513,429	453,113	407,278	370,912	353,775	409,931	414,103
Shares Outstanding	25,046	25,791	25,247	24,729	24,566	23,942	28,260	29,793
Statistical Record								
Return on Assets %	7.61	5.42	5.51	6.10	7.24	2.08	6.84	5.68
Return on Equity %	12.97	9.49	10.21	12.88	16.26	4.20	12.88	10.21
EBITDA Margin %	11.13	10.34	11.82	11.75	12.30	9.01	12.26	11.97
Net Margin %	4.46	3.29	3.21	3.43	3.82	1.25	3.96	3.60
Asset Turnover	1.71	1.65	1.72	1.78	1.89	1.66	1.73	1.58
Current Ratio	2.34	2.34	2.48	2.02	1.69	1.45	1.80	1.83
Debt to Equity	0.12	0.17	0.25	0.32	0.48	0.32	0.29	0.31
Price Range	47.00-36.84	40.93-27.34	38.91-29.30	30.92-22.93	25.42-17.56	27.00-17.25	34.88-21.88	29.88-23.00
P/E Ratio	17.60-13.80	22.61-15.10	22.75-17.13	15.38-11.41	10.82-7.47	45.76-29.24	19.38-12.15	20.75-15.97
Average Yield %	1.60	1.95	1.90	2.23	2.92	2.46	1.74	1.76

Address: 225 Main Street, Menasha, WI 54952-8003	**Web Site:** www.banta.com	**Auditors:** ERNST & YOUNG LLP
Telephone: (920) 751-7777	**Officers:** Stephanie A. Streeter - Chmn., Pres., C.E.O.	**Investor Contact:** 920-751-7777
Fax: (920) 751-7790	Ronald D. Kneezel - V.P., Sec., Gen. Couns.	**Transfer Agents:** American Stock Transfer & Trust Company, New York,

BARD (C.R.), INC.

*7 Year Price Score 159.51 *NYSE Composite Index=100 *12 Month Price Score 107.10

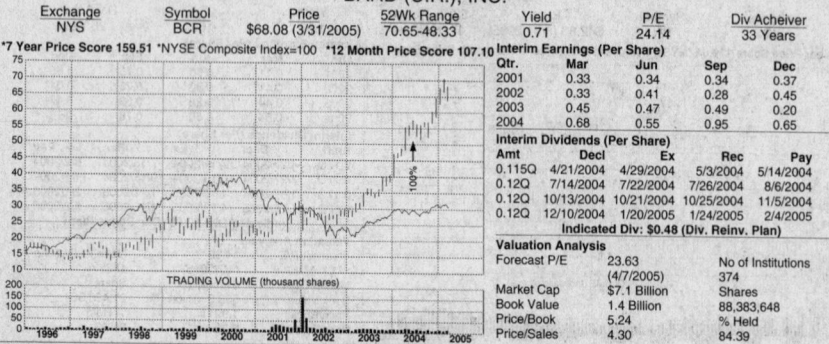

Interim Earnings (Per Share)

Qtr.	Mar	Jun	Sep	Dec
2001	0.33	0.34	0.34	0.37
2002	0.33	0.41	0.28	0.45
2003	0.45	0.47	0.49	0.20
2004	0.68	0.55	0.95	0.65

Interim Dividends (Per Share)

Amt	Decl	Ex	Rec	Pay
0.115Q	4/21/2004	4/29/2004	5/3/2004	5/14/2004
0.12Q	7/14/2004	7/22/2004	7/26/2004	8/6/2004
0.12Q	10/13/2004	10/21/2004	10/25/2004	11/5/2004
0.12Q	12/10/2004	1/20/2005	1/24/2005	2/4/2005

Indicated Div: $0.48 (Div. Reinv. Plan)

Valuation Analysis

Forecast P/E	23.63	No of Institutions	374
	(4/7/2005)	Shares	
Market Cap	$7.1 Billion	Shares	88,383,648
Book Value	1.4 Billion	% Held	
Price/Book	5.24		84.39
Price/Sales	4.30		

Business Summary: Medical Instruments & Equipment (MIC: 9.6 SIC: 841 NAIC: 39112)

C.R. Bard is a multinational developer, manufacturer and marketer of health care products. Co. engages in the design, manufacture, packaging, distribution and sale of medical, surgical, diagnostic and patient-care devices. Co. holds positions in the fields of vascular, urology, oncology and surgical specialty products. Co.'s products are marketed worldwide to hospitals, individual health care professionals, extended care facilities, alternate site facilities and the home, employing a combination of direct delivery and medical specialty distributors.

Recent Developments: For the year ended Dec 31 2004, net income increased 79.7% to $302,800 thousand from net income of $168,500 thousand a year earlier. Revenues were $1,656,100 thousand, up 15.6% from $1,433,100 thousand the year before. Total direct expense was $660,300 thousand versus $609,400 thousand in the prior year, an increase of 8.4%. Total indirect expense was $632,600 thousand versus $535,500 thousand in the prior year, an increase of 18.1%.

Prospects: Results are benefiting from steady revenue growth across Co.'s major product lines and geographies, particularly in its Vascular and Oncology product groups. Going forward, Co.'s outlook is strengthened by the combination of an expanded sales organization and innovative new products, which should continue to drive healthy levels of revenue growth in the upcoming quarters. Meanwhile, Co.'s success in improving its gross margin should continue to enable it increase its investment in product technology, strengthen its sales organization and enhance its long-term revenue growth profile.

Financial Data

(US$ in Thousands)	12/31/2004	12/31/2003	12/31/2002	12/31/2001	12/31/2000	12/31/1999	12/31/1998	12/31/1997
Earnings Per Share	2.82	1.60	1.47	1.38	1.04	1.14	2.25	0.63
Cash Flow Per Share	2.65	2.54	2.62	2.42	2.03	0.88	1.87	0.86
Tang Book Value Per Share	7.26	5.35	4.84	3.97	2.53	2.34	2.03	1.31
Dividends Per Share	0.470	0.450	0.430	0.420	0.410	0.390	0.370	0.350
Dividend Payout %	16.67	28.13	29.25	30.55	39.23	34.21	16.41	55.56
Income Statement								
Total Revenue	1,656,100	1,433,100	1,273,800	1,181,300	1,098,800	1,036,500	1,164,700	1,213,500
EBITDA	460,500	261,300	245,500	238,700	199,900	220,300	517,100	158,700
Depn & Amortn	54,700	44,700	41,000	40,000	49,600	49,100	58,700	57,300
Income Before Taxes	414,200	223,200	211,000	204,900	154,000	173,300	464,400	104,900
Income Taxes	111,400	54,700	56,000	61,700	47,100	55,200	212,100	32,600
Net Income	302,800	168,500	155,000	143,200	106,900	118,100	252,300	72,300
Average Shares	107,200	105,200	105,600	104,001	102,443	103,763	111,940	114,546
Balance Sheet								
Current Assets	1,054,000	875,100	758,000	647,400	526,600	529,100	488,500	563,500
Total Assets	2,009,100	1,692,000	1,416,700	1,231,100	1,089,200	1,126,400	1,079,800	1,279,300
Current Liabilities	390,300	421,900	316,900	234,500	224,500	352,500	302,800	310,600
Long-Term Obligations	151,400	151,500	152,200	156,400	204,300	158,400	160,000	340,700
Total Liabilities	649,000	646,300	536,300	442,400	475,300	552,100	512,200	706,200
Stockholders' Equity	1,360,100	1,045,700	880,400	788,700	613,900	574,300	567,600	573,100
Shares Outstanding	104,672	103,509	103,205	104,767	101,817	101,563	102,995	113,570
Statistical Record								
Return on Assets %	16.32	10.84	11.71	12.34	9.62	10.71	21.39	5.54
Return on Equity %	25.10	17.50	18.57	20.42	17.94	20.68	44.24	12.31
EBITDA Margin %	27.81	18.23	19.27	20.21	18.19	21.25	44.40	13.08
Net Margin %	18.28	11.76	12.17	12.12	9.73	11.39	21.66	5.96
Asset Turnover	0.89	0.92	0.96	1.02	0.99	0.94	0.99	0.93
Current Ratio	2.70	2.07	2.39	2.76	2.35	1.50	1.61	1.81
Debt to Equity	0.11	0.14	0.17	0.20	0.33	0.28	0.28	0.59
Price Range	64.58-40.20	40.63-27.41	32.25-23.13	32.26-21.00	27.34-17.63	29.56-21.13	24.75-14.34	19.00-13.25
P/E Ratio	22.90-14.26	25.39-17.13	21.94-15.73	23.37-15.21	26.29-16.95	25.93-18.53	11.00-6.38	30.16-21.03
Average Yield %	0.88	1.33	1.57	1.62	1.82	1.55	1.95	2.22

Address: 730 Central Avenue, Murray Hill, NJ 07974
Telephone: (908) 277-8000
Fax: (908) 277-8278

Web Site: www.crbard.com
Officers: Timothy M. Ring - Chmn., C.E.O. John H. Weiland - Pres., C.O.O.

Auditors: KPMG LLP
Investor Contact: 908-277-8139
Transfer Agents: EquiServe Trust Company, N.A., Providence, RI

BARNES & NOBLE INC

Exchange	Symbol	Price	52Wk Range	Yield	P/E
NYS	BKS	$34.49 (3/31/2005)	34.99-20.33	N/A	16.04

*7 Year Price Score 110.17 *NYSE Composite Index=100 *12 Month Price Score 117.23

TRADING VOLUME (thousand shares)

Interim Earnings (Per Share)

Qtr.	Apr	Jul	Oct	Jan
2001-02	(0.18)	(0.03)	(0.10)	1.24
2002-03	(0.25)	0.02	0.05	1.57
2003-04	(0.03)	0.20	0.14	1.76
2004-05	0.17	0.12	0.10	...

Interim Dividends (Per Share)

No Dividends Paid

Valuation Analysis

Forecast P/E	18.78	No of Institutions
	(4/7/2005)	220
Market Cap	$2.4 Billion	Shares
Book Value	1.3 Billion	49,651,760
Price/Book	1.82	% Held
Price/Sales	0.36	70.44

Business Summary: Retail - Miscellaneous (MIC: 5.11 SIC: 942 NAIC: 51211)

Barnes & Noble is a retailer of trade books, mass market paperbacks, children's books, off-price bargain books and magazines. As of Jan 31 2004, Co. operated 647 bookstores under the Barnes & Noble Booksellers, Bookstop and Bookstar names in 49 states. In addition, Co. operates 195 B. Dalton Bookseller stores, primarily in regional shopping malls. Through its approximate 65.0% interest in GameStop, Co. operated 1,514 video game and entertainment software stores under the GameStop, Babbage's, Software Etc. and FuncoLand names. Co. also conducts its e-commerce business through Barnes & Noble.com.

Recent Developments: For the quarter ended Oct 30 2004, net income decreased 24.9% to $7,642 from net income of $10,173 in the year-earlier quarter. Revenues were $1,459,014, up 14.9% from $1,270,072 the year before. Operating income was $20,749 versus an income of $31,509 in the prior-year quarter, a decrease of 34.1%. Total indirect expense was $372,919 versus $316,740 in the prior-year quarter, an increase of 17.7%.

Prospects: Co.'s near-term outlook appears challenging, reflecting slow same-store sales growth expectations at its regular and online stores. For the first quarter, Co. expects comparable store sales at Barnes & Noble stores to be in the low single digits. For the full year, same-store sales are expected to rise about 3.0%. Sales at Barnes & Noble.com are expected to increase at similar levels. First-quarter earnings are expected to be in a range of $0.11 to $0.13, and, for the full year, earnings should be in the range of $1.94 to $1.98. These projections reflect expense redundancies related to a new distribution center, which will reduce earnings by $0.08 per share.

Financial Data
(US$ in Thousands)

	9 Mos	6 Mos	3 Mos	01/31/2004	02/01/2003	02/02/2002	02/03/2001	01/29/2000
Earnings Per Share	2.15	2.19	2.27	2.07	1.39	0.94	(0.81)	1.75
Cash Flow Per Share	7.67	7.66	7.57	7.74	4.97	6.91	1.23	2.72
Tang Book Value Per Share	8.93	8.91	9.91	9.64	9.12	7.96	6.43	8.37
Income Statement								
Total Revenue	4,334,889	2,875,875	1,452,845	5,951,015	5,269,335	4,870,390	4,375,804	3,486,043
EBITDA	198,958	133,042	73,720	462,384	350,899	259,463	113,320	331,328
Depn & Amortn	139,545	92,128	45,475	166,545	151,586	150,118	146,317	112,693
Income Before Taxes	59,413	40,914	23,918	295,839	199,313	109,345	(32,997)	218,635
Income Taxes	23,528	16,342	9,541	120,554	80,223	45,378	18,969	89,637
Net Income	27,993	20,353	12,454	151,863	99,948	63,967	(51,966)	124,498
Average Shares	72,049	71,052	70,717	77,105	77,680	77,839	64,341	71,354
Balance Sheet								
Current Assets	2,184,919	1,895,316	2,049,860	2,193,499	1,886,868	1,590,994	1,455,253	1,241,519
Total Assets	3,661,004	3,354,070	3,360,310	3,507,294	2,995,427	2,623,220	2,557,476	2,413,791
Current Liabilities	1,611,365	1,293,485	1,272,756	1,441,841	1,231,448	1,140,228	935,075	922,851
Long-Term Obligations	245,000	257,400	300,000	300,000	300,000	449,000	666,900	431,600
Total Liabilities	2,340,198	2,037,936	2,082,130	2,020,348	1,766,686	1,735,110	1,779,799	1,567,431
Stockholders' Equity	1,320,806	1,316,134	1,278,180	1,259,659	1,027,790	888,110	777,677	846,360
Shares Outstanding	69,664	69,294	68,205	68,047	64,608	67,208	65,044	65,527
Statistical Record								
Return on Assets %	4.42	5.16	5.31	4.68	3.57	2.48	N.M.	5.91
Return on Equity %	13.16	13.69	14.45	13.31	10.46	7.70	N.M.	16.37
EBITDA Margin %	4.59	4.63	5.07	7.77	6.66	5.33	2.59	9.50
Net Margin %	0.65	0.71	0.86	2.55	1.90	1.31	N.M.	3.57
Asset Turnover	1.83	2.04	1.99	1.84	1.88	1.89	1.73	1.66
Current Ratio	1.36	1.47	1.61	1.52	1.53	1.40	1.56	1.35
Debt to Equity	0.19	0.20	0.23	0.24	0.29	0.51	0.86	0.51
Price Range	26.79-20.33	26.06-16.34	26.06-13.85	25.22-11.50	24.74-12.20	31.36-17.05	20.68-11.89	28.25-14.01
P/E Ratio	12.46-9.45	11.90-7.46	11.48-6.10	12.18-5.55	17.80-8.77	33.36-18.14	...	16.14-8.01

Address: 122 Fifth Avenue, New York, NY 10011	Web Site: www.barnesandnobleinc.com	Auditors: BDO SEIDMAN, LLP
Telephone: (212) 633-3300	Officers: Leonard Riggio - Chmn. Stephen Riggio - Vice-Chmn., C.E.O.	Investor Contact: 212-414-6104
Fax: (212) 366-5186		

BARR PHARMACEUTICALS INC

Exchange	Symbol	Price	52Wk Range	Yield	P/E
NYS	BRL	$48.83 (3/31/2005)	50.12-32.43	N/A	32.34

*7 Year Price Score 127.96 *NYSE Composite Index=100 *12 Month Price Score 106.64

Interim Earnings (Per Share)

Qtr.	Sep	Dec	Mar	Jun
2001-02	0.80	0.40	0.52	0.44
2002-03	0.41	0.42	0.44	0.35
2003-04	0.37	0.33	0.33	0.13
2004-05	0.49	0.56	...	...

Interim Dividends (Per Share)

Amt	Decl	Ex	Rec	Pay
50%	2/13/2004	3/16/2004	2/23/2004	3/15/2004

Valuation Analysis

Forecast P/E	17.88	No of Institutions
	(4/7/2005)	289
Market Cap	$5.0 Billion	Shares
Book Value	1.1 Billion	77,418,680
Price/Book	4.64	% Held
Price/Sales	4.46	75.44

TRADING VOLUME (thousand shares)

Business Summary: Pharmaceuticals (MIC: 9.1 SIC: 834 NAIC: 25412)

Barr Pharmaceuticals is a specialty pharmaceutical company that develops, manufactures and markets both generic and proprietary pharmaceutical products through its operating subsidiaries, Barr Laboratories and Duramed Pharmaceuticals. Co. markets generic products under the Barr label and almost all proprietary products under the Duramed label. As of Jun 30 2004, Co. manufactured and distributed more than 100 different dosage forms and strengths of over 70 different generic pharmaceutical products, including 19 oral contraceptive products. Also, Co. manufactures and distributes 11 proprietary pharmaceutical products, largely concentrated in the female healthcare arena.

Recent Developments: For the quarter ended Dec 31 2004, net income increased 69.3% to $59,387 thousand from net income of $35,069 thousand in the year-earlier quarter. Revenues were $257,369 thousand, down 31.2% from $374,124 thousand the year before. Operating income was $89,788 thousand versus an income of $49,348 thousand in the prior-year quarter, an increase of 81.9%. Total direct expense was $78,059 thousand versus $207,722 thousand in the prior-year quarter, a decrease of 62.4%. Total indirect expense was $89,522 thousand versus $117,054 thousand in the prior-year quarter, a decrease of 23.5%.

Prospects: Looking ahead, Co. expects diluted earnings per share for the fiscal year ending June 30 2005 to range from $2.35 to $2.45, with earnings in the second half of the year in the range of $1.30 to $1.40. The guidance for the balance of the fiscal year does not include potential costs and revenues associated with any business development activities or the favorable resolution of patent challenge litigation that may be completed by June 30 2005. Also, the guidance for the fiscal year does not include the impact from share repurchases, which may occur under Co.'s share repurchase program.

Financial Data
(US$ in Thousands)

	6 Mos	3 Mos	06/30/2004	06/30/2003	06/30/2002	06/30/2001	06/30/2000	06/30/1999
Earnings Per Share	1.51	1.27	1.15	1.62	2.06	0.74	0.53	0.93
Cash Flow Per Share	3.21	3.00	2.53	1.62	2.37	0.81	0.78	0.66
Tang Book Value Per Share	9.33	9.25	9.18	8.03	6.39	4.59	3.60	4.16
Income Statement								
Total Revenue	501,877	244,508	1,309,088	902,864	1,188,984	509,686	482,278	444,033
EBITDA	193,292	91,833	223,374	280,561	348,780	104,402	75,523	88,950
Depn & Amortn	21,210	9,989	32,059	22,713	15,290	10,846	10,420	9,306
Income Before Taxes	174,995	83,216	194,440	262,715	337,784	101,116	67,790	80,127
Income Taxes	63,473	31,081	71,337	95,149	125,405	38,629	25,448	30,877
Net Income	111,522	52,135	123,103	167,566	212,219	62,487	42,342	49,250
Average Shares	105,144	106,794	106,661	103,591	102,201	84,795	80,358	53,059
Balance Sheet								
Current Assets	835,906	837,318	878,246	847,504	637,668	436,774	315,408	248,140
Total Assets	1,352,378	1,329,080	1,333,269	1,180,937	888,554	543,394	423,853	347,890
Current Liabilities	213,836	200,570	207,645	274,787	177,455	151,560	112,516	101,277
Long-Term Obligations	27,016	31,602	32,355	34,027	42,634	24,899	28,084	30,008
Total Liabilities	272,013	273,447	291,223	312,942	222,022	177,752	141,685	134,183
Stockholders' Equity	1,080,365	1,055,633	1,042,046	867,995	666,532	365,642	282,168	213,707
Shares Outstanding	102,561	103,331	104,495	100,568	98,111	79,659	78,362	51,313
Statistical Record								
Return on Assets %	12.52	11.02	9.77	16.19	29.64	12.92	10.94	14.95
Return on Equity %	15.66	13.74	12.85	21.84	41.12	19.29	17.03	26.65
EBITDA Margin %	38.51	37.56	17.06	31.07	29.33	20.48	15.66	20.03
Net Margin %	22.22	21.32	9.40	18.56	17.85	12.26	8.78	11.09
Asset Turnover	0.88	1.00	1.04	0.87	1.66	1.05	1.25	1.35
Current Ratio	3.91	4.17	4.23	3.08	3.59	2.88	2.80	2.45
Debt to Equity	0.03	0.03	0.03	0.04	0.06	0.07	0.10	0.14
Price Range	53.49-32.43	56.49-32.43	56.49-33.15	43.68-22.44	39.72-26.93	34.44-19.56	19.92-8.46	14.54-7.41
P/E Ratio	35.42-21.48	44.48-25.54	49.12-28.83	26.96-13.85	19.28-13.07	46.55-26.43	37.58-15.97	15.63-7.96

Address: 400 Chestnut Ridge Road, Woodcliff Lake, NJ 07677-7668 Telephone: (201) 930 3300 Fax: (201) 930 3330	Web Site: www.barrlabs.com Officers: Bruce L. Downey - Chmn., C.E.O. Paul M. Bisaro - Pres., C.O.O.	Auditors: DELOITTE & TOUCHE LLP Investor Contact: 1-800-BARRLAB Transfer Agents: Continental Stock Transfer & Trust Company, New York

BAUSCH & LOMB, INC.

Exchange	Symbol	Price	52Wk Range	Yield	P/E
NYS	BOL	$73.30 (3/31/2005)	75.27-57.80	0.71	25.02

*7 Year Price Score 111.63 *NYSE Composite Index=100 *12 Month Price Score 104.36

Interim Earnings (Per Share)

Qtr.	Mar	Jun	Sep	Dec
2001	(0.02)	0.13	0.43	(0.15)
2002	0.16	0.40	0.17	0.60
2003	0.29	0.53	0.60	0.92
2004	0.43	0.76	0.79	0.93

Interim Dividends (Per Share)

Amt	Decl	Ex	Rec	Pay
0.13Q	4/27/2004	5/27/2004	6/1/2004	7/1/2004
0.13Q	7/20/2004	8/30/2004	9/1/2004	10/1/2004
0.13Q	11/2/2004	11/29/2004	12/1/2004	1/4/2005
0.13Q	2/22/2005	2/25/2005	3/1/2005	4/1/2005

Indicated Div: $0.52

Valuation Analysis

Forecast P/E	21.49	No of Institutions
	(4/7/2005)	251
Market Cap	$3.9 Billion	Shares
Book Value	1.4 Billion	48,742,564
Price/Book	2.73	% Held
Price/Sales	1.75	90.86

TRADING VOLUME (thousand shares)

Business Summary: Medical Instruments & Equipment (MIC: 9.6 SIC: 851 NAIC: 39115)

Bausch & Lomb is a developer of healthcare products for the eye. Co. operates five product categories. The contact lens category includes traditional, planned replacement disposable, daily disposable, rigid gas permeable, continuous wear and toric lenses. The lens care category includes Co.'s multipurpose solutions, enzyme cleaners and saline solutions. The pharmaceutical category includes generic and proprietary prescription pharmaceuticals and vision accessories. The cataract and vitreoretinal category includes products and equipment for cataract and vitreoretinal surgery. The refractive category includes lasers, microkeratomes, and other products and equipment used in refractive surgery.

Recent Developments: For the year ended Dec 25 2004, net income increased 27.2% to $159,600 thousand from net income of $125,500 thousand a year earlier. Revenues were $2,232,300 thousand, up 10.5% from $2,019,500 thousand the year before. Operating income was $279,600 thousand versus an income of $235,600 thousand in the prior year, an increase of 18.7%. Total direct expense was $934,900 thousand versus $858,000 thousand in the prior year, an increase of 9.0%. Total indirect expense was $1,017,800 thousand versus $925,900 thousand in the prior year, an increase of 9.9%.

Prospects: In 2005, Co. expects constant-currency revenues to grow 6.0% to 7.0%, with earnings per share of approximately $3.40 per share. Consistent with Co.'s ongoing operating objectives, it anticipates continued expansion in gross margins and further reductions in selling, general and administrative expenses as a percentage of sales, with investment in research and development growing at a higher rate than sales. As a result, further operating margin expansion is anticipated. Separately, first-quarter and first-half sales growth rates are expected to be lower than the full-year average pending scheduled product introductions in the second and third quarters of 2005.

Financial Data (US$ in Thousands)	12/25/2004	12/27/2003	12/28/2002	12/29/2001	12/30/2000	12/25/1999	12/26/1998	12/27/1997
Earnings Per Share	2.93	2.34	1.34	0.39	1.52	7.76	0.45	0.89
Cash Flow Per Share	5.34	4.69	4.41	3.43	6.09	3.91	2.63	3.90
Tang Book Value Per Share	9.13	5.20	2.87	2.48	4.18	11.05	1.52	7.45
Dividends Per Share	0.520	0.520	0.650	1.040	1.040	1.040	1.040	1.040
Dividend Payout %	17.75	22.22	48.51	266.67	68.42	13.40	231.11	116.85
Income Statement								
Total Revenue	2,232,300	2,019,500	1,816,700	1,711,900	1,772,400	1,756,100	2,362,800	1,915,700
EBITDA	420,400	376,100	299,200	298,400	376,900	429,600	395,000	286,000
Depn & Amortn	125,200	124,900	108,300	155,100	147,700	156,200	163,800	112,000
Income Before Taxes	246,800	197,000	137,000	85,000	160,700	185,000	130,400	118,000
Income Taxes	82,700	67,000	47,200	28,700	65,500	66,600	79,400	45,600
Net Income	159,600	125,500	72,500	21,200	83,400	444,800	25,200	49,400
Average Shares	54,504	53,491	53,997	53,715	54,724	58,639	56,367	55,654
Balance Sheet								
Current Assets	1,380,500	1,421,400	1,284,700	1,397,300	1,645,700	1,810,300	1,586,800	1,090,200
Total Assets	3,022,100	3,006,400	2,907,800	2,993,500	3,085,900	3,273,500	3,491,700	2,772,900
Current Liabilities	832,500	876,400	829,000	703,600	808,700	619,600	812,400	887,300
Long-Term Obligations	543,300	652,000	656,200	703,200	763,100	977,000	1,281,300	510,800
Total Liabilities	1,595,200	1,803,000	1,890,000	2,018,500	2,046,500	2,039,500	2,646,700	1,954,500
Stockholders' Equity	1,426,900	1,203,400	1,017,800	975,000	1,039,400	1,234,000	845,000	818,400
Shares Outstanding	53,239	52,619	53,969	53,613	53,473	56,763	56,827	55,209
Statistical Record								
Return on Assets %	5.31	4.26	2.46	0.70	2.58	13.19	0.81	1.84
Return on Equity %	12.17	11.33	7.30	2.11	7.22	42.91	3.04	5.83
EBITDA Margin %	18.83	18.62	16.47	17.43	21.26	24.46	16.72	14.93
Net Margin %	7.15	6.21	3.99	1.24	4.71	25.33	1.07	2.58
Asset Turnover	0.74	0.68	0.62	0.56	0.55	0.52	0.76	0.71
Current Ratio	1.66	1.62	1.55	1.99	2.03	2.92	1.95	1.23
Debt to Equity	0.38	0.54	0.64	0.72	0.73	0.79	1.52	0.62
Price Range	68.56-50.85	52.00-29.85	44.57-27.79	54.48-28.30	79.13-34.19	83.38-52.63	59.38-38.25	47.88-32.63
P/E Ratio	23.40-17.35	22.22-12.76	33.26-20.74	139.69-72.56	52.06-22.49	10.74-6.78	131.94-85.00	53.79-36.66
Average Yield %	0.85	1.31	1.84	2.67	1.91	1.56	1.24	2.60

Address: One Bausch & Lomb Place, Rochester, NY 14604-2701	Web Site: www.bausch.com	Auditors: PricewaterhouseCoopers LLP
Telephone: (585) 338-6000	Officers: Ronald L. Zarrella - Chmn., C.E.O. Alan H. Farnsworth - Sr. V.P., Pres., Europe, Middle East & Africa Region	Investor Contact: 585-338-5802
Fax: (585) 338-6007		Transfer Agents: Mellon Investor Services, LLC, South Hackensack, NJ

BAXTER INTERNATIONAL INC.

Exchange	Symbol	Price	52Wk Range	Yield	P/E
NYS	BAX	$33.98 (3/31/2005)	36.24-29.54	1.71	53.94

*7 Year Price Score 79.37   *NYSE Composite Index=100   *12 Month Price Score 99.24

Interim Earnings (Per Share)

Qtr.	Mar	Jun	Sep	Dec
2001	0.27	0.42	0.45	(0.13)
2002	0.41	0.32	0.51	0.02
2003	0.35	0.06	0.43	0.61
2004	0.29	(0.28)	0.45	0.17

Interim Dividends (Per Share)

Amt	Decl	Ex	Rec	Pay
0.582A	11/28/2001	12/12/2001	12/14/2001	1/7/2002
0.582A	11/18/2002	12/11/2002	12/13/2002	1/6/2003
0.582A	11/18/2003	12/10/2003	12/12/2003	1/5/2004
0.582A	11/16/2004	12/8/2004	12/10/2004	1/5/2005

Indicated Div: $0.58

Valuation Analysis

Forecast P/E	N/A	No of Institutions
Market Cap	$21.0 Billion	Shares
Book Value	3.7 Billion	486,657,280
Price/Book	5.67	% Held
Price/Sales	2.21	78.53

Business Summary: Medical Instruments & Equipment (MIC: 9.6 SIC: 841 NAIC: 39112)

Baxter International is a global medical products and services company engaged in medical devices, pharmaceuticals and biotechnology to assist health-care professionals and their patients with the treatment of complex medical conditions, including hemophilia, immune disorders, infectious diseases, cancer, kidney disease, trauma and other conditions. Co. operates in three segments: Medication Delivery, BioScience and Renal. Co.'s products are used by hospitals, clinical and medical research laboratories, blood and plasma collection centers, kidney dialysis centers, rehabilitation centers, nursing homes, doctors' offices and by patients at home under physician supervision.

Recent Developments: For the year ended Dec 31 2004, income from continuing operations decreased 57.8% to $383 million from income of $907 million a year earlier. Net income decreased 55.2% to $388 million from net income of $866 million a year earlier. Revenues were $9,509 million, up 6.8% from $8,904 million the year before. Total direct expense was $5,594 million versus $4,951 million in the prior year, an increase of 13.0%. Total indirect expense was $3,309 million versus $2,695 million in the prior year, an increase of 22.8%.

Prospects: For the first quarter of 2005, Co. expects organic sales growth of 3.0% to 4.0%, with diluted earnings per share from continuing operations of $0.33 to $0.35. For full-year 2005, Co. is forecasting organic sales growth of 2.0% to 4.0%, reflecting its decision to exit certain low margin businesses, which is expected to adversely impact sales growth by approximately 1.0%, or $125.0 million. Co. expects 2005 diluted earnings per share from continuing operations to be $1.82 to $1.90. Co. expects to generate cash flow from continuing operations of approximately $1.50 billion, or free cash flow of approximately $900.0 million in 2005, after $600.0 million of anticipated capital expenditures.

Financial Data
(US$ in Thousands)

	12/31/2004	12/31/2003	12/31/2002	12/31/2001	12/31/2000	12/31/1999	12/31/1998	12/31/1997
Earnings Per Share	0.63	1.45	1.26	1.00	1.24	1.35	0.55	0.53
Cash Flow Per Share	2.24	2.38	1.99	1.95	2.07	1.87	1.74	1.11
Tang Book Value Per Share	2.44	1.74	1.53	3.44	2.42	4.18	1.78	1.78
Dividends Per Share	0.582	0.582	0.582	0.582	0.582	0.582	0.582	0.569
Dividend Payout %	92.38	40.14	46.19	58.20	46.94	43.11	106.79	107.41
Income Statement								
Total Revenue	9,509,000	8,916,000	8,110,000	7,663,000	6,896,000	6,380,000	6,599,000	6,138,000
EBITDA	1,073,000	1,734,000	1,848,000	1,414,000	1,370,000	1,448,000	1,031,000	1,030,000
Depn & Amortn	544,000	497,000	400,000	381,000	339,000	309,000	321,000	344,000
Income Before Taxes	430,000	1,150,000	1,397,000	964,000	946,000	1,052,000	549,000	523,000
Income Taxes	47,000	228,000	364,000	300,000	208,000	273,000	234,000	223,000
Net Income	388,000	881,000	778,000	612,000	740,000	797,000	315,000	300,000
Average Shares	618,000	606,000	618,000	609,000	598,000	590,000	578,000	564,000
Balance Sheet								
Current Assets	6,019,000	5,437,000	5,160,000	3,977,000	3,651,000	3,819,000	4,651,000	3,870,000
Total Assets	14,147,000	13,779,000	12,478,000	10,343,000	8,733,000	9,644,000	10,085,000	8,707,000
Current Liabilities	4,286,000	3,819,000	3,851,000	3,294,000	3,372,000	2,700,000	2,988,000	2,557,000
Long-Term Obligations	3,933,000	4,421,000	4,398,000	2,486,000	1,726,000	2,601,000	3,096,000	2,635,000
Total Liabilities	10,442,000	10,456,000	9,539,000	6,586,000	6,074,000	6,296,000	7,246,000	6,088,000
Stockholders' Equity	3,705,000	3,323,000	2,939,000	3,757,000	2,659,000	3,348,000	2,839,000	2,619,000
Shares Outstanding	617,925	611,301	599,504	598,893	586,000	580,398	572,658	560,078
Statistical Record								
Return on Assets %	2.77	6.71	6.82	6.42	8.03	8.08	3.35	3.68
Return on Equity %	11.01	28.14	23.24	19.08	24.57	25.76	11.54	11.71
EBITDA Margin %	11.28	19.45	22.79	18.45	19.87	22.70	15.62	16.78
Net Margin %	4.08	9.88	9.59	7.99	10.73	12.49	4.77	4.89
Asset Turnover	0.68	0.68	0.71	0.80	0.75	0.65	0.70	0.75
Current Ratio	1.40	1.42	1.34	1.21	1.08	1.41	1.56	1.51
Debt to Equity	1.06	1.33	1.50	0.66	0.65	0.78	1.09	1.01
Price Range	34.59-28.76	31.20-18.56	59.60-24.22	55.50-40.75	44.44-24.79	36.33-28.07	31.57-23.29	28.73-19.43
P/E Ratio	54.90-45.65	21.52-12.80	47.30-19.22	55.50-40.75	35.84-19.99	26.91-20.80	57.40-42.35	54.21-36.67
Average Yield %	1.85	2.19	1.35	1.20	1.64	1.86	2.12	2.37

Address: One Baxter Parkway, Deerfield, IL 60015-4633 **Telephone:** (847) 948-2000 **Fax:** (847) 948-2964	**Web Site:** www.baxter.com **Officers:** Robert L. Parkinson Jr. - Chmn., C.E.O. John J. Greisch - Sr. V.P., C.F.O.	**Auditors:** PricewaterhouseCoopers LLP **Investor Contact:** 847-948-4551

BB&T CORP.

Exchange	Symbol	Price	52Wk Range	Yield	P/E	Div Acheiver
NYS	BBT	$39.08 (3/31/2005)	43.25-33.33	3.58	13.96	33 Years

*7 Year Price Score 95.42   ***NYSE Composite Index=100**   ***12 Month Price Score 94.07**

Interim Earnings (Per Share)

Qtr.	Mar	Jun	Sep	Dec
2001	0.53	0.54	0.48	0.61
2002	0.66	0.68	0.68	0.70
2003	0.69	0.67	0.21	0.56
2004	0.60	0.72	0.74	0.75

Interim Dividends (Per Share)

Amt	Decl	Ex	Rec	Pay
0.35Q	6/22/2004	7/14/2004	7/16/2004	8/2/2004
0.35Q	8/24/2004	10/13/2004	10/15/2004	11/1/2004
0.35Q	12/14/2004	1/12/2005	1/14/2005	2/1/2005
0.35Q	2/22/2005	4/13/2005	4/15/2005	5/2/2005

Indicated Div: $1.40 (Div. Reinv. Plan)

Valuation Analysis

Forecast P/E	12.73 (4/8/2005)	No of Institutions	397
Market Cap	$21.5 Billion	Shares	164,873,792
Book Value	10.9 Billion	% Held	30.06
Price/Book	1.98		
Price/Sales	3.23		

TRADING VOLUME (thousand shares)

Business Summary: Commercial Banking (MIC: 8.1 SIC: 021 NAIC: 22110)

BB&T, a multi-bank holding company with assets of $90.47 billion as of Dec 31 2003, operates more than 1,300 banking offices in the Carolinas, Virginia, West Virginia, Tennessee, Kentucky, Georgia, Maryland, Florida, Alabama, Indiana and Washington, D.C. Co.'s largest subsidiary is Branch Banking and Trust Company (BB&T-NC). BB&T-NC's subsidiaries include BB&T Leasing Corp., BB&T Investment Services, and BB&T Insurance Services. Co.'s other subsidiaries include Branch Banking and Trust Co. of South Carolina, Branch Banking and Trust Co. of Virginia, and Fidelity Service Corporation.

Recent Developments: For the year ended Dec 31 2004, net income increased 46.3% to $1,558,375 thousand from net income of $1,064,903 thousand a year earlier. Net interest income was $3,348,223 thousand, up 8.6% from $3,082,005 thousand the year before. Provision for loan losses was $249,269 thousand versus $247,585 thousand in the prior year, an increase of 0.7%. Non-interest income rose 16.0% to $2,119,271 thousand, while non-interest expense advanced 8.9% to $2,895,863 thousand.

Prospects: Looking ahead, Co. is optimistic about its outlook in 2005 as it works to further integrate new markets entered through past acquisitions. Separately, on Feb 16 2005, Co. announced that it agreed to acquire 70.0% ownership interest in Sterling Capital Management LLC of Charlotte, NC. Privately-held Sterling Capital Management, with more than $8.00 billion in assets under management, provides investment management services to institutional clients and high net worth individuals. The agreement if approved is expected to close in the second quarter of 2005.

Financial Data
(US$ in Thousands)

	12/31/2004	12/31/2003	12/31/2002	12/31/2001	12/31/2000	12/31/1999	12/31/1998	12/31/1997
Earnings Per Share	2.80	2.07	2.72	2.12	1.55	1.83	1.71	1.30
Cash Flow Per Share	5.49	7.47	1.73	0.21	0.62	5.06	0.61	0.97
Tang Book Value Per Share	11.33	10.92	12.04	13.50	11.91	9.66	9.51	8.22
Dividends Per Share	1.340	1.220	1.100	0.980	0.860	0.750	0.660	0.580
Dividend Payout %	47.86	58.94	40.44	46.23	55.48	40.98	38.60	44.62
Income Statement								
Interest Income	4,546,695	4,354,792	4,434,044	4,849,538	4,339,674	3,115,780	2,481,182	2,122,940
Interest Expense	1,198,472	1,272,787	1,686,584	2,415,053	2,322,046	1,534,065	1,233,778	1,023,415
Net Interest Income	3,348,223	3,082,005	2,747,460	2,434,485	2,017,628	1,581,715	1,247,404	1,099,525
Provision for Losses	249,269	248,000	263,700	224,318	127,431	92,097	80,310	89,850
Non-Interest Income	2,119,271	1,889,135	1,692,475	1,378,691	777,022	761,356	528,002	474,914
Non-Interest Expense	2,895,863	2,721,212	2,385,538	2,228,430	1,761,539	1,346,904	961,374	937,150
Income Before Taxes	2,322,362	1,617,030	1,790,697	1,360,428	905,680	904,070	733,722	547,439
Income Taxes	763,987	552,127	497,468	386,790	279,238	291,223	231,897	187,497
Net Income	1,558,375	1,064,903	1,303,009	973,638	626,442	612,847	501,825	359,942
Average Shares	556,041	514,082	478,792	459,269	398,915	335,298	293,571	276,440
Balance Sheet								
Net Loans & Leases	66,744,193	60,794,990	50,416,621	44,891,339	38,932,351	28,524,467	22,350,692	19,516,871
Total Assets	100,508,641	90,466,613	80,216,816	70,869,945	59,340,228	43,480,996	34,427,227	29,177,600
Total Deposits	67,699,337	59,349,785	51,280,016	44,733,275	38,014,501	27,251,142	23,046,907	20,210,116
Total Liabilities	89,634,167	80,531,882	72,828,902	64,719,736	54,554,303	40,281,837	31,668,679	26,939,963
Stockholders' Equity	10,874,474	9,934,731	7,387,914	6,150,209	4,785,925	3,199,159	2,758,548	2,237,637
Shares Outstanding	550,406	541,942	470,452	455,682	401,678	331,170	290,211	272,104
Statistical Record								
Return on Assets %	1.63	1.25	1.72	1.50	1.22	1.57	1.58	1.43
Return on Equity %	14.94	12.29	19.25	17.81	15.65	20.57	20.09	18.15
Net Interest Margin %	73.64	70.77	61.96	50.20	46.49	50.76	50.27	51.79
Efficiency Ratio %	43.44	43.58	38.94	35.78	34.43	34.74	31.95	36.07
Loans to Deposits	0.99	1.02	0.98	1.04	1.02	1.05	0.97	0.97
Price Range	43.25-33.33	39.66-31.15	39.23-31.26	38.48-31.42	38.25-22.00	40.44-27.31	40.63-27.31	32.50-17.63
P/E Ratio	15.45-11.90	19.16-15.05	14.42-11.49	18.15-14.82	24.68-14.19	22.10-14.92	23.76-15.97	25.00-13.56
Average Yield %	3.50	3.46	2.99	2.75	3.06	2.11	1.98	2.47

Address: 200 West Second Street, Winston-Salem, NC 27102 **Telephone:** (336) 733-2000 **Fax:** (336) 671-2399	**Web Site:** www.bbandt.com **Officers:** John A. Allison IV - Chmn., C.E.O. Scott E. Reed - Sr. Exec. V.P., C.F.O.	**Auditors:** PricewaterhouseCoopers LLP **Investor Contact:** 336-733-3058 **Transfer Agents:** Branch Banking & Trust Company, Wilson, NC

BEAR STEARNS COS., INC. (THE)

Exchange	Symbol	Price	52Wk Range	Yield	P/E
NYS	BSC	$99.90 (3/31/2005)	106.68-76.62	1.00	10.17

*7 Year Price Score 131.33 *NYSE Composite Index=100 *12 Month Price Score 102.54

TRADING VOLUME (thousand shares)

Interim Earnings (Per Share)

Qtr.	Feb	May	Aug	Nov
2002	1.29	2.59	1.23	1.37
2003	2.00	2.05	2.30	2.18
2004	2.57	2.49	2.09	2.60
2005	2.64	...	...	...

Interim Dividends (Per Share)

Amt	Decl	Ex	Rec	Pay
0.20Q	6/16/2004	7/14/2004	7/16/2004	7/30/2004
0.25Q	9/22/2004	10/13/2004	10/15/2004	10/29/2004
0.25Q	12/21/2004	1/12/2005	1/14/2005	1/28/2005
0.25Q	4/8/2005	4/15/2005	4/19/2005	4/29/2005

Indicated Div: $1.00

Valuation Analysis

Forecast P/E	10.29	No of Institutions	
	(4/13/2005)	376	
Market Cap	$11.3 Billion	Shares	
Book Value	9.5 Billion	71,828,672	
Price/Book	1.19	% Held	
Price/Sales	1.26	63.40	

Business Summary: Finance Intermediaries & Services (MIC: 8.7 SIC: 211 NAIC: 23120)

The Bear Stearns Companies is the parent company of Bear, Stearns and Company, a worldwide investment banking, securities trading and brokerage firm. The firm's business includes corporate finance and mergers and acquisitions, public finance, institutional equities and fixed income sales and trading, private client services and asset management. Through its wholly-owned subsidiary, Bear Stearns Securities, Co. provides professional and correspondent clearing services, in addition to clearing and settling Co.'s proprietary and customer transactions.

Recent Developments: For the year ended Nov 30 2004, Co. reported net income of $1,344,733 thousand compared with net income of $1,156,406 thousand the year before. Results for 2004 and 2003 included equity in earnings from affiliates of $1,226,680 thousand and $1,277,516 thousand, respectively. Total revenues rose 33.8% to $866,918 thousand from $647,835 thousand in 2003. Revenues from interest rose 16.3% to $487,089 thousand from $418,744 thousand the year before. Income before benefit from income taxes was $114,827 thousand compared with a loss of $122,195 thousand a year earlier.

Prospects: Co.'s businesses are well-positioned for coming market trends and poised for future success. Co.'s Capital Markets revenues are benefiting from increased domestic and international equity sales and trading, stronger risk arbitrage results and the consolidation of the specialist business, along with higher advisory, merger and acquisition and merchant banking revenues at its investment bank. Meanwhile, Global Clearing results are seeing higher levels of customer margin, free credit, stock borrow and customer short balances. Wealth Management is being positively affected by increasing private client service area commissions and higher assets under management in the asset management business.

Financial Data

(US$ in Thousands)	3 Mos	11/30/2004	11/30/2003	11/30/2002	11/30/2001	11/30/2000	11/26/1999	06/30/1999
Earnings Per Share	9.82	9.76	8.52	6.47	4.27	5.35	1.78	4.27
Cash Flow Per Share	(53.75)	(17.03)	(42.19)	(10.30)	45.94	(27.61)	(3.41)	1.42
Tang Book Value Per Share	80.17	82.31	67.58	56.88	48.26	44.54	34.97	33.07
Dividends Per Share	0.900	0.850	0.740	0.620	0.600	0.550	0.565	0.551
Dividend Payout %	9.16	8.71	8.69	9.58	14.05	10.28	31.72	12.91
Income Statement								
Interest Income	1,021,619	2,317,315	1,955,373	2,232,159	4,339,298	5,642,361	1,810,598	4,008,566
Commissions & Fees	...	2,326,724	1,982,538	1,944,454	1,888,856	2,229,091	854,029	1,853,210
Employee Costs	...	3,253,862	2,880,695	2,508,197	2,528,852	2,814,193	973,990	2,285,594
Interest Expense	784,709	1,609,019	1,400,953	1,762,580	3,793,998	4,800,891	1,531,787	3,379,914
Income Before Taxes	578,328	2,022,154	1,772,269	1,310,963	934,444	1,171,523	453,592	1,064,108
Income Taxes	199,523	677,421	615,863	432,618	309,479	398,340	167,778	391,060
Net Income	378,805	1,344,733	1,156,406	878,345	618,692	773,183	285,814	673,048
Average Shares	149,193	145,284	145,027	146,346	152,216	152,034	...	165,483
Balance Sheet								
Total Assets	268,429,074	255,949,894	212,168,110	184,854,423	185,530,228	171,166,473	162,037,962	153,894,340
Total Liabilities	258,910,176	246,959,022	204,135,522	177,909,840	179,139,201	165,012,185	156,596,015	148,438,831
Stockholders' Equity	9,518,898	8,990,872	7,470,088	6,382,083	5,628,527	5,654,288	4,941,947	4,955,509
Shares Outstanding	113,211	103,786	102,572	100,024	100,042	108,982	118,438	125,661
Statistical Record								
Return on Assets %	0.55	0.57	0.58	0.47	0.35	0.46	0.13	0.44
Return on Equity %	15.72	16.29	16.70	14.63	10.97	14.40	4.40	14.56
Net Interest Margin %	23.19	30.57	28.35	21.04	12.57	14.91	15.40	15.68
Price Range	106.68-76.62	98.55-71.00	82.55-58.65	67.39-51.92	64.04-42.06	72.13-36.94	45.65-33.27	55.22-25.28
P/E Ratio	10.86-7.80	10.10-7.27	9.69-6.88	10.42-8.02	15.00-9.85	13.48-6.90	25.65-18.69	12.93-5.92
Average Yield %	1.00	1.00	1.07	1.03	1.11	1.15	1.41	1.37

Address: 383 Madison Avenue, New York, NY 10179 **Telephone:** (212) 272 2000 **Fax:** (212) 272 4785	**Web Site:** www.bearstearns.com **Officers:** James E. Cayne - Chmn., C.E.O. Alan D. Schwartz - Co-Pres., Co-C.O.O.	**Auditors:** DELOITTE & TOUCHE LLP **Investor Contact:** 212-272-9251

BEARINGPOINT INC

Exchange	Symbol	Price	52Wk Range	Yield	P/E
NYS	BE	$8.77 (3/31/2005)	11.00-7.26	N/A	N/A

*7 Year Price Score N/A   *NYSE Composite Index=100   *12 Month Price Score 85.72

Interim Earnings (Per Share)

Qtr.	Sep	Dec	Mar	Jun
2002-03	0.09	0.09	0.06	(0.02)
Qtr.	Mar	Jun	Sep	Dec
2003	...	...	(0.02)	(0.65)
2004	0.01	0.08	0.06	...

Interim Dividends (Per Share)

No Dividends Paid

Valuation Analysis

Forecast P/E	N/A	No of Institutions
Market Cap	$1.7 Billion	Shares
Book Value	1.2 Billion	185,443,904
Price/Book	1.48	% Held
Price/Sales	0.75	93.09

TRADING VOLUME (thousand shares)

Business Summary: Accounting & Management Consulting Services (MIC: 12.2 SIC: 742 NAIC: 41512)

Bearingpoint is a business consulting, systems integration and managed services firm. Co. serves large companies, small and medium-sized businesses, government agencies and other organizations. Co. provides business and technology strategy, systems design and architecture, applications implementation, network, systems integration, and managed services. Co.'s offerings are designed to help its clients generate revenue, lower costs and access the information necessary to operate their business. Co. provides consulting services through four industry groups: Public Services, Financial Services, Communications and Content and Consumer, Industrial and Technology.

Recent Developments: For the quarter ended Sep 30 2004, Co. reported net income of $11,942 thousand compared with a net loss of $39,184 thousand in the corresponding quarter the year before. Revenue was $840,864 thousand, up 13.2% from $742,958 thousand in the equivalent period a year earlier. Gross margin was $173,455 thousand, or 20.6% of revenues, versus $742,958 thousand, or 11.7% of revenues, in 2003. Operating income amounted to $25,801 thousand compared with an operating loss of $50,291 thousand the year before.

Prospects: Co. continues to see a gradual improvement in information technology spending across numerous sectors. Recent top line gains were led by its Public Services segment, reflecting growth in both the Federal and State, Local and Education sectors, and its Financial Services segment, primarily due to strength in the Banking and Insurance sector. Thus, Co.'s utilization on a consolidated basis improved to 67.3% for the third quarter ended Sep 30, 2004 from 62.3% the previous year. Utilization for Co.'s international operations rose to 62.3% during the third quarter of 2004, up from 54.5% in 2003, while North American utilization increased to 70.7% during the same period, up from 69.0% last year.

Financial Data (US$ in Thousands)	9 Mos	6 Mos	3 Mos	12/31/2003	06/30/2003	06/30/2002	06/30/2001	06/30/2000
Earnings Per Share	(0.21)	(0.93)	(0.92)	(0.86)	0.22	(0.17)	(1.19)	(0.58)
Cash Flow Per Share	(0.30)	0.13	(0.07)	0.15	0.83	1.69	0.77	(3.56)
Tang Book Value Per Share	1.05	0.89	0.82	0.73	0.76	2.78	2.81	...
Income Statement								
Total Revenue	2,587,405	1,746,541	861,041	1,554,431	3,139,277	2,367,627	2,855,824	1,105,166
EBITDA	134,714	92,196	34,105	(119,208)	227,580	183,010	212,659	42,314
Depn & Amortn	56,237	38,983	19,850	37,141	115,785	49,320	61,022	20,649
Income Before Taxes	65,607	45,060	10,051	(162,936)	99,066	134,586	136,848	11,537
Income Taxes	36,331	27,726	7,898	2,831	57,759	81,524	101,897	29,339
Net Income	28,747	16,805	1,624	(165,767)	41,307	(26,898)	34,951	(17,802)
Average Shares	198,243	198,710	198,203	193,596	185,637	159,583	107,884	75,843
Balance Sheet								
Current Assets	1,071,499	1,037,861	938,619	862,281	760,852	647,213	704,759	641,192
Total Assets	2,319,984	2,283,362	2,188,210	2,129,447	2,049,812	895,131	999,635	925,230
Current Liabilities	770,211	790,005	628,727	629,396	520,117	283,295	354,109	466,203
Long-Term Obligations	226,921	230,054	298,060	238,883	268,812	...	1,846	42,383
Total Liabilities	1,138,989	1,153,953	1,058,209	997,789	860,159	293,261	367,523	538,902
Stockholders' Equity	1,180,995	1,129,409	1,130,001	1,131,658	1,189,653	601,870	632,112	(667,575)
Shares Outstanding	199,166	196,434	196,395	194,483	191,663	157,666	157,569	75,880
Statistical Record								
Return on Assets %	N.M.	0.76	0.08	N.M.	2.81	N.M.	3.63	N.M.
Return on Equity %	N.M.	1.49	0.14	N.M.	4.61	N.M.	...	...
EBITDA Margin %	5.21	5.28	3.96	N.M.	7.25	7.73	7.45	3.83
Net Margin %	1.11	0.96	0.19	N.M.	1.32	N.M.	1.22	N.M.
Asset Turnover	1.07	0.79	0.40	0.68	2.13	2.50	2.97	1.56
Current Ratio	1.39	1.31	1.49	1.37	1.46	2.28	1.99	1.38
Debt to Equity	0.19	0.20	0.26	0.21	0.23	...	N.M.	...
Price Range	11.25-7.26	11.25-7.78	11.25-5.98	11.07-7.78	13.58-5.32	21.17-9.41	23.48-10.91	...
P/E Ratio	...	...	...	...	61.73-24.18	...	...	...

Address: 1676 International Drive, McLean, VA 22102 Telephone: (703) 747-3000	Web Site: www.bearingpoint.com Officers: Roderick C. McGeary - Chmn. Harry L. You - C.E.O.	Auditors: PricewaterhouseCoopers LLP Investor Contact: (617) 988-1885

BECKMAN COULTER, INC.

Exchange	Symbol	Price	52Wk Range	Yield	P/E	Div Acheiver
NYS	BEC	$66.45 (3/31/2005)	72.02-52.21	0.84	20.70	13 Years

*7 Year Price Score 133.59 *NYSE Composite Index=100 *12 Month Price Score 105.24

Interim Earnings (Per Share)

Qtr.	Mar	Jun	Sep	Dec
2001	0.32	0.58	0.52	0.75
2002	0.43	0.64	0.49	0.52
2003	0.70	0.82	0.62	1.07
2004	0.54	0.88	0.87	0.91

Interim Dividends (Per Share)

Amt	Decl	Ex	Rec	Pay
0.11Q	4/7/2004	5/5/2004	5/7/2004	5/27/2004
0.13Q	7/26/2004	8/11/2004	8/13/2004	9/2/2004
0.13Q	10/11/2004	10/14/2004	10/18/2004	11/5/2004
0.14Q	1/28/2005	2/16/2005	2/18/2005	3/10/2005

Indicated Div: $0.56 (Div. Reinv. Plan)

Valuation Analysis

Forecast P/E	18.59	No of Institutions	
	(4/7/2005)	304	
Market Cap	$4.1 Billion	Shares	
Book Value	1.1 Billion	51,088,308	
Price/Book	3.74	% Held	
Price/Sales	1.70	82.36	

TRADING VOLUME (thousand shares)

Business Summary: Instruments and Related Products (MIC: 11.15 SIC: 826 NAIC: 34516)

Beckman Coulter designs, manufactures, and markets systems, which consist of instruments, chemistries, software and supplies that are designed to meet a variety of biomedical laboratory needs. Co.'s products are used in a range of applications from instruments used for medical research, clinical research and drug discovery to diagnostic systems. Co. operates in two segments: clinical diagnostics and biomedical research. Clinical diagnostics offers products that aid in the detection and monitoring of disease by means of laboratory evaluation and analysis of substances from patients. Biomedical research provides products for a wide range of applications based on the study of life processes.

Recent Developments: For the year ended Dec 31 2004, net income increased 1.8% to $210,900 thousand from net income of $207,200 thousand a year earlier. Revenues were $2,408,300 thousand, up 9.8% from $2,192,500 thousand the year before. Operating income was $333,700 thousand versus an income of $329,500 thousand in the prior year, an increase of 1.3%. Total direct expense was $1,269,300 thousand versus $1,144,800 thousand in the prior year, an increase of 10.9%. Total indirect expense was $805,300 thousand versus $718,200 thousand in the prior year, an increase of 12.1%.

Prospects: Co. continues to experience solid growth in sales, largely driven by its Clinical Diagnostics Division, which reported a 12.0% increase in sales versus the year before. Going forward, Co. is targeting full-year 2005 sales growth of between 7.0% and 9.0%, driven by a continued focus on its Clinical Diagnostic Division, and led by the accelerating adoption of laboratory automation, and the ongoing penetration of large laboratories with its UniCel® DxI 800 immunoassay system and the launch of new products for specialized testing. Furthermore, Co. is projecting diluted earnings per share in the range of $3.55 to $3.65 for 2005.

Financial Data
(US$ in Thousands)

	12/31/2004	12/31/2003	12/31/2002	12/31/2001	12/31/2000	12/31/1999	12/31/1998	12/31/1997
Earnings Per Share	3.21	3.21	2.08	2.16	2.03	1.78	0.57	(4.79)
Cash Flow Per Share	4.32	3.68	5.12	4.57	3.55	3.70	(0.03)	2.50
Tang Book Value Per Share	6.19	2.99	N.M.	N.M.	N.M.	N.M.	N.M.	N.M.
Dividends Per Share	0.480	0.400	0.350	0.340	0.325	0.320	0.305	0.300
Dividend Payout %	14.95	12.46	16.83	15.74	16.01	17.93	53.51	...
Income Statement								
Total Revenue	2,408,300	2,192,500	2,059,400	1,984,000	1,886,900	1,808,700	1,718,200	1,198,000
EBITDA	416,400	409,900	326,600	378,300	383,600	364,400	273,400	(119,500)
Depn & Amortn	115,200	106,800	109,800	126,400	136,100	143,700	152,400	109,100
Income Before Taxes	278,200	272,800	178,900	205,000	181,900	154,700	46,600	(251,900)
Income Taxes	67,300	65,600	43,400	63,500	56,400	48,700	13,100	12,500
Net Income	210,900	207,200	135,500	138,400	125,500	106,000	33,500	(264,400)
Average Shares	65,773	64,493	65,060	64,011	61,800	59,400	58,600	55,200
Balance Sheet								
Current Assets	1,279,600	1,161,200	1,056,200	1,035,600	927,800	966,400	956,600	976,700
Total Assets	2,795,000	2,558,200	2,263,600	2,178,000	2,018,200	2,110,800	2,133,300	2,331,000
Current Liabilities	613,300	578,200	611,600	509,900	501,100	575,900	719,300	894,900
Long-Term Obligations	611,700	625,600	626,600	760,300	862,800	980,700	982,200	1,181,300
Total Liabilities	1,700,700	1,660,500	1,671,500	1,659,800	1,674,300	1,882,900	2,006,400	2,249,200
Stockholders' Equity	1,094,300	897,700	592,100	518,200	343,900	227,900	126,900	81,800
Shares Outstanding	61,600	62,000	61,000	61,200	59,700	58,000	56,800	55,200
Statistical Record								
Return on Assets %	7.86	8.59	6.10	6.60	6.06	5.00	1.50	N.M.
Return on Equity %	21.12	27.82	24.41	32.11	43.78	59.75	32.10	N.M.
EBITDA Margin %	17.29	18.70	15.86	19.07	20.33	20.15	15.91	N.M.
Net Margin %	8.76	9.45	6.58	6.98	6.65	5.86	1.95	N.M.
Asset Turnover	0.90	0.91	0.93	0.95	0.91	0.85	0.77	0.73
Current Ratio	2.09	2.01	1.73	2.03	1.85	1.68	1.33	1.09
Debt to Equity	0.56	0.70	1.06	1.47	2.51	4.30	7.74	14.44
Price Range	67.70-49.99	51.31-28.50	52.47-25.78	47.01-34.50	41.94-23.66	27.56-20.00	31.81-20.00	26.06-18.78
P/E Ratio	21.09-15.57	15.98-8.88	25.23-12.39	21.76-15.97	20.66-11.65	15.48-11.24	55.81-35.09	...
Average Yield %	0.84	0.98	0.84	0.83	1.00	1.34	1.15	1.39

Address: 4300 N. Harbor Boulevard, Fullerton, CA 92835	Web Site: www.beckmancoulter.com	Auditors: KPMG LLP
Telephone: (714) 871-4848	**Officers:** Scott Garrett - Pres., C.E.O., C.O.O. James T. Glover - V.P., C.F.O.	**Investor Contact:** (714) 773-7620
Fax: (714) 773-8283		**Transfer Agents:** EquiServe Trust Company, N.A., Providence, RI

BECTON, DICKINSON AND CO.

Exchange	Symbol	Price	52Wk Range	Yield	P/E	Div Acheiver
NYS	BDX	$58.42 (3/31/2005)	59.98-46.41	1.23	28.78	32 Years

*7 Year Price Score 122.09 *NYSE Composite Index=100 *12 Month Price Score 104.04

Interim Earnings (Per Share)

Qtr.	Dec	Mar	Jun	Sep
2001-02	0.37	0.48	0.44	0.50
2002-03	0.43	0.54	0.49	0.61
2003-04	0.48	0.62	0.41	0.26
2004-05	0.75	...	...	...

Interim Dividends (Per Share)

Amt	Decl	Ex	Rec	Pay
0.15Q	5/25/2004	6/7/2004	6/9/2004	6/30/2004
0.15Q	7/27/2004	9/7/2004	9/9/2004	9/30/2004
0.18Q	11/23/2004	12/9/2004	12/13/2004	1/3/2005
0.18Q	2/1/2005	3/8/2005	3/10/2005	3/31/2005

Indicated Div: $0.72 (Div. Reinv. Plan)

Valuation Analysis

Forecast P/E	20.30 (4/7/2005)	No of Institutions 509
Market Cap	$14.8 Billion	Shares
Book Value	3.3 Billion	217,726,992
Price/Book	4.42	% Held
Price/Sales	2.95	86.09

Business Summary: Medical Instruments & Equipment (MIC: 9.6 SIC: 841 NAIC: 39112)

Becton, Dickinson and Co. is engaged principally in the manufacture and sale of a range of medical supplies, devices, laboratory equipment and diagnostic products used by healthcare institutions, life science researchers, clinical laboratories, industry and the general public. Co.'s operations consist of three worldwide business segments: BD Medical, BD Diagnostics and BD Biosciences. BD Medical includes products such as hypodermic syringes and needles for injection. BD Diagnostics includes products such as clinical and industrial microbiology, and sample collection products. BD Biosciences includes products and services for a variety of applications in life sciences.

Recent Developments: For the quarter ended Dec 31 2004, net income increased 55.8% to $195,351 thousand from net income of $125,402 thousand in the year-earlier quarter. Revenues were $1,288,369 thousand, up 8.7% from $1,185,120 thousand the year before. Operating income was $250,697 thousand versus an income of $168,480 thousand in the prior-year quarter, an increase of 48.8%. Total direct expense was $634,501 thousand versus $634,255 thousand in the prior-year quarter, an increase of 0.0%. Total indirect expense was $403,171 thousand versus $382,385 thousand in the prior-year quarter, an increase of 5.4%.

Prospects: Co. continues to perform well, supported by a combination of solid revenue growth across all segments and geographic regions, continued disciplined cost control and supply chain productivity. For the second quarter of 2005, Co. expects earnings from continuing operations will increase in the range of 3.0% to 5.0% from comparable 2004 levels to between $0.64 and $0.65 per diluted share. For full-year 2005, Co. expects earnings from continuing operations will increase in the range of 25.0% to 27.0% to between $2.76 and $2.81 per diluted share.

Financial Data (US$ in Thousands)	3 Mos	09/30/2004	09/30/2003	09/30/2002	09/30/2001	09/30/2000	09/30/1999	09/30/1998
Earnings Per Share	2.03	1.77	2.07	1.79	1.49	1.49	1.04	0.90
Cash Flow Per Share	4.54	4.35	3.56	3.24	3.03	2.43	1.73	2.04
Tang Book Value Per Share	9.06	8.01	7.60	6.48	7.16	5.70	4.76	4.65
Dividends Per Share	0.630	0.600	0.400	0.390	0.380	0.370	0.340	0.290
Dividend Payout %	30.99	33.90	19.32	21.79	25.50	24.83	32.69	32.22
Income Statement								
Total Revenue	1,288,369	4,934,745	4,527,940	4,033,069	3,754,302	3,618,334	3,418,412	3,116,873
EBITDA	342,522	1,035,487	1,003,889	901,204	937,864	882,386	703,570	625,955
Depn & Amortn	94,686	253,012	257,623	239,311	305,700	288,255	258,863	228,749
Income Before Taxes	238,714	752,868	709,706	628,589	576,750	519,934	372,655	340,866
Income Taxes	44,316	170,364	162,650	148,607	138,348	127,037	96,936	104,298
Net Income	195,351	467,402	547,056	479,982	401,652	392,897	275,719	236,568
Average Shares	261,970	263,337	263,635	268,183	268,833	263,239	264,580	262,128
Balance Sheet								
Current Assets	2,815,625	2,641,334	2,338,569	1,928,707	1,762,942	1,660,677	1,683,725	1,542,762
Total Assets	5,973,425	5,752,579	5,572,253	5,040,460	4,802,287	4,505,096	4,436,958	3,846,038
Current Liabilities	1,165,472	1,050,082	1,043,374	1,252,453	1,264,676	1,353,538	1,329,322	1,091,913
Long-Term Obligations	1,061,341	1,171,506	1,184,031	802,967	782,996	779,569	954,169	765,176
Total Liabilities	2,631,213	2,684,716	2,675,299	2,552,486	2,473,520	2,549,098	2,668,270	2,232,218
Stockholders' Equity	3,342,212	3,067,863	2,896,954	2,487,974	2,328,767	1,955,998	1,768,688	1,613,820
Shares Outstanding	252,915	249,334	251,133	255,529	259,236	253,496	250,797	247,843
Statistical Record								
Return on Assets %	9.25	8.23	10.31	9.75	8.63	8.76	6.66	6.83
Return on Equity %	16.77	15.63	20.32	19.93	18.75	21.04	16.30	15.78
EBITDA Margin %	26.59	20.98	22.17	22.35	24.98	24.39	20.58	20.08
Net Margin %	15.16	9.47	12.08	11.90	10.70	10.86	8.07	7.59
Asset Turnover	0.87	0.87	0.85	0.82	0.81	0.81	0.83	0.90
Current Ratio	2.42	2.52	2.24	1.54	1.39	1.23	1.27	1.41
Debt to Equity	0.32	0.38	0.41	0.32	0.34	0.40	0.54	0.47
Price Range	57.83-41.03	53.25-35.71	40.43-28.40	38.47-25.01	39.00-26.56	34.13-22.38	46.88-25.63	43.69-21.81
P/E Ratio	28.49-20.21	30.08-20.18	19.53-13.72	21.49-13.97	26.17-17.83	22.90-15.02	45.07-24.64	48.54-24.24
Average Yield %	1.26	1.31	1.17	1.14	1.12	1.35	0.95	0.87

Address: 1 Becton Drive, Franklin Lakes, NJ 07417-1880	Web Site: www.bd.com	Auditors: Ernst & Young LLP
Telephone: (201) 847-6800	Officers: Edward J. Ludwig - Chmn., Pres., C.E.O. John R. Considine - Exec. V.P., C.F.O.	Investor Contact: 800-284-6845
Fax: (201) 847-6475		Transfer Agents: EquiServe Trust Company, N.A., Jersey City, NJ

BELLSOUTH CORP.

Exchange	Symbol	Price	52Wk Range	Yield	P/E
NYS	BLS	$26.29 (3/31/2005)	28.80-24.82	4.11	10.15

*7 Year Price Score 65.04   *NYSE Composite Index=100   *12 Month Price Score 90.36

Interim Earnings (Per Share)

Qtr.	Mar	Jun	Sep	Dec
2001	0.47	0.47	...	0.42
2002	0.61	0.16	0.35	0.32
2003	0.66	0.51	0.51	0.43
2004	0.87	0.54	0.44	0.74

Interim Dividends (Per Share)

Amt	Decl	Ex	Rec	Pay
0.27Q	6/28/2004	7/9/2004	7/13/2004	8/2/2004
0.27Q	9/27/2004	10/7/2004	10/12/2004	11/1/2004
0.27Q	11/22/2004	1/11/2005	1/13/2005	2/1/2005
0.27Q	2/28/2005	4/12/2005	4/14/2005	5/2/2005
			Indicated Div: $1.08	

Valuation Analysis

Forecast P/E	16.32	No of Institutions	
	(4/7/2005)	727	
Market Cap	$48.1 Billion	Shares	
Book Value	23.1 Billion	1,045,388,032	
Price/Book	2.09	% Held	
Price/Sales	2.37	57.08	

TRADING VOLUME (thousand shares)

Business Summary: Communications (MIC: 10.1 SIC: 813 NAIC: 17110)

BellSouth is one of seven regional holding companies divested by AT&T on Jan 1 1984. Through its BellSouth Telecommunications subsidiary, Co. provides wireline communications services, including local exchange, network access and intraLATA long distance services in nine states throughout the southeastern region. Co.'s international operations consist primarily of wireless service providers operating in 14 countries in Latin America, Asia and Europe. As of Dec 31 2003, Co. owned 71.8 million access lines. Co. also owns 40.0% of Cingular Wireless, a provider of wireless voice and data communications services in the U.S., which has over 24.0 million U.S. wireless subscribers as of Dec 31 2003.

Recent Developments: For the year ended Dec 31 2003, income from continuing operations increased 0.4% to $3,488,000 thousand from income of $3,475,000 thousand a year earlier. Net income increased 195.1% to $3,904,000 thousand from net income of $1,323,000 thousand a year earlier. Revenues were $20,341,000 thousand, up 0.7% from $20,207,000 thousand the year before. Operating income was $5,557,000 thousand versus an income of $4,454,000 thousand in the prior year, an increase of 24.8%. Total direct expense was $6,991,000 thousand versus $6,670,000 thousand in the prior year, an increase of 4.8%. Total indirect expense was $7,793,000 thousand versus $9,083,000 thousand in the prior year, a decrease of 14.2%.

Prospects: Co.'s earnings reflect higher costs associated with restoration efforts following the adverse impact of four hurricanes in Florida in late 2004, severance-related expenses and a change in the calculation of the retiree medical benefit obligation. Also, Co.'s earnings related to Cingular Wireless are being affected by merger integration costs resulting from the acquisition of AT&T Wireless, higher gross customer additions and upgrades, lower service revenue, accelerated depreciation and acquisition-related financing costs. During the fourth quarter of 2004, Cingular Wireless added nearly 1.8 million customers, bringing its nationwide customer base to more than 49.0 million customers.

Financial Data

(US$ in Thousands)	12/31/2004	12/31/2003	12/31/2002	12/31/2001	12/31/2000	12/31/1999	12/31/1998	12/31/1997
Earnings Per Share	2.59	2.11	0.76	1.36	2.23	1.80	1.78	1.64
Cash Flow Per Share	3.70	4.62	4.41	4.27	4.57	4.32	3.93	3.55
Tang Book Value Per Share	11.73	9.33	8.05	7.51	6.81	5.86	6.79	6.66
Dividends Per Share	1.040	0.870	0.780	0.760	0.760	0.760	0.720	0.720
Dividend Payout %	40.15	41.23	102.63	55.88	34.08	42.22	40.45	43.90
Income Statement								
Total Revenue	20,300,000	22,635,000	22,440,000	24,130,000	26,151,000	25,224,000	23,123,000	20,561,000
EBITDA	9,438,000	10,827,000	10,406,000	10,114,000	12,861,000	11,189,000	10,945,000	10,146,000
Depn & Amortn	3,636,000	4,179,000	4,643,000	4,782,000	4,935,000	4,671,000	4,357,000	3,964,000
Income Before Taxes	5,186,000	5,600,000	4,575,000	4,017,000	6,598,000	5,488,000	5,751,000	5,421,000
Income Taxes	1,792,000	2,011,000	1,867,000	1,447,000	2,378,000	2,040,000	2,224,000	2,151,000
Net Income	4,758,000	3,904,000	1,423,000	2,570,000	4,220,000	3,448,000	3,527,000	3,261,000
Average Shares	1,836,000	1,852,000	1,876,000	1,887,000	1,891,000	1,916,000	1,984,000	1,990,000
Balance Sheet								
Net PPE	22,039,000	23,807,000	23,445,000	24,943,000	24,157,000	24,631,000	23,940,000	22,861,000
Total Assets	59,496,000	49,702,000	49,479,000	52,046,000	50,925,000	43,453,000	39,410,000	36,301,000
Long-Term Obligations	15,108,000	11,489,000	12,283,000	15,014,000	12,463,000	9,113,000	8,715,000	7,348,000
Total Liabilities	36,430,000	29,990,000	31,793,000	33,449,000	34,013,000	28,638,000	23,300,000	21,136,000
Stockholders' Equity	23,066,000	19,712,000	17,686,000	18,597,000	16,912,000	14,815,000	16,110,000	15,165,000
Shares Outstanding	1,831,000	1,830,000	1,860,000	1,877,000	1,872,000	1,883,000	1,950,000	1,984,000
Statistical Record								
Return on Assets %	8.69	7.87	2.80	4.99	8.92	8.32	9.32	9.47
Return on Equity %	22.18	20.88	7.84	14.48	26.53	22.30	22.55	22.95
EBITDA Margin %	46.49	47.83	46.37	41.91	49.18	44.36	47.33	49.35
Net Margin %	23.44	17.25	6.34	10.65	16.14	13.67	15.25	15.86
PPE Turnover	0.88	0.96	0.93	0.98	1.07	1.04	0.99	0.92
Asset Turnover	0.37	0.46	0.44	0.47	0.55	0.61	0.61	0.60
Debt to Equity	0.65	0.58	0.69	0.81	0.74	0.62	0.54	0.48
Price Range	30.67-24.82	29.25-20.05	40.45-18.36	44.69-36.97	52.31-35.81	50.81-40.06	49.88-27.41	28.97-19.50
P/E Ratio	11.84-9.58	13.86-9.50	53.22-24.16	32.86-27.18	23.46-16.06	28.23-22.26	28.02-15.40	17.66-11.89
Average Yield %	3.82	3.47	2.58	1.88	1.75	1.67	2.07	3.10

Address: 1155 Peachtree Street N.E., Room 15G03, Atlanta, GA 30309-3610
Telephone: (404) 249-2000
Fax: (404) 249-2071

Web Site: www.bellsouth.com
Officers: F. Duane Ackerman - Chmn., Pres., C.E.O. Rebecca M. Dunn - Sr. V.P., Corp. Compliance, Sec.

Auditors: PricewaterhouseCoopers LLP
Investor Contact: 800-631-6001
Transfer Agents: Mellon Investor Services, LLC, Ridgefield Park, NJ

BELO CORP.

Exchange	Symbol	Price	52Wk Range	Yield	P/E
NYS	BLC	$24.14 (3/31/2005)	29.50-21.22	1.66	21.36

*7 Year Price Score 101.37 *NYSE Composite Index=100 *12 Month Price Score 88.94

Interim Earnings (Per Share)

Qtr.	Mar	Jun	Sep	Dec
2001	0.01	...	...	...
2002	0.15	0.36	0.25	0.40
2003	0.14	0.34	0.27	0.36
2004	0.19	0.39	0.10	0.46

Interim Dividends (Per Share)

Amt	Decl	Ex	Rec	Pay
0.095Q	7/23/2004	8/11/2004	8/13/2004	9/3/2004
0.095Q	9/24/2004	11/9/2004	11/12/2004	12/3/2004
0.10Q	12/3/2004	2/9/2005	2/11/2005	3/4/2005
0.10Q	3/2/2005	5/11/2005	5/13/2005	6/3/2005

Indicated Div: $0.40

Valuation Analysis

Forecast P/E	20.74 (4/7/2005)	No of Institutions 189
Market Cap	$2.8 Billion	Shares 75,241,176
Book Value	1.6 Billion	% Held 76.50
Price/Book	1.69	
Price/Sales	1.83	

Business Summary: Media (MIC: 13.1 SIC: 711 NAIC: 11110)

Belo is a media company, with a diversified group of television broadcasting, newspaper publishing, interactive media and cable news operations in several markets and regions. Co. owns and operates 19 network-affiliated television stations; four daily newspapers, including The Dallas Morning News, The Providence Journal, The Press-Enterprise in Riverside, CA; and the Denton Record-Chronicle in Denton, TX; and three cable news channels and ownership interests in seven others. Co. also manages one television station through a local marketing agreement. Six of the Co.'s stations are in the top 15 U.S. television markets.

Recent Developments: For the year ended Dec 31 2004, net income increased 3.1% to $132,496 thousand from net income of $128,525 thousand a year earlier. Revenues were $1,510,234 thousand, up 5.2% from $1,436,011 thousand the year before. Operating income was $322,184 thousand versus an income of $310,251 thousand in the prior year, an increase of 3.8%. Total direct expense was $533,524 thousand versus $508,790 thousand in the prior year, an increase of 4.9%. Total indirect expense was $654,526 thousand versus $616,970 thousand in the prior year, an increase of 6.1%.

Prospects: Co. expects total revenue for the organization to increase in the low-to-mid single digit range for full-year 2005 with a low-single digit decrease in Television Group revenues and a mid-to-high single digit increase in Newspaper Group revenues. Excluding the $20.0 million charge to revenue in 2004 related to the circulation overstatement at The Dallas Morning News and an increase in 2005 of approximately $16.0 million in circulation revenue at The Morning News related to recommendations from the Circulation Review Team, Newspaper Group revenues are expected to increase in the low-to-mid single digits. For full-year 2005, earnings are expected to be in the range of $1.17 to $1.24 per share.

Financial Data

(US$ in Thousands)	12/31/2004	12/31/2003	12/31/2002	12/31/2001	12/31/2000	12/31/1999	12/31/1998	12/31/1997
Earnings Per Share	1.13	1.11	1.15	(0.02)	1.29	1.50	0.52	0.71
Cash Flow Per Share	2.40	2.27	2.81	1.51	2.16	1.87	1.90	2.22
Dividends Per Share	0.380	0.340	0.340	0.300	0.280	0.260	0.240	0.220
Dividend Payout %	33.63	30.63	26.09	...	21.71	17.33	46.15	30.99
Income Statement								
Total Revenue	1,510,234	1,436,011	1,427,764	1,364,578	1,588,812	1,433,982	1,407,345	1,248,381
EBITDA	404,115	403,298	423,594	317,447	584,586	556,022	397,540	379,893
Depn & Amortn	98,150	100,228	105,332	183,010	184,972	168,961	159,442	134,993
Income Before Taxes	215,801	209,460	213,454	21,763	266,834	276,453	130,460	154,122
Income Taxes	83,305	80,935	82,328	24,449	116,009	98,147	65,558	71,150
Net Income	132,496	128,525	131,126	(2,686)	150,825	178,306	64,902	82,972
Average Shares	117,272	115,487	113,638	109,816	117,198	119,177	124,836	117,122
Balance Sheet								
Current Assets	342,493	332,618	320,451	332,179	421,025	351,958	275,781	276,996
Total Assets	3,588,000	3,602,601	3,614,578	3,672,225	3,893,260	3,976,264	3,539,089	3,622,954
Current Liabilities	238,611	218,355	216,166	185,400	302,683	259,838	180,748	214,462
Long-Term Obligations	1,170,150	1,270,900	1,441,200	1,696,209	1,789,600	1,849,490	1,634,029	1,614,045
Total Liabilities	1,958,348	2,038,830	2,201,348	2,351,480	2,543,852	2,586,427	2,290,989	2,296,950
Stockholders' Equity	1,629,652	1,563,771	1,413,230	1,320,745	1,349,408	1,389,837	1,248,100	1,326,004
Shares Outstanding	114,333	115,024	112,758	110,382	109,853	118,658	118,925	124,694
Statistical Record								
Return on Assets %	3.68	3.56	3.60	N.M.	3.82	4.75	1.81	3.42
Return on Equity %	8.28	8.63	9.59	N.M.	10.98	13.52	5.04	9.78
EBITDA Margin %	26.76	28.08	29.67	23.26	36.79	38.77	28.25	30.43
Net Margin %	8.77	8.95	9.18	N.M.	9.49	12.43	4.61	6.65
Asset Turnover	0.42	0.40	0.39	0.36	0.40	0.38	0.39	0.52
Current Ratio	1.44	1.52	1.48	1.79	1.39	1.35	1.53	1.29
Debt to Equity	0.72	0.81	1.02	1.28	1.33	1.33	1.31	1.22
Price Range	29.50-21.22	28.55-18.85	24.30-18.30	19.95-15.37	19.94-12.31	23.44-16.38	28.38-14.56	28.06-16.75
P/E Ratio	26.11-18.78	25.72-16.98	21.13-15.91	...	15.46-9.54	15.63-10.92	54.57-28.00	39.52-23.59
Average Yield %	1.47	1.45	1.36	1.66	1.65	1.34	1.04	1.03

Address: P.O. Box 655237, Dallas, TX 75265-5237 **Telephone:** (214) 977-6606 **Fax:** (214) 977-6603	**Web Site:** www.belo.com **Officers:** Robert W. Decherd - Chmn., Pres., C.E.O. Dunia A. Shive - Exec. V.P., Media Oper.	**Auditors:** ERNST & YOUNG LLP **Investor Contact:** 214-977-6626 **Transfer Agents:** EquiServe Trust Company, N.A., Providence, RI

BEMIS, INC.

Exchange	Symbol	Price	52Wk Range	Yield	P/E	Div Acheiver
NYS	BMS	$31.12 (3/31/2005)	31.15-24.98	2.31	18.63	21 Years

*7 Year Price Score 109.66 ***NYSE Composite Index=100** ***12 Month Price Score 101.29**

TRADING VOLUME (thousand shares)

Interim Earnings (Per Share)

Qtr.	Mar	Jun	Sep	Dec
2001	0.28	0.34	0.34	0.36
2002	0.33	0.41	0.41	0.40
2003	0.33	0.36	0.32	0.36
2004	0.40	0.42	0.41	0.44

Interim Dividends (Per Share)

Amt	Decl	Ex	Rec	Pay
0.16Q	5/6/2004	5/14/2004	5/18/2004	6/1/2004
0.16Q	7/29/2004	8/16/2004	8/18/2004	9/1/2004
0.16Q	10/28/2004	11/15/2004	11/17/2004	12/1/2004
0.18Q	2/3/2005	2/14/2005	2/16/2005	3/1/2005

Indicated Div: $0.72 (Div. Reinv. Plan)

Valuation Analysis

Forecast P/E	16.67 (4/7/2005)	No of Institutions	263
Market Cap	$3.3 Billion	Shares	68,508,960
Book Value	1.3 Billion	% Held	
Price/Book	2.54	% Held	64.00
Price/Sales	1.17		

Business Summary: Paper Products (MIC: 11.11 SIC: 671 NAIC: 22221)

Bemis is a manufacturer of flexible packaging products and pressure-sensitive materials. Co.'s customers are in the U.S., Canada, and Europe with a growing presence in Asia Pacific, South America, and Mexico. In the flexible packaging segment, Co. primarily markets its products to the food industry, and, to a lesser extent, businesses such as chemical, agribusiness, medical, pharmaceutical, personal care products, tissue, batteries, electronics, automotive, construction, graphic industries, and other consumer goods. Pressure-Sensitive Materials are sold into label markets, graphic markets, and technical markets. As of Dec 31 2003, Co. manufactured from 53 facilities in ten countries.

Recent Developments: For the year ended Dec 31 2004, net income increased 22.3% to $179,967 thousand from net income of $147,145 thousand a year earlier. Revenues were $2,834,394 thousand, up 7.6% from $2,635,018 thousand the year before. Total direct expense was $2,238,694 thousand versus $2,101,537 thousand in the prior year, an increase of 6.5%. Total indirect expense was $327,267 thousand versus $299,597 thousand in the prior year, an increase of 9.2%.

Prospects: On Jan 5 2005, Co. acquired Dixie Toga, one of the largest packaging companies in South America, for about $250.0 million. Co. expects the acquisition to be modestly accretive to earnings in 2005. For the first quarter of 2005, Co. expects results to be comparable to the first quarter of 2004, excluding the potential impact of any gains or losses from the sale of restructured assets. For the full year 2005, Co. expects diluted earnings per share in the range of $1.82 to $1.90. Co. added that capital expenditures for 2005 are estimated to be $185.0 million to $200.0 million, substantially higher than 2004 levels due to its plans to expand its capacity in high demand product areas.

Financial Data

(US$ in Thousands)	12/31/2004	12/31/2003	12/31/2002	12/31/2001	12/31/2000	12/31/1999	12/31/1998	12/31/1997
Earnings Per Share	1.67	1.37	1.54	1.32	1.22	1.09	1.04	1.00
Cash Flow Per Share	2.53	2.93	2.71	3.01	1.97	1.77	2.08	1.36
Tang Book Value Per Share	7.48	5.81	4.11	4.39	4.76	5.51	4.88	4.62
Dividends Per Share	0.640	0.560	0.520	0.500	0.480	0.460	0.440	0.400
Dividend Payout %	38.32	40.88	33.77	37.88	39.34	42.20	42.11	40.00
Income Statement								
Total Revenue	2,834,394	2,635,018	2,369,038	2,293,104	2,164,583	1,918,025	1,848,004	1,877,237
EBITDA	425,549	367,440	386,246	351,572	319,632	283,592	270,842	253,840
Depn & Amortn	131,882	128,195	119,231	124,147	108,130	97,717	88,910	78,856
Income Before Taxes	293,667	239,245	267,015	227,425	211,502	185,875	181,932	174,984
Income Taxes	113,700	92,100	101,500	87,100	80,900	71,100	70,500	67,400
Net Income	179,967	147,145	165,515	140,325	130,602	114,775	111,432	107,584
Average Shares	107,942	107,733	107,492	106,243	107,106	105,314	106,648	107,760
Balance Sheet								
Current Assets	873,767	751,906	721,655	586,897	639,959	583,581	517,939	516,393
Total Assets	2,486,743	2,292,932	2,256,650	1,922,974	1,888,643	1,532,143	1,453,054	1,362,567
Current Liabilities	375,143	315,586	325,853	238,182	495,097	253,268	242,788	251,187
Long-Term Obligations	533,886	583,399	718,277	595,249	437,952	372,267	371,363	316,791
Total Liabilities	1,175,904	1,148,802	1,293,236	1,034,698	1,088,316	766,750	745,010	688,920
Stockholders' Equity	1,307,866	1,138,733	958,974	886,148	798,757	725,895	670,807	639,885
Shares Outstanding	106,947	106,242	105,887	105,739	105,204	104,378	104,538	105,936
Statistical Record								
Return on Assets %	7.51	6.47	7.92	7.36	7.61	7.69	7.92	8.50
Return on Equity %	14.67	14.03	17.94	16.66	17.09	16.44	17.00	17.83
EBITDA Margin %	15.01	13.94	16.30	15.33	14.77	14.79	14.66	13.52
Net Margin %	6.35	5.58	6.99	6.12	6.03	5.98	6.03	5.73
Asset Turnover	1.18	1.16	1.13	1.20	1.26	1.29	1.31	1.48
Current Ratio	2.33	2.38	2.21	2.46	1.29	2.30	2.13	2.06
Debt to Equity	0.41	0.51	0.75	0.67	0.55	0.51	0.55	0.50
Price Range	29.31-23.48	25.53-19.89	29.04-19.94	26.08-14.41	19.25-12.03	19.97-15.22	23.47-16.97	23.59-17.91
P/E Ratio	17.55-14.06	18.64-14.52	18.85-12.95	19.76-10.91	15.78-9.86	18.32-13.96	22.57-16.32	23.59-17.91
Average Yield %	2.42	2.47	2.03	2.50	2.93	2.57	2.16	1.91

Address: 222 South 9th Street, Suite 2300, Minneapolis, MN 55402-4099
Telephone: (612) 376-3000
Fax: (612) 340-6174

Web Site: www.bemis.com
Officers: John H. Roe - Chmn. Jeffrey H. Curler - Pres., C.E.O.

Auditors: PricewaterhouseCoopers LLP
Investor Contact: 612-376-3000
Transfer Agents: Wells Fargo Bank Minnesota, South St. Paul, MN

BERKLEY (W. R.) CORP.

Exchange	Symbol	Price	52Wk Range	Yield	P/E
NYS	BER	$33.07 (3/31/2005)	35.23-25.91	0.60	6.65

*7 Year Price Score 160.52 *NYSE Composite Index=100 ***12 Month Price Score 106.94**

TRADING VOLUME (thousand shares)

Interim Earnings (Per Share)

Qtr.	Mar	Jun	Sep	Dec
2001	0.16	0.14	(0.72)	(0.96)
2002	0.44	0.35	0.52	0.90
2003	0.83	1.10	0.87	1.08
2004	1.32	1.25	1.10	1.33

Interim Dividends (Per Share)

Amt	Decl	Ex	Rec	Pay
0.07Q	8/3/2004	9/15/2004	9/17/2004	10/1/2004
0.07Q	11/2/2004	12/13/2004	12/15/2004	1/3/2005
50%	3/14/2005	4/11/2005	3/24/2005	4/8/2005
0.05Q	3/14/2005	3/22/2005	3/24/2005	4/8/2005
		Indicated Div: $0.20		

Valuation Analysis

Forecast P/E	8.98	No of Institutions
	(4/7/2005)	226
Market Cap	$2.8 Billion	Shares
Book Value	2.1 Billion	66,104,772
Price/Book	1.32	% Held
Price/Sales	0.62	78.44

Business Summary: Insurance (MIC: 8.2 SIC: 331 NAIC: 24126)

Berkley (W.R.) is a holding company that operates in five segments of the property casualty insurance business: specialty lines of insurance, including excess and surplus lines and commercial transportation; alternative markets; reinsurance; regional commercial property casualty insurance, and international. Co.'s specialty insurance and reinsurance operations are conducted nationwide, as well as in the U.K. Co.'s alternative markets are conducted through the U.S. Regional insurance operations are conducted primarily in the Midwest, New England, Southern, excluding Florida, and mid-Atlantic regions of the U.S. International operations are conducted in Argentina and the Philippines.

Recent Developments: For the year ended Dec 31 2004, income from continuing operations increased 30.1% to $438,832 thousand from income of $337,220 thousand a year earlier. Revenues were $4,512,235 thousand, up 24.3% from $3,630,108 thousand the year before. Net premiums earned were $4,061,092 thousand versus $3,234,610 thousand in the prior year, an increase of 25.6%. Net investment income rose 38.7% to $291,295 thousand from $210,056 thousand a year ago.

Prospects: Co.'s recent cash flow position is strong. For instance, for the quarter ended Dec 31 2004, cash flow from operations increased 15.0% to $487.0 million compared with $424.0 million in the year-earlier period. Separately, Co. is optimistic about the environment and expects relative price stability in most parts of its marketplace. There is pressure on prices in some areas, but overall business conditions continue to look excellent. Based upon Co.'s historical performance and on current plans, estimates and expectations, it expects to continue to enjoy moderate growth and is confident that 2005 will result in after tax returns exceeding 20.0%.

Financial Data
(US$ in Thousands)

	12/31/2004	12/31/2003	12/31/2002	12/31/2001	12/31/2000	12/31/1999	12/31/1998	12/31/1997
Earnings Per Share	4.97	3.87	2.21	(1.40)	0.62	(0.64)	0.71	1.34
Cash Flow Per Share	19.24	16.82	12.57	2.32	(0.23)	0.84	3.46	4.50
Tang Book Value Per Share	24.33	19.43	20.86	11.59	10.56	8.94	13.16	13.14
Dividends Per Share	0.280	0.273	0.236	0.231	0.231	0.231	0.213	0.187
Dividend Payout %	5.63	7.06	10.67	...	37.41	...	30.19	13.91
Income Statement								
Premium Income	4,061,092	3,234,610	2,252,527	1,680,469	1,491,014	1,414,384	1,278,399	1,111,747
Total Revenue	4,512,235	3,630,108	2,566,084	1,941,797	1,781,287	1,673,668	1,582,517	1,400,310
Benefits & Claims	2,559,310	2,050,177	1,463,971	1,380,500	1,094,411	1,085,826	914,762	734,424
Income Before Taxes	638,513	489,304	259,433	(151,394)	40,851	(79,248)	62,781	129,241
Income Taxes	196,235	150,626	84,139	(56,661)	2,451	(45,766)	5,465	30,668
Net Income	438,105	337,220	175,045	(91,546)	36,238	(37,060)	46,195	91,219
Average Shares	88,181	87,063	79,384	68,748	58,479	58,335	65,508	67,916
Balance Sheet								
Total Assets	11,451,033	9,334,685	7,031,323	5,633,509	5,022,070	4,784,791	4,983,431	4,599,284
Total Liabilities	9,295,180	7,613,975	5,479,224	4,479,408	4,111,128	3,569,820	3,495,939	3,029,276
Stockholders' Equity	2,109,702	1,682,562	1,335,199	931,595	680,896	591,778	861,281	947,292
Shares Outstanding	84,272	83,537	61,166	74,791	57,726	57,637	59,634	66,528
Statistical Record								
Return on Assets %	4.20	4.12	2.76	N.M.	0.74	N.M.	0.96	2.10
Return on Equity %	23.04	22.35	15.44	N.M.	5.68	N.M.	5.11	9.99
Loss Ratio %	63.02	63.38	64.99	82.15	73.40	76.77	71.56	66.06
Net Margin %	9.71	9.29	6.82	(4.71)	2.03	(2.21)	2.92	6.51
Price Range	31.45-23.30	24.31-16.56	18.01-13.80	17.24-10.37	14.00-4.33	10.13-5.93	14.52-8.15	13.33-8.84
P/E Ratio	6.33-4.69	6.28-4.28	8.15-6.24	...	22.58-6.99	...	20.45-11.48	9.95-6.60
Average Yield %	1.01	1.29	1.46	1.76	3.10	3.13	1.83	1.69

Address: 475 Steamboat Road, Greenwich, CT 06830	**Web Site:** www.wrberkley.com	**Auditors:** KPMG LLP
Telephone: (203) 629-3000	**Officers:** William R. Berkley - Chmn., Pres., C.E.O.,	
Fax: (203) 629-3492	C.O.O. Eugene G. Ballard - Sr. V.P., C.F.O., Treas.	

BERKSHIRE HATHAWAY INC.

Exchange	Symbol	Price	52Wk Range	Yield	P/E
NYS	BRK A	$87000 (3/31/2005)	95650.00-81400.00	N/A	18.30

*7 Year Price Score 105.38 *NYSE Composite Index=100 *12 Month Price Score 95.04

TRADING VOLUME (thousand shares)

Interim Earnings (Per Share)

Qtr.	Mar	Jun	Sep	Dec
2001	397.00	506.00	(445.00)	63.00
2002	598.00	681.00	744.00	771.00
2003	1127.00	1452.00	1176.00	1554.00
2004	1008.00	834.00	739.00	2172.00

Interim Dividends (Per Share)

No Dividends Paid

Valuation Analysis

Forecast P/E	22.86	No of Institutions	
	(4/7/2005)	441	
Market Cap	$133.9 Billion	Shares	
Book Value	85.9 Billion	259,870	
Price/Book	1.56	% Held	
Price/Sales	1.80	20.51	

Business Summary: Insurance (MIC: 8.2 SIC: 331 NAIC: 24126)

Berkshire Hathaway is engaged in diverse business activities. As of Dec 31 2004, Co.'s insurance and reinsurance business activities were conducted through more than 50 domestic and foreign-based insurance companies including GEICO and General Re. Fruit of the Loom, Garan and H.H. Brown Shoe manufacture and distribute a variety of footwear and clothing products. Acme Building Brands and Benjamin Moore produce building and related materials. FlightSafety and NetJets provide training of aircraft and ship operators. Nebraska Furniture Mart, R.C. Willey Home Furnishings and Jordan's Furniture are retailers of home furnishings. Borsheim's and Helzberg Diamond Shops are retailers of fine jewelry.

Recent Developments: For the year ended Dec 31 2004, net income decreased 10.3% to $7,308,000 thousand from net income of $8,151,000 thousand a year earlier. Revenues were $68,869,000 thousand, up 15.5% from $59,603,000 thousand the year before. Net premiums earned were $21,085,000 thousand versus $21,493,000 thousand in the prior year, a decrease of 1.9%.

Prospects: Co.'s balance sheet reflects significant liquidity and a strong capital base. For instance, shareholders' equity at Dec 31 2004 totaled $85.90 billion, up 10.7% from $77.60 billion the year before. Separately, Co.'s underwriting insurance operations are being adversely affected by a decline in underwriting gains within General Re and Berkshire Hathaway Reinsurance Group. Also, Co.'s insurance operations are experiencing a decline in investment income in the absence of opportunities to invest cash balances into long-term instruments. However, Co.'s non-insurance businesses continue to perform fairly well.

Financial Data

(US$ in Thousands)	12/31/2004	12/31/2003	12/31/2002	12/31/2001	12/31/2000	12/31/1999	12/31/1998	12/31/1997
Earnings Per Share	4,753.00	5,309.00	2,795.00	521.00	2,185.00	1,025.00	2,262.00	1,542.00
Cash Flow Per Share	4,802.43	5,377.73	7,307.89	4,304.51	1,929.80	1,447.65	525.03	1,893.95
Tang Book Value Per Share	40,869.38	35,563.54	27,197.61	23,912.17	28,075.06	25,964.08	25,654.12	23,696.74
Income Statement								
Premium Income	21,085,000	21,493,000	19,182,000	17,905,000	19,343,000	14,306,000	5,481,000	4,761,000
Total Revenue	74,382,000	63,859,000	42,353,000	37,668,000	34,006,000	24,028,000	13,832,000	10,430,000
Benefits & Claims	14,823,000	14,927,000	15,269,000	18,398,000	17,332,000	12,518,000	4,040,000	3,420,000
Income Before Taxes	10,936,000	12,020,000	6,435,000	1,469,000	5,587,000	2,450,000	4,314,000	2,827,000
Income Taxes	3,569,000	3,805,000	2,134,000	620,000	2,018,000	852,000	1,457,000	898,000
Net Income	7,308,000	8,151,000	4,286,000	795,000	3,328,000	1,557,000	2,830,000	1,901,000
Balance Sheet								
Total Assets	188,874,000	180,559,000	169,544,000	162,752,000	135,792,000	131,416,000	122,237,000	56,110,900
Total Liabilities	102,216,000	102,218,000	104,116,000	103,453,000	72,799,000	72,232,000	63,190,000	24,199,200
Stockholders' Equity	85,900,000	77,596,000	64,037,000	57,950,000	61,724,000	57,761,000	57,403,000	31,455,200
Shares Outstanding	1,538	1,536	1,534	1,528	1,526	1,520	1,518	1,198
Statistical Record								
Return on Assets %	3.95	4.66	2.58	0.53	2.48	1.23	3.17	3.82
Return on Equity %	8.92	11.51	7.03	1.33	5.56	2.70	6.37	6.93
Loss Ratio %	70.30	69.45	79.60	102.75	89.60	87.50	73.71	71.83
Net Margin %	9.82	12.76	10.12	2.11	9.79	6.48	20.46	18.23
Price Range	95650-81400	84500-61200	78300-61500	75600-61400	71000-41300	80300-52600	80900-45900	48600-33200
P/E Ratio	20.12-17.13	15.92-11.53	28.01-22.00	145.11-117.85	32.49-18.90	78.34-51.32	35.76-20.29	31.52-21.53

Address: 1440 Kiewit Plaza, Omaha, NE 68131 Telephone: (402) 346 1400	Web Site: www.berkshirehathaway.com Officers: Warren E. Buffett - Chmn., C.E.O. Charles T. Munger - Vice-Chmn.	Auditors: Deloitte & Touche LLP Transfer Agents: Wells Fargo Bank

BEST BUY CO., INC.

Exchange	Symbol	Price	52Wk Range	Yield	P/E
NYS	BBY	$54.01 (3/31/2005)	62.00-44.27	0.81	20.15

*7 Year Price Score 119.62 *NYSE Composite Index=100 *12 Month Price Score 92.93

Interim Earnings (Per Share)

Qtr.	May	Aug	Nov	Feb
2001-02	0.17	0.26	0.25	1.08
2002-03	0.22	0.19	0.26	0.70
2003-04	(0.08)	0.42	0.37	1.43
2004-05	0.34	0.46	0.45	...

Interim Dividends (Per Share)

Amt	Decl	Ex	Rec	Pay
0.10Q	6/18/2004	7/2/2004	7/7/2004	7/28/2004
0.11Q	6/23/2004	10/4/2004	10/6/2004	10/27/2004
0.11Q	12/16/2004	1/3/2005	1/5/2005	1/26/2005
0.11Q	4/5/2005	4/18/2005	4/20/2005	5/11/2005
			Indicated Div: $0.44	

Valuation Analysis

Forecast P/E	16.49	No of Institutions	
	(4/7/2005)	534	
Market Cap	$17.7 Billion	Shares	
Book Value	4.0 Billion	226,452,928	
Price/Book	4.47	% Held	
Price/Sales	0.66	69.02	

Business Summary: Hospitality & Tourism (MIC: 5.1 SIC: 731 NAIC: 43112)

Best Buy Co. is a specialty retailer of consumer electronics, home-office products, entertainment software, appliances and related services. Co. operates two reportable segments: Domestic and International. The Domestic segment is comprised of the operations of U.S. Best Buy and Magnolia Audio Video. The International segment is comprised of Future Shop and Best Buy operations in Canada. At the end of fiscal 2004, Co. operated 608 U.S. Best Buy stores totaling approx. 26.4 million retail square feet; 22 Magnolia Audio Video stores totaling approx. 218,000 retail square feet; 108 Future Shop stores and 19 Canadian Best Buy stores totaling approx. 2.8 million retail square feet.

Recent Developments: For the quarter ended Nov 27 2004, net income increased 21.3% to $148,000 thousand from net income of $122,000 thousand in the year-earlier quarter. Revenues were $6,646,000 thousand, up 10.2% from $6,032,000 thousand the year before. Operating income was $233,000 thousand versus an income of $202,000 thousand in the prior-year quarter, an increase of 15.3%. Total indirect expense was $1,398,000 thousand versus $1,284,000 thousand in the prior-year quarter, an increase of 8.9%.

Prospects: Co.'s prospects appear constructive. For the quarter ended Feb 26 2005, Co. reported a comparable store sales gain of 3.1%, following a comparable sales gain of 9.9% for the prior-year's quarter. Co. attributed the positive sales results to an increase in the conversion rate, or the percentage of shoppers who leave the store with a purchase, and a higher average ticket, which offset a modest decrease in customer traffic. During the quarter ended Feb 26 2005, Co. opened 11 stores and closed two Magnolia Audio Video stores. Looking ahead, Co. anticipates continued growth in digital TVs, MP3 players, notebook computers and services, partially offset by declines from its analog businesses.

Financial Data (US$ in Thousands)	9 Mos	6 Mos	3 Mos	02/28/2004	03/01/2003	03/02/2002	03/03/2001	02/26/2000
Earnings Per Share	2.68	2.60	2.56	2.15	0.30	1.77	1.24	1.09
Cash Flow Per Share	5.63	4.24	3.93	4.39	2.33	5.01	2.56	2.49
Tang Book Value Per Share	10.30	9.49	9.17	8.96	7.04	5.48	4.60	3.65
Dividends Per Share	0.410	0.600	0.500	0.400	...	...	...	...
Dividend Payout %	15.28	23.04	19.54	18.60	...	...	...	...
Income Statement								
Total Revenue	18,206,000	11,555,000	5,475,000	24,547,000	20,946,000	19,597,000	15,326,552	12,494,023
EBITDA	971,000	632,000	287,000	1,689,000	1,320,000	1,246,000	771,677	648,800
Depn & Amortn	312,000	206,000	103,000	385,000	310,000	309,000	167,369	109,541
Income Before Taxes	666,000	427,000	184,000	1,296,000	1,014,000	936,000	641,479	562,570
Income Taxes	254,000	163,000	70,000	496,000	392,000	366,000	245,640	215,500
Net Income	412,000	264,000	114,000	705,000	99,000	570,000	395,839	347,070
Average Shares	331,900	329,300	329,800	328,000	324,800	322,500	318,987	318,870
Balance Sheet								
Current Assets	8,332,000	5,596,000	5,602,000	5,724,000	4,867,000	4,611,000	2,928,663	2,238,460
Total Assets	11,622,000	8,644,000	8,550,000	8,652,000	7,663,000	7,375,000	4,839,587	2,995,342
Current Liabilities	6,892,000	4,308,000	4,338,000	4,501,000	3,793,000	3,730,000	2,714,698	1,785,049
Long-Term Obligations	478,000	478,000	477,000	482,000	828,000	813,000	181,009	14,860
Total Liabilities	7,662,000	5,043,000	5,066,000	5,230,000	4,933,000	4,854,000	3,017,659	1,899,357
Stockholders' Equity	3,960,000	3,601,000	3,484,000	3,422,000	2,730,000	2,521,000	1,821,928	1,095,985
Shares Outstanding	328,075	324,397	324,845	324,648	321,966	319,128	312,207	300,568
Statistical Record								
Return on Assets %	8.13	10.46	10.75	8.67	1.32	9.36	9.94	12.64
Return on Equity %	25.29	26.21	27.01	22.98	3.78	26.32	26.69	32.22
EBITDA Margin %	5.33	5.47	5.24	6.88	6.30	6.36	5.03	5.19
Net Margin %	2.26	2.28	2.08	2.87	0.47	2.91	2.58	2.78
Asset Turnover	2.46	3.19	3.24	3.02	2.79	3.22	3.85	4.55
Current Ratio	1.21	1.30	1.29	1.27	1.28	1.24	1.08	1.25
Debt to Equity	0.12	0.13	0.14	0.14	0.30	0.32	0.10	0.01
Price Range	62.00-44.27	62.00-44.27	62.00-37.40	62.00-26.66	53.37-17.68	50.11-23.93	57.33-14.88	52.67-27.42
P/E Ratio	23.13-16.52	23.85-17.03	24.22-14.61	28.84-12.40	177.89-58.93	28.31-13.52	46.24-12.00	48.32-25.15
Average Yield %	0.78	1.15	0.99	0.87	...	...	...	...

Address: 7601 Penn Avenue South, Richfield , MN 55423-3645 Telephone: (612) 291-1000 Fax: (612) 292-4001	Web Site: www.bestbuy.com Officers: Richard M. Schulze - Chmn. Bradbury H. Anderson - Vice-Chmn., C.E.O.	Auditors: ERNST & YOUNG LLP Investor Contact: 612-291-6111

BIG LOTS, INC.

Exchange	Symbol	Price	52Wk Range	Yield	P/E
NYS	BLI	$12.02 (3/31/2005)	15.50-10.85	N/A	26.71

*7 Year Price Score 66.46   ***NYSE Composite Index=100**   ***12 Month Price Score 87.14**

Interim Earnings (Per Share)

Qtr.	Apr	Jul	Oct	Jan
2001-02	...	(0.09)	(0.14)	0.06
2002-03	0.11	0.03	(0.04)	0.57
2003-04	0.09	(0.07)	(0.05)	0.73
2004-05	0.06	(0.06)	(0.28)	...

Interim Dividends (Per Share)

No Dividends Paid

Valuation Analysis

Forecast P/E	20.32	No of Institutions
	(4/7/2005)	163
Market Cap	$1.4 Billion	Shares
Book Value	1.0 Billion	122,630,784
Price/Book	1.32	% Held
Price/Sales	0.31	N/A

Business Summary: Retail - General (MIC: 5.2 SIC: 311 NAIC: 52111)

Big Lots is a major retailer of close-out merchandise. As of Jan 31 2004, Co. operated a total of 1,430 stores in 45 states, including 1,385 stores under the name Big Lots and 45 stores under the name Big Lots Furniture. Co.'s stores offer substantial savings on a wide variety of name-brand consumer products, including food items, health and beauty aids, electronics, housewares, tools, paint, lawn and garden, hardware, sporting goods and toys. Co.'s wholesale operations are conducted through Big Lots Wholesale, Consolidated International and Wisconsin Toy.

Recent Developments: For the quarter ended Oct 30 2004, loss from continuing operations increased to $24,812 thousand from a loss of $5,118 thousand in the year-earlier quarter. Net loss increased to $31,460 thousand from a net loss of $6,377 thousand in the year-earlier quarter. Revenues were $980,027 thousand, up 3.4% from $948,117 thousand the year before. Operating loss was $26,038 thousand versus a loss of $4,727 thousand in the prior-year quarter. Total indirect expense was $396,815 thousand versus $374,515 thousand in the prior-year quarter, an increase of 6.0%.

Prospects: Sluggish customer traffic is being partially offset by positive average basket trends stemming from increased demand for Co.'s hardline products and home decorative merchandise. Co. is targeting first-quarter 2005 earnings in the range of $0.04 to $0.07 per diluted share, along with comparable-store sales growth of between 2.0% and 4.0%. Looking ahead, Co. is projecting full-year fiscal 2005 earnings in the range of $0.54 to $0.60 per diluted share, based on total sales growth of between 7.0% and 9.0% and a comparable-store sales increase in the range of 3.0% to 4.0%. Gross margins are expected to benefit from lower levels of clearance markdowns of seasonal merchandise and hanging apparel.

Financial Data

(US$ in Thousands)	9 Mos	6 Mos	3 Mos	01/31/2004	02/01/2003	02/02/2002	02/03/2001	01/29/2000
Earnings Per Share	0.45	0.68	0.67	0.69	0.66	(0.18)	(3.39)	0.85
Cash Flow Per Share	0.98	1.31	0.93	1.59	1.89	1.33	(2.72)	2.29
Tang Book Value Per Share	9.09	9.36	9.62	9.54	8.83	8.11	8.28	11.71
Dividends Per Share	...	...	...	...	...	0.010	...	...
Income Statement								
Total Revenue	2,994,175	2,014,148	1,019,198	4,174,383	3,868,550	3,433,321	3,277,088	4,700,217
EBITDA	56,366	55,045	37,300	221,962	228,161	41,727	247,756	270,882
Depn & Amortn	75,727	48,368	23,136	91,634	81,509	68,986	62,290	100,464
Income Before Taxes	(42,067)	(2,071)	9,912	114,946	126,541	(47,461)	162,519	145,116
Income Taxes	(16,674)	(1,490)	3,205	24,051	49,984	(18,747)	64,195	57,321
Net Income	(32,041)	(581)	6,707	81,175	76,557	(20,234)	(380,652)	96,110
Average Shares	112,403	114,686	118,294	117,253	116,707	113,660	112,414	112,952
Balance Sheet								
Current Assets	1,297,699	1,076,700	1,182,723	1,167,600	1,069,167	994,074	1,100,567	1,419,700
Total Assets	1,935,700	1,711,603	1,799,364	1,784,688	1,642,271	1,533,209	1,585,396	2,186,783
Current Liabilities	537,155	624,409	462,274	463,586	410,907	321,874	324,994	710,762
Long-Term Obligations	371,100	30,000	204,000	204,000	204,000	204,000	268,000	60,546
Total Liabilities	914,127	659,970	668,949	668,628	616,090	605,676	657,584	886,721
Stockholders' Equity	1,021,573	1,051,633	1,130,415	1,116,060	1,026,181	927,533	927,812	1,300,062
Shares Outstanding	112,446	112,323	117,473	116,927	116,165	114,398	112,079	111,000
Statistical Record								
Return on Assets %	2.84	4.62	4.50	4.75	4.84	N.M.	N.M.	4.56
Return on Equity %	5.19	7.50	7.16	7.60	7.86	N.M.	N.M.	7.77
EBITDA Margin %	1.88	2.73	3.66	5.32	5.90	1.22	7.56	5.76
Net Margin %	N.M.	N.M.	0.66	1.94	1.98	N.M.	N.M.	2.04
Asset Turnover	2.32	2.54	2.46	2.44	2.44	2.21	1.71	2.23
Current Ratio	2.42	1.72	2.56	2.52	2.60	3.09	3.39	2.00
Debt to Equity	0.36	0.03	0.18	0.18	0.20	0.22	0.29	0.05
Price Range	15.50-11.32	18.39-12.24	18.39-11.61	18.39-10.20	19.68-10.84	15.51-7.35	15.63-8.25	37.88-13.88
P/E Ratio	34.44-25.16	27.04-18.00	27.45-17.33	26.65-14.78	29.82-16.42	...	...	44.56-16.32
Average Yield %	...	...	...	...	...	0.09	...	...

Address: 300 Phillipi Road, P.O. Box 28512, Columbus, OH 43228-5311
Telephone: (614) 278-6800
Fax: (614) 278-6666

Web Site: www.biglots.com
Officers: Michael J. Potter - Chmn., Pres., C.E.O.
Brad A. Waite - Exec. V.P., H.R., & Loss Prevention

Auditors: DELOITTE & TOUCHE LLP
Investor Contact: 614-278-6622

BISYS GROUP, INC. (THE)

Exchange	Symbol	Price	52Wk Range	Yield	P/E
NYS	BSG	$15.68 (3/31/2005)	17.17-12.20	N/A	23.40

*7 Year Price Score 68.78   ***NYSE Composite Index=100**   ***12 Month Price Score 95.91**

Interim Earnings (Per Share)

Qtr.	Sep	Dec	Mar	Jun
2001-02	0.16	0.22	0.27	0.30
2002-03	0.14	0.24	0.27	0.28
2003-04	0.04	0.17	0.16	0.15
2004-05	0.18	0.18	...	...

Interim Dividends (Per Share)

Amt	Decl	Ex	Rec	Pay
2-for-1	9/21/2000	10/23/2000	10/6/2000	10/20/2000
100%	1/24/2002	2/25/2002	2/8/2002	2/22/2002

Valuation Analysis

Forecast P/E	18.69	No of Institutions
	(4/7/2005)	192
Market Cap	$1.9 Billion	Shares
Book Value	818.7 Million	110,074,344
Price/Book	2.31	% Held
Price/Sales	1.75	91.12

Business Summary: Miscellaneous Business Services (MIC: 12.8 SIC: 389 NAIC: 18210)

The Bisys Group supports clients with products and services provided through BISYS Investment Services, BISYS Insurance and Education Services, and BISYS Information Services. Co. distributes and administers mutual funds, hedge funds, private equity funds and other investment products; provides retirement plan recordkeeping services in partnership with financial institutions; and supports employers and IRA holders with ERISA plan documents and ancillary services. Co. also provides life and commercial property/casualty insurance distribution, training and education, and licensing and compliance products and services; and information processing and check imaging.

Recent Developments: For the quarter ended Dec 31 2004, net income increased 7.7% to $21,875 thousand from net income of $20,314 thousand in the year-earlier quarter. Revenues were $276,338 thousand, up 5.7% from $261,381 thousand the year before.

Prospects: Co.'s outlook appears constructive, reflecting in part recent top line growth and improved operating earnings from its Investment Services and Insurance Services segments. For example, for the quarter ended Dec 31 2004, Investment Services and Insurance Services revenues rose 7.9% and 10.3% to $149.2 million and $73.3 million, while segment operating earnings climbed 12.4% and 3.1% to $18.5 million and $14.3 million, respectively. Separately, on Jan 7 2005, Co. acquired RK Consulting, a New Jersey-based provider of investment fund administration services to the hedge fund and private equity industries, for cash consideration of approximately $83.0 million.

Financial Data
(US$ in Thousands)

	6 Mos	3 Mos	06/30/2004	06/30/2003	06/30/2002	06/30/2001	06/30/2000	06/30/1999
Earnings Per Share	0.67	0.66	0.53	0.92	0.94	0.70	0.61	0.34
Cash Flow Per Share	1.64	1.64	1.70	1.43	1.09	0.99	0.82	0.49
Tang Book Value Per Share	N.M.	N.M.	N.M.	N.M.	N.M.	0.01	1.56	0.86
Income Statement								
Total Revenue	544,467	268,129	1,037,302	958,419	865,705	701,757	571,401	472,676
EBITDA	108,924	54,881	187,098	241,688	240,576	189,399	146,632	98,552
Depn & Amortn	31,980	16,016	61,200	49,722	40,625	42,803	30,642	23,560
Income Before Taxes	68,673	34,494	108,194	175,295	187,849	140,694	116,039	76,192
Income Taxes	25,067	12,763	44,614	63,472	71,988	55,574	45,835	38,076
Net Income	43,606	21,731	63,580	111,823	115,861	85,120	70,204	38,116
Average Shares	119,698	120,575	120,890	121,721	123,859	120,650	113,972	111,744
Balance Sheet								
Current Assets	466,853	391,516	453,767	420,639	320,235	347,791	319,298	177,681
Total Assets	1,600,472	1,540,022	1,612,240	1,526,893	1,246,151	1,003,201	601,051	459,661
Current Liabilities	331,604	282,148	374,279	400,559	234,504	153,688	219,700	155,597
Long-Term Obligations	381,250	387,500	393,750	300,000	300,000	300,433	...	...
Total Liabilities	781,819	736,850	827,258	741,832	563,533	475,251	239,410	171,155
Stockholders' Equity	818,653	803,172	784,982	785,061	682,618	527,950	361,641	288,506
Shares Outstanding	120,372	120,717	120,677	120,133	119,880	116,844	111,228	108,360
Statistical Record								
Return on Assets %	4.95	5.22	4.04	8.06	10.30	10.61	13.20	9.60
Return on Equity %	9.94	10.02	8.08	15.24	19.14	19.14	21.54	14.47
EBITDA Margin %	20.01	20.47	18.04	25.22	27.79	26.99	25.66	20.85
Net Margin %	8.01	8.10	6.13	11.67	13.38	12.13	12.29	8.06
Asset Turnover	0.66	0.71	0.66	0.69	0.77	0.87	1.07	1.19
Current Ratio	1.41	1.39	1.21	1.05	1.37	2.26	1.45	1.14
Debt to Equity	0.47	0.48	0.50	0.38	0.44	0.57	...	...
Price Range	18.40-12.20	18.40-12.20	19.98-12.20	32.20-13.32	35.90-22.12	29.95-14.22	17.16-10.49	14.90-9.19
P/E Ratio	27.46-18.21	27.88-18.48	37.70-23.02	35.00-14.48	38.19-23.53	42.79-20.31	28.13-17.20	43.82-27.02

Address: 90 Park Avenue, New York, NY 10016 **Telephone:** (212) 907 6000 **Fax:** (212) 907 6001	**Web Site:** www.bisys.com **Officers:** Robert J. Casale - Chmn. Russell P. Fradin - Pres., C.E.O.	**Auditors:** PricewaterhouseCoopers LLP **Investor Contact:** 212-907-6000

BJ SERVICES CO.

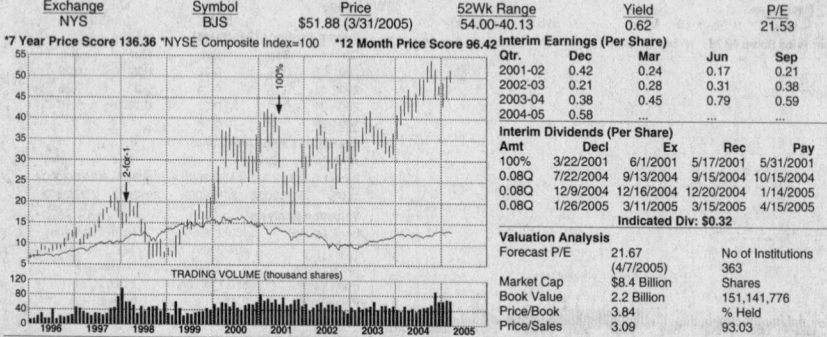

Exchange	Symbol	Price	52Wk Range	Yield	P/E
NYS	BJS	$51.88 (3/31/2005)	54.00-40.13	0.62	21.53

*7 Year Price Score 136.36 *NYSE Composite Index=100 *12 Month Price Score 96.42

Interim Earnings (Per Share)

Qtr.	Dec	Mar	Jun	Sep
2001-02	0.42	0.24	0.17	0.21
2002-03	0.21	0.28	0.31	0.38
2003-04	0.38	0.45	0.79	0.59
2004-05	0.58	...	...	...

Interim Dividends (Per Share)

Amt	Decl	Ex	Rec	Pay
100%	3/22/2001	6/1/2001	5/17/2001	5/31/2001
0.08Q	7/22/2004	9/13/2004	9/15/2004	10/15/2004
0.08Q	12/9/2004	12/16/2004	12/20/2004	1/14/2005
0.08Q	1/26/2005	3/11/2005	3/15/2005	4/15/2005

Indicated Div: $0.32

Valuation Analysis

Forecast P/E	21.67	No of Institutions	
	(4/7/2005)	363	
Market Cap	$8.4 Billion	Shares	
Book Value	2.2 Billion	151,141,776	
Price/Book	3.84	% Held	
Price/Sales	3.09	93.03	

Business Summary: Oil and Gas (MIC: 14.2 SIC: 389 NAIC: 13112)

BJ Services is engaged in providing pressure pumping and other oilfield services for the petroleum industry worldwide. Co.'s pressure pumping services consist of cementing and stimulation services used in the completion of new oil and natural gas wells and in remedial work on existing wells, both onshore and offshore. Other oilfield services include completion tools, completion fluids, casing and tubular services, production chemical services, and precommissioning, maintenance and turnaround services in the pipeline and process business, including pipeline inspection.

Recent Developments: For the quarter ended Dec 31 2004, net income increased 54.5% to $95,033 thousand from net income of $61,513 thousand in the year-earlier quarter. Revenues were $737,782 thousand, up 22.8% from $600,799 thousand the year before. Operating income was $130,138 thousand versus an income of $95,008 thousand in the prior-year quarter, an increase of 37.0%. Total direct expense was $550,086 thousand versus $457,730 thousand in the prior-year quarter, an increase of 20.2%. Total indirect expense was $55,682 thousand versus $47,305 thousand in the prior-year quarter, an increase of 17.7%.

Prospects: Co.'s top line growth is being driven by improvements from its North American pumping service business, which have helped offset revenue shortfalls from the North Sea stimulation vessel and its other service lines. All in all, Co. prospects appear constructive, due in large part to expectations of continued strong worldwide market activity. Accordingly, Co. is forecasting earnings for the quarter ended Mar 31 2005 in the range of $0.58 to $0.61 per diluted share. Moreover, Co. now expects its 2005 fiscal year earnings to be in the range of $2.30 to 2.40 per diluted share, up from its previous range of between $2.25 and $2.35 per diluted share.

Financial Data

(US$ in Thousands)	3 Mos	09/30/2004	09/30/2003	09/30/2002	09/30/2001	09/30/2000	09/30/1999	09/30/1998
Earnings Per Share	2.41	2.21	1.17	1.04	2.09	0.70	(0.21)	0.72
Cash Flow Per Share	3.47	3.29	2.07	2.19	3.16	1.29	0.46	1.91
Tang Book Value Per Share	8.06	7.46	4.87	3.48	5.57	4.20	2.72	2.82
Dividends Per Share	0.160	0.080	...	...	...	...	...	...
Dividend Payout %	6.65	3.62	...	...	...	...	...	...
Income Statement								
Total Revenue	737,782	2,600,986	2,142,877	1,865,796	2,233,520	1,555,389	1,131,334	1,527,468
EBITDA	173,086	656,721	409,692	364,580	644,865	295,693	85,648	288,488
Depn & Amortn	33,347	125,668	120,213	104,915	104,969	102,018	99,800	91,497
Income Before Taxes	138,734	520,737	275,672	252,694	529,181	175,283	(44,909)	172,054
Income Taxes	43,852	159,696	87,495	86,199	179,922	57,307	(15,221)	54,654
Net Income	95,033	361,041	188,177	166,495	349,259	117,976	(29,688)	117,400
Average Shares	165,213	163,414	161,257	160,736	167,080	168,700	141,578	162,526
Balance Sheet								
Current Assets	1,485,963	1,423,723	941,708	648,791	732,633	506,378	438,963	451,796
Total Assets	3,424,453	3,330,674	2,785,957	2,442,370	1,985,367	1,785,233	1,824,764	1,743,701
Current Liabilities	897,487	909,891	470,661	356,420	389,598	337,091	445,146	513,125
Long-Term Obligations	78,996	78,936	493,754	489,062	79,393	141,981	422,764	241,869
Total Liabilities	1,229,807	1,236,538	1,135,325	1,023,742	615,286	615,462	947,675	843,637
Stockholders' Equity	2,194,646	2,094,136	1,650,632	1,418,628	1,370,081	1,169,771	877,089	900,064
Shares Outstanding	162,458	161,868	158,306	156,795	160,484	165,296	142,356	140,868
Statistical Record								
Return on Assets %	12.58	11.77	7.20	7.52	18.53	6.52	N.M.	6.77
Return on Equity %	20.06	19.23	12.26	11.94	27.50	11.50	N.M.	12.62
EBITDA Margin %	23.46	25.25	19.12	19.54	28.87	19.01	7.57	18.89
Net Margin %	12.88	13.88	8.78	8.92	15.64	7.58	N.M.	7.69
Asset Turnover	0.87	0.85	0.82	0.84	1.18	0.86	0.63	0.88
Current Ratio	1.66	1.56	2.00	1.82	1.88	1.50	0.99	0.88
Debt to Equity	0.04	0.04	0.30	0.34	0.06	0.12	0.48	0.27
Price Range	54.00-35.25	52.90-30.90	41.95-24.90	38.65-17.12	42.33-14.87	37.77-13.78	19.50-6.63	22.14-6.31
P/E Ratio	22.41-14.63	23.94-13.98	35.85-21.28	37.16-16.46	20.25-7.11	53.95-19.69	...	30.75-8.77
Average Yield %	0.35	0.19	...	...	...	...	...	...

Address: 5500 Northwest Central Drive, Houston, TX 77092	Web Site: www.bjservices.com	Auditors: Deloitte & Touche LLP
Telephone: (713) 462-4239	Officers: J. W. Stewart - Chmn., Pres., C.E.O. Mark Airola - Chief Compliance Officer, Asst. Gen. Couns.	Investor Contact: 713-462-4239
Fax: (713) 895-5603		

BJ'S WHOLESALE CLUB, INC.

Exchange	Symbol	Price	52Wk Range	Yield	P/E
NYS	BJ	$31.06 (3/31/2005)	33.75-20.29	N/A	18.71

*7 Year Price Score 77.32   *NYSE Composite Index=100   *12 Month Price Score 107.17

Interim Earnings (Per Share)

Qtr.	Apr	Jul	Oct	Jan
2001-02	0.31	0.49	(0.46)	0.76
2002-03	0.32	0.50	0.33	0.69
2003-04	0.16	0.32	0.29	0.70
2004-05	0.23	0.40	0.33	...

Interim Dividends (Per Share)

No Dividends Paid

Valuation Analysis

Forecast P/E	17.09	No of Institutions	
	(4/7/2005)	224	
Market Cap	$2.2 Billion	Shares	
Book Value	904.4 Million	75,581,504	
Price/Book	2.39	% Held	
Price/Sales	0.30	N/A	

Business Summary: Retail - General (MIC: 5.2 SIC: 331 NAIC: 52990)

BJ's Wholesale Club sells brand name food and general merchandise at discounted prices through warehouse clubs in the eastern United States. As of Jan 31 2004, Co. operated 150 clubs in 16 states. In addition, Co. has gas stations in operation at 78 of its clubs, as well as pharmacies in 14 locations. Co. sells food items such as frozen foods, fresh meats, dairy products, dry grocery items, fresh produce and flowers, canned goods. General merchandise includes office supplies and equipment, consumer electronics, small appliances, auto accessories, tires, jewelry, housewares, health and beauty aids, computer software, books, greeting cards, apparel, tools, toys, and seasonal items.

Recent Developments: For the quarter ended Oct 30 2004, income from continuing operations increased 21.5% to $25,078 thousand from income of $20,633 thousand in the year-earlier quarter. Revenues were $1,797,687 thousand, up 9.9% from $1,636,007 thousand the year before. Operating income was $35,571 thousand versus an income of $32,464 thousand in the prior-year quarter, an increase of 9.6%. Total direct expense was $1,619,080 thousand versus $1,477,171 thousand in the prior-year quarter, an increase of 9.6%. Total indirect expense was $143,036 thousand versus $126,372 thousand in the prior-year quarter, an increase of 13.2%.

Prospects: Co.'s results going forward may benefit from its re-merchandising efforts, which include discontinuing or reducing pallet space for selected items and categories, including large exercise equipment; treadmills and weight sets; tools; tires; and certain stationery and electronics items. Co. has replaced them with generally faster-turning items, including additional beverages, paper goods, juices, salty snacks and international foods. Co. is also placing a greater focus on fresh foods, private brands and fashion. Separately, in Oct of 2004, Co. opened the first of two new test clubs in the Metro New York market exclusively for food service businesses under the name ProFoods Restaurant Supply.

Financial Data
(US$ in Thousands)

	9 Mos	6 Mos	3 Mos	01/31/2004	02/01/2003	02/02/2002	02/03/2001	01/29/2000
Earnings Per Share	1.66	1.62	1.54	1.47	1.84	1.11	1.77	1.47
Cash Flow Per Share	3.95	3.47	3.10	2.88	2.16	2.93	2.10	2.51
Tang Book Value Per Share	13.02	12.75	12.40	12.21	10.69	9.59	9.18	7.85
Income Statement								
Total Revenue	5,323,580	3,525,893	1,647,624	6,724,219	5,859,702	5,279,730	4,932,095	4,206,247
EBITDA	185,524	120,158	50,945	255,237	308,500	188,279	262,821	224,011
Depn & Amortn	73,376	48,671	24,413	87,050	73,113	61,680	54,953	46,476
Income Before Taxes	112,383	71,506	26,421	168,113	235,680	130,533	213,823	181,320
Income Taxes	42,926	27,127	10,171	63,318	89,871	48,185	82,322	70,171
Net Income	67,356	44,117	16,118	102,866	130,866	82,348	131,501	111,149
Average Shares	70,086	69,957	70,362	69,815	71,120	73,981	74,380	75,391
Balance Sheet								
Current Assets	1,027,205	953,433	885,400	908,720	767,070	752,818	694,571	580,683
Total Assets	1,838,042	1,748,819	1,686,761	1,721,109	1,480,957	1,421,884	1,233,734	1,073,448
Current Liabilities	813,071	745,580	712,714	761,433	650,028	625,000	514,643	447,207
Long-Term Obligations	12,434	14,042	14,576	15,088	18,727	63,700	1,828	2,050
Total Liabilities	933,676	862,464	824,187	868,888	740,154	735,317	568,819	496,050
Stockholders' Equity	904,366	886,355	862,574	852,221	740,803	686,567	664,915	577,398
Shares Outstanding	69,479	69,540	69,579	69,789	69,284	71,593	72,462	73,542
Statistical Record								
Return on Assets %	6.60	6.90	6.69	6.44	9.04	6.22	11.21	11.25
Return on Equity %	13.68	13.73	13.36	12.95	18.39	12.22	20.83	20.98
EBITDA Margin %	3.48	3.41	3.09	3.80	5.26	3.57	5.33	5.33
Net Margin %	1.27	1.25	0.98	1.53	2.23	1.56	2.67	2.64
Asset Turnover	4.11	4.31	4.29	4.21	4.05	3.99	4.21	4.26
Current Ratio	1.26	1.28	1.24	1.19	1.18	1.20	1.35	1.30
Debt to Equity	0.01	0.02	0.02	0.02	0.03	0.09	N.M.	N.M.
Price Range	29.47-20.29	27.18-17.24	27.18-14.21	27.18-9.38	47.35-15.40	56.97-40.35	42.95-26.75	38.75-20.72
P/E Ratio	17.75-12.22	16.78-10.64	17.65-9.23	18.49-6.38	25.73-8.37	51.32-36.35	24.27-15.11	26.36-14.09

Address: One Mercer Road, Natick, MA 01760
Telephone: (508) 651-7400
Fax: (508) 651-6114

Web Site: www.bjs.com
Officers: Herbert J. Zarkin - Chmn. Michael T. Wedge - Pres., C.E.O.

Auditors: PricewaterhouseCoopers LLP
Investor Contact: 508-651-6650

BLACK & DECKER CORP.

Exchange	Symbol	Price	52Wk Range	Yield	P/E
NYS	BDK	$78.99 (3/31/2005)	89.19-55.72	1.42	14.13

*7 Year Price Score 128.43 *NYSE Composite Index=100 *12 Month Price Score 104.43

Interim Earnings (Per Share)

Qtr.	Mar	Jun	Sep	Dec
2001	0.40	0.51	0.57	(0.16)
2002	0.41	0.81	0.68	0.94
2003	0.55	0.97	0.95	1.27
2004	1.09	1.50	1.37	1.63

Interim Dividends (Per Share)

Amt	Decl	Ex	Rec	Pay
0.21Q	4/27/2004	6/9/2004	6/11/2004	6/25/2004
0.21Q	7/19/2004	9/8/2004	9/10/2004	9/24/2004
0.21Q	10/27/2004	12/15/2004	12/17/2004	12/31/2004
0.28Q	2/10/2005	3/9/2005	3/11/2005	3/25/2005

Indicated Div: $1.12

Valuation Analysis

Forecast P/E	12.98 (4/7/2005)	No of Institutions 364
Market Cap	$6.5 Billion	Shares
Book Value	1.6 Billion	71,883,976
Price/Book	4.16	% Held
Price/Sales	1.20	87.55

TRADING VOLUME (thousand shares)

Business Summary: Industrial Machinery and Equipment (MIC: 11.5 SIC: 546 NAIC: 33991)

Black & Decker is a global manufacturer and marketer of power tools and accessories, hardware and home improvement products, and technology-based fastening systems. Co. produces corded and cordless electric power tools, lawn and garden tools, home products, accessories and attachments for power tools. Co. also provides product service and sells security hardware. In addition, Co. manufactures and sells plumbing products. Also, Co. produces an extensive line of metal and plastic fasteners and engineered fastening systems, including blind riveting, stud welding, assembly systems, specialty screws, prevailing torque nuts and assemblies, insert systems, and self-piercing riveting systems.

Recent Developments: For the year ended Dec 31 2004, income from continuing operations increased 53.6% to $441,100 thousand from income of $287,200 thousand a year earlier. Net income increased 55.6% to $456,000 thousand from net income of $293,000 thousand a year earlier. Revenues were $5,398,400 thousand, up 20.4% from $4,482,700 thousand the year before. Operating income was $629,200 thousand versus an income of $428,700 thousand in the prior year, an increase of 46.8%. Total direct expense was $3,432,900 thousand versus $2,887,100 thousand in the prior year, an increase of 18.9%. Total indirect expense was $1,336,300 thousand versus $1,166,900 thousand in the prior year, an increase of 14.5%.

Prospects: Demand for Co.'s products remains strong, and with tougher comparisons in mind, it is forecasting low to mid-single-digit sales growth, excluding currency translation and acquisitions. Including these factors, Co. expects a sales growth rate in the high teens. Operating margin in Co.'s existing business should increase modestly. Co. expects the Porter-Cable and Delta Tools Group acquisition to add $0.40 to earnings per share. As a result, Co. is projecting diluted earnings per share from continuing operations in the ranges of $5.95 to $6.10 for the full year and $1.05 to $1.10 for the first quarter of 2005.

Financial Data

(US$ in Thousands)	12/31/2004	12/31/2003	12/31/2002	12/31/2001	12/31/2000	12/31/1999	12/31/1998	12/31/1997
Earnings Per Share	5.59	3.75	2.84	1.33	3.34	3.40	(8.22)	2.35
Cash Flow Per Share	7.74	7.32	5.62	4.70	4.17	4.32	3.99	1.49
Tang Book Value Per Share	4.56	0.96	N.M.	0.51	N.M.	0.66	N.M.	N.M.
Dividends Per Share	0.840	0.570	0.480	0.480	0.480	0.480	0.480	0.480
Dividend Payout %	15.03	15.20	16.90	36.09	14.37	14.12	...	20.43
Income Statement								
Total Revenue	5,398,400	4,482,700	4,394,000	4,333,100	4,560,800	4,520,500	4,559,900	4,940,500
EBITDA	768,900	559,500	493,000	399,000	672,200	697,100	(318,700)	688,300
Depn & Amortn	142,500	133,400	127,800	159,400	163,400	160,000	155,200	214,200
Income Before Taxes	604,300	390,900	307,400	155,300	404,600	441,300	(588,300)	349,500
Income Taxes	163,200	103,700	77,700	47,300	122,600	141,000	166,500	122,300
Net Income	456,000	293,000	229,700	108,000	282,000	300,300	(754,800)	227,200
Average Shares	81,600	78,200	80,900	81,100	84,400	88,400	91,800	96,500
Balance Sheet								
Current Assets	2,927,200	2,203,000	2,193,900	1,892,300	1,962,000	1,911,400	1,751,800	2,078,800
Total Assets	5,530,800	4,222,500	4,130,500	4,014,200	4,089,700	4,012,700	3,852,500	5,360,700
Current Liabilities	1,792,600	1,312,100	1,453,400	1,070,600	1,632,300	1,572,700	1,374,700	1,372,600
Long-Term Obligations	1,200,600	915,600	927,600	1,191,400	798,500	847,100	1,148,900	1,623,700
Total Liabilities	3,972,100	3,376,000	3,530,900	3,263,200	3,397,300	3,211,600	3,278,500	3,569,300
Stockholders' Equity	1,558,700	846,500	599,600	751,000	692,400	801,100	574,000	1,791,400
Shares Outstanding	82,095	77,933	79,604	79,829	80,343	87,190	87,498	94,843
Statistical Record								
Return on Assets %	9.33	7.02	5.64	2.67	6.94	7.64	N.M.	4.32
Return on Equity %	37.81	40.52	34.01	14.96	37.66	43.68	N.M.	13.27
EBITDA Margin %	14.24	12.48	11.22	9.21	14.74	15.42	N.M.	13.93
Net Margin %	8.45	6.54	5.23	2.49	6.18	6.64	N.M.	4.60
Asset Turnover	1.10	1.07	1.08	1.07	1.12	1.15	0.99	0.94
Current Ratio	1.63	1.68	1.51	1.77	1.20	1.22	1.27	1.51
Debt to Equity	0.77	1.08	1.55	1.59	1.15	1.06	2.00	0.91
Price Range	89.19-48.25	49.65-33.76	50.00-35.50	46.37-29.01	52.25-28.44	63.31-42.00	65.19-38.31	43.06-29.75

Address: 701 East Joppa Road, Towson, MD 21286 **Telephone:** (410) 716 3900 **Fax:** (410) 716 2610	**Web Site:** www.bdk.com **Officers:** Nolan D. Archibald - Chmn., Pres., C.E.O. Paul A. Gustafson - Exec. V.P.	**Auditors:** ERNST & YOUNG LLP

BLACK HILLS CORPORATION

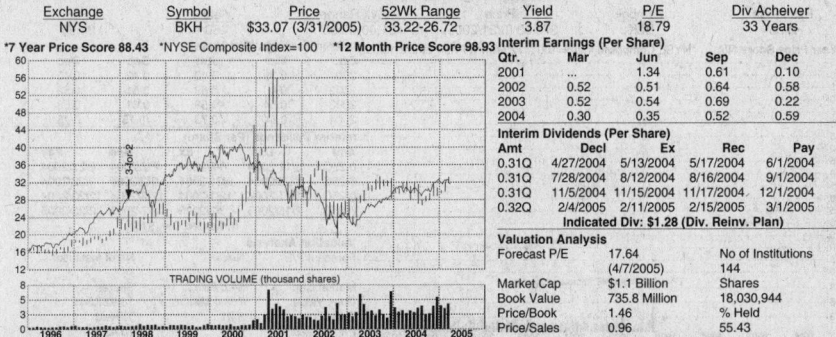

Exchange	Symbol	Price	52Wk Range	Yield	P/E	Div Achiever
NYS	BKH	$33.07 (3/31/2005)	33.22-26.72	3.87	18.79	33 Years

*7 Year Price Score 88.43 *NYSE Composite Index=100 *12 Month Price Score 98.93

Interim Earnings (Per Share)

Qtr.	Mar	Jun	Sep	Dec
2001	...	1.34	0.61	0.10
2002	0.52	0.51	0.64	0.58
2003	0.52	0.54	0.69	0.22
2004	0.30	0.35	0.52	0.59

Interim Dividends (Per Share)

Amt	Decl	Ex	Rec	Pay
0.31Q	4/27/2004	5/13/2004	5/17/2004	6/1/2004
0.31Q	7/28/2004	8/12/2004	8/16/2004	9/1/2004
0.31Q	11/5/2004	11/15/2004	11/17/2004.	12/1/2004
0.32Q	2/4/2005	2/11/2005	2/15/2005	3/1/2005

Indicated Div: $1.28 (Div. Reinv. Plan)

Valuation Analysis

Forecast P/E	17.64
	(4/7/2005)
Market Cap	$1.1 Billion
Book Value	735.8 Million
Price/Book	1.46
Price/Sales	0.96

No of Institutions	
144	
Shares	
18,030,944	
% Held	
55.43	

Business Summary: Electricity (MIC: 7.1 SIC: 911 NAIC: 21121)

Black Hills is an energy and communications company with three segments. Co.'s Wholesale Energy group generates and sells electricity, produces coal, natural gas and crude oil primarily in the Rocky Mountain region, and markets and transports fuel products. Co.'s Electric Utility group engages in the generation, transmission and distribution of electricity to about 61,000 customers in South Dakota, Wyoming and Montana. Co.'s Communications group offers broadband telecommunications services, including local and long distance telephone, expanded cable television, cable modem Internet access and high-speed data and video services to residential and business customers in part of South Dakota.

Recent Developments: For the year ended Dec 31 2004, net income decreased 5.3% to $57,973 thousand from net income of $61,222 thousand a year earlier. Revenues were $1,121,701 thousand, down 10.3% from $1,250,050 thousand the year before. Operating income was $133,919 thousand versus an income of $131,168 thousand in the prior year, an increase of 2.1%. Total direct expense was $987,782 thousand versus $1,118,882 thousand in the prior year, a decrease of 11.7%. Total indirect expense was $185,150 thousand versus $301,097 thousand in the prior year, a decrease of 38.5%.

Prospects: Going forward, Co. expects continued growth from oil and gas production and modest accretion from Cheyenne Light, Fuel & Power. Also, Co. expects modest improvement in communications results and an earnings increase from power generation due to a full year of contract revenues at the Las Vegas Cogeneration II facility and cost savings from integration efforts. However, Co. expects small decreases in earnings from Black Hills Power due to a planned maintenance outage of one of its coal-fired power plants, reduced oil marketing and transportation revenues and narrower margins from gas marketing. For 2005, Co. expects income from continuing operations in the range of $1.85 to $2.00 per share.

Financial Data
(US$ in Thousands)

	12/31/2004	12/31/2003	12/31/2002	12/31/2001	12/31/2000	12/31/1999	12/31/1998	12/31/1997
Earnings Per Share	1.76	1.97	2.26	3.42	2.37	1.73	1.19	1.49
Cash Flow Per Share	4.21	5.59	8.16	6.99	3.36	3.53	2.53	2.58
Tang Book Value Per Share	20.37	19.55	15.42	14.67	10.45	10.14	9.52	9.46
Dividends Per Share	1.240	1.200	1.160	1.120	1.080	1.040	1.000	0.947
Dividend Payout %	70.45	60.91	51.33	32.75	45.57	60.12	84.03	63.53
Income Statement								
Total Revenue	1,121,701	1,250,052	423,919	1,558,558	1,623,836	791,875	679,254	313,662
EBITDA	222,442	219,209	206,360	234,106	150,610	89,769	73,399	80,795
Depn & Amortn	87,833	80,791	69,738	54,051	32,864	25,067	24,037	22,311
Income Before Taxes	84,525	86,915	96,017	142,807	94,479	52,856	37,516	46,685
Income Taxes	26,704	29,920	29,662	50,544	30,358	15,789	11,708	14,326
Net Income	57,973	61,222	61,452	88,077	52,848	37,067	25,808	32,359
Average Shares	32,912	31,015	27,167	25,771	22,281	21,482	21,665	21,706
Balance Sheet								
Net PPE	1,445,732	1,442,422	1,677,877	1,238,224	794,281	464,189	389,607	401,127
Total Assets	2,056,163	2,063,225	2,035,169	1,658,767	1,320,320	674,806	559,417	508,741
Long-Term Obligations	733,581	868,459	618,862	415,798	307,092	160,700	162,030	163,360
Total Liabilities	1,320,398	1,353,478	1,500,006	1,143,603	1,037,974	458,200	352,751	303,338
Stockholders' Equity	735,765	709,747	535,163	515,164	282,346	216,606	206,666	205,403
Shares Outstanding	32,477	32,297	27,102	26,890	22,921	21,371	21,719	21,705
Statistical Record								
Return on Assets %	2.81	2.99	3.33	5.91	5.28	6.01	4.83	6.63
Return on Equity %	8.00	9.84	11.70	22.09	21.13	17.51	12.53	16.24
EBITDA Margin %	19.83	17.54	48.68	15.02	9.27	11.34	10.81	25.76
Net Margin %	5.17	4.90	14.50	5.65	3.25	4.68	3.80	10.32
PPE Turnover	0.77	0.80	0.29	1.53	2.57	1.85	1.72	0.78
Asset Turnover	0.54	0.61	0.23	1.05	1.62	1.28	1.27	0.64
Debt to Equity	1.00	1.22	1.16	0.81	1.09	0.74	0.78	0.80
Price Range	32.25-26.72	33.35-22.26	36.84-19.15	58.05-26.35	45.13-20.56	26.38-20.50	27.38-20.75	24.21-17.50
P/E Ratio	18.32-15.18	16.93-11.30	16.30-8.47	16.97-7.70	19.04-8.68	15.25-11.85	23.00-17.44	16.25-11.74
Average Yield %	4.17	4.08	3.99	2.86	4.17	4.51	4.21	4.88

Address: 625 Ninth Street, Rapid City, SD 57701	**Web Site:** www.blackhillscorp.com	**Auditors:** DELOITTE & TOUCHE LLP
Telephone: (605) 721-1700	**Officers:** Daniel P. Landguth - Chmn. David R. Emery - Pres., C.E.O.	**Investor Contact:** 605-721-1700
Fax: (605) 721-2597		**Transfer Agents:** Wells Fargo Shareowner Services

BLACKROCK, INC.

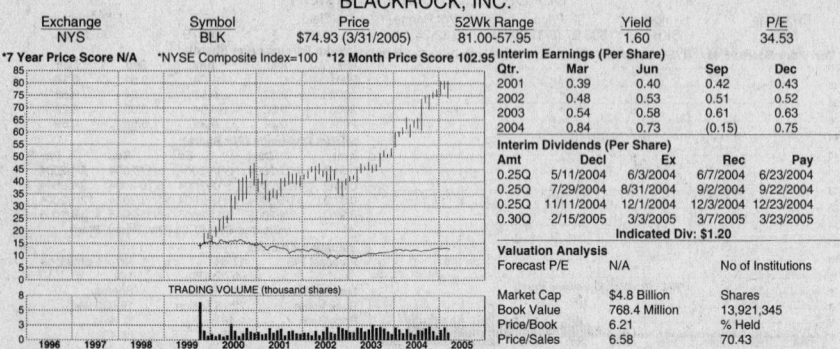

Exchange	Symbol	Price	52Wk Range	Yield	P/E
NYS	BLK	$74.93 (3/31/2005)	81.00-57.95	1.60	34.53

*7 Year Price Score N/A   *NYSE Composite Index=100   *12 Month Price Score 102.95

Interim Earnings (Per Share)

Qtr.	Mar	Jun	Sep	Dec
2001	0.39	0.40	0.42	0.43
2002	0.48	0.53	0.51	0.52
2003	0.54	0.58	0.61	0.63
2004	0.84	0.73	(0.15)	0.75

Interim Dividends (Per Share)

Amt	Decl	Ex	Rec	Pay
0.25Q	5/11/2004	6/3/2004	6/7/2004	6/23/2004
0.25Q	7/29/2004	8/31/2004	9/2/2004	9/22/2004
0.25Q	11/11/2004	12/1/2004	12/3/2004	12/23/2004
0.30Q	2/15/2005	3/3/2005	3/7/2005	3/23/2005
		Indicated Div: $1.20		

Valuation Analysis

Forecast P/E	N/A	No of Institutions
Market Cap	$4.8 Billion	Shares
Book Value	768.4 Million	13,921,345
Price/Book	6.21	% Held
Price/Sales	6.58	70.43

TRADING VOLUME (thousand shares)

Business Summary: Trusts & Holding Entities (MIC: 8.9 SIC: 726 NAIC: 25990)

BlackRock is an investment management firm with approximately $342.00 billion of assets under management as of Dec 31 2004. Co. manages fixed income, cash management, equity and alternative investment products on behalf of institutional and individual investors worldwide. Co. also offers investment tools, outsourcing and advisory services to institutional investors under the BlackRock Solutions® brand name. Co. is a majority owned indirect subsidiary of The PNC Financial Services Group, Inc. Co. is headquartered in New York City and has offices in Boston, Edinburgh, Hong Kong, Morristown, San Francisco, Singapore, Sydney, Tokyo and Wilmington.

Recent Developments: For the year ended Dec 31 2004, net income decreased 7.9% to $143,141 thousand from net income of $155,402 thousand a year earlier. Revenues were $725,311 thousand, up 21.2% from $598,212 thousand the year before.

Prospects: On Jan 19 2005, Co. provided full year 2005 diluted earnings per share guidance ranging from $2.83 to $3.13. Co. noted that its 2005 guidance reflects the estimated effect of Co.'s acquisition of SSRM Holdings, Inc. (SSR) including expected financing costs and one-time charges of about $0.09 per diluted share in the first quarter of 2005. On Jan 31 2005, Co. announced the completion of its acquisition of SSR from MetLife, Inc. SSRM Holdings is the holding company of State Street Research & Management Co. and SSR Realty Advisors. In addition, the employees and businesses of SSR will be integrated with, and operate under the names, BlackRock and BlackRock Realty Advisors.

Financial Data
(US$ in Thousands)

	12/31/2004	12/31/2003	12/31/2002	12/31/2001	12/31/2000	12/31/1999	12/31/1998	12/31/1997
Earnings Per Share	2.17	2.36	2.04	1.65	1.35	1.04	0.66	0.49
Cash Flow Per Share	3.62	2.78	2.66	2.60	1.70	2.04	1.00	...
Tang Book Value Per Share	9.18	8.13	6.96	4.72	2.75	1.35	N.M.	N.M.
Dividends Per Share	1.000	0.400	...	...	...	...	...	...
Dividend Payout %	46.08	16.95	...	...	...	...	...	...
Income Statement								
Total Revenue	725,311	598,212	576,977	533,144	476,872	380,981	339,482	205,473
Income Before Taxes	200,438	250,902	223,948	180,991	149,917	103,450	68,010	38,741
Income Taxes	52,264	95,247	90,699	73,557	62,556	44,033	32,395	16,655
Net Income	143,141	155,402	133,249	107,434	87,361	59,417	35,615	22,086
Average Shares	65,960	65,860	65,307	64,926	64,590	57,268	53,682	45,100
Balance Sheet								
Total Assets	1,145,235	967,223	864,188	684,478	537,003	447,582	440,784	335,507
Total Liabilities	359,714	252,676	229,534	198,361	168,762	167,056	334,593	290,544
Stockholders' Equity	768,352	713,308	634,654	486,117	368,241	280,526	106,191	44,963
Shares Outstanding	63,665	64,096	64,916	64,465	63,997	63,864	54,807	164
Statistical Record								
Return on Assets %	13.52	16.97	17.21	17.59	17.70	13.38	9.18	...
Return on Equity %	19.27	23.06	23.78	25.15	26.86	30.73	47.12	...
Price Range	77.51-53.11	53.53-39.40	47.35-34.30	44.22-31.82	47.50-15.75	19.19-12.81	...	...
P/E Ratio	35.72-24.47	22.68-16.69	23.21-16.81	26.80-19.28	35.19-11.67	18.45-12.32	...	...
Average Yield %	1.52	0.86	...	...	...	...	...	...

Address: 40 East 52nd Street, New York, NY 10022
Telephone: (212) 810-5300
Fax: (212) 754-3123

Web Site: www.blackrock.com
Officers: Laurence D. Fink - Chmn., C.E.O. Paul L. Audet - C.F.O., Managing Dir.

Auditors: DELOITTE & TOUCHE LLP
Investor Contact: 212-409-3555
Transfer Agents: Mellon Investor Services L.L.C., Ridgefield Park, NJ

BLOCK (H & R), INC.

Exchange	Symbol	Price	52Wk Range	Yield	P/E
NYS	HRB	$50.58 (3/31/2005)	53.30-44.77	1.74	16.21

*7 Year Price Score 121.12 *NYSE Composite Index=100 *12 Month Price Score 97.28

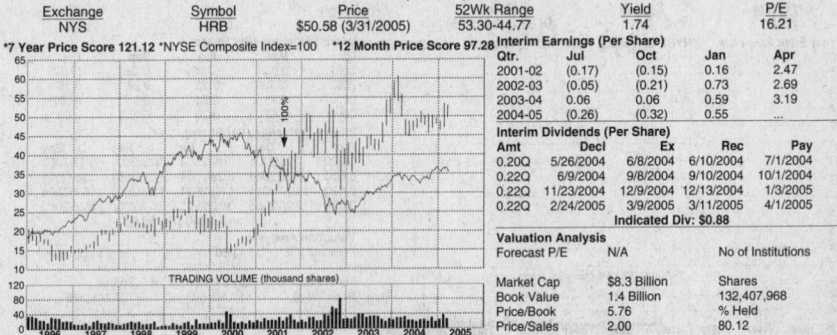

Interim Earnings (Per Share)

Qtr.	Jul	Oct	Jan	Apr
2001-02	(0.17)	(0.15)	0.16	2.47
2002-03	(0.05)	(0.21)	0.73	2.69
2003-04	0.06	0.06	0.59	3.19
2004-05	(0.26)	(0.32)	0.55	...

Interim Dividends (Per Share)

Amt	Decl	Ex	Rec	Pay
0.20Q	5/26/2004	6/8/2004	6/10/2004	7/1/2004
0.22Q	6/9/2004	9/8/2004	9/10/2004	10/1/2004
0.22Q	11/23/2004	12/9/2004	12/13/2004	1/3/2005
0.22Q	2/24/2005	3/9/2005	3/11/2005	4/1/2005
			Indicated Div: $0.88	

Valuation Analysis

Forecast P/E	N/A	No of Institutions	
Market Cap	$8.3 Billion	Shares	132,407,968
Book Value	1.4 Billion	% Held	80.12
Price/Book	5.76		
Price/Sales	2.00		

Business Summary: Personal Services (MIC: 5.15 SIC: 291 NAIC: 41213)

H&R Block is a provider of tax products and services and financial advice, investment and mortgage products and services, and business and consulting services. Co.'s tax services segments provide income tax return preparation services, electronic filing services and other services and products related to income tax return preparation to the general public in the United States, and also in Canada, Australia and the United Kingdom. Co. also offers investment services and securities products through H&R Block Financial Advisors, Inc. Co.'s mortgage services segment offers a range of home mortgage products and services through Option One Mortgage Corporation and H&R Block Mortgage Corporation.

Recent Developments: For the quarter ended Jan 31 2005, net income decreased 14.1% to $91,692 thousand from net income of $106,726 thousand in the year-earlier quarter. Revenues were $1,032,007 thousand, up 7.2% from $962,830 thousand the year before. Operating income was $131,951 thousand versus an income of $174,504 thousand in the prior-year quarter, a decrease of 24.4%. Total direct expense was $509,104 thousand versus $454,342 thousand in the prior-year quarter, an increase of 12.1%. Total indirect expense was $366,025 thousand versus $312,623 thousand in the prior-year quarter, an increase of 17.1%.

Prospects: Results are being negatively affected by aggressive pricing and increased competition in the mortgage market. However, Co. is making progress with its efforts to improve productivity and position its mortgage business for success as it transitions to a higher rate environment. Meanwhile, Co. will continue to focus on aggressively controlling origination costs and expand service capacity. Separately, Co. is enjoying a strong start to the current tax season as results through Feb 15 2005 show a 10.6% increase in total tax-preparation and related fees from a year earlier, which is being driven by an increase in average fees and new customer growth.

Financial Data
(US$ in Thousands)

	9 Mos	6 Mos	3 Mos	04/30/2004	04/30/2003	04/30/2002	04/30/2001	04/30/2000
Earnings Per Share	3.12	3.19	3.58	3.86	3.15	2.31	1.52	1.27
Cash Flow Per Share	1.96	4.38	3.11	5.22	3.85	4.05	1.61	2.57
Tang Book Value Per Share	0.18	N.M.	0.71	3.53	3.38	1.45	0.56	0.57
Dividends Per Share	0.840	0.820	0.800	0.780	0.700	0.630	0.588	0.537
Dividend Payout %	26.88	25.68	22.35	20.21	22.22	27.27	38.65	42.16
Income Statement								
Total Revenue	2,053,973	1,021,966	482,711	4,205,570	3,779,767	3,317,736	3,001,575	2,451,943
EBITDA	176,379	(43,067)	(17,093)	1,405,913	1,196,005	872,226	678,686	559,484
Depn & Amortn	183,184	115,421	55,471	241,756	208,928	155,386	205,608	147,218
Income Before Taxes	(6,805)	(158,488)	(72,564)	1,164,157	987,077	716,840	473,078	412,266
Income Taxes	(2,215)	(62,206)	(28,481)	459,901	407,013	282,435	196,330	160,371
Net Income	(4,590)	(96,282)	(44,083)	697,897	580,064	434,405	281,162	251,895
Average Shares	167,438	164,686	168,635	180,802	184,078	188,327	185,136	197,858
Balance Sheet								
Current Assets	3,621,186	2,483,040	2,205,221	2,961,299	2,747,361	2,245,143	2,271,206	3,863,543
Total Assets	6,141,121	4,896,858	4,614,762	5,380,026	4,603,905	4,230,791	4,121,624	5,699,350
Current Liabilities	3,402,355	2,281,714	2,151,126	2,472,043	1,897,196	1,879,702	1,988,402	3,520,449
Long-Term Obligations	928,529	931,781	546,196	545,811	822,302	868,387	870,974	872,396
Total Liabilities	4,692,471	3,582,191	3,099,656	3,483,017	2,940,196	2,861,371	2,947,883	4,480,761
Stockholders' Equity	1,448,650	1,314,667	1,515,106	1,897,009	1,663,709	1,369,420	1,173,741	1,218,589
Shares Outstanding	165,080	163,475	166,237	173,095	179,601	181,126	217,946	217,946
Statistical Record								
Return on Assets %	9.47	12.50	14.38	13.94	13.13	10.40	5.73	6.60
Return on Equity %	38.61	41.04	41.59	39.09	38.25	34.16	23.51	22.03
EBITDA Margin %	8.59	N.M.	N.M.	33.43	31.64	26.29	22.61	22.82
Net Margin %	N.M.	N.M.	N.M.	16.59	15.35	13.09	9.37	10.27
Asset Turnover	0.70	0.88	0.93	0.84	0.86	0.79	0.61	0.64
Current Ratio	1.06	1.09	1.03	1.20	1.45	1.19	1.14	1.10
Debt to Equity	0.64	0.71	0.36	0.29	0.49	0.63	0.74	0.72
Price Range	60.71-44.77	60.71-44.77	60.71-40.99	60.71-37.01	53.15-30.74	50.78-26.50	27.50-14.28	29.44-19.31
P/E Ratio	19.46-14.35	19.03-14.03	16.96-11.45	15.73-9.59	16.87-9.76	21.98-11.47	18.09-9.40	23.18-15.21
Average Yield %	1.71	1.63	1.63	1.64	1.64	1.63	3.10	2.31

Address: 4400 Main Street, Kansas City, MO 64111 **Telephone:** (816) 753-6900 **Fax:** (816) 932-8390	**Web Site:** www.hrblock.com **Officers:** Mark A. Ernst - Chmn., Pres., C.E.O. Jeffery W. Yabuki - Exec. V.P., C.O.O.	**Auditors:** KPMG LLP **Investor Contact:** 800-869-9220 Ext272 **Transfer Agents:** Mellon Investor Services LLC, Ridgefield Park, NJ

BLOCKBUSTER, INC.

Exchange	Symbol	Price	52Wk Range	Yield	P/E
NYS	BBI	$8.83 (3/31/2005)	17.50-6.78	0.91	N/A

*7 Year Price Score N/A　***NYSE Composite Index=100**　***12 Month Price Score 77.29**

TRADING VOLUME (thousand shares)

Interim Earnings (Per Share)

Qtr.	Mar	Jun	Sep	Dec
2001	0.03	(0.09)	(1.28)	(0.02)
2002	(9.72)	0.23	0.28	0.18
2003	0.45	0.34	0.35	(6.60)
2004	0.62	0.26	(7.82)	0.00

Interim Dividends (Per Share)

Amt	Decl	Ex	Rec	Pay
0.02Q	7/20/2004	8/19/2004	8/23/2004	9/13/2004
5.00Q	8/20/2004	8/25/2004	8/27/2004	9/3/2004
0.02Q	10/22/2004	11/4/2004	11/8/2004	11/29/2004
0.02Q	2/25/2005	3/10/2005	3/14/2005	3/28/2005

Indicated Div: $0.08

Valuation Analysis

Forecast P/E	13.30	No of Institutions
	(4/13/2005)	177
Market Cap	$1.6 Billion	Shares
Book Value	1.1 Billion	127,148,328
Price/Book	1.47	% Held
Price/Sales	0.27	70.20

Business Summary: Movies & Film (MIC: 13.2 SIC: 841 NAIC: 32230)

Blockbuster is a major renter of home videocassettes, DVDs and video games throughout the Americas, Europe, Asia and Australia. As of Dec 31 2003, Co. operated about 8,900 stores in the U.S., its territories and 27 other countries. Approximately 1,091 stores in the U.S. and 671 stores outside of the U.S. were operated by franchisees. Co.'s stores offer a wide selection of pre-recorded videos and DVDs for rent or purchase, along with video games for use with Sony PlayStation, Nintendo and other video game platforms. As of Mar 1 2004, Viacom International Inc. owned 81.5% of Co.'s Class A common stock and all of its Class B common stock.

Recent Developments: For the year ended Dec 31 2004, Co. reported a net loss of $1.25 billion compared with a loss from continuing operations of $974.3 million the year before. Results for 2004 included share-based compensation of $18.3 million versus Nil a year earlier. Results for 2003 excluded an accounting change charge of $4.4 million. Total revenues rose 2.4% to $6.05 billion from $5.91 billion a year earlier. Gross profit was $3.61 billion, or 59.7% of revenues, compared with $3.52 billion, or 59.6% of revenues, in 2003. Operating loss was $1.25 billion compared with a loss of $836.7 million the year before.

Prospects: On Feb 2 2005, Co. announced that it has filed a registration statement with the Securities and Exchange Commission for an exchange offer for all outstanding shares of Hollywood Entertainment Corporation at a value of $14.50 per share, comprised of $11.50 in cash and $3.00 in Blockbuster class A common stock. According to Co., the proposed transaction would be immediately accretive to its earnings per share and cash flow. Meanwhile, Co. expects total revenues for full-year 2005 to rise in the low-single digit range over 2004 as a result of growth in active members and growth in the store base. Co. also expects operating income for the full-year 2005 to be flat.

Financial Data
(US$ in Thousands)

	9 Mos	6 Mos	3 Mos	12/31/2003	12/31/2002	12/31/2001	12/31/2000	12/31/1999
Earnings Per Share	(13.47)	(5.37)	(5.29)	(5.46)	(8.96)	(1.37)	(0.43)	(0.44)
Cash Flow Per Share	6.72	7.11	7.83	7.86	8.13	7.94	7.53	7.32
Tang Book Value Per Share	N.M.	4.04	3.87	3.25	1.45	0.70	1.14	0.85
Dividends Per Share	5.080	0.080	0.080	0.080	0.080	0.080	0.080	0.020
Income Statement								
Total Revenue	4,334,300	2,924,300	1,503,100	5,911,700	5,565,900	5,156,700	4,960,100	4,463,500
EBITDA	(561,500)	690,500	376,300	(820,100)	573,800	20,900	536,500	513,800
Depn & Amortn	726,200	490,300	252,000	25,500	233,800	245,700	459,100	392,300
Income Before Taxes	(1,303,400)	193,000	120,400	(875,600)	294,600	(296,900)	(31,800)	5,400
Income Taxes	(46,400)	33,600	7,800	103,200	103,000	(56,100)	45,400	71,800
Net Income	(1,257,000)	159,400	112,600	(983,900)	(1,627,600)	(240,300)	(75,900)	(69,200)
Average Shares	181,100	181,600	182,000	180,100	181,600	175,600	175,000	156,100
Balance Sheet								
Current Assets	945,800	877,100	877,900	960,300	958,900	716,400	799,500	712,600
Total Assets	3,413,500	4,782,400	4,747,700	4,854,900	6,243,800	7,752,400	8,548,900	8,540,800
Current Liabilities	1,095,000	1,092,800	1,145,300	1,327,800	1,477,600	1,268,800	1,123,200	1,131,400
Long-Term Obligations	1,071,700	73,000	73,300	75,100	408,700	546,400	1,136,500	1,138,400
Total Liabilities	2,325,600	1,377,600	1,385,300	1,605,600	2,076,800	2,003,700	2,540,500	2,415,800
Stockholders' Equity	1,087,900	3,404,800	3,362,400	3,249,300	4,167,000	5,748,700	6,008,400	6,125,000
Shares Outstanding	181,100	181,100	181,100	180,900	176,800	176,800	175,000	175,000
Statistical Record								
EBITDA Margin %	N.M.	23.61	25.03	N.M.	10.31	0.41	10.82	11.51
Net Margin %	N.M.	5.45	7.49	N.M.	N.M.	N.M.	N.M.	N.M.
Asset Turnover	1.25	1.10	1.10	1.07	0.80	0.63	0.58	0.53
Current Ratio	0.86	0.80	0.77	0.72	0.65	0.56	0.71	0.63
Debt to Equity	0.99	0.02	0.02	0.02	0.10	0.10	0.19	0.19
Price Range	22.43-7.27	22.43-14.68	22.43-15.10	22.43-12.25	30.00-12.15	28.12-8.38	14.50-7.06	16.88-11.75
Average Yield %	32.09	0.45	0.44	0.46	0.34	0.43	0.79	0.14

Address: 1201 Elm Street, Dallas, TX 75270	Web Site: www.blockbuster.com	Auditors: PricewaterhouseCoopers LLP
Telephone: (214) 854-3000	Officers: John F. Antioco - Chmn., C.E.O. Larry J. Zine - Exec. V.P., C.F.O., Chief Admin. Officer	Investor Contact: 214-854-3863
Fax: (214) 854-4848		

BLYTH, INC.

Exchange	Symbol	Price	52Wk Range	Yield	P/E
NYS	BTH	$31.84 (3/31/2005)	35.84-27.81	1.32	17.99

*7 Year Price Score 98.32 *NYSE Composite Index=100 *12 Month Price Score 94.28

Interim Earnings (Per Share)

Qtr.	Apr	Jul	Oct	Jan
2001-02	0.33	0.27	0.55	0.29
2002-03	0.28	0.40	0.66	0.50
2003-04	0.42	0.24	0.76	0.45
2004-05	0.38	0.21	0.73	...

Interim Dividends (Per Share)

Amt	Decl	Ex	Rec	Pay
0.15S	9/4/2003	10/29/2003	10/31/2003	11/14/2003
0.17S	3/31/2004	4/28/2004	4/30/2004	5/14/2004
0.19S	9/9/2004	10/28/2004	11/1/2004	11/15/2004
0.21S	3/17/2005	4/27/2005	4/29/2005	5/13/2005

Indicated Div: $0.42

Valuation Analysis

Forecast P/E	13.79
	(4/7/2005)
Market Cap	$1.3 Billion
Book Value	459.4 Million
Price/Book	2.83
Price/Sales	0.83

No of Institutions	150
Shares	24,649,306
% Held	60.26

TRADING VOLUME (thousand shares)

Business Summary: Consumer Accessories (MIC: 4.6 SIC: 999 NAIC: 25998)

Blyth is a home expressions company that participates primarily in the home decor, seasonal decorations and gift industry. Co. designs, markets and distributes an extensive array of candles, home fragrance products, decorative accessories, seasonal decorations and household convenience items, as well as tabletop lighting and chafing fuel for the Away From Home or foodservice trade. Co. manufactures most of its candles and sources nearly all of its other products. Co.'s business segments include Direct Selling, Wholesale Home Fragrance, Wholesale Creative Expressions, and the Catalog & Internet.

Recent Developments: For the third quarter ended Oct 31 2004, net income declined 13.0% to $30.2 million compared with $34.8 million in the corresponding prior-year quarter. Results for 2003 included a restructuring and impairment charge of $767,000. Net sales increased 1.7% to $439.4 million from $431.9 million a year earlier. Gross profit rose 1.9% to $200.7 million from $196.9 million the year before. Operating profit amounted to $51.1 million versus $59.8 million in the previous year, a decrease of 14.6%.

Prospects: Co.'s outlook is mixed. On one hand, Co.'s European operations should continue to experience strong sales growth. However, Co.'s North American businesses will likely continue to face lower consumer and retailer demand. In response, Co. will remain focused on profitable growth through increased sales volume and cost management. For fiscal 2006, Co. expects earnings per share to be $2.35 to $2.40. This guidance assumes low single digit organic growth and takes into account the benefit from the July 2004 Dutch Tender Offer. Cash flow from operations is expected to exceed $130.0 million, with capital spending in the range of $20.0 million to $25.0 million.

Financial Data
(US$ in Thousands)

	9 Mos	6 Mos	3 Mos	01/31/2004	01/31/2003	01/31/2002	01/31/2001	01/31/2000
Earnings Per Share	1.77	1.79	1.83	1.88	1.83	1.44	1.66	1.89
Cash Flow Per Share	3.69	3.34	3.72	3.78	3.70	2.63	2.36	2.46
Tang Book Value Per Share	4.26	4.61	7.64	7.52	8.47	7.59	6.93	5.78
Dividends Per Share	0.360	0.320	0.320	0.280	0.220	0.200	0.200	...
Dividend Payout %	20.40	17.86	17.51	14.89	12.02	13.89	12.05	...
Income Statement								
Total Revenue	1,087,487	648,043	358,980	1,505,573	1,288,583	1,198,542	1,197,197	1,097,450
EBITDA	132,172	72,377	44,177	190,290	187,433	161,939	179,949	190,601
Depn & Amortn	26,080	17,756	9,048	35,954	30,212	36,246	33,383	28,107
Income Before Taxes	89,641	44,363	29,920	136,893	142,557	108,289	130,690	150,390
Income Taxes	32,398	17,243	12,195	50,377	53,032	40,283	49,975	57,543
Net Income	57,363	27,120	17,675	86,351	85,010	68,006	79,562	92,389
Average Shares	41,287	45,502	46,105	46,027	46,515	47,205	47,902	48,818
Balance Sheet								
Current Assets	576,347	497,173	616,193	606,739	472,437	423,872	373,707	321,862
Total Assets	1,128,060	1,021,993	1,143,010	1,127,963	886,658	794,312	763,470	713,096
Current Liabilities	337,977	256,055	211,917	206,199	153,623	138,647	149,294	130,605
Long-Term Obligations	271,158	271,153	275,409	275,743	165,079	160,230	167,316	176,587
Total Liabilities	668,677	586,222	546,261	538,993	347,194	326,249	341,676	332,882
Stockholders' Equity	459,383	435,771	596,749	588,970	539,464	468,063	421,794	380,214
Shares Outstanding	40,901	40,898	45,633	45,630	46,059	46,878	47,074	48,037
Statistical Record								
Return on Assets %	6.75	8.14	8.04	8.57	10.11	8.73	10.75	14.33
Return on Equity %	14.85	16.45	14.68	15.30	16.87	15.28	19.79	26.31
EBITDA Margin %	12.15	11.17	12.31	12.64	14.55	13.51	15.03	17.37
Net Margin %	5.27	4.18	4.92	5.74	6.60	5.67	6.65	8.42
Asset Turnover	1.36	1.55	1.48	1.49	1.53	1.54	1.62	1.70
Current Ratio	1.71	1.94	2.91	2.94	3.08	3.06	2.50	2.46
Debt to Equity	0.59	0.62	0.46	0.47	0.31	0.34	0.40	0.46
Price Range	35.84-27.98	35.84-26.15	34.37-25.79	33.50-23.71	32.51-20.90	25.81-18.40	33.09-21.44	34.56-21.50
P/E Ratio	20.25-15.81	20.02-14.61	18.78-14.09	17.82-12.61	17.77-11.42	17.92-12.78	19.94-12.91	18.29-11.38
Average Yield %	1.12	1.03	1.08	1.00	0.80	0.89	0.76	...

Address: One East Weaver Street, Greenwich, CT 06831-5118 **Telephone:** (203) 661-1926 **Fax:** (203) 661-1969	**Web Site:** www.blyth.com **Officers:** Robert B. Goergen - Chmn., Pres., C.E.O. Robert H. Barghaus - V.P., C.F.O.	**Auditors:** Deloitte & Touche LLP **Investor Contact:** 203-661-1926

BMC SOFTWARE, INC.

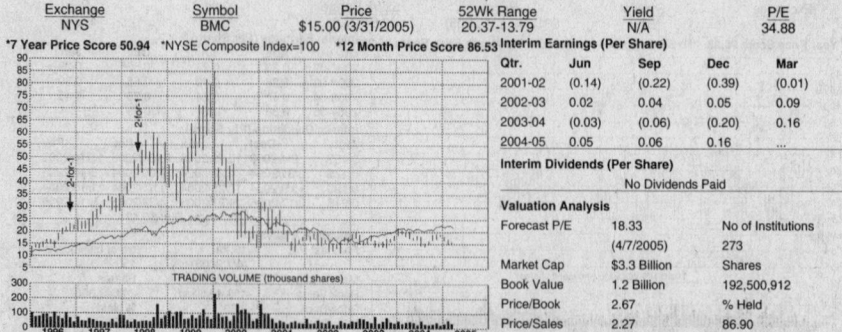

Exchange	Symbol	Price	52Wk Range	Yield	P/E
NYS	BMC	$15.00 (3/31/2005)	20.37-13.79	N/A	34.88

*7 Year Price Score 50.94   *NYSE Composite Index=100   *12 Month Price Score 86.53

Interim Earnings (Per Share)

Qtr.	Jun	Sep	Dec	Mar
2001-02	(0.14)	(0.22)	(0.39)	(0.01)
2002-03	0.02	0.04	0.05	0.09
2003-04	(0.03)	(0.06)	(0.20)	0.16
2004-05	0.05	0.06	0.16	...

Interim Dividends (Per Share)

No Dividends Paid

Valuation Analysis

Forecast P/E	18.33	No of Institutions	
	(4/7/2005)	273	
Market Cap	$3.3 Billion	Shares	
Book Value	1.2 Billion	192,500,912	
Price/Book	2.67	% Held	
Price/Sales	2.27	86.90	

TRADING VOLUME (thousand shares)

Business Summary: IT & Technology (MIC: 10.2 SIC: 372 NAIC: 11210)

BMC Software is an independent systems software vendor. Co. provides software products and services that allow companies to manage their information technology infrastructure from a business perspective. Co.'s portfolio of software spans from enterprise systems, applications, databases and service management. Co.'s software products are designed to help its customers manage their businesses through enterprise management services. As of Mar 31 2004, Co. managed its business through the following four business categories: Enterprise Data Management, Enterprise Systems Management, Remedy and Security and Other Solutions.

Recent Developments: For the quarter ended Dec 31 2004, net income was $36,400 thousand versus net loss of $44,400 thousand in the year-earlier quarter. Revenues were $386,800 thousand, up 3.2% from $374,800 thousand the year before. Operating income was $22,500 thousand versus a loss of $61,400 thousand in the prior-year quarter, a decrease of 136.6%. Total direct expense was $24,900 thousand versus $19,900 thousand in the prior-year quarter, an increase of 25.1%. Total indirect expense was $339,400 thousand versus $416,300 thousand in the prior-year quarter, a decrease of 18.5%.

Prospects: Co. is continuing to see sequential growth in its license bookings with its fiscal third quarter 2005 license booking up approximately 30.0% from the second quarter to $191.1 million. Co. is encouraged by its ability to meet its goals for revenue and earnings per share, as well as its deliverance of strong cash flow from operations. Co.'s Business Service Management strategy is helping customers meet compliance goals, and reduce costs, automate processes and run more efficient information technology organizations. Looking ahead to fiscal 2005, Co. expects revenues to be in the range of $1.48 billion to $1.49 billion and earnings to range from $0.69 to $0.74 per share, before special items.

Financial Data
(US$ in Thousands)

	9 Mos	6 Mos	3 Mos	03/31/2004	03/31/2003	03/31/2002	03/31/2001	03/31/2000
Earnings Per Share	0.43	0.07	(0.05)	(0.12)	0.20	(0.75)	0.17	0.96
Cash Flow Per Share	2.22	1.98	2.08	2.19	2.56	2.13	2.36	1.52
Tang Book Value Per Share	2.58	2.40	3.12	2.49	2.87	4.61	4.69	4.70
Income Statement								
Total Revenue	1,067,900	681,100	326,000	1,418,700	1,326,700	1,288,900	1,504,000	1,719,200
EBITDA	258,400	150,700	79,800	231,100	151,500	84,900	386,600	570,400
Depn & Amortn	159,700	102,500	49,500	259,400	82,200	315,000	314,900	235,600
Income Before Taxes	97,700	48,200	30,300	(29,400)	69,300	(230,500)	60,400	311,400
Income Taxes	37,900	24,800	19,600	(2,600)	21,300	(46,400)	18,000	68,900
Net Income	59,800	23,400	10,700	(26,800)	48,000	(184,100)	42,400	242,500
Average Shares	224,400	223,900	225,100	226,700	237,900	245,000	252,500	253,000
Balance Sheet								
Current Assets	1,225,500	1,075,200	1,386,900	1,424,900	1,098,200	996,800	902,700	896,200
Total Assets	3,153,400	3,002,200	2,933,800	3,044,800	2,845,500	2,676,200	3,033,900	2,962,100
Current Liabilities	1,068,700	973,100	900,000	986,900	838,800	680,600	829,000	883,900
Total Liabilities	1,910,400	1,783,800	1,729,000	1,829,600	1,462,100	1,169,600	1,218,600	1,181,200
Stockholders' Equity	1,243,000	1,218,400	1,204,800	1,215,200	1,383,400	1,506,600	1,815,300	1,780,900
Shares Outstanding	221,530	221,953	223,083	223,300	231,100	241,000	247,300	244,600
Statistical Record								
Return on Assets %	3.24	0.58	N.M.	N.M.	1.74	N.M.	1.41	9.22
Return on Equity %	7.83	1.31	N.M.	N.M.	3.32	N.M.	2.36	15.53
EBITDA Margin %	24.20	22.13	24.48	16.29	11.42	6.59	25.70	33.18
Net Margin %	5.60	3.44	3.28	N.M.	3.62	N.M.	2.82	14.11
Asset Turnover	0.49	0.51	0.50	0.48	0.48	0.45	0.50	0.65
Current Ratio	1.15	1.10	1.54	1.44	1.31	1.46	1.09	1.01
Price Range	21.60-13.79	21.60-13.31	21.60-13.31	21.60-13.31	19.75-11.20	29.10-11.90	49.81-13.63	85.19-30.19
P/E Ratio	50.23-32.07	308.57-190.14	...	...	98.75-56.00	...	293.01-80.15	88.74-31.45

Address: 2101 CityWest Boulevard, Houston, TX 77042-2827	Web Site: www.bmc.com	Auditors: Ernst & Young LLP
Telephone: (713) 918-8800	Officers: B. Garland Cupp - Chmn. Robert E. Beauchamp - Pres., C.E.O.	Investor Contact: 713-918-4233
Fax: (713) 918-8000		

BOEING CO. (THE)

Exchange	Symbol	Price	52Wk Range	Yield	P/E
NYS	BA	$58.46 (3/31/2005)	58.79-40.55	1.71	25.42

*7 Year Price Score 98.58   *NYSE Composite Index=100   *12 Month Price Score 101.27

Interim Earnings (Per Share)

Qtr.	Mar	Jun	Sep	Dec
2001	1.45	0.99	0.80	0.15
2002	(1.54)	0.96	0.46	0.73
2003	(0.60)	(0.24)	0.32	1.41
2004	0.77	0.75	0.56	0.23

Interim Dividends (Per Share)

Amt	Decl	Ex	Rec	Pay
0.20Q	5/3/2004	5/19/2004	5/21/2004	6/11/2004
0.20Q	6/28/2004	8/11/2004	8/13/2004	9/3/2004
0.20Q	10/25/2004	11/9/2004	11/12/2004	12/3/2004
0.25Q	12/13/2004	2/9/2005	2/11/2005	3/4/2005

Indicated Div: $1.00

Valuation Analysis

Forecast P/E	22.52	No of Institutions
	(4/6/2005)	597
Market Cap	$48.6 Billion	Shares
Book Value	11.3 Billion	546,743,168
Price/Book	4.31	% Held
Price/Sales	0.93	65.68

Business Summary: Aviation (MIC: 1.1 SIC: 721 NAIC: 36411)

The Boeing Company is a major aerospace company principally involved in the development, production and marketing of commercial aircraft and providing related support services mainly to commercial customers. Co. is also engaged in the research, development, production, modification and support of the following products and related systems: military aircraft, including fighter, transport and attack aircraft; helicopters; missiles; space systems; missile defense systems; satellites and satellite launching vehicles; rocket engines; and information and battle management systems.

Recent Developments: For the year ended Dec 31 2004, income from continuing operations increased 165.7% to $1,820 million from income of $685 million a year earlier. Net income increased 160.7% to $1,872 million from net income of $718 million a year earlier. Revenues were $52,457 million, up 4.4% from $50,256 million the year before. Operating income was $2,007 million versus an income of $398 million in the prior year, an increase of 404.3%. Total direct expense was $45,025 million versus $44,150 million in the prior year, an increase of 2.0%. Total indirect expense was $5,516 million versus $5,736 million in the prior year, a decrease of 3.8%.

Prospects: Defense and intelligence markets are expected to remain strong in 2005 and 2006; however, conditions in the commercial space market are expected to remain challenging. Global commercial airplane markets are improving with higher deliveries forecast for 2006 and further delivery recovery expected in 2007. Co. is targeting commercial airplane deliveries of 320 in 2005, rising to between 375 and 385 in 2006. For 2005, Co. expects revenues of about $58.00 billion and earnings of between $2.40 and $2.60 per share. Looking ahead, Co. anticipates revenue in the range of $62.00 billion to $63.00 billion in 2006, along with earnings of between $3.00 and $3.20 per share.

Financial Data (US$ in Thousands)	12/31/2004	12/31/2003	12/31/2002	12/31/2001	12/31/2000	12/31/1999	12/31/1998	12/31/1997
Earnings Per Share	2.30	0.89	0.61	3.41	2.44	2.49	1.15	(0.18)
Cash Flow Per Share	4.27	4.82	5.44	4.67	6.89	6.79	2.45	10.56
Tang Book Value Per Share	10.07	6.17	4.53	5.23	6.63	10.15	10.25	10.56
Dividends Per Share	0.770	0.680	0.680	0.680	0.560	0.560	0.560	0.560
Dividend Payout %	33.48	76.40	111.48	19.94	22.95	22.49	48.70	...
Income Statement								
Total Revenue	52,457,000	50,485,000	54,069,000	58,198,000	51,321,000	57,993,000	56,154,000	45,800,000
EBITDA	3,420,000	2,007,000	5,092,000	5,636,000	4,736,000	5,192,000	3,341,000	1,542,000
Depn & Amortn	1,125,000	1,099,000	1,182,000	1,422,000	1,292,000	1,437,000	1,491,000	1,370,000
Income Before Taxes	1,960,000	550,000	3,180,000	3,564,000	2,999,000	3,324,000	1,397,000	(341,000)
Income Taxes	140,000	(168,000)	861,000	738,000	871,000	1,015,000	277,000	(163,000)
Net Income	1,872,000	718,000	492,000	2,827,000	2,128,000	2,309,000	1,120,000	(178,000)
Average Shares	813,000	808,900	808,400	829,300	871,300	925,900	976,700	970,100
Balance Sheet								
Current Assets	15,100,000	17,258,000	16,855,000	16,206,000	15,864,000	15,712,000	16,375,000	19,263,000
Total Assets	53,963,000	53,035,000	52,342,000	48,343,000	42,028,000	36,147,000	36,672,000	38,024,000
Current Liabilities	20,835,000	18,448,000	19,810,000	20,486,000	18,289,000	13,656,000	13,422,000	14,152,000
Long-Term Obligations	10,879,000	13,299,000	12,589,000	10,866,000	7,567,000	5,980,000	6,103,000	6,123,000
Total Liabilities	42,677,000	44,896,000	44,646,000	37,518,000	31,008,000	24,685,000	24,356,000	25,071,000
Stockholders' Equity	11,286,000	8,139,000	7,696,000	10,825,000	11,020,000	11,462,000	12,316,000	12,953,000
Shares Outstanding	832,183	841,482	840,035	837,580	875,484	909,513	976,000	1,000,000
Statistical Record								
Return on Assets %	3.49	1.36	0.98	6.26	5.43	6.34	3.00	N.M.
Return on Equity %	19.22	9.07	5.31	25.88	18.88	19.42	8.86	N.M.
EBITDA Margin %	6.52	3.98	9.42	9.68	9.23	8.95	5.95	3.37
Net Margin %	3.57	1.42	0.91	4.86	4.15	3.98	1.99	N.M.
Asset Turnover	0.98	0.96	1.07	1.29	1.31	1.59	1.50	1.40
Current Ratio	0.72	0.94	0.85	0.79	0.87	1.15	1.22	1.36
Debt to Equity	0.96	1.63	1.64	1.00	0.69	0.52	0.50	0.47
Price Range	55.26-38.68	42.28-25.06	50.88-28.98	68.79-29.76	69.94-32.38	47.63-32.63	56.06-30.88	60.00-43.00
P/E Ratio	24.03-16.82	47.51-28.16	83.41-47.51	20.17-8.73	28.66-13.27	19.13-13.10	48.75-26.85	...
Average Yield %	1.62	2.04	1.71	1.31	1.16	1.37	1.29	1.06

Address: 100 North Riverside, Chicago, IL 60606-1596	Web Site: www.boeing.com	Auditors: Deloitte & Touche LLP
Telephone: (312) 544-2000	Officers: James A. Bell - Interim Pres., C.E.O., Exec. V.P., C.F.O. Laurette T. Koellner - Exec. V.P., Chief People & Admin. Officer	Investor Contact: 312-5442835
Fax: (206) 655-3987		Transfer Agents: EquiServe, Providence, RI

BORDERS GROUP, INC.

Exchange	Symbol	Price	52Wk Range	Yield	P/E
NYS	BGP	$26.62 (3/31/2005)	27.47-21.42	1.35	N/A

*7 Year Price Score 105.65 *NYSE Composite Index=100 *12 Month Price Score 101.51

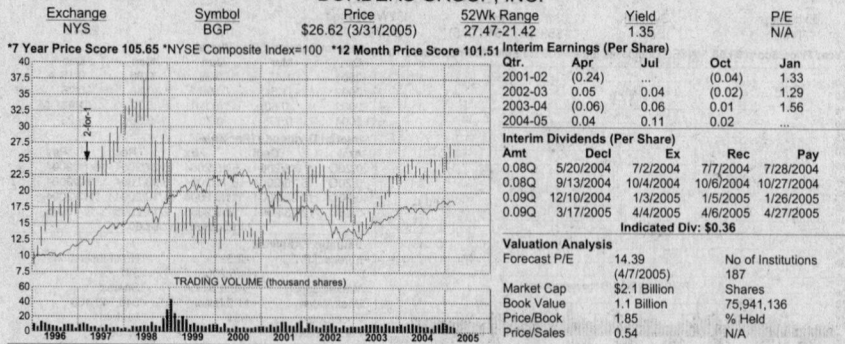

Interim Earnings (Per Share)

Qtr.	Apr	Jul	Oct	Jan
2001-02	(0.24)	...	(0.04)	1.33
2002-03	0.05	0.04	(0.02)	1.29
2003-04	(0.06)	0.06	0.01	1.56
2004-05	0.04	0.11	0.02	...

Interim Dividends (Per Share)

Amt	Decl	Ex	Rec	Pay
0.08Q	5/20/2004	7/2/2004	7/7/2004	7/28/2004
0.08Q	9/13/2004	10/4/2004	10/6/2004	10/27/2004
0.09Q	12/10/2004	1/3/2005	1/5/2005	1/26/2005
0.09Q	3/17/2005	4/4/2005	4/6/2005	4/27/2005

Indicated Div: $0.36

Valuation Analysis

Forecast P/E	14.39 (4/7/2005)	No of Institutions 187
Market Cap	$2.1 Billion	Shares 75,941,136
Book Value	1.1 Billion	% Held
Price/Book	1.85	
Price/Sales	0.54	N/A

Business Summary: Retail - Miscellaneous (MIC: 5.11 SIC: 942 NAIC: 51211)

Borders Group is the second largest operator of book, music and movie superstores and the largest operator of mall-based bookstores, based on both sales and number of stores. As of Jan 25 2004, Co. operated 445 superstores under the Borders name in the U.S. and 37 international stores in the United Kingdom, Australia, Puerto Rico, New Zealand and Singapore. Co. also operated 716 mall-based and other bookstores primarily under the Waldenbooks name in the U.S., and 36 bookstores under the Books etc. name in the United Kingdom, primarily in central London or in various airports.

Recent Developments: For the quarter ended Oct 24 2004, Co. reported a net loss of $1.5 million compared with net income of $0.5 million in the equivalent prior-year quarter. Revenues were $838.6 million, up 2.6% from $817.1 million the year before. Co. reported an operating loss of $0.3 million versus operating income of $3.0 million in the prior-year quarter. Total direct expense was $626.2 million, up 2.5% from $611.0 million in the prior-year quarter. Total indirect expense was $212.7 million versus $203.1 million in the prior-year quarter, an increase of 4.7%.

Prospects: Co.'s strategy for 2005 calls for continued growth and investment in the core Borders domestic superstore business through new and remodeled stores. In addition, Co. will focus on continued growth in sales and profitability within the International segment and ongoing initiatives to improve results in the Waldenbooks segment. Books will continue to highlight Co.'s customer offering and it expects to see strong results in other categories through the initial stages of cafe conversion to Seattle's Best Coffee and the addition of Paperchase gifts and stationery shops in Borders stores. Looking ahead to fiscal year 2005, Co. expects earnings to range from $1.85 to 1.92 per share.

Financial Data

(US$ in Thousands)	3 Mos	01/25/2004	01/26/2003	01/27/2002	01/28/2001	01/23/2000	01/24/1999	01/25/1998
Earnings Per Share	1.64	1.54	1.36	1.06	0.54	1.13	1.12	0.98
Cash Flow Per Share	2.83	2.89	2.36	3.29	1.74	2.24	2.17	1.94
Tang Book Value Per Share	13.09	13.40	11.86	10.61	9.58	8.76	7.84	6.48
Dividends Per Share	0.160	0.080	...	...	...	...	...	...
Dividend Payout %	9.76	5.19	...	...	...	...	...	...
Income Statement								
Total Revenue	838,100	3,731,000	3,513,000	3,387,900	3,271,200	2,999,200	2,595,000	2,266,000
EBITDA	30,900	309,700	291,000	253,200	230,400	250,900	234,000	192,800
Depn & Amortn	24,200	104,100	97,100	96,200	95,300	84,700	66,700	54,800
Income Before Taxes	4,800	196,900	181,300	142,600	122,000	148,300	151,100	130,800
Income Taxes	1,800	74,800	69,600	55,200	48,200	58,000	59,000	50,600
Net Income	3,000	120,000	111,700	87,400	43,600	90,300	92,100	80,200
Average Shares	79,800	77,900	82,033	82,724	80,288	80,218	82,503	82,241
Balance Sheet								
Current Assets	1,601,700	1,712,700	1,541,300	1,442,100	1,335,100	1,198,200	1,133,300	1,018,400
Total Assets	2,303,500	2,466,200	2,268,200	2,179,300	2,047,100	1,914,800	1,766,600	1,534,900
Current Liabilities	1,029,300	1,164,100	1,087,600	1,106,700	1,117,900	1,027,900	988,800	881,400
Long-Term Obligations	56,200	57,200	69,000	49,700	15,000	16,200	6,300	5,200
Total Liabilities	1,181,000	1,311,500	1,237,600	1,229,400	1,200,600	1,112,200	1,051,500	936,800
Stockholders' Equity	1,120,800	1,153,000	1,030,600	949,900	846,500	802,600	715,100	598,100
Shares Outstanding	77,762	78,273	78,731	81,202	78,649	77,687	77,695	75,395
Statistical Record								
Return on Assets %	5.73	5.08	5.04	4.15	2.17	4.92	5.59	5.86
Return on Equity %	11.97	11.02	11.31	9.76	5.20	11.93	14.07	14.50
EBITDA Margin %	3.69	8.30	8.28	7.47	7.04	8.37	9.02	8.51
Net Margin %	0.36	3.22	3.18	2.58	1.33	3.01	3.55	3.54
Asset Turnover	1.71	1.58	1.58	1.61	1.62	1.63	1.58	1.65
Current Ratio	1.56	1.47	1.42	1.30	1.19	1.17	1.15	1.16
Debt to Equity	0.05	0.05	0.07	0.05	0.02	0.02	0.01	0.01
Price Range	25.21-15.50	22.98-13.60	24.40-14.90	24.06-13.26	18.50-11.19	20.25-11.88	39.94-18.31	31.94-18.31
P/E Ratio	15.37-9.45	14.92-8.83	17.94-10.96	22.70-12.51	34.26-20.72	17.92-10.51	35.66-16.35	32.59-18.69
Average Yield %	0.78	0.44	...	...	...	...	...	...

Address: 100 Phoenix Drive, Ann Arbor, MI 48108-2202 Telephone: (734) 477-1100 Fax: (734) 477-4538	Web Site: www.bordersgroupinc.com Officers: Gregory P. Josefowicz - Chmn., Pres., C.E.O. Michael G. Spinozzi - Exec. V.P., Chief Mktg. Off.	Auditors: ERNST & YOUNG LLP

BORG WARNER INC

Exchange	Symbol	Price	52Wk Range	Yield	P/E
NYS	BWA	$48.68 (3/31/2005)	54.30-38.45	1.15	12.61

*7 Year Price Score 139.14 *NYSE Composite Index=100 *12 Month Price Score 103.49

Interim Earnings (Per Share)

Qtr.	Mar	Jun	Sep	Dec
2001	0.40	0.47	0.35	0.04
2002	(4.45)	0.85	0.59	0.76
2003	0.82	0.83	0.65	0.90
2004	0.91	0.97	0.79	1.19

Interim Dividends (Per Share)

Amt	Decl	Ex	Rec	Pay
0.125Q	4/21/2004	4/29/2004	5/3/2004	5/17/2004
0.125Q	7/21/2004	7/29/2004	8/2/2004	8/16/2004
0.125Q	10/20/2004	10/28/2004	11/1/2004	11/15/2004
0.14Q	11/10/2004	1/28/2005	2/1/2005	2/15/2005

Indicated Div: $0.56

Valuation Analysis

Forecast P/E	11.15	No of Institutions
	(4/7/2005)	217
Market Cap	$2.7 Billion	Shares
Book Value	1.5 Billion	49,227,064
Price/Book	1.79	% Held
Price/Sales	0.78	87.17

Business Summary: Automotive (MIC: 15.1 SIC: 714 NAIC: 36312)

BorgWarner is a supplier of engineered systems and components, primarily for automotive powertrain applications. The Engine group develops products to manage engines for fuel efficiency, reduced emissions and enhanced performance. Products include chain and chain systems, turbochargers, and emissions and thermal systems. The Drivetrain group develops transmission components and systems and torque management applications and systems. Torque management products include four-wheel drive and all-wheel drive transfer cases and systems to transfer torque with the drivetrain. Co. sells primarily to original equipment manufacturers of passenger cars, sport utility vehicles and light trucks.

Recent Developments: For the year ended Dec 31 2004, net income increased 24.8% to $218,300 thousand from net income of $174,900 thousand a year earlier. Revenues were $3,525,300 thousand, up 14.9% from $3,069,200 thousand the year before. Operating income was $309,100 thousand versus an income of $269,900 thousand in the prior year, an increase of 14.5%. Total direct expense was $2,874,200 thousand versus $2,482,500 thousand in the prior year, an increase of 15.8%. Total indirect expense was $342,700 thousand versus $317,600 thousand in the prior year, an increase of 7.9%.

Prospects: Looking ahead, Co. anticipates fuel-efficient engine and drivetrain technology to drive new business with the most rapid expansion through automakers. Meanwhile, Co. expects sales growth in the 8.0% to 10.0% range on its base business in 2005. Moreover, Co. expects 2005 earnings per share in a range of $4.30 to $4.55, which includes assumptions about Co.'s acquisition of Beru AG in a range of $0.15 to $0.30 per share, and expectations of $4.15 to $4.25 per share on its base business as a comparison to 2004 expectations. Co.'s acquisition of Beru AG, a supplier of ignition and sensor technology, will be consolidated within the BorgWarner Engine Group, beginning in the first quarter of 2005.

Financial Data

(US$ in Thousands)	12/31/2004	12/31/2003	12/31/2002	12/31/2001	12/31/2000	12/31/1999	12/31/1998	12/31/1997
Earnings Per Share	3.86	3.20	(2.22)	1.25	1.77	2.54	2.00	2.15
Cash Flow Per Share	7.61	5.67	4.91	3.72	5.71	6.64	2.82	3.53
Tang Book Value Per Share	11.95	7.40	2.90	N.M.	N.M.	N.M.	4.64	3.15
Dividends Per Share	0.500	0.360	0.300	0.300	0.300	0.300	0.300	0.300
Dividend Payout %	12.95	11.25	...	23.90	16.95	11.83	15.00	13.92
Income Statement								
Total Revenue	3,525,300	3,069,200	2,731,100	2,351,600	2,645,900	2,458,600	1,836,800	1,767,000
EBITDA	478,200	415,600	380,700	300,100	356,900	379,600	259,200	269,600
Depn & Amortn	139,900	125,600	109,200	146,200	145,500	123,400	91,600	87,100
Income Before Taxes	308,600	256,700	233,800	106,100	148,800	207,000	140,700	157,900
Income Taxes	81,200	73,200	77,200	39,700	54,800	74,700	46,000	54,700
Net Income	218,300	174,900	(119,100)	66,400	94,000	132,300	94,700	103,200
Average Shares	56,537	54,604	53,708	52,926	52,974	52,156	47,352	47,868
Balance Sheet								
Current Assets	1,074,300	824,600	566,500	441,300	410,600	558,300	376,100	306,900
Total Assets	3,529,100	3,038,900	2,682,900	2,770,900	2,765,900	2,970,700	1,846,100	1,736,300
Current Liabilities	663,800	470,300	451,200	455,000	529,900	659,800	454,100	395,200
Long-Term Obligations	568,000	634,000	632,300	701,400	740,400	846,300	248,500	270,400
Total Liabilities	1,972,500	1,761,300	1,687,000	1,655,300	1,668,500	1,904,400	1,060,300	1,021,900
Stockholders' Equity	1,534,200	1,260,400	981,400	1,104,200	1,087,100	1,057,500	777,300	693,700
Shares Outstanding	56,357	55,157	53,160	52,730	52,450	53,448	46,774	47,086
Statistical Record								
Return on Assets %	6.63	6.11	N.M.	2.40	3.27	5.49	5.29	6.14
Return on Equity %	15.58	15.60	N.M.	6.06	8.74	14.42	12.88	15.61
EBITDA Margin %	13.56	13.54	13.94	12.76	13.49	15.44	14.11	15.26
Net Margin %	6.19	5.70	N.M.	2.82	3.55	5.38	5.16	5.84
Asset Turnover	1.07	1.07	1.00	0.85	0.92	1.02	1.03	1.05
Current Ratio	1.62	1.75	1.26	0.97	0.77	0.85	0.83	0.78
Debt to Equity	0.37	0.50	0.64	0.64	0.68	0.80	0.32	0.39
Price Range	54.17-38.45	42.66-22.04	34.25-19.71	27.25-18.25	22.06-15.03	29.88-18.47	34.06-16.66	30.44-19.19
P/E Ratio	14.03-9.96	13.33-6.89	...	21.80-14.60	12.46-8.49	11.76-7.27	17.03-8.33	14.16-8.92
Average Yield %	1.11		1.08	1.32	1.65	1.25	1.17	1.23

Address: 3850 Hamlin Road, Auburn Hills, MI 48326	Web Site: www.bwauto.com	Auditors: Deloitte & Touche LLP
Telephone: (248) 754-9200	Officers: Timothy M. Manganello - Chmn., C.E.O. Robin J. Adams - Exec. V.P., C.F.O., Chief Admin. Officer	Investor Contact: 312-322-8683 Transfer Agents: Mellon Investor Services L.L.C., Ridgefield Park, NJ

BOSTON PROPERTIES, INC.

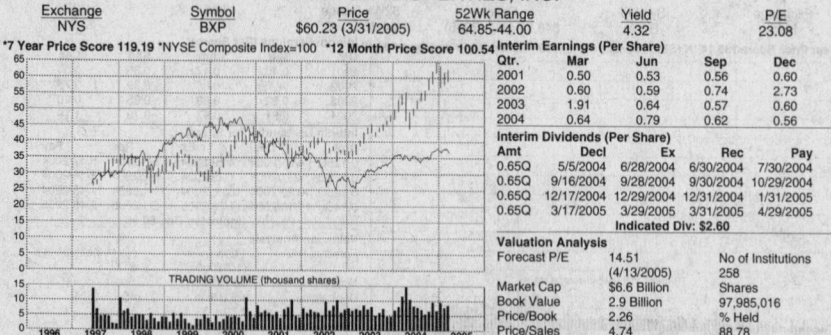

Exchange	Symbol	Price	52Wk Range	Yield	P/E
NYS	BXP	$60.23 (3/31/2005)	64.85-44.00	4.32	23.08

*7 Year Price Score 119.19 *NYSE Composite Index=100 *12 Month Price Score 100.54

Interim Earnings (Per Share)

Qtr.	Mar	Jun	Sep	Dec
2001	0.50	0.53	0.56	0.60
2002	0.60	0.59	0.74	2.73
2003	1.91	0.64	0.57	0.60
2004	0.64	0.79	0.62	0.56

Interim Dividends (Per Share)

Amt	Decl	Ex	Rec	Pay
0.65Q	5/5/2004	6/28/2004	6/30/2004	7/30/2004
0.65Q	9/16/2004	9/28/2004	9/30/2004	10/29/2004
0.65Q	12/17/2004	12/29/2004	12/31/2004	1/31/2005
0.65Q	3/17/2005	3/29/2005	3/31/2005	4/29/2005

Indicated Div: $2.60

Valuation Analysis

Forecast P/E	14.51	No of Institutions
	(4/13/2005)	258
Market Cap	$6.6 Billion	Shares
Book Value	2.9 Billion	97,985,016
Price/Book	2.26	% Held
Price/Sales	4.74	88.78

Business Summary: Property, Real Estate & Development (MIC: 8.3 SIC: 552 NAIC: 37210)

Boston Properties owns and develops office properties in the U.S. Co.'s properties are concentrated in four core markets: Boston, MA, Washington, D.C., midtown Manhattan and San Francisco, CA. As of Dec 31 2003, Co. owned or had interests in 140 properties totaling about 43.9 million net rentable square feet. Co.'s properties consisted of 131 office properties comprised of 103 Class A office properties (including three properties under construction) and 28 office/technical properties; four industrial properties; three hotels, and two retail properties. Co also owns or controls 43 parcels of land totaling 551.3 acres and structured parking for 31,098 vehicles.

Recent Developments: For the year ended Dec 31 2004, income from continuing operations increased 8.3% to $247,290 thousand from income of $228,412 thousand a year earlier. Net income decreased 22.3% to $284,017 thousand from net income of $365,322 thousand a year earlier. Revenues were $1,400,465 thousand, up 7.8% from $1,299,709 thousand the year before. Funds from Operations (FFO) for the year ended Dec 31 2004 were $459,500 thousand compared with FFO for the year ended Dec 31 2003 of $412,100 thousand, before the application of SFAS No. 133, Accounting for Derivative Instruments and Hedging Activities, as amended.

Prospects: For the first quarter of 2005, Co. is projecting diluted earnings per share (EPS) to be in the range of $0.49 to $0.51, with funds from operations of between $0.95 and $0.97 per share. For the first quarter, Co. is expecting its share of real estate depreciation and amortization to be approximately $0.46 per share. Looking ahead, for full-year 2005, Co. is forecasting diluted EPS of between $2.25 and $2.40, with funds from operations of between $4.10 and $4.25 per share. For the full year, Co. is projecting its share of real estate depreciation and amortization to be approximately $1.85 per share.

Financial Data

(US$ in Thousands)	12/31/2004	12/31/2003	12/31/2002	12/31/2001	12/31/2000	12/31/1999	12/31/1998	12/31/1997
Earnings Per Share	2.61	3.71	4.66	2.19	2.01	1.71	1.52	0.90
Cash Flow Per Share	4.02	5.04	4.70	4.66	4.74	4.58	3.54	...
Tang Book Value Per Share	26.61	24.43	22.65	19.32	19.02	15.57	14.93	4.52
Dividends Per Share	2.580	2.500	2.410	2.270	2.040	1.750	1.660	0.845
Dividend Payout %	98.85	67.39	51.72	103.65	101.49	102.34	109.21	93.89
Income Statement								
Property Income	1,293,292	1,219,165	1,173,785	1,007,610	858,942	765,417	487,577	139,641
Non-Property Income	107,173	90,463	61,038	25,368	20,411	21,147	26,270	6,002
Total Revenue	1,400,465	1,309,628	1,234,823	1,032,978	879,353	786,564	513,847	145,643
Depn & Amortn	252,941	210,477	186,429	150,163	133,150	120,059	75,418	21,719
Interest Expense	306,170	299,436	271,685	223,389	...	...	...	38,264
Net Income	284,017	365,322	444,383	208,032	152,998	119,776	93,112	35,151
Average Shares	108,762	98,486	94,612	92,200	72,741	66,776	61,308	39,108
Balance Sheet								
Total Assets	9,063,228	8,551,100	8,427,203	7,253,510	6,226,470	5,434,772	5,235,087	1,672,521
Long-Term Obligations	5,011,814	5,004,720	5,147,220	4,314,942	3,414,891	3,321,584	3,088,724	1,332,253
Total Liabilities	5,340,827	5,320,804	5,423,032	4,554,697	3,601,028	3,495,246	3,207,372	1,396,837
Stockholders' Equity	2,936,073	2,400,163	2,159,590	1,754,073	1,647,727	1,057,564	948,481	175,048
Shares Outstanding	110,320	98,230	95,362	90,780	86,630	67,910	63,528	38,694
Statistical Record								
Return on Assets %	3.22	4.30	5.67	3.09	2.62	2.25	2.70	...
Return on Equity %	10.62	16.02	22.71	12.23	11.28	11.94	16.57	...
Net Margin %	20.28	27.90	35.99	20.14	17.40	15.23	18.12	24.14
Price Range	64.85-44.00	48.34-34.99	41.55-33.93	43.31-34.33	44.75-29.81	37.13-27.50	35.94-23.88	34.38-26.06
P/E Ratio	24.85-16.86	13.03-9.43	8.92-7.28	19.78-15.68	22.26-14.83	21.71-16.08	23.64-15.71	38.19-28.96
Average Yield %	4.84	5.97	6.33	5.82	5.48	5.37	5.14	2.75

Address: 111 Huntington Avenue, Boston, MA 02199 **Telephone:** (617) 236 3300 **Fax:** (617) 536 3128	**Web Site:** www.bostonproperties.com **Officers:** Mortimer B. Zuckerman - Chmn. Edward H. Linde - Pres., C.E.O.	**Auditors:** PricewaterhouseCoopers LLP

BOSTON SCIENTIFIC CORP.

Exchange	Symbol	Price	52Wk Range	Yield	P/E
NYS	BSX	$29.29 (3/31/2005)	45.81-28.67	N/A	23.62

*7 Year Price Score 162.17 **NYSE Composite Index=100* ***12 Month Price Score 80.73**

Interim Earnings (Per Share)

Qtr.	Mar	Jun	Sep	Dec
2001	(0.01)	(0.22)	0.07	0.09
2002	0.10	0.03	0.20	0.13
2003	0.12	0.13	0.15	0.16
2004	0.23	0.36	0.30	0.35

Interim Dividends (Per Share)

No Dividends Paid

Valuation Analysis

Forecast P/E	14.62	No of Institutions
	(4/7/2005)	535
Market Cap	$24.5 Billion	Shares
Book Value	4.0 Billion	468,159,296
Price/Book	6.08	% Held
Price/Sales	4.35	55.82

Business Summary: Medical Instruments & Equipment (MIC: 9.6 SIC: 841 NAIC: 39112)

Boston Scientific is a developer, manufacturer and marketer of medical devices used in a broad range of interventional medical specialties, including cardiology, peripheral, neurovascular, electrophysiology, vascular surgery, endoscopy, oncology, urology and gynecology. Co.'s products are generally inserted into the human body through natural openings or small incisions in the skin and can be guided to most areas of the anatomy to diagnose and treat a wide range of medical problems. These less invasive procedures are designed to provide effect alternatives to traditional surgery by reducing procedural trauma, complexity, cost and recovery time.

Recent Developments: For the year ended Dec 31 2004, net income increased 125.0% to $1,062,000 thousand from net income of $472,000 thousand a year earlier. Revenues were $5,624,000 thousand, up 61.8% from $3,476,000 thousand the year before. Operating income was $1,574,000 thousand versus an income of $697,000 thousand in the prior year, an increase of 125.8%. Total direct expense was $1,292,000 thousand versus $961,000 thousand in the prior year, an increase of 34.4%. Total indirect expense was $2,758,000 thousand versus $1,818,000 thousand in the prior year, an increase of 51.7%.

Prospects: Co. continues to enjoy favorable results, supported by the strong market acceptance of its TAXUS® Express2™ paclitaxel-eluting coronary stent system. Also, Co. is benefiting from solid foreign currency fluctuations, which positively affected top-line growth by $155.0 million for the year ended Dec 31 2004. Separately, on Mar 4 2005, Co. announced that it has completed its acquisition of Advanced Stent Technologies, Inc. (AST), for an initial payment of $120.0 million payable in Co.'s stock, plus the possibility of future contingent payments. AST is a developer of stent and stent delivery systems designed to address anatomical needs of coronary artery disease in bifurcated vessels.

Financial Data

(US$ in Thousands)	12/31/2004	12/31/2003	12/31/2002	12/31/2001	12/31/2000	12/31/1999	12/31/1998	12/31/1997
Earnings Per Share	1.24	0.56	0.45	(0.07)	0.46	0.46	(0.34)	0.17
Cash Flow Per Share	2.15	0.96	0.90	0.61	0.91	0.90	0.33	0.10
Tang Book Value Per Share	0.82	0.49	0.12	N.M.	0.33	N.M.	N.M.	0.87
Income Statement								
Total Revenue	5,624,000	3,476,000	2,919,000	2,673,000	2,664,000	2,842,000	2,233,576	1,872,282
EBITDA	1,833,000	885,000	753,000	335,000	778,000	858,000	(79,136)	359,645
Depn & Amortn	275,000	196,000	161,000	232,000	181,000	178,000	128,605	86,692
Income Before Taxes	1,494,000	643,000	549,000	44,000	527,000	562,000	(275,314)	258,668
Income Taxes	432,000	171,000	176,000	98,000	154,000	191,000	(10,945)	98,254
Net Income	1,062,000	472,000	373,000	(54,000)	373,000	371,000	(264,369)	139,334
Average Shares	857,700	845,400	829,980	802,778	816,644	822,702	781,672	799,552
Balance Sheet								
Current Assets	3,289,000	1,880,000	1,208,000	1,106,000	992,000	1,055,000	1,266,627	1,064,021
Total Assets	8,170,000	5,699,000	4,450,000	3,974,000	3,427,000	3,572,000	3,892,711	1,967,807
Current Liabilities	2,605,000	1,393,000	923,000	831,000	819,000	1,055,000	1,619,658	808,011
Long-Term Obligations	1,139,000	1,172,000	847,000	973,000	574,000	678,000	1,363,822	46,235
Total Liabilities	4,145,000	2,837,000	1,983,000	1,959,000	1,492,000	1,848,000	3,071,574	981,575
Stockholders' Equity	4,025,000	2,862,000	2,467,000	2,015,000	1,935,000	1,724,000	821,137	986,232
Shares Outstanding	835,343	826,261	822,783	810,507	799,695	818,098	788,372	775,244
Statistical Record								
Return on Assets %	15.27	9.30	8.86	N.M.	10.63	9.94	N.M.	8.01
Return on Equity %	30.76	17.71	16.64	N.M.	20.33	29.15	N.M.	14.65
EBITDA Margin %	32.59	25.46	25.80	12.53	29.20	30.19	N.M.	19.21
Net Margin %	18.88	13.58	12.78	N.M.	14.00	13.05	N.M.	7.44
Asset Turnover	0.81	0.68	0.69	0.72	0.76	0.76	0.76	1.08
Current Ratio	1.26	1.35	1.31	1.33	1.21	1.00	0.78	1.32
Debt to Equity	0.28	0.41	0.34	0.48	0.30	0.39	1.66	0.05
Price Range	45.81-32.12	36.76-19.84	22.11-10.56	13.84-6.75	14.16-6.13	23.25-8.91	20.28-10.59	19.25-10.39
P/E Ratio	36.94-25.90	65.64-35.42	49.12-23.46	...	30.77-13.32	50.54-19.36	...	113.24-61.12

Address: One Boston Scientific Place, Natick, MA 01760-1537	Web Site: www.bsci.com	Auditors: Ernst & Young LLP
Telephone: (508) 650-8000	Officers: Peter M. Nicholas - Chmn. James R. Tobin - Pres., C.E.O.	
Fax: (508) 647-2200		

BOWATER INC.

Exchange	Symbol	Price	52Wk Range	Yield	P/E
NYS	BOW	$37.67 (3/31/2005)	45.99-34.79	2.12	N/A

*7 Year Price Score 74.71 ***NYSE Composite Index=100** ***12 Month Price Score 92.29**

Interim Earnings (Per Share)

Qtr.	Mar	Jun	Sep	Dec
2001	0.72	0.36	(0.04)	0.32
2002	0.22	(0.95)	(0.57)	(1.17)
2003	(1.26)	(0.45)	(1.00)	(0.89)
2004	(0.57)	(0.02)	(0.32)	(0.61)

Interim Dividends (Per Share)

Amt	Decl	Ex	Rec	Pay
0.20Q	5/12/2004	6/8/2004	6/10/2004	7/1/2004
0.20Q	7/28/2004	9/8/2004	9/10/2004	10/1/2004
0.20Q	11/10/2004	12/8/2004	12/10/2004	1/3/2005
0.20Q	1/26/2005	3/8/2005	3/10/2005	4/1/2005

Indicated Div: $0.80

Valuation Analysis

Forecast P/E	28.53	No of Institutions
	(4/7/2005)	175
Market Cap	$2.1 Billion	Shares
Book Value	1.5 Billion	61,107,812
Price/Book	1.40	% Held
Price/Sales	0.66	N/A

Business Summary: Paper Products (MIC: 11.11 SIC: 621 NAIC: 22122)

Bowater is engaged in the manufacture, sale and distribution of newsprint, uncoated specialty paper, coated groundwood paper, market pulp, lumber and timber. Co. operates facilities in the U.S., Canada and South Korea and, as of Dec 31 2004, Co.'s operations were supported by 1.4 million acres of timberlands owned or leased in the U.S. and Canada and 29.6 million acres of timber cutting rights on Crown-owned lands in Canada. Co. markets and distributes its products throughout the world. Co. operates through five divisions: the Newsprint Division, the Coated and Specialty Papers Division, the Pulp Division, the Forest Products Division and the Canadian Forest Products Division.

Recent Developments: For the year ended Dec 31 2004, net loss was $87,100 thousand versus net loss of $205,000 thousand a year earlier. Revenues were $3,190,300 thousand, up 17.2% from $2,721,100 thousand the year before. Operating income was $29,500 thousand versus a loss of $100,900 thousand in the prior year. Total direct expense was $2,346,400 thousand versus $2,194,000 thousand in the prior year, an increase of 6.9%. Total indirect expense was $814,400 thousand versus $628,000 thousand in the prior year, an increase of 29.7%.

Prospects: Top-line growth is being driven by improved pricing across all of Co.'s major product lines including newsprint, coated and specialty papers, partially offset by lower pulp and lumber prices. However, results are being negatively affected by sharply higher production costs stemming from a rise in the Canadian dollar, increased maintenance spending and higher energy and chemical costs. In addition, production of market pulp and newsprint is being hampered by downtime due to maintenance outages, capital projects, and other market-related reasons. Looking ahead, Co. anticipates further price increases and a strong rebound in earnings in 2005.

Financial Data
(US$$ in Thousands)

	12/31/2004	12/31/2003	12/31/2002	12/31/2001	12/31/2000	12/31/1999	12/31/1998	12/31/1997
Earnings Per Share	(1.52)	(3.60)	(2.50)	1.37	3.02	1.41	(0.44)	1.25
Cash Flow Per Share	2.14	0.36	0.72	7.03	7.94	2.71	5.76	4.86
Tang Book Value Per Share	12.16	14.15	16.56	21.60	18.50	14.80	15.98	27.89
Dividends Per Share	0.800	0.800	0.800	0.800	0.800	0.800	0.800	0.800
Dividend Payout %	...	...	...	58.39	26.49	56.74	...	64.00
Income Statement								
Total Revenue	3,190,300	2,721,100	2,581,100	2,449,200	2,500,300	2,134,700	1,995,000	1,484,503
EBITDA	378,800	230,300	248,200	647,100	654,000	575,000	327,300	305,220
Depn & Amortn	336,100	341,300	340,500	321,300	295,200	300,200	229,600	169,824
Income Before Taxes	(148,400)	(280,900)	(250,800)	193,500	239,200	155,800	16,800	89,483
Income Taxes	(54,800)	(70,100)	(100,500)	78,700	70,300	71,500	27,100	33,109
Net Income	(87,100)	(205,000)	(142,400)	73,200	159,400	78,700	(18,500)	53,691
Average Shares	57,200	57,000	56,900	53,300	52,800	55,000	47,600	40,812
Balance Sheet								
Current Assets	902,700	843,000	735,200	689,600	615,600	532,500	695,400	718,375
Total Assets	5,458,900	5,615,800	5,590,300	5,765,400	5,004,100	4,552,200	5,091,400	2,745,798
Current Liabilities	556,600	659,700	756,400	863,500	951,400	397,800	772,500	194,651
Long-Term Obligations	2,427,900	2,292,400	2,037,400	1,828,000	1,304,700	1,454,600	1,534,600	757,100
Total Liabilities	3,951,600	4,003,100	3,834,800	3,740,700	3,207,000	2,781,400	3,314,400	1,591,633
Stockholders' Equity	1,507,300	1,612,700	1,755,500	2,024,700	1,797,100	1,770,800	1,777,000	1,154,165
Shares Outstanding	55,830	55,437	55,279	54,704	50,277	60,828	51,936	40,474
Statistical Record								
Return on Assets %	N.M.	N.M.	N.M.	1.36	3.33	1.63	N.M.	1.91
Return on Equity %	N.M.	N.M.	N.M.	3.83	8.91	4.44	N.M.	4.62
EBITDA Margin %	11.87	8.46	9.62	26.42	26.16	26.94	16.41	20.56
Net Margin %	N.M.	N.M.	N.M.	2.99	6.38	3.69	N.M.	3.62
Asset Turnover	0.57	0.49	0.45	0.45	0.52	0.44	0.51	0.53
Current Ratio	1.62	1.28	0.97	0.80	0.65	1.34	0.90	3.69
Debt to Equity	1.61	1.42	1.16	0.90	0.73	0.82	0.86	0.66
Price Range	47.78-34.79	46.83-34.81	54.37-31.84	57.13-41.50	59.00-42.06	59.94-37.13	59.56-32.81	55.63-37.00
P/E Ratio	...	...	...	41.70-30.29	19.54-13.93	42.51-26.33	...	44.50-29.60
Average Yield %	1.96	1.97	1.78	1.68	1.58	1.63	1.73	1.74

Address: 55 East Camperdown Way, P.O. Box 1028, Greenville, SC 29602-1028 Telephone: (864) 271-7733 Fax: (864) 282-9482	Web Site: www.bowater.com Officers: Arnold M. Nemirow - Chmn., Pres., C.E.O. David G. Maffucci - Exec. V.P., Pres. Newsprint Division	Auditors: KPMG LLP

BOYD GAMING CORP.

Exchange	Symbol	Price	52Wk Range	Yield	P/E
NYS	BYD	$52.15 (3/31/2005)	57.50-21.79	0.65	36.73

*7 Year Price Score 233.16 *NYSE Composite Index=100 *12 Month Price Score 140.16

Interim Earnings (Per Share)

Qtr.	Mar	Jun	Sep	Dec
2001	0.10	0.14	0.07	0.10
2002	0.12	0.26	0.17	0.06
2003	0.25	0.07	0.12	0.19
2004	0.20	0.23	0.40	0.55

Interim Dividends (Per Share)

Amt	Decl	Ex	Rec	Pay
0.075Q	5/3/2004	5/12/2004	5/14/2004	6/1/2004
0.085Q	7/19/2004	8/11/2004	8/13/2004	9/1/2004
0.085Q	10/25/2004	11/9/2004	11/12/2004	12/1/2004
0.085Q	1/25/2005	2/9/2005	2/11/2005	3/1/2005
		Indicated Div: $0.34		

Valuation Analysis

Forecast P/E	26.60	No of Institutions
	(4/7/2005)	150
Market Cap	$4.6 Billion	Shares
Book Value	943.8 Million	30,896,226
Price/Book	4.84	% Held
Price/Sales	2.63	35.21

Business Summary: Sporting & Recreational (MIC: 13.5 SIC: 999 NAIC: 13210)

Boyd Gaming is a multi-jurisdictional gaming company that owns and operates twelve casino entertainment facilities located in five states. Co. operations include seven properties in or near Las Vegas, NV, including Stardust Resort and Casino, Sam's Town Hotel and Gambling Hall, Eldorado Casino, Jokers Wild Casino, California Hotel and Casino, Fremont Hotel and Casino, and Main Street Station Casino, Brewery and Hotel. Co. also owns and operates Sam's Town Hotel and Gambling Hall in Tunica County, MS, Par-A-Dice Hotel and Casino in East Peoria, IL, Treasure Chest Casino in New Orleans, LA, Blue Chip Casino in Michigan City, IN and Delta Downs Racetrack and Casino in Vinton, LA.

Recent Developments: For the year ended Dec 31 2004, net income increased 172.3% to $111,454 thousand from net income of $40,933 thousand a year earlier. Revenues were $1,734,058 thousand, up 38.4% from $1,253,070 thousand the year before. Operating income was $295,958 thousand versus an income of $148,800 thousand in the prior year, an increase of 98.9%. Total direct expense was $1,011,244 thousand versus $757,843 thousand in the prior year, an increase of 33.4%. Total indirect expense was $504,821 thousand versus $344,517 thousand in the prior year, an increase of 46.5%.

Prospects: Going forward, Co.'s long-term outlook appears solid. Trends in Las Vegas, NV continue to be robust, supported by growing demand and limited supply growth. Co. expects to increase its Las Vegas market share with the addition in 2005 of South Coast, which will serve the southern part of the metropolitan area. Meanwhile, Co. noted that construction has begun on the public space expansion in its Borgata Hotel Casino and Spa in Atlantic City, NJ, with completion scheduled for the second quarter of 2006. Co. added that the rooms expansion project is moving forward, with construction expected to commence in the fourth quarter 2005 and completion scheduled for the fourth quarter 2007.

Financial Data

(US$ in Thousands)	12/31/2004	12/31/2003	12/31/2002	12/31/2001	12/31/2000	12/31/1999	12/31/1998	12/31/1997
Earnings Per Share	1.42	0.62	0.61	0.40	1.01	0.62	0.46	0.08
Cash Flow Per Share	3.51	2.69	2.78	2.54	3.42	2.54	1.97	0.62
Tang Book Value Per Share	4.70	N.M.	N.M.	N.M.	N.M.	N.M.	0.40	N.M.
Dividends Per Share	0.320	0.150	...	...	...	...	...	...
Dividend Payout %	22.54	24.19	...	...	...	...	...	...
Income Statement								
Total Revenue	1,734,058	1,253,070	1,228,901	1,102,335	1,153,896	987,041	975,096	455,771
EBITDA	425,066	234,270	239,497	215,694	270,033	210,729	197,095	93,243
Depn & Amortn	136,126	94,224	90,077	99,811	90,480	74,118	73,407	35,097
Income Before Taxes	187,099	65,815	76,964	41,932	102,057	67,634	49,891	20,836
Income Taxes	75,645	24,882	28,740	16,982	39,292	27,595	21,291	8,736
Net Income	111,454	40,933	40,012	24,950	62,765	38,301	28,600	4,860
Average Shares	78,235	66,163	66,125	62,360	62,278	62,293	61,850	61,786
Balance Sheet								
Current Assets	262,055	159,631	263,940	130,888	128,571	142,619	141,745	124,699
Total Assets	3,919,032	1,872,997	1,912,990	1,754,913	1,577,614	1,443,981	1,146,256	1,152,415
Current Liabilities	322,304	200,301	177,536	167,083	157,017	136,930	117,653	112,342
Long-Term Obligations	2,304,343	1,097,589	1,227,324	1,143,358	1,016,813	982,149	774,890	842,932
Total Liabilities	2,975,262	1,431,744	1,504,429	1,401,176	1,247,836	1,177,002	918,950	955,274
Stockholders' Equity	943,770	441,253	408,561	353,737	329,778	266,979	227,306	197,141
Shares Outstanding	87,537	64,980	64,761	62,363	62,234	62,227	62,028	61,670
Statistical Record								
Return on Assets %	3.84	2.16	2.18	1.50	4.14	2.96	2.49	0.31
Return on Equity %	16.05	9.63	10.50	7.30	20.98	15.50	13.48	1.50
EBITDA Margin %	24.51	18.70	19.49	19.57	23.40	21.35	20.21	20.46
Net Margin %	6.43	3.27	3.26	2.26	5.44	3.88	2.93	1.07
Asset Turnover	0.60	0.66	0.67	0.66	0.76	0.76	0.85	0.29
Current Ratio	0.81	0.80	1.49	0.78	0.82	1.04	1.20	1.11
Debt to Equity	2.44	2.49	3.00	3.23	3.08	3.68	3.41	4.28
Price Range	42.26-15.75	18.30-11.42	18.67-6.48	6.50-3.26	6.00-3.31	7.06-3.13	8.19-2.69	9.00-5.06
P/E Ratio	29.76-11.09	29.52-18.42	30.61-10.62	16.25-8.15	5.94-3.28	11.39-5.04	17.80-5.84	112.50-63.28
Average Yield %	1.22	1.01	...	...	...	...	...	...

Address: 2950 Industrial Road, Las Vegas, NV 89109 **Telephone:** (702) 792-7200 **Fax:** (702) 792-7266	Web Site: www.boydgaming.com Officers: William S. Boyd - Chmn., C.E.O. Marianne Boyd Johnson - Vice-Chmn., Sr. V.P.	Auditors: Deloitte & Touche LLP Investor Contact: 702-792-7210

BRADY CORP.

*7 Year Price Score 129.08 *NYSE Composite Index=100 ***12 Month Price Score 117.11**

Interim Earnings (Per Share)

Qtr.	Oct	Jan	Apr	Jul
2001-02	0.17	0.13	0.18	0.70
2002-03	0.17	0.06	0.19	0.48
2003-04	0.22	0.17	0.34	1.39
2004-05	0.41	0.41	...	...

Interim Dividends (Per Share)

Amt	Decl	Ex	Rec	Pay
0.11Q	9/15/2004	10/6/2004	10/11/2004	11/1/2004
100%	11/18/2004	1/3/2005	12/10/2004	12/31/2004
0.11Q	11/18/2004	1/6/2005	1/10/2005	1/31/2005
0.11Q	2/15/2005	4/6/2005	4/8/2005	5/2/2005

Indicated Div: $0.44 (Div. Reinv. Plan)

Valuation Analysis

Forecast P/E	19.41	No of Institutions
	(4/7/2005)	126
Market Cap	$1.6 Billion	Shares
Book Value	459.4 Million	52,013,040
Price/Book	3.46	% Held
Price/Sales	2.09	N/A

Business Summary: Consumer Accessories (MIC: 4.6 SIC: 993 NAIC: 39950)

Brady is an international manufacturer and marketer of identification products and specialty materials. Co.'s products include labels and signs, printing systems and software, label-application and data-collection systems, safety devices and precision die-cut materials. Co.'s major products include identification applications and specialty tape products, including wire and cable markers, high-performance labels, laboratory identification products, stand-alone printing systems, bar-code and other software, graphics and workplace applications. Co. serves customers in electronics, telecommunications, manufacturing, electrical, construction, education and other industries.

Recent Developments: For the quarter ended Jan 31 2005, net income increased 156.2% to $20,579 thousand from net income of $8,033 thousand in the year-earlier quarter. Revenues were $196,216 thousand, up 28.3% from $152,948 thousand the year before. Operating income was $30,934 thousand an income of $11,643 thousand in the prior-year quarter, an increase of 165.7%. Total direct expense was $91,260 thousand versus $75,138 thousand in the prior-year quarter, an increase of 21.5%. Total indirect expense was $74,022 thousand versus $66,167 thousand in the prior-year quarter, an increase of 11.9%.

Prospects: Co. is seeing considerable strength in its end markets with all of its businesses and regions contributing to both sales and profitability. In addition, recent acquisitions continue meet or exceed expectations according to Co. As a result of improving profitability, Co. anticipates sales of $790.0 million to $810.0 million, with net income between $78.0 million and $80.0 million and earnings per share of $1.55 to $1.60 for fiscal 2005. This is up from Co.'s previous 2005 guidance of sales of $780.0 million to $800.0 million, net income of $66.0 million to $69.0 million and earnings per share of $1.35 to $1.41.

Financial Data

(US$ in Thousands)	6 Mos	3 Mos	07/31/2004	07/31/2003	07/31/2002	07/31/2001	07/31/2000	07/31/1999
Earnings Per Share	2.55	2.31	2.12	0.90	1.19	1.17	2.04	1.72
Cash Flow Per Share	2.20	1.92	0.89	0.60	0.59	0.58	0.53	0.68
Tang Book Value Per Share	1.92	1.37	1.69	4.47	4.61	4.44	4.13	4.09
Dividends Per Share	0.430	0.425	0.420	0.400	0.380	0.360	0.340	0.320
Dividend Payout %	16.89	18.41	19.86	44.69	32.07	30.90	16.71	18.66
Income Statement								
Total Revenue	396,635	200,419	671,219	554,866	516,962	545,944	541,077	470,862
EBITDA	76,756	38,851	91,748	50,347	59,847	67,854	94,542	80,376
Depn & Amortn	13,253	6,775	20,190	17,771	16,630	22,646	17,833	15,149
Income Before Taxes	59,327	29,937	70,327	32,455	43,135	44,790	76,131	64,782
Income Taxes	18,391	9,580	19,456	11,035	14,882	17,244	28,930	25,198
Net Income	40,936	20,357	50,871	21,420	28,253	27,546	47,201	39,584
Average Shares	49,988	49,230	95,624	93,508	93,358	92,428	91,732	90,731
Balance Sheet								
Current Assets	273,549	248,902	251,923	215,157	210,026	194,993	203,183	203,169
Total Assets	761,440	735,149	694,330	449,519	420,525	392,476	398,134	351,120
Current Liabilities	117,514	120,241	120,217	91,279	74,262	71,163	87,099	73,285
Long-Term Obligations	150,000	150,000	150,019	568	3,751	4,144	4,157	1,402
Total Liabilities	302,083	303,547	291,015	110,558	96,283	89,897	106,910	90,556
Stockholders' Equity	459,357	431,602	403,315	338,961	324,242	302,579	291,224	260,564
Shares Outstanding	49,129	48,651	48,160	46,618	46,242	45,828	45,462	45,209
Statistical Record								
Return on Assets %	11.74	10.10	8.87	4.92	6.95	6.97	12.57	11.94
Return on Equity %	17.75	15.49	13.67	6.46	9.01	9.28	17.06	16.03
EBITDA Margin %	19.35	19.38	13.67	9.07	11.58	12.43	17.47	17.07
Net Margin %	10.32	10.16	7.58	3.86	5.47	5.05	8.72	8.41
Asset Turnover	1.22	1.19	1.17	1.28	1.27	1.38	1.44	1.42
Current Ratio	2.33	2.07	2.10	2.36	2.83	2.74	2.33	2.77
Debt to Equity	0.33	0.35	0.37	N.M.	0.01	0.01	0.01	0.01
Price Range	32.13-17.45	27.49-17.30	23.10-15.90	17.70-12.89	20.30-13.65	19.47-13.88	17.91-12.38	17.50-8.19
P/E Ratio	12.60-6.84	11.90-7.49	10.90-7.50	19.67-14.32	17.06-11.47	16.64-11.86	8.78-6.07	10.17-4.76
Average Yield %	1.84	2.04	2.18	2.53	2.23	2.23	2.24	2.62

Address: 6555 West Good Hope Road, Milwaukee, WI 53223	Web Site: www.bradycorp.com	Auditors: Deloitte & Touche LLP
Telephone: (414) 358-6600	Officers: Frank M. Jaehnert - Pres., C.E.O. David R. Hawke - Exec. V.P.	Investor Contact: 414-438-6940
Fax: (414) 438-6910		Transfer Agents: Wells Fargo Bank Minnesota, N.A., St. Paul, MN

BRE PROPERTIES, INC.

Exchange	Symbol	Price	52Wk Range	Yield	P/E
NYS	BRE	$35.30 (3/31/2005)	42.31-30.75	5.67	29.17

*7 Year Price Score 106.64 *NYSE Composite Index=100 *12 Month Price Score 94.56

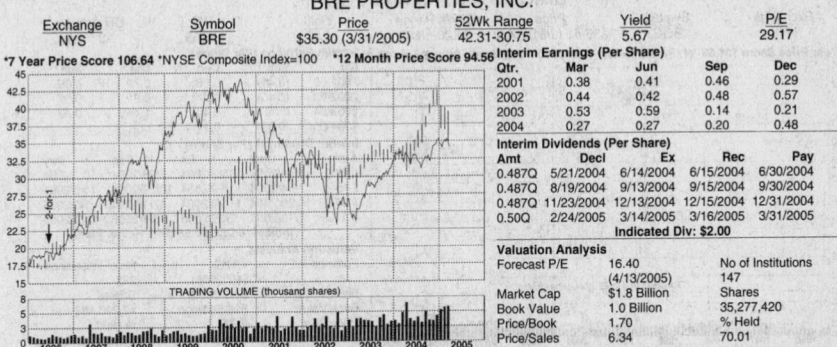

Interim Earnings (Per Share)

Qtr.	Mar	Jun	Sep	Dec
2001	0.38	0.41	0.46	0.29
2002	0.44	0.42	0.48	0.57
2003	0.53	0.59	0.14	0.21
2004	0.27	0.27	0.20	0.48

Interim Dividends (Per Share)

Amt	Decl	Ex	Rec	Pay
0.487Q	5/21/2004	6/14/2004	6/15/2004	6/30/2004
0.487Q	8/19/2004	9/13/2004	9/15/2004	9/30/2004
0.487Q	11/23/2004	12/13/2004	12/15/2004	12/31/2004
0.50Q	2/24/2005	3/14/2005	3/16/2005	3/31/2005
		Indicated Div: $2.00		

Valuation Analysis

Forecast P/E	16.40	No of Institutions	
	(4/13/2005)	147	
Market Cap	$1.8 Billion	Shares	
Book Value	1.0 Billion	35,277,420	
Price/Book	1.70	% Held	
Price/Sales	6.34	70.01	

Business Summary: Property, Real Estate & Development (MIC: 8.3 SIC: 798 NAIC: 25930)

BRE Properties-a real estate investment trust-develops, acquires and manages apartment communities convenient to its Residents' work, shopping, entertainment and transit in supply-constrained Western U.S. markets. BRE directly owns and operates 85 apartment communities totaling 23,685 units in California, Arizona, Washington, Utah and Colorado. As of Dec 31 2003, the Company has seven other properties in various stages of development and construction, totaling 1,660 units, and joint venture interests in two additional apartment communities, totaling 488 units.

Recent Developments: For the year ended Dec 31 2004, income from continuing operations decreased 11.4% to $45,304 thousand from income of $51,145 thousand a year earlier. Net income decreased 11.4% to $73,541 thousand from net income of $82,970 thousand a year earlier. Revenues were $280,642 thousand, up 9.5% from $256,230 thousand the year before. At Dec 31 2004, same-store average occupancy was 94.7% compared with 94.2% in the year-ago period. Funds from operation (FFO) for the year ended Dec 31 2004 amounted to $108,642 thousand compared with $103,690 thousand for the year ended Dec 31 2003.

Prospects: Co. believes funds from operations (FFO) per share results for 2005 will be affected by regional and national economic conditions, which may not generate material job growth during the year. Co. also noted that its operating results in 2005 will be affected by the level and timing of property acquisitions and dispositions, the delivery of apartment communities under construction, expense associated with litigation proceedings, costs related to the adoption of legislative and regulatory mandates, and the level, timing and costs associated with external capital formation. Thus, Co. estimates FFO for year 2005 will range from $2.17 to $2.27 per share, and earnings per share from $1.13 to $1.26.

Financial Data
(US$ in Thousands)

	12/31/2004	12/31/2003	12/31/2002	12/31/2001	12/31/2000	12/31/1999	12/31/1998	12/31/1997
Earnings Per Share	1.21	1.48	1.91	1.69	0.81	1.55	1.41	2.11
Cash Flow Per Share	2.71	2.42	2.99	2.97	2.72	2.54	2.26	1.79
Tang Book Value Per Share	20.76	16.64	15.75	15.96	16.28	17.27	17.30	16.95
Dividends Per Share	1.950	1.950	1.950	1.860	1.700	1.560	1.440	1.380
Dividend Payout %	161.16	131.76	102.09	110.06	209.88	100.65	102.13	65.40
Income Statement								
Property Income	267,997	260,660	255,814	243,538	235,723	234,253	203,245	128,678
Non-Property Income	12,645	14,483	16,003	20,138	17,754	...	...	9,083
Total Revenue	280,642	275,143	271,817	263,676	253,477	234,253	203,245	137,761
Depn & Amortn	64,212	53,352	47,535	40,328	37,425	35,524	27,763	17,938
Interest Expense	66,826	59,617	56,106	48,517	45,028	41,695	35,598	21,606
Net Income	73,541	83,128	95,809	83,377	41,303	73,216	60,644	76,197
Average Shares	50,825	47,445	47,770	48,510	48,270	47,760	46,110	36,610
Balance Sheet								
Total Assets	2,518,941	2,227,965	2,108,713	1,875,981	1,718,129	1,709,453	1,630,916	1,341,898
Long-Term Obligations	1,378,566	1,192,329	1,173,764	1,008,431	825,253	779,403	752,146	541,367
Total Liabilities	1,436,619	1,228,562	1,212,382	1,038,934	847,301	796,615	778,479	558,337
Stockholders' Equity	1,046,647	960,544	851,184	784,896	801,116	825,198	765,005	707,495
Shares Outstanding	50,418	49,992	45,870	45,807	45,895	44,679	44,221	41,740
Statistical Record								
Return on Assets %	3.09	3.83	4.81	4.64	2.40	4.38	4.08	7.17
Return on Equity %	7.31	9.18	11.71	10.51	5.07	9.21	8.24	13.01
Net Margin %	26.20	30.21	35.25	31.62	16.29	31.26	29.84	55.31
Price Range	42.31-30.75	34.84-28.34	34.25-27.38	32.90-26.75	33.63-21.38	25.78-20.53	27.92-21.38	29.02-22.97
P/E Ratio	34.97-25.41	23.54-19.15	17.93-14.34	19.47-15.83	41.51-26.40	16.63-13.24	19.80-15.16	13.75-10.89
Average Yield %	5.43	6.07	6.32	6.26	6.06	6.61	5.72	5.43

Address: 44 Montgomery Street, 36th Floor, San Francisco, CA 94104-4809 Telephone: (415) 445-6530 Fax: (415) 445-6505	Web Site: www.breproperties.com Officers: Frank C. McDowell - Vice-Chmn., C.E.O. Constance B. Moore - Pres., C.O.O.	Auditors: ERNST & YOUNG LLP

BRIGGS & STRATTON CORP.

Exchange	Symbol	Price	52Wk Range	Yield	P/E	Div Acheiver
NYS	BGG	$36.41 (3/31/2005)	44.20-33.59	1.87	15.56	13 Years

*7 Year Price Score 131.63 *NYSE Composite Index=100 *12 Month Price Score 92.82

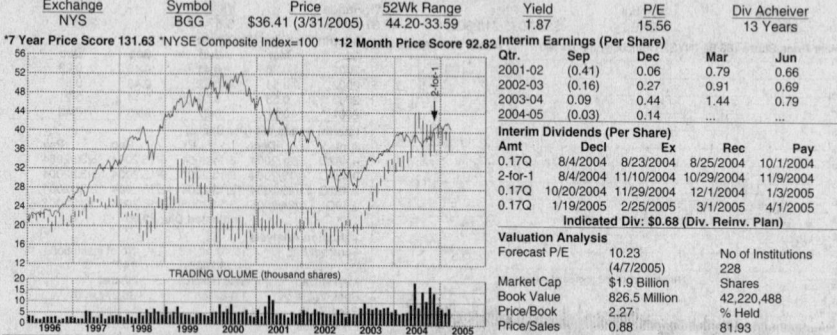

Interim Earnings (Per Share)

Qtr.	Sep	Dec	Mar	Jun
2001-02	(0.41)	0.06	0.79	0.66
2002-03	(0.16)	0.27	0.91	0.69
2003-04	0.09	0.44	1.44	0.79
2004-05	(0.03)	0.14	...	...

Interim Dividends (Per Share)

Amt	Decl	Ex	Rec	Pay
0.17Q	8/4/2004	8/23/2004	8/25/2004	10/1/2004
2-for-1	8/4/2004	11/10/2004	10/29/2004	11/9/2004
0.17Q	10/20/2004	11/29/2004	12/1/2004	1/3/2005
0.17Q	1/19/2005	2/25/2005	3/1/2005	4/1/2005

Indicated Div: $0.68 (Div. Reinv. Plan)

Valuation Analysis

Forecast P/E	10.23	No of Institutions
	(4/7/2005)	228
Market Cap	$1.9 Billion	Shares
Book Value	826.5 Million	42,220,488
Price/Book	2.27	% Held
Price/Sales	0.88	81.93

Business Summary: Industrial Machinery and Equipment (MIC: 11.5 SIC: 519 NAIC: 33618)

Briggs & Stratton is a producer of air cooled gasoline engines for outdoor power equipment. Co. designs, manufactures, markets and services these products for original equipment manufacturers (OEMs) worldwide. These engines are primarily aluminum alloy gasoline engines ranging from 3 to 31 horsepower. Co.'s engines are marketed under various brand names including Classic™, Sprint™, Quattro™, Quantum®, INTEK™, I/C®, Industrial Plus™ and Vanguard™. Additionally, through its wholly owned subsidiary, Briggs & Stratton Power Products Group, LLC, Co. designs, manufactures and markets portable generators, pressure washers and related accessories.

Recent Developments: For the quarter ended Dec 26 2004, net income decreased 65.8% to $7,060 thousand from net income of $20,635 thousand in the year-earlier quarter. Revenues were $503,700 thousand, up 21.1% from $415,984 thousand the year before. Operating income was $13,484 thousand versus an income of $38,676 thousand in the prior-year quarter, a decrease of 65.1%. Total direct expense was $397,558 thousand versus $325,138 thousand in the prior-year quarter, an increase of 22.3%. Total indirect expense was $92,658 thousand versus $52,170 thousand in the prior-year quarter, an increase of 77.6%.

Prospects: For the third quarter of fiscal 2005, Co. is targeting year-over-year sales growth of approximately 30.0%, along with net income growth in the range of 13.0% to 15.0%. Meanwhile, Co. expects to record an extraordinary gain of between $20.0 million and $30.0 million in the second half of fiscal 2005 related to its $125.0 million offer to buy the North American operations of Murray Inc. Co. also expects fiscal-2005 net income will be lowered by $3.0 million to $5.0 million as Co. absorbs some of Murray's operating losses. As a result, Co. is projecting full fiscal-2005 net income of between $143.0 million and $160.0 million.

Financial Data

(US$ in Thousands)	6 Mos	3 Mos	06/27/2004	06/29/2003	06/30/2002	07/01/2001	07/02/2000	06/27/1999
Earnings Per Share	2.34	2.64	2.77	1.75	1.18	1.11	2.98	2.26
Cash Flow Per Share	0.18	0.77	1.01	3.88	4.63	1.58	1.67	2.45
Tang Book Value Per Share	9.30	9.29	13.03	8.15	6.67	5.77	9.26	7.72
Dividends Per Share	0.670	0.665	0.660	0.640	0.630	0.620	0.600	0.580
Dividend Payout %	28.57	25.23	23.87	36.68	53.39	56.11	20.10	25.66
Income Statement								
Total Revenue	942,695	438,995	1,947,364	1,657,633	1,529,372	1,312,446	1,590,557	1,501,726
EBITDA	61,193	23,677	306,597	219,993	188,722	160,180	287,671	234,406
Depn & Amortn	35,837	17,886	66,898	63,526	65,968	59,711	51,370	49,604
Income Before Taxes	8,442	(2,328)	205,004	118,578	80,510	71,873	216,623	169,771
Income Taxes	2,870	(840)	68,890	37,940	27,390	23,860	80,150	63,670
Net Income	5,572	(1,488)	136,114	80,638	53,120	48,013	136,473	106,101
Average Shares	51,751	51,191	50,680	48,960	48,904	43,932	45,684	46,918
Balance Sheet								
Current Assets	1,018,395	838,394	981,993	807,147	669,944	613,430	471,997	459,146
Total Assets	1,933,897	1,748,350	1,637,153	1,475,193	1,349,033	1,296,195	930,245	875,885
Current Liabilities	510,367	328,961	300,561	301,395	266,023	242,182	312,778	282,502
Long-Term Obligations	360,941	360,752	360,562	503,397	499,022	508,134	98,512	113,307
Total Liabilities	1,107,431	922,660	819,558	960,206	899,387	873,443	520,780	509,975
Stockholders' Equity	826,466	825,690	817,595	514,987	449,646	422,752	409,465	365,910
Shares Outstanding	51,618	51,615	51,090	43,570	43,278	43,198	43,492	46,400
Statistical Record								
Return on Assets %	6.78	8.16	8.77	5.73	4.03	4.32	14.87	12.75
Return on Equity %	17.05	19.27	20.48	16.76	12.21	11.57	34.63	31.18
EBITDA Margin %	6.49	5.39	15.74	13.27	12.34	12.20	18.09	15.61
Net Margin %	0.59	N.M.	6.99	4.86	3.47	3.66	8.58	7.07
Asset Turnover	1.24	1.29	1.25	1.18	1.16	1.18	1.73	1.80
Current Ratio	2.00	2.55	3.27	2.68	2.52	2.53	1.51	1.63
Debt to Equity	0.44	0.44	0.44	0.98	1.11	1.20	0.24	0.31
Price Range	44.20-31.68	44.20-29.36	43.70-25.25	25.40-15.59	24.06-15.12	24.00-15.44	31.50-15.66	34.13-16.88
P/E Ratio	18.89-13.54	16.74-11.12	15.78-9.12	14.51-8.91	20.39-12.81	21.62-13.91	10.57-5.25	15.10-7.47
Average Yield %	1.79	1.85	2.01	3.16	3.12	3.10	2.44	2.35

Address: 12301 West Wirth Street, Wauwatosa, WI 53222	**Web Site:** www.briggsandstratton.com	**Auditors:** Deloitte & Touche LLP
Telephone: (414) 259-5333	**Officers:** John S. Shiely - Chmn., Pres., C.E.O. James E. Brenn - Sr. V.P., C.F.O.	**Investor Contact:** 414-259-5333
Fax: (414) 259-9594		**Transfer Agents:** National City Bank, Cleveland, OH

BRINKER INTERNATIONAL, INC.

Exchange	Symbol	Price	52Wk Range	Yield	P/E
NYS	EAT	$36.22 (3/31/2005)	39.52-29.49	N/A	28.52

*7 Year Price Score 115.16 *NYSE Composite Index=100 *12 Month Price Score 99.67

Interim Earnings (Per Share)

Qtr.	Sep	Dec	Mar	Jun
2001-02	0.39	0.35	0.34	0.44
2002-03	0.45	0.38	0.47	0.40
2003-04	0.45	0.45	0.01	0.66
2004-05	0.16	0.44	...	...

Interim Dividends (Per Share)

Amt	Decl	Ex	Rec	Pay
50%	12/8/2000	1/17/2001	1/3/2001	1/16/2001

Valuation Analysis

Forecast P/E	14.97	No of Institutions
	(4/7/2005)	234
Market Cap	$3.2 Billion	Shares
Book Value	925.7 Million	81,494,952
Price/Book	3.40	% Held
Price/Sales	0.84	92.34

Business Summary: Hospitality & Tourism (MIC: 5.1 SIC: 812 NAIC: 22110)

Brinker International operates and develops full-service restaurants. As of June 30 2004, Co. owned, operated or franchised 1,476 restaurants under the names Chili's Grill & Bar, Romano's Macaroni Grill, On The Border Mexican Grill & Cantina, Maggiano's Little Italy, Corner Bakery Cafe, Big Bowl Asian Kitchen, and Rockfish Seafood Grill. These restaurants range in price from casual to upscale and appeal to a variety of consumers with the different themes and menus. At June 30, 2004, Co.'s system of company-operated, jointly-developed an franchised units included 1,476 restaurants located in forty-nine states and throughout the world.

Recent Developments: For the quarter ended Dec 29 2004, net income decreased 4.5% to $41,403 thousand from net income of $43,359 thousand in the year-earlier quarter. Revenues were $950,793 thousand, up 7.3% from $886,490 thousand the year before. Operating income was $52,432 thousand versus an income of $68,005 thousand in the prior-year quarter, a decrease of 22.9%. Total direct expense was $805,134 thousand versus $736,459 thousand in the prior-year quarter, an increase of 9.3%. Total indirect expense was $93,227 thousand versus $82,026 thousand in the prior-year quarter, an increase of 13.7%.

Prospects: Top-line growth is being fueled primarily by new restaurant development and increases in comparable-store sales across all segments. For the third quarter of fiscal 2005, Co. anticipates revenue growth of between 6.0% and 8.0%. In addition, Co. is projecting earnings in the third quarter of between $0.63 and $0.65 per diluted share. Looking ahead, Co. is forecasting full-year fiscal 2005 earnings per diluted share in the range of $2.12 to $2.18, excluding one-time charges and gains. These estimates are based on comparable-store growth in the range of 1.0% to 3.0%.

Financial Data
(US$ in Thousands)

	6 Mos	3 Mos	06/30/2004	06/25/2003	06/26/2002	06/27/2001	06/28/2000	06/30/1999
Earnings Per Share	1.27	1.25	1.57	1.70	1.52	1.42	1.17	0.77
Cash Flow Per Share	4.92	4.77	4.93	4.64	4.00	2.50	2.74	1.92
Tang Book Value Per Share	9.08	7.73	9.58	9.76	8.04	7.66	6.99	5.94
Income Statement								
Total Revenue	1,861,271	910,478	3,707,486	3,285,394	2,887,111	2,473,656	2,159,837	1,870,554
EBITDA	162,233	64,206	434,301	435,910	383,530	331,906	285,059	222,165
Depn & Amortn	95,987	48,007	184,767	169,874	138,354	101,371	92,771	82,385
Income Before Taxes	52,046	9,080	237,931	253,587	231,849	221,927	181,542	130,539
Income Taxes	(3,266)	(5,639)	83,970	84,951	79,136	76,779	63,702	45,297
Net Income	55,312	14,719	153,961	168,636	152,713	145,148	117,840	78,835
Average Shares	96,471	90,930	97,939	99,135	100,565	102,098	101,115	102,184
Balance Sheet								
Current Assets	323,916	231,842	400,920	166,467	141,954	137,205	103,623	103,150
Total Assets	2,133,179	2,026,549	2,211,791	1,943,290	1,783,336	1,442,301	1,162,328	1,085,644
Current Liabilities	390,923	327,139	379,162	310,211	302,220	241,491	231,000	190,119
Long-Term Obligations	617,394	640,319	639,291	353,785	426,679	231,029	110,323	366,316
Total Liabilities	1,207,458	1,143,011	1,185,718	803,040	806,240	542,014	400,120	607,363
Stockholders' Equity	925,721	883,538	1,026,073	1,140,250	977,096	900,287	762,208	661,439
Shares Outstanding	87,017	96,688	90,647	97,854	97,440	99,509	98,799	98,849
Statistical Record								
Return on Assets %	5.84	6.10	7.29	9.08	9.49	11.18	10.51	7.48
Return on Equity %	11.68	11.98	13.98	15.97	16.31	17.51	16.60	12.36
EBITDA Margin %	8.72	7.05	11.71	13.27	13.28	13.42	13.20	11.88
Net Margin %	2.97	1.62	4.15	5.13	5.29	5.87	5.46	4.21
Asset Turnover	1.80	1.86	1.76	1.77	1.80	1.90	1.93	1.77
Current Ratio	0.83	0.71	1.06	0.54	0.47	0.57	0.45	0.54
Debt to Equity	0.67	0.72	0.62	0.31	0.44	0.26	0.14	0.55
Price Range	39.54-29.49	39.54-29.49	39.54-29.60	36.68-25.12	35.45-22.45	31.00-19.04	23.38-13.46	20.21-10.67
P/E Ratio	31.13-23.22	31.63-23.59	25.18-18.85	21.58-14.78	23.32-14.77	21.83-13.41	19.98-11.50	26.24-13.85

Address: 6820 LBJ Freeway, Dallas, TX 75240	Web Site: www.brinker.com	Auditors: KPMG LLP
Telephone: (972) 980-9917	Officers: Douglas H. Brooks - Chmn., Pres., C.E.O. Charles M. Sonsteby - Exec. V.P., C.F.O.	Investor Contact: 972-770-7228
Fax: (972) 770-9593		Transfer Agents: Mellom Investor Services LLC., Dallas, TX

BRINKS CO (THE)

Exchange	Symbol	Price	52Wk Range	Yield	P/E
NYS	BCO	$34.60 (3/31/2005)	39.91-26.41	0.29	15.73

*7 Year Price Score 118.42 *NYSE Composite Index=100 *12 Month Price Score 100.02

Interim Earnings (Per Share)

Qtr.	Mar	Jun	Sep	Dec
2001	0.34	0.07	0.17	(0.10)
2002	0.15	0.36	0.41	(0.44)
2003	(0.03)	0.11	0.94	(0.48)
2004	0.47	0.34	0.68	0.70

Interim Dividends (Per Share)

Amt	Decl	Ex	Rec	Pay
0.025Q	5/7/2004	5/13/2004	5/17/2004	6/1/2004
0.025Q	7/9/2004	8/12/2004	8/16/2004	9/1/2004
0.025Q	11/5/2004	11/12/2004	11/16/2004	12/1/2004
0.025Q	1/27/2005	2/4/2005	2/8/2005	3/1/2005
		Indicated Div: $0.10		

Valuation Analysis

Forecast P/E	N/A	No of Institutions
Market Cap	$2.0 Billion	Shares
Book Value	674.0 Million	47,789,492
Price/Book	2.91	% Held
Price/Sales	0.42	84.23

Business Summary: Stone, Clay, Glass, and Concrete Products (MIC: 11.2 SIC: 295 NAIC: 27992)

The Brink's Company is comprised of three operating segments. Brink's, Incorporated offers armored car transportation, ATM servicing, currency and deposit processing, coin sorting and wrapping, arranging the secure air transportation of valuables and the deploying and servicing of safes and safe control devices, including its patented CompuSafe® service. Brink's Home Security is engaged in marketing, selling, installing, monitoring and servicing electronic security systems in owner-occupied, single-family residences. BAX Global Inc. provides heavy transportation and supply chain management services through a global network, particularly for business-to-business shipping.

Recent Developments: For the year ended Dec 31 2004, income from continuing operations increased 452.7% to $100,600 thousand from income of $18,200 thousand a year earlier. Net income increased 313.3% to $121,500 thousand from net income of $29,400 thousand a year earlier. Revenues were $4,718,100 thousand, up 18.0% from $3,998,600 thousand the year before. Operating income was $189,900 thousand versus an income of $99,800 thousand in the prior year, an increase of 90.3%. Total indirect expense was $4,529,200 thousand versus $3,899,100 thousand in the prior year, an increase of 16.2%.

Prospects: For 2005, Co. will focus on further market penetration, including expansion of its products, services and value-added services. BAX Global should see further improvement from better market conditions in the U.S. and Europe as well as from winning new logistics and heavy freight business. At Brink's Inc., Co. expects to grow its traditional business lines, especially internationally, while expanding Cash Logistics and other value-added services. However, Co. expects that recent growth trends at Brink's will not continue in 2005 due to increased competition and tempered exchange rate gains. At Brink's Home Security, Co. will focus on increasing its presence on the commercial sector.

Financial Data

(US$ in Thousands)	12/31/2004	12/31/2003	12/31/2002	12/31/2001	12/31/2000	12/31/1999	12/31/1998	12/31/1997
Earnings Per Share	2.20	0.55	0.48	0.31	(5.12)	(4.74)	0.92	3.61
Cash Flow Per Share	5.12	5.66	4.63	6.17	7.27	4.90	3.49	4.07
Tang Book Value Per Share	7.31	4.63	2.82	4.62	4.69	6.28	5.49	5.48
Dividends Per Share	0.100	0.100	0.100	0.100	0.100	0.100	0.100	0.100
Dividend Payout %	4.55	18.18	20.83	32.26	...	...	10.87	2.77
Income Statement								
Total Revenue	4,718,100	3,998,600	3,776,700	3,624,200	3,834,112	4,089,150	3,746,882	3,394,398
EBITDA	328,700	236,100	261,000	295,300	232,818	248,925	272,005	298,082
Depn & Amortn	148,900	143,000	130,900	194,400	188,950	168,908	143,051	117,102
Income Before Taxes	161,500	73,900	110,200	73,200	4,629	47,449	95,210	158,255
Income Taxes	60,900	55,700	41,200	27,400	1,944	12,792	29,154	48,057
Net Income	121,500	29,400	26,100	16,600	(256,643)	34,657	66,056	110,198
Average Shares	55,300	53,200	52,400	51,400	50,146	68,081	66,812	66,886
Balance Sheet								
Current Assets	1,092,600	860,500	782,000	760,500	813,626	901,903	820,643	726,805
Total Assets	2,678,200	2,548,600	2,459,900	2,394,000	2,478,709	2,468,584	2,331,137	1,995,944
Current Liabilities	1,032,100	844,100	793,300	844,900	898,307	833,061	797,433	643,673
Long-Term Obligations	181,600	221,500	304,200	252,900	311,418	395,078	323,308	191,812
Total Liabilities	2,004,200	2,053,000	2,078,700	1,917,900	2,002,886	1,718,943	1,595,109	1,310,326
Stockholders' Equity	674,000	495,600	381,200	476,100	475,823	749,641	736,028	685,618
Shares Outstanding	56,700	54,300	54,300	54,300	51,778	71,772	70,972	69,914
Statistical Record								
Return on Assets %	4.64	1.17	1.08	0.68	N.M.	1.44	3.05	5.79
Return on Equity %	20.72	6.71	6.09	3.49	N.M.	4.67	9.29	17.05
EBITDA Margin %	6.97	5.90	6.91	8.15	6.07	6.09	7.26	8.78
Net Margin %	2.58	0.74	0.69	0.46	N.M.	0.85	1.76	3.25
Asset Turnover	1.80	1.60	1.56	1.49	1.55	1.70	1.73	1.78
Current Ratio	1.06	1.02	0.99	0.90	0.91	1.08	1.03	1.13
Debt to Equity	0.27	0.45	0.80	0.53	0.65	0.53	0.44	0.28
Price Range	39.91-22.61	23.21-12.36	28.31-17.74	25.20-16.88	22.00-10.94	31.88-18.38	42.63-28.13	41.50-25.25
P/E Ratio	18.14-10.28	42.20-22.47	58.98-36.96	81.29-54.45	...	...	46.33-30.57	11.50-6.99
Average Yield %	0.33	0.60	0.44	0.48	0.62	0.41	0.28	0.30

Address: 1801 Bayberry Court, Richmond, VA 23226-8100 **Telephone:** (804) 289-9600 **Fax:** (804) 289-9770	**Web Site:** www.brinkscompany.com **Officers:** Michael T. Dan - Chmn., Pres., C.E.O. James B. Hartough - V.P., Corp. Fin., Treas.	**Auditors:** KPMG LLP **Investor Contact:** 877-275-7488

BRISTOL-MYERS SQUIBB CO.

Exchange	Symbol	Price	52Wk Range	Yield	P/E
NYS	BMY	$25.46 (3/31/2005)	26.18-22.50	4.40	21.04

*7 Year Price Score 48.15   *NYSE Composite Index=100   *12 Month Price Score 94.00

TRADING VOLUME (thousand shares)

Interim Earnings (Per Share)

Qtr.	Mar	Jun	Sep	Dec
2001	0.68	0.61	0.63	0.75
2002	0.30	0.23	0.18	0.20
2003	0.39	0.45	0.45	0.29
2004	0.49	0.27	0.38	0.07

Interim Dividends (Per Share)

Amt	Decl	Ex	Rec	Pay
0.28Q	6/8/2004	6/30/2004	7/2/2004	8/2/2004
0.28Q	9/14/2004	9/29/2004	10/1/2004	11/1/2004
0.28Q	12/7/2004	1/5/2005	1/7/2005	2/1/2005
0.28Q	3/1/2005	3/30/2005	4/1/2005	5/2/2005

Indicated Div: $1.12

Valuation Analysis

Forecast P/E	18.21	No of Institutions	
	(4/7/2005)	934	
Market Cap	$49.6 Billion	Shares	
Book Value	10.2 Billion	1,289,863,424	
Price/Book	4.86	% Held	
Price/Sales	2.56	66.09	

Business Summary: Pharmaceuticals (MIC: 9.1 SIC: 834 NAIC: 25412)

Bristol-Myers Squibb, through its divisions and subsidiaries, discovers, develops, licenses, manufactures, markets, distributes and sells pharmaceuticals and other healthcare related products. The Pharmaceuticals segment discovers, develops, licenses, manufactures, markets, distributes and sells branded pharmaceuticals. The Oncology Therapeutics Network segment is a distributor of oncology drugs, supportive care products and related supplies. The Nutritionals segment, through Mead Johnson, manufactures, markets, distributes and sells infant formulas and other nutritional products. The Other Healthcare segment consists of ConvaTec, Medical Imaging and Consumer Medicines.

Recent Developments: For the year ended Dec 31 2004, income from continuing operations decreased 23.2% to $2,378 million from income of $3,097 million a year earlier. Net income decreased 23.1% to $2,388 million from net income of $3,106 million a year earlier. Revenues were $19,380 million, up 3.9% from $18,653 million the year before. Total direct expense was $5,989 million versus $5,406 million in the prior year, an increase of 10.8%. Total indirect expense was $9,514 million versus $8,539 million in the prior year, an increase of 11.4%.

Prospects: In the near term, Co. expects continued pressure from exclusivity losses on its earnings associated with the ongoing transition of its product portfolio. Meanwhile, Co. continues to be optimistic about two or three promising late stage pipeline compounds, muraglitazar, abatacept, and entecavir, two of which were recently filed, and Co. expects to complete the filing of the third in early 2005. Looking ahead, Co. expects full-diluted earnings from continuing operations to range from $1.35 to $1.45 per share for full-year 2005. Separately, in Jan 2005, Co. announced that it intends to divest its U.S. and Canadian consumer medicines business.

Financial Data

(US$ in Thousands)	12/31/2004	12/31/2003	12/31/2002	12/31/2001	12/31/2000	12/31/1999	12/31/1998	12/31/1997
Earnings Per Share	1.21	1.59	1.07	2.67	2.36	2.06	1.55	1.57
Cash Flow Per Share	1.63	1.81	0.49	2.78	2.36	2.25	2.07	1.24
Tang Book Value Per Share	1.76	1.66	1.14	1.70	3.96	3.61	3.01	2.82
Dividends Per Share	0.840	1.120	1.400	1.100	0.980	0.860	0.585	0.765
Dividend Payout %	69.42	70.44	130.84	41.20	41.53	41.75	37.74	48.73
Income Statement								
Total Revenue	19,380,000	20,894,000	18,119,000	19,423,000	18,216,000	20,222,000	18,284,000	16,701,000
EBITDA	5,532,000	5,695,000	3,665,000	3,816,000	6,175,000	6,468,000	4,960,000	5,085,000
Depn & Amortn	909,000	789,000	735,000	781,000	746,000	678,000	625,000	591,000
Income Before Taxes	4,418,000	4,694,000	2,647,000	2,986,000	5,478,000	5,767,000	4,268,000	4,482,000
Income Taxes	1,519,000	1,215,000	435,000	459,000	1,382,000	1,600,000	1,127,000	1,277,000
Net Income	2,388,000	3,106,000	2,066,000	5,245,000	4,711,000	4,167,000	3,141,000	3,205,000
Average Shares	1,976,000	1,950,000	1,942,000	1,965,000	1,997,000	2,027,000	2,031,000	2,042,000
Balance Sheet								
Current Assets	14,801,000	11,918,000	9,975,000	12,349,000	9,824,000	9,267,000	8,782,000	7,736,000
Total Assets	30,435,000	27,471,000	24,874,000	27,057,000	17,578,000	17,114,000	16,272,000	14,977,000
Current Liabilities	9,843,000	7,530,000	8,220,000	8,826,000	5,632,000	5,537,000	5,791,000	5,032,000
Long-Term Obligations	8,463,000	8,522,000	6,261,000	6,237,000	1,336,000	1,342,000	1,364,000	1,279,000
Total Liabilities	20,233,000	17,685,000	15,907,000	16,321,000	8,398,000	8,469,000	8,696,000	7,758,000
Stockholders' Equity	10,202,000	9,786,000	8,967,000	10,736,000	9,180,000	8,645,000	7,576,000	7,219,000
Shares Outstanding	1,947,000	1,939,983	1,936,829	1,935,620	1,953,535	1,980,806	1,988,000	1,986,000
Statistical Record								
Return on Assets %	8.23	11.87	7.96	23.50	27.08	24.96	20.10	21.61
Return on Equity %	23.83	33.13	20.97	52.67	52.71	51.38	42.46	46.49
EBITDA Margin %	28.54	27.26	20.23	19.65	33.90	31.98	27.13	30.45
Net Margin %	12.32	14.87	11.40	27.00	25.86	20.61	17.18	19.19
Asset Turnover	0.67	0.80	0.70	0.87	1.05	1.21	1.17	1.13
Current Ratio	1.50	1.58	1.21	1.40	1.74	1.67	1.52	1.54
Debt to Equity	0.83	0.87	0.70	0.58	0.15	0.16	0.18	0.18
Price Range	30.64-22.50	28.86-21.13	51.30-20.55	68.08-49.00	70.40-41.42	74.21-54.69	63.71-42.76	46.57-25.50
P/E Ratio	25.32-18.60	18.15-13.29	47.94-19.21	25.50-18.35	29.83-17.55	36.02-26.55	41.10-27.59	29.66-16.24
Average Yield %	3.34	4.44	4.51	1.98	1.77	1.33	1.13	2.11

Address: 345 Park Avenue, New York, NY 10154-0037	**Web Site:** www.bms.com	**Auditors:** PricewaterhouseCoopers LLP
Telephone: (212) 546-4000	**Officers:** Peter R. Dolan - Chmn., C.E.O. Donald J. Hayden Jr. - Exec. V.P., Pres., Americas	
Fax: (212) 546-4020		

BROWN & BROWN, INC.

| Exchange
NYS | Symbol
BRO | Price
$46.09 (3/31/2005) | 52Wk Range
48.25-38.32 | Yield
0.69 | P/E
24.78 | Div Acheiver
11 Years |

*7 Year Price Score 155.36 *NYSE Composite Index=100 *12 Month Price Score 100.36

Interim Earnings (Per Share)

Qtr.	Mar	Jun	Sep	Dec
2001	0.20	0.20	0.21	0.23
2002	0.31	0.31	0.29	0.31
2003	0.44	0.41	0.38	0.37
2004	0.53	0.46	0.43	0.44

Interim Dividends (Per Share)

Amt	Decl	Ex	Rec	Pay
0.07Q	4/22/2004	5/4/2004	5/6/2004	5/20/2004
0.07Q	7/21/2004	8/2/2004	8/4/2004	8/18/2004
0.08Q	10/20/2004	11/1/2004	11/3/2004	11/17/2004
0.08Q	1/19/2005	1/31/2005	2/2/2005	2/16/2005

Indicated Div: $0.32

Valuation Analysis

Forecast P/E	21.59 (4/7/2005)	No of Institutions 189
Market Cap	$3.2 Billion	Shares
Book Value	624.3 Million	44,584,188
Price/Book	5.11	% Held
Price/Sales	4.93	64.46

TRADING VOLUME (thousand shares)

Business Summary: Insurance (MIC: 8.2 SIC: 411 NAIC: 24210)

Brown & Brown is primarily engaged in the property and casualty business. Co.'s business is divided into four divisions. The Retail Division sells insurance products to commercial, professional and individual clients. The National Programs Division is comprised of two units: Professional Programs, which provides professional liability and related package products; and Special Programs, which markets targeted products and services for specific industries, trade groups and market niches. The Service Division provides third-party administration for workers' compensation and employee benefit markets. The Brokerage Division sells commercial insurance through independent agents and brokers.

Recent Developments: For the year ended Dec 31 2004, net income increased 16.8% to $128,843 thousand from net income of $110,322 thousand a year earlier. Revenues were $646,934 thousand, up 17.4% from $551,040 thousand the year before. Commissions and fees were $638,267 thousand, up 17.1% from $545,287 thousand in 2003. Investment income rose 90.1% to $2,715 thousand from $1,428 thousand a year earlier. Net other income increased 37.6% $5,962 thousand from $4,325 thousand the year before.

Prospects: Going forward, Co. will pursue its intermediate goal of achieving $1.00 billion in revenue and 40.0% in operating margin. Also, Co. will continue to focus on a large number of potential new acquisition opportunities it has in its pipeline. For instance, on Feb 11 2005, Co. agreed to acquire Hull & Company, Inc., an insurance wholesale company with 20 offices in nine states and annualized net retained revenues of about $63.0 million. On Feb 14 2005, Co. agreed to acquire Emerald Benefits, Inc. Emerald Benefits, with annualized revenues of about $3.8 million, is a retail insurance agency specializing in employee benefits in South Florida.

Financial Data
(US$ in Thousands)

	12/31/2004	12/31/2003	12/31/2002	12/31/2001	12/31/2000	12/31/1999	12/31/1998	12/31/1997
Earnings Per Share	1.86	1.60	1.22	0.85	0.58	0.50	0.43	0.37
Cash Flow Per Share	2.46	2.09	1.39	1.12	0.77	0.72	0.68	0.63
Tang Book Value Per Share	N.M.	0.40	0.17	N.M.	0.35	0.20	0.09	0.53
Dividends Per Share	0.290	0.242	0.200	0.160	0.135	0.115	0.102	0.088
Dividend Payout %	15.59	15.16	16.39	18.82	23.28	23.23	23.84	23.87
Income Statement								
Total Revenue	646,934	551,040	455,742	365,029	209,706	176,413	153,791	129,191
Income Before Taxes	206,949	176,482	134,664	90,478	53,978	44,208	37,485	31,638
Income Taxes	78,106	66,160	49,271	34,834	20,792	17,036	14,432	12,251
Net Income	128,843	110,322	83,122	53,913	33,186	27,172	23,053	19,387
Average Shares	69,444	68,897	68,043	63,222	57,326	54,944	53,724	52,350
Balance Sheet								
Total Assets	1,249,517	865,854	754,349	488,737	276,719	235,163	230,513	194,129
Total Liabilities	625,192	367,819	362,759	313,452	154,808	132,137	146,305	116,987
Stockholders' Equity	624,325	498,035	391,590	175,285	121,911	103,026	84,208	77,142
Shares Outstanding	69,159	68,561	68,178	63,194	57,398	54,880	53,992	52,428
Statistical Record								
Return on Assets %	12.15	13.62	13.37	14.09	12.93	11.67	10.86	10.37
Return on Equity %	22.90	24.80	29.33	36.28	29.43	29.02	28.58	26.85
Price Range	46.60-32.08	37.44-27.29	36.13-24.74	30.81-15.45	17.72-7.81	10.03-7.42	10.42-7.24	7.83-4.25
P/E Ratio	25.05-17.25	23.40-17.06	29.61-20.28	36.25-18.18	30.55-13.47	20.06-14.84	24.24-16.84	21.17-11.49
Average Yield %	0.72	0.76	0.63	0.71	1.09	1.31	1.15	1.56

Address: 220 South Ridgewood Ave., Daytona Beach, FL 32114
Telephone: (368) 252-9601

Web Site: www.bbinsurance.com
Officers: J. Hyatt Brown - Chmn., C.E.O. Jim W. Henderson - Pres., C.O.O., Asst. Treas.

Auditors: DELOITTE & TOUCHE LLP
Investor Contact: 904-239-7250
Transfer Agents: Wachovia Bank N.A., Charlotte, NC

BROWN-FORMAN CORP.

Exchange	Symbol	Price	52Wk Range	Yield	P/E	Div Acheiver
NYS	BF A	$55.05 (3/31/2005)	56.41-44.62	1.78	22.02	20 Years

*7 Year Price Score 119.18 *NYSE Composite Index=100 *12 Month Price Score 101.22

Interim Earnings (Per Share)

Qtr.	Jul	Oct	Jan	Apr
2001-02	0.28	0.58	0.42	0.38
2002-03	0.27	0.59	0.51	0.45
2003-04	0.26	0.72	0.66	0.47
2004-05	0.42	0.84	0.78	...

Interim Dividends (Per Share)

Amt	Decl	Ex	Rec	Pay
0.212Q	5/27/2004	6/3/2004	6/7/2004	7/1/2004
0.212Q	7/22/2004	9/2/2004	9/7/2004	10/1/2004
0.245Q	11/18/2004	12/2/2004	12/6/2004	1/1/2005
0.245Q	1/27/2005	3/8/2005	3/10/2005	4/1/2005
		Indicated Div: $0.98		

Valuation Analysis

Forecast P/E	20.39	No of Institutions	
	(4/7/2005)	58	
Market Cap	$6.7 Billion	Shares	
Book Value	1.2 Billion	38,249,928	
Price/Book	5.40	% Held	
Price/Sales	2.89	67.29	

TRADING VOLUME (thousand shares)

Business Summary: Food (MIC: 4.1 SIC: 084 NAIC: 12130)

Brown-Forman operates in two business segments: beverages and consumer durables. The beverages segment manufactures, bottles, imports, exports and markets a wide variety of alcoholic beverage brands. Co. also manufactures and markets new and used oak barrels. Co.'s principal beverage brands include: Jack Daniel's, Southern Comfort, Finlandia Vodka, Canadian Mist, Korbel champagnes, and Fetzer Vineyards, Bolla and Bel Arbor wines. The consumer durables segment sells fine china dinnerware, crystal stemware and giftware, stainless steel flatware, and silver-plated and metal giftware under the Lenox, Gorham and Dansk brand names, as well as Hartmann luggage.

Recent Developments: For the quarter ended Jan 31 2005, net income increased 19.4% to $96,100 thousand from net income of $80,500 thousand in the year-earlier quarter. Revenues were $630,500 thousand, up 6.4% from $592,600 thousand the year before. Operating income was $94,700 thousand versus an income of $126,900 thousand in the prior-year quarter, a decrease of 25.4%. Total direct expense was $255,200 thousand versus $249,000 thousand in the prior-year quarter, an increase of 2.5%. Total indirect expense was $280,600 thousand versus $216,700 thousand in the prior-year quarter, an increase of 29.5%.

Prospects: Global depletions of Co.'s Jack Daniel's are increasing due to growth in nearly all of its markets, particularly in the U.S., the U.K., Germany, South Africa and China. Jack Daniel's global profitability is benefiting from favorable currency exchange and underlying margin improvement. Underlying business trends for Co.'s premium spirits brands remain solid. For fiscal 2005, Co. expects earnings to range from $2.38 to $2.43 per diluted share, before the anticipated $0.36 to $0.38 per share gain from the sale of its Glenmorangie shareholding. Separately, Co. has agreed to acquire the remaining 20.0% of Finlandia Vodka Worldwide Ltd. from Altia Corporation for approximately $61.0 million.

Financial Data (US$ in Thousands)	9 Mos	6 Mos	3 Mos	04/30/2004	04/30/2003	04/30/2002	04/30/2001	04/30/2000
Earnings Per Share	2.50	2.38	2.27	2.11	1.81	1.67	1.70	1.59
Cash Flow Per Share	3.29	2.96	2.85	2.51	1.80	1.83	1.69	1.75
Tang Book Value Per Share	5.12	5.22	4.36	4.99	2.43	7.79	6.75	5.68
Dividends Per Share	0.882	0.850	0.825	0.800	0.725	0.680	0.640	0.605
Dividend Payout %	35.23	35.67	36.39	37.91	39.94	40.84	37.65	38.05
Income Statement								
Total Revenue	1,796,600	1,166,100	496,000	2,213,000	2,060,000	1,958,000	1,924,000	1,877,000
EBITDA	453,900	270,700	97,000	463,000	433,000	408,000	438,000	410,000
Depn & Amortn	43,800	28,900	14,100	56,000	55,000	55,000	64,000	62,000
Income Before Taxes	398,500	232,300	78,000	388,000	373,000	348,000	366,000	343,000
Income Taxes	147,900	77,800	26,100	130,000	128,000	120,000	133,000	125,000
Net Income	250,600	154,500	51,900	258,000	245,000	228,000	233,000	218,000
Average Shares	122,482	122,417	122,414	121,986	135,126	137,000	137,200	137,200
Balance Sheet								
Current Assets	1,310,900	1,276,000	1,086,000	1,083,000	1,068,000	1,029,000	994,000	1,020,000
Total Assets	2,622,200	2,563,700	2,372,700	2,376,000	2,264,000	2,016,000	1,939,000	1,802,000
Current Liabilities	489,200	483,700	368,200	369,000	548,000	495,000	538,000	522,000
Long-Term Obligations	600,800	601,100	630,200	630,000	629,000	40,000	40,000	41,000
Total Liabilities	1,381,000	1,360,900	1,279,400	1,291,000	1,424,000	705,000	752,000	754,000
Stockholders' Equity	1,241,200	1,202,800	1,093,300	1,085,000	840,000	1,311,000	1,187,000	1,048,000
Shares Outstanding	121,763	121,784	121,796	104,731	121,134	136,696	136,918	137,024
Statistical Record								
Return on Assets %	12.44	11.70	11.94	11.09	11.45	11.53	12.46	12.29
Return on Equity %	27.82	27.42	28.82	26.73	22.78	18.25	20.85	22.13
EBITDA Margin %	25.26	23.21	19.56	20.92	21.02	20.84	22.77	21.84
Net Margin %	13.95	13.25	10.46	11.66	11.89	11.64	12.11	11.61
Asset Turnover	0.94	0.92	0.96	0.95	0.96	0.99	1.03	1.06
Current Ratio	2.68	2.64	2.95	2.93	1.95	2.08	1.85	1.95
Debt to Equity	0.48	0.50	0.58	0.58	0.75	0.03	0.03	0.04
Price Range	51.90-44.62	51.90-43.01	51.90-39.50	51.90-38.51	40.25-30.16	39.20-30.32	34.75-24.56	34.50-21.00
P/E Ratio	20.76-17.85	21.81-18.07	22.86-17.40	24.60-18.25	22.24-16.66	23.47-18.16	20.44-14.45	21.70-13.21
Average Yield %	1.81	1.77	1.77	1.79	2.02	2.05	2.19	2.17

Address: 850 Dixie Highway, Louisville, KY 40210 **Telephone:** (502) 585-1100 **Fax:** (502) 774-7876	**Web Site:** www.brown-forman.com **Officers:** Owsley Brown II - Chmn., C.E.O. Michael B. Crutcher - Vice-Chmn., Sec., Gen. Couns.	**Auditors:** PricewaterhouseCoopers LLP **Transfer Agents:** National City Bank, Cleveland, OH

BRUNSWICK CORP.

Exchange	Symbol	Price	52Wk Range	Yield	P/E
NYS	BC	$46.85 (3/31/2005)	49.81-34.70	1.28	16.91

*7 Year Price Score 144.11 *NYSE Composite Index=100 *12 Month Price Score 98.52

Interim Earnings (Per Share)

Qtr.	Mar	Jun	Sep	Dec
2001	0.42	0.47	0.07	(0.03)
2002	0.15	0.51	0.26	0.22
2003	0.04	0.59	0.41	0.42
2004	0.50	0.93	0.75	0.59

Interim Dividends (Per Share)

Amt	Decl	Ex	Rec	Pay
0.125A	10/22/2001	11/21/2001	11/26/2001	12/14/2001
0.50A	10/23/2002	11/21/2002	11/25/2002	12/13/2002
0.50A	10/22/2003	11/21/2003	11/25/2003	12/12/2003
0.60A	10/25/2004	11/18/2004	11/22/2004	12/15/2004

Indicated Div: $0.60

Valuation Analysis

Forecast P/E	14.36	No of Institutions
	(4/7/2005)	291
Market Cap	$4.5 Billion	Shares
Book Value	1.7 Billion	82,392,888
Price/Book	2.65	% Held
Price/Sales	0.87	85.04

Business Summary: Shipping (MIC: 15.3 SIC: 732 NAIC: 33618)

Brunswick is a manufacturer of recreation brands. The Marine Engine segment consists of the Mercury Marine Group and Brunswick New Technologies. The Boat segment consists of the Brunswick Boat Group, which produces fiberglass pleasure boats, high-performance boats, offshore fishing boats, and aluminum fishing, pontoon and deck boats, and manufactures and distributes marine parts and accessories. The Fitness segment manufactures a full line of cardiovascular and strength-training equipment. The Bowling & Billiards segment consists of bowling products, capital equipment, and a full line of consumer and commercial billiards tables, air hockey tables, foosball tables and related accessories.

Recent Developments: For the year ended Dec 31 2004, net income increased 99.6% to $269,800 thousand from net income of $135,200 thousand a year earlier. Revenues were $5,229,300 thousand, up 26.7% from $4,128,700 thousand the year before. Operating income was $400,700 thousand versus an income of $221,400 thousand in the prior year, an increase of 81.0%. Total direct expense was $3,915,100 thousand versus $3,131,600 thousand in the prior year, an increase of 25.0%. Total indirect expense was $913,500 thousand versus $775,700 thousand in the prior year, an increase of 17.8%.

Prospects: For 2005, Co. should be well-positioned to take advantage of increased retail demand for marine products, which it estimates will be up in the mid-single digits for the industry. Moreover, Co. has a full complement of new products for introduction that is expected to drive marine sales up in the mid-teens. In the fitness and bowling & billiards segments, Co. anticipates mid-single digit sales growth. Meanwhile, increased volumes along with continued focus on effective cost management are expected to result in operating margin improvement of 70 to 100 basis points. Also, Co. estimates diluted earnings to range from $3.15 to $3.30 per share for 2005.

Financial Data

(US$ in Thousands)	12/31/2004	12/31/2003	12/31/2002	12/31/2001	12/31/2000	12/31/1999	12/31/1998	12/31/1997
Earnings Per Share	2.77	1.47	0.86	0.93	(1.08)	0.41	1.88	1.50
Cash Flow Per Share	4.33	4.33	4.59	3.77	2.89	3.25	4.36	2.64
Tang Book Value Per Share	7.84	6.77	5.90	5.78	6.40	6.99	5.35	4.75
Dividends Per Share	0.600	0.500	0.500	0.500	0.500	0.500	0.500	0.500
Dividend Payout %	21.66	34.01	58.14	53.76	...	121.95	26.60	33.33
Income Statement								
Total Revenue	5,229,300	4,128,700	3,711,900	3,370,800	3,811,900	4,283,800	3,945,200	3,657,400
EBITDA	581,200	392,700	353,300	345,500	539,700	281,600	506,200	444,400
Depn & Amortn	157,500	150,600	148,400	160,400	148,800	165,600	159,700	156,900
Income Before Taxes	378,500	201,100	161,600	132,200	323,300	55,000	283,800	236,200
Income Taxes	108,700	65,900	58,100	47,500	121,100	17,100	105,200	85,000
Net Income	269,800	135,200	78,400	81,800	(95,800)	37,900	186,300	150,500
Average Shares	97,300	91,900	90,700	88,100	88,700	92,600	99,000	100,300
Balance Sheet								
Current Assets	2,098,700	1,715,200	1,660,200	1,400,900	1,831,800	1,578,200	1,454,400	1,366,000
Total Assets	4,346,400	3,602,500*	3,407,100	3,157,500	3,396,500	3,354,800	3,351,500	3,241,400
Current Liabilities	1,253,800	1,101,800	1,005,600	902,700	1,247,900	1,088,400	1,036,400	948,200
Long-Term Obligations	728,400	583,800	589,500	600,200	601,800	622,500	635,400	645,500
Total Liabilities	2,634,100	2,279,500	2,305,300	2,046,600	2,329,400	2,054,600	2,040,200	1,926,400
Stockholders' Equity	1,712,300	1,323,000	1,101,800	1,110,900	1,067,100	1,300,200	1,311,300	1,315,000
Shares Outstanding	96,829	92,130	90,161	87,799	87,344	91,811	91,800	99,481
Statistical Record								
Return on Assets %	6.77	3.86	2.39	2.50	N.M.	1.13	5.65	4.98
Return on Equity %	17.73	11.15	7.09	7.51	N.M.	2.90	14.19	11.98
EBITDA Margin %	11.11	9.51	9.52	10.25	14.16	6.57	12.83	12.15
Net Margin %	5.16	3.27	2.11	2.43	N.M.	0.88	4.72	4.11
Asset Turnover	1.31	1.18	1.13	1.03	1.13	1.28	1.20	1.21
Current Ratio	1.67	1.56	1.65	1.55	1.47	1.45	1.40	1.44
Debt to Equity	0.43	0.44	0.54	0.54	0.56	0.48	0.48	0.49
Price Range	49.81-31.43	31.96-17.50	29.70-18.72	24.75-15.00	22.25-14.75	30.00-18.25	35.38-12.50	36.50-23.63
P/E Ratio	17.98-11.35	21.74-11.90	34.53-21.77	26.61-16.13	...	73.17-44.51	18.82-6.65	24.33-15.75
Average Yield %	1.46	2.05	2.08	2.43	2.70	2.10	2.02	1.65

Address: One North Field Court, Lake Forest, IL 60045-4811	**Web Site:** www.brunswick.com	**Auditors:** ERNST & YOUNG LLP
Telephone: (847) 735-4700	**Officers:** George W. Buckley - Chmn., C.E.O. Peter B. Hamilton - Vice-Chmn.	**Investor Contact:** 847-735-4204
Fax: (847) 735-4765		

BURLINGTON NORTHERN SANTA FE CORP.

Exchange	Symbol	Price	52Wk Range	Yield	P/E
NYS	BNI	$53.93 (3/31/2005)	55.69-31.50	1.26	25.68

*7 Year Price Score 114.02 *NYSE Composite Index=100 *12 Month Price Score 117.70

Interim Earnings (Per Share)

Qtr.	Mar	Jun	Sep	Dec
2001	0.34	0.50	0.58	0.46
2002	0.45	0.51	0.51	0.54
2003	0.50	0.54	0.55	0.61
2004	0.52	0.67	0.01	0.91

Interim Dividends (Per Share)

Amt	Decl	Ex	Rec	Pay
0.15Q	4/22/2004	6/8/2004	6/10/2004	7/1/2004
0.17Q	7/22/2004	9/8/2004	9/10/2004	10/1/2004
0.17Q	10/21/2004	12/9/2004	12/13/2004	1/3/2005
0.17Q	2/11/2005	3/9/2005	3/11/2005	4/1/2005

Indicated Div: $0.68

Valuation Analysis

Forecast P/E	15.57	No of Institutions	
	(4/7/2005)	491	
Market Cap	$20.3 Billion	Shares	
Book Value	9.3 Billion	290,540,320	
Price/Book	2.18	% Held	
Price/Sales	1.86	76.88	

Business Summary: Rail Transport (MIC: 15.5 SIC: 011 NAIC: 82111)

Burlington Northern Santa Fe is engaged primarily in the rail transportation business. As of Dec 31 2003, the rail operations of The Burlington Northern and Santa Fe Railway Company (BNSF Railway) operated a railroad system of approximately 32,500 route miles of track through 28 states and two Canadian provinces. Through one operating transportation services segment, BNSF Railway transports a range of products and commodities derived from manufacturing, agricultural and natural resource industries. These include Consumer Products, Industrial Products, Coal and Agricultural Products

Recent Developments: For the year ended Dec 31 2004, net income decreased 3.1% to $791,000 thousand from net income of $816,000 thousand a year earlier. Revenues were $10,946,000 thousand, up 16.3% from $9,413,000 thousand the year before. Operating income was $1,686,000 thousand versus an income of $1,665,000 thousand in the prior year, an increase of 1.3%. Total direct expense was $4,926,000 thousand versus $3,875,000 thousand in the prior year, an increase of 27.1%. Total indirect expense was $4,334,000 thousand versus $3,873,000 thousand in the prior year, an increase of 11.9%.

Prospects: Co. is benefiting from solid growth in freight revenues, which surged 19.0% to $2.92 billion during the fourth-quarter of 2004 from the year before. Co. noted that the increases in freight revenues is largely due to increased shipments in the areas of international intermodal, truckload, and perishables. Also, Co. is stronger shipment demand in the building products, petroleum products and construction products sectors, as well as coal. Additionally, freight shipments of agricultural products are being driven by increased export moves to the Pacific Northwest. This improvement in revenues, coupled with Co.'s continued focus on expense control initiatives, bodes well for future profitability.

Financial Data
(US$ in Thousands)

	12/31/2004	12/31/2003	12/31/2002	12/31/2001	12/31/2000	12/31/1999	12/31/1998	12/31/1997
Earnings Per Share	2.10	2.19	2.00	1.87	2.36	2.44	2.43	1.88
Cash Flow Per Share	6.41	6.19	5.57	5.67	5.61	5.23	4.71	3.91
Tang Book Value Per Share	24.71	22.87	21.11	20.35	19.10	17.98	16.52	14.53
Dividends Per Share	0.640	0.540	0.480	0.490	0.480	0.480	0.440	0.400
Dividend Payout %	30.48	24.66	24.00	26.20	20.34	19.67	18.11	21.28
Income Statement								
Total Revenue	10,946,000	9,413,000	8,979,000	9,208,000	9,205,000	9,100,000	8,941,000	8,413,000
EBITDA	2,694,000	2,561,000	2,575,000	2,554,000	2,933,000	3,103,000	3,035,000	2,518,000
Depn & Amortn	1,012,000	910,000	931,000	909,000	895,000	897,000	832,000	773,000
Income Before Taxes	1,273,000	1,231,000	1,216,000	1,182,000	1,585,000	1,819,000	1,849,000	1,404,000
Income Taxes	482,000	454,000	456,000	445,000	605,000	682,000	694,000	519,000
Net Income	791,000	816,000	760,000	731,000	980,000	1,137,000	1,155,000	885,000
Average Shares	376,600	372,300	380,800	390,700	415,200	466,800	476,200	471,000
Balance Sheet								
Total Assets	28,925,000	26,939,000	25,767,000	24,721,000	24,375,000	23,700,000	22,690,000	21,336,000
Long-Term Obligations	6,051,000	6,440,000	6,641,000	6,363,000	6,614,000	5,655,000	5,188,000	5,181,000
Total Liabilities	19,614,000	18,444,000	17,835,000	16,872,000	16,895,000	15,528,000	14,920,000	14,524,000
Stockholders' Equity	9,311,000	8,495,000	7,932,000	7,849,000	7,480,000	8,172,000	7,770,000	6,812,000
Shares Outstanding	376,812	371,460	375,778	385,777	391,592	454,559	470,475	468,912
Statistical Record								
Return on Assets %	2.82	3.10	3.01	2.98	4.07	4.90	5.25	4.30
Return on Equity %	8.86	9.93	9.63	9.54	12.49	14.26	15.84	13.84
EBITDA Margin %	24.61	27.21	28.68	27.74	31.86	34.10	33.94	29.93
Net Margin %	7.23	8.67	8.46	7.94	10.65	12.49	12.92	10.52
Asset Turnover	0.39	0.36	0.36	0.38	0.38	0.39	0.41	0.41
Price Range	48.67-30.06	32.44-23.62	31.30-23.78	33.80-23.45	29.13-19.25	37.81-23.13	35.58-27.38	33.65-23.63
P/E Ratio	23.18-14.31	14.81-10.79	15.65-11.89	18.07-12.54	12.34-8.16	15.50-9.48	14.64-11.27	17.90-12.57
Average Yield %	1.77	1.93	1.73	1.70	2.02	1.91	1.36	1.35

Address: 2650 Lou Menk Drive, Fort Worth, TX 76131-2830	Web Site: www.bnsf.com	Auditors: PricewaterhouseCoopers LLP
Telephone: (817) 333-2000	Officers: Matthew K. Rose - Chmn., Pres., C.E.O. Thomas N. Hund - Exec. V.P., C.F.O.	Investor Contact: 817-352-6452

145

BURLINGTON RESOURCES INC.

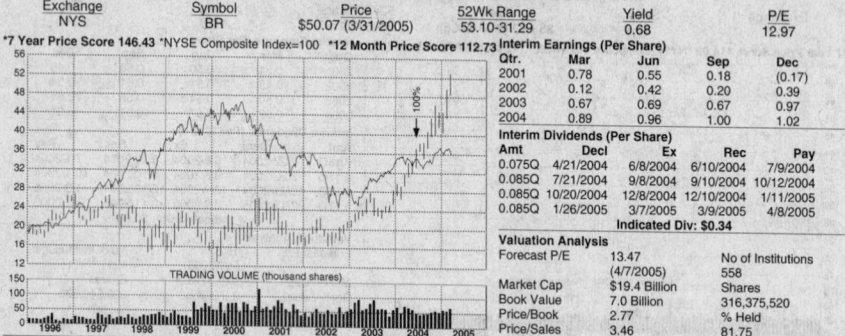

Exchange	Symbol	Price	52Wk Range	Yield	P/E
NYS	BR	$50.07 (3/31/2005)	53.10-31.29	0.68	12.97

*7 Year Price Score 146.43 *NYSE Composite Index=100 *12 Month Price Score 112.73

Interim Earnings (Per Share)

Qtr.	Mar	Jun	Sep	Dec
2001	0.78	0.55	0.18	(0.17)
2002	0.12	0.42	0.20	0.39
2003	0.67	0.69	0.67	0.97
2004	0.89	0.96	1.00	1.02

Interim Dividends (Per Share)

Amt	Decl	Ex	Rec	Pay
0.075Q	4/21/2004	6/8/2004	6/10/2004	7/9/2004
0.085Q	7/21/2004	9/8/2004	9/10/2004	10/12/2004
0.085Q	10/20/2004	12/8/2004	12/10/2004	1/11/2005
0.085Q	1/26/2005	3/7/2005	3/9/2005	4/8/2005

Indicated Div: $0.34

Valuation Analysis

Forecast P/E	13.47	No of Institutions	
	(4/7/2005)	558	
Market Cap	$19.4 Billion	Shares	
Book Value	7.0 Billion	316,375,520	
Price/Book	2.77	% Held	
Price/Sales	3.46	81.75	

Business Summary: Gas Utilities (MIC: 7.4 SIC: 922 NAIC: 86210)

Burlington Resources is a holding company engaged, through its principal subsidiaries, in the exploration for and the development, production and marketing of natural gas, crude oil and natural gas liquids. Co.'s principal subsidiaries include, Burlington Resources Oil & Gas LP, The Louisiana Land and Exploration Company, Burlington Resources Canada Ltd., Burlington Resources Canada (Hunter) Ltd., and their affiliated companies. At Dec 31 2003, total proved reserves were 11.80 trillion cubic feet of gas equivalents. In addition to its extensive North American operations, Co. has exploration, development and production operations in Northwest Europe, North Africa, China and South America.

Recent Developments: For the year ended Dec 31 2004, net income increased 27.1% to $1,527,000 thousand from net income of $1,201,000 thousand a year earlier. Revenues were $5,618,000 thousand, up 30.3% from $4,311,000 thousand the year before. Total direct expense was $453,000 thousand versus $408,000 thousand in the prior year, an increase of 11.0%. Total indirect expense was $2,820,000 thousand versus $2,247,000 thousand in the prior year, an increase of 25.5%.

Prospects: For the first quarter of 2005, Co. is targeting gas production of 900.0 million cubic feet equivalent per day (MMcfd) to 955.0 MMcfd in the U.S., 770.0 MMcfd to 800.0 MMcfd in Canada, and 180.0 MMcfd to 200.0 MMcfd in other international territories. Also, for the first quarter, Co. is projecting natural gas liquids production of a total of 64.5 thousand barrels of oil a day (Mbd) to 67.5 Mbd. Also for the first quarter, Co. is projecting crude oil production of 41.0 Mbd to 43.5 Mbd in U.S., 5.0 Mbd to 6.0 Mbd in Canada, and 39.0 Mbd to 45.0 Mbd in other international territories.

Financial Data

(US$ in Thousands)	12/31/2004	12/31/2003	12/31/2002	12/31/2001	12/31/2000	12/31/1999	12/31/1998	12/31/1997
Earnings Per Share	3.86	3.00	1.13	1.35	1.56	...	0.24	0.90
Cash Flow Per Share	8.74	6.38	3.85	5.09	3.69	2.55	2.18	3.17
Tang Book Value Per Share	15.36	11.48	7.52	6.83	8.70	7.51	9.93	8.53
Dividends Per Share	0.320	0.287	0.275	0.275	0.275	0.275	0.275	0.275
Dividend Payout %	8.29	9.58	24.44	20.37	17.63	...	114.58	30.73
Income Statement								
Total Revenue	5,618,000	4,311,000	2,964,000	3,326,000	3,147,000	2,065,000	1,637,000	2,000,000
EBITDA	3,723,000	2,757,000	1,676,000	1,827,000	1,868,000	865,000	777,000	1,091,000
Depn & Amortn	1,137,000	927,000	833,000	730,000	704,000	631,000	534,000	538,000
Income Before Taxes	2,304,000	1,570,000	569,000	907,000	967,000	23,000	95,000	411,000
Income Taxes	777,000	310,000	115,000	349,000	292,000	22,000	9,000	92,000
Net Income	1,527,000	1,201,000	454,000	561,000	675,000	1,000	86,000	319,000
Average Shares	395,000	400,000	404,000	416,000	432,000	434,000	356,000	356,000
Balance Sheet								
Current Assets	3,455,000	1,517,000	1,061,000	715,000	1,011,000	667,000	456,000	678,000
Total Assets	15,744,000	12,995,000	10,645,000	10,582,000	7,506,000	7,191,000	5,917,000	5,821,000
Current Liabilities	1,599,000	891,000	1,022,000	711,000	758,000	648,000	494,000	538,000
Long-Term Obligations	3,887,000	3,873,000	3,853,000	4,337,000	2,301,000	2,769,000	1,938,000	1,748,000
Total Liabilities	8,733,000	7,474,000	6,813,000	7,057,000	3,756,000	3,945,000	2,899,000	2,805,000
Stockholders' Equity	7,011,000	5,521,000	3,832,000	3,525,000	3,750,000	3,246,000	3,018,000	3,016,000
Shares Outstanding	387,941	395,297	402,878	401,585	431,137	431,939	303,910	353,418
Statistical Record								
Return on Assets %	10.60	10.16	4.28	6.20	9.16	0.02	1.47	6.29
Return on Equity %	24.30	25.68	12.34	15.42	19.24	0.03	2.85	11.93
EBITDA Margin %	66.27	63.95	56.55	54.93	59.36	41.89	47.46	54.55
Net Margin %	27.18	27.86	15.32	16.87	21.45	0.05	5.25	15.95
Asset Turnover	0.39	0.36	0.28	0.37	0.43	0.32	0.28	0.39
Current Ratio	2.16	1.70	1.04	1.01	1.33	1.03	0.92	1.26
Debt to Equity	0.55	0.70	1.01	1.23	0.61	0.85	0.64	0.58
Price Range	46.41-26.63	28.45-20.63	22.47-16.39	26.50-16.00	26.19-12.97	23.47-14.78	24.56-14.78	26.81-20.25
P/E Ratio	12.02-6.90	9.48-6.88	19.88-14.50	19.63-11.85	16.79-8.31	N.M.	102.34-61.59	29.79-22.50
Average Yield %	0.90	1.18	1.41	1.31	1.46	1.42	1.36	1.17

Address: 717 Texas Avenue, Suite 2100, Houston, TX 77002 **Telephone:** (713) 624-9500 **Fax:** (713) 624-9645	**Web Site:** www.br-inc.com **Officers:** Bobby S. Shackouls - Chmn., Pres., C.E.O. Randy L. Limbacher - Exec. V.P., C.O.O.	**Auditors:** PricewaterhouseCoopers LLP **Investor Contact:** 713-624-9548

CABLEVISION SYSTEMS CORP.

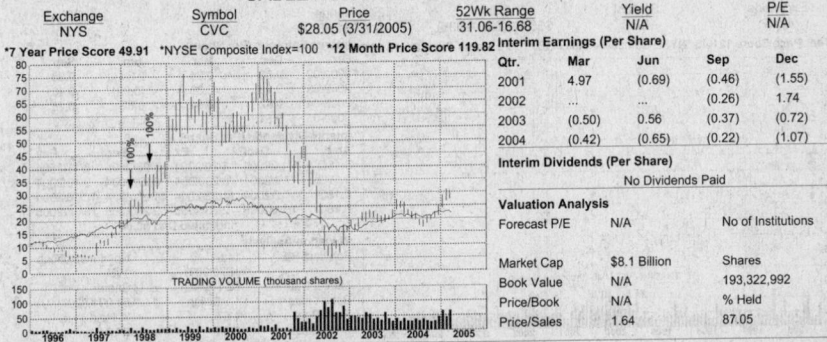

Exchange	Symbol	Price	52Wk Range	Yield	P/E
NYS	CVC	$28.05 (3/31/2005)	31.06-16.68	N/A	N/A

*7 Year Price Score 49.91 *NYSE Composite Index=100 *12 Month Price Score 119.82

Interim Earnings (Per Share)

Qtr.	Mar	Jun	Sep	Dec
2001	4.97	(0.69)	(0.46)	(1.55)
2002	...	...	(0.26)	1.74
2003	(0.50)	0.56	(0.37)	(0.72)
2004	(0.42)	(0.65)	(0.22)	(1.07)

Interim Dividends (Per Share)

No Dividends Paid

Valuation Analysis

Forecast P/E	N/A		No of Institutions
Market Cap	$8.1 Billion		Shares
Book Value	N/A		% Held
Price/Book	N/A		87.05
Price/Sales	1.64		

Shares: 193,322,992

Business Summary: Media (MIC: 13.1 SIC: 841 NAIC: 15120)

Cablevision Systems is the holding company for CSC Holdings, Inc. Through its subsidiary, Co. is a cable operator. Co. also has investments in cable programming networks, entertainment businesses and telecommunications companies. As of Dec 31, 2003, Co. served about 2.9 million cable TV subscribers in and around the New York City metropolitan area. Through Rainbow Media Holdings, Co. owns interests in and manages numerous national and regional programming networks, the Madison Square Garden sports and entertainment business and cable TV advertising sales companies. Through Cablevision Lightpath, Co. provides switched telephone services and high-speed Internet access to the business market.

Recent Developments: For the year ended Dec 31 2004, loss from continuing operations was $667,002 thousand compared with a loss of $283,116 thousand a year earlier. Net loss was $676,092 thousand versus net loss of $297,239 thousand a year earlier. Revenues were $5,028,622 thousand, up 20.1% from $4,186,141 thousand the year before. Operating loss was $59,437 thousand versus an income of $31,697 thousand in the prior year. Total direct expense was $2,414,624 thousand versus $1,956,157 thousand in the prior year, an increase of 23.4%. Total indirect expense was $2,673,435 thousand versus $2,198,287 thousand in the prior year, an increase of 21.6%.

Prospects: Moving forward, Co. is well positioned to continue reaping the benefits of its operating successes and improved financial position. For full-year 2005, for cable television, Co. expects basic video subscribers growth of 1.5% to 2.0%, revenue generating unit net additions of 1.0 million to 1.3 million, total revenue growth in the mid teens, adjusted operating cash flow growth in the mid teens, and capital expenditures of between $600.0 million and $650.0 million. In addition, for full-year 2005, for Rainbow Media, Co. is projecting AMC/IFC/WE total revenue growth in the range of mid to high single digit, and adjusted operating cash flow growth of between mid and high single digit.

Financial Data (US$ in Thousands)	12/31/2004	12/31/2003	12/31/2002	12/31/2001	12/31/2000	12/31/1999	12/31/1998	12/31/1997
Earnings Per Share	(2.36)	(1.04)	0.28	3.71	1.29	(5.12)	(3.16)	(0.12)
Cash Flow Per Share	2.13	1.59	1.33	(1.27)	0.71	1.75	2.82	2.73
Income Statement								
Total Revenue	4,932,864	4,177,148	4,003,407	4,404,546	4,411,048	3,942,985	3,265,143	1,949,358
EBITDA	955,208	1,470,914	768,455	2,908,531	...	...	...	...
Depn & Amortn	1,245,125	1,130,527	980,005	1,187,090	1,028,575	903,204	742,639	507,516
Income Before Taxes	(1,000,698)	(262,749)	(698,663)	1,195,465	...	...	...	...
Income Taxes	(333,696)	20,367	(137,814)	187,732	...	...	...	...
Net Income	(676,092)	(297,239)	90,112	1,007,733	229,253	(800,607)	(448,504)	136,663
Average Shares	287,085	285,486	331,959	177,172	173,913	156,503	142,016	99,608
Balance Sheet								
Current Assets	2,374,787	1,061,816	920,315	938,868	788,107	638,052	766,080	778,942
Total Assets	11,393,206	11,189,199	10,488,253	10,216,800	8,273,290	7,130,308	7,061,062	5,625,091
Current Liabilities	2,127,014	1,620,058	1,610,705	1,519,933	4,814,861	4,360,083	4,068,011	3,594,267
Long-Term Obligations	10,368,228	8,374,742	7,676,927	6,977,523	3,856,029	3,840,214	3,306,059	2,453,704
Total Liabilities	14,023,540	13,099,000	10,043,894	9,393,465	8,670,890	8,200,297	7,374,070	6,047,971
Stockholders' Equity	(2,630,334)	(1,989,802)	(1,723,832)	(1,585,906)	(2,529,879)	(3,067,083)	(2,611,685)	(2,378,773)
Shares Outstanding	287,803	286,809	280,134	270,092	174,921	173,210	151,494	100,284
Statistical Record								
Return on Assets %	N.M.	N.M.	0.87	10.90	2.97	N.M.	N.M.	3.16
EBITDA Margin %	19.36	35.21	19.20	66.03	...	...	...	...
Net Margin %	N.M.	N.M.	2.25	22.88	5.20	N.M.	N.M.	7.01
Asset Turnover	0.44	0.39	0.39	0.48	0.57	0.56	0.51	0.45
Current Ratio	1.12	0.66	0.57	0.62	0.16	0.15	0.19	0.22
Price Range	27.37-16.68	23.45-15.72	48.01-4.95	76.45-33.64	72.79-48.42	76.03-42.58	42.58-18.63	20.33-5.95
P/E Ratio	...	...	171.46-17.68	20.61-9.07	56.42-37.53	...	...	...

Address: 1111 Stewart Avenue, Bethpage, NY 11714-3581 **Telephone:** (516) 803-2300 **Fax:** (516) 803-2273	**Web Site:** www.cablevision.com **Officers:** Charles F. Dolan - Chmn. William J. Bell - Vice-Chmn.	**Auditors:** KPMG LLP **Investor Contact:** 516-803-2270 **Transfer Agents:** Mellon Investor Services

CABOT CORP.

Exchange	Symbol	Price	52Wk Range	Yield	P/E
NYS	CBT	$33.43 (3/31/2005)	40.70-31.65	1.91	17.50

*7 Year Price Score 121.45 *NYSE Composite Index=100   *12 Month Price Score 88.59

Interim Earnings (Per Share)

Qtr.	Dec	Mar	Jun	Sep
2001-02	0.53	0.36	0.28	0.33
2002-03	0.48	0.33	(0.09)	0.40
2003-04	0.42	0.54	0.62	0.25
2004-05	0.51	...	...	...

Interim Dividends (Per Share)

Amt	Decl	Ex	Rec	Pay
0.15Q	5/14/2004	5/26/2004	5/28/2004	6/11/2004
0.15Q	7/9/2004	8/25/2004	8/27/2004	9/10/2004
0.16Q	11/12/2004	11/23/2004	11/26/2004	12/10/2004
0.16Q	1/14/2005	2/23/2005	2/25/2005	3/11/2005

Indicated Div: $0.64

Valuation Analysis

Forecast P/E	14.01	No of Institutions	
	(4/7/2005)	195	
Market Cap	$2.1 Billion	Shares	
Book Value	1.3 Billion	51,091,820	
Price/Book	1.67	% Held	
Price/Sales	1.06	81.24	

Business Summary: Chemicals (MIC: 11.1 SIC: 895 NAIC: 25182)

Cabot is a global company with businesses in specialty chemicals, performance materials, and specialty fluids. Co. and its affiliates operate manufacturing facilities in the U.S. and more than 20 other countries. Co. manufactures, markets and distributes fine powders through four specialty chemical businesses: carbon black; fumed metal oxides; inkjet colorants; and aerogels. Carbon black is a form of elemental carbon, which is manufactured in a highly controlled process to produce particles and aggregates of varied structure and surface chemistry, resulting in many different performance characteristics for a wide variety of applications.

Recent Developments: For the quarter ended Dec 31 2004, net income increased 20.7% to $35,000 thousand from net income of $29,000 thousand in the year-earlier quarter. Revenues were $495,000 thousand, up 11.0% from $446,000 thousand the year before. Operating income was $48,000 thousand versus an income of $44,000 thousand in the prior-year quarter, an increase of 9.1%. Total direct expense was $378,000 thousand versus $339,000 thousand in the prior-year quarter, an increase of 11.5%. Total indirect expense was $69,000 thousand versus $63,000 thousand in the prior-year quarter, an increase of 9.5%.

Prospects: Going forward, Co. anticipates continued strong volumes in its chemicals business as well as substantial growth in both inkjet colorants and specialty fluids. Specifically, Co. continues to invest in its new businesses and anticipates that they will be growing contributors to Co.'s profitability. Additionally, Co. stated it is managing tight capacities within its carbon black and fumed metal oxides businesses and is encouraged by the strengthening of the economic environment in its areas of interest. Also, Co. anticipates modest gains in its super-metals business during the rest of fiscal 2005.

Financial Data

(US$ in Thousands)	3 Mos	09/30/2004	09/30/2003	09/30/2002	09/30/2001	09/30/2000	09/30/1999	09/30/1998
Earnings Per Share	1.91	1.82	1.14	1.50	1.66	6.20	1.31	1.61
Cash Flow Per Share	3.36	4.07	4.31	3.25	0.42	4.11	3.25	3.60
Tang Book Value Per Share	17.01	16.21	14.34	12.81	13.63	14.05	9.10	9.01
Dividends Per Share	0.610	0.600	0.540	0.520	0.480	0.440	0.440	0.420
Dividend Payout %	31.87	32.97	47.37	34.67	28.92	7.10	33.59	26.09
Income Statement								
Total Revenue	495,000	1,934,000	1,795,000	1,557,000	1,698,000	1,523,000	1,699,000	1,652,800
EBITDA	88,000	328,000	257,000	271,000	265,000	277,000	261,000	283,400
Depn & Amortn	35,000	134,000	135,000	109,000	115,000	120,000	125,000	115,400
Income Before Taxes	45,000	164,000	94,000	134,000	150,000	157,000	136,000	168,000
Income Taxes	9,000	39,000	17,000	30,000	42,000	57,000	49,000	60,500
Net Income	35,000	124,000	80,000	106,000	124,000	453,000	97,000	121,600
Average Shares	69,000	68,000	70,000	71,000	74,000	73,000	73,000	74,600
Balance Sheet								
Current Assets	1,262,000	1,173,000	1,140,000	959,000	968,000	1,190,000	659,000	618,900
Total Assets	2,537,000	2,426,000	2,308,000	2,067,000	1,919,000	2,134,000	1,842,000	1,805,200
Current Liabilities	493,000	372,000	352,000	286,000	291,000	494,000	450,000	536,300
Long-Term Obligations	391,000	506,000	516,000	495,000	419,000	329,000	419,000	316,300
Total Liabilities	1,224,000	1,235,000	1,229,000	1,090,000	969,000	1,087,000	1,136,000	1,099,700
Stockholders' Equity	1,260,000	1,191,000	1,079,000	977,000	950,000	1,047,000	706,000	705,500
Shares Outstanding	62,972	62,243	62,080	61,615	62,633	67,700	67,123	67,241
Statistical Record								
Return on Assets %	5.28	5.22	3.66	5.32	6.12	22.72	5.32	6.70
Return on Equity %	10.91	10.90	7.78	11.00	12.42	51.54	13.74	16.97
EBITDA Margin %	17.78	16.96	14.32	17.41	15.61	18.19	15.36	17.15
Net Margin %	7.07	6.41	4.46	6.81	7.30	29.74	5.71	7.36
Asset Turnover	0.81	0.81	0.82	0.78	0.84	0.76	0.93	0.91
Current Ratio	2.56	3.15	3.24	3.35	3.33	2.41	1.46	1.15
Debt to Equity	0.31	0.42	0.48	0.51	0.44	0.31	0.59	0.45
Price Range	40.70-30.32	40.70-27.08	30.60-19.53	41.87-21.00	41.35-18.56	22.02-10.57	18.08-11.40	22.36-12.51
P/E Ratio	21.31-15.87	22.36-14.88	26.84-17.13	27.91-14.00	24.91-11.18	3.55-1.70	13.80-8.70	13.89-7.77
Average Yield %	1.71	1.77	2.08	1.68	1.51	2.92	3.01	2.44

Address: Two Seaport Lane, Suite 1300, Boston, MA 02210-2019	Web Site: www.cabot-corp.com	Auditors: PricewaterhouseCoopers LLP
Telephone: (617) 345-0100	Officers: Kennett F. Burnes - Chmn., Pres., C.E.O. William J. Brady - Exec. V.P.	Investor Contact: 617-345-0100
Fax: (617) 242-6103		Transfer Agents: EquiServe Trust Company N.A., Providence, RI

CADENCE DESIGN SYSTEMS, INC.

Exchange	Symbol	Price	52Wk Range	Yield	P/E
NYS	CDN	$14.95 (3/31/2005)	15.18-11.55	N/A	59.80

7 Year Price Score 61.93 *NYSE Composite Index=100* **12 Month Price Score 96.47**

Interim Earnings (Per Share)

Qtr.	Mar	Jun	Sep	Dec
2001	0.01	(0.12)	0.50	0.15
2002	0.08	(0.18)	0.03	0.34
2003	(0.07)	(0.03)	(0.06)	0.09
2004	(0.03)	0.01	0.07	0.20

Interim Dividends (Per Share)

No Dividends Paid

Valuation Analysis

Forecast P/E	18.38	No of Institutions
	(4/13/2005)	212
Market Cap	$4.1 Billion	Shares
Book Value	1.7 Billion	249,103,584
Price/Book	2.39	% Held
Price/Sales	3.39	90.80

Business Summary: IT & Technology (MIC: 10.2 SIC: 372 NAIC: 11210)

Cadence Design Systems licenses electronic design automation, software, sells or leases hardware technology and provides design and methodology services. Co.'s range of products and services are used by electronic companies to design and develop complex integrated circuits and personal and commercial electronic systems. Co. has about 60 sales offices, design centers and research facilities around the world. Co. operates in three segments: products, services and maintenance. The products unit develops and markets software and hardware technologies. The maintenance unit services the ongoing, after-sale support requirements of those products. The services unit provides educational services.

Recent Developments: For the year ended Jan 2 2005, net income amounted to $74,474 thousand compared with a net loss of $17,566 thousand in the previous year. Results for 2004 and 2003 included pretax non-recurring charges of $22,542 thousand and $59,836 thousand, respectively. Revenues were $1,197,480 thousand, up 6.9% from $1,119,484 thousand the year before. Total costs and expenses slipped 3.0% to $1,096,308 thousand from $1,129,448 thousand in the previous year. Operating income was $101,172 thousand versus a loss of $9,964 thousand in the prior year.

Prospects: Co.'s pending acquisition of Verisity Ltd., a supplier of process automation applications for functional verification, is progressing as the two companies announced that the waiting period under the Hart-Scott-Rodino Antitrust Act relating to the proposed acquisition had expired on Feb 25 2005. The two companies signed a definitive agreement on Jan 12 2005 under which Co. agreed to acquire Verisity in an all-cash transaction for $12.00 in cash in exchange for each outstanding share of Verisity stock. Verisity presently maintains offices throughout Asia, Europe, and North America.

Financial Data
(US$ in Thousands)

	01/01/2005	01/03/2004	12/28/2002	12/29/2001	12/30/2000	01/01/2000	01/02/1999	01/03/1998
Earnings Per Share	0.25	(0.07)	0.27	0.55	0.19	(0.06)	0.14	0.77
Cash Flow Per Share	1.38	0.63	1.35	1.02	0.58	0.53	1.16	1.00
Tang Book Value Per Share	1.83	1.41	2.88	2.78	2.35	2.36	2.62	3.38
Income Statement								
Total Revenue	1,197,480	1,119,484	1,293,067	1,430,440	1,279,550	1,093,303	1,216,070	915,893
EBITDA	260,435	153,311	342,644	413,793	223,039	116,298	184,045	300,815
Depn & Amortn	173,385	182,302	181,875	175,530	157,203	129,788	78,243	56,637
Income Before Taxes	86,437	(30,565)	157,966	242,148	67,996	(11,380)	112,667	259,631
Income Taxes	11,963	(12,999)	86,017	100,861	18,019	2,695	80,685	77,889
Net Income	74,474	(17,566)	71,949	141,287	49,977	(14,075)	31,982	169,466
Average Shares	305,774	266,794	267,500	257,660	262,696	242,037	233,647	219,552
Balance Sheet								
Current Assets	1,069,915	842,241	758,643	634,922	556,848	479,912	579,710	609,059
Total Assets	2,989,839	2,817,902	2,438,261	1,730,030	1,477,321	1,459,659	1,405,958	1,023,850
Current Liabilities	548,958	481,928	511,890	472,391	491,574	421,558	327,912	268,795
Long-Term Obligations	420,000	420,061	52,659	1,476	3,298	25,024	136,380	1,599
Total Liabilities	1,289,869	1,245,621	778,956	608,683	567,856	473,510	548,479	296,753
Stockholders' Equity	1,699,970	1,572,281	1,659,305	1,121,347	909,465	986,149	857,479	727,097
Shares Outstanding	271,563	268,442	269,688	249,904	243,662	243,328	214,438	207,666
Statistical Record								
Return on Assets %	2.57	N.M.	3.46	8.83	3.41	N.M.	2.64	19.15
Return on Equity %	4.56	N.M.	5.19	13.95	5.29	N.M.	4.05	28.88
EBITDA Margin %	21.75	13.69	26.50	28.93	17.43	10.64	15.13	32.84
Net Margin %	6.22	N.M.	5.56	9.88	3.91	N.M.	2.63	18.50
Asset Turnover	0.41	0.42	0.62	0.89	0.87	0.77	1.00	1.04
Current Ratio	1.95	1.75	1.48	1.34	1.13	1.14	1.77	2.27
Debt to Equity	0.25	0.27	0.03	N.M.	N.M.	0.03	0.16	N.M.
Price Range	19.40-11.55	18.32-9.24	24.12-8.95	32.31-15.48	28.69-13.50	33.50-9.31	38.00-19.19	28.75-13.38
P/E Ratio	77.60-46.20	...	89.33-33.15	58.75-28.15	150.99-71.05	...	271.43-137.05	37.34-17.37

Address: 2655 Seely Avenue, Building 5, San Jose, CA 95134 Telephone: (408) 943-1234 Fax: (408) 943-0513	Web Site: www.cadence.com Officers: Donald L. Lucas - Chmn. H. Raymond Bingham - Exec. Chmn.	Auditors: KPMG LLP Investor Contact: 408-236-5972 Transfer Agents: Mellon Investor Services, South Hackensack, NJ

CAESARS ENTERTAINMENT INC

Exchange	Symbol	Price	52Wk Range	Yield	P/E
NYS	CZR	$19.79 (3/31/2005)	20.75-12.42	N/A	21.05

*7 Year Price Score N/A   *NYSE Composite Index=100   *12 Month Price Score 111.18

Interim Earnings (Per Share)

Qtr.	Mar	Jun	Sep	Dec
2001	0.15	0.16	(0.34)	(0.05)
2002	(3.09)	0.32	0.13	(0.07)
2003	0.14	0.14	0.16	(0.28)
2004	0.23	0.47	0.18	0.06

Interim Dividends (Per Share)

No Dividends Paid

Valuation Analysis

Forecast P/E	24.70	No of Institutions
	(4/7/2005)	235
Market Cap	$6.2 Billion	Shares
Book Value	3.5 Billion	227,324,752
Price/Book	1.78	% Held
Price/Sales	1.48	72.22

Business Summary: Hospitality & Tourism (MIC: 5.1 SIC: 011 NAIC: 21120)

Caesars Entertainment is primarily engaged in the ownership, operation and development of gaming facilities, and conducts its operations under the Caesars, Bally's, Flamingo, Grand Casinos, Hilton, Paris and Conrad brands. As of Dec 31 2003, Co. operated a total of 29 properties on four continents. As of Sep 30 2003, Co. had an 82.0%-owned and managed riverboat casino in Harrison County, IN, a 50.0%-owned and managed riverboat casino in Windsor, Canada, the casino operations of Caesars Palace at Sea, and two partially owned and managed casinos in Nova Scotia, Canada. Co. partially owns and manages two casino investments internationally, one in South Africa and one in Uruguay.

Recent Developments: For the year ended Dec 31 2004, net income increased 545.7% to $297 million from net income of $46 million a year earlier. Revenues were $4,206 million, up 6.6% from $3,945 million the year before. Operating income was $622 million versus an income of $434 million in the prior year, an increase of 43.3%. Total direct expense was $2,033 million versus $2,010 million in the prior year, an increase of 1.1%. Total indirect expense was $1,556 million versus $1,510 million in the prior year, an increase of 3.0%.

Prospects: Co. is performing well, supported by the strong performance of its Las Vegas, NV resorts and better than expected results in Atlantic City, NJ. Co. is also benefiting from major capital development projects it has completed in the past few years, including The Colosseum and The Roman Plaza at Caesars Palace, and the efficiency-enhancing technology tools Co. developed in its casinos, hotels, lounges and restaurants. Separately, on Mar 11 2005, Co. announced that stockholders of both companies approved an agreement to be acquired by Harrah's Operating Company, a wholly owned subsidiary of Harrah's Entertainment. Co. expects the transaction to close during the second quarter of 2005.

Financial Data

(US$ in Thousands)	12/31/2004	12/31/2003	12/31/2002	12/31/2001	12/31/2000	12/31/1999	12/31/1998	12/31/1997
Earnings Per Share	0.94	0.15	(2.71)	(0.08)	0.46	0.44	0.42	0.25
Cash Flow Per Share	2.31	2.05	2.35	2.13	2.49	1.71	1.22	1.43
Tang Book Value Per Share	8.90	7.45	7.06	6.49	6.52	6.01	7.63	7.22
Income Statement								
Total Revenue	4,206,000	4,455,000	4,652,000	4,581,000	4,896,000	3,176,000	2,305,000	2,572,000
EBITDA	1,051,000	915,000	1,102,000	922,000	1,223,000	722,000	550,000	435,000
Depn & Amortn	421,000	450,000	483,000	536,000	506,000	312,000	227,000	209,000
Income Before Taxes	349,000	132,000	264,000	(10,000)	265,000	253,000	223,000	134,000
Income Taxes	158,000	75,000	102,000	12,000	121,000	113,000	111,000	63,000
Net Income	297,000	46,000	(824,000)	(24,000)	143,000	136,000	109,000	67,000
Average Shares	316,000	304,000	304,000	299,000	301,000	309,000	263,000	266,000
Balance Sheet								
Current Assets	737,000	702,000	777,000	811,000	847,000	893,000	634,000	509,000
Total Assets	9,597,000	9,542,000	9,674,000	10,808,000	10,995,000	11,151,000	7,174,000	5,689,000
Current Liabilities	830,000	675,000	1,015,000	636,000	677,000	733,000	440,000	393,000
Long-Term Obligations	4,143,000	4,618,000	4,585,000	5,301,000	5,397,000	5,616,000	2,466,000	1,272,000
Total Liabilities	6,115,000	6,484,000	6,717,000	7,041,000	7,211,000	7,411,000	3,566,000	2,308,000
Stockholders' Equity	3,482,000	3,058,000	2,957,000	3,767,000	3,784,000	3,740,000	3,608,000	3,381,000
Shares Outstanding	313,800	303,800	300,600	301,300	297,600	304,000	303,000	288,000
Statistical Record								
Return on Assets %	3.10	0.48	N.M.	N.M.	1.29	1.48	1.69	1.20
Return on Equity %	9.06	1.53	N.M.	N.M.	3.79	3.70	3.12	2.05
EBITDA Margin %	24.99	20.54	23.69	20.13	24.98	22.73	23.86	16.91
Net Margin %	7.06	1.03	N.M.	N.M.	2.92	4.28	4.73	2.60
Asset Turnover	0.44	0.46	0.45	0.42	0.44	0.35	0.36	0.46
Current Ratio	0.89	1.04	0.77	1.28	1.25	1.22	1.44	1.30
Debt to Equity	1.19	1.51	1.55	1.43	1.43	1.50	0.68	0.38
Price Range	20.15-10.83	11.09-6.67	12.34-6.40	12.86-6.31	15.13-10.00	13.75-6.19	7.00-6.00	...
P/E Ratio	21.44-11.52	73.93-44.47	...	...	32.88-21.74	31.25-14.06	16.67-14.29	...

Address: 3930 Howard Hughes Parkway, Las Vegas, NV 89109 Telephone: (702) 699-5000 Fax: (702) 699-5121	Web Site: www.parkplace.com Officers: Stephen F. Bollenbach - Chmn. Clive S. Cummis - Vice-Chmn., Exec. V.P., Law & Corp. Affairs, Sec.	Auditors: Deloitte & Touche LLP Investor Contact: 702-699-5269

CALIFORNIA WATER SERVICE GROUP

			52Wk Range	Yield	P/E	Div Acheiver
Exchange	Symbol	Price	37.70-26.19	3.42	22.86	37 Years
NYS	CWT	$33.37 (3/31/2005)				

*7 Year Price Score 98.63 ***NYSE Composite Index=100** ***12 Month Price Score 103.45**

Interim Earnings (Per Share)

Qtr.	Mar	Jun	Sep	Dec
2001	0.01	0.37	0.39	0.20
2002	0.12	0.43	0.50	0.19
2003	(0.05)	0.30	0.53	0.42
2004	0.08	...	0.59	0.19

Interim Dividends (Per Share)

Amt	Decl	Ex	Rec	Pay
0.282Q	4/28/2004	5/6/2004	5/10/2004	5/21/2004
0.282Q	7/28/2004	8/5/2004	8/9/2004	8/20/2004
0.282Q	10/28/2004	11/4/2004	11/8/2004	11/19/2004
0.285Q	1/26/2005	2/3/2005	2/7/2005	2/18/2005

Indicated Div: $1.14 (Div. Reinv. Plan)

Valuation Analysis

Forecast P/E	N/A	No of Institutions
Market Cap	$612.9 Million	Shares
Book Value	291.1 Million	4,410,925
Price/Book	2.11	% Held
Price/Sales	1.94	24.01

Business Summary: Water Utilities (MIC: 7.2 SIC: 941 NAIC: 21310)

California Water Service Group is a utility water company that provides regulated and non-regulated water utility services to over 2.0 million customers in 99 communities in California, Washington, New Mexico and Hawaii as of Dec 31 2003. Co. is the parent company of California Water Service Company, Washington Water Service Company, New Mexico Water Service Company, Hawaii Water Service Company and CWS Utility Services. The sole business of Co. consists of the production, purchase, storage, purification, distribution and sale of water for domestic, industrial, public, and irrigation uses, and for fire protection. Annual water production totaled nearly 132.00 billion gallons for 2003.

Recent Developments: For the year ended Dec 31 2004, Co. reported net income of $26,026 thousand versus $19,417 thousand the year before. Operating revenues rose 13.9% to $315,567 thousand compared with $277,128 thousand a year earlier. Total direct operating expenses increased 10.0% to $206,150 thousand from $187,469 thousand in 2003. Total indirect operating expenses were $67,934 thousand, up 14.3% from $59,425 thousand the year before. Net operating income rose 37.2% to $41,483 thousand from $30,234 thousand in 2003.

Prospects: Co. stated that it will continue to pursue rate relief that reflects the higher costs of providing services. Co. noted that it received approval to raise rates on an annual basis by $4.1 million for step rate increases effective in Jan 2005. Also, Co. has received approval to collect $9.2 million related to balancing accounts. The collection periods vary by district and range from one to three years. Pending applications to the California Public Utilities Commission (CPUC) include 2004 general rate case filings totaling over $26.0 million for eight districts and corporate headquarters. Co. noted that it cannot predict the final amount or the timing of the CPUC's decisions on pending filings.

Financial Data
(US$ in Thousands)

	12/31/2004	12/31/2003	12/31/2002	12/31/2001	12/31/2000	12/31/1999	12/31/1998	12/31/1997
Earnings Per Share	1.46	1.21	1.25	0.97	1.31	1.53	1.45	1.83
Cash Flow Per Share	3.13	2.80	2.20	2.54	2.28	3.30	2.97	3.12
Tang Book Value Per Share	15.66	14.44	13.12	12.95	13.13	13.70	13.38	13.00
Dividends Per Share	1.130	1.125	1.120	1.115	1.100	1.085	1.070	1.055
Dividend Payout %	77.40	92.98	89.60	114.95	83.97	70.92	73.79	57.65
Income Statement								
Total Revenue	315,567	277,128	263,151	246,820	244,806	206,440	186,273	195,324
Depn & Amortn	26,114	23,256	21,238	19,226	18,368	15,802	14,563	13,670
Income Taxes	17,084	12,898	12,568	...	...	...	...	...
Net Income	26,026	19,417	19,073	14,965	19,963	19,919	18,395	23,305
Average Shares	17,674	15,893	15,185	15,285	15,173	12,936	12,619	12,619
Balance Sheet								
Net PPE	800,305	759,498	696,988	624,342	582,008	515,354	478,305	460,407
Total Assets	942,853	873,035	800,582	710,214	666,605	587,618	548,499	531,297
Long-Term Obligations	274,821	272,226	250,365	202,600	187,098	156,572	136,345	139,205
Total Liabilities	651,773	625,036	597,890	510,120	464,296	406,961	376,220	363,757
Stockholders' Equity	291,080	247,999	202,692	200,094	202,309	180,657	172,279	167,540
Shares Outstanding	18,367	16,932	15,182	15,182	15,146	12,936	12,619	12,619
Statistical Record								
Return on Assets %	2.86	2.32	2.52	2.17	3.17	3.51	3.41	4.47
Return on Equity %	9.63	8.62	9.47	7.44	10.40	11.29	10.83	14.33
Net Margin %	8.25	7.01	7.25	6.06	8.15	9.65	9.88	11.93
PPE Turnover	0.40	0.38	0.40	0.41	0.44	0.42	0.40	0.43
Asset Turnover	0.35	0.33	0.35	0.36	0.39	0.36	0.35	0.37
Debt to Equity	0.94	1.10	1.24	1.01	0.92	0.87	0.79	0.83
Price Range	37.70-26.19	30.97-23.65	26.69-21.60	28.60-23.38	30.94-21.69	31.88-22.94	32.75-21.00	29.53-18.81
P/E Ratio	25.82-17.94	25.60-19.55	21.35-17.28	29.48-24.10	23.62-16.56	20.83-14.99	22.59-14.48	16.14-10.28
Average Yield %	3.86	4.22	4.31	4.37	4.28	3.99	4.16	4.60

Address: 1720 North First Street, San Jose, CA 95112	**Web Site:** www.calwater.com	**Auditors:** KPMG LLP
Telephone: (408) 367 8200	**Officers:** Robert W. Foy - Chmn. Peter C. Nelson - Pres., C.E.O.	**Investor Contact:** 408-367-8200
Fax: (408) 437 9185		**Transfer Agents:** State Street Bank and Trust Company, Boston, MA

CALLAWAY GOLF CO.

Exchange	Symbol	Price	52Wk Range	Yield	P/E
NYS	ELY	$12.80 (3/31/2005)	19.95-9.28	2.19	N/A

*7 Year Price Score 72.93 ***NYSE Composite Index=100** ***12 Month Price Score 96.12**

Interim Earnings (Per Share)

Qtr.	Mar	Jun	Sep	Dec
2001	0.47	0.38	0.09	(0.10)
2002	0.46	0.55	0.11	(0.08)
2003	0.64	0.52	0.03	(0.51)
2004	0.59	0.20	(0.53)	(0.42)

Interim Dividends (Per Share)

Amt	Decl	Ex	Rec	Pay
0.07Q	5/25/2004	6/9/2004	6/11/2004	7/2/2004
0.07Q	8/25/2004	9/3/2004	9/8/2004	9/29/2004
0.07Q	11/23/2004	12/2/2004	12/6/2004	12/27/2004
0.07Q	3/3/2005	3/15/2005	3/17/2005	4/7/2005

Indicated Div: $0.28

Valuation Analysis

Forecast P/E	18.99	No of Institutions
	(4/7/2005)	157
Market Cap	$884.6 Million	Shares
Book Value	586.3 Million	62,466,192
Price/Book	1.51	% Held
Price/Sales	0.95	81.88

TRADING VOLUME (thousand shares)

Business Summary: Consumer Accessories (MIC: 4.6 SIC: 949 NAIC: 39920)

Callaway Golf manufactures golf clubs, golf balls, and sells golf accessories. Primary products include Big Bertha® Hawk Eye VFT® titanium metal woods, ERC Fusion and ERC Fusion+ drivers, ERC Forged titanium drivers, and ERC II Forged titanium metal woods, Great Big Bertha® II titanium metal woods, Great Big Bertha™ II+ titanium drivers, Big Bertha Steelhead Plus and Big Bertha Steelhead III metal woods, Big Bertha C4 drivers, Great Big Bertha Hawk Eye and Great Big Bertha Hawk Eye VFT Tungsten Injected™ titanium irons, Steelhead X-16 Pro Series stainless steel irons, and Odyssey® putters. The golf ball product line brand names include Top-Flite®, Strata®, and Ben Hogan® brands.

Recent Developments: For the year ended Dec 31 2004, net loss was $10,103 thousand versus net income of $45,523 thousand a year earlier. Revenues were $934,564 thousand, up 14.8% from $814,032 thousand the year before. Operating loss was $24,702 thousand versus an income of $65,855 thousand in the prior year. Total direct expense was $575,742 thousand versus $445,417 thousand in the prior year, an increase of 29.3%. Total indirect expense was $383,524 thousand versus $302,760 thousand in the prior year, an increase of 26.7%.

Prospects: Co.'s near-term prospect appear favorable, reflecting pricing initiatives taken mid-year 2004 to reduce inventory levels at retail prior to the start of 2005. Meanwhile, Co. has a wide range of new products to introduce across its brands for 2005. In addition to the Callaway Golf® Heavenwood® Hybrids, Big Bertha® Fusion® Irons, and the Odyssey® White Steel™ putters launched in late 2004, Co. has recently launched is new Big Bertha Titanium 454 Driver, X-18 and X-18™ Pro Series Irons, and the HX® Hot Golf Ball. These products will be supported by marketing plans developed in conjunction with Co.'s new advertising agency, Young & Rubicam.

Financial Data
(US$ in Thousands)

	12/31/2004	12/31/2003	12/31/2002	12/31/2001	12/31/2000	12/31/1999	12/31/1998	12/31/1997
Earnings Per Share	(0.15)	0.68	1.03	0.82	1.13	0.78	(0.38)	1.85
Cash Flow Per Share	0.13	1.80	2.09	1.43	1.30	2.36	0.44	2.42
Tang Book Value Per Share	5.88	6.27	5.57	5.05	5.38	4.98	4.33	4.97
Dividends Per Share	0.280	0.280	0.280	0.280	0.280	0.280	0.280	0.280
Dividend Payout %	...	41.18	27.18	34.15	24.78	35.90	...	15.14
Income Statement								
Total Revenue	934,564	814,032	792,064	816,163	837,627	714,471	697,621	842,927
EBITDA	27,641	113,901	150,971	137,211	171,095	128,968	(343)	233,173
Depn & Amortn	51,154	44,496	37,640	37,467	40,249	39,877	35,885	19,408
Income Before Taxes	(23,713)	67,883	111,671	98,192	129,322	85,497	(38,899)	213,765
Income Taxes	(13,610)	22,360	42,225	39,817	47,366	30,175	(12,335)	81,061
Net Income	(10,103)	45,523	69,446	58,375	80,999	55,322	(26,564)	132,704
Average Shares	67,721	66,471	67,274	71,314	71,412	70,397	69,463	71,698
Balance Sheet								
Current Assets	393,732	383,462	369,027	354,691	342,469	310,472	323,606	281,786
Total Assets	735,737	748,566	679,845	647,602	630,934	616,783	655,827	561,714
Current Liabilities	120,798	130,160	109,161	101,874	109,306	105,274	184,008	72,384
Long-Term Obligations	26	154	...	3,160	...	...	...	...
Total Liabilities	149,420	159,183	136,458	133,253	119,190	116,849	202,731	80,289
Stockholders' Equity	586,317	589,383	543,387	514,349	511,744	499,934	453,096	481,425
Shares Outstanding	69,111	66,862	75,805	77,755	74,142	76,302	75,098	74,252
Statistical Record								
Return on Assets %	N.M.	6.37	10.46	9.13	12.95	8.69	N.M.	26.81
Return on Equity %	N.M.	8.04	13.13	11.38	15.97	11.61	N.M.	31.46
EBITDA Margin %	2.96	13.99	19.06	16.81	20.43	18.05	N.M.	27.66
Net Margin %	N.M.	5.59	8.77	7.15	9.67	7.74	N.M.	15.74
Asset Turnover	1.26	1.14	1.19	1.28	1.34	1.12	1.15	1.70
Current Ratio	3.26	2.95	3.38	3.48	3.13	2.95	1.76	3.89
Debt to Equity	N.M.	N.M.	...	0.01	...	...	...	...
Price Range	19.95-9.28	17.07-10.50	20.40-9.55	27.01-12.21	20.56-11.00	18.00-9.31	33.25-9.56	38.38-26.13
P/E Ratio	...	25.10-15.44	19.81-9.27	32.94-14.89	18.20-9.73	23.08-11.94	...	20.74-14.12
Average Yield %	1.97	1.97	1.80	1.49	1.77	2.19	1.47	0.86

Address: 2180 Rutherford Road, Carlsbad, CA 92008-8815	Web Site: www.callawaygolf.com	Auditors: DELOITTE & TOUCHE LLP
Telephone: (760) 931-1771	Officers: Ronald A. Drapeau - Chmn., C.E.O. Patrice Hutin - Pres., C.O.O.	Investor Contact: 760-931-1771
Fax: (760) 931-8013		

CALPINE CORP.

Exchange	Symbol	Price	52Wk Range	Yield	P/E
NYS	CPN	$2.80 (3/31/2005)	4.94-2.32	N/A	N/A

*7 Year Price Score 22.17   *NYSE Composite Index=100   *12 Month Price Score 84.19

Interim Earnings (Per Share)

Qtr.	Mar	Jun	Sep	Dec
2001	0.30	0.32	0.88	0.30
2002	(0.24)	0.19	0.36	(0.12)
2003	(0.14)	(0.06)	0.51	0.30
2004	(0.17)	(0.07)	0.32	(0.64)

Interim Dividends (Per Share)

Amt	Decl	Ex	Rec	Pay
2-for-1	5/18/2000	6/9/2000	5/29/2000	6/8/2000
2-for-1	10/26/2000	11/15/2000	11/6/2000	11/14/2000

Valuation Analysis

Forecast P/E	0.00	No of Institutions	
	(4/13/2005)	272	
Market Cap	$1.5 Billion	Shares	
Book Value	4.6 Billion	377,799,488	
Price/Book	0.32	% Held	
Price/Sales	0.17	70.71	

TRADING VOLUME (thousand shares)

Business Summary: Electricity (MIC: 7.1 SIC: 911 NAIC: 21121)

Calpine is an independent power company engaged in the development, acquisition, ownership and operation of power generation facilities, and the sale of electricity predominantly in the U.S., but also in Canada and the U.K. Co. owns about 1.00 trillion cubic feet equivalent of proved natural gas reserves in Canada and the U.S. Co. also owns interests in 82 power plants having a net capacity of 19,319 megawatts (mw). Additionally, Co. has 18 gas-fired projects and three project expansions under construction having a net capacity of 10,702 mw. The completion of the new projects would give Co. interests in 100 power plants located in 23 states, three Canadian provinces and the U.K.

Recent Developments: For the year ended Dec 31 2004, Co. reported a loss from continuing operations of $440.8 million compared with income of $86.1 million a year earlier. Results for 2004 and 2003 included equipment cancellation and impairment costs of $42.4 million and $64.4 million, and long-term service agreement cancellation charges of $11.3 million and $16.4 million, respectively. Total revenue increased 4.0% to $9.23 billion from $8.87 billion the previous year. Income from operations decreased 98.9% to $5.7 million compared with $510.4 million the year before.

Prospects: For the year ended Dec 31 2005, Co. is expecting its loss per share to be in the range of $0.80 to $0.90. Also, Co. has outlined a program for 2005 that includes the completion of identified liquidity transactions, the repurchase of more than $1.00 billion of corporate debt, credit enhancement for Calpine Energy Services, additional power sales contracts, reductions in plant operating costs, turbine deployment and the expansion of its services business. The effect from these transactions has not been included in the aforementioned guidance. Meanwhile, Co. noted that as of Feb 24 2005 it was pursuing more than 22,000 megawatts of power sales opportunities throughout the North American market.

Financial Data

(US$ in Thousands)	9 Mos	6 Mos	3 Mos	12/31/2003	12/31/2002	12/31/2001	12/31/2000	12/31/1999
Earnings Per Share	0.09	0.56	0.58	0.71	0.33	1.87	1.10	0.43
Cash Flow Per Share	0.78	0.45	(0.11)	0.74	3.01	1.84	2.45	1.26
Tang Book Value Per Share	8.44	10.17	10.70	10.81	9.78	9.80	7.88	3.82
Income Statement								
Total Revenue	6,893,706	4,357,372	2,042,738	8,919,539	7,457,899	7,589,978	2,282,793	847,735
EBITDA	1,118,293	640,116	259,917	1,531,347	942,744	1,448,945	702,031	312,482
Depn & Amortn	598,855	397,143	197,183	735,341	542,176	369,870	141,594	87,210
Income Before Taxes	(256,753)	(269,498)	(179,998)	109,619	29,996	986,323	543,638	158,216
Income Taxes	(81,955)	(146,553)	(85,949)	(134)	(19,096)	345,261	218,951	61,973
Net Income	(84,871)	(99,890)	(71,192)	282,022	118,618	648,105	323,452	95,093
Average Shares	444,380	417,357	415,308	396,219	362,533	317,919	280,776	222,644
Balance Sheet								
Net PPE	20,620,243	21,031,174	20,736,669	20,081,052	18,850,967	15,384,990	7,459,055	2,866,447
Total Assets	28,430,919	27,441,762	27,362,038	27,303,932	23,226,992	21,309,295	9,737,257	3,991,606
Long-Term Obligations	17,084,864	17,597,599	17,193,652	17,095,769	12,462,309	11,824,417	4,430,357	2,006,190
Total Liabilities	23,420,432	22,490,310	22,413,322	22,271,787	18,065,906	17,128,313	6,340,417	2,694,556
Stockholders' Equity	4,638,541	4,600,891	4,583,362	4,621,253	3,851,914	3,010,569	2,236,774	964,632
Shares Outstanding	534,092	439,326	415,736	415,010	380,816	307,058	283,715	252,215
Statistical Record								
Return on Assets %	0.12	0.95	1.02	1.12	0.53	4.18	4.70	3.32
Return on Equity %	0.74	5.93	6.19	6.66	3.46	24.70	20.15	15.20
EBITDA Margin %	16.22	14.69	12.72	17.17	12.64	19.09	30.75	36.86
Net Margin %	(1.23)	(2.29)	(3.49)	3.16	1.59	8.54	14.17	11.22
PPE Turnover	0.43	0.43	0.44	0.46	0.44	0.66	0.44	0.43
Asset Turnover	0.32	0.33	0.34	0.35	0.33	0.49	0.33	0.30
Debt to Equity	3.68	3.82	3.75	3.70	3.24	3.93	1.98	2.08
Price Range	6.27-2.88	7.84-3.06	7.84-3.30	7.84-2.55	16.86-1.66	56.99-12.90	52.25-16.00	16.23-3.16
P/E Ratio	69.67-32.00	14.00-5.46	13.52-5.69	11.04-3.59	51.09-5.03	30.48-6.90	47.50-14.55	37.75-7.34

Address: 50 West San Fernando Street, San Jose, CA 95113-2429	**Web Site:** www.calpine.com	**Auditors:** PricewaterhouseCoopers LLP
Telephone: (408) 995-5115 **Fax:** (408) 995-0505	**Officers:** Peter Cartwright - Chmn., Pres., C.E.O. Ann B. Curtis - Vice-Chmn., Exec. V.P., Corp. Sec.	**Investor Contact:** 408-995-5115 Ext1125

CAMDEN PROPERTY TRUST

Exchange	Symbol	Price	52Wk Range	Yield	P/E
NYS	CPT	$47.03 (3/31/2005)	51.00-40.04	1.86	47.99

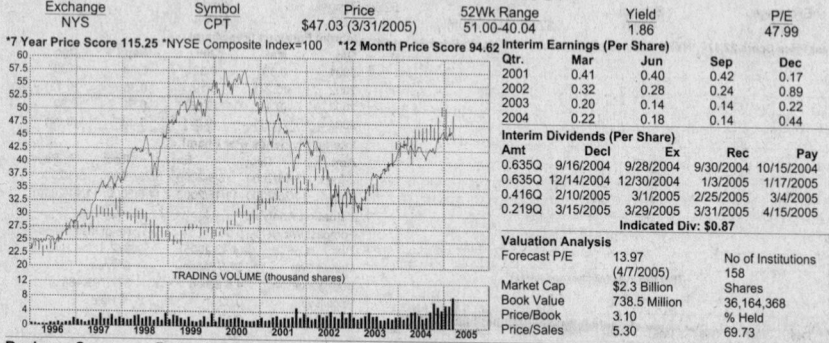

*7 Year Price Score 115.25 *NYSE Composite Index=100 *12 Month Price Score 94.62

Interim Earnings (Per Share)

Qtr.	Mar	Jun	Sep	Dec
2001	0.41	0.40	0.42	0.17
2002	0.32	0.28	0.24	0.89
2003	0.20	0.14	0.14	0.22
2004	0.22	0.18	0.14	0.44

Interim Dividends (Per Share)

Amt	Decl	Ex	Rec	Pay
0.635Q	9/16/2004	9/28/2004	9/30/2004	10/15/2004
0.635Q	12/14/2004	12/30/2004	1/3/2005	1/17/2005
0.416Q	2/10/2005	3/1/2005	2/25/2005	3/4/2005
0.219Q	3/15/2005	3/29/2005	3/31/2005	4/15/2005

Indicated Div: $0.87

Valuation Analysis

Forecast P/E	13.97 (4/7/2005)	No of Institutions 158
Market Cap	$2.3 Billion	Shares 36,164,368
Book Value	738.5 Million	% Held
Price/Book	3.10	69.73
Price/Sales	5.30	

Business Summary: Property, Real Estate & Development (MIC: 8.3 SIC: 798 NAIC: 25930)

Camden Property Trust is a self-administered and self-managed real estate investment trust. Co. is engaged in the ownership, development, construction, and management of multifamily apartment communities in ten states. As of Dec 31 2003, Co. owned interests in, operated or was developing 146 properties containing 52,346 apartment homes geographically dispersed in the Sunbelt and Midwestern markets, from Florida to California. At Dec 31 2003, Co. had two recently completed multifamily properties containing 786 apartment homes in lease-up. Two of Co.'s multifamily properties containing 1,002 apartment homes were under development at Dec 31 2003.

Recent Developments: For the year ended Dec 31 2004, income from continuing operations increased 13.8% to $30,556 thousand from income of $26,841 thousand a year earlier. Net income increased 40.5% to $41,341 thousand from net income of $29,430 thousand a year earlier. Revenues were $431,231 thousand, up 6.1% from $406,617 thousand the year before. Operating income was $42,689 thousand versus an income of $35,894 thousand in the prior year, an increase of 18.9%.

Prospects: Co. revised its guidance for fiscal 2005 as a result of a one-time gain of $24.2 million relating to its investment in Rent.com, which was acquired by eBay on Feb 23 2005. Accordingly, Co. now expects 2005 funds from operations of $3.39 to $3.59 per diluted share and earnings per share of $0.46 to $0.66 per diluted share, excluding any gains from property sales. Funds from operations for the first quarter of 2005 is expected to be $1.00 to $1.04 per diluted share, with earnings per share of $0.34 to $0.38 per diluted share, excluding any gains from property sales.

Financial Data (US$ in Thousands)	12/31/2004	12/31/2003	12/31/2002	12/31/2001	12/31/2000	12/31/1999	12/31/1998	12/31/1997
Earnings Per Share	0.98	0.71	1.73	1.41	1.63	1.23	1.12	1.41
Cash Flow Per Share	3.85	3.51	4.57	4.98	4.29	3.98	3.36	2.51
Tang Book Value Per Share	15.20	15.68	17.05	18.88	25.55	26.01	26.41	22.24
Dividends Per Share	2.540	2.540	2.540	2.440	2.250	2.080	2.020	1.960
Dividend Payout %	259.18	357.75	146.82	173.05	138.04	169.11	180.36	139.01
Income Statement								
Property Income	410,107	403,579	396,505	403,620	391,141	363,316	318,725	197,438
Non-Property Income	21,124	12,961	14,478	24,595	12,398	7,980	5,114	2,351
Total Revenue	431,231	416,540	410,983	428,215	403,539	371,296	323,839	199,789
Depn & Amortn	109,606	108,076	103,342	101,660	96,966	89,516	78,113	44,836
Interest Expense	79,214	75,414	71,499	69,841	69,036	57,856	50,467	28,537
Net Income	41,341	29,430	74,612	61,292	74,424	61,623	57,333	38,438
Average Shares	42,426	41,354	44,216	41,603	41,388	44,291	44,183	28,356
Balance Sheet								
Total Assets	2,629,364	2,625,561	2,609,899	2,449,665	2,430,881	2,487,932	2,347,982	1,323,620
Long-Term Obligations	1,576,405	1,509,677	1,427,016	1,207,047	1,138,117	1,165,090	1,002,568	480,754
Total Liabilities	1,731,282	1,644,291	1,569,717	1,325,335	1,244,371	1,270,999	1,102,235	543,706
Stockholders' Equity	738,515	784,885	839,453	918,251	974,183	1,016,675	1,170,388	710,564
Shares Outstanding	48,601	50,060	49,233	48,627	38,129	39,093	44,322	31,954
Statistical Record								
Return on Assets %	1.57	1.12	2.95	2.51	3.02	2.55	3.12	3.99
Return on Equity %	5.41	3.62	8.49	6.48	7.46	5.64	6.10	7.64
Net Margin %	9.59	7.07	18.15	14.31	18.44	16.60	17.70	19.24
Price Range	51.00-40.04	44.30-30.70	41.54-29.74	39.32-31.07	33.81-25.88	28.19-24.13	31.00-24.88	33.00-26.63
P/E Ratio	52.04-40.86	62.39-43.24	24.01-17.19	27.89-22.04	20.74-15.87	22.92-19.61	27.68-22.21	23.40-18.88
Average Yield %	5.60	6.97	7.14	6.98	7.74	7.83	7.08	6.64

| Address: 3 Greenway Plaza, Suite 1300, Houston, TX 77046
Telephone: (713) 354-2500
Fax: (713) 354-2710 | **Web Site:** www.camdenliving.com
Officers: Richard J. Campo - Chmn., C.E.O. D. Keith Oden - Pres., C.O.O. | **Auditors:** Deloitte & Touche LLP
Investor Contact: 713-354-2500
Transfer Agents: American Stock Transfer and Trust Company, New York, |

CAMPBELL SOUP CO.

Exchange NYS	Symbol CPB	Price $29.02 (3/31/2005)	52Wk Range 30.31-25.12	Yield 2.34	P/E 17.91

*7 Year Price Score 72.48   *NYSE Composite Index=100   *12 Month Price Score 97.00

Interim Earnings (Per Share)

Qtr.	Oct	Jan	Apr	Jul
2001-02	0.42	0.49	0.23	0.14
2002-03	0.39	0.56	0.31	0.18
2003-04	0.51	0.57	0.34	0.14
2004-05	0.56	0.57	...	...

Interim Dividends (Per Share)

Amt	Decl	Ex	Rec	Pay
0.158Q	6/24/2004	7/8/2004	7/12/2004	8/2/2004
0.17Q	9/23/2004	10/6/2004	10/11/2004	11/1/2004
0.17Q	11/18/2004	12/30/2004	1/3/2005	1/31/2005
0.17Q	3/24/2005	4/7/2005	4/11/2005	5/2/2005

Indicated Div: $0.68

Valuation Analysis

Forecast P/E	17.16	No of Institutions
	(4/7/2005)	284
Market Cap	$12.0 Billion	Shares
Book Value	1.3 Billion	164,124,864
Price/Book	8.93	% Held
Price/Sales	1.61	39.82

TRADING VOLUME (thousand shares)

Business Summary: Food (MIC: 4.1 SIC: 032 NAIC: 11422)

Campbell Soup is a manufacturer and marketer of convenience food products. Segments include North America Soup and Away From Home; North America Sauces and Beverages, which includes retail sales for Prego pasta sauces, Pace Mexican sauces, Franco-American canned pastas and gravies, V8 products, and Campbell's tomato juices; Biscuits and Confectionery, which includes all retail sales of Pepperidge Farm cookies, crackers, breads and frozen products in North America, Arnott's biscuits and crackers in Australia and Asia/Pacific, Arnott's Snackfoods salty snacks in Australia, and Godiva chocolates worldwide; and International Soup and Sauces, which comprises operations outside of North America.

Recent Developments: For the quarter ended Jan 30 2005, net income $235,000 thousand from net income of $235,000 thousand in the year-earlier quarter. Revenues were $2,223,000 thousand, up 5.9% from $2,100,000 thousand the year before. Operating income was $389,000 thousand versus an income of $389,000 0.0%. Total direct expense was $1,321,000 thousand versus $1,212,000 thousand in the prior-year quarter, an increase of 9.0%. Total indirect expense was $513,000 thousand versus $499,000 thousand in the prior-year quarter, an increase of 2.8%.

Prospects: Co. is pleased with its operating performance for the first half of fiscal 2005, and hopes to build on this momentum through the remainder of the year. Within the U.S. soup, sauces and beverages segment, "Campbell's Chunky" chili continues to perform well in the marketplace after a successful introduction in the first quarter. Also, Co.'s baking and snacking segment, Pepperidge Farm is seeing stronger sales across all three of its business segments, including bakery, cookies and crackers, and frozen. Co. confirmed its fiscal 2005 guidance for earnings per share to increase between 5.0% and 7.0%, excluding restructuring charges.

Financial Data (US$ in Thousands)	6 Mos	3 Mos	08/01/2004	08/03/2003	07/28/2002	07/29/2001	07/30/2000	08/01/1999
Earnings Per Share	1.62	1.62	1.57	1.45	1.28	1.55	1.65	1.63
Cash Flow Per Share	2.24	2.14	1.81	2.09	2.49	2.68	2.75	2.12
Dividends Per Share	0.655	0.642	0.630	0.630	0.630	0.900	0.900	0.885
Dividend Payout %	40.53	39.77	40.13	43.45	49.22	58.06	54.55	54.29
Income Statement								
Total Revenue	4,314,000	2,091,000	7,109,000	6,678,000	6,133,000	6,664,000	6,267,000	6,424,000
EBITDA	906,000	449,000	1,375,000	1,348,000	1,303,000	1,443,000	1,516,000	1,525,000
Depn & Amortn	136,000	68,000	260,000	243,000	319,000	249,000	251,000	255,000
Income Before Taxes	681,000	337,000	947,000	924,000	798,000	987,000	1,077,000	1,097,000
Income Taxes	216,000	107,000	300,000	298,000	273,000	338,000	363,000	373,000
Net Income	465,000	230,000	647,000	595,000	525,000	649,000	714,000	724,000
Average Shares	414,000	412,000	412,000	411,000	411,000	418,000	432,000	445,000
Balance Sheet								
Current Assets	1,674,000	1,869,000	1,481,000	1,290,000	1,199,000	1,221,000	1,168,000	1,294,000
Total Assets	7,074,000	7,228,000	6,675,000	6,205,000	5,721,000	5,927,000	5,196,000	5,522,000
Current Liabilities	2,219,000	2,602,000	2,339,000	2,783,000	2,678,000	3,120,000	3,032,000	3,146,000
Long-Term Obligations	2,552,000	2,565,000	2,543,000	2,543,000	2,249,000	2,243,000	1,218,000	1,330,000
Total Liabilities	5,735,000	6,111,000	5,801,000	5,818,000	5,835,000	6,174,000	5,059,000	5,287,000
Stockholders' Equity	1,339,000	1,117,000	874,000	387,000	(114,000)	(247,000)	137,000	235,000
Shares Outstanding	412,174	408,000	408,000	410,000	410,000	409,000	421,000	429,000
Statistical Record								
Return on Assets %	9.64	9.57	10.07	9.82	9.04	11.70	13.36	13.02
Return on Equity %	60.59	77.17	102.90	428.85	...	...	384.93	130.93
EBITDA Margin %	21.00	21.47	19.34	20.19	21.25	21.65	24.19	23.74
Net Margin %	10.78	11.00	9.10	8.91	8.56	9.74	11.39	11.27
Asset Turnover	1.07	1.05	1.11	1.10	1.06	1.20	1.17	1.15
Current Ratio	0.75	0.72	0.63	0.46	0.45	0.39	0.39	0.41
Debt to Equity	1.91	2.30	2.91	5.81	...	...	8.89	5.66
Price Range	30.31-25.12	28.60-25.12	28.60-23.56	26.39-19.79	31.25-21.94	34.75-24.69	46.63-25.81	59.13-38.81
P/E Ratio	18.71-15.51	17.65-15.51	18.22-15.01	18.20-13.65	24.41-17.14	22.42-15.93	28.26-15.64	36.27-23.81
Average Yield %	2.41	2.42	2.38	2.74	2.28	3.08	2.55	1.85

Address: 1 Campbell Place, Camden, NJ 08103-1799 Telephone: (856) 342-4800 Fax: (856) 342-3878	Web Site: www.campbellsoup.com Officers: George M. Sherman - Chmn. Douglas R. Conant - Pres., C.E.O.	Auditors: PricewaterhouseCoopers LLP Investor Contact: 856-342-6428 Transfer Agents: EquiServe Trust Company, Providence, RI

CAPITAL ONE FINANCIAL CORP.

Exchange	Symbol	Price	52Wk Range	Yield	P/E
NYS	COF	$74.77 (3/31/2005)	84.21-61.64	0.14	12.04

*7 Year Price Score 120.54 *NYSE Composite Index=100 *12 Month Price Score 97.57

Interim Earnings (Per Share)

Qtr.	Mar	Jun	Sep	Dec
2001	0.66	0.70	0.75	0.80
2002	0.83	0.92	1.13	1.05
2003	1.35	1.23	1.17	1.10
2004	1.84	1.64	1.97	0.76

Interim Dividends (Per Share)

Amt	Decl	Ex	Rec	Pay
0.027Q	5/3/2004	5/6/2004	5/10/2004	5/20/2004
0.027Q	7/30/2004	8/6/2004	8/10/2004	8/20/2004
0.027Q	10/29/2004	11/9/2004	11/12/2004	11/22/2004
0.027Q	1/31/2005	2/8/2005	2/10/2005	2/22/2005

Indicated Div: $0.11

Valuation Analysis

Forecast P/E	10.90	No of Institutions
	(4/7/2005)	478
Market Cap	$18.5 Billion	Shares
Book Value	8.4 Billion	199,329,872
Price/Book	2.20	% Held
Price/Sales	1.73	80.64

Business Summary: Credit & Lending (MIC: 8.6 SIC: 141 NAIC: 22291)

Capital One Financial is a holding company whose subsidiaries provide a variety of financial products and services to consumers. Co.'s subsidiary Capital One Bank offers credit card products. Capital One, F.S.B. provides certain consumer lending and deposit services, and Capital One Auto Finance, Inc. offers automobile and other motor vehicle financing products. Capital One Services provides various operating and administrative services. Co. is among the largest providers of MasterCard and Visa credit cards in the world. Co.'s subsidiaries collectively had 47.0 million managed accounts and $71.20 billion in managed outstanding loans as of Dec 31 2003.

Recent Developments: For the year ended Dec 31 2004, net income increased 35.9% to $1,543,482 thousand from net income of $1,135,842 thousand a year earlier. Net interest income was $3,002,978 thousand, up 7.8% from $2,785,089 thousand the year before. Provision for loan losses was $1,220,852 thousand versus $1,517,497 thousand in the prior year, a decrease of 19.5%. Non-interest income rose 8.9% to $5,900,157 thousand, while non-interest expense advanced 9.6% to $5,322,219 thousand.

Prospects: On Mar 6 2005, Co. announced an agreement to acquire Hibernia Corporation in a stock and cash transaction valued at approximately $5.30 billion. Upon closing, Hibernia National Bank will become a subsidiary of Co. Hibernia's leading market share in Louisiana and its promising Texas branch expansion should create a solid growth platform as Co. continues to expand, and also provide an additional source of lower cost funding. The transaction is expected to close in the third quarter of 2005. Co. expects to achieve cost savings and synergies of $135.0 million by 2007 and be accretive to earnings beginning in 2007. For 2005, Co expects earnings to range from $6.60 to $7.00 per diluted share.

Financial Data
(US$ in Thousands)

	12/31/2004	12/31/2003	12/31/2002	12/31/2001	12/31/2000	12/31/1999	12/31/1998	12/31/1997
Earnings Per Share	6.21	4.85	3.93	2.91	2.24	1.72	1.32	0.93
Cash Flow Per Share	19.16	9.02	10.35	6.04	7.09	6.44	3.97	2.57
Tang Book Value Per Share	33.98	25.75	20.44	15.33	9.94	7.69	6.45	4.55
Dividends Per Share	0.107	0.107	0.107	0.107	0.107	0.107	0.107	0.107
Dividend Payout %	1.72	2.20	2.71	3.67	4.76	6.20	8.08	11.43
Income Statement								
Interest Income	4,794,420	4,367,654	4,180,766	2,834,397	2,389,902	1,593,484	1,111,536	717,985
Interest Expense	1,791,442	1,582,565	1,461,654	1,171,007	801,017	540,882	424,284	334,847
Net Interest Income	3,002,978	2,785,089	2,719,112	1,663,390	1,588,885	1,052,602	687,252	383,138
Provision for Losses	1,220,852	1,517,497	2,149,328	989,836	718,170	382,948	267,028	262,837
Non-Interest Income	5,900,157	5,415,924	5,466,836	4,419,893	3,034,416	2,372,359	1,488,283	1,069,130
Non-Interest Expense	5,322,219	4,856,723	4,585,581	4,058,027	3,147,657	2,464,996	1,464,586	883,978
Income Before Taxes	2,360,064	1,826,793	1,451,039	1,035,420	757,474	577,017	443,921	305,453
Income Taxes	816,582	675,914	551,395	393,455	287,840	213,926	168,690	116,072
Net Income	1,543,482	1,135,842	899,644	641,965	469,634	363,091	275,231	189,381
Average Shares	248,767	234,103	228,744	220,576	209,449	210,683	208,765	202,953
Balance Sheet								
Net Loans & Leases	36,710,591	31,255,269	26,133,652	20,081,014	14,585,712	9,571,549	5,926,111	4,678,687
Total Assets	53,747,255	46,283,706	37,382,380	28,184,047	18,889,341	13,336,443	9,419,403	7,078,279
Total Deposits	25,636,802	22,416,332	17,325,965	12,838,968	8,379,025	3,783,809	1,999,979	1,313,654
Total Liabilities	45,359,066	40,231,895	32,759,209	24,860,569	16,926,827	11,820,836	8,148,997	6,087,356
Stockholders' Equity	8,388,189	6,051,811	4,623,171	3,323,478	1,962,514	1,515,607	1,270,406	893,259
Shares Outstanding	246,833	235,042	226,194	216,778	197,368	197,046	196,979	196,107
Statistical Record								
Return on Assets %	3.08	2.72	2.74	2.73	2.91	3.19	3.34	2.80
Return on Equity %	21.32	21.28	22.64	24.29	26.93	26.07	25.44	23.19
Net Interest Margin %	62.63	63.77	65.04	58.69	66.48	66.06	61.83	53.36
Efficiency Ratio %	49.77	49.64	47.53	55.94	58.03	62.16	56.33	49.46
Loans to Deposits	1.43	1.39	1.51	1.56	1.74	2.53	2.96	3.56
Price Range	84.21-60.23	64.12-25.38	65.75-24.70	72.06-39.95	71.75-33.06	59.35-36.00	42.85-17.44	18.06-10.46
P/E Ratio	13.56-9.70	13.22-5.23	16.73-6.28	24.76-13.73	32.03-14.76	34.51-20.93	32.47-13.21	19.42-11.25
Average Yield %	0.15	0.23	0.23	0.19	0.21	0.23	0.34	0.81

Address: 1680 Capital One Drive, Mclean, VA 22102 Telephone: (703) 720-1000	Web Site: www.capitalone.com Officers: Richard D. Fairbank - Chmn., Pres., C.E.O. Nigel W. Morris - Vice-Chmn.	Auditors: Ernst & Young LLP Investor Contact: 703-720-1000

CARDINAL HEALTH, INC.

Exchange NYS	Symbol CAH	Price $55.80 (3/31/2005)	52Wk Range 75.98-37.65	Yield 0.22	P/E 20.44

*7 Year Price Score 87.06   ***NYSE Composite Index=100**   ***12 Month Price Score 96.07**

Interim Earnings (Per Share)

Qtr.	Sep	Dec	Mar	Jun
2001-02	0.38	0.62	0.66	0.64
2002-03	0.64	0.82	0.84	0.81
2003-04	0.74	0.86	0.97	0.79
2004-05	0.49	0.49	...	...

Interim Dividends (Per Share)

Amt	Decl	Ex	Rec	Pay
0.03Q	5/5/2004	6/29/2004	7/1/2004	7/15/2004
0.03Q	8/4/2004	9/29/2004	10/1/2004	10/15/2004
0.03Q	12/8/2004	12/29/2004	1/1/2005	1/15/2005
0.03Q	2/2/2005	3/30/2005	4/1/2005	4/15/2005

Indicated Div: $0.12

Valuation Analysis

Forecast P/E	14.59	No of Institutions
	(4/7/2005)	505
Market Cap	$24.2 Billion	Shares
Book Value	8.6 Billion	356,880,192
Price/Book	2.82	% Held
Price/Sales	0.35	82.31

Business Summary: Pharmaceuticals (MIC: 9.1 SIC: 122 NAIC: 24210)

Cardinal Health is a holding company. Through its subsidiaries, Co. provides products and services to the healthcare industry, including pharmaceutical and other healthcare products distribution services and pharmaceutical-related products and services. Co. conducts its business within four business segments: Pharmaceutical Distribution and Provider Services, Medical Products and Services, Pharmaceutical Technologies and Services and Automation and Information Services. Co. also operates several specialty healthcare distribution businesses such as a pharmaceutical repackaging and distribution program for both independent and chain drugstore customers.

Recent Developments: For the quarter ended Dec 31 2004, income from continuing operations decreased 45.4% to $203,800 thousand from income of $373,600 thousand in the year-earlier quarter. Net income decreased 41.9% to $214,000 thousand from net income of $368,500 thousand in the year-earlier quarter. Revenues were $18,554,600 thousand, up 13.5% from $16,350,800 thousand the year before. Operating income was $320,800 thousand versus an income of $584,600 thousand in the prior-year quarter, a decrease of 45.1%. Total direct expense was $17,348,100 thousand versus $15,189,800 thousand in the prior-year quarter, an increase of 14.2%. Total indirect expense was $885,700 thousand versus $576,400 thousand in the prior-year quarter, an increase of 53.7%.

Prospects: Looking ahead, Co. is forecasting earnings before special items and non-recurring charges of $3.20 to $3.40 per share for fiscal 2005, a reduction from its prior projections due to uncertainty about branded pharmaceutical price increases, available inventory, and the short-term impact of its transition to fee-based distribution service agreements with drug makers. Co. added that 2005 results will also be hurt by continued delays in the installation of Pyxis committed contracts due to an organizational re-staffing. For fiscal 2006, Co. sees earnings growth coming in at a rate considerably above its long-term growth goal of mid-teens or better.

Financial Data
(US$ in Thousands)

	6 Mos	3 Mos	06/30/2004	06/30/2003	06/30/2002	06/30/2001	06/30/2000	06/30/1999
Earnings Per Share	2.73	3.10	3.35	3.10	2.30	1.88	1.59	1.09
Cash Flow Per Share	8.30	7.46	6.03	3.13	2.19	1.97	1.52	0.85
Tang Book Value Per Share	8.13	7.41	7.05	12.10	10.80	9.50	7.28	6.14
Dividends Per Share	0.120	0.120	0.120	0.105	0.100	0.085	0.070	0.067
Dividend Payout %	4.40	3.87	3.58	3.39	4.35	4.52	4.39	6.10
Income Statement								
Total Revenue	36,350,600	17,796,000	65,053,500	56,737,000	51,135,700	47,947,600	29,870,600	25,033,600
EBITDA	822,400	412,800	2,530,300	2,382,300	1,944,800	1,612,800	1,323,700	1,092,100
Depn & Amortn	198,200	92,500	291,900	255,700	243,500	280,600	245,900	233,500
Income Before Taxes	624,200	320,300	2,238,400	2,126,600	1,701,300	1,332,200	1,077,800	759,200
Income Taxes	202,600	102,500	713,700	714,700	575,000	474,800	398,100	302,900
Net Income	427,300	213,300	1,474,500	1,405,800	1,056,200	857,400	679,700	456,300
Average Shares	437,100	434,700	440,000	453,600	459,900	455,500	426,600	418,500
Balance Sheet								
Current Assets	13,311,000	13,787,000	13,057,900	13,249,600	11,906,600	10,716,300	6,870,600	5,146,600
Total Assets	21,789,000	22,269,100	21,369,100	18,521,400	16,438,000	14,642,400	10,264,900	8,289,000
Current Liabilities	9,689,300	9,992,300	9,369,400	7,314,400	6,810,400	6,574,800	4,261,500	2,959,000
Long-Term Obligations	2,384,600	2,892,600	2,834,700	2,471,900	2,207,100	1,871,000	1,485,800	1,223,900
Total Liabilities	13,229,500	14,050,100	13,392,800	10,763,300	10,045,000	9,205,300	6,283,700	4,826,000
Stockholders' Equity	8,559,500	8,219,000	7,976,300	7,758,100	6,393,000	5,437,100	3,981,200	3,463,000
Shares Outstanding	433,000	432,000	430,900	448,400	448,800	448,700	414,750	410,850
Statistical Record								
Return on Assets %	5.77	6.62	7.37	8.04	6.80	6.88	7.31	7.45
Return on Equity %	14.77	17.67	18.69	19.87	17.86	18.21	18.21	17.94
EBITDA Margin %	2.26	2.32	3.89	4.20	3.80	3.36	4.43	4.36
Net Margin %	1.18	1.20	2.27	2.48	2.07	1.79	2.28	1.82
Asset Turnover	3.36	3.29	3.25	3.25	3.29	3.85	3.21	4.09
Current Ratio	1.37	1.38	1.39	1.81	1.75	1.63	1.61	1.74
Debt to Equity	0.28	0.35	0.36	0.32	0.35	0.34	0.37	0.35
Price Range	75.98-37.65	75.98-42.33	75.98-54.75	71.16-49.08	76.60-60.80	77.00-45.27	49.33-24.79	53.67-36.56
P/E Ratio	27.83-13.79	24.51-13.65	22.68-16.34	22.95-15.83	33.30-26.43	40.96-24.08	31.03-15.59	49.24-33.54
Average Yield %	0.21	0.20	0.19	0.17	0.15	0.14	0.19	0.15

Address: 7000 Cardinal Place, Dublin, OH 43017 Telephone: (614) 757 5000 Fax: (614) 717 6000	Web Site: www.cardinal.com Officers: Robert D. Walter - Chmn., C.E.O. George L. Fotiades - Pres., C.O.O.	Auditors: Ernst & Young LLP

CAREMARK RX, INC.

Exchange	Symbol	Price	52Wk Range	Yield	P/E
NYS	CMX	$39.78 (3/31/2005)	42.02-27.80	N/A	27.82

*7 Year Price Score 179.84 *NYSE Composite Index=100 *12 Month Price Score 106.98

TRADING VOLUME (thousand shares)

Interim Earnings (Per Share)

Qtr.	Mar	Jun	Sep	Dec
2001	0.15	0.16	0.19	0.23
2002	0.24	0.27	0.31	2.19
2003	0.24	0.26	0.29	0.31
2004	0.29	0.30	0.37	0.46

Interim Dividends (Per Share)

No Dividends Paid

Valuation Analysis

Forecast P/E	21.55	No of Institutions
	(4/7/2005)	472
Market Cap	$18.9 Billion	Shares
Book Value	7.5 Billion	393,304,096
Price/Book	2.50	% Held
Price/Sales	0.73	86.06

Business Summary: Retail - Miscellaneous (MIC: 5.11 SIC: 912 NAIC: 46110)

Caremark Rx is a major pharmaceutical services company. Co.'s operations are conducted primarily through its Caremark Inc. and CaremarkPCS subsidiaries. Co.'s customers are mainly sponsors of health benefit plans (employers, unions, government employee groups, insurance companies and managed care organizations) and individuals located throughout the U.S. Co. dispenses pharmaceuticals to eligible participants in benefit plans maintained by its customers and utilizes its information systems to perform safety checks, drug interaction screening and generic substitution. During the year ended Dec 31 2004, Co. managed over 484.0 million prescriptions for individuals from over 2,000 organizations.

Recent Developments: For the year ended Dec 31 2004, revenues were $25,801,121 thousand, up 184.6% from $9,067,291 thousand the year before. Total direct expense was $24,192,434 thousand versus $8,299,190 thousand in the prior year, an increase of 191.5%. Total indirect expense was $579,992 thousand versus $240,829 thousand in the prior year, an increase of 140.8%.

Prospects: Co. expects 2005 revenue growth to be in the range of 25.0% to 28.0%. Additionally, Co. expects 2005 diluted earnings per share, before integration and other related expenses, to be in the range of $1.88 to $1.92 based on expected diluted shares outstanding of 464.0 million shares. Co. noted that it will continue to expense certain ongoing integration and expenses related to its Mar 24 2004 AdvancePCS acquisition as these costs are incurred. These expenses are not included in Co.'s earnings per share expectations for 2005. Separately, Co. expects first quarter 2005 diluted earnings per share, before integration and other related expenses, to be in the range of $0.42 to $0.43.

Financial Data

(US$ in Thousands)	12/31/2004	12/31/2003	12/31/2002	12/31/2001	12/31/2000	12/31/1999	12/31/1998	12/31/1997
Earnings Per Share	1.43	1.10	3.01	0.73	(0.82)	(0.74)	(6.64)	(4.42)
Cash Flow Per Share	3.89	2.23	1.74	1.27	1.07	0.45	0.44	0.43
Tang Book Value Per Share	N.M.	2.17	0.75	...	...	...	...	N.M.
Income Statement								
Total Revenue	25,801,121	9,067,291	6,805,348	5,614,029	4,430,144	3,307,806	2,634,017	6,331,151
EBITDA	1,121,474	529,793	363,763	232,904	138,538	86,193	74,334	(651,339)
Depn & Amortn	123,818	45,062	29,928	26,909	25,354	22,095	24,722	120,443
Income Before Taxes	997,656	484,731	333,835	205,995	113,184	64,098	49,612	(771,782)
Income Taxes	397,347	193,893	(494,962)	15,450	8,489	4,952	18,852	(78,040)
Net Income	600,309	290,838	791,294	177,328	(176,555)	(143,419)	(1,260,466)	(820,615)
Average Shares	420,296	264,781	263,305	262,237	214,025	194,950	189,927	185,830
Balance Sheet								
Current Assets	4,219,626	1,946,677	1,225,645	647,454	453,327	534,656	1,185,566	1,313,041
Total Assets	12,309,734	2,473,628	1,912,740	873,671	685,536	770,846	1,862,106	2,890,529
Current Liabilities	3,764,136	1,064,061	877,005	678,857	635,237	563,406	1,100,455	1,237,294
Long-Term Obligations	450,000	693,125	695,625	695,625	733,347	1,230,025	1,735,096	1,470,622
Total Liabilities	4,770,017	1,832,990	1,655,047	1,446,138	1,454,600	1,852,321	3,006,279	2,799,675
Stockholders' Equity	7,539,717	640,638	257,693	(772,467)	(969,064)	(1,281,475)	(1,144,173)	90,854
Shares Outstanding	474,578	268,578	263,005	226,180	230,755	191,140	199,032	188,449
Statistical Record								
Return on Assets %	8.10	13.26	56.80	22.75	N.M.	N.M.	N.M.	N.M.
Return on Equity %	14.64	64.75	...	...	...	...	...	N.M.
EBITDA Margin %	4.35	5.84	5.35	4.15	3.13	2.61	2.82	N.M.
Net Margin %	2.33	3.21	11.63	3.16	N.M.	N.M.	N.M.	N.M.
Asset Turnover	3.48	4.13	4.88	7.20	6.07	2.51	1.11	2.46
Current Ratio	1.12	1.83	1.40	0.95	0.71	0.95	1.08	1.06
Debt to Equity	0.06	1.08	2.70	...	...	...	...	16.19
Price Range	39.60-23.60	27.60-16.25	21.95-12.85	18.02-11.25	13.69-3.88	9.00-3.19	22.38-1.69	27.25-18.00
P/E Ratio	27.69-16.50	25.09-14.77	7.29-4.27	24.68-15.41	...	...	...	...

Address: 211 Commerce Street, Suite 800, Nashville, TN 37201 **Telephone:** (615) 743-6600	**Web Site:** www.caremarkrx.com **Officers:** Edwin Mac Crawford - Chmn., C.E.O. A.D. Frazier Jr. - Pres., C.O.O.	**Auditors:** KMPG LLP **Investor Contact:** 205-733-8996 **Transfer Agents:** Wachovia Bank, N.A., Charlotte, NC

CARLISLE COMPANIES INC.

Exchange	Symbol	Price	52Wk Range	Yield	P/E	Div Acheiver
NYS	CSL	$69.77 (3/31/2005)	72.43-55.25	1.32	27.47	28 Years

*7 Year Price Score 119.08 *NYSE Composite Index=100 *12 Month Price Score 102.07

Interim Earnings (Per Share)

Qtr.	Mar	Jun	Sep	Dec
2001	(0.33)	0.54	0.36	0.25
2002	0.42	0.81	0.65	(0.94)
2003	0.56	0.93	0.80	0.60
2004	0.76	1.19	0.92	(0.32)

Interim Dividends (Per Share)

Amt	Decl	Ex	Rec	Pay
0.22Q	5/5/2004	5/13/2004	5/17/2004	6/1/2004
0.23Q	8/2/2004	8/17/2004	8/19/2004	9/1/2004
0.23Q	11/3/2004	11/16/2004	11/18/2004	12/1/2004
0.23Q	2/2/2005	2/16/2005	2/18/2005	3/1/2005

Indicated Div: $0.92 (Div. Reinv. Plan)

Valuation Analysis

Forecast P/E	16.21	No of Institutions	
	(4/7/2005)	150	
Market Cap	$2.2 Billion	Shares	
Book Value	698.5 Million	20,690,454	
Price/Book	3.09	% Held	
Price/Sales	0.97	66.64	

Business Summary: Rubber Products (MIC: 11.6 SIC: 011 NAIC: 26211)

Carlisle is a manufacturing company. The Industrial Components segment manufactures non-automotive tires, wheels, transmission belts and accessories. Co. produces rubber and plastic automotive components and roofing membranes and FleeceBACK™ sheeting for flat roofs in its Automotive Components and Construction Materials segments. The Specialty Products segment manufactures heavy-duty friction and braking systems for trucks and heavy equipment. The General Industry produces aerospace wire, electronic cable and cable assemblies and interconnects, plastic foodservice permanentware and refrigerated truck bodies. The Transportation Products segment produces high-payload trailers and dump bodies.

Recent Developments: For the year ended Dec 31 2004, income from continuing operations increased 33.7% to $118,314 thousand from income of $88,484 thousand a year earlier. Net income decreased 10.5% to $79,612 thousand from net income of $88,920 thousand a year earlier. Revenues were $2,227,614 thousand, up 18.0% from $1,887,490 thousand the year before. Total direct expense was $1,804,486 thousand versus $1,526,295 thousand in the prior year, an increase of 18.2%. Total indirect expense was $237,991 thousand versus $221,295 thousand in the prior year, an increase of 7.5%.

Prospects: Earnings continue to show improvement, despite the dramatic rise in raw material costs and the high fees paid for Sarbanes-Oxley compliance. For instance, in Co.'s construction business, earnings improved 22.4% to $94.5 million, due largely to increased sales volume and selling price increases. Separately, in Jan 2005, Co. announced it would exit its automotive business, Carlisle Engineered Products. This disposition should enable Co. to focus on growing its core business units. Looking ahead, Co. expects earnings from continuing operations in the range of $4.10 to $4.25 per share for 2005.

Financial Data
(US$ in Thousands)

	12/31/2004	12/31/2003	12/31/2002	12/31/2001	12/31/2000	12/31/1999	12/31/1998	12/31/1997
Earnings Per Share	2.54	2.88	0.94	0.82	3.14	3.13	2.77	2.28
Cash Flow Per Share	3.59	3.81	7.43	7.37	4.13	4.51	3.21	2.74
Tang Book Value Per Share	12.94	10.37	8.09	6.72	9.79	10.63	8.85	7.48
Dividends Per Share	0.900	0.870	0.850	0.820	0.760	0.680	0.600	0.525
Dividend Payout %	35.43	30.21	90.43	100.00	24.20	21.73	21.66	23.03
Income Statement								
Total Revenue	2,227,614	2,108,164	1,971,280	1,849,477	1,771,067	1,611,256	1,517,494	1,260,550
EBITDA	238,329	206,560	184,645	131,005	238,432	222,051	208,205	172,041
Depn & Amortn	52,639	60,366	56,994	63,960	59,549	47,414	45,221	38,755
Income Before Taxes	170,340	131,733	110,500	37,925	150,865	155,483	140,269	116,784
Income Taxes	52,026	42,813	38,122	13,084	54,685	59,689	55,403	46,118
Net Income	79,612	88,920	28,625	24,841	96,180	95,794	84,866	70,666
Average Shares	31,409	30,863	30,583	30,450	30,599	30,635	30,674	31,025
Balance Sheet								
Current Assets	652,269	584,381	481,508	553,272	576,477	541,038	478,525	417,533
Total Assets	1,501,241	1,436,909	1,315,900	1,397,987	1,305,679	1,080,662	1,022,852	861,216
Current Liabilities	384,022	339,343	324,262	273,779	399,948	240,378	255,337	226,083
Long-Term Obligations	259,554	294,581	293,124	461,744	281,864	281,744	273,521	209,642
Total Liabilities	802,754	804,979	762,823	857,703	757,800	602,529	615,947	512,380
Stockholders' Equity	698,487	631,930	553,077	540,284	547,879	478,133	406,905	348,836
Shares Outstanding	30,896	30,991	30,597	30,263	30,251	30,127	30,178	30,351
Statistical Record								
Return on Assets %	5.40	6.46	2.11	1.84	8.04	9.11	9.01	8.81
Return on Equity %	11.94	15.01	5.24	4.57	18.70	21.65	22.46	21.53
EBITDA Margin %	10.70	9.80	9.37	7.08	13.46	13.78	13.72	13.65
Net Margin %	3.57	4.22	1.45	1.34	5.43	5.95	5.59	5.61
Asset Turnover	1.51	1.53	1.45	1.37	1.48	1.53	1.61	1.57
Current Ratio	1.70	1.72	1.48	2.02	1.44	2.25	1.87	1.85
Debt to Equity	0.37	0.47	0.53	0.85	0.51	0.59	0.67	0.60
Price Range	66.90-54.71	61.49-39.24	46.91-32.65	43.69-26.40	49.75-31.19	52.94-31.06	51.75-32.88	47.63-27.13
P/E Ratio	26.34-21.54	21.35-13.63	49.90-34.73	53.28-32.20	15.84-9.93	16.91-9.92	18.68-11.87	20.89-11.90
Average Yield %	1.49	1.87	2.12	2.33	1.86	1.60	1.34	1.42

Address: 13925 Ballantyne Corporate Place, Suite 400, Charlotte, NC 28277 **Telephone:** (704) 501-1100 **Fax:** (704) 501-1190	**Web Site:** www.carlisle.com **Officers:** Stephen P. Munn - Chmn. Richmond D. McKinnish - Pres., C.E.O.	**Auditors:** KPMG LLP **Investor Contact:** 704-501-1100 **Transfer Agents:** Computershare Investor Services, LLC., Chicago, IL

CARMAX INC.

Exchange	Symbol	Price	52Wk Range	Yield	P/E
NYS	KMX	$31.50 (3/31/2005)	33.60-18.45	N/A	31.82

*7 Year Price Score 142.56 *NYSE Composite Index=100 *12 Month Price Score 115.89

Interim Earnings (Per Share)

Qtr.	May	Aug	Nov	Feb
2001-02	0.25	0.25	0.17	0.16
2002-03	0.35	0.30	0.14	0.19
2003-04	0.34	0.37	0.18	0.21
2004-05	0.33	0.28	0.17	0.28

Interim Dividends (Per Share)

No Dividends Paid

Valuation Analysis

Forecast P/E	N/A	No of Institutions	
Market Cap	$3.3 Billion	Shares	
Book Value	769.2 Million	Shares	99,074,968
Price/Book	4.26	% Held	
Price/Sales	0.66		95.06

Business Summary: Retail - Automotive (MIC: 5.7 SIC: 521 NAIC: 41120)

Carmax is a major specialty retailer of used cars and light trucks. In addition, Co. sells new vehicles under franchise agreements with DaimlerChrysler, Mitsubishi, Nissan, Toyota, Ford and General Motors, operates a retail vehicle repair business, and a finance operation that provides prime-rated automobile installment loans. As of Mar 30 2004, Co. operated 50 used car superstores in 24 markets and 12 new car franchises, all of which are integrated or co-located with Co.'s used car superstores. During the twelve month period ended Feb 29 2004, Co. sold 245,740 vehicles, including 224,099 used cars.

Recent Developments: For the year ended Feb 28 2005, net income decreased 3.0% to $112.9 million from $116.5 million the year before. Results for 2005 and 2004 included gain on franchise dispositions of $633,000 and $2.3 million, respectively. Net sales operating revenues increased 14.4% to $5.26 billion from $4.60 billion a year earlier. The improvement in sales was primarily attributed to a rebound in sales growth in the second half of the fiscal year following the softness experienced in the first half of due to external market factors. Gross profit advanced 14.5% to $650.2 million from $570.9 million in 2004. CarMax Auto Finance income declined 2.7% to $82.7 million versus $85.0 million the year before.

Prospects: For the first quarter of fiscal 2006, Co. expects comp store used unit growth to be in the range of 9.0% to 12.0%, and earnings to be in the range of $0.35 to $0.38 per share. Co.'s sales trends thus far in the quarter have been healthy. In addition, Co. expects CarMax Auto Finance's (CAF) gain spread in the first quarter to be roughly 3.3%, compared with 3.8% in the first quarter of fiscal 2005. Separately, for fiscal 2006, Co. anticipates comp store used unit growth in the range of 5.0% to 9.0%. Also, for fiscal 2006, Co. currently expects earnings in the range of $1.20 to $1.30 per share. In addition, Co. expects CAF income to be slightly below the normalized range of 3.5% to 4.5%.

Financial Data

(US$ in Thousands)	9 Mos	6 Mos	3 Mos	02/29/2004	02/28/2003	02/28/2002	02/28/2001	02/29/2000
Earnings Per Share	0.99	1.00	1.08	1.10	0.91	0.82	0.43	0.01
Cash Flow Per Share	0.97	0.94	0.75	1.43	0.70	1.33	0.70	(1.05)
Tang Book Value Per Share	7.39	7.21	6.92	6.56	5.38	13.17	15.27	13.47
Income Statement								
Total Revenue	3,864,208	2,648,497	1,324,990	4,597,691	3,969,944	3,201,665	2,500,991	2,014,984
EBITDA	149,862	115,762	62,231	205,653	171,647	162,796	91,598	17,044
Depn & Amortn	13,413	8,895	4,313	16,303	14,950	16,340	18,116	15,241
Income Before Taxes	136,449	106,867	57,918	189,350	156,697	146,456	73,482	1,803
Income Taxes	53,215	41,678	22,588	72,900	61,895	55,654	27,918	685
Net Income	83,234	65,189	35,330	116,450	94,802	90,802	45,564	1,118
Average Shares	105,735	105,512	105,774	105,628	104,570	34,122	26,980	25,788
Balance Sheet								
Current Assets	737,547	766,575	836,493	773,481	708,745	577,703	492,907	425,670
Total Assets	1,125,059	1,097,694	1,123,257	1,037,017	917,617	720,222	710,953	675,495
Current Liabilities	228,245	232,062	288,664	242,398	248,103	223,392	225,937	196,123
Long-Term Obligations	111,940	100,000	100,000	100,000	100,000	...	83,057	121,257
Total Liabilities	355,823	347,241	403,753	356,264	363,048	234,743	319,450	330,506
Stockholders' Equity	769,236	750,453	719,504	680,753	554,569	485,479	391,503	344,989
Shares Outstanding	104,130	104,060	103,972	103,778	103,083	36,851	25,639	25,614
Statistical Record								
Return on Assets %	9.96	10.33	11.15	11.88	...	12.69	6.57	0.18
Return on Equity %	14.79	15.36	17.64	18.80	...	20.71	12.37	0.33
EBITDA Margin %	3.88	4.37	4.70	4.47	4.32	5.08	3.66	0.85
Net Margin %	2.15	2.46	2.67	2.53	2.39	2.84	1.82	0.06
Asset Turnover	4.69	4.68	4.55	4.69	...	4.47	3.61	3.22
Current Ratio	3.23	3.30	2.90	3.19	2.86	2.59	2.18	2.17
Debt to Equity	0.15	0.13	0.14	0.15	0.18	...	0.21	0.35
Price Range	35.39-18.45	39.25-18.45	39.25-21.60	39.25-12.65	33.30-13.52	28.51-5.05	5.50-1.63	6.56-1.44
P/E Ratio	35.75-18.64	39.25-18.45	36.34-20.00	35.68-11.50	36.59-14.86	34.77-6.16	12.79-3.78	656.25-143.75

Address: 4900 Cox Rd., Glen Allen, VA 23060	Web Site: www.carmax.com	Auditors: KPMG LLP
Telephone: (804) 747-0422	Officers: Richard L. Sharp - Chmn. W. Austin Ligon - Pres., C.E.O.	Investor Contact: 804-527-4000x2077
Fax: (804) 747-5848		

CARNIVAL CORP.

Exchange	Symbol	Price	52Wk Range	Yield	P/E
NYS	CCL	$51.81 (3/31/2005)	58.74-40.15	1.16	23.13

*7 Year Price Score 121.00 *NYSE Composite Index=100 *12 Month Price Score 102.56

Interim Earnings (Per Share)

Qtr.	Feb	May	Aug	Nov
2001	0.22	0.32	0.84	0.20
2002	0.22	0.33	0.85	0.33
2003	0.22	0.19	0.90	0.24
2004	0.25	0.41	1.23	0.34

Interim Dividends (Per Share)

Amt	Decl	Ex	Rec	Pay
0.125Q	4/27/2004	5/19/2004	5/21/2004	6/11/2004
0.125Q	7/20/2004	8/18/2004	8/20/2004	9/10/2004
0.15Q	10/25/2004	11/17/2004	11/19/2004	12/10/2004
0.15Q	1/19/2005	2/16/2005	2/18/2005	3/11/2005

Indicated Div: $0.60

Valuation Analysis

Forecast P/E	N/A	No of Institutions	
Market Cap	$41.7 Billion	Shares	447,100,864
Book Value	15.8 Billion	% Held	70.44
Price/Book	2.64		
Price/Sales	4.28		

Business Summary: Shipping (MIC: 15.3 SIC: 489 NAIC: 83212)

Carnival is a global cruise and vacation company. Co. has a portfolio of 12 cruise brands and cruises to all major destinations outside the Far East. The cruise brands are as follows: Carnival Cruise Lines, Princess Cruises, Holland America Line, Costa Cruises, P&O Cruises, AIDA, Cunard Line, Ocean Village, P&O Cruises Australia, Swan Hellenic, Seabourn Cruise Line, and Windstar Cruises. In addition to Co.'s cruise operations, Co. operates two tour companies under the brand names Holland America Tours and Princess Tours. The tour companies own about 17 hotels or lodges, over 500 motorcoaches, more than 20 domed railcars, two luxury dayboats, and sightseeing packages.

Recent Developments: For the year ended Nov 30 2004, net income increased 55.3% to $1,854,000 thousand from net income of $1,194,000 thousand a year earlier. Revenues were $9,727,000 thousand, up 44.8% from $6,718,000 thousand the year before. Total direct expense was $5,457,000 thousand versus $3,814,000 thousand in the prior year, an increase of 43.1%. Total indirect expense was $2,097,000 thousand versus $1,521,000 thousand in the prior year, an increase of 37.9%.

Prospects: Results are being positively affected by strong pricing and increased capacity, partially offset by higher fuel costs. During the first quarter of 2005, Co. introduced the 2,974-passenger Carnival Valor, which is operating seven-day Caribbean cruises from Miami, FL. Looking ahead, Co. expects that net revenue yields for the second quarter of 2005 will increase 6.0% to 7.0%, while net costs per available lower berth day are expected to grow 6.0% to 7.0%. Based on these estimates, Co. expects earnings per share for the second quarter to be in the range of $0.45 to $0.47. For the full year 2005, Co. is projecting earnings of about $2.70 per share.

Financial Data
(US$ in Thousands)

	11/30/2004	11/30/2003	11/30/2002	11/30/2001	11/30/2000	11/30/1999	11/30/1998	11/30/1997
Earnings Per Share	2.24	1.66	1.73	1.58	1.60	1.66	1.40	1.20
Cash Flow Per Share	4.00	2.69	2.50	2.12	2.13	...	...	...
Tang Book Value Per Share	13.85	11.83	11.48	10.13	8.37	8.86	6.46	5.71
Dividends Per Share	0.525	0.335	...	...	...	...	...	...
Dividend Payout %	23.44	20.18	...	...	...	...	...	...
Income Statement								
Total Revenue	9,727,000	6,718,000	4,368,269	4,535,751	3,778,542	3,497,470	3,009,306	2,447,468
EBITDA	3,001,000	1,996,000	...	...	...	...	...	...
Depn & Amortn	833,000	605,000	401,637	372,224	287,667	243,658	200,668	167,287
Income Before Taxes	1,901,000	1,223,000	...	...	...	...	...	...
Income Taxes	47,000	29,000	(56,562)	(12,257)	1,094	2,778	3,815	6,233
Net Income	1,854,000	1,194,000	1,015,941	926,200	965,458	1,027,240	835,885	666,050
Average Shares	851,000	724,000	588,056	586,862	601,912	616,000	598,448	596,548
Balance Sheet								
Current Assets	1,728,000	2,132,000	1,132,152	1,958,988	549,482	791,636	370,279	336,025
Total Assets	27,636,000	24,491,000	12,334,848	11,563,552	9,831,320	8,286,355	7,179,323	5,426,775
Current Liabilities	5,034,000	3,315,000	1,619,806	1,480,240	1,715,294	1,404,913	1,135,113	786,142
Long-Term Obligations	6,291,000	6,918,000	3,011,969	2,954,854	2,099,077	867,515	1,563,014	1,015,294
Total Liabilities	11,876,000	10,698,000	4,916,945	4,972,775	3,960,703	2,355,108	2,761,163	1,821,677
Stockholders' Equity	15,760,000	13,793,000	7,417,903	6,590,777	5,870,617	5,931,247	4,285,476	3,605,098
Shares Outstanding	804,000	798,000	586,788	586,171	617,568	616,966	595,448	594,408
Statistical Record								
Return on Assets %	7.09	6.48	8.50	8.66	10.63	13.28	13.26	12.65
Return on Equity %	12.51	11.26	14.50	14.87	16.32	20.11	21.19	20.07
EBITDA Margin %	30.85	29.71	...	...	...	...	...	...
Net Margin %	19.06	17.77	23.26	20.42	25.55	29.37	27.78	27.21
Asset Turnover	0.37	0.36	0.37	0.42	0.42	0.45	0.48	0.46
Current Ratio	0.34	0.64	0.70	1.32	0.32	0.56	0.33	0.43
Debt to Equity	0.40	0.50	0.41	0.45	0.35	0.15	0.36	0.28
Price Range	53.65-35.02	35.81-20.75	34.58-22.30	33.81-18.05	50.56-18.63	53.50-34.50	42.06-21.69	27.03-15.06
P/E Ratio	23.95-15.63	21.57-12.50	19.99-12.89	21.40-11.42	31.60-11.64	32.23-20.78	30.04-15.49	22.53-12.55
Average Yield %	1.17	1.13	...	...	...	...	...	...

Address: 3655 N.W. 87th Avenue, Miami, FL 33178-2428 Telephone: (305) 599 2600	Web Site: www.carnivalcorp.com Officers: Micky Arison - Chmn., C.E.O. Howard S. Frank - Vice-Chmn., C.O.O.	Auditors: PricewaterhouseCoopers LLP

CATALINA MARKETING CORP.

Exchange	Symbol	Price	52Wk Range	Yield	P/E
NYS	POS	$25.90 (3/31/2005)	30.52-16.43	1.16	32.78

*7 Year Price Score 75.02 *NYSE Composite Index=100 *12 Month Price Score 106.88

TRADING VOLUME (thousand shares)

Interim Earnings (Per Share)

Qtr.	Jun	Sep	Dec	Mar
2001-02	0.16	0.22	0.31	0.38
2002-03	0.19	0.19	0.31	0.31
2003-04	0.08	(0.21)	(0.07)	(0.17)
2004-05	0.21	0.39	0.36	...

Interim Dividends (Per Share)

Amt	Decl	Ex	Rec	Pay
200%	4/27/2000	8/18/2000	7/26/2000	8/17/2000
0.30A	9/1/2004	9/13/2004	9/15/2004	10/1/2004

Indicated Div: $0.30

Valuation Analysis

Forecast P/E	18.16	No of Institutions
	(4/7/2005)	159
Market Cap	$1.4 Billion	Shares
Book Value	222.1 Million	50,534,624
Price/Book	6.10	% Held
Price/Sales	3.07	96.60

Business Summary: Advertising, Marketing & PR (MIC: 12.4 SIC: 311 NAIC: 41810)

Catalina Marketing develops and distributes behavior-based communications for consumer packaged goods and pharmaceutical products manufacturers, marketers and retailers. Co.'s marketing solutions, including discount coupons, loyalty marketing programs, informative newsletters, sampling, advertising, in-store instant-win games and other incentives, are delivered directly to shoppers by various means. Co. reaches consumers using incentives, loyalty programs, and through direct mailings. As of Mar 31 2004, Co.'s installed store base was approximately 17,600 retail stores and about 11,900 pharmacies in the U.S., and over 5,500 retail international locations, primarily in Europe and Japan.

Recent Developments: For the quarter ended Dec 31 2004, income from continuing operations increased 34.7% to $20,403 thousand from income of $15,146 thousand in the year-earlier quarter. Net income was $18,971 thousand from net loss of $3,649 thousand in the year-earlier quarter. Revenues were $100,319 thousand, down 1.5% from $101,885 thousand the year before. Operating income was $32,552 thousand versus an income of $26,562 thousand in the prior-year quarter, an increase of 22.6%. Total direct expense was $26,200 thousand versus $32,479 thousand in the prior-year quarter, a decrease of 19.3%. Total indirect expense was $41,567 thousand versus $42,844 thousand in the prior-year quarter, a decrease of 3.0%.

Prospects: Co. noted that during fiscal year 2005, it renegotiated several significant retailer contracts that resulted in increased retailer fees in the third quarter of fiscal year 2005 versus the third quarter of last year. Further, since these contracts cover a term from one to five years and the higher fees have been established during the entire term of these specific retailers' contracts, future comparisons to the quarters prior to the third quarter of fiscal year 2005 will indicate higher costs. Separately, on Nov 29 2004, Co. announced that it has sold its Catalina Marketing Research Solutions division, concluding a series of four divestitures intended to sharpen its focus on its core assets.

Financial Data
(US$ in Thousands)

	9 Mos	6 Mos	3 Mos	03/31/2004	03/31/2003	03/31/2002	03/31/2001	03/31/2000
Earnings Per Share	0.79	0.36	(0.24)	(0.37)	1.00	1.08	1.00	0.89
Cash Flow Per Share	2.35	2.41	2.34	2.63	2.18	2.09	1.68	1.67
Tang Book Value Per Share	2.48	2.05	1.89	1.66	1.11	1.84	1.37	1.29
Dividends Per Share	0.300	0.300	...	...	...	...	...	...
Dividend Payout %	37.89	83.16	...	...	...	...	...	...
Income Statement								
Total Revenue	298,093	200,501	105,643	472,950	470,709	446,668	417,881	350,922
EBITDA	119,734	70,986	30,777	63,597	134,675	139,452	135,181	119,851
Depn & Amortn	33,598	22,337	12,198	48,546	43,268	42,048	43,243	35,175
Income Before Taxes	85,013	47,913	17,967	11,933	89,251	97,404	91,938	84,676
Income Taxes	32,394	18,251	7,041	30,436	34,153	35,552	34,945	34,041
Net Income	50,176	31,205	10,926	(19,273)	55,098	61,880	58,135	51,348
Average Shares	52,720	52,311	52,245	52,304	54,885	57,104	57,919	57,957
Balance Sheet								
Current Assets	196,704	183,672	165,742	158,997	112,438	127,278	118,028	115,372
Total Assets	394,389	385,780	381,070	386,809	422,421	403,802	388,048	303,752
Current Liabilities	92,810	108,241	141,003	157,023	137,193	117,342	128,424	142,285
Long-Term Obligations	61,804	62,660	29,913	29,908	49,926	16,469	38,764	10,814
Total Liabilities	172,275	185,654	185,488	201,233	205,512	148,934	176,451	162,707
Stockholders' Equity	222,114	200,126	194,668	184,662	215,995	254,868	211,597	141,045
Shares Outstanding	52,304	52,177	52,140	52,134	52,755	55,336	55,548	54,603
Statistical Record								
Return on Assets %	10.72	4.77	N.M.	N.M.	13.34	15.63	16.81	19.52
Return on Equity %	20.00	9.48	N.M.	N.M.	23.40	26.53	32.97	39.09
EBITDA Margin %	40.17	35.40	29.13	13.45	28.61	31.22	32.35	34.15
Net Margin %	16.83	15.56	10.34	N.M.	11.71	13.85	13.91	14.63
Asset Turnover	1.14	1.16	1.18	1.17	1.14	1.13	1.21	1.33
Current Ratio	2.12	1.70	1.18	1.01	0.82	1.08	0.92	0.81
Debt to Equity	0.28	0.31	0.15	0.16	0.23	0.06	0.18	0.08
Price Range	30.52-16.43	23.88-15.19	21.11-12.58	21.11-12.58	36.67-16.25	39.01-26.40	44.00-29.50	40.23-24.67
P/E Ratio	38.63-20.80	66.33-42.19	...	...	36.67-16.25	36.12-24.44	44.00-29.50	45.20-27.72
Average Yield %	1.42	1.60	...	...	...	...	...	...

Address: 200 Carillon Parkway, St. Petersburg, FL 33716-2325
Telephone: (727) 579-5000
Fax: (727) 570-8507

Web Site: www.catalinamarketing.com
Officers: Frederick W. Beinecke - Chmn. L. Richard Buell - C.E.O.

Auditors: PricewaterhouseCoopers LLP

CATERPILLAR INC.

Exchange	Symbol	Price	52Wk Range	Yield	P/E	Div Acheiver
NYS	CAT	$91.44 (3/31/2005)	99.96-69.62	1.79	15.90	11 Years

*7 Year Price Score 127.67 *NYSE Composite Index=100   *12 Month Price Score 104.88

Interim Earnings (Per Share)

Qtr.	Mar	Jun	Sep	Dec
2001	0.47	0.78	0.59	0.48
2002	0.23	0.58	0.61	0.88
2003	0.37	1.15	0.62	0.98
2004	1.16	1.55	1.41	1.56

Interim Dividends (Per Share)

Amt	Decl	Ex	Rec	Pay
0.37Q	4/14/2004	4/22/2004	4/26/2004	5/20/2004
0.41Q	6/9/2004	7/16/2004	7/20/2004	8/20/2004
0.41Q	10/13/2004	10/21/2004	10/25/2004	11/20/2004
0.41Q	12/8/2004	1/18/2005	1/20/2005	2/19/2005

Indicated Div: $1.64 (Div. Reinv. Plan)

Valuation Analysis

Forecast P/E	12.46	No of Institutions
	(4/7/2005)	644
Market Cap	$31.4 Billion	Shares
Book Value	7.5 Billion	255,230,208
Price/Book	4.20	% Held
Price/Sales	1.04	74.80

Business Summary: Industrial Machinery and Equipment (MIC: 11.5 SIC: 531 NAIC: 33120)

Caterpillar operates in three principal lines of business. The machinery division designs, manufactures and markets construction, mining, agricultural and forestry machinery. The engines division designs, manufactures and markets engines for Caterpillar machinery; electric power generation systems; on-highway trucks and locomotives; marine, petroleum, construction, industrial, agricultural, and other applications; and related parts. Engines range from 5 to over 22,000 horsepower, and turbines range from 1,600 to 19,500 horsepower. The financial products division consists primarily of Caterpillar Financial Services Corporation, Caterpillar Insurance Holdings, Inc. and their subsidiaries.

Recent Developments: For the year ended Dec 31 2004, net income increased 85.2% to $2,035,000 thousand from net income of $1,099,000 thousand a year earlier. Revenues were $30,251,000 thousand, up 32.9% from $22,763,000 thousand the year before. Operating income was $2,733,000 thousand versus an income of $1,688,000 thousand in the prior year, an increase of 61.9%. Total direct expense was $22,420,000 thousand versus $16,945,000 thousand in the prior year, an increase of 32.3%. Total indirect expense was $4,578,000 thousand versus $3,660,000 thousand in the prior year, an increase of 25.1%.

Prospects: Co.'s outlook appears encouraging, reflecting in part expectations of continued global economic growth. Accordingly, Co. expects 2005 sales and revenues to advance between 12.0% and 15.0% and profit per share to be up about 25.0% from 2004. Co. expects that its result for 2005 will benefit from improved price realization, increased volume, manufacturing efficiencies and a sharpened focus on its cost structure. Co. noted that it expects material cost pressures to continue for the first half of 2005, with some relief in the last six months. Thus, Co. expects the second half of 2005 to be stronger than the first half.

Financial Data (US$ in Thousands)	12/31/2004	12/31/2003	12/31/2002	12/31/2001	12/31/2000	12/31/1999	12/31/1998	12/31/1997
Earnings Per Share	5.75	3.13	2.30	2.32	3.02	2.63	4.11	4.37
Cash Flow Per Share	(11.63)	5.98	6.88	5.79	5.92	7.23	4.90	5.59
Tang Book Value Per Share	16.63	12.92	11.01	11.47	11.92	11.09	10.89	12.10
Dividends Per Share	1.560	1.420	1.400	1.380	1.330	1.250	1.100	0.900
Dividend Payout %	27.13	45.37	60.87	59.48	44.04	47.53	26.76	20.59
Income Statement								
Total Revenue	30,251,000	22,763,000	20,152,000	20,450,000	20,175,000	19,702,000	20,977,000	18,925,000
EBITDA	4,334,000	3,070,000	2,613,000	2,623,000	2,842,000	2,635,000	3,303,000	3,370,000
Depn & Amortn	1,397,000	1,347,000	1,220,000	1,169,000	1,022,000	945,000	865,000	738,000
Income Before Taxes	2,707,000	1,477,000	1,114,000	1,169,000	1,528,000	1,421,000	2,174,000	2,413,000
Income Taxes	731,000	398,000	312,000	367,000	447,000	455,000	665,000	796,000
Net Income	2,035,000	1,099,000	798,000	805,000	1,053,000	946,000	1,513,000	1,665,000
Average Shares	353,700	351,400	346,900	347,100	348,897	359,367	368,130	381,000
Balance Sheet								
Current Assets	20,856,000	16,791,000	14,628,000	13,400,000	12,521,000	11,734,000	11,459,000	9,814,000
Total Assets	43,091,000	36,465,000	32,851,000	30,657,000	28,464,000	26,635,000	25,128,000	20,756,000
Current Liabilities	16,210,000	12,621,000	11,344,000	10,276,000	8,568,000	8,178,000	7,565,000	6,379,000
Long-Term Obligations	15,837,000	14,078,000	11,596,000	11,291,000	11,334,000	9,928,000	9,404,000	6,942,000
Total Liabilities	35,624,000	30,387,000	27,379,000	25,046,000	22,864,000	21,170,000	19,997,000	16,077,000
Stockholders' Equity	7,467,000	6,078,000	5,472,000	5,611,000	5,600,000	5,465,000	5,131,000	4,679,000
Shares Outstanding	342,936	343,762	344,255	343,376	343,396	353,748	357,198	368,000
Statistical Record								
Return on Assets %	5.10	3.17	2.51	2.72	3.81	3.66	6.59	8.43
Return on Equity %	29.97	19.03	14.40	14.36	18.98	17.86	30.85	37.86
EBITDA Margin %	14.33	13.49	12.97	12.83	14.09	13.37	15.75	17.81
Net Margin %	6.73	4.83	3.96	3.94	5.22	4.80	7.21	8.80
Asset Turnover	0.76	0.66	0.63	0.69	0.73	0.76	0.91	0.96
Current Ratio	1.29	1.33	1.29	1.30	1.46	1.43	1.51	1.54
Debt to Equity	2.12	2.32	2.12	2.01	2.02	1.82	1.83	1.48

Address: 100 NE Adams Street, Peoria, IL 61629-7310	**Web Site:** www.CAT.com	**Auditors:** PricewaterhouseCoopers LLP
Telephone: (309) 675 1000	**Officers:** James W. Owens - Chmn., C.E.O. David B. Burritt - V.P., C.F.O.	**Investor Contact:** 309-675-4549
Fax: (309) 675 4332		**Transfer Agents:** Mellon Investor Services of South Hackensack, NJ

CBL & ASSOCIATES PROPERTIES, INC.

Exchange	Symbol	Price	52Wk Range	Yield	P/E	Div Acheiver
NYS	CBL	$71.51 (3/31/2005)	77.84-47.42	4.54	22.28	10 Years

*7 Year Price Score 148.76 *NYSE Composite Index=100 *12 Month Price Score 107.80

Interim Earnings (Per Share)

Qtr.	Mar	Jun	Sep	Dec
2001	0.60	0.47	0.32	0.73
2002	0.64	0.63	0.57	0.65
2003	0.74	0.68	0.65	1.93
2004	0.96	0.68	0.62	0.95

Interim Dividends (Per Share)

Amt	Decl	Ex	Rec	Pay
0.362Q	6/10/2004	6/28/2004	6/30/2004	7/16/2004
0.362Q	9/9/2004	9/28/2004	9/30/2004	10/15/2004
0.406Q	11/4/2004	12/29/2004	12/31/2004	1/14/2005
0.406Q	3/3/2005	3/29/2005	3/31/2005	4/15/2005

Indicated Div: $3.25

Valuation Analysis

Forecast P/E	12.79	No of Institutions
	(4/13/2005)	166
Market Cap	$2.2 Billion	Shares
Book Value	1.1 Billion	24,511,084
Price/Book	2.13	% Held
Price/Sales	2.95	78.06

Business Summary: Property, Real Estate & Development (MIC: 8.3 SIC: 798 NAIC: 25930)

CBL & Associates Properties is a self-managed, self-administered, fully-integrated real estate investment trust that is engaged in the ownership, development, acquisition, leasing, management and operation of regional shopping malls and community centers. Co.'s shopping center properties are located mostly in the southeast and midwest, as well as in select markets in other regions of the U.S. As of Dec 31 2003, Co. owned controlling interests in 56 regional malls; 21 associated centers, each adjacent to a regional shopping mall; 17 community centers and its corporate office building. Co. owned non-controlling interests in four regional malls, two associated centers and 42 community centers.

Recent Developments: For the year ended Dec 31 2004, net income decreased 16.0% to $121,111 thousand from net income of $144,139 thousand a year earlier. Results for 2004 included a loss of $3,080 thousand on the impairment of real estate assets. Revenues were $759,164 thousand, up 14.0% from $665,996 thousand the year before. Operating income was $344,492 thousand versus an income of $316,421 thousand in the prior year, an increase of 8.9%. Total direct operating expenses grew 11.9% to $115,345 thousand from $103,037 thousand in 2003. Total indirect operating expenses jumped 21.4% to $299,327 thousand from $246,538 thousand the year before.

Prospects: On Jan 12 2005, Co. announced that it has completed the third and final phase of the joint venture with Galileo America Inc., the U.S. affiliate of Australia-based Galileo America Shopping Trust. Co. contributed 90.0% interest in two power centers, one community center, and one community center expansion for total consideration of $58.6 million, including $12.1 million in assumed debt and $42.0 million in cash, net of closing costs. Meanwhile, Co. expects funds from operations to range from $5.66 to $5.74 per share for full-year 2005. The guidance assumes net operating income growth in the range of 2.0% to 3.0%.

Financial Data
(US$ in Thousands)

	12/31/2004	12/31/2003	12/31/2002	12/31/2001	12/31/2000	12/31/1999	12/31/1998	12/31/1997
Earnings Per Share	3.21	3.99	2.49	2.11	2.37	1.94	1.53	1.45
Cash Flow Per Share	10.98	9.16	9.55	6.67	4.72	4.63	3.70	2.55
Tang Book Value Per Share	33.64	27.61	24.87	20.38	17.35	16.96	16.91	13.75
Dividends Per Share	1.494	1.345	1.160	1.065	1.020	0.975	0.930	0.885
Dividend Payout %	46.53	33.71	46.59	50.47	43.04	50.26	60.78	61.03
Income Statement								
Property Income	739,066	653,355	583,236	539,569	351,400	313,412	251,936	174,929
Non-Property Income	20,098	14,176	15,858	4,806	5,088	4,191	2,704	2,675
Total Revenue	759,164	667,531	599,094	544,375	356,488	317,603	254,640	177,604
Depn & Amortn	141,707	119,176	101,937	89,444	61,910	55,240	45,357	33,363
Interest Expense	177,219	153,373	143,164	154,477	94,597	82,505	67,329	37,830
Net Income	121,111	144,139	84,906	60,908	65,722	54,595	40,499	34,941
Average Shares	32,002	31,193	29,668	25,833	25,021	24,834	24,340	24,151
Balance Sheet								
Total Assets	5,204,500	4,264,310	3,795,114	3,372,851	2,115,565	2,018,838	1,855,347	1,245,025
Long-Term Obligations	3,371,679	2,738,102	2,402,079	2,315,955	1,424,337	1,360,753	1,208,204	741,413
Total Liabilities	3,583,743	2,899,579	2,553,411	2,419,662	1,502,565	1,424,989	1,270,670	783,391
Stockholders' Equity	1,054,151	837,300	741,190	522,088	434,825	419,887	415,782	330,853
Shares Outstanding	31,333	30,323	29,797	25,616	25,067	24,755	24,591	24,064
Statistical Record								
Return on Assets %	2.55	3.58	2.37	2.22	3.17	2.82	2.61	3.08
Return on Equity %	12.77	18.26	13.44	12.73	15.34	13.07	10.85	11.58
Net Margin %	15.95	21.59	14.17	11.19	18.44	17.19	15.90	19.67
Price Range	76.63-47.42	57.38-37.56	40.89-31.50	31.85-25.13	25.88-20.13	27.00-19.44	26.88-23.38	27.63-22.63
P/E Ratio	23.87-14.77	14.38-9.41	16.42-12.65	15.09-11.91	10.92-8.49	13.92-10.02	17.57-15.28	19.05-15.60
Average Yield %	2.51	2.90	3.16	3.69	4.34	4.05	3.72	3.57

Address: 2030 Hamilton Place Blvd., Suite 500, Chattanooga, TN 37421-6000 **Telephone:** (423) 855 0001 **Fax:** (423) 855 8662	**Web Site:** www.cblproperties.com **Officers:** Charles B. Lebovitz - Chmn., C.E.O. John N. Foy - Vice-Chmn., C.F.O., Treas.	**Auditors:** Deloitte & Touche LLP

CEDAR FAIR, L.P.

Exchange	Symbol	Price	52Wk Range	Yield	P/E	Div Acheiver
NYS	FUN	$31.47 (3/31/2005)	34.97-28.86	5.85	21.41	17 Years

*7 Year Price Score 109.21 *NYSE Composite Index=100 *12 Month Price Score 96.18

Interim Earnings (Per Share)

Qtr.	Mar	Jun	Sep	Dec
2001	(0.60)	0.13	2.10	(0.50)
2002	(0.63)	0.40	2.01	(0.39)
2003	(0.62)	0.33	2.16	(0.21)
2004	(0.59)	0.25	2.02	(0.30)

Interim Dividends (Per Share)

Amt	Decl	Ex	Rec	Pay
0.45Q	6/24/2004	7/1/2004	7/6/2004	8/16/2004
0.45Q	9/23/2004	10/1/2004	10/5/2004	11/15/2004
0.45Q	12/16/2004	1/3/2005	1/5/2005	2/15/2005
0.46Q	3/7/2005	4/1/2005	4/5/2005	5/16/2005

Indicated Div: $1.84 (Div. Reinv. Plan)

Valuation Analysis

Forecast P/E	N/A	No of Institutions
Market Cap	$1.7 Billion	Shares
Book Value	N/A	11,176,841
Price/Book	N/A	% Held
Price/Sales	3.11	20.90

Business Summary: Sporting & Recreational (MIC: 13.5 SIC: 996 NAIC: 13110)

Cedar Fair is a limited partnership managed by Cedar Fair Management Company. As of Dec 31 2003, Co. owned and operated six amusement parks: Cedar Point on Lake Erie in Sandusky, OH; Knott's Berry Farm, located in Buena Park, CA; Dorney Park & Wildwater Kingdom, near Allentown, PA; Valleyfair, near Minneapolis, MN; Worlds of Fun in Kansas City, MO; and Michigan's Adventure, located near Muskegon, MI. Co.'s five water parks are located near San Diego and Palm Springs, CA, and adjacent to Cedar Point, Knott's Berry Farm and Worlds of Fun. Co. owns and operates four hotel facilities. Co. also operates Knott's Camp Snoopy at the Mall of America in Bloomington, MN under a management contract.

Recent Developments: For the year ended Dec 31 2004, net income decreased 8.8% to $78,315 thousand from net income of $85,888 thousand a year earlier. Revenues were $541,972 thousand, up 6.3% from $509,976 thousand the year before. Operating income was $117,830 thousand versus an income of $125,149 thousand in the prior year, a decrease of 5.8%. Total direct expense was $298,783 thousand versus $269,611 thousand in the prior year, an increase of 10.8%. Total indirect expense was $125,359 thousand versus $115,216 thousand in the prior year, an increase of 8.8%.

Prospects: Looking ahead to the 2005 season, Co. plans to invest $83.0 million in capital improvements at its 12 properties, including the addition of new roller coasters at Knott's Berry Farm and Dorney Park, as well as the introduction of a new water park at Geauga Lake. Co.'s capital projects are all proceeding on schedule and on budget, and should be ready for the 2005 season. Meanwhile, Co. anticipates full-year 2005 revenue growth of 6-8%, driven primarily by improvements in attendance and in-park guest per capita spending, as well as continued growth in accommodation revenues at its resort properties. In addition, Co. is targeting EBITDA in the range of $185.0 million to $195.0 million for 2005.

Financial Data

(US$ in Thousands)	12/31/2004	12/31/2003	12/31/2002	12/31/2001	12/31/2000	12/31/1999	12/31/1998	12/31/1997
Earnings Per Share	1.47	1.67	1.39	1.13	1.50	1.63	1.58	1.47
Cash Flow Per Share	2.84	2.67	2.90	2.46	2.22	2.39	2.52	2.10
Dividends Per Share	1.790	1.740	1.650	1.580	1.502	1.388	0.965	1.577
Dividend Payout %	121.77	104.19	118.71	139.82	100.17	85.12	61.08	107.31
Income Statement								
Total Revenue	541,972	509,976	502,851	477,256	472,920	438,001	419,500	264,137
EBITDA	172,983	172,569	155,225	141,043	155,088	151,837	144,673	97,831
Depn & Amortn	50,690	44,693	41,682	42,486	39,572	35,082	32,065	21,528
Income Before Taxes	97,030	103,806	88,576	74,414	94,159	101,384	97,948	68,458
Income Taxes	18,715	17,918	17,159	16,520	16,353	15,580	14,507	...
Net Income	78,315	85,888	71,417	57,894	77,806	85,804	83,441	68,458
Average Shares	53,315	51,334	51,263	51,113	51,679	52,390	52,414	46,265
Balance Sheet								
Current Assets	32,960	29,777	29,237	26,868	25,378	24,184	20,967	21,954
Total Assets	993,208	819,341	822,257	810,231	764,143	708,961	631,325	599,619
Current Liabilities	121,517	111,694	106,338	96,700	114,024	86,559	77,231	62,426
Long-Term Obligations	442,084	348,647	365,150	373,000	300,000	261,200	200,350	189,750
Total Liabilities	622,725	510,450	516,937	501,981	433,554	358,975	289,334	314,238
Shares Outstanding	53,480	50,673	50,549	50,514	50,813	51,798	51,980	52,403
Statistical Record								
Return on Assets %	8.62	10.46	8.75	7.35	10.53	12.80	13.56	15.15
EBITDA Margin %	31.92	33.84	30.87	29.55	32.79	34.67	34.49	37.04
Net Margin %	14.45	16.84	14.20	12.13	16.45	19.59	19.89	25.92
Asset Turnover	0.60	0.62	0.62	0.61	0.64	0.65	0.68	0.58
Current Ratio	0.27	0.27	0.27	0.28	0.22	0.28	0.27	0.35
Price Range	35.71-28.86	31.03-22.74	24.79-20.30	24.98-18.03	20.75-17.56	26.00-18.50	29.44-22.31	28.19-17.88
P/E Ratio	24.29-19.63	18.58-13.62	17.83-14.60	22.11-15.96	13.83-11.71	15.95-11.35	18.63-14.12	19.18-12.16
Average Yield %	5.69	6.51	7.10	7.50	8.05	6.07	3.66	7.29

Address: One Cedar Point Drive, Sandusky, OH 44870-5259	Web Site: www.cedarfair.com	Auditors: Price Waterhouse Coopers
Telephone: (419) 626-0830	**Officers:** Richard L. Kinzel - Chmn., Pres., C.E.O. Bruce A. Jackson - V.P., Fin., C.F.O.	**Investor Contact:** 419-627-2233
Fax: (419) 627-2234		**Transfer Agents:** American Stock Transfer & Trust Company, New York,

CENDANT CORP.

Exchange	Symbol	Price	52Wk Range	Yield	P/E
NYS	CD	$20.54 (3/31/2005)	23.90-19.08	1.75	10.48

*7 Year Price Score 110.87 ***NYSE Composite Index=100** ***12 Month Price Score 93.41**

Interim Earnings (Per Share)

Qtr.	Mar	Jun	Sep	Dec
2001	10.33	0.27	0.23	(10.10)
2002	0.34	0.01	0.24	0.23
2003	0.30	0.37	0.19	0.28
2004	0.42	0.66	0.56	0.33

Interim Dividends (Per Share)

Amt	Decl	Ex	Rec	Pay
0.07Q	4/20/2004	5/20/2004	5/24/2004	6/15/2004
0.09Q	7/20/2004	8/12/2004	8/16/2004	9/14/2004
0.09Q	10/19/2004	11/18/2004	11/22/2004	12/14/2004
0.09Q	1/24/2005	2/24/2005	2/28/2005	3/15/2005
		Indicated Div: $0.36		

Valuation Analysis

Forecast P/E	14.65 (4/7/2005)	No of Institutions 516
Market Cap	$21.6 Billion	Shares 829,067,776
Book Value	12.7 Billion	% Held
Price/Book	1.70	78.82
Price/Sales	1.09	

TRADING VOLUME (thousand shares)

Business Summary: Personal Services (MIC: 5.15 SIC: 299 NAIC: 12990)

Cendant is a diversified services provider. The Real Estate Services segment provides real estate brokerage services, mortgages and employee relocations. The Hospitality segment franchises hotels and facilitates vacation timeshare sales and exchanges. The Travel Distribution segment provides travel content and transaction processing services. The Financial Services segment provides enhancement packages to financial institutions, insurance-based products to consumers, loyalty programs to businesses and consumer discount membership programs. The Vehicle Services segment franchises vehicle rental businesses and provides fleet management and fuel card services.

Recent Developments: For the year ended Dec 31 2004, income from continuing operations increased 27.3% to $1,820,000 thousand from income of $1,430,000 thousand a year earlier. Net income increased 77.6% to $2,082,000 thousand from net income of $1,172,000 thousand a year earlier. Revenues were $19,785,000 thousand, up 9.8% from $18,015,000 thousand the year before.

Prospects: On Feb 28 2005, Co. acquired European online travel provider, ebookers plc, for about $350.0 million. This acquisition, together with Orbitz and the pending Gullivers acquisition, which is expected to close in April 2005, is part of Co.'s realignment plan to focus its core travel and real estate business. Going forward, Co. expects 2005 will be a transitional year as it integrates acquired businesses and reinvest the proceeds from divestitures. Accordingly, Co. expects revenue in the range of $17.64 billion to $18.2 billion in 2005, with earnings between $1.15 and $1.25 a share. For 2006, Co. expects earnings to climb to a range of $1.62 to $1.72 a share.

Financial Data

(US$ in Thousands)	12/31/2004	12/31/2003	12/31/2002	12/31/2001	12/31/2000	12/31/1999	12/31/1998	12/31/1997
Earnings Per Share	1.96	1.13	0.81	0.41	0.81	(0.07)	0.61	0.06
Cash Flow Per Share	5.24	7.08	1.23	3.20	1.91	4.04	0.95	0.78
Dividends Per Share	0.320	...	...	...	...	...	...	...
Dividend Payout %	16.33	...	...	...	...	...	...	...
Income Statement								
Total Revenue	19,785,000	18,192,000	14,088,000	8,950,000	3,930,000	5,402,000	5,283,800	5,314,700
EBITDA	4,762,000	4,366,000	3,793,000	2,927,000	1,452,000	495,000	1,897,600	2,291,000
Depn & Amortn	2,208,000	2,135,000	2,134,000	2,168,000	483,000	1,069,000	1,582,600	1,996,300
Income Before Taxes	2,554,000	2,231,000	1,659,000	759,000	969,000	(574,000)	315,000	294,700
Income Taxes	728,000	745,000	556,000	235,000	309,000	(406,000)	104,500	239,300
Net Income	2,082,000	1,172,000	846,000	385,000	602,000	(55,000)	539,600	55,400
Average Shares	1,064,000	1,040,000	1,043,000	917,000	762,000	751,000	880,400	851,700
Balance Sheet								
Current Assets	3,865,000	4,478,000	3,358,000	6,492,000	2,384,000	4,592,000	4,546,900	2,575,300
Total Assets	42,555,000	39,037,000	35,897,000	33,452,000	14,516,000	15,149,000	20,216,500	14,851,200
Current Liabilities	6,332,000	7,335,000	5,863,000	10,290,000	3,467,000	6,229,000	5,356,100	4,320,300
Long-Term Obligations	19,437,000	18,994,000	18,315,000	13,836,000	2,432,000	4,140,000	7,775,300	4,373,400
Total Liabilities	29,860,000	28,851,000	26,207,000	26,009,000	9,684,000	11,465,000	13,908,800	10,373,700
Stockholders' Equity	12,695,000	10,186,000	9,315,000	7,068,000	2,774,000	2,206,000	4,835,600	4,477,500
Shares Outstanding	1,051,326	1,008,844	1,031,765	977,708	737,888	706,548	833,281	831,788
Statistical Record								
Return on Assets %	5.09	3.13	2.44	1.61	4.05	N.M.	3.08	0.36
Return on Equity %	18.15	12.02	10.33	7.82	24.11	N.M.	11.59	1.11
EBITDA Margin %	24.07	24.00	26.92	32.70	36.95	9.16	35.91	43.11
Net Margin %	10.52	6.44	6.01	4.30	15.32	N.M.	10.21	1.04
Asset Turnover	0.48	0.49	0.41	0.37	0.26	0.31	0.30	0.35
Current Ratio	0.61	0.61	0.57	0.63	0.69	0.74	0.85	0.60
Debt to Equity	1.53	1.86	1.97	1.96	0.88	1.88	1.61	0.98
Price Range	23.90-19.08	21.26-9.99	19.06-8.62	20.52-9.18	25.32-8.10	25.32-13.88	39.44-7.15	32.77-19.07
P/E Ratio	12.19-9.74	18.81-8.84	23.53-10.64	50.06-22.38	31.26-10.00	...	64.66-11.72	546.16-317.76
Average Yield %	1.47	...	...	...	...	...	...	...

Address: 9 West 57th Street, New York, NY 10019 Telephone: (212) 413-1800 Fax: (212) 413-1924	Web Site: www.cendant.com Officers: Henry R. Silverman - Chmn., C.E.O. James E. Buckman - Vice-Chmn., Gen. Couns.	Auditors: Deloitte & Touche LLP Investor Contact: 212-413-1834

CENTERPOINT ENERGY, INC

Exchange	Symbol	Price	52Wk Range	Yield	P/E
NYS	CNP	$12.03 (3/31/2005)	12.61-10.02	3.33	N/A

*7 Year Price Score 51.40   *NYSE Composite Index=100   *12 Month Price Score 99.84

Interim Earnings (Per Share)

Qtr.	Mar	Jun	Sep	Dec
2002	...	...	(13.77)	(0.16)
2003	0.56	0.21	0.59	0.23
2004	0.24	0.19	(3.66)	0.77

Interim Dividends (Per Share)

Amt	Decl	Ex	Rec	Pay
0.10Q	7/29/2004	8/12/2004	8/16/2004	9/10/2004
0.10Q	11/15/2004	11/23/2004	11/26/2004	12/10/2004
0.10Q	1/26/2005	2/14/2005	2/16/2005	3/10/2005
0.10Q	3/3/2005	3/14/2005	3/16/2005	3/31/2005

Indicated Div: $0.40

Valuation Analysis

Forecast P/E	17.97	No of Institutions	
	(4/7/2005)	269	
Market Cap	$3.7 Billion	Shares	
Book Value	1.1 Billion	186,724,000	
Price/Book	3.35	% Held	
Price/Sales	0.44	60.53	

Business Summary: Electricity (MIC: 7.1 SIC: 911 NAIC: 21122)

CenterPoint Energy is a public utility holding company. Co. operates through two indirect wholly owned subsidiaries. CenterPoint Energy Houston Electric, LLC owns and operates Co.'s electric transmission and distribution business to retail electric providers serving about 1.9 million metered customers in the Texas Gulf Coast area. CenterPoint Energy Resources Corp., together with its subsidiaries, owns and operates Co.'s local gas distribution companies, interstate pipelines and gas gathering systems, provides various ancillary services, and offers variable and fixed price physical natural gas supplies to commercial and industrial customers and natural gas distributors.

Recent Developments: For the year ended Dec 31 2004, net loss was $904,704 thousand versus net income of $483,667 thousand a year earlier. Revenues were $8,510,428 thousand, up 9.3% from $7,789,681 thousand the year before. Operating income was $863,795 thousand versus an income of $1,355,413 thousand in the prior year, a decrease of 36.3%. Total indirect expense was $7,646,633 thousand versus $6,434,268 thousand in the prior year, an increase of 18.8%.

Prospects: Co. continues with the process of selling its generation assets. In December 2004, the first step of the transaction, the sale of the fossil assets, was completed, with Co. receiving $2.23 billion in cash. In the final step of the transaction, expected to take place in the first half of 2005 following Nuclear Regulatory Commission approval, Texas Genco LLC will acquire Co.'s nuclear generating assets. At that closing, Co. will receive a cash payment of $700.0 million. Looking ahead, Co. plans to continue to reduce its indebtedness and enhance the business performance of its core operations in 2005.

Financial Data

(US$ in Thousands)	12/31/2004	12/31/2003	12/31/2002	12/31/2001	12/31/2000
Earnings Per Share	(2.48)	1.58	(13.08)	3.35	1.56
Cash Flow Per Share	1.24	2.95	1.02	6.08	...
Tang Book Value Per Share	N.M.	N.M.	N.M.	16.29	...
Dividends Per Share	0.400	0.400	0.160	1.500	1.500
Dividend Payout %	...	25.32	...	44.78	96.15
Income Statement					
Total Revenue	8,510,428	9,760,124	7,922,498	10,656,357	10,374,202
EBITDA	926,117	1,464,688	1,905,508	1,927,470	1,737,324
Depn & Amortn	582,096	799,923	628,499	700,759	771,112
Income Before Taxes	344,021	664,765	594,309	675,177	456,238
Income Taxes	138,306	216,301	208,026	228,252	234,196
Net Income	(904,704)	483,667	(3,920,234)	980,559	447,500
Average Shares	359,506	306,220	299,644	292,193	287,273
Balance Sheet					
Net PPE	8,186,393	11,811,536	11,409,369	11,199,505	...
Total Assets	18,161,957	21,376,664	19,634,279	31,266,363	...
Long-Term Obligations	7,193,016	10,783,064	9,194,320	4,919,737	...
Total Liabilities	17,056,455	19,437,197	17,506,189	23,822,696	...
Stockholders' Equity	1,105,502	1,760,557	1,421,950	6,737,923	...
Shares Outstanding	308,045	306,297	305,017	302,944	299,914
Statistical Record					
Return on Assets %	N.M.	2.36	N.M.	...	...
Return on Equity %	N.M.	30.40	N.M.	...	...
EBITDA Margin %	10.88	15.01	24.05	18.09	16.75
Net Margin %	(10.63)	4.96	(49.48)	9.20	4.31
PPE Turnover	0.85	0.84	0.70	...	...
Asset Turnover	0.43	0.48	0.31	...	...
Debt to Equity	6.51	6.12	6.47	0.73	...
Price Range	12.21-9.69	10.11-4.50	21.81-4.39	40.64-19.21	39.15-16.15
P/E Ratio	...	6.40-2.85	...	12.13-5.73	25.10-10.35
Average Yield %	3.68	4.83	1.22	5.26	5.79

Address: 1111 Louisiana Street, Houston, TX 77002 Telephone: (713) 207-1111	Web Site: www.centerpointenergy.com Officers: Milton Carroll - Chmn. David M. McClanahan - Pres., C.E.O.	Auditors: Deloitte & Touche LLP Investor Contact: 713-207-6500 Transfer Agents: CenterPoint Energy Investor Services

CENTERPOINT PROPERTIES TRUST

Exchange	Symbol	Price	52Wk Range	Yield	P/E
NYS	CNT	$41.00 (3/31/2005)	48.83-33.98	4.17	22.28

*7 Year Price Score 136.49 *NYSE Composite Index=100 *12 Month Price Score 95.88

Interim Earnings (Per Share)

Qtr.	Mar	Jun	Sep	Dec
2001	0.25	0.30	0.31	(0.48)
2002	0.32	0.37	0.34	0.36
2003	0.33	0.36	0.37	0.57
2004	0.41	0.30	0.60	0.53

Interim Dividends (Per Share)

Amt	Decl	Ex	Rec	Pay
0.39Q	5/19/2004	7/14/2004	7/17/2004	7/22/2004
0.39Q	8/24/2004	10/19/2004	10/21/2004	11/1/2004
0.427Q	12/21/2004	1/25/2005	1/27/2005	2/8/2005
0.427Q	3/9/2005	4/12/2005	4/14/2005	4/25/2005

Indicated Div: $1.71

Valuation Analysis

Forecast P/E	16.17 (4/7/2005)	No of Institutions 129
Market Cap	$2.0 Billion	Shares 41,465,316
Book Value	607.0 Million	% Held
Price/Book	3.30	84.60
Price/Sales	12.55	

Business Summary: Property, Real Estate & Development (MIC: 8.3 SIC: 798 NAIC: 25930)

CenterPoint Properties Trust is a real estate investment trust that is focused primarily on industrial property within the Chicago region. Co. seeks to create value through the management, investment, development, and redevelopment of warehouse, distribution, light manufacturing, air freight and rail-related facilities. Co. also develops multi-facility industrial parks located near highways, airports and/or railroads. It currently owns and operates approximately 38 million square feet and the Company and its affiliates own or control an additional 3,185 acres of land upon which approximately 48 million square feet could be developed.

Recent Developments: For the year ended Dec 31 2004, net income increased 10.1% to $93,108 thousand from net income of $84,584 thousand a year earlier. Revenues were $159,772 thousand, up 13.7% from $140,543 thousand the year before.

Prospects: Co.'s results are benefiting from increasing investment and development. In January 2005, Co. acquired a 3.0 million square foot, eight-building industrial portfolio from HCA Commercial Real Estate for a gross purchase price of approximately $96.0 million. The buildings are located in submarkets of metropolitan Chicago and the weighted average lease term for the portfolio is approximately six years. Meanwhile, Co. has signed agreements to develop and sell two build-to-suit facilities totaling over 400,000 square feet at McCook Business Center in McCook, IL. Co.'s pipeline of value-added investments is robust and it sees growing demand at all of its major business parks under development.

Financial Data
(US$ in Thousands)

	12/31/2004	12/31/2003	12/31/2002	12/31/2001	12/31/2000	12/31/1999	12/31/1998	12/31/1997
Earnings Per Share	1.84	1.58	1.39	0.39	1.04	0.98	0.75	0.70
Cash Flow Per Share	1.62	1.61	1.28	1.62	1.70	1.86	1.55	1.06
Tang Book Value Per Share	12.41	10.33	11.42	11.29	11.99	11.30	10.22	10.13
Dividends Per Share	1.560	1.215	1.155	1.050	1.005	0.950	0.875	0.840
Dividend Payout %	84.78	76.90	83.39	272.73	96.17	96.94	116.67	119.15
Income Statement								
Property Income	158,826	160,105	155,804	159,242	158,293	136,282	110,298	81,638
Non-Property Income	946	1,318	896	4,325	186	2,654	2,810	4,320
Total Revenue	159,772	161,423	156,700	163,567	158,479	138,936	113,108	85,958
Depn & Amortn	45,552	39,665	37,713	37,767	35,109	29,331	23,235	16,078
Interest Expense	36,599	26,659	31,670	33,154	33,131	21,859	15,476	10,871
Income Before Taxes	9,261	30,758	44,460	30,752	...	...	...	...
Income Taxes	(1,017)	1,111	3,223	1,139	...	...	...	...
Net Income	93,108	84,584	75,392	27,997	54,686	48,760	36,458	27,630
Average Shares	49,157	47,488	47,166	46,344	42,758	41,719	40,203	37,894
Balance Sheet								
Total Assets	1,598,491	1,419,242	1,306,324	1,182,671	1,155,235	1,083,427	821,936	699,275
Long-Term Obligations	873,509	834,865	692,706	586,527	547,744	554,348	364,718	270,768
Total Liabilities	991,527	936,741	779,365	668,876	620,849	616,823	409,897	311,149
Stockholders' Equity	606,964	482,501	526,959	513,795	534,386	466,604	412,039	388,126
Shares Outstanding	48,900	46,691	46,134	45,507	44,567	41,299	40,303	38,330
Statistical Record								
Return on Assets %	6.15	6.21	6.06	2.40	4.87	5.12	4.79	4.80
Return on Equity %	17.05	16.76	14.49	5.34	10.90	11.10	9.11	8.69
Net Margin %	58.28	52.40	48.11	17.12	34.51	35.10	32.23	32.14
Price Range	48.83-33.98	38.41-27.05	29.75-24.35	25.50-22.52	23.88-17.22	18.81-15.53	18.44-15.34	18.53-14.25
P/E Ratio	26.54-18.46	24.31-17.12	21.40-17.52	65.37-57.76	22.96-16.56	19.20-15.85	24.58-20.46	26.47-20.36
Average Yield %	3.83	3.86	4.23	4.41	4.96	5.58	5.15	5.20

Address: 1808 Swift Road, Oak Brook, IL 60523-1501 **Telephone:** (630) 586-8000 **Fax:** (630) 586-8010	**Web Site:** www.CenterPoint-Prop.com **Officers:** Martin Barber - Co-Chmn. John S. Gates Jr. - Co.-Chmn., C.E.O.	**Auditors:** PricewaterhouseCoopers LLP **Investor Contact:** 630-586-8101

CENTEX CORP.

Exchange	Symbol	Price	52Wk Range	Yield	P/E
NYS	CTX	$57.27 (3/31/2005)	65.85-41.24	0.28	8.01

*7 Year Price Score 173.78 *NYSE Composite Index=100 *12 Month Price Score 111.09

Interim Earnings (Per Share)

Qtr.	Jun	Sep	Dec	Mar
2001-02	0.61	0.75	0.77	0.93
2002-03	0.69	0.92	1.25	1.56
2003-04	1.12	1.44	1.52	2.31
2004-05	1.35	1.61	1.91	...

Interim Dividends (Per Share)

Amt	Decl	Ex	Rec	Pay
0.04Q	5/27/2004	6/7/2004	6/9/2004	7/7/2004
0.04Q	7/22/2004	8/2/2004	8/4/2004	8/25/2004
0.04Q	10/20/2004	11/1/2004	11/3/2004	11/24/2004
0.04Q	2/15/2005	2/28/2005	3/2/2005	3/23/2005

Indicated Div: $0.16

Valuation Analysis

Forecast P/E	6.55	No of Institutions
	(4/7/2005)	325
Market Cap	$7.2 Billion	Shares
Book Value	3.8 Billion	107,677,320
Price/Book	1.88	% Held
Price/Sales	0.62	85.08

Business Summary: Building & General Construction (MIC: 3.2 SIC: 531 NAIC: 36115)

Centex is engaged in four business segments. Co.'s Home Building segment purchases and develops land and constructs and sells single-family homes, townhomes and condominiums. The Financial Services segment consists of home financing and the sale of title and other insurance coverages. The Construction Services segment manufactures, produces, distributes and sells cement, gypsum wallboard, recycled paperboard, aggregates and readymix concrete, and constructs buildings for both private and government interests. The Investment Real Estate segment acquires, develops and sells land, primarily for industrial, office, multi-family, retail, residential and mixed-use projects.

Recent Developments: For the quarter ended Dec 31 2004, net income increased 27.7% to $253,771 thousand from net income of $198,670 thousand in the year-earlier quarter. Revenues were $3,118,623 thousand, up 21.4% from $2,569,857 thousand the year before. Total indirect expense was $54,874 thousand versus $47,168 thousand in the prior-year quarter, an increase of 16.3%.

Prospects: Demand trends are favorable for Co. The overall demand for housing in the U.S. remains favorable, and is driven in the long-term by population growth, demographics, immigration, household formations and changes in home ownership rates. Short-term growth drivers such as mortgage rates, consumer confidence and employment levels can also impact housing demand. The highly fragmented homebuilding industry in the U.S. is in the early stages of consolidation. Co. believes industry consolidation will be an important trend over the next decade or more as large homebuilders seek to capitalize on the benefits of size, such as capital strength, more efficient operations and technological advantages.

Financial Data

(US$ in Thousands)	9 Mos	6 Mos	3 Mos	03/31/2004	03/31/2003	03/31/2002	03/31/2001	03/31/2000
Earnings Per Share	7.15	6.77	6.60	6.40	4.42	3.06	2.33	2.11
Cash Flow Per Share	(5.16)	0.47	4.74	5.57	(0.05)	0.67	(11.96)	7.23
Tang Book Value Per Share	28.44	26.10	24.43	22.79	19.13	14.44	11.60	9.83
Dividends Per Share	0.180	0.160	0.140	0.120	0.080	0.080	0.080	0.080
Dividend Payout %	2.52	2.36	2.12	1.88	1.81	2.62	3.44	3.79
Income Statement								
Total Revenue	8,869,602	5,750,979	2,766,073	10,363,391	9,117,241	7,748,430	6,710,735	5,956,366
EBITDA	1,078,002	656,768	299,802	1,250,690	908,064	709,424	476,840	465,832
Depn & Amortn	79,708	52,360	23,910	101,626	113,213	90,659	40,509	48,971
Income Before Taxes	998,294	604,408	275,892	1,149,064	794,851	618,765	436,331	416,861
Income Taxes	356,678	216,563	98,659	371,933	238,932	236,539	154,354	159,729
Net Income	641,616	387,845	177,233	827,686	555,919	382,226	281,977	257,132
Average Shares	132,547	130,981	130,926	129,392	126,116	125,058	121,321	121,857
Balance Sheet								
Current Assets	8,365,254	7,456,367	7,042,088	6,720,090	4,813,092	3,597,446	4,920,290	2,986,678
Total Assets	19,002,532	17,564,501	17,186,342	16,068,568	11,610,536	8,985,455	6,649,043	4,038,740
Current Liabilities	2,019,180	1,946,391	1,870,200	1,961,912	1,677,764	1,438,613	1,271,464	1,688,042
Long-Term Obligations	12,670,405	11,642,068	11,629,031	10,720,380	7,104,699	5,276,779	3,519,891	751,160
Total Liabilities	15,163,463	14,079,889	13,920,032	12,682,292	8,782,463	6,715,392	4,791,355	2,490,039
Stockholders' Equity	3,839,069	3,484,612	3,266,310	3,050,225	2,657,846	2,116,773	1,714,064	1,419,349
Shares Outstanding	126,139	123,987	123,514	122,660	119,478	122,342	119,858	118,776
Statistical Record								
Return on Assets %	5.43	5.45	5.87	5.96	5.40	4.89	5.28	6.12
Return on Equity %	26.95	27.63	28.60	28.92	23.29	19.96	18.00	19.60
EBITDA Margin %	12.15	11.42	10.84	12.07	9.96	9.16	7.11	7.82
Net Margin %	7.23	6.74	6.41	7.99	6.10	4.93	4.20	4.32
Asset Turnover	0.67	0.69	0.74	0.75	0.89	0.99	1.26	1.42
Current Ratio	4.14	3.83	3.77	3.43	2.87	2.50	3.87	1.77
Debt to Equity	3.30	3.34	3.56	3.51	2.67	2.49	2.05	0.53
Price Range	59.69-41.24	57.75-35.12	57.75-32.32	57.75-24.20	25.97-17.08	27.67-12.98	19.98-9.26	18.67-8.01
P/E Ratio	8.35-5.77	8.53-5.19	8.75-4.90	9.02-3.78	5.88-3.86	9.04-4.24	8.57-3.97	8.85-3.80
Average Yield %	0.37	0.34	0.32	0.30	0.35	0.34	0.57	0.62

Address: 2728 N. Harwood, Dallas, TX 75201-1516 **Telephone:** (214) 981-5000	**Web Site:** www.centex.com **Officers:** Timothy R. Eller - Chmn., Pres., C.E.O., C.O.O. Leldon E. Echols - Exec. V.P., C.F.O.	**Auditors:** ERNST & YOUNG LLP **Transfer Agents:** Mellon Investor Services LLC, Ridgefield Park, NJ

CENTURYTEL, INC.

Exchange	Symbol	Price	52Wk Range	Yield	P/E	Div Acheiver
NYS	CTL	$32.84 (3/31/2005)	35.49-26.51	0.73	13.63	31 Years

*7 Year Price Score 82.82 *NYSE Composite Index=100 *12 Month Price Score 97.86

Interim Earnings (Per Share)

Qtr.	Mar	Jun	Sep	Dec
2001	0.33	1.09	0.65	0.35
2002	0.50	0.55	4.26	0.30
2003	0.58	0.60	0.63	0.56
2004	0.58	0.60	0.63	0.60

Interim Dividends (Per Share)

Amt	Decl	Ex	Rec	Pay
0.058Q	5/27/2004	6/3/2004	6/7/2004	6/18/2004
0.058Q	8/24/2004	9/2/2004	9/7/2004	9/17/2004
0.058Q	11/18/2004	12/1/2004	12/3/2004	12/17/2004
0.06Q	2/22/2005	3/2/2005	3/4/2005	3/18/2005

Indicated Div: $0.24 (Div. Reinv. Plan)

Valuation Analysis

Forecast P/E	14.31	No of Institutions
	(4/7/2005)	307
Market Cap	$4.3 Billion	Shares
Book Value	3.4 Billion	111,198,464
Price/Book	1.27	% Held
Price/Sales	1.81	83.83

Business Summary: Communications (MIC: 10.1 SIC: 813 NAIC: 17110)

CenturyTel is a regional telecommunications company that is primarily engaged in providing local exchange telephone services. Co. also provides long distance, Internet access, fiber transport, competitive local exchange carrier, security monitoring, and other communications and business information services in certain local and regional markets. As of Dec 31 2003, Co.'s local exchange telephone subsidiaries operated approximately 2.4 million telephone access lines, primarily in rural, suburban and small urban areas in 22 states, with over 70.0% of these lines located in Wisconsin, Missouri, Alabama, Arkansas and Washington.

Recent Developments: For the year ended Dec 31 2004, net income decreased 2.2% to $337,244 thousand from net income of $344,707 thousand a year earlier. Revenues were $2,407,372 thousand, up 1.7% from $2,367,610 thousand the year before. Operating income was $753,953 thousand versus an income of $750,396 thousand in the prior year, an increase of 0.5%. Total indirect expense was $1,653,419 thousand versus $1,617,214 thousand in the prior year, an increase of 2.2%.

Prospects: On Feb 3 2004, Co. announced an agreement to purchase metro fiber networks in 16 markets, primarily in the central U.S., from KMC Telecom Holdings, Inc. for $65.0 million in cash, subject to purchase price adjustment. The purchase will add key markets to Co.'s LightCore footprint across Alabama, Indiana, Kansas, Louisiana, Michigan, Minnesota, Mississippi, Ohio, Tennessee, Texas and Wisconsin. In 2005, Co. believes it can continue to drive revenue growth from the further penetration of its bundled offerings and expansion in its fiber business. For full-year 2005, Co. expects earnings to be in the range of $2.20 to $2.35 per diluted share.

Financial Data

(US$ in Thousands)	12/31/2004	12/31/2003	12/31/2002	12/31/2001	12/31/2000	12/31/1999	12/31/1998	12/31/1997
Earnings Per Share	2.41	2.38	5.61	2.41	1.63	1.70	1.64	1.87
Cash Flow Per Share	6.95	7.44	5.62	4.73	4.00	2.94	3.41	2.20
Tang Book Value Per Share	N.M.	N.M.	N.M.	N.M.	N.M.	1.39	N.M.	N.M.
Dividends Per Share	0.230	0.220	0.210	0.200	0.190	0.180	0.173	0.164
Dividend Payout %	9.54	9.24	3.74	8.30	11.66	10.59	10.57	8.81
Income Statement								
Total Revenue	2,407,372	2,380,745	1,971,996	2,117,469	1,845,926	1,676,669	1,577,085	901,521
EBITDA	1,259,327	1,229,351	926,927	1,251,963	957,543	928,645	883,564	624,310
Depn & Amortn	500,904	470,641	411,626	473,384	388,056	348,816	328,554	159,495
Income Before Taxes	547,372	531,959	293,456	553,056	386,185	429,272	387,458	408,341
Income Taxes	210,128	187,252	103,537	210,025	154,711	189,503	158,701	152,363
Net Income	337,244	344,707	801,624	343,031	231,474	239,769	228,757	255,978
Average Shares	142,144	144,700	142,879	142,307	141,864	141,432	140,105	137,412
Balance Sheet								
Net PPE	3,341,401	3,455,481	3,531,645	2,999,563	2,959,293	2,256,458	2,351,453	2,258,563
Total Assets	7,796,953	7,895,852	7,770,408	6,318,684	6,393,290	4,705,407	4,935,455	4,709,401
Long-Term Obligations	2,762,019	3,109,302	3,578,132	2,087,500	3,050,292	2,078,311	2,558,000	2,609,541
Total Liabilities	4,387,188	4,417,336	4,682,404	3,981,304	4,361,211	2,857,415	3,403,973	3,886,709
Stockholders' Equity	3,409,765	3,478,516	3,088,004	2,337,380	2,032,079	1,847,992	1,531,482	1,300,272
Shares Outstanding	132,373	144,364	142,955	141,232	140,667	139,945	138,083	136,656
Statistical Record								
Return on Assets %	4.29	4.40	11.38	5.40	4.16	4.97	4.74	7.60
Return on Equity %	9.77	10.50	29.55	15.70	11.90	14.19	16.16	21.99
EBITDA Margin %	52.31	51.64	47.00	59.13	51.87	55.39	56.03	69.25
Net Margin %	14.01	14.48	40.65	16.20	12.54	14.30	14.51	28.39
PPE Turnover	0.71	0.68	0.60	0.71	0.71	0.73	0.68	0.53
Asset Turnover	0.31	0.30	0.28	0.33	0.33	0.35	0.33	0.27
Debt to Equity	0.81	0.89	1.16	0.89	1.50	1.12	1.67	2.01
Price Range	35.49-26.33	36.63-25.51	35.20-22.18	39.00-26.18	47.38-24.50	48.88-36.44	45.00-21.75	22.36-12.78
P/E Ratio	14.73-10.93	15.39-10.72	6.27-3.95	16.18-10.86	29.06-15.03	28.75-21.43	27.44-13.26	11.96-6.83
Average Yield %	0.74	0.69	0.71	0.64	0.57	0.43	0.56	1.02

Address: 100 CenturyTel Drive, Monroe, LA 71203	**Web Site:** www.centurytel.com	**Auditors:** KPMG LLP
Telephone: (318) 388-9000	**Officers:** Glen F. Post III - Chmn., C.E.O. Karen A. Puckett - Pres., C.O.O.	**Investor Contact:** 800 833-1188
Fax: (318) 789-8656		**Transfer Agents:** Computershare Investor Services, LLC, Chicago, IL

CERIDIAN CORP. (NEW)

Exchange	Symbol	Price	52Wk Range	Yield	P/E
NYS	CEN	$17.05 (3/31/2005)	23.30-16.70	N/A	28.90

*7 Year Price Score N/A   *NYSE Composite Index=100   *12 Month Price Score 85.53

Interim Earnings (Per Share)

Qtr.	Mar	Jun	Sep	Dec
2001	0.16	(0.08)	0.14	0.15
2002	0.12	0.16	0.15	0.19
2003	0.18	0.17	0.20	0.28
2004	0.16	0.03	0.12	...

Interim Dividends (Per Share)

No Dividends Paid

Valuation Analysis

Forecast P/E	29.93	No of Institutions	
	(4/13/2005)	182	
Market Cap	$2.5 Billion	Shares	
Book Value	1.3 Billion	137,970,864	
Price/Book	1.98	% Held	
Price/Sales	1.96	92.85	

TRADING VOLUME (thousand shares)

Business Summary: Accounting & Management Consulting Services (MIC: 12.2 SIC: 742 NAIC: 23430)

Ceridian is an information services company principally in the human resource, transportation and retail markets. Co.'s human resource solutions business enables customers to outsource a broad range of employment processes, from recruitment and applicant screening, to payroll, tax filing, human resource information systems, employee self-service, time and labor management, benefits administration, employee assistance and work-life programs. Co.'s human resource solutions operations are in the U.S., Canada and the U.K. Co.'s Comdata business provides transaction processing, financial services and regulatory compliance services primarily to the transportation and retail industries.

Recent Developments: For the quarter ended Sep 30 2004, net income declined 36.9% to $16.4 million compared with $26.0 million in the year-earlier quarter. Revenues advanced 10.7% to $334.3 million from $302.0 million the year before. Human Resource Solutions segment revenues advanced 8.7% to $241.7 million, reflecting strong installations, higher float balances, better retention, higher interest rates, a weaker dollar, and firming customer employment levels. Comdata segment revenues rose 16.2% to $92.6 million. Comparisons were made with restated results from the prior year.

Prospects: For the the fourth quarter of 2004, Co. anticipates revenue from its Human Resource Solutions business in the range of $277.0 million to $287.0 million, while revenue for its Comdata subsidiary of between $85.0 million and $88.0 million. Also, Co. expects fourth-quarter earnings in the range of $0.25 to $0.29 per share. Meanwhile, Co.'s Audit Committee has concluded that it is necessary to restate its financial results for the years 1999 through 2003, and the first quarter of 2004, to reflected accounting adjustments. The investigation by Co.'s external auditor is continuing. Separately, on Nov 1 2004, Comdata acquired Datamark Technologies, Inc. a provider of customer loyalty programs.

Financial Data (US$ in Thousands)	9 Mos	6 Mos	3 Mos	12/31/2003	12/31/2002	12/31/2001	12/31/2000	12/31/1999
Earnings Per Share	0.59	0.67	0.81	0.83	0.62	0.37	0.68	0.98
Cash Flow Per Share	0.91	0.96	1.05	0.54	1.11	1.25	1.85	1.37
Tang Book Value Per Share	1.26	1.00	0.77	0.86	0.06	N.M.	N.M.	N.M.
Income Statement								
Total Revenue	959,100	630,400	326,500	1,253,200	1,192,700	1,182,300	1,175,700	1,127,000
EBITDA	133,500	85,200	58,200	277,300	225,200	202,300	250,500	257,800
Depn & Amortn	62,700	41,400	20,800	85,100	75,900	105,400	87,600	72,200
Income Before Taxes	70,800	43,800	37,400	192,200	144,800	84,400	127,800	167,300
Income Taxes	24,500	15,400	13,100	67,400	51,100	34,900	48,300	62,900
Net Income	46,300	28,400	24,300	124,800	93,700	54,700	100,200	145,300
Average Shares	150,642	151,643	153,072	151,101	150,562	148,596	146,734	147,964
Balance Sheet								
Current Assets	785,400	756,700	692,500	663,200	681,900	615,600	715,400	601,100
Total Assets	5,417,300	5,065,100	5,755,200	5,188,700	4,458,400	4,037,000	2,088,000	1,988,500
Current Liabilities	458,200	429,000	383,400	349,000	420,700	417,000	473,900	426,400
Long-Term Obligations	108,800	144,800	155,800	157,000	191,500	236,400	500,300	611,100
Total Liabilities	4,129,800	3,820,000	4,494,400	3,916,800	3,331,600	2,975,900	1,151,800	1,176,300
Stockholders' Equity	1,287,500	1,245,100	1,260,800	1,271,900	1,126,800	1,061,100	936,200	812,200
Shares Outstanding	149,179	148,998	147,885	150,022	148,540	146,484	145,754	144,734
Statistical Record								
Return on Assets %	1.84	2.13	2.28	2.59	2.21	1.79	4.90	...
Return on Equity %	7.09	8.35	10.13	10.41	8.57	5.48	11.43	...
EBITDA Margin %	13.92	13.52	17.83	22.13	18.88	17.11	21.31	22.87
Net Margin %	4.83	4.51	7.44	9.96	7.86	4.63	8.52	12.89
Asset Turnover	0.27	0.27	0.24	0.26	0.28	0.39	0.58	...
Current Ratio	1.71	1.76	1.81	1.90	1.62	1.48	1.51	1.41
Debt to Equity	0.08	0.12	0.12	0.12	0.17	0.22	0.53	0.75
Price Range	23.30-17.24	23.30-16.92	22.33-13.55	21.71-12.77	22.86-12.15	20.42-14.14	...	...
P/E Ratio	39.49-29.22	34.78-25.25	27.57-16.73	26.16-15.39	36.87-19.60	55.19-38.22	...	...

Address: 3311 East Old Shakopee Road, Minneapolis, MN 55425-1640
Telephone: (952) 853-8100
Fax: (952) 853-3932

Web Site: www.ceridian.com
Officers: Ronald L. Turner - Chmn., Pres., C.E.O.
Robert H. Ewald - Exec. V.P., Pres., H.R. Solutions

Auditors: KPMG LLP
Investor Contact: 952-853-6022

CERTEGY, INC.

Exchange	Symbol	Price	52Wk Range	Yield	P/E
NYS	CEY	$34.62 (3/31/2005)	39.65-32.95	0.58	19.78

*7 Year Price Score N/A   *NYSE Composite Index=100   *12 Month Price Score 90.08

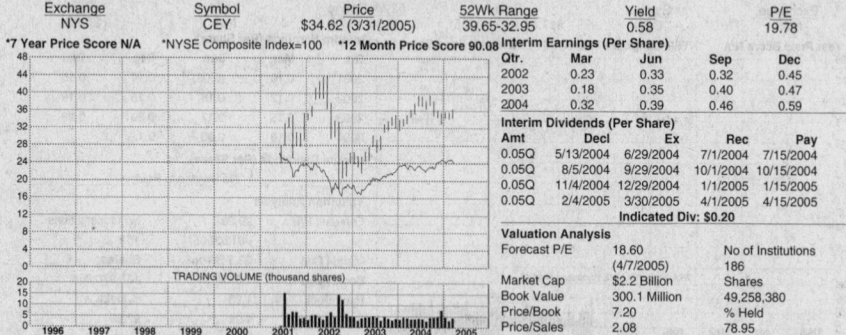

Interim Earnings (Per Share)

Qtr.	Mar	Jun	Sep	Dec
2002	0.23	0.33	0.32	0.45
2003	0.18	0.35	0.40	0.47
2004	0.32	0.39	0.46	0.59

Interim Dividends (Per Share)

Amt	Decl	Ex	Rec	Pay
0.05Q	5/13/2004	6/29/2004	7/1/2004	7/15/2004
0.05Q	8/5/2004	9/29/2004	10/1/2004	10/15/2004
0.05Q	11/4/2004	12/29/2004	1/1/2005	1/15/2005
0.05Q	2/4/2005	3/30/2005	4/1/2005	4/15/2005

Indicated Div: $0.20

Valuation Analysis

Forecast P/E	18.60	No of Institutions
	(4/7/2005)	186
Market Cap	$2.2 Billion	Shares
Book Value	300.1 Million	49,258,380
Price/Book	7.20	% Held
Price/Sales	2.08	78.95

Business Summary: Miscellaneous Business Services (MIC: 12.8 SIC: 323 NAIC: 61450)

Certegy provides credit, debit card and other transaction processing and check risk management services to financial institutions and merchants in the U.S. and internationally through two segments, Card Services and Check Services. Card Services provides card issuer services in the U.S., the U.K., Brazil, Chile, Australia, New Zealand, Ireland, Thailand, and the Caribbean. Card Services also provides merchant processing and e-banking services in the U.S. and card issuer software, support, and consulting services in numerous countries. Co.'s Check Service provides check risk management and related processing products and services to businesses accepting or cashing checks at the point-of-sale.

Recent Developments: For the year ended Dec 31 2004, net income increased 21.0% to $111,810 thousand from net income of $92,402 thousand a year earlier. Revenues were $1,039,506 thousand, up 12.8% from $921,734 thousand the year before. Operating income was $179,654 thousand versus an income of $148,215 thousand in the prior year, an increase of 21.2%. Total direct expense was $739,600 thousand versus $654,099 thousand in the prior year, an increase of 13.1%. Total indirect expense was $120,252 thousand versus $119,420 thousand in the prior year, an increase of 0.7%.

Prospects: Co.'s earnings guidance for 2005 include revenue growth of 10.0% to 12.0%, driven by low-double digit revenue growth in both Card Services and Check Services. Operating income growth of 12.0% to 14.0% over $168.6 million in 2004. Co. is expecting diluted earnings per share from continuing operations of $1.79 to $1.83, representing growth of 17.0% to 20.0% over $1.53 in 2004. Capital expenditures are expected to approximate $60.0 million to $65.0 million. In the first quarter of 2005, Co. expects to achieve revenue growth of approximately 10.0% and diluted earnings per share from continuing operations of $0.29 to $0.30.

Financial Data

(US$ in Thousands)	12/31/2004	12/31/2003	12/31/2002	12/31/2001	12/31/2000	12/31/1999	12/31/1998
Earnings Per Share	1.75	1.40	1.32	1.26	...	...	...
Cash Flow Per Share	2.30	2.12	1.86	1.51	...	...	...
Tang Book Value Per Share	0.59	0.58	N.M.	N.M.	...	...	...
Dividends Per Share	0.200	0.100	...	...	...	...	...
Dividend Payout %	11.43	7.14	...	...	...	...	...
Income Statement							
Total Revenue	1,039,506	1,015,464	1,007,968	851,123	778,562	681,172	566,120
EBITDA	234,604	204,207	192,118	197,850	191,166	165,554	130,747
Depn & Amortn	53,743	47,468	39,050	46,353	42,698	35,758	27,839
Income Before Taxes	167,947	148,789	145,948	144,297	147,167	128,895	102,375
Income Taxes	62,071	55,052	55,964	56,276	57,609	54,272	40,505
Net Income	111,810	92,402	89,984	87,076	88,462	74,629	61,090
Average Shares	63,966	65,870	69,033	69,063	...	...	...
Balance Sheet							
Current Assets	408,717	321,628	312,000	282,906	199,207	221,956	...
Total Assets	922,209	785,047	702,141	697,573	502,445	495,255	...
Current Liabilities	290,338	244,093	250,930	221,936	160,251	204,122	...
Long-Term Obligations	273,968	222,399	214,200	230,000	...	...	...
Total Liabilities	622,146	523,908	503,698	485,708	172,921	219,875	...
Stockholders' Equity	300,063	261,139	198,443	211,865	323,618	271,490	...
Shares Outstanding	62,383	64,352	66,396	68,836	...	...	...
Statistical Record							
Return on Assets %	13.06	12.43	12.86	14.51	17.68	...	...
Return on Equity %	39.74	40.21	43.86	32.52	29.65	...	...
EBITDA Margin %	22.57	20.11	19.06	23.25	24.55	24.30	23.10
Net Margin %	10.76	9.10	8.93	10.23	11.36	10.96	10.79
Asset Turnover	1.21	1.37	1.44	1.42	1.56	...	...
Current Ratio	1.41	1.32	1.24	1.27	1.24	1.09	...
Debt to Equity	0.91	0.85	1.08	1.09	...	...	...
Price Range	39.65-31.44	35.03-21.65	44.13-18.08	35.45-23.90	...	...	...
P/E Ratio	22.66-17.97	25.02-15.46	33.43-13.70	28.13-18.97	...	...	...
Average Yield %	0.56	0.35	...	...	...	...	...

Address: 100 Second Avenue South, Suite 1100S, St. Petersburg, FL 33701
Telephone: (727) 227-8000

Web Site: www.certegy.com
Officers: Lee A. Kennedy - Chmn., C.E.O. Larry J. Towe - Pres., C.O.O.

Auditors: Ernst & Young LLP
Investor Contact: 678-867-8004

CHARLES RIVER LABORATORIES INTERNATIONAL INC.

Exchange	Symbol	Price	52Wk Range	Yield	P/E
NYS	CRL	$47.04 (3/31/2005)	51.00-41.76	N/A	28.00

*7 Year Price Score N/A   *NYSE Composite Index=100   *12 Month Price Score 96.67

Interim Earnings (Per Share)

Qtr.	Mar	Jun	Sep	Dec
2001	0.17	0.21	0.23	0.19
2002	(0.03)	0.34	0.38	0.36
2003	0.40	0.42	0.40	0.42
2004	0.36	0.52	0.51	0.29

Interim Dividends (Per Share)

No Dividends Paid

Valuation Analysis

Forecast P/E	20.28	No of Institutions	
	(4/7/2005)	254	
Market Cap	$3.1 Billion	Shares	
Book Value	1.5 Billion	64,237,360	
Price/Book	2.10	% Held	
Price/Sales	4.04	97.17	

Business Summary: Biotechnology (MIC: 9.2 SIC: 836 NAIC: 25414)

Charles River Laboratories International is a global provider of critical research tools and integrated support services that assist in the drug discovery and development process.Co.'s Research Models and Services segment provides animal research models and related services required in research and development for new drugs, devices and therapies. The Preclinical Services segment provides in vitro and in vivo testing and services for new drug candidates. Co.'s Clinical Services segment consists of a Phase I-IV business, which includes a European Phase I clinic and an established international capability to manage Phase II-IV clinical studies.

Recent Developments: For the year ended Dec 25 2004, net income increased 12.0% to $89,792 thousand from net income of $80,151 thousand a year earlier. Revenues were $1,533,834 thousand, up 25.0% from $1,227,446 thousand the year before. Operating income was $160,323 thousand versus an income of $138,553 thousand in the prior year, an increase of 15.7%. Total direct expense was $468,351 thousand versus $380,058 thousand in the prior year, an increase of 23.2%. Total indirect expense was $138,243 thousand versus $95,112 thousand in the prior year, an increase of 45.3%.

Prospects: The robust demand for Co.'s essential products and services is continuing, making its prospects for 2005 appear bright. Co.'s acquisition of Inveresk has positioned it to more fully support its customers across more segments of the discovery and development pipeline. Co. is making progress in integrating the two companies. For 2005, Co. expects revenue growth in a range of 48.0% to 52.0%, which reflects the Inveresk acquisition as well as the strength in the market for outsourced drug discovery and development services. As a result of strong sales growth, efficiency improvements and operating synergies, Co. expects earnings in 2005 to range from $1.70 to $1.80 per diluted share.

Financial Data
(US$ in Thousands)

	12/25/2004	12/27/2003	12/28/2002	12/29/2001	12/30/2000	12/25/1999	12/26/1998	12/27/1997
Earnings Per Share	1.68	1.64	1.06	0.80	(0.35)	0.86	1.18	0.77
Cash Flow Per Share	3.74	2.73	3.00	1.74	1.20	1.90	1.89	...
Tang Book Value Per Share	N.M.	7.18	5.01	4.51	2.09	...	7.60	...
Income Statement								
Total Revenue	766,917	613,723	554,629	465,630	306,585	219,276	193,301	170,713
EBITDA	207,355	168,900	147,474	117,958	84,002	55,915	46,162	31,558
Depn & Amortn	46,309	29,564	23,986	27,115	18,870	12,999	10,895	9,703
Income Before Taxes	152,525	132,630	114,403	69,479	26,085	30,663	35,832	22,219
Income Taxes	61,156	51,063	43,572	27,095	7,837	15,561	14,123	8,499
Net Income	89,792	80,151	50,132	35,407	(11,224)	17,124	23,378	15,340
Average Shares	56,045	51,314	50,856	44,215	31,734	19,820	19,820	19,820
Balance Sheet								
Current Assets	510,306	370,888	278,092	210,154	119,737	90,073	97,214	...
Total Assets	2,626,835	799,554	701,344	571,362	410,608	363,056	234,254	...
Current Liabilities	349,115	114,351	113,369	98,532	64,320	69,736	62,387	...
Long-Term Obligations	605,980	185,683	192,484	155,867	202,500	382,501	1,192	...
Total Liabilities	1,144,538	324,755	325,401	268,864	280,351	459,696	65,689	...
Stockholders' Equity	1,472,505	464,623	357,376	289,510	116,927	(110,142)	168,259	...
Shares Outstanding	65,785	45,801	45,218	44,189	35,920	19,820	19,820	19,820
Statistical Record								
Return on Assets %	5.26	10.71	7.90	7.23	N.M.	5.75	...	...
Return on Equity %	9.30	19.56	15.54	17.47	N.M.	59.09	...	...
EBITDA Margin %	27.04	27.52	26.59	25.33	27.40	25.50	23.88	18.49
Net Margin %	11.71	13.06	9.04	7.60	N.M.	7.81	12.09	8.99
Asset Turnover	0.45	0.82	0.87	0.95	0.78	0.74	...	...
Current Ratio	1.46	3.24	2.45	2.13	1.86	1.29	1.56	...
Debt to Equity	0.41	0.40	0.54	0.54	1.73	...	0.01	...
Price Range	48.87-33.77	38.55-24.75	40.98-27.80	37.40-18.00	34.00-20.50	...	...	...
P/E Ratio	29.09-20.10	23.51-15.09	38.66-26.23	46.75-22.50	...	...	...	...

Address: 251 Ballardvale Street, Wilmington, MA 01887 Telephone: (978) 658-6000 Fax: (978) 658-7841	Web Site: www.criver.com Officers: James C. Foster - Chmn., Pres., C.E.O. Thomas F. Ackerman - Sr. V.P., C.F.O.	Auditors: PricewaterhouseCoopers LLP Investor Contact: 978-658-6000

CHESAPEAKE ENERGY CORP.

Exchange	Symbol	Price	52Wk Range	Yield	P/E
NYS	CHK	$21.94 (3/31/2005)	23.28-12.89	0.82	14.34

*7 Year Price Score 181.52 *NYSE Composite Index=100 *12 Month Price Score 119.59

Interim Earnings (Per Share)

Qtr.	Mar	Jun	Sep	Dec
2001	0.41	0.23	0.38	0.23
2002	(0.18)	0.13	0.08	0.13
2003	0.32	0.31	0.33	0.25
2004	0.38	0.31	0.29	0.55

Interim Dividends (Per Share)

Amt	Decl	Ex	Rec	Pay
0.045Q	6/9/2004	6/29/2004	7/1/2004	7/15/2004
0.045Q	9/20/2004	9/29/2004	10/1/2004	10/15/2004
0.045Q	12/21/2004	12/30/2004	1/3/2005	1/18/2005
0.045Q	3/11/2005	3/30/2005	4/1/2005	4/15/2005
			Indicated Div: $0.18	

Valuation Analysis

Forecast P/E	12.02	No of Institutions
	(4/7/2005)	339
Market Cap	$6.8 Billion	Shares
Book Value	3.2 Billion	208,222,288
Price/Book	2.16	% Held
Price/Sales	2.53	66.29

Business Summary: Oil and Gas (MIC: 14.2 SIC: 311 NAIC: 11111)

Chesapeake Energy is a holding company. Through its subsidiaries, Co. is engaged in the acquisition, exploration, and development of properties for the production of crude oil and natural gas from underground reservoirs and the marketing of natural gas and oil for other working interest owners in properties Co. operates. Chesapeake Energy Marketing, Inc., a wholly-owned subsidiary, provides marketing services, including commodity price structuring, contract administration and nomination services for Co. and its partners. At the end of 2004, Co. owned interests in approx. 20,000 producing oil and gas wells.

Recent Developments: For the year ended Dec 31 2004, net income increased 64.6% to $515,155 thousand from net income of $312,981 thousand a year earlier. Revenues were $2,709,268 thousand, up 57.8% from $1,717,432 thousand the year before. Operating income was $992,335 thousand versus an income of $675,255 thousand in the prior year, an increase of 47.0%. Total direct expense was $1,064,066 thousand versus $625,764 thousand in the prior year, an increase of 70.0%. Total indirect expense was $652,867 thousand versus $416,413 thousand in the prior year, an increase of 56.8%.

Prospects: Co.'s prospects are bright, reflecting higher production forecasts and strong demand for natural gas and oil. For 2005, Co. estimates its production will range from 478.00 billion cubic feet gas equivalent (bcfe) to 488.00 bcfe, up from 362.6 bcfe at the end of 2004. Co.'s production is being fueled by both organic drillbit growth and acquisition growth. In 2004, Co. added 1.70 trillion cubic feet equivalent (Tcfe) to its proved reserves to end the year with a total proved reserves of 4.90 Tcfe. Meanwhile, Co. is increasing its anticipated capital expenditures to a range of $1.40 billion to $1.50 billion due a planned increase in drilling activity on certain of its properties.

Financial Data

(US$ in Thousands)	12/31/2004	12/31/2003	12/31/2002	12/31/2001	12/31/2000	12/31/1999	12/31/1998	12/31/1997
Earnings Per Share	1.53	1.21	0.17	1.25	3.01	0.16	(9.97)	(0.45)
Cash Flow Per Share	5.71	4.48	2.59	3.41	2.43	1.49	1.00	1.31
Tang Book Value Per Share	8.57	5.45	3.99	3.75	1.84	...	...	3.77
Dividends Per Share	0.170	0.135	0.060	...	...	...	0.040	0.060
Dividend Payout %	11.11	11.16	35.29	...	...	...	...	...
Income Statement								
Total Revenue	2,709,268	1,717,432	737,751	969,051	627,952	354,946	377,946	232,864
EBITDA	1,588,122	1,043,173	414,697	719,313	391,274	219,020	(697,453)	48,737
Depn & Amortn	615,868	387,865	236,277	182,627	108,856	102,938	154,818	62,863
Income Before Taxes	804,926	500,952	67,140	438,365	196,162	35,030	(920,520)	(31,574)
Income Taxes	289,771	190,360	26,854	174,959	(259,408)	1,764	...	...
Net Income	515,155	312,981	40,286	217,406	455,570	33,266	(933,854)	(31,574)
Average Shares	305,718	258,567	172,714	173,981	151,564	102,038	94,911	70,835
Balance Sheet								
Current Assets	567,540	342,404	435,317	361,383	166,926	97,546	117,999	217,721
Total Assets	8,244,509	4,572,291	2,875,608	2,286,768	1,440,426	850,533	812,615	952,784
Current Liabilities	963,953	513,156	265,552	173,381	162,701	88,186	131,284	153,480
Long-Term Obligations	3,075,109	2,057,713	1,651,198	1,329,453	944,845	964,097	919,076	508,992
Total Liabilities	5,081,626	2,839,481	1,967,733	1,519,361	1,127,194	1,068,077	1,061,183	672,578
Stockholders' Equity	3,162,883	1,732,810	907,875	767,407	313,232	(217,544)	(248,568)	280,206
Shares Outstanding	311,868	216,784	190,144	164,742	153,030	95,002	96,710	74,298
Statistical Record								
Return on Assets %	8.02	8.40	1.56	11.67	39.66	4.00	N.M.	N.M.
Return on Equity %	20.99	23.70	4.81	40.24	949.60	...	N.M.	N.M.
EBITDA Margin %	58.62	60.74	56.21	74.23	62.31	61.71	N.M.	20.93
Net Margin %	19.01	18.22	5.46	22.43	72.55	9.37	N.M.	N.M.
Asset Turnover	0.42	0.46	0.29	0.52	0.55	0.43	0.43	0.20
Current Ratio	0.59	0.67	1.64	2.08	1.03	1.11	0.90	1.42
Debt to Equity	0.97	1.19	1.82	1.73	3.02	...	...	1.82
Price Range	18.13-11.90	13.95-7.40	8.55-5.15	10.97-4.99	10.25-2.06	3.94-0.75	7.63-0.75	31.50-7.00
P/E Ratio	11.85-7.78	11.53-6.12	50.29-30.29	8.78-3.99	3.41-0.69	24.61-4.69	...	...
Average Yield %	1.17	1.36	0.89	...	...	...	1.08	0.42

Address: 6100 North Western Avenue, Oklahoma City, OK 73118	**Web Site:** www.chkenergy.com	**Auditors:** PricewaterhouseCoopers LLP
Telephone: (405) 848-8000	**Officers:** Aubrey K. McClendon - Chmn., C.E.O.	**Investor Contact:** 405-879-9257
Fax: (405) 483-0573	Tom L. Ward - Pres., C.O.O.	

CHEVRONTEXACO CORP.

Exchange	Symbol	Price	52Wk Range	Yield	P/E	Div Acheiver
NYS	CVX	$58.31 (3/31/2005)	62.08-43.89	2.74	9.29	17 Years

*7 Year Price Score 102.75 *NYSE Composite Index=100 *12 Month Price Score 107.49

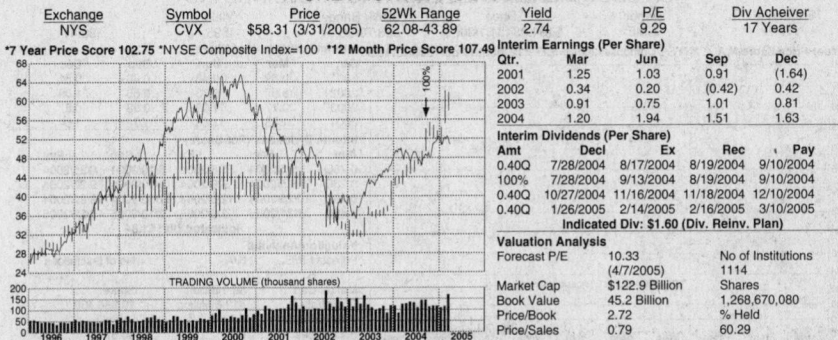

Interim Earnings (Per Share)

Qtr.	Mar	Jun	Sep	Dec
2001	1.25	1.03	0.91	(1.64)
2002	0.34	0.20	(0.42)	0.42
2003	0.91	0.75	1.01	0.81
2004	1.20	1.94	1.51	1.63

Interim Dividends (Per Share)

Amt	Decl	Ex	Rec	Pay
0.40Q	7/28/2004	8/17/2004	8/19/2004	9/10/2004
100%	7/28/2004	9/13/2004	8/19/2004	9/10/2004
0.40Q	10/27/2004	11/16/2004	11/18/2004	12/10/2004
0.40Q	1/26/2005	2/14/2005	2/16/2005	3/10/2005

Indicated Div: $1.60 (Div. Reinv. Plan)

Valuation Analysis

Forecast P/E	10.33	No of Institutions
	(4/7/2005)	1114
Market Cap	$122.9 Billion	Shares
Book Value	45.2 Billion	1,268,670,080
Price/Book	2.72	% Held
Price/Sales	0.79	60.29

TRADING VOLUME (thousand shares)

Business Summary: Oil and Gas (MIC: 14.2 SIC: 911 NAIC: 24110)

ChevronTexaco is a global energy company engaged in fully integrated petroleum operations, chemicals operations and coal mining activities. Co. also holds investments in power generation and gasification businesses. Petroleum operations consist of exploring for, developing and producing crude oil and natural gas; refining crude oil into finished petroleum products; marketing crude oil, natural gas and the many products derived from petroleum; and transporting crude oil, natural gas and petroleum products. As of Dec 31 2003, net proved reserves of natural gas were 20,191 billion cubic feet and net proved reserves of crude oil, condensate and natural gas liquids totaled 8,599 million barrels.

Recent Developments: For the year ended Dec 31 2004, net income increased 84.3% to $13,328 million from net income of $7,230 million a year earlier. Revenues were $155,300 million, up 28.1% from $121,277 million the year before. Total direct expense was $104,251 million versus $79,810 million in the prior year, an increase of 30.6%. Total indirect expense was $30,007 million versus $28,237 million in the prior year, an increase of 6.3%.

Prospects: Results are benefiting from higher prices for crude oil and natural gas, as well as increased demand for refined products, partially offset by a decline in production following asset sales and the impact of the four hurricanes in the U.S Gulf Coast region in 2004. On a segment basis, earnings in Co.'s downstream business are improved as it continues to experience higher industry demand and improved margins for refined products worldwide. In the upstream sector, Co. is seeing major progress in achieving its strategic objectives to grow profitably in its core areas of operation and to build a global gas business that will commercialize its significant international gas resource base.

Financial Data
(US$ in Thousands)

	12/31/2004	12/31/2003	12/31/2002	12/31/2001	12/31/2000	12/31/1999	12/31/1998	12/31/1997
Earnings Per Share	6.28	3.48	0.54	1.54	3.98	1.57	1.02	2.48
Cash Flow Per Share	6.92	5.80	4.68	5.40	6.65	3.41	2.85	3.49
Tang Book Value Per Share	21.47	16.97	14.79	15.91	15.54	13.52	12.90	13.32
Dividends Per Share	1.530	1.430	1.400	1.325	1.300	1.240	1.220	1.140
Dividend Payout %	24.36	41.09	261.68	85.76	32.62	78.98	119.61	46.06
Income Statement								
Total Revenue	155,300,000	121,761,000	99,049,000	106,245,000	52,129,000	36,586,000	30,557,000	41,950,000
EBITDA	25,892,000	18,628,000	9,952,000	16,183,000	12,578,000	6,986,000	4,559,000	8,114,000
Depn & Amortn	4,935,000	5,384,000	5,231,000	7,059,000	2,848,000	2,866,000	2,320,000	2,300,000
Income Before Taxes	20,551,000	12,770,000	4,156,000	8,291,000	9,270,000	3,648,000	1,834,000	5,502,000
Income Taxes	7,517,000	5,344,000	3,024,000	4,360,000	4,085,000	1,578,000	495,000	2,246,000
Net Income	13,328,000	7,230,000	1,132,000	3,288,000	5,185,000	2,070,000	1,339,000	3,256,000
Average Shares	2,122,000	2,128,000	2,126,800	2,125,800	1,302,200	1,319,000	1,314,200	1,316,800
Balance Sheet								
Current Assets	28,503,000	19,426,000	17,776,000	18,327,000	8,213,000	8,297,000	6,297,000	7,006,000
Total Assets	93,208,000	81,470,000	77,359,000	77,572,000	41,264,000	40,668,000	36,540,000	35,473,000
Current Liabilities	18,795,000	16,111,000	19,876,000	20,654,000	7,674,000	8,889,000	7,166,000	6,946,000
Long-Term Obligations	10,456,000	10,894,000	10,911,000	8,989,000	5,153,000	5,485,000	4,393,000	4,431,000
Total Liabilities	47,978,000	45,175,000	45,755,000	43,614,000	21,339,000	22,919,000	19,506,000	18,001,000
Stockholders' Equity	45,230,000	36,295,000	31,604,000	33,958,000	19,925,000	17,749,000	17,034,000	17,472,000
Shares Outstanding	2,107,120	2,138,295	2,136,273	2,134,441	1,282,120	1,312,692	1,320,000	1,311,800
Statistical Record								
Return on Assets %	15.22	9.10	1.46	5.53	12.62	5.36	3.72	9.26
Return on Equity %	32.61	21.30	3.45	12.20	27.45	11.90	7.76	19.68
EBITDA Margin %	16.67	15.30	10.05	15.23	24.13	19.09	14.92	19.34
Net Margin %	8.58	5.94	1.14	3.09	9.95	5.66	4.38	7.76
Asset Turnover	1.77	1.53	1.28	1.79	1.27	0.95	0.85	1.19
Current Ratio	1.52	1.21	0.89	0.89	1.07	0.93	0.88	1.01
Debt to Equity	0.23	0.30	0.35	0.26	0.26	0.31	0.26	0.25
Price Range	55.41-42.22	43.20-30.93	45.43-32.95	49.02-39.38	47.14-35.53	51.78-36.84	44.47-35.56	44.34-31.13
P/E Ratio	8.82-6.72	12.41-8.89	84.13-61.02	31.83-25.57	11.84-8.93	32.98-23.47	43.60-34.87	17.88-12.55
Average Yield %	3.20	4.04	3.51	2.98	3.07	2.76	3.00	3.06

Address: 6001 Bollinger Canyon Road, San Ramon, CA 94583-2324 Telephone: (925) 842-1000 Fax: (415) 894-6017	Web Site: www.chevrontexaco.com Officers: David J. O'Reilly - Chmn., C.E.O. Peter J. Robertson - Vice-Chmn.	Auditors: PricewaterhouseCoopers LLP Investor Contact: 415-894-5690 Transfer Agents: Mellon Investor Services LLC, Ridgefield Park, NJ

CHICAGO MERCANTILE EXCHANGE HOLDINGS INC

Exchange	Symbol	Price	52Wk Range	Yield	P/E
NYS	CME	$194.03 (3/31/2005)	228.70-96.74	0.95	30.41

*7 Year Price Score N/A   *NYSE Composite Index=100   *12 Month Price Score 115.95

Interim Earnings (Per Share)

Qtr.	Mar	Jun	Sep	Dec
2001	0.69	0.48	0.60	0.51
2002	0.57	0.73	0.65	1.09
2003	0.77	1.03	0.93	0.87
2004	1.35	1.66	1.72	1.64

Interim Dividends (Per Share)

Amt	Decl	Ex	Rec	Pay
0.26Q	5/5/2004	6/8/2004	6/10/2004	6/25/2004
0.26Q	8/5/2004	9/8/2004	9/10/2004	9/27/2004
0.26Q	10/25/2004	12/8/2004	12/10/2004	12/27/2004
0.46Q	1/31/2005	3/8/2005	3/10/2005	3/28/2005
			Indicated Div: $1.84	

Valuation Analysis

Forecast P/E	N/A	No of Institutions	
Market Cap	$6.6 Billion	Shares	19,386,460
Book Value	812.6 Million	% Held	56.67
Price/Book	8.14		
Price/Sales	9.02		

Business Summary: Finance Intermediaries & Services (MIC: 8.7 SIC: 231 NAIC: 23210)

Chicago Mercantile Exchange Holdings is in the market of futures contracts and options on futures contracts, often called derivatives. Co. brings together buyers and sellers of derivatives products on its open outcry trading floors, on the GLOBEX® electronic trading platform and through privately negotiated transactions that it clears. Co.'s key products include CME Eurodollar contracts and contracts based on major U.S. stock indexes, including the S&P 500® and the NASDAQ-100®. Co. also offers contracts for the principal foreign currencies and for a number of commodity products, including cattle, hogs and dairy .

Recent Developments: For the year ended Dec 31 2004, net income increased 79.8% to $219,555 thousand from net income of $122,132 thousand a year earlier. Revenues were $752,802 thousand, up 38.2% from $544,784 thousand the year before. Net investment income rose 57.1% to $14,520 thousand from $9,245 thousand a year ago. Clearing and transaction fees, which include clearing fees, CME Globex electronic trading fees and other volume-related charges increased 29.0% to $552,952 thousand, while clearing and transaction processing services revenue increased $54,130 thousand to $55,882 thousand.

Prospects: Results are benefiting from record volumes across all of Co.'s major product groups, spurred in large part by the growth of electronic trading. Co. noted that its average trading volume grew 33.0% during the fourth quarter to 3.1 million contracts per day, led by a 79.0% rise in foreign exchange products and higher interest-rate products, which rose 42.0%. Co.'s performance also reflects the significant first-year contribution generated from clearing Chicago Board of Trade transactions. Looking ahead, with average daily volume in February 2005 reaching 3.8 million contracts per day, Co. appears poised to benefit from ongoing growth trends within the industry as it reaches out to new markets.

Financial Data

(US$ in Thousands)	12/31/2004	12/31/2003	12/31/2002	12/31/2001	12/31/2000	12/31/1999
Earnings Per Share	6.38	3.60	3.13	2.37	(0.21)	0.09
Cash Flow Per Share	9.78	5.85	4.86	4.19	1.14	...
Tang Book Value Per Share	23.70	17.10	13.71	7.83	...	...
Dividends Per Share	1.040	0.630	...	...	...	...
Dividend Payout %	16.30	17.50	...	...	...	...
Income Statement						
Total Revenue	733,789	536,041	453,177	387,153	226,552	210,602
EBITDA	424,584	259,141	202,738	152,004	25,406	31,918
Depn & Amortn	56,928	53,016	48,509	37,639	33,489	25,274
Income Before Taxes	367,656	206,125	154,229	114,365	(8,083)	6,644
Income Taxes	148,101	83,993	60,162	46,063	(3,339)	1,855
Net Income	219,555	122,132	94,067	68,302	(5,909)	2,663
Average Shares	34,410	33,934	30,060	29,273	...	28,774
Balance Sheet						
Current Assets	2,694,865	4,723,379	3,215,131	1,946,110	267,432	...
Total Assets	2,857,466	4,872,636	3,355,016	2,068,881	381,444	...
Current Liabilities	2,025,623	4,287,975	2,889,494	1,801,845	198,294	...
Long-Term Obligations	...	...	2,328	6,650	6,063	...
Total Liabilities	2,044,869	4,309,641	2,908,877	1,818,512	217,773	...
Stockholders' Equity	812,597	562,995	446,139	250,369	163,671	...
Shares Outstanding	34,101	32,925	32,533	28,771	...	...
Statistical Record						
Return on Assets %	5.67	2.97	3.47	5.57	...	...
Return on Equity %	31.83	24.21	27.01	32.99	...	...
EBITDA Margin %	57.86	48.34	44.74	39.26	11.21	15.16
Net Margin %	29.92	22.78	20.76	17.64	N.M.	1.26
Asset Turnover	0.19	0.13	0.17	0.32	...	...
Current Ratio	1.33	1.10	1.11	1.08	1.35	...
Debt to Equity	...	...	0.01	0.03	0.04	...
Price Range	228.70-72.36	78.98-41.50	45.06-42.00	...	...	...
P/E Ratio	35.85-11.34	21.94-11.53	14.40-13.42	...	...	...
Average Yield %	0.77	1.02	...	...	...	...

Address: 20 South Wacker Drive, Chicago, IL 60606 **Telephone:** (312) 930-1000 **Fax:** (312) 466-4410	**Web Site:** www.cme.com **Officers:** Terrence A. Duffy - Chmn. William R. Shepard - Vice-Chmn.	**Auditors:** Ernst & Young LLP **Investor Contact:** 312-930-8491 **Transfer Agents:** Computershare Investor Services, Chicago, IL

CHICO'S FAS, INC.

Exchange	Symbol	Price	52Wk Range	Yield	P/E
NYS	CHS	$28.26 (3/31/2005)	29.87-16.95	N/A	N/A

*7 Year Price Score 227.01 *NYSE Composite Index=100 *12 Month Price Score 117.36

TRADING VOLUME (thousand shares)

Interim Earnings (Per Share)

Qtr.	Apr	Jul	Oct	Jan
2002-03	0.12	0.10	0.09	0.09
2003-04	0.13	0.14	0.15	0.14
2004-05	0.20	0.20	0.21	...

Interim Dividends (Per Share)

Amt	Decl	Ex	Rec	Pay
3-for-2	4/19/2001	5/17/2001	5/2/2001	5/16/2001
3-for-2	12/19/2001	1/22/2002	12/31/2001	1/18/2002
2-for-1	6/27/2002	7/30/2002	7/15/2002	7/29/2002
2-for-1	1/6/2005	2/23/2005	2/4/2005	2/22/2005

Valuation Analysis

Forecast P/E	27.92	No of Institutions
	(4/7/2005)	284
Market Cap	$5.0 Billion	Shares
Book Value	523.3 Million	185,113,360
Price/Book	9.64	% Held
Price/Sales	N/A	N/A

Business Summary: Retail - Apparel and Accessory Stores (MIC: 5.8 SIC: 621 NAIC: 48120)

Chico's FAS is a specialty retailer of exclusively designed, private label, sophisticated, casual-to-dressy clothing, complementary accessories and other non-clothing gift items under the Chico's and White House/Black Market brand names. The Chico's brand focuses on women who are 35 years old and up. The White House/Black Market brand focuses on women in the 25 to 45 age group. As of Mar 31 2004, Co. operated 559 retail stores, including those under the name of Chico's and White House/Black Market in 45 states, the District of Columbia, the Virgin Islands and Puerto Rico. Co. owns 403 Chico's front-line Co.-owned stores and 121 White House/Black Market stores. Co. has 12 franchise locations.

Recent Developments: For the three months ended Oct 31 2004, net income advanced 38.6% to $37.1 million from $26.8 million in the equivalent prior-year quarter. Net sales advanced 28.1% to $269.8 million from $210.6 million the previous year. Comparable-store sales for Co.-owned stores rose 6.1% year over year. Co-owned sales increased 29.1% to $260.4 million. Catalog and Internet sales rose 6.3% to $7.0 million, while sales to franshisees grew 3.8% to $2.4 million. Gross profit increased 30.0% to $168.2 million from $129.4 million in 2003. Operating income was $59.2 million, up 37.6% from $43.2 million the year before.

Prospects: Co.'s results are benefiting from the strength of brands, reflected by its strong growth in comparable-store sales in fiscal 2004. Going forward, Co.'s results should continue to benefit from its accelerated expansion plans. Co. opened 100 net new stores in fiscal 2004 and plans to open between 110 and 120 net new stores in fiscal 2005. Meanwhile, Co. has completed the White House / Black Market integration and completed the launch of its new intimate apparel line Soma by Chico's. This combination of actions should drive further earnings improvement in 2005 and beyond.

Financial Data

(US$ in Thousands)	9 Mos	6 Mos	01/31/2004	02/01/2003	02/02/2002	02/03/2001	01/29/2000	01/30/1999
Earnings Per Share	...	...	0.57	0.39	0.25	0.17	0.10	0.06
Cash Flow Per Share	...	...	0.84	0.65	0.41	0.25	0.11	...
Tang Book Value Per Share	2.39	2.22	1.60	1.41	0.88	0.54	0.34	0.23
Income Statement								
Total Revenue	781,331	511,558	768,499	531,108	378,085	259,446	155,002	106,742
EBITDA	196,510	129,311	183,874	122,936	77,943	51,341	28,113	17,542
Depn & Amortn	23,307	15,290	23,100	16,143	10,407	5,978	3,308	2,408
Income Before Taxes	174,576	114,774	161,662	107,676	68,043	45,772	24,983	14,983
Income Taxes	66,338	43,613	61,432	40,917	25,856	17,393	9,494	5,844
Net Income	108,238	71,161	100,230	66,759	42,187	28,379	15,489	9,139
Average Shares	180,238	180,378	176,284	172,064	167,556	163,330	159,129	153,538
Balance Sheet								
Current Assets	332,706	301,314	197,573	160,429	92,991	50,786	37,225	27,836
Total Assets	649,604	594,344	470,854	301,544	186,385	117,807	70,316	49,000
Current Liabilities	98,016	77,694	71,582	54,860	34,946	25,328	10,836	7,984
Long-Term Obligations	...	...	...	...	7,944	7,158	6,839	6,713
Total Liabilities	126,302	103,765	96,019	61,411	42,890	32,485	17,675	14,697
Stockholders' Equity	523,302	490,579	374,835	240,133	143,495	85,321	52,641	34,303
Shares Outstanding	178,596	178,814	175,074	170,564	163,162	157,464	154,156	151,074
Statistical Record								
Return on Assets %	...	...	26.02	27.44	27.81	29.68	26.03	...
Return on Equity %	...	...	32.69	34.90	36.98	40.47	35.73	...
EBITDA Margin %	25.15	25.28	23.93	23.15	20.62	19.79	18.14	16.43
Net Margin %	13.85	13.91	13.04	12.57	11.16	10.94	9.99	8.56
Asset Turnover	...	...	2.00	2.18	2.49	2.71	2.61	...
Current Ratio	3.39	3.88	2.76	2.92	2.66	2.01	3.44	3.49
Debt to Equity	...	...	...	...	0.06	0.08	0.13	0.20
Price Range	23.68-15.88	23.68-13.49	19.50-8.54	11.52-6.73	7.53-3.53	4.58-0.98	2.43-1.00	1.69-0.36
P/E Ratio			34.21-14.99	29.53-17.26	30.12-14.11	26.92-5.76	24.27-10.00	28.24-6.02

Address: 11215 Metro Parkway, Fort Myers, FL 33912 **Telephone:** (239) 277-6200 **Fax:** (239) 277-5237	**Web Site:** www.chicos.com **Officers:** Marvin J. Gralnick - Chmn. Scott A. Edmonds - Pres., C.E.O.	**Auditors:** ERNST & YOUNG LLP **Investor Contact:** 203-222-9013 **Transfer Agents:** The Registrar and Transfer Company, Cransford, NJ

CHITTENDEN CORP. (BURLINGTON, VT.)

Exchange	Symbol	Price	52Wk Range	Yield	P/E	Div Acheiver
NYS	CHZ	$26.07 (3/31/2005)	30.06-22.71	2.76	16.19	12 Years

*7 Year Price Score 107.86 *NYSE Composite Index=100 *12 Month Price Score 91.31

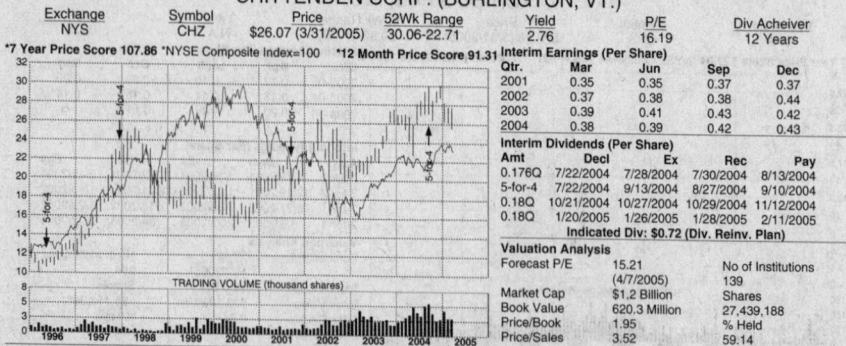

Interim Earnings (Per Share)

Qtr.	Mar	Jun	Sep	Dec
2001	0.35	0.35	0.37	0.37
2002	0.37	0.38	0.38	0.44
2003	0.39	0.41	0.43	0.42
2004	0.38	0.39	0.42	0.43

Interim Dividends (Per Share)

Amt	Decl	Ex	Rec	Pay
0.176Q	7/22/2004	7/28/2004	7/30/2004	8/13/2004
5-for-4	7/22/2004	9/13/2004	8/27/2004	9/10/2004
0.18Q	10/21/2004	10/27/2004	10/29/2004	11/12/2004
0.18Q	1/20/2005	1/26/2005	1/28/2005	2/11/2005

Indicated Div: $0.72 (Div. Reinv. Plan)

Valuation Analysis

Forecast P/E	15.21	No of Institutions
	(4/7/2005)	139
Market Cap	$1.2 Billion	Shares
Book Value	620.3 Million	27,439,188
Price/Book	1.95	% Held
Price/Sales	3.52	59.14

Business Summary: Commercial Banking (MIC: 8.1 SIC: 022 NAIC: 22110)

Chittenden is a bank holding company with assets totaling $5.90 billion as of Dec 31 2003. Through its subsidiaries, Co. is engaged in providing financial services. Co. offers a variety of lending services, including commercial loans and residential real estate loans. In addition, Co. offers acceptance of demand, savings, money market, cash management and time deposits. Co. also provides personal trust services, including services as executor, trustee, administrator, custodian and guardian. Corporate trust services are also provided, including services as trustee for pension and profit sharing plans. Asset management services are provided for personal and corporate trust clients.

Recent Developments: For the year ended Dec 31 2004, net income increased 0.4% to $75,127 thousand from net income of $74,799 thousand a year earlier. Net interest income was $225,498 thousand, up 3.4% from $218,063 thousand the year before. Provision for loan losses was $4,377 thousand versus $7,175 thousand in the prior year, a decrease of 39.0%. Non-interest income fell 24.3% to $73,405 thousand, while non-interest expense declined 7.8% to $176,372 thousand.

Prospects: Co. has completed its core data processing systems conversion and the acquisition of Granite Bank, which should contribute to solid results in 2005. Meanwhile, Co. is seeing double-digit growth in both commercial and commercial real estate loans. In addition, financings for commercial customers is also driving growth in Co.'s construction loan portfolio. Separately, Co. is experiencing strong deposit growth, reflecting higher levels of deposits from its commercial customers in its Vermont and New Hampshire franchises. Co.'s asset quality and net interest margins continue to improve as variable rate loans adjust due to the prime-rate increases.

Financial Data
(US$ in Thousands)

	12/31/2004	12/31/2003	12/31/2002	12/31/2001	12/31/2000	12/31/1999	12/31/1998	12/31/1997
Earnings Per Share	1.61	1.66	1.57	1.44	1.38	(0.06)	1.34	1.24
Cash Flow Per Share	2.33	3.53	1.02	2.31	1.67	2.50	1.57	1.73
Tang Book Value Per Share	8.02	7.17	8.66	7.55	7.31	7.76	7.34	6.59
Dividends Per Share	0.692	0.640	0.632	0.613	0.602	0.550	0.499	0.824
Dividend Payout %	42.98	38.65	40.31	42.56	43.72	...	37.32	66.39
Income Statement								
Interest Income	269,767	271,442	259,019	266,497	288,102	288,216	151,511	150,189
Interest Expense	44,269	53,379	66,404	96,192	121,030	113,235	60,508	59,545
Net Interest Income	225,498	218,063	192,615	170,305	167,072	174,981	91,003	90,644
Provision for Losses	4,377	7,175	8,331	8,041	8,700	8,700	5,100	4,050
Non-Interest Income	73,405	97,031	65,060	63,733	54,810	64,226	32,402	28,210
Non-Interest Expense	176,372	191,371	151,544	135,760	126,462	203,929	71,767	70,072
Income Before Taxes	118,154	116,548	97,800	90,237	86,720	26,578	46,538	44,732
Income Taxes	43,027	41,749	34,155	31,736	28,033	29,074	15,873	15,326
Net Income	75,127	74,799	63,645	58,501	58,687	(2,496)	30,665	29,406
Average Shares	46,731	45,150	40,618	40,683	42,625	44,743	22,942	23,697
Balance Sheet								
Net Loans & Leases	4,018,162	3,667,220	2,925,666	2,792,909	2,815,843	2,854,651	1,375,593	1,372,417
Total Assets	6,070,210	5,900,644	4,920,544	4,153,714	3,769,861	3,827,297	2,122,019	1,977,150
Total Deposits	5,038,730	4,969,891	4,126,092	3,669,846	3,292,407	3,204,098	1,890,754	1,757,545
Total Liabilities	5,449,953	5,320,693	4,501,752	3,783,060	3,427,795	3,464,837	1,946,872	1,814,877
Stockholders' Equity	620,257	579,951	418,792	370,654	342,066	362,460	175,147	162,273
Shares Outstanding	46,341	45,795	39,924	44,679	44,670	44,340	22,159	22,533
Statistical Record								
Return on Assets %	1.25	1.38	1.40	1.48	1.54	N.M.	1.50	1.48
Return on Equity %	12.48	14.98	16.12	16.42	16.61	N.M.	18.18	17.47
Net Interest Margin %	83.59	80.34	74.36	63.91	57.99	60.71	60.06	60.35
Efficiency Ratio %	51.39	51.94	46.76	41.11	36.88	57.86	39.02	39.28
Loans to Deposits	0.80	0.74	0.71	0.76	0.86	0.89	0.73	0.78
Price Range	30.06-22.71	27.52-19.89	27.34-18.97	23.00-17.80	20.16-14.64	21.52-16.80	25.28-16.56	22.98-11.84
P/E Ratio	18.67-14.11	16.58-11.98	17.42-12.08	15.97-12.36	14.61-10.61	...	18.87-12.36	18.53-9.55
Average Yield %	2.55	2.78	2.76	3.03	3.50	2.96	2.29	4.84

Address: Two Burlington Square, Burlington, VT 05401	Web Site: www.chittendencorp.com	Auditors: PricewaterhouseCoopers LLP
Telephone: (802) 658-4000	Officers: Paul A. Perrault - Chmn., Pres., C.E.O. Kirk W. Walters - Exec. V.P., C.F.O., Treas.	Investor Contact: 802 660 1412
Fax: (802) 660-1591		Transfer Agents: Computershare Investor Services, LLC, Chicago, IL

CHOICEPOINT, INC.

Exchange	Symbol	Price	52Wk Range	Yield	P/E
NYS	CPS	$40.11 (3/31/2005)	47.85-37.65	N/A	24.76

*7 Year Price Score 125.52 ***NYSE Composite Index=100** ***12 Month Price Score 89.82**

Interim Earnings (Per Share)

Qtr.	Mar	Jun	Sep	Dec
2001		---0.58---		
2002	0.31	0.27	0.35	0.36
2003	0.73	0.23	0.32	0.30
2004	0.37	0.40	0.43	0.43

Interim Dividends (Per Share)

Amt	Decl	Ex	Rec	Pay
2-for-1	10/20/1999	11/26/1999	11/10/1999	11/24/1999
3-for-2	1/31/2001	3/8/2001	2/16/2001	3/7/2001
33%	4/25/2002	6/7/2002	5/16/2002	6/6/2002

Valuation Analysis

Forecast P/E	22.35	No of Institutions	
	(4/7/2005)	257	
Market Cap	$3.5 Billion	Shares	
Book Value	983.7 Million	72,230,952	
Price/Book	3.60	% Held	
Price/Sales	3.85	80.29	

TRADING VOLUME (thousand shares)

Business Summary: Miscellaneous Business Services (MIC: 12.8 SIC: 323 NAIC: 24210)

ChoicePoint is a provider of identification and credential verification services. The Insurance services group provides insurers with claims history data, motor vehicle records, police records, credit information, modeling services, customized policy rating and issuance and software. The Business services and Government services groups provide background screenings and drug testing administration services, public record, background and relationship searches, vital records, tenant screening services, credential verification, due diligence information, Uniform Commercial Code searches and filings and DNA identification services. The Marketing services group provides direct marketing services.

Recent Developments: For the year ended Dec 31 2004, net income increased 4.2% to $147,955 thousand from net income of $141,992 thousand a year earlier. Revenues were $918,713 thousand, up 15.5% from $795,746 thousand the year before. Operating income was $241,778 thousand versus an income of $178,560 thousand in the prior year, an increase of 35.4%. Total direct expense was $492,122 thousand versus $447,543 thousand in the prior year, an increase of 10.0%. Total indirect expense was $184,813 thousand versus $169,643 thousand in the prior year, an increase of 8.9%.

Prospects: Based on recent business trends and acquisitions, Co. expects full year 2005 core revenue growth in the 15.0% to 18.0% range, and operating margins in the low-to-mid 27.0% range. During the quarter ended Dec 31 2004, Co. expanded its analytic capabilities in the Insurance Services segment and acquired two providers of rating services to insurance carriers and agents, InsurQuote, Inc. and Priority Data Systems, Inc. Co. also acquired certain assets of USAHire, LLC, an applicant tracking software provider. Subsequent to year end, Co. acquired i2 Limited, a provider of visual investigative and link analysis software for intelligence, law enforcement, military and large commercial applications.

Financial Data

(US$ in Thousands)	12/31/2004	12/31/2003	12/31/2002	12/31/2001	12/31/2000	12/31/1999	12/31/1998	12/31/1997
Earnings Per Share	1.62	1.58	1.01	0.58	0.52	0.49	0.44	0.36
Cash Flow Per Share	2.83	2.26	2.00	1.55	1.38	1.02	0.91	0.71
Tang Book Value Per Share	0.52	1.12	N.M.	0.02	0.10	N.M.	N.M.	N.M.
Income Statement								
Total Revenue	918,713	795,746	791,562	655,967	593,533	430,143	406,475	417,321
EBITDA	303,124	231,680	238,991	179,020	143,672	118,514	101,247	87,753
Depn & Amortn	61,346	53,120	45,759	59,512	53,619	37,913	31,032	27,638
Income Before Taxes	238,830	175,499	185,460	109,021	78,310	69,459	62,467	53,466
Income Taxes	90,875	67,391	71,217	58,687	34,488	30,070	27,048	24,522
Net Income	147,955	141,992	89,827	50,334	43,822	39,389	35,419	28,944
Average Shares	91,305	89,686	89,194	87,150	84,138	80,509	80,032	79,418
Balance Sheet								
Current Assets	218,377	203,952	205,335	212,670	178,329	155,841	143,606	146,119
Total Assets	1,287,476	1,021,284	979,010	832,392	704,439	532,872	534,199	359,971
Current Liabilities	223,668	178,481	202,696	284,689	106,339	88,362	124,960	77,238
Long-Term Obligations	17	1,835	97,059	2,390	141,638	187,195	191,697	95,457
Total Liabilities	303,817	230,789	356,403	347,571	303,370	329,961	374,627	232,226
Stockholders' Equity	983,659	790,495	622,607	484,821	401,069	202,911	159,572	127,745
Shares Outstanding	88,232	86,555	85,490	83,435	82,087	77,522	78,186	78,085
Statistical Record								
Return on Assets %	12.78	14.20	9.92	6.55	7.06	7.38	7.92	8.75
Return on Equity %	16.63	20.10	16.22	11.36	14.47	21.73	24.65	17.86
EBITDA Margin %	32.99	29.11	30.19	27.29	24.21	27.55	24.91	21.03
Net Margin %	16.10	17.84	11.35	7.67	7.38	9.16	8.71	6.94
Asset Turnover	0.79	0.80	0.87	0.85	0.96	0.81	0.91	1.26
Current Ratio	0.98	1.14	1.01	0.75	1.68	1.76	1.15	1.89
Debt to Equity	N.M.	N.M.	0.16	N.M.	0.35	0.92	1.20	0.75
Price Range	46.34-36.39	41.90-29.99	47.83-29.76	38.76-23.18	32.78-16.25	20.69-11.36	16.13-9.44	12.00-7.84
P/E Ratio	28.60-22.46	26.52-18.98	47.36-29.47	66.83-39.96	63.04-31.25	42.22-23.18	36.65-21.45	33.33-21.79

Address: 1000 Alderman Drive, Alpharetta, GA 30005
Telephone: (770) 752-6000
Fax: (770) 752-6250

Web Site: www.choicepoint.com
Officers: Derek V. Smith - Chmn., C.E.O. Douglas C. Curling - Pres., C.O.O.

Auditors: Deloitte & Touche LLP
Investor Contact: 770-752-6171
Transfer Agents: SunTrust Banks, Inc., Atlanta, GA

CHUBB CORP.

Exchange	Symbol	Price	52Wk Range	Yield	P/E	Div Acheiver
NYS	CB	$79.27 (3/31/2005)	80.95-64.00	2.17	9.90	40 Years

*7 Year Price Score 91.67   *NYSE Composite Index=100   *12 Month Price Score 101.12

Interim Earnings (Per Share)

Qtr.	Mar	Jun	Sep	Dec
2001	0.97	0.83	(1.40)	0.15
2002	1.15	1.20	(1.42)	0.33
2003	1.31	1.45	1.37	0.33
2004	1.88	1.85	1.88	2.40

Interim Dividends (Per Share)

Amt	Decl	Ex	Rec	Pay
0.39Q	6/4/2004	6/22/2004	6/24/2004	7/9/2004
0.39Q	9/9/2004	9/22/2004	9/24/2004	10/12/2004
0.39Q	12/2/2004	12/15/2004	12/17/2004	1/4/2005
0.43Q	3/4/2005	3/16/2005	3/18/2005	4/5/2005

Indicated Div: $1.72 (Div. Reinv. Plan)

Valuation Analysis

Forecast P/E	10.07 (4/7/2005)	No of Institutions	472
Market Cap	$15.3 Billion	Shares	166,066,720
Book Value	10.1 Billion	% Held	85.53
Price/Book	1.51		
Price/Sales	1.16		

TRADING VOLUME (thousand shares)

Business Summary: Insurance (MIC: 8.2 SIC: 331 NAIC: 24126)

Chubb is engaged in the property and casualty insurance business. Operations are divided into three strategic business units. Chubb Commercial Insurance specializes in commercial customer insurance products, including coverage for multiple peril, casualty, workers' compensation and property and marine. Chubb Specialty Insurance provides executive protection and professional liability products for privately and publicly owned companies. Chubb Specialty Insurance also includes Co.'s surety and accident businesses, as well as its reinsurance business. Chubb Personal Insurance offers products for individuals who require more coverage choices and higher limits than standard insurance policies.

Recent Developments: For the year ended Dec 31 2004, net income increased 91.4% to $1,548,400 thousand from net income of $808,800 thousand a year earlier. Revenues were $13,177,200 thousand, up 15.7% from $11,394,000 thousand the year before. Net premiums written climbed 8.8% to $12,052,900 thousand from $11,067,900 thousand in the previous year. Property and casualty income advanced 78.7% to $2,025,700 thousand from $1,133,400 thousand in 2003.

Prospects: Co. saw substantial improvement in its operating results for 2004, particularly in Chubb Personal Insurance, which had a solid year despite the worst hurricane season since 1992. For 2005, Co. anticipates net premium growth of 1.0% to 4.0%, a combined ratio between 91.0% and 94.0%, and growth of property and casualty investment income after taxes of 8.0% to 10.0%. Co. expects earnings to improve as it continues to focus on disciplined underwriting and expense management. Co. believes it can achieve full-year 2005 operating income in the range of $7.60 to $8.00 per share.

Financial Data
(US$ in Thousands)

	12/31/2004	12/31/2003	12/31/2002	12/31/2001	12/31/2000	12/31/1999	12/31/1998	12/31/1997
Earnings Per Share	8.01	4.46	1.29	0.63	4.01	3.66	4.19	4.39
Cash Flow Per Share	21.47	18.77	13.97	5.87	5.52	7.98	7.33	9.12
Tang Book Value Per Share	50.13	42.85	37.33	35.62	37.13	32.85	34.78	32.11
Dividends Per Share	1.560	1.440	1.400	1.360	1.320	1.283	1.240	1.160
Dividend Payout %	19.48	32.29	108.53	215.87	32.92	35.04	29.59	26.42
Income Statement								
Premium Income	11,635,700	10,182,500	8,085,300	6,656,400	6,145,900	5,652,000	5,303,800	5,157,400
Total Revenue	13,177,200	11,394,000	9,140,300	7,754,000	7,251,500	6,729,600	6,349,800	6,664,000
Income Before Taxes	2,068,200	933,600	168,400	(66,000)	851,000	710,100	849,700	974,100
Income Taxes	519,800	124,800	(54,500)	(177,500)	136,400	89,000	142,700	204,600
Net Income	1,548,400	808,800	222,900	111,500	714,600	621,100	707,000	769,500
Average Shares	193,200	181,300	172,900	175,800	178,300	169,800	168,600	176,200
Balance Sheet								
Total Assets	44,260,300	38,360,600	34,114,400	29,449,000	25,026,700	23,537,000	20,746,000	19,615,600
Total Liabilities	34,133,900	29,838,600	27,255,200	22,923,700	18,045,000	17,265,200	15,101,900	13,958,500
Stockholders' Equity	10,126,400	8,522,000	6,859,200	6,525,300	6,981,700	6,271,800	5,644,100	5,657,100
Shares Outstanding	192,676	187,963	171,201	170,071	174,919	175,489	162,267	176,200
Statistical Record								
Return on Assets %	3.74	2.23	0.70	0.41	2.93	2.81	3.50	3.89
Return on Equity %	16.56	10.52	3.33	1.65	10.75	10.42	12.51	13.84
Net Margin %	11.75	7.10	2.44	1.44	9.85	9.23	11.13	11.55
Price Range	77.00-64.00	69.24-42.45	78.20-52.20	83.44-58.59	90.00-44.75	75.94-45.50	88.25-57.00	78.13-51.25
P/E Ratio	9.61-7.99	15.52-9.52	60.62-40.47	132.44-93.00	22.44-11.16	20.75-12.43	21.06-13.60	17.80-11.67
Average Yield %	2.23	2.42	2.13	1.91	1.93	2.04	1.68	1.81

Address: 15 Mountain View Road, P.O. Box 1615, Warren, NJ 07061-1615 **Telephone:** (908) 903-2000 **Fax:** (908) 903-2003	Web Site: www.chubb.com **Officers:** John D. Finnegan - Chmn., Pres., C.E.O. Michael O'Reilly - Vice-Chmn., C.F.O., Chief Invest. Officer	**Auditors:** Ernst & Young LLP **Investor Contact:** 908-903-3579 **Transfer Agents:** EquiServe Trust Company, N.A., Jersey City, NJ

CHURCH & DWIGHT CO., INC.

Exchange	Symbol	Price	52Wk Range	Yield	P/E
NYS	CHD	$35.47 (3/31/2005)	36.52-27.15	0.68	26.08

*7 Year Price Score 140.12 *NYSE Composite Index=100   *12 Month Price Score 106.39

Interim Earnings (Per Share)

Qtr.	Mar	Jun	Sep	Dec
2001	0.20	0.22	0.25	0.10
2002	0.24	0.30	0.28	0.25
2003	0.33	0.39	0.31	0.25
2004	0.47	0.30	0.42	0.17

Interim Dividends (Per Share)

Amt	Decl	Ex	Rec	Pay
3-for-2	8/6/2004	9/2/2004	8/16/2004	9/1/2004
0.06Q	8/6/2004	8/12/2004	8/16/2004	9/1/2004
0.06Q	11/5/2004	11/10/2004	11/15/2004	12/1/2004
0.06Q	1/28/2005	2/3/2005	2/7/2005	3/1/2005
		Indicated Div: $0.24		

Valuation Analysis

Forecast P/E	20.03	No of Institutions	
	(4/7/2005)	196	
Market Cap	$2.2 Billion	Shares	
Book Value	560.0 Million	40,281,536	
Price/Book	4.00	% Held	
Price/Sales	1.53	63.56	

Business Summary: Chemicals (MIC: 11.1 SIC: 812 NAIC: 25181)

Church & Dwight manufactures and markets a broad range of household, personal care and specialty products under well-recognized brand names, including ARM & HAMMER and TROJAN. Co.'s business is divided into three primary segments, Consumer Domestic, Consumer International and Specialty Products. The Consumer Domestic segment includes household products for deodorizing and cleaning and laundry products. This segment also includes personal care products, such as TROJAN condoms, NAIR depilatories, FIRST RESPONSE and ANSWER home pregnancy and ovulation test kits, ARRID antiperspirant and ARM & HAMMER, MENTADENT, CLOSE-UP, PEPSODENT and AIM toothpastes.

Recent Developments: For the year ended Dec 31 2004, net income increased 9.7% to $88,808 thousand from net income of $80,961 thousand a year earlier. Revenues were $1,462,062 thousand, up 38.3% from $1,056,874 thousand the year before. Operating income was $171,753 thousand versus an income of $111,851 thousand in the prior year, an increase of 53.6%. Total direct expense was $928,674 thousand versus $738,883 thousand in the prior year, an increase of 25.7%. Total indirect expense was $361,635 thousand versus $206,140 thousand in the prior year, an increase of 75.4%.

Prospects: Co. appears poised for continued strong business growth in 2005, supported by several key steps it took during 2004, including the acquisition and integration of Armkel, the refinancing of its debt structure and a substantial second half increase in marketing and product development. Meanwhile, on the margin side, Co. will continue to work on a range of profit improvement strategies, including pricing, product mix and promotion efficiency, traditional supply chain optimization and other cost reduction programs. As a result, despite rising costs, Co. is confident it will be able to achieve its earnings objective of at least $1.70 per share.

Financial Data
(US$ in Thousands)

	12/31/2004	12/31/2003	12/31/2002	12/31/2001	12/31/2000	12/31/1999	12/31/1998	12/31/1997
Earnings Per Share	1.36	1.28	1.07	0.77	0.56	0.74	0.50	0.41
Cash Flow Per Share	3.14	1.95	1.92	0.71	1.78	1.10	0.83	0.28
Tang Book Value Per Share	N.M.	0.98	0.92	0.31	2.62	2.39	2.93	3.08
Dividends Per Share	0.227	0.207	0.200	0.193	0.187	0.173	0.160	0.153
Dividend Payout %	16.67	16.15	18.75	25.22	33.33	23.42	31.79	37.40
Income Statement								
Total Revenue	1,462,062	1,056,874	1,047,149	1,080,864	795,725	730,036	684,393	574,906
EBITDA	207,939	171,686	152,956	113,235	80,471	94,719	65,342	53,757
Depn & Amortn	39,093	30,224	27,890	27,843	23,454	19,256	16,503	14,158
Income Before Taxes	127,439	116,935	101,092	73,855	52,161	72,703	46,186	38,687
Income Taxes	38,631	35,974	34,402	26,871	18,315	26,821	15,897	14,181
Net Income	88,808	80,961	66,690	46,984	33,559	45,357	30,289	24,506
Average Shares	68,066	63,298	62,713	61,228	59,899	61,564	60,075	59,913
Balance Sheet								
Current Assets	493,796	289,222	285,436	293,207	162,527	175,783	166,808	149,443
Total Assets	1,877,998	1,119,611	988,241	949,085	455,632	476,306	391,438	351,014
Current Liabilities	357,539	232,054	191,167	196,016	149,138	140,608	124,237	126,231
Long-Term Obligations	754,706	331,149	352,488	406,564	20,136	58,107	29,630	6,815
Total Liabilities	1,317,968	681,123	640,595	666,782	220,982	249,573	196,600	171,673
Stockholders' Equity	560,030	438,494	347,646	282,303	234,650	226,733	194,838	179,341
Shares Outstanding	63,188	61,179	59,846	58,714	57,566	59,783	57,932	58,311
Statistical Record								
Return on Assets %	5.91	7.68	6.88	6.69	7.18	10.45	8.16	7.44
Return on Equity %	17.74	20.60	21.17	18.18	14.51	21.52	16.19	14.22
EBITDA Margin %	14.22	16.24	14.61	10.48	10.11	12.97	9.55	9.35
Net Margin %	6.07	7.66	6.37	4.35	4.22	6.21	4.43	4.26
Asset Turnover	0.97	1.00	1.08	1.54	1.70	1.68	1.84	1.74
Current Ratio	1.38	1.25	1.49	1.50	1.09	1.25	1.34	1.18
Debt to Equity	1.35	0.76	1.01	1.44	0.09	0.26	0.15	0.04
Price Range	33.62-25.78	27.65-18.73	23.93-17.27	18.96-13.21	18.21-9.88	20.13-11.17	11.98-8.90	10.63-7.29
P/E Ratio	24.72-18.96	21.60-14.63	22.36-16.14	24.62-17.15	32.51-17.63	27.20-15.09	23.96-17.79	25.91-17.78
Average Yield %	0.78	0.93	0.97	1.18	1.47	1.15	1.58	1.68

Address: 469 North Harrison Street, Princeton, NJ 08543-5297 Telephone: (609) 683-5900 Fax: (609) 497-7269	Web Site: www.churchdwight.com Officers: Robert A. Davies III - Chmn., Pres., C.E.O. Zvi Eiref - V.P., Fin., C.F.O.	Auditors: Deloitte & Touche LLP

CIGNA CORP.

Exchange	Symbol	Price	52Wk Range	Yield	P/E
NYS	CI	$89.30 (3/31/2005)	91.85-58.57	0.11	8.56

*7 Year Price Score 79.24   *NYSE Composite Index=100   *12 Month Price Score 113.48

Interim Earnings (Per Share)

Qtr.	Mar	Jun	Sep	Dec
2001	1.78	1.66	1.81	1.33
2002	1.52	1.50	(6.27)	0.33
2003	1.68	(0.38)	1.39	2.06
2004	0.55	3.67	2.34	3.88

Interim Dividends (Per Share)

Amt	Decl	Ex	Rec	Pay
0.025Q	4/28/2004	6/10/2004	6/14/2004	7/12/2004
0.025Q	7/28/2004	9/9/2004	9/13/2004	10/8/2004
0.025Q	10/27/2004	12/9/2004	12/13/2004	1/10/2005
0.025Q	2/24/2005	3/10/2005	3/14/2005	4/11/2005

Indicated Div: $0.10

Valuation Analysis

Forecast P/E	14.32	No of Institutions	
	(4/7/2005)	392	
Market Cap	$12.5 Billion	Shares	
Book Value	5.2 Billion	112,709,072	
Price/Book	2.40	% Held	
Price/Sales	0.69	85.68	

Business Summary: Insurance (MIC: 8.2 SIC: 324 NAIC: 24114)

CIGNA provides medical benefits through managed care and indemnity health care plans. Co. operates in four business segments. The Health Care segment includes HMO and Indemnity operations. The Disability and Life segment includes Co.'s group disability, life, and accident insurance operations that are managed separately from the health care operations. The International segment includes Co.'s life and health insurance and employee benefits businesses operating in selected international markets. The Co.'s remaining segments include the Reinsurance and Other segments.

Recent Developments:
For the year ended Dec 31 2004, income from continuing operations increased 170.0% to $1,577 million from income of $584 million a year earlier. Net income increased 127.5% to $1,438 million from net income of $632 million a year earlier. Revenues were $18,176 million, down 3.4% from $18,808 million the year before. Net premiums earned were $14,236 million versus $15,460 million in the prior year, a decrease of 7.9%. Net investment income fell 36.7% to $1,643 million from $2,594 million a year ago.

Prospects:
Co. outlook is positive, reflecting improvement in Co.'s Health Care business and ongoing profitable growth in its Disability and Life and International businesses. For 2005, Co. expects income from continuing operations before realized investments and special items in the range of $745.0 million to $815.0 million, including earnings of $520.0 million to $580.0 million from Health Care. For the first quarter, Co. expects income before realized investments and special items of $180.0 million to $210.0 million. Co.'s outlook includes first quarter membership declines of 8.0% to 9.0% from year-end 2004 levels. However, Co. anticipates membership will stabilize for the remainder of the year.

Financial Data
(US$ in Thousands)	12/31/2004	12/31/2003	12/31/2002	12/31/2001	12/31/2000	12/31/1999	12/31/1998	12/31/1997
Earnings Per Share	10.43	4.75	(2.83)	6.59	6.08	8.99	6.05	4.88
Cash Flow Per Share	10.49	16.52	9.47	7.34	10.51	9.34	2.97	5.60
Tang Book Value Per Share	25.59	20.62	16.12	22.94	23.26	24.71	28.12	24.95
Dividends Per Share	0.405	1.320	1.320	1.280	1.240	1.200	1.147	1.107
Dividend Payout %	3.88	27.79	...	19.42	20.39	13.35	18.95	22.68
Income Statement								
Premium Income	14,236,000	15,441,000	15,737,000	15,367,000	16,328,000	15,079,000	16,413,000	14,935,000
Total Revenue	18,176,000	18,808,000	19,348,000	19,115,000	19,994,000	18,781,000	21,437,000	20,038,000
Benefits & Claims	10,264,000	...	...	...	...	...	...	...
Income Before Taxes	2,375,000	903,000	(569,000)	1,497,000	1,497,000	1,219,000	2,010,000	1,650,000
Income Taxes	798,000	283,000	(172,000)	508,000	510,000	520,000	718,000	564,000
Net Income	1,438,000	668,000	(398,000)	989,000	987,000	1,774,000	1,292,000	1,086,000
Average Shares	137,884	140,606	148,687	150,036	159,810	197,248	213,447	223,000
Balance Sheet								
Total Assets	81,059,000	90,953,000	88,950,000	91,589,000	95,088,000	95,333,000	114,612,000	108,199,000
Total Liabilities	75,856,000	86,434,000	85,083,000	86,534,000	89,675,000	89,184,000	106,335,000	100,267,000
Stockholders' Equity	5,203,000	4,519,000	3,867,000	5,055,000	5,413,000	6,149,000	8,277,000	7,932,000
Shares Outstanding	140,000	140,591	139,370	141,553	152,005	169,697	205,650	216,000
Statistical Record								
Return on Assets %	1.67	0.74	N.M.	1.06	1.03	1.69	1.16	1.05
Return on Equity %	29.50	15.93	N.M.	18.90	17.03	24.59	15.94	14.35
Loss Ratio %	72.10	...	...	...	...	...	...	...
Net Margin %	7.91	3.55	(2.06)	5.17	4.94	9.45	6.03	5.42
Price Range	82.21-53.05	58.20-39.22	110.83-36.09	128.50-71.61	135.00-61.19	97.44-64.13	82.19-56.52	66.50-45.08
P/E Ratio	7.88-5.09	12.25-8.26	...	19.50-10.87	22.20-10.06	10.84-7.13	13.58-9.34	13.63-9.24
Average Yield %	0.62	2.76	1.61	1.33	1.31	1.42	1.69	1.98

Address: One Liberty Place, 1650 Market Street, Philadelphia, PA 19192-1550 Telephone: (215) 761-1000	Web Site: www.cigna.com Officers: H. Edward Hanway - Chmn., Pres., C.E.O. Michael W. Bell - Exec. V.P., C.F.O.	Auditors: PricewaterhouseCoopers LLP Transfer Agents: Mellon Investor Services, South Hackensack, NJ

CINCINNATI BELL INC (NEW)

Exchange	Symbol	Price	52Wk Range	Yield	P/E
NYS	CBB	$4.25 (3/31/2005)	4.71-3.26	N/A	20.24

*7 Year Price Score 25.32 ***NYSE Composite Index=100** ***12 Month Price Score 100.54**

Interim Earnings (Per Share)

Qtr.	Mar	Jun	Sep	Dec
2001	(0.17)	(0.14)	(0.14)	(0.91)
2002	0.83	(0.10)	0.01	(10.92)
2003	0.55	1.13	0.18	3.47
2004	0.03	0.05	0.06	0.07

Interim Dividends (Per Share)

No Dividends Paid

Valuation Analysis

Forecast P/E	N/A	No of Institutions
Market Cap	$1.0 Billion	Shares
Book Value	N/A	190,123,040
Price/Book	N/A	% Held
Price/Sales	0.86	77.12

TRADING VOLUME (thousand shares)

Business Summary: Communications (MIC: 10.1 SIC: 813 NAIC: 17110)

Cincinnati Bell is a provider of diversified telecommunications services whose primary business, as of Dec 31 2003, consisted of its Local and Wireless businesses. The Local segment provides local telephone service, network access, data transport, high-speed and dial-up Internet access, inter-lata toll, telecommunications equipment, installation and maintenance and other ancillary products and services to customers primarily in southwestern Ohio, northern Kentucky and southeastern Indiana. The Wireless segment includes the operations of Cincinnati Bell Wireless LLC, a joint venture with AT&T Wireless Services, in which Co. owns 80.1%.

Recent Developments: For the year ended Dec 31 2004, net income decreased 95.2% to $64,200 thousand from net income of $1,331,900 thousand a year earlier. Revenues were $1,207,100 thousand, down 22.5% from $1,557,800 thousand the year before. Operating income was $299,300 thousand versus an income of $684,000 thousand in the prior year, a decrease of 56.2%. Total direct expense was $481,400 thousand versus $681,500 thousand in the prior year, a decrease of 29.4%. Total indirect expense was $426,400 thousand versus $192,300 thousand in the prior year, an increase of 121.7%.

Prospects: Results are being hampered by lower telephone services revenue. However, digital subscriber line (DSL) growth and service bundling continue to help offset traditional access line losses. During 2004, Co. added 52,000 net subscribers to its Custom Connections super bundle, which offers local, long distance, wireless and/or DSL. This success, combined with its refinancing plan, strengthens Co.'s cash flows and should allow it to accelerate debt reduction and improve its future competitive strength. For full-year 2005, Co. expects revenue to decrease in the low single-digit range, with earnings before interest, tax, depreciation and amortization ranging from $480.0 million to $490.0 million.

Financial Data

(US$ in Thousands)	12/31/2004	12/31/2003	12/31/2002	12/31/2001	12/31/2000	12/31/1999	12/31/1998	12/31/1997
Earnings Per Share	0.21	5.36	(19.38)	(1.36)	(1.82)	0.20	1.08	(0.12)
Cash Flow Per Share	1.22	1.37	0.88	1.19	1.56	2.18	1.56	2.44
Tang Book Value Per Share	...	...	...	N.M.	N.M.	N.M.	0.28	2.83
Income Statement								
Total Revenue	1,207,100	1,557,800	2,155,900	2,350,500	2,050,100	1,131,100	885,100	1,756,800
EBITDA	491,300	821,100	(1,665,000)	356,600	81,200	314,000	261,400	517,800
Depn & Amortn	187,700	169,700	496,300	554,900	459,700	181,000	111,100	185,400
Income Before Taxes	100,300	417,200	(2,325,500)	(366,400)	(542,100)	71,300	126,100	296,900
Income Taxes	36,100	(828,800)	105,700	(80,200)	(165,600)	33,300	44,300	103,300
Net Income	64,200	1,331,900	(4,222,300)	(286,200)	(377,100)	31,400	149,900	(16,400)
Average Shares	250,500	253,300	218,400	217,400	211,700	150,700	138,200	137,700
Balance Sheet								
Net PPE	851,100	898,800	867,900	3,059,500	2,966,200	2,500,900	698,200	703,200
Total Assets	1,958,700	2,073,500	1,467,600	6,312,000	6,477,600	6,508,600	1,041,000	1,498,700
Long-Term Obligations	2,111,100	2,274,500	2,354,700	2,702,000	2,507,000	2,136,000	366,800	269,200
Total Liabilities	2,544,000	2,713,200	3,572,000	4,197,900	4,022,300	3,713,200	898,900	919,000
Stockholders' Equity	(624,500)	(679,400)	(2,548,300)	1,678,400	2,021,500	2,132,800	142,100	579,700
Shares Outstanding	245,401	244,561	218,690	218,067	215,529	200,872	136,382	136,100
Statistical Record								
Return on Assets %	3.18	75.23	N.M.	N.M.	N.M.	0.83	11.80	N.M.
Return on Equity %	...	...	...	N.M.	N.M.	2.76	41.54	N.M.
EBITDA Margin %	40.70	52.71	N.M.	15.17	3.96	27.76	29.53	29.47
Net Margin %	5.32	85.50	(195.85)	(12.18)	(18.39)	2.78	16.94	(0.93)
PPE Turnover	1.38	1.76	1.10	0.78	0.75	0.71	1.26	2.08
Asset Turnover	0.60	0.88	0.55	0.37	0.31	0.30	0.70	1.11
Debt to Equity	...	...	...	1.61	1.24	1.00	2.58	0.46
Price Range	5.89-3.26	7.25-3.51	10.55-1.15	28.75-7.79	40.50-20.00	36.94-15.44	15.62-8.80	13.70-9.59
P/E Ratio	28.05-15.52	1.35-0.65	...	...	...	184.69-77.19	14.46-8.15	...

Address: 201 East Fourth Street, Cincinnati, OH 45202 Telephone: (513) 397-9900	Web Site: Officers: Phillip R. Cox - Chmn. John F. Cassidy - Pres., C.E.O.	Auditors: PricewaterhouseCoopers LLP Investor Contact: 513-397-7877 Transfer Agents: Fifth Third Bank, Cincinnati, OH

CINERGY CORP

Exchange	Symbol	Price	52Wk Range	Yield	P/E
NYS	CIN	$40.52 (3/31/2005)	42.42-35.22	4.74	18.59

*7 Year Price Score 101.78 ***NYSE Composite Index=100** ***12 Month Price Score 95.29**

Interim Earnings (Per Share)

Qtr.	Mar	Jun	Sep	Dec
2001	0.75	0.51	0.80	0.69
2002	0.58	0.26	0.77	0.52
2003	0.95	0.47	0.62	0.59
2004	0.57	0.32	0.50	0.79

Interim Dividends (Per Share)

Amt	Decl	Ex	Rec	Pay
0.47Q	4/22/2004	4/29/2004	5/3/2004	5/15/2004
0.47Q	7/22/2004	7/29/2004	8/2/2004	8/15/2004
0.47Q	10/1/2004	10/7/2004	10/12/2004	11/15/2004
0.48Q	1/14/2005	1/28/2005	2/1/2005	2/15/2005

Indicated Div: $1.92

Valuation Analysis

Forecast P/E	14.03 (4/7/2005)	No of Institutions 341
Market Cap	$7.6 Billion	Shares
Book Value	4.1 Billion	117,936,560
Price/Book	1.85	% Held
Price/Sales	1.62	55.93

Business Summary: Electricity (MIC: 7.1 SIC: 931 NAIC: 21121)

Cinergy is the parent company of Cincinnati Gas & Electric and PSI Energy. Co. provides electricity, natural gas, and energy services through three business units. The Commercial segment manages, operates and maintains Co.'s wholesale generation and energy marketing and trading activities, primarily natural gas and electricity. The Regulated Businesses segment conducts electric generation and electric and gas transmission and distribution operations providing service to approximately 1.5 million customers. The Power Technology segment primarily manages Co.'s venture capital operations. At Dec 31 2004, Co.'s total electric capacity of its domestic generating plants was 13,331 megawatts.

Recent Developments: For the year ended Dec 31 2004, net income decreased 14.7% to $400,868 thousand from net income of $469,772 thousand a year earlier. Revenues were $4,687,950 thousand, up 6.2% from $4,415,877 thousand the year before. Operating income was $738,333 thousand versus an income of $810,822 thousand in the prior year, a decrease of 8.9%. Total direct expense was $3,235,283 thousand versus $2,956,438 thousand in the prior year, an increase of 9.4%. Total indirect expense was $714,334 thousand versus $648,617 thousand in the prior year, an increase of 10.1%.

Prospects: In 2004, Co. felt the adverse effects of rising emission allowance costs and has taken a number of steps to hedge future emission allowance risk exposure. Meanwhile, the Public Utilities Commission of Ohio has approved a rate stabilization plan for The Cincinnati Gas & Electric Co. that permits non-residential electric rates to increase in 2005 and residential electric rates to increase in 2006 to recover costs for environmental compliance, homeland security, taxes, fuel and emission allowances. Separately, Co. is conducting a feasibility study for constructing a commercial, integrated gasification combined cycle generating station using coal to produce 500 to 600 megawatts of electricity.

Financial Data

(US$ in Thousands)	12/31/2004	12/31/2003	12/31/2002	12/31/2001	12/31/2000	12/31/1999	12/31/1998	12/31/1997
Earnings Per Share	2.18	2.63	2.13	2.75	2.50	2.53	1.65	1.59
Cash Flow Per Share	4.59	5.36	5.96	4.36	3.89	2.16	4.58	4.78
Tang Book Value Per Share	21.63	20.50	19.18	17.98	17.54	16.70	16.02	16.10
Dividends Per Share	1.880	1.840	1.800	1.800	1.800	1.800	1.800	1.800
Dividend Payout %	86.24	69.96	84.51	65.45	72.00	71.15	109.09	113.21
Income Statement								
Total Revenue	4,687,950	4,415,877	11,960,081	12,922,537	8,421,964	5,937,888	5,876,294	4,352,843
EBITDA	1,240,326	1,269,065	1,221,566	1,348,485	1,254,032	1,206,367	953,774	...
Depn & Amortn	460,389	419,098	414,004	378,140	373,965	353,820	325,515	289,077
Income Before Taxes	504,699	581,365	557,656	702,218	655,608	617,769	384,672	...
Income Taxes	103,831	143,508	157,320	255,506	251,557	208,671	117,187	(35,937)
Net Income	400,868	469,772	360,576	442,279	399,466	403,641	260,968	253,238
Average Shares	183,531	178,473	167,047	161,047	160,000	158,863	159,000	...
Balance Sheet								
Net PPE	9,929,465	9,627,506	8,648,674	8,236,895	6,630,424	6,417,472	6,344,449	6,297,103
Total Assets	14,982,317	14,119,206	13,307,028	12,299,813	12,329,728	9,616,948	10,298,795	8,858,153
Long-Term Obligations	4,227,741	4,131,909	4,080,768	3,596,730	2,876,367	2,989,242	2,604,467	2,150,902
Total Liabilities	10,803,577	10,355,706	9,642,537	8,989,194	9,477,933	6,870,630	7,664,924	6,140,964
Stockholders' Equity	4,115,922	3,700,682	3,293,476	2,941,459	2,788,961	2,653,721	2,541,231	2,539,200
Shares Outstanding	187,524	178,336	168,663	159,402	158,967	158,923	158,664	157,745
Statistical Record								
Return on Assets %	2.75	3.43	2.82	3.59	3.63	4.05	2.72	2.86
Return on Equity %	10.23	13.43	11.57	15.44	14.64	15.54	10.27	9.89
EBITDA Margin %	26.46	28.74	10.21	10.44	14.89	20.32	16.23	...
Net Margin %	8.55	10.64	3.01	3.42	4.74	6.80	4.44	5.82
PPE Turnover	0.48	0.48	1.42	1.74	1.29	0.93	0.93	0.69
Asset Turnover	0.32	0.32	0.93	1.05	0.77	0.60	0.61	0.49
Debt to Equity	1.03	1.12	1.24	1.22	1.03	1.13	1.02	0.85
Price Range	42.42-35.22	38.81-30.32	36.98-26.86	35.41-28.70	35.19-20.13	34.50-23.75	38.69-31.00	39.00-32.13
P/E Ratio	19.46-16.16	14.76-11.53	17.36-12.61	12.88-10.44	14.08-8.05	13.64-9.39	23.45-18.79	24.53-20.20
Average Yield %	4.79	5.24	5.40	5.58	6.59	6.06	5.18	5.27

Address: 139 East Fourth Street, Cincinnati, OH 45202 **Telephone:** (513) 421-9500	**Web Site:** www.cinergy.com **Officers:** James E. Rogers - Chmn., Pres., C.E.O. Marc E. Manly - Exec. V.P., Chief Legal Officer	**Auditors:** Deloite & Touche LLP **Investor Contact:** 513-287-1083

CIRCUIT CITY STORES, INC.

Exchange	Symbol	Price	52Wk Range	Yield	P/E
NYS	CC	$16.05 (3/31/2005)	17.49-10.60	0.44	61.73

*7 Year Price Score 79.86   *NYSE Composite Index=100   *12 Month Price Score 102.10

Interim Earnings (Per Share)

Qtr.	May	Aug	Nov	Feb
2001-02	0.05	0.03	0.10	0.74
2002-03	0.08	0.04	(0.09)	0.36
2003-04	(0.21)	(0.60)	0.01	0.38
2004-05	(0.03)	(0.06)	(0.03)	...

Interim Dividends (Per Share)

Amt	Decl	Ex	Rec	Pay
0.018Q	6/16/2004	6/28/2004	6/30/2004	7/15/2004
0.018Q	9/15/2004	9/28/2004	9/30/2004	10/15/2004
0.018Q	12/15/2004	12/29/2004	12/31/2004	1/15/2005
0.018Q	3/15/2005	3/29/2005	3/31/2005	4/15/2005

Indicated Div: $0.07

Valuation Analysis

Forecast P/E	N/A		No of Institutions
Market Cap	$3.1 Billion		Shares
Book Value	2.1 Billion		173,343,344
Price/Book	1.49		% Held
Price/Sales	0.30		90.62

Business Summary: Hospitality & Tourism (MIC: 5.1 SIC: 731 NAIC: 43112)

Circuit City Stores is a national retailer of brand-name retailer of consumer electronics. As of June 15 2004, Co. operated 602 Superstores and five mall-based stores in 158 U.S. markets. In addition, Co.'s subsidiary, InterTAN, Inc., operated through about 1,000 retail stores and dealer outlets in Canada. Products offered include video equipment, such as television, digital satellite systems, DVD players, videocassette recorders, camcorders and cameras. Co. also offers home and portable audio systems and mobile electronics. Home office products include PCs, printers, peripherals, software and facsimile machines. Entertainment software products include video games, DVD movies and music.

Recent Developments: For the quarter ended Nov 30 2004, net loss decreased 135.2% to $5,900 thousand from net loss of $2,509 thousand in the year-earlier quarter. Revenues were $2,493,389 thousand, up 3.6% from $2,407,424 thousand the year before with comparable store merchandise sales decreasing 4.3%. Decreases in music and movie software sales accounted for about 160 basis points of the overall comparable store sales decline. A decrease in digital video service sales, principally driven by a business model change, accounted for about 120 basis points of the overall comparable store sales decrease. Total indirect expense fell 40.2% to $6,442 thousand versus $10,775 thousand in the prior-year quarter.

Prospects: On Feb 15 2005, Co. received an unsolicited letter from Highfields Capital Management LP indicating Highfields' interest in acquiring all of Co.'s outstanding shares at a price of $17.00 per share. Co. added that its directors would evaluate the proposal, as well as other available alternatives. Meanwhile, on Feb 16 2005, Co. announced it would close 19 superstores, five regional offices and a distribution center by the end of February as it attempts to improve its financial performance. The 19 stores had combined sales of $170.0 million for the year ended Dec 31 2004. Co. expects to incur expenses of about $30.0 million after tax in conjunction with the store and regional office closings.

Financial Data

(US$ in Thousands)	9 Mos	6 Mos	3 Mos	02/29/2004	02/28/2003	02/28/2002	02/28/2001	02/29/2000
Earnings Per Share	0.26	0.30	(0.23)	(0.43)	0.40	0.92	0.73	0.96
Cash Flow Per Share	2.93	1.12	1.02	(0.64)	(1.06)	3.52	0.68	2.63
Tang Book Value Per Share	9.40	9.53	9.74	10.91	11.15	11.13	10.13	9.33
Dividends Per Share	0.070	0.070	0.070	0.070	0.070	0.070	0.070	0.070
Dividend Payout %	27.36	23.34	...	...	17.50	7.61	9.59	7.29
Income Statement								
Total Revenue	6,905,003	4,411,614	2,066,588	9,745,445	9,953,530	12,791,468	12,959,028	12,614,390
EBITDA	84,647	50,322	28,315	210,124	245,337	519,284	412,447	676,922
Depn & Amortn	119,501	76,456	36,565	211,364	178,297	166,389	153,090	148,164
Income Before Taxes	(34,854)	(26,134)	(8,250)	(1,240)	67,040	352,895	259,357	528,758
Income Taxes	(12,304)	(9,484)	(3,016)	(453)	25,475	134,100	98,555	200,928
Net Income	(23,764)	(17,864)	(5,941)	(89,269)	106,084	218,795	160,802	197,590
Average Shares	191,135	195,350	199,429	205,865	247,904	241,217	232,810	230,109
Balance Sheet								
Current Assets	3,380,669	2,705,712	2,697,636	2,919,061	3,102,910	3,652,711	2,847,179	2,942,615
Total Assets	4,380,480	3,681,868	3,654,113	3,633,000	3,799,117	4,539,386	3,871,333	3,955,348
Current Liabilities	2,088,266	1,341,354	1,251,245	1,176,703	1,280,069	1,641,327	1,291,599	1,406,159
Long-Term Obligations	11,756	11,979	25,088	22,691	11,254	14,064	116,137	249,241
Total Liabilities	2,325,745	1,582,130	1,493,973	1,409,039	1,457,542	1,804,948	1,514,850	1,813,174
Stockholders' Equity	2,054,735	2,099,738	2,160,140	2,223,961	2,341,575	2,734,438	2,356,483	2,142,174
Shares Outstanding	191,249	195,183	199,300	203,899	209,954	245,676	232,659	229,482
Statistical Record								
Return on Assets %	1.20	1.65	N.M.	N.M.	2.54	5.20	4.11	5.33
Return on Equity %	2.50	2.87	N.M.	N.M.	4.18	8.60	7.15	9.74
EBITDA Margin %	1.23	1.14	1.37	2.16	2.46	4.06	3.18	5.37
Net Margin %	N.M.	N.M.	N.M.	N.M.	1.07	1.71	1.24	1.57
Asset Turnover	2.30	2.71	2.71	2.62	2.39	3.04	3.31	3.40
Current Ratio	1.62	2.02	2.16	2.48	2.42	2.23	2.20	2.09
Debt to Equity	0.01	0.01	0.01	0.01	N.M.	0.01	0.05	0.12
Price Range	17.49-8.84	14.10-8.84	13.02-6.44	13.02-4.27	16.24-4.13	19.93-6.58	40.94-6.35	34.30-17.27
P/E Ratio	67.27-34.00	47.00-29.47	N/A	N/A	40.61-10.32	21.66-7.16	56.08-8.70	35.73-17.99
Average Yield %	0.55	0.61	0.68	0.79	0.66	0.60	0.35	0.26

Address: 9950 Mayland Drive,	Web Site: www.circuitcity.com	Auditors: KPMG LLP
Richmond, VA 23233-1464	Officers: W. Alan McCollough - Chmn., C.E.O.	Investor Contact: 804-527-4000 x2077
Telephone: (804) 527-4000	Philip J. Schoonover - Pres.	

CIT GROUP INC. (DE)

Exchange	Symbol	Price	52Wk Range	Yield	P/E
NYS	CIT	$38.00 (3/31/2005)	46.07-33.28	1.37	10.86

*7 Year Price Score N/A *NYSE Composite Index=100 *12 Month Price Score 96.77

Interim Earnings (Per Share)

Qtr.	Mar	Jun	Sep	Dec
2003	0.60	0.65	0.69	0.72
2004	0.88	0.82	0.86	0.94

Interim Dividends (Per Share)

Amt	Decl	Ex	Rec	Pay
0.13Q	4/21/2004	5/12/2004	5/14/2004	5/28/2004
0.13Q	7/21/2004	8/11/2004	8/13/2004	8/30/2004
0.13Q	10/20/2004	11/10/2004	11/15/2004	11/30/2004
0.13Q	1/18/2005	2/11/2005	2/15/2005	2/28/2005

Indicated Div: $0.52

Valuation Analysis

Forecast P/E	9.89		No of Institutions
	(4/7/2005)		333
Market Cap	$8.0 Billion		Shares
Book Value	6.1 Billion		194,521,440
Price/Book	1.32		% Held
Price/Sales	2.11		92.26

Business Summary: Credit & Lending (MIC: 8.6 SIC: 153 NAIC: 32420)

CIT Group, with nearly $50.00 billion in assets under management as of Dec 31 2003, is a global source of financing and leasing capital and an advisor for companies across approximately 30 industries, including manufacturing, retailing, transportation, aerospace, construction, technology, communications, and various service-related industries. Co. operates extensively in the U.S. and Canada with strategic locations in Europe, Latin America, Australia and the Asia-Pacific region. Co. operates in five business segments: specialty finance, commercial finance, equipment finance, capital finance, and structured finance.

Recent Developments: For the year ended Dec 31 2004, net income increased 32.9% to $753,600 thousand from net income of $566,900 thousand a year earlier. Provision for loan losses was $214,200 thousand versus $387,300 thousand in the prior year, a decrease of 44.7%. Non-interest income rose 1.5% to $3,785,700 thousand, while non-interest expense advanced 13.0% to $1,088,200 thousand.

Prospects: On Feb 17 2005, Co. announced that it has completed its acquisition of Education Lending Group, Inc., a full-service education funding provider with a $4.00 billion portfolio and $1.50 billion of annual originations. Meanwhile, results are being positively affected by higher new business volumes across all operating segments and strong asset growth, particularly in the Specialty Finance and Capital Finance segments. In addition, Co. is taking steps to reposition its capital for higher returns, including the sale of its venture capital fund portfolio and the majority of its manufactured housing portfolio during the fourth quarter of 2004.

Financial Data

(US$ in Thousands)	12/31/2004	12/31/2003	12/31/2002	09/30/2002	09/30/2001	06/01/2001	12/31/2000	12/31/1999
Earnings Per Share	3.50	2.66	0.67	(31.66)	0.86	...	...	...
Cash Flow Per Share	7.65	10.33	...	...	...	...	...	...
Tang Book Value Per Share	25.94	23.17	21.18	20.67	19.04	...	...	...
Dividends Per Share	0.520	0.480	0.120	...	...	...	...	...
Dividend Payout %	14.86	18.05	17.91	...	...	...	...	...
Income Statement								
Total Revenue	3,785,700	3,729,500	971,700	4,342,800	1,676,500	2,298,800	5,248,400	2,565,900
EBITDA	2,236,700	2,023,900	513,300	(5,073,200)	972,400	813,700	2,372,300	1,019,000
Depn & Amortn	998,800	1,086,600	277,300	1,241,000	521,300	642,400	1,367,600	402,800
Income Before Taxes	1,237,900	937,300	236,000	(6,314,200)	451,100	171,300	1,004,700	616,200
Income Taxes	483,200	365,000	92,000	374,000	195,000	85,100	381,200	214,900
Net Income	753,600	566,900	141,300	(6,698,700)	252,500	81,300	611,600	389,400
Average Shares	215,054	213,143	...	...	...	...	...	...
Balance Sheet								
Current Assets	2,210,200	1,973,700	2,036,600	2,274,400	808,000	...	812,100	...
Total Assets	51,111,300	46,342,800	41,932,400	42,710,500	51,090,100	...	48,689,800	...
Current Liabilities	7,291,000	7,241,000	5,123,200	5,239,000	4,534,400	...	4,467,500	...
Long-Term Obligations	37,724,800	33,668,600	31,681,300	32,456,000	35,697,700	...	37,965,100	...
Total Liabilities	45,015,800	40,909,600	36,804,500	37,695,000	40,232,100	...	42,432,600	...
Stockholders' Equity	6,055,100	5,394,200	4,870,700	4,757,800	10,598,000	...	6,007,200	...
Shares Outstanding	210,440	211,805	211,805	211,573	211,573	...	...	...
Statistical Record								
Return on Assets %	1.54	1.28	0.24	N.M.	0.68	...	...	...
Return on Equity %	13.13	11.05	1.46	N.M.	4.07	...	...	...
EBITDA Margin %	59.08	54.27	52.82	N.M.	58.00	35.40	45.20	39.71
Net Margin %	19.91	15.20	14.54	N.M.	15.06	3.54	11.65	15.18
Asset Turnover	0.08	0.08	0.02	0.09	0.04	...	...	...
Current Ratio	0.30	0.27	0.40	0.43	0.18	...	0.18	...
Debt to Equity	6.23	6.24	6.50	6.82	3.37	...	6.32	...
Price Range	45.82-33.28	35.95-16.61	22.49-13.95	23.80-17.98				
P/E Ratio	13.09-9.51	13.52-6.24	33.57-20.82	...	...	...	...	...
Average Yield %	1.37	1.92	0.64	...	...	...	...	...

Address: 1 CIT Drive, Livingston, NJ 07039	Web Site: www.cit.com	Auditors: PricewaterhouseCoopers LLP
Telephone: (973) 740-5000	Officers: Jeffrey M. Peek - Chmn., C.E.O. Joseph M. Leone - Vice-Chmn., C.F.O.	

CITIGROUP INC

Exchange	Symbol	Price	52Wk Range	Yield	P/E	Div Acheiver
NYS	C	$44.94 (3/31/2005)	52.29-42.56	3.92	13.79	18 Years

*7 Year Price Score 100.08 *NYSE Composite Index=100 *12 Month Price Score 95.02

Interim Earnings (Per Share)

Qtr.	Mar	Jun	Sep	Dec
2001	0.69	0.69	0.61	0.74
2002	0.93	0.78	0.76	0.47
2003	0.79	0.83	0.90	0.91
2004	1.01	0.22	1.02	1.02

Interim Dividends (Per Share)

Amt	Decl	Ex	Rec	Pay
0.40Q	4/20/2004	4/29/2004	5/3/2004	5/28/2004
0.40Q	7/20/2004	7/29/2004	8/2/2004	8/27/2004
0.40Q	10/19/2004	10/28/2004	11/1/2004	11/24/2004
0.44Q	1/20/2005	2/3/2005	2/7/2005	2/25/2005

Indicated Div: $1.76 (Div. Reinv. Plan)

Valuation Analysis

Forecast P/E	10.59	No of Institutions
	(4/7/2005)	1309
Market Cap	$233.4 Billion	Shares
Book Value	109.3 Billion	3,386,324,992
Price/Book	2.14	% Held
Price/Sales	2.16	64.81

Business Summary: Commercial Banking (MIC: 8.1 SIC: 021 NAIC: 23930)

Citigroup is a bank holding company that provides financial services to consumers and corporations. Co.'s Global Consumer segment delivers banking, lending, insurance and investment services. Co.'s Global Corporate and Investment Bank segment provides corporations, governments, institutions and investors with financial products and services. Co.'s Private Client Services segment provides investment advice, financial planning and brokerage services. Co.'s Global Investment Management segment offers life insurance, annuity, asset management and personalized wealth management products and services. Proprietary Investment Activities include private equity investments and other investments.

Recent Developments: For the year ended Dec 31 2004, net income decreased 4.5% to $17,046 million from net income of $17,853 million a year earlier. Net interest income was $66,709 million, up 16.9% from $57,047 million the year before. Provision for loan losses was $6,233 million versus $8,046 million in the prior year, a decrease of 22.5%. Non-interest income rose 10.4% to $41,567 million, while non-interest expense advanced 32.7% to $51,974 million.

Prospects: Throughout 2005, Co. plans to implement many enhancements to its training, development, and compensation processes. Co. has increased its investment spending and executed several targeted acquisitions, which are enhancing its ability to reach and serve its global customer base. Co. is launching new card products and continues to expand its global branch network in retail banking and consumer finance. Meanwhile, in order to better serve its corporate customers, Co. is enhancing its electronic trading platforms, improving its capabilities in derivative products, and expanding its international direct custody business through direct investment and acquisitions.

Financial Data (US$ in Thousands)	12/31/2004	12/31/2003	12/31/2002	12/31/2001	12/31/2000	12/31/1999	12/31/1998	12/31/1997
Earnings Per Share	3.26	3.42	2.94	2.72	2.62	2.12	1.22	1.27
Cash Flow Per Share	(0.47)	(2.92)	5.13	5.28	0.54	2.06	1.08	0.30
Tang Book Value Per Share	11.72	10.75	9.70	15.57	12.84	10.64	8.94	6.99
Dividends Per Share	1.600	1.100	0.700	0.600	0.520	0.405	0.278	0.200
Dividend Payout %	49.08	32.16	23.81	22.06	19.85	19.08	22.84	15.75
Income Statement								
Interest Income	66,709,000	57,047,000	58,939,000	66,565,000	64,939,000	44,900,000	46,239,000	16,214,000
Premium Income	3,993,000	3,749,000	3,410,000	13,460,000	12,429,000	10,441,000	9,850,000	8,995,000
Interest Expense	22,086,000	17,271,000	21,248,000	31,965,000	36,638,000	24,768,000	27,495,000	...
Benefits & Claims	3,801,000	3,895,000	3,478,000	11,759,000	10,147,000	8,671,000	8,365,000	7,714,000
Income Before Taxes	24,182,000	26,333,000	20,537,000	21,897,000	21,143,000	15,948,000	9,269,000	5,012,000
Income Taxes	6,909,000	8,195,000	6,998,000	7,526,000	7,525,000	5,703,000	3,234,000	1,696,000
Net Income	17,046,000	17,853,000	15,276,000	14,126,000	13,519,000	9,867,000	5,807,000	3,104,000
Average Shares	5,207,399	5,193,599	5,166,199	5,146,999	5,122,199	4,591,331	4,630,398	2,359,800
Balance Sheet								
Total Assets	1,484,101,000	1,264,032,000	1,097,190,000	1,051,450,000	902,210,000	716,937,000	668,641,000	386,555,000
Total Liabilities	1,374,810,000	1,166,018,000	1,010,472,000	970,203,000	831,084,000	662,331,000	621,473,000	363,002,000
Stockholders' Equity	109,291,000	98,014,000	86,718,000	81,247,000	66,206,000	49,686,000	42,708,000	20,893,000
Shares Outstanding	5,194,642	5,156,949	5,140,824	5,118,688	5,022,221	4,490,031	4,515,998	2,290,000
Statistical Record								
Return on Assets %	1.24	1.51	1.42	1.45	1.67	1.42	1.10	1.15
Return on Equity %	16.40	19.33	18.19	19.16	23.27	21.36	18.26	18.27
Net Interest Margin %	66.89	69.72	63.95	51.98	43.58	44.84	40.54	...
Loss Ratio %	95.19	103.89	101.99	87.36	81.64	83.05	84.92	85.76
Price Range	52.29-42.56	49.00-31.42	48.55-25.21	52.57-33.95	54.97-33.61	40.61-23.20	33.78-14.90	26.92-18.72
P/E Ratio	16.04-13.06	14.33-9.19	16.51-8.57	19.33-12.48	20.98-12.83	19.16-10.94	27.68-12.22	21.20-14.74
Average Yield %	3.40	2.63	1.84	1.31	1.16	1.27	1.12	0.87

Address: 399 Park Avenue, New York, NY 10043
Telephone: (212) 559-1000
Fax: (212) 816-8913

Web Site: www.citigroup.com
Officers: Sanford I. Weill - Chmn. William R. Rhodes - Sr. Vice-Chmn.

Auditors: KPMG LLP
Investor Contact: 212-559-9446
Transfer Agents: Mellon Investor Services, LLC, Ridgefield Park, NJ

CITIZENS COMMUNICATIONS CO

Exchange	Symbol	Price	52Wk Range	Yield	P/E
NYS	CZN	$12.94 (3/31/2005)	14.75-12.10	7.73	56.26

*7 Year Price Score 98.50   *NYSE Composite Index=100   *12 Month Price Score 91.56

Interim Earnings (Per Share)

Qtr.	Mar	Jun	Sep	Dec
2001	0.07	(0.05)	(0.01)	(0.40)
2002	0.29	(0.15)	(2.49)	(0.08)
2003	0.45	0.12	0.04	0.05
2004	0.15	0.08	(0.04)	0.05

Interim Dividends (Per Share)

Amt	Decl	Ex	Rec	Pay
0.25Q	7/11/2004	8/16/2004	8/18/2004	9/2/2004
2.00Q	7/11/2004	8/16/2004	8/18/2004	9/2/2004
0.25Q	11/1/2004	12/8/2004	12/10/2004	12/31/2004
0.25Q	3/8/2005	3/16/2005	3/18/2005	3/31/2005

Indicated Div: $1.00

Valuation Analysis

Forecast P/E	27.78	No of Institutions	
	(4/7/2005)	276	
Market Cap	$4.4 Billion	Shares	248,688,000
Book Value	1.4 Billion	% Held	
Price/Book	3.23	73.10	
Price/Sales	2.00		

Business Summary: Communications (MIC: 10.1 SIC: 813 NAIC: 17110)

Citizens Communications is a telecommunications company providing wireline communications services to rural areas and small and medium-sized towns and cities as an incumbent local exchange carrier, or ILEC. Co. offers its ILEC services under the "Frontier" name. In addition, Co. provides competitive local exchange carrier, or CLEC, services to business customers and to other communications carriers in certain metropolitan areas in the western United States through Electric Lightwave, LLC, its wholly-owned subsidiary. Co. also provides electric distribution and generation services to primarily rural customers in Vermont.

Recent Developments: For the year ended Dec 31 2004, net income decreased 61.6% to $72,150 thousand from net income of $187,852 thousand a year earlier. Revenues were $2,192,980 thousand, down 10.3% from $2,444,938 thousand the year before. Operating income was $484,286 thousand versus an income of $557,612 thousand in the prior year, a decrease of 13.2%. Total direct expense was $205,166 thousand versus $369,689 thousand in the prior year, a decrease of 44.5%. Total indirect expense was $2,076,238 thousand versus $2,112,913 thousand in the prior year, a decrease of 1.7%.

Prospects: Increases in Co.'s data and enhanced service revenues is more than offsetting lower access services revenues, reduced long distance revenue and loss of access lines. Co.'s revenue generating units (which consist of access lines and high-speed Internet subscribers) are showing overall growth as it adds growing numbers of high-speed Internet customers. At the end of 2004, Co. had approximately 212,300 high-speed data subscribers, representing a 76.0% increase from the previous year. During 2004, Co. also retired or refinanced more than $1.20 billion of debt. Co. expects to save approximately $60.4 million in interest expense as a result of these transactions.

Financial Data

(US$ in Thousands)	12/31/2004	12/31/2003	12/31/2002	12/31/2001	12/31/2000	12/31/1999	12/31/1998	12/31/1997
Earnings Per Share	0.23	0.64	(2.43)	(0.38)	(0.11)	0.55	0.22	0.04
Cash Flow Per Share	2.35	2.59	2.27	1.90	1.17	1.33	1.01	0.89
Tang Book Value Per Share	N.M.	N.M.	N.M.	N.M.	4.09	7.30	6.90	6.58
Dividends Per Share	2.500	...	...	...	...	...	...	...
Dividend Payout %	1,086.96	...	...	...	...	...	...	...
Income Statement								
Total Revenue	2,192,980	2,444,938	2,669,332	2,456,993	1,802,358	1,087,428	1,542,372	1,393,619
EBITDA	1,037,263	1,207,309	(4,822)	939,141	524,980	537,326	458,024	368,834
Depn & Amortn	572,710	595,276	755,522	632,336	387,607	262,430	257,844	235,812
Income Before Taxes	85,529	195,509	(1,231,640)	(72,521)	(49,993)	187,924	87,941	23,693
Income Taxes	13,379	67,216	(414,874)	(14,805)	(16,132)	64,587	22,337	7,383
Net Income	72,150	187,852	(682,897)	(89,682)	(28,394)	144,486	57,060	10,100
Average Shares	309,183	302,436	284,573	273,721	266,931	262,392	259,621	260,824
Balance Sheet								
Net PPE	3,338,300	3,525,640	3,690,056	4,512,038	3,509,767	2,888,718	4,048,623	3,667,793
Total Assets	6,668,419	7,689,110	8,146,742	10,553,600	6,955,006	5,771,745	5,292,932	4,872,852
Long-Term Obligations	4,266,998	4,195,629	4,957,361	5,534,906	3,062,289	2,107,460	1,900,246	1,706,532
Total Liabilities	5,306,179	6,273,927	6,974,603	8,607,458	5,235,005	3,851,810	3,500,161	3,193,641
Stockholders' Equity	1,362,240	1,415,183	1,172,139	1,946,142	1,720,001	1,919,935	1,792,771	1,679,211
Shares Outstanding	339,633	284,709	282,482	281,289	265,768	262,924	259,885	255,049
Statistical Record								
Return on Assets %	1.00	2.37	N.M.	N.M.	N.M.	2.61	1.12	0.21
Return on Equity %	5.18	14.52	N.M.	N.M.	N.M.	7.78	3.29	0.60
EBITDA Margin %	47.30	49.38	N.M.	38.22	29.13	49.41	29.70	26.47
Net Margin %	3.29	7.68	(25.58)	(3.65)	(1.58)	13.29	3.70	0.72
PPE Turnover	0.64	0.68	0.65	0.61	0.56	0.31	0.40	0.41
Asset Turnover	0.30	0.31	0.29	0.28	0.28	0.20	0.30	0.30
Debt to Equity	3.13	2.96	4.23	2.84	1.78	1.10	1.06	1.02
Price Range	14.75-11.73	13.30-9.08	11.33-4.60	15.70-8.34	18.88-12.69	14.19-7.31	11.18-7.13	11.71-7.61
P/E Ratio	64.13-51.00	20.78-14.19	...	...	...	25.80-13.30	50.84-32.43	292.64-190.29
Average Yield %	19.00	...	...	...	...	...	...	...

Address: 3 High Ridge Park, Stamford, CT 06905-1390
Telephone: (203) 614-5600
Fax: (203) 614-4602

Web Site: www.czn.net
Officers: Leonard Tow - Chmn., C.E.O. Scott N. Schneider - Vice-Chmn., Pres., C.O.O.

Auditors: KPMG LLP

CITY NATIONAL CORP. (BEVERLY HILLS, CA)

Exchange	Symbol	Price	52Wk Range	Yield	P/E	Div Acheiver
NYS	CYN	$69.82 (3/31/2005)	70.91-58.09	2.06	17.28	10 Years

*7 Year Price Score 124.56 *NYSE Composite Index=100 ***12 Month Price Score 97.40**

Interim Earnings (Per Share)

Qtr.	Mar	Jun	Sep	Dec
2001	0.69	0.74	0.75	0.78
2002	0.87	0.88	0.94	0.87
2003	0.87	0.93	1.05	0.87
2004	1.00	1.03	1.04	0.97

Interim Dividends (Per Share)

Amt	Decl	Ex	Rec	Pay
0.32Q	4/28/2004	5/10/2004	5/12/2004	5/24/2004
0.32Q	7/28/2004	8/9/2004	8/11/2004	8/23/2004
0.32Q	10/27/2004	11/8/2004	11/10/2004	11/22/2004
0.36Q	1/20/2005	1/31/2005	2/2/2005	2/15/2005
		Indicated Div: $1.44		

Valuation Analysis

Forecast P/E	15.26 (4/7/2005)
Market Cap	$3.5 Billion
Book Value	1.3 Billion
Price/Book	2.57
Price/Sales	4.39
No of Institutions	222
Shares	30,042,108
% Held	60.59

Business Summary: Commercial Banking (MIC: 8.1 SIC: 021 NAIC: 22110)

City National, with assets of $13.02 billion as of Dec 31 2003, conducts its business through City National Bank. Co. provides private and business banking, investment, and trust services through 54 offices, including 12 full-service regional centers, in Southern California, the San Francisco Bay Area, and New York City. Co. offers a broad range of loans, deposit, cash management, international banking, and other services. Through City National Investments, Co. offers personal and employee benefit trust services, manages investments for clients and engages in securities sales and trading. Co. also manages and offers mutual funds under CNI Charter Funds.

Recent Developments: For the year ended Dec 31 2004, net income increased 10.5% to $206,322 thousand from net income of $186,677 thousand a year earlier. Net interest income was $545,888 thousand, up 6.1% from $514,615 thousand the year before. Provision for loan losses was Nil versus $29,000 thousand in the prior year. Non-interest income rose 4.0% to $184,265 thousand, while non-interest expense advanced 8.7% to $400,402 thousand.

Prospects: Going forward, Co. expects growth in net income per share for full year 2005 to be approximately 11.0% to 14.0% higher than net income per share for 2004. This is based on current economic conditions, business indicators and an expectation that the Fed Funds Rate will rise by an additional 75 basis points during 2005. Meanwhile, Co. expects average loans to grow at a rate faster than in 2004, while average deposits in 2005 are expected to grow at a slower rate than in 2004. Accordingly, Co. believes that a provision for credit losses will be required in 2005 as average loan balances grow.

Financial Data (US$ in Thousands)	12/31/2004	12/31/2003	12/31/2002	12/31/2001	12/31/2000	12/31/1999	12/31/1998	12/31/1997
Earnings Per Share	4.04	3.72	3.56	2.96	2.72	2.30	2.00	1.68
Cash Flow Per Share	4.23	5.71	3.72	3.06	3.98	2.45	2.90	2.05
Tang Book Value Per Share	21.27	18.65	17.42	14.81	11.50	9.78	10.61	9.83
Dividends Per Share	1.280	0.970	0.780	0.740	0.700	0.660	0.560	0.440
Dividend Payout %	31.68	26.08	21.91	25.00	25.74	28.70	28.00	26.19
Income Statement								
Interest Income	604,325	575,725	609,700	625,248	646,288	470,446	423,949	357,996
Interest Expense	58,437	61,110	94,444	191,094	239,772	148,441	130,278	104,328
Net Interest Income	545,888	514,615	515,256	434,154	406,516	322,005	293,671	253,668
Provision for Losses	...	29,000	67,000	35,000	21,500	...	...	...
Non-Interest Income	184,265	177,225	146,293	132,384	109,484	87,212	67,684	53,418
Non-Interest Expense	395,410	364,178	332,591	313,395	294,770	241,803	211,331	181,757
Income Before Taxes	329,751	294,623	261,958	218,143	199,730	167,414	150,024	125,329
Income Taxes	123,429	107,946	78,858	71,973	68,070	59,307	53,796	45,196
Net Income	206,322	186,677	183,100	146,170	131,660	108,107	96,228	80,133
Average Shares	51,074	50,198	51,389	49,376	48,393	46,938	48,141	47,809
Balance Sheet								
Net Loans & Leases	8,345,619	7,716,756	7,834,968	7,016,344	6,391,710	5,356,592	4,395,088	3,687,463
Total Assets	14,231,513	13,018,242	11,870,392	10,176,316	9,096,669	7,213,619	6,427,781	5,252,032
Total Deposits	11,986,915	10,937,063	9,839,698	8,131,202	7,408,670	5,669,409	4,887,402	4,228,348
Total Liabilities	12,856,616	11,772,942	10,760,433	9,285,739	8,353,021	6,641,973	5,865,978	4,743,362
Stockholders' Equity	1,348,535	1,219,256	1,109,959	890,577	743,648	571,646	561,803	508,670
Shares Outstanding	49,546	49,204	48,983	48,149	47,629	45,456	46,007	46,137
Statistical Record								
Return on Assets %	1.51	1.50	1.66	1.52	1.61	1.58	1.65	1.69
Return on Equity %	16.03	16.03	18.31	17.89	19.97	19.08	17.98	17.62
Net Interest Margin %	90.33	89.39	84.51	69.44	62.90	68.45	69.27	70.86
Efficiency Ratio %	50.14	48.37	43.99	41.37	39.00	43.36	42.99	44.18
Loans to Deposits	0.70	0.71	0.80	0.86	0.86	0.94	0.90	0.87
Price Range	70.75-57.93	64.00-39.25	56.14-40.40	49.38-33.91	40.75-25.88	41.63-30.38	41.63-26.56	36.94-20.75
P/E Ratio	17.51-14.34	17.20-10.55	15.77-11.35	16.68-11.46	14.98-9.51	18.10-13.21	20.81-13.28	21.99-12.35
Average Yield %	2.00	1.96	1.57	1.80	1.99	1.87	1.56	1.65

Address: City National Center, 400 North Roxbury Drive, Beverly Hills, CA 90210 **Telephone:** (310) 888-6000 **Fax:** (310) 888-6045	**Web Site:** www.cnb.com **Officers:** Bram Goldsmith - Chmn. Russell D. Goldsmith - Vice-Chmn., C.E.O.	**Auditors:** KPMG LLP **Investor Contact:** 310-888-6700 **Transfer Agents:** Continental Stock Transfer & Trust Co.

CLAIRE'S STORES, INC.

Exchange	Symbol	Price	52Wk Range	Yield	P/E
NYS	CLE	$23.04 (3/31/2005)	27.05-18.75	1.74	N/A

*7 Year Price Score 149.05 *NYSE Composite Index=100   *12 Month Price Score 93.36

TRADING VOLUME (thousand shares)

Interim Earnings (Per Share)

Qtr.	Apr	Jul	Oct	Jan
2003-04	0.16	0.23	0.26	0.53
2004-05	0.28	0.33	0.27	...

Interim Dividends (Per Share)

Amt	Decl	Ex	Rec	Pay
0.07Q	5/20/2004	6/4/2004	6/8/2004	6/18/2004
0.08Q	8/19/2004	9/2/2004	9/7/2004	9/17/2004
0.09Q	11/18/2004	12/3/2004	12/7/2004	12/17/2004
0.10Q	3/3/2005	3/10/2005	3/14/2005	3/24/2005
			Indicated Div: $0.40	

Valuation Analysis

Forecast P/E	14.20	No of Institutions
	(4/7/2005)	212
Market Cap	$2.3 Billion	Shares
Book Value	706.5 Million	80,346,208
Price/Book	3.23	% Held
Price/Sales	N/A	81.18

Business Summary: Retail - Apparel and Accessory Stores (MIC: 5.8 SIC: 632 NAIC: 48150)

Claire's Stores is a mall-based retailer of fashion accessories, including costume jewelry, hair ornaments and earrings, and apparel for pre-teens and teenagers, as well as young adults. Co.'s merchandise typically ranges in price between $2.00 and $20.00, with the average product priced at about $5.00. At Mar 31 2004, Co. operated 2,953 stores in all 50 states of the U.S., Puerto Rico, Canada, the Virgin Islands, the United Kingdom, Switzerland, Austria, Germany, France, Ireland and Japan. Co.'s stores operate primarily under the trade names Claire's Boutiques, Claire's Accessories, Icing by Claire's, Afterthoughts and The Icing.

Recent Developments: For the quarter ended Oct 30 2004, net income increased 7.5% to $27,158 thousand from net income of $25,253 thousand in the year-earlier quarter. Revenues were $296,702 thousand, up 12.3% from $264,146 thousand the year before. Total indirect expense was $117,177 thousand versus $104,059 thousand in the prior-year quarter, an increase of 12.6%.

Prospects: Co. views its fiscal-year 2006 as the starting point for its efforts to aggressively build the Claire's brand internationally. Co. noted that beyond expanding where it already owns stores, it will be opening company owned stores in at least two new countries over the latter half of fiscal 2006. Indeed, Co. stated that it sees significant opportunities in these markets and is already working to secure locations meeting its criteria. In addition, Co. noted that Claire's stores operated by its licensing partners in the Middle East and South Africa have been performing particularly well. Thus, Co. will accelerate new store openings in their respective territories in fiscal 2006.

Financial Data

(US$ in Thousands)	9 Mos	3 Mos	01/31/2004	02/01/2003	02/02/2002	02/03/2001	01/29/2000	01/30/1999
Earnings Per Share	...	1.29	1.17	0.80	0.20	0.65	0.85	0.61
Cash Flow Per Share	...	2.13	2.09	1.72	1.04	1.04	1.02	0.85
Tang Book Value Per Share	4.60	4.11	3.95	2.81	2.17	2.01	1.83	3.00
Dividends Per Share	0.270	0.180	0.140	0.080	0.080	0.060	0.080	0.075
Dividend Payout %	...	13.93	11.97	10.06	40.00	9.23	9.36	12.30
Income Statement								
Total Revenue	883,516	281,591	1,132,834	1,001,537	918,737	1,060,417	846,898	661,856
EBITDA	167,946	53,289	217,084	158,746	107,527	144,397	167,636	135,614
Depn & Amortn	33,879	10,946	42,662	38,623	42,931	44,149	28,841	21,878
Income Before Taxes	134,067	42,343	174,422	120,123	64,596	100,248	138,795	113,736
Income Taxes	46,468	14,651	59,384	42,144	23,470	35,273	50,860	42,084
Net Income	87,599	27,692	115,038	77,744	19,583	64,975	87,935	62,280
Average Shares	99,384	99,241	98,440	97,782	97,502	100,202	102,668	102,216
Balance Sheet								
Current Assets	427,731	377,372	360,023	321,608	214,424	259,779	290,018	239,618
Total Assets	895,924	825,287	805,924	728,527	611,575	668,534	702,099	394,272
Current Liabilities	153,112	144,962	143,326	141,010	82,536	100,097	96,855	69,091
Long-Term Obligations	...	...	...	70,000	110,104	151,374	192,000	...
Total Liabilities	189,453	175,964	173,474	227,273	207,387	268,834	303,313	80,054
Stockholders' Equity	706,471	649,323	632,450	501,254	404,188	399,700	398,786	314,218
Shares Outstanding	98,974	98,917	98,915	97,678	97,341	97,333	102,265	101,611
Statistical Record								
Return on Assets %	...	16.36	15.04	11.63	3.07	9.33	16.09	17.83
Return on Equity %	...	21.85	20.35	17.22	4.89	16.01	24.73	22.08
EBITDA Margin %	19.01	18.92	19.16	15.85	11.70	13.62	19.79	20.49
Net Margin %	9.91	9.83	10.15	7.76	2.13	6.13	10.38	9.41
Asset Turnover	...	1.51	1.48	1.50	1.44	1.52	1.55	1.89
Current Ratio	2.79	2.60	2.51	2.28	2.60	2.60	2.99	3.47
Debt to Equity	...	...	...	0.14	0.27	0.38	0.48	...
Price Range	26.25-18.06	23.20-12.68	23.20-10.56	13.15-8.22	11.32-5.84	12.38-7.91	16.56-7.50	11.88-7.50
P/E Ratio	...	17.98-9.83	19.83-9.03	16.44-10.28	56.63-29.22	19.04-12.16	19.49-8.82	19.47-12.30
Average Yield %	1.25	1.01	0.89	0.75	0.96	0.62	0.67	0.77

Address: 3 S.W. 129th Avenue, Pembroke Pines, FL 33027
Telephone: (954) 433-3900
Fax: (954) 433-3999

Web Site: www.clairestores.com
Officers: Marla Schaefer - Co-Chmn., Co-C.E.O. E. Bonnie Schaefer - Co-Chmn., Co-C.E.O.

Auditors: KPMG LLP
Investor Contact: 212-594-3127

CLARCOR INC.

Exchange	Symbol	Price	52Wk Range	Yield	P/E	Div Acheiver
NYS	CLC	$51.96 (3/31/2005)	56.00-40.99	0.98	20.62	24 Years

*7 Year Price Score 141.01 *NYSE Composite Index=100 *12 Month Price Score 104.20

Interim Earnings (Per Share)

Qtr.	Feb	May	Aug	Nov
2002	0.32	0.42	0.48	0.63
2003	0.38	0.51	0.56	0.69
2004	0.45	0.58	0.61	0.83
2005	0.50	...	...	...

Interim Dividends (Per Share)

Amt	Decl	Ex	Rec	Pay
0.128Q	9/20/2004	10/13/2004	10/15/2004	10/29/2004
0.128Q	12/13/2004	1/12/2005	1/14/2005	1/28/2005
0.128Q	3/21/2005	4/13/2005	4/15/2005	4/29/2005
2-for-1	3/21/2005	5/2/2005	4/15/2005	4/29/2005

Indicated Div: $0.51 (Div. Reinv. Plan)

Valuation Analysis

Forecast P/E	19.76	No of Institutions	
	(4/13/2005)	171	
Market Cap	$1.3 Billion	Shares	
Book Value	443.1 Million	20,386,556	
Price/Book	3.02	% Held	
Price/Sales	1.65	79.14	

Business Summary: Automotive (MIC: 15.1 SIC: 714 NAIC: 36399)

Clarcor manufactures filtration products and consumer and industrial packaging products. The Engine/Mobile Filtration segment includes filters for oil, air, fuel, coolants and hydraulic fluids for trucks, automobiles, construction, mining and industrial equipment, locomotives, marine and agricultural equipment. The Industrial/Environmental Filtration segment produces air and antimicrobial treated filters and high efficiency electronic air cleaners, specialty filters, industrial process liquid filters, pharmaceutical process and beverage filters, filtration systems, bilge separators and sand control filters. The Packaging segment includes a variety of containers and packaging items.

Recent Developments: For the quarter ended Feb 26 2005, net income increased 12.8% to $13,154 thousand from net income of $11,661 thousand in the year-earlier period. Revenues were $196,261 thousand, up 11.9% from $175,275 thousand the year before. Operating income was $21,080 thousand versus an income of $17,813 thousand in the prior-year quarter, an increase of 18.3%. Total direct expense was $139,242 thousand versus $123,788 thousand the year before, an increase of 12.4%. Total indirect expense was $35,939 thousand versus $33,671 thousand in the prior-year period, an increase of 6.7%.

Prospects: Operating margins reflect Co.'s ongoing efforts to improve the cost structure and manufacturing efficiencies of its Industrial/Environmental companies, placing it closer to its 2005 goal of a 10.0% annual operating margin for its Industrial/Environmental segment. Meanwhile, Co. expects capital expenditures for 2005 in the range of $25.0 to $30.0 million. Capital spending will be slated for the development of new products, including the development of new filter media, investing to expand the capabilities of its filtration research and technical centers and the completion of a new aviation fuel test facility in Greensboro, NC.

Financial Data
(US$ in Thousands)

	3 Mos	11/30/2004	11/30/2003	11/30/2002	11/30/2001	11/30/2000	11/27/1999	11/28/1998
Earnings Per Share	2.52	2.48	2.15	1.85	1.68	1.64	1.46	1.30
Cash Flow Per Share	2.76	2.91	3.50	3.42	2.58	2.21	1.62	1.75
Tang Book Value Per Share	11.47	10.96	9.80	7.74	6.40	5.75	4.98	6.90
Dividends Per Share	0.505	0.502	0.492	0.482	0.472	0.463	0.453	0.443
Dividend Payout %	20.00	20.26	22.91	26.08	28.13	28.20	30.99	34.04
Income Statement								
Total Revenue	196,261	787,686	741,358	715,563	666,964	652,148	477,869	426,773
EBITDA	26,326	118,272	106,576	96,822	97,200	95,402	73,269	64,780
Depn & Amortn	5,529	19,151	18,985	19,760	21,850	21,079	15,372	12,380
Income Before Taxes	20,768	99,060	86,059	71,450	65,734	63,487	55,615	51,347
Income Taxes	7,536	34,717	31,371	24,773	23,804	23,201	20,137	19,262
Net Income	13,154	63,997	54,552	46,601	41,893	40,237	35,412	32,079
Average Shares	26,160	25,753	25,372	25,171	24,892	24,506	24,313	24,648
Balance Sheet								
Current Assets	298,859	303,990	257,402	259,746	244,350	230,479	227,670	168,173
Total Assets	621,000	627,797	538,237	546,119	530,617	501,930	472,991	305,766
Current Liabilities	111,078	126,272	111,373	174,255	94,931	97,826	97,475	61,183
Long-Term Obligations	16,042	24,130	16,913	22,648	135,203	141,486	145,981	36,419
Total Liabilities	177,936	199,335	167,845	230,658	256,356	259,837	262,273	118,959
Stockholders' Equity	443,064	428,462	370,392	315,461	274,261	242,093	210,718	186,807
Shares Outstanding	25,759	25,611	25,309	24,918	24,626	24,381	24,019	23,949
Statistical Record								
Return on Assets %	11.22	10.95	10.06	8.66	8.11	8.16	9.12	10.94
Return on Equity %	15.91	15.98	15.91	15.80	16.23	17.58	17.87	17.97
EBITDA Margin %	13.41	15.02	14.38	13.53	14.57	14.63	15.33	15.18
Net Margin %	6.70	8.12	7.36	6.51	6.28	6.17	7.41	7.52
Asset Turnover	1.39	1.35	1.37	1.33	1.29	1.32	1.23	1.45
Current Ratio	2.69	2.41	2.31	1.49	2.57	2.36	2.34	2.75
Debt to Equity	0.04	0.06	0.05	0.07	0.49	0.58	0.69	0.19
Price Range	56.00-40.85	52.52-40.85	45.90-31.05	34.00-25.64	27.60-17.13	21.38-16.69	21.25-15.31	24.33-14.50
P/E Ratio	22.22-16.21	21.18-16.47	21.35-14.44	18.38-13.86	16.43-10.19	13.03-10.18	14.55-10.49	18.72-11.15
Average Yield %	1.07	1.12	1.31	1.61	1.94	2.47	2.45	2.29

Address: 840 Crescent Centre Drive, Suite 600, Franklin, TN 37067	Web Site: www.clarcor.com	Auditors: PricewaterhouseCoopers LLP
Telephone: (615) 771-3100	Officers: Norman E. Johnson - Chmn., Pres., C.E.O. William B. Walker - Vice-Chmn.	Transfer Agents: First Chicago Trust Company of New York, Jersey City, NJ

CLEAR CHANNEL COMMUNICATIONS, INC.

Exchange	Symbol	Price	52Wk Range	Yield	P/E
NYS	CCU	$34.47 (3/31/2005)	44.04-30.27	1.45	N/A

*7 Year Price Score 59.28   *NYSE Composite Index=100   *12 Month Price Score 88.75

Interim Earnings (Per Share)

Qtr.	Mar	Jun	Sep	Dec
2001	(0.53)	(0.40)	(0.39)	(0.61)
2002	(27.85)	0.39	0.34	0.33
2003	0.12	0.41	1.03	0.30
2004	0.19	0.41	0.44	(7.79)

Interim Dividends (Per Share)

Amt	Decl	Ex	Rec	Pay
0.10Q	4/28/2004	6/28/2004	6/30/2004	7/15/2004
0.125Q	7/21/2004	9/28/2004	9/30/2004	10/15/2004
0.125Q	10/20/2004	12/29/2004	12/31/2004	1/15/2005
0.125Q	2/16/2005	3/29/2005	3/31/2005	4/15/2005

Indicated Div: $0.50

Valuation Analysis

Forecast P/E	23.40		No of Institutions
	(4/7/2005)		406
Market Cap	$19.6 Billion		Shares
Book Value	9.5 Billion		435,270,816
Price/Book	2.06		% Held
Price/Sales	2.08		77.63

Business Summary: Advertising, Marketing & PR (MIC: 12.4 SIC: 313 NAIC: 41840)

Clear Channel Communications is a diversified media company with three reportable business segments. Co.'s radio broadcasting business included about 1,182 radio stations in the U.S. and equity interests in various international radio stations as of Dec 31 2003. Co.'s outdoor advertising segment included about 145,895 domestic and 641,680 international outdoor advertising displays, including billboards, street furniture and transit panels. Co.'s live entertainment business includes the operation, promotion, production and venue operation of live entertainment events. As of Dec 31 2003, Co. owned or operated 74 venues domestically and 29 venues internationally.

Recent Developments: For the year ended Dec 31 2004, net loss was $4,038,169,000 versus net income of $1,145,591,000 a year earlier. Revenues were $9,418,459,000, up 5.5% from $8,930,899,000 the year before. Operating income was $1,674,430,000 versus an income of $1,591,533,000 in the prior year, an increase of 5.2%. Total direct expense was $6,850,426,000 versus $6,488,856,000 in the prior year, an increase of 5.6%. Total indirect expense was $893,603,000 versus $850,510,000 in the prior year, an increase of 5.1%.

Prospects: Co. is beginning to experience growth in national advertising stemming from an increase in political advertising, as well as strength in consumer products, professional services and automotive advertisements. On Dec 15 2004, Co. announced that it will reduce commercial minutes on its stations by an average of 20.0% and begin selling more 30-second advertisements instead of the traditional 60-second spots in an effort to improve the quality of its radio programming. Co. noted that it is attracting new advertisers who have never used radio before, and consumers are reacting positively to the initiative to cut interruptions and shorten commercial lengths.

Financial Data
(US$ in Thousands)

	12/31/2004	12/31/2003	12/31/2002	12/31/2001	12/31/2000	12/31/1999	12/31/1998	12/31/1997
Earnings Per Share	(6.75)	1.85	(25.56)	(1.93)	0.57	0.22	0.22	0.34
Cash Flow Per Share	3.04	2.73	2.88	1.03	1.78	2.05	1.15	0.93
Tang Book Value Per Share	N.M.	N.M.	N.M.	N.M.	N.M.	N.M.	N.M.	N.M.
Dividends Per Share	0.450	0.200	...	...	...	...	0.35	N.M.
Dividend Payout %	...	10.81	...	...	...	...	...	...
Income Statement								
Total Revenue	9,418,459	8,930,899	8,421,055	7,970,003	5,345,306	2,678,160	1,350,940	697,068
EBITDA	2,425,946	2,984,745	2,271,731	1,873,560	2,497,706	1,129,364	556,025	293,360
Depn & Amortn	694,001	671,381	620,756	2,562,480	1,401,063	722,233	304,972	114,207
Income Before Taxes	1,364,192	1,925,364	1,218,189	(1,248,997)	713,539	220,213	117,922	104,077
Income Taxes	518,393	779,773	493,366	(104,971)	464,731	150,635	72,353	47,116
Net Income	(4,038,169)	1,145,591	(16,053,703)	(1,144,026)	248,808	72,470	54,031	63,576
Average Shares	598,275	620,770	627,440	591,965	438,711	324,408	249,123	183,030
Balance Sheet								
Current Assets	2,269,922	2,185,682	2,123,495	1,941,299	2,343,217	925,109	409,960	198,647
Total Assets	19,927,949	28,352,693	27,672,153	47,603,142	50,056,461	16,821,512	7,539,918	3,455,637
Current Liabilities	2,184,552	1,892,719	3,010,639	2,959,857	2,128,550	685,515	258,144	86,852
Long-Term Obligations	6,962,560	6,921,348	7,382,090	7,967,713	10,100,028	4,093,543	2,323,643	1,540,421
Total Liabilities	10,439,871	12,798,754	13,462,061	17,867,079	19,709,288	6,246,666	3,056,489	1,708,853
Stockholders' Equity	9,488,078	15,553,939	14,210,092	29,736,063	30,347,173	10,084,037	4,483,429	1,746,784
Shares Outstanding	567,264	615,893	613,100	597,990	585,650	338,609	263,698	196,389
Statistical Record								
Return on Assets %	N.M.	4.09	N.M.	N.M.	0.74	0.59	0.98	2.66
Return on Equity %	N.M.	7.70	N.M.	N.M.	1.23	0.99	1.73	5.63
EBITDA Margin %	25.76	33.42	26.98	23.51	46.73	42.17	41.16	42.08
Net Margin %	N.M.	12.83	N.M.	N.M.	4.65	2.71	4.00	9.12
Asset Turnover	0.39	0.32	0.22	0.16	0.16	0.22	0.25	0.29
Current Ratio	1.04	1.15	0.71	0.66	1.10	1.35	1.59	2.29
Debt to Equity	0.73	0.44	0.52	0.27	0.33	0.41	0.52	0.88
Price Range	47.37-30.27	47.00-32.35	53.98-22.62	67.00-36.80	95.38-45.75	90.25-53.13	61.75-36.13	39.72-17.13
P/E Ratio	...	25.41-17.49	...	...	167.32-80.26	410.23-241.48	280.68-164.20	116.82-50.37
Average Yield %	1.18	0.50	...	...	...	...	...	...

Address: 200 East Basse Road, San Antonio, TX 78209	Web Site: www.clearchannel.com	Auditors: Ernst & Young LLP
Telephone: (210) 822-2828	Officers: L. Lowry Mays - Chmn., C.E.O. Mark Pitman Mays - Pres., C.O.O.	Investor Contact: 210-822-2828
Fax: (210) 822-2299		

CLOROX CO.

Exchange	Symbol	Price	52Wk Range	Yield	P/E	Div Acheiver
NYS	CLX	$62.99 (3/31/2005)	63.00-48.91	1.78	11.07	28 Years

*7 Year Price Score 103.34 *NYSE Composite Index=100 *12 Month Price Score 102.88

Interim Earnings (Per Share)

Qtr.	Sep	Dec	Mar	Jun
2001-02	0.33	0.22	0.20	0.62
2002-03	0.65	0.40	0.50	0.67
2003-04	0.60	0.51	0.59	0.86
2004-05	0.57	3.68	...	...

Interim Dividends (Per Share)

Amt	Decl	Ex	Rec	Pay
0.27Q	5/19/2004	7/26/2004	7/28/2004	8/13/2004
0.27Q	9/15/2004	10/27/2004	10/29/2004	11/15/2004
0.28Q	11/17/2004	1/27/2005	1/31/2005	2/15/2005
0.28Q	3/16/2005	4/26/2005	4/28/2005	5/13/2005
		Indicated Div: $1.12 (Div. Reinv. Plan)		

Valuation Analysis

Forecast P/E	19.77	No of Institutions	
	(4/7/2005)	412	
Market Cap	$9.7 Billion	Shares	
Book Value	N/A	110,067,144	
Price/Book	N/A	% Held	
Price/Sales	2.19	71.76	

Business Summary: Chemicals (MIC: 11.1 SIC: 842 NAIC: 25612)

Clorox is engaged in the production and marketing of consumer products sold primarily through grocery, mass merchandise, club and other retail stores. Co. has three business segments: Household Products-North America, Specialty Products, and Household Products-Latin America/Other. Co.'s principal products include plastic bags, wraps and containers, home care cleaning products such as disinfecting sprays and wipes, toilet bowl cleaners, dilutable, spray and gel household cleaners, glass and surface cleaners, carpet cleaners, reusable cleaning cloths, drain openers and septic-system treatments, steel-wool soap pads and scrubber sponges, mildew removers, and soap scum and bathroom cleaners.

Recent Developments: For the quarter ended Dec 31 2004, income from continuing operations increased 34.7% to $136,000 thousand from income of $101,000 thousand in the year-earlier quarter. Net income increased 541.3% to $699,000 thousand from net income of $109,000 thousand in the year-earlier quarter. Revenues were $1,000,000 thousand, up 8.7% from $920,000 thousand the year before. Total direct expense was $569,000 thousand versus $527,000 thousand in the prior-year quarter, an increase of 8.0%. Total indirect expense was $249,000 thousand versus $234,000 thousand in the prior-year quarter, an increase of 6.4%.

Prospects: Results are benefiting from strong sales across nearly all of Co.'s business segments, most notably home care, Glad® trash bags, and the Latin America division. Meanwhile, top-line growth is being positively affected by strong shipments of new products, including Co.'s new Clorox ToiletWand disposable toilet cleaning system, and recent price increases on Glad trash bags and GladWare containers. Co. is considering raising prices on more products to help offset higher commodity costs. Looking ahead, Co. is targeting full fiscal-2005 sales growth in the range of 3.0% to 5.0%, along with earnings from continuing operations of between $2.70 and $2.80 per diluted share.

Financial Data

(US$ in Thousands)	6 Mos	3 Mos	06/30/2004	06/30/2003	06/30/2002	06/30/2001	06/30/2000	06/30/1999
Earnings Per Share	5.69	2.52	2.56	2.23	1.37	1.35	1.64	1.03
Cash Flow Per Share	5.20	4.57	4.24	3.68	3.78	3.16	2.78	2.50
Tang Book Value Per Share	...	1.43	0.77	N.M.	0.24	1.38	1.10	0.31
Dividends Per Share	1.080	1.080	1.080	0.880	0.840	0.840	0.800	0.720
Dividend Payout %	18.97	42.78	42.19	39.46	61.31	62.22	48.78	69.90
Income Statement								
Total Revenue	2,048,000	1,090,000	4,324,000	4,144,000	4,061,000	3,903,000	4,083,000	4,003,000
EBITDA	455,000	236,000	1,028,000	965,000	668,000	639,000	776,000	574,000
Depn & Amortn	94,000	47,000	162,000	138,000	135,000	74,000	66,000	54,000
Income Before Taxes	361,000	189,000	840,000	802,000	498,000	487,000	622,000	430,000
Income Taxes	116,000	66,000	294,000	288,000	176,000	162,000	228,000	184,000
Net Income	822,000	123,000	549,000	493,000	322,000	323,000	394,000	246,000
Average Shares	189,806	215,117	214,371	220,692	234,704	239,483	239,614	240,002
Balance Sheet								
Current Assets	1,047,000	1,130,000	1,043,000	951,000	1,002,000	1,103,000	1,454,000	1,116,000
Total Assets	3,710,000	3,772,000	3,834,000	3,652,000	3,630,000	3,995,000	4,353,000	4,132,000
Current Liabilities	1,469,000	1,095,000	1,268,000	1,451,000	1,225,000	1,069,000	1,541,000	1,368,000
Long-Term Obligations	2,124,000	474,000	475,000	495,000	678,000	685,000	590,000	702,000
Total Liabilities	4,167,000	2,128,000	2,294,000	2,437,000	2,276,000	2,095,000	2,559,000	2,562,000
Stockholders' Equity	(457,000)	1,644,000	1,540,000	1,215,000	1,354,000	1,900,000	1,794,000	1,570,000
Shares Outstanding	153,385	213,376	212,988	213,676	223,009	236,691	235,361	235,311
Statistical Record								
Return on Assets %	30.97	14.78	14.63	13.54	8.45	7.74	9.26	6.87
Return on Equity %	310.88	38.69	39.75	38.38	19.79	17.49	23.36	18.53
EBITDA Margin %	22.22	21.65	23.77	23.29	16.45	16.37	19.01	14.34
Net Margin %	40.14	11.28	12.70	11.90	7.93	8.28	9.65	6.15
Asset Turnover	1.21	1.19	1.15	1.14	1.07	0.94	0.96	1.12
Current Ratio	0.71	1.03	0.82	0.66	0.82	1.03	0.94	0.82
Debt to Equity	...	0.29	0.31	0.41	0.50	0.36	0.33	0.45
Price Range	59.16-46.83	54.68-45.20	53.95-42.00	48.24-32.18	47.62-34.64	47.94-30.06	56.97-29.88	66.16-39.75
P/E Ratio	10.40-8.23	21.70-17.94	21.07-16.41	21.63-14.43	34.76-25.28	35.51-22.27	34.74-18.22	64.23-38.59
Average Yield %	2.07	2.16	2.26	2.07	2.07		1.83	1.33

Address: 1221 Broadway, Oakland, CA 94612-1888	Web Site: www.clorox.com	Auditors: Ernst & Young LLP
Telephone: (510) 271-7000	Officers: R. W. Matschullat - Chmn. G. E. Johnston - Pres., C.E.O.	Transfer Agents: EquiServe Trust Company N.A., Providence, RI
Fax: (510) 832-1463		

CMS ENERGY CORP

Exchange	Symbol	Price	52Wk Range	Yield	P/E
NYS	CMS	$13.04 (3/31/2005)	13.38-7.90	N/A	20.38

*7 Year Price Score 37.28   *NYSE Composite Index=100   *12 Month Price Score 116.99

Interim Earnings (Per Share)

Qtr.	Mar	Jun	Sep	Dec
2001	0.85	0.40	(4.29)	(1.04)
2002	2.92	(0.56)	0.16	(6.88)
2003	0.51	(0.31)	(0.51)	(0.01)
2004	(0.07)	0.10	0.34	0.24

Interim Dividends (Per Share)

Dividend Payment Suspended

Valuation Analysis

Forecast P/E	15.29	No of Institutions	
	(4/7/2005)	236	
Market Cap	$2.5 Billion	Shares	
Book Value	2.4 Billion	153,305,696	
Price/Book	1.07	% Held	
Price/Sales	0.46	78.43	

TRADING VOLUME (thousand shares)

Business Summary: Electricity (MIC: 7.1 SIC: 931 NAIC: 21119)

CMS Energy is the holding company for Consumers Energy and CMS Enterprises. Co. operates in three reportable segments: electric utility, gas utility and enterprises. Consumers Energy provides regulated natural gas transportation, storage and distribution and electricity generation and distribution in the state of Michigan. Consumers Energy had approximately 1.8 million electric customers and 1.7 million gas customers as of Dec 31 2003. CMS Enterprises invests in, acquires, develops, constructs, manages, and operates non-utility power generation plants and natural gas facilities in the U.S. and select international markets, and also provides gas, oil and electric marketing services.

Recent Developments: For the year ended Dec 31 2004, income from continuing operations was $127 million compared with a loss of $42 million a year earlier. Net income was $121 million versus net loss of $43 million a year earlier. Revenues were $5,472 million, down 0.7% from $5,513 million the year before. Operating income was $593 million versus an income of $595 million in the prior year, a decrease of 0.3%. Total direct expense was $4,133 million versus $4,368 million in the prior year, a decrease of 5.4%. Total indirect expense was $861 million versus $714 million in the prior year, an increase of 20.6%.

Prospects: Co. has provided full-year 2005 reported earnings guidance of between $0.84 and $0.89 per share. Co. noted that its fourth quarter 2004 earnings included a benefit of $21.0 million, or $0.12 per share, as a result of a planned repatriation of $80.0 million from CMS Energy's foreign subsidiaries in 2005 and resulting lower deferred taxes due to the tax provisions of the American Jobs Creation Act. Co. anticipates that its foreign subsidiaries will repatriate additional cash in 2005 that will result in tax benefits in 2005. Co. stated that these benefits are included in its 2005 guidance and do not recur beyond 2005. Co. intends to invest the repatriated cash in its utility, Consumers Energy.

Financial Data

(US$ in Thousands)	12/31/2004	12/31/2003	12/31/2002	12/31/2001	12/31/2000	12/31/1999	12/31/1998	12/31/1997
Earnings Per Share	0.64	(0.30)	(4.46)	(4.17)	0.32	2.17	2.62	2.61
Cash Flow Per Share	2.35	(1.67)	2.90	3.19	3.99	8.33	5.04	6.84
Tang Book Value Per Share	10.51	9.68	7.86	8.31	12.13	13.49	19.19	19.59
Dividends Per Share	...	...	1.090	1.460	1.460	1.390	1.260	1.140
Dividend Payout %	...	...	...	...	456.25	64.06	48.09	43.68
Income Statement								
Total Revenue	5,472,000	5,513,000	8,687,000	9,597,000	8,998,000	6,103,000	5,141,000	4,787,000
EBITDA	1,210,000	1,083,000	528,000	921,000	1,365,000	1,490,000	1,213,000	1,212,000
Depn & Amortn	459,000	487,000	515,000	729,000	671,000	630,000	535,000	521,000
Income Before Taxes	122,000	15,000	(403,000)	(401,000)	104,000	341,000	342,000	385,000
Income Taxes	(5,000)	58,000	13,000	(73,000)	60,000	64,000	100,000	117,000
Net Income	121,000	(44,000)	(620,000)	(545,000)	36,000	277,000	285,000	268,000
Average Shares	172,100	150,400	139,000	130,800	113,100	114,700	107,200	98,700
Balance Sheet								
Net PPE	8,636,000	6,944,000	5,234,000	8,362,000	7,835,000	8,121,000	6,040,000	5,435,000
Total Assets	15,872,000	13,838,000	13,915,000	17,102,000	15,851,000	15,462,000	11,310,000	9,793,000
Long-Term Obligations	7,263,000	6,762,000	5,472,000	6,983,000	7,518,000	7,799,000	5,004,000	3,520,000
Total Liabilities	13,495,000	11,948,000	12,738,000	15,168,000	13,446,000	12,962,000	8,856,000	7,578,000
Stockholders' Equity	2,377,000	1,890,000	1,177,000	1,960,000	2,405,000	2,500,000	2,312,000	2,215,000
Shares Outstanding	194,997	161,100	144,100	132,989	121,201	116,038	108,104	100,900
Statistical Record								
Return on Assets %	0.81	N.M.	N.M.	N.M.	0.23	2.07	2.70	2.91
Return on Equity %	5.66	N.M.	N.M.	N.M.	1.46	11.51	12.59	12.54
EBITDA Margin %	22.11	19.64	6.08	9.60	15.17	24.41	23.59	25.32
Net Margin %	2.21	(0.80)	(7.14)	(5.68)	0.40	4.54	5.54	5.60
PPE Turnover	0.70	0.91	1.28	1.19	1.12	0.86	0.90	0.89
Asset Turnover	0.37	0.40	0.56	0.58	0.57	0.46	0.49	0.52
Debt to Equity	3.06	3.58	4.65	3.56	3.13	3.12	2.16	1.59
Price Range	10.53-7.90	10.59-3.49	24.62-5.79	31.75-19.89	31.69-16.44	48.44-30.50	49.94-39.00	44.06-31.63
P/E Ratio	16.45-12.34	...	...	...	99.02-51.37	22.32-14.06	19.06-14.89	16.88-12.12
Average Yield %	...	...	7.49	5.53	5.99	3.52	2.84	3.23

Address: One Energy Plaza, Jackson, MI 49201 **Telephone:** (517) 788-0550	**Web Site:** www.cmsenergy.com **Officers:** Kenneth Whipple - Chmn. S. Kinnie Smith Jr. - Vice-Chmn., Gen. Couns.	**Auditors:** Ernst & Young LLP **Investor Contact:** 517-788-1868

CNA FINANCIAL CORP.

Exchange	Symbol	Price	52Wk Range	Yield	P/E
NYS	CNA	$28.06 (3/31/2005)	30.49-22.17	N/A	19.09

*7 Year Price Score 72.26 *NYSE Composite Index=100 *12 Month Price Score 98.30

Interim Earnings (Per Share)

Qtr.	Mar	Jun	Sep	Dec
2001	1.61	(9.61)	(0.84)	0.33
2002	0.35	0.16	0.24	0.19
2003	0.30	0.25	(7.94)	0.81
2004	(0.55)	1.07	(0.17)	1.12

Interim Dividends (Per Share)

No Dividends Paid

Valuation Analysis

Forecast P/E	9.99	No of Institutions
	(4/7/2005)	117
Market Cap	$7.2 Billion	Shares
Book Value	9.2 Billion	254,533,728
Price/Book	0.78	% Held
Price/Sales	0.72	99.45

Business Summary: Insurance (MIC: 8.2 SIC: 331 NAIC: 24126)

CNA Financial is the nation's fourth largest commercial insurance writer and 11th largest property and casualty company, as of Dec 31 2003. Co. serves a wide variety of customers, including small, medium and large businesses; insurance companies; associations; professionals; and groups and individuals. Co.'s insurance products include property and casualty coverages; life, accident and health insurance; and retirement products and annuities. Co.'s services include risk management, information services, and claims administration. Co.'s products and services are marketed through independent agents, brokers, managing general agents and direct sales.

Recent Developments: For the year ended Dec 31 2004, net income was $441,000 thousand versus net loss of $1,433,000 thousand a year earlier. Revenues were $9,930,000 thousand, down 15.2% from $11,716,000 thousand the year before. Net premiums earned were $8,209,000 thousand versus $9,214,000 thousand in the prior year, a decrease of 10.9%. Net investment income rose 1.6% to $1,674,000 thousand from $1,647,000 thousand a year ago.

Prospects: After shedding non-core businesses and strengthening its balance sheet, Co. is turning its focus to growing its property and casualty operations. The transition is increasingly evident as operating results are benefiting from improved underwriting performance in the area of property and casualty. Also, Co. is seeing an improvement in net realized investment results largely due to higher investment gains from the fixed maturity securities portfolio. Operating results in the coming year should also benefit from the absence of losses on the sales of the Co.'s former Individual Life Insurance and Group Benefits businesses.

Financial Data (US$ in Thousands)	12/31/2004	12/31/2003	12/31/2002	12/31/2001	12/31/2000	12/31/1999	12/31/1998	12/31/1997
Earnings Per Share	1.47	(6.58)	0.68	(8.48)	6.61	(0.77)	1.49	5.17
Cash Flow Per Share	6.26	7.75	4.65	(3.09)	(7.46)	(14.35)	(5.13)	(1.04)
Tang Book Value Per Share	32.41	32.60	37.91	36.23	50.91	45.88	45.89	40.66
Income Statement								
Premium Income	8,209,000	9,214,000	10,213,000	9,365,000	11,474,000	13,282,000	13,375,000	13,362,000
Total Revenue	9,930,000	11,716,000	12,286,000	13,203,000	15,614,000	16,403,000	17,074,000	17,072,000
Benefits & Claims	6,446,000	9,916,000	8,392,000	11,383,000	9,831,000	11,900,000	11,717,000	11,268,000
Income Before Taxes	497,000	(2,352,000)	341,000	(2,305,000)	1,810,000	(11,000)	349,000	1,358,000
Income Taxes	29,000	(913,000)	68,000	(743,000)	568,000	(88,000)	47,000	392,000
Net Income	441,000	(1,433,000)	155,000	(1,644,000)	1,214,000	(130,000)	282,000	966,000
Average Shares	256,000	227,000	223,600	194,000	183,600	184,200	184,900	185,400
Balance Sheet								
Total Assets	62,500,000	68,503,000	61,731,000	65,968,000	62,068,000	61,219,000	62,432,000	61,269,000
Total Liabilities	53,018,000	59,295,000	52,074,000	57,377,000	52,204,000	52,086,000	52,998,000	52,960,000
Stockholders' Equity	9,207,000	8,952,000	9,401,000	8,367,000	9,647,000	8,938,000	9,157,000	8,309,000
Shares Outstanding	255,953	223,617	223,608	223,596	183,263	184,406	183,890	185,394
Statistical Record								
Return on Assets %	0.67	N.M.	0.24	N.M.	1.96	N.M.	0.46	1.59
Return on Equity %	4.84	N.M.	1.74	N.M.	13.03	N.M.	3.23	12.57
Loss Ratio %	78.52	107.62	82.17	121.55	85.68	89.59	87.60	84.33
Net Margin %	4.44	(12.23)	1.26	(12.45)	7.78	(0.79)	1.65	5.66
Price Range	30.49-22.17	26.90-19.00	30.86-22.32	39.90-24.35	41.44-24.75	45.31-33.31	53.17-35.19	43.92-32.29
P/E Ratio	20.74-15.08	...	45.38-32.82	...	6.27-3.74	...	35.68-23.62	8.49-6.25

Address: CNA Plaza, 333 South Wabash Avenue, Chicago, IL 60685 Telephone: (312) 822-5000 Fax: (312) 822-6419	Web Site: www.cna.com Officers: Bernard L. Hengesbaugh - Chmn. Stephen W. Lilienthal - C.E.O.	Auditors: Deloitte & Touche LLP Investor Contact: 312-822-7757

CNF, INC.

Exchange	Symbol	Price	52Wk Range	Yield	P/E
NYS	CNF	$46.79 (3/31/2005)	50.50-33.60	0.85	N/A

*7 Year Price Score 108.15 *NYSE Composite Index=100 *12 Month Price Score 100.81

Interim Earnings (Per Share)

Qtr.	Mar	Jun	Sep	Dec
2001	0.26	(4.67)	0.59	(4.45)
2002	0.35	0.37	0.61	0.41
2003	0.30	0.31	0.46	0.49
2004	0.45	0.64	(3.90)	0.57

Interim Dividends (Per Share)

Amt	Decl	Ex	Rec	Pay
0.10Q	4/26/2004	5/12/2004	5/14/2004	6/15/2004
0.10Q	6/28/2004	8/11/2004	8/13/2004	9/15/2004
0.10Q	9/27/2004	11/10/2004	11/15/2004	12/15/2004
0.10Q	1/24/2005	2/11/2005	2/15/2005	3/15/2005

Indicated Div: $0.40

Valuation Analysis

Forecast P/E	14.32	No of Institutions	
	(4/7/2005)	208	
Market Cap	$2.4 Billion	Shares	
Book Value	777.4 Million	43,045,952	
Price/Book	3.14	% Held	
Price/Sales	0.66	81.62	

Business Summary: Road Transport (MIC: 15.2 SIC: 213 NAIC: 84122)

CNF and its subsidiaries provide supply chain management services for business-to-business shipments by land, air and sea throughout the world. Co.'s principal businesses consist of Con-Way Transportation Services and Menlo Worldwide. Con-Way provides next-day, second-day and transcontinental freight trucking throughout the U.S., Canada, Puerto Rico and Mexico, as well as expedited transportation, air freight forwarding, contract logistics and warehousing, and truckload brokerage services. The Menlo Worldwide group of businesses includes logistics, time-definite domestic and international air freight and ocean forwarding services, customs brokerage, and other trade services.

Recent Developments: For the year ended Dec 31 2004, income from continuing operations increased 24.9% to $150,445 thousand from income of $120,485 thousand a year earlier. Net loss was $115,889 thousand versus net income of $92,024 thousand a year earlier. Revenues were $3,712,379 thousand, up 15.0% from $3,226,966 thousand the year before. Operating income was $284,167 thousand versus an income of $224,948 thousand in the prior year, an increase of 26.3%. Total direct expense was $2,953,665 thousand versus $2,549,467 thousand in the prior year, an increase of 15.9%. Total indirect expense was $474,547 thousand versus $452,551 thousand in the prior year, an increase of 4.9%.

Prospects: Co. is performing well, as cost-cutting and an improving economy helped to bolster the its bottom line. Separately, on Dec 19 2004, Co. completed the sale of its Menlo Worldwide Forwarding business to UPS for $150.0 million in cash, plus the assumption of $110.0 million in debt. This transaction, along with an improved balance sheet and cash flow increases from each of its profitable businesses, should provide additional flexibility for Co. to improve its competitiveness going forward. For the first quarter of 2005, Co. is projecting earnings from continuing operations in the range of $0.57 to $0.65 per diluted share.

Financial Data

(US$ in Thousands)	12/31/2004	12/31/2003	12/31/2002	12/31/2001	12/31/2000	12/31/1999	12/31/1998	12/31/1997
Earnings Per Share	(2.15)	1.57	1.74	(8.26)	2.36	3.35	2.45	2.19
Cash Flow Per Share	7.50	4.49	0.10	6.30	3.35	9.24	5.60	6.23
Tang Book Value Per Share	11.77	7.87	5.71	3.99	12.16	10.03	6.56	4.86
Dividends Per Share	0.400	0.400	0.400	0.400	0.400	0.400	0.400	0.400
Dividend Payout %	...	25.48	22.99	...	16.95	11.94	16.33	18.26
Income Statement								
Total Revenue	3,712,379	5,104,332	4,762,119	4,862,731	5,572,377	5,592,810	4,941,490	4,266,801
EBITDA	404,202	338,524	337,489	(465,142)	489,175	565,413	456,184	391,890
Depn & Amortn	117,684	152,437	167,687	202,799	198,007	202,319	173,146	130,523
Income Before Taxes	246,823	156,016	146,244	(695,933)	261,196	337,122	250,411	221,814
Income Taxes	96,378	63,992	32,035	(262,367)	109,880	146,648	111,433	100,925
Net Income	(115,889)	92,024	101,811	(394,591)	135,064	190,474	138,978	120,889
Average Shares	56,452	56,725	56,655	48,752	55,901	56,019	55,514	53,077
Balance Sheet								
Current Assets	1,514,895	1,316,679	1,268,488	1,327,846	1,240,335	1,200,233	1,100,361	1,009,387
Total Assets	2,496,401	2,749,852	2,739,761	2,990,020	3,244,941	3,049,010	2,689,412	2,421,496
Current Liabilities	712,831	809,595	873,054	883,975	958,909	1,049,154	907,482	806,138
Long-Term Obligations	601,344	536,314	1,004,844	565,815	534,649	433,446	467,635	473,488
Total Liabilities	1,719,034	1,806,044	1,896,763	2,226,933	2,058,019	1,956,062	1,788,057	1,638,393
Stockholders' Equity	777,367	818,808	717,998	638,087	1,061,922	967,948	776,355	658,103
Shares Outstanding	52,179	49,977	49,482	48,890	48,655	48,450	47,875	47,392
Statistical Record								
Return on Assets %	N.M.	3.35	3.55	N.M.	4.28	6.64	5.44	5.37
Return on Equity %	N.M.	11.98	15.02	N.M.	13.27	21.84	19.38	20.73
EBITDA Margin %	10.89	6.63	7.09	N.M.	8.78	10.11	9.23	9.18
Net Margin %	N.M.	1.80	2.14	N.M.	2.42	3.41	2.81	2.83
Asset Turnover	1.41	1.86	1.66	1.56	1.77	1.95	1.93	1.89
Current Ratio	2.13	1.63	1.45	1.50	1.29	1.14	1.21	1.25
Debt to Equity	0.77	0.65	1.40	0.89	0.50	0.45	0.60	0.72
Price Range	50.50-30.50	35.45-24.61	37.98-28.42	36.94-21.61	34.75-20.25	45.50-28.56	48.94-22.19	50.75-21.75
P/E Ratio	...	22.58-15.68	21.83-16.33	...	14.72-8.58	13.58-8.53	19.97-9.06	23.17-9.93
Average Yield %	1.01	1.31	1.23	1.35	1.45	1.03	1.05	1.17

Address: 3240 Hillview Avenue, Palo Alto, CA 94304	**Web Site:** www.cnf.com	**Auditors:** KMPG LLP
Telephone: (650) 494-2900	**Officers:** W. Keith Kennedy Jr. - Chmn. Gregory L. Quesnel - Pres., C.E.O.	**Investor Contact:** 650-813-5353
Fax: (650) 813-0160		

COACH, INC.

Exchange	Symbol	Price	52Wk Range	Yield	P/E
NYS	COH	$28.32 (3/31/2005)	29.75-18.06	N/A	34.11

*7 Year Price Score N/A *NYSE Composite Index=100 *12 Month Price Score 110.90

Interim Earnings (Per Share)

Qtr.	Sep	Dec	Mar	Jun
2001-02	0.04	0.12	0.03	0.04
2002-03	0.06	0.17	0.09	0.08
2003-04	0.11	0.25	0.15	0.17
2004-05	0.17	0.34	...	...

Interim Dividends (Per Share)

Amt	Decl	Ex	Rec	Pay
2-for-1	5/2/2002	7/5/2002	6/19/2002	7/3/2002
2-for-1	8/7/2003	10/2/2003	9/17/2003	10/1/2003
2-for-1	1/25/2005	4/5/2005	3/21/2005	4/4/2005

Valuation Analysis

Forecast P/E	N/A		No of Institutions
Market Cap	$10.8 Billion		Shares
Book Value	987.5 Million		162,399,232
Price/Book	10.95		% Held
Price/Sales	7.18		84.94

TRADING VOLUME (thousand shares)

Business Summary: Leather and Leather Products (MIC: 4.5 SIC: 172 NAIC: 16992)

Coach is a designer, producer and marketer of modern American classic accessories. Co.'s primary product offerings include handbags, women's and men's small leather goods, business cases, weekend and travel accessories, outerwear and related accessories. Together with its licensing partners, Coach also offers watches, footwear, eyewear and office furniture with the Coach brand name. Co.'s products are sold through a number of direct to consumer channels, which at the end of fiscal 2004 included: 174 North American retail stores; 76 North American factory stores; the Internet; and the Coach catalog.

Recent Developments: For the quarter ended Jan 1 2005, net income increased 40.5% to $134,123 thousand from net income of $95,438 thousand in the year-earlier quarter. Revenues were $531,759 thousand, up 29.2% from $411,513 thousand the year before. Operating income was $223,135 thousand versus an income of $160,704 thousand in the year-earlier quarter, an increase of 38.8%. Total direct expense was $128,791 thousand versus $106,370 thousand in the prior-year quarter, an increase of 21.1%. Total indirect expense was $179,833 thousand versus $144,439 thousand in the prior-year quarter, an increase of 24.5%.

Prospects: Co.'s spring season results are trending above plan. As a result, for the third quarter, Co. is targeting at least $400.0 million in sales and earnings per share of $0.43. For the fourth fiscal quarter, Co. is targeting at least $400.0 million in sales and earnings per share of $0.42. Co. continues to project U.S. comparable store sales gains of at least 10.0% in each channel for the second half of fiscal 2005, with sales in Japan rising at least 27.0% in constant currency with at least mid-single-digit same location sales growth. Co. expects full year 2005 sales and diluted earnings per share of over $1.67 billion and at least $1.89, respectively.

Financial Data (US$ in Thousands)	6 Mos	3 Mos	07/03/2004	06/28/2003	06/29/2002	06/30/2001	07/01/2000	07/03/1999
Earnings Per Share	0.83	0.73	0.68	0.40	0.23	0.19	0.14	0.06
Cash Flow Per Share	1.40	1.23	1.19	0.62	0.31	0.38	0.30	0.37
Tang Book Value Per Share	2.52	2.03	2.00	1.11	0.67	0.42	0.76	...
Income Statement								
Total Revenue	875,824	344,065	1,321,106	953,226	719,403	616,079	548,918	507,781
EBITDA	362,286	124,855	487,319	273,993	159,129	125,819	78,645	41,731
Depn & Amortn	27,716	13,420	42,854	30,231	25,494	24,131	22,628	22,256
Income Before Taxes	340,549	113,945	447,657	244,821	133,336	99,430	55,630	19,061
Income Taxes	129,408	43,299	167,866	90,585	47,325	35,400	17,027	2,346
Net Income	201,848	67,725	261,748	146,628	85,827	64,030	38,603	16,715
Average Shares	390,514	389,492	385,558	371,684	363,808	337,248	280,208	280,208
Balance Sheet								
Current Assets	910,878	795,864	705,616	448,538	287,588	151,567	133,688	126,620
Total Assets	1,407,136	1,102,690	1,028,658	617,652	440,571	258,711	296,653	282,088
Current Liabilities	337,983	244,990	181,938	161,461	159,428	104,448	79,599	74,935
Long-Term Obligations	3,270	3,270	3,420	3,535	3,615	3,690	3,735	3,775
Total Liabilities	419,674	312,619	246,372	190,723	180,215	110,397	83,845	78,926
Stockholders' Equity	987,462	790,071	782,286	426,929	260,356	148,314	212,808	203,162
Shares Outstanding	381,985	377,282	379,236	366,018	357,814	349,487	280,210	...
Statistical Record								
Return on Assets %	28.39	31.08	31.28	27.79	24.61	23.12	13.38	...
Return on Equity %	40.83	43.78	42.59	42.79	42.12	35.56	18.61	...
EBITDA Margin %	41.37	36.29	36.89	28.74	22.12	20.42	14.33	8.22
Net Margin %	23.05	19.68	19.81	15.38	11.93	10.39	7.03	3.29
Asset Turnover	1.33	1.53	1.58	1.81	2.06	2.22	1.90	...
Current Ratio	2.70	3.25	3.88	2.78	1.80	1.45	1.68	1.69
Debt to Equity	N.M.	N.M.	N.M.	0.01	0.01	0.02	0.02	0.02
Price Range	28.53-17.07	23.09-14.21	23.09-12.44	13.22-4.53	7.49-2.74	4.81-2.09	...	...
P/E Ratio	34.37-20.57	31.64-19.47	33.96-18.29	33.05-11.33	32.54-11.90	25.32-11.02	...	...

Address: 516 West 34th Street, New York, NY 10001	Web Site: www.coach.com	Auditors: Deloitte & Touche LLP
Telephone: (212) 594-1850	Officers: Lew Frankfort - Chmn., C.E.O. Keith Monda - Pres., C.O.O.	Investor Contact: 212-629-2618
Fax: (212) 594-1682		

COCA-COLA CO (THE)

*7 Year Price Score 71.77 *NYSE Composite Index=100 *12 Month Price Score 88.65

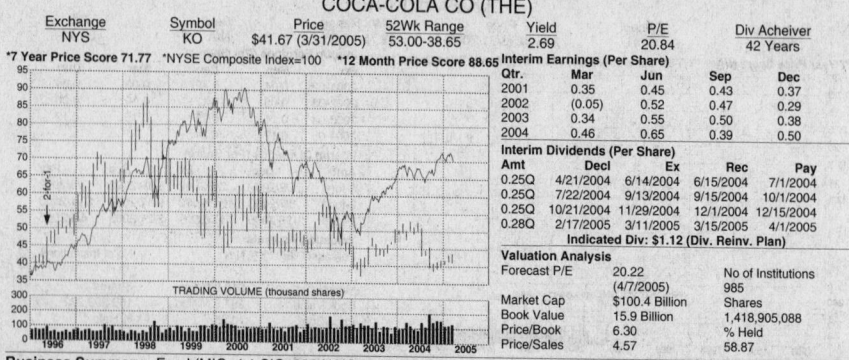

Interim Earnings (Per Share)

Qtr.	Mar	Jun	Sep	Dec
2001	0.35	0.45	0.43	0.37
2002	(0.05)	0.52	0.47	0.29
2003	0.34	0.55	0.50	0.38
2004	0.46	0.65	0.39	0.50

Interim Dividends (Per Share)

Amt	Decl	Ex	Rec	Pay
0.25Q	4/21/2004	6/14/2004	6/15/2004	7/1/2004
0.25Q	7/22/2004	9/13/2004	9/15/2004	10/1/2004
0.25Q	10/21/2004	11/29/2004	12/1/2004	12/15/2004
0.28Q	2/17/2005	3/11/2005	3/15/2005	4/1/2005

Indicated Div: $1.12 (Div. Reinv. Plan)

Valuation Analysis

Forecast P/E	20.22 (4/7/2005)	No of Institutions 985
Market Cap	$100.4 Billion	Shares
Book Value	15.9 Billion	1,418,905,088
Price/Book	6.30	% Held
Price/Sales	4.57	58.87

TRADING VOLUME (thousand shares)

Business Summary: Food (MIC: 4.1 SIC: 086 NAIC: 12111)

The Coca-Cola Company is engaged in the manufacturing, distributing and marketing of nonalcoholic beverage concentrates and syrups. Principal beverage products include: Coca-Cola, Coca-Cola Classic, Diet Coke, Vanilla Coke, Cherry Coke, Fanta, Sprite, Mr. Pibb, Mello Yellow, Barq's, Powerade, Fresca, Dasani plus other assorted diet and caffeine-free versions. Co. also produces, distributes and markets juice and juice-drink products. Brands include Minute Maid, Simply Orange orange juice, Odwalla super premium juices and drinks, Five Alive, Bacardi tropical fruit mixers (manufactured and marketed under a license from Bacardi & Company Limited) and Hi-C ready to serve fruit drinks.

Recent Developments: For the year ended Dec 31 2004, net income increased 11.5% to $4,847 million from net income of $4,347 million a year earlier. Revenues were $21,962 million, up 4.4% from $21,044 million the year before. Operating income was $5,698 million versus an income of $5,221 million in the prior year, an increase of 9.1%. Total direct expense was $7,638 million versus $7,762 million in the prior year, a decrease of 1.6%. Total indirect expense was $16,772 million versus $15,549 million in the prior year, an increase of 7.9%.

Prospects: Co. anticipates annual earnings per share growth in the high single-digits over the long term. However, Co. does not expect to hit this target in 2005 due to increased spending and continued weakness in certain markets. Co. plans to boost marketing spending during 2005 by approximately $350.0 million to $400.0 million with a major emphasis on its Diet Coke brand. Meanwhile, strong case volume growth in China, Brazil, Argentina, Spain, South Africa, Russia and Turkey is being partially offset by unit case volume declines in North America and Germany. Separately, during the first quarter of 2005, Co. plans to introduce Coca-Cola with Lime in the U.S.

Financial Data

(US$ in Thousands)	12/31/2004	12/31/2003	12/31/2002	12/31/2001	12/31/2000	12/31/1999	12/31/1998	12/31/1997
Earnings Per Share	2.00	1.77	1.23	1.60	0.88	0.98	1.42	1.64
Cash Flow Per Share	2.45	2.22	1.91	1.65	1.44	1.57	1.39	1.63
Tang Book Value Per Share	5.02	4.14	3.34	3.53	2.98	3.06	3.19	2.66
Dividends Per Share	1.000	0.880	0.800	0.720	0.680	0.640	0.600	0.560
Dividend Payout %	50.00	49.72	65.04	45.00	77.27	65.31	42.25	34.15
Income Statement								
Total Revenue	21,962,000	21,044,000	19,564,000	20,092,000	20,458,000	19,805,000	18,813,000	18,868,000
EBITDA	7,016,000	6,187,000	6,114,000	6,437,000	4,274,000	4,688,000	5,901,000	6,728,000
Depn & Amortn	755,000	690,000	625,000	803,000	773,000	792,000	645,000	626,000
Income Before Taxes	6,222,000	5,495,000	5,499,000	5,670,000	3,399,000	3,819,000	5,198,000	6,055,000
Income Taxes	1,375,000	1,148,000	1,523,000	1,691,000	1,222,000	1,388,000	1,665,000	1,926,000
Net Income	4,847,000	4,347,000	3,050,000	3,969,000	2,177,000	2,431,000	3,533,000	4,129,000
Average Shares	2,429,000	2,462,000	2,483,000	2,487,000	2,487,000	2,487,000	2,496,000	2,515,000
Balance Sheet								
Current Assets	12,094,000	8,396,000	7,352,000	7,171,000	6,620,000	6,480,000	6,380,000	5,969,000
Total Assets	31,327,000	27,342,000	24,501,000	22,417,000	20,834,000	21,623,000	19,145,000	16,940,000
Current Liabilities	10,971,000	7,886,000	7,341,000	8,429,000	9,321,000	9,856,000	8,640,000	7,379,000
Long-Term Obligations	1,157,000	2,517,000	2,701,000	1,219,000	835,000	854,000	687,000	801,000
Total Liabilities	15,392,000	13,252,000	12,701,000	11,051,000	11,518,000	12,110,000	10,742,000	9,629,000
Stockholders' Equity	15,935,000	14,090,000	11,800,000	11,366,000	9,316,000	9,513,000	8,403,000	7,311,000
Shares Outstanding	2,409,339	2,441,531	2,470,979	2,486,228	2,484,762	2,471,575	2,466,000	2,471,000
Statistical Record								
Return on Assets %	16.48	16.77	13.00	18.35	10.23	11.93	19.58	24.95
Return on Equity %	32.20	33.58	26.33	38.38	23.06	27.14	44.97	61.32
EBITDA Margin %	31.95	29.40	31.25	32.04	20.89	23.67	31.37	35.66
Net Margin %	22.07	20.66	15.59	19.75	10.64	12.27	18.78	21.88
Asset Turnover	0.75	0.81	0.83	0.93	0.96	0.97	1.04	1.14
Current Ratio	1.10	1.06	1.00	0.85	0.71	0.66	0.74	0.81
Debt to Equity	0.07	0.18	0.23	0.11	0.09	0.09	0.08	0.11
Price Range	53.00-38.65	50.75-37.07	57.64-43.47	60.82-42.85	66.88-43.31	70.50-47.56	87.94-56.19	71.88-51.88
P/E Ratio	26.50-19.32	28.67-20.94	46.86-35.34	38.01-26.78	75.99-49.22	71.94-48.53	61.93-39.57	43.83-31.63
Average Yield %	2.15	2.00	1.61	1.48	1.23	1.03	0.83	0.90

Address: One Coca-Cola Plaza, Atlanta, GA 30313
Telephone: (404) 676-2121
Fax: (404) 676-6792

Web Site: www.coca-cola.com
Officers: E. Neville Isdell - Chmn., C.E.O. Gary P. Fayard - Exec. V.P., C.F.O.

Auditors: Ernst & Young LLP
Investor Contact: 404-676-5766
Transfer Agents: EquiServe Trust Company, N.A., Providence, RI

COCA-COLA ENTERPRISES INC.

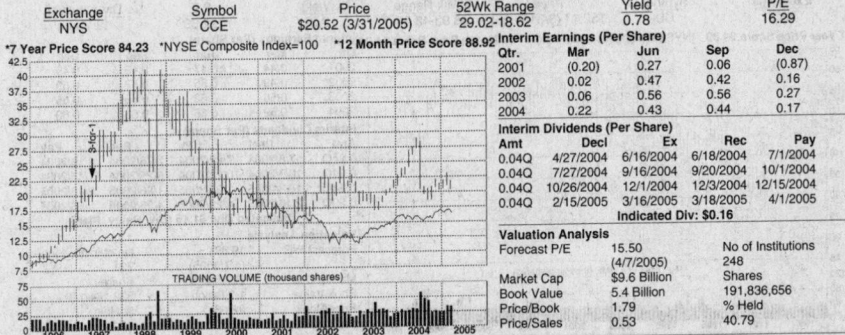

Exchange	Symbol	Price	52Wk Range	Yield	P/E
NYS	CCE	$20.52 (3/31/2005)	29.02-18.62	0.78	16.29

*7 Year Price Score 84.23   ***NYSE Composite Index=100**   ***12 Month Price Score 88.92**

Interim Earnings (Per Share)

Qtr.	Mar	Jun	Sep	Dec
2001	(0.20)	0.27	0.06	(0.87)
2002	0.02	0.47	0.42	0.16
2003	0.06	0.56	0.56	0.27
2004	0.22	0.43	0.44	0.17

Interim Dividends (Per Share)

Amt	Decl	Ex	Rec	Pay
0.04Q	4/27/2004	6/16/2004	6/18/2004	7/1/2004
0.04Q	7/27/2004	9/16/2004	9/20/2004	10/1/2004
0.04Q	10/26/2004	12/1/2004	12/3/2004	12/15/2004
0.04Q	2/15/2005	3/16/2005	3/18/2005	4/1/2005

Indicated Div: $0.16

Valuation Analysis

Forecast P/E	15.50	No of Institutions	
	(4/7/2005)	248	
Market Cap	$9.6 Billion	Shares	
Book Value	5.4 Billion	191,836,656	
Price/Book	1.79	% Held	
Price/Sales	0.53	40.79	

TRADING VOLUME (thousand shares)

Business Summary: Food (MIC: 4.1 SIC: 086 NAIC: 12111)

Coca-Cola Enterprises markets, produces, and distributes bottle and can nonalcoholic beverage products, primarily of The Coca-Cola Company. Products licensed to Co. through The Coca-Cola Company and its affiliates and joint ventures represented about 93.0% of total 2003 volume. As of Dec 31 2003, Co. distributed its bottle and can products to customers and consumers in the United States and Canada through license territories in 46 states in the United States, the District of Columbia, and the 10 provinces of Canada. Co. is also the sole licensed bottler for products of The Coca-Cola Company in Belgium, continental France, Great Britain, Luxembourg, Monaco, and the Netherlands.

Recent Developments: For the year ended Dec 31 2004, net income decreased 11.8% to $596,000 thousand from net income of $676,000 thousand a year earlier. Revenues were $18,158,000 thousand, up 4.8% from $17,330,000 thousand the year before. Operating income was $1,436,000 thousand versus an income of $1,577,000 thousand in the prior year, a decrease of 8.9%. Total direct expense was $10,771,000 thousand versus $10,165,000 thousand in the prior year, an increase of 6.0%. Total indirect expense was $5,951,000 thousand versus $5,588,000 thousand in the prior year, an increase of 6.5%.

Prospects: Results are being negatively affected by sluggish sales of Co.'s Coca-Cola Classic brand and other regular soft drinks as consumers, especially in the U.S., shift toward bottled waters, diet sodas, low-calorie juices and other healthier drinks. Going forward, results are expected to benefit from the introduction of new products, including Full Throttle, a new energy drink, and additional Dasani water flavors. Meanwhile, Co. is targeting first-quarter 2005 earnings of between $0.10 and $0.12 per share. Looking ahead, Co. anticipates full-year 2005 earnings per share in the range of the low to mid $1.30's.

Financial Data

(US$ in Thousands)	12/31/2004	12/31/2003	12/31/2002	12/31/2001	12/31/2000	12/31/1999	12/31/1998	12/31/1997
Earnings Per Share	1.26	1.46	1.07	(0.75)	0.54	0.13	0.35	0.43
Cash Flow Per Share	3.46	3.98	3.20	2.58	3.50	3.30	2.41	2.46
Tang Book Value Per Share	N.M.	N.M.	N.M.	6.25	6.67	6.83	5.95	4.61
Dividends Per Share	0.160	0.160	0.160	0.160	0.160	0.160	0.145	0.083
Dividend Payout %	12.70	10.96	14.95	...	29.63	123.08	41.43	19.38
Income Statement								
Total Revenue	18,158,000	17,330,000	16,889,000	15,700,000	14,750,000	14,406,000	13,414,000	11,278,000
EBITDA	2,655,000	2,744,000	2,412,000	1,956,000	2,385,000	2,187,000	1,990,000	1,660,000
Depn & Amortn	1,218,000	1,165,000	1,045,000	1,353,000	1,261,000	1,348,000	1,120,000	946,000
Income Before Taxes	818,000	972,000	705,000	(150,000)	333,000	88,000	169,000	178,000
Income Taxes	222,000	296,000	211,000	(131,000)	97,000	29,000	56,000	65,000
Net Income	596,000	676,000	494,000	(321,000)	236,000	59,000	142,000	171,000
Average Shares	473,000	461,000	458,000	432,000	429,000	436,000	406,000	396,000
Balance Sheet								
Current Assets	3,264,000	3,000,000	2,844,000	2,876,000	2,631,000	2,581,000	2,285,000	1,813,000
Total Assets	26,354,000	25,700,000	24,375,000	23,719,000	22,162,000	22,730,000	21,132,000	17,487,000
Current Liabilities	3,431,000	3,941,000	3,455,000	4,522,000	3,094,000	3,614,000	3,397,000	3,032,000
Long-Term Obligations	10,523,000	10,552,000	11,236,000	10,365,000	10,348,000	10,153,000	9,605,000	7,760,000
Total Liabilities	20,976,000	21,335,000	21,028,000	20,899,000	19,328,000	19,806,000	18,694,000	15,705,000
Stockholders' Equity	5,378,000	4,365,000	3,347,000	2,820,000	2,834,000	2,924,000	2,438,000	1,782,000
Shares Outstanding	469,650	455,754	449,700	445,115	418,068	421,317	401,455	386,554
Statistical Record								
Return on Assets %	2.28	2.70	2.05	N.M.	1.05	0.27	0.74	1.19
Return on Equity %	12.20	17.53	16.02	N.M.	8.17	2.20	6.73	10.26
EBITDA Margin %	14.62	15.83	14.28	12.46	16.17	15.18	14.84	14.72
Net Margin %	3.28	3.90	2.92	N.M.	1.60	0.41	1.06	1.52
Asset Turnover	0.70	0.69	0.70	0.68	0.66	0.66	0.69	0.79
Current Ratio	0.95	0.76	0.82	0.64	0.85	0.71	0.67	0.60
Debt to Equity	1.96	2.42	3.36	3.68	3.65	3.47	3.94	4.35
Price Range	29.02-18.62	23.02-17.05	24.46-16.13	23.64-14.09	29.19-14.63	37.31-16.94	41.13-22.88	35.56-15.88
P/E Ratio	23.03-14.78	15.77-11.68	22.86-15.07	...	54.05-27.08	287.02-130.29	117.50-65.36	82.70-36.92
Average Yield %	0.70	0.81	0.78	0.90	0.80	0.55	0.42	0.34

Address: 2500 Windy Ridge Parkway, Suite 700, Atlanta, GA 30339 **Telephone:** (770) 989-3000 **Fax:** (770) 989-3788	**Web Site:** www.cokecce.com **Officers:** Lowry F. Kline - Chmn. John R. Alm - Pres., C.E.O.	**Auditors:** Ernst & Young LLP **Investor Contact:** 770-989-3105 **Transfer Agents:** American Stock Transfer & Trust Co., New York, NY

COLGATE-PALMOLIVE CO.

Exchange	Symbol	Price	52Wk Range	Yield	P/E	Div Acheiver
NYS	CL	$52.17 (3/31/2005)	58.92-43.06	2.22	22.39	42 Years

*7 Year Price Score 84.80   *NYSE Composite Index=100   *12 Month Price Score 94.24

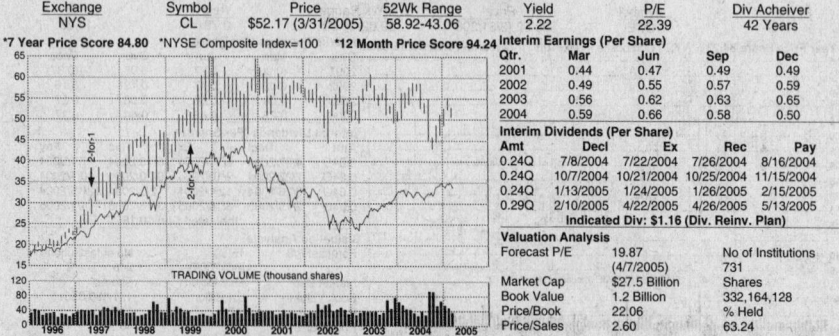

Interim Earnings (Per Share)

Qtr.	Mar	Jun	Sep	Dec
2001	0.44	0.47	0.49	0.49
2002	0.49	0.55	0.57	0.59
2003	0.56	0.62	0.63	0.65
2004	0.59	0.66	0.58	0.50

Interim Dividends (Per Share)

Amt	Decl	Ex	Rec	Pay
0.24Q	7/8/2004	7/22/2004	7/26/2004	8/16/2004
0.24Q	10/7/2004	10/21/2004	10/25/2004	11/15/2004
0.24Q	1/13/2005	1/24/2005	1/26/2005	2/15/2005
0.29Q	2/10/2005	4/22/2005	4/26/2005	5/13/2005

Indicated Div: $1.16 (Div. Reinv. Plan)

Valuation Analysis

Forecast P/E	19.87	No of Institutions	
	(4/7/2005)	731	
Market Cap	$27.5 Billion	Shares	
Book Value	1.2 Billion	332,164,128	
Price/Book	22.06	% Held	
Price/Sales	2.60	63.24	

Business Summary: Chemicals (MIC: 11.1 SIC: 844 NAIC: 25620)

Colgate-Palmolive is a consumer products company whose products are marketed in over 200 countries worldwide. Co. operates in two business segments. Co.'s oral, personal, household surface and fabric care segment include toothpaste, oral rinses and toothbrushes, hand soaps, shower gels, shampoos, deodorants, shave products, laundry and dishwashing detergents, cleansers and other similar items. Co.'s pet nutrition segment includes pet food products manufactured and marketed by Hill's Pet Nutrition. Principal global trademarks include Colgate, Palmolive, Kolynos, Sorriso, Mennen, Protex, Ajax, Soupline, Suavitel, Fab, Science Diet and Prescription Diet in addition to other regional trademarks.

Recent Developments: For the year ended Dec 31 2004, net income decreased 6.6% to $1,327,100 thousand from net income of $1,421,300 thousand a year earlier. Revenues were $10,584,200 thousand, up 6.9% from $9,903,400 thousand the year before. Operating income was $2,122,100 thousand versus an income of $2,166,000 thousand in the prior year, a decrease of 2.0%. Total direct expense was $4,747,200 thousand versus $4,456,100 thousand in the prior year, an increase of 6.5%. Total indirect expense was $3,680,300 thousand versus $3,260,700 thousand in the prior year, an increase of 12.9%.

Prospects: Looking ahead, Co. expects to continue to experience top-line growth momentum in 2005. Co.'s new product pipeline across all operating divisions is full and is being supported by aggressive levels of commercial spending. Also, Co. is pleased that its global restructuring program is on track and proceeding smoothly. Further, Co. is optimistic that it will reach its profit expectations in 2005 and that it is back on track to return to double-digit earnings growth in 2006. Meanwhile, Co. noted that its toothpaste market shares are up in more than 100 countries around the world including such competitive markets as the U.S., Mexico, China and Russia.

Financial Data

(US$ in Thousands)	12/31/2004	12/31/2003	12/31/2002	12/31/2001	12/31/2000	12/31/1999	12/31/1998	12/31/1997
Earnings Per Share	2.33	2.46	2.19	1.89	1.70	1.47	1.30	1.14
Cash Flow Per Share	3.30	3.29	2.97	2.87	2.66	2.22	2.00	1.86
Dividends Per Share	0.960	0.900	0.720	0.675	0.630	0.590	0.550	0.530
Dividend Payout %	41.20	36.59	32.88	35.71	37.06	40.14	42.15	46.70
Income Statement								
Total Revenue	10,584,200	9,903,400	9,294,300	9,427,800	9,357,900	9,118,200	8,971,600	9,056,700
EBITDA	2,449,900	2,481,500	2,309,600	2,171,000	2,078,300	1,906,400	1,753,300	1,605,700
Depn & Amortn	327,800	315,500	296,500	336,200	337,800	340,220	330,300	319,900
Income Before Taxes	2,002,400	2,041,900	1,870,300	1,668,700	1,567,200	1,394,600	1,250,100	1,102,300
Income Taxes	675,300	620,600	582,000	522,100	503,400	457,300	401,500	361,900
Net Income	1,327,100	1,421,300	1,288,300	1,146,600	1,063,800	937,300	848,600	740,400
Average Shares	569,300	578,800	589,100	607,700	627,300	638,800	648,400	650,200
Balance Sheet								
Current Assets	2,739,900	2,496,500	2,228,100	2,203,400	2,347,200	2,354,800	2,244,900	2,196,500
Total Assets	8,672,900	7,478,800	7,087,200	6,984,800	7,252,300	7,423,100	7,685,200	7,538,700
Current Liabilities	2,730,700	2,445,400	2,148,700	2,123,500	2,244,100	2,273,500	2,114,400	1,959,500
Long-Term Obligations	3,089,500	2,684,900	3,210,800	2,812,000	2,536,900	2,243,300	2,300,600	2,340,300
Total Liabilities	7,427,500	6,591,700	6,736,900	6,138,400	5,784,200	5,589,400	5,599,600	5,360,100
Stockholders' Equity	1,245,400	887,100	350,300	846,400	1,468,100	1,833,700	2,085,600	2,178,600
Shares Outstanding	526,625	533,697	536,001	550,722	566,655	578,863	585,420	591,280
Statistical Record								
Return on Assets %	16.39	19.52	18.31	16.11	14.46	12.41	11.15	9.59
Return on Equity %	124.12	229.72	215.31	99.08	64.26	47.83	39.80	35.15
EBITDA Margin %	23.15	25.06	24.85	23.03	22.21	20.91	19.54	17.73
Net Margin %	12.54	14.35	13.86	12.16	11.37	10.28	9.46	8.18
Asset Turnover	1.31	1.36	1.32	1.32	1.27	1.21	1.18	1.17
Current Ratio	1.00	1.02	1.04	1.04	1.05	1.04	1.06	1.12
Debt to Equity	2.48	3.03	9.17	3.32	1.73	1.22	1.10	1.07
Price Range	58.92-43.06	60.88-49.10	58.73-44.36	62.50-51.00	65.00-42.75	65.00-37.53	48.47-32.78	38.56-22.72
P/E Ratio	25.29-18.48	24.75-19.96	26.82-20.26	33.07-26.98	38.24-25.15	44.22-25.53	37.28-25.22	33.83-19.93
Average Yield %	1.82	1.64	1.33	1.19	1.13	1.18	1.31	1.72

Address: 300 Park Avenue, New York, NY 10022-7499	Web Site: www.colgate.com	Auditors: PricewaterhouseCoopers LLP
Telephone: (212) 310 2000	**Officers:** Reuben Mark - Chmn., C.E.O. Javier G. Teruel - Vice-Chmn.	**Investor Contact:** 212-310-3072
Fax: (212) 310 3284		**Transfer Agents:** EquiServe Trust Company, N.A., Providence, RI

COLLINS & AIKMAN CORP. (NEW)

Exchange	Symbol	Price	52Wk Range	Yield	P/E
NYS	CKC	$1.23 (3/31/2005)	6.56-0.95	N/A	N/A

*7 Year Price Score 33.63 *NYSE Composite Index=100 *12 Month Price Score 45.46

Interim Earnings (Per Share)

Qtr.	Mar	Jun	Sep	Dec
2001	(0.25)	0.28	(0.30)	(0.89)
2002	(0.10)	(0.29)	(0.54)	0.00
2003	(0.34)	0.13	(0.38)	(0.12)
2004	(0.28)	(0.35)	(0.67)	...

Interim Dividends (Per Share)

No Dividends Paid

Valuation Analysis

Forecast P/E	N/A	No of Institutions
Market Cap	$102.8 Million	Shares
Book Value	340.1 Million	25,339,416
Price/Book	0.30	% Held
Price/Sales	0.03	30.30

Business Summary: Textiles (MIC: 4.3 SIC: 273 NAIC: 14110)

Collins & Aikman designs, engineers and manufactures automotive interior components, including instrument panels, fully assembled cockpit modules, floor and acoustic systems, automotive fabric, interior trim, as well as exterior trim and convertible top systems. In North America, Co. manufactures components for about 90.0% of all light vehicle production platforms. Sales are diversified among all North American original equipment manufacturers (OEM), as well as Asian and European based global OEMs. Co. has more than 102 plants and facilities worldwide.

Recent Developments: For the quarter ended Sep 30 2004, net loss widened to $55.6 million from $32.1 million in the year-earlier quarter. Revenues were $864.8 million, down 4.1% from $902.2 million the year before. Operating income was $9.5 million versus an income of $8.3 million in the prior-year quarter, an increase of 14.5%. Total direct expense was $800.8 million versus $812.1 million in the prior-year quarter, a decrease of 1.4%. Total indirect expense was $54.5 million versus $81.8 million in the prior-year quarter, a decrease of 33.4%.

Prospects: Co.'s net sales have recently decreased primarily due to reduced volumes on several key North American programs and delays in new program launches that were scheduled to launch in the fourth quarter of 2004. Meanwhile, Co. is continuing to achieve solid marketing progress by adding new business bookings. These programs begin with model years incepting 2005 to 2008. A significant recent win included an instrument panel, cockpit and console program for a European customer. In addition, Co. has secured numerous contracts for its instrument panel, carpet and acoustic, accessory mat and plastic interior trim products.

Financial Data (US$ in Thousands)	9 Mos	6 Mos	3 Mos	12/31/2003	12/31/2002	12/31/2001	12/31/2000	12/25/1999
Earnings Per Share	(1.42)	(1.13)	(0.65)	(0.69)	(1.18)	(1.19)	0.17	(0.41)
Cash Flow Per Share	0.83	0.44	0.86	1.47	2.48	3.69	5.20	3.17
Income Statement								
Total Revenue	2,967,500	2,102,700	1,066,200	3,983,700	3,885,800	1,823,300	1,901,819	1,898,597
EBITDA	146,600	118,400	64,200	267,800	232,100	97,800	172,110	162,400
Depn & Amortn	112,700	73,500	37,000	140,200	117,000	81,800	74,706	71,474
Income Before Taxes	(125,600)	(56,600)	(23,400)	(61,000)	(33,800)	(68,300)	815	(1,119)
Income Taxes	(17,000)	(3,600)	(100)	(1,900)	17,500	(18,600)	2,252	246
Net Income	(108,600)	(53,000)	(23,300)	(57,500)	(53,500)	(46,200)	4,477	(10,215)
Average Shares	83,600	83,600	83,600	83,600	76,300	38,880	24,763	24,780
Balance Sheet								
Current Assets	654,500	677,700	725,200	655,900	803,300	744,500	424,885	465,366
Total Assets	3,196,700	3,161,800	3,252,000	3,191,200	3,157,100	2,993,400	1,280,290	1,348,890
Current Liabilities	895,200	871,000	944,000	925,300	929,400	769,100	389,729	362,255
Long-Term Obligations	1,361,200	1,313,700	1,310,400	1,237,700	1,255,200	1,282,400	799,677	884,550
Total Liabilities	2,856,600	2,786,600	2,841,900	2,750,900	2,635,700	2,471,000	1,435,276	1,500,011
Stockholders' Equity	340,100	375,200	410,100	440,300	397,500	374,700	(154,986)	(151,121)
Shares Outstanding	83,600	83,600	83,600	83,600	83,600	67,200	24,809	24,761
Statistical Record								
Return on Assets %	N.M.	N.M.	N.M.	N.M.	N.M.	N.M.	0.33	N.M.
EBITDA Margin %	4.94	5.63	6.02	6.72	5.97	5.36	9.05	8.55
Net Margin %	N.M.	N.M.	N.M.	N.M.	N.M.	N.M.	0.24	N.M.
Asset Turnover	1.24	1.25	1.24	1.26	1.26	0.85	1.42	1.39
Current Ratio	0.73	0.78	0.77	0.71	0.86	0.97	1.09	1.28
Debt to Equity	4.00	3.50	3.20	2.81	3.16	3.42	...	...
Price Range	6.76-2.43	6.76-2.09	6.76-2.09	4.83-2.09	28.38-2.45	25.75-8.95	17.50-7.19	19.06-10.00
P/E Ratio	...	...	...	...	...	...	102.94-42.28	...

Address: 250 Stephenson Highway, Troy, MI 48083 **Telephone:** (248) 824-2500 **Fax:** (248) 824-1532	**Web Site:** www.collinsaikman.com **Officers:** David A. Stockman - Chmn., C.E.O. J. Michael Stepp - Vice-Chmn.	**Auditors:** PricewaterhouseCoopers LLP

COLONIAL BANCGROUP INC.

Exchange	Symbol	Price	52Wk Range	Yield	P/E
NYS	CNB	$20.52 (3/31/2005)	22.45-16.78	2.97	15.43

*7 Year Price Score 121.17 *NYSE Composite Index=100 ***12 Month Price Score 96.44**

Interim Earnings (Per Share)

Qtr.	Mar	Jun	Sep	Dec
2001	0.26	0.27	0.27	0.26
2002	0.29	0.30	0.29	0.28
2003	0.29	0.30	0.31	0.30
2004	0.31	0.33	0.34	0.35

Interim Dividends (Per Share)

Amt	Decl	Ex	Rec	Pay
0.145Q	4/21/2004	4/28/2004	4/30/2004	5/14/2004
0.145Q	7/21/2004	7/28/2004	7/30/2004	8/13/2004
0.145Q	10/20/2004	10/27/2004	10/29/2004	11/12/2004
0.153Q	1/19/2005	1/26/2005	1/28/2005	2/11/2005

Indicated Div: $0.61

Valuation Analysis

Forecast P/E	13.97 (4/7/2005)	No of Institutions 200
Market Cap	$2.7 Billion	Shares 60,221,384
Book Value	1.4 Billion	% Held
Price/Book	1.97	41.38
Price/Sales	2.78	

TRADING VOLUME (thousand shares)

Business Summary: Commercial Banking (MIC: 8.1 SIC: 022 NAIC: 22110)

Colonial Bancgroup is a financial holding company, which allows it to affiliate with securities firms and insurance companies and to engage in other activities that are financial in nature, incidental to such financial activities, or complementary to such activities. Co.'s principal activity is to supervise and coordinate the business of its subsidiaries and to provide them with capital and services. Various statutory provisions and regulatory policies limit the amount of dividends Colonial Bank may pay without regulatory approval. As of Dec 31 2003, Co. operated 274 offices with $16.27 billion in assets in Alabama, Florida, Georgia, Nevada, Tennessee and Texas.

Recent Developments: For the year ended Dec 31 2004, net income increased 17.0% to $175,348 thousand from net income of $149,927 thousand a year earlier. Net interest income was $584,516 thousand, up 15.4% from $506,643 thousand the year before. Provision for loan losses was $26,994 thousand versus $37,378 thousand in the prior year, a decrease of 27.8%. Non-interest income rose 3.8% to $138,027 thousand, while non-interest expense advanced 14.6% to $426,579 thousand.

Prospects: Co. acquired Union Bank of Florida, headquartered in Sunrise, FL, and completed its merger into Colonial Bank on Feb 10 2005. The acquisition brings Co.'s Florida franchise to $6.70 billion in deposits and $10.20 billion in assets, or 54.0% of Co.'s total deposits and 51.0% of its total assets, respectively, in the Florida market. The Union transaction, coupled with Co.'s previously announced plan to acquire FFLC Bancorp, Inc. in Leesburg, FL, is expected to make Co. the fifth largest commercial bank in Florida once completed in the second quarter of 2005.

Financial Data
(US$ in Thousands)

	12/31/2004	12/31/2003	12/31/2002	12/31/2001	12/31/2000	12/31/1999	12/31/1998	12/31/1997
Earnings Per Share	1.33	1.20	1.16	1.06	1.01	1.06	0.49	0.89
Cash Flow Per Share	(0.33)	1.32	(1.43)	1.13	3.76	6.68	(3.72)	(0.04)
Tang Book Value Per Share	7.47	7.06	6.58	6.52	6.19	3.37	3.35	3.35
Dividends Per Share	0.580	0.560	0.520	0.480	0.440	0.380	0.340	0.300
Dividend Payout %	43.61	46.67	44.83	45.28	43.56	35.85	69.39	33.71
Income Statement								
Interest Income	848,017	780,808	783,431	902,167	897,761	775,934	693,542	497,987
Interest Expense	263,501	274,165	322,261	480,238	507,870	397,990	350,441	249,488
Net Interest Income	584,516	506,643	461,170	421,929	389,891	377,944	343,101	248,499
Provision for Losses	26,994	37,378	35,980	39,573	29,680	28,707	26,345	13,026
Non-Interest Income	138,027	127,449	102,352	93,709	75,299	142,239	125,258	87,759
Non-Interest Expense	429,870	369,551	312,779	284,168	249,982	301,552	355,412	200,131
Income Before Taxes	265,679	227,163	214,743	191,897	185,528	189,924	86,602	123,101
Income Taxes	90,331	77,236	73,872	69,181	67,732	-70,327	31,406	45,910
Net Income	175,348	149,927	140,025	122,103	112,731	119,597	55,196	77,191
Average Shares	132,315	125,289	120,648	115,881	111,472	113,252	112,431	86,872
Balance Sheet								
Net Loans & Leases	12,709,009	11,450,346	11,557,165	10,245,465	9,309,605	8,132,156	7,026,733	5,114,744
Total Assets	18,897,150	16,273,302	15,822,355	13,185,103	11,727,637	10,854,099	10,456,285	6,850,828
Total Deposits	11,646,612	9,768,592	9,319,735	8,322,979	8,143,017	7,967,978	7,446,153	5,255,830
Total Liabilities	17,503,535	15,094,997	14,750,919	12,320,329	10,970,785	10,158,920	9,816,478	6,356,574
Stockholders' Equity	1,393,615	1,178,305	1,071,436	864,774	756,852	695,179	639,807	494,254
Shares Outstanding	133,823	126,974	123,700	115,244	110,307	112,106	110,935	85,090
Statistical Record								
Return on Assets %	0.99	0.93	0.97	0.98	1.00	1.12	0.64	1.32
Return on Equity %	13.60	13.33	14.46	15.06	15.48	17.92	9.73	18.44
Net Interest Margin %	68.93	64.89	58.87	46.77	43.43	48.71	49.47	49.90
Efficiency Ratio %	43.60	40.69	35.31	28.53	25.69	32.84	43.41	34.17
Loans to Deposits	1.09	1.17	1.24	1.23	1.14	1.02	0.94	0.97
Price Range	22.45-16.52	17.47-10.75	16.11-11.01	14.98-10.75	11.25-8.31	15.00-10.19	18.78-10.38	17.53-9.34
P/E Ratio	16.88-12.42	14.56-8.96	13.89-9.49	14.13-10.14	11.14-8.23	14.15-9.61	38.33-21.17	19.70-10.50
Average Yield %	3.06	4.03	3.77	3.66	4.54	3.11	2.22	2.31

Address: One Commerce Street, Suite 800, Montgomery, AL 36104 Telephone: (334) 240-5000 Fax: (334) 240-5345	Web Site: www.colonialbank.com Officers: Robert E. Lowder - Chmn., C.E.O. W. Flake Oakley IV - Pres.	Auditors: PricewaterhouseCoopers LLP Investor Contact: 888-843-0622 Transfer Agents: SunTrust Bank, Atlanta, GA

COLONIAL PROPERTIES TRUST (AL)

Exchange	Symbol	Price	52Wk Range	Yield	P/E	Div Acheiver
NYS	CLP	$38.41 (3/31/2005)	42.44-33.93	7.03	26.49	10 Years

*7 Year Price Score 105.07 *NYSE Composite Index=100 *12 Month Price Score 89.48

Interim Earnings (Per Share)

Qtr.	Mar	Jun	Sep	Dec
2001	0.27	0.35	0.57	0.84
2002	0.60	0.97	0.53	0.48
2003	0.52	0.15	0.26	0.37
2004	0.50	0.24	0.18	0.54

Interim Dividends (Per Share)

Amt	Decl	Ex	Rec	Pay
0.67Q	4/22/2004	4/29/2004	5/3/2004	5/10/2004
0.67Q	7/20/2004	7/28/2004	7/30/2004	8/6/2004
0.67Q	10/19/2004	10/27/2004	10/29/2004	11/5/2004
0.675Q	1/21/2005	1/27/2005	1/31/2005	2/7/2005

Indicated Div: $2.70

Valuation Analysis

Forecast P/E	10.30	No of Institutions	
	(4/7/2005)	136	
Market Cap	$1.1 Billion	Shares	
Book Value	605.0 Million	18,152,120	
Price/Book	1.75	% Held	
Price/Sales	3.14	64.84	

TRADING VOLUME (thousand shares)

Business Summary: Property, Real Estate & Development (MIC: 8.3 SIC: 798 NAIC: 25930)

Colonial Properties is a self-administered equity real estate investment trust. Co. owns, develops and operates multifamily, office and retail properties in the Sunbelt region of the U.S. Co. is a fully-integrated real estate company, whose activities include ownership of a diversified portfolio of 112 wholly and partially-owned properties as of Dec 31 2003, located in Alabama, Florida, Georgia, Mississippi, North Carolina, South Carolina, Tennessee, Texas, and Virginia. Co. is the direct general partner of, and holds approx. 71.8% of the interests in, Colonial Realty Limited Partnership, a Delaware limited partnership.

Recent Developments: For the year ended Dec 31 2004, income from continuing operations decreased 20.9% to $22,810,000 from income of $28,848,000 a year earlier. Net income increased 4.5% to $54,618,000 from net income of $52,265,000 a year earlier. Revenues were $3,374,100,00, up 16.3% from $290,004,000 the year before. Operating income was $107,287,000 versus an income of $100,804,000 in the prior year, an increase of 6.4%.

Prospects: Co.'s top priorities in 2005 are to complete the acquisition of Cornerstone Realty Income Trust, integrate the two companies efficiently and execute its plans for asset dispositions and reinvestments. Co. has significant momentum in its multifamily and retail divisions, each with occupancy rates above 91.0%. Going forward, Co. expects to participate in anticipated growth of the economy and the recovery of the multifamily sector. For full-year 2005, Co. expects earnings per share to range from $4.45 to $4.53 per diluted share, and funds from operations to range between $3.68 and $3.76 per diluted share. Separately, Co. is reviewing bids on each of its malls being marketed for sale.

Financial Data (US$ in Thousands)	12/31/2004	12/31/2003	12/31/2002	12/31/2001	12/31/2000	12/31/1999	12/31/1998	12/31/1997
Earnings Per Share	1.45	1.29	2.58	2.02	1.82	1.83	1.59	1.53
Cash Flow Per Share	4.98	5.52	6.41	6.57	4.96	5.39	4.69	3.64
Tang Book Value Per Share	21.92	22.80	23.53	24.19	21.88	22.56	23.34	23.18
Dividends Per Share	2.680	2.660	2.640	2.520	2.400	2.320	2.200	2.080
Dividend Payout %	184.83	206.20	102.33	124.75	131.87	126.78	138.36	135.95
Income Statement								
Property Income	309,151	308,001	303,764	293,837	283,587	264,837	242,836	174,452
Non-Property Income	28,259	26,241	26,102	22,488	18,723	17,727	14,531	9,674
Total Revenue	337,410	334,242	329,866	316,325	302,310	282,564	257,367	184,126
Depn & Amortn	88,875	88,814	82,835	72,357	63,884	55,185	48,647	33,278
Interest Expense	78,933	66,666	65,265	71,397	71,855	57,211	52,063	40,496
Income Taxes	...	...	...	15	...	...	...	...
Net Income	54,618	52,265	73,377	55,609	49,590	55,776	50,222	31,948
Average Shares	27,462	25,232	22,408	20,792	21,249	24,478	24,641	19,808
Balance Sheet								
Total Assets	2,801,343	2,194,927	2,129,856	2,014,623	1,944,099	1,863,518	1,755,449	1,397,078
Long-Term Obligations	1,855,787	1,267,865	1,262,193	1,191,791	1,179,095	1,039,863	909,322	702,044
Total Liabilities	1,930,335	1,323,140	1,317,759	1,245,537	1,209,859	1,082,254	946,055	732,378
Stockholders' Equity	605,026	601,733	537,803	507,435	453,826	493,575	610,447	490,419
Shares Outstanding	27,599	26,394	22,850	20,976	20,742	21,872	26,147	21,152
Statistical Record								
Return on Assets %	2.18	2.42	3.54	2.81	2.60	3.08	3.19	2.72
Return on Equity %	9.03	9.17	14.04	11.57	10.44	10.10	9.12	8.30
Net Margin %	16.19	15.64	22.24	17.58	16.40	19.74	19.51	17.35
Price Range	42.44-33.93	40.31-30.77	38.95-31.15	31.60-25.20	28.63-22.69	28.63-22.00	32.13-24.38	31.88-26.88
P/E Ratio	29.27-23.40	31.25-23.85	15.10-12.07	15.64-12.48	15.73-12.47	15.64-12.02	20.20-15.33	20.83-17.57
Average Yield %	6.85	7.59	7.64	8.68	9.36	8.78	7.61	7.11

Address: 2101 Sixth Avenue North, Suite 750, Birmingham, AL 35203 **Telephone:** (205) 250-8700 **Fax:** (205) 250-8890	**Web Site:** www.colonialprop.com **Officers:** Thomas H. Lowder - Chmn., Pres., C.E.O. John P. Rigrish - Exec. V.P., Chief Admin. Officer	**Auditors:** PricewaterhouseCoopers LLP **Investor Contact:** 205-250-8880

COMERICA, INC.

Exchange	Symbol	Price	52Wk Range	Yield	P/E	Div Acheiver
NYS	CMA	$55.08 (3/31/2005)	63.46-51.02	3.99	12.63	21 Years

*7 Year Price Score 89.88 *NYSE Composite Index=100 *12 Month Price Score 91.93

Interim Earnings (Per Share)

Qtr.	Mar	Jun	Sep	Dec
2001	0.50	1.13	1.14	1.11
2002	1.20	1.03	0.14	1.18
2003	1.00	0.97	0.89	0.89
2004	0.92	1.10	1.13	1.21

Interim Dividends (Per Share)

Amt	Decl	Ex	Rec	Pay
0.52Q	5/18/2004	6/14/2004	6/15/2004	7/1/2004
0.52Q	7/27/2004	9/13/2004	9/15/2004	10/1/2004
0.52Q	11/23/2004	12/13/2004	12/15/2004	1/1/2005
0.55Q	1/25/2005	3/11/2005	3/15/2005	4/1/2005

Indicated Div: $2.20 (Div. Reinv. Plan)

Valuation Analysis

Forecast P/E	12.20	No of Institutions
	(4/7/2005)	385
Market Cap	$9.4 Billion	Shares
Book Value	5.1 Billion	118,839,296
Price/Book	1.84	% Held
Price/Sales	3.03	69.82

Business Summary: Commercial Banking (MIC: 8.1 SIC: 021 NAIC: 22110)

Comerica is a bank holding company with assets of $52.59 billion and total deposits of $41.46 billion as of Dec 31 2003. Co. operates banking subsidiaries in Michigan, Texas and California, banking operations in Florida, and businesses in several other states. Co. is a diversified financial services provider, offering a broad range of financial products and services for businesses and individuals. Through its subsidiaries, the Company has aligned its operations into three major lines of business: the Business Bank, the Individual Bank and the Investment Bank. Co. also has an investment services affiliate, Munder Capital Management, and operates banking subsidiaries in Canada and Mexico.

Recent Developments: For the year ended Dec 31 2004, net income increased 14.5% to $757,000 thousand from net income of $661,000 thousand a year earlier. Net interest income was $1,810,000 thousand, down 6.0% from $1,926,000 thousand the year before. Provision for loan losses was $64,000 thousand versus $377,000 thousand in the prior year, a decrease of 83.0%. Non-interest income fell 4.9% to $838,000 thousand, while non-interest expense advanced 0.7% to $1,493,000 thousand.

Prospects: Co. ended 2004 on a positive note, and expects improving business trends to continue to drive momentum in the coming year. Co. will remain focused on generating revenue growth through its investment in branches, technology and products. Also, operating results should continue to benefit from higher net interest income and improve cost controls. Meanwhile, Co.'s balance sheet reflects increases in both loans and deposits. Additionally, credit quality trends continue to improve in light of lower non-performing loans and should well-position Co. for favorable results in 2005.

Financial Data

(US$ in Thousands)	12/31/2004	12/31/2003	12/31/2002	12/31/2001	12/31/2000	12/31/1999	12/31/1998	12/31/1997
Earnings Per Share	4.36	3.75	3.40	3.88	4.63	4.14	3.72	3.19
Cash Flow Per Share	5.96	7.55	7.02	5.63	5.07	6.64	4.43	3.82
Tang Book Value Per Share	29.95	29.20	28.30	27.15	23.94	20.60	17.94	16.02
Dividends Per Share	2.080	2.000	1.920	1.760	1.600	1.440	1.280	1.147
Dividend Payout %	47.71	53.33	56.47	45.36	34.56	34.78	34.41	35.95
Income Statement								
Interest Income	2,237,000	2,412,000	2,797,000	3,393,547	3,261,636	2,672,710	2,616,774	2,647,403
Interest Expense	427,000	486,000	665,000	1,291,209	1,602,785	1,125,569	1,155,503	1,204,627
Net Interest Income	1,810,000	1,926,000	2,132,000	2,102,338	1,658,851	1,547,141	1,461,271	1,442,776
Provision for Losses	64,000	377,000	635,000	236,000	145,000	114,000	113,000	146,000
Non-Interest Income	857,000	887,000	900,000	803,332	825,890	716,888	603,148	527,952
Non-Interest Expense	1,493,000	1,483,000	1,515,000	1,559,033	1,188,370	1,116,957	1,020,044	1,007,986
Income Before Taxes	1,110,000	953,000	882,000	1,110,637	1,151,371	1,033,072	931,375	816,742
Income Taxes	353,000	292,000	281,000	401,059	402,045	360,483	324,299	286,266
Net Income	757,000	661,000	601,000	709,578	749,326	672,589	607,076	530,476
Average Shares	174,000	176,000	177,000	177,665	156,398	158,397	158,757	161,040
Balance Sheet								
Net Loans & Leases	40,170,000	39,499,000	41,490,000	40,541,248	35,522,235	32,216,808	30,152,454	28,470,897
Total Assets	51,766,000	52,592,000	53,301,000	50,731,973	41,985,185	38,653,332	36,600,831	36,292,398
Total Deposits	40,936,000	41,463,000	41,775,000	37,570,379	27,168,012	23,291,403	24,313,133	22,586,317
Total Liabilities	46,661,000	47,482,000	48,354,000	45,924,509	37,977,919	35,178,688	33,554,218	33,530,622
Stockholders' Equity	5,105,000	5,110,000	4,947,000	4,807,464	4,007,266	3,474,644	3,046,613	2,761,776
Shares Outstanding	170,475	175,000	174,775	177,074	156,943	156,517	155,881	156,815
Statistical Record								
Return on Assets %	1.45	1.25	1.16	1.53	1.85	1.79	1.67	1.50
Return on Equity %	14.78	13.15	12.32	16.10	19.98	20.63	20.90	19.73
Net Interest Margin %	80.91	79.85	76.22	61.95	50.86	57.89	55.84	54.50
Efficiency Ratio %	48.25	44.95	40.98	37.15	29.07	32.95	31.68	31.74
Loans to Deposits	0.98	0.95	0.99	1.08	1.31	1.38	1.24	1.26
Price Range	63.46-51.02	56.31-37.61	65.30-35.53	64.95-44.66	60.31-33.81	69.75-44.94	71.58-50.13	61.88-34.58
P/E Ratio	14.56-11.70	15.02-10.03	19.21-10.45	16.74-11.51	13.03-7.30	16.85-10.85	19.24-13.47	19.40-10.84
Average Yield %	3.62	4.33	3.47	3.11	3.29	2.45	1.99	2.48

Address: Comerica Tower at Detroit Center, 500 Woodward Avenue, MC 3391, Detroit, MI 48226-3509 **Telephone:** (313) 222 9743 **Fax:** (313) 222 6091	**Web Site:** www.comerica.com **Officers:** Ralph W. Babb Jr. - Chmn., Pres., C.E.O. Elizabeth S. Acton - Exec. V.P., C.F.O.	**Auditors:** ERNST & YOUNG LLP **Investor Contact:** 313-222-2840 **Transfer Agents:** Wells Fargo Shareowner Services, South St. Paul, MN

COMMERCE BANCORP, INC. (NJ)

Exchange	Symbol	Price	52Wk Range	Yield	P/E	Div Acheiver
NYS	CBH	$32.47 (3/31/2005)	33.38-24.12	1.36	19.92	13 Years

*7 Year Price Score 138.05 *NYSE Composite Index=100 *12 Month Price Score 96.42

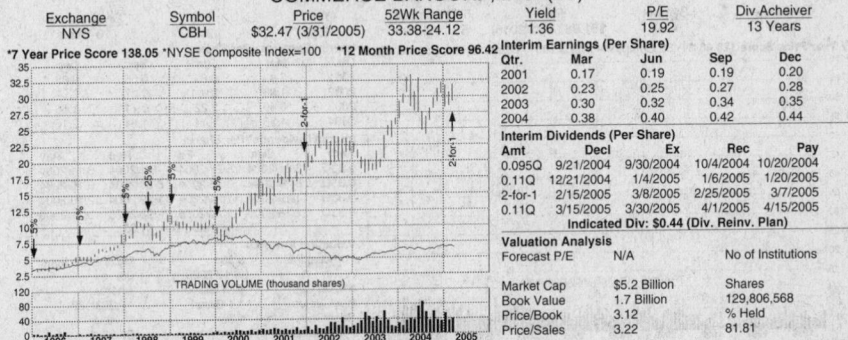

Interim Earnings (Per Share)

Qtr.	Mar	Jun	Sep	Dec
2001	0.17	0.19	0.19	0.20
2002	0.23	0.25	0.27	0.28
2003	0.30	0.32	0.34	0.35
2004	0.38	0.40	0.42	0.44

Interim Dividends (Per Share)

Amt	Decl	Ex	Rec	Pay
0.095Q	9/21/2004	9/30/2004	10/4/2004	10/20/2004
0.11Q	12/21/2004	1/4/2005	1/6/2005	1/20/2005
2-for-1	2/15/2005	3/8/2005	2/25/2005	3/7/2005
0.11Q	3/15/2005	3/30/2005	4/1/2005	4/15/2005

Indicated Div: $0.44 (Div. Reinv. Plan)

Valuation Analysis

Forecast P/E	N/A	No of Institutions
Market Cap	$5.2 Billion	Shares
Book Value	1.7 Billion	129,806,568
Price/Book	3.12	% Held
Price/Sales	3.22	81.81

Business Summary: Commercial Banking (MIC: 8.1 SIC: 021 NAIC: 22110)

Commerce Bancorp, with assets of $22.71 billion as of Dec 31 2003, is a bank holding company primarily serving the Metropolitan Philadelphia, New Jersey, Delaware and New York markets. Co. operates five bank subsidiaries, including Commerce Bank, Commerce Bank/Pennsylvania, Commerce Bank/Shore, Commerce Bank/Delaware, and Commerce Bank/North. As of Dec 31 2003, these banks provided a full range of retail and commercial banking services through 270 retail branch offices. Co. also operates Commerce Capital Markets, which is engaged in securities, investment banking and brokerage activities, and Commerce National Insurance Services, which operates an insurance brokerage agency.

Recent Developments: For the year ended Dec 31 2004, net income increased 40.7% to $273,418 thousand from net income of $194,287 thousand a year earlier. Net interest income was $1,017,785 thousand, up 34.7% from $755,866 thousand the year before. Provision for loan losses was $39,238 thousand versus $31,850 thousand in the prior year, an increase of 23.2%. Non-interest income rose 12.8% to $375,071 thousand, while non-interest expense advanced 23.0% to $938,778 thousand.

Prospects: On Jan 27 2005, Co. announced that it plans to build 55 plus new stores and create 1,800 career opportunities in its retail stores and support operations areas. Part of this year's growth includes expansion into three new markets, which include metro Washington/Baltimore, Connecticut and the Lehigh Valley in Pennsylvania. All of the new locations will offer seven-day-a-week branch banking and free checking along with other customer amenities such as free coin-counting machines. Moreover, Co. expects to continue adding new personnel by hiring approximately 10,000 new employees during the next five years.

Financial Data

(US$ in Thousands)	12/31/2004	12/31/2003	12/31/2002	12/31/2001	12/31/2000	12/31/1999	12/31/1998	12/31/1997
Earnings Per Share	1.63	1.30	1.02	0.76	0.62	0.54	0.47	0.40
Cash Flow Per Share	3.08	3.67	1.46	0.05	0.79	(0.03)	0.04	0.52
Tang Book Value Per Share	10.42	8.35	6.77	4.83	3.87	2.99	2.98	2.64
Dividends Per Share	0.380	0.330	0.300	0.275	0.242	0.207	0.218	0.138
Dividend Payout %	23.31	25.29	29.41	36.42	38.89	38.16	46.26	34.35
Income Statement								
Interest Income	1,238,291	915,631	755,371	604,367	505,300	386,448	289,280	244,177
Interest Expense	220,506	159,765	182,616	203,041	208,370	142,081	115,553	97,037
Net Interest Income	1,017,785	755,866	572,755	401,326	296,930	244,367	173,727	147,140
Provision for Losses	39,238	31,850	33,150	26,384	13,931	9,175	5,867	4,668
Non-Interest Income	375,071	332,478	257,466	196,805	150,760	114,596	88,947	57,374
Non-Interest Expense	938,778	763,392	579,168	420,036	315,357	252,523	181,967	137,929
Income Before Taxes	414,840	293,102	217,903	151,711	118,402	97,265	74,840	61,917
Income Taxes	141,422	98,815	73,088	48,689	38,355	31,305	25,522	21,592
Net Income	273,418	194,287	144,815	103,022	80,047	65,960	49,318	40,325
Average Shares	172,603	148,924	141,806	136,204	128,444	121,860	104,794	99,901
Balance Sheet								
Net Loans & Leases	9,318,991	7,328,519	5,731,856	4,516,431	3,638,580	2,922,706	1,904,954	1,390,028
Total Assets	30,501,645	22,712,180	16,403,981	11,363,703	8,296,516	6,635,793	4,894,065	3,938,967
Total Deposits	27,658,885	20,701,400	14,548,841	10,185,594	7,387,594	5,608,920	4,435,115	3,369,404
Total Liabilities	28,835,940	21,434,892	15,485,971	10,727,133	7,804,292	6,279,037	4,593,349	3,688,207
Stockholders' Equity	1,665,705	1,277,288	918,010	636,570	492,224	356,756	300,716	250,760
Shares Outstanding	159,840	153,012	135,666	131,665	127,045	119,377	100,821	92,058
Statistical Record								
Return on Assets %	1.02	0.99	1.04	1.05	1.07	1.14	1.12	1.19
Return on Equity %	18.53	17.70	18.63	18.25	18.81	20.06	17.89	18.66
Net Interest Margin %	82.19	82.55	75.82	66.40	58.76	63.23	60.05	60.26
Efficiency Ratio %	58.19	61.16	57.18	52.43	48.07	50.40	48.11	45.74
Loans to Deposits	0.34	0.35	0.39	0.44	0.49	0.52	0.43	0.41
Price Range	33.38-24.12	26.65-18.18	25.12-18.21	19.67-13.45	17.50-7.83	11.90-9.45	11.99-7.81	8.90-4.75
P/E Ratio	20.48-14.80	20.50-13.99	24.63-17.85	25.88-17.70	28.23-12.63	22.05-17.50	25.51-16.62	22.24-11.88

Address: Commerce Atrium, 1701 Route 70 East, Cherry Hill, NJ 08034-5400 Telephone: (856) 751-9000 Fax: (856) 751-9260	Web Site: www.commerceonline.com Officers: Vernon W. Hill II - Chmn., Pres., C.E.O. Peter M. Musumeci Jr. - Exec. V.P., Sr. Credit Officer, Treas., Asst. Sec.	Auditors: Ernst & Young LLP Investor Contact: 888-751-9000 Transfer Agents: Mellon Investor Services, LLP, New York, NY

COMMERCE GROUP, INC. (MA)

Exchange	Symbol	Price	52Wk Range	Yield	P/E	Div Acheiver
NYS	CGI	$61.98 (3/31/2005)	69.70-42.98	2.13	9.52	10 Years

*7 Year Price Score 128.48 *NYSE Composite Index=100 *12 Month Price Score 115.13

Interim Earnings (Per Share)

Qtr.	Mar	Jun	Sep	Dec
2001	0.43	0.83	0.65	0.83
2002	1.06	(0.01)	0.27	0.09
2003	0.40	2.22	0.71	1.66
2004	1.56	1.14	1.64	2.16

Interim Dividends (Per Share)

Amt	Decl	Ex	Rec	Pay
0.33Q	5/21/2004	5/27/2004	6/1/2004	6/11/2004
0.33Q	8/20/2004	8/26/2004	8/30/2004	9/10/2004
0.33Q	11/19/2004	11/24/2004	11/29/2004	12/10/2004
0.33Q	2/18/2005	2/24/2005	2/28/2005	3/11/2005

Indicated Div: $1.32

Valuation Analysis

Forecast P/E	9.88	No of Institutions
	(4/13/2005)	99
Market Cap	$2.1 Billion	Shares
Book Value	1.1 Billion	11,203,182
Price/Book	1.85	% Held
Price/Sales	1.14	33.38

Business Summary: Insurance (MIC: 8.2 SIC: 331 NAIC: 24126)

Commerce Group provides personal and commercial property and casualty insurance in Massachusetts and, to a lesser extent, in other states. Co.'s core product lines are personal and commercial automobile and homeowners insurance. In addition to its core product lines, Co. writes commercial multi-peril, inland marine, fire, general liability, and personal and commercial umbrella insurance. Co. writes insurance through its principal subsidiary, Commerce. Co. also writes insurance through three other subsidiaries, including Citation in Massachusetts; Commerce West in California and Oregon; and American Commerce, a wholly-owned subsidiary of ACIC Holding Co., Inc., in 16 states.

Recent Developments: For the year ended Dec 31 2004, net income increased 33.2% to $214,431 thousand from net income of $160,943 thousand a year earlier. Revenues were $1,806,571 thousand, up 10.1% from $1,640,822 thousand the year before. Net premiums earned were $1,638,833 thousand versus $1,445,628 thousand in the prior year, an increase of 13.4%. Net investment income rose 25.5% to $115,711 thousand from $92,183 thousand a year ago.

Prospects: Co.'s strong results reflect a significant decline in its operating combined ratio. The lower combined ratio is the result of a decrease in the loss ratio, partially offset by an increase in the underwriting ratio. The improvement in the loss ratio is the result of an increase in average earned premium revenue per automobile, a decline in the current year personal automobile physical damage claim frequency, more favorable loss reserve development and improved results from Commonwealth Automobile Reinsurers. Meanwhile, Co. underwriting ratio is being adversely affected by significantly higher accrued agents' profit sharing.

Financial Data

(US$ in Thousands)	12/31/2004	12/31/2003	12/31/2002	12/31/2001	12/31/2000	12/31/1999	12/31/1998	12/31/1997
Earnings Per Share	6.51	4.99	1.42	2.75	3.87	2.94	2.68	2.67
Cash Flow Per Share	9.87	8.13	6.94	3.16	4.32	3.57	1.81	2.22
Tang Book Value Per Share	33.45	28.40	24.53	24.44	23.08	18.73	18.57	18.03
Dividends Per Share	1.310	1.270	1.230	1.190	1.150	1.110	1.070	1.030
Dividend Payout %	20.12	25.45	86.62	43.27	29.72	37.76	39.93	38.58
Income Statement								
Premium Income	1,638,833	1,445,628	1,210,040	1,043,652	954,483	871,830	745,620	730,497
Total Revenue	1,806,571	1,640,822	1,257,119	1,153,838	1,099,480	987,540	852,330	841,313
Benefits & Claims	1,044,840	1,070,147	909,769	777,543	686,157	625,090	531,429	526,127
Income Before Taxes	304,186	219,305	52,026	115,425	170,066	128,790	124,467	127,695
Income Taxes	89,003	58,068	17,063	23,194	38,306	27,154	27,975	31,480
Net Income	214,431	160,943	46,755	93,094	132,080	102,588	96,492	96,215
Average Shares	32,952	32,254	33,028	33,794	34,121	34,940	36,042	36,044
Balance Sheet								
Total Assets	3,610,396	3,164,231	2,382,688	2,140,082	2,075,614	1,871,472	1,755,983	1,754,753
Total Liabilities	2,489,114	2,247,630	1,588,530	1,327,808	1,292,665	1,223,650	1,050,198	1,104,957
Stockholders' Equity	1,116,156	912,211	790,052	812,274	781,881	646,634	705,785	649,796
Shares Outstanding	33,322	32,060	32,116	33,130	33,753	34,359	38,000	36,042
Statistical Record								
Return on Assets %	6.31	5.80	2.07	4.42	6.67	5.66	5.50	5.61
Return on Equity %	21.09	18.91	5.84	11.68	18.44	15.17	14.24	15.56
Loss Ratio %	63.76	74.03	75.19	74.50	71.89	71.70	71.27	72.02
Net Margin %	11.87	9.81	3.72	8.07	12.01	10.39	11.32	11.44
Price Range	62.12-39.40	40.94-32.30	42.05-29.48	40.05-24.63	30.81-23.25	35.44-20.75	39.25-23.00	35.06-21.50
P/E Ratio	9.54-6.05	8.20-6.47	29.61-20.76	14.56-8.96	7.96-6.01	12.05-7.06	14.65-8.58	13.13-8.05
Average Yield %	2.69	3.40	3.31	3.46	4.24	4.41	3.24	3.83

Address: 211 Main Street, Webster, MA 01570 **Telephone:** (508) 943-9000	**Web Site:** www.commerceinsurance.com **Officers:** Arthur J. Remillard Jr. - Chmn., Pres., C.E.O. Gerald Fels - Exec. V.P., C.F.O.	**Auditors:** ERNST & YOUNG LLP **Transfer Agents:** EquiServe Trust Company N.A., Kansas City, MO

COMMERCIAL NET LEASE REALTY, INC.

Exchange	Symbol	Price	52Wk Range	Yield	P/E	Div Acheiver
NYS	NNN	$18.45 (3/31/2005)	21.20-15.49	7.05	16.04	15 Years

*7 Year Price Score 109.64 ***NYSE Composite Index=100** ***12 Month Price Score 97.22**

Interim Earnings (Per Share)

Qtr.	Mar	Jun	Sep	Dec
2001	0.38	0.34	0.23	(0.05)
2002	0.29	0.31	0.19	0.31
2003	0.23	0.28	0.32	0.30
2004	0.29	0.22	0.30	0.34

Interim Dividends (Per Share)

Amt	Decl	Ex	Rec	Pay
0.32Q	4/14/2004	4/28/2004	4/30/2004	5/14/2004
0.325Q	7/14/2004	7/28/2004	7/30/2004	8/13/2004
0.325Q	10/15/2004	10/27/2004	10/29/2004	11/15/2004
0.325Q	1/14/2005	1/27/2005	1/31/2005	2/15/2005

Indicated Div: $1.30 (Div. Reinv. Plan)

Valuation Analysis

Forecast P/E	12.51	No of Institutions	
	(4/7/2005)	126	
Market Cap	$960.8 Million	Shares	
Book Value	757.0 Million	22,575,692	
Price/Book	1.27	% Held	
Price/Sales	7.43	43.33	

Business Summary: Property, Real Estate & Development (MIC: 8.3 SIC: 798 NAIC: 25930)

Commercial Net Lease Realty is a fully integrated, self-administered real estate investment trust. Co. and its wholly-owned subsidiaries acquire, own, manage and indirectly, through investment interests, develop primarily single-tenant retail, office and industrial properties that are generally leased under long-term commercial net leases. As of Dec 31 2003, Co. owned 339 properties in 39 states that are generally leased to major retail businesses under long-term commercial net leases. These businesses include Academy, Barnes & Noble, Bennigan's, Best Buy, Borders, Eckerd, Jared Jewelers, OfficeMax, The Sports Authority and the United States of America.

Recent Developments: For the year ended Dec 31 2004, income from continuing operations increased 19.1% to $45,900 thousand from income of $38,525 thousand a year earlier. Net income increased 21.4% to $64,934 thousand from net income of $53,473 thousand a year earlier. Revenues were $129,309 thousand, up 24.8% from $103,614 thousand the year before. Operating income was $73,273 thousand versus an income of $58,894 thousand in the prior year, an increase of 24.4%.

Prospects: On Jan 18 2005, Co. announced that it has signed an agreement to acquire National Properties Corporation (NAPE). Total consideration, taking into account the special pre-closing dividend and including the assumption of debt, is estimated to be approximately $61.0 million based on Co.'s closing stock price on Jan 14 2005. Completion of the transaction is subject to customary closing conditions, including the approval of the holders of a majority of the outstanding shares of NAPE common stock. The acquisition is expected to be completed no later than the second quarter of 2005. NAPE currently owns 43 properties located in 12 states. These investment properties are leased to 17 corporations.

Financial Data
(US$ in Thousands)

	12/31/2004	12/31/2003	12/31/2002	12/31/2001	12/31/2000	12/31/1999	12/31/1998	12/31/1997
Earnings Per Share	1.15	1.13	1.09	0.91	1.26	1.16	1.10	1.25
Cash Flow Per Share	1.45	1.26	1.45	1.21	1.65	1.58	1.41	1.41
Tang Book Value Per Share	13.20	13.22	12.49	12.68	12.93	12.94	13.00	12.96
Dividends Per Share	1.290	1.280	1.270	1.260	1.245	1.240	1.230	1.200
Dividend Payout %	112.17	113.27	116.51	138.46	98.81	106.90	111.82	96.00
Income Statement								
Property Income	121,591	95,790	85,316	69,851	73,776	72,275	61,750	49,922
Non-Property Income	7,718	6,868	8,511	10,675	7,115	4,268	3,023	213
Total Revenue	129,309	102,658	93,827	80,526	80,891	76,543	64,773	50,135
Depn & Amortn	17,064	13,119	11,315	8,803	8,702	8,445	6,774	5,302
Interest Expense	32,463	27,731	26,720	24,952	26,528	21,920	13,460	11,478
Income Before Taxes	44,589	...	...	...	...	...	...	...
Income Taxes	(2,542)	...	...	...	...	...	...	397
Net Income	64,934	53,473	48,058	28,963	38,251	35,311	32,441	30,385
Average Shares	51,742	43,896	40,588	31,717	30,407	30,408	29,397	24,220
Balance Sheet								
Total Assets	1,300,048	1,208,310	954,108	1,006,628	761,611	749,789	685,595	537,014
Long-Term Obligations	506,341	437,338	345,689	327,933	258,681	242,271	154,807	56,736
Total Liabilities	541,022	477,556	404,967	441,988	367,710	358,427	301,705	174,870
Stockholders' Equity	756,998	730,754	549,141	564,640	393,901	391,362	383,890	362,144
Shares Outstanding	52,077	50,001	40,403	40,599	30,456	30,255	29,521	27,953
Statistical Record								
Return on Assets %	5.16	4.95	4.90	3.28	5.05	4.92	5.31	6.69
Return on Equity %	8.71	8.36	8.63	6.04	9.72	9.11	8.70	9.89
Net Margin %	50.22	52.09	51.22	35.97	47.29	46.13	50.08	60.61
Price Range	21.20-15.49	18.30-14.37	16.34-13.00	14.25-10.25	11.31-9.69	13.88-9.50	18.00-12.63	18.06-14.13
P/E Ratio	18.43-13.47	16.19-12.72	14.99-11.93	15.66-11.26	8.98-7.69	11.96-8.19	16.36-11.48	14.45-11.30
Average Yield %	7.06	7.70	8.50	9.97	11.94	10.38	7.92	7.66

Address: 450 South Orange Avenue, Suite 900, Orlando, FL 32801 **Telephone:** (407) 265-7348 **Fax:** (407) 423-2894	**Web Site:** www.cnlreit.com **Officers:** James M. Seneff Jr. - Chmn. Robert A. Bourne - Vice-Chmn.	**Auditors:** KPMG LLP **Investor Contact:** 407-265-7348 **Transfer Agents:** Wachovia Bank, N.A., Charlotte, NC

COMMSCOPE, INC.

Exchange	Symbol	Price	52Wk Range	Yield	P/E
NYS	CTV	$14.96 (3/31/2005)	22.52-14.09	N/A	13.01

*7 Year Price Score 78.10 ***NYSE Composite Index=100** ***12 Month Price Score 75.23**

TRADING VOLUME (thousand shares)

Interim Earnings (Per Share)

Qtr.	Mar	Jun	Sep	Dec
2001	0.32	0.11	0.12	(0.04)
2002	(0.03)	(0.69)	(0.32)	(0.07)
2003	(0.05)	(0.87)	0.02	(0.29)
2004	(0.27)	1.37	0.27	(0.23)

Interim Dividends (Per Share)

No Dividends Paid

Valuation Analysis

Forecast P/E	23.60	No of Institutions
	(4/7/2005)	160
Market Cap	$815.1 Million	Shares
Book Value	449.5 Million	57,766,800
Price/Book	1.81	% Held
Price/Sales	0.71	N/A

Business Summary: Communications (MIC: 10.1 SIC: 663 NAIC: 34220)

CommScope manufactures and sells cable for three broad product categories: cable television and other video applications, local area network applications, and wireless and other telecommunications applications. Co. is a worldwide designer, manufacturer and marketer of a broad line of coaxial cables and other high-performance electronic and fiber-optic cable products for cable television, telephony, Internet access and wireless communications. Co. is also a manufacturer of broadband cable for hybrid fiber coaxial applications. Co.'s products are used in cable television networks, telephone central offices, satellite television systems and security surveillance.

Recent Developments: For the year ended Dec 31 2004, net income was $75,755 thousand versus net loss of $70,560 thousand a year earlier. Revenues were $1,152,696 thousand, up 101.1% from $573,260 thousand the year before. Operating income was $5,906 thousand versus a loss of $8,954 thousand in the prior year. Total direct expense was $897,881 thousand versus $458,620 thousand in the prior year, an increase of 95.8%. Total indirect expense was $248,909 thousand versus $123,594 thousand in the prior year, an increase of 101.4%.

Prospects: Co. is benefiting from better than expected sales growth. However, ongoing cost pressures are negatively affecting operating margin. Accordingly, Co. is working to offset higher costs and improve under-performing product lines to strengthen its financial performance. Looking ahead, Co. expects sales of $1.20 billion to $1.30 billion, primarily driven by a modest increase in sales volume as well as price increases. Conversely, Co. believes material and selling, general and administrative costs will be somewhat higher than its earlier projections. Based on this revenue outlook, Co. expects operating margins will rise to the 5.0% to 5.5% level for full-year 2005.

Financial Data

(US$ in Thousands)	12/31/2004	12/31/2003	12/31/2002	12/31/2001	12/31/2000	12/31/1999	12/31/1998	12/31/1997
Earnings Per Share	1.15	(1.19)	(1.10)	0.52	1.60	1.31	0.79	0.70
Cash Flow Per Share	1.88	1.54	1.70	3.00	0.88	1.57	1.68	1.22
Tang Book Value Per Share	3.96	5.02	6.03	7.20	3.98	2.02	0.41	N.M.
Income Statement								
Total Revenue	1,152,696	573,260	598,467	738,498	950,026	748,914	571,733	599,216
EBITDA	57,051	24,919	21,192	99,729	178,533	144,419	99,766	96,676
Depn & Amortn	56,360	33,074	35,741	37,046	31,998	26,166	24,662	21,677
Income Before Taxes	(6,308)	(13,989)	(21,288)	55,213	136,880	108,627	60,214	61,514
Income Taxes	(7,019)	(5,174)	(7,858)	20,426	51,993	40,550	20,983	24,056
Net Income	75,755	(70,560)	(67,152)	27,865	84,887	68,077	39,231	37,458
Average Shares	67,685	59,231	61,171	53,500	56,047	52,050	49,521	49,238
Balance Sheet								
Current Assets	448,093	330,672	258,459	245,868	289,663	215,179	144,412	155,835
Total Assets	1,030,579	739,781	772,668	889,005	721,182	582,535	465,327	483,539
Current Liabilities	156,673	50,036	44,488	46,743	80,559	68,227	50,430	43,049
Long-Term Obligations	297,300	183,300	183,300	191,918	225,316	198,402	181,800	265,800
Total Liabilities	581,116	284,075	255,133	282,491	346,662	301,191	261,355	333,507
Stockholders' Equity	449,463	455,706	517,535	606,514	374,520	281,344	203,972	150,032
Shares Outstanding	54,487	59,318	59,219	61,688	51,263	50,889	50,254	49,109
Statistical Record								
Return on Assets %	8.53	N.M.	N.M.	3.46	12.99	12.99	8.27	7.78
Return on Equity %	16.69	N.M.	N.M.	5.68	25.81	28.05	22.16	13.78
EBITDA Margin %	4.95	4.35	3.54	13.50	18.79	19.28	17.45	16.13
Net Margin %	6.57	N.M.	N.M.	3.77	8.94	9.09	6.86	6.25
Asset Turnover	1.30	0.76	0.72	0.92	1.45	1.43	1.21	1.24
Current Ratio	2.86	6.61	5.81	5.26	3.60	3.15	2.86	3.62
Debt to Equity	0.66	0.40	0.35	0.32	0.60	0.71	0.89	1.77
Price Range	22.52-15.96	16.80-7.00	23.35-6.12	26.21-15.00	48.00-16.00	45.25-16.38	20.50-9.69	17.75-10.44
P/E Ratio	19.58-13.88	...	...	50.40-28.85	30.00-10.00	34.54-12.50	25.95-12.26	25.36-14.91

Address: 1100 CommScope Place S.E., Hickory, NC 28602 Telephone: (828) 324-2200 Fax: (828) 328-3400	Web Site: www.commscope.com Officers: Frank M. Drendel - Chmn., C.E.O. Brian D. Garrett - Pres., C.O.O.	Auditors: Deloitte & Touche LLP Investor Contact: 828-323-4848

COMMUNITY BANK SYSTEM, INC.

Exchange	Symbol	Price	52Wk Range	Yield	P/E	Div Acheiver
NYS	CBU	$22.91 (3/31/2005)	28.35-19.25	3.14	13.97	13 Years

*7 Year Price Score 126.15 *NYSE Composite Index=100 *12 Month Price Score 91.17

Interim Earnings (Per Share)

Qtr.	Mar	Jun	Sep	Dec
2001	0.28	0.09	0.28	0.20
2002	0.28	0.31	0.42	0.37
2003	0.38	0.38	0.44	0.30
2004	0.38	0.40	0.45	0.41

Interim Dividends (Per Share)

Amt	Decl	Ex	Rec	Pay
0.16Q	5/21/2004	6/14/2004	6/15/2004	7/9/2004
0.18Q	8/19/2004	9/13/2004	9/15/2004	10/11/2004
0.18Q	11/19/2004	12/13/2004	12/15/2004	1/10/2005
0.18Q	2/18/2005	3/11/2005	3/15/2005	4/11/2005

Indicated Div: $0.72 (Div. Reinv. Plan)

Valuation Analysis

Forecast P/E	13.80		No of Institutions
	(4/7/2005)		103
Market Cap	$702.0 Million		Shares
Book Value	474.6 Million		11,897,683
Price/Book	1.48		% Held
Price/Sales	2.73		39.25

Business Summary: Commercial Banking (MIC: 8.1 SIC: 021 NAIC: 22110)

Community Bank System is a bank holding company with $3.86 billion in assets and total deposits of $2.73 billion as of Dec 31 2003. As of Dec 31 2003, Co.'s wholly-owned community banking subsidiary, Community Bank, N.A., operated 126 customer facilities throughout 22 counties of Upstate New York and five counties of Northeastern Pennsylvania offering a range of commercial and retail banking services. Another Co. subsidiary, Benefit Plans Adminstrative Services, Inc., provides administration, consulting and actuarial services to sponsors of employee benefit plans.

Recent Developments: For the year ended Dec 31 2004, net income increased 24.3% to $50,196,000 from net income of $40,380,000 a year earlier. Net interest income was $151,043,000, up 14.6% from $131,828,000 the year before. Provision for loan losses was $8,750,000 versus $11,195,000 in the prior year, a decrease of 21.8%. Non-interest income rose 26.2% to $44,445,000, while non-interest expense advanced 16.7% to $119,899,000.

Prospects: Co.'s prospects appear decent, reflecting in part its recent results that have benefited from both acquired and organic growth in earning asset levels, strong growth in non-interest income and improved asset quality. Regarding its asset quality, Co. cited its enhanced credit risk management programs and continued emphasis on disciplined underwriting standards, as well as stabilizing economic conditions as positive factors. Separately, in Dec 2004, Co. completed the purchase of a branch office in Dansville, NY from HSBC Bank USA, N.A. Co. subsequently closed its own Dansville branch and consolidated all customer service activities into the former HSBC office.

Financial Data

(US$ in Thousands)	12/31/2004	12/31/2003	12/31/2002	12/31/2001	12/31/2000	12/31/1999	12/31/1998	12/31/1997
Earnings Per Share	1.64	1.50	1.47	0.81	1.43	1.21	1.02	1.01
Cash Flow Per Share	2.85	2.78	2.24	1.92	1.94	2.16	2.41	1.58
Tang Book Value Per Share	7.90	7.37	7.33	4.87	6.32	4.04	4.50	3.91
Dividends Per Share	0.680	0.610	0.560	0.540	0.520	0.480	0.430	0.380
Dividend Payout %	41.46	40.80	38.23	66.67	36.49	39.67	41.95	37.62
Income Statement								
Interest Income	212,795	191,129	204,870	197,850	145,221	123,888	122,938	117,628
Interest Expense	61,752	59,301	77,020	101,195	74,012	55,947	58,543	54,752
Net Interest Income	151,043	131,828	127,850	96,655	71,208	67,941	64,395	62,876
Provision for Losses	8,750	11,195	12,222	7,097	7,182	5,136	5,123	4,480
Non-Interest Income	44,445	34,981	32,600	29,083	20,989	15,487	17,040	11,808
Non-Interest Expense	119,899	102,461	95,824	89,039	55,989	52,733	51,876	45,799
Income Before Taxes	66,839	53,153	52,404	29,602	29,027	25,559	24,436	24,406
Income Taxes	16,643	12,773	13,887	8,891	8,708	7,923	8,902	8,844
Net Income	50,196	40,380	38,517	19,129	20,319	17,635	15,728	15,562
Average Shares	30,670	27,034	26,334	23,650	14,271	14,590	15,341	15,352
Balance Sheet								
Net Loans & Leases	2,326,715	2,099,414	1,780,574	1,708,969	1,084,112	995,802	904,779	830,778
Total Assets	4,393,831	3,855,397	3,434,204	3,210,833	2,022,635	1,840,702	1,680,689	1,633,742
Total Deposits	2,928,978	2,725,488	2,505,356	2,545,970	1,457,730	1,360,306	1,378,066	1,345,686
Total Liabilities	3,919,203	3,450,569	3,109,166	2,942,853	1,883,260	1,732,214	1,560,523	1,515,730
Stockholders' Equity	474,628	404,828	325,038	267,980	139,376	108,487	120,165	118,012
Shares Outstanding	30,641	28,330	25,957	25,805	13,986	14,592	14,592	15,173
Statistical Record								
Return on Assets %	1.21	1.11	1.16	0.73	1.05	1.00	0.95	1.05
Return on Equity %	11.38	11.07	12.99	9.39	16.35	15.43	13.21	13.69
Net Interest Margin %	70.98	68.97	62.41	48.85	49.03	54.84	52.38	53.45
Efficiency Ratio %	46.61	45.31	40.35	39.24	33.69	37.84	37.06	35.38
Loans to Deposits	0.79	0.77	0.71	0.67	0.74	0.73	0.66	0.62
Price Range	28.35-19.25	25.13-15.55	17.01-13.07	14.82-12.45	13.02-10.13	16.31-11.31	19.09-12.50	17.00-9.75
P/E Ratio	17.29-11.74	16.75-10.37	11.57-8.89	18.30-15.37	9.10-7.08	13.48-9.35	18.72-12.25	16.83-9.65
Average Yield %	2.84	3.07	3.67	3.95	4.55	3.73	2.73	2.94

Address: 5790 Widewaters Parkway, DeWitt, NY 13214-1883
Telephone: (315) 445-2282
Fax: (315) 445-2997

Web Site: www.communitybankna.com
Officers: James A. Gabriel - Chmn. Sanford A. Belden - Pres., C.E.O.

Auditors: PricewaterhouseCoopers LLP
Investor Contact: 315-445-2282
Transfer Agents: ChaseMellon Shareholder Services, L.L.C., Ridgefield

COMMUNITY HEALTH SYSTEMS, INC.

Exchange	Symbol	Price	52Wk Range	Yield	P/E
NYS	CYH	$34.91 (3/31/2005)	34.91-23.40	N/A	23.12

*7 Year Price Score N/A   *NYSE Composite Index=100   *12 Month Price Score 109.71

Interim Earnings (Per Share)

Qtr.	Mar	Jun	Sep	Dec
2001	0.13	0.11	0.11	0.15
2002	0.27	0.24	0.21	0.28
2003	0.33	0.30	0.31	0.35
2004	0.39	0.37	0.32	0.43

Interim Dividends (Per Share)

No Dividends Paid

Valuation Analysis

Forecast P/E	N/A	No of Institutions
Market Cap	$3.1 Billion	Shares
Book Value	1.2 Billion	85,198,936
Price/Book	2.47	% Held
Price/Sales	0.92	97.17

Business Summary: Hospitals & Health Care (MIC: 9.3 SIC: 062 NAIC: 22110)

Community Health Systems owns, leases and operates acute care hospitals that are the principal providers of primary healthcare services in non-urban communities in the U.S. Co.'s hospitals typically have 50 to 200 beds and are located in non-urban markets. Co.'s facilities, together with its medical staff, provide a range of inpatient and outpatient general hospital services and a variety of specialty services. As of Dec 31 2004, Co. owned, leased or operated 71 hospitals, geographically dispersed across 22 states, with an aggregate of 7,888 licensed beds.

Recent Developments: For the year ended Dec 31 2004, income from continuing operations increased 19.8% to $158,221 thousand from income of $132,049 thousand a year earlier. Net income increased 15.2% to $151,433 thousand from net income of $131,472 thousand a year earlier. Revenues were $3,332,641 thousand, up 19.2% from $2,796,766 thousand the year before. Operating income was $338,867 thousand versus an income of $291,358 thousand in the prior year, an increase of 16.3%. Total indirect expense was $2,992,196 thousand versus $2,503,421 thousand in the prior year, an increase of 19.5%.

Prospects: On Mar 1 2005, Co. announced the closing of the acquisition of Chestnut Hill Hospital, a 183-bed acute care general hospital located in northern Philadelphia from Chestnut HealthCare. The transaction also includes a rehabilitation facility and an assisted living facility. The University of Pennsylvania Health System will have a 15.0% minority interest. Separately, Co. recently agreed to sell the 74-bed Lakeview Community Hospital in Eufaula, AL, the 97-bed Troy Regional Hospital in Troy, AL, and the 75-bed Northeast Medical Center in Bonham, TX, to Attentus Healthcare Company. Looking ahead, Co. expects to grow its operating base and extend into new communities through acquisitions.

Financial Data (US$ in Thousands)	12/31/2004	12/31/2003	12/31/2002	12/31/2001	12/31/2000	12/31/1999	12/31/1998	12/31/1997
Earnings Per Share	1.51	1.30	1.00	0.50	0.14	(0.31)	(3.38)	(0.60)
Cash Flow Per Share	3.40	2.48	2.90	1.75	0.34	(0.22)	0.29	...
Tang Book Value Per Share	0.30	1.97	1.87	1.17	N.M.	N.M.	N.M.	
Income Statement								
Total Revenue	3,332,641	2,834,624	2,200,417	1,693,625	1,337,501	1,079,953	854,580	742,350
EBITDA	496,459	434,536	359,728	308,711	252,736	186,906	(18,652)	122,238
Depn & Amortn	158,380	143,766	118,218	119,668	97,624	81,651	76,500	69,157
Income Before Taxes	260,223	219,678	178,650	94,495	27,742	(11,236)	(196,343)	(36,672)
Income Taxes	102,002	88,206	73,392	45,944	18,173	5,553	(13,405)	(4,501)
Net Income	151,433	131,472	99,984	44,743	9,569	(16,789)	(183,290)	(32,171)
Average Shares	105,863	108,094	108,378	90,251	69,187	54,545	54,249	53,989
Balance Sheet								
Current Assets	815,449	696,080	647,726	494,559	408,577	300,496	230,111	...
Total Assets	3,632,608	3,350,211	2,809,496	2,460,664	2,213,837	1,895,084	1,747,016	...
Current Liabilities	362,359	398,064	318,430	299,572	240,873	235,277	226,688	...
Long-Term Obligations	1,804,868	1,444,981	1,173,929	980,083	1,201,590	1,407,604	1,246,594	...
Total Liabilities	2,392,617	1,999,622	1,595,191	1,344,999	1,457,663	1,665,376	1,500,190	...
Stockholders' Equity	1,239,991	1,350,589	1,214,305	1,115,665	756,174	229,708	246,826	...
Shares Outstanding	87,616	98,681	98,829	98,469	86,137	55,602	55,632	56,376
Statistical Record								
Return on Assets %	4.33	4.27	3.79	1.91	0.46	N.M.	...	...
Return on Equity %	11.66	10.25	8.58	4.78	1.94	N.M.	...	...
EBITDA Margin %	14.90	15.33	16.35	18.23	18.90	17.31	N.M.	16.47
Net Margin %	4.54	4.64	4.54	2.64	0.72	N.M.	N.M.	N.M.
Asset Turnover	0.95	0.92	0.84	0.72	0.65	0.59	...	...
Current Ratio	2.25	1.75	2.03	1.65	1.70	1.28	1.02	...
Debt to Equity	1.46	1.07	0.97	0.88	1.59	6.13	5.05	...
Price Range	30.73-23.40	27.40-16.88	29.90-19.40	34.25-22.00	36.55-13.69	...	...	...
P/E Ratio	20.35-15.50	21.08-12.98	29.90-19.40	68.50-44.00	261.07-97.71	...	...	...

Address: 155 Franklin Road, Suite 400, Brentwood, TN 37027 Telephone: (615) 373-9600	Web Site: www.chs.net Officers: Wayne T. Smith - Chmn., Pres., C.E.O. W. Larry Cash - Exec. V.P., C.F.O.	Auditors: Deloitte & Touche LLP Transfer Agents: Mellon Investor Services LLC, Atlanta, GA

COMPUTER ASSOCIATES INTERNATIONAL, INC.

Exchange	Symbol	Price	52Wk Range	Yield	P/E
NYS	CA	$27.10 (3/31/2005)	31.52-22.61	0.30	208.46

*7 Year Price Score 70.54 ***NYSE Composite Index=100** ***12 Month Price Score 93.84**

Interim Earnings (Per Share)

Qtr.	Jun	Sep	Dec	Mar
2001-02	(0.59)	(0.50)	(0.40)	(0.41)
2002-03	(0.11)	(0.09)	(0.08)	(0.18)
2003-04	0.02	(0.15)	0.04	0.14
2004-05	0.09	(0.16)	0.06	...

Interim Dividends (Per Share)

Amt	Decl	Ex	Rec	Pay
0.04S	5/13/2003	6/17/2003	6/19/2003	7/7/2003
0.04S	10/21/2003	12/18/2003	12/22/2003	1/7/2004
0.04S	6/16/2004	6/28/2004	6/30/2004	7/15/2004
0.04S	10/18/2004	12/16/2004	12/20/2004	1/5/2005

Indicated Div: $0.08

Valuation Analysis

Forecast P/E	27.37	No of Institutions
	(4/7/2005)	356
Market Cap	$16.0 Billion	Shares
Book Value	5.0 Billion	420,571,072
Price/Book	3.21	% Held
Price/Sales	4.64	71.12

Business Summary: IT & Technology (MIC: 10.2 SIC: 372 NAIC: 11210)

Computer Associates International is a business software company that delivers the end-to-end infrastructure to enable e-business through technology, education and services. Co. provides software applications for all types of businesses throughout the world. Co. has a portfolio of more than 200 patents worldwide and more than 800 patent applications pending, including enterprise management, database and application development, as well as products that provide the infrastructure for e-business and e-commerce over the Internet. Many of Co.'s products provide tools to measure and improve computer hardware and software performance and programmer productivity.

Recent Developments: For the quarter ended Dec 31 2004, net income increased 100.0% to $36,000 thousand from net income of $18,000 thousand in the year-earlier quarter. Revenues were $911,000 thousand, up 8.8% from $837,000 thousand the year before. Operating income was $81,000 thousand versus an income of $56,000 thousand in the prior-year quarter, an increase of 44.6%. Total direct expense was $169,000 thousand versus $170,000 thousand in the prior-year quarter, a decrease of 0.6%. Total indirect expense was $661,000 thousand versus $611,000 thousand in the prior-year quarter, an increase of 8.2%.

Prospects: Co. is performing generally well, boosted by its acquisition of Netegrity. Co.'s channel business also performed well, and its security business continues to be a strong, with more than 94.0% bookings growth. Going forward, Co.'s near-term outlook appears to be positive, reflecting limited-to-modest improvement in the current economic and information technology environments. For the fourth quarter, revenue is expected to be in the range of $900.0 million to $920.0 million, with earnings per share in the range of $0.07 to $0.08. For the full year, Co. expects revenue in the range of $3.53 billion to $3.55 billion, with earnings per share in the range of $0.06 to $0.07.

Financial Data
(US$ in Thousands)

	9 Mos	6 Mos	3 Mos	03/31/2004	03/31/2003	03/31/2002	03/31/2001	03/31/2000
Earnings Per Share	0.13	0.11	0.12	0.04	(0.46)	(1.91)	(1.02)	1.25
Cash Flow Per Share	2.33	2.31	2.36	2.20	2.28	2.17	2.38	2.90
Dividends Per Share	0.080	0.080	0.080	0.080	0.080	0.080	0.080	0.080
Dividend Payout %	62.28	73.02	65.77	200.00	...	...	...	6.40
Income Statement								
Total Revenue	2,626,000	1,715,000	860,000	3,276,000	3,116,000	2,964,000	4,198,000	6,103,000
EBITDA	460,000	234,000	252,000	660,000	421,000	(62,000)	788,000	2,523,000
Depn & Amortn	432,000	287,000	144,000	597,000	612,000	1,096,000	1,110,000	594,000
Income Before Taxes	(51,000)	(103,000)	82,000	(54,000)	(363,000)	(1,385,000)	(666,000)	1,590,000
Income Taxes	(46,000)	(62,000)	29,000	(18,000)	(96,000)	(283,000)	(75,000)	894,000
Net Income	(7,000)	(43,000)	53,000	25,000	(267,000)	(1,102,000)	(591,000)	696,000
Average Shares	595,000	587,000	615,000	580,000	575,000	577,000	582,000	557,000
Balance Sheet								
Current Assets	4,560,000	3,454,000	3,472,000	3,358,000	3,565,000	3,061,000	2,643,000	3,992,000
Total Assets	11,925,000	10,460,000	10,607,000	10,679,000	11,054,000	12,226,000	14,143,000	17,493,000
Current Liabilities	3,484,000	3,271,000	3,241,000	2,455,000	2,974,000	2,321,000	2,286,000	3,004,000
Long-Term Obligations	2,471,000	1,474,000	1,474,000	2,298,000	2,298,000	3,334,000	3,639,000	4,527,000
Total Liabilities	6,932,000	5,735,000	5,807,000	5,961,000	6,691,000	7,609,000	8,363,000	10,456,000
Stockholders' Equity	4,993,000	4,725,000	4,800,000	4,718,000	4,363,000	4,617,000	5,780,000	7,037,000
Shares Outstanding	591,357	585,642	585,344	582,594	576,272	577,180	575,697	589,392
Statistical Record								
Return on Assets %	0.65	0.58	0.67	0.23	N.M.	N.M.	N.M.	5.43
Return on Equity %	1.53	1.30	1.50	0.55	N.M.	N.M.	N.M.	14.21
EBITDA Margin %	17.52	13.64	29.30	20.15	13.51	N.M.	18.77	41.34
Net Margin %	N.M.	N.M.	6.16	0.76	N.M.	N.M.	N.M.	11.40
Asset Turnover	0.31	0.33	0.33	0.30	0.27	0.22	0.27	0.48
Current Ratio	1.31	1.06	1.07	1.37	1.20	1.32	1.16	1.33
Debt to Equity	0.49	0.31	0.31	0.49	0.53	0.72	0.63	0.64
Price Range	31.52-22.61	29.17-22.15	29.17-22.07	28.96-13.47	21.80-7.61	38.34-15.98	61.62-18.38	75.00-34.19
P/E Ratio	242.46-173.92	265.18-201.36	243.08-183.92	724.00-336.75	...	...	...	60.00-27.35
Average Yield %	0.30	0.31	0.31	0.34	0.57	0.26	0.23	0.14

Address: One Computer Associates Plaza, Islandia, NY 11749	**Web Site:** www.ca.com	**Auditors:** KPMG LLP
Telephone: (631) 342 6000	**Officers:** Lewis S. Ranieri - Chmn. John Swainson - Pres., C.E.O.	**Investor Contact:** 631-342-5601
Fax: (631) 342 5329		**Transfer Agents:** Mellon Investor Services, Ridgefield Park, NJ

COMPUTER SCIENCES CORP.

Exchange	Symbol	Price	52Wk Range	Yield	P/E
NYS	CSC	$45.85 (3/31/2005)	57.70-39.03	N/A	14.79

*7 Year Price Score 78.06 ***NYSE Composite Index=100** ***12 Month Price Score 92.41**

Interim Earnings (Per Share)

Qtr.	Jun	Sep	Dec	Mar
2001-02	0.28	0.40	0.51	0.82
2002-03	0.46	0.54	0.61	0.93
2003-04	0.49	0.57	0.68	1.01
2004-05	0.58	0.68	0.82	...

Interim Dividends (Per Share)

No Dividends Paid

Valuation Analysis

Forecast P/E	13.86	No of Institutions	
	(4/7/2005)	421	
Market Cap	$8.8 Billion	Shares	
Book Value	6.2 Billion	161,211,680	
Price/Book	1.41	% Held	
Price/Sales	0.58	84.36	

Business Summary: IT & Technology (MIC: 10.2 SIC: 373 NAIC: 41512)

Computer Sciences provides information technology (IT) outsourcing and IT and professional services to customers in the global commercial and U.S federal markets. Co.'s outsourcing services involve operating all or a portion of a customer's technology infrastructure, including systems analysis, applications development, network operations, desktop computing and data center management. Co.'s IT and professional services include systems integration, consulting and other professional services. Co also provides certain non-IT technical services, including aircraft maintenance, marine services and security services, primarily to U.S. federal customers.

Recent Developments: For the quarter ended Dec 31 2004, net income increased 22.7% to $157,500 thousand from net income of $128,400 thousand in the year-earlier quarter. Revenues were $3,516,800 thousand, up 5.6% from $3,329,500 thousand the year before. Total direct expense was $2,822,200 thousand versus $2,662,300 thousand in the prior-year quarter, an increase of 6.0%. Total indirect expense was $467,000 thousand versus $441,500 thousand in the prior-year quarter, an increase of 5.8%.

Prospects: On Feb 14 2005, Co. sold DynCorp International, DynMarine and selected DynCorp Technical Services contracts to Veritas Capital for about $850.0 million. This transaction should provide Co. with additional flexibility for several options, including pursuing large-scale outsourcing agreements and acquisitions of businesses enhancing or complementing its core operations. Going forward, Co. should be poised for continued growth for fiscal 2005 and beyond. Co. noted that new business wins during the third quarter totaled $5.30 billion. For fiscal 2005, Co. expects revenue of about $14.00 billion, with earnings per diluted share in the range of $3.12 to $3.18, including discontinued operations.

Financial Data

(US$ in Thousands)	9 Mos	6 Mos	3 Mos	04/02/2004	03/28/2003	03/29/2002	03/30/2001	03/31/2000
Earnings Per Share	3.10	2.96	2.85	2.75	2.54	2.01	1.37	2.37
Cash Flow Per Share	10.35	10.05	9.44	8.81	6.68	7.70	5.09	5.71
Tang Book Value Per Share	11.11	8.35	7.49	7.26	4.39	3.59	3.72	11.18
Income Statement								
Total Revenue	10,260,800	7,670,900	3,736,400	14,767,600	11,346,500	11,426,000	10,524,000	9,370,694
EBITDA	1,382,200	945,900	454,300	1,945,600	1,603,400	1,496,900	1,069,400	1,197,718
Depn & Amortn	781,500	517,400	254,600	1,038,100	857,500	857,600	649,300	545,723
Income Before Taxes	489,400	353,600	162,800	746,900	611,600	496,800	330,300	611,472
Income Taxes	148,600	112,700	52,400	227,500	171,400	152,700	97,100	208,600
Net Income	398,400	240,900	110,400	519,400	440,200	344,100	233,200	402,872
Average Shares	192,829	191,118	189,896	188,700	173,119	171,279	170,767	169,749
Balance Sheet								
Current Assets	6,182,400	5,270,000	4,781,100	4,867,200	4,088,100	3,304,200	3,204,000	2,766,335
Total Assets	13,099,400	12,329,100	11,815,900	11,804,000	10,433,200	8,610,500	8,174,800	5,874,124
Current Liabilities	4,344,900	3,996,000	3,227,700	3,253,200	2,987,200	2,708,000	3,588,900	1,983,966
Long-Term Obligations	1,804,600	1,806,000	2,306,000	2,306,400	2,204,900	1,873,100	1,029,400	652,367
Total Liabilities	6,894,900	6,545,400	6,234,300	6,300,300	5,826,800	4,986,900	4,959,600	2,830,150
Stockholders' Equity	6,204,500	5,783,700	5,581,600	5,503,700	4,606,400	3,623,600	3,215,200	3,043,974
Shares Outstanding	191,100	189,260	188,719	187,841	186,757	171,137	168,713	167,508
Statistical Record								
Return on Assets %	4.88	4.84	4.75	4.60	4.64	4.11	3.33	7.42
Return on Equity %	10.30	10.43	10.33	10.11	10.73	10.09	7.47	14.84
EBITDA Margin %	13.47	12.33	12.16	13.17	14.13	13.10	10.16	12.78
Net Margin %	3.88	3.14	2.95	3.52	3.88	3.01	2.22	4.30
Asset Turnover	1.26	1.32	1.32	1.31	1.19	1.37	1.50	1.73
Current Ratio	1.42	1.32	1.48	1.50	1.37	1.22	0.89	1.39
Debt to Equity	0.29	0.31	0.41	0.42	0.48	0.52	0.32	0.21
Price Range	57.70-39.03	48.63-38.14	46.68-36.84	46.68-28.52	49.58-24.56	52.85-30.11	96.56-30.42	94.63-53.81
P/E Ratio	18.61-12.59	16.43-12.89	16.38-12.93	16.97-10.37	19.52-9.67	26.29-14.98	70.48-22.20	39.93-22.71

Address: 2100 East Grand Avenue, El Segundo, CA 90245	Web Site: www.csc.com	Auditors: Deloitte & Touche LLP
Telephone: (310) 615-0311	Officers: Van B. Honeycutt - Chmn., C.E.O. Michael W. Laphen - Pres., C.O.O.	Investor Contact: 310-615-1680
Fax: (310) 640-2648		Transfer Agents: Mellon Investor Sevices, S.Hackkensack, NJ

CONAGRA FOODS, INC.

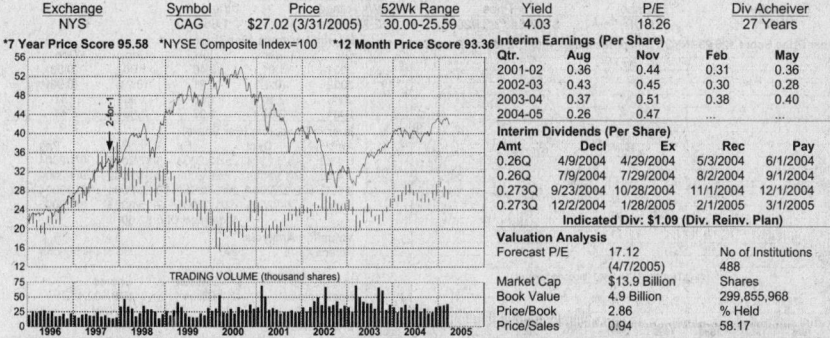

Exchange	Symbol	Price	52Wk Range	Yield	P/E	Div Acheiver
NYS	CAG	$27.02 (3/31/2005)	30.00-25.59	4.03	18.26	27 Years

*7 Year Price Score 95.58 *NYSE Composite Index=100 *12 Month Price Score 93.36

Interim Earnings (Per Share)

Qtr.	Aug	Nov	Feb	May
2001-02	0.36	0.44	0.31	0.36
2002-03	0.43	0.45	0.30	0.28
2003-04	0.37	0.51	0.38	0.40
2004-05	0.26	0.47	...	...

Interim Dividends (Per Share)

Amt	Decl	Ex	Rec	Pay
0.26Q	4/9/2004	4/29/2004	5/3/2004	6/1/2004
0.26Q	7/9/2004	7/29/2004	8/2/2004	9/1/2004
0.273Q	9/23/2004	10/28/2004	11/1/2004	12/1/2004
0.273Q	12/2/2004	1/28/2005	2/1/2005	3/1/2005

Indicated Div: $1.09 (Div. Reinv. Plan)

Valuation Analysis

Forecast P/E	17.12	No of Institutions	
	(4/7/2005)	488	
Market Cap	$13.9 Billion	Shares	
Book Value	4.9 Billion	299,855,968	
Price/Book	2.86	% Held	
Price/Sales	0.94	58.17	

Business Summary: Food (MIC: 4.1 SIC: 011 NAIC: 11611)

ConAgra Foods is a food company that operates in different areas of the food industry, with a focus on the sale of branded and value-added consumer products. Co.'s operations are classified into three segments. The Retail Products segment includes branded foods in the shelf-stable, frozen and refrigerated temperature classes. The Foodservice Products segment includes branded and customized food products, including meals, entrees, prepared potatoes, meats, seafood, sauces, and custom-manufactured culinary products. The Food Ingredients segment includes branded and commodity food ingredients, including milled grain ingredients, seasonings, blends and flavorings.

Recent Developments: For the quarter ended Nov 28 2004, net income decreased 10.3% to $242,300 thousand from net income of $270,100 thousand in the year-earlier quarter. Revenues were $4,116,200 thousand, up 8.2% from $3,804,800 thousand the year before. Total indirect expense was $441,700 thousand versus $477,700 thousand in the prior-year quarter, a decrease of 7.5%.

Prospects: Co. expects the second half of fiscal 2005 to show year-over-year profit growth, largely due to ongoing operational improvements. Co. is focused on marketing, operating, and information systems initiatives that will help expand profit margins over the long term. These activities will help Co. grow its top-line while operating an increasingly efficient supply chain that reflects low-cost manufacturing, purchasing, and logistics operations. Co.'s supply chain efficiency should be further enhanced by an ongoing program that drives an increased focus on higher-margin, higher-opportunity items, and phases out lower-margin items.

Financial Data

(US$ in Thousands)	6 Mos	3 Mos	05/30/2004	05/25/2003	05/26/2002	05/27/2001	05/28/2000	05/30/1999
Earnings Per Share	1.48	1.52	1.66	1.46	1.47	1.24	0.86	0.75
Cash Flow Per Share	1.54	1.30	1.40	1.35	4.48	0.24	1.46	2.52
Tang Book Value Per Share	0.43	0.06	0.41	N.M.	N.M.	N.M.	1.22	1.02
Dividends Per Share	1.053	1.040	1.028	0.978	0.930	0.878	0.789	0.692
Dividend Payout %	70.88	68.58	61.90	66.95	63.27	70.85	91.74	92.23
Income Statement								
Total Revenue	7,611,800	3,495,600	14,522,100	19,839,200	27,629,600	27,194,200	25,385,800	24,594,300
EBITDA	937,700	376,700	1,778,500	1,634,900	2,292,900	2,120,300	1,506,000	1,498,700
Depn & Amortn	174,000	88,900	352,300	396,700	623,200	592,900	536,500	499,800
Income Before Taxes	604,500	214,400	1,151,300	1,238,200	1,268,200	1,104,100	666,100	682,300
Income Taxes	227,900	81,100	355,300	436,000	483,200	421,600	253,100	323,900
Net Income	377,300	135,000	879,800	774,800	783,000	638,600	413,000	358,400
Average Shares	517,500	521,400	530,700	530,700	528,000	514,300	478,600	476,700
Balance Sheet								
Current Assets	5,487,100	4,903,400	5,144,900	6,059,600	6,433,900	7,362,600	5,966,500	5,656,100
Total Assets	14,202,100	14,021,800	14,230,100	15,071,400	15,496,200	16,480,800	12,295,800	12,146,100
Current Liabilities	3,651,100	2,954,000	3,001,600	3,803,400	4,313,400	6,935,600	5,489,200	5,386,400
Long-Term Obligations	4,589,300	5,287,400	5,280,700	5,395,200	5,743,700	4,109,500	2,566,800	2,543,100
Total Liabilities	9,341,400	9,361,400	9,390,600	10,449,700	11,188,000	12,497,600	9,331,700	9,237,300
Stockholders' Equity	4,860,700	4,660,400	4,839,500	4,621,700	4,308,200	3,983,200	2,964,100	2,908,800
Shares Outstanding	514,998	514,286	521,194	536,765	537,040	537,067	492,212	488,173
Statistical Record								
Return on Assets %	5.42	5.43	5.91	5.08	4.91	4.45	3.39	3.01
Return on Equity %	15.96	17.06	18.30	17.40	18.94	18.43	14.10	12.64
EBITDA Margin %	12.32	10.78	12.25	8.24	8.30	7.80	5.93	6.09
Net Margin %	4.96	3.86	6.06	3.91	2.83	2.35	1.63	1.46
Asset Turnover	1.03	0.98	0.98	1.30	1.73	1.90	2.08	2.07
Current Ratio	1.50	1.66	1.71	1.59	1.49	1.06	1.09	1.05
Debt to Equity	0.94	1.13	1.09	1.17	1.33	1.03	0.87	0.87
Price Range	29.34-24.50	29.34-21.15	29.34-21.15	27.65-19.65	25.64-19.02	26.13-17.99	28.06-15.50	34.25-23.25
P/E Ratio	19.82-16.55	19.30-13.91	17.67-12.74	18.94-13.46	17.44-12.94	21.07-14.51	32.63-18.02	45.67-31.00
Average Yield %	3.92	4.00	4.10	4.06	4.06	4.12	3.49	2.40

Address: One ConAgra Drive, Omaha, NE 68102-5001
Telephone: (402) 595-4000
Fax: (402) 978-4447

Web Site: www.conagrafoods.com
Officers: Bruce C. Rohde - Chmn., Pres., C.E.O. Dwight J. Goslee - Exec. V.P., Strategic Devel.

Auditors: Deloitte & Touche LLP
Investor Contact: 800-214-0349
Transfer Agents: Wells Fargo Shareowner Services, St. Paul, MN

CONOCOPHILLIPS

Exchange	Symbol	Price	52Wk Range	Yield	P/E
NYS	COP	$107.84 (3/31/2005)	112.32-68.69	1.85	9.30

*7 Year Price Score 126.23 ***NYSE Composite Index=100** ***12 Month Price Score 116.60**

Interim Earnings (Per Share)

Qtr.	Mar	Jun	Sep	Dec
2001	1.91	2.40	1.30	(0.03)
2002	(0.27)	0.91	(0.24)	(0.93)
2003	2.10	1.66	1.90	1.51
2004	2.33	2.97	2.86	3.44

Interim Dividends (Per Share)

Amt	Decl	Ex	Rec	Pay
0.43Q	5/5/2004	5/13/2004	5/17/2004	6/1/2004
0.43Q	7/15/2004	7/28/2004	7/31/2004	9/1/2004
0.50Q	9/22/2004	10/27/2004	10/29/2004	12/1/2004
0.50Q	2/4/2005	2/11/2005	2/15/2005	3/1/2005
		Indicated Div: $2.00		

Valuation Analysis

Forecast P/E	N/A	No of Institutions
Market Cap	$77.5 Billion	Shares
Book Value	42.7 Billion	549,602,112
Price/Book	1.81	% Held
Price/Sales	0.57	78.99

Business Summary: Oil and Gas (MIC: 14.2 SIC: 911 NAIC: 24110)

Conocophillips is an integrated global petroleum company. Co.'s exploration and production segment explores for and produces crude oil, natural gas, and natural gas liquids worldwide. The midstream segment, which includes Co.'s 30.3% equity investment in Duke Energy Field Services, gathers and processes natural gas and fractionates and markets natural gas liquids. The refining and marketing segment refines, markets and transports crude oil and petroleum products, primarily in the U.S., Europe and Asia. The chemicals segment manufactures and markets petrochemicals and plastics on a worldwide basis mainly through Co.'s 50.0% equity investment in Chevron Phillips Chemical Company LLC.

Recent Developments: For the year ended Dec 31 2004, income from continuing operations increased 76.5% to $8,107 from income of $4,593 a year earlier. Net income increased 71.7% to $8,129 from net income of $4,735 a year earlier. Revenues were $1,369,16, up 30.3% from $105,097 the year before. Total direct expense was $97,554 versus $74,619 in the prior year, an increase of 30.7%. Total indirect expense was $24,251 versus $21,053 in the prior year, an increase of 15.2%.

Prospects: On Feb 24 2005, Co. announced that it has agreed with Duke Energy to restructure the companies' ownership of Duke Energy Field Services (DEFS). The restructuring is expected to close in the second quarter of 2005, subject to necessary regulatory approvals. Co. is expected to increase its current 30.3% ownership in DEFS to 50.0% through a series of transactions. Separately, Co. expects 2005 production, including Canadian Syncrude, to increase to approximately 1.6 million barrels of oil equivalent per day, excluding the impacts of LUKOIL. Also, further increases are expected as expansion projects in the U.K. and Alaska are completed during the year.

Financial Data

(US$ in Thousands)	12/31/2004	12/31/2003	12/31/2002	12/31/2001	12/31/2000	12/31/1999	12/31/1998	12/31/1997
Earnings Per Share	11.60	6.91	(0.61)	5.63	7.26	2.39	0.91	3.61
Cash Flow Per Share	17.26	13.75	10.31	12.16	15.73	7.68	6.31	8.54
Tang Book Value Per Share	37.05	25.70	19.81	26.23	21.51	16.13	16.35	18.30
Dividends Per Share	1.790	1.630	1.480	1.400	1.360	1.360	1.360	1.340
Dividend Payout %	15.43	23.59	...	24.87	18.73	56.90	149.45	37.12
Income Statement								
Total Revenue	136,916,000	105,097,000	57,224,000	26,868,000	21,227,000	13,852,000	11,845,000	15,424,000
EBITDA	18,167,000	11,822,000	4,387,000	4,693,000	4,948,000	2,087,000	1,723,000	2,763,000
Depn & Amortn	3,798,000	3,485,000	2,223,000	1,391,000	1,179,000	902,000	1,302,000	863,000
Income Before Taxes	14,369,000	8,337,000	2,164,000	3,302,000	3,769,000	1,185,000	421,000	1,900,000
Income Taxes	6,262,000	3,744,000	1,450,000	1,659,000	1,907,000	576,000	184,000	941,000
Net Income	8,129,000	4,735,000	(295,000)	1,661,000	1,862,000	609,000	237,000	959,000
Average Shares	700,650	685,433	485,505	295,016	256,326	254,433	260,152	265,000
Balance Sheet								
Current Assets	15,021,000	11,192,000	10,903,000	4,363,000	2,606,000	2,773,000	2,349,000	2,648,000
Total Assets	92,861,000	82,455,000	76,836,000	35,217,000	20,509,000	15,201,000	14,216,000	13,860,000
Current Liabilities	15,586,000	14,011,000	12,816,000	4,542,000	3,492,000	2,520,000	2,132,000	2,445,000
Long-Term Obligations	14,370,000	16,340,000	18,917,000	8,645,000	6,622,000	4,271,000	4,106,000	2,775,000
Total Liabilities	49,033,000	47,247,000	46,318,000	20,227,000	13,766,000	10,002,000	9,347,000	8,396,000
Stockholders' Equity	42,723,000	34,366,000	29,517,000	14,340,000	6,093,000	4,549,000	4,219,000	4,814,000
Shares Outstanding	718,864	708,085	704,354	409,715	283,239	281,971	258,000	263,000
Statistical Record								
Return on Assets %	9.25	5.95	N.M.	5.96	10.40	4.14	1.69	7.00
Return on Equity %	21.03	14.82	N.M.	16.26	34.90	13.89	5.25	21.16
EBITDA Margin %	13.27	11.25	7.67	17.47	23.31	15.07	14.55	17.91
Net Margin %	5.94	4.51	N.M.	6.18	8.77	4.40	2.00	6.22
Asset Turnover	1.56	1.32	1.02	0.96	1.19	0.94	0.84	1.13
Current Ratio	0.96	0.80	0.85	0.96	0.75	1.10	1.10	1.08
Debt to Equity	0.34	0.48	0.64	0.60	1.09	0.94	0.97	0.58
Price Range	90.99-64.78	65.57-45.31	63.73-44.66	67.52-50.60	66.63-36.25	56.56-37.88	52.19-40.75	51.75-37.50
P/E Ratio	7.84-5.58	9.49-6.56	...	11.99-8.95	9.18-4.99	23.67-15.85	57.35-44.78	14.34-10.39
Average Yield %	2.35	3.02	2.71	2.45	2.60	2.84	2.93	2.96

Address: 600 North Dairy Ashford Road, Houston, TX 77079 Telephone: (281) 293 1000 Fax: (281) 661 7636	Web Site: www.phillips66.com Officers: Archie W. Dunham - Chmn. James J. Mulva - Pres., C.E.O.	Auditors: Ernst & Young LLP Investor Contact: 918-661-4757

CONSECO, INC.

Exchange	Symbol	Price	52Wk Range	Yield	P/E
NYS	CNO	$20.42 (3/31/2005)	23.76-15.74	N/A	12.53

*7 Year Price Score N/A *NYSE Composite Index=100 *12 Month Price Score 96.45

Interim Earnings (Per Share)

Qtr.	Mar	Jun	Sep	Dec
2002	(0.24)	(3.86)	(4.85)	1.27
2003	.....	0.67	......	......
2004	0.50	0.34	0.36	0.48

Interim Dividends (Per Share)

No Dividends Paid

Valuation Analysis

Forecast P/E	N/A	No of Institutions
Market Cap	$3.1 Billion	Shares
Book Value	3.9 Billion	142,147,344
Price/Book	0.79	% Held
Price/Sales	0.71	94.10

TRADING VOLUME (thousand shares)

1996 1997 1998 1999 2000 2001 2002 2003 2004 2005

Business Summary: Insurance (MIC: 8.2 SIC: 321 NAIC: 24114)

Conseco is a holding company. Through its subsidiaries, Co. is engaged in developing, marketing and administering supplemental health insurance, annuity, individual life insurance and other insurance products for a group of insurance companies that operate throughout the U.S. Co. sells its products through three distribution channels including career agents, professional independent producers, some of whom sell one or more of Co.'s product lines exclusively, and direct marketing. Co. conducts its business operations through two primary operating segments: Bankers Life and Conseco Insurance Group. Also, Co. operates a third segment comprised of businesses in run-off.

Recent Developments: For the year ended Dec 31 2004, net income was $294.8 million compared with net income of $96.3 million for the four months ended Dec 31 2003. Total revenue was $4,330.0 million versus $1,505.5 million in the previous year. Net premiums earned was $2,949.3 million versus $1,005.8 million in the prior year. Net investment income was $1,318.6 million versus $474.6 million a year earlier. Insurance policy benefit expenses amounted to $2,795.2 million versus $967.9 million the year before. Total benefits and expenses were $3,875.9 million versus $1,356.0 million in the previous year.

Prospects: Co. completed its financial transformation in 2004 and has posted solid earnings and strong cash flow since emerging from bankruptcy. This together with its successful equity offering and debt refinancing, has enabled it to begin 2005 with a strong financial position. Co. is well-positioned to accelerate its pace of productivity. Conseco Insurance Group (CIG) introduced a new cancer product in the second half of 2004, four new insurance products in the first quarter of 2005, and plans two new products in the second quarter of 2005. CIG is recruiting new agents in health and annuity lines that should fuel near-term sales growth. For 2005, Co. expects earnings of at least $1.68 per share.

Financial Data

(US$ in Thousands)	12/31/2004	12/31/2003	12/31/2002	12/31/2001	12/31/2000	12/31/1999	12/31/1998
Earnings Per Share	1.63	0.67	(22.67)	(1.24)	(3.69)	1.79	1.40
Cash Flow Per Share	7.90	4.39	3.75	3.92	3.69	5.51	3.14
Tang Book Value Per Share	21.41	8.22	...	1.62	0.27	3.51	3.82
Dividends Per Share	...	...	...	...	0.100	0.580	0.530
Dividend Payout %	...	...	...	...	...	32.40	37.86
Income Statement							
Premium Income	2,949,300	1,005,800	3,602,300	4,065,700	4,220,300	4,040,500	3,948,800
Total Revenue	4,330,000	1,505,500	4,418,300	8,108,100	8,296,400	8,335,700	7,716,000
Benefits & Claims	2,795,200	967,900	3,332,500	3,506,800	4,071,000	3,815,900	3,580,500
Income Before Taxes	454,100	149,500	(1,634,000)	(419,400)	(1,361,800)	1,150,900	1,045,700
Income Taxes	159,300	53,200	864,300	(115,800)	(376,200)	423,100	445,600
Net Income	294,800	96,300	(7,835,700)	(405,900)	(1,191,200)	595,000	467,100
Average Shares	155,930	143,486	345,807	338,145	325,953	332,893	332,701
Balance Sheet							
Total Assets	30,755,500	29,920,100	46,509,000	61,392,300	58,589,200	52,185,900	43,599,900
Total Liabilities	26,853,300	27,102,500	46,637,900	54,724,800	51,810,900	43,990,600	36,229,400
Stockholders' Equity	3,902,200	2,817,600	(2,050,400)	4,753,000	4,374,400	5,556,200	5,273,600
Shares Outstanding	151,057	100,115	346,007	344,743	325,318	327,678	315,844
Statistical Record							
Return on Assets %	0.97	0.25	N.M.	N.M.	N.M.	1.24	1.17
Return on Equity %	8.75	25.10	N.M.	N.M.	N.M.	10.99	10.19
Loss Ratio %	94.78	96.23	92.51	86.25	96.46	94.44	90.67
Net Margin %	6.81	6.40	(177.35)	(5.01)	(14.36)	7.14	6.05
Price Range	23.76-15.74	21.95-18.06	...	...	...	...	...
P/E Ratio	14.58-9.66	32.76-26.96	...	...	...	...	...

Address: 11825 N. Pennsylvania Street, Carmel, IN 46032 **Telephone:** (317) 817-6100 **Fax:** (317) 344-6452	**Web Site:** www.conseco.com **Officers:** Gary C. Wendt - Chmn. William J. Shea - Pres., C.E.O., C.O.O.	**Auditors:** PricewaterhouseCoopers LLP

CONSOL ENERGY INC

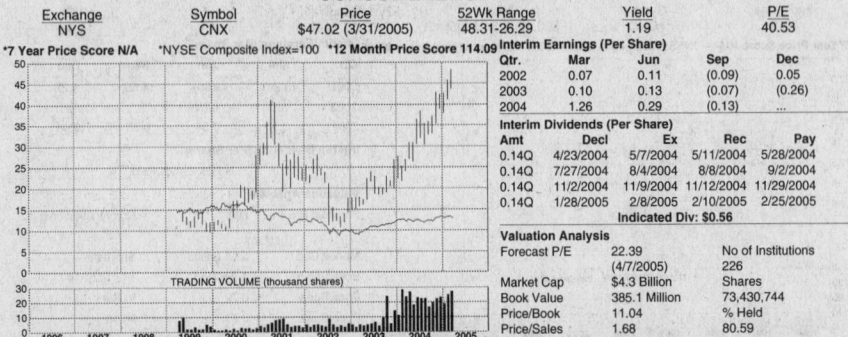

*7 Year Price Score N/A   *NYSE Composite Index=100   *12 Month Price Score 114.09

Interim Earnings (Per Share)

Qtr.	Mar	Jun	Sep	Dec
2002	0.07	0.11	(0.09)	0.05
2003	0.10	0.13	(0.07)	(0.26)
2004	1.26	0.29	(0.13)	...

Interim Dividends (Per Share)

Amt	Decl	Ex	Rec	Pay
0.14Q	4/23/2004	5/7/2004	5/11/2004	5/28/2004
0.14Q	7/27/2004	8/4/2004	8/8/2004	9/2/2004
0.14Q	11/2/2004	11/9/2004	11/12/2004	11/29/2004
0.14Q	1/28/2005	2/8/2005	2/10/2005	2/25/2005

Indicated Div: $0.56

Valuation Analysis

Forecast P/E	22.39	No of Institutions
	(4/7/2005)	226
Market Cap	$4.3 Billion	Shares
Book Value	385.1 Million	73,430,744
Price/Book	11.04	% Held
Price/Sales	1.68	80.59

TRADING VOLUME (thousand shares)

Business Summary: Coal Mining (MIC: 14.4 SIC: 222 NAIC: 12112)

CONSOL Energy is a multi-fuel energy producer and energy services provider that primarily serves the electric power generation industry in the U.S. That industry generates approximately two-thirds of its output by burning coal or gas, the two fuels Co. produces. Btu is a measure of energy required to raise the temperature of one pound of water by one degree Fahrenheit. At Dec 31 2003, Co. produced high-Btu bituminous coal from 20 mining complexes in the U.S. and Australia. In addition, Co. produces pipeline-quality coalbed methane gas from its coal properties in Pennsylvania, Virginia and West Virginia and conventional gas from its properties in Tennessee and Virginia.

Recent Developments: For the year ended Dec 31 2004, net income was $198,582 thousand versus net loss of $7,798 thousand a year earlier. Revenues were $2,776,749 thousand, up 24.9% from $2,222,466 thousand the year before. Total direct expense was $2,111,185 thousand versus $1,738,598 thousand in the prior year, an increase of 21.4%. Total indirect expense was $749,877 thousand versus $643,133 thousand in the prior year, an increase of 16.6%.

Prospects: In the first quarter of 2005, Co. is projecting coal and gas production of between 17.0 million tons and 18.0 million tons, and between 12.6 billions of cubic feet and 13.3 billions of cubic feet, respectively. For full-year 2005, Co. is forecasting gas volumes and coal production of between 50.0 billion cubic feet and 53.0 per billion cubic feet, and 68.0 million tons and 72.0 million tons, respectively. Co. expects coal in Northern Appalachia and Central Appalachia to be in tight supply, and coal inventories at power plants and at mines to be at the lowest levels in many years and, as a result, the pricing environment is expected to continue to improve.

Financial Data

(US$ in Thousands)	9 Mos	6 Mos	3 Mos	12/31/2003	12/31/2002	12/31/2001	06/30/2001	06/30/2000
Earnings Per Share	1.16	1.22	1.06	(0.10)	0.15	0.01	2.33	1.35
Cash Flow Per Share	2.86	3.66	4.79	4.66	4.19	0.79	5.54	3.70
Tang Book Value Per Share	4.26	4.50	0.16	N.M.	2.06	3.45	4.47	3.23
Dividends Per Share	0.560	0.560	0.560	0.560	0.840	1.120	1.120	1.120
Dividend Payout %	48.16	45.87	52.90	...	560.00	11,200.00	48.07	82.96
Income Statement								
Total Revenue	1,985,315	1,325,439	650,855	2,222,466	2,183,598	1,081,198	2,368,415	2,159,209
EBITDA	234,081	188,639	97,846	215,658	232,396	106,008	500,799	372,868
Depn & Amortn	188,504	124,696	62,558	249,165	272,819	125,628	260,464	266,321
Income Before Taxes	45,577	63,943	35,288	(33,507)	(40,423)	(19,620)	240,335	106,547
Income Taxes	6,036	4,828	7,542	(20,941)	(52,099)	(20,679)	56,685	(493)
Net Income	130,914	142,488	114,119	(7,798)	11,676	1,059	183,650	107,040
Average Shares	90,361	90,770	90,548	82,040	78,834	78,920	78,817	79,499
Balance Sheet								
Current Assets	501,076	562,791	543,081	470,840	622,837	570,254	565,861	577,728
Total Assets	4,167,579	4,196,753	4,320,036	4,318,978	4,293,160	4,297,594	3,894,971	3,866,311
Current Liabilities	735,752	693,975	859,324	824,599	814,433	640,748	933,973	952,802
Long-Term Obligations	424,652	424,974	424,975	441,912	488,431	472,669	231,028	300,605
Total Liabilities	3,782,494	3,790,762	3,932,876	4,028,341	4,131,113	4,026,035	3,543,324	3,612,132
Stockholders' Equity	385,085	405,991	387,160	290,637	162,047	271,559	351,647	254,179
Shares Outstanding	90,443	90,213	89,981	89,861	78,749	78,705	78,696	78,577
Statistical Record								
Return on Assets %	2.56	2.71	2.27	N.M.	0.27	0.02	4.73	2.76
Return on Equity %	30.42	40.92	36.03	N.M.	5.39	0.27	60.63	41.95
EBITDA Margin %	11.79	14.23	15.03	9.70	10.64	9.80	21.14	17.27
Net Margin %	6.59	10.75	17.53	N.M.	0.53	0.10	7.75	4.96
Asset Turnover	0.60	0.58	0.54	0.52	0.51	0.18	0.61	0.56
Current Ratio	0.68	0.81	0.63	0.57	0.76	0.89	0.61	0.61
Debt to Equity	1.10	1.05	1.10	1.52	3.01	1.74	0.66	1.18
Price Range	38.50-18.58	36.50-18.49	27.60-16.12	26.79-14.76	28.04-10.68	28.35-19.25	41.15-15.14	17.00-9.63
P/E Ratio	33.19-16.02	29.92-15.16	26.04-15.21	...	186.93-71.20	N.M.	17.66-6.50	12.59-7.13
Average Yield %	2.00	2.31	2.59	2.86	4.42	4.60	4.47	9.33

Address: 1800 Washington Road, Pittsburgh, PA 15241-1421 **Telephone:** (412) 831-4000 **Fax:** (412) 831-4103	Web Site: **Officers:** John L. Whitmire - Chmn. J. Brett Harvey - Pres., C.E.O.	**Auditors:** PricewaterhouseCoopers LLP

CONSOLIDATED EDISON, INC.

Exchange	Symbol	Price	52Wk Range	Yield	P/E	Div Acheiver
NYS	ED	$42.18 (3/31/2005)	45.59-37.26	5.41	18.58	30 Years

*7 Year Price Score 88.34   *NYSE Composite Index=100   *12 Month Price Score 94.60

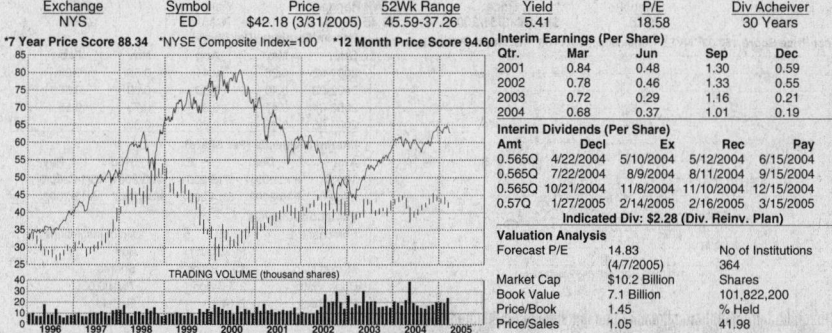

Interim Earnings (Per Share)

Qtr.	Mar	Jun	Sep	Dec
2001	0.84	0.48	1.30	0.59
2002	0.78	0.46	1.33	0.55
2003	0.72	0.29	1.16	0.21
2004	0.68	0.37	1.01	0.19

Interim Dividends (Per Share)

Amt	Decl	Ex	Rec	Pay
0.565Q	4/22/2004	5/10/2004	5/12/2004	6/15/2004
0.565Q	7/22/2004	8/9/2004	8/11/2004	9/15/2004
0.565Q	10/21/2004	11/8/2004	11/10/2004	12/15/2004
0.57Q	1/27/2005	2/14/2005	2/16/2005	3/15/2005
	Indicated Div: $2.28 (Div. Reinv. Plan)			

Valuation Analysis

Forecast P/E	14.83	No of Institutions
	(4/7/2005)	364
Market Cap	$10.2 Billion	Shares
Book Value	7.1 Billion	101,822,200
Price/Book	1.45	% Held
Price/Sales	1.05	41.98

Business Summary: Electricity (MIC: 7.1 SIC: 931 NAIC: 21121)

Consolidated Edison provides a range of energy-related products and services through six subsidiaries. Consolidated Edison Company of New York is a regulated utility providing electric, gas and steam service to New York City and Westchester County, New York. Orange and Rockland Utilities is a regulated utility serving customers in southeastern New York state and adjacent sections of northern New Jersey and northeastern Pennsylvania. Con Edison Solutions is a retail energy services company and Con Edison Energy is a wholesale energy supply company. Con Edison Development is an infrastructure development company and Con Edison Communications is a telecommunications infrastructure company.

Recent Developments: For the year ended Dec 31 2004, income from continuing operations was $537,000 thousand from income of $525,000 thousand in the previous year. Results for 2004 and 2003 excluded losses of discontinued operations of $12,000 and $109,000, respectively. Also, results for 2003 excluded an accounting change credit of $3,000 thousand. Revenues slipped to $9,758,000 thousand from $9,808,000 thousand the year before. Operating income decreased 10.9% to $931,000 thousand versus $1,044,000 thousand in 2003. Total direct expense rose 2.8% to $6,904,000 thousand from $6,715,000 thousand, while total indirect expense fell 6.2% to $1,923,000 from $2,049,000 thousand a year earlier.

Prospects: Co. expects its earnings for 2005 to be in the range of $2.75 to $2.90 a share. The forecast reflects the multi-year rate plans for gas and steam that took effect in Oct 2004 and a three-year electric rate plan that, subject to regulatory approval, is expected to take effect in Apr 2005. Construction expenditures are estimated at $1.60 billion per year for 2005 and 2006 and $1.70 billion for 2007, compared with $1.30 billion in 2004. Virtually all of the estimated construction expenditures are for Co.'s regulated utilities. Co. does not expect to issue new equity in 2005, other than an estimated $95.0 million to be issued through its dividend reinvestment and employee stock plans.

Financial Data
(US$ in Thousands)

	12/31/2004	12/31/2003	12/31/2002	12/31/2001	12/31/2000	12/31/1999	12/31/1998	12/31/1997
Earnings Per Share	2.27	2.38	3.02	3.21	2.74	3.13	3.04	2.95
Cash Flow Per Share	5.58	5.97	7.07	6.36	4.51	5.39	5.83	5.27
Tang Book Value Per Share	27.00	29.15	25.40	24.21	26.39	25.90	25.88	25.18
Dividends Per Share	2.260	2.240	2.220	2.200	2.180	2.140	2.120	2.100
Dividend Payout %	99.56	94.12	73.51	68.54	79.56	68.37	69.74	71.19
Income Statement								
Total Revenue	9,758,000	9,827,000	8,481,860	9,633,962	9,431,391	7,491,323	7,093,048	7,121,254
Depn & Amortn	551,000	529,000	494,553	526,235	586,407	526,182	518,514	502,779
Income Taxes	284,000	327,000	388,881	(21,922)	(10,622)	(26,891)	(2,229)	(3,190)
Net Income	537,000	528,000	646,036	682,242	582,835	700,615	712,742	694,479
Average Shares	236,400	221,800	214,049	212,919	212,186	223,442	234,308	235,082
Balance Sheet								
Net PPE	16,106,000	15,225,000	13,329,175	12,248,375	11,893,419	11,353,845	11,406,543	11,267,102
Total Assets	22,560,000	20,966,000	18,820,310	16,996,111	16,767,245	15,531,476	14,381,403	14,722,518
Long-Term Obligations	6,594,000	6,769,000	6,206,917	5,542,305	5,446,913	4,559,148	4,087,403	4,228,785
Total Liabilities	15,254,000	14,288,000	12,677,761	11,070,708	11,045,243	9,869,856	8,106,185	8,474,421
Stockholders' Equity	7,054,000	6,423,000	5,921,079	5,666,268	5,472,389	5,412,007	6,025,605	5,930,079
Shares Outstanding	242,514	202,629	213,932	212,146	188,816	192,452	232,833	235,490
Statistical Record								
Return on Assets %	2.46	2.65	3.61	4.04	3.60	4.68	4.90	4.83
Return on Equity %	7.95	8.55	11.15	12.25	10.68	12.25	11.92	11.91
Net Margin %	5.50	5.37	7.62	7.08	6.18	9.35	10.05	9.75
PPE Turnover	0.62	0.69	0.66	0.80	0.81	0.66	0.63	0.64
Asset Turnover	0.45	0.49	0.47	0.57	0.58	0.50	0.49	0.49
Debt to Equity	0.93	1.05	1.05	0.98	1.00	0.84	0.68	0.71
Price Range	45.59-37.26	45.99-37.00	45.10-33.58	42.18-32.38	39.25-26.19	52.88-33.75	55.94-39.56	41.31-27.25
P/E Ratio	20.08-16.41	19.32-15.55	14.93-11.12	13.14-10.09	14.32-9.56	16.89-10.78	18.40-13.01	14.00-9.24
Average Yield %	5.35	5.53	5.35	5.72	6.65	4.89	4.57	6.58

Address: 4 Irving Place, New York, NY 10003	**Web Site:** www.conedison.com	**Auditors:** PricewaterhouseCoopers LLP
Telephone: (212) 460-4600	**Officers:** Eugene R. McGrath - Chmn., Pres., C.E.O. Joan S. Freilich - Exec. V.P., C.F.O.	**Investor Contact:** 212-460-6611
Fax: (212) 475-0734		**Transfer Agents:** The Bank of New York, New York, NY

CONSTELLATION BRANDS INC

Exchange	Symbol	Price	52Wk Range	Yield	P/E
NYS	STZ	$52.87 (3/31/2005)	56.45-32.10	N/A	21.06

*7 Year Price Score 157.33 *NYSE Composite Index=100 *12 Month Price Score 119.66

Interim Earnings (Per Share)

Qtr.	May	Aug	Nov	Feb
2001-02	0.28	0.41	0.56	0.29
2002-03	0.40	0.53	0.69	0.56
2003-04	0.41	0.34	0.73	0.55
2004-05	0.45	0.69	0.83	...

Interim Dividends (Per Share)

Amt	Decl	Ex	Rec	Pay
100%	4/12/2001	5/15/2001	4/30/2001	5/14/2001
2-for-1	4/10/2002	5/14/2002	4/30/2002	5/13/2002

Valuation Analysis

Forecast P/E	17.08	No of Institutions
	(4/7/2005)	303
Market Cap	$5.7 Billion	Shares
Book Value	2.7 Billion	75,190,056
Price/Book	2.14	% Held
Price/Sales	1.46	78.02

Business Summary: Food (MIC: 4.1 SIC: 084 NAIC: 12130)

Constellation Brands is a producer, marketer and distributor of premier branded beverage alcohol products in the U.S. and the U.K. Co.'s business is broken into three segments: Constellation Wines (branded wine, and U.K. wholesale and other); Constellation Beers and Spirits (imported beer and distilled spirits); and Corporate Operations and Other. Co.'s key products include Corona Extra, Pacifico, St. Pauli Girl, Black Velvet, Fleischmann's, Mr. Boston, Simi, Estancia, Ravenswood, Blackstone, Banrock Station, Hardys, Nobilo, Alice White, Vendange, Almaden, Arbor Mist, Stowells, and Blackthorn.

Recent Developments: For the quarter ended Nov 30 2004, net income increased 17.0% to $96,893 thousand from net income of $82,840 thousand in the year-earlier quarter. Revenues were $1,085,711 thousand, up 10.0% from $987,248 thousand the year before. Operating income was $181,687 thousand versus an income of $161,195 thousand in the prior-year quarter, an increase of 12.7%. Total indirect expense was $131,977 thousand versus $121,421 thousand in the prior-year quarter, an increase of 8.7%.

Prospects: Looking ahead, for the fiscal years ending Feb 28 2005 and Feb 28 2006, Co. is projecting diluted earnings per share to be in the range of $2.29 to $2.34 and $2.77 to $2.92, respectively. Separately, on Dec 3 2004, Co. purchased a 40.0% ownership position in the premier Italian fine wine producer Ruffino, which is expected to fill its need for a product line that is in growing demand by American consumers. In addition, in late Dec 2004, Co. entered into a joint venture with jstar Brands to form "Planet 10 Spirits L.L.C." in order to create and market premium spirits brands in the U.S. Meanwhile, the integration of the Robert Mondavi business is underway.

Financial Data

(US$ in Thousands)	9 Mos	6 Mos	3 Mos	02/29/2004	02/28/2003	02/28/2002	02/28/2001	02/29/2000
Earnings Per Share	2.51	2.41	2.07	2.06	2.19	1.55	1.30	1.04
Cash Flow Per Share	2.23	2.84	2.80	3.37	2.63	2.49	1.41	2.04
Tang Book Value Per Share	3.31	1.57	0.79	0.86	0.77	N.M.	N.M.	N.M.
Income Statement								
Total Revenue	3,049,957	1,964,246	927,305	3,552,429	2,731,612	2,820,503	2,396,685	2,340,469
EBITDA	516,309	311,753	132,477	591,034	496,670	429,552	341,251	299,764
Depn & Amortn	67,421	44,991	21,994	101,954	56,347	85,404	70,383	64,723
Income Before Taxes	357,556	206,161	80,202	344,397	334,936	229,959	162,237	128,959
Income Taxes	128,720	74,218	28,873	123,983	131,630	91,984	64,895	51,584
Net Income	228,836	131,943	51,329	220,414	203,306	136,421	97,342	77,375
Average Shares	116,726	116,147	115,062	106,948	92,746	87,825	74,750	73,996
Balance Sheet								
Current Assets	2,548,127	2,294,596	2,180,235	2,071,471	1,330,101	1,231,248	1,190,989	995,997
Total Assets	6,079,884	5,655,650	5,549,074	5,558,673	3,196,330	3,069,385	2,512,169	2,348,791
Current Liabilities	1,327,573	1,203,268	1,167,341	1,029,802	585,208	595,210	427,160	438,217
Long-Term Obligations	1,716,685	1,720,588	1,736,159	1,778,853	1,191,631	1,293,183	1,307,437	1,237,135
Total Liabilities	3,410,641	3,274,481	3,238,391	3,181,054	2,021,346	2,113,649	1,895,901	1,827,951
Stockholders' Equity	2,669,243	2,381,169	2,310,683	2,377,619	1,174,984	955,736	616,268	520,840
Shares Outstanding	108,275	107,863	107,048	106,628	90,761	88,519	74,779	72,757
Statistical Record								
Return on Assets %	4.97	5.10	4.26	5.02	6.49	4.89	4.01	3.73
Return on Equity %	11.94	12.94	12.38	12.37	19.08	17.36	17.12	16.14
EBITDA Margin %	16.93	15.87	14.29	16.64	18.18	15.23	14.24	12.81
Net Margin %	7.50	6.72	5.54	6.20	7.44	4.84	4.06	3.31
Asset Turnover	0.67	0.70	0.68	0.81	0.87	1.01	0.99	1.13
Current Ratio	1.92	1.91	1.87	2.01	2.27	2.07	2.79	2.27
Debt to Equity	0.64	0.72	0.75	0.75	1.01	1.35	2.12	2.38
Price Range	44.99-30.72	39.49-29.11	36.14-26.97	35.57-22.00	32.00-22.36	27.18-15.67	17.14-10.64	15.13-10.73
P/E Ratio	17.92-12.24	16.39-12.08	17.46-13.03	17.27-10.68	14.61-10.21	17.53-10.11	13.18-8.19	14.54-10.32

Address: 370 Woodcliff Drive, Suite 300, Fairport, NY 14450 **Telephone:** (585) 218-3600 **Fax:** (585) 394-4839	**Web Site:** www.cbrands.com **Officers:** Richard Sands - Chmn., C.E.O. Robert Sands - Pres., C.O.O.	**Auditors:** KPMG LLP **Investor Contact:** 716-394-7900 **Transfer Agents:** Mellon Investor Services, Ridgefield Park, NJ

CONSTELLATION ENERGY GROUP, INC.

Exchange	Symbol	Price	52Wk Range	Yield	P/E
NYS	CEG	$51.70 (3/31/2005)	53.55-36.39	2.59	16.57

*7 Year Price Score 107.80 *NYSE Composite Index=100 *12 Month Price Score 113.06

Interim Earnings (Per Share)

Qtr.	Mar	Jun	Sep	Dec
2001	0.74	0.46	1.00	(1.63)
2002	1.40	0.50	0.92	0.39
2003	(0.80)	0.58	1.15	0.71
2004	0.39	0.76	1.19	0.76

Interim Dividends (Per Share)

Amt	Decl	Ex	Rec	Pay
0.285Q	4/23/2004	6/8/2004	6/10/2004	7/1/2004
0.285Q	7/23/2004	9/8/2004	9/10/2004	10/1/2004
0.285Q	10/25/2004	12/8/2004	12/10/2004	1/3/2005
0.335Q	1/27/2005	3/8/2005	3/10/2005	4/1/2005

Indicated Div: $1.34

Valuation Analysis

Forecast P/E	N/A	No of Institutions
Market Cap	$9.1 Billion	Shares
Book Value	4.7 Billion	113,944,056
Price/Book	1.93	% Held
Price/Sales	0.73	64.43

Business Summary: Electricity (MIC: 7.1 SIC: 931 NAIC: 21119)

Constellation Energy Group is a North American energy company that conducts its business through various subsidiaries including a merchant energy business and Baltimore Gas and Electric Company (BGE). Co.'s merchant energy business is a competitive provider of energy services for large customers in North America. BGE is a regulated electric transmission and distribution utility company and a regulated gas distribution utility company with a service territory that covers the City of Baltimore and all or part of ten counties in central Maryland. As of Dec 31 2003, Co. provided service to approximately 1.2 million electric customers and 617,500 natural gas customers.

Recent Developments: For the year ended Dec 31 2004, income from continuing operations increased 23.8% to $588,800 thousand from income of $475,700 thousand a year earlier. Net income increased 94.6% to $539,700 thousand from net income of $277,300 thousand a year earlier. Revenues were $12,549,700 thousand, up 29.5% from $9,687,800 thousand the year before. Operating income was $1,077,200 thousand versus an income of $1,066,300 thousand in the prior year, an increase of 1.0%. Total direct expense was $10,620,300 thousand versus $7,872,700 thousand in the prior year, an increase of 34.9%. Total indirect expense was $852,200 thousand versus $748,800 thousand in the prior year, an increase of 13.8%.

Prospects: Co.'s results are benefiting from NewEnergy's retail electric and gas business, which is its retail competitive supply operation, as well as the addition of the R. E. Ginna Nuclear Station. Co. completed its purchase of the Ginna nuclear facility on June 10 2004 from Rochester Gas & Electric Corporation (RG&E). Ginna consists of a 495 megawatt single-unit pressurized water reactor that entered service in 1970 and is licensed to operate until 2029. Co. will sell 90.0% of Ginna's output back to RG&E until June 2014 under a unit contingent power purchase agreement. Meanwhile, on Jan 28 2005, Co. established full-year 2005 earnings per share guidance of between $3.35 and $3.60.

Financial Data
(US$ in Thousands)

	12/31/2004	12/31/2003	12/31/2002	12/31/2001	12/31/2000	12/31/1999	12/31/1998	12/31/1997
Earnings Per Share	3.12	1.66	3.20	0.57	2.30	1.74	2.06	1.72
Cash Flow Per Share	6.30	6.49	6.21	3.57	5.66	4.54	5.53	4.92
Tang Book Value Per Share	25.99	23.18	22.73	23.48	20.95	20.05	19.98	19.43
Dividends Per Share	1.140	1.040	0.960	0.480	1.680	1.260	1.670	...
Dividend Payout %	36.54	62.65	30.00	84.21	73.04	72.41	81.07	...
Income Statement								
Total Revenue	12,549,700	9,703,000	4,703,000	3,928,300	3,878,500	3,786,200	3,358,100	3,307,600
EBITDA	1,752,000	1,685,400	1,664,700	828,000	1,371,600	1,273,700	1,176,200	1,067,600
Depn & Amortn	660,700	600,000	548,000	468,900	524,800	505,900	429,400	396,800
Income Before Taxes	761,000	745,200	835,200	120,300	575,400	512,800	505,900	440,800
Income Taxes	172,200	269,500	309,600	37,900	230,100	186,400	178,200	158,000
Net Income	539,700	277,300	525,600	90,900	345,300	260,100	327,700	282,800
Average Shares	173,100	166,700	164,200	160,700	150,000	149,600	148,500	147,700
Balance Sheet								
Net PPE	10,086,600	9,601,500	7,957,100	7,700,400	6,644,000	5,523,100	5,656,700	5,651,500
Total Assets	17,347,100	15,800,700	14,128,900	14,077,600	12,384,600	9,683,800	9,195,000	8,773,400
Long-Term Obligations	4,813,200	5,039,200	4,613,900	2,712,500	3,159,300	2,575,400	3,128,100	2,988,900
Total Liabilities	12,430,200	11,470,200	10,076,600	10,044,000	9,041,600	6,500,800	6,023,500	5,693,000
Stockholders' Equity	4,726,900	4,140,500	3,862,300	3,843,600	3,153,000	2,993,000	2,981,500	2,870,400
Shares Outstanding	176,333	167,819	164,842	163,707	150,531	149,245	149,246	147,700
Statistical Record								
Return on Assets %	3.25	1.85	3.73	0.69	3.12	2.76	3.65	3.26
Return on Equity %	12.14	6.93	13.64	2.60	11.21	8.71	11.20	9.88
EBITDA Margin %	13.96	17.37	35.40	21.08	35.36	33.64	35.03	32.28
Net Margin %	4.30	2.86	11.18	2.31	8.90	6.87	9.76	8.55
PPE Turnover	1.27	1.11	0.60	0.55	0.64	0.68	0.59	0.59
Asset Turnover	0.76	0.65	0.33	0.30	0.35	0.40	0.37	0.38
Debt to Equity	1.02	1.22	1.19	0.71	1.00	0.86	1.05	1.04
Price Range	44.76-36.39	39.50-25.56	32.26-20.61	49.95-22.00	51.39-27.56	31.44-25.06	35.25-29.56	34.13-25.00
P/E Ratio	14.35-11.66	23.80-15.40	10.08-6.44	87.63-38.60	22.35-11.98	18.07-14.40	17.11-14.35	19.84-14.53
Average Yield %	2.85	3.19	3.46	1.33	4.63	4.38	5.31	...

Address: 750 E. Pratt Street, Baltimore, MD 21202
Telephone: (410) 234-5000
Fax: (410) 234-5367

Web Site: www.constellationenergy.com
Officers: Mayo A. Shattuck III - Chmn., Pres., C.E.O. E. Follin Smith - Exec. V.P., C.F.O., Chief Admin. Officer

Auditors: PricewaterhouseCoopers LLP
Investor Contact: 410-783-3670

CONTINENTAL AIRLINES INC

Exchange	Symbol	Price	52Wk Range	Yield	P/E
NYS	CAL	$12.04 (3/31/2005)	13.96-7.85	N/A	N/A

*7 Year Price Score 31.31 *NYSE Composite Index=100 *12 Month Price Score 98.09

Interim Earnings (Per Share)

Qtr.	Mar	Jun	Sep	Dec
2001	0.16	0.74	0.05	(2.69)
2002	(2.61)	(2.18)	(0.58)	(1.66)
2003	(3.38)	1.10	1.83	0.72
2004	(1.88)	(0.26)	(0.24)	(3.17)

Interim Dividends (Per Share)

No Dividends Paid

Valuation Analysis

Forecast P/E	0.00		No of Institutions
	(4/7/2005)		141
Market Cap	$800.2 Million		Shares
Book Value	266.0 Million		65,161,816
Price/Book	3.01		% Held
Price/Sales	0.08		97.83

Business Summary: Aviation (MIC: 1.1 SIC: 512 NAIC: 81111)

Continental Airlines is a major United States air carrier engaged in the business of transporting passengers, cargo and mail. Co., together with its subsidiaries ExpressJet Airlines, Inc., which operates as Continental Express, and Continental Micronesia, Inc., flies to 127 domestic and 101 international destinations and offers additional connecting service through alliances with domestic and foreign carriers. Co. provides service to Europe, Mexico, Central America and South America, and through its Guam hub, provides service in the western Pacific, including Japan. Major hubs include Newark, NJ, Houston, TX, Cleveland, OH and Guam. At Dec. 31, 2003, Co. operated 579 aircraft.

Recent Developments: For the year ended Dec 31 2004, net loss was $363 million versus net income of $38 million a year earlier. Revenues were $9,744 million, up 9.9% from $8,870 million the year before. Operating loss was $229 million versus an income of $203 million in the prior year. Total direct expense was $3,538 million versus $3,344 million in the prior year, an increase of 5.8%. Total indirect expense was $6,435 million versus $5,323 million in the prior year, an increase of 20.9%.

Prospects: Co.'s prospect appear mixed. Co.'s earnings are being adversely affected by weak domestic yields and record-breaking fuel costs. However, Co. is continuing to focus on cost control efforts and has realized over $900.0 million of the $1.10 billion of previously announced revenue and cost savings initiatives. Separately, on Feb 28 2004, Co. reached a tentative agreement on new contracts covering its pilots, flight attendants, mechanics and dispatchers. The new contracts are expected to achieve additional annual cost savings of approximately $500.0 million. Co.'s actions taken in 2004 should position it to deliver stronger results in the future.

Financial Data
(US$ in Thousands)

	12/31/2004	12/31/2003	12/31/2002	12/31/2001	12/31/2000	12/31/1999	12/31/1998	12/31/1997
Earnings Per Share	(5.55)	0.58	(7.02)	(1.72)	5.45	6.20	5.02	4.99
Cash Flow Per Share	5.63	5.23	(1.21)	10.22	14.85	11.17	14.59	16.55
Tang Book Value Per Share	N.M.	N.M.	N.M.	2.03	1.35	7.06	0.19	N.M.
Income Statement								
Total Revenue	9,744,000	8,870,000	8,402,000	8,969,000	9,899,000	8,639,000	7,951,000	7,213,000
EBITDA	320,000	995,000	125,000	546,000	1,080,000	1,265,000	1,006,000	969,000
Depn & Amortn	414,000	444,000	444,000	467,000	402,000	360,000	294,000	254,000
Income Before Taxes	(440,000)	201,000	(615,000)	(114,000)	571,000	798,000	648,000	640,000
Income Taxes	(77,000)	114,000	(202,000)	(29,000)	222,000	310,000	248,000	237,000
Net Income	(363,000)	38,000	(451,000)	(95,000)	342,000	455,000	383,000	385,000
Average Shares	66,100	65,600	64,200	55,500	62,800	73,900	80,300	81,000
Balance Sheet								
Total Assets	10,545,000	10,649,000	10,740,000	9,791,000	9,201,000	8,223,000	7,086,000	5,830,000
Long-Term Obligations	5,167,000	5,558,000	5,222,000	4,198,000	3,374,000	3,055,000	2,480,000	1,568,000
Total Liabilities	10,279,000	9,857,000	9,720,000	8,387,000	7,349,000	6,630,000	5,782,000	4,672,000
Stockholders' Equity	266,000	792,000	767,000	1,161,000	1,160,000	1,593,000	1,193,000	916,000
Shares Outstanding	66,461	66,035	65,760	63,174	58,450	65,480	64,800	59,000
Statistical Record								
Return on Assets %	N.M.	0.36	N.M.	N.M.	3.91	5.94	5.93	6.98
Return on Equity %	N.M.	4.87	N.M.	N.M.	24.78	32.66	36.32	51.44
EBITDA Margin %	3.28	11.22	1.49	6.09	10.91	14.64	12.65	13.43
Net Margin %	(3.73)	0.43	(5.37)	(1.06)	3.45	5.27	4.82	5.34
Asset Turnover	0.92	0.83	0.82	0.94	1.13	1.13	1.23	1.31
Price Range	18.31-7.85	21.67-4.23	34.80-3.65	56.50-13.00	54.00-29.19	47.88-30.63	64.63-29.19	48.88-27.50
P/E Ratio	...	37.36-7.29	...	...	9.91-5.36	7.72-4.94	12.87-5.81	9.79-5.51

Address: 1600 Smith Street, Dept. HQSEO, Houston, TX 77002 Telephone: (713) 324 2950 Fax: (713) 520 6329	Web Site: www.flycontinental.com Officers: Lawrence W. Kellner - Chmn., C.E.O. Jeffrey Smisek - Pres.	Auditors: Ernst & Young LLP Investor Contact: 713-324-5242

CONVERGYS CORP.

Exchange	Symbol	Price	52Wk Range	Yield	P/E
NYS	CVG	$14.93 (3/31/2005)	16.80-12.42	N/A	19.39

*7 Year Price Score N/A   *NYSE Composite Index=100   *12 Month Price Score 96.14

Interim Earnings (Per Share)

Qtr.	Mar	Jun	Sep	Dec
2001	0.34	0.16	0.02	0.33
2002	0.35	0.35	0.34	(0.15)
2003	0.22	0.29	0.31	0.33
2004	0.22	0.20	0.21	0.14

Interim Dividends (Per Share)

No Dividends Paid

Valuation Analysis

Forecast P/E	14.59	No of Institutions	
	(4/7/2005)	223	
Market Cap	$2.6 Billion	Shares	
Book Value	1.3 Billion	103,243,344	
Price/Book	2.04	% Held	
Price/Sales	1.05	72.65	

Business Summary: IT & Technology (MIC: 10.2 SIC: 373 NAIC: 41512)

Convergys is a provider of outsourced, integrated billing and customer care software and services. Co. serves clients in the telecommunications, cable, broadband, satellite broadcasting, Internet services, technology, and financial services and other industries in more than 40 countries. Co. operates in two segments: the Information Management Group, which provides outsourced billing and information services and software, and the Customer Management Group, which provides outsourced marketing and customer support services and outsourced employee care services. At Dec 31 2004, Co. operated 63 contact centers with nearly 35,000 production workstations.

Recent Developments: For the year ended Dec 31 2004, net income decreased 35.0% to $111,500 thousand from net income of $171,600 thousand a year earlier. Revenues were $2,487,700 thousand, up 8.7% from $2,288,800 thousand the year before. Operating income was $185,500 thousand versus an income of $292,400 thousand in the prior year, a decrease of 36.6%. Total direct expense was $1,542,000 thousand versus $1,320,900 thousand in the prior year, an increase of 16.7%. Total indirect expense was $760,200 thousand versus $675,500 thousand in the prior year, an increase of 12.5%.

Prospects: Co. is delivering strong revenue growth as activity in its Customer Management group accelerates. Co. sees significant outsourcing opportunities in the pipeline and strong market acceptance of its service offerings. Meanwhile, Co.'s Information Management group continues to experience strong acceptance of its Infinys™ technology with new contract wins. Co. expects this growth momentum to continue in 2005. Separately, Co. expects its restructuring actions should be substantially completed by June 30 2005. Once complete, Co. expects annual savings in excess of $50.0 million. Beyond the restructuring, Co. continues to look for opportunities to improve its cost structure and operating margins.

Financial Data
(US$ in Thousands)

	12/31/2004	12/31/2003	12/31/2002	12/31/2001	12/31/2000	12/31/1999	12/31/1998	12/31/1997
Earnings Per Share	0.77	1.15	0.88	0.80	1.23	0.89	0.57	0.63
Cash Flow Per Share	1.38	2.49	2.64	1.98	1.17	3.05	1.03	0.93
Tang Book Value Per Share	2.12	2.13	2.28	3.03	2.41	1.13	0.29	1.85
Income Statement								
Total Revenue	2,487,700	2,288,800	2,286,200	2,320,600	2,162,500	1,762,900	1,447,200	987,500
EBITDA	324,900	402,500	392,500	451,200	510,700	385,300	265,800	197,000
Depn & Amortn	141,200	124,000	137,100	176,300	160,800	130,300	101,300	61,000
Income Before Taxes	173,400	271,600	244,400	254,900	317,000	222,500	130,600	130,600
Income Taxes	61,900	100,000	98,500	116,100	122,300	85,500	49,600	44,000
Net Income	111,500	171,600	145,900	138,800	194,700	137,000	81,000	86,600
Average Shares	145,400	148,800	166,100	174,400	158,000	154,500	142,900	137,000
Balance Sheet								
Current Assets	592,800	419,500	418,200	523,100	481,100	297,900	360,500	265,800
Total Assets	2,208,100	1,810,200	1,619,500	1,742,900	1,779,500	1,579,500	1,450,900	654,400
Current Liabilities	577,400	542,700	462,000	492,400	359,000	387,400	697,900	216,600
Long-Term Obligations	302,200	58,800	4,600	3,600	290,700	250,300	...	1,200
Total Liabilities	922,800	666,700	493,200	516,300	667,000	652,300	719,400	223,600
Stockholders' Equity	1,285,300	1,143,500	1,126,300	1,226,600	1,112,500	927,200	731,500	430,800
Shares Outstanding	175,300	174,600	173,400	172,200	154,400	153,000	151,950	137,000
Statistical Record								
Return on Assets %	5.53	10.01	8.68	7.88	11.56	9.04	7.69	13.60
Return on Equity %	9.16	15.12	12.40	11.87	19.04	16.52	13.94	21.79
EBITDA Margin %	13.06	17.59	17.17	19.44	23.62	21.86	18.37	19.95
Net Margin %	4.48	7.50	6.38	5.98	9.00	7.77	5.60	8.77
Asset Turnover	1.23	1.33	1.36	1.32	1.28	1.16	1.37	1.55
Current Ratio	1.03	0.77	0.91	1.06	1.34	0.77	0.52	1.23
Debt to Equity	0.24	0.05	N.M.	N.M.	0.26	0.27	...	N.M.
Price Range	19.48-12.42	20.60-11.35	37.96-12.60	49.99-24.80	55.13-28.00	31.50-14.56	22.56-9.88	...
P/E Ratio	25.30-16.13	17.91-9.87	43.14-14.32	62.49-31.00	44.82-22.76	35.39-16.36	39.58-17.32	...

Address: 201 East Fourth Street, Cincinnati, OH 45202 **Telephone:** (513) 723-7000 **Fax:** (513) 421-8624	**Web Site:** www.convergys.com **Officers:** James F. Orr - Chmn., Pres., C.E.O. Steven G. Rolls - Exec. V.P., Global Customer Mgmt., C.F.O.	**Auditors:** Ernst & Young LLP **Investor Contact:** 888-284-9900 **Transfer Agents:** The Fifth Third Bank, Corporate Trust Services, Cincinnati,

COOPER CAMERON CORP.

Exchange	Symbol	Price	52Wk Range	Yield	P/E
NYS	CAM	$57.21 (3/31/2005)	59.50-43.39	N/A	32.69

*7 Year Price Score 90.34   ***NYSE Composite Index=100**   ***12 Month Price Score 103.19**

Interim Earnings (Per Share)

Qtr.	Mar	Jun	Sep	Dec
2001	0.26	0.35	0.60	0.53
2002	0.35	0.40	0.37	(0.01)
2003	0.15	0.37	0.63	0.10
2004	0.31	0.35	0.55	0.54

Interim Dividends (Per Share)

No Dividends Paid

Valuation Analysis

Forecast P/E	25.01	No of Institutions
	(4/7/2005)	222
Market Cap	$3.0 Billion	Shares
Book Value	1.2 Billion	46,390,844
Price/Book	2.48	% Held
Price/Sales	1.45	85.86

Business Summary: Oil and Gas (MIC: 14.2 SIC: 533 NAIC: 33132)

Cooper Cameron is an international manufacturer of oil and gas pressure control equipment, including valves, wellheads, controls, chokes, blowout preventers and assembled systems for oil and gas drilling, production and transmission used in onshore, offshore and subsea applications. Co. is also a manufacturer of centrifugal air compressors, integral and separable gas compressors and turbochargers. During 2004, Co.'s operations were organized into three separate business segments: Cameron, Cooper Cameron Valves and Cooper Compression. In Feb 2004, Co. acquired Petreco International Inc., a supplier of oil and gas separation products.

Recent Developments: For the year ended Dec 31 2004, net income increased 35.9% to $94,415 thousand from net income of $69,450 thousand a year earlier. Revenues were $2,092,845 thousand, up 28.1% from $1,634,346 thousand the year before. Total direct expense was $1,560,268 thousand versus $1,181,650 thousand in the prior year, an increase of 32.0%. Total indirect expense was $386,779 thousand versus $372,134 thousand in the prior year, an increase of 3.9%.

Prospects: Co. is performing well, reflecting a better performance in subsea, the addition of Petreco and solid results in its surface product lines. Going forward, Co.'s outlook appears generally good, reflecting continued strength in the rig count and pipeline markets, coupled with progress in integrating the manufacturing facilities acquired in late 2004 into both CCV and Cameron's operations. For 2005, Co. expects earnings per share in the range of $0.35 to $0.40 for the first quarter and $2.20 and $2.35 for the full year. Capital expenditures during 2005 are expected to be about $70.0 million to $80 million.

Financial Data

(US$ in Thousands)	12/31/2004	12/31/2003	12/31/2002	12/31/2001	12/31/2000	12/31/1999	12/31/1998	12/31/1997
Earnings Per Share	1.75	1.25	1.10	1.75	0.50	0.78	2.48	2.53
Cash Flow Per Share	3.65	1.87	3.28	2.31	0.38	2.62	4.46	2.22
Tang Book Value Per Share	14.68	15.18	13.50	11.66	10.75	8.57	9.14	7.61
Income Statement								
Total Revenue	2,092,845	1,634,346	1,538,100	1,563,678	1,386,709	1,464,760	1,882,111	1,806,109
EBITDA	228,639	164,127	162,491	231,297	137,132	182,466	300,923	293,831
Depn & Amortn	82,841	83,565	77,907	83,095	75,321	83,716	72,474	65,862
Income Before Taxes	132,919	77,603	85,145	142,582	43,773	70,916	195,728	199,378
Income Taxes	38,504	20,362	24,676	44,237	16,113	27,914	59,572	58,796
Net Income	94,415	69,450	60,469	98,345	27,660	43,002	136,156	140,582
Average Shares	53,854	59,800	59,809	58,075	55,013	54,848	54,902	55,606
Balance Sheet								
Current Assets	1,205,324	1,147,701	1,017,861	964,986	687,986	704,573	966,260	960,789
Total Assets	2,356,430	2,140,685	1,997,670	1,875,052	1,493,873	1,470,719	1,823,603	1,643,230
Current Liabilities	528,260	679,919	374,810	377,771	346,031	421,826	529,842	528,795
Long-Term Obligations	458,355	204,061	462,942	459,142	188,060	195,860	364,363	328,824
Total Liabilities	1,128,183	1,003,962	956,367	951,771	651,594	756,641	1,043,318	1,001,179
Stockholders' Equity	1,228,247	1,136,723	1,041,303	923,281	842,279	714,078	780,285	642,051
Shares Outstanding	53,137	53,803	54,511	53,994	54,011	50,567	53,259	52,758
Statistical Record								
Return on Assets %	4.19	3.36	3.12	5.84	1.86	2.61	7.85	9.03
Return on Equity %	7.96	6.38	6.16	11.14	3.54	5.76	19.15	24.28
EBITDA Margin %	10.92	10.04	10.56	14.79	9.89	12.46	15.99	16.27
Net Margin %	4.51	4.25	3.93	6.29	1.99	2.94	7.23	7.78
Asset Turnover	0.93	0.79	0.79	0.93	0.93	0.89	1.09	1.16
Current Ratio	2.28	1.69	2.72	2.55	1.99	1.67	1.82	1.82
Debt to Equity	0.37	0.18	0.44	0.50	0.22	0.27	0.47	0.51
Price Range	56.20-41.10	55.24-41.80	59.30-36.87	73.00-29.15	83.88-43.69	49.00-22.75	71.00-21.75	80.63-30.88
P/E Ratio	32.11-23.49	44.19-33.44	53.91-33.52	41.71-16.66	167.75-87.38	62.82-29.17	28.63-8.77	31.87-12.20

Address: 1333 West Loop South, Suite 1700, Houston, TX 77027	Web Site: www.coopercameron.com	Auditors: Ernst & Young LLP
Telephone: (713) 513-3300	**Officers:** Sheldon R. Erikson - Chmn., Pres., C.E.O.	**Investor Contact:** 713-513-3344
Fax: (713) 513-3320	Franklin Myers - Sr. V.P., Fin., C.F.O.	**Transfer Agents:** EquiServe Trust Company N.A., Providence, RI

COOPER INDUSTRIES, LTD.

Exchange	Symbol	Price	52Wk Range	Yield	P/E
NYS	CBE	$71.52 (3/31/2005)	72.20-52.19	2.07	19.98

*7 Year Price Score 115.73 *NYSE Composite Index=100 *12 Month Price Score 105.77

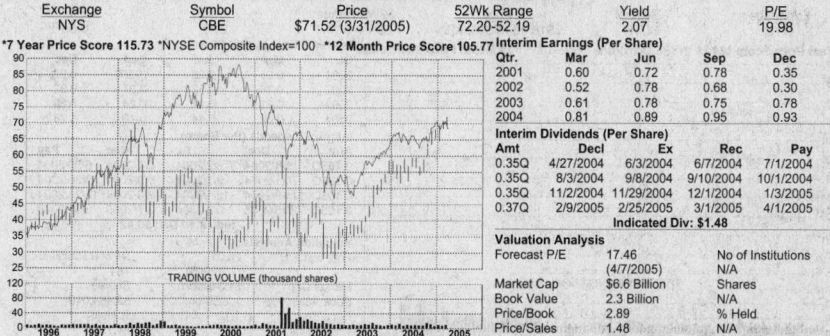

Interim Earnings (Per Share)

Qtr.	Mar	Jun	Sep	Dec
2001	0.60	0.72	0.78	0.35
2002	0.52	0.78	0.68	0.30
2003	0.61	0.78	0.75	0.78
2004	0.81	0.89	0.95	0.93

Interim Dividends (Per Share)

Amt	Decl	Ex	Rec	Pay
0.35Q	4/27/2004	6/3/2004	6/7/2004	7/1/2004
0.35Q	8/3/2004	9/8/2004	9/10/2004	10/1/2004
0.35Q	11/2/2004	11/29/2004	12/1/2004	1/3/2005
0.37Q	2/9/2005	2/25/2005	3/1/2005	4/1/2005

Indicated Div: $1.48

Valuation Analysis

Forecast P/E	17.46	No of Institutions
	(4/7/2005)	N/A
Market Cap	$6.6 Billion	Shares
Book Value	2.3 Billion	N/A
Price/Book	2.89	% Held
Price/Sales	1.48	N/A

Business Summary: Electrical (MIC: 11.14 SIC: 646 NAIC: 35122)

Cooper Industries operates in two business segments: The Electrical Products segment manufactures, markets and sells electrical and circuit protection products, including fittings, support systems, enclosures, wiring devices, plugs, receptacles, lighting fixtures, fuses, emergency lighting, fire detection systems and security products for use in residential, commercial and industrial construction, maintenance and repair applications. The Tools & Hardware segment manufactures, markets and sells hand tools for industrial, construction and consumer markets; automated assembly systems for industrial markets; and electric and pneumatic industrial power tools for general industry.

Recent Developments: For the year ended Dec 31 2004, net income increased 129.1% to $339,800 thousand from net income of $148,300 thousand a year earlier. Revenues were $4,462,900 thousand, up 9.9% from $4,061,400 thousand the year before. Operating income was $496,600 thousand versus an income of $392,000 thousand in the prior year, an increase of 26.7%. Total direct expense was $3,119,700 thousand versus $2,871,900 thousand in the prior year, an increase of 8.6%. Total indirect expense was $846,600 thousand versus $797,500 thousand in the prior year, an increase of 6.2%.

Prospects: Co.'s sales and orders are growing, margins are expanding and remain on an upward trend and its balance sheet has continued to strengthen. As Co. enters 2005, it is optimistic regarding conditions in most of its served markets. However, Co. also recognizes that residential construction markets have likely peaked and that cost pressures for certain commodity-based products will continue to be a challenge. That said, Co. remains confident that the disciplined execution of its key improvement initiatives will help it generate solid profitable growth. All things considered, Co. anticipates that its annual earnings for 2005 will increase between 10.0% and 15.0% compared with its 2004 results.

Financial Data

(US$ in Thousands)	12/31/2004	12/31/2003	12/31/2002	12/31/2001	12/31/2000	12/31/1999	12/31/1998	12/31/1997
Earnings Per Share	3.58	1.58	2.28	2.44	3.80	3.50	3.69	3.26
Cash Flow Per Share	5.11	4.80	5.15	4.49	5.36	4.27	2.94	4.21
Tang Book Value Per Share	1.56	0.66	0.07	0.69	N.M.	0.04	0.91	1.55
Dividends Per Share	1.400	1.400	0.700	1.400	1.400	1.320	1.320	1.320
Dividend Payout %	39.11	88.61	30.70	57.38	36.84	37.71	35.77	40.49
Income Statement								
Total Revenue	4,462,900	4,061,400	3,960,500	4,209,500	4,459,900	3,868,900	3,651,200	5,288,800
EBITDA	614,200	513,400	476,400	587,500	824,600	721,400	763,000	936,700
Depn & Amortn	117,600	121,400	121,700	186,400	174,400	147,600	137,500	219,600
Income Before Taxes	428,500	346,500	280,200	316,400	549,900	518,600	523,600	626,700
Income Taxes	88,700	72,200	66,500	55,100	192,500	186,700	187,700	232,100
Net Income	339,800	148,300	213,700	231,300	357,400	331,900	423,000	394,600
Average Shares	94,763	93,771	93,669	94,877	94,150	94,942	114,658	117,459
Balance Sheet								
Current Assets	2,218,600	1,960,800	1,689,000	1,651,200	1,735,100	1,466,600	1,417,300	2,136,700
Total Assets	5,340,800	4,965,500	4,687,900	4,611,400	4,789,300	4,143,400	3,779,100	6,052,500
Current Liabilities	1,827,600	1,021,500	959,500	1,106,100	1,173,600	1,085,800	970,700	1,385,100
Long-Term Obligations	698,600	1,336,700	1,280,700	1,107,000	1,300,800	894,500	774,500	1,272,200
Total Liabilities	3,054,300	2,847,100	2,685,500	2,588,200	2,885,100	2,400,300	2,215,500	3,475,900
Stockholders' Equity	2,286,500	2,118,200	2,002,400	2,023,200	1,904,200	1,743,100	1,563,600	2,576,600
Shares Outstanding	92,543	93,797	91,709	93,761	93,413	94,199	94,248	120,161
Statistical Record								
Return on Assets %	6.58	3.07	4.60	4.92	7.98	8.38	8.60	6.58
Return on Equity %	15.39	7.20	10.62	11.78	19.54	20.07	20.43	17.67
EBITDA Margin %	13.76	12.64	12.03	13.96	18.49	18.65	20.90	17.71
Net Margin %	7.61	3.65	5.40	5.49	8.01	8.58	11.59	7.46
Asset Turnover	0.86	0.84	0.85	0.90	1.00	0.98	0.74	0.88
Current Ratio	1.21	1.92	1.76	1.49	1.48	1.35	1.46	1.54
Debt to Equity	0.31	0.63	0.64	0.55	0.68	0.51	0.50	0.49
Price Range	68.25-51.56	58.70-34.06	45.97-27.95	60.25-31.85	45.94-30.19	56.25-39.75	69.94-37.94	57.44-40.75
P/E Ratio	19.06-14.40	37.15-21.56	20.16-12.26	24.69-13.05	12.09-7.94	16.07-11.36	18.95-10.28	17.62-12.50
Average Yield %	2.39	3.18	1.93	3.35	3.91	2.76	2.47	2.67

Address: 600 Travis, Suite 5800,	Web Site: www.cooperindustries.com	Auditors: Ernst & Young LLP
Houston, TX 77002	Officers: H. John Riley Jr. - Chmn., C.E.O Kirk S.	Investor Contact: (713) 209-8610
Telephone: (713) 209-8400	Hachigian - Pres., C.O.O.	
Fax: (713) 209-8996		

COOPER TIRE & RUBBER CO.

Exchange	Symbol	Price	52Wk Range	Yield	P/E
NYS	CTB	$18.36 (3/31/2005)	23.74-17.77	2.29	6.85

*7 Year Price Score 104.16 *NYSE Composite Index=100 ***12 Month Price Score 86.65**

Interim Earnings (Per Share)

Qtr.	Mar	Jun	Sep	Dec
2001	0.05	0.25	(0.27)	0.22
2002	0.36	0.52	0.31	0.32
2003	0.21	0.17	0.24	0.38
2004	0.32	0.44	0.13	1.78

Interim Dividends (Per Share)

Amt	Decl	Ex	Rec	Pay
0.105Q	5/4/2004	6/2/2004	6/4/2004	6/30/2004
0.105Q	7/21/2004	9/1/2004	9/3/2004	9/30/2004
0.105Q	11/19/2004	12/1/2004	12/3/2004	12/28/2004
0.105Q	2/15/2005	3/3/2005	3/7/2005	3/31/2005

Indicated Div: $0.42

Valuation Analysis

Forecast P/E	28.31 (4/7/2005)	No of Institutions 184
Market Cap	$1.3 Billion	Shares 59,454,040
Book Value	1.2 Billion	% Held
Price/Book	1.12	84.73
Price/Sales	0.63	

Business Summary: Rubber Products (MIC: 11.6 SIC: 011 NAIC: 26211)

Cooper Tire & Rubber is a leading manufacturer of replacement tires and original equipment automotive components. It is organized into two separate, reportable, business segments, Cooper Tire and Cooper-Standard Automotive. The Tire segment produces passenger car, light truck and motorcycle tires, and inner tubes, primarily for sale in the U.S. replacement market. This segment also manufactures radial medium truck tires and materials and equipment for the truck tire retread industry. The automotive segment manufactures automotive body sealing products and ranks among the top producers of noise, vibration and harshness control products and fluid handling systems for the automotive industry.

Recent Developments: For the year ended Dec 31 2004, income from continuing operations increased 0.4% to $27,446 thousand from income of $27,344 thousand a year earlier. Net income increased 172.7% to $201,372 thousand from net income of $73,835 thousand a year earlier. Revenues were $2,081,609 thousand, up 12.5% from $1,850,853 thousand the year before. Operating income was $63,224 thousand versus an income of $65,019 thousand in the prior year, a decrease of 2.8%. Total direct expense was $1,848,616 thousand versus $1,641,468 thousand in the prior year, an increase of 12.6%. Total indirect expense was $169,769 thousand versus $144,366 thousand in the prior year, an increase of 17.6%.

Prospects: On Jan 10 2005, Co. announced that it has entered an agreement to acquire an approximately 11.0% interest in Kumho Tire, a major tire manufacturer. The transaction is expected to be completed during the first quarter of 2005, subject to government and regulatory approvals. Meanwhile, near-term results will likely continue to be negatively affected by challenging industry conditions, higher raw material costs, and continuing capacity constraints. As a result, Co. anticipates first-quarter 2005 earnings of between $0.01 and $0.03 per share. Looking ahead, Co. expects margin improvement in the second half of 2005, driven by new product introductions and improved pricing.

Financial Data
(US$ in Thousands)

	12/31/2004	12/31/2003	12/31/2002	12/31/2001	12/31/2000	12/31/1999	12/31/1998	12/31/1997
Earnings Per Share	2.68	1.00	1.51	0.25	1.31	1.79	1.64	1.55
Cash Flow Per Share	1.37	3.18	4.65	3.71	3.13	2.78	2.64	2.66
Tang Book Value Per Share	15.30	7.48	6.99	6.64	7.07	7.15	11.45	10.58
Dividends Per Share	0.420	0.420	0.420	0.420	0.420	0.420	0.390	0.350
Dividend Payout %	15.67	42.00	27.81	168.00	32.06	23.46	23.78	22.58
Income Statement								
Total Revenue	2,081,609	3,514,399	3,329,957	3,154,702	3,472,372	2,196,343	1,879,760	1,814,411
EBITDA	173,445	367,936	432,317	306,845	446,398	365,519	315,340	304,911
Depn & Amortn	112,938	189,734	182,826	190,287	188,781	125,577	101,899	94,464
Income Before Taxes	35,006	114,110	177,197	29,158	160,156	215,497	198,217	194,792
Income Taxes	7,560	40,274	65,352	10,992	63,422	80,023	71,250	72,381
Net Income	201,372	73,836	111,845	18,166	96,734	135,474	126,967	122,411
Average Shares	75,185	74,203	74,024	72,558	73,584	75,837	77,598	79,128
Balance Sheet								
Current Assets	1,646,277	1,024,409	859,298	952,097	1,031,225	945,428	569,473	554,612
Total Assets	2,668,084	2,868,867	2,710,979	2,764,250	2,922,009	2,757,645	1,541,275	1,495,956
Current Liabilities	311,965	476,727	433,943	647,905	606,507	395,865	192,988	200,331
Long-Term Obligations	773,704	871,948	875,378	882,134	1,036,960	1,046,463	205,285	205,525
Total Liabilities	1,497,551	1,838,478	1,769,263	1,854,010	1,969,453	1,782,011	673,339	662,381
Stockholders' Equity	1,170,533	1,030,389	941,716	910,240	952,556	975,634	867,936	833,575
Shares Outstanding	71,139	73,964	73,557	72,599	72,543	75,809	75,791	78,760
Statistical Record								
Return on Assets %	7.25	2.65	4.09	0.64	3.40	6.30	8.36	8.84
Return on Equity %	18.25	7.49	12.08	1.95	10.01	14.70	14.92	15.11
EBITDA Margin %	8.33	10.47	12.98	9.73	12.86	16.64	16.78	16.80
Net Margin %	9.67	2.10	3.36	0.58	2.79	6.17	6.75	6.75
Asset Turnover	0.75	1.26	1.22	1.11	1.22	1.02	1.24	1.31
Current Ratio	5.28	2.15	1.98	1.47	1.70	2.39	2.95	2.77
Debt to Equity	0.66	0.85	0.93	0.97	1.09	1.07	0.24	0.25
Price Range	23.74-17.77	21.60-12.20	25.67-12.65	17.30-11.05	15.75-9.25	24.81-13.25	25.06-15.56	27.88-18.13
P/E Ratio	8.86-6.63	21.60-12.20	17.00-8.38	69.20-44.20	12.02-7.06	13.86-7.40	15.28-9.49	17.98-11.69
Average Yield %	1.99	2.53	2.27	3.04	3.60	2.11	1.86	1.56

Address: 701 Lima Avenue, Findlay, OH 45840 **Telephone:** (419) 423-1321 **Fax:** (419) 424-4305	**Web Site:** www.coopertire.com **Officers:** Thomas A. Dattilo - Chmn., Pres., C.E.O. Phillip G. Weaver - V.P., C.F.O.	**Auditors:** Ernst & Young LLP **Investor Contact:** 419-427-4768

CORNING, INC.

Exchange	Symbol	Price	52Wk Range	Yield	P/E
NYS	GLW	$11.13 (3/31/2005)	13.06-9.55	N/A	N/A

*7 Year Price Score 45.75   *NYSE Composite Index=100   *12 Month Price Score 91.74

TRADING VOLUME (thousand shares)

Interim Earnings (Per Share)

Qtr.	Mar	Jun	Sep	Dec
2001	0.14	(5.13)	(0.24)	(0.68)
2002	(0.10)	(0.39)	(0.25)	(0.65)
2003	(0.17)	(0.02)	0.02	(0.03)
2004	0.04	0.07	(1.78)	0.13

Interim Dividends (Per Share)

Dividend Payment Suspended

Valuation Analysis

Forecast P/E	19.33	No of Institutions	
	(4/7/2005)	500	
Market Cap	$15.7 Billion	Shares	
Book Value	3.8 Billion	925,576,448	
Price/Book	4.11	% Held	
Price/Sales	4.07	65.65	

Business Summary: Metal Works (MIC: 11.3 SIC: 357 NAIC: 34210)

Corning is a global, technology-based corporation that operates in two business segments. The Telecommunications segment produces optical fiber and cable and hardware and equipment products for the worldwide telecommunications industry. The Technologies segment manufactures specialized products with unique properties for customer applications utilizing glass, glass ceramic and polymer technologies. Businesses within this segment include liquid crystal display (LCD) glass for flat panel displays, environmental products, life science products, specialty materials products, and glass panels and funnels for televisions.

Recent Developments: For the year ended Dec 31 2004, loss from continuing operations was $2,185,000 thousand compared with a loss of $223,000 thousand a year earlier. Net loss was $2,165,000 thousand versus net loss of $223,000 thousand a year earlier. Revenues were $3,854,000 thousand, up 24.7% from $3,090,000 thousand the year before. Operating loss was $1,453,000 thousand versus a loss of $655,000 thousand in the prior year. Total direct expense was $2,439,000 thousand versus $2,241,000 thousand in the prior year, an increase of 8.8%. Total indirect expense was $2,868,000 thousand versus $1,504,000 thousand in the prior year, an increase of 90.7%.

Prospects: Co. is projecting first-quarter 2005 sales in the range of $980.0 million to $1.03 billion, with earnings of between $0.11 and $0.13 per share, before special items. In addition, Co. expects that foreign exchange rates will remain stable, and that its gross margin will be in the range of 37.0% to 38.0% for the quarter. Meanwhile, Co. plans to boost capital expenditures in 2005 to expand its capacity for manufacturing glass used in flat panel televisions. Co. is targeting capital expenditures of between $1.20 billion and $1.40 billion in 2005, with approximately 75.0% being used for liquid crystal display (LCD) expansion. Co. expects demand for LCD will grow by 40.0% to 60.0% in 2005.

Financial Data

(US$ in Thousands)	12/31/2004	12/31/2003	12/31/2002	12/31/2001	12/31/2000	12/31/1999	12/31/1998	12/31/1997
Earnings Per Share	(1.56)	(0.18)	(1.39)	(5.89)	0.48	0.65	0.56	0.62
Cash Flow Per Share	0.73	0.10	(0.31)	1.55	1.65	1.09	0.93	1.05
Tang Book Value Per Share	2.38	2.59	2.14	3.39	3.56	2.59	1.72	1.27
Dividends Per Share	...	...	...	0.120	0.240	0.240	0.240	0.240
Dividend Payout %	...	...	...	...	50.00	36.92	43.11	38.92
Income Statement								
Total Revenue	3,854,000	3,090,000	3,164,000	6,272,000	7,273,100	4,368,100	3,572,100	4,129,100
EBITDA	(1,253,400)	(120,000)	(1,921,000)	(4,946,000)	6,559,200	1,081,400	794,300	1,084,800
Depn & Amortn	210,600	517,000	661,000	1,080,000	5,761,200	380,700	298,000	321,600
Income Before Taxes	(1,580,000)	(759,000)	(2,720,000)	(6,111,000)	691,400	620,800	439,600	678,200
Income Taxes	1,031,000	(254,000)	(726,000)	(452,000)	407,100	188,600	132,800	227,200
Net Income	(2,165,000)	(223,000)	(1,302,000)	(5,498,000)	422,000	481,700	394,000	439,800
Average Shares	1,386,000	1,274,000	1,030,000	933,000	879,300	743,100	731,700	736,200
Balance Sheet								
Current Assets	3,281,000	2,694,000	3,825,000	4,107,000	4,634,400	1,782,500	1,310,300	1,424,200
Total Assets	9,710,000	10,752,000	11,548,000	12,793,000	17,525,700	6,012,200	4,981,900	4,811,400
Current Liabilities	2,336,000	1,553,000	1,680,000	1,994,000	1,948,700	1,488,000	1,074,700	1,017,300
Long-Term Obligations	2,214,000	2,668,000	3,963,000	4,461,000	3,966,400	1,288,700	998,300	1,134,100
Total Liabilities	5,865,000	5,288,000	6,857,000	7,379,000	6,892,800	3,785,000	3,476,300	3,564,900
Stockholders' Equity	3,816,000	5,464,000	4,691,000	5,414,000	10,632,900	2,227,200	1,505,600	1,246,500
Shares Outstanding	1,408,000	1,343,000	1,197,000	921,000	924,100	736,200	694,500	694,800
Statistical Record								
Return on Assets %	N.M.	N.M.	N.M.	N.M.	3.58	8.76	8.05	9.63
Return on Equity %	N.M.	N.M.	N.M.	N.M.	6.55	25.81	28.63	39.84
EBITDA Margin %	N.M.	N.M.	N.M.	N.M.	90.18	24.76	22.24	26.27
Net Margin %	N.M.	N.M.	N.M.	N.M.	5.80	11.03	11.03	10.65
Asset Turnover	0.38	0.28	0.26	0.41	0.62	0.79	0.73	0.90
Current Ratio	1.40	1.73	2.28	2.06	2.38	1.20	1.22	1.40
Debt to Equity	0.58	0.49	0.84	0.82	0.37	0.58	0.66	0.91
Price Range	13.78-9.55	12.01-3.31	10.70-1.10	70.13-7.01	113.33-34.58	42.98-15.00	15.00-7.83	21.67-11.33
P/E Ratio	...	...	...	...	236.11-72.05	66.12-23.08	26.79-13.99	34.95-18.28
Average Yield %	...	...	...	0.57	0.33	1.06	1.98	1.54

Address: One Riverfront Plaza, Corning, NY 14831-0001 **Telephone:** (607) 974-9000 **Fax:** (607) 974-8688	**Web Site:** www.corning.com **Officers:** James R. Houghton - Chmn., C.E.O. James B. Flaws - Vice-Chmn., C.F.O.	**Auditors:** PricewaterhouseCoopers LLP **Investor Contact:** 607-974-9000

COUNTRYWIDE FINANCIAL CORP

Exchange	Symbol	Price	52Wk Range	Yield	P/E
NYS	CFC	$32.46 (3/31/2005)	39.39-27.59	1.73	8.94

*7 Year Price Score 189.09 ***NYSE Composite Index=100** ***12 Month Price Score 94.82**

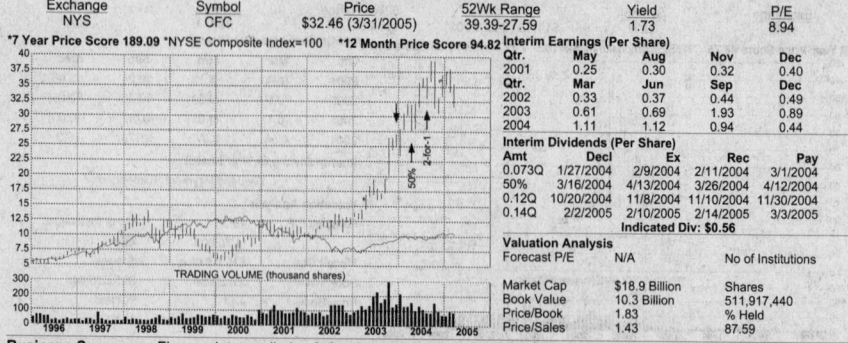

Interim Earnings (Per Share)

Qtr.	May	Aug	Nov	Dec
2001	0.25	0.30	0.32	0.40
Qtr.	Mar	Jun	Sep	Dec
2002	0.33	0.37	0.44	0.49
2003	0.61	0.69	1.93	0.89
2004	1.11	1.12	0.94	0.44

Interim Dividends (Per Share)

Amt	Decl	Ex	Rec	Pay
0.073Q	1/27/2004	2/9/2004	2/11/2004	3/1/2004
50%	3/16/2004	4/13/2004	3/26/2004	4/12/2004
0.12Q	10/20/2004	11/8/2004	11/10/2004	11/30/2004
0.14Q	2/2/2005	2/10/2005	2/14/2005	3/3/2005
		Indicated Div: $0.56		

Valuation Analysis

Forecast P/E	N/A	No of Institutions
Market Cap	$18.9 Billion	Shares
Book Value	10.3 Billion	511,917,440
Price/Book	1.83	% Held
Price/Sales	1.43	87.59

TRADING VOLUME (thousand shares)

Business Summary: Finance Intermediaries & Services (MIC: 8.7 SIC: 162 NAIC: 22292)

Countrywide Financial provides mortgage banking and diversified financial services. Mortgage banking businesses include loan production and servicing principally through Countrywide Home Loans, Inc. Also included in Co.'s mortgage banking segment is the LandSafe group of companies, which provide loan closing services. Co.'s diversified services encompass capital markets, banking, insurance, and global, largely through the activities of Countrywide Capital Markets, a mortgage-related investment banker; Countrywide Bank, a retail bank; Balboa Life and Casualty Group; Balboa Reinsurance, a captive mortgage reinsurance company; and Global Home Loans, a UK mortgage banking joint venture.

Recent Developments: For the year ended Dec 31 2004, net income decreased 7.4% to $2,197,574 thousand from net income of $2,372,950 thousand a year earlier. Provision for loan losses was $71,775 thousand versus $48,204 thousand in the prior year, an increase of 48.9%. Non-interest income fell 9.1% to $9,205,539 thousand, while non-interest expense advanced 21.4% to $4,580,551 thousand.

Prospects: Results are being adversely affected by a combination of market factors, including a flattening of the yield curve as 2-year and 10-year swap rates converged by 42 basis during the fourth quarter of 2004. However, Co. is achieving substantial growth in its Diversified Businesses, which is being fueled in large part by the continued growth of the Banking segment. This growth is being driven by loans originated and held for investment. Also, Co. is encouraged by an increase in purchase funding, reflecting its strategic initiative to increase volume in the less interest-rate sensitive purchase market. For 2005, Co. expects diluted earnings to range from $3.25 to $4.25 per share.

Financial Data

(US$ in Thousands)	12/31/2004	12/31/2003	12/31/2002	12/31/2001	02/28/2001	02/29/2000	02/28/1999	02/28/1998
Earnings Per Share	3.63	4.16	1.62	0.97	0.79	0.88	0.82	0.77
Cash Flow Per Share	5.83	(2.94)	(7.36)	(22.18)	(7.20)	5.39	(2.25)	(5.71)
Tang Book Value Per Share	2.22	1.78	N.M.	N.M.	N.M.	N.M.	N.M.	N.M.
Dividends Per Share	0.368	0.147	0.115	0.100	0.100	0.100	0.080	0.080
Dividend Payout %	10.15	3.55	7.09	10.28	12.74	11.36	9.73	10.36
Income Statement								
Interest Income	4,629,795	3,342,200	2,253,296	1,821,897	1,341,402	998,646	1,029,066	440,058
Interest Expense	2,608,338	1,940,207	1,461,066	1,474,719	1,348,242	930,294	983,829	424,341
Net Interest Income	2,021,457	1,401,993	792,230	347,178	(6,840)	68,352	45,237	15,717
Provision for Losses	71,775	...	...	...	...	...	...	...
Non-Interest Income	8,557,402	8,694,099	4,994,485	3,508,820	2,680,314	2,395,461	2,947,343	2,055,047
Non-Interest Expense	6,911,211	6,250,320	4,443,692	3,067,379	2,087,439	1,832,615	2,360,775	1,505,218
Income Before Taxes	3,595,873	3,845,772	1,343,023	788,619	586,035	631,198	631,805	565,546
Income Taxes	1,398,299	1,472,822	501,244	302,613	211,882	220,955	246,404	220,563
Net Income	2,197,574	2,372,950	841,779	486,006	374,153	410,243	385,401	344,983
Average Shares	605,722	571,125	518,894	499,170	476,138	466,750	468,178	446,102
Balance Sheet								
Net Loans & Leases	39,660,086	26,368,055	6,070,426	...	...	...	...	...
Total Assets	128,495,705	97,949,793	58,030,783	37,216,804	22,955,507	15,822,328	15,648,256	12,219,181
Total Deposits	20,013,208	9,327,671	3,114,271	...	...	...	...	...
Total Liabilities	118,185,629	88,865,077	52,369,650	32,629,162	18,896,243	12,434,449	12,629,371	9,631,238
Stockholders' Equity	10,310,076	8,084,716	5,161,133	4,087,642	3,559,264	2,887,879	2,518,885	2,087,943
Shares Outstanding	581,648	553,471	506,252	490,820	470,927	453,852	450,474	436,822
Statistical Record								
Return on Assets %	1.94	3.04	1.77	2.19	1.93	2.60	2.77	3.40
Return on Equity %	23.83	35.83	18.20	16.62	11.61	15.13	16.73	18.65
Net Interest Margin %	43.66	41.95	35.16	19.06	N.M.	6.84	4.40	3.57
Efficiency Ratio %	52.41	51.93	61.31	57.54	51.90	53.99	59.37	60.33
Loans to Deposits	1.98	2.83	1.95	...	...	...	...	...
Price Range	39.39-23.43	27.08-12.83	13.75-9.50	12.34-9.61	12.75-5.78	11.92-5.83	14.05-7.70	12.00-6.13
P/E Ratio	10.85-6.46	6.51-3.08	8.49-5.86	12.72-9.91	16.14-7.32	13.55-6.62	17.13-9.39	15.58-7.95
Average Yield %	1.13	0.81	0.98	0.93	1.10	1.17	0.69	0.92

Address: 4500 Park Granada Boulevard, Calabasas, CA 91302 **Telephone:** (818) 225-3000	**Web Site:** www.countrywide.com **Officers:** Angelo R. Mozilo - Chmn., C.E.O. Stanford L. Kurland - Pres., C.O.O.	**Auditors:** Grant Thornton LLP **Investor Contact:** 818-225-3550

COVANCE INC.

Exchange	Symbol	Price	52Wk Range	Yield	P/E
NYS	CVD	$47.61 (3/31/2005)	47.61-33.00	N/A	31.32

*7 Year Price Score 151.03 *NYSE Composite Index=100 ***12 Month Price Score 106.81**

Interim Earnings (Per Share)

Qtr.	Mar	Jun	Sep	Dec
2001	0.54	(0.05)	0.15	0.16
2002	0.19	0.21	0.36	0.27
2003	0.28	0.29	0.31	0.32
2004	0.34	0.36	0.39	0.43

Interim Dividends (Per Share)

No Dividends Paid

Valuation Analysis

Forecast P/E	25.03	No of Institutions
	(4/7/2005)	230
Market Cap	$3.0 Billion	Shares
Book Value	637.7 Million	51,592,648
Price/Book	4.65	% Held
Price/Sales	2.81	82.17

Business Summary: Biotechnology (MIC: 9.2 SIC: 731 NAIC: 41710)

Covance is a drug development services company that provides a range of early stage and late stage product development services to the pharmaceutical, biotechnology and medical device industries. Co. also provides services such as laboratory testing to the chemical, agrochemical and food industries. Co. has two business segments: early development services, which includes preclinical services and Phase I clinical services, and late-stage development services, which includes central laboratory, clinical development, periapproval, central electrocardiogram (ECG) diagnostic services, and healthcare economic and reimbursement services.

Recent Developments: For the year ended Dec 31 2004, net income increased 28.6% to $97,947 thousand from net income of $76,136 thousand a year earlier. Revenues were $1,056,397 thousand, up 8.4% from $974,210 thousand the year before. Operating income was $140,474 thousand versus an income of $116,575 thousand in the prior year, an increase of 20.5%. Total direct expense was $713,913 thousand versus $668,632 thousand in the prior year, an increase of 6.8%. Total indirect expense was $202,010 thousand versus $189,000 thousand in the prior year, an increase of 6.9%.

Prospects: Co. is performing well, reflecting a greater balance of revenue growth and operating margin performance between its Early Development and Late-Stage Development segments. Early Development's results were strong during the fourth quarter, with revenue growing 12.6% and operating margins at a solid 22.9%. These results were again led by Co.'s toxicology and chemistry offerings. Late-Stage Development achieved revenue growth of 10.6% and operating margin of 17.1%, with particularly strong performances in its health economics, periapproval, and central diagnostics service offerings. Looking ahead to 2005, Co. is targeting earnings per share in the range of $1.81 to $1.86.

Financial Data (US$ in Thousands)	12/31/2004	12/31/2003	12/31/2002	12/31/2001	12/31/2000	12/31/1999	12/31/1998	12/31/1997
Earnings Per Share	1.52	1.21	1.03	0.79	0.27	0.78	0.83	0.69
Cash Flow Per Share	2.60	2.27	2.12	1.13	0.85	1.35	1.10	1.34
Tang Book Value Per Share	9.33	8.11	6.19	4.86	3.19	3.12	2.62	1.84
Income Statement								
Total Revenue	1,056,397	974,210	924,697	855,877	868,087	828,980	731,574	590,651
EBITDA	186,590	161,716	133,706	132,909	98,222	134,669	129,229	108,370
Depn & Amortn	46,354	45,824	42,434	47,719	54,200	48,147	37,723	30,877
Income Before Taxes	142,526	115,701	90,441	78,342	24,971	76,460	84,145	69,179
Income Taxes	45,532	40,021	26,658	30,442	9,735	30,642	35,099	29,367
Net Income	97,947	76,136	63,783	47,900	15,236	45,818	48,608	39,754
Average Shares	64,644	63,081	61,641	60,430	57,492	58,680	58,774	57,463
Balance Sheet								
Current Assets	508,954	449,854	345,386	324,493	353,012	302,124	274,489	230,478
Total Assets	924,685	807,625	677,003	612,028	771,091	700,314	593,415	484,014
Current Liabilities	219,126	189,824	214,435	226,783	451,722	199,877	193,001	170,990
Long-Term Obligations	...	...	15,000	17,224	208,724	149,909	132,423	
Total Liabilities	286,999	243,644	245,336	267,083	505,340	437,662	368,400	326,957
Stockholders' Equity	637,686	563,981	431,667	344,945	265,751	262,652	225,015	157,057
Shares Outstanding	62,261	62,524	60,562	59,808	57,794	57,029	58,417	57,678
Statistical Record								
Return on Assets %	11.28	10.26	9.90	6.93	2.07	7.08	9.02	8.50
Return on Equity %	16.26	15.29	16.43	15.69	5.75	18.79	25.44	29.69
EBITDA Margin %	17.66	16.60	14.46	15.53	11.31	16.25	17.66	18.35
Net Margin %	9.27	7.82	6.90	5.60	1.76	5.53	6.64	6.73
Asset Turnover	1.22	1.31	1.43	1.24	1.18	1.28	1.36	1.26
Current Ratio	2.32	2.37	1.61	1.43	0.78	1.51	1.42	1.35
Debt to Equity	...	...	...	0.04	0.06	0.79	0.67	0.84
Price Range	41.40-26.25	27.55-16.90	24.63-12.71	25.30-10.56	16.25-6.88	32.88-8.31	29.31-17.81	22.63-14.75
P/E Ratio	27.24-17.27	22.77-13.97	23.91-12.34	32.03-13.37	60.19-25.46	42.15-10.66	35.32-21.46	32.79-21.38

Address: 210 Carnegie Center, Princeton, NJ 08540 **Telephone:** (609) 452-4440 **Fax:** (609) 452-9375	**Web Site:** www.covance.com **Officers:** Christopher A. Kuebler - Chmn., C.E.O. Joseph L. Herring - Pres., C.O.O.	**Auditors:** Ernst & Young LLP **Investor Contact:** 609-452-4953

COVENTRY HEALTH CARE INC.

Exchange	Symbol	Price	52Wk Range	Yield	P/E
NYS	CVH	$68.14 (3/31/2005)	68.18-38.44	N/A	18.32

*7 Year Price Score 212.05 *NYSE Composite Index=100 *12 Month Price Score 115.22

Interim Earnings (Per Share)

Qtr.	Mar	Jun	Sep	Dec
2001	0.19	0.20	0.21	0.22
2002	0.30	0.40	0.44	0.45
2003	0.55	0.70	0.74	0.76
2004	0.82	0.93	0.96	1.01

Interim Dividends (Per Share)

Amt	Decl	Ex	Rec	Pay
50%	12/23/2003	2/2/2004	1/9/2004	1/30/2004

Valuation Analysis

Forecast P/E	N/A		No of Institutions
Market Cap	$6.1 Billion		Shares
Book Value	1.2 Billion		99,029,040
Price/Book	5.07		% Held
Price/Sales	1.16		92.55

Business Summary: Professional Health Care Services (MIC: 9.4 SIC: 011 NAIC: 21491)

Coventry Health Care is a managed health care company with 2.5 million members as of Dec 31 2004. Co. operates health plans under the names Altius Health Plans, Carelink Health Plans, Coventry Health Care, Coventry Health and Life, Group Health Plan, HealthAmerica, HealthAssurance, HealthCare USA, OmniCare, PersonalCare, SouthCare, Southern Health and WellPath. Co. also operates a diversified portfolio of local market health plans serving 15 states, primarily in the Mid-Atlantic, Midwest and Southeast regions and are located in small to mid-sized metropolitan areas.

Recent Developments: For the year ended Dec 31 2004, net income increased 34.8% to $337,117 thousand from net income of $250,145 thousand a year earlier. Revenues were $5,311,969 thousand, up 17.1% from $4,535,143 thousand the year before. Net premiums earned were $5,198,599 thousand versus $4,442,445 thousand in the prior year, an increase of 17.0%.

Prospects: For the first quarter of 2005, Co. is projecting total revenues of $1.56 billion to $1.59 billion and earnings per share on a diluted basis of $1.05 to $1.07. For fiscal 2005, Co. is targeting risk revenues in the range of $5.80 billion to $5.90 billion, and management services revenues of $875.0 million to $925.0 million. Overall revenue for 2005 for the First Health businesses is expected to be between $885.0 million and $905.0 million on a full year basis. Due to the timing of the closing on Jan 28 2005, Co. expects to realize approximately 11/12 of the full year estimate in calendar year 2005 results. For fiscal 2005, Co. is targeting diluted earnings per share of $4.43 to $4.53.

Financial Data

(US$ in Thousands)	12/31/2004	12/31/2003	12/31/2002	12/31/2001	12/31/2000	12/31/1999	12/31/1998	12/31/1997
Earnings Per Share	3.72	2.75	1.59	0.83	0.62	0.46	(0.15)	0.24
Cash Flow Per Share	5.14	3.67	2.35	1.86	1.18	(0.13)	0.87	0.45
Tang Book Value Per Share	9.90	6.85	4.27	4.29	3.47	2.39	1.59	0.18
Income Statement								
Total Revenue	5,311,969	4,535,143	3,576,905	3,147,245	2,604,910	2,162,372	2,110,383	1,228,351
EBITDA	574,085	430,321	250,293	160,582	129,094	105,961	16,856	43,354
Depn & Amortn	47,094	37,257	24,552	25,900	27,026	28,200	25,800	12,735
Income Before Taxes	526,991	393,064	225,741	134,682	102,068	76,000	(17,510)	20,344
Income Taxes	189,874	142,919	80,138	51,153	40,728	32,565	(5,769)	8,422
Net Income	337,117	250,145	145,603	84,407	61,340	43,435	(11,741)	11,903
Average Shares	90,589	90,765	91,866	101,812	98,635	96,238	78,715	51,375
Balance Sheet								
Current Assets	973,027	533,967	424,275	578,518	506,500	483,405	591,045	237,124
Total Assets	2,340,600	1,981,736	1,643,440	1,451,273	1,239,036	1,081,583	1,090,593	469,331
Current Liabilities	931,820	854,880	800,712	751,545	632,163	522,886	565,853	260,861
Long-Term Obligations	170,500	170,500	175,000	...	...	...	46,358	85,719
Total Liabilities	1,128,174	1,052,738	997,403	762,194	638,606	554,103	654,054	351,513
Stockholders' Equity	1,212,426	928,998	646,037	689,079	600,430	480,385	436,539	117,818
Shares Outstanding	90,212	90,571	88,182	99,460	97,653	88,723	88,252	49,909
Statistical Record								
Return on Assets %	15.56	13.80	9.41	6.27	5.27	4.00	N.M.	2.59
Return on Equity %	31.40	31.76	21.81	13.09	11.32	9.47	N.M.	10.91
EBITDA Margin %	10.81	9.49	7.00	5.10	4.96	4.90	0.80	3.53
Net Margin %	6.35	5.52	4.07	2.68	2.35	2.01	N.M.	0.97
Asset Turnover	2.45	2.50	2.31	2.34	2.24	1.99	2.71	2.68
Current Ratio	1.04	0.62	0.53	0.77	0.80	0.92	1.04	0.91
Debt to Equity	0.14	0.18	0.27	...	...	...	0.11	0.73
Price Range	54.01-38.44	43.84-16.91	25.03-13.20	16.92-9.17	19.46-4.50	9.92-3.42	12.63-3.00	13.25-4.58
P/E Ratio	14.52-10.33	15.94-6.15	15.74-8.30	20.39-11.04	31.38-7.26	21.56-7.43	...	55.21-19.10

Address: 6705 Rockledge Drive, Suite 900, Bethesda, MD 20817 Telephone: (301) 581-0600 Fax: (301) 493-0742	Web Site: www.coventryhealth.com Officers: Allen F. Wise - Chmn. Dale B. Wolf - C.E.O.	Auditors: ERNST & YOUNG LLP

COX RADIO INC.

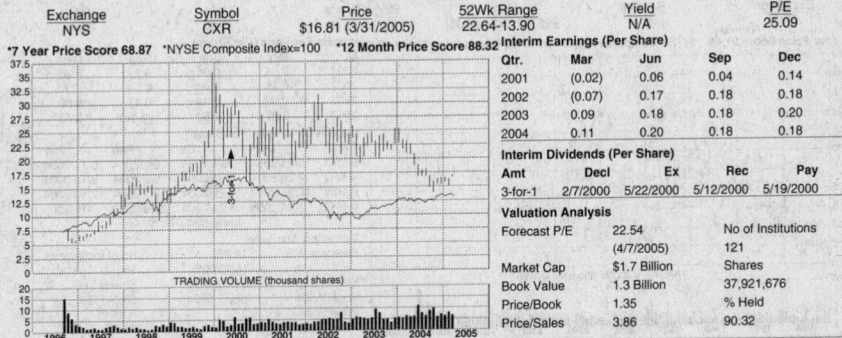

*7 Year Price Score 68.87 *NYSE Composite Index=100 *12 Month Price Score 88.32

Interim Earnings (Per Share)

Qtr.	Mar	Jun	Sep	Dec
2001	(0.02)	0.06	0.04	0.14
2002	(0.07)	0.17	0.18	0.18
2003	0.09	0.18	0.18	0.20
2004	0.11	0.20	0.18	0.18

Interim Dividends (Per Share)

Amt	Decl	Ex	Rec	Pay
3-for-1	2/7/2000	5/22/2000	5/12/2000	5/19/2000

Valuation Analysis

Forecast P/E	22.54	No of Institutions
	(4/7/2005)	121
Market Cap	$1.7 Billion	Shares
Book Value	1.3 Billion	37,921,676
Price/Book	1.35	% Held
Price/Sales	3.86	90.32

Business Summary: Media (MIC: 13.1 SIC: 832 NAIC: 15112)

Cox Radio is a radio broadcasting company with operations in the United States. As of Dec 31 2004, Co. owned, operated or provided sales services for 79 radio stations (66 FM and 13 AM) clustered in 18 markets including, Atlanta, GA, Birmingham, AL, Houston, TX, Jacksonville, FL, Miami, FL, Orlando, FL, San Antonio, TX and Tampa, FL. Co. operates three or more stations in 15 of its 18 markets. Co. operates a range of programming formats such as News/Talk, Classic Country, Traditional Hawaiian, Oldies, and Classic Rock in geographically diverse markets across the United States.

Recent Developments: For the year ended Dec 31 2004, net income increased 2.0% to $67,966 thousand from net income of $66,625 thousand a year earlier. Revenues were $438,213 thousand, up 2.9% from $425,873 thousand the year before. Operating income was $143,677 thousand versus an income of $139,092 thousand in the prior year, an increase of 3.3%. Total direct expense was $98,219 thousand versus $95,617 thousand in the prior year, an increase of 2.7%. Total indirect expense was $196,317 thousand versus $191,164 thousand in the prior year, an increase of 2.7%.

Prospects: Co. is pleased with its operating momentum at the end of 2004, and believes that it is well positioned for continued growth in the coming year. Moreover, Co. noted that it experienced a strong Jan month, and remained confident about its performance in Feb and Mar despite difficult revenue comparisons versus the year before. Going forward, Co. believes it will deliver low-single digit revenue growth for first quarter of fiscal 2005. Co. presently owns, operates or provides sales and marketing services for 79 stations clustered in 18 markets, including strategic major markets such as Atlanta, GA, Houston and San Antonio, TX and Miami, Orlando, and Tampa, FL.

Financial Data (US$ in Thousands)	12/31/2004	12/31/2003	12/31/2002	12/31/2001	12/31/2000	12/31/1999	12/31/1998	12/31/1997
Earnings Per Share	0.67	0.66	0.46	0.21	3.26	0.64	0.27	0.58
Cash Flow Per Share	0.74	1.00	1.06	0.95	0.72	0.65	0.55	0.50
Income Statement								
Total Revenue	438,213	425,873	420,592	395,303	369,404	300,494	261,213	199,572
EBITDA	155,216	150,427	150,019	137,244	609,992	146,698	85,377	111,351
Depn & Amortn	11,926	11,814	12,196	69,592	42,992	29,112	23,401	17,456
Income Before Taxes	112,902	105,046	98,173	20,171	534,484	94,826	45,054	84,531
Income Taxes	44,936	38,421	38,298	(1,307)	228,547	39,566	22,014	34,807
Net Income	67,966	66,625	45,941	20,691	305,937	55,260	23,040	49,724
Average Shares	100,758	100,542	100,532	100,188	93,936	86,637	86,556	85,482
Balance Sheet								
Current Assets	101,567	100,430	102,183	98,391	107,162	93,866	68,099	60,693
Total Assets	2,281,875	2,277,026	2,271,712	2,286,687	2,317,822	986,621	753,112	654,640
Current Liabilities	64,777	53,832	56,428	49,025	40,767	42,089	29,152	27,218
Long-Term Obligations	454,877	534,744	614,602	704,450	754,783	437,243	300,235	235,740
Total Liabilities	1,024,202	1,095,358	1,160,223	1,225,434	1,284,064	607,955	440,080	367,359
Stockholders' Equity	1,257,673	1,181,668	1,111,489	1,061,253	1,033,758	378,666	313,032	287,281
Shares Outstanding	100,710	100,323	100,183	100,003	99,427	86,748	85,648	85,227
Statistical Record								
Return on Assets %	2.97	2.93	2.02	0.90	18.47	6.35	3.27	10.85
Return on Equity %	5.56	5.81	4.23	1.98	43.20	15.98	7.68	19.01
EBITDA Margin %	35.42	35.32	35.67	34.72	165.13	48.82	32.68	55.79
Net Margin %	15.51	15.64	10.92	5.23	82.82	18.39	8.82	24.92
Asset Turnover	0.19	0.19	0.18	0.17	0.22	0.35	0.37	0.44
Current Ratio	1.57	1.87	1.81	2.01	2.63	2.23	2.34	2.23
Debt to Equity	0.36	0.45	0.55	0.66	0.73	1.15	0.96	0.82
Price Range	25.35-13.90	25.97-19.20	31.43-19.05	28.35-18.20	33.50-15.44	35.67-12.44	17.00-9.21	14.00-5.75
P/E Ratio	37.84-20.75	39.35-29.09	68.33-41.41	135.00-86.67	10.28-4.74	55.73-19.43	62.96-34.10	24.14-9.91

Address: 6205 Peachtree Dunwoody Road, Atlanta, GA 30328 **Telephone:** (678) 645-0000 **Fax:** (678) 843-5890	**Web Site:** www.coxradio.com **Officers:** James C. Kennedy - Chmn. Robert F. Neil - Pres., C.E.O.	**Auditors:** Deloitte & Touche LLP **Investor Contact:** 404-843-5000 **Transfer Agents:** Wachovia Bank N.A., Charlotte, NC

CRANE CO.

Exchange	Symbol	Price	52Wk Range	Yield	P/E
NYS	CR	$28.79 (3/31/2005)	34.33-25.95	1.39	N/A

*7 Year Price Score 97.14   *NYSE Composite Index=100   *12 Month Price Score 93.08

Interim Earnings (Per Share)

Qtr.	Mar	Jun	Sep	Dec
2001	0.34	0.54	0.30	0.30
2002	0.35	0.44	0.34	(0.85)
2003	0.28	0.44	0.47	0.56
2004	0.37	0.52	(3.48)	0.78

Interim Dividends (Per Share)

Amt	Decl	Ex	Rec	Pay
0.10Q	5/24/2004	6/1/2004	6/3/2004	6/11/2004
0.10Q	7/26/2004	8/31/2004	9/2/2004	9/10/2004
0.10Q	10/25/2004	11/29/2004	12/1/2004	12/10/2004
0.10Q	1/24/2005	2/24/2005	2/28/2005	3/10/2005

Indicated Div: $0.40

Valuation Analysis

Forecast P/E	12.86	No of Institutions
	(4/7/2005)	183
Market Cap	$1.7 Billion	Shares
Book Value	663.7 Million	38,041,320
Price/Book	2.57	% Held
Price/Sales	0.90	63.88

Business Summary: Metal Products (MIC: 11.4 SIC: 492 NAIC: 32912)

Crane is a manufacturer of engineered industrial products. Co.'s Fluid Handling segment manufactures and sells industrial valves and actuators; provides valve testing, service and parts; and manufactures and sells pumps and water treatment systems. The Aerospace segment includes pressure, fuel flow and position sensors and subsystems; and aircraft electrical power components and subsystems. The Engineered Materials segment includes the manufacture of fiberglass reinforced plastic panels. The Merchandising Systems segment manufactures vending machines, and coin changers and validators. The Controls segment includes ride-leveling, air-suspension control valves for heavy trucks and trailers.

Recent Developments: For the year ended Dec 31 2004, net loss was $105,421 thousand versus net income of $104,303 thousand a year earlier. Revenues were $1,890,335 thousand, up 15.5% from $1,635,991 thousand the year before. Operating loss was $161,490 thousand versus an income of $169,012 thousand in the prior year. Total direct expense was $1,298,874 thousand versus $1,105,566 thousand in the prior year, an increase of 17.5%. Total indirect expense was $752,951 thousand versus $361,413 thousand in the prior year, an increase of 108.3%.

Prospects: Co. is seeing market improvement in most of its end markets. However, higher material costs are affecting margins in Engineered Materials, Fluid Handling and, to a lesser extent, Merchandising Systems segments. Aerospace and Electronics segment margins remain under pressure from the mix of original equipment manufacturer/aftermarket sales and higher engineering costs for new programs, as well as lower sales volume levels of Electronics products. Nevertheless, Co. increased it full-year 2005 earnings per share guidance from the previously disclosed range of $2.05 to $2.15 to a revised guidance range of $2.10 to $2.25, reflecting lower anticipated interest expense in the coming year.

Financial Data
(US$ in Thousands)

	12/31/2004	12/31/2003	12/31/2002	12/31/2001	12/31/2000	12/31/1999	12/31/1998	12/31/1997
Earnings Per Share	(1.78)	1.75	(0.19)	1.47	2.02	1.70	2.00	1.63
Cash Flow Per Share	1.87	2.74	3.31	3.30	2.47	3.15	2.80	2.18
Tang Book Value Per Share	0.34	3.24	3.24	3.87	4.11	3.10	3.33	3.81
Dividends Per Share	0.400	0.400	0.400	0.400	0.400	0.400	0.367	0.333
Dividend Payout %	...	22.86	...	27.21	19.80	23.53	18.33	20.49
Income Statement								
Total Revenue	1,890,335	1,635,991	1,516,347	1,587,180	1,491,190	1,553,657	2,268,505	2,036,831
EBITDA	(90,659)	224,013	88,858	230,551	266,385	235,179	301,144	251,982
Depn & Amortn	55,716	54,025	49,790	74,610	55,281	61,280	61,458	55,400
Income Before Taxes	(168,170)	151,164	24,453	135,817	190,360	155,795	214,641	175,837
Income Taxes	(62,749)	46,861	7,825	47,197	66,631	54,897	76,203	63,066
Net Income	(105,421)	104,303	(11,448)	88,620	123,729	114,570	138,438	112,771
Average Shares	59,251	59,716	59,728	60,355	61,399	67,460	69,368	69,384
Balance Sheet								
Current Assets	702,806	661,776	509,477	523,257	500,152	505,160	698,966	607,753
Total Assets	2,116,508	1,811,776	1,413,696	1,292,115	1,143,851	1,175,447	1,454,674	1,185,893
Current Liabilities	410,014	418,574	288,425	249,139	231,977	233,515	351,162	295,812
Long-Term Obligations	296,592	295,861	205,318	302,368	213,790	286,772	359,090	260,716
Total Liabilities	1,452,814	1,025,525	764,634	640,820	537,088	607,337	811,440	653,349
Stockholders' Equity	663,694	786,251	649,062	651,295	606,763	568,110	643,234	532,544
Shares Outstanding	59,203	59,676	59,447	59,689	60,426	62,802	68,495	68,313
Statistical Record								
Return on Assets %	N.M.	6.47	N.M.	7.28	10.64	8.71	10.49	9.92
Return on Equity %	N.M.	14.53	N.M.	14.09	21.00	18.92	23.55	22.66
EBITDA Margin %	N.M.	13.69	5.86	14.53	17.86	15.14	13.27	12.37
Net Margin %	N.M.	6.38	N.M.	5.58	8.30	7.37	6.10	5.54
Asset Turnover	0.96	1.01	1.12	1.30	1.28	1.18	1.72	1.79
Current Ratio	1.71	1.58	1.77	2.10	2.16	2.16	1.99	2.05
Debt to Equity	0.45	0.38	0.32	0.46	0.35	0.50	0.56	0.49
Price Range	34.33-25.95	30.75-15.23	28.95-18.08	31.80-20.48	29.06-18.63	30.64-16.42	35.87-20.90	29.90-17.60
P/E Ratio	...	17.57-8.70	...	21.63-13.93	14.39-9.22	18.02-9.66	17.94-10.45	18.34-10.80
Average Yield %	1.34	1.77	1.71	1.50	1.68	1.65	1.24	1.34

Address: 100 First Stamford Place, Stamford, CT 06092	**Web Site:** www.craneco.com	**Auditors:** Deloitte & Touche LLP
Telephone: (203) 363 7300	**Officers:** Robert S. Evans - Chmn. Eric C. Fast - Pres., C.E.O.	**Investor Contact:** 1-888-272-6327
Fax: (203) 363 7295		

CRESCENT REAL ESTATE EQUITIES CO

Exchange	Symbol	Price	52Wk Range	Yield	P/E
NYS	CEI	$16.34 (3/31/2005)	19.09-15.05	9.18	11.51

*7 Year Price Score 71.84   ***NYSE Composite Index=100**   ***12 Month Price Score 93.90**

Interim Earnings (Per Share)

Qtr.	Mar	Jun	Sep	Dec
2001	0.26	0.10	0.17	(0.70)
2002	0.11	0.07	0.20	0.26
2003	(0.19)	(0.06)	(0.03)	0.29
2004	(0.19)	(0.18)	(0.19)	1.97

Interim Dividends (Per Share)

Amt	Decl	Ex	Rec	Pay
0.375Q	4/16/2004	4/28/2004	4/30/2004	5/14/2004
0.375Q	7/15/2004	7/28/2004	7/30/2004	8/13/2004
0.375Q	10/15/2004	10/27/2004	10/29/2004	11/15/2004
0.375Q	1/14/2005	1/27/2005	1/31/2005	2/15/2005
		Indicated Div: $1.50		

Valuation Analysis

Forecast P/E	12.51	No of Institutions
	(4/7/2005)	175
Market Cap	$1.6 Billion	Shares
Book Value	1.3 Billion	59,016,568
Price/Book	1.25	% Held
Price/Sales	1.66	59.12

Business Summary: Property, Real Estate & Development (MIC: 8.3 SIC: 798 NAIC: 25930)

Crescent Real Estate Equities operates as a real estate investment trust and provides management, leasing and development services. Co. operates in four investment segments: Office, Resorts and Hotels, Residential Development and Temperature-controlled Logistics. The resort and hotel segment is comprised of six luxury and destination fitness resorts and spas and four upscale business-class hotel properties. The residential development segment consists of four residential corporations that own 23 properties through joint venture or partnership agreements. The temperature-controlled logistics segment consists of 87 facilities.

Recent Developments: For the year ended Dec 31 2004, income from continuing operations increased 480.0% to $165,004 thousand from income of $28,448 thousand a year earlier. Net income increased 564.6% to $172,936 thousand from net income of $26,022 thousand a year earlier. Revenues were $1,289,958 thousand, up 18.0% from $1,093,429 thousand the year before.

Prospects: Co. continues to make progress towards improving its long-term earnings growth. For instance, Co. purchased three office properties in December 2004 and one in February 2005. Out of the four new office properties, two are in new markets, Atlanta, GA and Seattle, WA. These markets share similar characteristics with Co.'s other office markets in that they rank high on the list to benefit from future employment growth. Going forward, Co. expects continued improvement in the economy in 2005. Accordingly, Co. is cautiously optimistic that its overall portfolio occupancy will be more than 90.0% leased by year-end 2005.

Financial Data

(US$ in Thousands)	12/31/2004	12/31/2003	12/31/2002	12/31/2001	12/31/2000	12/31/1999	12/31/1998	12/31/1997
Earnings Per Share	1.42	...	0.63	(0.17)	2.02	(0.06)	1.21	1.20
Cash Flow Per Share	0.96	1.25	2.44	1.98	2.16	2.18	2.32	2.26
Tang Book Value Per Share	6.88	8.14	8.25	9.77	12.57	15.28	17.84	18.62
Dividends Per Share	1.500	1.500	1.500	2.025	2.200	2.200	1.690	1.295
Dividend Payout %	105.63	...	238.10	...	108.91	...	139.67	107.92
Income Statement								
Property Income	978,761	949,244	1,003,345	655,864	693,521	720,821	671,655	430,383
Non-Property Income	...	...	13,058	40,190	24,884	25,458	26,688	16,990
Total Revenue	978,761	949,244	1,016,403	696,054	718,405	746,279	698,343	447,373
Depn & Amortn	176,686	168,129	153,469	135,484	133,336	141,940	124,568	77,925
Interest Expense	176,771	172,116	179,212	182,410	203,197	192,033	152,214	86,441
Income Taxes	(12,937)	26,325	(4,922)	...	...	...	...	...
Net Income	172,936	26,022	87,708	(4,659)	248,122	10,959	165,600	117,341
Average Shares	99,244	98,928	103,731	109,140	128,731	137,892	127,402	97,847
Balance Sheet								
Total Assets	4,037,764	4,318,522	4,288,399	4,142,149	4,531,769	4,950,561	5,043,447	4,179,980
Long-Term Obligations	2,152,255	2,558,699	2,382,910	2,214,094	2,271,895	2,598,929	2,318,156	1,710,124
Total Liabilities	2,574,603	2,940,889	2,758,812	2,434,162	2,462,937	2,769,913	2,467,600	1,837,382
Stockholders' Equity	1,300,250	1,221,804	1,354,813	1,405,940	1,731,327	2,056,774	2,422,545	2,197,317
Shares Outstanding	99,420	99,274	124,280	123,396	121,818	121,537	124,555	117,977
Statistical Record								
Return on Assets %	4.13	0.60	2.08	N.M.	5.22	0.22	3.59	3.97
Return on Equity %	13.68	2.02	6.35	N.M.	13.06	0.49	7.17	7.66
Net Margin %	17.67	2.74	8.63	(0.67)	34.54	1.47	23.71	26.23
Price Range	19.09-15.05	17.51-13.75	20.15-13.61	25.00-16.77	23.31-15.88	24.94-15.44	40.00-21.06	40.50-25.25
P/E Ratio	13.44-10.60	N.M.	31.98-21.60	...	11.54-7.86	...	33.06-17.41	33.75-21.04
Average Yield %	8.93	9.65	8.58	9.24	10.89	10.57	5.58	4.13

Address: 777 Main Street, Suite 2100, Fort Worth, TX 76102 **Telephone:** (817) 321 2100 **Fax:** (817) 321 2000	**Web Site:** www.crescent.com **Officers:** Richard E. Rainwater - Chmn. Dennis H. Alberts - Pres., C.O.O.	**Auditors:** ERNST & YOUNG LLP

CROMPTON CORP

Exchange	Symbol	Price	52Wk Range	Yield	P/E
NYS	CK	$14.60 (3/31/2005)	15.65-5.36	1.37	N/A

*7 Year Price Score 67.89   *NYSE Composite Index=100   *12 Month Price Score 140.80

Interim Earnings (Per Share)

Qtr.	Mar	Jun	Sep	Dec
2001	0.14	0.12	(0.60)	(0.76)
2002	0.06	(0.06)	0.11	0.02
2003	0.05	(0.08)	0.72	(0.51)
2004	0.53	0.01	(0.35)	(0.49)

Interim Dividends (Per Share)

Amt	Decl	Ex	Rec	Pay
0.05Q	4/27/2004	5/5/2004	5/7/2004	5/28/2004
0.05Q	7/20/2004	8/4/2004	8/6/2004	8/27/2004
0.05Q	10/18/2004	10/27/2004	10/29/2004	11/19/2004
0.05Q	1/24/2005	2/2/2005	2/4/2005	2/25/2005
		Indicated Div: $0.20		

Valuation Analysis

Forecast P/E	25.54	No of Institutions
	(4/7/2005)	148
Market Cap	$1.7 Billion	Shares
Book Value	329.0 Million	97,778,704
Price/Book	5.20	% Held
Price/Sales	0.67	83.44

Business Summary: Chemicals (MIC: 11.1 SIC: 869 NAIC: 24690)

Crompton manufactures and markets a variety of polymer and specialty products. Most of Co.'s products are sold to industrial customers for use as additives, ingredients or intermediates that impart particular characteristics to the customers' end products. Co.'s products are currently marketed in more than 120 countries and serve a variety of end use markets including tires, agriculture, automobiles, textiles, plastics, lubricants, petrochemicals, leather, construction, recreation, mining, packaging, home furnishings, personal care, appliances and paper.

Recent Developments: For the year ended Dec 31 2004, loss from continuing operations was $36,732 thousand compared with a loss of $118,651 thousand a year earlier. Net loss was $34,590 thousand versus net income of $18,954 thousand a year earlier. Revenues were $2,549,762 thousand, up 16.7% from $2,185,043 thousand the year before. Operating loss was $59,931 thousand versus a loss of $35,018 thousand in the prior year. Total direct expense was $1,907,226 thousand versus $1,616,092 thousand in the prior year, an increase of 18.0%. Total indirect expense was $716,576 thousand versus $617,138 thousand in the prior year, an increase of 16.1%.

Prospects: On Mar 9 2005, Co. and Great Lakes Chemical Corporation (GLK) announced that they have entered into a definitive merger agreement under which Co. will acquire GLK in an all-stock transaction. Under terms of the agreement, GLK shareholders will receive 2.2232 shares of Crompton common stock for each share of GLK common stock they hold. The new company would be owned 51.0% by Co. shareholders and 49.0% by GLK shareholders on a fully diluted basis. Co. expects the transaction, which is expected to close by mid-2005, will be accretive to the combined company's 2006 earnings per share and cash flow per share.

Financial Data

(US$ in Thousands)	12/31/2004	12/31/2003	12/31/2002	12/31/2001	12/31/2000	12/31/1999	12/31/1998	12/31/1997
Earnings Per Share	(0.30)	0.17	(2.45)	(1.10)	0.78	(2.10)	2.14	1.15
Cash Flow Per Share	0.32	(0.13)	1.78	1.64	1.54	1.06	2.30	2.94
Dividends Per Share	0.200	0.200	0.200	0.200	0.200	0.050	...	0.050
Dividend Payout %	...	117.65	...	...	25.64	...	...	4.35
Income Statement								
Total Revenue	2,549,762	2,185,043	2,546,872	2,718,798	3,038,430	2,092,358	1,796,119	1,851,180
EBITDA	121,142	70,987	257,539	106,831	444,821	70,064	457,772	331,951
Depn & Amortn	126,100	136,087	146,550	185,560	181,971	116,660	80,536	79,856
Income Before Taxes	(83,399)	(154,753)	9,285	(188,606)	142,374	(116,429)	298,716	148,746
Income Taxes	(46,667)	(36,102)	(6,189)	(64,662)	53,101	42,922	115,493	56,675
Net Income	(34,590)	18,954	(283,507)	(123,944)	89,273	(175,038)	161,755	86,829
Average Shares	114,736	112,531	115,656	113,061	115,165	83,507	75,700	75,358
Balance Sheet								
Current Assets	996,338	810,454	777,134	815,074	1,076,895	1,119,753	597,756	715,049
Total Assets	2,678,709	2,529,182	2,840,815	3,232,188	3,528,327	3,726,618	1,408,893	1,548,820
Current Liabilities	709,169	701,245	681,490	682,618	715,463	977,970	394,372	363,088
Long-Term Obligations	862,251	754,018	1,261,847	1,392,833	1,479,394	1,309,812	646,857	896,291
Total Liabilities	2,349,729	2,226,473	2,640,932	2,684,647	2,774,351	2,966,706	1,342,190	1,568,910
Stockholders' Equity	328,980	302,709	199,883	547,541	753,976	759,912	66,703	(20,090)
Shares Outstanding	117,185	114,492	113,854	113,057	112,474	116,835	71,964	73,608
Statistical Record								
Return on Assets %	N.M.	0.71	N.M.	N.M.	2.45	N.M.	10.94	...
Return on Equity %	N.M.	7.54	N.M.	N.M.	11.76	N.M.	694.03	...
EBITDA Margin %	4.75	3.25	10.11	3.93	14.64	3.35	25.49	17.93
Net Margin %	N.M.	0.87	N.M.	N.M.	2.94	N.M.	9.01	4.69
Asset Turnover	0.98	0.81	0.84	0.80	0.84	0.81	1.21	...
Current Ratio	1.40	1.16	1.14	1.19	1.51	1.14	1.52	1.97
Debt to Equity	2.62	2.49	6.31	2.54	1.96	1.72	9.70	...
Price Range	11.80-5.36	7.56-3.68	12.90-5.68	12.19-6.27	13.94-7.06	20.88-7.56	31.88-13.00	27.00-18.25
P/E Ratio	...	44.47-21.65	...	...	17.87-9.05	...	14.89-6.07	23.48-15.87
Average Yield %	2.64	3.38	2.01	2.06	1.92	0.31	...	0.22

Address: 199 Benson Road, Middlebury, CT 06749 Telephone: (203) 573-2000	Web Site: www.cromptoncorp.com Officers: Vincent A. Calarco - Chmn. Robert L. Wood - Pres., C.E.O.	Auditors: KPMG LLP Investor Contact: 203-573-2000

CROWN CASTLE INTERNATIONAL CORP

Exchange	Symbol	Price	52Wk Range	Yield	P/E
NYS	CCI	$16.06 (3/31/2005)	17.47-12.63	N/A	15.75

*7 Year Price Score N/A   *NYSE Composite Index=100   *12 Month Price Score 99.27

Interim Earnings (Per Share)

Qtr.	Mar	Jun	Sep	Dec
2001	(0.41)	(0.49)	(0.60)	(0.57)
2002	(0.56)	(0.49)	(0.16)	(0.02)
2003	(0.38)	(0.47)	(0.50)	(0.73)
2004	(0.34)	(0.22)	2.02	(0.44)

Interim Dividends (Per Share)

No Dividends Paid

Valuation Analysis

Forecast P/E	0.00	No of Institutions
	(4/13/2005)	194
Market Cap	$3.6 Billion	Shares
Book Value	2.1 Billion	204,346,672
Price/Book	1.69	% Held
Price/Sales	4.50	91.39

TRADING VOLUME (thousand shares)

Business Summary: Communications (MIC: 10.1 SIC: 899 NAIC: 17212)

Crown Castle International owns, operates and leases towers and co-locatable rooftop sites, and transmission networks for wireless communications and broadcast transmission. Co. also provides complementary services to its customers, including network design, radio frequency engineering, site acquisition, site development and construction, antenna installation and network management and maintenance. As of Dec 31 2003, Co. owned, leased or managed 15,517 sites, including 10,642 sites in the U.S. and Puerto Rico, 3,487 sites in the U.K., and 1,388 sites in Australia.

Recent Developments: For the year ended Dec 31 2004, Co. reported a loss of $306.9 million, before income from discontinued operations of $542.0 million, versus a loss of $464.8 million, before income from discontinued operations of $10.5 million and a $551,000 accounting change charge, in the prior year. Net revenues climbed 8.8% to $603.9 million from $555.1 million the year before. Site rental revenues advanced 11.3% to $537.5 million, while network services and other revenues slipped 8.2% to $66.4 million. Operating loss was $27.2 million versus an operating loss of $75.4 million a year earlier. Comparisons were made with restated prior-year results.

Prospects: While Co.'s outlook for 2005 is currently based on a lower level of new leasing activity than achieved in 2004, Co. continues to see positive signs from its customers in the U.S., which may result in additional revenue. Further, as of Jan 1 2005, more than 95.0% of Co.'s 2005 outlook for site rental revenue was under contract, demonstrating the inherent predictability of the tower business. Meanwhile, Co. continues to focus its efforts on maximizing recurring cash flow per share and exploring opportunities to refinance a significant portion of its indebtedness. Co. hopes to complete these refinancing activities during the second quarter.

Financial Data
(US$ in Thousands)

	9 Mos	6 Mos	3 Mos	12/31/2003	12/31/2002	12/31/2001	12/31/2000	12/31/1999
Earnings Per Share	0.74	(1.78)	(2.03)	(2.09)	(1.16)	(2.08)	(1.48)	(0.96)
Cash Flow Per Share	0.70	0.82	1.28	1.20	0.96	0.62	0.92	0.70
Tang Book Value Per Share	8.32	7.31	3.31	3.52	5.28	6.00	6.58	6.49
Income Statement								
Total Revenue	442,594	293,548	248,487	930,348	901,533	898,951	649,165	345,759
EBITDA	4,252	(4,297)	30,116	(62,266)	39,185	(22,504)	36,472	38,790
Depn & Amortn	190,909	128,117	87,782	324,152	301,928	328,491	238,796	130,106
Income Before Taxes	(186,657)	(132,414)	(57,666)	(386,418)	(262,743)	(350,995)	(202,324)	(91,316)
Income Taxes	481	337	5,955	7,518	12,276	16,478	246	275
Net Income	356,772	(104,561)	(64,967)	(398,365)	(272,521)	(366,167)	(204,786)	(96,761)
Average Shares	222,841	221,853	219,294	216,947	218,028	214,246	178,588	131,466
Balance Sheet								
Current Assets	989,245	2,328,805	355,102	641,760	867,081	1,216,061	772,134	662,045
Total Assets	4,972,678	6,370,206	6,446,880	6,737,591	6,892,601	7,375,458	6,439,841	3,836,650
Current Liabilities	172,814	1,790,657	396,872	643,530	360,769	411,453	324,876	131,281
Long-Term Obligations	1,898,847	1,898,752	3,138,866	3,182,850	3,212,710	3,394,011	2,602,687	1,542,343
Total Liabilities	2,125,698	3,742,212	3,757,900	4,038,143	3,756,706	3,963,013	3,020,917	1,740,688
Stockholders' Equity	2,128,098	1,912,923	1,971,626	1,984,413	2,208,498	2,364,648	2,420,862	1,617,747
Shares Outstanding	223,591	225,296	222,154	220,758	215,983	218,804	198,912	157,414
Statistical Record								
Return on Assets %	3.68	N.M.	N.M.	N.M.	N.M.	N.M.	N.M.	N.M.
Return on Equity %	10.16	N.M.	N.M.	N.M.	N.M.	N.M.	N.M.	N.M.
EBITDA Margin %	0.96	N.M.	12.12	N.M.	4.35	N.M.	5.62	11.22
Net Margin %	80.61	N.M.	N.M.	N.M.	N.M.	N.M.	N.M.	N.M.
Asset Turnover	0.14	0.13	0.15	0.14	0.13	0.13	0.13	0.13
Current Ratio	5.72	1.30	0.89	1.00	2.40	2.96	2.38	5.04
Debt to Equity	0.89	0.99	1.59	1.60	1.45	1.44	1.08	0.95
Price Range	16.23-9.41	16.23-7.77	13.85-5.50	12.96-3.26	11.49-1.02	29.63-7.51	42.44-22.44	32.38-15.13
P/E Ratio	21.93-12.72	...	...	...	...	...	...	...

Address: 510 Bering Drive, Suite 500, Houston, TX 77057-1457
Telephone: (713) 570-3000
Fax: (713) 570-3100

Web Site: www.crowncastle.com
Officers: J. Landis Martin - Chmn. John P. Kelly - Pres., C.E.O.

Auditors: KPMG LLP
Investor Contact: 713-529-6600

CROWN HOLDINGS INC

Exchange	Symbol	Price	52Wk Range	Yield	P/E
NYS	CCK	$15.56 (3/31/2005)	17.07-8.13	N/A	51.87

*7 Year Price Score 66.55   *NYSE Composite Index=100   *12 Month Price Score 127.47

Interim Earnings (Per Share)

Qtr.	Mar	Jun	Sep	Dec
2001	(0.37)	0.04	(0.10)	(7.31)
2002	(0.43)	0.48	0.45	(1.70)
2003	(0.21)	0.43	0.04	(0.32)
2004	(0.11)	0.20	0.35	(0.17)

Interim Dividends (Per Share)

No Dividends Paid

Valuation Analysis

Forecast P/E	N/A	No of Institutions
Market Cap	$2.6 Billion	Shares
Book Value	277.0 Million	132,793,592
Price/Book	9.30	% Held
Price/Sales	0.36	79.58

TRADING VOLUME (thousand shares)

Business Summary: Metal Products (MIC: 11.4 SIC: 411 NAIC: 32431)

Crown Holdings is a global company that designs, manufactures and sells packaging products for consumer goods with 186 plants along with sales and service facilities throughout 42 countries as of Dec 31 2003. Co.'s products include steel and aluminum cans for food, beverage, household and other consumer products and a wide variety of metal and plastic caps, closures and dispensing systems. Co.'s business is organized on the basis of geographic regions with three reportable segments: Americas, Europe, and Asia-Pacific. The Americas includes the U.S., Canada and Central and South America. Europe includes Europe, Africa and the Middle East. Asia-Pacific includes China and Southeast Asia.

Recent Developments: For the year ended Dec 31 2004, net income was $51,000 thousand versus net loss of $32,000 thousand a year earlier. Revenues were $7,199,000 thousand, up 8.6% from $6,630,000 thousand the year before. Total direct expense was $6,292,000 thousand versus $5,865,000 thousand in the prior year, an increase of 7.3%. Total indirect expense was $405,000 thousand versus $400,000 thousand in the prior year, an increase of 1.2%.

Prospects: Co.'s near-term outlook appears reasonably positive, reflecting progress in its efforts to improve productivity, effective cost containment, closely managed working capital, increased cash flow and debt reduction. Also, Co. is benefiting from its geographic diversity, with more than 70.0% of 2004 net sales generated outside the U.S. Meanwhile, profit margin continues to show improvement, led by increased operating efficiencies, stronger foreign currencies and solid volumes. Separately, Co. announced that it plans to substantially increase beverage can production capacity in the Middle East. The plan is expected to bring an additional 1.50 billion cans of capacity to the region.

Financial Data

(US$ in Thousands)	12/31/2004	12/31/2003	12/31/2002	12/31/2001	12/31/2000	12/31/1999	12/31/1998	12/31/1997
Earnings Per Share	0.30	(0.19)	(8.38)	(7.74)	(1.40)	1.36	0.71	2.10
Cash Flow Per Share	2.44	2.64	2.89	2.47	2.14	6.77	5.40	3.13
Dividends Per Share	...	...	...	...	1.000	1.000	1.000	1.000
Dividend Payout %	...	...	...	...	...	73.53	140.85	47.62
Income Statement								
Total Revenue	7,199,000	6,630,000	6,792,000	7,187,000	7,289,000	7,732,000	8,300,000	8,494,600
EBITDA	822,000	813,000	561,000	492,000	651,000	1,173,000	1,076,000	1,336,900
Depn & Amortn	308,000	326,000	375,000	499,000	495,000	522,000	533,000	540,000
Income Before Taxes	161,000	119,000	(145,000)	(444,000)	(217,000)	309,000	180,000	457,000
Income Taxes	82,000	95,000	30,000	528,000	(58,000)	105,000	74,000	147,700
Net Income	51,000	(32,000)	(1,205,000)	(972,000)	(174,000)	181,000	105,000	294,000
Average Shares	168,800	164,700	143,800	125,600	126,800	129,800	132,900	140,300
Balance Sheet								
Current Assets	2,343,000	2,122,000	2,024,000	2,422,000	2,913,000	2,841,000	3,168,000	3,147,200
Total Assets	8,125,000	7,773,000	7,505,000	9,620,000	11,159,000	11,545,000	12,469,000	12,305,700
Current Liabilities	2,080,000	2,036,000	2,270,000	2,506,000	2,261,000	3,414,000	4,710,000	4,049,300
Long-Term Obligations	3,796,000	3,709,000	3,388,000	4,475,000	5,049,000	3,573,000	3,188,000	3,301,400
Total Liabilities	7,848,000	7,633,000	7,592,000	8,816,000	9,050,000	8,654,000	9,494,000	8,776,500
Stockholders' Equity	277,000	140,000	(87,000)	804,000	2,109,000	2,891,000	2,975,000	3,529,200
Shares Outstanding	165,559	165,024	159,430	125,702	125,621	121,081	122,337	128,399
Statistical Record								
Return on Assets %	0.64	N.M.	N.M.	N.M.	N.M.	1.51	0.85	2.36
Return on Equity %	24.39	N.M.	N.M.	N.M.	N.M.	6.17	3.23	8.29
EBITDA Margin %	11.42	12.26	8.26	6.85	8.93	15.17	12.96	15.74
Net Margin %	0.71	N.M.	N.M.	N.M.	N.M.	2.34	1.27	3.46
Asset Turnover	0.90	0.87	0.79	0.69	0.64	0.64	0.67	0.68
Current Ratio	1.13	1.04	0.89	0.97	1.29	0.83	0.67	0.78
Debt to Equity	13.70	26.49	...	5.57	2.39	1.24	1.07	0.94
Price Range	14.02-8.13	9.50-4.61	12.25-2.54	9.63-0.92	23.63-3.13	36.06-19.81	55.00-24.38	59.13-44.50
P/E Ratio	46.73-27.10	...	...	...	...	26.52-14.57	77.46-34.33	28.15-21.19
Average Yield %	...	...	...	...	7.20	3.58	2.34	1.92

Address: One Crown Way, Philadelphia, PA 19154 **Telephone:** (215) 698-5100 **Fax:** (215) 676-7245	**Web Site:** www.crowncork.com **Officers:** John W. Conway - Chmn., Pres., C.E.O. Alan W. Rutherford - Vice-Chmn., Exec. V.P., C.F.O.	**Auditors:** PricewaterhouseCoopers LLP **Investor Contact:** 215-552-3770

CSX CORP.

Exchange	Symbol	Price	52Wk Range	Yield	P/E
NYS	CSX	$41.65 (3/31/2005)	43.32-29.43	0.96	27.40

*7 Year Price Score 87.19 *NYSE Composite Index=100 *12 Month Price Score 109.59

Interim Earnings (Per Share)

Qtr.	Mar	Jun	Sep	Dec
2001	0.10	0.51	0.47	0.31
2002	0.12	0.63	0.60	0.64
2003	0.46	0.59	(0.48)	0.57
2004	0.14	0.55	0.57	0.26

Interim Dividends (Per Share)

Amt	Decl	Ex	Rec	Pay
0.10Q	5/5/2004	5/21/2004	5/25/2004	6/15/2004
0.10Q	7/14/2004	8/23/2004	8/25/2004	9/15/2004
0.10Q	10/20/2004	11/22/2004	11/24/2004	12/15/2004
0.10Q	2/9/2005	2/23/2005	2/25/2005	3/15/2005

Indicated Div: $0.40

Valuation Analysis

Forecast P/E	16.05	No of Institutions
	(4/7/2005)	308
Market Cap	$9.0 Billion	Shares
Book Value	6.8 Billion	172,234,928
Price/Book	1.32	% Held
Price/Sales	1.12	79.88

Business Summary: Rail Transport (MIC: 15.5 SIC: 011 NAIC: 82111)

CSX is a freight transportation company with principal business units providing rail, intermodal, and international terminal operations. The rail system, CSX Transportation Inc., operated over a more than 23,000 route-mile network in 23 states, the District of Columbia and two Canadian provinces, as of Dec 31 2003. CSX Intermodal Inc. operates a network of dedicated intermodal facilities across North America. CSX World Terminals operates container-freight terminal facilities in Asia, Europe, Australia, Latin America and the U.S. As of Dec 31 2003, Co and Norfolk Southern, through a jointly-owned acquisition entity, held economic interests in Conrail of 42.0% and 58.0%, respectively.

Recent Developments: For the year ended Dec 31 2004, income from continuing operations increased 205.1% to $418 million from income of $137 million a year earlier. Net income increased 37.8% to $339 million from net income of $246 million a year earlier. Revenues were $8,020 million, up 6.0% from $7,566 million the year before. Operating income was $1,000 million versus an income of $520 million in the prior year, an increase of 92.3%. Total direct expense was $6,246 million versus $6,070 million in the prior year, an increase of 2.9%. Total indirect expense was $774 million versus $976 million in the prior year, a decrease of 20.7%.

Prospects: On Feb 22 2005, Co. announced that it has completed the sale of its international terminal business, CSX World Terminals, to Dubai Ports International for approximately $1.14 billion in cash. The sale of these operations will help Co. sharpen its focus on growing its core surface transportation business. Meanwhile, Co. is benefiting from an improved business climate and continued strong demand for rail transportation. Separately, Co. is taking steps to improve its customer service and cost structure, which should allow it to capitalize even more on both growth and yield.

Financial Data
(US$ in Thousands)

	12/31/2004	12/26/2003	12/27/2002	12/28/2001	12/29/2000	12/31/1999	12/25/1998	12/26/1997
Earnings Per Share	1.52	1.14	1.99	1.38	2.67	0.01	2.51	3.72
Cash Flow Per Share	6.62	3.77	5.31	3.92	3.38	5.00	4.76	7.44
Tang Book Value Per Share	31.60	30.00	29.07	28.64	28.28	26.35	27.08	26.41
Dividends Per Share	0.400	0.400	0.400	0.800	1.200	1.200	1.200	1.080
Dividend Payout %	26.32	35.09	20.10	57.97	44.94	12,000.00	47.81	29.03
Income Statement								
Total Revenue	8,020,000	7,793,000	8,152,000	8,110,000	8,191,000	10,811,000	9,898,000	10,621,000
EBITDA	1,781,000	1,305,000	1,817,000	1,588,000	1,420,000	1,281,000	1,909,000	2,280,000
Depn & Amortn	730,000	643,000	649,000	622,000	600,000	621,000	630,000	646,000
Income Before Taxes	637,000	265,000	723,000	448,000	277,000	139,000	773,000	1,183,000
Income Taxes	219,000	76,000	256,000	155,000	91,000	88,000	236,000	384,000
Net Income	339,000	246,000	424,000	293,000	565,000	2,000	537,000	799,000
Average Shares	225,030	214,396	213,512	212,409	211,314	212,696	214,196	214,445
Balance Sheet								
Total Assets	24,581,000	21,760,000	20,951,000	20,801,000	20,491,000	20,720,000	20,427,000	19,957,000
Long-Term Obligations	6,234,000	6,886,000	6,519,000	5,839,000	5,810,000	6,196,000	6,432,000	6,416,000
Total Liabilities	17,770,000	15,307,000	14,710,000	14,681,000	14,474,000	14,964,000	14,547,000	14,191,000
Stockholders' Equity	6,811,000	6,453,000	6,241,000	6,120,000	6,017,000	5,756,000	5,880,000	5,766,000
Shares Outstanding	215,529	215,071	214,686	213,688	212,738	218,445	217,119	218,310
Statistical Record								
Return on Assets %	1.44	1.16	2.04	1.42	2.75	0.01	2.67	4.34
Return on Equity %	5.03	3.89	6.88	4.84	9.62	0.03	9.25	14.89
EBITDA Margin %	22.21	16.75	22.29	19.58	17.34	11.85	19.29	21.47
Net Margin %	4.23	3.16	5.20	3.61	6.90	0.02	5.43	7.52
Asset Turnover	0.34	0.37	0.39	0.39	0.40	0.52	0.49	0.58
Price Range	40.32-29.22	36.00-25.91	41.10-25.57	40.61-25.69	32.56-19.56	53.44-29.00	60.44-37.50	61.75-41.75
P/E Ratio	26.53-19.22	31.58-22.73	20.65-12.85	29.43-18.61	12.20-7.33	N.M.	24.08-14.94	16.60-11.22
Average Yield %	1.21	1.31	1.19	2.34	4.98	2.83	2.52	2.06

Address: 500 Water Street, 15th floor, Jacksonville, FL 32202
Telephone: (904) 359-3200

Web Site: www.csx.com
Officers: Michael J. Ward - Chmn., Pres., C.E.O.
Oscar Munoz - Exec. V.P., C.F.O.

Auditors: ERNST & YOUNG LLP
Investor Contact: 904-366-4242

235

CULLEN/FROST BANKERS, INC.

Exchange	Symbol	Price	52Wk Range	Yield	P/E	Div Acheiver
NYS	CFR	$45.15 (3/31/2005)	49.00-41.17	2.35	16.97	11 Years

*7 Year Price Score 117.01 *NYSE Composite Index=100 *12 Month Price Score 95.31

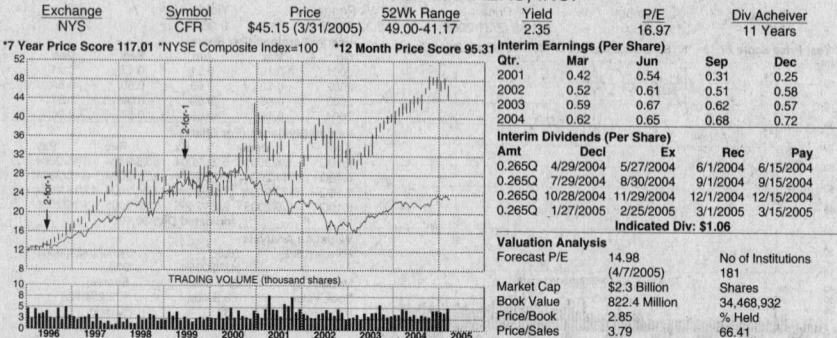

Interim Earnings (Per Share)

Qtr.	Mar	Jun	Sep	Dec
2001	0.42	0.54	0.31	0.25
2002	0.52	0.61	0.51	0.58
2003	0.59	0.67	0.62	0.57
2004	0.62	0.65	0.68	0.72

Interim Dividends (Per Share)

Amt	Decl	Ex	Rec	Pay
0.265Q	4/29/2004	5/27/2004	6/1/2004	6/15/2004
0.265Q	7/29/2004	8/30/2004	9/1/2004	9/15/2004
0.265Q	10/28/2004	11/29/2004	12/1/2004	12/15/2004
0.265Q	1/27/2005	2/25/2005	3/1/2005	3/15/2005

Indicated Div: $1.06

Valuation Analysis

Forecast P/E	14.98 (4/7/2005)	No of Institutions 181
Market Cap	$2.3 Billion	Shares 34,468,932
Book Value	822.4 Million	% Held 66.41
Price/Book	2.85	
Price/Sales	3.79	

Business Summary: Commercial Banking (MIC: 8.1 SIC: 029 NAIC: 22110)

Cullen/Frost Bankers is a financial holding company offering a broad range of banking and financial services to retail and commercial customers throughout Texas. As of Dec 31 2004, Co. operated 78 financial centers in Texas through its wholly-owned subsidiary, The Frost National Bank. In addition to general commercial banking, Co.'s other product and services include trust and investment management, investment banking, insurance brokerage, leasing, asset-based lending, treasury management and item processing. As of Dec 31 2004, Co. had consolidated total assets of $9.95 billion and total deposits of $8.11 billion.

Recent Developments: For the year ended Dec 31 2004, net income increased 8.3% to $141,325 thousand from net income of $130,501 thousand a year earlier. Net interest income was $331,375 thousand, up 5.6% from $313,654 thousand the year before. Provision for loan losses was $2,500 thousand versus $10,544 thousand in the prior year, a decrease of 76.3%. Non-interest income rose 4.5% to $225,110 thousand, while non-interest expense advanced 5.8% to $345,030 thousand.

Prospects: Net interest income growth is benefiting from improving economic conditions and rising interest rates, along with an increase in average earning assets. Meanwhile, earnings are benefiting from continued growth of non-interest income, which is being fueled by higher trust fees and insurance fees, due primarily to Co.'s acquisition of the Sammons Group during the third quarter of 2004. Separately, higher non-interest expenses are resulting from increases in salaries and employment benefits. Looking ahead, results are expected to continue to be positively effected by Co.'s strong sales efforts and improvements in asset quality.

Financial Data

(US$ in Thousands)	12/31/2004	12/31/2003	12/31/2002	12/31/2001	12/31/2000	12/31/1999	12/31/1998	12/31/1997
Earnings Per Share	2.66	2.48	2.23	1.52	2.03	1.78	1.39	1.38
Cash Flow Per Share	2.49	3.93	5.34	1.91	2.48	2.56	2.17	0.98
Tang Book Value Per Share	13.59	12.65	11.40	11.58	11.14	9.64	9.60	9.17
Dividends Per Share	1.035	0.940	0.875	0.840	0.760	0.675	0.575	0.480
Dividend Payout %	38.91	37.90	39.24	55.26	37.44	37.92	41.52	34.91
Income Statement								
Interest Income	393,544	368,946	389,898	460,976	512,331	447,580	428,091	324,715
Interest Expense	62,106	55,188	75,865	144,759	189,568	150,602	160,118	127,471
Net Interest Income	331,438	313,758	314,033	316,217	322,763	296,978	267,973	197,244
Provision for Losses	2,500	10,544	22,546	40,031	14,103	12,427	10,393	7,900
Non-Interest Income	225,110	215,361	200,709	192,891	170,865	157,085	138,666	109,332
Non-Interest Expense	345,030	326,035	312,142	352,606	313,280	293,015	278,506	199,956
Income Before Taxes	209,018	192,540	180,054	116,471	166,245	148,621	117,740	98,720
Income Taxes	67,693	62,039	57,821	38,565	57,428	50,979	42,095	35,235
Net Income	141,325	130,501	116,986	80,916	108,817	97,642	75,645	63,485
Average Shares	53,140	52,658	52,423	53,348	53,657	54,746	54,678	46,130
Balance Sheet								
Net Loans & Leases	5,089,181	4,507,245	4,436,329	4,445,727	4,471,380	4,108,383	3,592,987	2,601,676
Total Assets	9,952,787	9,672,114	9,552,318	8,369,584	7,660,372	6,996,680	6,869,605	5,230,588
Total Deposits	8,105,678	8,068,857	7,628,143	7,098,007	6,499,690	5,953,832	5,845,487	4,483,911
Total Liabilities	9,130,392	8,902,110	8,848,528	7,774,665	7,087,346	6,487,369	6,356,686	4,822,183
Stockholders' Equity	822,395	770,004	703,790	594,919	573,026	509,311	512,919	408,405
Shares Outstanding	51,923	51,776	51,295	51,355	51,430	52,823	53,426	44,530
Statistical Record								
Return on Assets %	1.44	1.36	1.31	1.01	1.48	1.41	1.25	1.25
Return on Equity %	17.70	17.71	18.02	13.86	20.05	19.10	16.42	16.13
Net Interest Margin %	84.22	85.04	80.54	68.60	63.40	66.35	62.60	60.74
Efficiency Ratio %	55.77	55.80	52.85	53.93	45.86	48.46	49.14	46.07
Loans to Deposits	0.63	0.56	0.58	0.63	0.69	0.69	0.61	0.58
Price Range	49.00-38.90	41.00-29.40	40.04-29.40	41.19-23.84	43.19-19.63	29.94-23.00	30.41-20.78	31.09-16.50
P/E Ratio	18.42-14.62	16.53-11.85	17.96-13.18	27.10-15.68	21.27-9.67	16.82-12.92	21.88-14.95	22.53-11.96
Average Yield %	2.35	2.69	2.53	2.54	2.69	2.58	2.14	2.23

Address: 100 W. Houston Street, San Antonio, TX 78205 Telephone: (210) 220-4011 Fax: (210) 220-5578	Web Site: www.frostbank.com Officers: Tom C. Frost - Sr. Chmn. Richard W. Evans Jr. - Chmn., C.E.O.	Auditors: Ernst & Young LLP Transfer Agents: Bank of New York, New York, NY

CUMMINS, INC.

Exchange	Symbol	Price	52Wk Range	Yield	P/E
NYS	CMI	$70.35 (3/31/2005)	84.42-54.40	1.71	9.52

*7 Year Price Score 135.14 *NYSE Composite Index=100 *12 Month Price Score 98.45

Interim Earnings (Per Share)

Qtr.	Mar	Jun	Sep	Dec
2001	(0.68)	(2.14)	0.08	0.08
2002	(0.75)	0.33	0.96	1.53
2003	(0.79)	0.34	0.60	1.09
2004	0.76	1.76	2.40	2.44

Interim Dividends (Per Share)

Amt	Decl	Ex	Rec	Pay
0.30Q	7/13/2004	8/16/2004	8/18/2004	9/1/2004
0.30Q	10/12/2004	11/12/2004	11/16/2004	12/1/2004
0.30Q	2/15/2005	2/17/2005	2/22/2005	3/1/2005
0.30Q	4/5/2005	5/13/2005	5/17/2005	6/1/2005
		Indicated Div: $1.20		

Valuation Analysis

Forecast P/E	8.39	No of Institutions	
	(4/7/2005)	262	
Market Cap	$3.2 Billion	Shares	
Book Value	1.4 Billion	40,690,784	
Price/Book	2.31	% Held	
Price/Sales	0.38	87.84	

Business Summary: Industrial Machinery and Equipment (MIC: 11.5 SIC: 519 NAIC: 33618)

Cummins designs, manufactures, distributes and services diesel and natural gas engines, electric power generation systems and engine-related products, including filtration and emissions solutions, fuel systems, controls and air handling systems. The Engine Group offers diesel engines for heavy-duty trucks, medium-duty trucks, and bus and light commercial vehicles. The Power Generation Group offers diesel, natural gas, and gasoline-fueled power generation sets. The Filtration Group and Other segment produces filters, silencers and intake and exhaust systems. The International Distributor Group consists of 18 wholly-owned and two joint venture retail distributors that sell Co.'s products.

Recent Developments: For the year ended Dec 31 2004, net income increased 600.0% to $350 million from net income of $50 million a year earlier. Revenues were $8,438 million, up 34.0% from $6,296 million the year before. Total direct expense was $6,758 million versus $5,173 million in the prior year, an increase of 30.6%. Total indirect expense was $1,145 million versus $960 million in the prior year, an increase of 19.3%.

Prospects: Co. continues to benefit from improving market conditions, particularly in the North American heavy-duty truck engine market, and its geographic diversification. Moreover, stronger earnings have generated a significant amount of cash, which should allow Co. to reduce its debt further in the coming year, including paying down $255.0 million in debt during the first quarter. Co. expects to earn between $1.50 to $1.60 a share in the first quarter of 2005 and between $8.00 to $8.30 a share for the full-year of 2005. In addition, Co. expects to invest between $220.0 million and $240.0 million in capital expenditures in 2005 to increase manufacturing capacity and fund growth.

Financial Data

(US$ in Thousands)	12/31/2004	12/31/2003	12/31/2002	12/31/2001	12/31/2000	12/31/1999	12/31/1998	12/31/1997
Earnings Per Share	7.39	1.27	2.13	(2.66)	0.20	4.13	(0.55)	5.48
Cash Flow Per Share	14.51	4.02	5.00	3.76	10.13	8.02	7.04	5.24
Tang Book Value Per Share	20.72	12.01	9.66	16.47	23.72	25.66	21.14	33.49
Dividends Per Share	1.200	1.200	1.200	1.200	1.200	1.125	1.100	1.075
Dividend Payout %	16.24	94.49	56.34	...	600.00	27.24	...	19.62
Income Statement								
Total Revenue	8,438,000	6,296,000	5,853,000	5,681,000	6,597,000	6,639,000	6,266,000	5,625,000
EBITDA	773,000	354,000	347,000	...	316,000	522,000	264,000	470,000
Depn & Amortn	240,000	186,000	219,000	231,000	240,000	233,000	199,000	158,000
Income Before Taxes	432,000	91,000	78,000	...	3,000	221,000	(6,000)	286,000
Income Taxes	56,000	12,000	(38,000)	(42,000)	(19,000)	55,000	4,000	74,000
Net Income	350,000	50,000	82,000	(102,000)	8,000	160,000	(21,000)	212,000
Average Shares	49,200	39,500	38,800	38,300	38,200	38,600	38,500	38,700
Balance Sheet								
Current Assets	3,273,000	2,130,000	1,982,000	1,635,000	1,830,000	2,180,000	1,876,000	1,710,000
Total Assets	6,527,000	5,126,000	4,837,000	4,335,000	4,500,000	4,697,000	4,542,000	3,765,000
Current Liabilities	2,197,000	1,391,000	1,329,000	970,000	1,223,000	1,314,000	1,071,000	1,055,000
Long-Term Obligations	1,299,000	1,380,000	999,000	915,000	1,032,000	1,092,000	1,137,000	522,000
Total Liabilities	4,918,000	4,054,000	3,904,000	3,227,000	3,092,000	3,194,000	3,208,000	2,290,000
Stockholders' Equity	1,401,000	949,000	841,000	1,025,000	1,336,000	1,429,000	1,272,000	1,422,000
Shares Outstanding	46,000	42,700	41,600	41,400	41,400	41,500	42,000	42,100
Statistical Record								
Return on Assets %	5.99	1.00	1.79	N.M.	0.17	3.46	N.M.	5.94
Return on Equity %	29.71	5.59	8.79	N.M.	0.58	11.85	N.M.	15.51
EBITDA Margin %	9.16	5.62	5.93	...	4.79	7.86	4.21	8.36
Net Margin %	4.15	0.79	1.40	N.M.	0.12	2.41	N.M.	3.77
Asset Turnover	1.44	1.26	1.28	1.29	1.43	1.44	1.51	1.58
Current Ratio	1.49	1.53	1.49	1.69	1.50	1.66	1.75	1.62
Debt to Equity	0.93	1.45	1.19	0.89	0.77	0.76	0.89	0.37
Price Range	84.42-48.70	52.30-22.21	50.19-19.69	45.32-29.31	49.63-27.23	64.88-35.25	62.06-28.94	82.44-44.75
P/E Ratio	11.42-6.59	41.18-17.49	23.56-9.24	...	248.13-136.17	15.71-8.54	...	15.04-8.17
Average Yield %	1.87	3.20	3.52	3.14	3.46	2.33	2.31	1.69

Address: 500 Jackson Street, Columbus, IN 47202 Telephone: (812) 377-5000 Fax: (812) 377-4937	Web Site: www.cummins.com Officers: Theodore M. Solso - Chmn., C.E.O. F. Joseph Loughrey - Exec. V.P., Pres., Engine Business	Auditors: PricewatehouseCoopers LLP Investor Contact: 812-377-3121

CVS CORP. (DE)

Exchange	Symbol	Price	52Wk Range	Yield	P/E
NYS	CVS	$52.62 (3/31/2005)	53.45-34.78	0.55	23.92

*7 Year Price Score 95.39 *NYSE Composite Index=100 *12 Month Price Score 106.59

Interim Earnings (Per Share)

Qtr.	Mar	Jun	Sep	Dec
2001	0.54	0.48	0.30	(0.32)
2002	0.43	0.43	0.40	0.49
2003	0.48	0.49	0.46	0.64
2004	0.59	0.56	0.44	0.61

Interim Dividends (Per Share)

Amt	Decl	Ex	Rec	Pay
0.066Q	7/7/2004	7/20/2004	7/22/2004	8/2/2004
0.066Q	9/14/2004	10/20/2004	10/22/2004	11/1/2004
0.072Q	1/5/2005	1/20/2005	1/24/2005	2/4/2005
0.072Q	3/2/2005	4/20/2005	4/22/2005	5/2/2005

Indicated Div: $0.29

Valuation Analysis

Forecast P/E	19.36 (4/7/2005)	No of Institutions	582
Market Cap	$21.1 Billion	Shares	335,617,280
Book Value	7.0 Billion	% Held	82.96
Price/Book	3.02		
Price/Sales	0.69		

Business Summary: Retail - Miscellaneous (MIC: 5.11 SIC: 912 NAIC: 46110)

CVS operates a chain of 4,179 retail and specialty pharmacy stores in 32 states and the District of Columbia as of Jan 3 2004. In addition to prescription drugs and services, Co.'s stores offer a broad selection of general merchandise, including over-the-counter drugs, greeting cards, film and photo-finishing services, beauty and cosmetics, seasonal merchandise and convenience foods. Co. also operates a pharmacy benefit management business that provides services including plan design and administration, formulary management, mail order pharmacy services, claims processing and generic substitution.

Recent Developments: For the year ended Jan 1 2005, net income increased 8.4% to $918,800 thousand from net income of $847,300 thousand a year earlier. Revenues were $30,594,300 thousand, up 15.1% from $26,588,000 thousand the year before. Operating income was $1,454,700 thousand versus an income of $1,423,600 thousand in the prior year, an increase of 2.2%. Total direct expense was $22,563,100 thousand versus $19,725,000 thousand in the prior year, an increase of 14.4%. Total indirect expense was $6,576,500 thousand versus $5,439,400 thousand in the prior year, an increase of 20.9%.

Prospects: Co.'s sales are benefiting from the acquisition of 1,268 Eckerd drugstores on July 31 2004, as well as Eckerd's pharmacy benefit management (PBM) and mail order pharmacy business. The acquisition of stores in Florida and Texas, along with a significant PBM has solidified Co.'s competitive position in the industry. Sales are also benefiting from higher pharmacy same-store sales. Co. has made significant progress toward integrating the acquired stores, and it is on track to complete the integration by July 2005. Meanwhile, Co.'s gross margins are being positively affected by the increasing usage of generic drugs and a better mix of front-end sales.

Financial Data

(US$ in Thousands)	01/01/2005	01/03/2004	12/28/2002	12/29/2001	12/30/2000	01/01/2000	12/31/1998	12/31/1997
Earnings Per Share	2.20	2.06	1.75	1.00	1.83	1.55	0.98	0.07
Cash Flow Per Share	2.30	2.42	3.08	1.74	2.00	1.68	0.57	(0.81)
Tang Book Value Per Share	9.96	11.35	9.45	8.90	8.20	6.88	5.40	3.96
Dividends Per Share	0.265	0.230	0.230	0.230	0.230	0.230	0.225	0.220
Dividend Payout %	12.05	11.17	13.14	23.00	12.57	14.84	22.93	314.29
Income Statement								
Total Revenue	30,594,300	26,588,000	24,181,500	22,241,400	20,087,500	18,098,300	15,273,600	12,738,200
EBITDA	1,951,500	1,765,300	1,516,500	1,091,400	1,619,300	1,413,400	1,021,900	426,000
Depn & Amortn	496,800	341,700	310,300	320,800	296,600	277,900	249,700	226,200
Income Before Taxes	1,396,400	1,375,500	1,155,800	709,600	1,243,400	1,076,400	711,300	155,000
Income Taxes	477,600	528,200	439,200	296,400	497,400	441,300	314,900	117,700
Net Income	918,800	847,300	716,600	413,200	746,000	635,100	396,400	37,700
Average Shares	415,440	407,700	405,300	408,300	408,000	408,900	405,200	346,000
Balance Sheet								
Current Assets	7,919,500	6,496,500	5,982,100	5,454,100	4,936,600	4,608,000	4,349,200	3,685,000
Total Assets	14,546,800	10,543,100	9,645,300	8,628,200	7,949,500	7,275,400	6,736,200	5,636,900
Current Liabilities	4,858,800	3,489,200	3,105,900	3,065,900	2,964,100	2,889,900	3,183,300	2,855,000
Long-Term Obligations	1,925,900	753,100	1,076,300	810,400	536,800	558,500	275,700	272,600
Total Liabilities	7,559,600	4,521,300	4,448,300	4,061,300	3,644,900	3,595,700	3,625,600	3,275,500
Stockholders' Equity	6,987,200	6,021,800	5,197,000	4,566,900	4,304,600	3,679,700	3,110,600	2,361,400
Shares Outstanding	400,959	395,384	393,071	390,887	392,322	391,996	390,211	344,800
Statistical Record								
Return on Assets %	7.34	8.26	7.86	5.00	9.83	9.04	6.41	0.89
Return on Equity %	14.16	14.86	14.72	9.34	18.74	18.65	14.49	2.09
EBITDA Margin %	6.38	6.64	6.27	4.91	8.06	7.81	6.69	3.34
Net Margin %	3.00	3.19	2.96	1.86	3.71	3.51	2.60	0.30
Asset Turnover	2.45	2.59	2.65	2.69	2.65	2.58	2.47	3.01
Current Ratio	1.63	1.86	1.93	1.78	1.67	1.59	1.37	1.29
Debt to Equity	0.28	0.13	0.21	0.18	0.12	0.15	0.09	0.12
Price Range	46.90-34.21	37.46-21.99	35.58-23.99	62.10-23.28	59.94-28.00	56.44-30.31	55.69-31.09	34.47-19.69
P/E Ratio	21.32-15.55	18.18-10.67	20.33-13.71	62.10-23.28	32.75-15.30	36.41-19.56	56.82-31.73	492.41-281.25
Average Yield %	0.65	0.79	0.78	0.52	0.54	0.50	0.55	0.83

Address: One CVS Drive, Woonsocket, RI 02895	Web Site: www.cvs.com	Auditors: KPMG LLP
Telephone: (401) 765-1500	Officers: Thomas M. Ryan - Chmn., Pres., C.E.O. David B. Rickard - Exec. V.P., C.F.O., Chief Admin. Officer	Investor Contact: 800 201 0938
Fax: (401) 762-2137		

CYPRESS SEMICONDUCTOR CORP.

Exchange	Symbol	Price	52Wk Range	Yield	P/E
NYS	CY	$12.60 (3/31/2005)	21.30-8.60	N/A	74.12

*7 Year Price Score 55.43   *NYSE Composite Index=100   *12 Month Price Score 101.04

Interim Earnings (Per Share)

Qtr.	Mar	Jun	Sep	Dec
2001	0.08	(0.14)	(2.92)	(0.33)
2002	(0.33)	(0.23)	(0.45)	(1.02)
2003	(0.27)	(0.10)	0.12	0.19
2004	0.16	0.13	0.02	(0.16)

Interim Dividends (Per Share)

No Dividends Paid

Valuation Analysis

Forecast P/E	90.62	No of Institutions
	(4/7/2005)	205
Market Cap	$1.6 Billion	Shares
Book Value	660.4 Million	97,177,120
Price/Book	2.45	% Held
Price/Sales	1.71	77.28

Business Summary: IT & Technology (MIC: 10.2 SIC: 674 NAIC: 34413)

Cypress Semiconductor designs, develops, manufactures and markets high-performance digital and mixed-signal integrated circuits for the networking, wireless infrastructure and handsets, computation, consumer, automotive, and industrial markets. Co. is organized into three reportable business segments - Memory, Non-Memory and SunPower. Co.'s Memory business designs and produces static random access memories. Co.'s Non-Memory business targets the networking, wireless infrastructure and handsets, computation, consumer, automotive, industrial and other markets. In addition, Co. designs and manufactures high-performance silicon solar cells through its SunPower subsidiary.

Recent Developments: For the year ended Jan 2 2005, net income was $24,698 thousand versus net loss of $5,331 thousand a year earlier. Revenues were $948,438 thousand, up 13.3% from $836,756 thousand the year before. Operating loss was $1,382 thousand versus a loss of $8,304 thousand in the prior year. Total direct expense was $492,058 thousand versus $435,749 thousand in the prior year, an increase of 12.9%. Total indirect expense was $457,762 thousand versus $409,311 thousand in the prior year, an increase of 11.8%.

Prospects: In light of recent disappointing operating performance, Co. is taking decisive action to return to profitability quickly, including actions to reduce its cost structure and improve its end-market orientation, as well as an organizational restructure and a reduction in force of approximately 200 employees worldwide. Co. is also merging its Timing Technology Division and Personal Communications Division into a new, market-oriented Consumer and Computation Division. Separately, Co. recently announced that it has signed and closed a definitive agreement to acquire SMaL Camera Technologies, a designer of digital imaging applications for a variety of business and consumer applications.

Financial Data

(US$ in Thousands)	01/02/2005	12/28/2003	12/29/2002	12/30/2001	12/31/2000	01/02/2000	01/03/1999	12/29/1997
Earnings Per Share	0.17	(0.04)	(2.02)	(3.28)	2.03	0.81	(1.24)	0.21
Cash Flow Per Share	1.23	0.82	0.18	0.77	4.31	1.59	1.10	1.42
Tang Book Value Per Share	1.66	1.61	2.12	3.06	8.86	6.32	5.76	7.10
Income Statement								
Total Revenue	948,438	836,756	774,746	819,192	1,287,787	705,487	486,841	544,356
EBITDA	173,694	177,396	(37,522)	(221,267)	539,214	212,911	(1,301)	142,590
Depn & Amortn	175,332	179,228	210,753	249,000	145,411	107,423	112,702	111,361
Income Before Taxes	(1,877)	(2,509)	(246,260)	(444,437)	370,170	95,871	(124,856)	24,032
Income Taxes	(26,575)	2,822	2,838	(32,680)	92,862	4,817	(14,006)	5,613
Net Income	24,698	(5,331)	(249,098)	(407,412)	277,308	91,054	(110,850)	18,419
Average Shares	134,592	121,509	123,112	124,135	144,228	111,735	89,338	94,648
Balance Sheet								
Current Assets	563,880	518,395	513,947	626,835	1,282,786	537,395	283,689	398,080
Total Assets	1,572,994	1,567,497	1,572,648	1,886,436	2,361,754	1,117,224	756,299	956,270
Current Liabilities	233,610	210,679	199,760	254,502	299,427	192,765	99,609	93,053
Long-Term Obligations	606,688	684,260	468,900	517,700	570,500	160,000	160,000	175,000
Total Liabilities	912,636	998,309	899,025	1,018,008	1,034,086	419,249	267,198	312,794
Stockholders' Equity	660,358	569,188	673,623	868,428	1,327,668	697,975	489,101	643,476
Shares Outstanding	128,493	120,483	123,743	121,495	125,659	110,516	84,859	90,684
Statistical Record								
Return on Assets %	1.55	N.M.	N.M.	N.M.	15.99	9.75	N.M.	2.11
Return on Equity %	3.95	N.M.	N.M.	N.M.	27.45	15.38	N.M.	3.20
EBITDA Margin %	18.31	21.20	N.M.	N.M.	41.87	30.18	N.M.	26.19
Net Margin %	2.60	N.M.	N.M.	N.M.	21.53	12.91	N.M.	3.38
Asset Turnover	0.59	0.53	0.45	0.39	0.74	0.76	0.56	0.62
Current Ratio	2.41	2.46	2.57	2.46	4.28	2.79	2.85	4.28
Debt to Equity	0.92	1.20	0.70	0.60	0.43	0.23	0.33	0.27
Price Range	23.68-8.60	23.06-5.11	25.04-3.81	28.61-13.91	57.75-18.81	33.44-8.06	11.63-6.06	18.56-7.75
P/E Ratio	139.29-50.59	...	...	...	28.45-9.27	41.28-9.95	...	88.39-36.90

Address: 3901 North First Street, San Jose, CA 95134-1599	**Web Site:** www.cypress.com	**Auditors:** PricewaterhouseCoopers LLI
Telephone: (408) 943-2600	**Officers:** T. J. Rodgers - Pres., C.E.O. Antonio R. Alvarez - Exec. V.P., Memory Products Div.	**Transfer Agents:** EquiServe, L.P., Canton, MA
Fax: (408) 943-2741		

CYTEC INDUSTRIES, INC.

*7 Year Price Score 122.12 *NYSE Composite Index=100 *12 Month Price Score 103.43

Interim Earnings (Per Share)

Qtr.	Mar	Jun	Sep	Dec
2001	0.41	0.50	0.63	0.17
2002	0.17	0.52	0.78	0.49
2003	0.38	0.64	0.55	0.38
2004	0.78	0.72	0.23	1.09

Interim Dividends (Per Share)

Amt	Decl	Ex	Rec	Pay
0.10Q	4/22/2004	5/6/2004	5/10/2004	5/25/2004
0.10Q	7/23/2004	8/6/2004	8/10/2004	8/25/2004
0.10Q	10/21/2004	11/8/2004	11/10/2004	11/26/2004
0.10Q	1/20/2005	2/8/2005	2/10/2005	2/25/2005
		Indicated Div: $0.40		

Valuation Analysis

Forecast P/E	16.00	No of Institutions	
	(4/7/2005)	192	
Market Cap	$2.2 Billion	Shares	
Book Value	906.5 Million	34,446,264	
Price/Book	2.38	% Held	
Price/Sales	1.26	86.33	

Business Summary: Chemicals (MIC: 11.1 SIC: 169 NAIC: 25998)

Cytec Industries is a global specialty chemicals and specialty materials company. Co. serves major markets for aerospace, automotive and industrial coatings, chemical intermediates, mining, plastics and water treatment. Co.'s Water and Industrial Process Chemicals segment mainly includes water treatment chemicals, mining chemicals and phosphine and phosphorous specialties. Performance Products mainly include coatings, amino resins and specialty additives, performance chemicals and polymer additives. Specialty Materials mainly include advanced composites and film adhesives. Building Block Chemicals principally include acrylonitrile, hydrocyanic acid, acrylamide, sulfuric acid and melamine.

Recent Developments: For the year ended Dec 31 2004, net income increased 62.9% to $126,100 thousand from net income of $77,400 thousand a year earlier. Revenues were $1,721,300 thousand, up 17.0% from $1,471,800 thousand the year before. Operating income was $159,600 thousand versus an income of $141,100 thousand in the prior year, an increase of 13.1%. Total direct expense was $1,311,200 thousand versus $1,114,900 thousand in the prior year, an increase of 17.6%. Total indirect expense was $250,500 thousand versus $215,800 thousand in the prior year, an increase of 16.1%.

Prospects: Co.'s outlook is tempered by higher raw material and energy costs. Co. noted that costs for oil and natural gas have not subsided and many raw materials are in short supply. Thus, Co. is continuing its selling price initiatives but has indicated that it is still catching up to the rising trend of raw material costs. Meanwhile, Co. views the global demand outlook as positive. Separately, on Mar 1 2005, Co. announced that it has completed its acquisition of UCB's Surface Specialties business in a transaction valued at $1.80 billion. In conjunction with this transaction, Co. has agreed to divest Surface Specialties' amino resin product line during 2005, and to use the proceeds to reduce debt.

Financial Data

(US$ in Thousands)	12/31/2004	12/31/2003	12/31/2002	12/31/2001	12/31/2000	12/31/1999	12/31/1998	12/31/1997
Earnings Per Share	2.84	1.93	1.96	1.71	4.15	2.73	2.68	2.39
Cash Flow Per Share	4.22	3.40	5.36	3.54	2.62	4.64	3.41	2.90
Tang Book Value Per Share	12.48	8.87	6.43	6.58	5.77	2.66	1.88	2.03
Dividends Per Share	0.400	...	...	...	...	...	...	...
Dividend Payout %	14.08	...	...	...	...	...	...	...
Income Statement								
Total Revenue	1,721,300	1,471,800	1,346,200	1,387,100	1,492,500	1,412,500	1,444,500	1,290,600
EBITDA	280,500	236,200	210,400	211,000	392,800	295,000	307,500	234,200
Depn & Amortn	98,800	93,600	83,700	90,300	96,600	95,100	87,200	78,800
Income Before Taxes	164,300	126,400	110,200	101,100	271,100	173,000	197,900	149,700
Income Taxes	38,200	35,400	30,900	34,900	93,500	51,700	73,200	149,700
Net Income	126,100	77,400	79,300	71,100	177,600	121,300	124,700	113,600
Average Shares	40,829	40,158	40,512	41,590	42,745	44,505	46,480	47,554
Balance Sheet								
Current Assets	904,800	711,400	604,800	509,900	567,800	491,100	477,600	452,800
Total Assets	2,226,100	2,025,900	1,751,500	1,650,400	1,719,400	1,759,900	1,730,600	1,614,100
Current Liabilities	496,700	336,500	430,800	282,000	358,900	366,100	394,400	375,000
Long-Term Obligations	300,100	416,200	216,000	314,700	311,200	422,500	419,500	324,000
Total Liabilities	1,319,600	1,270,500	1,128,600	1,013,500	1,103,200	1,254,100	1,299,600	1,226,700
Stockholders' Equity	906,500	755,400	622,900	636,900	616,200	505,800	431,000	387,400
Shares Outstanding	39,834	38,992	38,799	39,621	40,166	41,609	43,190	45,137
Statistical Record								
Return on Assets %	5.92	4.10	4.66	4.22	10.18	6.95	7.46	7.90
Return on Equity %	15.13	11.23	12.59	11.35	31.57	25.90	30.47	32.37
EBITDA Margin %	16.30	16.05	15.63	15.21	26.32	20.88	21.29	18.15
Net Margin %	7.33	5.26	5.89	5.13	11.90	8.59	8.63	8.80
Asset Turnover	0.81	0.78	0.79	0.82	0.86	0.81	0.86	0.90
Current Ratio	1.82	2.11	1.40	1.81	1.58	1.34	1.21	1.21
Debt to Equity	0.33	0.55	0.35	0.49	0.51	0.84	0.97	0.84
Price Range	51.73-32.97	38.76-25.98	33.58-19.34	38.31-21.27	39.94-22.50	31.50-20.00	58.31-15.13	50.63-34.75
P/E Ratio	18.21-11.61	20.08-13.46	17.13-9.87	22.40-12.44	9.62-5.42	11.54-7.33	21.76-5.64	21.18-14.54
Average Yield %	0.94	...	...	...	...	...	...	...

DANA CORP.

Exchange	Symbol	Price	52Wk Range	Yield	P/E
NYS	DCN	$12.79 (3/31/2005)	21.90-12.35	3.75	23.69

*7 Year Price Score 62.50   *NYSE Composite Index=100   *12 Month Price Score 76.49

Interim Earnings (Per Share)

Qtr.	Mar	Jun	Sep	Dec
2001	(0.18)	0.10	0.08	(2.01)
2002	(1.54)	0.35	0.02	(0.06)
2003	0.28	0.35	0.41	0.45
2004	0.42	0.72	0.27	(0.89)

Interim Dividends (Per Share)

Amt	Decl	Ex	Rec	Pay
0.12Q	4/20/2004	5/27/2004	6/1/2004	6/15/2004
0.12Q	7/20/2004	8/30/2004	9/1/2004	9/15/2004
0.12Q	10/19/2004	11/29/2004	12/1/2004	12/15/2004
0.12Q	2/15/2005	2/25/2005	3/1/2005	3/15/2005
		Indicated Div: $0.48		

Valuation Analysis

Forecast P/E	10.13	No of Institutions
	(4/7/2005)	218
Market Cap	$1.9 Billion	Shares
Book Value	2.4 Billion	110,826,768
Price/Book	0.79	% Held
Price/Sales	0.21	73.81

Business Summary: Automotive (MIC: 15.1 SIC: 714 NAIC: 36399)

Dana is an independent suppliers of vehicle components for original equipment and distribution markets. Automotive Systems Group manufactures drivetrain modules, systems and components, consisting of axles, driveshafts, structures and chassis products, for the automotive and light vehicle markets, as well as driveshafts for the commercial vehicle market. Engine and Fluid Management Group produces sealing, thermal management, fluid transfer, and engine power products. Heavy Vehicle Technologies and Systems Group manufactures and sells axles, brakes, driveshafts, chassis and suspension modules, ride controls and related modules and systems, transaxles, transmissions and electronic controls.

Recent Developments: For the year ended Dec 31 2004, income from continuing operations decreased 45.7% to $95,000 thousand from income of $175,000 thousand a year earlier. Net income decreased 63.1% to $82,000 thousand from net income of $222,000 thousand a year earlier. Revenues were $8,990,000 thousand, up 11.4% from $8,067,000 thousand the year before. Total direct expense was $8,333,000 thousand versus $7,245,000 thousand in the prior year, an increase of 15.0%. Total indirect expense was $576,000 thousand versus $520,000 thousand in the prior year, an increase of 10.8%.

Prospects: Co. believes that raw material costs will continue to affect results in the near term. However, as Co. moves into 2005, it can expect more of an offsetting benefit from its cost reduction programs. These include the consolidation of its purchasing function, the accelerated deployment of lean manufacturing techniques, and the standardization of administrative processes throughout the company. Co. expects earnings to be lower in the first half of 2005 compared to last year mainly due to higher raw material prices. Therefore, Co. is anticipating first-quarter earnings of $0.17 to $0.23 per share. Co.'s full-year earnings guidance is $1.40 to $1.62 per share.

Financial Data

(US$ in Thousands)	12/31/2004	12/31/2003	12/31/2002	12/31/2001	12/31/2000	12/31/1999	12/31/1998	12/31/1997
Earnings Per Share	0.54	1.49	(1.22)	(2.01)	2.18	3.08	3.20	1.94
Cash Flow Per Share	0.37	2.26	3.52	4.31	6.46	3.68	...	5.71
Tang Book Value Per Share	12.29	10.04	6.15	7.52	11.21	12.01	11.32	15.89
Dividends Per Share	0.480	0.090	0.040	0.940	1.240	1.240	1.140	1.040
Dividend Payout %	88.89	6.04	N.M.	N.M.	56.88	40.26	35.63	53.61
Income Statement								
Total Revenue	8,990,000	8,067,000	9,694,000	10,469,000	12,691,000	13,353,000	12,838,700	12,402,400
EBITDA	442,000	696,000	729,000	374,000	1,310,000	1,535,000	1,587,500	1,305,900
Depn & Amortn	361,000	394,000	478,000	548,000	523,000	519,000	487,700	450,300
Income Before Taxes	(136,000)	81,000	(9,000)	(483,000)	464,000	737,000	820,200	604,200
Income Taxes	(196,000)	(49,000)	(27,000)	(161,000)	171,000	251,000	315,600	293,800
Net Income	82,000	222,000	(182,000)	(298,000)	334,000	513,000	534,100	320,100
Average Shares	150,704	148,891	148,841	149,084	153,000	166,497	167,000	164,600
Balance Sheet								
Current Assets	3,468,000	4,533,000	4,118,000	3,797,000	4,323,000	4,801,000	4,337,000	4,285,300
Total Assets	9,047,000	9,617,000	9,553,000	10,207,000	11,236,000	11,123,000	10,137,500	9,511,100
Current Liabilities	2,689,000	2,965,000	2,824,000	3,489,000	4,331,000	3,888,000	3,986,600	3,794,000
Long-Term Obligations	2,054,000	2,605,000	3,215,000	3,008,000	2,649,000	2,732,000	1,717,900	1,789,800
Total Liabilities	6,612,000	7,567,000	8,071,000	8,249,000	8,608,000	8,166,000	7,198,300	6,908,700
Stockholders' Equity	2,435,000	2,050,000	1,482,000	1,958,000	2,628,000	2,957,000	2,939,200	2,602,400
Shares Outstanding	149,881	148,627	148,557	148,530	148,000	163,151	165,700	163,800
Statistical Record								
Return on Assets %	0.88	2.32	N.M.	N.M.	2.97	4.83	5.27	4.09
Return on Equity %	3.65	12.57	N.M.	N.M.	12.71	17.40	18.17	15.88
EBITDA Margin %	4.92	8.63	7.52	3.57	10.32	11.50	12.36	10.53
Net Margin %	0.91	2.75	N.M.	N.M.	2.63	3.84	4.16	2.58
Asset Turnover	0.96	0.84	0.98	0.98	1.13	1.26	1.26	1.58
Current Ratio	1.29	1.53	1.46	1.09	1.00	1.23	1.09	1.13
Debt to Equity	0.84	1.27	2.17	1.54	1.01	0.92	0.58	0.69
Price Range	22.95-14.10	18.40-6.31	22.67-9.28	26.57-10.55	31.50-13.00	52.75-26.56	61.19-32.00	53.88-30.63
P/E Ratio	42.50-26.11	12.35-4.23	N/A	N/A	14.45-5.96	17.13-8.62	19.12-10.00	27.77-15.79
Average Yield %	2.55	0.71	0.25	5.15	5.24	3.12	2.35	2.60

Address: 4500 Dorr Street, Toledo, OH 43615	Web Site: www.dana.com	Auditors: PricewaterhouseCoopers LLP
Telephone: (419) 535-4500	Officers: Michael J. Burns - Chmn., Pres., C.E.O. Robert C. Richter - V.P., C.F.O.	Investor Contact: 800-537-8823
Fax: (419) 535-4643		

DANAHER CORP.

Exchange	Symbol	Price	52Wk Range	Yield	P/E	Div Acheiver
NYS	DHR	$53.41 (3/31/2005)	58.64-44.48	0.11	23.22	11 Years

*7 Year Price Score 136.55 *NYSE Composite Index=100 *12 Month Price Score 97.33

Interim Earnings (Per Share)

Qtr.	Mar	Jun	Sep	Dec
2001	0.28	0.32	0.29	0.12
2002	(0.29)	0.33	0.37	0.52
2003	0.33	0.40	0.44	0.53
2004	0.45	0.56	0.62	0.67

Interim Dividends (Per Share)

Amt	Decl	Ex	Rec	Pay
0.015Q	6/18/2004	6/23/2004	6/25/2004	7/30/2004
0.015Q	9/17/2004	9/22/2004	9/24/2004	10/29/2004
0.015Q	12/20/2004	12/29/2004	12/31/2004	1/28/2005
0.015Q	3/21/2005	3/22/2005	3/25/2005	4/29/2005

Indicated Div: $0.06

Valuation Analysis

Forecast P/E	19.21	No of Institutions
	(4/7/2005)	491
Market Cap	$16.5 Billion	Shares
Book Value	4.6 Billion	211,739,136
Price/Book	3.57	% Held
Price/Sales	2.39	68.48

Business Summary: Metal Products (MIC: 11.4 SIC: 429 NAIC: 32510)

Danaher conducts its operations through two business segments: Process/Environmental Controls and Tools & Components. The Process/Environmental Controls segment encompasses five strategic platforms (Motion, Environmental, Electronic Test, Medical Technologies and Product Identification) and three focused niche businesses (Power Quality, Aerospace and Defense, and Industrial Controls). The Tools & Components segment encompasses one strategic platform, Mechanics' Hand Tools, and five focused niche businesses. Products are distributed by Co.'s sales personnel and independent representatives to distributors, end-users, and original equipment manufacturers.

Recent Developments: For the year ended Dec 31 2004, net income increased 39.0% to $746,000 thousand from net income of $536,834 thousand a year earlier. Revenues were $6,889,301 thousand, up 30.1% from $5,293,876 thousand the year before. Operating income was $1,105,133 thousand versus an income of $845,995 thousand in the prior year, an increase of 30.6%. Total direct expense was $3,996,636 thousand versus $3,154,809 thousand in the prior year, an increase of 26.7%. Total indirect expense was $1,787,532 thousand versus $1,293,072 thousand in the prior year, an increase of 38.2%.

Prospects: On Dec 23 2004, Co. agreed to acquire LEM Instruments, a producer of electrical measurement products used in both commercial and industrial applications, for about $57.0 million in cash. The acquisition is expected to close in the first quarter of 2005. In January 2005, Co. announced it would expand its reporting to three segments, including Professional Instrumentation, Industrial Technologies and Tools and Components. The Industrial Technologies segment will include the motion and product identification platforms as well as focused niche businesses previously included in the Process/Environmental Controls segment. For 2005, Co. anticipates earnings in the range of $2.62 to $2.72 per share.

Financial Data

(US$ in Thousands)	12/31/2004	12/31/2003	12/31/2002	12/31/2001	12/31/2000	12/31/1999	12/31/1998	12/31/1997
Earnings Per Share	2.30	1.69	0.94	1.00	1.12	0.90	0.66	0.64
Cash Flow Per Share	3.33	2.81	2.36	2.12	1.79	1.48	1.23	1.18
Tang Book Value Per Share	N.M.	0.99	0.01	N.M.	0.28	1.46	0.25	0.30
Dividends Per Share	0.058	0.050	0.045	0.040	0.035	0.030	0.028	0.025
Dividend Payout %	2.50	2.97	4.79	3.98	3.14	3.35	4.17	3.89
Income Statement								
Total Revenue	6,889,301	5,293,876	4,577,232	3,782,444	3,777,777	3,197,238	2,910,038	2,050,968
EBITDA	1,261,261	979,431	830,687	680,401	701,870	572,648	434,693	343,001
Depn & Amortn	156,128	133,436	129,565	178,390	149,721	126,419	108,651	76,116
Income Before Taxes	1,057,717	797,035	657,468	476,264	522,924	429,562	301,111	253,781
Income Taxes	311,717	260,201	223,327	178,599	198,711	167,938	118,165	98,975
Net Income	746,000	536,834	290,391	297,665	324,213	261,624	182,946	154,806
Average Shares	327,701	323,140	316,964	303,696	290,998	292,178	277,770	241,024
Balance Sheet								
Current Assets	2,918,690	2,942,151	2,387,266	1,874,615	1,474,306	1,202,117	886,904	618,339
Total Assets	8,493,893	6,890,050	6,029,145	4,820,483	4,031,679	3,047,071	2,738,715	1,879,717
Current Liabilities	2,202,286	1,380,903	1,265,312	1,017,294	1,018,540	708,786	688,705	524,235
Long-Term Obligations	925,535	1,284,498	1,197,422	1,119,333	713,557	341,037	412,918	162,720
Total Liabilities	3,874,211	3,243,341	3,019,546	2,591,897	2,089,346	1,338,317	1,386,884	962,836
Stockholders' Equity	4,619,682	3,646,709	3,009,599	2,228,586	1,942,333	1,708,754	1,351,831	916,881
Shares Outstanding	308,920	307,362	305,064	286,628	284,026	284,880	270,214	210,880
Statistical Record								
Return on Assets %	9.67	8.31	5.35	6.73	9.14	9.04	7.92	8.49
Return on Equity %	18.00	16.13	11.09	14.27	17.71	17.10	16.13	18.03
EBITDA Margin %	18.31	18.50	18.15	17.99	18.58	17.91	14.94	16.72
Net Margin %	10.83	10.14	6.34	7.87	8.58	8.18	6.29	7.55
Asset Turnover	0.89	0.82	0.84	0.85	1.06	1.11	1.26	1.13
Current Ratio	1.33	2.13	1.89	1.84	1.45	1.70	1.29	1.18
Debt to Equity	0.20	0.35	0.40	0.50	0.37	0.20	0.31	0.18
Price Range	58.64-43.99	45.98-30.23	37.66-26.62	33.84-22.77	34.34-18.56	34.28-21.56	27.16-14.69	15.94-9.91
P/E Ratio	25.50-19.13	27.20-17.88	40.07-28.32	33.84-22.77	30.66-16.57	38.09-23.96	41.15-22.25	24.90-15.48
Average Yield %	0.12	0.14	0.14	0.14	0.14	0.11	0.14	0.20

Address: 2099 Pennsylvania Ave. NW, 12th Floor, Washington, DC 20006-1813	**Web Site:** www.danaher.com	**Auditors:** Ernst & Young LLP
Telephone: (202) 828 0850	**Officers:** Steven M. Rales - Chmn. H. Lawrence Culp Jr. - Pres., C.E.O.	**Investor Contact:** 202-828-0850
Fax: (202) 828 0860		**Transfer Agents:** SunTrust Bank

DARDEN RESTAURANTS, INC.

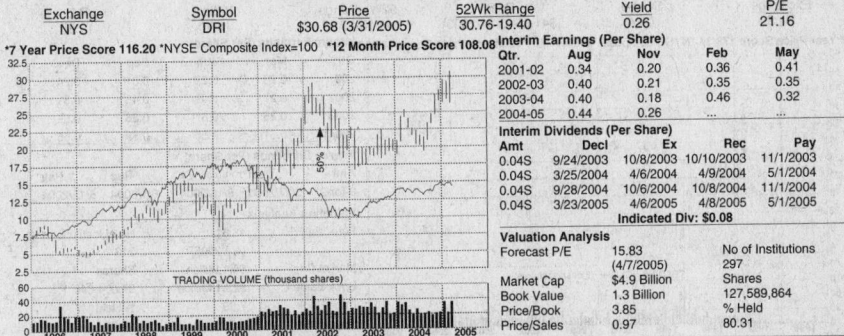

Exchange	Symbol	Price	52Wk Range	Yield	P/E
NYS	DRI	$30.68 (3/31/2005)	30.76-19.40	0.26	21.16

*7 Year Price Score 116.20 *NYSE Composite Index=100 *12 Month Price Score 108.08

Interim Earnings (Per Share)

Qtr.	Aug	Nov	Feb	May
2001-02	0.34	0.20	0.36	0.41
2002-03	0.40	0.21	0.35	0.35
2003-04	0.40	0.18	0.46	0.32
2004-05	0.44	0.26	...	...

Interim Dividends (Per Share)

Amt	Decl	Ex	Rec	Pay
0.04S	9/24/2003	10/8/2003	10/10/2003	11/1/2003
0.04S	3/25/2004	4/6/2004	4/9/2004	5/1/2004
0.04S	9/28/2004	10/6/2004	10/8/2004	11/1/2004
0.04S	3/23/2005	4/6/2005	4/8/2005	5/1/2005

Indicated Div: $0.08

Valuation Analysis

Forecast P/E	15.83	No of Institutions
	(4/7/2005)	297
Market Cap	$4.9 Billion	Shares
Book Value	1.3 Billion	127,589,864
Price/Book	3.85	% Held
Price/Sales	0.97	80.31

TRADING VOLUME (thousand shares)

Business Summary: Hospitality & Tourism (MIC: 5.1 SIC: 812 NAIC: 22110)

Darden Restaurants is engaged in the casual dining restaurant business. As of May 30, 2004, Co. operated 1,325 restaurants in the United States and Canada. In the United States, Co. operates 1,288 restaurants in 49 states, including 649 Red Lobster®, 537 Olive Garden®, 32 Bahama Breeze®, 69 Smokey Bones Barbeque & Grill and one Seasons 52 restaurants. In Canada, Co. operates 37 restaurants, including 31 Red Lobster and six Olive Garden restaurants. Red Lobster is a full-service, seafood-specialty restaurant. The Olive Garden is a full-service Italian restaurant. Bahama Breeze has a Caribbean theme. Smokey Bones BBQ Sports Bar restaurant combines barbecue with sports entertainment.

Recent Developments: For the quarter ended Nov 28 2004, net income increased 43.0% to $42,975 thousand from net income of $30,053 thousand in the year-earlier quarter. Revenues were $1,229,373 thousand, up 7.6% from $1,142,543 thousand the year before. Total indirect expense was $183,961 thousand versus $172,368 thousand in the prior-year quarter, an increase of 6.7%.

Prospects: Co. continues to experience strong sales and earnings growth at its core casual dining concepts. Olive Garden sales are benefiting from strong same-store sales growth and revenue from several net new restaurants, while Red Lobster is being positively affected by solid same-store sales increases. Co.'s increases sales, combined with lower selling, general and administrative and depreciation and amortization expenses as a percentage of sales is driving significant growth in operating profit. For fiscal-year 2005, Co. expects to deliver diluted net earnings per share growth in the range of 31.0% to 33.0%. Meanwhile, Co.'s Smokey Bones expects to open a total of 35 restaurants in fiscal 2005.

Financial Data

(US$ in Thousands)	6 Mos	3 Mos	05/30/2004	05/25/2003	05/26/2002	05/27/2001	05/28/2000	05/30/1999
Earnings Per Share	1.45	1.39	1.36	1.31	1.30	1.06	0.89	0.66
Cash Flow Per Share	3.90	3.11	3.16	3.00	2.92	2.35	1.75	1.70
Tang Book Value Per Share	7.97	8.09	7.86	7.25	6.56	5.76	5.18	4.81
Dividends Per Share	0.080	0.080	0.080	0.080	0.053	0.053	0.053	0.053
Dividend Payout %	5.52	5.76	5.88	6.11	4.10	5.03	5.97	8.08
Income Statement								
Total Revenue	2,508,017	1,278,644	5,003,355	4,654,971	4,368,701	4,021,157	3,701,256	3,458,107
EBITDA	304,560	176,164	600,312	588,464	573,301	485,777	432,654	365,621
Depn & Amortn	111,135	55,311	216,655	198,119	173,407	153,895	136,359	130,206
Income Before Taxes	171,454	109,889	339,998	347,748	363,309	301,218	273,907	215,875
Income Taxes	57,467	37,764	108,536	115,488	125,521	104,218	97,202	75,337
Net Income	113,987	72,125	231,462	232,260	237,788	197,000	176,705	140,538
Average Shares	163,400	163,200	169,700	177,400	183,500	185,700	197,850	212,100
Balance Sheet								
Current Assets	411,674	366,662	346,307	325,629	449,531	328,142	290,460	327,737
Total Assets	2,887,918	2,809,431	2,780,348	2,664,633	2,529,736	2,218,458	1,971,423	1,905,660
Current Liabilities	849,898	688,778	683,481	639,909	601,014	554,258	606,887	534,215
Long-Term Obligations	502,574	652,672	653,349	658,086	662,506	517,927	304,073	314,065
Total Liabilities	1,621,199	1,537,055	1,534,578	1,468,442	1,400,859	1,183,216	1,010,953	941,624
Stockholders' Equity	1,266,719	1,272,376	1,245,770	1,196,191	1,128,877	1,035,242	960,470	964,036
Shares Outstanding	158,868	157,217	158,431	164,950	172,135	176,070	183,288	198,180
Statistical Record								
Return on Assets %	8.48	8.35	8.36	8.97	10.04	9.43	9.14	7.24
Return on Equity %	18.96	18.44	18.65	20.03	22.04	19.80	18.41	14.21
EBITDA Margin %	12.14	13.78	12.00	12.64	13.12	12.08	11.69	10.57
Net Margin %	4.54	5.64	4.63	4.99	5.44	4.90	4.77	4.06
Asset Turnover	1.76	1.77	1.81	1.80	1.85	1.92	1.91	1.78
Current Ratio	0.48	0.53	0.51	0.51	0.75	0.59	0.48	0.61
Debt to Equity	0.40	0.51	0.52	0.55	0.59	0.50	0.32	0.33
Price Range	27.50-19.00	25.37-18.39	25.37-18.39	27.40-16.80	29.33-16.01	19.51-10.46	15.21-8.38	15.50-9.54
P/E Ratio	18.97-13.10	18.25-13.23	18.65-13.52	20.92-12.82	22.56-12.31	18.40-9.87	17.09-9.41	23.48-14.46
Average Yield %	0.36	0.37	0.38	0.37	0.24	0.37	0.44	0.44

Address: 5900 Lake Ellenor Drive, Orlando, FL 32809 Telephone: (407) 245-4000	Web Site: www.darden.com Officers: Joe R. Lee - Chmn. Andrew H. Madsen - Pres., C.O.O.	Auditors: KPMG LLP Investor Contact: 800-832-7336 Transfer Agents: Wachovia Bank National Association

DAVITA INC.

Exchange	Symbol	Price	52Wk Range	Yield	P/E
NYS	DVA	$41.85 (3/31/2005)	44.10-27.38	N/A	19.38

*7 Year Price Score 178.37 *NYSE Composite Index=100 *12 Month Price Score 115.90

Interim Earnings (Per Share)

Qtr.	Mar	Jun	Sep	Dec
2001	0.23	0.22	0.31	0.24
2002	0.27	0.09	0.48	0.51
2003	0.35	0.37	0.36	0.59
2004	0.51	0.50	0.59	0.55

Interim Dividends (Per Share)

Amt	Decl	Ex	Rec	Pay
3-for-2	5/17/2004	6/16/2004	6/1/2004	6/15/2004

Valuation Analysis

Forecast P/E	18.61	No of Institutions
	(4/7/2005)	213
Market Cap	$4.1 Billion	Shares
Book Value	523.1 Million	87,804,848
Price/Book	7.89	% Held
Price/Sales	1.79	89.96

Business Summary: Diagnostic Services (MIC: 9.5 SIC: 092 NAIC: 21999)

DaVita is a provider of dialysis services in the U.S. for patients suffering from chronic kidney failure, also known as end stage renal disease, or ESRD. As of Dec 31 2004, Co. operated or provided administrative services to approximately 660 outpatient dialysis centers located in 37 states and the District of Columbia, serving approximately 54,000 patients. Throughout its network of outpatient dialysis centers, Co. also provides training, supplies and on-call support services to its peritoneal dialysis patients. Additionally, Co. provides acute inpatient dialysis services in approximately 370 hospitals.

Recent Developments: For the year ended Dec 31 2004, net income increased 26.4% to $222,254 thousand from net income of $175,791 thousand a year earlier. Revenues were $2,298,595 thousand, up 14.0% from $2,016,418 thousand the year before. Operating income was $410,123 thousand versus an income of $378,535 thousand in the prior year, an increase of 8.3%. Total direct expense was $1,555,070 thousand versus $1,360,556 thousand in the prior year, an increase of 14.3%. Total indirect expense was $333,402 thousand versus $277,327 thousand in the prior year, an increase of 20.2%.

Prospects: On Feb 8 2005, Co. announced 2005 guidance that included an expected increase in operating income of 2.0% to 6% over 2004, exclusive of the effects of its proposed Gambro Healthcare acquisition and related debt financing, as well as the anticipated expensing of stock options in accordance with FASB No. 123R. On Dec 6 2004, Co. entered into an agreement to acquire Gambro Healthcare, Inc., a U.S. dialysis service provider, for a purchase price of approximately $3.05 billion in cash. In connection with the Gambro acquisition Co. stated that it will be assessing financing alternatives, which could include closing some or all of the financing in advance of the closing of the acquisition.

Financial Data
(US$ in Thousands)

	12/31/2004	12/31/2003	12/31/2002	12/31/2001	12/31/2000	12/31/1999	12/31/1998	12/31/1997
Earnings Per Share	2.16	1.66	1.31	1.01	0.11	(1.21)	(0.03)	0.55
Cash Flow Per Share	4.24	3.11	3.17	2.17	2.51	1.39	0.15	0.09
Income Statement								
Total Revenue	2,298,595	2,016,418	1,854,632	1,650,753	1,486,302	1,445,351	1,204,894	438,205
EBITDA	500,962	429,781	452,488	418,585	273,177	41,452	233,846	106,982
Depn & Amortn	86,666	74,687	64,665	105,209	111,605	112,481	92,028	27,124
Income Before Taxes	361,884	288,266	316,187	240,938	44,935	(181,826)	64,085	66,620
Income Taxes	139,630	112,475	129,500	104,600	27,960	(34,570)	41,580	25,141
Net Income	222,254	175,791	157,329	137,315	13,485	(147,256)	(4,298)	36,977
Average Shares	102,861	113,760	135,720	155,181	124,735	121,728	122,551	67,953
Balance Sheet								
Current Assets	868,720	605,058	544,526	474,664	397,875	654,748	559,542	186,050
Total Assets	2,511,959	1,945,530	1,775,693	1,662,683	1,596,632	2,056,718	1,915,581	695,340
Current Liabilities	441,735	362,820	292,601	298,681	249,527	1,698,544	174,464	39,776
Long-Term Obligations	1,322,468	1,117,002	1,311,252	811,190	974,006	5,696	1,225,781	356,563
Total Liabilities	1,988,825	1,638,659	1,705,429	1,159,046	1,247,264	1,730,314	1,433,769	421,668
Stockholders' Equity	523,134	306,871	70,264	503,637	349,368	326,404	481,812	273,672
Shares Outstanding	98,566	96,754	90,988	126,780	123,203	121,789	121,544	66,884
Statistical Record								
Return on Assets %	9.94	9.45	9.15	8.43	0.74	N.M.	N.M.	6.92
Return on Equity %	53.41	93.22	54.83	32.20	3.98	N.M.	N.M.	14.65
EBITDA Margin %	21.79	21.31	24.40	25.36	18.38	2.87	19.41	24.41
Net Margin %	9.67	8.72	8.48	8.32	0.91	N.M.	N.M.	8.44
Asset Turnover	1.03	1.08	1.08	1.01	0.81	0.73	0.92	0.82
Current Ratio	1.97	1.67	1.86	1.59	1.59	0.39	3.21	4.68
Debt to Equity	2.53	3.64	18.66	1.61	2.79	0.02	2.54	1.30
Price Range	39.62-25.33	26.67-13.01	17.42-12.97	16.30-9.73	11.67-1.71	19.71-3.92	24.08-12.67	22.29-11.25
P/E Ratio	18.34-11.73	16.06-7.84	13.30-9.90	16.14-9.64	106.06-15.53	...	...	40.53-20.45

Address: 21250 Hawthorne Blvd., Suite 800, Torrance, CA 90503-5517
Telephone: (310) 792-2600
Fax: (310) 792-8928

Web Site: www.davita.com
Officers: Kent J. Thiry - Chmn., C.E.O. Denise K. Fletcher - Sr. V.P., C.F.O.

Auditors: KPMG LLP
Investor Contact: 800-310-4872

DEAN FOODS CO.

Exchange	Symbol	Price	52Wk Range	Yield	P/E
NYS	DF	$34.30 (3/31/2005)	37.44-28.46	N/A	19.27

*7 Year Price Score 132.67 *NYSE Composite Index=100 *12 Month Price Score 94.64

Interim Earnings (Per Share)

Qtr.	Mar	Jun	Sep	Dec
2001	0.25	0.37	0.32	0.25
2002	0.08	0.48	0.45	0.19
2003	0.43	0.54	0.76	0.54
2004	0.43	0.47	0.25	0.63

Interim Dividends (Per Share)

Amt	Decl	Ex	Rec	Pay
2-for-1	2/21/2002	4/24/2002	4/8/2002	4/24/2002
3-for-2	5/8/2003	6/10/2003	5/23/2003	6/9/2003

Valuation Analysis

Forecast P/E	15.48	No of Institutions
	(4/7/2005)	271
Market Cap	$5.1 Billion	Shares
Book Value	2.7 Billion	117,282,656
Price/Book	1.92	% Held
Price/Sales	0.47	78.11

TRADING VOLUME (thousand shares)

Business Summary: Food (MIC: 4.1 SIC: 024 NAIC: 11520)

Dean Foods is a major processor and distributor of food and beverage products. Co. produces a full line of Co.-branded and private-label dairy products including milk and milk-based beverages, ice cream, coffee creamers, half-and-half, whipping cream, whipped toppings, sour cream, cottage cheese, yogurt, dips, dressings and soy milk. National brand names include International Delight®, Hershey's®, Land O'Lakes®, Folger's®, Jakada®, Marie's®, Dean's®, Silk® and Sun Soy®. Co. is also a supplier of pickles and other specialty food products, juice, juice drinks and water.

Recent Developments: For the year ended Dec 31 2004, net income decreased 19.8% to $285,374 thousand from net income of $355,703 thousand a year earlier. Revenues were $10,822,285 thousand, up 17.8% from $9,184,616 thousand the year before. Operating income was $666,893 thousand versus an income of $765,985 thousand in the prior year, a decrease of 12.9%. Total direct expense was $8,257,756 thousand versus $6,808,207 thousand in the prior year, an increase of 21.3%. Total indirect expense was $1,897,636 thousand versus $1,610,424 thousand in the prior year, an increase of 17.8%.

Prospects: On Jan 27 2005, Co. announced that it intends to pursue a tax-free spin-off of its Specialty Foods Group business to its shareholders. The transaction will create a publicly traded private label and regionally branded consumer packaged goods company with approximately 1,700 employees. The transaction is expected to be completed by the third quarter of 2005. Meanwhile, Co. continues to see robust growth at its Branded Products group, White Wave Foods. In addition, Co.'s Dairy group is continuing to expand its market presence with volume growth of fresh fluid milk and cream. For 2005, Co. expects revenues of about $10.60 billion and earning in the range of $2.20 to $2.30 per share.

Financial Data

(US$ in Thousands)	12/31/2004	12/31/2003	12/31/2002	12/31/2001	12/31/2000	12/31/1999	12/31/1998	12/31/1997
Earnings Per Share	1.78	2.27	1.21	1.19	1.27	1.04	1.19	0.30
Cash Flow Per Share	3.40	3.60	4.86	3.67	3.51	2.88	1.96	1.54
Income Statement								
Total Revenue	10,822,285	9,184,616	8,991,464	6,230,116	5,756,303	4,481,999	3,320,940	1,794,876
EBITDA	890,693	946,575	792,464	487,437	491,534	358,981	308,312	163,976
Depn & Amortn	223,547	191,885	173,994	154,887	144,983	116,645	91,779	44,607
Income Before Taxes	462,376	573,556	420,785	230,763	233,965	193,103	164,451	82,705
Income Taxes	177,002	217,853	152,988	83,739	90,303	75,463	59,823	43,375
Net Income	285,374	355,703	175,416	109,830	118,719	109,731	131,606	28,764
Average Shares	160,704	160,695	163,163	110,676	110,013	128,575	125,896	94,047
Balance Sheet								
Current Assets	1,596,424	1,400,881	1,311,146	1,482,184	817,931	639,407	813,899	396,076
Total Assets	7,756,368	6,992,536	6,582,266	6,731,897	3,780,478	2,658,922	3,013,783	1,403,462
Current Liabilities	1,106,426	1,170,393	1,192,948	1,174,963	699,908	479,117	559,071	232,873
Long-Term Obligations	3,116,032	2,611,356	2,554,482	2,971,525	1,225,045	689,397	893,077	777,813
Total Liabilities	5,095,231	4,449,723	4,938,973	5,256,017	3,181,646	2,074,950	2,358,012	1,044,152
Stockholders' Equity	2,661,137	2,542,813	1,643,293	1,475,880	598,832	583,972	655,771	359,310
Shares Outstanding	149,222	154,993	132,961	131,809	81,856	87,862	100,794	91,389
Statistical Record								
Return on Assets %	3.86	5.24	2.64	2.09	3.68	3.87	5.96	3.22
Return on Equity %	10.94	16.99	11.25	10.59	20.02	17.70	25.93	12.70
EBITDA Margin %	8.23	10.31	8.81	7.82	8.54	8.01	9.28	9.14
Net Margin %	2.64	3.87	1.95	1.76	2.06	2.45	3.96	1.60
Asset Turnover	1.46	1.35	1.35	1.19	1.78	1.58	1.50	2.01
Current Ratio	1.44	1.20	1.10	1.26	1.17	1.33	1.46	1.70
Debt to Equity	1.17	1.03	1.55	2.01	2.05	1.18	1.36	2.16
Price Range	37.44-28.46	33.52-24.73	26.81-18.61	24.16-14.38	17.34-12.08	16.98-9.96	22.19-8.63	20.38-6.50
P/E Ratio	21.03-15.99	14.77-10.90	22.15-15.38	20.30-12.08	13.66-9.51	16.33-9.58	18.64-7.25	67.92-21.67

Address: 2515 McKinney Avenue, Suite 1200, Dallas, TX 75201
Telephone: (214) 303-3400
Fax: (214) 528-9929

Web Site: www.deanfoods.com
Officers: Gregg L. Engles - Chmn., C.E.O. Barry A. Fromberg - Exec. V.P., C.F.O.

Auditors: Deloitte & Touche LLP
Transfer Agents: Computershare Investor Services

DEERE & CO.

Exchange	Symbol	Price	52Wk Range	Yield	P/E
NYS	DE	$67.13 (3/31/2005)	74.85-57.60	1.85	11.67

*7 Year Price Score 122.14 *NYSE Composite Index=100 ***12 Month Price Score 95.79**

Interim Earnings (Per Share)

Qtr.	Jan	Apr	Jul	Oct
2001-02	(0.16)	0.59	0.61	0.29
2002-03	0.28	1.07	1.02	0.27
2003-04	0.68	1.88	1.58	1.42
2004-05	0.89	...	...	...

Interim Dividends (Per Share)

Amt	Decl	Ex	Rec	Pay
0.28Q	5/26/2004	6/28/2004	6/30/2004	8/2/2004
0.28Q	8/25/2004	9/28/2004	9/30/2004	11/1/2004
0.28Q	12/1/2004	12/29/2004	12/31/2004	2/1/2005
0.31Q	2/23/2005	3/29/2005	3/31/2005	5/2/2005

Indicated Div: $1.24

Valuation Analysis

Forecast P/E	11.07 (4/7/2005)	No of Institutions 467
Market Cap	$16.5 Billion	Shares 196,707,200
Book Value	6.5 Billion	% Held
Price/Book	2.55	79.80
Price/Sales	0.80	

Business Summary: Industrial Machinery and Equipment (MIC: 11.5 SIC: 523 NAIC: 33111)

Deere & Company operates four major business segments. The agricultural equipment segment manufactures and distributes a full line of farm equipment and service parts. The commercial and consumer equipment segment manufactures and distributes equipment and service parts for commercial and residential uses. The construction and forestry segment manufactures, distributes to dealers and sells at retail a broad range of machines and service parts used in construction, earthmoving, material handling and timber harvesting. The credit segment primarily finances sales and leases by Co. dealers of new and used agricultural, commercial and consumer, and construction and forestry equipment.

Recent Developments: For the quarter ended Jan 31 2005, net income increased 30.4% to $222,800 thousand from net income of $170,800 thousand in the year-earlier quarter. Revenues were $4,127,100 thousand, up 18.5% from $3,483,800 thousand the year before. Total direct expense was $2,918,000 thousand versus $2,445,100 thousand in the prior-year quarter, an increase of 19.3%. Total indirect expense was $696,500 thousand versus $629,100 thousand in the prior-year quarter, an increase of 10.7%.

Prospects: Positive customer response is expected to continue driving Co.'s performance in 2005. In addition, Co. is having success expanding its market position on a global basis. For full-year 2005 and the second quarter of 2005, excluding the impact of currency translation, company equipment sales are expected to increase by 6.0% to 8.0% and 9.0% to 11.0%, respectively. Currency is forecast to add about two percentage points to sales for both periods. Production levels are expected to be down slightly for the year but up 3.0% to 5.0% for the second quarter. Net income is forecast to be around $1.50 billion for the full year and in the range of $500.0 million to $525.0 million for the quarter.

Financial Data

(US$ in Thousands)	3 Mos	10/31/2004	10/31/2003	10/31/2002	10/31/2001	10/31/2000	10/31/1999	10/31/1998
Earnings Per Share	5.75	5.56	2.64	1.33	(0.27)	2.06	1.02	4.16
Cash Flow Per Share	4.01	4.69	6.39	7.89	4.74	4.60	6.16	1.71
Tang Book Value Per Share	22.28	21.86	11.81	9.49	13.14	15.56	16.25	16.63
Dividends Per Share	1.120	1.060	0.880	0.880	0.880	0.880	0.880	0.880
Dividend Payout %	19.48	19.06	33.33	66.17	...	42.72	86.27	21.15
Income Statement								
Total Revenue	4,127,100	19,986,100	15,534,600	13,947,000	13,292,900	13,136,800	11,750,900	13,821,500
EBITDA	672,900	3,326,800	1,910,800	1,593,800	1,088,900	2,101,900	1,435,000	2,497,400
Depn & Amortn	160,300	621,000	311,000	354,000	348,000	647,900	513,300	418,000
Income Before Taxes	345,500	2,113,700	971,300	602,700	(24,800)	777,500	365,100	1,560,000
Income Taxes	119,800	708,500	336,900	258,300	17,700	293,800	134,700	553,900
Net Income	222,800	1,406,100	643,100	319,200	(64,000)	485,500	239,200	1,021,400
Average Shares	251,000	253,100	243,300	240,900	236,800	236,000	234,400	245,700
Balance Sheet								
Current Assets	20,799,500	20,547,000	19,307,100	16,869,200	15,538,800	14,043,100	12,203,100	13,428,600
Total Assets	28,948,100	28,754,000	26,258,000	23,768,000	22,663,100	20,469,400	17,578,200	18,001,500
Current Liabilities	7,897,200	7,753,000	7,767,500	7,730,700	9,356,200	8,824,700	7,081,500	8,351,100
Long-Term Obligations	10,954,700	11,090,000	10,404,000	8,950,000	6,561,000	4,764,000	3,806,000	2,792,000
Total Liabilities	22,450,000	22,361,200	22,255,900	20,604,800	18,670,900	16,167,500	13,483,900	13,921,700
Stockholders' Equity	6,498,100	6,392,800	4,002,100	3,163,200	3,992,200	4,301,900	4,094,300	4,079,800
Shares Outstanding	246,505	246,859	243,521	238,894	237,331	234,555	233,804	232,310
Statistical Record								
Return on Assets %	5.28	5.10	2.57	1.37	N.M.	2.55	1.34	5.95
Return on Equity %	26.95	26.98	17.95	8.92	N.M.	11.53	5.85	24.83
EBITDA Margin %	16.30	16.65	12.30	11.43	8.19	16.00	12.21	18.07
Net Margin %	5.40	7.04	4.14	2.29	N.M.	3.70	2.04	7.39
Asset Turnover	0.75	0.72	0.62	0.60	0.62	0.69	0.66	0.81
Current Ratio	2.63	2.65	2.49	2.18	1.66	1.59	1.72	1.61
Debt to Equity	1.69	1.73	2.60	2.83	1.64	1.11	0.93	0.68
Price Range	74.85-57.60	74.85-57.60	60.62-37.96	49.78-36.99	46.63-34.60	49.56-30.38	45.13-29.75	63.00-28.69
P/E Ratio	13.02-10.02	13.46-10.36	22.96-14.38	37.43-27.81	...	24.06-14.75	44.24-29.17	15.14-6.90
Average Yield %	1.69	1.64	1.86	1.98	2.19	2.26	2.34	1.78

Address: One John Deere Place, Moline, IL 61265 Telephone: (309) 765-8000 Fax: (309) 765-9929	Web Site: www.johndeere.com Officers: Robert W. Lane - Chmn., Pres., C.E.O. Nathan J. Jones - Sr. V.P., C.F.O.	Auditors: Deloitte & Touche LLP Investor Contact: 309-765-4491

DEL MONTE FOODS CO.

Exchange	Symbol	Price	52Wk Range	Yield	P/E
NYS	DLM	$10.85 (3/31/2005)	11.62-9.90	N/A	15.07

*7 Year Price Score N/A   *NYSE Composite Index=100   *12 Month Price Score 94.24

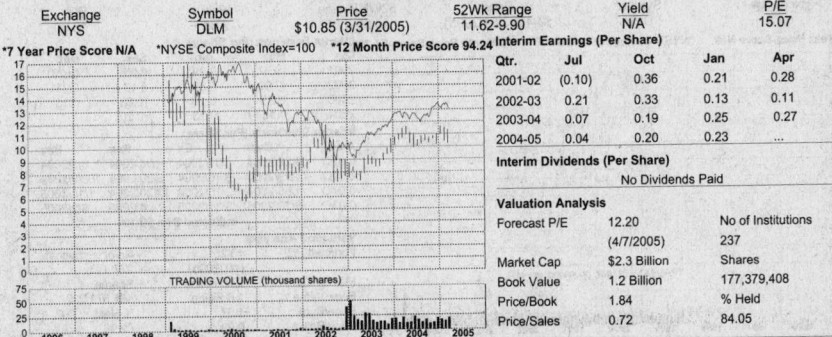

Interim Earnings (Per Share)

Qtr.	Jul	Oct	Jan	Apr
2001-02	(0.10)	0.36	0.21	0.28
2002-03	0.21	0.33	0.13	0.11
2003-04	0.07	0.19	0.25	0.27
2004-05	0.04	0.20	0.23	...

Interim Dividends (Per Share)

No Dividends Paid

Valuation Analysis

Forecast P/E	12.20	No of Institutions	237
	(4/7/2005)		
Market Cap	$2.3 Billion	Shares	
Book Value	1.2 Billion		177,379,408
Price/Book	1.84	% Held	
Price/Sales	0.72		84.05

Business Summary: Food (MIC: 4.1 SIC: 033 NAIC: 11421)

Del Monte Foods and its consolidated subsidiaries are engaged in the production, distribution and marketing of branded and private label food and pet products for the U.S. retail market, with food brands, such as Del Monte, StarKist, Contadina, S&W, College Inn and other brand names and foods and snacks for pets, with brands including 9Lives, Kibbles 'n Bits, Pup-Peroni, Snausages, Pounce and other brand names. The majority of Co.'s products are sold nationwide in all channels serving retail markets, mass merchandisers, the U.S. military, certain export markets, the foodservice industry and food processors.

Recent Developments: For the quarter ended Jan 30 2005, income from continuing operations decreased 6.9% to $48,600 thousand from income of $52,200 thousand in the year-earlier quarter. Net income decreased 9.3% to $48,500 thousand from net income of $53,500 thousand in the year-earlier quarter. Revenues were $861,300 thousand, up 6.2% from $811,100 thousand. Operating income was $104,400 thousand with an income of $115,100 thousand in the prior-year quarter, a decrease of 9.3%. Total direct expense was $629,100 thousand with $583,900 thousand in the prior-year quarter, an increase of 7.7%. Total indirect expense was $127,800 thousand with $112,100 thousand in the prior-year quarter, an increase of 14.0%.

Prospects: Top-line growth is being driven by higher volume from new product introductions, increased marketing support, strength in the pet food and private-label soup segments, and increased pricing. Meanwhile, earnings continue to be hampered by inflationary cost pressures in steel and energy, logistics and other transportation-related costs, as well as higher fish costs. Co. anticipates these higher cost levels to continue to hamper results over the next 12 to 18 months. Looking ahead, Co. expects fiscal 2005 sales growth of between 2.0% and 3.0%, along with earnings from continuing operations in the range of $0.65 to $0.70 per diluted share.

Financial Data
(US$ in Thousands)

	9 Mos	6 Mos	3 Mos	05/02/2004	04/27/2003	06/30/2002	06/30/2001	06/30/2000
Earnings Per Share	0.72	0.74	0.74	0.78	0.76	0.73	0.26	2.42
Cash Flow Per Share	1.18	1.18	1.05	1.28	2.84	3.24	1.72	(0.14)
Income Statement								
Total Revenue	2,333,900	1,472,600	626,000	3,129,900	2,171,100	1,322,400	1,512,000	1,462,100
EBITDA	304,200	177,000	60,900	469,700	296,900	146,900	168,000	186,100
Depn & Amortn	68,200	45,300	22,400	89,500	50,500	33,500	36,700	39,600
Income Before Taxes	159,600	81,200	13,900	251,200	201,100	55,900	56,700	79,400
Income Taxes	60,600	30,800	5,300	90,500	67,600	16,100	16,700	(53,600)
Net Income	98,600	50,100	8,500	164,600	133,500	38,500	13,800	128,700
Average Shares	212,708	212,066	211,860	211,212	176,494	53,048	52,767	53,097
Balance Sheet								
Current Assets	1,371,100	1,546,100	1,362,400	1,225,700	1,139,400	589,000	622,500	577,800
Total Assets	3,579,500	3,766,300	3,583,900	3,459,700	3,544,900	1,070,000	1,124,100	1,040,700
Current Liabilities	422,500	690,600	549,300	434,300	444,500	261,600	231,500	428,000
Long-Term Obligations	1,363,900	1,365,800	1,367,600	1,369,500	1,635,300	587,400	709,800	443,000
Total Liabilities	2,336,000	2,577,500	2,442,800	2,330,800	2,595,500	1,038,300	1,099,200	1,030,100
Stockholders' Equity	1,243,500	1,188,800	1,141,100	1,128,900	949,400	31,700	24,900	10,600
Shares Outstanding	211,022	210,739	209,778	209,691	209,303	52,299	52,260	52,219
Statistical Record								
Return on Assets %	4.13	4.08	4.33	4.62	5.85	3.51	1.27	13.42
Return on Equity %	13.12	14.21	14.81	15.58	27.52	136.04	77.75	...
EBITDA Margin %	13.03	12.02	9.73	15.01	13.68	11.11	11.11	12.73
Net Margin %	4.22	3.40	1.36	5.26	6.15	2.91	0.91	8.80
Asset Turnover	0.87	0.82	0.86	0.88	0.95	1.21	1.40	1.52
Current Ratio	3.25	2.24	2.48	2.82	2.56	2.25	2.69	1.35
Debt to Equity	1.10	1.15	1.20	1.21	1.72	18.53	28.51	41.79
Price Range	11.62-9.90	11.62-9.40	11.62-8.40	11.62-7.87	11.85-7.12	11.96-7.47	11.50-5.69	16.88-6.81
P/E Ratio	16.14-13.75	15.70-12.70	15.70-11.35	14.90-10.09	15.59-9.37	16.38-10.23	44.23-21.87	6.97-2.82

Address: One Market @ The Landmark, San Francisco, CA 94105	Web Site: www.delmonte.com	Auditors: KPMG LLP
Telephone: (415) 247-3000	**Officers:** Richard G. Wolford - Chmn., Pres., C.E.O. David L. Meyers - Exec. V.P., Admin., C.F.O.	**Investor Contact:** 415-247-3382
Fax: (415) 247-3565		**Transfer Agents:** Bank of New York, New York, NY

DELPHI CORP.

Interim Earnings (Per Share)

Qtr.	Mar	Jun	Sep	Dec
2001	(0.77)	0.29	0.05	(0.23)
2002	(0.09)	0.39	0.10	0.21
2003	0.23	0.16	(0.63)	0.15
2004	0.10	0.23	(0.20)	...

Interim Dividends (Per Share)

Amt	Decl	Ex	Rec	Pay
0.07Q	6/22/2004	7/1/2004	7/6/2004	8/3/2004
0.07Q	9/9/2004	9/16/2004	9/20/2004	10/19/2004
0.07Q	12/8/2004	12/16/2004	12/20/2004	1/18/2005
0.03Q	3/23/2005	3/31/2005	4/4/2005	5/2/2005

Indicated Div: $0.12

Valuation Analysis

Forecast P/E	15.25	No of Institutions	
	(4/7/2005)	277	
Market Cap	$2.5 Billion	Shares	465,571,232
Book Value	1.6 Billion	% Held	82.96
Price/Book	1.57		
Price/Sales	0.09		

Business Summary: Automotive (MIC: 15.1 SIC: 714 NAIC: 36399)

Delphi is a supplier of vehicle electronics, transportation components, integrated systems and modules. Co. operates its business along three reporting segments: Dynamics, Propulsion & Thermal Sector, which includes selected businesses from Co.'s energy and engine management systems, chassis, steering and thermal systems product lines; Electrical, Electronics, Safety & Interior Sector, which includes selected businesses from Co.'s automotive electronics, audio, consumer and aftermarket products, communication systems, safety and power and signal distribution systems product lines; and Automotive Holdings Group, comprised of underperforming product lines and plant sites.

Recent Developments: For the three months ended Sep 30 2004, Co. reported a net loss of $114.0 million compared with a net loss of $353.0 million in the corresponding year-earlier period. Co. noted that it continues to be challenged by commodity cost increases, most notably steel and petroleum-based resin products. Total net sales rose 1.3% to $6.65 billion from $6.56 billion the previous year. Non-GM revenues were $3.16 billion, or 47.4% of sales, an increase of 19.7% from the third quarter of 2003. Co. posted an operating loss of $114.0 million versus an operating loss of $528.0 million the year before.

Prospects: Co.'s outlook is somewhat uncertain. Co. noted that calendar year 2005 is presenting it with a number of competitive challenges, including expected revenue volatility from North America, Asia, and Europe. Also, Co. cited commodities, troubled supplier situations and the unpredictability of attrition as factors making its ability to forecast its cost structure difficult on a quarterly basis. Meanwhile, Co. continues to move forward with cost-saving initiatives. For the first quarter ended Mar 31 2005, Co.'s recommended revenue range is from $6.80 billion to $7.00 billion at the Eurodollar to U.S. dollar rate of 1.34. Co. noted that non-GM revenue are likely to exceed 50.0% of sales.

Financial Data

(US$ in Thousands)	6 Mos	3 Mos	12/31/2003	12/31/2002	12/31/2001	12/31/2000	12/31/1999	12/31/1998
Earnings Per Share	(0.14)	(0.22)	(0.10)	0.61	(0.66)	1.88	1.95	(0.20)
Cash Flow Per Share	1.65	1.33	1.32	3.70	2.43	0.48	(2.20)	1.83
Tang Book Value Per Share	N.M.	N.M.	N.M.	1.04	4.13	6.73	5.69	0.02
Dividends Per Share	0.210	0.350	0.280	0.280	0.280	0.280	0.210	...
Dividend Payout %	...	...	...	45.90	...	14.89	10.77	...
Income Statement								
Total Revenue	14,960,000	7,411,000	28,096,000	27,427,000	26,088,000	29,139,000	29,192,000	28,479,000
EBITDA	891,000	408,000	1,143,000	1,689,000	811,000	2,738,000	2,613,000	1,056,000
Depn & Amortn	561,000	279,000	1,110,000	988,000	1,150,000	936,000	856,000	1,102,000
Income Before Taxes	219,000	70,000	(142,000)	531,000	(528,000)	1,667,000	1,721,000	(266,000)
Income Taxes	34,000	16,000	(86,000)	188,000	(158,000)	605,000	638,000	(173,000)
Net Income	185,000	54,000	(56,000)	343,000	(370,000)	1,062,000	1,083,000	(93,000)
Average Shares	562,432	563,622	560,114	562,431	560,041	563,568	554,633	465,000
Balance Sheet								
Current Assets	8,006,000	8,697,000	8,046,000	7,542,000	7,498,000	8,603,000	9,811,000	6,405,000
Total Assets	20,755,000	21,532,000	20,904,000	19,316,000	18,602,000	18,521,000	18,350,000	15,506,000
Current Liabilities	5,830,000	6,855,000	6,191,000	5,860,000	5,850,000	6,243,000	6,737,000	4,061,000
Long-Term Obligations	2,432,000	2,434,000	2,434,000	2,084,000	2,083,000	1,623,000	1,640,000	3,137,000
Total Liabilities	19,150,000	19,979,000	19,334,000	18,037,000	16,290,000	14,755,000	15,150,000	15,497,000
Stockholders' Equity	1,605,000	1,553,000	1,570,000	1,279,000	2,312,000	3,766,000	3,200,000	9,000
Shares Outstanding	561,200	560,300	560,314	558,100	560,200	559,800	562,000	565,000
Statistical Record								
Return on Assets %	N.M.	N.M.	N.M.	1.81	N.M.	5.74	6.40	N.M.
Return on Equity %	N.M.	N.M.	N.M.	19.10	N.M.	30.41	67.50	...
EBITDA Margin %	5.96	5.51	4.07	6.16	3.11	9.40	8.95	3.71
Net Margin %	1.24	0.73	N.M.	1.25	N.M.	3.64	3.71	N.M.
Asset Turnover	1.42	1.38	1.40	1.45	1.41	1.58	1.72	1.87
Current Ratio	1.37	1.27	1.30	1.29	1.28	1.38	1.46	1.58
Debt to Equity	1.52	1.57	1.55	1.63	0.90	0.43	0.51	348.56
Price Range	11.67-8.02	11.67-6.83	10.21-6.53	17.24-6.70	17.50-10.30	21.13-10.94	21.69-14.38	...
P/E Ratio	...	...	...	28.26-10.98	...	11.24-5.82	11.12-7.37	...
Average Yield %	2.17	3.81	3.27	2.33	1.97	1.76	1.18	...

Address: 5725 Delphi Drive, Troy, MI 48098	**Web Site:** www.delphi.com	**Auditors:** Deloitte & Touche LLP
Telephone: (248) 813-2000	**Officers:** J. T. Battenberg III - Chmn., C.E.O. David B. Wohleen - Vice-Chm.	**Investor Contact:** 877 733 5374
Fax: (248) 813-2670		

DELTA AIR LINES, INC. (DE)

Exchange	Symbol	Price	52Wk Range	Yield	P/E
NYS	DAL	$4.05 (3/31/2005)	8.56-2.93	N/A	N/A

*7 Year Price Score 14.82   *NYSE Composite Index=100   *12 Month Price Score 81.28

Interim Earnings (Per Share)

Qtr.	Mar	Jun	Sep	Dec
2001	(1.11)	(0.76)	(2.13)	(5.99)
2002	(3.25)	(1.54)	(2.67)	(2.98)
2003	(3.81)	1.40	(1.36)	(2.69)
2004	(3.12)	(15.79)	(5.16)	(17.01)

Interim Dividends (Per Share)

Dividend Payment Suspended

Valuation Analysis

Forecast P/E	0.00	No of Institutions
	(4/7/2005)	195
Market Cap	$566.3 Million	Shares
Book Value	N/A	157,094,592
Price/Book	N/A	% Held
Price/Sales	0.04	N/A

Business Summary: Aviation (MIC: 1.1 SIC: 512 NAIC: 81111)

Delta Air Lines is a major air carrier providing scheduled passenger and cargo service through a network of routes throughout the U.S. and abroad. Co. is the second-largest airline in terms of passengers flown, and the third-largest airline based on operating revenues and revenue passenger miles flown. Delta, Song, Delta Express, Delta Shuttle, the Delta Connection carriers and Delta's Worldwide Partners operate 7,318 flights each day to 487 cities in 82 countries. Co.'s hub airports are located in Atlanta, GA, Cincinnati, OH, Dallas/Fort Worth, TX and Salt Lake City, UT. As of Dec 31 2003, Co. operated a fleet of 833 aircraft.

Recent Developments: For the year ended Dec 31 2004, net loss was $5,198 million versus net loss of $773 million a year earlier. Revenues were $15,002 million, up 6.5% from $14,087 million the year before. Operating loss was $3,308 million versus a loss of $785 million in the prior year. Total direct expense was $7,680 million versus $6,359 million in the prior year, an increase of 20.8%. Total indirect expense was $10,630 million versus $8,513 million in the prior year, an increase of 24.9%.

Prospects: Co. estimates that its funding obligation in 2005 for its defined benefit pension and defined contribution plans will be approximately $400.0 million to $450.0 million. Capital expenditures for the Mar 2005 quarter are estimated to be approximately $289.0 million, including approximately $147.0 million for aircraft. All of Co.'s regional jet aircraft deliveries in 2005 will be financed under existing agreements. The remaining mainline aircraft to be delivered in 2005 are scheduled to be sold to a third party immediately upon delivery from the manufacturer, pursuant to a previously announced agreement.

Financial Data
(US$ in Thousands)

	12/31/2004	12/31/2003	12/31/2002	12/31/2001	12/31/2000	06/30/2000	06/30/1999	06/30/1998
Earnings Per Share	(41.07)	(6.40)	(10.44)	(9.99)	6.28	9.42	7.20	6.34
Cash Flow Per Share	(8.82)	3.67	2.31	1.92	15.53	18.21	20.50	19.54
Tang Book Value Per Share	...	...	N.M.	12.84	25.14	21.09	25.63	20.65
Dividends Per Share	...	0.050	0.100	0.100	0.100	0.100	0.100	0.100
Dividend Payout %	...	...	...	...	1.59	1.06	1.39	1.58
Income Statement								
Total Revenue	15,002,000	13,303,000	13,305,000	13,879,000	16,741,000	15,888,000	14,711,000	14,138,000
EBITDA	(1,961,000)	737,000	(211,000)	(171,000)	3,007,000	3,626,000	2,888,000	2,578,000
Depn & Amortn	1,244,000	1,230,000	1,181,000	1,283,000	1,187,000	1,146,000	961,000	861,000
Income Before Taxes	(3,992,000)	(1,189,000)	(2,002,000)	(1,864,000)	1,549,000	2,283,000	1,826,000	1,648,000
Income Taxes	1,206,000	(416,000)	(730,000)	(648,000)	621,000	914,000	725,000	647,000
Net Income	(5,198,000)	(773,000)	(1,272,000)	(1,216,000)	828,000	1,303,000	1,101,000	1,001,000
Average Shares	127,000	123,400	123,300	123,100	131,000	137,900	152,300	157,200
Balance Sheet								
Total Assets	21,801,000	26,356,000	24,720,000	23,605,000	21,931,000	20,566,000	16,544,000	14,603,000
Long-Term Obligations	13,005,000	11,538,000	10,174,000	8,347,000	5,896,000	4,525,000	1,952,000	1,782,000
Total Liabilities	27,320,000	26,740,000	23,563,000	19,581,000	16,354,000	15,479,000	11,901,000	10,405,000
Stockholders' Equity	(5,796,000)	(659,000)	893,000	3,769,000	5,343,000	4,873,000	4,448,000	4,023,000
Shares Outstanding	139,830	123,544	123,359	123,246	123,013	122,639	138,600	176,000
Statistical Record								
Return on Assets %	N.M.	N.M.	N.M.	N.M.	2.86	7.00	7.07	7.32
Return on Equity %	...	N.M.	N.M.	N.M.	11.22	27.88	25.99	28.48
EBITDA Margin %	N.M.	5.54	N.M.	N.M.	17.96	22.82	19.63	18.23
Net Margin %	(34.65)	(5.81)	(9.56)	(8.76)	4.95	8.20	7.48	7.08
Asset Turnover	0.62	0.52	0.55	0.61	0.58	0.85	0.94	1.03
Price Range	13.03-2.93	15.85-6.75	38.59-6.50	52.75-20.64	57.50-40.38	63.13-43.63	71.56-41.34	64.69-41.00
P/E Ratio	...	...	...	...	9.16-6.43	6.70-4.63	9.94-5.74	10.20-6.47
Average Yield %	...	0.41	0.47	0.26	0.21	0.19	0.17	0.18

Address: Hartsfield Atlanta International Airport, 1030 Delta Blvd, Atlanta, GA 30320-6001 **Telephone:** (404) 715 2600 **Fax:** (404) 715 5042	**Web Site:** www.delta.com **Officers:** Gerald Grinstein - C.E.O. Michael J. Palumbo - Exec. V.P., C.F.O.	**Auditors:** Deloitte & Touche LLP **Transfer Agents:** Wells Fargo Shareowner Services

DELUXE CORP.

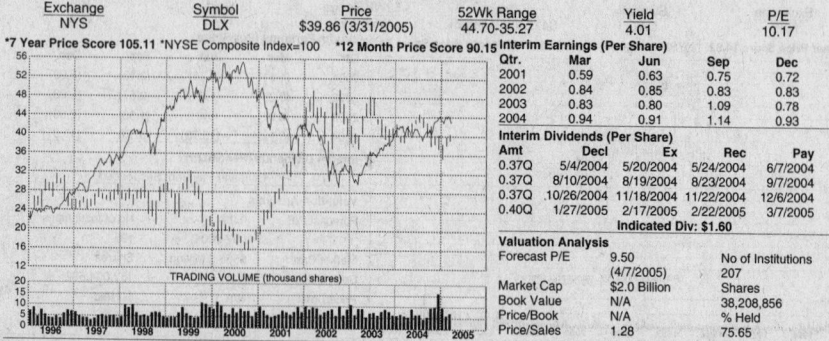

Exchange	Symbol	Price	52Wk Range	Yield	P/E
NYS	DLX	$39.86 (3/31/2005)	44.70-35.27	4.01	10.17

*7 Year Price Score 105.11 *NYSE Composite Index=100 *12 Month Price Score 90.15

Interim Earnings (Per Share)

Qtr.	Mar	Jun	Sep	Dec
2001	0.59	0.63	0.75	0.72
2002	0.84	0.85	0.83	0.83
2003	0.83	0.80	1.09	0.78
2004	0.94	0.91	1.14	0.93

Interim Dividends (Per Share)

Amt	Decl	Ex	Rec	Pay
0.37Q	5/4/2004	5/20/2004	5/24/2004	6/7/2004
0.37Q	8/10/2004	8/19/2004	8/23/2004	9/7/2004
0.37Q	10/26/2004	11/18/2004	11/22/2004	12/6/2004
0.40Q	1/27/2005	2/17/2005	2/22/2005	3/7/2005

Indicated Div: $1.60

Valuation Analysis

Forecast P/E	9.50	No of Institutions	
	(4/7/2005)	207	
Market Cap	$2.0 Billion	Shares	
Book Value	N/A		38,208,856
Price/Book	N/A	% Held	
Price/Sales	1.28		75.65

Business Summary: Printing (MIC: 13.4 SIC: 782 NAIC: 23118)

Deluxe provides personal and business checks, business forms, labels, self-inking stamps, fraud prevention services and customer retention programs to banks, credit unions, financial services companies, consumers and small businesses. Co. reaches clients and customers through a number of distribution channels: the Internet, direct mail, the telephone and a nationwide sales force. Co. operates in three business segments: Financial Services; Direct Checks; and Business Services. Co. has facilities in the U.S., India, Canada and the U.K. Co.'s products and services are sold primarily in the U.S.

Recent Developments: For the year ended Dec 31 2004, income from continuing operations increased 3.2% to $198,648 thousand from income of $192,472 thousand a year earlier. Net income increased 2.9% to $197,991 thousand from net income of $192,472 thousand a year earlier. Revenues were $1,567,015 thousand, up 26.2% from $1,242,141 thousand the year before. Operating income was $347,912 thousand versus an income of $318,921 thousand in the prior year, an increase of 9.1%. Total direct expense was $535,949 thousand versus $425,965 thousand in the prior year, an increase of 25.8%. Total indirect expense was $683,154 thousand versus $497,255 thousand in the prior year, an increase of 37.4%.

Prospects: Co. is experiencing strong operating results, which includes contributions from the New England Business Services acquisition. Small Business Services is outperforming Co.'s expectations in delivering on anticipated integration cost synergies, and is also benefiting from cost management efforts. Co. will continue to focus on the integration process and implementing its plan for Small Business Services in 2005. Co. expects growth in this segment in 2006 and 2007 due to a larger customer base, expanded products and services, and additional synergy cost efficiencies. For full-year 2005, Co. expects earnings of approximately $3.30 per diluted share.

Financial Data

(US$ in Thousands)	12/31/2004	12/31/2003	12/31/2002	12/31/2001	12/31/2000	12/31/1999	12/31/1998	12/31/1997
Earnings Per Share	3.92	3.49	3.36	2.69	2.24	2.64	1.80	0.55
Cash Flow Per Share	6.12	3.33	4.09	3.96	3.50	2.88	3.66	3.61
Tang Book Value Per Share	...	...	N.M.	N.M.	0.55	2.89	5.15	5.44
Dividends Per Share	1.480	1.480	1.480	1.480	1.480	1.480	1.480	1.480
Dividend Payout %	37.76	42.41	44.05	55.02	66.07	56.06	82.22	269.09
Income Statement								
Total Revenue	1,567,015	1,242,141	1,283,983	1,278,375	1,262,712	1,650,500	1,931,796	1,919,366
EBITDA	442,210	378,334	403,331	374,732	352,836	417,071	340,597	221,241
Depn & Amortn	93,856	60,082	58,205	73,982	68,570	83,910	85,784	97,269
Income Before Taxes	316,873	299,380	340,722	297,534	273,429	324,655	246,540	115,150
Income Taxes	118,225	106,908	126,448	111,634	103,957	121,633	101,132	70,478
Net Income	197,991	192,472	214,274	185,900	161,936	203,022	145,408	44,672
Average Shares	50,549	55,228	63,747	69,115	72,420	77,009	80,855	81,957
Balance Sheet								
Current Assets	240,386	78,928	199,646	83,972	208,768	418,749	619,232	512,613
Total Assets	1,499,079	562,960	668,973	537,721	649,469	992,643	1,203,034	1,148,364
Current Liabilities	571,198	387,839	214,779	367,124	305,173	404,666	451,936	381,555
Long-Term Obligations	953,848	380,620	306,589	10,084	10,201	115,542	106,321	109,986
Total Liabilities	1,677,570	861,043	604,657	459,116	386,661	575,335	594,124	538,116
Stockholders' Equity	(178,491)	(298,083)	64,316	78,605	262,808	417,308	608,910	610,248
Shares Outstanding	50,265	50,173	61,445	64,101	72,555	72,019	80,481	81,326
Statistical Record								
Return on Assets %	19.15	31.25	35.51	31.32	19.67	18.49	12.37	3.84
Return on Equity %	...	...	299.85	108.90	47.49	39.57	23.85	6.75
EBITDA Margin %	28.22	30.46	31.41	29.31	27.94	25.27	17.63	11.53
Net Margin %	12.63	15.50	16.69	14.54	12.82	12.30	7.53	2.33
Asset Turnover	1.52	2.02	2.13	2.15	1.53	1.50	1.64	1.65
Current Ratio	0.42	0.20	0.93	0.23	0.68	1.03	1.37	1.34
Debt to Equity	...	...	4.77	0.13	0.04	0.28	0.17	0.18
Price Range	44.70-37.33	48.35-37.22	49.75-33.37	42.19-19.17	23.19-15.89	32.38-19.79	30.33-21.09	29.48-23.99
P/E Ratio	11.40-9.52	13.85-10.66	14.81-9.93	15.68-7.13	10.35-7.09	12.27-7.50	16.85-11.72	53.61-43.61
Average Yield %	3.60	3.51	3.37	4.99	7.78	5.52	5.54	5.61

Address: 3680 Victoria Street North, Shoreview, MN 55126-2966 **Telephone:** (651) 483-7111 **Fax:** (651) 483-7337	**Web Site:** www.deluxe.com **Officers:** Lawrence J. Mosner - Chmn., C.E.O. Ronald E. Eilers - Pres., C.O.O.	**Auditors:** PricewaterhouseCoopers LLP **Investor Contact:** 651-483-7358

DEVELOPERS DIVERSIFIED REALTY CORP.

Exchange	Symbol	Price	52Wk Range	Yield	P/E
NYS	DDR	$39.75 (3/31/2005)	45.85-31.47	5.43	17.75

*7 Year Price Score 149.57 *NYSE Composite Index=100 *12 Month Price Score 98.63

Interim Earnings (Per Share)

Qtr.	Mar	Jun	Sep	Dec
2001	0.29	0.40	0.24	0.24
2002	0.27	0.25	0.28	0.36
2003	0.37	0.66	0.28	0.95
2004	0.46	0.77	0.30	0.72

Interim Dividends (Per Share)

Amt	Decl	Ex	Rec	Pay
0.46Q	5/19/2004	6/17/2004	6/21/2004	7/6/2004
0.51Q	7/7/2004	9/16/2004	9/20/2004	10/4/2004
0.51Q	12/1/2004	12/22/2004	12/27/2004	1/6/2005
0.54Q	2/21/2005	3/17/2005	3/21/2005	4/4/2005
		Indicated Div: $2.16		

Valuation Analysis

Forecast P/E	12.21	No of Institutions	
	(4/7/2005)	233	
Market Cap	$4.3 Billion	Shares	
Book Value	2.6 Billion	80,082,688	
Price/Book	1.68	% Held	
Price/Sales	7.17	73.85	

Business Summary: Property, Real Estate & Development (MIC: 8.3 SIC: 798 NAIC: 25930)

Developers Diversified Realty is a self-administered and self-managed real estate investment trust primarily engaged in the business of acquiring, developing, redeveloping, owning, leasing and managing shopping centers and business centers. At Feb 27 2004, Co.'s portfolio included 347 shopping centers and 34 business centers, including 127 properties which are owned through joint ventures, and over 550 undeveloped acres primarily located adjacent to certain of the shopping centers. The shopping centers consist of 331 community shopping centers, 12 enclosed mini-malls and four lifestyle centers.

Recent Developments: For the year ended Dec 31 2004, income from continuing operations increased 7.4% to $177,826,000 from income of $165,643,000 a year earlier. Net income increased 12.3% to $269,762,000 from net income of $240,261,000 a year earlier. Revenues were $5,989,330,00, up 28.6% from $465,732,000 the year before. Operating income was $270,616,000 versus an income of $213,591,000 in the prior year, an increase of 26.7%.

Prospects: On Feb 28 2005, Co. announced it had sold interests in two community shopping centers located in Brookfield, WI and Brentwood, TN to Co.'s joint venture with Macquarie DDR Trust (MDT), an international investment bank and advisor and manager of specialized real estate funds in Australia. The two properties have a total purchase price of $51.6 million, which equates to a 7.4% cap rate. Co. also anticipates that over the next two months, MDT will acquire six additional community shopping centers, comprised of eight individual retail assets, from Co.'s consolidated portfolio for approximately $235.0 million subject to approval. This proposed pricing equates to a cap rate of about 7.25%.

Financial Data
(US$ in Thousands)

	12/31/2004	12/31/2003	12/31/2002	12/31/2001	12/31/2000	12/31/1999	12/31/1998	12/31/1997
Earnings Per Share	2.24	2.27	1.16	1.17	1.31	0.95	0.98	1.02
Cash Flow Per Share	3.02	3.21	3.30	3.16	2.61	2.50	2.41	1.82
Tang Book Value Per Share	16.90	12.35	9.63	8.92	8.75	9.22	9.77	9.38
Dividends Per Share	1.940	1.690	1.520	1.480	1.440	1.400	1.310	1.260
Dividend Payout %	86.61	74.45	131.03	126.50	109.92	147.37	133.67	122.93
Income Statement								
Property Income	568,631	446,231	333,569	294,209	262,685	241,625	213,999	158,718
Non-Property Income	30,302	29,866	23,674	28,030	23,108	22,308	14,169	10,322
Total Revenue	598,933	476,097	357,243	322,239	285,793	263,933	228,168	169,040
Depn & Amortn	139,947	101,733	82,200	66,915	56,083	53,968	44,654	33,712
Interest Expense	129,659	89,678	76,831	81,770	77,030	68,023	57,196	35,558
Income Taxes	1,469	...	...	...	...	...	...	...
Net Income	269,762	240,261	101,970	92,372	100,833	87,397	77,922	67,522
Average Shares	99,024	84,188	64,837	55,834	56,176	63,468	58,509	52,124
Balance Sheet								
Total Assets	5,583,547	3,941,151	2,776,852	2,497,207	2,332,021	2,320,860	2,126,524	1,391,918
Long-Term Obligations	2,718,690	2,083,131	1,498,798	1,308,301	1,227,575	1,152,051	1,000,481	668,521
Total Liabilities	3,029,228	2,327,081	1,831,291	1,663,193	1,312,469	1,252,604	1,082,811	722,868
Stockholders' Equity	2,554,319	1,614,070	945,561	834,014	783,750	852,345	902,785	669,050
Shares Outstanding	108,082	86,433	66,608	59,454	54,880	59,503	61,289	55,376
Statistical Record								
Return on Assets %	5.65	7.15	3.87	3.83	4.32	3.93	4.43	5.71
Return on Equity %	12.91	18.77	11.46	11.42	12.29	9.96	9.91	11.86
Net Margin %	45.04	50.46	28.54	28.67	35.28	33.11	34.15	39.94
Price Range	45.85-31.47	33.60-21.28	23.47-18.20	19.20-12.94	16.13-11.31	18.44-12.44	21.16-16.38	20.63-17.50
P/E Ratio	20.47-14.05	14.80-9.37	20.23-15.69	16.41-11.06	12.31-8.64	19.41-13.09	21.59-16.71	20.22-17.16
Average Yield %	5.17	6.12	7.10	8.86	10.51	9.27	9.26	6.59

Address: 3300 Enterprise Parkway, Beachwood, OH 44122	Web Site: www.ddrc.com	Auditors: PricewaterhouseCoopers LLP
Telephone: (216) 755-5500	**Officers:** Scott A. Wolstein - Chmn., C.E.O. David M. Jacobstein - Pres., C.O.O.	**Investor Contact:** 216-755-5500
Fax: (216) 755-1500		

DEVRY INC.

Exchange	Symbol	Price	52Wk Range	Yield	P/E
NYS	DV	$18.92 (3/31/2005)	32.20-14.22	N/A	46.15

*7 Year Price Score 72.41   ***NYSE Composite Index=100**   ***12 Month Price Score 79.23**

Interim Earnings (Per Share)

Qtr.	Sep	Dec	Mar	Jun
2001-02	0.20	0.26	0.26	0.23
2002-03	0.16	0.33	0.21	0.17
2003-04	0.15	0.22	0.23	0.22
2004-05	0.06	0.08	...	

Interim Dividends (Per Share)

No Dividends Paid

Valuation Analysis

Forecast P/E	31.79	No of Institutions
	(4/7/2005)	150
Market Cap	$1.3 Billion	Shares
Book Value	488.1 Million	55,420,788
Price/Book	2.73	% Held
Price/Sales	2.14	78.76

Business Summary: Vocational Education Services (MIC: 6.2 SIC: 299 NAIC: 11519)

DeVry operates an international system of degree-granting, career-oriented higher education schools and an international training firm. Devry University offers various undergraduate degrees in business, technology and management. The university's Keller Graduate School of Management offers graduate degree programs. Ross University, through its schools of Medicine and Veterinary Medicine, offer both doctor of medicine and doctor of veterinary medicine degrees. Becker Professional Review is an international training firm that offers preparatory coursework for the Certified Public Accountant, Certified Management Accountant and Chartered Financial Analyst exams.

Recent Developments: For the quarter ended Dec 31 2004, net income decreased 62.4% to $5,856 thousand from net income of $15,578 thousand in the year-earlier quarter. Revenues were $194,522 thousand, down 2.2% from $198,806 thousand the year before. Total direct expense was $108,236 thousand versus $104,635 thousand in the prior-year quarter, an increase of 3.4%. Total indirect expense was $76,663 thousand versus $70,156 thousand in the prior-year quarter, an increase of 9.3%.

Prospects: Co.'s results are being adversely affected by both a reduction in full-time campus enrollments during the 2004 fall term and increasing levels of part-time students at DeVry University Online and at DeVry University Centers. In addition, Co.'s earnings are being negatively affected by charges related to voluntary and involuntary work force reductions. These reductions are expected to reduce the costs of operations beginning in fiscal 2006. Meanwhile, Co. continues to execute its plan to improve products and services and address marketing and recruitment deficiencies. Co. believes that these activities will positively influence undergraduate enrollments in fiscal 2006.

Financial Data
(US$ in Thousands)

	6 Mos	3 Mos	06/30/2004	06/30/2003	06/30/2002	06/30/2001	06/30/2000	06/30/1999
Earnings Per Share	0.41	0.73	0.82	0.87	0.95	0.82	0.68	0.55
Cash Flow Per Share	1.05	0.35	1.91	1.40	1.65	1.22	1.02	0.79
Tang Book Value Per Share	1.77	1.64	1.54	0.45	3.94	2.95	2.17	1.98
Income Statement								
Total Revenue	382,918	188,396	784,885	679,579	648,134	568,177	506,824	420,635
EBITDA	38,055	16,579	143,762	128,069	144,972	126,459	104,734	81,194
Depn & Amortn	27,211	13,267	54,572	40,332	33,536	30,144	25,251	17,784
Income Before Taxes	10,844	3,312	81,356	86,457	110,629	95,915	78,074	63,110
Income Taxes	2,498	822	23,295	33,459	43,574	38,139	30,293	24,280
Net Income	10,156	4,300	58,061	61,148	67,055	57,776	47,781	38,830
Average Shares	70,507	70,677	70,757	70,336	70,594	70,662	70,390	70,454
Balance Sheet								
Current Assets	264,574	227,732	208,875	169,687	117,827	88,627	81,964	78,941
Total Assets	934,232	895,681	884,132	856,644	467,628	391,675	327,079	260,691
Current Liabilities	224,951	178,271	156,649	138,511	103,692	94,382	89,185	74,043
Long-Term Obligations	190,000	200,000	215,000	275,000	...	...	...	...
Total Liabilities	446,285	413,214	405,875	440,977	114,082	107,004	101,940	85,386
Stockholders' Equity	488,087	482,467	478,257	415,667	353,546	284,671	225,139	175,305
Shares Outstanding	70,368	70,365	70,021	70,021	69,898	69,755	69,642	69,414
Statistical Record								
Return on Assets %	3.13	0.48	6.65	9.23	15.61	16.08	16.21	16.03
Return on Equity %	6.25	0.89	12.95	15.90	21.01	22.67	23.80	24.93
EBITDA Margin %	9.94	8.80	18.32	18.85	22.37	22.26	20.66	19.30
Net Margin %	2.65	2.28	7.40	9.00	10.35	10.17	9.43	9.23
Asset Turnover	0.67	0.21	0.90	1.03	1.51	1.58	1.72	1.74
Current Ratio	1.18	1.28	1.33	1.23	1.14	0.94	0.92	1.07
Debt to Equity	0.39	0.41	0.45	0.66	...	...	...	...
Price Range	32.20-14.22	32.20-18.10	32.20-22.01	26.20-13.58	39.99-22.84	41.31-26.44	30.50-15.88	30.63-17.00
P/E Ratio	78.54-34.68	44.11-24.79	39.27-26.84	30.11-15.61	42.09-24.04	50.38-32.24	44.85-23.35	55.68-30.91

Address: One Tower Lane, Suite 1000, Oakbrook Terrace, IL 60181 **Telephone:** (630) 571-7700 **Fax:** (630) 571-0317	**Web Site:** www.devry.com **Officers:** Dennis J. Keller - Chmn., Co-C.E.O. Ronald L. Taylor - Pres., Co-C.E.O., C.O.O.	**Auditors:** PricewaterhouseCoopers LLP **Investor Contact:** 630-574-1949 **Transfer Agents:** Computershares Investor Services, L.L.C., Chicago, IL

DIAMOND OFFSHORE DRILLING, INC.

Exchange	Symbol	Price	52Wk Range	Yield	P/E
NYS	DO	$49.90 (3/31/2005)	50.89-21.55	0.50	N/A

*7 Year Price Score 92.50 *NYSE Composite Index=100 *12 Month Price Score 137.42

Interim Earnings (Per Share)

Qtr.	Mar	Jun	Sep	Dec
2001	0.27	0.32	0.38	0.29
2002	0.17	0.09	0.16	0.05
2003	(0.17)	(0.13)	(0.09)	0.01
2004	(0.08)	(0.08)	0.02	0.08

Interim Dividends (Per Share)

Amt	Decl	Ex	Rec	Pay
0.063Q	4/16/2004	4/29/2004	5/3/2004	6/1/2004
0.063Q	7/16/2004	7/29/2004	8/2/2004	9/1/2004
0.063Q	10/15/2004	10/28/2004	11/1/2004	12/1/2004
0.063Q	1/25/2005	1/28/2005	2/1/2005	3/1/2005

Indicated Div: $0.25

Valuation Analysis

Forecast P/E	34.14	No of Institutions
	(4/7/2005)	182
Market Cap	$6.4 Billion	Shares
Book Value	1.6 Billion	134,512,736
Price/Book	3.95	% Held
Price/Sales	7.88	N/A

Business Summary: Oil and Gas (MIC: 14.2 SIC: 381 NAIC: 13111)

Diamond Offshore Drilling is engaged principally in the contract drilling of offshore oil and gas wells. Co.'s fleet offers a range of services worldwide in various markets, including the deep water, harsh environment, conventional semisubmersible and the jack-up market. As of Dec 31 2003, Co.'s fleet of 45 offshore rigs consisted of 30 semisubmersibles, 14 jack-ups and one drillship. Principal markets for Co.'s operations are the U.S. Gulf of Mexico, the United Kingdom sector of the North Sea, South America, Africa, Australia and Southeast Asia.

Recent Developments: For the year ended Dec 31 2004, net loss was $7,243 thousand versus net loss of $48,414 thousand a year earlier. Revenues were $814,662 thousand, up 19.6% from $680,941 thousand the year before. Operating income was $3,928 thousand versus a loss of $38,323 thousand in the prior year. Total indirect expense was $807,508 thousand versus $720,602 thousand in the prior year, an increase of 12.1%.

Prospects: Co.'s outlook is encouraging. For instance, Co.'s drilling rigs continued to improve in the fourth quarter of 2004 and early in 2005. Particular strength was evident in the Gulf of Mexico (GOM) and the Southeast Asia floater markets, where effective industry utilization is near 100.0%. The market for jack-up rigs in the GOM has also continued to improve, with dayrates for Co.'s 300-ft. units in the high $40,000s to low $50,000s and dayrates for its 350-ft. jack-ups in the mid $50,000s range. Additionally, Co. recently signed two letters of intent for contracts totaling about $243.0 million and covering a total of 1,315 days. Both contracts are expected to commence in the second half of 2005.

Financial Data

(US$ in Thousands)	12/31/2004	12/31/2003	12/31/2002	12/31/2001	12/31/2000	12/31/1999	12/31/1998	12/31/1997
Earnings Per Share	(0.06)	(0.37)	0.47	1.26	0.53	1.11	2.66	1.93
Cash Flow Per Share	1.61	1.25	2.14	2.81	1.48	2.93	3.96	2.86
Tang Book Value Per Share	12.65	12.81	13.68	13.74	12.86	13.02	11.81	10.17
Dividends Per Share	0.250	0.438	0.500	0.500	0.500	0.500	0.500	0.140
Dividend Payout %	...	...	106.38	39.68	94.34	45.05	18.80	7.25
Income Statement								
Total Revenue	814,662	680,941	752,561	885,349	659,436	821,024	1,208,801	956,093
EBITDA	210,553	149,967	283,781	435,868	226,107	358,094	704,945	529,743
Depn & Amortn	196,034	192,283	193,791	185,980	154,493	143,504	130,792	108,791
Income Before Taxes	(3,533)	(54,237)	96,174	272,365	110,867	240,363	590,231	430,061
Income Taxes	3,710	(5,823)	33,654	90,820	38,586	84,292	206,572	151,456
Net Income	(7,243)	(48,414)	62,520	173,823	72,281	156,071	383,659	278,605
Average Shares	129,021	130,253	140,713	149,294	145,050	145,698	147,896	147,489
Balance Sheet								
Current Assets	1,195,681	835,263	1,033,756	1,427,415	1,100,957	860,292	938,424	718,775
Total Assets	3,379,386	3,135,019	3,258,765	3,502,517	3,079,506	2,681,029	2,609,716	2,298,561
Current Liabilities	613,907	100,000	118,402	335,016	123,013	135,401	160,401	131,245
Long-Term Obligations	709,413	928,030	924,475	920,636	856,559	400,000	400,000	400,000
Total Liabilities	1,753,558	1,454,539	1,451,251	1,649,371	1,311,653	838,807	854,458	763,034
Stockholders' Equity	1,625,828	1,680,480	1,807,514	1,853,146	1,767,853	1,842,222	1,755,258	1,535,527
Shares Outstanding	128,567	130,336	130,334	132,053	133,150	135,824	139,333	139,309
Statistical Record								
Return on Assets %	N.M.	N.M.	1.85	5.28	2.50	5.90	15.63	14.39
Return on Equity %	N.M.	N.M.	3.42	9.60	3.99	8.68	23.32	20.41
EBITDA Margin %	25.85	22.02	37.71	49.23	34.29	43.62	58.32	55.41
Net Margin %	N.M.	N.M.	8.31	19.63	10.96	19.01	31.74	29.14
Asset Turnover	0.25	0.21	0.22	0.27	0.23	0.31	0.49	0.49
Current Ratio	1.95	8.35	8.73	4.26	8.95	6.35	5.85	5.48
Debt to Equity	0.44	0.55	0.51	0.50	0.48	0.22	0.23	0.26
Price Range	40.29-20.48	23.62-17.15	34.74-17.90	45.04-23.43	47.13-26.50	40.44-20.50	54.63-20.69	66.75-27.69
P/E Ratio	...	...	73.91-38.09	35.75-18.60	88.92-50.00	36.43-18.47	20.54-7.78	34.59-14.35
Average Yield %	0.92	2.18	1.91	1.47	1.35	1.65	1.37	0.33

Address: 15415 Katy Freeway, Houston, TX 77094	**Web Site:** www.diamondoffshore.com	**Auditors:** Deloitte & Touche LLP
Telephone: (281) 492-5300	**Officers:** James S. Tisch - Chmn., C.E.O. Lawrence R. Dickerson - Pres., C.O.O.	**Investor Contact:** 281-492-5393
Fax: (281) 492-5316		

DIEBOLD, INC.

Exchange	Symbol	Price	52Wk Range	Yield	P/E	Div Acheiver
NYS	DBD	$54.85 (3/31/2005)	57.51-44.85	1.49	21.59	51 Years

*7 Year Price Score 118.42 *NYSE Composite Index=100 *12 Month Price Score 99.97

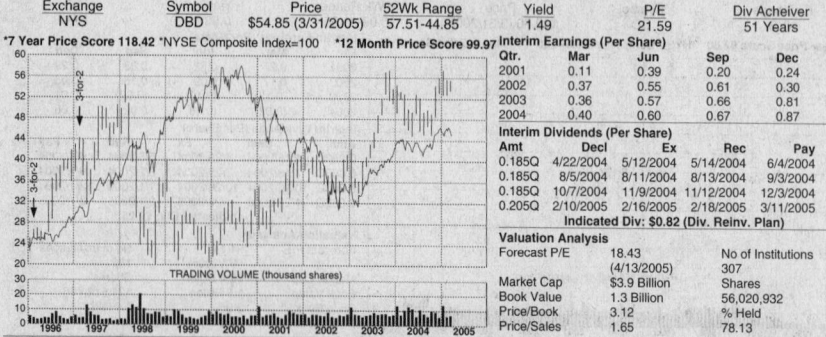

Interim Earnings (Per Share)

Qtr.	Mar	Jun	Sep	Dec
2001	0.11	0.39	0.20	0.24
2002	0.37	0.55	0.61	0.30
2003	0.36	0.57	0.66	0.81
2004	0.40	0.60	0.67	0.87

Interim Dividends (Per Share)

Amt	Decl	Ex	Rec	Pay
0.185Q	4/22/2004	5/12/2004	5/14/2004	6/4/2004
0.185Q	8/5/2004	8/11/2004	8/13/2004	9/3/2004
0.185Q	10/7/2004	11/9/2004	11/12/2004	12/3/2004
0.205Q	2/10/2005	2/16/2005	2/18/2005	3/11/2005

Indicated Div: $0.82 (Div. Reinv. Plan)

Valuation Analysis

Forecast P/E	18.43	No of Institutions
	(4/13/2005)	307
Market Cap	$3.9 Billion	Shares
Book Value	1.3 Billion	56,020,932
Price/Book	3.12	% Held
Price/Sales	1.65	78.13

Business Summary: Office Equipment Supplies (MIC: 11.12 SIC: 578 NAIC: 33313)

Diebold develops, manufactures, sells and services self-service transaction systems, electronic and physical security systems, software and various products used to equip bank facilities to global financial and commercial markets and electronic voting terminals and solutions to the government. Co.'s primary customers include banks and financial institutions, as well as hospitals, colleges and universities, public libraries, government agencies, utilities and various retail outlets. Sales of systems and equipment are made directly to customers by Co.' sales personnel and by manufacturer's representatives and distributors.

Recent Developments: For the year ended Dec 31 2004, net income increased 5.3% to $183,957 thousand from net income of $174,776 thousand a year earlier. Revenues were $2,380,910 thousand, up 12.9% from $2,109,673 thousand the year before. Operating income was $276,974 thousand versus an income of $257,357 thousand in the prior year, an increase of 7.6%. Total direct expense was $1,702,526 thousand versus $1,483,977 thousand in the prior year, an increase of 14.7%. Total indirect expense was $401,410 thousand versus $368,339 thousand in the prior year, an increase of 9.0%.

Prospects: Co. is encouraged by its continued strong order growth in financial self-service and security. Also, Co. is pleased with the performance in U.S. product and service margins excluding election losses. However, Co. is disappointed with margins in Western Europe, where Opteva has not fully completed customer certifications. Co. is making significant strides in achieving certification for Opteva in Western Europe and anticipates key certifications will be achieved by the end of the first quarter. Meanwhile, Co. continues to experience significant pricing pressures. Accordingly, Co. will take aggressive actions in 2005 to better align its resources and cost structure to become more competitive.

Financial Data

(US$ in Thousands)	12/31/2004	12/31/2003	12/31/2002	12/31/2001	12/31/2000	12/31/1999	12/31/1998	12/31/1997
Earnings Per Share	2.54	2.40	1.37	0.93	1.92	1.85	1.10	1.76
Cash Flow Per Share	3.22	2.90	2.27	2.16	2.04	2.72	2.57	1.61
Tang Book Value Per Share	11.84	11.24	9.32	8.79	8.94	9.63	9.87	9.69
Dividends Per Share	0.740	0.680	0.660	0.640	0.620	0.600	0.560	0.500
Dividend Payout %	29.13	28.33	48.18	68.82	32.29	32.43	50.91	28.41
Income Statement								
Total Revenue	2,380,910	2,109,673	1,940,163	1,760,297	1,743,608	1,259,177	1,185,707	1,226,936
EBITDA	354,583	330,609	306,526	157,960	257,939	236,047	145,456	204,360
Depn & Amortn	74,983	64,301	61,296	45,453	35,901	34,709	25,649	18,701
Income Before Taxes	268,943	257,023	218,551	99,839	204,357	201,338	119,807	185,659
Income Taxes	84,986	82,247	86,250	32,946	67,438	72,482	43,659	63,143
Net Income	183,957	174,776	99,154	66,893	136,919	128,856	76,148	122,516
Average Shares	72,534	72,924	72,297	71,783	71,479	69,562	69,310	69,490
Balance Sheet								
Current Assets	1,234,632	1,105,159	924,888	952,426	804,363	647,936	543,548	549,837
Total Assets	2,135,552	1,900,502	1,625,081	1,651,913	1,585,427	1,298,831	1,004,188	991,050
Current Liabilities	728,623	618,653	564,962	658,018	566,792	382,407	235,533	242,080
Long-Term Obligations	...	...	...	20,800	20,800	20,800	20,800	20,800
Total Liabilities	875,077	752,264	684,258	748,803	649,361	454,436	305,065	322,469
Stockholders' Equity	1,260,475	1,148,238	940,823	903,110	936,066	844,395	699,123	668,581
Shares Outstanding	71,592	72,649	72,111	71,356	71,547	71,096	68,880	69,005
Statistical Record								
Return on Assets %	9.09	9.91	6.05	4.13	9.47	11.19	7.63	13.24
Return on Equity %	15.23	16.73	10.75	7.27	15.34	16.70	11.14	19.69
EBITDA Margin %	14.89	15.67	15.80	8.97	14.79	18.75	12.27	16.66
Net Margin %	7.73	8.28	5.11	3.80	7.85	10.23	6.42	9.99
Asset Turnover	1.18	1.20	1.18	1.09	1.21	1.09	1.19	1.33
Current Ratio	1.69	1.79	1.64	1.45	1.42	1.69	2.31	2.27
Debt to Equity	...	...	...	0.02	0.02	0.02	0.03	0.03
Price Range	56.06-44.85	57.43-33.94	42.41-31.00	41.00-25.96	34.56-21.63	39.88-20.50	54.50-20.13	50.63-31.50
P/E Ratio	22.07-17.66	23.93-14.14	30.96-22.63	44.09-27.91	18.00-11.26	21.55-11.08	49.55-18.30	28.76-17.90
Average Yield %	1.48	1.52	1.76	1.93	2.24	2.22	1.59	1.16

Address: 5995 Mayfair Road, North Canton, OH 44720-8077	**Web Site:** www.diebold.com	**Auditors:** KPMG LLP
Telephone: (330) 490-4000	**Officers:** Walden W. O'Dell - Chmn., C.E.O. Eric C. Evans - Pres., C.O.O.	**Investor Contact:** 330-490-5900
Fax: (330) 588-3794		**Transfer Agents:** The Bank of New York, New York, NY

DILLARD'S INC.

Exchange	Symbol	Price	52Wk Range	Yield	P/E
NYS	DDS	$26.90 (3/31/2005)	27.54-15.54	0.59	37.89

*7 Year Price Score 91.40 *NYSE Composite Index=100 *12 Month Price Score 105.10

Interim Earnings (Per Share)

Qtr.	Apr	Jul	Oct	Jan
2001-02	0.34	(0.22)	(0.48)	1.63
2002-03	0.69	0.08	(0.06)	0.84
2003-04	0.29	(0.60)	(0.19)	0.61
2004-05	0.64	(0.31)	(0.23)	...

Interim Dividends (Per Share)

Amt	Decl	Ex	Rec	Pay
0.04Q	5/25/2004	6/28/2004	6/30/2004	8/2/2004
0.04Q	9/7/2004	9/28/2004	9/30/2004	11/1/2004
0.04Q	12/6/2004	12/29/2004	12/31/2004	2/1/2005
0.04Q	3/11/2005	3/29/2005	3/31/2005	5/2/2005

Indicated Div: $0.16

Valuation Analysis

Forecast P/E	28.23 (4/7/2005)	No of Institutions	192
Market Cap	$2.2 Billion	Shares	68,041,216
Book Value	2.2 Billion	% Held	87.10
Price/Book	1.00		
Price/Sales	0.28		

Business Summary: Retail - General (MIC: 5.2 SIC: 311 NAIC: 52111)

Dillard's operates a chain of retail department stores located primarily in the Southwest, Southeast and Midwest regions of the United States. As of Jan 31 2004, Co. operated 328 stores in 29 states. Co. offers merchandise aimed at middle to upper-middle income consumers, with an emphasis on brand names, fashion-oriented apparel, cosmetics, accessories, and home furnishings. Co.'s major product categories include cosmetics, women's and juniors' clothing, children's clothing, men's clothing and accessories, shoes, accessories and lingerie, and home products.

Recent Developments: For the quarter ended Oct 30 2004, net loss decreased 18.0% to $18,688 thousand from net loss of $15,835 thousand in the year-earlier quarter. Revenues were $1,755,147 thousand, down 3.6% from $1,820,436 thousand the year before. Total indirect expense was $643,452 thousand versus $645,128 thousand in the prior-year quarter, a decrease of 0.3%.

Prospects: Co.'s outlook appears mixed. For the 13 weeks ended Jan 29 2005, sales were unchanged on a percentage basis in both total and comparable stores. However, Co. noted that gross margin for the period improved 140 basis points as a percentage of sales as a result of its efforts to strengthen its merchandise mix. Gross margin gains were driven by higher levels of markups combined with lower levels of markdowns. Separately, Co. has announced plans to close its Harding Mall location in Nashville, TN and its Westgate Shopping Center location in Cleveland in the spring of 2005. Co. plans to open nine new Dillard's locations during 2005.

Financial Data
(US$ in Thousands)

	9 Mos	6 Mos	3 Mos	01/31/2004	02/01/2003	02/02/2002	02/03/2001	01/29/2000
Earnings Per Share	0.71	0.74	0.46	0.11	(4.67)	0.85	(0.06)	1.55
Cash Flow Per Share	6.38	5.88	7.55	5.18	4.24	7.35	8.60	6.76
Tang Book Value Per Share	26.43	26.54	26.95	26.35	26.25	25.02	24.05	22.50
Dividends Per Share	0.160	0.160	0.160	0.160	0.160	0.160	0.160	0.160
Dividend Payout %	22.60	21.52	34.54	145.45	...	18.82	...	10.32
Income Statement								
Total Revenue	5,397,081	3,641,934	1,911,879	7,863,668	8,233,939	8,388,339	8,817,785	8,921,237
EBITDA	240,656	194,107	159,539	494,260	699,585	615,670	671,279	816,389
Depn & Amortn	226,521	150,769	75,532	297,201	305,545	313,711	306,096	295,874
Income Before Taxes	14,135	43,338	84,007	15,994	211,100	111,571	140,860	283,949
Income Taxes	5,090	15,605	30,245	6,650	74,800	45,785	44,030	120,220
Net Income	9,045	27,733	53,762	9,344	(398,405)	71,798	(5,850)	163,729
Average Shares	82,894	83,738	83,871	83,900	85,316	84,020	91,171	105,617
Balance Sheet								
Current Assets	3,309,357	2,875,006	3,155,526	3,023,691	3,130,251	2,814,510	2,842,948	3,423,725
Total Assets	6,659,664	6,230,001	6,510,177	6,411,097	6,675,932	7,074,559	7,199,309	7,918,204
Current Liabilities	2,116,073	1,224,139	1,393,796	1,336,087	886,461	928,071	876,697	810,594
Long-Term Obligations	1,366,776	1,772,223	1,869,165	1,872,776	2,211,606	2,145,036	2,396,577	2,919,275
Total Liabilities	4,452,205	3,963,097	4,222,381	4,174,000	4,411,736	4,406,162	4,569,489	5,085,370
Stockholders' Equity	2,207,459	2,266,904	2,287,796	2,237,097	2,264,196	2,668,397	2,629,820	2,832,834
Shares Outstanding	82,127	84,026	83,516	83,490	84,757	83,887	85,000	98,778
Statistical Record								
Return on Assets %	0.88	0.98	0.58	0.14	N.M.	1.01	N.M.	2.04
Return on Equity %	2.73	2.79	1.71	0.42	N.M.	2.72	N.M.	5.79
EBITDA Margin %	4.46	5.33	8.34	6.29	8.50	7.34	7.61	9.15
Net Margin %	0.17	0.76	2.81	0.12	N.M.	0.86	N.M.	1.84
Asset Turnover	1.14	1.23	1.17	1.21	1.20	1.18	1.15	1.11
Current Ratio	1.56	2.35	2.26	2.26	3.53	3.03	3.24	4.22
Debt to Equity	0.62	0.78	0.82	0.84	0.98	0.80	0.91	1.03
Price Range	23.76-14.46	23.76-13.98	19.16-12.77	17.86-12.49	30.47-12.94	22.00-12.63	19.75-9.50	36.56-18.00
P/E Ratio	33.46-20.37	32.11-18.89	41.65-27.76	62.36-113.55	...	25.88-14.86	...	23.59-11.61
Average Yield %	0.85	0.92	1.02	1.09	0.74	0.98	1.16	0.63

Address: 1600 Cantrell Road, Little Rock, AR 72201
Telephone: (501) 376 5200
Fax: (501) 376 5917

Web Site: www.dillards.com
Officers: William Dillard II - Chmn., C.E.O. Alex Dillard - Pres.

Auditors: Deloitte & Touche LLP
Investor Contact: 501-376-5965

DISNEY (WALT) CO. (THE)

Exchange	Symbol	Price	52Wk Range	Yield	P/E
NYS	DIS	$28.73 (3/31/2005)	29.88-20.89	N/A	25.42

*7 Year Price Score 80.25   *NYSE Composite Index=100   *12 Month Price Score 104.82

Interim Earnings (Per Share)

Qtr.	Dec	Mar	Jun	Sep
2002-03	0.13	0.11	0.20	0.19
2003-04	0.33	0.26	0.29	0.24
2004-05	0.35	...	...	...

Interim Dividends (Per Share)

Dividend Payment Suspended

Valuation Analysis

Forecast P/E	21.95	No of Institutions
	(4/7/2005)	855
Market Cap	$57.4 Billion	Shares
Book Value	26.3 Billion	1,354,368,768
Price/Book	2.18	% Held
Price/Sales	1.87	66.15

Business Summary: Sporting & Recreational (MIC: 13.5 SIC: 996 NAIC: 13110)

The Walt Disney Company, together with its subsidiaries, is a entertainment company with operations in four business segments: Media Networks, Parks and Resorts, Studio Entertainment and Consumer Products. Co. is an international entertainment company. Co.'s Media Networks division includes its broadcasting and cable networks. The Studio Entertainment division includes theatrical films and home video. The Parks and Resorts division includes Walt Disney World Resort, Disney Regional Entertainment, and Anaheim Sports, Inc. The Consumer Products division includes character merchandise and publications licensing, The Disney Stores, and books and magazines.

Recent Developments: For the quarter ended Jan 1 2005, net income increased 5.1% to $723,000 thousand from net income of $688,000 thousand in the year-earlier quarter. Revenues were $8,666,000 thousand, up 1.4% from $8,549,000 thousand the year before. Total direct expense was $7,492,000 thousand versus $7,384,000 thousand in the prior-year quarter, an increase of 1.5%.

Prospects: Results are being positively affected by improved profitability from the Media Networks and Parks and Resorts segments, partially offset by lower earnings in the Studio Entertainment segment due primarily to a decline in DVD sales. Meanwhile, Co. anticipates double-digit earnings growth in 2005, driven by improved ratings at ABC, continued strong ESPN performance, and increased theme park attendance. Looking ahead, results may benefit from Co.'s efforts to grow its international operations. Co. is taking steps to launch its Disney Channel television programming in India, China, and eventually Russia. In addition, Co. plans to open a new theme park in Hong Kong later in 2005.

Financial Data

(US$ in Thousands)	3 Mos	09/30/2004	09/30/2003	09/30/2002	09/30/2001	09/30/2000	09/30/1999	09/30/1998
Earnings Per Share	1.13	1.12	0.62	0.60	(0.02)	0.57	0.62	0.89
Cash Flow Per Share	2.19	2.13	1.42	1.12	1.43	3.03	2.72	2.51
Tang Book Value Per Share	3.29	3.15	2.01	1.78	4.03	3.78	2.55	1.35
Dividends Per Share	...	...	...	0.210	0.210	0.210	0.052	0.193
Dividend Payout %	...	...	...	35.00	N.M.	36.84	8.47	21.72
Income Statement								
Total Revenue	8,666,000	30,752,000	27,061,000	25,329,000	25,269,000	25,402,000	23,402,000	22,976,000
EBITDA	2,380,000	5,566,000	4,124,000	3,232,000	3,037,000	5,386,000	4,233,000	5,019,000
Depn & Amortn	1,098,000	1,210,000	1,077,000	1,042,000	1,754,000	2,195,000	1,307,000	1,240,000
Income Before Taxes	1,142,000	3,739,000	2,254,000	2,190,000	1,283,000	2,633,000	2,314,000	3,157,000
Income Taxes	393,000	1,197,000	789,000	853,000	1,059,000	1,606,000	1,014,000	1,307,000
Net Income	723,000	2,345,000	1,267,000	1,236,000	(158,000)	920,000	1,300,000	1,850,000
Average Shares	2,107,000	2,106,000	2,067,000	2,044,000	2,143,000	2,148,000	2,083,000	2,079,000
Balance Sheet								
Current Assets	10,378,000	9,369,000	8,314,000	7,849,000	7,029,000	10,007,000	10,200,000	9,375,000
Total Assets	55,449,000	53,902,000	49,988,000	50,045,000	43,699,000	45,027,000	43,679,000	41,378,000
Current Liabilities	11,264,000	11,059,000	8,669,000	7,819,000	6,219,000	8,402,000	7,707,000	7,525,000
Long-Term Obligations	10,309,000	9,734,000	10,987,000	12,825,000	8,940,000	6,959,000	9,278,000	9,562,000
Total Liabilities	29,113,000	27,821,000	26,197,000	26,600,000	21,027,000	20,927,000	22,704,000	21,990,000
Stockholders' Equity	26,336,000	26,081,000	23,791,000	23,445,000	22,672,000	24,100,000	20,975,000	19,388,000
Shares Outstanding	1,998,000	1,998,400	2,013,300	2,018,600	2,018,600	2,114,300	2,071,000	2,690,000
Statistical Record								
Return on Assets %	4.43	4.50	2.53	2.64	N.M.	2.07	3.06	4.67
Return on Equity %	9.40	9.38	5.36	5.36	N.M.	4.07	6.44	10.09
EBITDA Margin %	27.46	18.10	15.24	12.76	12.02	21.20	18.09	21.84
Net Margin %	8.34	7.63	4.68	4.88	N.M.	3.62	5.56	8.05
Asset Turnover	0.57	0.59	0.54	0.54	0.57	0.57	0.55	0.58
Current Ratio	0.92	0.85	0.96	1.00	1.13	1.19	1.32	1.25
Debt to Equity	0.39	0.37	0.46	0.55	0.39	0.29	0.44	0.49
Price Range	28.00-20.89	28.00-20.17	22.56-14.14	25.00-13.77	41.38-16.98	43.63-23.50	38.00-23.50	42.38-24.44
P/E Ratio	24.78-18.49	25.00-18.01	36.39-22.81	41.67-22.95	N/A	76.54-41.23	61.29-37.90	47.61-27.46
Average Yield %	...	...	...	1.03	0.70	0.59	0.17	0.57

Address: 500 South Buena Vista Street, Burbank, CA 91521 **Telephone:** (818) 560-1000	**Web Site:** www.disney.com **Officers:** George J. Mitchell - Chmn. Michael D. Eisner - C.E.O.	**Auditors:** PricewaterhouseCoopers LLP

DOLLAR GENERAL CORP. (TN)

Exchange	Symbol	Price	52Wk Range	Yield	P/E
NYS	DG	$21.91 (3/31/2005)	22.50-17.32	0.73	23.31

*7 Year Price Score 93.83   *NYSE Composite Index=100   *12 Month Price Score 101.71

Interim Earnings (Per Share)

Qtr.	Apr	Jul	Oct	Jan
2001-02	0.11	0.08	0.14	0.29
2002-03	0.14	0.13	0.20	0.32
2003-04	0.18	0.18	0.23	0.30
2004-05	0.20	0.22	0.22	...

Interim Dividends (Per Share)

Amt	Decl	Ex	Rec	Pay
0.04Q	5/25/2004	6/29/2004	7/1/2004	7/15/2004
0.04Q	8/24/2004	9/28/2004	9/30/2004	10/14/2004
0.04Q	12/1/2004	12/28/2004	12/30/2004	1/13/2005
0.04Q	3/16/2005	3/29/2005	3/31/2005	4/14/2005

Indicated Div: $0.16

Valuation Analysis

Forecast P/E	18.76 (4/7/2005)	No of Institutions	299
Market Cap	$7.2 Billion	Shares	231,532,752
Book Value	1.6 Billion	% Held	70.66
Price/Book	4.55		
Price/Sales	0.96		

Business Summary: Retail - General (MIC: 5.2 SIC: 331 NAIC: 52990)

Dollar General sells general merchandise through a chain of 6,817 stores in 29 states as of Feb 27 2004. Co. also operates seven distribution centers in Florida, Kentucky, Mississippi, Missouri, Ohio, Oklahoma and Virginia. Co. offers hard goods, including health and beauty aids, home cleaning supplies, housewares, stationery, and seasonal goods. Co. also markets soft goods, including apparel for the whole family, shoes, and domestics. Co. also sells manufacturers' overruns, closeouts, and "irregulars" at a discount from regular prices. Co. emphasizes even-dollar pricing of its merchandise, most of which is priced at $10 or less.

Recent Developments: For the quarter ended Oct 29 2004, net income decreased 8.7% to $71,126 thousand from net income of $77,903 thousand in the year-earlier quarter. Revenues were $1,879,187 thousand, up 11.5% from $1,685,346 thousand the year before. Operating income was $113,956 thousand versus an income of $131,346 thousand in the prior-year quarter, a decrease of 13.2%. Total indirect expense was $440,029 thousand versus $385,551 thousand in the prior-year quarter, an increase of 14.1%.

Prospects: Co. expects diluted earnings per share of between $1.14 and $1.19 for fiscal 2005, including a charge of about $0.01 per share in the second half of 2005 relating to the expensing of stock options. Co.'s operating initiatives for 2005 include opening approximately 730 new stores, including at least 30 Dollar General Market stores, and continuing its western expansion and expanding the Market concept to new geographic areas; completing construction of the Jonesville, SC distribution center, scheduled to open in June 2005; identifying the location for and begin construction of its ninth distribution center; and improving inventory management, including maintaining high store in-stock levels.

Financial Data

(US$ in Thousands)	9 Mos	6 Mos	3 Mos	01/30/2004	01/31/2003	02/01/2002	02/02/2001	01/28/2000
Earnings Per Share	0.94	0.95	0.91	0.89	0.79	0.62	0.21	0.65
Cash Flow Per Share	1.13	1.29	1.71	1.55	1.31	0.80	0.64	0.46
Tang Book Value Per Share	4.81	4.69	4.51	4.69	3.86	3.13	2.60	2.80
Dividends Per Share	0.155	0.150	0.145	0.140	0.128	0.128	0.122	0.097
Dividend Payout %	16.45	15.76	15.90	15.73	16.20	20.65	57.90	15.01
Income Statement								
Total Revenue	5,463,389	3,584,202	1,747,959	6,871,992	6,100,404	5,322,895	4,550,571	3,887,964
EBITDA	459,514	303,373	154,186	663,662	592,224	496,578	265,403	413,246
Depn & Amortn	122,882	80,697	39,636	152,399	134,959	122,967	111,399	63,944
Income Before Taxes	319,785	212,193	108,108	479,760	414,626	327,822	108,647	344,145
Income Taxes	109,488	73,022	40,259	178,760	149,680	120,309	38,005	124,718
Net Income	210,297	139,171	67,849	301,000	264,946	207,513	70,642	219,427
Average Shares	330,313	330,298	337,257	337,636	335,050	335,017	333,858	336,962
Balance Sheet								
Current Assets	1,722,234	1,586,642	1,629,658	1,652,215	1,323,908	1,556,047	1,124,927	1,095,535
Total Assets	2,828,017	2,655,005	2,673,769	2,652,709	2,333,153	2,552,385	2,282,462	1,450,941
Current Liabilities	848,659	780,869	853,417	743,802	664,501	1,133,551	537,935	472,297
Long-Term Obligations	321,194	259,000	261,621	265,337	330,337	339,470	720,764	1,200
Total Liabilities	1,250,527	1,116,129	1,185,686	1,075,789	1,045,085	1,510,667	1,420,699	525,020
Stockholders' Equity	1,577,490	1,538,876	1,488,083	1,576,920	1,288,068	1,041,718	861,763	925,921
Shares Outstanding	327,668	328,399	329,695	336,190	333,340	332,606	331,198	330,865
Statistical Record								
Return on Assets %	11.59	12.77	12.29	12.11	10.88	8.61	3.72	16.53
Return on Equity %	20.39	21.80	21.88	21.07	22.81	21.86	7.78	26.64
EBITDA Margin %	8.41	8.46	8.82	9.66	9.71	9.33	5.83	10.63
Net Margin %	3.85	3.88	3.88	4.38	4.34	3.90	1.55	5.64
Asset Turnover	2.75	2.89	2.81	2.76	2.50	2.21	2.40	2.93
Current Ratio	2.03	2.03	1.91	2.22	1.99	1.37	2.09	2.32
Debt to Equity	0.20	0.17	0.18	0.17	0.26	0.33	0.84	N.M.
Price Range	23.10-17.32	23.10-17.32	23.10-14.54	22.94-9.78	19.46-10.68	23.88-11.25	23.06-13.50	25.80-15.60
P/E Ratio	24.57-18.43	24.32-18.23	25.38-15.98	25.78-10.99	24.63-13.52	38.52-18.15	109.82-64.29	39.69-24.00
Average Yield %	0.77	0.74	0.73	0.78	0.85	0.75	0.67	0.46

Address: 100 Mission Ridge, Goodlettsville, TN 37072 **Telephone:** (615) 855-4000 **Fax:** (615) 855-5527	**Web Site:** www.dollargeneral.com **Officers:** David A. Perdue Jr. - Chmn., C.E.O. Lawrence V. Jackson - Pres., C.O.O.	**Auditors:** Ernst & Young LLP **Investor Contact:** 615-855-5525

DOMINION RESOURCES INC

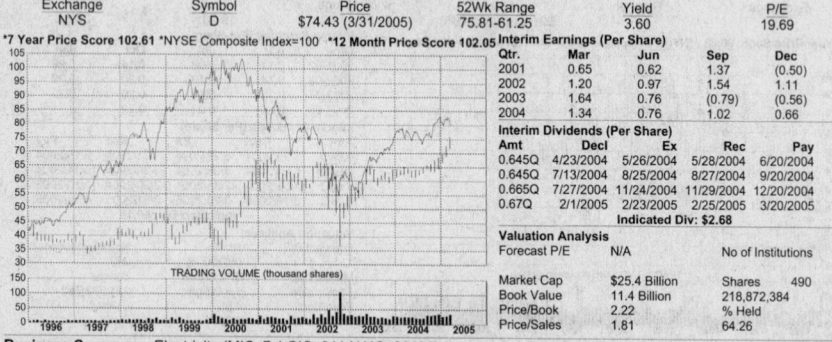

Exchange	Symbol	Price	52Wk Range	Yield	P/E
NYS	D	$74.43 (3/31/2005)	75.81-61.25	3.60	19.69

*7 Year Price Score 102.61 *NYSE Composite Index=100 *12 Month Price Score 102.05

Interim Earnings (Per Share)

Qtr.	Mar	Jun	Sep	Dec
2001	0.65	0.62	1.37	(0.50)
2002	1.20	0.97	1.54	1.11
2003	1.64	0.76	(0.79)	(0.56)
2004	1.34	0.76	1.02	0.66

Interim Dividends (Per Share)

Amt	Decl	Ex	Rec	Pay
0.645Q	4/23/2004	5/26/2004	5/28/2004	6/20/2004
0.645Q	7/13/2004	8/25/2004	8/27/2004	9/20/2004
0.665Q	7/27/2004	11/24/2004	11/29/2004	12/20/2004
0.67Q	2/1/2005	2/23/2005	2/25/2005	3/20/2005
		Indicated Div: $2.68		

Valuation Analysis

Forecast P/E	N/A	No of Institutions
Market Cap	$25.4 Billion	Shares 490
Book Value	11.4 Billion	218,872,384
Price/Book	2.22	% Held
Price/Sales	1.81	64.26

Business Summary: Electricity (MIC: 7.1 SIC: 911 NAIC: 21121)

Dominion Resources is a fully integrated gas and electric holding company with operations conducted through four business lines. Dominion Energy manages Co.'s electric and gas transmission operations, certain gas production and storage operations, energy trading, marketing, hedging and arbitrage activities. Dominion Delivery manages Co.'s electric and gas distribution systems and customer services operations, as well as retail energy marketing operations. Dominion Exploration and Production manages Co.'s gas and oil exploration, development and production operations. Dominion Generation manages the generation of Co.'s electric utility and merchant fleet and its power purchase agreements.

Recent Developments: For the year ended Dec 31 2004, net income increased 292.8% to $1,249,000 thousand from net income of $318,000 thousand a year earlier. Revenues were $13,972,000 thousand, up 15.7% from $12,078,000 thousand the year before. Operating income was $2,717,000 thousand versus an income of $2,561,000 thousand in the prior year, an increase of 6.1%. Total direct expense was $6,683,000 thousand versus $4,917,000 thousand in the prior year, an increase of 35.9%. Total indirect expense was $4,572,000 thousand versus $4,600,000 thousand in the prior year, a decrease of 0.6%.

Prospects: On Mar 4 2005, Co. agreed to sell UBS Investment Bank 76.40 billion cubic feet of natural gas. Under the terms of the volumetric production payment (VPP) agreement, Co. will receive $424.4 million in cash for a fixed-term overriding royalty interest in more than 2,900 producing natural gas wells. Co., which plans to use proceeds from the deal to pay down debt, will retain control of the properties. Going forward, Co. expects to produce first-quarter 2005 operating earnings in the range of $1.35 to $1.45 per share. Co. noted that it expects a $40.0 million to $45.0 million charge related to the pending acquisition of the Panda non-utility power plant, expected to close in the first quarter.

Financial Data

(US$ in Thousands)	12/31/2004	12/31/2003	12/31/2002	12/31/2001	12/31/2000	12/31/1999	12/31/1998	12/31/1997
Earnings Per Share	3.78	1.00	4.82	2.15	1.85	1.48	2.75	2.15
Cash Flow Per Share	8.60	7.42	8.71	9.65	5.69	6.56	6.19	6.82
Tang Book Value Per Share	20.93	19.19	18.18	15.71	14.20	24.80	26.56	16.55
Dividends Per Share	2.600	2.580	2.580	2.580	2.580	2.580	2.580	2.580
Dividend Payout %	68.78	258.00	53.53	120.00	139.46	174.32	93.82	120.00
Income Statement								
Total Revenue	13,972,000	12,078,000	10,218,000	10,558,000	9,260,000	5,520,000	6,086,200	7,677,600
EBITDA	4,320,000	3,729,000	4,248,000	3,135,000	2,826,000	2,133,000	2,277,800	2,211,900
Depn & Amortn	1,433,000	1,334,000	1,379,000	1,322,000	1,268,000	798,000	826,200	905,700
Income Before Taxes	1,964,000	1,546,000	2,043,000	914,000	600,000	828,000	868,900	678,800
Income Taxes	700,000	597,000	681,000	370,000	183,000	259,000	306,000	233,000
Net Income	1,249,000	318,000	1,362,000	544,000	436,000	296,000	535,600	399,200
Average Shares	330,500	318,800	281,000	252,500	235,900	191,400	194,900	...
Balance Sheet								
Net PPE	26,716,000	25,850,000	20,257,000	18,681,000	14,849,000	10,764,000	10,636,600	12,532,600
Total Assets	45,446,000	44,186,000	37,909,000	34,369,000	29,348,000	17,747,000	17,517,000	20,192,700
Long-Term Obligations	15,507,000	15,776,000	12,060,000	12,119,000	10,101,000	6,936,000	5,070,900	7,196,000
Total Liabilities	33,763,000	33,391,000	26,042,000	24,485,000	21,461,000	12,002,000	10,816,200	13,675,300
Stockholders' Equity	11,426,000	10,538,000	10,213,000	8,368,000	6,992,000	4,752,000	5,315,900	5,040,500
Shares Outstanding	340,591	325,000	308,000	264,700	245,800	186,300	194,500	187,800
Statistical Record								
Return on Assets %	2.78	0.77	3.77	1.71	1.85	1.68	2.84	2.27
Return on Equity %	11.34	3.06	14.66	7.08	7.40	5.88	10.34	8.01
EBITDA Margin %	30.92	30.87	41.57	29.69	30.52	38.64	37.43	28.81
Net Margin %	8.94	2.63	13.33	5.15	4.71	5.36	8.80	5.20
PPE Turnover	0.53	0.52	0.52	0.63	0.72	0.52	0.53	0.67
Asset Turnover	0.31	0.29	0.28	0.33	0.39	0.31	0.32	0.44
Debt to Equity	1.36	1.50	1.18	1.45	1.44	1.46	0.95	1.43
Price Range	68.45-61.25	65.66-51.84	66.85-36.49	69.56-56.00	67.25-35.13	48.63-36.94	48.19-38.50	42.69-33.38
P/E Ratio	18.11-16.20	65.66-51.84	13.87-7.57	32.35-26.05	36.35-18.99	32.85-24.96	17.52-14.00	19.85-15.52
Average Yield %	4.05	4.33	4.44	4.14	5.32	5.94	6.10	6.89

Address: 120 Tredegar Street, Richmond, VA 23219	Web Site: www.dom.com	Auditors: Deloitte & Touche LLP
Telephone: (804) 819-2000	Officers: Thomas E. Capps - Chmn., C.E.O. Thomas F. Farrell II - Pres., C.O.O.	Investor Contact: 804-819-2150
Fax: (804) 775-5819		Transfer Agents: Dominion Resources Services, Inc

DONALDSON CO. INC.

Exchange	Symbol	Price	52Wk Range	Yield	P/E
NYS	DCI	$32.28 (3/31/2005)	33.97-25.24	0.74	26.03

*7 Year Price Score 143.57 *NYSE Composite Index=100 *12 Month Price Score 101.27

Interim Earnings (Per Share)

Qtr.	Oct	Jan	Apr	Jul
2001-02	0.22	0.23	0.23	0.28
2002-03	0.25	0.23	0.28	0.29
2003-04	0.28	0.28	0.33	0.29
2004-05	0.31	0.31	...	...

Interim Dividends (Per Share)

Amt	Decl	Ex	Rec	Pay
0.055Q	5/19/2004	6/3/2004	6/7/2004	6/17/2004
0.055Q	7/30/2004	8/18/2004	8/20/2004	9/10/2004
0.06Q	11/19/2004	11/24/2004	11/29/2004	12/10/2004
0.06Q	1/21/2005	2/16/2005	2/18/2005	3/11/2005

Indicated Div: $0.24

Valuation Analysis

Forecast P/E	23.36	No of Institutions
	(4/7/2005)	206
Market Cap	$2.7 Billion	Shares
Book Value	537.0 Million	53,223,960
Price/Book	5.03	% Held
Price/Sales	1.79	63.75

Business Summary: Industrial Machinery and Equipment (MIC: 11.5 SIC: 564 NAIC: 33412)

Donaldson Company is a worldwide manufacturer of filtration systems and replacement parts. Co.'s product mix includes air and liquid filters and exhaust and emission control products for mobile equipment; in-plant air cleaning systems; compressed air purification systems; air intake systems for industrial gas turbines; and specialized filters for such diverse applications as computer disk drives, aircraft passenger cabins and semiconductor processing. Co. has two reporting segments: Engine Products and Industrial Products. Products are manufactured at over 30 plants around the world and through three joint venture. Products sold to original equipment manufacturers and directly to end users.

Recent Developments: For the quarter ended Jan 31 2005, net income increased 6.9% to $26,716 thousand from net income of $24,999 thousand in the year-earlier quarter. Revenues were $388,424 thousand, up 16.9% from $332,210 thousand the year before. Operating income was $36,971 thousand versus an income of $34,543 thousand in the prior-year quarter, an increase of 7.0%. Total direct expense was $267,168 thousand versus $228,774 thousand in the prior-year quarter, an increase of 16.8%. Total indirect expense was $84,285 thousand versus $68,893 thousand in the prior-year quarter, an increase of 22.3%.

Prospects: Given that its efforts to recover the recent steel price increases are substantially completed, Co. believes it is poised for increasing profits and margins going forward. For 2005, Co. expects growth in sales of both engine products and industrial products in the low teens. In its engine segment, Co. expects North American heavy-duty new truck build rates to remain at their current high levels throughout the remainder of fiscal 2005 as truck manufacturers are near capacity. With respect to its industrial business, backlogs indicate second-half shipments should be stronger than first-half shipments. As a result, Co. expects full-year gas turbine sales to match fiscal 2004's total.

Financial Data

(US$ in Thousands)	6 Mos	3 Mos	07/31/2004	07/31/2003	07/31/2002	07/31/2001	07/31/2000	07/31/1999
Earnings Per Share	1.24	1.21	1.18	1.05	0.95	0.83	0.76	0.66
Cash Flow Per Share	1.61	1.59	1.34	1.69	1.75	0.93	0.96	1.07
Tang Book Value Per Share	4.91	4.63	5.03	3.40	3.18	2.94	2.42	2.84
Dividends Per Share	0.225	0.212	0.205	0.175	0.155	0.147	0.135	0.115
Dividend Payout %	18.20	17.61	17.37	16.59	16.32	17.77	17.88	17.56
Income Statement								
Total Revenue	761,330	372,906	1,414,980	1,218,252	1,126,005	1,137,015	1,092,294	944,139
EBITDA	100,396	50,591	188,345	174,013	157,300	155,113	144,539	123,889
Depn & Amortn	22,009	11,041	41,555	37,557	31,751	38,577	34,326	27,686
Income Before Taxes	74,123	37,526	141,836	130,567	119,018	104,928	100,333	89,210
Income Taxes	20,013	10,132	35,519	35,253	32,135	29,380	30,100	26,763
Net Income	54,110	27,394	106,317	95,314	86,883	75,548	70,233	62,447
Average Shares	87,269	88,038	90,429	90,469	91,428	91,224	93,328	95,586
Balance Sheet								
Current Assets	620,525	589,287	557,380	454,705	456,484	407,227	375,479	311,477
Total Assets	1,086,374	1,041,512	1,001,609	881,997	850,131	706,830	669,657	528,358
Current Liabilities	326,898	360,923	275,524	214,076	272,790	217,279	235,722	151,144
Long-Term Obligations	111,729	70,196	70,856	105,156	105,019	99,259	92,645	86,691
Total Liabilities	549,381	537,132	452,316	434,604	467,510	387,737	389,492	265,595
Stockholders' Equity	536,993	504,380	549,293	447,393	382,621	319,093	280,165	262,763
Shares Outstanding	83,638	83,357	86,281	99,311	87,829	88,765	89,315	92,394
Statistical Record								
Return on Assets %	10.76	10.98	11.26	11.01	11.16	10.98	11.69	12.15
Return on Equity %	20.88	22.02	21.28	22.97	24.76	25.21	25.80	24.09
EBITDA Margin %	13.19	13.57	13.31	14.28	13.97	13.64	13.23	13.12
Net Margin %	7.11	7.35	7.51	7.82	7.72	6.64	6.43	6.61
Asset Turnover	1.48	1.48	1.50	1.41	1.45	1.65	1.82	1.84
Current Ratio	1.90	1.63	2.02	2.12	1.67	1.87	1.59	2.06
Debt to Equity	0.21	0.14	0.13	0.24	0.27	0.31	0.33	0.33
Price Range	33.97-25.24	30.52-25.24	30.52-23.63	24.41-15.43	22.30-13.47	16.48-9.59	12.41-9.56	12.94-7.25
P/E Ratio	27.40-20.35	25.23-20.86	25.87-20.02	23.25-14.70	23.47-14.17	19.85-11.56	16.32-12.58	19.60-10.98
Average Yield %	0.79	0.76	0.74	0.94	0.86	1.14	1.22	1.15

Address: 1400 West 94th Street, Minneapolis, MN 55431
Telephone: (952) 887-3131
Fax: (952) 887-3155

Web Site: www.donaldson.com
Officers: William G. Van Dyke - Chmn. William M. Cook - Pres., C.E.O.

Auditors: PricewatehouseCoopers LLP
Investor Contact: 651-450-4064

DONNELLEY (R.R.) & SONS CO.

Exchange	Symbol	Price	52Wk Range	Yield	P/E	Div Acheiver
NYS	RRD	$31.62 (3/31/2005)	35.29-28.50	3.29	35.93	35 Years

*7 Year Price Score 93.30   *NYSE Composite Index=100   *12 Month Price Score 94.73

Interim Earnings (Per Share)

Qtr.	Mar	Jun	Sep	Dec
2001	0.12	0.05	0.36	(0.32)
2002	0.20	0.22	0.42	0.42
2003	0.05	0.17	0.47	0.85
2004	(0.39)	(0.06)	0.51	0.67

Interim Dividends (Per Share)

Amt	Decl	Ex	Rec	Pay
0.26Q	7/22/2004	8/5/2004	8/9/2004	9/1/2004
0.26Q	9/30/2004	11/4/2004	11/8/2004	12/1/2004
0.26Q	1/27/2005	2/8/2005	2/10/2005	3/1/2005
0.26Q	3/24/2005	5/6/2005	5/10/2005	6/1/2005

Indicated Div: $1.04 (Div. Reinv. Plan)

Valuation Analysis

Forecast P/E	N/A	No of Institutions 367
Market Cap	$7.0 Billion	Shares
Book Value	4.0 Billion	186,413,744
Price/Book	1.76	% Held
Price/Sales	0.98	86.54

Business Summary: Printing (MIC: 13.4 SIC: 752 NAIC: 23110)

R. R. Donnelley & Sons is engaged in preparing, producing and delivering integrated communications services designed to produce, manage and deliver its customers' content, regardless of the communications medium. Co.'s services include content creation, digital content management, production and distribution. Co. operates primarily in three business segments: print, logistics and financial. Co. serves the following end-markets: magazines, catalogs and retail, telecommunications, book publishing premedia, financial services, direct mail, international, and logistics.

Recent Developments: For the year ended Dec 31 2004, income from continuing operations increased 40.5% to $264,900 thousand from income of $188,500 thousand a year earlier. Net income increased 1.0% to $178,300 thousand from net income of $176,500 thousand a year earlier. Revenues were $7,156,400 thousand, up 71.1% from $4,182,600 thousand the year before. Operating income was $459,200 thousand versus an income of $292,700 thousand in the prior year, an increase of 56.9%. Total direct expense was $5,269,600 thousand versus $3,085,600 thousand in the prior year, an increase of 70.8%. Total indirect expense was $1,427,600 thousand versus $804,300 thousand in the prior year, an increase of 77.5%.

Prospects: In December 2004, Co. announced plans to divest its Peak business and, accordingly, will report this business as a discontinued operation effective with the fourth quarter of 2004. Co.'s Peak business provides integration, maintenance and consulting services related to automatic identification and data collection systems and hardware. The business reported a loss of $5.8 million, on sales of $135.2 million, for the nine months ended Sep 30 2004. Looking ahead, Co. expects full-year 2005 earnings from continuing operations of about $1.95 per share.

Financial Data

(US$ in Thousands)	12/31/2004	12/31/2003	12/31/2002	12/31/2001	12/31/2000	12/31/1999	12/31/1998	12/31/1997
Earnings Per Share	0.88	1.54	1.24	0.21	2.17	2.38	2.08	0.89
Cash Flow Per Share	4.05	3.13	3.62	4.70	6.04	4.93	5.25	5.09
Tang Book Value Per Share	3.81	5.14	4.51	3.92	5.06	6.01	6.85	8.31
Dividends Per Share	1.040	1.020	0.980	0.940	0.900	0.860	0.820	0.780
Dividend Payout %	118.18	66.23	79.03	447.62	41.47	36.13	39.42	87.64
Income Statement								
Total Revenue	7,156,400	4,787,162	4,754,937	5,297,760	5,764,335	5,183,408	5,018,436	4,850,033
EBITDA	828,200	564,641	562,050	524,800	914,025	969,075	955,274	764,975
Depn & Amortn	385,500	306,005	323,499	378,723	390,402	374,382	367,803	370,445
Income Before Taxes	356,800	208,277	175,733	74,894	433,984	506,529	509,305	303,765
Income Taxes	92,600	31,768	33,496	49,906	167,084	195,014	214,725	97,240
Net Income	178,300	176,509	142,237	24,988	266,900	308,314	294,580	130,631
Average Shares	204,200	114,302	114,372	118,498	123,093	129,566	141,865	147,508
Balance Sheet								
Current Assets	2,600,600	999,510	866,439	940,194	1,206,449	1,229,850	1,144,993	1,146,571
Total Assets	8,553,700	3,188,950	3,151,772	3,400,017	3,914,202	3,853,464	3,787,819	4,134,166
Current Liabilities	1,487,300	883,582	954,730	984,290	1,190,561	1,203,463	898,300	812,622
Long-Term Obligations	1,581,200	752,497	752,870	881,318	739,190	748,498	998,978	1,153,226
Total Liabilities	4,567,100	2,205,798	2,237,178	2,511,610	2,681,654	2,715,206	2,486,941	2,542,669
Stockholders' Equity	3,986,600	983,152	914,594	888,407	1,232,548	1,138,258	1,300,878	1,591,497
Shares Outstanding	222,400	113,674	113,124	113,121	140,889	123,237	134,322	145,118
Statistical Record								
Return on Assets %	3.03	5.57	4.34	0.68	6.85	8.07	7.44	2.91
Return on Equity %	7.16	18.60	15.78	2.36	22.45	25.28	20.37	8.11
EBITDA Margin %	11.57	11.79	11.82	9.91	15.86	18.70	19.04	15.77
Net Margin %	2.49	3.69	2.99	0.47	4.63	5.95	5.87	2.69
Asset Turnover	1.22	1.51	1.45	1.45	1.48	1.36	1.27	1.08
Current Ratio	1.75	1.13	0.91	0.96	1.01	1.02	1.27	1.41
Debt to Equity	0.40	0.77	0.82	0.99	0.60	0.66	0.77	0.72
Price Range	35.29-27.95	30.15-17.05	31.96-19.06	31.62-24.83	27.00-19.00	43.81-22.81	47.75-34.00	41.06-29.63
P/E Ratio	40.10-31.76	19.58-11.07	25.77-15.37	150.57-118.24	12.44-8.76	18.41-9.59	22.96-16.35	46.14-33.29
Average Yield %	3.32	4.29	3.70	3.33	3.88	2.65	1.98	2.22

Address: 77 West Wacker Drive, Chicago, IL 60601 Telephone: (312) 326 8000 Fax: (312) 326 8543	Web Site: www.rrdonnelley.com Officers: William L. Davis - Pres. Mark A. Angelson - C.E.O.	Auditors: Deloite & Touche LLP Investor Contact: 312-326-8313 Transfer Agents: EquiServe Trust Company, N.A., Jersey City, NJ

DORAL FINANCIAL CORP.

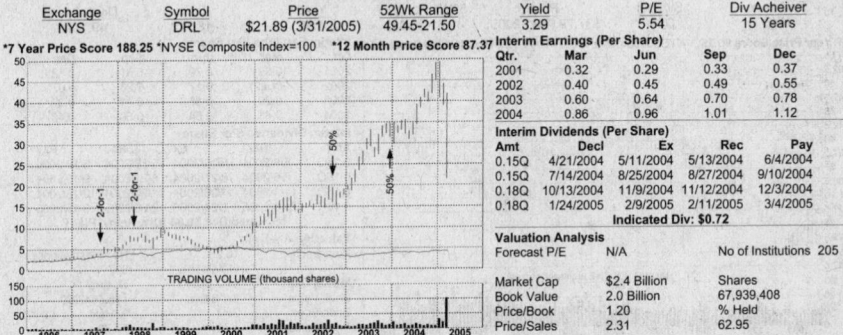

Exchange	Symbol	Price	52Wk Range	Yield	P/E	Div Acheiver
NYS	DRL	$21.89 (3/31/2005)	49.45-21.50	3.29	5.54	15 Years

*7 Year Price Score 188.25 *NYSE Composite Index=100   *12 Month Price Score 87.37

Interim Earnings (Per Share)

Qtr.	Mar	Jun	Sep	Dec
2001	0.32	0.29	0.33	0.37
2002	0.40	0.45	0.49	0.55
2003	0.60	0.64	0.70	0.78
2004	0.86	0.96	1.01	1.12

Interim Dividends (Per Share)

Amt	Decl	Ex	Rec	Pay
0.15Q	4/21/2004	5/11/2004	5/13/2004	6/4/2004
0.15Q	7/14/2004	8/25/2004	8/27/2004	9/10/2004
0.18Q	10/13/2004	11/9/2004	11/12/2004	12/3/2004
0.18Q	1/24/2005	2/9/2005	2/11/2005	3/4/2005

Indicated Div: $0.72

Valuation Analysis

Forecast P/E	N/A	No of Institutions 205
Market Cap	$2.4 Billion	Shares
Book Value	2.0 Billion	67,939,408
Price/Book	1.20	% Held
Price/Sales	2.31	62.95

Business Summary: Finance Intermediaries & Services (MIC: 8.7 SIC: 162 NAIC: 22292)

Doral Financial is a diversified financial services company engaged in mortgage banking, commercial banking, institutional broker-dealer activities and insurance agency activities. Co.'s activities are principally conducted in Puerto Rico and in the New York City metropolitan area. As of Dec 31 2003, Doral Bank, Co.'s Puerto Rico banking subsidiary, operated 37 branches in Puerto Rico, concentrated in the greater San Juan metropolitan area and the Island's northeast region. As of Dec 31 2003, Co. had consolidated assets of $10.39 billion and deposits of $2.97 billion.

Recent Developments: For the quarter ended Dec 31 2004, net income increased 52.3% to $489,625 thousand from net income of $321,299 thousand in the year-earlier quarter. Net interest income was $265,898 thousand, up 46.5% from $181,480 thousand the year before. Provision for loan losses was $5,507 thousand versus $14,085 thousand in the prior-year quarter, an decrease of 61.0%. Non-interest income rose 9.3% to $450,384 thousand, while non-interest expense advanced 12.5% to $209,052 thousand.

Prospects: For 2005, Co. anticipates an increase in tax-exempt AAA rated Mortgage-Backed Securities and U.S. Treasuries with the resulting increase in tax-exempt interest income, as a result of deploying Co.'s capital and cash positions. Additionally, Co. sees another year of strong residential mortgage loan production and an increase in secured real estate commercial loans and other loan products at Co.'s banking entities. Also, Co. expects continued demand of new housing loans including the growing government-sponsored affordable housing loans, and continued strong production of refinancing loans for debt consolidation purposes which are highly profitable for Co.

Financial Data

(US$ in Thousands)	12/31/2004	12/31/2003	12/31/2002	12/31/2001	12/31/2000	12/31/1999	12/31/1998	12/31/1997
Earnings Per Share	3.95	2.72	1.89	1.31	0.82	0.67	0.56	0.24
Cash Flow Per Share	(4.20)	2.98	(11.62)	(4.99)	(4.50)	(4.46)	(10.01)	(5.25)
Tang Book Value Per Share	12.97	9.45	7.58	5.92	3.89	4.11	2.90	2.18
Dividends Per Share	0.600	0.400	0.280	0.211	0.169	0.133	0.102	0.086
Dividend Payout %	15.19	14.71	14.79	16.10	20.54	20.00	18.25	36.32
Income Statement								
Interest Income	570,847	452,570	415,600	356,095	325,545	211,679	148,051	90,131
Interest Expense	304,949	271,090	263,178	271,668	283,241	161,795	114,786	61,438
Net Interest Income	265,898	181,480	152,422	84,427	42,304	49,884	33,265	28,693
Provision for Losses	5,507	14,085	7,429	4,445	4,078	2,626	883	600
Non-Interest Income	450,384	411,772	255,393	191,132	164,585	126,911	88,340	45,286
Non-Interest Expense	209,052	185,802	139,410	112,854	106,659	97,556	60,883	35,582
Income Before Taxes	501,723	393,365	260,976	158,260	96,152	76,613	59,839	37,797
Income Taxes	12,098	72,066	40,008	20,338	11,496	8,687	7,007	5,249
Net Income	489,625	321,299	220,968	143,851	84,656	67,926	52,832	20,231
Average Shares	119,744	110,434	109,438	102,381	94,710	95,448	94,338	87,139
Balance Sheet								
Net Loans & Leases	1,752,490	1,410,849	1,022,342	644,113	398,191	231,184	166,987	133,055
Total Assets	15,102,401	10,393,996	8,421,689	6,694,283	5,463,386	4,537,343	2,918,113	1,857,789
Total Deposits	3,643,080	2,971,272	2,217,211	1,669,909	1,303,525	1,010,424	533,113	300,494
Total Liabilities	13,129,632	8,801,556	7,376,718	5,932,163	4,957,676	4,152,361	2,648,554	1,670,834
Stockholders' Equity	1,972,769	1,592,440	1,044,971	762,120	505,710	384,982	269,559	186,955
Shares Outstanding	107,908	107,903	107,761	107,573	95,384	90,965	90,965	82,788
Statistical Record								
Return on Assets %	3.83	3.42	2.92	2.37	1.69	1.82	2.21	1.37
Return on Equity %	27.39	24.36	24.46	22.69	18.96	20.76	23.15	11.99
Net Interest Margin %	46.58	40.10	36.68	23.71	12.99	23.57	22.47	31.83
Efficiency Ratio %	20.47	21.50	20.78	20.62	21.76	28.81	25.76	26.28
Loans to Deposits	0.48	0.47	0.46	0.39	0.31	0.23	0.31	0.44
Price Range	49.25-29.87	34.67-18.73	19.94-13.68	17.50-9.97	11.36-3.89	9.83-4.72	10.08-4.67	5.67-2.72
P/E Ratio	12.47-7.56	12.75-6.89	10.55-7.24	13.36-7.61	13.86-4.74	14.68-7.05	18.01-8.33	23.61-11.34
Average Yield %	1.60	1.45	1.69	1.53	2.80	1.87	1.43	2.28

Address: 1451 Franklin D. Roosevelt Avenue, San Juan, PR 00920-2717 **Telephone:** (787) 474-6700	**Web Site:** www.doralfinancial.com **Officers:** Salomon Levis - Chmn., C.E.O. Zoila Lewis - Pres., C.O.O.	**Auditors:** PricewaterhouseCoopers LLP **Investor Contact:** 212-329-3729 **Transfer Agents:** Mellon Investor Services, LLC, Ridgefield Park, NJ

DOVER CORP.

Exchange	Symbol	Price	52Wk Range	Yield	P/E	Div Acheiver
NYS	DOV	$37.79 (3/31/2005)	42.61-36.03	1.69	18.71	49 Years

*7 Year Price Score 90.75   ***NYSE Composite Index=100**   ***12 Month Price Score 91.05**

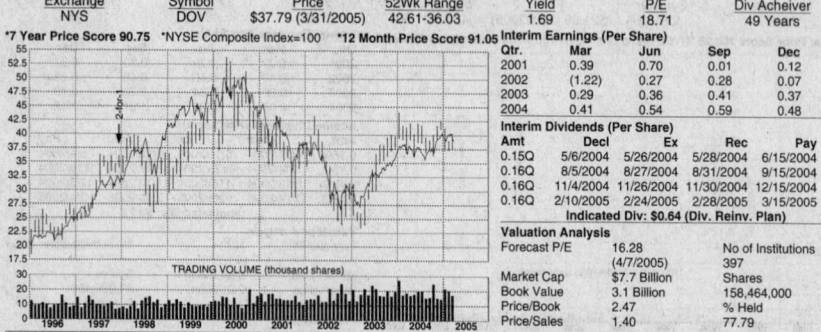

Interim Earnings (Per Share)

Qtr.	Mar	Jun	Sep	Dec
2001	0.39	0.70	0.01	0.12
2002	(1.22)	0.27	0.28	0.07
2003	0.29	0.36	0.41	0.37
2004	0.41	0.54	0.59	0.48

Interim Dividends (Per Share)

Amt	Decl	Ex	Rec	Pay
0.15Q	5/6/2004	5/26/2004	5/28/2004	6/15/2004
0.16Q	8/5/2004	8/27/2004	8/31/2004	9/15/2004
0.16Q	11/4/2004	11/26/2004	11/30/2004	12/15/2004
0.16Q	2/10/2005	2/24/2005	2/28/2005	3/15/2005

Indicated Div: $0.64 (Div. Reinv. Plan)

Valuation Analysis

Forecast P/E	16.28 (4/7/2005)	No of Institutions 397
Market Cap	$7.7 Billion	Shares 158,464,000
Book Value	3.1 Billion	% Held 77.79
Price/Book	2.47	
Price/Sales	1.40	

Business Summary: Industrial Machinery and Equipment (MIC: 11.5 SIC: 531 NAIC: 33120)

Dover is a diversified industrial manufacturing corporation made up of 52 operating companies. Dover Diversified's products include packaging and printing machinery, heat transfer equipment, food refrigeration and display cases as well as products for use in the defense, aerospace and automotive industries. Dover Industries makes products for use in the waste handling, bulk transport, automotive service, commercial food service and packaging, welding, cash dispenser and construction industries. Dover Technologies' products include automated assembly and testing equipment, specialized electronic components and industrial printers. Dover Resources manufactures products for various industries.

Recent Developments: For the year ended Dec 31 2004, income from continuing operations increased 43.4% to $409,140 thousand from income of $285,216 thousand a year earlier. Net income increased 40.9% to $412,755 thousand from net income of $292,927 thousand a year earlier. Revenues were $5,488,112 thousand, up 24.4% from $4,413,296 thousand the year before. Operating income was $612,202 thousand versus an income of $443,758 thousand in the prior year, an increase of 38.0%. Total direct expense was $3,593,748 thousand versus $2,892,874 thousand in the prior year, an increase of 24.2%. Total indirect expense was $1,282,162 thousand versus $1,076,664 thousand in the prior year, an increase of 19.1%.

Prospects: Co. continues to perform well, reflecting sales increases at 11 of the 12 companies. In particular, Hill Phoenix, Crenlo, PMI, Sargent, Tranter PHE and SWEP all had solid results, and, together with a strong finish at Belvac, generated most of the earnings growth in 2004. Going forward, given the current strong backlogs coupled with its new product initiatives, responsive customer service and expanding focus on global sourcing, Co. remains optimistic about its outlook for 2005. However, Co. does not anticipate as significant an increase as it had experienced in 2004 as many of Co.'s core technology companies face more uncertain market conditions.

Financial Data

(US$ in Thousands)	12/31/2004	12/31/2003	12/31/2002	12/31/2001	12/31/2000	12/31/1999	12/31/1998	12/31/1997
Earnings Per Share	2.02	1.44	(0.60)	1.22	2.54	4.41	1.69	1.79
Cash Flow Per Share	2.93	2.93	1.95	3.35	2.73	2.21	2.19	2.07
Tang Book Value Per Share	2.16	2.70	2.65	1.97	1.82	1.10	2.14	2.71
Dividends Per Share	0.620	0.570	0.540	0.520	0.480	0.440	0.400	0.360
Dividend Payout %	30.69	39.58	...	42.62	18.90	9.98	23.67	20.11
Income Statement								
Total Revenue	5,488,112	4,413,296	4,183,664	4,459,695	5,400,717	4,446,420	3,977,666	4,547,656
EBITDA	774,281	585,367	495,523	533,677	1,064,194	833,121	702,771	824,469
Depn & Amortn	160,845	151,309	161,003	219,963	203,384	183,244	167,687	170,663
Income Before Taxes	552,146	371,892	269,691	238,434	772,315	615,004	488,646	616,836
Income Taxes	143,006	86,676	58,542	71,595	239,108	209,950	162,249	211,405
Net Income	412,755	292,927	(121,261)	248,537	519,612	928,992	378,845	405,431
Average Shares	204,786	203,614	203,346	204,013	204,677	210,679	224,386	226,815
Balance Sheet								
Current Assets	2,149,947	1,849,640	1,658,001	1,654,928	1,974,849	1,611,562	1,304,524	1,591,345
Total Assets	5,792,179	5,133,752	4,437,385	4,602,202	4,892,116	4,131,940	3,627,276	3,277,524
Current Liabilities	1,355,976	910,801	696,938	819,171	1,604,640	1,334,865	989,747	1,196,573
Long-Term Obligations	753,063	1,003,915	1,030,299	1,033,243	631,846	608,025	610,090	262,630
Total Liabilities	2,673,497	2,391,081	2,042,762	2,082,663	2,450,541	2,093,184	1,716,392	1,573,940
Stockholders' Equity	3,118,682	2,742,671	2,394,623	2,519,539	2,441,575	2,038,756	1,910,884	1,703,584
Shares Outstanding	203,496	202,912	202,402	202,579	203,183	204,628	220,407	234,507
Statistical Record								
Return on Assets %	7.53	6.12	N.M.	5.24	11.48	23.95	10.97	12.93
Return on Equity %	14.05	11.40	N.M.	10.02	23.13	47.04	20.96	25.39
EBITDA Margin %	14.11	13.26	11.84	11.97	19.70	18.74	17.67	18.13
Net Margin %	7.52	6.64	N.M.	5.57	9.62	20.89	9.52	8.92
Asset Turnover	1.00	0.92	0.93	0.94	1.19	1.15	1.15	1.45
Current Ratio	1.59	2.03	2.38	2.02	1.23	1.21	1.32	1.33
Debt to Equity	0.24	0.37	0.43	0.41	0.26	0.30	0.32	0.15
Price Range	44.02-36.03	40.08-23.35	43.31-23.91	43.32-28.77	53.81-36.00	47.50-29.50	39.81-25.94	36.31-24.38
P/E Ratio	21.79-17.84	27.83-16.22	...	35.51-23.58	21.19-14.17	10.77-6.69	23.56-15.35	20.29-13.62
Average Yield %	1.56	1.76	1.63	1.39	1.07	1.14	1.17	1.18

Address: 280 Park Avenue, New York, NY 10017	Web Site: www.dovercorporation.com	Auditors: PricewaterhouseCoopers LLP
Telephone: (212) 922-1640	Officers: Thomas L. Reece - Chmn. Ronald L. Hoffman - Pres., C.E.O.	Investor Contact: 212-922-1640
Fax: (212) 922-1656		Transfer Agents: Mellon Investor Services, Ridgefield Park, NJ

DOW CHEMICAL CO.

Exchange	Symbol	Price	52Wk Range	Yield	P/E
NYS	DOW	$49.85 (3/31/2005)	56.42-36.86	2.69	17.01

*7 Year Price Score 109.04 *NYSE Composite Index=100 *12 Month Price Score 109.68

TRADING VOLUME (thousand shares)

Interim Earnings (Per Share)

Qtr.	Mar	Jun	Sep	Dec
2001	(0.76)	0.31	0.06	(0.04)
2002	0.11	0.26	0.14	(0.88)
2003	0.08	0.43	0.36	1.00
2004	0.50	0.72	0.65	1.06

Interim Dividends (Per Share)

Amt	Decl	Ex	Rec	Pay
0.335Q	5/13/2004	6/28/2004	6/30/2004	7/30/2004
0.335Q	9/9/2004	9/28/2004	9/30/2004	10/29/2004
0.335Q	12/9/2004	12/29/2004	12/31/2004	1/28/2005
0.335Q	2/10/2005	3/29/2005	3/31/2005	4/29/2005
			Indicated Div: $1.34	

Valuation Analysis

Forecast P/E	11.09	No of Institutions
	(4/7/2005)	730
Market Cap	$47.5 Billion	Shares
Book Value	12.3 Billion	660,053,056
Price/Book	3.87	% Held
Price/Sales	1.18	70.00

Business Summary: Chemicals (MIC: 11.1 SIC: 821 NAIC: 25211)

Dow is a diversified manufacturer of basic and performance chemical, plastic, and agricultural products that serve numerous consumer markets in 175 countries, including food, transportation, health and medicine, personal and home care, and building and construction. Co. conducts its worldwide operations through global businesses, which are reported in six operating segments: Performance Plastics, Performance Chemicals, Agricultural Sciences, Plastics, Chemicals, and Hydrocarbons and Energy. As of Dec 31 2004, Co. had 165 manufacturing sites in 37 countries and supplied more than 3,300 products.

Recent Developments: For the year ended Dec 31 2004, net income increased 61.7% to $2,797 million from net income of $1,730 million a year earlier. Revenues were $40,161 million, up 23.1% from $32,632 million the year before. Total direct expense was $34,244 million versus $28,177 million in the prior year, an increase of 21.5%. Total indirect expense was $2,519 million versus $2,436 million in the prior year, an increase of 3.4%.

Prospects: Co. is performing well, as global economic growth is driving higher demand for chemicals and plastics, and providing support for margin expansion. However, feedstock and energy costs remain high and volatile, increasing by over 50.0% versus the fourth quarter of 2003. For 2005, Co. expects that continued global economic growth will further improve chemical industry demand. However, the high and volatile feedstock and energy costs that have characterized this industry for the past two years are expected to continue. As a result, Co. will focus on financial discipline, lowering the total cost to serve customers and price/volume management in order to improve its financial performance.

Financial Data

(US$ in Thousands)	12/31/2004	12/31/2003	12/31/2002	12/31/2001	12/31/2000	12/31/1999	12/31/1998	12/31/1997
Earnings Per Share	2.93	1.87	(0.37)	(0.43)	2.22	1.98	5.76	2.57
Cash Flow Per Share	2.83	4.11	2.32	1.98	1.79	4.53	13.18	5.28
Tang Book Value Per Share	9.01	5.79	4.19	7.58	10.77	9.69	26.26	8.67
Dividends Per Share	1.340	1.340	1.340	1.295	1.160	1.160	1.160	1.120
Dividend Payout %	45.73	71.66	...	...	52.25	58.59	20.14	43.64
Income Statement								
Total Revenue	40,161,000	32,632,000	27,609,000	27,805,000	23,008,000	19,989,000	18,441,000	20,018,000
EBITDA	6,442,000	4,303,000	1,831,000	1,808,000	4,468,000	3,744,000	3,642,000	4,494,000
Depn & Amortn	1,985,000	1,816,000	1,745,000	1,773,000	1,679,000	1,268,000	1,276,000	1,269,000
Income Before Taxes	3,796,000	1,751,000	(622,000)	(613,000)	2,401,000	2,166,000	2,012,000	2,948,000
Income Taxes	877,000	(82,000)	(280,000)	(228,000)	823,000	766,000	685,000	1,041,000
Net Income	2,797,000	1,730,000	(338,000)	(385,000)	1,513,000	1,331,000	1,304,000	1,802,000
Average Shares	953,800	926,100	910,500	901,800	683,000	673,300	227,300	704,400
Balance Sheet								
Current Assets	15,890,000	13,002,000	11,681,000	10,308,000	9,260,000	8,847,000	8,040,000	8,640,000
Total Assets	45,885,000	41,891,000	39,562,000	35,515,000	27,645,000	25,499,000	23,830,000	24,040,000
Current Liabilities	10,506,000	9,534,000	8,856,000	8,125,000	7,873,000	6,295,000	6,842,000	7,340,000
Long-Term Obligations	11,629,000	11,763,000	11,659,000	9,266,000	4,865,000	5,022,000	4,051,000	4,196,000
Total Liabilities	33,615,000	32,716,000	31,936,000	25,522,000	18,459,000	17,176,000	16,401,000	16,414,000
Stockholders' Equity	12,270,000	9,175,000	7,626,000	9,993,000	9,186,000	8,323,000	7,429,000	7,626,000
Shares Outstanding	952,926	927,448	912,656	904,837	677,503	669,844	220,376	676,404
Statistical Record								
Return on Assets %	6.36	4.25	N.M.	N.M.	5.68	5.40	5.45	7.40
Return on Equity %	26.01	20.59	N.M.	N.M.	17.24	16.90	17.32	23.13
EBITDA Margin %	16.04	13.19	6.63	6.50	19.42	18.73	19.75	22.45
Net Margin %	6.96	5.30	N.M.	N.M.	6.58	6.66	7.07	9.00
Asset Turnover	0.91	0.80	0.74	0.88	0.86	0.81	0.77	0.82
Current Ratio	1.51	1.36	1.32	1.27	1.18	1.41	1.18	1.18
Debt to Equity	0.95	1.28	1.53	0.93	0.53	0.60	0.55	0.55
Price Range	51.02-36.86	42.00-25.16	36.75-24.50	39.58-29.45	46.67-23.38	45.65-28.92	33.83-25.50	33.83-25.71
P/E Ratio	17.41-12.58	22.46-13.45	...	...	21.02-10.53	23.05-14.60	5.87-4.43	13.16-10.00
Average Yield %	3.16	4.11	4.42	3.77	3.49	3.04	3.75	3.83

Address: 2030 Dow Center, Midland, MI 48674 **Telephone:** (989) 636-1000 **Fax:** (989) 636-3518	**Web Site:** www.dow.com **Officers:** William S. Stavropoulos - Chmn. Anthony J. Carbone - Vice-Chmn.	**Auditors:** Deloitte & Touche LLP **Investor Contact:** 989-636-8193

263

DOW JONES & CO., INC

Exchange	Symbol	Price	52Wk Range	Yield	P/E
NYS	DJ	$37.37 (3/31/2005)	49.43-37.02	2.68	30.88

*7 Year Price Score 72.15 ***NYSE Composite Index=100** ***12 Month Price Score 83.29**

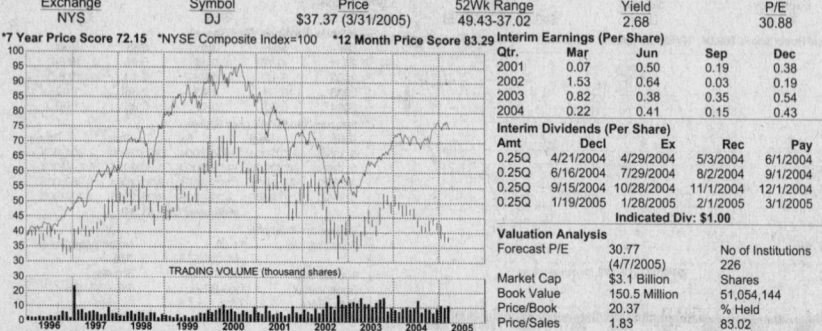

Interim Earnings (Per Share)

Qtr.	Mar	Jun	Sep	Dec
2001	0.07	0.50	0.19	0.38
2002	1.53	0.64	0.03	0.19
2003	0.82	0.38	0.35	0.54
2004	0.22	0.41	0.15	0.43

Interim Dividends (Per Share)

Amt	Decl	Ex	Rec	Pay
0.25Q	4/21/2004	4/29/2004	5/3/2004	6/1/2004
0.25Q	6/16/2004	7/29/2004	8/2/2004	9/1/2004
0.25Q	9/15/2004	10/28/2004	11/1/2004	12/1/2004
0.25Q	1/19/2005	1/28/2005	2/1/2005	3/1/2005

Indicated Div: $1.00

Valuation Analysis

Forecast P/E	30.77	No of Institutions
	(4/7/2005)	226
Market Cap	$3.1 Billion	Shares
Book Value	150.5 Million	51,054,144
Price/Book	20.37	% Held
Price/Sales	1.83	83.02

Business Summary: Media (MIC: 13.1 SIC: 711 NAIC: 11110)

Dow Jones is a global provider of business and financial news and information. The print publishing segment contains The Wall Street Journal, and its international editions in Europe and Asia; Barron's; Smart Money magazines; Dow Jones interactive publishing; The Far Eastern Economic Review; and television operations. The electronic publishing segment includes the Dow Jones newswires, Consumer Electronic Publishing and Dow Jones Indexes/Ventures. Community newspapers published by Ottaway Newspapers, Inc. include 15 general interest dailies. Co. is also the co-owner with Reuters Group of Factiva, with Hearst of SmartMoney and with NBC of the CNBC television operations in Asia and Europe.

Recent Developments: For the year ended Dec 31 2004, net income decreased 41.6% to $99,548 thousand from net income of $170,599 thousand a year earlier. Revenues were $1,671,458 thousand, up 7.9% from $1,548,485 thousand the year before. Operating income was $162,174 thousand versus an income of $142,913 thousand in the prior year, an increase of 13.5%. Total direct expense was $815,731 thousand versus $777,437 thousand in the prior year, an increase of 4.9%. Total indirect expense was $693,553 thousand versus $628,135 thousand in the prior year, an increase of 10.4%.

Prospects: On Jan 24 2005, Co. closed its acquisition of MarketWatch, a provider of business news, financial information and analytical tools, for about $528.0 million. The acquisition accelerates the growth of Co.'s growing online operations by adding the MarketWatch brand that reaches a complementary, but larger, audience for online business and financial news. The acquisition will also expand the advertising-targeting capabilities that Co. offers advertisers. Separately, Co. is cautiously optimistic about its outlook as it focuses on controlling its costs and improving its products. For the first quarter of 2005, Co. expects earnings per share to be in the range of $0.05 to $0.08.

Financial Data

(US$ in Thousands)	12/31/2004	12/31/2003	12/31/2002	12/31/2001	12/31/2000	12/31/1999	12/31/1998	12/31/1997
Earnings Per Share	1.21	2.08	2.40	1.14	(1.35)	2.99	0.09	(8.36)
Cash Flow Per Share	3.07	2.70	1.74	3.99	5.07	3.28	3.23	4.79
Tang Book Value Per Share	N.M.	N.M.	N.M.	N.M.	0.98	5.24	4.60	4.07
Dividends Per Share	1.000	1.000	1.000	1.000	1.000	0.960	0.960	0.960
Dividend Payout %	82.64	48.08	41.67	87.72	N.M.	32.11	N.M.	N.M.
Income Statement								
Total Revenue	1,671,458	1,548,485	1,559,173	1,773,083	2,202,618	2,001,835	2,158,106	2,572,518
EBITDA	265,059	329,702	370,351	205,901	186,300	526,984	221,290	(493,783)
Depn & Amortn	105,234	106,014	109,738	105,713	107,885	103,669	142,439	250,734
Income Before Taxes	156,085	220,858	257,530	99,688	76,378	418,046	71,658	(763,884)
Income Taxes	58,578	51,704	63,741	10,794	196,957	145,501	63,083	37,796
Net Income	99,548	170,599	201,506	98,220	(118,962)	272,429	8,362	(802,132)
Average Shares	82,285	81,950	83,917	86,258	87,854	91,151	96,404	95,993
Balance Sheet								
Current Assets	253,914	245,879	250,604	245,959	368,243	455,989	434,989	506,553
Total Assets	1,380,203	1,304,154	1,207,659	1,298,340	1,362,056	1,530,559	1,484,022	1,919,734
Current Liabilities	716,518	613,523	622,479	601,893	587,224	578,530	592,497	672,395
Long-Term Obligations	135,845	153,110	92,937	173,958	150,865	149,945	149,889	228,806
Total Liabilities	1,225,830	1,167,914	1,176,527	1,252,694	1,194,695	977,069	974,682	1,138,912
Stockholders' Equity	150,543	129,661	30,571	41,777	158,768	553,490	509,340	780,822
Shares Outstanding	82,044	81,708	81,916	84,631	86,829	89,820	91,969	96,670
Statistical Record								
Return on Assets %	7.40	13.58	16.08	7.38	N.M.	18.07	0.49	N.M.
Return on Equity %	70.86	212.94	557.05	97.95	N.M.	51.26	1.30	N.M.
EBITDA Margin %	15.86	21.29	23.75	11.61	8.46	26.33	10.25	N.M.
Net Margin %	5.96	11.02	12.92	5.54	N.M.	13.61	0.39	N.M.
Asset Turnover	1.24	1.23	1.24	1.33	1.52	1.33	1.27	1.10
Current Ratio	0.35	0.40	0.40	0.41	0.63	0.79	0.73	0.75
Debt to Equity	0.90	1.18	3.04	4.16	0.95	0.27	0.29	0.29
Price Range	52.65-39.96	53.03-33.75	60.03-31.05	63.90-44.05	76.75-53.38	70.13-44.00	58.50-42.00	55.56-33.88
P/E Ratio	43.51-33.02	25.50-16.23	25.01-12.94	56.05-38.64	N/A	23.45-14.72	650.00-466.67	N/A
Average Yield %	2.21	2.30	2.11	1.84	1.55	1.80	1.91	2.22

Address: 200 Liberty Street, New York, NY 10281	**Web Site:** www.dowjones.com	**Auditors:** PricewaterhouseCoopers LLP
Telephone: (212) 416-2000	**Officers:** Peter R. Kann - Chmn., C.E.O. Richard F. Zannino - Exec. V.P., C.O.O.	**Investor Contact:** 609-520-5660
Fax: (212) 416-2829		

DPL INC.

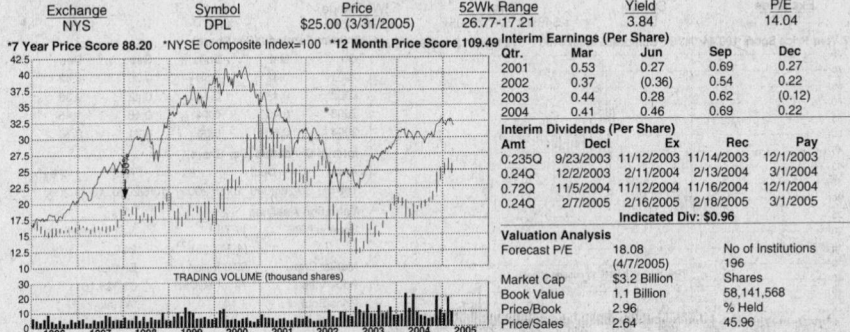

Exchange	Symbol	Price	52Wk Range	Yield	P/E
NYS	DPL	$25.00 (3/31/2005)	26.77-17.21	3.84	14.04

*7 Year Price Score 88.20   *NYSE Composite Index=100   *12 Month Price Score 109.49

Interim Earnings (Per Share)

Qtr.	Mar	Jun	Sep	Dec
2001	0.53	0.27	0.69	0.27
2002	0.37	(0.36)	0.54	0.22
2003	0.44	0.28	0.62	(0.12)
2004	0.41	0.46	0.69	0.22

Interim Dividends (Per Share)

Amt	Decl	Ex	Rec	Pay
0.235Q	9/23/2003	11/12/2003	11/14/2003	12/1/2003
0.24Q	12/2/2003	2/11/2004	2/13/2004	3/1/2004
0.72Q	11/5/2004	11/12/2004	11/16/2004	12/1/2004
0.24Q	2/7/2005	2/16/2005	2/18/2005	3/1/2005

Indicated Div: $0.96

Valuation Analysis

Forecast P/E	18.08	No of Institutions
	(4/7/2005)	196
Market Cap	$3.2 Billion	Shares
Book Value	1.1 Billion	58,141,568
Price/Book	2.96	% Held
Price/Sales	2.64	45.96

Business Summary: Electricity (MIC: 7.1 SIC: 931 NAIC: 21121)

DPL is engaged in the acquisition and holding of securities of corporations for investment purposes. Co.'s principal subsidiary is The Dayton Power and Light Company ("DP&L"). DP&L sells electricity and natural gas to residential, commercial and governmental customers in a 6,000 square mile area of West Central Ohio. Electricity for DP&L's 24 county service area is generated at eight power plants and is distributed to more than 500,000 customers. Principal industries served include automotive, food processing, paper, plastic manufacuring, and defense.

Recent Developments: For the year ended Dec 31 2004, net income increased 46.3% to $217,300 thousand from net income of $148,500 thousand a year earlier. Revenues were $1,199,900 thousand, up 0.7% from $1,191,000 thousand the year before. Operating income was $336,500 thousand versus an income of $371,900 thousand in the prior year, a decrease of 9.5%. Total direct expense was $613,300 thousand versus $522,300 thousand in the prior year, an increase of 17.4%. Total indirect expense was $106,000 thousand versus $157,900 thousand in the prior year, a decrease of 32.9%.

Prospects: Co. expects to spend approximately $800.0 million in capital expenditures in the utility business over the next four years, including expenditures of $175.0 million in fiscal 2005. Weather-adjusted utility revenues are expected to increase approximately 3.0% in fiscal 2005, with approximately half of this increase from organic growth. Additionally, Co. has long-term fuel supply agreements that provide for 83.0% of fuel supply in 2005 and 60.0% in 2006. Fuel and purchased power costs in 2005 are estimated to increase 7.0% to 10.0% compared with 2004. Co. expects utility only earnings for 2005 to be $0.95 to $1.05 per share.

Financial Data
(US$ in Thousands)

	12/31/2004	12/31/2003	12/31/2002	12/31/2001	12/31/2000	12/31/1999	12/31/1998	12/31/1997
Earnings Per Share	1.78	1.22	0.72	1.71	1.83	1.35	1.24	1.20
Cash Flow Per Share	1.10	2.92	2.63	2.60	1.68	2.62	2.03	2.25
Tang Book Value Per Share	8.25	7.13	6.56	6.49	6.98	9.20	8.58	8.03
Dividends Per Share	0.960	0.940	0.940	0.940	0.940	0.940	0.940	0.907
Dividend Payout %	53.93	77.05	130.56	54.97	51.37	69.63	75.81	75.56
Income Statement								
Total Revenue	1,199,900	1,191,000	1,186,400	1,199,600	1,436,900	1,338,900	1,379,600	1,355,800
EBITDA	647,900	584,600	474,600	648,000	733,700	603,900	563,400	518,500
Depn & Amortn	144,800	187,900	182,200	174,200	151,900	162,300	160,100	144,400
Income Before Taxes	342,900	215,000	137,600	336,800	441,500	332,100	309,500	286,800
Income Taxes	125,600	83,500	50,300	121,300	156,600	127,900	120,400	105,400
Net Income	217,300	148,500	87,300	216,500	243,500	204,200	189,100	181,400
Average Shares	122,200	121,700	121,900	126,600	132,900	151,400	152,800	151,400
Balance Sheet								
Net PPE	2,530,100	2,573,900	2,502,700	2,482,300	2,267,000	2,266,800	22,383,700	2,256,200
Total Assets	4,165,500	4,444,700	4,176,100	4,253,500	4,436,000	4,340,440	3,855,900	3,585,200
Long-Term Obligations	2,117,300	1,954,700	2,142,400	2,150,800	1,758,500	1,336,600	1,065,900	971,000
Total Liabilities	3,098,500	3,519,400	3,323,400	3,409,500	3,520,700	2,865,900	2,449,300	2,276,300
Stockholders' Equity	1,067,000	925,300	852,800	844,000	915,300	1,474,500	1,406,600	1,308,900
Shares Outstanding	126,501	126,501	126,501	126,501	127,774	157,801	161,265	160,203
Statistical Record								
Return on Assets %	5.03	3.45	2.07	4.98	5.53	4.98	5.08	5.18
Return on Equity %	21.75	16.70	10.29	24.61	20.32	14.18	13.93	14.33
EBITDA Margin %	54.00	49.08	40.00	54.02	51.06	45.10	40.84	38.24
Net Margin %	18.11	12.47	7.36	18.05	16.95	15.25	13.71	13.38
PPE Turnover	0.47	0.47	0.48	0.51	0.63	0.11	0.11	0.60
Asset Turnover	0.28	0.28	0.28	0.28	0.33	0.33	0.37	0.39
Debt to Equity	1.98	2.11	2.51	2.55	1.92	0.91	0.76	0.74
Price Range	25.36-17.21	21.15-11.95	27.19-13.75	32.38-22.30	33.69-16.63	21.69-16.38	21.63-16.94	19.17-15.33
P/E Ratio	14.25-9.67	17.34-9.80	37.76-19.10	18.93-13.04	18.41-9.08	16.06-12.13	17.44-13.66	15.97-12.78
Average Yield %	4.72	5.95	4.53	3.52	3.81	5.09	5.02	5.54

Address: 1065 Woodman Drive, Dayton, OH 45432	**Web Site:** www.dplinc.com	**Auditors:** KPMG
Telephone: (937) 224-6000	**Officers:** Robert D. Biggs - Exec. Chmn. W. August Hillenbrand - Vice-Chmn.	**Investor Contact:** 800-322-9244
Fax: (937) 224-6500		**Transfer Agents:** EquiServe, Providence, RI

DST SYSTEMS INC. (DE)

Exchange	Symbol	Price	52Wk Range	Yield	P/E
NYS	DST	$46.18 (3/31/2005)	52.25-42.49	N/A	17.83

*7 Year Price Score 100.44 *NYSE Composite Index=100 *12 Month Price Score 94.14

TRADING VOLUME (thousand shares)

Interim Earnings (Per Share)

Qtr.	Mar	Jun	Sep	Dec
2001	0.42	0.58	0.39	0.42
2002	0.48	0.44	0.42	0.38
2003*	0.43	0.44	0.45	1.45
2004	0.60	0.60	0.61	0.79

Interim Dividends (Per Share)

Amt	Decl	Ex	Rec	Pay
100%	9/26/2000	10/20/2000	10/6/2000	10/19/2000

Valuation Analysis

Forecast P/E	17.75	No of Institutions
	(4/7/2005)	244
Market Cap	$3.8 Billion	Shares
Book Value	745.8 Million	63,525,184
Price/Book	5.14	% Held
Price/Sales	1.58	76.34

Business Summary: Communications (MIC: 10.1 SIC: 375 NAIC: 18111)

DST Systems provides information processing and software services and products. The Financial Services segment provides information processing and computer software services and products primarily to mutual funds, investment managers, corporations, insurance companies, banks, brokers and financial planners. The Output Solutions segment provides integrated print and electronic communication products and services. The Customer Management segment provides customer management, billing and marketing products and services to the video/broadband, direct broadcast satellite, wire-line and Internet Protocol telephony, Internet and utility markets.

Recent Developments: For the year ended Dec 31 2004, net income decreased 30.5% to $222,800 thousand from net income of $320,800 thousand a year earlier. Revenues were $2,428,600 thousand, up 0.5% from $2,416,300 thousand the year before. Operating income was $315,700 thousand versus an income of $307,500 thousand in the prior year, an increase of 2.7%. Total direct expense was $1,954,400 thousand versus $1,958,400 thousand in the prior year, a decrease of 0.2%. Total indirect expense was $158,500 thousand versus $150,400 thousand in the prior year, an increase of 5.4%.

Prospects: During the fourth quarter of 2004, Co.'s Financial Services segment received commitments from three new clients with a total of 1.2 million shareowner accounts. Subsequent to the fourth quarter of 2004, Co. received additional commitments from five new mutual fund clients with a total of 7.2 million shareowner accounts and one insurance client with 200,000 401(k) participants. Co. expects these conversions will take place throughout 2005. Co. continues to pursue 19 potential new clients with a combined total of about 18.0 million to 20.0 million accounts. Separately, Co. expects the sale of its EquiServe unit to to close in the first quarter 2005, following necessary regulatory approvals.

Financial Data
(US$ in Thousands)

	12/31/2004	12/31/2003	12/31/2002	12/31/2001	12/31/2000	12/31/1999	12/31/1998	12/31/1997
Earnings Per Share	2.59	2.77	1.72	1.81	1.67	1.06	0.56	0.59
Cash Flow Per Share	4.73	3.24	3.28	3.00	2.66	2.00	2.19	1.29
Tang Book Value Per Share	6.46	3.56	8.63	10.58	12.48	11.38	8.80	7.92
Income Statement								
Total Revenue	2,428,600	2,416,300	2,383,800	1,660,000	1,362,100	1,203,300	1,096,100	650,678
EBITDA	534,600	606,200	474,000	520,400	471,200	342,600	232,900	175,781
Depn & Amortn	157,300	149,200	144,000	159,400	128,900	123,100	108,700	79,402
Income Before Taxes	322,000	430,100	316,600	353,500	336,700	214,300	115,600	88,709
Income Taxes	99,200	109,300	107,600	125,300	120,900	76,900	44,300	29,178
Net Income	222,800	320,800	209,000	228,200	215,800	138,100	71,600	58,997
Average Shares	86,100	116,000	121,700	126,000	129,400	129,600	128,600	99,676
Balance Sheet								
Current Assets	796,000	681,800	665,100	604,800	590,700	464,500	375,800	231,324
Total Assets	3,383,400	3,198,600	2,744,200	2,704,000	2,552,400	2,326,300	1,897,000	1,355,404
Current Liabilities	713,500	572,200	546,500	471,400	356,200	285,800	268,600	140,993
Long-Term Obligations	1,373,700	1,437,800	379,500	243,400	68,700	44,400	49,700	92,005
Total Liabilities	2,637,600	2,514,900	1,322,200	1,231,600	986,600	862,700	730,000	518,314
Stockholders' Equity	745,800	683,700	1,422,000	1,472,400	1,565,800	1,463,600	1,166,200	835,710
Shares Outstanding	83,000	83,900	119,600	120,400	121,800	124,800	125,834	98,086
Statistical Record								
Return on Assets %	6.75	10.80	7.67	8.68	8.82	6.54	4.40	4.76
Return on Equity %	31.09	30.47	14.44	15.02	14.21	10.50	7.15	7.71
EBITDA Margin %	22.01	25.09	19.88	31.35	34.59	28.47	21.25	27.02
Net Margin %	9.17	13.28	8.77	13.75	15.84	11.48	6.53	9.07
Asset Turnover	0.74	0.81	0.88	0.63	0.56	0.57	0.67	0.53
Current Ratio	1.12	1.19	1.22	1.28	1.66	1.63	1.40	1.64
Debt to Equity	1.84	2.10	0.27	0.17	0.04	0.03	0.04	0.11
Price Range	52.25-41.30	41.90-24.30	50.50-24.37	66.25-39.90	74.06-26.69	38.16-25.59	34.97-17.91	22.28-12.13
P/E Ratio	20.17-15.95	15.13-8.77	29.36-14.17	36.60-22.04	44.35-15.98	36.00-24.15	62.44-31.98	37.76-20.55

Address: 333 West 11th Street, Kansas City, MO 64105	Web Site: www.dstsystems.com	Auditors: PricewaterhouseCoopers LLP
Telephone: (816) 435 1000	Officers: Thomas A. McDonnell - Pres., C.E.O.	
Fax: (816) 435 8630	Thomas A. McCullough - Exec. V.P., C.O.O.	

DTE ENERGY CO.

Exchange	Symbol	Price	52Wk Range	Yield	P/E
NYS	DTE	$45.48 (3/31/2005)	46.66-38.19	4.53	18.27

*7 Year Price Score 90.06   *NYSE Composite Index=100   *12 Month Price Score 99.24

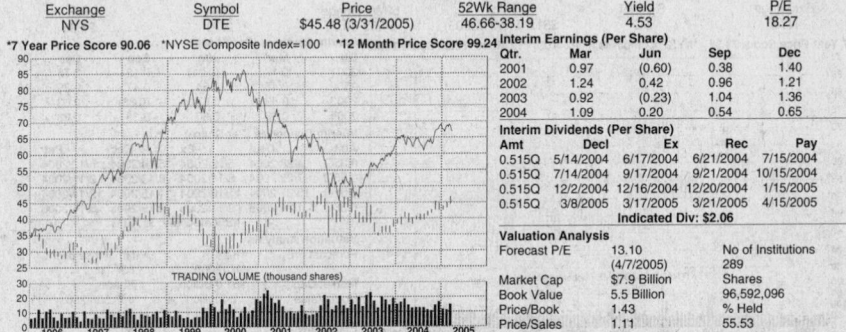

Interim Earnings (Per Share)

Qtr.	Mar	Jun	Sep	Dec
2001	0.97	(0.60)	0.38	1.40
2002	1.24	0.42	0.96	1.21
2003	0.92	(0.23)	1.04	1.36
2004	1.09	0.20	0.54	0.65

Interim Dividends (Per Share)

Amt	Decl	Ex	Rec	Pay
0.515Q	5/14/2004	6/17/2004	6/21/2004	7/15/2004
0.515Q	7/14/2004	9/17/2004	9/21/2004	10/15/2004
0.515Q	12/2/2004	12/16/2004	12/20/2004	1/15/2005
0.515Q	3/8/2005	3/17/2005	3/21/2005	4/15/2005
			Indicated Div: $2.06	

Valuation Analysis

Forecast P/E	13.10	No of Institutions
	(4/7/2005)	289
Market Cap	$7.9 Billion	Shares
Book Value	5.5 Billion	96,592,096
Price/Book	1.43	% Held
Price/Sales	1.11	55.53

Business Summary: Electricity (MIC: 7.1 SIC: 911 NAIC: 21122)

DTE Energy is a holding company whose principal subsidiary is Detroit Edison Co. Detroit Edison supplied energy to 2.1 million customers in Southeastern Michigan as of Dec 31 2003. Co. added a second subsidiary in 2001, MichCon. MichCon served 1.2 million customers across Michigan as of Dec 31 2003. Eight wholly-owned subsidiaries, along with various affiliates of Co., are engaged in non-regulated businesses, including energy-related services and products. Such services and products include the operations of a pulverized coal facility and a coke oven battery, coal sales and brokering, energy technologies, real estate development, power marketing and specialty engineering services.

Recent Developments: For the year ended Dec 31 2004, income from continuing operations decreased 7.7% to $443,000 thousand from income of $480,000 thousand a year earlier. Net income decreased 17.3% to $431,000 thousand from net income of $521,000 thousand a year earlier. Revenues were $7,114,000 thousand, up 1.0% from $7,041,000 thousand the year before. Operating income was $846,000 thousand versus an income of $747,000 thousand in the prior year, an increase of 13.3%. Total direct expense was $5,427,000 thousand versus $5,350,000 thousand in the prior year, an increase of 1.4%. Total indirect expense was $841,000 thousand versus $944,000 thousand in the prior year, a decrease of 10.9%.

Prospects: Co. anticipates 2005 to be a brighter year as its electric rate restructuring proposal and the resolution of MichCon's rate case is expected to bring its utilities back to financial health and provide a sustainable and stable regulatory structure. Co. also plans to continue its strategy of growing its non-utility businesses while maintaining a strong balance sheet. Operationally, Co. will focus on effectively redeploying the $1.65 billion in cash that Co. expects its non-utility businesses to generate from 2005 to 2008 into corporate debt reduction, investments in non-utility businesses and stock repurchases. Co. expects earnings of $3.30 to $3.60 per diluted share in 2005.

Financial Data

(US$ in Thousands)	12/31/2004	12/31/2003	12/31/2002	12/31/2001	12/31/2000	12/31/1999	12/31/1998	12/31/1997
Earnings Per Share	2.49	3.09	3.83	2.16	3.27	3.33	3.05	2.88
Cash Flow Per Share	5.75	5.66	5.94	5.30	7.59	7.57	5.99	6.94
Tang Book Value Per Share	19.98	19.10	14.61	18.13	28.15	26.95	25.50	24.55
Dividends Per Share	2.060	2.060	2.060	2.060	2.060	2.060	2.060	2.060
Dividend Payout %	82.73	66.67	53.79	95.37	63.00	61.86	67.54	71.53
Income Statement								
Total Revenue	7,114,000	7,041,000	6,749,000	7,849,000	5,597,000	4,728,000	4,221,000	3,764,000
EBITDA	1,603,000	1,557,000	1,851,000	1,482,000	1,571,000	1,618,000	1,577,000	1,631,000
Depn & Amortn	744,000	691,000	759,000	795,000	758,000	735,000	661,000	660,000
Income Before Taxes	396,000	357,000	573,000	219,000	477,000	543,000	597,000	674,000
Income Taxes	165,000	(123,000)	(59,000)	(110,000)	9,000	60,000	154,000	257,000
Net Income	431,000	521,000	632,000	332,000	468,000	483,000	443,000	417,000
Average Shares	173,300	168,300	164,767	154,000	143,000	145,000	145,000	145,000
Balance Sheet								
Net PPE	10,491,000	10,324,000	9,813,000	9,543,000	7,387,000	7,148,000	6,943,000	8,934,000
Total Assets	21,297,000	20,753,000	19,238,000	19,228,000	12,662,000	12,316,000	12,088,000	11,223,000
Long-Term Obligations	7,606,000	7,669,000	7,514,000	7,654,000	4,062,000	4,052,000	4,323,000	3,914,000
Total Liabilities	15,749,000	15,466,000	14,402,000	14,365,000	8,647,000	8,407,000	8,390,000	7,517,000
Stockholders' Equity	5,548,000	5,287,000	4,565,000	4,589,000	4,015,000	3,909,000	3,698,000	3,706,000
Shares Outstanding	174,209	168,606	167,462	142,651	142,651	145,041	145,000	145,098
Statistical Record								
Return on Assets %	2.04	2.61	3.29	2.08	3.74	3.96	3.80	3.75
Return on Equity %	7.93	10.58	13.81	7.72	11.78	12.70	11.97	11.66
EBITDA Margin %	22.53	22.11	27.43	18.88	28.07	34.22	37.36	43.33
Net Margin %	6.06	7.40	9.36	4.23	8.36	10.22	10.50	11.08
PPE Turnover	0.68	0.70	0.70	0.93	0.77	0.67	0.53	0.42
Asset Turnover	0.34	0.35	0.35	0.49	0.45	0.39	0.36	0.34
Debt to Equity	1.37	1.45	1.65	1.67	1.01	1.04	1.17	1.06
Price Range	45.30-38.07	49.28-34.54	47.68-34.10	46.68-33.75	39.19-29.19	44.31-31.19	49.06-33.88	34.69-26.25
P/E Ratio	18.19-15.29	15.95-11.18	12.45-8.90	21.61-15.62	11.98-8.93	13.31-9.37	16.09-11.11	12.04-9.11
Average Yield %	5.04	5.27	4.78	4.97	6.09	5.32	5.09	6.93

Address: 2000 2nd Avenue, Room 2412, Detroit, MI 48226-1279 **Telephone:** (313) 235-4000	**Web Site:** www.dteenergy.com **Officers:** Anthony F. Earley Jr. - Chmn., C.E.O., C.O.O. Gerard M. Anderson - Pres.	**Auditors:** Deloitte & Touche LLP **Investor Contact:** 313-235-8030

DU PONT (E.I.) DE NEMOURS & CO

Exchange	Symbol	Price	52Wk Range	Yield	P/E
NYS	DD	$51.24 (3/31/2005)	54.55-40.21	2.73	28.95

*7 Year Price Score 78.37 ***NYSE Composite Index=100** ***12 Month Price Score 106.51**

TRADING VOLUME (thousand shares)

Interim Earnings (Per Share)

Qtr.	Mar	Jun	Sep	Dec
2001	0.47	(0.21)	0.13	3.76
2002	0.48	0.54	0.47	0.35
2003	0.53	0.67	(0.88)	0.63
2004	0.66	0.50	0.33	0.28

Interim Dividends (Per Share)

Amt	Decl	Ex	Rec	Pay
0.35Q	4/28/2004	5/12/2004	5/14/2004	6/12/2004
0.35Q	7/28/2004	8/11/2004	8/13/2004	9/11/2004
0.35Q	10/27/2004	11/10/2004	11/15/2004	12/14/2004
0.35Q	1/26/2005	2/11/2005	2/15/2005	3/14/2005
		Indicated Div: $1.40		

Valuation Analysis

Forecast P/E	18.28	No of Institutions	
	(4/7/2005)	835	
Market Cap	$51.0 Billion	Shares	
Book Value	11.4 Billion	603,568,256	
Price/Book	4.48	% Held	
Price/Sales	1.82	60.54	

Business Summary: Chemicals (MIC: 11.1 SIC: 821 NAIC: 25211)

E.I. du Pont de Nemours provides science and technology products for a range of industries including high-performance materials, synthetic fibers, electronics, specialty chemicals, agriculture and biotechnology. Co. has a portfolio of trademarks and brands, including Lycra®, Teflon®, Stainmaster®, Kevlar®, Pioneer®, Tyvek®, Dacron®, Cordura®, Corian®, CoolMax® and Tactel®. Co. operates in the following segments: agricultural and nutrition, coatings and color technologies, electronic and communication technologies, performance materials; and safety and protection.

Recent Developments: For the year ended Dec 31 2004, net income increased 82.9% to $1,780,000 thousand from net income of $973,000 thousand a year earlier. Revenues were $27,995,000 thousand, up 1.0% from $27,730,000 thousand the year before. Total direct expense was $20,416,000 thousand versus $20,759,000 thousand in the prior year, a decrease of 1.7%. Total indirect expense was $5,775,000 thousand versus $6,543,000 thousand in the prior year, a decrease of 11.7%.

Prospects: For 2005, sales from new products are expected to increase to 33.0% of total sales as Co. continues to introduce new products and realizes the full advantage of new products introduced in the previous four years. Raw material costs are expected to increase above 2004 levels, due mainly to elevated prices for oil and natural gas. However, Co. expects to improve operating margins through its cost improvement program and higher sale prices. In addition, Co. plans to increase sales in emerging markets, particularly Asia, and continue to focus on productivity gains. Accordingly, Co. is confident it can achieve full-year earnings of between $2.65 and $2.85 per share, excluding charges.

Financial Data

(US$ in Thousands)	12/31/2004	12/31/2003	12/31/2002	12/31/2001	12/31/2000	12/31/1999	12/31/1998	12/31/1997
Earnings Per Share	1.77	0.96	(1.11)	4.16	2.19	6.99	3.90	2.08
Cash Flow Per Share	3.23	2.60	2.06	2.33	4.85	4.46	3.66	6.18
Tang Book Value Per Share	6.25	4.63	4.58	7.30	4.50	3.72	9.90	8.63
Dividends Per Share	1.400	1.400	1.400	1.400	1.400	1.400	1.365	1.230
Dividend Payout %	79.10	145.83	...	33.65	63.93	20.03	35.00	59.13
Income Statement								
Total Revenue	27,995,000	27,730,000	24,522,000	25,370,000	29,202,000	27,892,000	25,748,000	46,653,000
EBITDA	2,789,000	1,727,000	3,639,000	8,598,000	5,307,000	3,380,000	4,173,000	7,065,000
Depn & Amortn	1,347,000	1,584,000	1,515,000	1,754,000	1,860,000	1,690,000	1,560,000	2,385,000
Income Before Taxes	1,442,000	143,000	2,124,000	6,844,000	3,447,000	1,690,000	2,613,000	4,680,000
Income Taxes	(329,000)	(930,000)	185,000	2,467,000	1,072,000	1,410,000	941,000	2,275,000
Net Income	1,780,000	973,000	(1,103,000)	4,339,000	2,314,000	7,690,000	4,480,000	2,405,000
Average Shares	1,003,392	1,000,010	998,737	1,041,164	1,051,042	1,097,970	1,145,000	1,150,000
Balance Sheet								
Current Assets	15,211,000	18,462,000	13,459,000	14,801,000	11,656,000	12,653,000	9,236,000	11,874,000
Total Assets	35,632,000	37,039,000	34,621,000	40,319,000	39,426,000	40,777,000	38,536,000	42,942,000
Current Liabilities	7,939,000	13,043,000	7,096,000	8,067,000	9,255,000	11,228,000	11,610,000	14,070,000
Long-Term Obligations	5,548,000	4,301,000	5,647,000	5,350,000	6,658,000	6,625,000	4,495,000	5,929,000
Total Liabilities	23,145,000	26,761,000	23,135,000	23,443,000	25,747,000	27,385,000	24,175,000	31,002,000
Stockholders' Equity	11,377,000	9,781,000	9,063,000	14,452,000	13,299,000	12,875,000	13,954,000	11,270,000
Shares Outstanding	994,340	997,284	993,940	1,001,953	1,042,931	1,052,473	1,126,000	1,130,000
Statistical Record								
Return on Assets %	4.89	2.72	N.M.	10.88	5.75	19.39	11.00	5.94
Return on Equity %	16.78	10.33	N.M.	31.27	17.63	57.33	35.52	21.88
EBITDA Margin %	9.96	6.23	14.84	33.89	18.17	12.12	16.21	15.14
Net Margin %	6.36	3.51	N.M.	17.10	7.92	27.57	17.40	5.16
Asset Turnover	0.77	0.77	0.65	0.64	0.73	0.70	0.63	1.15
Current Ratio	1.92	1.42	1.90	1.83	1.26	1.13	0.80	0.84
Debt to Equity	0.49	0.44	0.62	0.37	0.50	0.51	0.32	0.53
Price Range	49.15-40.21	45.94-35.11	49.09-36.07	49.70-33.61	71.63-38.50	74.88-50.25	82.75-51.75	69.00-47.06
P/E Ratio	27.77-22.72	47.85-36.57	...	11.95-8.08	32.71-17.58	10.71-7.19	21.22-13.27	33.17-22.63
Average Yield %	3.21	3.38	3.24	3.22	2.86	2.20	2.13	2.11

Address: 1007 Market Street, Wilmington, DE 19898 Telephone: (302) 774-1000 Fax: (302) 774-0748	Web Site: www.dupont.com Officers: Charles O. Holliday Jr. - Chmn., C.E.O. Richard R. Goodmanson - Exec. V.P., C.O.O.	Auditors: PricewaterhouseCoopers LLP Investor Contact: 302-774-4994

DUKE ENERGY CORP.

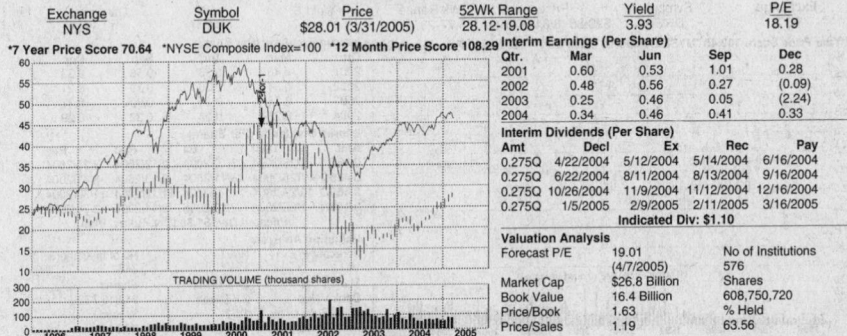

Exchange	Symbol	Price	52Wk Range	Yield	P/E
NYS	DUK	$28.01 (3/31/2005)	28.12-19.08	3.93	18.19

*7 Year Price Score 70.64 *NYSE Composite Index=100 *12 Month Price Score 108.29

Interim Earnings (Per Share)

Qtr.	Mar	Jun	Sep	Dec
2001	0.60	0.53	1.01	0.28
2002	0.48	0.56	0.27	(0.09)
2003	0.25	0.46	0.05	(2.24)
2004	0.34	0.46	0.41	0.33

Interim Dividends (Per Share)

Amt	Decl	Ex	Rec	Pay
0.275Q	4/22/2004	5/12/2004	5/14/2004	6/16/2004
0.275Q	6/22/2004	8/11/2004	8/13/2004	9/16/2004
0.275Q	10/26/2004	11/9/2004	11/12/2004	12/16/2004
0.275Q	1/5/2005	2/9/2005	2/11/2005	3/16/2005

Indicated Div: $1.10

Valuation Analysis

Forecast P/E	19.01 (4/7/2005)	No of Institutions 576
Market Cap	$26.8 Billion	Shares 608,750,720
Book Value	16.4 Billion	% Held 63.56
Price/Book	1.63	
Price/Sales	1.19	

Business Summary: Electricity (MIC: 7.1 SIC: 911 NAIC: 21122)

Duke Energy is a diversified multinational energy-services corporation that conducts business through four subsidiaries. The Franchised Electric Group generates, transmits, distributes and sells electricity in central and western North Carolina and western South Carolina. The Natural Gas Transmission Group provides transportation and storage of natural gas for customers throughout the East Coast and Southern U.S. and in Canada. The Field Services Group gathers, compresses, treats, processes, transports, trades and markets, and stores natural gas. Duke Energy North America develops, operates and manages merchant power generation facilities.

Recent Developments: For the year ended Dec 31 2004, income from continuing operations was $1,232,000 thousand compared with a loss of $1,003,000 thousand a year earlier. Net income was $1,490,000 thousand versus net loss of $1,323,000 thousand a year earlier. Revenues were $22,503,000 thousand, up 1.9% from $22,080,000 thousand the year before. Operating income was $3,014,000 thousand versus a loss of $853,000 thousand in the prior year. Total direct expense was $17,001,000 thousand versus $17,290,000 thousand in the prior year, a decrease of 1.7%. Total indirect expense was $2,488,000 thousand versus $5,643,000 thousand in the prior year, a decrease of 55.9%.

Prospects: Co. approved a plan to repurchase up to $2.50 billion in common stock periodically over the next three years. This repurchase plan will be funded in part by a restructuring of Co.'s ownership interest in Duke Energy Field Services (DEFS) with ConocoPhillips to a 50-50 joint venture, subject to U.S. and Canadian regulatory approvals. The plan reflects Co.'s strategy to monetize some of its assets, reduce risks and generate cash during a high commodity price environment. The plan will be funded by the sale by DEFS of the general partner of TEPPCO to EPCO for $1.10 billion and the sale by Co. of its 2.5 million limited partner units in TEPPCO for roughly $100.0 million.

Financial Data

(US$ in Thousands)

	12/31/2004	12/31/2003	12/31/2002	12/31/2001	12/31/2000	12/31/1999	12/31/1998	12/31/1997
Earnings Per Share	1.54	(1.48)	1.22	2.44	2.38	2.04	1.70	1.25
Cash Flow Per Share	4.43	4.35	5.42	5.99	3.02	3.68	3.23	2.97
Tang Book Value Per Share	12.85	10.74	12.51	14.10	11.49	11.14	10.54	9.78
Dividends Per Share	1.100	1.100	1.100	1.100	1.100	1.100	1.100	1.080
Dividend Payout %	71.43	...	90.16	45.08	46.22	54.05	64.71	86.40
Income Statement								
Total Revenue	22,503,000	22,529,000	15,663,000	59,503,000	49,318,000	21,742,000	17,610,000	16,308,900
EBITDA	5,158,000	1,655,000	4,454,000	5,379,000	5,055,000	3,052,000	3,606,000	3,067,600
Depn & Amortn	2,037,000	1,987,000	1,692,000	1,450,000	1,348,000	1,151,000	1,055,000	982,500
Income Before Taxes	1,772,000	(1,712,000)	1,652,000	3,144,000	2,796,000	1,300,000	2,037,000	1,613,300
Income Taxes	540,000	(707,000)	618,000	1,150,000	1,020,000	453,000	777,000	638,900
Net Income	1,490,000	(1,323,000)	1,034,000	1,898,000	1,776,000	1,507,000	1,252,000	974,400
Average Shares	966,000	903,000	838,100	767,000	739,400	730,000	724,000	723,400
Balance Sheet								
Net PPE	33,506,000	34,986,000	36,219,000	28,415,000	24,469,000	20,995,000	16,875,000	15,735,900
Total Assets	55,470,000	56,203,000	60,966,000	48,375,000	58,176,000	33,409,000	26,806,000	24,028,800
Long-Term Obligations	16,932,000	20,622,000	20,221,000	12,321,000	11,019,000	8,683,000	6,272,000	6,530,000
Total Liabilities	39,029,000	42,455,000	46,022,000	35,686,000	48,120,000	24,411,000	18,656,000	16,489,100
Stockholders' Equity	16,441,000	13,748,000	14,944,000	12,689,000	10,056,000	8,998,000	8,150,000	7,539,700
Shares Outstanding	957,000	911,000	895,000	777,000	739,000	732,000	726,000	719,900
Statistical Record								
Return on Assets %	2.66	N.M.	1.89	3.56	3.87	5.01	4.93	5.20
Return on Equity %	9.84	N.M.	7.48	16.69	18.59	17.58	15.96	15.68
EBITDA Margin %	22.92	7.35	28.44	9.04	10.25	14.04	20.48	18.81
Net Margin %	6.62	(5.87)	6.60	3.19	3.60	6.93	7.11	5.97
PPE Turnover	0.66	0.63	0.48	2.25	2.16	1.15	1.08	1.28
Asset Turnover	0.40	0.38	0.29	1.12	1.07	0.72	0.69	0.87
Debt to Equity	1.03	1.50	1.35	0.97	1.10	0.96	0.77	0.87
Price Range	26.05-19.08	21.35-12.32	39.80-16.56	47.48-32.94	44.97-23.19	32.34-23.53	35.34-26.72	28.09-21.06
P/E Ratio	16.92-12.39	...	32.62-13.57	19.46-13.50	18.89-9.74	15.85-11.53	20.79-15.72	22.48-16.85
Average Yield %	4.98	6.31	3.83	2.75	3.32	3.93	3.69	4.53

Address: 526 South Church Street, Charlotte, NC 28202-1803 **Telephone:** (704) 594-6200 **Fax:** (704) 382-0230	**Web Site:** www.duke-energy.com **Officers:** Paul M. Anderson - Chmn., C.E.O. Fred J. Fowler - Pres., C.O.O.	**Auditors:** Deloitte & Touche LLP **Investor Contact:** 800-488-3853 **Transfer Agents:** Duke Energy, Charlotte, NC

269

DUKE REALTY CORP.

Exchange	Symbol	Price	52Wk Range	Yield	P/E	Div Acheiver
NYS	DRE	$29.85 (3/31/2005)	35.77-28.76	6.23	28.16	11 Years

*7 Year Price Score 109.48 *NYSE Composite Index=100 *12 Month Price Score 90.33

Interim Earnings (Per Share)

Qtr.	Mar	Jun	Sep	Dec
2001	0.45	0.38	0.58	0.33
2002	0.34	0.36	0.29	0.21
2003	0.28	0.25	0.30	0.37
2004	0.23	0.24	0.30	0.29

Interim Dividends (Per Share)

Amt	Decl	Ex	Rec	Pay
0.46Q	1/28/2004	2/10/2004	2/12/2004	2/27/2004
0.465Q	7/28/2004	8/11/2004	8/13/2004	8/31/2004
0.465Q	10/27/2004	11/9/2004	11/12/2004	11/30/2004
0.465Q	1/26/2005	2/10/2005	2/14/2005	2/28/2005

Indicated Div: $1.86 (Div. Reinv. Plan)

Valuation Analysis

Forecast P/E	N/A	No of Institutions
		247
Market Cap	$4.3 Billion	Shares
Book Value	2.8 Billion	94,813,336
Price/Book	1.51	% Held
Price/Sales	3.66	66.34

Business Summary: Property, Real Estate & Development (MIC: 8.3 SIC: 798 NAIC: 25930)

Duke Realty is a self-administered and self-managed real estate investment trust company that focuses on major cities in the Midwest and the Southeast. As of Dec. 31, 2003, Co.'s 899 rental properties encompass over 109.0 million rentable square feet and are leased by approximately 4,100 tenants whose businesses include manufacturing, retailing, wholesale trade, distribution and professional services. Co. also owns or controls nearly 3,800 acres of unencumbered land ready for development. Through its service operations, Co. also provides, on a fee basis, leasing, property and asset management, development, construction, build-to-suit, and other tenant-related services.

Recent Developments: For the year ended Dec 31 2004, income from continuing operations decreased 9.9% to $163,201 thousand from income of $181,186 thousand a year earlier. Net income decreased 5.3% to $188,701 thousand from net income of $199,232 thousand a year earlier. Revenues were $1,165,999 thousand, up 11.1% from $1,049,796 thousand the year before. Operating income was $163,031 thousand versus an income of $180,638 thousand in the prior year, a decrease of 9.7%.

Prospects: Co.'s outlook appears promising with $80.0 million in new business booked in the fourth quarter of 2004 and continued improvements in profitability. Including projects under development, Co.'s total portfolio at the end of the fourth quarter of 2004 consisted of 893 properties totaling more than 114.0 million square feet that were 89.7% leased. Looking ahead to fiscal 2005, Co. expects funds from operations to follow a normal seasonal pattern with the first quarter typically being Co.'s slowest period. Co. remains comfortable with funds from operations in the range of $2.43 to $2.55 for the year, and $0.56 to $0.58 for the first quarter of 2005.

Financial Data
(US$ in Thousands)

	12/31/2004	12/31/2003	12/31/2002	12/31/2001	12/31/2000	12/31/1999	12/31/1998	12/31/1997
Earnings Per Share	1.06	1.19	1.19	1.75	1.66	1.32	1.12	0.98
Cash Flow Per Share	2.67	2.72	4.25	3.34	3.53	3.27	2.74	2.40
Tang Book Value Per Share	15.18	15.57	16.11	16.56	16.45	16.36	14.20	13.36
Dividends Per Share	1.850	1.830	1.810	1.760	1.640	1.460	1.280	1.105
Dividend Payout %	174.53	153.78	152.10	100.57	98.80	110.61	114.29	112.76
Income Statement								
Property Income	744,065	706,722	684,311	691,958	697,270	523,950	337,768	220,970
Non-Property Income	421,934	343,074	268,319	341,695	97,355	65,644	35,573	31,110
Total Revenue	1,165,999	1,049,796	952,630	1,033,653	794,625	589,594	373,341	252,080
Depn & Amortn	233,486	199,860	179,346	164,303	163,415	112,643	70,128	46,174
Interest Expense	135,130	129,160	117,073	113,830	133,948	86,757	60,217	40,296
Net Income	188,701	199,232	206,325	282,409	261,939	182,240	110,704	78,484
Average Shares	157,062	151,141	150,839	151,710	147,441	120,511	92,468	74,993
Balance Sheet								
Total Assets	5,896,643	5,561,249	5,348,823	5,330,033	5,460,036	5,486,238	2,853,653	2,176,214
Long-Term Obligations	2,518,704	2,335,536	2,106,285	1,814,856	1,973,215	2,113,476	1,007,317	720,119
Total Liabilities	2,875,661	2,681,706	2,424,002	2,149,834	2,311,829	2,383,897	1,176,812	834,169
Stockholders' Equity	2,825,869	2,666,749	2,616,180	2,785,009	2,712,890	2,668,596	1,570,112	1,234,681
Shares Outstanding	142,894	136,594	135,007	131,416	127,932	125,823	86,053	76,065
Statistical Record								
Return on Assets %	3.28	3.65	3.86	5.23	4.77	4.37	4.40	4.44
Return on Equity %	6.85	7.54	7.64	10.27	9.71	8.60	7.89	7.89
Net Margin %	16.18	18.98	21.66	27.32	32.96	30.91	29.65	31.13
Price Range	35.77-28.76	31.75-24.50	28.95-22.42	25.97-22.00	25.75-17.88	23.94-16.81	24.94-19.81	24.88-17.44
P/E Ratio	33.75-27.13	26.68-20.59	24.33-18.84	14.84-12.57	15.51-10.77	18.13-12.74	22.27-17.69	25.38-17.79
Average Yield %	5.68	6.53	7.15	7.36	7.45	6.85	5.56	5.28

Address: 600 East 96th Street, Suite 100, Indianapolis, IN 46240 Telephone: (317) 808-6000 Fax: (317) 808-6770	Web Site: www.dukerealty.com Officers: Thomas L. Hefner - Chmn., C.E.O. Dennis D. Oklak - Pres., C.O.O.	Auditors: KPMG LLP Investor Contact: 317-808-6005 Transfer Agents: American Stock Transfer & Trust Company, New York

DUN & BRADSTREET CORP (DE) (NEW)

Exchange	Symbol	Price	52Wk Range	Yield	P/E
NYS	DNB	$61.45 (3/31/2005)	62.69-51.45	N/A	21.19

*7 Year Price Score N/A ***NYSE Composite Index=100** ***12 Month Price Score 99.33**

TRADING VOLUME (thousand shares)

Interim Earnings (Per Share)

Qtr.	Mar	Jun	Sep	Dec
2001	0.37	0.44	0.36	0.70
2002	0.46	0.13	0.43	0.84
2003	0.48	0.46	0.38	0.98
2004	0.66	0.54	0.65	1.04

Interim Dividends (Per Share)

No Dividends Paid

Valuation Analysis

Forecast P/E	N/A	No of Institutions 245
Market Cap	$4.2 Billion	Shares
Book Value	54.2 Million	57,726,420
Price/Book	77.79	% Held
Price/Sales	2.98	83.62

Business Summary: Miscellaneous Business Services (MIC: 12.8 SIC: 389 NAIC: 18111)

Dun & Bradstreet collects and organizes business information. The foundation of Co.'s product offerings is its database containing information on over 83.0 million public and private business entities located in more than 200 countries. Co.'s Risk Management Solutions products are designed for credit and transaction risk management, while its Sales & Marketing Solutions products are intended to help clients find and retain customers. Supply Management Solutions products are designed to manage customer and vendor relationships. E-Business Solutions consists of Hoover's, Inc., a provider of information on companies, primarily to sales, marketing and business development professionals.

Recent Developments: For the year ended Dec 31 2004, net income increased 21.4% to $211,800 thousand from net income of $174,500 thousand a year earlier. Revenues were $1,414,000 thousand, up 2.0% from $1,386,400 thousand the year before. Operating income was $318,800 thousand versus an income of $291,800 thousand in the prior year, an increase of 9.3%. Total direct expense was $403,900 thousand versus $433,300 thousand in the prior year, a decrease of 6.8%. Total indirect expense was $691,300 thousand versus $661,300 thousand in the prior year, an increase of 4.5%.

Prospects: Looking ahead to full-year 2005, Co. is forecasting core revenue growth of 6.0% to 8.0%, before the effect of foreign exchange, and operating income growth, before non-core gains and charges, of 11.0% to 14.0%. For fiscal 2005, Co. expects diluted earnings per share to be between $3.39 and $3.49, before non-core gains and charges, representing 14.0% to 17.0% growth. This guidance includes the effect of the new share repurchase program. In addition, Co. expects full-year 2005 free cash flow to be between $265.0 million and $280.0 million, before the impact of any payments made in connection with its legacy tax matters.

Financial Data (US$ in Thousands)	12/31/2004	12/31/2003	12/31/2002	12/31/2001	12/31/2000	12/31/1999	12/31/1998	12/31/1997
Earnings Per Share	2.90	2.30	1.87	1.88	2.52	3.12	3.26	2.14
Cash Flow Per Share	3.79	3.21	2.86	2.73	0.29	4.24	4.47	...
Income Statement								
Total Revenue	1,414,000	1,386,400	1,275,600	1,308,800	1,417,600	1,407,700	1,420,500	1,353,600
EBITDA	398,600	358,800	339,900	363,200	267,600	275,400	289,200	303,000
Depn & Amortn	47,300	64,000	84,200	94,500	111,200	127,900	126,200	115,800
Income Before Taxes	340,800	280,400	239,200	257,800	151,700	145,400	157,300	135,700
Income Taxes	129,200	106,200	94,100	101,100	78,100	64,100	71,100	42,500
Net Income	211,800	174,500	143,400	153,200	206,600	256,000	280,100	184,000
Average Shares	73,104	75,826	76,874	81,510	81,994	82,142	85,851	86,276
Balance Sheet								
Current Assets	762,100	730,800	614,200	580,200	538,600	606,700	585,500	...
Total Assets	1,635,500	1,624,700	1,527,700	1,431,200	1,423,600	1,574,800	1,574,700	...
Current Liabilities	713,600	735,900	718,100	662,700	743,100	1,037,000	1,008,700	...
Long-Term Obligations	300,000	299,900	299,900	299,600	...	...	...	...
Total Liabilities	1,581,300	1,576,300	1,546,500	1,452,100	1,474,600	1,991,400	1,945,700	...
Stockholders' Equity	54,200	48,400	(18,800)	(20,900)	(51,000)	(416,600)	(371,000)	...
Shares Outstanding	68,613	72,253	74,358	76,878	80,154	80,411	82,527	...
Statistical Record								
Return on Assets %	12.96	11.07	9.69	10.73	13.74	16.26	...	...
Return on Equity %	411.74	360.54	...	...	...	...	...	...
EBITDA Margin %	28.19	25.88	26.65	27.75	18.88	19.56	20.36	22.38
Net Margin %	14.98	12.59	11.24	11.71	14.57	18.19	19.72	13.59
Asset Turnover	0.87	0.88	0.86	0.92	0.94	0.89	...	...
Current Ratio	1.07	0.99	0.86	0.88	0.72	0.59	0.58	...
Debt to Equity	5.54	6.20	...	...	...	...	...	...
Price Range	60.37-48.18	50.71-32.62	43.08-28.32	36.25-21.23	26.94-13.50	...	...	...
P/E Ratio	20.82-16.61	22.05-14.18	23.04-15.14	19.28-11.29	10.69-5.36	...	...	...

Address: 103 JFK Parkway, Short hills, NJ 07078 Telephone: (973) 921-5500	Web Site: www.dnb.com Officers: Allan Z. Loren - Chmn., C.E.O. Steven W. Alesio - Pres., C.E.O.	Auditors: PricewaterhouseCoopers LLP

DUQUESNE LIGHT HOLDINGS INC

Exchange	Symbol	Price	52Wk Range	Yield	P/E
NYS	DQE	$17.92 (3/31/2005)	19.70-17.01	5.58	9.28

*7 Year Price Score 59.49   *NYSE Composite Index=100   *12 Month Price Score 92.66

TRADING VOLUME (thousand shares)

Interim Earnings (Per Share)

Qtr.	Mar	Jun	Sep	Dec
2001	0.22	(2.17)	0.40	(1.22)
2002	0.29	(1.69)	0.36	(0.65)
2003	0.39	0.45	0.40	1.05
2004	0.28	0.31	0.30	...

Interim Dividends (Per Share)

Amt	Decl	Ex	Rec	Pay
0.25Q	5/27/2004	6/8/2004	6/10/2004	7/1/2004
0.25Q	7/22/2004	9/8/2004	9/10/2004	10/1/2004
0.25Q	11/19/2004	12/8/2004	12/10/2004	1/1/2005
0.25Q	2/17/2005	3/8/2005	3/10/2005	4/1/2005

Indicated Div: $1.00

Valuation Analysis

Forecast P/E	14.98 (4/7/2005)	No of Institutions	162
Market Cap	$1.4 Billion	Shares	43,346,288
Book Value	606.2 Million	% Held	56.38
Price/Book	2.27		
Price/Sales	1.53		

Business Summary: Electricity (MIC: 7.1 SIC: 911 NAIC: 21121)

Duquesne Light Holdings is a multi-utility delivery and services company providing electricity, water and communications to more than one million customers throughout the U.S. Duquesne Light, Co.'s largest subsidiary, is an electric utility engaged in the supply, transmission and distribution of electric energy. Co.'s expanded business lines include propane distribution, communication systems, and financing and insurance services for Co. and various affiliates. Co.'s other subsidiaries are DQE Capital Corp., DQE Energy Services, Inc., DQE Financial Corp., and DQE Communications, Inc.

Recent Developments: For the quarter ended Sep 30 2004, income from continuing operations decreased 22.5% to $23,400 thousand from income of $30,200 thousand in the year-earlier quarter. Net income decreased 22.9% to $23,600 thousand from net income of $30,600 thousand in the year-earlier quarter. Revenues were $242,800 thousand, down 1.3% from $246,000 thousand the year before. Operating income was $40,200 thousand versus income of $49,000 thousand in the prior-year quarter, a decrease of 18.0%. Total direct expense grew 1.5% to $159,700 thousand from $162,100 thousand a year earlier. Total indirect expense was $42,900 thousand versus $34,900 thousand in the prior-year quarter, an increase of 22.9%.

Prospects: On Sep 30 2004, Co. notified WPS Resources Corporation (WPS) that it was terminating the asset sale agreement dated as of Oct 23 2003, pursuant to which it would have acquired WPS' Sunbury generation station for approximately $120.0 million. A condition precedent to Co.'s obligation to complete the acquisition was approval of its rate and related generation supply plan for 2005 through 2010 by the Pennsylvania Public Utility Commission (PUC). Co. did not receive such reasonably satisfactory approval from the PUC. Nevertheless, Co. has reaffirmed its 2005 earnings guidance of $90.0 million to $95.0 million, or $1.16 to $1.22 per share, from continuing operations.

Financial Data

(US$ in Thousands)	9 Mos	6 Mos	3 Mos	12/31/2003	12/31/2002	12/31/2001	12/31/2000	12/31/1999
Earnings Per Share	1.93	2.04	2.18	2.29	(3.28)	(2.75)	2.39	2.62
Cash Flow Per Share	1.16	3.66	3.64	3.59	3.95	4.78	5.21	4.48
Tang Book Value Per Share	7.90	7.80	7.71	7.63	6.09	9.09	14.02	18.78
Dividends Per Share	1.000	1.000	1.000	1.000	1.340	1.680	1.620	1.540
Dividend Payout %	51.85	49.12	45.98	43.67	...	...	67.78	58.78
Income Statement								
Total Revenue	678,800	436,000	217,100	902,800	1,019,400	1,296,082	1,327,604	1,341,201
EBITDA	137,400	90,500	45,300	285,600	316,500	311,780	711,152	727,634
Depn & Amortn	62,100	41,100	20,400	100,300	186,400	416,800	379,136	256,789
Income Before Taxes	75,300	49,400	24,900	110,900	46,600	(209,462)	208,406	312,138
Income Taxes	12,200	7,200	3,200	17,700	19,900	(56,081)	70,350	110,722
Net Income	68,800	45,200	21,800	175,900	(214,600)	(153,381)	153,551	201,416
Average Shares	78,300	78,200	78,000	77,600	65,700	55,888	65,002	77,676
Balance Sheet								
Net PPE	1,449,300	1,444,600	1,439,500	1,437,300	1,425,500	1,688,325	1,707,071	1,828,067
Total Assets	2,698,000	2,709,900	2,587,400	2,540,800	2,811,300	3,225,909	3,865,973	5,608,992
Long-Term Obligations	958,000	1,055,000	932,300	977,500	1,082,000	1,198,759	1,349,298	1,649,940
Total Liabilities	1,945,400	1,967,600	1,930,300	1,894,700	2,115,500	2,474,612	2,840,814	3,988,945
Stockholders' Equity	606,200	596,100	585,700	575,400	452,600	508,461	783,745	1,347,865
Shares Outstanding	76,723	76,427	75,994	75,423	74,344	55,908	55,885	71,766
Statistical Record								
Return on Assets %	5.54	5.72	6.25	6.57	N.M.	N.M.	3.23	3.71
Return on Equity %	26.82	28.99	31.88	34.22	N.M.	N.M.	14.37	14.22
EBITDA Margin %	20.24	20.76	20.87	31.63	31.05	24.06	53.57	54.25
Net Margin %	10.14	10.37	10.04	19.48	(21.05)	(11.83)	11.57	15.02
PPE Turnover	0.62	0.63	0.63	0.63	0.65	0.76	0.75	0.76
Asset Turnover	0.33	0.33	0.33	0.34	0.34	0.37	0.28	0.25
Debt to Equity	1.58	1.77	1.59	1.70	2.39	2.36	1.72	1.22
Price Range	20.44-15.41	20.44-13.81	20.44-12.09	18.39-12.09	22.20-11.29	33.15-16.68	48.50-30.75	44.19-33.88
P/E Ratio	10.59-7.98	10.02-6.77	9.38-5.55	8.03-5.28	...	...	20.29-12.87	16.87-12.93
Average Yield %	5.44	5.76	6.16	6.65	7.95	7.02	4.06	3.89

Address: 411 Seventh Avenue, Pittsburgh, PA 15219 **Telephone:** (412) 393-6000 **Fax:** (412) 393-6065	**Web Site:** www.dqe.com **Officers:** Morgan K. O'Brien - Pres., C.E.O. Joseph G. Belechak - Sr. V.P., C.O.O.	**Auditors:** Deloitte & Touche LLP **Investor Contact:** 412-393-6167

DYCOM INDUSTRIES, INC.

Exchange	Symbol	Price	52Wk Range	Yield	P/E
NYS	DY	$22.99 (3/31/2005)	35.39-21.30	N/A	22.54

7 Year Price Score 98.70 *NYSE Composite Index=100 *12 Month Price Score 86.51

Interim Earnings (Per Share)
Qtr.	Oct	Jan	Apr	Jul
2001-02	0.19	0.12	0.17	(1.23)
2002-03	0.09	(0.02)	0.06	0.24
2003-04	0.29	0.34	0.23	0.34
2004-05	0.32	0.15	...	...

Interim Dividends (Per Share)
Amt	Decl	Ex	Rec	Pay
3-for-2	1/20/2000	2/17/2000	2/2/2000	2/16/2000

Valuation Analysis
Forecast P/E	20.40	No of Institutions
	(4/7/2005)	184
Market Cap	$1.1 Billion	Shares
Book Value	546.7 Million	42,742,712
Price/Book	2.05	% Held
Price/Sales	1.18	87.56

Business Summary: Construction - Public Infrastructure (MIC: 3.1 SIC: 623 NAIC: 37130)

Dycom Industries is a provider of specialty contracting services, including engineering, construction, installation, and maintenance services to telecommunications providers throughout the United States. Co. provides a range of telecommunications infrastructure services including the engineering, placement and maintenance of aerial, underground, and buried fiber-optic, coaxial and copper cable systems owned by local and long distance communications carriers and cable television multiple system operators. Additionally, Co. provides similar services related to the installation of integrated voice, data, and video local and wide area networks within buildings.

Recent Developments: For the quarter ended Jan 29 2005, net income decreased 55.2% to $7,373,590 from net income of $16,442,142 in the year-earlier quarter. Revenues were $224,538,572 , up 14.3% from $196,368,974 the year before. Total direct expense was $181,986,298 versus $151,224,328 in the prior-year quarter, an increase of 20.3%. Total indirect expense was $31,731,199 versus $29,870,776 in the prior-year quarter, an increase of 6.2%.

Prospects: A nonrecurring gain in fiscal 2004 is subtracting from earnings. For instance, for the quarter ended Jan 29 2005, Co. reported a nonrecurring items of nil versus a gain of $11.4 million in 2004 related to the sale of long-term accounts receivable. Separately, for the third quarter of fiscal 2005, Co. is projecting revenue to be in the range of $235.0 million to $250.0 million, with diluted earnings per share of between $0.23 and $0.28. For the fourth quarter of fiscal 2005, Co. is forecasting revenue to range from $275.0 million to $295.0 million, with diluted earnings per share to range from $0.35 to $0.45.

Financial Data
(US$ in Thousands)	6 Mos	3 Mos	07/31/2004	07/26/2003	07/27/2002	07/28/2001	07/29/2000	07/31/1999
Earnings Per Share	1.02	1.21	1.20	0.36	(2.73)	1.44	1.54	1.03
Cash Flow Per Share	2.01	2.16	2.53	0.53	1.45	3.15	1.83	1.08
Tang Book Value Per Share	5.91	5.67	5.34	7.15	6.76	7.32	6.97	5.93
Income Statement								
Total Revenue	487,704	263,166	872,716	618,183	624,021	826,746	806,270	473,453
EBITDA	61,912	37,108	139,435	68,229	9,633	140,604	137,545	80,756
Depn & Amortn	24,065	11,265	42,066	39,074	38,844	40,117	31,759	20,143
Income Before Taxes	37,993	25,796	97,180	30,455	(26,259)	104,983	109,233	60,612
Income Taxes	14,998	10,176	38,547	13,306	9,508	43,573	44,201	24,162
Net Income	22,994	15,621	58,633	17,149	(123,027)	61,411	65,032	36,450
Average Shares	49,343	49,169	48,819	47,886	45,049	42,770	42,314	35,185
Balance Sheet								
Current Assets	284,508	293,686	276,033	305,473	256,736	309,368	324,429	241,129
Total Assets	668,322	668,141	651,835	536,543	514,553	575,696	514,000	384,550
Current Liabilities	93,948	103,445	102,478	70,734	70,551	84,948	114,759	78,606
Long-Term Obligations	5,078	6,292	7,094	20	30	6,796	9,106	9,982
Total Liabilities	121,651	132,531	132,874	86,203	83,256	106,815	136,022	97,259
Stockholders' Equity	546,671	535,610	518,961	450,340	431,297	468,881	377,978	287,291
Shares Outstanding	48,813	48,621	48,596	47,986	47,846	42,964	41,900	38,441
Statistical Record								
Return on Assets %	7.41	9.66	9.71	3.27	N.M.	11.30	14.51	13.23
Return on Equity %	9.76	11.84	11.90	3.90	N.M.	14.54	19.60	18.90
EBITDA Margin %	12.69	14.10	15.98	11.04	1.54	17.01	17.06	17.06
Net Margin %	4.71	5.94	6.72	2.77	N.M.	7.43	8.07	7.70
Asset Turnover	1.40	1.51	1.44	1.18	1.15	1.52	1.80	1.72
Current Ratio	3.03	2.84	2.69	4.32	3.64	3.64	2.83	3.07
Debt to Equity	0.01	0.01	0.01	N.M.	N.M.	0.01	0.02	0.03
Price Range	35.39-21.30	33.04-21.30	29.35-16.43	17.92-8.59	21.89-8.89	55.50-10.50	56.81-20.71	37.33-11.92
P/E Ratio	34.70-20.88	27.31-17.60	24.46-13.69	49.78-23.86	...	38.54-7.29	36.89-13.45	36.25-11.57

Address: 4440 PGA Boulevard, Suite 500, Palm Beach Gardens, FL 33410-6542
Telephone: (561) 627 7171
Fax: (561) 627 7709

Web Site: www.dycomind.com
Officers: Steven E. Nielsen - Chmn., Pres., C.E.O. Timothy Estes - Exec. V.P., C.O.O.

Auditors: Deloitte & Touche LLP
Investor Contact: 561-627-7171

DYNEGY INC

Exchange	Symbol	Price	52Wk Range	Yield	P/E
NYS	DYN	$3.91 (3/31/2005)	5.86-3.62	N/A	N/A

*7 Year Price Score 21.19   *NYSE Composite Index=100   *12 Month Price Score 88.74

Interim Earnings (Per Share)

Qtr.	Mar	Jun	Sep	Dec
2001	0.41	0.43	0.85	0.21
2002	(0.41)	(0.92)	(4.92)	(2.38)
2003	0.17	(1.00)	2.65	(0.86)
2004	0.15	0.01	0.16	(0.42)

Interim Dividends (Per Share)

Dividend Payment Suspended

Valuation Analysis

Forecast P/E	0.00 (4/7/2005)	No of Institutions	216
Market Cap	$1.5 Billion	Shares	
Book Value	1.9 Billion		171,948,272
Price/Book	0.80	% Held	
Price/Sales	0.24		45.17

TRADING VOLUME (thousand shares)

Business Summary: Oil and Gas (MIC: 14.2 SIC: 311 NAIC: 11111)

Dynegy is a holding company and conducts substantially all of its business operations through its subsidiaries. Co.'s business operations are focused primarily in three areas of the energy industry: power generation; natural gas liquids; and regulated energy delivery. Co.'s power generation segment is engaged in the production and sale of electric power from its owned and leased facilities. The natural gas liquids segment consists of its midstream asset operations, located principally in Texas, Louisiana and New Mexico, and its North American natural gas liquids marketing business. The regulated energy delivery segment consists of our Illinois Power Company.

Recent Developments: For the year ended Dec 31 2004, loss from continuing operations was $10,000 thousand compared with a loss of $713,000 thousand a year earlier. Net loss was $15,000 thousand versus net loss of $692,000 thousand a year earlier. Revenues were $6,153,000 thousand, up 6.3% from $5,787,000 thousand the year before. Operating income was $192,000 thousand versus a loss of $594,000 thousand in the prior year. Total direct expense was $5,214,000 thousand versus $5,074,000 thousand in the prior year, an increase of 2.8%. Total indirect expense was $747,000 thousand versus $1,307,000 thousand in the prior year, a decrease of 42.8%.

Prospects: For 2005, Co. expects a net loss of $335 million to $319 million. This guidance includes a one-time, pre-tax charge Co. expects to realize from its acquisition of Sithe Energies and the related tax benefit. Co. expects operating cash flow in 2005 to be in the range of $200.0 million to $215.0 million. Separately, on Mar 7 2005, Co. entered into a comprehensive, Midwest generation system settlement resolving the environmental litigation related to its Baldwin Energy Complex in Illinois. Under the agreement reached with regulators, Co. will spend $545.0 million over the next seven years on a number of pollution-reduction efforts. The sum also includes a $9.0 million fine to the EPA.

Financial Data

(US$ in Thousands)	12/31/2004	12/31/2003	12/31/2002	12/31/2001	12/31/2000	12/31/1999	12/31/1998	12/31/1997
Earnings Per Share	(0.10)	1.35	(8.38)	1.90	1.48	0.46	0.33	(0.34)
Cash Flow Per Share	0.01	2.34	(0.07)	2.49	1.45	0.03	0.83	0.92
Tang Book Value Per Share	4.85	5.04	4.57	8.79	6.30	3.95	3.46	3.12
Dividends Per Share	...	...	0.150	0.300	0.247	...	...	0.025
Dividend Payout %	...	...	...	15.79	16.71	...	...	...
Income Statement								
Total Revenue	6,153,000	5,787,000	5,553,000	42,242,000	29,445,000	15,429,976	14,257,997	13,378,380
EBITDA	737,000	362,000	(1,610,000)	1,623,000	1,370,000	413,015	333,688	285,708
Depn & Amortn	356,000	525,000	613,000	449,000	357,000	108,325	100,005	372,148
Income Before Taxes	(99,000)	(672,000)	(2,582,000)	915,000	762,000	226,526	158,691	(149,895)
Income Taxes	(89,000)	(198,000)	(627,000)	269,000	261,000	74,677	50,338	62,210
Net Income	(15,000)	(453,000)	(2,737,000)	648,000	501,000	151,849	108,353	(102,485)
Average Shares	504,000	423,000	418,000	340,000	315,000	333,950	329,210	334,018
Balance Sheet								
Current Assets	2,752,000	3,030,000	7,586,000	9,507,000	10,150,000	2,805,080	2,117,241	2,018,780
Total Assets	9,852,000	13,293,000	20,030,000	24,874,000	21,406,000	6,525,171	5,264,237	4,516,903
Current Liabilities	1,802,000	2,576,000	6,748,000	8,555,000	9,405,000	2,538,523	2,026,323	1,753,094
Long-Term Obligations	4,332,000	5,893,000	5,454,000	4,124,000	3,433,000	1,333,926	1,046,890	1,002,054
Total Liabilities	7,479,000	10,716,000	16,374,000	17,396,000	16,444,000	5,015,689	3,936,174	3,297,778
Stockholders' Equity	1,867,000	2,045,000	2,087,000	4,719,000	3,598,000	1,309,482	1,128,063	1,019,125
Shares Outstanding	381,903	375,562	370,062	355,218	332,651	312,596	304,194	302,284
Statistical Record								
Return on Assets %	N.M.	N.M.	N.M.	2.80	3.58	2.58	2.22	N.M.
Return on Equity %	N.M.	N.M.	N.M.	15.58	20.36	12.46	10.09	N.M.
EBITDA Margin %	11.98	6.26	N.M.	3.84	4.65	2.68	2.34	2.14
Net Margin %	N.M.	N.M.	N.M.	1.53	1.70	0.98	0.76	N.M.
Asset Turnover	0.53	0.35	0.25	1.83	2.10	2.62	2.92	3.07
Current Ratio	1.53	1.18	1.12	1.11	1.08	1.11	1.04	1.15
Debt to Equity	2.32	2.88	2.61	0.87	0.95	1.02	0.93	0.98
Price Range	5.86-3.46	5.23-1.18	32.00-0.51	57.95-20.90	57.58-17.19	17.38-10.47	15.47-11.94	13.75-10.13
P/E Ratio	...	3.87-0.87	...	30.50-11.00	38.91-11.61	37.77-22.76	46.88-36.17	...
Average Yield %	...	...	1.36	0.68	0.65	...	...	0.22

Address: 1000 Louisiana, Suite 5800, Houston, TX 77002 Telephone: (713) 507-6400 Fax: (713) 507-6888	Web Site: www.dynegy.com Officers: Daniel L. Dienstbier - Chmn. Bruce A. Williamson - Pres., C.E.O.	Auditors: PricewaterhouseCoopers LLP Investor Contact: 713-507-6466

E* TRADE FINANCIAL CORP

Exchange	Symbol	Price	52Wk Range	Yield	P/E
NYS	ET	$12.00 (3/31/2005)	15.00-9.73	N/A	12.12

*7 Year Price Score 80.24   *NYSE Composite Index=100   *12 Month Price Score 97.58

Interim Earnings (Per Share)

Qtr.	Mar	Jun	Sep	Dec
2001	(0.02)	(0.03)	(0.72)	0.08
2002	(0.80)	0.09	0.06	0.11
2003	0.06	0.03	0.17	0.29
2004	0.23	0.31	0.21	0.24

Interim Dividends (Per Share)

No Dividends Paid

Valuation Analysis

Forecast P/E	N/A	No of Institutions	286
Market Cap	$4.4 Billion	Shares	
Book Value	2.2 Billion	239,721,360	
Price/Book	1.99	% Held	
Price/Sales	2.14	64.68	

Business Summary: Commercial Banking (MIC: 8.1 SIC: 021 NAIC: 23999)

E*Trade Financial is a financial services holding company. Co.'s retail customers are offered an array of trading, investing, banking and lending products, including personal access through its E*TRADE FINANCIAL Centers. Co. also offers, either alone or with its partners, branded retail brokerage websites in the U.S., Australia, Canada, Denmark, Germany, Hong Kong, Iceland, Japan, Korea, Sweden and the UK. Institutional brokerage products and services include execution services, direct market access to exchanges through a web-based platform, cross-border trading and independent research. Co. also provides corporate clients with employee stock plan administration and options management tools.

Recent Developments: For the year ended Dec 31 2004, net income leapt 71.4% to $350.9 million compared with $204.7 million a year earlier. Results excluded income of $29.6 million in 2004 and a loss of $1.7 million in 2003 from discontinued operations. The improvement in earnings was primarily attributed to an increase in Co.'s brokerage and banking revenues, a decline in expenses excluding interest, most significant of which, was the decrease in facility restructuring and other exit charges, and a decline in the amount of gains on sales of its investment in Softbank Investment, partially offset by losses from the early retirement debt. Total net revenues rose 6.2% to $1.53 billion from $1.44 billion a year ago.

Prospects: In 2005, Co. realigned its organizational structure and operations around its retail and institutional customers. Co. noted that for retail, the realignment will integrate the management and operations of its brokerage, banking and lending businesses in an effort to provide integrated product and service offerings. For institutional, the realignment will integrate the management and operations of balance sheet management, market making and institutional sales trading. Co. also intends to raise marketing spending in 2005, targeting certain customer segments. Co. noted that for these customer segments, the marketing will be focused on increasing customer usage and aggregating customer assets.

Financial Data

(US$ in Thousands)	12/31/2004	12/31/2003	12/31/2002	12/31/2001	12/31/2000	09/30/2000	09/30/1999	09/30/1998
Earnings Per Share	0.99	0.55	(0.52)	(0.73)	...	0.06	(0.23)	(0.01)
Cash Flow Per Share	4.44	1.92	5.34	(0.77)	0.23	(0.46)	(0.45)	(0.18)
Tang Book Value Per Share	4.60	3.74	2.69	2.55	...	4.51	3.81	3.14
Income Statement								
Total Revenue	2,076,562	2,008,360	1,901,702	2,062,115	569,032	1,973,183	621,402	245,282
EBITDA	559,493	351,672	237,737	(270,430)	15,190	139,528	(59,164)	10,848
Depn & Amortn	4,654	2,287	8,712	9,142	7,811	22,764	32,372	12,513
Income Before Taxes	514,006	310,354	193,940	(310,255)	3,229	104,449	(91,536)	(1,665)
Income Taxes	162,183	112,388	85,121	(39,934)	1,905	85,478	(37,098)	(953)
Net Income	380,483	203,027	(186,405)	(241,532)	1,353	19,152	(54,438)	(712)
Average Shares	405,389	367,361	361,051	332,370	321,430	319,336	235,926	169,140
Balance Sheet								
Current Assets	5,408,856	5,789,276	3,820,272	3,846,478	...	6,843,813	3,332,947	1,851,238
Total Assets	31,032,583	26,049,216	21,534,248	18,172,414	...	17,317,437	3,926,980	1,968,918
Current Liabilities	25,917,399	21,864,070	17,452,641	14,390,017	...	12,671,331	2,847,468	1,184,917
Long-Term Obligations	2,384,879	1,899,780	2,010,027	1,684,759	...	2,287,000	...	...
Total Liabilities	28,804,381	24,130,922	19,885,094	16,531,997	...	15,429,073	3,013,313	1,258,682
Stockholders' Equity	2,228,202	1,918,294	1,505,789	1,570,914	...	1,856,833	913,667	710,236
Shares Outstanding	369,623	366,636	358,044	347,592	...	304,504	239,822	226,413
Statistical Record								
Return on Assets %	1.33	0.85	N.M.	N.M.	...	0.18	N.M.	N.M.
Return on Equity %	18.30	11.86	N.M.	N.M.	...	1.38	N.M.	N.M.
EBITDA Margin %	26.94	17.51	12.50	N.M.	2.67	7.07	N.M.	4.42
Net Margin %	18.32	10.11	N.M.	N.M.	0.24	0.97	N.M.	N.M.
Asset Turnover	0.07	0.08	0.10	0.11	...	0.19	0.21	0.17
Current Ratio	0.21	0.26	0.22	0.27	...	0.54	1.17	1.56
Debt to Equity	1.07	0.99	1.33	1.07	...	1.23	...	...
Price Range	15.15-9.73	12.74-3.70	12.31-2.95	14.94-4.83	15.88-6.75	39.19-13.94	62.75-3.01	11.75-4.16
P/E Ratio	15.30-9.83	23.16-6.73	N/A	N/A	N.M.	653.13-232.29	N/A	N/A

Address: 4500 Bohannon Drive, Menlo Park, CA 94025	**Web Site:** www.etrade.com	**Auditors:** Deloitte & Touche LLP
Telephone: (650) 331-6000	**Officers:** George Hayter - Chmn. R. Jarrett Lilien - Pres., C.O.O.	**Investor Contact:** 650-331-5397
Fax: (650) 842-2552		

EASTGROUP PROPERTIES, INC.

Exchange	Symbol	Price	52Wk Range	Yield	P/E	Div Achiever
NYS	EGP	$37.70 (3/31/2005)	39.67-28.01	5.15	38.47	12 Years

*7 Year Price Score 121.53 *NYSE Composite Index=100 *12 Month Price Score 102.64

Interim Earnings (Per Share)

Qtr.	Mar	Jun	Sep	Dec
2001	0.27	0.53	0.38	0.32
2002	0.22	0.27	0.16	0.18
2003	0.17	0.21	0.13	0.20
2004	0.21	0.22	0.32	0.24

Interim Dividends (Per Share)

Amt	Decl	Ex	Rec	Pay
0.48Q	5/27/2004	6/16/2004	6/18/2004	6/30/2004
0.48Q	9/2/2004	9/15/2004	9/17/2004	9/30/2004
0.48Q	12/3/2004	12/15/2004	12/17/2004	12/30/2004
0.485Q	3/15/2005	3/22/2005	3/25/2005	3/31/2005

Indicated Div: $1.94 (Div. Reinv. Plan)

Valuation Analysis

Forecast P/E	14.25	No of Institutions
	(4/7/2005)	108
Market Cap	$793.9 Million	Shares
Book Value	351.8 Million	13,387,729
Price/Book	2.26	% Held
Price/Sales	6.92	63.50

Business Summary: Property, Real Estate & Development (MIC: 8.3 SIC: 798 NAIC: 25930)

Eastgroup Properties is a self-administered, equity real estate investment trust focused on the acquisition, operation and development of industrial properties in the major Sunbelt markets throughout the U.S. with an emphasis in the states of Arizona, California, Florida and Texas. Co.'s strategy for growth is based on ownership of premier distribution facilities generally clustered near major transportation features in supply constrained submarkets. As of Dec 31 2003, Co.'s portfolio includes 19.4 million square feet with an additional 746,000 square feet under development.

Recent Developments: For the year ended Dec 31 2004, income from continuing operations increased 7.9% to $21,572 thousand from income of $19,995 thousand a year earlier. Net income increased 14.1% to $23,327 thousand from net income of $20,445 thousand a year earlier. Revenues were $114,684 thousand, up 6.6% from $107,595 thousand the year before. Total expenses climbed 6.2% to $93,112 thousand from $87,600 thousand in 2003.

Prospects: Co. estimates that funds from operations (FFO) per share for full-year 2005 will range from $2.59 to $2.71. Also, Co. expects that earnings per share for 2005 should range between $0.86 and $0.98. Co. noted that its projections were based on assumptions that include 2005 average occupancy of between 90.0% and 92.0%; same store property net operating income (PNOI) increases of 1.2% to 4.4%; existing development contributions of $0.14 per share in PNOI; acquisitions, net of dispositions, of $25.0 million to $30.0 million during 2005; no lease termination fees; floating rate bank debt at an average rate of 4.0%; and new fixed rate debt of $50.0 million on Jul 1 2005 at 6.0%.

Financial Data
(US$ in Thousands)

	12/31/2004	12/31/2003	12/31/2002	12/31/2001	12/31/2000	12/31/1999	12/31/1998	12/31/1997
Earnings Per Share	0.98	0.70	0.84	1.51	1.68	1.99	1.66	1.56
Cash Flow Per Share	2.76	2.84	3.39	3.23	3.38	2.91	1.81	1.80
Tang Book Value Per Share	14.98	16.05	15.40	16.48	16.84	16.76	16.25	15.88
Dividends Per Share	1.920	1.900	1.880	1.800	1.580	1.480	1.400	1.337
Dividend Payout %	195.92	271.43	223.81	119.21	94.05	74.37	84.34	85.68
Income Statement								
Property Income	114,051	107,771	103,048	100,560	93,906	83,320	74,312	49,791
Non-Property Income	633	670	2,762	4,735	4,197	2,916	2,416	3,831
Total Revenue	114,684	108,441	105,810	105,295	98,103	86,236	76,728	53,622
Depn & Amortn	30,059	32,397	30,818	27,413	23,821	20,178	16,574	10,409
Interest Expense	20,481	19,015	17,387	17,823	18,570	17,688	16,948	10,551
Net Income	23,327	20,445	23,626	34,182	36,512	38,355	29,336	20,779
Average Shares	21,088	18,194	16,237	16,046	15,798	17,362	16,432	13,338
Balance Sheet								
Total Assets	768,664	729,267	702,341	683,782	666,205	632,151	567,548	413,127
Long-Term Obligations	303,674	285,722	248,343	205,014	168,709	148,665	122,494	105,380
Total Liabilities	414,974	360,518	344,097	311,333	289,116	260,499	248,821	155,812
Stockholders' Equity	351,806	366,945	356,485	370,710	375,392	369,312	316,024	257,315
Shares Outstanding	21,059	20,853	16,104	15,912	15,849	15,555	16,307	16,205
Statistical Record								
Return on Assets %	3.11	2.86	3.41	5.06	5.61	6.39	5.98	5.98
Return on Equity %	6.47	5.65	6.50	9.16	9.78	11.19	10.23	10.32
Net Margin %	20.34	18.85	22.33	32.46	37.22	44.48	38.23	38.75
Price Range	38.59-28.01	32.90-23.88	26.35-22.40	23.90-20.19	23.88-17.56	21.13-15.75	22.06-16.69	22.88-17.75
P/E Ratio	39.38-28.58	47.00-34.11	31.37-26.67	15.83-13.37	14.21-10.45	10.62-7.91	13.29-10.05	14.66-11.38
Average Yield %	5.70	6.93	7.61	8.10	7.55	8.09	7.14	6.71

Address: 300 One Jackson Place, 188 East Capitol Street, Jackson, MS 39201-2195 **Telephone:** (601) 354 3555 **Fax:** (601) 352 1441	**Web Site:** www.eastgroup.net **Officers:** Leland R. Speed - Chmn. David H. Hoster II - Pres., C.E.O.	**Auditors:** KPMG LLP **Transfer Agents:** First Chicago Trust Company of New York, Jersey City, NJ

EASTMAN CHEMICAL CO.

Exchange	Symbol	Price	52Wk Range	Yield	P/E
NYS	EMN	$59.00 (3/31/2005)	61.36-42.26	2.98	27.06

*7 Year Price Score 93.80   *NYSE Composite Index=100   ***12 Month Price Score 109.15**

Interim Earnings (Per Share)

Qtr.	Mar	Jun	Sep	Dec
2001	0.48	(1.92)	0.31	(1.20)
2002	0.07	0.58	0.31	(0.17)
2003	0.27	0.46	(4.35)	0.12
2004	(0.07)	1.07	0.49	0.69

Interim Dividends (Per Share)

Amt	Decl	Ex	Rec	Pay
0.44Q	5/6/2004	6/14/2004	6/15/2004	7/1/2004
0.44Q	8/5/2004	9/13/2004	9/15/2004	10/1/2004
0.44Q	12/2/2004	12/13/2004	12/15/2004	1/3/2005
0.44Q	3/3/2005	3/11/2005	3/15/2005	4/1/2005

Indicated Div: $1.76

Valuation Analysis

Forecast P/E	13.86	No of Institutions
	(4/7/2005)	285
Market Cap	$4.7 Billion	Shares
Book Value	1.2 Billion	65,690,724
Price/Book	3.95	% Held
Price/Sales	0.71	82.80

Business Summary: Chemicals (MIC: 11.1 SIC: 821 NAIC: 25211)

Eastman Chemical manufactures and sells a broad range of plastics, chemicals and fibers. Co. is the largest producer of polyethlene terephthalate (PET) polymers for packaging based on capacity share. As of Dec 31 2003, Co. had 35 manufacturing sites in 16 countries that supply major chemicals, fibers and plastics products. Co. operates in three divisions. The Eastman division includes the coatings, adhesives, specialty polymers, and inks segment; the Performance Chemicals and Intermediates segment; and the Specialty Plastics segment. The Voridian division includes the Polymers segment and the Fibers segment. The Developing Businesses division includes developing new businesses.

Recent Developments: For the year ended Dec 31 2004, net income was $170 million versus net loss of $270 million a year earlier. Revenues were $6,580 million, up 13.4% from $5,800 million the year before. Operating income was $175 million versus a loss of $267 million in the prior year. Total direct expense was $5,602 million versus $4,990 million in the prior year, an increase of 12.3%. Total indirect expense was $810 million versus $1,110 million in the prior year, a decrease of 27.0%.

Prospects: On Jan 27 2005, Co. announced that it has entered into an agreement with Danisco A/S, under which Danisco will acquire all of Co.'s common and preferred shares in Genencor International, Inc., for approximately $419.0 million in cash, comprised of $15.00 per share for the common stock and $44.0 million for the preferred stock. Co.expects to complete the transaction by May 31 2005, at the latest. Going forward, Co. expects sales volume to remain strong throughout, but also anticipates that key raw material and energy costs will escalate during the first quarter of 2005. Also, Co. expects to implement selling price increases in order to recover its margin over raw material and energy costs.

Financial Data

(US$ in Thousands)	12/31/2004	12/31/2003	12/31/2002	12/31/2001	12/31/2000	12/31/1999	12/31/1998	12/31/1997
Earnings Per Share	2.18	(3.50)	0.79	(2.33)	3.94	0.61	3.13	3.63
Cash Flow Per Share	6.35	3.16	10.39	5.61	10.79	9.51	9.25	8.94
Tang Book Value Per Share	10.67	8.97	9.02	9.92	15.64	16.81	24.42	22.47
Dividends Per Share	1.760	1.760	1.760	1.760	1.760	1.760	1.760	1.760
Dividend Payout %	80.73	...	222.78	...	44.67	288.52	56.23	48.48
Income Statement								
Total Revenue	6,580,000	5,800,000	5,320,000	5,384,000	5,292,000	4,590,000	4,481,000	4,678,000
EBITDA	501,000	110,000	603,000	278,000	1,005,000	581,000	807,000	860,000
Depn & Amortn	322,000	367,000	397,000	435,000	418,000	383,000	351,000	327,000
Income Before Taxes	64,000	(381,000)	84,000	(297,000)	452,000	72,000	360,000	446,000
Income Taxes	(106,000)	(108,000)	5,000	(118,000)	149,000	24,000	111,000	160,000
Net Income	170,000	(270,000)	61,000	(179,000)	303,000	48,000	249,000	286,000
Average Shares	78,300	77,100	77,100	76,800	77,000	78,400	79,500	78,800
Balance Sheet								
Current Assets	1,768,000	2,010,000	1,529,000	1,458,000	1,523,000	1,489,000	1,415,000	1,490,000
Total Assets	5,872,000	6,230,000	6,273,000	6,086,000	6,550,000	6,303,000	5,876,000	5,778,000
Current Liabilities	1,099,000	1,477,000	1,224,000	958,000	1,258,000	1,608,000	985,000	954,000
Long-Term Obligations	2,061,000	2,089,000	2,054,000	2,143,000	1,914,000	1,506,000	1,649,000	1,714,000
Total Liabilities	4,688,000	5,187,000	5,002,000	4,708,000	4,738,000	4,544,000	3,942,000	4,025,000
Stockholders' Equity	1,184,000	1,043,000	1,271,000	1,378,000	1,812,000	1,759,000	1,934,000	1,753,000
Shares Outstanding	79,213	77,244	77,346	76,979	76,743	78,090	79,200	78,000
Statistical Record								
Return on Assets %	2.80	N.M.	0.99	N.M.	4.70	0.79	4.27	5.18
Return on Equity %	15.23	N.M.	4.61	N.M.	16.92	2.60	13.51	16.86
EBITDA Margin %	7.61	1.90	11.33	5.16	18.99	12.66	18.01	18.38
Net Margin %	2.58	N.M.	1.15	N.M.	5.73	1.05	5.56	6.11
Asset Turnover	1.08	0.93	0.86	0.85	0.82	0.75	0.77	0.85
Current Ratio	1.61	1.36	1.25	1.52	1.21	0.93	1.44	1.56
Debt to Equity	1.74	2.00	1.62	1.56	1.06	0.86	0.85	0.98
Price Range	57.97-38.00	39.53-27.89	49.04-35.35	55.25-30.25	54.13-34.19	59.81-36.69	72.94-44.19	64.50-51.00
P/E Ratio	26.59-17.43	...	62.08-44.75	...	13.74-8.68	98.05-60.14	23.30-14.12	17.77-14.05
Average Yield %	3.88	5.26	4.15	3.95	3.97	3.76	2.92	3.03

Address: 100 N. Eastman Road, Kingsport, TN 37660	Web Site: www.eastman.com	Auditors: PricewaterhouseCoopers LLP
Telephone: (423) 229-2000	Officers: J. Brian Ferguson - Chmn., C.E.O. James P. Rogers - Exec. V.P.	Investor Contact: 423-229-8692
Fax: (423) 224-0208		

EASTMAN KODAK CO.

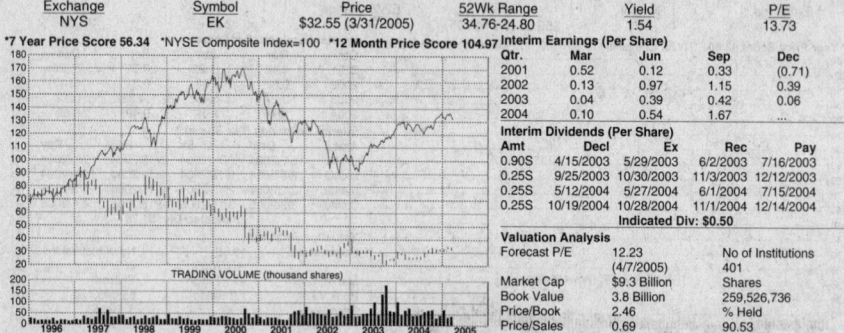

Exchange	Symbol	Price	52Wk Range	Yield	P/E
NYS	EK	$32.55 (3/31/2005)	34.76-24.80	1.54	13.73

*7 Year Price Score 56.34   *NYSE Composite Index=100   *12 Month Price Score 104.97

Interim Earnings (Per Share)

Qtr.	Mar	Jun	Sep	Dec
2001	0.52	0.12	0.33	(0.71)
2002	0.13	0.97	1.15	0.39
2003	0.04	0.39	0.42	0.06
2004	0.10	0.54	1.67	...

Interim Dividends (Per Share)

Amt	Decl	Ex	Rec	Pay
0.90S	4/15/2003	5/29/2003	6/2/2003	7/16/2003
0.25S	9/25/2003	10/30/2003	11/3/2003	12/12/2003
0.25S	5/12/2004	5/27/2004	6/1/2004	7/15/2004
0.25S	10/19/2004	10/28/2004	11/1/2004	12/14/2004
		Indicated Div: $0.50		

Valuation Analysis

Forecast P/E	12.23 (4/7/2005)	No of Institutions	401
Market Cap	$9.3 Billion	Shares	259,526,736
Book Value	3.8 Billion	% Held	90.53
Price/Book	2.46		
Price/Sales	0.69		

TRADING VOLUME (thousand shares)

Business Summary: Consumer Accessories (MIC: 4.6 SIC: 861 NAIC: 25992)

Eastman Kodak develops, manufactures, and markets traditional and digital imaging products and services. Co. operates in five business segments. The Digital and Film Imaging Systems segment includes consumer and professional imaging, entertainment and digital and applied imaging products. The Health Imaging segment includes health imaging products, systems and services. The Graphic Communications Group includes on-demand color printing and networking publishing systems. The Commercial Imaging group includes image capture, output and storage. Co.'s other group includes organic light emitting diode displays, imaging solutions and optical products.

Recent Developments: For the quarter ended Sep 30 2004, income from continuing operations decreased 60.9% to $45 million from income of $115 million in the year-earlier quarter. Net income increased 292.6% to $479 million from net income of $122 million in the year-earlier quarter. Revenues were $3,364 million, up 0.5% from $3,346 million the year before. Operating loss was $4 million versus operating income of $131 million in the prior-year quarter. Total direct expense was $2,289 million versus $2,241 million in the prior-year quarter, an increase of 2.1%. Total indirect expense was $1,079 million versus $974 million in the prior-year quarter, an increase of 10.8%.

Prospects: On Jan 31 2005, Co. announced that it has entered into a definitive agreement to acquire Creo, a premier supplier of prepress systems used by commercial printers worldwide. Under the terms of the agreement, Co. will pay approximately $980.0 million in cash for all the outstanding shares of Creo, on a fully diluted basis. The transaction, which has been approved by Co. and Creo's respective boards of directors, is to be carried out by statutory plan of arrangement under Canadian law and is subject to regulatory approvals, the approval of Creo's shareholders, and court approval. For 2006, Co. expects that Creo will add at least $0.05 to per share operational earnings.

Financial Data
(US$ in Thousands)

	9 Mos	6 Mos	3 Mos	12/31/2003	12/31/2002	12/31/2001	12/31/2000	12/31/1999
Earnings Per Share	2.37	1.12	0.97	0.92	2.64	0.26	4.59	4.33
Cash Flow Per Share	4.39	5.03	5.26	5.74	7.56	7.11	3.21	6.08
Tang Book Value Per Share	8.17	6.42	6.29	5.53	6.28	6.69	8.54	9.44
Dividends Per Share	0.500	0.500	1.150	1.150	1.800	1.770	1.760	1.760
Dividend Payout %	21.10	44.83	119.08	125.00	68.18	680.77	38.34	40.65
Income Statement								
Total Revenue	9,752,000	6,388,000	2,919,000	13,317,000	12,835,000	13,234,000	13,994,000	14,089,000
EBITDA	891,000	631,000	226,000	1,145,000	1,931,000	1,236,000	3,199,000	3,169,000
Depn & Amortn	701,000	457,000	214,000	830,000	818,000	919,000	889,000	918,000
Income Before Taxes	60,000	87,000	(32,000)	172,000	946,000	108,000	2,132,000	2,109,000
Income Taxes	(144,000)	(72,000)	(48,000)	(66,000)	153,000	32,000	725,000	717,000
Net Income	661,000	182,000	28,000	265,000	770,000	76,000	1,407,000	1,392,000
Average Shares	286,700	286,600	287,000	286,600	291,700	291,000	306,600	321,500
Balance Sheet								
Current Assets	5,942,000	5,275,000	4,862,000	5,455,000	4,534,000	4,683,000	5,491,000	5,444,000
Total Assets	15,110,000	14,720,000	14,433,000	14,818,000	13,369,000	13,362,000	14,212,000	14,370,000
Current Liabilities	5,352,000	5,363,000	4,876,000	5,307,000	5,377,000	5,354,000	6,215,000	5,769,000
Long-Term Obligations	1,953,000	1,997,000	2,256,000	2,302,000	1,164,000	1,666,000	1,166,000	936,000
Total Liabilities	11,319,000	11,449,000	11,215,000	11,554,000	10,592,000	10,468,000	10,784,000	10,458,000
Stockholders' Equity	3,791,000	3,271,000	3,218,000	3,264,000	2,777,000	2,894,000	3,428,000	3,912,000
Shares Outstanding	286,679	286,605	286,000	286,580	285,933	290,929	290,484	310,420
Statistical Record								
Return on Assets %	4.66	2.23	2.02	1.88	5.76	0.55	9.82	9.57
Return on Equity %	20.25	10.50	9.20	8.77	27.16	2.40	38.23	35.24
EBITDA Margin %	9.14	9.88	7.74	8.60	15.04	9.34	22.86	22.49
Net Margin %	6.78	2.85	0.96	1.99	6.00	0.57	10.05	9.88
Asset Turnover	0.93	0.94	0.97	0.94	0.96	0.96	0.98	0.97
Current Ratio	1.11	0.98	1.00	1.03	0.84	0.87	0.88	0.94
Debt to Equity	0.52	0.61	0.70	0.71	0.42	0.58	0.34	0.24
Price Range	32.22-20.50	30.95-20.50	31.99-20.50	40.24-20.50	38.22-25.86	49.21-24.65	66.25-36.44	79.63-57.38
P/E Ratio	13.59-8.65	27.63-18.30	32.98-21.13	43.74-22.28	14.48-9.80	189.27-94.81	14.43-7.94	18.39-13.25
Average Yield %	1.90	1.92	4.23	4.07	5.76	4.37	3.21	2.53

Address: 343 State Street, Rochester, NY 14650
Telephone: (585) 724 4000
Fax: (716) 724 0663

Web Site: www.kodak.com
Officers: Daniel A. Carp - Chmn., C.E.O. Antonio M. Perez - Pres., C.O.O.

Auditors: PricewaterhouseCoopers LLP

EATON CORP.

Exchange	Symbol	Price	52Wk Range	Yield	P/E
NYS	ETN	$65.40 (3/31/2005)	72.36-55.19	1.90	15.84

*7 Year Price Score 135.89 *NYSE Composite Index=100 ***12 Month Price Score 98.87**

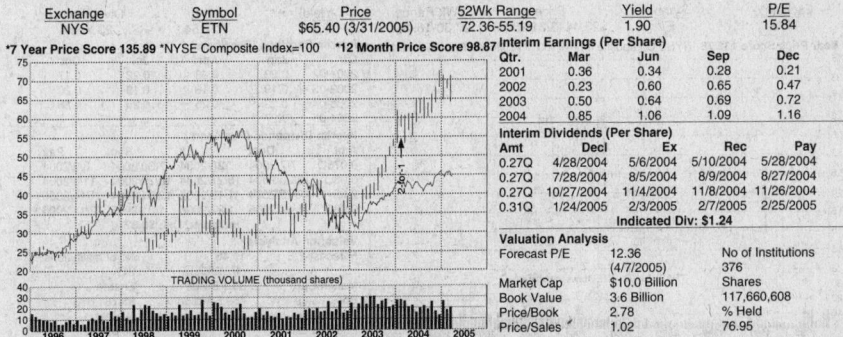

Interim Earnings (Per Share)

Qtr.	Mar	Jun	Sep	Dec
2001	0.36	0.34	0.28	0.21
2002	0.23	0.60	0.65	0.47
2003	0.50	0.64	0.69	0.72
2004	0.85	1.06	1.09	1.16

Interim Dividends (Per Share)

Amt	Decl	Ex	Rec	Pay
0.27Q	4/28/2004	5/6/2004	5/10/2004	5/28/2004
0.27Q	7/28/2004	8/5/2004	8/9/2004	8/27/2004
0.27Q	10/27/2004	11/4/2004	11/8/2004	11/26/2004
0.31Q	1/24/2005	2/3/2005	2/7/2005	2/25/2005

Indicated Div: $1.24

Valuation Analysis

Forecast P/E	12.36 (4/7/2005)	No of Institutions 376
Market Cap	$10.0 Billion	Shares 117,660,608
Book Value	3.6 Billion	% Held 76.95
Price/Book	2.78	
Price/Sales	1.02	

Business Summary: Electrical (MIC: 11.14 SIC: 699 NAIC: 35999)

Eaton is a global diversified industrial manufacturer. Co. is engaged in the design and manufacture of fluid power systems; electrical power quality, distribution and control; automotive engine air management and powertrain controls for fuel economy; and intelligent drivetrain systems for fuel economy and safety in trucks. Co.'s operations are divided into four business segments: Fluid, Electrical, Automotive and Truck. As of Dec 31 2003, Co.'s total backlog is approximately $1.30 billion. Also, Co. sold products in more than 100 countries as of Dec 31 2003.

Recent Developments: For the year ended Dec 31 2004, net income increased 67.9% to $648 million from net income of $386 million a year earlier. Revenues were $9,817 million, up 21.8% from $8,061 million the year before. Total direct expense was $7,082 million versus $5,897 million in the prior year, an increase of 20.1%. Total indirect expense was $1,863 million versus $1,574 million in the prior year, an increase of 18.4%.

Prospects: Co. anticipates first-quarter 2005 net income in the range of $1.10 to $1.20 per share. Looking ahead, Co. is projecting full-year 2005 sales growth of approximately 12.0% to 14.0%, or between $11.00 billion and $11.20 billion, including incremental sales of about $500.0 million from joint ventures and acquisitions. Also, Co. is targeting net income per share in the range of $4.90 to $5.10 for 2005, along with free cash flow of between $600.0 million and $700.0 million, after capital expenditures of approximately $400.0 million. Separately, on Feb 1 2005, Co. announced that it has entered into an agreement to acquire Pigozzi S.A., a producer of agricultural powertrain products in Brazil.

Financial Data

(US$ in Thousands)	12/31/2004	12/31/2003	12/31/2002	12/31/2001	12/31/2000	12/31/1999	12/31/1998	12/31/1997
Earnings Per Share	4.13	2.56	1.96	1.20	3.12	4.18	2.40	2.62
Cash Flow Per Share	5.46	5.91	6.37	5.51	3.60	4.70	4.50	4.95
Tang Book Value Per Share	3.45	3.14	N.M.	0.29	N.M.	0.64	7.17	7.37
Dividends Per Share	1.080	0.920	0.880	0.880	0.880	0.880	0.880	0.860
Dividend Payout %	26.15	35.94	44.90	73.64	28.21	21.05	36.67	32.82
Income Statement								
Total Revenue	9,817,000	8,061,000	7,209,000	7,299,000	8,309,000	8,402,000	6,625,000	7,563,000
EBITDA	1,259,000	989,000	879,000	869,000	1,191,000	1,540,000	904,000	1,089,000
Depn & Amortn	400,000	394,000	376,000	449,000	462,000	425,000	331,000	342,000
Income Before Taxes	781,000	508,000	399,000	278,000	552,000	963,000	485,000	668,000
Income Taxes	133,000	122,000	118,000	109,000	189,000	346,000	136,000	204,000
Net Income	648,000	386,000	281,000	169,000	453,000	617,000	349,000	410,000
Average Shares	157,100	150,500	143,400	141,000	145,200	147,400	145,400	156,000
Balance Sheet								
Current Assets	3,182,000	3,093,000	2,457,000	2,387,000	2,571,000	2,782,000	1,982,000	2,055,000
Total Assets	9,075,000	8,223,000	7,138,000	7,646,000	8,180,000	8,437,000	5,665,000	5,465,000
Current Liabilities	2,262,000	2,126,000	1,734,000	1,669,000	2,107,000	2,649,000	1,516,000	1,357,000
Long-Term Obligations	1,734,000	1,651,000	1,887,000	2,252,000	2,447,000	1,915,000	1,191,000	1,272,000
Total Liabilities	5,469,000	5,106,000	4,836,000	5,171,000	5,770,000	5,813,000	3,608,000	3,394,000
Stockholders' Equity	3,606,000	3,117,000	2,302,000	2,475,000	2,410,000	2,624,000	2,057,000	2,071,000
Shares Outstanding	153,300	153,000	141,200	139,000	136,600	148,000	144,000	150,000
Statistical Record								
Return on Assets %	7.47	5.03	3.80	2.14	5.44	8.75	6.27	7.61
Return on Equity %	19.22	14.25	11.76	6.92	17.95	26.36	16.91	19.38
EBITDA Margin %	12.82	12.27	12.19	11.91	14.33	18.33	13.65	14.40
Net Margin %	6.60	4.79	3.90	2.32	5.45	7.34	5.27	5.42
Asset Turnover	1.13	1.05	0.98	0.92	1.00	1.19	1.19	1.40
Current Ratio	1.41	1.45	1.42	1.43	1.22	1.05	1.31	1.51
Debt to Equity	0.48	0.53	0.82	0.91	1.02	0.73	0.58	0.61
Price Range	72.36-53.24	54.33-33.45	43.92-29.68	40.09-28.73	36.45-25.39	44.12-27.47	42.34-25.21	44.33-29.27
P/E Ratio	17.52-12.89	21.22-13.06	22.41-15.14	33.41-23.95	11.68-8.14	10.55-6.57	17.64-10.50	16.92-11.17
Average Yield %	1.75	2.16	2.36	2.49	2.89	2.49	2.60	2.38

Address: Eaton Center, 1111 Superior Avenue, Cleveland, OH 44114-2584 Telephone: (216) 523-5000 Fax: (216) 479-7092	Web Site: www.eaton.com Officers: Alexander M. Cutler - Chmn., Pres., C.E.O. Richard H. Fearon - Exec. V.P., Chief Fin. & Planning Officer	Auditors: Ernst & Young LLP Investor Contact: 888-328-6647

EATON VANCE CORP

Exchange	Symbol	Price	52Wk Range	Yield	P/E	Div Acheiver
NYS	EV	$23.44 (3/31/2005)	27.30-16.46	1.37	22.54	23 Years

*7 Year Price Score 132.78 *NYSE Composite Index=100 *12 Month Price Score 110.56

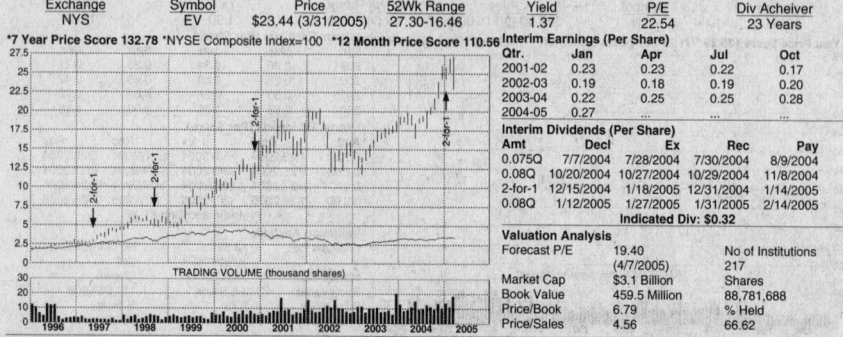

Interim Earnings (Per Share)

Qtr.	Jan	Apr	Jul	Oct
2001-02	0.23	0.23	0.22	0.17
2002-03	0.19	0.18	0.19	0.20
2003-04	0.22	0.25	0.25	0.28
2004-05	0.27	...	...	...

Interim Dividends (Per Share)

Amt	Decl	Ex	Rec	Pay
0.075Q	7/7/2004	7/28/2004	7/30/2004	8/9/2004
0.08Q	10/20/2004	10/27/2004	10/29/2004	11/8/2004
2-for-1	12/15/2004	1/18/2005	12/31/2004	1/14/2005
0.08Q	1/12/2005	1/27/2005	1/31/2005	2/14/2005

Indicated Div: $0.32

Valuation Analysis

Forecast P/E	19.40 (4/7/2005)	No of Institutions	217
Market Cap	$3.1 Billion	Shares	88,781,688
Book Value	459.5 Million	% Held	66.62
Price/Book	6.79		
Price/Sales	4.56		

Business Summary: Wealth Management (MIC: 8.8 SIC: 282 NAIC: 23930)

Eaton Vance is engaged in the provision of investment advisory and distribution services to mutual funds and other investment funds, and investment management and counseling services to individual high-net-worth investors, family offices and institutional clients. Co. operates in one business segment, namely as an investment adviser managing fund and separate account assets. Co. provides investment advisory or administration services to over 150 funds, 1,300 separately managed individual and institutional accounts, and participates in more than 40 retail managed account broker/dealer programs.

Recent Developments: For the quarter ended Jan 31 2005, Co. reported net income of $38,409,000 compared with net income of $30,813,000 in the equivalent period a year earlier. Total revenue rose 15.8% to $181,781,000 from $156,973,000 in the corresponding quarter the year before. Operating income was $62,859,000, up 25.5% from $50,103,000 in the comparable 2004 period. Results for 2005 and 2004 included gains on investment of $10,000 and $5,000, respectively. Also, results included a foreign currency gain of $22,000 in 2005 and a foreign currency loss of $18,000 in 2004.

Prospects: Results are benefiting from Co.'s successful closed-end fund offerings as net fund and separate account inflows were $1.30 billion in the first quarter of fiscal 2005. Also, revenues are benefiting from higher average assets under management, which amounted to $98.00 billion at the end of the first quarter of 2005, up 17.2% from the year before. The improvement in assets under managements reflects the positive effects of long-term fund and separate account net inflows, market price appreciation and $1.90 billion of separate accounts acquired from Deutsche Bank in July 2004.

Financial Data
(US$ in Thousands)

	3 Mos	10/31/2004	10/31/2003	10/31/2002	10/31/2001	10/31/2000	10/31/1999	10/31/1998
Earnings Per Share	1.04	1.00	0.76	0.85	0.80	0.79	0.11	0.20
Cash Flow Per Share	1.37	0.87	0.32	0.97	1.02	0.52	0.15	0.07
Tang Book Value Per Share	2.46	2.37	2.06	1.92	1.40	1.82	1.37	1.47
Dividends Per Share	0.295	0.275	0.200	0.149	0.126	0.101	0.080	0.064
Dividend Payout %	28.30	27.64	26.49	17.50	15.78	12.82	74.42	31.48
Income Statement								
Total Revenue	181,781	661,813	523,133	522,985	486,372	429,566	429,566	249,987
Income Before Taxes	63,239	221,658	164,858	186,241	178,666	187,179	85,910	50,038
Income Taxes	23,368	79,797	57,700	65,184	62,469	71,128	33,505	19,515
Net Income	38,409	138,943	106,123	121,057	116,020	116,051	15,798	30,523
Average Shares	143,711	139,578	140,750	142,824	144,600	146,444	148,988	151,028
Balance Sheet								
Total Assets	709,574	743,566	658,702	616,619	675,301	432,989	358,229	380,260
Total Liabilities	211,571	226,190	234,734	242,919	373,210	178,039	163,961	168,451
Stockholders' Equity	459,497	449,506	416,277	372,302	301,126	254,950	194,268	211,809
Shares Outstanding	133,182	133,581	136,810	138,514	137,233	139,087	141,039	142,663
Statistical Record								
Return on Assets %	20.81	19.76	16.64	18.74	20.94	29.25	4.28	7.95
Return on Equity %	33.10	32.01	26.91	35.95	41.73	51.53	7.78	13.93
Price Range	26.07-16.46	21.81-16.46	17.80-11.70	20.36-11.98	19.10-11.16	13.69-8.47	9.72-4.75	6.19-4.05
P/E Ratio	25.07-15.83	21.81-16.46	23.42-15.39	23.95-14.09	23.88-13.95	17.33-10.72	88.35-43.18	30.94-20.23
Average Yield %	1.44	1.45	1.30	0.90	0.81	0.94	1.20	1.21

Address: 255 State Street, Boston, MA 02109
Telephone: (617) 482-8260
Fax: (617) 482-2396

Web Site: www.eatonvance.com
Officers: James B. Hawkes - Chmn., Pres., C.E.O. Thomas E. Faust Jr. - Exec. V.P., Chief Investment Officer

Auditors: Deloitte & Touche LLP
Investor Contact: 617-482-8260
Transfer Agents: EquiServe Trust Company, N.A., Kansas City, MO

ECOLAB, INC.

Exchange	Symbol	Price	52Wk Range	Yield	P/E	Div Acheiver
NYS	ECL	$33.05 (3/31/2005)	35.26-28.05	1.06	27.77	12 Years

7 Year Price Score 122.29 **NYSE Composite Index=100** **12 Month Price Score 95.29**

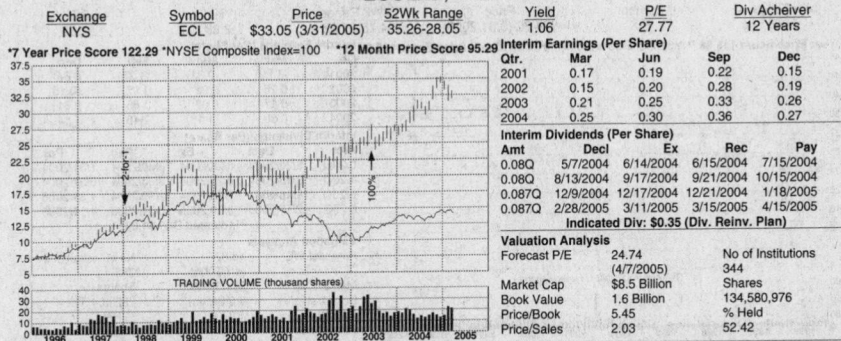

Interim Earnings (Per Share)

Qtr.	Mar	Jun	Sep	Dec
2001	0.17	0.19	0.22	0.15
2002	0.15	0.20	0.28	0.19
2003	0.21	0.25	0.33	0.26
2004	0.25	0.30	0.36	0.27

Interim Dividends (Per Share)

Amt	Decl	Ex	Rec	Pay
0.08Q	5/7/2004	6/14/2004	6/15/2004	7/15/2004
0.08Q	8/13/2004	9/17/2004	9/21/2004	10/15/2004
0.087Q	12/9/2004	12/17/2004	12/21/2004	1/18/2005
0.087Q	2/28/2005	3/11/2005	3/15/2005	4/15/2005
Indicated Div: $0.35 (Div. Reinv. Plan)				

Valuation Analysis

Forecast P/E	24.74	No of Institutions	
	(4/7/2005)	344	
Market Cap	$8.5 Billion	Shares	
Book Value	1.6 Billion	134,580,976	
Price/Book	5.45	% Held	
Price/Sales	2.03	52.42	

Business Summary: Chemicals (MIC: 11.1 SIC: 842 NAIC: 25612)

Ecolab develops and markets products and services for the hospitality, foodservice, institutional and industrial markets. Co. operates in three business segments. The Cleaning and Sanitizing segment consists of seven business units and offers cleaners, sanitizers, detergents, lubricants, chemical cleaning, animal health, water treatment, infection control and janitorial products. Other U.S. Services consists of two business units focused on the elimination and prevention of pests, and the manufacturing of dishwashing and customized machines for the foodservice industry. The International segment serves customers in Europe, Asia Pacific, Canada, Latin America, the Middle East and Africa.

Recent Developments: For the year ended Dec 31 2004, net income increased 11.9% to $310,488 thousand from net income of $277,348 thousand a year earlier. Revenues were $4,184,933 thousand, up 11.2% from $3,761,819 thousand the year before. Operating income was $534,122 thousand versus an income of $482,658 thousand in the prior year, an increase of 10.7%. Total direct expense was $2,031,280 thousand versus $1,845,202 thousand in the prior year, an increase of 10.1%. Total indirect expense was $1,619,531 thousand versus $1,433,959 thousand in the prior year, an increase of 12.9%.

Prospects: Co.'s outlook is positive, aided by continued domestic and international sales growth. However, rising raw material costs, weak economies in Europe and currency changes may force Co. to take actions, including raising prices and focused costs savings. For the first quarter of 2005, Co. expects both domestic and international operations to increase over 2004 levels. Gross margins are expected to be in the range of 51.0% to 52.0% of sales, and selling, general and administrative expenses are expected to be in the 39.0% range. Earnings per share are expected to be in the range of $0.27 to $0.29. For the full year, Co. expects earnings per share will be in the range $1.30 to $1.34.

Financial Data (US$ in Thousands)	12/31/2004	12/31/2003	12/31/2002	12/31/2001	12/31/2000	12/31/1999	12/31/1998	12/31/1997
Earnings Per Share	1.19	1.06	0.80	0.72	0.78	0.66	0.72	0.50
Cash Flow Per Share	2.26	2.04	1.64	1.43	1.23	1.13	0.91	0.91
Tang Book Value Per Share	1.33	1.14	0.83	0.41	1.77	1.98	1.75	1.30
Dividends Per Share	0.328	0.297	0.275	0.263	0.245	0.218	0.195	0.168
Dividend Payout %	27.52	28.07	34.38	36.21	31.41	33.21	27.08	33.50
Income Statement								
Total Revenue	4,184,933	3,761,819	3,403,585	2,354,723	2,264,313	2,080,012	1,888,226	1,640,352
EBITDA	769,345	716,475	607,606	481,169	491,575	424,481	383,951	319,383
Depn & Amortn	235,223	222,712	211,740	162,990	148,436	134,530	121,971	100,879
Income Before Taxes	488,778	448,418	351,971	289,745	318,534	267,238	240,238	205,867
Income Taxes	178,290	171,070	140,081	117,408	129,495	109,769	101,782	85,345
Net Income	310,488	277,348	209,770	188,170	206,127	175,786	192,506	133,955
Average Shares	261,776	262,737	261,574	259,856	263,892	268,838	268,094	267,644
Balance Sheet								
Current Assets	1,279,066	1,150,340	1,015,937	929,583	600,568	577,321	503,514	509,501
Total Assets	3,716,174	3,228,918	2,878,429	2,525,000	1,714,011	1,585,946	1,470,995	1,416,299
Current Liabilities	939,547	851,942	866,350	827,952	532,034	470,674	399,791	404,464
Long-Term Obligations	645,425	604,441	539,743	512,280	234,377	169,014	227,041	259,384
Total Liabilities	2,153,655	1,933,492	1,778,678	1,644,648	957,004	823,930	780,454	864,598
Stockholders' Equity	1,562,519	1,295,426	1,099,751	880,352	757,007	762,016	690,541	551,701
Shares Outstanding	257,541	257,416	259,880	255,800	254,322	258,832	258,958	258,254
Statistical Record								
Return on Assets %	8.92	9.08	7.76	8.88	12.46	11.50	13.33	10.21
Return on Equity %	21.67	23.16	21.19	22.98	27.07	24.20	30.99	25.00
EBITDA Margin %	18.38	19.05	17.85	20.43	21.71	20.41	20.33	19.47
Net Margin %	7.42	7.37	6.16	7.99	9.10	8.45	10.20	8.17
Asset Turnover	1.20	1.23	1.26	1.11	1.37	1.36	1.31	1.25
Current Ratio	1.36	1.35	1.17	1.12	1.13	1.23	1.26	1.26
Debt to Equity	0.41	0.47	0.49	0.58	0.31	0.22	0.33	0.47
Price Range	35.26-26.22	27.91-23.36	25.07-18.36	21.97-15.48	22.34-14.13	22.09-16.06	18.84-13.42	13.91-9.13
P/E Ratio	29.63-22.03	26.33-22.04	31.34-22.96	30.51-21.51	28.65-18.11	33.48-24.34	26.17-18.64	27.81-18.25
Average Yield %	1.08	1.16	1.22	1.33	1.31	1.13	1.30	1.51

Address: 370 Wabasha Street North, St. Paul, MN 55102-1390 Telephone: (651) 293-2233 Fax: (612) 225-3080	Web Site: www.ecolab.com Officers: Allan L. Schuman - Chmn., C.E.O. Douglas M. Baker Jr. - Pres., C.O.O.	Auditors: PricewaterhouseCoopers LLP Investor Contact: 612-293-2809 Transfer Agents: EquiServe Trust Company, N.A., Providence, RI

EDISON INTERNATIONAL

Exchange	Symbol	Price	52Wk Range	Yield	P/E
NYS	EIX	$34.72 (3/31/2005)	34.75-21.97	2.88	12.53

*7 Year Price Score 115.86 ***NYSE Composite Index=100** ***12 Month Price Score 108.08**

Interim Earnings (Per Share)

Qtr.	Mar	Jun	Sep	Dec
2001	(1.89)	(0.31)	(1.27)	6.64
2002	0.26	2.02	1.07	(0.15)
2003	0.17	0.07	1.65	0.61
2004	0.30	(1.15)	2.46	1.14

Interim Dividends (Per Share)

Amt	Decl	Ex	Rec	Pay
0.20Q	5/20/2004	6/28/2004	6/30/2004	7/31/2004
0.20Q	9/16/2004	9/28/2004	9/30/2004	10/31/2004
0.25Q	11/18/2004	12/28/2004	12/30/2004	1/31/2005
0.25Q	2/17/2005	3/29/2005	3/31/2005	4/30/2005
			Indicated Div: $1.00	

Valuation Analysis

Forecast P/E	15.82 (4/7/2005)	No of Institutions	282
Market Cap	$11.3 Billion	Shares	232,404,592
Book Value	6.0 Billion	% Held	71.33
Price/Book	1.87		
Price/Sales	1.11		

Business Summary: Electricity (MIC: 7.1 SIC: 911 NAIC: 21122)

Edison International, through its subsidiary Southern California Edison (SCE), provides electric service to a 50,000-square-mile area of Central and Southern California, which includes some 800 cities and communities, with a population of more than 12.0 million people. Co.'s nonutility businesses are Edison Mission Energy (EME), which is engaged in developing, acquiring, owning or leasing, and operating electric power generation facilities worldwide; Edison Capital, a provider of capital and financial services for energy and infrastructure projects; and Edison Enterprises, which provides integrated energy services, utility outsourcing, and consumer products and services.

Recent Developments: For the year ended Dec 31 2004, net income increased 11.6% to $916,000 thousand from net income of $821,000 thousand a year earlier. Revenues were $10,199,000 thousand, down 5.0% from $10,732,000 thousand the year before. Operating income was $1,100,000 thousand versus an income of $1,455,000 thousand in the prior year, a decrease of 24.4%. Total direct expense was $6,902,000 thousand versus $7,739,000 thousand in the prior year, a decrease of 10.8%. Total indirect expense was $2,197,000 thousand versus $1,538,000 thousand in the prior year, an increase of 42.8%.

Prospects: On Dec 16 2004, Co. and its subsidiary, Edison Mission Energy (EME), announced that EME has completed the sale of its international power generation portfolio, owned by a Dutch holding company which EME refers to as BV, to the consortium of International Power plc and Mitsui & Co., Ltd. Consideration from the sale of the BV was approximately $2.00 billion, representing a base purchase price of $2.30 billion after adjustments. Together with the closing of the sale of its interest in Contact Energy, completed Sep 30 2004, the sale by EME of its international assets is complete and has resulted thus far in the receipt of total cash proceeds in the amount of $2.70 billion.

Financial Data

(US$ in Thousands)	12/31/2004	12/31/2003	12/31/2002	12/31/2001	12/31/2000	12/31/1999	12/31/1998	12/31/1997
Earnings Per Share	2.77	2.50	3.20	3.17	(5.84)	1.79	1.84	1.73
Cash Flow Per Share	4.89	10.14	7.14	9.12	4.22	6.07	4.07	5.34
Tang Book Value Per Share	18.57	13.86	11.59	8.10	7.43	15.01	14.55	14.71
Dividends Per Share	1.050	0.200	...	...	1.110	0.810	1.040	1.000
Dividend Payout %	37.91	8.00	...	...	n.m.	45.25	56.52	57.80
Income Statement								
Total Revenue	10,199,000	12,135,000	11,488,000	11,436,000	11,717,000	9,670,000	10,208,000	9,235,000
EBITDA	1,365,000	2,326,000	2,922,000	5,723,000	(1,436,000)	1,178,000		
Depn & Amortn	98,000	108,000	113,000	92,000	168,000	112,000	169,000	88,000
Income Before Taxes	282,000	992,000	1,526,000	4,049,000	(2,992,000)	917,000	1,123,000	1,237,000
Income Taxes	(92,000)	213,000	391,000	1,647,000	(1,049,000)	294,000	455,000	537,000
Net Income	916,000	821,000	1,077,000	1,035,000	(1,943,000)	623,000	668,000	700,000
Average Shares	331,000	329,000	328,000	326,000	333,000	349,000	364,000	405,000
Balance Sheet								
Net PPE	13,475,000	12,587,000	8,247,000	8,013,000	7,819,000	7,331,000	7,254,000	10,939,000
Total Assets	33,269,000	34,962,000	33,284,000	36,774,000	35,100,000	36,229,000	24,698,000	25,101,000
Long-Term Obligations	9,678,000	11,787,000	11,557,000	12,674,000	12,150,000	13,391,000	8,008,000	8,871,000
Total Liabilities	26,778,000	28,933,000	27,064,000	31,824,000	31,152,000	29,350,000	19,048,000	18,956,000
Stockholders' Equity	6,049,000	5,383,000	4,437,000	3,272,000	2,420,000	5,211,000	5,099,000	5,527,000
Shares Outstanding	325,811	325,811	325,811	325,811	325,811	347,207	350,553	375,764
Statistical Record								
Return on Assets %	2.68	2.41	3.07	2.88	N.M.	2.05	2.68	2.82
Return on Equity %	15.98	16.72	27.94	36.37	N.M.	12.09	12.57	11.74
EBITDA Margin %	13.38	19.17	25.44	50.04	N.M.	12.18	...	...
Net Margin %	8.98	6.77	9.38	9.05	(16.58)	6.44	6.54	7.58
PPE Turnover	0.78	1.16	1.41	1.44	1.54	1.33	1.12	0.82
Asset Turnover	0.30	0.36	0.33	0.32	0.33	0.32	0.41	0.37
Debt to Equity	1.60	2.19	2.60	3.87	5.02	2.57	1.57	1.61
Price Range	32.43-21.53	21.98-11.06	19.50-7.85	15.94-8.25	29.50-14.94	29.63-22.06	30.94-25.19	27.63-19.50
P/E Ratio	11.71-7.77	8.79-4.42	6.09-2.45	5.03-2.60	n.a.	16.55-12.33	16.81-13.69	15.97-11.27
Average Yield %	4.05	1.21	...	...	5.17	3.09	3.71	4.19

Address: 2244 Walnut Grove Avenue, Suite 369, Rosemead, CA 91770 **Telephone:** (626) 302 2222 **Fax:** (626) 302 9935	**Web Site:** www.edison.com **Officers:** John E. Bryson - Chmn., Pres., C.E.O. Theodore F. Craver Jr. - Exec. V.P., C.F.O., Treas.	**Auditors:** PricewaterhouseCoopers LLP

EDWARDS (A.G.), INC.

Exchange	Symbol	Price	52Wk Range	Yield	P/E
NYS	AGE	$44.80 (3/31/2005)	45.11-31.45	1.43	18.82

*7 Year Price Score 86.98 ***NYSE Composite Index=100** ***12 Month Price Score 106.64**

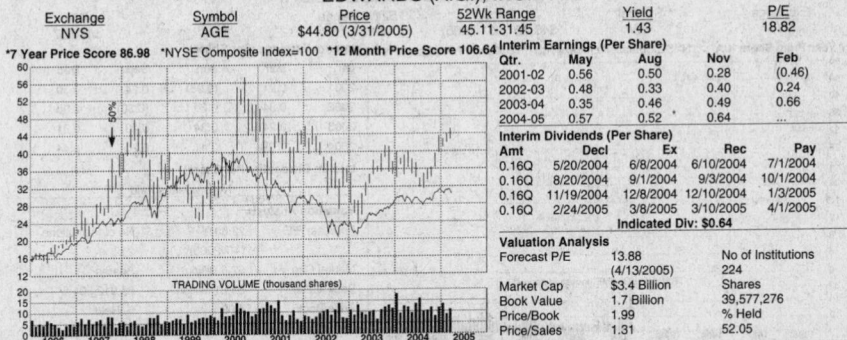

Interim Earnings (Per Share)

Qtr.	May	Aug	Nov	Feb
2001-02	0.56	0.50	0.28	(0.46)
2002-03	0.48	0.33	0.40	0.24
2003-04	0.35	0.46	0.49	0.66
2004-05	0.57	0.52	0.64	...

Interim Dividends (Per Share)

Amt	Decl	Ex	Rec	Pay
0.16Q	5/20/2004	6/8/2004	6/10/2004	7/1/2004
0.16Q	8/20/2004	9/1/2004	9/3/2004	10/1/2004
0.16Q	11/19/2004	12/8/2004	12/10/2004	1/3/2005
0.16Q	2/24/2005	3/8/2005	3/10/2005	4/1/2005
		Indicated Div: $0.64		

Valuation Analysis

Forecast P/E	13.88	No of Institutions
	(4/13/2005)	224
Market Cap	$3.4 Billion	Shares
Book Value	1.7 Billion	39,577,276
Price/Book	1.99	% Held
Price/Sales	1.31	52.05

Business Summary: Finance Intermediaries & Services (MIC: 8.7 SIC: 211 NAIC: 23120)

A.G. Edwards is a holding co. whose subsidiaries provide securities and commodities brokerage, investment banking, trust, asset management, and insurance services. As of Feb 29 2004, Co.'s subsidiary, A.G. Edwards & Sons, operated more than 700 locations in 49 states, the District of Columbia, London, England, and Geneva, Switzerland. A.G. Edwards & Sons provides a full range of financial products and services to individual and institutional investors and offers investment banking services to corporate, governmental and municipal clients. Co. is a member of all major securities exchanges in the U.S., the National Association of Securities Dealers and the Securities Investor Protection Corp.

Recent Developments: For the quarter ended Nov 30 2004, net income increased 23.8% to $49,173 thousand from net income of $39,717 thousand in the year-earlier quarter. Revenues were $639,216 thousand, up 1.5% from $629,724 thousand the year before. Net revenues after interest expenses rose 1.4% to $637,989 thousand from $629,321 thousand in 2003. Compensation and benefits expense was $411,574 thousand, up 2.7% from $400,878 thousand a year earlier. Total other operating expenses were $148,558 thousand, down 11.4% from $167,595 thousand the previous year.

Prospects: Earnings were adversely affected by a decrease in client activity in individual equities as well as a charge of $10.0 million for occupancy and equipment expenses. This was partially offset by a credit of $8.0 million in other expenses to correctly recognize state-registration fees for Co.'s financial consultants over the registration period. Going into fiscal 2006, Co. is excited to begin the next phase of its branding initiative. With a new campaign that will begin in mid-April, Co. will enhance awareness of its brand. The positive feedback Co. has already received from its clients and financial consultants makes it confident that its branding effort is leading it in the right direction.

Financial Data
(US$ in Thousands)

	9 Mos	6 Mos	3 Mos	02/29/2004	02/28/2003	02/28/2002	02/28/2001	02/29/2000
Earnings Per Share	2.38	2.23	2.17	1.97	1.46	0.88	3.43	4.08
Cash Flow Per Share	4.72	1.61	3.00	2.68	4.32	11.57	9.54	(1.63)
Tang Book Value Per Share	22.53	22.37	22.38	22.08	20.92	20.42	20.29	19.69
Dividends Per Share	0.640	0.640	0.640	0.640	0.640	0.640	0.640	0.600
Dividend Payout %	26.86	28.64	29.43	32.49	43.84	72.73	18.66	14.71
Income Statement								
Total Revenue	1,920,576	1,281,360	661,881	2,498,874	2,199,215	2,363,801	2,839,148	2,819,007
Income Before Taxes	214,307	136,450	73,326	245,274	171,434	92,058	455,154	623,115
Income Taxes	78,242	49,558	27,062	85,789	52,606	20,557	167,677	240,194
Net Income	136,065	86,892	46,264	159,485	118,828	71,501	287,477	382,921
Average Shares	77,844	79,156	80,951	80,990	81,177	81,282	83,925	93,814
Balance Sheet								
Total Assets	4,105,297	4,001,300	4,110,942	4,435,059	3,980,094	4,187,170	4,859,984	5,347,587
Total Liabilities	2,392,559	2,280,968	2,328,661	2,656,740	2,291,557	2,539,374	3,233,640	3,630,465
Stockholders' Equity	1,712,738	1,720,332	1,782,281	1,778,319	1,688,537	1,647,796	1,626,344	1,717,122
Shares Outstanding	76,033	76,919	79,639	80,526	80,725	80,695	80,137	87,209
Statistical Record								
Return on Assets %	4.58	4.48	4.42	3.78	2.91	1.58	5.63	8.35
Return on Equity %	11.02	10.66	10.27	9.18	7.12	4.37	17.20	22.83
Price Range	40.15-31.45	41.36-31.45	41.36-32.69	41.36-23.60	45.90-25.92	46.76-30.87	57.25-31.69	37.06-24.44
P/E Ratio	16.87-13.21	18.55-14.10	19.06-15.06	20.99-11.98	31.44-17.75	53.14-35.08	16.69-9.24	9.08-5.99
Average Yield %	1.78	1.74	1.72	1.84	1.79	1.56	1.45	1.97

Address: One North Jefferson Avenue, St. Louis, MO 63103
Telephone: (314) 955-3000
Fax: (314) 955-5913

Web Site: www.agedwards.com
Officers: Robert L. Bagby - Chmn., C.E.O. Ronald J. Kessler - Vice-Chmn.

Auditors: Deloitte & Touche LLP

EDWARDS LIFESCIENCES CORP

Exchange	Symbol	Price	52Wk Range	Yield	P/E
NYS	EW	$43.22 (3/31/2005)	44.28-31.88	N/A	1440.67

*7 Year Price Score N/A   ***NYSE Composite Index=100**   ***12 Month Price Score 107.51**

Interim Earnings (Per Share)

Qtr.	Mar	Jun	Sep	Dec
2001	0.21	(0.95)	0.24	0.30
2002	0.34	0.50	(0.30)	0.36
2003	0.24	0.34	0.40	0.31
2004	(1.04)	0.41	0.20	0.44

Interim Dividends (Per Share)

No Dividends Paid

Valuation Analysis

Forecast P/E	22.60	No of Institutions	
	(4/7/2005)	212	
Market Cap	$2.6 Billion	Shares	
Book Value	628.1 Million	55,912,504	
Price/Book	4.09	% Held	
Price/Sales	2.76	93.84	

Business Summary: Pharmaceuticals (MIC: 9.1 SIC: 834 NAIC: 25412)

Edwards Lifesciences develops products and technologies designed to treat advanced cardiovascular disease. Co. focuses on four main cardiovascular disease states: heart valve disease, coronary artery disease, peripheral vascular disease and congestive heart failure. Co.'s products are sold in approximately 100 countries under proprietary brands including, Carpentier-Edwards, Cosgrove-Edwards, Fogarty, LifeStent, PERIMOUNT and Swan-Ganz. The products and technologies provided by Co. to treat cardiovascular disease are categorized into five main areas: cardiac surgery, critical care, vascular, perfusion and other distributed products.

Recent Developments: For the year ended Dec 31 2004, net income decreased 97.8% to $1,700 thousand from net income of $79,000 thousand a year earlier. Revenues were $931,500 thousand, up 8.3% from $860,500 thousand the year before. Total direct expense was $370,200 thousand versus $359,400 thousand in the prior year, an increase of 3.0%. Total indirect expense was $517,400 thousand versus $399,800 thousand in the prior year, an increase of 29.4%.

Prospects: Looking ahead, Co. expects sales for 2005 in the range of $980.0 million to $1.02 billion, with gross profit margin growing by more than 100 basis points. Earnings per share are expected to be about $0.45 for the first quarter and between $1.85 and $1.95 for the full year, excluding charges. Separately, on Jan 26 2005, Co. announced that it is realigning its business in Japan as part of its efforts to focus on its core cardiovascular businesses. This initiative includes selling the cardiopulmonary products business in Japan to Terumo Corp. for between $10.0 million and $20 million. Co. also is exiting its pacemaker distribution business in Japan and restructuring its Japanese operations.

Financial Data

(US$ in Thousands)	12/31/2004	12/31/2003	12/31/2002	12/31/2001	12/31/2000	12/31/1999	12/31/1998	12/31/1997
Earnings Per Share	0.03	1.29	0.91	(0.19)	(4.81)	...	...	...
Cash Flow Per Share	3.02	2.07	2.04	1.71	2.34	...	...	...
Tang Book Value Per Share	2.32	3.63	2.39	0.96	N.M.	...	...	...
Income Statement								
Total Revenue	931,500	860,500	704,000	692,000	804,000	905,000	865,000	879,000
EBITDA	98,600	150,100	106,600	60,000	(174,000)	197,000	175,000	65,000
Depn & Amortn	54,300	44,100	39,100	46,000	65,000	84,000	82,000	80,000
Income Before Taxes	30,100	92,800	56,000	(9,000)	(259,000)	113,000	93,000	(15,000)
Income Taxes	28,400	13,800	300	1,000	13,000	31,000	31,000	37,000
Net Income	1,700	79,000	55,700	(11,000)	(272,000)	82,000	62,000	(52,000)
Average Shares	62,000	61,100	61,300	59,000	58,400	...	...	...
Balance Sheet								
Current Assets	367,500	360,200	326,400	293,000	282,000	356,000	353,000	...
Total Assets	1,112,700	1,101,400	1,008,200	973,000	1,088,000	1,437,000	1,483,000	...
Current Liabilities	195,400	167,200	197,900	184,000	219,000	156,000	157,000	...
Long-Term Obligations	267,100	255,800	245,500	310,000	367,000	...	...	...
Total Liabilities	484,600	466,300	468,800	514,000	648,000	213,000	212,000	...
Stockholders' Equity	628,100	635,100	539,400	459,000	440,000	1,224,000	1,271,000	...
Shares Outstanding	59,438	59,480	60,177	59,327	58,668	...	...	...
Statistical Record								
Return on Assets %	0.15	7.49	5.62	N.M.	N.M.	5.62	...	...
Return on Equity %	0.27	13.45	11.16	N.M.	N.M.	6.57	...	...
EBITDA Margin %	10.59	17.44	15.14	8.67	N.M.	21.77	20.23	7.39
Net Margin %	0.18	9.18	7.91	N.M.	N.M.	9.06	7.17	N.M.
Asset Turnover	0.84	0.82	0.71	0.67	0.64	0.62	...	...
Current Ratio	1.88	2.15	1.65	1.59	1.29	2.28	2.25	...
Debt to Equity	0.43	0.40	0.46	0.68	0.83	...	...	...
Price Range	42.26-29.61	32.52-24.44	29.53-18.57	28.76-16.88	26.25-13.00	...	...	...
P/E Ratio	N.M.	25.21-18.95	32.45-20.41	...	...	...	...	...

Address: One Edwards Way, Irvine, CA 92614	Web Site: www.edwards.com	Auditors: PricewaterhouseCoopers LLP
Telephone: (949) 250-2500	Officers: Michael A. Mussallem - Chmn., C.E.O.	
Fax: (949) 250-2525	Corinne H. Lyle - Corp. V.P., C.F.O., Treas.	

EL PASO CORP.

Exchange	Symbol	Price	52Wk Range	Yield	P/E
NYS	EP	$10.58 (3/31/2005)	12.99-6.76	1.51	N/A

*7 Year Price Score 25.84   *NYSE Composite Index=100   *12 Month Price Score 118.90

Interim Earnings (Per Share)

Qtr.	Mar	Jun	Sep	Dec
2001	(0.80)	(0.18)	0.41	0.74
2002	0.72	(0.08)	(0.12)	(3.11)
2003	(0.66)	(1.99)	(0.24)	(0.33)
2004	(0.32)	0.03	(0.33)	...

Interim Dividends (Per Share)

Amt	Decl	Ex	Rec	Pay
0.04Q	4/29/2004	6/2/2004	6/4/2004	7/6/2004
0.04Q	7/16/2004	9/1/2004	9/3/2004	10/4/2004
0.04Q	11/18/2004	12/1/2004	12/3/2004	1/3/2005
0.04Q	2/18/2005	3/2/2005	3/4/2005	4/4/2005
		Indicated Div: $0.16		

Valuation Analysis

		No of Institutions
Forecast P/E	0.00	336
	(4/7/2005)	Shares
Market Cap	$6.8 Billion	497,007,904
Book Value	4.0 Billion	% Held
Price/Book	1.69	77.27
Price/Sales	1.12	

Business Summary: Gas Utilities (MIC: 7.4 SIC: 922 NAIC: 86210)

El Paso provides natural gas and related energy products in a safe, efficient, dependable manner. Co. operates through four business segments: Pipelines segment provides natural gas transmission, storage and related services and owns or has interests in approximately 58,000 miles of interstate natural gas pipelines in the U.S. and internationally; Production segment is engaged in the exploration for, and the acquisition, development and production of natural gas, oil and natural gas liquids; Field Services segment includes gathering and processing of natural gas; and Merchant Energy segment consists of a Global Power division, an Energy Marketing and Trading division.

Recent Developments: For the quarter ended Sep 30 2004, Co. posted a loss from continuing operations of $202.0 million versus income of $65.0 million a year earlier. Results for 2004 and 2003 included losses on long-lived assets of $550.0 million and $54.0 million, respectively. Operating revenue fell 16.6% to $1.43 billion from $1.71 billion the previous year. Regulated segment earnings before interest expense and income taxes (EBIT), which is comprised of Co.'s Pipelines business, slid 11.0% to $268.0 million. Unregulated segment EBIT, which includes Co.'s Production, Marketing and Trading, Power, and Field Services business, fell 45.5% to $334.0 million. Comparisons were made with restated prior-year results.

Prospects: Co. announced the it sold for $74.5 million its membership interests in two subsidiaries that own and operate natural gas gathering systems and a cryogenic processing plant to Enterprise Products Partners L.P. Meanwhile, Co. recently acquired two exploration and production properties in east Texas and south Texas for $211.0 million. The properties add about 124.00 billion cubic feet equivalent of proved reserves and 29.0 million cubic feet equivalent per day of average net production. Separately, Co. executed new power purchase agreements for its Rio Negro and Manaus power plants in Brazil. In addition, Co. will transfer ownership of the plants to Manaus Energia in January 2008.

Financial Data (US$ in Thousands)	9 Mos	6 Mos	3 Mos	12/31/2003	12/31/2002	12/31/2001	12/31/2000	12/31/1999
Earnings Per Share	(0.95)	(0.86)	(2.86)	(3.23)	(2.62)	0.18	2.73	(1.12)
Cash Flow Per Share	1.60	2.51	4.76	3.90	0.78	8.16	(4.51)	2.20
Tang Book Value Per Share	5.61	5.02	5.08	5.36	11.69	17.63	15.20	10.47
Dividends Per Share	0.160	0.160	0.160	0.160	0.870	0.850	0.824	0.800
Dividend Payout %	...	...	...	...	...	472.22	30.18	...
Income Statement								
Total Revenue	4,510,000	3,081,000	1,585,000	6,711,000	12,194,000	57,475,000	21,950,000	10,581,000
EBITDA	1,907,000	1,366,000	510,000	1,794,000	1,021,000			
Depn & Amortn	808,000	538,000	283,000	1,207,000	1,405,000	1,359,000	589,000	618,000
Income Before Taxes	(130,000)	(5,000)	(195,000)	(1,200,000)	(1,784,000)	182,000	286,000	(81,000)
Income Taxes	124,000	47,000	(44,000)	(584,000)	(495,000)	93,000	652,000	(255,000)
Net Income	(404,000)	(190,000)	(206,000)	(1,928,000)	(1,467,000)	516,000	243,000	228,000
Average Shares	639,000	639,000	638,000	597,000	560,000			
Balance Sheet								
Net PPE	18,625,000	18,349,000	18,156,000	18,594,000	23,610,000	24,591,000	11,659,000	10,261,000
Total Assets	31,795,000	32,727,000	35,215,000	37,084,000	46,224,000	48,171,000	27,445,000	5,223,000
Long-Term Obligations	17,673,000	18,259,000	19,681,000	20,275,000	16,307,000	13,184,000	5,949,000	
Total Liabilities	27,397,000	27,973,000	30,451,000	32,163,000	34,427,000	34,802,000	21,818,000	12,017,000
Stockholders' Equity	4,032,000	4,306,000	4,330,000	4,474,000	8,377,000	9,356,000	3,569,000	2,947,000
Shares Outstanding	643,433	642,937	640,856	632,201	599,568	530,734	234,780	229,596
Statistical Record								
Return on Assets %	N.M.	N.M.	N.M.	N.M.	N.M.	0.25	2.95	N.M.
Return on Equity %	N.M.	N.M.	N.M.	N.M.	N.M.	1.44	19.96	N.M.
EBITDA Margin %	42.28	44.34	32.18	26.73	8.37	...	...	...
Net Margin %	(8.96)	(6.17)	(13.00)	(28.73)	(12.03)	0.16	2.97	(2.41)
PPE Turnover	0.29	0.30	0.31	0.32	0.51	3.17	2.00	1.20
Asset Turnover	0.16	0.16	0.16	0.16	0.26	1.52	0.99	0.79
Debt to Equity	4.38	4.24	4.55	4.53	1.95	1.41	1.67	1.77
Price Range	9.71-6.13	9.71-6.13	9.71-6.04	9.96-3.45	46.77-5.30	74.50-38.60	73.19-31.25	42.00-31.00
P/E Ratio	...	...	...	...	..413.89-214.44	26.81-11.45	...	...
Average Yield %	2.12	2.14	2.10	2.20	3.62	1.51	1.63	2.20

Address: 1001 Louisiana Street, Houston, TX 77002 Telephone: (713) 420-2600 Fax: (713) 420-4417	Web Site: www.elpaso.com Officers: Ronald L. Kuehn Jr. - Chmn. Douglas L. Foshee - Pres., C.E.O.	Auditors: PricewaterhouseCoopers LLP Investor Contact: 713-420-5855 Transfer Agents: Fleet National Bank c/o EquiServe, Providence, RI

ELECTRONIC DATA SYSTEMS CORP. (NEW)

Exchange	Symbol	Price	52Wk Range	Yield	P/E
NYS	EDS	$20.67 (3/31/2005)	23.35-15.79	0.97	N/A

7 Year Price Score 41.31 **NYSE Composite Index=100** **12 Month Price Score 96.93**

TRADING VOLUME (thousand shares)

Interim Earnings (Per Share)

Qtr.	Mar	Jun	Sep	Dec
2001	0.93	0.62	0.44	0.82
2002	0.72	0.64	0.18	0.74
2003	(0.26)	0.28	(0.08)	(0.79)
2004	(0.02)	0.54	(0.30)	...

Interim Dividends (Per Share)

Amt	Decl	Ex	Rec	Pay
0.15Q	4/23/2004	5/12/2004	5/14/2004	6/10/2004
0.05Q	7/27/2004	8/11/2004	8/13/2004	9/10/2004
0.05Q	10/21/2004	11/10/2004	11/15/2004	12/10/2004
0.05Q	2/2/2005	2/11/2005	2/15/2005	3/10/2005

Indicated Div: $0.20

Valuation Analysis

Forecast P/E	73.68	No of Institutions
	(4/7/2005)	334
Market Cap	$10.6 Billion	Shares
Book Value	7.3 Billion	458,473,504
Price/Book	1.46	% Held
Price/Sales	0.51	89.22

Business Summary: IT & Technology (MIC: 10.2 SIC: 374 NAIC: 18210)

Electronic Data Systems is a global provider of information technology and business process outsourcing services. Infrastructure services delivers hosting, storage, desktop, helpdesk, security and privacy and communications services. Application services helps organizations plan, develop, integrate and manage custom applications. Business process outsourcing enables clients to achieve economies of scale by leveraging a shared-services model. A.T. Kearney provides clients with management consulting services and executive searches. UGS PLM Solutions is a global provider of product data management, collaboration and product design software applications.

Recent Developments: For the quarter ended Sep 30 2004, loss from continuing operations was $169 million compared with a loss of $35 million in the year-earlier quarter. Net loss amounted to $153 million versus a net loss of $16 million in the year-earlier quarter. Revenues were $4,945 million, down 1.0% from $4,993 million the year before. Operating loss amounted to $202 million versus income of $27 million in the prior-year quarter. Total direct costs were $4,745 million, an increase of 4.0%. Total indirect costs were unchanged at $402 million versus the prior-year period.

Prospects: In Jan 2005, Co. and Towers Perrin announced an agreement to form a new company to deliver a range of human resources (HR) outsourcing services to enterprises, HR departments, employees and retirees. Co. will own 85.0% of the new company, with Towers Perrin owning the balance. Co. will pay about $420.0 million to Towers Perrin as a part of the agreement, which is expected to close by Mar 31 2005. Separately, Co. expects full-year 2005 revenue of $20.00 billion to $21.00 billion, and earnings per share (EPS) of $0.50 to $0.60. Co.'s EPS guidance does not include the effect of new accounting rules for expensing stock options or expected changes in its long-term incentive compensation strategy.

Financial Data
(US$ in Thousands)

	9 Mos	6 Mos	3 Mos	12/31/2003	12/31/2002	12/31/2001	12/31/2000	12/31/1999
Earnings Per Share	(0.56)	(0.18)	(0.57)	(3.55)	2.28	2.81	2.40	0.85
Cash Flow Per Share	3.03	2.50	2.68	2.89	4.69	3.66	3.33	4.24
Tang Book Value Per Share	5.43	5.13	1.96	N.M.	3.22	3.06	4.53	3.93
Dividends Per Share	0.500	0.600	0.600	0.600	0.600	0.600	0.600	0.600
Dividend Payout %	...	...	...	...	26.32	21.35	25.00	70.59
Income Statement								
Total Revenue	15,381,000	10,436,000	5,198,000	21,476,000	21,502,000	21,543,000	19,226,800	18,534,200
EBITDA	1,273,000	(42,000)	(39,000)	1,575,000	3,226,000	3,928,000	3,440,700	2,243,500
Depn & Amortn	1,496,000	...	...	1,663,000	1,443,000	1,482,000	1,431,200	1,435,800
Income Before Taxes	(480,000)	(235,000)	(39,000)	(389,000)	1,525,000	2,199,000	1,800,000	657,700
Income Taxes	(141,000)	(65,000)	(1,000)	(137,000)	518,000	812,000	656,700	236,800
Net Income	105,000	258,000	(12,000)	(1,698,000)	1,116,000	1,363,000	1,143,300	420,900
Average Shares	511,000	497,000	482,000	479,000	489,000	484,000	476,400	498,000
Balance Sheet								
Current Assets	8,802,000	8,196,000	8,148,000	6,823,000	9,385,000	7,374,000	6,166,700	5,877,700
Total Assets	17,901,000	17,486,000	17,843,000	18,280,000	18,880,000	16,353,000	12,700,300	12,522,300
Current Liabilities	5,751,000	5,492,000	7,128,000	7,473,000	6,129,000	4,367,000	4,318,300	4,996,000
Long-Term Obligations	3,410,000	3,376,000	3,580,000	3,488,000	4,148,000	4,692,000	2,585,600	2,215,700
Total Liabilities	10,623,000	10,329,000	12,231,000	12,566,000	11,858,000	9,907,000	7,561,600	7,987,700
Stockholders' Equity	7,278,000	7,157,000	5,612,000	5,714,000	7,022,000	6,446,000	5,138,700	4,534,600
Shares Outstanding	513,159	508,457	484,571	480,604	476,872	477,315	465,298	466,192
Statistical Record								
Return on Assets %	N.M.	N.M.	N.M.	N.M.	6.33	9.38	9.04	3.50
Return on Equity %	N.M.	N.M.	N.M.	N.M.	16.57	23.53	23.57	8.05
EBITDA Margin %	8.28	N.M.	N.M.	7.33	15.00	18.23	17.90	12.10
Net Margin %	0.68	2.47	N.M.	N.M.	5.19	6.33	5.95	2.27
Asset Turnover	1.14	1.13	1.19	1.16	1.22	1.48	1.52	1.54
Current Ratio	1.53	1.49	1.14	0.91	1.53	1.69	1.43	1.18
Debt to Equity	0.47	0.47	0.64	0.61	0.59	0.73	0.50	0.49
Price Range	25.22-15.79	25.22-15.79	25.22-16.27	24.56-14.45	68.55-11.27	71.88-53.12	75.00-39.00	70.00-45.00
P/E Ratio	...	...	...	...	30.07-4.94	25.58-18.90	31.25-16.25	82.35-52.94
Average Yield %	2.50	2.87	2.83	2.98	1.48	0.97	1.08	1.08

Address: 5400 Legacy Drive, Plano, TX 75024 -3199	Web Site: www.eds.com	Auditors: KPMG LLP
Telephone: (972) 604-6000	Officers: Michael H. Jordan - Chmn., C.E.O. Jeffrey M. Heller - Pres., C.O.O.	Investor Contact: 888-610-1122
Fax: (972) 605-6796		

EMC CORP. (MA)

Exchange	Symbol	Price	52Wk Range	Yield	P/E
NYS	EMC	$12.32 (3/31/2005)	14.87-9.37	N/A	34.22

*7 Year Price Score 40.53 *NYSE Composite Index=100 *12 Month Price Score 97.90

Interim Earnings (Per Share)
Qtr.	Mar	Jun	Sep	Dec
2001	0.18	0.05	(0.43)	(0.03)
2002	(0.03)	0.00	0.01	(0.03)
2003	0.02	0.04	0.07	0.10
2004	0.06	0.08	0.09	0.13

Interim Dividends (Per Share)
Amt	Decl	Ex	Rec	Pay
100%	2/25/1999	6/1/1999	5/14/1999	5/28/1999
100%	5/3/2000	6/5/2000	5/19/2000	6/2/2000
0.00U	1/12/2001	2/8/2001	1/24/2001	2/7/2001

Valuation Analysis
Forecast P/E	N/A
No of Institutions	650
Market Cap	$29.6 Billion
Shares	1,566,762,496
Book Value	11.5 Billion
% Held	65.17
Price/Book	2.57
Price/Sales	3.60

Business Summary: IT & Technology (MIC: 10.2 SIC: 572 NAIC: 34112)

EMC designs, manufactures and markets a range of storage platforms and software offerings, as well as related services that enable its customers to store, manage, protect and share electronic information. These integrated applications create an enterprise information infrastructure. Co.'s products are sold to customers who use a range of computing platforms for key applications, including transaction processing, enterprise resource planning, customer relationship management, data warehousing, electronic commerce and Web hosting. Co.'s information storage systems include its Symmetrix systems, CLARiiON systems, NetWin and Celerra systems, Centera systems, and Connectrix systems.

Recent Developments: For the year ended Dec 31 2004, net income increased 75.6% to $871,189 thousand from net income of $496,108 thousand a year earlier. Revenues were $8,229,488 thousand, up 32.0% from $6,236,808 the year before. Operating income was $1,043,993 thousand versus an income of $401,157 thousand in the prior year, an increase of 160.2%. Total direct expense was $4,014,881 thousand versus $3,394,750 thousand in the prior year, an increase of 18.3%. Total indirect expense was $3,170,614 thousand versus $2,440,901 thousand in the prior year, an increase of 29.9%.

Prospects: Revenues reflect greater demand for Co.'s products and services, contributions from the acquisitions of Documentum, LEGATO and VMware and the positive impact of improved distribution channels, broadened product offerings and favorable foreign currency exchange rates. Going forward, Co. plans to focus its efforts in 2005 on improving its operating and gross margins and expanding its product offerings. Co. expects its revenues for 2005 to grow at approximately twice the rate of the storage and information management IT markets, which Co. estimates will grow around 7.0% to 8.0%.

Financial Data
(US$ in Thousands)

	12/31/2004	12/31/2003	12/31/2002	12/31/2001	12/31/2000	12/31/1999	12/31/1998	12/31/1997
Earnings Per Share	0.36	0.22	(0.05)	(0.23)	0.79	0.46	0.37	0.26
Cash Flow Per Share	0.87	0.69	0.66	0.74	0.97	0.67	0.43	0.26
Tang Book Value Per Share	3.22	3.19	3.21	3.42	3.72	2.38	1.65	1.20
Income Statement								
Total Revenue	8,229,488	6,236,808	5,438,352	7,090,633	8,872,816	6,715,610	3,973,735	2,937,860
EBITDA	1,695,446	1,002,253	238,128	(17,497)	2,895,251	1,752,413	1,236,623	869,757
Depn & Amortn	502,900	428,200	523,200	548,200	439,449	361,758	158,614	136,257
Income Before Taxes	1,185,030	571,023	(296,487)	(577,035)	2,441,198	1,357,165	1,057,818	718,037
Income Taxes	313,841	74,915	(177,781)	(69,323)	659,123	346,595	264,455	179,509
Net Income	871,189	496,108	(118,706)	(507,712)	1,782,075	1,010,570	793,363	538,528
Average Shares	2,450,570	2,237,656	2,206,294	2,211,273	2,245,203	2,219,064	2,156,704	2,102,000
Balance Sheet								
Current Assets	4,830,926	4,687,304	4,217,248	4,923,242	6,100,051	4,320,396	3,104,813	2,627,026
Total Assets	15,422,906	14,092,860	9,590,447	9,889,635	10,628,342	7,173,288	4,568,571	3,490,109
Current Liabilities	2,948,700	2,546,529	2,041,650	2,179,414	2,113,647	1,397,915	653,193	505,870
Long-Term Obligations	128,456	129,966	...	...	14,457	686,609	538,896	558,454
Total Liabilities	3,899,619	3,208,139	2,364,445	2,288,815	2,451,133	2,221,502	1,244,435	1,113,808
Stockholders' Equity	11,523,287	10,884,721	7,226,002	7,600,820	8,177,209	4,951,786	3,324,136	2,376,301
Shares Outstanding	2,404,969	2,414,739	2,185,375	2,220,382	2,195,489	2,078,550	2,014,532	1,988,232
Statistical Record								
Return on Assets %	5.89	4.19	N.M.	N.M.	19.97	17.21	19.69	18.62
Return on Equity %	7.75	5.48	N.M.	N.M.	27.07	24.42	27.84	26.84
EBITDA Margin %	20.60	16.07	4.38	N.M.	32.63	26.09	31.12	29.61
Net Margin %	10.59	7.95	N.M.	N.M.	20.08	15.05	19.97	18.33
Asset Turnover	0.56	0.53	0.56	0.69	0.99	1.14	0.99	1.02
Current Ratio	1.64	1.84	2.07	2.26	2.89	3.09	4.75	5.19
Debt to Equity	0.01	0.01	...	...	N.M.	0.14	0.16	0.24
Price Range	15.59-9.37	14.49-6.14	17.37-3.83	78.37-11.00	101.29-47.09	54.11-20.85	20.85-6.18	7.97-3.94
P/E Ratio	43.31-26.03	65.86-27.91	...	...	128.21-59.61	117.63-45.32	56.34-16.70	30.66-15.15

Address: 176 South Street, Hopkinton, MA 01748
Telephone: (508) 435-1000
Fax: (508) 435-5222

Web Site: www.emc.com
Officers: Michael C. Ruettgers - Chmn. Joseph M. Tucci - Pres., C.E.O.

Auditors: PricewaterhouseCoopers LLP
Investor Contact: 508-293-7137

EMCOR GROUP, INC.

Exchange	Symbol	Price	52Wk Range	Yield	P/E
NYS	EME	$46.82 (3/31/2005)	49.05-36.38	N/A	21.98

*7 Year Price Score 104.95 *NYSE Composite Index=100 *12 Month Price Score 101.90

Interim Earnings (Per Share)

Qtr.	Mar	Jun	Sep	Dec
2001	0.44	0.81	1.00	1.15
2002	0.47	0.96	1.26	1.38
2003	0.21	0.53	0.42	0.17
2004	0.37	0.09	0.99	0.67

Interim Dividends (Per Share)

No Dividends Paid

Valuation Analysis

Forecast P/E	20.57	No of Institutions	
	(4/7/2005)	124	
Market Cap	$713.4 Million	Shares	
Book Value	562.4 Million	16,047,220	
Price/Book	1.27	% Held	
Price/Sales	0.15	N/A	

Business Summary: Building & General Construction (MIC: 3.2 SIC: 731 NAIC: 38210)

EMCOR Group specializes in the design, integration, installation, start-up, operation and maintenance of systems for generation and distribution of electrical power; lighting systems; low-voltage systems; voice and data communications systems; heating, ventilation, air conditioning, refrigeration and clean-room process ventilation systems; and plumbing, process and high-purity piping systems. Co. provides services to a broad range of commercial, industrial, utility, and institutional customers through approximately 70 principal operating subsidiaries, joint ventures and a majority-owned interest in a limited liability company in the United States, at Dec 31 2003.

Recent Developments: For the year ended Dec 31 2004, net income increased 61.0% to $33,207 thousand from net income of $20,621 thousand a year earlier. Revenues were $4,747,880 thousand, up 4.7% from $4,534,646 thousand the year before. Operating income was $42,129 thousand versus an income of $47,057 thousand in the prior year, a decrease of 10.5%. Total direct expense was $4,300,978 thousand versus $4,052,192 thousand in the prior year, an increase of 6.1%. Total indirect expense was $404,773 thousand versus $435,397 thousand in the prior year, a decrease of 7.0%.

Prospects: Based on Co.'s contract backlog and continued project selectivity, Co. is projecting revenue in 2005 to be $4.40 billion to $4.60 billion. Profitability in 2005 is expected to be enhanced by improved performance in Co.'s mechanical segment combined with a better environment for the mobile services operations within its facilities services business. For 2005, Co. is forecasting earnings per share in the range of $2.00 to $2.40. While the trajectory of any economic cycle is difficult to predict, if growth in demand for Co.'s higher value-added services accelerates, it has sufficient capacity to deploy and drive its earnings growth at a faster pace.

Financial Data

(US$ in Thousands)	12/31/2004	12/31/2003	12/31/2002	12/31/2001	12/31/2000	12/31/1999	12/31/1998	12/31/1997
Earnings Per Share	2.13	1.33	4.07	3.40	2.95	2.21	1.11	0.74
Cash Flow Per Share	3.58	0.09	10.40	6.26	8.73	3.66	3.45	2.68
Tang Book Value Per Share	17.34	14.71	12.44	24.70	15.84	11.00	12.19	9.94
Income Statement								
Total Revenue	4,747,880	4,534,646	3,968,051	3,419,854	3,460,204	2,893,962	2,210,374	1,950,868
EBITDA	64,542	69,687	130,551	106,882	95,026	72,184	47,804	35,606
Depn & Amortn	24,383	24,535	16,126	18,200	16,101	14,093	10,580	8,192
Income Before Taxes	33,162	36,916	112,326	89,474	71,587	49,678	29,741	15,462
Income Taxes	(45)	16,295	49,424	39,462	31,498	21,857	12,649	6,881
Net Income	33,207	20,621	62,902	50,012	40,089	27,821	12,315	7,577
Average Shares	15,566	15,461	15,457	15,240	14,943	14,444	13,629	10,175
Balance Sheet								
Current Assets	1,425,571	1,389,156	1,334,935	1,217,324	1,138,760	927,987	731,969	622,661
Total Assets	1,817,969	1,795,247	1,758,491	1,349,664	1,261,864	1,056,489	801,002	660,654
Current Liabilities	1,162,373	1,178,457	1,179,875	854,261	852,387	717,582	511,917	456,595
Long-Term Obligations	1,332	561	905	848	115,878	116,003	117,274	63,212
Total Liabilities	1,255,608	1,273,891	1,268,621	927,731	1,028,361	886,240	681,186	565,331
Stockholders' Equity	562,361	521,356	489,870	421,933	233,503	170,249	119,816	95,323
Shares Outstanding	15,236	15,032	14,918	14,815	10,470	9,295	9,830	9,590
Statistical Record								
Return on Assets %	1.83	1.16	4.05	3.83	3.45	3.00	1.69	1.19
Return on Equity %	6.11	4.08	13.80	15.26	19.80	19.18	11.45	8.46
EBITDA Margin %	1.36	1.54	3.29	3.13	2.75	2.49	2.16	1.83
Net Margin %	0.70	0.45	1.59	1.46	1.16	0.96	0.56	0.39
Asset Turnover	2.62	2.55	2.55	2.62	2.98	3.12	3.02	3.06
Current Ratio	1.23	1.18	1.13	1.43	1.34	1.29	1.43	1.36
Debt to Equity	N.M.	N.M.	N.M.	N.M.	0.50	0.68	0.98	0.66
Price Range	46.89-34.46	54.73-33.29	63.60-44.15	48.15-24.69	27.38-17.56	25.63-16.13	23.00-12.75	22.13-12.88
P/E Ratio	22.01-16.18	41.15-25.03	15.63-10.85	14.16-7.26	9.28-5.95	11.60-7.30	20.72-11.49	29.90-17.40

Address: 301 Merritt Seven Corporate Park, Norwalk, CT 06851-1060
Telephone: (203) 849-7800
Fax: (203) 849-7900

Web Site: www.emcorgroup.com
Officers: Frank T. MacInnis - Chmn., Pres., C.E.O. Sheldon I. Cammaker - Exec. V.P., Sec., Gen. Couns.

Auditors: ERNST & YOUNG LLP
Investor Contact: 203-849-7938

EMERSON ELECTRIC CO.

Exchange	Symbol	Price	52Wk Range	Yield	P/E	Div Achiever
NYS	EMR	$64.93 (3/31/2005)	70.44-56.56	2.56	21.01	48 Years

*7 Year Price Score 92.22   *NYSE Composite Index=100   *12 Month Price Score 97.30

Interim Earnings (Per Share)

Qtr.	Dec	Mar	Jun	Sep
2001-02	0.61	0.65	0.68	0.59
2002-03	0.52	0.56	0.85	0.66
2003-04	0.58	0.75	0.81	0.84
2004-05	0.70	...	...	...

Interim Dividends (Per Share)

Amt	Decl	Ex	Rec	Pay
0.40Q	5/4/2004	5/12/2004	5/14/2004	6/10/2004
0.40Q	8/3/2004	8/11/2004	8/13/2004	9/10/2004
0.415Q	11/2/2004	11/9/2004	11/12/2004	12/10/2004
0.415Q	2/1/2005	2/9/2005	2/11/2005	3/10/2005

Indicated Div: $1.66 (Div. Reinv. Plan)

Valuation Analysis

Forecast P/E	18.90	No of Institutions	
	(4/7/2005)	800	
Market Cap	$27.2 Billion	Shares	
Book Value	7.7 Billion	301,306,176	
Price/Book	3.56	% Held	
Price/Sales	1.71	71.86	

TRADING VOLUME (thousand shares)

Business Summary: Electrical (MIC: 11.14 SIC: 621 NAIC: 35312)

Emerson designs and supplies product technology and delivers engineering services in a range of industrial, commercial and consumer markets around the world. Co. is organized into five business segments, based on the nature of the products and services rendered. These segments are Process Management, Industrial Automation, Network Power, Climate Technologies, and Appliance and Tools. Through these segments Co. provides goods and services to allow customer to improve plant efficiency, quality control, power optimization, and storage capabilities. Co. operates under various trade and brand names in each of its segments.

Recent Developments: For the quarter ended Dec 31 2004, net income increased 21.7% to $297,000 thousand from net income of $244,000 thousand in the year-earlier quarter. Revenues were $3,970,000 thousand, up 10.3% from $3,600,000 thousand the year before. Total direct expense was $2,558,000 thousand versus $2,318,000 thousand in the prior-year quarter, an increase of 10.4%. Total indirect expense was $872,000 thousand versus $790,000 thousand in the prior-year quarter, an increase of 10.4%.

Prospects: Co. is benefiting from sales volume leverage and its previous restructuring actions, which are offsetting higher material costs and the dilution from the Marconi acquisition. Going forward, Co. expects that its shift to best-cost manufacturing, together with its aggressive sourcing initiatives, productivity improvements, and price increases will allow it to deliver improvement in operating margins in the coming quarters. Meanwhile, the acceleration of underlying orders in Asia and Latin America, combined with solid demand in the U.S., should help drive sales growth between 8.0% and 11.0% for fiscal 2005 and allow Co. to deliver 10.0% to 15.0% earnings per share growth.

Financial Data

(US$ in Thousands)	3 Mos	09/30/2004	09/30/2003	09/30/2002	09/30/2001	09/30/2000	09/30/1999	09/30/1998
Earnings Per Share	3.09	2.98	2.59	0.29	2.40	3.30	3.00	2.77
Cash Flow Per Share	5.23	5.27	4.13	4.34	4.01	4.29	4.17	3.76
Tang Book Value Per Share	4.58	4.72	3.60	1.98	2.22	2.53	4.43	4.79
Dividends Per Share	1.615	1.600	1.570	1.550	1.530	1.430	1.300	1.180
Dividend Payout %	52.24	53.69	60.62	534.48	63.75	43.33	43.33	42.60
Income Statement								
Total Revenue	3,970,000	15,615,000	13,958,000	13,824,000	15,479,600	15,544,800	14,269,500	13,447,200
EBITDA	625,000	2,619,000	2,179,000	2,339,000	2,601,400	3,144,400	2,848,100	2,637,700
Depn & Amortn	137,000	557,000	534,000	541,000	708,500	678,500	637,500	562,500
Income Before Taxes	434,000	1,852,000	1,414,000	1,565,000	1,588,600	2,178,300	2,020,900	1,923,500
Income Taxes	137,000	595,000	401,000	505,000	556,800	755,900	707,300	694,900
Net Income	297,000	1,257,000	1,089,000	122,000	1,031,800	1,422,400	1,313,600	1,228,600
Average Shares	421,900	422,200	420,900	420,900	429,500	431,400	438,400	444,100
Balance Sheet								
Current Assets	6,841,000	6,416,000	5,500,000	4,961,000	5,320,100	5,482,700	5,124,400	5,001,300
Total Assets	16,956,000	16,361,000	15,194,000	14,545,000	15,046,400	15,164,300	13,623,500	12,659,800
Current Liabilities	4,749,000	4,339,000	3,417,000	4,400,000	5,379,100	5,218,800	4,590,400	4,021,700
Long-Term Obligations	2,886,000	3,136,000	3,733,000	2,990,000	2,255,600	2,247,700	1,317,100	1,056,600
Total Liabilities	9,301,000	9,123,000	8,734,000	8,804,000	8,932,400	8,761,500	7,443,000	6,856,500
Stockholders' Equity	7,655,000	7,238,000	6,460,000	5,741,000	6,114,000	6,402,800	6,180,500	5,803,300
Shares Outstanding	419,585	419,428	421,154	420,709	419,625	427,476	433,044	438,224
Statistical Record								
Return on Assets %	8.00	7.95	7.32	0.82	6.83	9.85	10.00	10.19
Return on Equity %	18.17	18.30	17.85	2.06	16.49	22.55	21.92	21.89
EBITDA Margin %	15.74	16.77	15.61	16.92	16.81	20.23	19.96	19.62
Net Margin %	7.48	8.05	7.80	0.88	6.67	9.15	9.21	9.14
Asset Turnover	0.98	0.99	0.94	0.93	1.02	1.08	1.09	1.11
Current Ratio	1.44	1.48	1.61	1.13	0.99	1.05	1.12	1.24
Debt to Equity	0.38	0.43	0.58	0.52	0.37	0.35	0.21	0.18
Price Range	70.44-56.56	68.46-52.65	56.79-42.42	65.51-43.20	78.81-45.80	70.19-41.13	70.94-51.81	67.13-51.56
P/E Ratio	22.80-18.30	22.97-17.67	21.93-16.38	225.90-148.97	32.84-19.08	21.27-12.46	23.65-17.27	24.23-18.61
Average Yield %	2.56	2.62	3.11	2.88	2.34	2.47	2.09	1.96

Address: 8000 W. Florissant Avenue, St. Louis, MO 63136	Web Site: www.gotoemerson.com	Auditors: KPMG LLP
Telephone: (314) 553-2000	Officers: David N. Farr - Chmn., C.E.O. James G. Berges - Pres.	Investor Contact: 314-553-2197
Fax: (314) 553-3527		Transfer Agents: EquiServe Trust Company, N.A., Providence, RI

ENERGEN CORP.

Exchange	Symbol	Price	52Wk Range	Yield	P/E	Div Acheiver
NYS	EGN	$66.60 (3/31/2005)	67.95-40.30	1.20	19.08	22 Years

*7 Year Price Score 151.80 *NYSE Composite Index=100 *12 Month Price Score 114.46

Interim Earnings (Per Share)

Qtr.	Mar	Jun	Sep	Dec
2002	1.24	0.37	0.01	0.47
2003	1.56	0.66	0.33	0.57
2004	1.65	0.61	0.37	0.86

Interim Dividends (Per Share)

Amt	Decl	Ex	Rec	Pay
0.185Q	4/28/2004	5/12/2004	5/14/2004	6/1/2004
0.193Q	7/22/2004	8/11/2004	8/13/2004	9/1/2004
0.193Q	10/27/2004	11/10/2004	11/15/2004	12/1/2004
0.20Q	1/26/2005	2/11/2005	2/15/2005	3/1/2005

Indicated Div: $0.80 (Div. Reinv. Plan)

Valuation Analysis

Forecast P/E	15.15	No of Institutions
	(4/7/2005)	203
Market Cap	$2.4 Billion	Shares
Book Value	803.7 Million	24,597,786
Price/Book	3.03	% Held
Price/Sales	2.60	67.15

Business Summary: Gas Utilities (MIC: 7.4 SIC: 924 NAIC: 21210)

Energen is a diversified energy holding company engaged primarily in the acquisition, development, exploration and production of oil, natural gas and natural gas liquids in the continental U.S. and in the purchase, distribution, and sale of natural gas, principally in central and north Alabama. Alagasco, Co.'s principal subsidiary, is the largest natural gas distribution utility in Alabama, and services a territory that includes approximately 185 cities and communities in 28 counties. The oil and gas exploration and production arm of Co. is Energen Resources, which conducts its activities onshore in North America.

Recent Developments: For the year ended Dec 31 2004, income from continuing operations increased 15.6% to $127,450 thousand from income of $110,265 thousand a year earlier. Net income increased 15.2% to $127,463 thousand from net income of $110,654 thousand a year earlier. Revenues were $937,384 thousand, up 11.3% from $842,221 thousand the year before. Operating income was $245,076 thousand versus an income of $217,888 thousand in the prior year, an increase of 12.5%. Total direct expense was $494,113 thousand versus $442,042 thousand in the prior year, an increase of 11.8%. Total indirect expense was $198,195 thousand versus $182,291 thousand in the prior year, an increase of 8.7%.

Prospects: Results are benefiting from higher prices for natural gas, oil and natural gas liquids (NGL). Meanwhile, Co. is projecting full-year 2005 earnings of between $4.25 and $4.45 per share. This earnings guidance for 2005 assumes that prices applicable to Co.'s unhedged production will average $6.00 per thousand cubic feet (Mcf) of natural gas, $32.00 per barrel of oil, and $0.53 per gallon of NGL. Looking ahead, Co. is targeting full-year 2006 earnings per share in the range of $4.65 to $4.85. This earnings guidance assumes that prices applicable to Co.'s unhedged production will average $6.15 per Mcf of natural gas, $35.00 per barrel of oil, and $0.58 per gallon of NGL.

Financial Data

(US$ in Thousands)	12/31/2004	12/31/2003	12/31/2002	12/31/2001	09/30/2001	09/30/2000	09/30/1999	09/30/1998
Earnings Per Share	3.49	3.10	2.03	0.12	2.18	1.75	1.38	1.23
Cash Flow Per Share	8.00	6.86	6.35	0.54	5.09	3.48	4.41	4.25
Tang Book Value Per Share	21.97	19.30	16.77	15.18	15.61	13.21	12.09	11.23
Dividends Per Share	0.755	0.730	0.710	0.690	0.685	0.665	0.645	0.625
Dividend Payout %	21.63	23.55	34.98	575.00	31.42	38.00	46.74	50.81
Income Statement								
Total Revenue	937,384	842,221	677,175	146,164	784,973	555,595	497,517	502,627
EBITDA	366,766	334,440	245,575	36,013	212,917	184,649	167,333	145,028
Depn & Amortn	120,960	117,785	110,767	25,184	86,975	87,073	88,615	80,999
Income Before Taxes	203,063	174,393	91,095	195	83,872	59,807	41,545	34,028
Income Taxes	75,613	64,128	20,509	(3,384)	15,976	6,789	135	(2,221)
Net Income	127,463	110,654	68,639	3,658	67,896	53,018	41,410	36,249
Average Shares	36,558	35,716	33,838	31,277	31,083	30,359`	29,920	29,437
Balance Sheet								
Net PPE	1,783,059	1,433,451	1,256,803	1,005,679	998,334	907,829	861,107	756,344
Total Assets	2,181,739	1,781,432	1,530,891	1,240,356	1,223,879	1,203,041	1,184,895	993,455
Long-Term Obligations	612,891	552,842	512,954	544,133	544,110	353,932	371,824	372,782
Total Liabilities	1,378,073	1,082,400	948,081	766,151	743,112	802,181	823,391	664,206
Stockholders' Equity	803,666	699,032	582,810	474,205	480,767	400,860	361,504	329,249
Shares Outstanding	36,582	36,223	34,745	31,248	30,799	30,350	29,903	29,326
Statistical Record								
Return on Assets %	6.41	6.68	4.95	0.24	5.60	4.43	3.80	3.79
Return on Equity %	16.92	17.26	12.99	0.67	15.40	13.87	11.99	11.50
EBITDA Margin %	39.13	39.71	36.26	24.64	27.12	33.23	33.63	28.85
Net Margin %	13.60	13.14	10.14	2.50	8.65	9.54	8.32	7.21
PPE Turnover	0.58	0.63	0.60	0.12	0.82	0.63	0.62	0.71
Asset Turnover	0.47	0.51	0.49	0.10	0.65	0.46	0.46	0.53
Debt to Equity	0.76	0.79	0.88	1.15	1.13	0.88	1.03	1.13
Price Range	59.80-39.99	41.96-28.23	29.80-21.86	25.20-22.00	39.71-22.21	30.05-14.75	20.25-13.63	22.31-15.56
P/E Ratio	17.13-11.46	13.54-9.11	14.68-10.77	210.00-183.33	18.22-10.19	17.17-8.43	14.67-9.87	18.14-12.65
Average Yield %	1.60	2.14	2.76	2.91	2.27	3.36	3.62	3.24

Address: 605 Richard Arrington Jr. Blvd. N., Birmingham, AL 35203-2707
Telephone: (205) 326-2700
Fax: (205) 326-2704

Web Site: www.energen.com
Officers: William Michael Warren Jr. - Chmn., Pres., C.E.O. Geoffrey C. Ketcham - Exec. V.P., C.F.O., Treas.

Auditors: PricewaterhouseCoopers LLP
Investor Contact: 800-654-3206
Transfer Agents: EquiServe Trust Company, N.A., Providence, RI

ENERGIZER HOLDINGS, INC.

Exchange NYS	Symbol ENR	Price $59.80 (3/31/2005)	52Wk Range 61.00-37.60	Yield N/A	P/E 17.18

*7 Year Price Score N/A ***NYSE Composite Index=100** ***12 Month Price Score 116.40**

Interim Earnings (Per Share)

Qtr.	Dec	Mar	Jun	Sep
2001-02	0.76	0.21	0.43	0.61
2002-03	0.95	0.37	0.20	0.38
2003-04	1.32	0.63	0.46	0.78
2004-05	1.62	...	...	...

Interim Dividends (Per Share)

No Dividends Paid

Valuation Analysis

Forecast P/E	16.17	No of Institutions
	(4/7/2005)	216
Market Cap	$4.2 Billion	Shares
Book Value	675.2 Million	52,412,840
Price/Book	6.26	% Held
Price/Sales	1.47	74.12

TRADING VOLUME (thousand shares)

1996 1997 1998 1999 2000 2001 2002 2003 2004 2005

Business Summary: Electrical (MIC: 11.14 SIC: 692 NAIC: 35912)

Energizer Holdings is a manufacturer of primary batteries, flashlights and men's and women's wet-shave products. Co.'s products are marketed and sold in more than 150 countries. Co.'s subsidiaries manufacture and/or market a line of primary alkaline and carbon zinc batteries, miniature batteries, specialty photo lithium batteries, rechargeable batteries, and flashlights and other lighting products. Through its Schick-Wilkinson Sword wet shave business, Co. manufactures and markets a range of razor systems and disposable shave products for men and women, as well as shaving products such as lotions and shaving creams, and, at a facility in the United Kingdom, ceremonial swords.

Recent Developments: For the quarter ended Dec 31 2004, net income increased 5.8% to $121,700 thousand from net income of $115,000 thousand in the year-earlier quarter. Revenues were $875,900 thousand, up 7.9% from $811,700 thousand before. Total direct expense was $430,500 thousand versus $402,500 thousand in the prior-year quarter, an increase of 7.0%. Total indirect expense was $255,300 thousand versus $236,300 thousand in the prior-year quarter, an increase of 8.0%.

Prospects: Co. is performing well, supported by new products launched over the past two years, including QUATTRO and Intuition shaving systems and Energizer e2 Lithium AAA batteries. However, this is being partially offset by unfavorable pricing and product mix of non-Energizer branded products and the continuing shift to larger pack sizes. Co. is also experiencing higher costs for raw materials. Although such increases have been more than offset by other cost savings and, additionally in the battery business, favorable production efficiencies and high production levels, Co. is uncertain whether these costs savings will fully offset further increases in material costs for the remainder of the year.

Financial Data (US$ in Thousands)	3 Mos	09/30/2004	09/30/2003	09/30/2002	09/30/2001	09/30/2000	09/30/1999	09/30/1998
Earnings Per Share	3.48	3.21	1.93	2.01	(0.42)	1.88	...	...
Cash Flow Per Share	5.36	6.01	5.15	2.23	3.44	3.57	...	...
Tang Book Value Per Share	N.M.	N.M.	1.99	6.71	5.42	5.11	...	...
Income Statement								
Total Revenue	875,900	2,812,700	2,232,500	1,739,700	1,694,200	1,914,300	1,872,300	1,921,800
EBITDA	179,100	504,600	349,000	356,900	144,500	388,700	350,700	374,800
Depn & Amortn	...	115,800	83,200	57,400	79,800	82,000	94,900	101,200
Income Before Taxes	179,100	358,000	237,600	278,400	31,500	279,200	248,200	262,500
Income Taxes	57,400	90,600	67,700	92,000	70,500	99,000	85,200	54,300
Net Income	121,700	267,400	169,900	186,400	(39,000)	181,400	83,200	164,700
Average Shares	75,200	83,400	88,200	94,100	94,100	96,300	...	...
Balance Sheet								
Current Assets	1,503,100	1,376,700	1,243,100	887,900	783,300	930,300	974,000	997,200
Total Assets	3,078,400	2,915,700	2,732,100	1,588,100	1,497,600	1,793,500	1,833,700	2,077,600
Current Liabilities	914,200	907,900	727,500	534,600	495,200	528,600	495,900	518,700
Long-Term Obligations	1,108,900	1,059,600	913,600	160,000	225,000	370,000	1,900	1,300
Total Liabilities	2,403,200	2,333,500	1,924,100	883,300	889,700	1,055,300	520,800	546,300
Stockholders' Equity	675,200	582,200	808,000	704,800	607,900	738,200	1,312,900	1,531,300
Shares Outstanding	70,710	72,902	85,077	88,455	91,718	95,552	...	...
Statistical Record								
Return on Assets %	9.26	9.44	7.87	12.08	N.M.	9.97	4.25	...
Return on Equity %	36.06	38.36	22.46	28.40	N.M.	17.64	5.85	...
EBITDA Margin %	20.45	17.94	15.63	20.52	8.53	20.31	18.73	19.50
Net Margin %	13.89	9.51	7.61	10.71	N.M.	9.48	4.44	8.57
Asset Turnover	0.97	0.99	1.03	1.13	1.03	1.05	0.96	...
Current Ratio	1.64	1.52	1.71	1.66	1.58	1.76	1.96	1.92
Debt to Equity	1.64	1.82	1.13	0.23	0.37	0.50	N.M.	N.M.
Price Range	49.93-36.87	48.10-35.89	38.20-22.94	31.90-15.52	26.46-15.01	24.50-14.88	...	...
P/E Ratio	14.35-10.59	14.98-11.18	19.79-11.89	15.87-7.72	N/A	13.03-7.91	...	...

Address: 533 Maryville University Drive, St. Louis, MO 63141 Telephone: (314) 985-2000	Web Site: www.energizer.com Officers: William P. Stiritz - Chmn. Ward M. Klein - Pres., C.E.O., C.O.O.	Auditors: PricewaterhouseCoopers LLP Investor Contact: 314-982-2013 Transfer Agents: Continental Stock Transfer & Trust Company, New York,

ENERGY EAST CORP.

Exchange	Symbol	Price	52Wk Range	Yield	P/E
NYS	EAS	$26.22 (3/31/2005)	27.01-22.15	4.20	16.92

*7 Year Price Score 95.95   *NYSE Composite Index=100   *12 Month Price Score 96.79

Interim Earnings (Per Share)

Qtr.	Mar	Jun	Sep	Dec
2001	0.98	0.23	(0.18)	0.57
2002	0.90	0.05	0.16	0.38
2003	0.93	0.19	(0.04)	0.36
2004	0.82	0.26	0.11	...

Interim Dividends (Per Share)

Amt	Decl	Ex	Rec	Pay
0.26Q	4/8/2004	4/16/2004	4/20/2004	5/15/2004
0.26Q	7/9/2004	7/16/2004	7/20/2004	8/15/2004
0.275Q	10/7/2004	10/15/2004	10/19/2004	11/15/2004
0.275Q	1/7/2005	1/14/2005	1/19/2005	2/15/2005

Indicated Div: $1.10

Valuation Analysis

Forecast P/E	16.10	No of Institutions
	(4/7/2005)	201
Market Cap	$3.9 Billion	Shares
Book Value	2.7 Billion	71,802,144
Price/Book	1.44	% Held
Price/Sales	0.80	48.81

TRADING VOLUME (thousand shares)

Business Summary: Electricity (MIC: 7.1 SIC: 931 NAIC: 21121)

Energy East, through its subsidiaries, is engaged in the energy delivery business consisting primarily of its regulated electricity transmission, distribution and generation operations in upstate New York and Maine and its regulated natural gas transportation, storage and distribution operations in upstate New York, Connecticut, Maine and Massachusetts. As of Dec 31 2003, Co. served 1.8 million electric customers and 900,000 natural gas customers. Other businesses include a non-utility generating company, retail energy marketing companies, telecommunication assets, a district heating and cooling system, and a regulated liquefied natural gas peaking plant.

Recent Developments: For the quarter ended Sep 30 2004, income from continuing operations increased 715.5% to $17,500 thousand from income of $2,146 thousand in the year-earlier quarter. Revenues were $967,805 thousand, up 8.8% from $890,276 thousand the year before. Operating income was $91,422 thousand versus $72,270 thousand in the prior-year quarter, an increase of 26.5%. Total direct expense was $753,344 thousand versus $681,698 thousand in the prior-year quarter, an increase of 10.5%. Total indirect expense was $106,625 thousand versus $136,308 thousand in the prior-year quarter, a decrease of 21.8%.

Prospects: Results are benefiting largely from the RG&E Electric and Natural Gas Rate Agreements and the sale of Ginna, as well as lower financing costs and savings from integration and efficiency initiatives. However, a number of factors are tempering these benefits, including lower income from gas operations, higher stock option expense and higher depreciation due to electric plant additions. Going forward, Co. should continue to be well positioned for growth in the next several quarters. Through the use of internal cash flow and proceeds from the sale of the Ginna nuclear plant and numerous non-utility businesses to pay down debt, Co. expects to achieve that goal in the near future.

Financial Data

(US$ in Thousands)

	9 Mos	6 Mos	3 Mos	12/31/2003	12/31/2002	12/31/2001	12/31/2000	12/31/1999
Earnings Per Share	1.55	1.40	1.33	1.44	1.44	1.61	2.06	1.88
Cash Flow Per Share	2.50	3.49	3.68	3.31	3.13	1.16	1.99	(1.09)
Tang Book Value Per Share	7.79	7.75	7.73	7.11	6.53	7.57	6.49	12.84
Dividends Per Share	1.030	1.020	1.010	1.000	0.960	0.920	0.880	0.840
Dividend Payout %	66.62	72.83	76.06	69.44	66.67	57.14	42.72	44.68
Income Statement								
Total Revenue	3,598,055	2,666,758	1,586,091	4,593,819	4,008,918	3,759,787	2,959,520	2,278,608
EBITDA	827,814	676,675	354,028	1,032,584	800,656	763,295	711,388	1,222,788
Depn & Amortn	224,130	169,934	85,498	419,237	255,782	204,281	165,524	639,069
Income Before Taxes	401,573	369,294	198,540	335,074	287,127	341,986	393,361	450,811
Income Taxes	220,319	205,803	77,988	127,687	98,524	154,379	156,682	214,494
Net Income	174,591	158,618	120,552	210,446	188,603	187,607	235,034	218,751
Average Shares	146,807	146,596	146,428	145,730	131,117	116,708	114,213	116,316
Balance Sheet								
Net PPE	5,633,166	5,617,899	5,763,004	5,778,109	4,801,839	3,626,432	3,632,928	2,139,829
Total Assets	10,717,348	10,668,028	11,393,913	11,306,432	10,269,879	7,269,232	7,003,633	3,769,397
Long-Term Obligations	3,863,462	3,907,681	3,997,783	3,994,096	3,351,959	2,471,278	2,346,814	1,235,089
Total Liabilities	8,000,187	7,956,619	8,637,612	8,643,013	7,348,305	5,099,682	5,243,787	2,355,284
Stockholders' Equity	2,670,490	2,664,785	2,665,259	2,572,324	2,460,612	1,781,177	1,716,522	1,403,954
Shares Outstanding	146,910	146,706	146,484	146,262	144,392	116,718	117,656	109,343
Statistical Record								
Return on Assets %	2.14	1.93	1.76	1.95	2.15	2.63	4.35	5.06
Return on Equity %	8.76	7.87	7.44	8.36	8.89	10.73	15.02	14.03
EBITDA Margin %	23.01	25.37	22.32	22.48	19.97	20.30	24.04	53.66
Net Margin %	4.85	5.95	7.60	4.58	4.70	4.99	7.94	9.60
PPE Turnover	0.91	0.89	0.88	0.87	0.95	1.04	1.02	0.76
Asset Turnover	0.45	0.45	0.43	0.43	0.46	0.53	0.55	0.53
Debt to Equity	1.45	1.47	1.50	1.55	1.36	1.39	1.37	0.88
Price Range	25.85-21.67	25.85-19.40	25.49-17.80	23.71-17.46	23.10-17.25	21.99-17.23	23.44-18.00	28.41-20.75
P/E Ratio	16.68-13.98	18.46-13.86	19.17-13.38	16.47-12.13	16.04-11.98	13.66-10.70	11.38-8.74	15.11-11.04
Average Yield %	4.34	4.46	4.62	4.79	4.58	4.68	4.22	3.27

Address: P. O. Box 12904, Albany, NY 12212-2904	**Web Site:** www.energyeast.com	**Auditors:** PricewaterhouseCoopers LLP
Telephone: (518) 434-3049	**Officers:** Wesley W. von Schack - Chmn., Pres., C.E.O. Kenneth M. Jasinski - Exec. V.P., C.F.O.	**Investor Contact:** 607-347-2561

ENGELHARD CORP.

Exchange	Symbol	Price	52Wk Range	Yield	P/E
NYS	EC	$30.03 (3/31/2005)	32.49-26.70	1.60	15.97

*7 Year Price Score 106.40 *NYSE Composite Index=100 *12 Month Price Score 94.24

Interim Earnings (Per Share)

Qtr.	Mar	Jun	Sep	Dec
2001	0.37	0.45	0.43	0.46
2002	0.40	0.46	0.02	0.43
2003	0.44	0.43	0.47	0.50
2004	0.40	0.54	0.48	0.44

Interim Dividends (Per Share)

Amt	Decl	Ex	Rec	Pay
0.11Q	5/6/2004	6/14/2004	6/15/2004	6/30/2004
0.11Q	8/5/2004	9/13/2004	9/15/2004	9/30/2004
0.11Q	10/7/2004	12/13/2004	12/15/2004	12/31/2004
0.12Q	2/3/2005	3/11/2005	3/15/2005	3/31/2005

Indicated Div: $0.48

Valuation Analysis

Forecast P/E	15.11
	(4/7/2005)
Market Cap	$3.7 Billion
Book Value	1.4 Billion
Price/Book	2.59
Price/Sales	0.88

No of Institutions	232
Shares	106,268,136
% Held	86.97

TRADING VOLUME (thousand shares)

Business Summary: Chemicals (MIC: 11.1 SIC: 819 NAIC: 31419)

Engelhard develops, manufactures and markets technologies based on surface and materials science for a wide range of industrial customers. Co. operates in four business units: Environmental Technologies, Process Technologies, Appearance and Performance Technologies, and Materials Services. The Environmental Technologies unit provides emission-control technologies and systems. The Process Technologies unit supplies advanced chemical-process catalysts, additives and sorbents. The Appearance and Performance Technologies unit provides pigments and performance additives. The Materials Services provides certain precious metals, base metals and related services.

Recent Developments: For the year ended Dec 31 2004, net income increased 0.6% to $235,528 thousand from net income of $234,223 thousand a year earlier. Revenues were $4,166,420 thousand, up 12.2% from $3,714,493 thousand the year before. Operating income was $273,479 thousand versus an income of $281,573 thousand in the prior year, a decrease of 2.9%. Total direct expense was $3,496,606 thousand versus $3,080,408 thousand in the prior year, an increase of 13.5%. Total indirect expense was $396,335 thousand versus $352,512 thousand in the prior year, an increase of 12.4%.

Prospects: Co. expects modest growth in net earnings per share in 2005. Co. expects balanced performance across its technology segments and ongoing productivity initiatives to provide a strong underlying financial base. This should more than offset expected increases in pension and medical expenses and costs associated with a new requirement to expense employee stock options. For full-year 2005, Co. expects earnings to range from $1.90 to $2.00 per share. Separately, on Mar 1 2005, Co. announced its offer to acquire a majority stake in Coletica, S.A., a developer of performance-based, skin-care compounds and related technologies for the cosmetics and personal care industries.

Financial Data (US$ in Thousands)	12/31/2004	12/31/2003	12/31/2002	12/31/2001	12/31/2000	12/31/1999	12/31/1998	12/31/1997
Earnings Per Share	1.88	1.84	1.31	1.71	1.31	1.47	1.29	0.33
Cash Flow Per Share	2.62	5.03	2.36	2.66	1.42	2.64	1.23	1.36
Tang Book Value Per Share	8.89	8.12	6.32	5.44	4.51	3.49	4.02	3.95
Dividends Per Share	0.440	0.410	0.400	0.400	0.400	0.400	0.400	0.380
Dividend Payout %	23.40	22.28	30.53	23.39	30.53	27.21	31.01	115.15
Income Statement								
Total Revenue	4,166,420	3,714,493	3,753,571	5,096,926	5,542,648	4,404,942	4,174,553	3,630,653
EBITDA	439,085	448,613	376,896	457,735	425,395	452,297	420,381	226,654
Depn & Amortn	128,687	127,672	113,562	108,517	117,059	111,624	100,931	88,066
Income Before Taxes	291,899	300,646	237,924	305,224	245,687	284,118	260,563	85,812
Income Taxes	56,371	64,154	66,516	79,663	77,391	86,656	73,479	38,034
Net Income	235,528	234,223	171,408	225,561	168,296	197,462	187,084	47,778
Average Shares	125,350	127,267	130,450	132,155	128,141	134,590	145,366	145,937
Balance Sheet								
Current Assets	1,589,449	1,393,560	1,566,041	1,493,747	1,741,705	1,388,324	1,359,967	1,255,172
Total Assets	3,178,592	2,933,003	3,020,714	2,995,549	3,166,832	2,903,963	2,866,319	2,586,323
Current Liabilities	929,667	948,015	1,386,247	1,500,800	1,826,699	1,455,841	1,270,445	1,240,136
Long-Term Obligations	513,680	390,565	247,805	237,853	248,566	499,466	497,393	373,574
Total Liabilities	1,764,280	1,647,604	1,943,547	1,992,043	2,292,265	2,139,573	1,964,762	1,801,063
Stockholders' Equity	1,414,312	1,285,399	1,077,167	1,003,506	874,567	764,390	901,557	785,260
Shares Outstanding	121,902	124,410	127,358	129,075	126,633	125,881	143,287	144,492
Statistical Record								
Return on Assets %	7.69	7.87	5.70	7.32	5.53	6.84	6.86	1.88
Return on Equity %	17.40	19.83	16.48	24.02	20.48	23.71	22.18	5.90
EBITDA Margin %	10.54	12.08	10.04	8.98	7.67	10.27	10.07	6.24
Net Margin %	5.65	6.31	4.57	4.43	3.04	4.48	4.48	1.32
Asset Turnover	1.36	1.25	1.25	1.65	1.82	1.53	1.53	1.43
Current Ratio	1.71	1.47	1.13	1.00	0.95	0.95	1.07	1.01
Debt to Equity	0.36	0.30	0.23	0.24	0.28	0.65	0.55	0.48
Price Range	32.49-26.70	30.40-19.41	32.70-21.51	28.73-19.27	21.06-13.06	23.44-16.63	22.81-16.06	23.75-17.19
P/E Ratio	17.28-14.20	16.52-10.55	24.96-16.42	16.80-11.27	16.08-9.97	15.94-11.31	17.68-12.45	71.97-52.08
Average Yield %	1.50	1.61	1.49	1.57	2.29	2.06	2.06	1.86

Address: 101 Wood Avenue, Iselin, NJ 08830	Web Site: www.engelhard.com	Auditors: ERNST & YOUNG LLP
Telephone: (732) 205-5000	Officers: Barry W. Perry - Chmn., C.E.O. Michael A. Sperduto - V.P., C.F.O.	Investor Contact: 732-205-6106
Fax: (732) 632-9253		

ENSCO INTERNATIONAL INC.

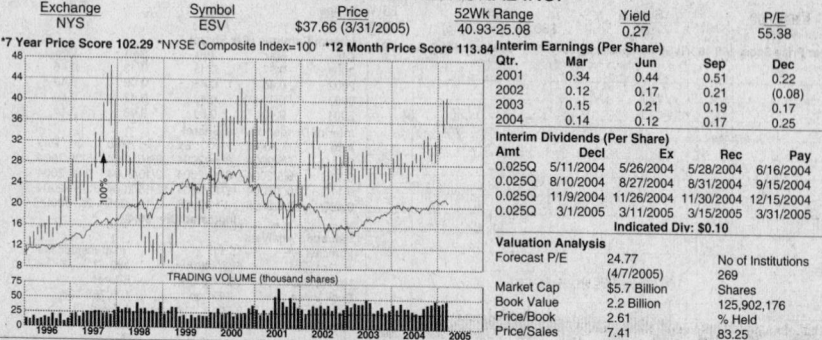

Exchange	Symbol	Price	52Wk Range	Yield	P/E
NYS	ESV	$37.66 (3/31/2005)	40.93-25.08	0.27	55.38

*7 Year Price Score 102.29 *NYSE Composite Index=100 *12 Month Price Score 113.84

Interim Earnings (Per Share)

Qtr.	Mar	Jun	Sep	Dec
2001	0.34	0.44	0.51	0.22
2002	0.12	0.17	0.21	(0.08)
2003	0.15	0.21	0.19	0.17
2004	0.14	0.12	0.17	0.25

Interim Dividends (Per Share)

Amt	Decl	Ex	Rec	Pay
0.025Q	5/11/2004	5/26/2004	5/28/2004	6/16/2004
0.025Q	8/10/2004	8/27/2004	8/31/2004	9/15/2004
0.025Q	11/9/2004	11/26/2004	11/30/2004	12/15/2004
0.025Q	3/1/2005	3/11/2005	3/15/2005	3/31/2005

Indicated Div: $0.10

Valuation Analysis

Forecast P/E	24.77	No of Institutions	
	(4/7/2005)	269	
Market Cap	$5.7 Billion	Shares	125,902,176
Book Value	2.2 Billion	% Held	83.25
Price/Book	2.61		
Price/Sales	7.41		

Business Summary: Oil and Gas (MIC: 14.2 SIC: 381 NAIC: 13111)

ENSCO International is an international offshore contract drilling company. Co. is engaged, through a number of subsidiaries, in the drilling of offshore oil and gas wells in domestic and international markets under contracts with major international, government-owned and independent oil and gas companies. As of Feb 29 2004, Co.'s fleet of offshore drilling rigs included 43 jackup rigs, seven barge rigs, five platform rigs and one semisubmersible rig. Co.'s operations are concentrated in the geographic regions of North America, Europe/Africa, Asia Pacific and South America/Caribbean.

Recent Developments: For the year ended Dec 31 2004, income from continuing operations decreased 5.1% to $103,500 thousand from income of $109,100 thousand a year earlier. Net income decreased 5.1% to $102,800 thousand from net income of $108,300 thousand a year earlier. Revenues were $768,000 thousand, down 1.7% from $781,200 thousand the year before. Operating income was $172,100 thousand versus an income of $183,800 thousand in the prior year, a decrease of 6.4%. Total direct expense was $425,500 thousand versus $445,200 thousand in the prior year, a decrease of 4.4%. Total indirect expense was $170,400 thousand versus $152,200 thousand in the prior year, an increase of 12.0%.

Prospects: Co. is seeing strength in the offshore drilling market, its rate structure is improving and its contract backlog is increasing on a global basis. Co. noted that its Asia and Pacific Rim market is showing particular strength, and that two of its jackup rigs recently secured long term commitments in Saudia Arabia, at rates considerably above prior commitments. Rate structures are improving in Europe and Africa, with recent fixtures for standard North Sea jackup work in the range of $70,000 to $75,000 per day. Co. estimates several of its jackup rigs in the region will experience downtime during the first half of 2005. This could result in about 100 idle rig days in the first quarter of 2005.

Financial Data

(US$ in Thousands)	12/31/2004	12/31/2003	12/31/2002	12/31/2001	12/31/2000	12/31/1999	12/31/1998	12/31/1997
Earnings Per Share	0.68	0.72	0.42	1.50	0.61	0.05	1.81	1.64
Cash Flow Per Share	1.71	1.96	1.49	3.08	1.00	0.84	3.21	2.39
Tang Book Value Per Share	12.18	11.55	10.85	9.93	8.82	9.05	9.08	7.57
Dividends Per Share	0.100	0.100	0.100	0.100	0.100	0.100	0.100	0.050
Dividend Payout %	14.71	13.89	23.81	6.67	16.39	200.00	5.52	3.05
Income Statement								
Total Revenue	768,000	790,800	698,100	817,400	533,800	363,700	813,200	815,100
EBITDA	322,800	323,200	249,100	451,000	237,200	119,000	487,200	503,200
Depn & Amortn	150,400	140,600	136,000	134,600	105,700	108,200	93,600	113,400
Income Before Taxes	139,500	149,300	87,100	291,900	125,200	5,200	382,500	375,800
Income Taxes	36,000	42,100	27,800	84,600	39,800	(2,900)	123,800	137,800
Net Income	102,800	108,300	59,300	207,300	85,400	6,700	253,900	233,900
Average Shares	150,600	150,100	141,400	137,900	139,300	137,700	140,600	142,900
Balance Sheet								
Current Assets	493,700	543,300	387,500	461,300	288,700	272,800	476,300	447,100
Total Assets	3,322,000	3,183,000	3,061,500	2,323,800	2,108,000	1,978,000	1,992,800	1,772,000
Current Liabilities	215,800	187,400	198,300	149,300	117,100	134,800	159,400	130,900
Long-Term Obligations	527,100	549,900	547,500	462,400	422,200	371,200	375,500	400,800
Total Liabilities	1,140,100	1,101,900	1,094,500	883,600	779,100	737,000	747,800	695,300
Stockholders' Equity	2,181,900	2,081,100	1,967,000	1,440,200	1,328,900	1,241,000	1,245,000	1,076,700
Shares Outstanding	151,100	150,500	149,000	134,600	138,500	137,200	137,100	142,200
Statistical Record								
Return on Assets %	3.15	3.47	2.20	9.36	4.17	0.34	13.49	15.15
Return on Equity %	4.81	5.35	3.48	14.97	6.63	0.54	21.87	24.33
EBITDA Margin %	42.03	40.87	35.68	55.17	44.44	32.72	59.91	61.73
Net Margin %	13.39	13.69	8.49	25.36	16.00	1.84	31.22	28.70
Asset Turnover	0.24	0.25	0.26	0.37	0.26	0.18	1.84	0.53
Current Ratio	2.29	2.90	1.95	3.09	2.47	2.02	2.99	3.42
Debt to Equity	0.24	0.26	0.28	0.32	0.32	0.30	0.30	0.37
Price Range	33.75-25.08	30.90-24.01	35.36-21.04	44.44-13.20	42.50-21.25	24.31-8.81	33.50-8.75	46.56-20.44
P/E Ratio	49.63-36.88	42.92-33.35	84.19-50.10	29.63-8.80	69.67-34.84	486.25-176.25	18.51-4.83	28.39-12.46
Average Yield %	0.34	0.37	0.36	0.37	0.30	0.58	0.51	0.17

Address: 500 North Akard Street, Suite 4300, Dallas, TX 75201-3331	Web Site: www.enscous.com	Auditors: KPMG LLP
Telephone: (214) 397-3000	Officers: Carl F. Thorne - Chmn., C.E.O. James W. Swent - Sr. V.P., C.F.O.	
Fax: (214) 855-0300		

ENTERCOM COMMUNICATIONS CORP

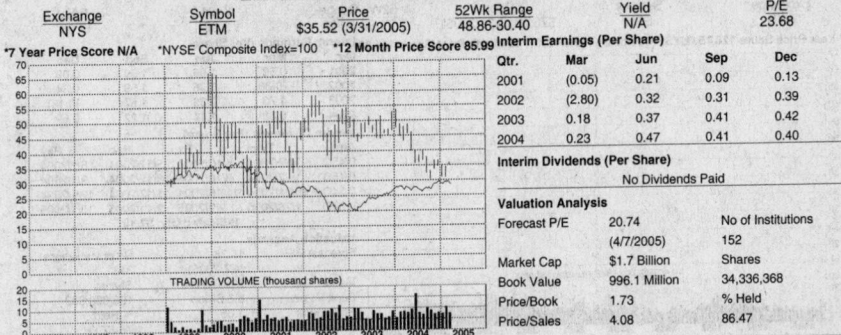

Exchange	Symbol	Price	52Wk Range	Yield	P/E
NYS	ETM	$35.52 (3/31/2005)	48.86-30.40	N/A	23.68

*7 Year Price Score N/A   *NYSE Composite Index=100   *12 Month Price Score 85.99

Interim Earnings (Per Share)

Qtr.	Mar	Jun	Sep	Dec
2001	(0.05)	0.21	0.09	0.13
2002	(2.80)	0.32	0.31	0.39
2003	0.18	0.37	0.41	0.42
2004	0.23	0.47	0.41	0.40

Interim Dividends (Per Share)

No Dividends Paid

Valuation Analysis

Forecast P/E	20.74	No of Institutions
	(4/7/2005)	152
Market Cap	$1.7 Billion	Shares
Book Value	996.1 Million	34,336,368
Price/Book	1.73	% Held
Price/Sales	4.08	86.47

Business Summary: Media (MIC: 13.1 SIC: 832 NAIC: 15112)

Entercom Communications is the fourth largest radio broadcasting company in the United States, based on 2003 net revenue. As of Dec 31 2003, Co. operated in 19 markets, including Boston, MA; Seattle, WA; Denver, CO; Portland, OR; Sacramento, CA; Kansas City, MO; Milwaukee, WI; Norfolk, VA; New Orleans, LA; Memphis, TN; Buffalo, NY; Greensboro, NC; Rochester, NY; Greenville/Spartanburg, SC; Wilkes-Barre/Scranton, PA; Wichita, KS; Madison, WI; Gainesville/Ocala and Longview/Kelso, FL.

Recent Developments: For the year ended Dec 31 2004, net income increased 5.4% to $75,634 thousand from net income of $71,780 thousand a year earlier. Revenues were $423,455 thousand, up 5.6% from $401,056 thousand the year before. Operating income was $145,196 thousand versus an income of $140,234 thousand in the prior year, an increase of 3.5%. Total indirect expense was $278,259 thousand versus $260,822 thousand in the prior year, an increase of 6.7%.

Prospects: Results are being positively affected by strong same-station revenue growth, improved market conditions both nationally and locally, along with increasing demand for 30-second and 15-second commercials as a result of research presented to advertisers by Co. on the effectiveness of such ads. Meanwhile, during the fourth quarter of 2004, Co. entered into an agreement to sell its four radio stations located in Longview, WA, for $2.2 million in cash. This transaction is expected to be completed in the first quarter of 2005. Separately, Co. expects an increase in net revenue of approximately 5.0% for the first quarter of 2005.

Financial Data (US$ in Thousands)	12/31/2004	12/31/2003	12/31/2002	12/31/2001	12/31/2000	12/31/1999	12/31/1998	09/30/1998
Earnings Per Share	1.50	1.39	(1.67)	0.38	1.04	(1.61)	0.64	0.06
Cash Flow Per Share	2.61	2.56	2.13	1.88	1.53	1.07	0.36	1.04
Income Statement								
Total Revenue	423,455	401,056	391,289	332,897	352,025	215,001	47,363	132,998
EBITDA	161,844	150,962	132,623	103,858	159,773	70,447	53,709	37,211
Depn & Amortn	16,996	15,740	16,270	46,509	43,475	21,564	4,358	13,066
Income Before Taxes	123,523	115,212	93,353	30,028	79,050	40,954	43,765	9,892
Income Taxes	47,889	43,432	37,529	12,194	31,796	100,913	310	453
Net Income	75,634	71,780	(83,052)	17,268	47,254	(60,877)	43,455	7,063
Average Shares	50,534	51,607	49,765	45,994	45,613	38,237	24,104	22,239
Balance Sheet								
Current Assets	105,460	105,354	187,439	87,780	90,938	70,420	126,566	51,125
Total Assets	1,667,961	1,577,052	1,568,530	1,438,740	1,473,928	1,396,048	681,034	522,945
Current Liabilities	25,783	91,454	73,032	53,581	27,781	27,530	25,142	16,761
Long-Term Obligations	483,259	329,027	394,044	363,934	461,249	465,760	427,543	321,037
Total Liabilities	671,888	545,442	553,025	557,859	613,227	584,437	455,567	339,975
Stockholders' Equity	996,073	1,031,610	890,505	755,881	735,701	686,611	225,467	182,970
Shares Outstanding	48,635	51,431	49,859	45,353	45,239	45,179	21,533	21,534
Statistical Record								
Return on Assets %	4.65	4.56	N.M.	1.19	3.28	N.M.	6.64	1.59
Return on Equity %	7.44	7.47	N.M.	2.32	6.63	N.M.	17.16	3.90
EBITDA Margin %	38.22	37.64	33.89	31.20	45.39	32.77	113.40	27.98
Net Margin %	17.86	17.90	N.M.	5.19	13.42	N.M.	91.75	5.31
Asset Turnover	0.26	0.25	0.26	0.23	0.24	0.21	0.07	0.30
Current Ratio	4.09	1.15	2.57	1.64	3.27	2.56	5.03	3.05
Debt to Equity	0.49	0.32	0.44	0.48	0.63	0.68	1.90	1.75
Price Range	53.80-30.40	53.07-43.07	58.65-36.88	53.75-31.05	66.56-25.63	66.50-28.88	...	...
P/E Ratio	35.87-20.27	38.18-30.99	...	141.45-81.71	64.00-24.64	...	...

Address: 401 City Avenue, Suite 409, Bala Cynwyd, PA 19004 **Telephone:** (610) 660-5610 **Fax:** (610) 660-5620	**Web Site:** www.entercom.com **Officers:** Joseph M. Field - Chmn., C.E.O. David J. Field - Pres., C.O.O.	**Auditors:** PricewaterhouseCoopers LLP **Investor Contact:** 610-660-5647

ENTERGY CORP.

Exchange	Symbol	Price	52Wk Range	Yield	P/E
NYS	ETR	$70.66 (3/31/2005)	71.90-50.68	3.06	17.98

*7 Year Price Score 128.75 *NYSE Composite Index=100 *12 Month Price Score 104.98

Interim Earnings (Per Share)

Qtr.	Mar	Jun	Sep	Dec
2001	0.69	1.06	1.39	0.09
2002	(0.36)	1.06	1.59	0.34
2003	1.73	0.89	1.57	(0.18)
2004	0.88	1.14	1.22	0.69

Interim Dividends (Per Share)

Amt	Decl	Ex	Rec	Pay
0.45Q	4/7/2004	5/10/2004	5/12/2004	6/1/2004
0.45Q	8/2/2004	8/10/2004	8/12/2004	9/1/2004
0.54Q	10/21/2004	11/15/2004	11/17/2004	12/1/2004
0.54Q	1/28/2005	2/9/2005	2/11/2005	3/1/2005

Indicated Div: $2.16

Valuation Analysis

Forecast P/E	15.36	No of Institutions	
	(4/7/2005)	348	
Market Cap	$15.3 Billion	Shares	
Book Value	8.3 Billion	166,500,832	
Price/Book	1.85	% Held	
Price/Sales	1.51	78.12	

Business Summary: Electricity (MIC: 7.1 SIC: 911 NAIC: 21113)

Entergy is a public utility holding company engaged principally in power production, distribution operations, and related diversified services. Through Entergy-Koch, L.P., it is a provider of wholesale energy marketing and trading services. Co. has five wholly-owned domestic retail electric utility subsidiaries: Entergy Arkansas, Entergy Gulf States, Entergy Louisiana, Entergy Mississippi, and Entergy New Orleans. As of Dec 31 2003, these utility companies provided retail electric service to approximately 2.6 million customers primarily in portions of the states of Arkansas, Louisiana, Mississippi, and Texas.

Recent Developments: For the year ended Dec 31 2004, net income decreased 1.8% to $933,049 thousand from net income of $950,467 thousand a year earlier. Revenues were $10,123,724 thousand, up 10.1% from $9,194,920 thousand the year before. Operating income was $1,653,564 thousand versus an income of $1,484,555 thousand in the prior year, an increase of 11.4%. Total direct expense was $7,255,292 thousand versus $6,467,964 thousand in the prior year, an increase of 12.2%. Total indirect expense was $1,214,868 thousand versus $1,242,401 thousand in the prior year, a decrease of 2.2%.

Prospects: Co.'s results are benefiting from a return to more normal weather, which is allowing the utility operations to demonstrate the underlying strength of the business and the operational improvements that have been made. Utility, Parent and Other operational results are benefiting from strong sales growth. Meanwhile, Co. recently completed the sales of Entergy-Koch Trading and Gulf South Pipeline which will produce total cash proceeds of more than $1.00 billion. Separately, Co.'s Entergy Nuclear signed new contracts that is raising the average price for its energy contracts by $2.00 per megawatt hour. For full-year 2005, Co. expects earnings to range from $4.60 to $4.85 per share.

Financial Data

(US$ in Thousands)	12/31/2004	12/31/2003	12/31/2002	12/31/2001	12/31/2000	12/31/1999	12/31/1998	12/31/1997
Earnings Per Share	3.93	4.01	2.64	3.23	2.97	2.25	3.00	1.03
Cash Flow Per Share	12.88	8.84	9.78	10.03	8.66	5.33	6.81	7.18
Tang Book Value Per Share	36.52	36.38	33.54	33.78	31.89	29.78	28.82	27.23
Dividends Per Share	1.890	1.600	1.340	1.275	1.215	1.200	1.500	1.800
Dividend Payout %	48.09	39.90	50.76	39.47	40.91	53.33	50.00	174.76
Income Statement								
Total Revenue	10,123,724	9,194,920	8,305,035	9,620,899	10,016,148	8,773,228	11,494,772	9,561,721
EBITDA	2,823,102	2,806,396	2,386,233	2,644,662	2,544,429	2,355,672	3,064,482	3,015,004
Depn & Amortn	1,045,122	996,603	869,638	740,805	816,001	867,216	1,222,231	1,401,811
Income Before Taxes	1,298,957	1,303,467	917,010	1,182,718	1,189,836	951,693	1,052,364	772,240
Income Taxes	365,908	490,074	293,938	455,693	478,921	356,667	266,735	471,341
Net Income	933,049	950,467	623,072	750,507	710,915	595,026	785,629	300,899
Average Shares	231,193	231,146	227,303	224,733	228,541	245,326	246,572	240,298
Balance Sheet								
Net PPE	18,695,631	18,298,797	17,194,952	17,264,028	16,496,625	15,500,756	15,328,582	18,132,828
Total Assets	28,310,777	28,554,210	26,947,969	25,910,311	25,565,227	22,985,087	22,848,023	27,000,700
Long-Term Obligations	7,162,891	7,476,838	7,242,942	7,502,113	7,933,966	6,816,047	6,816,826	9,304,325
Total Liabilities	19,648,734	19,516,215	18,536,068	17,878,769	17,946,116	15,092,580	14,870,005	19,118,724
Stockholders' Equity	8,296,687	8,703,658	7,838,237	7,456,020	7,338,353	7,457,857	7,445,495	7,031,971
Shares Outstanding	216,829	228,897	222,421	220,732	219,604	239,036	246,620	245,842
Statistical Record								
Return on Assets %	3.27	3.42	2.36	2.92	2.92	2.60	3.15	1.20
Return on Equity %	10.95	11.49	8.15	10.15	9.58	7.99	10.85	4.27
EBITDA Margin %	27.89	30.52	28.73	27.49	25.40	26.85	26.66	31.53
Net Margin %	9.22	10.34	7.50	7.80	7.10	6.78	6.83	3.15
PPE Turnover	0.55	0.52	0.48	0.57	0.62	0.57	0.69	0.56
Asset Turnover	0.36	0.33	0.31	0.37	0.41	0.38	0.46	0.38
Debt to Equity	0.86	0.86	0.92	1.01	1.08	0.91	0.92	1.32
Price Range	68.16-50.68	57.14-42.85	46.70-33.18	44.48-33.66	43.25-16.69	33.13-23.88	32.44-23.44	29.94-22.75
P/E Ratio	17.34-12.90	14.25-10.69	17.69-12.57	13.77-10.42	14.56-5.62	14.72-10.61	10.81-7.81	29.07-22.09
Average Yield %	3.19	3.15	3.16	3.31	4.07	4.05	5.25	6.94

Address: 639 Loyola Avenue, New Orleans, LA 70113	Web Site: www.entergy.com	Auditors: DELOITTE & TOUCHE LLP
Telephone: (504) 576 4000	Officers: Robert v. d. Luft - Chmn. J. Wayne Leonard - C.E.O.	
Fax: (504) 576 4428		

ENTERPRISE PRODUCTS PARTNERS L.P.

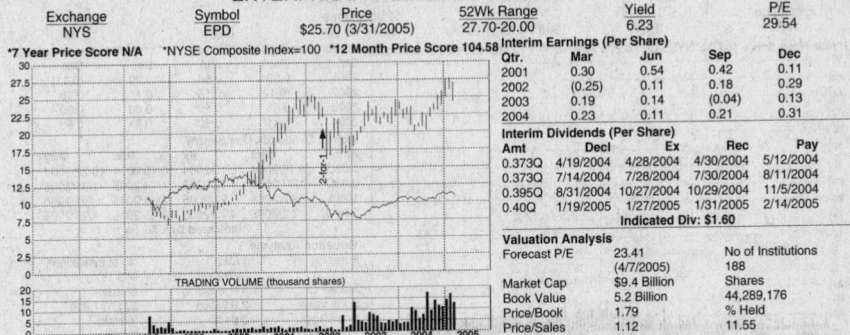

Exchange	Symbol	Price	52Wk Range	Yield	P/E
NYS	EPD	$25.70 (3/31/2005)	27.70-20.00	6.23	29.54

*7 Year Price Score N/A   *NYSE Composite Index=100   *12 Month Price Score 104.58

Interim Earnings (Per Share)

Qtr.	Mar	Jun	Sep	Dec
2001	0.30	0.54	0.42	0.11
2002	(0.25)	0.11	0.18	0.29
2003	0.19	0.14	(0.04)	0.13
2004	0.23	0.11	0.21	0.31

Interim Dividends (Per Share)

Amt	Decl	Ex	Rec	Pay
0.373Q	4/19/2004	4/28/2004	4/30/2004	5/12/2004
0.373Q	7/14/2004	7/28/2004	7/30/2004	8/11/2004
0.395Q	8/31/2004	10/27/2004	10/29/2004	11/5/2004
0.40Q	1/19/2005	1/27/2005	1/31/2005	2/14/2005

Indicated Div: $1.60

Valuation Analysis

Forecast P/E	23.41	No of Institutions
	(4/7/2005)	188
Market Cap	$9.4 Billion	Shares
Book Value	5.2 Billion	44,289,176
Price/Book	1.79	% Held
Price/Sales	1.12	11.55

TRADING VOLUME (thousand shares)

Business Summary: Oil and Gas (MIC: 14.2 SIC: 311 NAIC: 11111)

Enterprise Products Partners is a provider of midstream energy services to producers and consumers of natural gas and natural gas liquids (NGLs). Co. has five operating segments: Fractionation, which primarily includes NGL fractionation, isomerization services, and propylene fractionation; Pipelines, which consists of liquids and natural gas pipeline systems, storage and import/export terminal services; Processing, which includes the natural gas processing business and NGL merchant activities; and Octane Enhancement, which represents Co.'s equity interest in a facility that produces motor gasoline additives. Co.'s Other segment consists primarily of fee-based marketing services.

Recent Developments: For the year ended Dec 31 2004, net income increased 156.6% to $268,261 thousand from net income of $104,546 thousand a year earlier. Revenues were $8,321,202 thousand, up 55.6% from $5,346,431 thousand the year before. Operating income was $422,994 thousand versus an income of $248,104 thousand in the prior year, an increase of 70.5%. Total direct expense was $7,904,336 thousand versus $5,046,777 thousand in the prior year, an increase of 56.6%. Total indirect expense was $93,135 thousand versus $75,180 thousand in the prior year, an increase of 24.1%.

Prospects: On Feb 28 2005, Co. announced certain of its affiliates have acquired interests in the Dixie Pipeline Company increasing its total ownership interest to 66.0% from 20.0%. In separate transactions, Co. purchased a 26.0% interest from an affiliate of ChevronTexaco for $40.0 million, and a 20.0% interest from an affiliate of ConocoPhillips for $31.0 million. Meanwhile, drilling activity in the major producing areas, including the deepwater Gulf of Mexico, Rocky Mountains and San Juan, and the improving economy have increased demand for Co. integrated midstream energy services. Over the next two years, Co. expects large volumes of new production to flow into its integrated system of assets.

Financial Data (US$ in Thousands)	12/31/2004	12/31/2003	12/31/2002	12/31/2001	12/31/2000	12/31/1999	12/31/1998	12/31/1997
Earnings Per Share	0.87	0.41	0.48	1.39	1.32	0.82	0.09	0.05
Cash Flow Per Share	1.42	2.12	2.12	2.03	2.68	1.27	...	...
Tang Book Value Per Share	10.40	6.06	4.51	5.36	8.96	7.90	4.16	...
Dividends Per Share	1.513	1.442	1.327	1.156	1.025	0.900	0.160	...
Dividend Payout %	173.85	351.83	276.56	83.48	77.65	109.76	188.24	...
Income Statement								
Total Revenue	8,321,202	5,346,431	3,584,783	3,179,727	3,073,139	1,346,456	738,902	1,020,281
EBITDA	621,913	369,557	294,134	...	...	...	...	...
Depn & Amortn	198,887	115,825	94,925	51,903	41,016	25,315	19,194	17,684
Income Before Taxes	269,369	113,698	100,081	...	...	...	...	...
Income Taxes	3,761	5,293	1,634	...	...	...	...	...
Net Income	268,261	104,546	95,500	242,178	220,506	120,295	10,077	52,163
Average Shares	266,045	206,367	176,490	170,786	164,887	145,577	...	...
Balance Sheet								
Current Assets	1,440,723	687,183	637,568	518,775	581,392	384,538	137,693	127,034
Total Assets	11,315,461	4,802,814	4,230,272	2,431,193	1,951,521	1,494,952	741,037	697,713
Current Liabilities	1,585,879	1,096,876	721,356	409,216	586,379	531,120	82,771	167,344
Long-Term Obligations	4,266,236	1,899,548	2,231,463	855,278	404,000	166,000	90,000	215,334
Total Liabilities	5,986,676	3,096,861	3,029,368	1,284,271	1,015,562	705,487	178,501	385,828
Stockholders' Equity	5,222,310	1,671,604	1,188,681	1,135,391	926,554	781,523	556,911	...
Shares Outstanding	363,870	217,780	183,809	174,214	93,049	91,105	133,926	...
Statistical Record								
Return on Assets %	3.32	2.31	2.87	11.05	12.76	10.76	...	...
Return on Equity %	7.76	7.31	8.22	23.49	25.75	17.98	...	...
EBITDA Margin %	7.47	6.91	8.21	...	...	...	...	...
Net Margin %	3.22	1.96	2.66	7.62	7.18	8.93	1.36	5.11
Asset Turnover	1.03	1.18	1.08	1.45	1.78	1.20	...	...
Current Ratio	0.91	0.63	0.88	1.27	0.99	0.72	1.66	0.76
Debt to Equity	0.82	1.14	1.88	0.75	0.44	0.21	0.16	...
Price Range	25.86-20.00	24.70-18.01	25.35-16.25	25.98-13.44	15.81-9.13	10.19-7.44	10.78-7.00	...
P/E Ratio	29.72-22.99	60.24-43.93	52.81-33.85	18.69-9.67	11.98-6.91	12.42-9.07	119.79-77.78	...
Average Yield %	6.70	6.65	6.26	5.68	8.84	9.91	1.87	...

Address: 2727 North Loop West, Suite 700, Houston, TX 77008-1037 Telephone: (713) 880-6500 Fax: (713) 880-6668	Web Site: www.epplp.com Officers: Dan L. Duncan - Chmn. O. S. Andras - Pres., C.E.O.	Auditors: Deloitte & Touche LLP Transfer Agents: Mellon Investor Services, LLC

EOG RESOURCES, INC.

Exchange	Symbol	Price	52Wk Range	Yield	P/E
NYS	EOG	$48.74 (3/31/2005)	48.74-22.80	0.33	18.89

*7 Year Price Score 154.08 *NYSE Composite Index=100 *12 Month Price Score 123.51

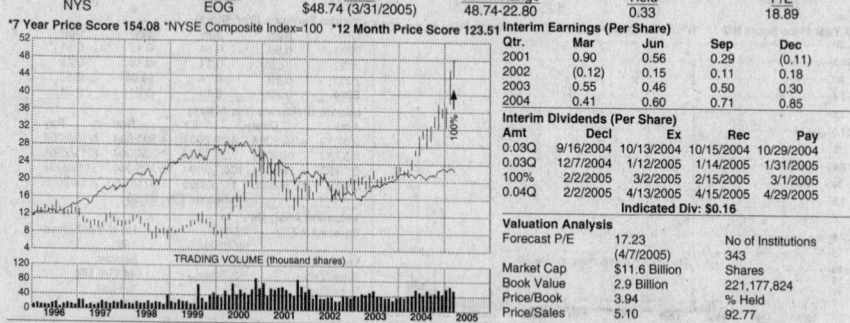

Interim Earnings (Per Share)

Qtr.	Mar	Jun	Sep	Dec
2001	0.90	0.56	0.29	(0.11)
2002	(0.12)	0.15	0.11	0.18
2003	0.55	0.46	0.50	0.30
2004	0.41	0.60	0.71	0.85

Interim Dividends (Per Share)

Amt	Decl	Ex	Rec	Pay
0.03Q	9/16/2004	10/13/2004	10/15/2004	10/29/2004
0.03Q	12/7/2004	1/12/2005	1/14/2005	1/31/2005
100%	2/2/2005	3/2/2005	2/15/2005	3/1/2005
0.04Q	2/2/2005	4/13/2005	4/15/2005	4/29/2005

Indicated Div: $0.16

Valuation Analysis

Forecast P/E	17.23	No of Institutions
	(4/7/2005)	343
Market Cap	$11.6 Billion	Shares
Book Value	2.9 Billion	221,177,824
Price/Book	3.94	% Held
Price/Sales	5.10	92.77

Business Summary: Oil and Gas (MIC: 14.2 SIC: 311 NAIC: 13112)

EOG Resources is engaged in the exploration for, and the development, production and marketing of natural gas and crude oil primarily in major producing basins in the United States, as well as in Canada and Trinidad and, to a lesser extent, selected other international areas, including the United Kingdom North Sea. As of Dec 31 2003, Co.'s estimated net proved natural gas reserves were 4,645.00 billion cubic feet and estimated net proved crude oil, condensate and natural gas liquids reserves were 95.0 million barrels. As of Dec 31 2003, approximately 49.0% of Co.'s reserves were located in the United States, 27.0% in Trinidad, 23.0% in Canada and 1.0% in the United Kingdom North Sea.

Recent Developments: For the year ended Dec 31 2004, net income increased 45.3% to $624,855 thousand from net income of $430,145 thousand a year earlier. Revenues were $2,271,225 thousand, up 30.2% from $1,744,675 thousand the year before. Operating income was $979,195 thousand versus an income of $697,314 thousand in the prior year, an increase of 40.4%. Total indirect expense was $1,292,030 thousand versus $1,047,361 thousand in the prior year, an increase of 23.4%.

Prospects: Co.'s operations in the U.S. and Canada have expanded considerably over the past few years, with Co. seeing an aggregate increase of 5.0% in natural gas production and a 7.2% increase in total production in these regions during 2004. Looking ahead, Co. is optimistic that it is well positioned to achieve its production growth targets in the coming year. Accordingly, Co. expects to achieve 13.5% organic production growth in 2005, which includes an 11.0% increase in natural gas production from its operations in the U.S. and Canada. To achieve this, Co. is budgeting approximately $1.60 billion for capital expenditures in the coming year.

Financial Data

(US$ in Thousands)	12/31/2004	12/31/2003	12/31/2002	12/31/2001	12/31/2000	12/31/1999	12/31/1998	12/31/1997
Earnings Per Share	2.58	1.80	0.33	1.65	1.62	2.00	0.18	0.39
Cash Flow Per Share	6.16	5.76	2.90	5.17	4.13	1.57	1.31	1.69
Tang Book Value Per Share	11.97	8.95	6.64	6.48	5.28	4.12	4.16	4.13
Dividends Per Share	0.115	0.090	0.080	0.077	0.065	0.060	0.060	0.060
Dividend Payout %	4.47	5.00	24.62	4.70	4.01	3.01	33.33	15.58
Income Statement								
Total Revenue	2,271,225	1,744,675	1,095,036	1,654,887	1,489,895	801,406	769,188	783,501
EBITDA	1,493,543	1,154,430	577,362	1,068,954	1,064,589	1,089,408	380,623	426,021
Depn & Amortn	504,403	441,843	398,036	392,399	370,026	459,877	271,762	234,834
Income Before Taxes	926,012	653,876	119,672	631,445	633,557	567,712	60,282	163,470
Income Taxes	301,157	216,600	32,499	232,829	236,626	(1,382)	4,111	41,500
Net Income	624,855	430,145	87,173	398,616	396,931	569,094	56,171	121,970
Average Shares	238,376	233,038	234,490	234,976	238,204	284,704	310,108	316,320
Balance Sheet								
Current Assets	586,803	396,014	394,792	272,421	394,427	200,501	246,350	282,035
Total Assets	5,798,923	4,749,015	3,814,006	3,414,044	3,000,815	2,610,793	3,018,095	2,723,355
Current Liabilities	632,204	476,519	276,351	310,847	369,678	218,618	262,634	290,997
Long-Term Obligations	1,077,622	1,108,872	1,145,132	855,969	859,000	990,306	1,142,779	741,275
Total Liabilities	2,853,499	2,525,634	2,141,611	1,771,358	1,619,890	1,481,182	1,737,791	1,442,306
Stockholders' Equity	2,945,424	2,223,381	1,672,395	1,642,686	1,380,925	1,129,611	1,280,304	1,281,049
Shares Outstanding	237,854	231,283	229,440	230,903	233,808	238,209	307,448	310,128
Statistical Record								
Return on Assets %	11.82	10.05	2.41	12.43	14.11	20.22	1.96	4.71
Return on Equity %	24.11	22.08	5.26	26.37	31.53	47.23	4.39	9.58
EBITDA Margin %	65.76	66.17	52.73	64.59	71.45	135.94	49.48	54.37
Net Margin %	27.51	24.65	7.96	24.09	26.64	71.01	7.30	15.57
Asset Turnover	0.43	0.41	0.30	0.52	0.53	0.28	0.27	0.30
Current Ratio	0.93	0.83	1.43	0.88	1.07	0.92	0.94	0.97
Debt to Equity	0.37	0.50	0.68	0.52	0.62	0.88	0.89	0.58
Price Range	37.91-21.45	23.61-18.00	21.89-15.47	26.78-13.32	28.22-6.94	12.63-7.56	11.94-6.44	13.31-8.75
P/E Ratio	14.70-8.31	13.11-10.00	66.32-46.86	16.23-8.07	17.42-4.28	6.31-3.78	66.32-35.76	34.13-22.44
Average Yield %	0.40	0.44	0.43	0.40	0.42	0.62	0.64	0.57

Address: 333 Clay Street, Suite 4200, Houston, TX 77002-7361 **Telephone:** (713) 651-7000	**Web Site:** www.eogresources.com **Officers:** Mark G. Papa - Chmn., C.E.O. Edmund P. Segner III - Pres., Chief of Staff	**Auditors:** DELOITTE & TOUCHE LLP **Investor Contact:** 713-651-7000 **Transfer Agents:** EquiServe Trust Company, N.A.

EQUIFAX, INC.

Exchange	Symbol	Price	52Wk Range	Yield	P/E
NYS	EFX	$30.69 (3/31/2005)	31.32-23.25	0.39	17.44

*7 Year Price Score 103.48 *NYSE Composite Index=100 *12 Month Price Score 106.50

Interim Earnings (Per Share)

Qtr.	Mar	Jun	Sep	Dec
2001	0.35	0.21	0.26	0.06
2002	0.30	0.34	0.28	0.37
2003	0.32	0.31	0.38	0.21
2004	0.38	0.55	0.40	0.44

Interim Dividends (Per Share)

Amt	Decl	Ex	Rec	Pay
0.02Q	1/30/2004	2/19/2004	2/23/2004	3/15/2004
0.03Q	4/28/2004	5/21/2004	5/25/2004	6/15/2004
0.03Q	8/9/2004	8/23/2004	8/25/2004	9/15/2004
0.03Q	2/8/2005	2/17/2005	2/22/2005	3/15/2005
		Indicated Div: $0.12		

Valuation Analysis

Forecast P/E	17.84	No of Institutions
	(4/7/2005)	282
Market Cap	$4.0 Billion	Shares
Book Value	523.6 Million	99,671,472
Price/Book	7.58	% Held
Price/Sales	3.12	73.94

TRADING VOLUME (thousand shares)

Business Summary: Miscellaneous Business Services (MIC: 12.8 SIC: 323 NAIC: 61450)

Equifax collects, organizes and manages various types of credit, financial, public record, demographic, and marketing information regarding individuals and businesses. Co.'s products and services include consumer credit information, information database management, marketing information, business credit information, decisioning and analytical tools, and identity verification services which businesses use to make informed decisions about extending credit or service, managing portfolio risk, and develop marketing strategies for consumers and small businesses. Co. also provides products to enable consumers to manage and protect their financial affairs. Co. operates in 13 countries.

Recent Developments: For the year ended Dec 31 2004, income from continuing operations increased 31.3% to $237,300 thousand from income of $180,700 thousand a year earlier. Net income increased 42.3% to $234,700 thousand from net income of $164,900 thousand a year earlier. Revenues were $1,272,800 thousand, up 5.1% from $1,210,700 thousand the year before. Operating income was $375,800 thousand versus an income of $314,200 thousand in the prior year, an increase of 19.6%. Total direct expense was $531,500 thousand versus $499,700 thousand in the prior year, an increase of 6.4%. Total indirect expense was $365,500 thousand versus $396,800 thousand in the prior year, a decrease of 7.9%.

Prospects: On Feb 7 2005, Co. announced that it has entered into an agreement to acquire APPRO Systems, Inc., a developer of technologies for consumer, commercial and retail banking lending operations, for approximately $92.0 million in cash. The transaction is expected to be completed within 90 days. Looking ahead, Co. anticipates full-year 2005 revenue growth in the range of 6.0% to 9.0%, or about $1.35 billion to $1.39 billion, along with earnings of between $1.69 and $1.76 per share. In addition, Co. expects free cash flow from continuing operations in the range of $255.0 million to $275.0 million in 2005, and capital expenditures of between $60.0 million and $70.0 million.

Financial Data (US$ in Thousands)	12/31/2004	12/31/2003	12/31/2002	12/31/2001	12/31/2000	12/31/1999	12/31/1998	12/31/1997
Earnings Per Share	1.76	1.21	1.29	0.88	1.68	1.55	1.34	1.24
Cash Flow Per Share	2.35	2.16	1.83	1.86	2.11	2.36	2.04	1.46
Dividends Per Share	0.110	0.080	0.080	0.225	0.370	0.362	0.352	0.345
Dividend Payout %	6.25	6.61	6.20	25.57	22.02	23.39	26.31	27.82
Income Statement								
Total Revenue	1,272,800	1,225,400	1,109,300	1,139,000	1,965,881	1,772,694	1,620,978	1,366,087
EBITDA	501,200	375,600	436,600	356,600	610,103	552,158	473,771	421,004
Depn & Amortn	81,100	52,900	80,500	106,200	148,783	125,263	103,825	77,069
Income Before Taxes	385,200	283,100	314,900	202,600	385,369	365,924	327,245	323,138
Income Taxes	147,900	104,600	123,600	85,300	157,347	150,047	133,812	137,613
Net Income	234,700	164,900	178,000	122,500	228,022	215,877	193,433	183,737
Average Shares	133,500	136,700	138,500	139,000	136,016	139,603	144,403	147,818
Balance Sheet								
Current Assets	299,600	285,900	285,600	358,000	604,909	609,433	520,365	400,932
Total Assets	1,557,200	1,553,300	1,506,900	1,422,600	2,069,637	1,839,781	1,828,795	1,177,104
Current Liabilities	456,900	354,800	427,900	275,900	426,224	504,795	419,179	327,609
Long-Term Obligations	398,500	663,000	690,600	693,600	993,569	933,708	869,486	339,301
Total Liabilities	1,033,600	1,181,800	1,285,900	1,179,100	1,686,059	1,624,156	1,462,329	827,707
Stockholders' Equity	523,600	371,500	221,000	243,500	383,578	215,625	366,466	349,397
Shares Outstanding	129,400	132,700	135,700	136,200	135,835	134,001	140,042	142,609
Statistical Record								
Return on Assets %	15.05	10.78	12.15	7.02	11.63	11.77	12.87	14.82
Return on Equity %	52.30	55.66	76.64	39.07	75.90	74.17	54.04	47.46
EBITDA Margin %	39.38	30.65	39.36	31.31	31.03	31.15	29.23	30.82
Net Margin %	18.44	13.46	16.05	10.76	11.60	12.18	11.93	13.45
Asset Turnover	0.82	0.80	0.76	0.65	1.00	0.97	1.08	1.10
Current Ratio	0.66	0.81	0.67	1.30	1.42	1.21	1.24	1.22
Debt to Equity	0.76	1.78	3.12	2.85	2.59	4.33	2.37	0.97
Price Range	28.38-23.25	27.45-18.21	30.89-19.61	27.00-16.54	20.94-11.76	23.46-12.17	26.60-18.76	21.13-14.17
P/E Ratio	16.13-13.21	22.69-15.05	23.95-15.20	30.68-18.79	12.46-7.00	15.13-7.85	19.85-14.00	17.04-11.42
Average Yield %	0.43	0.35	0.32	1.06	2.38	1.98	1.59	1.97

Address: 1550 Peachtree Street, N.W., Atlanta, GA 30309	**Web Site:** www.equifax.com	**Auditors:** ERNST & YOUNG LLP
Telephone: (404) 885-8000	**Officers:** Thomas F. Chapman - Chmn., C.E.O. Mark E. Miller - Pres., C.O.O.	**Investor Contact:** 404-885-8000
Fax: (404) 885-8682		

EQUITABLE RESOURCES, INC.

Exchange	Symbol	Price	52Wk Range	Yield	P/E
NYS	EQT	$57.44 (3/31/2005)	60.88-44.28	2.65	12.94

*7 Year Price Score 144.55 ***NYSE Composite Index=100** ***12 Month Price Score 101.49**

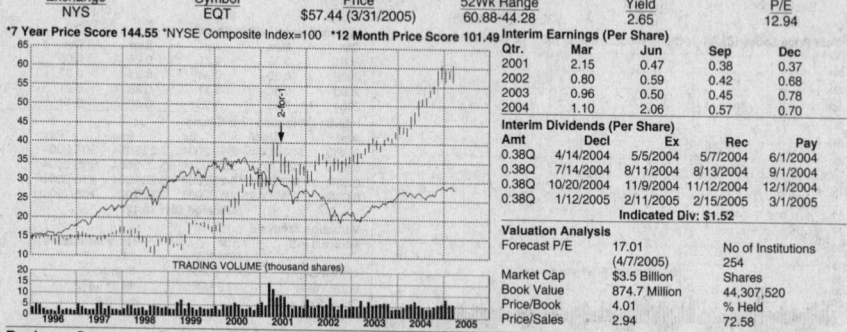

Interim Earnings (Per Share)

Qtr.	Mar	Jun	Sep	Dec
2001	2.15	0.47	0.38	0.37
2002	0.80	0.59	0.42	0.68
2003	0.96	0.50	0.45	0.78
2004	1.10	2.06	0.57	0.70

Interim Dividends (Per Share)

Amt	Decl	Ex	Rec	Pay
0.38Q	4/14/2004	5/5/2004	5/7/2004	6/1/2004
0.38Q	7/14/2004	8/11/2004	8/13/2004	9/1/2004
0.38Q	10/20/2004	11/9/2004	11/12/2004	12/1/2004
0.38Q	1/12/2005	2/11/2005	2/15/2005	3/1/2005

Indicated Div: $1.52

Valuation Analysis

Forecast P/E	17.01
	(4/7/2005)
Market Cap	$3.5 Billion
Book Value	874.7 Million
Price/Book	4.01
Price/Sales	2.94

No of Institutions	254
Shares	44,307,520
% Held	72.58

Business Summary: Gas Utilities (MIC: 7.4 SIC: 923 NAIC: 21210)

Equitable Resources is an integrated energy company operating through three business segments: Equitable Supply, Equitable Utilities and NORESCO. The production segment's operations include exploration and production activities in the East (Appalachian) and Gulf regions, as well as Appalachian area natural gas gathering and liquids processing. The utilities segment's activities are comprised of Co.'s natural gas supply, natural gas transmission and distribution operations and energy-management services for customers throughout the U.S. Co. also has energy-service management projects in selected international markets.

Recent Developments: For the year ended Dec 31 2004, net income increased 64.6% to $279,854 thousand from net income of $170,001 thousand a year earlier. Revenues were $1,191,609 thousand, up 13.8% from $1,047,277 thousand the year before. Operating income was $304,651 thousand versus an income of $302,217 thousand in the prior year, an increase of 0.8%. Total direct expense was $519,140 thousand versus $428,706 thousand in the prior year, an increase of 21.1%. Total indirect expense was $367,818 thousand versus $316,354 thousand in the prior year, an increase of 16.3%.

Prospects: In January 2005, Co. completed its acquisition of the remaining 99.0% limited partnership interest in Eastern Seven Partners, L.P. for $57.5 million in cash and the assumption of liabilities totaling $47.3 million. The acquisition will add approximately 30 billion cubic feet equivalent of reserves. Meanwhile, Co. plans to sell some non-core producing properties during the first half of 2005. Separately, Co. is reiterating its diluted earnings per share guidance for full-year 2005 of between $3.45 and $3.50. This earnings guidance assumes $5.50 per MMbtu average NYMEX natural gas price and normal weather. In addition, Co. is projecting capital expenditures of $293.0 million in 2005.

Financial Data

(US$ in Thousands)	12/31/2004	12/31/2003	12/31/2002	12/31/2001	12/31/2000	12/31/1999	12/31/1998	12/31/1997
Earnings Per Share	4.44	2.68	2.41	2.30	1.60	1.00	(0.59)	1.08
Cash Flow Per Share	2.85	1.95	3.39	2.02	5.53	2.55	0.88	1.59
Tang Book Value Per Share	13.49	14.65	11.66	12.35	9.73	8.84	8.93	10.25
Dividends Per Share	1.440	0.970	0.670	0.627	0.590	0.590	0.590	0.590
Dividend Payout %	32.43	36.19	27.80	27.28	36.88	58.71	...	54.63
Income Statement								
Total Revenue	1,191,609	1,047,277	1,069,068	1,764,491	1,652,218	1,062,738	882,625	2,151,015
EBITDA	556,533	380,933	339,845	355,670	338,011	...	80,390	264,947
Depn & Amortn	84,738	79,818	72,840	75,041	99,006	123,822	89,521	95,067
Income Before Taxes	422,548	255,349	228,218	239,531	163,344	...	(49,433)	124,202
Income Taxes	142,694	81,792	77,592	87,723	57,171	39,356	(22,381)	46,145
Net Income	279,854	170,001	154,107	151,808	106,173	69,130	(44,119)	78,057
Average Shares	63,101	63,358	64,016	66,075	66,332	68,674	73,666	72,232
Balance Sheet								
Net PPE	1,879,787	1,766,782	1,561,815	1,414,277	1,419,429	1,221,431	1,198,070	1,506,495
Total Assets	3,196,546	2,939,892	2,436,891	2,518,747	2,455,850	1,789,574	1,854,247	2,411,010
Long-Term Obligations	617,769	632,147	447,000	271,250	287,789	298,350	281,350	417,564
Total Liabilities	2,321,874	1,974,552	1,533,252	1,547,593	1,637,155	1,021,764	1,020,828	1,587,490
Stockholders' Equity	874,672	965,340	778,639	846,154	693,695	642,810	708,419	823,520
Shares Outstanding	61,031	62,367	62,342	63,870	65,078	65,460	71,712	73,858
Statistical Record								
Return on Assets %	9.10	6.32	6.22	6.10	4.99	3.79	N.M.	3.46
Return on Equity %	30.34	19.50	18.97	19.72	15.84	10.23	N.M.	9.97
EBITDA Margin %	46.70	36.37	31.79	20.16	20.46	...	9.11	12.32
Net Margin %	23.49	16.23	14.42	8.60	6.43	6.50	(5.00)	3.63
PPE Turnover	0.65	0.63	0.72	1.25	1.25	0.88	0.65	1.44
Asset Turnover	0.39	0.39	0.43	0.71	0.78	0.58	0.41	0.95
Debt to Equity	0.71	0.65	0.57	0.32	0.41	0.46	0.40	0.51
Price Range	60.74-42.15	43.25-34.68	37.48-29.40	40.08-27.20	33.38-16.47	19.50-11.69	17.69-10.47	17.69-13.94
P/E Ratio	13.68-9.49	16.14-12.94	15.55-12.20	17.42-11.83	20.86-10.29	19.50-11.69	...	16.38-12.91
Average Yield %	2.88	2.47	1.95	1.89	2.37	3.65	4.06	3.87

Address: One Oxford Centre, 301 Grant Street, Suite 3300, Pittsburgh, PA 15219 Telephone: (412) 553 5700 Fax: (412) 553 5732	Web Site: www.eqt.com Officers: Murry S. Gerber - Chmn., Pres., C.E.O. David L. Porges - Vice-Chmn., Exec. V.P., Fin. & Admin.	Auditors: Ernst & Young LLP Investor Contact: 412-553-7833

EQUITY OFFICE PROPERTIES TRUST

Exchange	Symbol	Price	52Wk Range	Yield	P/E
NYS	EOP	$30.13 (3/31/2005)	30.99-24.59	6.64	125.54

*7 Year Price Score 87.17   *NYSE Composite Index=100   *12 Month Price Score 99.48

Interim Earnings (Per Share)

Qtr.	Mar	Jun	Sep	Dec
2001	0.39	0.40	0.49	0.26
2002	0.48	0.40	0.40	(1.11)
2003	0.35	0.37	0.28	0.50
2004	0.16	0.25	(0.32)	0.15

Interim Dividends (Per Share)

Amt	Decl	Ex	Rec	Pay
0.50Q	6/15/2004	6/28/2004	6/30/2004	7/15/2004
0.50Q	9/15/2004	9/28/2004	9/30/2004	10/15/2004
0.50Q	12/1/2004	12/13/2004	12/15/2004	12/31/2004
0.50Q	3/15/2005	3/29/2005	3/31/2005	4/15/2005
		Indicated Div: $2.00		

Valuation Analysis

Forecast P/E	11.77	No of Institutions	
	(4/7/2005)	386	
Market Cap	$12.2 Billion	Shares	
Book Value	9.3 Billion	313,850,368	
Price/Book	1.31	% Held	
Price/Sales	3.81	77.70	

Business Summary: Property, Real Estate & Development (MIC: 8.3 SIC: 798 NAIC: 25930)

Equity Office Properties Trust is the largest publicly-held owner and operator of office properties in the United States, based upon equity market capitalization and square footage. As of Dec 31 2003, Co. had a portfolio of 684 office properties comprising about 122.3 million square feet of commercial office space in 18 states and the District of Columbia, 75 industrial properties comprising about 5.8 million square feet and about 400,000 square feet of office properties under development. In addition to its development pipeline, Co. owns various undeveloped land parcels on which about 12.0 million square feet of office space could be developed.

Recent Developments: For the year ended Dec 31 2004, income from continuing operations decreased 70.1% to $155,716 thousand from income of $520,865 thousand a year earlier. Net income decreased 79.0% to $137,307 thousand from net income of $655,062 thousand a year earlier. Revenues were $3,195,851 thousand, up 1.9% from $3,137,151 thousand the year before. Operating income was $921,687 thousand versus an income of $1,234,333 thousand in the prior year, a decrease of 25.3%.

Prospects: On Feb 2 2005, Co. updated its outlook. Co. now expects full-year 2005 diluted earnings per share of between $0.65 and $0.80, and diluted funds from operations of $2.50 to $2.65. Co.'s guidance does not include the effects of future acquisitions or gains or losses from dispositions, or the effects of any future impairments that could arise as a result of either asset sales or market conditions. Consequently, on Mar 4 2005, Co. announced a series of dispositions, including 12 office buildings in suburban Philadelphia for total proceeds of about $159.0 million. Co. noted that with these transactions, it has exited the Philadelphia market except for a minority interest in two properties.

Financial Data
(US$ in Thousands)

	12/31/2004	12/31/2003	12/31/2002	12/31/2001	12/31/2000	12/31/1999	12/31/1998	12/31/1997
Earnings Per Share	0.24	1.50	0.17	1.55	1.52	1.48	1.24	0.43
Cash Flow Per Share	3.01	2.82	3.35	3.45	3.26	2.81	3.00	1.17
Tang Book Value Per Share	22.43	24.31	24.83	25.20	24.28	24.69	24.76	24.87
Dividends Per Share	2.000	2.000	2.000	1.900	1.740	1.580	1.380	0.560
Dividend Payout %	833.33	133.33	n.m.	122.58	114.47	106.76	111.29	130.23
Income Statement								
Property Income	3,104,652	3,090,828	3,336,191	3,002,594	2,169,099	1,886,758	1,632,675	403,389
Non-Property Income	91,199	104,804	169,891	127,554	95,144	55,485	47,024	9,579
Total Revenue	3,195,851	3,195,632	3,506,082	3,130,148	2,264,243	1,942,243	1,679,699	412,968
Depn & Amortn	804,506	716,841	687,853	578,015	433,724	361,986	308,880	70,346
Interest Expense	850,722	827,335	815,015	734,061	535,533	418,688	345,015	80,853
Income Before Taxes	108,243	457,773	730,958	627,019	470,860	431,353	349,029	71,712
Income Taxes	2,012	5,373	9,394	8,837	...	...	...	...
Net Income	137,307	655,062	770,215	618,182	470,860	431,353	349,029	71,712
Average Shares	450,997	452,561	469,138	411,986	318,997	291,157	283,974	180,014
Balance Sheet								
Total Assets	24,671,539	24,189,010	25,246,783	25,808,422	18,794,253	14,046,058	14,261,291	11,751,672
Long-Term Obligations	12,261,459	11,144,801	11,565,541	11,744,325	8,751,994	5,398,918	4,809,405	2,243,017
Total Liabilities	13,853,340	12,454,042	12,728,959	12,895,706	9,508,784	6,336,531	6,472,613	4,591,697
Stockholders' Equity	9,271,282	10,059,864	11,085,472	11,308,366	8,067,073	6,826,073	7,050,963	6,405,157
Shares Outstanding	403,842	400,460	411,200	414,548	306,966	251,582	259,902	249,528
Statistical Record								
Return on Assets %	0.56	2.65	3.02	2.77	2.86	3.05	2.68	0.92
Return on Equity %	1.42	6.20	6.88	6.38	6.31	6.22	5.19	1.76
Net Margin %	4.30	20.50	21.97	19.75	20.80	22.21	20.78	17.37
Price Range	30.14-24.59	29.10-23.47	31.36-23.21	32.99-26.70	33.19-23.44	29.25-21.00	31.88-20.75	34.69-26.06
P/E Ratio	125.58-102.46	19.40-15.65	184.47-136.53	21.28-17.23	21.83-15.42	19.76-14.19	25.71-16.73	80.67-60.61
Average Yield %	7.21	7.48	7.21	6.37	6.17	6.08	5.13	1.81

Address: Two North Riverside Plaza, Suite 2100, Chicago, IL 60606	**Web Site:** www.equityoffice.com	**Auditors:** Ernst & Young LLP
Telephone: (312) 466-3300	**Officers:** Samuel Zell - Chmn. Richard D. Kincaid - Pres., C.E.O.	**Investor Contact:** 800-692-5304
Fax: (312) 466-0332		**Transfer Agents:** EquiServe, Providence, RI

EQUITY RESIDENTIAL

Exchange	Symbol	Price	52Wk Range	Yield	P/E
NYS	EQR	$32.21 (3/31/2005)	36.57-27.29	5.37	21.76

*7 Year Price Score 105.03 *NYSE Composite Index=100 *12 Month Price Score 95.91

Interim Earnings (Per Share)

Qtr.	Mar	Jun	Sep	Dec
2001	0.40	0.28	0.26	0.43
2002	0.28	0.32	0.23	0.35
2003	0.41	0.41	0.41	0.32
2004	0.35	0.39	0.26	0.48

Interim Dividends (Per Share)

Amt	Decl	Ex	Rec	Pay
0.433Q	5/19/2004	6/16/2004	6/18/2004	7/9/2004
0.433Q	8/23/2004	9/15/2004	9/17/2004	10/8/2004
0.433Q	11/22/2004	12/15/2004	12/17/2004	1/14/2005
0.433Q	2/21/2005	3/16/2005	3/18/2005	4/8/2005

Indicated Div: $1.73

Valuation Analysis

Forecast P/E	N/A	No of Institutions
Market Cap	$9.2 Billion	Shares 312
Book Value	5.1 Billion	240,486,976
Price/Book	1.81	% Held
Price/Sales	4.86	84.07

Business Summary: Property, Real Estate & Development (MIC: 8.3 SIC: 798 NAIC: 25930)

Equity Residential is a self-administered and self-managed equity real estate investment trust. Co., through its subsidiaries, is engaged in the acquisition, disposition, ownership, management and operation of multifamily properties. As of Dec 31 2003, Co. owned or had investments in 968 properties in 34 states consisting of 207,506 units.

Recent Developments: For the year ended Dec 31 2004, income from continuing operations decreased 14.3% to $135,276 thousand from income of $157,867 thousand a year earlier. Net income decreased 9.7% to $472,329 thousand from net income of $523,311 thousand a year earlier. Revenues were $1,889,501 thousand, up 10.8% from $1,706,020 thousand the year before. Operating income was $526,685 thousand versus an income of $530,264 thousand in the prior year, a decrease of 0.7%.

Prospects: Co. is performing well. For instance, revenues in the majority of Co.'s markets increased primarily as a result of decreased concessions. On the transaction front, Co. took advantage of strong prices and sold nearly $1.00 billion in assets in unfavorable markets and invested $900.0 million in assets and markets with greater long-term potential. In 2005, Co. expects to see a continued improvement in fundamentals and revenues, as well as a positive impact from the its actions to reposition its portfolio. For the first quarter of 2005, Co. expects funds from operations of $0.73 to $0.75 per share. For the full year, Co. expects funds from operations of $2.43 to $2.53 per share.

Financial Data
(US$ in Thousands)

	12/31/2004	12/31/2003	12/31/2002	12/31/2001	12/31/2000	12/31/1999	12/31/1998	12/31/1997
Earnings Per Share	1.48	1.55	1.18	1.36	1.67	1.15	0.81	0.88
Cash Flow Per Share	2.56	2.75	3.27	3.33	3.21	3.21	2.66	2.52
Tang Book Value Per Share	15.46	15.54	15.57	16.59	16.47	16.46	16.58	14.86
Dividends Per Share	1.750	1.750	1.750	1.750	1.750	1.750	0.438	1.275
Dividend Payout %	118.24	112.90	148.31	128.68	104.79	152.84	53.68	144.89
Income Statement								
Property Income	1,878,262	1,808,925	1,969,617	2,132,460	1,987,362	1,711,738	1,293,560	707,733
Non-Property Income	11,239	14,373	24,436	38,183	42,978	41,380	43,889	39,588
Total Revenue	1,889,501	1,823,298	1,994,053	2,170,643	2,030,340	1,753,118	1,337,449	747,321
Depn & Amortn	504,076	477,990	477,582	471,721	451,344	410,272	299,653	155,714
Interest Expense	349,314	332,629	337,489	355,250	382,946	337,189	246,585	121,324
Income Before Taxes	474,329	543,347	421,313	473,585	549,951	330,333	255,032	176,014
Net Income	472,329	543,847	421,313	473,585	549,451	393,881	258,206	176,592
Average Shares	303,871	297,041	297,969	295,552	291,266	271,310	225,156	148,502
Balance Sheet								
Total Assets	12,645,275	11,466,893	11,810,917	12,235,625	12,263,966	11,715,689	10,700,260	7,094,631
Long-Term Obligations	6,459,806	5,360,489	5,523,699	5,742,758	5,706,152	5,473,868	4,680,527	2,948,323
Total Liabilities	7,037,165	5,850,523	6,002,491	6,185,853	6,031,801	5,753,776	4,938,439	3,131,236
Stockholders' Equity	5,072,528	5,015,441	5,197,123	5,413,950	5,619,547	5,504,934	5,330,447	3,689,991
Shares Outstanding	285,076	277,643	271,095	265,232	265,232	254,901	236,460	178,170
Statistical Record								
Return on Assets %	3.91	4.67	3.50	3.87	4.57	3.51	2.90	3.50
Return on Equity %	9.34	10.65	7.94	8.58	9.85	7.27	5.72	9.77
Net Margin %	25.00	29.83	21.13	21.82	27.06	22.47	19.31	23.63
Price Range	36.57-27.29	30.05-23.24	30.90-21.91	30.35-24.82	28.59-19.53	23.97-19.22	26.06-17.47	27.41-20.31
P/E Ratio	24.71-18.44	19.39-14.99	26.19-18.57	22.32-18.25	17.12-11.70	20.84-16.71	32.18-21.57	31.14-23.08
Average Yield %	5.69	6.45	6.53	6.42	7.59	8.21	1.92	5.33

Address: Two North Riverside Plaza, Chicago, IL 60606 Telephone: (312) 474-1300 Fax: (312) 454-8703	Web Site: www.eqityapartments.com Officers: Samuel Zell - Chmn. Bruce W. Duncan - Pres., C.E.O.	Auditors: Ernst & Young LLP Investor Contact: 312-466-3779 Transfer Agents: EquiServe Trust Company, NA Providence, RI

ESSEX PROPERTY TRUST, INC.

Exchange	Symbol	Price	52Wk Range	Yield	P/E	Div Acheiver
NYS	ESS	$69.10 (3/31/2005)	85.11-60.05	4.69	20.57	10 Years

*7 Year Price Score 125.46 ***NYSE Composite Index=100** ***12 Month Price Score 94.34**

Interim Earnings (Per Share)

Qtr.	Mar	Jun	Sep	Dec
2001	0.59	0.61	0.79	0.80
2002	0.61	1.14	0.57	0.50
2003	0.48	0.50	0.43	0.28
2004	0.26	0.23	1.49	1.38

Interim Dividends (Per Share)

Amt	Decl	Ex	Rec	Pay
0.79Q	5/13/2004	6/28/2004	6/30/2004	7/15/2004
0.79Q	9/17/2004	9/28/2004	9/30/2004	10/15/2004
0.79Q	12/14/2004	12/29/2004	12/31/2004	1/15/2005
0.81Q	2/24/2005	3/29/2005	3/31/2005	4/15/2005
		Indicated Div: $3.24		

Valuation Analysis

Forecast P/E	15.59	No of Institutions	
	(4/7/2005)	136	
Market Cap	$1.6 Billion	Shares	
Book Value	578.5 Million	19,967,398	
Price/Book	2.74	% Held	
Price/Sales	5.81	87.01	

Business Summary: Property, Real Estate & Development (MIC: 8.3 SIC: 798 NAIC: 25930)

Essex Property Trust is engaged in the ownership, acquisition, development and management of multifamily apartment communities. 121 properties (comprising 26,012 apartment units), of which 14,943 units are located in Southern California, 4,605 units are located in Northern California, 5,886 of which are located in the Pacific Northwest, and 578 are located in other areas. In addition, Co. has an ownership interest in other real estate assets consisting of five recreational vehicle parks (comprising 1,717 spaces), four office buildings (totaling approximately 63,540 square feet) and two manufactured housing communities (containing 607 sites).

Recent Developments: For the quarter ended Dec 31 2004, income from continuing operations increased 235.5% to $78,976 thousand from income of $33,527 thousand in the year-earlier quarter. Net income increased 227.1% to $79,693 thousand from net income of $35,090 thousand in the year-earlier quarter. Revenues were $283,483 thousand, up 12.6% from $251,576 thousand the year before.

Prospects: During the quarter ended Dec 31 2004, Co. acquired four multifamily communities aggregating 645 units for a combined contract price of about $109.9 million, utilizing a portion of the proceeds from the sale of its investment in Coronado at Newport North, a 732-unit multifamily community located in Newport Beach, CA. Separately, on Feb 2 2005, Co. announced that it has acquired Cedar Terrace Apartments, a 180-unit apartment community, located in Bellevue, WA, for consideration of about $22.3 million. Co. noted that it does not anticipate any material effect from development transactions to Funds From Operations (FFO) in 2005. Thus, Co. has reiterated its 2005 FFO mid-point guidance of $4.41.

Financial Data

(US$ in Thousands)	9 Mos	6 Mos	3 Mos	12/31/2003	12/31/2002	12/31/2001	12/31/2000	12/31/1999
Earnings Per Share	2.26	1.20	1.46	1.70	2.82	2.59	2.37	2.36
Cash Flow Per Share	5.11	4.91	4.79	4.81	4.63	5.36	5.04	4.77
Tang Book Value Per Share	24.12	23.28	23.83	24.74	23.41	20.98	21.27	21.48
Dividends Per Share	3.150	3.140	3.130	3.120	3.080	2.800	2.380	2.150
Dividend Payout %	139.57	262.69	213.72	183.53	109.22	108.11	100.42	91.10
Income Statement								
Property Income	209,071	136,639	66,331	222,868	177,265	183,482	167,771	140,427
Non-Property Income	...	5,708	3,475	11,582	22,857	22,152	10,969	5,618
Total Revenue	209,071	142,347	69,806	234,450	200,122	205,634	178,740	146,045
Depn & Amortn	55,595	36,873	18,705	50,417	37,841	36,952	31,404	26,716
Interest Expense	45,785	29,391	14,310	42,751	35,012	39,105	30,384	21,268
Income Before Taxes	...	...	...	60,139	68,718	69,156	64,200	52,092
Net Income	47,180	12,150	6,450	37,947	52,874	48,545	44,353	43,564
Average Shares	23,205	23,128	23,104	21,678	18,725	18,768	18,657	18,491
Balance Sheet								
Total Assets	2,149,125	2,153,304	2,089,796	1,728,564	1,619,734	1,329,458	1,281,849	1,062,313
Long-Term Obligations	1,263,444	1,253,767	1,166,492	832,229	804,063	638,660	595,535	384,108
Total Liabilities	1,334,859	1,308,521	1,230,256	895,064	865,890	691,379	652,044	436,331
Stockholders' Equity	578,459	558,881	570,194	589,701	491,314	386,599	391,675	387,693
Shares Outstanding	22,943	22,935	22,880	22,825	20,983	18,428	18,417	18,049
Statistical Record								
Return on Assets %	2.88	1.54	1.83	2.27	3.59	3.72	3.77	4.37
Return on Equity %	10.13	5.59	6.43	7.02	12.05	12.48	11.35	11.21
Net Margin %	22.57	8.54	9.24	16.19	26.42	23.61	24.81	29.83
Price Range	74.89-59.88	69.22-57.25	66.60-52.25	66.08-49.50	55.75-45.23	55.94-43.20	57.75-32.81	35.38-26.13
P/E Ratio	33.14-26.50	57.68-47.71	45.62-35.79	38.87-29.12	19.77-16.04	21.60-16.68	24.37-13.84	14.99-11.07
Average Yield %	4.82	4.98	5.11	5.36	6.11	5.26	5.36	6.77

Address: 925 East Meadow Drive, Palo Alto, CA 94303	Web Site: www.essexpropertytrust.com	Auditors: KPMG LLP
Telephone: (650) 494-3700	Officers: George M. Marcus - Chmn. Keith R.	Investor Contact: 650-849-1600
Fax: (650) 494-8743	Guericke - Vice-Chmn., Pres., C.E.O.	

EXELON CORP.

Exchange	Symbol	Price	52Wk Range	Yield	P/E
NYS	EXC	$45.89 (3/31/2005)	46.85-31.29	3.49	16.51

*7 Year Price Score 124.40 *NYSE Composite Index=100 *12 Month Price Score 109.02

TRADING VOLUME (thousand shares)

Interim Earnings (Per Share)

Qtr.	Mar	Jun	Sep	Dec
2001	0.61	0.48	0.63	0.48
2002	0.01	0.75	0.85	0.61
2003	0.56	0.57	(0.16)	0.41
2004	0.61	0.78	0.85	0.53

Interim Dividends (Per Share)

Amt	Decl	Ex	Rec	Pay
0.275Q	4/27/2004	5/12/2004	5/15/2004	6/10/2004
0.305Q	7/28/2004	8/11/2004	8/15/2004	9/10/2004
0.40Q	10/21/2004	11/10/2004	11/15/2004	12/10/2004
0.40Q	1/25/2005	2/11/2005	2/15/2005	3/10/2005

Indicated Div: $1.60

Valuation Analysis

Forecast P/E	15.02	No of Institutions	
	(4/7/2005)	510	
Market Cap	$30.6 Billion	Shares	
Book Value	9.4 Billion	426,307,616	
Price/Book	3.25	% Held	
Price/Sales	2.11	64.34	

Business Summary: Electricity (MIC: 7.1 SIC: 931 NAIC: 21122)

Exelon is a holding company that operates through its subsidiaries in three business segments, energy delivery, generation and enterprises. The energy delivery unit consists of the regulated electricity, distribution and transmission services of Commonwealth Edison, PECO Energy and the regulated sale of natural gas and distribution services by PECO. The generation business consists of the owned and contracted for electric generating facilities and energy marketing operations of Exelon Generation and a 50.0% interest in Sithe Energies. The enterprise unit consists primarily of the energy services business of Exelon Services, Exelon Thermal Holdings and F&M Holdings.

Recent Developments: For the year ended Dec 31 2004, net income increased 106.0% to $1,864,000 thousand from net income of $905,000 thousand a year earlier. Revenues were $14,515,000 thousand, down 8.2% from $15,812,000 thousand the year before. Operating income was $3,433,000 thousand versus an income of $2,277,000 thousand in the prior year, an increase of 50.8%. Total direct expense was $9,058,000 thousand versus $11,828,000 thousand in the prior year, a decrease of 23.4%. Total indirect expense was $2,024,000 thousand versus $1,707,000 thousand in the prior year, an increase of 18.6%.

Prospects: On Feb 4 2005, Co. and Public Service Enterprise Group (PSEG) announced that they have made four major regulatory filings relating to their planned merger. In addition, with respect to fossil fuel facilities, the companies propose to divest a total of 2,900 megawatt (MW), including about 1,000 MW of peaking capacity and 1,900 MW of mid-merit capacity, of which at least 550 MW must be coal fired. The companies have proposed that the sale of this generating capacity will occur as soon as possible within 18 months following close of the merger. On Dec 20 2004, Co. entered into an agreement to be acquired by PSEG, a public electric and gas utility company located primarily in New Jersey.

Financial Data

(US$ in Thousands)	12/31/2004	12/31/2003	12/31/2002	12/31/2001	12/31/2000	12/31/1999	12/31/1998	12/31/1997
Earnings Per Share	2.78	1.38	2.22	2.21	1.44	1.45	1.12	(3.40)
Cash Flow Per Share	6.64	5.19	5.61	5.65	2.71	2.26	3.21	2.33
Tang Book Value Per Share	5.87	5.77	4.25	4.51	5.95	4.56	6.80	6.13
Dividends Per Share	1.255	0.960	0.880	0.910	0.454	0.500	0.500	0.900
Dividend Payout %	45.14	69.82	39.64	41.08	31.65	34.60	44.84	...
Income Statement								
Total Revenue	14,515,000	15,812,000	14,955,000	15,140,000	7,499,000	5,436,753	5,210,482	4,617,901
EBITDA	4,722,000	3,131,000	4,974,000	4,903,000	1,973,000	1,358,353	1,224,731	1,041,284
Depn & Amortn	1,305,000	1,126,000	1,340,000	1,449,000	458,000	(14,301)	41,857	39,100
Income Before Taxes	2,512,000	1,124,000	2,668,000	2,347,000	907,000	976,984	852,032	629,327
Income Taxes	692,000	331,000	998,000	931,000	341,000	357,998	319,654	292,769
Net Income	1,864,000	905,000	1,440,000	1,428,000	586,000	582,414	512,724	(1,497,106)
Average Shares	669,000	658,000	650,000	644,000	408,000	395,232	447,808	445,086
Balance Sheet								
Net PPE	21,482,000	20,630,000	17,134,000	13,742,000	12,936,000	5,045,008	4,764,013	4,670,724
Total Assets	42,770,000	41,941,000	37,478,000	34,821,000	34,597,000	13,119,509	12,048,363	12,356,568
Long-Term Obligations	12,148,000	13,489,000	13,127,000	12,876,000	12,958,000	5,969,113	3,004,889	3,973,266
Total Liabilities	33,218,000	33,351,000	29,064,000	25,978,000	26,752,000	11,025,315	8,411,494	9,047,580
Stockholders' Equity	9,423,000	8,503,000	7,742,000	8,230,000	7,215,000	1,910,480	3,057,342	2,726,731
Shares Outstanding	666,688	656,365	646,625	642,013	340,957	362,543	449,368	445,094
Statistical Record								
Return on Assets %	4.39	2.28	3.98	4.11	2.45	4.63	4.20	N.M.
Return on Equity %	20.74	11.14	18.03	18.49	12.81	23.45	17.73	N.M.
EBITDA Margin %	32.53	19.80	33.26	32.38	26.31	24.98	23.51	22.55
Net Margin %	12.84	5.72	9.63	9.43	7.81	10.71	9.84	(32.42)
PPE Turnover	0.69	0.84	0.97	1.14	0.83	1.11	1.10	0.59
Asset Turnover	0.34	0.40	0.41	0.44	0.31	0.43	0.43	0.33
Debt to Equity	1.29	1.59	1.70	1.56	1.80	3.12	0.98	1.46
Price Range	44.70-31.29	33.18-23.41	28.46-20.18	34.90-20.52	35.42-16.81	25.00-15.75	21.09-9.47	13.00-9.50
P/E Ratio	16.08-11.26	24.04-16.97	12.82-9.09	15.79-9.29	24.60-11.68	17.24-10.86	18.83-8.45	...
Average Yield %	3.51	3.36	3.52	3.25	1.89	2.45	3.37	8.06

Address: 10 South Dearborn Street, 37th Floor, P.O. Box 805379, Chicago, IL 60680-5379
Telephone: (312) 394-7398

Web Site: www.exeloncorp.com
Officers: John W. Rowe - Chmn., Pres., C.E.O.
Pamela B. Strobel - Exec. V.P., Chief Admin. Officer

Auditors: PricewaterhouseCoopers LLP
Investor Contact: 312-394-4321

EXXON MOBIL CORP.

Exchange	Symbol	Price	52Wk Range	Yield	P/E	Div Acheiver
NYS	XOM	$59.60 (3/31/2005)	63.57-41.52	1.81	15.32	22 Years

*7 Year Price Score 104.90 *NYSE Composite Index=100 *12 Month Price Score 113.02

Interim Earnings (Per Share)

Qtr.	Mar	Jun	Sep	Dec
2001	0.71	0.65	0.46	0.39
2002	0.30	0.38	0.39	0.60
2003	1.05	0.62	0.55	1.01
2004	0.83	0.88	0.88	1.30

Interim Dividends (Per Share)

Amt	Decl	Ex	Rec	Pay
0.27Q	4/28/2004	5/11/2004	5/13/2004	6/10/2004
0.27Q	7/28/2004	8/11/2004	8/13/2004	9/10/2004
0.27Q	10/27/2004	11/9/2004	11/12/2004	12/10/2004
0.27Q	1/26/2005	2/8/2005	2/10/2005	3/10/2005

Indicated Div: $1.08 (Div. Reinv. Plan)

Valuation Analysis

Forecast P/E	14.68	No of Institutions
	(4/7/2005)	1289
Market Cap	$381.5 Billion	Shares
Book Value	101.8 Billion	3,306,151,936
Price/Book	3.75	% Held
Price/Sales	1.28	51.78

TRADING VOLUME (thousand shares)

Business Summary: Oil and Gas (MIC: 14.2 SIC: 911 NAIC: 24110)

Exxon Mobil's principal business is energy, involving exploration for, and production of, crude oil and natural gas, manufacturing of petroleum products and transportation and sale of crude oil, natural gas and petroleum products. Co. is a major manufacturer and marketer of basic petrochemicals, including olefins, aromatics, polyethylene and polypropylene plastics and a wide variety of specialty products. Co. also has interests in electric power generation facilities. As of Dec 31 2003, worldwide proved developed and undeveloped reserves were: crude oil and natural gas liquids, 12,075 million barrels; and natural gas, 54,769 billion cubic feet.

Recent Developments: For the year ended Dec 30 2004, net income increased 17.8% to $25,330 million from net income of $21,510 million a year earlier. Revenues were $298,035 million, up 20.8% from $246,738 million the year before. Total direct expense was $139,224 million versus $107,658 million in the prior year, an increase of 29.3%. Total indirect expense was $116,156 million versus $106,213 million in the prior year, an increase of 9.4%.

Prospects: Co. is experiencing strong performance across each of its operating segments. Co.'s Upstream earnings are benefiting from higher liquids and natural gas realizations, with higher liquids production in both West Africa and Norway and higher average crude and natural gas prices. Meanwhile, Co.'s Downstream earnings are being positively affected by stronger worldwide refining margins and higher refinery throughput. Co.'s Chemical earnings are up due to better margins, higher volumes and favorable foreign exchange effects. Separately, Co. is continuing to actively invest in capital spending and exploration projects.

Financial Data

(US$ in Thousands)	12/31/2004	12/31/2003	12/31/2002	12/31/2001	12/31/2000	12/31/1999	12/31/1998	12/31/1997
Earnings Per Share	3.89	3.23	1.68	2.21	2.52	1.13	1.29	1.69
Cash Flow Per Share	6.24	4.30	3.15	3.33	3.29	2.17	2.28	2.97
Tang Book Value Per Share	15.90	13.69	11.13	10.74	10.21	9.12	8.99	8.85
Dividends Per Share	1.060	0.980	0.920	0.910	0.880	0.835	0.820	0.813
Dividend Payout %	27.25	30.34	54.76	41.18	34.92	74.22	63.57	48.22
Income Statement								
Total Revenue	298,035,000	246,738,000	204,506,000	213,488,000	232,748,000	185,527,000	117,772,000	137,242,000
EBITDA	51,646,000	41,220,000	26,218,000	32,356,000	35,800,000	20,149,000	14,496,000	18,687,000
Depn & Amortn	9,767,000	9,047,000	8,310,000	7,944,000	8,130,000	8,304,000	5,340,000	5,474,000
Income Before Taxes	41,241,000	31,966,000	17,510,000	24,119,000	27,081,000	11,150,000	9,056,000	12,798,000
Income Taxes	15,911,000	11,006,000	6,499,000	9,014,000	11,091,000	3,240,000	2,616,000	4,338,000
Net Income	25,330,000	21,510,000	11,460,000	15,320,000	17,720,000	7,910,000	6,370,000	8,460,000
Average Shares	6,519,001	6,662,001	6,803,001	6,941,001	7,034,001	6,906,001	4,855,999	5,009,999
Balance Sheet								
Current Assets	60,377,000	45,960,000	38,291,000	35,681,000	40,399,000	31,141,000	17,593,000	21,192,000
Total Assets	195,256,000	174,278,000	152,644,000	143,174,000	149,000,000	144,521,000	92,630,000	96,064,000
Current Liabilities	42,981,000	38,386,000	33,175,000	30,114,000	38,191,000	38,733,000	19,412,000	19,654,000
Long-Term Obligations	5,013,000	4,756,000	6,655,000	7,099,000	7,280,000	8,402,000	4,530,000	7,050,000
Total Liabilities	93,500,000	84,363,000	78,047,000	70,013,000	78,243,000	81,055,000	48,880,000	52,404,000
Stockholders' Equity	101,756,000	89,915,000	74,597,000	73,161,000	70,757,000	63,466,000	43,750,000	43,660,000
Shares Outstanding	6,400,999	6,568,001	6,700,001	6,809,001	6,930,001	6,959,785	4,855,999	4,913,999
Statistical Record								
Return on Assets %	13.67	13.16	7.75	10.49	12.04	6.67	6.75	8.83
Return on Equity %	26.36	26.15	15.51	21.29	26.33	14.76	14.57	19.40
EBITDA Margin %	17.33	16.71	12.82	15.16	15.38	10.86	12.31	13.62
Net Margin %	8.50	8.72	5.60	7.18	7.61	4.26	5.41	6.16
Asset Turnover	1.61	1.51	1.38	1.46	1.58	1.56	1.25	1.43
Current Ratio	1.40	1.20	1.15	1.18	1.06	0.80	0.91	1.08
Debt to Equity	0.05	0.05	0.09	0.10	0.10	0.13	0.10	0.16
Price Range	51.97-40.10	41.00-31.82	44.38-30.27	45.77-35.83	47.22-35.53	43.22-32.41	38.28-29.06	33.41-24.50
P/E Ratio	13.36-10.31	12.69-9.85	26.42-18.02	20.71-16.21	18.74-14.10	38.25-28.68	29.68-22.53	19.77-14.50
Average Yield %	2.34	2.71	2.44	2.20	2.12	2.18	2.37	2.77

Address: 5959 Las Colinas Boulevard, Irving, TX 75039-2298 **Telephone:** (972) 444-1000 **Fax:** (972) 444-1348	**Web Site:** www.exxonmobil.com **Officers:** Lee R. Raymond - Chmn., C.E.O. Harry J. Longwell - Exec. V.P.	**Auditors:** PricewaterhouseCoopers LLP **Transfer Agents:** EquiServe Trust Company, N.A., Providence, RI

F.N.B. CORP (PA)

Exchange	Symbol	Price	52Wk Range	Yield	P/E	Div Acheiver
NYS	FNB	$19.15 (3/31/2005)	22.72-18.72	4.80	14.84	20 Years

*7 Year Price Score 124.92 *NYSE Composite Index=100 *12 Month Price Score 87.95

Interim Earnings (Per Share)

Qtr.	Mar	Jun	Sep	Dec
2001	0.22	0.37	0.46	0.47
2002	(0.19)	0.50	0.51	0.51
2003	0.50	0.53	0.01	0.22
2004	0.34	0.32	0.31	0.31

Interim Dividends (Per Share)

Amt	Decl	Ex	Rec	Pay
0.23Q	5/12/2004	5/27/2004	6/1/2004	6/15/2004
0.23Q	8/18/2004	8/30/2004	9/1/2004	9/15/2004
0.23Q	11/10/2004	11/29/2004	12/1/2004	12/15/2004
0.23Q	2/16/2005	2/25/2005	3/1/2005	3/15/2005

Indicated Div: $0.92 (Div. Reinv. Plan)

Valuation Analysis

Forecast P/E N/A No of Institutions

Market Cap	$958.6 Million	Shares
Book Value	324.1 Million	16,970,132
Price/Book	2.96	% Held
Price/Sales	2.88	30.23

Business Summary: Commercial Banking (MIC: 8.1 SIC: 021 NAIC: 22110)

F.N.B., with assets of $8.31 billion as of Dec 31 2003, is a financial holding company that provides a full range of financial services to consumers and small- to medium-size businesses in its market areas. Co.'s bank subsidiaries offer traditional full-service commercial banking services, including commercial and individual demand and time deposit accounts and commercial, mortgage and individual installment loans. In addition, Co.'s bank subsidiaries offer various alternative investment products, including mutual funds and annuities. The consumer finance subsidiary offers personal installment loans to individuals and purchase installment sales finance from retail merchants.

Recent Developments: For the year ended Dec 31 2004, net income increased 5.1% to $61,795 thousand from net income of $58,789 thousand a year earlier. Net interest income was $170,058 thousand, up 0.0% from $170,029 thousand the year before. Provision for loan losses was $16,280 thousand versus $17,155 thousand in the prior year, a decrease of 5.1%. Non-interest income rose 14.7% to $78,141 thousand, while non-interest expense declined 23.4% to $139,891 thousand.

Prospects: Results in 2005 are expected to benefit from ongoing market share growth stemming primarily from Co.'s aggressive acquisition activity. Co.'s acquisition of NSD Bancorp, Inc. is anticipated to be completed in February 2005 following approval by NSD shareholders. NSD's principal subsidiary, NorthSide Bank is an independent community bank operating eleven full-service branches in the Pittsburgh, PA area. Separately, on Oct 8 2004, Co. completed its acquisition of Pennsylvania-based Slippery Rock Financial Corporation, the parent company of First National Bank of Slippery Rock.

Financial Data

(US$ in Thousands)	12/31/2004	12/31/2003	12/31/2002	12/31/2001	12/31/2000	12/31/1999	12/31/1998	12/31/1997
Earnings Per Share	1.29	1.25	1.34	1.52	1.62	1.48	1.32	1.63
Cash Flow Per Share	2.23	2.17	1.05	1.36	2.17	2.78	(1.02)	2.50
Tang Book Value Per Share	4.79	8.73	11.08	13.02	12.51	11.35	11.77	11.61
Dividends Per Share	0.920	0.930	0.810	0.69	0.65	0.62	0.58	0.50
Dividend Payout %	71.32	74.36	60.32	45.39	40.12	41.89	43.94	30.67
Income Statement								
Interest Income	254,448	423,313	426,784	296,693	290,936	254,916	235,985	195,508
Interest Expense	84,390	129,836	145,671	125,667	135,308	106,467	103,385	84,478
Net Interest Income	170,058	293,477	281,113	171,026	155,628	148,449	132,600	111,030
Provision for Losses	16,280	24,339	19,094	12,915	10,877	9,240	7,255	10,585
Non-Interest Income	78,141	130,571	120,873	82,799	55,645	46,928	31,745	23,113
Non-Interest Expense	142,587	315,323	289,444	174,830	137,501	129,679	109,174	88,208
Income Before Taxes	89,332	84,386	93,448	66,080	62,895	56,458	47,916	35,350
Income Taxes	27,537	25,597	30,113	21,508	20,119	17,163	16,044	11,036
Net Income	61,795	58,789	63,335	44,572	42,776	39,295	31,872	33,123
Average Shares	48,012	46,972	47,073	29,311	25,484	26,468	24,265	20,322
Balance Sheet								
Net Loans & Leases	3,338,994	5,634,336	5,152,098	3,161,659	2,923,336	2,767,463	2,298,834	1,858,214
Total Assets	5,027,009	8,308,310	7,090,232	4,129,087	3,886,548	3,706,184	3,250,695	2,649,494
Total Deposits	3,598,087	6,159,499	5,426,157	3,292,392	3,102,937	2,909,434	2,708,572	2,192,713
Total Liabilities	4,702,907	7,701,401	6,491,636	3,759,890	3,565,304	3,415,869	2,978,537	2,418,858
Stockholders' Equity	324,102	606,909	598,596	369,197	321,244	290,315	272,158	230,636
Shares Outstanding	50,058	46,313	46,055	28,346	25,541	25,385	22,928	19,612
Statistical Record								
Return on Assets %	0.92	0.76	1.13	1.11	1.12	1.13	1.08	1.51
Return on Equity %	13.24	9.75	13.09	12.91	13.95	13.97	12.68	17.19
Net Interest Margin %	66.83	69.33	65.87	57.64	53.49	58.23	56.19	56.79
Efficiency Ratio %	42.87	56.93	52.85	46.07	39.67	42.96	40.78	40.35
Loans to Deposits	0.93	0.91	0.95	0.96	0.94	0.95	0.85	0.85
Price Range	22.77-18.80	18.80-13.58	16.03-12.39	13.52-9.85	10.42-7.96	12.22-9.14	15.89-10.18	15.33-8.67
P/E Ratio	17.65-14.57	15.04-10.87	11.96-9.24	8.89-6.48	6.43-4.92	8.25-6.18	12.04-7.71	9.41-5.32
Average Yield %	4.40	5.75	5.62	5.91	7.07	5.81	4.45	4.17

Address: 2150 Goodlette Road North, Naples, FL 34102 Telephone: (239) 262-7600	Web Site: www.fnbcorporation.com Officers: Peter Mortensen - Chmn. Stephen J. Gurgovits - Pres., C.E.O.	Auditors: Ernst & Young LLP Investor Contact: 239-659-9894 Transfer Agents: F.N.B. Shareholder Services, Naples, FL

FAIR ISAAC CORP

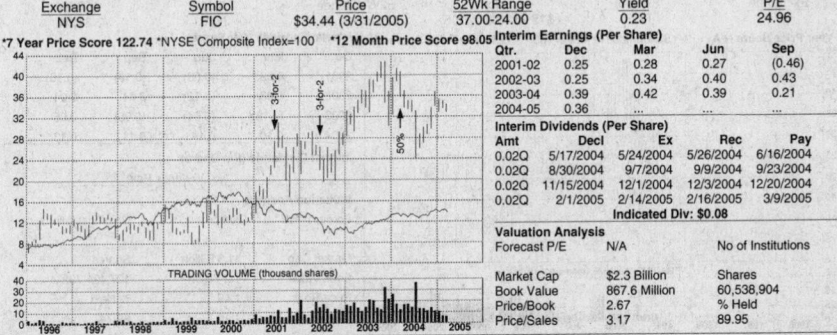

Exchange	Symbol	Price	52Wk Range	Yield	P/E
NYS	FIC	$34.44 (3/31/2005)	37.00-24.00	0.23	24.96

*7 Year Price Score 122.74 *NYSE Composite Index=100 *12 Month Price Score 98.05

Interim Earnings (Per Share)

Qtr.	Dec	Mar	Jun	Sep
2001-02	0.25	0.28	0.27	(0.46)
2002-03	0.25	0.34	0.40	0.43
2003-04	0.39	0.42	0.39	0.21
2004-05	0.36	...	...	...

Interim Dividends (Per Share)

Amt	Decl	Ex	Rec	Pay
0.02Q	5/17/2004	5/24/2004	5/26/2004	6/16/2004
0.02Q	8/30/2004	9/7/2004	9/9/2004	9/23/2004
0.02Q	11/15/2004	12/1/2004	12/3/2004	12/20/2004
0.02Q	2/1/2005	2/14/2005	2/16/2005	3/9/2005

Indicated Div: $0.08

Valuation Analysis

Forecast P/E	N/A	No of Institutions	
Market Cap	$2.3 Billion	Shares	60,538,904
Book Value	867.6 Million	% Held	89.95
Price/Book	2.67		
Price/Sales	3.17		

Business Summary: Miscellaneous Business Services (MIC: 12.8 SIC: 389 NAIC: 16110)

Fair Isaac provides products and services that enable businesses to automate and improve decisions. Co. provides predictive modeling, decision analytics, business intelligence management, and decision management systems. Co. assists businesses to make decisions in the areas of customer targeting and acquisition, customer origination, customer management, fraud and collections, as well as helping businesses improve the speed and consistency of non-customer decisions such as processing. Co. is organized into four reporting segments: Strategy Machine™ Solutions; Scoring Solution; Professional Services; and Analytic Software Tools.

Recent Developments: For the quarter ended Dec 31 2004, net income decreased 3.1% to $27,861 thousand from net income of $28,761 thousand in the year-earlier quarter. Revenues were $195,546 thousand, up 15.5% from $169,341 thousand the year before. Operating income was $44,426 thousand versus an income of $47,578 thousand in the prior-year quarter, a decrease of 6.6%. Total direct expense was $69,770 thousand versus $59,535 thousand in the prior-year quarter, an increase of 17.2%. Total indirect expense was $81,350 thousand versus $62,228 thousand in the prior-year quarter, an increase of 30.7%.

Prospects: Co. believes that it is off to a solid start in achieving its 2005 objectives as revenues are higher for each of its four business segments, and first-quarter new bookings amounted to $115.4 million. Co. noted that it is seeing considerable revenues momentum from its Strategy Machine Solutions unit primarily resulting from revenues generated by its collections and recovery and mortgage banking applications associated with the acquisition of London Bridge and increased revenues from fraud protection application products. Also, Co.'s Scoring Solutions segment revenues are being bolstered mostly by an increase in revenues derived from risk scoring services at credit reporting agencies.

Financial Data
(US$ in Thousands)

	3 Mos	09/30/2004	09/30/2003	09/30/2002	09/30/2001	09/30/2000	09/30/1999	09/30/1998
Earnings Per Share	1.38	1.41	1.41	0.32	0.89	0.56	0.62	0.50
Cash Flow Per Share	3.07	2.84	2.42	1.88	1.43	0.76	0.89	0.89
Tang Book Value Per Share	0.73	1.31	4.26	5.97	5.21	3.88	3.09	2.61
Dividends Per Share	0.073	0.067	0.053	0.044	0.027	0.024	0.024	0.024
Dividend Payout %	5.33	4.73	3.77	13.89	3.01	4.23	3.83	4.76
Income Statement								
Total Revenue	195,546	706,206	629,295	392,418	329,148	297,985	276,931	245,545
EBITDA	58,996	224,714	219,850	79,028	96,263	64,496	65,070	55,453
Depn & Amortn	13,913	48,955	44,653	30,833	25,072	21,461	17,431	14,948
Income Before Taxes	44,756	168,815	172,140	53,098	76,853	47,070	50,600	42,105
Income Taxes	16,895	66,027	64,983	35,214	30,741	19,439	20,620	17,778
Net Income	27,861	102,788	107,157	17,884	46,112	27,631	29,980	24,327
Average Shares	80,056	73,032	75,973	56,325	51,883	49,392	48,478	48,812
Balance Sheet								
Current Assets	486,981	466,101	667,872	428,174	134,261	137,212	101,327	102,613
Total Assets	1,430,801	1,444,779	1,495,173	1,212,513	317,013	241,288	210,353	189,614
Current Liabilities	151,867	120,316	98,362	90,209	39,637	36,518	45,442	47,761
Long-Term Obligations	400,000	400,000	541,364	139,922	...	...	364	789
Total Liabilities	563,173	528,308	645,631	239,041	45,241	42,287	53,854	56,163
Stockholders' Equity	867,628	916,471	849,542	973,472	271,772	199,001	156,499	133,451
Shares Outstanding	67,190	69,579	69,867	75,997	50,934	49,069	47,183	47,190
Statistical Record								
Return on Assets %	6.80	6.97	7.92	2.34	16.52	12.20	14.99	14.53
Return on Equity %	11.52	11.61	11.76	2.87	19.59	15.50	20.68	20.56
EBITDA Margin %	30.17	31.82	34.94	20.14	29.25	21.64	23.50	22.58
Net Margin %	14.25	14.55	17.03	4.56	14.01	9.27	10.83	9.91
Asset Turnover	0.49	0.48	0.46	0.51	1.18	1.32	1.38	1.47
Current Ratio	3.21	3.87	6.79	4.75	3.39	3.76	2.23	2.15
Debt to Equity	0.46	0.44	0.64	0.14	...	...	N.M.	0.01
Price Range	41.33-24.00	42.65-24.00	40.63-19.87	29.33-16.79	30.98-11.37	16.43-8.30	15.56-7.87	13.63-8.59
P/E Ratio	29.95-17.39	30.25-17.02	28.82-14.09	91.67-52.47	34.81-12.78	29.33-14.81	25.09-12.69	27.26-17.19
Average Yield %	0.22	0.19	0.21	0.18	0.14	0.18	0.21	0.22

Address: 901 Marquette Avenue, Suite 3200, Minneapolis, MN 55402-3232 **Telephone:** (612) 758-5200	**Web Site:** www.fairisaac.com **Officers:** Thomas G. Grudnowski - Pres., C.E.O. Charles M. Osborne - V.P., C.F.O.	**Auditors:** KPMG LLP **Investor Contact:** 415-491-7122 **Transfer Agents:** Mellon Investor Services, San Francisco, CA

FAIRCHILD SEMICONDUCTOR INTERNATIONAL, INC.

Exchange	Symbol	Price	52Wk Range	Yield	P/E
NYS	FCS	$15.33 (3/31/2005)	25.62-11.99	N/A	31.94

*7 Year Price Score N/A   *NYSE Composite Index=100   *12 Month Price Score 92.46

TRADING VOLUME (thousand shares)

Interim Earnings (Per Share)

Qtr.	Mar	Jun	Sep	Dec
2001	0.02	(0.08)	(0.19)	(0.16)
2002	0.03	(0.12)	0.04	0.04
2003	(0.15)	(0.54)	(0.05)	0.05
2004	0.10	0.14	0.11	0.13

Interim Dividends (Per Share)

No Dividends Paid

Valuation Analysis

Forecast P/E	N/A	No of Institutions
Market Cap	$1.8 Billion	Shares
Book Value	1.2 Billion	107,421,792
Price/Book	1.49	% Held
Price/Sales	1.14	89.74

Business Summary: IT & Technology (MIC: 10.2 SIC: 674 NAIC: 34413)

Fairchild Semiconductor International supplies semiconductors for the communications, computing, consumer, industrial, and automotive markets. The analog and mixed signal segment's products monitor, interpret and control continuously variable functions. The discrete segment's products perform power switching, power conditioning and signal amplification in electronic circuits. The logic and memory segment product's perform a variety of functions in a system mostly in the interface between larger application-specific integrated circuits, microprocessors, memory components or connectors. Other products include optoelectronics such as optocouplers, infrared devices, LED lamps and displays.

Recent Developments: For the year ended Dec 26 2004, net income was $59,200 thousand versus net loss of $81,500 thousand a year earlier. Revenues were $1,603,100 thousand, up 14.9% from $1,395,800 thousand the year before. Operating income was $134,700 thousand versus a loss of $18,900 thousand in the prior year. Total direct expense was $1,154,800 thousand versus $1,088,000 thousand in the prior year, an increase of 6.1%. Total indirect expense was $313,600 thousand versus $326,700 thousand in the prior year, a decrease of 4.0%.

Prospects: As a result of continued strength in the computing, consumer and industrial markets, Co. is seeing its strongest demand for power products going into notebook, storage, TV, DVD, set-top box, power supply and battery charger applications. Additionally, demand for Co.'s low power switches in support of the notebook and ultra-portable end markets is stronger. Co. noted that it is seeing less pricing pressure on bookings for its power analog and high power switches, which are in tighter supply. Meanwhile, new product design wins bode well for Co.'s business growth. For instance, Co. won designs in power supply applications for the computing end market at a number of large Asian customers.

Financial Data

(US$ in Thousands)	12/26/2004	12/28/2003	12/29/2002	12/30/2001	12/31/2000	12/26/1999	05/30/1999	05/31/1998
Earnings Per Share	0.48	(0.69)	(0.02)	(0.42)	2.69	0.23	(1.97)	...
Cash Flow Per Share	2.05	1.08	1.27	1.57	3.85	0.92	0.70	...
Tang Book Value Per Share	7.09	6.26	6.64	3.28	5.43	N.M.	...	...
Income Statement								
Total Revenue	1,603,100	1,395,800	1,411,900	1,407,700	1,783,200	786,200	735,100	789,200
EBITDA	301,400	140,600	241,700	203,600	479,800	164,800	56,300	172,100
Depn & Amortn	175,100	182,900	171,500	179,100	151,100	82,300	103,700	84,800
Income Before Taxes	72,800	(108,500)	(16,400)	(64,100)	270,700	26,300	(119,200)	32,800
Income Taxes	13,600	(27,000)	(13,900)	(22,400)	(2,400)	5,000	(5,100)	10,700
Net Income	59,200	(81,500)	(2,500)	(41,700)	273,100	21,300	(114,100)	20,600
Average Shares	123,500	117,500	108,100	99,600	101,400	83,700	62,900	...
Balance Sheet								
Current Assets	1,032,400	984,000	1,020,300	874,800	876,400	459,000	406,400	209,500
Total Assets	2,376,500	2,258,500	2,288,100	2,149,200	1,837,500	1,137,600	1,095,700	635,700
Current Liabilities	286,600	247,700	206,900	199,300	292,200	206,700	198,700	144,500
Long-Term Obligations	845,200	848,600	852,800	1,138,100	705,200	717,200	1,045,900	526,700
Total Liabilities	1,147,400	1,110,800	1,072,900	1,341,200	999,800	924,400	1,246,000	671,800
Stockholders' Equity	1,229,100	1,147,700	1,215,200	808,000	837,700	213,200	(240,400)	(116,600)
Shares Outstanding	119,577	118,285	117,005	99,965	99,324	88,789	62,967	62,874
Statistical Record								
Return on Assets %	2.56	N.M.	N.M.	N.M.	18.06	1.53	N.M.	3.40
Return on Equity %	5.00	N.M.	N.M.	N.M.	51.13	28.04	...	...
EBITDA Margin %	18.80	10.07	17.12	14.46	26.91	20.96	7.66	21.81
Net Margin %	3.69	N.M.	N.M.	N.M.	15.32	2.71	N.M.	2.61
Asset Turnover	0.69	0.62	0.64	0.71	1.18	0.56	0.85	1.30
Current Ratio	3.60	3.97	4.93	4.39	3.00	2.22	2.05	1.45
Debt to Equity	0.69	0.74	0.70	1.41	0.84	3.36	...	...
Price Range	28.00-11.99	26.78-10.11	31.85-6.94	27.75-12.17	48.44-11.81	34.00-18.50	...	...
P/E Ratio	58.33-24.98	...	...	...	18.01-4.39	147.83-80.43	...	...

Address: 82 Running Hill Road, South Portland, ME 04106	Web Site: www.fairchildsemi.com	Auditors: KPMG LLP
Telephone: (207) 775-8100	Officers: Kirk P. Pond - Chmn., Pres., C.E.O. Joseph R. Martin - Vice Chmn., Exec. V.P.	Investor Contact: 207-775-8660
Fax: (207) 761-3415		

FAMILY DOLLAR STORES, INC.

Exchange	Symbol	Price	52Wk Range	Yield	P/E	Div Acheiver
NYS	FDO	$30.36 (3/31/2005)	35.95-25.60	1.25	20.38	28 Years

*7 Year Price Score 97.41   ***NYSE Composite Index=100**   ***12 Month Price Score 99.79**

Interim Earnings (Per Share)

Qtr.	Nov	Feb	May	Aug
2001-02	0.29	0.37	0.35	0.24
2002-03	0.33	0.42	0.40	0.28
2003-04	0.37	0.47	0.43	0.26
2004-05	0.33	...	...	...

Interim Dividends (Per Share)

Amt	Decl	Ex	Rec	Pay
0.085Q	5/14/2004	6/14/2004	6/15/2004	7/15/2004
0.085Q	8/17/2004	9/13/2004	9/15/2004	10/15/2004
0.085Q	11/2/2004	12/13/2004	12/15/2004	1/14/2005
0.095Q	1/20/2005	3/11/2005	3/15/2005	4/15/2005

Indicated Div: $0.38

Valuation Analysis

Forecast P/E	19.82	No of Institutions	
	(4/7/2005)	254	
Market Cap	$5.1 Billion	Shares	
Book Value	1.4 Billion	144,393,360	
Price/Book	3.62	% Held	
Price/Sales	0.94	86.10	

Business Summary: Retail - General (MIC: 5.2 SIC: 331 NAIC: 52990)

Family Dollar Stores is engaged in the operation of a chain of self-service retail discount stores. The stores offer a variety of hardlines and softlines merchandise. Hardlines merchandise includes primarily household chemicals and paper products, candy, snacks and other foods, health and beauty aids, electronics, housewares and giftware, pet food and supplies, toys, stationery and school supplies, seasonal goods, hardware and automotive supplies. Softlines merchandise includes men's, women's, boys', girls' and infants' clothing, shoes, and domestic items such as blankets, sheets and towels. As of Oct 1 2004, Co. operated 5,481 stores in 44 states and the District of Columbia.

Recent Developments: For the quarter ended Nov 27 2004, net income decreased 14.1% to $55,355,000 from net income of $64,452,000 in the year-earlier quarter. Revenues were $1,380,245,000, up 10.9% from $1,244,683,000 the year before. Total direct expense climbed 13.1% to $919,893,000 from $813,358,000 a year earlier. Total indirect expense was $373,724,000 versus $329,826,000 in the prior-year quarter, an increase of 13.3%.

Prospects: Co. is benefiting from higher sales in existing stores and in new stores opened as part of the store expansion project. Co. plans on opening between 500 and 560 stores and closing 60 to 70 stores in fiscal 2005. Under its urban initiative, Co. is investing in process changes, technology and people in stores in its major urban markets. Co. expects the initiative to improve operating performance, including higher sales and lower shrinkage, in over 1,000 stores in 30 large urban markets this year. Also, Co. is continuing with its initiative to install perishable food coolers in at least 500 stores this year. For fiscal 2005, Co. expects earnings to range from $1.53 to $1.55 per diluted share.

Financial Data
(US$ in Thousands)

	3 Mos	08/28/2004	08/30/2003	08/31/2002	09/01/2001	08/26/2000	08/28/1999	08/29/1998
Earnings Per Share	1.49	1.53	1.43	1.25	1.10	1.00	0.81	0.60
Cash Flow Per Share	2.00	2.21	1.72	2.34	0.95	1.07	0.64	1.24
Tang Book Value Per Share	8.40	8.13	7.61	6.66	5.57	4.66	4.00	3.36
Dividends Per Share	0.330	0.320	0.280	0.250	0.230	0.210	0.190	0.170
Dividend Payout %	22.09	20.92	19.58	20.00	20.91	21.00	23.46	28.33
Income Statement								
Total Revenue	1,380,245	5,281,888	4,750,171	4,162,652	3,665,362	3,132,639	2,751,181	2,361,930
EBITDA	111,844	512,098	478,040	418,636	366,107	325,421	266,468	200,831
Depn & Amortn	25,216	97,883	88,315	77,015	67,685	54,509	43,788	34,843
Income Before Taxes	86,628	414,215	389,725	341,621	298,422	270,911	222,679	165,988
Income Taxes	31,273	151,530	142,250	124,692	108,917	98,894	82,600	62,700
Net Income	55,355	262,685	247,475	216,929	189,505	172,017	140,079	103,288
Average Shares	168,008	171,624	173,354	174,049	172,774	172,648	172,511	173,223
Balance Sheet								
Current Assets	1,268,289	1,225,308	1,156,492	1,055,859	807,265	750,673	719,955	646,630
Total Assets	2,227,417	2,167,422	1,985,695	1,754,619	1,399,745	1,243,714	1,095,252	942,180
Current Liabilities	724,455	713,551	595,331	530,780	390,294	412,017	378,546	343,275
Total Liabilities	819,510	807,022	674,726	599,671	440,730	445,750	404,601	364,029
Stockholders' Equity	1,407,907	1,360,400	1,310,969	1,154,948	959,015	797,964	690,651	578,151
Shares Outstanding	167,687	167,396	172,208	173,329	172,035	171,131	172,750	172,203
Statistical Record								
Return on Assets %	11.93	12.72	13.27	13.79	14.11	14.75	13.79	12.06
Return on Equity %	18.31	19.78	20.13	20.58	21.22	23.17	22.14	19.26
EBITDA Margin %	8.10	9.70	10.06	10.06	9.99	10.39	9.69	8.50
Net Margin %	4.01	4.97	5.21	5.21	5.17	5.49	5.09	4.37
Asset Turnover	2.55	2.56	2.55	2.65	2.73	2.69	2.71	2.76
Current Ratio	1.75	1.72	1.94	1.99	2.07	1.82	1.90	1.88
Price Range	39.39-25.60	43.61-25.60	40.25-24.16	36.86-24.56	30.09-16.88	33.25-14.38	25.56-12.69	21.31-10.63
P/E Ratio	26.44-17.18	28.50-16.73	28.15-16.90	29.49-19.65	27.35-15.34	23.25-14.38	31.56-15.66	35.52-17.71
Average Yield %	1.05	0.92	0.87	0.80	0.96	1.13	0.92	1.07

Address: 10401 Old Monroe Road, Matthews, NC 28105	**Web Site:** www.familydollar.com	**Auditors:** PricewaterhouseCoopers LLP
Telephone: (704) 847-6961	**Officers:** Howard R. Levine - Chmn., C.E.O. R. James Kelly - Vice-Chmn., C.F.O., Admin. Officer	**Investor Contact:** 704-847-6961
Fax: (704) 847-5534		**Transfer Agents:** Mellon Investor Services LLC, Ridgefield Park, NJ

FANNIE MAE

Exchange	Symbol	Price	52Wk Range	Yield	P/E	Div Acheiver
NYS	FNM	$54.45 (3/31/2005)	77.54-53.96	1.91	6.90	19 Years

*7 Year Price Score 83.76   *NYSE Composite Index=100   *12 Month Price Score 80.81

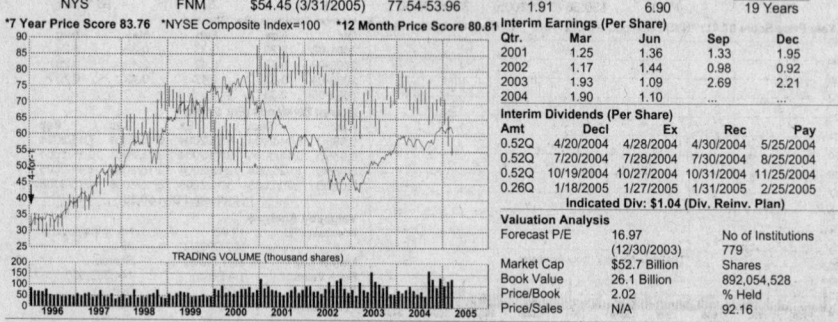

Interim Earnings (Per Share)

Qtr.	Mar	Jun	Sep	Dec
2001	1.25	1.36	1.33	1.95
2002	1.17	1.44	0.98	0.92
2003	1.93	1.09	2.69	2.21
2004	1.90	1.10	...	...

Interim Dividends (Per Share)

Amt	Decl	Ex	Rec	Pay
0.52Q	4/20/2004	4/28/2004	4/30/2004	5/25/2004
0.52Q	7/20/2004	7/28/2004	7/30/2004	8/25/2004
0.52Q	10/19/2004	10/27/2004	10/31/2004	11/25/2004
0.26Q	1/18/2005	1/27/2005	1/31/2005	2/25/2005
	Indicated Div: $1.04 (Div. Reinv. Plan)			

Valuation Analysis

Forecast P/E	16.97	No of Institutions	
	(12/30/2003)	779	
Market Cap	$52.7 Billion	Shares	
Book Value	26.1 Billion	892,054,528	
Price/Book	2.02	% Held	
Price/Sales	N/A	92.16	

Business Summary: Credit & Lending (MIC: 8.6 SIC: 111 NAIC: 22292)

Fannie Mae is a federally chartered, private, shareholder-owned co., and an investor in home mortgage loans in the U.S. Co. operates in the secondary mortgage market by purchasing mortgages and mortgage-related securities, including mortgage-related securities guaranteed by Co., from primary market institutions, such as commercial banks, savings and loan associations, mortgage cos., and other investors. Co. provides additional liquidity in the secondary mortgage market by issuing and guaranteeing mortgage-related securities. Co. provides liquidity in the secondary mortgage market through Co.'s two primary business segments: the Portfolio Investment business and the Credit Guaranty business.

Recent Developments: For the quarter ended June 30 2004, net income totaled $1.11 billion, up 0.9% compared with $1.10 billion in the corresponding prior-year quarter. Results for 2004 and 2003 included a $23.5 million gain and a $739.8 million loss, respectively, from the retirement of debt, and purchased options expenses of $1.98 billion and $1.88 billion. Net interest income fell 11.1% to $3.11 billion, while net interest margin dropped 26 basis points to 1.04%. Guaranty fee income climbed 3.9% to $656.7 million, driven by a 13.6% rise in average outstanding mortgage-backed security growth, partially offset by a 1.8 basis point decline in the effective guaranty fee rate on that business.

Prospects: On Sep 20 2004, the Office of Federal Housing Enterprise Oversight (OFHEO) delivered its report to Co. of its findings to date of the agency's special examination. The OFHEO report raises a number of questions and concerns about Co.'s accounting policies and practices with respect to Financial Accounting Standard (FAS) No. 91, Accounting for Nonrefundable Fees and Costs Associated with Originating or Acquiring Loans and Initial Direct Costs of Leases and FAS No. 133, Accounting for Derivative Instruments and Hedging Activities. Co. continues to believe that its current accounting policies and applications of the aforementioned are consistent with generally accepted accounting principles.

Financial Data
(US$ in Thousands)

	6 Mos	3 Mos	12/31/2003	12/31/2002	12/31/2001	12/31/2000	12/31/1999	12/31/1998
Earnings Per Share	7.89	7.88	7.91	4.53	5.72	4.29	3.72	3.23
Cash Flow Per Share	7.39	4.97	19.98	12.24	14.70	12.44	11.58	7.48
Tang Book Value Per Share	22.74	17.21	18.83	13.76	15.86	18.58	16.02	13.95
Dividends Per Share	1.940	1.810	1.680	1.320	1.200	1.120	1.080	0.960
Dividend Payout %	24.59	22.97	21.24	29.14	20.98	26.11	29.03	29.72
Income Statement								
Interest Income	24,399,000	12,344,000	50,920,000	50,853,000	49,170,000	42,781,000	35,495,000	29,995,000
Interest Expense	18,090,000	9,148,000	37,351,000	40,287,000	41,080,000	37,107,000	30,601,000	25,885,000
Net Interest Income	6,309,000	3,196,000	13,569,000	10,566,000	8,090,000	5,674,000	4,894,000	4,110,000
Provision for Losses	20,000	32,000	100,000	128,000	(115,000)	(120,000)	(120,000)	(50,000)
Non-Interest Income	1,226,000	739,000	2,848,000	2,048,000	1,633,000	1,307,000	1,473,000	1,504,000
Non-Interest Expense	770,000	410,000	3,631,000	5,764,000	1,354,000	905,000	800,000	708,000
Income Before Taxes	3,839,000	2,558,000	10,413,000	6,048,000	8,291,000	5,982,000	5,440,000	4,645,000
Income Taxes	827,000	659,000	2,693,000	1,429,000	2,224,000	1,566,000	1,519,000	1,201,000
Net Income	3,012,000	1,899,000	7,905,000	4,619,000	5,894,000	4,448,000	3,912,000	3,418,000
Average Shares	970,000	975,000	981,000	997,000	1,006,000	1,009,000	1,031,000	1,037,000
Balance Sheet								
Net Loans & Leases	239,673,000	237,788,000	240,582,000	186,055,000	705,167,000	607,399,000	522,780,000	415,223,000
Total Assets	989,341,000	995,268,000	1,001,009,569,000	887,515,000	799,791,000	675,072,000	575,167,000	485,014,000
Total Liabilities	963,220,000	974,463,000	987,196,000	871,227,000	781,673,000	654,234,000	557,538,000	469,561,000
Stockholders' Equity	26,121,000	20,805,000	22,373,000	16,288,000	18,118,000	20,838,000	17,629,000	15,453,000
Shares Outstanding	968,000	970,000	970,000	989,000	997,000	999,000	1,019,000	1,025,000
Statistical Record								
Return on Assets %	0.30	0.19	0.83	0.55	0.80	0.71	0.74	0.78
Return on Equity %	12.46	8.82	40.89	26.85	30.26	23.06	23.65	23.37
Net Interest Margin %	25.82	25.89	26.65	20.78	16.45	13.26	13.79	13.70
Efficiency Ratio %	2.87	3.13	6.75	10.90	2.67	2.05	2.16	2.25
Price Range	79.88-60.40	79.88-60.40	75.37-58.93	83.15-59.54	87.49-72.95	87.81-48.38	75.00-59.00	75.94-56.31
P/E Ratio	10.12-7.66	10.14-7.66	9.53-7.45	18.36-13.14	15.30-12.75	20.47-11.28	20.16-15.86	23.51-17.43
Average Yield %	2.73	2.54	2.45	1.78	1.50	1.78	1.60	1.51

Address: 3900 Wisconsin Avenue, NW, Washington, DC 20016-2892 **Telephone:** (202) 752-7000 **Fax:** (202) 752-4934	**Web Site:** www.fanniemae.com **Officers:** Stephen B. Ashley - Non-Exec. Chmn. Daniel H. Mudd - Vice-Chmn., Interim C.E.O., C.O.O.	**Auditors:** KPMG LLP **Investor Contact:** 202-752-7115 **Transfer Agents:** Equiserve Trust Company NA., Providence RI

FEDERAL REALTY INVESTMENT TRUST (MD)

Exchange	Symbol	Price	52Wk Range	Yield	P/E	Div Acheiver
NYS	FRT	$48.35 (3/31/2005)	52.55-34.73	4.18	34.29	37 Years

*7 Year Price Score 139.15 *NYSE Composite Index=100 *12 Month Price Score 101.84

Interim Earnings (Per Share)
Qtr.	Mar	Jun	Sep	Dec
2001	0.32	0.51	0.33	0.36
2002	(0.15)	0.74	0.31	(0.07)
2003	0.26	0.29	0.44	0.67
2004	0.28	0.45	0.30	0.37

Interim Dividends (Per Share)
Amt	Decl	Ex	Rec	Pay
0.49Q	6/10/2004	6/22/2004	6/24/2004	7/15/2004
0.505Q	9/7/2004	9/22/2004	9/24/2004	10/15/2004
0.505Q	12/14/2004	12/30/2004	1/3/2005	1/17/2005
0.505Q	3/3/2005	3/14/2005	3/16/2005	4/15/2005

Indicated Div: $2.02 (Div. Reinv. Plan)

Valuation Analysis
Forecast P/E	15.92	No of Institutions
	(4/7/2005)	169
Market Cap	$2.5 Billion	Shares
Book Value	790.5 Million	39,173,864
Price/Book	3.19	% Held
Price/Sales	6.39	74.69

Business Summary: Property, Real Estate & Development (MIC: 8.3 SIC: 798 NAIC: 25930)
Federal Realty Investment Trust specializes in the ownership, management, development and redevelopment of high quality retail and mixed-use properties. As of Dec 31 2003, Co. owned or had an interest in 62 community and neighborhood shopping centers comprising about 13.5 million square feet, primarily located in densely populated and affluent communities throughout the Northeast and Mid-Atlantic U.S. In addition, Co. owned 49 urban and retail mixed-use properties comprising over 2.7 million square feet and one apartment complex, primarily located in strategic metropolitan markets in the Northeast and Mid-Atlantic regions and California. As of Dec 31 2003, Co.'s properties were 93.1% leased.

Recent Developments: For the year ended Dec 31 2004, income from continuing operations decreased 3.2% to $68,974 thousand from income of $71,236 thousand a year earlier. Net income decreased 10.9% to $84,156 thousand from net income of $94,497 thousand a year earlier. Revenues were $394,274 thousand, up 11.8% from $352,567 thousand the year before. Rental income rose 9.9% to $371,856 thousand, while other property income jumped 68.2% to $17,503 thousand a year earlier. Operating income rose 4.4% to $156,491 thousand from $149,864 thousand in 2003.

Prospects: Co.'s leasing activity, effective identification and execution of redevelopment opportunities, and acquisition capacity for its own portfolio and its joint venture should support growth in 2005 and beyond. For 2005, Co. anticipates funds from operations in the range of $3.01 to $3.04 per diluted share, and expects net income ranging from $1.41 to $1.44 per diluted share. Meanwhile, Co. recently announced the acquisition of a 126,000 square foot supermarket-anchored shopping center in the Boston metropolitan area for $16.5 million. The property, Atlantic Plaza in North Reading, MA, was acquired for the Trust's joint venture with Clarion Lion Properties Fund. Atlantic Plaza is 100.0% leased.

Financial Data
(US$ in Thousands)

	12/31/2004	12/31/2003	12/31/2002	12/31/2001	12/31/2000	12/31/1999	12/31/1998	12/31/1997
Earnings Per Share	1.41	1.59	0.85	1.52	1.35	1.02	0.94	1.14
Cash Flow Per Share	3.15	2.58	2.86	2.77	2.73	2.58	2.31	1.88
Tang Book Value Per Share	12.57	11.31	9.40	8.92	9.31	10.00	10.73	11.59
Dividends Per Share	1.990	1.950	1.930	1.900	1.84	1.77	1.75	1.69
Dividend Payout %	141.13	122.64	227.06	125.00	136.30	173.53	186.17	148.25
Income Statement								
Property Income	389,359	352,497	313,678	293,912	271,749	257,064	232,533	198,234
Non-Property Income	4,915	5,379	5,156	6,590	7,532	7,649	5,945	6,037
Total Revenue	394,274	357,876	318,834	300,502	279,281	264,713	238,478	204,271
Depn & Amortn	90,438	74,616	64,529	59,914	53,259	50,011	46,047	41,399
Interest Expense	85,058	75,232	65,054	69,313	66,418	61,492	55,125	47,288
Net Income	84,156	94,497	55,287	68,756	60,523	48,443	44,960	46,504
Average Shares	51,547	48,619	42,882	40,266	39,910	40,638	40,080	38,988
Balance Sheet								
Total Assets	2,266,896	2,143,435	1,999,378	1,837,978	1,621,079	1,534,048	1,484,317	1,316,573
Long-Term Obligations	979,006	949,357	1,003,212	935,625	809,200	757,862	583,769	551,862
Total Liabilities	1,457,408	1,422,479	1,325,725	1,212,572	1,105,504	986,891	908,828	727,011
Stockholders' Equity	790,534	691,374	644,287	592,388	467,654	501,827	529,947	553,810
Shares Outstanding	52,136	49,200	43,535	40,071	39,469	40,201	40,080	39,148
Statistical Record								
Return on Assets %	3.81	4.56	2.88	3.98	3.83	3.21	3.21	3.95
Return on Equity %	11.33	14.15	8.94	12.97	12.45	9.39	8.30	9.87
Net Margin %	21.34	26.40	17.34	22.88	21.67	18.30	18.85	22.77
Price Range	52.55-34.73	39.80-26.75	28.75-22.93	23.71-18.98	22.31-17.88	24.50-16.63	25.88-19.56	28.63-24.63
P/E Ratio	37.27-24.63	25.03-16.82	33.82-26.98	15.60-12.49	16.53-13.24	24.02-16.30	27.53-20.81	25.11-21.60
Average Yield %	4.57	5.81	7.32	9.03	9.16	8.61	7.70	6.35

Address: 1626 East Jefferson Street, Rockville, MD 20852-4041 **Telephone:** (301) 998-8100 **Fax:** (301) 998-3700	**Web Site:** www.federalrealty.com **Officers:** Mark Ordan - Chmn. Donald C. Wood - Pres., C.E.O., C.O.O.	**Auditors:** Grant Thornton LLP **Transfer Agents:** American Stock Transfer & Trust Company, New York, NY

FEDERAL SIGNAL CORP.

Exchange	Symbol	Price	52Wk Range	Yield	P/E
NYS	FSS	$15.17 (3/31/2005)	20.43-14.56	1.58	N/A

*7 Year Price Score 74.68   *NYSE Composite Index=100   *12 Month Price Score 83.45

Interim Earnings (Per Share)

Qtr.	Mar	Jun	Sep	Dec
2001	0.26	0.37	0.20	0.22
2002	0.04	0.24	0.28	0.28
2003	0.14	0.20	0.21	0.24
2004	0.05	(0.14)	(0.08)	0.13

Interim Dividends (Per Share)

Amt	Decl	Ex	Rec	Pay
0.10Q	4/30/2004	6/14/2004	6/15/2004	7/5/2004
0.10Q	7/22/2004	9/13/2004	9/15/2004	10/4/2004
0.10Q	10/21/2004	12/13/2004	12/15/2004	1/4/2005
0.06Q	2/14/2005	3/11/2005	3/15/2005	4/4/2005

Indicated Div: $0.24 (Div. Reinv. Plan)

Valuation Analysis

Forecast P/E	21.50 (4/7/2005)	No of Institutions	142
Market Cap	$731.2 Million	Shares	36,993,972
Book Value	412.7 Million	% Held	76.85
Price/Book	1.77		
Price/Sales	0.64		

Business Summary: Automotive (MIC: 15.1 SIC: 711 NAIC: 36120)

Federal Signal is a worldwide manufacturer and supplier of street cleaning, vacuum loader and refuse collection vehicles; fire rescue vehicles; safety, signaling and communication equipment and tooling products. Co. operates manufacturing facilities in 52 plants around the world in 12 countries serving customers in North America, South America, Europe and Asia. Co. also provides customer and dealer financing to support the sale of its vehicles. Products manufactured and services rendered by Co. are divided into four major operating groups: Environmental Products, Fire Rescue, Safety Products and Tool.

Recent Developments: For the year ended Dec 31 2004, loss from continuing operations was $12,700,000 compared with an income of $35,100,000 a year earlier. Net loss was $2,300,000 versus net income of $37,300,000 a year earlier. Revenues were $11,390,000,00, down 1.0% from $1,150,700,000 the year before. Operating loss was $500,000 versus an income of $61,700,000 in the prior year. Total direct expense was $895,700,000 versus $849,800,000 in the prior year, an increase of 5.4%. Total indirect expense was $243,800,000 versus $239,200,000 in the prior year, an increase of 1.9%.

Prospects: Co.'s outlook is tempered by recent losses incurred by its Fire Rescue Group and refuse truck body operations. On the positive side, Co. has completed the closure of its Preble, NY fire rescue plant and has moved the build of stainless steel trucks into its Ocala, FL plant. Also, Co. expects to complete the consolidation of its refuse truck body production into a single plant by early 2005. Meanwhile, Co. has announced two divestitures that should further its efforts to sharpen its focus on, and grow its core businesses. On Dec 15 2004, Co. announced the sale of Justrite Manufacturing Company, L.L.C., and on Dec 3 2004, Co. announced the sale of Technical Tooling, Inc.

Financial Data
(US$ in Thousands)

	12/31/2004	12/31/2003	12/31/2002	12/31/2001	12/31/2000	12/31/1999	12/31/1998	12/31/1997
Earnings Per Share	(0.05)	0.78	0.83	1.05	1.26	1.25	1.30	1.29
Cash Flow Per Share	1.09	1.57	1.92	2.10	1.41	1.26	1.66	1.42
Tang Book Value Per Share	1.25	1.17	1.04	1.74	1.82	1.67	1.98	2.45
Dividends Per Share	0.400	0.700	0.800	0.780	0.760	0.740	0.710	0.670
Dividend Payout %	...	89.74	96.39	74.29	60.32	59.20	54.62	51.94
Income Statement								
Total Revenue	1,139,000	1,206,798	1,057,201	1,072,175	1,106,127	1,061,896	1,002,787	924,912
EBITDA	17,900	90,202	105,172	121,080	144,872	134,972	129,156	122,555
Depn & Amortn	22,400	24,435	23,995	30,258	29,057	27,237	23,586	20,545
Income Before Taxes	(25,300)	46,017	61,102	64,454	84,414	84,396	86,234	84,847
Income Taxes	(12,600)	8,345	14,923	17,864	26,759	26,859	26,838	25,878
Net Income	(2,300)	37,303	38,195	47,573	57,537	57,537	59,396	58,969
Average Shares	48,100	47,984	45,939	45,443	45,521	45,958	45,846	45,840
Balance Sheet								
Current Assets	418,400	403,552	394,817	342,325	348,936	346,137	311,207	268,622
Total Assets	1,125,900	1,186,409	1,168,410	1,015,614	991,118	960,961	835,999	727,905
Current Liabilities	229,700	284,370	221,884	179,430	288,920	269,463	195,193	227,029
Long-Term Obligations	394,100	395,477	481,566	446,595	316,932	307,020	288,812	177,523
Total Liabilities	713,200	763,359	769,601	655,305	633,687	606,928	514,217	428,133
Stockholders' Equity	412,700	422,509	398,065	359,436	357,431	354,033	321,782	299,772
Shares Outstanding	48,200	47,918	47,660	45,129	45,304	46,114	45,329	45,606
Statistical Record								
Return on Assets %	N.M.	3.17	3.50	4.74	5.88	6.40	7.60	8.24
Return on Equity %	N.M.	9.09	10.08	13.27	16.13	17.03	19.11	20.60
EBITDA Margin %	1.57	7.47	9.95	11.29	13.10	12.71	12.88	13.25
Net Margin %	N.M.	3.09	3.61	4.44	5.20	5.42	5.92	6.38
Asset Turnover	0.98	1.02	0.97	1.07	1.13	1.18	1.28	1.29
Current Ratio	1.82	1.42	1.78	1.91	1.21	1.18	1.28	1.29
Debt to Equity	0.95	0.94	1.21	1.24	0.89	0.87	0.90	0.59
Price Range	20.43-15.96	20.70-13.67	26.75-16.16	24.50-17.25	23.88-14.88	27.38-15.13	27.38-20.25	27.25-20.19
P/E Ratio	...	26.54-17.53	32.23-19.47	23.33-16.43	18.95-11.81	21.90-12.10	21.06-15.58	21.12-15.65
Average Yield %	2.20	4.14	3.69	3.64	3.95	3.46	3.10	2.69

Address: 1415 West 22nd Street, Oak Brook, IL 60523-2004	Web Site: www.federalsignal.com	Auditors: Ernst & Young LLP
Telephone: (630) 954-2000	Officers: Robert D. Welding - Pres., C.E.O. Stephanie K. Kushner - V.P., C.F.O.	Investor Contact: 630-954-2000
Fax: (630) 954-2030		Transfer Agents: National City Bank, Cleveland, OH

FEDERATED DEPARTMENT STORES, INC. (DE)

Exchange	Symbol	Price	52Wk Range	Yield	P/E
NYS	FD	$63.64 (3/31/2005)	64.45-43.11	0.85	16.62

*7 Year Price Score 105.97 *NYSE Composite Index=100 *12 Month Price Score 108.13

TRADING VOLUME (thousand shares)

Interim Earnings (Per Share)

Qtr.	Apr	Jul	Oct	Jan
2001-02	0.29	0.55	0.02	(2.24)
2002-03	0.43	1.39	0.54	1.75
2003-04	0.24	0.64	0.36	2.46
2004-05	0.52	0.43	0.42	...

Interim Dividends (Per Share)

Amt	Decl	Ex	Rec	Pay
0.135Q	5/21/2004	6/14/2004	6/15/2004	7/1/2004
0.135Q	8/27/2004	9/13/2004	9/15/2004	10/1/2004
0.135Q	10/21/2004	12/13/2004	12/15/2004	1/3/2005
0.135Q	2/25/2005	3/11/2005	3/15/2005	4/1/2005

Indicated Div: $0.54

Valuation Analysis

Forecast P/E	N/A	No of Institutions
Market Cap	$10.8 Billion	Shares
Book Value	5.5 Billion	160,406,080
Price/Book	1.94	% Held
Price/Sales	0.69	94.80

Business Summary: Retail - General (MIC: 5.2 SIC: 311 NAIC: 52111)

Federated Department Stores, as of Jan 31 2004, operated more than 393 department stores and 66 furniture galleries and other specialty stores. The stores are located in 34 states, Puerto Rico and Guam under the names of Macy's, Bloomingdale's, Bon-Macy's, Lazarus-Macy's, Goldsmith's-Macy's, Rich's-Macy's and Burdines-Macy's. Co.'s stores sell men's, women's and children's apparel and accessories, cosmetics, home furnishings, and other consumer goods, and are diversified by size of store, merchandising character, and character of community served. Co. also operates direct-to-customer catalog and e-commerce subsidiaries under the names of Bloomingdale's By Mail and macys.com.

Recent Developments: For the quarter ended Oct 30 2004, net income increased 10.4% to $74,000 thousand from net income of $67,000 thousand in the year-earlier quarter. Revenues were $3,491,000 thousand, up 0.1% from $3,486,000 thousand the year before. Operating income was $175,000 thousand versus an income of $173,000 thousand in the prior-year quarter, an increase of 1.2%. Total indirect expense was $1,216,000 thousand versus $1,222,000 thousand in the prior-year quarter, a decrease of 0.5%.

Prospects: On Feb 28 2005, Co. announced that it has entered in an agreement to acquire The May Department Stores Company for total equity value of approximately $11.00 billion. Pursuant to the transaction, each share of May will be converted into the right to receive $17.75 per share of cash and 0.3115 shares of Co.'s stock. In addition, Co. will assume May debt that was approximately $6.00 billion at year-end, for a total consideration of approximately $17.00 billion. Upon completion, Co. will operate more than 950 department stores, along with approximately 700 bridal and formalwear stores. Co. expects the transaction to be completed in the third quarter of 2005.

Financial Data
(US$ in Thousands)

	9 Mos	6 Mos	3 Mos	01/31/2004	02/01/2003	02/02/2002	02/03/2001	01/29/2000
Earnings Per Share	3.83	3.78	3.98	3.71	4.12	(1.38)	(0.90)	3.62
Cash Flow Per Share	7.79	7.65	7.91	8.65	5.94	7.05	6.17	6.02
Tang Book Value Per Share	29.01	30.15	30.07	29.69	26.93	24.31	24.93	19.89
Dividends Per Share	0.520	0.510	0.500	0.375	...	...	...	...
Dividend Payout %	13.56	13.50	12.55	10.11	...	...	...	...
Income Statement								
Total Revenue	10,556,000	7,065,000	3,517,000	15,264,000	15,435,000	15,651,000	18,407,000	17,716,000
EBITDA	1,175,000	821,000	394,000	2,054,000	2,028,000	1,800,000	1,290,000	2,446,000
Depn & Amortn	538,000	359,000	178,000	713,000	685,000	696,000	740,000	745,000
Income Before Taxes	403,000	283,000	156,000	1,084,000	1,048,000	780,000	113,000	1,346,000
Income Taxes	154,000	108,000	60,000	391,000	410,000	262,000	297,000	551,000
Net Income	249,000	175,000	96,000	693,000	818,000	(276,000)	(184,000)	795,000
Average Shares	174,400	182,000	180,500	186,600	198,700	199,600	204,800	219,600
Balance Sheet								
Current Assets	7,735,000	7,134,000	7,632,000	7,452,000	7,154,000	7,280,000	8,700,000	8,522,000
Total Assets	14,624,000	14,065,000	14,623,000	14,550,000	14,441,000	15,044,000	17,012,000	17,692,000
Current Liabilities	4,376,000	3,555,000	3,822,000	3,883,000	3,601,000	3,714,000	4,869,000	4,552,000
Long-Term Obligations	3,038,000	3,040,000	3,149,000	3,151,000	3,408,000	3,859,000	4,374,000	4,589,000
Total Liabilities	9,076,000	8,219,000	8,577,000	8,610,000	8,679,000	9,480,000	11,190,000	11,140,000
Stockholders' Equity	5,548,000	5,846,000	6,046,000	5,940,000	5,762,000	5,564,000	5,822,000	6,552,000
Shares Outstanding	169,205	172,697	179,806	178,500	190,200	200,800	197,600	242,200
Statistical Record								
Return on Assets %	4.83	4.99	5.12	4.79	5.56	N.M.	N.M.	5.12
Return on Equity %	12.77	12.16	12.69	11.88	14.48	N.M.	N.M.	13.00
EBITDA Margin %	11.13	11.62	11.20	13.46	13.14	11.50	7.01	13.81
Net Margin %	2.36	2.48	2.73	4.54	5.30	N.M.	N.M.	4.49
Asset Turnover	1.07	1.11	1.07	1.06	1.05	0.98	1.04	1.14
Current Ratio	1.77	2.01	2.00	1.92	1.99	1.96	1.79	1.87
Debt to Equity	0.55	0.52	0.52	0.53	0.59	0.69	0.75	0.70
Price Range	55.05-43.11	55.05-38.55	55.05-30.07	50.17-23.91	44.00-25.64	49.26-26.60	45.50-23.50	56.88-36.56
P/E Ratio	14.37-11.26	14.56-10.20	13.83-7.56	13.52-6.44	10.68-6.22	...	...	15.71-10.10
Average Yield %	1.08	1.07	1.13	0.97	...	...	...	...

Address: 151 West 34th Street, New York, NY 10001	**Web Site:** www.federated-fds.com	**Auditors:** KPMG LLP
Telephone: (212) 494-1602	**Officers:** Terry J. Lundgren - Chmn., Pres., C.E.O. Thomas G. Cody - Vice-Chmn., Legal, H.R., Internal Audit & External Affairs	**Investor Contact:** 513-579-7780
Fax: (212) 494-1838		**Transfer Agents:** Bank of New York, New York, NY

FEDERATED INVESTORS INC (PA)

Exchange	Symbol	Price	52Wk Range	Yield	P/E
NYS	FII	$28.31 (3/31/2005)	32.14-26.88	1.77	17.26

*7 Year Price Score N/A *NYSE Composite Index=100 *12 Month Price Score 91.69

Interim Earnings (Per Share)

Qtr.	Mar	Jun	Sep	Dec
2001	0.35	0.36	0.36	0.34
2002	0.44	0.45	0.43	0.42
2003	0.43	0.44	0.46	0.39
2004	0.46	0.46	0.43	0.29

Interim Dividends (Per Share)

Amt	Decl	Ex	Rec	Pay
0.102Q	4/19/2004	5/5/2004	5/7/2004	5/14/2004
0.102Q	8/4/2004	8/4/2004	8/6/2004	8/13/2004
0.125Q	10/28/2004	11/4/2004	11/8/2004	11/15/2004
0.125Q	2/3/2005	2/16/2005	2/18/2005	2/28/2005

Indicated Div: $0.50

Valuation Analysis

Forecast P/E	15.29 (4/7/2005)	No of Institutions	212
Market Cap	$3.0 Billion	Shares	61,164,104
Book Value	457.8 Million	% Held	57.22
Price/Book	6.62		
Price/Sales	3.58		

Business Summary: Wealth Management (MIC: 8.8 SIC: 282 NAIC: 23930)

Federated Investors and its subsidiaries provide of investment management and related financial services. Co. sponsors, markets and provides investment-related services to various investment products, including mutual funds and separately managed accounts. As of Dec 31 2003, Co. had $197.90 billion assets under management in 136 mutual funds and various separate accounts. These funds are offered through 5,900 institutions and intermediaries, including corporations, government entities, insurance companies, foundations, and endowments. Co. also provides mutual fund administrative services to its managed funds and to funds sponsored by third parties, where Co. acts as fund distributor.

Recent Developments: For the year ended Dec 31 2004, income from continuing operations decreased 4.8% to $179,058 thousand from income of $188,061 thousand a year earlier. Net income decreased 5.4% to $181,179 thousand from net income of $191,485 thousand a year earlier. Revenues were $846,964 thousand, up 6.4% from $795,773 thousand the year before.

Prospects: Given the challenging interest-rate environment, Co. continues to focus on growing its customer base for cash management. In addition, Co. is pursuing growth initiatives in a number of other areas, including acquisitions, the accelerated growth of equity assets in its managed account business and the continued investment in equity management employees. Separately, in the fourth quarter of 2004, Co. agreed to purchase the cash management business of Alliance Capital Management Holding LP. In connection with the transaction, up to $25.00 billion in assets from money market funds will be transferred to Co. in 2005.

Financial Data

(US$ in Thousands)	12/31/2004	12/31/2003	12/31/2002	12/31/2001	12/31/2000	12/31/1999	12/31/1998	12/31/1997
Earnings Per Share	1.64	1.71	1.74	1.40	1.27	0.96	0.71	0.40
Cash Flow Per Share	2.75	2.31	1.98	2.44	1.44	1.06	0.49	0.12
Tang Book Value Per Share	1.36	1.56	0.94	0.22	0.86	0.62	0.28	...
Dividends Per Share	0.414	0.297	0.217	0.175	0.139	0.109	0.049	...
Dividend Payout %	25.24	17.37	12.47	12.50	10.92	11.39	6.92	...
Income Statement								
Total Revenue	846,964	823,248	711,069	715,777	680,768	601,098	522,127	403,719
Income Before Taxes	289,264	299,600	315,714	269,603	242,522	194,881	145,934	81,983
Income Taxes	110,206	108,115	111,954	96,887	87,162	70,861	53,565	30,957
Net Income	181,179	191,485	203,760	168,447	155,360	124,020	92,369	50,577
Average Shares	110,410	112,059	117,304	119,992	122,295	129,085	125,496	125,496
Balance Sheet								
Total Assets	954,688	879,228	530,007	431,553	704,750	673,193	580,020	337,156
Total Liabilities	496,349	482,815	188,710	194,093	556,344	553,785	490,643	377,800
Stockholders' Equity	457,753	395,853	340,717	237,097	147,868	118,812	88,706	(41,110)
Shares Outstanding	107,008	108,664	112,560	115,369	117,129	122,571	129,297	125,149
Statistical Record								
Return on Assets %	19.70	27.18	42.38	29.65	22.49	19.79	20.14	17.31
Return on Equity %	42.33	51.99	70.53	87.51	116.20	119.53	388.14	...
Price Range	33.59-26.88	31.68-24.20	35.16-23.62	32.41-24.06	31.19-12.63	13.50-10.38	13.21-7.38	...
P/E Ratio	20.48-16.39	18.53-14.15	20.21-13.57	23.15-17.19	24.56-9.94	14.06-10.81	18.60-10.39	...
Average Yield %	1.38	1.08	0.72	0.60	0.64	0.92	0.44	...

Address: Federated Investors Tower, Pittsburgh, PA 15222-3779 **Telephone:** (412) 288-1900 **Fax:** (412) 288-2919	**Web Site:** www.federatedinvestors.com **Officers:** John F. Donahue - Chmn. John W. McGonigle - Vice-Chmn., Exec. V.P., Chief Legal Officer, Sec.	**Auditors:** Ernst & Young LLP **Investor Contact:** 412-288-1054

FEDEX CORP

Exchange	Symbol	Price	52Wk Range	Yield	P/E
NYS	FDX	$93.95 (3/31/2005)	101.55-70.55	0.30	20.34

*7 Year Price Score 140.14 *NYSE Composite Index=100 *12 Month Price Score 104.44

Interim Earnings (Per Share)

Qtr.	Aug	Nov	Feb	May
2001-02	0.36	0.81	0.39	0.78
2002-03	0.53	0.81	0.49	0.89
2003-04	0.42	0.30	0.68	1.36
2004-05	1.08	1.15	1.03	...

Interim Dividends (Per Share)

Amt	Decl	Ex	Rec	Pay
0.07Q	5/28/2004	6/8/2004	6/10/2004	7/1/2004
0.07Q	8/20/2004	9/8/2004	9/10/2004	10/1/2004
0.07Q	11/22/2004	12/9/2004	12/13/2004	1/3/2005
0.07Q	2/18/2005	3/9/2005	3/11/2005	4/1/2005

Indicated Div: $0.28

Valuation Analysis

Forecast P/E	16.67	No of Institutions
	(4/14/2005)	574
Market Cap	$28.4 Billion	Shares
Book Value	9.1 Billion	221,425,680
Price/Book	3.11	% Held
Price/Sales	0.99	73.49

Business Summary: Aviation (MIC: 1.1 SIC: 512 NAIC: 81112)

FedEx is a global provider of transportation, e-commerce and business services. Co.'s principal operating subsidiaries are FedEx Express, an express transportation company; FedEx Ground Package System, a provider of small-package ground delivery service; FedEx Freight, a provider of regional less-than-truckload freight services; FedEx Custom Critical, a provider of time-specific, critical shipments in North America; FedEx Trade Networks, a provider of international trade services, including customs brokerage and global cargo distribution; and FedEx Kinko's, a provider of document solutions and business services through a network of more than 1,200 locations as of May 31 2004.

Recent Developments: For the quarter ended Feb 28 2005, net income jumped 53.1% to $317.0 million compared with $207.0 million in the year-earlier quarter. Total revenue advanced 21.1% to $7.34 billion from $6.06 billion a year earlier. Total average daily package volume at FedEx Express and FedEx Ground combined grew more than 10.0% year over year, led by double-digit growth in ground and FedEx International Priority® shipments. FedEx Freight average daily less-than-truckload shipment volume increased 9.0% from a year ago. FedEx Express, FedEx Ground and FedEx Freight each reported solid yield improvement. Operating income surged 40.3% to $552.0 million versus $372.0 million a year earlier.

Prospects: Co. is optimistic regarding its outlook, citing solid business momentum and strong customer demand. Co. noted that total average daily package volume at FedEx Express and FedEx Ground combined grew more than 10.0% year over year for the third quarter ended Feb 28 2005, led by double-digit growth in ground and FedEx International Priority® shipments. FedEx Freight average daily less-than-truckload shipment volume rose 9.0%. Also, during the third quarter, operating income benefited from the timing of adjustments to Co.'s indexed fuel surcharges. However, Co. cautioned that should the recent trend of fuel cost increases continue, fourth quarter margins could be negatively affected.

Financial Data (US$ in Thousands)	9 Mos	6 Mos	3 Mos	05/31/2004	05/31/2003	05/31/2002	05/31/2001	05/31/2000
Earnings Per Share	4.62	4.26	3.42	2.76	2.74	2.34	1.99	2.32
Cash Flow Per Share	10.75	9.95	10.59	10.07	6.28	7.48	7.08	5.56
Tang Book Value Per Share	20.81	19.81	18.59	17.45	20.85	18.38	16.20	14.35
Dividends Per Share	0.270	0.260	0.240	0.220	0.200	...	...	...
Dividend Payout %	5.84	6.10	7.02	7.97	7.30	...	...	...
Income Statement								
Total Revenue	21,648,000	14,309,000	6,975,000	24,710,000	22,487,000	20,607,000	19,629,040	18,256,945
EBITDA	2,804,000	1,888,000	933,000	2,810,000	2,807,000	2,663,000	2,347,300	2,398,663
Depn & Amortn	1,091,000	723,000	360,000	1,375,000	1,351,000	1,364,000	1,275,774	1,154,863
Income Before Taxes	1,602,000	1,088,000	534,000	1,319,000	1,338,000	1,160,000	927,573	1,137,740
Income Taxes	601,000	404,000	204,000	481,000	508,000	435,000	343,202	449,404
Net Income	1,001,000	684,000	330,000	838,000	830,000	710,000	584,371	688,336
Average Shares	308,000	307,000	305,000	304,000	303,000	303,000	293,179	296,326
Balance Sheet								
Total Assets	20,375,000	20,037,000	19,379,000	19,134,000	15,385,000	13,812,000	13,340,012	11,527,111
Long-Term Obligations	2,441,000	2,740,000	2,744,000	2,837,000	1,709,000	1,800,000	1,900,119	1,776,253
Total Liabilities	11,253,000	11,241,000	10,990,000	11,098,000	8,097,000	7,267,000	7,439,592	6,741,868
Stockholders' Equity	9,122,000	8,796,000	8,389,000	8,036,000	7,288,000	6,545,000	5,900,420	4,785,243
Shares Outstanding	302,074	301,000	300,571	299,995	298,593	298,191	297,328	298,573
Statistical Record								
Return on Assets %	7.30	7.18	5.96	4.84	5.69	5.23	4.70	6.19
Return on Equity %	16.90	16.05	13.22	10.91	12.00	11.41	10.94	14.53
EBITDA Margin %	12.95	13.19	13.38	11.37	12.48	12.92	11.96	13.14
Net Margin %	4.62	4.78	4.73	3.39	3.69	3.45	2.98	3.77
Asset Turnover	1.48	1.51	1.49	1.43	1.54	1.52	1.58	1.64
Price Range	100.53-66.20	95.71-64.92	82.81-63.79	77.16-59.70	63.98-42.80	61.22-34.45	49.85-33.94	56.88-31.06
P/E Ratio	21.76-14.33	22.47-15.24	24.21-18.65	27.96-21.63	23.35-15.62	26.16-14.72	25.05-17.05	24.52-13.39
Average Yield %	0.32	0.34	0.32	0.32	0.38	...	...	...

Address: 942 South Shady Grove Road, Memphis, TN 38120 Telephone: (901) 818-7500 Fax: (901) 346-1013	Web Site: www.fedex.com Officers: Fredrick W. Smith - Chmn., Pres., C.E.O. Alan B. Graf Jr. - Exec. V.P., C.F.O.	Auditors: ERNST & YOUNG LLP Investor Contact: 901-818-7200

FERRO CORP.

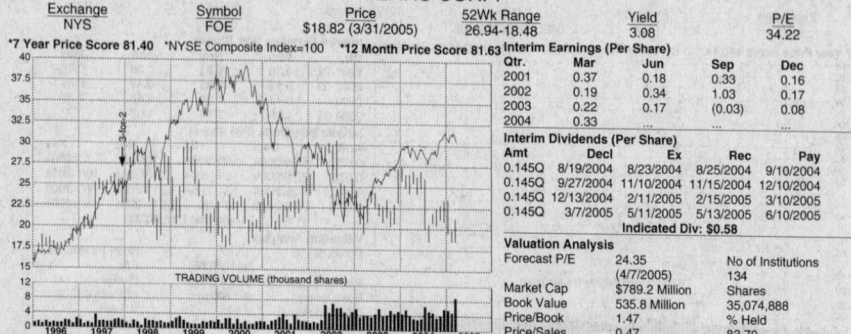

Exchange	Symbol	Price	52Wk Range	Yield	P/E
NYS	FOE	$18.82 (3/31/2005)	26.94-18.48	3.08	34.22

*7 Year Price Score 81.40   *NYSE Composite Index=100   *12 Month Price Score 81.63

Interim Earnings (Per Share)

Qtr.	Mar	Jun	Sep	Dec
2001	0.37	0.18	0.33	0.16
2002	0.19	0.34	1.03	0.17
2003	0.22	0.17	(0.03)	0.08
2004	0.33	...	...	...

Interim Dividends (Per Share)

Amt	Decl	Ex	Rec	Pay
0.145Q	8/19/2004	8/23/2004	8/25/2004	9/10/2004
0.145Q	9/27/2004	11/10/2004	11/15/2004	12/10/2004
0.145Q	12/13/2004	2/11/2005	2/15/2005	3/10/2005
0.145Q	3/7/2005	5/11/2005	5/13/2005	6/10/2005

Indicated Div: $0.58

Valuation Analysis

Forecast P/E	24.35	No of Institutions	
	(4/7/2005)	134	
Market Cap	$789.2 Million	Shares	35,074,888
Book Value	535.8 Million	% Held	
Price/Book	1.47	83.70	
Price/Sales	0.47		

Business Summary: Chemicals (MIC: 11.1 SIC: 851 NAIC: 25510)

Ferro is a global producer of an array of performance materials sold to a broad range of manufacturers in approximately 30 markets throughout the world. Co. operates in two segments: Coatings and Performance Chemicals. Coatings products include ceramics and color, industrial coatings and electronic materials. Performance Chemicals consists of polymer additives, performance and fine chemicals, plastic compounds and plastic colorants. Co.'s products are used in the markets of building and renovation, major appliances, automotive, household furnishings, transportation, industrial products, telecommunications, and pharmaceuticals.

Recent Developments: For the three months ended Mar 31 2004, net income jumped 52.2% to $14.4 million compared with income from continuing operations of $9.5 million in the corresponding quarter of 2003. Results for 2004 and 2003 included net foreign currency losses of $1.7 million and $1.2 million, respectively. Results for 2003 excluded gains of $69.0 million from discontinued operations. Total net sales were $451.7 million, up 12.4% from $401.8 million in the prior-year period. Sales benefited from improved macro economic conditions in North America, stronger demand in most key end markets, favorable foreign currency exchange rates and increased product prices.

Prospects: Co. stated that the investigative procedures undertaken in Jul 2004, the follow-up of additional procedures requested by KPMG, and the analysis of potential restatements of previously-issued financial statements, have delayed Co.'s issuance of financial statements for the second and third quarters of 2004. Meanwhile, Co. expects that the slowdown in demand from the electronics market will be temporary with demand improving in the second quarter of 2005. On a cautionary note, Co. noted that raw material cost increases continue to be an issue although it has seen some recent moderation. Co. stated that it has also taken a more aggressive approach to raising prices to offset these cost issues.

Financial Data
(US$ in Thousands)

	3 Mos	12/31/2003	12/31/2002	12/31/2001	12/31/2000	12/31/1999	12/31/1998	12/31/1997
Earnings Per Share	0.55	0.43	1.79	1.04	1.92	1.85	1.67	(1.08)
Cash Flow Per Share	2.03	2.10	4.41	6.41	3.30	3.61	2.20	3.42
Tang Book Value Per Share	2.72	0.82	N.M.	N.M.	1.24	3.78	4.59	3.97
Dividends Per Share	0.580	0.580	0.580	0.580	0.580	0.550	0.495	0.430
Dividend Payout %	105.81	134.88	32.40	55.77	30.21	29.73	29.64	...
Income Statement								
Total Revenue	451,740	1,622,370	1,528,454	1,501,059	1,447,284	1,355,283	1,361,844	1,381,280
EBITDA	28,059	129,383	151,291	160,549	190,363	181,404	165,951	6,382
Depn & Amortn	...	70,385	61,900	63,700	50,343	48,501	43,122	44,975
Income Before Taxes	19,253	24,243	48,580	61,466	116,615	116,114	110,481	(48,470)
Income Taxes	4,862	6,863	14,833	22,269	43,476	43,099	41,199	(11,193)
Net Income	14,391	19,551	73,723	39,197	73,139	73,015	69,282	(37,277)
Average Shares	43,747	41,090	41,008	37,118	37,663	38,807	40,479	38,132
Balance Sheet								
Current Assets	621,392	582,043	485,585	600,580	443,228	490,529	456,893	427,030
Total Assets	1,771,473	1,751,226	1,604,473	1,732,559	1,127,005	971,750	849,165	785,679
Current Liabilities	424,114	413,095	404,167	405,226	365,095	337,633	282,556	277,707
Long-Term Obligations	507,895	516,236	443,552	829,740	350,781	236,794	156,283	102,020
Total Liabilities	1,235,632	1,225,305	1,131,977	1,432,173	817,847	674,755	565,904	512,528
Stockholders' Equity	535,841	525,921	472,496	300,386	309,158	296,995	283,261	273,151
Shares Outstanding	41,932	41,457	40,516	34,336	-34,164	35,169	35,327	37,323
Statistical Record								
Return on Assets %	1.44	1.17	4.42	2.74	6.95	8.02	8.48	N.M.
Return on Equity %	4.78	3.92	19.08	12.86	24.07	25.17	24.90	N.M.
EBITDA Margin %	6.21	7.97	9.90	10.70	13.15	13.38	12.19	0.46
Net Margin %	3.19	1.21	4.82	2.61	5.05	5.39	5.09	N.M.
Asset Turnover	0.98	0.97	0.92	1.05	1.38	1.49	1.67	1.67
Current Ratio	1.47	1.41	1.20	1.48	1.21	1.45	1.62	1.54
Debt to Equity	0.95	0.98	0.94	2.76	1.13	0.80	0.55	0.37
Price Range	27.44-20.25	27.21-19.32	30.55-21.47	26.11-19.79	23.88-17.63	30.00-19.31	29.88-18.38	26.29-18.75
P/E Ratio	49.89-36.82	63.28-44.93	17.07-11.99	25.11-19.03	12.43-9.18	16.22-10.44	17.89-11.00	...
Average Yield %	2.47	2.58	2.18	2.58	2.77	2.28	1.95	1.85

Address: 1000 Lakeside Ave., Cleveland, OH 44114
Telephone: (216) 641-8580
Fax: (216) 696-6930

Web Site: www.ferro.com
Officers: Hector R. Ortino - Chmn., C.E.O. James C. Bays - V.P., Gen. Couns.

Auditors: KPMG LLP
Investor Contact: 216-875-7155
Transfer Agents: National City Bank, Cleveland, OH

FIDELITY NATIONAL FINANCIAL, INC.

Exchange	Symbol	Price	52Wk Range	Yield	P/E	Div Acheiver
NYS	FNF	$32.94 (3/31/2005)	46.77-32.00	3.04	7.82	17 Years

*7 Year Price Score 158.57 *NYSE Composite Index=100 *12 Month Price Score 99.40

Interim Earnings (Per Share)

Qtr.	Mar	Jun	Sep	Dec
2001	0.34	0.63	0.63	0.69
2002	0.75	0.82	1.05	1.29
2003	1.05	1.62	1.81	1.13
2004	0.88	1.26	1.09	0.98

Interim Dividends (Per Share)

Amt	Decl	Ex	Rec	Pay
0.18Q	7/21/2004	8/16/2004	8/18/2004	9/1/2004
0.25Q	9/7/2004	11/15/2004	11/17/2004	12/1/2004
0.25Q	1/26/2005	3/8/2005	3/10/2005	3/24/2005
10.00Q	3/9/2005	3/29/2005	3/21/2005	3/28/2005
		Indicated Div: $1.00		

Valuation Analysis

Forecast P/E	12.45	No of Institutions
	(4/7/2005)	319
Market Cap	$5.7 Billion	Shares
Book Value	4.7 Billion	105,648,304
Price/Book	1.21	% Held
Price/Sales	0.69	60.56

Business Summary: Insurance (MIC: 8.2 SIC: 361 NAIC: 24127)

Fidelity National Financial, through its principal subsidiaries, is a major U.S. title insurance and diversified real estate-related services company. As of Dec 31 2003, Co. provided title insurance in 49 states, the District of Columbia, Guam, Puerto Rico, the U.S. Virgin Islands and in Canada and Mexico. Co. also provides information-based technology applications and processing services to financial institutions and the mortgage and financial services industries. Co.'s reporting segments include title and escrow, financial institution software and services, lender outsourcing solutions, information services, specialty insurance, and corporate and other.

Recent Developments: For the year ended Dec 31 2004, net income decreased 14.0% to $740,962 thousand from net income of $861,820 thousand a year earlier. Revenues were $8,296,002 thousand, up 7.5% from $7,715,215 thousand the year before. Net premiums earned were $4,978,584 thousand versus $4,873,482 thousand in the prior year, an increase of 2.2%. Total expenses jumped 12.9% to $7,111,911 thousand from $6,294,576 thousand in 2003.

Prospects: Near-term prospects appear moderately favorable, as Co. noted that order volumes remain strong by historical standards. However, open orders slowed significantly during the 2004 holiday season, which will likely impact closing volumes in the first quarter of 2005. Meanwhile, Co. is optimistic about both the strength of the mortgage markets and the level of mortgage interest rates. Separately, Co.'s subsidiary, Fidelity National Information Services, Inc. entered into a definitive stock purchase agreement to sell an approximately 25.0% minority in common stock to an investment group led by Thomas H. Lee Partners, L.P. and Texas Pacific Group for a total purchase price of about $500.0 million.

Financial Data
(US$ in Thousands)

	12/31/2004	12/31/2003	12/31/2002	12/31/2001	12/31/2000	12/31/1999	12/31/1998	12/31/1997
Earnings Per Share	4.21	5.63	3.91	2.29	1.07	1.36	1.94	1.09
Cash Flow Per Share	6.83	8.65	6.21	3.31	1.64	1.01	1.54	2.50
Tang Book Value Per Share	4.57	6.84	9.55	12.65	10.53	9.56	8.25	5.95
Dividends Per Share	0.790	0.633	0.292	0.246	0.240	0.228	0.153	0.139
Dividend Payout %	18.76	11.24	7.47	10.74	22.45	16.74	7.88	12.73
Income Statement								
Premium Income	4,978,584	4,873,482	3,547,729	2,694,479	1,946,159	939,452	910,278	533,220
Total Revenue	8,296,002	7,715,215	5,082,640	3,874,107	2,741,994	1,352,204	1,288,465	746,712
Income Before Taxes	1,184,091	1,420,639	851,300	518,641	194,140	...	...	...
Income Taxes	438,114	539,843	306,468	207,456	85,825	46,975	69,442	31,959
Net Income	740,962	861,820	531,717	305,476	108,315	70,853	105,692	39,771
Average Shares	176,000	153,171	135,870	133,189	101,382	52,135	55,692	39,316
Balance Sheet								
Total Assets	9,270,535	7,295,339	5,245,744	4,415,998	3,833,985	1,029,173	969,470	600,559
Total Liabilities	4,551,570	3,407,145	2,860,011	2,729,962	2,721,656	592,066	571,198	400,626
Stockholders' Equity	4,700,091	3,873,359	2,253,936	1,638,870	1,106,737	432,494	396,740	196,319
Shares Outstanding	172,555	164,840	131,594	129,592	105,117	45,234	48,074	32,967
Statistical Record								
Return on Assets %	8.92	13.74	11.01	7.41	4.44	7.09	13.46	7.17
Return on Equity %	17.24	28.13	27.32	22.25	14.04	17.09	35.64	25.95
Net Margin %	8.93	11.17	10.46	7.89	3.95	5.24	8.20	5.33
Price Range	45.67-33.34	35.25-22.36	24.44-15.78	22.20-12.08	23.67-7.14	18.33-8.26	23.53-13.28	17.08-5.71
P/E Ratio	10.85-7.92	6.26-3.97	6.25-4.04	9.69-5.28	22.12-6.67	13.48-6.08	12.13-6.85	15.67-5.24
Average Yield %	2.08	2.34	1.44	1.50	2.12	2.12	0.83	1.57

Address: 601 Riverside Avenue, Jacksonville, FL 32204 Telephone: (904) 854-8100	Web Site: www.fnf.com Officers: William P. Foley II - Chmn., C.E.O. Frank P. Willey - Vice-Chmn.	Auditors: KPMG LLP Investor Contact: 904-854-8120 Transfer Agents: EquiServe Trust Company, N.A., Providence, RI

FIRST AMERICAN CORP (THE)

Exchange	Symbol	Price	52Wk Range	Yield	P/E
NYS	FAF	$32.94 (3/31/2005)	37.67-24.60	2.19	8.60

*7 Year Price Score 112.74 ***NYSE Composite Index=100** ***12 Month Price Score 107.21**

Interim Earnings (Per Share)

Qtr.	Mar	Jun	Sep	Dec
2001	0.27	0.75	0.55	0.68
2002	0.57	0.51	0.84	1.01
2003	1.05	1.47	1.62	1.07
2004	0.62	1.27	1.17	0.76

Interim Dividends (Per Share)

Amt	Decl	Ex	Rec	Pay
0.15Q	5/14/2004	6/28/2004	6/30/2004	7/15/2004
0.15Q	8/26/2004	9/28/2004	9/30/2004	10/15/2004
0.15Q	12/9/2004	12/29/2004	12/31/2004	1/14/2005
0.18Q	2/24/2005	3/29/2005	3/31/2005	4/15/2005

Indicated Div: $0.72

Valuation Analysis

Forecast P/E	N/A	No of Institutions
Market Cap	$3.0 Billion	Shares
Book Value	2.5 Billion	53,101,616
Price/Book	1.20	% Held
Price/Sales	0.44	57.19

Business Summary: Insurance (MIC: 8.2 SIC: 361 NAIC: 24127)

The First American, through its subsidiaries, is engaged in the business of providing business information and related products and services. Co. has seven segments that fall within two primary business groups, financial services and information technology. The financial services group provides title insurance, specialty insurance and trust and other services. The information technology group specializes in providing mortgage information, property information, credit information and screening information. As of Dec 31 2003, Co. had approximately 1,400 offices throughout the United States and abroad.

Recent Developments: For the year ended Dec 31 2004, net income decreased 22.6% to $349,099,000 from net income of $451,022,000 a year earlier. Revenues were $67,223,260,00, up 8.2% from $6,213,714,000 the year before.

Prospects: Co. intends to continue to pursue key initiatives in an effort to maintain strong profits in 2005 despite a weaker mortgage application market. These initiatives are expected to create opportunities for margin expansion, include Co.'s bundling alternatives of multiple products and services to the mortgage industry, FAST technology to enhance production efficiencies and streamline information, and strategic acquisitions to expand data capabilities and to increase market share. Thus, on Feb 24 2005, Co. announced the acquisition of privately held United General Financial Services, Inc., and its subsidiary companies, including United General Title Insurance Company. Terms were not disclosed.

Financial Data

(US$ in Thousands)	12/31/2004	12/31/2003	12/31/2002	12/31/2001	12/31/2000	12/31/1999	12/31/1998	12/31/1997
Earnings Per Share	3.83	5.22	2.92	2.27	1.24	0.50	3.32	1.21
Cash Flow Per Share	7.83	10.83	7.55	5.83	2.21	2.68	6.29	2.13
Tang Book Value Per Share	9.52	7.95	10.87	9.78	8.20	8.17	9.28	5.35
Dividends Per Share	0.600	0.500	0.340	0.270	0.240	0.240	0.220	0.169
Dividend Payout %	15.67	9.58	11.64	11.89	19.35	48.00	6.63	13.92
Income Statement								
Total Revenue	6,722,326	6,213,714	4,704,209	3,750,723	2,934,255	2,988,169	2,877,328	1,887,461
EBITDA	806,262	953,146	546,736	437,888	240,212	247,003	421,226	144,358
Depn & Amortn	128,978	114,424	96,829	108,348	86,336	77,031	59,804	38,149
Income Before Taxes	677,284	838,722	449,907	329,540	153,876	169,972	361,422	106,209
Income Taxes	243,200	292,000	149,900	117,500	54,700	62,300	127,700	41,500
Net Income	349,099	451,022	234,367	167,268	82,223	33,003	198,710	64,709
Average Shares	91,895	87,775	82,567	75,834	66,050	66,351	59,822	53,355
Balance Sheet								
Current Assets	1,903,527	1,518,510	1,238,231	945,927	556,454	571,665	599,536	338,577
Total Assets	6,208,365	4,892,111	3,398,045	2,837,263	2,199,737	2,116,414	1,784,790	1,168,144
Current Liabilities	1,283,190	899,612	625,060	477,797	348,856	361,541	346,845	234,595
Long-Term Obligations	732,770	553,888	425,705	415,341	219,838	196,815	130,193	41,973
Total Liabilities	3,744,801	3,012,591	2,033,456	1,732,811	1,329,500	1,300,423	1,052,875	756,732
Stockholders' Equity	2,463,564	1,879,520	1,364,589	1,104,452	870,237	815,991	731,915	411,412
Shares Outstanding	90,058	78,826	73,636	68,694	63,887	65,068	60,332	52,122
Statistical Record								
Return on Assets %	6.27	10.88	7.52	6.64	3.80	1.69	13.46	6.03
Return on Equity %	16.03	27.81	18.98	16.94	9.73	4.26	34.76	16.94
EBITDA Margin %	11.99	15.34	11.62	11.67	8.19	8.27	14.64	7.65
Net Margin %	5.19	7.26	4.98	4.46	2.80	1.10	6.91	3.43
Asset Turnover	1.21	1.50	1.51	1.49	1.36	1.53	1.95	1.76
Current Ratio	1.48	1.69	1.98	1.98	1.60	1.58	1.73	1.44
Debt to Equity	0.30	0.29	0.31	0.38	0.25	0.24	0.18	0.10
Price Range	35.14-24.60	30.64-21.72	23.10-16.54	34.91-16.51	32.88-10.69	34.81-11.50	41.38-16.08	16.42-6.97
P/E Ratio	9.17-6.42	5.87-4.16	7.91-5.66	15.38-7.27	26.51-8.62	69.63-23.00	12.46-4.84	13.57-5.76
Average Yield %	2.04	1.95	1.65	1.24	1.45	1.34	0.82	1.63

Address: 1 First American Way, Santa Ana, CA 92707-5913
Telephone: (714) 800-3000

Web Site: www.firstam.com
Officers: Parker S. Kennedy - Chmn., C.E.O. Craig I. DeRoy - Pres.

Auditors: PricewaterhouseCoopers LLP
Investor Contact: 800-854-3643 xt 391!

FIRST COMMONWEALTH FINANCIAL CORP. (INDIANA, PA)

Exchange	Symbol	Price	52Wk Range	Yield	P/E	Div Acheiver
NYS	FCF	$13.70 (3/31/2005)	15.76-12.01	4.82	23.62	17 Years

*7 Year Price Score 97.16   *NYSE Composite Index=100   ***12 Month Price Score 93.73**

Interim Earnings (Per Share)

Qtr.	Mar	Jun	Sep	Dec
2001	0.21	0.21	0.22	0.23
2002	0.13	0.19	0.21	0.22
2003	0.23	0.23	0.23	0.21
2004	0.22	0.18	(0.04)	0.24

Interim Dividends (Per Share)

Amt	Decl	Ex	Rec	Pay
0.16Q	6/15/2004	6/28/2004	6/30/2004	7/15/2004
0.16Q	9/21/2004	9/28/2004	9/30/2004	10/15/2004
0.165Q	12/21/2004	12/29/2004	12/31/2004	1/14/2005
0.165Q	3/15/2005	3/29/2005	3/31/2005	4/15/2005

Indicated Div: $0.66 (Div. Reinv. Plan)

Valuation Analysis

Forecast P/E	N/A	No of Institutions
Market Cap	$957.2 Million	Shares
Book Value	532.0 Million	14,928,414
Price/Book	1.80	% Held
Price/Sales	2.94	21.36

TRADING VOLUME (thousand shares)

Business Summary: Commercial Banking (MIC: 8.1 SIC: 021 NAIC: 22110)

First Commonwealth Financial is a financial services holding company with $5.19 billion in assets, as of Dec 31 2003. Co. operates 91 community banking offices in Pennsylvania through First Commonwealth Bank, a Pennsylvania chartered bank. Financial services and insurance products are also provided by First Commonwealth Trust, First Commonwealth Financial Advisors, and First Commonwealth Insurance Agency. Co. also operates First Commonwealth Systems, a data processing subsidiary, First Commonwealth Professional Resources, a support services subsidiary, and jointly owns Commonwealth Trust Credit Life Insurance, a credit life reinsurance company.

Recent Developments: For the year ended Dec 31 2004, net income decreased 27.5% to $38,652 thousand from net income of $53,300 thousand a year earlier. Net interest income was $167,335 thousand, up 16.6% from $143,532 thousand the year before. Provision for loan losses was $8,070 thousand versus $12,770 thousand in the prior year, a decrease of 36.8%. Non-interest income rose 2.3% to $43,572 thousand, while non-interest expense advanced 46.1% to $164,555 thousand.

Prospects: Operating results for fiscal 2004 reflect a penalty of $29.4 million for the prepayment of $440.0 million of Federal Home Loan Bank (FHLB) long-term borrowings. Although the penalty reduced short-term profitability, the outcome of the refinancing is expected to expand the maturity distribution of Co.'s FHLB advances in an effort to minimize the impact of the maturities on any one year. It is also expected to improve net interest margin through lower interest costs on FHLB advances. Co.'s net interest margin was 3.30% for fiscal year 2004 compared with 3.47% in 2003.

Financial Data

(US$ in Thousands)	12/31/2004	12/31/2003	12/31/2002	12/31/2001	12/31/2000	12/31/1999	12/31/1998	12/31/1997
Earnings Per Share	0.58	0.90	0.74	0.86	0.82	0.88	0.54	0.69
Cash Flow Per Share	0.59	0.97	0.99	0.80	1.15	0.87	0.86	0.81
Tang Book Value Per Share	5.59	6.55	6.67	6.33	5.74	4.93	5.74	6.17
Dividends Per Share	0.645	0.625	0.605	0.585	0.565	0.515	0.445	0.410
Dividend Payout %	111.21	69.44	81.76	68.02	68.90	58.52	82.41	58.99
Income Statement								
Interest Income	278,025	243,773	275,568	308,891	311,882	297,507	283,421	199,811
Interest Expense	110,690	100,241	122,673	167,170	174,539	152,653	148,282	102,753
Net Interest Income	167,335	143,532	152,895	141,721	137,343	144,854	135,139	97,058
Provision for Losses	8,070	12,770	12,223	11,495	10,030	9,450	15,049	6,929
Non-Interest Income	47,649	48,444	37,206	40,224	33,683	30,853	26,338	19,843
Non-Interest Expense	164,555	112,655	125,441	105,007	99,461	93,615	100,201	65,909
Income Before Taxes	42,359	66,551	52,437	65,443	61,535	72,642	46,227	44,063
Income Taxes	3,707	13,251	8,911	15,254	14,289	19,612	12,229	13,529
Net Income	38,652	53,300	43,526	50,189	47,246	53,030	33,374	30,534
Average Shares	66,487	59,387	58,742	58,118	57,618	60,569	61,666	43,932
Balance Sheet								
Net Loans & Leases	3,473,770	2,787,497	2,574,138	2,533,777	2,457,226	2,466,520	2,342,546	1,901,137
Total Assets	6,198,478	5,189,195	4,524,743	4,583,530	4,372,312	4,340,846	4,096,789	2,929,315
Total Deposits	3,844,475	3,288,275	3,044,124	3,093,150	3,064,146	2,948,829	2,931,131	2,242,478
Total Liabilities	5,666,500	4,758,249	4,123,353	4,213,464	4,038,156	4,054,163	3,741,384	2,657,481
Stockholders' Equity	531,978	430,946	401,390	370,066	334,156	286,683	355,405	271,834
Shares Outstanding	69,868	60,712	58,962	58,451	58,195	58,142	61,876	44,092
Statistical Record								
Return on Assets %	0.68	1.10	0.96	1.12	1.08	1.26	0.95	1.11
Return on Equity %	8.01	12.81	11.28	14.25	15.18	16.52	10.64	11.45
Net Interest Margin %	60.19	58.88	55.48	45.88	44.04	48.69	47.68	48.57
Efficiency Ratio %	50.53	38.55	40.11	30.08	28.78	28.51	32.35	30.01
Loans to Deposits	0.90	0.85	0.85	0.82	0.80	0.84	0.80	0.85
Price Range	15.76-12.01	14.98-11.50	14.12-10.84	15.00-9.50	12.00-8.63	14.31-10.16	17.53-11.50	17.53-8.63
P/E Ratio	27.17-20.71	16.64-12.78	19.08-14.65	17.44-11.05	14.63-10.52	16.26-11.54	32.47-21.30	25.41-12.50
Average Yield %	4.60	4.82	4.87	5.03	5.72	4.34	3.30	3.88

Address: Old Courthouse Square, 22 North Sixth Street, Indiana, PA 15701 Telephone: (724) 349-7220	Web Site: www.fcbanking.com Officers: E. James Trimarchi - Chmn. Johnston A. Glass - Vice-Chmn.	Auditors: ERNST & YOUNG LLP Investor Contact: 800-331-4107 Transfer Agents: The Bank of New York, New York, NY

FIRST DATA CORP

Exchange	Symbol	Price	52Wk Range	Yield	P/E
NYS	FDC	$39.31 (3/31/2005)	46.45-39.12	0.61	17.63

*7 Year Price Score 117.18 *NYSE Composite Index=100 *12 Month Price Score 88.77

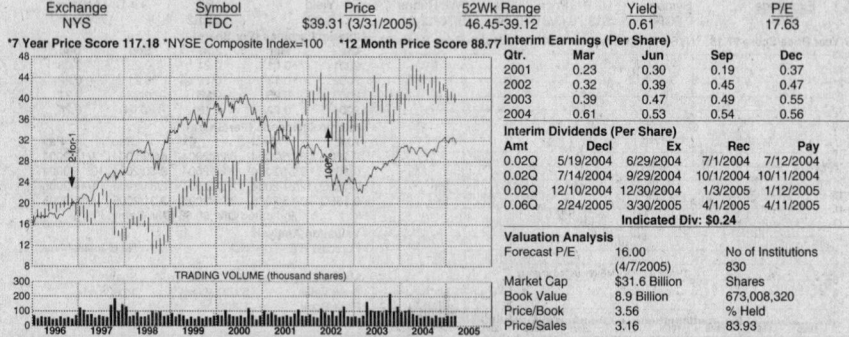

Interim Earnings (Per Share)

Qtr.	Mar	Jun	Sep	Dec
2001	0.23	0.30	0.19	0.37
2002	0.32	0.39	0.45	0.47
2003	0.39	0.47	0.49	0.55
2004	0.61	0.53	0.54	0.56

Interim Dividends (Per Share)

Amt	Decl	Ex	Rec	Pay
0.02Q	5/19/2004	6/29/2004	7/1/2004	7/12/2004
0.02Q	7/14/2004	9/29/2004	10/1/2004	10/11/2004
0.02Q	12/10/2004	12/30/2004	1/3/2005	1/12/2005
0.06Q	2/24/2005	3/30/2005	4/1/2005	4/11/2005
		Indicated Div: $0.24		

Valuation Analysis

Forecast P/E	16.00	No of Institutions	
	(4/7/2005)	830	
Market Cap	$31.6 Billion	Shares	
Book Value	8.9 Billion	673,008,320	
Price/Book	3.56	% Held	
Price/Sales	3.16	83.93	

Business Summary: IT & Technology (MIC: 10.2 SIC: 374 NAIC: 18210)

First Data operates electronic commerce and payment services businesses. Co.'s Payment Services segment provides money transfer and bill payment services through its Western Union and Orlandi Valuta money transfer agent networks that consist of approximately 219,000 agent locations in more than 195 countries and territories as of Dec 31 2004. Co.'s Merchant Services segment provides merchant and network acquiring and transaction processing services, automated teller machine processing and check guarantee and verification services. Co.'s Card Issuing Services segment provides credit, debit, private-label, smart and stored-value card and debit network issuing and processing services.

Recent Developments: For the year ended Dec 31 2004, income from continuing operations increased 34.0% to $1,867,800 thousand from income of $1,394,000 thousand a year earlier. Net income increased 33.1% to $1,875,200 thousand from net income of $1,408,700 thousand a year earlier. Non-interest income fell 8.7% to $680,900 thousand, while non-interest expense advanced 27.9% to $2,742,800 thousand.

Prospects: For 2005, Co. has indicated that it will focus on driving strong internal growth, executing on its Concord integration and seeking acquisitions that compliment its core strengths. Consequently, Co. expects full-year 2005 earnings per share in the range of $2.34 to $2.43, excluding $0.11 in planned estimated integration expenses. Co. noted that this range does not include any effect from expensing stock options. Separately, on Jan 12 2005 Co. announced that it has completed the acquisition of the credit card processing business unit of FinecoBank S.p.A., part of Capitalia Group. Co. expects the acquisition to expand and reinforce its operations in Italy.

Financial Data
(US$ in Thousands)

	12/31/2004	12/31/2003	12/31/2002	12/31/2001	12/31/2000	12/31/1999	12/31/1998	12/31/1997
Earnings Per Share	2.23	1.88	1.61	1.10	1.13	1.38	0.52	0.40
Cash Flow Per Share	2.82	2.70	2.53	1.81	1.45	1.54	1.43	1.32
Tang Book Value Per Share	N.M.	N.M.	N.M.	N.M.	0.19	0.51	N.M.	N.M.
Dividends Per Share	0.080	0.080	0.070	0.040	0.050	0.040	0.040	0.040
Dividend Payout %	3.59	4.26	4.35	3.64	4.44	2.90	7.69	10.13
Income Statement								
Total Revenue	10,013,200	8,400,200	7,636,200	6,450,800	5,705,200	5,539,800	5,117,600	5,234,500
EBITDA	3,343,100	2,507,700	2,304,900	1,969,400	1,996,300	2,547,000	1,407,100	1,357,100
Depn & Amortn	738,200	569,300	538,500	638,400	588,800	617,800	591,100	534,200
Income Before Taxes	2,493,200	1,838,800	1,654,300	1,211,400	1,308,300	1,825,400	711,900	706,400
Income Taxes	674,700	463,900	432,200	336,800	378,700	625,700	246,200	349,700
Net Income	1,875,200	1,408,700	1,237,900	871,900	929,600	1,199,700	465,700	356,700
Average Shares	840,200	749,200	771,800	795,000	828,200	870,200	896,600	933,800
Balance Sheet								
Current Assets	18,397,100	17,484,000	18,904,900	15,080,800	11,606,200	11,506,800	11,129,700	9,730,300
Total Assets	32,718,800	25,585,600	26,591,200	21,912,200	17,295,100	17,004,800	16,587,000	15,315,200
Current Liabilities	18,340,100	17,077,800	18,490,500	14,143,400	11,986,800	11,676,200	11,173,500	9,899,700
Long-Term Obligations	3,703,000	2,915,900	2,561,800	2,684,800	975,200	1,072,000	1,129,400	1,134,400
Total Liabilities	23,832,700	21,538,300	22,434,900	18,392,300	13,567,400	13,097,100	12,831,100	11,657,900
Stockholders' Equity	8,886,100	4,047,300	4,156,300	3,519,900	3,727,700	3,907,700	3,755,900	3,657,300
Shares Outstanding	804,000	716,500	752,800	761,000	835,800	835,800	871,000	893,800
Statistical Record								
Return on Assets %	6.41	5.40	5.10	4.45	5.41	7.14	2.92	2.41
Return on Equity %	28.92	34.34	32.25	24.06	24.28	31.31	12.56	9.68
EBITDA Margin %	33.39	29.85	30.18	30.53	34.99	45.98	27.50	25.93
Net Margin %	18.73	16.77	16.21	13.52	16.29	21.66	9.10	6.81
Asset Turnover	0.34	0.32	0.31	0.33	0.33	0.33	0.32	0.35
Current Ratio	1.00	1.02	1.02	1.07	0.97	0.99	1.00	0.98
Debt to Equity	0.42	0.72	0.62	0.76	0.26	0.27	0.30	0.31
Price Range	46.45-38.13	44.50-31.34	45.00-25.65	39.97-25.13	28.16-18.75	25.41-15.94	17.97-10.34	22.72-12.84
P/E Ratio	20.83-17.10	23.67-16.67	27.95-15.93	36.34-22.84	24.92-16.59	18.41-11.55	34.56-19.89	56.80-32.11
Average Yield %	0.19	0.21	0.19	0.12	0.21	0.18	0.27	0.22

Address: 6200 South Quebec Street, Greenwood Village, CO 80111	**Web Site:** www.firstdata.com	**Auditors:** Ernst & Young LLP
Telephone: (303) 967-8000	**Officers:** Charles T. Fote - Chmn., Pres., C.E.O.	**Investor Contact:** 303-967-6756
Fax: (303) 967-6262	Christina Gold - Sr. Exec. V.P.	

FIRST HORIZON NATIONAL CORP

Exchange	Symbol	Price	52Wk Range	Yield	P/E
NYS	FHN	$40.79 (3/31/2005)	48.01-40.00	4.22	11.52

*7 Year Price Score 106.15 *NYSE Composite Index=100 *12 Month Price Score 90.43

Interim Earnings (Per Share)

Qtr.	Mar	Jun	Sep	Dec
2001	0.41	0.65	0.68	0.68
2002	0.67	0.69	0.73	0.80
2003	0.91	0.90	0.91	0.90
2004	0.92	0.92	0.89	0.81

Interim Dividends (Per Share)

Amt	Decl	Ex	Rec	Pay
0.40Q	1/20/2004	3/10/2004	3/12/2004	4/1/2004
0.40Q	4/20/2004	6/9/2004	6/11/2004	7/1/2004
0.40Q	7/20/2004	9/8/2004	9/10/2004	10/1/2004
0.43Q	10/20/2004	12/15/2004	12/17/2004	1/1/2005
		Indicated Div: $1.72		

Valuation Analysis

Forecast P/E	11.41	No of Institutions
	(4/7/2005)	309
Market Cap	$5.0 Billion	Shares
Book Value	2.0 Billion	58,197,244
Price/Book	2.47	% Held
Price/Sales	1.99	46.97

TRADING VOLUME (thousand shares)

Business Summary: Commercial Banking (MIC: 8.1 SIC: 021 NAIC: 22110)

First Tennessee National, the parent company of First Tennessee Bank, held assets of $24.47 billion as of Dec 31 2003. Co. ranked second in terms of total assets among Tennessee-headquartered bank holding companies and ranked 33rd nationally. Co. provides diversified financial services though five business segments: First Tennessee Banking Group, First Horizon, FTN Financial, Transaction Processing and Corporate. First Horizon includes home loans, equity lending and money centers; FTN Financial includes capital markets, equity research, and investment banking; and Transaction Processing includes credit card merchant processing and nationwide payment processing.

Recent Developments: For the year ended Dec 31 2004, net income decreased 4.0% to $454,408 thousand from net income of $473,309 thousand a year earlier. Net interest income was $856,311 thousand, up 6.3% from $805,784 thousand the year before. Provision for loan losses was $48,348 thousand versus $86,698 thousand in the prior year, a decrease of 44.2%. Non-interest income fell 17.6% to $1,356,186 thousand, while non-interest expense declined 9.8% to $1,501,316 thousand.

Prospects: Looking ahead, Co. expects to resume earnings per share growth in 2005, now that retail/commercial banking has rebalanced to nearly 80.0% of its pre-tax earnings and national expansion initiatives continue to progress. While Co. may experience short-term favorable and unfavorable volatility in its earnings stream, Co. believes that over the long term it will continue to operate at a level consistent with high-performing growth and maintain return on equity at solid levels. Co. has been able to accomplish this goal over the last three and five year periods as demonstrated by its average annual earnings per share growth of 14.0% and its average annual return on equity of greater than 20.0%.

Financial Data
(US$ in Thousands)

	12/31/2004	12/31/2003	12/31/2002	12/31/2001	12/31/2000	12/31/1999	12/31/1998	12/31/1997
Earnings Per Share	3.54	3.62	2.89	2.42	1.77	1.85	1.72	1.50
Cash Flow Per Share	(2.54)	18.79	(6.14)	(8.80)	3.75	15.30	(24.53)	(3.58)
Tang Book Value Per Share	6.33	7.06	8.41	4.99	4.03	2.17	2.34	3.38
Dividends Per Share	1.630	1.300	1.050	0.910	0.880	0.790	0.685	0.615
Dividend Payout %	46.05	35.91	36.33	37.60	49.72	42.70	39.83	41.00
Income Statement								
Interest Income	1,166,802	1,053,370	1,039,093	1,198,871	1,363,046	1,207,164	1,133,777	941,293
Interest Expense	310,491	247,586	286,581	512,596	764,695	617,654	593,238	458,197
Net Interest Income	856,311	805,784	752,512	686,275	598,351	589,510	540,539	483,096
Provision for Losses	48,348	86,698	92,184	93,493	67,353	57,923	51,351	51,115
Non-Interest Income	1,363,186	1,640,014	1,541,065	1,259,636	1,063,420	1,123,104	985,503	668,130
Non-Interest Expense	1,504,340	1,640,102	1,643,334	1,358,748	1,257,416	1,275,252	1,121,769	785,044
Income Before Taxes	666,809	718,998	558,059	493,670	337,002	379,439	352,922	315,067
Income Taxes	212,401	245,689	181,608	164,068	104,421	131,906	126,542	117,595
Net Income	454,408	473,309	376,451	318,209	232,581	247,533	226,380	197,472
Average Shares	128,436	130,876	130,221	131,537	131,663	133,978	131,862	131,987
Balance Sheet								
Net Loans & Leases	16,269,514	13,830,192	11,201,147	10,127,770	10,095,754	9,223,555	8,421,051	8,185,491
Total Assets	29,771,683	24,506,690	23,823,095	20,616,791	18,555,086	18,373,390	18,733,961	14,387,897
Total Deposits	19,782,167	15,679,971	15,713,903	13,606,334	12,188,691	11,358,701	11,723,039	9,671,779
Total Liabilities	27,730,242	22,615,920	21,987,523	18,994,842	17,032,502	17,031,923	17,534,427	13,333,801
Stockholders' Equity	2,040,983	1,890,318	1,691,180	1,477,762	1,384,156	1,241,467	1,099,534	954,096
Shares Outstanding	123,531	124,834	125,600	125,865	128,744	129,878	128,974	128,209
Statistical Record								
Return on Assets %	1.67	1.96	1.69	1.62	1.26	1.33	1.37	1.44
Return on Equity %	23.05	26.43	23.76	22.24	17.67	21.15	22.05	20.69
Net Interest Margin %	73.39	76.50	72.42	57.24	43.90	48.83	47.68	51.32
Efficiency Ratio %	59.46	60.89	63.69	55.27	51.82	54.73	52.93	48.78
Loans to Deposits	0.82	0.88	0.71	0.74	0.83	0.81	0.72	0.85
Price Range	48.01-41.59	47.98-35.94	40.45-30.05	37.25-27.38	29.06-16.06	45.19-27.56	38.06-23.81	33.75-18.38
P/E Ratio	13.56-11.75	13.25-9.93	14.00-10.40	15.39-11.31	16.42-9.07	24.43-14.90	22.13-13.84	22.50-12.25
Average Yield %	3.67	3.10	2.89	2.72	4.13	2.20	2.17	2.44

Address: 165 Madison Avenue, Memphis, TN 38103 Telephone: (901) 523-4444 Fax: (901) 523-4030	Web Site: www.firstTennessee.com Officers: J. Kenneth Glass - Chmn., Pres., C.E.O. John H. Hamilton - Exec. V.P., Product Mgmt. & Delivery Serv.	Auditors: KPMG LLP Investor Contact: 901-523-4068

FIRSTENERGY CORP.

Exchange NYS	Symbol FE	Price $41.95 (3/31/2005)	52Wk Range 43.15-36.88	Yield 3.93	P/E 15.71

*7 Year Price Score 107.48 *NYSE Composite Index=100   *12 Month Price Score 95.71

Interim Earnings (Per Share)

Qtr.	Mar	Jun	Sep	Dec
2001	0.45	0.67	1.06	0.63
2002	0.40	0.79	1.05	(0.10)
2003	0.82	(0.20)	0.51	0.34
2004	0.53	0.62	0.91	0.61

Interim Dividends (Per Share)

Amt	Decl	Ex	Rec	Pay
0.375Q	7/20/2004	8/4/2004	8/6/2004	9/1/2004
0.375Q	10/19/2004	11/3/2004	11/5/2004	12/1/2004
0.412Q	11/30/2004	2/3/2005	2/7/2005	3/1/2005
0.412Q	3/15/2005	5/4/2005	5/6/2005	6/1/2005
		Indicated Div: $1.65		

Valuation Analysis

Forecast P/E	15.02 (4/7/2005)	No of Institutions 317
Market Cap	$13.8 Billion	Shares
Book Value	8.6 Billion	226,445,008
Price/Book	1.61	% Held
Price/Sales	1.11	68.65

Business Summary: Electricity (MIC: 7.1 SIC: 911 NAIC: 21122)

FirstEnergy has eight electric utility operating companies: Ohio Edison, Pennsylvania Power, The Cleveland Electric Illuminating Company, Metropolitan Edison, Pennsylvania Electric, American Transmission Systems, Toledo Edison and Jersey Central Power & Light. Co.'s subsidiaries and affiliates provide a wide range of energy and energy-related products and services, including the generation and sale of electricity; exploration and production of oil and natural gas; transmission and marketing of natural gas; mechanical and electricity contracting and construction; energy management; and telecommunications.

Recent Developments: For the year ended Dec 31 2004, income from continuing operations increased 106.0% to $873,779 thousand from income of $424,249 thousand a year earlier. Net income increased 107.7% to $878,175 thousand from net income of $422,764 thousand a year earlier. Revenues were $12,453,046 thousand, up 6.7% from $11,674,888 thousand the year before. Total direct expense was $7,771,365 thousand versus $7,760,944 thousand in the prior year, an increase of 0.1%. Total indirect expense was $2,470,203 thousand versus $2,440,728 thousand in the prior year, an increase of 1.2%.

Prospects: Co. continues to benefit from the operating performance of its generation fleet, which is enabling it to take advantage of sales opportunities in the wholesale market. Other factor's favorably affecting earnings include improved power generation margins, lower operating costs in most business units, higher investment income, the return to service of the Davis-Besse nuclear power station and the approval of Co.s' rate stabilization plan in Ohio. Also, Co. has made considerable progress in improving its financial flexibility through an aggressive debt reduction and refinancing program. For instance, Co. retired about $1.00 billion in debt in 2004, and restructured an additional $1.80 billlion.

Financial Data

(US$ in Thousands)	12/31/2004	12/31/2003	12/31/2002	12/31/2001	12/31/2000	12/31/1999	12/31/1998	12/31/1997
Earnings Per Share	2.67	1.39	2.14	2.81	2.69	2.50	1.95	1.94
Cash Flow Per Share	5.72	6.43	6.53	5.58	6.76	6.55	5.10	5.44
Tang Book Value Per Share	7.70	6.55	4.11	6.04	11.42	10.47	9.62	8.91
Dividends Per Share	1.500	1.500	1.500	1.500	1.500	1.500	1.500	1.500
Dividend Payout %	56.18	107.91	70.09	53.38	55.76	60.00	76.92	77.32
Income Statement								
Total Revenue	12,453,046	12,307,047	12,151,997	7,999,362	7,028,961	6,319,647	5,861,285	2,821,435
Depn & Amortn	1,832,623	1,331,484	1,169,818	975,801	1,035,379	1,032,174	822,294	535,825
Income Taxes	670,922	405,959	549,476	474,457	376,802	394,827	321,699	183,798
Net Income	878,175	422,764	629,280	646,447	598,970	568,299	410,874	305,774
Average Shares	328,982	304,972	294,421	230,430	222,444	227,227	226,373	...
Balance Sheet								
Net PPE	13,478,356	13,268,922	12,679,813	12,428,429	7,575,076	9,093,341	9,242,574	9,573,210
Total Assets	31,067,944	32,909,948	33,580,773	37,351,513	17,941,294	18,224,047	18,063,507	18,080,795
Long-Term Obligations	10,013,349	9,789,066	10,872,216	11,433,313	5,742,048	6,001,264	6,352,359	6,969,835
Total Liabilities	22,478,650	24,620,607	26,460,724	29,952,914	13,288,168	13,660,157	13,614,349	13,921,197
Stockholders' Equity	8,589,294	8,289,341	7,120,049	7,398,599	4,653,126	4,563,890	4,449,158	4,159,598
Shares Outstanding	329,836	329,836	297,636	297,636	224,531	232,454	237,069	230,207
Statistical Record								
Return on Assets %	2.74	1.27	1.77	2.34	3.30	3.13	2.27	2.25
Return on Equity %	10.38	5.49	8.67	10.73	12.96	12.61	9.55	9.18
Net Margin %	7.05	3.44	5.18	8.08	8.52	8.99	7.01	10.84
PPE Turnover	0.93	0.95	0.97	0.80	0.84	0.69	0.62	0.37
Asset Turnover	0.39	0.37	0.34	0.29	0.39	0.35	0.32	0.21
Debt to Equity	1.17	1.18	1.53	1.55	1.23	1.31	1.43	1.68
Price Range	43.15-35.20	38.50-27.65	38.65-25.05	36.88-25.81	31.88-18.19	33.00-22.56	33.88-27.50	29.00-19.63
P/E Ratio	16.16-13.18	27.70-19.89	18.06-11.71	13.12-9.19	11.85-6.76	13.20-9.03	17.37-14.10	14.95-10.12
Average Yield %	3.83	4.54	4.56	4.83	6.09	5.28	4.99	6.57

Address: 76 South Main Street, Akron, OH 44308-1890 Telephone: (800) 736 3402 Fax: (330) 384 3772	Web Site: www.firstenergycorp.com Officers: George M. Smart - Chmn. Anthony J. Alexander - Pres., C.E.O.	Auditors: PricewaterhouseCoopers LLP Investor Contact: 330-384-5500

FISHER SCIENTIFIC INTERNATIONAL INC.

Exchange	Symbol	Price	52Wk Range	Yield	P/E
NYS	FSH	$56.92 (3/31/2005)	64.75-53.26	N/A	31.62

*7 Year Price Score 150.88 *NYSE Composite Index=100   *12 Month Price Score 96.57

TRADING VOLUME (thousand shares)

Interim Earnings (Per Share)

Qtr.	Mar	Jun	Sep	Dec
2001	(0.59)	0.23	0.30	0.21
2002	0.34	0.35	0.52	0.46
2003	(0.02)	0.57	0.47	0.27
2004	0.51	0.65	0.10	0.69

Interim Dividends (Per Share)

No Dividends Paid

Valuation Analysis

Forecast P/E	15.99	No of Institutions
	(4/7/2005)	335
Market Cap	$6.8 Billion	Shares
Book Value	3.9 Billion	119,284,440
Price/Book	1.75	% Held
Price/Sales	1.45	99.71

Business Summary: Engineering Services (MIC: 12.1 SIC: 049 NAIC: 23460)

Fisher Scientific International is a provider of products and services to the global scientific research and U.S. clinical laboratory markets. Co.'s customers include pharmaceutical and biotechnology companies, colleges and universities, medical research institutions, hospitals and reference labs, and quality control, process control and research and development laboratories. Co. offers more than 600,000 products and services to more than 350,000 customers located in 145 countries. Co. operates in three business segments: scientific products and services, healthcare products and services and laboratory workstations.

Recent Developments: For the year ended Dec 31 2004, net income increased 112.2% to $166,400 thousand from net income of $78,400 thousand a year earlier. Revenues were $4,662,700 thousand, up 30.8% from $3,564,400 thousand the year before. Operating income was $287,000 thousand versus an income of $258,600 thousand in the prior year, an increase of 11.0%. Total direct expense was $3,285,600 thousand versus $2,624,900 thousand in the prior year, an increase of 25.2%. Total indirect expense was $1,090,100 thousand versus $680,900 thousand in the prior year, an increase of 60.1%.

Prospects: On Mar 8 2005, Co. announced that it has signed a definitive agreement to sell Atos Medical AB, a manufacturer of ear, nose and throat medical devices with 2004 sales totaling $35.0 million, to Nordic Capital for $110.0 million in cash. The transaction is subject to customary closing conditions. Co. expects to complete the transaction by the beginning of the second quarter. For 2005, Co. expects full-year revenue growth, excluding foreign-exchange effects, of approximately 20.0% to 22.0% and operating margins of 13.3% to 13.5%. Also, for 2005, Co. reaffirmed its forecast of earnings per share of $3.45 to $3.60, which includes approximately $0.23 of intangible amortization expense.

Financial Data (US$ in Thousands)	12/31/2004	12/31/2003	12/31/2002	12/31/2001	12/31/2000	12/31/1999	12/31/1998	12/31/1997
Earnings Per Share	1.80	1.29	0.87	0.31	0.51	0.55	(1.24)	(1.50)
Cash Flow Per Share	4.54	3.83	2.92	3.21	2.67	3.03	...	...
Tang Book Value Per Share	N.M.	N.M.	N.M.	N.M.	...	...	...	3.57
Dividends Per Share	...	...	...	...	...	...	...	0.060
Income Statement								
Total Revenue	4,662,700	3,564,400	3,238,400	2,880,000	2,622,300	2,469,700	2,252,300	2,175,300
EBITDA	440,500	263,700	307,700	211,800	200,500	224,400	83,000	64,900
Depn & Amortn	143,300	82,800	74,900	82,000	63,600	62,400	53,000	47,000
Income Before Taxes	192,400	96,100	141,500	30,300	37,800	57,800	(60,300)	(5,100)
Income Taxes	26,000	17,700	44,800	13,900	15,100	34,400	(10,800)	25,400
Net Income	166,400	78,400	50,600	16,400	22,700	23,400	(49,500)	(30,500)
Average Shares	92,200	60,600	57,900	53,000	44,400	42,800	40,000	20,300
Balance Sheet								
Current Assets	1,691,000	1,010,800	769,400	757,800	650,600	634,800	561,100	592,400
Total Assets	8,090,200	2,859,400	1,871,400	1,839,200	1,385,700	1,402,600	1,357,600	1,176,500
Current Liabilities	967,700	648,500	583,300	637,700	507,800	519,500	453,200	354,900
Long-Term Obligations	2,309,200	1,386,100	921,800	956,100	991,100	1,011,100	1,022,000	267,800
Total Liabilities	4,220,200	2,284,000	1,737,900	1,815,900	1,697,400	1,733,200	1,682,300	829,400
Stockholders' Equity	3,870,000	575,400	133,500	23,300	(311,700)	(330,600)	(324,700)	347,100
Shares Outstanding	118,673	62,955	54,638	54,157	40,116	40,052	40,034	20,356
Statistical Record								
Return on Assets %	3.03	2.74	2.70	1.02	1.62	1.70	...	...
Return on Equity %	7.47	13.63	37.90	70.39	...	...	...	...
EBITDA Margin %	9.45	7.40	9.50	7.35	7.65	9.09	3.69	2.98
Net Margin %	3.57	2.20	1.56	0.57	0.87	0.95	N.M.	N.M.
Asset Turnover	0.85	1.25	1.73	1.79	1.88	1.79	...	...
Current Ratio	1.75	1.56	1.32	1.19	1.28	1.22	1.24	1.67
Debt to Equity	0.60	2.41	6.90	41.03	...	...	...	0.77
Price Range	62.60-39.76	42.24-26.19	32.95-23.25	39.88-21.70	49.63-20.06	43.00-16.38	20.19-9.55	10.18-7.10
P/E Ratio	34.78-22.09	32.74-20.30	37.87-26.72	128.63-70.00	97.30-39.34	78.18-29.77	...	...
Average Yield %	...	...	...	...	...	...	...	0.66

Address: One Liberty Lane, Hampton, NH 03842 **Telephone:** (603) 926-5911 **Fax:** (603) 929-2449	**Web Site:** www.fisherscientific.com **Officers:** Paul M. Montrone - Chmn., C.E.O. Paul M. Meister - Vice-Chmn.	**Auditors:** Deloitte & Touche LLP **Investor Contact:** 603-929-2381

FLORIDA ROCK INDUSTRIES, INC.

Exchange	Symbol	Price	52Wk Range	Yield	P/E
NYS	FRK	$58.82 (3/31/2005)	64.35-36.65	1.36	23.34

*7 Year Price Score 169.64 *NYSE Composite Index=100 *12 Month Price Score 115.56

Interim Earnings (Per Share)

Qtr.	Dec	Mar	Jun	Sep
2001-02	0.37	0.29	0.44	0.48
2002-03	0.29	0.37	0.53	0.55
2003-04	0.73	0.56	0.75	0.54
2004-05	0.68	...	...	...

Interim Dividends (Per Share)

Amt	Decl	Ex	Rec	Pay
0.20Q	8/4/2004	9/15/2004	9/17/2004	10/1/2004
1.00Q	8/4/2004	9/15/2004	9/17/2004	10/1/2004
0.20Q	12/1/2004	12/15/2004	12/17/2004	1/3/2005
0.20Q	1/26/2005	3/11/2005	3/15/2005	4/1/2005

Indicated Div: $0.80

Valuation Analysis

Forecast P/E N/A No of Institutions

Market Cap	$2.6 Billion	Shares	
Book Value	644.0 Million		22,463,564
Price/Book	3.96	% Held	
Price/Sales	2.63		51.76

Business Summary: Stone, Clay, Glass, and Concrete Products (MIC: 11.2 SIC: 273 NAIC: 27320)

Florida Rock Industries is a provider of construction aggregates, concentrating its operations in the southeastern and mid-Atlantic states. Operations are divided into three business segments: construction aggregates is engaged in the mining, processing, distribution and sale of sand, gravel and crushed stone; concrete products is engaged in production and sale of ready-mix concrete, concrete block and pre-stressed concrete, as well as sales of other building materials; cement and calcium products is engaged in the production and sale of Portland and masonry cement and the sale of calcium products to the animal feed and roofing industries.

Recent Developments: For the quarter ended Dec 31 2004, net income decreased 6.4% to $30,087 thousand from net income of $32,128 thousand in the year-earlier quarter. Revenues were $250,928 thousand, up 11.3% from $225,392 thousand the year before. Operating income was $46,947 thousand versus an income of $49,517 thousand in the prior-year quarter, a decrease of 5.2%. Total indirect expense was $22,592 thousand versus $9,286 thousand in the prior-year quarter, an increase of 143.3%.

Prospects: The adverse impact of four hurricanes in Aug and Sep 2004 suppressed market demand and interfered with Co.'s rail distribution of crushed stone products in Florida. However, business performance now appears to be improving as most of Co.'s Florida operating facilities are back to pre-hurricane performance levels. Meanwhile, Co. remains optimistic about the growth opportunities in its respective markets. Co. noted that residential construction should remain its stronger driver of operating performance, but remains vulnerable to any material increases in mortgage rates. Separately, higher volumes and improved pricing in the concrete segment should benefit operating profit margin.

Financial Data

(US$ in Thousands)	3 Mos	09/30/2004	09/30/2003	09/30/2002	09/30/2001	09/30/2000	09/30/1999	09/30/1998
Earnings Per Share	2.52	2.58	1.74	1.59	1.61	1.40	1.08	0.90
Cash Flow Per Share	4.48	4.44	3.09	3.38	2.92	2.16	2.52	1.72
Tang Book Value Per Share	11.42	10.90	9.89	10.64	9.24	7.90	6.86	6.85
Dividends Per Share	1.733	1.700	0.367	0.247	0.223	0.189	0.156	0.111
Dividend Payout %	68.68	65.89	21.07	15.55	13.84	13.49	14.46	12.38
Income Statement								
Total Revenue	250,928	948,519	746,059	723,724	715,695	647,753	579,302	492,467
EBITDA	63,769	242,921	178,775	174,884	179,049	152,476	111,043	93,064
Depn & Amortn	15,882	63,628	63,126	66,152	62,603	51,960	38,497	33,433
Income Before Taxes	47,530	177,953	116,308	106,320	106,920	92,153	71,848	59,977
Income Taxes	17,443	64,283	40,707	37,425	37,636	32,439	25,291	21,117
Net Income	30,087	113,670	75,934	68,895	69,284	59,714	46,557	38,860
Average Shares	44,313	44,088	43,642	43,429	42,930	42,678	43,375	43,206
Balance Sheet								
Current Assets	169,959	198,336	190,094	126,587	156,258	123,348	122,465	100,607
Total Assets	920,189	934,929	886,154	733,349	755,120	690,045	604,168	451,556
Current Liabilities	120,696	158,901	95,723	87,181	86,270	80,717	107,566	74,786
Long-Term Obligations	41,575	41,927	118,964	43,695	138,456	163,620	96,989	23,935
Total Liabilities	276,207	314,049	311,732	222,702	308,922	310,096	265,910	151,670
Stockholders' Equity	643,982	620,880	574,422	510,647	446,198	379,949	338,258	299,886
Shares Outstanding	43,401	43,347	43,078	42,867	42,357	41,799	42,447	42,448
Statistical Record								
Return on Assets %	12.32	12.45	9.38	9.26	9.59	9.20	8.82	9.32
Return on Equity %	17.90	18.97	14.00	14.40	16.77	16.58	14.59	13.77
EBITDA Margin %	25.41	25.61	23.96	24.16	25.02	23.54	19.17	18.90
Net Margin %	11.99	11.98	10.18	9.52	9.68	9.22	8.04	7.89
Asset Turnover	1.07	1.04	0.92	0.97	0.99	1.00	1.10	1.18
Current Ratio	1.41	1.25	1.99	1.45	1.81	1.53	1.14	1.35
Debt to Equity	0.06	0.07	0.21	0.09	0.31	0.43	0.29	0.08
Price Range	59.53-36.56	49.58-33.07	35.49-19.37	29.41-18.72	24.52-14.50	18.78-12.44	20.22-10.06	13.97-8.81
P/E Ratio	23.62-14.51	19.22-12.82	20.39-11.13	18.50-11.77	15.23-9.01	13.41-8.89	18.72-9.31	15.52-9.78
Average Yield %	3.86	4.16	1.39	1.03	1.18	1.22	1.05	0.93

Address: 155 East 21st Street, Jacksonville, FL 32206	Web Site: www.flarock.com	Auditors: Deloitte & Touche LLP
Telephone: (904) 355-1781	Officers: Edward L. Baker - Chmn. John D. Baker II - Pres., C.E.O.	Transfer Agents: Wachovia Bank, N.A., Charlotte, NC
Fax: (904) 355-0817		

FLOWSERVE CORP.

Exchange	Symbol	Price	52Wk Range	Yield	P/E
NYS	FLS	$25.87 (3/31/2005)	27.79-19.80	N/A	23.73

7 Year Price Score 98.95   **NYSE Composite Index=100**   **12 Month Price Score 99.09**

TRADING VOLUME (thousand shares)

Interim Earnings (Per Share)

Qtr.	Mar	Jun	Sep	Dec
2001	(0.22)	0.07	0.15	0.42
2002	0.28	0.27	0.17	0.31
2003	0.15	0.24	0.19	0.38
2004	0.19	0.33	...	...

Interim Dividends (Per Share)

Dividend Payment Suspended

Valuation Analysis

Forecast P/E	19.92	No of Institutions	
	(4/7/2005)	169	
Market Cap	$1.4 Billion	Shares	
Book Value	834.9 Million	49,824,512	
Price/Book	1.70	% Held	
Price/Sales	0.58	90.14	

Business Summary: Industrial Machinery and Equipment (MIC: 11.5 SIC: 561 NAIC: 33911)

Flowserve is a manufacturer and aftermarket service provider of comprehensive flow control systems. Co. develops and manufactures precision-engineered flow control equipment for critical service applications. The flow control system components include pumps, valves and mechanical seals. Co.'s products and services are used in several industries, including petroleum, chemical, power generation and water treatment. Co. operates mainly through three business segments. The Pump Division supplies engineered and industrial pumps. The Flow Control Division supplies valves and related products. The Flow Solutions Division provides mechanical seals and aftermarket services.

Recent Developments: For the second quarter ended June 30 2004, net income advanced 20.3% to $18.4 million compared with $15.3 million in the equivalent 2003 quarter. Results for 2004 and 2003 included losses on optional prepayments of debt of $100,000 and $500,000, respectively. Results for 2003 also included integration expense of $5.7 million and restructuring expense of $800,000. Sales increased 6.5% to $654.6 million from $614.4 million a year earlier, primarily due to growth in the Flowserve Pump and Flow Solutions divisions. Gross profit climbed 8.0% to $196.3 million from $181.7 million the year before. Operating income rose 7.4% to $49.6 million from $46.2 million in 2003.

Prospects: Co. now plans to file Form 10-Q reports for the second and third quarters of 2004 and its 2004 Form 10-K report in or shortly before the third quarter of 2005. Co. expects to report new material control weaknesses arising from its ongoing assessment and expects to receive an adverse opinion on the operating effectiveness of its internal controls from its external auditors. In addition, Co. has certain internal control issues in its recordkeeping and other control procedures that have been identified during a pending IRS audit. Meanwhile, Co. announced that it is planning to divest the non-core service operations, collectively called General Services, of its Flow Control Division.

Financial Data

(US$ in Thousands)	3 Mos	12/31/2003	12/31/2002	12/31/2001	12/31/2000	12/31/1999	12/31/1998	12/31/1997
Earnings Per Share	1.00	0.96	1.02	(0.04)	0.35	0.32	1.23	1.26
Cash Flow Per Share	3.20	3.34	4.80	(1.24)	0.46	2.16	1.36	2.20
Tang Book Value Per Share	N.M.	N.M.	N.M.	N.M.	N.M.	5.66	6.73	7.77
Dividends Per Share	...	...	...	...	...	0.560	0.560	0.560
Dividend Payout %	...	...	...	...	...	175.00	45.53	44.44
Income Statement								
Total Revenue	611,350	2,404,371	2,251,331	1,917,507	1,538,293	1,061,272	1,083,086	1,152,196
EBITDA	56,271	226,677	250,316	224,292	150,542	73,348	125,631	141,997
Depn & Amortn	20,004	72,621	65,313	80,591	57,037	39,599	39,299	38,933
Income Before Taxes	16,437	73,835	92,070	25,629	23,184	18,245	73,157	89,789
Income Taxes	6,150	20,947	31,674	9,275	7,876	6,068	25,502	38,223
Net Income	10,287	52,888	53,025	(1,497)	13,241	12,117	48,875	51,566
Average Shares	55,429	55,250	52,193	38,719	37,842	37,856	39,898	40,896
Balance Sheet								
Current Assets	1,087,705	1,091,034	1,031,032	898,139	898,052	453,788	487,290	514,664
Total Assets	2,795,580	2,800,653	2,607,665	2,051,975	2,110,143	838,151	870,197	880,025
Current Liabilities	644,057	632,658	492,010	416,771	434,017	195,660	219,126	230,444
Long-Term Obligations	857,694	879,766	1,055,748	996,222	1,111,108	198,010	186,292	128,936
Total Liabilities	1,960,645	1,979,905	1,851,975	1,640,956	1,805,232	529,877	525,433	484,752
Stockholders' Equity	834,935	820,748	755,690	411,019	304,911	308,274	344,764	395,273
Shares Outstanding	54,825	54,839	54,850	44,792	37,436	37,413	37,667	40,603
Statistical Record								
Return on Assets %	2.03	1.96	2.28	N.M.	0.90	1.43	5.59	7.90
Return on Equity %	6.84	6.71	9.09	N.M.	4.31	3.73	13.21	17.33
EBITDA Margin %	9.20	9.43	11.12	11.70	9.79	6.91	11.60	12.32
Net Margin %	1.68	2.20	2.36	N.M.	0.86	1.15	4.51	4.48
Asset Turnover	0.91	0.89	0.97	0.92	1.04	1.24	1.24	1.77
Current Ratio	1.69	1.72	2.10	2.15	2.07	2.32	2.22	2.23
Debt to Equity	1.03	1.07	1.40	2.42	3.64	0.64	0.54	0.33
Price Range	22.62-11.24	22.62-10.70	34.90-7.90	32.90-19.33	23.00-10.56	21.50-15.13	33.31-15.63	36.31-21.63
P/E Ratio	22.62-11.24	23.56-11.15	34.22-7.75	...	65.71-30.18	67.19-47.27	27.08-12.70	28.82-17.16
Average Yield %	...	...	...	...	...	3.23	2.30	1.99

Address: 5215 N. O'Connor Blvd., Suite 2300, Irving, TX 75039-5421	**Web Site:** www.flowserve.com	**Auditors:** PricewaterhouseCoopers LLP
Telephone: (972) 443-6500	**Officers:** C. Scott Greer - Chmn., Pres., C.E.O.	**Investor Contact:** 972-443-6500
Fax: (972) 443-6800	Andrew J. Beall - V.P., Pres., Flow Solutions Div.	**Transfer Agents:** National City Bank, Cleveland, OH

FLUOR CORP.

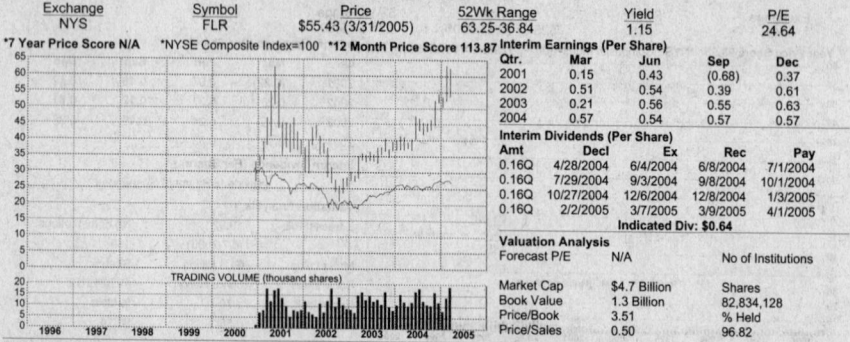

Exchange	Symbol	Price	52Wk Range	Yield	P/E
NYS	FLR	$55.43 (3/31/2005)	63.25-36.84	1.15	24.64

*7 Year Price Score N/A   *NYSE Composite Index=100   *12 Month Price Score 113.87

Interim Earnings (Per Share)

Qtr.	Mar	Jun	Sep	Dec
2001	0.15	0.43	(0.68)	0.37
2002	0.51	0.54	0.39	0.61
2003	0.21	0.56	0.55	0.63
2004	0.57	0.54	0.57	0.57

Interim Dividends (Per Share)

Amt	Decl	Ex	Rec	Pay
0.16Q	4/28/2004	6/4/2004	6/8/2004	7/1/2004
0.16Q	7/29/2004	9/3/2004	9/8/2004	10/1/2004
0.16Q	10/27/2004	12/6/2004	12/8/2004	1/3/2005
0.16Q	2/2/2005	3/7/2005	3/9/2005	4/1/2005

Indicated Div: $0.64

Valuation Analysis

Forecast P/E	N/A	No of Institutions	
Market Cap	$4.7 Billion	Shares	82,834,128
Book Value	1.3 Billion	% Held	96.82
Price/Book	3.51		
Price/Sales	0.50		

Business Summary: Construction - Public Infrastructure (MIC: 3.1 SIC: 629 NAIC: 41330)

Fluor is a holding company that provides professional services on a global basis in the fields of engineering, procurement, construction and maintenance. Co. has five principal operating segments: Oil and Gas, Industrial and Infrastructure, Government, Global Services and Power. Fluor Constructors International, which is organized and operates separately from Co.'s segments, provides unionized management, construction and management services in the U.S. and Canada, independently and as a subcontractor on projects to its segments. Co.'s customer industries range from oil and gas to the U.S. federal government. Co. also performs operations and maintenance activities for industrial clients.

Recent Developments: For the year ended Dec 31 2004, net income increased 18.6% to $186,695 thousand from net income of $157,450 thousand a year earlier. Revenues were $9,380,277 thousand, up 6.5% from $8,805,703 thousand the year before. Total direct expense was $8,960,236 thousand versus $8,399,477 thousand in the prior year, an increase of 6.7%. Total indirect expense was $141,465 thousand versus $142,388 thousand in the prior year, an increase of 0.7%.

Prospects: Co. continues to see a favorable outlook for new project prospects in 2005. Co. is well positioned to capitalize on strengthening trends in capital spending trends across a number of its markets. Strong backlog levels are expected to result in continued strong revenue and earnings growth over the next several years. During 2004, Co. began work on a significant number of new multi-year projects. Given the profit lag associated with the slow ramp-up of new projects and variability associated with the timing of future new awards, Co. is projecting full-year 2005 earnings in the range of $2.30 to $2.60 per share.

Financial Data

(US$ in Thousands)	12/31/2004	12/31/2003	12/31/2002	12/31/2001	12/31/2000	10/31/2000	10/31/1999	10/31/1998
Earnings Per Share	2.25	1.95	2.05	0.25	(0.05)	1.62	1.37	2.97
Cash Flow Per Share	(1.00)	(3.77)	2.61	8.71	(0.63)	1.88	6.18	...
Tang Book Value Per Share	14.89	12.51	10.76	9.57	8.49	19.96	19.27	...
Dividends Per Share	0.640	0.640	0.640	0.640	...	...	...	...
Dividend Payout %	28.44	32.82	31.22	256.00	...	...	...	...
Income Statement								
Total Revenue	9,380,277	8,805,703	9,958,956	8,972,161	1,866,519	9,970,154	11,334,355	12,377,476
EBITDA	369,541	344,437	332,063	303,407	20,558	468,605	396,968	505,469
Depn & Amortn	91,888	79,676	77,989	117,179	22,698	311,688	318,204	288,870
Income Before Taxes	281,158	267,981	260,524	185,320	(7,102)	142,221	76,581	222,748
Income Taxes	94,463	88,526	90,548	57,554	(3,079)	42,375	49,898	86,834
Net Income	186,695	157,450	163,615	19,410	(4,023)	123,949	104,187	235,344
Average Shares	82,795	80,539	79,853	79,157	74,098	75,256	75,929	79,135
Balance Sheet								
Current Assets	2,723,314	2,213,644	1,941,465	1,851,327	1,382,258	1,447,793	1,910,171	...
Total Assets	3,969,557	3,449,482	3,142,151	3,091,162	2,700,561	3,652,734	4,886,117	...
Current Liabilities	1,763,981	1,829,138	1,756,171	1,811,418	1,648,081	1,620,375	2,204,310	...
Long-Term Obligations	347,649	44,652	17,613	17,594	17,576	17,573	317,555	...
Total Liabilities	2,633,765	2,367,948	2,258,284	2,301,896	2,067,484	2,043,477	3,304,745	...
Stockholders' Equity	1,335,792	1,081,534	883,867	789,266	633,077	1,609,257	1,581,372	...
Shares Outstanding	84,538	82,102	80,188	80,106	74,609	75,743	76,034	75,573
Statistical Record								
Return on Assets %	5.02	4.78	5.25	0.67	N.M.	2.90	...	...
Return on Equity %	15.40	16.02	19.56	2.73	N.M.	7.75	...	...
EBITDA Margin %	3.94	3.91	3.33	3.38	1.10	4.70	3.50	4.08
Net Margin %	1.99	1.79	1.64	0.22	N.M.	1.24	0.92	1.90
Asset Turnover	2.52	2.67	3.20	3.10	0.42	2.33	...	...
Current Ratio	1.54	1.21	1.11	1.02	0.84	0.89	0.87	...
Debt to Equity	0.26	0.04	0.02	0.02	0.03	0.01	0.20	...
Price Range	54.54-36.84	40.54-27.18	44.57-20.94	62.65-31.82	33.19-27.06	...	...	...
P/E Ratio	24.24-16.37	20.79-13.94	21.74-10.21	250.60-127.28	...	...	...	...
Average Yield %	1.49	1.85	1.97	1.51	...	...	...	...

Address: One Enterprise Drive, Aliso Viejo, CA 92656 Telephone: (949) 349-2000	Web Site: www.fluor.com Officers: Alan L. Boeckmann - Chmn., C.E.O. H. Steven Gilbert - Sr. V.P., Human Res., Admin.	Auditors: Ernst & Young LLP Investor Contact: 949-349-3909

FMC CORP.

Exchange	Symbol	Price	52Wk Range	Yield	P/E
NYS	FMC	$53.45 (3/31/2005)	55.93-38.69	N/A	12.49

*7 Year Price Score 118.16 *NYSE Composite Index=100 ***12 Month Price Score 102.92**

Interim Earnings (Per Share)

Qtr.	Mar	Jun	Sep	Dec
2001	(0.86)	(9.62)	0.66	(1.03)
2002	0.28	0.57	0.79	0.21
2003	0.05	0.61	(0.10)	0.18
2004	0.15	0.82	0.78	2.51

Interim Dividends (Per Share)

No Dividends Paid

Valuation Analysis

Forecast P/E	13.03	No of Institutions	
	(4/7/2005)	187	
Market Cap	$2.0 Billion	Shares	
Book Value	876.2 Million	32,770,792	
Price/Book	2.26	% Held	
Price/Sales	0.96	88.50	

Business Summary: Machinery Supply Retail (MIC: 12.9 SIC: 084 NAIC: 33294)

FMC is a diversified chemical company that serves agricultural, industrial and consumer markets globally. Co. is divided into three operating segments: Agricultural Products, Specialty Chemicals and Industrial Chemicals. Agricultural Products focus on insecticides, which are used to enhance crop yield and quality by controlling a spectrum of pests, and on herbicides, which are used to reduce the need for manual or mechanical weeding. Specialty Chemicals consists of Co.'s BioPolymer and lithium businesses and focused on food ingredients. Industrial Chemicals manufactures a wide range of inorganic materials, including soda ash, hydrogen peroxide, specialty peroxygens and phosphorus chemicals.

Recent Developments: For the year ended Dec 31 2004, income from continuing operations increased 341.2% to $175,600 thousand from income of $39,800 thousand a year earlier. Net income increased 504.5% to $160,200 thousand from net income of $26,500 thousand a year earlier. Revenues were $2,051,200 thousand, up 6.8% from $1,921,400 thousand the year before. Total direct expense was $1,474,200 thousand versus $1,400,500 thousand in the prior year, an increase of 5.3%. Total indirect expense was $351,700 thousand versus $319,200 thousand in the prior year, an increase of 10.2%.

Prospects: Co. is targeting first-quarter 2005 earnings before restructuring and other charges of between $0.55 and $0.65 per diluted share. Near-term results should benefit from continued strong demand in Brazil, a shift of North America demand into 2005, and the recovery in Industrial Chemicals segment. Looking ahead, Co. anticipates double-digit growth in earnings per share before restructuring and other income and charges, resulting in full-year 2005 earnings of between $3.70 and $3.90 per diluted share. Earnings growth is expected to be fueled by a significant recovery in selling prices in the Industrial Chemicals segment and continued growth in the Specialty Chemicals segment.

Financial Data (US$ in Thousands)	12/31/2004	12/31/2003	12/31/2002	12/31/2001	12/31/2000	12/31/1999	12/31/1998	12/31/1997
Earnings Per Share	4.28	0.75	1.92	(10.86)	3.50	6.57	3.05	4.41
Cash Flow Per Share	5.79	4.79	3.19	(6.74)	8.10	18.63	11.20	25.59
Tang Book Value Per Share	19.08	12.25	7.88	3.27	9.98	7.84	10.10	9.74
Income Statement								
Total Revenue	2,051,200	1,921,400	1,852,900	1,943,000	3,925,500	4,273,600	4,378,400	4,312,600
EBITDA	343,800	254,800	276,900	(283,000)	504,200	571,800	564,400	287,500
Depn & Amortn	134,300	124,600	118,800	131,600	188,900	190,800	206,600	238,400
Income Before Taxes	131,100	38,000	86,500	(472,900)	222,600	274,300	249,500	(59,700)
Income Taxes	(44,500)	(1,800)	17,400	(166,600)	45,300	58,300	64,200	(35,200)
Net Income	160,200	26,500	65,800	(337,700)	110,600	212,600	106,500	162,400
Average Shares	37,351	35,591	34,343	31,052	31,576	32,377	34,939	36,805
Balance Sheet								
Current Assets	1,072,700	1,009,700	1,175,700	820,300	1,329,800	1,416,500	1,681,700	1,715,600
Total Assets	2,978,400	2,828,800	2,872,000	2,477,200	3,745,900	3,995,800	4,166,400	4,113,100
Current Liabilities	820,100	727,500	874,600	1,079,200	1,399,900	1,576,000	1,411,900	1,464,500
Long-Term Obligations	822,200	1,033,400	1,035,900	651,800	872,100	945,100	1,326,400	1,140,200
Total Liabilities	2,102,200	2,240,500	2,466,000	2,258,400	2,945,500	3,252,200	3,437,000	3,352,500
Stockholders' Equity	876,200	588,300	406,000	218,800	800,400	743,600	729,400	760,600
Shares Outstanding	37,028	35,261	35,072	31,305	30,644	30,363	32,703	34,924
Statistical Record								
Return on Assets %	5.50	0.93	2.46	N.M.	2.85	5.21	2.57	3.57
Return on Equity %	21.82	5.33	21.06	N.M.	14.29	28.87	14.30	20.09
EBITDA Margin %	16.76	13.26	14.94	N.M.	12.84	13.38	12.89	6.67
Net Margin %	7.81	1.38	3.55	N.M.	2.82	4.97	2.43	3.77
Asset Turnover	0.70	0.67	0.69	0.62	1.01	1.05	1.06	0.95
Current Ratio	1.31	1.39	1.34	0.76	0.95	0.90	1.19	1.17
Debt to Equity	0.94	1.76	2.55	2.98	1.09	1.27	1.82	1.50
Price Range	50.00-33.16	34.85-14.38	41.92-23.46	43.87-24.62	40.10-24.49	38.98-20.79	43.01-25.60	47.54-31.28
P/E Ratio	11.68-7.75	46.47-19.17	21.83-12.22	...	11.46-7.00	5.93-3.16	14.10-8.39	10.78-7.09

Address: 1735 Market Street, Philadelphia, PA 19103 **Telephone:** (215) 299-6000 **Fax:** (215) 299-6618	**Web Site:** www.fmc.com **Officers:** William G. Walter - Chmn., Pres., C.E.O. W. Kim Foster - Sr. V.P., C.F.O.	**Auditors:** KPMG LLP **Investor Contact:** 312-861-6921

FMC TECHNOLOGIES, INC.

Exchange	Symbol	Price	52Wk Range	Yield	P/E
NYS	FTI	$33.18 (3/31/2005)	35.87-24.93	N/A	19.75

*7 Year Price Score N/A   ***NYSE Composite Index=100**   ***12 Month Price Score 102.78**

Interim Earnings (Per Share)

Qtr.	Mar	Jun	Sep	Dec
2001	(0.09)	0.15	0.17	0.33
2002	(2.89)	0.27	0.25	0.38
2003	0.14	0.34	0.30	0.34
2004	0.20	0.35	0.32	0.82

Interim Dividends (Per Share)

No Dividends Paid

Valuation Analysis

Forecast P/E	22.00	No of Institutions	
	(4/7/2005)	174	
Market Cap	$2.3 Billion	Shares	
Book Value	662.2 Million	61,867,796	
Price/Book	3.44	% Held	
Price/Sales	0.82	89.51	

TRADING VOLUME (thousand shares)

1996 1997 1998 1999 2000 2001 2002 2003 2004 2005

Business Summary: Oil and Gas (MIC: 14.2 SIC: 533 NAIC: 33132)

FMC Technologies designs, manufactures and services systems and products through four segments. Energy Production Systems is a supplier of systems and services used in the offshore, particularly deepwater, exploration and production of crude oil and natural gas. Energy Processing Systems is a provider of specialized systems and products to customers involved in the production, transportation and processing of crude oil, natural gas and refined petroleum-based products. FoodTech is a supplier of food handling and processing systems and products to industrial food processing companies. Airport Systems provides equipment and services for airlines, airports and air freight companies.

Recent Developments: For the year ended Dec 31 2004, net income increased 69.4% to $116,700 thousand from net income of $68,900 thousand a year earlier. Revenues were $2,767,700 thousand, up 20.0% from $2,307,100 thousand the year before. Total direct expense was $2,266,300 thousand versus $1,843,600 thousand in the prior year, an increase of 22.9%. Total indirect expense was $397,300 thousand versus $357,900 thousand in the prior year, an increase of 11.0%.

Prospects: Results are being driven by demand for Co.'s subsea systems business, as well as its surface and fluid control businesses, which is benefiting from increased drilling activity. For 2005, Co. should continue to benefit from strong growth in its Energy Production Systems and Energy Processing Systems segments. However, the FoodTech segment is anticipated to be flat to slightly up, reflecting the impact of the 2004 Florida hurricanes in the citrus business. Co. estimates that full-year 2005 earnings per diluted share will be in the range of $1.30 to $1.50.

Financial Data

(US$ in Thousands)	12/31/2004	12/31/2003	12/31/2002	12/31/2001	12/31/2000	12/31/1999	12/31/1998
Earnings Per Share	1.68	1.13	(1.94)	0.53	0.92	...	...
Cash Flow Per Share	1.87	2.20	1.74	1.06	...	...	...
Tang Book Value Per Share	6.89	3.62	2.81	1.09	0.26	...	...
Income Statement							
Total Revenue	2,767,700	2,307,100	2,071,500	1,927,900	1,875,200	1,953,100	2,185,500
EBITDA	267,800	192,100	162,500	122,500	154,000	171,800	194,300
Depn & Amortn	101,900	76,600	59,700	47,900	59,100	62,300	66,600
Income Before Taxes	159,000	106,600	90,300	63,500	90,600	110,000	125,800
Income Taxes	42,300	31,000	26,200	24,100	22,700	33,500	38,600
Net Income	116,700	75,600	(129,700)	34,700	67,900	71,000	87,200
Average Shares	69,300	66,900	66,824	65,923	...	...	...
Balance Sheet							
Current Assets	1,217,100	949,400	818,400	755,100	693,300	658,400	...
Total Assets	1,893,900	1,590,600	1,372,500	1,437,900	1,373,700	1,473,200	...
Current Liabilities	995,400	845,100	734,000	680,800	569,800	576,400	...
Long-Term Obligations	160,400	201,100	175,400	194,100	...	...	...
Total Liabilities	1,231,700	1,161,300	1,068,700	1,019,700	736,100	751,000	...
Stockholders' Equity	662,200	429,300	303,800	418,200	637,600	722,200	...
Shares Outstanding	68,697	66,200	65,500	65,005	1,000,000	...	...
Statistical Record							
Return on Assets %	6.68	5.10	N.M.	2.47	4.76	...	...
Return on Equity %	21.32	20.62	N.M.	6.57	9.96	...	...
EBITDA Margin %	9.68	8.33	7.84	6.35	8.21	8.80	8.89
Net Margin %	4.22	3.28	N.M.	1.80	3.62	3.64	3.99
Asset Turnover	1.58	1.56	1.47	1.37	1.31	...	...
Current Ratio	1.22	1.12	1.11	1.11	1.22	1.14	...
Debt to Equity	0.24	0.47	0.58	0.46	...	...	...
Price Range	34.46-23.04	24.53-18.17	23.60-14.46	22.00-11.31	...	...	...
P/E Ratio	20.51-13.71	21.71-16.08	...	41.51-21.34	...	...	...

Address: 1803 Gears Road, Houston, TX 77067	Web Site: www.fmctechnologies.com	Auditors: KPMG LLP
Telephone: (281) 591-4000	Officers: Joseph H. Netherland - Chmn., Pres., C.E.O. Peter D. Kinnear - Exec. V.P.	Investor Contact: 312-861-6414

FOOT LOCKER, INC.

Exchange	Symbol	Price	52Wk Range	Yield	P/E
NYS	FL	$29.30 (3/31/2005)	29.58-20.07	1.02	16.46

*7 Year Price Score 143.83 ***NYSE Composite Index=100** ***12 Month Price Score 104.63**

TRADING VOLUME (thousand shares)

Interim Earnings (Per Share)

Qtr.	Apr	Jul	Oct	Jan
2001-02	0.27	(0.10)	0.23	0.24
2002-03	0.14	0.21	0.31	0.39
2003-04	0.26	0.24	0.41	0.47
2004-05	0.31	0.53	0.47	...

Interim Dividends (Per Share)

Amt	Decl	Ex	Rec	Pay
0.06Q	5/26/2004	7/14/2004	7/16/2004	7/30/2004
0.06Q	8/18/2004	10/13/2004	10/15/2004	10/29/2004
0.075Q	11/17/2004	1/12/2005	1/14/2005	1/28/2005
0.075Q	2/16/2005	4/13/2005	4/15/2005	4/29/2005

Indicated Div: $0.30

Valuation Analysis

Forecast P/E	14.93 (4/7/2005)	No of Institutions	237
Market Cap	$4.6 Billion	Shares	133,335,824
Book Value	1.7 Billion	% Held	85.52
Price/Book	2.62		
Price/Sales	0.88		

Business Summary: Retail - Apparel and Accessory Stores (MIC: 5.8 SIC: 661 NAIC: 16213)

Foot Locker is a global retailer of athletic footwear and apparel, operating as of Jan 31, 2004, 3,610 primarily mall-based stores in North America, Europe and Australia. Co., through its subsidiaries, operates in two reportable segments — Athletic Stores and Direct-to-Customers. The Athletic Stores segment includes Foot Locker, Lady Foot Locker, Kids Foot Locker and Champs Sports. The Direct-to-Customers segment reflects Footlocker.com, Inc., which sells, through its affiliates, including Eastbay, Inc., to customers through catalogs and Internet websites.

Recent Developments: For the quarter ended Oct 30 2004, net income increased 19.4% to $74,000 thousand from net income of $62,000 thousand in the year-earlier quarter. Revenues were $1,366,000 thousand, up 14.4% from $1,194,000 thousand the year before. Total indirect expense was $308,000 thousand versus $287,000 thousand in the prior-year quarter, an increase of 7.3%.

Prospects: Looking ahead, Co. is seeking to build upon the momentum of generating solid sales and earnings per share increases in 2005. Accordingly, Co. expects a comparable-store sales increase in the low-to-mid single digit range and earnings per share growth of 10.0% to 20.0%. Moreover, Co. has planned capital expenditures at $170.0 million for 2005, including the opening of up to 100 new stores and remodeling/relocating of 275 stores. Meanwhile, Co. is benefiting from strong cash flow, which is being used to fund acquisitions, support its capital expenditure program, reduce liabilities and increase cash dividends to its shareholders.

Financial Data

(US$ in Thousands)	9 Mos	6 Mos	3 Mos	01/31/2004	02/01/2003	02/02/2002	02/03/2001	01/29/2000
Earnings Per Share	1.78	1.72	1.43	1.39	1.05	0.64	(1.73)	0.35
Cash Flow Per Share	1.16	2.01	1.86	1.87	2.47	1.32	1.77	0.61
Tang Book Value Per Share	8.56	8.09	8.13	7.94	6.34	6.13	6.28	7.18
Dividends Per Share	0.240	0.210	0.180	0.150	0.030	...	...	...
Dividend Payout %	13.45	12.19	12.56	10.79	2.86	...	...	...
Income Statement								
Total Revenue	3,820,000	2,454,000	1,186,000	4,779,000	4,509,000	4,379,000	4,356,000	4,647,000
EBITDA	365,000	210,000	112,000	489,000	421,000	353,000	349,000	267,000
Depn & Amortn	109,000	71,000	34,000	147,000	149,000	154,000	151,000	182,000
Income Before Taxes	244,000	131,000	74,000	324,000	246,000	175,000	176,000	28,000
Income Taxes	78,000	39,000	27,000	115,000	84,000	64,000	69,000	11,000
Net Income	204,000	130,000	48,000	207,000	153,000	92,000	(240,000)	48,000
Average Shares	157,400	157,100	156,200	152,900	150,800	146,900	139,100	138,800
Balance Sheet								
Current Assets	1,695,000	1,723,000	1,596,000	1,519,000	1,284,000	1,114,000	1,000,000	1,089,000
Total Assets	3,106,000	3,106,000	2,760,000	2,689,000	2,486,000	2,290,000	2,232,000	2,515,000
Current Liabilities	691,000	797,000	808,000	545,000	572,000	539,000	629,000	777,000
Long-Term Obligations	346,000	339,000	182,000	335,000	356,000	365,000	259,000	312,000
Total Liabilities	1,361,000	1,454,000	1,345,000	1,314,000	1,376,000	1,298,000	1,219,000	1,376,000
Stockholders' Equity	1,745,000	1,652,000	1,415,000	1,375,000	1,110,000	992,000	1,013,000	1,139,000
Shares Outstanding	155,906	155,655	145,423	143,952	141,075	139,911	138,491	137,665
Statistical Record								
Return on Assets %	9.50	9.25	8.22	8.02	6.42	4.08	N.M.	1.79
Return on Equity %	18.34	18.52	16.93	16.71	14.60	9.20	N.M.	4.42
EBITDA Margin %	9.55	8.56	9.44	10.23	9.34	8.06	8.01	5.75
Net Margin %	5.34	5.30	4.05	4.33	3.39	2.10	N.M.	1.03
Asset Turnover	1.78	1.75	1.83	1.85	1.89	1.94	1.81	1.73
Current Ratio	2.45	2.16	1.98	2.79	2.24	2.07	1.59	1.40
Debt to Equity	0.20	0.21	0.13	0.24	0.32	0.37	0.26	0.27
Price Range	27.00-17.90	27.00-13.99	27.00-10.34	25.64-9.52	17.84-8.49	18.98-10.60	16.38-5.31	11.75-3.56

Address: 112 West 34th Street, New York, NY 10120 **Telephone:** (212) 720-3700 **Fax:** (212) 553-7026	**Web Site:** www.footlocker-inc.com **Officers:** Matthew D. Serra - Chmn., Pres., C.E.O. Bruce L. Hartman - Exec. V.P., C.F.O.	**Auditors:** KPMG LLP

FORD MOTOR CO. (DE)

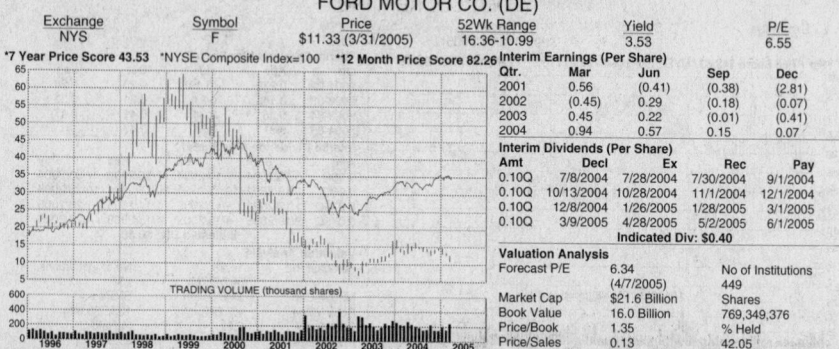

Exchange	Symbol	Price	52Wk Range	Yield	P/E
NYS	F	$11.33 (3/31/2005)	16.36-10.99	3.53	6.55

*7 Year Price Score 43.53 *NYSE Composite Index=100 *12 Month Price Score 82.26

Interim Earnings (Per Share)

Qtr.	Mar	Jun	Sep	Dec
2001	0.56	(0.41)	(0.38)	(2.81)
2002	(0.45)	0.29	(0.18)	(0.07)
2003	0.45	0.22	(0.01)	(0.41)
2004	0.94	0.57	0.15	0.07

Interim Dividends (Per Share)

Amt	Decl	Ex	Rec	Pay
0.10Q	7/8/2004	7/28/2004	7/30/2004	9/1/2004
0.10Q	10/13/2004	10/28/2004	11/1/2004	12/1/2004
0.10Q	12/8/2004	1/26/2005	1/28/2005	3/1/2005
0.10Q	3/9/2005	4/28/2005	5/2/2005	6/1/2005

Indicated Div: $0.40

Valuation Analysis

Forecast P/E	6.34	No of Institutions
	(4/7/2005)	449
Market Cap	$21.6 Billion	Shares
Book Value	16.0 Billion	769,349,376
Price/Book	1.35	% Held
Price/Sales	0.13	42.05

Business Summary: Automotive (MIC: 15.1 SIC: 711 NAIC: 36111)

Ford Motor is a global automaker. Co.'s automotive brands include Aston Martin, Ford, Jaguar, Land Rover, Lincoln, Mercury and Volvo. Co.'s Automotive segment engages in the design, manufacture, sale and service of cars, trucks, vehicle components and systems. The segment also provides after-the-sale vehicle services and products, such as maintenance, and light repair, heavy repair, collision, vehicle accessories and extended repair service products. Co.'s Financial Services segment operates through Ford Motor Credit Company and The Hertz Corporation, and engages in vehicle-related financing, leasing and insurance and rental of vehicles and equipment. Co. also owns 33.4% of Mazda Motor Corp.

Recent Developments: For the year ended Dec 31 2004, income from continuing operations increased 302.9% to $3,634,000 thousand from income of $902,000 thousand a year earlier. Net income increased 604.4% to $3,487,000 thousand from net income of $495,000 thousand a year earlier. Revenues were $171,652,000 thousand, up 4.5% from $164,338,000 thousand the year before. Total direct expense was $135,856,000 thousand versus $129,685,000 thousand in the prior year, an increase of 4.8%. Total indirect expense was $19,285,000 thousand versus $21,150,000 thousand in the prior year, a decrease of 8.8%.

Prospects: New products, such as the Ford Mustang, Ford GT, Ford Five Hundred, Ford Freestyle and Ford Hybrid Escape are expected to improve Co.'s U.S. market share going forward. These new vehicles are a part of the largest product roll-out in Co.'s history, which will continue into 2005. Meanwhile, Co. recently announced its 2005 guidance of earnings per share of $1.75 to $1.95, based on total company pre-tax profit in the range of $5.00 billion to $5.70 billion, excluding special items. Also, Co. anticipates first-quarter earnings per share in 2005 of $0.25 to $0.35, excluding special items.

Financial Data

(US$ in Thousands)	12/31/2004	12/31/2003	12/31/2002	12/31/2001	12/31/2000	12/31/1999	12/31/1998	12/31/1997
Earnings Per Share	1.73	0.27	(0.54)	(3.02)	2.30	5.86	17.76	5.62
Cash Flow Per Share	12.34	11.04	10.24	12.57	22.84	24.64	19.11	23.14
Tang Book Value Per Share	4.60	2.40	N.M.	4.31	10.14	22.83	19.32	25.55
Dividends Per Share	0.400	0.400	0.400	1.050	0.300	1.880	1.720	1.645
Dividend Payout %	23.12	148.15	...	...	13.04	32.08	9.68	29.27
Income Statement								
Total Revenue	171,652,000	164,196,000	162,586,000	162,412,000	170,064,000	162,558,000	144,416,000	153,627,000
EBITDA	18,358,000	13,696,000	13,880,000	11,411,000	32,497,000	33,867,000	47,259,000	33,906,000
Depn & Amortn	6,434,000	5,506,000	4,937,000	8,913,000	14,849,000	15,193,000	14,329,000	13,583,000
Income Before Taxes	4,853,000	1,370,000	953,000	(7,584,000)	8,234,000	11,026,000	25,396,000	10,939,000
Income Taxes	937,000	135,000	302,000	(2,151,000)	2,705,000	3,670,000	3,176,000	3,741,000
Net Income	3,487,000	495,000	(980,000)	(5,453,000)	3,467,000	7,237,000	22,071,000	6,920,000
Average Shares	2,126,000	1,843,000	1,829,000	1,810,000	1,504,000	1,233,000	1,237,000	1,224,000
Balance Sheet								
Current Assets	58,071,000	60,152,000	47,834,000	36,260,000	39,310,000	45,679,000	39,860,000	38,465,000
Total Assets	305,341,000	315,920,000	295,222,000	276,543,000	284,421,000	276,229,000	237,545,000	279,097,000
Current Liabilities	124,248,000	116,000,000	94,576,000	98,568,000	119,240,000	121,482,000	106,872,000	125,119,000
Long-Term Obligations	106,540,000	119,751,000	120,136,000	120,758,000	98,887,000	78,059,000	64,181,000	80,245,000
Total Liabilities	289,296,000	304,269,000	289,632,000	268,757,000	265,811,000	248,692,000	214,136,000	248,363,000
Stockholders' Equity	16,045,000	11,651,000	5,590,000	7,786,000	18,610,000	27,537,000	23,409,000	30,734,000
Shares Outstanding	1,908,000	1,831,388	1,831,219	1,806,608	1,835,050	1,206,420	1,211,649	1,203,000
Statistical Record								
Return on Assets %	1.12	0.16	N.M.	N.M.	1.23	2.82	8.54	2.55
Return on Equity %	25.11	5.74	N.M.	N.M.	14.98	28.41	81.53	24.07
EBITDA Margin %	10.69	8.34	8.54	7.03	19.11	20.83	32.72	22.07
Net Margin %	2.03	0.30	N.M.	N.M.	2.04	4.45	15.28	4.50
Asset Turnover	0.55	0.54	0.57	0.58	0.61	0.63	0.56	0.57
Current Ratio	0.47	0.52	0.51	0.37	0.33	0.38	0.37	0.31
Debt to Equity	6.64	10.28	21.49	15.51	5.31	2.83	2.74	2.61
Price Range	17.10-12.70	16.79-6.60	18.19-7.15	30.71-14.93	54.80-22.13	64.05-44.54	58.34-27.83	31.73-19.56
P/E Ratio	9.88-7.34	62.19-24.44	...	...	23.83-9.62	10.93-7.60	3.29-1.57	5.65-3.48
Average Yield %	2.77	3.73	3.02	4.49	0.79	3.52	3.76	6.58

Address: One American Road, Dearborn, MI 48126	Web Site: www.ford.com	Auditors: PricewaterhouseCoopers LLP
Telephone: (313) 322-3000	Officers: William Clay Ford Jr. - Chmn., C.E.O.	Investor Contact: 313-323-8220
Fax: (313) 222-4177	James J. Padilla - Pres.	Transfer Agents: First Chicago Trust Company of New York

FOREST CITY ENTERPRISES, INC.

Exchange	Symbol	Price	52Wk Range	Yield	P/E	Div Acheiver
NYS	FCE A	$63.80 (3/31/2005)	65.51-50.00	0.63	44.00	10 Years

*7 Year Price Score 146.54 ***NYSE Composite Index=100** ***12 Month Price Score 105.32**

TRADING VOLUME (thousand shares)

Interim Earnings (Per Share)

Qtr.	Apr	Jul	Oct	Jan
2001-02	0.20	0.33	1.38	0.23
2002-03	0.20	0.25	0.18	0.34
2003-04	0.29	0.13	0.52	(0.10)
2004-05	0.14	0.68	0.73	

Interim Dividends (Per Share)

Amt	Decl	Ex	Rec	Pay
0.10Q	9/8/2004	11/29/2004	12/1/2004	12/15/2004
0.20Q	12/9/2004	12/30/2004	1/3/2005	1/18/2005
0.10Q	12/9/2004	2/25/2005	3/1/2005	3/15/2005
0.10Q	3/24/2005	5/27/2005	6/1/2005	6/15/2005

Indicated Div: $0.40

Valuation Analysis

Forecast P/E	12.93	No of Institutions
	(4/7/2005)	108
Market Cap	$3.2 Billion	Shares
Book Value	810.2 Million	25,993,070
Price/Book	3.94	% Held
Price/Sales	2.94	70.25

Business Summary: Property, Real Estate & Development (MIC: 8.3 SIC: 512 NAIC: 36220)

Forest City Enterprises is engaged in the ownership, development, management and acquisition of commercial and residential real estate properties in 20 states and the District of Columbia. Co. operates through four strategic business units. The Commercial Group, Co.'s largest business unit, owns, develops, acquires and operates regional malls, specialty/urban retail centers, office buildings, hotels and mixed-use projects. The Residential Group owns, develops, acquires and operates residential rental properties. The Land Development Group acquires and sells both land and developed lots to residential, commercial and industrial customers. The Lumber Trading Group is a lumber wholesaler.

Recent Developments: For the quarter ended Oct 31 2004, income from continuing operations decreased 16.8% to $16,799 thousand from income of $20,200 thousand in the year-earlier quarter. Net income increased 43.8% to $37,340 thousand from net income of $25,972 thousand in the year-earlier quarter. Results for 2004 included a loss on the early extinguishment of debt $1,275 thousand. Revenues from rental operations rose 8.5% to $256,108 thousand from $236,043 thousand in the corresponding period the year before.

Prospects: Co. is continuing to expand its presence in its core market of New York City/Philadelphia, California, Boston, Greater Washington, D.C./Baltimore, and Denver. Co.'s business strategy is to concentrate on high-growth, high-barrier-to-entry urban markets where it has access to large, complex commercial, residential and mixed-use projects. Meanwhile, given favorable market conditions and low interest rates, Co. is pursuing development of condominiums in selected markets with high demand for upscale urban homes. Looking ahead, Co.'s robust development pipeline should continue to fuel earnings growth in the coming years.

Financial Data (US$ in Thousands)	9 Mos	6 Mos	3 Mos	01/31/2004	01/31/2003	01/31/2002	01/31/2001	01/31/2000
Earnings Per Share	1.45	1.23	0.69	0.84	0.97	2.17	2.01	0.90
Cash Flow Per Share	6.36	4.29	2.99	2.98	4.33	1.69	4.57	2.82
Tang Book Value Per Share	16.20	15.71	15.13	14.98	14.22	13.39	10.13	8.58
Dividends Per Share	0.370	0.360	0.330	0.300	0.220	0.177	0.147	0.120
Dividend Payout %	25.50	29.17	47.92	35.71	22.68	8.14	7.28	13.33
Income Statement								
Property Income	...	522,275	248,444	898,339	791,806	738,508	658,369	...
Non-Property Income	...	66,498	40,137	123,249	135,744	168,062	136,416	...
Total Revenue	762,152	588,773	288,581	1,021,588	927,550	906,570	794,785	793,071
Depn & Amortn	124,501	85,425	40,947	127,631	115,001	97,842	98,364	88,144
Interest Expense	182,519	120,963	59,942	198,122	177,237	178,580	182,544	159,719
Income Before Taxes	109,161	86,737	19,610	77,052	81,998	159,957	117,348	64,849
Income Taxes	36,262	28,507	5,499	28,799	31,826	63,487	22,312	24,319
Net Income	79,366	42,026	7,203	42,669	48,831	103,029	91,637	40,802
Average Shares	50,919	50,867	50,870	50,572	50,178	47,386	45,500	45,229
Balance Sheet								
Total Assets	7,255,887	7,194,174	6,843,455	5,895,072	5,077,209	4,417,646	4,030,470	3,814,474
Long-Term Obligations	5,123,698	5,063,924	4,776,590	4,010,827	3,371,757	2,894,998	2,849,812	2,749,380
Total Liabilities	6,331,646	6,329,540	6,005,535	5,097,687	4,292,171	3,687,256	3,495,744	3,427,968
Stockholders' Equity	810,182	785,974	756,802	748,911	705,972	662,513	456,636	386,506
Shares Outstanding	49,996	50,026	50,026	49,986	49,655	49,463	45,096	45,046
Statistical Record								
Return on Assets %	1.15	1.01	0.59	0.78	1.03	2.44	2.33	1.13
Return on Equity %	9.60	8.34	4.75	5.87	7.14	18.41	21.68	11.36
Net Margin %	10.41	7.14	2.50	4.18	5.26	11.36	11.53	5.14
Price Range	56.00-44.31	54.60-40.00	54.60-36.55	52.00-30.95	40.27-29.00	40.90-27.27	27.71-16.67	18.92-13.50
P/E Ratio	38.62-30.56	44.39-32.52	79.13-52.97	61.90-36.85	41.52-29.90	18.85-12.57	13.79-8.29	21.02-15.00
Average Yield %	0.72	0.74	0.72	0.74	0.63	0.54	0.66	0.72

Address: Terminal Tower, 50 Public Square, Suite 1100, Cleveland, OH 44113 **Telephone:** (216) 621-6060 **Fax:** (216) 362-2692	**Web Site:** www.fceinc.com **Officers:** Albert B. Ratner - Co-Chmn. Samuel H. Miller - Co-Chmn., Treas.	**Auditors:** PricewaterhouseCoopers LLP **Investor Contact:** 216-416-3215

FOREST LABORATORIES, INC.

Exchange	Symbol	Price	52Wk Range	Yield	P/E
NYS	FRX	$36.95 (3/31/2005)	75.20-36.47	N/A	14.96

*7 Year Price Score 123.45 *NYSE Composite Index=100 *12 Month Price Score 78.16

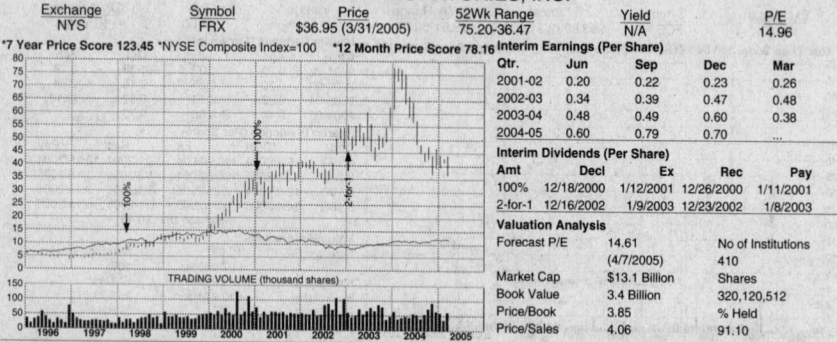

Interim Earnings (Per Share)

Qtr.	Jun	Sep	Dec	Mar
2001-02	0.20	0.22	0.23	0.26
2002-03	0.34	0.39	0.47	0.48
2003-04	0.48	0.49	0.60	0.38
2004-05	0.60	0.79	0.70	...

Interim Dividends (Per Share)

Amt	Decl	Ex	Rec	Pay
100%	12/18/2000	1/12/2001	12/26/2000	1/11/2001
2-for-1	12/16/2002	1/9/2003	12/23/2002	1/8/2003

Valuation Analysis

Forecast P/E	14.61	No of Institutions	
	(4/7/2005)	410	
Market Cap	$13.1 Billion	Shares	
Book Value	3.4 Billion	320,120,512	
Price/Book	3.85	% Held	
Price/Sales	4.06	91.10	

Business Summary: Pharmaceuticals (MIC: 9.1 SIC: 834 NAIC: 25412)

Forest Laboratories develops, manufactures and sells ethical drug products which require a physician's prescription, as well as non-prescription pharmaceutical products sold over-the-counter. Co. products include Namenda™, for the treatment of moderate to severe Alzheimer's disease; Lexapro®, for the treatment of major depression; Celexa™, for the treatment of depression; Neramexane™, for various CNS disorders; Milnacipran™, for the treatment of Fibromyalgia Syndrome; CCR1™, a specific chemokine receptor involved in the inflammation process; Benicar™, for the treatment of hypertension; Lercanidipine™, for lowering blood pressure; and Tiazac®, for the treatment of angina and hypertension.

Recent Developments: For the quarter ended Dec 31 2004, net income increased 15.3% to $260,805,000 from net income of $226,118,000 in the year-earlier quarter. Revenues were $832,343,000 , up 17.7% from $707,181,000 the year before. Total direct expense was $176,431,000 versus $160,866,000 in the prior-year quarter, an increase of 9.7%. Total indirect expense was $320,256,000 versus $258,450,000 in the prior-year quarter, an increase of 23.9%.

Prospects: All of Co.'s principal promoted brands are exhibiting strong growth, which is expected to continue in the future. Co.'s co-promotion agreement with Sankyo Pharma for Benicar® and Benicar HCT™ saw its first quarter of profitable results in the third quarter of fiscal 2005 , which Co. expects to substantially increase going forward. In addition, Co.'s partner, Merck Sante, received Federal Drug Administration marketing approval for Campral®, a glutamate modulator for the treatment of alcohol dependence, which Co. began to market in January 2005. Given the continuing underlying strength of its promoted brands, Co. anticipates earnings for fiscal-year 2005 to be approximately $2.60 per share.

Financial Data

(US$ in Thousands)	9 Mos	6 Mos	3 Mos	03/31/2004	03/31/2003	03/31/2002	03/31/2001	03/31/2000
Earnings Per Share	2.47	2.36	2.06	1.95	1.66	0.91	0.59	0.32
Cash Flow Per Share	2.75	2.64	2.23	1.71	2.02	1.20	0.52	0.51
Tang Book Value Per Share	8.78	9.26	8.67	8.03	5.66	3.75	2.64	1.79
Income Statement								
Total Revenue	2,506,403	1,674,060	792,826	2,680,274	2,245,806	1,601,824	1,205,174	899,301
EBITDA	1,020,819	678,801	297,279	959,013	841,688	484,498	309,350	165,678
Depn & Amortn	18,871	12,509	6,242	22,191	21,119	14,320	10,623	8,231
Income Before Taxes	1,001,948	666,292	291,037	936,822	820,569	470,178	298,727	157,447
Income Taxes	215,898	141,047	61,118	200,948	198,581	132,224	83,631	44,759
Net Income	786,050	525,245	229,919	735,874	621,988	337,954	215,096	112,688
Average Shares	371,638	375,226	380,943	376,779	373,702	370,484	365,968	351,780
Balance Sheet								
Current Assets	2,812,342	3,126,621	2,858,480	2,916,234	2,255,333	1,195,112	884,149	645,233
Total Assets	3,919,843	4,286,667	4,045,323	3,862,736	2,918,107	1,951,873	1,446,930	1,097,642
Current Liabilities	512,662	583,771	550,563	604,754	564,397	324,980	223,618	211,090
Total Liabilities	514,193	585,387	552,328	606,872	566,289	326,784	224,816	212,952
Stockholders' Equity	3,405,650	3,701,280	3,492,995	3,255,864	2,351,818	1,625,089	1,222,114	884,690
Shares Outstanding	354,934	368,366	370,080	369,527	363,472	358,512	353,202	338,644
Statistical Record								
Return on Assets %	25.07	23.81	22.05	21.65	25.54	19.89	16.91	11.39
Return on Equity %	28.88	27.67	25.89	26.17	31.28	23.74	20.42	13.80
EBITDA Margin %	40.73	40.55	37.50	35.78	37.48	30.25	25.67	18.42
Net Margin %	31.36	31.38	29.00	27.46	27.70	21.10	17.85	12.53
Asset Turnover	0.87	0.83	0.80	0.79	0.92	0.94	0.95	0.91
Current Ratio	5.49	5.36	5.19	4.82	4.00	3.68	3.95	3.06
Price Range	77.59-36.80	77.59-41.98	77.59-42.00	77.59-42.00	55.50-33.00	42.05-26.93	35.48-18.91	21.13-10.53
P/E Ratio	31.41-14.90	32.88-17.79	37.67-20.39	39.79-21.54	33.43-19.88	46.21-29.59	60.13-32.04	66.02-32.91

Address: 909 Third Avenue, New York, NY 10022-4731	Web Site: www.forestlaboratories.com	Auditors: BDO Seidman, LLP
Telephone: (212) 421-7850	Officers: Howard Solomon - Chmn., C.EO. Kenneth E. Goodman - Pres., C.O.O.	
Fax: (212) 750-9152		

FOREST OIL CORP.

Exchange	Symbol	Price	52Wk Range	Yield	P/E
NYS	FST	$40.50 (3/31/2005)	42.50-24.02	N/A	19.19

*7 Year Price Score 99.05 ***NYSE Composite Index=100** ***12 Month Price Score 119.68**

Interim Earnings (Per Share)

Qtr.	Mar	Jun	Sep	Dec
2001	1.60	1.01	0.03	(0.57)
2002	(0.04)	0.23	0.06	0.19
2003	0.80	0.48	0.54	(0.06)
2004	0.35	0.50	0.53	0.73

Interim Dividends (Per Share)

No Dividends Paid

Valuation Analysis

Forecast P/E	N/A	No of Institutions	
Market Cap	$2.4 Billion	Shares	52,456,048
Book Value	1.5 Billion	% Held	86.78
Price/Book	1.64		
Price/Sales	2.65		

Business Summary: Oil and Gas (MIC: 14.2 SIC: 311 NAIC: 11111)

Forest Oil is an independent oil and gas company engaged in the acquisition, exploration, development and production of natural gas and liquids in North America and selected international locations. In 2003, Co. operated in five business units: the Gulf Coast, Western United States, Alaska, Canada and International. As of Dec 31 2003, Co.'s proved reserves and producing properties were all located in North America. At Dec 31 2003, approximately 88.0% of Co.'s proved oil and gas reserves were in the United States and approximately 12.0% in Canada. As of Dec 31 2003, Co.'s estimated proved reserves were 1,296 billion cubic feet equivalent, of which about 62.0% was natural gas.

Recent Developments: For the year ended Dec 31 2004, income from continuing operations increased 36.5% to $123,126 thousand from income of $90,228 thousand a year earlier. Net income increased 38.7% to $122,551 thousand from net income of $88,351 thousand a year earlier. Revenues were $912,898 thousand, up 38.9% from $657,178 thousand the year before. Operating income was $258,287 thousand versus an income of $201,169 thousand in the prior year, an increase of 28.4%. Total direct expense was $238,194 thousand versus $154,170 thousand in the prior year, an increase of 54.5%. Total indirect expense was $416,417 thousand versus $301,839 thousand in the prior year, an increase of 38.0%.

Prospects: On Feb 28 2005, Co. announced that it has agreed to acquire a private company whose primary asset is an operated working interest of 83.0% in the Buffalo Wallow Field and approximately 33,300 gross acres primarily in Hemphill and Wheeler Counties, Texas. Under the terms of the transaction, Co. will pay about $200.0 million in cash for the company's equity and assume about $30.0 million of debt. The acquisition, which is expected to be completed on Mar 31 2005, subject to customary closing conditions, should add production of between 7 and 8 billion cubic feet equivalent (Bcfe) in 2005, along with 15 to 16 Bcfe in 2006.

Financial Data
(US$ in Thousands)

	12/31/2004	12/31/2003	12/31/2002	12/31/2001	12/31/2000	12/31/1999	12/31/1998	12/31/1997
Earnings Per Share	2.11	1.75	0.44	2.11	2.64	0.40	(4.68)	(0.27)
Cash Flow Per Share	9.95	7.72	4.05	10.45	6.60	2.31	2.19	1.80
Tang Book Value Per Share	23.51	22.14	19.32	19.48	17.41	5.52	3.28	6.49
Income Statement								
Total Revenue	912,898	657,178	475,694	1,018,379	913,058	357,258	321,819	339,641
EBITDA	610,899	428,107	276,899	466,667	410,940	147,531	(83,611)	108,718
Depn & Amortn	351,185	233,902	187,663	227,826	213,997	89,531	101,007	80,933
Income Before Taxes	201,870	144,864	38,803	188,931	136,674	17,127	(223,604)	6,382
Income Taxes	78,744	54,636	14,317	79,577	6,066	(2,514)	(25,818)	3,293
Net Income	122,551	88,351	21,276	103,743	130,608	19,043	(191,590)	(9,270)
Average Shares	58,089	50,353	48,207	49,282	47,977	48,268	40,910	34,961
Balance Sheet								
Current Assets	283,468	215,360	160,471	201,965	238,828	71,358	61,376	88,560
Total Assets	3,122,505	2,683,548	1,924,681	1,796,369	1,752,378	800,052	759,736	647,782
Current Liabilities	323,615	273,109	191,675	240,298	239,937	86,175	61,028	66,498
Long-Term Obligations	888,819	929,971	767,219	594,178	622,234	371,680	505,450	254,760
Total Liabilities	1,650,358	1,497,750	1,003,470	872,426	893,412	481,068	590,745	385,955
Stockholders' Equity	1,472,147	1,185,798	921,211	923,943	858,966	318,984	168,991	261,827
Shares Outstanding	59,693	53,555	47,024	46,744	48,229	53,778	44,637	36,320
Statistical Record								
Return on Assets %	4.21	3.83	1.14	5.85	10.21	2.44	N.M.	N.M.
Return on Equity %	9.20	8.39	2.31	11.64	22.11	7.80	N.M.	N.M.
EBITDA Margin %	66.92	65.14	58.21	45.82	45.01	41.30	N.M.	32.01
Net Margin %	13.42	13.44	4.47	10.19	14.30	5.33	N.M.	N.M.
Asset Turnover	0.31	0.29	0.26	0.57	0.71	0.46	0.46	0.56
Current Ratio	0.88	0.79	0.84	0.84	1.00	0.83	1.01	1.33
Debt to Equity	0.60	0.78	0.83	0.64	0.72	1.17	2.99	0.97
Price Range	34.03-23.47	29.35-19.99	32.35-20.92	37.29-23.45	36.88-14.50	36.00-10.88	33.00-15.38	37.75-24.50
P/E Ratio	16.13-11.12	16.77-11.42	73.52-47.55	17.67-11.11	13.97-5.49	90.00-27.19	...	...

Address: 1600 Broadway, Suite 2200, Denver, CO 80202	Web Site: www.forestoil.com	Auditors: KPMG LLP
Telephone: (303) 812-1400	Officers: Forrest E. Hoglund - Chmn. H. Craig Clark - Pres., C.E.O.	Investor Contact: 303-812-1610
Fax: (303) 812-1400		

FORTUNE BRANDS INC

Exchange	Symbol	Price	52Wk Range	Yield	P/E
NYS	FO	$80.63 (3/31/2005)	84.90-69.01	1.64	15.42

*7 Year Price Score 142.13 *NYSE Composite Index=100 *12 Month Price Score 100.83

Interim Earnings (Per Share)

Qtr.	Mar	Jun	Sep	Dec
2001	0.39	0.66	0.60	0.84
2002	0.55	1.27	0.73	0.86
2003	0.66	1.18	0.97	1.04
2004	0.92	1.11	1.52	1.67

Interim Dividends (Per Share)

Amt	Decl	Ex	Rec	Pay
0.30Q	4/27/2004	5/10/2004	5/12/2004	6/1/2004
0.33Q	7/27/2004	8/9/2004	8/11/2004	9/1/2004
0.33Q	9/28/2004	11/8/2004	11/10/2004	12/1/2004
0.33Q	1/28/2005	2/7/2005	2/9/2005	3/1/2005

Indicated Div: $1.32

Valuation Analysis

Forecast P/E	16.27	No of Institutions	
	(4/7/2005)	493	
Market Cap	$11.6 Billion	Shares	
Book Value	3.2 Billion	89,437,792	
Price/Book	3.62	% Held	
Price/Sales	1.59	61.73	

Business Summary: Metal Products (MIC: 11.4 SIC: 429 NAIC: 32510)

Fortune Brands is an international consumer products holding company. Home and hardware brands include Moen faucets, Master locks, Aristokraft, Schrock, Diamond and Omega cabinets, Therma-Tru door systems, and Waterloo tool storage sold by units of Fortune Brands Home & Hardware. Office brands include Day-Timer, Kensington, Wilson Jones and Swingline sold by units of ACCO World. Acushnet's golf brands include Titleist, Cobra and Footjoy. Spirit and wine brands sold by units of Jim Beam Brands Worldwide include Jim Beam and Knob Creek bourbons, DeKuyper cordials, The Dalmore single malt scotch, Vox vodka and Geyser Peak and Wild Horse wines.

Recent Developments: For the year ended Dec 31 2004, net income increased 35.3% to $783,800 thousand from net income of $579,200 thousand a year earlier. Revenues were $7,320,900 thousand, up 17.8% from $6,214,500 thousand the year before. Operating income was $1,123,300 thousand versus an income of $917,500 thousand in the prior year, an increase of 22.4%. Total direct expense was $4,352,200 thousand versus $3,675,300 thousand in the prior year, an increase of 18.4%. Total indirect expense was $1,845,400 thousand versus $1,621,700 thousand in the prior year, an increase of 13.8%.

Prospects: Looking ahead, results are expected to benefit from new product introductions, expanded customer relationships, along with supply chain efficiencies. In addition, Co. anticipates growing sales and gaining market share in the home and hardware business as it ramps up its new Thomasville line of products at Home Depot and its Diamond Reflections branded products at Lowes. Meanwhile, Co. is projecting first quarter and full-year 2005 double-digit growth in diluted earnings per share, excluding one-time charges or gains. Also, Co. is targeting 2005 free cash flow of between $450.0 million and $500.0 million after dividends and capital expenditures.

Financial Data

(US$ in Thousands)	12/31/2004	12/31/2003	12/31/2002	12/31/2001	12/31/2000	12/31/1999	12/31/1998	12/31/1997
Earnings Per Share	5.23	3.86	3.41	2.49	(0.88)	(5.35)	1.49	0.56
Cash Flow Per Share	5.44	5.43	5.27	4.24	2.99	2.93	2.35	2.48
Tang Book Value Per Share	N.M.	N.M.	N.M.	2.06	0.89	0.59	1.91	2.91
Dividends Per Share	1.260	1.140	1.020	0.970	0.930	0.890	0.850	1.410
Dividend Payout %	24.09	29.53	29.91	38.96	...	...	57.05	251.79
Income Statement								
Total Revenue	7,320,900	6,214,500	5,677,700	5,678,700	5,844,500	5,524,700	5,240,900	4,844,500
EBITDA	1,391,300	1,140,100	994,100	807,400	409,400	(383,400)	865,700	499,100
Depn & Amortn	221,000	192,600	178,700	218,700	236,700	230,500	251,100	242,700
Income Before Taxes	1,085,600	884,400	756,200	491,900	38,900	(720,700)	511,900	139,700
Income Taxes	283,000	289,200	214,200	94,400	176,600	169,900	218,300	98,200
Net Income	783,800	579,200	525,600	386,000	(137,700)	(890,600)	263,100	98,500
Average Shares	149,900	150,300	154,000	155,300	157,600	166,600	176,200	173,300
Balance Sheet								
Current Assets	2,641,900	2,281,600	1,903,100	1,969,600	2,264,500	2,312,800	2,265,300	2,095,600
Total Assets	7,883,600	7,444,900	5,822,200	5,300,900	5,764,100	6,417,100	7,359,700	6,942,500
Current Liabilities	2,036,000	2,133,500	1,514,700	1,258,400	2,039,900	2,002,900	1,844,600	1,768,500
Long-Term Obligations	1,239,500	1,242,600	841,700	950,300	1,151,800	1,204,800	981,700	739,100
Total Liabilities	4,300,600	4,355,900	3,110,100	2,807,400	3,628,200	3,678,900	3,262,200	2,925,400
Stockholders' Equity	3,209,600	2,719,500	2,313,200	2,102,700	2,135,900	2,738,200	4,097,500	4,017,100
Shares Outstanding	144,285	146,264	146,990	147,997	153,508	229,600	170,884	114,142
Statistical Record								
Return on Assets %	10.20	8.73	9.45	6.98	N.M.	N.M.	3.68	1.20
Return on Equity %	26.37	23.02	23.80	18.21	N.M.	N.M.	6.48	2.56
EBITDA Margin %	19.00	18.35	17.51	14.22	7.00	N.M.	16.52	10.30
Net Margin %	10.71	9.32	9.26	6.80	N.M.	N.M.	5.02	2.03
Asset Turnover	0.95	0.94	1.02	1.03	0.96	0.80	0.73	0.59
Current Ratio	1.30	1.07	1.26	1.57	1.11	1.15	1.23	1.18
Debt to Equity	0.39	0.46	0.36	0.45	0.54	0.44	0.24	0.18
Price Range	78.90-66.94	71.49-40.70	57.67-37.48	40.20-29.06	33.06-19.44	44.63-29.75	42.06-26.31	37.56-31.00
P/E Ratio	15.09-12.80	18.52-10.54	16.91-10.99	16.14-11.67	...	...	28.23-17.66	67.08-55.36
Average Yield %	1.72	2.11	2.07	2.75	3.55	...	2.44	2.38	4.13

Address: 300 Tower Parkway,	Web Site: www.fortunebrands.com	Auditors: PricewaterhouseCoopers LLP
Lincolnshire, IL 60069-3640	Officers: Norman H. Wesley - Chmn., C.E.O. Mark	Investor Contact: 847-484-4410
Telephone: (847) 484-4400	Hausberg - Sr. V.P., Fin., Treas.	Transfer Agents: Bank of New York,
Fax: (847) 478-0073		New York, NY

FPL GROUP, INC.

Exchange	Symbol	Price	52Wk Range	Yield	P/E
NYS	FPL	$40.15 (3/31/2005)	40.90-30.48	3.54	16.32

*7 Year Price Score 100.64 *NYSE Composite Index=100 *12 Month Price Score 105.53

TRADING VOLUME (thousand shares)

Interim Earnings (Per Share)

Qtr.	Mar	Jun	Sep	Dec
2001	0.33	0.65	0.99	0.34
2002	(0.17)	0.73	0.29	0.36
2003	0.50	0.67	0.93	0.41
2004	0.39	0.71	0.88	0.47

Interim Dividends (Per Share)

Amt	Decl	Ex	Rec	Pay
0.34Q	7/23/2004	8/25/2004	8/27/2004	9/15/2004
0.34Q	10/15/2004	11/23/2004	11/26/2004	12/15/2004
0.355Q	2/18/2005	3/2/2005	3/4/2005	3/15/2005
2-for-1	2/18/2005	3/16/2005	3/4/2005	3/15/2005

Indicated Div: $1.42

Valuation Analysis

Forecast P/E	15.67	No of Institutions
	(4/7/2005)	517
Market Cap	$14.9 Billion	Shares
Book Value	7.5 Billion	265,395,264
Price/Book	1.98	% Held
Price/Sales	1.42	71.22

Business Summary: Electricity (MIC: 7.1 SIC: 911 NAIC: 21121)

FPL Group is a holding company whose principal operating subsidiary, Florida Power & Light Company, is engaged in the generation, transmission, distribution and sale of electric energy. Co. supplies service throughout most of the east and lower west coasts of Florida. As of Dec 31 2004, Florida Power & Light Company served about 4.2 million customer accounts. FPL Energy is a limited liability company that owns, develops, constructs, manages and operates domestic electric-generating facilities in wholesale energy markets. At Dec 31 2004, FPL Energy had net generating capability totaling 11,520 megawatts, all of which consisted of ownership interests in operating independent power projects.

Recent Developments: For the year ended Dec 31 2004, net income decreased 0.3% to $887,000 thousand from net income of $890,000 thousand a year earlier. Revenues were $10,522,000 thousand, up 9.3% from $9,630,000 thousand the year before. Operating income was $1,472,000 thousand versus an income of $1,531,000 thousand in the prior year, a decrease of 3.9%. Total direct expense was $6,889,000 thousand versus $6,165,000 thousand in the prior year, an increase of 11.7%. Total indirect expense was $2,161,000 thousand versus $1,934,000 thousand in the prior year, an increase of 11.7%.

Prospects: On Jan 21 2005, Co. reaffirmed its earnings guidance for full-year 2005 of $5.00 to $5.20 per share excluding the cumulative effect of adopting new accounting standards, as well as the mark-to-market effect of non-qualifying hedges. Co. stated that its forecast for 2005 reflects continued customer growth at Florida Power & Light and normal weather at both the utility and FPL Energy. Co. said that it expects earnings contributions from Florida Power & Light in the range of $3.95 to $4.10, from FPL Energy of $1.30 to $1.45, and a negative effect from corporate and other of $0.30 to $0.35 per share.

Financial Data

(US$ in Thousands)	12/31/2004	12/31/2003	12/31/2002	12/31/2001	12/31/2000	12/31/1999	12/31/1998	12/31/1997
Earnings Per Share	2.46	2.50	1.37	2.31	2.07	2.04	1.93	1.78
Cash Flow Per Share	7.37	6.35	6.76	5.76	2.86	4.57	5.04	4.62
Tang Book Value Per Share	20.24	18.93	17.46	17.09	15.91	15.04	14.18	13.33
Dividends Per Share	1.300	1.200	1.160	1.120	1.080	1.040	1.000	0.960
Dividend Payout %	52.95	48.00	84.98	48.48	52.17	51.11	51.95	53.78
Income Statement								
Total Revenue	10,522,000	9,630,000	8,311,000	8,475,000	7,082,000	6,438,000	6,661,000	6,369,000
EBITDA	2,852,000	2,758,000	2,158,000	2,467,000	2,350,000	2,282,000	2,549,000	2,274,000
Depn & Amortn	1,246,000	1,118,000	908,000	983,000	1,032,000	1,040,000	1,284,000	1,061,000
Income Before Taxes	1,154,000	1,261,000	939,000	1,160,000	1,040,000	1,020,000	943,000	922,000
Income Taxes	267,000	368,000	244,000	379,000	336,000	323,000	279,000	304,000
Net Income	887,000	890,000	473,000	781,000	704,000	697,000	664,000	618,000
Average Shares	361,600	356,400	346,600	337,800	340,000	342,000	346,000	346,000
Balance Sheet								
Net PPE	21,226,000	20,297,000	14,304,000	11,662,000	9,934,000	9,264,000	8,555,000	9,354,000
Total Assets	28,333,000	26,935,000	19,790,000	17,463,000	15,300,000	13,441,000	12,029,000	12,449,000
Long-Term Obligations	8,027,000	8,723,000	5,790,000	4,858,000	3,976,000	3,478,000	2,347,000	2,949,000
Total Liabilities	20,796,000	19,963,000	13,174,000	11,222,000	9,481,000	7,845,000	6,677,000	7,378,000
Stockholders' Equity	7,537,000	6,972,000	6,616,000	6,241,000	5,819,000	5,596,000	5,352,000	5,071,000
Shares Outstanding	372,351	368,000	366,000	352,000	351,532	357,109	361,424	363,524
Statistical Record								
Return on Assets %	3.20	3.81	2.54	4.77	4.89	5.47	5.43	5.01
Return on Equity %	12.19	13.10	7.36	12.95	12.30	12.73	12.74	12.42
EBITDA Margin %	27.11	28.64	25.97	29.11	33.18	35.45	38.27	35.70
Net Margin %	8.43	9.24	5.69	9.22	9.94	10.83	9.97	9.70
PPE Turnover	0.51	0.56	0.64	0.78	0.74	0.72	0.74	0.68
Asset Turnover	0.38	0.41	0.45	0.52	0.49	0.51	0.54	0.52
Debt to Equity	1.07	1.25	0.88	0.78	0.68	0.62	0.44	0.58
Price Range	37.98-30.48	33.91-27.10	32.45-23.15	35.13-25.95	36.25-18.41	30.81-20.94	36.00-28.22	29.88-21.50
P/E Ratio	15.44-12.39	13.57-10.84	23.69-16.90	15.21-11.23	17.51-8.89	15.10-10.26	18.65-14.62	16.78-12.08
Average Yield %	3.89	3.88	4.06	3.87	4.10	3.92	3.20	3.99

Address: 700 Universe Boulevard, Juno Beach, FL 33408	Web Site: www.fplgroup.com	Auditors: Deloitte & Touche LLP
Telephone: (561) 694-4000	Officers: Lewis Hay III - Chmn., Pres., C.E.O. Moray P. Dewhurst - V.P., Fin., C.F.O.	
Fax: (561) 694-4620		

FRANKLIN RESOURCES, INC.

Exchange	Symbol	Price	52Wk Range	Yield	P/E	Div Acheiver
NYS	BEN	$68.65 (3/31/2005)	73.24-47.37	0.58	22.73	15 Years

*7 Year Price Score 120.54 *NYSE Composite Index=100 *12 Month Price Score 109.88

Interim Earnings (Per Share)

Qtr.	Dec	Mar	Jun	Sep
2001-02	0.45	0.46	0.48	0.26
2002-03	0.43	0.43	0.52	0.60
2003-04	0.69	0.68	0.69	0.74
2004-05	0.92	...	...	...

Interim Dividends (Per Share)

Amt	Decl	Ex	Rec	Pay
0.085Q	9/24/2004	9/30/2004	10/4/2004	10/15/2004
0.10Q	12/16/2004	12/29/2004	12/31/2004	1/14/2005
0.10Q	3/15/2005	3/29/2005	3/31/2005	4/15/2005
2.00Q	3/15/2005	3/29/2005	3/31/2005	4/15/2005

Indicated Div: $0.40 (Div. Reinv. Plan)

Valuation Analysis

Forecast P/E	18.13 (4/7/2005)	No of Institutions	367
Market Cap	$17.2 Billion	Shares	118,912,608
Book Value	5.3 Billion	% Held	47.49
Price/Book	3.22		
Price/Sales	4.76		

Business Summary: Wealth Management (MIC: 8.8 SIC: 282 NAIC: 23930)

Franklin Resources is a bank holding company and a financial services company. Through its wholly-owned direct and indirect subsidiary companies, Co. provides a range of investment advisory, investment management and related services to open-end and closed-end investment companies, institutional accounts, high net-worth families, individuals and separate accounts in the United States and internationally. Co. also provides investment management and related services to a number of closed-end investment companies. As of Sep 30 2004, Co.'s subsidiaries had $361.90 billion in assets under management.

Recent Developments: For the quarter ended Dec 31 2004, net income increased 39.3% to $240.0 million from net income of $172.3 million in the corresponding prior-year quarter. Revenues advanced 21.8% to $986.0 million from $809.7 million a year earlier. Investment management fees climbed 24.6% to $566.5 million, and underwriting and distribution fees rose 23.2% to $340.4 million. Shareholder servicing fees increased 3.0% to $63.2 million, while other revenues fell 12.3% to $15.4 million. Operating income grew 34.7% to $300.1 million from $222.9 million the year before.

Prospects: Co. is performing well, due largely to asset growth from both market appreciation and inflows. During the first quarter of fiscal 2005, assets under management rose 19.5% to $402.20 billion from $336.70 billion the previous year. Separately, in Dec 2004, Co. agreed to pay an additional $20.0 million to the SEC to settle charges against two of its units for failing to fully disclose payments to brokerage firms for promoting fund shares. Meanwhile, Franklin Templeton Investments, the unit that runs Co.'s Canadian mutual funds, continues to provide information to the Ontario Securities Commission in response to possible enforcement action against the unit stemming from alleged market timing.

Financial Data

(US$ in Thousands)	3 Mos	09/30/2004	09/30/2003	09/30/2002	09/30/2001	09/30/2000	09/30/1999	09/30/1998
Earnings Per Share	3.02	2.80	1.97	1.65	1.91	2.28	1.69	1.98
Cash Flow Per Share	4.30	3.78	2.16	2.82	2.19	2.84	2.32	2.74
Tang Book Value Per Share	13.11	12.23	9.31	8.69	7.63	7.37	5.79	4.08
Dividends Per Share	0.355	0.415	0.295	0.275	0.255	0.240	0.220	0.200
Dividend Payout %	11.75	14.82	14.97	16.67	13.35	10.53	13.02	10.10
Income Statement								
Total Revenue	986,022	3,438,208	2,624,448	2,518,532	2,354,843	2,340,140	2,262,497	2,577,272
Income Before Taxes	335,649	993,866	700,203	578,275	637,790	739,591	574,084	676,284
Income Taxes	95,660	291,981	197,373	145,552	153,069	177,502	147,373	175,834
Net Income	239,989	706,664	502,830	432,723	484,721	562,089	426,711	500,450
Average Shares	262,629	252,152	254,681	262,054	253,663	246,624	252,757	252,941
Balance Sheet								
Total Assets	8,451,248	8,228,135	6,970,749	6,422,738	6,265,650	4,042,443	3,666,790	3,480,049
Total Liabilities	3,019,346	3,045,262	2,660,641	2,155,792	2,287,754	1,076,950	1,009,796	1,199,282
Stockholders' Equity	5,339,332	5,106,784	4,310,108	4,266,946	3,977,896	2,965,493	2,656,994	2,280,767
Shares Outstanding	250,242	249,680	245,931	258,555	260,797	243,730	251,006	251,742
Statistical Record								
Return on Assets %	9.74	9.27	7.51	6.82	9.40	14.54	11.94	15.22
Return on Equity %	15.55	14.97	11.73	10.50	13.96	19.94	17.28	24.21
Price Range	70.75-47.37	60.05-43.56	46.80-28.18	44.13-30.97	47.83-31.90	44.72-25.19	45.00-27.25	57.31-26.38
P/E Ratio	23.43-15.69	21.45-15.56	23.76-14.30	26.75-18.77	25.04-16.70	19.61-11.05	26.63-16.12	28.95-13.32
Average Yield %	0.64	0.80	0.82	0.73	0.62	0.73	0.61	0.43

Address: One Franklin Parkway, San Mateo, CA 94403	Web Site: www.frk.com	Auditors: PricewaterhouseCoopers LLP
Telephone: (650) 312-2000	Officers: Charles B. Johnson - Chmn. Harmon E. Burns - Vice-Chmn.	Investor Contact: 800-632-2350
Fax: (650) 312-3655		Transfer Agents: Bank of New York

FREDDIE MAC

Exchange	Symbol	Price	52Wk Range	Yield	P/E	Div Acheiver
NYS	FRE	$63.20 (3/31/2005)	73.70-56.93	2.22	9.46	14 Years

*7 Year Price Score 95.92 ***NYSE Composite Index=100** ***12 Month Price Score 92.08**

TRADING VOLUME (thousand shares)

Interim Earnings (Per Share)

Qtr.	Mar	Jun	Sep	Dec
2000	0.81	0.83	0.86	0.89
2001	1.13	1.24	1.40	1.87
2002	1.94	1.50	2.13	8.61
2003			-6.68-	

Interim Dividends (Per Share)

Amt	Decl	Ex	Rec	Pay
0.30Q	6/4/2004	6/10/2004	6/14/2004	6/30/2004
0.30Q	9/10/2004	9/16/2004	9/20/2004	9/30/2004
0.30Q	12/3/2004	12/9/2004	12/13/2004	12/31/2004
0.35Q	3/4/2005	3/10/2005	3/14/2005	3/31/2005

Indicated Div: $1.40 (Div. Reinv. Plan)

Valuation Analysis

Forecast P/E	16.34	No of Institutions
	(4/7/2005)	566
Market Cap	$43.5 Billion	Shares
Book Value	31.5 Billion	621,063,552
Price/Book	1.38	% Held
Price/Sales	1.14	89.50

Business Summary: Credit & Lending (MIC: 8.6 SIC: 111 NAIC: 22292)

Freddie Mac purchases conventional residential mortgages from mortgage lending institutions and finances most of its purchases with sales of guaranteed mortgage securities called Mortgage Participation Certificates for which Co. ultimately assumes the risk of borrower default. Co. also maintains an investment portfolio that consists principally of federal funds sold, reverse repurchase agreements and tax-advantaged and other short-term investments. Co.'s financial performance is driven primarily by the growth of its total servicing portfolio, the mix of sold versus retained portfolios, the spreads earned on the sold and retained portfolios and mortgage default costs.

Recent Developments: For the year ended Dec 31 2004, net income fell 41.3% to $2.83 billion compared with $4.82 billion in the previous year. Results for 2004 and 2003 included losses on investment activity of $348.0 million and $1.11 billion, and losses on debt retirement of $327.0 million and $1.78 billion, respectively. Results also included a loss of $4.48 billion in 2004 and a gain of $39.0 million in 2003 on derivatives. Net interest income decreased 3.8% to $9.14 billion from $9.50 billion a year earlier. Total interest income declined 4.0% to $35.60 billion, while total interest expense inched up 0.2% to $9.14 billion.

Prospects: Co. is making significant progress in increasing its market share, streamlining operations and seizing business opportunities. While operating in a challenging, lower-growth environment, Co. believes it can continue to produce value for investors and home owners. For 2005, Co. expects to report net interest income materially lower than 2004, primarily due to compression in net interest margins on its existing portfolio and lower nominal margins on floating-rate mortgage-related security purchases. However, this decrease should be significantly offset by lower losses in non-interest income/loss, assuming current forward rates are realized.

Financial Data
(US$ in Thousands)

	12/31/2003	12/31/2002	12/31/2001	12/31/2000	12/31/1999	12/31/1998	12/31/1997	12/31/1996
Earnings Per Share	6.68	14.18	5.64	3.40	2.96	2.31	1.88	1.65
Cash Flow Per Share	6.52	24.53	25.61	20.95	(17.82)	(11.01)	7.95	(2.51)
Tang Book Value Per Share	39.03	38.87	15.50	16.81	11.98	11.55	8.74	9.62
Dividends Per Share	1.040	0.880	0.800	0.680	0.600	0.480	0.400	0.350
Dividend Payout %	15.57	6.21	14.18	20.00	20.27	20.78	21.28	21.21
Income Statement								
Interest Income	37,098,000	38,476,000	34,288,000	28,350,000	22,753,000	16,638,000	13,001,000	10,783,000
Interest Expense	26,509,000	26,564,000	28,808,000	25,512,000	20,213,000	14,711,000	11,370,000	9,241,000
Net Interest Income	10,589,000	11,912,000	5,480,000	2,838,000	2,540,000	1,927,000	1,631,000	1,542,000
Provision for Losses	10,000	128,000	45,000	40,000	60,000	190,000	310,000	320,000
Non-Interest Income	1,102,000	(68,000)	1,639,000	1,489,000	1,405,000	1,307,000	1,298,000	1,249,000
Non-Interest Expense	2,211,000	1,737,000	1,020,000	883,000	834,000	791,000	755,000	758,000
Income Before Taxes	7,018,000	14,803,000	6,300,000	3,534,000	3,161,000	2,356,000	1,964,000	1,797,000
Income Taxes	2,202,000	4,713,000	1,927,000	995,000	943,000	656,000	569,000	539,000
Net Income	4,816,000	10,090,000	4,147,000	2,547,000	2,223,000	1,700,000	1,395,000	1,243,000
Average Shares	688,675	695,116	696,876	696,448	700,211	684,658	692,000	...
Balance Sheet								
Net Loans & Leases	660,357,000	589,722,000	494,259,000	385,117,000	322,569,000	255,348,000	164,250,000	137,520,000
Total Assets	803,449,000	752,249,000	617,340,000	459,297,000	386,684,000	321,421,000	194,597,000	173,866,000
Total Liabilities	770,033,000	718,610,000	598,367,000	443,865,000	374,602,000	309,978,000	186,154,000	166,271,000
Stockholders' Equity	31,487,000	31,330,000	15,373,000	14,837,000	11,525,000	10,835,000	7,521,000	6,731,000
Shares Outstanding	688,573	687,376	695,304	692,584	695,091	695,179	679,000	695,000
Statistical Record								
Return on Assets %	0.62	1.47	0.77	0.60	0.63	0.66	0.76	0.80
Return on Equity %	15.33	43.21	27.45	19.27	19.88	18.52	19.58	19.69
Net Interest Margin %	28.54	30.96	15.98	10.01	11.16	11.58	12.55	14.30
Efficiency Ratio %	5.79	4.52	2.84	2.96	3.45	4.41	5.28	6.30
Price Range	64.73-47.35	68.60-53.98	70.79-60.00	69.00-37.69	64.63-45.75	65.13-39.50	43.38-27.03	28.66-19.44
P/E Ratio	9.69-7.09	4.84-3.81	12.55-10.64	20.29-11.08	21.83-15.46	28.19-17.10	23.07-14.38	17.37-11.78
Average Yield %	1.88	1.41	1.22	1.41	1.08	0.98	1.18	1.54

Address: 8200 Jones Branch Drive, McLean, VA 22102-3110 Telephone: (703) 903 2000 Fax: (703) 903-2759	Web Site: www.freddiemac.com Officers: Richard F. Syron - Chmn., C.E.O. Eugene M. McQuade - Pres., C.O.O.	Auditors: PricewaterhouseCoopers LLP Investor Contact: 800 373 3343 Transfer Agents: EquiServe Trust Company, N.A., Jersey City, NJ

FREEPORT-MCMORAN COPPER & GOLD INC.

Exchange	Symbol	Price	52Wk Range	Yield	P/E
NYS	FCX	$39.61 (3/31/2005)	43.73-28.40	2.52	46.60

*7 Year Price Score 157.80 *NYSE Composite Index=100 *12 Month Price Score 101.99

Interim Earnings (Per Share)

Qtr.	Mar	Jun	Sep	Dec
2001	0.26	0.25	0.03	(0.01)
2002	(0.03)	0.04	0.39	0.47
2003	0.33	0.37	0.29	0.01
2004	(0.10)	(0.30)	0.10	1.15

Interim Dividends (Per Share)

Amt	Decl	Ex	Rec	Pay
0.25Q	1/4/2005	1/12/2005	1/14/2005	2/1/2005
0.25Q	2/2/2005	3/11/2005	3/15/2005	3/31/2005
0.25Q	2/2/2005	3/11/2005	3/15/2005	3/31/2005
0.25Q	4/5/2005	4/13/2005	4/15/2005	5/1/2005
			Indicated Div: $1.00	

Valuation Analysis

Forecast P/E	11.52	No of Institutions
	(4/7/2005)	335
Market Cap	$7.1 Billion	Shares
Book Value	1.2 Billion	163,951,936
Price/Book	6.09	% Held
Price/Sales	2.99	91.30

Business Summary: Non-Precious Metals (MIC: 14.3 SIC: 021 NAIC: 12234)

Freeport-McMoRan Copper & Gold is a holding company. Through its subsidiaries, Co. is engaged in the exploration, development, mining and processing of ore containing copper, gold and silver in Irian Jaya, Indonesia. Co.'s operations are located in the remote rugged highlands of the Sudirman Mountain Range in the province of Papua, Indonesia, which is located on the western half of the island of New Guinea. Co. also smelts and refines copper concentrates in Spain and markets the refined copper products. In addition, Co. operates a copper smelter and refinery in Gresik, Indonesia. As of Dec 31 2003, proven reserves included 39.70 billion pounds of copper and 46.6 million ounces of gold.

Recent Developments: For the year ended Dec 31 2004, net income increased 11.3% to $202,267 thousand from net income of $181,660 thousand a year earlier. Revenues were $2,371,866 thousand, up 7.2% from $2,212,165 thousand the year before. Operating income was $703,576 thousand versus an income of $823,308 thousand in the prior year, a decrease of 14.5%. Total direct expense was $1,656,699 thousand versus $1,302,129 thousand in the prior year, an increase of 27.2%. Total indirect expense was $11,591 thousand versus $86,728 thousand in the prior year, a decrease of 86.6%.

Prospects: Co. was once again successful in 2004 in adding to its reserves and pursuing additional exploration opportunities to enhance the value of its business. With estimated 2005 sales of 1.50 billion pounds of copper and 2.9 million ounces of gold, representing increases of 50.0% for copper and 100.0% for gold from 2004 levels, Co. should be well positioned to generate improved financial results in the coming year. Meanwhile, capital expenditures for 2005 are expected to total $180.0 million for the full year, up from $141.0 million for the same period in 2004.

Financial Data

(US$ in Thousands)	12/31/2004	12/31/2003	12/31/2002	12/31/2001	12/31/2000	12/31/1999	12/31/1998	12/31/1997
Earnings Per Share	0.85	0.97	0.87	0.53	0.26	0.61	0.67	1.06
Cash Flow Per Share	1.87	3.67	3.54	3.54	3.34	3.46	2.73	2.61
Tang Book Value Per Share	0.36	4.23	...	...	...	...	...	...
Dividends Per Share	1.100	0.270	0.99	0.89	0.92	0.81	0.200	0.900
Dividend Payout %	129.41	27.84	113.79	167.92	353.85	132.79	29.85	84.91
Income Statement								
Total Revenue	2,371,866	2,212,165	1,910,462	1,838,866	1,868,610	1,887,328	1,757,132	2,000,904
EBITDA	937,396	1,027,791	893,346	816,260	762,142	868,116	844,421	882,341
Depn & Amortn	214,909	246,999	272,475	283,889	283,556	293,213	277,407	213,855
Income Before Taxes	574,384	583,775	449,662	358,776	273,240	380,834	361,426	516,766
Income Taxes	330,680	338,053	245,518	202,979	159,573	195,653	361,426	516,766
Net Income	202,267	181,660	164,654	113,025	76,987	136,467	170,566	231,315
Average Shares	184,923	159,102	146,418	144,938	154,519	164,567	175,354	197,653
Balance Sheet								
Current Assets	1,459,947	1,100,133	637,980	548,270	569,122	564,454	545,894	463,089
Total Assets	5,086,995	4,718,366	4,192,193	4,211,929	3,950,741	4,082,916	4,192,634	4,152,209
Current Liabilities	697,562	631,782	537,873	628,427	633,912	515,067	518,487	475,665
Long-Term Obligations	1,873,692	2,075,934	1,961,278	2,133,180	1,987,731	4,066,940	4,657,978	4,616,260
Total Liabilities	3,923,346	3,942,382	3,925,367	4,107,485	3,912,810	5,919,506	6,418,207	6,181,447
Stockholders' Equity	1,163,649	775,984	266,826	104,444	37,931	196,880	103,416	278,892
Shares Outstanding	178,990	183,367	144,909	143,975	144,041	163,496	164,308	184,255
Statistical Record								
Return on Assets %	4.11	4.08	3.92	2.68	1.91	2.45	3.69	6.11
Return on Equity %	20.80	34.84	88.70	108.22	65.39	69.31	80.48	51.37
EBITDA Margin %	39.52	46.46	46.76	44.39	40.79	46.00	48.06	44.10
Net Margin %	8.53	8.21	8.62	6.15	4.12	7.23	8.76	12.25
Asset Turnover	0.48	0.50	0.45	0.44	0.46	0.46	0.42	0.50
Current Ratio	2.09	1.74	1.19	0.87	0.90	1.10	1.05	0.97
Debt to Equity	1.61	2.68	7.35	20.42	52.40	20.66	45.04	16.55
Price Range	44.45-28.40	46.24-16.01	20.80-10.48	16.98-8.71	21.19-6.75	21.13-9.19	21.06-9.94	34.13-15.06
P/E Ratio	52.29-33.41	47.67-16.51	23.91-12.05	32.04-15.68	81.49-25.96	34.63-15.06	31.44-14.83	32.19-14.21
Average Yield %	3.00	1.01	6.33	7.17	8.37	5.48	1.36	3.24

Address: 1615 Poydras Street, New Orleans, LA 70112	Web Site: www.fcx.com	Auditors: ERNST & YOUNG LLP
Telephone: (504) 582-4000	**Officers:** James R. Moffett - Chmn., C.E.O. B. M. Rankin Jr. - Vice-Chmn.	**Investor Contact:** 504-582-4000
Fax: (504) 582-1847		

FRIEDMAN BILLINGS RAMSEY GROUP INC

Exchange	Symbol	Price	52Wk Range	Yield	P/E
NYS	FBR	$15.87 (3/31/2005)	27.42-15.42	8.57	7.67

*7 Year Price Score 143.19 *NYSE Composite Index=100 *12 Month Price Score 89.97

Interim Earnings (Per Share)

Qtr.	Mar	Jun	Sep	Dec
2001	(0.12)	0.10	(0.49)	0.22
2002	0.23	0.36	0.31	0.20
2003	0.12	0.43	0.41	0.52
2004	0.54	0.48	0.55	0.51

Interim Dividends (Per Share)

Amt	Decl	Ex	Rec	Pay
0.34Q	9/9/2004	9/28/2004	9/30/2004	10/29/2004
0.34Q	12/9/2004	12/29/2004	12/31/2004	1/28/2005
0.05Q	12/9/2004	12/29/2004	12/31/2004	1/28/2005
0.34Q	3/17/2005	3/29/2005	3/31/2005	4/29/2005

Indicated Div: $1.36

Valuation Analysis

Forecast P/E N/A

		No of Institutions
Market Cap	$2.7 Billion	Shares
Book Value	1.6 Billion	82,256,176
Price/Book	1.70	% Held
Price/Sales	2.55	56.63

Business Summary: Finance Intermediaries & Services (MIC: 8.7 SIC: 211 NAIC: 23120)

Friedman Billings Ramsey Group was formed through the combination of Friedman, Billings, Ramsey Group (old) and FBR Investment on Mar 31 2003. Co. is a national investment bank that provides investment banking, institutional brokerage, asset management and private client services through its operating subsidiaries and invests in mortgage-backed securities and merchant banking opportunities. Co. focuses capital and financial expertise on six industry sectors: financial services, real estate, technology, healthcare, energy and diversified industries. Co. is headquartered in the Washington, D.C. metropolitan area, with offices in 13 states throughout the eastern region, London and Vienna.

Recent Developments: For the year ended Dec 31 2004, net income jumped 73.6% to $349.6 million compared with $201.4 million the year before. Total revenues leapt 67.4% to $1.05 billion from $628.5 million a year earlier. The improvement in results was primarily driven by strong results achieved in Co.'s investment banking, institutional brokerage and asset management businesses. Within the investment banking business, Co. added bankers to its capital markets platform. Further, the improvement in results reflect Co.'s success in maintaining client relationships while expanding its client base into new areas. In particular, Co. is excited about its success with financial sponsor groups.

Prospects: With the planned acquisition of First NLC Financial Services, a rapidly growing non-conforming mortgage lender, Co. believes it can shift approximately 70.0% of the equity it currently deploys in the agency mortgage-backed securities strategy into non-conforming mortgages during 2005. This would result in approximately $700.0 million of its equity capital invested in non-conforming mortgages with a total balance of approximately $10.50 billion, all substantially match-funded to mitigate interest rate risk. Co.'s current judgment is that this portfolio can achieve a return on equity in excess of 25.0% in the current environment.

Financial Data
(US$ in Thousands)

	12/31/2004	12/31/2003	12/31/2002	12/31/2001	12/31/2000	12/31/1999	12/31/1998	12/31/1997
Earnings Per Share	2.07	1.63	1.10	(0.27)	0.36	(0.14)	(0.33)	1.48
Cash Flow Per Share	2.31	1.87	1.09	0.56	0.16	0.03	(1.75)	1.92
Tang Book Value Per Share	8.62	8.57	4.51	3.36	4.34	3.86	5.28	6.20
Dividends Per Share	1.530	1.360	...	...	...	...	...	...
Dividend Payout %	73.91	83.44	...	...	...	...	...	...
Income Statement								
Total Revenue	1,052,102	628,525	268,203	160,789	180,890	138,966	122,868	256,135
Income Before Taxes	408,720	246,005	55,441	(15,622)	22,245	(6,971)	(16,209)	57,136
Income Taxes	59,161	44,591	3,035	(1,760)	4,163	...	...	(2,402)
Net Income	349,559	201,414	53,283	(12,714)	18,082	(6,971)	(16,209)	59,539
Average Shares	168,489	123,307	48,442	47,465	50,682	48,872	49,723	40,275
Balance Sheet								
Total Assets	12,928,288	11,333,613	406,185	291,958	252,219	226,356	205,116	359,327
Total Liabilities	11,349,764	9,779,274	161,020	106,647	37,663	37,387	18,214	132,680
Stockholders' Equity	1,578,524	1,554,339	245,165	185,311	214,556	188,969	186,902	226,646
Shares Outstanding	168,896	166,893	50,455	49,604	49,380	48,960	35,402	36,577
Statistical Record								
Return on Assets %	2.87	3.43	15.26	N.M.	7.54	N.M.	N.M.	24.56
Return on Equity %	22.25	22.39	24.76	N.M.	8.94	N.M.	N.M.	43.19
Price Range	28.02-15.89	23.64-7.98	12.73-5.19	7.79-4.50	18.00-5.56	19.88-4.94	21.00-3.75	20.50-17.94
P/E Ratio	13.54-7.68	14.50-4.90	11.57-4.72	...	50.00-15.45	...	...	13.85-12.12
Average Yield %	7.42	9.48	...	...	...	...	...	...

Address: 1001 Nineteenth Street North, Arlington, VA 22209 Telephone: (703) 312 9500	Web Site: www.fbr.com Officers: Emanuel J. Friedman - Co-Chmn., Co-C.E.O. Eric F. Billings - Co-Chmn., Co- C.E.O.	Auditors: PricewatehouseCoopers LLP Investor Contact: 703-469-1080

FULLER (H.B.) COMPANY

Exchange	Symbol	Price	52Wk Range	Yield	P/E	Div Acheiver
NYS	FUL	$29.00 (3/31/2005)	29.10-25.34	1.59	22.31	37 Years

*7 Year Price Score 90.81 *NYSE Composite Index=100 *12 Month Price Score 91.96

Interim Earnings (Per Share)

Qtr.	Feb	May	Aug	Nov
2002	0.02	0.28	0.32	0.36
2003	0.11	0.34	0.43	0.47
2004	0.16	0.41	0.33	0.34
2005	0.22	...	...	...

Interim Dividends (Per Share)

Amt	Decl	Ex	Rec	Pay
0.115Q	4/15/2004	4/27/2004	4/29/2004	5/13/2004
0.115Q	7/9/2004	7/20/2004	7/22/2004	8/5/2004
0.115Q	9/30/2004	10/12/2004	10/14/2004	10/28/2004
0.115Q	1/28/2005	2/9/2005	2/11/2005	2/25/2005

Indicated Div: $0.46 (Div. Reinv. Plan)

Valuation Analysis

Forecast P/E	19.85	No of Institutions
	(4/13/2005)	130
Market Cap	$834.8 Million	Shares
Book Value	556.5 Million	21,491,162
Price/Book	1.50	% Held
Price/Sales	0.58	75.00

Business Summary: Chemicals (MIC: 11.1 SIC: 891 NAIC: 25520)

H.B. Fuller and its subsidiaries manufacture and market adhesives and specialty chemical products globally, with sales operations in 33 countries in North America, Europe, Latin America and the Asia/Pacific region. Co.'s products, in thousands of formulations, are sold to customers in a wide range of industries. Also, Co. is a producer and supplier of specialty chemical products for a variety of applications such as ceramic tile installation, HVAC insulation installation, powder coatings applied to metal surfaces such as office furniture, appliances and lawn and garden equipment, specialty hot melt adhesives for packaging applications, and liquid paint sold through retail outlets.

Recent Developments: For the quarter ended Feb 26 2005, net income jumped 40.9% to $6.5 million compared with $4.6 million in the year-earlier quarter. Results for 2005 and 2004 included gains of $1.8 million and $34,000, respectively, from sales of fixed assets. Net revenue advanced 10.8% to $353.0 million from $318.6 million a year earlier. The improvement in revenues was primarily attributed to pricing increases of 4.4% and growth in volumes of 1.4%, while acquisitions added 2.7% and positive currency effects contributed 2.3%. Gross profit climbed 5.7% to $90.7 million, or 25.7% of net revenue, from $85.8 million, or 26.9% of net revenue.

Prospects: Co. is seeing progress in its business, particularly with regard to pricing. The limited availability of raw materials and extraordinary rise in their cost is requiring Co. to be active in passing through these costs to customers. Although Co. is making headway with respect to the run-up in raw material costs, these pressures are expected to continue in the first half of 2005. As a result, Co. expects fiscal 2005 earnings to be slightly better than fiscal 2004, before charges for Co.'s Chilean operations. Separately, Co. is entering into joint ventures with Sekisui Chemical Company in Japan and China. The two will merge their Japanese adhesives businesses to form Sekisui-Fuller Company, Ltd.

Financial Data
(US$ in Thousands)

	3 Mos	11/27/2004	11/29/2003	11/30/2002	12/01/2001	12/02/2000	11/27/1999	11/28/1998
Earnings Per Share	1.30	1.23	1.35	0.98	1.57	1.74	1.55	0.57
Cash Flow Per Share	4.23	4.35	2.12	2.94	3.22	2.76	4.13	1.90
Tang Book Value Per Share	15.49	15.24	14.52	12.59	12.37	11.07	9.88	8.51
Dividends Per Share	0.460	0.458	0.448	0.438	0.427	0.417	0.407	0.393
Dividend Payout %	35.34	37.20	33.15	44.64	27.23	23.99	26.29	68.26
Income Statement								
Total Revenue	352,987	1,409,606	1,287,331	1,256,210	1,274,059	1,352,562	1,364,458	1,347,241
EBITDA	25,748	103,549	104,218	97,203	117,871	129,070	125,202	82,327
Depn & Amortn	13,918	56,030	54,136	57,544	54,401	52,165	50,776	49,541
Income Before Taxes	8,500	48,298	50,808	40,312	63,470	76,905	74,426	32,786
Income Taxes	2,720	14,713	14,307	12,973	19,833	28,455	31,807	18,826
Net Income	6,501	35,603	38,619	28,176	44,439	49,163	43,370	15,990
Average Shares	28,962	28,909	28,694	28,601	28,330	28,206	27,956	27,688
Balance Sheet								
Current Assets	513,758	553,650	448,492	408,874	403,873	435,064	440,143	457,900
Total Assets	1,087,820	1,135,359	1,007,588	961,439	966,173	1,010,361	1,025,615	1,046,169
Current Liabilities	245,564	293,449	200,026	214,846	204,163	226,725	265,920	285,160
Long-Term Obligations	137,747	138,149	161,047	161,763	203,001	250,464	263,714	300,074
Total Liabilities	531,355	582,300	498,250	513,109	532,147	605,651	649,235	704,765
Stockholders' Equity	556,465	553,059	509,338	448,330	434,026	404,710	376,380	341,404
Shares Outstanding	28,787	28,641	28,435	28,362	28,280	28,240	28,080	27,965
Statistical Record								
Return on Assets %	3.57	3.33	3.93	2.93	4.51	4.75	4.20	1.63
Return on Equity %	6.99	6.72	8.09	6.40	10.63	12.38	12.12	4.71
EBITDA Margin %	7.29	7.35	8.10	7.74	9.25	9.54	9.18	6.11
Net Margin %	1.84	2.53	3.00	2.24	3.49	3.63	3.18	1.19
Asset Turnover	1.38	1.32	1.31	1.31	1.29	1.31	1.32	1.38
Current Ratio	2.09	1.89	2.24	1.90	1.98	1.92	1.66	1.61
Debt to Equity	0.25	0.25	0.32	0.36	0.47	0.62	0.70	0.88
Price Range	29.10-24.84	30.19-24.84	29.50-20.00	32.50-24.54	30.95-16.59	34.25-14.34	36.09-19.19	32.41-17.25
P/E Ratio	22.38-19.11	24.54-20.20	21.85-14.81	33.16-25.04	19.71-10.57	19.68-8.24	23.29-12.38	56.85-30.26
Average Yield %	1.69	1.67	1.83	1.53	1.85	1.92	1.43	1.51

Address: 1200 Willow Lake Boulevard, St. Paul, Vadnais Heights, MN 55110-5101
Telephone: (651) 236-5900
Fax: (651) 236-5161

Web Site: www.hbfuller.com
Officers: Albert P. L. Stroucken - Chmn., Pres., C.E.O. John A. Feenan - Sr. V.P., C.F.O.

Auditors: PricewaterhouseCoopers LLP
Investor Contact: 651-236-5150
Transfer Agents: Wells Fargo Shareowner Services, Minnesota, MN

FURNITURE BRANDS INTERNATIONAL INC.

Exchange	Symbol	Price	52Wk Range	Yield	P/E
NYS	FBN	$21.81 (3/31/2005)	33.68-21.00	2.75	13.14

*7 Year Price Score 85.85 ***NYSE Composite Index=100** ***12 Month Price Score 88.54**

TRADING VOLUME (thousand shares)

Interim Earnings (Per Share)
Qtr.	Mar	Jun	Sep	Dec
2001	0.39	0.03	0.27	0.44
2002	0.58	0.57	0.44	0.52
2003	0.52	0.42	0.34	0.40
2004	0.58	0.30	0.36	0.42

Interim Dividends (Per Share)
Amt	Decl	Ex	Rec	Pay
0.125Q	4/29/2004	5/6/2004	5/10/2004	5/28/2004
0.125Q	7/29/2004	8/5/2004	8/9/2004	8/27/2004
0.15Q	10/28/2004	11/4/2004	11/8/2004	11/26/2004
0.15Q	1/27/2005	2/3/2005	2/7/2005	2/28/2005
			Indicated Div: $0.60	

Valuation Analysis
Forecast P/E	12.14	No of Institutions
	(4/7/2005)	169
Market Cap	$1.2 Billion	Shares
Book Value	957.5 Million	52,287,776
Price/Book	1.21	% Held
Price/Sales	0.47	92.57

Business Summary: Chemicals (MIC: 11.1 SIC: 519 NAIC: 37125)

Furniture Brands International is a manufacturer of residential furniture in the U.S. Co. markets its products across a broad spectrum of price categories and distributes them through an extensive system of independently owned national, regional and local retailers. Co. manufactures and distributes case goods, consisting of bedroom, dining room and living room furniture; stationary upholstery products, consisting of sofas, loveseats, sectionals and chairs; occasional furniture, consisting of wood tables, accent pieces, home entertainment centers and home office furniture; recliners, motion furniture and sleep sofas; and accessories.

Recent Developments: For the year ended Dec 31 2004, net income decreased 3.2% to $91,567 thousand from net income of $94,573 thousand a year earlier. Revenues were $2,447,430 thousand, up 0.5% from $2,434,130 thousand the year before. Operating income was $155,656 thousand versus an income of $165,126 thousand in the prior year, a decrease of 5.7%. Total direct expense was $1,781,037 thousand versus $1,777,814 thousand in the prior year, an increase of 0.2%. Total indirect expense was $510,737 thousand versus $491,190 thousand in the prior year, an increase of 4.0%.

Prospects: As Co. moves forward in achieving greater control over its distribution channels and consumer discretionary spending picks up as a result of an improving domestic economy, Co. believes it can return to meaningful sales growth. However, Co.'s sales expectations for the first quarter of 2005 reflect the current weakness in incoming orders versus the prior year. Co. expects first quarter sales to be down 4.0% to 5.0% from last year's performance and net earnings to be in the range of $0.45 to $0.49 per diluted share, including an estimated $0.03 per share in restructuring and impairment charges. Meanwhile, Co. continues to generate strong cash flow from operations.

Financial Data
(US$ in Thousands)	12/31/2004	12/31/2003	12/31/2002	12/31/2001	12/31/2000	12/31/1999	12/31/1998	12/31/1997
Earnings Per Share	1.66	1.68	2.11	1.13	2.10	2.14	1.82	1.15
Cash Flow Per Share	1.96	3.09	2.03	3.67	2.66	2.91	2.52	1.84
Tang Book Value Per Share	11.36	10.96	9.24	7.18	5.92	3.46	1.86	N.M.
Dividends Per Share	0.525	0.125	...	...	...	...	...	...
Dividend Payout %	31.63	7.44	...	...	...	...	...	...
Income Statement								
Total Revenue	2,447,430	2,367,738	2,397,709	1,891,313	2,116,239	2,088,112	1,960,250	1,808,276
EBITDA	205,869	218,813	254,202	164,601	259,941	270,469	250,167	205,096
Depn & Amortn	49,050	50,923	49,266	55,767	58,155	56,528	55,469	55,995
Income Before Taxes	142,640	149,224	184,424	87,694	165,997	176,764	152,143	107,254
Income Taxes	51,073	54,651	65,593	29,664	57,574	64,854	54,205	40,201
Net Income	91,567	94,573	118,831	58,030	105,901	111,910	97,938	67,053
Average Shares	55,219	56,255	56,386	51,324	50,442	52,334	53,809	58,473
Balance Sheet								
Current Assets	908,125	886,052	849,459	778,715	691,581	671,900	675,873	618,509
Total Assets	1,587,759	1,578,259	1,567,402	1,503,489	1,304,838	1,288,834	1,303,204	1,257,236
Current Liabilities	197,010	182,819	197,364	175,295	143,118	153,864	166,725	136,221
Long-Term Obligations	302,400	303,200	374,800	454,400	462,000	535,100	589,200	667,800
Total Liabilities	630,276	611,357	697,887	743,830	720,933	814,637	889,695	933,914
Stockholders' Equity	957,483	966,902	869,515	759,659	583,905	474,197	413,509	323,322
Shares Outstanding	53,216	55,946	55,649	54,612	49,675	49,370	51,752	52,004
Statistical Record								
Return on Assets %	5.77	6.01	7.74	4.13	8.14	8.63	7.65	5.31
Return on Equity %	9.49	10.30	14.59	8.64	19.96	25.21	26.58	18.05
EBITDA Margin %	8.41	9.24	10.60	8.70	12.28	12.95	12.76	11.34
Net Margin %	3.74	3.99	4.96	3.07	5.00	5.36	5.00	3.71
Asset Turnover	1.54	1.51	1.56	1.35	1.63	1.61	1.53	1.43
Current Ratio	4.61	4.85	4.30	4.44	4.83	4.37	4.05	4.54
Debt to Equity	0.32	0.31	0.43	0.60	0.79	1.13	1.42	2.07
Price Range	34.97-21.00	29.33-18.17	42.30-19.02	32.41-18.25	22.00-14.06	27.88-17.06	33.69-13.50	21.13-13.88
P/E Ratio	21.07-12.65	17.46-10.82	20.05-9.01	28.68-16.15	10.48-6.70	13.03-7.97	18.51-7.42	18.37-12.07
Average Yield %	1.97	0.52	...	...	...	...	...	...

Address: 101 South Hanley Road, St. Louis, MO 63105-3493 **Telephone:** (314) 863-1100 **Fax:** (314) 863-5306	**Web Site:** www.furniturebrands.com **Officers:** Wilbert G. Holliman - Chmn., C.E.O. Lynn Chipperfield - Sr. V.P., Chief Admin. Officer	**Auditors:** KPMG LLP **Investor Contact:** 314 863-1100

GALLAGHER (ARTHUR J.) & CO.

Exchange	Symbol	Price	52Wk Range	Yield	P/E	Div Acheiver
NYS	AJG	$28.80 (3/31/2005)	33.96-27.06	3.89	14.47	20 Years

*7 Year Price Score 109.80 ***NYSE Composite Index=100** ***12 Month Price Score 89.24**

TRADING VOLUME (thousand shares)

Interim Earnings (Per Share)

Qtr.	Mar	Jun	Sep	Dec
2001	0.27	0.26	0.47	0.36
2002	0.37	0.37	0.26	0.36
2003	0.13	0.39	0.52	0.53
2004	0.41	0.49	0.57	0.51

Interim Dividends (Per Share)

Amt	Decl	Ex	Rec	Pay
0.25Q	5/18/2004	6/28/2004	6/30/2004	7/15/2004
0.25Q	7/22/2004	9/28/2004	9/30/2004	10/15/2004
0.25Q	10/21/2004	12/29/2004	12/31/2004	1/14/2005
0.28Q	1/19/2005	3/29/2005	3/31/2005	4/15/2005

Indicated Div: $1.12

Valuation Analysis

Forecast P/E	14.05	No of Institutions
	(4/7/2005)	235
Market Cap	$2.7 Billion	Shares
Book Value	761.0 Million	62,528,424
Price/Book	3.49	% Held
Price/Sales	1.79	67.87

Business Summary: Insurance (MIC: 8.2 SIC: 411 NAIC: 24210)

Arthur J. Gallagher & Co. is engaged in providing insurance brokerage, risk management and related services to clients in the U.S. and abroad. Co.'s principal activity is the negotiation and placement of insurance for its clients. Co. also specializes in furnishing risk management services. Risk management involves assisting clients in analyzing risks and determining whether proper protection is best obtained through the purchase of insurance or through retention of all or a portion of those risks, and the adoption of corporate risk management policies and cost-effective loss control and prevention programs. Co. also has a financial services group that manages its investment portfolio.

Recent Developments: For the year ended Dec 31 2004, net income increased 28.9% to $188.5 million from net income of $146.2 million in the previous year. Total revenues advanced 17.1% to $1.48 billion from $1.26 billion a year earlier. Brokerage segment revenues climbed 9.2% to $926.4 million, while Risk Management segment revenues grew 15.8% to $372.6 million. Financial Services segment revenue jumped 93.7% to $181.3 million. Total cost and expenses increased 16.3% to $1.24 billion from $1.07 billion the year before.

Prospects: On Jan 24 2005, Co. announced that it has combined the operations of its two U.S. reinsurance brokerage subsidiaries, Arthur J. Gallagher Intermediaries, Inc. in New York and John P. Woods & Co., Inc. in New Jersey, to form Gallagher RE, Inc. Subsequently, Gallagher RE acquired certain reinsurance brokerage assets in Minnesota and Alabama from JLT Re Solutions, Inc., which will help expand its reinsurance coverage beyond primarily East Coast states. Meanwhile, Co. continues to expand its insurance brokerage business through acquisitions. Co. acquired Horton Insurance Agency, Inc. on Jan 20 2005, as well as Marine Insurance Service, LLC on Jan 14 2005.

Financial Data

(US$ in Thousands)	12/31/2004	12/31/2003	12/31/2002	12/31/2001	12/31/2000	12/31/1999	12/31/1998	12/31/1997
Earnings Per Share	1.99	1.57	1.41	1.39	1.05	0.88	0.78	0.78
Cash Flow Per Share	3.02	2.54	1.71	1.54	1.73	0.87	0.81	1.00
Tang Book Value Per Share	4.20	4.40	4.44	3.60	3.75	3.14	2.69	2.31
Dividends Per Share	1.000	0.720	0.600	0.520	0.460	0.400	0.350	0.310
Dividend Payout %	50.25	45.86	42.55	37.41	43.81	45.45	45.16	39.62
Income Statement								
Total Revenue	1,480,300	1,263,800	1,101,222	910,043	740,596	605,836	540,655	488,028
Income Before Taxes	235,500	193,300	185,342	141,853	125,394	104,235	84,529	80,782
Income Taxes	47,000	47,100	55,603	16,597	37,618	36,482	28,028	27,466
Net Income	188,500	146,200	129,739	125,256	87,776	67,753	56,501	53,316
Average Shares	94,500	93,300	91,861	90,127	83,924	77,132	72,824	68,152
Balance Sheet								
Total Assets	3,237,900	2,901,600	2,463,574	1,471,823	1,062,298	884,146	746,010	641,752
Total Liabilities	2,476,900	2,282,500	1,935,419	1,100,210	747,926	641,679	543,542	477,845
Stockholders' Equity	761,000	619,100	528,155	371,613	314,372	242,467	202,468	163,907
Shares Outstanding	92,100	90,000	88,548	85,111	79,497	73,680	70,580	66,364
Statistical Record								
Return on Assets %	6.12	5.45	6.59	9.89	8.99	8.31	8.14	8.65
Return on Equity %	27.24	25.49	28.84	36.52	31.44	30.46	30.84	35.73
Price Range	33.96-27.06	32.65-23.45	36.86-22.10	38.30-22.00	33.66-11.75	16.19-10.59	11.59-8.44	9.56-7.47
P/E Ratio	17.07-13.60	20.80-14.94	26.14-15.67	27.55-15.83	32.05-11.19	18.39-12.04	14.86-10.82	12.26-9.58
Average Yield %	3.17	2.63	1.94	1.77	2.13	3.17	3.36	3.66

Address: Two Pierce Place, Itasca, IL 60143-3141 **Telephone:** (630) 773-3800 **Fax:** (630) 285-4000	**Web Site:** www.ajg.com **Officers:** Robert E. Gallagher - Chmn. J. Patrick Gallagher Jr. - Pres., C.E.O.	**Auditors:** Ernst & Young LLP **Transfer Agents:** Computershare Investor Services, Chicago, IL

GANNETT CO., INC.

Exchange	Symbol	Price	52Wk Range	Yield	P/E	Div Acheiver
NYS	GCI	$79.08 (3/31/2005)	91.00-78.43	1.37	16.07	33 Years

*7 Year Price Score 99.87 ***NYSE Composite Index=100** ***12 Month Price Score 89.17**

Interim Earnings (Per Share)

Qtr.	Mar	Jun	Sep	Dec
2001	0.66	0.88	0.66	0.93
2002	0.91	1.13	0.99	1.29
2003	0.93	1.20	1.03	1.31
2004	1.00	1.30	1.18	1.45

Interim Dividends (Per Share)

Amt	Decl	Ex	Rec	Pay
0.25Q	5/4/2004	6/2/2004	6/4/2004	7/1/2004
0.27Q	8/4/2004	9/8/2004	9/10/2004	10/1/2004
0.27Q	10/26/2004	12/15/2004	12/17/2004	1/3/2005
0.27Q	2/22/2005	3/2/2005	3/4/2005	4/1/2005

Indicated Div: $1.08 (Div. Reinv. Plan)

Valuation Analysis

Forecast P/E	15.21 (4/7/2005)	No of Institutions 654
Market Cap	$20.1 Billion	Shares 201,438,080
Book Value	8.2 Billion	% Held 79.87
Price/Book	2.46	
Price/Sales	2.72	

Business Summary: Media (MIC: 13.1 SIC: 711 NAIC: 11110)

Gannett is a news and information company that publishes newspapers and operates broadcasting stations. Co. is also engaged in marketing, commercial printing, a newswire service, data services, and news programming. Co. has operations in 43 states, the District of Columbia, Guam, the U.K., and in certain European and Asian markets. Co. is the largest U.S. newspaper group in terms of circulation, with 100 daily newspapers, including USA Today, more than 500 non-daily publications and USA Weekend, a weekly newspaper magazine. In the U.K., Co.'s subsidiary Newsquest publishes nearly 300 titles, including 17 daily newspapers. Co. owns and operates 22 television stations in major markets.

Recent Developments: For the year ended Dec 26 2004, net income increased 8.7% to $1,317,186 thousand from net income of $1,211,213 thousand a year earlier. Revenues were $7,381,283 thousand, up 10.0% from $6,711,115 thousand the year before. Operating income was $2,147,679 thousand versus an income of $1,981,018 thousand in the prior year, an increase of 8.4%. Total direct expense was $3,821,435 thousand versus $3,453,769 thousand in the prior year, an increase of 10.6%. Total indirect expense was $1,412,169 thousand versus $1,276,328 thousand in the prior year, an increase of 10.6%.

Prospects: Co. strong revenue performance is helping it achieve record operating results, despite an uneven advertising environment. Co.'s results reflect strong revenue growth in its broadcasting segment, which is being driven by significant levels of advertising. Co. is also seeing solid revenue growth in the newspaper segment due, in part, to higher demand for local and classified advertising. In the U.K., Newsquest is continuing to post improved results which also are benefiting from a favorable exchange rate. However, higher newsprint expense and certain employee benefit costs are tempering the growth in Co.'s results.

Financial Data (US$ in Thousands)	12/26/2004	12/28/2003	12/29/2002	12/30/2001	12/31/2000	12/26/1999	12/27/1998	12/28/1997
Earnings Per Share	4.92	4.46	4.31	3.12	6.41	3.40	3.50	2.50
Cash Flow Per Share	6.01	5.50	3.88	4.96	1.85	4.12	3.44	3.14
Tang Book Value Per Share	N.M.	N.M.	N.M.	N.M.	N.M.	N.M.	0.66	N.M.
Dividends Per Share	1.040	0.980	0.940	0.900	0.860	0.820	0.780	0.740
Dividend Payout %	21.14	21.97	21.81	28.85	13.42	24.12	22.29	29.60
Income Statement								
Total Revenue	7,381,283	6,711,115	6,422,249	6,344,245	6,222,318	5,260,190	5,121,291	4,729,491
EBITDA	2,375,506	2,205,909	2,129,883	2,031,552	2,176,774	1,896,158	2,039,713	1,601,777
Depn & Amortn	244,021	231,532	222,444	443,777	375,915	280,091	310,206	301,073
Income Before Taxes	1,995,386	1,840,313	1,764,528	1,370,597	1,608,840	1,527,187	1,669,413	1,208,979
Income Taxes	678,200	629,100	604,400	539,400	636,900	607,800	669,500	496,300
Net Income	1,317,186	1,211,213	1,160,128	831,197	1,719,077	957,928	999,913	712,679
Average Shares	267,590	271,872	269,286	266,833	268,118	281,608	285,711	285,610
Balance Sheet								
Current Assets	1,370,695	1,223,261	1,133,079	1,178,198	1,302,336	1,075,222	906,385	884,634
Total Assets	15,399,251	14,706,239	13,733,014	13,096,101	12,980,411	9,006,446	6,979,480	6,890,351
Current Liabilities	1,005,450	961,837	958,625	1,127,737	1,174,001	883,778	727,967	767,501
Long-Term Obligations	4,607,743	3,834,511	4,547,265	5,080,025	5,747,856	2,463,250	1,306,859	1,740,534
Total Liabilities	7,143,888	6,190,819	6,821,219	7,360,179	7,877,001	4,376,800	2,999,656	3,410,615
Stockholders' Equity	8,164,002	8,422,981	6,911,795	5,735,922	5,103,410	4,629,646	3,979,824	3,479,736
Shares Outstanding	254,344	272,417	267,909	265,797	264,271	277,926	279,001	283,874
Statistical Record								
Return on Assets %	8.77	8.54	8.67	6.39	15.38	12.02	14.46	10.85
Return on Equity %	15.93	15.84	18.40	15.38	34.75	22.31	26.88	22.42
EBITDA Margin %	32.18	32.87	33.16	32.02	34.98	36.05	39.83	33.87
Net Margin %	17.84	18.05	18.06	13.10	27.63	18.21	19.52	15.07
Asset Turnover	0.49	0.47	0.48	0.49	0.56	0.66	0.74	0.72
Current Ratio	1.36	1.27	1.18	1.04	1.11	1.22	1.25	1.15
Debt to Equity	0.56	0.46	0.66	0.89	1.13	0.53	0.33	0.50
Price Range	91.00-78.99	88.93-67.68	79.87-63.39	71.10-55.55	83.25-48.69	79.31-61.81	74.69-48.94	61.00-35.81
P/E Ratio	18.50-16.05	19.94-15.17	18.53-14.71	22.79-17.80	12.99-7.60	23.33-18.18	21.34-13.98	24.40-14.33
Average Yield %	1.22	1.27	1.28	1.40	1.40	1.17	1.22	1.55

Address: 7950 Jones Branch Drive, McLean, VA 22107-0910 Telephone: (703) 854-6000 Fax: (703) 364-0855	Web Site: www.gannett.com Officers: Douglas H. McCorkindale - Chmn., Pres., C.E.O. Gracia C. Martore - Sr. V.P., C.F.O.	Auditors: PricewaterhouseCoopers LLP Investor Contact: 703-854-6918 Transfer Agents: Wells Fargo Bank Minnesota, N.A., St. Paul, MN

GARTNER, INC.

Exchange	Symbol	Price	52Wk Range	Yield	P/E
NYS	IT	$9.57 (3/31/2005)	13.38-9.16	N/A	73.62

*7 Year Price Score 73.43   ***NYSE Composite Index=100**   ***12 Month Price Score 78.84**   Interim Earnings (Per Share)

TRADING VOLUME (thousand shares)

Interim Earnings (Per Share)

Qtr.	Mar	Jun	Sep	Dec
2002	.....	.....	(0.18)	.....
2003	(0.02)	0.13	0.07	0.05
2004	0.00	0.08	0.00	0.04

Interim Dividends (Per Share)

No Dividends Paid

Valuation Analysis

Forecast P/E	28.78	No of Institutions
	(4/13/2005)	121
Market Cap	$1.1 Billion	Shares
Book Value	130.0 Million	51,396,200
Price/Book	8.22	% Held
Price/Sales	1.20	57.42

Business Summary: Accounting & Management Consulting Services (MIC: 12.2 SIC: 741 NAIC: 41710)

Gartner is a provider of research and analysis on information technology, computer hardware, software, communications and related technology industries. Co. provides comprehensive coverage of the information technology industry to about 10,000 client organizations. Research unit offers products that highlight industry developments, review products and technologies, provide market research, and analyze industry trends. Consulting unit consists of consulting and services that provide assessments of cost performance, efficiency and quality. Events unit consists of vendor and user focused expositions and conferences.

Recent Developments: For the year ended Dec 31 2004, net income fell 29.7% to $5.0 million compared with $16.6 million the year before. Results included a loss of $3.0 in 2004 and a gain of $4.7 million in 2003 from investments. Total revenues advanced 4.1% to $893.8 million from $858.4 million a year earlier. On a segment basis, research revenue grew 2.9% to $480.5 million, with research contract value amounting to $509.0 million, up 5.6% from $482.0 million at Dec 31 2003. Consulting revenue increased slightly by 0.3% to $138.4 million, while events revenue climbed 14.5% to $15.5 million. Operating income declined 10.8% to $42.4 million from $47.5 million the year before.

Prospects: For full-year 2005, Co. is targeting total revenue of approximately $916.0 million to $942.0 million, driven by its Research segment which is expected to earn revenues of approximately $485.0 million to $495.0 million. Moreover, Co. is targeting earnings before taxes, depreciation and amortization of $85.0 million to $95.0 million, and earnings per share of $0.15 to $0.24. In the first quarter of 2005, Co. expects to record special charges of $10.0 million to $20.0 million related to the restructuring of international operations and severance. Longer term, Co. expects the recent launch of initiatives to begin producing results in 2005 and to have a material impact on earnings in 2006.

Financial Data
(US$ in Thousands)

	12/31/2004	12/31/2003	12/31/2002	09/30/2002	09/30/2001	09/30/2000	09/30/1999	09/30/1998
Earnings Per Share	0.13	0.26	(0.18)	0.47	(0.77)	0.29	0.84	0.84
Cash Flow Per Share	0.39	1.50	0.01	1.74	0.86	0.87	1.26	0.98
Tang Book Value Per Share	N.M.	1.11		...	...	N.M.	N.M.	2.28
Income Statement								
Total Revenue	893,821	858,446	229,814	907,174	952,042	858,671	734,234	641,957
EBITDA	64,116	91,257	(3,087)	139,080	64,623	137,157	162,628	168,830
Depn & Amortn	28,337	38,595	11,628	44,453	53,240	56,156	31,633	27,266
Income Before Taxes	34,462	35,556	(20,022)	73,603	(9,392)	56,101	31,633	27,266
Income Taxes	17,573	11,863	(5,604)	25,025	(9,172)	56,101	139,247	151,121
Net Income	16,889	23,693	(14,418)	48,578	(66,203)	28,826	50,976	62,774
Average Shares	126,326	92,579	81,379	130,882	85,862	89,529	88,271	88,347
Balance Sheet								
Current Assets	487,845	549,477	459,265	455,033	448,821	512,868	432,184	511,079
Total Assets	861,194	917,264	827,403	824,850	839,002	1,002,965	803,444	832,871
Current Liabilities	529,198	491,133	457,877	437,342	527,514	587,339	473,621	414,835
Long-Term Obligations	150,000	...	351,539	346,300	326,200	307,254	250,000	...
Total Liabilities	731,146	541,518	856,104	829,740	873,520	928,145	728,958	417,933
Stockholders' Equity	130,048	375,746	(28,701)	(4,890)	(34,518)	74,820	74,486	414,938
Shares Outstanding	111,765	129,999	80,509	82,012	83,664	86,302	89,247	113,719
Statistical Record								
Return on Assets %	1.89	2.72	N.M.	5.84	N.M.	2.82	10.79	11.95
Return on Equity %	6.66	13.65	...	...	N.M.	34.13	36.07	25.80
EBITDA Margin %	7.17	10.63	N.M.	15.33	6.79	15.97	22.15	26.30
Net Margin %	1.89	2.76	N.M.	5.35	N.M.	2.98	12.02	13.76
Asset Turnover	1.00	0.98	0.22	1.09	N.M.			
Current Ratio	0.92	1.12	1.00	1.04	1.03	0.95	0.90	0.87
Debt to Equity	1.15				0.85	0.87	0.91	1.23
Price Range	13.38-11.00	13.52-6.86	10.51-6.11	13.48-7.75	12.31-5.97	22.19-9.75	25.63-16.00	40.81-20.88
P/E Ratio	102.92-84.62	52.00-26.38	...	28.68-16.49		76.51-33.62	30.51-19.05	48.59-24.85

Address: P.O. Box 10212, 56 Top Gallant Road, Stamford, CT 06904-2212
Telephone: (203) 316-1111
Fax: (203) 316-1100

Web Site: www.gartner.com
Officers: Michael D. Fleisher - Chmn., Pres., C.E.O. Christopher Lafond - Exec. V.P., C.F.O.

Auditors: KPMG LLP
Investor Contact: 203-316-6768

GATEWAY INC

Exchange	Symbol	Price	52Wk Range	Yield	P/E
NYS	GTW	$4.03 (3/31/2005)	6.92-3.67	N/A	N/A

*7 Year Price Score 20.38 ***NYSE Composite Index=100** ***12 Month Price Score 84.96**

Interim Earnings (Per Share)

Qtr.	Mar	Jun	Sep	Dec
2001	(1.56)	(0.06)	(1.61)	0.03
2002	(0.39)	(0.19)	(0.15)	(0.22)
2003	(0.22)	(0.22)	(0.43)	(0.35)
2004	(0.51)	(0.91)	(0.16)	0.13

Interim Dividends (Per Share)

No Dividends Paid

Valuation Analysis

Forecast P/E	N/A	No of Institutions	
Market Cap	$1.5 Billion	Shares	
Book Value	245.0 Million		
Price/Book	6.12	% Held	
Price/Sales	0.41	40.22	150,291,456

TRADING VOLUME (thousand shares)

Business Summary: IT & Technology (MIC: 10.2 SIC: 571 NAIC: 34111)

Gateway provides a broad range of personal computers, consumer electronics products, enterprise systems, communication tools, applications, training and related services. Co. offers a wide range of plasma, LCD and rear projection TVs, digital cameras, other consumer electronics products, and enterprise systems, which integrate with and complement its line of PCs, along with a full complement of related products and services. Co. is also a supplier of PCs to large corporate, small and medium businesses and government and educational institutions. Co. sells its products through its Web site, telephone call centers, and through a limited number of third-party channels.

Recent Developments: For the year ended Dec 31 2004, net loss was $567,618 thousand versus net loss of $514,812 thousand a year earlier. Revenues were $3,649,734 thousand, up 7.3% from $3,402,364 thousand the year before. Operating loss was $601,978 thousand versus a loss of $510,575 thousand in the prior year. Total direct expense was $3,342,662 thousand versus $2,938,800 thousand in the prior year, an increase of 13.7%. Total indirect expense was $909,050 thousand versus $974,139 thousand in the prior year, a decrease of 6.7%.

Prospects: Co. continues to benefit from efforts to simplify processes, increase productivity and expand distribution of its products. With the integration of eMachines and restructuring initiatives largely complete, Co. is looking to make strides toward its goal of long-term, sustainable profitability. For 2005, Co. will look to further leverage its model and lower its selling, general and administrative expense structure to achieve growth across all of its segments. Co. expects first quarter 2005 revenue in the range of $810.0 to $850.0 million, consistent with sales mix shifts between segments and in-line with previously announced full-year 2005 revenue guidance of $4.00 billion to $4.25 billion.

Financial Data (US$ in Thousands)	12/31/2004	12/31/2003	12/31/2002	12/31/2001	12/31/2000	12/31/1999	12/31/1998	12/31/1997
Earnings Per Share	(1.45)	(1.62)	(0.95)	(3.20)	0.73	1.32	1.09	0.35
Cash Flow Per Share	(1.19)	0.22	(0.08)	(0.84)	0.90	2.33	2.92	1.44
Tang Book Value Per Share	N.M.	1.57	3.16	4.10	6.85	6.15	4.08	2.62
Income Statement								
Total Revenue	3,649,734	3,402,364	4,171,325	6,079,524	9,600,600	8,645,561	7,467,925	6,293,680
EBITDA	(469,506)	(327,274)	(316,288)	(1,090,337)	597,684	797,584	646,772	290,394
Depn & Amortn	112,225	163,973	159,458	199,976	189,084	134,105	105,524	86,774
Income Before Taxes	(581,731)	(491,247)	(475,746)	(1,290,313)	408,600	663,479	541,248	203,620
Income Taxes	(14,113)	23,565	(178,028)	(275,900)	155,266	235,535	194,849	93,823
Net Income	(567,618)	(514,812)	(297,718)	(1,033,915)	241,483	427,944	346,399	109,797
Average Shares	391,115	324,160	324,020	323,289	331,320	324,421	317,858	312,402
Balance Sheet								
Current Assets	1,399,617	1,663,477	1,955,372	2,122,924	2,267,060	2,696,805	2,228,186	1,544,683
Total Assets	1,771,787	2,028,438	2,509,407	2,986,857	4,152,544	3,954,688	2,890,380	2,039,271
Current Liabilities	1,122,652	999,004	940,349	1,146,028	1,631,034	1,809,710	1,429,674	1,003,906
Long-Term Obligations	300,000	...	...	...	...	2,998	3,360	7,240
Total Liabilities	1,526,750	1,108,700	1,067,467	1,228,664	1,772,205	1,937,570	1,546,005	1,109,227
Stockholders' Equity	245,037	722,018	1,246,518	1,565,084	2,380,339	2,017,118	1,344,375	930,044
Shares Outstanding	372,216	324,392	324,072	323,973	323,403	319,286	313,138	308,256
Statistical Record								
Return on Assets %	N.M.	N.M.	N.M.	N.M.	5.94	12.50	14.05	5.91
Return on Equity %	N.M.	N.M.	N.M.	N.M.	10.95	25.46	30.46	12.58
EBITDA Margin %	N.M.	N.M.	N.M.	N.M.	6.23	9.23	8.66	4.61
Net Margin %	N.M.	N.M.	N.M.	N.M.	2.52	4.95	4.64	1.74
Asset Turnover	1.92	1.50	1.52	1.70	2.36	2.53	3.03	3.39
Current Ratio	1.25	1.67	2.08	1.85	1.39	1.49	1.56	1.54
Debt to Equity	1.22	...	...	...	...	N.M.	N.M.	0.01
Price Range	6.92-3.67	6.76-2.04	10.25-2.69	23.69-4.65	73.00-16.82	82.50-25.59	33.56-16.25	22.38-11.91
P/E Ratio	...	...	...	...	100.00-23.04	62.50-19.39	30.79-14.91	63.93-34.02

Address: 14303 Gateway Place, Poway, CA 92064	Web Site: www.gateway.com	Auditors: PricewaterhouseCoopers LLP
Telephone: (858) 848-3401	Officers: Theodore W. Waitt - Chmn. John Heubusch - Asst. Chmn.	Investor Contact: 800-846-4503
Fax: (858) 799-3459		

GATX CORP.

Exchange	Symbol	Price	52Wk Range	Yield	P/E
NYS	GMT	$33.19 (3/31/2005)	33.30-21.56	2.41	10.92

*7 Year Price Score 73.68   ***NYSE Composite Index=100**   ***12 Month Price Score 105.34**

Interim Earnings (Per Share)

Qtr.	Mar	Jun	Sep	Dec
2001	3.45	0.44	(0.15)	(0.24)
2002	0.51	0.42	0.39	(0.61)
2003	0.04	0.50	0.46	0.56
2004	0.46	0.71	0.78	1.12

Interim Dividends (Per Share)

Amt	Decl	Ex	Rec	Pay
0.20Q	4/23/2004	6/14/2004	6/15/2004	6/30/2004
0.20Q	7/23/2004	9/13/2004	9/15/2004	9/30/2004
0.20Q	10/1/2004	12/13/2004	12/15/2004	12/31/2004
0.20Q	2/4/2005	2/23/2005	2/25/2005	3/31/2005

Indicated Div: $0.80

Valuation Analysis

Forecast P/E	N/A	No of Institutions
Market Cap	$1.6 Billion	Shares
Book Value	1.1 Billion	46,126,964
Price/Book	1.52	% Held
Price/Sales	1.41	93.30

TRADING VOLUME (thousand shares)

Business Summary: Rail Transport (MIC: 15.5 SIC: 741 NAIC: 88210)

GATX specializes in railcar and locomotive leasing, aircraft operating leasing, information technology leasing, and financing other large ticket equipment. Co. provides its services primarily through four operating segments: GATX Rail, GATX Air, GATX Technology Services and GATX Specialty Finance. As of Dec 31 2003, GATX Rail's owned worldwide fleet, including rail and specialty owned cars, totaled approximately 125,000 railcars. Co. also has an ownership interest in approximately 27,000 railcars worldwide through rail and specialty's investments in affiliated companies.

Recent Developments: For the year ended Dec 31 2004, income from continuing operations increased 156.9% to $158,500 thousand from income of $61,700 a year earlier. Net income increased 120.5% to $169,600 thousand from net income of $76,900 thousand a year earlier. Revenues were $1,166,200 thousand, up 12.8% from $1,033,600 thousand the year before. Total direct expense was $129,200 thousand versus $112,300 thousand in the prior year, an increase of 15.0%. Total indirect expense was $713,100 thousand versus $734,800 thousand in the prior year, a decrease of 3.0%.

Prospects: On Dec 16 2004, Co. completed the sale of its Staten Island property to 380 Development, LLC, a majority-owned subsidiary of International Speedway Corp., for approximately $99.0 million. Meanwhile, Co. has acquired the remaining interest in Locomotive Leasing Partners from the Electro-Motive Division of General Motors, resulting in 100.0% ownership of the fleet of 486 locomotives by GATX Rail. Terms of this transaction were not disclosed. Looking ahead to 2005, Co. is focused on capitalizing on investment opportunities, improving its credit profile and strengthening its earnings. For 2005, Co. expects earnings from continuing operations to range from $1.60 to $1.70 per diluted share.

Financial Data

(US$ in Thousands)	12/31/2004	12/31/2003	12/31/2002	12/31/2001	12/31/2000	12/31/1999	12/31/1998	12/31/1997
Earnings Per Share	3.04	1.56	...	3.51	1.37	3.01	2.62	(1.27)
Cash Flow Per Share	6.09	8.31	8.99	7.33	9.37	7.20	6.90	6.46
Tang Book Value Per Share	19.93	16.13	15.07	16.79	16.25	17.20	14.87	13.39
Dividends Per Share	0.800	1.280	1.280	1.240	1.200	1.100	1.000	0.920
Dividend Payout %	26.32	82.05	...	35.33	87.59	36.54	38.17	...
Income Statement								
Total Revenue	1,166,200	1,242,700	1,274,300	1,488,600	1,311,800	1,773,000	1,763,100	1,701,900
EBITDA	596,900	624,600	631,700	671,400	630,900	794,300	665,000	387,400
Depn & Amortn	207,800	321,800	368,100	415,900	334,800	308,200	267,500	252,300
Income Before Taxes	226,700	102,900	39,000	5,600	53,500	253,900	162,600	(87,300)
Income Taxes	68,200	26,000	10,000	(1,900)	22,700	102,600	74,300	(5,500)
Net Income	169,600	76,900	300	172,900	66,600	151,300	131,900	(50,900)
Average Shares	60,002	49,222	49,177	49,202	48,753	50,301	50,426	45,084
Balance Sheet								
Current Assets	553,400	1,066,000	1,534,800	1,830,300	1,684,500	1,144,100	1,032,400	1,168,500
Total Assets	5,612,900	6,080,600	6,428,300	6,109,700	6,263,700	5,866,800	4,939,300	4,947,800
Current Liabilities	378,200	370,700	426,600	658,900	1,016,200	815,500	707,000	805,200
Long-Term Obligations	3,132,100	3,823,900	4,212,800	3,788,500	3,752,300	3,432,600	2,821,700	2,819,400
Total Liabilities	4,532,000	5,191,700	5,626,700	5,227,900	5,474,200	5,030,800	4,206,400	4,292,400
Stockholders' Equity	1,080,900	888,900	801,600	881,800	789,500	836,000	732,900	655,400
Shares Outstanding	49,530	49,246	49,048	48,756	48,599	48,599	49,284	48,942
Statistical Record								
Return on Assets %	2.89	1.23	0.00	2.79	1.10	2.80	2.67	N.M.
Return on Equity %	17.17	9.10	0.04	20.69	8.17	19.29	19.00	N.M.
EBITDA Margin %	51.18	50.26	49.57	45.10	48.09	44.80	37.72	22.76
Net Margin %	14.54	6.19	0.02	11.61	5.08	8.53	7.48	N.M.
Asset Turnover	0.20	0.20	0.20	0.24	0.22	0.33	0.36	0.35
Current Ratio	1.46	2.88	3.60	2.78	1.66	1.40	1.46	1.45
Debt to Equity	2.90	4.30	5.26	4.30	4.75	4.11	3.85	4.30
Price Range	30.05-20.51	28.68-13.68	35.55-16.45	49.19-25.68	49.88-28.56	40.69-29.25	45.94-26.38	36.28-23.81
P/E Ratio	9.88-6.75	18.38-8.77	N.M.	14.01-7.32	36.41-20.85	13.52-9.72	17.53-10.07	...
Average Yield %	3.12	5.41	4.69	3.26	3.16	3.12	2.65	3.16

Address: 500 West Monroe Street, Chicago, IL 60661-3676	Web Site: www.gatx.com	Auditors: ERNST & YOUNG LLP
Telephone: (312) 621-6200	Officers: Ronald H. Zech - Chmn., Pres., C.E.O.	Investor Contact: 312-621-6633
Fax: (312) 621-6665	Brian A. Kenney - Sr. V.P., C.F.O.	

GENENTECH, INC.

Exchange	Symbol	Price	52Wk Range	Yield	P/E
NYS	DNA	$56.61 (3/31/2005)	66.00-42.87	N/A	77.55

*7 Year Price Score 154.56 *NYSE Composite Index=100 ***12 Month Price Score 88.01**

Interim Earnings (Per Share)

Qtr.	Mar	Jun	Sep	Dec
2001	0.03	0.04	0.04	0.04
2002	0.09	(0.20)	0.09	0.09
2003	0.14	0.13	0.14	0.12
2004	0.17	0.16	0.21	0.20

Interim Dividends (Per Share)

Amt	Decl	Ex	Rec	Pay
2-for-1	10/25/1999	11/3/1999	10/29/1999	11/2/1999
100%	10/5/2000	10/25/2000	10/17/2000	10/24/2000
100%	3/3/2004	5/13/2004	4/28/2004	5/12/2004

Valuation Analysis

Forecast P/E	52.43	No of Institutions
	(4/7/2005)	402
Market Cap	$59.3 Billion	Shares
Book Value	6.8 Billion	414,275,456
Price/Book	8.74	% Held
Price/Sales	12.83	39.59

TRADING VOLUME (thousand shares)

Business Summary: Pharmaceuticals (MIC: 9.1 SIC: 834 NAIC: 25412)

Genentech is a biotechnology company that uses human genetic information to discover, develop, manufacture and market human pharmaceuticals. Co. manufactures and markets ten protein-based pharmaceuticals including Protropin®, used for growth hormone deficiency (GHD) in children; Herceptin®, for the treatment of one type of metastic breast cancer; Activase®, which dissolves blood clots that cause strokes and heart attacks; Rituxan®, a single-agent therapy for the treatment of a certain type of non-Hodgkins lymphoma; Pulmozyme®, used for treatment of cystic fibrosis; Nutropin® and Nutropin AQ®, used for GHD in children and adults. Nutropin Depot™, for treatment of GHD in children.

Recent Developments: For the year ended Dec 31 2004, net income increased 39.5% to $784,816 thousand from net income of $562,527 thousand a year earlier. Revenues were $4,621,157 thousand, up 40.0% from $3,300,327 thousand the year before. Operating income was $1,136,819 thousand versus an income of $804,715 thousand in the prior year, an increase of 41.3%. Total direct expense was $672,526 thousand versus $480,123 thousand in the prior year, an increase of 40.1%. Total indirect expense was $2,811,812 thousand versus $2,015,489 thousand in the prior year, an increase of 39.5%.

Prospects: Co.'s near-term prospects appears favorable as results are being driven by four new product launches over a 16-month period. For instance, 2004 operating revenues increased by $1.30 billion over 2003's level and more than doubled from 2001. Meanwhile, Co.'s emphasis on research and development has helped to build a pipeline that includes more than 30 projects in development, and is expected to result in continued growth and the achievement of its Horizon 2010 goals. In addition, Co. is pleased with its development programs focused on combination therapies, which should potentially bring new treatments to patients.

Financial Data
(US$ in Thousands)

	12/31/2004	12/31/2003	12/31/2002	12/31/2001	12/31/2000	12/31/1999	12/31/1998	12/31/1997
Earnings Per Share	0.73	0.53	0.06	0.14	(0.07)	(1.12)	0.17	0.13
Cash Flow Per Share	1.13	1.20	0.57	0.46	0.18	(0.01)	0.35	0.12
Tang Book Value Per Share	4.58	4.19	3.00	3.32	2.80	2.13	2.30	2.04
Income Statement								
Total Revenue	4,621,157	3,300,327	2,719,246	2,212,277	1,736,356	1,421,378	1,150,943	1,016,748
EBITDA	1,489,516	1,117,406	304,749	711,086	459,073	(1,059,566)	330,752	235,328
Depn & Amortn	353,200	295,400	275,000	428,100	455,100	281,360	78,101	65,533
Income Before Taxes	1,219,416	897,506	29,749	282,986	3,973	(1,340,926)	252,651	169,795
Income Taxes	434,600	287,324	(34,038)	127,112	20,414	(196,398)	70,742	40,751
Net Income	784,816	562,527	63,787	150,236	(74,241)	(1,144,528)	181,909	129,044
Average Shares	1,079,209	1,057,620	1,048,816	1,070,582	1,044,358	1,025,720	1,038,976	1,011,176
Balance Sheet								
Current Assets	3,422,757	2,756,830	2,082,784	2,209,352	1,788,811	1,326,507	1,241,958	1,193,918
Total Assets	9,403,395	8,736,171	6,777,319	7,134,847	6,711,813	6,554,441	2,855,402	2,507,612
Current Liabilities	1,243,266	873,031	646,660	651,755	448,681	484,127	291,327	289,557
Long-Term Obligations	412,250	412,250	...	...	149,692	149,708	149,990	150,000
Total Liabilities	2,621,205	2,215,873	1,438,435	1,215,028	1,037,610	1,271,636	511,557	476,387
Stockholders' Equity	6,782,190	6,520,298	5,338,884	5,919,819	5,674,203	5,282,805	2,343,845	2,031,225
Shares Outstanding	1,047,126	1,049,484	1,025,620	1,056,626	1,050,953	1,032,441	1,016,920	993,824
Statistical Record								
Return on Assets %	8.63	7.25	0.92	2.17	N.M.	N.M.	6.78	5.45
Return on Equity %	11.77	9.49	1.13	2.59	N.M.	N.M.	8.32	6.73
EBITDA Margin %	32.23	33.86	11.21	32.14	26.44	N.M.	28.74	23.15
Net Margin %	16.98	17.04	2.35	6.79	N.M.	N.M.	15.81	12.69
Asset Turnover	0.51	0.43	0.39	0.32	0.26	0.30	0.43	0.43
Current Ratio	2.75	3.16	3.22	3.39	3.99	2.74	4.26	4.12
Debt to Equity	0.06	0.06	...	...	0.03	0.03	0.06	0.07
Price Range	66.00-42.87	47.58-16.13	27.23-12.75	40.00-19.32	58.63-23.06	34.81-9.43	9.96-7.45	7.58-6.69
P/E Ratio	90.40-58.73	89.76-30.43	453.75-212.50	285.71-138.04	...	...	58.59-43.80	58.29-51.44

Address: 1 DNA Way, South San Francisco, CA 94080-4990	Web Site: www.gene.com	Auditors: Ernst & Young LLP
Telephone: (650) 225-1000	Officers: Arthur D. Levinson - Chmn., Pres., C.E.O.	Investor Contact: 650-225-8852
Fax: (650) 225-8326	Louis J. Lavigne Jr. - Exec. V.P., C.F.O.	Transfer Agents: EquiServe, LP

GENERAL DYNAMICS CORP.

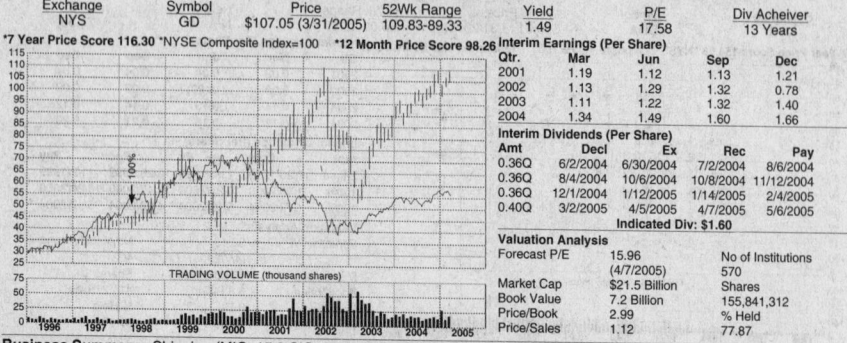

Exchange	Symbol	Price	52Wk Range	Yield	P/E	Div Acheiver
NYS	GD	$107.05 (3/31/2005)	109.83-89.33	1.49	17.58	13 Years

7 Year Price Score 116.30 *NYSE Composite Index=100 *12 Month Price Score 98.26

Interim Earnings (Per Share)

Qtr.	Mar	Jun	Sep	Dec
2001	1.19	1.12	1.13	1.21
2002	1.13	1.29	1.32	0.78
2003	1.11	1.22	1.32	1.40
2004	1.34	1.49	1.60	1.66

Interim Dividends (Per Share)

Amt	Decl	Ex	Rec	Pay
0.36Q	6/2/2004	6/30/2004	7/2/2004	8/6/2004
0.36Q	8/4/2004	10/6/2004	10/8/2004	11/12/2004
0.36Q	12/1/2004	1/12/2005	1/14/2005	2/4/2005
0.40Q	3/2/2005	4/5/2005	4/7/2005	5/6/2005
			Indicated Div: $1.60	

Valuation Analysis

Forecast P/E	15.96		No of Institutions
	(4/7/2005)		570
Market Cap	$21.5 Billion		Shares
Book Value	7.2 Billion		155,841,312
Price/Book	2.99		% Held
Price/Sales	1.12		77.87

TRADING VOLUME (thousand shares)

Business Summary: Shipping (MIC: 15.3 SIC: 731 NAIC: 36611)

General Dynamics is a major defense contractor operating in four business segments. Information Systems and Technology provides defense and commercial customers with infrastructure and systems integration skills required to process, communicate and manage information. Marine Systems provides the U.S. Navy with combat vessels. Aerospace designs and develops technologically advanced business jet aircraft. Combat Systems provides systems integration, design, and production for armored vehicles, armaments, munitions and components. Other businesses consist of a coal mining operation, an aggregates operation and a leasing operation for liquefied natural gas tankers.

Recent Developments: For the year ended Dec 31 2004, income from continuing operations increased 22.5% to $1,203 million from income of $982 million a year earlier. Net income increased 22.2% to $1,227 million from net income of $1,004 million a year earlier. Revenues were $19,178 million, up 17.2% from $16,369 million the year before. Operating income was $1,941 million versus an income of $1,445 million in the prior year, an increase of 34.3%. Total indirect expense was $17,237 million versus $14,924 million in the prior year, an increase of 15.5%.

Prospects: Co. is experiencing increasing earnings and operating margins in three out of four of its major business groups, and the growth of funded backlog across all four of its groups bodes well for its future. Looking ahead to 2005, Co. anticipates continuing solid performance from Combat Systems and Information Systems & Technology, margin improvement in Marine Systems and continuing improvement at Gulfstream. Co. expects 2005 earnings per share from continuing operations to increase between 11.0% and 13.0%. Co. also expects free cash flow from operations to approximate net earnings.

Financial Data
(US$ in Thousands)

	12/31/2004	12/31/2003	12/31/2002	12/31/2001	12/31/2000	12/31/1999	12/31/1998	12/31/1997
Earnings Per Share	6.09	5.04	4.52	4.65	4.48	4.36	2.86	2.50
Cash Flow Per Share	9.01	8.71	5.59	5.48	5.34	5.08	2.94	4.42
Tang Book Value Per Share	N.M.	N.M.	5.62	3.84	6.43	3.27	5.46	5.64
Dividends Per Share	1.400	1.260	1.180	1.100	1.020	0.940	0.865	0.820
Dividend Payout %	22.99	25.00	26.11	23.66	22.77	21.56	30.24	32.80
Income Statement								
Total Revenue	19,178,000	16,617,000	13,829,000	12,163,000	10,356,000	8,959,000	4,970,000	4,062,000
EBITDA	2,259,000	1,747,000	1,842,000	1,751,000	1,548,000	1,360,000	671,000	534,000
Depn & Amortn	326,000	277,000	213,000	271,000	226,000	200,000	126,000	91,000
Income Before Taxes	1,785,000	1,372,000	1,584,000	1,424,000	1,262,000	1,126,000	549,000	479,000
Income Taxes	582,000	375,000	533,000	481,000	361,000	246,000	185,000	163,000
Net Income	1,227,000	1,004,000	917,000	943,000	901,000	880,000	364,000	316,000
Average Shares	201,467	199,152	202,852	202,907	201,262	202,057	127,000	127,000
Balance Sheet								
Current Assets	7,287,000	6,394,000	5,098,000	4,893,000	3,551,000	3,491,000	1,873,000	1,689,000
Total Assets	17,544,000	16,183,000	11,731,000	11,069,000	7,987,000	7,774,000	4,572,000	4,091,000
Current Liabilities	5,374,000	5,616,000	4,582,000	4,579,000	2,901,000	3,453,000	1,461,000	1,291,000
Long-Term Obligations	3,291,000	3,296,000	718,000	724,000	162,000	169,000	249,000	257,000
Total Liabilities	10,355,000	10,262,000	6,532,000	6,541,000	4,167,000	4,603,000	2,353,000	2,176,000
Stockholders' Equity	7,189,000	5,921,000	5,199,000	4,528,000	3,820,000	3,171,000	2,219,000	1,915,000
Shares Outstanding	201,033	197,966	200,993	200,746	200,502	201,013	127,000	126,000
Statistical Record								
Return on Assets %	7.26	7.19	8.04	9.90	11.40	14.26	8.40	8.55
Return on Equity %	18.67	18.06	18.85	22.59	25.71	32.65	17.61	17.42
EBITDA Margin %	11.78	10.51	13.32	14.40	14.95	15.18	13.50	13.15
Net Margin %	6.40	6.04	6.63	7.75	8.70	9.82	7.32	7.78
Asset Turnover	1.13	1.19	1.21	1.28	1.31	1.45	1.15	1.10
Current Ratio	1.36	1.14	1.11	1.07	1.22	1.01	1.28	1.31
Debt to Equity	0.46	0.56	0.14	0.16	0.04	0.05	0.11	0.13
Price Range	109.83-86.10	90.39-52.37	110.58-74.57	94.99-61.00	78.00-37.00	74.81-46.94	61.25-40.38	44.97-31.63
P/E Ratio	18.03-14.14	17.93-10.39	24.46-16.50	20.43-13.12	17.41-8.26	17.16-10.77	21.42-14.12	17.99-12.65
Average Yield %	1.44	1.72	1.34	1.43	1.76	1.53	1.80	2.12

Address: 2941 Fairview Park Drive, Suite 100, Falls Church, VA 22042-4153 **Telephone:** (703) 876-3000 **Fax:** (703) 876-3125	Web Site: www.generaldynamics.com **Officers:** Nicholas D. Chabraja - Chmn., C.E.O. Michael W. Toner - Exec. V.P., Group Exec., Marine Systems	Auditors: KPMG LLP **Investor Contact:** 703-876-3195 **Transfer Agents:** EquiServe Trust Company, N.A., Jersey City, NJ

GENERAL ELECTRIC CO.

Exchange	Symbol	Price	52Wk Range	Yield	P/E	Div Acheiver
NYS	GE	$36.06 (3/31/2005)	37.48-29.95	2.44	22.68	29 Years

*7 Year Price Score 79.10   *NYSE Composite Index=100   *12 Month Price Score 98.62

Interim Earnings (Per Share)

Qtr.	Mar	Jun	Sep	Dec
2001	0.26	0.39	0.33	0.40
2002	0.25	0.44	0.41	0.31
2003	0.30	0.38	0.36	0.45
2004	0.32	0.38	0.38	0.51

Interim Dividends (Per Share)

Amt	Decl	Ex	Rec	Pay
0.20Q	6/11/2004	6/24/2004	6/28/2004	7/26/2004
0.20Q	9/17/2004	9/23/2004	9/27/2004	10/25/2004
0.22Q	12/10/2004	12/22/2004	12/27/2004	1/25/2005
0.22Q	2/11/2005	2/24/2005	2/28/2005	4/25/2005

Indicated Div: $0.88 (Div. Reinv. Plan)

Valuation Analysis

Forecast P/E	19.72	No of Institutions	
	(4/7/2005)	1349	
Market Cap	$381.7 Billion	Shares	
Book Value	110.3 Billion		5,777,798,656
Price/Book	3.46	% Held	
Price/Sales	2.51	54.51	

Business Summary: Electrical (MIC: 11.14 SIC: 641 NAIC: 35110)

General Electric is engaged in developing, manufacturing and marketing a wide variety of products for the generation, transmission, distribution, control and utilization of electricity. Co.'s operating segments include: Commercial Finance, Consumer Finance, Energy, Healthcare, Infrastructure, Transportation, NBC, Advanced Materials, Consumer and Industrial, Equipment Services and Insurance. Co.'s products include major appliances; lighting products; industrial automation products; medical diagnostic imaging equipment; motors; electrical distribution and control equipment; locomotives; power generation and delivery products; nuclear power support services and fuel assemblies.

Recent Developments: For the year ended Dec 31 2004, net income increased 10.6% to $16,593 million from net income of $15,002 million a year earlier. Revenues were $152,363 million, up 13.5% from $134,187 million the year before. Total direct expense was $77,386 million versus $67,575 million in the prior year, an increase of 14.5%. Total indirect expense was $38,148 million versus $31,821 million in the prior year, an increase of 19.9%.

Prospects: Co. has completed its strategic repositioning and returned to double-digit earnings growth. Co. is benefiting from strong execution of its growth initiatives and an improving global economy. In addition, Co. has made good progress on its portfolio, exceeding its synergy goals for the Amersham and Universal acquisitions, adding capabilities to its water, security and key financial service units, and executing several dispositions, including the initial public offering of Genworth and the sale of 60.0% of Gecis, Co.'s global business processing operation. As a result, Co. anticipates achieving 10.0% to 15.0% annual earnings growth with strong cash flow generation in 2005 and 2006.

Financial Data

(US$ in Thousands)	12/31/2004	12/31/2003	12/31/2002	12/31/2001	12/31/2000	12/31/1999	12/31/1998	12/31/1997
Earnings Per Share	1.59	1.49	1.41	1.37	1.27	1.07	0.93	0.82
Cash Flow Per Share	3.50	3.02	2.96	3.24	2.29	2.50	1.97	1.45
Tang Book Value Per Share	2.55	2.40	1.76	2.33	2.32	1.68	1.55	1.56
Dividends Per Share	0.820	0.770	0.730	0.660	0.570	0.487	0.417	0.360
Dividend Payout %	51.57	51.68	51.77	48.18	44.88	45.36	44.64	43.90
Income Statement								
Total Revenue	152,363,000	134,187,000	131,698,000	125,913,000	129,853,000	111,630,000	100,469,000	90,840,000
EBITDA	28,491,000	26,860,000	24,889,000	26,790,000	26,182,000	22,268,000	19,337,000	16,448,000
Depn & Amortn	8,385,000	6,956,000	5,998,000	7,089,000	7,736,000	6,691,000	5,860,000	5,269,000
Income Before Taxes	20,106,000	19,904,000	18,891,000	19,701,000	18,446,000	15,577,000	13,477,000	11,179,000
Income Taxes	3,513,000	4,315,000	3,758,000	5,573,000	5,711,000	4,860,000	4,181,000	2,976,000
Net Income	16,593,000	15,002,000	14,118,000	13,684,000	12,735,000	10,717,000	9,296,000	8,203,000
Average Shares	10,445,000	10,075,000	10,028,000	10,052,000	10,057,000	9,996,000	9,990,000	10,035,000
Balance Sheet								
Current Assets	39,339,000	32,148,000	28,838,000	27,237,000	25,509,000	24,092,000	18,590,000	20,680,000
Total Assets	750,330,000	647,483,000	575,244,000	495,023,000	437,006,000	405,200,000	355,935,000	304,012,000
Current Liabilities	206,280,000	176,530,000	181,827,000	198,904,000	156,112,000	161,216,000	141,579,000	120,668,000
Long-Term Obligations	213,161,000	170,004,000	140,632,000	79,806,000	82,132,000	71,427,000	59,663,000	46,603,000
Total Liabilities	623,663,000	562,523,000	506,065,000	434,984,000	381,578,000	357,429,000	312,780,000	265,892,000
Stockholders' Equity	110,284,000	79,180,000	63,706,000	54,824,000	50,492,000	42,557,000	38,880,000	34,438,000
Shares Outstanding	10,586,358	10,063,120	9,969,894	9,925,938	9,932,006	9,854,529	9,813,000	9,795,000
Statistical Record								
Return on Assets %	2.37	2.45	2.64	2.94	3.02	2.82	2.82	2.85
Return on Equity %	17.47	21.00	23.82	25.99	27.30	26.32	25.36	25.02
EBITDA Margin %	18.70	20.02	18.90	21.28	20.16	19.95	19.25	18.11
Net Margin %	10.89	11.18	10.72	10.87	9.81	9.60	9.25	9.03
Asset Turnover	0.22	0.22	0.25	0.27	0.31	0.29	0.30	0.32
Current Ratio	0.19	0.18	0.16	0.14	0.16	0.15	0.13	0.17
Debt to Equity	1.93	2.15	2.21	1.46	1.63	1.68	1.53	1.35
Price Range	37.48-29.18	32.11-22.17	41.55-22.00	53.40-30.37	60.00-41.71	53.17-32.00	34.42-23.85	25.13-16.27
P/E Ratio	23.57-18.35	21.55-14.88	29.47-15.60	38.98-22.17	47.24-32.84	49.69-29.91	37.01-25.65	30.64-19.84
Average Yield %	2.49	2.75	2.34	1.52	1.10	1.21	1.27	1.73

Address: 3135 Easton Turnpike, Fairfield, CT 06828-0001 **Telephone:** (203) 373 2211 **Fax:** (203) 373 3131	**Web Site:** www.ge.com **Officers:** Jeffrey R. Immelt - Chmn., C.E.O. Dennis D. Dammerman - Vice-Chmn.	**Auditors:** KPMG LLP **Investor Contact:** 203-373-2816 **Transfer Agents:** GE Share Owner Services, c/o The Bank of New York,

GENERAL GROWTH PROPERTIES, INC. (DE)

Exchange	Symbol	Price	52Wk Range	Yield	P/E	Div Acheiver
NYS	GGP	$34.10 (3/31/2005)	37.54-25.51	4.22	28.18	11 Years

*7 Year Price Score 160.37 *NYSE Composite Index=100 *12 Month Price Score 101.07

Interim Earnings (Per Share)

Qtr.	Mar	Jun	Sep	Dec
2001	0.13	(0.16)	0.16	0.27
2002	0.17	0.19	0.24	0.39
2003	0.24	0.23	0.29	1.12
2004	0.27	0.23	0.29	0.42

Interim Dividends (Per Share)

Amt	Decl	Ex	Rec	Pay
0.30Q	7/2/2004	7/13/2004	7/15/2004	7/30/2004
0.36Q	8/20/2004	10/13/2004	10/15/2004	10/29/2004
0.36Q	1/7/2005	1/12/2005	1/17/2005	1/31/2005
0.36Q	4/4/2005	4/13/2005	4/15/2005	4/29/2005

Indicated Div: $1.44 (Div. Reinv. Plan)

Valuation Analysis

Forecast P/E	N/A		No of Institutions
Market Cap	$8.0 Billion		Shares
Book Value	2.1 Billion		186,622,768
Price/Book	3.73		% Held
Price/Sales	4.44		85.33

Business Summary: Property, Real Estate & Development (MIC: 8.3 SIC: 798 NAIC: 25930)

General Growth Properties is primarily engaged in the ownership, operation, management, leasing, acquisition, development and expansion of regional mall and community shopping centers in the United States. As of Dec 31 2003, Co.'s portfolio is comprised primarily of 162 operating retail properties (regional malls or community centers). Co. also has certain office space associated with Co.'s retail properties and approximately 1.4 million square feet of commercial/industrial space at 6 former JP Realty properties. The 162 operating retail properties are shopping centers with a variety of smaller Mall Stores.

Recent Developments: For the year ended Dec 31 2004, income from continuing operations decreased 0.7% to $253,652 thousand from income of $255,563 thousand a year earlier. Net income increased 1.7% to $267,852 thousand from net income of $263,411 thousand a year earlier. Revenues were $1,802,845 thousand, up 42.8% from $1,262,791 thousand the year before. Operating income was $742,275 thousand versus an income of $548,400 thousand in the prior year, an increase of 35.4%.

Prospects: Co.'s prospects appear favorable, reflecting recent solid operating trends. For instance, comparable net operating income from consolidated properties for the fourth quarter ended Dec 31 2004 increased by 8.0% compared with the same period last year. Also, mall shop occupancy increased to 92.1% at Dec 31 2004 versus 91.3% at Dec 31 2003. For consolidated properties, average rent per square foot for new/renewal leases signed during 2004 was $33.53 versus $31.83 for 2003. Accordingly, Co.'s funds from operations guidance for 2005 is estimated to be $3.13 per share. Separately, on Nov 12 2004, Co. completed its acquisition of The Rouse Company.

Financial Data
(US$ in Thousands)

	12/31/2004	12/31/2003	12/31/2002	12/31/2001	12/31/2000	12/31/1999	12/31/1998	12/31/1997
Earnings Per Share	1.21	1.22	0.98	0.43	0.73	0.55	0.49	0.91
Cash Flow Per Share	3.41	2.88	2.47	1.31	1.98	1.61	0.93	0.88
Tang Book Value Per Share	9.13	7.69	6.39	6.37	5.98	5.98	5.01	5.40
Dividends Per Share	1.260	1.020	0.890	0.747	0.680	0.647	0.470	0.600
Dividend Payout %	104.13	83.61	90.51	175.00	93.58	116.87	96.58	65.93
Income Statement								
Property Income	1,588,496	1,150,315	871,559	713,316	682,109	595,142	416,105	281,097
Non-Property Income	214,349	120,413	108,907	90,393	16,658	17,200	10,471	10,050
Total Revenue	1,802,845	1,270,728	980,466	803,709	698,767	612,342	426,576	291,147
Depn & Amortn	377,056	240,234	185,124	152,878	126,689	112,874	75,227	48,508
Interest Expense	472,185	278,543	218,935	214,277	218,075	185,984	125,851	78,775
Income Taxes	2,383	...	...	...	...	...	...	...
Net Income	267,852	263,411	209,258	92,310	137,948	101,125	66,445	89,551
Average Shares	220,149	215,079	212,553	158,721	156,288	138,093	109,146	98,520
Balance Sheet								
Total Assets	25,718,625	9,582,897	7,280,822	5,646,807	5,284,104	4,954,895	4,027,474	2,097,719
Long-Term Obligations	20,310,947	6,649,490	4,592,311	3,398,207	3,244,126	3,119,534	2,648,776	1,275,785
Total Liabilities	22,621,032	7,008,664	4,900,850	3,570,562	3,478,028	3,333,097	2,804,836	1,336,746
Stockholders' Equity	2,143,150	1,670,409	1,196,525	1,183,386	938,418	927,758	585,707	498,505
Shares Outstanding	234,724	217,293	187,191	185,771	156,843	155,092	117,003	92,367
Statistical Record								
Return on Assets %	1.51	3.12	3.24	1.69	2.69	2.25	2.17	4.65
Return on Equity %	14.01	18.38	17.59	8.70	14.74	13.36	12.26	21.61
Net Margin %	14.86	20.73	21.34	11.49	19.74	16.51	15.58	30.76
Price Range	36.63-25.51	27.89-16.09	17.33-12.91	13.39-11.00	12.06-8.94	12.85-8.35	12.90-10.96	12.67-10.17
P/E Ratio	30.27-21.08	22.86-13.19	17.69-13.17	31.15-25.58	16.52-12.24	23.37-15.19	26.32-22.36	13.92-11.17
Average Yield %	4.07	4.78	5.74	6.10	6.47	5.85	3.90	5.38

Address: 110 North Wacker Drive, Suite 3100, Chicago, IL 60606 Telephone: (312) 960-5000 Fax: (312) 960-5475	Web Site: www.generalgrowth.com Officers: Matthew Bucksbaum - Chmn. Robert Michaels - Pres., C.O.O.	Auditors: DELOITTE & TOUCHE LLP Transfer Agents: Mellon Investor Services, LLC, South Hackensack, NJ

GENERAL MILLS, INC.

Exchange	Symbol	Price	52Wk Range	Yield	P/E
NYS	GIS	$49.15 (3/31/2005)	53.36-43.30	2.52	17.87

*7 Year Price Score 96.22 *NYSE Composite Index=100 *12 Month Price Score 100.82

TRADING VOLUME (thousand shares)

Interim Earnings (Per Share)

Qtr.	Aug	Nov	Feb	May
2001-02	0.64	0.41	0.22	0.12
2002-03	0.47	0.73	0.63	0.59
2003-04	0.59	0.81	0.63	0.72
2004-05	0.47	0.97	...	...

Interim Dividends (Per Share)

Amt	Decl	Ex	Rec	Pay
0.31Q	6/28/2004	7/8/2004	7/12/2004	8/2/2004
0.31Q	9/27/2004	10/6/2004	10/11/2004	11/1/2004
0.31Q	12/13/2004	1/6/2005	1/10/2005	2/1/2005
0.31Q	2/28/2005	4/7/2005	4/11/2005	5/2/2005

Indicated Div: $1.24

Valuation Analysis

Forecast P/E	15.81	No of Institutions	576
	(4/7/2005)		
Market Cap	$17.9 Billion	Shares	259,335,776
Book Value	5.0 Billion	% Held	71.04
Price/Book	3.59		
Price/Sales	1.62		

Business Summary: Food (MIC: 4.1 SIC: 043 NAIC: 11230)

General Mills is a producer of packaged consumer foods. Co.'s U.S. Retail segment consists of cereals, meals, refrigerated and frozen dough products, baking products, snacks, yogurt and organic foods. The Bakeries and Foodservice segment consists of products marketed to retail and wholesale bakeries and offered to the commercial and noncommercial foodservice sectors throughout the U.S. and Canada, such as restaurants and business and school cafeterias. The International segment is made up of retail business outside the U.S. and foodservice business outside of the U.S. and Canada. Products include Cheerios, Wheaties, Total, Betty Crocker, Gold Medal, Yoplait, Chex and Colombo.

Recent Developments: For the quarter ended Nov 28 2004, net income increased 19.2% to $367,000 thousand from net income of $308,000 thousand in the year-earlier quarter. Revenues were $3,168,000 thousand, up 3.5% from $3,060,000 thousand the year before. Total indirect expense was $640,000 thousand versus $686,000 thousand in the prior-year quarter, a decrease of 6.7%.

Prospects: On Feb 28 2005, Co. announced that its 40.5% ownership interest in the Snack Ventures Europe joint venture has been redeemed for $750.0 million. The redemption ends the European snack joint venture between Co. and PepsiCo. Co. reaffirmed that it will use net cash proceeds from this transaction, estimated at $710.0 million, to reduce debt. Co. is also targeting $675.0 million of operating cash for debt reduction in 2005. In the second half of fiscal 2005, Co.'s plans call for continuing contributions from both productivity and pricing. In particular, Co. expects its list price increases and higher merchandised price points to be increasingly reflected at retail.

Financial Data

(US$ in Thousands)	6 Mos	3 Mos	05/30/2004	05/25/2003	05/26/2002	05/27/2001	05/28/2000	05/30/1999
Earnings Per Share	2.75	2.58	2.75	2.43	1.34	2.28	2.00	1.70
Cash Flow Per Share	4.60	4.08	3.83	4.43	2.77	2.60	2.31	2.25
Dividends Per Share	1.170	1.135	1.100	1.100	1.100	1.100	1.100	1.080
Dividend Payout %	42.57	44.05	40.00	45.27	82.09	48.25	55.00	63.53
Income Statement								
Total Revenue	5,753,000	2,585,000	11,070,000	10,506,000	7,949,000	7,077,700	6,700,200	6,246,100
EBITDA	1,213,000	...	2,416,000	2,228,000	1,379,000	1,427,500	1,307,700	1,160,300
Depn & Amortn	221,000	108,000	399,000	365,000	296,000	223,100	208,800	194,200
Income Before Taxes	754,000	...	1,509,000	1,316,000	667,000	998,300	947,000	846,700
Income Taxes	254,000	83,000	528,000	460,000	239,000	349,900	335,900	304,000
Net Income	550,000	183,000	1,055,000	917,000	458,000	665,100	614,400	534,500
Average Shares	377,000	387,000	384,000	378,000	342,000	292,000	307,300	314,600
Balance Sheet								
Current Assets	3,307,000	3,124,000	3,215,000	3,179,000	3,437,000	1,408,200	1,190,300	1,102,500
Total Assets	18,649,000	18,351,000	18,448,000	18,227,000	16,540,000	5,091,200	4,573,700	4,140,700
Current Liabilities	2,355,000	2,523,000	2,757,000	3,444,000	5,747,000	2,208,800	2,529,100	1,700,300
Long-Term Obligations	7,429,000	7,426,000	7,410,000	7,516,000	5,591,000	2,221,000	1,760,300	1,702,400
Total Liabilities	12,531,000	12,679,000	12,901,000	13,752,000	12,811,000	5,039,000	4,862,500	3,976,500
Stockholders' Equity	4,983,000	5,373,000	5,248,000	4,175,000	3,576,000	52,200	(288,800)	164,200
Shares Outstanding	364,000	380,000	379,000	370,000	367,000	285,200	285,400	304,000
Statistical Record								
Return on Assets %	5.63	5.39	5.66	5.29	4.25	13.80	14.14	13.40
Return on Equity %	21.67	20.26	22.03	23.73	25.32	...	...	302.47
EBITDA Margin %	21.08	...	21.82	21.21	17.35	20.17	19.52	18.58
Net Margin %	9.56	7.08	9.53	8.73	5.76	9.40	9.17	8.56
Asset Turnover	0.59	0.60	0.59	0.61	0.74	1.47	1.54	1.57
Current Ratio	1.40	1.24	1.17	0.92	0.60	0.64	0.47	0.65
Debt to Equity	1.49	1.38	1.41	1.80	1.56	42.55	...	10.37
Price Range	49.13-43.30	49.13-43.86	49.66-43.86	48.00-38.40	52.86-42.30	46.13-31.69	43.59-30.06	42.13-30.06
P/E Ratio	17.87-15.75	19.04-17.00	18.06-15.95	19.75-15.80	39.45-31.57	20.23-13.90	21.80-15.03	24.78-17.68
Average Yield %	2.55	2.46	2.38	2.50	2.38	2.80	2.90	2.94

Address: Number One General Mills Boulevard, Minneapolis, MN 55426-1348 **Telephone:** (763) 764-7600 **Fax:** (763) 764-7384	**Web Site:** www.generalmills.com **Officers:** Stephen W. Sanger - Chmn., C.E.O. Stephen R. Demeritt - Vice-Chmn.	**Auditors:** KPMG LLP **Investor Contact:** 763-764-2607

GENERAL MOTORS CORP

Exchange	Symbol	Price	52Wk Range	Yield	P/E
NYS	GM	$29.39 (3/31/2005)	49.50-28.35	6.81	5.94

*7 Year Price Score 65.78   *NYSE Composite Index=100   *12 Month Price Score 77.93

Interim Earnings (Per Share)

Qtr.	Mar	Jun	Sep	Dec
2001	0.53	1.03	(0.41)	0.62
2002	0.57	2.43	(1.42)	1.77
2003	2.71	1.58	0.79	(0.03)
2004	2.25	2.36	0.78	(0.44)

Interim Dividends (Per Share)

Amt	Decl	Ex	Rec	Pay
0.50Q	5/4/2004	5/12/2004	5/14/2004	6/10/2004
0.50Q	8/3/2004	8/11/2004	8/13/2004	9/10/2004
0.50Q	10/29/2004	11/4/2004	11/8/2004	12/10/2004
0.50Q	2/1/2005	2/9/2005	2/11/2005	3/10/2005

Indicated Div: $2.00

Valuation Analysis

Forecast P/E	29.33	No of Institutions
	(4/7/2005)	482
Market Cap	$16.6 Billion	Shares
Book Value	27.7 Billion	437,103,904
Price/Book	0.60	% Held
Price/Sales	0.09	77.39

Business Summary: Automotive (MIC: 15.1 SIC: 711 NAIC: 36111)

General Motors designs, manufactures, and markets vehicles in North America under the following nameplates: Chevrolet, Pontiac, GMC, Oldsmobile, Buick, Cadillac, and Saturn. Co. also operates outside North America with vehicles designed, manufactured and marketed under the following nameplates: Opel, Vauxhall, Holden, Saab, Buick, Chevrolet, GMC, and Cadillac. Co. also provides financial services, including consumer vehicle financing, automotive dealership and other commercial financing, residential and commercial mortgage services, automobile service contracts, personal automobile insurance coverage and selected commercial insurance coverage.

Recent Developments: For the year ended Dec 31 2004, net income decreased 26.6% to $2,805,000 thousand from net income of $3,822,000 thousand a year earlier. Revenues were $193,517,000 thousand, up 4.1% from $185,837,000 thousand the year before. Total direct expense was $159,951,000 thousand versus $152,435,000 thousand in the prior year, an increase of 4.9%. Total indirect expense was $20,394,000 thousand versus $20,957,000 thousand in the prior year, a decrease of 2.7%.

Prospects: Co. had a solid finish to 2004 as sales volumes for its newest vehicles gained momentum. Additionally, Co. is continuing to make progress in the key areas of productivity, quality and cost reduction. In 2005, Co.'s product portfolio includes a number of new high-volume vehicles that are continuing to ramp such as the Pontiac G6 and Chevrolet Cobalt. Meanwhile, Co. expects to introduce the Pontiac Solstice, Chevrolet HHR, and Cadillac DTS in 2005. Looking ahead to 2005, Co. expects earnings to range from $4.00 to $5.00 per share, before special items. For 2005, Co. expects higher global sales volumes, $2.00 billion in operating cash flow and capital expenditures of about $8.00 billion.

Financial Data
(US$ in Thousands)

	12/31/2004	12/31/2003	12/31/2002	12/31/2001	12/31/2000	12/31/1999	12/31/1998	12/31/1997
Earnings Per Share	4.95	7.14	3.35	1.77	6.68	9.18	4.18	8.62
Cash Flow Per Share	8.38	4.58	11.56	6.42	15.59	35.20	22.22	20.02
Tang Book Value Per Share	40.35	36.49	N.M.	N.M.	10.80	16.02	6.25	7.57
Dividends Per Share	2.000	2.000	2.000	2.000	2.000	2.000	2.000	2.000
Dividend Payout %	40.40	28.01	59.70	112.99	29.94	21.79	47.85	23.20
Income Statement								
Total Revenue	193,517,000	185,524,000	186,763,000	177,260,000	184,632,000	176,558,000	161,315,000	178,174,000
EBITDA	23,761,000	28,025,000	15,807,000	23,016,000	30,127,000	29,115,000	23,706,000	24,769,000
Depn & Amortn	10,589,000	15,580,000	12,938,000	12,908,000	13,411,000	12,318,000	12,201,000	10,942,000
Income Before Taxes	1,192,000	2,981,000	2,080,000	1,518,000	7,164,000	9,047,000	4,612,000	7,714,000
Income Taxes	(911,000)	731,000	533,000	768,000	2,393,000	3,118,000	1,463,000	1,069,000
Net Income	2,805,000	3,822,000	1,736,000	601,000	4,452,000	6,002,000	2,956,000	6,698,000
Average Shares	1,557,000	1,669,000	1,481,500	1,432,000	1,291,000	780,000	783,000	832,000
Balance Sheet								
Current Assets	91,213,000	86,261,000	63,956,000	47,186,000	42,312,000	42,621,000	44,509,000	42,579,000
Total Assets	479,603,000	448,507,000	370,782,000	323,969,000	303,100,000	274,730,000	257,389,000	228,888,000
Current Liabilities	129,013,000	32,930,000	104,084,000	129,373,000	142,298,000	126,355,000	116,178,000	101,401,000
Long-Term Obligations	207,174,000	271,756,000	134,272,000	104,638,000	65,704,000	62,745,000	52,574,000	42,565,000
Total Liabilities	451,480,000	422,932,000	363,134,000	303,516,000	272,079,000	253,272,000	241,518,000	210,433,000
Stockholders' Equity	27,726,000	25,268,000	6,814,000	19,707,000	30,175,000	20,644,000	14,984,000	17,506,000
Shares Outstanding	565,132	561,997	1,518,732	1,436,549	1,423,468	756,527	761,168	797,342
Statistical Record								
Return on Assets %	0.60	0.93	0.50	0.19	1.54	2.26	1.22	2.97
Return on Equity %	10.56	23.83	13.09	2.41	17.47	33.69	18.20	32.73
EBITDA Margin %	12.28	15.11	8.46	12.98	16.32	16.49	14.70	13.90
Net Margin %	1.45	2.06	0.93	0.34	2.41	3.40	1.83	3.76
Asset Turnover	0.42	0.45	0.54	0.57	0.64	0.66	0.66	0.79
Current Ratio	0.71	2.62	0.61	0.36	0.30	0.34	0.38	0.42
Debt to Equity	7.47	10.75	19.71	5.31	2.18	3.04	3.51	2.43
Price Range	55.00-37.04	53.70-29.92	68.02-31.01	67.04-40.10	93.63-48.81	77.54-58.62	62.86-41.56	55.86-41.44
P/E Ratio	11.11-7.48	7.52-4.19	20.30-9.26	37.88-22.66	14.02-7.31	8.45-6.39	15.04-9.94	6.48-4.81
Average Yield %	4.50	5.17	4.07	3.73	2.89	2.91	3.64	4.23

Address: 300 Renaissance Center, Detroit, MI 48265-3000	Web Site: www.gm.com	Auditors: Deloitte & Touche LLP
Telephone: (313) 556-5000	Officers: G. Richard Wagoner Jr. - Chmn., C.E.O.	Investor Contact: 212-418-6270
Fax: (313) 556-5108	John M. Devine - Vice-Chmn., C.F.O.	Transfer Agents: BankBoston c/o Boston EquiServe Trust Co., Boston,

GENUINE PARTS CO.

Exchange	Symbol	Price	52Wk Range	Yield	P/E	Div Acheiver
NYS	GPC	$43.49 (3/31/2005)	44.70-32.72	2.87	19.33	48 Years

*7 Year Price Score 108.30 ***NYSE Composite Index=100** ***12 Month Price Score 101.52**

Interim Earnings (Per Share)

Qtr.	Mar	Jun	Sep	Dec
2001	0.52	0.55	0.51	0.14
2002	(1.76)	0.55	0.54	0.51
2003	0.39	0.52	0.51	0.49
2004	0.57	0.58	0.56	0.54

Interim Dividends (Per Share)

Amt	Decl	Ex	Rec	Pay
0.30Q	4/19/2004	6/9/2004	6/11/2004	7/1/2004
0.30Q	8/16/2004	9/8/2004	9/10/2004	10/1/2004
0.30Q	11/15/2004	12/8/2004	12/10/2004	1/3/2005
0.313Q	2/21/2005	3/9/2005	3/11/2005	4/1/2005

Indicated Div: $1.25 (Div. Reinv. Plan)

Valuation Analysis

Forecast P/E	17.87	No of Institutions
	(4/7/2005)	350
Market Cap	$7.6 Billion	Shares
Book Value	2.5 Billion	122,257,216
Price/Book	2.99	% Held
Price/Sales	0.84	69.97

Business Summary: Retail - Automotive (MIC: 5.7 SIC: 013 NAIC: 23120)

Genuine Parts is a service distribution and sales organization. Co.'s Automotive Parts group distributes automotive replacement parts and accessory items to independent and company-owned NAPA auto parts stores. The Industrial Parts group's Motion Industries distributes industrial bearings and power transmission replacement parts, including hydraulic and pneumatic products, material handling equipment and agricultural and irrigation equipment. The Office Products group's S. P. Richards Company distributes a line of office and business-related products. The Electrical and Electronic Materials Group's EIS distributes a range of materials and products for electrical and electronic apparatus.

Recent Developments: For the year ended Dec 31 2004, net income increased 18.4% to $395,552 thousand from net income of $334,101 thousand a year earlier. Revenues were $9,097,267 thousand, up 7.7% from $8,449,300 thousand the year before. Total direct expense was $6,267,544 thousand versus $5,826,684 thousand in the prior year, an increase of 7.6%. Total indirect expense was $2,193,804 thousand versus $2,050,873 thousand in the prior year, an increase of 7.0%.

Prospects: Prospects appear favorable as sales are stronger in all four of Co.'s business segments. Also, Co. continues to see improvement in the area of gross margin, operating expenses as a percentage of sales and operating margin. Moreover, Co.'s financial flexibility appears much stronger with the generation of $555.0 million in operating cash flow and total debt reduced by $125.1 million during the 12 months ended Dec 31 2004. Looking ahead, Co. will strive to pick up the revenue pace in the coming year, as it believes all the plans are in place to build upon the favorable momentum experienced in 2004.

Financial Data

(US$ in Thousands)	12/31/2004	12/31/2003	12/31/2002	12/31/2001	12/31/2000	12/31/1999	12/31/1998	12/31/1997
Earnings Per Share	2.25	1.91	(0.16)	1.71	2.20	2.11	1.98	1.90
Cash Flow Per Share	3.17	2.31	1.56	1.93	1.79	2.05	1.58	1.40
Tang Book Value Per Share	14.21	12.95	11.88	10.97	10.50	9.80	9.52	10.39
Dividends Per Share	1.200	1.180	1.160	1.140	1.100	1.040	1.000	0.960
Dividend Payout %	53.33	61.78	...	66.67	50.00	49.29	50.51	50.53
Income Statement								
Total Revenue	9,097,267	8,449,300	8,258,927	8,220,668	8,369,857	7,981,687	6,614,032	6,005,245
EBITDA	698,126	640,756	675,887	581,806	739,053	718,034	658,422	624,467
Depn & Amortn	62,207	69,013	70,151	85,793	92,303	89,967	69,305	58,867
Income Before Taxes	635,919	571,743	605,736	496,013	646,750	628,067	589,117	565,600
Income Taxes	240,367	218,101	238,236	198,866	261,427	250,445	233,323	223,203
Net Income	395,552	334,101	(27,590)	297,147	385,323	377,622	355,794	342,397
Average Shares	175,660	174,480	175,104	173,633	175,327	179,238	180,081	180,165
Balance Sheet								
Current Assets	3,633,484	3,417,626	3,335,775	3,146,212	3,019,481	2,895,203	2,683,357	2,093,551
Total Assets	4,455,247	4,116,497	4,019,843	4,206,646	4,142,114	3,929,672	3,600,380	2,754,363
Current Liabilities	1,132,715	1,016,931	1,069,718	919,181	988,313	916,012	818,409	556,938
Long-Term Obligations	500,000	625,108	674,796	835,580	770,581	702,417	588,640	209,490
Total Liabilities	1,910,870	1,804,214	1,889,834	1,861,523	1,881,308	1,752,155	1,547,048	894,895
Stockholders' Equity	2,544,377	2,312,283	2,130,009	2,345,123	2,260,806	2,177,517	2,053,332	1,859,468
Shares Outstanding	174,964	174,045	174,380	173,473	172,389	177,275	179,505	178,948
Statistical Record								
Return on Assets %	9.20	8.21	N.M.	7.12	9.52	10.03	11.20	12.98
Return on Equity %	16.24	15.04	N.M.	12.90	17.32	17.85	18.19	19.07
EBITDA Margin %	7.67	7.58	8.18	7.08	8.83	9.00	9.95	10.40
Net Margin %	4.35	3.95	N.M.	3.61	4.60	4.73	5.38	5.70
Asset Turnover	2.12	2.08	2.01	1.97	2.07	2.12	2.08	2.28
Current Ratio	3.21	3.36	3.12	3.42	3.06	3.16	3.28	3.76
Debt to Equity	0.20	0.27	0.32	0.36	0.34	0.32	0.29	0.11
Price Range	44.06-32.13	33.66-27.43	38.08-27.64	37.44-24.26	26.44-18.63	35.75-23.13	38.13-29.38	35.63-28.92
P/E Ratio	19.58-14.28	17.62-14.36	...	21.89-14.19	12.02-8.47	16.94-10.96	19.26-14.84	18.75-15.22
Average Yield %	3.20	3.74	3.48	3.78	4.98	3.49	2.95	2.99

Address: 2999 Circle 75 Parkway, Atlanta, GA 30339	Web Site: www.genpt.com	Auditors: Ernst & Young LLP
Telephone: (770) 953-1700	Officers: Larry L. Prince - Chmn. Thomas C. Gallagher - Pres., C.E.O.	Investor Contact: 770-953-1700
Fax: (770) 956-2211		Transfer Agents: Sun Trust Bank, Atlanta, GA

GEORGIA-PACIFIC CORP.

Exchange	Symbol	Price	52Wk Range	Yield	P/E
NYS	GP	$35.49 (3/31/2005)	37.85-31.75	1.97	14.97

*7 Year Price Score 99.04   *NYSE Composite Index=100   *12 Month Price Score 93.87

TRADING VOLUME (thousand shares)

Interim Earnings (Per Share)

Qtr.	Mar	Jun	Sep	Dec
2001	(0.61)	0.13	(0.80)	(0.82)
2002	0.26	(0.36)	0.27	(0.95)
2003	(0.11)	0.25	0.75	0.12
2004	0.57	0.84	0.91	0.06

Interim Dividends (Per Share)

Amt	Decl	Ex	Rec	Pay
0.125	7/30/2004	8/5/2004	8/9/2004	8/19/2004
0.125	11/5/2004	11/17/2004	11/19/2004	11/29/2004
0.125	2/3/2005	2/10/2005	2/14/2005	2/24/2005

Valuation Analysis

Forecast P/E	N/A	No of Institutions	
Market Cap	$9.1 Billion	Shares	
Book Value	6.2 Billion	198,599,248	
Price/Book	1.47	% Held	
Price/Sales	0.46	76.44	

Business Summary: Paper Products (MIC: 11.11 SIC: 611 NAIC: 22110)

Georgia-Pacific is broadly engaged in four business operations: the manufacture of tissue products (including bath tissue, paper towels, and napkins) and disposable tabletop products (including disposable cups, plates and cutlery); the manufacture of containerboard and packaging (including linerboard, medium, kraft and corrugated packaging); the manufacture of bleached pulp and paper (including paper, market and fluff pulp, and bleached board) and the manufacture and distribution of building products (including plywood, oriented strand board, various industrial wood products, and softwood and hardwood lumber, and certain non-wood items including gypsum board, chemicals and other products).

Recent Developments: For the year ended Jan 1 2005, income from continuing operations increased 93.2% to $626 million from income of $324 million a year earlier. Net income increased 145.3% to $623 million from net income of $254 million a year earlier.0% from $19,656 million the year before. Operating income was $1,624 million versus an income of $1,252 million in the prior year, an increase of 29.7%. Total direct expense was $14,831 million versus $15,376 million in the prior year, a decrease of 3.5%. Total indirect expense was $3,362 million versus $3,152 million in the prior year, an increase of 6.7%.

Prospects: Co. is encouraged by the implementation of its strategy to improve and separate its brands in its North America Consumer Products segment. Internationally, continuing cost reduction initiatives in Europe are helping Co.'s consumer products business by offsetting lower prices and inflation. Meanwhile, Co.'s Building Products Manufacturing segment is seeing strong demand for its structural panels as residential housing demand remains strong and commercial construction conditions continue to improve. In 2005, Co. expects to continue to improve its financial strength and flexibility by reducing debt, increasing cash flow and improving returns on capital.

Financial Data
(US$ in Thousands)

	01/01/2005	01/03/2004	12/28/2002	12/29/2001	12/30/2000	01/01/2000	12/31/1998	12/31/1997
Earnings Per Share	2.37	1.01	(3.09)	(2.10)	1.94	4.07	0.85	0.85
Cash Flow Per Share	5.79	7.09	4.26	6.53	9.91	8.28	8.58	6.14
Tang Book Value Per Share	N.M.	N.M.	N.M.	N.M.	N.M.	6.84	7.91	10.26
Dividends Per Share	0.500	0.50	0.50	0.500	0.500	0.500	0.500	1.000
Dividend Payout %	21.10	49.50	...	...	25.77	12.29	58.48	116.96
Income Statement								
Total Revenue	19,656,000	20,255,000	23,271,000	25,016,000	22,218,000	17,977,000	13,336,000	13,094,000
EBITDA	2,569,000	2,213,000	1,363,000	2,131,000	2,388,000	3,137,000	1,745,000	1,548,000
Depn & Amortn	945,000	1,045,000	1,030,000	1,346,000	937,000	821,000	811,000	848,000
Income Before Taxes	923,000	335,000	(508,000)	(295,000)	812,000	1,821,000	491,000	235,000
Income Taxes	297,000	109,000	(318,000)	181,000	307,000	705,000	202,000	106,000
Net Income	623,000	254,000	(735,000)	(407,000)	505,000	1,116,000	274,000	69,000
Average Shares	262,806	251,400	237,600	227,600	176,900	175,900	182,400	182,200
Balance Sheet								
Current Assets	3,947,000	4,598,000	4,706,000	5,460,000	6,288,000	4,559,000	2,645,000	2,916,000
Total Assets	23,072,000	24,405,000	24,629,000	26,364,000	30,882,000	16,897,000	12,700,000	12,950,000
Current Liabilities	3,616,000	4,423,000	4,045,000	5,810,000	6,082,000	4,191,000	2,648,000	3,020,000
Long-Term Obligations	8,070,000	9,170,000	10,185,000	10,221,000	13,490,000	5,484,000	4,125,000	3,713,000
Total Liabilities	16,847,000	19,011,000	20,069,000	21,459,000	25,160,000	13,022,000	9,576,000	9,476,000
Stockholders' Equity	6,225,000	5,394,000	4,560,000	4,905,000	5,722,000	3,875,000	3,124,000	3,474,000
Shares Outstanding	256,992	252,980	250,238	230,095	224,884	172,207	183,040	182,792
Statistical Record								
Return on Assets %	2.63	1.02	N.M.	N.M.	2.12	7.52	2.14	0.54
Return on Equity %	10.75	5.02	N.M.	N.M.	10.55	31.80	8.31	1.97
EBITDA Margin %	13.07	10.93	5.86	8.52	10.75	17.45	13.08	11.82
Net Margin %	3.17	1.25	N.M.	N.M.	2.27	6.21	2.05	0.53
Asset Turnover	0.83	0.81	0.92	0.88	0.93	1.21	1.04	1.02
Current Ratio	1.09	1.04	1.16	0.94	1.03	1.09	1.00	0.97
Debt to Equity	1.30	1.70	2.23	2.08	2.36	1.42	1.32	1.07
Price Range	37.85-26.68	30.87-13.07	31.49-10.09	37.20-26.14	50.63-21.25	53.50-29.28	39.75-18.88	37.95-25.15
P/E Ratio	15.97-11.26	30.56-12.94	...	...	26.10-10.95	13.14-7.19	46.76-22.21	44.65-29.59
Average Yield %	1.47	...	0.56	1.58	1.59	1.18	1.73	3.31

Address: 133 Peachtree Street, N.E., Atlanta, GA 30303 **Telephone:** (404) 652-4000	**Web Site:** www.gp.com **Officers:** Alston D. Correll - Chmn., C.E.O. Lee M. Thomas - Pres., C.O.O.	**Auditors:** ERNST & YOUNG LLP

GETTY IMAGES, INC.

Exchange	Symbol	Price	52Wk Range	Yield	P/E
NYS	GYI	$71.11 (3/31/2005)	74.89-50.71	N/A	41.34

*7 Year Price Score 155.83 *NYSE Composite Index=100 *12 Month Price Score 110.84

TRADING VOLUME (thousand shares)

Interim Earnings (Per Share)

Qtr.	Mar	Jun	Sep	Dec
2001	(0.28)	(0.46)	(0.35)	(0.75)
2002	0.05	0.08	0.13	0.14
2003	0.23	0.23	0.16	0.49
2004	0.43	0.41	0.44	0.44

Interim Dividends (Per Share)

No Dividends Paid

Valuation Analysis

Forecast P/E	34.80	No of Institutions
	(4/7/2005)	209
Market Cap	$4.3 Billion	Shares
Book Value	1.1 Billion	55,414,304
Price/Book	4.06	% Held
Price/Sales	6.94	90.82

Business Summary: Miscellaneous Business Services (MIC: 12.8 SIC: 389 NAIC: 18111)

Getty Images is a global provider of imagery and related products and related services. Co. delivers its products digitally via the Internet and CD-ROMs, serving customers in more than 100 countries. Co. provides imagery to creative professionals at advertising agencies, graphic design firms, corporations and film and broadcasting companies; editorial customers involved in newspaper, magazine, book, CD-ROM and online publishing; and corporate marketing departments and other business customers. Co. offers its customers a variety of visual content, including creative, or stock imagery, editorial photography (news, sports, entertainment and archival imagery), illustrations and related services.

Recent Developments: For the year ended Dec 31 2004, net income increased 66.6% to $106,650 thousand from net income of $64,017 thousand a year earlier. Revenues were $622,427 thousand, up 19.0% from $523,196 thousand the year before. Operating income was $168,267 thousand versus an income of $103,269 thousand in the prior year, an increase of 62.9%. Total direct expense was $172,684 thousand versus $148,343 thousand in the prior year, an increase of 16.4%. Total indirect expense was $281,476 thousand versus $271,584 thousand in the prior year, an increase of 3.6%.

Prospects: On Jan 27 2005, Co. provided first quarter 2005 revenue guidance of $175.0 million to $180.0 million, and earnings per diluted share guidance of $0.51 to $0.54. For full-year 2005, Co. increased its outlook and now expects revenue in the range of $705.0 million to $715.0 million and earnings per diluted share of $2.10 to $2.20. The number of fully diluted shares assumed in the guidance is approximately 64.0 million for both the first quarter and full year. Co. noted that its guidance for 2005 does not include the effect of expensing share-based compensation, which becomes mandatory in its quarter ended Sep 30 2005 pursuant to Financial Accounting Standards Board Statement No.123R.

Financial Data

(US$ in Thousands)	12/31/2004	12/31/2003	12/31/2002	12/31/2001	12/31/2000	12/31/1999	12/31/1998	12/31/1997
Earnings Per Share	1.72	1.11	0.39	(1.84)	(3.40)	(1.94)	(1.25)	0.11
Cash Flow Per Share	3.42	2.85	1.99	0.88	0.76	0.15	0.25	0.35
Tang Book Value Per Share	6.92	3.77	0.86	N.M.	N.M.	3.04	0.59	1.37
Income Statement								
Total Revenue	622,427	523,196	463,011	450,985	484,846	247,840	185,084	100,797
EBITDA	228,184	154,779	125,864	56,843	15,714	25,092	21,513	18,208
Depn & Amortn	59,450	61,400	76,013	140,300	168,200	90,000	51,400	11,500
Income Before Taxes	174,039	87,716	36,087	(98,662)	(164,151)	(69,493)	(32,873)	7,895
Income Taxes	67,389	23,699	14,619	(3,350)	5,567	(1,660)	2,680	3,873
Net Income	106,650	64,017	21,468	(95,312)	(169,334)	(67,833)	(36,383)	4,022
Average Shares	62,031	57,496	55,455	51,723	49,708	35,049	29,160	38,765
Balance Sheet								
Current Assets	631,862	407,509	212,989	150,641	204,025	209,075	69,209	60,504
Total Assets	1,451,584	1,224,084	1,025,055	993,081	1,100,636	939,569	462,863	171,638
Current Liabilities	113,780	115,083	111,078	137,366	142,662	92,076	46,582	37,442
Long-Term Obligations	265,000	265,011	244,739	256,215	274,427	101,802	72,354	14,657
Total Liabilities	388,472	388,278	357,102	393,581	417,089	193,878	118,936	52,099
Stockholders' Equity	1,063,112	835,806	667,953	599,500	683,547	745,691	343,927	119,539
Shares Outstanding	60,735	57,325	53,887	51,924	50,806	45,266	30,575	38,317
Statistical Record								
Return on Assets %	7.95	5.69	2.13	N.M.	N.M.	N.M.	N.M.	3.01
Return on Equity %	11.20	8.51	3.39	N.M.	N.M.	N.M.	N.M.	4.33
EBITDA Margin %	36.66	29.58	27.18	12.60	3.24	10.12	11.62	18.06
Net Margin %	17.13	12.24	4.64	N.M.	N.M.	N.M.	N.M.	3.99
Asset Turnover	0.46	0.47	0.46	0.43	0.47	0.35	0.58	0.75
Current Ratio	5.55	3.54	1.92	1.10	1.43	2.27	1.49	1.62
Debt to Equity	0.25	0.32	0.37	0.43	0.40	0.14	0.21	0.12
Price Range	69.30-47.50	50.74-25.80	38.11-13.80	37.00-9.29	60.50-23.47	51.88-16.25	27.50-8.88	...
P/E Ratio	40.29-27.62	45.71-23.24	97.72-35.38	...	...	...	...	...

Address: 601 N. 34th Street, Seattle, WA 98103	Web Site: www.gettyimages.com	Auditors: PricewaterhouseCoopers LLP
Telephone: (206) 925-5000	Officers: Mark H. Getty - Chmn. Mark Torrance - Vice-Chmn.	Investor Contact: 206-925-5000
Fax: (206) 925-5001		

GILLETTE CO., (THE)

Exchange	Symbol	Price	52Wk Range	Yield	P/E
NYS	G	$50.48 (3/31/2005)	51.60-37.95	1.29	30.05

*7 Year Price Score 97.82 *NYSE Composite Index=100 ***12 Month Price Score 106.94**

Interim Earnings (Per Share)

Qtr.	Mar	Jun	Sep	Dec
2001	0.17	0.22	0.28	0.19
2002	0.21	0.28	0.33	0.33
2003	0.25	0.33	0.41	0.36
2004	0.37	0.42	0.47	0.42

Interim Dividends (Per Share)

Amt	Decl	Ex	Rec	Pay
0.163Q	6/17/2004	7/29/2004	8/2/2004	9/3/2004
0.163Q	10/21/2004	10/28/2004	11/1/2004	12/3/2004
0.163Q	12/16/2004	1/28/2005	2/1/2005	3/4/2005
0.163Q	3/10/2005	4/28/2005	5/2/2005	6/3/2005
			Indicated Div: $0.65	

Valuation Analysis

Forecast P/E	27.01	No of Institutions	
	(4/7/2005)	721	
Market Cap	$50.0 Billion	Shares	
Book Value	2.8 Billion	724,961,664	
Price/Book	17.62	% Held	
Price/Sales	4.77	73.13	

Business Summary: Metal Products (MIC: 11.4 SIC: 423 NAIC: 32212)

Gillette manufactures and sells a variety of consumer products. Co.'s five primary businesses are: Blades and Razors, which include male shaving systems sold under the Mach3, SensorExcel and TracII brands, and female shaving franchises sold under the Gillette for Women Venus, Sensor Excel for Women, Sensor for Women brands; Duracell, which include the Duracell Ultra and CopperTop alkaline batteries; Oral Care which include toothbrushes sold under the Braun and Oral-B brands; Braun, which includes electric shavers under the Braun brand; Personal Care, which includes shaving preparations and related items sold under the Gillette, Satin Care, Right Guard, Soft & Dri and Dry Idea brands.

Recent Developments:
For the year ended Dec 31 2004, net income increased 22.1% to $1,691,000 thousand from net income of $1,385,000 thousand a year earlier. Revenues were $10,477,000 thousand, up 13.2% from $9,252,000 thousand the year before. Operating income was $2,465,000 thousand versus an income of $2,003,000 thousand in the prior year, an increase of 23.1%. Total direct expense was $4,264,000 thousand versus $3,897,000 thousand in the prior year, an increase of 9.4%. Total indirect expense was $3,748,000 thousand versus $3,352,000 thousand in the prior year, an increase of 11.8%.

Prospects:
On Jan 28 2005, Co. announced that it has signed an agreement to be acquired by The Procter & Gamble Company (P&G) for approximately $57.00 billion of P&G common stock. The transaction, which is subject to certain conditions including shareholder and regulatory approvals, is expected to be completed in fall 2005. Meanwhile, results are being positively affected by strong demand for recently introduced products in Co.'s shaving, oral care and personal care businesses. Results in 2005 are expected to benefit from the launch of several new trade-up products, including two new women's razors, Venus Vibrance and Venus Disposable.

Financial Data

(US$ in Thousands)	12/31/2004	12/31/2003	12/31/2002	12/31/2001	12/31/2000	12/31/1999	12/31/1998	12/31/1997
Earnings Per Share	1.68	1.35	1.15	0.86	0.37	1.14	0.95	1.25
Cash Flow Per Share	2.24	2.59	1.97	1.98	1.52	1.45	1.15	1.14
Tang Value Per Share	1.24	0.70	0.86	0.74	0.33	0.58	1.81	2.07
Dividends Per Share	0.650	0.650	0.650	0.650	0.635	0.570	0.487	0.412
Dividend Payout %	38.69	48.15	56.52	75.58	171.62	50.00	51.32	33.13
Income Statement								
Total Revenue	10,477,000	9,252,000	8,453,000	8,961,000	9,295,000	9,897,000	10,056,000	10,062,000
EBITDA	3,031,000	2,584,000	2,311,000	1,992,000	2,041,000	2,559,000	2,214,000	2,712,000
Depn & Amortn	610,000	578,000	500,000	509,000	535,000	500,000	459,000	422,000
Income Before Taxes	2,384,000	1,964,000	1,752,000	1,342,000	1,288,000	1,930,000	1,669,000	2,221,000
Income Taxes	693,000	589,000	543,000	432,000	467,000	670,000	588,000	794,000
Net Income	1,691,000	1,385,000	1,216,000	910,000	392,000	1,260,000	1,081,000	1,427,000
Average Shares	1,007,000	1,024,000	1,059,000	1,058,000	1,063,000	1,111,000	1,144,000	1,148,000
Balance Sheet								
Current Assets	4,068,000	3,650,000	3,797,000	4,455,000	4,682,000	5,132,000	5,440,000	4,690,000
Total Assets	10,731,000	9,955,000	9,863,000	9,969,000	10,402,000	11,786,000	11,902,000	10,864,000
Current Liabilities	4,203,000	3,658,000	3,488,000	4,838,000	5,471,000	4,180,000	3,478,000	2,641,000
Long-Term Obligations	2,142,000	2,453,000	2,457,000	1,654,000	1,650,000	2,931,000	2,256,000	1,476,000
Total Liabilities	7,895,000	7,731,000	7,603,000	7,832,000	8,478,000	8,726,000	7,359,000	6,023,000
Stockholders' Equity	2,836,000	2,224,000	2,260,000	2,137,000	1,924,000	3,060,000	4,543,000	4,841,000
Shares Outstanding	990,000	1,007,000	1,044,000	1,056,000	1,053,000	1,065,000	1,105,000	1,120,938
Statistical Record								
Return on Assets %	16.30	13.98	12.26	8.93	3.52	10.64	9.50	13.40
Return on Equity %	66.66	61.78	55.31	44.82	15.69	33.14	23.04	30.58
EBITDA Margin %	28.93	27.93	27.34	22.23	21.96	25.86	22.02	26.95
Net Margin %	16.14	14.97	14.39	10.16	4.22	12.73	10.75	14.18
Asset Turnover	1.01	0.93	0.85	0.88	0.84	0.84	0.88	0.94
Current Ratio	0.97	1.00	1.09	0.92	0.86	1.23	1.56	1.78
Debt to Equity	0.76	1.10	1.09	0.77	0.86	0.96	0.50	0.30
Price Range	45.53-35.88	36.73-28.08	37.09-27.77	36.31-25.62	42.50-27.63	64.25-33.44	62.56-36.25	52.25-36.31
P/E Ratio	27.10-21.36	27.21-20.80	32.25-24.15	42.22-29.79	114.86-74.66	56.36-29.33	65.86-38.16	41.80-29.05
Average Yield %	1.60	2.03	2.00	2.12	1.86	1.22	0.95	0.94

Address: Prudential Tower Building, Boston, MA 02199 Telephone: (617) 421-7000 Fax: (617) 421-7123	Web Site: www.gillette.com Officers: James M. Kilts - Chmn., Pres., C.E.O. Edward F. DeGraan - Vice-Chmn.	Auditors: KPMG LLP Investor Contact: (617) 421-7000

GLATFELTER

Exchange	Symbol	Price	52Wk Range	Yield	P/E
NYS	GLT	$14.75 (3/31/2005)	15.47-10.68	2.44	11.61

*7 Year Price Score 84.32 ***NYSE Composite Index=100** ***12 Month Price Score 101.51**

Interim Earnings (Per Share)

Qtr.	Mar	Jun	Sep	Dec
2001	0.36	(0.53)	0.11	0.22
2002	0.26	0.17	0.30	0.13
2003	0.61	0.01	(0.15)	(0.17)
2004	0.83	(0.04)	0.05	0.43

Interim Dividends (Per Share)

Amt	Decl	Ex	Rec	Pay
0.09Q	6/17/2004	7/7/2004	7/9/2004	8/2/2004
0.09Q	9/15/2004	10/6/2004	10/8/2004	11/1/2004
0.09Q	12/15/2004	1/7/2005	1/11/2005	2/1/2005
0.09Q	3/9/2005	4/6/2005	4/8/2005	5/1/2005

Indicated Div: $0.36

Valuation Analysis

Forecast P/E	14.67	No of Institutions
	(4/7/2005)	139
Market Cap	$648.3 Million	Shares
Book Value	420.4 Million	36,674,400
Price/Book	1.54	% Held
Price/Sales	1.17	83.42

Business Summary: Paper Products (MIC: 11.11 SIC: 621 NAIC: 22121)

Glatfelter is a global manufacturer of specialty papers and engineered products. Co. is organized into three business units including Engineered Products, Long-Fiber and Overlay Papers, and Printing and Converting Papers. Also, Co. supplies tobacco papers to fulfill obligations of a supply agreement entered into related to the sale of its Ecusta division. The agreement expires in mid-2004. Co.'s products are marketed in many countries including the U.S., either through wholesale paper merchants, brokers and agents or directly to customers. At Dec 31 2003, Co.'s manufacturing facilities were located in Spring Grove, PA and Neenah, WI as well as Germany, France and the Philippines.

Recent Developments: For the year ended Dec 31 2004, net income increased 343.1% to $56,102 thousand from net income of $12,661 thousand a year earlier. Revenues were $553,477 thousand, up 1.9% from $543,233 thousand the year before. Operating income was $103,394 thousand versus an income of $34,250 thousand in the prior year, an increase of 201.9%. Total direct expense was $461,063 thousand versus $463,687 thousand in the prior year, a decrease of 0.6%. Total indirect expense was $21,805 thousand versus $45,296 thousand in the prior year, a decrease of 51.9%.

Prospects: Sales growth is being driven by increased volume in Co.'s Long Fiber & Overlay Papers business, due primarily to strong demand from the food and beverage market, as well as improved product pricing in Co.'s North American markets. Meanwhile, results in 2005 are expected to be positively affected by strategic cost-control initiatives that Co. began implementing during the second quarter of 2004 in North America. Cost savings generated by this restructuring program, which is expected to be completed by the end of the first quarter of 2005, should offset the raw material price increases Co. is experiencing in the market.

Financial Data

(US$ in Thousands)	12/31/2004	12/31/2003	12/31/2002	12/31/2001	12/31/2000	12/31/1999	12/31/1998	12/31/1997
Earnings Per Share	1.27	0.29	0.86	0.16	1.04	0.98	0.86	1.07
Cash Flow Per Share	0.90	1.07	1.71	1.50	2.44	1.94	2.39	2.02
Tang Book Value Per Share	9.56	8.48	8.57	8.27	8.79	8.48	8.17	8.08
Dividends Per Share	0.360	0.440	0.875	0.700	0.700	0.700	0.700	0.700
Dividend Payout %	28.35	151.72	101.74	437.50	67.31	71.43	81.40	65.42
Income Statement								
Total Revenue	553,477	543,233	553,637	652,539	739,812	695,806	717,705	587,212
EBITDA	153,734	88,894	117,827	56,708	114,709	112,918	106,470	109,373
Depn & Amortn	51,598	56,029	45,190	44,988	46,106	47,766	47,738	35,796
Income Before Taxes	90,763	20,416	59,065	11,720	68,603	65,152	58,732	73,577
Income Taxes	34,661	7,430	21,470	4,762	24,603	23,727	22,599	28,293
Net Income	56,102	12,661	37,595	6,958	44,000	41,425	36,133	45,284
Average Shares	44,023	43,760	43,791	42,846	42,483	42,431	42,202	42,442
Balance Sheet								
Current Assets	198,452	171,702	176,380	240,428	286,624	268,127	241,908	376,479
Total Assets	1,052,270	1,027,019	957,028	960,724	1,013,191	1,003,780	990,738	937,583
Current Liabilities	104,007	112,470	97,948	209,315	119,184	132,631	126,876	288,885
Long-Term Obligations	207,277	248,469	218,709	152,593	300,245	301,380	325,381	150,000
Total Liabilities	631,900	655,588	583,195	607,255	640,488	645,656	646,809	597,167
Stockholders' Equity	420,370	371,431	373,833	353,469	372,703	358,124	343,929	340,416
Shares Outstanding	43,949	43,782	43,644	42,750	42,390	42,246	42,085	42,150
Statistical Record								
Return on Assets %	5.38	1.28	3.92	0.70	4.35	4.15	3.75	5.48
Return on Equity %	14.13	3.40	10.34	1.92	12.01	11.80	10.56	13.49
EBITDA Margin %	27.78	16.36	21.28	8.69	15.51	16.23	14.83	18.63
Net Margin %	10.14	2.33	6.79	1.07	5.95	5.95	5.03	7.71
Asset Turnover	0.53	0.55	0.58	0.58	0.66	0.73	0.70	0.74	0.71
Current Ratio	1.91	1.53	1.80	1.15	2.40	2.02	1.91	1.30
Debt to Equity	0.49	0.67	0.59	0.43	0.81	0.84	0.95	0.44
Price Range	15.47-10.64	15.37-9.75	19.20-10.65	16.37-11.80	14.56-9.88	16.44-9.63	19.06-11.38	22.63-15.50
P/E Ratio	12.18-8.38	53.00-33.62	22.33-12.38	102.31-73.75	14.00-9.50	16.77-9.82	22.17-13.23	21.14-14.49
Average Yield %	2.87	3.53	5.70	4.92	6.17	5.24	4.55	3.82

Address: 96 South George Street, Suite 500, York, PA 17401	**Web Site:** www.glatfelter.com	**Auditors:** Deloitte & Touche LLP
Telephone: (717) 225-4711	**Officers:** George H. Glatfelter II - Chmn., C.E.O.	
Fax: (717) 225-6834	John C. van Roden Jr. - Sr. V.P., C.F.O.	

GLOBAL PAYMENTS, INC.

Exchange	Symbol	Price	52Wk Range	Yield	P/E
NYS	GPN	$64.49 (3/31/2005)	64.49-41.83	0.25	30.28

*7 Year Price Score N/A   *NYSE Composite Index=100   *12 Month Price Score 106.38

Interim Earnings (Per Share)

Qtr.	Aug	Nov	Feb	May
2001-02	0.34	0.31	0.27	(0.29)
2002-03	0.39	0.36	0.32	0.34
2003-04	0.41	0.38	0.42	0.38
2004-05	0.62	0.59	0.54	...

Interim Dividends (Per Share)

Amt	Decl	Ex	Rec	Pay
0.04Q	5/3/2004	5/13/2004	5/17/2004	5/31/2004
0.04Q	8/3/2004	8/13/2004	8/17/2004	8/31/2004
0.04Q	11/2/2004	11/12/2004	11/16/2004	11/30/2004
0.04Q	2/1/2005	2/10/2005	2/14/2005	2/28/2005

Indicated Div: $0.16

Valuation Analysis

Forecast P/E	N/A	No of Institutions
Market Cap	$2.5 Billion	Shares
Book Value	555.4 Million	36,706,396
Price/Book	4.52	% Held
Price/Sales	3.31	94.79

Business Summary: Communications (MIC: 10.1 SIC: 822 NAIC: 34417)

Global Payments Inc. is a payments company. As a high volume payments processor of electronic transactions, Co. enables consumers, corporations, government agencies and other profit and non-profit business enterprises to facilitate payments to purchase goods and services or further other economic goals. Co. markets it products and services throughout the United States, Canada and Europe, and Co. also conducts business in the Latin America through Co.'s money transfer product offering. Co.'s products and services primarily target customers in many vertical industries including government, professional services, restaurants, universities, utilities, gaming, retail and health care.

Recent Developments: For the quarter ended Feb 28 2005, net income increased 31.0% to $21.6 million from $16.5 million in the equivalent 2004 quarter. Revenues were $195.5 million, up 20.3% from $162.6 million in the year earlier quarter. The improvement in results was primarily driven by higher-than-anticipated growth from Co.'s Central and Eastern European operations and from its consumer money transfer channel. In addition, Co.'s core domestic direct channel outpaced its expectations, largely due to strong growth from its independent sales organizations. Operating income climbed 25.6% to $38.2 million from $30.4 million a year earlier.

Prospects: Co.'s prospects appear favorable, due in part to solid growth from its Central and Eastern European operations as well as from its consumer money transfer channel. In addition, Co. noted that its core domestic direct channel is benefiting from strong growth from its independent sales organizations, while its Canadian direct channel has been aided by a higher-than-anticipated effect of re-pricing initiatives and the Canadian currency exchange rate. Accordingly, on Mar 21 2005 Co. increased its fiscal 2005 annual revenue guidance to a range of $774.0 million to $781.0 million, and its fiscal 2005 annual diluted earnings per share guidance to a range of $2.31 to $2.35.

Financial Data

(US$ in Thousands)	9 Mos	6 Mos	3 Mos	05/31/2004	05/31/2003	05/31/2002	05/31/2001	05/31/2000
Earnings Per Share	2.13	2.01	1.80	1.60	1.41	0.63	0.82	1.24
Cash Flow Per Share	5.46	2.65	2.14	2.45	0.96	4.39	2.75	1.55
Tang Book Value Per Share	0.09	N.M.	N.M.	N.M.	1.81	0.09	N.M.	N.M.
Dividends Per Share	0.160	0.160	0.160	0.160	0.160	0.160	0.040	...
Dividend Payout %	7.51	7.98	8.91	10.00	11.35	25.40	4.88	...
Income Statement								
Total Revenue	576,666	381,140	192,591	629,320	516,084	462,826	353,195	340,033
EBITDA	143,552	97,879	49,078	135,249	117,205	94,034	60,240	73,800
Depn & Amortn	33,394	22,044	10,668	35,500	32,061	29,571	21,756	20,028
Income Before Taxes	110,158	75,835	38,410	99,749	85,144	64,463	38,484	53,772
Income Taxes	40,759	28,059	14,212	37,306	31,844	24,624	14,816	20,725
Net Income	69,399	47,776	24,198	62,443	53,300	23,840	23,668	33,047
Average Shares	40,103	39,801	39,220	38,955	37,824	38,009	28,916	...
Balance Sheet								
Current Assets	165,631	216,908	209,193	203,204	128,203	79,457	136,498	80,225
Total Assets	831,153	865,951	843,521	832,895	484,234	431,418	458,604	287,946
Current Liabilities	179,237	249,443	275,361	286,072	62,861	97,005	132,484	137,653
Long-Term Obligations	1,087	1,420	3,500	12,947	3,251	4,711	1,974	4,332
Total Liabilities	259,390	322,746	341,533	360,343	94,567	109,889	148,730	149,679
Stockholders' Equity	555,368	526,066	484,506	449,422	366,426	296,288	271,022	119,795
Shares Outstanding	38,945	38,722	38,454	38,068	37,132	36,787	36,477	35,634
Statistical Record								
Return on Assets %	10.06	10.06	10.49	9.46	11.64	5.36	6.34	11.41
Return on Equity %	17.21	16.95	16.32	15.27	16.09	8.40	12.11	29.07
EBITDA Margin %	24.89	25.68	25.48	21.49	22.71	20.32	17.06	21.70
Net Margin %	12.03	12.54	12.56	9.92	10.33	5.15	6.70	9.72
Asset Turnover	0.90	0.92	1.01	0.95	1.13	1.04	0.95	1.17
Current Ratio	0.92	0.87	0.76	0.71	2.04	0.82	1.03	0.58
Debt to Equity	N.M.	N.M.	0.01	0.03	0.01	0.02	0.01	0.04
Price Range	59.95-41.83	57.38-41.83	51.13-36.00	51.13-31.95	36.47-22.47	38.42-23.05	26.50-15.00	...
P/E Ratio	28.15-19.64	28.55-20.81	28.41-20.00	31.96-19.97	25.87-15.94	60.98-36.59	32.32-18.29	...
Average Yield %	0.32	0.34	0.36	0.38	0.55	0.34	...	...

Address: 10 Glenlake Parkway, North Tower, Atlanta, GA 30328-3495 Telephone: (770) 829-8234	Web Site: www.globalpaymentsinc.com Officers: Paul R. Garcia - Chmn., Pres., C.E.O. James G. Kelly - Sr. Exec. V.P., C.F.O.	Auditors: DELOITTE & TOUCHE LLP Transfer Agents: SunTrust Bank

GOLDEN WEST FINANCIAL CORP.

Exchange	Symbol	Price	52Wk Range	Yield	P/E	Div Acheiver
NYS	GDW	$60.50 (3/31/2005)	66.94-49.88	0.40	14.65	21 Years

*7 Year Price Score 152.33 *NYSE Composite Index=100 ***12 Month Price Score 101.26**

Interim Earnings (Per Share)

Qtr.	Mar	Jun	Sep	Dec
2001	0.53	0.65	0.64	0.71
2002	0.76	0.72	0.78	0.80
2003	0.83	0.88	0.92	0.94
2004	0.96	1.02	1.04	1.10

Interim Dividends (Per Share)

Amt	Decl	Ex	Rec	Pay
0.05Q	4/27/2004	5/12/2004	5/15/2004	6/10/2004
0.05Q	7/26/2004	8/11/2004	8/15/2004	9/10/2004
0.06Q	10/21/2004	11/10/2004	11/15/2004	12/10/2004
0.06Q	1/27/2005	2/11/2005	2/15/2005	3/10/2005
		Indicated Div: $0.24		

Valuation Analysis

Forecast P/E	12.99	No of Institutions	
	(4/7/2005)	349	
Market Cap	$18.5 Billion	Shares	
Book Value	7.3 Billion	215,213,136	
Price/Book	2.55	% Held	
Price/Sales	4.15	70.12	

Business Summary: Other Depository Banking (MIC: 8.5 SIC: 035 NAIC: 22120)

Golden West Financial, with assets of $82.55 billion as of Dec 31 2003, is the holding company of World Savings Bank, FSB, a federally chartered savings and lending institution. As of Dec 31 2003, Co. operated 479 savings and lending offices in 38 states under the World name. Also, Co. has two other subsidiaries, Atlas Advisers and Atlas Securities, which provide services to Atlas Assets, a registered open-end management investment company sponsored by Co. Atlas Advisers is a registered investment adviser and the investment manager of Atlas Assets' portfolios. Atlas Securities is a registered broker-dealer and the sole distributor of Atlas Fund shares.

Recent Developments: For the year ended Dec 31 2004, net income increased 15.7% to $1,279,721 thousand from net income of $1,106,099 thousand a year earlier. Net interest income was $2,618,605 thousand, up 18.6% from $2,208,384 thousand the year before. Provision for loan losses was $3,401 thousand versus $11,864 thousand in the prior year, a decrease of 71.3%. Non-interest income fell 6.2% to $293,923 thousand, while non-interest expense advanced 16.7% to $833,058 thousand.

Prospects: Earnings growth is being driven by rapid loan growth, as Co.'s loan originations rose to an all-time high of $49.00 billion in 2004. Interest rates on Co.'s primary loan product, the adjustable-rate mortgage (ARM) remained low and stable in 2004, while the cost of a borrower's other alternative, a fixed-rate mortgage, has been more volatile. Furthermore, some of the benefits from the increased size of the loan portfolio are being offset by a decline in Co.'s primary spread, which is the difference in what Co. earns on its loans and investments and what Co. pays for savings and borrowings.

Financial Data
(US$ in Thousands)

	12/31/2004	12/31/2003	12/31/2002	12/31/2001	12/31/2000	12/31/1999	12/31/1998	12/31/1997
Earnings Per Share	4.13	3.57	3.06	2.54	1.71	1.44	1.25	1.02
Cash Flow Per Share	5.48	8.71	4.41	4.00	2.04	1.54	1.89	1.08
Tang Book Value Per Share	23.73	19.55	16.37	13.77	11.64	9.90	9.16	7.88
Dividends Per Share	0.210	0.177	0.151	0.130	0.110	0.096	0.086	0.076
Dividend Payout %	5.08	4.97	4.94	5.13	6.45	6.71	6.85	7.42
Income Statement								
Interest Income	4,178,856	3,528,344	3,497,034	4,209,612	3,796,540	2,825,845	2,962,553	2,832,497
Interest Expense	1,560,251	1,319,960	1,566,740	2,578,280	2,645,372	1,822,360	1,995,231	1,942,002
Net Interest Income	2,618,605	2,208,384	1,930,294	1,631,332	1,151,168	1,003,485	967,322	890,495
Provision for Losses	3,401	11,864	21,170	22,265	9,195	(2,089)	11,260	57,609
Non-Interest Income	293,923	313,330	247,000	236,739	160,820	143,302	137,613	81,268
Non-Interest Expense	840,126	720,515	601,494	513,802	424,847	386,147	354,507	326,959
Income Before Taxes	2,069,001	1,789,335	1,554,630	1,332,004	877,946	762,729	739,168	587,195
Income Taxes	789,280	683,236	596,351	513,181	332,155	282,750	292,077	233,057
Net Income	1,279,721	1,106,099	958,279	812,805	545,791	479,979	434,580	354,138
Average Shares	310,119	309,974	313,364	320,716	320,555	333,902	346,923	346,638
Balance Sheet								
Net Loans & Leases	100,559,179	74,205,578	58,268,899	41,065,375	33,762,643	27,919,817	25,721,288	33,260,709
Total Assets	106,888,541	82,549,890	68,405,828	58,586,271	55,703,969	42,142,205	38,468,729	39,590,271
Total Deposits	52,965,311	46,726,965	41,038,797	34,472,585	30,047,919	27,714,910	26,219,095	24,109,717
Total Liabilities	99,613,665	76,602,622	63,380,578	54,302,081	52,016,682	38,947,351	35,344,411	36,892,240
Stockholders' Equity	7,274,876	5,947,268	5,025,250	4,284,190	3,687,287	3,194,854	3,124,318	2,698,031
Shares Outstanding	306,524	304,238	307,042	311,063	316,820	322,715	341,166	342,414
Statistical Record								
Return on Assets %	1.35	1.47	1.51	1.42	1.11	1.19	1.11	0.92
Return on Equity %	19.30	20.16	20.59	20.39	15.82	15.19	14.93	14.03
Net Interest Margin %	62.66	62.59	55.20	38.75	30.32	35.51	32.65	31.44
Efficiency Ratio %	18.78	18.76	16.07	11.56	10.74	13.01	11.44	11.22
Loans to Deposits	1.90	1.59	1.42	1.19	1.12	1.01	0.98	1.38
Price Range	61.90-49.33	51.73-34.84	36.49-28.95	35.00-23.57	34.72-13.59	19.01-14.64	19.04-12.06	16.30-9.98
P/E Ratio	14.99-11.94	14.49-9.76	11.92-9.46	13.78-9.28	20.30-7.95	13.20-10.16	15.23-9.65	15.98-9.78
Average Yield %	0.38	0.41	0.42	0.46	0.45	0.52	0.59	0.59

Address: 1901 Harrison Street, Oakland, CA 94612	Web Site: www.gdw.com	Auditors: Deloitte & Touche LLP
Telephone: (510) 446-3420	Officers: Herbert M. Sandler - Co-Chmn., Co-C.E.O.	Investor Contact: 510-446-3614
Fax: (510) 446-3072	Marion O. Sandler - Co-Chmn., Co-C.E.O.	Transfer Agents: Mellon Investor Services, LLC, San Francisco, CA

GOLDMAN SACHS GROUP, INC.

Exchange	Symbol	Price	52Wk Range	Yield	P/E
NYS	GS	$109.99 (3/31/2005)	112.80-83.86	0.91	12.33

*7 Year Price Score N/A   *NYSE Composite Index=100   *12 Month Price Score 103.77

Interim Earnings (Per Share)

Qtr.	Feb	May	Aug	Nov
2002	0.98	1.06	1.00	0.99
2003	1.29	1.36	1.32	1.89
2004	2.50	2.31	1.74	2.36

Interim Dividends (Per Share)

Amt	Decl	Ex	Rec	Pay
0.12Q	9/24/2002	10/24/2002	10/28/2002	11/25/2002
0.12Q	12/19/2002	1/24/2003	1/28/2003	2/27/2003
0.12Q	3/20/2003	4/25/2003	4/29/2003	5/29/2003
0.25Q	6/20/2003	7/25/2003	7/29/2003	8/28/2003

Indicated Div: $1.00

Valuation Analysis

Forecast P/E	11.25	No of Institutions	
	(4/7/2005)	679	
Market Cap	$52.9 Billion	Shares	
Book Value	25.1 Billion	314,541,152	
Price/Book	2.11	% Held	
Price/Sales	1.77	65.22	

Business Summary: Finance Intermediaries & Services (MIC: 8.7 SIC: 211 NAIC: 23110)

Goldman Sachs Group is a global investment banking, securities and investment management firm.Co.'s activities are divided into three segments: Investment Banking provides a range of investment banking services to corporations, financial institutions, governments and individuals; Trading and Principal Investments facilitates customer transactions with corporations, financial institutions, governments and individuals; Asset Management and Securities Services offers an array of investment strategies, advice and planning across all major asset classes and provides prime brokerage, financing services and securities lending services.

Recent Developments: For the year ended Nov 30 2004, net income increased 51.5% to $4,553 million from net income of $3,005 million a year earlier. Revenues were $29,839 million, up 26.3% from $23,623 million the year before. Net investment income rose 40.1% to $11,984 million from $8,555 million a year ago.

Prospects: Co.'s outlook appears favorable, reflecting in part recent broad-based top line gains. For instance, for the three months ended Feb 25 2005, net revenues in Investment Banking advanced 17.0% to $893.0 million, led by higher Financial Advisory and Underwriting revenues, the latter due to higher net revenues in debt underwriting. Net revenues in Trading and Principal Investment rose 6.3% to $4.38 billion, driven by gains in Fixed Income, Currency and Commodities. Lastly, net revenues in Asset Management and Securities Services grew 8.2% to $1.13 billion, reflecting higher Securities Services net revenues mainly due to sharply higher customer balances in securities lending and margin lending.

Financial Data

(US$ in Thousands)	11/26/2004	11/28/2003	11/29/2002	11/30/2001	11/24/2000	11/26/1999	11/27/1998	11/28/1997
Earnings Per Share	8.92	5.87	4.03	4.26	6.00	5.57	...	...
Cash Flow Per Share	(68.85)	(32.14)	(20.39)	(29.29)	23.04	(26.53)	...	...
Tang Book Value Per Share	42.02	35.20	40.18	38.28	34.19	22.98	...	...
Dividends Per Share	1.000	0.740	0.480	0.480	0.480	0.240	...	...
Dividend Payout %	11.21	12.61	11.91	11.27	8.00	4.31	...	...
Income Statement								
Interest Income	11,914,000	10,751,000	11,269,000	16,620,000	17,396,000	12,722,000	15,010,000	14,087,000
Interest Expense	8,888,000	7,600,000	8,868,000	15,327,000	16,410,000	12,018,000	13,958,000	12,986,000
Net Interest Income	3,026,000	3,151,000	2,401,000	1,293,000	986,000	704,000	1,052,000	1,101,000
Non-Interest Income	17,925,000	12,872,000	11,585,000	14,518,000	15,604,000	12,641,000	7,468,000	6,346,000
Non-Interest Expense	14,275,000	11,578,000	10,733,000	12,115,000	11,570,000	11,353,000	5,599,000	4,433,000
Income Before Taxes	6,676,000	4,445,000	3,253,000	3,696,000	5,020,000	1,992,000	2,921,000	3,014,000
Income Taxes	2,123,000	1,440,000	1,139,000	1,386,000	1,953,000	(716,000)	493,000	268,000
Net Income	4,553,000	3,005,000	2,114,000	2,310,000	3,067,000	2,708,000	2,428,000	2,746,000
Average Shares	510,500	511,900	525,100	541,800	511,500	485,804	...	...
Balance Sheet								
Total Assets	531,379,000	403,799,000	355,574,000	312,218,000	289,760,000	250,491,000	217,380,000	178,401,000
Total Liabilities	506,300,000	382,167,000	336,571,000	293,987,000	273,230,000	240,346,000	210,996,000	171,864,000
Stockholders' Equity	25,079,000	21,632,000	19,003,000	18,231,000	16,530,000	10,145,000	...	...
Shares Outstanding	480,959	473,014	472,941	476,229	483,474	441,421	508,000	...
Statistical Record								
Return on Assets %	0.98	0.79	0.63	0.76	1.14	1.16	1.23	...
Return on Equity %	19.55	14.83	11.39	13.08	23.06	...	...	...
Net Interest Margin %	25.40	29.31	21.31	7.78	5.67	5.53	7.01	7.82
Efficiency Ratio %	47.84	49.01	46.96	38.91	35.06	44.76	24.91	21.70
Price Range	109.05-83.86	96.98-62.85	96.75-59.28	118.62-65.75	132.00-69.81	82.81-55.81	...	...
P/E Ratio	12.23-9.40	16.52-10.71	24.01-14.71	27.85-15.43	22.00-11.64	14.87-10.02	...	...
Average Yield %	1.04	0.92	0.61	0.53	0.50	0.36	...	...

Address: 85 Broad Street, New York, NY 10004	**Web Site:** www.gs.com	**Auditors:** PricewaterhouseCoopers LLP
Telephone: (212) 902-1000	**Officers:** Henry M. Paulson Jr. - Chmn., C.E.O.	**Investor Contact:** 212-357-2674
Fax: (212) 902-3000	Robert S. Kaplan - Vice-Chmn.	

GOODRICH CORP.

Exchange	Symbol	Price	52Wk Range	Yield	P/E
NYS	GR	$38.29 (3/31/2005)	38.98-27.03	2.09	26.78

*7 Year Price Score 90.57 *NYSE Composite Index=100 *12 Month Price Score 107.58

Interim Earnings (Per Share)

Qtr.	Mar	Jun	Sep	Dec
2001	1.62	0.78	0.83	(0.48)
2002	0.49	0.45	0.45	0.10
2003	0.25	0.12	0.29	0.19
2004	0.38	0.32	0.41	0.30

Interim Dividends (Per Share)

Amt	Decl	Ex	Rec	Pay
0.20Q	4/27/2004	6/3/2004	6/7/2004	7/1/2004
0.20Q	7/28/2004	9/2/2004	9/7/2004	10/1/2004
0.20Q	10/19/2004	12/2/2004	12/6/2004	1/3/2005
0.20Q	2/22/2005	3/3/2005	3/7/2005	4/1/2005

Indicated Div: $0.80

Valuation Analysis

Forecast P/E	22.21	No of Institutions
	(4/7/2005)	252
Market Cap	$4.6 Billion	Shares
Book Value	1.3 Billion	98,041,504
Price/Book	3.40	% Held
Price/Sales	0.97	82.00

Business Summary: Aviation (MIC: 1.1 SIC: 728 NAIC: 36413)

Goodrich is a global supplier of components, systems and services. Co. is organized into three business units: airframe systems, engine systems and electronic systems. Airframe systems provides systems and components related to aircraft taxi, take-off, landing and stopping. Engine Systems includes the aerostructures business unit, a supplier of nacelles, pylons, thrust reversers and related aircraft engine housing components. Engine Systems also produces engine and fuel controls, pumps, fuel delivery systems, and structural and rotating components. Electronic Systems produces a range of products that provide flight performance measurements, flight management, and control and safety data.

Recent Developments: For the year ended Dec 31 2004, income from continuing operations increased 305.2% to $156,000 thousand from income of $38,500 thousand a year earlier. Net income increased 71.5% to $172,200 thousand from net income of $100,400 thousand a year earlier. Revenues were $4,724,500 thousand, up 7.8% from $4,382,900 thousand the year before. Operating income was $399,800 thousand versus an income of $245,000 thousand in the prior year, an increase of 63.2%. Total direct expense was $3,507,100 thousand versus $3,365,900 thousand in the prior year, an increase of 4.2%. Total indirect expense was $817,600 thousand versus $772,000 thousand in the prior year, an increase of 5.9%.

Prospects: Looking ahead, Co. anticipates full-year 2005 sales in the range of $5.00 billion to $5.10 billion, representing year-over-year growth of between 6.0% and 8.0%. Meanwhile, Co. is projecting diluted earnings per share for full-year 2005 to be between $1.60 and $1.80, along with capital expenditures in the range of $190.0 million to $210.0 million. Separately, on Feb 11 2005, Co. announced that it has been awarded a contract by Airbus to build engine housings and thrust reversers for its planned A350 aircraft that is expected to enter into service in 2010. The contract is expected to generate approximately $6.00 billion in original equipment and aftermarket sales for Co. over 20 years.

Financial Data

(US$ in Thousands)	12/31/2004	12/31/2003	12/31/2002	12/31/2001	12/31/2000	12/31/1999	12/31/1998	12/31/1997
Earnings Per Share	1.43	0.85	1.14	2.76	3.04	1.53	3.02	2.41
Cash Flow Per Share	3.49	4.71	5.20	3.71	2.19	3.39	4.88	2.95
Tang Book Value Per Share	N.M.	N.M.	N.M.	4.67	3.48	1.41	9.63	11.35
Dividends Per Share	0.800	0.800	0.875	1.100	1.100	1.100	1.100	1.100
Dividend Payout %	55.94	94.12	76.75	39.86	36.18	71.90	36.42	45.64
Income Statement								
Total Revenue	4,724,500	4,382,900	3,910,200	4,184,500	4,363,800	5,537,500	3,950,800	3,373,000
EBITDA	562,000	437,800	526,700	539,200	759,400	698,600	624,100	417,600
Depn & Amortn	222,900	219,100	183,500	173,800	192,500	230,600	165,400	138,800
Income Before Taxes	199,300	69,200	269,600	281,700	461,400	334,500	384,900	217,800
Income Taxes	43,400	22,800	93,200	94,300	156,700	146,500	146,300	94,100
Net Income	172,200	100,400	117,900	289,200	325,900	169,600	226,500	178,200
Average Shares	120,300	118,200	105,500	106,900	109,100	110,700	75,000	74,600
Balance Sheet								
Current Assets	2,356,800	2,087,100	2,008,100	1,921,300	3,080,300	2,100,500	1,614,500	1,401,300
Total Assets	6,217,500	5,889,900	5,989,600	4,638,100	5,717,500	5,455,600	4,192,600	3,493,900
Current Liabilities	1,564,500	1,400,900	1,554,200	1,158,600	2,147,300	1,510,900	990,800	934,900
Long-Term Obligations	1,899,400	2,136,600	2,129,000	1,307,200	1,316,200	1,516,900	995,200	564,300
Total Liabilities	4,874,600	4,696,400	4,931,300	3,151,700	4,217,100	3,891,100	2,469,400	1,948,200
Stockholders' Equity	1,342,900	1,193,500	932,900	1,361,400	1,226,600	1,293,200	1,599,600	1,422,600
Shares Outstanding	119,143	117,725	117,061	101,697	102,330	110,232	74,400	72,700
Statistical Record								
Return on Assets %	2.84	1.69	2.22	5.59	5.82	3.52	5.89	5.79
Return on Equity %	13.54	9.44	10.28	22.35	25.80	11.73	14.99	14.41
EBITDA Margin %	11.90	9.99	13.47	12.89	17.40	12.62	15.80	12.38
Net Margin %	3.64	2.29	3.02	6.91	7.47	3.06	5.73	5.28
Asset Turnover	0.78	0.74	0.74	0.81	0.78	1.15	1.03	1.10
Current Ratio	1.51	1.49	1.29	1.66	1.43	1.39	1.63	1.50
Debt to Equity	1.41	1.79	2.28	0.96	1.07	1.17	0.62	0.40
Price Range	33.55-26.75	30.09-13.51	32.85-14.38	42.62-16.47	41.24-21.19	43.34-20.23	52.79-26.07	46.35-34.07
P/E Ratio	23.46-18.71	35.40-15.89	28.82-12.61	15.44-5.97	13.56-6.97	28.33-13.22	17.48-8.63	19.23-14.14
Average Yield %	2.63	3.77	3.62	3.43	3.41	3.32	2.70	2.69

Address: Four Coliseum Centre, 2730 West Tyvola Road, Charlotte, NC 28217-4578
Telephone: (704) 423-7000
Fax: (704) 423-7075

Web Site: www.goodrich.com
Officers: Marshall O. Larsen - Chmn., Pres., C.E.O. Ulrich Schmidt - Exec. V.P., C.F.O.

Auditors: Ernst & Young LLP
Investor Contact: 704-423-5517

GOODYEAR TIRE & RUBBER CO.

Exchange	Symbol	Price	52Wk Range	Yield	P/E
NYS	GT	$13.35 (3/31/2005)	16.00-7.85	N/A	21.19

*7 Year Price Score 38.42   *NYSE Composite Index=100   *12 Month Price Score 116.03

Interim Earnings (Per Share)

Qtr.	Mar	Jun	Sep	Dec
2001	(0.30)	0.05	0.06	(1.08)
2002	(0.39)	0.18	0.20	(6.62)
2003	(0.93)	(0.42)	(0.60)	(2.68)
2004	(0.44)	0.14	0.21	0.70

Interim Dividends (Per Share)

Dividend Payment Suspended

Valuation Analysis

Forecast P/E	17.92	No of Institutions	
	(4/7/2005)	243	
Market Cap	$2.3 Billion	Shares	
Book Value	72.8 Million	132,413,240	
Price/Book	32.20	% Held	
Price/Sales	0.13	75.33	

Business Summary: Rubber Products (MIC: 11.6 SIC: 011 NAIC: 26211)

Goodyear Tire & Rubber is a global manufacturer of tires and rubber products, engaging in operations in most regions of the world. Co.'s principal business is the development, manufacture, distribution and sale of tires for most applications. Co. also manufactures and markets several lines of rubber and other products for the transportation industry and various other industrial and consumer markets; and synthetic rubber and rubber-related chemicals for various applications. In addition, Co. provides automotive repair and other services at retail and commercial outlets and sells various other products.

Recent Developments: For the year ended Dec 31 2004, net income was $114,800 thousand versus net loss of $807,400 thousand a year earlier. Revenues were $18,370,400 thousand, up 21.5% from $15,122,100 thousand the year before. Total direct expense was $14,709,200 thousand versus $12,499,000 thousand in the prior year, an increase of 17.7%. Total indirect expense was $2,888,700 thousand versus $2,665,700 thousand in the prior year, an increase of 8.4%.

Prospects: On Feb 28 2005, Co. announced that it had reached agreement with Titan Tire Corporation, a subsidiary of Titan International, Inc., to sell its North American farm tire assets, including its manufacturing plant, property and equipment in Freeport, IL, and inventories, pending approvals. The sale, which also would include a licensing agreement with Titan to manufacture and sell Co. branded farm tires in North America, is valued at approximately $100.0 million. Co. believes this agreement is important in that it allows Co. to sell a non-core asset, but allows continued access to the same Co. branded tires from a company that considers the farm business as core.

Financial Data

(US$ in Thousands)	12/31/2004	12/31/2003	12/31/2002	12/31/2001	12/31/2000	12/31/1999	12/31/1998	12/31/1997
Earnings Per Share	0.63	(4.58)	(6.62)	(1.27)	0.25	1.52	4.31	3.53
Cash Flow Per Share	4.09	(1.75)	4.05	7.92	3.24	4.06	2.80	6.80
Tang Book Value Per Share	N.M.	...	N.M.	14.06	18.49	19.83	24.02	21.63
Dividends Per Share	...	0.480	0.480	1.020	1.200	1.200	1.200	1.140
Dividend Payout %	...	...	...	...	480.00	78.95	27.84	32.29
Income Statement								
Total Revenue	18,370,400	15,119,000	13,850,000	14,147,200	14,417,100	12,880,600	12,626,300	13,155,100
EBITDA	1,371,900	273,800	807,400	642,600	957,800	1,041,500	1,625,500	1,365,800
Depn & Amortn	714,800	693,300	602,800	636,700	630,300	581,700	487,800	469,300
Income Before Taxes	322,700	(689,900)	(17,900)	(273,000)	58,800	296,700	1,002,700	800,000
Income Taxes	207,900	112,200	1,087,900	(69,400)	18,500	55,600	285,700	241,300
Net Income	114,800	(802,100)	(1,105,800)	(203,600)	40,300	241,100	682,300	558,700
Average Shares	192,258	175,314	167,020	159,955	158,764	158,939	158,307	158,000
Balance Sheet								
Current Assets	8,631,700	6,988,100	5,226,700	5,255,000	5,467,200	5,261,200	4,529,100	4,163,900
Total Assets	16,533,300	15,005,500	13,146,600	13,512,900	13,568,000	13,102,600	10,589,300	9,917,400
Current Liabilities	5,113,100	3,685,500	4,071,400	3,326,500	4,225,900	3,959,900	3,276,500	3,251,000
Long-Term Obligations	4,449,100	4,826,200	2,989,000	3,203,600	2,349,600	2,347,900	1,186,500	844,500
Total Liabilities	16,460,500	15,018,600	12,496,000	10,648,900	10,065,000	9,485,500	6,843,500	6,521,900
Stockholders' Equity	72,800	(13,100)	650,600	2,864,000	3,503,000	3,617,100	3,745,800	3,395,500
Shares Outstanding	175,619	175,326	175,307	163,165	157,603	156,335	155,943	157,000
Statistical Record								
Return on Assets %	0.73	N.M.	N.M.	N.M.	0.30	2.04	6.65	5.70
Return on Equity %	383.54	N.M.	N.M.	N.M.	1.13	6.55	19.11	16.74
EBITDA Margin %	7.47	1.81	5.83	4.54	6.64	8.09	12.87	10.38
Net Margin %	0.62	N.M.	N.M.	N.M.	0.28	1.87	5.40	4.25
Asset Turnover	1.16	1.07	1.04	1.04	1.08	1.09	1.23	1.34
Current Ratio	1.69	1.90	1.28	1.58	1.29	1.33	1.38	1.28
Debt to Equity	61.11	...	4.59	1.12	0.67	0.65	0.32	0.25
Price Range	15.01-7.09	8.10-3.57	28.31-6.60	31.64-17.72	29.88-15.60	66.75-25.50	75.75-46.31	70.50-50.13
P/E Ratio	23.83-11.25	...	...	...	119.50-62.40	43.91-16.78	17.58-10.75	19.97-14.20
Average Yield %	...	7.84	2.81	4.15	5.31	2.40	1.96	1.91

Address: 1144 East Market Street, Akron, OH 44316-0001
Telephone: (330) 796-2121
Fax: (330) 796-4099

Web Site: www.goodyear.com
Officers: Robert J. Keegan - Chmn., Pres., C.E.O.
Richard J. Kramer - Exec. V.P., C.F.O.

Auditors: PricewaterhouseCoopers LLP
Investor Contact: 216-796-8576
Transfer Agents: EquiServe Trust Company, N.A., Providence, RI

GRACO INC.

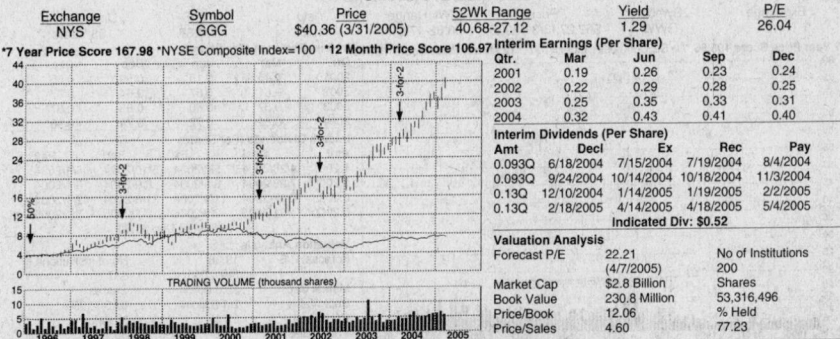

Exchange	Symbol	Price	52Wk Range	Yield	P/E
NYS	GGG	$40.36 (3/31/2005)	40.68-27.12	1.29	26.04

*7 Year Price Score 167.98 *NYSE Composite Index=100 *12 Month Price Score 106.97

Interim Earnings (Per Share)

Qtr.	Mar	Jun	Sep	Dec
2001	0.19	0.26	0.23	0.24
2002	0.22	0.29	0.28	0.25
2003	0.25	0.35	0.33	0.31
2004	0.32	0.43	0.41	0.40

Interim Dividends (Per Share)

Amt	Decl	Ex	Rec	Pay
0.093Q	6/18/2004	7/15/2004	7/19/2004	8/4/2004
0.093Q	9/24/2004	10/14/2004	10/18/2004	11/3/2004
0.13Q	12/10/2004	1/14/2005	1/19/2005	2/2/2005
0.13Q	2/18/2005	4/14/2005	4/18/2005	5/4/2005
		Indicated Div: $0.52		

Valuation Analysis

Forecast P/E	22.21	No of Institutions	
	(4/7/2005)	200	
Market Cap	$2.8 Billion	Shares	
Book Value	230.8 Million	53,316,496	
Price/Book	12.06	% Held	
Price/Sales	4.60	77.23	

Business Summary: Industrial Machinery and Equipment (MIC: 11.5 SIC: 561 NAIC: 33911)

Graco supplies equipment for the management of fluids in vehicle lubrication, industrial and commercial applications. Co. serves customers in the global manufacturing, process, construction and maintenance industries. Co. designs, manufactures and markets systems and equipment to move, measure, proportion, control, dispense and spray a variety of fluids and viscous materials. The industrial/automotive unit provides equipment for sealants and adhesives, process, finishing, protective coatings and automotive refinishing. The contractor equipment unit designs and markets sprayers for paint and coatings. Lubrication equipment provides products for the lubrication and maintenance of vehicles.

Recent Developments: For the year ended Dec 31 2004, net income increased 25.3% to $108,681 thousand from net income of $86,713 thousand a year earlier. Revenues were $605,032 thousand, up 13.1% from $535,098 thousand the year before. Operating income was $161,531 thousand versus an income of $128,833 thousand in the prior year, an increase of 25.4%. Total direct expense was $276,622 thousand versus $252,296 thousand in the prior year, an increase of 9.6%. Total indirect expense was $166,879 thousand versus $153,969 thousand in the prior year, an increase of 8.4%.

Prospects: On Feb 4 2005 Co. announced that it had purchased, from affiliates of PMC Global, Inc. of Sun Valley California, the stock of Gusmer Corporation, based in Lakewood, NJ, for $45.0 million cash. In a related transaction, Co. also acquired the stock of Gusmer Europe S.L., based in Vilanova, Spain, for $20.0 million cash. Gusmer Corporation and Gusmer Europe S.L. (Gusmer) had combined sales of approx. $43.0 million in 2004. Gusmer is a designer and manufacturer of specialized two-component dispense equipment systems, as well as replacement parts used in the operation of its equipment.

Financial Data

(US$ in Thousands)	12/31/2004	12/26/2003	12/27/2002	12/28/2001	12/29/2000	12/31/1999	12/25/1998	12/26/1997
Earnings Per Share	1.55	1.23	1.05	0.92	1.01	0.84	0.60	0.51
Cash Flow Per Share	1.75	1.59	1.35	1.29	1.17	1.09	1.00	0.42
Tang Book Value Per Share	3.08	2.17	3.28	2.28	2.43	0.91	0.14	1.83
Dividends Per Share	1.873	0.220	0.196	0.178	0.166	0.130	0.130	0.111
Dividend Payout %	120.85	17.84	18.68	19.32	16.45	15.49	21.89	21.83
Income Statement								
Total Revenue	605,032	535,098	487,048	472,819	494,373	442,474	432,185	413,897
EBITDA	178,879	147,143	130,419	117,207	125,487	110,558	90,418	77,876
Depn & Amortn	17,600	18,747	18,080	18,494	15,452	14,701	13,736	13,494
Income Before Taxes	160,781	127,913	111,725	97,466	105,908	88,841	71,363	63,516
Income Taxes	52,100	41,200	36,100	32,200	35,800	29,500	24,100	18,800
Net Income	108,681	86,713	75,625	65,266	70,108	59,341	47,263	44,716
Average Shares	70,251	70,416	72,307	70,832	69,536	70,422	79,471	88,310
Balance Sheet								
Current Assets	227,226	256,106	240,524	155,497	143,742	137,989	131,320	156,292
Total Assets	371,714	397,390	355,850	276,113	237,976	236,033	233,702	264,532
Current Liabilities	96,773	187,947	80,214	73,253	81,841	78,263	82,966	68,980
Long-Term Obligations	...	...	...	...	18,050	65,695	112,582	6,163
Total Liabilities	140,877	227,580	110,444	102,373	127,121	173,093	224,389	107,023
Stockholders' Equity	230,837	169,810	245,406	173,740	110,855	62,940	9,313	157,509
Shares Outstanding	68,979	69,060	71,299	70,004	45,615	68,903	67,826	86,241
Statistical Record								
Return on Assets %	27.80	23.09	24.00	25.46	29.66	24.86	19.02	17.50
Return on Equity %	53.38	41.88	36.18	45.99	80.90	161.60	56.82	31.63
EBITDA Margin %	29.57	27.50	26.78	24.79	25.38	24.99	20.92	18.82
Net Margin %	17.96	16.21	15.53	13.80	14.18	13.41	10.94	10.80
Asset Turnover	1.55	1.42	1.55	1.84	2.09	1.85	1.74	1.62
Current Ratio	2.35	1.36	3.00	2.12	1.76	1.76	1.58	2.27
Debt to Equity	...	...	...	...	0.16	1.04	12.09	0.04
Price Range	37.70-26.43	26.99-17.12	20.32-15.27	17.16-10.82	12.30-8.59	10.63-5.93	10.72-6.04	7.81-4.67
P/E Ratio	24.32-17.05	21.95-13.92	19.36-14.54	18.65-11.76	12.17-8.51	12.65-7.05	17.87-10.06	15.32-9.15
Average Yield %	6.07	0.99	1.09	1.31	1.69	1.47	1.52	1.77

Address: 88 - 11th Avenue Northeast, Minneapolis, MN 55413 Telephone: (612) 623-6000 Fax: (612) 623-6777	Web Site: www.graco.com Officers: L. R. Mitau - Chmn. David A. Roberts - Pres., C.E.O.	Auditors: Deloitte & Touche LLP Investor Contact: 612-623-6659

GRAINGER (W.W.) INC.

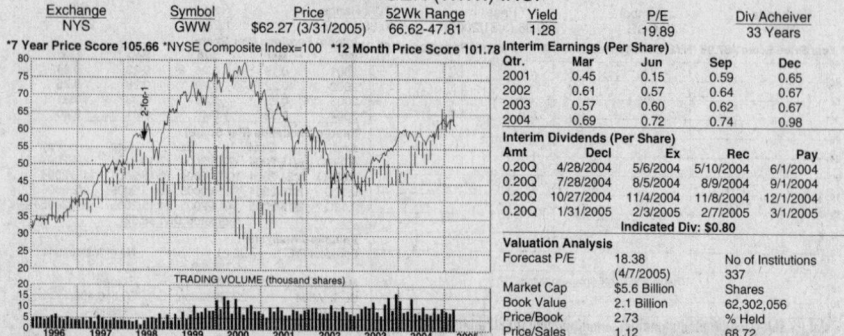

Exchange	Symbol	Price	52Wk Range	Yield	P/E	Div Acheiver
NYS	GWW	$62.27 (3/31/2005)	66.62-47.81	1.28	19.89	33 Years

*7 Year Price Score 105.66 *NYSE Composite Index=100 *12 Month Price Score 101.78

Interim Earnings (Per Share)

Qtr.	Mar	Jun	Sep	Dec
2001	0.45	0.15	0.59	0.65
2002	0.61	0.57	0.64	0.67
2003	0.57	0.60	0.62	0.67
2004	0.69	0.72	0.74	0.98

Interim Dividends (Per Share)

Amt	Decl	Ex	Rec	Pay
0.20Q	4/28/2004	5/6/2004	5/10/2004	6/1/2004
0.20Q	7/28/2004	8/5/2004	8/9/2004	9/1/2004
0.20Q	10/27/2004	11/4/2004	11/8/2004	12/1/2004
0.20Q	1/31/2005	2/3/2005	2/7/2005	3/1/2005

Indicated Div: $0.80

Valuation Analysis

Forecast P/E	18.38	No of Institutions	
	(4/7/2005)	337	
Market Cap	$5.6 Billion	Shares	
Book Value	2.1 Billion		62,302,056
Price/Book	2.73	% Held	
Price/Sales	1.12		68.72

Business Summary: Engineering Services (MIC: 12.1 SIC: 063 NAIC: 23610)

W.W. Grainger is primarily a supplier of facilities maintenance products in North America through its Branch-based Distribution segment, which includes a network of 575 branches in the U.S., Canada, and Mexico, 17 distribution facilities, and multiple Web sites. Co.'s Lab Safety segment is a direct marketer of safety and other industrial products to U.S. and Canadian businesses. Co.'s Integrated Supply segment offers customers on-site outsourcing services, including business process reengineering, inventory and tool crib management, purchasing management and information management.

Recent Developments: For the year ended Dec 31 2004, net income increased 26.4% to $286,923 thousand from net income of $226,971 thousand a year earlier. Revenues were $5,049,785 thousand, up 8.2% from $4,667,014 thousand the year before. Operating income was $439,530 thousand versus an income of $387,261 thousand in the prior year, an increase of 13.5%. Total direct expense was $3,143,133 thousand versus $2,975,513 thousand in the prior year, an increase of 5.6%. Total indirect expense was $1,467,122 thousand versus $1,304,240 thousand in the prior year, an increase of 12.5%.

Prospects: Results are being positively affected by strong demand from the manufacturing and commercial sectors stemming from improving economic conditions in the U.S. Looking ahead, Co. is projecting full-year 2005 sales growth of between 8.0% and 11.0%, along with earnings in the range of $3.20 to $3.45 per share. In 2005, Co. plans to expand into additional markets, improve product availability, and increase its sales coverage. Separately, on Jan 10 2005, Co. announced that its Lab Safety Supply unit has agreed to acquire AW Direct Inc., a marketer of general towing and work truck equipment and accessories to customers in the auto service, utilities, government and construction markets.

Financial Data

(US$ in Thousands)	12/31/2004	12/31/2003	12/31/2002	12/31/2001	12/31/2000	12/31/1999	12/31/1998	12/31/1997
Earnings Per Share	3.13	2.46	2.24	1.84	2.05	1.92	2.44	2.27
Cash Flow Per Share	4.49	4.34	3.30	5.48	2.92	0.32	3.48	4.24
Tang Book Value Per Share	20.44	18.20	16.59	15.09	14.08	13.47	11.39	11.13
Dividends Per Share	0.785	0.735	0.715	0.695	0.670	0.630	0.585	0.530
Dividend Payout %	25.08	29.88	31.92	37.77	32.68	32.81	23.98	23.35
Income Statement								
Total Revenue	5,049,785	4,667,014	4,643,898	4,754,317	4,977,044	4,533,853	4,341,269	4,136,560
EBITDA	541,407	474,011	492,915	408,336	461,000	415,967	484,804	471,852
Depn & Amortn	98,256	90,253	93,488	103,209	106,893	98,227	78,865	79,651
Income Before Taxes	445,139	381,090	397,837	297,280	331,595	303,750	400,847	389,636
Income Taxes	158,216	154,119	162,349	122,750	138,692	123,019	162,343	157,803
Net Income	286,923	226,971	211,567	174,530	192,903	180,731	238,504	231,833
Average Shares	91,673	92,394	94,303	94,727	94,223	94,315	97,846	102,178
Balance Sheet								
Current Assets	1,754,713	1,633,413	1,484,947	1,392,611	1,483,002	1,471,145	1,206,365	1,182,988
Total Assets	2,809,573	2,624,678	2,437,448	2,331,246	2,459,601	2,564,826	2,103,902	1,997,821
Current Liabilities	662,434	706,640	586,266	553,811	747,324	870,534	664,493	533,881
Long-Term Obligations	...	4,895	119,693	118,219	125,258	124,928	122,883	131,201
Total Liabilities	741,603	779,543	769,750	728,057	922,215	1,084,297	825,161	703,160
Stockholders' Equity	2,067,970	1,845,135	1,667,698	1,603,189	1,537,386	1,480,529	1,278,741	1,294,661
Shares Outstanding	90,597	91,020	91,568	93,344	93,932	93,381	93,505	97,722
Statistical Record								
Return on Assets %	10.53	8.97	8.87	7.29	7.66	7.74	11.63	11.26
Return on Equity %	14.62	12.92	12.94	11.11	12.75	13.10	18.54	16.82
EBITDA Margin %	10.72	10.16	10.61	8.59	9.26	9.17	11.17	11.41
Net Margin %	5.68	4.86	4.56	3.67	3.88	3.99	5.49	5.60
Asset Turnover	1.85	1.84	1.95	1.98	1.98	1.94	2.12	2.01
Current Ratio	2.65	2.31	2.53	2.51	1.98	1.69	1.82	2.22
Debt to Equity	...	N.M.	0.07	0.07	0.08	0.08	0.10	0.10
Price Range	66.62-45.17	53.11-41.93	59.27-39.82	48.52-30.23	56.00-24.63	58.06-37.13	54.47-37.63	49.00-36.06
P/E Ratio	21.28-14.43	21.59-17.04	26.46-17.78	26.37-16.43	27.32-12.01	30.24-19.34	22.32-15.42	21.59-15.89
Average Yield %	1.46	1.56	1.42	1.72	1.75	1.34	1.24	1.25

Address: 100 Grainger Parkway, Lake Forest, IL 60045-5201 Telephone: (847) 535-1000 Fax: (847) 535-0878	Web Site: www.grainger.com Officers: Richard L. Keyser - Chmn., C.E.O. James T. Ryan - Exec. V.P., Mktg., Sales, & Services	Auditors: GRANT THORNTON LLP Investor Contact: 847-535-1000 Transfer Agents: BankBoston, N.A. c/o EquiServe, Boston, MA

GRANITE CONSTRUCTION INC.

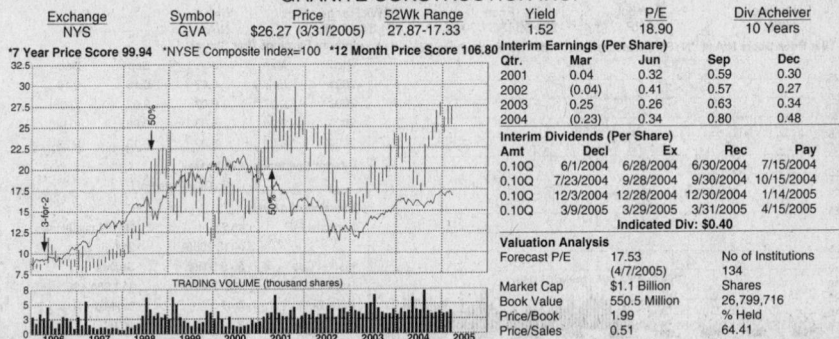

Exchange	Symbol	Price	52Wk Range	Yield	P/E	Div Acheiver
NYS	GVA	$26.27 (3/31/2005)	27.87-17.33	1.52	18.90	10 Years

7 Year Price Score 99.94 **NYSE Composite Index=100** **12 Month Price Score 106.80**

Interim Earnings (Per Share)

Qtr.	Mar	Jun	Sep	Dec
2001	0.04	0.32	0.59	0.30
2002	(0.04)	0.41	0.57	0.27
2003	0.25	0.26	0.63	0.34
2004	(0.23)	0.34	0.80	0.48

Interim Dividends (Per Share)

Amt	Decl	Ex	Rec	Pay
0.10Q	6/1/2004	6/28/2004	6/30/2004	7/15/2004
0.10Q	7/23/2004	9/28/2004	9/30/2004	10/15/2004
0.10Q	12/3/2004	12/28/2004	12/30/2004	1/14/2005
0.10Q	3/9/2005	3/29/2005	3/31/2005	4/15/2005

Indicated Div: $0.40

Valuation Analysis

Forecast P/E	17.53		No of Institutions
	(4/7/2005)		134
Market Cap	$1.1 Billion		Shares
Book Value	550.5 Million		26,799,716
Price/Book	1.99		% Held
Price/Sales	0.51		64.41

TRADING VOLUME (thousand shares)

Business Summary: Construction - Public Infrastructure (MIC: 3.1 SIC: 611 NAIC: 37310)

Granite Construction is a heavy civil construction contractor that serves both public and private sector clients in the U.S. Within the public sector, Co. primarily concentrates on infrastructure projects, including the construction of roads, highways, bridges, mass transit facilities and airports. Within the private sector, Co. performs site preparation services for buildings, plants, subdivisions and other facilities. Co. owns and leases substantial aggregate reserves and owns 158 construction materials processing plants. Co. also maintains a large fleet of heavy construction equipment.

Recent Developments: For the year ended Dec 31 2004, net income decreased 5.8% to $57,007 thousand from net income of $60,504 thousand a year earlier. Revenues were $2,136,212 thousand, up 15.8% from $1,844,491 thousand the year before. Operating income was $83,552 thousand versus an income of $79,285 thousand in the prior year, an increase of 5.4%. Total direct expense was $1,914,191 thousand versus $1,618,041 thousand in the prior year, an increase of 18.3%. Total indirect expense was $295,504 thousand versus $299,044 thousand in the prior year, a decrease of 1.2%.

Prospects: Co. continues to perform well. In particular, Co. is encouraged with the strength of its private development market, which supported its construction business in the West and drove the demand for its construction materials. Co. expects this trend to continue in 2005. However, bottom line results from Co.'s Heavy Construction Division are being hampered by profit forecasts on several projects that were revised downward as a result of increased estimated costs to complete. While it has some underperforming projects yet to complete, Co. believes that its focus on improving gross margins, coupled with a healthy backlog of $1.90 billion should lead to improved financial results going forward.

Financial Data

(US$ in Thousands)	12/31/2004	12/31/2003	12/31/2002	12/31/2001	12/31/2000	12/31/1999	12/31/1998	12/31/1997
Earnings Per Share	1.39	1.48	1.21	1.24	1.38	1.31	1.13	0.69
Cash Flow Per Share	1.96	1.93	2.60	3.13	1.89	2.56	2.41	1.61
Tang Book Value Per Share	13.23	12.16	11.03	10.19	9.24	8.09	7.26	6.26
Dividends Per Share	0.400	0.400	0.320	0.320	0.307	0.267	0.200	0.160
Dividend Payout %	28.78	27.03	26.45	25.81	22.22	20.41	17.65	23.30
Income Statement								
Total Revenue	2,136,212	1,844,491	1,764,742	1,547,994	1,348,325	1,328,774	1,226,100	1,028,205
EBITDA	162,623	171,324	146,319	134,510	140,703	133,349	116,116	84,270
Depn & Amortn	68,470	71,644	64,466	54,990	50,525	47,197	41,410	40,518
Income Before Taxes	94,924	97,525	82,739	81,497	92,870	86,043	75,011	44,178
Income Taxes	28,477	35,304	29,951	30,969	37,055	33,127	28,504	16,346
Net Income	57,007	60,504	49,279	50,528	55,815	52,916	46,507	27,832
Average Shares	41,031	40,808	40,723	40,711	40,409	40,444	41,008	40,413
Balance Sheet								
Current Assets	825,338	618,651	547,895	586,916	411,628	402,321	370,808	314,283
Total Assets	1,277,954	1,060,410	983,819	929,684	711,142	679,572	626,571	551,809
Current Liabilities	469,411	348,704	327,499	338,503	231,577	258,664	228,360	210,373
Long-Term Obligations	148,503	126,708	132,380	131,391	63,891	64,853	69,137	58,396
Total Liabilities	727,480	555,519	528,950	511,182	333,378	351,840	325,289	294,375
Stockholders' Equity	550,474	504,891	454,869	418,502	377,764	327,732	301,282	257,434
Shares Outstanding	41,612	41,528	41,257	41,089	40,881	40,493	41,473	41,098
Statistical Record								
Return on Assets %	4.86	5.92	5.15	6.16	8.00	8.10	7.89	5.43
Return on Equity %	10.77	12.61	11.28	12.69	15.78	16.83	16.65	11.34
EBITDA Margin %	7.61	9.29	8.29	8.69	10.44	10.04	9.47	8.20
Net Margin %	2.67	3.28	2.79	3.26	4.14	3.98	3.79	2.71
Asset Turnover	1.82	1.80	1.84	1.89	1.93	2.03	2.08	2.01
Current Ratio	1.76	1.77	1.67	1.73	1.78	1.56	1.62	1.49
Debt to Equity	0.27	0.25	0.29	0.31	0.17	0.20	0.23	0.23
Price Range	27.87-17.33	24.25-13.89	25.30-13.98	30.50-19.33	20.50-11.75	24.67-11.38	22.58-9.56	10.94-7.78
P/E Ratio	20.05-12.47	16.39-9.39	20.91-11.55	24.60-15.59	14.86-8.51	18.83-8.68	19.99-8.46	15.86-11.27
Average Yield %	1.78	2.16	1.57	1.31	1.85	1.59	1.29	1.71

Address: 585 W. Beach Street, Box 50085, Watsonville, CA 95077-5085 **Telephone:** (831) 761-7500 **Fax:** (408) 722-9657	**Web Site:** www.graniteconstruction.com **Officers:** David H. Watts - Chmn. William G. Dorey - Pres., C.E.O.	**Auditors:** PricewaterhouseCoopers LLP **Investor Contact:** 831-761-4741

GRANT PRIDECO INC

Exchange	Symbol	Price	52Wk Range	Yield	P/E
NYS	GRP	$24.16 (3/31/2005)	24.84-14.55	N/A	49.31

*7 Year Price Score N/A   ***NYSE Composite Index=100**   ***12 Month Price Score 110.71**

TRADING VOLUME (thousand shares)

Interim Earnings (Per Share)

Qtr.	Mar	Jun	Sep	Dec
2001	(0.20)	0.13	0.16	0.16
2002	0.07	0.03	0.02	(0.06)
2003	0.03	0.03	0.06	(0.08)
2004	0.09	0.02	0.15	0.23

Interim Dividends (Per Share)

No Dividends Paid

Valuation Analysis

Forecast P/E	45.72	No of Institutions
	(4/13/2005)	211
Market Cap	$3.0 Billion	Shares
Book Value	668.5 Million	111,984,496
Price/Book	4.47	% Held
Price/Sales	3.18	90.63

Business Summary: Oil and Gas (MIC: 14.2 SIC: 381 NAIC: 33132)

Grant Prideco is a manufacturer and supplier of oilfield drill pipe and other drill stem products, and a North American provider of high-performance premium connections and tubular products. Co.'s drill stem products are used to drill oil and gas wells, while its premium connections and tubular products are primarily used in drilling and completing oil and gas wells. Co.'s drilling products are manufactured in the U.S., China, Italy, Mexico, Singapore, Austria, and Indonesia. These products are sold and serviced through over 16 sales and service facilities worldwide. Co. also provides a variety of products and services to the worldwide offshore and deepwater market.

Recent Developments: For the year ended Dec 31 2004, income from continuing operations was $64.8 million compared with income of $4.7 million a year earlier. Results for 2003 included fixed asset write-downs from Co.'s manufacturing rationalization program of $24.9 million, asset impairments of $6.4 million related to two technology joint ventures, and transition costs of $800,000 associated with its ReedHycalog acquisition in Dec 2002. Revenues advanced 17.6% to $945.6 million from $803.8 million the previous year, reflecting gains from across each of Co.'s three primary operating segments.

Prospects: Co. is experiencing higher revenues in all of its segments due to strong industry demand. Also, Co.'s margins are benefiting from increased pricing across all of its segments, coupled with benefits from the Drilling Products and Services segment's rationalization program and the Tubular Technology and Services segment's restructuring program. Improved efficiency at Co.'s Drill Bits segment, following a shift in capacity between plants, should produce cost savings in 2005. Looking ahead, Co. anticipates the continued strong drilling environment will drive pricing and volumes higher in 2005. Earnings for 2005 are expected to range from $0.95 to $1.05 per share.

Financial Data

(US$ in Thousands)	9 Mos	6 Mos	3 Mos	12/31/2003	12/31/2002	12/31/2001	12/31/2000	12/31/1999
Earnings Per Share	0.18	0.09	0.10	0.04	0.06	0.25	(0.15)	(0.33)
Cash Flow Per Share	0.78	0.63	0.47	0.66	1.07	0.37	(0.30)	0.64
Tang Book Value Per Share	1.86	1.64	1.57	1.43	1.29	2.18	1.84	...
Income Statement								
Total Revenue	695,032	444,772	229,797	838,456	639,748	740,127	498,481	286,370
EBITDA	129,256	80,457	40,156	102,835	81,476	108,285	26,997	(2,638)
Depn & Amortn	31,778	21,761	10,809	46,032	31,100	36,500	31,842	30,514
Income Before Taxes	66,136	37,706	18,852	12,932	23,325	44,718	(21,850)	(44,495)
Income Taxes	21,162	12,759	6,919	4,526	7,228	15,651	(7,365)	(11,199)
Net Income	31,645	12,923	10,673	5,190	6,634	28,090	(16,485)	(33,511)
Average Shares	126,603	125,383	124,262	123,401	112,854	110,884	109,000	101,245
Balance Sheet								
Current Assets	560,113	519,705	532,114	510,863	522,234	392,363	377,033	272,038
Total Assets	1,309,565	1,260,951	1,275,979	1,262,061	1,315,349	915,598	892,564	734,575
Current Liabilities	192,120	169,815	183,582	166,255	181,979	186,181	178,585	107,401
Long-Term Obligations	391,037	404,829	410,684	426,853	478,846	205,024	219,104	124,276
Total Liabilities	641,023	628,095	651,816	655,947	726,477	446,631	461,061	280,719
Stockholders' Equity	668,542	632,856	624,163	606,114	588,872	468,967	431,503	453,856
Shares Outstanding	123,559	122,725	122,204	120,715	120,473	109,125	108,492	...
Statistical Record								
Return on Assets %	1.66	0.80	0.92	0.40	0.59	3.11	N.M.	...
Return on Equity %	3.38	1.65	1.94	0.87	1.25	6.24	N.M.	...
EBITDA Margin %	18.60	18.09	17.47	12.26	12.74	14.63	5.42	N.M.
Net Margin %	4.55	2.91	4.64	0.62	1.04	3.80	N.M.	N.M.
Asset Turnover	0.72	0.71	0.68	0.65	0.57	0.82	0.61	...
Current Ratio	2.92	3.06	2.90	3.07	2.87	2.11	2.11	2.53
Debt to Equity	0.58	0.64	0.66	0.70	0.81	0.44	0.51	0.27
Price Range	20.66-10.09	18.49-10.01	15.58-10.01	14.74-10.01	16.50-8.35	24.04-5.68	25.88-14.13	...
P/E Ratio	114.78-56.06	205.44-111.22	155.80-100.10	368.50-250.25	275.00-139.17	96.16-22.72	...	...

Address: 1330 Post Oak Blvd., Suite 2700, Houston, TX 77056
Telephone: (832) 681-8000
Fax: (832) 297-8525

Web Site: www.grantprideco.com
Officers: Michael McShane - Chmn., Pres., C.E.O. William G. Chunn - Exec. V.P., Oper.

Auditors: Ernst & Young LLP
Transfer Agents: American Stock Transfer & Trust Company, New York, NY

GREAT LAKES CHEMICAL CORP.

Exchange	Symbol	Price	52Wk Range	Yield	P/E
NYS	GLK	$32.12 (3/31/2005)	34.34-22.31	1.25	26.11

*7 Year Price Score 74.17   *NYSE Composite Index=100   *12 Month Price Score 100.76

Interim Earnings (Per Share)

Qtr.	Mar	Jun	Sep	Dec
2001	0.40	(3.06)	(2.12)	(0.99)
2002	(0.03)	2.11	0.25	0.15
2003	(0.02)	0.38	(0.54)	(0.84)
2004	(0.10)	0.27	1.04	0.02

Interim Dividends (Per Share)

Amt	Decl	Ex	Rec	Pay
0.095Q	5/6/2004	6/29/2004	7/1/2004	7/30/2004
0.095Q	9/9/2004	9/29/2004	10/1/2004	10/29/2004
0.10Q	12/2/2004	12/29/2004	1/1/2005	1/31/2005
0.10Q	2/7/2005	3/30/2005	4/1/2005	4/29/2005

Indicated Div: $0.40

Valuation Analysis

Forecast P/E	25.60	No of Institutions
	(4/7/2005)	167
Market Cap	$1.7 Billion	Shares
Book Value	875.5 Million	49,197,680
Price/Book	1.89	% Held
Price/Sales	1.03	95.65

Business Summary: Chemicals (MIC: 11.1 SIC: 899 NAIC: 25998)

Great Lakes Chemical is engaged in the delivery of specialty chemical solutions and consumer products. Co.'s products and services help treat and purify water, keep surfaces in and around the home shining, protect against and extinguish fire, and enhance the stability and performance of a wide range of consumer products, such as computers, electronics, automobiles, packaging, building materials and furniture. Co. serves customers and markets through an integrated network of research, production, sales, distribution and technical services facilities. Co. is organized into three global business units: polymer additives, specialty products and performance chemicals.

Recent Developments: For the year ended Dec 31 2004, income from continuing operations was $19,900 thousand compared with a loss of $40,100 thousand a year earlier. Net income was $62,900 thousand versus net loss of $51,400 thousand a year earlier. Revenues were $1,603,700 thousand, up 12.5% from $1,425,900 thousand the year before. Operating income was $52,800 thousand versus a loss of $62,200 thousand in the prior year. Total direct expense was $1,277,400 thousand versus $1,165,800 thousand in the prior year, an increase of 9.6%. Total indirect expense was $286,800 thousand versus $321,700 thousand in the prior year, a decrease of 10.8%.

Prospects: Co.'s near term outlook appears mixed. For instance, Co.'s operating results are showing considerable improvement on a year-over-year basis due to a stronger performance in the Industrial Performance Products segment. However, these gains are being partially offset by a decline in earnings in Co.'s Consumer Products segment and the timing of costs incurred at the corporate level. Going forward, Co. will continue to focus on restoring operating margins to support reinvestment levels. On the consumer side, pricing momentum is gaining traction, and Co.'s targeted pricing gains in this business should enable it to absorb the significant expected increase in raw materials and packaging costs.

Financial Data

(US$ in Thousands)	12/31/2004	12/31/2003	12/31/2002	12/31/2001	12/31/2000	12/31/1999	12/31/1998	12/31/1997
Earnings Per Share	1.23	(1.02)	2.48	(5.76)	2.42	2.41	1.50	0.94
Cash Flow Per Share	0.46	1.87	2.88	3.72	3.92	4.54	10.28	4.28
Tang Book Value Per Share	11.46	9.38	11.34	9.44	13.38	13.74	16.07	20.23
Dividends Per Share	0.385	0.365	0.340	0.320	0.320	0.323	0.400	0.630
Dividend Payout %	31.30	...	13.71	...	13.22	13.38	26.67	67.02
Income Statement								
Total Revenue	1,603,700	1,464,600	1,401,500	1,594,700	1,670,500	1,453,300	1,394,300	1,311,227
EBITDA	125,400	31,500	176,400	(222,100)	265,000	264,900	149,700	190,858
Depn & Amortn	96,700	94,700	80,100	100,700	100,100	89,500	83,500	73,688
Income Before Taxes	3,500	(89,000)	68,700	(356,900)	164,900	175,400	66,200	117,170
Income Taxes	(16,400)	(55,100)	21,300	(67,400)	37,900	35,800	9,800	45,400
Net Income	62,900	(51,400)	125,000	(289,500)	127,000	139,600	89,000	56,945
Average Shares	51,100	50,400	50,300	50,300	52,500	58,000	59,200	60,297
Balance Sheet								
Current Assets	919,000	760,400	847,100	681,400	1,007,800	1,167,500	995,600	668,546
Total Assets	1,801,500	1,693,200	1,717,700	1,687,600	2,134,400	2,261,000	2,004,600	2,270,391
Current Liabilities	364,300	402,900	418,200	452,700	384,800	311,200	346,600	304,356
Long-Term Obligations	428,900	427,600	432,600	527,800	688,200	883,400	515,300	561,455
Total Liabilities	926,000	949,700	972,000	1,074,100	1,184,700	1,266,900	950,300	962,948
Stockholders' Equity	875,500	743,500	745,700	613,500	949,700	994,100	1,054,300	1,307,443
Shares Outstanding	51,500	50,600	50,200	50,200	50,300	54,400	58,400	58,944
Statistical Record								
Return on Assets %	3.59	N.M.	7.34	N.M.	5.76	6.55	4.16	2.31
Return on Equity %	7.75	N.M.	18.39	N.M.	13.03	13.63	7.54	4.08
EBITDA Margin %	7.82	2.15	12.59	N.M.	15.86	18.23	10.74	14.56
Net Margin %	3.92	N.M.	8.92	N.M.	7.60	9.61	6.38	4.34
Asset Turnover	0.92	0.86	0.82	0.83	0.76	0.68	0.65	0.53
Current Ratio	2.52	1.89	2.03	1.51	2.62	3.75	2.87	2.20
Debt to Equity	0.49	0.58	0.58	0.86	0.72	0.89	0.49	0.43
Price Range	29.62-22.27	27.50-20.11	29.00-21.64	37.13-20.95	39.63-26.63	49.38-33.31	47.09-36.21	47.09-36.32
P/E Ratio	24.08-18.11	...	11.69-8.73	...	16.37-11.00	20.49-13.82	31.39-24.14	50.09-38.64
Average Yield %	1.50	1.64	1.35	1.11	1.01	0.79	0.98	1.53

Address: 9025 North River Road, Suite 400, Indianapolis, IN 46240 Telephone: (317) 715-3000 Fax: (317) 715-3060	Web Site: www.greatlakes.com Officers: John J. Gallagher III - Acting C.E.O. Larry J. Bloom - Exec. V.P., Chief Strategy Officer	Auditors: Ernst & Young LLP Investor Contact: 317-715-3027

GREAT PLAINS ENERGY, INC.

Exchange	Symbol	Price	52Wk Range	Yield	P/E
NYS	GXP	$30.58 (3/31/2005)	34.36-28.17	5.43	12.79

*7 Year Price Score 96.83 ***NYSE Composite Index=100** ***12 Month Price Score 94.89**

TRADING VOLUME (thousand shares)

Interim Earnings (Per Share)

Qtr.	Mar	Jun	Sep	Dec
2001	0.20	0.58	0.89	(2.09)
2002	(0.05)	0.57	1.11	0.41
2003	0.20	0.73	1.20	(0.07)
2004	0.39	0.59	1.02	0.37

Interim Dividends (Per Share)

Amt	Decl	Ex	Rec	Pay
0.415Q	5/4/2004	5/26/2004	5/28/2004	6/21/2004
0.415Q	8/3/2004	8/25/2004	8/27/2004	9/20/2004
0.415Q	11/2/2004	11/24/2004	11/29/2004	12/20/2004
0.415Q	2/1/2005	2/24/2005	2/28/2005	3/21/2005

Indicated Div: $1.66

Valuation Analysis

Forecast P/E	14.48 (4/7/2005)	No of Institutions	197
Market Cap	$2.3 Billion	Shares	30,604,712
Book Value	1.2 Billion	% Held	41.11
Price/Book	1.93		
Price/Sales	0.92		

Business Summary: Industrial Machinery and Equipment (MIC: 11.5 SIC: 568 NAIC: 33613)

Great Plains Energy is a diversified public utility holding company which operates through three reportable segments: Kansas City Power & Light (KCP&L), an integrated, regulated electric utility in the states of Missouri and Kansas, that provides electricity to retail customers; Strategic Energy LLC, which provides retail electricity services and operates in several electricity markets offering retail choice, including California, Massachusetts, Michigan, New Jersey, New York, Ohio, Pennsylvania and Texas; and KLT Gas Inc., which explores for, develops and produces unconventional natural gas resources.

Recent Developments: For the year ended Dec 31 2004, income from continuing operations decreased 8.5% to $173,535 thousand from income of $189,702 thousand a year earlier. Net income increased 24.8% to $180,811 thousand from net income of $144,923 thousand a year earlier. Revenues were $2,464,018 thousand, up 14.7% from $2,148,045 thousand the year before. Operating income was $2,145,217 thousand versus an income of $1,780,777 thousand in the prior year, an increase of 20.5%. Total direct expense was $1,887,257 thousand versus $1,563,256 thousand in the prior year, an increase of 20.7%. Total indirect expense was $247,694 thousand versus $264,927 thousand in the prior year, a decrease of 6.5%.

Prospects: For 2005, Co. is anticipating ongoing earnings in the range of $2.05 to $2.20 per share. This projection reflects a significant projected increase in 2005 fuel costs at Kansas City Power & Light (KCP&L) segment; lower anticipated 2005 margins at Strategic Energy segment; expiration of a portion of the Co.'s investment tax credits in 2005, a full year's recognition of additional shares outstanding from its June 2004 stock offering; and the absence of the 2004 impact of the lower composite tax rate on deferred tax balances. These factors are projected to more than offset projected retail load growth and expense savings at KCP&L as well as substantially lower holding company costs in 2005.

Financial Data

(US$ in Thousands)	12/31/2004	12/31/2003	12/31/2002	12/31/2001	12/31/2000	12/31/1999	12/31/1998	12/31/1997
Earnings Per Share	2.39	2.07	1.99	(0.42)	2.54	1.26	1.89	1.18
Cash Flow Per Share	5.22	5.58	5.38	4.51	3.13	2.59	4.89	3.37
Tang Book Value Per Share	15.35	13.82	13.58	12.59	14.88	13.97	14.41	14.19
Dividends Per Share	1.660	1.660	1.660	1.660	1.660	1.660	1.640	1.620
Dividend Payout %	69.46	80.19	83.42		65.35	131.75	86.77	137.29
Income Statement								
Total Revenue	2,464,018	2,149,496	1,861,882	1,461,918	1,115,868	897,393	938,941	895,943
EBITDA	486,473	452,970	443,765	219,988	417,028	...	...	...
Depn & Amortn	176,057	167,672	177,198	192,613	159,545	146,473	143,669	137,325
Income Before Taxes	227,386	209,127	177,473	(75,957)	181,797	...	...	...
Income Taxes	54,451	55,514	48,285	(35,914)	53,166	3,180	32,800	8,079
Net Income	180,811	144,923	126,188	(24,171)	158,704	81,915	120,722	76,560
Average Shares	72,092	69,248	62,623	61,864	61,864	61,898	61,884	62,895
Balance Sheet								
Net PPE	2,734,450	2,700,934	2,604,069	2,623,714	2,527,790	2,298,895	2,316,448	2,323,555
Total Assets	3,798,901	3,665,287	3,506,739	3,464,402	3,293,891	2,990,142	3,012,364	3,058,033
Long-Term Obligations	956,460	1,158,345	974,335	778,686	1,041,847	685,884	749,283	934,007
Total Liabilities	2,618,307	2,668,993	2,528,269	2,645,687	2,333,539	2,086,498	2,031,562	2,090,613
Stockholders' Equity	1,180,594	996,294	978,470	818,715	960,352	903,644	980,802	967,420
Shares Outstanding	74,365	69,255	69,196	61,908	61,908	61,908	61,909	61,909
Statistical Record								
Return on Assets %	4.83	4.04	3.62	N.M.	5.04	2.73	3.98	2.56
Return on Equity %	16.57	14.68	14.04	N.M.	16.98	8.69	12.39	7.78
EBITDA Margin %	19.74	21.07	23.83	15.05	37.37	...	...	...
Net Margin %	7.34	6.74	6.78	(1.65)	14.22	9.13	12.86	8.55
PPE Turnover	0.90	0.81	0.71	0.57	0.46	0.39	0.40	0.38
Asset Turnover	0.66	0.60	0.53	0.43	0.35	0.30	0.31	0.30
Debt to Equity	0.81	1.16	1.00	0.95	1.08	0.76	0.76	0.97
Price Range	35.29-28.17	32.60-21.77	26.60-16.62	27.35-23.50	29.00-21.25	29.63-21.06	31.50-28.19	29.94-27.38
P/E Ratio	14.77-11.79	15.75-10.52	13.37-8.35	...	11.42-8.37	23.51-16.72	16.67-14.91	25.37-23.20
Average Yield %	5.36	5.99	7.35	6.59	6.55	6.57	5.53	5.64

Address: 1201 Walnut Street, P.O. Box 418679, Kansas City, MO 64106-2124 Telephone: (816) 556-2200 Fax: (816) 556-2924	Web Site: www.greatplainsenergy.com Officers: Michael J. Chesser - Chmn., C.E.O. William H. Downey - Pres., C.O.O.	Auditors: DELOITTE & TOUCHE LLP Investor Contact: 816-556-2053

GROUP 1 AUTOMOTIVE, INC.

Exchange	Symbol	Price	52Wk Range	Yield	P/E
NYS	GPI	$26.30 (3/31/2005)	37.75-25.71	N/A	22.29

*7 Year Price Score 106.61 *NYSE Composite Index=100 *12 Month Price Score 86.74

Interim Earnings (Per Share)

Qtr.	Mar	Jun	Sep	Dec
2001	0.47	0.68	0.75	0.69
2002	0.64	0.78	0.84	0.54
2003	0.64	0.86	0.92	0.84
2004	0.45	0.67	(0.42)	0.47

Interim Dividends (Per Share)

No Dividends Paid

Valuation Analysis

Forecast P/E	8.78	No of Institutions
	(4/7/2005)	97
Market Cap	$613.0 Billion	Shares
Book Value	567.2 Million	16,320,115
Price/Book	1080.88	% Held
Price/Sales	112.80	69.45

Business Summary: Retail - Automotive (MIC: 5.7 SIC: 511 NAIC: 41110)

Group 1 Automotive operates in the automotive retailing industry. Co., through its dealerships and Internet sites, sells new and used vehicles, provides maintenance and repair services, sells replacement parts and arranges related financing, vehicle service and insurance contracts. Co. sells 30 American, Asian and European brands of economy, family, sports and luxury cars, light trucks and sport utility vehicles. As of Mar 1 2004, Co. owned 82 dealerships, comprised of 122 franchises and 29 collision service centers, located in California, Colorado, Florida, Georgia, Louisiana, Massachusetts, New Jersey, New Mexico, Oklahoma and Texas.

Recent Developments: For the year ended Dec 31 2004, net income decreased 63.5% to $27,781,000 from net income of $76,126,000 a year earlier. Revenues were $54,350,330,00, up 20.3% from $4,518,560,000 the year before. Total direct expense was $9,206,534,000 versus $7,590,298,000 in the prior year, an increase of 21.3%. Total indirect expense was $732,615,000 versus $574,208,000 in the prior year, an increase of 27.6%.

Prospects: In January 2005, Co. completed the acquisition of new Dodge and Chrysler franchises in Tulsa, OK. In 2005, Co. will focus on integrating the franchises acquired in 2004. As a result, Co.'s 2005 acquisition target is $300.0 million in aggregate anticipated annual revenues versus the $1.20 billion acquired in 2004. Meanwhile, oversupply of domestic new vehicles remains a major concern. Until inventories more closely match consumer demand, Co. believes that most of its markets will remain highly competitive, pressures on gross margins will continue and sales will be driven by automakers' incentive programs. For full-year 2005, Co. expects earnings of $2.95 to $3.05 per diluted share.

Financial Data
(US$ in Thousands)

	12/31/2004	12/31/2003	12/31/2002	12/31/2001	12/31/2000	12/31/1999	12/31/1998	12/31/1997
Earnings Per Share	1.18	3.26	2.80	2.59	1.88	1.55	1.16	0.76
Cash Flow Per Share	3.50	3.57	3.21	4.32	4.46	3.54	1.40	n.m
Tang Book Value Per Share	0.57	5.67	3.36	4.84	N.M.	N.M.	0.69	4.25
Income Statement								
Total Revenue	5,435,033	4,518,560	4,214,364	3,996,374	3,586,146	2,508,324	1,630,057	403,967
EBITDA	108,436	162,344	148,518	146,936	134,900	96,752	58,511	11,397
Depn & Amortn	15,836	14,381	11,940	15,716	16,038	10,616	6,426	1,020
Income Before Taxes	47,952	113,072	107,282	89,422	65,826	55,689	35,221	6,391
Income Taxes	20,171	36,946	40,217	33,980	25,014	22,174	14,502	573
Net Income	27,781	76,126	67,065	55,442	40,812	33,515	20,719	5,818
Average Shares	23,494	23,346	23,968	21,415	21,709	21,558	17,904	15,098
Balance Sheet								
Current Assets	1,205,215	930,923	903,038	661,932	720,539	553,423	326,922	161,682
Total Assets	1,947,220	1,488,165	1,423,765	1,054,425	1,099,553	842,910	477,710	213,149
Current Liabilities	1,049,762	654,393	809,283	507,219	665,770	473,295	278,671	111,473
Long-Term Obligations	156,747	230,178	83,222	95,499	140,393	113,174	42,821	7,053
Total Liabilities	1,380,046	970,056	980,348	662,182	852,137	610,881	341,526	123,778
Stockholders' Equity	567,174	518,109	443,417	392,243	247,416	232,029	136,184	89,372
Shares Outstanding	23,310	22,451	22,240	22,686	19,765	22,722	18,230	14,663
Statistical Record								
Return on Assets %	1.61	5.23	5.41	5.15	4.19	5.08	6.00	2.73
Return on Equity %	5.11	15.83	16.05	17.33	16.98	18.20	18.37	6.51
EBITDA Margin %	2.00	3.59	3.52	3.68	3.76	3.86	3.59	2.82
Net Margin %	0.51	1.68	1.59	1.39	1.14	1.34	1.27	1.44
Asset Turnover	3.16	3.10	3.40	3.71	3.68	3.80	4.72	1.90
Current Ratio	1.15	1.42	1.12	1.31	1.08	1.17	1.17	1.45
Debt to Equity	0.28	0.44	0.19	0.24	0.57	0.49	0.31	0.08
Price Range	38.25-26.68	40.05-20.11	50.15-18.92	34.50-8.19	16.50-8.13	29.00-12.94	26.00-8.75	13.94-8.13
P/E Ratio	32.42-22.61	12.29-6.17	17.91-6.76	13.32-3.16	8.78-4.32	18.71-8.35	22.41-7.54	18.34-10.69

Address: 950 Echo Lane, Suite 100, Houston, TX 77024 **Telephone:** (713) 647-5700 **Fax:** (713) 647-5858	**Web Site:** www.group1auto.com **Officers:** B. B. Hollingsworth Jr. - Chmn., Pres., C.E.O. Scott L. Thompson - Exec. V.P., C.F.O., Treas.	**Auditors:** Ernst & Young LLP **Transfer Agents:** Mellon Investor Services LLC, Dallas, TX

GTECH HOLDINGS CORP.

Exchange	Symbol	Price	52Wk Range	Yield	P/E
NYS	GTK	$23.53 (3/31/2005)	31.93-19.79	1.44	15.79

*7 Year Price Score 169.78 *NYSE Composite Index=100   *12 Month Price Score 88.72

Interim Earnings (Per Share)

Qtr.	May	Aug	Nov	Feb
2001-02	0.15	0.14	0.18	0.09
2002-03	0.25	0.33	0.28	0.36
2003-04	0.34	0.37	0.34	0.36
2004-05	0.40	0.40	0.35	...

Interim Dividends (Per Share)

Amt	Decl	Ex	Rec	Pay
0.085Q	6/22/2004	6/29/2004	7/1/2004	7/30/2004
0.085Q	10/1/2004	10/13/2004	10/15/2004	10/29/2004
0.085Q	1/4/2005	1/12/2005	1/14/2005	1/28/2005
0.085Q	4/5/2005	4/13/2005	4/15/2005	4/29/2005
		Indicated Div: $0.34		

Valuation Analysis

Forecast P/E	15.52	No of Institutions	
	(4/7/2005)	218	
Market Cap	$2.7 Billion	Shares	
Book Value	634.8 Million	111,755,936	
Price/Book	4.29	% Held	
Price/Sales	2.30	96.51	

Business Summary: IT & Technology (MIC: 10.2 SIC: 379 NAIC: 13290)

Gtech Holdings, a global information technology company providing software, network and professional services that power transaction processing solutions, is the operator of highly-secure on-line lottery transaction processing systems. As of Feb 28 2004, GTECH, the wholly-owned subsidiary of Co., operated on-line lottery systems for, or supplied equipment and services to, 27 of the 41 on-line lottery authorities in the U.S. and 57 of the 113 international on-line lottery authorities. Co. offers its customers a range of lottery technology services, including the design, assembly, installation, operation, maintenance and marketing of on-line lottery systems and instant ticket support systems.

Recent Developments: For the quarter ended Nov 27 2004, net income decreased 0.0% to $45,855 thousand from net income of $45,867 thousand in the year-earlier quarter. Revenues were $315,647 thousand, up 23.8% from $254,922 thousand the year before. Operating income was $72,751 thousand versus an income of $68,744 thousand in the prior-year quarter, an increase of 5.8%. Total direct expense was $200,149 thousand versus $145,085 thousand in the prior-year quarter, an increase of 38.0%. Total indirect expense was $42,747 thousand versus $41,093 thousand in the prior-year quarter, an increase of 4.0%.

Prospects: For full-year fiscal 2005, Co. expects total revenue growth of approximately 19.0%, with service revenue growth in the range of 6.0% to 7.0%. Co. expects product sales to be in the range of $240.0 million to $250.0 million. Moreover, Co. expects service margins to be approximately 40.0%, with product margins in the range of 34.0% to 36.0%. Based on Co.'s current operational outlook, it now expects diluted earnings per share for fiscal 2005 to be in the range of $1.46 to $1.48. Based upon the preliminary outlook, for fiscal 2006, Co. expects product sales in the range of $215.0 million to $235.0 million and diluted earnings per share in the range of $1.53 to $1.58.

Financial Data
(US$ in Thousands)

	9 Mos	6 Mos	3 Mos	02/28/2004	02/22/2003	02/23/2002	02/24/2001	02/26/2000
Earnings Per Share	1.49	1.48	1.45	1.42	1.22	0.56	0.31	0.65
Cash Flow Per Share	3.25	3.47	3.72	3.50	2.92	2.93	1.83	1.60
Tang Book Value Per Share	1.97	1.60	1.51	2.92	1.77	0.75	1.40	1.19
Dividends Per Share	0.340	0.340	0.340	0.255	...	...	...	...
Dividend Payout %	22.85	22.94	23.44	17.96	...	...	...	...
Income Statement								
Total Revenue	919,367	603,720	280,205	1,051,330	978,790	1,009,701	936,543	1,010,798
EBITDA	362,072	248,111	123,116	415,039	374,681	308,205	266,699	366,876
Depn & Amortn	115,484	73,014	35,012	119,059	138,185	168,543	174,395	185,376
Income Before Taxes	237,803	169,358	85,103	290,794	229,066	122,236	70,735	155,977
Income Taxes	85,252	62,662	31,488	107,594	87,045	46,450	27,587	62,392
Net Income	152,551	106,696	53,615	183,200	142,021	68,026	43,148	93,585
Average Shares	131,435	132,743	134,978	130,288	116,782	120,636	138,620	145,040
Balance Sheet								
Current Assets	609,096	331,016	370,586	613,402	348,597	278,030	337,828	239,200
Total Assets	1,862,503	1,522,352	1,539,499	1,559,131	949,929	853,829	938,160	891,023
Current Liabilities	296,813	298,601	352,484	418,172	304,630	289,478	272,555	210,947
Long-Term Obligations	754,888	474,099	453,463	463,215	287,088	329,715	316,961	349,400
Total Liabilities	1,227,716	940,198	951,288	996,842	634,363	650,874	623,798	594,447
Stockholders' Equity	634,787	582,154	588,211	562,289	315,566	202,955	314,362	296,576
Shares Outstanding	115,648	115,621	117,986	118,395	113,276	114,982	137,030	139,216
Statistical Record								
Return on Assets %	11.79	15.23	15.17	14.37	15.79	7.61	4.73	10.63
Return on Equity %	34.33	38.86	39.94	41.06	54.93	26.37	14.16	32.33
EBITDA Margin %	39.38	41.10	43.94	39.48	38.28	30.52	28.48	36.30
Net Margin %	16.59	17.67	19.13	17.43	14.51	6.74	4.61	9.26
Asset Turnover	0.71	0.87	0.85	0.82	1.09	1.13	1.03	1.15
Current Ratio	2.05	1.11	1.05	1.47	1.14	0.96	1.24	1.13
Debt to Equity	1.19	0.81	0.77	0.82	0.91	1.62	1.01	1.18
Price Range	31.93-19.79	31.93-19.79	31.93-16.91	29.61-13.50	15.10-9.20	12.81-6.46	6.75-3.89	6.95-4.88

Address: 55 Technology Way, West Greenwich, RI 02817	Web Site: www.gtech.com	Auditors: Ernst & Young LLP
Telephone: (401) 392-1000	Officers: Robert M. Dewey Jr. - Chmn. W. Bruce Turner - Pres., C.E.O.	Investor Contact: 401-392-6980
Fax: (401) 392-1234		Transfer Agents: Bank of New York, New York, NY

GUIDANT CORP.

Exchange	Symbol	Price	52Wk Range	Yield	P/E
NYS	GDT	$73.90 (3/31/2005)	74.95-50.55	0.54	45.34

*7 Year Price Score 112.49 *NYSE Composite Index=100 *12 Month Price Score 106.73

Interim Earnings (Per Share)

Qtr.	Mar	Jun	Sep	Dec
2001	0.36	0.38	0.40	0.44
2002	0.45	0.67	0.57	0.31
2003	0.30	(0.32)	0.41	0.66
2004	0.44	0.39	0.48	0.32

Interim Dividends (Per Share)

Amt	Decl	Ex	Rec	Pay
0.10Q	5/17/2004	5/27/2004	6/1/2004	6/15/2004
0.10Q	8/17/2004	8/30/2004	9/1/2004	9/15/2004
0.10Q	10/18/2004	11/29/2004	12/1/2004	12/15/2004
0.10Q	2/14/2005	2/25/2005	3/1/2005	3/15/2005

Indicated Div: $0.40

Valuation Analysis

Forecast P/E	28.37	No of Institutions
	(4/7/2005)	556
Market Cap	$23.7 Billion	Shares
Book Value	3.7 Billion	258,738,912
Price/Book	6.33	% Held
Price/Sales	6.29	80.20

TRADING VOLUME (thousand shares)

Business Summary: Medical Instruments & Equipment (MIC: 9.6 SIC: 841 NAIC: 39112)

Guidant designs, develops, manufactures and markets implantable cardioverter defibrillator systems used to detect and treat abnormally fast heart rhythms (tachycardia), implantable pacemaker systems used to manage slow or irregular heart rhythms (bradycardia), implantable cardiac resynchronization therapy cardioverter defibrillator and pacemaker systems used to treat heart failure and provide backup therapy for tachycardia and bradycardia, coronary and noncoronary stent systems, angioplasty dialation catheters, intravascular radiotherapy systems and related accessories for the treatment of artery and biliary structure disease, and products for emerging therapies.

Recent Developments: For the year ended Dec 31 2004, income from continuing operations increased 36.7% to $573,000 thousand from income of $419,300 thousand a year earlier. Net income increased 58.6% to $524,000 thousand from net income of $330,300 thousand a year earlier. Revenues were $3,765,600 thousand, up 3.3% from $3,644,800 thousand the year before. Total direct expense was $921,600 thousand versus $877,400 thousand in the prior year, an increase of 5.0%. Total indirect expense was $1,892,800 thousand versus $1,787,700 thousand in the prior year, an increase of 5.9%.

Prospects: Co.'s outlook is generally positive, reflecting strong growth in the implantable defibrillator market, a moderation in its coronary stent revenue erosion, and continued acceleration of its emerging businesses. Separately, on Dec 16 2004, Co. agreed to be acquired by Johnson & Johnson in a transaction valued at about $25.40 billion. Under the terms of the agreement, each share of Co.'s common stock will be exchanged for $30.40 in cash and $45.60 in Johnson & Johnson common stock. The deal, approved by both boards, still must be approved by U.S. and European regulators as well as by Co.'s shareholders. Co. expects to hold a meeting for shareholder approval in the Spring of 2005.

Financial Data

(US$ in Thousands)	12/31/2004	12/31/2003	12/31/2002	12/31/2001	12/31/2000	12/31/1999	12/31/1998	12/31/1997
Earnings Per Share	1.63	1.06	2.00	1.58	1.21	1.10	(0.01)	0.48
Cash Flow Per Share	3.63	1.33	3.46	2.27	2.14	1.19	0.96	0.68
Tang Book Value Per Share	9.55	6.60	5.58	3.05	1.75	0.65	1.02	1.30
Dividends Per Share	0.400	0.240	...	...	...	...	0.025	0.025
Dividend Payout %	24.54	22.64	...	...	...	...	...	5.15
Income Statement								
Total Revenue	3,765,600	3,698,800	3,239,600	2,707,600	2,548,700	2,352,300	1,897,000	1,328,200
EBITDA	1,042,300	629,400	970,800	839,700	783,600	703,300	215,800	334,300
Depn & Amortn	172,900	150,700	127,600	141,000	133,100	119,700	72,900	66,000
Income Before Taxes	877,800	485,000	839,200	667,200	595,800	528,000	127,600	248,800
Income Taxes	304,800	59,500	227,400	183,200	221,500	183,500	129,800	98,800
Net Income	524,000	330,300	611,800	484,000	374,300	341,200	(2,200)	145,300
Average Shares	321,240	312,520	305,990	306,220	310,110	310,890	294,590	299,780
Balance Sheet								
Current Assets	3,707,900	3,079,900	2,303,200	1,548,300	1,162,300	916,100	763,500	625,100
Total Assets	5,372,200	4,640,100	3,716,100	2,916,800	2,521,400	2,250,200	1,569,500	1,225,000
Current Liabilities	1,028,700	1,062,400	865,800	789,100	709,200	738,500	587,200	541,300
Long-Term Obligations	357,200	698,300	361,700	460,000	508,900	527,700	390,000	80,000
Total Liabilities	1,630,100	1,926,800	1,394,300	1,371,000	1,337,900	1,382,900	1,015,600	643,200
Stockholders' Equity	3,742,100	2,713,300	2,321,800	1,545,800	1,183,500	867,300	553,900	581,800
Shares Outstanding	320,692	308,971	306,604	305,153	308,476	306,839	301,176	301,492
Statistical Record								
Return on Assets %	10.44	7.91	18.45	17.80	15.65	17.87	N.M.	13.04
Return on Equity %	16.19	13.12	31.64	35.47	36.40	48.02	N.M.	28.21
EBITDA Margin %	27.68	17.02	29.97	31.01	30.75	29.90	11.38	25.17
Net Margin %	13.92	8.93	18.89	17.88	14.69	14.50	N.M.	10.94
Asset Turnover	0.75	0.89	0.98	1.00	1.07	1.23	1.36	1.19
Current Ratio	3.60	2.90	2.66	1.96	1.64	1.24	1.30	1.15
Debt to Equity	0.10	0.26	0.16	0.30	0.43	0.61	0.70	0.14
Price Range	73.75-50.55	60.37-29.11	49.90-26.00	53.44-27.99	73.44-44.63	69.00-43.88	55.97-26.19	33.56-13.53
P/E Ratio	45.25-31.01	56.95-27.46	24.95-13.00	33.82-17.72	60.69-36.88	62.73-39.89	...	69.92-28.19
Average Yield %	0.64	0.55	...	...	...	...	0.07	0.11

Address: 111 Monument Circle, 29th Floor, Indianapolis, IN 46204-5129
Telephone: (317) 971-2000
Fax: (317) 971-2040

Web Site: www.guidant.com
Officers: Ronald W. Dollens - Pres., C.E.O. Keith E. Brauer - V.P., Fin., C.F.O.

Auditors: Ernst & Young LLP

HALLIBURTON CO. (HOLDING CO.)

Exchange	Symbol	Price	52Wk Range	Yield	P/E
NYS	HAL	$43.25 (3/31/2005)	44.80-27.30	1.16	N/A

*7 Year Price Score 93.21   *NYSE Composite Index=100   *12 Month Price Score 113.42

Interim Earnings (Per Share)

Qtr.	Mar	Jun	Sep	Dec
2001	0.25	0.89	0.42	0.32
2002	0.05	(1.15)	0.22	(1.43)
2003	0.10	0.06	0.13	(2.17)
2004	(0.15)	(1.52)	(0.09)	(0.46)

Interim Dividends (Per Share)

Amt	Decl	Ex	Rec	Pay
0.125Q	5/19/2004	6/1/2004	6/3/2004	6/24/2004
0.125Q	7/15/2004	8/31/2004	9/2/2004	9/23/2004
0.125Q	10/21/2004	11/29/2004	12/1/2004	12/22/2004
0.125Q	2/16/2005	3/1/2005	3/3/2005	3/24/2005
		Indicated Div: $0.50		

Valuation Analysis

Forecast P/E	23.15	No of Institutions	
	(4/7/2005)	462	
Market Cap	$19.1 Billion	Shares	
Book Value	3.9 Billion	359,230,496	
Price/Book	4.86	% Held	
Price/Sales	0.93	71.21	

TRADING VOLUME (thousand shares)

Business Summary: Construction - Public Infrastructure (MIC: 3.1 SIC: 611 NAIC: 37310)

Halliburton provides a variety of services, products, maintenance, engineering and construction to energy, industrial and governmental customers worldwide. Co.'s Energy Services Group provides a range of services and products for the exploration, development and production of oil and gas. The Energy Services Group is comprised of the drilling and formation evaluation segment, the fluids segment, the production optimization segment, and the Landmark and other energy services segment. Co.'s Engineering and Construction Group segment, operating as KBR, provides a range of services to energy and industrial customers and governmental entities worldwide.

Recent Developments: For the year ended Dec 31 2004, income from continuing operations increased 13.6% to $385,000 thousand from income of $339,000 thousand a year earlier. Net loss was $979,000 thousand versus net loss of $820,000 thousand a year earlier. Revenues were $20,466,000 thousand, up 25.8% from $16,271,000 thousand the year before. Operating income was $837,000 thousand versus an income of $720,000 thousand in the prior year, an increase of 16.2%. Total direct expense was $19,323,000 thousand versus $15,268,000 thousand in the prior year, an increase of 26.6%. Total indirect expense was $306,000 thousand versus $283,000 thousand in the prior year, an increase of 8.1%.

Prospects: Prospects are mixed as Co. continues to experience lower activity on government services projects in the Middle East with KBR. Co. noted that KBR's backlog at Dec 31 2004 was $8.40 billion, down approximately $900.0 million from Sep 30 2004. Conversely, Co. is seeing growing revenue momentum within its Energy Services Group, supported by increased drilling and exploration activity both in the U.S. and abroad. Looking ahead, Co. expects customer spending in this area to continue to increase in 2005 and beyond. Co. also recently noted that its asbestos exposure has ended with the recent settlement with asbestos claimants.

Financial Data

(US$ in Thousands)	12/31/2004	12/31/2003	12/31/2002	12/31/2001	12/31/2000	12/31/1999	12/31/1998	12/31/1997
Earnings Per Share	(2.22)	(1.88)	(2.31)	1.88	1.12	0.99	(0.03)	1.75
Cash Flow Per Share	2.12	(1.79)	3.62	2.40	(0.13)	0.53	1.03	2.15
Tang Book Value Per Share	7.10	4.28	6.50	9.29	7.80	7.96	7.48	8.62
Dividends Per Share	0.500	0.500	0.500	0.500	0.500	0.500	0.500	0.500
Dividend Payout %	...	...	...	26.60	44.64	50.51	...	28.57
Income Statement								
Total Revenue	20,466,000	16,271,000	12,572,000	13,046,000	11,944,000	14,898,000	17,353,100	8,818,600
EBITDA	1,345,000	1,239,000	358,000	1,605,000	959,000	1,222,000	974,800	1,106,800
Depn & Amortn	509,000	518,000	505,000	531,000	503,000	599,000	587,000	309,500
Income Before Taxes	651,000	612,000	(228,000)	954,000	335,000	555,000	278,800	766,300
Income Taxes	241,000	234,000	80,000	384,000	129,000	214,000	244,400	300,000
Net Income	(979,000)	(820,000)	(998,000)	809,000	501,000	438,000	(14,700)	454,400
Average Shares	441,000	437,000	432,000	430,000	446,000	443,000	438,800	259,500
Balance Sheet								
Current Assets	9,962,000	7,919,000	5,560,000	5,573,000	5,568,000	6,022,000	6,083,100	2,971,600
Total Assets	15,796,000	15,463,000	12,844,000	10,966,000	10,103,000	10,728,000	11,112,000	5,603,000
Current Liabilities	7,064,000	6,542,000	3,272,000	2,908,000	3,826,000	3,693,000	4,003,700	1,772,900
Long-Term Obligations	3,593,000	3,415,000	1,181,000	1,403,000	1,049,000	1,056,000	1,369,700	538,900
Total Liabilities	11,756,000	12,816,000	9,286,000	6,214,000	6,175,000	6,441,000	7,050,800	3,018,300
Stockholders' Equity	3,932,000	2,547,000	3,558,000	4,752,000	3,928,000	4,287,000	4,061,200	2,584,700
Shares Outstanding	442,000	439,000	436,000	434,000	427,000	442,000	440,000	262,300
Statistical Record								
Return on Assets %	N.M.	N.M.	N.M.	7.68	4.80	4.01	N.M.	9.05
Return on Equity %	N.M.	N.M.	N.M.	18.64	12.16	10.49	N.M.	19.16
EBITDA Margin %	6.57	7.61	2.85	12.30	8.03	8.20	5.62	12.55
Net Margin %	N.M.	N.M.	N.M.	6.20	4.19	2.94	N.M.	5.15
Asset Turnover	1.31	1.15	1.06	1.24	1.14	1.36	2.08	1.76
Current Ratio	1.41	1.21	1.70	1.92	1.46	1.63	1.52	1.68
Debt to Equity	0.91	1.34	0.33	0.30	0.27	0.25	0.34	0.21
Price Range	41.35-26.00	27.12-17.78	21.00-9.10	49.20-12.00	54.69-33.38	51.44-28.25	57.00-26.19	62.69-30.00
P/E Ratio	...	...	...	26.17-6.38	48.83-29.80	51.96-28.54	...	35.82-17.14
Average Yield %	1.57	2.22	3.20	1.51	1.16	1.26	1.24	1.16

Address: 5 Houston Center, 1401 McKinney, Suite 2400, Houston, TX 77010 Telephone: (713) 676-3011	Web Site: www.halliburton.com Officers: David J. Lesar - Chmn., Pres., C.E.O. C. Christpher Gaut - Exec. V.P., C.F.O.	Auditors: KPMG LLP Investor Contact: 214-978-2691

HANOVER COMPRESSOR CO. (HOLDING CO.)

Exchange	Symbol	Price	52Wk Range	Yield	P/E
NYS	HC	$12.07 (3/31/2005)	14.72-10.26	N/A	N/A

*7 Year Price Score 60.96   *NYSE Composite Index=100   *12 Month Price Score 97.41

Interim Earnings (Per Share)

Qtr.	Mar	Jun	Sep	Dec
2001	0.26	0.31	0.29	0.09
2002	0.06	(0.70)	0.11	(0.94)
2003	(0.66)	0.00	(1.35)	(0.88)
2004	(0.11)	(0.11)	(0.06)	(0.24)

Interim Dividends (Per Share)

No Dividends Paid

Valuation Analysis

Forecast P/E	0.00	No of Institutions
	(4/7/2005)	146
Market Cap	$1.0 Billion	Shares
Book Value	760.1 Million	66,528,504
Price/Book	1.38	% Held
Price/Sales	0.88	76.42

Business Summary: General Construction Supplies & Services (MIC: 3.3 SIC: 359 NAIC: 32412)

Hanover Compressor is engaged in the global natural gas compression business and is also a provider of service, fabrication and equipment for oil and natural gas processing and transportation applications. Co. sells and rents this equipment and provides operation and maintenance services, for both customer-owned equipment and its fleet of rental equipment. Co.'s maintenance business, together with its parts and service business, provides outsourcing services to customers that own their own equipment. Co. also fabricates compressor and oil and gas production and processing equipment and provides gas processing and treating, and oilfield power generation services.

Recent Developments: For the year ended Dec 31 2004, loss from continuing operations was $54,091 thousand compared with a loss of $117,488 thousand a year earlier. Net loss was $44,006 thousand versus net loss of $208,259 thousand a year earlier. Revenues were $1,188,595 thousand, up 10.6% from $1,075,080 thousand the year before. Total direct expense was $731,545 thousand versus $686,819 thousand in the prior year, an increase of 6.5%. Total indirect expense was $344,211 thousand versus $407,491 thousand in the prior year, a decrease of 15.5%.

Prospects: Looking ahead, Co. indicated that it intends to focus on improving its operating margins and fleet utilization, reducing interest costs through continued debt reduction, while growing its business prudently. Co.'s compression horsepower utilization rate as of Dec 31 2004, on a total horsepower basis, was about 81.9%, an increase over utilization of approximately 81.5% at Sep 30 2004 and 80.9% at Dec 31 2003. Thus, for 2005 Co. anticipates earnings before interest, taxes, depreciation and amortization from continuing operations to be between $280.0 million and $320.0 million. Co. also anticipates capital expenditures for 2005 to be in the $125.0 million to $150.0 million range.

Financial Data (US$ in Thousands)	12/31/2004	12/31/2003	12/31/2002	12/31/2001	12/31/2000	12/31/1999	12/31/1998	12/31/1997
Earnings Per Share	(0.52)	(2.57)	(1.46)	0.95	0.88	1.32	1.01	0.66
Cash Flow Per Share	1.55	2.03	2.46	2.13	0.12	2.39	1.10	1.26
Tang Book Value Per Share	6.57	6.88	8.96	10.07	7.49	12.84	11.08	10.16
Income Statement								
Total Revenue	1,188,595	1,095,350	1,028,810	1,078,209	603,829	317,028	281,957	198,798
EBITDA	145,976	64,834	58,762	196,344	141,272	100,923	86,790	57,856
Depn & Amortn	175,300	172,600	151,181	78,934	47,802	37,337	37,154	28,439
Income Before Taxes	(29,324)	(107,766)	(92,419)	117,410	93,470	63,586	49,636	29,417
Income Taxes	24,767	784	(17,576)	44,609	34,771	23,145	19,259	11,314
Net Income	(44,006)	(208,259)	(116,068)	72,637	58,699	40,441	30,377	18,103
Average Shares	84,792	81,123	79,500	81,175	71,192	30,527	30,091	27,345
Balance Sheet								
Current Assets	548,838	544,002	581,088	615,854	498,255	192,532	165,056	94,789
Total Assets	2,762,163	2,918,466	2,154,029	2,272,966	1,289,521	756,510	614,590	506,452
Current Liabilities	245,728	288,760	369,003	340,030	188,313	84,566	51,792	36,762
Long-Term Obligations	1,637,080	1,746,793	521,203	504,260	110,935	69,681	156,943	158,838
Total Liabilities	1,983,330	2,136,350	1,140,010	1,143,513	563,278	301,103	297,877	218,181
Stockholders' Equity	760,055	753,488	927,626	1,043,203	639,993	369,157	316,713	288,271
Shares Outstanding	86,992	82,396	80,562	79,228	66,454	28,752	28,590	28,367
Statistical Record								
Return on Assets %	N.M.	N.M.	N.M.	4.08	5.72	5.90	5.42	4.27
Return on Equity %	N.M.	N.M.	N.M.	8.63	11.60	11.79	10.04	7.78
EBITDA Margin %	12.28	5.92	5.71	18.21	23.40	31.83	30.78	29.10
Net Margin %	N.M.	N.M.	N.M.	6.74	9.72	12.76	10.77	9.11
Asset Turnover	0.42	0.43	0.46	0.61	0.59	0.46	0.50	0.47
Current Ratio	2.23	1.88	1.57	1.81	2.65	2.28	3.19	2.58
Debt to Equity	2.15	2.32	0.56	0.48	0.17	0.19	0.50	0.55
Price Range	14.60-10.26	12.19-6.00	25.26-6.60	41.75-19.45	45.13-17.00	19.06-9.78	14.63-8.84	13.00-8.91
P/E Ratio	...	...	...	43.95-20.47	51.28-19.32	14.44-7.41	14.48-8.76	19.70-13.49

Address: 12001 North Houston Rosslyn, Houston, TX 77086
Telephone: (281) 447-8787
Fax: (281) 441-0821

Web Site: www.hanover-co.com
Officers: John E. Jackson - C.F.O. Chad C. Deaton - Pres., C.E.O.

Auditors: PricewaterhouseCoopers LLP
Investor Contact: 281-447-8787
Transfer Agents: Mellon Shareholder Services, LLC, South Hackensack, NY

HARLEY-DAVIDSON, INC.

Exchange	Symbol	Price	52Wk Range	Yield	P/E	Div Acheiver
NYS	HDI	$57.76 (3/31/2005)	62.97-52.54	0.87	19.25	11 Years

*7 Year Price Score 119.52 *NYSE Composite Index=100 *12 Month Price Score 95.51

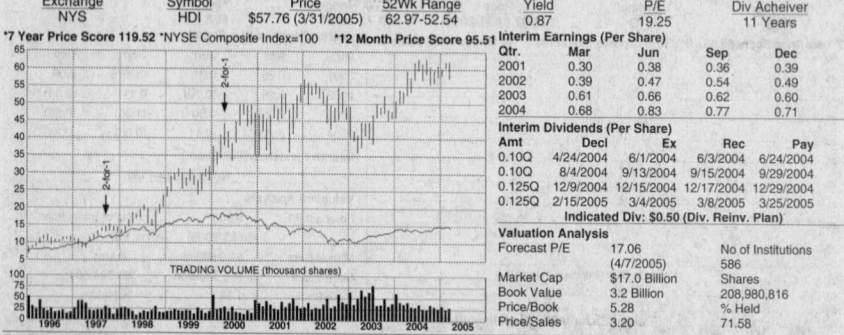

Interim Earnings (Per Share)

Qtr.	Mar	Jun	Sep	Dec
2001	0.30	0.38	0.36	0.39
2002	0.39	0.47	0.54	0.49
2003	0.61	0.66	0.62	0.60
2004	0.68	0.83	0.77	0.71

Interim Dividends (Per Share)

Amt	Decl	Ex	Rec	Pay
0.10Q	4/24/2004	6/1/2004	6/3/2004	6/24/2004
0.10Q	8/4/2004	9/13/2004	9/15/2004	9/29/2004
0.125Q	12/9/2004	12/15/2004	12/17/2004	12/29/2004
0.125Q	2/15/2005	3/4/2005	3/8/2005	3/25/2005

Indicated Div: $0.50 (Div. Reinv. Plan)

Valuation Analysis

Forecast P/E	17.06 (4/7/2005)
Market Cap	$17.0 Billion
Book Value	3.2 Billion
Price/Book	5.28
Price/Sales	3.20

No of Institutions	586
Shares	208,980,816
% Held	71.58

Business Summary: Automotive (MIC: 15.1 SIC: 751 NAIC: 36991)

Harley-Davidson is a motorcycle manufacturer. Co.'s Motorcycles and Related Products segment designs, manufactures and sells primarily heavyweight touring, custom and performance motorcycles as well as a full line of motorcycle parts, accessories, clothing and collectibles. Co.'s motorcycle brands include Harley-Davidson® and Buell®. The Financial Services segment, consisting of Co.'s subsidiary Harley-Davidson Financial Services, Inc. and its subsidiaries, provides financing and servicing of wholesale inventory receivables and retail loans, primarily for the purchase of motorcycles, as well as property/casualty insurance and extended service contracts through certain unaffiliated carriers.

Recent Developments: For the year ended Dec 31 2004, net income increased 16.9% to $889,766 thousand from net income of $760,928 thousand a year earlier. Revenues were $5,320,452 thousand, up 8.5% from $4,903,733 thousand the year before. Operating income was $1,361,491 thousand versus an income of $1,149,264 thousand in the prior year, an increase of 18.5%. Total direct expense was $3,232,317 thousand versus $3,070,294 thousand in the prior year, an increase of 5.3%. Total indirect expense was $726,644 thousand versus $684,175 thousand in the prior year, an increase of 6.2%.

Prospects: Results continue to improve as Co. increases motorcycle availability to obtain higher customer satisfaction and by stimulating interest among perspective customers. U.S. retail sales for Harley-Davidson motorcycles more than 7.0% in 2004. Co. expects to continue to grow in 2005 and ship 339,000 Harley-Davidson motorcycles during the year to support this growth. This is consistent with Co.'s established goals of satisfying demand for 400,000 motorcycles in 2007 and generating an annual earnings growth rate in the mid-teens. In addition, Co. expects growth for parts and accessories revenue to be slightly higher and general merchandise revenue to be lower than motorcycle unit growth.

Financial Data
(US$ in Thousands)

	12/31/2004	12/31/2003	12/31/2002	12/31/2001	12/31/2000	12/31/1999	12/31/1998	12/31/1997
Earnings Per Share	3.00	2.50	1.90	1.43	1.13	0.86	0.69	0.56
Cash Flow Per Share	3.28	3.10	2.58	2.50	1.86	1.37	1.04	1.02
Tang Book Value Per Share	10.73	9.63	7.21	5.64	4.47	3.65	3.20	2.59
Dividends Per Share	0.405	0.195	0.135	0.115	0.098	0.087	0.077	0.068
Dividend Payout %	13.50	7.80	7.11	8.04	8.63	10.12	11.23	11.95
Income Statement								
Total Revenue	5,320,452	4,903,733	4,302,470	3,544,959	2,943,543	2,480,624	2,084,167	1,774,924
EBITDA	1,570,497	1,339,865	1,045,064	809,038	664,321	526,601	419,823	338,609
Depn & Amortn	214,112	196,918	175,778	153,061	133,348	113,822	87,422	70,178
Income Before Taxes	1,379,486	1,166,035	885,827	673,455	548,556	420,793	336,229	276,302
Income Taxes	489,720	405,107	305,610	235,709	200,843	153,592	122,729	102,232
Net Income	889,766	760,928	580,217	437,746	347,713	267,201	213,500	174,070
Average Shares	296,852	304,470	305,158	306,248	307,470	309,714	309,406	307,896
Balance Sheet								
Current Assets	3,266,272	2,729,127	2,066,586	1,665,264	1,297,264	948,994	844,963	704,021
Total Assets	5,483,293	4,923,088	3,861,217	3,118,495	2,436,404	2,112,077	1,920,209	1,598,901
Current Liabilities	1,172,696	955,773	990,052	716,110	497,743	518,154	468,515	361,688
Long-Term Obligations	800,000	670,000	380,000	380,000	355,000	280,000	280,000	280,000
Total Liabilities	2,264,822	1,965,396	1,628,302	1,362,212	1,030,749	950,997	890,298	772,233
Stockholders' Equity	3,218,471	2,957,692	2,232,915	1,756,283	1,405,655	1,161,080	1,029,911	826,668
Shares Outstanding	294,310	301,510	302,662	302,789	302,070	302,722	305,862	304,650
Statistical Record								
Return on Assets %	17.05	17.32	16.63	15.76	15.25	13.25	12.13	11.93
Return on Equity %	28.73	29.32	29.09	27.69	27.02	24.39	23.00	23.37
EBITDA Margin %	29.52	27.32	24.29	22.82	22.57	21.23	20.14	19.08
Net Margin %	16.72	15.52	13.49	12.35	11.81	10.77	10.24	9.81
Asset Turnover	1.02	1.12	1.23	1.28	1.29	1.23	1.18	1.22
Current Ratio	2.79	2.86	2.09	2.33	2.61	1.83	1.80	1.95
Debt to Equity	0.25	0.23	0.17	0.22	0.25	0.24	0.27	0.34
Price Range	62.97-46.00	52.45-35.95	57.00-42.83	55.66-35.19	50.00-29.63	32.03-23.22	23.69-12.56	15.38-8.47
P/E Ratio	20.99-15.33	20.98-14.38	30.00-22.54	38.92-24.61	44.25-26.22	37.25-27.00	34.33-18.21	27.46-15.12
Average Yield %	0.71	0.44	0.27	0.25	0.24	0.31	0.45	0.56

Address: 3700 West Juneau Avenue, Milwaukee, WI 53208 **Telephone:** (414) 342-4680 **Fax:** (414) 343-4621	**Web Site:** www.harley-davidson.com **Officers:** Jeffrey L. Bleustein - Chmn., C.E.O. James M. Brostowitz - V.P., Treas., Contr.	**Auditors:** Ernst & Young LLP **Investor Contact:** 877-437-8625 **Transfer Agents:** Computershare Investor Services, LLC, Chicago, IL

HARMAN INTERNATIONAL INDUSTRIES, INC.

Exchange	Symbol	Price	52Wk Range	Yield	P/E
NYS	HAR	$88.46 (3/31/2005)	130.72-71.44	0.06	31.82

*7 Year Price Score 251.11 *NYSE Composite Index=100   *12 Month Price Score 98.65

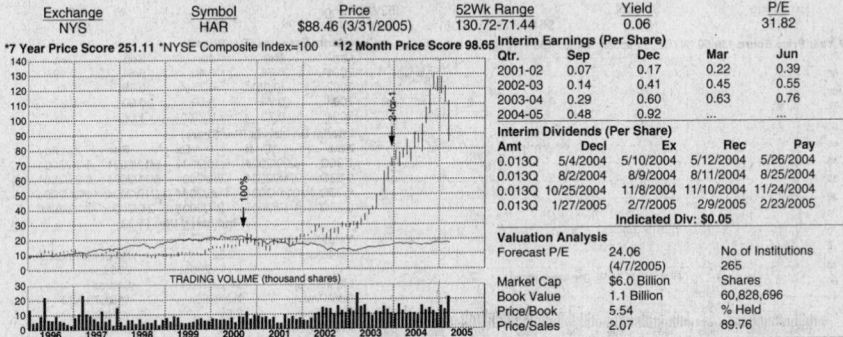

Interim Earnings (Per Share)

Qtr.	Sep	Dec	Mar	Jun
2001-02	0.07	0.17	0.22	0.39
2002-03	0.14	0.41	0.45	0.55
2003-04	0.29	0.60	0.63	0.76
2004-05	0.48	0.92	...	...

Interim Dividends (Per Share)

Amt	Decl	Ex	Rec	Pay
0.013Q	5/4/2004	5/10/2004	5/12/2004	5/26/2004
0.013Q	8/2/2004	8/9/2004	8/11/2004	8/25/2004
0.013Q	10/25/2004	11/8/2004	11/10/2004	11/24/2004
0.013Q	1/27/2005	2/7/2005	2/9/2005	2/23/2005

Indicated Div: $0.05

Valuation Analysis

Forecast P/E	24.06	No of Institutions	
	(4/7/2005)	265	
Market Cap	$6.0 Billion	Shares	60,828,696
Book Value	1.1 Billion	% Held	89.76
Price/Book	5.54		
Price/Sales	2.07		

Business Summary: Electrical (MIC: 11.14 SIC: 651 NAIC: 34310)

Harman International is engaged in the manufacture of audio and electronic products for consumer and professional use. Co.'s businesses are organized into the Consumer Systems group and Professional Group. Consumer Systems Group designs, manufactures and markets loudspeakers and audio, video and electronic products systems for home, vehicle, and computer applications. Professional Group designs, manufactures and markets loudspeakers, microphones, electronics and systems used by audio professionals in concert halls, stadiums, airports and other buildings and for recording, broadcast, cinema and music reproduction applications.

Recent Developments: For the quarter ended Dec 31 2004, net income increased 57.8% to $65,425 thousand from net income of $41,472 thousand in the year-earlier quarter. Revenues were $788,587 thousand, up 14.0% from $691,611 thousand the year before. Operating income was $99,512 thousand versus an income of $65,891 thousand in the prior-year quarter, an increase of 51.0%. Total direct expense was $510,097 thousand versus $472,297 thousand in the prior-year quarter, an increase of 8.0%. Total indirect expense was $178,978 thousand versus $153,423 thousand in the prior-year quarter, an increase of 16.7%.

Prospects: Co. is seeing steady growth within its Consumer Systems Group, fueled by increased sales of automotive infotainment systems and increased sales of branded automotive audio systems. Meanwhile, during the second quarter, Co. acquired QNX Software Systems, a provider of real time operating system software, development tools, and services for embedded design systems, for about $139.0 million. The acquisition further strengthens Co.'s software capabilities and enables it to develop the next generation of infotainment systems for car, home and computer applications. Accordingly, Co. now expects earnings for 2005 of $3.00 per share. For fiscal 2006, Co. expects earnings per share of $3.55.

Financial Data

(US$ in Thousands)	6 Mos	3 Mos	06/30/2004	06/30/2003	06/30/2002	06/30/2001	06/30/2000	06/30/1999
Earnings Per Share	2.78	2.46	2.27	1.55	0.85	0.48	1.03	0.16
Cash Flow Per Share	6.96	7.15	7.31	3.87	2.89	0.84	2.82	1.82
Tang Book Value Per Share	10.41	10.15	9.43	6.66	5.03	4.33	4.69	4.61
Dividends Per Share	0.050	0.050	0.050	0.050	0.050	0.050	0.050	0.050
Dividend Payout %	1.80	2.03	2.20	3.23	5.88	10.42	4.85	30.77
Income Statement								
Total Revenue	1,480,293	691,706	2,711,374	2,228,519	1,826,188	1,716,547	1,677,939	1,500,135
EBITDA	218,721	85,826	350,759	253,637	180,667	137,250	185,954	104,868
Depn & Amortn	61,498	27,416	106,032	88,545	78,084	67,201	64,618	66,780
Income Before Taxes	151,256	55,043	227,520	142,471	80,177	45,099	102,829	14,447
Income Taxes	52,159	21,371	69,637	37,043	22,602	12,703	29,923	2,706
Net Income	99,097	33,672	157,883	105,428	57,513	32,364	72,838	11,723
Average Shares	70,942	70,227	69,487	68,048	67,806	67,474	70,600	72,244
Balance Sheet								
Current Assets	1,137,087	1,199,554	1,204,035	967,624	876,763	708,871	671,026	646,609
Total Assets	2,139,717	1,995,830	1,988,810	1,703,658	1,480,280	1,162,385	1,137,505	1,065,755
Current Liabilities	643,318	660,719	662,354	487,410	433,471	350,155	361,381	286,821
Long-Term Obligations	335,450	339,039	387,616	497,759	470,424	343,822	254,818	280,414
Total Liabilities	1,057,778	1,066,287	1,113,814	1,047,873	953,651	739,443	651,172	597,568
Stockholders' Equity	1,081,939	929,543	874,996	655,785	526,629	422,942	486,333	468,187
Shares Outstanding	67,741	66,506	66,090	65,219	65,046	64,121	68,125	71,028
Statistical Record								
Return on Assets %	9.80	9.18	8.53	6.62	4.35	2.81	6.59	1.07
Return on Equity %	21.09	21.19	20.57	17.83	12.11	7.12	15.22	2.39
EBITDA Margin %	14.78	12.41	12.94	11.38	9.89	8.00	11.08	6.99
Net Margin %	6.69	4.87	5.82	4.73	3.15	1.89	4.34	0.78
Asset Turnover	1.45	1.50	1.46	1.40	1.38	1.49	1.52	1.37
Current Ratio	1.77	1.82	1.82	1.99	2.02	2.02	1.86	2.25
Debt to Equity	0.31	0.36	0.44	0.76	0.89	0.81	0.52	0.60
Price Range	130.72-68.31	107.75-49.17	91.00-39.32	39.79-19.14	30.32-15.45	24.00-12.40	16.81-9.45	11.67-7.88
P/E Ratio	47.02-24.57	43.80-19.99	40.09-17.32	25.67-12.35	35.68-18.17	50.00-25.83	16.32-9.18	72.95-49.22
Average Yield %	0.05	0.06	0.08	0.17	0.22	0.29	0.38	0.51

Address: 1101 Pennsylvania Avenue, NW, Suite 1010, Washington, DC 20004 Telephone: (202) 393-1101 Fax: (202) 393-3064	Web Site: www.harman.com Officers: Sidney Harman - Exec. Chmn. Bernard A. Girod - Vice-Chmn., C.E.O.	Auditors: KPMG LLP Transfer Agents: Mellon Investor Services, Los Angeles, CA

HARRAH'S ENTERTAINMENT, INC.

Exchange	Symbol	Price	52Wk Range	Yield	P/E
NYS	HET	$64.58 (3/31/2005)	69.74-44.20	2.04	19.81

*7 Year Price Score 139.50 *NYSE Composite Index=100   *12 Month Price Score 108.05

Interim Earnings (Per Share)

Qtr.	Mar	Jun	Sep	Dec
2001	0.38	0.40	0.54	0.49
2002	(0.05)	0.75	0.89	0.48
2003	0.74	0.69	0.90	0.32
2004	0.73	0.79	1.06	0.68

Interim Dividends (Per Share)

Amt	Decl	Ex	Rec	Pay
0.30Q	4/29/2004	5/10/2004	5/12/2004	5/26/2004
0.33Q	7/15/2004	8/9/2004	8/11/2004	8/25/2004
0.33Q	10/20/2004	11/8/2004	11/10/2004	11/24/2004
0.33Q	1/19/2005	2/7/2005	2/9/2005	2/23/2005

Indicated Div: $1.32

Valuation Analysis

Forecast P/E	20.82	No of Institutions
	(4/13/2005)	336
Market Cap	$7.2 Billion	Shares
Book Value	2.0 Billion	119,078,632
Price/Book	3.69	% Held
Price/Sales	1.58	N/A

Business Summary: Sporting & Recreational (MIC: 13.5 SIC: 999 NAIC: 13210)

Harrah's Entertainment, as of Feb 4 2004, operated 25 casinos nationwide under the Harrah's, Showboat, Rio, and Player brand names. Co. conducts its business through a wholly-owned subsidiary, Harrah's Operating Company, Inc. (HOC). Co.'s principal asset is the stock of HOC, which holds, directly or indirectly through subsidiaries, substantially all of the assets of Co.'s businesses. Co.'s U.S. markets include Atlantic City, Las Vegas, Reno, Shreveport, North Kansas City, Laughlin and others. Co. competes in all four segments of the casino industry: traditional land-based casinos, riverboat and dockside casinos, limited stakes casinos and casinos for Indian communities.

Recent Developments: For the year ended Dec 31 2004, income from continuing operations was $329.5 million compared with income of $261.1 million a year earlier. Results for 2004 included merger and integration costs for Co.'s Caesars Entertainment, Inc. acquisition of $2.3 million. Results for 2003 included losses from the early extinguishment of debt of $19.1 million. Net revenues rose 15.2% to $4.55 billion from $3.95 billion in 2003. Co. attributed the increased revenue primarily to the acquisition of Horseshoe Gaming on Jul 1 2004, strong results from its properties in Southern Nevada and organic growth at most of its properties. Income from operations was $791.1 million, 16.5% higher than the year before.

Prospects: Co. is performing well, supported by strong market conditions and robust cross-market play at Co.'s three Southern Nevada properties. However, this was partially offset by a month-long labor strike at Co.'s two Atlantic City, NV properties. Going forward, Co.'s implementation of marketing and customer-service initiatives, such as Total Rewards 2, strategic capital investments in existing properties and the acquisition of Horseshoe Gaming Holding Corp. should set the stage for sustainable long-term growth. Meanwhile, Co. remains optimistic that it will be able to complete its acquisition of Caesars Entertainment, Inc. in the second quarter of 2005.

Financial Data

(US$ in Thousands)	9 Mos	6 Mos	3 Mos	12/31/2003	12/31/2002	12/31/2001	12/31/2000	12/31/1999
Earnings Per Share	2.90	2.73	2.63	2.65	2.07	1.81	(0.10)	1.62
Cash Flow Per Share	7.96	6.22	7.12	6.77	6.64	6.82	4.66	4.08
Tang Book Value Per Share	N.M.	4.68	5.12	4.65	2.50	1.88	4.04	5.88
Dividends Per Share	1.230	1.200	0.900	0.600	...	...	...	...
Dividend Payout %	42.46	43.95	34.19	22.64	...	...	...	...
Income Statement								
Total Revenue	3,359,261	2,238,172	1,109,166	4,322,722	4,136,393	3,709,040	3,471,150	3,024,428
EBITDA	893,540	568,263	274,645	1,052,694	1,113,874	941,856	568,714	711,465
Depn & Amortn	262,022	173,739	84,372	342,557	331,696	332,672	282,110	218,299
Income Before Taxes	436,015	277,424	132,027	475,718	535,900	348,343	17,839	359,583
Income Taxes	160,073	101,431	48,206	172,201	197,292	126,737	15,415	128,914
Net Income	290,753	171,968	81,731	292,623	235,029	208,967	(12,060)	208,470
Average Shares	112,513	113,573	112,614	110,403	113,534	115,708	117,190	128,748
Balance Sheet								
Current Assets	696,103	667,482	618,391	684,637	686,237	617,698	583,433	486,669
Total Assets	8,303,952	6,693,622	6,662,201	6,578,844	6,350,049	6,128,582	5,166,085	4,766,847
Current Liabilities	796,147	690,802	660,003	582,962	626,455	568,908	778,503	371,571
Long-Term Obligations	4,956,007	3,563,949	3,580,095	3,671,889	3,763,066	3,719,443	2,835,846	2,540,268
Total Liabilities	6,313,148	4,788,652	4,778,862	4,790,415	4,839,000	4,723,147	3,877,653	3,261,621
Stockholders' Equity	1,958,098	1,871,380	1,851,536	1,738,440	1,471,008	1,374,113	1,269,718	1,486,277
Shares Outstanding	111,956	111,909	112,428	110,889	109,708	112,322	115,952	124,379
Statistical Record								
Return on Assets %	4.42	4.68	4.52	4.53	3.77	3.70	N.M.	5.18
Return on Equity %	17.74	17.41	17.18	18.24	16.52	15.81	N.M.	17.84
EBITDA Margin %	26.60	25.39	24.76	24.35	26.93	25.39	16.38	23.52
Net Margin %	8.66	7.68	7.37	6.77	5.68	5.63	N.M.	6.89
Asset Turnover	0.62	0.67	0.67	0.67	0.66	0.66	0.70	0.75
Current Ratio	0.87	0.97	0.94	1.17	1.10	1.09	0.75	1.31
Debt to Equity	2.53	1.90	1.93	2.11	2.56	2.71	2.23	1.71
Price Range	57.42-41.10	57.42-39.50	55.28-34.71	49.77-30.75	50.95-35.61	38.08-22.93	29.75-17.38	29.75-14.38
P/E Ratio	19.80-14.17	21.03-14.47	21.02-13.20	18.78-11.60	24.61-17.20	21.04-12.67	...	18.36-8.87
Average Yield %	2.46	2.49	2.01	1.48	...	...	...	...

Address: One Harrah's Court, Las Vegas, NV 89119	**Web Site:** www.harrahs.com	**Auditors:** Deloitte & Touche LLP
Telephone: (702) 407-6000	**Officers:** Gary W. Loveman - Chmn., Pres., C.E.O. Charles L. Atwood - Sr. V.P., C.F.O.	**Transfer Agents:** The Bank of New York, New York , NY

HARRIS CORP.

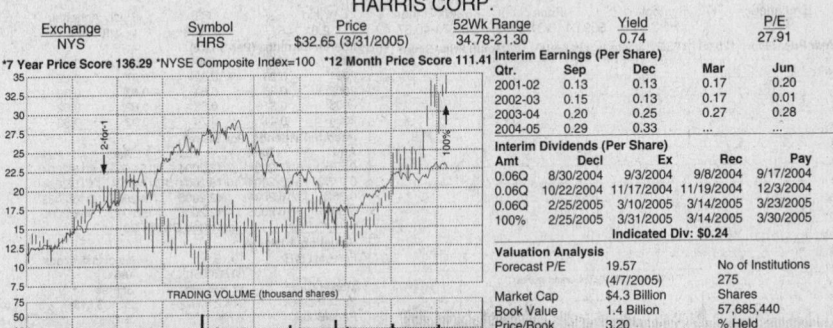

Exchange	Symbol	Price	52Wk Range	Yield	P/E
NYS	HRS	$32.65 (3/31/2005)	34.78-21.30	0.74	27.91

*7 Year Price Score 136.29 *NYSE Composite Index=100 ***12 Month Price Score 111.41**

Interim Earnings (Per Share)

Qtr.	Sep	Dec	Mar	Jun
2001-02	0.13	0.13	0.17	0.20
2002-03	0.15	0.13	0.17	0.01
2003-04	0.20	0.25	0.27	0.28
2004-05	0.29	0.33	...	...

Interim Dividends (Per Share)

Amt	Decl	Ex	Rec	Pay
0.06Q	8/30/2004	9/3/2004	9/8/2004	9/17/2004
0.06Q	10/22/2004	11/17/2004	11/19/2004	12/3/2004
0.06Q	2/25/2005	3/10/2005	3/14/2005	3/23/2005
100%	2/25/2005	3/31/2005	3/14/2005	3/30/2005

Indicated Div: $0.24

Valuation Analysis

Forecast P/E	19.57	No of Institutions	
	(4/7/2005)	275	
Market Cap	$4.3 Billion	Shares	
Book Value	1.4 Billion	57,685,440	
Price/Book	3.20	% Held	
Price/Sales	1.57	86.66	

Business Summary: Instruments and Related Products (MIC: 11.15 SIC: 812 NAIC: 34511)

Harris, along with its subsidiaries, is an international communications technology company focused on providing assured communications™ products, systems and services for government and commercial customers. Co. structures its operations around the following four business segments: Government Communications Systems, RF Communications, Microwave Communications and Broadcast Communications. Co.'s operating divisions serve markets for government communications, tactical radio, broadcast, and microwave systems. As of July 2 2004, Co. sold its products in more than 150 countries. .

Recent Developments: For the quarter ended Dec 31 2004, net income increased 36.3% to $45,100 thousand from net income of $33,100 thousand in the year-earlier quarter. Revenues were $737,200 thousand, up 24.1% from $593,900 thousand the year before. Total direct expense was $540,200 thousand versus $440,400 thousand in the prior-year quarter, an increase of 22.7%. Total indirect expense was $127,200 thousand versus $104,900 thousand in the prior-year quarter, an increase of 21.3%.

Prospects: Going forward, Co. expects to benefit from a growing pipeline in its RF Communications business. For instance, in the domestic market, the anticipated supplemental U.S. defense budget is expected to provide immediate additional radio funding for the U.S. Army's Modularity program, as well as requirements for the U.S. Marine Corps, Army Reserve, and National Guard. Co. is also encouraged by solid growth in its Broadcast business, and the expanded market presence and opportunities expected from the acquisition of Encoda. As a result, Co. raised its fiscal year 2005 earnings guidance to a range of $2.85 to $2.95 per diluted share.

Financial Data

(US$ in Thousands)	6 Mos	3 Mos	07/02/2004	06/27/2003	06/28/2002	06/29/2001	06/30/2000	07/02/1999
Earnings Per Share	1.17	1.07	1.00	0.45	0.63	0.16	0.13	0.34
Cash Flow Per Share	1.72	1.44	2.01	1.15	1.57	(0.20)	0.45	1.60
Tang Book Value Per Share	5.13	7.85	7.95	7.19	7.04	6.83	8.76	9.52
Dividends Per Share	0.220	0.210	0.200	0.160	0.100	0.100	0.195	0.480
Dividend Payout %	18.84	19.54	20.10	35.56	16.00	62.50	156.00	143.28
Income Statement								
Total Revenue	1,406,600	669,400	2,518,600	2,092,700	1,875,800	1,955,100	1,807,400	1,743,500
EBITDA	159,400	75,200	253,400	165,300	193,600	173,600	104,900	138,000
Depn & Amortn	27,500	12,600	55,100	56,400	55,100	79,700	68,600	63,500
Income Before Taxes	123,800	58,900	180,000	90,100	125,100	72,400	38,500	78,000
Income Taxes	38,600	18,800	54,300	30,600	42,500	51,000	13,500	28,100
Net Income	85,200	40,100	132,800	59,500	82,600	21,400	18,000	53,100
Average Shares	141,800	140,800	133,800	132,800	132,600	134,000	146,800	159,400
Balance Sheet								
Current Assets	1,196,400	1,482,600	1,553,800	1,357,700	1,153,500	1,222,000	1,629,000	1,031,400
Total Assets	2,325,500	2,224,500	2,225,800	2,080,300	1,858,500	1,959,900	2,326,900	2,958,600
Current Liabilities	552,800	492,400	542,800	495,500	425,600	460,300	555,900	807,300
Long-Term Obligations	401,400	401,400	401,400	401,600	283,000	384,400	382,600	514,500
Total Liabilities	968,900	897,900	947,000	897,100	708,600	844,700	952,600	1,369,100
Stockholders' Equity	1,356,600	1,326,600	1,278,800	1,183,200	1,149,900	1,115,200	1,374,300	1,589,500
Shares Outstanding	133,121	133,448	132,688	132,782	132,684	131,692	137,915	159,301
Statistical Record								
Return on Assets %	7.16	6.66	6.07	3.03	4.34	1.00	0.68	1.58
Return on Equity %	12.34	11.45	10.61	5.11	7.31	1.72	1.22	3.33
EBITDA Margin %	11.33	11.23	10.06	7.90	10.32	8.88	5.80	7.92
Net Margin %	6.06	5.99	5.27	2.84	4.40	1.09	1.00	3.05
Asset Turnover	1.24	1.19	1.15	1.07	0.99	0.91	0.69	0.52
Current Ratio	2.16	3.01	2.86	2.74	2.71	2.65	2.93	1.28
Debt to Equity	0.30	0.30	0.31	0.34	0.25	0.34	0.28	0.32
Price Range	34.12-18.98	28.06-17.70	25.38-14.61	18.34-12.15	19.25-12.89	18.69-10.61	19.50-8.86	18.73-11.61
P/E Ratio	29.16-16.22	26.22-16.55	25.38-14.61	40.76-27.00	30.56-20.45	116.80-66.28	150.00-68.17	55.09-34.16
Average Yield %	0.87	0.94	0.99	1.07	0.61	0.70	1.41	3.16

Address: 1025 West NASA Boulevard, Melbourne, FL 32919 Telephone: (321) 727-9100 Fax: (321) 724-3973	Web Site: www.harris.com Officers: Howard L. Lance - Chmn., Pres., C.E.O. Bryan R. Roub - Sr. V.P., C.F.O.	Auditors: Ernst & Young LLP Investor Contact: 321-727-9383 Transfer Agents: Mellon Investor Services LLC, Ridgefield Park, NJ

HARSCO CORP.

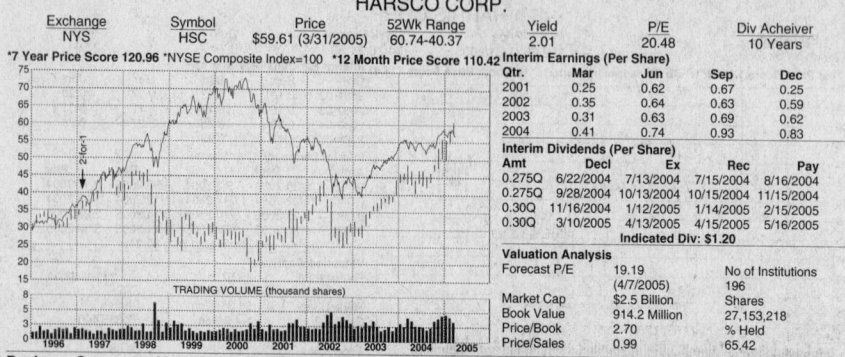

*7 Year Price Score 120.96 *NYSE Composite Index=100 ***12 Month Price Score 110.42**

Interim Earnings (Per Share)

Qtr.	Mar	Jun	Sep	Dec
2001	0.25	0.62	0.67	0.25
2002	0.35	0.64	0.63	0.59
2003	0.31	0.63	0.69	0.62
2004	0.41	0.74	0.93	0.83

Interim Dividends (Per Share)

Amt	Decl	Ex	Rec	Pay
0.275Q	6/22/2004	7/13/2004	7/15/2004	8/16/2004
0.275Q	9/28/2004	10/13/2004	10/15/2004	11/15/2004
0.30Q	11/16/2004	1/12/2005	1/14/2005	2/15/2005
0.30Q	3/10/2005	4/13/2005	4/15/2005	5/16/2005

Indicated Div: $1.20

Valuation Analysis

Forecast P/E	19.19 (4/7/2005)	No of Institutions 196
Market Cap	$2.5 Billion	Shares
Book Value	914.2 Million	27,153,218
Price/Book	2.70	% Held
Price/Sales	0.99	65.42

TRADING VOLUME (thousand shares)

Business Summary: Metal Products (MIC: 11.4 SIC: 449 NAIC: 32312)

Harsco is a diversified multinational provider of industrial services and engineered products. Operations are divided into three primary segments. The Mill Services segment includes the MultiServ Division and provides outsourced, on-site mill services to the global steel and metals industries. The Access Services segment includes the SGB Group and Patent Construction Systems divisions and provides scaffolding, shoring, forming and other access solutions. The Gas Technologies segment's manufacturing and service facilities comprise an integrated manufacturing network for gas containment and control products.

Recent Developments: For the year ended Dec 31 2004, income from continuing operations increased 30.5% to $113,540 thousand from income of $86,999 thousand a year earlier. Net income increased 31.4% to $121,211 thousand from net income of $92,217 thousand a year earlier. Revenues were $2,502,059 thousand, up 18.1% from $2,118,516 thousand the year before. Operating income was $209,849 thousand versus an income of $173,892 thousand in the prior year, an increase of 20.7%. Total direct expense was $1,916,384 thousand versus $1,604,373 thousand in the prior year, an increase of 19.4%. Total indirect expense was $375,826 thousand versus $340,251 thousand in the prior year, an increase of 10.5%.

Prospects: Co. expects continued growth into 2005, as the overall outlook for each of its business units is encouraging. Supported by strong levels of cash flow, Co. expects to make further growth investments in new long-term, high renewal-rate service contracts for the Mill Services business and for growth in the Access Services and Track Technologies rail services businesses. Also, Co. will continue to give consideration to bolt-on acquisitions to further enhance its industrial services growth. For 2005, Co. expects earnings from continuing operations to range from $3.05 to $3.15 per diluted share.

Financial Data
(US$ in Thousands)

	12/31/2004	12/31/2003	12/31/2002	12/31/2001	12/31/2000	12/31/1999	12/31/1998	12/31/1997
Earnings Per Share	2.91	2.25	2.21	1.79	2.42	2.21	2.34	5.67
Cash Flow Per Share	6.56	6.46	6.29	6.03	6.47	5.23	4.15	3.05
Tang Book Value Per Share	11.61	9.03	6.59	8.32	7.66	9.77	9.74	12.71
Dividends Per Share	1.100	1.050	1.000	0.960	0.940	0.900	0.880	0.800
Dividend Payout %	37.80	46.67	45.25	53.63	38.84	40.72	37.61	14.11
Income Statement								
Total Revenue	2,502,059	2,118,516	1,976,732	2,108,474	2,004,741	1,720,811	1,735,394	1,629,121
EBITDA	394,348	343,148	331,995	338,294	351,807	305,589	323,282	296,427
Depn & Amortn	184,371	168,935	155,661	176,531	159,099	135,853	131,381	116,539
Income Before Taxes	171,239	135,902	136,699	113,795	148,591	147,430	179,775	171,611
Income Taxes	49,034	41,708	42,240	36,982	46,805	51,599	67,361	65,213
Net Income	121,211	92,217	90,106	71,725	96,803	90,713	107,513	278,832
Average Shares	41,598	40,973	40,680	40,066	40,022	41,017	45,910	49,192
Balance Sheet								
Current Assets	924,924	764,351	702,402	716,067	726,415	612,955	587,441	713,652
Total Assets	2,389,756	2,138,035	1,999,297	2,090,766	2,180,948	1,659,823	1,623,581	1,477,188
Current Liabilities	578,397	495,075	473,580	474,674	536,179	430,516	474,822	372,492
Long-Term Obligations	594,747	584,425	605,613	720,197	774,450	418,504	309,131	198,898
Total Liabilities	1,475,566	1,361,047	1,354,757	1,404,593	1,506,769	1,009,702	938,282	695,486
Stockholders' Equity	914,190	776,988	644,540	686,173	674,179	650,121	685,299	781,702
Shares Outstanding	41,431	40,866	40,539	39,984	39,805	40,071	42,250	46,746
Statistical Record								
Return on Assets %	5.34	4.46	4.41	3.36	5.03	5.53	6.93	19.91
Return on Equity %	14.30	12.97	13.54	10.55	14.58	13.59	14.66	38.12
EBITDA Margin %	15.76	16.20	16.80	16.04	17.55	17.76	18.63	18.20
Net Margin %	4.84	4.35	4.56	3.40	4.83	5.27	6.20	17.12
Asset Turnover	1.10	1.02	0.97	0.99	1.04	1.05	1.12	1.16
Current Ratio	1.60	1.54	1.48	1.51	1.35	1.42	1.24	1.92
Debt to Equity	0.65	0.75	0.94	1.05	1.15	0.64	0.45	0.25
Price Range	56.01-40.37	44.27-27.74	44.00-24.86	35.91-23.82	31.75-17.69	34.13-23.44	46.69-24.31	47.13-33.56
P/E Ratio	19.25-13.87	19.68-12.33	19.91-11.25	20.06-13.31	13.12-7.31	15.44-10.61	19.95-10.39	8.31-5.92
Average Yield %	2.38	2.96	2.98	3.29	3.61	3.10	2.23	2.00

Address: 350 Poplar Church Road, Camp Hill, PA 17011 **Telephone:** (717) 763-7064 **Fax:** (717) 763-6424	**Web Site:** www.harsco.com **Officers:** Derek C. Hathaway - Chmn., Pres., C.E.O. G. D. H. Butler - Sr. V.P., Oper.	**Auditors:** PricewaterhouseCoopers LLP **Investor Contact:** 717-975-5677

HARTE-HANKS, INC.

Exchange	Symbol	Price	52Wk Range	Yield	P/E
NYS	HHS	$27.56 (3/31/2005)	27.62-22.61	0.73	24.83

*7 Year Price Score 116.47 ***NYSE Composite Index=100** ***12 Month Price Score 99.60**

Interim Earnings (Per Share)

Qtr.	Mar	Jun	Sep	Dec
2001	0.19	0.21	0.21	0.21
2002	0.21	0.25	0.24	0.26
2003	0.18	0.26	0.26	0.28
2004	0.21	0.29	0.29	0.32

Interim Dividends (Per Share)

Amt	Decl	Ex	Rec	Pay
0.04Q	5/18/2004	5/27/2004	6/1/2004	6/15/2004
0.04Q	8/24/2004	9/1/2004	9/6/2004	9/15/2004
0.04Q	11/22/2004	12/2/2004	12/6/2004	12/15/2004
0.05Q	1/31/2005	2/25/2005	3/1/2005	3/15/2005
		Indicated Div: $0.20		

Valuation Analysis

Forecast P/E	21.69	No of Institutions	
	(4/7/2005)	162	
Market Cap	$2.3 Billion	Shares	
Book Value	571.8 Million	49,015,840	
Price/Book	4.10	% Held	
Price/Sales	2.27	57.92	

Business Summary: Non-Media Publishing (MIC: 13.3 SIC: 741 NAIC: 11140)

Harte-Hanks is a direct and targeted marketing company that provides direct marketing services and shopper advertising opportunities to a wide range of local, regional, national and international consumer and business-to-business marketers. Co.'s direct marketing business operates both nationally and internationally, while its shopper business operates in selected local and regional markets in California and Florida. Direct marketing offers a complete range of specialized, coordinated and integrated direct and interactive marketing services from a single source. Shoppers offer advertisers a targeted local advertising system, with virtually 100.0% penetration in their area of distribution.

Recent Developments: For the year ended Dec 31 2004, net income increased 11.7% to $97,568 thousand from net income of $87,362 thousand a year earlier. Revenues were $1,030,461 thousand, up 9.1% from $944,576 thousand the year before. Operating income was $165,295 thousand versus an income of $146,487 thousand in the prior year, an increase of 12.8%. Total direct expense was $361,298 thousand versus $334,359 thousand in the prior year, an increase of 8.1%. Total indirect expense was $503,868 thousand versus $463,730 thousand in the prior year, an increase of 8.7%.

Prospects: Results are benefiting from solid shopper growth fueled by strong performances in real estate, financial services, and employment-related advertising. Results are being positively affected by Co.'s direct marketing business, which experienced revenue growth of 11.9% and operating income up 26.9% during the fourth quarter over the prior year. Co. noted that four of its five vertical markets, high tech/telecom, select, retail and heath care markets showed double-digit growth rates, while financial services sales were essentially flat. Looking ahead, Co. is optimistic about its outlook and expects to deliver similar growth in 2005, excluding stock option expenses, as it achieved in 2004.

Financial Data

(US$ in Thousands)	12/31/2004	12/31/2003	12/31/2002	12/31/2001	12/31/2000	12/31/1999	12/31/1998	12/31/1997
Earnings Per Share	1.11	0.97	0.96	0.82	0.79	0.67	0.60	2.91
Cash Flow Per Share	1.77	1.40	1.53	1.61	1.09	1.10	(1.56)	0.84
Tang Book Value Per Share	1.31	1.32	1.03	1.22	1.15	1.64	2.68	2.88
Dividends Per Share	0.160	0.120	0.098	0.080	0.067	0.053	0.040	0.027
Dividend Payout %	14.41	12.37	10.24	9.76	8.47	7.92	6.67	0.92
Income Statement								
Total Revenue	1,030,461	944,576	908,777	917,928	960,773	829,752	748,546	638,349
EBITDA	192,416	174,625	181,012	183,936	180,195	152,286	131,855	99,357
Depn & Amortn	28,769	30,033	32,728	48,920	43,720	34,788	28,977	22,461
Income Before Taxes	162,968	143,905	147,350	132,438	136,859	122,811	116,159	75,119
Income Taxes	65,400	56,543	56,605	52,754	54,973	49,870	47,788	30,848
Net Income	97,568	87,362	90,745	79,684	81,886	72,941	68,371	335,748
Average Shares	87,806	89,982	94,872	97,174	104,479	108,216	114,085	115,500
Balance Sheet								
Current Assets	250,497	217,297	198,612	202,807	235,873	220,133	325,813	613,139
Total Assets	828,353	759,130	736,732	771,049	807,105	769,427	715,213	954,923
Current Liabilities	182,192	134,072	121,761	121,774	149,964	154,017	116,484	371,349
Long-Term Obligations	...	5,000	16,300	48,312	65,370	5,000	...	...
Total Liabilities	256,554	203,532	204,199	218,683	256,102	191,809	138,122	388,686
Stockholders' Equity	571,799	555,598	532,533	552,366	551,003	577,618	577,091	566,237
Shares Outstanding	84,981	87,492	90,204	93,212	97,028	102,159	106,887	109,791
Statistical Record								
Return on Assets %	12.26	11.68	12.04	10.10	10.36	9.83	8.19	43.40
Return on Equity %	17.26	16.06	16.73	14.44	14.47	12.63	11.96	82.00
EBITDA Margin %	18.67	18.49	19.92	20.04	18.76	18.35	17.61	15.56
Net Margin %	9.47	9.25	9.99	8.68	8.52	8.79	9.13	52.60
Asset Turnover	1.29	1.26	1.21	1.16	1.22	1.12	0.90	0.83
Current Ratio	1.37	1.62	1.63	1.67	1.57	1.43	2.80	1.65
Debt to Equity	...	0.01	0.03	0.09	0.12	0.01	...	...
Price Range	26.87-21.50	22.13-17.33	22.30-16.18	18.78-13.73	18.75-13.29	19.17-13.04	19.00-11.58	12.79-8.58
P/E Ratio	24.21-19.37	22.81-17.87	23.23-16.85	22.90-16.74	23.73-16.82	28.61-19.47	31.67-19.31	4.40-2.95
Average Yield %	0.67	0.63	0.50	0.51	0.42	0.33	0.26	0.26

Address: 200 Concord Plaza Drive, San Antonio, TX 78216
Telephone: (210) 829-9000
Fax: (210) 829-9403

Web Site: www.harte-hanks.com
Officers: Larry D. Franklin - Chmn. Houston H. Harte - Vice-Chmn.

Auditors: KPMG LLP
Investor Contact: 210-829-9140

HARTFORD FINANCIAL SERVICES GROUP INC.

Exchange	Symbol	Price	52Wk Range	Yield	P/E
NYS	HIG	$68.56 (3/31/2005)	73.76-53.29	1.69	9.63

*7 Year Price Score 98.20 ***NYSE Composite Index=100** ***12 Month Price Score 101.06**

TRADING VOLUME (thousand shares)

Interim Earnings (Per Share)

Qtr.	Mar	Jun	Sep	Dec
2001	1.02	0.94	(0.43)	0.58
2002	1.17	0.74	1.06	1.01
2003	(5.46)	1.88	1.20	1.70
2004	1.93	1.46	1.66	2.08

Interim Dividends (Per Share)

Amt	Decl	Ex	Rec	Pay
0.28Q	5/20/2004	5/27/2004	6/1/2004	7/1/2004
0.28Q	7/22/2004	8/30/2004	9/1/2004	10/1/2004
0.29Q	10/21/2004	11/29/2004	12/1/2004	1/3/2005
0.29Q	2/17/2005	2/25/2005	3/1/2005	4/1/2005

Indicated Div: $1.16

Valuation Analysis

Forecast P/E	9.22	No of Institutions
	(4/13/2005)	466
Market Cap	$20.2 Billion	Shares
Book Value	14.2 Billion	265,387,936
Price/Book	1.42	% Held
Price/Sales	0.89	89.75

Business Summary: Insurance (MIC: 8.2 SIC: 411 NAIC: 24210)

Hartford Financial Services Group is a diversified insurance and financial services company. Co.'s Life segment provides retail and institutional investment products; life insurance for wealth protection; accumulation and transfer needs, group benefits products; and fixed and variable annuity products through its international business. Co.'s Property & Casualty segment provides workers' compensation, property, automobile, liability, umbrella, specialty casualty, marine, agricultural and bond coverages to commercial accounts; professional liability coverage and directors and officers liability coverage; automobile, homeowners and home-based business coverage; and insurance related services.

Recent Developments: For the year ended Dec 31 2004, net income amounted to $2.12 billion compared with a net loss of $91.0 million a year earlier. Results for 2004 and 2003 included after-tax net realized capital gains of $178.0 million and $191.0 million, respectively. Results for 2004 included tax benefits of $216.0 million stemming from the favorable resolution of various tax items relating to prior tax years. Results for 2003 also included an after-tax charge of $1.70 billion for an increase in asbestos reserves. Revenues rose 21.1% to $22.69 billion from $18.73 billion the year before. Operating income was $1.97 billion compared with a loss of $253.0 million the year before.

Prospects: Co. now expects 2005 earnings per diluted share of between $7.25 and $7.55, up from its prior guidance of $7.15 to $7.45. The revision reflects in part the higher level of U.S. equity markets at year end 2004 and Co.'s expectation that the recent favorable property loss frequency will persist for at least a short time into 2005. Co.'s 2005 guidance assumes total annual equity market return of 9.0% from levels at the end of 2004; continued written premium growth in business insurance and personal lines; and stable underwriting returns in personal lines, slightly decreased underwriting returns in business insurance and stable underwriting returns in the specialty commercial insurance segment.

Financial Data

(US$ in Thousands)	12/31/2004	12/31/2003	12/31/2002	12/31/2001	12/31/2000	12/31/1999	12/31/1998	12/31/1997
Earnings Per Share	7.12	(0.33)	3.97	2.10	4.34	3.79	4.30	5.58
Cash Flow Per Share	8.99	14.30	10.62	9.69	10.62	3.96	3.90	8.67
Tang Book Value Per Share	42.55	35.00	35.31	29.81	32.98	25.16	28.25	25.78
Dividends Per Share	1.130	1.090	1.050	1.010	0.970	0.920	0.850	0.800
Dividend Payout %	15.87	...	26.45	48.10	22.35	24.27	19.77	14.34
Income Statement								
Total Revenue	22,693,000	18,733,000	15,907,000	15,147,000	14,703,000	13,528,000	15,022,000	13,305,000
EBITDA	5,625,000	2,080,000	3,413,000	2,640,000	...	1,293,000	1,578,000	1,788,000
Depn & Amortn	3,102,000	2,630,000	2,345,000	2,286,000	2,276,000	58,000	103,000	85,000
Income Before Taxes	2,523,000	(550,000)	1,068,000	354,000	...	1,235,000	1,475,000	1,703,000
Income Taxes	385,000	(459,000)	68,000	(195,000)	390,000	287,000	388,000	334,000
Net Income	2,115,000	(91,000)	1,000,000	507,000	974,000	862,000	1,015,000	1,888,000
Average Shares	297,000	272,400	251,800	241,400	224,400	227,500	236,200	238,000
Balance Sheet								
Current Assets	10,561,000	9,505,000	8,083,000	7,947,000	7,101,000	6,726,000	6,934,000	12,852,000
Total Assets	259,735,000	225,853,000	182,043,000	181,238,000	171,532,000	167,051,000	150,632,000	131,743,000
Current Liabilities	621,000	1,050,000	315,000	599,000	235,000	31,000	31,000	291,000
Long-Term Obligations	4,308,000	4,613,000	2,596,000	1,965,000	1,862,000	1,548,000	1,548,000	1,482,000
Total Liabilities	245,497,000	214,214,000	171,309,000	172,225,000	164,068,000	161,156,000	143,744,000	125,261,000
Stockholders' Equity	14,238,000	11,639,000	10,734,000	9,013,000	7,464,000	5,466,000	6,423,000	6,085,000
Shares Outstanding	294,208	283,379	255,240	245,536	226,290	217,226	227,395	236,000
Statistical Record								
Return on Assets %	0.87	N.M.	0.55	0.29	0.57	0.54	0.72	1.57
Return on Equity %	16.30	N.M.	10.13	6.15	15.02	14.50	16.23	35.61
EBITDA Margin %	24.79	11.10	21.46	17.43	...	9.56	10.50	13.44
Net Margin %	9.32	N.M.	6.29	3.35	6.62	6.37	6.76	14.19
Asset Turnover	0.09	0.09	0.09	0.09	0.09	0.09	0.11	0.11
Current Ratio	17.01	9.05	25.66	13.27	30.22	216.97	223.68	44.16
Debt to Equity	0.30	0.40	0.24	0.22	0.25	0.28	0.24	0.24
Price Range	69.31-53.29	59.03-32.30	69.97-37.38	70.46-50.10	79.31-29.38	65.06-37.31	59.56-38.19	46.78-32.81
P/E Ratio	9.73-7.48	...	17.62-9.42	33.55-23.86	18.27-6.77	17.17-9.84	13.85-8.88	8.38-5.88
Average Yield %	1.77	2.26	1.87	1.63	1.70	1.74	1.64	2.00

Address: Hartford Plaza, Hartford, CT 06115-1900	**Web Site:** www.thehartford.com	**Auditors:** Deloitte & Touche LLP
Telephone: (860) 547-5000	**Officers:** Ramani Ayer - Chmn., Pres., C.E.O. David M. Johnson - Exec. V.P., C.F.O.	**Investor Contact:** 860-547-2537
Fax: (860) 720-6097		

HASBRO, INC.

Exchange	Symbol	Price	52Wk Range	Yield	P/E
NYS	HAS	$20.45 (3/31/2005)	23.33-17.00	1.76	21.30

*7 Year Price Score 90.41   *NYSE Composite Index=100   *12 Month Price Score 100.01

Interim Earnings (Per Share)

Qtr.	Mar	Jun	Sep	Dec
2001	(0.15)	(0.11)	0.29	0.31
2002	(0.10)	(0.15)	0.32	0.36
2003	0.01	0.06	0.38	0.43
2004	0.03	0.06	0.45	0.42

Interim Dividends (Per Share)

Amt	Decl	Ex	Rec	Pay
0.06Q	5/20/2004	7/29/2004	8/2/2004	8/16/2004
0.06Q	7/28/2004	10/28/2004	11/1/2004	11/15/2004
0.06Q	12/16/2004	1/28/2005	2/1/2005	2/15/2005
0.09Q	2/17/2005	4/28/2005	5/2/2005	5/16/2005

Indicated Div: $0.36

Valuation Analysis

Forecast P/E	16.28	No of Institutions	
	(4/7/2005)	220	
Market Cap	$3.6 Billion	Shares	
Book Value	1.6 Billion	155,593,232	
Price/Book	2.21	% Held	
Price/Sales	1.21	87.63	

Business Summary: Consumer Accessories (MIC: 4.6 SIC: 944 NAIC: 39932)

Hasbro provides children's and family leisure time and entertainment products and services, including the design, manufacture and marketing of games and toys ranging from traditional to high-tech. Co.'s product lines include Playskool®, Tonka®, Super Soaker®, Milton Bradley®, Parker Brothers®, Tiger™, and Wizards of the Coast®. Toys and games include G.I. Joe®, Transformers®, Tonka® Trucks, Easy-Bake® Oven, Play-Doh®, Lite-Brite®, Spirograph®, Star Wars®, Super Soaker®, Nerf®, The Game of Life®, Battleship® Scrabble®, Monopoly®, Koosh® and Micro Machines®.

Recent Developments: For the year ended Dec 30 2004, net income increased 24.3% to $195,977 thousand from net income of $157,664 thousand a year earlier. Revenues were $2,997,510 thousand, down 4.5% from $3,138,657 thousand the year before. Operating income was $293,012 thousand versus an income of $344,616 thousand in the prior year, a decrease of 15.0%. Total direct expense was $1,251,657 thousand versus $1,287,962 thousand in the prior year, a decrease of 2.8%. Total indirect expense was $1,452,841 thousand versus $1,506,079 thousand in the prior year, a decrease of 3.5%.

Prospects: Top-line results reflect a soft retail environment in the fourth quarter, as well as a disappointing performance in the U. S. Toys segment, primarily related to softness in Co.'s boys business, including BEYBLADE, and low margins on higher volume VIDEONOW products. As a result, Co. took actions in the fourth quarter, primarily in the U. S. Toys segment, to reduce its expenses going forward and position it more favorably in the fastest growing areas of its business. Looking ahead, Co. plans to focus on consumer electronics for tweens, toys tied to the release of Star Wars Episode III in May 2005, as well as new Transformers and GI Joe lines, which are tied into new television programming.

Financial Data (US$ in Thousands)	12/26/2004	12/28/2003	12/29/2002	12/30/2001	12/31/2000	12/26/1999	12/27/1998	12/28/1997
Earnings Per Share	0.96	0.88	(0.98)	0.35	(0.82)	0.93	1.00	0.68
Cash Flow Per Share	2.04	2.62	2.75	2.17	0.91	2.01	0.64	2.84
Tang Book Value Per Share	3.00	1.32	0.08	N.M.	N.M.	N.M.	1.92	4.36
Dividends Per Share	0.210	0.120	0.120	0.120	0.240	0.233	0.213	0.204
Dividend Payout %	21.88	13.64	...	34.29	...	25.09	21.33	30.07
Income Statement								
Total Revenue	2,997,510	3,138,657	2,816,230	2,856,339	3,787,215	4,232,263	3,304,454	3,188,559
EBITDA	437,966	460,649	365,425	425,786	152,656	620,509	508,788	398,595
Depn & Amortn	146,180	164,123	183,838	225,899	264,221	277,324	169,199	166,584
Income Before Taxes	260,088	244,064	104,088	96,199	(225,986)	273,845	303,478	204,525
Income Taxes	64,111	69,049	29,030	35,401	(81,355)	84,892	97,113	69,539
Net Income	195,977	157,664	(170,674)	59,732	(144,631)	188,953	206,365	134,986
Average Shares	196,048	178,484	185,063	173,018	176,437	202,103	205,420	206,353
Balance Sheet								
Current Assets	1,718,222	1,509,263	1,431,624	1,368,618	1,580,213	2,131,652	1,789,986	1,573,874
Total Assets	3,240,660	3,163,376	3,142,881	3,368,979	3,828,459	4,463,348	3,793,845	2,899,727
Current Liabilities	1,148,611	930,055	966,850	758,591	1,239,812	2,071,327	1,366,300	1,003,546
Long-Term Obligations	302,698	686,871	857,274	1,165,649	1,167,838	420,654	407,180	...
Total Liabilities	1,600,936	1,758,136	1,951,515	2,016,115	2,501,053	2,584,373	1,849,050	1,061,600
Stockholders' Equity	1,639,724	1,405,240	1,191,366	1,352,864	1,327,406	1,878,975	1,944,795	1,838,117
Shares Outstanding	177,315	175,499	173,169	172,958	172,441	192,984	209,700	200,161
Statistical Record								
Return on Assets %	6.14	5.01	N.M.	1.66	N.M.	4.59	6.18	4.86
Return on Equity %	12.91	12.18	N.M.	4.47	N.M.	9.91	10.94	7.80
EBITDA Margin %	14.61	14.68	12.98	14.91	4.03	14.66	15.40	12.50
Net Margin %	6.54	5.02	N.M.	2.09	N.M.	4.46	6.25	4.23
Asset Turnover	0.94	1.00	0.87	0.80	0.90	1.03	0.99	1.15
Current Ratio	1.50	1.62	1.48	1.80	1.27	1.03	1.31	1.57
Debt to Equity	0.18	0.49	0.72	0.86	0.88	0.22	0.21	...
Price Range	23.33-17.00	22.48-11.21	16.97-10.06	18.22-10.31	18.94-9.13	36.50-17.19	27.29-19.04	23.92-15.18
P/E Ratio	24.30-17.71	25.55-12.74	...	52.06-29.46	...	39.25-18.48	27.29-19.04	35.17-22.92
Average Yield %	1.08			0.88	0.82	1.72	0.91	0.90	1.09

Address: 1027 Newport Avenue, Pawtucket, RI 02862 **Telephone:** (401) 431-8697 **Fax:** (401) 727-5544	**Web Site:** www.hasbro.com **Officers:** Alan G. Hassenfeld - Chmn. Alfred J. Verrecchia - Pres., C.E.O.	**Auditors:** KPMG LLP **Investor Contact:** 401-431-8697

HAVERTY FURNITURE COS., INC.

Exchange	Symbol	Price	52Wk Range	Yield	P/E	Div Acheiver
NYS	HVT A	$15.38 (3/31/2005)	21.60-15.38	1.50	15.54	34 Years

*7 Year Price Score N/A   *NYSE Composite Index=100   ***12 Month Price Score 86.35**

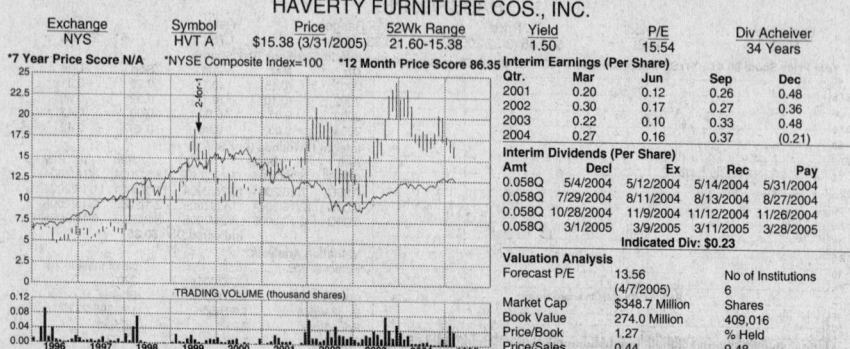

Interim Earnings (Per Share)

Qtr.	Mar	Jun	Sep	Dec
2001	0.20	0.12	0.26	0.48
2002	0.30	0.17	0.27	0.36
2003	0.22	0.10	0.33	0.48
2004	0.27	0.16	0.37	(0.21)

Interim Dividends (Per Share)

Amt	Decl	Ex	Rec	Pay
0.058Q	5/4/2004	5/12/2004	5/14/2004	5/31/2004
0.058Q	7/29/2004	8/11/2004	8/13/2004	8/27/2004
0.058Q	10/28/2004	11/9/2004	11/12/2004	11/26/2004
0.058Q	3/1/2005	3/9/2005	3/11/2005	3/28/2005

Indicated Div: $0.23

Valuation Analysis

Forecast P/E	13.56	No of Institutions
	(4/7/2005)	6
Market Cap	$348.7 Million	Shares
Book Value	274.0 Million	409,016
Price/Book	1.27	% Held
Price/Sales	0.44	9.48

TRADING VOLUME (thousand shares)

Business Summary: Retail - Furniture & Home Furnishings (MIC: 5.9 SIC: 712 NAIC: 42110)

Haverty Furniture Companies is a full-service home furnishings retailer with 113 stores in 15 southern and central states as of Dec 31 2003. Co.'s stores, primarily targeted at middle and upper-middle income families, offer a wide selection of well-known brand names of furniture, such as Broyhill, Lane, Bernhardt, La-Z-Boy, Sealy and Serta. Co. also carries merchandise that bears the Havertys brand. Co. offers a revolving charge credit plan with credit limits determined through its on-line credit approval system and an additional credit program outsourced to a third-party finance company.

Recent Developments: For the year ended Dec 31 2004, net income decreased 10.2% to $22,754 thousand from net income of $25,331 thousand a year earlier. Revenues were $788,664 thousand, up 5.0% from $751,027 thousand the year before. Total direct expense was $386,789 thousand versus $378,985 thousand in the prior year, an increase of 2.1%. Total indirect expense was $367,616 thousand versus $331,600 thousand in the prior year, an increase of 10.9%.

Prospects: Co. is benefiting from solid revenue growth in all product categories with greater consumer focus on bedding and recliners. Co. is able to fulfill customer orders at a greater pace due in part to improvements in its distribution methods. Meanwhile, Co. is targeting several new markets for future expansion as it looks to bring quality, fashionable home furnishings to more consumers. Separately, Co. announced the acquisition of land in the growing southeastern suburbs of metro-Atlanta near Stonecrest Mall for a new store to open late in 2005. Co. believes the strength of its merchandising gives it an advantage in gaining market share in Atlanta.

Financial Data

(US$ in Thousands)	12/31/2004	12/31/2003	12/31/2002	12/31/2001	12/31/2000	12/31/1999	12/31/1998	12/31/1997
Earnings Per Share	0.99	1.13	1.10	1.06	1.15	1.19	0.72	0.57
Cash Flow Per Share	2.70	3.73	3.94	1.43	0.80	3.15	2.42	1.06
Tang Book Value Per Share	12.08	11.28	10.30	9.45	8.64	7.81	7.08	6.79
Dividends Per Share	0.250	0.235	0.220	0.210	0.203	0.190	0.165	0.160
Dividend Payout %	25.25	20.80	20.00	19.81	17.61	15.97	22.92	28.07
Income Statement								
Total Revenue	788,664	751,027	713,010	689,178	693,575	633,721	557,258	506,118
EBITDA	58,802	59,796	61,367	63,160	71,306	69,116	53,750	48,909
Depn & Amortn	19,145	17,199	15,903	16,239	15,738	14,844	14,272	13,792
Income Before Taxes	36,174	38,725	38,903	36,340	43,861	42,870	26,295	20,787
Income Taxes	13,420	14,444	14,588	13,630	16,010	15,470	9,460	7,400
Net Income	22,754	25,331	24,315	22,710	24,495	27,400	16,835	13,387
Average Shares	23,083	22,437	22,145	21,502	21,203	22,982	23,404	23,340
Balance Sheet								
Current Assets	230,422	256,485	263,825	305,755	295,992	271,678	278,177	289,629
Total Assets	457,566	433,202	404,839	460,905	448,163	404,648	392,901	406,514
Current Liabilities	126,096	104,196	101,520	123,903	95,520	98,434	70,467	132,908
Long-Term Obligations	44,228	65,402	69,821	131,559	170,369	134,687	161,778	111,489
Total Liabilities	183,610	180,466	179,958	259,507	268,788	235,855	234,843	246,960
Stockholders' Equity	273,956	252,736	224,881	201,398	179,375	168,793	158,058	159,554
Shares Outstanding	22,674	22,409	21,832	21,302	20,773	21,610	22,330	23,482
Statistical Record								
Return on Assets %	5.09	6.05	5.62	5.00	5.73	6.87	4.21	3.32
Return on Equity %	8.62	10.61	11.41	11.93	14.03	16.77	10.60	8.62
EBITDA Margin %	7.46	7.96	8.61	9.16	10.28	10.91	9.65	9.66
Net Margin %	2.89	3.37	3.41	3.30	3.53	4.32	3.02	2.65
Asset Turnover	1.77	1.79	1.65	1.52	1.62	1.59	1.39	1.26
Current Ratio	1.83	2.46	2.60	2.47	3.10	2.76	3.95	2.18
Debt to Equity	0.16	0.26	0.31	0.65	0.95	0.80	1.02	0.70
Price Range	23.49-16.10	24.30-9.75	21.25-10.05	16.40-10.00	13.19-9.56	18.50-9.63	12.72-6.38	7.25-5.31
P/E Ratio	23.73-16.26	21.50-8.63	19.32-9.14	15.47-9.43	11.47-8.32	15.55-8.09	17.66-8.85	12.72-9.32
Average Yield %	1.30	1.46	1.41	1.49	1.77	1.36	1.69	2.56

Address: 780 Johnson Ferry Road, Suite 800, Atlanta, GA 30342
Telephone: (404) 443-2900

Web Site: www.havertys.com
Officers: Clarence H. Ridley - Chmn. Clarence H. Smith - Pres., C.E.O.

Auditors: Ernst & Young LLP
Investor Contact: 404-443-2900
Transfer Agents: SunTrust Bank, Atlanta, GA

HAWAIIAN ELECTRIC INDUSTRIES, INC.

Exchange	Symbol	Price	52Wk Range	Yield	P/E
NYS	HE	$25.52 (3/31/2005)	29.76-23.07	4.86	18.49

*7 Year Price Score 110.72 *NYSE Composite Index=100 *12 Month Price Score 94.26

Interim Earnings (Per Share)

Qtr.	Mar	Jun	Sep	Dec
2001	0.41	0.38	0.11	0.34
2002	0.38	0.42	0.45	0.38
2003	0.33	0.29	0.41	0.50
2004	0.40	0.14	0.53	0.31

Interim Dividends (Per Share)

Amt	Decl	Ex	Rec	Pay
0.31Q	4/20/2004	5/6/2004	5/10/2004	6/10/2004
0.31Q	7/20/2004	8/6/2004	8/10/2004	9/10/2004
0.31Q	10/26/2004	11/8/2004	11/10/2004	12/10/2004
0.31Q	1/25/2005	2/14/2005	2/16/2005	3/10/2005
		Indicated Div: $1.24		

Valuation Analysis

Forecast P/E	16.61	No of Institutions
	(4/7/2005)	183
Market Cap	$2.1 Billion	Shares
Book Value	1.2 Billion	25,683,280
Price/Book	1.70	% Held
Price/Sales	1.07	31.82

Business Summary: Electricity (MIC: 7.1 SIC: 911 NAIC: 21121)

Hawaiian Electric Industries is a holding company engaged in the electric utility and banking businesses operating primarily in Hawaii. Hawaiian Electric Company, Inc. and its operating subsidiaries, Maui Electric Company, Limited and Hawaii Electric Light Company, Inc., provide electricity to 93.0% of the Hawaii electric public utility market through over 400,000 residential, commercial and large light and power accounts on Oahu, Hawaii, Maui, Lanai and Molokai. American Savings Bank, F.S.B. (ASB), with assets of $6.50 billion at Dec 31 2003, offers a wide range of personal and business services to nearly 600,000 accounts through a network of 68 branch offices.

Recent Developments: For the year ended Dec 31 2004, income from continuing operations decreased 8.7% to $107,739 thousand from income of $118,048 thousand a year earlier. Net income decreased 4.0% to $109,652 thousand from net income of $114,178 thousand a year earlier. Revenues were $1,924,057 thousand, up 8.0% from $1,781,316 thousand the year before. Operating income was $270,960 thousand versus an income of $263,567 thousand in the prior year, an increase of 2.8%. Total direct expense was $1,376,768 thousand versus $1,220,120 thousand in the prior year, an increase of 12.8%. Total indirect expense was $17,019 thousand versus $19,064 thousand in the prior year, a decrease of 10.7%.

Prospects: Results are being positively affected by increased earnings from Co.'s utility operations reflecting kilowatthour sales growth, which is being driven by increases in usage and the number of customers, particularly residential customers. Meanwhile, bank earnings continue to benefit from strong asset quality. Co. noted that delinquent and nonaccrual loans and charge-offs are well below historical norms due to considerable momentum in Hawaii's residential real estate market and business conditions. During 2004, Co. reduced its allowance for possible loan losses by $8.4 million.

Financial Data

(US$ in Thousands)	12/31/2004	12/31/2003	12/31/2002	12/31/2001	12/31/2000	12/31/1999	12/31/1998	12/31/1997
Earnings Per Share	1.38	1.52	1.62	1.24	0.70	1.50	1.32	1.38
Cash Flow Per Share	3.06	3.19	3.37	3.84	4.01	3.25	3.43	2.28
Tang Book Value Per Share	13.88	13.12	12.89	11.63	11.21	11.50	11.08	10.85
Dividends Per Share	1.240	1.240	1.240	1.240	1.240	1.240	1.240	1.220
Dividend Payout %	89.86	81.31	76.54	100.40	177.14	82.67	93.94	88.73
Income Statement								
Total Revenue	1,924,057	1,781,316	1,653,701	1,727,277	1,719,024	1,523,290	1,485,165	1,463,979
EBITDA	403,613	400,192	393,339	371,915	263,624	342,940	328,986	305,549
Depn & Amortn	128,760	150,399	140,993	129,544	120,939	123,001	112,796	105,349
Income Before Taxes	200,219	182,415	181,909	165,903	66,986	149,884	151,581	141,783
Income Taxes	92,480	64,367	63,692	58,157	21,242	56,990	56,953	55,341
Net Income	109,652	114,178	118,217	83,705	45,744	96,847	84,811	86,442
Average Shares	79,719	74,974	72,954	67,884	65,374	64,582	64,258	62,940
Balance Sheet								
Net PPE	2,422,303	2,311,888	2,079,325	2,067,503	2,091,345	2,066,195	2,093,398	2,019,558
Total Assets	9,610,627	9,201,158	8,876,503	8,517,943	8,469,322	8,291,026	8,199,260	7,953,882
Long-Term Obligations	2,154,966	2,081,473	2,282,522	2,178,521	2,337,816	2,166,610	1,705,179	1,539,049
Total Liabilities	8,365,277	7,877,721	7,595,797	7,353,872	7,395,018	7,208,193	7,087,240	6,905,138
Stockholders' Equity	1,210,945	1,089,031	1,046,300	929,665	839,059	847,586	826,972	814,681
Shares Outstanding	80,687	75,837	73,618	71,200	65,982	64,426	64,232	63,790
Statistical Record								
Return on Assets %	1.16	1.26	1.36	0.99	0.54	1.17	1.05	1.24
Return on Equity %	9.51	10.69	11.97	9.47	5.41	11.57	10.33	10.89
EBITDA Margin %	20.98	22.47	23.79	21.53	15.34	22.51	22.15	20.87
Net Margin %	5.70	6.41	7.15	4.85	2.66	6.36	5.71	5.90
PPE Turnover	0.81	0.81	0.80	0.83	0.82	0.73	0.72	0.74
Asset Turnover	0.20	0.20	0.19	0.20	0.20	0.18	0.18	0.21
Debt to Equity	1.78	1.91	2.18	2.34	2.79	2.56	2.06	1.89
Price Range	29.54-23.07	23.91-19.45	24.33-17.73	20.54-16.84	18.75-13.91	20.22-14.16	21.28-18.38	20.63-16.50
P/E Ratio	21.41-16.72	15.73-12.80	15.02-10.94	16.56-13.58	26.79-19.87	13.48-9.44	16.12-13.92	14.95-11.96
Average Yield %	4.76	5.72	5.69	6.58	7.54	7.11	6.25	6.73

Address: 900 Richards Street, Honolulu, HI 96813 **Telephone:** (808) 543-5662 **Fax:** (808) 543-7966	**Web Site:** www.hei.com **Officers:** Robert F. Clarke - Chmn., Pres., C.E.O. Eric K. Yeaman - V.P., C.F.O., Treas.	**Auditors:** KPMG LLP **Investor Contact:** 808-543-7385

HCA, INC.

Exchange	Symbol	Price	52Wk Range	Yield	P/E
NYS	HCA	$53.57 (3/31/2005)	53.57-35.00	1.12	20.76

*7 Year Price Score 99.07 *NYSE Composite Index=100 *12 Month Price Score 109.74

Interim Earnings (Per Share)

Qtr.	Mar	Jun	Sep	Dec
2001	0.59	0.48	0.48	0.09
2002	0.74	0.66	0.38	(0.19)
2003	0.90	0.47	0.61	0.63
2004	0.69	0.72	0.47	0.70

Interim Dividends (Per Share)

Amt	Decl	Ex	Rec	Pay
0.13Q	5/27/2004	7/28/2004	8/1/2004	9/1/2004
0.13Q	9/23/2004	10/28/2004	11/1/2004	12/1/2004
0.13Q	11/18/2004	1/28/2005	2/1/2005	3/1/2005
0.15Q	2/1/2005	4/27/2005	5/1/2005	6/1/2005
		Indicated Div: $0.60		

Valuation Analysis

Forecast P/E   N/A   No of Institutions

Market Cap	$22.6 Billion	Shares
Book Value	4.4 Billion	325,476,064
Price/Book	5.14	% Held
Price/Sales	0.96	75.11

Business Summary: Hospitals & Health Care (MIC: 9.3 SIC: 062 NAIC: 22110)

HCA is a holding company whose subsidiaries own and operate hospitals and related health care entities. At Dec 31 2003, these affiliates owned and operated 191 hospitals and 83 freestanding surgery centers. Affiliates of Co. are also partners in several 50/50 joint ventures that own and operate six hospitals and four ambulatory surgery centers. Co.'s facilities are located in 23 U.S. states, London, England and Geneva, Switzerland. Co. integrates fragmented providers and services (such as hospitals, physicians, outpatient centers, psychiatric facilities and home-health agencies) to create local healthcare networks.

Recent Developments: For the year ended Dec 31 2004, net income decreased 6.5% to $1,246 million from net income of $1,332 million a year earlier. Revenues were $23,502 million, up 7.8% from $21,808 million the year before. Total direct expense was $3,901 million versus $3,522 million in the prior year, an increase of 10.8%. Total indirect expense was $17,147 million versus $15,807 million in the prior year, an increase of 8.5%.

Prospects: Co. continues to build an infrastructure in order to operate its existing outpatient services more efficiently and to develop new opportunities in the outpatient setting. During 2004, Co. opened or acquired five new surgery centers and formed or restructured partnerships at five centers that had been managed by hospitals, bringing its total to 91 ambulatory surgery centers in 16 states. Co. has also begun to develop new outpatient business, particularly in the areas of imaging and surgery. Co. expects it will acquire or develop 5 to 10 surgery centers and 15 to 25 imaging centers over the next year. Separately, Co. expects full-year 2005 earnings in the range of $2.75 to $2.90 per share.

Financial Data

(US$ in Thousands)	12/31/2004	12/31/2003	12/31/2002	12/31/2001	12/31/2000	12/31/1999	12/31/1998	12/31/1997
Earnings Per Share	2.58	2.61	1.59	1.65	0.39	1.11	0.59	(0.46)
Cash Flow Per Share	6.39	4.32	5.37	2.70	2.78	2.09	2.98	2.25
Tang Book Value Per Share	4.42	7.60	7.21	5.32	4.14	5.84	7.27	5.82
Dividends Per Share	0.410	0.080	0.080	0.080	0.080	0.080	0.080	0.080
Dividend Payout %	15.89	3.07	5.03	4.85	20.51	7.21	13.56	...
Income Statement								
Total Revenue	23,502,000	21,808,000	19,729,000	17,953,000	16,670,000	16,657,000	18,681,000	18,819,000
EBITDA	3,786,000	3,759,000	2,911,000	3,089,000	2,108,000	2,792,000	2,889,000	2,119,000
Depn & Amortn	1,250,000	1,112,000	1,010,000	1,048,000	1,033,000	1,094,000	1,247,000	1,238,000
Income Before Taxes	1,973,000	2,156,000	1,455,000	1,505,000	516,000	1,227,000	1,081,000	388,000
Income Taxes	727,000	824,000	622,000	602,000	297,000	570,000	549,000	206,000
Net Income	1,246,000	1,332,000	833,000	886,000	219,000	657,000	379,000	(305,000)
Average Shares	483,663	510,874	525,219	538,177	567,685	591,029	646,649	663,000
Balance Sheet								
Current Assets	4,683,000	4,822,000	4,505,000	4,141,000	4,453,000	3,597,000	3,863,000	4,423,000
Total Assets	21,465,000	21,063,000	18,741,000	17,730,000	17,568,000	16,885,000	19,429,000	22,002,000
Current Liabilities	3,174,000	3,168,000	3,739,000	3,184,000	4,141,000	3,332,000	3,559,000	2,773,000
Long-Term Obligations	10,044,000	8,042,000	6,497,000	6,553,000	5,631,000	5,284,000	5,685,000	9,276,000
Total Liabilities	17,058,000	14,854,000	13,039,000	12,968,000	13,163,000	11,268,000	11,848,000	14,752,000
Stockholders' Equity	4,407,000	6,209,000	5,702,000	4,762,000	4,405,000	5,617,000	7,581,000	7,250,000
Shares Outstanding	422,642	490,717	514,176	509,297	542,991	564,272	642,578	641,000
Statistical Record								
Return on Assets %	5.84	6.69	4.57	5.02	1.27	3.62	1.83	N.M.
Return on Equity %	23.41	22.37	15.92	19.33	4.36	9.96	5.11	N.M.
EBITDA Margin %	16.11	17.24	14.75	17.21	12.65	16.76	15.46	11.26
Net Margin %	5.30	6.11	4.22	4.94	1.31	3.94	2.03	N.M.
Asset Turnover	1.10	1.10	1.08	1.02	0.97	0.92	0.90	0.87
Current Ratio	1.48	1.52	1.20	1.30	1.08	1.08	1.09	1.60
Debt to Equity	2.28	1.30	1.14	1.38	1.28	0.94	0.75	1.28
Price Range	46.30-35.00	43.75-27.85	51.90-36.94	46.90-34.21	44.62-19.31	29.31-16.60	32.67-16.72	42.88-25.80
P/E Ratio	17.95-13.57	16.76-10.67	32.64-23.23	28.42-20.73	114.41-49.52	26.41-14.96	55.37-28.34	...
Average Yield %	1.02	0.21	0.18	0.20	0.25	0.35	0.31	0.24

Address: One Park Plaza, Nashville, TN 37203
Telephone: (615) 344-9551
Fax: (615) 320-2266

Web Site: www.hcahealthcare.com
Officers: Jack O. Bovender Jr. - Chmn., C.E.O.
Richard M. Bracken - Pres., C.O.O.

Auditors: Ernst & Young LLP
Investor Contact: 615-344-1199

HCC INSURANCE HOLDINGS, INC.

Exchange	Symbol	Price	52Wk Range	Yield	P/E
NYS	HCC	$36.16 (3/31/2005)	38.96-27.94	0.94	14.64

*7 Year Price Score 114.61 *NYSE Composite Index=100 ***12 Month Price Score 104.64**

Interim Earnings (Per Share)

Qtr.	Mar	Jun	Sep	Dec
2001	0.28	0.34	(0.49)	0.40
2002	0.37	0.43	0.39	0.50
2003	0.48	0.54	0.59	0.62
2004	0.68	0.71	0.24	0.84

Interim Dividends (Per Share)

Amt	Decl	Ex	Rec	Pay
0.075Q	3/29/2004	3/30/2004	4/1/2004	4/14/2004
0.075Q	6/7/2004	6/30/2004	7/2/2004	7/16/2004
0.085Q	9/15/2004	9/29/2004	10/1/2004	10/15/2004
0.085Q	12/20/2004	12/30/2004	1/3/2005	1/17/2005

Indicated Div: $0.34

Valuation Analysis

Forecast P/E	11.15	No of Institutions
	(4/7/2005)	192
Market Cap	$2.5 Billion	Shares
Book Value	1.3 Billion	64,353,432
Price/Book	1.86	% Held
Price/Sales	1.92	92.25

TRADING VOLUME (thousand shares)

Business Summary: Insurance (MIC: 8.2 SIC: 331 NAIC: 24126)

HCC Insurance Holdings provides group life, accident and health and property and casualty insurance coverages, underwriting agency and intermediary services both to commercial customers and individuals. Co. concentrates its activities in selected narrowly defined specialty lines of business. Co. operates primarily in the U.S., the U.K. and Spain, although some of its operations have a broader international scope. Co. underwrites insurance both on a direct basis, where it insures a risk in exchange for a premium, and on a reinsurance basis, where it insures all or a portion of another insurance company's risk in exchange for all or a portion of the premium.

Recent Developments: For the year ended Dec 31 2004, income from continuing operations increased 48.8% to $159,021,000 from income of $106,877,000 a year earlier. Net income increased 13.6% to $163,025,000 from net income of $143,561,000 a year earlier. Revenues were $12,831,540,00, up 36.2% from $941,964,000 the year before. Net premiums earned were $1,010,692,000 versus $738,272,000 in the prior year, an increase of 36.9%.

Prospects: Co. is providing fiscal 2005 net earnings guidance with a range between $3.15 and $3.25 per diluted share. This represents 28.0% earnings per diluted share growth and a 17.0% return on shareholders' equity at the bottom end of the range, despite dilution from the equity offering in Dec 2004 and the expensing of stock options. Co. expects total revenue to increase approximately 20.0% in 2005, predominantly due to growth of net earned premium by 25.0% and investment income by 25.0%. Co.'s combined ratio is expected to be approximate 88.0% without any consideration for potential catastrophe activity during the coming year.

Financial Data
(US$ in Thousands)

	12/31/2004	12/31/2003	12/31/2002	12/31/2001	12/31/2000	12/31/1999	12/31/1998	12/31/1997
Earnings Per Share	2.47	2.23	1.68	0.51	1.06	0.51	1.48	1.07
Cash Flow Per Share	10.29	8.35	2.81	1.81	2.64	0.83	1.04	1.19
Tang Book Value Per Share	12.93	10.32	8.78	7.07	5.23	3.97	7.29	7.92
Dividends Per Share	0.320	0.280	0.255	0.245	0.270	0.200	0.160	0.120
Dividend Payout %	12.96	12.56	15.18	48.04	25.47	39.22	10.81	11.21
Income Statement								
Premium Income	1,010,692	738,272	505,521	342,787	267,647	141,362	143,100	163,090
Total Revenue	1,283,154	941,964	669,382	505,461	466,167	341,871	308,034	273,410
Benefits & Claims	645,230	488,652	306,491	267,390	198,470	109,650	91,302	96,514
Income Before Taxes	240,753	166,734	163,179	60,383	92,646	37,394	107,486	73,048
Income Taxes	81,732	59,857	57,351	30,186	37,202	12,271	35,208	23,297
Net Income	163,025	143,561	105,828	30,197	53,431	25,123	72,278	49,751
Average Shares	65,884	64,383	62,936	59,619	50,622	49,649	48,936	46,609
Balance Sheet								
Total Assets	5,933,437	4,864,296	3,704,151	3,219,120	2,742,976	2,650,623	1,709,069	1,222,763
Total Liabilities	4,609,772	3,817,376	2,821,244	2,455,667	2,213,541	2,193,195	1,269,206	857,283
Stockholders' Equity	1,323,665	1,046,920	882,907	763,453	529,435	457,428	439,863	365,480
Shares Outstanding	68,038	63,964	62,358	61,438	50,345	48,839	48,252	46,159
Statistical Record								
Return on Assets %	3.01	3.35	3.06	1.01	1.98	1.15	4.93	5.05
Return on Equity %	13.72	14.88	12.86	4.67	10.80	5.60	17.95	16.41
Loss Ratio %	63.84	66.19	60.63	78.00	74.15	77.57	63.80	59.18
Net Margin %	12.71	15.24	15.81	5.97	11.46	7.35	23.46	18.20
Price Range	34.56-27.94	31.94-22.49	28.72-19.78	29.01-20.50	26.94-11.06	24.94-8.50	23.63-16.25	32.06-18.75
P/E Ratio	13.99-11.31	14.32-10.09	17.10-11.77	56.88-40.20	25.41-10.44	48.90-16.67	15.96-10.98	29.96-17.52
Average Yield %	1.01	0.99	1.01	0.96	1.52	1.14	0.80	0.47

Address: 13403 Northwest Freeway, Houston, TX 77040-6094 Telephone: (713) 690-7300 Fax: (713) 462-2401	Web Site: Officers: Stephen L. Way - Chmn., Pres., C.E.O. Edward H. Ellis Jr. - Exec. V.P., C.F.O., Chief Acctg. Officer	Auditors: PricewaterhouseCoopers LLP

HEALTH CARE PROPERTY INVESTORS, INC.

Exchange	Symbol	Price	52Wk Range	Yield	P/E	Div Achiever
NYS	HCP	$23.47 (3/31/2005)	28.85-21.68	7.16	21.14	19 Years

*7 Year Price Score 116.79 ***NYSE Composite Index=100** ***12 Month Price Score 91.30**

Interim Earnings (Per Share)

Qtr.	Mar	Jun	Sep	Dec
2001	0.20	0.27	0.16	0.27
2002	0.21	0.29	0.27	0.20
2003	0.18	0.17	0.30	0.32
2004	0.31	0.27	0.22	0.31

Interim Dividends (Per Share)

Amt	Decl	Ex	Rec	Pay
0.417Q	4/26/2004	5/4/2004	5/6/2004	5/21/2004
0.417Q	7/23/2004	8/2/2004	8/4/2004	8/19/2004
0.417Q	10/27/2004	11/4/2004	11/8/2004	11/19/2004
0.42Q	1/31/2005	2/3/2005	2/7/2005	2/18/2005

Indicated Div: $1.68 (Div. Reinv. Plan)

Valuation Analysis

Forecast P/E	12.91	No of Institutions
	(4/7/2005)	239
Market Cap	$3.1 Billion	Shares
Book Value	1.4 Billion	65,303,636
Price/Book	2.21	% Held
Price/Sales	7.32	48.67

Business Summary: Property, Real Estate & Development (MIC: 8.3 SIC: 798 NAIC: 25930)

Health Care Property Investors is a real estate investment trust that invests in healthcare-related facilities throughout the United States, including long-term care facilities, congregate care and assisted living facilities, acute care and rehabilitation hospitals, medical office buildings and physician group practice clinics. Co.'s investment portfolio as of Dec 31 2003 included 554 facilities in 44 states. Co.'s investments included 173 long-term care facilities, 124 retirement and assisted living facilities, 196 medical office buildings, 31 hospitals and 30 other health care facilities.

Recent Developments: For the year ended Dec 31 2004, income from continuing operations increased 8.2% to $157,846 thousand from income of $145,942 thousand a year earlier. Net income increased 6.6% to $169,040 thousand from net income of $158,585 thousand a year earlier. Revenues were $428,684 thousand, up 13.9% from $376,304 thousand the year before. Operating income was $170,050 thousand versus an income of $155,693 thousand in the prior year, an increase of 9.2%.

Prospects: Co. continues to refine its portfolio. For instance, during the fourth quarter of 2004, Co. made investments of about $117.0 million, increasing its aggregate investments, including development properties placed in service, for the full year of 2004 to about $538.0 million. The fourth-quarter investments included the purchase of three medical office buildings, a 42.0% condominium interest in a fourth medical office building and one retail/garage building. Also during the fourth quarter, Co. sold properties valued at approximately $170.0 million, principally comprised of medical office buildings.

Financial Data
(US$ in Thousands)

	12/31/2004	12/31/2003	12/31/2002	12/31/2001	12/31/2000	12/31/1999	12/31/1998	12/31/1997
Earnings Per Share	1.11	0.97	0.96	0.89	1.06	1.13	1.27	1.10
Cash Flow Per Share	2.06	2.06	1.94	1.86	2.01	1.78	1.83	1.52
Tang Book Value Per Share	8.49	8.82	8.46	8.62	8.55	9.00	6.58	6.36
Dividends Per Share	1.670	1.660	1.630	1.550	1.470	1.390	1.310	1.230
Dividend Payout %	150.45	171.13	168.91	174.16	138.03	123.56	103.15	112.33
Income Statement								
Property Income	388,631	348,649	331,737	310,602	306,830	199,570	138,439	113,920
Non-Property Income	40,053	51,534	27,839	21,858	22,977	25,223	23,110	14,583
Total Revenue	428,684	400,183	359,576	332,460	329,807	224,793	161,549	128,503
Depn & Amortn	99,342	87,551	82,259	84,098	72,590	44,789	29,577	22,667
Interest Expense	89,136	90,749	77,952	78,489	86,747	57,701	36,753	28,825
Net Income	169,040	158,585	137,380	121,166	133,767	96,225	87,167	64,789
Average Shares	133,362	126,130	116,294	107,950	102,200	69,722	67,328	57,988
Balance Sheet								
Total Assets	3,102,634	3,035,957	2,748,417	2,431,153	2,398,703	2,469,390	1,356,612	940,964
Long-Term Obligations	1,486,206	1,407,284	1,333,848	1,057,752	1,158,928	1,179,507	709,045	452,858
Total Liabilities	1,561,411	1,595,340	1,467,528	1,184,429	1,254,148	1,269,133	761,193	498,695
Stockholders' Equity	1,419,442	1,440,617	1,280,889	1,246,724	1,144,555	1,200,257	595,419	442,269
Shares Outstanding	133,658	131,039	118,939	112,773	101,747	102,842	61,974	60,432
Statistical Record								
Return on Assets %	5.49	5.48	5.30	5.02	5.48	5.03	7.59	7.65
Return on Equity %	11.79	11.65	10.87	10.13	11.38	10.72	16.80	16.63
Net Margin %	39.43	39.63	38.21	36.45	40.56	42.81	53.96	50.42
Price Range	29.09-21.68	25.63-16.68	22.43-18.11	19.51-14.78	15.25-11.84	16.47-10.97	19.63-14.44	20.16-16.00
P/E Ratio	26.21-19.53	26.42-17.19	23.36-18.86	21.92-16.61	14.39-11.17	14.57-9.71	15.45-11.37	18.32-14.55
Average Yield %	6.43	8.01	8.00	8.87	10.77	10.09	7.57	6.83

Address: 4675 MacArthur Court, Suite 900, Newport Beach, CA 92660 **Telephone:** (949) 221-0600 **Fax:** (949) 221-0607	**Web Site:** www.hcpi.com **Officers:** Kenneth B. Roath - Chmn. James F. Flaherty III - Pres., C.E.O.	**Auditors:** Ernst & Young LLP **Investor Contact:** 949-221-0600 **Transfer Agents:** The Bank of New York, New York, NY

HEALTH MANAGEMENT ASSOCIATES, INC.

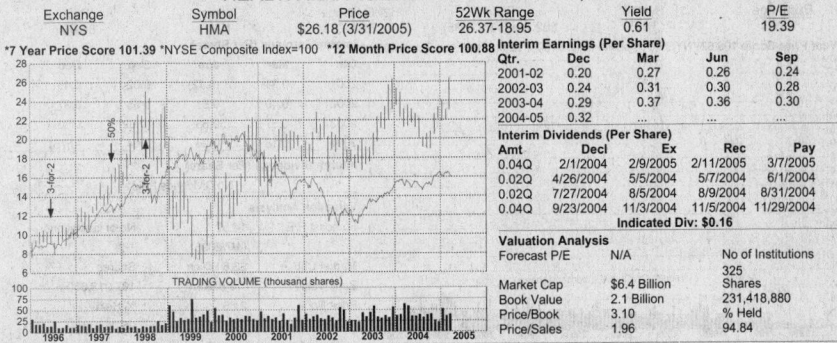

Exchange	Symbol	Price	52Wk Range	Yield	P/E
NYS	HMA	$26.18 (3/31/2005)	26.37-18.95	0.61	19.39

*7 Year Price Score 101.39 *NYSE Composite Index=100 *12 Month Price Score 100.88

Interim Earnings (Per Share)
Qtr.	Dec	Mar	Jun	Sep
2001-02	0.20	0.27	0.26	0.24
2002-03	0.24	0.31	0.30	0.28
2003-04	0.29	0.37	0.36	0.30
2004-05	0.32	...	...	...

Interim Dividends (Per Share)
Amt	Decl	Ex	Rec	Pay
0.04Q	2/1/2004	2/9/2005	2/11/2005	3/7/2005
0.02Q	4/26/2004	5/5/2004	5/7/2004	6/1/2004
0.02Q	7/27/2004	8/5/2004	8/9/2004	8/31/2004
0.04Q	9/23/2004	11/3/2004	11/5/2004	11/29/2004
			Indicated Div: $0.16	

Valuation Analysis
Forecast P/E	N/A	No of Institutions 325
Market Cap	$6.4 Billion	Shares
Book Value	2.1 Billion	231,418,880
Price/Book	3.10	% Held
Price/Sales	1.96	94.84

Business Summary: Hospitals & Health Care (MIC: 9.3 SIC: 062 NAIC: 22110)

Health Management Associates, through its subsidiaries, owns and operates general acute care hospitals and psychiatric hospitals in non-urban communities. As of Sep 30 2004, Co. operated 52 hospitals, consisting of 50 acute care hospitals with a total of 7,286 licensed beds and two psychiatric hospitals with a total of 178 licensed beds. Co. operates facilities located in Alabama, Arkansas, Florida, Georgia, Kentucky, Mississippi, Missouri, North Carolina, Oklahoma, Pennsylvania, South Carolina, Tennessee, Texas, Virginia, Washington and West Virginia. Co. provides both inpatient and outpatient services in its hospitals.

Recent Developments: For the quarter ended Dec 31 2004, net income increased 10.4% to $78,752 thousand from net income of $71,311 thousand in the year-earlier quarter. Revenues were $822,181 thousand, up 8.7% from $756,553 thousand the year before. Total indirect expense was $690,761 thousand versus $635,410 thousand in the prior-year quarter, an increase of 8.7%.

Prospects: Effective Feb 1 2005, Co. completed the acquisition of three hospitals from Bon Secours Health System, Inc. They include the 312-bed Bon Secours Venice Hospital, located in Venice, FL, the 212-bed Bon Secours St. Joseph's Hospital, located in Port Charlotte, FL, and the 133-bed Bon Secours St. Mary's Hospital in Norton, VA. The Venice and St. Joseph's hospitals are located in southwest Florida in areas that Co. believes will continue to need additional health care services, notably in the delivery of services to favorable demographic segments. Co. stated that with this acquisition, it will be in the range of its fiscal 2005 acquisition objective of acquiring between four and six hospitals.

Financial Data
(US$ in Thousands)	3 Mos	09/30/2004	09/30/2003	09/30/2002	09/30/2001	09/30/2000	09/30/1999	09/30/1998
Earnings Per Share	1.35	1.32	1.13	0.97	0.76	0.68	0.59	0.54
Cash Flow Per Share	2.13	1.88	1.40	1.47	1.19	0.73	0.67	0.47
Tang Book Value Per Share	5.36	5.05	5.16	4.24	4.08	3.27	2.89	2.82
Dividends Per Share	0.100	0.080	0.080	...	...	...	...	...
Dividend Payout %	7.43	6.06	7.08	...	...	...	...	...
Income Statement								
Total Revenue	822,181	3,205,885	2,560,576	2,262,601	1,879,801	1,577,767	1,355,707	1,138,802
EBITDA	164,135	661,395	568,600	500,990	411,597	350,494	307,931	275,716
Depn & Amortn	36,595	134,915	109,864	95,328	90,646	74,499	61,278	50,437
Income Before Taxes	127,540	526,480	458,736	405,662	320,951	275,995	246,653	225,279
Income Taxes	48,788	201,381	175,312	159,226	125,973	108,328	96,808	88,435
Net Income	78,752	325,099	283,424	246,436	194,978	167,667	149,845	136,844
Average Shares	247,379	246,826	255,884	260,641	264,351	247,277	255,067	255,575
Balance Sheet								
Current Assets	1,017,740	941,594	1,093,336	695,786	565,231	486,963	425,472	308,707
Total Assets	3,632,199	3,507,288	2,979,487	2,364,317	1,941,577	1,772,065	1,517,300	1,112,105
Current Liabilities	343,440	320,131	272,963	273,743	188,087	169,782	175,221	120,546
Long-Term Obligations	927,212	925,518	924,713	650,159	428,990	520,151	401,522	134,217
Total Liabilities	1,569,234	1,529,278	1,342,412	1,017,565	687,928	741,999	626,777	355,280
Stockholders' Equity	2,062,965	1,978,010	1,637,075	1,346,752	1,253,649	1,030,066	890,523	756,825
Shares Outstanding	243,989	243,481	240,205	238,567	245,435	255,357	253,405	251,558
Statistical Record								
Return on Assets %	9.50	10.00	10.61	11.45	10.50	10.17	11.40	14.88
Return on Equity %	17.45	17.94	19.00	18.95	17.08	17.41	18.19	20.78
EBITDA Margin %	19.96	20.63	22.21	22.14	21.90	22.21	22.71	24.21
Net Margin %	9.58	10.14	11.07	10.89	10.37	10.63	11.05	12.02
Asset Turnover	0.94	0.99	0.96	1.05	1.01	0.96	1.03	1.24
Current Ratio	2.96	2.94	4.01	2.54	3.01	2.87	2.43	2.56
Debt to Equity	0.45	0.47	0.56	0.48	0.34	0.50	0.45	0.18
Price Range	25.33-18.95	26.29-19.00	22.80-16.69	22.87-16.53	22.31-13.96	20.81-7.00	23.50-7.38	25.06-14.06
P/E Ratio	18.76-14.04	19.92-14.39	20.18-14.77	23.58-17.04	29.36-18.37	30.61-10.29	39.83-12.50	46.41-26.03
Average Yield %	0.46	0.36	0.42	...	...	...	...	...

Address: 5811 Pelican Bay Boulevard, Suite 500, Naples, FL 34108-2710 Telephone: (239) 598-3131	Web Site: www.hma-corp.com Officers: William J. Schoen - Chmn. Joseph V. Vumbacco - Pres., C.E.O.	Auditors: Ernst & Young LLP Investor Contact: 941-598-3131

HEALTH NET, INC.

Exchange	Symbol	Price	52Wk Range	Yield	P/E
NYS	HNT	$32.71 (3/31/2005)	32.71-22.23	N/A	86.08

*7 Year Price Score 106.62 *NYSE Composite Index=100 *12 Month Price Score 106.40

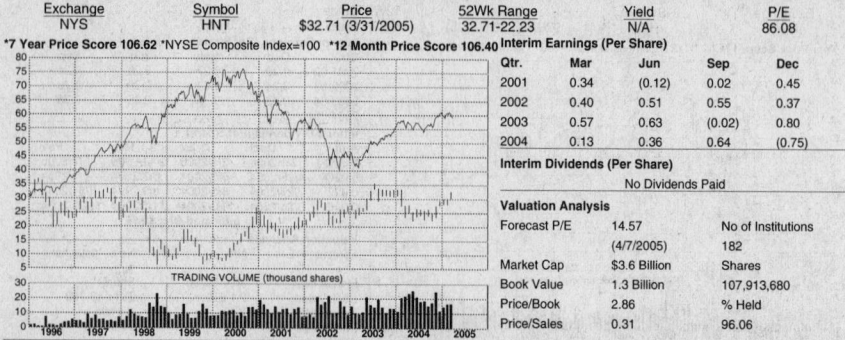

Interim Earnings (Per Share)

Qtr.	Mar	Jun	Sep	Dec
2001	0.34	(0.12)	0.02	0.45
2002	0.40	0.51	0.55	0.37
2003	0.57	0.63	(0.02)	0.80
2004	0.13	0.36	0.64	(0.75)

Interim Dividends (Per Share)

No Dividends Paid

Valuation Analysis

Forecast P/E	14.57		No of Institutions
	(4/7/2005)		182
Market Cap	$3.6 Billion		Shares
Book Value	1.3 Billion		107,913,680
Price/Book	2.86		% Held
Price/Sales	0.31		96.06

Business Summary: Diagnostic Services (MIC: 9.5 SIC: 099 NAIC: 21491)

Health Net is a managed care organization that administers the delivery of managed healthcare services. Co.'s health maintenance organizations, insured preferred provider organizations and point-of-service plans provide health benefits to approximately 5.3 million individuals in 14 states through group, individual, Medicare, Medicaid and TRICARE programs as of Dec 31 2003. Co. also offers managed health care products related to behavioral health and prescription drugs. Additionally, Co. offers health and life insurance and indemnity products, as well as auxiliary non-health products such as life and accidental death and disability insurance, in 36 states and the District of Columbia.

Recent Developments: For the year ended Dec 31 2004, net income decreased 81.8% to $42,604 thousand from net income of $234,030 thousand a year earlier. Revenues were $11,646,393 thousand, up 5.3% from $11,064,702 thousand the year before. Net premiums earned were $9,560,244 thousand versus $9,093,219 thousand in the prior year, an increase of 5.1%. Net investment income fell 2.0% to $58,147 thousand from $59,332 thousand a year ago.

Prospects: Co.'s focus on pricing, which should enhance its position for 2005, continues to result in lower commercial enrollment. Co. noted that commercial enrollment, including both at-risk and Administrative Services Only membership, was down 3.3% for the quarter ended Dec 31 2004 versus the third quarter of 2004. Co. expects that commercial enrollment will be down modestly overall for 2005. However, Co. expects to gain membership in several markets in the second half of the year. Consequently, Co. believes its earnings per diluted share for full year 2005 will be between $2.30 and $2.50. Co. believes that its earnings per diluted share in the first quarter of 2005 will be between $0.50 and $0.55.

Financial Data

(US$ in Thousands)	12/31/2004	12/31/2003	12/31/2002	12/31/2001	12/31/2000	12/31/1999	12/31/1998	12/31/1997
Earnings Per Share	0.38	1.98	1.82	0.69	1.33	1.16	(1.35)	(1.52)
Cash Flow Per Share	(0.49)	3.27	3.38	4.44	2.98	2.43	0.83	(1.02)
Tang Book Value Per Share	4.74	4.80	4.35	2.94	1.61	N.M.	N.M.	N.M.
Income Statement								
Total Revenue	11,646,393	11,064,702	10,201,543	10,064,460	9,076,555	8,706,219	8,896,076	7,235,019
EBITDA	111,704	575,648	426,687	236,045	368,646	356,049	(126,054)	9,152
Depn & Amortn	44,288	58,677	70,192	98,695	105,899	112,041	128,100	98,400
Income Before Taxes	67,416	516,971	356,495	137,350	262,747	244,008	(254,154)	(89,248)
Income Taxes	24,812	193,891	118,928	50,821	99,124	96,226	(88,996)	(21,418)
Net Income	42,604	234,030	228,626	86,529	163,623	142,365	(165,158)	(187,084)
Average Shares	113,038	118,278	126,004	125,186	123,453	122,343	121,974	123,821
Balance Sheet								
Current Assets	2,492,314	2,412,480	2,372,404	2,341,943	2,399,554	2,347,793	2,239,884	2,409,693
Total Assets	3,653,194	3,549,276	3,466,677	3,559,647	3,670,116	3,696,481	3,929,541	4,076,350
Current Liabilities	1,861,156	1,773,705	1,702,050	1,755,526	1,811,081	1,730,329	1,825,431	1,764,672
Long-Term Obligations	397,760	398,963	398,821	593,860	766,450	1,039,352	1,254,278	1,308,979
Total Liabilities	2,380,314	2,255,051	2,157,628	2,394,135	2,608,985	2,805,282	3,185,499	3,180,376
Stockholders' Equity	1,272,880	1,294,225	1,309,049	1,165,512	1,061,131	891,199	744,042	895,974
Shares Outstanding	111,277	113,427	120,642	123,685	122,800	122,373	122,216	121,553
Statistical Record								
Return on Assets %	1.18	6.67	6.51	2.39	4.43	3.73	N.M.	N.M.
Return on Equity %	3.31	17.98	18.48	7.77	16.72	17.41	N.M.	N.M.
EBITDA Margin %	0.96	5.20	4.18	2.35	4.06	4.09	N.M.	0.13
Net Margin %	0.37	2.12	2.24	0.86	1.80	1.64	N.M.	N.M.
Asset Turnover	3.23	3.15	2.90	2.78	2.46	2.28	2.22	2.74
Current Ratio	1.34	1.36	1.39	1.33	1.32	1.36	1.23	1.37
Debt to Equity	0.31	0.31	0.30	0.51	0.72	1.17	1.69	1.46
Price Range	33.46-22.23	35.62-23.06	29.65-20.61	25.63-16.13	26.88-7.69	19.06-6.50	32.13-6.31	33.69-22.25
P/E Ratio	88.05-58.50	17.99-11.65	16.29-11.32	37.14-23.38	20.21-5.78	16.43-5.60	...	...

Address: 21650 Oxnard Street,	Web Site: www.healthnet.com	Auditors: Deloitte & Touche LLP
Woodland Hills, CA 91367	Officers: Jay M. Gellert - Pres., C.E.O. Marvin P.	Investor Contact: 818-676-6978
Telephone: (818) 676-6000	Rich - Exec. V.P., Fin., Oper.	Transfer Agents: Computershare
Fax: (818) 676-6000		Investor Services

HEALTHCARE REALTY TRUST, INC.

Exchange	Symbol	Price	52Wk Range	Yield	P/E	Div Acheiver
NYS	HR	$36.44 (3/31/2005)	43.66-32.87	7.14	25.31	11 Years

*7 Year Price Score 119.50 *NYSE Composite Index=100 ***12 Month Price Score 89.91**

Interim Earnings (Per Share)

Qtr.	Mar	Jun	Sep	Dec
2001	0.47	0.44	0.45	0.45
2002	0.44	0.50	0.44	0.17
2003	0.45	0.42	0.42	0.40
2004	0.42	0.37	0.31	0.34

Interim Dividends (Per Share)

Amt	Decl	Ex	Rec	Pay
0.635Q	4/27/2004	5/12/2004	5/14/2004	6/3/2004
0.64Q	7/27/2004	8/12/2004	8/16/2004	9/2/2004
0.645Q	10/26/2004	11/10/2004	11/15/2004	12/2/2004
0.65Q	1/25/2005	2/10/2005	2/14/2005	3/3/2005

Indicated Div: $2.60 (Div. Reinv. Plan)

Valuation Analysis

Forecast P/E	13.56	No of Institutions
	(4/7/2005)	172
Market Cap	$1.7 Billion	Shares
Book Value	1.0 Billion	27,215,148
Price/Book	1.69	% Held
Price/Sales	8.06	57.07

Business Summary: Property, Real Estate & Development (MIC: 8.3 SIC: 798 NAIC: 25930)

Healthcare Realty Trust is a self-managed and self-administered real estate investment trust (REIT) that integrates owning, acquiring, managing and developing real estate properties and mortgages associated with the delivery of healthcare services throughout the U.S. Co. focuses predominantly on outpatient healthcare facilities, which are designed to provide medical services outside of traditional impatient hospital or nursing home settings. As of Dec 31 2003, Co. had investments of $1.70 billion in 218 properties and mortgages located in 30 states, and affiliated with 61 healthcare-related entities.

Recent Developments: For the year ended Dec 31 2004, income from continuing operations declined 8.2% to $57.6 million compared with $62.8 million in the previous year. Earnings for 2004 and 2003 excluded income from discontinued operations of $5.8 million and $62.8 million, respectively. Results for 2004 included a charge for an adjustment to amortization of deferred compensation of $2.4 million. Total revenues advanced 23.3% to $227.2 million from $184.2 million a year earlier. Total costs and expenses jumped 39.6% to $169.5 million from $121.4 million the year before.

Prospects: Results are being negatively affected by the application of Financial Accounting Standards Board (FASB) Statement No. 141 in accounting for the acquisition of real estate operations. FASB Statement No. 141 requires that the purchase price of these real estate operations be allocated between the land, the physical building as if the building was vacant when acquired and the lease intangible assets acquired. The purchase price allocated to the lease intangible assets is amortized over the remaining lease term, typically one to five years. This has reduced net income more notably in 2004 than prior years due to Co.'s increased volume of acquisitions, which totaled $299.0 million during 2004.

Financial Data

(US$ in Thousands)	9 Mos	6 Mos	3 Mos	12/31/2003	12/31/2002	12/31/2001	12/31/2000	12/31/1999
Earnings Per Share	1.50	1.61	1.66	1.69	1.55	1.81	1.82	1.99
Cash Flow Per Share	2.55	2.36	1.95	2.36	2.66	2.29	3.16	2.34
Tang Book Value Per Share	21.61	20.54	20.79	21.07	21.72	24.41	25.00	25.44
Dividends Per Share	2.530	2.510	2.490	2.470	2.390	2.310	2.230	2.150
Dividend Payout %	169.16	156.34	150.42	146.15	154.19	127.62	122.53	108.04
Income Statement								
Property Income	147,812	99,367	47,956	177,470	177,800	173,461	167,465	156,733
Non-Property Income	22,781	7,580	3,708	14,527	16,727	21,077	27,873	30,524
Total Revenue	170,593	106,947	51,664	191,997	194,527	194,538	195,338	187,257
Depn & Amortn	40,006	24,763	11,935	46,162	46,558	45,129	42,938	42,378
Interest Expense	32,470	20,755	8,973	34,601	34,195	38,110	42,995	38,603
Net Income	47,375	33,437	17,812	70,507	70,091	79,887	79,801	86,027
Average Shares	45,692	42,414	42,379	41,780	41,606	40,463	40,301	39,810
Balance Sheet								
Total Assets	1,807,296	1,691,697	1,647,813	1,525,710	1,489,546	1,555,910	1,587,076	1,607,964
Long-Term Obligations	720,865	764,198	716,872	590,281	545,063	505,222	536,781	563,884
Total Liabilities	776,984	807,220	752,998	623,432	581,347	543,823	579,039	590,061
Stockholders' Equity	1,030,312	884,477	894,815	902,278	908,199	1,012,087	1,008,037	1,017,903
Shares Outstanding	47,682	43,065	43,046	42,823	41,823	41,465	40,314	40,004
Statistical Record								
Return on Assets %	3.85	4.26	4.44	4.68	4.60	5.08	4.98	5.34
Return on Equity %	6.60	7.59	7.74	7.79	7.30	7.91	7.86	8.45
Net Margin %	27.77	31.27	34.48	36.72	36.03	41.06	40.85	45.94
Price Range	43.66-31.98	43.66-29.15	42.83-24.42	36.45-24.42	32.15-27.28	28.25-21.38	21.44-15.50	22.81-14.69
P/E Ratio	29.11-21.32	27.12-18.11	25.80-14.71	21.57-14.45	20.74-17.60	15.61-11.81	11.78-8.52	11.46-7.38
Average Yield %	6.84	7.06	7.43	8.06	7.94	9.14	12.24	10.90

Address: 3310 West End Avenue, Suite 700, Nashville, TN 37203 **Telephone:** (615) 269-8175 **Fax:** (615) 269-8461	**Web Site:** www.healthcarerealty.com **Officers:** David R. Emery - Chmn., C.E.O. Scott W. Holmes - Sr. V.P., C.F.O.	**Auditors:** Ernst & Young LLP **Investor Contact:** 781-575-3400 **Transfer Agents:** EquiServe , Providence, RI

HEARST-ARGYLE TELEVISION INC.

Exchange	Symbol	Price	52Wk Range	Yield	P/E
NYS	HTV	$25.50 (3/31/2005)	27.68-22.63	1.10	19.62

*7 Year Price Score 89.27 *NYSE Composite Index=100 *12 Month Price Score 93.24

Interim Earnings (Per Share)

Qtr.	Mar	Jun	Sep	Dec
2001	0.22	0.10	(0.07)	0.08
2002	0.15	0.33	0.27	0.40
2003	0.11	0.29	0.24	0.36
2004	0.19	0.37	0.32	0.41

Interim Dividends (Per Share)

Amt	Decl	Ex	Rec	Pay
0.06Q	6/25/2004	6/30/2004	7/5/2004	7/15/2004
0.06Q	9/22/2004	10/1/2004	10/5/2004	10/15/2004
0.07Q	12/1/2004	1/3/2005	1/5/2005	1/15/2005
0.07Q	3/31/2005	4/1/2005	4/5/2005	4/15/2005

Indicated Div: $0.28

Valuation Analysis

Forecast P/E	25.20 (4/7/2005)	No of Institutions 119
Market Cap	$2.5 Billion	Shares 23,078,596
Book Value	1.8 Billion	% Held
Price/Book	1.40	24.84
Price/Sales	3.16	

Business Summary: Media (MIC: 13.1 SIC: 833 NAIC: 15112)

Hearst-Argyle Television owned or managed 28 television stations reaching approximately 18.2% of television households in the U.S. as of Dec. 31, 2004. Co.'s 13 ABC-affiliated television stations, which cover 8.4% of U.S. television households, comprise the largest ABC affiliate group. Co.'s 10 NBC-affiliated television stations, which cover 7.3% of U.S. television households, comprise the second largest NBC affiliate group. Co. also owns two CBS-affiliated television stations and one WB station, and manages one UPN station and one independent station. In addition, Co. also manages two radio stations.

Recent Developments: For the year ended Dec 31 2004, net income increased 31.5% to $123,942,000 from net income of $94,221,000 a year earlier. Revenues were $7,798,790,00, up 13.6% from $686,775,000 the year before. Operating income was $284,751,000 versus an income of $218,822,000 in the prior year, an increase of 30.1%. Total indirect expense was $495,128,000 versus $467,953,000 in the prior year, an increase of 5.8%.

Prospects: For 2005, Co. is focused on maximizing new revenue opportunities to help counter the non-election year political advertising cycle. Nevertheless, Co. estimates that first quarter 2005 total revenue will be 4.0% to 5.0% below the comparable period in 2004, which reflects the absence of approximately $10.0 million from political advertising and a $2.5 million reduction in network compensation. Conversely, revenues from Co.'s core categories, including automotive, packaged goods, pharmaceuticals, fast foods, beverages, furniture and retail categories, is expected to increase by approximately 3.5% in the first quarter of 2005.

Financial Data
(US$ in Thousands)

	12/31/2004	12/31/2003	12/31/2002	12/31/2001	12/31/2000	12/31/1999	12/31/1998	12/31/1997
Earnings Per Share	1.30	1.00	1.15	0.32	0.47	0.37	0.88	0.14
Cash Flow Per Share	2.10	1.93	2.23	1.81	2.04	1.67	2.50	0.78
Dividends Per Share	0.180	0.060	...	...	...	...	...	...
Dividend Payout %	13.85	6.00	...	...	...	...	...	...
Income Statement								
Total Revenue	779,879	686,775	721,311	641,876	747,281	661,386	407,313	146,440
EBITDA	333,075	275,182	291,268	344,356	378,738	343,653	220,798	82,929
Depn & Amortn	50,376	55,437	43,607	187,096	183,667	168,048	78,764	26,802
Income Before Taxes	200,294	136,530	174,218	57,662	78,908	68,713	102,479	40,297
Income Taxes	76,352	42,309	66,201	27,101	36,438	33,311	42,796	16,419
Net Income	123,942	94,221	108,017	31,087	44,925	32,310	48,857	7,666
Average Shares	101,406	92,990	92,550	92,000	92,457	83,229	53,699	48,752
Balance Sheet								
Current Assets	306,506	284,672	216,196	209,947	232,285	237,134	515,249	227,243
Total Assets	3,842,140	3,799,087	3,762,925	3,779,705	3,817,989	3,913,227	1,421,140	1,044,109
Current Liabilities	137,908	130,418	130,679	131,640	123,748	123,665	90,468	71,868
Long-Term Obligations	1,016,242	1,088,595	1,946,756	2,320,410	2,896,984	3,127,192	1,685,192	980,000
Total Liabilities	2,077,052	2,126,705	1,983,663	2,113,091	2,373,613	2,496,436	1,096,750	717,455
Stockholders' Equity	1,753,837	1,672,382	1,579,262	1,466,614	1,444,376	1,416,791	324,390	326,654
Shares Outstanding	96,510	92,766	92,364	91,827	91,925	94,783	52,137	53,828
Statistical Record								
Return on Assets %	3.24	2.49	2.86	0.82	1.16	1.21	3.96	1.12
Return on Equity %	7.22	5.80	7.09	2.14	3.13	3.71	15.01	3.36
EBITDA Margin %	42.71	40.07	40.38	53.65	50.68	51.96	54.21	56.63
Net Margin %	15.89	13.72	14.98	4.84	6.01	4.89	11.99	5.23
Asset Turnover	0.20	0.18	0.19	0.17	0.19	0.25	0.33	0.21
Current Ratio	2.22	2.18	1.65	1.59	1.88	1.92	5.70	3.16
Debt to Equity	0.58	0.65	1.23	1.58	2.01	2.21	5.19	3.00
Price Range	28.95-22.63	27.61-20.11	27.49-18.90	24.25-16.70	29.06-17.13	34.25-20.31	40.00-24.38	32.50-22.50
P/E Ratio	22.27-17.41	27.61-20.11	23.90-16.43	75.78-52.19	61.84-36.44	92.57-54.90	45.45-27.70	232.14-160.71
Average Yield %	0.70	0.25	...	...	...	...	...	...

Address: 888 Seventh Avenue, New York, NY 10106	Web Site: www.hearstargyle.com	Auditors: Deloitte & Touche LLP
Telephone: (212) 887-6800	Officers: Victor F. Ganzi - Chmn. David J. Barrett - Pres., C.E.O.	Investor Contact: 212-887-6827
Fax: (212) 887-6875		

HEINZ (H.J.) CO.

Exchange	Symbol	Price	52Wk Range	Yield	P/E
NYS	HNZ	$36.84 (3/31/2005)	39.20-34.57	3.09	17.38

*7 Year Price Score 83.71   ***NYSE Composite Index=100**   ***12 Month Price Score 92.31**

Interim Earnings (Per Share)

Qtr.	Jul	Oct	Jan	Apr
2001-02	0.57	0.59	0.57	0.63
2002-03	0.50	0.60	0.43	0.29
2003-04	0.60	0.54	0.57	0.57
2004-05	0.55	0.56	0.43	...

Interim Dividends (Per Share)

Amt	Decl	Ex	Rec	Pay
0.285Q	6/9/2004	6/22/2004	6/24/2004	7/10/2004
0.285Q	9/8/2004	9/21/2004	9/23/2004	10/10/2004
0.285Q	11/10/2004	12/21/2004	12/23/2004	1/10/2005
0.285Q	3/9/2005	3/22/2005	3/24/2005	4/10/2005

Indicated Div: $1.14 (Div. Reinv. Plan)

Valuation Analysis

Forecast P/E	14.98		No of Institutions
	(4/7/2005)		508
Market Cap	$12.9 Billion		Shares
Book Value	2.3 Billion		221,325,040
Price/Book	5.56		% Held
Price/Sales	1.46		63.22

TRADING VOLUME (thousand shares)

Business Summary: Food (MIC: 4.1 SIC: 099 NAIC: 11941)

H.J. Heinz and its subsidiaries manufacture and market an extensive line of processed food products throughout the world. Co.'s principal products include ketchup, condiments and sauces, frozen food, soups, beans and pasta meals, tuna and other seafood products, infant food and other processed food products. Major U.S. brands include Heinz, Classico, Quality Chef, Yoshida, Jack Daniels™, Catelli, Wyler's, Diana Sauce, Bell 'Orto, Bella Rosa, Pablum, Chef Francisco, Domani, Dianne's, Ore-Ida, Bagel Bites, Weight Watchers™, Boston Market™, Smart Ones, Hot Bites, and Poppers. Overseas, well-known brands include Plasmon, Pudliszki, Orlando, Wattie's, Olivine, Farley's, ABC, and Champs.

Recent Developments: For the quarter ended Jan 26 2005, net income decreased 24.6% to $152,411 thousand from net income of $202,237 thousand in the year-earlier quarter. Revenues were $2,261,219 thousand, up 7.8% from $2,097,181 thousand the year before. Operating income was $329,568 thousand versus an income of $355,367 thousand in the prior-year quarter, a decrease of 7.3%. Total direct expense was $1,441,306 thousand versus $1,317,934 thousand in the prior-year quarter, an increase of 9.4%. Total indirect expense was $490,345 thousand versus $423,880 thousand in the prior-year quarter, an increase of 15.7%.

Prospects: Top-line growth is benefiting from strong sales in Co.'s North American businesses, especially its U.S. Consumer Products. However, this growth is being offset by increased commodity and fuel costs, lower pricing and substantially higher supply chain costs in the European seafood business. Co. noted it is reviewing options to realign and simplify its European business. Looking ahead to the balance of fiscal 2005, Co. remains on track with its full-year earnings per share target, excluding special charges, of $2.32 to $2.42, with an expectation toward the lower end of the range. For the full year, operating free cash flow is expected to be in the range of $750.0 million to $850.0 million.

Financial Data

(US$ in Thousands)	9 Mos	6 Mos	3 Mos	04/28/2004	04/30/2003	05/01/2002	05/02/2001	05/03/2000
Earnings Per Share	2.12	2.26	2.24	2.29	1.60	2.36	1.36	2.47
Cash Flow Per Share	2.69	3.25	3.34	3.56	2.59	2.55	1.46	1.50
Dividends Per Share	1.125	1.110	1.095	1.080	1.485	1.607	1.545	1.445
Dividend Payout %	53.16	49.20	48.96	47.16	92.81	68.11	113.60	58.50
Income Statement								
Total Revenue	6,463,805	4,202,586	2,003,026	8,414,538	8,236,836	9,431,000	9,430,422	9,407,949
EBITDA	1,112,697	793,254	392,354	1,591,008	1,275,908	1,847,111	1,282,489	2,014,577
Depn & Amortn	184,700	119,312	59,083	233,943	214,728	301,697	299,166	306,483
Income Before Taxes	777,349	576,640	286,586	1,168,551	868,731	1,278,590	673,058	1,463,676
Income Taxes	246,714	184,525	91,750	389,618	313,372	444,701	178,140	573,123
Net Income	546,212	393,801	194,836	804,273	566,285	833,889	478,012	890,553
Average Shares	353,842	354,145	354,977	354,372	354,144	352,871	351,041	360,095
Balance Sheet								
Current Assets	3,531,446	4,027,149	3,557,226	3,610,796	3,284,320	3,373,566	3,116,814	3,169,949
Total Assets	9,952,867	10,447,979	9,760,486	9,877,189	9,224,751	10,278,354	9,035,150	8,850,657
Current Liabilities	1,814,933	2,580,074	2,249,770	2,469,068	1,926,134	2,509,169	3,655,097	2,126,070
Long-Term Obligations	4,689,436	4,676,639	4,523,797	4,537,980	4,776,143	4,642,968	3,014,853	3,935,826
Total Liabilities	7,631,977	8,282,355	7,793,257	7,983,000	8,025,594	8,559,738	7,661,423	7,254,801
Stockholders' Equity	2,320,890	2,165,624	1,967,229	1,894,189	1,199,157	1,718,616	1,373,727	1,595,856
Shares Outstanding	350,060	349,329	349,448	351,957	351,448	350,904	348,948	347,443
Statistical Record								
Return on Assets %	7.50	8.00	8.37	8.44	5.82	8.66	5.36	10.37
Return on Equity %	36.18	42.87	47.36	52.14	38.92	54.08	32.28	51.56
EBITDA Margin %	17.21	18.88	19.59	18.91	15.49	19.59	13.60	21.41
Net Margin %	8.45	9.37	9.73	9.56	6.88	8.84	5.07	9.47
Asset Turnover	0.89	0.87	0.91	0.88	0.85	0.98	1.06	1.10
Current Ratio	1.95	1.56	1.58	1.46	1.71	1.34	0.85	1.49
Debt to Equity	2.02	2.16	2.30	2.40	3.98	2.70	2.19	2.47
Price Range	39.20-34.57	39.20-34.57	39.20-31.98	38.95-29.71	38.91-27.31	42.31-34.34	42.91-31.93	48.54-27.99
P/E Ratio	18.49-16.31	17.35-15.30	17.50-14.28	17.01-12.97	24.32-17.07	17.93-14.55	31.55-23.48	19.65-11.33
Average Yield %	3.01	3.01	3.03	3.09	4.56	4.27	4.18	3.78

Address: 600 Grant Street, Pittsburgh, PA 15219	Web Site: www.heinz.com	Auditors: PricewaterhouseCoopers LLP
Telephone: (412) 456-5700	Officers: William R. Johnson - Chmn., Pres., C.E.O.	Investor Contact: 412-456-6034
Fax: (412) 456-6128	Joseph Jimenez - Exec. V.P.	Transfer Agents: Mellon Investor Services LLC, Ridgefield Park, NJ

HELMERICH & PAYNE, INC.

Exchange	Symbol	Price	52Wk Range	Yield	P/E	Div Acheiver
NYS	HP	$39.69 (3/31/2005)	41.10-24.01	0.83	52.92	28 Years

*7 Year Price Score 106.40 *NYSE Composite Index=100 *12 Month Price Score 120.88

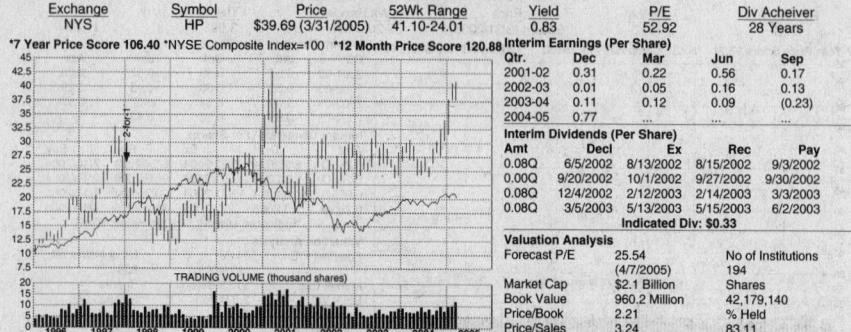

Interim Earnings (Per Share)

Qtr.	Dec	Mar	Jun	Sep
2001-02	0.31	0.22	0.56	0.17
2002-03	0.01	0.05	0.16	0.13
2003-04	0.11	0.12	0.09	(0.23)
2004-05	0.77	...	...	...

Interim Dividends (Per Share)

Amt	Decl	Ex	Rec	Pay
0.08Q	6/5/2002	8/13/2002	8/15/2002	9/3/2002
0.00Q	9/20/2002	10/1/2002	9/27/2002	9/30/2002
0.08Q	12/4/2002	2/12/2003	2/14/2003	3/3/2003
0.08Q	3/5/2003	5/13/2003	5/15/2003	6/2/2003

Indicated Div: $0.33

Valuation Analysis

Forecast P/E	25.54	No of Institutions	
	(4/7/2005)	194	
Market Cap	$2.1 Billion	Shares	
Book Value	960.2 Million	42,179,140	
Price/Book	2.21	% Held	
Price/Sales	3.24	83.11	

Business Summary: Oil and Gas (MIC: 14.2 SIC: 381 NAIC: 13111)

Helmerich & Payne is engaged in contract drilling of oil and gas wells for others. Co. is also engaged in the ownership, development, and operation of commercial real estate. Co. is organized into two separate autonomous operating entities being contract drilling and real estate. Both businesses operate independently of the other. Both the contract drilling and real estate businesses are conducted through wholly-owned subsidiaries. Operating decentralization is balanced by a centralized finance division, which handles all accounting, data processing, budgeting, insurance, cash management, and related activities.

Recent Developments: For the quarter ended Dec 31 2004, net income increased 496.7% to $39,310 thousand from net income of $6,588 thousand in the year-earlier quarter. Revenues were $174,679 thousand, up 30.1% from $134,273 thousand the year before. Operating income was $30,919 thousand versus an income of $9,122 thousand in the prior-year quarter, an increase of 238.9%. Total indirect expense was $143,760 thousand versus $125,151 thousand in the prior-year quarter, an increase of 14.9%.

Prospects: Co. results are encouraging, as tightening U.S. rig supply has translated into meaningful improvements in dayrates and margins. During the first quarter of fiscal 2005, average U.S. land rig revenues and cash margins were up by $926 and $1,340 per day, respectively, over the fourth quarter of 2004. Cash margins averaged $5,563 per rig day versus $3,414 per rig day during the first quarter of 2004. U.S. land rig utilization was 92.0%, an increase from 81.0% utilization recorded the year before. Going forward, Co. expects these conditions in the U.S. will continue and that international rig activity will likely improve if crude oil and natural gas prices remain within recent price ranges.

Financial Data

(US$ in Thousands)	3 Mos	09/30/2004	09/30/2003	09/30/2002	09/30/2001	09/30/2000	09/30/1999	09/30/1998
Earnings Per Share	0.75	0.09	0.35	1.26	2.84	1.64	0.86	2.00
Cash Flow Per Share	2.83	2.68	1.93	3.05	5.57	4.06	3.22	2.27
Tang Book Value Per Share	17.94	18.12	18.29	17.90	20.59	19.12	17.09	16.06
Dividends Per Share	0.325	0.323	0.320	0.305	0.300	0.285	0.280	0.275
Dividend Payout %	43.41	358.33	91.43	24.21	10.56	17.38	32.56	13.75
Income Statement								
Total Revenue	174,679	620,928	515,284	510,928	826,854	631,095	564,319	636,640
EBITDA	...	115,130	128,924	154,769	323,857	252,225	182,152	242,864
Depn & Amortn	23,265	94,435	82,693	62,569	88,787	112,386	110,733	89,702
Income Before Taxes	...	8,000	33,942	91,220	235,102	136,763	64,938	152,220
Income Taxes	27,130	4,365	14,649	40,573	93,027	57,684	25,706	56,677
Net Income	39,310	4,359	17,873	63,517	144,254	82,300	42,788	101,154
Average Shares	51,256	50,833	50,596	50,345	50,772	50,035	49,817	50,565
Balance Sheet								
Current Assets	352,239	245,886	197,531	178,751	331,412	265,144	160,624	184,345
Total Assets	1,473,092	1,406,844	1,415,835	1,227,313	1,364,507	1,259,492	1,109,699	1,090,430
Current Liabilities	58,342	59,903	88,618	72,899	121,221	78,894	71,904	125,484
Long-Term Obligations	200,000	200,000	200,000	100,000	50,000	50,000	50,000	50,000
Total Liabilities	512,923	492,734	498,584	332,143	338,030	303,789	261,590	297,282
Stockholders' Equity	960,169	914,110	917,251	895,170	1,026,477	955,703	848,109	793,148
Shares Outstanding	53,529	50,445	50,140	50,010	49,852	49,980	49,625	49,383
Statistical Record								
Return on Assets %	2.61	0.31	1.35	4.90	10.99	6.93	3.89	9.52
Return on Equity %	4.03	0.47	1.97	6.61	14.56	9.10	5.21	12.86
EBITDA Margin %	...	18.54	25.02	30.29	39.17	39.97	32.28	38.15
Net Margin %	22.50	0.70	3.47	12.43	17.45	13.04	7.58	15.89
Asset Turnover	0.45	0.44	0.39	0.39	0.63	0.53	0.51	0.60
Current Ratio	6.04	4.10	2.23	2.45	2.73	3.36	2.23	1.47
Debt to Equity	0.21	0.22	0.22	0.11	0.05	0.05	0.06	0.06
Price Range	34.16-24.01	30.61-23.57	32.34-23.57	31.42-18.40	42.84-17.38	28.19-14.00	22.10-11.76	32.92-11.90
P/E Ratio	45.55-32.01	340.11-264.11	92.40-67.34	24.93-14.60	15.08-6.12	17.19-8.54	25.70-13.68	16.46-5.95
Average Yield %	1.16	1.20	1.17	1.24	1.05	1.34	1.70	1.29

Address: 1437 South Boulder Avenue, Suite 1400, Tulsa, OK 74119 **Telephone:** (918) 742-5531 **Fax:** (918) 742-0237	**Web Site:** www.hpinc.com **Officers:** W. H. Helmerich III - Chmn. Hans C. Helmerich - Pres., C.E.O.	**Auditors:** Ernst & Young LLP **Investor Contact:** 918-742-5531 **Transfer Agents:** UMB Bank, Kansas City, MO

HERCULES INC.

Exchange	Symbol	Price	52Wk Range	Yield	P/E
NYS	HPC	$14.49 (3/31/2005)	15.24-9.99	N/A	57.96

*7 Year Price Score 64.30   *NYSE Composite Index=100   ***12 Month Price Score 102.66**

TRADING VOLUME (thousand shares)

Interim Earnings (Per Share)

Qtr.	Mar	Jun	Sep	Dec
2001	(0.09)	0.21	(0.66)	0.00
2002	(5.32)	(0.10)	(0.32)	0.09
2003	(0.14)	0.29	0.17	0.10
2004	0.24	0.04	(0.47)	0.45

Interim Dividends (Per Share)

No Dividends Paid

Valuation Analysis

Forecast P/E	N/A	No of Institutions
Market Cap	$1.6 Billion	Shares
Book Value	97.0 Million	99,763,760
Price/Book	16.75	% Held
Price/Sales	0.81	88.32

Business Summary: Chemicals (MIC: 11.1 SIC: 899 NAIC: 25998)

Hercules is a manufacturer and marketer of specialty chemicals and related services for a broad range of business, consumer and industrial applications. Co. has significant operations in North America, Europe, Asia and Latin America, and product sales in over 50 countries. Co.'s principal products are chemicals used by the paper industry to increase paper and paperboard performance and enhance the manufacturing process; water-soluble polymers; polypropylene and polypropylene/polyethylene bicomponent fibers; and specialty resins. Co. serves the pulp and paper, paints and adhesives, construction materials, food, pharmaceutical and personal care, and industrial specialties markets.

Recent Developments: For the year ended Dec 31 2004, net income decreased 40.0% to $27,000 thousand from net income of $45,000 thousand a year earlier. Revenues were $1,997,000 thousand, up 8.2% from $1,846,000 thousand the year before. Operating income was $227,000 thousand versus an income of $255,000 thousand in the prior year, a decrease of 11.0%. Total direct expense was $1,310,000 thousand versus $1,167,000 thousand in the prior year, an increase of 12.3%. Total indirect expense was $460,000 thousand versus $424,000 thousand in the prior year, an increase of 8.5%.

Prospects: Escalating raw material costs temper Co.'s prospects. Co. noted that overall, volumes remain strong; however, rising raw material costs, especially polypropylene, have affected its bottom-line results. Looking ahead, Co. expects a continued solid performance from its Aqualon unit and improving operating profit from its Pulp and Paper unit. Also, Co. expects that polypropylene costs in its FiberVisions unit will remain at historically high levels, but noted that costs should flatten out in 2005. Meanwhile, Co. has instituted price hikes across its businesses to help offset higher raw material costs and continued with cost savings and productivity initiatives to raise its profitability.

Financial Data
(US$ in Thousands)

	12/31/2004	12/31/2003	12/31/2002	12/31/2001	12/31/2000	12/31/1999	12/31/1998	12/31/1997
Earnings Per Share	0.25	0.42	(5.65)	(0.54)	0.91	1.62	0.10	3.13
Cash Flow Per Share	1.12	0.21	(1.99)	1.01	0.65	2.71	1.88	1.89
Tang Book Value Per Share	N.M.	N.M.	...	N.M.	N.M.	N.M.	N.M.	7.18
Dividends Per Share	...	...	...	...	0.620	1.080	1.080	1.000
Dividend Payout %	...	...	...	...	68.13	66.67	1,080.00	31.95
Income Statement								
Total Revenue	1,997,000	1,846,000	1,705,000	2,620,000	3,152,000	3,248,000	2,145,000	1,866,000
EBITDA	221,000	307,000	123,000	397,000	535,000	643,000	252,000	679,000
Depn & Amortn	83,000	81,000	82,000	178,000	212,000	223,000	108,000	76,000
Income Before Taxes	29,000	95,000	(55,000)	23,000	164,000	243,000	77,000	593,000
Income Taxes	2,000	21,000	(4,000)	72,000	66,000	75,000	68,000	269,000
Net Income	27,000	45,000	(616,000)	(58,000)	98,000	168,000	9,000	319,000
Average Shares	109,000	107,900	109,100	108,200	107,400	103,900	97,400	102,400
Balance Sheet								
Current Assets	772,000	820,000	907,000	842,000	1,022,000	1,338,000	1,240,000	689,000
Total Assets	2,710,000	2,766,000	2,693,000	5,049,000	5,309,000	5,896,000	5,833,000	2,411,000
Current Liabilities	477,000	457,000	616,000	917,000	922,000	1,559,000	1,317,000	799,000
Long-Term Obligations	1,210,000	1,326,000	738,000	1,959,000	2,342,000	1,777,000	3,096,000	419,000
Total Liabilities	2,613,000	2,700,000	2,192,000	3,713,000	3,871,000	4,041,000	5,074,000	1,721,000
Stockholders' Equity	97,000	66,000	(123,000)	712,000	816,000	863,000	559,000	690,000
Shares Outstanding	112,141	110,991	109,369	108,787	107,542	106,389	100,828	96,068
Statistical Record								
Return on Assets %	0.98	1.65	N.M.	N.M.	1.74	2.86	0.22	13.30
Return on Equity %	33.04	...	N.M.	N.M.	11.64	23.63	1.44	40.46
EBITDA Margin %	11.07	16.63	7.21	15.15	16.97	19.80	11.75	36.39
Net Margin %	1.35	2.44	N.M.	N.M.	3.11	5.17	0.42	17.10
Asset Turnover	0.73	0.68	0.44	0.51	0.56	0.55	0.52	0.78
Current Ratio	1.62	1.79	1.47	0.92	1.11	0.86	0.94	0.86
Debt to Equity	12.47	20.09	...	2.75	2.87	2.06	5.54	0.61
Price Range	15.09-9.99	12.40-7.60	13.68-8.67	19.94-6.94	27.88-11.63	40.38-22.50	50.06-25.56	54.50-38.75
P/E Ratio	60.36-39.96	29.52-18.10	...	...	30.63-12.77	24.92-13.89	500.63-255.63	17.41-12.38
Average Yield %	...	...	...	...	3.77	3.55	2.73	2.12

Address: Hercules Plaza, 1313 North Market Street, Wilmington, DE 19894-0001
Telephone: (302) 594-5000
Fax: (302) 594-5400

Web Site: www.herc.com
Officers: John K. Wulff - Chmn. Craig A. Rogerson - Pres., C.E.O.

Auditors: PricewaterhouseCoopers LLP
Investor Contact: 302-594-6491

HERSHEY FOODS CORP.

Exchange	Symbol	Price	52Wk Range	Yield	P/E	Div Acheiver
NYS	HSY	$60.46 (3/31/2005)	64.42-40.90	1.46	26.29	30 Years

*7 Year Price Score 127.21 *NYSE Composite Index=100 *12 Month Price Score 112.93

Interim Earnings (Per Share)

Qtr.	Mar	Jun	Sep	Dec
2001	0.28	0.19	0.44	(0.17)
2002	0.32	0.23	0.45	0.48
2003	0.36	0.27	0.55	0.55
2004	0.41	0.56	0.66	0.68

Interim Dividends (Per Share)

Amt	Decl	Ex	Rec	Pay
0.198Q	4/28/2004	5/21/2004	5/25/2004	6/15/2004
0.22Q	7/28/2004	8/23/2004	8/25/2004	9/15/2004
0.22Q	10/5/2004	11/22/2004	11/24/2004	12/15/2004
0.22Q	2/15/2005	2/23/2005	2/25/2005	3/15/2005

Indicated Div: $0.88 (Div. Reinv. Plan)

Valuation Analysis

Forecast P/E	25.83 (4/7/2005)	No of Institutions	437
Market Cap	$14.9 Billion	Shares	107,055,192
Book Value	1.1 Billion	% Held	57.87
Price/Book	13.69		
Price/Sales	3.37		

Business Summary: Food (MIC: 4.1 SIC: 066 NAIC: 11320)

Hershey Foods is engaged in the manufacture, distribution and sale of consumer food products including: chocolate and non-chocolate confectionery products sold in the form of bar goods, bagged items and boxed items; and grocery products sold in the form of baking ingredients, chocolate drink mixes, peanut butter, dessert toppings and beverages. Co.'s products are marketed in over 90 countries worldwide under more than 50 brands. Principal confectionery brands include: Hershey's®, Reese's®, Mr. Goodbar®, Jolly Rancher®, Kit Kat®, Milk Duds®, Whoppers®, York®, Twizzlers®, Super Bubble®, Ice Breakers®, Breath Savers® and Care*free®.

Recent Developments: For the year ended Dec 31 2004, net income increased 29.1% to $590,879 thousand from net income of $457,584 thousand a year earlier. Revenues were $4,429,248 thousand, up 6.2% from $4,172,551 thousand the year before. Operating income was $902,177 thousand versus an income of $796,356 thousand in the prior year, an increase of 13.3%. Total direct expense was $2,679,531 thousand versus $2,544,726 thousand in the prior year, an increase of 5.3%. Total indirect expense was $847,540 thousand versus $831,469 thousand in the prior year, an increase of 1.9%.

Prospects: On Dec 16 2004, Co. announced an average 5.8% wholesale price increase on its standard candy bars, king-size bars, six-pack and vending-machine lines effective immediately. Co. also announced it would raise the cost of packed chocolates by an average of 4.1% effective Feb 14 2005. All told, the changes apply to about half of Co.'s domestic confectionery and translate into a 3.0% price increase over its entire domestic product line. For 2005, Co. expects organic net sales to grow near the top of its long-term objective of 3.0% to 4.0%, before the benefit of the business acquisitions completed in 2004. Earnings per share are expected to increase within its long-range goal of 9.0% to 11.0%.

Financial Data
(US$ in Thousands)

	12/31/2004	12/31/2003	12/31/2002	12/31/2001	12/31/2000	12/31/1999	12/31/1998	12/31/1997
Earnings Per Share	2.30	1.73	1.47	0.75	1.21	1.63	1.17	1.12
Cash Flow Per Share	3.13	2.26	2.29	2.59	1.50	1.17	1.36	1.60
Tang Book Value Per Share	2.03	3.29	3.55	2.16	2.57	2.34	1.79	1.05
Dividends Per Share	0.835	0.723	0.630	0.583	0.540	0.500	0.460	0.420
Dividend Payout %	36.30	41.76	42.86	77.67	44.63	30.67	39.32	37.67
Income Statement								
Total Revenue	4,429,248	4,172,551	4,120,317	4,557,241	4,220,976	3,970,924	4,435,615	4,302,236
EBITDA	1,091,842	976,923	876,195	603,128	798,614	965,453	800,824	782,960
Depn & Amortn	189,665	180,567	177,908	190,494	175,964	163,308	158,161	152,750
Income Before Taxes	835,644	732,827	637,565	343,541	546,639	727,874	557,006	553,955
Income Taxes	244,765	267,875	233,987	136,385	212,096	267,564	216,118	217,704
Net Income	590,879	457,584	403,578	207,156	334,543	460,310	340,888	336,251
Average Shares	256,827	264,532	275,429	275,392	276,730	282,600	291,126	302,032
Balance Sheet								
Current Assets	1,182,441	1,131,569	1,263,618	1,167,541	1,295,348	1,279,980	1,133,966	1,034,814
Total Assets	3,797,531	3,582,540	3,480,551	3,247,430	3,447,764	3,346,652	3,404,098	3,291,236
Current Liabilities	1,285,382	585,810	546,940	604,444	766,901	712,829	814,824	795,715
Long-Term Obligations	690,602	968,499	851,800	876,972	877,654	878,213	879,103	1,029,136
Total Liabilities	2,708,229	2,302,674	2,108,848	2,100,226	2,272,728	2,248,025	2,361,797	2,438,430
Stockholders' Equity	1,089,302	1,279,866	1,371,703	1,147,204	1,175,036	1,098,627	1,042,301	852,806
Shares Outstanding	246,587	259,059	268,440	332,145	272,563	276,919	286,294	285,864
Statistical Record								
Return on Assets %	15.97	12.96	12.00	6.19	9.82	13.64	10.18	10.38
Return on Equity %	49.74	34.51	32.04	17.84	29.35	43.00	35.98	33.39
EBITDA Margin %	24.65	23.41	21.27	13.23	18.92	24.31	18.05	18.20
Net Margin %	13.34	10.97	9.79	4.55	7.93	11.59	7.69	7.82
Asset Turnover	1.20	1.18	1.22	1.36	1.24	1.18	1.32	1.33
Current Ratio	0.92	1.93	2.31	1.93	1.69	1.80	1.39	1.30
Debt to Equity	0.63	0.76	0.62	0.76	0.75	0.80	0.84	1.21
Price Range	56.58-37.42	39.26-30.65	39.74-28.68	34.66-28.50	32.81-18.88	32.00-23.16	38.03-29.91	31.66-21.19
P/E Ratio	24.60-16.27	22.69-17.72	27.04-19.51	46.21-38.00	27.12-15.60	19.63-14.21	32.51-25.56	28.26-18.92
Average Yield %	1.82	2.05	1.86	1.85	2.20	1.82	1.36	1.57

Address: 100 Crystal A Drive, Hershey, PA 17033
Telephone: (717) 534-6799
Fax: (717) 531-6161

Web Site: www.hersheys.com
Officers: Richard H. Lenny - Chmn., Pres., C.E.O. David J. West - Sr. V.P., C.F.O.

Auditors: KPMG LLP
Investor Contact: (800) 539-0291
Transfer Agents: Mellon Investor Services, LLC, Ridgefield Park, NJ

HEWITT ASSOCIATES INC

Exchange	Symbol	Price	52Wk Range	Yield	P/E
NYS	HEW	$26.60 (3/31/2005)	32.60-24.50	N/A	21.63

7 Year Price Score N/A   *NYSE Composite Index=100   *12 Month Price Score 94.92

Interim Earnings (Per Share)

Qtr.	Dec	Mar	Jun	Sep
2001-02	...	...	(0.51)	0.24
2002-03	0.15	0.24	0.27	0.30
2003-04	0.30	0.31	0.30	0.34
2004-05	0.28	...	...	...

Interim Dividends (Per Share)

No Dividends Paid

Valuation Analysis

Forecast P/E	N/A	No of Institutions
Market Cap	$3.2 Billion	Shares
Book Value	1.5 Billion	47,712,280
Price/Book	2.06	% Held
Price/Sales	1.31	39.26

TRADING VOLUME (thousand shares)

Business Summary: Accounting & Management Consulting Services (MIC: 12.2 SIC: 742 NAIC: 41612)

Hewitt Associates is a provider of human resources outsourcing and consulting services. Co.'s has two principal business segments: Outsourcing - Co.'s benefits outsourcing services include health and welfare, defined contribution and defined benefit. Co.'s outsourcing service offering includes payroll administration, allows Co. to provide its clients with a stand-alone payroll service and enables Co. to offer a range of human resources outsourcing services; Consulting - Co. provides consulting and actuarial services covering the design, implementation, communication and operation of health and welfare, compensation and retirement plans and broader human resources programs and processes.

Recent Developments: For the quarter ended Dec 31 2004, net income increased 15.9% to $34,025 thousand from net income of $29,363 thousand in the year-earlier quarter. Revenues were $725,288 thousand, up 31.7% from $550,689 thousand the year before. Operating income was $61,733 thousand versus an income of $55,930 thousand in the prior-year quarter, an increase of 10.4%. Total indirect expense was $663,555 thousand versus $494,759 thousand in the prior-year quarter, an increase of 34.1%.

Prospects: On Mar 9 2005, Co. revised its fiscal 2005 earnings outlook. Co. now expects core earnings of $145.0 million to $150.0 million for fiscal 2005, compared with its previous guidance of $152.0 million to $156.0 million. Co. stated that the revised outlook is due to a number of factors, including lower margins on benefits outsourcing services; one-time charges of approximately $8.0 million related to the termination of an acquired client relationship; a higher mix of lower margin revenues within Outsourcing; and modestly lower Consulting revenues versus expectations. Co. anticipates that these factors will be partially offset by lower variable compensation expenses.

Financial Data
(US$ in Thousands)

	3 Mos	09/30/2004	09/30/2003	09/30/2002	09/30/2001	09/30/2000	09/30/1999
Earnings Per Share	1.23	1.25	0.97	(0.27)	...	...	...
Cash Flow Per Share	2.09	2.50	2.94	2.94	...	...	...
Tang Book Value Per Share	3.97	3.87	2.32	1.64	2.93	...	...
Income Statement							
Total Revenue	725,288	2,262,227	2,031,293	1,750,079	1,502,093	1,306,059	1,090,286
EBITDA	97,670	341,369	292,411	333,843	292,844	284,163	240,847
Depn & Amortn	36,832	118,218	114,394	96,610	96,995	91,429	77,486
Income Before Taxes	57,669	207,859	160,641	223,426	183,182	181,675	155,875
Income Taxes	23,644	85,015	66,364	33,053	...	...	...
Net Income	34,025	122,844	94,277	190,373	183,182	181,675	155,875
Average Shares	119,598	97,950	96,832	85,301	...	...	...
Balance Sheet							
Current Assets	1,118,974	901,053	743,230	579,616	454,222	421,231	...
Total Assets	2,647,249	1,807,974	1,597,806	1,219,346	701,357	703,319	...
Current Liabilities	560,674	483,393	453,014	383,168	246,905	283,044	...
Long-Term Obligations	305,151	201,235	218,754	235,913	172,446	153,122	...
Total Liabilities	1,108,113	948,621	907,745	686,781	441,986	460,624	...
Stockholders' Equity	1,539,136	859,353	690,061	532,565	259,371	242,695	...
Shares Outstanding	119,315	98,579	98,217	98,457	88,507	...	...
Statistical Record							
Return on Assets %	5.91	7.19	6.69	19.82	26.08	...	...
Return on Equity %	11.12	15.81	15.42	48.08	72.97	...	...
EBITDA Margin %	13.47	15.09	14.40	19.08	19.50	21.76	22.09
Net Margin %	4.69	5.43	4.64	10.88	12.20	13.91	14.30
Asset Turnover	1.13	1.32	1.44	1.82	2.14	...	...
Current Ratio	2.00	1.86	1.64	1.51	1.84	1.49	...
Debt to Equity	0.20	0.23	0.32	0.44	0.66	0.63	...
Price Range	35.53-24.50	35.53-23.72	35.20-20.70	31.01-21.53	...	...	...
P/E Ratio	28.89-19.92	28.42-18.98	36.29-21.34	...	...	...	...

Address: 100 Half Day Road, Lincolnshire, IL 60069 Telephone: (847) 295-5000	Web Site: www.hewitt.com Officers: Dale L. Gifford - Chmn., C.E.O. Dan A. DeCanniere - C.F.O.	Auditors: Ernst & Young LLP

HEWLETT-PACKARD CO. (DE)

Exchange	Symbol	Price	52Wk Range	Yield	P/E
NYS	HPQ	$21.94 (3/31/2005)	23.64-16.50	1.46	18.75

*7 Year Price Score 63.21 *NYSE Composite Index=100 *12 Month Price Score 96.05

TRADING VOLUME (thousand shares)

Interim Earnings (Per Share)

Qtr.	Jan	Apr	Jul	Oct
2001-02	0.25	0.13	(0.67)	0.20
2002-03	0.24	0.22	0.10	0.28
2003-04	0.30	0.29	0.19	0.37
2004-05	0.32	...	...	...

Interim Dividends (Per Share)

Amt	Decl	Ex	Rec	Pay
0.08Q	5/28/2004	6/14/2004	6/16/2004	7/7/2004
0.08Q	7/16/2004	9/13/2004	9/15/2004	10/6/2004
0.08Q	11/19/2004	12/13/2004	12/15/2004	1/5/2005
0.08Q	1/18/2005	3/14/2005	3/16/2005	4/7/2005

Indicated Div: $0.32

Valuation Analysis

Forecast P/E	14.37	No of Institutions
	(4/7/2005)	815
Market Cap	$63.7 Billion	Shares
Book Value	37.7 Billion	1,937,384,064
Price/Book	1.69	% Held
Price/Sales	0.78	66.91

Business Summary: IT & Technology (MIC: 10.2 SIC: 571 NAIC: 34111)

Hewlett-Packard is a global provider of products, technologies, solutions and services to consumers and businesses. Co.'s offerings span information technology infrastructure and storage, personal computing and other access devices, multi-vendor services including maintenance, consulting and integration and outsourcing, and imaging and printing. Co.'s products and services are available worldwide. Co.'s operations are organized into seven business segments: the Personal Systems Group, the Imaging and Printing Group, Enterprise Storage and Servers, HP Services, HP Financial Services, Software and Corporate Investments.

Recent Developments: For the quarter ended Jan 31 2005, net income increased 0.7% to $943,000 thousand from net income of $936,000 thousand in the year-earlier quarter. Revenues were $21,454,000 thousand, up 9.9% from $19,514,000 thousand the year before. Operating income was $1,165,000 thousand versus an income of $1,143,000 thousand in the prior-year quarter, an increase of 1.9%. Total direct expense was $16,480,000 thousand versus $14,651,000 thousand in the prior-year quarter, an increase of 12.5%. Total indirect expense was $3,752,000 thousand versus $3,680,000 thousand in the prior-year quarter, an increase of 2.0%.

Prospects: Co.'s prospects appear mixed. On the positive side, Co. is experiencing decent top line growth from across each of its business segments. Geographically, for the first quarter ended Jan 31 2005, on a year-over-year basis, revenue in Europe, the Middle East and Africa (EMEA) grew approximately 12.0% to $9.30 billion, in Americas rose 6.0% to $8.90 billion and in Asia Pacific/Japan grew 15.0% to $3.30 billion. On a consolidated basis, when adjusted for the effects of currency, first quarter 2005 revenue grew about 5.0% year-over- year. However, Co.'s outlook is tempered by its lackluster operating margin, which declined to 5.4% for the first quarter of 2005 from 5.9% in the year-ago period.

Financial Data

(US$ in Thousands)	3 Mos	10/31/2004	10/31/2003	10/31/2002	10/31/2001	10/31/2000	10/31/1999	10/31/1998
Earnings Per Share	1.17	1.15	0.83	(0.36)	0.21	1.80	1.67	1.39
Cash Flow Per Share	2.22	1.68	1.99	2.18	1.32	1.74	1.53	2.63
Tang Book Value Per Share	6.18	6.06	6.08	5.36	6.81	7.30	9.11	8.33
Dividends Per Share	0.320	0.320	0.320	0.320	0.320	0.320	0.320	0.300
Dividend Payout %	27.43	27.83	38.55	...	152.38	17.78	19.16	21.66
Income Statement								
Total Revenue	21,454,000	79,905,000	73,061,000	56,588,000	45,226,000	48,782,000	42,370,000	47,061,000
EBITDA	1,662,000	6,599,000	5,451,000	1,050,000	2,071,000	6,250,000	5,712,000	6,195,000
Depn & Amortn	612,000	2,403,000	2,563,000	2,102,000	1,369,000	1,368,000	1,316,000	1,869,000
Income Before Taxes	1,050,000	4,196,000	2,888,000	(1,052,000)	702,000	4,625,000	4,194,000	4,091,000
Income Taxes	107,000	699,000	349,000	(129,000)	78,000	1,064,000	1,090,000	1,146,000
Net Income	943,000	3,497,000	2,539,000	(903,000)	408,000	3,697,000	3,491,000	2,945,000
Average Shares	2,936,000	3,055,000	3,063,000	2,499,000	1,974,000	2,077,000	2,104,000	2,144,000
Balance Sheet								
Current Assets	41,715,000	42,901,000	40,996,000	36,075,000	21,305,000	23,244,000	21,642,000	21,584,000
Total Assets	75,143,000	76,138,000	74,708,000	70,710,000	32,584,000	34,009,000	35,297,000	33,673,000
Current Liabilities	27,573,000	28,588,000	26,630,000	24,310,000	13,964,000	15,197,000	14,321,000	13,473,000
Long-Term Obligations	4,408,000	4,623,000	6,494,000	6,035,000	3,729,000	3,402,000	1,764,000	2,063,000
Total Liabilities	37,417,000	38,574,000	36,962,000	34,448,000	18,631,000	19,800,000	17,002,000	16,754,000
Stockholders' Equity	37,726,000	37,564,000	37,746,000	36,262,000	13,953,000	14,209,000	18,295,000	16,919,000
Shares Outstanding	2,902,000	2,911,000	3,043,000	3,043,733	1,939,000	1,947,312	2,009,192	2,030,000
Statistical Record								
Return on Assets %	4.71	4.62	3.49	N.M.	1.23	10.64	10.12	9.00
Return on Equity %	9.20	9.26	6.86	N.M.	2.90	22.69	19.83	17.81
EBITDA Margin %	7.75	8.26	7.46	1.86	4.58	12.81	13.48	13.16
Net Margin %	4.40	4.38	3.48	N.M.	0.90	7.58	8.24	6.26
Asset Turnover	1.10	1.06	1.00	1.10	1.36	1.40	1.23	1.44
Current Ratio	1.51	1.50	1.54	1.48	1.53	1.53	1.51	1.60
Debt to Equity	0.12	0.12	0.17	0.17	0.27	0.24	0.10	0.12
Price Range	24.12-16.50	26.12-16.50	23.52-14.85	23.53-11.16	47.44-14.50	67.44-28.20	45.37-22.56	31.86-18.95
P/E Ratio	20.62-14.10	22.71-14.35	28.34-17.89	...	225.89-69.05	37.47-15.67	27.17-13.51	22.92-13.64
Average Yield %	1.57	1.52	1.69	1.82	1.13	0.64	0.99	1.27

Address: 3000 Hanover Street, Palo Alto, CA 94304-1112	Web Site: www.hp.com	Auditors: ERNST & YOUNG LLP
Telephone: (650) 857-1501	Officers: Patricia C. Dunn - Chmn. Robert P. Wayman - Exec. V.P., C.F.O., Interim C.E.O.	Investor Contact: 866-438-4771
Fax: (650) 857-5518		Transfer Agents: ComputerShare Investor Services, Chicago, IL

HIBERNIA CORP.

Exchange	Symbol	Price	52Wk Range	Yield	P/E	Div Acheiver
NYS	HIB	$32.01 (3/31/2005)	32.95-21.72	2.50	17.21	11 Years

*7 Year Price Score 125.48 ***NYSE Composite Index=100** ***12 Month Price Score 98.96**

Interim Earnings (Per Share)

Qtr.	Mar	Jun	Sep	Dec
2001	0.31	0.34	0.35	0.36
2002	0.37	0.39	0.40	0.41
2003	0.36	0.39	0.44	0.45
2004	0.42	0.47	0.49	0.49

Interim Dividends (Per Share)

Amt	Decl	Ex	Rec	Pay
0.18Q	4/21/2004	4/29/2004	5/3/2004	5/20/2004
0.20Q	7/21/2004	7/29/2004	8/2/2004	8/20/2004
0.20Q	10/27/2004	11/4/2004	11/8/2004	11/22/2004
0.20Q	1/25/2005	2/2/2005	2/4/2005	2/22/2005

Indicated Div: $0.80 (Div. Reinv. Plan)

Valuation Analysis

Forecast P/E	15.69	No of Institutions
	(4/7/2005)	241
Market Cap	$5.0 Billion	Shares
Book Value	1.9 Billion	84,576,568
Price/Book	2.56	% Held
Price/Sales	3.58	54.51

Business Summary: Commercial Banking (MIC: 8.1 SIC: 021 NAIC: 22110)

Hibernia is a bank holding company headquartered in Louisiana. As of Dec 31 2003, Co. had assets of $18.60 billion and deposits of $14.20 billion with 259 locations in 34 Louisiana parishes, 18 Texas counties and two Mississippi counties. Co. conducts its business through its sole depository institution subsidiary, Hibernia National Bank. In addition, Co. offers financial products and services, including retail, small business, commercial, international, mortgage and private banking; leasing; investment banking; corporate finance; treasury management; and insurance.

Recent Developments: For the year ended Dec 31 2004, net income increased 13.4% to $292,954 thousand from net income of $258,336 thousand a year earlier. Net interest income was $750,673 thousand, up 11.9% from $670,753 thousand the year before. Provision for loan losses was $48,250 thousand versus $60,050 thousand in the prior year, a decrease of 19.7%. Non-interest income rose 10.7% to $387,426 thousand, while non-interest expense advanced 13.6% to $622,556 thousand.

Prospects: Co. continues to benefit from its expansion plans. Loans at Dec 31 2004 were $15.70 billion, up 22.0% from $12.90 billion a year earlier. Co. added that its acquisition of Coastal Bancorp contributed about $2.00 billion in loans and, combined with its Texas branch-building program, more than doubled the number of Co.'s locations in 2004 to more than 100. Co. plans to open about 20 new branches in Houston and Dallas-Fort Worth, TX in 2005. Meanwhile, the board of directors has authorized an additional $150.0 million to extend the de novo program beyond 2005. By the end of 2007, Co. expects to have opened about 70 offices as part of the de novo program.

Financial Data
(US$ in Thousands)

	12/31/2004	12/31/2003	12/31/2002	12/31/2001	12/31/2000	12/31/1999	12/31/1998	12/31/1997
Earnings Per Share	1.86	1.64	1.56	1.35	1.04	1.06	1.10	0.98
Cash Flow Per Share	3.97	4.96	3.24	(0.53)	1.86	3.07	1.56	1.18
Tang Book Value Per Share	10.12	9.26	8.51	9.81	8.83	7.96	7.79	7.15
Dividends Per Share	0.760	0.630	0.570	0.530	0.490	0.435	0.375	0.330
Dividend Payout %	40.86	38.41	36.54	39.26	47.12	41.04	34.09	33.67
Income Statement								
Interest Income	1,002,433	910,305	987,094	1,159,400	1,217,319	1,055,325	953,722	750,082
Interest Expense	251,760	239,552	282,857	494,729	606,760	470,520	423,188	322,325
Net Interest Income	750,673	670,753	704,237	664,671	610,559	584,805	530,534	427,757
Provision for Losses	48,250	60,050	80,625	97,250	120,650	87,800	26,000	620
Non-Interest Income	387,426	350,083	352,905	318,124	248,685	214,703	184,935	145,431
Non-Interest Expense	640,131	564,383	593,697	548,295	476,078	440,921	416,584	361,944
Income Before Taxes	449,718	396,403	382,820	337,250	262,516	270,787	272,885	210,624
Income Taxes	174,263	154,304	132,963	118,452	91,883	95,684	94,256	73,235
Net Income	292,954	258,336	249,857	218,798	170,633	175,103	178,629	137,389
Average Shares	157,498	157,600	160,057	159,236	158,020	158,902	156,165	133,325
Balance Sheet								
Net Loans & Leases	15,491,642	12,669,711	11,279,447	11,045,216	11,946,425	10,700,604	9,878,206	7,472,711
Total Assets	22,308,088	18,560,442	17,392,661	16,618,176	16,698,046	15,314,179	14,011,531	11,023,038
Total Deposits	17,378,946	14,159,519	13,481,022	12,953,112	12,692,732	11,855,903	10,603,006	8,633,329
Total Liabilities	20,366,191	16,782,957	15,711,799	15,058,397	15,218,395	13,938,664	12,693,430	9,972,724
Stockholders' Equity	1,941,897	1,777,485	1,680,862	1,559,779	1,479,651	1,375,515	1,318,101	1,050,314
Shares Outstanding	155,245	155,261	157,412	159,066	157,729	160,324	156,400	133,001
Statistical Record								
Return on Assets %	1.43	1.44	1.47	1.31	1.06	1.19	1.43	1.35
Return on Equity %	15.71	14.94	15.42	14.40	11.92	13.00	15.08	13.83
Net Interest Margin %	74.89	73.68	71.34	57.33	50.16	55.41	55.63	57.03
Efficiency Ratio %	46.06	44.78	44.31	37.11	32.47	34.72	36.59	40.42
Loans to Deposits	0.89	0.89	0.84	0.85	0.94	0.90	0.93	0.87
Price Range	29.98-21.72	23.69-16.47	21.60-16.80	19.23-11.88	13.75-8.75	17.38-10.38	21.94-13.06	19.38-12.38
P/E Ratio	16.12-11.68	14.45-10.04	13.85-10.77	14.24-8.80	13.22-8.41	16.39-9.79	19.94-11.88	19.77-12.63
Average Yield %	3.03	3.18	2.95	3.34	4.33	3.12	2.05	2.18

Address: 313 Carondelet Street, New Orleans, LA 70130	Web Site: www.hibernia.com	Auditors: Ernst & Young LLP
Telephone: (504) 533-2831	Officers: E. R. Campbell - Vice-Chmn. Paul J. Bonitatibus - Pres., Consumer & Buss. Banking	Investor Contact: 504-533-2180
Fax: (504) 586-2199		Transfer Agents: Mellon Investor Services, Ridgefield Park, NJ

HIGHWOODS PROPERTIES, INC.

Exchange	Symbol	Price	52Wk Range	Yield	P/E
NYS	HIW	$26.82 (3/31/2005)	27.95-20.85	6.34	92.48

*7 Year Price Score 85.68 *NYSE Composite Index=100 *12 Month Price Score 98.46

Interim Earnings (Per Share)

Qtr.	Mar	Jun	Sep	Dec
2001	0.54	0.51	0.49	0.29
2002	0.36	0.39	0.12	(0.37)
2003	0.06	0.05	0.26	0.10
2004	(0.03)	(0.04)	0.26	...

Interim Dividends (Per Share)

Amt	Decl	Ex	Rec	Pay
0.425Q	4/29/2004	5/6/2004	5/10/2004	6/4/2004
0.425Q	7/27/2004	8/5/2004	8/9/2004	9/3/2004
0.425Q	10/26/2004	11/4/2004	11/8/2004	12/3/2004
0.425Q	1/25/2005	2/3/2005	2/7/2005	3/4/2005

Indicated Div: $1.70

Valuation Analysis

Forecast P/E	0.00	No of Institutions
	(4/7/2005)	164
Market Cap	$1.4 Billion	Shares
Book Value	1.4 Billion	38,964,656
Price/Book	1.02	% Held
Price/Sales	3.23	72.54

Business Summary: Property, Real Estate & Development (MIC: 8.3 SIC: 798 NAIC: 25930)

Highwoods Properties is a self-administered and self-managed equity real estate investment trust that owns and operates suburban office, industrial and retail properties in the southeastern and midwestern U.S. Co. conducts substantially all of its activities through Highwoods Realty Limited Partnership and at Dec 31 2003, Co. owned 88.9% of the common units in Highwoods Realty. As of Dec 31 2003, Co. owned 465 in-service office, industrial and retail properties; owned an interest of 50.0% or less in 65 in-service office and industrial properties; owned 1,305 acres of undeveloped land suitable for future development; and was developing an additional seven properties.

Recent Developments: For the three months ended Sep 30 2004, income from continuing operations was $20.4 million compared with income of $23.9 million in the corresponding year-earlier period. Results for 2004 included a gain of $14.4 million related to a settlement of a bankruptcy claim. Results for 2003 included a gain of $16.3 million on the extinguishment of co-venture obligations. Rental and other revenues declined 6.2% to $114.3 million from $121.8 million the previous year. Funds from operations decreased 3.6% to $43.2 million from $44.8 million the year before.

Prospects: Co. is optimistic that its strategies will enable it to achieve its performance targets for 2005. These strategies include selling non-core land, expanding its build-to-suit and infill development pipeline, disposing of non-differentiating properties and reducing outstanding debt. Separately, Co. expects funds from operations (FFO) per share to be in the range of $2.25 to $2.35 for 2005, with occupancy rates between 88.0% and 90.0%. Co. added that in light of the uncertainty related to US Airways' continuing operations, its guidance does not include any anticipated revenue from this customer. If US Airways fulfills its lease obligations, this would increase 2005 FFO by about $0.05 per share.

Financial Data
(US$ in Thousands)

	9 Mos	6 Mos	3 Mos	12/31/2003	12/31/2002	12/31/2001	12/31/2000	12/31/1999
Earnings Per Share	0.29	0.29	0.38	0.47	1.17	1.83	1.70	1.71
Cash Flow Per Share	2.88	2.90	2.84	2.88	3.79	4.57	4.32	3.79
Tang Book Value Per Share	19.39	19.54	20.39	20.82	22.10	23.22	23.98	24.54
Dividends Per Share	1.700	1.700	1.700	1.860	2.340	2.310	2.250	2.190
Dividend Payout %	588.41	591.98	448.02	395.74	200.00	126.23	132.35	128.07
Income Statement								
Property Income	...	...	108,622	422,062	454,220	506,850	543,383	564,465
Non-Property Income	351,088	238,675	...	...	...	33,765	23,048	20,470
Total Revenue	351,088	238,675	108,622	422,062	454,220	540,615	566,431	584,935
Depn & Amortn	110,590	75,871	38,271	135,792	130,850	124,108	122,516	115,170
Interest Expense	90,570	62,774	26,912	114,271	110,527	108,501	112,827	117,134
Net Income	31,903	10,344	5,884	55,695	93,461	131,211	133,487	138,093
Average Shares	54,002	53,274	53,542	53,409	53,485	54,571	59,347	61,529
Balance Sheet								
Total Assets	3,316,145	3,332,662	3,508,523	3,326,809	3,395,369	3,648,286	3,701,602	4,016,197
Long-Term Obligations	1,600,627	1,603,485	1,767,239	1,558,758	1,528,720	1,719,230	1,587,019	1,766,117
Total Liabilities	1,777,236	1,784,360	1,875,438	1,670,530	1,649,334	1,839,465	1,696,843	1,878,062
Stockholders' Equity	1,419,134	1,427,294	1,471,201	1,491,029	1,557,472	1,605,640	1,791,545	1,892,470
Shares Outstanding	53,713	53,716	53,631	53,474	53,400	52,891	58,124	60,918
Statistical Record								
Return on Assets %	1.36	1.36	1.46	1.66	2.65	3.57	3.45	3.32
Return on Equity %	3.13	3.10	3.35	3.65	5.91	7.72	7.23	7.29
Net Margin %	9.09	4.33	5.42	13.20	20.58	24.27	23.57	23.61
Price Range	27.64-20.85	27.64-20.85	27.64-20.17	26.02-20.00	29.36-18.70	26.67-23.45	27.19-20.25	27.69-20.25
P/E Ratio	95.31-71.90	95.31-71.90	72.74-53.08	55.36-42.55	25.09-15.98	14.57-12.81	15.99-11.91	16.19-11.84
Average Yield %	6.92	6.99	7.10	8.18	9.42	9.18	9.66	8.95

Address: 3100 Smoketree Court, Suite 600, Raleigh, NC 27604 Telephone: (919) 872-4924 Fax: (919) 873-088	Web Site: www.highwoods.com Officers: O. Temple Sloan Jr. - Chmn. John L. Turner - Vice-Chmn.	Auditors: Ernst & Young LLP Investor Contact: 919-872-4924

HILB ROGAL & HOBBS CO

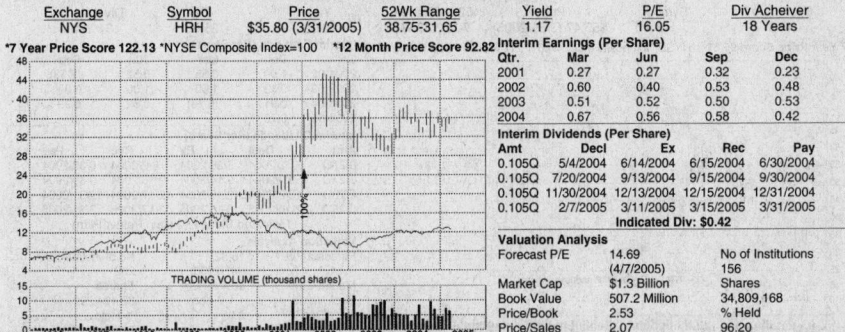

Exchange	Symbol	Price	52Wk Range	Yield	P/E	Div Acheiver
NYS	HRH	$35.80 (3/31/2005)	38.75-31.65	1.17	16.05	18 Years

*7 Year Price Score 122.13 *NYSE Composite Index=100 *12 Month Price Score 92.82

Interim Earnings (Per Share)

Qtr.	Mar	Jun	Sep	Dec
2001	0.27	0.27	0.32	0.23
2002	0.60	0.40	0.53	0.48
2003	0.51	0.52	0.50	0.53
2004	0.67	0.56	0.58	0.42

Interim Dividends (Per Share)

Amt	Decl	Ex	Rec	Pay
0.105Q	5/4/2004	6/14/2004	6/15/2004	6/30/2004
0.105Q	7/20/2004	9/13/2004	9/15/2004	9/30/2004
0.105Q	11/30/2004	12/13/2004	12/15/2004	12/31/2004
0.105Q	2/7/2005	3/11/2005	3/15/2005	3/31/2005

Indicated Div: $0.42

Valuation Analysis

Forecast P/E	14.69 (4/7/2005)	No of Institutions 156
Market Cap	$1.3 Billion	Shares 34,809,168
Book Value	507.2 Million	% Held
Price/Book	2.53	96.20
Price/Sales	2.07	

Business Summary: Insurance (MIC: 8.2 SIC: 411 NAIC: 24210)

Hilb, Rogal & Hamilton serves as an intermediary between its clients and insurance companies that underwrite client risks. Co. assists clients in managing their risks in areas such as property and casualty, executive and employee benefits and other areas of specialized exposure. Co. has offices located throughout the U.S. and London, England. Co.'s client base ranges from personal to large national accounts and is primarily comprised of middle-market and top-tier commercial and industrial accounts. Co. also advises clients on risk management and employee benefits and provides claims administration and loss control consulting services to clients.

Recent Developments: For the year ended Dec 31 2004, Co. reported net income increased 8.6% to $81,414,000 from net income of $74,954,000 a year earlier. Results for 2004 included a loss on the early extinguishment of debt of $1,557,000, while results for 2003 included a retirement benefit of $5,195,000. Revenues were $619,603,000, up 9.9% from $563,647,000 the year before. Commission and fees rose 9.7% to $609,660,000 from $555,732,000, while investment income increased to $3,176,000 from $3,151,000 a year earlier. Other revenues jumped 42.0% to $6,767,000 from $4,764,000 the year before.

Prospects: Co. continues to benefit from recent acquisitions and net new business, partially offset by a softening rate environment and declines in contingent and override levels. Also, Co. is experiencing the unfavorable affect of higher legal, compliance, and claim expenses and continued investment in its major accounts initiative. Meanwhile, legal and regulatory developments and sharp declines in premium rates continue to pose challenges for the insurance brokerage industry into 2005. However, these conditions are creating opportunities for Co. to compete for major account and middle-market prospects. Looking ahead, Co. remains focused on meeting its current five-year strategic growth plan.

Financial Data
(US$ in Thousands)

	12/31/2004	12/31/2003	12/31/2002	12/31/2001	12/31/2000	12/31/1999	12/31/1998	12/31/1997
Earnings Per Share	2.23	2.06	2.01	1.07	0.77	0.72	0.59	0.48
Cash Flow Per Share	3.19	3.19	2.51	2.27	1.83	0.67	0.79	0.80
Dividends Per Share	0.407	0.367	0.357	0.347	0.338	0.328	0.318	0.310
Dividend Payout %	18.27	17.84	17.79	32.48	43.83	45.49	53.81	63.92
Income Statement								
Total Revenue	619,603	563,647	452,726	330,267	262,119	227,226	175,364	173,709
Income Before Taxes	137,977	124,901	103,257	56,730	39,737	33,069	25,364	21,845
Income Taxes	56,563	49,947	42,082	24,381	17,610	13,583	10,418	9,055
Net Income	81,414	74,954	65,119	32,349	21,802	19,486	14,945	12,790
Average Shares	36,493	36,304	29,240	27,411	29,783	28,014	25,417	26,430
Balance Sheet								
Total Assets	1,277,999	1,049,227	833,024	499,301	353,371	317,981	188,066	181,607
Total Liabilities	770,843	614,960	522,376	356,500	265,149	246,806	142,355	130,268
Stockholders' Equity	507,156	434,267	310,648	142,801	88,222	71,176	45,710	51,339
Shares Outstanding	35,886	35,446	33,484	28,310	26,560	26,117	24,234	25,626
Statistical Record								
Return on Assets %	6.98	7.96	9.78	7.59	6.48	7.70	8.09	7.05
Return on Equity %	17.25	20.12	28.72	28.00	27.28	33.34	30.80	23.99
Price Range	38.75-31.49	43.85-28.34	45.40-27.75	31.08-16.97	20.97-12.91	14.56-7.78	9.94-7.75	9.69-6.31
P/E Ratio	17.38-14.12	21.29-13.76	22.59-13.81	29.05-15.86	27.23-16.76	20.23-10.81	16.84-13.14	20.18-13.15
Average Yield %	1.16	1.12	0.93	1.56	1.98	3.02	3.52	3.92

Address: 4951 Lake Brook Drive, Suite 500, Glen Allen, VA 23060
Telephone: (804) 747-6500
Fax: (804) 747-6046

Web Site: www.hrh.com
Officers: Martin L. Vaughan III - Chmn., C.E.O.
Robert B. Lockhart - Pres., C.O.O.

Auditors: Ernst & Young LLP
Investor Contact: 804-747-6500
Transfer Agents: Mellon Investor Services, LLC, Ridgefield Park, NJ

HILLENBRAND INDUSTRIES, INC.

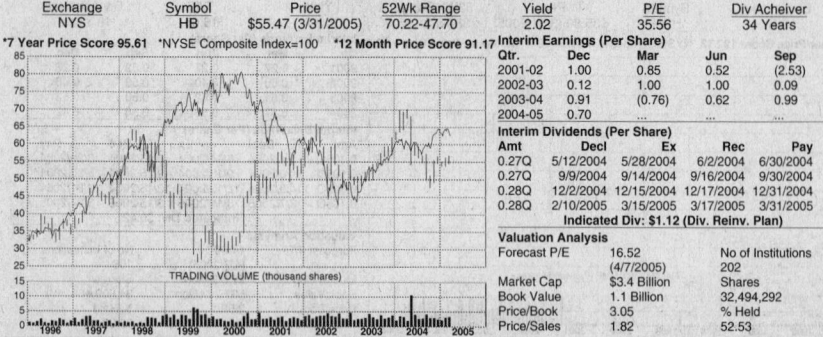

Exchange	Symbol	Price	52Wk Range	Yield	P/E	Div Acheiver
NYS	HB	$55.47 (3/31/2005)	70.22-47.70	2.02	35.56	34 Years

*7 Year Price Score 95.61   *NYSE Composite Index=100   *12 Month Price Score 91.17

Interim Earnings (Per Share)

Qtr.	Dec	Mar	Jun	Sep
2001-02	1.00	0.85	0.52	(2.53)
2002-03	0.12	1.00	1.00	0.09
2003-04	0.91	(0.76)	0.62	0.99
2004-05	0.70	...	...	...

Interim Dividends (Per Share)

Amt	Decl	Ex	Rec	Pay
0.27Q	5/12/2004	5/28/2004	6/2/2004	6/30/2004
0.27Q	9/9/2004	9/14/2004	9/16/2004	9/30/2004
0.28Q	12/2/2004	12/15/2004	12/17/2004	12/31/2004
0.28Q	2/10/2005	3/15/2005	3/17/2005	3/31/2005

Indicated Div: $1.12 (Div. Reinv. Plan)

Valuation Analysis

Forecast P/E	16.52 (4/7/2005)	No of Institutions	202
Market Cap	$3.4 Billion	Shares	32,494,292
Book Value	1.1 Billion	% Held	52.53
Price/Book	3.05		
Price/Sales	1.82		

Business Summary: Hospitals & Health Care (MIC: 9.3 SIC: 599 NAIC: 39995)

Hillenbrand Industries is a holding company for its two major operating businesses serving the health care and funeral services industries in the United States and abroad. Hill-Rom is a manufacturer of equipment for the health care industry, a provider of associated systems for wound, pulmonary and circulatory care and provides biomedical equipment rentals and other services to enhance the operational efficiency and asset utilization of health care facilities. Batesville Casket serves the funeral services industry and is a manufacturer of caskets and cremation-related products.

Recent Developments: For the quarter ended Dec 31 2004, net income decreased 22.8% to $44,000 thousand from net income of $57,000 thousand in the year-earlier quarter. Revenues were $475,000 thousand, up 12.6% from $422,000 thousand the year before. Operating income was $66,000 thousand versus an income of $73,000 thousand in the prior-year quarter, a decrease of 9.6%. Total direct expense was $255,000 thousand versus $219,000 thousand in the prior-year quarter, an increase of 16.4%. Total indirect expense was $154,000 thousand versus $146,000 thousand in the prior-year quarter, an increase of 5.5%.

Prospects: Co. is making progress in several key areas that support its 2005 goals of high single-digit revenue and low double-digit earnings growth. However, gross margin performance continues to be challenging, primary due to lower sales volumes at Batesville Casket and at Hill-Rom's rental business. In order to return margins to acceptable levels, Co.'s focus over the next few quarters will be to continue to manage costs and increase efficiencies at all its U.S. businesses, and to return its European operations to profitability. Co. expects 2005 income from continuing operations to reach $339.0 million to $349.0 million, or $3.40 to $3.50 per share, on revenue of $1.93 billion to $1.98 billion.

Financial Data

(US$ in Thousands)	3 Mos	09/30/2004	09/30/2003	09/30/2002	12/01/2001	12/02/2000	11/27/1999	11/28/1998
Earnings Per Share	1.56	1.75	2.22	(0.16)	2.71	2.44	1.87	2.73
Cash Flow Per Share	7.03	5.58	6.06	6.31	7.10	4.63	2.27	2.57
Tang Book Value Per Share	9.38	8.81	15.79	12.72	13.24	10.42	10.17	11.29
Dividends Per Share	1.090	1.080	1.000	0.977	0.840	0.800	0.780	0.720
Dividend Payout %	69.95	61.71	45.05	...	31.00	32.79	41.71	26.37
Income Statement								
Total Revenue	475,000	1,829,000	2,042,000	1,757,000	2,107,000	2,096,000	2,047,000	2,001,000
EBITDA	102,000	387,000	374,000	43,000	246,000	267,000	222,000	320,000
Depn & Amortn	29,000	64,000	73,000	64,000	...	...	...	...
Income Before Taxes	69,000	308,000	282,000	(35,000)	223,000	240,000	195,000	293,000
Income Taxes	25,000	120,000	100,000	(25,000)	53,000	86,000	71,000	109,000
Net Income	44,000	110,000	138,000	(10,000)	170,000	154,000	124,000	184,000
Average Shares	62,689	62,725	62,184	62,921	62,814	62,913	66,295	67,577
Balance Sheet								
Current Assets	781,000	739,000	708,000	958,000	868,000	724,000	782,000	858,000
Total Assets	2,034,000	1,992,000	5,412,000	5,442,000	5,049,000	4,597,000	4,433,000	4,280,000
Current Liabilities	302,000	313,000	367,000	551,000	320,000	282,000	371,000	375,000
Long-Term Obligations	356,000	360,000	155,000	322,000	305,000	302,000	302,000	303,000
Total Liabilities	906,000	896,000	4,253,000	4,443,000	4,023,000	3,766,000	3,595,000	3,328,000
Stockholders' Equity	1,128,000	1,096,000	1,159,000	999,000	1,026,000	831,000	838,000	952,000
Shares Outstanding	62,028	61,953	61,814	61,702	62,466	62,404	63,546	66,759
Statistical Record								
Return on Assets %	2.62	2.96	2.54	N.M.	3.53	3.36	2.85	4.55
Return on Equity %	8.41	9.73	12.79	N.M.	18.36	18.16	13.89	20.08
EBITDA Margin %	21.47	21.16	18.32	2.45	11.68	12.74	10.85	15.99
Net Margin %	9.26	6.01	6.76	N.M.	8.07	7.35	6.06	9.20
Asset Turnover	0.51	0.49	0.38	0.40	0.44	0.46	0.47	0.49
Current Ratio	2.59	2.36	1.93	1.74	2.71	2.57	2.11	2.29
Debt to Equity	0.32	0.33	0.13	0.32	0.30	0.36	0.36	0.32
Price Range	70.22-47.70	70.22-49.76	57.64-46.91	65.99-48.75	58.10-43.88	51.00-29.06	56.88-26.38	64.38-44.56
P/E Ratio	45.01-30.58	40.13-28.43	25.96-21.13	...	21.44-16.19	20.90-11.91	30.41-14.10	23.58-16.32
Average Yield %	1.85	1.80	1.95	1.69	1.62	2.28	1.89	1.26

Address: 700 State Route 46 East, Batesville, IN 47006-8835 **Telephone:** (812) 934-7000 **Fax:** (812) 934-7364	**Web Site:** www.hillenbrand.com **Officers:** Ray J. Hillenbrand - Chmn. Rolf A. Classon - Vice-Chmn.	**Auditors:** PricewaterhouseCoopers LLP **Investor Contact:** 812-934-8400 **Transfer Agents:** Computershare Investor Services, Chicago, IL

HILTON HOTELS CORP.

Exchange	Symbol	Price	52Wk Range	Yield	P/E
NYS	HLT	$22.35 (3/31/2005)	23.26-16.25	0.36	37.25

*7 Year Price Score 122.31 *NYSE Composite Index=100 *12 Month Price Score 104.56

Interim Earnings (Per Share)

Qtr.	Mar	Jun	Sep	Dec
2001	0.15	0.23	0.06	0.01
2002	0.09	0.20	0.13	0.11
2003	0.02	0.14	0.09	0.17
2004	0.10	0.19	0.16	0.16

Interim Dividends (Per Share)

Amt	Decl	Ex	Rec	Pay
0.02Q	5/27/2004	6/9/2004	6/11/2004	6/25/2004
0.02Q	7/22/2004	9/1/2004	9/3/2004	9/10/2004
0.02Q	11/12/2004	12/1/2004	12/3/2004	12/17/2004
0.02Q	1/27/2005	3/2/2005	3/4/2005	3/18/2005

Indicated Div: $0.08

Valuation Analysis

Forecast P/E	30.60	No of Institutions
	(4/7/2005)	328
Market Cap	$8.7 Billion	Shares
Book Value	2.6 Billion	303,245,856
Price/Book	3.39	% Held
Price/Sales	2.10	78.82

Business Summary: Hospitality & Tourism (MIC: 5.1 SIC: 011 NAIC: 21110)

Hilton Hotels Corp. is engaged in the ownership, management and development of hotels, resorts and timeshare properties and the franchising of lodging properties. Co.'s hotel brands include Hilton®, Hilton Garden Inn, Doubletree, Embassy Suites, Hampton, Homewood Suites by Hilton and Conrad. In addition, Co. develops and operates timeshare resorts through Hilton Grand Vacations Company. As of Dec 31 2003, Co.'s system contained 2,173 properties, totaling over 348,000 rooms. Co. owned an interest in and operated 122 hotels, leased seven hotels, managed 206 hotels owned by others and franchised 1,808 hotels. Co. also managed or franchised 30 timeshare properties.

Recent Developments: For the year ended Dec 31 2003, net income decreased 17.2% to $164,000 thousand from net income of $198,000 thousand a year earlier. Revenues were $3,819,000 thousand, up 0.1% from $3,816,000 thousand the year before. Operating income was $515,000 thousand versus an income of $603,000 thousand in the prior year, a decrease of 14.6%. Total direct expense was $1,931,000 thousand versus $1,857,000 thousand in the prior year, an increase of 4.0%. Total indirect expense was $1,407,000 thousand versus $1,387,000 thousand in the prior year, an increase of 1.4%.

Prospects: Co. is optimistic regarding its prospects for 2005, citing its expectations of a favorable economic environment and continuation of strong hotel demand among business, group and leisure travelers, coupled with limited new full-service hotel supply growth. Accordingly, Co. estimates full-year 2005 total revenue of $4.50 billion to $4.53 billion, comparable owned hotel revenue per available room (RevPAR) gains of between 7.5% and 8.5%, and diluted earnings per share in the low $0.70 range. Co. stated that it expects to add 130 to 150 hotels and 16,000 to 20,000 rooms to its system in 2005. Co. also reaffirmed 2005 anticipated total capital spending of approximately $430.0 million.

Financial Data

(US$ in Thousands)	12/31/2004	12/31/2003	12/31/2002	12/31/2001	12/31/2000	12/31/1999	12/31/1998	12/31/1997
Earnings Per Share	0.60	0.43	0.53	0.45	0.73	0.65	1.12	0.94
Cash Flow Per Share	1.42	1.30	1.80	1.59	1.59	1.05	1.56	2.39
Tang Book Value Per Share	0.63	N.M.	N.M.	N.M.	N.M.	N.M.	0.72	8.25
Dividends Per Share	0.080	0.080	0.080	0.080	0.080	0.080	0.320	0.320
Dividend Payout %	13.33	18.60	15.09	17.78	10.96	12.31	28.57	34.04
Income Statement								
Total Revenue	4,146,000	3,819,000	3,847,000	3,050,000	3,451,000	2,150,000	1,769,000	5,316,000
EBITDA	1,012,000	885,000	989,000	1,053,000	1,338,000	742,000	604,000	941,000
Depn & Amortn	339,000	347,000	357,000	401,000	390,000	190,000	127,000	303,000
Income Before Taxes	373,000	223,000	285,000	250,000	479,000	313,000	336,000	448,000
Income Taxes	127,000	53,000	81,000	77,000	200,000	130,000	136,000	187,000
Net Income	238,000	164,000	198,000	166,000	272,000	174,000	297,000	250,000
Average Shares	418,000	393,000	401,000	394,000	391,633	209,195	278,000	281,231
Balance Sheet								
Current Assets	1,106,000	1,020,000	630,000	996,000	840,000	763,000	469,000	1,011,000
Total Assets	8,242,000	8,178,000	8,348,000	8,785,000	9,140,000	9,253,000	3,944,000	7,826,000
Current Liabilities	629,000	895,000	575,000	902,000	646,000	629,000	506,000	941,000
Long-Term Obligations	3,633,000	3,801,000	4,554,000	4,950,000	5,693,000	6,085,000	3,037,000	2,709,000
Total Liabilities	5,674,000	5,939,000	6,295,000	7,002,000	7,498,000	7,838,000	3,757,000	4,443,000
Stockholders' Equity	2,568,000	2,239,000	2,053,000	1,783,000	1,642,000	1,415,000	187,000	3,383,000
Shares Outstanding	389,000	381,000	376,000	369,000	369,000	368,000	261,000	249,000
Statistical Record								
Return on Assets %	2.89	1.98	2.31	1.85	2.95	2.64	5.05	3.25
Return on Equity %	9.88	7.64	10.32	9.69	17.75	21.72	16.64	7.58
EBITDA Margin %	24.41	23.17	25.71	34.52	38.77	34.51	34.14	17.70
Net Margin %	5.74	4.29	5.15	5.44	7.88	8.09	16.79	4.70
Asset Turnover	0.50	0.46	0.45	0.34	0.37	0.33	0.30	0.69
Current Ratio	1.76	1.14	1.10	1.10	1.30	1.21	0.93	1.07
Debt to Equity	1.41	1.70	2.22	2.78	3.47	4.30	16.24	0.80
Price Range	22.85-15.14	17.35-10.55	17.01-10.00	13.36-6.70	11.81-6.38	16.81-8.50	23.21-9.29	23.58-16.17
P/E Ratio	38.08-25.23	40.35-24.53	32.09-18.87	29.69-14.89	16.18-8.73	25.87-13.08	20.72-8.30	25.09-17.20
Average Yield %	0.44	0.57	0.63	0.73	0.88	0.63	1.85	1.66

Address: 9336 Civic Center Dr.,	Web Site: www.hilton.com	Auditors: Ernst & Young LLP
Beverly Hills, CA 90210	Officers: Barron Hilton - Chmn. Stephen F.	Investor Contact: (310) 205-4030
Telephone: (310) 278-4321	Bollenbach - Pres., C.E.O.	Transfer Agents: Bank of New York,
Fax: (310) 205-7824		New York, NY

HNI CORP

Exchange	Symbol	Price	52Wk Range	Yield	P/E	Div Acheiver
NYS	HNI	$44.95 (3/31/2005)	45.39-36.80	1.38	22.82	16 Years

*7 Year Price Score 120.32 ***NYSE Composite Index=100** ***12 Month Price Score 98.63**

Interim Earnings (Per Share)

Qtr.	Mar	Jun	Sep	Dec
2001	0.31	0.07	0.48	0.40
2002	0.27	0.34	0.46	0.48
2003	0.27	0.35	0.59	0.47
2004	0.38	0.44	0.65	0.50

Interim Dividends (Per Share)

Amt	Decl	Ex	Rec	Pay
0.14Q	5/4/2004	5/12/2004	5/14/2004	6/1/2004
0.14Q	8/2/2004	8/10/2004	8/12/2004	9/1/2004
0.14Q	11/12/2004	11/18/2004	11/22/2004	12/1/2004
0.155Q	2/16/2005	2/23/2005	2/25/2005	3/1/2005

Indicated Div: $0.62

Valuation Analysis

Forecast P/E	19.88 (4/7/2005)	No of Institutions 139
Market Cap	$2.5 Billion	Shares
Book Value	669.2 Million	27,657,876
Price/Book	3.71	% Held
Price/Sales	1.19	50.20

Business Summary: Chemicals (MIC: 11.1 SIC: 522 NAIC: 37214)

HNI manufactures and markets office furniture and hearth products. Co.'s office furniture products are in four categories: storage, seating, office systems, and desks and related products. The office products are sold to dealers, wholesalers, warehouse clubs, retail superstores, end-user customers, and federal and state governments. Co.'s hearth products include wood-burning, pellet-burning, gas-burning and electric factory-built fireplaces, fireplace inserts, stoves, gas logs, and accessories. The hearth products are sold through a national system of dealers, wholesalers, large regional contractors and Co.-owned retail outlets. Co. has locations in the U.S., Canada and Mexico.

Recent Developments: For the year ended Jan 1 2005, net income increased 15.8% to $113,582 thousand from net income of $98,105 thousand a year earlier. Revenues were $2,093,447 thousand, up 19.2% from $1,755,728 thousand the year before. Operating income was $178,412 thousand versus an income of $149,961 thousand in the prior year, an increase of 19.0%. Total direct expense was $1,342,143 thousand versus $1,116,513 thousand in the prior year, an increase of 20.2%. Total indirect expense was $572,892 thousand versus $489,254 thousand in the prior year, an increase of 17.1%.

Prospects: Results are benefiting from strong growth trends in the office furniture and hearth products markets. Meanwhile, incremental increases in steel and other material costs are expected to continue to pressure margins in the first quarter of 2005. However, full-year 2005 margins are expected to be comparable to margins in 2004 as Co. continues to implement price increases and other initiatives designed to reduce costs and improve productivity. Co. has announced additional price increases that will become effective through the first half of 2005 and are anticipated to generate approximately 3.0% to 5.0% in annualized price realization.

Financial Data

(US$ in Thousands)	01/01/2005	01/03/2004	12/28/2002	12/29/2001	12/30/2000	01/01/2000	01/02/1999	01/03/1998
Earnings Per Share	1.97	1.68	1.55	1.26	1.77	1.44	1.72	1.45
Cash Flow Per Share	3.41	2.39	3.45	3.87	3.42	2.57	2.39	2.33
Tang Book Value Per Share	8.04	8.89	7.79	6.45	5.97	6.45	5.77	4.59
Dividends Per Share	0.560	0.520	0.500	0.480	0.440	0.380	0.320	0.280
Dividend Payout %	28.43	30.95	32.26	38.10	24.86	26.39	18.60	19.31
Income Statement								
Total Revenue	2,093,447	1,755,728	1,692,622	1,792,438	2,046,286	1,789,281	1,696,433	1,362,713
EBITDA	245,115	222,733	211,445	204,477	257,080	211,896	232,176	180,769
Depn & Amortn	66,703	72,772	68,755	81,385	79,046	65,453	52,999	35,610
Income Before Taxes	178,869	150,931	140,554	116,261	165,964	137,575	170,109	139,128
Income Taxes	65,287	52,826	49,194	41,854	59,747	50,215	63,796	52,173
Net Income	113,582	98,105	91,360	74,407	106,217	87,360	106,313	86,955
Average Shares	57,577	58,545	59,040	59,087	60,140	...	...	...
Balance Sheet								
Current Assets	374,579	462,122	405,054	319,657	330,141	316,556	290,329	295,150
Total Assets	1,021,657	1,021,826	1,020,552	961,891	1,022,470	906,723	864,469	754,673
Current Liabilities	266,250	245,816	298,680	230,443	264,868	225,123	217,438	200,759
Long-Term Obligations	3,645	4,126	9,837	80,830	128,285	124,173	135,563	134,511
Total Liabilities	352,494	311,937	373,659	369,211	449,128	405,452	402,447	373,011
Stockholders' Equity	669,163	709,889	646,893	592,680	573,342	501,271	462,022	381,662
Shares Outstanding	55,303	58,238	58,373	58,672	59,796	60,171	61,290	61,659
Statistical Record								
Return on Assets %	11.15	9.45	9.24	7.52	11.04	9.89	13.17	13.49
Return on Equity %	16.52	14.23	14.78	12.80	19.82	18.19	25.27	26.98
EBITDA Margin %	11.71	12.69	12.49	11.41	12.56	11.84	13.69	13.27
Net Margin %	5.43	5.59	5.40	4.15	5.19	4.88	6.27	6.38
Asset Turnover	2.05	1.69	1.71	1.81	2.13	2.03	2.10	2.11
Current Ratio	1.41	1.88	1.36	1.39	1.25	1.41	1.34	1.47
Debt to Equity	0.01	0.01	0.02	0.14	0.22	0.25	0.29	0.35
Price Range	45.71-35.40	43.87-24.67	30.64-23.37	28.82-19.96	27.81-16.00	29.75-18.88	36.88-20.00	32.00-16.63
P/E Ratio	23.20-17.97	26.11-14.68	19.77-15.08	22.87-15.84	15.71-9.04	20.66-13.11	21.44-11.63	22.07-11.47
Average Yield %	1.39	1.57	1.83	1.95	1.87	1.63	1.12	1.15

| Address: 414 East Third Street, P.O. Box 1109, Muscatine, IA 52761-0071
Telephone: (563) 264-7400
Fax: (563) 264-7217 | Web Site: www.honi.com
Officers: Jack D. Michaels - Chmn., Pres., C.E.O.
Stanley A. Askren - Pres.,, Chief, Oper. Officer | Auditors: PricewaterhouseCoopers LLP
Investor Contact: 563-264-7400
Transfer Agents: Computershare Investor Services, LLC, Chicago, IL |

HOLLY CORP.

Exchange	Symbol	Price	52Wk Range	Yield	P/E	Div Acheiver
NYS	HOC	$37.27 (3/31/2005)	39.17-15.93	0.86	14.28	11 Years

*7 Year Price Score 211.72 *NYSE Composite Index=100 *12 Month Price Score 136.63

Interim Earnings (Per Share)

Qtr.	Oct	Jan	Apr	Dec
2003	— — — — — 1.44 — — — — — —			
Qtr.	Mar	Jun	Sep	Dec
2004	0.44	1.56	0.36	0.24

Interim Dividends (Per Share)

Amt	Decl	Ex	Rec	Pay
100%	8/2/2004	8/31/2004	8/16/2004	8/30/2004
0.08Q	8/2/2004	9/16/2004	9/20/2004	10/4/2004
0.08Q	12/10/2004	12/23/2004	12/28/2004	1/4/2005
0.08Q	3/14/2005	3/23/2005	3/28/2005	4/4/2005
		Indicated Div: $0.32		

Valuation Analysis

Forecast P/E	15.79	No of Institutions	
	(4/7/2005)	106	
Market Cap	$1.2 Billion	Shares	
Book Value	339.9 Million	22,919,400	
Price/Book	3.43	% Held	
Price/Sales	0.52	72.55	

Business Summary: Oil and Gas (MIC: 14.2 SIC: 911 NAIC: 24110)

Holly is an indepedent petroleum refiner. The Refining segment refines crude oil and markets wholesale refined products, such as gasoline, diesel fuel and jet fuel, and includes refineries in New Mexico, Utah, and Montana. Co. also owns and operates or owns interests in thirteen refined products storage terminals in New Mexico, Texas, Utah, Montana, Washington, Idaho and Arizona. Also, Co. owns or leases about 2,000 miles of pipeline located principally in west Texas and New Mexico. The Pipeline Transportation segment uses 500 miles of the pipeline and owns a 70.0% interest in Rio Grande Pipeline Company, which transports liquid petroleum gases to Mexico.

Recent Developments: For the year ended Dec 31 2004, net income increased 82.1% to $83,879 thousand from net income of $46,053 thousand a year earlier. Revenues were $2,246,373 thousand, up 60.1% from $1,403,244 thousand the year before. Operating income was $145,514 thousand versus an income of $60,067 thousand in the prior year, an increase of 142.3%. Total direct expense was $1,835,997 thousand versus $1,155,858 thousand in the prior year, an increase of 58.8%. Total indirect expense was $264,862 thousand versus $187,319 thousand in the prior year, an increase of 41.4%.

Prospects: Looking ahead, Co. will continue to focus on improving its profit potential through the execution of its previously-announced value-added refinery initiatives for 2005 and will continue to deploy capital to improve the profitability of its existing operations. Co. believes that it is well positioned to continue to prosper in the current industry environment, where for the foreseeable future, strong demand for refined products appears likely to test refinery supply. Meanwhile, Co. will look to leverage its financial strengths through the pursuit of strategic acquisitions and organic growth opportunities.

Financial Data

(US$ in Thousands)	12/31/2004	12/31/2003	12/31/2002	07/31/2002	07/31/2001	07/31/2000	07/31/1999	07/31/1998
Earnings Per Share	2.61	1.44	0.17	1.00	2.38	0.35	0.60	0.46
Cash Flow Per Share	5.27	2.28	(0.20)	1.36	3.48	1.45	1.44	1.16
Tang Book Value Per Share	10.35	8.32	7.23	7.34	6.52	4.29	3.90	3.46
Dividends Per Share	0.290	0.220	0.215	0.205	0.185	0.170	0.160	0.150
Dividend Payout %	11.11	15.28	126.47	20.40	7.76	47.89	26.45	32.61
Income Statement								
Total Revenue	2,246,373	1,403,244	448,637	888,906	1,142,130	965,946	597,986	590,299
EBITDA	178,102	112,312	20,842	80,020	151,689	51,283	67,296	56,970
Depn & Amortn	40,481	36,275	11,726	27,699	27,327	27,496	26,358	24,379
Income Before Taxes	138,469	74,359	8,517	50,896	121,895	18,634	33,159	24,866
Income Taxes	54,590	28,306	3,114	18,867	48,445	7,189	13,222	9,699
Net Income	83,879	46,053	5,403	32,029	73,450	11,445	19,937	15,167
Average Shares	32,170	32,032	31,804	31,942	30,774	32,260	33,016	33,016
Balance Sheet								
Current Assets	572,906	336,406	254,347	278,844	284,130	267,104	194,778	154,387
Total Assets	982,713	708,892	515,793	502,306	490,429	464,362	390,982	349,857
Current Liabilities	424,264	364,667	241,902	218,971	226,399	266,741	180,927	139,594
Long-Term Obligations	25,000	8,571	17,143	25,714	34,286	42,857	56,595	70,341
Total Liabilities	485,247	425,808	287,299	273,750	288,695	334,781	262,102	235,508
Stockholders' Equity	339,916	268,609	228,494	228,556	201,734	129,581	128,880	114,349
Shares Outstanding	31,294	31,028	31,035	31,122	30,961	30,203	33,016	33,016
Statistical Record								
Return on Assets %	9.89	7.52	0.76	6.45	15.39	2.67	5.38	4.34
Return on Equity %	27.49	18.53	1.77	14.89	44.34	8.83	16.39	13.82
EBITDA Margin %	7.93	8.00	4.65	9.00	13.28	5.31	11.25	9.65
Net Margin %	3.73	3.28	1.20	3.60	6.43	1.18	3.33	2.57
Asset Turnover	2.65	2.29	0.63	1.79	2.39	2.25	1.61	1.69
Current Ratio	1.35	0.92	1.05	1.27	1.25	1.00	1.08	1.11
Debt to Equity	0.07	0.03	0.08	0.11	0.17	0.33	0.44	0.62
Price Range	28.43-13.60	14.99-10.00	11.49-7.50	10.57-7.33	12.49-3.00	3.81-2.34	6.50-3.11	8.22-6.03
P/E Ratio	10.89-5.21	10.41-6.94	67.59-44.12	10.57-7.33	5.25-1.26	10.89-6.70	10.83-5.18	17.87-13.11
Average Yield %	1.48	1.72	2.36	2.27	3.29	5.24	4.18	2.20

Address: 100 Crescent Court, Suite 1600, Dallas, TX 75201-6927	**Web Site:** www.hollycorp.com	**Auditors:** ERNST & YOUNG LLP
Telephone: (214) 871-3555	**Officers:** Lamar Norsworthy - Chmn., C.E.O.	**Transfer Agents:** American Stock Transfer & Trust Company, New York, NY
Fax: (214) 871-3566	Matthew P. Clifton - Pres.	

HOME DEPOT, INC.

Exchange	Symbol	Price	52Wk Range	Yield	P/E	Div Acheiver
NYS	HD	$38.24 (3/31/2005)	43.79-32.88	1.05	17.23	17 Years

*7 Year Price Score 82.46 *NYSE Composite Index=100 *12 Month Price Score 97.34

Interim Earnings (Per Share)

Qtr.	Apr	Jul	Oct	Jan
2001-02	0.27	0.39	0.33	0.30
2002-03	0.36	0.50	0.40	0.30
2003-04	0.39	0.56	0.50	0.42
2004-05	0.49	0.70	0.60	...

Interim Dividends (Per Share)

Amt	Decl	Ex	Rec	Pay
0.085Q	5/26/2004	6/8/2004	6/10/2004	6/24/2004
0.085Q	8/6/2004	8/31/2004	9/2/2004	9/16/2004
0.085Q	11/18/2004	11/30/2004	12/2/2004	12/16/2004
0.10Q	2/24/2005	3/8/2005	3/10/2005	3/24/2005

Indicated Div: $0.40 (Div. Reinv. Plan)

Valuation Analysis

Forecast P/E	14.99	No of Institutions
	(4/7/2005)	1057
Market Cap	$91.0 Billion	Shares
Book Value	23.7 Billion	1,381,075,328
Price/Book	3.83	% Held
Price/Sales	1.27	62.89

Business Summary: Retail - Hardware (MIC: 5.6 SIC: 211 NAIC: 44110)

The Home Depot operated 1,707 retail warehouse stores as of Feb 1 2004 in the United States, Canada and Mexico that offer a wide assortment of building materials and home improvement products. The average Home Depot store has about 107,000 square feet of interior floor space and about 22,000 square feet of additional outdoor selling area for landscaping supplies. Co. also operates 54 EXPO Design Center stores that sell products and services primarily for home decorating and remodeling projects, 11 Home Depot Landscape Supply stores, five Home Depot Supply stores, and two Home Depot Floor Store outlets.

Recent Developments: For the quarter ended Oct 31 2004, net income increased 14.8% to $1,317,000 thousand from net income of $1,147,000 thousand in the year-earlier quarter. Revenues were $18,772,000 thousand, up 13.1% from $16,598,000 thousand the year before. Operating income was $2,056,000 thousand versus an income of $1,823,000 thousand in the prior-year quarter, an increase of 12.8%. Total indirect expense was $4,196,000 thousand versus $3,370,000 thousand in the prior-year quarter, an increase of 24.5%.

Prospects: Looking ahead, Co. expects fiscal year 2005 sales to grow between 9.0% to 12.0% and that earnings per share will grow between 10.0% and 14.0%. Additionally, Co. plans to add 175 new stores and continue its investment in store modernization and technology through a capital spending plan of $3.70 billion. Separately, Co. announced that it has formed a new strategic partnership with LG Electronics to bring a third line of home appliances to Co.'s product offerings in the second quarter of 2005. The product line will include laundry systems, refrigerators, dishwashers, air conditioners and microwave ovens, among others.

Financial Data

(US$ in Thousands)	9 Mos	6 Mos	3 Mos	02/01/2004	02/02/2003	02/03/2002	01/28/2001	01/30/2000
Earnings Per Share	2.22	2.12	1.97	1.88	1.56	1.29	1.10	1.00
Cash Flow Per Share	3.10	3.48	3.10	2.87	2.06	2.51	1.21	1.09
Tang Book Value Per Share	9.39	9.61	9.66	9.56	8.39	7.53	6.32	5.22
Dividends Per Share	0.310	0.295	0.270	0.260	0.210	0.170	0.160	0.113
Dividend Payout %	13.99	13.94	13.68	13.83	13.46	13.18	14.55	11.33
Income Statement								
Total Revenue	56,282,000	37,510,000	17,550,000	64,816,000	58,247,000	53,553,000	45,738,000	38,434,000
EBITDA	7,230,000	4,839,000	2,058,000	7,922,000	6,733,000	5,696,000	4,792,000	4,258,000
Depn & Amortn	971,000	636,000	312,000	1,076,000	903,000	764,000	601,000	463,000
Income Before Taxes	6,256,000	4,196,000	1,742,000	6,843,000	5,872,000	4,957,000	4,217,000	3,804,000
Income Taxes	2,296,000	1,553,000	644,000	2,539,000	2,208,000	1,913,000	1,636,000	1,484,000
Net Income	3,960,000	2,643,000	1,098,000	4,304,000	3,664,000	3,044,000	2,581,000	2,320,000
Average Shares	2,199,000	2,214,000	2,250,000	2,289,000	2,344,000	2,353,000	2,352,000	2,342,000
Balance Sheet								
Current Assets	15,727,000	15,467,000	16,289,000	13,328,000	11,917,000	10,361,000	7,777,000	6,390,000
Total Assets	39,631,000	38,331,000	37,948,000	34,437,000	30,011,000	26,394,000	21,385,000	17,081,000
Current Liabilities	11,811,000	12,927,000	12,712,000	9,554,000	8,035,000	6,501,000	4,385,000	3,656,000
Long-Term Obligations	2,151,000	1,124,000	1,126,000	856,000	1,321,000	1,250,000	1,545,000	750,000
Total Liabilities	15,884,000	15,881,000	15,526,000	12,030,000	10,209,000	8,312,000	6,381,000	4,740,000
Stockholders' Equity	23,747,000	22,450,000	22,422,000	22,407,000	19,802,000	18,082,000	15,004,000	12,341,000
Shares Outstanding	2,381,000	2,194,000	2,235,000	2,257,000	2,293,000	2,345,888	2,323,747	2,304,317
Statistical Record								
Return on Assets %	13.13	13.04	12.57	13.39	13.03	12.54	13.46	15.23
Return on Equity %	21.40	21.43	20.90	20.45	19.40	18.10	18.93	22.07
EBITDA Margin %	12.85	12.90	11.73	12.22	11.56	10.64	10.48	11.08
Net Margin %	7.04	7.05	6.26	6.64	6.29	5.68	5.64	6.04
Asset Turnover	1.91	1.90	1.88	2.02	2.07	2.21	2.38	2.52
Current Ratio	1.33	1.20	1.28	1.40	1.48	1.59	1.77	1.75
Debt to Equity	0.09	0.05	0.05	0.04	0.07	0.07	0.10	0.06
Price Range	41.16-32.88	37.52-30.36	37.52-28.07	37.52-20.70	52.07-20.53	53.45-32.80	68.50-34.88	68.75-36.17
P/E Ratio	18.54-14.81	17.70-14.32	19.05-14.25	19.96-11.01	33.38-13.16	41.43-25.43	62.27-31.70	68.75-36.17
Average Yield %	0.86	0.84	0.79	0.83	0.60	0.37	0.31	0.25

Address: 2455 Paces Ferry Road N.W., Atlanta, GA 30339-4024	**Web Site:** www.homedepot.com	**Auditors:** KPMG LLP
Telephone: (770) 433-8211	**Officers:** Robert L. Nardelli - Chmn. Pres., C.E.O.	**Investor Contact:** 770-384-4388
Fax: (770) 431-2707	Carol B. Tome - Exec. V.P., C.F.O.	**Transfer Agents:** EquiServe Trust Company, N.A., Providence, RI

HOME PROPERTIES INC

Exchange	Symbol	Price	52Wk Range	Yield	P/E	Div Acheiver
NYS	HME	$38.80 (3/31/2005)	43.92-36.85	6.49	32.88	10 Years

*7 Year Price Score 107.79 *NYSE Composite Index=100 *12 Month Price Score 94.05

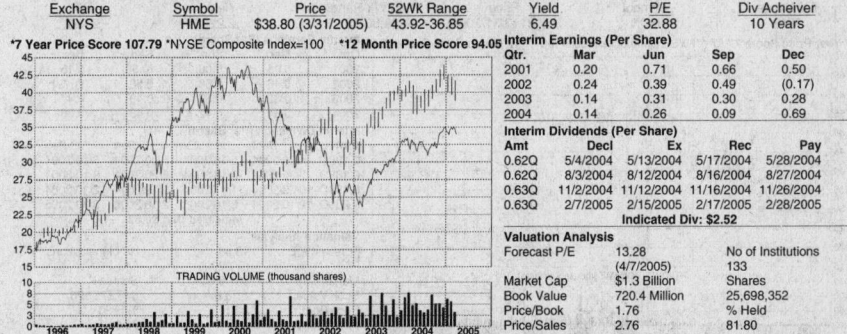

Interim Earnings (Per Share)

Qtr.	Mar	Jun	Sep	Dec
2001	0.20	0.71	0.66	0.50
2002	0.24	0.39	0.49	(0.17)
2003	0.14	0.31	0.30	0.28
2004	0.14	0.26	0.09	0.69

Interim Dividends (Per Share)

Amt	Decl	Ex	Rec	Pay
0.62Q	5/4/2004	5/13/2004	5/17/2004	5/28/2004
0.62Q	8/3/2004	8/12/2004	8/16/2004	8/27/2004
0.63Q	11/2/2004	11/12/2004	11/16/2004	11/26/2004
0.63Q	2/7/2005	2/15/2005	2/17/2005	2/28/2005

Indicated Div: $2.52

Valuation Analysis

Forecast P/E	13.28 (4/7/2005)	No of Institutions 133
Market Cap	$1.3 Billion	Shares 25,698,352
Book Value	720.4 Million	% Held
Price/Book	1.76	81.80
Price/Sales	2.76	

Business Summary: Property, Real Estate & Development (MIC: 8.3 SIC: 798 NAIC: 25930)

Home Properties is a self-administered and self-managed real estate investment trust that owns, operates, acquires and rehabilitates apartment communities in the Northeastern, Mid-Atlantic and Midwestern U.S. Co. conducts its business through Home Properties of New York, L.P., a New York limited partnership in which Co. held a 67.7% partnership interest as of Dec. 31 2003 and two management companies, Home Properties Management, Inc. and Home Properties Resident Services, Inc. As of Dec 31 2003, Co. operated 197 communities with 48,080 apartment units.

Recent Developments: For the year ended Dec 31 2004, income from continuing operations decreased 1.5% to $36,147 thousand from income of $36,701 thousand a year earlier. Net income increased 12.5% to $47,022 thousand from net income of $41,798 thousand a year earlier. Revenues were $458,330 thousand, up 9.1% from $420,030 thousand the year before. Income from operations was $50,322 thousand, down 4.2% from $52,558 thousand the year before.

Prospects: Co. is benefiting from continued improvements in rental rates, total revenues and net operating income. However, occupancy levels at Co.'s apartment communities continue to be challenged by the lack of meaningful job growth and lower home mortgage rates. Meanwhile, Co.'s exit from the affordable business is expected to favorably affect bottom-line results in the long term. Specifically, Co. will be able to focus its efforts on the core business of owning and managing market-rate apartment communities. Additionally, On Jan 13 2005, Co. announced it had acquired a 204 unit apartment complex called Ridgeview Chase for a purchase price of $19.7 million.

Financial Data

(US$ in Thousands)	12/31/2004	12/31/2003	12/31/2002	12/31/2001	12/31/2000	12/31/1999	12/31/1998	12/31/1997
Earnings Per Share	1.18	1.03	0.96	2.11	1.41	1.34	1.33	0.84
Cash Flow Per Share	4.82	4.99	5.51	6.71	6.15	4.84	4.36	3.68
Tang Book Value Per Share	19.48	20.53	20.67	21.10	19.50	22.81	20.52	16.25
Dividends Per Share	2.490	2.450	2.410	2.310	2.160	1.970	1.830	1.740
Dividend Payout %	211.02	237.86	251.04	109.48	153.19	147.01	137.59	207.14
Income Statement								
Property Income	455,023	429,618	392,620	362,233	310,249	224,469	141,171	66,224
Non-Property Income	3,307	4,886	2,942	5,290	8,799	9,994	8,072	3,473
Total Revenue	458,330	434,504	395,562	367,523	319,048	234,463	149,243	69,697
Depn & Amortn	98,051	79,279	68,799	65,521	52,995	38,066	24,405	11,938
Interest Expense	90,506	85,110	77,314	66,446	56,792	39,558	23,980	11,967
Net Income	47,022	41,798	44,939	64,506	41,456	26,282	18,688	6,390
Average Shares	33,314	29,575	26,335	22,227	20,755	18,800	14,022	7,588
Balance Sheet								
Total Assets	2,816,796	2,513,317	2,456,266	2,063,789	1,871,888	1,503,617	1,012,235	543,823
Long-Term Obligations	1,644,722	1,380,696	1,300,807	960,358	832,783	618,901	418,942	210,096
Total Liabilities	1,785,599	1,441,510	1,396,963	1,052,606	882,083	706,614	445,570	235,544
Stockholders' Equity	720,422	741,263	726,242	620,596	569,528	497,123	361,956	151,432
Shares Outstanding	32,625	31,966	27,027	24,010	21,565	19,598	17,635	9,318
Statistical Record								
Return on Assets %	1.76	1.68	1.99	3.28	2.45	2.09	2.40	1.61
Return on Equity %	6.42	5.70	6.67	10.84	7.75	6.12	7.28	5.45
Net Margin %	10.26	9.62	11.36	17.55	12.99	11.21	12.52	9.17
Price Range	43.92-36.85	40.92-31.19	37.94-28.90	33.14-26.13	31.56-25.56	29.06-22.38	27.94-21.56	28.06-20.38
P/E Ratio	37.22-31.23	39.73-30.28	39.52-30.10	15.71-12.38	22.38-18.13	21.69-16.70	21.01-16.21	33.41-24.26
Average Yield %	6.23	6.76	7.16	7.81	7.68	7.54	7.09	7.27

Address: 850 Clinton Square, Rochester, NY 14604
Telephone: (585) 546-4900
Fax: (585) 546-5433

Web Site: www.homeproperties.com
Officers: Norman P. Leenhouts - Co-Chmn. Nelson B. Leenhouts - Co-Chmn.

Auditors: PricewaterhouseCoopers LLP
Investor Contact: 716-546-4900

HONEYWELL INTERNATIONAL, INC.

Exchange	Symbol	Price	52Wk Range	Yield	P/E
NYS	HON	$37.21 (3/31/2005)	39.30-32.23	2.22	24.97

*7 Year Price Score 77.87 *NYSE Composite Index=100 *12 Month Price Score 98.33

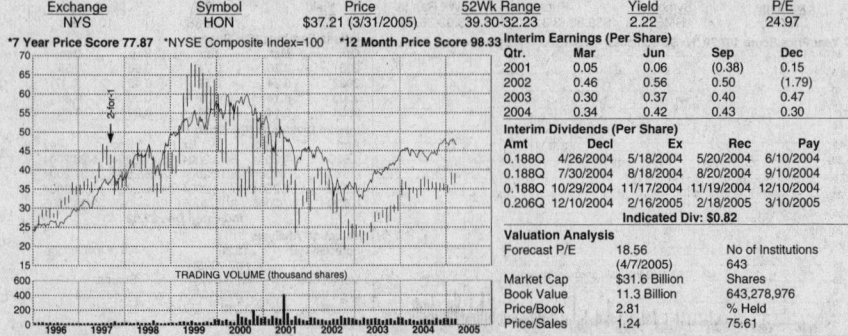

Interim Earnings (Per Share)

Qtr.	Mar	Jun	Sep	Dec
2001	0.05	0.06	(0.38)	0.15
2002	0.46	0.56	0.50	(1.79)
2003	0.30	0.37	0.40	0.47
2004	0.34	0.42	0.43	0.30

Interim Dividends (Per Share)

Amt	Decl	Ex	Rec	Pay
0.188Q	4/26/2004	5/18/2004	5/20/2004	6/10/2004
0.188Q	7/30/2004	8/18/2004	8/20/2004	9/10/2004
0.188Q	10/29/2004	11/17/2004	11/19/2004	12/10/2004
0.206Q	12/10/2004	2/16/2005	2/18/2005	3/10/2005
		Indicated Div: $0.82		

Valuation Analysis

Forecast P/E	18.56	No of Institutions
	(4/7/2005)	643
Market Cap	$31.6 Billion	Shares
Book Value	11.3 Billion	643,278,976
Price/Book	2.81	% Held
Price/Sales	1.24	75.61

Business Summary: Automotive (MIC: 15.1 SIC: 714 NAIC: 36399)

Honeywell International is a diversified technology and manufacturing company, serving customers worldwide with aerospace products and services, control, sensing and security technologies for buildings, homes and industry, turbochargers, automotive products, specialty chemicals, fibers, and electronic and advanced materials. Co. has four reportable segments: Aerospace, Automation and Control Solutions, Specialty Materials and Transportation Systems. Co. is engaged in manufacturing, sales and research and development mainly in the U.S., Europe, Canada, Asia and Latin America. U.S. exports and foreign manufactured products are significant to Co.'s operations.

Recent Developments: For the year ended Dec 31 2004, net income decreased 3.2% to $1,281,000 thousand from net income of $1,324,000 thousand a year earlier. Revenues were $25,601,000 thousand, up 10.8% from $23,103,000 thousand the year before. Total direct expense was $20,585,000 thousand versus $18,235,000 thousand in the prior year, an increase of 12.9%. Total indirect expense was $3,179,000 thousand versus $2,912,000 thousand in the prior year, an increase of 9.2%.

Prospects: Co. is experiencing strong organic growth in each of its operating segments and is exceeding its sales, earnings and cash targets. Co. is continuing to see improvements in its end markets and results from its investments in growth initiatives. Co.'s Aerospace business is benefiting from new contracts on Boeing's 7E7 Dreamliner, continuing growth in its strong defense business and increases in global flying hours. Meanwhile, Co. has agreed to acquire Novar plc for approximately $2.40 billion. The acquisition will bolster Co.'s Automation and Control Solutions business and is expected to be accretive to earnings in 2005.

Financial Data

(US$ in Thousands)	12/31/2004	12/31/2003	12/31/2002	12/31/2001	12/31/2000	12/31/1999	12/31/1998	12/31/1997
Earnings Per Share	1.49	1.54	(0.27)	(0.12)	2.05	1.90	2.32	2.02
Cash Flow Per Share	2.62	2.55	2.90	2.46	2.48	3.00	2.13	2.31
Tang Book Value Per Share	4.70	4.46	2.52	3.45	4.72	4.95	4.11	3.51
Dividends Per Share	0.750	0.750	0.750	0.750	0.750	0.680	0.600	0.520
Dividend Payout %	50.34	48.70	...	...	36.59	35.79	25.86	25.74
Income Statement								
Total Revenue	25,601,000	23,103,000	22,274,000	23,652,000	25,023,000	23,735,000	15,128,000	14,472,000
EBITDA	2,661,000	2,636,000	129,000	902,000	3,874,000	3,394,000	2,714,000	2,500,000
Depn & Amortn	650,000	661,000	730,000	919,000	995,000	881,000	609,000	609,000
Income Before Taxes	1,680,000	1,640,000	(945,000)	(422,000)	2,398,000	2,248,000	1,943,000	1,716,000
Income Taxes	399,000	296,000	(725,000)	(323,000)	739,000	707,000	612,000	546,000
Net Income	1,281,000	1,324,000	(220,000)	(99,000)	1,659,000	1,541,000	1,331,000	1,170,000
Average Shares	862,333	862,095	820,292	812,273	809,468	808,990	574,377	579,869
Balance Sheet								
Current Assets	12,820,000	11,523,000	10,195,000	9,894,000	10,661,000	10,422,000	5,593,000	5,573,000
Total Assets	31,062,000	29,344,000	27,559,000	24,226,000	25,175,000	23,527,000	15,560,000	13,707,000
Current Liabilities	8,739,000	6,783,000	6,574,000	6,220,000	7,214,000	8,272,000	5,185,000	4,436,000
Long-Term Obligations	4,069,000	4,961,000	4,719,000	4,731,000	3,941,000	2,457,000	1,476,000	1,215,000
Total Liabilities	19,810,000	18,615,000	18,634,000	15,056,000	15,468,000	14,928,000	10,263,000	9,321,000
Stockholders' Equity	11,252,000	10,729,000	8,925,000	9,170,000	9,707,000	8,599,000	5,297,000	4,386,000
Shares Outstanding	850,013	862,330	854,493	814,966	807,291	795,133	558,466	558,343
Statistical Record								
Return on Assets %	4.23	4.65	N.M.	N.M.	6.79	7.88	9.10	8.82
Return on Equity %	11.62	13.47	N.M.	N.M.	18.08	22.18	27.49	27.32
EBITDA Margin %	10.39	11.41	0.58	3.81	15.48	14.30	17.94	17.27
Net Margin %	5.00	5.73	N.M.	N.M.	6.63	6.49	8.80	8.08
Asset Turnover	0.85	0.81	0.86	0.96	1.02	1.21	1.03	1.09
Current Ratio	1.47	1.70	1.55	1.59	1.48	1.26	1.08	1.26
Debt to Equity	0.36	0.46	0.53	0.52	0.41	0.29	0.28	0.28
Price Range	38.11-31.75	33.43-20.73	40.76-19.20	53.50-23.59	59.88-33.00	68.06-39.00	47.13-33.00	46.84-33.50
P/E Ratio	25.58-21.31	21.71-13.46	...	...	29.21-16.10	35.82-20.53	20.31-14.22	23.19-16.58
Average Yield %	2.13	2.81	2.38	1.91	1.63	1.21	1.46	1.34

Address: 101 Columbia Road, P.O. Box 4000, Morristown, NJ 07962-2497 Telephone: (973) 455 2000 Fax: (973) 455 4807	Web Site: www.honeywell.com Officers: David M. Cote - Chmn., C.E.O. David J. Anderson - Sr. V.P., C.F.O.	Auditors: PricewaterhouseCoopers LLP Investor Contact: 973-455-4732

HORACE MANN EDUCATORS CORP.

Exchange	Symbol	Price	52Wk Range	Yield	P/E
NYS	HMN	$17.74 (3/31/2005)	19.28-15.08	2.37	15.03

*7 Year Price Score 75.51 *NYSE Composite Index=100 *12 Month Price Score 97.98

Interim Earnings (Per Share)

Qtr.	Mar	Jun	Sep	Dec
2001	0.41	(0.12)	0.22	0.12
2002	0.38	(0.47)	0.02	0.33
2003	0.19	0.05	(0.34)	0.54
2004	0.51	0.44	(0.30)	...

Interim Dividends (Per Share)

Amt	Decl	Ex	Rec	Pay
0.105Q	5/25/2004	6/14/2004	6/15/2004	6/30/2004
0.105Q	9/14/2004	9/22/2004	9/24/2004	9/30/2004
0.105Q	12/10/2004	12/16/2004	12/20/2004	12/30/2004
0.105Q	3/8/2005	3/16/2005	3/18/2005	3/30/2005
			Indicated Div: $0.42	

Valuation Analysis

Forecast P/E	15.77 (4/13/2005)	No of Institutions 124
Market Cap	$759.2 Million	Shares 42,975,124
Book Value	545.9 Million	% Held
Price/Book	1.39	N/A
Price/Sales	0.86	

Business Summary: Insurance (MIC: 8.2 SIC: 331 NAIC: 24126)

Horace Mann Educators is an insurance holding company. Through its subsidiaries, Co. markets and underwrites personal lines of property and casualty and life insurance and retirement annuities in the U.S. The primary products of Co.'s property and casualty lines are private passenger automobile and homeowners insurance. Co.'s principal insurance subsidiaries are Horace Mann Insurance, Teachers Insurance, Horace Mann Life Insurance, Horace Mann Property & Casualty Insurance, and Horace Mann Lloyds. Co. markets its products primarily to educators and other employees of public schools. Co. sells and services its products primarily through an exclusive sales force of full-time agents.

Recent Developments: For the year ended Dec 31 2004, net income more than doubled to $56,313 thousand compared with $18,975 thousand in the previous year. Results for 2003 included pre-tax restructuring charges of $408 thousand. Revenues rose 2.8% to $878,349 thousand from $853,748 thousand the year before. Net premiums earned grew 4.8% to $674,704 thousand in 2003. Total benefits, losses, and expenses fell 3.2% to $808,592 thousand from $834,569 thousand in the prior year.

Prospects: Co. is benefiting from solid earnings growth despite the negative affect of four hurricanes, which drove a higher level of catastrophe costs in 2004. Meanwhile, Co.'s underlying non-catastrophe property and casualty results continue to gain traction, benefiting from additional underwriting and pricing actions taken over the last several quarters, ongoing improvements in claims processes, cost containment initiatives, and a continuing low level of non-catastrophe claim frequencies. Going forward, Co.'s underlying 2004 results support a preliminary estimate of full-year 2005 net income before realized investment gains and losses of between $1.55 and $1.65 per share.

Financial Data
(US$ in Thousands)

	9 Mos	6 Mos	3 Mos	12/31/2003	12/31/2002	12/31/2001	12/31/2000	12/31/1999
Earnings Per Share	1.18	1.15	0.76	0.44	0.28	0.63	0.51	1.07
Cash Flow Per Share	4.08	4.01	3.73	2.75	4.04	3.66	3.04	3.59
Tang Book Value Per Share	11.65	10.66	12.39	10.67	10.53	9.17	8.29	7.26
Dividends Per Share	0.420	0.420	0.420	0.420	0.420	0.420	0.420	0.383
Dividend Payout %	35.47	36.40	55.30	95.45	150.00	66.67	82.35	35.75
Income Statement								
Premium Income	501,771	336,660	167,563	643,536	625,233	615,242	598,714	595,128
Total Revenue	654,494	436,604	221,441	853,748	771,874	804,490	781,204	775,426
Benefits & Claims	377,852	218,428	111,455	518,978	450,866	475,583	466,048	416,186
Income Before Taxes	37,016	57,150	30,587	19,179	7,665	28,342	9,721	93,354
Income Taxes	9,032	16,522	8,896	204	(3,668)	2,755	(11,120)	48,849
Net Income	27,984	40,628	21,691	18,975	11,333	25,587	20,841	44,505
Average Shares	43,022	42,968	42,934	42,904	41,199	40,877	40,966	41,708
Balance Sheet								
Total Assets	5,752,959	5,420,070	5,518,972	4,972,988	4,512,289	4,489,026	4,420,580	4,253,846
Total Liabilities	5,207,062	4,916,675	4,942,424	4,442,513	3,983,447	4,029,836	3,992,587	3,853,704
Stockholders' Equity	545,897	503,395	576,548	530,475	528,842	459,190	427,993	400,142
Shares Outstanding	42,794	42,759	42,722	42,721	42,691	40,735	40,517	41,033
Statistical Record								
Return on Assets %	0.92	0.94	0.62	0.40	0.25	0.57	0.48	1.03
Return on Equity %	9.42	9.07	5.81	3.58	2.29	5.77	5.02	9.93
Loss Ratio %	75.30	64.88	66.52	80.64	72.11	77.30	77.84	69.93
Net Margin %	4.28	9.31	9.80	2.22	1.47	3.18	2.67	5.74
Price Range	17.58-12.94	17.48-12.94	16.75-12.94	16.75-12.50	23.95-13.70	22.09-15.30	21.88-12.44	32.00-19.50
P/E Ratio	14.90-10.97	15.20-11.25	22.04-17.03	38.07-28.41	85.54-48.93	35.06-24.29	42.89-24.39	29.91-18.22
Average Yield %	2.69	2.75	2.83	2.88	2.28	2.23	2.61	1.49

Address: 1 Horace Mann Plaza, Springfield, IL 62715-0001
Telephone: (217) 789-2500
Fax: (217) 788-5137

Web Site: www.horacemann.com
Officers: Joseph J. Melone - Chmn. Louis G. Lower II - Pres., C.E.O.

Auditors: KPMG LLP
Investor Contact: 217-789-2500
Transfer Agents: American Stock Transfer & Trust Co. New York, NY

HORMEL FOODS CORP.

Exchange	Symbol	Price	52Wk Range	Yield	P/E	Div Acheiver
NYS	HRL	$31.11 (3/31/2005)	32.24-26.00	1.67	18.19	37 Years

*7 Year Price Score 114.82 ***NYSE Composite Index=100** ***12 Month Price Score 98.34**

TRADING VOLUME (thousand shares)

Interim Earnings (Per Share)

Qtr.	Jan	Apr	Jul	Oct
2001-02	0.36	0.23	0.27	0.49
2002-03	0.34	0.24	0.25	0.50
2003-04	0.37	0.38	0.40	0.50
2004-05	0.46	...	...	...

Interim Dividends (Per Share)

Amt	Decl	Ex	Rec	Pay
0.113Q	5/24/2004	7/21/2004	7/24/2004	8/15/2004
0.113Q	9/20/2004	10/20/2004	10/23/2004	11/15/2004
0.13Q	11/22/2004	1/19/2005	1/22/2005	2/15/2005
0.13Q	3/29/2005	4/20/2005	4/23/2005	5/15/2005

Indicated Div: $0.52 (Div. Reinv. Plan)

Valuation Analysis

Forecast P/E	17.63	No of Institutions
	(4/7/2005)	197
Market Cap	$4.3 Billion	Shares
Book Value	1.5 Billion	37,453,196
Price/Book	2.96	% Held
Price/Sales	0.89	27.11

Business Summary: Food (MIC: 4.1 SIC: 011 NAIC: 11611)

Hormel Foods is primarily engaged in the production of a variety of meat and food products and the marketing of those products throughout the United States. Although pork and turkey remain the major raw materials for Co. products, Co. has emphasized for several years the manufacture and distribution of branded, consumer packaged items rather than the commodity fresh meat business. Co.'s business is reported in five segments: Grocery Products, Refrigerated Foods, Jennie-O Turkey Store, Specialty Foods, and All Other. Co.'s products primarily consist of meat and other food products. The meat products are sold fresh, frozen, cured, smoked, cooked and canned.

Recent Developments: For the quarter ended Jan 30 2005, net income increased 24.4% to $64,474 thousand from net income of $51,826 thousand in the year-earlier quarter. Revenues were $1,271,431 thousand, up 12.0% from $1,135,533 thousand the year before. Operating income was $104,601 thousand versus an income of $85,224 thousand in the prior-year quarter, an increase of 22.7%. Total direct expense was $959,618 thousand versus $863,757 thousand in the prior-year quarter, an increase of 11.1%. Total indirect expense was $210,139 thousand versus $188,258 thousand in the prior-year quarter, an increase of 11.6%.

Prospects: On Dec 30 2004, Co. announced that it has acquired, for the purchase price of about $186.0 million, all of the stock of Clougherty Packing Company, a privately held pork processor and creator of the FARMER JOHN brand of pork products. Also, on Jan 31 2005, Co. announced the acquisition of Arriba Foods Inc., a manufacturer and marketer of Mexican food products, for $47.0 million in cash. Arriba's products are marketed under the Manny's, Gringo Pete's and Mexican Accent brands and are expected to strengthen Co.'s presence in the ethnic products category. Both acquisitions are expected to be immediately accretive to Co.'s respective Refrigerated Foods and Grocery Products business segments.

Financial Data

(US$ in Thousands)	3 Mos	10/30/2004	10/25/2003	10/26/2002	10/27/2001	10/28/2000	10/30/1999	10/31/1998
Earnings Per Share	1.71	1.65	1.33	1.35	1.30	1.20	1.11	0.93
Cash Flow Per Share	2.43	2.09	1.83	2.36	2.32	1.08	1.65	1.51
Tang Book Value Per Share	6.50	6.43	5.36	5.41	4.45	5.64	5.20	4.82
Dividends Per Share	0.468	0.450	0.420	0.390	0.370	0.350	0.330	0.320
Dividend Payout %	27.33	27.27	31.58	28.89	28.46	29.17	29.73	34.59
Income Statement								
Total Revenue	1,271,431	4,779,875	4,200,328	3,910,314	4,124,112	3,675,132	3,357,757	3,261,045
EBITDA	135,366	486,452	409,215	408,633	403,160	345,173	329,875	291,301
Depn & Amortn	26,160	94,745	88,020	83,238	90,193	65,886	64,656	60,273
Income Before Taxes	102,432	364,565	289,331	293,970	285,014	264,381	251,473	217,336
Income Taxes	37,958	132,902	103,552	104,648	102,573	94,164	88,035	78,045
Net Income	64,474	231,663	185,779	189,322	182,441	170,217	163,438	139,291
Average Shares	139,626	140,179	139,710	140,292	140,125	141,523	147,010	150,406
Balance Sheet								
Current Assets	943,332	1,029,403	823,974	962,170	883,281	711,109	800,143	717,365
Total Assets	2,605,404	2,533,968	2,393,121	2,220,196	2,162,698	1,641,940	1,685,585	1,555,892
Current Liabilities	488,424	464,366	441,990	410,111	420,203	342,625	385,407	267,651
Long-Term Obligations	361,495	361,510	395,273	409,648	462,407	145,928	184,723	204,874
Total Liabilities	1,154,843	1,134,720	1,140,386	1,104,941	1,166,817	768,063	844,443	742,577
Stockholders' Equity	1,450,561	1,399,248	1,252,735	1,115,255	995,881	873,877	841,142	813,315
Shares Outstanding	138,175	137,875	138,596	138,411	138,663	138,569	142,724	146,992
Statistical Record								
Return on Assets %	9.57	9.25	8.08	8.66	9.62	10.26	10.11	8.89
Return on Equity %	17.47	17.19	15.73	17.98	19.57	19.90	19.81	16.97
EBITDA Margin %	10.65	10.18	9.74	10.45	9.78	9.39	9.82	8.93
Net Margin %	5.07	4.85	4.42	4.84	4.42	4.63	4.87	4.27
Asset Turnover	1.92	1.91	1.83	1.79	2.17	2.21	2.08	2.08
Current Ratio	1.93	2.22	1.86	2.35	2.10	2.08	2.08	2.68
Debt to Equity	0.25	0.26	0.32	0.37	0.46	0.17	0.22	0.25
Price Range	31.87-26.00	31.63-23.80	24.98-20.18	28.03-20.50	26.39-16.75	22.28-14.13	22.63-14.78	19.50-13.09
P/E Ratio	18.64-15.20	19.17-14.42	18.78-15.17	20.76-15.19	20.30-12.88	18.57-11.77	20.38-13.32	20.97-14.08
Average Yield %	1.61	1.60	1.85	1.58	1.73	2.00	1.77	1.97

Address: 1 Hormel Place, Austin, MN 55912-3680	**Web Site:** www.hormel.com	**Auditors:** Ernst & Young LLP
Telephone: (507) 437-5611	**Officers:** Joel W. Johnson - Chmn., C.E.O. Jeffrey M. Ettinger - Pres., C.O.O.	**Investor Contact:** 507-437-5007
Fax: (507) 437-5489		**Transfer Agents:** Wells Fargo Bank Minnesota, N.A., South St. Paul, MN

HORTON (D.R.) INC.

Exchange	Symbol	Price	52Wk Range	Yield	P/E
NYS	DHI	$29.24 (3/31/2005)	34.13-19.18	0.92	11.70

*7 Year Price Score 196.03 ***NYSE Composite Index=100** ***12 Month Price Score 117.33**

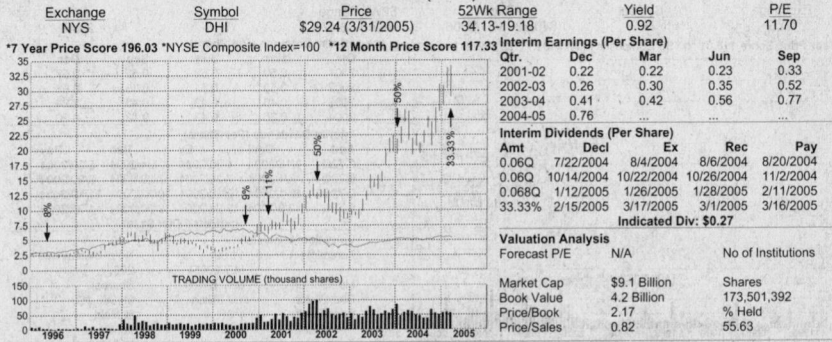

Interim Earnings (Per Share)

Qtr.	Dec	Mar	Jun	Sep
2001-02	0.22	0.22	0.23	0.33
2002-03	0.26	0.30	0.35	0.52
2003-04	0.41	0.42	0.56	0.77
2004-05	0.76	...	...	...

Interim Dividends (Per Share)

Amt	Decl	Ex	Rec	Pay
0.06Q	7/22/2004	8/4/2004	8/6/2004	8/20/2004
0.06Q	10/14/2004	10/22/2004	10/26/2004	11/2/2004
0.068Q	1/12/2005	1/26/2005	1/28/2005	2/11/2005
33.33%	2/15/2005	3/17/2005	3/1/2005	3/16/2005

Indicated Div: $0.27

Valuation Analysis

Forecast P/E	N/A	No of Institutions
Market Cap	$9.1 Billion	Shares
Book Value	4.2 Billion	173,501,392
Price/Book	2.17	% Held
Price/Sales	0.82	55.63

Business Summary: Building & General Construction (MIC: 3.2 SIC: 531 NAIC: 36115)

D.R. Horton is a national homebuilder. Co. constructs and sells single-family homes, designed principally for first-time and move-up homebuyers, through its operating divisions in 21 states and 63 metropolitan markets of the United States, primarily under the name of D.R. Horton, America's Builder. Through its financial services operations, Co. provides mortgage banking and title agency services to homebuyers in many of its homebuilding markets. Co.'s subsidiary title companies serve as title insurance agents by providing title insurance policies, examination and closing services, primarily to purchasers of homes built and sold by Co.

Recent Developments: For the quarter ended Dec 31 2004, net income increased 29.8% to $241,000 thousand from net income of $185,600 thousand in the year-earlier quarter. Revenues were $2,520,100 thousand, up 14.3% from $2,204,500 thousand the year before. Total direct expense was $1,847,100 thousand versus $1,670,300 thousand in the prior-year quarter, an increase of 10.6%. Total indirect expense was $278,800 thousand versus $230,900 thousand in the prior-year quarter, an increase of 20.7%.

Prospects: Co.'s continued sales momentum combined with its strong backlog, provides a solid foundation for achieving improved revenues and earnings in fiscal year 2005. Co.'s backlog was $4.78 billion at Dec 31 2004, up 34.4% from $3.55 billion the year before, and Co.'s sales contract backlog was 17,405 units, up 20.2%. In light of encouraging prospects, Co. is raising its guidance for fiscal 2005 to a range of $4.75 to $4.90. This range represents a 16.0% to 19.0% increase in earnings per share over the $4.11 reported in fiscal year 2004, and is based on projected consolidated revenues of more than $12.50 billion (approximately 50,000 homes closed).

Financial Data

(US$ in Thousands)	3 Mos	09/30/2004	09/30/2003	09/30/2002	09/30/2001	09/30/2000	09/30/1999	09/30/1998
Earnings Per Share	2.50	2.16	1.44	1.00	0.78	0.59	0.48	0.30
Cash Flow Per Share	(2.65)	(0.95)	1.00	(0.24)	(0.17)	(0.33)	(0.53)	(0.45)
Tang Book Value Per Share	11.59	7.61	5.55	4.04	3.38	2.66	2.10	1.70
Dividends Per Share	0.240	0.215	0.135	0.097	0.060	0.041	0.031	0.024
Dividend Payout %	9.60	9.96	9.41	9.62	7.74	7.00	6.43	8.01
Income Statement								
Total Revenue	2,520,100	10,840,800	8,728,100	6,738,831	4,455,514	3,653,695	3,156,211	2,176,941
EBITDA	406,800	1,644,300	1,061,461	693,657	449,147	339,332	289,101	171,147
Depn & Amortn	15,000	55,500	45,861	40,645	36,062	24,492	20,842	9,828
Income Before Taxes	391,800	1,582,900	1,008,162	647,507	407,797	309,224	263,826	159,099
Income Taxes	150,800	607,800	382,207	242,815	152,924	117,505	103,999	65,719
Net Income	241,000	975,100	625,955	404,692	257,009	191,719	159,827	93,380
Average Shares	317,066	451,428	437,165	404,682	329,798	324,522	331,624	321,933
Balance Sheet								
Current Assets	7,850,300	7,085,400	5,665,200	4,447,413	3,043,657	2,263,556	1,994,676	1,434,787
Total Assets	9,698,700	8,985,200	7,279,377	6,017,527	3,652,190	2,694,577	2,361,808	1,667,835
Current Liabilities	406,100	946,600	397,978	391,355	182,641	98,817	104,350	28,497
Long-Term Obligations	3,926,800	3,006,500	2,565,145	2,486,976	1,701,689	1,245,586	1,086,273	826,007
Total Liabilities	5,300,900	4,858,100	4,112,216	3,726,719	2,393,079	1,719,750	1,559,397	1,114,953
Stockholders' Equity	4,190,100	3,960,700	3,031,260	2,269,863	1,250,247	969,563	797,609	549,436
Shares Outstanding	311,663	444,525	442,189	418,585	329,577	321,035	325,546	289,530
Statistical Record								
Return on Assets %	12.19	11.96	9.42	8.37	8.10	7.56	7.93	7.82
Return on Equity %	27.79	27.82	23.62	22.99	23.16	21.64	23.73	22.99
EBITDA Margin %	16.14	15.17	12.16	10.29	10.08	9.29	9.16	7.86
Net Margin %	9.56	8.99	7.17	6.01	5.77	5.25	5.06	4.29
Asset Turnover	1.32	1.33	1.31	1.39	1.40	1.44	1.57	1.82
Current Ratio	19.33	7.49	14.23	11.36	16.66	22.91	19.12	50.35
Debt to Equity	0.94	0.76	0.85	1.10	1.36	1.28	1.36	1.50
Price Range	31.02-19.18	26.79-16.35	16.43-8.03	14.37-6.79	9.93-4.82	5.70-2.84	6.34-3.20	6.73-4.13
P/E Ratio	12.41-7.67	12.40-7.57	11.41-5.58	14.37-6.79	12.73-6.18	9.66-4.82	13.20-6.67	22.44-13.78
Average Yield %	1.04	0.98	1.16	0.88	0.85	1.08	0.65	0.45

Address: 301 Commerce St., Suite 500, Fort Worth, TX 76102 **Telephone:** (817) 390-8200	**Web Site:** www.drhorton.com **Officers:** Donald R. Horton - Chmn. Donald J. Tomnitz - Vice-Chmn., Pres., C.E.O.	**Auditors:** Ernst & Young LLP **Investor Contact:** 817-390-8200 **Transfer Agents:** American Stock Transfer & Trust Co., New York, NY

HOSPITALITY PROPERTIES TRUST

Exchange	Symbol	Price	52Wk Range	Yield	P/E
NYS	HPT	$40.38 (3/31/2005)	46.90-36.17	7.13	23.48

*7 Year Price Score 118.01 *NYSE Composite Index=100 *12 Month Price Score 91.98

Interim Earnings (Per Share)

Qtr.	Mar	Jun	Sep	Dec
2001	0.50	0.52	0.52	0.57
2002	0.50	0.54	0.53	0.58
2003	0.46	0.43	0.43	2.24
2004	0.36	0.43	0.43	0.50

Interim Dividends (Per Share)

Amt	Decl	Ex	Rec	Pay
0.72Q	4/16/2004	4/30/2004	5/4/2004	5/20/2004
0.72Q	7/1/2004	7/20/2004	7/22/2004	8/20/2004
0.72Q	10/1/2004	10/20/2004	10/22/2004	11/19/2004
0.72Q	12/9/2004	12/28/2004	12/30/2004	1/31/2005
			Indicated Div: $2.88	

Valuation Analysis

Forecast P/E	11.09	No of Institutions
	(4/7/2005)	206
Market Cap	$2.7 Billion	Shares
Book Value	1.7 Billion	32,565,160
Price/Book	1.61	% Held
Price/Sales	4.20	48.46

Business Summary: Property, Real Estate & Development (MIC: 8.3 SIC: 798 NAIC: 25930)

Hospitality Properties Trust is a real estate investment trust that buys and owns hotels that are leased to or operated by unaffiliated hotel companies. As of Dec 31 2003, Co. owned 286 hotels with 38,577 rooms or suites located in 38 states in the United States. Co.'s hotels are operated as Marriott Hotels and Resorts®, Courtyard by Marriott®, Residence Inn by Marriott®, Staybridge Suites by Holiday Inn®, AmeriSuites®, Candlewood Suites®, Primesm Hotels and Resorts, Homestead Studio Suites®, TownePlace Suites by Marriott® or SpringHill Suites by Marriott®.

Recent Developments: For the year ended Dec 31 2004, net income decreased 46.6% to $127,091 thousand from net income of $238,213 thousand a year earlier. Revenues were $645,368 thousand, up 16.7% from $552,801 thousand the year before. Operating income was $126,888 thousand versus an income of $238,213 thousand in the prior year, a decrease of 46.7%.

Prospects: Co. is performing well, supported by an expanding economy and limited new hotel supply. During the fourth quarter, revenue per available room (RevPAR) improved to $55.65 versus $52.18 in the year-earlier period. Separately, in December 2004, Co. agreed to purchase 13 hotels for $450.0 million. The 13 hotels to be purchased include four full service luxury InterContinental Hotels, four full service upscale Crowne Plaza Hotels, three full service Holiday Inn Hotels and two upscale, extended stay, all suites Staybridge Suites Hotels. Co. anticipates the acquisitions to be completed during the first quarter of 2005.

Financial Data

(US$ in Thousands)	12/31/2004	12/31/2003	12/31/2002	12/31/2001	12/31/2000	12/31/1999	12/31/1998	12/31/1997
Earnings Per Share	1.72	3.57	2.15	2.12	2.24	2.13	1.92	2.15
Cash Flow Per Share	3.35	3.51	3.36	3.48	3.33	3.26	3.18	2.95
Tang Book Value Per Share	23.85	23.81	23.81	24.51	24.98	25.64	25.74	25.92
Dividends Per Share	2.880	3.600	2.860	2.820	2.770	2.060	2.620	2.450
Dividend Payout %	167.44	100.84	133.02	133.02	123.66	96.71	136.46	113.95
Income Statement								
Total Revenue	645,368	552,801	348,706	303,877	263,023	237,218	174,961	114,132
Depn & Amortn	117,627	107,343	99,124	93,812	86,371	76,930	57,356	33,289
Net Income	127,091	238,213	142,202	131,956	126,271	111,929	81,341	59,153
Average Shares	66,503	62,576	62,538	58,986	56,466	52,566	42,317	...
Balance Sheet								
Current Assets	54,405	62,183	54,144	78,875	51,907	99,588	48,259	94,516
Total Assets	2,689,425	2,761,601	2,403,756	2,354,964	2,220,909	2,194,852	1,837,638	1,313,256
Current Liabilities	228,265	221,703	272,029	265,700	258,150	247,491	238,177	180,363
Long-Term Obligations	697,505	826,126	473,965	464,781	464,748	414,780	414,753	125,000
Total Liabilities	1,003,552	1,116,073	758,736	750,445	737,969	675,137	663,781	305,363
Stockholders' Equity	1,685,873	1,645,528	1,645,020	1,604,519	1,482,940	1,519,715	1,173,857	1,007,893
Shares Outstanding	67,203	62,587	62,547	62,515	56,472	56,449	45,596	38,878
Statistical Record								
Return on Assets %	4.65	9.22	5.98	5.77	5.70	5.55	5.16	5.41
Return on Equity %	7.61	14.48	8.75	8.55	8.39	8.31	7.46	7.16
Net Margin %	19.69	43.09	40.78	43.42	48.01	47.18	46.49	51.83
Asset Turnover	0.24	0.21	0.15	0.13	0.12	0.12	0.11	0.10
Current Ratio	0.24	0.28	0.20	0.30	0.20	0.40	0.20	0.52
Debt to Equity	0.41	0.50	0.29	0.29	0.31	0.27	0.35	0.12
Price Range	46.90-36.17	42.08-27.89	36.50-28.02	30.00-20.95	25.25-18.56	29.63-18.00	36.00-24.13	38.31-28.38
P/E Ratio	27.27-21.03	11.79-7.81	16.98-13.03	14.15-9.88	11.27-8.29	13.91-8.45	18.75-12.57	17.82-13.20
Average Yield %	6.79	10.91	8.59	10.55	12.54	8.27	8.53	7.52

Address: 400 Centre Street, Newton, MA 02458
Telephone: (617) 964-8389
Fax: (617) 969-5730

Web Site: www.hptreit.com
Officers: John G. Murray - Pres., C.O.O. Mark L. Kleifges - C.F.O., Treas.

Auditors: Ernst & Young LLP

HOST MARRIOTT CORP (NEW)

Exchange	Symbol	Price	52Wk Range	Yield	P/E
NYS	HMT	$16.56 (3/31/2005)	17.30-11.37	1.93	N/A

*7 Year Price Score 107.10 *NYSE Composite Index=100 *12 Month Price Score 106.16

Interim Earnings (Per Share)

Qtr.	Mar	Jun	Aug	Dec
2001	0.12	0.16	(0.06)	(0.13)
2002	(0.03)	0.06	(0.18)	(0.04)
2003	(0.16)	(0.09)	(0.35)	0.54
2004	(0.12)	0.02	(0.17)	0.16

Interim Dividends (Per Share)

Amt	Decl	Ex	Rec	Pay
0.26Q	6/18/2001	6/27/2001	6/29/2001	7/13/2001
0.26Q	9/19/2001	9/26/2001	9/28/2001	10/12/2001
0.05Q	9/8/2004	11/26/2004	11/30/2004	12/20/2004
0.08Q	3/21/2005	3/29/2005	3/31/2005	4/15/2005

Indicated Div: $0.32

Valuation Analysis

Forecast P/E	N/A	No of Institutions
Market Cap	$5.8 Billion	Shares
Book Value	2.4 Billion	316,156,704
Price/Book	2.42	% Held
Price/Sales	1.59	90.72

Business Summary: Property, Real Estate & Development (MIC: 8.3 SIC: 798 NAIC: 21110)

Host Marriott is a lodging real estate company. As of Feb 15 2004, Co.'s lodging portfolio consisted of 113 upper-upscale and luxury full-service hotels containing approximately 57,000 rooms and primarily operated under premium brands, such as Marriott, Ritz-Carlton, Hyatt, Four Seasons, Westin and Hilton. Co.'s portfolio is geographically diverse with hotels in most of the major metropolitan areas in 28 states, Washington, D.C., Toronto and Calgary, Canada and Mexico City, Mexico. In addition to its hotels, Co. maintains investments in a joint venture and partnerships that in the aggregate own four full-service hotels, 120 limited-service hotels, the Tiburon Golf Club and other investments.

Recent Developments: For the year ended Dec 31 2004, loss from continuing operations was $64 million compared with a loss of $238 million a year earlier. Net loss was nil versus net income of $14 million a year earlier. Revenues were $3,640 million, up 10.7% from $3,288 million the year before. Operating income was $407 million versus an income of $299 million in the prior year, an increase of 36.1%.

Prospects: Co. expects comparable hotel revenue per available room (RevPAR) for the first quarter and full year 2005 to increase approximately 6.0% to 8.0% and 6.5% to 8.5%, respectively. Co. expects comparable hotel adjusted operating profit margins to increase 100 basis points to 150 basis points. Based upon this guidance, Co. estimates that net income should be approximately $46.0 million to $52.0 million for the first quarter and $100.0 million to $136.0 million for the full year, with earnings per diluted share of approximately $0.10 to $0.12 for the first quarter and $0.18 to $0.28 for the full year of 2005.

Financial Data
(US$ in Thousands)

	12/31/2004	12/31/2003	12/31/2002	12/31/2001	12/31/2000	12/31/1999	12/31/1998	01/02/1998
Earnings Per Share	(0.12)	(0.07)	(0.19)	0.08	0.63	0.92	0.27	0.24
Cash Flow Per Share	1.06	1.33	1.48	0.96	2.18	1.40	1.59	2.29
Tang Book Value Per Share	5.87	5.61	4.82	4.83	5.54	5.80	5.13	5.89
Dividends Per Share	0.050	...	...	0.780	0.910	0.840	...	...
Dividend Payout %	...	...	...	975.00	144.44	91.30	...	...
Income Statement								
Property Income	106,000	100,000	101,000	126,000	1,390,000	1,295,000	...	1,130,000
Non-Property Income	3,534,000	3,348,000	3,579,000	3,628,000	83,000	81,000	3,513,000	17,000
Total Revenue	3,640,000	3,448,000	3,680,000	3,754,000	1,473,000	1,376,000	3,513,000	1,147,000
Depn & Amortn	370,000	384,000	372,000	374,000	327,000	289,000	239,000	236,000
Interest Expense	483,000	491,000	466,000	460,000	433,000	430,000	335,000	302,000
Income Before Taxes	(74,000)	(237,000)	(23,000)	61,000	61,000	180,000	174,000	83,000
Income Taxes	(10,000)	(12,000)	6,000	8,000	(98,000)	(16,000)	(20,000)	36,000
Net Income	...	14,000	(16,000)	51,000	156,000	211,000	47,000	50,000
Average Shares	337,300	281,000	263,000	288,400	289,000	308,100	256,400	208,200
Balance Sheet								
Total Assets	8,421,000	8,592,000	8,316,000	8,338,000	8,396,000	8,202,000	8,268,000	6,526,000
Long-Term Obligations	5,523,000	5,486,000	5,638,000	5,602,000	5,322,000	5,069,000	5,131,000	3,783,000
Total Liabilities	5,818,000	5,762,000	6,008,000	6,044,000	6,015,000	5,692,000	5,892,000	4,776,000
Stockholders' Equity	2,395,000	2,136,000	1,610,000	1,609,000	1,421,000	1,505,000	1,311,000	1,200,000
Shares Outstanding	350,300	320,300	263,700	263,200	221,300	225,600	255,600	203,800
Statistical Record								
Return on Assets %	...	0.17	N.M.	0.61	1.87	2.56	0.64	0.86
Return on Equity %	...	0.75	N.M.	3.37	10.63	14.99	3.76	4.31
Net Margin %	...	0.41	(0.43)	1.36	10.59	15.33	1.34	4.36
Price Range	17.30-11.37	12.32-6.10	12.05-7.75	13.89-6.45	12.94-8.06	14.75-7.75	19.01-8.89	21.06-13.78
P/E Ratio	...	...	...	173.63-80.63	20.54-12.80	16.03-8.42	70.39-32.93	87.76-57.43
Average Yield %	0.38	...	...	6.90	8.93	7.75	...	...

Address: 6903 Rockledge Drive, Suite 1500, Bethesda, MD 20817	**Web Site:** www.hostmarriott.com	**Auditors:** KPMG LLP
Telephone: (240) 744-1000	**Officers:** Richard E. Marriott - Chmn. Christopher J. Nassetts - Pres., C.E.O.	**Transfer Agents:** EquiServe Trust Company, NA Providence , RI
Fax: (240) 380-6338		

HOVNANIAN ENTERPRISES, INC.

Exchange	Symbol	Price	52Wk Range	Yield	P/E
NYS	HOV	$51.00 (3/31/2005)	59.10-29.33	N/A	8.98

*7 Year Price Score 220.52 ***NYSE Composite Index=100** ***12 Month Price Score 123.41**

TRADING VOLUME (thousand shares)

Interim Earnings (Per Share)

Qtr.	Jan	Apr	Jul	Oct
2001-02	0.30	0.40	0.60	0.83
2002-03	0.68	0.80	1.05	1.40
2003-04	0.87	1.06	1.33	2.05
2004-05	1.25	...	...	...

Interim Dividends (Per Share)

Amt	Decl	Ex	Rec	Pay
100%	3/8/2004	3/29/2004	3/19/2004	3/26/2004

Valuation Analysis

Forecast P/E	7.52	No of Institutions
	(4/7/2005)	181
Market Cap	$3.1 Billion	Shares
Book Value	1.3 Billion	30,250,060
Price/Book	2.45	% Held
Price/Sales	0.71	65.00

Business Summary: Building & General Construction (MIC: 3.2 SIC: 531 NAIC: 36115)

Hovnanian Enterprises is engaged in designing, constructing, marketing and selling single-family detached homes, attached townhomes and condominiums, mid-rise and high-rise condominiums, urban infill and active adult homes in planned residential developments. Co. consists of two operating groups: homebuilding and financial services. Co.'s financial services group provides mortgage loans and title services to its homebuilding customers. As of Oct 31 2004, Co. offers homes for sale in 275 communities in 24 markets in 13 states throughout the United States.

Recent Developments: For the quarter ended Jan 31 2005, net income increased 41.2% to $81,482 thousand from net income of $57,711 thousand in the year-earlier quarter. Revenues were $1,058,146 thousand, up 36.5% from $775,215 thousand the year before. Total direct expense was $796,085 thousand versus $586,337 thousand in the prior-year quarter, an increase of 35.8%. Total indirect expense was $125,202 thousand versus $91,183 thousand in the prior-year quarter, an increase of 37.3%.

Prospects: On Mar 2 2005, Co. announced that it has acquired the operations of Town & Country Homes, a privately-held homebuilder and land developer headquartered in Lombard, IL, for an undisclosed purchase price paid in cash. Concurrently, Co. entered into a joint venture agreement with affiliates of Blackstone Real Estate Advisors in New York to own and develop Town & Country's existing residential communities. Town & Country expects to deliver approximately 2,000 homes in calendar year 2005, with total revenues of approximately $640.0 million. Co.'s broad product offering continues to capitalize on the demographic trends that are driving housing demand in its markets.

Financial Data
(US$ in Thousands)

	3 Mos	10/31/2004	10/31/2003	10/31/2002	10/31/2001	10/31/2000	10/31/1999	10/31/1998
Earnings Per Share	5.68	5.35	3.92	2.14	1.15	0.75	0.69	0.58
Cash Flow Per Share	(2.48)	(3.03)	(3.14)	4.09	0.69	(1.38)	0.82	1.43
Tang Book Value Per Share	18.39	16.93	11.32	7.86	6.74	6.21	5.33	4.67
Income Statement								
Total Revenue	1,058,146	4,160,403	3,201,857	2,551,106	1,741,963	1,137,807	948,287	941,947
EBITDA	143,614	584,884	426,612	233,131	118,282	60,754	56,931	45,585
Depn & Amortn	11,708	35,112	15,094	6,506	11,928	8,936	6,314	4,293
Income Before Taxes	131,906	549,772	411,518	226,625	106,354	51,818	50,617	41,292
Income Taxes	50,424	201,091	154,138	88,347	42,668	18,655	19,674	15,141
Net Income	81,482	348,681	257,380	137,696	63,686	33,163	30,075	25,403
Average Shares	65,419	65,133	65,538	64,310	55,584	44,086	43,804	44,032
Balance Sheet								
Current Assets	2,872,172	2,736,542	1,929,357	1,464,430	911,580	759,323	634,192	460,758
Total Assets	3,315,229	3,156,267	2,332,371	1,678,128	1,064,258	873,541	712,861	589,102
Current Liabilities	272,177	548,513	404,734	353,824	180,273	132,539	182,633	154,327
Long-Term Obligations	1,383,036	1,256,792	1,013,382	761,755	508,339	477,643	293,802	233,383
Total Liabilities	1,912,502	1,805,305	1,418,116	1,115,579	688,612	610,182	476,435	387,710
Stockholders' Equity	1,277,070	1,192,394	819,712	562,549	375,646	263,359	236,426	201,392
Shares Outstanding	61,355	61,086	60,097	61,105	55,753	42,410	44,318	43,120
Statistical Record								
Return on Assets %	12.46	12.67	12.84	10.04	6.57	4.17	4.62	4.14
Return on Equity %	34.16	34.56	37.24	29.35	19.93	13.23	13.74	13.36
EBITDA Margin %	13.57	14.06	13.32	9.14	6.79	5.34	6.00	4.84
Net Margin %	7.70	8.38	8.04	5.40	3.66	2.91	3.17	2.70
Asset Turnover	1.49	1.51	1.60	1.86	1.80	1.43	1.46	1.54
Current Ratio	10.55	4.99	4.77	4.14	5.06	5.73	3.47	2.99
Debt to Equity	1.08	1.05	1.24	1.35	1.35	1.81	1.24	1.16
Price Range	52.24-29.33	48.31-29.33	41.28-14.36	20.00-5.58	9.60-3.59	3.91-2.75	4.63-3.00	5.69-3.19
P/E Ratio	9.20-5.16	9.03-5.48	10.53-3.66	9.35-2.61	8.35-3.13	5.21-3.67	6.70-4.35	9.81-5.50

Address: 10 Highway 35, P.O. Box 500, Red Bank, NJ 07701 **Telephone:** (732) 747-7800 **Fax:** (732) 747-7159	Web Site: www.khov.com **Officers:** Kevork S. Hovnanian - Chmn. Ara K. Hovnanian - Pres., C.E.O.	Auditors: Ernst & Young LLP **Investor Contact:** 732-747-7800 **Transfer Agents:** National City Bank, Cleveland, OH

HRPT PROPERTIES TRUST

Exchange	Symbol	Price	52Wk Range	Yield	P/E
NYS	HRP	$11.91 (3/31/2005)	13.05-8.85	7.05	18.05

*7 Year Price Score 95.87 *NYSE Composite Index=100 *12 Month Price Score 103.74

Interim Earnings (Per Share)

Qtr.	Mar	Jun	Sep	Dec
2001	0.18	0.16	0.11	0.06
2002	0.13	0.17	0.16	0.15
2003	0.12	0.12	0.09	0.17
2004	0.22	0.13	0.14	0.17

Interim Dividends (Per Share)

Amt	Decl	Ex	Rec	Pay
0.21Q	7/7/2004	7/21/2004	7/23/2004	8/25/2004
0.21Q	10/5/2004	10/20/2004	10/22/2004	11/22/2004
0.21Q	1/10/2005	1/19/2005	1/21/2005	2/23/2005
0.21Q	4/5/2005	4/20/2005	4/22/2005	5/23/2005
		Indicated Div: $0.84		

Valuation Analysis

Forecast P/E	9.62	No of Institutions	
	(4/13/2005)	166	
Market Cap	$2.1 Billion	Shares	
Book Value	2.3 Billion	96,394,768	
Price/Book	0.92	% Held	
Price/Sales	3.50	54.36	

TRADING VOLUME (thousand shares)

Business Summary: Property, Real Estate & Development (MIC: 8.3 SIC: 798 NAIC: 25930)

HRPT Properties Trust is a real estate investment trust (REIT). As of Dec 31 2003, Co. owned 238 office buildings with approximately 35.8 million sq. ft. that are located throughout the United States. Co. also owns minority equity positions in two former subsidiary REITs: Senior Housing Properties Trust and Hospitality Properties Trust. Co.'s day-to-day operations are conducted by Reit Management & Research LLC (RMR), its investment manager. RMR originates and presents investment opportunities to Co.'s board of trustees. RMR also provides property management services to Co. and an RMR affiliate provides garage management services at one of Co.'s properties.

Recent Developments: For the year ended Dec 31 2004, net income increased 42.3% to $162,829 thousand from net income of $114,446 thousand a year earlier. Rental income improved 20.5% to $603,229 thousand from $500,316 thousand in the previous year. Total expenses jumped 19.6% to $365,403 thousand from $305,424 thousand in 2003. Operating income was $237,826 thousand versus an income of $194,892 thousand in the prior year, an increase of 22.0%.

Prospects: Going forward, Co. expects improving results following the acquisition 136 buildings in 2004 with 8.3 million square feet. On Feb 17 2005, Co. announced an agreement to purchase 188 acres of industrial lands in Oahu, from the Estate of James Campbell and its affiliates for $115.5 million. The land to be acquired is located on the southwest coast of Oahu, about 20 miles from downtown Honolulu and are part of the James Campbell Industrial Park. The lands contain 41 parcels that are currently 95.0% leased to 60 tenants with average remaining lease terms of approximately 15 years. Co. expects the purchase to be completed before the end of 2005.

Financial Data

(US$ in Thousands)	12/31/2004	12/31/2003	12/31/2002	12/31/2001	12/31/2000	12/31/1999	12/31/1998	12/31/1997
Earnings Per Share	0.66	0.50	0.61	0.51	1.08	0.86	1.21	1.24
Cash Flow Per Share	1.18	1.47	1.39	1.11	1.17	1.70	1.62	2.01
Tang Book Value Per Share	10.29	10.71	11.20	11.36	11.59	11.54	13.89	12.81
Dividends Per Share	0.820	0.800	0.800	0.800	1.040	1.460	1.510	1.450
Dividend Payout %	124.24	160.00	131.15	156.86	96.30	169.77	124.79	116.94
Income Statement								
Property Income	603,229	500,316	413,790	387,561	400,976	416,198	340,851	188,000
Non-Property Income	...	411	3,176	6,611	4,030	11,343	15,703	20,863
Total Revenue	603,229	500,727	416,966	394,172	405,006	427,541	356,554	208,863
Depn & Amortn	119,728	98,153	74,026	66,663	64,030	73,529	60,836	40,029
Interest Expense	118,212	101,144	86,360	87,075	100,074	87,470	64,326	36,766
Net Income	162,829	114,446	106,763	82,804	142,272	113,862	144,516	114,000
Average Shares	176,157	136,270	128,817	130,253	131,937	131,843	119,867	92,168
Balance Sheet								
Total Assets	4,813,330	4,013,244	3,206,340	2,805,426	2,900,143	2,953,308	3,064,057	2,135,963
Long-Term Obligations	2,355,031	1,876,821	1,215,977	1,097,217	1,302,950	1,349,890	1,132,081	787,879
Total Liabilities	2,506,136	2,001,593	1,280,067	1,148,926	1,370,931	1,430,841	1,236,264	869,703
Stockholders' Equity	2,307,194	2,011,651	1,926,273	1,656,500	1,529,212	1,522,467	1,827,793	1,266,260
Shares Outstanding	177,316	142,773	128,825	128,808	131,948	131,908	131,547	98,853
Statistical Record								
Return on Assets %	3.68	3.17	3.55	2.90	4.85	3.78	5.56	6.77
Return on Equity %	7.52	5.81	5.96	5.20	9.30	6.80	9.34	11.55
Net Margin %	26.99	22.86	25.60	21.01	35.13	26.63	40.53	54.58
Price Range	12.96-8.85	10.30-8.18	9.37-7.19	9.93-7.73	10.35-6.14	13.29-7.37	17.88-11.95	17.61-15.05
P/E Ratio	19.64-13.41	20.60-16.36	15.36-11.79	19.46-15.17	9.58-5.68	15.45-8.58	14.78-9.88	14.20-12.14
Average Yield %	7.65	8.78	9.39	9.48	14.05	12.96	9.87	9.01

Address: 400 Centre Street, Newton, MA 02458
Telephone: (617) 332-3990
Fax: (617) 332-2261

Web Site: www.hrpreit.com
Officers: John A. Mannix - Pres., C.O.O. John C. Popeo - C.F.O., Treas., Sec.

Auditors: Ernst & Young LLP
Investor Contact: 617-332-3990

HUBBELL INC.

Exchange	Symbol	Price	52Wk Range	Yield	P/E
NYS	HUB A	$46.92 (3/31/2005)	49.65-38.41	2.81	18.69

*7 Year Price Score 109.81 *NYSE Composite Index=100* ***12 Month Price Score 102.15**

TRADING VOLUME (thousand shares)

Interim Earnings (Per Share)

Qtr.	Mar	Jun	Sep	Dec
2001	0.36	0.37	0.33	(0.24)
2002	0.33	0.51	0.52	0.45
2003	0.36	0.40	0.57	0.58
2004	0.56	0.51	0.67	0.77

Interim Dividends (Per Share)

Amt	Decl	Ex	Rec	Pay
0.33Q	6/9/2004	6/17/2004	6/21/2004	7/12/2004
0.33Q	9/15/2004	9/23/2004	9/27/2004	10/12/2004
0.33Q	12/7/2004	12/16/2004	12/20/2004	1/11/2005
0.33Q	2/18/2005	3/10/2005	3/14/2005	4/11/2005

Indicated Div: $1.32

Valuation Analysis

Forecast P/E	17.58	No of Institutions	
	(4/7/2005)	44	
Market Cap	$2.9 Billion	Shares	
Book Value	944.3 Million	6,881,447	
Price/Book	3.04	% Held	
Price/Sales	1.44	73.59	

Business Summary: Electrical (MIC: 11.14 SIC: 646 NAIC: 35122)

Hubbell produces electrical and electronic products for the commercial, industrial, utility, and telecommunications markets. The Electrical segment sells wiring device products, lighting fixtures and controls, fittings, switches and outlet boxes, enclosures, wire management products and voice and data signal processing components. The Power segment manufactures construction, switching and protection products, hot line tools, grounding equipment, cover ups, fasteners, cable accessories, cutouts and connectors. The Industrial Technology segment makes test and measurement equipment, high-voltage power supplies and variable tranformers, industrial controls and specialized communications systems.

Recent Developments: For the year ended Dec 31 2004, net income increased 34.4% to $154,700 thousand from net income of $115,100 thousand a year earlier. Revenues were $1,993,000 thousand, up 12.6% from $1,770,700 thousand the year before. Operating income was $212,600 thousand versus an income of $171,900 thousand in the prior year, an increase of 23.7%. Total direct expense was $1,431,100 thousand versus $1,289,200 thousand in the prior year, an increase of 11.0%. Total indirect expense was $349,300 thousand versus $309,600 thousand in the prior year, an increase of 12.8%.

Prospects: Co.'s outlook for 2005 appears constructive, reflecting expected continued growth across its key markets. Going forward, Co. indicated that it will maintain its focus on its operational initiatives that include lean manufacturing and working capital efficiency. Co. also will seek to extend its product lines, while seeking complementary acquisitions at reasonable prices. Co. noted that its restructuring initiatives for 2005 will entail expense of between $20.0 million and $30.0 million, pre-tax, primarily in its lighting operations. Accordingly, Co. expects full-year 2005 earnings per share, excluding restructuring expense, to be in the $2.65 to $2.95 range.

Financial Data

(US$ in Thousands)	12/31/2004	12/31/2003	12/31/2002	12/31/2001	12/31/2000	12/31/1999	12/31/1998	12/31/1997
Earnings Per Share	2.51	1.91	1.38	0.82	2.25	2.21	2.50	1.89
Cash Flow Per Share	3.04	4.09	3.04	3.40	2.02	2.70	2.88	2.21
Tang Book Value Per Share	10.09	8.41	7.25	7.98	8.64	9.56	9.27	9.54
Dividends Per Share	1.320	1.320	1.320	1.320	1.310	1.270	1.220	1.130
Dividend Payout %	52.59	69.11	95.65	160.98	58.22	57.47	48.80	59.79
Income Statement								
Total Revenue	1,993,000	1,770,700	1,587,800	1,312,200	1,424,100	1,451,800	1,424,600	1,378,831
EBITDA	266,600	228,700	194,600	124,300	258,900	265,700	288,500	230,706
Depn & Amortn	48,900	52,600	49,800	53,000	54,900	52,800	48,100	43,215
Income Before Taxes	197,300	155,500	127,000	55,800	184,300	197,000	230,500	180,168
Income Taxes	42,600	40,400	18,400	7,500	46,100	51,200	61,100	49,850
Net Income	154,700	115,100	83,200	48,300	138,200	145,800	169,400	130,318
Average Shares	61,600	60,100	59,700	58,900	61,300	65,900	67,700	68,843
Balance Sheet								
Current Assets	892,400	709,300	596,300	508,300	620,000	552,800	564,800	596,173
Total Assets	1,642,400	1,499,400	1,410,300	1,205,400	1,454,500	1,399,200	1,390,400	1,284,784
Current Liabilities	409,300	288,400	254,700	283,900	489,400	343,400	345,000	256,301
Long-Term Obligations	199,100	298,800	298,700	99,800	99,700	99,600	99,600	99,519
Total Liabilities	698,100	669,700	666,100	468,900	685,000	543,400	549,800	454,528
Stockholders' Equity	944,300	829,700	744,200	736,500	769,500	855,800	840,600	830,256
Shares Outstanding	61,214	60,278	59,241	58,719	58,757	64,252	65,600	67,027
Statistical Record								
Return on Assets %	9.82	7.91	6.36	3.63	9.66	10.45	12.66	10.55
Return on Equity %	17.39	14.63	11.24	6.41	16.96	17.19	20.28	16.57
EBITDA Margin %	13.39	12.92	12.26	9.47	18.18	18.30	20.25	16.73
Net Margin %	7.76	6.50	5.24	3.68	9.70	10.04	11.89	9.45
Asset Turnover	1.27	1.22	1.21	0.99	1.00	1.04	1.07	1.12
Current Ratio	2.18	2.46	2.34	1.79	1.27	1.61	1.64	2.33
Debt to Equity	0.21	0.36	0.40	0.14	0.13	0.12	0.12	0.12
Price Range	48.36-36.92	42.84-26.95	35.00-25.26	29.65-23.59	28.13-21.56	44.94-26.00	48.81-34.25	47.19-37.50
P/E Ratio	19.27-14.71	22.43-14.11	25.36-18.30	36.16-28.77	12.50-9.58	20.33-11.76	19.53-13.70	24.97-19.84
Average Yield %	3.17	3.81	4.27	4.83	5.26	3.51	2.83	2.65

Address: 584 Derby-Milford Road, Orange, CT 06477-4024
Telephone: (203) 799-4100
Fax: (203) 799-4333

Web Site: www.hubbell.com
Officers: G. Jackson Ratcliffe - Chmn. Timothy H. Powers - Pres., C.E.O.

Auditors: PricewaterhouseCoopers LLP
Transfer Agents: Mellon Investors Services LLC, Ridgefield Park, NJ

HUDSON UNITED BANCORP

Exchange	Symbol	Price	52Wk Range	Yield	P/E	Div Acheiver
NYS	HU	$35.25 (3/31/2005)	41.64-33.09	4.20	12.37	14 Years

*7 Year Price Score 108.95 *NYSE Composite Index=100 ***12 Month Price Score 90.14**

Interim Earnings (Per Share)

Qtr.	Mar	Jun	Sep	Dec
2001	0.46	0.49	0.51	0.54
2002	0.93	0.56	0.60	0.63
2003	0.63	0.65	0.68	0.54
2004	0.69	0.70	0.72	0.73

Interim Dividends (Per Share)

Amt	Decl	Ex	Rec	Pay
0.33Q	4/22/2004	5/12/2004	5/14/2004	6/1/2004
0.35Q	7/28/2004	8/11/2004	8/13/2004	9/1/2004
0.35Q	10/22/2004	11/9/2004	11/12/2004	12/1/2004
0.37Q	1/25/2005	2/16/2005	2/18/2005	3/1/2005

Indicated Div: $1.48 (Div. Reinv. Plan)

Valuation Analysis

Forecast P/E	11.57	No of Institutions
	(4/7/2005)	167
Market Cap	$1.6 Billion	Shares
Book Value	531.6 Million	23,529,248
Price/Book	2.98	% Held
Price/Sales	2.78	52.28

Business Summary: Commercial Banking (MIC: 8.1 SIC: 022 NAIC: 22110)

Hudson United Bancorp is a bank holding company. Co. directly owns Hudson United Bank, a full-service commercial bank that operated 205 offices, as of Dec 31 2003, throughout the state of New Jersey; in the Hudson Valley area of New York State; in New York City; in southern Connecticut; and in Philadelphia and surrounding areas in Pennsylvania. Co. also directly owns six additional subsidiaries, which are HUBCO Capital Trust I, HUBCO Capital Trust II, JBI Capital Trust I, Hudson United Capital Trust I, Hudson United Capital Trust II and Jefferson Delaware Inc. As of Dec 31 2003, Co., through its subsidiaries, had total deposits of $6.24 billion and total assets of $8.10 billion.

Recent Developments: For the year ended Dec 31 2004, net income increased 14.0% to $128,083 thousand from net income of $112,321 thousand a year earlier. Net interest income was $315,652 thousand, up 5.5% from $299,258 thousand the year before. Provision for loan losses was $29,700 thousand versus $52,000 thousand in the prior year, a decrease of 42.9%. Non-interest income rose 17.5% to $156,327 thousand, while non-interest expense advanced 10.7% to $281,287 thousand.

Prospects: Co. continues to show a steady trend of growth in commercial loans, commercial mortgage and credit card receivables. The growth in these higher yielding assets should continue to allow Co. to achieve strong earnings growth. Also, Co.'s bottom-line is benefiting from lower interest expense on deposits, partially offset in part by yields on new loans being originated in a lower interest rate environment. Interest income on securities is growing due to an increase in the average volume being partially offset by a decline in average yield. For fiscal 2005, Co. is forecasting earnings to be in the range of $3.00 to $3.10 per share.

Financial Data

(US$ in Thousands)	12/31/2004	12/31/2003	12/31/2002	12/31/2001	12/31/2000	12/31/1999	12/31/1998	12/31/1997
Earnings Per Share	2.85	2.50	2.72	2.00	0.92	1.18	0.49	1.80
Cash Flow Per Share	3.13	4.00	6.00	0.73	3.44	2.81	5.37	3.11
Tang Book Value Per Share	9.51	7.91	7.38	6.50	5.58	7.07	8.25	6.32
Dividends Per Share	1.360	1.180	1.100	1.010	0.932	0.883	0.778	0.646
Dividend Payout %	47.72	47.20	40.44	50.50	101.28	74.68	157.32	35.88
Income Statement								
Interest Income	414,434	394,129	430,003	470,363	608,309	644,576	468,547	218,041
Interest Expense	98,782	94,871	129,246	184,997	288,583	301,510	214,353	77,797
Net Interest Income	315,652	299,258	300,757	285,366	319,726	343,066	254,194	140,244
Provision for Losses	14,850	26,000	51,333	34,147	24,000	52,200	14,374	7,327
Non-Interest Income	156,327	133,045	185,122	109,425	31,095	88,698	33,299	41,107
Non-Interest Expense	283,706	256,295	247,126	227,240	250,031	271,287	232,096	93,593
Income Before Taxes	173,423	150,008	187,420	133,404	76,790	108,277	41,023	80,431
Income Taxes	45,340	37,687	64,214	38,943	26,969	38,939	17,872	31,117
Net Income	128,083	112,321	123,206	94,461	49,821	69,338	23,151	49,314
Average Shares	44,944	44,892	45,349	47,160	54,186	58,566	47,241	27,357
Balance Sheet								
Net Loans & Leases	4,766,385	4,591,909	4,267,546	4,374,556	5,182,343	5,571,759	3,333,311	1,736,598
Total Assets	9,079,042	8,100,658	7,651,261	6,999,535	6,817,226	9,686,286	6,778,661	3,046,505
Total Deposits	6,344,198	6,243,359	6,199,701	5,983,545	5,813,267	6,455,345	5,051,390	2,314,399
Total Liabilities	8,547,392	7,642,468	7,218,735	6,615,631	6,448,753	9,167,120	6,321,846	2,710,365
Stockholders' Equity	531,650	458,190	432,526	383,904	368,473	519,166	456,815	186,140
Shares Outstanding	44,982	44,798	45,023	45,814	47,964	57,085	45,786	25,571
Statistical Record								
Return on Assets %	1.49	1.43	1.68	1.37	0.60	0.84	0.47	1.60
Return on Equity %	25.81	25.22	30.18	25.11	11.19	14.21	7.20	25.13
Net Interest Margin %	76.16	75.93	69.94	60.67	52.56	53.22	54.25	64.32
Efficiency Ratio %	49.71	48.62	40.17	39.19	39.10	37.00	46.25	36.12
Loans to Deposits	0.75	0.74	0.69	0.73	0.89	0.86	0.66	0.75
Price Range	41.64-33.09	40.39-29.80	32.85-23.30	29.33-20.00	25.11-16.42	31.77-22.73	33.53-19.09	33.53-18.41
P/E Ratio	14.61-11.61	16.16-11.92	12.08-8.57	14.66-10.00	27.30-17.85	26.93-19.26	68.42-38.95	18.63-10.23
Average Yield %	3.64	3.43	3.71	4.06	4.54	3.14	2.76	2.64

Address: 1000 Macarthur Boulevard, Mahwah, NJ 07430 Telephone: (201) 236-2600 Fax: (201) 236-2649	Web Site: www.hudsonunitedbank.com Officers: Kenneth T. Neilson - Chmn., Pres., C.E.O. James Mayo - Exec. V.P., Oper. & Technology	Auditors: Ernst & Young LLP Investor Contact: 201-236-2803 Transfer Agents: American Stock Transfer Company, New York, NY

HUGHES SUPPLY INC.

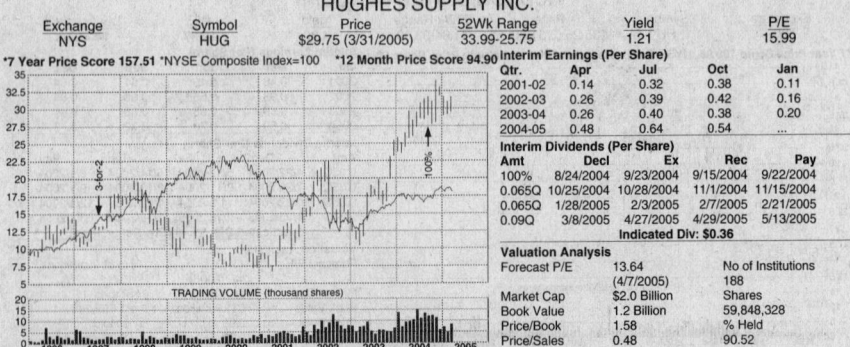

Exchange	Symbol	Price	52Wk Range	Yield	P/E
NYS	HUG	$29.75 (3/31/2005)	33.99-25.75	1.21	15.99

*7 Year Price Score 157.51 ***NYSE Composite Index=100** ***12 Month Price Score 94.90**

Interim Earnings (Per Share)

Qtr.	Apr	Jul	Oct	Jan
2001-02	0.14	0.32	0.38	0.11
2002-03	0.26	0.39	0.42	0.16
2003-04	0.26	0.40	0.38	0.20
2004-05	0.48	0.64	0.54	...

Interim Dividends (Per Share)

Amt	Decl	Ex	Rec	Pay
100%	8/24/2004	9/23/2004	9/15/2004	9/22/2004
0.065Q	10/25/2004	10/28/2004	11/1/2004	11/15/2004
0.065Q	1/28/2005	2/3/2005	2/7/2005	2/21/2005
0.09Q	3/8/2005	4/27/2005	4/29/2005	5/13/2005

Indicated Div: $0.36

Valuation Analysis

Forecast P/E	13.64 (4/7/2005)	No of Institutions	188
Market Cap	$2.0 Billion	Shares	59,848,328
Book Value	1.2 Billion	% Held	90.52
Price/Book	1.58		
Price/Sales	0.48		

Business Summary: Engineering Services (MIC: 12.1 SIC: 063 NAIC: 23610)

Hughes Supply is engaged in wholesale distribution of a broad range of materials, equipment and supplies primarily to the construction industry. As of Jan 30 2004, Co. distributed over 350,000 products from 486 locations in 38 states. These products are used by its customers in new construction for commercial, residential, infrastructure and industrial applications and for replacement and renovation projects. Major product lines distributed by Co. include electrical, plumbing, water and sewer, air conditioning and heating, industrial pipe, valves and fittings, building materials, electric utilities, and water systems.

Recent Developments: For the quarter ended Oct 29 2004, net income increased 89.9% to $33,800 thousand from net income of $17,800 thousand in the year-earlier quarter. Revenues were $1,167,500 thousand, up 35.8% from $859,500 thousand the year before. Operating income was $61,300 thousand versus an income of $34,000 thousand in the prior-year quarter, an increase of 80.3%. Total indirect expense was $212,600 thousand versus $159,500 thousand in the prior-year quarter, an increase of 33.3%.

Prospects: Co. is encouraged by strengthening demand in both the commercial construction and the industrial end markets. Also, residential activity continues to be strong in the geographic markets in which Co. operates. Accordingly, Co. expects business demand to continue to be good in the near-term, with stable to moderately increasing commodity prices. For the first quarter of fiscal 2006 ending Apr 30 2005, Co. expects revenues to range from $1.24 billion to $1.26 billllion, an increase of 24.0% to 26.0% over the prior year, with organic sales growth of 7.0% to 8.0%. First quarter diluted earnings per share are expected to range from $0.50 to $0.52, an incrase of 4.0% to 10.0%.

Financial Data

(US$ in Thousands)	9 Mos	6 Mos	3 Mos	01/30/2004	01/31/2003	01/25/2002	01/26/2001	01/28/2000
Earnings Per Share	1.86	1.70	1.46	1.23	1.23	0.94	0.98	1.40
Cash Flow Per Share	1.85	1.72	2.89	3.19	2.38	3.13	1.43	0.72
Tang Book Value Per Share	8.84	7.05	7.02	6.58	6.85	6.96	6.77	5.92
Dividends Per Share	0.245	0.215	0.215	0.150	0.177	0.170	0.170	0.170
Dividend Payout %	13.18	12.65	14.70	12.20	14.49	18.09	17.26	12.14
Income Statement								
Total Revenue	3,303,400	2,135,900	992,800	3,253,400	3,066,341	3,037,708	3,310,163	2,994,877
EBITDA	210,500	139,300	59,200	147,100	151,832	141,724	156,277	171,036
Depn & Amortn	22,900	14,900	6,900	18,000	23,268	31,093	32,312	29,629
Income Before Taxes	166,000	110,600	46,000	94,500	98,239	74,686	80,677	109,602
Income Taxes	63,000	41,400	16,200	36,800	40,155	30,621	34,162	43,731
Net Income	103,000	69,200	29,800	57,700	58,084	44,065	46,515	65,871
Average Shares	63,000	62,000	61,800	47,000	47,330	46,848	47,168	47,094
Balance Sheet								
Current Assets	1,617,900	1,337,500	1,168,200	1,041,000	931,534	863,440	980,891	957,778
Total Assets	2,487,200	2,203,900	1,958,200	1,881,300	1,436,342	1,293,262	1,400,277	1,369,014
Current Liabilities	636,800	588,300	543,800	437,400	372,752	275,165	301,761	300,278
Long-Term Obligations	534,300	449,600	301,700	368,700	378,076	403,671	516,168	535,000
Total Liabilities	1,254,200	1,121,700	917,600	869,300	791,490	698,789	830,242	846,570
Stockholders' Equity	1,233,000	1,082,200	1,040,600	1,012,000	644,852	594,473	570,035	522,444
Shares Outstanding	65,615	61,204	61,333	61,157	47,380	47,500	47,269	47,160
Statistical Record								
Return on Assets %	5.59	5.22	4.38	3.49	4.19	3.28	3.37	5.30
Return on Equity %	11.75	11.05	8.98	6.98	9.22	7.59	8.54	13.13
EBITDA Margin %	6.37	6.52	5.96	4.52	4.95	4.67	4.72	5.71
Net Margin %	3.12	3.24	3.00	1.77	1.89	1.45	1.41	2.20
Asset Turnover	2.04	2.05	2.01	1.97	2.21	2.26	2.40	2.41
Current Ratio	2.54	2.27	2.15	2.38	2.50	3.14	3.25	3.19
Debt to Equity	0.43	0.42	0.29	0.36	0.59	0.68	0.91	1.02
Price Range	31.66-19.11	30.77-16.23	29.65-13.93	25.88-10.39	22.49-12.37	15.81-6.72	10.65-7.21	14.97-8.97
P/E Ratio	17.02-10.27	18.10-9.54	20.31-9.54	21.04-8.44	18.28-10.06	16.82-7.15	10.87-7.35	10.69-6.41
Average Yield %	0.92	0.90	1.02	0.85	1.05	1.54	1.90	1.43

Address: One Hughes Way, Orlando, FL 32805 **Telephone:** (407) 841 4755 **Fax:** (407) 649 1670	**Web Site:** www.hughessupply.com **Officers:** David H. Hughes - Chmn. Thomas I. Morgan - Pres., C.E.O.	**Auditors:** PricewaterhouseCoopers LLP **Investor Contact:** 407-841-4755

HUMANA INC.

Exchange	Symbol	Price	52Wk Range	Yield	P/E
NYS	HUM	$31.94 (3/31/2005)	34.86-15.55	N/A	18.57

*7 Year Price Score 128.95 *NYSE Composite Index=100 *12 Month Price Score 135.38

Interim Earnings (Per Share)

Qtr.	Mar	Jun	Sep	Dec
2001	0.16	0.15	0.18	0.21
2002	0.28	0.27	0.31	(0.01)
2003	0.20	0.43	0.38	0.40
2004	0.41	0.50	0.52	0.29

Interim Dividends (Per Share)

No Dividends Paid

Valuation Analysis

Forecast P/E	15.74	No of Institutions	
	(4/7/2005)	278	
Market Cap	$5.1 Billion	Shares	
Book Value	2.1 Billion	124,572,032	
Price/Book	2.45	% Held	
Price/Sales	0.39	77.46	

Business Summary: Insurance (MIC: 8.2 SIC: 324 NAIC: 24114)

Humana offers health insurance coverage and related services through a variety of traditional and Internet-based plans, for employer groups, government-sponsored programs and individuals. As of Dec 31 2003, Co. had approximately 1.7 million members in its specialty products programs and approximately 463,300 contracts with physicians, hospitals, dentists and other providers to provide health care to its members. Operations are divided into two segments. The Commercial segment includes three lines of business: fully insured medical, administrative services only and specialty. The Government segment includes three lines of business, Medicare+Choice, Medicaid and TRICARE business.

Recent Developments: For the year ended Dec 31 2004, net income increased 22.3% to $280,012 thousand from net income of $228,934 thousand a year earlier. Revenues were $13,104,325 thousand, up 7.2% from $12,226,311 thousand the year before. Net premiums earned were $12,689,432 thousand versus $11,825,283 thousand in the prior year, an increase of 7.3%.

Prospects: On Feb 16 2005, Co. announced that it has completed its acquisition of CarePlus Health Plans of Florida, which provides Medicare HMO Advantage plans and benefits to 50,000 people eligible for Medicare in Miami-Dade, Broward and Palm Beach counties in Florida. The acquisition is expected to be immediately accretive to earnings at an annual rate of approximately $0.15 to $0.18 per diluted share during the first 12 months. Co. is raising its first-quarter 2005 earnings guidance to a range of $0.61 to $0.63 per share. Looking ahead, Co. is targeting full-year 2005 consolidated revenues of about $14.50 billion and earnings of $2.20 per diluted share.

Financial Data
(US$ in Thousands)

	12/31/2004	12/31/2003	12/31/2002	12/31/2001	12/31/2000	12/31/1999	12/31/1998	12/31/1997
Earnings Per Share	1.72	1.41	0.85	0.70	0.54	(2.28)	0.77	1.05
Cash Flow Per Share	2.16	2.60	1.97	0.91	0.24	1.30	0.46	1.77
Tang Book Value Per Share	7.52	6.54	5.09	4.33	3.37	2.76	3.01	1.69
Income Statement								
Premium Income	12,689,432	11,825,283	10,930,397	9,938,961	10,395,000	9,959,000	9,597,000	7,880,000
Total Revenue	13,104,325	12,226,311	11,261,181	10,194,886	10,514,000	10,113,000	9,781,000	8,036,000
Income Before Taxes	415,850	344,716	209,934	183,080	114,000	(404,000)	203,000	270,000
Income Taxes	135,838	115,782	67,179	65,909	24,000	(22,000)	74,000	97,000
Net Income	280,012	228,934	142,755	117,171	90,000	(382,000)	129,000	173,000
Average Shares	162,456	161,960	167,801	167,308	166,931	167,555	168,000	165,800
Balance Sheet								
Total Assets	5,657,617	5,293,323	4,600,030	4,403,638	4,167,000	4,900,000	5,496,000	5,418,000
Total Liabilities	3,567,493	3,457,374	2,993,556	2,895,689	2,807,000	3,632,000	3,808,000	3,917,000
Stockholders' Equity	2,090,124	1,835,949	1,606,474	1,507,949	1,360,000	1,268,000	1,688,000	1,501,000
Shares Outstanding	160,266	161,890	162,972	168,811	169,066	167,514	166,000	164,100
Statistical Record								
Return on Assets %	5.10	4.63	3.17	2.73	1.98	N.M.	2.36	4.04
Return on Equity %	14.23	13.30	9.17	8.17	6.83	N.M.	8.09	12.39
Net Margin %	2.14	1.87	1.27	1.15	0.86	(3.78)	1.32	2.15
Price Range	30.02-15.55	23.29-8.68	17.09-9.87	14.94-8.58	15.38-4.75	20.75-5.88	31.88-12.88	24.94-17.75
P/E Ratio	17.45-9.04	16.52-6.16	20.11-11.61	21.34-12.26	28.47-8.80	...	41.40-16.72	23.75-16.90

Address: 500 West Main Street, Louisville, KY 40202 **Telephone:** (502) 580-1000 **Fax:** (502) 580-1441	**Web Site:** www.humana.com **Officers:** David A. Jones - Chmn. David A. Jones Jr. - Vice-Chmn.	**Auditors:** PricewaterhouseCoopers LLP **Investor Contact:** 502-580-3644

IDACORP, INC.

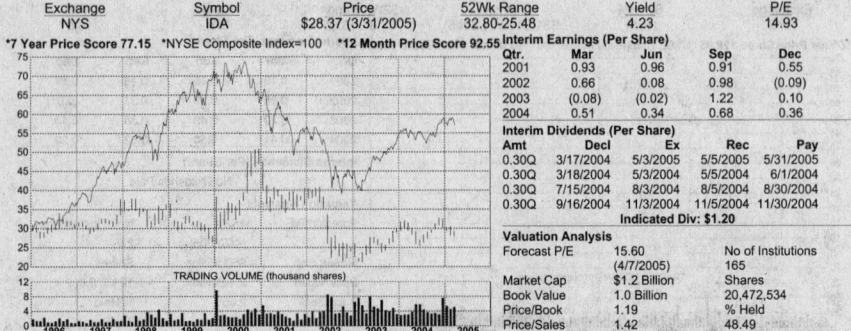

Exchange	Symbol	Price	52Wk Range	Yield	P/E
NYS	IDA	$28.37 (3/31/2005)	32.80-25.48	4.23	14.93

*7 Year Price Score 77.15 ***NYSE Composite Index=100** ***12 Month Price Score 92.55**

Interim Earnings (Per Share)

Qtr.	Mar	Jun	Sep	Dec
2001	0.93	0.96	0.91	0.55
2002	0.66	0.08	0.98	(0.09)
2003	(0.08)	(0.02)	1.22	0.10
2004	0.51	0.34	0.68	0.36

Interim Dividends (Per Share)

Amt	Decl	Ex	Rec	Pay
0.30Q	3/17/2004	5/3/2005	5/5/2005	5/31/2005
0.30Q	3/18/2004	5/3/2004	5/5/2004	6/1/2004
0.30Q	7/15/2004	8/3/2004	8/5/2004	8/30/2004
0.30Q	9/16/2004	11/3/2004	11/5/2004	11/30/2004

Indicated Div: $1.20

Valuation Analysis

Forecast P/E	15.60	No of Institutions
	(4/7/2005)	165
Market Cap	$1.2 Billion	Shares
Book Value	1.0 Billion	20,472,534
Price/Book	1.19	% Held
Price/Sales	1.42	48.49

Business Summary: Electricity (MIC: 7.1 SIC: 911 NAIC: 21121)

Idacorp is a holding company comprised of Idaho Power Company (IPC), a regulated electric utility; IDACORP Financial, an investment vehicle that makes investments primarily in low-income housing projects; IdaTech, a developer of fully integrated fuel cell systems; IDACOMM, a subsidiary providing telecommunications services and high-speed Internet access technologies, and its subsidiary Velocitus, a commercial and residential Internet service provider; and Ida-West Energy, a manager of independent power projects. As of Dec 31 2004, IPC supplied electric energy to approximately 440,000 general business customers.

Recent Developments: For the year ended Dec 31 2004, net income increased 56.7% to $72,983 thousand from net income of $46,578 thousand a year earlier. Revenues were $844,491 thousand, up 2.6% from $823,002 thousand the year before. Operating income was $93,251 thousand versus an income of $84,062 thousand in the prior year, an increase of 10.9%. Total direct expense was $751,240 thousand versus $738,940 thousand in the prior year, an increase of 1.7%. Total indirect expense was $37,341 thousand versus $77,914 thousand in the prior year, a decrease of 52.1%.

Prospects: The Feb 14 2005 hydrological survey shows Snake River Basin snow pack levels at 65.0% of average. Due to such factors as depleted reservoir levels upstream of the Idaho Power hydroelectric system, dry soil conditions, and the expected timing of the spring runoff, the Northwest River Forecast Center currently projects 2.6 million acre-feet (maf) of water will flow into Brownlee Reservoir during the April-through-July period, down from 3.2 maf in 2004. Generation from Idaho Power's hydroelectric facilities is expected to be 5.9 million megawatt-hours (MWh) in 2005 versus 6.0 million MWh in 2004 and normal generation of 9.2 million MWh.

Financial Data

(US$ in Thousands)	12/31/2004	12/31/2003	12/31/2002	12/31/2001	12/31/2000	12/31/1999	12/31/1998	12/31/1997
Earnings Per Share	1.90	1.22	1.63	3.35	3.72	2.43	2.37	2.32
Cash Flow Per Share	5.06	8.15	9.21	(0.21)	3.55	6.13	4.52	4.57
Tang Book Value Per Share	23.88	22.62	23.01	23.19	21.85	20.02	19.42	18.93
Dividends Per Share	1.200	1.695	1.860	1.860	1.860	1.860	1.860	1.860
Dividend Payout %	63.16	138.93	114.11	55.52	50.00	76.54	78.48	80.17
Income Statement								
Total Revenue	844,491	823,002	928,800	5,648,000	1,019,353	658,336	1,121,976	748,503
EBITDA	230,721	216,031	197,348	372,000	375,665	294,040	280,726	274,313
Depn & Amortn	124,192	129,070	122,831	111,000	103,971	95,436	87,143	80,485
Income Before Taxes	48,213	25,459	10,525	190,000	210,701	137,021	133,806	133,570
Income Taxes	(24,770)	(21,119)	(51,147)	65,000	70,818	45,672	44,630	46,472
Net Income	72,983	46,578	61,672	125,000	139,883	91,349	89,176	87,098
Average Shares	38,361	38,186	37,729	37,387	37,556	37,612	37,612	37,612
Balance Sheet								
Net PPE	2,209,462	2,088,319	1,906,498	1,886,000	1,805,036	1,745,683	1,711,509	1,716,927
Total Assets	3,234,172	3,101,726	3,252,638	3,642,000	4,639,258	2,636,993	2,451,620	2,451,816
Long-Term Obligations	979,549	945,834	898,676	843,000	864,114	821,558	815,937	746,142
Total Liabilities	2,225,886	2,237,445	2,377,811	2,771,000	3,818,447	1,884,023	1,721,223	1,739,998
Stockholders' Equity	1,008,286	864,281	874,827	871,000	820,811	752,970	730,397	711,818
Shares Outstanding	42,217	38,206	38,017	37,562	37,567	37,612	37,612	37,612
Statistical Record								
Return on Assets %	2.30	1.47	1.79	3.02	3.83	3.59	3.64	3.64
Return on Equity %	7.77	5.36	7.07	14.78	17.73	12.32	12.37	12.39
EBITDA Margin %	27.32	26.25	21.25	6.59	36.85	44.66	25.02	36.65
Net Margin %	8.64	5.66	6.64	2.21	13.72	13.88	7.95	11.64
PPE Turnover	0.39	0.41	0.49	3.06	0.57	0.38	0.65	0.44
Asset Turnover	0.27	0.26	0.27	1.36	0.28	0.26	0.46	0.31
Debt to Equity	0.97	1.09	1.03	0.97	1.05	1.09	1.12	1.05
Price Range	32.80-25.48	30.00-21.09	40.82-21.36	47.50-34.10	50.88-26.00	36.50-26.38	37.81-30.13	37.75-28.63
P/E Ratio	17.26-13.41	24.59-17.29	25.04-13.10	14.18-10.18	13.68-6.99	15.02-10.85	15.95-12.71	16.27-12.34
Average Yield %	4.08	6.68	6.05	4.88	4.87	6.02	5.43	5.92

Address: 1221 W. Idaho Street, Boise, ID 83702-5627	**Web Site:** www.idacorpinc.com	**Auditors:** Deloitte & Touche LLP
Telephone: (208) 388-2200	**Officers:** Jon H. Miller - Chmn. Jan B. Packwood - Pres., C.E.O.	
Fax: (208) 388-6916		

IDT CORP.

Exchange	Symbol	Price	52Wk Range	Yield	P/E
NYS	IDT	$14.79 (3/31/2005)	20.44-13.50	N/A	N/A

*7 Year Price Score N/A *NYSE Composite Index=100 ***12 Month Price Score 87.88**

TRADING VOLUME (thousand shares)

Interim Earnings (Per Share)

Qtr.	Oct	Jan	Apr	Jul
2001-02	(2.22)	(0.23)	(0.64)	(0.98)
2002-03	(0.05)	(0.16)	(0.12)	0.10
2003-04	(0.17)	0.20	(0.84)	(0.25)
2004-05	(0.12)	(0.19)	...	

Interim Dividends (Per Share)

No Dividends Paid

Valuation Analysis

Forecast P/E	64.91	No of Institutions	
	(4/7/2005)	98	
Market Cap	$1.5 Billion	Shares	
Book Value	987.6 Million	41,005,196	
Price/Book	1.47	% Held	
Price/Sales	0.60	55.78	

Business Summary: IT & Technology (MIC: 10.2 SIC: 373 NAIC: 41512)

IDT is a telecommunications and entertainment company. Co.'s telecommunications offerings are prepaid debit and rechargeable calling cards, wholesale carrier services and consumer local and long distance phone services. Co.'s entertainment business is comprised of complementary operations and investments that enable us to acquire, develop, finance and produce animated entertainment programming and to distribute home entertainment content to the mass market. Co. also operates various media-related businesses including brochure distribution and radio operations.

Recent Developments: For the quarter ended Jan 31 2005, net loss was $17,725,000 versus net income of $18,416,000 in the year-earlier quarter. Revenues were $608,846,000, up 15.5% from $526,973,000 the year before. Operating loss was $24,581,000 versus a loss of $16,157,000 in the prior-year quarter, an increase of 52.1%. Total direct expense was $447,515,000 versus $396,054,000 in the prior-year quarter, an increase of 13.0%. Total indirect expense was $185,912,000 versus $147,076,000 in the prior-year quarter, an increase of 26.4%.

Prospects: Co. recently announced that Liberty Media will exchange all of its direct and indirect interests in Net2Phone for about 3.8 million newly issued shares of Co.'s class B common stock. At the close of this transaction Co. will own 41.2% of Net2Phone and have voting control. Liberty Media will own 17.2% of Co. Separately, Co.'s Telecom revenue is benefiting from gains in its retail services, which is being partially offset by weaker wholesale telecom sales. Meanwhile, IDT Entertainment's results are being positively affected by the acquisitions of Anchor Bay Entertainment, Mainframe Entertainment and Manga Entertainment. Co. expects entertainment fiscal 2005 revenues of nearly $200.0 million.

Financial Data

(US$ in Thousands)	6 Mos	3 Mos	07/31/2004	07/31/2003	07/31/2002	07/31/2001	07/31/2000	07/31/1999
Earnings Per Share	(1.39)	(1.01)	(1.09)	(0.22)	(4.04)	7.12	6.14	(0.70)
Cash Flow Per Share	0.32	0.81	0.87	0.51	0.29	0.38	(2.20)	(0.55)
Tang Book Value Per Share	8.85	9.09	9.04	10.15	10.22	12.21	8.21	5.11
Income Statement								
Total Revenue	1,238,565	629,719	2,216,905	1,834,547	1,531,614	1,230,950	1,093,912	732,184
EBITDA	...	...	25,740	18,359	(214,382)	755,063	477,144	63,945
Depn & Amortn	52,675	24,379	99,868	89,309	66,016	60,351	91,481	41,989
Income Before Taxes	...	...	(51,813)	(44,855)	(258,641)	747,480	392,893	20,728
Income Taxes	7,517	3,966	9,581	(70,373)	(124,345)	209,395	218,403	17,850
Net Income	(29,458)	(11,733)	(95,711)	(17,517)	(303,349)	532,359	230,850	2,917
Average Shares	95,635	95,208	87,920	80,176	75,108	74,786	37,619	33,529
Balance Sheet								
Current Assets	1,295,955	1,278,622	1,330,408	1,228,322	1,201,423	1,243,732	641,893	292,198
Total Assets	1,870,508	1,864,561	1,874,357	1,732,342	1,607,920	1,881,338	1,219,055	515,336
Current Liabilities	548,062	507,459	525,364	467,767	392,975	328,339	293,963	112,784
Long-Term Obligations	28,757	33,567	31,810	45,084	45,398	50,179	56,114	128,715
Total Liabilities	756,029	734,388	750,429	687,468	683,434	783,934	519,559	241,499
Stockholders' Equity	987,598	997,510	991,233	897,527	869,530	1,075,985	468,188	253,405
Shares Outstanding	98,167	96,419	96,076	81,986	79,376	71,900	35,929	34,012
Statistical Record								
Return on Assets %	N.M.	N.M.	N.M.	N.M.	N.M.	34.34	26.55	0.63
Return on Equity %	N.M.	N.M.	N.M.	N.M.	N.M.	68.95	63.81	1.19
EBITDA Margin %	...	...	1.16	1.00	N.M.	61.34	43.62	8.73
Net Margin %	N.M.	N.M.	N.M.	N.M.	N.M.	43.25	21.10	0.40
Asset Turnover	1.29	1.30	1.23	1.10	0.88	0.79	1.26	1.57
Current Ratio	2.36	2.52	2.53	2.63	3.06	3.79	2.18	2.59
Debt to Equity	0.03	0.03	0.03	0.05	0.05	0.05	0.12	0.51
Price Range	22.40-13.50	23.80-13.50	23.80-15.65	18.50-13.82	20.10-8.51	14.00-10.75	...	...
P/E Ratio	...	...	...	...	...	1.97-1.51	...	...

Address: 520 Broad Street, Newark, NJ 07102	**Web Site:** www.idt.net	**Auditors:** Ernst & Young LLP
Telephone: (973) 438-1000	**Officers:** Howard S. Jonas - Chmn. James A. Courter - Vice-Chmn., C.E.O.	**Investor Contact:** 201-928-2975
Fax: (973) 438-1609		**Transfer Agents:** American Stock Transfer & Trust Co., New York, NY

IKON OFFICE SOLUTIONS, INC.

Exchange	Symbol	Price	52Wk Range	Yield	P/E
NYS	IKN	$9.89 (3/31/2005)	12.90-9.89	1.62	18.66

*7 Year Price Score 100.16 *NYSE Composite Index=100 *12 Month Price Score 88.03

Interim Earnings (Per Share)

Qtr.	Dec	Mar	Jun	Sep
2001-02	0.22	0.24	0.28	0.25
2002-03	0.21	0.23	0.10	0.21
2003-04	0.18	0.19	0.05	0.17
2004-05	0.12	...	...	...

Interim Dividends (Per Share)

Amt	Decl	Ex	Rec	Pay
0.04Q	4/27/2004	5/20/2004	5/24/2004	6/10/2004
0.04Q	7/27/2004	8/19/2004	8/23/2004	9/10/2004
0.04Q	10/28/2004	11/18/2004	11/22/2004	12/10/2004
0.04Q	1/27/2005	2/17/2005	2/22/2005	3/10/2005

Indicated Div: $0.16

Valuation Analysis

Forecast P/E	15.22 (4/7/2005)	No of Institutions 124
Market Cap	$1.4 Billion	Shares
Book Value	1.8 Billion	123,706,088
Price/Book	0.79	% Held
Price/Sales	0.30	87.96

Business Summary: IT & Technology (MIC: 10.2 SIC: 045 NAIC: 23430)

Ikon Office Solutions integrates imaging systems and services that are designed to help businesses manage document workflow and increase efficiency. As an independent distribution channel for copier and printer technologies, Co. provides systems from manufacturers such as Canon, Ricoh, Konica Minolta, EFI, and HP, and document management software and service support through its team of worldwide service professionals. Co. also provides document management services, including outsourcing and professional services, on-site copy and mailroom management, fleet management, off-site digital printing solutions, and customized workflow and imaging application development.

Recent Developments: For the quarter ended Dec 31 2004, net income decreased 39.9% to $16,627 thousand from net income of $27,664 thousand in the year-earlier quarter. Revenues were $1,095,651 thousand, down 3.6% from $1,136,479 thousand the year before. Operating income was $37,451 thousand versus an income of $54,598 thousand in the prior-year quarter, a decrease of 31.4%. Total direct expense was $692,557 thousand versus $670,475 thousand in the prior-year quarter, an increase of 3.3%. Total indirect expense was $357,755 thousand versus $376,468 thousand in the prior-year quarter, a decrease of 5.0%.

Prospects: Although Co. is absorbing weakness in North American equipment sales and off-site managed services, these challenges are being offset by solid results in customer services, professional services and on-site managed services. On-site managed services are benefiting from new multiyear contracts and a stronger base of recurring revenue. In addition, Co.'s European operations are delivering strong revenue growth and operating margin expansion. Going forward Co. expects to improve its sales coverage model and invest in future operational improvements. For fiscal 2005, Co. expects earnings to range from $0.63 to $0.68 per share.

Financial Data

(US$ in Thousands)	3 Mos	09/30/2004	09/30/2003	09/30/2002	09/30/2001	09/30/2000	09/30/1999	09/30/1998
Earnings Per Share	0.53	0.60	0.75	0.99	0.11	0.20	0.23	(0.76)
Cash Flow Per Share	(2.47)	(2.57)	3.03	3.33	2.89	2.50	3.04	1.99
Tang Book Value Per Share	3.19	3.09	2.58	2.08	0.97	0.87	0.50	N.M.
Dividends Per Share	0.160	0.160	0.160	0.160	0.160	0.160	0.160	0.160
Dividend Payout %	30.31	26.67	21.33	16.16	145.45	80.00	69.57	...
Income Statement								
Total Revenue	1,095,651	4,649,820	4,710,912	4,827,502	5,273,479	5,446,945	5,522,144	5,628,663
EBITDA	57,978	264,412	347,864	424,636	315,737	346,748	347,480	199,006
Depn & Amortn	20,527	92,368	112,458	131,047	178,568	195,094	196,864	202,525
Income Before Taxes	24,648	123,986	186,373	239,200	67,796	81,833	79,391	(74,187)
Income Taxes	8,021	32,432	70,356	88,866	53,791	55,873	45,555	8,863
Net Income	16,627	91,554	116,017	150,334	15,205	29,082	33,836	(83,050)
Average Shares	143,951	169,282	167,802	155,084	144,408	148,327	149,003	135,145
Balance Sheet								
Current Assets	1,951,248	2,084,740	2,662,498	2,626,430	2,514,637	2,512,543	2,233,901	2,259,446
Total Assets	4,368,147	4,537,907	6,639,507	6,472,618	6,290,992	6,362,585	5,801,313	5,748,796
Current Liabilities	1,106,948	1,256,943	2,237,376	2,167,684	2,265,126	2,308,531	2,047,591	1,754,853
Long-Term Obligations	1,126,466	1,164,725	1,982,558	2,090,178	1,965,716	1,561,734	1,747,990	2,086,862
Total Liabilities	2,603,052	2,812,297	5,004,055	4,937,672	4,895,414	4,470,917	4,340,773	4,321,508
Stockholders' Equity	1,765,095	1,725,610	1,635,452	1,534,946	1,395,578	1,441,092	1,460,540	1,427,288
Shares Outstanding	140,381	142,133	146,368	144,024	141,776	141,698	149,218	137,015
Statistical Record								
Return on Assets %	1.47	1.63	1.77	2.36	0.24	0.48	0.59	N.M.
Return on Equity %	4.63	5.43	7.32	10.26	1.07	2.00	2.34	N.M.
EBITDA Margin %	5.29	5.69	7.38	8.80	5.99	6.37	6.29	3.54
Net Margin %	1.52	1.97	2.46	3.11	0.29	0.53	0.61	N.M.
Asset Turnover	0.84	0.83	0.72	0.76	0.83	0.89	0.96	1.02
Current Ratio	1.76	1.66	1.19	1.21	1.11	1.09	1.09	1.29
Debt to Equity	0.64	0.67	1.21	1.36	1.41	1.08	1.20	1.46
Price Range	13.17-10.15	13.17-7.31	9.26-6.40	14.24-6.65	9.80-2.31	10.69-3.88	16.25-6.94	36.25-5.25
P/E Ratio	24.85-19.15	21.95-12.18	12.35-8.53	14.38-6.72	89.09-21.02	53.44-19.38	70.65-30.16	...
Average Yield %	1.37	1.45	2.09	1.52	2.86	2.62	1.32	0.67

Address: 70 Valley Stream Parkway, Malvern, PA 19355 Telephone: (610) 296-8000 Fax: (610) 408-7026	Web Site: www.ikon.com Officers: Matthew J. Espe - Chmn., Pres., C.E.O. Brian D. Edwards - Sr. V.P., North American Sales	Auditors: PricewaterhouseCoopers LLP Investor Contact: 610-408-7196 Transfer Agents: National City Bank, Cleveland, OH

ILLINOIS TOOL WORKS, INC.

Exchange	Symbol	Price	52Wk Range	Yield	P/E	Div Acheiver
NYS	ITW	$89.53 (3/31/2005)	95.99-78.87	1.25	20.39	42 Years

*7 Year Price Score 112.29 *NYSE Composite Index=100 *12 Month Price Score 92.96

Interim Earnings (Per Share)

Qtr.	Mar	Jun	Sep	Dec
2001	0.60	0.76	0.65	0.62
2002	(0.08)	0.87	0.80	0.72
2003	0.63	0.90	0.87	0.92
2004	0.93	1.16	1.09	1.20

Interim Dividends (Per Share)

Amt	Decl	Ex	Rec	Pay
0.24Q	5/7/2004	6/28/2004	6/30/2004	7/19/2004
0.28Q	8/6/2004	9/28/2004	9/30/2004	10/18/2004
0.28Q	10/29/2004	12/29/2004	12/31/2004	1/24/2005
0.28Q	2/16/2005	3/29/2005	3/31/2005	4/18/2005

Indicated Div: $1.12 (Div. Reinv. Plan)

Valuation Analysis

Forecast P/E	17.75	No of Institutions	
	(4/7/2005)	637	
Market Cap	$26.2 Billion	Shares	
Book Value	7.6 Billion	229,622,720	
Price/Book	3.43	% Held	
Price/Sales	2.23	78.57	

Business Summary: Plastics (MIC: 11.7 SIC: 089 NAIC: 26199)

Illinois Tool Works is a global manufacturer of engineered products and specialty systems, and has 625 operations in 44 countries that are organized into five segments. Engineered Products - North America segment and Engineered Products - International segment manufacture short lead-time plastic and metal components and fasteners, and specialty products. Specialty Systems - North America segment and Specialty Systems - International segment design and manufacture longer lead-time machinery and related consumables, and specialty equipment. The Leasing and Investments segment invests in mortgage entities, and leases telecommunications, aircraft, air traffic control and other equipment.

Recent Developments: For the year ended Dec 31 2004, net income increased 30.8% to $1,338,694 thousand from net income of $1,023,680 thousand a year earlier. Revenues were $11,731,425 thousand, up 16.9% from $10,035,623 thousand in the prior year. Operating income was $2,056,613 thousand versus an income of $1,633,458 thousand in the prior year, an increase of 25.9%. Total direct expense was $7,591,246 thousand versus $6,527,692 thousand in the prior year, an increase of 16.3%. Total indirect expense was $2,083,566 thousand versus $1,874,473 thousand in the prior year, an increase of 11.2%.

Prospects: Looking forward, Co. noted that while it remains optimistic regarding its earnings prospects for 2005, it is forecasting some slowing in end markets and, as a result, a base revenue growth range of 4.0% to 6.0% for the full year. As a result of this anticipated base revenue slowdown and expected year-over-year declines in Leasing and Investments as well as currency related income, Co. is forecasting an earnings range of $4.96 to $5.16 for income per diluted share from continuing operations. Co. noted that this increase in earnings range reflects its continuation of its share repurchase program. Co. plans to repurchase 12.1 million shares as part of the second and final phase of the program.

Financial Data

(US$ in Thousands)	12/31/2004	12/31/2003	12/31/2002	12/31/2001	12/31/2000	12/31/1999	12/31/1998	12/31/1997
Earnings Per Share	4.39	3.32	2.31	2.63	3.15	2.76	2.67	2.33
Cash Flow Per Share	5.05	4.46	4.21	4.44	3.71	3.45	2.89	...
Tang Book Value Per Share	15.17	16.44	13.13	10.83	9.55	9.27	8.59	8.14
Dividends Per Share	1.040	0.940	0.900	0.840	0.760	0.660	0.540	0.455
Dividend Payout %	23.69	28.31	38.96	31.94	24.13	23.91	20.22	19.53
Income Statement								
Total Revenue	11,731,425	10,035,623	9,467,740	9,292,791	9,983,577	9,333,185	5,647,889	5,220,433
EBITDA	2,396,308	1,922,705	1,790,193	1,669,032	1,948,078	1,745,946	1,263,783	1,103,352
Depn & Amortn	353,283	302,090	305,752	386,308	413,370	343,284	199,712	174,210
Income Before Taxes	1,999,405	1,576,114	1,433,560	1,230,849	1,478,180	1,352,712	1,059,584	924,351
Income Taxes	659,680	535,900	501,750	428,440	520,200	511,600	386,800	337,400
Net Income	1,338,694	1,023,680	712,592	805,659	957,980	841,112	672,784	586,951
Average Shares	304,851	308,750	308,045	306,306	304,414	304,649	252,443	251,760
Balance Sheet								
Current Assets	4,322,198	4,783,202	3,878,809	3,163,244	3,329,061	3,272,931	1,834,473	1,858,642
Total Assets	11,351,934	11,193,321	10,623,101	9,822,349	9,603,456	9,060,259	6,118,162	5,394,756
Current Liabilities	1,850,971	1,488,903	1,567,162	1,518,158	1,817,610	2,045,361	1,222,009	1,157,880
Long-Term Obligations	921,098	920,360	1,460,381	1,267,141	1,549,038	1,360,746	947,008	854,328
Total Liabilities	3,724,324	3,319,035	3,974,030	3,781,611	4,202,469	4,244,836	2,780,127	2,588,302
Stockholders' Equity	7,627,610	7,874,286	6,649,071	6,040,738	5,400,987	4,815,423	3,338,035	2,806,454
Shares Outstanding	292,228	308,636	306,582	304,926	305,448	300,568	250,128	249,598
Statistical Record								
Return on Assets %	11.84	9.38	6.97	8.29	10.24	11.08	11.69	...
Return on Equity %	17.22	14.10	11.23	14.08	18.70	20.63	21.90	...
EBITDA Margin %	20.43	19.16	18.91	17.96	19.51	18.71	22.38	21.14
Net Margin %	11.41	10.20	7.53	8.67	9.60	9.01	11.91	11.24
Asset Turnover	1.04	0.92	0.93	0.96	1.07	1.23	0.98	...
Current Ratio	2.34	3.21	2.48	2.08	1.83	1.60	1.50	1.61
Debt to Equity	0.12	0.12	0.22	0.21	0.29	0.28	0.28	0.30
Price Range	95.99-73.42	84.15-55.15	77.38-55.73	71.20-49.15	68.31-51.06	81.75-58.00	71.81-45.38	60.13-38.38
P/E Ratio	21.87-16.72	25.35-16.61	33.50-24.13	27.07-18.69	21.69-16.21	29.62-21.01	26.90-16.99	25.80-16.47
Average Yield %	1.18	1.39	1.33	1.34	1.30	0.93	0.89	0.94

Address: 3600 West Lake Avenue, Glenview, IL 60025-5811 Telephone: (847) 724-7500 Fax: (847) 657-4261	Web Site: www.itw.com Officers: W. James Farrell - Chmn., C.E.O. Frank S. Ptak - Vice-Chmn.	Auditors: DELOITTE & TOUCHE LLP Transfer Agents: Computershare Investor Service, L.L.C., Chicago, IL

IMATION CORP.

Exchange	Symbol	Price	52Wk Range	Yield	P/E
NYS	IMN	$34.75 (3/31/2005)	43.62-29.81	1.15	41.37

*7 Year Price Score 109.76 *NYSE Composite Index=100 *12 Month Price Score 89.86

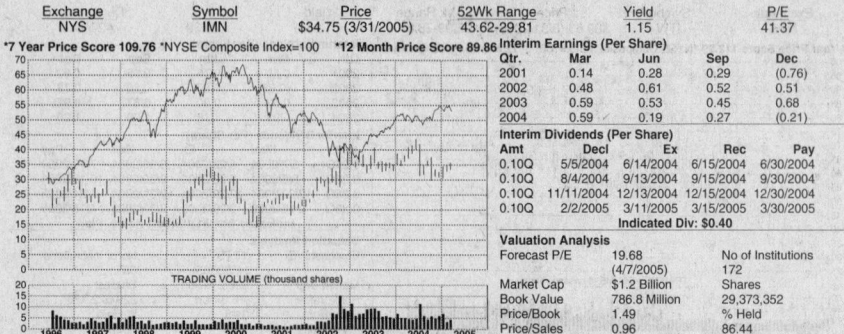

Interim Earnings (Per Share)

Qtr.	Mar	Jun	Sep	Dec
2001	0.14	0.28	0.29	(0.76)
2002	0.48	0.61	0.52	0.51
2003	0.59	0.53	0.45	0.68
2004	0.59	0.19	0.27	(0.21)

Interim Dividends (Per Share)

Amt	Decl	Ex	Rec	Pay
0.10Q	5/5/2004	6/14/2004	6/15/2004	6/30/2004
0.10Q	8/4/2004	9/13/2004	9/15/2004	9/30/2004
0.10Q	11/11/2004	12/13/2004	12/15/2004	12/30/2004
0.10Q	2/2/2005	3/11/2005	3/15/2005	3/30/2005
			Indicated Div: $0.40	

Valuation Analysis

Forecast P/E	19.68	No of Institutions	
	(4/7/2005)	172	
Market Cap	$1.2 Billion	Shares	
Book Value	786.8 Million	29,373,352	
Price/Book	1.49	% Held	
Price/Sales	0.96	86.44	

Business Summary: IT & Technology (MIC: 10.2 SIC: 374 NAIC: 18210)

Imation is primarily engaged in the development, manufacture, sourcing, marketing and distribution of recordable magnetic, optical and solid state flash memory storage media products, for users of digital information technology in more than 100 countries around the world. These removable storage media products are used in conjunction with hardware devices, including tape libraries, floppy disk and optical disc drives, certain consumer electronic devices, and desktop and laptop computers developed and sold by other companies. Co. operates through its Data Storage and Information Management and Specialty Papers operating segments.

Recent Developments: For the year ended Dec 31 2004, income from continuing operations decreased 48.3% to $42,300 thousand from income of $81,800 thousand a year earlier. Net income decreased 63.5% to $29,900 thousand from net income of $82,000 thousand a year earlier. Revenues were $1,219,300 thousand, up 4.8% from $1,163,500 thousand the year before. Operating income was $53,900 thousand versus an income of $119,600 thousand in the prior year, a decrease of 54.9%. Total direct expense was $919,400 thousand versus $828,800 thousand in the prior year, an increase of 10.9%. Total indirect expense was $246,000 thousand versus $215,100 thousand in the prior year, an increase of 14.4%.

Prospects: Co. is targeting total revenue growth for full-year 2005 of 3.0% to 5.0%, or to a range of $1.26 billion to $1.28 billion. Additionally, for full-year 2005, Co. is targeting operating income of between $87.0 million and $92.0 million. Co. noted that in 2004, it reported operating income of $53.9 million including charges of $25.2 million from restructuring and other items. Thus, Co. is hopeful that full-year 2005 operating income will grow between 10.0% and 16.0% over the $79.1 million as adjusted to eliminate the 2004 restructuring and other items. Fully diluted earnings per share, on a 35.0% tax rate, is targeted between $1.75 and $1.82 for full-year 2005.

Financial Data

(US$ in Thousands)	12/31/2004	12/31/2003	12/31/2002	12/31/2001	12/31/2000	12/31/1999	12/31/1998	12/31/1997
Earnings Per Share	0.84	2.26	2.11	(0.05)	(0.13)	1.17	1.45	(4.54)
Cash Flow Per Share	3.65	2.28	3.45	3.68	5.46	2.27	(0.16)	3.36
Tang Book Value Per Share	22.30	22.33	20.55	18.13	18.21	17.21	15.48	14.03
Dividends Per Share	0.380	0.240	...	...	...	...	...	...
Dividend Payout %	45.24	10.62	...	...	...	...	...	...
Income Statement								
Total Revenue	1,219,300	1,163,500	1,066,700	1,176,500	1,234,900	1,412,600	2,046,500	2,201,800
EBITDA	95,000	156,500	144,000	36,300	83,700	159,100	259,800	(42,800)
Depn & Amortn	46,300	39,000	38,700	54,100	122,300	87,700	129,400	147,500
Income Before Taxes	53,200	122,100	112,600	(6,800)	(26,300)	69,300	109,900	(206,000)
Income Taxes	10,900	40,300	39,400	(5,100)	(25,300)	27,000	52,800	(25,900)
Net Income	29,900	82,000	75,100	(1,700)	(4,400)	43,900	57,100	(180,100)
Average Shares	35,600	36,300	35,600	34,800	35,100	37,600	39,500	39,700
Balance Sheet								
Current Assets	786,000	838,400	842,200	756,900	686,200	771,400	919,900	1,104,400
Total Assets	1,110,600	1,172,800	1,119,900	1,053,700	987,900	1,127,600	1,322,200	1,665,500
Current Liabilities	275,200	297,200	310,000	347,200	291,100	357,200	422,100	565,500
Long-Term Obligations	...	...	...	...	...	1,100	32,700	319,700
Total Liabilities	323,800	352,500	381,400	398,000	325,400	402,300	561,100	983,300
Stockholders' Equity	786,800	820,300	738,500	655,700	662,500	725,300	761,100	682,200
Shares Outstanding	33,700	35,400	35,500	35,300	35,200	37,200	41,000	40,581
Statistical Record								
Return on Assets %	2.61	7.15	6.91	N.M.	N.M.	3.58	3.82	N.M.
Return on Equity %	3.71	10.52	10.77	N.M.	N.M.	5.91	7.91	N.M.
EBITDA Margin %	7.79	13.45	13.50	3.09	6.78	11.26	12.69	N.M.
Net Margin %	2.45	7.05	7.04	N.M.	N.M.	3.11	2.79	N.M.
Asset Turnover	1.07	1.01	0.98	1.15	1.16	1.15	1.37	1.36
Current Ratio	2.86	2.82	2.72	2.18	2.36	2.16	2.18	1.95
Debt to Equity	...	...	...	...	...	N.M.	0.04	0.47
Price Range	43.62-29.81	40.80-32.25	42.25-21.07	25.40-14.94	33.56-14.19	34.25-15.06	19.69-13.56	30.38-15.56
P/E Ratio	51.93-35.49	18.05-14.27	20.02-9.99	...	...	29.27-12.87	13.58-9.35	...
Average Yield %	1.05	0.67	...	...	...	...	...	...

Address: 1 Imation Place, Oakdale, MN 55128-3414	**Web Site:** www.imation.com	**Auditors:** PricewaterhouseCoopers LLP
Telephone: (651) 704-4000	**Officers:** Bruce A. Henderson - Chmn. Linda W. Hart - Vice-Chmn., C.E.O.	**Investor Contact:** 651-704-3475
Fax: (800) 537-4675		

IMS HEALTH, INC.

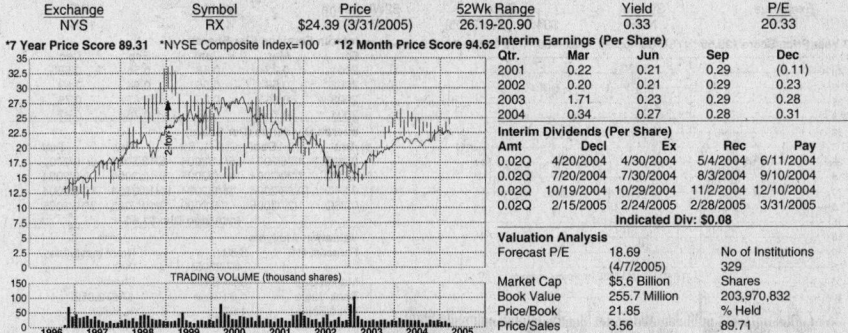

Business Summary: IT & Technology (MIC: 10.2 SIC: 374 NAIC: 18210)

IMS Health is a global provider of information solutions to the pharmaceutical and healthcare industries. Co. operates in more than 100 countries and provides market information, sales management and decision-support services to the pharmaceutical and healthcare industries. Co.'s key products include sales management information to optimize sales force productivity, marketing effectiveness research for prescription and over-the-counter pharmaceutical products, consulting and other services. Co. also owns a venture capital unit, Enterprise Associates, LLC, which is focused on investments in emerging businesses, and a 25.9% equity interest in The TriZetto Group, Inc. at Dec 31 2003. .

Recent Developments: For the year ended Dec 31 2004, net income decreased 55.3% to $285,422 thousand from net income of $638,945 thousand a year earlier. Revenues were $1,569,045 thousand, up 13.6% from $1,381,761 thousand the year before. Operating income was $386,461 thousand versus an income of $361,492 thousand in the prior year, an increase of 6.9%. Total direct expense was $664,053 thousand versus $575,834 thousand in the prior year, an increase of 15.3%. Total indirect expense was $518,531 thousand versus $444,435 thousand in the prior year, an increase of 16.7%.

Prospects: Co. appears optimistic regarding its prospects for 2005, reflecting recent business improvement across its operations. Specifically, Co. cited double-digit revenue gains experienced by both its Europe and Asia Pacific regions during 2004. Looking forward, Co.'s long-term goals include achieving top line growth of between 8.0% and 13.0%, and earnings per share growth matching or exceeding revenue growth. To help achieve these goals, Co. has identified five areas that it views as attractive emerging marketplace opportunities, including Japan, China, Consumer Health, Biotech, and Government.

Financial Data
(US$ in Thousands)

	12/31/2004	12/31/2003	12/31/2002	12/31/2001	12/31/2000	12/31/1999	12/31/1998	12/31/1997
Earnings Per Share	1.20	2.58	0.93	0.62	0.40	0.86	0.66	0.93
Cash Flow Per Share	1.71	1.53	1.31	1.10	0.51	1.11	0.71	0.79
Tang Book Value Per Share	N.M.	N.M.	N.M.	N.M.	N.M.	N.M.	0.92	1.90
Dividends Per Share	0.080	0.080	0.080	0.080	0.080	0.080	0.030	...
Dividend Payout %	6.67	3.10	8.60	12.90	20.00	9.30	4.55	...
Income Statement								
Total Revenue	1,569,045	1,381,761	1,428,097	1,332,923	1,424,359	1,397,989	1,186,513	1,059,559
EBITDA	519,653	410,631	492,173	261,985	366,621	448,250	348,637	400,669
Depn & Amortn	93,534	75,132	61,782	69,178	92,000	100,443	96,358	88,651
Income Before Taxes	414,439	324,323	423,510	183,801	261,313	348,442	270,661	322,474
Income Taxes	129,181	165,954	130,404	38,415	140,412	98,076	92,196	88,358
Net Income	285,422	638,945	266,115	185,426	120,816	276,061	220,558	312,350
Average Shares	237,705	247,263	286,663	300,147	300,038	319,561	335,770	334,980
Balance Sheet								
Current Assets	936,519	778,929	827,264	656,845	568,517	607,450	634,477	629,757
Total Assets	1,890,736	1,644,338	1,618,528	1,367,554	1,243,007	1,450,756	1,731,519	1,502,089
Current Liabilities	554,121	836,625	678,583	635,491	827,156	723,403	550,318	397,289
Long-Term Obligations	626,670	152,050	325,000	150,000	...	...	...	...
Total Liabilities	1,533,016	1,352,908	1,216,912	1,004,169	1,004,125	832,175	906,249	700,519
Stockholders' Equity	255,714	189,577	222,256	218,366	103,540	493,706	825,270	801,570
Shares Outstanding	229,129	238,339	281,065	294,088	291,339	302,143	318,741	324,188
Statistical Record								
Return on Assets %	16.10	39.16	17.82	14.21	8.95	17.35	13.64	18.96
Return on Equity %	127.85	310.29	120.79	115.21	40.35	41.86	27.11	37.31
EBITDA Margin %	33.12	29.72	34.46	19.65	25.74	32.06	29.38	37.81
Net Margin %	18.19	46.24	18.63	13.91	8.48	19.75	18.59	29.48
Asset Turnover	0.89	0.85	0.96	1.02	1.05	0.88	0.73	0.64
Current Ratio	1.69	0.93	1.22	1.03	0.69	0.84	1.15	1.59
Debt to Equity	2.45	0.80	1.46	0.69	...	...	...	...
Price Range	26.60-20.90	25.01-14.17	22.45-13.25	30.20-18.99	28.56-14.33	33.76-20.61	33.32-17.47	18.05-11.48
P/E Ratio	22.17-17.42	9.69-5.49	24.14-14.25	48.71-30.63	71.41-35.83	39.26-23.96	50.49-26.47	19.41-12.34
Average Yield %	0.33	0.43	0.44	0.31	0.40	0.30	0.12	...

Address: 1499 Post Road, Fairfield, CT 06824	Web Site: www.imshealth.com	Auditors: PricewaterhouseCoopers LLP
Telephone: (203) 319-4700	**Officers:** David M. Thomas - Chmn. David R. Carlucci - Pres., C.E.O.	**Transfer Agents:** American Stock Transfer and Trust Company
Fax: (203) 222-4201		

INDYMAC BANCORP INC

Exchange	Symbol	Price	52Wk Range	Yield	P/E
NYS	NDE	$34.00 (3/31/2005)	39.05-29.92	4.24	12.41

*7 Year Price Score 129.56 *NYSE Composite Index=100 *12 Month Price Score 99.72

Interim Earnings (Per Share)

Qtr.	Mar	Jun	Sep	Dec
2001	0.23	0.48	0.55	0.58
2002	0.58	0.56	0.64	0.63
2003	0.66	0.75	0.87	0.75
2004	0.70	0.38	0.78	0.87

Interim Dividends (Per Share)

Amt	Decl	Ex	Rec	Pay
0.30Q	4/28/2004	5/11/2004	5/13/2004	6/10/2004
0.32Q	7/30/2004	8/10/2004	8/12/2004	9/9/2004
0.34Q	10/28/2004	11/8/2004	11/10/2004	12/9/2004
0.36Q	1/27/2005	2/8/2005	2/10/2005	3/10/2005

Indicated Div: $1.44

Valuation Analysis

Forecast P/E	8.63	No of Institutions
	(4/7/2005)	200
Market Cap	$2.1 Billion	Shares
Book Value	1.3 Billion	47,672,352
Price/Book	1.67	% Held
Price/Sales	1.79	76.69

Business Summary: Other Depository Banking (MIC: 8.5 SIC: 035 NAIC: 51112)

IndyMac Bancorp is the holding company for IndyMac Bank, an Internet-based mortgage banker with proprietary systems to facilitate automated underwriting and risk-based pricing on a nationwide basis. Co.'s mortgage banking group offers multi-channel distribution of its mortgage products and services through a nationwide network of mortgage brokers, mortgage bankers and community financial institutions in addition to programs offered directly to consumers and through realtors and home builders. Co. also provides community lending services though its limited Southern California branch system.

Recent Developments: For the year ended Dec 31 2004, net income decreased 0.5% to $170,522 thousand from net income of $171,303 thousand a year earlier. Net interest income was $405,062 thousand, up 30.3% from $310,937 thousand the year before. Provision for loan losses was $8,170 thousand versus $19,700 thousand in the prior year, a decrease of 58.5%. Non-interest income fell 2.3% to $407,482 thousand, while non-interest expense advanced 22.7% to $522,078 thousand.

Prospects: Co.'s results reflect strong performance as the mortgage industry transitions to more normal levels of production. While industry volumes have declined recently, Co.'s volumes have increased, producing growth in overall market share. Co.'s market share success is the result of its customer base being predominantly comprised of mortgage brokers and mortgage bankers with strong ties to Realtors and the purchase market, a product mix that is generally less interest rate sensitive, and a significant expansion of its geographic presence, sales force and customers nationwide. Looking ahead to 2005, Co. anticipates earnings of about $3.93 per share, including the effects of stock option expensing.

Financial Data
(US$ in Thousands)

	12/31/2004	12/31/2003	12/31/2002	12/31/2001	12/31/2000	12/31/1999	12/31/1998	12/31/1997
Earnings Per Share	2.74	3.01	2.41	1.84	1.69	1.48	0.48	0.43
Cash Flow Per Share	(86.00)	8.10	(15.74)	(19.35)	(12.66)	9.03	(1.26)	(14.61)
Tang Book Value Per Share	8.74	9.51	9.39	8.09	7.69	11.02	10.85	11.11
Dividends Per Share	1.210	0.550	...	...	...	1.740	1.890	1.710
Dividend Payout %	44.16	18.27	...	...	...	117.57	393.75	397.67
Income Statement								
Interest Income	767,608	575,841	477,104	544,940	438,403	346,614	528,825	360,901
Interest Expense	362,546	264,904	267,816	340,941	283,355	185,623	355,359	242,372
Net Interest Income	405,062	310,937	209,288	203,999	155,048	160,991	173,466	118,529
Provision for Losses	8,170	19,700	16,154	22,022	15,974	16,446	35,892	18,622
Non-Interest Income	407,482	416,902	382,172	317,540	198,024	3,875	(16,266)	8,315
Non-Interest Expense	522,078	425,457	345,146	283,748	177,761	34,600	29,286	26,341
Income Before Taxes	282,296	282,682	230,160	216,547	141,080	...	...	...
Income Taxes	111,507	111,379	86,767	89,974	59,254	...	...	...
Net Income	170,522	171,303	143,393	116,388	117,926	115,929	33,790	24,295
Average Shares	62,152	56,926	59,592	63,191	69,787	78,290	70,092	56,454
Balance Sheet								
Net Loans & Leases	11,195,325	10,022,433	6,189,331	5,076,049	3,983,127	2,802,218	3,834,108	4,481,598
Total Assets	16,825,644	13,240,391	9,574,454	7,497,311	5,740,204	3,726,522	4,851,152	5,849,110
Total Deposits	5,743,479	4,350,773	3,140,502	3,238,864	797,935	...	...	...
Total Liabilities	15,561,673	12,222,960	8,724,489	6,535,886	5,012,311	2,898,992	4,029,049	5,145,216
Stockholders' Equity	1,263,971	1,017,431	849,965	845,138	727,893	827,530	822,103	703,894
Shares Outstanding	61,995	56,760	54,829	60,366	62,176	75,076	75,794	63,352
Statistical Record								
Return on Assets %	1.13	1.50	1.68	1.76	2.48	2.70	0.63	0.53
Return on Equity %	14.91	18.35	16.92	14.80	15.12	14.06	4.43	4.06
Net Interest Margin %	52.77	54.00	43.87	37.44	35.37	46.45	32.80	32.84
Efficiency Ratio %	44.43	42.86	40.17	32.90	27.93	9.87	5.71	7.13
Loans to Deposits	1.95	2.30	1.97	1.57	4.99	...	...	...
Price Range	37.82-29.41	30.83-17.75	26.75-16.57	29.59-21.62	29.50-10.59	17.00-10.06	27.13-8.75	25.81-19.38
P/E Ratio	13.80-10.73	10.24-5.90	11.10-6.88	16.08-11.75	17.46-6.21	11.49-6.80	56.51-18.23	60.03-45.06
Average Yield %	3.65	2.32	...	...	...	13.18	9.27	7.63

Address: 155 North Lake Avenue, Pasadena, CA 91101-7211
Telephone: (626) 535-5901
Fax: (626) 535-8203

Web Site: www.indymacbank.com
Officers: Michael W. Perry - Chmn., C.E.O. Scott Keys - Exec. V.P., C.F.O.

Auditors: Ernst & Young LLP
Investor Contact: 800-669-2300 x5019

INGERSOLL-RAND CO. LTD.

Exchange	Symbol	Price	52Wk Range	Yield	P/E
NYS	IR	$79.65 (3/31/2005)	87.33-60.96	1.26	17.09

*7 Year Price Score 120.25 ***NYSE Composite Index=100** ***12 Month Price Score 106.90**

Interim Earnings (Per Share)

Qtr.	Mar	Jun	Sep	Dec
2001	0.31	0.38	0.20	0.59
2002	0.48	0.63	0.53	1.07
2003	0.90	0.81	0.88	1.14
2004	1.02	1.63	...	...

Interim Dividends (Per Share)

Amt	Decl	Ex	Rec	Pay
0.19Q	2/4/2004	2/12/2004	2/17/2004	3/1/2004
0.19Q	4/7/2004	5/13/2004	5/17/2004	6/1/2004
0.25Q	8/4/2004	8/13/2004	8/17/2004	9/1/2004
0.25Q	2/2/2005	2/11/2005	2/15/2005	3/1/2005
		Indicated Div: $1.00		

TRADING VOLUME (thousand shares)

Valuation Analysis

Forecast P/E	16.98	No of Institutions
	(4/7/2005)	N/A
Market Cap	$13.8 Billion	Shares
Book Value	4.8 Billion	N/A
Price/Book	2.90	% Held
Price/Sales	1.36	N/A

Business Summary: Industrial Machinery and Equipment (MIC: 11.5 SIC: 569 NAIC: 33999)

Ingersoll-Rand is engaged in four operating segments. Climate Control manufactures Thermo King temperature control units and Hussmann refrigerated display cases. Industrial Solutions offers air and gas compressors, gas and steam turbines, microturbines, industrial tools and generators. Infrastructure manufactures Bobcat compact equipment, Blaw-Know and ABG pavers, Ingersoll-Rand compactors, drilling equipment and portable power products, and Club Car golf and utility vehicles. Lastly, Security and Safety manufactures locks and locksets, door closers, exit devices, steel doors and frames, power-operated doors, architectural columns and biometric and electronic access control technologies.

Recent Developments: For the year ended Dec 31 2004, income from continuing operations leapt 55.7% to $829.8 million compared with income of $532.8 million a year earlier. Results for 2003 included restructuring charges of $3.2 million. Results for 2004 and 2003 excluded income from discontinued operations of $388.9 million and $111.7 million, respectively. Revenues advanced 13.9% to $9.39 billion from $8.25 billion the year before. Operating income climbed 42.2% to $1.12 billion from $787.6 million a year earlier. Results reflect Co.'s completion of the process of aligning and strengthening its portfolio to capitalize on growth opportunities in global markets.

Prospects: First-quarter 2005 earnings from continuing operations are expected to increase by 25.0% to 36.0% to $1.15 to $1.25 per share from a year ago with earnings in the range of $1.10 to $1.20 per share versus $1.02 for the first quarter of 2004. Based on the expected macro-economic environment, Co. expects organic revenue growth of 6.0% to 8.0% for 2005. Operating margins will improve based on higher volumes and ongoing productivity actions. Full-year 2005 earnings from continuing operations are expected to increase by 20.0% to 26.0%, to $5.65 to $5.95 per share versus $4.73 per share in 2004. Diluted earnings per share from total operations for full-year 2005 is expected to be $5.45 to $5.75.

Financial Data

(US$ in Thousands)	6 Mos	3 Mos	12/31/2003	12/31/2002	12/31/2001	12/31/2000	12/31/1999	12/31/1998
Earnings Per Share	4.66	3.84	3.74	(1.02)	1.48	4.12	3.57	3.08
Cash Flow Per Share	3.62	2.61	1.41	3.55	3.64	4.79	5.11	5.49
Dividends Per Share	0.760	0.740	0.720	0.680	...	...	...	...
Dividend Payout %	16.31	19.27	19.25	...	...	...	...	...
Income Statement								
Total Revenue	5,005,900	2,292,000	9,876,200	8,951,300	9,682,000	8,798,200	7,666,700	8,291,500
EBITDA	666,100	280,600	1,058,200	823,900	858,800	1,380,400	1,320,300	1,297,600
Depn & Amortn	101,200	48,900	194,000	205,900	362,500	297,000	272,400	282,600
Income Before Taxes	484,100	190,800	687,700	387,700	243,300	829,300	844,800	789,200
Income Taxes	68,700	25,800	94,200	20,300	(2,900)	283,100	299,900	280,100
Net Income	465,700	179,500	644,500	(173,500)	246,200	669,400	591,100	509,100
Average Shares	175,300	176,600	172,400	170,200	166,300	162,410	165,752	165,482
Balance Sheet								
Current Assets	3,580,900	3,508,400	3,538,600	4,112,400	3,187,800	3,322,800	2,868,300	2,427,600
Total Assets	10,589,400	10,594,000	10,664,900	10,809,600	11,063,700	10,528,500	8,400,200	8,309,500
Current Liabilities	2,803,500	3,000,100	3,053,000	3,798,100	2,851,000	3,966,600	1,738,900	1,848,800
Long-Term Obligations	1,366,600	1,522,800	1,518,600	2,092,100	2,900,700	1,540,100	2,113,300	2,166,000
Total Liabilities	5,829,400	6,102,300	6,171,600	7,331,400	7,147,100	6,630,800	4,914,700	5,199,500
Stockholders' Equity	4,760,000	4,491,700	4,493,300	3,478,200	3,916,600	3,495,200	3,083,000	2,707,500
Shares Outstanding	173,316	173,294	174,453	169,228	168,003	160,566	163,128	164,389
Statistical Record								
Return on Assets %	7.84	6.52	6.00	N.M.	2.28	7.05	7.07	6.09
Return on Equity %	18.96	16.53	16.17	N.M.	6.64	20.30	20.42	20.17
EBITDA Margin %	13.31	12.24	10.71	9.20	8.87	15.69	17.22	15.65
Net Margin %	9.30	7.83	6.53	N.M.	2.54	7.61	7.71	6.14
Asset Turnover	0.98	0.97	0.92	0.82	0.90	0.93	0.92	0.99
Current Ratio	1.28	1.17	1.16	1.08	1.12	0.84	1.65	1.31
Debt to Equity	0.29	0.34	0.34	0.60	0.74	0.44	0.69	0.80
Price Range	72.68-47.26	72.25-38.55	68.04-35.23	54.16-29.84	49.95-31.02	57.25-30.50	71.44-45.00	53.50-35.00
P/E Ratio	15.60-10.14	18.82-10.04	18.19-9.42	...	33.75-20.96	13.90-7.40	20.01-12.61	17.37-11.36
Average Yield %	1.22	1.31	1.44	1.57	...	...	...	...

Address: Clarendon House, 2 Church Street, Hamilton, 07677 **Telephone:** (441) 295-2838	**Web Site:** www.ingersoll-rand.com **Officers:** Herbert L. Henkel - Chmn., Pres., C.E.O. Timothy E. Scofield - Sr. V.P., C.F.O.	**Auditors:** PricewaterhouseCoopers LLP **Investor Contact:** 201-573-3113

INGRAM MICRO INC.

Exchange	Symbol	Price	52Wk Range	Yield	P/E
NYS	IM	$16.67 (3/31/2005)	20.80-11.93	N/A	12.08

*7 Year Price Score 73.33   *NYSE Composite Index=100   *12 Month Price Score 101.24

Interim Earnings (Per Share)

Qtr.	Mar	Jun	Sep	Dec
2001	0.18	(0.08)	(0.09)	0.03
2002	(1.74)	0.06	(0.06)	(0.07)
2003	0.07	0.08	0.53	0.30
2004	0.24	0.16	0.49	0.49

Interim Dividends (Per Share)

No Dividends Paid

Valuation Analysis

Forecast P/E	12.87	No of Institutions	
	(4/7/2005)	170	
Market Cap	$2.6 Billion	Shares	
Book Value	2.2 Billion	119,482,288	
Price/Book	1.18	% Held	
Price/Sales	0.10	75.09	

Business Summary: IT & Technology (MIC: 10.2 SIC: 045 NAIC: 23430)

Ingram Micro is a worldwide distributor of information technology products and services. Co. markets computer hardware, networking equipment, and software products to reseller customers in more than 100 countries. Co. also provides logistics and fulfillment services to vendor and reseller customers. Co. offers more than 280,000 products, including desktop and notebook personal computers, servers, workstations, mass storage devices, CD-ROM drives, monitors, printers, scanners, and modems. Co. also provides a range of outsourcing programs, including tailored financing programs, channel assembly, systems configuration, and marketing programs.

Recent Developments: For the year ended Jan 1 2005, net income increased 47.4% to $219,901 thousand from net income of $149,201 thousand a year earlier. Revenues were $25,462,071 thousand, up 12.6% from $22,613,017 thousand the year before. Operating income was $283,367 thousand versus an income of $156,193 thousand in the prior year, an increase of 81.4%. Total direct expense was $24,060,029 thousand versus $21,389,529 thousand in the prior year, an increase of 12.5%. Total indirect expense was $1,118,675 thousand versus $1,067,295 thousand in the prior year, an increase of 4.8%.

Prospects: Co. is experiencing renewed sales growth due to organic growth in its existing operation, particularly Europe, as well as from additional revenues from the former Tech Pacific business acquired in November 2004. Demand continues to be generally solid throughout the world, with some pockets of increasing competition and economic softness in certain markets. Co. expects to maintain or enhance market share through strategic initiatives to spur both sales and income, while expanding its reach into new technologies and markets. For the first quarter of 2005, Co. expects sales to range from $7.00 billion to $7.20 billion, with net income ranging from $0.28 to $0.30 per diluted share.

Financial Data

(US$ in Thousands)	01/01/2005	01/03/2004	12/28/2002	12/29/2001	12/30/2000	01/01/2000	01/02/1999	01/03/1998
Earnings Per Share	1.38	0.98	(1.81)	0.04	1.52	1.24	1.64	1.32
Cash Flow Per Share	2.33	(0.62)	1.59	1.95	5.78	4.01	(2.01)	(4.69)
Tang Book Value Per Share	10.59	10.72	9.30	9.12	9.87	10.46	8.22	6.53
Income Statement								
Total Revenue	25,462,071	22,613,017	22,459,265	25,186,933	30,715,149	28,068,642	22,034,038	16,581,539
EBITDA	351,088	217,827	128,593	170,283	551,218	485,447	541,331	408,340
Depn & Amortn	57,657	78,519	98,763	114,980	108,510	97,601	67,942	47,835
Income Before Taxes	263,276	115,794	8,998	15,935	362,509	290,493	406,860	326,489
Income Taxes	43,375	(33,407)	3,329	6,588	138,756	110,852	161,685	131,463
Net Income	219,901	149,201	(275,192)	6,737	226,173	183,419	245,175	193,640
Average Shares	159,680	152,308	152,145	150,047	148,640	147,784	149,537	146,307
Balance Sheet								
Current Assets	6,082,162	4,968,093	4,600,386	4,456,846	5,770,084	6,968,929	6,031,550	4,445,994
Total Assets	6,926,737	5,474,162	5,144,354	5,302,007	6,608,982	8,271,927	6,733,404	4,932,151
Current Liabilities	4,313,213	3,340,108	3,186,869	3,139,617	4,117,965	4,670,606	3,599,650	2,729,385
Long-Term Obligations	346,183	239,909	241,052	205,304	502,844	1,317,115	1,681,478	1,119,262
Total Liabilities	4,685,927	3,601,213	3,508,365	3,434,709	4,734,590	6,301,282	5,326,333	3,872,490
Stockholders' Equity	2,240,810	1,872,949	1,635,989	1,867,298	1,874,392	1,966,845	1,399,257	1,038,206
Shares Outstanding	158,737	151,963	150,778	149,024	146,207	144,493	141,980	137,081
Statistical Record								
Return on Assets %	3.56	2.76	N.M.	0.11	3.05	2.45	4.21	4.59
Return on Equity %	10.72	8.37	N.M.	0.36	11.81	10.93	20.17	20.45
EBITDA Margin %	1.38	0.96	0.57	0.68	1.79	1.73	2.46	2.46
Net Margin %	0.86	0.66	N.M.	0.03	0.74	0.65	1.11	1.17
Asset Turnover	4.12	4.19	4.31	4.24	4.14	3.75	3.79	3.93
Current Ratio	1.41	1.49	1.44	1.42	1.40	1.49	1.68	1.63
Debt to Equity	0.15	0.13	0.15	0.11	0.27	0.67	1.20	1.08
Price Range	20.80-11.93	16.00-9.52	18.70-10.30	17.36-10.81	20.94-10.50	35.88-10.00	54.00-26.94	33.56-19.38
P/E Ratio	15.07-8.64	16.33-9.71		434.00-270.31	13.77-6.91	28.93-8.06	32.93-16.43	25.43-14.68

Address: 1600 E. St. Andrew Place, Santa Ana, CA 92705 Telephone: (714) 566-1000 Fax: (714) 566-7604	Web Site: www.ingrammicro.com Officers: Kent B. Foster - Chmn., C.E.O. Kevin M. Murai - Pres.	Auditors: Price Waterhouse Coopers LL Investor Contact: 714-382-4400

INTERNATIONAL BUSINESS MACHINES CORP.

Exchange	Symbol	Price	52Wk Range	Yield	P/E
NYS	IBM	$91.38 (3/31/2005)	98.58-82.21	0.79	18.54

7 Year Price Score 82.00 *NYSE Composite Index=100 *12 Month Price Score 95.49

Interim Earnings (Per Share)

Qtr.	Mar	Jun	Sep	Dec
2001	0.98	1.15	0.90	1.32
2002	0.68	0.03	0.76	0.59
2003	0.79	0.97	1.02	1.55
2004	0.95	1.16	1.06	1.79

Interim Dividends (Per Share)

Amt	Decl	Ex	Rec	Pay
0.18Q	4/27/2004	5/6/2004	5/10/2004	6/10/2004
0.18Q	7/27/2004	8/6/2004	8/10/2004	9/10/2004
0.18Q	10/26/2004	11/8/2004	11/10/2004	12/10/2004
0.18Q	1/25/2005	2/8/2005	2/10/2005	3/10/2005

Indicated Div: $0.72

Valuation Analysis

Forecast P/E	15.99	No of Institutions
	(4/7/2005)	1172
Market Cap	$150.4 Billion	Shares
Book Value	29.7 Billion	910,279,872
Price/Book	5.06	% Held
Price/Sales	1.56	55.76

Business Summary: IT & Technology (MIC: 10.2 SIC: 571 NAIC: 34111)

International Business Machines provides information technology services, software, systems, products, financing and technologies. Operations include global services, systems & technology, software and global financing. The global services unit includes outsourcing and consulting contracts and integrated technology services. The systems & technology unit provides computing power and storage applications. The personal systems group provides sales of personal computers, business and computing solutions for retail stores and advanced printing capabilities for large enterprise clients and small and medium-sized businesses. The software unit consists of middleware and operating systems software.

Recent Developments: For the year ended Dec 31 2004, income from continuing operations increased 11.0% to $8,448,000 thousand from income of $7,613,000 thousand a year earlier. Net income increased 11.2% to $8,430,000 thousand from net income of $7,583,000 thousand a year earlier. Revenues were $96,293,000 thousand, up 8.0% from $89,131,000 thousand the year before. Total direct expense was $60,261,000 thousand versus $56,113,000 thousand in the prior year, an increase of 7.4%. Total indirect expense was $25,057,000 thousand versus $22,929,000 thousand in the prior year, an increase of 9.3%.

Prospects: Co. is leveraging its industry expertise, advanced technologies, and economies of scale, to help customers transform their business processes. Co. has made substantial investments to expand its existing capabilities in four areas, Business Transformation Outsourcing, Engineering and Technology Services, Strategy and Change Consulting, and Business Performance Management Software. Co. is comfortable with the expected 11.0% earnings growth for 2005, which is consistent with its longer-term model. On Dec 7 2004, Co. announced an agreement to sell its Personal Computing division to Lenovo Group Limited for at least $650.0 million in cash and up to $600.0 million in Lenovo common stock.

Financial Data
(US$ in Thousands)

	12/31/2004	12/31/2003	12/31/2002	12/31/2001	12/31/2000	12/31/1999	12/31/1998	12/31/1997
Earnings Per Share	4.93	4.32	2.06	4.35	4.44	4.12	3.29	3.00
Cash Flow Per Share	9.17	8.46	8.10	8.23	5.25	5.59	4.96	4.51
Tang Book Value Per Share	11.86	11.54	10.03	12.40	10.63	10.28	9.53	9.19
Dividends Per Share	0.700	0.630	0.590	0.550	0.510	0.470	0.430	0.388
Dividend Payout %	14.20	14.58	28.64	12.64	11.49	11.41	13.09	12.90
Income Statement								
Total Revenue	96,293,000	89,131,000	81,186,000	85,866,000	88,396,000	87,548,000	81,667,000	78,508,000
EBITDA	16,902,000	15,783,000	12,162,000	16,011,000	17,246,000	19,069,000	14,745,000	14,773,000
Depn & Amortn	4,915,000	4,916,000	4,493,000	4,820,000	4,995,000	6,585,000	4,992,000	5,018,000
Income Before Taxes	12,028,000	10,874,000	7,524,000	10,953,000	11,534,000	11,757,000	9,040,000	9,027,000
Income Taxes	3,580,000	3,261,000	2,190,000	3,230,000	3,441,000	4,045,000	2,712,000	2,934,000
Net Income	8,430,000	7,583,000	3,579,000	7,723,000	8,093,000	7,712,000	6,328,000	6,093,000
Average Shares	1,708,872	1,756,090	1,730,941	1,771,230	1,812,118	1,871,074	1,920,000	2,022,000
Balance Sheet								
Current Assets	46,970,000	44,998,000	41,652,000	42,461,000	43,880,000	43,155,000	42,360,000	40,418,000
Total Assets	109,183,000	104,457,000	96,484,000	88,313,000	88,349,000	87,495,000	86,100,000	81,499,000
Current Liabilities	39,798,000	37,900,000	34,550,000	35,119,000	36,406,000	39,578,000	36,827,000	33,507,000
Long-Term Obligations	14,828,000	16,986,000	19,986,000	15,963,000	18,371,000	14,124,000	15,508,000	13,696,000
Total Liabilities	79,436,000	76,593,000	73,702,000	64,699,000	67,725,000	66,984,000	66,667,000	61,683,000
Stockholders' Equity	29,747,000	27,864,000	22,782,000	23,614,000	20,624,000	20,511,000	19,433,000	19,816,000
Shares Outstanding	1,645,592	1,694,508	1,722,366	1,723,193	1,762,899	1,804,216	1,852,000	1,936,000
Statistical Record								
Return on Assets %	7.87	7.55	3.87	8.74	9.18	8.89	7.55	7.49
Return on Equity %	29.19	29.95	15.43	34.92	39.24	38.61	32.25	29.40
EBITDA Margin %	17.55	17.71	14.98	18.65	19.51	21.78	18.06	18.82
Net Margin %	8.75	8.51	4.41	8.99	9.16	8.81	7.75	7.76
Asset Turnover	0.90	0.89	0.88	0.97	1.00	1.01	0.97	0.97
Current Ratio	1.18	1.19	1.21	1.21	1.21	1.09	1.15	1.21
Debt to Equity	0.50	0.61	0.88	0.68	0.89	0.69	0.80	0.69
Price Range	100.19-82.21	93.98-75.18	125.60-55.07	123.89-84.81	133.63-81.56	137.88-81.38	94.63-48.06	56.44-32.31
P/E Ratio	20.32-16.68	21.75-17.40	60.97-26.73	28.48-19.50	30.10-18.37	33.46-19.75	28.76-14.61	18.81-10.77
Average Yield %	0.77	0.74	0.70	0.51	0.46	0.44	0.69	0.86

Address: One New Orchard Road, Armonk, NY 10504	**Web Site:** www.ibm.com	**Auditors:** Ernst & Young LLP
Telephone: (914) 499-1900	**Officers:** Samuel J. Palmisano - Chmn., Pres., C.E.O.	**Investor Contact:** 888-421-8860
Fax: (914) 765-4190	John R. Joyce - Sr. V.P., C.F.O.	

INTERNATIONAL FLAVORS & FRAGRANCES INC.

Exchange	Symbol	Price	52Wk Range	Yield	P/E
NYS	IFF	$39.50 (3/31/2005)	43.05-34.66	1.77	19.27

*7 Year Price Score 97.43   ***NYSE Composite Index=100**   ***12 Month Price Score 98.69**

Interim Earnings (Per Share)

Qtr.	Mar	Jun	Sep	Dec
2001	0.21	0.34	0.35	0.31
2002	0.44	0.47	0.52	0.41
2003	0.34	0.54	0.54	0.41
2004	0.59	0.59	0.44	0.42

Interim Dividends (Per Share)

Amt	Decl	Ex	Rec	Pay
0.175Q	5/12/2004	6/22/2004	6/24/2004	7/8/2004
0.175Q	9/10/2004	9/21/2004	9/23/2004	10/7/2004
0.175Q	12/15/2004	12/21/2004	12/23/2004	1/10/2005
0.175Q	3/8/2005	3/18/2005	3/22/2005	4/7/2005

Indicated Div: $0.70

Valuation Analysis

Forecast P/E	16.80	No of Institutions
	(4/7/2005)	230
Market Cap	$3.7 Billion	Shares
Book Value	910.5 Million	70,804,632
Price/Book	4.11	% Held
Price/Sales	1.84	74.91

Business Summary: Chemicals (MIC: 11.1 SIC: 869 NAIC: 25199)

International Flavors & Fragrances is a creator and manufacturer of flavor and fragrance products used by other manufacturers to impart or improve flavor or fragrance in a variety of consumer products. Fragrance products are sold principally to manufacturers of perfumes, cosmetics, toiletries, hair care products, deodorants, soaps, detergents and air care products. Flavor products are sold principally to manufacturers of prepared foods, beverages, dairy foods, pharmaceuticals and confectionery products. As of Dec 31 2003, Co. produced more than 35,000 unique compounds annually of which 60.0% are flavors and 40.0% fragrances.

Recent Developments: For the year ended Dec 31 2004, net income increased 13.6% to $196,071 thousand from net income of $172,597 thousand a year earlier. Revenues were $2,033,653 thousand, up 6.9% from $1,901,520 thousand the year before. Total direct expense was $1,160,235 thousand versus $1,092,456 thousand in the prior year, an increase of 6.2%. Total indirect expense was $563,139 thousand versus $523,290 thousand in the prior year, an increase of 7.6%.

Prospects: Co. expects 2005 local currency sales to increase in the low-single digits versus 2004 sales. However, for comparison purposes, 2004 sales include $58.0 million of sales attributable to the European fruit preparations business. Excluding fruit sales from the 2004 comparative, Co. expects 2005 local currency sales to increase in the low to mid-single digits in comparison to 2004. Co. expects earnings per share for 2005 to be in the range of $2.34 to $2.41 compared with $2.05 in 2004. Excluding restructuring and other charges recorded in 2004, this performance represents an expected increase in earnings per share of between 3.0% and 6.0% over the comparable 2004 results of $2.27 per share.

Financial Data

(US$ in Thousands)	12/31/2004	12/31/2003	12/31/2002	12/31/2001	12/31/2000	12/31/1999	12/31/1998	12/31/1997
Earnings Per Share	2.05	1.83	1.84	1.20	1.22	1.53	1.90	1.99
Cash Flow Per Share	3.13	2.88	2.57	1.90	2.66	1.85	2.02	2.19
Tang Book Value Per Share	1.28	N.M.	N.M.	N.M.	N.M.	8.19	8.91	9.17
Dividends Per Share	0.685	0.630	0.600	0.600	1.290	1.520	1.490	1.450
Dividend Payout %	33.41	34.43	32.61	50.00	105.74	99.35	78.42	72.86
Income Statement								
Total Revenue	2,033,653	1,901,520	1,809,249	1,843,766	1,462,795	1,439,499	1,407,349	1,426,791
EBITDA	371,998	338,581	350,875	311,270	253,471	299,834	360,074	390,469
Depn & Amortn	90,996	86,721	84,458	123,493	69,344	56,369	49,006	50,278
Income Before Taxes	281,002	251,860	266,417	187,777	184,127	243,465	311,068	340,191
Income Taxes	84,931	79,263	90,473	71,775	61,122	81,465	107,283	121,962
Net Income	196,071	172,597	175,944	116,002	123,005	162,000	203,785	218,229
Average Shares	95,418	94,419	95,873	96,819	101,093	105,943	107,430	109,625
Balance Sheet								
Current Assets	961,370	902,672	866,749	896,361	1,018,940	835,414	848,028	935,459
Total Assets	2,363,294	2,306,892	2,232,694	2,268,051	2,489,033	1,401,495	1,388,064	1,422,261
Current Liabilities	399,522	526,045	359,497	560,214	1,179,017	369,702	272,908	264,861
Long-Term Obligations	668,969	690,231	1,007,085	939,404	417,402	3,832	4,341	5,114
Total Liabilities	1,452,807	1,564,261	1,658,016	1,743,881	1,857,774	542,998	443,013	421,773
Stockholders' Equity	910,487	742,631	574,678	524,170	631,259	858,497	945,051	1,000,488
Shares Outstanding	94,672	93,729	94,254	94,764	97,426	104,821	106,046	109,131
Statistical Record								
Return on Assets %	8.37	7.60	7.82	4.88	6.31	11.61	14.50	14.90
Return on Equity %	23.66	26.20	32.02	20.08	16.47	17.96	20.95	21.01
EBITDA Margin %	18.29	17.81	19.39	16.88	17.33	20.83	25.59	27.37
Net Margin %	9.64	9.08	9.72	6.29	8.41	11.25	14.48	15.30
Asset Turnover	0.87	0.84	0.80	0.78	0.75	1.03	1.00	0.97
Current Ratio	2.41	1.72	2.41	1.60	0.86	2.26	3.11	3.53
Debt to Equity	0.73	0.93	1.75	1.79	0.66	N.M.	N.M.	0.01
Price Range	43.05-33.25	36.57-29.66	37.32-27.42	31.45-20.21	37.63-15.13	47.13-34.25	51.50-32.81	53.25-40.50
P/E Ratio	21.00-16.22	19.98-16.21	20.28-14.90	26.21-16.84	30.84-12.40	30.80-22.39	27.11-17.27	26.76-20.35
Average Yield %	1.82	1.96	1.83	2.31	4.63	3.79	3.45	3.04

Address: 521 West 57th Street, New York, NY 10019-2960 **Telephone:** (212) 765-5500 **Fax:** (212) 708-7132	**Web Site:** www.iff.com **Officers:** Richard A. Goldstein - Chmn., C.E.O. Julian W. Boyden - Exec. V.P., New Bus. Devel.	**Auditors:** PricewaterhouseCoopers LLP

INTERNATIONAL GAME TECHNOLOGY

Exchange	Symbol	Price	52Wk Range	Yield	P/E
NYS	IGT	$26.66 (3/31/2005)	46.82-26.23	1.80	22.59

*7 Year Price Score 177.72 *NYSE Composite Index=100 *12 Month Price Score 81.07

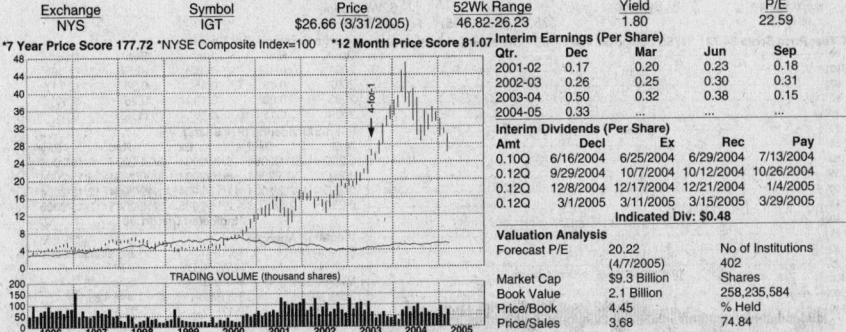

Interim Earnings (Per Share)

Qtr.	Dec	Mar	Jun	Sep
2001-02	0.17	0.20	0.23	0.18
2002-03	0.26	0.25	0.30	0.31
2003-04	0.50	0.32	0.38	0.15
2004-05	0.33	...	...	...

Interim Dividends (Per Share)

Amt	Decl	Ex	Rec	Pay
0.10Q	6/16/2004	6/25/2004	6/29/2004	7/13/2004
0.12Q	9/29/2004	10/7/2004	10/12/2004	10/26/2004
0.12Q	12/8/2004	12/17/2004	12/21/2004	1/4/2005
0.12Q	3/1/2005	3/11/2005	3/15/2005	3/29/2005

Indicated Div: $0.48

Valuation Analysis

Forecast P/E	20.22	No of Institutions
	(4/7/2005)	402
Market Cap	$9.3 Billion	Shares
Book Value	2.1 Billion	258,235,584
Price/Book	4.45	% Held
Price/Sales	3.68	74.84

Business Summary: Industrial Machinery and Equipment (MIC: 11.5 SIC: 559 NAIC: 33319)

International Game Technology is engaged in the design, development, manufacturing, distribution and sales of computerized gaming machines and systems products in all jurisdictions where gaming is legal. Co. redefined its business segments under a reorganization of management responsibilities to cover all products in geographical areas. The two operating segments consist of the North America Division and the International Division. The North America Division encompasses Co.'s operations in the US and Canada, including the IGT Systems group. The International Division oversees Co.'s efforts abroad in Australia, New Zealand, Europe, Latin America, South Africa, the UK and Japan.

Recent Developments: For the quarter ended Dec 31 2004, net income decreased 30.6% to $122,444 thousand from net income of $176,324 thousand in the year-earlier quarter. Revenues were $641,205 thousand, up 5.5% from $608,061 thousand the year before. Operating income was $189,723 thousand versus an income of $202,243 thousand in the prior-year quarter, a decrease of 6.2%. Total direct expense was $328,182 thousand versus $286,995 thousand in the prior-year quarter, an increase of 14.4%. Total indirect expense was $123,300 thousand versus $118,823 thousand in the prior-year quarter, an increase of 3.8%.

Prospects: Looking ahead, results are expected to be positively affected by the launch of several new MegaJackpots® products later this year. Meanwhile, Co. continues to expand its operations geographically. On Feb 15 2005, Co. announced that has formed a new division, IGT-Asia, that will be located in Macau to help service the rapidly growing Asian gaming markets. Separately, on Jan 5 2005, Co. announced that it has formed a new subsidiary, IGT-Canada, Inc., through the acquisition of its Canadian distributor, Hi-Tech Gaming, that will support sales and service for customers throughout Canada.

Financial Data

(US$ in Thousands)	3 Mos	09/30/2004	09/30/2003	09/28/2002	09/29/2001	09/30/2000	10/02/1999	09/30/1998
Earnings Per Share	1.18	1.34	1.11	0.79	0.70	0.50	0.16	0.33
Cash Flow Per Share	1.87	1.79	1.24	1.50	0.67	0.42	0.65	0.24
Tang Book Value Per Share	2.26	1.97	1.41	0.54	0.40	N.M.	0.26	0.94
Dividends Per Share	0.440	0.300	0.175	...	...	...	0.015	0.030
Dividend Payout %	37.40	22.39	15.77	...	...	...	9.68	9.02
Income Statement								
Total Revenue	641,205	2,484,752	2,128,137	1,847,568	1,199,209	1,004,395	929,662	824,123
EBITDA	233,301	833,976	796,477	656,486	455,040	350,567	170,962	271,703
Depn & Amortn	42,482	149,809	133,987	146,101	63,348	54,387	52,330	41,468
Income Before Taxes	191,319	653,416	598,564	444,171	339,472	244,987	101,393	234,532
Income Taxes	68,875	223,663	223,257	167,453	125,537	88,195	36,081	82,086
Net Income	122,444	488,677	390,727	271,165	213,935	156,792	62,058	152,446
Average Shares	374,103	370,892	351,316	344,196	306,100	312,916	400,952	458,812
Balance Sheet								
Current Assets	1,662,589	1,509,704	2,078,228	1,195,022	967,674	814,226	975,240	670,543
Total Assets	4,009,408	3,872,964	4,185,231	3,315,818	1,923,439	1,623,716	1,765,060	1,543,628
Current Liabilities	590,153	560,009	945,081	511,059	370,899	258,993	212,556	200,540
Long-Term Obligations	794,402	791,848	1,146,759	971,375	984,742	991,507	990,436	322,510
Total Liabilities	1,930,581	1,896,315	2,497,753	1,874,011	1,627,326	1,527,131	1,522,842	1,002,352
Stockholders' Equity	2,078,827	1,976,649	1,687,478	1,433,144	296,113	96,585	242,218	541,276
Shares Outstanding	346,978	346,090	345,542	347,305	291,729	290,275	349,421	435,461
Statistical Record								
Return on Assets %	10.38	12.10	10.36	10.38	12.10	9.28	3.73	11.05
Return on Equity %	22.05	26.60	24.91	31.45	109.26	92.81	15.76	28.73
EBITDA Margin %	36.38	33.56	37.43	35.53	37.95	34.90	18.39	32.97
Net Margin %	19.10	19.67	18.36	14.68	17.84	15.61	6.68	18.50
Asset Turnover	0.60	0.62	0.56	0.71	0.68	0.59	0.56	0.60
Current Ratio	2.82	2.70	2.20	2.34	2.61	3.14	4.59	3.34
Debt to Equity	0.38	0.40	0.68	0.68	3.33	10.27	4.09	0.60
Price Range	46.82-28.72	46.82-28.09	28.87-16.31	17.76-10.28	16.33-8.20	8.63-4.36	6.13-3.59	7.14-4.63
P/E Ratio	39.68-24.34	34.94-20.96	26.01-14.69	22.48-13.01	23.33-11.72	17.25-8.72	38.28-22.46	21.64-14.02
Average Yield %	1.21	0.84	0.81	...	...	...	0.31	0.49

Address: 9295 Prototype Drive, Reno, NV 89521	Web Site: www.igt.com	Auditors: Deloitte & Touche LLP
Telephone: (775) 448-7777	Officers: Thomas J. Matthews - Chmn., C.E.O.	Investor Contact: 775-448-0880
Fax: (775) 448-0719	Maureen T. Mullarkay - Exec. V.P., C.F.O., Treas.	Transfer Agents: The Bank of New York, New York, NY

INTERNATIONAL PAPER CO.

Exchange	Symbol	Price	52Wk Range	Yield	P/E
NYS	IP	$36.79 (3/31/2005)	44.70-35.74	2.72	N/A

*7 Year Price Score 84.72   ***NYSE Composite Index=100**   ***12 Month Price Score 87.44**

Interim Earnings (Per Share)

Qtr.	Mar	Jun	Sep	Dec
2001	(0.09)	(0.65)	(0.57)	(1.19)
2002	0.13	0.45	0.30	(2.71)
2003	0.09	0.19	0.25	0.10
2004	0.15	0.40	(1.13)	0.51

Interim Dividends (Per Share)

Amt	Decl	Ex	Rec	Pay
0.25Q	5/11/2004	5/19/2004	5/21/2004	6/15/2004
0.25Q	7/13/2004	8/18/2004	8/20/2004	9/15/2004
0.25Q	10/12/2004	11/17/2004	11/19/2004	12/15/2004
0.25Q	2/8/2005	2/16/2005	2/18/2005	3/15/2005
		Indicated Div: $1.00		

Valuation Analysis

Forecast P/E	18.18 (4/7/2005)
Market Cap	$17.9 Billion
Book Value	8.3 Billion
Price/Book	2.17
Price/Sales	0.70

No of Institutions	471
Shares	445,126,144
% Held	90.78

TRADING VOLUME (thousand shares)

Business Summary: Paper Products (MIC: 11.11 SIC: 621 NAIC: 22121)

International Paper is a global paper and forest products company with an extensive distribution system. Co.'s businesses include paper, packaging and forest products. As of Dec 31 2003, Co. had operations in over 40 countries and exported its products to more than 120 nations. Co.'s primary markets and manufacturing and distribution operations are in the U.S., Canada, Europe, the Pacific Rim and South America. Co. produces printing and writing papers, pulp, tissue, paperboard and packaging and wood products. Co. manufactures specialty chemicals and specialty panels and laminated products.

Recent Developments: For the year ended Dec 31 2004, income from continuing operations increased 62.6% to $478 million from income of $294 million a year earlier. Net loss was $35 million versus net income of $302 million a year earlier. Revenues were $25,548 million, up 6.6% from $23,955 million the year before. Total direct expense was $18,996 million versus $17,878 million in the prior year, an increase of 6.3%. Total indirect expense was $5,221 million versus $5,053 million in the prior year, an increase of 3.3%.

Prospects: Co.'s near-term outlook is mixed. On the positive side, Co. is beginning to see conditions improving. For instance, after a slow month in January, Co.'s order activity is picking up, and its average price realizations are moving up on coated paper, some grades of printing papers, bleached board and pulp. However, Co.'s profit margins and earnings are expected to be under pressure, as the raw material cost environment continues to be severe. In addition, Co. expects higher benefit-related costs, and the investment it is making to improve its supply chain to be somewhat higher in the first quarter.

Financial Data

(US$ in Thousands)	12/31/2004	12/31/2003	12/31/2002	12/31/2001	12/31/2000	12/31/1999	12/31/1998	12/31/1997
Earnings Per Share	(0.07)	0.63	(1.83)	(2.50)	0.32	0.44	0.77	(0.50)
Cash Flow Per Share	4.90	3.80	4.35	3.55	5.39	4.18	5.46	4.11
Tang Book Value Per Share	6.69	6.01	4.31	7.78	11.89	18.65	20.44	20.36
Dividends Per Share	1.000	1.000	1.000	1.000	1.000	1.000	1.000	1.000
Dividend Payout %	...	158.73	...	...	312.50	227.27	129.87	...
Income Statement								
Total Revenue	25,548,000	25,179,000	24,976,000	26,363,000	28,180,000	24,573,000	19,541,000	20,096,000
EBITDA	1,489,000	1,112,000	1,154,000	1,534,000	3,455,000	2,509,000	2,074,000	1,764,000
Depn & Amortn	...	...	...	1,870,000	1,916,000	1,520,000	1,186,000	1,258,000
Income Before Taxes	746,000	346,000	371,000	(1,265,000)	723,000	448,000	392,000	16,000
Income Taxes	206,000	(92,000)	(54,000)	(270,000)	117,000	86,000	80,000	38,000
Net Income	(35,000)	302,000	(880,000)	(1,204,000)	142,000	183,000	236,000	(151,000)
Average Shares	488,400	481,100	483,000	481,600	450,000	416,100	306,300	301,000
Balance Sheet								
Current Assets	9,319,000	9,337,000	7,738,000	8,312,000	10,455,000	7,241,000	6,010,000	5,945,000
Total Assets	34,217,000	35,525,000	33,792,000	37,158,000	42,109,000	30,268,000	26,356,000	26,754,000
Current Liabilities	4,872,000	6,803,000	4,579,000	5,374,000	7,413,000	4,382,000	3,636,000	4,880,000
Long-Term Obligations	14,132,000	13,450,000	13,042,000	12,457,000	12,648,000	7,520,000	6,407,000	7,154,000
Total Liabilities	25,963,000	27,288,000	26,418,000	26,867,000	30,075,000	19,964,000	17,454,000	18,044,000
Stockholders' Equity	8,254,000	8,237,000	7,374,000	10,291,000	12,034,000	10,304,000	8,902,000	8,710,000
Shares Outstanding	487,479	481,500	479,100	481,600	481,500	413,400	307,100	302,200
Statistical Record								
Return on Assets %	N.M.	0.87	N.M.	N.M.	0.39	0.65	0.89	N.M.
Return on Equity %	N.M.	3.87	N.M.	N.M.	1.27	1.91	2.68	N.M.
EBITDA Margin %	5.83	4.42	4.62	5.82	12.26	10.21	10.61	8.78
Net Margin %	N.M.	1.20	N.M.	N.M.	0.50	0.74	1.21	N.M.
Asset Turnover	0.73	0.73	0.70	0.67	0.78	0.87	0.74	0.73
Current Ratio	1.91	1.37	1.69	1.55	1.41	1.65	1.65	1.22
Debt to Equity	1.71	1.63	1.77	1.21	1.05	0.73	0.72	0.82
Price Range	44.98-37.80	43.12-33.44	46.05-31.45	42.63-32.36	58.63-26.81	57.88-39.56	55.19-37.00	59.94-39.00
P/E Ratio	...	68.44-53.08	...	...	183.20-83.79	131.53-89.91	71.67-48.05	...
Average Yield %	2.40	2.66	2.52	2.63	2.71	2.01	2.17	2.08

Address: 400 Atlantic Street, Stamford, CT 06921
Telephone: (203) 541-8000
Fax: (203) 541-8255

Web Site: www.internationalpaper.com
Officers: John V. Faraci - Chmn., C.E.O. Robert M. Amen - Pres.

Auditors: Deloitte & Touche LLP
Investor Contact: 203-541-8625

INTERNATIONAL RECTIFIER CORP.

Exchange	Symbol	Price	52Wk Range	Yield	P/E
NYS	IRF	$45.50 (3/31/2005)	49.11-31.39	N/A	24.07

*7 Year Price Score 109.47 *NYSE Composite Index=100 *12 Month Price Score 101.46

TRADING VOLUME (thousand shares)

Interim Earnings (Per Share)

Qtr.	Sep	Dec	Mar	Jun
2001-02	0.15	0.17	0.19	0.25
2002-03	0.17	(1.90)	0.11	0.21
2003-04	0.25	0.25	0.39	0.42
2004-05	0.53	0.55	...	...

Interim Dividends (Per Share)

No Dividends Paid

Valuation Analysis

Forecast P/E	15.58	No of Institutions	
	(4/7/2005)	219	
Market Cap	$3.1 Billion	Shares	
Book Value	1.3 Billion	49,149,824	
Price/Book	2.35	% Held	
Price/Sales	2.61	72.61	

Business Summary: IT & Technology (MIC: 10.2 SIC: 674 NAIC: 34413)

International Rectifier is a designer, manufacturer and marketer of power management products and a supplier of a type of power semiconductor called a MOSFET (a metal oxide semiconductor field effect transistor). Power semiconductors process electricity into a form more usable by electrical products. Co.'s products are used in end-markets, including information technology, automotive, consumer electronics, aerospace/defense and industrial. Co.'s design centers are located throughout the world, including the United States, Canada, the United Kingdom, Denmark, Italy, France, Germany and Singapore.

Recent Developments: For the quarter ended Dec 31 2004, net income increased 134.0% to $39,514 thousand from net income of $16,888 thousand in the year-earlier quarter. Revenues were $298,560 thousand, up 18.3% from $252,314 thousand the year before. Total direct expense was $169,179 thousand versus $157,431 thousand in the prior-year quarter, an increase of 7.5%. Total indirect expense was $76,842 thousand versus $72,017 thousand in the prior-year quarter, an increase of 6.7%.

Prospects: Co.'s focus on proprietary products continues to drive its margin expansion. Going forward, over the next six quarters, Co. will continue to expand its proprietary product portfolio and plan to reach greater than 50.0% gross margins. This will involve a follow-on divestiture or discontinuation of $150.0 million in annual revenues that no longer add value to its business objectives. For the first quarter of 2005, revenues are expected to be flat to down 6.0% sequentially from the fourth quarter. Co. noted that it has more than 80.0% backlog coverage of its target revenue for the quarter. Co. expects overall gross margin to be flat sequentially plus or minus 1.0 percentage point.

Financial Data
(US$ in Thousands)

	6 Mos	3 Mos	06/30/2004	06/30/2003	06/30/2002	06/30/2001	06/30/2000	06/30/1999
Earnings Per Share	1.89	1.59	1.31	(1.40)	0.75	1.35	1.19	(0.11)
Cash Flow Per Share	3.21	2.77	2.48	2.02	0.81	3.32	1.75	1.88
Tang Book Value Per Share	16.49	15.82	15.61	13.11	13.64	14.13	13.70	7.65
Income Statement								
Total Revenue	610,785	312,225	1,060,500	864,443	720,229	978,585	753,327	545,371
EBITDA	142,464	71,923	177,219	(69,805)	123,218	167,712	163,489	88,438
Depn & Amortn	37,054	18,361	57,123	57,064	63,906	71,054	55,937	46,162
Income Before Taxes	103,044	51,845	118,284	(126,198)	65,811	118,381	101,540	31,156
Income Taxes	25,950	14,265	28,514	(36,559)	17,111	30,732	28,431	10,780
Net Income	77,094	37,580	89,770	(89,639)	48,700	87,649	68,337	(5,778)
Average Shares	76,490	75,711	68,363	63,982	65,271	64,800	57,662	51,788
Balance Sheet								
Current Assets	1,075,818	989,485	953,210	874,839	729,254	1,209,181	591,623	306,274
Total Assets	2,147,160	2,056,294	2,017,006	1,821,852	1,813,182	1,746,462	1,025,970	709,085
Current Liabilities	244,207	227,222	215,036	211,733	170,267	195,975	150,160	140,632
Long-Term Obligations	555,969	561,034	560,019	579,379	566,841	552,751	4,589	158,418
Total Liabilities	834,877	816,590	812,794	809,613	754,537	766,805	181,904	312,811
Stockholders' Equity	1,312,283	1,239,704	1,204,212	1,012,239	1,058,645	979,657	844,066	396,274
Shares Outstanding	67,688	66,738	66,358	64,185	63,698	63,132	61,594	51,781
Statistical Record								
Return on Assets %	6.59	5.71	4.66	N.M.	2.74	6.32	7.86	N.M.
Return on Equity %	10.97	9.68	8.08	N.M.	4.78	9.61	10.99	N.M.
EBITDA Margin %	23.32	23.04	16.71	N.M.	17.11	17.14	21.70	16.22
Net Margin %	12.62	12.04	8.46	N.M.	6.76	8.96	9.07	N.M.
Asset Turnover	0.59	0.59	0.55	0.48	0.40	0.71	0.87	0.75
Current Ratio	4.41	4.35	4.43	4.13	4.28	6.17	3.94	2.18
Debt to Equity	0.42	0.45	0.47	0.57	0.54	0.56	0.01	0.40
Price Range	54.50-31.39	56.25-31.39	56.25-26.82	28.53-11.12	49.69-24.75	67.78-28.00	57.56-12.25	13.31-4.25
P/E Ratio	28.84-16.61	35.38-19.74	42.94-20.47	...	66.25-33.00	50.21-20.74	48.37-10.29	...

Address: 233 Kansas Street, El Segundo, CA 90245
Telephone: (310) 726 8000
Fax: (310) 322 3332

Web Site: www.irf.com
Officers: Eric Lidow - Chmn. Alexander Lidow - C.E.O.

Auditors: PricewaterhouseCoopers LLP
Investor Contact: 310-726-8512
Transfer Agents: Mellon Investor Services, South Hackensack, NJ

INTERNATIONAL STEEL GROUP INC

Exchange	Symbol	Price	52Wk Range	Yield	P/E
NYS	ISG	$39.50 (3/31/2005)	41.92-26.42	N/A	3.95

*7 Year Price Score N/A ***NYSE Composite Index=100 *12 Month Price Score 108.01**

Interim Earnings (Per Share)

Qtr.	Mar	Jun	Sep	Dec
2003	(0.03)	(0.37)	(0.24)	(0.60)
2004	0.68	0.92	2.51	5.84

Interim Dividends (Per Share)

No Dividends Paid

Valuation Analysis

Forecast P/E	N/A	No of Institutions
Market Cap	$3.9 Billion	Shares
Book Value	2.0 Billion	58,189,552
Price/Book	1.96	% Held
Price/Sales	0.44	58.17

TRADING VOLUME (thousand shares)

Business Summary: Metal Works (MIC: 11.3 SIC: 312 NAIC: 31111)

International Steel Group is an integrated steel producer in North America. Co. has annual raw steel production capabilities of about 23 million net tons and ships a variety of steel products from 13 major steel producing and finishing facilities in eight states. Co. operates principally in one segment of business, carbon steel, and substantially all of its operations are in the United States. Co.'s principal products include a range of hot-rolled, cold-rolled and coated sheets, tin mill products, carbon and alloy plates, wire rod, rail products and semi-finished shapes to serve the automotive, construction, pipe and tube, appliance, container and machinery markets.

Recent Developments: For the year ended Dec 31 2004, net income was $1,027,400 thousand versus net loss of $23,500 thousand a year earlier. Revenues were $9,015,900 thousand, up 121.5% from $4,070,000 thousand the year before. Operating income was $815,300 thousand versus an income of $3,500 thousand in the prior year, an increase of 23194.3%. Total direct expense was $7,827,900 thousand versus $3,836,900 thousand in the prior year, an increase of 104.0%. Total indirect expense was $389,700 thousand versus $229,600 thousand in the prior year, an increase of 69.7%.

Prospects: Co. is experiencing fairly good underlying demand across most market segments. Meanwhile, Co. noted that customer inventories in early 2005 are at relatively high levels, especially at service centers. However, the inventories continue to be consumed. First-quarter 2005 shipments are expected to be about 4.0 million tons, while average sales per ton shipped is expected to increase modestly. Costs per ton shipped in the first quarter should be about the same as in the fourth quarter of 2004, reflecting the absence of any major equipment outages planned during the quarter. In addition, Co. anticipates lower natural gas and scrap costs will be offset by higher prices for iron ore and coal.

Financial Data

(US$ in Thousands)	12/31/2004	12/31/2003	12/31/2002
Earnings Per Share	9.99	(1.26)	0.99
Cash Flow Per Share	7.02	3.75	...
Tang Book Value Per Share	20.16	9.74	4.37
Income Statement			
Total Revenue	9,015,900	4,070,000	933,100
EBITDA	884,800	28,600	125,000
Depn & Amortn	129,100	76,000	11,000
Income Before Taxes	755,700	(47,400)	114,000
Income Taxes	(271,700)	(23,900)	45,900
Net Income	1,027,400	(23,500)	68,100
Average Shares	103,000	77,100	68,900
Balance Sheet			
Current Assets	2,930,500	1,707,400	394,300
Total Assets	4,488,600	2,635,000	668,100
Current Liabilities	1,381,000	831,500	234,100
Long-Term Obligations	806,800	575,500	68,400
Total Liabilities	2,484,500	1,685,800	363,900
Stockholders' Equity	2,004,100	949,200	304,200
Shares Outstanding	99,394	97,470	69,663
Statistical Record			
Return on Assets %	28.77	N.M.	...
Return on Equity %	69.39	N.M.	...
EBITDA Margin %	9.81	0.70	13.40
Net Margin %	11.40	N.M.	7.30
Asset Turnover	2.52	2.46	...
Current Ratio	2.12	2.05	1.68
Debt to Equity	0.40	0.61	0.22
Price Range	43.10-26.42	41.55-35.20	...
P/E Ratio	4.31-2.64	...	...

Address: 4020 Kinross Lakes Parkway, Richfield , OH 44286-9000 **Telephone:** (330) 659-9100	**Web Site:** www.intlsteel.com **Officers:** Wilbur L. Ross - Chmn. Rodney B. Mott - Pres., C.E.O.	**Auditors:** KPMG LLP **Transfer Agents:** Registrar and Transfer Company, Cranford , NJ

INTERPUBLIC GROUP OF COS., INC.

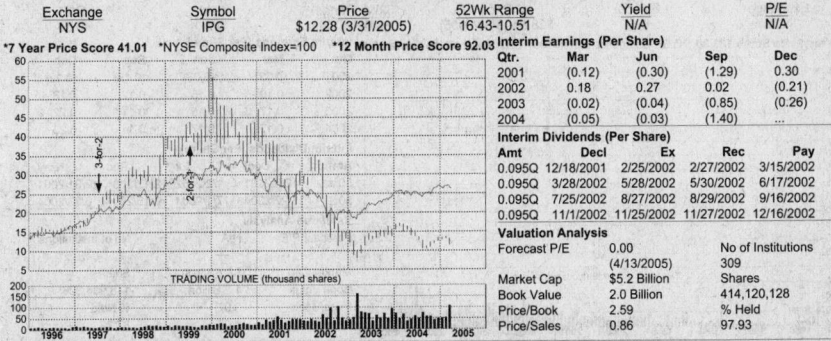

Exchange	Symbol	Price	52Wk Range	Yield	P/E
NYS	IPG	$12.28 (3/31/2005)	16.43-10.51	N/A	N/A

*7 Year Price Score 41.01 ***NYSE Composite Index=100** ***12 Month Price Score 92.03**

Interim Earnings (Per Share)

Qtr.	Mar	Jun	Sep	Dec
2001	(0.12)	(0.30)	(1.29)	0.30
2002	0.18	0.27	0.02	(0.21)
2003	(0.02)	(0.04)	(0.85)	(0.26)
2004	(0.05)	(0.03)	(1.40)	...

Interim Dividends (Per Share)

Amt	Decl	Ex	Rec	Pay
0.095Q	12/18/2001	2/25/2002	2/27/2002	3/15/2002
0.095Q	3/28/2002	5/28/2002	5/30/2002	6/17/2002
0.095Q	7/25/2002	8/27/2002	8/29/2002	9/16/2002
0.095Q	11/1/2002	11/25/2002	11/27/2002	12/16/2002

Valuation Analysis

Forecast P/E	0.00	No of Institutions
	(4/13/2005)	309
Market Cap	$5.2 Billion	Shares
Book Value	2.0 Billion	414,120,128
Price/Book	2.59	% Held
Price/Sales	0.86	97.93

Business Summary: Advertising, Marketing & PR (MIC: 12.4 SIC: 311 NAIC: 41810)

Interpublic Group of Companies is a large organization of advertising agencies and marketing services companies. Its four global operating groups are McCann-Erickson WorldGroup, The Partnership, FCB Group, and Interpublic Sports and Entertainment Group. Major global brands include Draft, Foote, Cone & Belding Worldwide, Golin/Harris International, Initiative Media, Jack Morton Worldwide, Lowe & Partners Worldwide, McCann-Erickson, Octagon, Universal McCann, and Weber Shandwick Worldwide. Co. also offers advertising agency services through association arrangements with local agencies in various parts of the world.

Recent Developments: For the quarter ended Sep 30 2004, loss from continuing operations amounted to $584.9 million versus a loss of $416.2 million in the year-earlier quarter. Net loss amounted to $578.4 million versus a net loss of $327.1 million in the year-earlier quarter. Revenues were $1,508.8 million, up 6.3% from $1,418.9 million the year before. Operating loss was $420.2 million versus a loss of $171.1 million in the prior-year quarter.

Prospects: Co.'s outlook is mixed. On one hand, organic growth should continue to benefit from efforts to promote collaborative, business-building activity. During the first nine months of 2004, Co. generated an additional 215 active projects, representing an anticipated $154.0 million in annualized revenue, of which $67.7 million has already been realized. However, these positive developments may continue to be adversely affected by ongoing restructuring efforts and higher costs. Looking ahead, Co. will continue to focus on making progress in organic growth and other turnaround metrics. Co. is confident that it will be able to achieve its turnaround objectives by mid-2006.

Financial Data

(US$ in Thousands)	9 Mos	6 Mos	3 Mos	12/31/2003	12/31/2002	12/31/2001	12/31/2000	12/31/1999
Earnings Per Share	(1.74)	(1.18)	(1.20)	(1.17)	0.26	(1.37)	1.15	1.11
Cash Flow Per Share	1.20	1.02	1.06	1.30	2.32	0.40	0.99	2.02
Dividends Per Share	...	...	...	...	0.380	0.380	0.370	0.330
Dividend Payout %	...	...	...	...	146.15	...	32.17	29.73
Income Statement								
Total Revenue	4,448,000	2,939,200	1,395,100	5,863,400	6,203,600	6,726,800	5,625,845	4,427,303
EBITDA	(232,900)	167,400	48,600	142,800	681,700	48,500	1,066,558	867,418
Depn & Amortn	173,500	119,100	61,100	277,900	300,500	451,200	299,541	215,939
Income Before Taxes	(492,500)	(9,100)	(41,900)	(269,000)	265,400	(524,300)	657,906	585,057
Income Taxes	105,200	6,600	(26,800)	254,000	140,300	(43,900)	273,034	236,339
Net Income	(600,700)	(22,300)	(16,900)	(451,700)	99,500	(505,300)	358,658	321,921
Average Shares	415,400	414,600	413,300	385,500	381,300	369,000	312,653	289,548
Balance Sheet								
Current Assets	6,737,200	7,127,300	6,747,200	7,349,700	6,322,300	6,467,200	6,026,053	5,767,844
Total Assets	11,202,300	12,156,200	11,700,500	12,234,500	11,793,700	11,514,700	10,238,222	8,727,255
Current Liabilities	6,171,200	6,597,700	6,138,900	6,624,500	7,089,800	6,433,900	6,106,080	5,636,929
Long-Term Obligations	2,188,900	2,189,300	2,190,600	2,191,700	1,817,700	2,480,600	1,505,061	867,262
Total Liabilities	9,200,500	9,593,800	9,133,400	9,628,600	9,693,700	9,535,400	8,191,866	7,099,184
Stockholders' Equity	2,001,800	2,562,400	2,567,100	2,605,900	2,100,000	1,979,300	2,046,356	1,628,071
Shares Outstanding	422,400	422,000	417,900	418,100	386,200	378,500	314,672	287,567
Statistical Record								
Return on Assets %	N.M.	N.M.	N.M.	N.M.	0.85	N.M.	3.77	4.11
Return on Equity %	N.M.	N.M.	N.M.	N.M.	4.88	N.M.	19.47	22.25
EBITDA Margin %	N.M.	5.70	3.48	2.44	10.99	0.72	18.96	19.59
Net Margin %	N.M.	N.M.	N.M.	N.M.	1.60	N.M.	6.38	7.27
Asset Turnover	0.54	0.49	0.50	0.49	0.53	0.62	0.59	0.57
Current Ratio	1.09	1.08	1.10	1.11	0.89	1.01	0.99	1.02
Debt to Equity	1.09	0.85	0.85	0.84	0.87	1.25	0.74	0.53
Price Range	17.19-10.51	17.19-12.94	17.19-9.30	16.41-8.01	34.89-11.25	47.19-19.30	57.69-33.06	58.06-34.59
P/E Ratio	...	...	...	...	134.19-43.27	...	50.16-28.75	52.31-31.17
Average Yield %	...	...	...	...	1.62	1.20	0.88	0.81

Address: 1271 Avenue of the Americas, New York, NY 10020 **Telephone:** (212) 399-8000 **Fax:** (212) 399-8130	**Web Site:** www.interpublic.com **Officers:** David A. Bell - Chmn., Pres., C.E.O. Christopher Coughlin - Exec. V.P., C.F.O., C.O.O.	**Auditors:** PricewaterhouseCoopers LLP **Investor Contact:** 212-399-8208

IRON MOUNTAIN INC (PA) (NEW)

Exchange	Symbol	Price	52Wk Range	Yield	P/E
NYS	IRM	$28.84 (3/31/2005)	35.05-27.02	N/A	40.06

*7 Year Price Score 133.30 ***NYSE Composite Index=100** ***12 Month Price Score 86.44**

Interim Earnings (Per Share)

Qtr.	Mar	Jun	Sep	Dec
2001	0.03	(0.08)	(0.18)	(0.12)
2002	0.10	0.15	0.12	0.13
2003	0.17	0.15	0.11	0.22
2004	0.17	0.17	0.14	0.23

Interim Dividends (Per Share)

Amt	Decl	Ex	Rec	Pay
50%	12/5/2001	1/2/2002	12/17/2001	12/31/2001
50%	5/27/2004	7/1/2004	6/15/2004	6/30/2004

Valuation Analysis

Forecast P/E	N/A	No of Institutions	
Market Cap	$3.7 Billion	Shares	
Book Value	1.2 Billion		113,936,336
Price/Book	3.07	% Held	
Price/Sales	2.06		87.72

TRADING VOLUME (thousand shares)

Business Summary: Road Transport (MIC: 15.2 SIC: 225 NAIC: 93110)

Iron Mountain provides records and information management and related services. Customers include commercial, legal, banking, healthcare, accounting, insurance, entertainment and government organizations. Co.'s records management business provides storage for all major media, digital archiving services, secure shredding services and specialized services for vital records, film and sound and regulated industries. Co.'s data protection services include: disaster preparedness planning support, secure off-site vaulting of data backup media, electronic vaulting for on-line data backup and recovery and intellectual property escrow services to protect and manage proprietary information.

Recent Developments: For the year ended Dec 31 2004, net income increased 11.3% to $94,191 thousand from net income of $84,637 thousand a year earlier. Revenues were $1,817,589 thousand, up 21.1% from $1,501,329 thousand the year before. Operating income was $344,496 thousand versus an income of $304,893 thousand in the prior year, an increase of 13.0%. Total direct expense was $823,899 thousand versus $680,747 thousand in the prior year, an increase of 21.0%. Total indirect expense was $649,194 thousand versus $515,689 thousand in the prior year, an increase of 25.9%.

Prospects: For the quarter ending Mar 31 2005, Co. is forecasting revenues to be in the range of $485.0 million to $495.0 million, with operating income of between $78.0 million and $85.0 million. First quarter depreciation and amortization spending is expected to be approximately $45.0 million. For the year ending Dec 31 2005, Co. is projecting revenues to be in the range of $1.95 billion to $2.02 billion, with operating income of between $341.0 million and $360.0 million. Full-year 2005 depreciation and amortization spending is expected to be between $179.0 million and $185.0 million. Capital expenditures for the year are expected to be in the range of $220.0 million to $250.0 million.

Financial Data

(US$ in Thousands)	12/31/2004	12/31/2003	12/31/2002	12/31/2001	12/31/2000	12/31/1999	12/31/1998	12/31/1997
Earnings Per Share	0.72	0.65	0.45	(0.35)	(0.23)	(0.19)	(0.18)	(0.31)
Cash Flow Per Share	2.36	2.26	2.01	1.28	1.31	0.74	0.65	0.42
Income Statement								
Total Revenue	1,817,589	1,501,329	1,318,497	1,171,116	986,371	519,549	270,300	183,517
EBITDA	519,759	442,029	371,342	285,132	229,348	131,669	72,357	50,122
Depn & Amortn	167,275	134,572	114,761	158,521	129,405	67,403	37,165	22,597
Income Before Taxes	166,735	156,989	119,949	(8,131)	(18,032)	9,841	(7,672)	(1,737)
Income Taxes	69,574	66,730	49,295	26,036	9,125	10,579	3,318	7,424
Net Income	94,191	84,637	58,292	(44,057)	(27,825)	(14,219)	(10,990)	(15,197)
Average Shares	131,176	130,077	129,106	125,499	119,531	75,026	62,388	49,691
Balance Sheet								
Current Assets	501,154	471,583	367,040	309,317	236,668	143,664	51,962	32,189
Total Assets	4,442,387	3,892,099	3,230,655	2,859,906	2,659,096	1,317,212	666,458	394,713
Current Liabilities	515,463	584,745	427,902	359,009	314,053	150,348	68,109	45,095
Long-Term Obligations	2,438,587	1,974,147	1,662,365	1,460,843	1,314,342	603,057	514,352	277,767
Total Liabilities	3,223,819	2,825,985	2,285,794	1,973,947	1,734,638	828,458	603,363	335,390
Stockholders' Equity	1,218,568	1,066,114	944,861	885,959	924,458	488,754	63,095	59,323
Shares Outstanding	129,817	128,362	127,574	126,441	124,379	79,800	63,249	61,174
Statistical Record								
Return on Assets %	2.25	2.38	1.91	N.M.	N.M.	N.M.	N.M.	N.M.
Return on Equity %	8.22	8.42	6.37	N.M.	N.M.	N.M.	N.M.	N.M.
EBITDA Margin %	28.60	29.44	28.16	24.35	23.25	25.34	26.77	27.31
Net Margin %	5.18	5.64	4.42	N.M.	N.M.	N.M.	N.M.	N.M.
Asset Turnover	0.43	0.42	0.43	0.42	0.49	0.52	0.51	0.58
Current Ratio	0.97	0.81	0.86	0.86	0.75	0.96	0.76	0.71
Debt to Equity	2.00	1.85	1.76	1.65	1.42	1.23	8.15	4.68
Price Range	35.05-26.14	26.87-20.70	22.37-14.29	20.28-14.67	17.47-12.97	17.47-11.31	16.03-9.48	11.70-6.89
P/E Ratio	48.68-36.31	41.34-31.85	49.70-31.75	...	...	...	...	...

Address: 745 Atlantic Ave., Boston, MA 02111	Web Site: www.ironmountain.com	Auditors: DELOITTE & TOUCHE LLP
Telephone: (617) 535-4766	Officers: C. Richard Reese - Chmn., Pres., C.E.O. John F. Kenny Jr. - Exec. V.P., C.F.O.	Investor Contact: 617-535-4799
Fax: (617) 350-7881		

IRWIN FINANCIAL CORP. (COLUMBUS, IN)

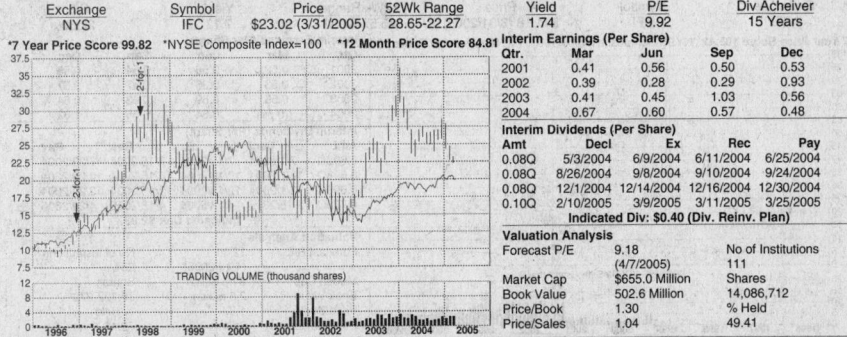

Exchange	Symbol	Price	52Wk Range	Yield	P/E	Div Acheiver
NYS	IFC	$23.02 (3/31/2005)	28.65-22.27	1.74	9.92	15 Years

*7 Year Price Score 99.82 ***NYSE Composite Index=100** ***12 Month Price Score 84.81**

Interim Earnings (Per Share)

Qtr.	Mar	Jun	Sep	Dec
2001	0.41	0.56	0.50	0.53
2002	0.39	0.28	0.29	0.93
2003	0.41	0.45	1.03	0.56
2004	0.67	0.60	0.57	0.48

Interim Dividends (Per Share)

Amt	Decl	Ex	Rec	Pay
0.08Q	5/3/2004	6/9/2004	6/11/2004	6/25/2004
0.08Q	8/26/2004	9/8/2004	9/10/2004	9/24/2004
0.08Q	12/1/2004	12/14/2004	12/16/2004	12/30/2004
0.10Q	2/10/2005	3/9/2005	3/11/2005	3/25/2005

Indicated Div: $0.40 (Div. Reinv. Plan)

Valuation Analysis

Forecast P/E	9.18	No of Institutions
	(4/7/2005)	111
Market Cap	$655.0 Million	Shares
Book Value	502.6 Million	14,086,712
Price/Book	1.30	% Held
Price/Sales	1.04	49.41

TRADING VOLUME (thousand shares)

Business Summary: Commercial Banking (MIC: 8.1 SIC: 022 NAIC: 22110)

Irwin Financial is a diversified financial services company with $4.99 billion in assets at Dec 31 2003. Co.'s major lines of business are: mortgage banking, commercial banking, home equity lending, commercial finance and venture capital. Direct and indirect major subsidiaries include Irwin Union Bank and Trust, a commercial bank, which together with Irwin Union Bank, F.S.B., a federal savings bank, conduct Co.'s commercial banking activities; Irwin Mortgage Corporation, a mortgage banking company; Irwin Home Equity Corporation, a consumer home equity lending company; Irwin Commercial Finance Corporation, a commercial finance subsidiary; and IrwinVentures LLC, a venture capital company.

Recent Developments: For the year ended Dec 31 2004, net income decreased 4.0% to $69,904,000 from net income of $72,817,000 a year earlier. Net interest income was $252,078,000, down 7.3% from $271,885,000 the year before. Provision for loan losses was $14,195,000 versus $47,583,000 in the prior year, a decrease of 70.2%. Non-interest income fell 6.2% to $287,050,000, while non-interest expense declined 1.2% to $407,235,000.

Prospects: Top-line results are being hampered by lower revenues from Co.'s mortgage banking operations, reflecting a combination of lower earning assets, reduced gains on secondary market activities, and lower net recovery of mortgage servicing impairment. Looking ahead, Co. expects long-term interest rate increases during 2005 will help boost the value of its mortgage servicing assets. This anticipated increase in servicing values, coupled with portfolio growth and stable credit quality, should help drive earnings growth in 2005. However, Co. noted that if interest rates do not rise in the near term, it expects that net income will fall significantly below expectations for the first quarter of 2005.

Financial Data
(US$ in Thousands)

	12/31/2004	12/31/2003	12/31/2002	12/31/2001	12/31/2000	12/31/1999	12/31/1998	12/31/1997
Earnings Per Share	2.32	2.45	1.89	2.00	1.67	1.51	1.38	1.08
Cash Flow Per Share	0.55	21.38	(24.11)	(12.84)	(4.87)	21.38	(18.60)	(4.17)
Tang Book Value Per Share	17.67	15.36	12.98	10.84	8.97	7.55	6.70	5.82
Dividends Per Share	0.320	0.280	0.270	0.260	0.240	0.200	0.160	0.140
Dividend Payout %	13.79	11.43	14.29	13.00	14.37	13.25	11.59	13.02
Income Statement								
Interest Income	344,303	370,984	311,442	268,233	184,530	126,613	122,386	99,441
Interest Expense	92,225	99,099	97,795	121,084	93,534	54,794	59,202	44,582
Net Interest Income	252,078	271,885	213,647	147,149	90,996	71,819	63,184	54,859
Provision for Losses	14,195	47,583	43,996	17,505	5,403	4,443	5,995	6,238
Non-Interest Income	287,050	329,299	257,433	271,391	211,711	204,069	243,729	174,564
Non-Interest Expense	407,235	435,199	340,853	327,420	237,962	214,111	245,436	176,534
Income Before Taxes	117,698	118,402	86,231	73,615	59,342	57,334	55,482	46,652
Income Taxes	47,794	45,585	33,398	28,624	23,676	19,481	20,354	17,734
Net Income	69,904	72,817	53,328	45,516	...	37,853	35,128	28,918
Average Shares	31,278	30,850	29,675	24,173	21,593	21,886	22,139	22,722
Balance Sheet								
Net Loans & Leases	3,405,997	3,096,769	2,764,340	2,115,464	1,221,793	724,869	547,103	602,281
Total Assets	5,239,341	4,988,359	4,884,722	3,439,795	2,422,429	1,680,847	1,946,179	1,496,794
Total Deposits	3,395,263	2,899,662	2,694,344	2,309,018	1,443,330	870,318	1,009,211	719,596
Total Liabilities	4,736,697	4,556,099	4,523,311	3,207,472	2,232,504	1,473,480	1,752,947	1,320,884
Stockholders' Equity	502,644	432,260	360,555	232,323	189,925	159,296	145,233	127,983
Shares Outstanding	28,452	28,134	27,771	21,305	21,025	21,104	21,672	22,000
Statistical Record								
Return on Assets %	1.36	1.48	1.28	1.55	...	2.09	2.04	2.07
Return on Equity %	14.91	18.37	17.99	21.56	...	24.86	25.71	23.43
Net Interest Margin %	73.21	73.29	68.60	54.86	49.31	56.72	51.63	55.17
Efficiency Ratio %	64.50	62.15	59.92	60.68	60.05	64.75	67.04	64.43
Loans to Deposits	1.00	1.07	1.03	0.92	0.85	0.83	0.54	0.84
Price Range	35.95-23.20	31.99-16.10	20.36-13.90	27.50-14.51	21.38-13.50	28.31-17.81	36.00-20.13	21.50-12.34
P/E Ratio	15.50-10.00	13.06-6.57	10.77-7.35	13.75-7.25	12.80-8.08	18.75-11.80	26.09-14.58	19.91-11.43
Average Yield %	1.18	1.20	1.58	1.22	1.52	0.90	0.60	0.88

Address: 500 Washington Street,	Web Site: www.irwinfinancial.com	Auditors: PricewaterhouseCoopers LLP
Columbus, IN 47201	Officers: William I. Miller - Chmn., C.E.O. Thomas	Investor Contact: 812-376-1020
Telephone: (812) 376 1909	D. Washburn - Exec. V.P.	Transfer Agents: Mellon Investor
Fax: (812) 376 1709		Services, LLC, Ridgefield Park, NJ

ISTAR FINANCIAL INC

Exchange	Symbol	Price	52Wk Range	Yield	P/E
NYS	SFI	$41.18 (3/31/2005)	45.57-34.50	7.12	22.50

*7 Year Price Score 105.12 *NYSE Composite Index=100 *12 Month Price Score 96.82

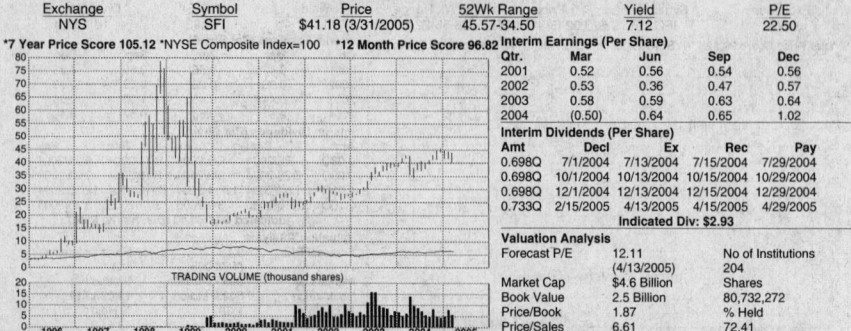

Interim Earnings (Per Share)

Qtr.	Mar	Jun	Sep	Dec
2001	0.52	0.56	0.54	0.56
2002	0.53	0.36	0.47	0.57
2003	0.58	0.59	0.63	0.64
2004	(0.50)	0.64	0.65	1.02

Interim Dividends (Per Share)

Amt	Decl	Ex	Rec	Pay
0.698Q	7/1/2004	7/13/2004	7/15/2004	7/29/2004
0.698Q	10/1/2004	10/13/2004	10/15/2004	10/29/2004
0.698Q	12/1/2004	12/13/2004	12/15/2004	12/29/2004
0.733Q	2/15/2005	4/13/2005	4/15/2005	4/29/2005
		Indicated Div: $2.93		

Valuation Analysis

Forecast P/E	12.11	No of Institutions
	(4/13/2005)	204
Market Cap	$4.6 Billion	Shares
Book Value	2.5 Billion	80,732,272
Price/Book	1.87	% Held
Price/Sales	6.61	72.41

Business Summary: Property, Real Estate & Development (MIC: 8.3 SIC: 798 NAIC: 25930)

iStar Financial is a publicly traded finance company focused on the commercial real estate industry. Co. provides custom-tailored financing to high-end private and corporate owners of real estate, including senior and junior mortgage debt, senior and mezzanine corporate capital, and corporate net lease financing. Co., which is taxed as a real estate investment trust ("REIT"), seeks to deliver strong dividends and superior risk-adjusted returns on equity to shareholders by providing innovative and value added financing solutions to its customers.

Recent Developments: For the year ended Dec 31 2004, income from continuing operations decreased 24.9% to $198,953 thousand from income of $264,817 thousand a year earlier. Net income decreased 10.9% to $260,447 thousand from net income of $292,157 thousand a year earlier. Revenues were $694,424 thousand, up 21.2% from $573,111 thousand the year before. Total costs and expenses jumped 63.8% to $497,664 thousand from $303,761 thousand in 2003.

Prospects: On Mar 3 2005, Co. announced that it has completed the acquisition of Falcon Financial Investment Trust for an aggregate purchase price of approximately $120.0 million. The acquisition expands Co.'s current investment activities in AutoStar, which is the first of what Co. expects to be a series of iStar-branded platforms that deliver customized on-balance sheet approach to financing underserved and real estate-intensive businesses. Looking ahead, Co. expects diluted earnings per share of $2.25 to $2.60, based on expected net asset growth of $3.00 billion in 2005.

Financial Data
(US$ in Thousands)

	12/31/2004	12/31/2003	12/31/2002	12/31/2001	12/31/2000	12/31/1999	12/31/1998	12/31/1997
Earnings Per Share	1.83	2.43	1.93	2.19	2.10	0.25	1.36	0.00
Cash Flow Per Share	3.29	3.37	3.88	3.07	2.25	2.12	1.32	...
Tang Book Value Per Share	22.03	22.53	20.64	20.46	20.86	21.20	18.52	0.14
Dividends Per Share	2.790	2.650	2.520	2.450	2.400	1.860	1.140	...
Dividend Payout %	152.46	109.05	130.57	111.87	114.29	744.00	83.82	...
Income Statement								
Interest Income	353,799	304,394	255,631	254,119	268,011	209,848	112,914	896
Interest Expense	231,027	194,999	185,375	170,121	173,891	91,184	44,697	...
Net Interest Income	122,772	109,395	70,256	83,998	94,120	118,664	68,217	...
Non-Interest Income	340,625	302,155	270,093	230,057	203,811	54,949	15,182	991
Non-Interest Expense	253,546	121,943	118,273	83,168	82,393	134,686	23,442	461
Net Income	260,447	292,157	215,270	229,912	217,586	38,886	59,903	11
Average Shares	112,464	104,101	92,649	88,234	86,151	60,393	43,460	...
Balance Sheet								
Net Loans & Leases	3,788,340	3,393,635	...	...	...	...	...	...
Total Assets	7,220,237	6,660,590	5,611,697	4,378,560	4,034,775	3,813,552	2,059,616	13,441
Total Liabilities	4,745,749	4,240,256	3,583,816	2,588,132	2,240,666	2,009,644	1,088,888	1,915
Stockholders' Equity	2,455,242	2,415,228	2,025,300	1,787,778	1,787,885	1,801,343	970,728	6,351
Shares Outstanding	111,432	107,215	98,114	87,387	85,726	84,985	52,407	45,300
Statistical Record								
Return on Assets %	3.74	4.76	4.31	5.47	5.53	1.32	5.78	...
Return on Equity %	10.67	13.16	11.29	12.86	12.09	2.81	12.26	...
Net Interest Margin %	34.70	35.94	27.48	33.05	35.12	56.55	60.42	...
Efficiency Ratio %	36.51	20.10	22.50	17.18	17.46	50.86	18.30	24.43
Price Range	45.57-34.50	40.00-27.05	31.45-24.59	28.46-19.19	22.44-16.63	74.58-16.69	78.75-25.76	36.06-9.20
P/E Ratio	24.90-18.85	16.46-11.13	16.30-12.74	13.00-8.76	10.68-7.92	298.32-66.75	57.90-18.94	N.M.
Average Yield %	6.91	7.75	8.99	9.82	12.40	4.73	2.71	...

Address: 1114 Avenue of the Americas, 27th Floor, New York, NY 10036 **Telephone:** (212) 930-9400 **Fax:** (212) 930-9494	**Web Site:** www.istarfinancial.com **Officers:** Jay Sugarman - Chmn., C.E.O. Jay S. Nydick - Pres.	**Auditors:** PricewaterhouseCoopers LLP **Transfer Agents:** Equiserve, Inc., Jersey City, NJ

ITT EDUCATIONAL SERVICES, INC.

Exchange	Symbol	Price	52Wk Range	Yield	P/E
NYS	ESI	$48.50 (3/31/2005)	50.90-30.88	N/A	30.12

*7 Year Price Score 154.50 ***NYSE Composite Index=100** ***12 Month Price Score 110.73**

Interim Earnings (Per Share)

Qtr.	Mar	Jun	Sep	Dec
2001	0.10	0.11	0.19	0.31
2002	0.14	0.15	0.26	0.40
2003	0.19	0.21	0.34	0.52
2004	0.19	0.30	0.39	0.72

Interim Dividends (Per Share)

Amt	Decl	Ex	Rec	Pay
100%	5/13/2002	6/6/2002	5/28/2002	6/5/2002

Valuation Analysis

Forecast P/E	21.24 (4/7/2005)	No of Institutions 183
Market Cap	$2.2 Billion	Shares
Book Value	235.1 Million	46,722,068
Price/Book	9.49	% Held
Price/Sales	3.61	N/A

Business Summary: Schools and Universities (MIC: 6.1 SIC: 222 NAIC: 11210)

ITT Educational Services is a provider of technology-oriented post-secondary degree programs in the U.S. As of Dec 31 2004, Co. operated 77 institutes in 30 states. Co. designs its education programs, after consultation with employers, to help graduates prepare for careers in various fields involving their areas of study. As of Dec 31 2004, Co. offered 17 degree programs and several diploma programs in various fields of study to more than 40,000 students. All of Co.'s institutes offers programs involving information technology, electronics technology and drafting and design. Fifty institutes offer a program involving business, and forty institutes offer a program involving criminal justice.

Recent Developments: For the year ended Dec 31 2004, net income increased 27.9% to $75,263 thousand from net income of $58,858 thousand a year earlier. Revenues were $617,834 thousand, up 18.2% from $522,856 thousand the year before. Operating income was $119,548 thousand versus an income of $94,521 thousand in the prior year, an increase of 26.5%. Total direct expense was $298,747 thousand versus $280,006 thousand in the prior year, an increase of 6.7%. Total indirect expense was $199,539 thousand versus $148,329 thousand in the prior year, an increase of 34.5%.

Prospects: Co. is performing well, supported by strong demand for its new bachelor degree programs in business and criminal justice. During the fourth quarter, 39 ITT Technical Institutes started classes in one or more of the new bachelor degree programs in Business Administration, Business Accounting Technology and Criminal Justice. Meanwhile, two new ITT Technical Institutes opened in the fourth quarter of 2004 in Kansas City, MS and Kennesaw, GA. In addition, Co. closed two ITT Technical Institutes in California. Co. noted it plans to open up to four new ITT Technical Institutes and as many as four additional learning sites in 2005.

Financial Data (US$ in Thousands)	12/31/2004	12/31/2003	12/31/2002	12/31/2001	12/31/2000	12/31/1999	12/31/1998	12/31/1997
Earnings Per Share	1.61	1.27	0.94	0.70	0.51	0.47	0.26	0.35
Cash Flow Per Share	2.97	3.37	2.77	1.00	1.18	1.13	(0.12)	0.26
Tang Book Value Per Share	5.11	3.22	1.97	1.69	1.38	1.17	1.89	1.63
Income Statement								
Total Revenue	617,834	522,856	464,946	410,551	347,524	316,370	291,375	261,664
EBITDA	141,631	117,706	89,426	70,133	56,234	47,907	27,918	34,162
Depn & Amortn	18,249	21,190	21,117	18,527	14,519	11,150	9,282	7,939
Income Before Taxes	123,382	96,516	70,993	54,314	44,422	39,153	23,965	31,788
Income Taxes	48,119	37,658	27,139	20,600	16,937	14,802	10,024	12,665
Net Income	75,263	58,858	43,854	33,714	24,709	23,528	13,941	19,123
Average Shares	46,808	46,280	46,793	48,216	48,370	50,760	54,372	54,210
Balance Sheet								
Current Assets	372,781	256,646	173,266	134,210	92,570	89,082	138,758	112,958
Total Assets	493,389	363,270	247,707	195,399	150,896	131,002	175,571	145,914
Current Liabilities	233,101	202,337	142,495	108,393	79,926	68,622	70,241	55,946
Total Liabilities	258,315	217,146	158,683	117,211	86,210	73,231	73,715	58,099
Stockholders' Equity	235,074	146,124	89,024	78,188	64,686	57,771	101,856	87,815
Shares Outstanding	45,993	45,430	45,082	46,320	46,993	49,230	54,022	54,000
Statistical Record								
Return on Assets %	17.52	19.27	19.79	19.47	17.48	15.35	8.67	13.58
Return on Equity %	39.38	50.06	52.45	47.19	40.25	29.48	14.70	24.44
EBITDA Margin %	22.92	22.51	19.23	17.08	16.18	15.14	9.58	13.06
Net Margin %	12.18	11.26	9.43	8.21	7.11	7.44	4.78	7.31
Asset Turnover	1.44	1.71	2.10	2.37	2.46	2.06	1.81	1.86
Current Ratio	1.60	1.27	1.22	1.24	1.16	1.30	1.98	2.02
Price Range	59.46-28.29	56.03-23.26	26.25-14.50	22.70-9.28	14.09-6.00	20.06-7.53	17.84-10.69	13.50-9.69
P/E Ratio	36.93-17.57	44.12-18.31	27.92-15.43	32.43-13.26	27.63-11.76	42.69-16.02	68.63-41.11	38.57-27.68

Address: 13000 North Meridian Street, Carmel, IN 46032-1404
Telephone: (317) 706-9200
Fax: (317) 594-4382

Web Site: www.itt-tech.edu
Officers: Rene R. Champagne - Chmn., C.E.O. Kevin M. Modany - Sr. V.P., C.F.O.

Auditors: PricewaterhouseCoopers LLP

ITT INDUSTRIES INC.

Exchange	Symbol	Price	52Wk Range	Yield	P/E
NYS	ITT	$90.24 (3/31/2005)	91.56-75.57	0.80	19.70

*7 Year Price Score 134.93 *NYSE Composite Index=100 ***12 Month Price Score 100.57**

Interim Earnings (Per Share)

Qtr.	Mar	Jun	Sep	Dec
2001	0.65	0.84	0.75	0.81
2002	0.77	0.99	1.28	1.01
2003	0.92	1.06	1.16	1.15
2004	0.94	1.18	1.16	1.29

Interim Dividends (Per Share)

Amt	Decl	Ex	Rec	Pay
0.17Q	5/11/2004	5/19/2004	5/21/2004	7/1/2004
0.17Q	7/13/2004	8/25/2004	8/27/2004	10/1/2004
0.17Q	10/5/2004	11/17/2004	11/19/2004	1/1/2005
0.18Q	2/8/2005	3/9/2005	3/11/2005	4/1/2005

Indicated Div: $0.72

Valuation Analysis

Forecast P/E	17.64	No of Institutions	
	(4/7/2005)	356	
Market Cap	$8.3 Billion	Shares	
Book Value	2.3 Billion	74,550,416	
Price/Book	3.55	% Held	
Price/Sales	1.23	80.79	

Business Summary: Automotive (MIC: 15.1 SIC: 594 NAIC: 33996)

ITT Industries operates in four business segments. Fluid Technology provides fluid systems and products for the water, wastewater, treatment, Industrial and other markets. Defense Electronics & Services serves military and government agencies with products such as air traffic control systems, jamming devices, digital combat radios and night vision devices. Motion & Flow Control produces engineered valves and switches, products, fluid handling materials and specialty shock absorbers and friction materials. Electronic Components consist of products and services for communications, industrial, medical, transportation, military/aerospace, commercial aircraft, computer, and consumer uses.

Recent Developments: For the year ended Dec 31 2004, income from continuing operations increased 11.0% to $437,500 thousand from income of $394,000 thousand a year earlier. Net income increased 7.0% to $432,300 thousand from net income of $403,900 thousand a year earlier. Revenues were $6,764,100 thousand, up 20.6% from $5,610,800 thousand the year before. Operating income was $634,900 thousand versus an income of $533,200 thousand in the prior year, an increase of 19.1%. Total direct expense was $5,100,400 thousand versus $4,230,300 thousand in the prior year, an increase of 20.6%. Total indirect expense was $1,028,800 thousand versus $847,300 thousand in the prior year, an increase of 21.4%.

Prospects: Co.'s outlook is solid, due largely to the momentum being generated by its ITT Management System, which includes its Value-Based Six Sigma initiative. Co. noted that it has begun taking additional steps, ranging from the realignment of its infrastructure to global sourcing, all in an effort to ensure that its costs are in line to achieve its stated earnings target of $7.00 to $8.00 per share by 2008. Beyond its planned Value-Based Six Sigma savings initiative, Co.'s goal is to reduce costs by an additional $25.0 million per year. For full-year 2005, Co. is targeting revenue in the range of $7.15 billion to $7.43 billion, with earnings per share between $5.00 and $5.15.

Financial Data
(US$ in Thousands)

	12/31/2004	12/31/2003	12/31/2002	12/31/2001	12/31/2000	12/31/1999	12/31/1998	12/31/1997
Earnings Per Share	4.58	4.29	4.06	3.05	2.94	2.53	13.55	0.89
Cash Flow Per Share	5.71	6.25	6.54	5.41	4.70	3.85	1.67	6.61
Tang Book Value Per Share	N.M.	1.56	N.M.	N.M.	N.M.	N.M.	4.53	N.M.
Dividends Per Share	0.680	0.640	0.600	0.600	0.600	0.600	0.600	0.600
Dividend Payout %	14.85	14.92	14.78	19.67	20.41	23.72	4.43	67.42
Income Statement								
Total Revenue	6,764,100	5,626,600	4,985,300	4,675,700	4,829,400	4,632,200	4,492,700	8,777,100
EBITDA	836,500	708,600	712,600	608,300	696,900	635,600	161,400	756,000
Depn & Amortn	198,600	188,000	171,400	212,900	201,800	181,100	195,600	436,400
Income Before Taxes	610,000	530,700	508,800	333,400	419,900	369,700	(160,000)	186,400
Income Taxes	172,500	139,800	128,900	116,700	155,400	136,800	(62,400)	72,700
Net Income	432,300	403,900	379,900	276,700	264,500	232,900	1,532,500	108,100
Average Shares	94,400	94,100	93,600	90,600	90,000	92,000	113,100	121,000
Balance Sheet								
Current Assets	2,329,200	2,105,500	1,700,500	1,458,800	1,506,300	1,628,300	2,382,400	2,377,400
Total Assets	7,276,700	5,937,600	5,389,600	4,508,400	4,611,400	4,529,800	5,048,800	6,220,500
Current Liabilities	2,445,800	1,686,600	1,730,200	1,896,600	2,232,700	2,110,400	2,150,800	3,544,900
Long-Term Obligations	542,800	460,900	492,200	456,400	408,400	478,800	515,500	532,200
Total Liabilities	4,933,700	4,089,900	4,252,300	3,132,600	3,400,200	3,430,700	3,748,800	5,398,200
Stockholders' Equity	2,343,000	1,847,700	1,137,300	1,375,800	1,211,200	1,099,100	1,300,000	822,300
Shares Outstanding	92,289	92,271	91,824	88,786	87,915	88,000	96,000	118,400
Statistical Record								
Return on Assets %	6.53	7.13	7.68	6.07	5.77	4.86	27.20	1.85
Return on Equity %	20.58	27.06	30.23	21.39	22.83	19.42	144.42	13.33
EBITDA Margin %	12.37	12.59	14.29	13.01	14.43	13.72	3.59	8.61
Net Margin %	6.39	7.18	7.62	5.92	5.48	5.03	34.11	1.23
Asset Turnover	1.02	0.99	1.01	1.03	1.05	0.97	0.80	1.50
Current Ratio	0.95	1.25	0.98	0.77	0.67	0.77	1.11	0.67
Debt to Equity	0.23	0.25	0.43	0.33	0.34	0.44	0.40	0.65
Price Range	86.40-71.32	74.21-50.68	70.60-47.25	51.30-36.60	39.13-23.25	41.50-31.31	40.13-28.44	33.25-22.25
P/E Ratio	18.86-15.57	17.30-11.81	17.39-11.64	16.82-12.00	13.31-7.91	16.40-12.38	2.96-2.10	37.36-25.00
Average Yield %	0.86	1.03	0.96	1.35	1.89	1.63	1.71	2.16

Address: 4 West Red Oak Lane, White Plains, NY 10604 **Telephone:** (914) 641-2000 **Fax:** (914) 696-2950	**Web Site:** www.itt.com **Officers:** Steven R. Loranger - Chmn., Pres., C.E.O. Edward W. Williams - Sr. V.P., C.F.O.	**Auditors:** Deloitte & Touche LLP **Investor Contact:** 914-641-2000 **Transfer Agents:** Bank of New York, New York, NY

JPMORGAN CHASE & CO.

Exchange	Symbol	Price	52Wk Range	Yield	P/E
NYS	JPM	$34.60 (3/31/2005)	42.26-34.58	3.93	22.32

*7 Year Price Score 79.82   *NYSE Composite Index=100   *12 Month Price Score 89.50

Interim Earnings (Per Share)

Qtr.	Mar	Jun	Sep	Dec
2001	0.58	0.18	0.22	(0.17)
2002	0.48	0.50	0.01	(0.20)
2003	0.69	0.89	0.78	0.89
2004	0.92	(0.27)	0.39	0.49

Interim Dividends (Per Share)

Amt	Decl	Ex	Rec	Pay
0.34Q	4/20/2004	7/1/2004	7/6/2004	7/31/2004
0.34Q	9/21/2004	10/4/2004	10/6/2004	10/31/2004
0.34Q	12/14/2004	1/4/2005	1/6/2005	1/31/2005
0.34Q	3/15/2005	4/4/2005	4/6/2005	4/30/2005

Indicated Div: $1.36

Valuation Analysis

Forecast P/E	11.53	No of Institutions
	(4/7/2005)	1115
Market Cap	$123.0 Billion	Shares
Book Value	105.7 Billion	2,287,544,320
Price/Book	1.16	% Held
Price/Sales	2.16	64.37

Business Summary: Commercial Banking (MIC: 8.1 SIC: 021 NAIC: 22110)

JPMorgan Chase & Company is a global financial services firm with assets of $770.91 billion at Dec 31 2003. Co. conducts investment banking, financial services for consumers and businesses, financial transaction processing, investment management, private banking and private equity. Co.'s activities are organized into five major business franchises: Investment Bank, Treasury and Securities Services, Investment Management & Private Banking, JPMorgan Partners and Retail and Middle Market Financial Services. Co. is a global financial services firm with operations in over 50 countries.

Recent Developments: For the year ended Dec 31 2004, net income decreased 33.5% to $4,466 million from net income of $6,719 million a year earlier. Net interest income was $16,761 million, up 29.3% from $12,965 million the year before. Provision for loan losses was $2,544 million versus $1,540 million in the prior year, an increase of 65.2%. Non-interest income rose 29.0% to $26,336 million, while non-interest expense advanced 57.6% to $32,835 million.

Prospects: On Jan 7 2005, Co. announced that it has signed an agreement with Vastera, a provider of global trade management solutions, whereby Vastera will be acquired by and combined with the Logistics and Trade Services businesses of its Treasury Services unit. Under the agreement, Vastera shareholders will receive $3.00 for each outstanding share of Vastera common stock they own, for a total transaction value of approximately $129.0 million. Completion of the merger is subject to Vastera shareholder and various banking and other customary regulatory approvals. Vastera's solutions automate the required trade management processes associated with the physical movement of goods internationally.

Financial Data

(US$ in Thousands)	12/31/2004	12/31/2003	12/31/2002	12/31/2001	12/31/2000	12/31/1999	12/31/1998	12/31/1997
Earnings Per Share	1.55	3.24	0.80	0.80	2.86	4.18	2.83	2.68
Cash Flow Per Share	(7.82)	7.27	(12.67)	(1.58)	(7.24)	(2.72)	2.83	4.29
Tang Book Value Per Share	13.34	14.76	14.21	12.54	12.96	18.29	17.93	15.84
Dividends Per Share	1.360	1.360	1.360	1.340	1.233	1.060	0.927	0.807
Dividend Payout %	87.74	41.98	170.00	167.50	43.12	25.36	32.78	30.14
Income Statement								
Interest Income	30,595,000	23,444,000	25,284,000	32,181,000	36,643,000	20,237,000	22,289,000	21,756,000
Interest Expense	13,834,000	11,107,000	13,758,000	21,379,000	27,131,000	11,493,000	13,723,000	13,598,000
Net Interest Income	16,761,000	12,337,000	11,526,000	10,802,000	9,512,000	8,744,000	8,566,000	8,158,000
Provision for Losses	2,544,000	1,540,000	4,331,000	3,185,000	1,377,000	1,621,000	1,343,000	804,000
Non-Interest Income	26,336,000	20,919,000	18,088,000	18,248,000	23,422,000	13,473,000	10,090,000	8,625,000
Non-Interest Expense	34,359,000	21,688,000	22,764,000	23,299,000	22,824,000	12,221,000	11,383,000	10,069,000
Income Before Taxes	6,194,000	10,028,000	2,519,000	2,566,000	8,733,000	8,375,000	5,930,000	5,910,000
Income Taxes	1,728,000	3,309,000	856,000	847,000	3,006,000	2,929,000	2,148,000	2,202,000
Net Income	4,466,000	6,719,000	1,663,000	1,694,000	5,727,000	5,446,000	3,782,000	3,708,000
Average Shares	2,850,600	2,055,000	2,009,000	1,972,400	1,969,000	1,285,500	1,303,950	1,317,600
Balance Sheet								
Net Loans & Leases	394,794,000	214,995,000	211,014,000	212,920,000	212,385,000	172,702,000	169,202,000	164,830,000
Total Assets	1,157,248,000	770,912,000	758,800,000	693,575,000	715,348,000	406,105,000	365,875,000	365,521,000
Total Deposits	521,456,000	326,492,000	304,753,000	293,650,000	279,365,000	241,745,000	212,437,000	193,688,000
Total Liabilities	1,051,595,000	724,758,000	716,494,000	651,926,000	672,460,000	381,938,000	341,487,000	343,229,000
Stockholders' Equity	105,653,000	46,154,000	42,306,000	41,099,000	42,338,000	23,617,000	23,838,000	21,742,000
Shares Outstanding	3,556,191	2,042,620	1,998,706	1,973,400	1,928,490	1,240,756	1,271,850	1,262,892
Statistical Record								
Return on Assets %	0.46	0.88	0.23	0.24	1.02	1.41	1.03	1.06
Return on Equity %	5.87	15.19	3.99	4.06	17.32	22.95	16.59	17.35
Net Interest Margin %	54.78	52.62	45.59	33.57	25.96	43.21	38.43	37.50
Efficiency Ratio %	60.35	48.89	52.49	46.20	38.00	36.25	35.16	33.14
Loans to Deposits	0.76	0.66	0.69	0.73	0.76	0.71	0.80	0.85
Price Range	43.01-35.19	37.30-20.75	39.14-15.45	55.98-30.82	65.67-36.88	59.29-44.33	51.33-26.83	42.13-28.46
P/E Ratio	27.75-22.70	11.51-6.40	48.92-19.31	69.97-38.52	22.96-12.89	14.18-10.61	18.14-9.48	15.72-10.62
Average Yield %	3.52	4.35	4.71	3.10	2.50	2.00	2.23	2.32

Address: 270 Park Avenue, New York, NY 10017
Telephone: (212) 270 6000
Fax: (212) 270 1648

Web Site: www.jpmorganchase.com
Officers: William B. Harrison Jr. - Chmn., C.E.O. Dina Dublon - Exec. V.P., C.F.O.

Auditors: PricewaterhouseCoopers LLP
Investor Contact: 212-270-7318

JABIL CIRCUIT, INC.

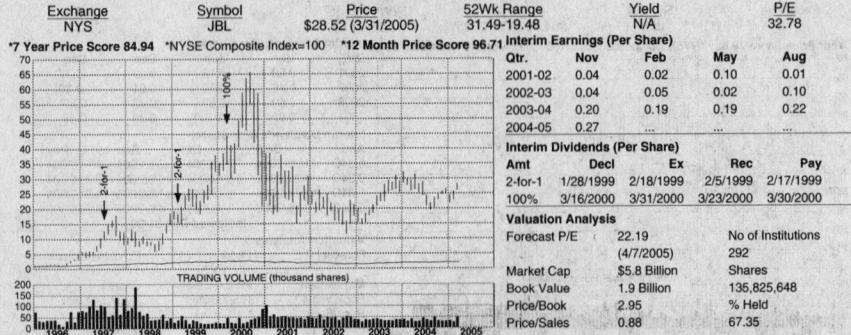

Exchange	Symbol	Price	52Wk Range	Yield	P/E
NYS	JBL	$28.52 (3/31/2005)	31.49-19.48	N/A	32.78

*7 Year Price Score 84.94 *NYSE Composite Index=100 *12 Month Price Score 96.71

Interim Earnings (Per Share)

Qtr.	Nov	Feb	May	Aug
2001-02	0.04	0.02	0.10	0.01
2002-03	0.04	0.05	0.02	0.10
2003-04	0.20	0.19	0.19	0.22
2004-05	0.27	...	...	...

Interim Dividends (Per Share)

Amt	Decl	Ex	Rec	Pay
2-for-1	1/28/1999	2/18/1999	2/5/1999	2/17/1999
100%	3/16/2000	3/31/2000	3/23/2000	3/30/2000

Valuation Analysis

Forecast P/E	22.19	No of Institutions	
	(4/7/2005)	292	
Market Cap	$5.8 Billion	Shares	
Book Value	1.9 Billion	135,825,648	
Price/Book	2.95	% Held	
Price/Sales	0.88	67.35	

Business Summary: Electrical (MIC: 11.14 SIC: 672 NAIC: 34412)

Jabil Circuit designs and manufactures electronic circuit board assemblies and systems for original equipment manufacturers in the automotive, computing and storage, consumer products, instrumentation and medical, networking, peripherals and telecommunications industries. Co. serves its customers with dedicated work cell business units that are capable of providing customers with varying combinations of services. Services include integrated design and engineering; component selection, sourcing and procurement; automated assembly; design and implementation of product testing; parallel global production; systems assembly and direct order fulfillment; and repair and warranty.

Recent Developments: For the quarter ended Nov 30 2004, net income increased 31.6% to $55,915 thousand from net income of $42,496 thousand in the year-earlier quarter. Revenues were $1,833,375 thousand, up 21.5% from $1,508,994 thousand the year before. Operating income was $70,305 thousand versus an income of $53,036 thousand in the prior-year quarter, an increase of 32.6%. Total direct expense was $1,678,517 thousand versus $1,375,545 thousand in the prior-year quarter, an increase of 22.0%. Total indirect expense was $84,553 thousand versus $80,413 thousand in the prior-year quarter, an increase of 5.1%.

Prospects: On Mar 11 2005, Co. announced that it has completed the acquisition of the electronics manufacturing business of Varian, Inc. for approximately $195.0 million. The acquisition will allow Co. to continue to grow and expand its focus on the medical, military/aerospace and instrumentation business sectors. The transaction should be accretive to earnings during fiscal year 2005. Co. expects fiscal 2005 growth in revenue and earnings per share of approximately 20.0% and 25.0%. For fiscal 2005, Co. anticipates net revenue of approximately $7.50 billion and earnings in the range of $1.09 to $1.11 per diluted share.

Financial Data

(US$ in Thousands)	3 Mos	08/31/2004	08/31/2003	08/31/2002	08/31/2001	08/31/2000	08/31/1999	08/31/1998
Earnings Per Share	0.87	0.81	0.21	0.17	0.59	0.78	0.56	0.37
Cash Flow Per Share	1.99	2.25	1.33	2.81	0.95	0.20	0.69	0.66
Tang Book Value Per Share	7.87	7.29	6.06	6.63	6.43	6.68	3.32	1.67
Income Statement								
Total Revenue	1,833,375	6,252,897	4,729,482	3,545,466	4,330,655	3,558,321	2,000,346	1,277,374
EBITDA	124,317	431,354	271,523	236,363	319,162	312,253	197,207	120,806
Depn & Amortn	54,012	221,709	224,470	188,313	155,400	99,337	55,978	35,702
Income Before Taxes	66,784	197,513	36,954	44,756	166,148	212,696	139,537	81,980
Income Taxes	10,869	30,613	(6,053)	10,041	47,631	67,048	48,063	25,047
Net Income	55,915	166,900	43,007	34,715	118,517	145,648	91,474	56,933
Average Shares	205,843	205,849	202,103	200,782	202,223	187,448	163,656	154,302
Balance Sheet								
Current Assets	2,579,471	2,182,675	2,093,947	1,588,344	1,446,798	1,387,270	587,900	290,379
Total Assets	3,775,176	3,329,356	3,244,745	2,547,906	2,357,578	2,018,192	920,651	526,703
Current Liabilities	1,480,223	1,159,084	1,263,218	593,382	504,775	691,975	330,797	186,719
Long-Term Obligations	294,993	305,194	297,018	354,668	361,667	25,000	33,333	81,667
Total Liabilities	1,826,987	1,510,016	1,656,269	1,040,940	943,502	748,009	374,819	278,337
Stockholders' Equity	1,948,189	1,819,340	1,588,476	1,506,966	1,414,076	1,270,183	545,832	248,366
Shares Outstanding	201,685	201,298	199,345	197,950	196,871	190,250	164,454	149,072
Statistical Record								
Return on Assets %	4.93	5.06	1.48	1.42	5.42	9.88	12.64	12.21
Return on Equity %	9.96	9.77	2.78	2.38	8.83	16.00	23.04	26.49
EBITDA Margin %	6.78	6.90	5.74	6.67	7.37	8.78	9.86	9.46
Net Margin %	3.05	2.67	0.91	0.98	2.74	4.09	4.57	4.46
Asset Turnover	1.80	1.90	1.63	1.45	1.98	2.00	2.76	2.74
Current Ratio	1.74	1.88	1.66	2.68	2.87	2.00	1.78	1.56
Debt to Equity	0.15	0.17	0.19	0.24	0.26	0.02	0.06	0.33
Price Range	32.35-19.48	32.35-19.48	28.15-11.53	30.71-14.96	65.84-18.12	63.78-22.00	26.88-5.88	17.88-5.88
P/E Ratio	37.18-22.39	39.94-24.05	134.05-54.90	180.65-88.00	111.60-30.71	81.77-28.21	47.99-10.49	48.31-15.88

Address: 10560 Dr. Martin Luther King, Jr. Street North, St. Petersburg, FL 33716 Telephone: (727) 577-9749 Fax: (727) 579-8529	Web Site: www.jabil.com Officers: William D. Morean - Chmn. Thomas A. Sansone - Vice-Chmn.	Auditors: KPMG LLP Investor Contact: 727-803-3349

JACOBS ENGINEERING GROUP, INC.

Exchange	Symbol	Price	52Wk Range	Yield	P/E
NYS	JEC	$51.92 (3/31/2005)	56.40-37.21	N/A	23.49

*7 Year Price Score 125.76 ***NYSE Composite Index=100** ***12 Month Price Score 113.57**

Interim Earnings (Per Share)

Qtr.	Dec	Mar	Jun	Sep
2001-02	0.47	0.49	0.50	0.52
2002-03	0.54	0.56	0.58	0.59
2003-04	0.59	0.61	0.52	0.53
2004-05	0.56	...	...	...

Interim Dividends (Per Share)

Amt	Decl	Ex	Rec	Pay
100%	2/12/2002	4/2/2002	3/1/2002	4/1/2002

Valuation Analysis

Forecast P/E	20.26	No of Institutions	
	(4/7/2005)	259	
Market Cap	$2.9 Billion	Shares	
Book Value	1.0 Billion	46,241,864	
Price/Book	2.83	% Held	
Price/Sales	0.62	81.32	

Business Summary: Construction - Public Infrastructure (MIC: 3.1 SIC: 629 NAIC: 36210)

Jacobs Engineering Group is a professional services firm in the United States. Co.'s business focuses on providing a range of technical, professional, and construction services to a number of industrial, commercial, and governmental clients around the world. Co. provides project services (which include engineering, design, architectural, and similar services); process, scientific, and systems consulting services; operations and maintenance services; and, construction services (which include direct-hire construction and construction management services). Co. provides its services through offices and subsidiaries located in North America, Europe, Asia, and Australia.

Recent Developments: For the quarter ended Dec 31 2004, net income decreased 3.8% to $32,530 thousand from net income of $33,800 thousand in the year-earlier quarter. Revenues were $1,283,300 thousand, up 13.1% from $1,135,129 thousand the year before. Operating income was $52,719 thousand versus an income of $52,418 thousand in the prior-year quarter, an increase of 0.6%. Total direct expense was $1,094,562 thousand versus $972,867 thousand in the prior-year quarter, an increase of 12.5%. Total indirect expense was $136,019 thousand versus $109,844 thousand in the prior-year quarter, an increase of 23.8%.

Prospects: Co. is enjoying positive earnings momentum. Co. is particularly pleased with the growth in its backlog during the quarter, which includes important wins from clients in the oil and gas, refining, and federal programs markets. Co.'s backlog at Dec 31 2004 totaled $8.00 billion, including a technical professional services component of $4.50 billion. This compares to total backlog and technical professional services backlog of $7.10 billion and $3.50 billion, respectively, at Dec 31 2003. Given this backlog level, Co. reaffirmed its earnings guidance in the range of $2.40 to $2.70 per share for fiscal 2005, and in the range of $0.58 to $0.63 per share for the second quarter.

Financial Data

(US$ in Thousands)	3 Mos	09/30/2004	09/30/2003	09/30/2002	09/30/2001	09/30/2000	09/30/1999	09/30/1998
Earnings Per Share	2.21	2.25	2.27	1.98	1.61	0.96	1.24	1.04
Cash Flow Per Share	1.95	1.56	2.68	2.97	0.28	1.55	1.58	1.76
Tang Book Value Per Share	8.66	7.20	7.99	5.45	5.10	4.29	3.89	5.74
Income Statement								
Total Revenue	1,283,300	4,594,235	4,615,601	4,555,661	3,956,993	3,418,942	2,875,007	2,101,145
EBITDA	63,374	233,078	234,185	208,978	185,145	128,879	141,844	109,027
Depn & Amortn	11,460	34,154	35,350	35,087	38,952	40,098	31,586	22,979
Income Before Taxes	50,829	198,424	196,939	168,754	138,206	81,322	104,522	88,784
Income Taxes	18,299	69,449	68,929	59,064	50,446	30,341	39,077	34,399
Net Income	32,530	128,975	128,010	109,690	87,760	50,981	65,445	54,385
Average Shares	57,950	57,433	56,392	55,396	54,496	52,946	52,956	52,192
Balance Sheet								
Current Assets	1,216,995	1,083,513	970,097	974,903	946,159	851,023	729,620	566,007
Total Assets	2,206,427	2,071,044	1,670,510	1,673,984	1,557,040	1,384,376	1,220,186	807,489
Current Liabilities	759,386	685,914	611,414	740,417	700,659	683,863	584,982	368,348
Long-Term Obligations	112,141	78,758	17,806	85,732	164,308	146,820	135,371	26,221
Total Liabilities	1,167,053	1,066,017	828,427	984,371	965,239	888,833	771,469	436,084
Stockholders' Equity	1,039,374	1,005,027	842,083	689,613	591,801	495,543	448,717	371,405
Shares Outstanding	56,750	56,698	55,836	54,765	53,744	52,772	52,285	51,225
Statistical Record								
Return on Assets %	6.48	6.88	7.65	6.79	5.97	3.90	6.46	7.01
Return on Equity %	13.26	13.93	16.71	17.12	16.14	10.77	15.96	15.63
EBITDA Margin %	4.94	5.07	5.07	4.59	4.68	3.77	4.93	5.19
Net Margin %	2.53	2.81	2.77	2.41	2.22	1.49	2.28	2.59
Asset Turnover	2.41	2.45	2.76	2.82	2.69	2.62	2.84	2.71
Current Ratio	1.60	1.58	1.59	1.32	1.35	1.24	1.25	1.54
Debt to Equity	0.11	0.08	0.02	0.12	0.28	0.30	0.30	0.07
Price Range	48.01-37.21	49.70-37.21	48.46-26.29	42.58-29.20	37.67-19.06	20.16-13.47	21.25-13.63	17.06-12.44
P/E Ratio	21.72-16.84	22.09-16.54	21.36-11.58	21.51-14.75	23.40-11.84	21.00-14.03	17.14-10.99	16.41-11.96

Address: 1111 South Arroyo Parkway, Pasadena, CA 91105 Telephone: (626) 578-3500 Fax: (626) 578-6967	Web Site: www.jacobs.com Officers: Noel G. Watson - Chmn., C.E.O. Craig L. Martin - Pres.	Auditors: Ernst & Young LLP Investor Contact: 818-449-2171

JANUS CAPITAL GROUP INC

*7 Year Price Score N/A   ***NYSE Composite Index=100**   ***12 Month Price Score 88.83**

Interim Earnings (Per Share)

Qtr.	Mar	Jun	Sep	Dec
2001	0.48	0.39	0.11	0.32
2002	0.42	0.30	(0.60)	0.26
2003	0.17	0.21	0.22	3.54
2004	(0.08)	0.56	0.22	0.03

Interim Dividends (Per Share)

Amt	Decl	Ex	Rec	Pay
0.01A	12/5/2001	1/11/2002	1/15/2002	1/31/2002
0.04A	5/9/2002	7/11/2002	7/15/2002	7/31/2002
0.04A	5/12/2003	7/11/2003	7/15/2003	7/31/2003
0.04A	5/13/2004	7/13/2004	7/15/2004	7/30/2004

Indicated Div: $0.04

Valuation Analysis

Forecast P/E	24.86	No of Institutions
	(4/13/2005)	233
Market Cap	$3.3 Billion	Shares
Book Value	2.7 Billion	198,562,992
Price/Book	1.20	% Held
Price/Sales	3.24	85.98

Business Summary: Accounting & Management Consulting Services (MIC: 12.2 SIC: 741 NAIC: 23930)

Janus Capital Group and its consolidated subsidiaries sponsor, market and provide investment advisory, distribution and administrative services primarily to mutual funds in both domestic and international markets. As of Dec 31 2003, Co. managed $151.50 billion in assets across multiple investment disciplines. Co. consists of Janus Capital Management, Enhanced Investment Technologies, Bay Isle Financial and Capital Group Partners. Co. owns 30.0% of Perkins, Wolf, McDonnell and Company, which is a subadvisor for certain Janus value products, and approximately 9.0% of DST Systems.

Recent Developments: For the year ended Dec 31 2004, net income decreased 82.0% to $169,500 thousand from net income of $942,700 thousand a year earlier. Non-interest income fell 23.8% to $1,238,800 thousand, while non-interest expense advanced 8.1% to $901,400 thousand. Total operating expenses climbed 17.9% to $898,900 thousand from $761,600 thousand the year before. Operating income dropped 52.0% to $111,900 thousand from $233,100 thousand in 2003.

Prospects: Co. continues to place emphasis on delivering strong fund performance and stabilizing assets under management. As a result, Co. is pleased with the significant progress it is making on the performance front, as well as the improving trend in its flows. Meanwhile, Co. will look to capitalize on several actions taken in 2004 to improve net flows which include investing in brand advertising, expanding its distribution efforts by adding seasonal sales professionals. Co. remains confident that these measures benefit net flows in 2005. Separately, Co. recently introduced to new diversified mutual funds, including the Janus Triton Fund and Janus Research Fund.

Financial Data
(US$ in Thousands)

	12/31/2004	12/31/2003	12/31/2002	12/31/2001	12/31/2000	12/31/1999
Earnings Per Share	0.73	4.14	0.38	1.31	2.90	1.38
Cash Flow Per Share	(0.04)	1.14	1.27	2.28	3.28	...
Tang Book Value Per Share	1.43	1.00	N.M.	1.46	4.04	...
Dividends Per Share	0.040	0.040	0.050	0.040	0.010	...
Dividend Payout %	5.48	0.97	13.16	3.05	0.34	...
Income Statement						
Total Revenue	1,010,800	994,700	1,144,800	1,555,700	2,248,100	1,212,300
Income Before Taxes	265,600	894,600	319,500	620,000	1,202,400	586,500
Income Taxes	92,200	(65,400)	231,800	217,700	427,000	216,100
Net Income	169,500	949,900	84,700	302,300	663,700	313,100
Average Shares	231,900	229,500	224,200	224,424	225,423	223,000
Balance Sheet						
Total Assets	3,767,600	4,332,200	3,321,700	3,391,600	1,581,000	...
Total Liabilities	1,028,000	1,667,900	1,810,200	2,005,000	449,900	...
Stockholders' Equity	2,734,500	2,661,200	1,508,000	1,363,300	1,057,800	...
Shares Outstanding	234,436	239,200	222,544	222,101	218,909	...
Statistical Record						
Return on Assets %	4.17	24.82	2.52	12.16	...	...
Return on Equity %	6.27	45.57	5.90	24.97	...	...
Price Range	17.70-12.73	18.55-9.86	28.91-9.08	46.00-18.55	53.94-32.50	...
P/E Ratio	24.25-17.44	4.48-2.38	76.08-23.89	35.11-14.16	18.60-11.21	...
Average Yield %	0.26	0.28	0.27	0.13	0.02	...

Address: 100 Fillmore Street, Denver, CO 64105	**Web Site:** www.janus.com	**Auditors:** Deloitte & Touche LLP
Telephone: (303) 333-3863	**Officers:** Landon H. Rowland - Chmn., Pres., C.E.O.	**Investor Contact:** 303-394-7311
	Mark B. Whiston - Vice-Chmn., Pres., C.E.O.	

JEFFERIES GROUP, INC. (NEW)

Exchange	Symbol	Price	52Wk Range	Yield	P/E
NYS	JEF	$37.68 (3/31/2005)	42.93-28.38	1.27	18.93

*7 Year Price Score N/A   ***NYSE Composite Index=100**   ***12 Month Price Score 99.72**

TRADING VOLUME (thousand shares)

Interim Earnings (Per Share)

Qtr.	Mar	Jun	Sep	Dec
2001	0.32	0.33	0.20	0.30
2002	0.33	0.32	0.22	0.28
2003	0.25	0.32	0.35	0.50
2004	0.51	0.50	0.51	...

Interim Dividends (Per Share)

Amt	Decl	Ex	Rec	Pay
0.08Q	4/12/2004	5/12/2004	5/14/2004	6/15/2004
0.10Q	7/13/2004	8/12/2004	8/16/2004	9/15/2004
0.10Q	10/19/2004	11/10/2004	11/15/2004	12/15/2004
0.12Q	1/20/2005	2/11/2005	2/15/2005	3/15/2005

Indicated Div: $0.48

Valuation Analysis

Forecast P/E	18.71	No of Institutions
	(4/13/2005)	154
Market Cap	$2.1 Billion	Shares
Book Value	968.1 Million	32,676,316
Price/Book	2.21	% Held
Price/Sales	1.87	57.15

Business Summary: Finance Intermediaries & Services (MIC: 8.7 SIC: 211 NAIC: 23110)

Jefferies Group and its subsidiaries operate as a full-service investment bank and institutional securities firm focused on the middle market. Co. offers financial advisory, capital raising, mergers and acquisitions, and restructuring services to small and mid-cap companies and provides trade execution in equity, high yield, convertible and international securities, as well as research and asset management capabilities, to institutional investors. Co. also offers correspondent clearing, prime brokerage, private client services and securities lending services.

Recent Developments: For the quarter ended Dec 31 2004, net income advanced 56.2% to $131,366 thousand from net income of $84,051 thousand in the previous year. Revenues were $1,198,639 thousand, up 29.3% from $926,716 thousand the year before. Total non-interest expense increased 21.3% to $831,256 thousand versus $685,081 thousand a year earlier. Interest expense jumped 44.5% to $140,394 thousand from $97,102 thousand in 2003.

Prospects: Co.'s near-term outlook is being boosted by its platform growth and diversification. For instance, for the year ended Dec 31 2004, net income jumped 56.3% to $131.4 million versus $84.1 million the year before. Also, asset management fees and investment income from managed funds rocketed 147.7% to $81.2 million versus $32.8 million last year. Further, investment banking revenues leapt 53.7% to $352.8 million compared with $229.6 million the year before. In addition, interest income advanced 31.3% to $134.5 million versus $102.4 million the year before. Also, other revenues grew 25.9% to $13.2 million year over year. Going forward, Co. will continue to investment in its platform.

Financial Data

(US$ in Thousands)	9 Mos	6 Mos	3 Mos	12/31/2003	12/31/2002	12/31/2001	12/31/2000	12/31/1999
Earnings Per Share	1.99	1.86	1.68	1.42	1.14	1.14	1.13	1.27
Cash Flow Per Share	(1.46)	3.67	1.04	2.78	(3.36)	2.32	(0.96)	1.24
Tang Book Value Per Share	15.15	12.96	14.09	13.01	10.65	10.54	9.28	8.26
Dividends Per Share	0.340	0.320	0.265	0.210	0.100	0.100	0.100	0.100
Dividend Payout %	17.05	17.17	15.75	14.79	8.81	8.77	8.85	7.84
Income Statement								
Interest Income	85,132	49,184	24,739	102,403	92,027	131,408	172,124	115,425
Interest Expense	93,206	53,890	24,587	97,102	80,087	114,709	144,460	96,496
Net Interest Income	(8,074)	(4,706)	152	5,301	11,940	16,699	27,664	18,929
Non-Interest Income	788,234	531,080	278,355	824,313	662,749	653,583	589,739	524,722
Non-Interest Expense	609,315	410,479	217,288	685,081	570,997	567,630	522,010	459,556
Income Before Taxes	170,845	115,895	61,219	144,533	103,692	102,652	95,393	84,095
Income Taxes	63,980	42,464	21,257	52,851	41,121	43,113	40,412	35,256
Net Income	95,970	63,695	31,909	84,051	62,571	59,539	54,981	61,727
Average Shares	63,867	63,927	63,078	59,266	55,020	52,264	48,670	47,984
Balance Sheet								
Total Assets	14,084,052	13,058,203	11,045,626	10,992,283	6,898,691	5,344,737	3,957,869	2,896,252
Total Liabilities	13,115,902	12,108,554	10,142,477	10,153,912	6,270,174	4,779,081	3,499,422	2,499,675
Stockholders' Equity	968,150	949,649	903,149	838,371	628,517	565,656	458,447	396,577
Shares Outstanding	56,872	65,043	56,808	56,702	53,904	53,671	49,376	47,999
Statistical Record								
Return on Assets %	1.01	1.03	1.00	0.94	1.02	1.28	1.60	2.21
Return on Equity %	14.84	14.09	13.04	11.46	10.48	11.63	12.83	16.88
Net Interest Margin %	N.M.	N.M.	0.61	5.18	12.97	12.71	16.07	16.40
Efficiency Ratio %	67.84	69.70	71.69	73.93	75.65	72.31	68.52	71.79
Price Range	39.01-28.38	39.01-23.98	39.01-17.98	33.50-16.58	25.55-16.81	21.20-12.95	15.91-9.59	15.03-9.25
P/E Ratio	19.60-14.26	20.97-12.89	23.22-10.70	23.59-11.68	22.41-14.75	18.60-11.36	14.08-8.49	11.84-7.28
Average Yield %	1.02	0.99	0.90	0.82	0.46	0.61	0.82	0.84

Address: 520 Madison Avenue, 12th Floor, New York, NY 10022 **Telephone:** (212) 284 2550 **Fax:** (212) 284-2111	**Web Site:** www.jefco.com **Officers:** Richard B. Handler - Chmn., C.E.O. John C. Shaw Jr. - Pres., C.O.O.	**Auditors:** KPMG LLP **Investor Contact:** 310-444-5618

JEFFERSON-PILOT CORP.

Exchange	Symbol	Price	52Wk Range	Yield	P/E	Div Acheiver
NYS	JP	$49.05 (3/31/2005)	55.89-46.56	3.40	12.51	37 Years

*7 Year Price Score 94.64   ***NYSE Composite Index=100**   ***12 Month Price Score 91.66**

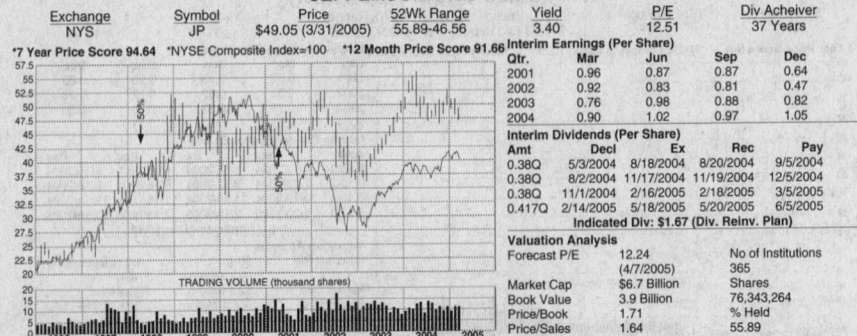

Interim Earnings (Per Share)

Qtr.	Mar	Jun	Sep	Dec
2001	0.96	0.87	0.87	0.64
2002	0.92	0.83	0.81	0.47
2003	0.76	0.98	0.88	0.82
2004	0.90	1.02	0.97	1.05

Interim Dividends (Per Share)

Amt	Decl	Ex	Rec	Pay
0.38Q	5/3/2004	8/18/2004	8/20/2004	9/5/2004
0.38Q	8/2/2004	11/17/2004	11/19/2004	12/5/2004
0.38Q	11/1/2004	2/16/2005	2/18/2005	3/5/2005
0.417Q	2/14/2005	5/18/2005	5/20/2005	6/5/2005

Indicated Div: $1.67 (Div. Reinv. Plan)

Valuation Analysis

Forecast P/E	12.24	No of Institutions	
	(4/7/2005)	365	
Market Cap	$6.7 Billion	Shares	
Book Value	3.9 Billion	76,343,264	
Price/Book	1.71	% Held	
Price/Sales	1.64	55.89	

Business Summary: Insurance (MIC: 8.2 SIC: 311 NAIC: 24113)

Jefferson-Pilot is a holding company that conducts insurance, investment, broadcasting and other business through its subsidiaries. Jefferson-Pilot Life Insurance Company, Jefferson Pilot Financial Insurance Company, and Jefferson Pilot LifeAmerica Insurance Company, together known as Jefferson Pilot Financial, offer full lines of individual and group life insurance products as well as annuity and investment products. As of Dec 31 2003, Jefferson-Pilot Communications Company owned and operated three network television stations and 17 radio stations, and produced and syndicated sports programming.

Recent Developments: For the year ended Dec 31 2004, net income increased 11.0% to $546 million from net income of $492 million a year earlier. Revenues were $4,102 million, up 14.8% from $3,573 million the year before. Net premiums earned were $1,293 million versus $951 million in the prior year, an increase of 36.0%. Net investment income amounted to $1,672 million from $1,657 million a year earlier. Results included realized investment gains of $41 million in 2004 and realized investment losses of $47 million in 2003.

Prospects: Co.'s Annuity and Investment Products segment is experiencing a challenging environment for its life insurance and annuity businesses. Continued low investment yields are having a broad effect on Co.'s business in the form of reduced investment spreads on life and annuity products and above-trend surrenders of some older annuity contracts. Separately, Co.'s Benefit Partners segment continues to build its business profitably through internal growth, and the successful integration of the Canada Life business. Meanwhile, Co. believes its Jefferson-Pilot Communications segment's solid performance continues to demonstrate its ability to conceive and implement profitable strategies.

Financial Data
(US$ in Thousands)

	12/31/2004	12/31/2003	12/31/2002	12/31/2001	12/31/2000	12/31/1999	12/31/1998	12/31/1997
Earnings Per Share	3.92	3.44	3.04	3.34	3.29	2.95	2.61	2.31
Cash Flow Per Share	7.16	3.79	2.91	4.86	3.23	3.05	2.73	4.07
Tang Book Value Per Share	26.47	24.85	22.61	20.53	18.38	15.80	17.77	15.73
Dividends Per Share	1.470	1.293	1.183	1.072	0.960	0.857	0.768	0.693
Dividend Payout %	37.50	37.57	38.90	32.09	29.21	29.07	29.45	30.00
Income Statement								
Premium Income	1,293,000	951,000	1,564,000	1,424,000	1,365,000	903,000	1,049,000	1,135,000
Total Revenue	4,102,000	3,573,000	3,480,000	3,330,000	3,238,000	2,561,000	2,610,000	2,578,000
Benefits & Claims	2,287,000	2,005,000	1,999,000	1,796,000	1,660,000	1,208,000	1,307,000	1,399,000
Income Before Taxes	840,000	738,000	710,000	800,000	814,000	751,000	670,000	591,000
Income Taxes	277,000	246,000	235,000	263,000	277,000	256,000	226,000	195,000
Net Income	546,000	492,000	475,000	538,000	537,000	495,000	444,000	396,000
Average Shares	139,213	142,867	148,222	153,411	155,922	159,348	160,578	160,188
Balance Sheet								
Total Assets	35,105,000	32,696,000	30,609,000	28,996,000	27,321,000	26,446,000	24,338,000	23,131,000
Total Liabilities	31,171,000	28,890,000	26,769,000	25,305,000	23,862,000	23,393,000	20,983,000	20,046,000
Stockholders' Equity	3,934,000	3,806,000	3,540,000	3,391,000	3,159,000	2,753,000	3,052,000	2,732,000
Shares Outstanding	136,819	140,610	142,799	150,007	154,305	155,016	158,844	159,417
Statistical Record								
Return on Assets %	1.61	1.55	1.59	1.91	1.99	1.95	1.87	1.95
Return on Equity %	14.07	13.40	13.71	16.43	18.12	17.05	15.35	15.75
Loss Ratio %	176.88	210.83	127.81	126.12	121.61	133.78	124.59	123.26
Net Margin %	13.31	13.77	13.65	16.16	16.58	19.33	17.01	15.36
Price Range	55.89-46.56	50.65-36.20	52.60-36.53	48.95-39.60	50.29-33.63	52.92-41.21	52.21-32.89	38.47-23.11
P/E Ratio	14.26-11.88	14.72-10.52	17.30-12.02	14.66-11.86	15.29-10.22	17.94-13.97	20.00-12.60	16.65-10.00
Average Yield %	2.91	3.03	2.63	2.37	2.28	1.85	1.74	2.32

Address: 100 North Greene Street, Greensboro, NC 27401 **Telephone:** (336) 691 3000 **Fax:** (336) 691 3938	Web Site: www.jpfinancial.com **Officers:** Dennis R. Glass - Pres., C.E.O. Theresa M. Stone - Exec. V.P., C.F.O.	Auditors: Ernst & Young LLP **Investor Contact:** 336-691-3379 **Transfer Agents:** Wachovia Bank, Charlotte, NC

JOHNSON CONTROLS INC

Exchange	Symbol	Price	52Wk Range	Yield	P/E	Div Acheiver
NYS	JCI	$55.76 (3/31/2005)	63.83-51.16	1.79	13.15	29 Years

*7 Year Price Score 124.95 *NYSE Composite Index=100 *12 Month Price Score 94.63

Interim Earnings (Per Share)

Qtr.	Dec	Mar	Jun	Sep
2001-02	0.64	0.60	0.93	1.01
2002-03	0.74	0.70	1.00	1.16
2003-04	0.86	0.82	1.15	1.41
2004-05	0.87	...	...	...

Interim Dividends (Per Share)

Amt	Decl	Ex	Rec	Pay
0.225Q	5/26/2004	6/9/2004	6/11/2004	6/30/2004
0.225Q	7/28/2004	9/8/2004	9/10/2004	9/30/2004
0.25Q	11/17/2004	12/13/2004	12/15/2004	1/3/2005
0.25Q	1/26/2005	3/9/2005	3/11/2005	3/31/2005

Indicated Div: $1.00 (Div. Reinv. Plan)

Valuation Analysis

Forecast P/E	12.32 (4/7/2005)	No of Institutions	459
Market Cap	$10.7 Billion	Shares	127,150,336
Book Value	5.6 Billion	% Held	66.51
Price/Book	1.91		
Price/Sales	0.39		

Business Summary: Miscellaneous Business Services (MIC: 12.8 SIC: 531 NAIC: 61790)

Johnson Controls provided installed building control systems and technical and facility management services, including comfort, energy and security management for the non-residential buildings market. Co. conducts its business in two operating segments: The Automotive Group which designs and manufactures products and systems for passenger cars and light trucks, including vans and SUVs and the Controls Group which provides installed control systems and technical and facility management services which improve the comfort, fire-safety, security, productivity, energy efficiency, and cost-effectiveness of non-residential buildings.

Recent Developments: For the quarter ended Dec 31 2004, income from continuing operations increased 0.8% to $160,500 thousand from income of $159,200 thousand in the year-earlier quarter. Net income increased 2.4% to $168,400 thousand from net income of $164,500 thousand in the year-earlier quarter. Revenues were $6,975,500 thousand, up 10.8% from the year before. Operating income was $245,400 thousand versus $253,500 thousand in the prior-year quarter, a decrease of 3.2%. Total direct expense was $6,132,700 thousand versus $5,447,300 thousand in the prior-year quarter, an increase of 12.6%. Total indirect expense was $597,400 thousand versus $592,100 thousand in the prior-year quarter, an increase of 0.9%.

Prospects: On Feb 11 2005, Co. announced an agreement to sell its Johnson Controls World Services (JCWS) subsidiary to IAP Worldwide Services based in Irmo, SC. IAP will pay approximately $260.0 million in cash for JCWS, subject to normal adjustments. JCWS had sales of approximately $770.0 million in fiscal 2004. The parties expect to complete the transaction in the next few weeks. JCWS intends to continue to fully support its existing federal projects and accounts throughout the process. Separately, Co. confirmed its outlook for the full year of 2005, including sales growth of 8.0% to 10.0% and double-digit increases in operating and net income.

Financial Data

(US$ in Thousands)	3 Mos	09/30/2004	09/30/2003	09/30/2002	09/30/2001	09/30/2000	09/30/1999	09/30/1998
Earnings Per Share	4.24	4.24	3.60	3.17	2.56	2.54	2.24	1.81
Cash Flow Per Share	7.71	7.91	4.30	5.59	5.60	4.34	5.95	3.30
Tang Book Value Per Share	7.98	5.81	3.80	2.24	3.51	1.82	0.22	N.M.
Dividends Per Share	0.925	0.900	0.720	0.660	0.620	0.560	0.500	0.460
Dividend Payout %	21.81	21.23	20.00	20.79	24.27	22.00	22.32	25.34
Income Statement								
Total Revenue	6,975,500	26,553,400	22,646,000	20,103,400	18,427,200	17,154,600	16,139,400	12,586,800
EBITDA	421,100	1,925,300	1,718,800	1,632,800	1,493,000	1,429,000	1,351,500	1,119,700
Depn & Amortn	164,500	616,400	557,800	516,200	515,900	461,800	445,600	384,200
Income Before Taxes	230,100	1,212,100	1,057,500	1,006,000	867,100	855,700	769,900	616,800
Income Taxes	48,600	315,700	327,800	347,600	335,500	338,900	311,700	256,000
Net Income	168,400	817,500	682,900	600,500	478,300	472,400	419,600	337,700
Average Shares	193,600	192,600	189,200	188,200	186,000	183,800	184,200	183,200
Balance Sheet								
Current Assets	6,856,100	6,376,800	5,620,300	4,946,200	4,544,000	4,277,200	3,848,500	3,404,200
Total Assets	15,676,600	15,090,800	13,127,300	11,165,300	9,911,500	9,428,000	8,614,200	7,942,100
Current Liabilities	6,623,400	6,601,600	5,584,100	4,806,200	4,579,700	4,510,000	4,266,600	4,288,400
Long-Term Obligations	1,668,500	1,630,600	1,776,900	1,826,600	1,394,800	1,315,300	1,283,300	997,500
Total Liabilities	10,095,000	9,884,500	8,866,000	7,665,600	6,926,100	6,851,900	6,344,200	6,000,700
Stockholders' Equity	5,581,600	5,206,300	4,261,300	3,499,700	2,985,400	2,576,100	2,270,000	1,941,400
Shares Outstanding	191,174	190,320	180,310	177,760	174,997	171,978	170,790	169,400
Statistical Record								
Return on Assets %	5.59	5.78	5.62	5.70	4.95	5.22	5.07	4.83
Return on Equity %	16.13	17.22	17.60	18.52	17.20	19.44	19.93	18.61
EBITDA Margin %	6.04	7.25	7.59	8.12	8.10	8.33	8.37	8.90
Net Margin %	2.41	3.08	3.02	2.99	2.60	2.75	2.60	2.68
Asset Turnover	1.84	1.88	1.86	1.91	1.91	1.90	1.95	1.80
Current Ratio	1.04	0.97	1.01	1.03	0.99	0.95	0.90	0.79
Debt to Equity	0.30	0.31	0.42	0.52	0.47	0.51	0.57	0.51
Price Range	63.83-51.16	60.90-47.30	50.34-35.26	46.52-32.75	40.77-23.84	35.19-23.50	37.56-20.97	30.50-21.38
P/E Ratio	15.05-12.07	14.36-11.16	13.98-9.79	14.68-10.33	15.93-9.31	13.85-9.25	16.77-9.36	16.85-11.81
Average Yield %	1.62	1.62	1.71	1.61	1.88	1.99	1.59	1.77

Address: 5757 North Green Bay Avenue, P.O. Box 591, Milwaukee, WI 53201
Telephone: (414) 524-1200
Fax: (414) 524-3200

Web Site: www.johnsoncontrols.com
Officers: John M. Barth - Chmn., Pres., C.E.O. Stephen A. Roell - Exec. V.P., C.F.O.

Auditors: PricewaterhouseCoopers LLP
Investor Contact: 414-524-2363
Transfer Agents: Firstar Trust Company, Milwaukee, WI

JOHNSON & JOHNSON

Exchange	Symbol	Price	52Wk Range	Yield	P/E	Div Achiever
NYS	JNJ	$67.16 (3/31/2005)	68.44-50.52	1.70	23.65	42 Years

*7 Year Price Score 99.76 *NYSE Composite Index=100 *12 Month Price Score 105.27

Interim Earnings (Per Share)

Qtr.	Mar	Jun	Sep	Dec
2001	0.53	0.48	0.49	0.36
2002	0.59	0.54	0.57	0.46
2003	0.69	0.40	0.69	0.62
2004	0.83	0.82	0.78	0.41

Interim Dividends (Per Share)

Amt	Decl	Ex	Rec	Pay
0.285Q	4/22/2004	5/14/2004	5/18/2004	6/8/2004
0.285Q	7/20/2004	8/13/2004	8/17/2004	9/7/2004
0.285Q	10/22/2004	11/12/2004	11/16/2004	12/7/2004
0.285Q	1/4/2005	2/11/2005	2/15/2005	3/8/2005
	Indicated Div: $1.14 (Div. Reinv. Plan)			

Valuation Analysis

Forecast P/E	20.30 (4/7/2005)	No of Institutions	1322
Market Cap	$199.5 Billion	Shares	1,897,025,280
Book Value	31.8 Billion	% Held	63.79
Price/Book	6.27		
Price/Sales	4.21		

Business Summary: Pharmaceuticals (MIC: 9.1 SIC: 834 NAIC: 25412)

Johnson & Johnson is engaged in the manufacture and sale of a broad range of products in the health care field. The Pharmaceutical segment consists of prescription drugs in the antifungal, anti-infective, cardiovascular, dermatology, gastrointestinal, hematology, immunology, neurology, oncology, pain management, psychotropic and urology fields. The Medical Devices and Diagnostics segment includes products used by or under the direction of health care professionals. The Consumer segment manufactures and markets products used in the baby and child care, skin care, oral and wound care and women's health care fields, as well as nutritional and over-the-counter pharmaceutical products.

Recent Developments: For the year ended Jan 2 2005, net income increased 18.2% to $8,509 million from net income of $7,197 million a year earlier. Revenues were $47,348 million, up 13.1% from $41,862 million the year before. Total direct expense was $13,422 million versus $12,176 million in the prior year, an increase of 10.2%. Total indirect expense was $21,081 million versus $19,733 million in the prior year, an increase of 6.8%.

Prospects: On Dec 15 2004, Co. announced that it has entered into a definitive agreement to acquire Guidant, a global company engaged in the treatment of cardiac and vascular disease. While the transaction is projected to close during the third quarter of 2005, it is subject to clearance under the Hart-Scott-Rodino Antitrust Improvements Act, the European Union merger control regulation, and other customary closing conditions. The agreement will also require the approval of Guidant's shareholders. The transaction is valued at an estimated net acquisition cost of $23.90 billion.

Financial Data

(US$ in Thousands)	01/02/2005	12/28/2003	12/29/2002	12/30/2001	12/31/2000	01/02/2000	01/03/1999	12/28/1997
Earnings Per Share	2.84	2.40	2.16	1.84	1.70	1.47	1.12	1.21
Cash Flow Per Share	3.69	3.58	2.73	2.93	2.37	2.05	1.79	1.63
Tang Book Value Per Share	6.72	5.17	4.53	4.97	4.15	3.11	2.37	3.38
Dividends Per Share	1.095	0.925	0.795	0.700	0.620	0.545	0.485	0.425
Dividend Payout %	38.56	38.54	36.81	38.04	36.47	37.07	43.50	35.27
Income Statement								
Total Revenue	47,348,000	41,862,000	36,298,000	33,004,000	29,139,000	27,471,000	23,657,000	22,629,000
EBITDA	14,933,000	12,192,000	10,900,000	9,200,000	7,904,000	7,148,000	5,363,000	5,560,000
Depn & Amortn	2,103,000	1,854,000	1,705,000	1,605,000	1,515,000	1,444,000	1,246,000	1,067,000
Income Before Taxes	12,838,000	10,308,000	9,291,000	7,898,000	6,622,000	5,753,000	4,269,000	4,576,000
Income Taxes	4,329,000	3,111,000	2,694,000	2,230,000	1,822,000	1,586,000	1,210,000	1,273,000
Net Income	8,509,000	7,197,000	6,597,000	5,668,000	4,800,000	4,167,000	3,059,000	3,303,000
Average Shares	3,003,500	3,008,100	3,054,100	3,099,300	2,834,800	2,836,400	2,743,200	2,739,800
Balance Sheet								
Current Assets	27,320,000	22,995,000	19,266,000	18,473,000	15,450,000	13,200,000	11,132,000	10,563,000
Total Assets	53,317,000	48,263,000	40,556,000	38,488,000	31,321,000	29,163,000	26,211,000	21,453,000
Current Liabilities	13,927,000	13,448,000	11,449,000	8,044,000	7,140,000	7,454,000	8,162,000	5,283,000
Long-Term Obligations	2,565,000	2,955,000	2,022,000	2,217,000	2,037,000	2,450,000	1,269,000	1,126,000
Total Liabilities	21,504,000	21,394,000	17,859,000	14,255,000	12,513,000	12,950,000	12,621,000	9,094,000
Stockholders' Equity	31,813,000	26,869,000	22,697,000	24,233,000	18,808,000	16,213,000	13,590,000	12,359,000
Shares Outstanding	2,971,023	2,967,973	2,968,295	3,047,215	2,781,874	2,779,366	2,688,000	2,690,000
Statistical Record								
Return on Assets %	16.48	16.25	16.74	16.28	15.92	15.09	12.63	15.98
Return on Equity %	28.53	29.12	28.19	26.41	27.49	28.04	23.20	28.56
EBITDA Margin %	31.54	29.12	30.03	27.88	27.13	26.02	22.67	24.57
Net Margin %	17.97	17.19	18.17	17.17	16.47	15.17	12.93	14.60
Asset Turnover	0.92	0.95	0.92	0.95	0.97	0.99	0.98	1.09
Current Ratio	1.96	1.71	1.68	2.30	2.16	1.77	1.36	2.00
Debt to Equity	0.08	0.11	0.09	0.09	0.11	0.15	0.09	0.09
Price Range	63.76-49.50	58.67-48.73	65.49-41.85	60.97-41.63	52.53-34.25	53.06-38.50	44.50-32.00	33.47-24.88
P/E Ratio	22.45-17.43	24.45-20.30	30.32-19.38	33.14-22.62	30.90-20.15	36.10-26.19	39.73-28.57	27.66-20.56
Average Yield %	1.96	1.76	1.38	1.35	1.39	1.16	1.29	1.43

Address: One Johnson & Johnson Plaza, New Brunswick, NJ 08933 **Telephone:** (732) 524 0400 **Fax:** (732) 214 0332	**Web Site:** www.jnj.com **Officers:** William C. Weldon - Chmn., C.E.O. Robert J. Darretta - Vice-Chmn., C.F.O.	**Auditors:** PricewaterhouseCoopers LLP **Investor Contact:** 800-950-5089 **Transfer Agents:** EquiServe Trust Company, N.A., Providence, RI

JONES APPAREL GROUP, INC.

*7 Year Price Score 96.91   *NYSE Composite Index=100   *12 Month Price Score 85.45

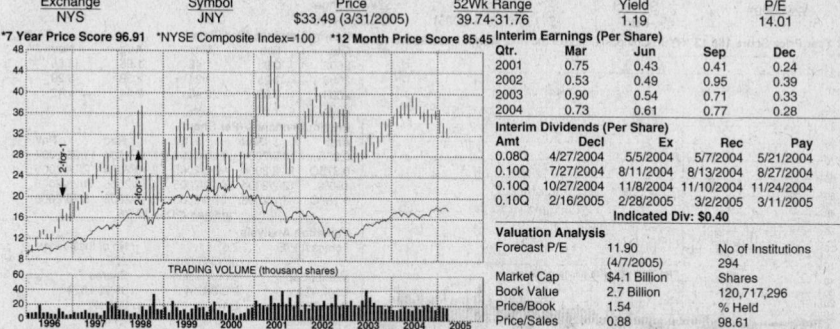

Interim Earnings (Per Share)

Qtr.	Mar	Jun	Sep	Dec
2001	0.75	0.43	0.41	0.24
2002	0.53	0.49	0.95	0.39
2003	0.90	0.54	0.71	0.33
2004	0.73	0.61	0.77	0.28

Interim Dividends (Per Share)

Amt	Decl	Ex	Rec	Pay
0.08Q	4/27/2004	5/5/2004	5/7/2004	5/21/2004
0.10Q	7/27/2004	8/11/2004	8/13/2004	8/27/2004
0.10Q	10/27/2004	11/8/2004	11/10/2004	11/24/2004
0.10Q	2/16/2005	2/28/2005	3/2/2005	3/11/2005

Indicated Div: $0.40

Valuation Analysis

Forecast P/E	11.90	No of Institutions
	(4/7/2005)	294
Market Cap	$4.1 Billion	Shares
Book Value	2.7 Billion	120,717,296
Price/Book	1.54	% Held
Price/Sales	0.88	98.61

Business Summary: Apparel (MIC: 4.4 SIC: 331 NAIC: 15232)

Jones Apparel Group is a designer and marketer of branded apparel, footwear and accessories. Co.'s nationally recognized brands include: Jones New York, Polo Jeans Company licensed from Polo Ralph Lauren Corporation, Evan-Picone, Norton McNaughton, Gloria Vanderbilt, Erika, l.e.i., Energie, Nine West, Easy Spirit, Enzo Angiolini, Bandolino, Napier, Judith Jack, Kasper, Anne Klein, Albert Nipon and LeSuit. Co. also markets costume jewelry under the Tommy Hilfiger brand licensed from Tommy Hilfiger Corporation and the Givenchy brand licensed from Givenchy Corporation, and footwear and accessories under the ESPRIT brand licensed from Esprit Europe, B.V.

Recent Developments: For the year ended Dec 31 2004, net income decreased 8.2% to $301,800 thousand from net income of $328,600 thousand a year earlier. Revenues were $4,649,700 thousand, up 6.3% from $4,375,300 thousand the year before. Operating income was $528,400 thousand versus an income of $579,800 thousand in the prior year, a decrease of 8.9%. Total direct expense was $2,944,400 thousand versus $2,738,600 thousand in the prior year, an increase of 7.5%. Total indirect expense was $1,176,900 thousand versus $1,056,900 thousand in the prior year, an increase of 11.4%.

Prospects: Co. enters 2005 cautiously optimistic that the overall retail environment will improve. For fiscal 2005, Co. is forecasting total revenues in the range of $5.30 billion to $5.35 billion with an operating profit margin in the range of 11.4% to 12.0%. For fiscal 2005, Co. expects earnings per share from $2.75 to $2.90 up from $2.39 per share in 2004. This forecast reflects Co.'s cautious outlook and includes the projected results of Barneys New York, along with the incremental interest expense associated with the $750.0 million senior note financing completed Nov 22 2004. Co. anticipates 2005 full year operating cash flow to be in a range of $450.0 million to $475.0 million.

Financial Data

(US$ in Thousands)	12/31/2004	12/31/2003	12/31/2002	12/31/2001	12/31/2000	12/31/1999	12/31/1998	12/31/1997
Earnings Per Share	2.39	2.48	2.36	1.82	2.48	1.60	1.47	1.13
Cash Flow Per Share	3.73	3.57	5.59	4.56	2.84	2.17	2.21	1.07
Tang Book Value Per Share	N.M.	0.98	0.66	0.03	0.16	N.M.	2.33	3.96
Dividends Per Share	0.360	0.160	...	...	...	...	...	...
Dividend Payout %	15.06	6.45	...	...	...	...	...	...
Income Statement								
Total Revenue	4,649,700	4,375,300	4,340,900	4,073,100	4,142,700	3,150,700	1,685,229	1,387,471
EBITDA	641,200	681,800	680,400	611,800	713,900	453,600	283,081	211,231
Depn & Amortn	109,000	99,500	88,800	131,900	109,300	75,400	21,226	14,594
Income Before Taxes	482,900	527,000	533,500	399,800	503,100	314,600	251,811	194,609
Income Taxes	181,100	198,400	201,200	163,600	201,200	126,200	96,947	72,884
Net Income	301,800	328,600	318,500	236,200	301,900	188,400	154,864	121,725
Average Shares	126,500	136,500	139,000	133,700	121,900	118,000	105,128	107,810
Balance Sheet								
Current Assets	1,296,200	1,455,900	1,318,200	1,141,000	1,181,700	1,130,600	631,843	440,771
Total Assets	4,550,800	4,187,700	3,852,600	3,373,500	2,979,200	2,792,000	1,188,672	580,767
Current Liabilities	683,900	629,000	427,300	378,200	886,800	661,400	173,888	110,202
Long-Term Obligations	1,016,600	835,100	978,100	976,600	576,200	834,200	414,653	27,290
Total Liabilities	1,896,900	1,649,900	1,549,100	1,468,100	1,502,000	1,551,000	594,323	143,599
Stockholders' Equity	2,653,900	2,537,800	2,303,500	1,905,400	1,477,200	1,241,000	594,349	435,632
Shares Outstanding	122,200	126,200	128,400	125,700	120,100	122,600	103,494	102,188
Statistical Record								
Return on Assets %	6.89	8.17	8.82	7.44	10.43	9.47	17.50	22.78
Return on Equity %	11.59	13.57	15.13	13.97	22.15	20.53	30.07	29.97
EBITDA Margin %	13.79	15.58	15.67	15.02	17.23	14.40	16.80	15.22
Net Margin %	6.49	7.51	7.34	5.80	7.29	5.98	9.19	8.77
Asset Turnover	1.06	1.09	1.20	1.28	1.43	1.58	1.90	2.60
Current Ratio	1.90	2.31	3.08	3.02	1.33	1.71	3.63	4.00
Debt to Equity	0.38	0.33	0.42	0.51	0.39	0.67	0.70	0.06
Price Range	39.74-33.46	36.98-26.80	41.31-27.07	47.21-24.65	35.00-20.56	35.06-22.06	37.50-16.44	28.31-16.06
P/E Ratio	16.63-14.00	14.91-10.81	17.50-11.47	25.94-13.54	14.11-8.29	21.91-13.79	25.51-11.18	25.06-14.21
Average Yield %	0.99	0.52	...	...	...	...	...	...

Address: 250 Rittenhouse Circle, Keystone Park, Bristol, PA 19007 Telephone: (215) 785-4000 Fax: (215) 785-1228	Web Site: www.jny.com Officers: Sidney Kimmel - Chmn. Peter Boneparth - Pres., C.E.O.	Auditors: BDO Seidman, LLP

KB HOME

Exchange	Symbol	Price	52Wk Range	Yield	P/E
NYS	KBH	$117.46 (3/31/2005)	126.38-61.06	0.64	10.61

*7 Year Price Score 168.13 *NYSE Composite Index=100 *12 Month Price Score 129.91

Interim Earnings (Per Share)

Qtr.	Feb	May	Aug	Nov
2002	0.95	1.42	1.95	2.86
2003	1.25	1.94	2.33	3.29
2004	0.88	2.40	2.84	4.42
2005	1.41	...	...	...

Interim Dividends (Per Share)

Amt	Decl	Ex	Rec	Pay
0.25Q	10/7/2004	11/8/2004	11/11/2004	11/25/2004
0.375Q	12/2/2004	2/8/2005	2/10/2005	2/24/2005
100%	12/2/2004	4/29/2005	4/18/2005	4/28/2005
0.188Q	4/7/2005	5/10/2005	5/12/2005	5/26/2005

Indicated Div: $0.75

Valuation Analysis

Forecast P/E	7.51 (4/13/2005)	No of Institutions	272
Market Cap	$11.2 Billion	Shares	35,709,624
Book Value	2.2 Billion	% Held	74.80
Price/Book	5.14		
Price/Sales	1.53		

Business Summary: Building & General Construction (MIC: 3.2 SIC: 521 NAIC: 36115)

KB Home is engaged in the acquisition and development of land primarily for residential purposes and offers a variety of homes that are designed to appeal to a wide range of buyers, including first-time, move-up and active adult homebuyers. Domestically, Co. had operating divisions in 10 states serving 31 markets as of Nov 30 2003. Internationally, Co. operates in France through its majority-owned subsidiary, Kaufman & Broad S.A. In addition to constructing homes, Kaufman builds commercial projects and high-density residential properties. Co.'s mortgage banking subsidiary, KB Home Mortgage Company, provides mortgage banking services primarily to domestic homebuyers.

Recent Developments: For the year ended Nov 30 2004, net income advanced 29.7% to $480.9 million compared with $370.8 million in the previous year. Total revenues climbed 20.5% to $ 7.05 billion from $5.85 billion a year earlier. Construction revenues grew 21.3% to $7.01 billion, while mortgage banking revenues fell 40.9% to $44.4 million. Operating income from construction activities jumped 37.6% to $774.7 million from $562.9 million the year before. Mortgage banking income dropped 40.9% to $8.7 million from $35.8 million in 2003.

Prospects: Prospects appear favorable as Co. continues to enjoy solid growth in both its markets in the U.S. and France. Co. is looking to build on this positive momentum in the coming year by investing in its businesses to drive profitable long-term growth primarily through de novo expansion. Co. plans to finance its expansion goals through the recently announced issuance of $300.0 million in 5-7/8% senior notes. The funding raised from the issuance will be used to further improve Co.'s capital structure and reduce borrowing costs. Also, Co. is raising its 2005 earnings guidance from $14.00 to $14.50 per diluted share, an anticipated 27.0% increase over 2004 diluted earnings per share.

Financial Data

(US$ in Thousands)	3 Mos	11/30/2004	11/30/2003	11/30/2002	11/30/2001	11/30/2000	11/30/1999	11/30/1998
Earnings Per Share	11.07	11.40	8.80	7.15	5.50	5.24	3.08	2.32
Cash Flow Per Share	(4.20)	(2.86)	11.73	8.60	1.23	1.65	2.28	(0.32)
Tang Book Value Per Share	20.25	38.69	29.25	22.51	17.90	10.54	9.79	10.73
Dividends Per Share	1.125	1.000	0.300	0.300	0.300	0.300	0.300	0.300
Dividend Payout %	10.16	8.77	3.41	4.20	5.45	5.73	9.74	12.93
Income Statement								
Total Revenue	1,636,120	7,052,684	5,850,554	5,030,816	4,574,184	3,930,858	3,836,295	2,449,362
EBITDA	193,360	755,801	597,522	517,135	407,172	365,667	287,155	182,294
Depn & Amortn	5,880	23,863	23,278	19,328	45,142	42,310	39,752	18,060
Income Before Taxes	186,044	717,702	553,464	469,250	324,517	297,660	226,869	146,567
Income Taxes	63,300	236,800	182,700	154,900	110,300	87,700	79,400	51,300
Net Income	122,744	480,902	370,764	314,350	214,217	209,960	147,469	95,267
Average Shares	87,096	42,178	42,123	43,954	38,919	40,069	47,831	41,033
Balance Sheet								
Current Assets	5,430,432	5,042,150	3,671,399	3,507,008	3,275,554	2,431,544	2,188,635	1,646,490
Total Assets	6,259,567	5,835,956	4,235,859	4,025,540	3,692,866	2,828,921	2,664,235	1,860,204
Current Liabilities	844,591	794,075	586,245	521,341	479,568	322,672	338,239	220,304
Long-Term Obligations	2,389,995	2,048,247	1,393,005	1,688,706	1,706,009	1,403,202	1,227,309	818,523
Total Liabilities	4,071,284	3,780,275	2,643,008	2,751,189	2,600,385	2,174,162	1,987,652	1,385,693
Stockholders' Equity	2,188,283	2,055,681	1,592,851	1,274,351	1,092,481	654,759	676,583	474,511
Shares Outstanding	95,755	46,688	46,628	47,974	50,377	42,949	48,090	39,992
Statistical Record								
Return on Assets %	9.73	9.52	8.98	8.15	6.57	7.62	6.52	5.81
Return on Equity %	27.36	26.29	25.86	26.56	24.52	31.45	25.62	22.22
EBITDA Margin %	11.82	10.72	10.21	10.28	8.90	9.30	7.49	7.44
Net Margin %	7.50	6.82	6.34	6.25	4.68	5.34	3.84	3.89
Asset Turnover	1.35	1.40	1.42	1.30	1.40	1.43	1.70	1.49
Current Ratio	6.43	6.35	6.26	6.73	6.83	7.54	6.47	7.47
Debt to Equity	1.09	1.00	0.87	1.33	1.56	2.14	1.81	1.72
Price Range	126.38-61.06	91.41-61.06	71.74-41.08	52.90-33.38	37.06-24.89	32.38-16.88	30.38-17.75	34.81-17.50
P/E Ratio	11.42-5.52	8.02-5.36	8.15-4.67	7.40-4.67	6.74-4.53	6.18-3.22	9.86-5.76	15.01-7.54
Average Yield %	1.38	1.38	0.55	0.66	0.99	1.33	1.26	1.12

Address: 10990 Wilshire Boulevard, Los Angeles, CA 90024 Telephone: (310) 231 4000 Fax: (310) 231 4222	Web Site: www.kbhome.com Officers: Bruce Karatz - Chmn., C.E.O. Jeffrey T. Mezger - Exec. V.P., C.O.O.	Auditors: Ernst & Young LLP Investor Contact: 310-231-4000

KEANE, INC.

Exchange	Symbol	Price	52Wk Range	Yield	P/E
NYS	KEA	$13.03 (3/31/2005)	16.35-12.60	N/A	27.15

*7 Year Price Score 61.78 *NYSE Composite Index=100 ***12 Month Price Score 85.69**

TRADING VOLUME (thousand shares)

Interim Earnings (Per Share)

Qtr.	Mar	Jun	Sep	Dec
2001	0.12	0.10	0.08	(0.05)
2002	0.07	0.07	0.05	(0.09)
2003	0.15	0.10	0.09	0.10
2004	0.09	0.13	0.13	0.14

Interim Dividends (Per Share)

No Dividends Paid

Valuation Analysis

Forecast P/E	19.10	No of Institutions	
	(4/7/2005)	150	
Market Cap	$810.3 Million	Shares	
Book Value	461.7 Million	43,352,288	
Price/Book	1.75	% Held	
Price/Sales	0.89	69.51	

Business Summary: Accounting & Management Consulting Services (MIC: 12.2 SIC: 741 NAIC: 41512)

Keane is a provider of information technology and business consulting services. Co. helps clients plan, build and manage applications software through its business consulting, application development and integration, and application development and management outsourcing services. Co. also optimizes clients' internal processes through business process outsourcing services through Worldzen, a majority owned subsidiary. Co. delivers information technology services through an integrated network of local branch offices in North America and the U.K., and through advanced development centers in the U.S., Canada and India.

Recent Developments: For the year ended Dec 31 2004, net income increased 10.5% to $32,282,000 from net income of $29,222,000 a year earlier. Operating income was $51,433,000 versus an income of $42,180,000 in the prior year, an increase of 21.9%. Total direct expense was $637,240,000 versus $554,375,000 in the prior year, an increase of 14.9%. Total indirect expense was $222,870,000 versus $208,421,000 in the prior year, an increase of 6.9%.

Prospects: For the first quarter of 2005, Co. is projecting revenues to be in the range of $230.0 million to $240.0 million, with earnings per share (EPS) to be in the range of $0.09 to $0.11. These estimates include the dilutive impact of approximately $0.01 associated with Co.'s convertible debentures and exclude the impact associated with expensing of equity-based compensation. Separately, for fiscal year 2005, Co. estimates revenues to be in the range of $1.00 billion to $1.05 billion, with EPS to be in the range of $.54 to $.58. These estimates include the dilutive impact associated with Co.'s convertible debentures and exclude the impact associated with expensing of equity-based compensation.

Financial Data
(US$ in Thousands)

	12/31/2004	12/31/2003	12/31/2002	12/31/2001	12/31/2000	12/31/1999	12/31/1998	12/31/1997
Earnings Per Share	0.48	0.44	0.11	0.25	0.29	1.01	1.33	0.68
Cash Flow Per Share	0.83	1.18	0.77	1.21	1.38	1.51	0.93	0.48
Tang Book Value Per Share	1.49	1.49	1.82	2.97	3.47	4.54	4.58	3.22
Income Statement								
Total Revenue	911,543	804,976	873,203	779,159	871,956	1,041,092	1,076,198	654,395
EBITDA	85,890	79,852	41,343	55,629	63,765	154,332	195,337	102,209
Depn & Amortn	28,700	27,000	27,452	26,113	28,991	31,519	21,018	21,442
Income Before Taxes	51,508	48,696	13,636	29,221	34,186	122,813	174,156	80,605
Income Taxes	19,226	19,474	5,455	11,834	13,832	49,739	77,807	34,656
Net Income	32,282	29,222	8,181	17,387	20,354	73,074	96,349	45,949
Average Shares	71,807	66,423	74,406	69,396	69,993	72,395	72,284	67,517
Balance Sheet								
Current Assets	342,134	332,312	236,121	312,550	294,629	297,460	312,267	200,104
Total Assets	804,194	797,987	685,674	679,903	463,594	514,825	457,560	306,310
Current Liabilities	115,815	103,126	125,087	110,871	81,332	89,267	91,800	58,781
Long-Term Obligations	150,017	150,193	772	1,203	2,380	2,759	1,976	188
Total Liabilities	336,465	331,313	195,090	150,730	92,917	92,026	93,776	58,969
Stockholders' Equity	461,703	458,132	490,584	529,173	370,677	422,799	363,784	247,341
Shares Outstanding	62,183	63,344	69,520	75,508	72,730	72,370	71,648	66,560
Statistical Record								
Return on Assets %	4.02	3.94	1.20	3.04	4.15	15.03	25.23	16.97
Return on Equity %	7.00	6.16	1.60	3.86	5.12	18.58	31.53	20.70
EBITDA Margin %	9.42	9.92	4.73	7.14	7.31	14.82	18.15	15.62
Net Margin %	3.54	3.63	0.94	2.23	2.33	7.02	8.95	7.02
Asset Turnover	1.13	1.09	1.28	1.36	1.78	2.14	2.82	2.42
Current Ratio	2.95	3.22	1.89	2.82	3.62	3.33	3.40	3.40
Debt to Equity	0.32	0.33	N.M.	N.M.	0.01	0.01	0.01	N.M.
Price Range	18.00-12.75	15.13-6.90	19.05-5.64	22.00-9.76	32.13-9.75	42.50-18.00	60.94-28.13	40.69-14.88
P/E Ratio	37.50-26.56	34.39-15.68	173.18-51.27	88.00-39.04	110.78-33.62	42.08-17.82	45.82-21.15	59.83-21.88

Address: 100 City Square, Boston, MA 02129	Web Site: www.keane.com	Auditors: Ernst & Young LLP
Telephone: (617) 241-9200	Officers: John F. Keane Sr. - Chmn. Brian T. Keane - Pres., C.E.O.	Investor Contact: 800-75-KEANE
Fax: (617) 241-9507		

KELLOGG CO

Exchange	Symbol	Price	52Wk Range	Yield	P/E
NYS	K	$43.27 (3/31/2005)	45.29-39.18	2.33	20.22

*7 Year Price Score 108.12 *NYSE Composite Index=100 ***12 Month Price Score 95.66**

Interim Earnings (Per Share)

Qtr.	Mar	Jun	Sep	Dec
2001	0.21	0.28	0.37	0.30
2002	0.37	0.42	0.49	0.46
2003	0.40	0.50	0.56	0.46
2004	0.53	0.57	0.59	0.45

Interim Dividends (Per Share)

Amt	Decl	Ex	Rec	Pay
0.253Q	4/27/2004	5/27/2004	6/1/2004	6/15/2004
0.253Q	7/16/2004	8/27/2004	8/31/2004	9/15/2004
0.253Q	10/22/2004	11/23/2004	11/26/2004	12/15/2004
0.253Q	2/18/2005	2/25/2005	3/1/2005	3/15/2005

Indicated Div: $1.01

Valuation Analysis

Forecast P/E	18.33	No of Institutions	
	(4/7/2005)	405	
Market Cap	$17.9 Billion	Shares	
Book Value	2.3 Billion	325,042,368	
Price/Book	7.92	% Held	
Price/Sales	1.86	78.44	

Business Summary: Food (MIC: 4.1 SIC: 043 NAIC: 11230)

Kellogg is a manufacturer and marketer of ready-to-eat cereal products and convenience foods such as cookies, crackers, toaster pastries, cereal bars, frozen waffles, and meat alternatives. Co.'s cereal products are generally marketed under the Kellogg's name and are sold principally to the grocery trade through direct sales forces for resale to consumers. Other products are marketed under brands such as Keebler, Pop-Tarts, Eggo, Cheez-It, Nutri-Grain, Rice Krispies, Murray, Austin, Morningstar Farms, Famous Amos, Carr's, Ready Crust, and Kashi. Co.'s products are manufactured in 17 countries and distributed in 180 countries in Asia, Australia, Europe, Africa and Latin America.

Recent Developments: For the year ended Jan 1 2005, net income increased 13.1% to $890,600 thousand from net income of $787,100 thousand a year earlier. Revenues were $9,613,900 thousand, up 9.1% from $8,811,500 thousand the year before. Operating income was $1,681,100 thousand versus an income of $1,544,100 thousand in the prior year, an increase of 8.9%. Total direct expense was $5,298,700 thousand versus $4,898,900 thousand in the prior year, an increase of 8.2%. Total indirect expense was $2,634,100 thousand versus $2,368,500 thousand in the prior year, an increase of 11.2%.

Prospects: Top-line results are being positively affected by strong demand in North America for snacks such as Co.'s new French toast-flavored Pop Tarts, All-Bran cereal bars, and Cheez-It crackers. In addition, sales growth is being driven by increased sales of both cereal and snacks in Mexico. Meanwhile, Co. is experiencing weak sales of its Keebler cookies and expects challenging conditions to persist throughout the current year. In an effort to drive earnings growth, Co. is focusing on promoting higher-priced cereals such as Special K with real fruit and implementing cost-reduction initiatives. Looking ahead, co. is targeting full-year 2005 earnings in the range of $2.28 to $2.32 per share.

Financial Data (US$ in Thousands)	01/01/2005	12/27/2003	12/28/2002	12/31/2001	12/31/2000	12/31/1999	12/31/1998	12/31/1997
Earnings Per Share	2.14	1.92	1.75	1.16	1.45	0.83	1.23	1.32
Cash Flow Per Share	2.93	2.88	2.47	2.79	2.17	1.96	1.76	2.12
Tang Book Value Per Share	N.M.	N.M.	N.M.	N.M.	1.21	1.18	1.26	1.49
Dividends Per Share	1.010	1.010	1.010	1.010	0.990	0.960	0.920	0.870
Dividend Payout %	47.20	52.60	57.71	87.07	68.28	115.66	74.80	65.91
Income Statement								
Total Revenue	9,613,900	8,811,500	8,304,100	8,853,300	6,954,700	6,984,200	6,762,100	6,830,100
EBITDA	2,084,500	1,913,700	1,883,900	1,594,200	1,295,800	943,500	1,180,100	1,300,100
Depn & Amortn	410,000	372,800	348,400	438,600	290,600	288,000	278,100	287,300
Income Before Taxes	1,365,900	1,169,500	1,144,300	804,100	867,700	536,700	782,500	904,500
Income Taxes	475,300	382,400	423,400	322,100	280,000	198,400	279,900	340,500
Net Income	890,600	787,100	720,900	473,600	587,700	338,300	502,600	546,000
Average Shares	416,400	410,500	411,500	407,200	405,600	405,700	408,600	414,100
Balance Sheet								
Current Assets	2,121,800	1,797,200	1,763,400	1,902,000	1,606,800	1,569,200	1,496,500	1,467,700
Total Assets	10,790,400	10,230,800	10,219,300	10,368,600	4,896,300	4,808,700	5,051,500	4,877,600
Current Liabilities	2,846,000	2,766,000	3,014,900	2,207,600	2,492,600	1,587,800	1,718,500	1,657,300
Long-Term Obligations	3,892,600	4,265,400	4,519,400	5,619,000	709,200	1,612,800	1,614,500	1,415,400
Total Liabilities	8,533,200	8,787,600	9,324,100	9,497,100	3,998,800	3,995,500	4,161,700	3,880,100
Stockholders' Equity	2,257,200	1,443,200	895,100	871,500	897,500	813,200	889,800	997,500
Shares Outstanding	413,022	409,699	407,852	406,611	405,638	405,500	405,000	410,800
Statistical Record								
Return on Assets %	8.34	7.72	7.06	6.21	12.08	6.86	10.12	11.00
Return on Equity %	47.36	67.51	82.29	53.54	68.52	39.73	53.26	47.90
EBITDA Margin %	21.68	21.72	22.69	18.01	18.63	13.51	17.45	19.03
Net Margin %	9.26	8.93	8.68	5.35	8.45	4.84	7.43	7.99
Asset Turnover	0.90	0.86	0.81	1.16	1.43	1.42	1.36	1.38
Current Ratio	0.75	0.65	0.58	0.86	0.64	0.99	0.87	0.89
Debt to Equity	1.72	2.96	5.05	6.45	0.79	1.98	1.81	1.42
Price Range	45.24-37.20	37.80-28.02	36.89-29.35	33.56-25.00	31.31-21.00	42.06-30.19	49.69-29.56	50.31-32.19
P/E Ratio	21.14-17.38	19.69-14.59	21.08-16.77	28.93-21.55	21.59-14.48	50.68-36.37	40.40-24.03	38.12-24.38
Average Yield %	2.44	3.02	3.00	3.55	3.83	2.69	2.38	2.14

Address: One Kellogg Square, P.O. Box 3599, Battle Creek, MI 49016-3599 **Telephone:** (269) 961-2000 **Fax:** (616) 961-2871	**Web Site:** www.kelloggcompany.com **Officers:** Carlos M. Gutierrez - Chmn., C.E.O. David Mackay - Pres., C.O.O.	**Auditors:** PricewaterhouseCoopers LLP **Investor Contact:** 269-961-6365

KING PHARMACEUTICALS, INC.

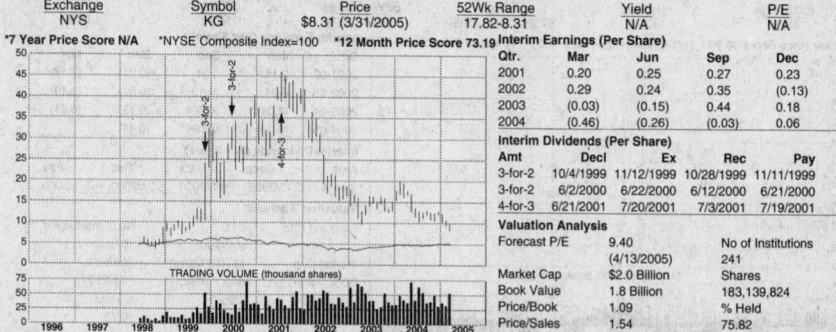

Exchange	Symbol	Price	52Wk Range	Yield	P/E
NYS	KG	$8.31 (3/31/2005)	17.82-8.31	N/A	N/A

*7 Year Price Score N/A *NYSE Composite Index=100 *12 Month Price Score 73.19

Interim Earnings (Per Share)

Qtr.	Mar	Jun	Sep	Dec
2001	0.20	0.25	0.27	0.23
2002	0.29	0.24	0.35	(0.13)
2003	(0.03)	(0.15)	0.44	0.18
2004	(0.46)	(0.26)	(0.03)	0.06

Interim Dividends (Per Share)

Amt	Decl	Ex	Rec	Pay
3-for-2	10/4/1999	11/12/1999	10/28/1999	11/11/1999
3-for-2	6/2/2000	6/22/2000	6/12/2000	6/21/2000
4-for-3	6/21/2001	7/20/2001	7/3/2001	7/19/2001

Valuation Analysis

Forecast P/E	9.40	No of Institutions
	(4/13/2005)	241
Market Cap	$2.0 Billion	Shares
Book Value	1.8 Billion	183,139,824
Price/Book	1.09	% Held
Price/Sales	1.54	75.82

Business Summary: Pharmaceuticals (MIC: 9.1 SIC: 834 NAIC: 25412)

King Pharmaceuticals is a vertically integrated pharmaceutical company that researches, develops, manufactures, markets and sells primarily branded prescription pharmaceutical products. Co. markets its branded pharmaceutical products to general/family practitioners, internal medicine physicians, cardiologists, endocrinologists, pediatricians and hospitals. Co.'s pharmaceutical products can be divided into five therapeutic areas: cardiovascular, anti-infectives, vaccines and biologicals, thyroid-disorder drugs and women's health. Co. also provides contract manufacturing for a number of pharmaceutical and biotechnology companies.

Recent Developments: For the year ended Dec 31 2004, Co. reported a loss from continuing operations of $50.6 million compared with income of $97.4 million in the prior year. Results for 2004 and 2003 excluded losses from discontinued operations of $109.7 million and $5.5 million, respectively. Results for 2004 and 2003 included net acquisition-related, restructuring, impairment and other non-recurring charges of $173.7 million and $306.6 million, respectively. Results for 2004 also included a Medicaid related charge of $65.0 million and Mylan transaction costs of $9.1 million. Total revenues decreased 12.6% to $1.30 billion from $1.49 billion a year earlier.

Prospects: On Feb 27 2005, Co. and Mylan Laboratories Inc. announced that the companies have mutually agreed to terminate the agreement pursuant to which Mylan was to acquire Co. Meanwhile, Co.'s outlook appears somewhat uncertain. Co.'s revenues declined during the fourth quarter and the twelve months ended Dec 31 2004 compared with the same periods last year primarily due to sharp wholesale inventory reductions of the Co.'s branded pharmaceutical products. Co. noted that these reductions were due to its implementation of wholesale inventory management agreements in early 2004. Co. expects that these reductions will not be substantially complete until the end of the first quarter of 2005.

Financial Data

(US$ in Thousands)	12/31/2004	12/31/2003	12/31/2002	12/31/2001	12/31/2000	12/31/1999	12/31/1998	12/31/1997
Earnings Per Share	(0.66)	0.44	0.74	0.93	0.29	0.47	0.23	0.08
Cash Flow Per Share	1.08	1.81	1.87	1.21	0.83	0.84	0.06	0.06
Tang Book Value Per Share	1.83	0.68	2.90	3.51	1.16	N.M.	N.M.	N.M.
Income Statement								
Total Revenue	1,304,364	1,521,388	1,128,335	872,262	620,243	348,271	163,463	47,909
EBITDA	110,696	312,298	317,658	420,545	258,725	157,827	65,566	15,724
Depn & Amortn	162,116	128,662	59,971	47,966	41,942	29,748	9,983	2,395
Income Before Taxes	(58,034)	177,089	267,663	370,870	191,684	73,046	40,717	10,580
Income Taxes	(7,412)	71,233	85,143	138,006	87,103	27,392	15,396	3,968
Net Income	(160,288)	105,856	182,520	217,936	64,509	44,949	20,910	6,612
Average Shares	241,475	241,526	245,698	233,906	217,771	97,183	90,383	78,809
Balance Sheet								
Current Assets	1,127,063	946,303	1,261,702	1,237,559	317,243	130,673	75,610	22,812
Total Assets	2,924,156	3,177,734	2,750,660	2,506,611	1,282,395	805,689	668,171	104,863
Current Liabilities	688,930	668,849	369,964	151,443	105,082	89,750	44,523	23,236
Long-Term Obligations	345,000	345,000	345,093	346,397	99,005	553,355	514,486	48,289
Total Liabilities	1,075,366	1,135,554	819,477	598,327	294,662	657,253	566,735	75,529
Stockholders' Equity	1,848,790	2,042,180	1,931,183	1,908,284	987,733	148,436	101,436	29,334
Shares Outstanding	241,706	241,190	240,624	247,692	170,841	96,411	96,314	83,999
Statistical Record								
Return on Assets %	N.M.	3.57	6.94	11.50	6.16	6.10	5.41	9.17
Return on Equity %	N.M.	5.33	9.51	15.05	11.32	35.98	31.98	29.37
EBITDA Margin %	8.49	20.53	28.15	48.21	41.71	45.32	40.11	32.82
Net Margin %	N.M.	6.96	16.18	24.99	10.40	12.91	12.79	13.80
Asset Turnover	0.43	0.51	0.43	0.46	0.59	0.47	0.42	0.66
Current Ratio	1.64	1.41	3.41	8.17	3.02	1.46	1.70	0.98
Debt to Equity	0.19	0.17	0.18	0.18	0.10	3.73	5.07	1.65
Price Range	19.96-10.37	17.94-9.69	42.13-15.35	46.05-25.79	40.45-15.75	32.63-6.63	8.79-3.65	...
P/E Ratio	...	40.77-22.02	56.93-20.74	49.52-27.73	139.49-54.31	69.41-14.10	38.22-15.85	...

Address: 501 Fifth Street, Bristol, TN 37620	**Web Site:** www.kingpharm.com	**Auditors:** PricewaterhouseCoopers LLP
Telephone: (423) 989-8000	**Officers:** Brian A. Markison - Pres., C.E.O. John A. Bellamy - Exec. V.P., Legal Affairs, Gen. Couns.	
Fax: (423) 274-8677		

KEMET CORP.

Exchange	Symbol	Price	52Wk Range	Yield	P/E
NYS	KEM	$7.75 (3/31/2005)	14.94-7.58	N/A	N/A

*7 Year Price Score 56.99 *NYSE Composite Index=100 *12 Month Price Score 79.33

Interim Earnings (Per Share)

Qtr.	Jun	Sep	Dec	Mar
2001-02	0.15	0.01	(0.31)	(0.17)
2002-03	0.04	(0.13)	(0.37)	(0.19)
2003-04	(0.04)	(0.50)	(0.15)	(0.61)
2004-05	(0.02)	(0.09)	(0.45)	...

Interim Dividends (Per Share)

Amt	Decl	Ex	Rec	Pay
2-for-1	5/15/2000	6/2/2000	5/24/2000	6/1/2000

Valuation Analysis

Forecast P/E	0.00	No of Institutions	
	(4/7/2005)	167	
Market Cap	$670.6 Million	Shares	
Book Value	640.1 Million	69,863,272	
Price/Book	1.05	% Held	
Price/Sales	1.53	80.73	

TRADING VOLUME (thousand shares)

Business Summary: Electrical (MIC: 11.14 SIC: 675 NAIC: 34414)

KEMET is a manufacturer of tantalum and multilayer ceramic capacitors, and solid aluminum capacitors. Capacitors are electronic components that store, filter, and regulate electrical energy and current flow and are one of the essential passive components used on circuit boards. Capacitors are used in a variety of electronic applications and products, including communication systems, data processing equipment, personal computers, cellular phones, automotive electronic systems, military and aerospace systems, and consumer electronics. During fiscal year 2004, Co. shipped approximately 27.10 billion capacitors.

Recent Developments: For the quarter ended Dec 31 2004, net loss increased 197.3% to $38,861 thousand from net loss of $13,072 thousand in the year-earlier quarter. Revenues were $95,503 thousand, down 14.2% from $111,335 thousand the year before. Operating loss was $38,154 thousand versus a loss of $19,274 thousand in the prior-year quarter, an increase of 98.0%. Total direct expense was $95,813 thousand versus $103,605 thousand in the prior-year quarter, a decrease of 7.5%. Total indirect expense was $37,844 thousand versus $27,004 thousand in the prior-year quarter, an increase of 40.1%.

Prospects: Co. results continue to be negatively affected by an inventory correction cycle in its industry, especially at its distribution customers which represent approximately one half of its revenue. However, Co. is encouraged that recent order rates are showing improvement, tempered by the fact that its distributors' inventories may decline further. Going forward, Co. will continue to move all of its commodity production to lower cost regions in fiscal 2005. Also, Co. has implemented other initiatives such as its six sigma programs to further reduce cost and improve quality.

Financial Data
(US$ in Thousands)

	9 Mos	6 Mos	3 Mos	03/31/2004	03/31/2003	03/31/2002	03/31/2001	03/31/2000
Earnings Per Share	(1.16)	(0.87)	(1.27)	(1.30)	(0.65)	(0.32)	4.00	0.85
Cash Flow Per Share	(0.39)	(0.32)	(0.07)	0.44	0.51	(0.40)	4.43	2.20
Tang Book Value Per Share	6.89	7.32	7.38	7.39	8.72	9.46	9.79	5.76
Income Statement								
Total Revenue	323,908	228,405	122,383	433,882	447,332	508,555	1,406,147	822,095
EBITDA	2,711	(8,940)	15,692	(155,703)	(87,113)	(43,803)	622,695	168,319
Depn & Amortn	49,617	...	17,443	...	...	...	63,601	55,699
Income Before Taxes	(46,865)	(8,777)	(1,464)	(158,328)	(87,894)	(40,730)	568,300	105,564
Income Taxes	1,312	539	387	(46,353)	(31,906)	(13,441)	215,954	35,445
Net Income	(48,177)	(9,316)	(1,851)	(111,975)	(55,988)	(27,289)	352,346	70,119
Average Shares	86,525	86,506	86,494	86,412	86,167	85,773	88,181	82,411
Balance Sheet								
Current Assets	296,138	289,142	292,271	409,044	547,784	567,161	745,129	449,295
Total Assets	893,457	931,283	949,427	969,808	1,101,010	1,171,714	1,366,530	927,256
Current Liabilities	92,399	87,773	86,452	95,313	84,249	112,385	285,074	189,141
Long-Term Obligations	100,000	100,000	100,000	100,000	100,000	100,000	100,000	100,000
Total Liabilities	253,331	253,953	266,464	285,330	307,735	316,669	480,354	379,800
Stockholders' Equity	640,126	677,330	682,963	684,478	793,275	855,045	886,176	547,456
Shares Outstanding	86,531	86,511	86,498	86,468	86,239	85,923	86,019	87,025
Statistical Record								
Return on Assets %	N.M.	N.M.	N.M.	N.M.	N.M.	N.M.	30.72	8.79
Return on Equity %	N.M.	N.M.	N.M.	N.M.	N.M.	N.M.	49.15	16.24
EBITDA Margin %	0.84	N.M.	12.82	N.M.	N.M.	N.M.	44.28	20.47
Net Margin %	N.M.	N.M.	N.M.	N.M.	N.M.	N.M.	25.06	8.53
Asset Turnover	0.46	0.46	0.44	0.42	0.39	0.40	1.23	1.03
Current Ratio	3.20	3.29	3.38	4.29	6.50	5.05	2.61	2.38
Debt to Equity	0.16	0.15	0.15	0.15	0.13	0.12	0.11	0.18
Price Range	16.62-7.58	16.62-7.94	16.62-9.98	16.62-7.69	22.08-6.29	22.33-14.20	41.53-14.63	38.31-5.75
P/E Ratio	...	...	...	...	...	...	10.38-3.66	45.07-6.76

Address: 2835 Kemet Way, Simpsonville, SC 29681 **Telephone:** (864) 963-6300 **Fax:** (864) 963-6322	**Web Site:** www.kemet.com **Officers:** Frank G. Brandenberg - Chmn. James P. McClintock - Pres., C.O.O.	**Auditors:** KPMG LLP **Investor Contact:** 864-963-6300

KENNAMETAL INC.

| Exchange
NYS | Symbol
KMT | Price
$47.49 (3/31/2005) | 52Wk Range
52.58-40.54 | Yield
1.43 | P/E
16.84 |

*7 Year Price Score 115.48 *NYSE Composite Index=100 *12 Month Price Score 98.71

Interim Earnings (Per Share)

Qtr.	Sep	Dec	Mar	Jun
2001-02	0.40	(0.08)	0.42	(7.44)
2002-03	0.31	0.07	0.27	(0.14)
2003-04	0.24	0.30	0.66	0.82
2004-05	0.61	0.74	...	...

Interim Dividends (Per Share)

Amt	Decl	Ex	Rec	Pay
0.17Q	1/28/2004	2/6/2004	2/10/2004	2/25/2004
0.17Q	7/28/2004	8/6/2004	8/10/2004	8/25/2004
0.17Q	10/27/2004	11/8/2004	11/10/2004	11/22/2004
0.17Q	1/26/2005	2/4/2005	2/8/2005	2/23/2005
		Indicated Div: $0.68		

Valuation Analysis

Forecast P/E	12.79	No of Institutions
	(4/7/2005)	194
Market Cap	$1.8 Billion	Shares
Book Value	1.0 Billion	33,098,780
Price/Book	1.77	% Held
Price/Sales	0.83	88.25

Business Summary: Industrial Machinery and Equipment (MIC: 11.5 SIC: 541 NAIC: 33512)

Kennametal specializes in developing and manufacturing metalworking tools and wear-resistant parts. Co.'s metalworking tools are made of cemented tungsten carbides, ceramics, cermets, high-speed steel and other hard materials. Co. also manufactures and markets a line of toolholders, toolholding systems and rotary cutting tools by machining and fabricating steel bars and other metal alloys. Co. is a supplier of metalworking consumables and related products in the U.S. and Europe. Co. also manufactures tungsten carbide products used in engineered applications, mining and highway construction, including circuit board drills, compacts and metallurgical powders.

Recent Developments: For the quarter ended Dec 31 2004, net income increased 158.7% to $28,181 thousand from net income of $10,892 thousand in the year-earlier quarter. Revenues were $556,218 thousand, up 20.7% from $460,778 thousand the year before. Operating income was $41,267 thousand versus an income of $19,303 thousand in the prior-year quarter, an increase of 113.8%. Total direct expense was $374,804 thousand versus $313,146 thousand in the prior-year quarter, an increase of 19.7%. Total indirect expense was $140,147 thousand versus $128,329 thousand in the prior-year quarter, an increase of 9.2%.

Prospects: On Mar 1 2005, Co. announced that it has completed its acquisition of Extrude Home Corporation, a worldwide supplier of engineered component process technology, for approximately $137.0 million. The acquisition is expected to be modestly accretive to earnings beginning in the June quarter of fiscal 2005. For the third quarter of fiscal 2005, organic sales, which exclude foreign currency fluctuations and acquisitions, are projected to increase between 8.0% and 10.0% year over year, while Co. is targeting earnings in the range of $0.80 to $0.85 per share. For fiscal 2005, organic sales are expected to grow 11.0% to 13.0%, while earnings are expected to be between $3.05 and $3.15 per share.

Financial Data

(US$ in Thousands)	6 Mos	3 Mos	06/30/2004	06/30/2003	06/30/2002	06/30/2001	06/30/2000	06/30/1999
Earnings Per Share	2.82	2.39	2.02	0.51	(6.70)	1.73	1.70	1.31
Cash Flow Per Share	5.59	5.42	4.97	5.16	4.98	6.14	7.29	7.57
Tang Book Value Per Share	12.31	10.20	9.42	6.98	9.94	5.58	3.90	1.98
Dividends Per Share	0.680	0.680	0.680	0.680	0.680	0.680	0.680	0.680
Dividend Payout %	24.09	28.49	33.66	133.33	...	39.31	40.00	51.91
Income Statement								
Total Revenue	1,087,654	531,436	1,971,441	1,758,957	1,583,742	1,807,896	1,853,663	1,902,916
EBITDA	117,599	58,951	202,513	154,535	165,307	242,007	257,136	242,995
Depn & Amortn	31,609	15,468	65,955	84,079	73,629	97,297	101,646	95,991
Income Before Taxes	73,413	37,027	110,674	34,290	59,051	94,329	100,411	78,410
Income Taxes	20,607	13,330	35,500	14,300	18,900	37,300	43,700	32,900
Net Income	50,901	22,720	73,578	18,130	(211,908)	53,288	51,710	39,116
Average Shares	38,016	37,363	36,473	35,479	31,627	30,749	30,364	29,960
Balance Sheet								
Current Assets	845,374	820,187	796,945	764,679	637,384	681,196	758,558	750,448
Total Assets	2,028,140	1,970,023	1,938,663	1,779,092	1,523,611	1,825,442	1,982,942	2,043,648
Current Liabilities	397,921	483,485	489,382	336,347	262,100	294,485	361,155	376,866
Long-Term Obligations	376,268	318,989	313,400	514,932	387,887	582,585	637,686	717,852
Total Liabilities	1,005,384	1,028,214	1,035,279	1,038,635	798,978	1,018,812	1,147,582	1,245,012
Stockholders' Equity	1,003,507	924,432	887,152	721,577	713,962	796,769	780,254	745,131
Shares Outstanding	37,407	37,071	36,633	35,473	34,810	30,841	30,523	30,067
Statistical Record								
Return on Assets %	5.44	4.63	3.95	1.10	N.M.	2.80	2.56	1.87
Return on Equity %	11.65	10.46	9.12	2.53	N.M.	6.76	6.76	5.28
EBITDA Margin %	10.81	11.09	10.27	8.79	10.44	13.39	13.87	12.77
Net Margin %	4.68	4.28	3.73	1.03	N.M.	2.95	2.79	2.06
Asset Turnover	1.12	1.09	1.06	1.07	0.95	0.95	0.92	0.91
Current Ratio	2.12	1.70	1.63	2.27	2.43	2.31	2.10	1.99
Debt to Equity	0.37	0.35	0.35	0.71	0.54	0.73	0.82	0.96
Price Range	52.58-38.54	45.80-36.88	45.80-33.59	35.85-27.45	42.98-29.72	37.10-21.42	33.63-19.31	43.75-16.50
P/E Ratio	18.65-13.67	19.16-15.43	22.67-16.63	70.29-53.82	...	21.45-12.38	19.78-11.36	33.40-12.60
Average Yield %	1.54	1.64	1.68	2.11	1.78	2.38	2.51	2.75

| **Address:** World Headquarters, 1600 Technology Way, P.O. Box 231, Latrobe, PA 15650-0231
Telephone: (724) 539-5000
Fax: (724) 539-4710 | **Web Site:** www.kennametal.com
Officers: Markos I. Tambakeras - Chmn., Pres., C.E.O. Carlos M. Cardoso - Exec. V.P., C.O.O. | **Auditors:** PricewaterhouseCoopers LLP
Investor Contact: 724-539-6141
Transfer Agents: Mellon Investor Services, LLC, Ridgefield Park, NJ |

KERR-MCGEE CORP.

Business Summary: Oil and Gas (MIC: 14.2 SIC: 311 NAIC: 11111)

Kerr-McGee is an energy and inorganic chemical company with worldwide operations and assets of more than $14 billion. The company is focused on two core businesses - oil and gas exploration and production and the production and marketing of titanium dioxide pigment (TiO2). Kerr-McGee produces oil and natural gas from four core areas of operations - the Gulf of Mexico, onshore United States, the U.K. sector of the North Sea and China's Bohai Bay. As of Dec 31 2003, proven developed and undeveloped reserves were as follows: crude oil, condensate and natural gas liquids totaled 496.0 million barrels; natural gas totaled 3,181 billion cubic feet.

Recent Developments: For the year ended Dec 31 2004, income from continuing operations increased 57.2% to $415 million from income of $264 million a year earlier. Net income increased 84.5% to $404 million from net income of $219 million a year earlier. Revenues were $5,157 million, up 26.4% from $4,080 million the year before. Operating income was $711 million versus an income of $516 million in the prior year, an increase of 37.8%. Total direct expense was $1,953 million versus $1,563 million in the prior year, an increase of 25.0%. Total indirect expense was $2,248 million versus $1,750 million in the prior year, an increase of 28.5%.

Prospects: Co. expects to achieve record production in 2005, with volumes forecasted to increase in the range of 13.0% to 18.0% year over year. In addition, Co. is confident it will boost reserves in 2005 with its capital and exploratory program, which includes identified low-risk exploitation opportunities in the Rockies and appraisals of 2004 discoveries in Alaska, Brazil and China. Also, Co. has confirmed rigs for its aggressive onshore and offshore drilling programs and plans to move more of its large inventory of probable and possible resources into the proved reserve category throughout the year. Separately, Co. is considering the sale of its chemical unit that produces titanium dioxide.

Financial Data

(US$ in Thousands)	12/31/2004	12/31/2003	12/31/2002	12/31/2001	12/31/2000	12/31/1999	12/31/1998	12/31/1997
Earnings Per Share	3.11	2.17	(4.84)	4.74	8.37	1.64	1.06	4.04
Cash Flow Per Share	16.19	15.16	14.43	11.77	18.91	8.25	2.11	11.85
Tang Book Value Per Share	26.53	22.60	21.72	28.13	27.87	17.17	28.23	29.88
Dividends Per Share	1.800	1.800	1.800	1.800	1.800	1.800	1.800	1.800
Dividend Payout %	57.88	82.95	...	37.97	21.51	109.76	169.81	44.55
Income Statement								
Total Revenue	5,157,000	4,185,000	3,700,000	3,638,000	4,121,000	2,696,000	1,396,000	1,711,000
EBITDA	1,819,000	1,277,000	182,000	1,561,000	2,002,000	891,000	(111,000)	536,000
Depn & Amortn	1,154,000	839,000	844,000	779,000	732,000	648,000	298,000	271,000
Income Before Taxes	671,000	443,000	(657,000)	804,000	1,299,000	257,000	(375,000)	277,000
Income Taxes	256,000	189,000	(46,000)	298,000	457,000	111,000	(148,000)	83,000
Net Income	404,000	219,000	(485,000)	486,000	842,000	142,000	50,000	194,000
Average Shares	136,919	110,683	100,330	107,111	103,987	86,497	47,000	48,000
Balance Sheet								
Current Assets	1,887,000	1,757,000	1,290,000	1,367,000	1,315,000	1,161,000	751,000	689,000
Total Assets	14,518,000	10,174,000	9,909,000	10,961,000	7,666,000	5,899,000	3,341,000	3,096,000
Current Liabilities	2,505,000	2,232,000	1,610,000	1,174,000	1,349,000	840,000	536,000	523,000
Long-Term Obligations	3,236,000	3,081,000	3,798,000	4,540,000	2,244,000	2,496,000	901,000	552,000
Total Liabilities	9,200,000	7,538,000	7,373,000	7,787,000	5,033,000	4,407,000	2,008,000	1,656,000
Stockholders' Equity	5,318,000	2,636,000	2,536,000	3,174,000	2,633,000	1,492,000	1,333,000	1,440,000
Shares Outstanding	151,889	100,860	100,383	100,185	94,484	86,483	47,000	48,000
Statistical Record								
Return on Assets %	3.26	2.18	N.M.	5.22	12.38	3.07	1.55	6.24
Return on Equity %	10.13	8.47	N.M.	16.74	40.71	10.05	3.61	13.82
EBITDA Margin %	35.27	30.51	4.92	42.91	48.58	33.05	N.M.	31.33
Net Margin %	7.83	5.23	N.M.	13.36	20.43	5.27	3.58	11.34
Asset Turnover	0.42	0.42	0.35	0.39	0.61	0.58	0.43	0.55
Current Ratio	0.75	0.79	0.80	1.16	0.97	1.38	1.40	1.32
Debt to Equity	0.61	1.17	1.50	1.43	0.85	1.67	0.68	0.38
Price Range	62.79-46.49	48.27-38.26	63.33-38.34	73.39-47.73	69.13-40.75	62.00-28.63	72.50-36.25	74.63-56.00
P/E Ratio	20.19-14.95	22.24-17.63		15.48-10.07	8.26-4.87	37.80-17.45	68.40-34.20	18.47-13.86
Average Yield %	3.38	4.17	3.53	2.89	3.04	3.80	3.30	2.77

Address: Kerr-McGee Center, 123 Robert S. Kerr Ave., P.O. Box 25861, Oklahoma City, OK 73125 Telephone: (405) 270 1313 Fax: (405) 270 3123	Web Site: www.kerr-mcgee.com Officers: Luke R. Corbett - Chmn., C.E.O. Kenneth W. Crouch - Exec. V.P.	Auditors: Ernst & Young LLP Investor Contact: 866-378-9899

KEYCORP (NEW)

Exchange	Symbol	Price	52Wk Range	Yield	P/E	Div Achiever
NYS	KEY	$32.45 (3/31/2005)	34.46-28.43	4.01	14.11	25 Years

*7 Year Price Score 99.04   *NYSE Composite Index=100   ***12 Month Price Score 96.58**

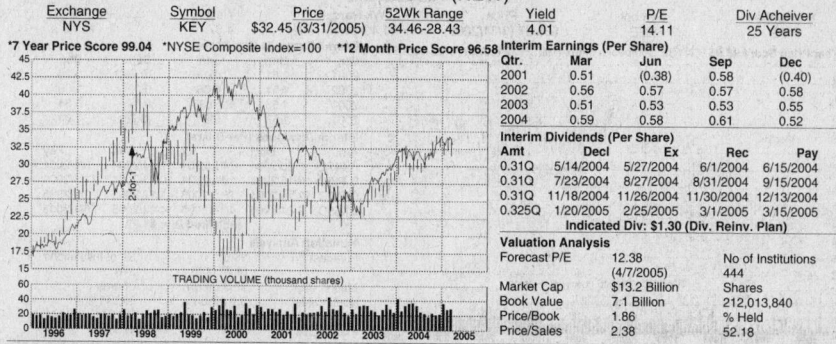

Interim Earnings (Per Share)

Qtr.	Mar	Jun	Sep	Dec
2001	0.51	(0.38)	0.58	(0.40)
2002	0.56	0.57	0.57	0.58
2003	0.51	0.53	0.53	0.55
2004	0.59	0.58	0.61	0.52

Interim Dividends (Per Share)

Amt	Decl	Ex	Rec	Pay
0.31Q	5/14/2004	5/27/2004	6/1/2004	6/15/2004
0.31Q	7/23/2004	8/27/2004	8/31/2004	9/15/2004
0.31Q	11/18/2004	11/26/2004	11/30/2004	12/13/2004
0.325Q	1/20/2005	2/25/2005	3/1/2005	3/15/2005

Indicated Div: $1.30 (Div. Reinv. Plan)

Valuation Analysis

Forecast P/E	12.38	No of Institutions
	(4/7/2005)	444
Market Cap	$13.2 Billion	Shares
Book Value	7.1 Billion	212,013,840
Price/Book	1.86	% Held
Price/Sales	2.38	52.18

Business Summary: Commercial Banking (MIC: 8.1 SIC: 021 NAIC: 22110)

KeyCorp is a multi-line financial services company, with assets of $84.49 billion as of Dec 31 2003. Co. provides investment management, retail and commercial banking, consumer finance, and investment banking products and services to individuals and companies throughout the United States and, for certain businesses, internationally. As of Dec 31 2003, Co. operates nationwide through 906 KeyCenters and offices, a network of 2,167 ATMs, telephone banking centers, and a Web site named Key.com that provides account access and financial products 24 hours a day.

Recent Developments: For the year ended Dec 31 2004, net income increased 5.6% to $954,000 thousand from net income of $903,000 thousand a year earlier. Net interest income was $2,637,000 thousand, down 3.2% from $2,725,000 thousand the year before. Provision for loan losses was $185,000 thousand versus $501,000 thousand in the prior year, a decrease of 63.1%. Non-interest income fell 0.8% to $1,746,000 thousand, while non-interest expense advanced 2.5% to $2,810,000 thousand.

Prospects: Co.'s operating results reflect its continued focus on revenue growth and improved asset quality. Higher levels of both net interest income and noninterest income are being supported by continued growth in commercial loan balances as well as strengthening financial markets. Also, Co.'s asset quality continues to strengthen as nonperforming loans are down. For the first quarter of 2005, Co. expects earnings to be in the range of $0.60 to $0.63 per share, and for the full year of 2005, Co.'s expectation is for earnings to be in the range of $2.55 to $2.65 per share.

Financial Data

(US$ in Thousands)	12/31/2004	12/31/2003	12/31/2002	12/31/2001	12/31/2000	12/31/1999	12/31/1998	12/31/1997
Earnings Per Share	2.30	2.12	2.27	0.31	2.30	2.45	2.23	2.07
Cash Flow Per Share	3.95	2.97	3.43	3.99	3.65	4.14	4.08	0.56
Tang Book Value Per Share	13.91	13.88	13.35	11.85	12.42	11.14	10.30	9.14
Dividends Per Share	1.240	1.220	1.200	1.180	1.120	1.040	0.940	0.840
Dividend Payout %	53.91	57.55	52.86	380.65	48.70	42.45	42.15	40.58
Income Statement								
Interest Income	3,818,000	3,970,000	4,366,000	5,627,000	6,277,000	5,695,000	5,525,000	5,262,000
Interest Expense	1,181,000	1,245,000	1,617,000	2,802,000	3,547,000	2,908,000	2,841,000	2,468,000
Net Interest Income	2,637,000	2,725,000	2,749,000	2,825,000	2,730,000	2,787,000	2,684,000	2,794,000
Provision for Losses	185,000	501,000	553,000	1,350,000	490,000	348,000	297,000	320,000
Non-Interest Income	1,746,000	1,760,000	1,769,000	1,725,000	2,194,000	2,294,000	1,575,000	1,306,000
Non-Interest Expense	2,810,000	2,742,000	2,653,000	2,941,000	2,917,000	3,049,000	2,483,000	2,435,000
Income Before Taxes	1,388,000	1,242,000	1,312,000	259,000	1,517,000	1,684,000	1,479,000	1,345,000
Income Taxes	434,000	339,000	336,000	102,000	515,000	577,000	483,000	426,000
Net Income	954,000	903,000	976,000	132,000	1,002,000	1,107,000	996,000	919,000
Average Shares	415,430	426,157	430,703	429,573	435,573	452,363	447,437	444,544
Balance Sheet								
Net Loans & Leases	67,326,000	61,305,000	61,005,000	61,632,000	65,904,000	63,292,000	61,112,000	52,480,000
Total Assets	90,739,000	84,487,000	85,202,000	80,938,000	87,270,000	83,395,000	80,020,000	73,699,000
Total Deposits	57,842,000	50,858,000	49,346,000	44,795,000	48,649,000	43,233,000	42,583,000	45,073,000
Total Liabilities	83,622,000	77,518,000	78,367,000	74,783,000	80,647,000	77,006,000	73,853,000	67,768,000
Stockholders' Equity	7,117,000	6,969,000	6,835,000	6,155,000	6,623,000	6,389,000	6,167,000	5,181,000
Shares Outstanding	407,569	416,494	423,943	424,005	423,254	443,427	452,452	438,064
Statistical Record								
Return on Assets %	1.09	1.06	1.17	0.16	1.17	1.35	1.30	1.30
Return on Equity %	13.51	13.08	15.03	2.07	15.36	17.63	17.55	18.27
Net Interest Margin %	69.07	68.64	62.96	50.20	43.49	48.94	48.58	53.10
Efficiency Ratio %	50.50	47.85	43.24	40.00	34.44	38.16	34.97	37.07
Loans to Deposits	1.16	1.21	1.24	1.38	1.35	1.46	1.44	1.16
Price Range	34.46-28.43	29.32-22.52	29.00-21.30	28.44-20.75	28.25-15.69	36.94-21.19	43.13-24.94	36.44-24.19
P/E Ratio	14.98-12.36	13.83-10.62	12.78-9.38	91.73-66.94	12.28-6.82	15.08-8.65	19.34-11.18	17.60-11.68
Average Yield %	3.97	4.71	4.66	4.75	5.36	3.48	2.77	2.88

Address: 127 Public Square, Cleveland, OH 44114-1306	Web Site: www.key.com	Auditors: Ernst & Young LLP
Telephone: (216) 689-6300	Officers: Henry L. Meyer III - Chmn., Pres., C.E.O.	Investor Contact: (216) 689-4520
Fax: (216) 689-3595	Thomas C. Stevens - Vice-Chmn., Chief Admin. Officer, Sec.	Transfer Agents: Computershare Investor Services, Chicago, IL

KEYSPAN CORP.

Exchange	Symbol	Price	52Wk Range	Yield	P/E
NYS	KSE	$38.97 (3/31/2005)	41.41-34.15	4.67	13.72

*7 Year Price Score 98.05 *NYSE Composite Index=100 *12 Month Price Score 96.75

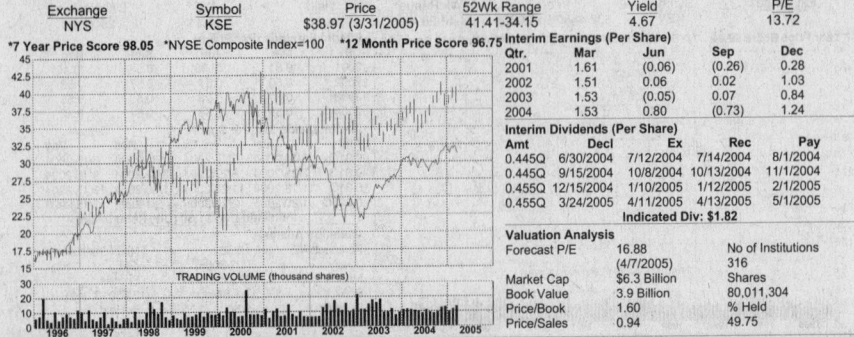

Interim Earnings (Per Share)

Qtr.	Mar	Jun	Sep	Dec
2001	1.61	(0.26)	(0.26)	0.28
2002	1.51	0.06	0.02	1.03
2003	1.53	(0.05)	0.07	0.84
2004	1.53	0.80	(0.73)	1.24

Interim Dividends (Per Share)

Amt	Decl	Ex	Rec	Pay
0.445Q	6/30/2004	7/12/2004	7/14/2004	8/1/2004
0.445Q	9/15/2004	10/8/2004	10/13/2004	11/1/2004
0.455Q	12/15/2004	1/10/2005	1/12/2005	2/1/2005
0.455Q	3/24/2005	4/11/2005	4/13/2005	5/1/2005
		Indicated Div: $1.82		

Valuation Analysis

Forecast P/E	16.88 (4/7/2005)	No of Institutions 316
Market Cap	$6.3 Billion	Shares 80,011,304
Book Value	3.9 Billion	% Held 49.75
Price/Book	1.60	
Price/Sales	0.94	

Business Summary: Gas Utilities (MIC: 7.4 SIC: 924 NAIC: 21210)

KeySpan, through its subsidiaries, is primarily engaged in gas distribution and electric services. Co.'s gas distribution business consists of six regulated subsidiaries that operate in New York, Massachusetts and New Hampshire and serve about 2.6 million gas customers as of Dec 31 2004. The electric services segment operates Long Island's electric system under contract with the Long Island Power Authority. Co.'s other subsidiaries are involved in gas production; gas storage; liquefied natural gas storage; wholesale and retail electric marketing; appliance service; a minimum amount of fiber optic services; and engineering and consulting services.

Recent Developments: For the year ended Dec 31 2004, income from continuing operations increased 44.3% to $614,713 thousand from income of $426,069 thousand a year earlier. Net income increased 19.9% to $463,665 thousand from net income of $386,730 thousand a year earlier. Revenues were $6,650,466 thousand, up 1.8% from $6,535,524 thousand the year before. Operating income was $935,270 thousand versus an income of $1,047,629 thousand in the prior year, a decrease of 10.7%. Total direct expense was $4,771,816 thousand versus $4,532,327 thousand in the prior year, an increase of 5.3%. Total indirect expense was $989,916 thousand versus $974,782 thousand in the prior year, an increase of 1.6%.

Prospects: In 2004, Co. divested its non-core investments in Houston Exploration and KeySpan Canada, while creating significant value, and has announced the pending sale of its final non-core asset in Ireland. Separately, based on its strategic review of the Energy Services segment, Co. completed its exit of its mechanical contracting activities by mid-February 2005. Co. is using its proceeds from asset sales to invest in its gas and electric businesses and to strengthen its balance sheet. Looking ahead to 2005, Co. expects earning to be in the range of $2.30 to $2.40 per share, excluding special items.

Financial Data

(US$ in Thousands)	12/31/2004	12/31/2003	12/31/2002	12/31/2001	12/31/2000	12/31/1999	12/31/1998	03/31/1998
Earnings Per Share	2.84	2.39	2.61	1.56	2.10	1.62	(1.34)	2.56
Cash Flow Per Share	4.67	7.49	5.73	6.44	3.34	4.25	(1.80)	5.55
Tang Book Value Per Share	13.79	11.60	8.11	7.95	7.06	18.37	21.63	21.88
Dividends Per Share	1.780	1.780	1.780	1.780	1.780	1.780	0.742	...
Dividend Payout %	62.68	74.48	68.20	114.10	84.76	109.88	...	...
Income Statement								
Total Revenue	6,650,466	6,915,161	5,970,666	6,633,115	5,121,490	2,954,613	1,721,852	3,124,094
EBITDA	1,823,264	1,583,260	1,437,289	1,358,667	1,042,349	800,098	266,646	938,066
Depn & Amortn	549,495	564,213	514,613	559,138	335,106	253,440	254,859	159,497
Income Before Taxes	1,193,417	1,082,277	622,744	903,309	941,401	761,127	27,685	1,065,931
Income Taxes	729,752	695,547	636,045	659,617	640,594	502,516	194,618	703,697
Net Income	463,665	386,730	377,688	243,692	300,807	258,611	(166,933)	362,240
Average Shares	161,277	159,232	142,300	139,221	134,357	138,526	145,767	121,415
Balance Sheet								
Net PPE	7,067,924	8,894,303	7,217,600	6,605,931	6,358,297	4,240,012	3,778,265	3,814,081
Total Assets	13,364,130	14,626,784	12,614,306	11,789,606	11,550,121	6,730,691	6,895,102	11,900,725
Long-Term Obligations	4,418,729	5,611,432	5,224,081	4,697,649	4,274,938	1,682,702	1,619,067	4,381,949
Total Liabilities	9,436,086	10,371,719	9,355,444	8,622,544	8,524,902	3,851,605	3,354,670	8,675,678
Stockholders' Equity	3,914,410	3,745,516	3,028,441	2,974,679	2,900,021	2,799,364	3,470,881	3,225,047
Shares Outstanding	160,818	159,664	142,424	139,429	137,014	133,866	130,420	121,681
Statistical Record								
Return on Assets %	3.30	2.84	3.10	2.09	3.28	3.80	N.M.	3.05
Return on Equity %	12.07	11.42	12.58	8.30	10.53	8.25	...	...
EBITDA Margin %	27.42	22.90	24.07	20.48	20.35	27.08	15.49	30.03
Net Margin %	6.97	5.59	6.33	3.67	5.87	8.75	(9.69)	11.60
PPE Turnover	0.83	0.86	0.86	1.02	0.96	0.74	0.46	0.82
Asset Turnover	0.47	0.51	0.49	0.57	0.56	0.43	0.10	0.26
Debt to Equity	1.13	1.50	1.73	1.58	1.47	0.60	0.47	1.36
Price Range	41.41-34.15	38.00-31.42	38.03-29.17	40.82-29.35	43.00-20.31	31.00-22.63	33.81-25.81	31.56-22.38
P/E Ratio	14.58-12.02	15.90-13.15	14.57-11.18	26.17-18.81	20.48-9.67	19.14-13.97	...	12.33-8.74
Average Yield %	4.74	5.18	5.11	4.98	5.72	6.54	2.52	...

Address: 175 East Old Country Road, Hicksville, NY 11801 **Telephone:** (631) 755-6650 **Fax:** (718) 545-2293	**Web Site:** www.keyspanenergy.com **Officers:** Robert B. Catell - Chmn., C.E.O. Robert J. Fani - Pres., C.O.O.	**Auditors:** Deloitte & Touche LLP **Investor Contact:** 718-403-3265 **Transfer Agents:** EquiServe Trust Company, NA, Jersey City, NJ

KIMBERLY-CLARK CORP.

Exchange	Symbol	Price	52Wk Range	Yield	P/E	Div Acheiver
NYS	KMB	$65.73 (3/31/2005)	68.15-58.04	2.74	18.21	30 Years

*7 Year Price Score 96.81 ***NYSE Composite Index=100** ***12 Month Price Score 96.25**

Interim Earnings (Per Share)

Qtr.	Mar	Jun	Sep	Dec
2001	0.81	0.78	0.79	0.65
2002	0.84	0.81	0.85	0.72
2003	0.78	0.82	0.83	0.91
2004	0.91	0.90	0.89	0.91

Interim Dividends (Per Share)

Amt	Decl	Ex	Rec	Pay
0.40Q	5/3/2004	6/2/2004	6/4/2004	7/2/2004
0.40Q	8/2/2004	9/8/2004	9/10/2004	10/4/2004
0.40Q	11/16/2004	12/8/2004	12/10/2004	1/4/2005
0.45Q	2/23/2005	3/2/2005	3/4/2005	4/4/2005

Indicated Div: $1.80 (Div. Reinv. Plan)

Valuation Analysis

Forecast P/E	17.22 (4/7/2005)	No of Institutions 754
Market Cap	$31.7 Billion	Shares
Book Value	6.6 Billion	356,084,320
Price/Book	4.79	% Held
Price/Sales	2.10	73.99

TRADING VOLUME (thousand shares)

Business Summary: Paper Products (MIC: 11.11 SIC: 621 NAIC: 22121)

Kimberly-Clark is engaged in the manufacturing and marketing of health and hygiene products. The Personal Care segment manufactures disposable diapers, training and youth pants and swimpants and feminine and incontinence care products. The Consumer Tissue segment manufactures facial and bathroom tissue, paper towels and napkins for household use and wet wipes. The Business-to-Business segment manufactures facial and bathroom tissue, paper towels, wipers and napkins for away-from-home use, health care products; and printing papers. Brands include Huggies, Pull-Ups, Little Swimmers, GoodNites, Kotex, Lightdays, Depend, Kleenex, Scott, Cottonelle, Viva, Scottex, Kimberly-Clark and Kimwipes.

Recent Developments: For the year ended Dec 31 2004, income from continuing operations increased 7.7% to $1,770,400 thousand from income of $1,643,600 thousand a year earlier. Net income increased 6.3% to $1,800,200 thousand from net income of $1,694,200 thousand a year earlier. Revenues were $15,083,200 thousand, up 7.5% from $14,026,300 thousand the year before. Operating income was $2,506,400 thousand versus an income of $2,331,600 thousand in the prior year, an increase of 7.5%. Total direct expense was $10,014,700 thousand versus $9,231,900 thousand in the prior year, an increase of 8.5%. Total indirect expense was $2,562,100 thousand versus $2,462,800 thousand in the prior year, an increase of 4.0%.

Prospects: Co. will continue to execute its global business plan in 2005 and remains comfortable with its previous guidance. Co. is targeting sales growth of 3.0% to 5.0%, consistent with its long-term objective. Based on Co.'s plans to drive innovation, it believes the gain will come largely from improvement in sales volumes, with price, mix and currency about flat. Co. expects to deliver earnings of $3.70 to $3.85 per share for the year, representing mid to high single-digit growth compared with net income from continuing operations of $3.55 in 2004.

Financial Data

(US$ in Thousands)	12/31/2004	12/31/2003	12/31/2002	12/31/2001	12/31/2000	12/31/1999	12/31/1998	12/31/1997
Earnings Per Share	3.61	3.33	3.22	3.02	3.31	3.09	2.11	1.61
Cash Flow Per Share	5.49	5.15	4.69	4.26	3.94	3.98	3.62	2.53
Tang Book Value Per Share	8.13	8.21	6.65	7.10	7.04	7.12	6.13	6.35
Dividends Per Share	1.600	1.360	1.200	1.120	1.080	1.040	1.000	0.960
Dividend Payout %	44.32	40.84	37.27	37.09	32.63	33.66	47.39	59.63
Income Statement								
Total Revenue	15,083,200	14,348,000	13,566,300	14,524,400	13,982,000	13,006,800	12,297,800	12,546,600
EBITDA	3,148,300	3,065,700	3,182,400	3,077,800	3,307,200	3,063,400	2,379,900	1,811,800
Depn & Amortn	800,300	758,800	718,600	739,600	673,400	628,000	579,400	490,900
Income Before Taxes	2,203,400	2,157,000	2,297,400	2,164,400	2,436,000	2,251,700	1,626,100	1,187,500
Income Taxes	483,900	514,200	666,600	645,700	758,500	730,200	561,900	433,100
Net Income	1,800,200	1,694,200	1,674,600	1,609,900	1,800,600	1,668,100	1,165,800	901,500
Average Shares	499,200	508,600	520,000	533,200	543,800	540,100	553,100	559,300
Balance Sheet								
Current Assets	4,961,900	4,438,100	4,273,900	3,922,200	3,789,900	3,561,800	3,366,900	3,489,000
Total Assets	17,018,000	16,779,900	15,585,800	15,007,600	14,479,800	12,815,500	11,510,300	11,266,000
Current Liabilities	4,537,200	3,918,700	4,038,300	4,168,300	4,573,900	3,845,800	3,790,700	3,706,300
Long-Term Obligations	2,298,000	2,733,700	2,844,700	2,424,000	2,000,600	1,926,600	2,068,200	1,803,900
Total Liabilities	9,665,600	9,445,700	9,382,000	8,822,300	8,712,500	7,722,400	7,623,100	7,140,700
Stockholders' Equity	6,629,500	6,766,300	5,650,300	5,646,900	5,767,300	5,093,100	3,887,200	4,125,300
Shares Outstanding	482,903	501,589	510,800	521,000	533,400	540,600	538,300	556,300
Statistical Record								
Return on Assets %	10.62	10.47	10.95	10.92	13.16	13.71	10.24	7.80
Return on Equity %	26.80	27.29	29.65	28.21	33.07	37.15	29.10	20.94
EBITDA Margin %	20.87	21.37	23.46	21.19	23.65	23.55	19.35	14.44
Net Margin %	11.94	11.81	12.34	11.08	12.88	12.82	9.48	7.19
Asset Turnover	0.89	0.89	0.89	0.99	1.02	1.07	1.08	1.09
Current Ratio	1.09	1.13	1.06	0.94	0.83	0.93	0.89	0.94
Debt to Equity	0.35	0.40	0.50	0.43	0.35	0.38	0.53	0.44
Price Range	66.98-55.52	58.10-42.66	65.34-45.28	70.58-51.36	70.59-44.61	67.10-44.98	57.95-36.75	55.30-43.87
P/E Ratio	18.56-15.38	17.45-12.81	20.29-14.06	23.37-17.01	21.33-13.48	21.72-14.56	27.46-17.42	34.35-27.25
Average Yield %	2.56	2.76	2.08	1.86	1.85	1.87	2.10	1.93

Address: P.O. Box 619100, Dallas, TX 75261-9100 **Telephone:** (972) 281 1200	**Web Site:** www.kimberly-clark.com **Officers:** Thomas J. Falk - Chmn., Pres., C.E.O. Mark A. Buthman - Sr. V.P., C.F.O.	**Auditors:** Deloitte & Touche LLP **Investor Contact:** 800-639-1352 **Transfer Agents:** EquiServe Trust Company, N.A., Providence, RI

KIMCO REALTY CORP.

Exchange	Symbol	Price	52Wk Range	Yield	P/E	Div Acheiver
NYS	KIM	$53.90 (3/31/2005)	58.94-40.55	4.53	21.47	12 Years

*7 Year Price Score 131.08 ***NYSE Composite Index=100** ***12 Month Price Score 99.51**

Interim Earnings (Per Share)

Qtr.	Mar	Jun	Sep	Dec
2001	0.51	0.55	0.54	0.56
2002	0.53	0.54	0.53	0.56
2003	0.63	0.46	0.80	0.72
2004	0.61	0.61	0.67	0.63

Interim Dividends (Per Share)

Amt	Decl	Ex	Rec	Pay
0.57Q	6/15/2004	7/1/2004	7/6/2004	7/15/2004
0.57Q	9/15/2004	10/1/2004	10/5/2004	10/15/2004
0.61Q	10/26/2004	12/30/2004	1/3/2005	1/18/2005
0.61Q	3/15/2005	4/1/2005	4/5/2005	4/15/2005

Indicated Div: $2.44 (Div. Reinv. Plan)

Valuation Analysis

Forecast P/E	13.92	No of Institutions
	(4/7/2005)	238
Market Cap	$6.1 Billion	Shares
Book Value	2.2 Billion	66,666,580
Price/Book	2.71	% Held
Price/Sales	11.72	59.26

Business Summary: Property, Real Estate & Development (MIC: 8.3 SIC: 798 NAIC: 25930)

Kimco Realty is an owner and operator of neighborhood and community shopping centers. As of Feb 5 2004, Co. had interests in 699 properties totaling approximately 102.6 million square feet of leasable space located in 41 states, Canada and Mexico. Co.'s portfolio includes properties relating to the Kimco Income REIT, a joint venture arrangement with institutional investors established for the purpose of investing in retail properties financed primarily with individual non-recourse mortgages debt. Co.'s ownership interests also include the RioCan Venture and Kimco Retail Opportunity Portfolio and other properties or portfolios where Co. also retains management.

Recent Developments: For the year ended Dec 31 2004, Co. reported income from continuing operations of $281,637 thousand compared with income of $242,747 thousand a year earlier. Net income decreased 3.5% to $297,137 thousand from net income of $307,879 thousand a year earlier. Results for 2004 and 2003 included gains of $12,434 thousand and $10,497 thousand, respectively, from the sale of development properties. Revenues from rental properties was $516,967 thousand, up 9.3% from $473,047 thousand the year before.

Prospects: On Dec 21 2004, Co. announced that PL Retail LLC, a joint venture between Co. and clients of DRA Advisors LLC, has completed the $1.20 billion acquisition of Price Legacy Corporation. The joint venture acquired 33 neighborhood and community shopping centers totaling 7.7 million square feet of gross leasable area. The properties are located primarily in California, Florida and Arizona. Co. will manage the properties on behalf of the joint venture and earn property management fees and leasing commissions. Meanwhile, Co. continues to benefit from increased portfolio occupancy, reflecting new leasing, acquisition activity, and property sales.

Financial Data
(US$ in Thousands)

	12/31/2004	12/31/2003	12/31/2002	12/31/2001	12/31/2000	12/31/1999	12/31/1998	12/31/1997
Earnings Per Share	2.51	2.62	2.16	2.16	1.91	1.64	1.29	1.19
Cash Flow Per Share	3.27	2.88	2.67	2.98	2.70	2.61	2.11	2.23
Tang Book Value Per Share	19.89	19.30	18.23	18.28	17.98	17.59	17.56	12.25
Dividends Per Share	2.320	2.190	2.100	1.960	2.253	1.640	1.373	1.180
Dividend Payout %	92.43	83.59	97.22	90.74	118.18	100.00	106.73	99.44
Income Statement								
Property Income	516,967	479,664	450,829	468,616	459,407	433,880	338,798	198,929
Total Revenue	516,967	479,664	450,829	468,616	459,407	433,880	338,798	198,929
Depn & Amortn	102,872	89,068	76,674	74,209	71,129	67,416	51,348	30,053
Interest Expense	107,726	102,709	86,896	...	...	...	...	...
Income Before Taxes	226,397	200,889	261,474	255,914	...	176,778	...	...
Income Taxes	3,919	1,516	12,904	19,376	...	...	...	...
Net Income	297,137	307,879	245,668	236,538	205,025	176,778	122,266	85,836
Average Shares	113,572	108,770	105,969	101,163	93,653	91,466	75,960	56,775
Balance Sheet								
Total Assets	4,749,597	4,603,925	3,756,878	3,384,779	3,171,348	3,007,476	3,051,178	1,343,890
Long-Term Obligations	509,697	468,698	274,732	292,829	245,413	212,321	434,311	121,364
Total Liabilities	2,406,306	2,368,162	1,755,610	1,486,320	1,453,242	1,388,912	1,453,204	596,039
Stockholders' Equity	2,236,400	2,135,846	1,907,328	1,890,084	1,704,339	1,605,435	1,585,019	743,319
Shares Outstanding	112,426	110,623	104,601	103,352	94,717	91,193	90,200	60,592
Statistical Record								
Return on Assets %	6.34	7.36	6.88	7.22	6.62	5.84	5.56	7.25
Return on Equity %	13.55	15.23	12.94	13.16	12.36	11.08	10.50	12.73
Net Margin %	57.48	64.19	54.49	50.48	44.63	40.74	36.09	43.15
Price Range	58.94-40.55	45.86-30.50	33.61-28.01	34.00-27.27	29.75-22.04	26.92-20.83	27.38-22.42	23.75-20.33
P/E Ratio	23.48-16.16	17.50-11.64	15.56-12.97	15.74-12.62	15.58-11.54	16.41-12.70	21.22-17.38	19.96-17.09
Average Yield %	4.75	5.70	6.68	6.43	8.57	6.65	5.54	5.34

Address: 3333 New Hyde Park Road, Suite 100, New Hyde Park, NY 11042-0020	**Web Site:** www.kimcorealty.com	**Auditors:** PricewaterhouseCoopers LLP
	Officers: Milton Cooper - Chmn., C.E.O. Michael J. Flynn - Vice-Chmn., Pres., C.O.O.	**Investor Contact:** 516-869-9000
Telephone: (516) 869-9000		**Transfer Agents:** The Bank of New York, New York, NY
Fax: (516) 869 9001		

KINDRED HEALTHCARE INC

Exchange	Symbol	Price	52Wk Range	Yield	P/E
NYS	KND	$35.10 (3/31/2005)	35.10-22.82	N/A	21.02

*7 Year Price Score N/A   *NYSE Composite Index=100   *12 Month Price Score 111.65

TRADING VOLUME (thousand shares)

Interim Earnings (Per Share)

Qtr.	Mar	Sep	Sep	Dec
2002	0.47	0.60	(0.29)	0.14
2003	(0.38)	(1.25)	0.34	(0.86)
2004	0.32	0.52	0.37	0.46

Interim Dividends (Per Share)

Amt	Decl	Ex	Rec	Pay
2-for-1				

Valuation Analysis

Forecast P/E	16.10	No of Institutions	
	(4/7/2005)	140	
Market Cap	$1.3 Billion	Shares	
Book Value	719.8 Million	41,938,352	
Price/Book	1.81	% Held	
Price/Sales	0.37	N/A	

Business Summary: Hospitals & Health Care (MIC: 9.3 SIC: 059 NAIC: 23110)

Kindred Healthcare provides long-term healthcare services primarily through the operation of nursing centers, hospitals and institutional pharmacies. Co. is organized into two operating divisions: the health services division, which operates nursing centers and a rehabilitation therapy business and the hospital division, which operates hospitals and an institutional pharmacy business. As of Mar 31 2004, Co.'s health services division operated 254 nursing centers, with 32,812 licensed beds in 30 states, and a rehabilitation therapy business. Co.'s hospital division operated 68 hospitals, with 5,323 licensed beds in 23 states.

Recent Developments: For the year ended Dec 31 2004, income from continuing operations increased 63.3% to $85,923 thousand from income of $52,623 thousand a year earlier. Net income was $70,580 thousand versus net loss of $75,336 thousand a year earlier. Revenues were $3,531,223 thousand, up 9.3% from $3,229,722 thousand the year before. Total indirect expense was $3,379,758 thousand versus $3,136,280 thousand in the prior year, an increase of 7.8%.

Prospects: Co.'s strong fourth quarter results for 2004 provides it with great operational momentum as it heads into the coming year. Meanwhile, Co. reaffirmed its 2005 guidance for consolidated revenues to approximate $3.80 billion, and operating income, or earnings before interest, income taxes, depreciation and rents, to be in the range of $535.0 million to $545.0 million. Professional liability costs are expected to range from $90.0 million to $100.0 million, while depreciation and net interest costs of about $100.0 million. Net income from continuing operations is expected to range from $95.0 million to $101.0 million, with diluted earnings per share in the range of $2.10 to $2.25.

Financial Data
(US$ in Thousands)

	12/31/2004	12/31/2003	12/31/2002	12/31/2001	03/31/2001	12/31/2000	12/31/1999	12/31/1998
Earnings Per Share	1.67	(2.15)	0.96	1.42	3.29	(0.39)	(4.92)	(4.76)
Cash Flow Per Share	7.47	3.42	7.16	4.60	1.03	1.32	1.64	2.36
Tang Book Value Per Share	18.51	15.58	15.39	13.65	...	...	...	N.M.
Income Statement								
Total Revenue	3,531,223	3,284,019	3,357,822	2,329,019	752,409	2,888,542	2,665,641	2,999,739
EBITDA	256,891	184,560	154,222	162,449	82,330	82,394	(509,111)	(265,184)
Depn & Amortn	98,691	89,129	78,134	56,917	18,645	73,545	93,196	124,617
Income Before Taxes	145,386	85,109	61,715	83,792	49,685	(51,582)	(682,749)	(496,809)
Income Taxes	59,463	35,655	28,389	36,450	500	2,000	500	76,099
Net Income	70,580	(75,336)	34,753	51,655	471,976	(53,582)	(692,172)	(650,845)
Average Shares	42,403	35,048	36,002	36,516	143,312	140,458	140,812	136,686
Balance Sheet								
Current Assets	874,343	843,087	920,316	831,973	...	695,852	591,884	628,478
Total Assets	1,593,293	1,585,414	1,644,178	1,508,874	...	1,334,414	1,235,974	1,717,890
Current Liabilities	577,766	577,880	582,156	515,126	...	428,691	396,873	1,311,047
Long-Term Obligations	32,544	139,397	162,008	212,269	...	...	...	6,600
Total Liabilities	873,508	987,849	1,012,550	918,393	...	1,767,266	1,614,283	1,404,645
Stockholders' Equity	719,785	597,565	631,628	590,481	...	(432,852)	(378,309)	313,245
Shares Outstanding	37,189	36,340	35,298	35,366	...	140,522	140,556	140,292
Statistical Record								
Return on Assets %	4.43	N.M.	2.20	3.63	...	N.M.	N.M.	N.M.
Return on Equity %	10.69	N.M.	5.69	65.54	...	...	...	N.M.
EBITDA Margin %	7.27	5.62	4.59	6.97	10.94	2.85	N.M.	N.M.
Net Margin %	2.00	N.M.	1.03	2.22	62.73	N.M.	N.M.	N.M.
Asset Turnover	2.22	2.03	2.13	1.64	...	2.24	1.80	1.19
Current Ratio	1.51	1.46	1.58	1.62	...	1.62	1.49	0.48
Debt to Equity	0.05	0.23	0.26	0.36	...	...	...	0.02
Price Range	30.56-22.82	26.53-5.49	26.00-5.99	32.50-15.50	...	...	...	...
P/E Ratio	18.30-13.67	...	27.08-6.24	22.89-10.92	...	...	...	...

Address: 680 South Fourth Street, Louisville, KY 40202-2412 **Telephone:** (502) 596-7300	**Web Site:** www.kindredhealthcare.com **Officers:** Edward L. Kuntz - Chmn. Paul J. Diaz - Pres., C.E.O.	**Auditors:** PricewaterhouseCoopers LLP **Transfer Agents:** National City Bank., Cleveland OH

KINDER MORGAN ENERGY PARTNERS, L.P.

Exchange	Symbol	Price	52Wk Range	Yield	P/E
NYS	KMP	$45.00 (3/31/2005)	47.65-38.33	6.38	20.27

*7 Year Price Score 122.11 *NYSE Composite Index=100 *12 Month Price Score 97.06

Interim Earnings (Per Share)

Qtr.	Mar	Jun	Sep	Dec
2001	0.45	0.36	0.37	0.40
2002	0.48	0.48	0.50	0.50
2003	0.52	0.48	0.49	0.51
2004	0.52	0.51	0.59	0.60

Interim Dividends (Per Share)

Amt	Decl	Ex	Rec	Pay
0.69Q	4/21/2004	4/28/2004	4/30/2004	5/14/2004
0.71Q	7/21/2004	7/28/2004	7/30/2004	8/13/2004
0.73Q	10/20/2004	10/27/2004	10/29/2004	11/12/2004
0.74Q	1/18/2005	1/27/2005	1/31/2005	2/14/2005

Indicated Div: $2.87

Valuation Analysis

Forecast P/E	20.14	No of Institutions
	(4/7/2005)	251
Market Cap	$9.3 Billion	Shares
Book Value	N/A	26,653,256
Price/Book	N/A	% Held
Price/Sales	1.17	18.06

Business Summary: Oil and Gas (MIC: 14.2 SIC: 612 NAIC: 86110)

Kinder Morgan Energy Partner is a publicly-traded pipeline limited partnership that owns an independent refined petroleum products pipeline system in the U.S. Co. owns or operates more than 10,000 miles of pipelines and 39 associated terminals. Co.'s pipelines transport gasoline and other petroleum products as well as natural gas. Co. transports, stores and sells up to 7.80 billion cubic feet per day of natural gas and has over 15,000 miles of natural gas transmission pipelines, plus natural gas gathering and storage facilities. Co. also produces, transports and markets carbon dioxide and has over 1,100 miles of pipelines that transport carbon dioxide to oil fields.

Recent Developments: For the year ended Dec 31 2004, net income increased 19.3% to $831,578 thousand from net income of $697,337 thousand a year earlier. Revenues were $7,932,861 thousand, up 19.8% from $6,624,322 thousand the year before. Operating income was $973,996 thousand versus an income of $806,689 thousand in the prior year, an increase of 20.7%. Total direct expense was $6,418,363 thousand versus $5,385,953 thousand in the prior year, an increase of 19.2%. Total indirect expense was $540,502 thousand versus $431,680 thousand in the prior year, an increase of 25.2%.

Prospects: Co. is benefiting from its solid asset position, which generated cash flow to support distributions of more than $975.0 million for 2004. Co. attributes this growth to strong internal growth and contributions from acquisitions. Co. invested approximately $574.0 million in capital expansion projects in 2004 and made acquisitions totaling more than $600.0 million. Going forward, Co. expects to declare cash distributions of $3.13 per limited partner unit for full-year 2005. The 2005 outlook represents 9.0% growth over the declared distribution of $2.87 per unit for 2004. Also, Co. is optimistic about its chances of making accretive acquisitions in 2005.

Financial Data

(US$ in Thousands)	12/31/2004	12/31/2003	12/31/2002	12/31/2001	12/31/2000	12/31/1999	12/31/1998	12/31/1997
Earnings Per Share	2.22	2.00	1.96	1.56	1.34	1.28	0.88	0.51
Cash Flow Per Share	5.85	4.15	5.06	3.78	2.38	1.87	1.67	1.19
Dividends Per Share	2.810	2.575	2.360	2.075	1.600	1.095	1.192	0.815
Dividend Payout %	126.58	128.75	120.41	133.01	119.85	85.21	136.29	159.80
Income Statement								
Total Revenue	7,932,861	6,624,322	4,237,057	2,946,676	816,442	428,749	322,617	73,932
EBITDA	1,338,387	1,114,836	977,736	781,261	476,391	298,051	194,710	39,669
Depn & Amortn	294,201	222,976	177,616	151,088	90,825	50,723	37,321	10,067
Income Before Taxes	851,304	710,503	623,660	458,716	292,282	194,723	118,789	16,997
Income Taxes	19,726	16,631	15,283	16,373	13,934	9,826	1,572	(740)
Net Income	831,578	697,337	608,377	442,343	278,348	182,302	103,606	17,737
Average Shares	197,038	185,494	172,186	154,110	126,212	97,984	80,240	26,822
Balance Sheet								
Net PPE	8,168,680	7,091,558	6,244,242	5,082,612	3,306,305	2,578,313	1,763,386	244,967
Total Assets	10,552,942	9,139,182	8,353,576	6,732,666	4,625,210	3,228,738	2,152,272	312,906
Long-Term Obligations	4,852,563	4,438,142	3,826,489	2,231,574	1,255,453	989,101	611,571	146,824
Total Liabilities	6,656,422	5,628,255	4,937,647	3,573,632	2,508,143	1,453,940	791,609	162,682
Shares Outstanding	207,008	189,039	180,910	165,804	129,716	96,930	97,644	28,222
Statistical Record								
Return on Assets %	8.42	7.97	8.07	7.79	7.07	6.78	8.41	5.75
EBITDA Margin %	16.87	16.83	23.08	26.51	58.35	69.52	60.35	53.66
Net Margin %	10.48	10.53	14.36	15.01	34.09	42.52	32.11	23.99
PPE Turnover	1.04	0.99	0.75	0.70	0.28	0.20	0.32	0.31
Asset Turnover	0.80	0.76	0.56	0.52	0.21	0.16	0.26	0.24
Price Range	49.27-38.33	49.69-34.25	38.65-28.00	39.05-26.13	28.16-18.56	22.69-16.56	19.06-14.56	19.91-6.88
P/E Ratio	22.19-17.27	24.84-17.13	19.72-14.29	25.03-16.75	21.01-13.85	17.72-12.94	21.66-16.55	39.03-13.48
Average Yield %	6.33	6.43	7.09	6.08	7.47	5.60	6.79	5.95

Address: 500 Dallas Street, Suite 1000, Houston, TX 77002 **Telephone:** (713) 369-9000	**Web Site:** www.kindermorgan.com **Officers:** Richard D. Kinder - Chmn., C.E.O. Michael C. Morgan - Pres.	**Auditors:** PricewaterhouseCoopers LLP **Investor Contact:** 713-369-9490

KINDER MORGAN, INC. (KS)

Exchange	Symbol	Price	52Wk Range	Yield	P/E
NYS	KMI	$75.70 (3/31/2005)	81.31-56.91	3.70	18.11

*7 Year Price Score 128.78 *NYSE Composite Index=100 *12 Month Price Score 109.60

Interim Earnings (Per Share)

Qtr.	Mar	Jun	Sep	Dec
2001	0.37	0.41	0.48	0.60
2002	0.71	0.59	0.66	0.50
2003	0.90	0.76	0.77	0.65
2004	1.02	0.84	0.90	1.43

Interim Dividends (Per Share)

Amt	Decl	Ex	Rec	Pay
0.563Q	1/21/2004	1/28/2004	1/30/2004	2/13/2004
0.563Q	4/21/2004	4/28/2004	4/30/2004	5/14/2004
0.563Q	10/20/2004	10/27/2004	10/29/2004	11/12/2004
0.70Q	1/18/2005	1/27/2005	1/31/2005	2/14/2005
		Indicated Div: $2.80		

Valuation Analysis

Forecast P/E	18.04	No of Institutions
	(4/7/2005)	343
Market Cap	$9.4 Billion	Shares
Book Value	2.9 Billion	74,141,728
Price/Book	3.26	% Held
Price/Sales	8.03	60.08

Business Summary: Gas Utilities (MIC: 7.4 SIC: 923 NAIC: 21210)

Kinder Morgan is an energy storage and transportation provider. As of Dec 31 2003, Co. operated more than 35,000 miles of natural gas and products pipelines and about 80 terminals. Co. owns the general partner interest of Kinder Morgan Energy Partners, L.P., which is a pipeline limited partnership. Co.'s Natural Gas Pipeline Company of America (NGPL) segment includes an interstate natural gas pipeline system with about 9,900 miles of pipelines and associated storage facilities; and TransColorado Gas Transmission Company, a 300-mile interstate natural gas pipeline in western Colorado and northwest New Mexico. Co. also owns interests in and operates a retail natural gas distribution business.

Recent Developments: For the year ended Dec 31 2004, net income increased 36.8% to $522,080 thousand from net income of $381,704 thousand a year earlier. Revenues were $1,164,933 thousand, up 6.1% from $1,097,897 thousand the year before. Operating income was $397,928 thousand versus an income of $356,093 thousand in the prior year, an increase of 11.7%. Total direct expense was $507,920 thousand versus $477,449 thousand in the prior year, an increase of 6.4%. Total indirect expense was $259,085 thousand versus $264,355 thousand in the prior year, a decrease of 2.0%.

Prospects: In 2005 and beyond, Co. plans to remain focused on owning and operating predominantly fee-based, mid-stream energy assets in strategic markets that are integral to helping meet the growing demand for energy products across the U.S. Meanwhile, for 2005, Co. raised its earnings guidance to approximately $4.22 per share, up slightly from the prior estimate of $4.20. The 2005 guidance represents an 11.0% growth over 2004 earnings per share of $3.81. These expectations include contributions from assets presently owned by Kinder Morgan and do not include any benefits from acquisitions. Additionally, Co. expects cash flow in 2005 of approximately $620.0 million.

Financial Data

(US$ in Thousands)	12/31/2004	12/31/2003	12/31/2002	12/31/2001	12/31/2000	12/31/1999	12/31/1998	12/31/1997
Earnings Per Share	4.18	3.08	2.45	1.86	1.32	(3.01)	0.92	1.63
Cash Flow Per Share	5.19	4.79	3.63	3.79	1.46	3.89	1.49	2.09
Tang Book Value Per Share	23.19	21.62	19.35	18.24	15.70	14.79	17.74	12.63
Dividends Per Share	2.250	1.100	0.300	0.200	0.200	0.650	0.760	0.727
Dividend Payout %	53.83	35.71	12.24	10.75	15.15	...	82.61	44.49
Income Statement								
Total Revenue	1,164,933	1,097,897	1,015,255	1,054,918	2,713,737	1,745,481	4,387,843	2,145,118
EBITDA	1,029,094	894,376	713,510	731,726	657,762	641,433	443,440	212,647
Depn & Amortn	118,742	117,528	106,496	108,290	108,165	144,268	97,999	55,994
Income Before Taxes	755,221	626,304	445,079	407,236	306,442	245,179	98,261	113,158
Income Taxes	226,711	244,600	135,912	168,601	122,727	90,527	38,272	35,661
Net Income	522,080	381,704	302,725	225,070	151,981	(241,444)	59,989	77,497
Average Shares	124,938	123,824	123,402	121,326	115,030	80,358	64,635	47,307
Balance Sheet								
Net PPE	5,851,965	6,083,937	6,048,107	5,703,952	5,724,617	5,789,564	7,023,176	1,420,975
Total Assets	10,116,901	10,036,711	10,102,750	9,533,085	8,418,105	9,540,283	9,612,212	2,305,805
Long-Term Obligations	2,629,793	3,209,329	2,991,770	2,404,967	2,478,983	3,293,326	3,300,025	553,816
Total Liabilities	7,252,147	7,370,594	7,747,753	7,273,088	6,620,684	7,874,442	8,388,391	1,692,673
Stockholders' Equity	2,864,754	2,666,117	2,354,997	2,259,997	1,797,421	1,665,841	1,216,821	606,132
Shares Outstanding	123,532	123,316	121,693	123,926	114,482	112,666	68,597	47,994
Statistical Record								
Return on Assets %	5.17	3.79	3.08	2.51	1.69	N.M.	1.01	3.94
Return on Equity %	18.83	15.20	13.12	11.09	8.75	N.M.	6.58	13.77
EBITDA Margin %	88.34	81.46	70.28	69.36	24.24	36.75	10.11	9.91
Net Margin %	44.82	34.77	29.82	21.34	5.60	(13.83)	1.37	3.61
PPE Turnover	0.19	0.18	0.17	0.18	0.47	0.27	1.04	1.75
Asset Turnover	0.12	0.11	0.10	0.12	0.30	0.18	0.74	1.09
Debt to Equity	0.92	1.20	1.27	1.06	1.38	1.98	2.71	0.91
Price Range	73.57-56.91	59.10-42.27	56.99-32.15	59.75-43.31	54.25-20.19	24.25-12.19	40.33-22.92	36.00-24.17
P/E Ratio	17.60-13.61	19.19-13.72	23.26-13.12	32.12-23.29	41.10-15.29	...	43.84-24.91	22.09-14.83
Average Yield %	3.61	2.17	0.69	0.38	0.58	3.16	2.27	2.59

Address: 500 Dallas Street, Suite 1000, Houston, TX 77002 **Telephone:** (713) 369-9000 **Fax:** (713) 495-2817	Web Site: www.kindermorgan.com **Officers:** Richard D. Kinder - Chmn., Pres., C.E.O. C. Park Shaper - Exec. V.P., C.F.O.	Auditors: PricewaterhouseCoopers LLP **Investor Contact:** 713-369-9490

KNIGHT-RIDDER, INC.

Exchange	Symbol	Price	52Wk Range	Yield	P/E
NYS	KRI	$67.25 (3/31/2005)	79.63-62.48	2.05	16.28

*7 Year Price Score 98.28   *NYSE Composite Index=100   *12 Month Price Score 89.80

Interim Earnings (Per Share)

Qtr.	Mar	Jun	Sep	Dec
2001	0.47	0.15	0.65	0.88
2002	0.60	0.90	0.67	1.15
2003	0.62	0.95	0.85	1.22
2004	0.70	1.08	0.99	1.37

Interim Dividends (Per Share)

Amt	Decl	Ex	Rec	Pay
0.32Q	5/4/2004	5/17/2004	5/19/2004	6/1/2004
0.345Q	7/27/2004	8/9/2004	8/11/2004	8/23/2004
0.345Q	10/26/2004	11/8/2004	11/10/2004	11/22/2004
0.345Q	2/1/2005	2/14/2005	2/16/2005	2/28/2005

Indicated Div: $1.38

Valuation Analysis

Forecast P/E	16.45		No of Institutions
	(4/7/2005)		263
Market Cap	$5.1 Billion		Shares
Book Value	1.4 Billion		65,533,336
Price/Book	3.54		% Held
Price/Sales	1.70		86.80

TRADING VOLUME (thousand shares)

Business Summary: Media (MIC: 13.1 SIC: 711 NAIC: 11110)

Knight-Ridder is a U.S. newspaper publisher, with products in print and on-line. Co. publishes 31 daily newspapers in 28 U.S. markets, with a readership of 8.7 million daily and 12.6 million on Sunday. Co. also has investments in a variety of Internet and technology companies and two newsprint companies. Co.'s Internet operation, Knight Ridder Digital, develops and manages its on-line properties, including RealCities.com, a national network of city and regional destination sites in 105 U.S. markets. Some of the larger newspapers include The Philadelphia Inquirer, Philadelphia Daily News, The Miami Herald, el Nuevo Herald, and The Kansas City Star.

Recent Developments: For the year ended Dec 26 2004, net income increased 10.2% to $326,243 thousand from net income of $296,071 thousand a year earlier. Revenues were $3,014,149 thousand, up 2.3% from $2,945,991 thousand the year before. Operating income was $585,240 thousand versus an income of $567,607 thousand in the prior year, an increase of 3.1%. Total direct expense was $396,075 thousand versus $383,099 thousand in the prior year, an increase of 3.4%. Total indirect expense was $2,032,834 thousand versus $1,995,285 thousand in the prior year, an increase of 1.9%.

Prospects: Co.'s outlook appears satisfactory. Co. indicated on Jan 26 2005 that it is on track to achieve mid to high single-digit earnings per share growth for 2005. However, Co. noted that it expects first quarter 2005 comparisons will be challenging due to overall revenue growth being weakest in that period; the Easter shift, which benefited the first quarter last year, will benefit the second quarter this year; and a number of new revenue initiatives with ramp-up expenses that will launch in the first quarter of 2005. Separately, on Feb 15 2005, Co. announced the acquisition of five daily free-distribution newspapers in the Peninsula south of San Francisco. Terms were not disclosed.

Financial Data

(US$ in Thousands)	12/26/2004	12/28/2003	12/29/2002	12/30/2001	12/31/2000	12/26/1999	12/27/1998	12/28/1997
Earnings Per Share	4.13	3.63	3.04	2.16	3.53	3.49	3.73	4.08
Cash Flow Per Share	5.89	5.56	5.15	6.35	5.45	6.34	3.78	2.63
Dividends Per Share	1.330	1.180	1.020	1.000	0.920	0.890	0.800	0.800
Dividend Payout %	32.20	32.51	33.55	46.30	26.06	25.50	21.45	19.61
Income Statement								
Total Revenue	3,014,149	2,945,991	2,841,594	2,900,209	3,211,767	3,228,225	3,091,919	2,876,785
EBITDA	650,782	642,889	645,023	589,905	825,756	847,187	773,905	929,347
Depn & Amortn	99,868	111,410	122,483	184,572	187,597	189,354	167,985	141,613
Income Before Taxes	501,294	463,014	448,670	307,399	525,290	568,015	507,916	693,852
Income Taxes	175,051	166,943	166,943	122,575	210,927	228,076	202,285	297,348
Net Income	326,243	296,071	257,448	184,824	314,363	339,939	365,857	413,015
Average Shares	78,950	81,477	84,726	85,694	89,105	97,460	98,176	101,314
Balance Sheet								
Current Assets	549,795	525,949	539,153	535,571	576,094	570,304	525,691	641,115
Total Assets	4,222,278	4,096,679	4,164,658	4,213,376	4,243,526	4,192,334	4,257,097	4,355,142
Current Liabilities	479,806	454,934	466,718	480,032	508,360	497,141	653,756	598,656
Long-Term Obligations	1,497,907	1,433,560	1,521,008	1,573,255	1,591,910	1,260,814	1,329,001	1,599,133
Total Liabilities	2,773,547	2,607,124	2,699,888	2,651,768	2,699,610	2,406,779	2,591,864	2,802,194
Stockholders' Equity	1,447,156	1,489,245	1,461,479	1,560,288	1,541,470	1,780,684	1,662,731	1,551,673
Shares Outstanding	76,256	79,239	81,593	83,977	73,995	79,611	78,328	81,598
Statistical Record								
Return on Assets %	7.86	7.19	6.16	4.38	7.33	8.07	8.52	11.42
Return on Equity %	22.28	20.12	17.09	11.95	18.62	19.80	22.83	30.87
EBITDA Margin %	21.59	21.82	22.70	20.34	25.71	26.24	25.03	32.31
Net Margin %	10.82	10.05	9.06	6.37	9.79	10.53	11.83	14.36
Asset Turnover	0.73	0.72	0.68	0.69	0.75	0.77	0.72	0.80
Current Ratio	1.15	1.16	1.16	1.12	1.13	1.15	0.80	1.07
Debt to Equity	1.04	0.96	1.04	1.01	1.03	0.71	0.80	1.03
Price Range	79.63-62.48	76.12-58.50	69.96-51.64	65.17-52.25	59.56-44.25	63.50-46.00	59.13-41.00	56.94-36.50
P/E Ratio	19.28-15.13	20.97-16.12	23.01-16.99	30.17-24.19	16.87-12.54	18.19-13.18	15.85-10.99	13.96-8.95
Average Yield %	1.87	1.75	1.62	1.72	1.78	1.66	1.51	1.73

Address: 50 W. San Fernando Street, Suite 1500, San Jose, CA 95113	**Web Site:** www.knightridder.com	**Auditors:** Ernst & Young LLP
Telephone: (408) 938-7700	**Officers:** P. Anthony Ridder - Chmn., C.E.O. Gary R. Effren - Sr. V.P., Fin.	**Investor Contact:** 408-938-7838
Fax: (408) 938-7755		

KOHL'S CORP.

Exchange	Symbol	Price	52Wk Range	Yield	P/E
NYS	KSS	$51.63 (3/31/2005)	53.70-40.96	N/A	24.35

*7 Year Price Score 82.14 *NYSE Composite Index=100 *12 Month Price Score 97.13

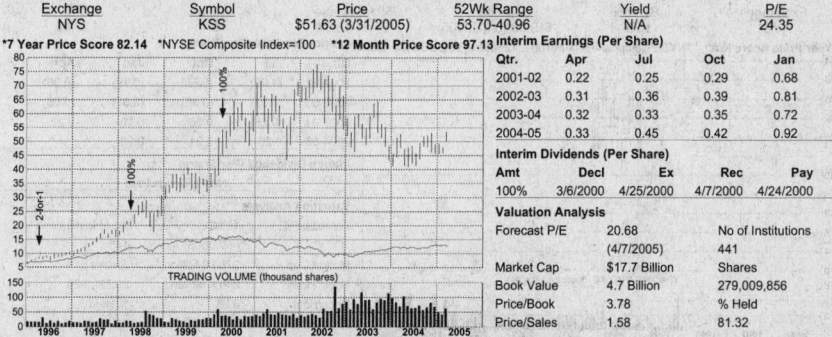

Interim Earnings (Per Share)

Qtr.	Apr	Jul	Oct	Jan
2001-02	0.22	0.25	0.29	0.68
2002-03	0.31	0.36	0.39	0.81
2003-04	0.32	0.33	0.35	0.72
2004-05	0.33	0.45	0.42	0.92

Interim Dividends (Per Share)

Amt	Decl	Ex	Rec	Pay
100%	3/6/2000	4/25/2000	4/7/2000	4/24/2000

Valuation Analysis

Forecast P/E	20.68	No of Institutions	
	(4/7/2005)	441	
Market Cap	$17.7 Billion	Shares	
Book Value	4.7 Billion	279,009,856	
Price/Book	3.78	% Held	
Price/Sales	1.58	81.32	

TRADING VOLUME (thousand shares)

Business Summary: Retail - General (MIC: 5.2 SIC: 311 NAIC: 52111)

Kohl's operates family-oriented, specialty department stores. As of Apr 1 2004, Co. operated 563 stores in 37 states. Co.'s stores feature quality, national brand merchandise including moderately-priced apparel, shoes, accessories, soft home products, such as towels, sheets and pillows, and housewares targeted to middle-income customers shopping for their families and homes. In addition, Co. operates seven distribution centers located in California, Missouri, New York, Ohio, Texas, Virginia, and Wisconsin.

Recent Developments: For the year ended Jan 29 2005, net income increased 25.7% to $730,380 thousand from net income of $580,897 thousand a year earlier. Revenues were $11,700,619 thousand, up 13.8% from $10,282,094 thousand the year before. Operating income was $1,236,702 thousand versus an income of $1,006,802 thousand in the prior year, an increase of 22.8%. Total direct expense was $7,586,992 thousand versus $6,887,033 thousand in the prior year, an increase of 10.2%. Total indirect expense was $2,876,925 thousand versus $2,388,259 thousand in the prior year, an increase of 20.5%.

Prospects: In fiscal 2005, Co. plans to open roughly 95 stores, split evenly between new market entries and fill-ins in existing markets. In the Spring season, Co. will open approximately 33 stores, including seven stores each in the northeast, midwest and southeast regions and four stores each in the mid-Atlantic, southwest and southcentral regions of the U.S. In 2005, Co. intends to focus on creating an improved shopping experience through improvements in merchandise content and new improvements in merchandise presentation. Also, Co. will look to drive market share gains through differentiation in its marketing.

Financial Data

(US$ in Thousands)	9 Mos	6 Mos	3 Mos	01/31/2004	02/01/2003	02/02/2002	02/03/2001	01/29/2000
Earnings Per Share	1.92	1.85	1.73	1.72	1.87	1.45	1.10	0.77
Cash Flow Per Share	2.72	3.17	2.82	2.23	1.99	1.63	1.11	0.34
Tang Book Value Per Share	12.96	12.45	11.98	11.60	9.85	7.78	6.21	4.70
Income Statement								
Total Revenue	7,621,913	4,878,031	2,380,173	10,282,094	9,120,287	7,488,654	6,151,996	4,557,112
EBITDA	918,649	600,651	264,192	1,230,889	1,257,420	983,674	760,265	527,130
Depn & Amortn	209,044	137,268	66,235	207,585	167,037	133,699	108,950	78,855
Income Before Taxes	664,547	433,396	182,953	950,373	1,034,374	799,864	605,114	421,112
Income Taxes	251,202	163,827	69,159	359,221	390,993	304,188	232,966	162,970
Net Income	413,345	269,569	113,794	591,152	643,381	495,676	372,148	258,142
Average Shares	344,896	344,195	343,858	344,907	346,728	344,944	338,075	333,856
Balance Sheet								
Current Assets	4,155,674	3,259,188	3,206,873	3,024,839	3,284,094	2,464,044	1,921,897	1,366,523
Total Assets	8,344,674	7,272,590	7,003,512	6,698,450	6,315,503	4,929,586	3,855,154	2,914,662
Current Liabilities	2,160,795	1,341,873	1,252,130	1,122,357	1,507,992	879,971	723,297	634,412
Long-Term Obligations	1,104,283	1,091,421	1,088,663	1,075,973	1,058,784	1,095,420	803,081	494,993
Total Liabilities	3,661,253	2,784,435	2,676,761	2,507,111	2,803,586	2,138,180	1,652,515	1,229,159
Stockholders' Equity	4,683,421	4,488,155	4,326,751	4,191,339	3,511,917	2,791,406	2,202,639	1,685,503
Shares Outstanding	343,090	341,121	340,955	340,141	337,322	335,138	332,167	326,197
Statistical Record								
Return on Assets %	8.54	9.48	8.97	9.11	11.47	11.32	10.82	10.67
Return on Equity %	15.35	15.43	14.90	15.39	20.47	19.91	18.83	18.18
EBITDA Margin %	12.05	12.31	11.10	11.97	13.79	13.14	12.36	11.57
Net Margin %	5.42	5.53	4.78	5.75	7.05	6.62	6.05	5.66
Asset Turnover	1.45	1.61	1.59	1.58	1.63	1.71	1.79	1.88
Current Ratio	1.92	2.43	2.56	2.70	2.18	2.80	2.66	2.15
Debt to Equity	0.24	0.24	0.25	0.26	0.30	0.39	0.36	0.29
Price Range	56.09-40.96	64.49-40.96	64.49-41.20	64.49-41.20	77.75-49.45	71.82-43.30	71.00-34.53	40.63-31.28
P/E Ratio	29.21-21.33	34.86-22.14	37.28-23.82	37.49-23.95	41.58-26.44	49.53-29.86	64.55-31.39	52.76-40.63

Address: N56 W17000 Ridgewood Drive, Menomonee Falls, WI 53051-5660 Telephone: (262) 703 7000 Fax: (262) 703 6373	Web Site: www.kohls.com Officers: R. Lawrence Montgomery - Chmn., C.E.O. Kevin Mansell - Pres.	Auditors: Ernst & Young LLP Investor Contact: 262-703-1893

KORN/FERRY INTERNATIONAL (DE)

Exchange	Symbol	Price	52Wk Range	Yield	P/E
NYS	KFY	$19.03 (3/31/2005)	21.61-13.07	N/A	22.13

*7 Year Price Score N/A *NYSE Composite Index=100 *12 Month Price Score 100.19

Interim Earnings (Per Share)

Qtr.	Jul	Oct	Jan	Apr
2001-02	(1.25)	(0.82)	(0.19)	(0.36)
2002-03	(0.02)	(0.48)	(0.07)	(0.05)
2003-04	(0.25)	0.06	0.10	0.22
2004-05	0.20	0.21	0.23	...

Interim Dividends (Per Share)

No Dividends Paid

Valuation Analysis

Forecast P/E	16.92	No of Institutions	
	(4/7/2005)	145	
Market Cap	$780.0 Million	Shares	
Book Value	240.4 Million		30,592,928
Price/Book	3.24	% Held	
Price/Sales	1.74		76.50

Business Summary: Human Resources Services (MIC: 12.6 SIC: 361 NAIC: 41612)

Korn/Ferry International and its subsidiaries are engaged in the business of providing executive recruitment, middle-management recruitment and consulting and related services globally on a retained basis. Executive search, Co.'s core business, focuses on board level, chief executive and other senior executive positions for clients predominantly in the consumer, financial services, industrial, life sciences and technology industries. Futurestep, Co.'s middle-management recruitment business, creates customized recruitment strategies based on clients' individual workforce needs. At Apr 30 2004, the Futurestep database contained over 1.0 million recruitment candidates.

Recent Developments: For the quarter ended Jan 31 2005, net income increased 152.9% to $9,824,000 from net income of $3,885,000 in the year-earlier quarter. Revenues were $123,622,000 , up 42.6% from $86,685,000 the year before. Operating income was $17,104,000 versus an income of $6,246,000 in the prior-year quarter, an increase of 173.8%. Total indirect expense was $106,518,000 versus $80,439,000 in the prior-year quarter, an increase of 32.4%.

Prospects: Results are being positively affected by increased demand for Co.'s recruitment and leadership development services across all of its geographic regions. Going forward, Co. is focusing on expanding its non-search services, such as outsource applications, management consulting and leadership development. Co. hopes these non-search services will account for approximately 25.0% of revenues in three years, up from about 15.0% of revenues at the end of 2004. Meanwhile, Co. estimates that fourth quarter fiscal 2005 fee revenue is likely to be in the range of $115.0 million to $122.0 million, assuming constant foreign exchange rates, along with earnings in the range of $0.22 to $0.25 per share.

Financial Data

(US$ in Thousands)	9 Mos	6 Mos	3 Mos	04/30/2004	04/30/2003	04/30/2002	04/30/2001	04/30/2000
Earnings Per Share	0.86	0.73	0.58	0.13	(0.63)	(2.62)	0.81	0.82
Cash Flow Per Share	1.72	1.26	0.83	0.82	0.65	(1.59)	1.70	2.05
Tang Book Value Per Share	3.24	2.89	2.58	2.16	1.90	2.47	3.79	3.66
Income Statement								
Total Revenue	345,346	221,724	108,183	350,703	338,466	393,891	653,777	500,743
EBITDA	55,517	35,211	17,229	27,599	4,046	(85,717)	94,710	75,540
Depn & Amortn	6,723	4,382	2,242	10,030	16,161	17,482	26,990	13,333
Income Before Taxes	40,773	25,557	12,434	7,666	(22,637)	(111,720)	60,299	57,771
Income Taxes	15,288	9,391	4,486	3,218	2,040	(12,328)	25,326	24,126
Net Income	26,905	17,081	8,371	5,403	(22,902)	(98,251)	31,013	30,811
Average Shares	46,974	46,262	45,861	39,202	37,576	37,547	38,478	37,680
Balance Sheet								
Current Assets	262,200	222,170	186,182	182,712	161,635	171,895	226,402	267,838
Total Assets	494,163	440,000	398,738	394,686	369,013	377,574	500,329	475,994
Current Liabilities	130,844	104,290	78,927	94,418	88,962	146,285	171,194	184,790
Long-Term Obligations	44,901	44,852	45,195	44,400	41,364	1,634	11,842	16,916
Total Liabilities	253,717	225,165	199,614	213,804	192,952	198,277	226,877	241,550
Stockholders' Equity	240,446	214,835	199,124	180,882	166,455	179,297	270,166	231,224
Shares Outstanding	40,990	39,074	39,012	38,170	37,590	37,869	37,516	36,748
Statistical Record								
Return on Assets %	8.25	7.55	6.31	1.41	N.M.	N.M.	6.35	7.88
Return on Equity %	17.24	15.74	13.00	3.10	N.M.	N.M.	12.37	15.21
EBITDA Margin %	16.08	15.88	15.93	7.87	1.20	N.M.	14.49	15.09
Net Margin %	7.79	7.70	7.74	1.54	N.M.	N.M.	4.74	6.15
Asset Turnover	1.04	1.05	1.03	0.92	0.91	0.90	1.34	1.28
Current Ratio	2.00	2.13	2.36	1.94	1.82	1.18	1.32	1.45
Debt to Equity	0.19	0.21	0.23	0.25	0.25	0.01	0.04	0.07
Price Range	21.61-11.97	19.99-8.74	19.65-8.21	16.58-6.74	11.60-5.70	23.78-5.84	39.94-15.53	42.44-11.88
P/E Ratio	25.13-13.92	27.38-11.97	33.88-14.16	127.54-51.85	...	...	49.31-19.17	51.75-14.48

Address: 1800 Century Park East, Suite 900, Los Angeles, CA 90067	**Web Site:** www.kornferry.com	**Auditors:** ERNST & YOUNG LLP
Telephone: (310) 552 1834	**Officers:** Paul C. Reilly - Chmn., C.E.O. Gary D. Burnison - Exec. V.P., C.F.O., C.O.O.	**Investor Contact:** 310-226-2613
Fax: (310) 553 8640		

KRAFT FOODS, INC.

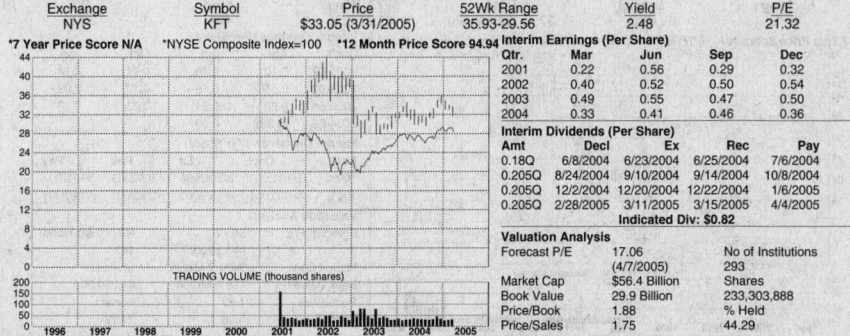

Exchange	Symbol	Price	52Wk Range	Yield	P/E
NYS	KFT	$33.05 (3/31/2005)	35.93-29.56	2.48	21.32

*7 Year Price Score N/A   *NYSE Composite Index=100   *12 Month Price Score 94.94

Interim Earnings (Per Share)

Qtr.	Mar	Jun	Sep	Dec
2001	0.22	0.56	0.29	0.32
2002	0.40	0.52	0.50	0.54
2003	0.49	0.55	0.47	0.50
2004	0.33	0.41	0.46	0.36

Interim Dividends (Per Share)

Amt	Decl	Ex	Rec	Pay
0.18Q	6/8/2004	6/23/2004	6/25/2004	7/6/2004
0.205Q	8/24/2004	9/10/2004	9/14/2004	10/8/2004
0.205Q	12/2/2004	12/20/2004	12/22/2004	1/6/2005
0.205Q	2/28/2005	3/11/2005	3/15/2005	4/4/2005
		Indicated Div: $0.82		

Valuation Analysis

Forecast P/E	17.06 (4/7/2005)	No of Institutions 293
Market Cap	$56.4 Billion	Shares 233,303,888
Book Value	29.9 Billion	% Held
Price/Book	1.88	44.29
Price/Sales	1.75	

Business Summary: Retail - Food & Beverage (MIC: 5.3 SIC: 141 NAIC: 24410)

Kraft Foods is a holding company, which manufactures and markets branded foods and beverages through its wholly-owned subsidiaries, Kraft Foods North America, Inc. and Kraft Foods International, Inc. As of Dec 31 2003, Co. had operations in 68 countries and sold its products in more than 150 countries. Co.'s products include Kraft cheese, Jacobs and Maxwell House coffees, Nabisco cookies and crackers, Philadelphia cream cheese, Oscar Mayer meats, Post cereals and Milka chocolates. As of Dec 31 2003, Altria Group, Inc. owned approximately 84.6% of Co.'s outstanding common stock.

Recent Developments: For the year ended Dec 31 2004, net income decreased 21.0% to $2,669 million from net income of $3,379 million a year earlier. Revenues were $32,168 million, up 5.5% from $30,498 million the year before. Operating income was $4,612 million versus an income of $5,860 million in the prior year, a decrease of 21.3%. Total direct expense was $20,281 million versus $18,531 million in the prior year, an increase of 9.4%. Total indirect expense was $7,275 million versus $6,107 million in the prior year, an increase of 19.1%.

Prospects: On Mar 16 2005, Co. announced plans to launch its proprietary Tassimo Hot Beverage System in the U.S. in the fall of 2005. The new brewing system, part of the "on-demand" coffee category, provides a menu of beverages that can be made at home in less than one minute. Co. has already launched the new brand in France, the U.K. and Switzerland, making this a growth opportunity with global potential. Separately, on Nov 15 2004, Co. announced the sale of substantially all of its sugar confectionery business for about $1.50 billion. The proposed sale includes the Life Savers, Creme Savers, Altoids, Trolli and Sugus brands. The transaction is expected to close by the second quarter 2005.

Financial Data
(US$ in Thousands)

	12/31/2004	12/31/2003	12/31/2002	12/31/2001	12/31/2000	12/31/1999	12/31/1998
Earnings Per Share	1.55	2.01	1.96	1.17	1.38	1.20	1.12
Cash Flow Per Share	2.34	2.39	2.15	2.07	2.23	1.85	...
Dividends Per Share	0.770	0.660	0.560	0.260	...	...	...
Dividend Payout %	49.68	32.84	28.57	22.22	...	...	...
Income Statement							
Total Revenue	32,168,000	31,010,000	29,723,000	33,875,000	26,532,000	26,797,000	27,311,000
EBITDA	5,491,000	6,824,000	6,830,000	6,526,000	5,046,000	4,609,000	4,573,000
Depn & Amortn	879,000	813,000	716,000	1,642,000	1,034,000	1,030,000	1,038,000
Income Before Taxes	3,946,000	5,346,000	5,267,000	3,447,000	3,415,000	3,040,000	2,999,000
Income Taxes	1,274,000	1,866,000	1,869,000	1,565,000	1,414,000	1,287,000	1,367,000
Net Income	2,665,000	3,476,000	3,394,000	1,882,000	2,001,000	1,753,000	1,632,000
Average Shares	1,714,000	1,728,000	1,736,000	1,610,000	1,455,000	1,455,000	1,455,000
Balance Sheet							
Current Assets	9,722,000	8,124,000	7,456,000	7,006,000	7,152,000	5,890,000	...
Total Assets	59,928,000	59,285,000	57,100,000	55,798,000	52,071,000	30,336,000	...
Current Liabilities	9,078,000	7,861,000	7,169,000	8,875,000	7,590,000	5,373,000	...
Long-Term Obligations	9,723,000	11,591,000	10,416,000	8,134,000	2,695,000	433,000	...
Total Liabilities	30,017,000	30,755,000	31,268,000	32,320,000	38,023,000	16,875,000	...
Stockholders' Equity	29,911,000	28,530,000	25,832,000	23,478,000	14,048,000	13,461,000	...
Shares Outstanding	1,705,355	1,721,937	1,730,619	1,735,000	1,455,000	1,455,000	...
Statistical Record							
Return on Assets %	4.46	5.97	6.01	3.49	4.84	...	...
Return on Equity %	9.10	12.79	13.77	10.03	14.51	...	...
EBITDA Margin %	17.07	22.01	22.98	19.26	19.02	17.20	16.74
Net Margin %	8.28	11.21	11.42	5.56	7.54	6.54	5.98
Asset Turnover	0.54	0.53	0.53	0.63	0.64	...	...
Current Ratio	1.07	1.03	1.04	0.79	0.94	1.10	...
Debt to Equity	0.33	0.41	0.40	0.35	0.19	0.03	...
Price Range	35.93-29.56	39.20-26.99	43.84-33.01	35.39-29.94	...	...	...
P/E Ratio	23.18-19.07	19.50-13.43	22.37-16.84	30.25-25.59	...	...	...
Average Yield %	2.39	2.14	1.45	0.80	...	...	...

Address: Three Lakes Drive, Northfield, IL 60093-2753
Telephone: (847) 646-2000
Fax: (847) 646-6005

Web Site: www.kraft.com
Officers: Roger K. Deromedi - C.E.O. James P. Dollive - Exec. V.P., C.F.O.

Auditors: PricewaterhouseCoopers LLP
Investor Contact: 847-646-3194
Transfer Agents: EquiServe Trust Co,. NA, Providence, RI

KRISPY KREME DOUGHNUTS INC

Exchange	Symbol	Price	52Wk Range	Yield	P/E
NYS	KKD	$7.63 (3/31/2005)	35.01-5.36	N/A	38.15

*7 Year Price Score N/A   *NYSE Composite Index=100   *12 Month Price Score 43.69

Interim Earnings (Per Share)

Qtr.	Apr	Jul	Oct	Jan
2001-02	0.10	0.10	0.11	0.14
2002-03	0.15	0.15	0.17	0.09
2003-04	0.22	0.21	0.23	0.26
2004-05	(0.38)	0.09	...	...

Interim Dividends (Per Share)

Amt	Decl	Ex	Rec	Pay
100%	2/13/2001	3/20/2001	3/5/2001	3/19/2001
100%	5/17/2001	6/15/2001	5/29/2001	6/14/2001

Valuation Analysis

Forecast P/E	56.77	No of Institutions
	(4/13/2005)	143
Market Cap	$471.2 Million	Shares
Book Value	439.5 Million	44,290,300
Price/Book	1.07	% Held
Price/Sales	0.66	71.72

Business Summary: Retail - Food & Beverage (MIC: 5.3 SIC: 461 NAIC: 11811)

Krispy Kreme Doughnuts is a retailer of more than 20 varieties of doughnuts, including Co.'s signature Hot Original Glazed, as well as coffee and other beverages and bakery items. As of Feb 1 2004, Co. operated 357 Co.-owned and franchised stores in 43 states, Canada, Australia, the United kingdom and Mexico. Each of Co.'s stores has the capacity, depending on equipment size, to produce from 4,000 dozen to over 10,000 dozen doughnuts daily. In addition, Co. sells fresh doughnuts, both packaged and unpackaged, to a variety of retail customers, such as supermarkets, convenience stores and other food service and institutional accounts.

Recent Developments: Co. has delayed reporting any further earnings information while it restates financial statements for fiscal 2004. For the quarter ended Aug 1 2004, income from continuing operations decreased 53.5% to $6,244 thousand from income of $13,440 thousand in the year-earlier quarter. Net income decreased 55.7% to $5,764 thousand from net income of $13,001 thousand in the year-earlier quarter. Revenues were $177,448 thousand, up 11.5% from $159,176 thousand the year before. Operating income was $11,840 thousand versus an income of $25,007 thousand in the prior-year quarter, a decrease of 52.7%. Total indirect expense was $165,608 thousand versus $134,169 thousand in 2003, an increase of 23.4%.

Prospects: On Mar 16 2005, Co. was served with a purported class action lawsuit that asserts claims under the Employee Retirement Income Security Act. Co. noted that an adverse outcome of this action could have a material adverse effect on its results of operations and financial condition. Separately, on Mar 25 2005, Co. announced that the lenders under its credit facility have agreed to extend until Apr 11 2005 the date on which an event of default would occur by reason of its failure to deliver financial statements for the quarter ended Oct 31 2004. If Co. is able to obtain a new lending group for new credit facilities, it will repay in full the current lenders.

Financial Data

(US$ in Thousands)	6 Mos	3 Mos	02/01/2004	02/02/2003	02/03/2002	01/28/2001	01/30/2000	01/31/1999
Earnings Per Share	0.20	0.32	0.92	0.56	0.45	0.28	3.19	(1.92)
Cash Flow Per Share	1.78	1.78	1.62	0.93	0.66	0.62	4.82	7.10
Tang Book Value Per Share	4.27	4.15	3.99	3.99	3.15	2.42	25.56	22.62
Dividends Per Share	...	...	...	...	...	...	...	3,250
Income Statement								
Total Revenue	361,804	184,356	665,592	491,549	394,354	300,715	220,243	180,880
EBITDA	42,059	23,909	117,888	66,859	47,862	28,522	15,384	325
Depn & Amortn	12,458	6,130	19,723	12,271	7,959	6,457	4,546	4,278
Income Before Taxes	27,204	16,522	94,677	54,773	42,546	23,783	9,606	(5,279)
Income Taxes	11,113	6,675	37,590	21,295	16,168	9,058	3,650	(2,112)
Net Income	(18,674)	(24,438)	57,087	33,478	26,378	14,725	5,956	(3,167)
Average Shares	63,351	63,573	62,388	59,492	58,443	53,655	1,963	1,649
Balance Sheet								
Current Assets	165,173	151,214	138,644	141,128	101,769	67,611	41,038	33,780
Total Assets	661,608	654,483	660,664	410,487	255,376	171,493	104,958	93,312
Current Liabilities	69,739	63,306	53,493	59,687	52,533	38,168	29,586	25,393
Long-Term Obligations	112,135	130,469	135,056	57,188	3,912	...	20,502	18,620
Total Liabilities	219,516	221,017	206,134	131,942	65,218	44,697	57,203	51,065
Stockholders' Equity	439,499	430,651	452,207	273,352	187,667	125,679	47,755	42,247
Shares Outstanding	61,754	61,408	61,286	56,295	54,271	51,832	1,868	1,868
Statistical Record								
Return on Assets %	2.03	3.50	10.69	10.08	12.16	10.68	6.02	...
Return on Equity %	3.10	5.14	15.78	14.56	16.56	17.03	13.27	...
EBITDA Margin %	11.62	12.97	17.71	13.60	12.14	9.48	6.99	0.18
Net Margin %	N.M.	N.M.	8.58	6.81	6.69	4.90	2.70	N.M.
Asset Turnover	1.17	1.25	1.25	1.48	1.82	2.18	2.23	...
Current Ratio	2.37	2.39	2.59	2.36	1.94	1.77	1.39	1.33
Debt to Equity	0.26	0.30	0.30	0.21	0.02	...	0.43	0.44
Price Range	49.37-15.71	49.37-30.60	49.37-28.11	43.27-28.52	45.75-15.13	26.25-9.20	...	...
P/E Ratio	246.85-78.55	154.28-95.63	53.66-30.55	77.27-50.93	101.67-33.61	93.75-32.87	...	...

Address: 370 Knollwood Street, Suite 500, Winston-Salem, NC 27103	Web Site: www.krispykreme.com	Auditors: PricewaterhouseCoopers LLP
Telephone: (336) 725 2981	Officers: James H. Morgan - Chmn. Steven G.	
Fax: (336) 733 3794	Panagos - Pres., C.O.O.	

KROGER CO.

Exchange	Symbol	Price	52Wk Range	Yield	P/E
NYS	KR	$16.03 (3/31/2005)	18.20-14.73	N/A	55.28

*7 Year Price Score 68.03 ***NYSE Composite Index=100** ***12 Month Price Score 95.89**

Interim Earnings (Per Share)

Qtr.	May	Aug	Nov	Jan
2001-02	0.36	0.31	0.16	0.42
2002-03	0.45	0.33	0.33	0.42
2003-04	0.46	0.25	0.15	(0.44)
2004-05	0.35	0.19	0.19	...

Interim Dividends (Per Share)

No Dividends Paid

Valuation Analysis

Forecast P/E	13.18 (4/7/2005)	No of Institutions 338
Market Cap	$11.7 Billion	Shares
Book Value	4.3 Billion	563,855,936
Price/Book	2.71	% Held
Price/Sales	0.21	77.01

Business Summary: Retail - Food & Beverage (MIC: 5.3 SIC: 411 NAIC: 45110)

Kroger operated 2,532 supermarkets in 32 states as of Jan 31 2004, principally under the Kroger, Fred Meyer, Ralphs, Smith's, King Soopers, Dillons, Fry's and Fry's Marketplace, City Market, Food 4 Less and QFC banners. Most stores include floral, seafood, pharmacy, bakery and other specialty departments. Co. operates 802 convenience stores under the names: Kwik Shop, Quick Stop, Tom Thumb, Turkey Hill Minit Markets, Loaf 'N Jug, and Mini-Mart. Co. also operates 440 fine jewelry stores, under the banners of Fred Meyer, Merksamer, Fox's, Littman, and Barclay Jewelers, 466 supermarket fuel centers, and 42 food processing plants.

Recent Developments: For the quarter ended Nov 6 2004, net income increased 30.0% to $143 million from net income of $110 million in the year-earlier quarter. Revenues were $12,854 million, up 5.9% from $12,141 million the year before. Operating income was $337 million versus an income of $324 million in the prior-year quarter, an increase of 4.0%. Total direct expense was $9,632 million versus $9,016 million in the prior-year quarter, an increase of 6.8%. Total indirect expense was $2,885 million versus $2,801 million in the prior-year quarter, an increase of 3.0%.

Prospects: Co.'s prospects appear encouraging, reflecting recent positive identical food-store sales comparisons. For instance, for the third quarter ended Nov 6 2004 identical food-store sales, including fuel, increased 3.2% and, excluding fuel, increased 1.8%. Co. noted that Ralphs and Food 4 Less stores in southern California together accounted for 0.1% of this increase. Meanwhile, Co. opened, expanded, relocated or acquired 30 food stores; remodeled 33 stores; and closed 20 stores during the third quarter of 2004. Total food store square footage increased 1.2% over the prior year. Capital expenditures totaled $429.0 million.

Financial Data

(US$ in Thousands)	9 Mos	6 Mos	3 Mos	01/31/2004	02/01/2003	02/02/2002	02/03/2001	01/29/2000
Earnings Per Share	0.29	0.25	0.31	0.42	1.52	1.26	1.04	0.73
Cash Flow Per Share	3.22	3.01	3.01	2.97	4.10	2.93	2.73	...
Tang Book Value Per Share	1.64	1.54	1.37	1.18	0.36	N.M.	N.M.	N.M.
Income Statement								
Total Revenue	42,739,000	29,885,000	16,905,000	53,791,000	51,760,000	50,098,000	49,000,000	45,352,000
EBITDA	2,256,000	1,633,000	961,000	2,583,000	3,660,000	3,435,000	3,191,000	2,742,000
Depn & Amortn	949,000	662,000	372,000	1,209,000	1,087,000	1,076,000	1,008,000	961,000
Income Before Taxes	865,000	646,000	417,000	770,000	1,973,000	1,711,000	1,508,000	1,129,000
Income Taxes	317,000	241,000	154,000	455,000	740,000	668,000	628,000	491,000
Net Income	548,000	405,000	263,000	315,000	1,205,000	1,043,000	877,000	628,000
Average Shares	742,000	744,000	749,000	754,000	791,000	825,000	846,000	858,000
Balance Sheet								
Current Assets	6,197,000	5,562,000	5,838,000	5,619,000	5,566,000	5,512,000	5,416,000	5,531,000
Total Assets	21,091,000	20,284,000	20,477,000	20,184,000	20,102,000	19,087,000	18,190,000	17,966,000
Current Liabilities	6,408,000	6,140,000	6,046,000	5,586,000	5,608,000	5,485,000	5,591,000	5,728,000
Long-Term Obligations	7,613,000	7,299,000	7,757,000	8,116,000	8,222,000	8,412,000	8,210,000	8,045,000
Total Liabilities	16,754,000	16,015,000	16,337,000	16,173,000	16,252,000	15,585,000	15,101,000	15,283,000
Stockholders' Equity	4,337,000	4,269,000	4,140,000	4,011,000	3,850,000	3,502,000	3,089,000	2,683,000
Shares Outstanding	732,000	736,000	738,000	743,000	758,000	894,000	815,000	835,000
Statistical Record								
Return on Assets %	1.02	0.89	1.13	1.57	6.17	5.61	4.77	...
Return on Equity %	4.94	4.26	5.58	8.04	32.87	31.74	29.90	...
EBITDA Margin %	5.28	5.46	5.68	4.80	7.07	6.86	6.51	6.05
Net Margin %	1.28	1.36	1.56	0.59	2.33	2.08	1.79	1.38
Asset Turnover	2.68	2.73	2.70	2.68	2.65	2.70	2.67	...
Current Ratio	0.97	0.91	0.97	1.01	0.99	1.00	0.97	0.97
Debt to Equity	1.76	1.71	1.87	2.02	2.14	2.40	2.66	3.00
Price Range	19.46-14.73	19.60-14.97	19.60-15.10	19.60-12.13	23.48-11.41	27.36-19.92	27.06-14.19	34.38-14.94
P/E Ratio	67.10-50.79	78.40-59.88	63.23-48.71	46.67-28.88	15.45-7.51	21.71-15.81	26.02-13.64	47.09-20.46

Address: 1014 Vine Street, Cincinnati, OH 45202 **Telephone:** (513) 762-4000 **Fax:** (513) 762-1400	**Web Site:** www.kroger.com **Officers:** David B. Dillon - Chmn., C.E.O. W. Rodney McMullen - Vice-Chmn.	**Auditors:** PricewaterhouseCoopers LLP **Investor Contact:** 513-762-4969 **Transfer Agents:** Bank of New York, New York, NY

L-3 COMMUNICATIONS HOLDINGS, INC.

Exchange	Symbol	Price	52Wk Range	Yield	P/E
NYS	LLL	$71.02 (3/31/2005)	76.87-56.50	0.70	21.33

*7 Year Price Score N/A   *NYSE Composite Index=100   *12 Month Price Score 101.63

Interim Earnings (Per Share)

Qtr.	Mar	Jun	Sep	Dec
2001	0.20	0.30	0.41	0.56
2002	0.35	0.38	0.62	0.81
2003	0.50	0.53	0.74	0.94
2004	0.67	0.81	0.93	0.92

Interim Dividends (Per Share)

Amt	Decl	Ex	Rec	Pay
0.10Q	4/27/2004	5/13/2004	5/17/2004	6/15/2004
0.10Q	7/14/2004	8/13/2004	8/17/2004	9/15/2004
0.10Q	10/12/2004	11/15/2004	11/17/2004	12/15/2004
0.125Q	2/10/2005	2/17/2005	2/22/2005	3/15/2005

Indicated Div: $0.50

Valuation Analysis

Forecast P/E	17.95 (4/13/2005)	No of Institutions 468
Market Cap	$8.2 Billion	Shares 91,097,480
Book Value	3.8 Billion	% Held 78.30
Price/Book	2.16	
Price/Sales	1.19	

Business Summary: Communications (MIC: 10.1 SIC: 663 NAIC: 34220)

L-3 Communications Holdings is a supplier of a range of products used in a number of aerospace and defense platforms. Co. is also a supplier of subsystems on many platforms, including those for secure communication networks, mobile satellite communications, information security systems, shipboard communications, naval power systems, fuzes and safety and arming devices for missiles and munitions, microwave assemblies for radars and missiles, telemetry and instrumentation and airport security systems. Co. is also a prime system contractor for aircraft modernization and maintenance, Intelligence, Surveillance and Reconnaissance (ISR) collection platforms, and simulation and training.

Recent Developments: For the year ended Dec 31 2004, net income advanced 37.5% to $381.9 million compared with $277.6 million in the previous year. Results for 2004 and 2003 included losses on the retirement of debt of $5.0 million and $11.2 million, respectively. Total sales climbed 36.3% to $6.90 billion from $5.06 billion a year earlier. Sales from contracts, primarily with the U.S. Government jumped 39.8% to $6.16 billion, while commercial sales increased 12.4% to $741.4 million. Operating income expanded 28.8% to $748.6 million from $581.0 million the year before.

Prospects: Co. expects that for 2005 U.S. defense spending will remain strong as the DoD continues to focus on transforming the military and upgrading its assets. So, Co. expects 2005 sales exceeding $8.00 billion, with growth in excess of 17.0%, versus 2004, including organic sales growth of at least 10.0%, with the remaining growth coming from business acquisitions. Co.'s estimates includes its recent agreements to acquire the Marine Controls division of CAE, the Boeing Electron Dynamics Devices business and the General Dynamics Propulsion Systems business, which are slated to close during the first quarter of 2005. Full-year 2005 diluted earnings per share are expected to range from $3.95 to $4.05.

Financial Data
(US$ in Thousands)

	12/31/2004	12/31/2003	12/31/2002	12/31/2001	12/31/2000	12/31/1999	12/31/1998	12/31/1997
Earnings Per Share	3.33	2.71	1.93	1.48	1.19	0.88	0.63	0.30
Cash Flow Per Share	5.74	4.75	3.66	2.31	1.70	1.54	1.72	1.85
Dividends Per Share	0.400	...	...	...	...	...	...	...
Dividend Payout %	12.01	...	...	...	...	...	...	...
Income Statement								
Total Revenue	6,896,997	5,061,594	4,011,229	2,347,422	1,910,061	1,405,462	1,037,045	546,525
EBITDA	868,180	669,896	535,954	355,580	298,596	213,642	143,268	75,153
Depn & Amortn	126,144	103,400	83,252	82,968	71,485	57,622	42,919	23,707
Income Before Taxes	596,688	433,813	330,210	186,222	134,079	95,430	53,450	22,992
Income Taxes	214,808	156,173	117,885	70,764	51,352	36,741	20,899	10,687
Net Income	381,880	277,640	178,097	115,458	82,727	58,689	32,551	12,305
Average Shares	117,372	106,068	97,413	85,438	69,906	67,032	51,800	40,024
Balance Sheet								
Current Assets	2,808,324	1,937,702	1,639,374	1,238,585	829,570	567,707	405,367	267,377
Total Assets	7,780,765	6,492,890	5,242,308	3,335,433	2,463,544	1,633,771	1,285,396	703,404
Current Liabilities	1,175,840	924,212	696,639	524,277	468,669	318,306	247,534	135,567
Long-Term Obligations	2,189,806	2,457,300	1,847,752	1,315,252	1,095,000	605,000	605,000	392,000
Total Liabilities	3,903,468	3,842,183	2,966,865	2,051,644	1,770,975	1,050,596	985,422	589,737
Stockholders' Equity	3,799,761	2,574,496	2,202,202	1,213,892	692,569	583,175	299,974	113,667
Shares Outstanding	115,681	97,077	94,577	78,496	67,213	65,589	54,804	34,112
Statistical Record								
Return on Assets %	5.34	4.73	4.15	3.98	4.03	4.02	3.27	1.90
Return on Equity %	11.95	11.62	10.43	12.11	12.93	13.29	15.74	4.19
EBITDA Margin %	12.59	13.23	13.36	15.15	15.63	15.20	13.82	13.75
Net Margin %	5.54	5.49	4.44	4.92	4.33	4.18	3.14	2.25
Asset Turnover	0.96	0.86	0.94	0.81	0.93	0.96	1.04	0.84
Current Ratio	2.39	2.10	2.35	2.36	1.77	1.78	1.64	1.97
Debt to Equity	0.58	0.95	0.84	1.08	1.58	1.04	2.02	3.45
Price Range	76.87-49.80	51.60-35.60	65.98-41.09	48.23-31.24	38.78-17.84	26.44-17.41	24.09-13.31	...
P/E Ratio	23.08-14.95	19.04-13.14	34.19-21.29	32.59-21.11	32.59-14.99	30.04-19.78	38.24-21.13	...
Average Yield %	0.64	...	...	...	...	...	...	...

Address: 600 Third Avenue, New York, NY 10016 **Telephone:** (212) 697-1111 **Fax:** (212) 867-5249	**Web Site:** www.L-3Com.com **Officers:** Frank C. Lanza - Chmn., C.E.O. Robert V. LaPenta - Pres., C.F.O.	**Auditors:** PricewaterhouseCoopers LLP **Investor Contact:** 212-697-1111

LA-Z-BOY INC.

Exchange	Symbol	Price	52Wk Range	Yield	P/E	Div Acheiver
NYS	LZB	$13.93 (3/31/2005)	22.50-12.95	3.16	N/A	23 Years

*7 Year Price Score 72.52 *NYSE Composite Index=100 ***12 Month Price Score 83.37**

Interim Earnings (Per Share)

Qtr.	Jul	Oct	Jan	Apr
2001-02	0.05	0.20	0.35	0.41
2002-03	(0.68)	0.50	0.41	0.44
2003-04	0.11	0.28	0.29	(0.78)
2004-05	(0.07)	0.17	0.21	...

Interim Dividends (Per Share)

Amt	Decl	Ex	Rec	Pay
0.11Q	5/4/2004	5/26/2004	5/28/2004	6/10/2004
0.11Q	8/10/2004	8/26/2004	8/30/2004	9/10/2004
0.11Q	11/9/2004	11/23/2004	11/26/2004	12/10/2004
0.11Q	2/8/2005	2/23/2005	2/25/2005	3/10/2005

Indicated Div: $0.44 (Div. Reinv. Plan)

Valuation Analysis

Forecast P/E	11.98 (4/7/2005)	No of Institutions	138
Market Cap	$726.7 Million	Shares	38,495,096
Book Value	526.2 Million	% Held	73.79
Price/Book	1.38		
Price/Sales	0.35		

Business Summary: Chemicals (MIC: 11.1 SIC: 511 NAIC: 37121)

La-Z-Boy is a furniture manufacturer and import distributor. Co. is comprised of two business groups: upholstery and casegoods. The upholstery segment includes recliners, sofas, chairs, sleeper sofas, loveseats and ottomans. The casegoods segment includes tables, chairs, dressers, headboards and accent pieces. In addition to upholstery and wood, Co. markets contract furniture to the hospitality, healthcare and assisted living industries. Brand names include La-Z-Boy, England, Sam Moore, Bauhaus, Pennsylvania House, Clayton Marcus, Kincaid, Hammary, Alexvale, American Drew, La-Z-Boy Contract Furniture, American of Martinsville, Drew and Lea.

Recent Developments: For the quarter ended Jan 22 2005, net income decreased 27.4% to $11,092 thousand from net income of $15,279 thousand in the year-earlier quarter. Revenues were $518,160 thousand, up 5.3% from $492,167 thousand the year before. Operating income was $20,254 thousand versus an income of $26,040 thousand in the prior-year quarter, a decrease of 22.2%. Total direct expense was $791,990 thousand versus $768,218 thousand in the prior-year quarter, an increase of 3.1%. Total indirect expense was $101,911 thousand versus $82,018 thousand in the prior-year quarter, an increase of 24.3%.

Prospects: Co. continues to face soft market conditions at the retail level. Also, operating margins remain weak in light of continued pressure from increased raw material pricing. However, Co. has begun to see some improvement in its margin trend as the impact of recent price increases take effect. Looking ahead, Co. expects sales for the fourth quarter of fiscal 2005 to be flat to slightly up compared with the prior year's quarter. Co. anticipates earnings for the fourth quarter to be in the range of $0.26 to $0.30 per diluted share, which includes restructuring charges of $0.01 and up to a $0.02 per share potential loss from the consolidation of variable interest entities.

Financial Data

(US$ in Thousands)	9 Mos	6 Mos	3 Mos	04/24/2004	04/26/2003	04/27/2002	04/28/2001	04/29/2000
Earnings Per Share	(0.47)	(0.39)	(0.28)	(0.11)	0.63	1.01	1.13	1.60
Cash Flow Per Share	0.58	0.68	2.10	2.49	2.19	2.20	1.92	1.06
Tang Book Value Per Share	8.24	8.10	8.01	8.19	8.36	8.15	7.40	6.70
Dividends Per Share	0.430	0.420	0.410	0.400	0.400	0.360	0.350	0.320
Dividend Payout %	...	...	...	...	63.49	35.64	30.97	20.00
Income Statement								
Total Revenue	1,518,201	1,000,041	466,371	1,998,876	2,111,830	2,153,952	2,256,197	1,717,420
EBITDA	54,021	26,292	3,435	62,653	196,202	141,625	173,922	178,334
Depn & Amortn	21,154	14,000	6,908	29,112	30,695	43,988	45,697	30,342
Income Before Taxes	25,367	7,476	(5,682)	22,288	154,997	88,936	112,044	140,313
Income Taxes	9,640	2,841	(2,159)	19,760	58,899	27,185	43,708	52,699
Net Income	16,429	5,337	(3,523)	(5,796)	36,316	61,751	68,336	87,614
Average Shares	52,193	52,101	51,967	53,679	57,435	61,125	60,692	54,860
Balance Sheet								
Current Assets	636,704	676,729	624,921	653,674	679,494	671,692	708,776	692,369
Total Assets	1,027,495	1,061,957	1,011,199	1,047,496	1,123,066	1,160,776	1,222,503	1,218,297
Current Liabilities	209,042	250,412	206,367	283,321	214,587	226,893	249,915	237,006
Long-Term Obligations	229,158	231,652	232,833	181,807	222,371	139,386	199,419	236,094
Total Liabilities	501,342	543,669	498,815	525,168	513,127	447,254	527,357	555,205
Stockholders' Equity	526,153	518,288	512,384	522,328	609,939	713,522	695,146	663,092
Shares Outstanding	52,166	52,087	52,002	52,031	55,027	59,953	60,501	61,328
Statistical Record								
Return on Assets %	N.M.	N.M.	N.M.	N.M.	3.19	5.20	5.61	9.33
Return on Equity %	N.M.	N.M.	N.M.	N.M.	5.50	8.79	10.09	15.99
EBITDA Margin %	3.56	2.63	0.74	3.13	9.29	6.58	7.71	10.38
Net Margin %	1.08	0.53	N.M.	N.M.	1.72	2.87	3.03	5.10
Asset Turnover	2.00	1.91	1.95	1.85	1.85	1.81	1.85	1.83
Current Ratio	3.05	2.70	3.03	2.31	3.17	2.96	2.84	2.92
Debt to Equity	0.44	0.45	0.45	0.35	0.36	0.20	0.29	0.36
Price Range	23.50-12.95	23.50-13.00	24.12-16.63	24.12-18.90	30.04-16.45	30.88-15.16	18.50-13.44	24.44-13.69
P/E Ratio	...	...	...	...	47.68-26.11	30.57-15.01	16.37-11.89	15.27-8.55
Average Yield %	2.43	2.20	1.98	1.86	1.74	1.71	2.21	1.67

Address: 1284 North Telegraph Road, Monroe, MI 48162 Telephone: (734) 241-1444 Fax: (734) 241-4422	Web Site: www.la-z-boy.com Officers: Patrick H. Norton - Chmn. Kurt L. Darrow - Pres., C.E.O.	Auditors: PricewaterhouseCoopers LLP Investor Contact: 734-241-4414 Transfer Agents: EquiServe Trust Company, N.A., Providence, RI

LABORATORY CORP. OF AMERICA HOLDINGS

Exchange	Symbol	Price	52Wk Range	Yield	P/E
NYS	LH	$48.20 (3/31/2005)	50.10-36.80	N/A	19.67

*7 Year Price Score 137.63 *NYSE Composite Index=100 *12 Month Price Score 101.54

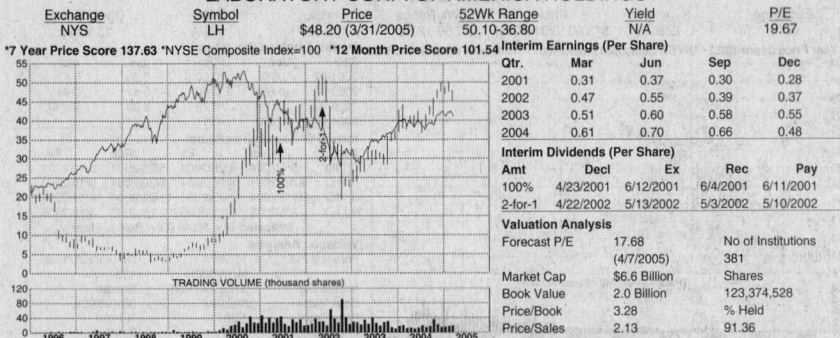

Interim Earnings (Per Share)

Qtr.	Mar	Jun	Sep	Dec
2001	0.31	0.37	0.30	0.28
2002	0.47	0.55	0.39	0.37
2003	0.51	0.60	0.58	0.55
2004	0.61	0.70	0.66	0.48

Interim Dividends (Per Share)

Amt	Decl	Ex	Rec	Pay
100%	4/23/2001	6/12/2001	6/4/2001	6/11/2001
2-for-1	4/22/2002	5/13/2002	5/3/2002	5/10/2002

Valuation Analysis

Forecast P/E	17.68	No of Institutions	
	(4/7/2005)	381	
Market Cap	$6.6 Billion	Shares	
Book Value	2.0 Billion	123,374,528	
Price/Book	3.28	% Held	
Price/Sales	2.13	91.36	

Business Summary: Diagnostic Services (MIC: 9.5 SIC: 071 NAIC: 21511)

Laboratory Corp. of America Holdings is an independent clinical laboratory. Through a national network of laboratories, Co. offers more than 4,400 different clinical laboratory tests that are used by the medical profession in routine testing, patient diagnosis, and in the monitoring and treatment of disease. In addition, Co. has developed specialty and niche businesses based on certain types of specialized testing capabilities and client requirements, such as oncology testing, HIV genotyping and phenotyping, diagnostic genetics and clinical research trials. Co. has a network of 31 primary labs and over 1,200 service sites, consisting of branches, patient service centers and STAT labs.

Recent Developments: For the year ended Dec 31 2004, net income increased 13.1% to $363000 thousand from net income of $321000 thousand a year earlier. Revenues were $3084800 thousand, up 4.9% from $2939400 thousand the year before. Operating income was $598400 thousand versus an income of $533700 thousand in the prior year, an increase of 12.1%. Total direct expense was $1795500 thousand versus $1714800 thousand in the prior year, an increase of 4.7%. Total indirect expense was $690900 thousand versus $6909000%.

Prospects: Revenues are benefiting from improved testing volume, measured by accessions, and an improvement in price per accession. Co.'s significant generation of free cash flow has allowed it to continue to repurchase shares, as well as complete the strategic acquisition of US LABS on Feb 3 2005. The acquisition of US LABS provides both an important anatomical pathology base in California and a facility capable of launching a genomics and esoteric platform in the West. Meanwhile, Co.'s existing genomic, esoteric and anatomical pathology testing businesses are poised for continued growth, and Co. remains focused on its strategic priorities related to customer retention and managed care.

Financial Data
(US$ in Thousands)

	12/31/2004	12/31/2003	12/31/2002	12/31/2001	12/31/2000	12/31/1999	12/31/1998	12/31/1997
Earnings Per Share	2.45	2.22	1.77	1.27	0.81	0.30	0.50	(2.65)
Cash Flow Per Share	3.85	3.92	3.12	2.28	2.61	3.56	2.51	2.93
Tang Book Value Per Share	1.04	0.27	2.67	0.83	0.08	N.M.	N.M.	N.M.
Income Statement								
Total Revenue	3,084,800	2,939,400	2,507,700	2,199,800	1,919,300	1,698,700	1,612,600	1,579,900
EBITDA	787,000	710,500	544,600	458,000	334,200	232,500	211,800	(5,200)
Depn & Amortn	135,600	129,200	96,800	101,100	89,600	84,500	84,200	86,800
Income Before Taxes	615,300	540,400	432,300	332,300	207,600	105,500	81,500	(161,300)
Income Taxes	252,300	219,400	177,700	149,600	95,500	40,100	12,700	(54,400)
Net Income	363,000	321,000	254,600	179,500	112,100	65,400	68,800	(106,900)
Average Shares	150,700	144,756	144,197	141,077	96,299	51,508	49,938	49,296
Balance Sheet								
Current Assets	740,000	657,900	596,700	624,500	511,700	499,500	519,100	527,600
Total Assets	3,600,900	3,414,900	2,611,800	1,929,600	1,666,900	1,590,200	1,640,900	1,658,500
Current Liabilities	300,800	757,600	228,800	201,200	311,900	245,600	251,400	196,600
Long-Term Obligations	892,200	360,700	521,500	508,900	353,700	482,800	575,500	689,600
Total Liabilities	1,601,600	1,519,000	1,000,100	844,200	789,500	1,414,700	1,486,500	1,529,400
Stockholders' Equity	1,999,300	1,895,900	1,611,700	1,085,400	877,400	175,500	154,400	129,100
Shares Outstanding	136,200	143,333	147,741	141,107	139,478	51,515	50,112	49,417
Statistical Record								
Return on Assets %	10.32	10.65	11.21	9.98	6.86	4.05	4.17	N.M.
Return on Equity %	18.59	18.30	18.88	18.29	21.24	39.65	48.54	N.M.
EBITDA Margin %	25.51	24.17	21.72	20.82	17.41	13.69	13.13	N.M.
Net Margin %	11.77	10.92	10.15	8.16	5.84	3.85	4.27	N.M.
Asset Turnover	0.88	0.98	1.10	1.22	1.18	1.05	0.98	0.88
Current Ratio	2.46	0.87	2.61	3.10	1.64	2.03	2.06	2.68
Debt to Equity	0.45	0.19	0.32	0.47	0.40	2.75	3.73	5.34
Price Range	50.00-36.80	37.10-23.24	51.98-19.19	45.40-27.95	45.00-8.13	9.38-3.28	6.56-2.81	10.00-3.44
P/E Ratio	20.41-15.02	16.71-10.47	29.37-10.84	35.75-22.01	55.56-10.03	31.25-10.94	13.13-5.63	...

Address: 358 South Main Street, Burlington, NC 27215 **Telephone:** (336) 229-1127 **Fax:** (336) 229-7717	**Web Site:** www.labcorp.com **Officers:** Thomas P. Mac Mahon - Chmn., Pres., C.E.O. Wesley R. Elingburg - Exec. V.P., C.F.O., Treas.	**Auditors:** PricewaterhouseCoopers LLP **Investor Contact:** 336-436-4855

LABRANCHE & CO., INC.

Exchange	Symbol	Price	52Wk Range	Yield	P/E
NYS	LAB	$9.30 (3/31/2005)	11.21-7.09	N/A	N/A

7 Year Price Score N/A   *NYSE Composite Index=100   *12 Month Price Score 103.45

TRADING VOLUME (thousand shares)

Interim Earnings (Per Share)

Qtr.	Mar	Jun	Sep	Dec
2001	0.40	0.29	0.15	0.30
2002	0.43	0.22	0.33	0.36
2003	0.07	0.18	0.04	(3.37)
2004	0.11	(0.43)	(0.61)	0.15

Interim Dividends (Per Share)

Dividend Payment Suspended

Valuation Analysis

Forecast P/E	26.40 (4/13/2005)	No of Institutions 117
Market Cap	$562.9 Million	Shares 44,494,768
Book Value	693.0 Million	% Held
Price/Book	0.81	
Price/Sales	1.76	73.40

Business Summary: Finance Intermediaries & Services (MIC: 8.7 SIC: 211 NAIC: 23120)

LaBranche & Co. is a holding company that owns all the outstanding stock of Henderson Brothers, which is a clearing broker for customers of several introducing brokers and provides direct access floor brokerage services to institutional customers. As a NYSE specialist, Co.'s role is to maintain a fair and orderly market in its specialist stocks. As of Dec 31 2003, Co. is the specialist for more than 650 companies, nine of which are in the Dow Jones Industrial Average, 30 of which are in the S&P 100 Index and 103 of which are S&P 500 Index companies. Co. also acts as the specialist in over 200 options.

Recent Developments: For the year ended Dec 31 2004, Co. reported a net loss of $43.8 million compared with a net loss of $179.4 million in the previous year. Results for 2004 and 2003 included net gains on non-marketable investments of $25.0 million and $1.1 million, goodwill impairment charges of $37.6 million and $170.3 million, and exchange memberships impairments of $18.3 million and $515,000, respectively. Results also included a premium charge for the repurchase of debt of $49.0 million in 2004 and a charge for restitution and fines of $63.5 million in 2003. Total revenues increased 4.3% to $319.0 million from $306.0 million a year earlier.

Prospects: Co.'s outlook appears satisfactory, reflecting recent solid top line growth. For example, total revenue climbed 18.1% to $83.8 million for the three months ended Dec 31 2004, driven by higher net gains on principal transactions, commissions and other revenues. Meanwhile, total expenses for the period, excluding restitution and fines and goodwill impairment charges in the comparable year-ago period, increased 11.1% to $69.8 million from $62.8 million, due primarily to increased employee compensation and related benefits expenses, higher interest expense, and increased exchange, clearing and brokerage fees.

Financial Data
(US$ in Thousands)

	12/31/2004	12/31/2003	12/31/2002	12/31/2001	12/31/2000	12/31/1999	12/31/1998	12/31/1997
Earnings Per Share	(0.77)	(3.08)	1.34	1.13	1.69	0.72	...	...
Cash Flow Per Share	(2.09)	7.70	1.62	(2.18)	0.59	(0.36)	...	...
Tang Book Value Per Share	0.93	0.81	0.85	N.M.	N.M.	1.78	...	...
Dividends Per Share	...	0.240	...	...	...	...	...	...
Income Statement								
Total Revenue	319,047	305,989	452,845	424,130	344,809	201,037	126,411	67,630
Income Before Taxes	(55,825)	(185,396)	166,124	156,711	166,577	52,933	32,855	17,715
Income Taxes	(12,045)	(6,007)	78,898	85,124	84,654	23,899	3,900	1,881
Net Income	(43,780)	(179,389)	87,226	71,587	81,923	29,034	28,955	15,834
Average Shares	59,905	59,614	59,939	56,948	48,581	40,443	...	...
Balance Sheet								
Total Assets	2,055,097	1,959,602	1,912,802	2,000,837	1,004,122	505,125	272,180	157,739
Total Liabilities	1,361,755	1,186,316	923,114	1,072,479	633,221	253,153	157,534	99,385
Stockholders' Equity	692,986	772,964	989,688	928,358	370,901	251,972	...	...
Shares Outstanding	60,532	59,791	59,504	58,733	49,069	45,875	...	...
Statistical Record								
Return on Assets %	N.M.	N.M.	4.46	4.76	10.83	7.47	13.47	...
Return on Equity %	N.M.	N.M.	9.10	11.02	26.23	...	...	...
Price Range	12.10-7.09	26.99-7.60	36.11-17.50	51.03-19.50	39.63-11.13	14.50-9.38	...	...
P/E Ratio	...	...	26.95-13.06	45.16-17.26	23.45-6.58	20.14-13.02	...	...
Average Yield %	...	1.38	...	...	...	...	...	...

Address: One Exchange Plaza, New York, NY 10006
Telephone: (212) 425-1144
Fax: (212) 344-1469

Web Site: www.labranche.com
Officers: George M.L. LaBranche - Chmn., Pres., C.E.O. S. Lawrence Prendergast - Exec. V.P., Fin.

Auditors: KPMG LLP
Investor Contact: 212-820-0437

LAFARGE NORTH AMERICA, INC.

Exchange	Symbol	Price	52Wk Range	Yield	P/E
NYS	LAF	$58.45 (3/31/2005)	63.75-40.65	1.51	15.14

*7 Year Price Score 119.88 *NYSE Composite Index=100 *12 Month Price Score 114.18

Interim Earnings (Per Share)

Qtr.	Mar	Jun	Sep	Dec
2001	(0.92)	1.19	1.80	1.12
2002	(0.74)	1.44	1.94	0.98
2003	(1.19)	1.00	3.04	0.91
2004	(0.96)	1.34	2.16	1.28

Interim Dividends (Per Share)

Amt	Decl	Ex	Rec	Pay
0.20Q	5/4/2004	5/13/2004	5/17/2004	6/1/2004
0.22Q	8/3/2004	8/12/2004	8/16/2004	9/1/2004
0.22Q	11/2/2004	11/10/2004	11/15/2004	12/1/2004
0.22Q	2/4/2005	2/11/2005	2/15/2005	3/1/2005
		Indicated Div: $0.88		

Valuation Analysis

Forecast P/E	12.74 (4/7/2005)	No of Institutions	171
Market Cap	$4.1 Billion	Shares	27,464,588
Book Value	3.1 Billion	% Held	36.73
Price/Book	1.33		
Price/Sales	1.10		

Business Summary: Stone, Clay, Glass, and Concrete Products (MIC: 11.2 SIC: 241 NAIC: 27310)

Lafarge North America is a major supplier of cement and ready-mixed concrete in North America. Co. also produces construction aggregates such as crushed stone, sand and gravel, and is a manufacturer of gypsum drywall. Co. has over 1,000 operations doing business in most states and throughout Canada, where it conducts business through its subsidiary, Lafarge Canada Inc. Co.'s products are used in the construction of such diverse projects as roads, offices, factories, hospitals, department stores, sports stadiums, banks, museums, high-rise apartments, amusement parks, swimming pools and bridges.

Recent Developments: For the year ended Dec 31 2004, net income increased 5.3% to $295,501 thousand from net income of $280,557 thousand a year earlier. Revenues were $3,763,268 thousand, up 13.4% from $3,318,936 thousand the year before. Total direct expense was $3,108,597 thousand versus $2,773,693 thousand in the prior year, an increase of 12.1%. Total indirect expense was $402,974 thousand versus $353,056 thousand in the prior year, an increase of 14.1%.

Prospects: Results reflect sustained construction activity in both the U.S. and Canada, helped by solid economic growth and low interest rates. In addition, favorable weather both at the beginning and end of the year resulted in strong volumes in the first and fourth quarters, typically low seasons in the construction business. Pricing trends also continued to be positive, and successful price increases in most of Co.'s product lines were achieved in the majority of its markets. Looking ahead, Co. expects the continuation of solid demand and a favorable pricing environment in most of its markets. However, Co. cautioned that it expects to experience cost pressures, especially escalating energy prices.

Financial Data

(US$ in Thousands)	12/31/2004	12/31/2003	12/31/2002	12/31/2001	12/31/2000	12/31/1999	12/31/1998	12/31/1997
Earnings Per Share	3.86	3.79	3.64	3.21	3.51	3.77	3.24	2.54
Cash Flow Per Share	4.44	5.54	5.82	5.87	6.64	5.49	5.22	4.72
Tang Book Value Per Share	35.53	30.01	23.81	21.67	21.03	18.50	14.19	16.47
Dividends Per Share	0.840	0.700	0.600	0.600	0.600	0.600	0.510	0.420
Dividend Payout %	21.76	18.47	16.48	18.69	17.09	15.92	15.74	16.54
Income Statement								
Total Revenue	3,763,268	3,318,936	3,251,555	3,323,020	2,787,629	2,654,361	2,448,205	1,806,351
EBITDA	685,190	594,247	594,382	588,208	599,046	649,889	563,829	407,202
Depn & Amortn	211,300	189,900	182,154	194,160	168,294	168,272	156,782	106,304
Income Before Taxes	441,399	350,645	369,157	346,156	403,829	436,786	379,824	294,234
Income Taxes	145,898	133,198	100,782	112,066	146,462	161,412	144,324	112,258
Net Income	295,501	280,557	268,375	234,090	257,367	275,374	235,500	181,976
Average Shares	76,653	74,014	73,814	72,910	73,379	73,022	72,665	71,780
Balance Sheet								
Current Assets	1,971,070	1,666,214	1,258,640	1,184,008	1,076,585	1,135,501	937,891	815,968
Total Assets	5,404,135	4,766,664	4,234,228	4,117,601	3,902,584	3,304,246	2,904,797	1,899,057
Current Liabilities	1,082,535	583,245	660,741	838,583	740,479	510,243	414,977	295,732
Long-Term Obligations	470,838	715,391	671,048	674,616	687,448	719,781	751,151	132,337
Total Liabilities	2,291,276	2,107,022	2,074,577	2,120,540	2,010,415	1,581,362	1,489,623	643,369
Stockholders' Equity	3,112,859	2,659,642	2,159,651	1,997,061	1,892,169	1,722,884	1,415,174	1,255,688
Shares Outstanding	70,600	69,400	68,900	67,890	67,492	73,200	72,300	71,780
Statistical Record								
Return on Assets %	5.79	6.23	6.43	5.84	7.12	8.87	9.80	9.80
Return on Equity %	10.21	11.64	12.91	12.04	14.20	17.55	17.63	15.38
EBITDA Margin %	18.21	17.90	18.28	17.70	21.49	24.48	23.03	22.54
Net Margin %	7.85	8.45	8.25	7.04	9.23	10.37	9.62	10.07
Asset Turnover	0.74	0.74	0.78	0.83	0.77	0.85	1.02	0.97
Current Ratio	1.82	2.86	1.90	1.41	1.45	2.23	2.26	2.76
Debt to Equity	0.15	0.27	0.31	0.34	0.36	0.42	0.53	0.11
Price Range	51.55-39.80	40.85-26.46	44.70-26.06	39.00-22.69	27.75-16.75	40.69-25.94	41.88-24.31	33.56-20.13
P/E Ratio	13.35-10.31	10.78-6.98	12.28-7.16	12.15-7.07	7.91-4.77	10.79-6.88	12.92-7.50	13.21-7.92
Average Yield %	1.88	2.13	1.66	1.81	2.64	1.89	1.44	1.57

Address: 12950 Worldgate Dr, Suite 500, Herndon, VA 20170	Web Site: www.lafargenorthamerica.com	Auditors: Ernst & Young LLP
Telephone: (703) 480-3600	Officers: Bertrand P. Collomb - Chmn. Bernard L. Kasriel - Vice-Chmn.	Investor Contact: 703 480-3600

LAIDLAW INTERNATIONAL INC

Exchange	Symbol	Price	52Wk Range	Yield	P/E
NYS	LI	$20.80 (3/31/2005)	23.00-12.01	N/A	31.52

*7 Year Price Score N/A   *NYSE Composite Index=100   *12 Month Price Score 120.50

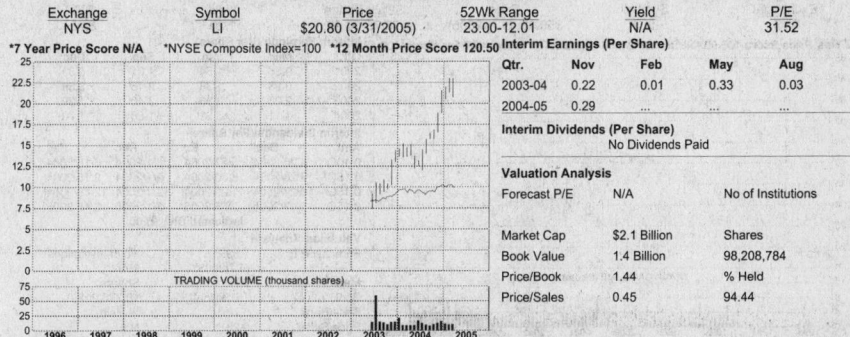

Interim Earnings (Per Share)

Qtr.	Nov	Feb	May	Aug
2003-04	0.22	0.01	0.33	0.03
2004-05	0.29	...	...	...

Interim Dividends (Per Share)
No Dividends Paid

Valuation Analysis

Forecast P/E	N/A	No of Institutions
Market Cap	$2.1 Billion	Shares
Book Value	1.4 Billion	98,208,784
Price/Book	1.44	% Held
Price/Sales	0.45	94.44

Business Summary: Urban Transport (MIC: 15.6 SIC: 111 NAIC: 85210)

Laidlaw International is a holding company engaged in transportation and healthcare services. Co.'s education services segment provides school bus transportation through school buses and special education vehicles throughout Canada and the U.S. Co.'s public transit services segment provides municipal and paratransit bus transportation within the U.S. Co.'s Greyhound segment provides inter-city, tourism and small parcel bus transportation throughout North America. Co.'s healthcare transportation services segment provides healthcare related transportation services in the U.S. Co.'s emergency management services segment provides emergency department physician services throughout the U.S.

Recent Developments: For the quarter ended Nov 30 2004, net income increased 34.5% to $30,400 thousand from net income of $22,600 thousand in the year-earlier quarter. Revenues were $1,227,300 thousand, up 1.4% from $1,210,300 thousand the year before. Operating income was $80,100 thousand versus an income of $69,500 thousand in the prior-year quarter, an increase of 15.3%. Total indirect expense was $1,147,200 thousand versus $1,140,800 thousand in the prior-year quarter, an increase of 0.6%.

Prospects: On Feb 10 2005, Co. announced that it has completed the sale of its healthcare companies, American Medical Response and EmCare, to Emergency Medical Services L.P., an affiliate of Onex Corporation, for net cash proceeds of $775.0 million. Co. plans to use the proceeds to retire outstanding debt and purchase all or some of the 3.8 million shares of its common stock held in a trust for the benefit of the Greyhound U.S. Pension Plans. Looking ahead, consolidated revenue for fiscal 2005 is expected to be flat to up 2.0% compared with fiscal 2004. In addition, Co. is projecting net capital expenditures for fiscal 2005 of approximately $240.0 million to $250.0 million.

Financial Data

(US$ in Thousands)	3 Mos	08/31/2004	08/31/2003	05/31/2003	08/31/2002	08/31/2001
Earnings Per Share	0.66	0.59	(0.10)	(3.72)	0.05	4.37
Cash Flow Per Share	3.96	3.89	1.87	0.86	1.33	...
Tang Book Value Per Share	11.08	9.96	8.58	...	N.M.	...
Income Statement						
Total Revenue	1,227,300	4,631,400	997,100	3,485,700	4,432,100	4,418,300
EBITDA	162,700	507,100	63,700	1,246,000	391,600	328,900
Depn & Amortn	81,200	283,500	52,100	229,300	358,800	350,300
Income Before Taxes	51,100	94,000	(19,900)	997,100	5,100	(292,300)
Income Taxes	20,700	32,300	(10,000)	4,500	(9,800)	(45,800)
Net Income	30,400	61,700	(9,900)	(1,212,800)	14,900	1,425,900
Average Shares	104,100	103,800	100,000	325,900	325,900	325,900
Balance Sheet						
Current Assets	1,100,500	1,031,900	948,000	...	1,116,600	...
Total Assets	3,983,500	3,905,200	3,852,700	...	6,211,800	...
Current Liabilities	664,000	686,600	694,800	...	634,100	...
Long-Term Obligations	1,129,400	1,114,200	1,145,100	...	204,400	...
Total Liabilities	2,535,200	2,528,700	2,562,400	...	5,257,700	...
Stockholders' Equity	1,448,300	1,376,500	1,290,300	...	954,100	...
Shares Outstanding	100,200	103,806	103,777	325,927	325,927	325,927
Statistical Record						
Return on Assets %	1.75	1.59	N.M.	...	...	...
Return on Equity %	4.99	4.61	N.M.	...	...	...
EBITDA Margin %	13.26	10.95	6.39	35.75	8.84	7.44
Net Margin %	2.48	1.33	N.M.	N.M.	0.34	32.27
Asset Turnover	1.16	1.19	0.20	...	...	...
Current Ratio	1.66	1.50	1.36	...	1.76	...
Debt to Equity	0.78	0.81	0.89	...	0.21	...
Price Range	18.90-12.01	15.70-9.45	10.52-7.44	...	...	...
P/E Ratio	28.64-18.20	26.61-16.02	...	...	...	...

Address: 55 Shuman Boulevard, Suite 400, Naperville, IL 60563 **Telephone:** (630) 848-3000	**Web Site:** www.laidlaw.com **Officers:** Kevin E. Benson - Pres., C.E.O. Douglas A. Carty - Sr. V.P., C.F.O.	**Auditors:** PricewaterhouseCoopers LLP

LANDAMERICA FINANCIAL GROUP, INC.

Exchange	Symbol	Price	52Wk Range	Yield	P/E
NYS	LFG	$50.03 (3/31/2005)	56.75-36.28	1.20	6.25

*7 Year Price Score 106.90 *NYSE Composite Index=100 *12 Month Price Score 106.40

Interim Earnings (Per Share)

Qtr.	Mar	Jun	Sep	Dec
2001	0.36	1.54	1.01	0.33
2002	0.93	1.38	2.15	3.59
2003	2.28	3.33	3.40	1.29
2004	1.11	3.32	1.88	1.70

Interim Dividends (Per Share)

Amt	Decl	Ex	Rec	Pay
0.10Q	4/28/2004	5/27/2004	6/1/2004	6/15/2004
0.15Q	7/28/2004	8/30/2004	9/1/2004	9/15/2004
0.15Q	10/27/2004	11/29/2004	12/1/2004	12/15/2004
0.15Q	2/17/2005	2/25/2005	3/1/2005	3/15/2005

Indicated Div: $0.60

Valuation Analysis

Forecast P/E	7.69	No of Institutions
	(4/7/2005)	153
Market Cap	$898.7 Million	Shares
Book Value	1.2 Billion	18,776,212
Price/Book	0.78	% Held
Price/Sales	0.26	N/A

Business Summary: Insurance (MIC: 8.2 SIC: 361 NAIC: 24127)

LandAmerica Financial Group is a holding company. Co., through its subsidiaries, provides products and services that are used to facilitate the purchase, sale, transfer and financing of residential and commercial real estate. Co. is one of the largest title insurance underwriters in the U.S. based on title premium revenues. Co. also conducts business in Mexico, Canada, the Caribbean and Latin America. In addition to the issuance of title insurance policies, Co. provides a range of other services for residential and commercial real estate transactions including title search, examination, document preparation, escrow and closing.

Recent Developments: For the year ended Dec 31 2004, net income decreased 23.8% to $146,300 thousand from net income of $192,100 thousand a year earlier. Revenues were $3,522,100 thousand, up 3.4% from $3,406,000 thousand the year before. Net premiums earned were $3,444,500 thousand versus $3,345,400 thousand in the prior year, an increase of 3.0%.

Prospects: Co. continues to actively implement the acquisition portion of its strategy to provide a broad array of services focused on the real estate transaction, while managing its ongoing operations in an environment with significantly reduced mortgage origination volumes. With its lower overall business volumes in residential refinancing, Co. continues to remain vigilant in managing the cost structure of its business. During the fourth quarter of 2004, Co. acquired LoanCare Servicing Center, one of the largest mortgage subservicers in the United States, and 3 Arch Financial Services Corporation, which expanded Co.'s presence in default management services.

Financial Data

(US$ in Thousands)	12/31/2004	12/31/2003	12/31/2002	12/31/2001	12/31/2000	12/31/1999	12/31/1998	12/31/1997
Earnings Per Share	8.01	10.31	8.04	3.24	(6.60)	2.79	5.05	2.84
Cash Flow Per Share	14.11	16.56	12.37	7.99	6.46	7.21	11.69	2.11
Tang Book Value Per Share	20.58	24.51	36.08	28.88	20.05	15.19	16.14	26.18
Dividends Per Share	0.500	0.340	0.240	0.200	0.200	0.200	0.200	0.200
Dividend Payout %	6.24	3.30	2.99	6.17	...	7.17	3.96	7.04
Income Statement								
Total Revenue	3,522,100	3,406,002	2,586,550	2,170,477	1,802,405	2,048,013	1,848,870	639,099
Income Before Taxes	226,100	296,940	229,772	94,165	(128,137)	84,870	146,302	40,469
Income Taxes	79,800	104,820	80,420	33,899	(47,371)	30,553	53,274	14,312
Net Income	146,300	192,120	149,352	60,266	(80,766)	54,317	93,028	26,157
Average Shares	18,264	18,636	18,580	18,617	13,397	19,503	18,421	9,224
Balance Sheet								
Total Assets	3,290,000	2,717,460	1,910,832	1,707,481	1,618,957	1,657,921	1,692,358	554,693
Total Liabilities	2,138,900	1,672,982	1,047,212	979,988	954,857	927,218	921,169	262,289
Stockholders' Equity	1,151,100	1,044,478	863,620	727,493	664,100	730,703	771,189	292,404
Shares Outstanding	17,962	18,814	18,348	18,583	13,518	13,680	15,295	8,965
Statistical Record								
Return on Assets %	4.86	8.30	8.26	3.62	N.M.	3.24	8.28	4.86
Return on Equity %	13.29	20.14	18.77	8.66	N.M.	7.23	17.49	9.43
Price Range	57.12-36.28	53.01-35.45	37.75-25.70	49.99-23.74	41.69-16.19	58.75-15.56	63.69-31.19	33.25-16.75
P/E Ratio	7.13-4.53	5.14-3.44	4.70-3.20	15.43-7.33	...	21.06-5.58	12.61-6.18	11.71-5.90
Average Yield %	1.10	0.76	0.74	0.62	0.84	0.70	0.40	0.83

Address: 101 Gateway Centre Parkway, Richmond, VA 23235-5153 **Telephone:** (804) 267 8000 **Fax:** (804) 267 8833	**Web Site:** www.landam.com **Officers:** Charles H. Foster Jr. - Chmn. Janet A. Alpert - Vice-Chmn.	**Auditors:** Ernst & Young LLP **Investor Contact:** 804-267-8114

LAUDER (ESTEE) COS., INC. (THE)

Exchange	Symbol	Price	52Wk Range	Yield	P/E
NYS	EL	$44.98 (3/31/2005)	48.80-40.00	0.89	25.85

*7 Year Price Score 97.39   *NYSE Composite Index=100   *12 Month Price Score 92.20

Interim Earnings (Per Share)

Qtr.	Sep	Dec	Mar	Jun
2001-02	0.38	0.35	0.19	(0.13)
2002-03	0.29	0.44	0.33	0.20
2003-04	0.33	0.41	0.42	0.31
2004-05	0.41	0.60	...	...

Interim Dividends (Per Share)

Amt	Decl	Ex	Rec	Pay
0.05A	5/14/2002	6/12/2002	6/14/2002	7/2/2002
0.20A	10/30/2002	12/10/2002	12/12/2002	1/3/2003
0.30A	11/5/2003	12/12/2003	12/16/2003	1/6/2004
0.40A	11/3/2004	12/8/2004	12/10/2004	12/28/2004

Indicated Div: $0.40

Valuation Analysis

Forecast P/E	N/A	No of Institutions
Market Cap	$10.1 Billion	Shares
Book Value	1.8 Billion	104,246,752
Price/Book	5.63	% Held
Price/Sales	1.67	77.68

Business Summary: Chemicals (MIC: 11.1 SIC: 844 NAIC: 25620)

Estee Lauder Companies manufactures and markets quality skin care, makeup, fragrance and hair care products. Co.'s products are sold in over 130 countries and territories under the following well-recognized brand names: Estée Lauder, Clinique, Aramis, Prescriptives, Origins, M.A.C, Bobbi Brown, La Mer, Aveda, Stila, Jo Malone, Bumble and bumble, Darphin and Rodan + Fields. Co. is also the global licensee for fragrances and cosmetics sold under the Tommy Hilfiger, Donna Karan, kate spade and Michael Kors brands. Co. sells its products principally through limited distribution channels to complement the images associated with its brands.

Recent Developments: For the quarter ended Dec 31 2004, net income increased 44.5% to $138,300 thousand from net income of $95,700 thousand in the year-earlier quarter. Revenues were $1,750,300 thousand, up 8.1% from $1,619,100 thousand the year before. Operating income was $230,500 thousand versus an income of $219,000 thousand in the prior-year quarter, an increase of 5.3%. Total indirect expense was $1,071,800 thousand versus $987,400 thousand in the prior-year quarter, an increase of 8.5%.

Prospects: Co. continues to focus on investing in new brands, new channels and new geographic distribution to drive future growth. Thus, Co. expects net sales for the second half of fiscal 2005 to grow about 9.0%, including a currency translation benefit of about 2.0%, versus fiscal 2004's second half. Geographic region net sales growth in constant currency is expected to be led by the Americas and Europe, the Middle East & Africa, followed by Asia/Pacific. On a product category basis, in constant currency, hair care and fragrance are expected to be the leading growth categories, followed by skin care and makeup. Co. expects to achieve diluted earnings per share of $0.87 to $0.92 for the second half.

Financial Data

(US$ in Thousands)	6 Mos	3 Mos	06/30/2004	06/30/2003	06/30/2002	06/30/2001	06/30/2000	06/30/1999
Earnings Per Share	1.74	1.55	1.48	1.26	0.70	1.16	1.20	1.03
Cash Flow Per Share	2.59	2.69	2.93	2.36	2.17	1.28	1.86	1.49
Tang Book Value Per Share	4.63	4.36	4.35	2.91	3.23	2.64	1.77	1.33
Dividends Per Share	0.400	0.300	0.300	0.200	0.200	0.200	0.200	0.177
Dividend Payout %	23.05	19.41	·20.27	15.87	28.57	17.24	16.67	17.23
Income Statement								
Total Revenue	3,254,400	1,504,100	5,790,400	5,117,600	4,743,700	4,608,100	4,440,300	3,961,500
EBITDA	480,300	202,200	835,700	669,900	503,400	658,500	662,600	574,200
Depn & Amortn	94,500	46,900	191,700	174,800	162,000	162,900	146,800	117,300
Income Before Taxes	378,400	151,200	616,900	487,000	331,600	483,300	498,700	440,200
Income Taxes	141,500	56,000	232,600	160,500	114,400	174,000	184,600	167,300
Net Income	233,300	95,000	342,100	319,800	191,900	305,200	314,100	272,900
Average Shares	229,200	231,200	231,600	234,700	241,100	242,200	242,500	241,200
Balance Sheet								
Current Assets	2,404,500	2,267,800	2,199,200	1,844,900	1,927,600	1,738,900	1,618,500	1,570,200
Total Assets	3,954,800	3,774,300	3,708,100	3,349,900	3,416,500	3,218,800	3,043,300	2,746,700
Current Liabilities	1,465,600	1,365,300	1,322,000	1,053,600	959,600	856,700	901,800	862,200
Long-Term Obligations	472,800	472,600	461,500	283,600	403,900	410,900	418,400	422,500
Total Liabilities	2,136,800	2,025,600	1,959,100	1,554,000	1,594,600	1,506,700	1,523,000	1,462,200
Stockholders' Equity	1,801,300	1,736,400	1,733,500	1,423,600	1,461,900	1,352,100	1,160,300	924,500
Shares Outstanding	225,267	225,719	227,527	227,456	237,602	238,855	237,861	237,160
Statistical Record								
Return on Assets %	10.14	9.61	9.67	9.45	5.78	9.75	10.82	10.38
Return on Equity %	23.70	22.16	21.61	22.17	13.64	24.30	30.05	33.67
EBITDA Margin %	14.76	13.44	14.43	13.09	10.61	14.29	14.92	14.49
Net Margin %	7.17	6.32	5.91	6.25	4.05	6.62	7.07	6.89
Asset Turnover	1.53	1.59	1.64	1.51	1.43	1.47	1.53	1.51
Current Ratio	1.64	1.66	1.66	1.75	2.01	2.03	1.79	1.82
Debt to Equity	0.26	0.27	0.27	0.20	0.28	0.30	0.36	0.46
Price Range	48.80-38.17	48.80-34.10	48.78-32.88	35.94-25.75	43.45-29.51	49.42-34.30	56.00-39.06	50.13-24.53
P/E Ratio	28.05-21.94	31.48-22.00	32.96-22.22	28.52-20.44	62.07-42.16	42.61-29.57	46.67-32.55	48.67-23.82
Average Yield %	0.91	0.71	0.76	0.67	0.57	0.49	0.43	0.46

Address: 767 Fifth Avenue, New York, NY 10153 **Telephone:** (212) 572 4200	**Web Site:** www.elcompanies.com **Officers:** Leonard A. Lauder - Chmn. William P. Lauder - Pres., C.E.O.	**Auditors:** KPMG LLP

LEAR CORP.

Exchange	Symbol	Price	52Wk Range	Yield	P/E
NYS	LEA	$44.36 (3/31/2005)	65.90-43.96	2.25	7.69

*7 Year Price Score 113.95 *NYSE Composite Index=100 *12 Month Price Score 84.16

Interim Earnings (Per Share)

Qtr.	Mar	Jun	Sep	Dec
2001	0.22	0.70	0.24	(0.75)
2002	0.70	1.27	0.91	1.76
2003	1.01	1.54	1.10	1.90
2004	1.30	1.65	1.32	1.51

Interim Dividends (Per Share)

Amt	Decl	Ex	Rec	Pay
0.20Q	5/13/2004	5/26/2004	5/28/2004	6/14/2004
0.20Q	8/13/2004	8/25/2004	8/27/2004	9/13/2004
0.20Q	11/11/2004	11/23/2004	11/26/2004	12/13/2004
0.25Q	1/13/2005	2/23/2005	2/25/2005	3/14/2005
			Indicated Div: $1.00	

Valuation Analysis

Forecast P/E	10.61	No of Institutions	
	(4/7/2005)	243	
Market Cap	$3.0 Billion	Shares	
Book Value	2.7 Billion	63,877,424	
Price/Book	1.10	% Held	
Price/Sales	0.18	95.15	

Business Summary: Retail - Automotive (MIC: 5.7 SIC: 013 NAIC: 23120)

Lear is an automotive interior systems supplier. Co. has three reportable operating segments: Seating, Interior, and Electronic and Electrical. The Seating segment includes seat systems and components. The Interior segment includes flooring and acoustic systems, door panels, instrument panels and cockpit systems, overhead systems and other interior products. The Electronic and Electrical segment includes electrical and electronic distribution systems, primarily wire harnesses, wireless systems and interior control systems. Co.'s major customers include General Motors, Ford, DaimlerChrysler, BMW, Fiat, PSA, Volkswagen, Renault/Nissan, Toyota and Subaru.

Recent Developments: For the year ended Dec 31 2004, net income increased 11.0% to $422,200 thousand from net income of $380,500 thousand a year earlier. Revenues were $16,960,000 thousand, up 7.7% from $15,746,700 thousand the year before. Total direct expense was $15,557,900 thousand versus $14,400,300 thousand in the prior year, an increase of 8.0%. Total indirect expense was $633,700 thousand versus $573,600 thousand in the prior year, an increase of 10.5%.

Prospects: Challenging industry conditions in both of Co.'s major markets is adversely affecting near-term results. However, Co.'s longer-term outlook remains positive, supported by its $3.80 billion three-year sales backlog and strong operating fundamentals. Assuming 2005 production of 15.7 million to 16.0 million units in North America and 18.3 million to 18.6 million units in Europe, Co. expects net sales of $17.60 billion to $18.00 billion due to the addition of new business globally. Net income is expected to range from $5.00 to $6.00 per share. However, since the beginning of 2005, production schedules have continued to decline, and Co. is seeing cost pressures from its supply base.

Financial Data

(US$ in Thousands)	12/31/2004	12/31/2003	12/31/2002	12/31/2001	12/31/2000	12/31/1999	12/31/1998	12/31/1997
Earnings Per Share	5.77	5.55	0.19	0.40	4.17	3.80	1.70	3.04
Cash Flow Per Share	9.87	8.79	8.34	12.97	11.52	8.37	4.26	6.78
Dividends Per Share	0.800	0.200	...	...	...	...	...	...
Dividend Payout %	13.86	3.60	...	...	...	...	...	...
Income Statement								
Total Revenue	16,960,000	15,746,700	14,424,600	13,624,700	14,072,800	12,428,800	9,059,400	7,342,900
EBITDA	1,084,900	1,042,800	992,000	757,300	1,192,600	1,019,000	545,000	631,200
Depn & Amortn	355,100	321,800	301,000	392,200	392,200	340,900	219,700	184,400
Income Before Taxes	564,300	534,400	480,500	110,400	484,200	443,000	214,800	345,800
Income Taxes	128,000	153,700	157,000	68,700	197,300	174,000	93,900	143,100
Net Income	422,200	380,500	13,000	26,300	274,700	257,100	115,500	207,200
Average Shares	74,727	68,533	67,057	65,305	65,840	67,743	68,023	68,249
Balance Sheet								
Current Assets	4,372,000	3,375,400	2,507,700	2,366,800	2,828,000	3,154,200	2,198,000	1,614,900
Total Assets	9,944,400	8,571,000	7,483,000	7,579,200	8,375,500	8,717,600	5,677,300	4,459,100
Current Liabilities	4,647,900	3,582,100	3,045,200	3,182,800	3,371,600	3,487,400	2,497,500	1,854,000
Long-Term Obligations	1,866,900	2,057,200	2,132,800	2,293,900	2,852,100	3,324,800	1,463,400	1,063,100
Total Liabilities	7,214,300	6,313,500	5,820,700	6,020,100	6,774,700	7,252,300	4,377,300	3,252,100
Stockholders' Equity	2,730,100	2,257,500	1,662,300	1,559,100	1,600,800	1,465,300	1,300,000	1,207,000
Shares Outstanding	67,416	68,533	65,737	64,253	63,554	66,599	66,684	56,642
Statistical Record								
Return on Assets %	4.55	4.74	0.17	0.33	3.21	3.57	2.28	5.01
Return on Equity %	16.88	19.41	0.81	1.66	17.87	18.59	9.21	18.62
EBITDA Margin %	6.40	6.62	6.88	5.56	8.47	8.20	6.02	8.60
Net Margin %	2.49	2.42	0.09	0.19	1.95	2.07	1.27	2.82
Asset Turnover	1.83	1.96	1.92	1.71	1.64	1.73	1.79	1.77
Current Ratio	0.94	0.94	0.82	0.74	0.84	0.90	0.88	0.87
Debt to Equity	0.68	0.91	1.28	1.47	1.78	2.27	1.13	0.88
Price Range	68.88-49.73	63.12-33.06	52.49-33.15	42.14-24.42	35.44-19.94	53.00-29.13	57.44-30.56	51.25-33.38
P/E Ratio	11.94-8.62	11.37-5.96	276.26-174.47	105.35-61.05	8.50-4.78	13.95-7.66	33.79-17.98	16.86-10.98
Average Yield %	1.36	0.42	...	...	...	...	...	...

Address: 21557 Telegraph Road,	Web Site: www.lear.com	Auditors: Ernst & Young LLP
Southfield, MI 48086-5008	Officers: Robert E. Rossiter - Chmn., Pres., C.E.O.	Investor Contact: 800-413-5327
Telephone: (248) 447-1500	James H. Vandenberghe - Vice-Chmn.	Transfer Agents: The Bank of New York

LEE ENTERPRISES, INC.

Exchange	Symbol	Price	52Wk Range	Yield	P/E
NYS	LEE	$43.40 (3/31/2005)	49.70-42.77	1.66	22.14

*7 Year Price Score 117.02 ***NYSE Composite Index=100** ***12 Month Price Score 89.52**

TRADING VOLUME (thousand shares)

Interim Earnings (Per Share)

Qtr.	Dec	Mar	Jun	Sep
2001-02	0.41	0.30	0.72	0.42
2002-03	0.51	0.33	0.48	0.43
2003-04	0.55	0.35	0.54	0.47
2004-05	0.60	...	...	...

Interim Dividends (Per Share)

Amt	Decl	Ex	Rec	Pay
0.18Q	5/21/2004	5/27/2004	6/1/2004	7/1/2004
0.18Q	8/16/2004	8/30/2004	9/1/2004	10/1/2004
0.18Q	11/17/2004	11/29/2004	12/1/2004	1/3/2005
0.18Q	2/23/2005	2/25/2005	3/1/2005	4/1/2005

Indicated Div: $0.72

Valuation Analysis

Forecast P/E	21.15 (4/7/2005)	No of Institutions 159
Market Cap	$2.0 Billion	Shares 32,551,144
Book Value	898.3 Million	% Held 71.75
Price/Book	2.19	
Price/Sales	2.84	

Business Summary: Media (MIC: 13.1 SIC: 711 NAIC: 11110)

Lee Enterprises directly, and through its ownership of associated companies, publishes 44 daily newspapers in 19 states and more than 200 weekly, classified and specialty publications, along with associated online services as of Sep 30 2004. Co. also owns 50.0% of Madison Newspapers. Co.'s online activities are comprised of Web sites supporting each of its daily newspapers and certain of its other publications. Co. also owns 81.0% of Townnews.com, an Internet service company, which provides Web infrastructure for more than 800 daily and weekly newspapers, and shoppers. In addition, Co. has minority investments in two Internet service companies, PowerOne Media and CityXpress Corp.

Recent Developments: For the quarter ended Dec 31 2004, net income increased 10.3% to $27,011 thousand from net income of $24,479 thousand in the year-earlier quarter. Revenues were $184,084 thousand, up 6.4% from $172,984 thousand the year before. Operating income was $42,903 thousand versus an income of $39,587 thousand in the prior-year quarter, an increase of 8.4%. Total indirect expense was $141,181 thousand versus $133,397 thousand in the prior-year quarter, an increase of 5.8%.

Prospects: On Jan 30 2005, Co. announced that it has entered into a definitive agreement to acquire Pulitzer Inc. for a cash purchase price of $64.00 per share, with enterprise value totaling $1.46 billion. Pulitzer operates 14 daily newspapers, including the St. Louis Post-Dispatch. Pulitzer also operates more than 100 weekly newspapers, shoppers, and niche publications as well as online sites in all of its markets. Co. expects the transaction to be dilutive to earnings by an estimated $0.08 to $0.10 per diluted share in fiscal 2005, excluding one-time transition costs and assuming a May 31 2005 closing. Dilution to earnings per share is estimated to be approximately 10.0% to 11.0% in fiscal 2006.

Financial Data

(US$ in Thousands)	3 Mos	09/30/2004	09/30/2003	09/30/2002	09/30/2001	09/30/2000	09/30/1999	09/30/1998
Earnings Per Share	1.96	1.91	1.75	1.85	7.13	1.89	1.52	1.37
Cash Flow Per Share	...	2.91	3.17	2.62	2.45	2.88	2.21	2.25
Tang Book Value Per Share	N.M.	N.M.	N.M.	N.M.	8.43	1.43	N.M.	N.M.
Dividends Per Share	0.720	0.720	0.680	0.680	0.680	0.640	0.600	0.560
Dividend Payout %	36.81	37.70	38.86	36.76	9.54	33.86	39.47	40.88
Income Statement								
Total Revenue	184,084	683,324	656,741	525,896	441,153	431,513	536,333	517,293
EBITDA	54,163	194,287	183,554	155,879	108,007	148,925	157,226	150,423
Depn & Amortn	11,506	48,027	46,616	35,050	32,158	29,326	39,748	37,576
Income Before Taxes	42,935	134,661	121,523	111,059	92,434	110,215	106,535	100,132
Income Taxes	15,924	48,192	43,462	30,030	32,977	40,340	38,562	37,899
Net Income	27,011	86,071	78,041	81,975	314,228	83,663	67,973	62,233
Average Shares	45,243	45,092	44,316	44,351	44,089	44,360	44,861	45,557
Balance Sheet								
Current Assets	100,277	92,857	89,885	104,027	537,677	251,566	102,543	99,591
Total Assets	1,407,962	1,403,844	1,421,377	1,463,830	1,000,397	746,233	679,513	660,585
Current Liabilities	105,200	105,481	134,551	108,749	125,139	117,627	79,448	98,061
Long-Term Obligations	185,000	202,000	268,600	394,700	161,800	173,400	187,005	186,028
Total Liabilities	509,709	527,001	619,221	722,574	318,453	351,066	325,184	340,826
Stockholders' Equity	898,253	876,843	802,156	741,256	681,944	395,167	354,329	319,759
Shares Outstanding	45,368	45,217	44,621	44,311	44,038	43,810	44,259	44,350
Statistical Record								
Return on Assets %	6.27	6.08	5.41	6.65	35.98	11.70	10.14	9.49
Return on Equity %	10.26	10.22	10.11	11.52	58.35	22.26	20.17	19.47
EBITDA Margin %	29.42	28.43	27.95	29.64	24.48	34.51	29.31	29.08
Net Margin %	14.67	12.60	11.88	15.59	71.23	19.39	12.67	12.03
Asset Turnover	0.49	0.48	0.46	0.43	0.51	0.64	0.80	0.79
Current Ratio	0.95	0.88	0.67	0.96	4.30	2.14	1.29	1.02
Debt to Equity	0.21	0.23	0.33	0.53	0.24	0.44	0.53	0.58
Price Range	49.70-43.49	49.70-38.67	40.49-30.23	39.76-29.02	34.70-25.25	31.94-19.88	31.50-23.00	33.81-23.56
P/E Ratio	25.36-22.19	26.02-20.25	23.14-17.27	21.49-15.69	4.87-3.54	16.90-10.52	20.72-15.13	24.68-17.20
Average Yield %	1.55	1.59	1.94	1.93	2.20	2.47	2.12	1.92

Address: 201 N. Harrison Street, Suite 600, Davenport, IA 52801 **Telephone:** (563) 383-2100 **Fax:** (563) 326-2972	**Web Site:** www.lee.net **Officers:** Mary E. Junck - Chmn., Pres., C.E.O. Rosanne M. Cheeseman - V.P., Sales & Mktg.	**Auditors:** Deloitte & Touche LLP **Investor Contact:** 563-383-2163

LEGG MASON, INC.

Exchange	Symbol	Price	52Wk Range	Yield	P/E	Div Acheiver
NYS	LM	$78.14 (3/31/2005)	84.12-48.97	0.77	23.33	21 Years

*7 Year Price Score 151.57 *NYSE Composite Index=100 *12 Month Price Score 115.72

Interim Earnings (Per Share)

Qtr.	Jun	Sep	Dec	Mar
2001-02	0.35	0.30	0.40	0.45
2002-03	0.47	0.44	0.47	0.47
2003-04	0.55	0.62	0.71	0.81
2004-05	0.76	0.81	0.98	...

Interim Dividends (Per Share)

Amt	Decl	Ex	Rec	Pay
3-for-2	7/20/2004	9/27/2004	9/8/2004	9/24/2004
0.15Q	7/20/2004	10/5/2004	10/7/2004	10/25/2004
0.15Q	10/19/2004	12/6/2004	12/8/2004	1/3/2005
0.15Q	1/18/2005	3/1/2005	3/3/2005	4/4/2005

Indicated Div: $0.60

Valuation Analysis

Forecast P/E	17.71	No of Institutions
	(4/7/2005)	323
Market Cap	$8.3 Billion	Shares
Book Value	2.2 Billion	80,702,920
Price/Book	3.83	% Held
Price/Sales	3.49	74.22

Business Summary: Finance Intermediaries & Services (MIC: 8.7 SIC: 211 NAIC: 23120)

Legg Mason is a holding company. Through its subsidiaries, Co. is engaged in providing asset management, securities brokerage, investment banking and other related financial services to individuals, institutions, corporations, governments and government agencies. Co. operate through three business segments: Asset Management, Private Client and Capital Markets; however, in reporting Co. results, Co. includes a fourth segment - Corporate.

Recent Developments: For the quarter ended Dec 31 2004, net income increased 39.4% to $112,710 thousand from net income of $80,833 thousand in the year-earlier quarter. Revenues were $658,278 thousand, up 26.3% from $521,166 thousand the year before. Investment advisory and related fees increased 32.7% to $433,114 thousand from $326,458 thousand, while commissions rose 8.8% to $92,821 thousand versus $85,307 thousand the year before. Principal transactions slipped to 1.6% to $39,302 thousand from $39,922 thousand in 2003.

Prospects: Co.'s revenues and earnings are benefiting from record net flows in its assets under management which is driving higher investment advisory and related fees. The higher investment advisory and related fees are primarily a result of increases in revenues at Private Capital Management, Western Asset, Royce and Legg Mason Capital Management, and to higher fee-based revenues in Co.'s Private Client group. Separately, on Dec 31 2004, Co. completed its acquisition of the assets of the New York City, Philadelphia, Cincinnati and Chicago offices of Scudder Private Investment Counsel from Deutsche Bank. Co. has secured long-term employment contracts from all of the related portfolio managers.

Financial Data

(US$ in Thousands)	9 Mos	6 Mos	3 Mos	03/31/2004	03/31/2003	03/31/2002	03/31/2001	03/31/2000
Earnings Per Share	3.35	3.09	2.90	2.71	1.85	1.49	1.53	1.55
Cash Flow Per Share	3.98	5.55	2.71	1.88	3.09	0.88	2.34	1.93
Tang Book Value Per Share	6.68	3.23	2.39	6.50	3.32	1.52	8.26	7.07
Dividends Per Share	0.500	0.300	0.400	0.373	0.287	0.260	0.233	0.203
Dividend Payout %	14.91	9.71	13.79	13.79	15.47	17.41	15.22	13.09
Income Statement								
Total Revenue	1,798,721	1,140,443	554,927	2,004,267	1,615,382	1,578,612	1,536,253	1,370,804
Income Before Taxes	468,659	287,381	138,701	472,309	308,321	253,249	265,820	239,141
Income Taxes	177,873	109,305	52,287	181,701	117,412	100,313	109,590	96,616
Net Income	290,786	178,076	86,414	297,764	190,909	152,936	156,230	142,525
Average Shares	116,401	114,742	115,569	110,769	103,140	102,393	101,874	91,180
Balance Sheet								
Total Assets	7,733,227	7,027,971	7,496,423	7,262,981	6,067,450	5,939,614	4,687,626	4,785,053
Total Liabilities	5,569,888	5,299,649	5,847,490	5,703,371	4,819,493	4,855,066	3,759,906	4,033,124
Stockholders' Equity	2,163,339	1,728,322	1,648,933	1,559,610	1,247,957	1,084,548	927,720	751,929
Shares Outstanding	105,923	100,765	100,740	99,823	97,241	96,665	94,274	87,898
Statistical Record								
Return on Assets %	5.25	5.17	4.74	4.46	3.18	2.88	3.30	3.44
Return on Equity %	20.92	22.41	21.86	21.15	16.37	15.20	18.60	21.76
Price Range	73.26-48.97	66.07-48.13	66.07-43.30	63.22-32.49	37.98-25.44	37.87-23.83	39.96-23.96	32.67-20.83
P/E Ratio	21.87-14.62	21.38-15.58	22.78-14.93	23.33-11.99	20.53-13.75	25.41-16.00	26.12-15.66	21.08-13.44
Average Yield %	0.84	0.53	0.73	0.75	0.89	0.82	0.70	0.83

Address: 100 Light Street, Baltimore, MD 21202
Telephone: (410) 539-0000
Fax: (410) 539-8010

Web Site: www.leggmason.com
Officers: Raymond A. Mason - Chmn., Pres., C.E.O.
Timothy C. Scheve - Sr. Exec. V.P.

Auditors: PricewaterhouseCoopers LLP
Investor Contact: 410-539-0000
Transfer Agents: Wachovia Bank, N.A., Charlotte, NC

LEGGETT & PLATT, INC.

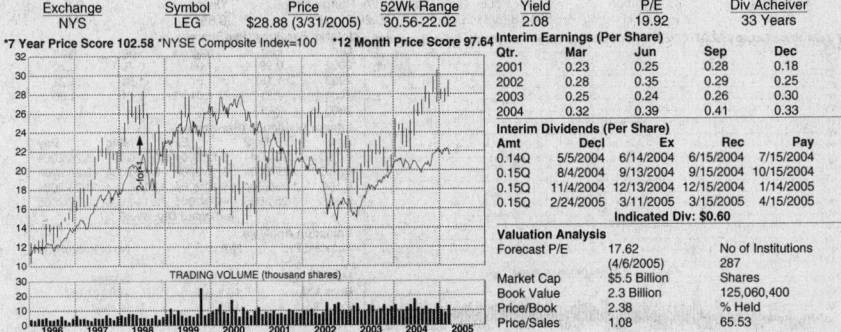

Exchange	Symbol	Price	52Wk Range	Yield	P/E	Div Acheiver
NYS	LEG	$28.88 (3/31/2005)	30.56-22.02	2.08	19.92	33 Years

*7 Year Price Score 102.58 *NYSE Composite Index=100 **12 Month Price Score 97.64

Interim Earnings (Per Share)

Qtr.	Mar	Jun	Sep	Dec
2001	0.23	0.25	0.28	0.18
2002	0.28	0.35	0.29	0.25
2003	0.25	0.24	0.26	0.30
2004	0.32	0.39	0.41	0.33

Interim Dividends (Per Share)

Amt	Decl	Ex	Rec	Pay
0.14Q	5/5/2004	6/14/2004	6/15/2004	7/15/2004
0.15Q	8/4/2004	9/13/2004	9/15/2004	10/15/2004
0.15Q	11/4/2004	12/13/2004	12/15/2004	1/14/2005
0.15Q	2/24/2005	3/11/2005	3/15/2005	4/15/2005

Indicated Div: $0.60

Valuation Analysis

Forecast P/E	17.62	No of Institutions
	(4/6/2005)	287
Market Cap	$5.5 Billion	Shares
Book Value	2.3 Billion	125,060,400
Price/Book	2.38	% Held
Price/Sales	1.08	65.53

Business Summary: Chemicals (MIC: 11.1 SIC: 515 NAIC: 37121)

Leggett & Platt is primarily engaged in the manufacture of engineered components and products that are used in homes, offices, retail stores, and automobiles. Products include: retail store fixtures and point of purchase displays; components for residential furniture and bedding; components for office furniture; non-automotive aluminum die castings; drawn steel wire; automotive seat support and lumbar systems; and bedding industry machinery for wire forming, sewing and quilting. Operations consist of 29 business units, which are organized into 11 groups that make up five business segments.

Recent Developments: For the year ended Dec 31 2004, net income increased 38.6% to $285,400 thousand from net income of $205,900 thousand a year earlier. Revenues were $5,085,500 thousand, up 15.9% from $4,388,200 thousand the year before. Operating income was $461,700 thousand versus an income of $355,300 thousand in the prior year, an increase of 29.9%. Total direct expense was $4,169,700 thousand versus $3,616,500 thousand in the prior year, an increase of 15.3%. Total indirect expense was $470,700 thousand versus $418,300 thousand in the prior year, an increase of 12.5%.

Prospects: Co.'s earnings are being driven by asset sales, a lower tax rate, sales growth and full production at its steel mill. Offsets include unit volume declines in some product lines (primarily innersprings and wire) and significant inventory expenses. However, Co. expects the impact of these two negative factors to diminish considerably in the first quarter of 2005. Co. expects first-quarter earnings of $0.33 to $0.38 a share on sales roughly flat versus the fourth quarter of 2004. For the full year of 2005, Co. expects earnings of $1.50 to $1.70 a share, on sales growth of 6.0% to 10.0% above 2004 levels.

Financial Data (US$ in Thousands)	12/31/2004	12/31/2003	12/31/2002	12/31/2001	12/31/2000	12/31/1999	12/31/1998	12/31/1997
Earnings Per Share	1.45	1.05	1.17	0.94	1.32	1.45	1.24	1.08
Cash Flow Per Share	1.75	2.01	2.29	2.68	2.21	1.87	1.80	1.52
Tang Book Value Per Share	6.37	5.62	5.36	4.81	4.58	4.50	4.59	3.88
Dividends Per Share	0.580	0.540	0.500	0.480	0.420	0.360	0.315	0.270
Dividend Payout %	40.00	51.43	42.74	51.06	31.82	24.83	25.40	25.00
Income Statement								
Total Revenue	5,085,500	4,388,200	4,271,800	4,113,800	4,276,300	3,779,000	3,370,400	2,909,200
EBITDA	638,900	522,300	565,200	547,800	654,100	651,800	557,000	470,700
Depn & Amortn	177,200	167,000	164,600	196,600	173,300	149,300	127,900	105,600
Income Before Taxes	422,600	315,100	363,500	297,300	418,600	462,600	395,600	333,300
Income Taxes	137,200	109,200	130,400	109,700	154,500	172,100	147,600	125,000
Net Income	285,400	205,900	233,100	187,600	264,100	290,500	248,000	208,300
Average Shares	196,875	196,953	199,795	200,434	200,388	200,938	200,669	193,190
Balance Sheet								
Current Assets	2,064,800	1,819,400	1,488,000	1,421,900	1,405,300	1,256,200	1,137,100	944,600
Total Assets	4,197,200	3,889,700	3,501,100	3,412,900	3,373,200	2,977,500	2,535,300	2,106,300
Current Liabilities	959,600	625,900	598,000	457,000	476,600	431,500	401,400	372,500
Long-Term Obligations	779,400	1,012,200	808,600	977,600	988,400	787,400	574,100	466,200
Total Liabilities	1,884,100	1,775,700	1,524,200	1,546,300	1,579,400	1,331,300	1,098,500	932,300
Stockholders' Equity	2,313,100	2,114,000	1,976,900	1,866,600	1,793,800	1,646,200	1,436,800	1,174,000
Shares Outstanding	190,886	192,102	194,498	196,298	196,097	196,880	197,683	192,754
Statistical Record								
Return on Assets %	7.04	5.57	6.74	5.53	8.29	10.54	10.69	10.91
Return on Equity %	12.86	10.07	12.13	10.25	15.31	18.85	19.00	19.70
EBITDA Margin %	12.56	11.90	13.23	13.32	15.30	17.25	16.53	16.18
Net Margin %	5.61	4.69	5.46	4.56	6.18	7.69	7.36	7.16
Asset Turnover	1.25	1.19	1.24	1.21	1.34	1.37	1.45	1.52
Current Ratio	2.15	2.91	2.49	3.11	2.95	2.91	2.83	2.54
Debt to Equity	0.34	0.48	0.41	0.52	0.55	0.48	0.40	0.40
Price Range	30.56-21.35	23.57-17.40	27.16-18.90	24.23-17.00	22.25-14.25	27.88-18.81	28.44-17.13	23.53-15.81
P/E Ratio	21.08-14.72	22.45-16.57	23.21-16.15	25.78-18.09	16.86-10.80	19.22-12.97	22.93-13.81	21.79-14.64
Average Yield %	2.25	2.58	2.13	2.26	2.35	1.58	1.30	1.36

Address: No. 1 Leggett Road, Carthage, MO 64836	Web Site: www.leggett.com	Auditors: PricewaterhouseCoopers LLP
Telephone: (417) 358 8131	Officers: Felix E. Wright - Chmn., C.E.O. David S. Haffner - Pres., C.O.O.	Investor Contact: 417-358-8131
Fax: (417) 358 8449		Transfer Agents: U.M.B. Bank, Kansas City, MO

LEHMAN BROTHERS HOLDINGS INC

Exchange	Symbol	Price	52Wk Range	Yield	P/E
NYS	LEH	$94.16 (3/31/2005)	96.20-67.65	0.85	10.96

*7 Year Price Score 122.01 *NYSE Composite Index=100 *12 Month Price Score 106.41

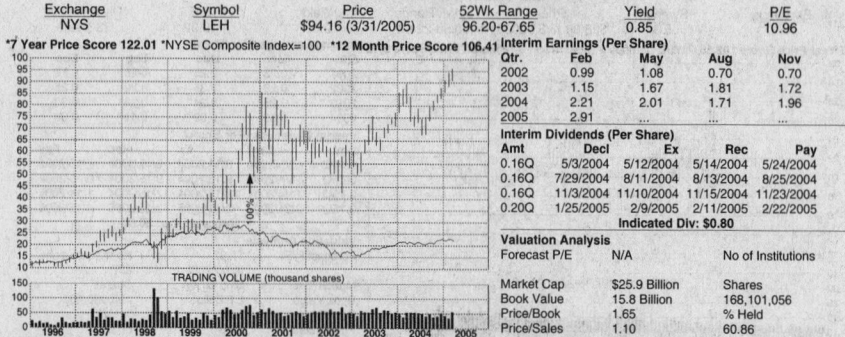

Interim Earnings (Per Share)

Qtr.	Feb	May	Aug	Nov
2002	0.99	1.08	0.70	0.70
2003	1.15	1.67	1.81	1.72
2004	2.21	2.01	1.71	1.96
2005	2.91	...	...	...

Interim Dividends (Per Share)

Amt	Decl	Ex	Rec	Pay
0.16Q	5/3/2004	5/12/2004	5/14/2004	5/24/2004
0.16Q	7/29/2004	8/11/2004	8/13/2004	8/25/2004
0.16Q	11/3/2004	11/10/2004	11/15/2004	11/23/2004
0.20Q	1/25/2005	2/9/2005	2/11/2005	2/22/2005
		Indicated Div: $0.80		

Valuation Analysis

Forecast P/E	N/A	No of Institutions	
Market Cap	$25.9 Billion	Shares	
Book Value	15.8 Billion		168,101,056
Price/Book	1.65	% Held	
Price/Sales	1.10		60.86

Business Summary: Finance Intermediaries & Services (MIC: 8.7 SIC: 211 NAIC: 23999)

Lehman Brothers Holdings, with assets of $357.17 billion as of Nov 30 2004, is a global investment bank, serving institutional, corporate, government and high-net-worth individual clients and customers. Co. provides an array of equities and fixed income sales, trading and research, investment banking services and investment management and advisory services. Through its subsidiaries, Co. is a global market-maker in major equity and fixed income products. Co.'s principal business activities are investment banking, capital markets and investment management.

Recent Developments: For the year ended Nov 30 2004, net income advanced 39.4% to $2.37 billion compared with $1.70 billion in the previous year. Results for 2004 and 2003 included real estate reconfiguration charges of $19.0 million and $77.0 million, respectively. Earnings benefited from the increased scale of Co.'s asset management business and the growth of its mortgage origination platform through several business acquisitions. Net revenues jumped 33.9% to $11.58 billion from $8.65 billion a year earlier.Total revenues climbed 22.9% to $21.25 billion, while interest expense increased 12.0% to $9.67 billion. Total non-interest expenses grew 31.9% to $8.06 billion from $6.11 billion the year before.

Prospects: Co.'s prospects are enhanced by the recent solid results from across its operating segments. For example, for the quarter ended Nov 30 2004, Investment Banking revenues rose 27.5% to $608.0 million, fueled by a 95.0% increase in merger and acquisition advisory fees, and higher revenues from debt origination activity. Also, Capital Markets net revenues grew 17.8% to $1.82 billion, driven by strength from Fixed Income and a rebound in Equity Capital Markets activity. Lastly, Co. posted higher net revenues from its Client Services segment, due in part to improved results from the Asset Management business as assets under management rose to $136.70 billion from $120.10 billion last year.

Financial Data
(US$ in Thousands)

	3 Mos	11/30/2004	11/30/2003	11/30/2002	11/30/2001	11/30/2000	11/30/1999	11/30/1998
Earnings Per Share	8.59	7.90	6.35	3.47	4.38	6.38	4.08	2.60
Cash Flow Per Share	(23.74)	(39.61)	10.37	99.67	27.47	(60.27)	25.70	(41.57)
Tang Book Value Per Share	40.43	37.54	32.13	34.74	31.96	29.19	22.75	19.04
Dividends Per Share	0.680	0.640	0.480	0.360	0.280	0.220	0.180	0.150
Dividend Payout %	7.92	8.10	7.56	10.37	6.39	3.45	4.42	5.78
Income Statement								
Interest Income	3,884,000	11,032,000	9,942,000	11,728,000	16,470,000	19,440,000	14,251,000	16,542,000
Interest Expense	3,581,000	9,674,000	8,640,000	10,626,000	15,656,000	18,740,000	13,649,000	15,781,000
Net Interest Income	303,000	1,358,000	1,302,000	1,102,000	814,000	700,000	602,000	761,000
Non-Interest Income	3,507,000	10,218,000	7,345,000	5,053,000	5,922,000	7,007,000	4,738,000	3,352,000
Non-Interest Expense	2,504,000	8,058,000	6,111,000	4,676,000	4,988,000	5,128,000	3,709,000	3,061,000
Income Before Taxes	1,306,000	...	...	...	...	...	...	...
Income Taxes	431,000	1,125,000	765,000	368,000	437,000	748,000	457,000	316,000
Net Income	875,000	2,369,000	1,699,000	975,000	1,255,000	1,775,000	1,132,000	736,000
Average Shares	294,000	290,700	259,900	261,200	265,300	264,200	258,600	250,000
Balance Sheet								
Total Assets	363,692,000	357,168,000	312,061,000	260,336,000	247,816,000	224,720,000	192,244,000	153,890,000
Total Liabilities	347,938,000	342,248,000	297,577,000	250,684,000	238,647,000	216,079,000	185,251,000	148,477,000
Stockholders' Equity	15,754,000	14,920,000	13,174,000	8,942,000	8,459,000	7,781,000	6,283,000	5,413,000
Shares Outstanding	275,429	274,159	266,679	231,131	237,534	236,395	239,826	228,000
Statistical Record								
Return on Assets %	0.74	0.71	0.59	0.38	0.53	0.85	0.65	0.48
Return on Equity %	17.43	16.82	15.36	11.21	15.46	25.17	19.36	14.81
Net Interest Margin %	7.80	12.31	13.10	9.40	4.94	3.60	4.22	4.60
Efficiency Ratio %	33.88	37.92	35.35	27.86	22.28	19.39	19.53	15.39
Price Range	94.38-67.65	89.50-67.65	75.80-50.37	69.52-42.59	85.72-46.64	80.00-31.06	41.94-20.44	42.50-12.38
P/E Ratio	10.99-7.88	11.33-8.56	11.94-7.93	20.03-12.27	19.57-10.65	12.54-4.87	10.28-5.01	16.35-4.76
Average Yield %	0.85	0.82	0.75	0.60	0.41	0.44	0.63	0.51

Address: 745 Seventh Avenue, New York, NY 10019 **Telephone:** (212) 526-7000 **Fax:** (212) 526-3738	**Web Site:** www.lehman.com **Officers:** Richard S. Fuld Jr. - Chmn., C.E.O. Thomas A. Russo - Vice-Chmn., Chief Legal Officer	**Auditors:** Ernst & Young LLP **Investor Contact:** 212-526-0858

LENNAR CORP.

Exchange	Symbol	Price	52Wk Range	Yield	P/E
NYS	LEN	$56.68 (3/31/2005)	62.30-40.99	0.97	9.94

*7 Year Price Score 176.31 *NYSE Composite Index=100 *12 Month Price Score 111.58

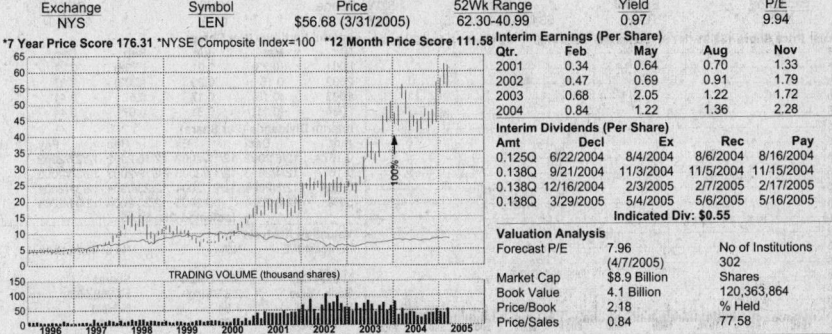

Interim Earnings (Per Share)

Qtr.	Feb	May	Aug	Nov
2001	0.34	0.64	0.70	1.33
2002	0.47	0.69	0.91	1.79
2003	0.68	2.05	1.22	1.72
2004	0.84	1.22	1.36	2.28

Interim Dividends (Per Share)

Amt	Decl	Ex	Rec	Pay
0.125Q	6/22/2004	8/4/2004	8/6/2004	8/16/2004
0.138Q	9/21/2004	11/3/2004	11/5/2004	11/15/2004
0.138Q	12/16/2004	2/3/2005	2/7/2005	2/17/2005
0.138Q	3/29/2005	5/4/2005	5/6/2005	5/16/2005

Indicated Div: $0.55

Valuation Analysis

Forecast P/E	7.96	No of Institutions
	(4/7/2005)	302
Market Cap	$8.9 Billion	Shares
Book Value	4.1 Billion	120,363,864
Price/Book	2.18	% Held
Price/Sales	0.84	77.58

Business Summary: Building & General Construction (MIC: 3.2 SIC: 521 NAIC: 36115)

Lennar is a homebuilder and a provider of financial services. Co.'s homebuilding operations include the sale and construction of single-family attached and detached homes, as well as the purchase, development and sale of residential land directly and through unconsolidated entities in which it has investments. Co. operates primarily under the Lennar and U.S. Home brand names. Co.'s financial services operations provide mortgage financing, title insurance, closing services and insurance agency services for both buyers of its homes and others. Co. also provides high-speed Internet and cable television services to residents of communities it develop and to others.

Recent Developments: For the year ended Nov 30 2004, net income increased 25.8% to $945,619 thousand from net income of $751,391 thousand a year earlier. Revenues were $10,504,899 thousand, up 17.9% from $8,907,619 thousand the year before. Total direct expense was $8,993,304 thousand versus $7,692,877 thousand in the prior year, an increase of 16.9%. Total indirect expense was $141,722 thousand versus $111,488 thousand in the prior year, an increase of 27.1%.

Prospects: Co.'s prospects appear solid. On Feb 17 2005, Co. announced that, through a joint venture, it placed the winning bid to purchase Heritage Fields, a former Marine Corps base in Irvine, CA. The winning bid was $650.0 million to acquire the 3,700 acre, mixed-use, master-planned community, which includes approximately 3,400 homesites, commercial and retail properties. Co. anticipates new home deliveries beginning in fiscal 2008. Also, on Feb 14 2005, Co. announced that it will acquire, directly from Roseland Property Company and through joint ventures with Roseland, a portfolio of 15 properties located along the Hudson River waterfront facing mid-town Manhattan and in the greater Boston area.

Financial Data (US$ in Thousands)	11/30/2004	11/30/2003	11/30/2002	11/30/2001	11/30/2000	11/30/1999	11/30/1998	11/30/1997
Earnings Per Share	5.70	4.65	3.86	3.00	1.82	1.37	1.25	1.12
Cash Flow Per Share	1.75	3.94	1.60	0.47	4.15	1.04	0.57	(1.20)
Tang Book Value Per Share	25.94	20.68	17.17	12.96	9.79	7.61	6.15	4.13
Dividends Per Share	0.512	0.144	0.025	0.025	0.025	0.025	0.025	0.044
Dividend Payout %	8.99	3.09	0.65	0.83	1.37	1.82	2.01	3.92
Income Statement								
Total Revenue	10,504,899	8,907,619	7,319,802	6,029,301	4,706,968	3,118,514	2,416,865	1,303,082
EBITDA	1,592,353	1,282,965	948,098	748,093	431,088	333,207	264,493	94,766
Depn & Amortn	73,286	75,911	72,389	68,670	55,453	47,730	24,379	9,039
Income Before Taxes	1,519,067	1,207,054	875,709	679,423	375,635	285,477	240,114	85,727
Income Taxes	573,448	455,663	330,580	261,578	146,498	112,763	96,046	35,122
Net Income	945,619	751,391	545,129	417,845	229,137	172,714	144,068	84,431
Average Shares	167,340	163,352	142,852	141,158	128,998	130,070	117,248	75,836
Balance Sheet								
Current Assets	6,617,827	4,917,769	4,017,172	3,264,899	2,631,481	1,368,969	1,257,033	894,547
Total Assets	9,165,280	6,775,432	5,755,633	4,714,426	3,777,914	2,057,647	1,917,834	1,343,284
Current Liabilities	222,769	45,214	...	...	...	...	33,440	22,634
Long-Term Obligations	2,021,014	1,552,217	1,585,309	1,505,255	1,254,650	523,661	565,522	574,759
Total Liabilities	5,112,308	3,511,658	3,526,476	3,055,164	2,549,334	1,176,148	1,202,169	904,285
Stockholders' Equity	4,052,972	3,263,774	2,229,157	1,659,262	1,228,580	881,499	715,665	438,999
Shares Outstanding	156,230	157,836	129,826	128,030	125,462	115,834	116,302	106,320
Statistical Record								
Return on Assets %	11.83	11.99	10.41	9.84	7.83	8.69	8.84	5.43
Return on Equity %	25.78	27.36	28.04	28.94	21.66	21.63	24.95	14.88
EBITDA Margin %	15.16	14.40	12.95	12.41	9.16	10.68	10.94	7.27
Net Margin %	9.00	8.44	7.45	6.93	4.87	5.54	5.96	6.48
Asset Turnover	1.31	1.42	1.40	1.42	1.61	1.57	1.48	0.84
Current Ratio	29.71	108.77	...	...	...	...	37.59	39.52
Debt to Equity	0.50	0.48	0.71	0.91	1.02	0.59	0.79	1.31
Price Range	56.01-40.99	49.20-22.18	28.80-16.92	22.55-14.42	15.78-7.05	12.54-6.06	16.38-6.99	9.58-4.25
P/E Ratio	9.83-7.19	10.58-4.77	7.46-4.38	7.52-4.81	8.67-3.87	9.15-4.42	13.10-5.60	8.55-3.80
Average Yield %	1.11	0.45	0.10	0.14	0.25	0.26	0.21	0.77

Address: 700 Northwest 107th Avenue, Miami, FL 33172	**Web Site:** www.lennar.com	**Auditors:** Deloitte & Touche LLP
Telephone: (305) 559-4000	**Officers:** Robert J. Strudler - Chmn. Stuart A. Miller - Pres., C.E.O.	**Investor Contact:** 305-559-4000
Fax: (305) 227-7115		

LEUCADIA NATIONAL CORP.

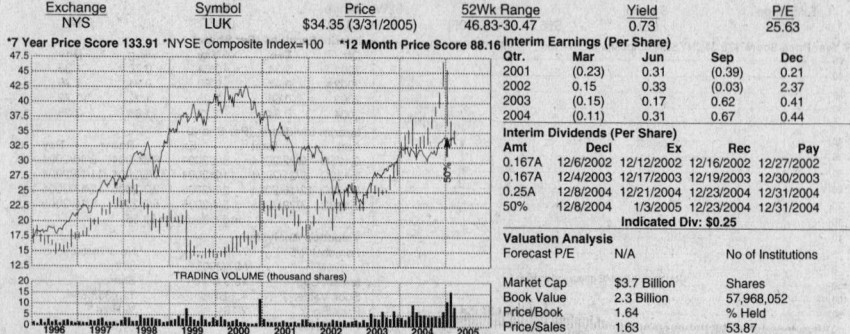

Exchange	Symbol	Price	52Wk Range	Yield	P/E
NYS	LUK	$34.35 (3/31/2005)	46.83-30.47	0.73	25.63

*7 Year Price Score 133.91 *NYSE Composite Index=100 *12 Month Price Score 88.16

Interim Earnings (Per Share)

Qtr.	Mar	Jun	Sep	Dec
2001	(0.23)	0.31	(0.39)	0.21
2002	0.15	0.33	(0.03)	2.37
2003	(0.15)	0.17	0.62	0.41
2004	(0.11)	0.31	0.67	0.44

Interim Dividends (Per Share)

Amt	Decl	Ex	Rec	Pay
0.167A	12/6/2002	12/12/2002	12/16/2002	12/27/2002
0.167A	12/4/2003	12/17/2003	12/19/2003	12/30/2003
0.25A	12/8/2004	12/21/2004	12/23/2004	12/31/2004
50%	12/8/2004	1/3/2005	12/23/2004	12/31/2004

Indicated Div: $0.25

Valuation Analysis

Forecast P/E	N/A	No of Institutions
Market Cap	$3.7 Billion	Shares
Book Value	2.3 Billion	57,968,052
Price/Book	1.64	% Held
Price/Sales	1.63	53.87

Business Summary: Commercial Banking (MIC: 8.1 SIC: 021 NAIC: 24126)

Leucadia National is a holding company engaged in a variety of businesses, including telecommunications, principally through its subsidiary, WilTel Communications Group, which owns or leases and operates a nationwide inter-city fiber-optic network; healthcare services, through Symphony Health Services; and banking and lending, principally through American Investment Bank; In addition, Co is engaged in manufacturing, through its Plastics Division; real estate activities; winery operations; and property and casualty reinsurance, primarily in the U.S. Co. also is involved in the development of a copper mine in Spain through its 72.1% interest in MK Resources Company as of Dec 31 2004.

Recent Developments: For the year ended Dec 31 2004, income from continuing operations increased 77.0% to $151,956 thousand from income of $85,875 thousand a year earlier. Net income increased 49.9% to $145,500 thousand from net income of $97,054 thousand a year earlier. Revenues were $2,262,111 thousand, up 312.1% from $548,971 thousand the year before. Total direct expense was $1,390,636 thousand versus $267,931 thousand in the prior year, an increase of 419.0%. Total indirect expense was $719,403 thousand versus $269,791 thousand in the prior year, an increase of 166.7%.

Prospects: Co. continues to benefit from solid revenues from its telecommunication operations, reflecting contributions from the acquisition of WilTel in 2003. Much of the revenue momentum is primarily associated with WilTel's business with SBC, its largest customer, which is benefiting from growth in voice products. However, WilTel's non-SBC related business continues to reflect excess telecommunications capacity in the marketplace, which has resulted in low prices and a competitive environment. In addition, SBC's announcement to migrate its business to AT&T is expected to have a significant adverse affect on WilTel's future revenues and profitability.

Financial Data
(US$ in Thousands)

	12/31/2004	12/31/2003	12/31/2002	12/31/2001	12/31/2000	12/31/1999	12/31/1998	12/31/1997
Earnings Per Share	1.34	1.05	1.92	(0.09)	1.39	2.41	0.57	7.09
Cash Flow Per Share	0.64	(0.27)	0.66	(0.28)	(1.75)	1.04	(1.22)	(1.61)
Tang Book Value Per Share	20.98	19.48	17.01	14.41	14.52	13.17	19.93	19.45
Dividends Per Share	0.250	0.167	0.167	0.167	0.167	9.053	...	0.167
Dividend Payout %	18.66	15.92	8.68	...	11.96	375.14	...	2.35
Income Statement								
Total Revenue	2,262,111	556,375	241,805	375,298	715,487	706,632	530,506	643,476
Depn & Amortn	235,916	61,099	16,197	5,367	49,149	47,908	48,348	69,227
Income Taxes	(20,192)	(44,201)	(144,865)	(16,648)	72,756	44,521	(25,073)	(10,251)
Net Income	145,500	97,054	161,623	(7,508)	116,008	215,042	54,343	661,815
Average Shares	107,471	92,551	83,500	82,963	83,293	89,028	95,265	93,307
Balance Sheet								
Current Assets	2,059,949	1,350,363	826,022	993,049	1,370,179	1,210,555	1,341,061	1,566,267
Total Assets	4,800,403	4,397,164	2,541,778	2,577,239	3,143,637	3,070,227	3,958,951	4,500,369
Current Liabilities	659,337	657,328	132,181	223,754	385,056	436,491	337,694	403,981
Long-Term Obligations	1,483,504	1,154,878	233,073	343,276	374,523	483,309	722,601	352,872
Total Liabilities	2,523,475	2,245,435	898,744	1,268,522	1,826,284	1,833,135	1,996,320	2,477,096
Stockholders' Equity	2,258,653	2,134,161	1,534,525	1,195,453	1,204,241	1,121,988	1,853,159	1,863,531
Shares Outstanding	107,600	106,235	87,402	82,977	82,945	85,202	92,977	95,818
Statistical Record								
Return on Assets %	3.16	2.80	6.31	N.M.	3.72	6.12	1.28	13.65
Return on Equity %	6.61	5.29	11.84	N.M.	9.95	14.46	2.92	44.39
Net Margin %	6.43	17.44	66.84	N.M.	16.21	30.43	10.24	102.85
Asset Turnover	0.49	0.16	0.09	0.13	0.23	0.20	0.13	0.13
Current Ratio	3.12	2.05	6.25	4.44	3.56	2.77	3.97	3.88
Debt to Equity	0.66	0.54	0.15	0.29	0.31	0.43	0.39	0.19
Price Range	46.83-30.47	30.73-21.93	26.62-18.65	23.63-17.57	24.63-14.00	21.92-13.67	27.04-17.96	24.33-17.17
P/E Ratio	34.95-22.74	29.27-20.89	13.86-9.71	...	17.72-10.07	9.09-5.67	47.44-31.51	3.43-2.42
Average Yield %	0.70	0.66	0.73	0.79	1.01	53.62	...	0.80

Address: 315 Park Avenue South, New York, NY 10010-3607 Telephone: (212) 460-1900 Fax: (212) 598-4869	Web Site: www.leucadia.com Officers: Ian M. Cumming - Chmn. Joseph S. Steinberg - Pres.	Auditors: PricewaterhouseCoopers LLP Investor Contact: 212-460-1900

LEXINGTON CORPORATE PROPERTIES TRUST

Exchange	Symbol	Price	52Wk Range	Yield	P/E	Div Acheiver
NYS	LXP	$21.94 (3/31/2005)	23.56-17.30	6.56	27.43	10 Years

*7 Year Price Score 119.25 *NYSE Composite Index=100   *12 Month Price Score 98.06

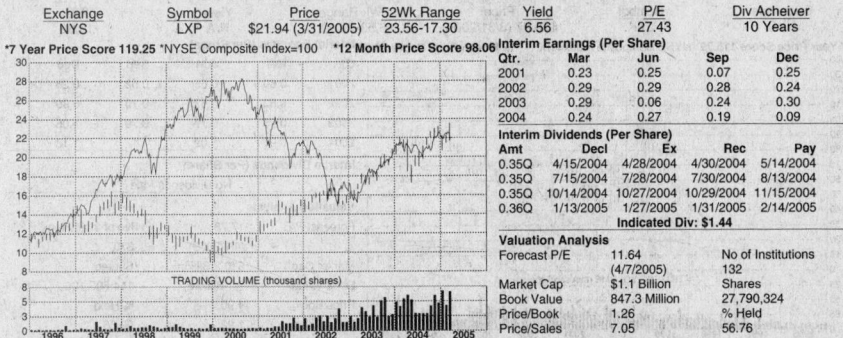

Interim Earnings (Per Share)

Qtr.	Mar	Jun	Sep	Dec
2001	0.23	0.25	0.07	0.25
2002	0.29	0.29	0.28	0.24
2003	0.29	0.06	0.24	0.30
2004	0.24	0.27	0.19	0.09

Interim Dividends (Per Share)

Amt	Decl	Ex	Rec	Pay
0.35Q	4/15/2004	4/28/2004	4/30/2004	5/14/2004
0.35Q	7/15/2004	7/28/2004	7/30/2004	8/13/2004
0.35Q	10/14/2004	10/27/2004	10/29/2004	11/15/2004
0.36Q	1/13/2005	1/27/2005	1/31/2005	2/14/2005
			Indicated Div: $1.44	

Valuation Analysis

Forecast P/E	11.64	No of Institutions
	(4/7/2005)	132
Market Cap	$1.1 Billion	Shares
Book Value	847.3 Million	27,790,324
Price/Book	1.26	% Held
Price/Sales	7.05	56.76

TRADING VOLUME (thousand shares)

Business Summary: Property, Real Estate & Development (MIC: 8.3 SIC: 798 NAIC: 25930)

Lexington Corporate Properties Trust is a self-managed and self-administered real estate investment trust that acquires, owns and manages a geographically diverse portfolio of net leased office, industrial and retail properties and provides investment advisory and asset management services to institutional investors in the net lease area. As of Dec 31 2003, Co.'s real property portfolio consisted of 118 properties or interests located in 35 states, including warehousing, distribution and manufacturing facilities, office buildings and retail properties. Co. manages its real estate and credit risk through geographic, industry, tenant and lease maturity diversification.

Recent Developments: For the year ended Dec 31 2004, income from continuing operations increased 57.9% to $43.7 million compared with $27.7 million in the previous year. Earnings for 2004 and 2003 excluded income from discontinued operations of $1.1 million and $6.0 million, respectively. Results included a tenant bankruptcy write-off of $2.9 million in 2004 and a debt retirement charge of $7.5 million in 2003. Total revenues advanced 36.3% to $151.2 million from $111.0 million a year earlier.

Prospects: On Dec 30 2004, Co. announced that one of its joint venture programs acquired a newly constructed office building/call center facility located in Wilmington, NC for approximately $20.0 million. This acquisition increased total volume for fiscal 2004 to about $900.0 million. Going forward, Co. is actively working on several acquisitions that it expects to close during the first quarter of 2005. Further, Co. intends to continue pursuing opportunities that enhance its portfolio in terms of tenant credit quality, lease term, market and tenant industry diversification, and total return potential. Co. expects to generate funds from operations per share of $1.85 to $1.90 for fiscal 2005.

Financial Data (US$ in Thousands)	12/31/2004	12/31/2003	12/31/2002	12/31/2001	12/31/2000	12/31/1999	12/31/1998	12/31/1997
Earnings Per Share	0.80	0.88	1.09	0.77	1.10	1.08	0.78	0.32
Cash Flow Per Share	1.95	2.11	2.15	2.28	2.41	2.36	1.90	2.08
Tang Book Value Per Share	12.03	12.02	11.09	9.89	8.78	8.87	9.14	9.58
Dividends Per Share	1.400	1.340	1.320	1.270	1.220	1.200	1.170	1.160
Dividend Payout %	175.00	152.27	121.10	164.94	110.91	111.11	150.00	362.50
Income Statement								
Property Income	146,340	111,658	93,884	78,402	76,824	75,760	62,846	42,493
Non-Property Income	4,885	8,862	6,735	4,460	3,181	1,540	2,271	1,076
Total Revenue	151,225	120,520	100,619	82,862	80,005	77,300	65,117	43,569
Depn & Amortn	41,710	29,572	23,375	19,952	19,010	18,991	16,070	11,484
Income Before Taxes	41,860	34,812	...	...	27,967	...	...	...
Income Taxes	1,181	...	...	...	...	...	...	...
Net Income	44,807	33,649	30,595	18,062	21,952	21,347	15,737	8,593
Average Shares	52,048	39,493	32,602	19,862	24,714	24,945	21,983	11,639
Balance Sheet								
Total Assets	1,697,086	1,207,411	902,471	822,153	668,377	656,481	647,007	467,115
Long-Term Obligations	765,144	455,940	460,517	445,771	345,505	301,333	302,252	222,533
Total Liabilities	793,037	564,534	508,840	469,403	400,502	385,203	367,482	232,040
Stockholders' Equity	847,290	579,848	332,976	266,713	174,885	176,797	180,775	182,466
Shares Outstanding	48,621	40,682	30,030	24,507	17,151	17,193	17,103	16,510
Statistical Record								
Return on Assets %	3.08	3.19	3.55	2.42	3.30	3.28	2.83	2.21
Return on Equity %	6.26	7.37	10.20	8.18	12.45	11.94	8.66	6.25
Net Margin %	29.63	27.92	30.41	21.80	27.44	27.62	24.17	19.72
Price Range	23.23-17.30	20.85-15.63	16.75-14.25	15.56-11.94	12.25-9.00	12.88-9.00	16.25-10.88	16.50-12.13
P/E Ratio	29.04-21.63	23.69-17.76	15.37-13.07	20.21-15.50	11.14-8.18	11.92-8.33	20.83-13.94	51.56-37.89
Average Yield %	6.70	7.41	8.40	9.13	11.11	10.67	8.55	8.18

Address: One Penn Plaza, Suite 4015, New York, NY 10119-4015 Telephone: (212) 692-7200	Web Site: www.lxp.com Officers: E. Robert Roskind - Chmn. T. Wilson Eglin - Pres., C.E.O., C.O.O.	Auditors: KPMG LLP

LEXMARK INTERNATIONAL, INC.

Exchange	Symbol	Price	52Wk Range	Yield	P/E
NYS	LXK	$79.97 (3/31/2005)	96.53-77.90	N/A	18.68

*7 Year Price Score 115.79 *NYSE Composite Index=100 *12 Month Price Score 86.90

Interim Earnings (Per Share)

Qtr.	Mar	Jun	Sep	Dec
2001	0.60	0.65	0.52	0.28
2002	0.53	0.67	0.70	0.90
2003	0.73	0.77	0.79	1.05
2004	0.91	1.02	1.17	1.18

Interim Dividends (Per Share)

No Dividends Paid

Valuation Analysis

Forecast P/E	17.78	No of Institutions	
	(4/7/2005)	370	
Market Cap	$10.2 Billion	Shares	
Book Value	2.1 Billion	114,803,120	
Price/Book	4.90	% Held	
Price/Sales	1.92	90.66	

Business Summary: Office Equipment Supplies (MIC: 11.12 SIC: 577 NAIC: 34119)

Lexmark International is a developer, manufacturer and supplier of printing and imaging devices for offices and homes. Co.'s products include laser printers, inkjet printers, multifunction devices, associated supplies and services. Co. also sells dot matrix printers for printing single and multi-part forms by business users and develops, manufactures and markets a line of other office imaging products. The principal customers for Co.'s products are dealers, retailers and distributors worldwide. Co.'s products are sold in more than 150 countries in North and South America, Europe, the Middle East, Africa, Asia, the Pacific Rim and the Caribbean.

Recent Developments: For the year ended Dec 31 2004, net income increased 29.5% to $568,700 thousand from net income of $439,200 thousand a year earlier. Revenues were $5,313,800 thousand, up 11.8% from $4,754,700 thousand the year before. Operating income was $732,100 thousand versus an income of $593,900 thousand in the prior year, an increase of 23.3%. Total direct expense was $3,522,400 thousand versus $3,209,600 thousand in the prior year, an increase of 9.7%. Total indirect expense was $1,059,300 thousand versus $951,200 thousand in the prior year, an increase of 11.4%.

Prospects: Improvement in Co.'s gross profit margin to 32.0% for the quarter ended Dec 31 2004 compared with 31.9% a year earlier supports Co.'s satisfactory near-term prospects. Accordingly, for the first quarter ended Mar 31 2005, Co. expects a year-over-year revenue growth rate of mid- to high-single digits and earnings per share of $0.95 to $1.05. Looking ahead, Co. believes that the strength of its product line and its supplies-driven business model will keep it well positioned for continued growth. However, Co. noted that uncertainty in the economy and the potential for aggressive price competition continue.

Financial Data

(US$ in Thousands)	12/31/2004	12/31/2003	12/31/2002	12/31/2001	12/31/2000	12/31/1999	12/31/1998	12/31/1997
Earnings Per Share	4.28	3.34	2.79	2.05	2.13	2.32	1.70	0.99
Cash Flow Per Share	5.96	5.84	6.35	1.51	3.70	3.10	2.17	1.93
Tang Book Value Per Share	16.32	12.78	8.57	8.25	7.89	6.42	4.41	3.71
Income Statement								
Total Revenue	5,313,800	4,754,700	4,356,400	4,142,800	3,807,000	3,452,300	3,020,600	2,493,500
EBITDA	866,900	742,000	642,800	458,200	500,400	549,700	452,000	343,000
Depn & Amortn	134,900	148,900	138,200	125,600	91,200	80,100	75,600	77,500
Income Before Taxes	746,500	593,500	495,600	317,800	396,400	458,900	365,400	254,700
Income Taxes	177,800	154,300	128,900	44,200	111,000	140,400	122,400	91,700
Net Income	568,700	439,200	366,700	273,600	285,400	318,500	243,000	149,000
Average Shares	132,900	131,400	131,600	133,800	134,300	137,546	142,801	150,337
Balance Sheet								
Current Assets	3,000,900	2,443,800	1,798,800	1,493,100	1,243,700	1,088,700	1,020,000	776,100
Total Assets	4,124,300	3,450,400	2,808,100	2,449,900	2,073,200	1,702,600	1,483,400	1,208,200
Current Liabilities	1,467,500	1,183,300	1,099,000	931,100	979,000	735,500	605,700	547,500
Long-Term Obligations	149,500	149,300	149,200	149,100	148,900	148,700	148,700	57,000
Total Liabilities	2,041,400	1,807,400	1,726,500	1,374,000	1,296,200	1,043,500	905,300	707,500
Stockholders' Equity	2,082,900	1,643,000	1,081,600	1,075,900	777,000	659,100	578,100	500,700
Shares Outstanding	127,600	128,600	126,200	130,400	98,514	102,679	130,982	135,080
Statistical Record								
Return on Assets %	14.97	14.04	13.95	12.10	15.08	19.99	18.06	12.26
Return on Equity %	30.44	32.24	33.99	29.53	39.64	51.49	45.05	28.63
EBITDA Margin %	16.31	15.61	14.76	11.06	13.14	15.92	14.96	13.76
Net Margin %	10.70	9.24	8.42	6.60	7.50	9.23	8.04	5.98
Asset Turnover	1.40	1.52	1.66	1.83	2.01	2.17	2.24	2.05
Current Ratio	2.04	2.07	1.64	1.60	1.27	1.48	1.68	1.42
Debt to Equity	0.07	0.09	0.14	0.14	0.19	0.23	0.26	0.11
Price Range	96.53-76.32	78.64-57.41	67.27-42.47	69.66-41.13	130.75-29.50	101.88-42.78	50.25-17.88	19.00-10.63
P/E Ratio	22.55-17.83	23.54-17.19	24.11-15.22	33.98-20.06	61.38-13.85	43.91-18.44	29.56-10.51	19.19-10.73

Address: One Lexmark Centre Drive, Lexington, KY 40550 Telephone: (859) 232-2000 Fax: (859) 232-3120	Web Site: www.lexmark.com Officers: Paul J. Curlander - Chmn., C.E.O. Gary E. Morin - Exec. V.P., C.F.O.	Auditors: PricewaterhouseCoopers LLP Investor Contact: 859-232-5934

LIBERTY MEDIA CORP. (NEW)

Exchange	Symbol	Price	52Wk Range	Yield	P/E
NYS	L	$10.37 (3/31/2005)	11.05-8.44	N/A	518.50

*7 Year Price Score 71.47   *NYSE Composite Index=100   *12 Month Price Score 101.01

Interim Earnings (Per Share)

Qtr.	Mar	Jun	Sep	Dec
2001	(0.06)	(0.82)	(0.08)	(1.44)
2002	(0.57)	(1.20)	(0.03)	(1.26)
2003	0.05	(0.17)	0.02	(0.33)
2004	...	(0.11)	0.13	0.00

Interim Dividends (Per Share)

No Dividends Paid

Valuation Analysis

Forecast P/E	N/A		No of Institutions
Market Cap	$29.0 Billion		Shares
Book Value	24.6 Billion		2,008,236,160
Price/Book	1.18		% Held
Price/Sales	3.78		74.96

Business Summary: Media (MIC: 13.1 SIC: 841 NAIC: 12110)

Liberty Media is a holding company that is primarily engaged in electronic retailing, international cable television distribution, telephony and programming, and the production, acquisition and distribution through all available formats and media of branded entertainment, educational and informational programming and software. As of Dec 31 2003, Co. operated in the U.S., Europe, South America and Asia. Co.'s principal assets include interests in QVC, Inc., Starz Encore Group LLC, Ascent Media Group, Inc., Discovery Communications, Inc., UnitedGlobalCom, Inc., Jupiter Telecommunications Co., Ltd., Court Television Network, Game Show Network, InterActiveCorp and The News Corporation Limited.

Recent Developments: For the year ended Dec 31 2004, income from continuing operations was $161 million compared with a loss of $1,225 million a year earlier. Net income was $46 million versus net loss of $1,222 million a year earlier. Revenues were $7,682 million, up 105.5% from $3,738 million the year before. Operating income was $742 million versus a loss of $939 million in the prior year. Total direct expense was $3,594 million versus $1,258 million in the prior year, an increase of 185.7%. Total indirect expense was $3,346 million versus $3,419 million in the prior year, a decrease of 2.1%.

Prospects: For full-year 2005, Co. expects revenues in its QVC segment to increase by the high single digit percentage and operating cash flow and operating income to increase by the low double digit percentage. Also, Co. expects revenues for full-year 2005 at its Starz Entertainment Group to range from $1.00 billion to $1.05 billion, with operating cash flow between $150.0 million and $170.0 million and operating income to range from $64.0 million and $84.0 million. Lastly, full-year revenues at Co.'s Discovery Communications segment is expected to increase by the mid-teen percentage and operating cash flow by the low double digit percentage.

Financial Data
(US$ in Thousands)

	12/31/2004	12/31/2003	12/31/2002	12/31/2001	12/31/2000	12/31/1999	02/28/1999	12/31/1998
Earnings Per Share	0.02	(0.44)	(2.06)	(2.40)	...	...	...	...
Cash Flow Per Share	0.32	...	...	...	...	...	...	...
Tang Book Value Per Share	3.10	4.13	6.36	8.02	7,981,000.00	9,541,000.00	...	2,777,000.00
Income Statement								
Total Revenue	7,682,000	4,028,000	2,084,000	2,059,000	1,526,000	729,000	235,000	1,359,000
EBITDA	1,675,000	199,000	(4,394,000)	(9,373,000)	5,858,000	(2,222,000)	184,000	1,303,000
Depn & Amortn	736,000	510,000	384,000	984,000	853,000	562,000	22,000	129,000
Income Before Taxes	324,000	(850,000)	(5,201,000)	(10,882,000)	4,759,000	(3,072,000)	137,000	1,070,000
Income Taxes	158,000	374,000	(1,702,000)	(3,908,000)	2,190,000	(1,097,000)	211,000	461,000
Net Income	46,000	(1,222,000)	(5,330,000)	(6,203,000)	2,569,000	(1,975,000)	(70,000)	622,000
Average Shares	2,856,000	...	...	...	...	...	...	...
Balance Sheet								
Current Assets	4,788,000	6,419,000	4,500,000	3,531,000	2,954,000	3,368,000	...	1,029,000
Total Assets	50,181,000	54,013,000	39,685,000	48,539,000	54,176,000	58,650,000	...	15,783,000
Current Liabilities	3,207,000	2,836,000	2,027,000	2,780,000	2,962,000	3,370,000	...	838,000
Long-Term Obligations	8,566,000	9,482,000	4,316,000	4,764,000	5,269,000	2,723,000	...	1,912,000
Total Liabilities	25,296,000	24,878,000	14,752,000	18,283,000	19,604,000	20,219,000	...	6,421,000
Stockholders' Equity	24,586,000	28,842,000	24,682,000	30,123,000	34,224,000	38,408,000	...	9,230,000
Shares Outstanding	2,799,958	2,886,936	2,688,998	2,590,173	3	3	...	3
Statistical Record								
Return on Assets %	0.09	N.M.	N.M.	N.M.	4.54	N.M.	...	...
Return on Equity %	0.17	N.M.	N.M.	N.M.	7.05	N.M.	...	...
EBITDA Margin %	21.80	4.94	N.M.	N.M.	383.88	N.M.	78.30	95.88
Net Margin %	0.60	N.M.	N.M.	N.M.	168.35	N.M.	N.M.	45.77
Asset Turnover	0.15	0.09	0.05	0.04	0.03	0.02	...	...
Current Ratio	1.49	2.26	2.22	1.27	1.00	1.00	...	1.23
Debt to Equity	0.35	0.33	0.17	0.16	0.15	0.07	...	0.21
Price Range	11.05-8.44	10.10-7.13	12.31-5.21	14.70-9.07	24.90-8.90	23.52-10.78	11.57-9.26	9.54-4.65
P/E Ratio	552.50-422.00	...	...	...	...	...	...	...

Address: 12300 Liberty Boulevard, Englewood, CO 80112 **Telephone:** (720) 875-5400	**Web Site:** **Officers:** John C. Malone - Chmn. Robert R. Bennett - Pres., C.E.O.	**Auditors:** KPMG LLP

LIBERTY PROPERTY TRUST

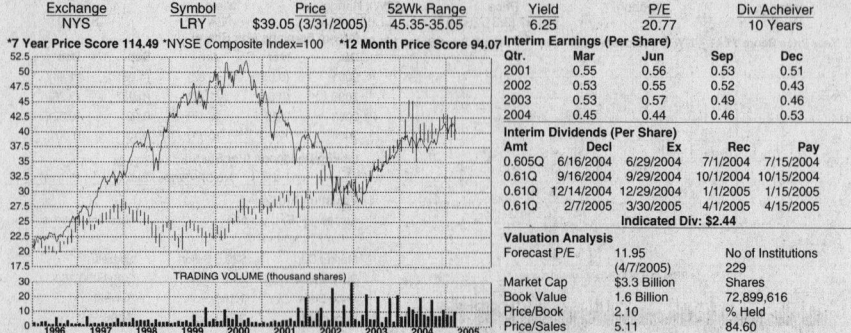

Exchange	Symbol	Price	52Wk Range	Yield	P/E	Div Acheiver
NYS	LRY	$39.05 (3/31/2005)	45.35-35.05	6.25	20.77	10 Years

*7 Year Price Score 114.49 ***NYSE Composite Index=100** ***12 Month Price Score 94.07**

Interim Earnings (Per Share)

Qtr.	Mar	Jun	Sep	Dec
2001	0.55	0.56	0.53	0.51
2002	0.53	0.55	0.52	0.43
2003	0.53	0.57	0.49	0.46
2004	0.45	0.44	0.46	0.53

Interim Dividends (Per Share)

Amt	Decl	Ex	Rec	Pay
0.605Q	6/16/2004	6/29/2004	7/1/2004	7/15/2004
0.61Q	9/16/2004	9/29/2004	10/1/2004	10/15/2004
0.61Q	12/14/2004	12/29/2004	1/1/2005	1/15/2005
0.61Q	2/7/2005	3/30/2005	4/1/2005	4/15/2005

Indicated Div: $2.44

Valuation Analysis

Forecast P/E	11.95 (4/7/2005)	No of Institutions 229
Market Cap	$3.3 Billion	Shares 72,899,616
Book Value	1.6 Billion	% Held 84.60
Price/Book	2.10	
Price/Sales	5.11	

Business Summary: Property, Real Estate & Development (MIC: 8.3 SIC: 798 NAIC: 25930)

Liberty Property Trust is a self-administered and self- managed Maryland real estate investment trust (REIT). Substantially all of Co.'s assets are owned directly or indirectly, and substantially all of Co.'s operations are conducted directly or indirectly, by its subsidiary, Liberty Property Limited Partnership, a Pennsylvania limited partnership. As of December 31, 2003, Co.'s portfolio consisted of 673 industrial and office properties totaling approximately 53.7 million square feet. In addition, Co. had 15 properties under development and, together with the Properties in Operation, and owned 1,079 acres of land.

Recent Developments: For the year ended Dec 31 2004, income from continuing operations decreased 0.4% to $148,697 thousand from income of $149,318 thousand a year earlier. Net income decreased 1.3% to $161,443 thousand from net income of $163,610 thousand a year earlier. Revenues were $655,355 thousand, up 5.7% from $620,282 thousand the year before. Operating income was $285,175 thousand versus an income of $285,110 thousand in the prior year, an increase of 0.0%.

Prospects: During 2004, Co. acquired 20 properties, including seven in the fourth quarter, for approximately $235.8 million. These properties, which contain 3.9 million square feet, were 68.6% leased at Dec 31 2004, yielding 6.1%, and are expected to produce a stabilized yield of 9.1%. Separately, in January 2005, Co. began construction on Comcast Center, a $435.0 million, 1.2 million square foot, 57-story office tower in Center City, Philadelphia, PA. The project will provide a new headquarters for Comcast Corporation and will be available for occupancy beginning in the fall of 2007. Looking ahead, Co. is projecting full-year 2005 funds from operations in the range of $3.20 to $3.35 per share.

Financial Data

(US$ in Thousands)	12/31/2004	12/31/2003	12/31/2002	12/31/2001	12/31/2000	12/31/1999	12/31/1998	12/31/1997
Earnings Per Share	1.88	2.05	2.02	2.15	2.17	1.95	1.59	1.38
Cash Flow Per Share	3.45	3.32	3.93	4.27	3.56	3.19	3.59	3.13
Tang Book Value Per Share	18.63	18.61	17.69	17.68	17.59	17.53	17.46	15.84
Dividends Per Share	2.430	2.410	2.380	2.320	2.180	1.940	1.740	1.660
Dividend Payout %	129.26	117.56	117.82	107.91	100.46	99.49	109.43	120.29
Income Statement								
Property Income	655,355	625,032	597,430	580,308	528,589	466,522	382,980	225,361
Non-Property Income	...	...	8,599	6,857	4,374	5,976	4,113	7,156
Total Revenue	655,355	625,032	606,029	587,165	532,963	472,498	387,093	232,517
Depn & Amortn	141,015	127,115	114,870	106,642	97,360	89,415	72,394	48,119
Interest Expense	123,352	123,907	116,625	112,006	108,295	99,663	78,617	53,888
Net Income	161,443	163,610	161,665	166,537	159,271	141,324	108,615	60,444
Average Shares	86,024	79,868	76,272	73,580	68,173	66,727	61,315	40,806
Balance Sheet								
Total Assets	4,162,827	3,834,008	3,627,061	3,552,825	3,396,355	3,118,133	2,933,371	2,094,337
Long-Term Obligations	2,133,171	1,885,866	1,866,187	1,753,131	1,703,896	1,491,238	1,423,843	960,134
Total Liabilities	2,358,702	2,081,444	2,067,033	1,935,009	1,876,781	1,636,015	1,565,081	1,054,064
Stockholders' Equity	1,596,259	1,544,897	1,351,589	1,423,422	1,320,805	1,294,607	1,267,036	955,595
Shares Outstanding	85,675	83,012	76,425	73,661	68,212	66,971	65,645	52,693
Statistical Record								
Return on Assets %	4.03	4.39	4.50	4.79	4.88	4.67	4.32	3.72
Return on Equity %	10.25	11.30	11.65	12.14	12.15	11.03	9.77	9.08
Net Margin %	24.63	26.18	26.68	28.36	29.88	29.91	28.06	26.00
Price Range	45.47-35.05	38.90-29.31	35.17-27.60	31.10-25.75	28.97-22.00	25.38-20.38	28.56-20.81	28.88-23.63
P/E Ratio	24.19-18.64	18.98-14.30	17.41-13.66	14.47-11.98	13.35-10.14	13.01-10.45	17.96-13.09	20.92-17.12
Average Yield %	6.04	7.10	7.60	8.15	8.50	8.34	6.93	6.46

Address: 65 Valley Stream Parkway, Suite 100, Malvern, PA 19355
Telephone: (610) 648-1700
Fax: (610) 644-4129

Web Site: www.libertyproperty.com
Officers: William P. Hankowsky - Chmn., Pres., C.E.O., Chief Invest. Officer George J. Alburger Jr. - Exec. V.P., C.F.O.

Auditors: Ernst & Young LLP
Investor Contact: 610-648-1704
Transfer Agents: EquiServe Trust Company, N.A., Providence, RI

486

LILLY (ELI) & CO.

Exchange	Symbol	Price	52Wk Range	Yield	P/E	Div Acheiver
NYS	LLY	$52.10 (3/31/2005)	76.26-50.44	2.92	31.39	37 Years

*7 Year Price Score 74.36   ***NYSE Composite Index=100**   ***12 Month Price Score 82.67**

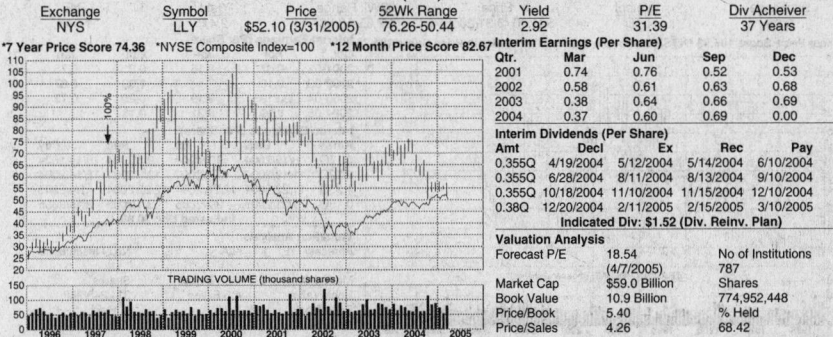

Interim Earnings (Per Share)

Qtr.	Mar	Jun	Sep	Dec
2001	0.74	0.76	0.52	0.53
2002	0.58	0.61	0.63	0.68
2003	0.38	0.64	0.66	0.69
2004	0.37	0.60	0.69	0.00

Interim Dividends (Per Share)

Amt	Decl	Ex	Rec	Pay
0.355Q	4/19/2004	5/12/2004	5/14/2004	6/10/2004
0.355Q	6/28/2004	8/11/2004	8/13/2004	9/10/2004
0.355Q	10/18/2004	11/10/2004	11/15/2004	12/10/2004
0.38Q	12/20/2004	2/11/2005	2/15/2005	3/10/2005
	Indicated Div: $1.52 (Div. Reinv. Plan)			

Valuation Analysis

Forecast P/E	18.54 (4/7/2005)
Market Cap	$59.0 Billion
Book Value	10.9 Billion
Price/Book	5.40
Price/Sales	4.26
No of Institutions	787
Shares	774,952,448
% Held	68.42

TRADING VOLUME (thousand shares)

Business Summary: Pharmaceuticals (MIC: 9.1 SIC: 834 NAIC: 25412)

Eli Lilly discovers, develops, manufactures, and sells pharmaceuticals and animal health products. Neuroscience products include Prozac®, Zyprexa®, Strattera™ Darvon®, Permax®, Symbyax® and Sarafem™. Endocrine products include Humulin®, Humalog®, Humalog Mix 75/25®, Actos®, Evista®, Forteo® and Humatrope®. Oncology products include Gemzar® and Alimta®. Animal Health products include Tylan®, Rumensin®, Coban®, Monteban®, Maxiban®, Apralan®, Micotil®, Pulmotil®, Surmax®, Optaflexx® and Paylean®. Cardiovascular products, consist primarily of ReoPro®, Dobutrex®, Xigris® and Cynt®. Anti-infective products include Ceclor®, Keflex®, Keftab®, Lorabid®, and Vancocin®, and other products.

Recent Developments: For the year ended Dec 31 2004, net income decreased 29.3% to $1,810,100 thousand from net income of $2,560,800 thousand a year earlier. Revenues were $13,857,900 thousand, up 10.1% from $12,582,500 thousand the year before. Total direct expense was $3,223,900 thousand versus $2,675,100 thousand in the prior year, an increase of 20.5%. Total indirect expense was $7,367,500 thousand versus $6,405,600 thousand in the prior year, an increase of 15.0%.

Prospects: For the first quarter of 2005, Co. expects earnings per share of $0.65 to $0.67, up from an adjusted $0.64 per share a year ago. Excluding incremental equity compensation expense, earnings per share will be $0.71 to $0.73 per share, up from $0.70 a year ago. For the full year of 2005, Co. expects sales to grow 8.0% to 10.0% (with sales acceleration in the second half), gross margins as a percent of sales to decline by roughly 50 basis points to 75 basis points, marketing and administrative expenses to grow in the low-single digits, research and development expense to grow in the mid-single digits and other income to contribute approximately $175.0 million to $225.0 million.

Financial Data

(US$ in Thousands)	12/31/2004	12/31/2003	12/31/2002	12/31/2001	12/31/2000	12/31/1999	12/31/1998	12/31/1997
Earnings Per Share	1.66	2.37	2.50	2.55	2.79	2.46	1.87	(0.35)
Cash Flow Per Share	2.64	3.39	1.92	3.40	3.44	2.41	2.40	2.18
Tang Book Value Per Share	9.65	8.69	7.37	6.32	5.37	4.49	2.86	2.79
Dividends Per Share	1.420	1.340	1.240	1.120	1.040	0.920	0.800	0.740
Dividend Payout %	85.54	56.54	49.60	43.92	37.28	37.40	42.78	...
Income Statement								
Total Revenue	13,857,900	12,582,500	11,077,500	11,542,500	10,862,200	10,002,900	9,236,800	8,517,600
EBITDA	3,539,400	3,810,200	3,950,700	4,007,000	4,294,500	3,685,100	3,155,400	1,254,100
Depn & Amortn	597,500	548,500	493,000	454,900	435,800	439,700	490,400	509,800
Income Before Taxes	2,941,900	3,261,700	3,457,700	3,552,100	3,858,700	3,245,400	2,665,000	510,200
Income Taxes	1,131,800	700,900	749,800	742,700	800,900	698,700	568,700	895,300
Net Income	1,810,100	2,560,800	2,707,900	2,780,000	3,057,800	2,721,000	2,097,900	(385,100)
Average Shares	1,088,936	1,082,230	1,085,088	1,090,793	1,097,725	1,106,055	1,121,486	1,101,099
Balance Sheet								
Current Assets	12,835,800	8,758,700	7,804,100	6,938,900	7,943,000	7,055,500	5,406,800	5,320,700
Total Assets	24,867,000	21,678,100	19,042,000	16,434,100	14,690,800	12,825,200	12,595,500	12,577,400
Current Liabilities	7,593,700	5,550,600	5,063,500	5,203,000	4,960,700	3,935,400	4,607,200	4,191,600
Long-Term Obligations	4,491,900	4,687,800	4,358,200	3,132,100	2,633,700	2,811,900	2,185,500	2,326,100
Total Liabilities	13,947,100	11,913,300	10,768,400	9,330,100	8,643,900	7,812,200	8,165,900	7,771,800
Stockholders' Equity	10,919,900	9,764,800	8,273,600	7,104,000	6,046,900	5,013,000	4,429,600	4,645,600
Shares Outstanding	1,131,942	1,123,725	1,122,443	1,123,348	1,125,560	1,090,238	1,019,090	1,110,522
Statistical Record								
Return on Assets %	7.76	12.58	15.27	17.86	22.16	21.41	16.67	N.M.
Return on Equity %	17.45	28.39	35.22	42.28	55.14	57.63	46.23	N.M.
EBITDA Margin %	25.54	30.28	35.66	34.72	39.54	36.84	34.16	14.72
Net Margin %	13.06	20.35	24.45	24.08	28.15	27.20	22.71	N.M.
Asset Turnover	0.59	0.62	0.62	0.74	0.79	0.79	0.73	0.63
Current Ratio	1.69	1.58	1.54	1.33	1.60	1.79	1.17	1.27
Debt to Equity	0.41	0.48	0.53	0.44	0.44	0.56	0.49	0.50
Price Range	76.26-50.44	73.89-53.70	80.69-48.15	91.50-72.59	108.56-54.50	97.44-61.50	90.88-58.25	69.94-36.25
P/E Ratio	45.94-30.39	31.18-22.66	32.28-19.26	35.88-28.47	38.91-19.53	39.61-25.00	48.60-31.15	...
Average Yield %	2.15	2.11	1.91	1.40	1.32	1.21	1.12	1.41

Address: Lilly Corporate Center, Indianapolis, IN 46285 **Telephone:** (317) 276-2000 **Fax:** (317) 276-6331	**Web Site:** www.lilly.com **Officers:** Sidney Taurel - Chmn., Pres., C.E.O. Charles E. Golden - Exec. V.P., C.F.O.	**Auditors:** Ernst & Young LLP **Investor Contact:** 317-276-2506 **Transfer Agents:** Norwest Shareowner Services, South St. Paul, MN

LIMITED BRANDS INC.

Exchange	Symbol	Price	52Wk Range	Yield	P/E
NYS	LTD	$24.30 (3/31/2005)	27.83-18.56	2.47	17.48

*7 Year Price Score 105.53 *NYSE Composite Index=100 *12 Month Price Score 101.75

Interim Earnings (Per Share)

Qtr.	Apr	Jul	Oct	Jan
2001-02	0.07	0.16	0.21	0.75
2002-03	0.10	...	0.03	0.67
2003-04	0.19	0.19	0.25	0.73
2004-05	0.19	0.31	0.16	...

Interim Dividends (Per Share)

Amt	Decl	Ex	Rec	Pay
0.12Q	8/19/2004	9/1/2004	9/3/2004	9/14/2004
0.12Q	11/19/2004	12/1/2004	12/3/2004	12/14/2004
1.23Q	11/22/2004	12/20/2004	12/22/2004	1/4/2005
0.15Q	1/31/2005	3/2/2005	3/4/2005	3/15/2005

Indicated Div: $0.60

Valuation Analysis

Forecast P/E	N/A	No of Institutions
Market Cap	$9.9 Billion	Shares
Book Value	4.5 Billion	314,348,768
Price/Book	2.21	% Held
Price/Sales	1.06	77.34

Business Summary: Retail - Apparel and Accessory Stores (MIC: 5.8 SIC: 621 NAIC: 48120)

Limited Brands operated 3,911 specialty retail stores as of Jan 31 2004. Co. sells women's intimate and other apparel, personal care products and accessories under the Victoria's Secret brand name and sold through its stores and catalogue and e-commerce operations. Co. also sells personal care products and accessories and home fragrance products under the Bath & Body Works and White Barn Candle Company brand names, along with women's and men's apparel through its Express and Limited stores. Co. also operates a Henri Bendel store in New York City featuring high-income fashions. As of Jan 31 2004, Co. owned about 23% of Galyan's Trading Co., which offers merchandise for sports enthusiasts.

Recent Developments: For the quarter ended Oct 30 2004, net income decreased 39.6% to $78,345 thousand from net income of $129,674 thousand in the year-earlier quarter. Revenues were $1,890,855 thousand, up 2.4% from $1,846,770 thousand the year before. Operating income was $53,145 thousand versus an income of $42,172 thousand in the prior-year quarter, an increase of 26.0%. Total indirect expense was $560,440 thousand versus $553,281 thousand in the prior-year quarter, an increase of 1.3%.

Prospects: Co.'s near-term outlook appears somewhat uncertain. On the positive side, Co.'s comparable store sales for the fourth quarter ended Jan 29 2005 increased 2.0%, aided by increases from Victoria's Secret and Victoria's Secret Beauty, Victoria's Secret Direct, Bath & Body Works and The White Barn Candle Co., and Limited Brands. However, these gains were offset to a certain degree by declines from Express and The Limited. Looking ahead, Co. expects full-year 2005 earnings growth of between 13.0% and 15.0% compared with 2004's adjusted $1.40 per share.

Financial Data
(US$ in Thousands)

	9 Mos	6 Mos	3 Mos	01/31/2004	02/01/2003	02/02/2002	02/03/2001	01/29/2000
Earnings Per Share	1.39	1.48	1.36	1.36	0.96	1.19	0.96	1.00
Cash Flow Per Share	2.15	2.40	1.97	2.05	1.56	2.27	1.77	1.34
Tang Book Value Per Share	6.68	5.69	5.54	6.71	5.93	6.04	5.44	4.99
Dividends Per Share	0.460	0.440	0.420	0.400	0.300	0.300	0.300	0.300
Dividend Payout %	33.03	29.69	30.84	29.41	31.25	25.21	31.25	30.00
Income Statement								
Total Revenue	6,079,890	4,189,035	1,978,203	8,934,000	8,445,000	9,363,000	10,104,606	9,723,334
EBITDA	739,519	558,531	235,881	1,448,000	1,148,000	1,215,000	1,088,295	1,182,499
Depn & Amortn	227,217	152,685	75,575	283,000	310,000	277,000	271,146	272,443
Income Before Taxes	498,934	398,589	156,637	1,166,000	837,000	904,000	758,905	831,759
Income Taxes	176,000	154,000	60,000	449,000	341,000	385,000	331,000	371,000
Net Income	322,934	244,589	96,637	717,000	502,000	519,000	427,905	460,759
Average Shares	479,898	480,296	515,439	526,000	522,000	435,000	443,048	455,564
Balance Sheet								
Current Assets	4,083,920	3,553,454	3,302,784	4,433,000	3,606,000	2,682,000	2,067,798	2,246,277
Total Assets	7,501,035	6,945,665	6,696,609	7,873,000	7,246,000	4,719,000	4,088,122	4,087,689
Current Liabilities	1,321,782	1,335,234	1,119,954	1,392,000	1,259,000	1,319,000	1,000,185	1,238,206
Long-Term Obligations	1,146,483	648,293	648,256	648,000	547,000	250,000	400,000	400,000
Total Liabilities	3,041,277	2,527,748	2,328,180	2,607,000	2,386,000	1,975,000	1,771,667	1,940,612
Stockholders' Equity	4,459,758	4,417,917	4,368,429	5,266,000	4,860,000	2,744,000	2,316,455	2,147,077
Shares Outstanding	406,425	469,399	472,300	524,000	523,000	429,000	425,943	429,928
Statistical Record								
Return on Assets %	9.64	10.81	10.39	9.51	8.41	11.82	10.30	10.70
Return on Equity %	15.20	16.43	15.49	14.20	13.24	20.57	18.86	21.10
EBITDA Margin %	12.16	13.33	11.92	16.21	13.59	12.98	10.77	12.16
Net Margin %	5.31	5.84	4.89	8.03	5.94	5.54	4.23	4.74
Asset Turnover	1.26	1.32	1.32	1.19	1.42	2.13	2.43	2.26
Current Ratio	3.09	2.66	2.95	3.18	2.86	2.03	2.07	1.81
Debt to Equity	0.26	0.15	0.15	0.12	0.11	0.09	0.17	0.19
Price Range	24.78-17.17	21.45-14.90	21.45-13.08	18.39-11.05	22.25-12.20	19.77-9.42	27.75-14.59	23.63-15.25
P/E Ratio	17.83-12.35	14.49-10.07	15.77-9.62	13.52-8.13	23.18-12.71	16.61-7.92	28.91-15.20	23.63-15.25
Average Yield %	2.34	2.39	2.42	2.56	1.77	1.98	1.43	1.51

Address: Three Limited Parkway, P.O. Box 16000, Columbus, OH 43216	Web Site: www.limited.com	Auditors: Ernst & Young LLP
Telephone: (614) 415-7000	**Officers:** Leslie H. Wexner - Chmn., C.E.O. Leonard A. Schlesinger - Vice-Chmn., C.O.O.	**Investor Contact:** 614-479-7000
Fax: (614) 479-7440		

LINCOLN NATIONAL CORP. (ID)

Exchange	Symbol	Price	52Wk Range	Yield	P/E	Div Acheiver
NYS	LNC	$45.14 (3/31/2005)	49.95-41.71	3.23	11.43	21 Years

*7 Year Price Score 92.26   *NYSE Composite Index=100   *12 Month Price Score 95.17

Interim Earnings (Per Share)

Qtr.	Mar	Jun	Sep	Dec
2001	0.83	0.74	0.61	0.87
2002	0.49	0.81	(0.68)	0.34
2003	0.23	0.80	0.74	1.08
2004	0.72	1.04	1.12	1.07

Interim Dividends (Per Share)

Amt	Decl	Ex	Rec	Pay
0.35Q	5/13/2004	7/7/2004	7/9/2004	8/1/2004
0.35Q	9/9/2004	10/6/2004	10/8/2004	11/1/2004
0.365Q	11/11/2004	1/6/2005	1/10/2005	2/1/2005
0.365Q	3/10/2005	4/7/2005	4/11/2005	5/1/2005

Indicated Div: $1.46 (Div. Reinv. Plan)

Valuation Analysis

Forecast P/E	10.93
	(4/7/2005)
Market Cap	$7.8 Billion
Book Value	6.2 Billion
Price/Book	1.27
Price/Sales	1.46

No of Institutions	412
Shares	128,441,744
% Held	73.67

Business Summary: Insurance (MIC: 8.2 SIC: 311 NAIC: 24113)

Lincoln National operates multiple insurance and investment management businesses, divided into four business segments. The Lincoln Retirement segment provides fixed and variable annuities products to the individual annuities and employer-sponsored markets. The Life Insurance segment provides life insurance products designed specifically for the high net-worth and affluent markets. The Investment Management segment provides investment products and services to both individual and institutional investors. The Lincoln UK segment provides life insurance products in the United Kingdom.

Recent Developments: For the year ended Dec 31 2004, net income increased 38.1% to $707,009 thousand from net income of $511,936 thousand a year earlier. Revenues were $5,371,274 thousand, up 1.7% from $5,283,881 thousand the year before. Net premiums earned were $298,904 thousand versus $280,951 thousand in the prior year, an increase of 6.4%. Net investment income rose 2.5% to $2,704,129 thousand from $2,638,526 thousand a year ago.

Prospects: Co. has been success in growing gross deposits and net flows across multiple products and markets while also achieving improvements in operating earnings and return on equity. Recent operating results validate Co.'s keen focus on product, distribution, brand and risk management. Also, Co. is achieving much improved results in its investment management retail deposits and total net flows. Going forward, income from commercial mortgage loan prepayment and bond make-whole premiums should continue to contribute to strong Life and Retirement returns.

Financial Data (US$ in Thousands)	12/31/2004	12/31/2003	12/31/2002	12/31/2001	12/31/2000	12/31/1999	12/31/1998	12/31/1997
Earnings Per Share	3.95	2.85	0.49	3.05	3.19	2.30	2.51	4.49
Cash Flow Per Share	6.29	5.89	2.68	6.64	10.35	8.27	6.63	5.42
Tang Book Value Per Share	22.26	18.77	15.62	14.11	11.06	5.59	10.16	19.38
Dividends Per Share	3.000	3.000	3.000	3.000	3.000	3.000	3.000	3.000
Dividend Payout %	75.95	105.26	612.24	98.36	94.04	130.43	119.52	66.82
Income Statement								
Premium, Income	298,904	280,951	315,943	1,704,002	1,813,111	1,881,515	1,620,629	1,328,735
Total Revenue	5,371,274	5,283,881	4,635,462	6,380,638	6,851,507	6,803,700	6,087,063	4,898,479
Benefits & Claims	2,303,652	2,428,523	2,859,505	3,409,740	3,557,160	3,805,024	3,328,865	3,191,733
Income Before Taxes	1,035,658	1,047,563	1,624	764,139	836,291	569,964	697,398	34,881
Income Taxes	304,147	280,408	(89,966)	158,362	214,898	109,610	187,623	12,651
Net Income	707,009	511,936	91,590	590,211	621,393	460,354	509,775	933,988
Average Shares	179,017	179,441	185,596	193,303	194,920	200,417	203,262	207,992
Balance Sheet								
Total Assets	116,219,265	106,744,868	93,133,422	98,001,304	99,844,059	103,095,733	93,836,260	77,174,708
Total Liabilities	110,043,676	100,933,243	87,837,155	92,737,820	94,889,975	98,831,865	88,448,319	72,191,793
Stockholders' Equity	6,175,589	5,811,625	5,296,267	5,263,484	4,954,084	4,263,868	5,387,941	4,982,915
Shares Outstanding	173,557	178,212	177,307	186,943	190,748	195,494	202,112	201,718
Statistical Record								
Return on Assets %	0.63	0.51	0.10	0.60	0.61	0.47	0.60	1.25
Return on Equity %	11.76	9.22	1.73	11.55	13.45	9.54	9.83	19.76
Loss Ratio %	770.70	864.39	905.07	200.10	196.19	202.23	205.41	240.21
Net Margin %	13.16	9.69	1.98	9.25	9.07	6.77	8.37	19.07
Price Range	49.95-40.17	41.32-25.17	53.50-25.17	52.55-39.10	56.13-23.19	57.31-36.50	48.78-34.38	39.06-24.75
P/E Ratio	12.65-10.17	14.50-8.83	109.18-51.37	17.23-12.82	17.59-7.27	24.92-15.87	19.43-13.70	8.70-5.51
Average Yield %	6.60	8.65	7.34	6.46	7.43	6.49	7.04	9.41

Address: 1500 Market Street, Suite 3900, Philadelphia, PA 19102-2112 Telephone: (215) 448-1400	Web Site: www.lfg.com Officers: Jon A. Boscia - Chmn., C.E.O. Richard C. Vaughan - Exec. V.P., C.F.O.	Auditors: ERNST & YOUNG LLP Investor Contact: 215-448-1422 Transfer Agents: First Chicago Trust Company of New York, Jersey City, NJ

LIZ CLAIBORNE, INC.

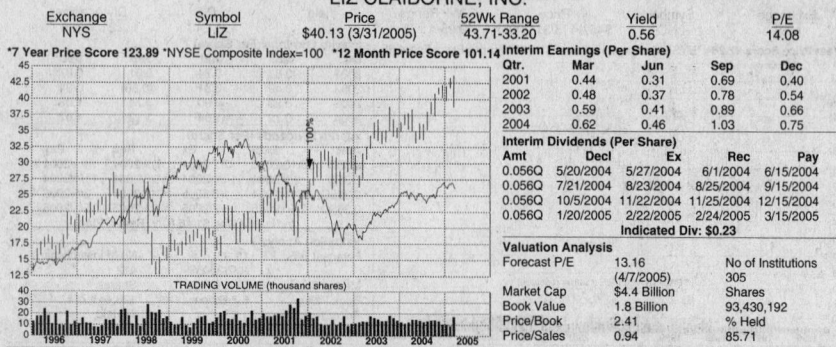

Exchange	Symbol	Price	52Wk Range	Yield	P/E
NYS	LIZ	$40.13 (3/31/2005)	43.71-33.20	0.56	14.08

*7 Year Price Score 123.89 *NYSE Composite Index=100 *12 Month Price Score 101.14

Interim Earnings (Per Share)

Qtr.	Mar	Jun	Sep	Dec
2001	0.44	0.31	0.69	0.40
2002	0.48	0.37	0.78	0.54
2003	0.59	0.41	0.89	0.66
2004	0.62	0.46	1.03	0.75

Interim Dividends (Per Share)

Amt	Decl	Ex	Rec	Pay
0.056Q	5/20/2004	5/27/2004	6/1/2004	6/15/2004
0.056Q	7/21/2004	8/23/2004	8/25/2004	9/15/2004
0.056Q	10/5/2004	11/22/2004	11/25/2004	12/15/2004
0.056Q	1/20/2005	2/22/2005	2/24/2005	3/15/2005

Indicated Div: $0.23

Valuation Analysis

Forecast P/E	13.16	No of Institutions
	(4/7/2005)	305
Market Cap	$4.4 Billion	Shares
Book Value	1.8 Billion	93,430,192
Price/Book	2.41	% Held
Price/Sales	0.94	85.71

Business Summary: Apparel (MIC: 4.4 SIC: 339 NAIC: 15239)

Liz Claiborne designs and markets branded women's and men's apparel, accessories and fragrance products. Co.'s brands include Axcess, Bora Bora, Claiborne, Crazy Horse, Curve, Dana Buchman, Elisabeth, Ellen Tracy, Emma James, ENYCE, First Issue, Intuitions, J.H. Collectibles, Jane Street, Juicy Couture, Laundry by Shelli Segal, Liz Claiborne, Lucky Brand, Mambo, Marvella, Mexx, Monet, Monet 2, Realities, Sigrid Olsen, Spark, Trifari and Villager. Co. also holds various licenses under the following trademarks: DKNY® Jeans, DKNY® Active, CITY DKNY®, Kenneth Cole New York, Reaction Ke

Recent Developments: For the year ended Jan 1 2005, net income increased 12.1% to $313,569 thousand from net income of $279,693 thousand a year earlier. Revenues were $4,632,828 thousand, up 9.2% from $4,241,115 thousand the year before. Operating income was $502,746 thousand versus an income of $470,790 thousand in the prior year, an increase of 6.8%. Total direct expense was $2,490,266 thousand versus $2,351,324 thousand in the prior year, an increase of 5.9%. Total indirect expense was $1,639,816 thousand versus $1,419,001 thousand in the prior year, an increase of 15.6%.

Prospects: Co. is focused on solid execution and disciplined inventory management. For the first quarter of 2005, Co. is projecting sales growth of 7.0% to 9.0%, with earnings per share in the range of $0.63 to $0.66. Separately, for fiscal 2005, based on current visibility, Co. is forecasting a sales increase of 6.0% to 8.0%, with diluted earnings per share in the range of $2.96 to $3.02, including the impact resulting from the planned adoption in the third quarter of 2005 of an accounting change for share-based payment, estimated to be $0.10 to $0.12, as well as the shift in the composition of its 2005 equity-based management compensation toward restricted stock and away from stock options.

Financial Data

(US$ in Thousands)	01/01/2005	01/03/2004	12/28/2002	12/29/2001	12/30/2000	01/01/2000	01/02/1999	01/03/1998
Earnings Per Share	2.85	2.55	2.16	1.83	1.72	1.56	1.28	1.31
Cash Flow Per Share	4.24	3.59	4.01	3.17	2.52	2.39	1.01	1.02
Tang Book Value Per Share	7.13	6.73	5.43	5.71	5.45	5.95	7.30	6.97
Dividends Per Share	0.225	0.225	0.225	0.225	0.225	0.225	0.225	0.225
Dividend Payout %	7.89	8.82	10.42	12.30	13.12	14.42	17.51	17.11
Income Statement								
Total Revenue	4,632,828	4,241,115	3,717,503	3,448,522	3,104,141	2,806,548	2,535,268	2,412,601
EBITDA	627,982	573,881	483,965	429,697	387,380	369,422	322,462	339,168
Depn & Amortn	115,634	104,981	96,395	101,491	77,033	67,836	55,785	46,024
Income Before Taxes	480,197	438,391	362,446	300,089	288,430	301,586	266,677	293,144
Income Taxes	166,628	158,698	131,281	108,032	103,835	109,144	97,300	108,500
Net Income	313,569	279,693	231,165	192,057	184,595	192,442	169,377	184,644
Average Shares	109,886	109,619	107,196	105,051	107,494	123,440	131,694	140,382
Balance Sheet								
Current Assets	1,509,141	1,348,401	1,203,171	1,106,026	910,576	858,609	1,075,293	1,057,420
Total Assets	3,029,752	2,606,999	2,296,318	1,951,255	1,512,159	1,411,801	1,392,791	1,305,285
Current Liabilities	637,601	526,642	590,980	447,314	357,904	352,311	363,351	327,657
Long-Term Obligations	484,516	440,303	377,725	387,345	269,219	116,085	...	...
Total Liabilities	1,204,443	1,019,180	1,002,527	886,973	673,142	506,507	380,887	338,199
Stockholders' Equity	1,811,789	1,577,971	1,286,361	1,056,161	834,285	902,169	981,110	921,627
Shares Outstanding	108,734	109,571	107,035	105,224	102,418	113,440	127,901	132,196
Statistical Record								
Return on Assets %	11.16	11.22	10.91	11.12	12.66	13.76	12.59	13.52
Return on Equity %	18.55	19.21	19.79	20.37	21.32	20.49	17.85	18.71
EBITDA Margin %	13.56	13.53	13.02	12.46	12.48	13.16	12.72	14.06
Net Margin %	6.77	6.59	6.22	5.57	5.95	6.86	6.68	7.65
Asset Turnover	1.65	1.70	1.76	2.00	2.13	2.01	1.88	1.77
Current Ratio	2.37	2.56	2.04	2.47	2.54	2.44	2.96	3.23
Debt to Equity	0.27	0.28	0.29	0.37	0.32	0.13	...	...
Price Range	42.21-33.20	38.82-26.31	32.65-24.22	27.14-18.63	23.59-15.63	20.00-15.50	27.38-12.75	28.59-19.38
P/E Ratio	14.81-11.65	15.22-10.32	15.12-11.21	14.83-10.18	13.72-9.08	12.82-9.94	21.39-9.96	21.83-14.79
Average Yield %	0.60	0.68	0.77	0.93	1.11	1.26	1.11	0.96

Address: 1441 Broadway, New York, NY 10018 **Telephone:** (212) 354-4900	**Web Site:** www.lizclaiborne.com **Officers:** Paul R. Charron - Chmn., C.E.O. Angela J. Ahrendts - Exec. V.P.	**Auditors:** DELOITTE & TOUCHE LLP **Transfer Agents:** First Chicago Trust Company of New York, Jersey City, NJ

LOCKHEED MARTIN CORP.

Exchange	Symbol	Price	52Wk Range	Yield	P/E
NYS	LMT	$61.06 (3/31/2005)	61.62-45.64	1.64	21.58

*7 Year Price Score 104.38 *NYSE Composite Index=100 *12 Month Price Score 102.15

Interim Earnings (Per Share)

Qtr.	Mar	Jun	Sep	Dec
2001	0.25	0.33	0.49	(3.49)
2002	0.49	0.75	0.64	(0.77)
2003	0.55	0.54	0.48	0.77
2004	0.65	0.66	0.69	0.83

Interim Dividends (Per Share)

Amt	Decl	Ex	Rec	Pay
0.22Q	4/22/2004	5/27/2004	6/1/2004	6/30/2004
0.22Q	8/5/2004	8/30/2004	9/1/2004	9/30/2004
0.25Q	9/23/2004	11/29/2004	12/1/2004	12/30/2004
0.25Q	1/27/2005	2/25/2005	3/1/2005	3/31/2005

Indicated Div: $1.00

Valuation Analysis

Forecast P/E	18.71	No of Institutions
	(4/7/2005)	456
Market Cap	$26.7 Billion	Shares
Book Value	7.0 Billion	456,084,384
Price/Book	3.81	% Held
Price/Sales	0.75	N/A

Business Summary: Defense (MIC: 1.2 SIC: 761 NAIC: 36414)

Lockheed Martin designs, develops, manufactures, integrates, operates and supports advanced technology systems, products, and services for customers in domestic and international defense, civil, and commercial markets, with Co.'s principal customers being agencies of the U.S. Government. Business areas include aeronautics, space, systems integration, and technology services. Co. is a major defense, Department of Energy, and NASA contractor. Co. operates in five principal business segments: Aeronautics, Electronic Systems, Space Systems, Integrated Systems & Solutions, and Information & Technology Services.

Recent Developments: For the year ended Dec 31 2004, net income increased 20.2% to $1,266 million from net income of $1,053 million a year earlier. Revenues were $35,526 million, up 11.6% from $31,824 million the year before. Operating income was $2,089 million versus an income of $2,019 million in the prior year, an increase of 3.5%. Total direct expense was $33,558 million versus $29,848 million in the prior year, an increase of 12.4%.

Prospects: Co. recently completed the acquisition of STASYS Limited, a U.K.-based technology and consulting firm specializing in network communications and defense interoperability. Also, Co.has entered into a definitive agreement to acquire The SYTEX Group, Inc. based in Doylestown, PA, which provides information technology applications and technical support services to the U.S. Department of Defense and other federal agencies. Co. has agreed to pay net consideration of $462.0 million after taking $13.0 million of net cash being acquired. Co.'s guidance for 2005 includes net sales and diluted earnings per share in the ranges of $36.00 billion to $37.50 billion and $3.05 to $3.30, respectively.

Financial Data

(US$ in Thousands)	12/31/2004	12/31/2003	12/31/2002	12/31/2001	12/31/2000	12/31/1999	12/31/1998	12/31/1997
Earnings Per Share	2.83	2.34	1.11	(2.42)	(1.29)	0.99	2.63	3.04
Cash Flow Per Share	6.58	4.05	5.14	4.27	5.02	2.82	5.39	3.26
Dividends Per Share	0.910	0.580	0.440	0.440	0.440	0.880	0.820	0.800
Dividend Payout %	32.16	24.79	39.64	...	...	88.89	31.18	26.27
Income Statement								
Total Revenue	35,526,000	31,824,000	26,578,000	23,990,000	25,329,000	25,530,000	26,266,000	28,069,000
EBITDA	2,641,000	2,553,000	1,669,000	1,620,000	2,084,000	2,945,000	3,489,000	3,791,000
Depn & Amortn	656,000	609,000	558,000	823,000	968,000	969,000	1,005,000	1,052,000
Income Before Taxes	1,664,000	1,532,000	577,000	188,000	286,000	1,200,000	1,661,000	1,937,000
Income Taxes	398,000	479,000	44,000	109,000	710,000	463,000	660,000	637,000
Net Income	1,266,000	1,053,000	500,000	(1,046,000)	(519,000)	382,000	1,001,000	1,300,000
Average Shares	447,100	450,000	452,000	432,500	400,800	384,100	381,100	427,000
Balance Sheet								
Current Assets	8,953,000	9,401,000	10,626,000	10,778,000	11,259,000	10,696,000	10,611,000	10,105,000
Total Assets	25,554,000	26,175,000	25,758,000	27,654,000	30,349,000	30,012,000	28,744,000	28,361,000
Current Liabilities	8,566,000	8,893,000	9,821,000	9,689,000	10,175,000	8,812,000	10,267,000	9,189,000
Long-Term Obligations	5,104,000	6,072,000	6,217,000	7,422,000	9,065,000	11,427,000	8,957,000	10,528,000
Total Liabilities	18,533,000	19,419,000	19,893,000	21,211,000	23,189,000	23,651,000	22,607,000	23,185,000
Stockholders' Equity	7,021,000	6,756,000	5,865,000	6,443,000	7,160,000	6,361,000	6,137,000	5,176,000
Shares Outstanding	438,000	446,500	455,709	441,000	431,000	398,164	393,000	388,000
Statistical Record								
Return on Assets %	4.88	4.06	1.87	N.M.	N.M.	1.30	3.51	4.51
Return on Equity %	18.33	16.69	8.12	N.M.	N.M.	6.11	17.70	21.61
EBITDA Margin %	7.43	8.02	6.28	6.75	8.23	11.54	13.28	13.51
Net Margin %	3.56	3.31	1.88	N.M.	N.M.	1.50	3.81	4.63
Asset Turnover	1.37	1.23	1.00	0.83	0.84	0.87	0.92	0.97
Current Ratio	1.05	1.06	1.08	1.11	1.11	1.21	1.03	1.10
Debt to Equity	0.73	0.90	1.06	1.15	1.27	1.80	1.46	2.03
Price Range	61.62-43.82	58.85-41.13	71.43-46.24	49.92-31.73	35.85-16.63	44.56-17.38	58.50-41.66	56.00-39.63
P/E Ratio	21.77-15.48	25.15-17.58	64.35-41.66	...	...	45.01-17.55	22.24-15.84	18.42-13.03
Average Yield %	1.75	1.20	0.75	1.11	1.69	2.59	1.56	1.67

Address: 6801 Rockledge Drive, Bethesda, MD 20817-1877 **Telephone:** (301) 897-6000 **Fax:** (301) 897-6083	**Web Site:** www.lockheedmartin.com **Officers:** Robert J. Stevens - Pres., C.E.O., C.O.O. Christopher E. Kubasik - Exec. V.P., C.F.O.	**Auditors:** Ernst & Young LLP **Investor Contact:** 301-897-6455

LOEWS CORP.

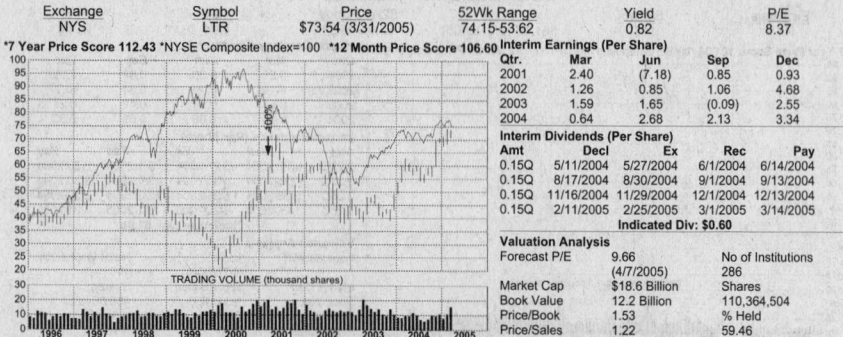

Exchange	Symbol	Price	52Wk Range	Yield	P/E
NYS	LTR	$73.54 (3/31/2005)	74.15-53.62	0.82	8.37

*7 Year Price Score 112.43 *NYSE Composite Index=100 *12 Month Price Score 106.60

Interim Earnings (Per Share)

Qtr.	Mar	Jun	Sep	Dec
2001	2.40	(7.18)	0.85	0.93
2002	1.26	0.85	1.06	4.68
2003	1.59	1.65	(0.09)	2.55
2004	0.64	2.68	2.13	3.34

Interim Dividends (Per Share)

Amt	Decl	Ex	Rec	Pay
0.15Q	5/11/2004	5/27/2004	6/1/2004	6/14/2004
0.15Q	8/17/2004	8/30/2004	9/1/2004	9/13/2004
0.15Q	11/16/2004	11/29/2004	12/1/2004	12/13/2004
0.15Q	2/11/2005	2/25/2005	3/1/2005	3/14/2005
			Indicated Div: $0.60	

Valuation Analysis

Forecast P/E	9.66	No of Institutions	
	(4/7/2005)	286	
Market Cap	$18.6 Billion	Shares	
Book Value	12.2 Billion	110,364,504	
Price/Book	1.53	% Held	
Price/Sales	1.22	59.46	

Business Summary: Insurance (MIC: 8.2 SIC: 331 NAIC: 24126)

Loews is a highly diversified company that operates primarily in the cigarette and insurance businesses. Co. produces and sells cigarettes through its wholly-owned subsidiary Lorillard. Brand names include Newport, Kent, True, Maverick and Old Gold. As of Dec 31 2003, Co. owned 90% of CNA Financial, which has operations in property and casualty insurance. Another wholly-owned subsidiary is Loews Hotels Holding, which owns and operates 20 Loews Hotels. Co. also holds a 97% interest in Bulova and a 54% interest in Diamond Offshore Drilling, which operates 45 offshore drilling rigs.

Recent Developments: For the year ended Dec 31 2004, net income was $1,231,300 thousand versus net loss of $610,700 thousand a year earlier. Revenues were $15,242,300 thousand, down 7.4% from $16,461,000 thousand the year before. Net premiums earned were $8,205,000 thousand versus $9,209,800 thousand in the prior year, a decrease of 10.9%.

Prospects: In a transaction previously announced on Nov 22 2004, Co.'s wholly-owned subsidiary, Boardwalk Pipelines, has completed the acquisition of Gulf South Pipeline from Entergy-Koch in a transaction valued at $1.14 billion. Gulf South Pipeline owns and operates an 8,000-mile interstate natural gas pipeline, gathering and storage system located in the U.S. Gulf Coast. Gulf South is headquartered in Houston with field offices located in Texas, Louisiana, Mississippi, Alabama and Florida. The Gulf South pipeline system is comprised of approximately 6,800 miles of interstate transmission pipeline, 1,200 miles of gathering pipeline and 68.5 billion cubic feet of working gas storage capacity.

Financial Data

(US$ in Thousands)	12/31/2004	12/31/2003	12/31/2002	12/31/2001	12/31/2000	12/31/1999	12/31/1998	12/31/1997
Earnings Per Share	8.79	(1.15)	7.61	(3.02)	18.88	3.35	4.06	6.90
Cash Flow Per Share	11.53	12.25	7.86	2.76	(4.68)	(16.37)	(2.06)	1.98
Tang Book Value Per Share	46.89	44.13	49.07	48.70	109.64	91.58	86.26	77.51
Dividends Per Share	0.600	0.600	0.600	0.575	0.500	0.500	0.500	0.500
Dividend Payout %	6.83	...	7.88	...	2.65	14.93	12.32	7.25
Income Statement								
Total Revenue	15,242,300	16,461,000	17,495,400	19,417,200	21,337,800	21,465,200	21,208,300	20,138,800
EBITDA	2,475,400	(878,000)	2,095,700	(422,400)	3,548,900	1,596,500	1,666,300	2,143,100
Depn & Amortn	329,300	192,000	139,000	58,700	(13,900)	298,000	219,700	226,500
Income Before Taxes	1,822,000	(1,378,400)	1,647,100	(813,100)	3,205,900	944,200	1,077,400	1,593,200
Income Taxes	533,800	(534,100)	582,000	(175,400)	1,106,900	305,500	354,500	495,300
Net Income	1,231,300	(610,700)	912,000	(589,100)	1,876,700	363,200	464,800	793,600
Average Shares	243,990	227,190	227,740	195,328	99,366	108,533	114,539	115,000
Balance Sheet								
Current Assets	27,333,900	31,913,300	26,948,100	26,368,900	24,597,100	21,030,400	22,145,400	22,577,900
Total Assets	73,749,500	77,880,900	70,519,600	75,251,100	70,877,100	69,463,700	70,906,400	69,577,100
Current Liabilities	5,566,700	6,021,500	4,114,800	5,690,900	2,279,800	2,163,900	1,740,300	1,711,900
Long-Term Obligations	5,980,200	5,820,200	5,651,900	5,920,300	6,040,000	5,706,300	5,966,700	5,752,600
Total Liabilities	59,883,800	65,155,000	57,389,100	63,628,400	57,478,100	57,135,700	58,227,900	57,522,600
Stockholders' Equity	12,183,300	11,054,300	11,235,200	9,649,300	11,191,100	9,977,700	10,201,200	9,665,100
Shares Outstanding	253,551	243,412	225,351	191,493	98,614	104,480	112,582	115,000
Statistical Record								
Return on Assets %	1.62	N.M.	1.25	N.M.	2.67	0.52	0.66	1.16
Return on Equity %	10.57	N.M.	8.73	N.M.	17.68	3.60	4.68	8.63
EBITDA Margin %	16.24	N.M.	11.98	N.M.	16.63	7.44	7.86	10.64
Net Margin %	8.08	N.M.	5.21	N.M.	8.80	1.69	2.19	3.94
Asset Turnover	0.20	0.22	0.24	0.27	0.30	0.31	0.30	0.29
Current Ratio	4.91	5.30	6.55	4.63	10.79	9.72	12.73	13.19
Debt to Equity	0.49	0.53	0.50	0.61	0.54	0.57	0.58	0.60

Address: 667 Madison Avenue, New York, NY 10021-8087 Telephone: (212) 521-2000 Fax: (212) 521-2498	Web Site: www.loews.com Officers: Preston R. Tisch - Chmn. James S. Tisch - Pres., C.E.O.	Auditors: Deloitte & Touche LLP

LONGS DRUG STORES CORP.

Exchange	Symbol	Price	52Wk Range	Yield	P/E
NYS	LDG	$34.22 (3/31/2005)	34.22-18.83	1.64	39.79

*7 Year Price Score 82.60   *NYSE Composite Index=100   *12 Month Price Score 108.70

Interim Earnings (Per Share)

Qtr.	Apr	Jul	Oct	Jan
2001-02	0.31	0.30	0.07	0.58
2002-03	(0.36)	0.29	0.08	0.17
2003-04	0.16	0.14	0.14	0.35
2004-05	0.25	0.09	0.17	...

Interim Dividends (Per Share)

Amt	Decl	Ex	Rec	Pay
0.14Q	5/25/2004	5/27/2004	6/1/2004	7/12/2004
0.14Q	8/24/2004	8/27/2004	8/31/2004	10/11/2004
0.14Q	11/16/2004	11/26/2004	11/30/2004	1/10/2005
0.14Q	3/1/2005	3/4/2005	3/8/2005	4/11/2005

Indicated Div: $0.56

Valuation Analysis

Forecast P/E	30.19	No of Institutions
	(4/7/2005)	133
Market Cap	$1.3 Billion	Shares
Book Value	719.8 Million	27,448,036
Price/Book	1.79	% Held
Price/Sales	0.28	72.82

Business Summary: Retail - Miscellaneous (MIC: 5.11 SIC: 912 NAIC: 46110)

Longs Drug Stores operated a chain of 470 drug stores, as of Jan 29 2004, located in California, Hawaii, Washington, Nevada, Colorado, and Oregon. Co.'s stores, which range in size from 15,000 to 30,000 square feet, operate under the following names, Longs, Longs Drugs, Longs Drug Stores, Longs Pharmacy and Longs Express. Co.'s core merchandise segments include prescription drugs, over-the-counter medications, health care products, photo and photo processing, cosmetics, greeting cards, food and beverage items, housewares, toiletries, mail centers and seasonal merchandise. Co. also provides pharmacy benefit management services through its wholly-owned subsidiary, RxAmerica LLC.

Recent Developments: For the quarter ended Oct 28 2004, net income increased 19.1% to $6,229 thousand from net income of $5,230 thousand in the year-earlier quarter. Revenues were $1,100,897 thousand, up 1.3% from $1,087,293 thousand the year before. Operating income was $12,477 thousand versus an income of $11,954 thousand in the prior-year quarter, an increase of 4.4%. Total indirect expense was $275,235 thousand versus $262,050 thousand in the prior-year quarter, an increase of 5.0%.

Prospects: For the full year ended Jan 26 2006, Co. estimates that total sales will grow between 1.0% and 3.0% and same-store sales will be flat to up 2.0% compared with last year. Consequently, Co.'s goal is to achieve net income, excluding the expensing of stock options, of $1.27 to $1.35 per diluted share in fiscal 2006. For the first quarter ended Apr 28 2005, Co. estimates that total sales will be flat to negative 2.0% and same-store sales will be flat to negative 2.0% versus the first quarter of last year. Thus, Co.'s goal is to achieve net income in the range of $0.27 to $0.32 per diluted share in the first quarter of 2006.

Financial Data

(US$ in Thousands)	9 Mos	6 Mos	3 Mos	01/29/2004	01/30/2003	01/31/2002	01/25/2001	01/27/2000
Earnings Per Share	0.86	0.83	0.88	0.79	0.18	1.25	1.19	1.76
Cash Flow Per Share	3.47	2.60	3.65	3.29	1.14	5.31	5.13	2.66
Tang Book Value Per Share	16.79	16.72	16.74	16.66	16.34	15.75	14.70	14.37
Dividends Per Share	0.560	0.560	0.560	0.560	0.560	0.560	0.560	0.560
Dividend Payout %	65.00	67.35	63.51	70.89	311.11	44.80	47.06	31.82
Income Statement								
Total Revenue	3,411,075	2,310,178	1,159,696	4,526,524	4,426,273	4,304,734	4,027,132	3,672,413
EBITDA	104,388	71,163	39,934	142,996	135,415	167,474	159,844	174,620
Depn & Amortn	64,518	43,770	21,517	83,595	77,736	78,193	69,283	56,102
Income Before Taxes	29,245	20,231	14,819	46,022	44,644	75,265	74,284	113,874
Income Taxes	10,391	7,606	5,572	16,258	13,317	28,097	29,400	44,900
Net Income	18,854	12,625	9,247	29,764	6,702	47,168	44,884	68,974
Average Shares	37,577	37,555	37,450	37,454	38,223	37,751	37,843	39,090
Balance Sheet								
Current Assets	756,496	704,339	730,788	736,515	662,661	684,414	608,141	582,175
Total Assets	1,467,951	1,412,872	1,437,508	1,442,112	1,352,071	1,411,591	1,353,667	1,270,323
Current Liabilities	514,507	489,947	567,762	562,938	420,098	447,754	448,694	351,895
Long-Term Obligations	175,688	164,688	109,688	114,558	181,429	198,774	198,060	181,180
Total Liabilities	748,156	699,407	724,941	728,191	635,601	690,018	669,872	567,629
Stockholders' Equity	719,795	713,465	712,567	713,921	716,470	721,573	683,795	702,694
Shares Outstanding	37,600	37,370	37,258	37,544	38,501	37,977	37,367	39,385
Statistical Record								
Return on Assets %	2.24	2.27	2.39	2.14	0.49	3.36	3.43	6.03
Return on Equity %	4.55	4.43	4.71	4.17	0.93	6.60	6.49	10.31
EBITDA Margin %	3.06	3.08	3.44	3.16	3.06	3.89	3.97	4.75
Net Margin %	0.55	0.55	0.80	0.66	0.15	1.10	1.11	1.88
Asset Turnover	3.21	3.36	3.30	3.25	3.21	3.06	3.08	3.21
Current Ratio	1.47	1.44	1.29	1.31	1.58	1.53	1.36	1.65
Debt to Equity	0.24	0.23	0.15	0.16	0.25	0.28	0.29	0.26
Price Range	26.10-17.75	25.10-17.75	25.10-14.24	25.10-13.44	32.09-19.66	31.81-20.40	24.88-16.56	39.38-21.50
P/E Ratio	30.35-20.64	30.24-21.39	28.52-16.18	31.77-17.01	178.28-109.22	25.45-16.32	20.90-13.92	22.37-12.22
Average Yield %	2.51	2.59	2.75	2.89	2.25	2.24	2.70	1.80

Address: 141 North Civic Drive, Walnut Creek, CA 94596 Telephone: (925) 937-1170 Fax: (925) 210-6886	Web Site: www.longs.com Officers: Warren F. Bryant - Chmn., Pres., C.E.O. Steven F. McCann - Exec. V.P., C.F.O., Treas.	Auditors: Deloitte & Touche LLP Investor Contact: 925-979-3979

LONGVIEW FIBRE CO.

Exchange	Symbol	Price	52Wk Range	Yield	P/E
NYS	LFB	$18.76 (3/31/2005)	19.50-10.07	0.43	36.78

*7 Year Price Score 105.27 *NYSE Composite Index=100   *12 Month Price Score 109.39

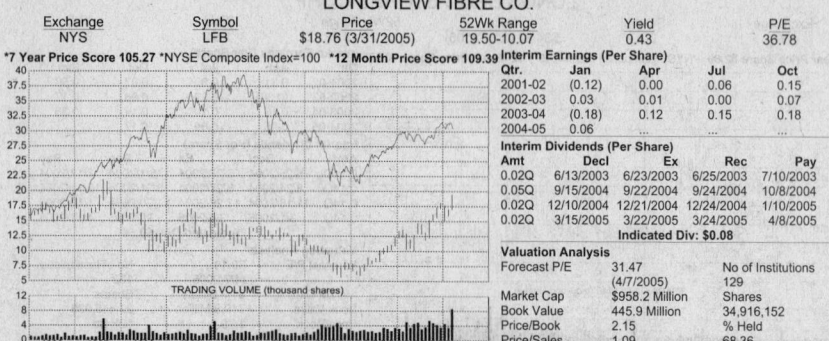

Interim Earnings (Per Share)

Qtr.	Jan	Apr	Jul	Oct
2001-02	(0.12)	0.00	0.06	0.15
2002-03	0.03	0.01	0.00	0.07
2003-04	(0.18)	0.12	0.15	0.18
2004-05	0.06	...	...	...

Interim Dividends (Per Share)

Amt	Decl	Ex	Rec	Pay
0.02Q	6/13/2003	6/23/2003	6/25/2003	7/10/2003
0.05Q	9/15/2004	9/22/2004	9/24/2004	10/8/2004
0.02Q	12/10/2004	12/21/2004	12/24/2004	1/10/2005
0.02Q	3/15/2005	3/22/2005	3/24/2005	4/8/2005

Indicated Div: $0.08

Valuation Analysis

Forecast P/E	31.47	No of Institutions
	(4/7/2005)	129
Market Cap	$958.2 Million	Shares
Book Value	445.9 Million	34,916,152
Price/Book	2.15	% Held
Price/Sales	1.09	68.36

Business Summary: Paper Products (MIC: 11.11 SIC: 621 NAIC: 22121)

Longview Fibre is a diversified timberlands manager and a specialty paper and container manufacturer. Using sustainable forestry methods, Co. manages approximately 585,000 acres of softwood timberlands predominantly located in western Washington and Oregon, primarily for the sale of logs to the U.S. and Japanese markets. Co.'s manufacturing facilities include one of the largest pulp-paper mills in North America at Longview, WA; a network of 15 converting plants in 12 states; and a sawmill in central Washington. Co.'s products include: logs; corrugated and solid-fiber containers; commodity and specialty Kraft paper; paperboard; dimension and specialty lumber; and paper bags.

Recent Developments: For the quarter ended Jan 31 2005, net income was $3,312 thousand versus net loss of $9,283 thousand in the year-earlier quarter. Revenues were $448,160 thousand, up 31.9% from $339,854 thousand the year before. Operating income was $14,119 thousand versus a loss of $5,363 thousand in the prior-year quarter, an increase of 363.3%. Total direct expense was $188,214 thousand versus $155,853 thousand in the prior-year quarter, an increase of 20.8%. Total indirect expense was $21,747 thousand versus $19,437 thousand in the prior-year quarter, an increase of 11.9%.

Prospects: Bottom line results are benefiting from improved demand and pricing conditions in each of Co.'s three operating segments year over year. Looking ahead, Co. expects several favorable factors to benefit the second quarter, including a continuation of the economic recovery in the U.S. and inventories that appear to be in line with current and anticipated demand. Recent incoming orders for paper and paperboard, combined with limited downtime for repairs in Feb 2005, indicate a likely second quarter utilization rate of between 82.0% and 87.0% at Co.'s Longview mill, which should improve costs and profitability.

Financial Data

(US$ in Thousands)	3 Mos	10/31/2004	10/31/2003	10/31/2002	10/31/2001	10/31/2000	10/31/1999	10/31/1998
Earnings Per Share	0.51	0.27	0.10	0.10	0.48	0.73	0.39	(0.13)
Cash Flow Per Share	2.08	1.79	1.88	1.25	2.16	2.17	2.27	1.34
Tang Book Value Per Share	8.73	8.69	8.46	8.40	8.33	8.38	8.14	8.03
Dividends Per Share	0.070	0.050	0.040	0.030	0.480	0.480	0.280	0.540
Dividend Payout %	13.76	18.52	40.00	30.00	100.00	65.75	71.79	...
Income Statement								
Total Revenue	224,080	831,166	773,337	769,281	875,955	876,298	774,349	753,244
EBITDA	34,951	139,724	129,573	121,981	148,379	165,989	153,949	117,423
Depn & Amortn	20,409	79,518	78,247	75,783	71,566	67,382	84,243	92,896
Income Before Taxes	5,257	22,901	8,554	3,333	37,667	58,947	31,484	(14,152)
Income Taxes	1,945	9,000	3,200	(1,800)	13,000	21,300	11,500	(7,500)
Net Income	3,312	13,901	5,354	5,133	24,667	37,647	19,984	(6,652)
Average Shares	51,077	51,076	51,076	51,076	51,151	51,576	51,676	
Balance Sheet								
Current Assets	193,274	201,696	170,861	181,920	189,882	205,048	192,720	197,838
Total Assets	1,253,265	1,270,930	1,255,404	1,306,442	1,324,448	1,276,690	1,212,753	1,263,343
Current Liabilities	110,441	143,430	130,252	144,804	151,823	162,670	124,719	142,520
Long-Term Obligations	452,179	442,148	463,003	510,195	540,400	490,900	495,900	547,018
Total Liabilities	807,321	827,276	823,097	877,446	899,053	844,648	792,290	848,394
Stockholders' Equity	445,944	443,654	432,307	428,996	425,395	432,042	420,463	414,949
Shares Outstanding	51,076	51,076	51,076	51,076	51,076	51,576	51,676	51,677
Statistical Record								
Return on Assets %	2.13	1.10	0.42	0.39	1.90	3.02	1.61	N.M.
Return on Equity %	6.08	3.17	1.24	1.20	5.75	8.81	4.78	N.M.
EBITDA Margin %	15.60	16.81	16.76	15.86	16.94	18.94	19.88	15.59
Net Margin %	1.48	1.67	0.69	0.67	2.82	4.30	2.58	N.M.
Asset Turnover	0.71	0.66	0.60	0.58	0.67	0.70	0.63	0.60
Current Ratio	1.75	1.41	1.31	1.26	1.25	1.26	1.55	1.39
Debt to Equity	1.01	1.00	1.07	1.19	1.27	1.14	1.18	1.32
Price Range	18.14-10.07	16.15-10.07	10.93-5.91	12.75-5.60	14.13-9.10	16.38-10.75	17.06-9.69	17.31-9.75
P/E Ratio	35.57-19.75	59.81-37.30	109.30-59.10	127.50-56.00	29.43-18.96	22.43-14.73	43.75-24.84	...
Average Yield %	0.50	0.40	0.49	0.31	3.78	3.75	2.15	3.70

Address: 300 Fibre Way, Longview, WA 98632	**Web Site:** www.longviewfibre.com	**Auditors:** PricewaterhouseCoopers LLP
Telephone: (360) 425-1550	**Officers:** Richard H. Wollenberg - Chmn., Pres., C.E.O. Lisa J. McLaughlin - Sr. V.P. Fin, Treas., Sec.	**Transfer Agents:** LaSalle Bank, N.A., Chicago, IL
Fax: (360) 575-5934		

LOUISIANA-PACIFIC CORP.

Exchange	Symbol	Price	52Wk Range	Yield	P/E
NYS	LPX	$25.14 (3/31/2005)	28.55-21.37	1.59	6.55

*7 Year Price Score 141.39 *NYSE Composite Index=100 *12 Month Price Score 99.04

Interim Earnings (Per Share)

Qtr.	Mar	Jun	Sep	Dec
2001	(0.86)	(0.09)	(0.02)	(0.68)
2002	(0.03)	(0.13)	0.03	(0.40)
2003	0.01	(0.16)	1.17	1.53
2004	0.98	1.75	0.98	0.12

Interim Dividends (Per Share)

Amt	Decl	Ex	Rec	Pay
0.075Q	5/3/2004	5/13/2004	5/17/2004	6/1/2004
0.075Q	8/2/2004	8/13/2004	8/17/2004	9/1/2004
0.10Q	11/8/2004	11/12/2004	11/16/2004	12/1/2004
0.10Q	2/3/2005	2/10/2005	2/14/2005	3/1/2005

Indicated Div: $0.40

Valuation Analysis

Forecast P/E	10.45		No of Institutions
	(4/7/2005)		244
Market Cap	$2.8 Billion		Shares
Book Value	1.8 Billion		92,976,640
Price/Book	1.57		% Held
Price/Sales	0.97		83.94

Business Summary: Wood Products (MIC: 11.9 SIC: 421 NAIC: 21113)

Louisiana-Pacific is a manufacturer and distributor of building materials. The Oriented Strand Board (OSB) segment manufactures and distributes OSB. The Composite Wood Products segment produces and markets SmartSide® siding and related accessories, hardboard siding and specialty OSB. The Plastic Building Products segment produces and markets vinyl siding and related accessories, composite decking and moulding products. The Engineered Wood Products segment manufactures and distributes I-joists and laminated veneer lumber and other related products. The Other Products segment is comprised of products that are not individually significant.

Recent Developments: For the year ended Dec 31 2004, income from continuing operations increased 48.6% to $423,500 thousand from income of $284,900 thousand a year earlier. Net income increased 54.4% to $420,700 thousand from net income of $272,500 thousand a year earlier. Revenues were $2,849,400 thousand, up 24.9% from $2,280,700 thousand the year before. Operating income was $750,900 thousand versus an income of $572,000 thousand in the prior naic, an increase of 31.3%. Total direct expense was $1,741,700 thousand versus $1,512,200 thousand in the prior year, an increase of 15.2%. Total indirect expense was $356,800 thousand versus $180,500 thousand in the prior year, an increase of 97.7%.

Prospects: On Dec 8 2004, Co. announced it has signed a memorandum of understanding with Clarke County, AL, the Clarke County Industrial Development Board, and the State of Alabama to build an oriented strand board mill. The industrial facility will be developed and constructed on about 820.0 acres of land near Thomasville, AL. Pending execution of a project agreement, Co. has production start-up slated for late 2007. Separately, Co. believes the fundamentals are in place to support another strong year in building product sales. With the quality of Co.'s assets and the investments it has made to improve operations and expand capacity, it is in a good position to take advantage of this environment.

Financial Data

(US$ in Thousands)	12/31/2004	12/31/2003	12/31/2002	12/31/2001	12/31/2000	12/31/1999	12/31/1998	12/31/1997
Earnings Per Share	3.84	2.56	(0.59)	(1.64)	(0.13)	2.04	0.02	(0.94)
Cash Flow Per Share	5.54	4.83	0.85	1.42	0.79	4.45	1.13	0.81
Tang Book Value Per Share	13.48	8.60	5.78	7.48	9.28	9.64	10.84	11.02
Dividends Per Share	0.300	...	...	0.240	0.560	0.560	0.560	0.560
Dividend Payout %	7.81	...	...	...	...	27.45	2,800.00	...
Income Statement								
Total Revenue	2,849,400	2,300,200	1,942,700	2,359,700	2,932,800	2,878,600	2,297,100	2,402,500
EBITDA	719,100	569,800	174,000	(59,100)	209,300	525,200	170,600	21,800
Depn & Amortn	...	...	131,900	170,200	184,400	156,300	143,800	142,800
Income Before Taxes	699,400	515,200	(20,900)	(289,100)	(18,200)	357,000	14,000	(150,000)
Income Taxes	279,700	233,100	4,300	(112,400)	(11,500)	139,500	15,800	(43,600)
Net Income	420,700	272,500	(62,000)	(171,600)	(13,800)	216,800	2,000	(101,800)
Average Shares	109,600	106,500	104,600	104,400	104,100	106,200	108,600	108,450
Balance Sheet								
Current Assets	1,604,100	1,325,200	491,300	493,100	654,100	739,400	612,100	596,800
Total Assets	3,450,600	3,204,400	2,773,100	3,016,800	3,374,700	3,488,200	2,519,100	2,578,400
Current Liabilities	440,000	289,600	273,300	309,500	378,200	540,700	366,600	319,300
Long-Term Obligations	622,500	1,020,700	1,070,100	1,152,000	1,183,800	1,014,800	459,800	572,300
Total Liabilities	1,682,800	1,880,500	1,767,100	1,935,900	2,079,500	2,128,200	1,296,300	1,292,200
Stockholders' Equity	1,767,800	1,310,900	1,006,000	1,080,900	1,295,200	1,360,000	1,222,800	1,286,200
Shares Outstanding	110,141	106,462	104,584	104,578	104,360	104,968	107,273	109,628
Statistical Record								
Return on Assets %	12.61	9.12	N.M.	N.M.	N.M.	7.22	0.08	N.M.
Return on Equity %	27.26	23.52	N.M.	N.M.	N.M.	16.79	0.16	N.M.
EBITDA Margin %	25.24	24.77	8.96	N.M.	7.14	18.24	7.43	0.91
Net Margin %	14.76	11.85	N.M.	N.M.	N.M.	7.53	0.09	N.M.
Asset Turnover	0.85	0.77	0.67	0.74	0.85	0.96	0.90	0.93
Current Ratio	3.65	4.58	1.80	1.59	1.73	1.37	1.67	1.87
Debt to Equity	0.35	0.78	1.06	1.07	0.91	0.75	0.38	0.44
Price Range	27.99-17.88	19.10-7.30	12.48-5.40	13.84-5.80	15.38-7.06	24.50-11.63	24.19-16.63	25.56-17.63
P/E Ratio	7.29-4.66	7.46-2.85	...	...	...	12.01-5.70	N.M.	...
Average Yield %	1.25	...	...	2.41	5.08	3.02	2.79	2.66

Address: 414 Union Street, Suite 2000, Nashville, TN 37219	**Web Site:** www.LPcorp.com	**Auditors:** Deloitte & Touche LLP
Telephone: (615) 986-5600	**Officers:** Mark A. Suwyn - Chmn., C.E.O. Richard W. Frost - Exec. V.P., Commodity Prods, Procurement & Engrg.	**Investor Contact:** 503-221-0800

LOWE'S COS., INC.

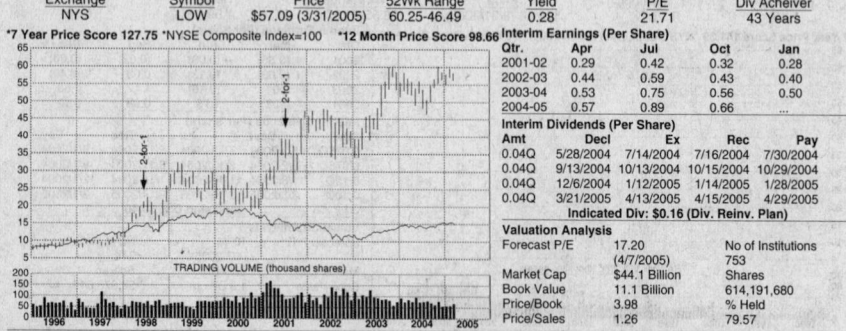

Exchange	Symbol	Price	52Wk Range	Yield	P/E	Div Acheiver
NYS	LOW	$57.09 (3/31/2005)	60.25-46.49	0.28	21.71	43 Years

*7 Year Price Score 127.75 *NYSE Composite Index=100 *12 Month Price Score 98.66

Interim Earnings (Per Share)

Qtr.	Apr	Jul	Oct	Jan
2001-02	0.29	0.42	0.32	0.28
2002-03	0.44	0.59	0.43	0.40
2003-04	0.53	0.75	0.56	0.50
2004-05	0.57	0.89	0.66	...

Interim Dividends (Per Share)

Amt	Decl	Ex	Rec	Pay
0.04Q	5/28/2004	7/14/2004	7/16/2004	7/30/2004
0.04Q	9/13/2004	10/13/2004	10/15/2004	10/29/2004
0.04Q	12/6/2004	1/12/2005	1/14/2005	1/28/2005
0.04Q	3/21/2005	4/13/2005	4/15/2005	4/29/2005

Indicated Div: $0.16 (Div. Reinv. Plan)

Valuation Analysis

Forecast P/E	17.20	No of Institutions
	(4/7/2005)	753
Market Cap	$44.1 Billion	Shares
Book Value	11.1 Billion	614,191,680
Price/Book	3.98	% Held
Price/Sales	1.26	79.57

Business Summary: Retail - Hardware (MIC: 5.6 SIC: 211 NAIC: 44110)

Lowe's Companies is a major worldwide retailer of home improvement products, with a specific emphasis on retail do-it-yourself and commercial business customers. Co. specializes in offering products and services for home improvement, home decor, home maintenance, home repair and remodeling and maintenance of commercial buildings. As of Jan 30 2004, Co. operated 952 stores in 45 states representing 108.8 million square feet of selling space. Each store is stocked with more than 40,000 separate items, while Co.'s special order program features more than 400,000 additional items.

Recent Developments: For the quarter ended Oct 29 2004, net income increased 15.5% to $522,000 thousand from net income of $452,000 thousand in the year-earlier quarter. Revenues were $9,064,000 thousand, up 16.2% from $7,802,000 thousand the year before. Comparable-store sales increased 5.2% year over year. Total indirect expense was $2,160,000 thousand versus $1,679,000 thousand in the prior-year quarter, an increase of 28.6%.

Prospects: Results should benefit from Co.'s aggressive store expansion program and comparable-store sales growth. For the first quarter of fiscal 2005, Co. anticipates opening 28 stores and expects sales growth of about 15.0% year over year. In addition, Co. is projecting first-quarter earnings of between $0.75 and $0.77 per diluted share. Looking ahead, Co. expects to open 150 stores in fiscal 2005 reflecting total square footage growth of 13.0% to 14.0%. Total sales are expected to increase approximately 17.0% for the year, while comparable-store sales are forecast to increase by about 5.0%. Diluted earnings per share of $3.25 to $3.34 are expected for the fiscal year ending Feb 3 2006.

Financial Data

(US$ in Thousands)	9 Mos	6 Mos	3 Mos	01/30/2004	01/31/2003	02/01/2002	02/02/2001	01/28/2000
Earnings Per Share	2.63	2.53	2.39	2.34	1.85	1.30	1.05	0.88
Cash Flow Per Share	4.04	4.03	4.11	3.88	3.47	2.09	1.45	1.54
Tang Book Value Per Share	14.36	13.66	13.42	13.09	10.62	8.60	7.17	6.14
Dividends Per Share	0.141	0.131	0.116	0.110	0.085	0.077	0.070	0.063
Dividend Payout %	5.35	5.16	4.84	4.70	4.59	5.96	6.64	7.14
Income Statement								
Total Revenue	27,914,000	18,850,000	8,681,000	30,838,000	26,491,000	22,111,108	18,778,559	15,905,595
EBITDA	3,528,000	2,408,000	1,000,000	3,959,000	3,186,000	2,331,890	1,811,776	1,485,791
Depn & Amortn	663,000	433,000	213,000	781,000	645,000	534,102	409,511	337,822
Income Before Taxes	2,732,000	1,882,000	739,000	2,998,000	2,359,000	1,624,251	1,281,440	1,063,117
Income Taxes	1,051,000	723,000	284,000	1,136,000	888,000	600,989	471,569	390,322
Net Income	1,681,000	1,159,000	455,000	1,877,000	1,471,000	1,023,262	809,871	672,795
Average Shares	792,000	796,000	808,000	806,000	800,000	794,597	768,950	767,708
Balance Sheet								
Current Assets	6,753,000	6,502,000	8,085,000	6,687,000	5,568,000	4,920,392	4,175,013	3,709,541
Total Assets	20,512,000	19,732,000	20,778,000	19,042,000	16,109,000	13,736,219	11,375,754	9,012,323
Current Liabilities	4,909,000	4,733,000	5,871,000	4,368,000	3,578,000	3,016,830	2,928,585	2,385,954
Long-Term Obligations	3,661,000	3,664,000	3,668,000	3,678,000	3,736,000	3,734,011	2,697,669	1,726,579
Total Liabilities	9,427,000	9,185,000	10,272,000	8,733,000	7,807,000	7,061,777	5,880,869	4,316,852
Stockholders' Equity	11,085,000	10,547,000	10,506,000	10,309,000	8,302,000	6,674,442	5,494,885	4,695,471
Shares Outstanding	772,000	772,000	783,000	787,300	781,900	775,714	766,484	764,718
Statistical Record								
Return on Assets %	10.69	10.72	9.91	10.71	9.88	8.17	7.82	8.79
Return on Equity %	19.99	20.34	19.92	20.23	19.70	16.86	15.64	17.23
EBITDA Margin %	12.64	12.77	11.52	12.84	12.03	10.55	9.65	9.34
Net Margin %	6.02	6.15	5.24	6.09	5.55	4.63	4.31	4.23
Asset Turnover	1.78	1.79	1.67	1.76	1.78	1.77	1.81	2.08
Current Ratio	1.38	1.37	1.38	1.53	1.56	1.63	1.43	1.55
Debt to Equity	0.33	0.35	0.35	0.36	0.45	0.56	0.49	0.37
Price Range	60.05-46.49	60.05-45.81	60.05-39.00	60.05-34.01	48.10-33.50	47.50-25.00	31.75-18.72	32.56-21.50
P/E Ratio	22.83-17.68	23.74-18.11	25.13-16.32	25.66-14.53	26.00-18.11	36.54-19.23	30.24-17.83	37.00-24.43
Average Yield %	0.26	0.24	0.22	0.23	0.20	0.22	0.30	0.23

Address: 1000 Lowe's Boulevard, Mooresville, NC 28117 **Telephone:** (704) 758-1000	**Web Site:** www.lowes.com **Officers:** Robert A. Niblock - Chmn., Pres., C.E.O. Dale C. Pond - Sr. Exec. V.P., Merchandising & Mktg.	**Auditors:** Deloitte & Touche LLP **Investor Contact:** 704-758-2033 **Transfer Agents:** EquiServe Trust Company, NA, Canton, MA

LSI LOGIC CORP.

Exchange	Symbol	Price	52Wk Range	Yield	P/E
NYS	LSI	$5.59 (3/31/2005)	9.91-4.03	N/A	N/A

*7 Year Price Score 30.55   *NYSE Composite Index=100   *12 Month Price Score 93.61

Interim Earnings (Per Share)

Qtr.	Mar	Jun	Sep	Dec
2001	(0.10)	(0.91)	1.09	(0.68)
2002	(0.47)	(0.17)	(0.07)	(0.08)
2003	(0.33)	(0.43)	(0.08)	0.02
2004	0.02	0.02	(0.73)	(0.52)

Interim Dividends (Per Share)

Amt	Decl	Ex	Rec	Pay
2-for-1	1/26/2000	2/17/2000	2/4/2000	2/16/2000

Valuation Analysis

Forecast P/E	16.24	No of Institutions	
	(4/7/2005)	259	
Market Cap	$2.2 Billion	Shares	
Book Value	1.6 Billion	199,596,784	
Price/Book	1.34	% Held	
Price/Sales	1.27	51.47	

Business Summary: IT & Technology (MIC: 10.2 SIC: 674 NAIC: 34413)

LSI Logic designs, develops, manufactures and markets complex, high-performance integrated circuits and storage systems. The semiconductor segment uses advanced process technology and design methodologies to produce complex integrated circuits. These system-on-a-chip products include both application specific integrated circuits and application specific standard products. Semiconductor products also include redundant array of independent disks, host bus adapters and related products and services. The Storage Systems segment provides modular, high-performance, disk storage systems and sub-assemblies to server and storage original equipment manufacturers.

Recent Developments: For the year ended Dec 31 2004, net loss was $463,531 thousand versus net loss of $308,547 thousand a year earlier. Revenues were $1,700,164 thousand, up 0.4% from $1,693,070 thousand the year before. Operating loss was $436,349 thousand versus a loss of $272,616 thousand in the prior year. Total direct expense was $964,556 thousand versus $1,015,865 thousand in the prior year, a decrease of 5.1%. Total indirect expense was $1,171,957 thousand versus $949,821 thousand in the prior year, an increase of 23.4%.

Prospects: Co.'s outlook appears challenging, due in part to recent lackluster revenue growth. On the positive side, Co. believes that its top line results going forward will benefit from its positions in several high-growth sectors, including DVD recorders, Ultra320 SCSI controllers, Serial Attached SCSI, Fibre Channel, redundant array of independent disks (RAID) adapters and its RapidChip® Platform application specific integrated circuits (ASICs). Meanwhile, Co. expects revenue for the first quarter ended Mar 31 2005 in the range of $400.0 million to $415.0 million. Capital spending is projected to be about $20.0 million in the first quarter of 2005, and approximately $80.0 million in total for 2005.

Financial Data

(US$ in Thousands)	12/31/2004	12/31/2003	12/31/2002	12/31/2001	12/31/2000	12/31/1999	12/31/1998	12/31/1997
Earnings Per Share	(1.21)	(0.82)	(0.79)	(2.84)	0.70	0.23	(0.47)	0.56
Cash Flow Per Share	0.24	0.50	0.41	0.34	1.81	1.52	0.81	1.44
Tang Book Value Per Share	1.33	2.39	2.80	3.15	5.96	5.21	4.16	5.59
Income Statement								
Total Revenue	1,700,164	1,693,070	1,816,938	1,784,923	2,737,667	2,089,444	1,490,701	1,290,275
EBITDA	(229,124)	35,066	188,202	(348,588)	866,397	631,362	110,034	392,056
Depn & Amortn	185,055	288,749	426,629	637,189	445,074	367,157	225,205	166,396
Income Before Taxes	(439,499)	(284,386)	(290,404)	(1,030,355)	379,750	224,217	(123,648)	224,163
Income Taxes	24,000	24,000	1,750	(39,198)	142,959	65,030	7,916	62,748
Net Income	(463,531)	(308,547)	(292,440)	(991,955)	236,600	67,174	(131,632)	159,248
Average Shares	384,070	377,781	370,529	349,280	354,337	325,088	281,598	288,054
Balance Sheet								
Current Assets	1,365,287	1,390,037	1,626,053	1,768,968	2,072,240	1,288,284	819,503	870,461
Total Assets	2,874,001	3,447,901	4,142,737	4,625,772	4,197,487	3,206,605	2,799,997	2,126,912
Current Liabilities	396,280	391,251	397,811	509,985	626,934	475,331	592,844	438,231
Long-Term Obligations	781,846	865,606	1,241,217	...	...	...	...	...
Total Liabilities	1,255,696	1,397,953	1,835,876	2,140,020	1,693,608	1,344,563	1,284,624	555,742
Stockholders' Equity	1,618,046	2,042,450	2,300,355	2,479,885	2,498,137	1,855,832	1,510,135	1,565,973
Shares Outstanding	387,490	381,491	375,096	368,446	321,523	299,572	282,838	280,322
Statistical Record								
Return on Assets %	N.M.	N.M.	N.M.	N.M.	6.37	2.24	N.M.	7.81
Return on Equity %	N.M.	N.M.	N.M.	N.M.	10.84	3.99	N.M.	11.05
EBITDA Margin %	N.M.	2.07	10.36	N.M.	31.65	30.22	7.38	30.39
Net Margin %	N.M.	N.M.	N.M.	N.M.	8.64	3.21	N.M.	12.34
Asset Turnover	0.54	0.45	0.41	0.40	0.74	0.70	0.61	0.63
Current Ratio	3.45	3.55	4.09	3.47	3.31	2.71	1.38	1.99
Debt to Equity	0.48	0.42	0.54	...	...	...	...	...
Price Range	11.45-4.03	11.96-3.97	18.58-4.14	24.99-10.80	88.25-16.43	35.63-8.06	14.50-5.56	23.25-9.59
P/E Ratio	...	...	...	...	126.07-23.47	154.89-35.05	...	41.52-17.13

Address: 1621 Barber Lane, Milpitas, CA 95035	Web Site: www.lsilogic.com	Auditors: PricewaterhouseCoopers LLP
Telephone: (408) 433-8000	Officers: Wilfred J. Corrigan - Chmn., C.E.O. Bryon Look - Exec. V.P., C.F.O.	Investor Contact: 408-954-4710
Fax: (408) 433-3220		

LUBRIZOL CORP.

Exchange	Symbol	Price	52Wk Range	Yield	P/E
NYS	LZ	$40.64 (3/31/2005)	43.39-30.68	2.56	24.34

*7 Year Price Score 101.40 *NYSE Composite Index=100 *12 Month Price Score 106.75

Interim Earnings (Per Share)

Qtr.	Mar	Jun	Sep	Dec
2001	0.36	0.62	0.44	0.41
2002	0.58	0.66	0.71	0.49
2003	0.50	0.57	0.47	0.21
2004	0.72	0.08	0.61	0.26

Interim Dividends (Per Share)

Amt	Decl	Ex	Rec	Pay
0.26Q	4/26/2004	5/6/2004	5/10/2004	6/10/2004
0.26Q	7/26/2004	8/6/2004	8/10/2004	9/10/2004
0.26Q	9/27/2004	11/8/2004	11/10/2004	12/10/2004
0.26Q	12/13/2004	2/8/2005	2/10/2005	3/10/2005

Indicated Div: $1.04

Valuation Analysis

Forecast P/E	14.69	No of Institutions	
	(4/7/2005)	228	
Market Cap	$2.7 Billion	Shares	
Book Value	1.5 Billion	56,323,832	
Price/Book	1.78	% Held	
Price/Sales	0.86	83.66	

Business Summary: Chemicals (MIC: 11.1 SIC: 861 NAIC: 25191)

Lubrizol is a global provider of specialty chemicals and materials for a wide variety of markets and end-use applications, such as lubricant additives for engine oils, other transportation-related fluids and industrial lubricants, as well as fuel additives for gasoline and diesel fuel. In addition, Co. makes ingredients and additives for personal care products and pharmaceuticals; specialty materials, including plastics technology; performance coatings in the form of specialty resins and additives; and additives for the food and beverage industry. Co. operates in two business segments: Lubricant Additives, also known as Lubrizol Additives, and Specialty Chemicals, also known as Noveon.

Recent Developments: For the year ended Dec 31 2004, net income increased 3.0% to $93,500 thousand from net income of $90,800 thousand a year earlier. Revenues were $3,159,500 thousand, up 54.0% from $2,052,100 thousand the year before. Total direct expense was $2,359,500 thousand versus $1,507,800 thousand in the prior year, an increase of 56.5%. Total indirect expense was $586,000 thousand versus $397,200 thousand in the prior year, an increase of 47.5%.

Prospects: For the first quarter of 2005, Co. expects earnings per share (EPS) to be in the range of $0.66 to $0.72, including about half the 2005 restructuring charges. For full-year 2005, Co. is projecting EPS to be in the range of $2.72 to $2.87, including restructuring charges of about $0.03 per share related to the closure of the its U.K. manufacturing plant. Excluding the restructuring charges, EPS are projected to be $0.67 to $0.73, with EPS for the year of $2.75 to $2.90. Even with 29.0% more shares outstanding, the first quarter of 2005 projection exceeds EPS year over year, excluding a 2004 currency forward contract gain related to Co.'s acquisition of hyperdispersants.

Financial Data

(US$ in Thousands)	12/31/2004	12/31/2003	12/31/2002	12/31/2001	12/31/2000	12/31/1999	12/31/1998	12/31/1997
Earnings Per Share	1.67	1.75	2.29	1.83	2.22	2.25	1.27	2.66
Cash Flow Per Share	5.88	3.77	4.75	3.82	4.25	5.30	2.77	4.05
Tang Book Value Per Share	N.M.	13.22	12.78	11.86	11.34	11.75	11.04	14.31
Dividends Per Share	1.040	1.040	1.040	1.040	1.040	1.040	1.040	1.010
Dividend Payout %	62.28	59.43	45.41	56.83	46.85	46.22	81.89	37.97
Income Statement								
Total Revenue	3,159,500	2,052,123	1,983,867	1,844,644	1,775,780	1,748,003	1,617,919	1,673,782
EBITDA	373,600	250,809	292,820	257,035	289,440	316,912	220,057	324,579
Depn & Amortn	154,700	100,423	95,831	98,832	100,834	99,720	88,047	87,217
Income Before Taxes	146,600	129,071	180,388	139,949	170,348	195,350	118,814	231,147
Income Taxes	53,100	38,297	54,116	45,833	52,339	72,358	47,614	76,278
Net Income	93,500	90,774	118,487	94,116	118,009	122,992	71,200	154,869
Average Shares	56,000	51,884	51,794	51,494	53,220	54,716	56,122	58,229
Balance Sheet								
Current Assets	1,598,000	937,848	909,779	756,724	727,908	780,442	687,470	657,076
Total Assets	4,566,300	1,942,316	1,860,137	1,662,319	1,659,490	1,682,354	1,643,237	1,462,292
Current Liabilities	657,300	299,477	307,741	259,214	282,246	311,300	270,028	261,930
Long-Term Obligations	1,964,100	386,726	384,845	388,111	378,783	365,372	390,394	182,165
Total Liabilities	2,989,200	937,730	937,497	856,550	874,739	892,230	874,119	646,844
Stockholders' Equity	1,523,500	953,305	869,252	773,192	752,281	790,124	769,118	815,448
Shares Outstanding	66,778	51,588	51,457	51,152	51,307	54,477	54,548	56,966
Statistical Record								
Return on Assets %	2.87	4.77	6.73	5.67	7.04	7.40	4.59	10.81
Return on Equity %	7.53	9.96	14.43	12.34	15.26	15.78	8.99	18.95
EBITDA Margin %	11.82	12.22	14.76	13.93	16.30	18.13	13.60	19.39
Net Margin %	2.96	4.42	5.97	5.10	6.65	7.04	4.40	9.25
Asset Turnover	0.97	1.08	1.13	1.11	1.06	1.05	1.04	1.17
Current Ratio	2.43	3.13	2.96	2.92	2.58	2.51	2.55	2.51
Debt to Equity	1.29	0.41	0.44	0.50	0.50	0.46	0.51	0.22
Price Range	37.36-29.86	34.23-26.92	35.84-26.21	37.08-24.44	33.50-18.56	30.94-18.81	39.06-22.56	46.94-30.38
P/E Ratio	22.37-17.88	19.56-15.38	15.65-11.45	20.26-13.35	15.09-8.36	13.75-8.36	30.76-17.77	17.65-11.42
Average Yield %	3.09	3.33	3.25	3.31	4.33	3.99	3.29	2.65

Address: 29400 Lakeland Blvd., Wickliffe, OH 44092-2298 **Telephone:** (440) 943-4200 **Fax:** (440) 943-5337	**Web Site:** www.lubrizol.com **Officers:** James L. Hambrick - Chmn., Pres., C.E.O. Joseph W. Bauer - V.P., Gen. Couns.	**Auditors:** DELOITTE & TOUCHE LLP **Investor Contact:** 440-943-4200 **Transfer Agents:** American Stock Transfer & Trust Company, New York.

LUCENT TECHNOLOGIES INC.

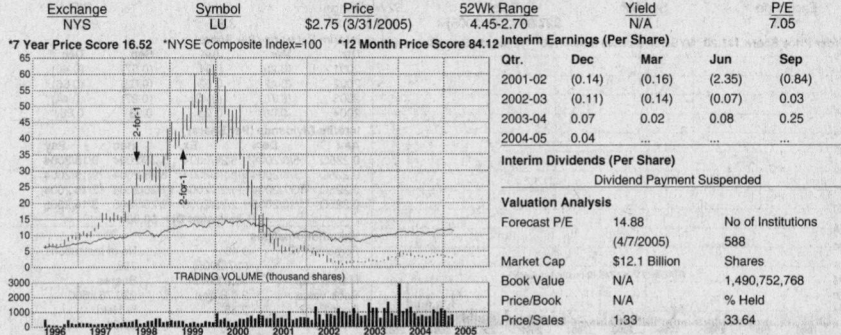

Exchange	Symbol	Price	52Wk Range	Yield	P/E
NYS	LU	$2.75 (3/31/2005)	4.45-2.70	N/A	7.05

*7 Year Price Score 16.52   *NYSE Composite Index=100   *12 Month Price Score 84.12

Interim Earnings (Per Share)

Qtr.	Dec	Mar	Jun	Sep
2001-02	(0.14)	(0.16)	(2.35)	(0.84)
2002-03	(0.11)	(0.14)	(0.07)	0.03
2003-04	0.07	0.02	0.08	0.25
2004-05	0.04	...	...	...

Interim Dividends (Per Share)

Dividend Payment Suspended

Valuation Analysis

Forecast P/E	14.88	No of Institutions
	(4/7/2005)	588
Market Cap	$12.1 Billion	Shares
Book Value	N/A	1,490,752,768
Price/Book	N/A	% Held
Price/Sales	1.33	33.64

Business Summary: Communications (MIC: 10.1 SIC: 813 NAIC: 17110)

Lucent Technologies designs and delivers systems, services and software for communications service providers. Co.'s three segments are Integrated Network Solutions, Mobility Solutions and Lucent Worldwide Services. INS provides a range of software and wireline equipment related to voice networking (primarily consisting of switching products and voice messaging products), data and network management and optical networking. Mobility provides software and wireless equipment to support radio access and core networks. Services provides deployment, maintenance, professional and managed services in support of both Co.'s product offerings as well as multi-vendor networks.

Recent Developments: For the quarter ended Dec 31 2004, net income decreased 48.5% to $174 million from net income of $338 million in the year-earlier quarter. Revenues were $2,335 million, up 3.4% from $2,259 million the year before. Operating income was $319 million versus an income of $271 million in the prior-year quarter, an increase of 17.7%. Total direct expense was $1,351 million versus $1,340 million in the prior-year quarter, an increase of 0.8%. Total indirect expense was $665 million versus $648 million in the prior-year quarter, an increase of 2.6%.

Prospects: As the transformation of networks continues, customers are increasingly focused on deploying new Internet Protocol-based, revenue-generating services that will differentiate their businesses. Meanwhile, industry consolidation and increased competition continue to drive customers to invest in areas important for next-generation networks. Co. continues to achieve strong results in its mobility business where the migration to 3G is ramping up. Separately, while the wireline market remains a challenge in the near term, Co. continues to execute on a long-term strategy of investing in areas critical to convergence such as next-generation optical, VoIP, broadband access, and mobile high-speed data.

Financial Data

(US$ in Thousands)	3 Mos	09/30/2004	09/30/2003	09/30/2002	09/30/2001	09/30/2000	09/30/1999	09/30/1998
Earnings Per Share	0.39	0.42	(0.29)	(3.49)	(4.77)	0.37	1.52	0.36
Cash Flow Per Share	0.13	0.15	(0.24)	(0.22)	(1.01)	0.09	(0.09)	0.52
Tang Book Value Per Share	...	...	...	...	2.80	4.59	4.27	1.99
Dividends Per Share	...	...	...	...	0.060	0.080	0.080	0.077
Dividend Payout %	...	...	...	...	...	21.62	5.26	21.23
Income Statement								
Total Revenue	2,335,000	9,045,000	8,470,000	12,321,000	21,294,000	33,813,000	38,303,000	30,147,000
EBITDA	438,000	1,928,000	242,000	(5,331,000)	(17,105,000)	5,544,000	7,531,000	3,875,000
Depn & Amortn	165,000	693,000	978,000	1,470,000	2,536,000	2,318,000	1,806,000	1,334,000
Income Before Taxes	184,000	1,063,000	(1,003,000)	(7,069,000)	(19,904,000)	3,003,000	5,443,000	2,306,000
Income Taxes	10,000	(939,000)	(233,000)	4,757,000	(5,734,000)	1,322,000	1,985,000	1,336,000
Net Income	174,000	2,002,000	(770,000)	(11,753,000)	(16,198,000)	1,219,000	4,766,000	970,000
Average Shares	4,997,999	5,312,999	3,950,000	3,426,700	3,400,700	3,325,900	3,142,700	2,666,800
Balance Sheet								
Current Assets	7,603,000	8,231,000	7,833,000	9,155,000	16,103,000	21,490,000	21,931,000	14,078,000
Total Assets	16,687,000	16,963,000	15,765,000	17,791,000	33,664,000	48,792,000	38,775,000	26,720,000
Current Liabilities	3,682,000	4,466,000	5,015,000	6,326,000	10,169,000	10,877,000	11,778,000	10,428,000
Long-Term Obligations	4,810,000	4,837,000	4,439,000	3,236,000	3,274,000	3,076,000	4,162,000	2,409,000
Total Liabilities	17,404,000	18,342,000	19,136,000	20,845,000	20,807,000	22,620,000	25,191,000	21,186,000
Stockholders' Equity	(717,000)	(1,379,000)	(4,239,000)	(4,734,000)	11,023,000	26,172,000	13,584,000	5,534,000
Shares Outstanding	4,415,999	4,394,999	4,169,000	3,490,310	3,414,168	3,384,332	3,071,751	2,632,000
Statistical Record								
Return on Assets %	11.44	12.20	N.M.	N.M.	N.M.	2.78	14.55	3.84
Return on Equity %	...	...	...	N.M.	N.M.	6.12	49.86	21.75
EBITDA Margin %	18.76	21.32	2.86	N.M.	N.M.	16.40	19.66	12.85
Net Margin %	7.45	22.13	N.M.	N.M.	N.M.	3.61	12.44	3.22
Asset Turnover	0.57	0.55	0.50	0.48	0.52	0.77	1.17	1.19
Current Ratio	2.06	1.84	1.56	1.45	1.58	1.98	1.86	1.35
Debt to Equity	...	...	...	...	0.30	0.12	0.31	0.44
Price Range	4.75-2.70	4.75-2.14	2.55-0.58	7.02-0.76	27.17-4.34	63.02-22.12	60.08-21.83	39.16-13.97
P/E Ratio	12.18-6.92	11.31-5.10	...	...	...	170.32-59.77	39.52-14.36	108.77-38.79
Average Yield %	...	...	...	...	0.58	0.18	0.19	0.33

Address: 600 Mountain Avenue, Murray Hill, NJ 07974 **Telephone:** (908) 582-8500 **Fax:** (908) 582-7826	**Web Site:** www.lucent.com **Officers:** Patricia F. Russo - Chmn., C.E.O. William T. O'Shea - Exec. V.P., Strategy & Bus. Devel.	**Auditors:** PricewaterhouseCoopers LLP

LYONDELL CHEMICAL CO

Exchange	Symbol	Price	52Wk Range	Yield	P/E
NYS	LYO	$27.92 (3/31/2005)	35.25-14.84	3.22	96.28

*7 Year Price Score 115.20 *NYSE Composite Index=100 *12 Month Price Score 129.90

Interim Earnings (Per Share)

Qtr.	Mar	Jun	Sep	Dec
2001	(0.29)	0.04	(0.57)	(0.46)
2002	(0.47)	0.02	(0.02)	(0.66)
2003	(0.70)	(0.43)	(0.27)	(0.44)
2004	(0.08)	0.02	0.28	0.08

Interim Dividends (Per Share)

Amt	Decl	Ex	Rec	Pay
0.225Q	5/6/2004	5/21/2004	5/25/2004	6/15/2004
0.225Q	7/8/2004	8/23/2004	8/25/2004	9/15/2004
0.225Q	10/7/2004	11/23/2004	11/26/2004	12/15/2004
0.225Q	1/20/2005	2/23/2005	2/25/2005	3/15/2005
		Indicated Div: $0.90		

Valuation Analysis

Forecast P/E	9.46	No of Institutions
	(4/7/2005)	256
Market Cap	$6.8 Billion	Shares
Book Value	2.7 Billion	220,761,600
Price/Book	2.55	% Held
Price/Sales	1.14	89.91

Business Summary: Oil and Gas (MIC: 14.2 SIC: 911 NAIC: 24110)

Lyondell Chemical is a global chemical company. Co. manufactures and markets a variety of basic chemicals and gasoline blending components, primarily propylene oxide and its derivatives, including propylene glycol, propylene glycol ethers and butanediol, co-products styrene monomer and tertiary butyl alcohol and its derivative, methyl tertiary butyl ether, as well as toluene diisocyanate, which are collectively known as Co.'s intermediate chemicals and derivatives business. As of Dec 31 2004, Co. held a 58.75% participation interest in Lyondell-Citgo Refining, which produces refined petroleum products, and a 70.5% interest in Equistar Chemicals.

Recent Developments: For the year ended Dec 31 2004, net income was $54,000 thousand versus net loss of $302,000 thousand a year earlier. Operating income was $105,000 thousand versus a loss of $1,000 thousand in the prior year. Total direct expense was $5,475,000 thousand versus $3,599,000 thousand in the prior year, an increase of 52.1%. Total indirect expense was $388,000 thousand versus $203,000 thousand in the prior year, an increase of 91.1%.

Prospects: Business conditions continue to appear positive for the majority of Co.'s products and it continues to benefit from particularly strong economics from its crude oil-related ethylene facilities. Supply/demand conditions for the majority of its products have strengthened, and Co. expects this strengthening to continue throughout 2005. However, volatile and elevated energy prices and resultant raw material prices continue to be a concern. Overall, Co. believes that 2005 will be characterized by additional tightening of supply/demand and strengthening margins. Operationally, Co. intends to focus on taking advantage of these conditions. Financially, Co. remains focused on debt reduction.

Financial Data

(US$ in Thousands)	12/31/2004	12/31/2003	12/31/2002	12/31/2001	12/31/2000	12/31/1999	12/31/1998	12/31/1997
Earnings Per Share	0.29	(1.84)	(1.10)	(1.28)	3.71	(1.10)	0.67	3.58
Cash Flow Per Share	2.08	0.63	2.16	1.69	0.52	2.91	3.37	3.36
Tang Book Value Per Share	N.M.	N.M.	N.M.	N.M.	N.M.	N.M.	N.M.	7.74
Dividends Per Share	0.900	0.900	0.900	0.900	0.900	0.900	0.900	0.900
Dividend Payout %	310.34	...	...	...	24.26	...	134.33	25.14
Income Statement								
Total Revenue	5,968,000	3,801,000	3,262,000	3,226,000	4,036,000	3,693,000	1,703,000	3,010,000
EBITDA	815,000	161,000	426,000	417,000	1,416,000	784,000	467,000	601,000
Depn & Amortn	289,000	250,000	244,000	269,000	261,000	299,000	116,000	84,000
Income Before Taxes	77,000	(481,000)	(191,000)	(221,000)	693,000	(104,000)	89,000	456,000
Income Taxes	23,000	(179,000)	(58,000)	(76,000)	223,000	(24,000)	37,000	170,000
Net Income	54,000	(302,000)	(148,000)	(150,000)	437,000	(115,000)	52,000	286,000
Average Shares	186,000	164,288	133,943	117,563	117,778	103,115	78,000	80,000
Balance Sheet								
Current Assets	4,457,000	1,359,000	1,171,000	1,207,000	1,345,000	1,886,000	1,326,000	103,000
Total Assets	15,928,000	7,633,000	7,448,000	6,703,000	7,047,000	9,498,000	9,225,000	1,559,000
Current Liabilities	2,295,000	699,000	624,000	559,000	734,000	1,021,000	2,337,000	308,000
Long-Term Obligations	7,555,000	4,151,000	3,926,000	3,846,000	3,844,000	6,046,000	5,391,000	345,000
Total Liabilities	13,255,000	6,477,000	6,269,000	5,954,000	5,902,000	8,491,000	8,651,000	940,000
Stockholders' Equity	2,673,000	1,156,000	1,179,000	749,000	1,145,000	1,007,000	574,000	619,000
Shares Outstanding	243,684	176,792	160,413	117,563	117,560	117,571	77,000	80,000
Statistical Record								
Return on Assets %	0.46	N.M.	N.M.	N.M.	5.27	N.M.	0.96	11.83
Return on Equity %	2.81	N.M.	N.M.	N.M.	40.50	N.M.	8.72	54.48
EBITDA Margin %	13.66	4.24	13.06	12.93	35.08	21.23	27.42	19.97
Net Margin %	0.90	N.M.	N.M.	N.M.	10.83	N.M.	3.05	9.50
Asset Turnover	0.51	0.50	0.46	0.47	0.49	0.39	0.32	1.25
Current Ratio	1.94	1.94	1.88	2.16	1.83	1.85	0.57	0.33
Debt to Equity	2.83	3.59	3.33	5.13	3.36	6.00	9.39	0.56
Price Range	29.27-14.84	17.03-11.11	17.47-10.35	17.84-10.05	19.50-8.56	22.31-11.25	36.13-16.06	27.06-18.75
P/E Ratio	100.93-51.17	...	...	...	5.26-2.31	...	53.92-23.97	7.56-5.24
Average Yield %	4.64	6.45	6.32	6.10	6.38	5.71	3.50	3.74

Address: 1221 McKinney St., Suite 700, Houston, TX 77010 **Telephone:** (713) 652-7200 **Fax:** (713) 652-4563	**Web Site:** www.lyondell.com **Officers:** William T. Butler - Chmn. Dan F. Smith - Pres., C.E.O.	**Auditors:** PricewaterhouseCoopers LLP **Investor Contact:** 713-309-7141

M & T BANK CORP

Exchange	Symbol	Price	52Wk Range	Yield	P/E	Div Acheiver
NYS	MTB	$102.06 (3/31/2005)	108.01-83.37	1.57	17.01	24 Years

*7 Year Price Score 118.04 *NYSE Composite Index=100 *12 Month Price Score 97.08

Interim Earnings (Per Share)

Qtr.	Mar	Jun	Sep	Dec
2001	0.85	0.94	0.98	1.05
2002	1.25	1.26	1.23	1.32
2003	1.23	1.10	1.28	1.36
2004	1.30	1.53	1.56	1.61

Interim Dividends (Per Share)

Amt	Decl	Ex	Rec	Pay
0.40Q	4/20/2004	5/27/2004	6/1/2004	6/30/2004
0.40Q	7/27/2004	8/31/2004	9/2/2004	9/30/2004
0.40Q	10/27/2004	11/29/2004	12/1/2004	12/31/2004
0.40Q	2/17/2005	2/24/2005	2/28/2005	3/31/2005

Indicated Div: $1.60 (Div. Reinv. Plan)

Valuation Analysis

Forecast P/E	15.36	No of Institutions
	(4/7/2005)	266
Market Cap	$11.8 Billion	Shares
Book Value	5.7 Billion	74,007,744
Price/Book	2.05	% Held
Price/Sales	3.63	64.31

Business Summary: Commercial Banking (MIC: 8.1 SIC: 022 NAIC: 22110)

M&T Bank, with assets of $49.83 billion as of Dec 31 2003, is a bank holding company with two wholly-owned bank subsidiaries, Manufacturers and Traders Trust and M&T Bank, National Association. The banks collectively offer commercial banking, trust and investment services to their customers. Through its subsidiaries, Co. provides individuals, corporations and institutions with operations in the following six segments: Commercial Banking, Commercial Real Estate, Discretionary Portfolio, Residential Mortgage Banking, Retail Banking, and Other operations.

Recent Developments: For the year ended Dec 31 2004, net income increased 25.9% to $722,521 thousand from net income of $573,942 thousand a year earlier. Net interest income was $1,734,572 thousand, up 8.5% from $1,598,755 thousand the year before. Provision for loan losses was $95,000 thousand versus $131,000 thousand in the prior year, a decrease of 27.5%. Non-interest income rose 13.5% to $942,969 thousand, while non-interest expense advanced 4.7% to $1,516,018 thousand.

Prospects: Co.'s net interest income is benefiting from higher average earning assets, reflecting solid growth in average loans outstanding and average investment securities. However, net interest margin is being adversely affected primarily by lower yields earned on loans and investment securities. Meanwhile, Co.'s non-interest income is being positively affected by higher levels of service charges on deposit accounts and letter of credit and other credit-related fees, which is offsetting lower mortgage revenues. Co. continues to be encouraged by lower levels of net charge-offs and non-performing loans. Looking ahead to 2005, Co. expects earnings to range from $6.60 to $6.80 per diluted share.

Financial Data
(US$ in Thousands)

	12/31/2004	12/31/2003	12/31/2002	12/31/2001	12/31/2000	12/31/1999	12/31/1998	12/31/1997
Earnings Per Share	6.00	4.95	5.07	3.82	3.44	3.28	2.62	2.53
Cash Flow Per Share	6.14	10.94	6.90	1.61	4.29	7.78	0.48	5.42
Tang Book Value Per Share	23.08	21.42	21.36	17.84	16.10	14.88	13.72	15.59
Dividends Per Share	1.600	1.200	1.050	1.000	0.625	0.450	0.380	0.320
Dividend Payout %	26.67	24.24	20.71	26.18	18.17	13.71	14.53	12.67
Income Statement								
Interest Income	2,298,732	2,126,565	1,842,099	2,101,885	1,772,784	1,478,631	1,351,794	1,064,961
Interest Expense	564,160	527,810	594,514	943,597	918,597	719,234	687,503	508,093
Net Interest Income	1,734,572	1,598,755	1,247,585	1,158,288	854,187	759,397	664,291	556,868
Provision for Losses	95,000	131,000	122,000	103,500	38,000	44,500	43,200	46,000
Non-Interest Income	942,969	831,095	511,931	477,426	324,672	282,375	270,595	193,067
Non-Interest Expense	1,516,018	1,448,180	921,032	948,318	694,453	578,958	566,123	421,776
Income Before Taxes	1,066,523	850,670	716,484	583,896	446,406	418,314	325,563	282,159
Income Taxes	344,002	276,728	231,392	205,821	160,250	152,688	117,589	105,918
Net Income	722,521	573,942	485,092	378,075	286,156	265,626	207,974	176,241
Average Shares	120,406	115,932	95,663	99,024	83,171	80,900	79,500	69,770
Balance Sheet								
Net Loans & Leases	37,771,613	35,158,377	25,291,312	24,762,752	22,368,111	17,090,606	15,485,183	11,221,912
Total Assets	52,938,721	49,826,081	33,174,525	31,450,196	28,949,456	22,409,115	20,583,891	14,002,935
Total Deposits	35,429,473	33,114,944	21,664,923	21,580,400	20,232,673	15,373,620	14,737,152	11,163,158
Total Liabilities	47,209,107	44,108,871	29,992,702	28,510,745	26,248,971	20,612,069	18,981,525	12,972,669
Stockholders' Equity	5,729,614	5,717,210	3,181,823	2,939,451	2,700,485	1,797,046	1,602,366	1,030,266
Shares Outstanding	115,227	120,106	92,028	93,683	93,244	77,238	76,980	66,100
Statistical Record								
Return on Assets %	1.40	1.38	1.50	1.25	1.11	1.24	1.20	1.31
Return on Equity %	12.59	12.90	15.85	13.41	12.69	15.63	15.80	18.21
Net Interest Margin %	75.46	75.18	67.73	55.11	48.18	51.36	49.14	52.29
Efficiency Ratio %	46.77	48.96	39.13	36.77	33.11	32.88	34.89	33.53
Loans to Deposits	1.07	1.06	1.17	1.15	1.11	1.11	1.05	1.01
Price Range	108.01-83.37	98.55-75.69	89.94-68.00	81.23-61.09	68.00-36.40	56.66-41.00	57.52-41.00	46.50-28.10
P/E Ratio	18.00-13.90	19.91-15.29	17.74-13.41	21.26-15.99	19.77-10.58	17.27-12.50	21.96-15.65	18.38-11.11
Average Yield %	1.69	1.39	1.30	1.39	1.34	0.91	0.77	0.90

Address: One M&T Plaza, 5th Floor, Buffalo, NY 14203	Web Site: www.mandtbank.com	Auditors: PricewaterhouseCoopers LLP
Telephone: (716) 842-5445	Officers: Robert G. Wilmers - Chmn., Pres., CEO	Transfer Agents: Registrar and
Fax: (716) 842-5177	Carl L. Campbell - Vice-Chmn.	Transfer Company, Cranford, NJ

MACERICH CO. (THE)

Exchange	Symbol	Price	52Wk Range	Yield	P/E	Div Acheiver
NYS	MAC	$53.28 (3/31/2005)	64.66-39.75	4.88	38.06	10 Years

*7 Year Price Score 146.83 ***NYSE Composite Index=100** ***12 Month Price Score 100.01**

TRADING VOLUME (thousand shares)

Interim Earnings (Per Share)

Qtr.	Mar	Jun	Sep	Dec
2001	0.19	0.20	0.27	1.05
2002	0.50	(0.04)	0.32	0.85
2003	0.37	0.55	0.69	0.45
2004	0.31	0.29	0.29	0.51

Interim Dividends (Per Share)

Amt	Decl	Ex	Rec	Pay
0.61Q	4/29/2004	5/18/2004	5/20/2004	6/10/2004
0.61Q	7/30/2004	8/18/2004	8/20/2004	9/10/2004
0.65Q	10/29/2004	11/10/2004	11/15/2004	12/9/2004
0.65Q	2/7/2005	2/18/2005	2/23/2005	3/8/2005

Indicated Div: $2.60

Valuation Analysis

Forecast P/E	12.89	No of Institutions
	(4/7/2005)	185
Market Cap	$3.1 Billion	Shares
Book Value	913.5 Million	55,589,400
Price/Book	3.43	% Held
Price/Sales	5.72	93.78

Business Summary: Property, Real Estate & Development (MIC: 8.3 SIC: 798 NAIC: 25930)

Macerich is a self-administered and self-managed real estate investment trust involved in the acquisition, ownership, development, redevelopment, management and leasing of regional malls and community centers located throughout the United States. Co. is the sole general partner of, and owns an 82.0% ownership interest in, The Macerich Partnership. As of Dec 31 2003, Co. owned or had an ownership interest in 58 regional malls, 18 community centers and two development properties aggregating approximately 58.0 million square feet. Co. conducts all of its operations through the Operating Partnership and its management companies.

Recent Developments: For the year ended Dec 31 2004, income from continuing operations decreased 23.0% to $98,653 thousand from income of $128,154 thousand a year earlier. Net income decreased 28.4% to $91,633 thousand from net income of $128,034 thousand a year earlier. Revenues were $547,268 thousand, up 13.2% from $483,577 thousand the year before.

Prospects: On Dec 23 2004, Co. announced that it has signed a definitive agreement to acquire Wilmorite Properties, Inc. and Wilmorite Holdings L.P. for a total purchase price of about $2.33 billion. Wilmorite's portfolio includes interests in 11 regional malls and two open-air community centers, with 13.4 million square feet of space located in Connecticut, New York, New Jersey, Kentucky and Virginia. About 5.0 million square feet of gross leaseable area is located at three regional malls: Tysons Corner Center in McLean, VA, Freehold Raceway Mall in Freehold, NJ and Danbury Fair Mall in Danbury, CT. Co. expects the transaction to close in Mar 2005 and to be neutral to funds from operation in 2005.

Financial Data

(US$ in Thousands)	12/31/2004	12/31/2003	12/31/2002	12/31/2001	12/31/2000	12/31/1999	12/31/1998	12/31/1997
Earnings Per Share	1.40	2.09	1.62	1.72	1.11	2.99	1.06	0.85
Cash Flow Per Share	3.31	4.88	5.52	4.16	3.55	4.10	2.77	3.03
Tang Book Value Per Share	12.83	14.42	15.49	10.27	10.78	18.20	17.03	8.32
Dividends Per Share	2.480	2.320	2.220	2.140	2.060	1.965	1.865	1.780
Dividend Payout %	177.14	111.00	137.04	124.42	185.59	65.72	175.94	209.41
Income Statement								
Property Income	528,099	468,255	366,883	323,038	311,919	318,800	279,306	218,009
Non-Property Income	19,169	17,749	12,041	11,535	8,173	8,644	4,555	3,205
Total Revenue	547,268	486,004	378,924	334,573	320,092	327,444	283,861	221,214
Depn & Amortn	145,573	106,794	77,767	66,016	61,680	61,574	52,506	41,568
Interest Expense	146,327	132,512	122,934	109,646	108,447	113,348	91,433	66,407
Net Income	91,633	128,034	81,382	77,723	56,929	129,011	44,075	22,046
Average Shares	73,099	75,198	50,066	44,963	45,050	60,893	43,628	38,403
Balance Sheet								
Total Assets	4,637,096	4,145,593	3,662,080	2,294,502	2,337,242	2,404,293	2,322,056	1,505,002
Long-Term Obligations	2,337,120	1,916,798	1,743,108	1,364,660	1,403,595	1,400,456	1,370,118	1,067,959
Total Liabilities	3,403,314	2,855,559	2,395,449	1,584,226	1,607,134	1,626,408	1,579,119	1,188,244
Stockholders' Equity	913,533	953,485	797,798	348,954	362,272	620,286	577,413	216,295
Shares Outstanding	58,785	57,902	51,490	33,981	33,612	34,072	33,902	26,005
Statistical Record								
Return on Assets %	2.08	3.28	2.73	3.36	2.39	5.46	2.30	1.64
Return on Equity %	9.79	14.62	14.19	21.86	11.56	21.54	11.11	9.71
Net Margin %	16.74	26.34	21.48	23.23	17.79	39.40	15.53	9.97
Price Range	64.66-39.75	44.50-28.82	31.48-26.30	26.60-18.75	24.75-18.44	27.06-17.81	30.00-23.25	29.56-25.06
P/E Ratio	46.19-28.39	21.29-13.79	19.43-16.23	15.47-10.90	22.30-16.61	9.05-5.96	28.30-21.93	34.78-29.49
Average Yield %	4.86	6.46	7.59	9.26	9.69	8.37	6.82	6.45

Address: 401 Wilshire Boulevard, Suite 700, Santa Monica, CA 90401	Web Site: www.macerich.com	Auditors: Deloitte & Touche LLP
Telephone: (310) 394-6000	Officers: Mace Siegel - Chmn. Dana K. Anderson - Vice-Chmn.	
Fax: (310) 395-2791		

MACK CALI REALTY CORP

Exchange	Symbol	Price	52Wk Range	Yield	P/E
NYS	CLI	$42.35 (3/31/2005)	47.00-35.20	5.95	25.67

*7 Year Price Score 112.85 *NYSE Composite Index=100   *12 Month Price Score 95.40

Interim Earnings (Per Share)

Qtr.	Mar	Jun	Sep	Dec
2001	0.29	0.98	0.43	0.58
2002	0.70	0.61	0.59	0.52
2003	0.52	0.58	0.84	0.47
2004	0.44	0.26	0.46	0.49

Interim Dividends (Per Share)

Amt	Decl	Ex	Rec	Pay
0.63Q	6/17/2004	7/1/2004	7/6/2004	7/19/2004
0.63Q	9/14/2004	10/1/2004	10/5/2004	10/18/2004
0.63Q	12/7/2004	1/3/2005	1/5/2005	1/18/2005
0.63Q	3/24/2005	4/1/2005	4/5/2005	4/18/2005

Indicated Div: $2.52

Valuation Analysis

Forecast P/E	11.59	No of Institutions
	(4/7/2005)	215
Market Cap	$2.6 Billion	Shares
Book Value	1.5 Billion	50,652,224
Price/Book	1.67	% Held
Price/Sales	4.39	82.44

Business Summary: Property, Real Estate & Development (MIC: 8.3 SIC: 798 NAIC: 25930)

Mack-Cali Realty is a fully-integrated, self-administered and self-managed real estate investment trust that owns and operates a portfolio comprised of office and office/flex properties located primarily in the Northeast. As of Dec 31 2003, Co. owned or had interests in 263 properties, totaling about 28.3 million square feet, plus developable land. The properties were comprised of: 154 office buildings and 97 office/flex buildings totaling about 27.8 million square feet, six industrial/warehouse buildings totaling 387,400 square feet, two stand-alone retail properties totaling approximately 17,300 square feet, two land leases, a mixed use retail property and a 350-room hotel.

Recent Developments: For the year ended Dec 31 2004, income from continuing operations decreased 26.1% to $98,739 thousand from income of $133,598 thousand a year earlier. Net income decreased 28.4% to $102,453 thousand from net income of $143,053 thousand a year earlier. Revenues were $588,991 thousand, up 3.5% from $569,273 thousand the year before.

Prospects: Co. has made several acquisitions recently. In Dec. Co. acquired three office buildings totaling 279,811 square feet (sq. ft.) in Parsippany, NJ for $30.8 million. In addition, Co. purchased a 125,783 sq. ft. six-story class A office building in Bala Cynwyd, PA for $18.6 million. On Mar 2 2005, Co. completed its acquisition of all the interests in a 1.2 million sq. ft. class A 42-story office tower on the Jersey City waterfront for $329.0 million. Looking ahead to full-year 2005, Co. anticipates net income will be in the range of $1.51 to $1.71 per diluted share and expects funds from operations to range from $3.45 to $3.65 per diluted share.

Financial Data

(US$ in Thousands)	12/31/2004	12/31/2003	12/31/2002	12/31/2001	12/31/2000	12/31/1999	12/31/1998	12/31/1997
Earnings Per Share	1.65	2.43	2.43	2.32	3.10	2.04	2.07	0.04
Cash Flow Per Share	3.94	3.82	3.85	4.70	3.09	4.17	3.74	2.50
Tang Book Value Per Share	24.90	25.52	25.37	25.26	24.64	24.67	24.86	23.22
Dividends Per Share	2.520	2.520	2.490	2.450	2.350	2.810	1.550	1.900
Dividend Payout %	152.73	103.70	102.47	105.60	75.81	137.75	74.88	4,750.00
Income Statement								
Property Income	575,860	567,403	549,474	562,640	549,681	532,035	479,509	237,345
Non-Property Income	13,131	18,843	20,140	21,708	26,472	19,449	14,190	12,456
Total Revenue	588,991	586,246	569,614	584,348	576,153	551,484	493,699	249,801
Depn & Amortn	140,226	126,405	115,951	97,940	98,114	91,606	80,496	50,334
Interest Expense	109,649	116,311	107,823	112,003	105,394	102,960	88,043	39,078
Net Income	102,453	143,053	139,722	131,659	185,338	119,739	116,578	1,405
Average Shares	68,743	65,990	65,427	64,775	73,070	67,133	63,893	44,156
Balance Sheet								
Total Assets	3,850,165	3,749,570	3,796,429	3,746,770	3,676,977	3,629,601	3,452,194	2,593,444
Long-Term Obligations	1,702,300	1,628,584	1,752,372	1,700,150	1,628,512	1,490,175	1,420,931	972,650
Total Liabilities	1,877,096	1,779,983	1,912,199	1,867,938	1,774,239	1,648,844	1,526,974	1,056,759
Stockholders' Equity	1,545,111	1,541,488	1,454,194	1,432,588	1,453,290	1,441,882	1,423,907	1,157,440
Shares Outstanding	61,038	59,420	57,318	56,712	58,980	58,446	57,266	49,856
Statistical Record								
Return on Assets %	2.69	3.79	3.70	3.55	5.06	3.38	3.86	0.08
Return on Equity %	6.62	9.55	9.68	9.12	12.77	8.36	9.03	0.15
Net Margin %	17.39	24.40	24.53	22.53	32.17	21.71	23.61	0.56
Price Range	47.00-35.20	41.75-27.35	35.59-27.91	31.92-25.58	28.75-22.88	33.06-23.25	41.00-26.25	42.69-28.75
P/E Ratio	28.48-21.33	17.18-11.26	14.65-11.49	13.76-11.03	9.27-7.38	16.21-11.40	19.81-12.68	N.M.
Average Yield %	5.99	7.28	7.82	8.63	8.95	9.87	4.55	5.45

Address: 11 Commerce Drive, Cranford, NJ 07016-3599 Telephone: (908) 272 8000 Fax: (908) 272 6755	Web Site: www.mack-cali.com Officers: William L. Mack - Chmn. Mitchell E. Hersh - C.E.O.	Auditors: PricewaterhouseCoopers LLP

MANDALAY RESORT GROUP

Exchange	Symbol	Price	52Wk Range	Yield	P/E
NYS	MBG	$70.49 (3/31/2005)	70.90-50.97	1.53	20.26

*7 Year Price Score 186.36 ***NYSE Composite Index=100** ***12 Month Price Score 98.61**

Interim Earnings (Per Share)

Qtr.	Apr	Jul	Oct	Jan
2001-02	0.61	0.40	0.32	(0.64)
2002-03	0.68	0.41	0.47	0.09
2003-04	0.69	0.67	0.63	0.33
2004-05	1.30	0.86	0.99	...

Interim Dividends (Per Share)

Amt	Decl	Ex	Rec	Pay
0.25Q	8/27/2003	10/10/2003	10/15/2003	11/1/2003
0.27Q	12/2/2003	1/13/2004	1/15/2004	2/2/2004
0.27Q	3/3/2004	4/14/2004	4/16/2004	5/3/2004
0.27Q	6/2/2004	7/13/2004	7/15/2004	8/2/2004
		Indicated Div: $1.08		

Valuation Analysis

Forecast P/E	17.85	No of Institutions	
	(4/7/2005)	228	
Market Cap	$4.8 Billion	Shares	
Book Value	1.3 Billion	53,887,424	
Price/Book	3.80	% Held	
Price/Sales	1.72	79.80	

Business Summary: Sporting & Recreational (MIC: 13.5 SIC: 999 NAIC: 13210)

Mandalay Resort Group, as of Dec 31 2003, owned and operated eleven properties in Nevada: Mandalay Bay, Luxor, Excalibur, Circus Circus, and Slots-A-Fun in Las Vegas; Circus Circus-Reno; Colorado Belle and Edgewater in Laughlin; Gold Strike and Nevada Landing in Jean and Railroad Pass in Henderson. Co. also owns and operates Gold Strike in Tunica County, MS. Co. owns 50% interests in Silver Legacy in Reno, Monte Carlo in Las Vegas, and Grand Victoria in Elgin, IL. Co. owns a 53.5% interest in and operates MotorCity in Detroit, MI. Co. caters to high volume business by providing moderately-priced rooms, food and alternative entertainment with gaming activity for family-oriented vacationers.

Recent Developments: For the quarter ended Oct 31 2004, net income increased 65.1% to $67,107 thousand from net income of $40,642 thousand in the year-earlier quarter. Revenues were $720,323 thousand, up 15.1% from $625,620 thousand the year before. Operating income was $167,034 thousand versus an income of $124,009 thousand in the prior-year quarter, an increase of 34.7%. Total indirect expense was $186,530 thousand versus $171,845 thousand in the prior-year quarter, an increase of 8.5%.

Prospects: Co.'s pending acquisition of MGM MIRAGE is progressing on track as the Federal Trade Commission (FTC) completed its review of the transaction and voted unanimously to grant clearance for the deal proceed. The transaction is still subject to customary closing conditions and receipt of state regulatory approvals. Co. anticipates the transaction will be completed in the first quarter of 2005. Co.'s acquisition of MGM Mirage will add 11 casino resorts located in Nevada, Mississippi and Michigan to its existing portfolio, as well as investments in three other casino resorts in Nevada, New Jersey and the UK.

Financial Data (US$ in Thousands)	9 Mos	6 Mos	3 Mos	01/31/2004	01/31/2003	01/31/2002	01/31/2001	01/31/2000
Earnings Per Share	3.48	3.11	2.92	2.31	1.65	0.71	1.50	0.46
Cash Flow Per Share	7.58	7.60	6.76	6.72	5.18	4.92	5.55	2.26
Tang Book Value Per Share	16.56	15.48	14.78	13.43	11.66	12.76	8.98	8.81
Dividends Per Share	0.810	1.060	1.020	0.750	...	...	...	...
Dividend Payout %	23.30	34.05	34.90	32.47	...	...	...	...
Income Statement								
Total Revenue	2,163,531	1,443,208	729,368	2,491,099	2,354,118	2,461,799	2,524,224	2,050,898
EBITDA	...	...	...	609,174	554,615	538,810	646,159	452,278
Depn & Amortn	142,164	96,163	50,024	175,531	144,995	216,001	217,984	172,407
Income Before Taxes	...	...	...	232,318	195,334	93,006	194,392	103,116
Income Taxes	116,859	81,130	47,210	82,471	77,869	39,962	74,692	38,959
Net Income	212,649	145,542	87,328	149,847	115,603	53,044	119,700	42,163
Average Shares	68,075	68,126	66,974	64,881	70,158	74,459	79,701	91,896
Balance Sheet								
Current Assets	365,696	365,519	350,805	349,867	311,404	266,987	286,630	281,539
Total Assets	4,751,318	4,765,598	4,782,621	4,782,496	4,354,664	4,037,034	4,248,266	4,329,476
Current Liabilities	326,977	346,435	333,749	330,951	317,377	309,241	296,675	244,619
Long-Term Obligations	2,725,036	2,792,060	2,868,800	3,001,975	2,763,593	2,482,087	2,623,597	2,691,292
Total Liabilities	3,449,392	3,535,449	3,601,770	3,709,003	3,453,148	3,100,063	3,198,001	3,166,792
Stockholders' Equity	1,254,105	1,180,809	1,132,501	1,030,270	882,929	940,609	1,068,940	1,187,780
Shares Outstanding	67,531	67,506	67,463	65,411	62,572	68,355	76,276	89,869
Statistical Record								
Return on Assets %	4.96	4.43	4.19	3.28	2.76	1.28	2.78	1.03
Return on Equity %	20.74	20.16	19.65	15.66	12.68	5.28	10.58	3.60
EBITDA Margin %	...	...	...	24.45	23.56	21.89	25.60	22.05
Net Margin %	9.83	10.08	11.97	6.02	4.91	2.15	4.74	2.06
Asset Turnover	0.58	0.57	0.56	0.55	0.56	0.59	0.59	0.50
Current Ratio	1.12	1.06	1.05	1.06	0.98	0.86	0.97	1.15
Debt to Equity	2.17	2.36	2.53	2.91	3.13	2.64	2.45	2.27
Price Range	70.23-39.25	70.23-34.76	61.60-25.95	48.61-23.71	36.30-23.99	27.65-14.54	28.17-12.94	25.94-12.94
P/E Ratio	20.18-11.28	22.58-11.18	21.10-8.89	21.04-10.26	22.00-14.54	38.94-20.48	18.78-8.63	56.39-28.13
Average Yield %	1.41	2.12	2.43	2.14	...	...	...	...

Address: 3950 Las Vegas Boulevard South, Las Vegas, NV 89119 Telephone: (702) 632-6700 Fax: (702) 634-3450	Web Site: www.mandalayresortgroup.com Officers: Michael S. Ensign - Chmn., C.E.O., C.O.O. William A. Richardson - Vice-Chmn.	Auditors: Deloitte & Touche LLP Investor Contact: 702-632-6708

MANITOWOC CO., INC.

Exchange	Symbol	Price	52Wk Range	Yield	P/E
NYS	MTW	$40.39 (3/31/2005)	42.25-29.45	0.69	28.24

*7 Year Price Score 102.89 ***NYSE Composite Index=100** ***12 Month Price Score 106.38**

TRADING VOLUME (thousand shares)

Interim Earnings (Per Share)

Qtr.	Mar	Jun	Sep	Dec
2001	0.40	0.60	0.51	0.35
2002	0.27	0.81	0.57	(0.98)
2003	0.02	0.05	0.27	(0.21)
2004	0.21	0.56	0.47	0.19

Interim Dividends (Per Share)

Amt	Decl	Ex	Rec	Pay
0.28Q	10/14/2002	11/27/2002	12/2/2002	12/9/2002
0.28Q	10/29/2003	11/26/2003	12/1/2003	12/10/2003
0.28Q	10/26/2004	11/29/2004	12/1/2004	12/10/2004
0.07Q	2/25/2005	3/3/2005	3/7/2005	3/14/2005
		Indicated Div: $0.28		

Valuation Analysis

Forecast P/E	17.67	No of Institutions
	(4/12/2005)	166
Market Cap	$1.2 Billion	Shares
Book Value	518.9 Million	23,772,276
Price/Book	2.33	% Held
Price/Sales	0.62	79.30

Business Summary: Industrial Machinery and Equipment (MIC: 11.5 SIC: 531 NAIC: 33120)

Manitowoc Company is a diversified industrial manufacturer of cranes, foodservice equipment and mid-size commercial, research and military ships. The crane business designs, manufactures and markets lattice-boom crawler cranes, mobile telescopic cranes, tower cranes, and boom trucks. The foodservice business designs, manufactures and markets full product lines of ice making machines, walk-in and reach-in refrigerator/freezers, fountain beverage delivery systems and other foodservice refrigeration products. The marine service business provides new construction, ship repair and maintenance services for freshwater and saltwater vessels from four shipyards on the U.S. Great Lakes.

Recent Developments: For the year ended Dec 31 2004, net income increased 1002.8% to $39,138 thousand from net income of $3,549 thousand a year earlier. Revenues were $1,964,101 thousand, up 25.0% from $1,570,856 thousand the year before. Operating income was $107,897 thousand versus an income of $85,882 thousand in the prior year, an increase of 25.6%. Total direct expense was $1,582,131 thousand versus $1,238,122 thousand in the prior year, an increase of 27.8%. Total indirect expense was $274,073 thousand versus $259,749 thousand in the prior year, an increase of 5.5%.

Prospects: Co.'s Crane segment is experiencing improved sales, earnings and margins due to its globalization efforts, as well as its cost-reduction initiatives and price increases to offset rising steel prices. Worldwide demand remains strong for Co.'s tower cranes, mobile telescopic cranes, and boom trucks, and its crawler cranes are doing well outside of North America. Co. plans to build a new manufacturing facility in China to help meet growing crane demand in Asia. In its Foodservice segment, Co. expects cost-cutting and outsourcing efforts, along with price increases to help offset cost increases in 2005. For 2005, Co. expects earnings in the range of $2.00 to $2.20 per share.

Financial Data

(US$ in Thousands)	12/31/2004	12/31/2003	12/31/2002	12/31/2001	12/31/2000	12/31/1999	12/31/1998	12/31/1997
Earnings Per Share	1.43	0.13	(0.80)	1.86	2.40	2.55	1.97	1.39
Cash Flow Per Share	2.11	5.68	3.75	4.39	2.53	3.98	2.19	1.68
Dividends Per Share	0.280	0.280	0.280	0.300	0.300	0.300	0.300	0.298
Dividend Payout %	19.58	215.38	N.M.	16.13	12.50	11.76	15.25	21.40
Income Statement								
Total Revenue	1,964,101	1,593,186	1,406,577	1,116,580	873,272	805,491	694,822	545,864
EBITDA	159,984	127,897	149,821	150,526	128,681	133,509	105,763	75,759
Depn & Amortn	53,960	48,356	35,078	33,359	18,053	16,713	14,610	11,712
Income Before Taxes	49,129	22,606	62,780	79,689	96,120	106,006	81,412	57,817
Income Taxes	9,335	4,069	22,601	30,817	35,852	39,222	30,032	21,394
Net Income	39,138	3,549	(20,502)	45,548	60,268	66,784	51,380	36,423
Average Shares	27,377	26,702	25,781	24,548	25,122	26,200	26,125	26,097
Balance Sheet								
Current Assets	845,961	646,089	647,164	331,090	223,507	190,998	190,877	145,516
Total Assets	1,928,136	1,602,581	1,577,123	1,080,812	642,530	530,240	481,014	396,368
Current Liabilities	652,680	545,224	460,398	296,161	239,490	189,308	198,112	170,812
Long-Term Obligations	512,236	567,084	623,547	446,522	137,668	79,223	79,834	66,359
Total Liabilities	1,409,207	1,304,157	1,282,008	817,017	408,761	298,064	308,462	267,750
Stockholders' Equity	518,929	298,424	295,115	263,795	233,769	232,176	172,552	128,618
Shares Outstanding	29,949	26,572	24,053	24,053	24,259	26,088	36,747	36,747
Statistical Record								
Return on Assets %	2.21	0.22	N.M.	5.29	10.25	13.21	11.71	10.20
Return on Equity %	9.55	1.20	N.M.	18.31	25.80	33.00	34.12	31.82
EBITDA Margin %	8.15	8.03	10.65	13.48	14.74	16.57	15.22	13.88
Net Margin %	1.99	0.22	N.M.	4.08	6.90	8.29	7.39	6.67
Asset Turnover	1.11	1.00	1.06	1.30	1.49	1.59	1.58	1.53
Current Ratio	1.30	1.18	1.41	1.12	0.93	1.01	0.96	0.85
Debt to Equity	0.99	1.90	2.11	1.69	0.59	0.34	0.46	0.52
Price Range	39.20-27.59	31.75-16.78	43.70-23.00	32.80-22.78	34.44-17.94	42.38-24.42	31.13-16.58	26.63-14.89
P/E Ratio	27.41-19.29	244.23-129.08	N/A	17.63-12.25	14.35-7.47	16.62-9.58	15.80-8.42	19.15-10.71
Average Yield %	0.85	1.27	0.85	1.08	1.11	0.92	1.22	1.47

Address: 500 South 16th St., Manitowoc, WI 54221-0066 **Telephone:** (920) 684-4410 **Fax:** (920) 683-8129	**Web Site:** www.manitowoc.com **Officers:** Terry D. Growcock - Chmn., C.E.O. Mary Ellen Bowers - Exec. V.P., Corp. Devel.	**Auditors:** PricewaterhouseCoopers LLP **Investor Contact:** 920-683-8122

MANOR CARE, INC. (NEW)

Exchange	Symbol	Price	52Wk Range	Yield	P/E
NYS	HCR	$36.36 (3/31/2005)	36.36-29.51	1.65	19.14

*7 Year Price Score 112.59 *NYSE Composite Index=100 *12 Month Price Score 97.20

Interim Earnings (Per Share)

Qtr.	Mar	Jun	Sep	Dec
2001	0.24	0.30	0.30	(0.17)
2002	0.33	0.38	0.38	0.24
2003	0.33	0.21	0.35	0.42
2004	0.46	0.45	0.45	0.55

Interim Dividends (Per Share)

Amt	Decl	Ex	Rec	Pay
0.14Q	4/23/2004	5/5/2004	5/7/2004	5/21/2004
0.14Q	7/23/2004	8/5/2004	8/9/2004	8/23/2004
0.14Q	10/22/2004	11/4/2004	11/8/2004	11/22/2004
0.15Q	1/28/2005	2/10/2005	2/14/2005	2/28/2005

Indicated Div: $0.60

Valuation Analysis

Forecast P/E	16.84	No of Institutions
	(4/7/2005)	230
Market Cap	$3.1 Billion	Shares
Book Value	984.2 Million	72,491,352
Price/Book	3.18	% Held
Price/Sales	0.97	84.11

Business Summary: Hospitals & Health Care (MIC: 9.3 SIC: 051 NAIC: 23110)

Manor Care provides a range of health care services, including skilled nursing care, assisted living, subacute medical and rehabilitation care, rehabilitation therapy, hospice care, home health care and management services for subacute care and rehabilitation therapy. The most significant portion of Co.'s business relates to long-term care, including skilled nursing care and assisted living. On Dec 31 2003, Co. operated 293 skilled nursing facilities and 70 assisted living facilities in 32 states with 62.0% of its facilities located in Florida, Illinois, Michigan, Ohio and Pennsylvania.

Recent Developments: For the year ended Dec 31 2004, net income increased 41.4% to $168,222 thousand from net income of $119,007 thousand a year earlier. Revenues were $3,208,867 thousand, up 5.9% from $3,029,441 thousand the year before. Operating income was $292,610 thousand versus an income of $219,531 thousand in the prior year, an increase of 33.3%. Total indirect expense was $2,916,257 thousand versus $2,809,910 thousand in the prior year, an increase of 3.8%.

Prospects: Co. is focused on managing its general and professional liability costs, which is helping to keep costs related to patient liability claims stable. Following Co.'s semiannual actuarial review in the fourth quarter, it was determined that these efforts would enable it to once again lower its accrual rate by approximately $1.0 million per quarter. Meanwhile, Co. believes that there is still more work to do in the tort reform arena in support of its internal efforts. National tort reform remains a key issue in U.S. politics, and Co. stated that it will continue to support these efforts as well as initiatives in states key to its operations.

Financial Data

(US$ in Thousands)	12/31/2004	12/31/2003	12/31/2002	12/31/2001	12/31/2000	12/31/1999	12/31/1998	12/31/1997
Earnings Per Share	1.90	1.31	1.31	0.66	0.38	(0.41)	(0.03)	1.51
Cash Flow Per Share	3.79	3.35	2.89	2.78	2.05	1.27	1.41	1.63
Tang Book Value Per Share	10.26	9.86	9.68	9.28	8.86	8.71	10.85	6.78
Dividends Per Share	0.560	0.250	...	...	...	...	...	...
Dividend Payout %	29.47	19.08	...	...	...	...	...	...
Income Statement								
Total Revenue	3,208,867	3,029,441	2,905,448	2,694,056	2,380,578	2,135,345	2,209,087	891,963
EBITDA	425,120	...	375,230	308,951	243,610	67,596	141,351	154,233
Depn & Amortn	127,821	128,810	124,895	128,159	121,208	115,910	119,329	37,709
Income Before Taxes	254,879	...	212,684	129,992	61,669	(102,396)	(24,565)	101,185
Income Taxes	86,657	71,405	80,820	61,502	21,489	(47,238)	21,597	31,064
Net Income	168,222	119,007	130,550	68,490	39,055	(43,658)	(2,933)	70,121
Average Shares	88,725	91,119	99,328	103,685	103,126	107,627	108,958	46,515
Balance Sheet								
Current Assets	540,367	585,399	510,817	589,630	504,879	431,151	417,756	170,751
Total Assets	2,340,698	2,396,711	2,306,932	2,424,071	2,358,468	2,280,866	2,715,140	936,351
Current Liabilities	402,254	387,502	641,864	391,359	472,545	408,649	503,711	121,324
Long-Term Obligations	555,275	659,181	373,112	715,830	644,054	687,502	693,180	292,951
Total Liabilities	1,356,539	1,421,606	1,290,885	1,377,533	1,345,739	1,300,829	1,515,972	502,345
Stockholders' Equity	984,159	975,105	1,016,047	1,046,538	1,012,729	980,037	1,199,168	434,006
Shares Outstanding	86,000	89,000	95,000	102,300	102,667	102,365	103,100	44,223
Statistical Record								
Return on Assets %	7.08	5.06	5.52	2.86	1.68	N.M.	N.M.	8.06
Return on Equity %	17.13	11.95	12.66	6.65	3.91	N.M.	N.M.	16.96
EBITDA Margin %	13.25	...	12.91	11.47	10.23	3.17	6.40	17.29
Net Margin %	5.24	3.93	4.49	2.54	1.64	N.M.	N.M.	7.86
Asset Turnover	1.35	1.29	1.23	1.13	1.02	0.85	1.21	1.03
Current Ratio	1.34	1.51	0.80	1.51	1.07	1.06	0.83	1.41
Debt to Equity	0.56	0.68	0.37	0.68	0.64	0.70	0.58	0.67
Price Range	37.02-29.51	35.74-17.65	26.72-18.06	33.90-18.06	20.75-6.69	33.13-14.13	47.31-23.94	41.94-25.63
P/E Ratio	19.48-15.53	27.28-13.47	20.40-13.79	51.36-27.37	54.61-17.60	N.A.	N.A..	27.77-16.97
Average Yield %	1.70	0.98	...	...	...	...	...	...

Address: 333 N. Summit Street, Toledo, OH 43604-2617	Web Site: www.hcr-manorcare.com	Auditors: Ernst & Young LLP
Telephone: (419) 252-5500	Officers: Paul A. Ormond - Chmn., Pres., C.E.O. M. Keith Weikel - Sr. Exec. V.P., C.O.O.	
Fax: (419) 247-1364		

MANPOWER INC. (WI)

Exchange	Symbol	Price	52Wk Range	Yield	P/E
NYS	MAN	$43.52 (3/31/2005)	50.77-38.71	0.92	16.80

*7 Year Price Score 112.57 *NYSE Composite Index=100 *12 Month Price Score 89.38

TRADING VOLUME (thousand shares)

Interim Earnings (Per Share)

Qtr.	Mar	Jun	Sep	Dec
2001	0.35	0.45	0.48	0.34
2002	0.09	0.33	0.52	0.52
2003	0.19	0.37	0.56	0.62
2004	0.45	0.56	0.89	0.68

Interim Dividends (Per Share)

Amt	Decl	Ex	Rec	Pay
0.10S	4/29/2003	5/30/2003	6/3/2003	6/16/2003
0.10S	10/29/2003	11/28/2003	12/2/2003	12/15/2003
0.10S	4/27/2004	6/1/2004	6/3/2004	6/14/2004
0.20S	11/1/2004	12/2/2004	12/6/2004	12/15/2004

Indicated Div: $0.40

Valuation Analysis

Forecast P/E	15.42	No of Institutions
	(4/7/2005)	261
Market Cap	$3.9 Billion	Shares
Book Value	2.2 Billion	79,559,904
Price/Book	1.81	% Held
Price/Sales	0.26	88.50

Business Summary: Personal Services (MIC: 5.15 SIC: 299 NAIC: 61330)

Manpower engages in global staffing with over 4,000 offices in 66 countries. Co. provides human resource services, including: permanent, temporary and contract employee recruitment; employee assessment; training; internal audit, accounting, technology and tax services; and organizational consulting services under the Manpower and Supplay names. Co.'s Brooks Street Bureau is a U.K. provider of secretarial, office, and light industrial recruitment. Elan is an information technology and technical recruiter. Jefferson Wells International is a provider of internal audit, accounting, technology and tax services. The Empower Group provides organizational performance consulting services worldwide.

Recent Developments: For the year ended Dec 31 2004, net income increased 78.4% to $245,700 thousand from net income of $137,700 thousand a year earlier. Revenues were $14,930,000 thousand, up 22.5% from $12,184,500 thousand the year before. Operating income was $395,800 thousand versus an income of $257,900 thousand in the prior year, an increase of 53.5%. Total direct expense was $12,141,900 thousand versus $10,047,700 thousand in the prior year, an increase of 20.8%. Total indirect expense was $2,392,300 thousand versus $1,878,900 thousand in the prior year, an increase of 27.3%.

Prospects: Co. is encouraged with its recent operating performance, supported by considerable contributions from its European operations and Jefferson Wells, its financial professional services unit. Co. is also pleased with the performance of Right Management Consultants, its career transition and organizational consulting unit, which enhanced its ability to compete effectively in the industry. Based on Co.'s unique service mix, designed to meet customer needs throughout the employment and business cycle, it should be well-positioned to move forward in 2005. Looking ahead to the first quarter of 2005, Co. anticipates earnings per diluted share to range from $0.34 to $0.37.

Financial Data

(US$ in Thousands)	12/31/2004	12/31/2003	12/31/2002	12/31/2001	12/31/2000	12/31/1999	12/31/1998	12/31/1997
Earnings Per Share	2.59	1.74	1.46	1.62	2.22	1.91	0.93	1.97
Cash Flow Per Share	2.10	2.88	2.98	1.79	2.07	(0.01)	3.31	0.31
Tang Book Value Per Share	9.71	9.36	5.89	4.38	6.50	7.39	8.48	7.69
Dividends Per Share	0.300	0.200	0.200	0.200	0.200	0.200	0.190	0.170
Dividend Payout %	11.58	11.49	13.70	12.35	9.01	10.47	20.43	8.63
Income Statement								
Total Revenue	14,930,000	12,184,500	10,610,900	10,483,800	10,842,800	9,770,100	8,814,272	7,258,504
EBITDA	499,800	327,500	294,100	306,900	359,700	278,800	180,096	293,884
Depn & Amortn	94,300	72,000	72,700	80,200	66,800	63,700	55,550	41,623
Income Before Taxes	369,500	222,100	188,000	197,900	265,200	205,800	113,770	249,208
Income Taxes	123,800	84,400	74,800	73,400	94,000	55,800	38,106	85,328
Net Income	245,700	137,700	113,200	124,500	171,200	150,000	75,664	163,880
Average Shares	96,800	79,300	77,700	77,000	77,100	78,700	80,101	83,380
Balance Sheet								
Current Assets	4,017,500	3,237,100	2,653,300	2,314,400	2,396,700	2,257,300	1,961,562	1,686,901
Total Assets	5,843,100	4,384,900	3,701,700	3,238,600	3,041,600	2,718,700	2,381,100	2,047,030
Current Liabilities	2,601,900	1,877,900	1,562,300	1,290,600	1,522,200	1,418,100	1,311,056	1,004,677
Long-Term Obligations	676,100	829,600	799,000	811,100	491,600	357,500	154,594	189,785
Total Liabilities	3,669,100	3,074,600	2,701,800	2,424,300	2,301,200	2,068,100	1,712,162	1,429,467
Stockholders' Equity	2,174,000	1,310,300	999,900	814,300	740,400	650,600	668,938	617,563
Shares Outstanding	90,290	78,659	77,098	76,128	75,772	75,986	78,930	80,346
Statistical Record								
Return on Assets %	4.79	3.41	3.26	3.96	5.93	5.88	3.42	8.63
Return on Equity %	14.06	11.92	12.48	16.02	24.55	22.74	11.76	26.90
EBITDA Margin %	3.35	2.69	2.77	2.93	3.32	2.85	2.04	4.05
Net Margin %	1.65	1.13	1.07	1.19	1.58	1.54	0.86	2.26
Asset Turnover	2.91	3.01	3.06	3.34	3.75	3.83	3.98	3.82
Current Ratio	1.54	1.72	1.70	1.79	1.57	1.59	1.50	1.68
Debt to Equity	0.31	0.63	0.80	1.00	0.66	0.55	0.23	0.31
Price Range	50.77-38.71	47.54-27.50	42.97-25.00	37.56-24.35	39.81-26.75	38.69-21.00	44.88-19.38	50.38-30.00
P/E Ratio	19.60-14.95	27.32-15.80	29.43-17.12	23.19-15.03	17.93-12.05	20.26-10.99	48.25-20.83	25.57-15.23
Average Yield %	0.65	0.54	0.56	0.64	0.58	0.75	0.60	0.43

Address: 5301 N. Ironwood Road, Milwaukee, WI 53217 **Telephone:** (414) 961 1000 **Fax:** (414) 332 0796	**Web Site:** www.manpower.com **Officers:** Jeffery A. Joerres - Chmn., Pres., C.E.O. Michael J. Van Handel - Exec. V.P., C.F.O., Sec.	**Auditors:** PricewaterhouseCoopers LLP

MARATHON OIL CORP.

Exchange	Symbol	Price	52Wk Range	Yield	P/E
NYS	MRO	$46.92 (3/31/2005)	48.76-32.22	2.39	12.58

*7 Year Price Score 111.39 *NYSE Composite Index=100 *12 Month Price Score 109.81

Interim Earnings (Per Share)

Qtr.	Mar	Jun	Sep	Dec
2001	1.62	1.88	0.62	(2.90)
2002	0.22	0.54	0.28	0.62
2003	0.99	0.80	0.90	1.57
2004	0.83	1.02	0.64	1.25

Interim Dividends (Per Share)

Amt	Decl	Ex	Rec	Pay
0.25Q	4/28/2004	5/17/2004	5/19/2004	6/10/2004
0.25Q	7/28/2004	8/16/2004	8/18/2004	9/10/2004
0.28Q	10/27/2004	11/15/2004	11/17/2004	12/10/2004
0.28Q	1/24/2005	2/14/2005	2/16/2005	3/10/2005

Indicated Div: $1.12

Valuation Analysis

Forecast P/E	N/A	No of Institutions	
Market Cap	$16.3 Billion	Shares	279,949,952
Book Value	8.1 Billion	% Held	80.67
Price/Book	2.01		
Price/Sales	0.33		

Business Summary: Oil and Gas (MIC: 14.2 SIC: 382 NAIC: 13112)

Marathon Oil is engaged in worldwide exploration and production of crude oil and natural gas; domestic refining, marketing and transportation of crude oil and petroleum products primarily through its 62.0%-owned subsidiary, Marathon Ashland Petroleum LLC (MAP); and other energy related businesses. As of Dec 31 2003, Co. was conducting exploration and development activities in nine countries, including Angola, Canada, Equatorial Guinea, Gabon, Ireland, Norway, Russia, the United Kingdom and the United States. Net estimated developed and undeveloped proved reserves as of 12/31/03 were: liquid hydrocarbons, 578.0 million barrels; natural gas, 2.78 trillion cubic feet.

Recent Developments: For the year ended Dec 31 2004, income from continuing operations increased 24.2% to $1,257,000 thousand from income of $1,012,000 thousand a year earlier. Net income decreased 4.5% to $1,261,000 thousand from net income of $1,321,000 thousand a year earlier. Revenues were $49,907,000 thousand, up 21.0% from $41,234,000 thousand the year before. Operating income was $2,670,000 thousand versus an income of $2,084,000 thousand in the prior year, an increase of 28.1%. Total direct expense was $30,740,000 thousand versus $24,918,000 thousandthe prior year, an increase of 23.4%. Total indirect expense was $16,497,000 thousand versus $14,232,000 thousand the prior year, an increase of 15.9%.

Prospects: Despite the adverse effects of the hurricanes in the Gulf of Mexico in 2004 and delays associated with Co.'s liquids expansion projects in Equatorial Guinea, Co.'s three business segments saw improved profitability in 2004 over the year before. Co. attributes this improvement to the continued success of its exploration program, with saw six discoveries during 2004 in Norway, Angola, the Gulf of Mexico and Equatorial Guinea. Meanwhile, Co. estimates its 2005 production will average approximately 325,000 to 350,000 barrels of oil equivalent per day (boepd), excluding the impact of any acquisitions, dispositions or potential reentry into Libya.

Financial Data

(US$ in Thousands)	12/31/2004	12/31/2003	12/31/2002	12/31/2001	12/31/2000	12/31/1999	12/31/1998	12/31/1997
Earnings Per Share	3.73	4.26	1.66	1.22	1.39	2.11	1.05	1.58
Cash Flow Per Share	11.05	8.90	7.76	11.76	10.11	...	4.88	4.33
Tang Book Value Per Share	22.36	18.37	15.13	15.97	15.72	15.50	13.95	12.52
Dividends Per Share	1.030	0.960	0.920	0.920	...	...	0.840	0.760
Dividend Payout %	27.61	22.54	55.42	75.41	...	...	80.00	48.10
Income Statement								
Total Revenue	49,907,000	41,234,000	31,720,000	33,066,000	33,859,000	24,327,000	22,075,000	15,754,000
EBITDA	3,395,000	2,970,000	2,402,000	3,480,000	2,393,000	2,203,000	1,634,000	1,590,000
Depn & Amortn	1,217,000	1,175,000	1,201,000	1,236,000	1,245,000	950,000	941,000	664,000
Income Before Taxes	1,984,000	1,596,000	925,000	2,077,000	914,000	978,000	452,000	672,000
Income Taxes	727,000	584,000	389,000	759,000	482,000	324,000	142,000	216,000
Net Income	1,261,000	1,321,000	516,000	157,000	432,000	654,000	310,000	456,000
Average Shares	338,253	310,326	309,951	309,510	311,761	309,696	293,000	291,000
Balance Sheet								
Current Assets	8,867,000	6,040,000	4,479,000	4,411,000	4,985,000	4,102,000	2,976,000	2,018,000
Total Assets	23,423,000	19,482,000	17,812,000	16,129,000	15,232,000	15,705,000	14,544,000	10,565,000
Current Liabilities	5,253,000	4,207,000	3,659,000	3,468,000	4,012,000	3,149,000	2,610,000	2,262,000
Long-Term Obligations	4,057,000	4,085,000	4,410,000	3,432,000	1,937,000	3,320,000	3,456,000	2,476,000
Total Liabilities	12,622,000	11,396,000	12,730,000	11,189,000	10,387,000	10,905,000	10,232,000	6,947,000
Stockholders' Equity	8,111,000	6,075,000	5,082,000	4,940,000	4,845,000	4,800,000	4,312,000	3,618,000
Shares Outstanding	346,697	310,421	309,873	309,395	308,266	309,696	309,000	289,000
Statistical Record								
Return on Assets %	5.86	7.08	3.04	1.00	2.79	...	2.47	4.40
Return on Equity %	17.73	23.68	10.30	3.21	8.93	...	7.82	13.11
EBITDA Margin %	6.80	7.20	7.57	10.52	7.07	9.06	7.40	10.09
Net Margin %	2.53	3.20	1.63	0.47	1.28	2.69	1.40	2.89
Asset Turnover	2.32	2.21	1.87	2.11	2.18	...	1.76	1.52
Current Ratio	1.69	1.44	1.22	1.27	1.24	1.30	1.14	0.89
Debt to Equity	0.50	0.67	0.87	0.69	0.40	0.69	0.80	0.68
Price Range	42.13-30.78	33.37-20.20	30.02-19.00	33.44-25.28	29.81-21.25	33.25-20.00	38.56-26.00	38.75-23.88
P/E Ratio	11.29-8.25	7.83-4.74	18.08-11.45	27.41-20.72	21.45-15.29	15.76-9.48	36.73-24.76	24.53-15.11
Average Yield %	2.87	3.68	3.64	3.17	...	...	2.52	2.47

Address: 5555 San Felipe Road, Houston, TX 77056-2723 **Telephone:** (713) 629-6600	**Web Site:** www.marathon.com **Officers:** Thomas J. Usher - Chmn. Clarence P. Cazalot Jr. - Pres., C.E.O.	**Auditors:** PricewaterhouseCoopers **Investor Contact:** 713-296-4114

MARKEL CORP (HOLDING CO)

Exchange	Symbol	Price	52Wk Range	Yield	P/E
NYS	MKL	$345.21 (3/31/2005)	367.91-269.20	N/A	21.04

*7 Year Price Score 128.78 *NYSE Composite Index=100   *12 Month Price Score 105.31

Interim Earnings (Per Share)

Qtr.	Mar	Jun	Sep	Dec
2001	1.04	0.09	(10.58)	(4.88)
2002	1.73	2.36	0.88	2.68
2003	3.70	5.97	(1.68)	4.53
2004	4.29	5.99	1.40	4.73

Interim Dividends (Per Share)

No Dividends Paid

Valuation Analysis

Forecast P/E	14.21	No of Institutions
	(4/7/2005)	151
Market Cap	$3.4 Billion	Shares
Book Value	1.7 Billion	7,088,905
Price/Book	2.05	% Held
Price/Sales	1.50	72.04

Business Summary: Insurance (MIC: 8.2 SIC: 331 NAIC: 24126)

Markel sells specialty insurance products and programs to a variety of niche markets. Co. operates in three segments. The Excess and Surplus Lines segment writes property and casualty insurance for nonstandard and hard-to-place risks, including catastrophe-exposed property, professional liability, product liability, general liability, commercial umbrella and other coverages. The Specialty Admitted segment writes risks that are unique and hard-to-place in the standard market but remain with an admitted insurance company for marketing and regulatory reasons. The London Insurance Market segment writes specialty property, casualty, marine and aviation insurance on a direct and reinsurance basis.

Recent Developments: For the year ended Dec 31 2004, net income increased 34.0% to $165,412 thousand from net income of $123,477 thousand a year earlier. Revenues were $2,262,058 thousand, up 8.1% from $2,091,904 thousand the year before. Net premiums earned were $2,053,887 thousand versus $1,864,251 thousand in the prior year, an increase of 10.2%. Net investment income rose 11.7% to $204,032 thousand from $182,608 thousand a year ago.

Prospects: Co.'s results are benefiting from strong underwriting profits on its core business and exceptional investment returns, demonstrating its continuing commitment and ability to grow book value per share. Gross written premiums have declined primarily due to increasing competition across many product lines and Co.'s re-underwriting of various books of business. While Co. anticipates further pricing pressures in 2005, it will focus on new product development, client relations, and underwriting profitability. Separately, Co. completed the sale of Corifrance, its reinsurance subsidiary, on Jan 11 2005.

Financial Data
(US$ in Thousands)

	12/31/2004	12/31/2003	12/31/2002	12/31/2001	12/31/2000	12/31/1999	12/31/1998	12/31/1997
Earnings Per Share	16.41	12.52	7.65	(14.73)	(3.99)	7.20	10.17	8.92
Cash Flow Per Share	69.94	64.16	51.64	19.27	12.86	0.10	7.25	12.52
Tang Book Value Per Share	133.72	104.09	81.13	72.61	47.66	52.07	70.63	58.36
Income Statement								
Premium Income	2,053,887	1,864,251	1,549,016	1,206,684	938,543	437,196	333,267	332,878
Total Revenue	2,262,058	2,091,904	1,770,195	1,397,412	1,094,483	524,321	426,001	419,047
Benefits & Claims	1,308,343	1,269,522	1,114,610	1,049,421	731,531	283,630	203,336	210,061
Income Before Taxes	224,045	181,584	117,693	(182,198)	(51,806)	53,440	75,385	66,351
Income Taxes	58,633	58,107	42,369	(56,481)	(24,214)	12,826	18,092	15,924
Net Income	165,412	123,477	75,324	(125,717)	(27,592)	40,614	57,293	50,427
Average Shares	10,190	9,861	9,852	8,534	6,920	5,638	5,636	5,652
Balance Sheet								
Total Assets	9,397,586	8,532,233	7,408,560	6,440,628	5,473,153	2,455,305	1,921,264	1,870,100
Total Liabilities	7,741,083	7,149,954	6,249,449	5,355,520	4,720,781	2,071,886	1,495,963	1,513,296
Stockholders' Equity	1,656,503	1,382,279	1,159,111	1,085,108	752,372	383,419	425,301	356,804
Shares Outstanding	9,847	9,846	9,832	9,819	7,330	5,590	5,522	5,474
Statistical Record								
Return on Assets %	1.84	1.55	1.09	N.M.	N.M.	1.86	3.02	2.90
Return on Equity %	10.86	9.72	6.71	N.M.	N.M.	10.04	14.65	16.13
Loss Ratio %	63.70	68.10	71.96	86.97	77.94	64.87	61.01	63.10
Net Margin %	7.31	5.90	4.26	(9.00)	(2.52)	7.75	13.45	12.03
Price Range	364.00-253.51	279.00-202.40	221.00-171.50	210.15-160.88	181.00-113.50	192.00-145.00	185.00-132.75	161.00-89.00
P/E Ratio	22.18-15.45	22.28-16.17	28.89-22.42	N.A.	N.A.	26.67-20.14	18.19-13.05	18.05-9.98

Address: 4521 Highwoods Parkway, Glen Allen, VA 23060-6148
Telephone: (804) 747-0136
Fax: (804) 965-1600

Web Site: www.markelcorp.com
Officers: Alan I. Kirshner - Chmn., C.E.O. Anthony F. Markel - Pres., C.O.O.

Auditors: KPMG LLP
Investor Contact: 800-446-6671
Transfer Agents: Wachovia Bank, N.A.

MARRIOTT INTERNATIONAL, INC. (NEW)

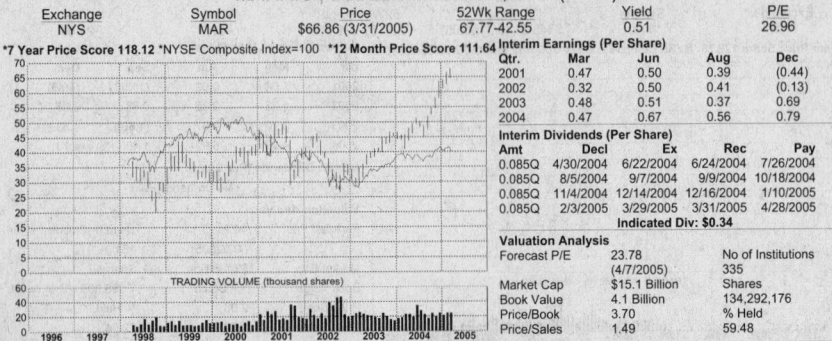

Exchange	Symbol	Price	52Wk Range	Yield	P/E
NYS	MAR	$66.86 (3/31/2005)	67.77-42.55	0.51	26.96

*7 Year Price Score 118.12 *NYSE Composite Index=100 ***12 Month Price Score 111.64**

Interim Earnings (Per Share)

Qtr.	Mar	Jun	Aug	Dec
2001	0.47	0.50	0.39	(0.44)
2002	0.32	0.50	0.41	(0.13)
2003	0.48	0.51	0.37	0.69
2004	0.47	0.67	0.56	0.79

Interim Dividends (Per Share)

Amt	Decl	Ex	Rec	Pay
0.085Q	4/30/2004	6/22/2004	6/24/2004	7/26/2004
0.085Q	8/5/2004	9/7/2004	9/9/2004	10/18/2004
0.085Q	11/4/2004	12/14/2004	12/16/2004	1/10/2005
0.085Q	2/3/2005	3/29/2005	3/31/2005	4/28/2005

Indicated Div: $0.34

Valuation Analysis

Forecast P/E	23.78	No of Institutions
	(4/7/2005)	335
Market Cap	$15.1 Billion	Shares
Book Value	4.1 Billion	134,292,176
Price/Book	3.70	% Held
Price/Sales	1.49	59.48

Business Summary: Hospitality & Tourism (MIC: 5.1 SIC: 011 NAIC: 21110)

Marriott International operates and franchises hotels and lodging facilities with 2,718 hotels and timeshare resorts in the U.S. and 68 other countries as of Jan 2 2004. Co. operates and franchises full-service hotels under the Marriott, Marriott Conference Centers, JW Marriott, The Ritz-Carlton, Renaissance, Ramada International, and Bulgari brands; Timeshare under the Marriott Vacation Club International, Horizons, The Ritz-Carlton Club and Marriott Grand Residence Club names; select-service lodging under the Courtyard, Fairfield Inn and SpringHill Suites brands; and extended-stay lodging under the Residence Inn, TownePlace Suites, Marriot ExecuStay and Mariott Executive Apartments brands.

Recent Developments: For the year ended Jan 2 2004, income from continuing operations decreased 19.9% to $476 million from income of $594 million a year earlier. Net income decreased 15.8% to $502 million from net income of $596 million a year earlier. Revenues were $9,014 million, down 10.7% from $10,099 million the year before. Total direct expense was $8,637 million versus $9,622 million in the prior year, a decrease of 10.2%.

Prospects: An improving economic climate is increasing demand for hotels, driving room rates and property profitability higher. Accordingly, Co. believes its market share will continue to increase in 2005, as it plans to add 25,000 to 30,000 new rooms to its worldwide system. Further, Co. estimates North American revenue per available room (REVPAR) growth for 2005 of 7.0% to 9.0% with a 1.5% to 2.0% improvement in house profit margins. Under these assumptions, Co. expects total fee revenues to range from $990.0 million to $1.01 billion in 2005, an increase of 13.0% to 16.0%, and earnings per share to range between $2.73 and $2.83.

Financial Data
(US$ in Thousands)

	12/31/2004	01/02/2004	01/03/2003	12/28/2001	12/29/2000	12/31/1999	01/01/1999	01/02/1998
Earnings Per Share	2.48	2.05	1.10	0.92	1.89	1.51	1.46	1.19
Cash Flow Per Share	3.94	1.82	2.11	1.65	3.54	2.88	...	2.06
Tang Book Value Per Share	11.72	10.33	9.14	7.12	5.95	4.42	3.36	4.45
Dividends Per Share	0.330	0.295	0.275	0.255	0.235	0.215	0.195	...
Dividend Payout %	13.31	14.39	25.00	27.72	12.43	14.24	13.36	...
Income Statement								
Total Revenue	10,099,000	9,014,000	8,441,000	10,152,000	10,017,000	8,739,000	7,968,000	9,046,000
EBITDA	773,000	629,000	622,000	607,000	997,000	828,000	766,000	647,000
Depn & Amortn	166,000	160,000	187,000	222,000	195,000	162,000	140,000	126,000
Income Before Taxes	654,000	488,000	471,000	370,000	757,000	637,000	632,000	531,000
Income Taxes	100,000	(43,000)	32,000	134,000	278,000	237,000	242,000	207,000
Net Income	596,000	502,000	277,000	236,000	479,000	400,000	390,000	324,000
Average Shares	240,500	245,400	254,600	256,700	254,000	247,500	273,100	278,000
Balance Sheet								
Current Assets	1,946,000	1,235,000	1,744,000	2,130,000	1,415,000	1,600,000	1,333,000	1,367,000
Total Assets	8,668,000	8,177,000	8,296,000	9,107,000	8,237,000	7,324,000	6,233,000	5,557,000
Current Liabilities	2,356,000	1,770,000	2,207,000	1,802,000	1,917,000	1,743,000	1,412,000	1,639,000
Long-Term Obligations	836,000	1,391,000	1,553,000	2,815,000	2,016,000	1,676,000	1,267,000	422,000
Total Liabilities	4,587,000	4,339,000	4,723,000	5,629,000	4,970,000	4,416,000	3,663,000	2,971,000
Stockholders' Equity	4,081,000	3,838,000	3,573,000	3,478,000	3,267,000	2,908,000	2,570,000	2,586,000
Shares Outstanding	225,769	231,200	235,900	240,700	241,000	246,300	255,600	255,600
Statistical Record								
Return on Assets %	7.10	6.11	3.13	2.73	6.17	5.92	...	6.66
Return on Equity %	15.09	13.58	7.73	7.02	15.56	14.64	...	16.12
EBITDA Margin %	7.65	6.98	7.37	5.98	9.95	9.47	9.61	7.15
Net Margin %	5.90	5.57	3.28	2.32	4.78	4.58	4.89	3.58
Asset Turnover	1.20	1.10	0.95	1.17	1.29	1.29	...	1.86
Current Ratio	0.83	0.70	0.79	1.18	0.74	0.92	0.94	0.83
Debt to Equity	0.20	0.36	0.43	0.81	0.62	0.58	0.49	0.16
Price Range	63.55-40.79	46.77-28.85	46.34-26.63	49.68-28.95	42.69-26.63	43.94-29.50	37.19-19.88	...
P/E Ratio	25.63-16.45	22.81-14.07	42.13-24.05	54.00-31.47	22.59-14.09	29.10-19.54	25.47-13.61	...
Average Yield %	0.67	0.76	0.75	0.61	0.66	0.61	0.64	...

Address: 10400 Fernwood Road, Bethesda, MD 20817
Telephone: (301) 380-3000

Web Site: www.marriott.com
Officers: J. W. Marriott Jr. - Chmn., C.E.O. William J. Shaw - Pres., C.O.O.

Auditors: Ernst & Young LLP
Investor Contact: 301 380-6500

MARSH & MCLENNAN COS., INC.

Exchange	Symbol	Price	52Wk Range	Yield	P/E	Div Acheiver
NYS	MMC	$30.42 (3/31/2005)	47.00-24.10	2.24	92.18	43 Years

7 Year Price Score 74.05 ***NYSE Composite Index=100** **12 Month Price Score 77.42**

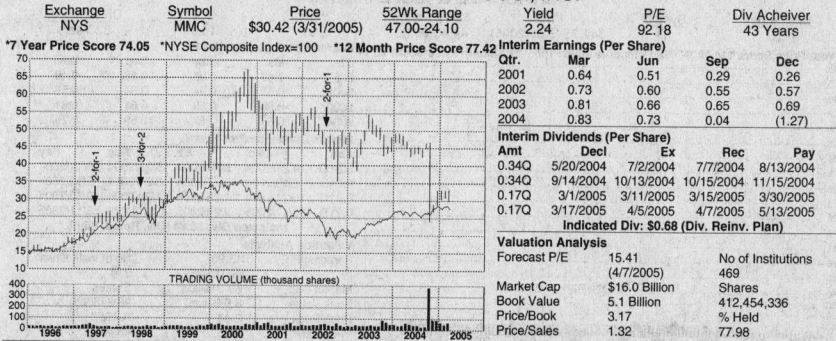

Interim Earnings (Per Share)

Qtr.	Mar	Jun	Sep	Dec
2001	0.64	0.51	0.29	0.26
2002	0.73	0.60	0.55	0.57
2003	0.81	0.66	0.65	0.69
2004	0.83	0.73	0.04	(1.27)

Interim Dividends (Per Share)

Amt	Decl	Ex	Rec	Pay
0.34Q	5/20/2004	7/2/2004	7/7/2004	8/13/2004
0.34Q	9/14/2004	10/13/2004	10/15/2004	11/15/2004
0.17Q	3/1/2005	3/11/2005	3/15/2005	3/30/2005
0.17Q	3/17/2005	4/5/2005	4/7/2005	5/13/2005

Indicated Div: $0.68 (Div. Reinv. Plan)

Valuation Analysis

Forecast P/E	15.41	No of Institutions
	(4/7/2005)	469
Market Cap	$16.0 Billion	Shares
Book Value	5.1 Billion	412,454,336
Price/Book	3.17	% Held
Price/Sales	1.32	77.98

Business Summary: Insurance (MIC: 8.2 SIC: 411 NAIC: 24210)

Marsh & McLennan Companies is engaged in the worldwide business of providing retail and wholesale insurance services, principally as a broker or consultant for insurers, insurance underwriters and other brokers. Co.'s subsidiaries include Marsh, a risk and insurance services firm; Putnam Investments, one of the largest investment management companies in the U.S.; and Mercer Consulting Group, a major global provider of consulting services. Other subsidiaries render advisory services in the area of employee benefits and compensation consulting, management consulting, economic consulting and environmental consulting.

Recent Developments: For the year ended Dec 31 2004, net income decreased 88.6% to $176,000 thousand from net income of $1,540,000 thousand a year earlier. Results for 2004 and 2003 included one-time charges of $969,000 thousand and $10,000 thousand, respectively, related primarily to regulatory settlements. Revenues were $12,159,000 thousand, up 5.3% from $11,544,000 thousand the year before. Operating income slid 74.0% to $648,000 thousand from $2,496,000 thousand the previous year.

Prospects: On Jan 31 2005, Co. announced it would establish an $850.0 million fund associated with a settlement with the New York State Attorney General and the New York State Insurance Department. Under the agreement, on June 1 2005 and 2006, respectively, Co. will pay $255.0 million into the fund. On June 1 2007 and 2008, respectively, Co. will pay $170.0 million into the fund. Going forward, Co. will focus on restructuring its operations, improving efficiencies and eliminating unprofitable accounts. Once fully implemented, these initiatives should lead to annual expense savings exceeding $375.0 million.

Financial Data

(US$ in Thousands)	12/31/2004	12/31/2003	12/31/2002	12/31/2001	12/31/2000	12/31/1999	12/31/1998	12/31/1997
Earnings Per Share	0.33	2.81	2.45	1.70	2.05	1.31	1.49	0.80
Cash Flow Per Share	3.92	3.50	2.37	2.50	2.50	1.90	2.21	0.85
Tang Book Value Per Share	N.M.	N.M.	N.M.	N.M.	N.M.	N.M.	N.M.	1.53
Dividends Per Share	0.990	1.490	1.090	1.030	0.950	0.850	0.733	0.633
Dividend Payout %	300.00	53.02	44.49	60.77	46.34	64.89	49.22	79.49
Income Statement								
Total Revenue	12,159,000	11,588,000	10,440,000	9,943,000	10,157,000	9,157,000	7,190,000	6,008,600
Income Before Taxes	450,000	2,335,000	2,133,000	1,590,000	1,955,000	1,247,000	1,305,000	662,400
Income Taxes	259,000	770,000	747,000	599,000	753,000	521,000	509,000	263,000
Net Income	176,000	1,540,000	1,365,000	974,000	1,181,000	726,000	796,000	399,400
Average Shares	535,000	548,000	557,000	572,000	568,000	544,000	528,000	501,600
Balance Sheet								
Total Assets	18,337,000	15,053,000	13,855,000	13,293,000	13,769,000	13,021,000	11,871,000	7,914,200
Total Liabilities	13,281,000	9,602,000	8,837,000	8,120,000	8,541,000	8,851,000	8,212,000	4,715,400
Stockholders' Equity	5,056,000	5,451,000	5,018,000	5,173,000	5,228,000	4,170,000	3,659,000	3,198,800
Shares Outstanding	526,809	526,736	538,199	548,654	552,052	534,051	514,000	509,850
Statistical Record								
Return on Assets %	1.05	10.65	10.06	7.20	8.79	5.83	8.05	6.41
Return on Equity %	3.34	29.42	26.79	18.73	25.06	18.55	23.21	15.70
Price Range	49.30-24.10	54.74-38.52	56.85-35.53	58.56-40.25	67.44-36.50	48.16-28.72	32.00-22.25	26.58-17.23
P/E Ratio	149.39-73.03	19.48-13.71	23.20-14.50	34.45-23.68	32.90-17.80	36.76-21.92	21.48-14.93	33.23-21.54
Average Yield %	2.36	3.17	2.23	2.04	1.75	2.04	2.82	2.83

Address: 1166 Avenue Of The Americas, New York, NY 10036 Telephone: (212) 345-5000 Fax: (212) 345-4809	Web Site: www.mmc.com Officers: Michael G. Cherkasky - Pres., C.E.O. Sandra S. Wijnberg - Sr. V.P., C.F.O.	Auditors: DELOITTE & TOUCHE LLP Investor Contact: 212-345-5475 Transfer Agents: The Bank of New York, New York, NY

MARSHALL & ILSLEY CORP.

Exchange	Symbol	Price	52Wk Range	Yield	P/E	Div Acheiver
NYS	MI	$41.75 (3/31/2005)	44.43-36.60	2.01	15.07	32 Years

*7 Year Price Score 114.12 *NYSE Composite Index=100 ***12 Month Price Score 95.11**

Interim Earnings (Per Share)

Qtr.	Mar	Jun	Sep	Dec
2001	0.40	0.28	0.38	0.49
2002	0.53	0.54	0.54	0.55
2003	0.56	0.59	0.61	0.61
2004	0.65	0.67	0.69	0.76

Interim Dividends (Per Share)

Amt	Decl	Ex	Rec	Pay
0.21Q	4/27/2004	5/26/2004	5/28/2004	6/11/2004
0.21Q	8/19/2004	8/27/2004	8/31/2004	9/10/2004
0.21Q	10/21/2004	11/26/2004	11/30/2004	12/10/2004
0.21Q	2/17/2005	2/25/2005	3/1/2005	3/11/2005

Indicated Div: $0.84 (Div. Reinv. Plan)

Valuation Analysis

Forecast P/E	13.96
	(4/7/2005)
Market Cap	$9.5 Billion
Book Value	3.9 Billion
Price/Book	2.44
Price/Sales	3.05

No of Institutions	310
Shares	98,843,920
% Held	43.45

Business Summary: Commercial Banking (MIC: 8.1 SIC: 021 NAIC: 22110)

Marshall & Ilsley, a multibank holding company with assets of $34.40 billion as of Dec 31 2003, is headquartered in Milwaukee, WI. Co. has 199 banking offices in Wisconsin, 28 locations throughout Arizona, 11 offices in Minnesota, six offices in Missouri, two offices in Florida, one office in Nevada and one office in Illinois, as well as on the Internet. Co. also provides trust services, residential mortgage banking, capital markets, brokerage and insurance, commercial leasing and commercial mortgage banking. Co.'s principal subsidiary is Metavante Corporation, a provider of integrated financial transaction processing, outsourcing services, software, and consulting services.

Recent Developments: For the year ended Dec 31 2004, net income increased 15.3% to $627,086 thousand from net income of $544,105 thousand a year earlier. Net interest income was $1,131,992 thousand, up 7.1% from $1,057,286 thousand the year before. Provision for loan losses was $37,963 thousand versus $62,993 thousand in the prior year, a decrease of 39.7%. Non-interest income rose 22.2% to $1,419,324 thousand, while non-interest expense advanced 9.9% to $1,595,558 thousand.

Prospects: On Feb 9 2005, Metavante Corporation, Co.'s financial technology subsidiary, announced that it completed the acquisition of Clark, NJ-based Prime Associates, Inc., an international provider of software, data and services that address the regulatory and compliance mandate of financial institutions such as anti-money laundering regulations. The acquisition is in line with Co.'s direction to offer technology and consulting services to all segments of the financial services industry. Terms of the transaction were not disclosed. Meanwhile, Co. is benefiting from favorable earnings results, largely due to total loan growth and a decrease in nonperforming loans.

Financial Data

(US$ in Thousands)	12/31/2004	12/31/2003	12/31/2002	12/31/2001	12/31/2000	12/31/1999	12/31/1998	12/31/1997
Earnings Per Share	2.77	2.38	2.16	1.54	1.45	1.57	1.30	1.21
Cash Flow Per Share	4.51	4.57	4.41	1.13	4.79	2.97	1.28	1.42
Tang Book Value Per Share	7.76	9.96	8.61	9.16	9.22	8.27	8.99	9.45
Dividends Per Share	0.810	0.700	0.625	0.568	0.517	0.470	0.430	0.393
Dividend Payout %	29.24	29.41	28.94	36.73	35.81	29.94	32.95	32.44
Income Statement								
Interest Income	1,665,790	1,529,920	1,567,336	1,709,107	1,747,982	1,496,584	1,434,044	1,143,670
Interest Expense	533,798	472,634	561,038	866,328	1,074,976	791,303	757,974	579,623
Net Interest Income	1,131,992	1,057,286	1,006,298	842,779	673,006	705,281	676,070	564,047
Provision for Losses	37,963	62,993	74,416	54,115	30,352	25,419	27,090	17,253
Non-Interest Income	1,446,495	1,215,801	1,082,688	1,002,812	928,352	845,774	756,333	598,858
Non-Interest Expense	1,595,558	1,451,707	1,295,978	1,290,431	1,100,656	997,697	940,028	775,401
Income Before Taxes	944,966	758,387	718,592	501,045	470,350	527,939	465,285	370,251
Income Taxes	317,880	214,282	238,265	163,124	152,948	173,428	163,962	125,107
Net Income	627,086	544,105	480,327	337,485	315,123	354,511	301,323	245,144
Average Shares	226,551	228,285	222,048	218,264	217,766	226,010	230,480	203,020
Balance Sheet								
Net Loans & Leases	29,097,000	24,800,756	23,570,437	19,027,174	17,351,972	16,109,199	13,770,114	12,339,463
Total Assets	40,437,402	34,372,643	32,874,642	27,253,734	26,077,739	24,369,723	21,566,293	19,477,452
Total Deposits	26,455,087	22,270,105	20,393,706	16,493,047	19,248,627	16,435,163	15,919,919	14,355,998
Total Liabilities	36,547,588	31,043,950	29,837,974	24,760,766	23,835,550	22,252,797	19,322,514	17,557,381
Stockholders' Equity	3,889,814	3,328,693	3,036,668	2,492,968	2,242,189	2,116,926	2,243,779	1,920,071
Shares Outstanding	227,340	223,226	226,232	207,897	205,693	211,632	212,206	203,074
Statistical Record								
Return on Assets %	1.67	1.62	1.60	1.27	1.25	1.54	1.47	1.43
Return on Equity %	17.33	17.10	17.37	14.25	14.42	16.26	14.47	15.41
Net Interest Margin %	67.96	69.11	64.20	49.31	38.50	47.13	47.14	49.32
Efficiency Ratio %	51.27	52.87	48.90	47.58	41.13	42.59	42.92	44.50
Loans to Deposits	1.10	1.11	1.16	1.15	0.90	0.98	0.86	0.86
Price Range	44.43-36.18	38.40-25.07	31.95-23.25	32.06-24.02	31.41-19.31	35.97-27.38	31.06-20.25	31.06-16.38
P/E Ratio	16.04-13.06	16.13-10.53	14.79-10.76	20.82-15.60	21.66-13.32	22.91-17.44	23.89-15.58	25.67-13.53
Average Yield %	2.04	2.26	2.11	2.06	2.16	1.50	1.60	1.78

Address: 770 North Water Street, Milwaukee, WI 53202
Telephone: (414) 765-7700
Fax: (414) 765-8026

Web Site: www.micorp.com
Officers: Dennis J. Kuester - Chmn., Pres., C.E.O. John M. Presley - Sr. V.P., C.F.O.

Auditors: Deloitte & Touche LLP
Transfer Agents: Continental Stock Transfer & Trust Company, New York, NY

MARTIN MARIETTA MATERIALS, INC.

Exchange	Symbol	Price	52Wk Range	Yield	P/E	Div Achiever
NYS	MLM	$55.92 (3/31/2005)	57.84-41.66	1.43	21.02	10 Years

*7 Year Price Score 94.27 ***NYSE Composite Index=100** ***12 Month Price Score 109.39**

TRADING VOLUME (thousand shares)

Interim Earnings (Per Share)

Qtr.	Mar	Jun	Sep	Dec
2001	(0.10)	0.82	0.95	0.51
2002	(0.22)	1.09	0.80	0.10
2003	(0.43)	0.81	0.93	0.60
2004	(0.14)	0.92	1.11	0.77

Interim Dividends (Per Share)

Amt	Decl	Ex	Rec	Pay
0.18Q	5/26/2004	5/28/2004	6/2/2004	6/30/2004
0.20Q	8/18/2004	8/30/2004	9/1/2004	9/30/2004
0.20Q	11/18/2004	11/29/2004	12/1/2004	12/31/2004
0.20Q	2/3/2005	2/25/2005	3/1/2005	3/31/2005
		Indicated Div: $0.80		

Valuation Analysis

Forecast P/E	18.52	No of Institutions	
	(4/7/2005)	189	
Market Cap	$2.6 Billion	Shares	
Book Value	1.2 Billion	43,962,688	
Price/Book	2.29	% Held	
Price/Sales	1.50	93.21	

Business Summary: Construction - Public Infrastructure (MIC: 3.1 SIC: 611 NAIC: 37310)

Martin Marietta Materials is principally engaged in the aggregates business used in the construction of highways, and in domestic commercial and residential construction. As of Dec 31 2004, Co.'s aggregates and asphalt products and ready-mixed concrete were sold from a network of 308 quarries, distribution facilities and plants to customers in 28 states, Canada and the Caribbean. Also, Co. has a Specialty Products segment that produces magnesia-based chemicals products used in industrial, agricultural and environmental applications; dolomitic lime sold for the steel industry; and structural composite products used in a variety of industries.

Recent Developments: For the year ended Dec 31 2004, income from continuing operations increased 19.5% to $128,179 thousand from income of $107,241 thousand a year earlier. Net income increased 38.0% to $129,163 thousand from net income of $93,623 thousand a year earlier. Revenues were $1,759,613 thousand, up 4.5% from $1,684,548 thousand the year before. Operating income was $226,592 thousand versus an income of $195,455 thousand in the prior year, an increase of 15.9%. Total direct expense was $1,417,423 thousand versus $1,375,019 thousand in the prior year, an increase of 3.1%. Total indirect expense was $115,598 thousand versus $114,074 thousand in the prior year, an increase of 1.3%.

Prospects: Results are being positively affected by strong price increases in the Aggregates segment along with Co.'s efforts to reduce costs and improve efficiencies. Meanwhile, robust sales growth in the Magnesia Specialties segment is being driven by strong lime sales to the steel industry and increased chemical sales to a variety of end users. Separately, Co. is targeting first-quarter 2005 results of between earnings of $0.05 per share and a loss of $0.10 per share. Looking to full-year 2005, Co. expects earnings of between $2.85 and $3.20 per diluted share. For 2005, aggregates shipment volume is expected to increase 2.0% to 4.0%, while aggregates pricing is projected to grow 3.0% to 4.0%.

Financial Data

(US$ in Thousands)	12/31/2004	12/31/2003	12/31/2002	12/31/2001	12/31/2000	12/31/1999	12/31/1998	12/31/1997
Earnings Per Share	2.66	1.91	1.77	2.19	2.39	2.68	2.48	2.13
Cash Flow Per Share	5.53	5.67	4.18	5.28	4.54	4.79	4.79	4.24
Tang Book Value Per Share	11.99	10.83	9.70	8.55	9.70	7.86	6.25	8.37
Dividends Per Share	0.760	0.690	0.580	0.560	0.540	0.520	0.500	0.480
Dividend Payout %	28.57	36.13	32.77	25.57	22.59	19.40	20.16	22.54
Income Statement								
Total Revenue	1,759,613	1,711,453	1,692,437	1,718,050	1,517,517	1,258,827	1,057,691	900,863
EBITDA	359,849	324,324	326,994	359,866	347,089	358,478	296,666	247,831
Depn & Amortn	132,173	139,606	138,696	154,635	136,373	124,754	98,765	79,720
Income Before Taxes	184,722	142,131	144,270	158,439	168,821	194,313	174,142	151,212
Income Taxes	56,543	41,047	46,455	53,077	56,794	68,532	58,529	52,683
Net Income	129,163	93,623	86,305	105,362	112,027	125,781	115,613	98,529
Average Shares	48,534	49,136	48,858	48,066	46,948	46,947	46,707	46,238
Balance Sheet								
Current Assets	624,253	621,519	526,149	496,232	425,001	403,365	369,388	322,012
Total Assets	2,355,852	2,330,093	2,258,530	2,224,580	1,841,439	1,742,574	1,588,589	1,105,713
Current Liabilities	203,813	220,164	197,827	192,037	189,113	182,696	152,233	108,235
Long-Term Obligations	713,661	717,073	733,471	797,385	601,580	602,011	602,113	310,675
Total Liabilities	1,202,425	1,200,246	1,175,520	1,202,368	978,153	968,568	920,890	543,877
Stockholders' Equity	1,153,427	1,129,847	1,083,010	1,022,212	863,286	774,006	667,699	561,836
Shares Outstanding	47,306	48,670	48,847	48,559	46,783	46,715	46,642	46,211
Statistical Record								
Return on Assets %	5.50	4.08	3.85	5.18	6.23	7.55	8.58	10.51
Return on Equity %	11.28	8.46	8.20	11.18	13.65	17.45	18.81	18.90
EBITDA Margin %	20.45	18.95	19.32	20.95	22.87	28.48	28.05	27.51
Net Margin %	7.34	5.47	5.10	6.13	7.38	9.99	10.93	10.94
Asset Turnover	0.75	0.75	0.76	0.85	0.84	0.76	0.79	0.96
Current Ratio	3.06	2.82	2.66	2.58	2.25	2.21	2.43	2.98
Debt to Equity	0.62	0.63	0.68	0.78	0.70	0.78	0.90	0.55
Price Range	53.66-41.66	47.78-26.15	48.12-27.45	51.27-36.00	54.25-32.25	67.75-36.00	62.19-36.00	37.00-23.25
P/E Ratio	20.17-15.66	25.02-13.69	27.19-15.51	23.41-16.44	22.70-13.49	25.28-13.43	25.08-14.52	17.37-10.92
Average Yield %	1.66	1.97	1.56	1.27	1.27	1.03	1.11	1.54

Address: 2710 Wycliff Road, Raleigh, NC 27607-3033	Web Site: www.martinmarietta.com	Auditors: Ernst & Young LLP
Telephone: (919) 781-4550	Officers: Stephen P. Zelnak Jr. - Chmn., Pres., C.E.O. Philip J. Sipling - Exec. V.P.	Investor Contact: 919-783-4658
Fax: (919) 783-4552		

MARVEL ENTERPRISES, INC.

Exchange	Symbol	Price	52Wk Range	Yield	P/E
NYS	MVL	$20.00 (3/31/2005)	21.55-12.45	N/A	18.18

*7 Year Price Score 196.50 *NYSE Composite Index=100 *12 Month Price Score 97.81

Interim Earnings (Per Share)

Qtr.	Mar	Jun	Sep	Dec
2001	(0.25)	(0.22)	(0.10)	0.36
2002	(0.07)	0.07	0.11	(0.84)
2003	0.38	0.28	0.57	0.11
2004	0.27	0.25	0.30	0.27

Interim Dividends (Per Share)

No Dividends Paid

Valuation Analysis

Forecast P/E	17.73		No of Institutions
	(4/13/2005)		153
Market Cap	$2.1 Billion		Shares
Book Value	546.5 Million		71,326,912
Price/Book	3.85		% Held
Price/Sales	4.09		67.70

Business Summary: Consumer Accessories (MIC: 4.6 SIC: 942 NAIC: 39931)

Marvel Enterprises is a character-based entertainment company with a proprietary library of over 5,000 characters, including Spider-Man, the X-Men, The Incredible Hulk, Daredevil, Captain America, Fantastic Four, and others. Co.'s business is divided into three operating segments. Marvel Licensing relates to the licensing of Co.'s characters for use in a wide variety of products, including toys, electronic games, apparel, as well as in feature films and television programs. Marvel Publishing creates and publishes comic books and trade paperbacks principally in North America. Toy Biz designs, develops, markets and distributes a limited line of toys worldwide.

Recent Developments: For the year ended Dec 31 2004, net income declined 17.7% to $124.9 million compared with $151.6 million in the previous year. Net sales jumped 47.7% to $513.5 million from $347.6 million a year earlier, reflecting higher licensing revenues, increased toy segment sales and increased sales of comic books. Growth in licensing primarily resulted from the consolidation of Co.'s joint venture sales and strong growth in international licensing. The Toy segment increase resulted from strong sales of toys based on the Spider-Man 2 movie. Gross profit advanced 32.0% to $353.9 million versus $268.2 million the year before. Operating income increased 34.2% to $224.4 million from $167.2 million in 2003.

Prospects: Results continue to reflect the expanding global power of the Marvel brand and an increase in consumer and media products based on its characters. Additionally, Co. continues to make strides in extending its development pipeline for entertainment projects. As a result, Co. has been able to improve the economic terms for new media and consumer product projects. Looking ahead, Co. reiterated its forecast for 2005, expecting first-quarter sales of between $88.0 million and $98.0 million, with earnings in the range of $0.25 to $0.29 per share. For full-year 2005, Co. forecast sales of between $370.0 million and $390.0 million, with earnings in the range of $1.07 to $1.12 per share.

Financial Data (US$ in Thousands)	12/31/2004	12/31/2003	12/31/2002	12/31/2001	12/31/2000	12/31/1999	12/31/1998	12/31/1997
Earnings Per Share	1.10	1.34	(0.79)	(0.21)	(2.09)	(0.95)	(0.82)	(0.71)
Cash Flow Per Share	1.50	1.70	1.30	0.17	(0.48)	0.02	0.66	0.28
Tang Book Value Per Share	1.95	1.17	N.M.	N.M.	N.M.	N.M.	N.M.	2.37
Income Statement								
Total Revenue	513,468	347,626	299,046	181,224	231,651	319,645	232,076	150,812
EBITDA	231,142	173,428	86,445	31,996	(104)	48,234	7,639	(28,706)
Depn & Amortn	3,783	4,338	5,772	29,323	54,663	43,935	26,423	20,168
Income Before Taxes	206,872	150,372	38,676	(26,501)	(86,668)	(27,778)	(28,224)	(49,650)
Income Taxes	64,631	(1,276)	11,902	647	2,927	4,482	4,386	(20,185)
Net Income	124,877	151,648	22,610	5,265	(89,858)	(33,791)	(32,610)	(29,465)
Average Shares	113,957	113,439	57,771	51,483	50,500	50,299	43,759	41,619
Balance Sheet								
Current Assets	295,668	335,007	122,615	100,227	113,443	172,909	172,584	116,432
Total Assets	714,814	741,857	517,519	517,570	555,284	654,637	689,904	150,366
Current Liabilities	153,437	120,809	90,011	71,301	71,703	80,990	305,976	42,385
Long-Term Obligations	...	150,962	150,962	181,790	250,000	250,000	...	...
Total Liabilities	168,314	272,407	241,870	267,637	321,703	332,084	333,900	42,385
Stockholders' Equity	546,500	469,450	242,869	41,958	31,396	135,763	183,624	107,981
Shares Outstanding	105,101	108,615	91,710	52,150	50,553	50,335	50,178	41,619
Statistical Record								
Return on Assets %	17.10	24.08	4.37	0.98	N.M.	N.M.	N.M.	N.M.
Return on Equity %	24.52	42.58	15.88	14.36	N.M.	N.M.	N.M.	N.M.
EBITDA Margin %	45.02	49.89	28.91	17.66	N.M.	15.09	3.29	N.M.
Net Margin %	24.32	43.62	7.56	2.91	N.M.	N.M.	N.M.	N.M.
Asset Turnover	0.70	0.55	0.58	0.34	0.38	0.48	0.55	0.94
Current Ratio	1.93	2.77	1.36	1.41	1.58	2.13	0.56	2.75
Debt to Equity	...	0.32	0.62	4.33	7.96	1.84	...	...
Price Range	23.56-12.45	21.09-5.99	6.27-2.37	2.77-0.96	4.92-0.96	6.42-3.17	7.33-3.00	13.33-5.04
P/E Ratio	21.42-11.32	15.74-4.47	...	...	...	...	...	...

Address: 10 East 40th Street, New York, NY 10016 Telephone: (212) 576-4000	Web Site: www.marvel.com Officers: Morton E. Handel - Chmn. Isaac Perlmutter - Vice-Chmn., C.E.O.	Auditors: Ernst & Young LLP

MASCO CORP.

Exchange	Symbol	Price	52Wk Range	Yield	P/E	Div Achiever
NYS	MAS	$34.67 (3/31/2005)	38.03-26.94	2.31	17.69	46 Years

*7 Year Price Score 109.09 *NYSE Composite Index=100 *12 Month Price Score 98.63

Interim Earnings (Per Share)

Qtr.	Mar	Jun	Sep	Dec
2001	0.25	0.30	(0.39)	0.27
2002	0.31	0.43	0.24	0.37
2003	0.32	0.46	0.65	0.20
2004	0.36	0.58	0.80	0.23

Interim Dividends (Per Share)

Amt	Decl	Ex	Rec	Pay
0.16Q	6/25/2004	7/7/2004	7/9/2004	8/9/2004
0.18Q	9/13/2004	10/6/2004	10/8/2004	11/8/2004
0.18Q	12/8/2004	1/5/2005	1/7/2005	2/7/2005
0.20Q	3/22/2005	4/6/2005	4/8/2005	5/9/2005

Indicated Div: $0.80 (Div. Reinv. Plan)

Valuation Analysis

Forecast P/E	13.86 (4/7/2005)	No of Institutions 489
Market Cap	$15.5 Billion	Shares
Book Value	5.4 Billion	365,203,008
Price/Book	2.86	% Held
Price/Sales	1.28	82.03

Business Summary: Metal Products (MIC: 11.4 SIC: 432 NAIC: 37122)

Masco is engaged in the manufacture and sale of cabinets and related products, plumbing products, architectural coatings and other specialty home improvement and building products. These products are sold to the home improvement and home construction markets through mass merchandisers, hardware stores, home centers, builders, distributors and other outlets for consumers and builders. Co.'s brand names and tradenames include the following: Kraftmaid®, Merillat®, Mill's Pride®, Quality Cabinets®, Delta®, Peerless®, Newport Brass®, Behr®, Premium Plus®, Masterchem®, Franklin Brass®, Ginger®, Bath Unlimited®, Milgard®, Griffin™, and Cambrian™.

Recent Developments: For the year ended Dec 31 2004, income from continuing operations increased 17.7% to $930,000 thousand from income from continuing operations of $790,000 thousand a year earlier. Revenues were $12,074,000 thousand, up 14.2% from $10,571,000 thousand the year before. Gross profit totaled $3,718,000 thousand, or 30.8% of revenues, compared with $3,214,000 thousand, or 30.7% of revenues, the previous year. Operating income climbed 5.7% to $1,569,000 thousand from $1,484,000 thousand in the prior year.

Prospects: For first quarter 2005, Co. is projecting earnings from continuing operations, seasonally the lowest quarter of the year, to be in a range of $0.44 to $0.47 per common share, compared with first quarter 2004 earnings from continuing operations of $0.52 per common share, which included $0.03 per common share of income related to the Behr litigation and $0.07 per common share of previously disclosed other income, principally net gains from the sale of financial investments. Based on current business trends, Co. is projecting full-year 2005 earnings from continuing operations in a range of $2.40 to $2.50 per common share.

Financial Data

(US$ in Thousands)	12/31/2004	12/31/2003	12/31/2002	12/31/2001	12/31/2000	12/31/1999	12/31/1998	12/31/1997
Earnings Per Share	1.96	1.64	1.15	0.42	1.31	1.28	1.39	1.15
Cash Flow Per Share	3.26	2.97	2.53	2.10	1.66	1.13	1.26	1.27
Tang Book Value Per Share	1.54	1.35	1.31	1.30	2.78	3.14	4.99	4.53
Dividends Per Share	0.660	0.580	0.545	0.525	0.490	0.450	0.430	0.305
Dividend Payout %	33.67	35.37	47.39	125.00	37.40	35.16	30.94	26.52
Income Statement								
Total Revenue	12,074,000	10,936,000	9,419,400	8,358,000	7,243,000	6,307,000	4,345,000	3,760,000
EBITDA	1,958,000	1,702,000	1,462,440	773,860	1,262,630	1,153,790	930,220	779,200
Depn & Amortn	229,000	232,000	200,600	269,500	238,300	181,800	136,300	116,000
Income Before Taxes	1,518,000	1,216,000	1,031,000	300,700	893,400	904,100	755,000	630,900
Income Taxes	569,000	463,000	348,900	102,200	301,700	334,500	279,000	248,500
Net Income	893,000	806,000	589,700	198,500	591,700	569,600	476,000	382,400
Average Shares	456,000	491,000	514,100	474,900	451,800	446,200	343,700	337,600
Balance Sheet								
Current Assets	4,402,000	3,804,000	3,949,770	2,626,920	2,308,160	2,109,780	1,862,620	1,626,720
Total Assets	12,541,000	12,149,000	12,050,430	9,183,330	7,744,000	6,634,920	5,167,350	4,333,760
Current Liabilities	2,147,000	2,099,000	1,932,450	1,236,560	1,078,050	846,430	846,580	620,000
Long-Term Obligations	4,187,000	3,848,000	4,316,470	3,627,630	3,018,240	2,431,270	1,391,420	1,321,470
Total Liabilities	7,118,000	6,693,000	6,756,590	5,063,500	4,317,940	3,498,420	2,438,770	2,104,740
Stockholders' Equity	5,423,000	5,456,000	5,293,840	4,119,830	3,426,060	3,136,500	2,728,580	2,229,020
Shares Outstanding	446,720	458,380	488,890	459,050	444,750	443,510	339,330	331,140
Statistical Record								
Return on Assets %	7.21	6.66	5.55	2.35	8.21	9.65	10.02	9.52
Return on Equity %	16.37	15.00	12.53	5.26	17.98	19.42	19.20	18.80
EBITDA Margin %	16.22	15.56	15.53	9.26	17.43	18.29	21.41	20.72
Net Margin %	7.40	7.37	6.26	2.37	8.17	9.03	10.96	10.17
Asset Turnover	0.98	0.90	0.89	0.99	1.00	1.07	0.91	0.94
Current Ratio	2.05	1.81	2.04	2.12	2.14	2.49	2.20	2.62
Debt to Equity	0.77	0.71	0.82	0.88	0.88	0.78	0.51	0.59
Price Range	36.80-26.02	28.31-16.82	29.08-17.68	26.49-18.00	25.69-14.81	33.50-23.00	32.50-21.13	26.53-17.06
P/E Ratio	18.78-13.28	17.26-10.26	25.29-15.37	63.07-42.86	19.61-11.31	26.17-17.97	23.38-15.20	23.07-14.84
Average Yield %	2.13	2.50	2.24	2.24	2.46	1.55	1.55	1.47

Address: 21001 Van Born Road, Taylor, MI 48180 **Telephone:** (313) 274 7400 **Fax:** (313) 792 6135	**Web Site:** www.masco.com **Officers:** Richard A. Manoogian - Chmn., C.E.O. Alan H. Barry - Pres., C.O.O.	**Auditors:** PricewaterhouseCoopers LLP **Investor Contact:** 313-274-7400 **Transfer Agents:** Bank of New York, New York, NY

MATTEL INC

Exchange	Symbol	Price	52Wk Range	Yield	P/E
NYS	MAT	$21.35 (3/31/2005)	21.42-15.98	2.11	15.81

*7 Year Price Score 77.85   *NYSE Composite Index=100   *12 Month Price Score 104.85

Interim Earnings (Per Share)

Qtr.	Mar	Jun	Sep	Dec
2001	(0.08)	(0.01)	0.46	0.31
2002	(0.59)	0.04	0.63	0.42
2003	0.07	0.05	0.61	0.49
2004	0.02	0.06	0.61	0.67

Interim Dividends (Per Share)

Amt	Decl	Ex	Rec	Pay
0.05A	11/9/2001	11/21/2001	11/26/2001	12/12/2001
0.05A	11/13/2002	11/22/2002	11/26/2002	12/12/2002
0.40A	11/21/2003	12/4/2003	12/8/2003	12/23/2003
0.45A	11/18/2004	12/1/2004	12/3/2004	12/17/2004

Indicated Div: $0.45

Valuation Analysis

Forecast P/E	16.06	No of Institutions	
	(4/7/2005)	332	
Market Cap	$8.9 Billion	Shares	
Book Value	2.4 Billion	374,070,912	
Price/Book	3.72	% Held	
Price/Sales	1.74	89.77	

Business Summary: Consumer Accessories (MIC: 4.6 SIC: 942 NAIC: 39931)

Mattel designs, manufactures, and markets a variety of toy products worldwide through sales to retailers and directly to consumers. Co.'s portfolio of products are grouped into three groups. Mattel Brands include Barbie®, Polly Pocket!™ and ello™, Hot Wheels®, Matchbox® and Tyco® R/C vehicles and playsets and Nickelodeon®, Harry Potter™, Yu-Gi-oh!™, and games and puzzles. Fisher Price Brands include Fisher-Price®, Power Wheels®, Sesame Street®, Little People®, Disney preschool and plush, Winnie the Pooh, Rescue Heroes™, Barney™, See 'N Say®, Dora the Explorer™, PowerTouch™ and View-Master®. American Girl Brands include American Girl Today®, The American Girls Collection® and Bitty Baby®.

Recent Developments: For the year ended Dec 31 2004, net income increased 6.5% to $572,723 thousand from net income of $537,632 thousand a year earlier. Revenues were $5,102,786 thousand, up 2.9% from $4,960,100 thousand the year before. Operating income was $730,817 thousand versus an income of $785,710 thousand in the prior year, a decrease of 7.0%. Total direct expense was $2,692,061 thousand versus $2,530,617 thousand in the prior year, an increase of 6.4%. Total indirect expense was $1,679,908 thousand versus $1,643,773 thousand in the prior year, an increase of 2.2%.

Prospects: Despite a challenging retail environment, Co. finished 2004 with solid momentum in its sales performance, which it hopes to build on in the coming year. Also, Co. made good progress on two of its key goals, including re-invigorating the Barbie® brand and building on its success in the learning category. Co. noted that its core brands, including Hot Wheels®, Fisher-Price® and American Girl®, continue to be the key drivers behind its revenue performance, and that its debt-to-total capital ratio of 20.6% at the end of 2004 is in line with its long-term goal. Co. ended fiscal 2004 with more than $1.10 billion in cash, which is consistent with the level on hand at the end of fiscal 2003.

Financial Data

(US$ in Thousands)	12/31/2004	12/31/2003	12/31/2002	12/31/2001	12/31/2000	12/31/1999	12/31/1998	12/31/1997
Earnings Per Share	1.35	1.22	0.52	0.68	(1.01)	(0.21)	1.10	0.93
Cash Flow Per Share	1.36	1.38	2.65	1.76	1.30	0.14	1.88	1.63
Tang Book Value Per Share	3.92	3.49	2.96	1.46	0.62	1.35	1.98	4.38
Dividends Per Share	0.450	0.400	0.050	0.050	0.270	0.350	0.310	0.270
Dividend Payout %	33.33	32.79	9.62	7.35	...	...	28.18	29.03
Income Statement								
Total Revenue	5,102,786	4,960,100	4,885,340	4,804,062	4,669,942	5,514,950	4,781,892	4,834,616
EBITDA	936,813	986,284	909,598	837,298	623,041	332,543	786,941	705,123
Depn & Amortn	182,478	183,819	191,928	252,156	244,638	291,677	211,045	189,911
Income Before Taxes	696,254	740,854	621,497	430,010	225,424	(110,743)	465,063	425,082
Income Taxes	123,531	203,222	166,455	119,090	55,247	(28,370)	132,799	135,288
Net Income	572,723	537,632	230,101	298,919	(430,969)	(82,373)	332,264	285,184
Average Shares	423,093	442,231	441,292	436,166	427,126	414,186	303,243	295,653
Balance Sheet								
Current Assets	2,637,150	2,394,856	2,388,964	2,092,596	1,751,497	2,420,027	2,057,810	2,461,736
Total Assets	4,756,492	4,510,950	4,459,659	4,540,561	4,313,397	5,127,022	4,262,165	3,803,791
Current Liabilities	1,727,171	1,467,746	1,648,753	1,596,981	1,502,407	1,817,524	1,317,211	1,173,424
Long-Term Obligations	400,000	589,130	640,070	1,020,919	1,242,396	1,183,835	983,507	664,073
Total Liabilities	2,370,680	2,294,729	2,480,947	2,802,103	2,910,299	3,164,335	2,441,967	1,981,721
Stockholders' Equity	2,385,812	2,216,221	1,978,712	1,738,458	1,403,098	1,962,687	1,820,198	1,822,070
Shares Outstanding	415,400	428,500	430,500	430,900	426,000	421,600	286,100	291,600
Statistical Record								
Return on Assets %	12.33	11.99	5.11	6.75	N.M.	N.M.	8.24	8.52
Return on Equity %	24.82	25.63	12.38	19.03	N.M.	N.M.	18.24	17.44
EBITDA Margin %	18.36	19.88	18.62	17.43	13.34	6.03	16.46	14.58
Net Margin %	11.22	10.84	4.71	6.22	N.M.	N.M.	6.95	5.90
Asset Turnover	1.10	1.11	1.09	1.09	0.99	1.17	1.19	1.44
Current Ratio	1.53	1.63	1.45	1.31	1.17	1.33	1.56	2.10
Debt to Equity	0.17	0.27	0.32	0.59	0.89	0.60	0.54	0.36
Price Range	19.50-15.98	23.05-18.80	22.20-15.75	19.75-13.70	15.00-9.06	29.00-11.81	45.63-21.69	41.38-24.00
P/E Ratio	14.44-11.84	18.89-15.41	42.69-30.29	29.04-20.15	...	...	41.48-19.72	44.49-25.81
Average Yield %	2.49	1.97	0.26	0.29	2.26	1.62	0.83	0.85

Address: 333 Continental Boulevard, El Segundo, CA 90245-5012	**Web Site:** www.service.mattel.com	**Auditors:** PricewaterhouseCoopers LLP
Telephone: (310) 252-2000	**Officers:** Robert A. Eckert - Chmn., C.E.O. Tom A. Debrowski - Exec. V.P., Worldwide Oper.	**Investor Contact:** 310-252-2000
Fax: (310) 252-3671		

MAXTOR CORP.(NEW)

Exchange	Symbol	Price	52Wk Range	Yield	P/E
NYS	MXO	$5.32 (3/31/2005)	8.53-2.89	N/A	N/A

*7 Year Price Score N/A   *NYSE Composite Index=100   *12 Month Price Score 93.84

Interim Earnings (Per Share)

Qtr.	Mar	Jun	Sep	Dec
2001	0.01	(1.35)	(0.69)	(0.66)
2002	(0.27)	(0.46)	(0.68)	0.02
2003	0.11	0.03	0.12	0.15
2004	0.04	(0.11)	(0.38)	(0.28)

Interim Dividends (Per Share)

No Dividends Paid

Valuation Analysis

Forecast P/E	0.00 (4/7/2005)	No of Institutions 156
Market Cap	$1.3 Billion	Shares
Book Value	583.4 Million	205,571,072
Price/Book	2.28	% Held
Price/Sales	0.35	81.25

TRADING VOLUME (thousand shares)

Business Summary: IT & Technology (MIC: 10.2 SIC: 572 NAIC: 34112)

Maxtor is a provider of hard disk drives for a range of applications, including desktop computers, high-performance Intel-based servers, near-line storage systems and consumer electronics. The desktop products are marketed under the DiamondMax®, MaXLine® and Fireball® brand names and consist of 3.5-inch disk drives with storage capabilities that range from 40 to 300 gigabytes. Co. also provides a line of high-end 3.5-inch hard disk drives for use in high-performance, storage-intensive applications such as workstations, enterprise servers and storage subsystems. These Intel-based server products are marketed under the Atlas brand name and provide storage capacities of 18.4 to 147.1 gigabytes.

Recent Developments: For the year ended Dec 27 2003, income from continuing operations was $100,460 thousand compared with a loss of $260,566 thousand a year earlier. Net income was $102,671 thousand versus net loss of $334,067 thousand a year earlier. Revenues were $4,086,443 thousand, up 8.1% from $3,779,514 thousand the year before. Operating income was $130,021 thousand versus a loss of $243,828 thousand in the prior year. Total direct expense was $3,385,390 thousand versus $3,382,099 thousand in the prior year, an increase of 0.1%. Total indirect expense was $571,032 thousand versus $641,243 thousand in the prior year, a decrease of 10.9%.

Prospects: Co. is seeing stronger demand in the desktop and enterprise markets, stable pricing and lean channel inventory. However, Co.'s core results continue to reflect an uncompetitive cost and expense structure, primarily on its desktop business. As a result, Co. has developed and begun to execute a 100 Day Plan to rationalize the product roadmap, improve its cost structure, reduce its operating expenses. Co. has prioritized product development for 2005, eliminating uncompetitive programs and increasing funding for small form factor drive development. In addition, Co. anticipates reducing U.S. headcount by up to 200 over the course of 2005.

Financial Data

(US$ in Thousands)	12/25/2004	12/27/2003	12/28/2002	12/29/2001	12/30/2000	01/01/2000	12/26/1998	12/27/1997
Earnings Per Share	(0.73)	0.41	(1.40)	(3.12)	0.27	(0.48)	0.47	...
Cash Flow Per Share	(0.02)	0.63	(0.12)	0.12	1.14	1.07	7.54	(9.81)
Tang Book Value Per Share	0.34	N.M.	N.M.	N.M.	2.23	2.12	1.80	...
Income Statement								
Total Revenue	3,796,328	4,086,443	3,779,514	3,797,031	2,704,859	2,486,123	2,408,528	1,424,320
EBITDA	26,936	371,308	10,734	(274,450)	139,248	51,453	141,723	(6,712)
Depn & Amortn	182,000	241,900	242,180	343,421	92,042	86,337	74,203	65,642
Income Before Taxes	(182,180)	103,964	(258,391)	(643,016)	33,475	(48,607)	38,736	(108,856)
Income Taxes	(261)	3,504	2,175	3,382	1,673	1,541	7,563	1,035
Net Income	(181,919)	102,671	(334,067)	(646,398)	31,802	(50,148)	31,173	(109,891)
Average Shares	247,671	251,135	239,474	206,911	119,115	105,503	65,814	15,125
Balance Sheet								
Current Assets	1,238,707	1,490,069	1,023,345	1,256,853	801,412	701,730	743,777	440,698
Total Assets	2,114,453	2,722,226	2,360,834	2,715,464	1,024,919	906,335	863,413	555,472
Current Liabilities	1,090,187	1,262,968	1,166,644	1,169,781	628,922	537,195	548,935	552,205
Long-Term Obligations	382,570	355,809	206,343	244,458	92,259	113,770	145,046	224,313
Total Liabilities	1,531,041	2,001,717	1,768,513	1,815,281	721,181	650,965	693,981	776,518
Stockholders' Equity	583,412	720,509	592,321	900,183	303,738	255,370	169,432	(221,046)
Shares Outstanding	250,167	246,001	242,507	236,977	116,205	94,293	94,293	15,125
Statistical Record								
Return on Assets %	N.M.	4.05	N.M.	N.M.	3.30	N.M.	4.41	N.M.
Return on Equity %	N.M.	15.68	N.M.	N.M.	11.41	N.M.	...	...
EBITDA Margin %	0.71	9.09	0.28	N.M.	5.15	2.07	5.88	N.M.
Net Margin %	N.M.	2.51	N.M.	N.M.	1.18	N.M.	1.29	N.M.
Asset Turnover	1.57	1.61	1.49	2.04	2.81	2.76	3.40	3.31
Current Ratio	1.14	1.18	0.88	1.07	1.27	1.31	1.35	0.80
Debt to Equity	0.66	0.49	0.35	0.27	0.30	0.45	0.86	...
Price Range	12.40-2.89	15.30-4.85	7.70-1.89	8.36-3.57	14.69-5.34	19.56-4.53	15.63-6.81	...
P/E Ratio	...	37.32-11.83	...	...	54.40-19.79	...	33.24-14.49	...

Address: 500 McCarthy Blvd., Milpitas, CA 95035
Telephone: (408) 894-5000
Fax: (408) 432-4510

Web Site: www.maxtor.com
Officers: Chong Sup Park - Chmn., C.E.O. Michael J. Wingert - Pres., C.O.O.

Auditors: PricewaterhouseCoopers LLP
Investor Contact: 408-894-5000
Transfer Agents: Bank of New York

MAY DEPARTMENT STORES CO. (THE)

Exchange	Symbol	Price	52Wk Range	Yield	P/E	Div Acheiver
NYS	MAY	$37.02 (3/31/2005)	37.36-23.95	2.65	18.42	29 Years

*7 Year Price Score 78.33 *NYSE Composite Index=100 *12 Month Price Score 111.47

Interim Earnings (Per Share)

Qtr.	Apr	Jul	Oct	Jan
2001-02	0.34	0.35	0.16	1.36
2002-03	0.23	0.22	0.05	1.26
2003-04	0.23	(0.39)	0.15	1.42
2004-05	0.24	0.33	0.02	...

Interim Dividends (Per Share)

Amt	Decl	Ex	Rec	Pay
0.242Q	8/20/2004	8/30/2004	9/1/2004	9/15/2004
0.242Q	11/12/2004	11/29/2004	12/1/2004	12/15/2004
0.245Q	2/10/2005	2/25/2005	3/1/2005	3/15/2005
0.245Q	3/18/2005	5/27/2005	6/1/2005	6/15/2005

Indicated Div: $0.98 (Div. Reinv. Plan)

Valuation Analysis

Forecast P/E	18.02	No of Institutions
	(4/7/2005)	368
Market Cap	$10.8 Billion	Shares
Book Value	4.2 Billion	276,041,696
Price/Book	2.58	% Held
Price/Sales	0.78	94.54

TRADING VOLUME (thousand shares)

Business Summary: Retail - General (MIC: 5.2 SIC: 311 NAIC: 52111)

The May Department Stores operated 444 department stores in 36 states and the District of Columbia as of Jan 31 2004 under the following names: Lord & Taylor, Filene's, Kaufmann's, Robinsons-May, Meier & Frank, Hecht's, Strawbridge's, Foley's, Famous-Barr, L.S. Ayers, and The Jones Store. Co. is also a major retailer of bridal gowns and bridal-related merchandise through David's Bridal, Inc. and Priscilla of Boston, Inc., and provides tuxedo rental services through After Hours Formalwear, Inc. At Jan 31 2004, Co. operated 210 David's Bridal stores in 44 states and Puerto Rico, 460 After Hours Formalwear stores in 30 states, and ten Priscilla of Boston stores in nine states.

Recent Developments: For the 13 weeks ended Oct 30 2004, net income dropped 83.0% to $8.0 million compared with $47.0 million in the corresponding quarter of 2003. Results for 2004 and 2003 included restructuring costs of $1.0 million and $5.0 million, respectively. Results for 2003 also included restructuring markdowns of $1.0 million. Net sales were $3.48 billion, up 17.0% from $2.98 billion the year before. Net sales included merchandise sales and lease department income. Store-for-store sales decreased 3.4% for the quarter. Sales for the quarter were good in selected merchandise categories.

Prospects: Co. is implementing a number of strategic initiatives that are designed to increase its sales and earnings in 2005. For instance, Co. continues to improve its in-store shopping experience by reducing inventory levels, in an effort to make stores more open and easier to shop, and by installing upgraded point-of-sale equipment, directional signage and price checkers. Also, this should result in additional markdowns and ensure that Co. is well-positioned for receipt of spring merchandise. Meanwhile, Co. will look to maintain its aggressive pursuit of the younger customer, while continuing to serve the needs of the baby boomer, its core customer.

Financial Data
(US$ in Thousands)

	9 Mos	6 Mos	3 Mos	01/31/2004	02/01/2003	02/02/2002	02/03/2001	01/29/2000
Earnings Per Share	2.01	2.14	1.42	1.41	1.76	2.21	2.62	2.60
Cash Flow Per Share	5.16	5.78	5.67	5.79	5.08	5.57	4.32	4.62
Tang Book Value Per Share	3.17	3.31	8.76	8.72	8.39	7.76	8.53	9.51
Dividends Per Share	0.968	0.965	0.963	0.960	0.950	0.940	0.930	0.890
Dividend Payout %	48.09	45.18	67.66	68.09	53.98	42.53	35.50	34.23
Income Statement								
Total Revenue	9,402,000	5,919,000	2,963,000	13,343,000	13,491,000	14,175,000	14,511,000	13,866,000
EBITDA	754,000	566,000	261,000	1,521,000	1,722,000	2,052,000	2,258,000	2,279,000
Depn & Amortn	460,000	285,000	140,000	564,000	557,000	559,000	511,000	469,000
Income Before Taxes	294,000	281,000	121,000	639,000	820,000	1,144,000	1,402,000	1,523,000
Income Taxes	109,000	104,000	45,000	205,000	278,000	438,000	544,000	596,000
Net Income	185,000	177,000	76,000	434,000	542,000	703,000	858,000	927,000
Average Shares	292,800	307,900	308,300	307,000	307,900	317,600	327,700	355,600
Balance Sheet								
Current Assets	6,023,000	5,551,000	5,088,000	5,143,000	4,722,000	4,925,000	5,270,000	5,115,000
Total Assets	15,619,000	15,134,000	11,984,000	12,097,000	11,936,000	11,920,000	11,574,000	10,935,000
Current Liabilities	4,135,000	3,574,000	2,468,000	2,685,000	2,666,000	2,538,000	2,214,000	2,415,000
Long-Term Obligations	5,786,000	5,794,000	3,788,000	3,797,000	4,035,000	4,403,000	4,534,000	3,560,000
Total Liabilities	11,434,000	10,893,000	7,766,000	7,906,000	7,901,000	8,079,000	7,719,000	6,858,000
Stockholders' Equity	4,185,000	4,241,000	4,218,000	4,191,000	4,035,000	3,841,000	3,855,000	4,077,000
Shares Outstanding	291,985	291,435	290,844	288,800	288,300	287,200	298,200	325,500
Statistical Record								
Return on Assets %	4.42	4.86	3.64	3.62	4.56	6.00	7.50	8.66
Return on Equity %	15.24	16.00	10.63	10.58	13.80	18.32	21.28	23.49
EBITDA Margin %	8.02	9.56	8.81	11.40	12.76	14.48	15.56	16.44
Net Margin %	1.97	2.99	2.56	3.25	4.02	4.96	5.91	6.69
Asset Turnover	1.01	1.01	1.12	1.11	1.13	1.21	1.27	1.30
Current Ratio	1.46	1.55	2.06	1.92	1.77	1.94	2.38	2.12
Debt to Equity	1.38	1.37	0.90	0.91	1.00	1.15	1.18	0.87
Price Range	36.31-23.95	36.31-24.12	36.31-20.10	33.61-18.01	37.60-20.43	41.25-27.98	38.95-19.63	45.00-29.56
P/E Ratio	18.06-11.92	16.97-11.27	25.57-14.15	23.84-12.77	21.36-11.61	18.67-12.66	14.87-7.49	17.31-11.37
Average Yield %	3.32	3.29	3.45	3.91	3.22	2.71	3.41	2.34

Address: 611 Olive Street, St. Louis, MO 63101-1799	**Web Site:** www.maycompany.com	**Auditors:** Deloite & Touche LLP
Telephone: (314) 342 6300	**Officers:** John L. Dunham - Interim Chmn., Pres., C.E.O. William P. McNamara - Vice-Chmn.	**Investor Contact:** 314-342-6413
Fax: (314) 444 6869		**Transfer Agents:** The Bank of New York, New York, NY

MAYTAG CORP.

Exchange	Symbol	Price	52Wk Range	Yield	P/E
NYS	MYG	$13.97 (3/31/2005)	31.95-13.31	5.15	N/A

*7 Year Price Score 49.57   *NYSE Composite Index=100   *12 Month Price Score 68.09

Interim Earnings (Per Share)

Qtr.	Mar	Jun	Sep	Dec
2001	0.96	1.08	(0.38)	(0.27)
2002	0.73	0.86	0.78	0.04
2003	0.44	0.32	0.46	0.31
2004	0.49	(0.52)	0.09	(0.17)

Interim Dividends (Per Share)

Amt	Decl	Ex	Rec	Pay
0.18Q	5/13/2004	5/27/2004	6/1/2004	6/15/2004
0.18Q	8/12/2004	8/30/2004	9/1/2004	9/15/2004
0.18Q	11/11/2004	11/29/2004	12/1/2004	12/15/2004
0.18Q	2/10/2005	2/25/2005	3/1/2005	3/15/2005

Indicated Div: $0.72

Valuation Analysis

Forecast P/E	11.72 (4/7/2005)	No of Institutions 222
Market Cap	$1.1 Billion	Shares
Book Value	N.M.	68,632,272
Price/Book	N.M.	% Held
Price/Sales	0.23	86.32

Business Summary: Electrical (MIC: 11.14 SIC: 639 NAIC: 35228)

Maytag is a manufacturer of home and commercial appliances. Co.'s products are sold to customers throughout North America and international markets. Co. operates in three business segments: major appliances, housewares, and commercial products. The Major Appliances segment includes Maytag Appliances, Maytag Services and Maytag International. The Housewares segment includes Hoover Floor Care and Maytage Housewares. The Commercial Products segment, which includes Dixie-Narco Vending, Maytag Specialty and Maytag Commercial Laundry, provides commercial cooking and vending equipment to distributors, soft drink bottlers and restaurant chains and dealers.

Recent Developments: For the year ended Jan 1 2005, loss from continuing operations was $9,345 thousand compared with an income of $114,378 thousand a year earlier. Net loss was $9,006 thousand versus net income of $120,133 thousand a year earlier. Revenues were $4,721,538 thousand, down 1.5% from $4,791,866 thousand the year before. Operating income was $40,348 thousand versus an income of $228,293 thousand in the prior year, a decrease of 82.3%. Total direct expense was $4,061,319 thousand versus $3,932,335 thousand in the prior year, an increase of 3.3%. Total indirect expense was $619,871 thousand versus $631,238 thousand in the prior year, a decrease of 1.8%.

Prospects: Co. is taking actions to improve its operating performance going forward. For instance, Co. is expecting to benefit in 2005 from its "One Company" restructuring, which consolidates Hoover floor care, Maytag Appliances and its corporate organizations. However, Co. is lowering its earnings guidance for 2005 as a result of lower revenue generation in the fourth quarter 2004 and recent distribution announcements that occurred in January. Co. expects reported earnings per share in 2005 to be in the range of $1.10 to $1.30, including about $0.05 in restructuring charges.

Financial Data

(US$ in Thousands)	01/01/2005	01/03/2004	12/31/2002	12/31/2001	12/31/2000	12/31/1999	12/31/1998	12/31/1997
Earnings Per Share	(0.11)	1.53	2.40	1.41	2.44	3.66	2.99	1.84
Cash Flow Per Share	3.44	4.48	4.69	5.24	4.82	5.34	5.87	3.70
Tang Book Value Per Share	N.M.	N.M.	N.M.	N.M.	N.M.	0.00	0.93	1.92
Dividends Per Share	0.720	0.720	0.720	0.720	0.720	0.720	0.680	0.640
Dividend Payout %	...	47.06	30.00	51.06	29.51	19.67	22.74	34.78
Income Statement								
Total Revenue	4,721,538	4,791,866	4,666,031	4,323,713	4,247,504	4,323,673	4,069,290	3,407,911
EBITDA	204,738	391,308	521,754	435,887	556,429	737,503	682,204	497,713
Depn & Amortn	169,782	165,785	163,708	158,975	160,337	147,393	148,554	138,163
Income Before Taxes	(21,318)	172,760	295,656	212,084	331,959	530,851	470,885	300,555
Income Taxes	(11,973)	58,382	100,523	30,089	115,200	195,100	176,100	109,800
Net Income	(9,006)	120,133	188,794	47,736	200,967	328,528	280,610	180,290
Average Shares	79,078	78,746	78,504	78,565	82,425	89,731	93,973	98,055
Balance Sheet								
Current Assets	1,445,497	1,304,323	1,323,599	1,369,544	1,076,559	1,021,516	968,862	934,717
Total Assets	3,020,024	3,024,140	3,104,249	3,156,151	2,668,924	2,636,487	2,587,663	2,514,154
Current Liabilities	910,663	983,790	1,163,740	1,074,493	971,687	853,023	790,697	566,638
Long-Term Obligations	972,568	874,832	738,767	932,065	451,336	337,764	446,505	549,524
Total Liabilities	3,095,048	2,958,329	3,062,110	3,032,463	2,082,185	1,839,159	1,906,044	1,724,622
Stockholders' Equity	(75,024)	65,811	42,139	23,546	21,676	427,380	507,564	615,809
Shares Outstanding	79,413	78,739	78,288	76,864	76,240	82,524	89,218	95,011
Statistical Record								
Return on Assets %	N.M.	3.89	6.03	1.64	7.56	12.58	11.00	7.44
Return on Equity %	...	220.76	574.85	211.12	89.26	70.28	49.96	30.31
EBITDA Margin %	4.34	8.17	11.18	10.08	13.10	17.06	16.76	14.60
Net Margin %	N.M.	2.51	4.05	1.10	4.73	7.60	6.90	5.29
Asset Turnover	1.57	1.55	1.49	1.48	1.60	1.66	1.60	1.41
Current Ratio	1.59	1.33	1.14	1.27	1.11	1.20	1.23	1.65
Debt to Equity	...	13.29	17.53	39.58	20.82	0.79	0.88	0.89
Price Range	31.95-15.81	30.05-18.74	47.59-19.15	37.01-23.50	48.00-25.25	74.00-32.38	64.38-36.44	37.31-19.75
P/E Ratio	...	19.64-12.25	19.83-7.98	26.25-16.67	19.67-10.35	20.22-8.85	21.53-12.19	20.28-10.73
Average Yield %	3.04	2.91	2.08	2.28	2.12	1.25	1.41	2.35

Address: 403 West Fourth Street North, Newton, IA 50208
Telephone: (641) 792-7000
Fax: (641) 787-8376

Web Site: www.maytagcorp.com
Officers: Ralph F. Hake - Chmn., C.E.O. George C. Moore - Exec. V.P., C.F.O.

Auditors: Ernst & Young LLP
Investor Contact: 641-787-8136

MBIA INC.

Exchange	Symbol	Price	52Wk Range	Yield	P/E	Div Acheiver
NYS	MBI	$52.28 (3/31/2005)	64.86-52.28	2.14	9.29	17 Years

*7 Year Price Score 104.64 *NYSE Composite Index=100 *12 Month Price Score 91.73

Interim Earnings (Per Share)

Qtr.	Mar	Jun	Sep	Dec
2001	0.78	0.96	1.03	1.05
2002	1.03	0.97	1.11	0.81
2003	1.54	1.51	1.31	1.25
2004	1.42	1.48	1.29	1.44

Interim Dividends (Per Share)

Amt	Decl	Ex	Rec	Pay
0.24Q	6/11/2004	6/23/2004	6/25/2004	7/15/2004
0.24Q	9/10/2004	9/22/2004	9/24/2004	10/15/2004
0.24Q	12/10/2004	12/21/2004	12/23/2004	1/18/2005
0.28Q	3/10/2005	3/23/2005	3/28/2005	4/15/2005

Indicated Div: $1.12

Valuation Analysis

Forecast P/E	9.48	No of Institutions
	(4/7/2005)	403
Market Cap	$7.3 Billion	Shares
Book Value	6.6 Billion	134,678,752
Price/Book	1.11	% Held
Price/Sales	3.64	97.85

Business Summary: Insurance (MIC: 8.2 SIC: 351 NAIC: 24130)

MBIA is engaged in providing financial guarantee insurance, investment management services and municipal and other services to public finance clients and structured finance clients on a global basis. Financial guarantee insurance provides an unconditional and irrevocable guarantee of the payment of the principal of, and interest or other amounts owing on, insured obligations when due. Co. conducts its financial guarantee business through its wholly-owned subsidiary, MBIA Insurance Corporation. Co. also owns MBIA Assurance S.A., a French insurance company, which writes financial guarantee insurance in the member countries of the European Union.

Recent Developments: For the year ended Dec 31 2004, income from continuing operations decreased 0.1% to $812,728 thousand from income of $813,812 thousand a year earlier. Net income decreased 0.1% to $815,304 thousand from net income of $815,916 thousand a year earlier. Revenues were $1,423,392 thousand, up 2.7% from $1,385,493 thousand the year before. Net premiums earned were $822,467 thousand versus $739,871 thousand in the prior year, an increase of 11.2%. Net investment income rose 26.6% to $577,977 thousand from $456,693 thousand a year ago.

Prospects: Going forward, Co. expects a challenging market environment characterized by tight credit spreads and increased levels of competition to continue in 2005. However, Co. believes that it has a solid pipeline across most of its product lines. For 2005, Co. expects operating earnings per share, excluding refundings, to increase by 10.0% to 12.0%, but then return to the 12.0% to 14.0% growth range in 2006-2007. Co. anticipates operating return on equity (ROE) will be at the lower end of the 12.0% to 14.0% range in 2005 due to its strong capital position and the projected decline in refunding volume. For 2006 and 2007, Co. expects operating ROE will improve and be within the 12.0% to 14.0% range.

Financial Data

(US$ in Thousands)	12/31/2004	12/31/2003	12/31/2002	12/31/2001	12/31/2000	12/31/1999	12/31/1998	12/31/1997
Earnings Per Share	5.63	5.61	3.92	3.82	3.55	2.13	2.88	2.81
Cash Flow Per Share	6.34	6.82	5.95	4.87	4.32	2.97	4.59	3.66
Tang Book Value Per Share	46.63	42.88	37.32	31.56	27.86	22.79	24.59	21.82
Dividends Per Share	0.960	0.800	0.680	0.600	0.547	0.537	0.527	0.513
Dividend Payout %	17.05	14.26	17.35	15.71	15.38	25.23	18.29	18.25
Income Statement								
Premium Income	822,467	732,997	588,509	523,870	446,353	442,796	424,550	297,377
Total Revenue	2,001,369	1,688,881	1,217,358	1,135,785	1,024,570	964,421	921,047	653,982
Benefits & Claims	81,880	72,888	61,688	56,651	51,291	198,454	34,683	18,673
Income Before Taxes	1,129,913	1,148,640	792,581	790,984	714,857	387,883	565,038	479,569
Income Taxes	317,185	335,055	205,763	207,826	186,220	67,353	132,310	105,393
Net Income	815,304	813,585	579,087	570,091	528,637	320,530	432,728	374,176
Average Shares	144,799	144,980	147,574	149,282	148,668	150,603	150,244	133,120
Balance Sheet								
Total Assets	33,027,410	30,267,734	18,852,101	16,199,685	13,894,338	12,263,899	11,796,564	9,810,762
Total Liabilities	26,448,339	24,008,719	13,358,750	11,417,047	9,670,925	8,750,798	8,004,347	6,762,509
Stockholders' Equity	6,579,071	6,259,015	5,493,351	4,782,638	4,223,413	3,513,101	3,792,217	3,048,253
Shares Outstanding	139,391	143,875	144,773	148,434	147,845	149,328	149,322	134,191
Statistical Record								
Return on Assets %	2.57	3.31	3.30	3.79	4.03	2.66	4.01	4.07
Return on Equity %	12.67	13.85	11.27	12.66	13.63	8.78	12.65	13.54
Loss Ratio %	9.96	9.94	10.48	10.81	11.49	44.82	8.17	6.28
Net Margin %	40.74	48.17	47.57	50.19	51.60	33.24	46.98	57.22
Price Range	67.13-53.67	60.08-34.64	59.65-35.32	57.25-39.21	49.96-24.42	47.71-30.38	53.46-31.67	44.83-30.58
P/E Ratio	11.92-9.53	10.71-6.17	15.22-9.01	14.99-10.26	14.07-6.88	22.40-14.26	18.56-11.00	15.95-10.88
Average Yield %	1.61	1.61	1.37	1.18	1.44	1.38	1.17	1.38

Address: 113 King Street, Armonk, NY 10504	**Web Site:** www.mbia.com	**Auditors:** PricewaterhouseCoopers LLP
Telephone: (914) 273-4545	**Officers:** Joseph W. Brown Jr. - Chmn., C.E.O. Gary C. Dunton - Pres., C.O.O.	**Investor Contact:** 914-765-3648
Fax: (914) 765-3163		**Transfer Agents:** Wells Fargo Shareowner Services, St. Paul, MN

MBNA CORP.

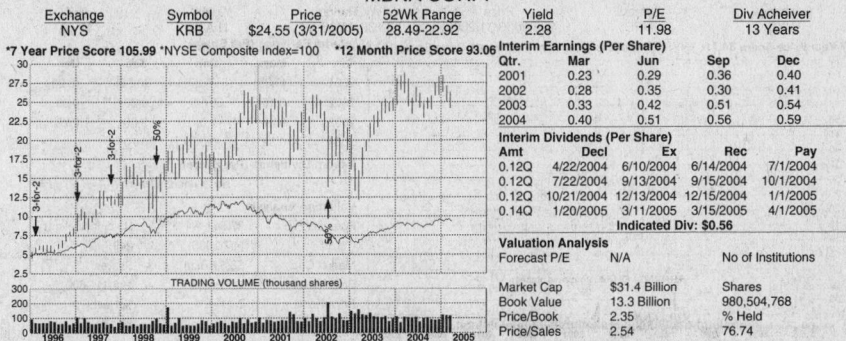

Exchange	Symbol	Price	52Wk Range	Yield	P/E	Div Acheiver
NYS	KRB	$24.55 (3/31/2005)	28.49-22.92	2.28	11.98	13 Years

*7 Year Price Score 105.99 *NYSE Composite Index=100 ***12 Month Price Score 93.06**

Interim Earnings (Per Share)

Qtr.	Mar	Jun	Sep	Dec
2001	0.23	0.29	0.36	0.40
2002	0.28	0.35	0.30	0.41
2003	0.33	0.42	0.51	0.54
2004	0.40	0.51	0.56	0.59

Interim Dividends (Per Share)

Amt	Decl	Ex	Rec	Pay
0.12Q	4/22/2004	6/10/2004	6/14/2004	7/1/2004
0.12Q	7/22/2004	9/13/2004	9/15/2004	10/1/2004
0.12Q	10/21/2004	12/13/2004	12/15/2004	1/1/2005
0.14Q	1/20/2005	3/11/2005	3/15/2005	4/1/2005

Indicated Div: $0.56

Valuation Analysis

Forecast P/E N/A No of Institutions

Market Cap	$31.4 Billion	Shares
Book Value	13.3 Billion	980,504,768
Price/Book	2.35	% Held
Price/Sales	2.54	76.74

TRADING VOLUME (thousand shares)

Business Summary: Commercial Banking (MIC: 8.1 SIC: 021 NAIC: 22110)

MBNA is a registered bank holding company, with assets of $59.13 billion as of Dec 31 2003. Co. is the parent of MBNA America Bank, N.A., which has two wholly-owned foreign bank subsidiaries, MBNA Europe Bank and MBNA Canada Bank. MBNA.com, provides credit card, consumer loan, retail deposit, travel and shopping services. Co. is an independent credit card lender and an issuer of affinity credit cards, marketed primarily to members of associations and customers of financial institutions. Co. offers credit cards in the U.S., the U.K., Ireland, Canada and Spain. In addition to its credit card lending, Co. also makes other consumer loans and offers insurance and deposit products.

Recent Developments: For the year ended Dec 31 2004, net income increased 14.5% to $2,677,296 thousand from net income of $2,338,104 a year earlier. Net interest income was $2,433,904 thousand, up 7.2% from $2,271,114 thousand the year before. Provision for loan losses was $1,146,855 thousand versus $1,392,701 thousand in the prior year, a decrease of 17.7%. Non-interest income rose 5.5% to $8,258,386 thousand, while non-interest expense advanced 7.7% to $5,516,703 thousand.

Prospects: Co. recently announced it will incur a one-time restructuring charge in the first quarter of 2005 to cover expenses associated with its voluntary early retirement program and voluntary employee severance program. The charge is expected to total approximately $300.0 million to $350.0 million pre-tax, and the resulting anticipated pre-tax expense savings of the program is approximately $150.0 million in 2005 and $200.0 million in 2006. Following the end of the voluntary early retirement and severance programs, Co. will undertake a review of its operations and look for opportunities to consolidate some of its facilities.

Financial Data

(US$ in Thousands)	12/31/2004	12/31/2003	12/31/2002	12/31/2001	12/31/2000	12/31/1999	12/31/1998	12/31/1997
Earnings Per Share	2.05	1.79	1.34	1.28	1.02	0.81	0.65	0.51
Cash Flow Per Share	3.62	3.03	3.60	2.14	(0.20)	1.17	0.45	0.11
Tang Book Value Per Share	7.63	6.20	4.63	4.08	3.03	3.49	2.12	1.75
Dividends Per Share	0.480	0.360	0.273	0.240	0.213	0.187	0.160	0.142
Dividend Payout %	23.41	20.11	20.40	18.75	20.91	23.14	24.74	27.83
Income Statement								
Interest Income	4,068,619	3,858,884	3,678,070	3,205,102	2,775,679	2,262,271	1,966,172	1,711,013
Interest Expense	1,531,818	1,508,511	1,603,495	1,814,065	1,691,727	1,328,506	1,223,833	1,018,623
Net Interest Income	2,536,801	2,350,373	2,074,575	1,391,037	1,083,952	933,765	742,339	692,390
Provision for Losses	1,146,855	1,392,701	1,340,157	1,140,615	409,017	408,914	310,039	260,040
Non-Interest Income	8,258,386	7,825,480	6,752,903	6,939,619	5,093,174	4,207,821	3,228,969	2,812,879
Non-Interest Expense	5,516,703	5,124,147	4,701,925	4,474,831	3,647,702	3,077,708	2,407,204	2,223,121
Income Before Taxes	4,131,629	3,659,005	2,785,416	2,715,210	2,120,407	1,654,964	1,254,065	2,044,216
Income Taxes	1,454,333	1,320,901	1,019,462	1,020,919	807,875	630,541	477,799	399,608
Net Income	2,677,296	2,338,104	1,765,954	1,694,291	1,312,532	1,024,423	776,266	622,500
Average Shares	1,297,178	1,295,142	1,277,787	1,314,229	1,269,796	1,255,557	1,184,131	1,184,701
Balance Sheet								
Net Loans & Leases	32,622,292	19,323,656	16,585,582	13,870,193	11,296,336	7,615,134	11,559,188	8,099,400
Total Assets	61,714,140	59,113,355	52,856,746	45,447,945	38,678,096	30,859,132	25,806,260	21,305,513
Total Deposits	31,239,504	31,836,081	30,616,216	27,094,745	24,343,595	18,714,753	15,407,040	12,913,213
Total Liabilities	48,390,888	48,000,315	43,755,427	37,649,227	32,050,818	26,659,689	23,415,225	19,335,463
Stockholders' Equity	13,323,252	11,113,040	9,101,319	7,798,718	6,627,278	4,199,443	2,391,035	1,970,050
Shares Outstanding	1,277,671	1,277,597	1,277,671	1,277,671	1,277,705	1,202,671	1,127,693	1,127,673
Statistical Record								
Return on Assets %	4.42	4.18	3.59	4.03	3.76	3.62	3.30	3.25
Return on Equity %	21.85	23.13	20.90	23.49	24.18	31.09	35.60	33.88
Net Interest Margin %	62.35	60.91	56.40	43.40	39.05	41.28	37.76	40.47
Efficiency Ratio %	44.75	43.85	45.08	44.11	46.36	47.57	46.34	49.14
Loans to Deposits	1.04	0.61	0.54	0.51	0.46	0.41	0.75	0.63
Price Range	28.78-22.92	25.45-12.15	25.97-13.40	26.04-16.70	26.54-13.33	21.67-13.96	16.92-9.17	13.39-8.07
P/E Ratio	14.04-11.18	14.22-6.79	19.38-10.30	20.35-13.05	26.02-13.07	26.75-17.23	26.03-14.10	26.25-15.83
Average Yield %	1.86	1.74	1.26	1.06	1.06	1.07	1.11	1.29

Address: 1100 North King Street, Wilmington, DE 19884-0141 Telephone: (302) 456-8588 Fax: (302) 456-8541	Web Site: www.mbna.com Officers: Randolph D. Lerner Esq. - Chmn. Richard K. Struthers - Vice-Chmn., Chief Loan Officer	Auditors: Ernst & Young LLP Investor Contact: 800-362-6255 Transfer Agents: National City Bank, Cleveland, OH

MCAFEE INC

Exchange	Symbol	Price	52Wk Range	Yield	P/E
NYS	MFE	$22.56 (3/31/2005)	33.39-15.68	N/A	16.59

*7 Year Price Score 84.71   *NYSE Composite Index=100   *12 Month Price Score 103.63

TRADING VOLUME (thousand shares)

Interim Earnings (Per Share)

Qtr.	Mar	Jun	Sep	Dec
2001	(0.35)	(0.27)	(0.08)	(0.03)
2002	0.10	0.14	0.06	0.50
2003	0.07	0.02	0.06	0.28
2004	0.32	0.06	0.70	...

Interim Dividends (Per Share)

No Dividends Paid

Valuation Analysis

Forecast P/E	37.54	No of Institutions	249
	(4/7/2005)		
Market Cap	$3.6 Billion	Shares	
Book Value	1.1 Billion		136,415,600
Price/Book	3.37	% Held	
Price/Sales	3.85		85.16

Business Summary: IT & Technology (MIC: 10.2 SIC: 372 NAIC: 11210)

McAfee is engaged as a provider of computer security solutions designed to prevent intrusions on networks and computer systems. Co. offers two families of products, McAfee System Protection Solutions, for desktop computers and servers, and McAfee Network Protection Solutions, for corporate networks. Co.'s computer security solutions are offered primarily to large enterprises, governments, small and medium-sized businesses and consumer users. Co. operates its business in five geographic regions including North America, Europe, the Middle East and Africa, or EMEA, Japan, the Asia-Pacific and Latin America.

Recent Developments: For the quarter ended Sep 30 2004, net income increased 996.6% to $118,148 thousand from net income of $10,774 thousand in the year-earlier quarter. Revenues were $221,633 thousand, down 2.7% from $227,775 thousand the year before. Operating income was $210,717 thousand versus an income of $10,093 thousand in the prior-year quarter, an increase of 1987.8%. Total direct expense was $34,273 thousand versus $37,935 thousand in the prior-year quarter, a decrease of 9.7%. Total indirect expense was $-23,357 thousand versus $179,747 thousand in the prior-year quarter, a decrease of 113%.

Prospects: Operating results are starting reflect benefits from steps taken by Co. over the last several months to streamline its business. For full-year 2005, Co. is raising revenue guidance to between $920.0 million and $960.0 million and non-GAAP net earnings to between $1.10 and $1.15 per share. Separately, Co. announced the sale of McAfee Research assets to SPARTA and expects the transaction to close in the second quarter of 2005. Co. remains committed to code and vulnerability research through the McAfee Anti-virus and Vulnerability Emergency Response Team.

Financial Data

(US$ in Thousands)	9 Mos	6 Mos	3 Mos	12/31/2003	12/31/2002	12/31/2001	12/31/2000	12/31/1999
Earnings Per Share	1.36	0.72	0.68	0.43	0.80	(0.73)	(0.74)	(1.15)
Cash Flow Per Share	1.71	1.60	1.34	0.97	1.31	1.06	0.19	(0.17)
Tang Book Value Per Share	3.69	2.00	2.61	2.09	2.55	1.85	2.16	2.92
Income Statement								
Total Revenue	666,389	444,756	216,624	936,336	1,043,044	834,478	745,692	683,668
EBITDA	346,381	130,022	94,907	135,925	183,802	41,368	(7,655)	(49,166)
Depn & Amortn	53,531	36,629	18,171	62,800	53,895	108,054	90,096	81,492
Income Before Taxes	292,850	93,393	76,736	73,125	129,907	(91,383)	(97,751)	(130,658)
Income Taxes	106,532	25,223	20,718	13,220	(274)	11,409	9,924	29,243
Net Income	186,318	68,170	56,018	70,242	128,312	(100,650)	(102,721)	(159,901)
Average Shares	172,103	163,925	186,564	164,489	176,249	137,847	138,072	138,695
Balance Sheet								
Current Assets	886,075	948,214	1,043,385	961,253	1,194,146	1,082,787	620,692	675,789
Total Assets	1,919,136	2,110,478	2,184,412	2,120,498	2,045,487	1,627,132	1,384,848	1,479,394
Current Liabilities	561,370	922,054	881,088	545,485	881,943	541,034	423,699	390,124
Long-Term Obligations	...	...	...	347,397	356,013	578,850	395,969	...
Total Liabilities	854,162	1,264,780	1,215,365	1,232,409	1,275,319	1,165,034	855,130	809,971
Stockholders' Equity	1,064,974	845,698	969,047	888,089	770,168	444,787	518,651	660,106
Shares Outstanding	159,280	155,685	164,412	161,721	157,926	140,699	138,089	139,419
Statistical Record								
Return on Assets %	11.67	5.94	5.62	3.37	6.99	N.M.	N.M.	N.M.
Return on Equity %	24.15	14.58	12.95	8.47	21.12	N.M.	N.M.	N.M.
EBITDA Margin %	51.98	29.23	43.81	14.52	17.62	4.96	N.M.	N.M.
Net Margin %	27.96	15.33	25.86	7.50	12.30	N.M.	N.M.	N.M.
Asset Turnover	0.48	0.46	0.46	0.45	0.57	0.55	0.52	0.45
Current Ratio	1.58	1.03	1.18	1.76	1.35	2.00	1.46	1.73
Debt to Equity	...	...	...	0.39	0.46	1.30	0.76	...
Price Range	20.10-12.95	19.75-10.75	18.50-10.75	20.28-10.75	30.26-8.45	27.27-4.19	36.69-4.13	66.25-11.06
P/E Ratio	14.78-9.52	27.43-14.93	27.21-15.81	47.16-25.00	37.83-10.56	N.A.	N.A.	N.A.

Address: 3965 Freedom Circle, Santa Clara, CA 95054	**Web Site:** www.networkassociates.com	**Auditors:** PricewaterhouseCoopers LLP
Telephone: (408) 988-3832	**Officers:** George Samenuk - Chmn., C.E.O. Gene Hodges - Pres.	
Fax: (408) 970-9727		

MCCLATCHY CO. (THE)

Exchange	Symbol	Price	52Wk Range	Yield	P/E
NYS	MNI	$74.16 (3/31/2005)	75.47-67.31	0.70	22.27

*7 Year Price Score 124.53 ***NYSE Composite Index=100** ***12 Month Price Score 96.18**

Interim Earnings (Per Share)

Qtr.	Mar	Jun	Sep	Dec
2001	0.23	0.27	0.31	0.46
2002	0.51	0.78	0.71	0.84
2003	0.55	0.94	0.77	0.98
2004	0.62	0.86	0.83	1.02

Interim Dividends (Per Share)

Amt	Decl	Ex	Rec	Pay
0.12Q	5/19/2004	6/14/2004	6/16/2004	7/1/2004
0.13Q	7/28/2004	9/13/2004	9/15/2004	10/1/2004
0.13Q	11/30/2004	12/13/2004	12/15/2004	1/3/2005
0.13Q	1/25/2005	3/14/2005	3/16/2005	4/1/2005
		Indicated Div: $0.52		

Valuation Analysis

Forecast P/E	21.28	No of Institutions
	(4/7/2005)	116
Market Cap	$3.4 Billion	Shares
Book Value	1.4 Billion	17,805,814
Price/Book	2.42	% Held
Price/Sales	2.96	87.58

Business Summary: Media (MIC: 13.1 SIC: 711 NAIC: 11110)

McClatchy owns and publishes 24 newspapers with a combined circulation of 1.4 million daily and 1.9 million Sunday. Co. has operations in the following regions: California, the Northwest (Alaska and Washington), the Carolinas, and Minnesota. Co.'s newspapers range from large dailies serving metropolitan areas to non-daily newspapers serving small communities. Another business owned by Co. includes Nando Media, Co.'s national online publishing operation. In addition, Co. has a 13.5% interest in Ponderay Newsprint, a general partnership that owns and operates a newsprint mill in Washington State.

Recent Developments: For the year ended Dec 26 2004, net income increased 3.8% to $155,876 thousand from net income of $150,222 thousand a year earlier. Revenues were $1,163,376 thousand, up 5.8% from $1,099,391 thousand the year before. Operating income was $269,309 thousand versus an income of $248,941 thousand in the prior year, an increase of 8.2%. Total indirect expense was $894,067 thousand versus $850,450 thousand in the prior year, an increase of 5.1%.

Prospects: Prospects appear promising as Co. continues to benefit from steady advertising demand. Co. noted that advertising revenues, particularly in retail advertising, are better than expected, helping to propel earnings per share growth. Also, Co. is benefiting from favorable growth in on-line advertising and direct marketing advertising, which continues to fuel top-line growth. For 2005, Co. expects business patterns to be similar to those experienced in 2004. While the economy appears to be healthy, advertising spending continues to be sporadic in selected markets. Co. expects overall advertising revenue growth to be in the low to mid-single-digit range in the first quarter of 2005.

Financial Data

(US$ in Thousands)	12/26/2004	12/28/2003	12/29/2002	12/30/2001	12/31/2000	12/26/1999	12/27/1998	12/31/1997
Earnings Per Share	3.33	3.23	2.84	1.27	1.97	1.83	1.41	1.80
Cash Flow Per Share	4.02	3.93	3.71	4.34	3.98	3.66	3.15	3.09
Tang Book Value Per Share	2.39	N.M.	N.M.	N.M.	N.M.	N.M.	N.M.	4.50
Dividends Per Share	0.500	0.440	0.400	0.400	0.400	0.380	0.380	0.380
Dividend Payout %	15.02	13.62	14.08	31.50	20.30	20.77	26.95	21.11
Income Statement								
Total Revenue	1,163,376	1,099,391	1,081,898	1,080,053	1,142,124	1,087,947	968,651	641,950
EBITDA	333,188	318,888	318,244	276,550	347,710	336,356	281,479	178,369
Depn & Amortn	66,532	70,139	75,265	111,803	112,013	110,353	96,556	53,411
Income Before Taxes	257,561	230,659	216,885	120,702	171,020	160,261	122,103	116,260
Income Taxes	101,685	86,462	85,669	62,705	82,090	77,729	61,052	47,461
Net Income	155,876	150,222	131,216	57,997	88,930	82,532	61,051	68,799
Average Shares	46,815	46,456	46,178	45,616	45,243	45,015	43,349	38,155
Balance Sheet								
Current Assets	203,763	188,458	248,201	248,367	235,538	215,619	200,539	122,795
Total Assets	2,049,400	1,875,298	1,980,651	2,104,160	2,165,658	2,204,028	2,246,725	853,781
Current Liabilities	156,890	296,654	250,840	307,703	227,335	233,454	220,390	98,443
Long-Term Obligations	267,200	204,923	471,615	594,714	778,102	878,166	1,004,000	94,000
Total Liabilities	626,396	659,281	923,322	1,105,995	1,206,807	1,324,362	1,439,720	289,112
Stockholders' Equity	1,423,004	1,216,017	1,057,329	998,165	958,851	879,666	807,005	564,669
Shares Outstanding	46,464	46,280	46,015	45,593	45,244	44,957	44,790	38,107
Statistical Record								
Return on Assets %	7.97	7.81	6.44	2.72	4.00	3.72	3.98	7.96
Return on Equity %	11.85	13.25	12.80	5.94	9.52	9.81	9.00	12.89
EBITDA Margin %	28.64	29.01	29.42	25.61	30.44	30.92	29.06	27.79
Net Margin %	13.40	13.66	12.13	5.37	7.79	7.59	6.30	10.72
Asset Turnover	0.59	0.57	0.53	0.51	0.51	0.49	0.63	0.74
Current Ratio	1.30	0.64	0.99	0.81	1.04	0.92	0.91	1.25
Debt to Equity	0.19	0.17	0.45	0.60	0.81	1.00	1.24	0.17
Price Range	73.75-67.31	68.25-51.59	64.25-46.25	48.96-37.50	44.88-28.94	43.38-29.19	38.06-25.19	34.81-23.63
P/E Ratio	22.15-20.21	21.13-15.97	22.62-16.29	38.55-29.53	22.78-14.69	23.70-15.95	26.99-17.86	19.34-13.13
Average Yield %	0.71	0.74	0.69	0.96	1.12	1.08	1.23	1.32

Address: 2100 Q Street, Sacramento, CA 95816-6899
Telephone: (916) 321 1846
Fax: (916) 321 1964

Web Site: www.mcclatchy.com
Officers: Gary B. Pruitt - Chmn., Pres., C.E.O. Patrick J. Talamantes - V.P., Fin., C.F.O.

Auditors: Deloitte & Touche LLP
Investor Contact: 916-321-1846

MCCORMICK & CO., INC.

Exchange	Symbol	Price	52Wk Range	Yield	P/E	Div Acheiver
NYS	MKC	$34.43 (3/31/2005)	39.06-32.25	1.86	22.80	18 Years

*7 Year Price Score 135.71 *NYSE Composite Index=100 *12 Month Price Score 96.67

Interim Earnings (Per Share)
Qtr.	Feb	May	Aug	Nov
2002	0.24	0.24	0.25	0.54
2003	0.25	0.28	0.36	0.59
2004	0.27	0.30	0.33	0.62
2005	0.26	...	...	...

Interim Dividends (Per Share)
Amt	Decl	Ex	Rec	Pay
0.14Q	6/22/2004	6/30/2004	7/2/2004	7/16/2004
0.14Q	9/28/2004	10/6/2004	10/8/2004	10/22/2004
0.16Q	11/23/2004	12/29/2004	12/31/2004	1/21/2005
0.16Q	3/23/2005	3/31/2005	4/4/2005	4/15/2005

Indicated Div: $0.64

Valuation Analysis
Forecast P/E	N/A	No of Institutions
Market Cap	$4.7 Billion	Shares
Book Value	904.5 Million	87,776,760
Price/Book	5.15	% Held
Price/Sales	1.82	72.66

Business Summary: Food (MIC: 4.1 SIC: 099 NAIC: 11942)

McCormick & Company is a specialty food company. Co. manufactures, markets and distributes spices, herbs, seasonings and other flavors to the food industry. Co.'s consumer segment sells seasoning blends, spices, herbs, extracts, sauces, marinades and specialty foods to the consumer food market under a variety of brands, including "McCormick" and "Zatarain's" in the U.S., "Ducros" and "Silvo" in continental Europe, "Club House" in Canada and "Schwartz" in the U.K. Co.'s industrial segment sells blended seasonings, spices and herbs, condiments, compound flavors and extracts, and coating systems to food processors, restaurants, distributors, warehouse clubs and institutional operations.

Recent Developments: For the three months ended Feb 28 2005, net income decreased 5.4% to $36.0 million compared with $38.1 million in the comparable year-earlier period. Results for 2005 and 2004 included special charges of $1.3 million and $69,000, respectively. Net sales rose 5.5% to $603.6 million from $572.4 million the previous year. Co. stated that higher volume, pricing and product mix contributed 3.0% of the increase, of which 2.0% was attributable to its 2004 acquisition of Silvo. Favorable foreign exchange rates added 2.0%. Gross profit amounted to $228.2 million, or 37.8% of net sales, versus $221.7 million, or 38.7% of net sales.

Prospects: Results are benefiting from higher volumes, favorable foreign currency exchange rates, additional sales from recent acquisitions, and improved pricing. Increased volumes are being driven by new product launches, expanded distribution and more effective marketing. Meanwhile, earnings are being positively affected by the implementation of cost-reduction initiatives, which are expected to generate costs savings of $25.0 million in 2005 and $30.0 million in 2006. Looking ahead, Co. is projecting fiscal 2005 sales growth of between 4.0% and 7.0%. In addition, Co. is targeting fiscal 2005 earnings in the range of $1.70 to $1.74 per share.

Financial Data
(US$ in Thousands)	3 Mos	11/30/2004	11/30/2003	11/30/2002	11/30/2001	11/30/2000	11/30/1999	11/30/1998
Earnings Per Share	1.51	1.52	1.48	1.26	1.04	0.99	0.71	0.70
Cash Flow Per Share	2.53	2.54	1.40	1.60	1.48	1.46	1.61	0.98
Tang Book Value Per Share	0.56	0.45	0.28	0.62	N.M.	N.M.	1.70	1.57
Dividends Per Share	0.580	0.560	0.460	0.420	0.400	0.380	0.340	0.320
Dividend Payout %	38.41	36.84	31.08	33.33	38.28	38.38	47.55	45.39
Income Statement								
Total Revenue	603,623	2,526,200	2,269,600	2,320,000	2,218,500	2,123,500	2,006,900	1,881,100
EBITDA	75,653	406,800	373,900	345,200	315,700	287,000	239,800	244,200
Depn & Amortn	17,641	72,000	65,300	66,800	73,000	61,300	57,400	54,800
Income Before Taxes	46,928	293,800	270,000	234,800	190,400	186,000	150,000	152,500
Income Taxes	15,017	89,000	83,400	74,300	62,900	66,600	60,100	54,900
Net Income	36,035	214,500	210,800	179,800	146,600	137,500	103,300	103,800
Average Shares	140,457	141,300	142,600	142,300	140,200	139,200	144,000	147,600
Balance Sheet								
Current Assets	775,484	864,000	762,100	724,600	635,800	620,000	490,600	503,800
Total Assets	2,276,675	2,369,600	2,148,200	1,930,800	1,772,000	1,659,900	1,188,800	1,259,100
Current Liabilities	850,674	772,700	712,700	673,400	713,700	1,027,200	470,600	518,000
Long-Term Obligations	295,524	465,000	448,600	453,900	454,100	160,200	241,400	250,400
Total Liabilities	1,339,922	1,448,900	1,370,800	1,338,500	1,308,900	1,300,600	806,400	871,000
Stockholders' Equity	904,547	889,700	755,200	592,300	463,100	359,300	382,400	388,100
Shares Outstanding	135,213	135,500	137,200	140,000	138,400	136,600	140,800	145,000
Statistical Record								
Return on Assets %	9.57	9.47	10.34	9.71	8.54	9.63	8.44	8.25
Return on Equity %	24.38	26.01	31.29	34.07	35.65	36.98	26.81	26.57
EBITDA Margin %	12.53	16.10	16.47	14.88	14.23	13.52	11.95	12.98
Net Margin %	5.97	8.49	9.29	7.75	6.61	6.48	5.15	5.52
Asset Turnover	1.15	1.12	1.11	1.25	1.29	1.49	1.64	1.50
Current Ratio	0.91	1.12	1.07	1.08	0.89	0.60	1.04	0.97
Debt to Equity	0.33	0.52	0.59	0.77	0.98	0.45	0.63	0.65
Price Range	39.06-31.00	37.41-28.84	30.21-22.10	26.93-20.36	23.00-17.13	18.63-12.03	17.25-13.38	18.03-13.19
P/E Ratio	25.87-20.53	24.61-18.97	20.41-14.93	21.37-16.16	22.11-16.47	18.81-12.15	24.30-18.84	25.76-18.84
Average Yield %	1.65	1.68	1.79	1.78	1.95	2.48	2.16	2.05

Address: 18 Loveton Circle, P.O Box 6000, Sparks, MD 21152 **Telephone:** (410) 771-7301 **Fax:** (410) 771-7462	**Web Site:** www.mccormick.com **Officers:** Robert J. Lawless - Chmn., Pres., C.E.O. Francis A. Contino - Exec. V.P., Strategic Planning, C.F.O.	**Auditors:** Ernst & Young LLP **Investor Contact:** 410-771-7244 **Transfer Agents:** Wells Fargo Bank Minnesota, N.A., St. Paul, MN

MCDONALD'S CORP

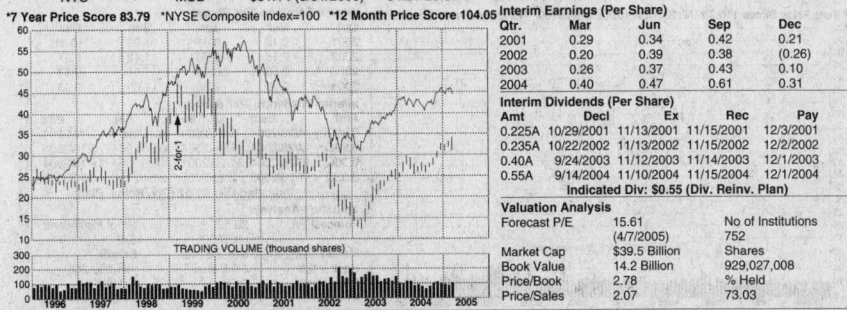

Exchange	Symbol	Price	52Wk Range	Yield	P/E	Div Acheiver
NYS	MCD	$31.14 (3/31/2005)	34.21-25.31	1.77	17.40	28 Years

*7 Year Price Score 83.79 *NYSE Composite Index=100 *12 Month Price Score 104.05

Interim Earnings (Per Share)

Qtr.	Mar	Jun	Sep	Dec
2001	0.29	0.34	0.42	0.21
2002	0.20	0.39	0.38	(0.26)
2003	0.26	0.37	0.43	0.10
2004	0.40	0.47	0.61	0.31

Interim Dividends (Per Share)

Amt	Decl	Ex	Rec	Pay
0.225A	10/29/2001	11/13/2001	11/15/2001	12/3/2001
0.235A	10/22/2002	11/13/2002	11/15/2002	12/2/2002
0.40A	9/24/2003	11/12/2003	11/14/2003	12/1/2003
0.55A	9/14/2004	11/10/2004	11/15/2004	12/1/2004

Indicated Div: $0.55 (Div. Reinv. Plan)

Valuation Analysis

Forecast P/E	15.61	No of Institutions
	(4/7/2005)	752
Market Cap	$39.5 Billion	Shares
Book Value	14.2 Billion	929,027,008
Price/Book	2.78	% Held
Price/Sales	2.07	73.03

TRADING VOLUME (thousand shares)

Business Summary: Hospitality & Tourism (MIC: 5.1 SIC: 812 NAIC: 22211)

McDonald's develops, licenses, leases and services a worldwide system of restaurants in more than 100 countries. Co.'s menu includes hamburgers, cheeseburgers, the Big Mac, Quarter Pounder with Cheese, Big N' Tasty, Filet-O-Fish, Chicken McNuggets, several chicken sandwiches, french fries, salads, milk shakes, McFlurry desserts, ice cream sundaes and cones, pies, cookies and beverages. As of Dec 31 2003, there were approx. 18,000 units operated by franchisees, more than 8,000 units operated by Co., and about 4,000 units operated by affiliates. Co. also operates Boston Market and Chipotle Mexican Grill in the U.S. and has a minority ownership interest in U.K.-based Pret A Manger.

Recent Developments: For the year ended Dec 31 2004, net income increased 54.9% to $2,278,500 thousand from net income of $1,471,400 thousand a year earlier. Revenues were $19,064,700 thousand, up 11.2% from $17,140,500 thousand the year prior. Operating income was $3,540,500 thousand versus an income of $2,832,200 thousand in the prior year, an increase of 25.0%. Total direct expense was $4,852,700 thousand versus $4,314,800 thousand in the prior year, an increase of 12.5%. Total indirect expense was $10,731,500 thousand versus $10,030,400 thousand in the prior year, an increase of 7.0%.

Prospects: Strong performance at Co.'s domestic stores is being driven by the introduction of new products, extended hours of operation, cashless payments, and increased advertising. Co. is planning several new product launches in 2005, including a "robust" coffee blend and a line of premium chicken sandwiches. Co. also plans to introduce gift cards at the end of the year and is taking steps to expand the number of stores open 24 hours a day. Looking ahead, Co. is projecting full-year 2005 revenue growth of between 3.0% and 5.0%, along with operating income growth in the range of 6.0% to 7.0%. In addition, Co. expects to add about 350 net new McDonald's restaurants in 2005.

Financial Data

(US$ in Thousands)	12/31/2004	12/31/2003	12/31/2002	12/31/2001	12/31/2000	12/31/1999	12/31/1998	12/31/1997
Earnings Per Share	1.79	1.15	0.70	1.25	1.46	1.39	1.10	1.15
Cash Flow Per Share	3.09	2.57	2.27	2.08	2.07	2.22	2.03	1.77
Tang Book Value Per Share	9.74	8.18	6.88	6.30	5.95	6.20	6.26	4.83
Dividends Per Share	0.550	0.400	0.235	0.225	0.215	0.195	0.176	0.161
Dividend Payout %	30.73	34.78	33.57	18.00	14.73	14.03	16.02	14.08
Income Statement								
Total Revenue	19,064,700	17,140,500	15,405,700	14,870,000	14,243,000	13,259,300	12,421,400	11,408,800
EBITDA	4,761,800	3,882,600	3,087,000	3,868,400	4,322,900	4,236,700	3,602,300	3,565,500
Depn & Amortn	1,201,000	1,148,200	1,050,800	1,086,300	1,010,700	956,300	881,100	793,800
Income Before Taxes	3,202,400	2,346,400	1,662,100	2,329,700	2,882,300	2,884,100	2,307,400	2,407,300
Income Taxes	923,900	838,200	670,000	693,100	905,000	936,200	757,300	764,800
Net Income	2,278,500	1,471,400	893,500	1,636,600	1,977,300	1,947,900	1,550,100	1,642,500
Average Shares	1,273,700	1,276,500	1,281,500	1,309,300	1,356,500	1,404,200	1,405,700	1,410,200
Balance Sheet								
Current Assets	2,857,800	1,885,400	1,715,400	1,819,300	1,662,400	1,572,300	1,309,400	1,142,300
Total Assets	27,837,500	25,525,100	23,970,500	22,534,500	21,683,500	20,983,200	19,784,400	18,241,500
Current Liabilities	3,520,500	2,485,800	2,422,300	2,248,300	2,360,900	3,274,300	2,497,100	2,984,500
Long-Term Obligations	8,357,300	9,342,500	9,703,600	8,555,500	7,843,900	5,632,400	6,188,600	4,834,100
Total Liabilities	13,636,000	13,543,200	13,689,600	13,046,100	12,479,100	11,344,100	10,319,700	9,389,900
Stockholders' Equity	14,201,500	11,981,900	10,280,900	9,488,400	9,204,400	9,639,100	9,464,700	8,851,600
Shares Outstanding	1,269,900	1,261,900	1,268,200	1,280,700	1,304,900	1,350,800	1,356,200	1,660,600
Statistical Record								
Return on Assets %	8.52	5.95	3.84	7.40	9.24	9.56	8.15	9.22
Return on Equity %	17.36	13.22	9.04	17.51	20.93	20.39	16.93	18.70
EBITDA Margin %	24.98	22.65	20.04	26.01	30.35	31.95	29.00	31.25
Net Margin %	11.95	8.58	5.80	11.01	13.88	14.69	12.48	14.40
Asset Turnover	0.71	0.69	0.66	0.67	0.67	0.65	0.65	0.64
Current Ratio	0.81	0.76	0.71	0.81	0.70	0.48	0.52	0.38
Debt to Equity	0.59	0.78	0.94	0.90	0.85	0.58	0.65	0.55
Price Range	32.66-24.64	26.56-12.38	30.65-15.48	34.69-25.00	42.75-27.00	48.38-37.66	39.16-22.69	27.34-21.63
P/E Ratio	18.25-13.77	23.10-10.77	43.79-22.11	27.75-20.00	29.28-18.49	34.80-27.09	35.60-20.63	23.78-18.80
Average Yield %	1.98	1.98	0.97	0.79	0.64	0.46	0.57	0.67

Address: McDonald's Plaza, Oak Brook, IL 60523	Web Site: www.mcdonalds.com	Auditors: Ernst & Young LLP
Telephone: (630) 623-3000	Officers: Andrew J. McKenna - Chmn. Jim Skinner - Vice-Chmn., C.E.O.	Investor Contact: 630-623-7428
Fax: (630) 623-5027		Transfer Agents: First Chicago Trust Company, Jersey City, NJ

MCGRAW-HILL COS., INC. (THE)

Exchange	Symbol	Price	52Wk Range	Yield	P/E	Div Achiever
NYS	MHP	$87.25 (3/31/2005)	95.91-73.09	1.51	22.26	31 Years

*7 Year Price Score 116.38 *NYSE Composite Index=100 *12 Month Price Score 103.31

Interim Earnings (Per Share)

Qtr.	Mar	Jun	Sep	Dec
2001	0.10	0.61	1.22	(0.01)
2002	0.15	0.70	1.42	0.67
2003	0.50	0.74	1.51	0.83
2004	0.39	0.86	1.69	0.98

Interim Dividends (Per Share)

Amt	Decl	Ex	Rec	Pay
0.30Q	4/28/2004	5/24/2004	5/26/2004	6/10/2004
0.30Q	7/28/2004	8/24/2004	8/26/2004	9/10/2004
0.30Q	10/28/2004	11/23/2004	11/26/2004	12/10/2004
0.33Q	1/26/2005	2/22/2005	2/24/2005	3/10/2005

Indicated Div: $1.32 (Div. Reinv. Plan)

Valuation Analysis

Forecast P/E	20.52	No of Institutions
	(4/7/2005)	542
Market Cap	$16.6 Billion	Shares
Book Value	3.0 Billion	141,299,248
Price/Book	5.55	% Held
Price/Sales	3.15	74.26

TRADING VOLUME (thousand shares)

Business Summary: Non-Media Publishing (MIC: 13.3 SIC: 731 NAIC: 11130)

McGraw-Hill, a multimedia publishing and information services company, serves worldwide markets in education, finance and business information. As of Dec 31 2003, Co. operated more than 322 offices in 33 countries. Co. provides information in print through books, newsletters, and magazines, including Business Week; on-line over electronic networks; over the air by television, satellite and FM sideband; and on software, videotape, facsimile and compact disks. Among Co.'s business units are Standard & Poor's Financial Information Services and Standard & Poor's Ratings Services divisions.

Recent Developments: For the year ended Dec 31 2004, income from continuing operations increased 10.0% to $756,410 thousand from income of $687,811 thousand a year earlier. Net income increased 9.9% to $755,823 thousand from net income of $687,650 thousand a year earlier. Revenues were $5,250,538 thousand, up 7.4% from $4,890,320 thousand the year before. Operating income was $1,174,690 thousand versus an income of $1,137,374 thousand in the prior year, an increase of 3.3%. Total direct expense was $2,046,645 thousand versus $2,018,450 thousand in the prior year, an increase of 1.4%. Total indirect expense was $3,933,759 thousand versus $3,648,895 thousand in the prior year, an increase of 7.8%.

Prospects: Co. is benefiting from profitable returns in its Information and Media Services segment, largely due to an improvement in advertising. Also, Co. is benefiting from rigorous cost controls, and as a result, its operating margin is expanding. Separately, Co. is having solid growth in the California reading adoption, stimulated, in part, by new Reading First funding, a program as part of the No Child Left Behind Act to ensure children can read at or above grade level by the end of the third grade. Going forward, Co. expects year-over-year double-digit growth in earnings per share from continuing operations for 2005.

Financial Data

(US$ in Thousands)	12/31/2004	12/31/2003	12/31/2002	12/31/2001	12/31/2000	12/31/1999	12/31/1998	12/31/1997
Earnings Per Share	3.92	3.58	2.96	1.92	2.06	2.14	1.67	1.46
Cash Flow Per Share	5.59	7.26	5.92	5.52	3.63	3.61	3.83	1.88
Tang Book Value Per Share	5.43	4.49	1.88	0.18	0.33	2.24	1.48	0.64
Dividends Per Share	1.200	1.080	1.020	0.980	0.940	0.860	0.782	0.720
Dividend Payout %	30.61	30.17	34.46	51.04	45.63	40.19	46.86	49.48
Income Statement								
Total Revenue	5,250,538	4,827,857	4,787,668	4,645,535	4,280,968	3,991,997	3,729,145	3,534,095
EBITDA	1,299,458	1,255,027	1,055,960	850,485	973,891	877,683	738,081	646,993
Depn & Amortn	124,768	117,653	128,378	180,357	153,708	137,696	129,698	123,185
Income Before Taxes	1,168,905	1,130,277	905,065	615,058	767,342	697,974	560,422	471,266
Income Taxes	412,495	442,466	328,305	238,027	295,426	272,210	218,565	180,591
Net Income	755,823	687,650	576,760	377,031	403,794	425,764	333,141	290,675
Average Shares	192,912	192,005	194,573	195,873	196,072	198,557	199,104	199,504
Balance Sheet								
Current Assets	2,447,830	2,256,152	1,674,307	1,812,947	1,801,690	1,553,725	1,428,761	1,464,421
Total Assets	5,862,989	5,394,068	5,032,182	5,161,191	4,931,444	4,088,797	3,788,144	3,724,474
Current Liabilities	1,968,662	1,993,734	1,775,291	1,876,393	1,780,785	1,525,453	1,291,451	1,206,242
Long-Term Obligations	513	389	458,923	833,571	817,529	354,775	452,097	607,030
Total Liabilities	2,878,476	2,837,017	2,866,360	3,307,306	3,170,400	2,397,304	2,236,336	2,289,823
Stockholders' Equity	2,984,513	2,557,051	2,165,822	1,853,885	1,761,044	1,691,493	1,551,808	1,434,651
Shares Outstanding	189,813	190,396	191,832	193,218	194,285	195,708	197,111	198,204
Statistical Record								
Return on Assets %	13.39	13.19	11.32	7.47	8.93	10.81	8.87	7.89
Return on Equity %	27.20	29.12	28.70	20.86	23.33	26.25	22.31	20.79
EBITDA Margin %	24.75	26.00	22.06	18.31	22.75	21.99	19.79	18.31
Net Margin %	14.40	14.24	12.05	8.12	9.43	10.67	8.93	8.22
Asset Turnover	0.93	0.93	0.94	0.92	0.95	1.01	0.99	0.96
Current Ratio	1.24	1.13	0.94	0.97	1.01	1.02	1.11	1.21
Debt to Equity	N.M.	N.M.	0.21	0.45	0.46	0.21	0.29	0.42
Price Range	91.86-69.50	69.92-52.50	68.89-51.15	70.45-49.30	67.13-42.75	62.25-47.63	51.53-34.72	37.31-22.69
P/E Ratio	23.43-17.73	19.53-14.66	23.27-17.28	36.69-25.68	32.58-20.75	29.09-22.25	30.86-20.79	25.56-15.54
Average Yield %	1.53	1.76	1.63	1.62	1.69	1.58	1.94	2.42

Address: 1221 Avenue Of The Americas, New York, NY 10020-1095	**Web Site:** www.mcgraw-hill.com	**Auditors:** Ernst & Young LLP
Telephone: (212) 512-2000	**Officers:** Harold McGraw III - Chmn., Pres., C.E.O. Robert J. Bahash - Exec. V.P., C.F.O.	**Investor Contact:** 212-512-4321
Fax: (212) 512-2305		**Transfer Agents:** Mellon Investor Services, South Hackensack, NJ

MCKESSON CORP. (NEW)

Exchange	Symbol	Price	52Wk Range	Yield	P/E
NYS	MCK	$37.75 (3/31/2005)	38.41-22.98	0.64	N/A

*7 Year Price Score 73.09   *NYSE Composite Index=100   *12 Month Price Score 108.47

Interim Earnings (Per Share)

Qtr.	Jun	Sep	Dec	Mar
2001-02	0.37	0.27	0.37	0.43
2002-03	0.39	0.42	0.46	0.61
2003-04	0.53	0.53	0.41	0.73
2004-05	0.55	0.29	(2.26)	...

Interim Dividends (Per Share)

Amt	Decl	Ex	Rec	Pay
0.06Q	5/26/2004	6/7/2004	6/9/2004	7/1/2004
0.06Q	7/28/2004	8/30/2004	9/1/2004	10/1/2004
0.06Q	10/28/2004	11/29/2004	12/1/2004	1/3/2005
0.06Q	1/26/2005	2/25/2005	3/1/2005	4/1/2005
		Indicated Div: $0.24		

Valuation Analysis

Forecast P/E	N/A	No of Institutions
Market Cap	$11.1 Billion	Shares
Book Value	4.9 Billion	243,564,400
Price/Book	2.26	% Held
Price/Sales	0.14	82.51

TRADING VOLUME (thousand shares)

Business Summary: Pharmaceuticals (MIC: 9.1 SIC: 122 NAIC: 24210)

McKesson provides products and services to the healthcare industry. The Pharmaceutical Solutions segment distributes ethical and proprietary drugs and health and beauty care products in North America. This segment also provides automated pharmaceutical dispensing systems, medical management and specialty pharmaceutical products and services, and patient and payor services, consulting and outsourcing services. The Medical-Surgical Solutions segment distributes medical-surgical supplies and equipment, and provides logistics within the U.S. The Information Solutions segment provides software, support and services to healthcare organizations throughout North America and Europe.

Recent Developments: For the quarter ended Dec 31 2004, net loss was $665,400 thousand versus net income of $120,200 thousand in the year-earlier quarter. Revenues were $20,781,900 thousand, up 14.0% from $18,231,900 thousand the year before. Operating loss was $965,400 thousand versus an income of $184,500 thousand in the prior-year quarter, a decrease of 623.3%. Total indirect expense was $1,806,000 thousand versus $571,000 thousand in the prior-year quarter, an increase of 216.3%.

Prospects: In Jan 2005, Co. announced a settlement agreement that represents a major positive step in resolving the securities litigation and removing the resulting uncertainty hanging over the organization for the past six years. Separately, Co. is making progress in securing more predictable compensation from manufacturers and its Pharmaceutical Solutions revenue is seeing strong growth reflecting new customer agreements that previously took effect. For fiscal year 2005, Co. expect earnings to range from $2.05 to $2.15 per diluted share, before the affect of the securities litigation charge. Co. continues to expect significantly higher operating cash flow versus $563.0 million in fiscal 2004.

Financial Data

(US$ in Thousands)	9 Mos	6 Mos	3 Mos	03/31/2004	03/31/2003	03/31/2002	03/31/2001	03/31/2000
Earnings Per Share	(0.70)	1.98	2.21	2.19	1.88	1.43	(0.17)	2.57
Cash Flow Per Share	4.64	4.21	2.24	1.94	2.40	1.15	1.25	(1.47)
Tang Book Value Per Share	11.11	13.24	12.91	12.66	10.57	9.81	8.55	8.47
Dividends Per Share	0.240	0.240	0.240	0.240	0.240	0.240	0.240	0.240
Dividend Payout %	N.M.	12.15	10.84	10.96	12.77	16.78	N.M.	9.34
Income Statement								
Total Revenue	59,902,800	39,120,900	19,186,600	69,506,100	57,120,800	50,006,000	42,010,000	36,734,200
EBITDA	(344,300)	543,000	337,000	1,235,200	1,155,700	927,800	261,900	514,400
Depn & Amortn	185,800	123,500	61,300	232,100	203,700	207,500	246,100	201,300
Income Before Taxes	(620,500)	359,700	246,100	911,400	861,600	607,400	15,800	313,100
Income Taxes	(204,800)	110,000	82,500	264,900	293,300	182,600	52,300	122,300
Net Income	(415,700)	249,700	163,600	646,500	555,400	418,600	(48,300)	723,700
Average Shares	293,800	300,000	300,100	298,600	298,800	298,100	283,100	281,300
Balance Sheet								
Current Assets	15,309,400	14,636,400	13,816,300	13,004,200	11,253,600	10,698,700	9,164,000	7,965,500
Total Assets	18,684,200	17,965,700	17,143,400	16,240,200	14,353,400	13,324,000	11,529,900	10,372,900
Current Liabilities	12,048,100	10,731,700	10,012,400	9,456,100	7,974,400	7,588,000	6,549,700	5,121,800
Long-Term Obligations	1,201,800	1,205,100	1,205,200	1,209,800	1,290,700	1,288,400	1,035,600	1,243,800
Total Liabilities	13,759,500	12,433,600	11,720,400	11,074,900	9,824,900	9,383,900	8,037,000	6,807,100
Stockholders' Equity	4,924,700	5,532,100	5,423,000	5,165,300	4,528,500	3,940,100	3,492,900	3,565,800
Shares Outstanding	295,200	293,900	293,600	290,300	291,200	287,900	283,983	281,100
Statistical Record								
Return on Assets %	N.M.	3.50	4.09	4.21	4.01	3.37	N.M.	7.42
Return on Equity %	N.M.	11.23	12.93	13.30	13.12	11.26	N.M.	22.39
EBITDA Margin %	N.M.	1.39	1.76	1.78	2.02	1.86	0.62	1.40
Net Margin %	N.M.	0.64	0.85	0.93	0.97	0.84	N.M.	1.97
Asset Turnover	4.48	4.50	4.51	4.53	4.13	4.02	3.84	3.77
Current Ratio	1.27	1.36	1.38	1.38	1.41	1.41	1.40	1.56
Debt to Equity	0.24	0.22	0.22	0.23	0.29	0.33	0.30	0.35
Price Range	35.80-22.98	35.80-25.65	36.47-27.31	36.94-23.60	41.81-22.99	41.45-25.34	35.89-16.06	68.19-18.25
P/E Ratio	...	18.08-12.95	16.50-12.36	16.87-10.78	22.24-12.23	28.99-17.72	N.A.	26.53-7.10
Average Yield %	0.80	0.78	0.75	0.78	0.78	0.67	0.90	0.81

Address: One Post Street, San Francisco, CA 94104
Telephone: (415) 983-8300
Fax: (415) 983-8453

Web Site: www.mckhboc.com
Officers: John H. Hammergren - Chmn., Pres., C.E.O. Jeffrey C. Campbell - Exec. V.P., C.F.O.

Auditors: Ernst & Young LLP
Investor Contact: 415-983-7153
Transfer Agents: The Bank of New York, New York, NY

M.D.C. HOLDINGS, INC.

Exchange	Symbol	Price	52Wk Range	Yield	P/E
NYS	MDC	$69.65 (3/31/2005)	80.76-43.75	0.86	7.92

*7 Year Price Score 194.83 *NYSE Composite Index=100 ***12 Month Price Score 121.12**

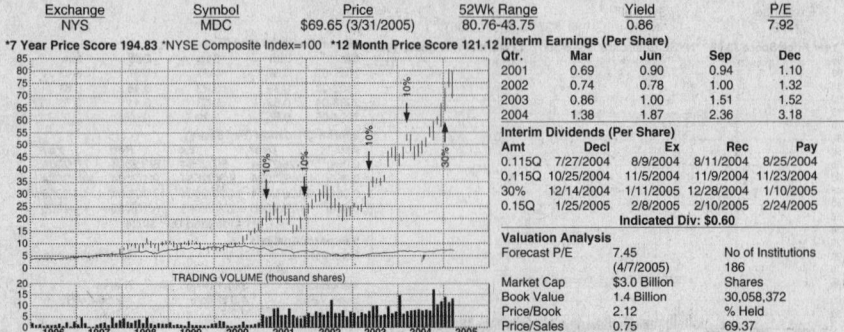

Interim Earnings (Per Share)

Qtr.	Mar	Jun	Sep	Dec
2001	0.69	0.90	0.94	1.10
2002	0.74	0.78	1.00	1.32
2003	0.86	1.00	1.51	1.52
2004	1.38	1.87	2.36	3.18

Interim Dividends (Per Share)

Amt	Decl	Ex	Rec	Pay
0.115Q	7/27/2004	8/9/2004	8/11/2004	8/25/2004
0.115Q	10/25/2004	11/5/2004	11/9/2004	11/23/2004
30%	12/14/2004	1/11/2005	12/28/2004	1/10/2005
0.15Q	1/25/2005	2/8/2005	2/10/2005	2/24/2005

Indicated Div: $0.60

Valuation Analysis

Forecast P/E	7.45		No of Institutions
	(4/7/2005)		186
Market Cap	$3.0 Billion		Shares
Book Value	1.4 Billion		30,058,372
Price/Book	2.12		% Held
Price/Sales	0.75		69.37

Business Summary: Finance Intermediaries & Services (MIC: 8.7 SIC: 162 NAIC: 36115)

M.D.C. Holdings is engaged in owning and managing subsidiary companies that build and sell homes under the name Richmond American Homes. Co. also provides mortgage financing, primarily for its homebuyers, through its wholly-owned subsidiary, HomeAmerican Mortgage. Co. has representation in Colorado, Northern Virginia, suburban Maryland, Phoenix, AZ, Tucson, AZ, Las Vegas, NV and Salt Lake City, UT; and was among the top ten homebuilders in Northern and Southern California. Co. also had a growing presence in Dallas/Fort Worth, TX and recently entered the Houston, TX, Philadelphia/Delaware Valley, PA, West Florida, Jacksonville, FL and Chicago, IL markets.

Recent Developments: For the year ended Dec 31 2004, net income increased 84.3% to $391,165 thousand from net income of $212,229 thousand a year earlier. Revenues were $4,009,072 thousand, up 37.3% from $2,920,070 thousand the year before. Total direct expense was $3,270,574 thousand versus $2,497,146 thousand in the prior year, an increase of 31.0%. Total indirect expense was $101,584 thousand versus $74,701 thousand in the prior year, an increase of 36.0%.

Prospects: Co. intends to expand its home closings by growing the current number of its active communities to nearly 300 before the end of 2005. Active communities in Arizona and California should expand by more than 50.0% from current levels in each market. Annual increases of more than 15.0% are expected in Nevada, Colorado and Jacksonville and Co. should see several communities coming on line for each of its new operations in Chicago, Tampa and the Delaware Valley. Separately, Co. has acquired the right to purchase about 1,200 finished lots in the Central Valley of CA from Del Valle Homes. The lot acquisitions should contribute 50 home closings in 2005 and more than 350 home closings in 2006.

Financial Data

(US$ in Thousands)	12/31/2004	12/31/2003	12/31/2002	12/31/2001	12/31/2000	12/31/1999	12/31/1998	12/31/1997
Earnings Per Share	8.79	4.90	3.83	3.64	2.95	2.28	0.95	0.62
Cash Flow Per Share	(0.56)	2.02	(3.95)	2.24	(1.55)	(0.10)	0.03	0.61
Tang Book Value Per Share	32.57	24.05	19.26	15.63	11.95	10.07	7.84	7.46
Dividends Per Share	0.434	0.283	0.197	0.153	0.126	0.105	0.079	0.063
Dividend Payout %	4.93	5.78	5.14	4.20	4.27	4.60	8.31	10.10
Income Statement								
Total Revenue	4,009,072	2,920,070	2,318,524	2,125,874	1,751,545	1,567,638	1,263,209	969,562
EBITDA	646,914	383,900	300,951	282,832	224,993	166,298	104,080	55,138
Depn & Amortn	10,000	35,677	26,907	27,445	21,792	17,845	20,228	15,050
Income Before Taxes	636,914	348,223	274,044	255,387	203,201	148,453	83,852	39,327
Income Taxes	245,749	135,994	106,739	99,672	79,898	59,061	32,284	15,122
Net Income	391,165	212,229	167,305	155,715	123,303	89,392	36,254	22,026
Average Shares	44,498	43,333	43,657	42,835	41,772	39,201	39,115	37,891
Balance Sheet								
Current Assets	2,451,950	1,719,497	1,300,442	984,174	889,528	716,826	559,324	481,222
Total Assets	2,790,044	1,969,800	1,595,180	1,190,956	1,061,598	877,008	714,013	621,770
Current Liabilities	624,913	456,180	471,623	362,622	404,924	313,596	241,543	203,594
Long-Term Obligations	746,310	497,700	322,990	174,503	174,444	174,389	174,339	188,583
Total Liabilities	1,371,223	953,880	794,613	537,125	579,368	487,985	415,882	392,177
Stockholders' Equity	1,418,821	1,015,920	800,567	653,831	482,230	389,023	298,131	229,593
Shares Outstanding	43,255	42,233	41,572	41,819	40,366	38,613	38,035	30,778
Statistical Record								
Return on Assets %	16.39	11.91	12.01	13.83	12.69	11.24	5.43	3.56
Return on Equity %	32.04	23.37	23.01	27.41	28.23	26.02	13.74	9.93
EBITDA Margin %	16.14	13.15	12.98	13.30	12.85	10.61	8.24	5.69
Net Margin %	9.76	7.27	7.22	7.32	7.04	5.70	2.87	2.27
Asset Turnover	1.68	1.64	1.66	1.89	1.80	1.97	1.89	1.56
Current Ratio	3.92	3.77	2.76	2.71	2.20	2.29	2.32	2.36
Debt to Equity	0.53	0.49	0.40	0.27	0.36	0.45	0.58	0.82
Price Range	66.93-41.28	49.44-22.84	33.57-19.07	26.85-14.19	17.86-7.09	11.49-7.22	12.35-6.86	7.98-4.14
P/E Ratio	7.61-4.70	10.09-4.66	8.76-4.98	7.38-3.90	6.06-2.40	5.04-3.17	13.00-7.22	12.87-6.67
Average Yield %	0.84	0.82	0.74	0.76	1.13	1.11	0.84	1.21

Address: 3600 South Yosemite Street, Suite 900, Denver, CO 80237	Web Site: www.richmondamerican.com	Auditors: Ernst & Young LLP
Telephone: (303) 773-1100	**Officers:** Larry A. Mizel - Chmn., C.E.O. David D. Mandarich - Pres., C.O.O.	**Investor Contact:** 303-773-1100 x8679
Fax: (303) 793-2760		

MDU RESOURCES GROUP INC.

Exchange	Symbol	Price	52Wk Range	Yield	P/E	Div Acheiver
NYS	MDU	$27.62 (3/31/2005)	28.47-22.06	2.61	15.69	14 Years

*7 Year Price Score 113.80 *NYSE Composite Index=100 *12 Month Price Score 100.36

Interim Earnings (Per Share)

Qtr.	Mar	Jun	Sep	Dec
2001	0.33	0.42	0.49	0.28
2002	0.23	0.23	0.50	0.42
2003	0.18	0.39	0.58	0.40
2004	0.20	0.50	0.60	0.45

Interim Dividends (Per Share)

Amt	Decl	Ex	Rec	Pay
0.17Q	5/13/2004	6/8/2004	6/10/2004	7/1/2004
0.18Q	8/12/2004	9/7/2004	9/9/2004	10/1/2004
0.18Q	11/11/2004	12/7/2004	12/9/2004	1/1/2005
0.18Q	2/17/2005	3/8/2005	3/10/2005	4/1/2005

Indicated Div: $0.72 (Div. Reinv. Plan)

Valuation Analysis

Forecast P/E	14.58	No of Institutions	
	(4/7/2005)	220	
Market Cap	$3.3 Billion	Shares	
Book Value	1.7 Billion	43,938,868	
Price/Book	1.94	% Held	
Price/Sales	1.20	37.14	

Business Summary: Construction - Public Infrastructure (MIC: 3.1 SIC: 611 NAIC: 37310)

MDU Resources Group is a diversified natural resource company operating through six reportable segments. Co.'s electric and natural gas distribution segments include the operations of Montana- Dakota and Great Plains Natural Gas Co. The utility services segment includes all the operations of Utility Services, Inc. The pipeline and energy services segment includes WBI Holdings' natural gas transportation, underground storage, gathering services, and energy-related management services. The natural gas and oil production segment includes the operations of WBI Holdings. The construction materials and mining segment includes the results of Knife River's operations.

Recent Developments: For the year ended Dec 31 2004, net income increased 18.1% to $207,067 thousand from net income of $175,324 thousand a year earlier. Revenues were $2,719,257 thousand, up 15.6% from $2,352,189 thousand the year before. Operating income was $320,718 thousand versus an income of $312,072 thousand in the prior year, an increase of 2.8%. Total direct expense was $2,086,982 thousand versus $1,771,530 thousand in the prior year, an increase of 17.8%. Total indirect expense was $311,557 thousand versus $268,587 thousand in the prior year, an increase of 16.0%.

Prospects: Results are being positively affected by strong operating performance in Co.'s natural gas and oil production segment, driven by improved pricing, increased natural gas production, and additions to the reserve base. Meanwhile, significant growth in Co.'s independent power production business is being fueled by expanded operations both domestically and internationally. For 2005, Co. is projecting earnings in the range of $1.70 to $1.90 per share. In addition, Co. anticipates investing about $445.0 million in capital expenditures during 2005. Looking ahead, Co.'s long-term compound annual growth target for earnings per share from operations are in the range of 6.0% to 9.0%.

Financial Data

(US$ in Thousands)	12/31/2004	12/31/2003	12/31/2002	12/31/2001	12/31/2000	12/31/1999	12/31/1998	12/31/1997
Earnings Per Share	1.76	1.55	1.38	1.53	1.20	1.01	0.44	0.83
Cash Flow Per Share	3.71	3.75	3.08	3.45	2.25	1.89	1.83	2.13
Tang Book Value Per Share	12.21	9.20	8.25	10.60	9.03	7.83	6.92	5.92
Dividends Per Share	0.700	0.660	0.627	0.600	0.573	0.547	0.522	0.502
Dividend Payout %	39.77	42.58	45.41	39.30	47.78	53.95	118.69	60.75
Income Statement								
Total Revenue	2,719,257	2,352,189	2,031,537	2,223,632	1,873,671	1,279,809	896,627	607,674
EBITDA	567,248	522,616	437,650	440,006	339,599	251,214	159,651	181,336
Depn & Amortn	208,770	188,337	157,961	139,917	110,888	81,818	77,786	65,767
Income Before Taxes	301,041	281,485	234,674	254,190	180,678	133,390	51,592	85,360
Income Taxes	93,974	98,572	86,230	98,341	69,650	49,310	17,485	30,743
Net Income	207,067	175,324	148,444	155,849	111,028	84,080	34,107	54,617
Average Shares	117,411	112,460	106,863	101,803	92,085	82,305	76,255	65,217
Balance Sheet								
Net PPE	2,572,705	2,222,293	1,924,886	1,809,318	1,601,014	1,248,176	1,120,615	839,536
Total Assets	3,733,521	3,380,592	2,937,249	2,623,071	2,312,959	1,766,303	1,488,713	1,113,892
Long-Term Obligations	873,441	939,450	819,558	783,709	728,166	563,545	413,264	298,561
Total Liabilities	2,052,508	1,929,956	1,638,504	1,498,300	1,416,899	1,081,770	922,871	712,596
Stockholders' Equity	1,681,013	1,450,636	1,298,745	1,124,771	896,060	684,533	565,842	402,996
Shares Outstanding	118,226	113,357	111,063	104,665	97,542	85,557	79,549	65,572
Statistical Record								
Return on Assets %	5.81	5.55	5.34	6.31	5.43	5.17	2.62	4.96
Return on Equity %	13.19	12.75	12.25	15.42	14.01	13.45	7.04	14.18
EBITDA Margin %	20.86	22.22	21.54	19.79	18.12	19.63	17.81	29.84
Net Margin %	7.61	7.45	7.31	7.01	5.93	6.57	3.80	8.99
PPE Turnover	1.13	1.13	1.09	1.30	1.31	1.08	0.91	0.76
Asset Turnover	0.76	0.74	0.73	0.90	0.92	0.79	0.69	0.55
Debt to Equity	0.52	0.65	0.63	0.70	0.81	0.82	0.73	0.74
Price Range	27.46-22.06	24.25-16.69	22.23-12.47	26.82-15.20	22.00-12.00	17.96-12.83	18.83-12.67	14.86-9.44
P/E Ratio	15.60-12.53	15.65-10.77	16.11-9.03	17.53-9.93	18.33-10.00	17.78-12.71	42.80-28.79	17.90-11.38
Average Yield %	2.86	3.15	3.55	2.96	3.61	3.57	3.28	4.54

Address: Schuchart Building, 918 East Divide Avenue, P.O. Box 5650, Bismarck, ND 58506-5650 **Telephone:** (701) 222-7900 **Fax:** (701) 222-7607	**Web Site:** www.mdu.com **Officers:** Martin A. White - Chmn., Pres., C.E.O. Warren L. Robinson - Exec. V.P., C.F.O.	**Auditors:** Deloitte & Touche LLP **Investor Contact:** 800-437-8000 x7621 **Transfer Agents:** Wells Fargo Bank Minnesota, N.A. Shareowner Services, St. Paul, MN

MEADWESTVACO CORP.

Exchange	Symbol	Price	52Wk Range	Yield	P/E
NYS	MWV	$31.82 (3/31/2005)	34.23-25.60	2.89	N/A

*7 Year Price Score 93.93 ***NYSE Composite Index=100** ***12 Month Price Score 96.10**

Interim Earnings (Per Share)

Qtr.	Jan	Apr	Jul	Dec
2000-01	— — — — — — (0.21)— — — — — —			

Qtr.	Mar	Jun	Sep	Dec
2002	(0.37)	(0.04)	(0.01)	0.22
2003	(0.38)	(0.04)	0.14	0.25
2004	(0.01)	0.24	0.52	(2.48)

Interim Dividends (Per Share)

Amt	Decl	Ex	Rec	Pay
0.23Q	4/27/2004	5/5/2004	5/7/2004	6/1/2004
0.23Q	6/22/2004	8/4/2004	8/6/2004	9/1/2004
0.23Q	10/26/2004	11/3/2004	11/5/2004	12/1/2004
0.23Q	1/25/2005	2/2/2005	2/4/2005	3/1/2005

Indicated Div: $0.92

Valuation Analysis

Forecast P/E	21.20	No of Institutions
	(4/7/2005)	310
Market Cap	$6.5 Billion	Shares
Book Value	4.3 Billion	147,359,808
Price/Book	1.50	% Held
Price/Sales	0.79	72.23

Business Summary: Paper Products (MIC: 11.11 SIC: 621 NAIC: 22130)

MeadWestvaco is a global producer of packaging, coated and specialty papers, consumer and office products, and specialty chemicals. The Packaging segment produces paperboard, linerboard and kraft and packaging for consumer products. The Paper segment manufactures and distributes coated, carbonless and specialty papers, and also includes Co.'s panelboard investment. The Consumer and Office Products segment produces and distributes school, office, envelopes, and time-management products to retailers and commercial distributors. The Specialty Chemicals segment produces activated carbon products; resins and lignin-based surfactants; and tall oil fatty acid, rosin and derivative products.

Recent Developments: For the year ended Dec 31 2004, net loss was $349,000 thousand versus net income of $18,000 thousand a year earlier. Revenues were $8,227,000 thousand, up 8.9% from $7,553,000 thousand the year before. Total direct expense was $7,029,000 thousand versus $6,556,000 thousand in the prior year, an increase of 7.2%. Total indirect expense was $882,000 thousand versus $865,000 thousand in the prior year, an increase of 2.0%.

Prospects: On Jan 18 2005, Co. announced that it has reached a definitive agreement to sell its papers business and associated assets for $2.30 billion to a new company controlled by Cerberus Capital Management L.P., a private, New York-based investment firm. The proceeds will be used to improve capital structure to focus on profitable growth opportunities in the global packaging markets. The sale is expected to be completed in the second quarter of 2005. Going forward, Co. expects its markets to remain firm, with continued price realization in paperboard and coated paper. Also, Co. expects earnings in its packaging and consumer and office segments to be affected by the normal seasonal slowdown.

Financial Data

(US$ in Thousands)	12/31/2004	12/31/2003	12/31/2002	12/31/2001	10/31/2001	10/31/2000	10/31/1999	10/31/1998
Earnings Per Share	(1.73)	(0.03)	(2.02)	(0.21)	0.87	2.44	1.11	1.30
Cash Flow Per Share	4.65	2.31	2.57	0.29	2.49	5.78	4.12	4.01
Tang Book Value Per Share	16.47	17.95	18.42	17.11	17.21	23.17	21.65	22.39
Dividends Per Share	0.920	0.920	0.920	0.220	0.880	0.880	0.880	0.880
Dividend Payout %	N.M.	N.M.	N.M.	N.M.	101.15	36.07	79.28	67.69
Income Statement								
Total Revenue	8,227,000	7,553,000	7,242,000	600,400	3,983,622	3,719,931	2,831,233	2,904,664
EBITDA	478,000	920,000	908,000	55,000	673,593	909,665	551,984	595,556
Depn & Amortn	666,000	670,000	626,000	60,700	347,444	313,948	280,470	280,981
Income Before Taxes	(454,000)	(29,000)	(15,000)	(38,600)	118,510	403,572	147,976	204,413
Income Taxes	(105,000)	(27,000)	(12,000)	(16,900)	30,300	148,900	36,800	72,400
Net Income	(349,000)	(6,000)	(389,000)	(21,700)	88,210	245,869	111,176	132,013
Average Shares	201,900	200,400	192,100	102,600	101,564	100,916	100,495	101,788
Balance Sheet								
Current Assets	2,562,000	2,426,000	2,431,000	1,033,600	1,015,670	1,063,677	738,008	739,192
Total Assets	11,681,000	12,487,000	12,921,000	6,828,300	6,786,989	6,569,903	4,896,692	5,008,668
Current Liabilities	1,751,000	1,501,000	1,620,000	725,800	701,051	566,918	425,114	467,125
Long-Term Obligations	3,427,000	3,969,000	4,233,000	2,697,200	2,660,467	2,686,674	...	...
Total Liabilities	7,364,000	7,719,000	8,090,000	4,513,100	4,446,136	4,237,310	2,725,404	2,762,220
Stockholders' Equity	4,317,000	4,768,000	4,831,000	2,315,200	2,340,853	2,332,593	2,171,288	2,246,448
Shares Outstanding	203,930	200,897	200,039	102,554	103,170	100,662	100,293	100,326
Statistical Record								
Return on Assets %	N.M.	N.M.	N.M.	N.M.	1.32	4.28	2.24	2.66
Return on Equity %	N.M.	N.M.	N.M.	N.M.	3.77	10.89	5.03	5.83
EBITDA Margin %	5.81	12.18	12.54	9.16	16.91	24.45	19.50	20.50
Net Margin %	N.M.	N.M.	N.M.	N.M.	2.21	6.61	3.93	4.54
Asset Turnover	0.68	0.59	0.73	0.08	0.60	0.65	0.57	0.59
Current Ratio	1.46	1.62	1.50	1.42	1.45	1.88	1.74	1.58
Debt to Equity	0.79	0.83	0.88	1.16	1.14	1.15	...	...
Price Range	34.23-25.60	29.75-21.69	36.40-15.70	29.08-24.55	31.92-22.90	34.69-24.50	32.38-21.00	34.00-21.25
P/E Ratio	N.A.	N/A	N/A	N/A	36.69-26.32	14.22-10.04	29.17-18.92	26.15-16.35
Average Yield %	3.12	3.68	3.32	0.80	3.34	3.02	3.24	3.04

Address: One High Ridge Park, Stamford, CT 06905	**Web Site:** www.meadwestvaco.com	**Auditors:** PricewaterhouseCoopers LLP
Telephone: (203) 461-7400	**Officers:** John A. Luke Jr. - Chmn., C.E.O. James A. Buzzard - Pres.	**Investor Contact:** 203-461-7500

MEDCO HEALTH SOLUTIONS, INC.

Exchange	Symbol	Price	52Wk Range	Yield	P/E
NYS	MHS	$49.57 (3/31/2005)	50.00-30.00	N/A	28.33

*7 Year Price Score N/A   *NYSE Composite Index=100   *12 Month Price Score 114.84

TRADING VOLUME (thousand shares)

Interim Earnings (Per Share)

Qtr.	Mar	Jun	Sep	Dec
2002	------------	1.34	------------	
2003	0.38	0.39	0.37	0.43
2004	0.38	0.46	0.43	0.48

Interim Dividends (Per Share)

No Dividends Paid

Valuation Analysis

Forecast P/E	22.29	No of Institutions
	(4/13/2005)	480
Market Cap	$13.6 Billion	Shares
Book Value	5.7 Billion	198,339,264
Price/Book	2.38	% Held
Price/Sales	0.38	72.03

Business Summary: Retail - Miscellaneous (MIC: 5.11 SIC: 912 NAIC: 46110)

Medco Health Solutions is a pharmacy benefits manager. Co. assists its clients in moderating the cost and enhancing the quality of prescription drug benefits provided to more than 60.0 million Americans nationwide. Co. accomplishes this primarily by negotiating competitive rebates and discounts from pharmaceutical manufacturers, obtaining competitive discounts from retail pharmacies and administering prescriptions filled through Co.'s national networks of retail pharmacies or Co.'s own home delivery pharmacies. Co.'s clients include private and public-sector employers and healthcare organizations.

Recent Developments: For the year ended Dec 25 2004, net income increased 13.1% to $481.6 million compared with $425.8 million a year earlier. Total net revenues advanced 3.2% to $35.35 billion from $34.26 billion in the previous year. Retail product revenue decreased 4.5% to $21.63 billion, mainly due to a 8.5% decrease in retail volume resulting from client terminations and lower prescription drug utilization from plan design changes in support of mail order. Mail order product revenue increased 19.0% to $13.39 billion, primarily due to a 12.3% increase in mail order volume, reflecting higher utilization from plan design changes encouraging the use of mail order as well as volumes from new clients.

Prospects: On Feb 23 2005, Co. announced a definitive agreement to acquire Accredo Health, Incorporated in a cash and stock transaction valued at the time of the announcement at $43.33 per share, or $2.20 billion. The combined company expects to achieve annual pre-tax operating synergies of more than $40.0 million in 2006 primarily through operating leverage and cross-selling opportunities. The acquisition should create a strong platform for Co.'s future growth in the specialty pharmacy market. Meanwhile, Co. continues to expect full-year 2005 diluted earnings on a U.S. GAAP basis to be in the range of $1.94 to $2.03 per share, representing an 11.0% to 16.0% increase over 2004.

Financial Data

(US$ in Thousands)	12/25/2004	12/27/2003	12/28/2002	12/29/2001	12/30/2000
Earnings Per Share	1.75	1.57	1.34	0.95	0.80
Cash Flow Per Share	2.62	4.17	1.75	2.45	...
Tang Book Value Per Share	0.98	N.M.	3.37	1.70	...
Income Statement					
Total Revenue	35,351,900	34,264,500	32,958,500	29,070,600	22,266,300
EBITDA	1,183,800	1,012,000	877,700	841,200	736,700
Depn & Amortn	377,500	283,300	257,400	322,900	289,200
Income Before Taxes	806,300	728,700	620,300	518,300	447,500
Income Taxes	324,700	302,900	258,700	261,700	230,700
Net Income	481,600	425,800	361,600	256,600	216,800
Average Shares	274,700	270,800	270,000	270,000	270,000
Balance Sheet					
Current Assets	4,320,400	3,760,300	3,226,400	2,533,800	...
Total Assets	10,541,500	10,263,000	9,922,500	9,251,800	...
Current Liabilities	2,644,500	2,605,300	2,054,900	1,809,400	...
Long-Term Obligations	1,092,900	1,346,100	...	...	...
Total Liabilities	4,822,100	5,183,000	3,286,900	2,983,500	...
Stockholders' Equity	5,719,400	5,080,000	6,635,600	6,268,300	...
Shares Outstanding	274,436	270,532	270,000	270,000	...
Statistical Record					
Return on Assets %	4.64	4.23	3.78	...	...
Return on Equity %	8.94	7.29	5.62	...	...
EBITDA Margin %	3.35	2.95	2.66	2.89	3.31
Net Margin %	1.36	1.24	1.10	0.88	0.97
Asset Turnover	3.41	3.40	3.45	...	...
Current Ratio	1.63	1.44	1.57	1.40	...
Debt to Equity	0.19	0.26	...	...	...
Price Range	40.25-30.00	37.75-20.50	...	...	...
P/E Ratio	23.00-17.14	24.04-13.06	...	...	...

Address: 100 Parsons Pond Drive, Franklin Lakes, NJ 07417-2603 **Telephone:** (201) 269-3400	**Web Site:** www.medco.com **Officers:** David B. Snow Jr. - Chmn., Pres., C.E.O. Kenneth O. Klepper - Exec. V.P., C.O.O.	**Auditors:** PricewaterhouseCoopers LLP **Investor Contact:** 201-269-6187

MEDIA GENERAL, INC.

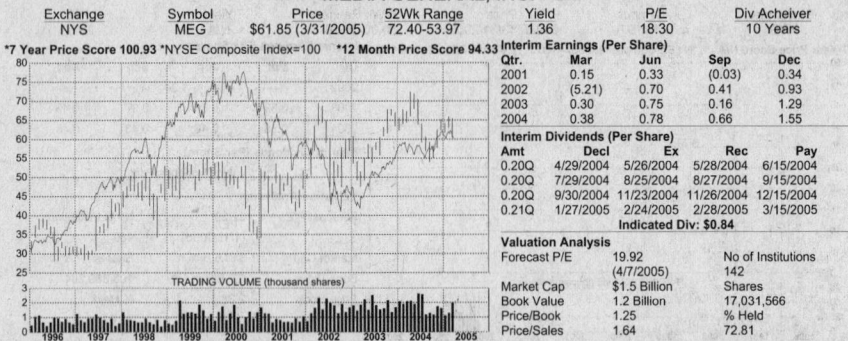

Exchange	Symbol	Price	52Wk Range	Yield	P/E	Div Acheiver
NYS	MEG	$61.85 (3/31/2005)	72.40-53.97	1.36	18.30	10 Years

*7 Year Price Score 100.93 *NYSE Composite Index=100 *12 Month Price Score 94.33

Interim Earnings (Per Share)

Qtr.	Mar	Jun	Sep	Dec
2001	0.15	0.33	(0.03)	0.34
2002	(5.21)	0.70	0.41	0.93
2003	0.30	0.75	0.16	1.29
2004	0.38	0.78	0.66	1.55

Interim Dividends (Per Share)

Amt	Decl	Ex	Rec	Pay
0.20Q	4/29/2004	5/26/2004	5/28/2004	6/15/2004
0.20Q	7/29/2004	8/25/2004	8/27/2004	9/15/2004
0.20Q	9/30/2004	11/23/2004	11/26/2004	12/15/2004
0.21Q	1/27/2005	2/24/2005	2/28/2005	3/15/2005
		Indicated Div: $0.84		

Valuation Analysis

Forecast P/E	19.92	No of Institutions
	(4/7/2005)	142
Market Cap	$1.5 Billion	Shares
Book Value	1.2 Billion	17,031,566
Price/Book	1.25	% Held
Price/Sales	1.64	72.81

Business Summary: Media (MIC: 13.1 SIC: 711 NAIC: 11110)

Media General is an independent, publicly-owned communications company with interests in newspapers, television stations, interactive media, and diversified information services. Co.'s publishing assets include The Tampa Tribune, the Richmond Times-Dispatch, the Winston-Salem Journal, and 22 other daily newspapers in Virginia, North Carolina, Florida, Alabama and South Carolina, as well as nearly 100 other periodicals and a 20.0% interest in The Denver Post. Co.'s 26 network-affiliated television stations reach more than 30.0% of the television households in the Southeast, and nearly 8.0% of those in the U.S. Co.'s interactive media offerings include more than 50 on-line enterprises.

Recent Developments: For the year ended Dec 26 2004, net income increased 36.6% to $80,185 thousand from net income of $58,685 thousand a year earlier. Revenues were $900,420 thousand, up 7.5% from $837,423 thousand the year before. Operating income was $149,332 thousand versus an income of $122,276 thousand in the prior year, an increase of 22.1%. Total direct expense was $375,752 thousand versus $356,694 thousand in the prior year, an increase of 5.3%. Total indirect expense was $375,336 thousand versus $358,453 thousand in the prior year, an increase of 4.7%.

Prospects: For the first quarter of 2005, Co. expects Publishing Division revenues to continue to show growth similar to that of the fourth quarter of 2004. Classified revenues are estimated to maintain their growth trends with solid gains in employment advertising, and the division expects year-over-year improvement in the Retail and National categories. The Broadcast Division, as expected, will face certain challenges. However, new revenue development initiatives are expected to drive revenue growth of approximately 2.0%. Also, events such as the NCAA March Madness basketball games should benefit advertising in the first quarter of 2005.

Financial Data

(US$ in Thousands)	12/26/2004	12/28/2003	12/29/2002	12/30/2001	12/31/2000	12/26/1999	12/27/1998	12/28/1997
Earnings Per Share	3.38	2.50	(3.14)	0.79	2.22	32.78	2.63	(0.40)
Cash Flow Per Share	5.94	5.34	7.54	5.49	(15.33)	4.70	5.29	4.54
Tang Book Value Per Share	N.M.	N.M.	N.M.	N.M.	N.M.	11.92	N.M.	N.M.
Dividends Per Share	0.800	0.760	0.720	0.680	0.640	0.600	0.560	0.530
Dividend Payout %	23.67	30.40	N.M.	86.08	28.83	1.83	21.29	N.M.
Income Statement								
Total Revenue	900,420	837,423	836,800	807,176	830,601	795,408	973,978	909,987
EBITDA	219,003	187,074	201,519	198,925	250,777	259,496	277,425	250,065
Depn & Amortn	60,643	58,804	65,495	113,732	105,293	97,532	100,201	98,316
Income Before Taxes	127,278	93,846	88,150	30,946	102,926	115,410	111,175	86,307
Income Taxes	47,093	34,800	34,731	13,022	39,369	45,463	40,301	33,797
Net Income	80,185	58,685	(72,917)	18,204	53,719	881,316	70,874	(10,490)
Average Shares	23,729	23,408	23,236	22,956	24,189	26,885	26,914	26,694
Balance Sheet								
Current Assets	170,847	162,621	160,552	163,038	172,880	796,734	176,226	165,927
Total Assets	2,368,812	2,386,755	2,347,011	2,534,059	2,561,282	2,340,374	1,917,346	1,814,201
Current Liabilities	126,871	114,403	111,501	100,497	114,541	629,188	147,097	131,211
Long-Term Obligations	95,320	627,289	642,937	777,662	822,077	46,838	928,101	900,000
Total Liabilities	747,083	1,279,294	1,287,757	1,370,391	1,389,360	1,009,472	1,439,997	1,395,975
Stockholders' Equity	1,183,769	1,107,461	1,059,254	1,163,668	1,171,922	1,330,902	477,349	418,226
Shares Outstanding	23,830	23,545	23,208	22,976	22,714	26,468	26,771	26,729
Statistical Record								
Return on Assets %	3.38	2.49	N.M.	0.72	2.16	41.51	3.81	N.M.
Return on Equity %	7.02	5.43	N.M.	1.56	4.22	97.74	15.87	N.M.
EBITDA Margin %	24.32	22.34	24.08	24.64	30.19	32.62	28.48	27.48
Net Margin %	8.91	7.01	N.M.	2.26	6.47	110.80	7.28	N.M.
Asset Turnover	0.38	0.35	0.34	0.32	0.33	0.37	0.52	0.64
Current Ratio	1.35	1.42	1.44	1.62	1.51	1.27	1.20	1.26
Debt to Equity	0.08	0.57	0.61	0.67	0.70	0.04	1.94	2.15
Price Range	72.40-53.97	67.88-47.53	69.49-47.38	53.50-34.09	54.19-33.98	55.50-44.38	51.38-34.25	44.38-28.38
P/E Ratio	21.42-15.97	27.15-19.01	N.A.	67.72-43.15	24.41-15.31	1.69-1.35	19.53-13.02	N.A.
Average Yield %	1.27	1.31	1.26	1.45	1.36	1.19	1.21	1.51

Address: 333 East Franklin Street, Richmond, VA 23219	Web Site: www.mediageneral.com	Auditors: Ernst & Young LLP
Telephone: (804) 649-6000	Officers: J. Stewart Bryan III - Chmn., C.E.O.	Investor Contact: 804-649-6000
Fax: (804) 649-6898	Marshall N. Morton - Vice-Chmn., C.F.O.	

MEDICIS PHARMACEUTICAL CORP.

Exchange	Symbol	Price	52Wk Range	Yield	P/E
NYS	MRX	$29.98 (3/31/2005)	44.81-28.86	0.40	28.28

*7 Year Price Score 126.15 *NYSE Composite Index=100 *12 Month Price Score 83.38

Interim Earnings (Per Share)

Qtr.	Sep	Dec	Mar	Jun
2001-02	0.22	0.14	0.25	0.19
2002-03	0.21	0.28	0.18	0.25
2003-04	(0.50)	0.23	0.33	0.40
2004-05	0.02	0.31	...	...

Interim Dividends (Per Share)

Amt	Decl	Ex	Rec	Pay
0.025Q	6/10/2004	6/29/2004	7/1/2004	7/30/2004
0.03Q	9/14/2004	9/29/2004	10/1/2004	10/29/2004
0.03Q	12/14/2004	12/30/2004	1/3/2005	1/31/2005
0.03Q	3/16/2005	3/30/2005	4/1/2005	4/29/2005

Indicated Div: $0.12

Valuation Analysis

Forecast P/E	18.07 (4/7/2005)	No of Institutions 212
Market Cap	$1.6 Billion	Shares
Book Value	444.8 Million	57,948,232
Price/Book	3.66	% Held
Price/Sales	4.66	N/A

TRADING VOLUME (thousand shares)

Business Summary: Pharmaceuticals (MIC: 9.1 SIC: 834 NAIC: 25412)

Medicis Pharmaceutical is a specialty pharmaceutical company. Co. is engaged in the development and marketing of products in the United States for the treatment of dermatological, aesthetic and podiatric conditions in the United States and Canada. Co. offers a range of products addressing various conditions including acne, fungal infections, rosacea, hyperpigmentation, photoaging, psoriasis, eczema, skin and skin-structure infections, seborrheic dermatitis and cosmesis (improvement in the texture and appearance of skin). As of June 30 2004, Co. offers 13 branded products. Co.'s core brands are Dynacin®, Loprox®, Omnicef®, Plexion®, Restylane®, and Triaz®.

Recent Developments: For the quarter ended Dec 31 2004, net income increased 48.2% to $20,201,000 from net income of $13,627,000 in the year-earlier quarter. Revenues were $92,349,000 , up 30.7% from $70,633,000 the year before. Operating income was $31,535,000 versus an income of $20,801,000 in the prior-year quarter, an increase of 51.6%. Total direct expense was $13,438,000 versus $11,237,000 in the prior-year quarter, an increase of 19.6%. Total indirect expense was $47,376,000 versus $38,595,000 in the prior-year quarter, an increase of 22.8%.

Prospects: Co. is performing well, highlighted by solid growth of RESTYLANE®, LOPROX® Shampoo and DYNACIN® Tablets, along with the introduction of its PLEXION® Cleansing Cloths. These core products represented about 78.0% of total revenue during the second quarter. Looking ahead to the second half of fiscal 2005, Co. anticipates introducing at least one new product from its research and development pipeline. As a result, Co. raised its fiscal 2005 financial guidance. Co. now expects revenue of about $376.0 million, and earnings per share of about $1.43, excluding special charges. For the third quarter of fiscal 2005, Co. expects revenue of about $95.0 million, with earnings of about $0.36 per share.

Financial Data

(US$ in Thousands)	6 Mos	3 Mos	06/30/2004	06/30/2003	06/30/2002	06/30/2001	06/30/2000	06/30/1999
Earnings Per Share	1.06	0.98	0.52	0.91	0.80	0.64	0.70	0.70
Cash Flow Per Share	2.43	1.89	2.29	1.56	1.21	1.17	0.71	0.45
Tang Book Value Per Share	2.02	2.61	3.39	2.89	4.40	5.89	5.02	4.27
Dividends Per Share	0.110	0.105	0.100	0.025	...	...	...	...
Dividend Payout %	10.41	10.74	19.23	2.75	...	...	...	...
Income Statement								
Total Revenue	181,167	88,818	303,722	247,539	212,807	167,801	139,099	116,871
EBITDA	44,351	6,961	73,652	94,726	82,613	53,506	65,586	63,754
Depn & Amortn	11,552	5,697	26,737	16,788	12,162	9,686	10,080	7,792
Income Before Taxes	32,551	1,118	46,157	77,660	78,984	59,325	67,382	65,640
Income Taxes	11,328	95	15,317	26,404	28,960	18,905	24,388	24,203
Net Income	21,223	1,023	30,840	51,256	50,024	40,420	42,994	41,437
Average Shares	70,843	60,268	59,258	56,422	62,810	63,387	60,997	58,924
Balance Sheet								
Current Assets	632,028	683,191	733,863	645,628	658,473	398,879	351,288	335,420
Total Assets	979,871	1,025,598	1,078,384	936,990	876,273	548,696	495,340	467,338
Current Liabilities	79,637	71,617	67,120	68,847	47,214	40,411	38,987	56,980
Long-Term Obligations	453,065	453,065	453,067	400,000	400,000	...	...	...
Total Liabilities	535,045	524,682	523,081	475,869	447,214	45,242	57,900	93,762
Stockholders' Equity	444,826	500,916	555,303	461,121	429,059	503,454	437,439	373,576
Shares Outstanding	54,356	66,613	66,177	63,267	55,485	60,486	58,984	57,324
Statistical Record								
Return on Assets %	6.64	5.88	3.05	5.65	7.02	7.74	8.91	10.11
Return on Equity %	14.37	12.54	6.05	11.52	10.73	8.59	10.57	11.87
EBITDA Margin %	24.48	7.84	24.25	38.27	38.82	31.89	47.15	54.55
Net Margin %	11.71	1.15	10.15	20.71	23.51	24.09	30.91	35.46
Asset Turnover	0.36	0.33	0.30	0.27	0.30	0.32	0.29	0.29
Current Ratio	7.94	9.54	10.93	9.38	13.95	9.87	9.01	5.89
Debt to Equity	1.02	0.90	0.82	0.87	0.93	...	...	...
Price Range	44.81-33.07	44.81-27.91	44.81-27.47	30.50-17.16	32.30-20.38	36.81-18.00	31.50-10.13	23.71-10.44

Address: 8125 North Hayden Road, Scottsdale, AZ 85258-2463 Telephone: (602) 808 8800 Fax: (602) 808 0822	Web Site: www.medicis.com Officers: Jonah Shacknai - Chmn., C.E.O. Mark A. Prygocki Sr. - Exec. V.P., C.F.O., Treas., Sec.	Auditors: Ernst & Young LLP Investor Contact: 602-808-3854 Transfer Agents: Wells Fargo Shareowner Services, St. Paul, MN

MEDTRONIC, INC.

Exchange	Symbol	Price	52Wk Range	Yield	P/E	Div Acheiver
NYS	MDT	$50.95 (3/31/2005)	54.92-46.40	0.66	28.95	27 Years

*7 Year Price Score 97.30 *NYSE Composite Index=100 *12 Month Price Score 97.83

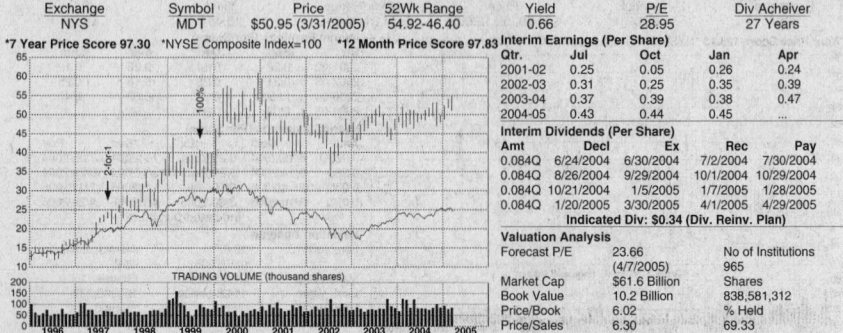

Interim Earnings (Per Share)

Qtr.	Jul	Oct	Jan	Apr
2001-02	0.25	0.05	0.26	0.24
2002-03	0.31	0.25	0.35	0.39
2003-04	0.37	0.39	0.38	0.47
2004-05	0.43	0.44	0.45	...

Interim Dividends (Per Share)

Amt	Decl	Ex	Rec	Pay
0.084Q	6/24/2004	6/30/2004	7/2/2004	7/30/2004
0.084Q	8/26/2004	9/29/2004	10/1/2004	10/29/2004
0.084Q	10/21/2004	1/5/2005	1/7/2005	1/28/2005
0.084Q	1/20/2005	3/30/2005	4/1/2005	4/29/2005

Indicated Div: $0.34 (Div. Reinv. Plan)

Valuation Analysis

Forecast P/E	23.66	No of Institutions
	(4/7/2005)	965
Market Cap	$61.6 Billion	Shares
Book Value	10.2 Billion	838,581,312
Price/Book	6.02	% Held
Price/Sales	6.30	69.33

Business Summary: Medical Instruments & Equipment (MIC: 9.6 SIC: 845 NAIC: 34510)

Medtronic operates in five business segments that manufacture and sell device-based medical therapies. Cardiac Rhythm Management offers physicians and their patients a variety of products to treat heart rhythm disorders. Cardiac Surgery offers a broad range of products for use by cardiac surgeons in the operating room. The Vascular segment offers minimally invasive products for the treatment of coronary vascular disease. The Neurological and Diabetes segment offers products for the treatment of neurological disorders. The Spinal and Ear, Nose & Throat segment offers a range of products and therapies to treat a variety of disorders of the cranium, spine, ear, nose and throat.

Recent Developments: For the quarter ended Jan 28 2005, net income increased 17.3% to $544,100 thousand from net income of $463,900 thousand in the year-earlier quarter. Revenues were $2,530,700 thousand, up 15.4% from $2,193,800 thousand the year before. Total direct expense was $605,600 thousand versus $538,400 thousand in the prior-year quarter, an increase of 12.5%. Total indirect expense was $1,079,500 thousand versus $908,400 thousand in the prior-year quarter, an increase of 18.8%.

Prospects: Co. is benefiting from sequential revenue increases in all of its business lines, and continues to enjoy particularly favorable results from its two largest product lines, implantable cardioverter-defibrillators (ICD) and spinal products. Meanwhile, new product introductions, combined with recently expanded indications and reimbursement coverage for ICD therapy, should bode well for continued strong performance. Separately, Co. continues to prepare for CE Mark approval and European commercialization of the Endeavor™ Drug Eluting Coronary Stent system.

Financial Data

(US$ in Thousands)	9 Mos	6 Mos	3 Mos	04/30/2004	04/25/2003	04/26/2002	04/27/2001	04/30/2000
Earnings Per Share	1.76	1.69	1.64	1.60	1.30	0.80	0.85	0.90
Cash Flow Per Share	2.44	2.49	2.39	2.31	1.71	1.32	1.54	0.87
Tang Book Value Per Share	4.06	3.86	3.50	3.18	2.21	1.10	3.53	2.61
Dividends Per Share	0.324	0.313	0.301	0.290	0.250	0.230	0.200	0.160
Dividend Payout %	18.38	18.44	18.32	18.13	19.23	28.75	23.57	17.78
Income Statement								
Total Revenue	7,276,600	4,745,900	2,346,100	9,087,200	7,665,200	6,410,800	5,551,800	5,014,600
EBITDA	2,579,500	1,712,900	851,900	3,236,700	2,756,600	1,860,600	1,772,500	1,856,900
Depn & Amortn	339,300	223,700	110,100	442,600	408,100	329,800	297,300	243,300
Income Before Taxes	2,264,600	1,500,600	746,100	2,796,900	2,341,300	1,524,200	1,549,400	1,629,000
Income Taxes	655,100	435,200	216,400	837,600	741,500	540,200	503,400	530,500
Net Income	1,609,500	1,065,400	529,700	1,959,300	1,599,800	984,000	1,046,000	1,098,500
Average Shares	1,219,100	1,220,700	1,220,200	1,225,200	1,227,900	1,224,400	1,226,000	1,220,800
Balance Sheet								
Current Assets	6,728,200	6,369,600	5,873,700	5,312,700	4,605,500	3,488,000	3,756,800	3,013,400
Total Assets	15,695,400	15,180,300	14,557,000	14,110,800	12,320,800	10,904,500	7,038,900	5,669,400
Current Liabilities	2,655,900	2,487,600	4,298,300	4,240,600	1,813,300	3,984,900	1,359,300	991,500
Long-Term Obligations	1,974,900	1,974,800	1,600	1,100	1,980,300	9,500	13,300	14,100
Total Liabilities	5,463,300	5,255,000	5,108,900	5,033,800	4,414,400	4,473,400	1,529,400	1,177,900
Stockholders' Equity	10,232,100	9,925,300	9,448,100	9,077,000	7,906,400	6,431,100	5,509,500	4,491,500
Shares Outstanding	1,209,520	1,208,725	1,210,281	1,209,459	1,218,128	1,215,208	1,209,514	1,197,698
Statistical Record								
Return on Assets %	14.72	14.73	14.77	14.59	13.81	11.00	16.60	20.79
Return on Equity %	22.66	22.69	22.78	22.70	22.38	16.53	21.09	26.90
EBITDA Margin %	35.45	36.09	36.31	35.62	35.96	29.02	31.93	37.03
Net Margin %	22.12	22.45	22.58	21.56	20.87	15.35	18.84	21.91
Asset Turnover	0.67	0.67	0.68	0.68	0.66	0.72	0.88	0.95
Current Ratio	2.53	2.56	1.37	1.25	2.54	0.88	2.76	3.04
Debt to Equity	0.19	0.20	N.M.	N.M.	0.25	N.M.	N.M.	N.M.
Price Range	53.28-46.40	53.19-43.36	52.65-43.36	52.65-43.36	48.95-33.74	51.24-38.99	61.00-40.71	57.69-31.31
P/E Ratio	30.27-26.36	31.47-25.66	32.10-26.44	32.91-27.10	37.65-25.95	64.05-48.74	71.76-47.89	64.10-34.79
Average Yield %	0.65	0.64	0.62	0.60	0.57	0.51	0.39	0.40

Address: 710 Medtronic Parkway,	Web Site: www.medtronic.com	Auditors: PricewaterhouseCoopers LLP
Minneapolis, MN 55432	Officers: Arthur D. Collins Jr. - Chmn., C.E.O.	Investor Contact: 763-505-2692
Telephone: (763) 514-4000	William A. Hawkins - Pres., C.O.O.	Transfer Agents: Wells Fargo Bank
Fax: (763) 514-4000		Minnesota N.A., St. Paul, MN

MELLON FINANCIAL CORP.

Exchange	Symbol	Price	52Wk Range	Yield	P/E
NYS	MEL	$28.54 (3/31/2005)	32.61-26.54	2.52	15.18

*7 Year Price Score 74.34   ***NYSE Composite Index=100**   ***12 Month Price Score 92.83**

Interim Earnings (Per Share)

Qtr.	Mar	Jun	Sep	Dec
2001	0.54	0.12	0.40	1.70
2002	0.48	0.25	0.44	0.38
2003	0.37	0.41	0.42	0.43
2004	0.57	0.42	0.43	0.46

Interim Dividends (Per Share)

Amt	Decl	Ex	Rec	Pay
0.16Q	1/20/2004	1/28/2004	1/30/2004	2/13/2004
0.18Q	7/20/2004	7/28/2004	7/30/2004	8/13/2004
0.18Q	10/19/2004	10/27/2004	10/29/2004	11/15/2004
0.18Q	1/19/2005	1/27/2005	1/31/2005	2/15/2005

Indicated Div: $0.72

Valuation Analysis

Forecast P/E	15.11	No of Institutions	
	(4/7/2005)	433	
Market Cap	$12.1 Billion	Shares	
Book Value	4.1 Billion	292,073,792	
Price/Book	2.95	% Held	
Price/Sales	2.45	68.94	

Business Summary: Commercial Banking (MIC: 8.1 SIC: 021 NAIC: 22110)

Mellon Financial, with assets of $33.98 billion as of Dec 31 2003, is a provider of wealth management and global asset management for individual and institutional investors, as well as global investment services for businesses and institutions. Co. offers an array of banking services for individuals and small, mid-size and large businesses in selected geographies. Its asset management companies, which include The Dreyfus Corp. and Founders Asset Management in the U.S., Newton Management in the U.K., and Standish Mellon Asset Management, provide investment products. In addition, Co. provides retirement and employee benefits consulting through Mellon Human Resources & Investor Solutions.

Recent Developments: For the year ended Dec 31 2004, income from continuing operations increased 18.3% to $800,000 thousand from income of $676,000 thousand a year earlier. Net income increased 13.6% to $796,000 thousand from net income of $701,000 thousand a year earlier. Net interest income was $458,000 thousand, down 19.6% from $570,000 thousand the year before. Provision for loan losses was $11,000 thousand versus $7,000 thousand in the prior year, an increase of 257.1%. Non-interest income rose 10.8% to $4,064,000 thousand, while non-interest expense advanced 4.3% to $3,376,000 thousand.

Prospects: On Feb 28 2005, Co. announced it completed its previously announced acquisition of DPM, a Somerset, NJ-based hedge fund administrator that serves 91 clients with assets of approximately $30.00 billion. Separately, for the first quarter of 2005, net interest revenue is expected to be at the mid to upper end of a $115.0 million to $120.0 million range on a fully taxable equivalent basis, assuming a gradual and measured increase in interest rates and allowing for tactical investment securities decisions. During 2005, Co. will continue to be focus on generating organic revenue growth, delivering positive operating leverage and investing in its businesses.

Financial Data

(US$ in Thousands)	12/31/2004	12/31/2003	12/31/2002	12/31/2001	12/31/2000	12/31/1999	12/31/1998	12/31/1997
Earnings Per Share	1.88	1.63	1.55	2.76	2.03	1.85	1.63	1.44
Cash Flow Per Share	2.01	1.85	(0.17)	6.61	1.46	5.04	1.19	1.01
Tang Book Value Per Share	3.86	3.30	2.82	3.66	4.34	3.72	2.05	2.27
Dividends Per Share	0.700	0.570	0.490	0.820	0.860	0.780	0.705	0.645
Dividend Payout %	37.23	34.97	31.61	29.71	42.36	42.16	43.38	44.79
Income Statement								
Interest Income	862,000	917,000	1,056,000	1,397,000	2,829,000	2,759,000	2,892,000	2,716,000
Interest Expense	404,000	348,000	446,000	823,000	1,501,000	1,329,000	1,401,000	1,249,000
Net Interest Income	458,000	569,000	610,000	574,000	1,328,000	1,430,000	1,491,000	1,467,000
Provision for Losses	(11,000)	7,000	172,000	(4,000)	45,000	45,000	60,000	148,000
Non-Interest Income	4,064,000	3,633,000	3,681,000	2,658,000	3,150,000	3,227,000	2,922,000	2,418,000
Non-Interest Expense	3,376,000	3,207,000	3,126,000	2,561,000	2,851,000	3,049,000	3,013,000	2,568,000
Income Before Taxes	1,157,000	988,000	993,000	675,000	1,582,000	1,563,000	1,340,000	1,169,000
Income Taxes	357,000	311,000	326,000	239,000	575,000	574,000	470,000	398,000
Net Income	796,000	701,000	682,000	1,318,000	1,007,000	963,000	870,000	771,000
Average Shares	424,287	430,718	439,189	477,712	496,825	521,986	530,000	522,000
Balance Sheet								
Net Loans & Leases	6,656,000	7,364,000	8,311,000	8,414,000	25,976,000	29,845,000	31,597,000	28,667,000
Total Assets	37,115,000	33,983,000	36,231,000	34,360,000	50,364,000	47,946,000	50,777,000	44,892,000
Total Deposits	23,591,000	20,843,000	22,657,000	20,715,000	36,890,000	33,421,000	34,383,000	31,305,000
Total Liabilities	33,013,000	30,281,000	32,836,000	30,878,000	46,212,000	42,939,000	45,265,000	40,056,000
Stockholders' Equity	4,102,000	3,702,000	3,395,000	3,482,000	4,152,000	4,016,000	4,521,000	3,845,000
Shares Outstanding	423,353	427,032	430,781	446,508	486,738	500,623	524,000	508,000
Statistical Record								
Return on Assets %	2.23	2.00	1.93	3.11	2.04	1.95	1.82	1.76
Return on Equity %	20.34	19.75	19.83	34.53	24.59	22.56	20.80	20.31
Net Interest Margin %	53.13	62.05	57.77	41.09	46.94	51.83	51.56	54.01
Efficiency Ratio %	68.53	70.48	65.99	63.16	47.68	50.94	51.82	50.02
Loans to Deposits	0.28	0.35	0.37	0.41	0.70	0.89	0.92	0.92
Price Range	33.93-26.54	33.62-20.30	40.80-20.94	50.75-30.25	51.31-27.50	39.88-31.31	39.00-24.50	31.72-17.44
P/E Ratio	18.05-14.12	20.63-12.45	26.32-13.51	18.39-10.96	25.28-13.55	21.55-16.93	23.93-15.03	22.03-12.11
Average Yield %	2.34	2.06	1.53	2.02	2.23	2.24	2.20	2.76

Address: One Mellon Center,	Web Site: www.mellon.com	Auditors: KPMG LLP
Pittsburgh, PA 15258-0001	Officers: Martin G. McGuinn - Chmn., C.E.O. Steven	Investor Contact: 412-234-5601
Telephone: (412) 234-5000	G. Elliott - Sr. Vice-Chmn.	
Fax: (412) 234-6283		

MEMC ELECTRONIC MATERIALS, INC.

Exchange	Symbol	Price	52Wk Range	Yield	P/E
NYS	WFR	$13.45 (3/31/2005)	14.56-7.39	N/A	13.19

*7 Year Price Score 89.05 *NYSE Composite Index=100 *12 Month Price Score 118.62

Interim Earnings (Per Share)

Qtr.	Mar	Jun	Sep	Dec
2001	(0.25)	(5.10)	(0.97)	5.85
2002	(0.26)	0.07	(0.25)	0.37
2003	0.09	0.13	0.16	0.15
2004	0.16	0.27	0.27	0.31

Interim Dividends (Per Share)

No Dividends Paid

Valuation Analysis

Forecast P/E	12.07	No of Institutions	
	(4/7/2005)	147	
Market Cap	$2.8 Billion	Shares	
Book Value	442.9 Million	99,701,368	
Price/Book	6.33	% Held	
Price/Sales	2.73	47.73	

Business Summary: IT & Technology (MIC: 10.2 SIC: 674 NAIC: 34413)

MEMC Electronic Materials is engaged in the production of wafers for the semiconductor industry. Co. provides wafers in sizes ranging from 100mm to 300mm and in three categories: prime polished, epitaxial, and test/monitor. Co.'s wafers are used as a starting material for the manufacture of various types of semiconductor devices, including microprocessor, memory, logic and power devices. In turn, these devices are used in computers, cellular phones and other mobile electronic devices, automobiles and other products. Co.'s principal customers include memory, microprocessor and applications specific integrated circuit manufacturers, as well as foundries.

Recent Developments: For the year ended Dec 31 2004, net income increased 94.0% to $226,201 thousand from net income of $116,617 thousand a year earlier. Revenues were $1,027,958 thousand, up 31.6% from $781,100 thousand the year before. Operating income was $260,488 thousand versus an income of $142,619 thousand in the prior year, an increase of 82.6%. Total direct expense was $658,543 thousand versus $548,344 thousand in the prior year, an increase of 20.1%. Total indirect expense was $108,927 thousand versus $90,137 thousand in the prior year, an increase of 20.8%.

Prospects: While 2005 is expected to be a strong growth year, Co. continues to see the effects of short-term inventory adjustments in the semiconductor industry. As a result, Co. anticipates its sales and margins in first quarter will be flat versus the fourth quarter of 2004. In the meantime, Co.'s 300mm expansion program is proceeding well. By the end of the first quarter, Co. anticipates crossing over the 150,000 wafers per month mark of 300mm capacity. This should keep Co. on track to achieve its goal of 350,000 wafers per month capacity by the end of 2006. Co. noted it anticipates the first 300mm wafers from its Taisil facility will be available in the third quarter of 2005.

Financial Data

(US$ in Thousands)	12/31/2004	12/31/2003	12/31/2002	12/31/2001	11/13/2001	12/31/2000	12/31/1999	12/31/1998
Earnings Per Share	1.02	0.53	(0.17)	(0.48)	(7.03)	(0.62)	(2.43)	(7.80)
Cash Flow Per Share	1.36	0.63	0.59	(0.07)	(0.33)	0.75	(1.66)	(0.83)
Tang Book Value Per Share	2.13	0.94	...	...	...	4.61	5.55	8.66
Income Statement								
Total Revenue	1,027,958	781,100	687,180	58,846	559,007	871,637	693,594	758,916
EBITDA	251,175	192,577	120,247	(28,664)	(18,649)	169,221	10,501	(173,800)
Depn & Amortn	44,135	31,049	34,160	5,271	169,341	173,085	159,081	155,874
Income Before Taxes	198,531	155,887	19,567	(36,018)	(259,666)	(77,827)	(212,648)	(373,215)
Income Taxes	(40,119)	36,864	16,712	1,576	239,352	(21,013)	(65,921)	(89,394)
Net Income	226,201	116,617	(5,070)	(29,397)	(489,025)	(43,390)	(151,481)	(316,332)
Average Shares	221,047	218,719	129,810	69,612	69,612	69,596	62,224	40,580
Balance Sheet								
Current Assets	390,330	365,345	363,708	264,030	...	410,407	275,920	299,138
Total Assets	1,009,942	726,752	631,682	549,334	...	1,890,566	1,724,581	1,773,714
Current Liabilities	215,624	244,054	286,073	221,699	...	323,625	189,614	258,644
Long-Term Obligations	116,082	59,251	160,998	144,743	...	942,972	869,759	871,163
Total Liabilities	520,565	469,002	598,366	518,500	...	1,449,734	1,248,453	1,326,432
Stockholders' Equity	442,898	193,623	(24,680)	(20,249)	...	366,419	432,791	399,040
Shares Outstanding	208,393	207,002	195,532	69,612	...	69,612	69,534	40,507
Statistical Record								
Return on Assets %	25.98	17.17	N.M.	N.M.	...	N.M.	N.M.	N.M.
Return on Equity %	70.88	138.05	N.M.	...	...	N.M.	N.M.	N.M.
EBITDA Margin %	24.43	24.65	17.50	N.M.	N.M.	19.41	1.51	N.M.
Net Margin %	22.00	14.93	N.M.	N.M.	N.M.	N.M.	N.M.	N.M.
Asset Turnover	1.18	1.15	1.16	0.05	...	0.48	0.40	0.43
Current Ratio	1.81	1.50	1.27	1.19	...	1.27	1.46	1.16
Debt to Equity	0.26	0.31	...	...	...	2.57	2.01	2.18
Price Range	13.25-7.39	14.25-7.15	10.12-2.89	4.57-3.31	11.74-1.05	23.75-6.94	21.50-5.50	19.00-3.00
P/E Ratio	12.99-7.25	26.89-13.49	N.A.	N.A.	N.A.	N.A.	N.A.	N.A.

Address: 501 Pearl Drive, St. Peters, MO 63376	Web Site: www.memc.com	Auditors: KPMG LLP
Telephone: (636) 474-5000	Officers: John Marren - Chmn. Nabeel Gareeb - Pres., C.E.O.	Investor Contact: 636-279-5000
Fax: (636) 474-5158		Transfer Agents: ComputerShare Investor Services, Chicago, IL

MERCK & CO., INC

Exchange	Symbol	Price	52Wk Range	Yield	P/E	Div Acheiver
NYS	MRK	$32.37 (3/31/2005)	48.37-26.00	4.70	12.40	21 Years

*7 Year Price Score 55.77 *NYSE Composite Index=100 *12 Month Price Score 76.85

Interim Earnings (Per Share)

Qtr.	Mar	Jun	Sep	Dec
2001	0.71	0.78	0.84	0.81
2002	0.71	0.77	0.83	0.83
2003	0.76	0.83	0.82	0.62
2004	0.73	0.79	0.60	0.50

Interim Dividends (Per Share)

Amt	Decl	Ex	Rec	Pay
0.37Q	5/25/2004	6/2/2004	6/4/2004	7/1/2004
0.38Q	7/27/2004	9/1/2004	9/3/2004	10/1/2004
0.38Q	11/23/2004	12/1/2004	12/3/2004	1/3/2005
0.38Q	2/22/2005	3/2/2005	3/4/2005	4/1/2005
Indicated Div: $1.52 (Div. Reinv. Plan)				

Valuation Analysis

Forecast P/E	13.38	No of Institutions
	(4/7/2005)	1008
Market Cap	$71.5 Billion	Shares
Book Value	17.3 Billion	1,286,763,648
Price/Book	4.14	% Held
Price/Sales	3.12	58.28

Business Summary: Pharmaceuticals (MIC: 9.1 SIC: 834 NAIC: 25412)

Merck & Co. is a research-driven pharmaceutical company that discovers, develops, manufactures and markets human and animal health products, directly and through its joint ventures. Co.'s products include therapeutic and preventive agents, generally sold by prescription, for the treatment of human disorders. Among these products are Zocor, a cholesterol-lowering medicine, Fosamax, a treatment for osteoporosis, Vioxx, a prescription arthritis medicine, Singulair, for the treatment of chronic asthma, and Cozaar and Hyzaar for the treatment of high blood pressure.

Recent Developments: For the year ended Dec 31 2004, net income decreased 14.9% to $5,813,400 thousand from net income of $6,830,900 thousand a year earlier. Revenues were $22,938,600 thousand, up 2.0% from $22,485,900 thousand the year before. Total direct expense was $4,959,800 thousand versus $4,436,900 thousand in the prior year, an increase of 11.8%. Total indirect expense was $11,356,500 thousand versus $9,674,800 thousand in the prior year, an increase of 17.4%.

Prospects: On Sep 30 2004, Co. announced the voluntary worldwide withdrawal of VIOXX, its arthritis and acute pain medication, and plans to vigorously defend against VIOXX-related lawsuits, including taking cases to trial. In response to the withdrawal, Co. has accelerated its cost structure reduction plan, which is expected to result in $2.00 billion in savings through 2008. Co. plans to submit its three Phase III vaccines for U.S. Food and Drug Administration approval in 2005. These vaccines should provide significant new opportunities for Co. in the pediatric, adolescent and adult vaccines markets. Looking ahead, Co. expects full-year 2005 earnings of $2.42 to $2.52 per share.

Financial Data

(US$ in Thousands)	12/31/2004	12/31/2003	12/31/2002	12/31/2001	12/31/2000	12/31/1999	12/31/1998	12/31/1997
Earnings Per Share	2.61	3.03	3.14	3.14	2.90	2.45	2.15	1.87
Cash Flow Per Share	3.95	3.77	4.22	3.97	3.32	2.61	2.24	2.62
Tang Book Value Per Share	7.03	6.13	4.88	3.77	3.23	2.43	1.91	2.44
Dividends Per Share	1.500	1.460	1.420	1.380	1.260	1.120	0.990	0.870
Dividend Payout %	57.47	48.18	45.22	43.95	43.45	45.71	46.05	46.52
Income Statement								
Total Revenue	22,938,600	22,485,900	51,790,300	47,715,700	40,363,200	32,714,000	26,898,200	23,636,900
EBITDA	9,418,800	10,408,000	11,673,400	11,841,000	11,115,200	9,716,500	9,046,100	7,207,500
Depn & Amortn	1,450,700	1,314,200	1,488,300	1,463,800	1,277,300	1,144,800	1,015,100	837,100
Income Before Taxes	7,974,500	9,051,600	10,213,600	10,402,600	9,824,100	8,619,500	8,133,100	6,462,300
Income Taxes	2,161,100	2,462,000	3,064,100	3,120,800	3,002,400	2,729,000	2,884,900	1,848,200
Net Income	5,813,400	6,830,900	7,149,500	7,281,800	6,821,700	5,890,500	5,248,200	4,614,100
Average Shares	2,226,400	2,253,100	2,277,000	2,322,300	2,353,200	2,404,600	2,441,100	2,469,400
Balance Sheet								
Current Assets	13,475,200	11,527,200	14,833,900	12,961,600	13,353,400	11,259,200	10,228,500	8,213,000
Total Assets	42,572,800	40,587,500	47,561,200	44,006,700	39,910,400	35,634,900	31,853,400	25,811,900
Current Liabilities	11,744,100	9,569,600	12,375,200	11,544,200	9,709,600	8,758,800	6,068,800	5,568,600
Long-Term Obligations	4,691,500	5,096,000	4,879,000	4,798,600	3,600,700	3,143,900	3,220,800	1,346,500
Total Liabilities	25,284,600	25,011,100	29,360,700	27,956,600	25,078,000	22,393,300	19,051,600	13,198,400
Stockholders' Equity	17,288,200	15,576,400	18,200,500	16,050,100	14,832,400	13,241,600	12,801,800	12,613,500
Shares Outstanding	2,208,639	2,221,764	2,244,983	2,272,729	2,307,599	2,329,078	2,360,453	2,387,296
Statistical Record								
Return on Assets %	13.94	15.50	15.62	17.35	18.01	17.46	18.20	18.42
Return on Equity %	35.28	40.45	41.75	47.16	48.47	45.24	41.30	37.54
EBITDA Margin %	41.06	46.29	22.54	24.82	27.54	29.70	33.63	30.49
Net Margin %	25.34	30.38	13.80	15.26	16.90	18.01	19.51	19.52
Asset Turnover	0.55	0.51	1.13	1.14	1.07	0.97	0.93	0.94
Current Ratio	1.15	1.20	1.20	1.12	1.38	1.29	1.69	1.47
Debt to Equity	0.27	0.33	0.27	0.30	0.24	0.24	0.25	0.11
Price Range	49.08-26.00	59.85-40.60	60.92-36.96	88.02-54.11	89.80-51.05	81.75-57.67	75.18-48.68	50.78-37.68
P/E Ratio	18.80-9.96	19.75-13.40	19.40-11.77	28.03-17.23	30.96-17.60	33.37-23.54	34.97-22.64	27.16-20.15
Average Yield %	3.57	2.84	2.77	2.05	1.81	1.62	1.63	1.95

Address: P.O. Box 100, One Merck Drive, Whitehouse Station, NJ 08889-0100 Telephone: (908) 423-1000 Fax: (908) 735-1500	Web Site: www.merck.com Officers: Raymond V. Gilmartin - Chmn., Pres., C.E.O. Judy C. Lewent - Exec. V.P., C.F.O.	Auditors: PricewaterhouseCoppers LLP Investor Contact: 908-423-5881 Transfer Agents: Wells Fargo Bank Minnesota, N.A., South St. Paul, MN

MERCURY GENERAL CORP.

Exchange	Symbol	Price	52Wk Range	Yield	P/E	Div Acheiver
NYS	MCY	$55.26 (3/31/2005)	59.98-46.98	3.11	10.55	18 Years

*7 Year Price Score 109.83 *NYSE Composite Index=100 *12 Month Price Score 97.70

Interim Earnings (Per Share)

Qtr.	Mar	Jun	Sep	Dec
2001	0.45	0.49	0.59	0.41
2002	0.53	0.02	0.34	0.32
2003	0.77	0.80	0.91	0.90
2004	1.26	1.43	1.19	1.36

Interim Dividends (Per Share)

Amt	Decl	Ex	Rec	Pay
0.37Q	5/2/2004	6/14/2004	6/15/2004	6/30/2004
0.37Q	8/2/2004	9/13/2004	9/15/2004	9/30/2004
0.37Q	10/29/2004	12/13/2004	12/15/2004	12/29/2004
0.43Q	1/28/2005	3/11/2005	3/15/2005	3/31/2005

Indicated Div: $1.72

Valuation Analysis

Forecast P/E	11.24	No of Institutions
	(4/7/2005)	170
Market Cap	$3.0 Billion	Shares
Book Value	1.5 Billion	21,650,192
Price/Book	2.06	% Held
Price/Sales	1.13	39.70

Business Summary: Insurance (MIC: 8.2 SIC: 331 NAIC: 24126)

Mercury General, through its subsidiaries, engages primarily in writing all risk classifications of automobile insurance in a number of states, principally in California. Co. offers automobile policyholders the following types of coverage: bodily injury liability, underinsured and uninsured motorist, personal injury protection, property damage liability, comprehensive, collision and other hazards specified in the policy. Co. sells its policies through independent agents in California, Florida, Georgia, Illinois, New York, Texas, Oklahoma, New Jersey and Virginia. In addition, Co. writes other lines of insurance in various states, including mechanical breakdown and homeowners insurance.

Recent Developments: For the year ended Dec 31 2004, net income increased 55.3% to $286,208 thousand from net income of $184,321 thousand a year earlier. Revenues were $2,668,157 thousand, up 17.8% from $2,265,517 thousand the year before. Net premiums earned were $2,528,636 thousand versus $2,145,047 thousand in the prior year, an increase of 17.9%. Net investment income rose 4.9% to $109,681 thousand from $104,520 thousand the previous year.

Prospects: In late 2004, Co. began writing private passenger automobile insurance in Michigan and Nevada, making it the 12 and 13 states in which Co. writes automobile insurance. Separately, Co. is expecting a higher loss frequency in the first quarter of 2005 versus the year before. This is due largely to the state of California experiencing precipitation levels that were significantly higher than average in Jan 2005. Consequently, the number of losses reported in the California homeowners line of business was more than double the number reported in Jan 2004, and the number of California automobile losses reported in Jan 2005 was approx. 10.0% more than the number reported in Jan 2004.

Financial Data
(US$ in Thousands)

	12/31/2004	12/31/2003	12/31/2002	12/31/2001	12/31/2000	12/31/1999	12/31/1998	12/31/1997
Earnings Per Share	5.24	3.38	1.21	1.94	2.02	2.44	3.21	2.82
Cash Flow Per Share	8.58	8.17	6.31	3.68	2.82	3.46	3.50	4.88
Tang Book Value Per Share	26.77	23.07	20.21	19.71	19.06	16.71	16.78	14.51
Dividends Per Share	1.480	1.320	1.200	1.060	0.960	0.840	0.700	0.580
Dividend Payout %	28.24	39.05	99.17	54.64	47.52	34.43	21.81	20.57
Income Statement								
Premium Income	2,528,636	2,145,047	1,741,527	1,380,561	1,249,259	1,188,307	1,121,584	1,031,280
Total Revenue	2,668,157	2,265,517	1,786,271	1,506,980	1,366,018	1,280,676	1,222,123	1,127,946
Benefits & Claims	1,582,254	1,452,051	1,268,243	1,010,439	901,781	789,103	684,468	654,729
Income Before Taxes	407,843	245,801	60,668	124,809	128,555	168,539	235,280	209,779
Income Taxes	121,635	61,480	(5,437)	19,470	19,189	34,830	57,754	53,473
Net Income	286,208	184,321	66,105	105,339	109,366	133,709	177,526	156,306
Average Shares	54,633	54,547	54,502	54,382	54,258	54,815	55,354	55,383
Balance Sheet								
Total Assets	3,609,743	3,119,766	2,645,296	2,316,540	2,142,263	1,906,367	1,877,025	1,725,532
Total Liabilities	2,150,195	1,864,263	1,546,510	1,246,829	1,109,358	996,776	959,650	925,940
Stockholders' Equity	1,459,548	1,255,503	1,098,786	1,069,711	1,032,905	909,591	917,375	799,592
Shares Outstanding	54,514	54,424	54,361	54,276	54,193	54,425	54,684	55,125
Statistical Record								
Return on Assets %	8.48	6.39	2.66	4.72	5.39	7.07	9.86	9.94
Return on Equity %	21.03	15.66	6.10	10.02	11.23	14.64	20.68	21.70
Loss Ratio %	62.57	67.69	72.82	73.19	72.19	66.41	61.03	63.49
Net Margin %	10.73	8.14	3.70	6.99	8.01	10.44	14.53	13.86
Price Range	59.98-46.44	48.58-34.30	50.63-37.37	43.85-32.21	43.88-21.25	45.50-21.06	69.44-33.25	55.25-26.19
P/E Ratio	11.45-8.86	14.37-10.15	41.84-30.88	22.60-16.60	21.72-10.52	18.65-8.63	21.63-10.36	19.59-9.29
Average Yield %	2.90	3.07	2.74	2.83	3.44	3.44	1.36	1.52

Address: 4484 Wilshire Boulevard, Los Angeles, CA 90010 **Telephone:** (323) 937-1060 **Fax:** (323) 857-7116	**Web Site:** www.mercuryinsurance.com **Officers:** George Joseph - Chmn., C.E.O. Gabriel Tirador - Pres., C.O.O.	**Auditors:** KPMG LLP **Investor Contact:** 800-900-6729 **Transfer Agents:** The Bank of New York, New York, NY

MEREDITH CORP.

Exchange	Symbol	Price	52Wk Range	Yield	P/E	Div Acheiver
NYS	MDP	$46.75 (3/31/2005)	55.75-45.89	1.20	19.56	11 Years

*7 Year Price Score 109.93 *NYSE Composite Index=100 *12 Month Price Score 85.52

Interim Earnings (Per Share)

Qtr.	Sep	Dec	Mar	Jun
2001-02	0.17	0.17	0.35	1.10
2002-03	(1.36)	0.38	0.50	0.58
2003-04	0.39	0.39	0.65	0.71
2004-05	0.50	0.54	...	...

Interim Dividends (Per Share)

Amt	Decl	Ex	Rec	Pay
0.12Q	5/12/2004	5/26/2004	5/28/2004	6/15/2004
0.12Q	8/11/2004	8/27/2004	8/31/2004	9/15/2004
0.12Q	11/8/2004	11/26/2004	11/30/2004	12/15/2004
0.14Q	1/31/2005	2/24/2005	2/28/2005	3/15/2005

Indicated Div: $0.56

Valuation Analysis

Forecast P/E	16.18	No of Institutions
	(4/7/2005)	192
Market Cap	$2.3 Billion	Shares
Book Value	621.3 Million	34,903,000
Price/Book	3.76	% Held
Price/Sales	1.97	86.56

Business Summary: Media (MIC: 13.1 SIC: 721 NAIC: 11120)

Meredith is engaged in magazine and book publishing, television broadcasting, integrated marketing, and interactive media. The publishing segment consists of 17 magazine brands, including Better Homes and Gardens, Ladies' Home Journal, and American Baby, as well as 160 special interest publications; book publishing with nearly 300 books in print; integrated marketing relationships; a consumer database; an Internet presence, including 24 web sites and strategic alliances with Internet destinations; brand licensing relationships; and other related operations. The broadcasting segment includes the operations of 12 network-affiliated television stations located across the continental U.S.

Recent Developments: For the quarter ended Dec 31 2004, net income increased 57.9% to $27,715 thousand from net income of $17,557 thousand in the year-earlier quarter. Revenues were $294,553 thousand, up 5.1% from $280,379 thousand the year before. Operating income was $48,701 thousand versus an income of $34,323 thousand in the prior-year quarter, an increase of 41.9%. Total indirect expense was $122,439 thousand versus $124,337 thousand in the prior-year quarter, a decrease of 1.5%.

Prospects: Looking ahead, Co. anticipates option-adjusted earnings per share of $0.67 to $0.69 and $2.50, for the third quarter and full-year of fiscal 2005, respectively. Additionally, for the third quarter of fiscal 2005, Broadcast pacings, which are a snapshot in time and change frequently, are currently running up in the low single digits. Co. expects the Publishing Group to grow operating profit in the mid to high single digits in the third quarter due to strong results from its integrated marketing operations, increased circulation profit, and prudent cost management. Publishing advertising revenues are expected to be down in the low single digits, reflecting the uncertain advertising climate.

Financial Data

(US$ in Thousands)	6 Mos	3 Mos	06/30/2004	06/30/2003	06/30/2002	06/30/2001	06/30/2000	06/30/1999
Earnings Per Share	2.39	2.25	2.14	0.10	1.79	1.39	1.35	1.67
Cash Flow Per Share	3.27	3.82	3.40	3.47	2.83	2.74	2.88	2.58
Dividends Per Share	0.480	0.455	0.430	0.370	0.350	0.330	0.310	0.290
Dividend Payout %	20.06	20.26	20.09	370.00	19.55	23.74	22.96	17.37
Income Statement								
Total Revenue	583,416	288,863	1,161,652	1,080,104	987,829	1,053,213	1,097,165	1,036,122
EBITDA	109,873	55,203	269,428	244,554	275,431	243,800	248,951	256,074
Depn & Amortn	17,199	8,445	66,314	68,786	93,770	95,699	87,614	82,612
Income Before Taxes	82,772	41,803	180,613	148,559	149,072	116,200	127,586	152,175
Income Taxes	32,033	16,179	69,897	57,491	57,691	44,928	56,556	62,518
Net Income	51,632	25,624	110,716	5,319	91,381	71,272	71,030	89,657
Average Shares	51,469	51,658	51,689	51,093	50,921	51,354	52,774	53,761
Balance Sheet								
Current Assets	310,481	329,690	314,014	268,429	272,211	291,082	288,799	256,175
Total Assets	1,507,255	1,490,561	1,465,927	1,436,721	1,460,264	1,437,747	1,439,773	1,423,396
Current Liabilities	435,079	440,426	370,961	297,199	307,406	371,406	358,701	344,115
Long-Term Obligations	175,000	175,000	225,000	375,000	385,000	400,000	455,000	485,000
Total Liabilities	885,945	908,369	877,197	935,956	952,547	989,839	1,017,264	1,010,091
Stockholders' Equity	621,310	582,192	588,730	500,765	507,717	447,908	379,844	360,158
Shares Outstanding	49,979	49,999	50,484	50,149	49,575	49,791	49,209	50,284
Statistical Record								
Return on Assets %	8.39	7.89	7.61	0.37	6.31	4.95	4.95	7.20
Return on Equity %	21.57	21.19	20.27	1.05	19.12	17.22	19.14	25.26
EBITDA Margin %	18.83	19.11	23.19	22.64	27.88	23.15	22.69	24.71
Net Margin %	8.85	8.87	9.53	0.49	9.25	6.77	6.47	8.65
Asset Turnover	0.81	0.80	0.80	0.75	0.68	0.73	0.76	0.83
Current Ratio	0.71	0.75	0.85	0.90	0.89	0.78	0.81	0.74
Debt to Equity	0.28	0.30	0.38	0.75	0.76	0.89	1.20	1.35
Price Range	55.75-48.81	55.75-46.17	55.75-44.00	47.58-34.09	44.75-27.20	38.52-27.19	41.94-22.44	48.25-27.19
P/E Ratio	23.33-20.42	24.78-20.52	26.05-20.56	475.80-340.90	25.00-15.20	27.71-19.56	31.06-16.62	28.89-16.28
Average Yield %	0.93	0.90	0.87	0.89	0.94	1.00	0.92	0.80

Address: 1716 Locust Street, Des Moines, IA 50309-3023
Telephone: (515) 284-3000
Fax: (515) 284-2700

Web Site: www.meredith.com
Officers: William T. Kerr - Chmn., C.E.O. Stephen M. Lacy - Pres., C.O.O.

Auditors: KPMG LLP
Investor Contact: 800-284-4236
Transfer Agents: Boston EquiServe, Boston, MA

MERRILL LYNCH & CO INC

Exchange	Symbol	Price	52Wk Range	Yield	P/E
NYS	MER	$56.60 (3/31/2005)	61.55-47.53	1.13	12.92

*7 Year Price Score 97.24   ***NYSE Composite Index=100**   ***12 Month Price Score 99.49**

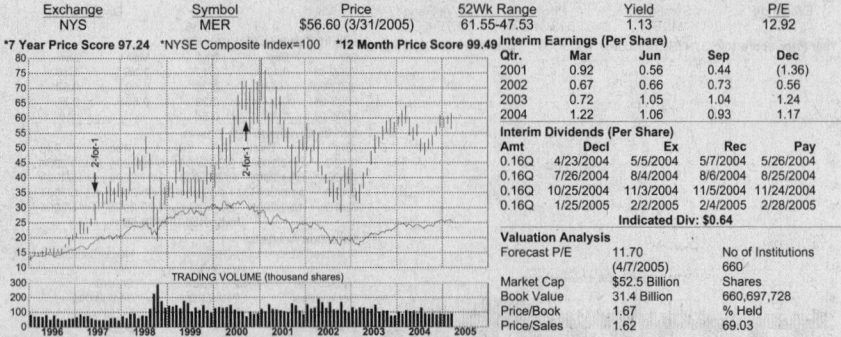

Interim Earnings (Per Share)

Qtr.	Mar	Jun	Sep	Dec
2001	0.92	0.56	0.44	(1.36)
2002	0.67	0.66	0.73	0.56
2003	0.72	1.05	1.04	1.24
2004	1.22	1.06	0.93	1.17

Interim Dividends (Per Share)

Amt	Decl	Ex	Rec	Pay
0.16Q	4/23/2004	5/5/2004	5/7/2004	5/26/2004
0.16Q	7/26/2004	8/4/2004	8/6/2004	8/25/2004
0.16Q	10/25/2004	11/3/2004	11/5/2004	11/24/2004
0.16Q	1/25/2005	2/2/2005	2/4/2005	2/28/2005

Indicated Div: $0.64

Valuation Analysis

Forecast P/E	11.70	No of Institutions	
	(4/7/2005)	660	
Market Cap	$52.5 Billion	Shares	
Book Value	31.4 Billion	660,697,728	
Price/Book	1.67	% Held	
Price/Sales	1.62	69.03	

Business Summary: Finance Intermediaries & Services (MIC: 8.7 SIC: 211 NAIC: 23999)

Merrill Lynch & Company provides broker-dealer, investment banking, financing, wealth management, advisory, asset management, insurance, lending and related products and services on a global basis. Merrill Lynch, Pierce, Fenner & Smith, a major subsidiary of Co., is a broker and a dealer in various financial instruments, and an investment banker. Co. reports in three business segments: the Global Markets and Investment Banking, Global Private Client, and Merrill Lynch Investment Managers. As of Dec 31 2003, client assets totaled approximately $1.50 trillion, including $500.00 billion under management.

Recent Developments: For the year ended Dec 31 2004, net income increased 15.6% to $4,436,000 thousand from net income of $3,836,000 thousand a year earlier. Revenues were $22,023,000 thousand, up 10.8% from $19,868,000 thousand the year before. Net investment income rose 394.3% to $346,000 thousand from $70,000 thousand a year ago.

Prospects: Co. is encouraged by the strong financial and operating performance in 2004. Each of Co.'s three major businesses turned in an impressive performance, delivering strong results and making progress toward enhancing their ability to grow. Global Markets and Investment Banking is benefiting from initiatives to better position its equity markets franchise, broaden its footprint in commodities and capitalize on strong client relationships. Global Private Client is benefiting from the growing ranks of its financial advisors and solid net inflows into annuitized products. Merrill Lynch Investment Managers' results are being positively affected by broader distribution of its products.

Financial Data

(US$ in Thousands)	12/31/2004	12/26/2003	12/27/2002	12/28/2001	12/29/2000	12/31/1999	12/25/1998	12/26/1997
Earnings Per Share	4.38	4.05	2.63	0.57	4.11	3.09	1.50	2.42
Cash Flow Per Share	(14.30)	10.56	22.61	7.68	1.64	0.24	14.62	(26.82)
Tang Book Value Per Share	26.48	23.69	20.76	18.39	16.67	10.09	6.09	3.65
Dividends Per Share	0.640	0.640	0.640	0.640	0.605	0.525	0.460	0.375
Dividend Payout %	14.61	15.80	24.33	112.28	14.72	17.02	30.67	15.53
Income Statement								
Interest Income	14,973,000	11,678,000	13,178,000	20,143,000	21,196,000	15,097,000	19,314,000	17,087,000
Commissions & Fees	8,138,000	7,024,000	7,070,000	8,805,000	11,026,000	9,948,000	9,063,000	7,416,000
Employee Costs	10,596,000	9,570,000	9,426,000	11,269,000	13,730,000	11,153,000	9,199,000	7,962,000
Interest Expense	10,444,000	7,591,000	9,645,000	16,877,000	18,085,000	13,010,000	18,306,000	16,062,000
Income Taxes	1,400,000	1,470,000	1,053,000	609,000	1,738,000	1,265,000	713,000	1,097,000
Net Income	4,436,000	3,988,000	2,513,000	573,000	3,784,000	2,618,000	1,259,000	1,906,000
Average Shares	1,003,779	975,524	942,222	938,555	911,416	836,262	812,600	773,498
Balance Sheet								
Total Assets	648,059,000	494,518,000	447,928,000	419,419,000	407,200,000	328,071,000	299,804,000	292,819,000
Total Liabilities	616,689,000	464,197,000	422,395,000	396,716,000	386,182,000	312,544,000	287,045,000	283,863,000
Stockholders' Equity	31,370,000	27,651,000	22,875,000	20,008,000	18,304,000	12,802,000	10,132,000	8,329,000
Shares Outstanding	928,036	945,910	867,290	843,473	807,954	735,530	712,568	670,164
Statistical Record								
Return on Assets %	0.76	0.85	0.58	0.14	1.03	0.82	0.43	0.76
Return on Equity %	14.79	15.83	11.75	3.00	24.40	22.46	13.68	25.11
Net Interest Margin %	30.25	35.00	26.81	16.21	14.68	13.82	5.22	6.00
Price Range	64.25-47.53	59.86-31.57	58.36-28.43	80.00-36.01	72.94-36.72	49.97-31.84	53.97-18.88	38.91-19.91
P/E Ratio	14.67-10.85	14.78-7.80	22.19-10.81	140.35-63.18	17.75-8.93	16.17-10.31	35.98-12.58	16.08-8.23
Average Yield %	1.15	1.36	1.51	1.12	1.05	1.36	1.21	1.29

Address: 4 World Financial Center, New York, NY 10080 Telephone: (212) 449-1000 Fax: (212) 449-7461	Web Site: www.ml.com Officers: E. Stanley O'Neal - Chmn., Pres., C.E.O. Thomas H. Patrick - Exec. Vice-Chmn., Fin., Admin.	Auditors: Deloitte & Touche LLP Investor Contact: 866-607-1234

METLIFE INC

Exchange	Symbol	Price	52Wk Range	Yield	P/E
NYS	MET	$39.10 (3/31/2005)	41.37-33.21	1.18	10.71

*7 Year Price Score N/A   *NYSE Composite Index=100   *12 Month Price Score 99.05

Interim Earnings (Per Share)

Qtr.	Mar	Jun	Sep	Dec
2001	0.37	0.41	0.21	(0.37)
2002	0.44	0.53	0.45	0.78
2003	0.47	0.79	0.75	0.90
2004	0.69	1.25	0.92	0.68

Interim Dividends (Per Share)

Amt	Decl	Ex	Rec	Pay
0.20A	10/23/2001	11/2/2001	11/6/2001	12/14/2001
0.21A	10/22/2002	11/6/2002	11/8/2002	12/13/2002
0.23A	10/21/2003	11/5/2003	11/7/2003	12/15/2003
0.46A	9/28/2004	11/3/2004	11/5/2004	12/13/2004

Indicated Div: $0.46

Valuation Analysis

Forecast P/E	10.98 (4/7/2005)	No of Institutions	373
Market Cap	$28.6 Billion	Shares	336,883,360
Book Value	22.8 Billion	% Held	45.96
Price/Book	1.25		
Price/Sales	0.73		

Business Summary: Insurance (MIC: 8.2 SIC: 411 NAIC: 24210)

MetLife is a provider of insurance and other financial services to individual and institutional customers. Co. offers life insurance, annuities, automobile and homeowners insurance and mutual funds to individuals, as well as group insurance, reinsurance, and retirement and savings products and services to corporations and other institutions. As of Dec 31 2003, Co. serves about 13.0 million households in the U.S. and provides benefits to about 37.0 million employees and family members through their plan sponsors, including 88 of the FORTUNE 100 largest companies. Co. also has direct international insurance operations in 10 countries serving about 8.0 million customers.

Recent Developments: For the year ended Dec 31 2004, income from continuing operations increased 42.6% to $2,708 million from income of $1,899 million a year earlier. Net income increased 24.4% to $2,758 million from net income of $2,217 million a year earlier. Revenues were $39,014 million, up 10.4% from $35,325 million the year before. Net premiums earned were $25,216 million versus $23,169 million in the prior year, an increase of 8.8%. Net investment income rose 7.6% to $12,418 million from $11,539 million a year ago.

Prospects: On Jan 31 2005, Co. announced that it has entered into an agreement to acquire Travelers Life & Annuity Co. from Citigroup Inc., along with substantially all of Citigroup's international insurance businesses, for approximately $11.50 billion, subject to closing adjustments. As a result of the transaction, Co.'s international operations will likely grow significantly in terms of revenue and earnings, types of products offered, and in the number of countries in which it operates. Co. expects that the transaction will be immediately accretive and will boost earnings per share by approximately 4.0% to 6.0% in 2006. The acquisition is expected to close in the summer of 2005.

Financial Data
(US$ in Thousands)

	12/31/2004	12/31/2003	12/31/2002	12/31/2001	12/31/2000	12/31/1999	12/31/1998
Earnings Per Share	3.65	2.94	2.20	0.62	1.49	...	...
Cash Flow Per Share	10.73	9.98	7.09	6.48	1.71	...	...
Tang Book Value Per Share	31.16	27.93	24.83	22.45	22.31	18.11	...
Dividends Per Share	0.460	0.230	0.210	0.200	0.200	...	...
Dividend Payout %	12.60	7.82	9.55	32.26	13.42	...	...
Income Statement							
Premium Income	25,216,000	23,169,000	21,225,000	19,101,000	18,137,000	13,526,000	12,863,000
Total Revenue	39,014,000	35,789,000	33,147,000	31,928,000	31,947,000	25,426,000	27,106,000
Benefits & Claims	22,662,000	20,848,000	19,523,000	18,454,000	17,220,000	...	...
Income Before Taxes	3,779,000	2,630,000	1,671,000	739,000	1,416,000	1,435,000	2,087,000
Income Taxes	1,071,000	687,000	516,000	266,000	463,000	593,000	740,000
Net Income	2,758,000	2,217,000	1,605,000	473,000	953,000	617,000	1,343,000
Average Shares	754,833	746,844	729,201	767,017	788,508	...	...
Balance Sheet							
Total Assets	356,808,000	326,841,000	277,385,000	256,898,000	255,018,000	225,232,000	215,346,000
Total Liabilities	333,984,000	305,692,000	258,735,000	239,580,000	237,539,000	124,955,000	124,203,000
Stockholders' Equity	22,824,000	21,149,000	17,385,000	16,062,000	16,389,000	13,690,000	14,867,000
Shares Outstanding	732,487	757,186	700,278	715,507	734,597	755,903	...
Statistical Record							
Return on Assets %	0.80	0.73	0.60	0.18	0.40	0.28	...
Return on Equity %	12.51	11.51	9.60	2.92	6.32	4.32	...
Loss Ratio %	89.87	89.98	91.98	96.61	94.94	...	...
Net Margin %	7.07	6.19	4.84	1.48	2.98	2.43	4.95
Price Range	41.18-32.63	33.92-24.01	34.58-20.75	34.88-25.20	36.50-15.13	...	...
P/E Ratio	11.28-8.94	11.54-8.17	15.72-9.43	56.25-40.65	24.50-10.15	N.A.	N.A.
Average Yield %	1.27	0.80	0.74	0.67	0.85	N.A.	N.A.

Address: One Madison Avenue, New York, NY 10010-3690 Telephone: (212) 578-2211	Web Site: www.metlife.com Officers: Robert H. Benmosche - Chmn., Pres., C.E.O. Stewart G. Nagler - Vice-Chmn., C.F.O.	Auditors: Deloitte & Touche LLP

METTLER-TOLEDO INTERNATIONAL, INC.

Exchange	Symbol	Price	52Wk Range	Yield	P/E
NYS	MTD	$47.50 (3/31/2005)	53.00-40.50	N/A	20.04

*7 Year Price Score 109.33 *NYSE Composite Index=100 *12 Month Price Score 98.93

Interim Earnings (Per Share)

Qtr.	Mar	Jun	Sep	Dec
2001	0.34	0.16	0.48	0.70
2002	0.41	0.61	0.51	0.69
2003	0.29	0.57	0.53	0.73
2004	0.41	0.62	0.54	0.80

Interim Dividends (Per Share)

No Dividends Paid

Valuation Analysis

Forecast P/E	17.41	No of Institutions
	(4/7/2005)	151
Market Cap	$2.1 Billion	Shares
Book Value	720.9 Million	38,762,728
Price/Book	2.86	% Held
Price/Sales	1.47	89.59

Business Summary: Instruments and Related Products (MIC: 11.15 SIC: 826 NAIC: 34516)

Mettler-Toledo International is a supplier of precision instruments and services. Co. manufactures weighing instruments for use in laboratory, industrial, packaging, logistics and food retailing applications. Co. also manufactures related analytical instruments, and provides automated chemistry applications used in drug and chemical compound discovery and development. In addition, Co. manufactures metal detection and other end-of-line inspection systems used in production and packaging, and provides devices for use in certain process analytics applications. Co.'s primary manufacturing facilities are located in Switzerland, the U.S., Germany, the U.K. and China.

Recent Developments: For the year ended Dec 31 2004, net income increased 12.6% to $107,957 thousand from net income of $95,838 thousand a year earlier. Revenues were $2,808,908 thousand, up 7.7% from $2,608,862 thousand the year before. Total direct expense was $722,047 thousand versus $686,255 thousand in the prior year, an increase of 5.2%. Total indirect expense was $515,253 thousand versus $462,549 thousand in the prior year, an increase of 11.4%.

Prospects: Co.'s results are benefiting from improving sales and operating efficiency. Co.'s gross margins are improving, reflecting the continued focus on reducing costs and its efforts to bring additional value to its product and service offerings. Although the economic environment for 2005 remains uncertain, Co. currently sees improving conditions in Europe and the U.S. and expects China to continue to generate growth, albeit at a slower pace than in 2004. Going forward, Co. sees its franchise as fundamentally solid with strong market positions, a promising technology portfolio and a productive global sales and service network.

Financial Data (US$ in Thousands)	12/31/2004	12/31/2003	12/31/2002	12/31/2001	12/31/2000	12/31/1999	12/31/1998	12/31/1997
Earnings Per Share	2.37	2.11	2.21	1.68	1.66	1.16	0.92	(2.06)
Cash Flow Per Share	3.74	2.64	2.61	2.50	2.17	2.37	1.88	1.76
Tang Book Value Per Share	3.71	2.36	N.M.	N.M.	N.M.	N.M.	N.M.	N.M.
Income Statement								
Total Revenue	1,404,454	1,304,431	1,213,707	1,148,022	1,095,547	1,065,473	935,658	878,415
EBITDA	197,880	179,950	162,343	172,568	161,893	137,156	114,399	61,807
Depn & Amortn	30,768	28,886	34,724	36,972	33,254	35,299	32,226	31,835
Income Before Taxes	154,224	136,911	110,410	118,434	108,605	79,877	59,535	(5,952)
Income Taxes	46,267	41,073	9,989	46,170	38,510	31,398	20,999	17,489
Net Income	107,957	95,838	100,421	72,264	70,119	48,101	37,625	(65,106)
Average Shares	45,483	45,508	45,370	42,978	42,141	41,295	40,682	31,617
Balance Sheet								
Current Assets	552,357	505,537	475,727	431,758	423,339	387,945	358,230	309,882
Total Assets	1,480,072	1,387,276	1,303,393	1,189,412	887,582	820,973	820,441	749,313
Current Liabilities	348,246	327,909	367,664	347,587	349,153	336,175	293,429	263,583
Long-Term Obligations	196,290	223,239	262,093	309,479	237,807	249,721	340,246	340,334
Total Liabilities	759,186	733,280	801,007	801,228	708,742	708,958	762,442	720,365
Stockholders' Equity	720,886	653,996	502,386	388,184	178,840	112,015	53,835	25,399
Shares Outstanding	43,366	44,582	44,384	44,145	39,372	38,674	38,400	38,336
Statistical Record								
Return on Assets %	7.51	7.12	8.06	6.96	8.19	5.86	4.79	N.M.
Return on Equity %	15.66	16.58	22.55	25.49	48.08	58.01	94.97	N.M.
EBITDA Margin %	14.09	13.80	13.38	15.03	14.78	12.87	12.23	7.04
Net Margin %	7.69	7.35	8.27	6.29	6.40	4.51	4.02	N.M.
Asset Turnover	0.98	0.97	0.97	1.11	1.28	1.30	1.19	1.15
Current Ratio	1.59	1.54	1.29	1.24	1.21	1.15	1.22	1.18
Debt to Equity	0.27	0.34	0.52	0.80	1.33	2.23	6.32	13.40
Price Range	51.97-40.50	42.73-28.90	51.85-25.77	53.06-37.90	55.63-31.88	38.63-20.44	28.06-16.44	18.50-14.88
P/E Ratio	21.93-17.09	20.25-13.70	23.46-11.66	31.58-22.56	33.51-19.20	33.30-17.62	30.50-17.87	...

Address: Im Langacher, P.O. Box MT-100, Greifensee
Telephone: (44) 944 22 11
Fax: (1) 944 24 70

Web Site: www.mt.com
Officers: Robert F. Spoerry - Chmn., Pres., C.E.O. William P. Donnelly - C.F.O.

Auditors: PricewaterhouseCoopers AG
Investor Contact: 614-438-4748
Transfer Agents: Mellon Investor Services, Ridgefield Park, NJ

MGIC INVESTMENT CORP. (MILWAUKEE, WI)

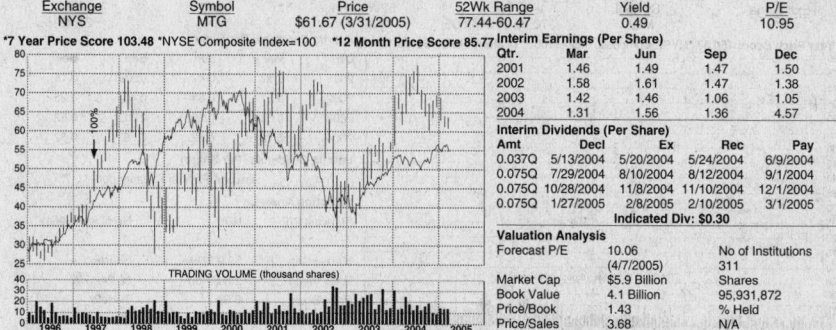

Exchange	Symbol	Price	52Wk Range	Yield	P/E
NYS	MTG	$61.67 (3/31/2005)	77.44-60.47	0.49	10.95

*7 Year Price Score 103.48 *NYSE Composite Index=100 *12 Month Price Score 85.77

Interim Earnings (Per Share)

Qtr.	Mar	Jun	Sep	Dec
2001	1.46	1.49	1.47	1.50
2002	1.58	1.61	1.47	1.38
2003	1.42	1.46	1.06	1.05
2004	1.31	1.56	1.36	4.57

Interim Dividends (Per Share)

Amt	Decl	Ex	Rec	Pay
0.037Q	5/13/2004	5/20/2004	5/24/2004	6/9/2004
0.075Q	7/29/2004	8/10/2004	8/12/2004	9/1/2004
0.075Q	10/28/2004	11/8/2004	11/10/2004	12/1/2004
0.075Q	1/27/2005	2/8/2005	2/10/2005	3/1/2005

Indicated Div: $0.30

Valuation Analysis

Forecast P/E	10.06	No of Institutions
	(4/7/2005)	311
Market Cap	$5.9 Billion	Shares
Book Value	4.1 Billion	95,931,872
Price/Book	1.43	% Held
Price/Sales	3.68	N/A

Business Summary: Insurance (MIC: 8.2 SIC: 351 NAIC: 24130)

MGIC Investment is a holding company which, through its subsidiary, Mortgage Guaranty Insurance, is a provider of private mortgage insurance coverage in the U.S. to mortgage bankers, savings institutions, commercial banks, mortgage brokers, credit unions and other lenders. Private mortgage insurance covers residential first mortgage loans and expands home ownership opportunities. Private mortgage insurance also facilitates the sale of low down-payment mortgage loans in the secondary mortgage market, principally to Freddie Mac and Fannie Mae. As of Dec 31 2003, Co. had about $189.63 billion in primary insurance in force covering approximately 1.6 million mortgages.

Recent Developments: For the year ended Dec 31 2004, net income increased 12.0% to $553,186 thousand from net income of $493,879 thousand a year earlier. Revenues were $1,612,693 thousand, down 4.3% from $1,685,411 thousand the year before. Net premiums earned were $1,329,428 thousand versus $1,366,011 thousand in the prior year, a decrease of 2.7%.

Prospects: Decreases in premiums earned and a decline in other revenues are contributing to Co.'s lower revenues. Earnings are benefiting from improved credit loss performance, higher contributions from joint ventures and lower operating expenses, partially offset by the expected decline in earned premiums. Separately, Co. noted that the mix of business it writes may affect the likelihood of gains or losses occurring. For instance, Co. has decided to broaden its reach into emerging markets by adding staff and additional resources to its Emerging Markets unit. It is expected that more than half of domestic growth in homeownership over the next several decades will come from the emerging markets.

Financial Data (US$ in Thousands)	12/31/2004	12/31/2003	12/31/2002	12/31/2001	12/31/2000	12/31/1999	12/31/1998	12/31/1997
Earnings Per Share	5.63	4.99	6.04	5.93	5.05	4.30	3.39	2.75
Cash Flow Per Share	5.72	6.95	5.91	5.85	5.17	4.21	3.75	3.20
Tang Book Value Per Share	43.05	38.58	33.87	28.47	23.07	16.79	15.05	13.07
Dividends Per Share	0.225	0.113	0.100	0.100	0.100	0.100	0.100	0.095
Dividend Payout %	4.00	2.25	1.66	1.69	1.98	2.33	2.95	3.45
Income Statement								
Premium Income	1,329,428	1,366,011	1,182,098	1,042,267	890,091	792,581	763,284	708,744
Total Revenue	1,612,693	1,685,411	1,565,803	1,357,841	1,110,341	996,755	971,666	868,272
Benefits & Claims	700,999	766,028	365,752	160,814	91,723	97,196	211,354	242,362
Income Before Taxes	591,777	575,797	897,642	931,910	788,801	681,010	554,585	465,373
Income Taxes	159,348	146,027	268,451	292,773	246,802	210,809	169,120	141,623
Net Income	553,186	493,879	629,191	639,137	541,999	470,201	385,465	323,750
Average Shares	98,245	99,022	104,214	107,795	107,260	109,258	113,582	117,924
Balance Sheet								
Total Assets	6,380,691	5,917,387	5,300,303	4,567,012	3,857,781	3,104,393	3,050,541	2,617,687
Total Liabilities	2,237,052	2,120,485	1,905,111	1,546,825	1,392,899	1,328,404	1,409,950	1,130,905
Stockholders' Equity	4,143,639	3,796,902	3,395,192	3,020,187	2,464,882	1,775,989	1,640,591	1,486,782
Shares Outstanding	96,260	98,412	100,251	106,086	106,825	105,798	109,003	113,792
Statistical Record								
Return on Assets %	8.97	8.81	12.75	15.17	15.53	15.28	13.60	13.38
Return on Equity %	13.90	13.73	19.62	23.30	25.49	27.52	24.65	22.70
Loss Ratio %	52.73	56.08	30.94	15.43	10.30	12.26	27.69	34.20
Net Margin %	34.30	29.30	40.18	47.07	48.81	47.17	39.67	37.29
Price Range	77.44-56.32	58.50-35.80	73.62-33.87	77.00-51.63	71.50-32.13	61.56-33.19	73.69-27.81	66.50-35.38
P/E Ratio	13.75-10.00	11.72-7.17	12.19-5.61	12.98-8.71	14.16-6.36	14.32-7.72	21.74-8.20	24.18-12.86
Average Yield %	0.33	0.23	0.17	0.16	0.19	0.22	0.18	0.20

Address: 250 East Kilbourn Avenue, Milwaukee, WI 53202 Telephone: (414) 347-6480 Fax: (414) 347-6696	Web Site: www.mgic.com Officers: Curt S. Culver - Pres., C.E.O. J. Michael Lauer - Exec. V.P., C.F.O.	Auditors: PricewaterhouseCoopers LLP Investor Contact: 414-347-6596

MGM MIRAGE

Exchange	Symbol	Price	52Wk Range	Yield	P/E
NYS	MGG	$70.82 (3/31/2005)	79.21-40.20	N/A	24.85

*7 Year Price Score 150.37 *NYSE Composite Index=100 *12 Month Price Score 125.13

Interim Earnings (Per Share)

Qtr.	Mar	Jun	Sep	Dec
2001	0.52	0.47	(0.09)	0.15
2002	0.51	0.63	0.43	0.25
2003	0.33	0.35	0.31	0.62
2004	0.72	0.72	0.89	0.52

Interim Dividends (Per Share)

Dividend Payment Suspended

Valuation Analysis

Forecast P/E	N/A	No of Institutions	
Market Cap	$9.9 Billion	Shares	
Book Value	2.8 Billion	% Held	
Price/Book	3.59		
Price/Sales	2.35	38.97	

TRADING VOLUME (thousand shares)

Business Summary: Sporting & Recreational (MIC: 13.5 SIC: 996 NAIC: 13110)

MGM Mirage is a holding company. Co., through its wholly owned subsidiaries, owns and operates hotel, casino and entertainment resorts. Co. owns and operates the following casino resorts on the Las Vegas Strip in Las Vegas, Nevada: Bellagio, MGM Grand Las Vegas, The Mirage, Treasure Island ("TI"), New York-New York and the Boardwalk Hotel and Casino. Co. owns a 50% interest in the joint venture that owns and operates the Monte Carlo Resort & Casino, also located on the Las Vegas Strip. Co. owns three resorts in Primm, Nevada at the California/Nevada state line – Whiskey Pete's, Buffalo Bill's and the Primm Valley Resort, as well as two championship golf courses.

Recent Developments: For the year ended Dec 31 2004, income from continuing operations increased 51.9% to $349,856 thousand from income of $230,273 thousand a year earlier. Net income increased 69.2% to $412,332 thousand from net income of $243,697 thousand a year earlier. Revenues were $4,238,104 thousand, up 9.7% from $3,862,743 thousand the year before. Operating income was $950,860 thousand versus an income of $699,729 thousand in the prior year, an increase of 35.9%. Total direct expense was $2,292,895 thousand versus $2,141,228 thousand in the prior year, an increase of 7.1%. Total indirect expense was $1,114,007 thousand versus $1,075,398 thousand in the prior year, an increase of 3.6%.

Prospects: Going forward, Co. expects revenue-available-per- room growth to be in the 10.0% range in the first quarter of 2005, driven by a solid convention and events calendar. Property-level earnings before interest taxes depreciation amortization is expected to increase over the prior year due to the expected continued strength in hotel results and solid gaming volumes. The Bellagio expansion will also contribute to the positive comparison. As a result, Co. supports the current earnings consensus for the first quarter of $0.74 per share. Separately, on Feb 25 2005, Co. announced that the Nevada Gaming Commission approved the proposed merger between Co. and Mandalay Resort Group.

Financial Data
(US$ in Thousands)	12/31/2004	12/31/2003	12/31/2002	12/31/2001	12/31/2000	12/31/1999	12/31/1998	12/31/1997
Earnings Per Share	2.85	1.61	1.83	1.06	1.09	0.72	0.61	0.94
Cash Flow Per Share	5.92	4.72	5.25	5.00	5.61	2.49	1.54	1.60
Tang Book Value Per Share	18.08	15.84	15.58	15.30	14.63	8.76	8.91	9.17
Dividends Per Share	...	...	...	...	0.100	...	...	...
Dividend Payout %	...	...	...	...	9.17	...	...	...
Income Statement								
Total Revenue	4,238,104	3,908,816	4,031,295	4,009,618	3,232,590	1,391,650	773,863	827,597
EBITDA	1,362,793	1,139,271	1,185,171	1,044,562	861,413	337,636	208,081	255,537
Depn & Amortn	434,256	448,763	427,150	421,231	324,438	128,714	78,561	65,371
Income Before Taxes	555,815	353,704	466,314	277,589	275,040	150,153	109,528	180,301
Income Taxes	205,959	116,592	173,551	106,996	108,880	55,029	40,580	65,045
Net Income	412,332	243,697	292,435	169,815	160,744	86,058	68,948	111,018
Average Shares	144,666	151,592	159,940	160,822	147,901	120,086	112,684	117,670
Balance Sheet								
Current Assets	820,202	757,621	605,410	661,927	795,644	269,913	208,080	170,791
Total Assets	11,115,029	10,709,710	10,504,985	10,497,443	10,734,601	2,760,743	1,773,794	1,398,374
Current Liabilities	927,977	765,059	750,068	887,910	1,233,205	290,090	189,365	181,490
Long-Term Obligations	5,458,848	5,521,890	5,213,778	5,295,313	5,355,412	1,323,853	537,664	51,688
Total Liabilities	8,343,325	8,175,922	7,840,841	7,986,743	8,352,156	1,726,897	809,413	296,752
Stockholders' Equity	2,771,704	2,533,788	2,664,144	2,510,700	2,382,445	1,033,846	964,381	1,101,622
Shares Outstanding	140,369	143,096	154,574	157,396	159,130	113,880	104,066	115,970
Statistical Record								
Return on Assets %	3.77	2.30	2.78	1.60	2.38	3.80	4.35	8.27
Return on Equity %	15.50	9.38	11.30	6.94	9.38	8.61	6.67	10.70
EBITDA Margin %	32.16	29.15	29.40	26.05	26.65	24.26	26.89	30.88
Net Margin %	9.73	6.23	7.25	4.24	4.97	6.18	8.91	13.41
Asset Turnover	0.39	0.37	0.38	0.38	0.48	0.61	0.49	0.62
Current Ratio	0.88	0.99	0.81	0.75	0.65	0.93	1.10	0.94
Debt to Equity	1.97	2.18	1.96	2.11	2.25	1.28	0.56	0.05
Price Range	73.08-37.22	38.38-24.48	41.85-28.40	32.73-17.76	38.19-19.00	27.19-13.56	19.59-11.47	22.41-16.19
P/E Ratio	25.64-13.06	23.84-15.20	22.87-15.52	30.88-16.75	35.03-17.43	37.76-18.84	32.12-18.80	23.84-17.22
Average Yield %	...	...	...	...	0.34	...	...	...

Address: 3600 Las Vegas Boulevard South, Las Vegas, NV 89109 **Telephone:** (702) 693-7120 **Fax:** (702) 693-8626	**Web Site:** www.mgmmirage.com **Officers:** J. Terrence Lanni - Chmn., C.E.O. James J. Murren - Pres., C.F.O., Treas.	**Auditors:** Deloitte & Touche LLP **Investor Contact:** 702-891-3333

MICHAELS STORES, INC.

Exchange	Symbol	Price	52Wk Range	Yield	P/E
NYS	MIK	$36.30 (3/31/2005)	36.30-22.70	0.77	26.12

*7 Year Price Score 166.67 *NYSE Composite Index=100 *12 Month Price Score 108.18

Interim Earnings (Per Share)

Qtr.	Apr	Jul	Oct	Jan
2001-02	0.06	0.04	0.10	0.47
2002-03	0.14	0.16	0.23	0.47
2003-04	0.15	0.17	0.27	0.68
2004-05	0.21	0.19	0.31	...

Interim Dividends (Per Share)

Amt	Decl	Ex	Rec	Pay
0.07Q	9/16/2004	9/23/2004	9/27/2004	10/29/2004
100%	9/17/2004	10/13/2004	9/27/2004	10/12/2004
0.07Q	12/1/2004	1/12/2005	1/17/2005	1/31/2005
0.07Q	3/15/2005	4/13/2005	4/15/2005	4/29/2005

Indicated Div: $0.28

Valuation Analysis

Forecast P/E	20.38	No of Institutions
	(4/7/2005)	225
Market Cap	$4.9 Billion	Shares
Book Value	1.2 Billion	116,276,096
Price/Book	4.10	% Held
Price/Sales	1.50	86.27

Business Summary: Retail - Sporting, Toys & Hobby (MIC: 5.12 SIC: 945 NAIC: 51120)

Michaels Stores is a national specialty retailer providing materials, ideas and education for creative activities. As of Mar 24 2004, Co. owned and operated 812 Michaels stores in the U.S. and Canada, offering arts and crafts supplies and products for the do-it-yourself home decorator and 158 Aaron Brothers stores, offering photo frames, a line of ready-made frames, custom frames and art supplies. Co. also had two ReCollections stores, its scrapbooking and paper crafting retail concepts in Texas. In addition, Co. had two Star Wholesale stores, offering merchandise to interior decorators/designers, wedding/event planners, florists, hotels, restaurants and commercial display companies.

Recent Developments: For the quarter ended Oct 30 2004, net income increased 11.2% to $42,488 thousand from net income of $38,208 thousand in the year-earlier quarter. Revenues were $799,905 thousand, up 5.9% from $755,246 thousand the year before. Operating income was $72,772 thousand versus an income of $63,599 thousand in the prior-year quarter, an increase of 14.4%. Total indirect expense was $727,133 thousand versus $691,647 thousand in the prior-year quarter, an increase of 5.1%.

Prospects: Going forward, Co. expects same-store sales to increase 3.0% to 5.0% and total sales to increase 8.0% to 10.0%. Also, operating margin is expected to grow 60 to 80 basis points driven by both gross margin expansion and selling, general and administration expense leverage. Moreover, diluted earnings per share are anticipated to increase 15.0% to 20.0% over fiscal 2004 results. Meanwhile, the implementation of Co.'s automated replenishment system completed in June 2004, combined with the implementation of its perpetual inventory system, continue to be significant sales and profit generating tools. These tools should continue to drive same-store sales growth and gross margin expansion.

Financial Data
(US$ in Thousands)

	9 Mos	6 Mos	3 Mos	01/31/2004	02/01/2003	02/02/2002	02/03/2001	01/29/2000
Earnings Per Share	1.39	1.35	1.33	1.27	1.00	0.67	0.57	0.50
Cash Flow Per Share	2.98	2.73	2.38	2.16	0.82	1.37	1.09	0.53
Tang Book Value Per Share	7.99	7.85	7.91	7.73	6.64	5.39	4.58	3.68
Dividends Per Share	0.240	0.220	0.210	0.150	...	...	...	...
Dividend Payout %	17.29	16.33	15.77	11.81				
Income Statement								
Total Revenue	2,208,691	1,408,786	725,852	3,091,256	2,856,373	2,530,727	2,249,440	1,882,522
EBITDA	241,110	144,984	74,605	389,321	350,791	250,236	218,042	184,251
Depn & Amortn	66,050	43,773	21,776	83,869	79,328	69,411	65,947	59,206
Income Before Taxes	159,621	90,814	47,501	285,190	250,389	159,912	134,069	102,391
Income Taxes	61,055	34,736	18,169	107,345	102,659	65,564	53,628	40,090
Net Income	98,566	56,078	29,332	177,845	140,297	89,030	78,589	62,301
Average Shares	138,796	139,280	139,692	139,858	141,100	133,864	137,112	131,940
Balance Sheet								
Current Assets	1,422,910	1,328,699	1,349,028	1,283,372	1,066,440	950,063	729,816	722,987
Total Assets	1,949,113	1,855,189	1,871,388	1,801,647	1,560,973	1,414,633	1,158,436	1,096,703
Current Liabilities	485,337	406,206	404,494	369,480	299,454	351,207	289,008	270,976
Long-Term Obligations	200,000	200,000	200,000	200,000	200,000	200,000	125,000	221,940
Total Liabilities	754,143	673,617	670,919	634,349	548,946	590,069	453,790	529,905
Stockholders' Equity	1,194,970	1,181,572	1,200,469	1,167,298	1,012,027	824,564	704,646	566,798
Shares Outstanding	135,093	135,774	137,173	135,995	134,933	131,394	127,347	120,256
Statistical Record								
Return on Assets %	10.42	10.73	10.74	10.61	9.46	6.94	6.86	6.07
Return on Equity %	16.90	17.05	16.87	16.37	15.32	11.68	12.16	11.92
EBITDA Margin %	10.92	10.29	10.28	12.59	12.28	9.89	9.69	9.79
Net Margin %	4.46	3.98	4.04	5.75	4.91	3.52	3.49	3.31
Asset Turnover	1.77	1.84	1.82	1.84	1.93	1.97	1.96	1.83
Current Ratio	2.93	3.27	3.34	3.47	3.56	2.71	2.53	2.67
Debt to Equity	0.17	0.17	0.17	0.17	0.20	0.24	0.18	0.39
Price Range	30.58-20.71	27.95-17.66	26.16-15.45	25.27-10.15	24.32-14.71	17.50-6.86	12.02-4.80	8.75-4.09
P/E Ratio	22.00-14.90	20.71-13.08	19.67-11.62	19.90-7.99	24.32-14.71	26.12-10.24	21.08-8.42	17.50-8.19
Average Yield %	0.95	0.94	0.97	0.79	...	...	...	...

Address: 8000 Bent Branch Drive, Irving, TX 75063 **Telephone:** (972) 409-1300 **Fax:** (972) 409-1555	**Web Site:** www.michaels.com **Officers:** Charles J. Wyly Jr. - Chmn. Sam Wyly - Vice-Chmn.	**Auditors:** Ernst & Young LLP **Investor Contact:** 888-515-MIKE

MICRON TECHNOLOGY INC.

Exchange	Symbol	Price	52Wk Range	Yield	P/E
NYS	MU	$10.34 (3/31/2005)	17.96-10.06	N/A	22.48

*7 Year Price Score 40.80 *NYSE Composite Index=100 *12 Month Price Score 81.59

Interim Earnings (Per Share)

Qtr.	Nov	Feb	May	Aug
2001-02	(0.44)	(0.05)	(0.04)	(0.98)
2002-03	(0.52)	(1.02)	(0.36)	(0.21)
2003-04	0.00	(0.04)	0.13	0.14
2004-05	0.23	...	...	...

Interim Dividends (Per Share)

Amt	Decl	Ex	Rec	Pay
100%	3/29/2000	5/2/2000	4/18/2000	5/1/2000

Valuation Analysis

Forecast P/E	16.26	No of Institutions
	(4/7/2005)	281
Market Cap	$6.3 Billion	Shares
Book Value	5.8 Billion	522,495,968
Price/Book	1.10	% Held
Price/Sales	1.39	85.12

TRADING VOLUME (thousand shares)

Business Summary: IT & Technology (MIC: 10.2 SIC: 674 NAIC: 34413)

Micron Technology manufactures and markets dynamic random access memory (DRAM), flash memory and complementary metal-oxide semiconductor (CMOS) image sensors. Co.'s products are used in a broad range of electronic devices, including consumer and industrial products. DRAM products are high density, low-cost-per-bit, random access memory devices that provide high-speed data storage and retrieval. Flash memory products are re-writeable, non-volatile semiconductor devices that retain memory content when the power is off. CMOS image sensors are semiconductor devices that capture and process images into pictures or video for a variety of consumer and industrial applications.

Recent Developments: For the year ended Sep 2 2004, net income was $157.2 million compared with a net loss of $1.27 billion in 2003. Results for 2004 and 2003 included a restructuring credit of $22.5 million and a charge of $109.2 million, respectively. Net sales advanced 42.5% to $4.40 billion compared with $3.09 billion a year earlier, as a result of an approximate 15.0% higher per megabit average selling price for semiconductor memory. Semiconductor memory production, which is measured in megabits, was approximately 23.0% higher in fiscal 2004 than in fiscal 2003. Gross margin improved to $1.31 billion versus a loss of $20.7 million the year before.

Prospects: Co. expects that near-term growth in megabit production will be affected by an increase in wafers allocated to Double Data Rate 2 (DDR2) Synchronous DRAM products, CMOS image sensors, Specialty memory products and Flash memory products. Co. noted that the gross margin percentage for DDR2 products is lower than its average as DDR2 products have not yet reached mature manufacturing yields. Separately, in order to develop new product and process technologies, support future growth, achieve operating efficiencies and maintain product quality, Co. continues to invest in manufacturing technologies, facilities and capital equipment, research and development, and product and process technologies.

Financial Data
(US$ in Thousands)

	3 Mos	09/02/2004	08/28/2003	08/29/2002	08/30/2001	08/31/2000	09/02/1999	09/03/1998
Earnings Per Share	0.46	0.24	(2.11)	(1.51)	(1.05)	2.56	(0.13)	(0.55)
Cash Flow Per Share	1.85	1.78	0.47	0.96	1.34	3.76	1.63	0.44
Tang Book Value Per Share	8.99	8.73	7.68	9.93	11.59	10.96	7.44	6.11
Income Statement								
Total Revenue	1,260,300	4,404,200	3,091,300	2,589,000	3,935,900	7,336,300	3,764,000	3,011,900
EBITDA	485,700	1,469,400	27,100	141,600	5,800	3,271,600	745,500	255,400
Depn & Amortn	312,100	1,216,600	1,208,900	1,174,600	1,084,400	963,100	790,500	590,700
Income Before Taxes	169,100	232,000	(1,200,200)	(998,500)	(959,500)	2,317,000	(91,500)	(335,200)
Income Taxes	14,200	74,800	73,000	(91,500)	(446,000)	796,700	(36,000)	(118,800)
Net Income	154,900	157,200	(1,273,200)	(907,000)	(625,000)	1,504,200	(68,900)	(233,700)
Average Shares	700,500	645,700	607,500	601,500	592,400	605,400	521,400	424,400
Balance Sheet								
Current Assets	2,689,600	2,638,700	2,037,000	2,118,800	3,137,700	4,904,400	2,830,000	1,499,200
Total Assets	7,892,600	7,760,600	7,158,200	7,555,400	8,363,200	9,631,500	6,965,200	4,688,300
Current Liabilities	1,127,200	972,100	993,000	752,700	687,000	1,647,500	922,000	740,300
Long-Term Obligations	825,200	1,027,900	997,100	360,800	445,000	933,700	1,527,500	757,300
Total Liabilities	2,113,200	2,145,200	2,120,700	1,188,800	1,228,400	3,000,200	2,832,800	1,843,200
Stockholders' Equity	5,779,400	5,614,800	4,971,000	6,306,400	7,134,800	6,432,000	3,964,100	2,693,000
Shares Outstanding	612,700	611,500	609,900	602,900	598,400	567,300	504,400	427,000
Statistical Record								
Return on Assets %	4.03	2.07	N.M.	N.M.	N.M.	18.18	N.M.	N.M.
Return on Equity %	5.55	2.92	N.M.	N.M.	N.M.	29.02	N.M.	N.M.
EBITDA Margin %	38.54	33.36	0.88	5.47	0.15	44.59	19.81	8.48
Net Margin %	12.29	3.57	N.M.	N.M.	N.M.	20.50	N.M.	N.M.
Asset Turnover	0.59	0.58	0.42	0.33	0.44	0.89	0.65	0.62
Current Ratio	2.39	2.71	2.05	2.81	4.57	2.98	3.07	2.03
Debt to Equity	0.14	0.18	0.20	0.06	0.06	0.15	0.39	0.28
Price Range	17.96-11.06	17.96-11.06	18.76-6.76	39.50-17.25	81.50-28.56	96.56-29.75	39.75-12.44	22.34-10.06
P/E Ratio	39.04-24.04	74.83-46.08	N.A.	N.A.	N.A.	37.72-11.62	N.A.	N.A.

Address: 8000 South Federal Way, P.O. Box 6, Boise, ID 83716-9632 **Telephone:** (208) 368-4000 **Fax:** (208) 368-4435	**Web Site:** www.micron.com **Officers:** Steven R. Appleton - Chmn., Pres., C.E.O. Kipp A. Bedard - V.P., Investor Relations	**Auditors:** PricewaterhouseCoopers LLP **Investor Contact:** 208-368-4400 **Transfer Agents:** Wells Fargo Shareowner Services, South St. Paul,

546

MILLIPORE CORP

Exchange	Symbol	Price	52Wk Range	Yield	P/E
NYS	MIL	$43.40 (3/31/2005)	56.37-43.11	N/A	20.67

*7 Year Price Score 102.37 *NYSE Composite Index=100 *12 Month Price Score 83.82

TRADING VOLUME (thousand shares)

Interim Earnings (Per Share)

Qtr.	Mar	Jun	Sep	Dec
2001	0.11	(0.18)	0.33	0.39
2002	0.46	0.46	0.39	0.41
2003	0.44	0.46	0.50	0.67
2004	0.55	0.57	0.50	0.49

Interim Dividends (Per Share)

Dividend Payment Suspended

Valuation Analysis

Forecast P/E	17.88	No of Institutions
	(4/7/2005)	237
Market Cap	$2.2 Billion	Shares
Book Value	638.9 Million	45,865,988
Price/Book	3.38	% Held
Price/Sales	2.45	92.02

Business Summary: Instruments and Related Products (MIC: 11.15 SIC: 826 NAIC: 34516)

Millipore is a multinational bioscience company that provides technologies, tools and services for the discovery, development and production of therapeutic drugs and for other purposes. Co. serves customers in the worldwide biotechnology, life science research and other bioscience markets with a variety of products and services used in the purification, separation and analysis of fluids. Co.'s products are based on a variety of enabling technologies, including its membrane filtration and chromatography technologies. Co. operates through three segments: BioPharmaceutical, Laboratory Water and Life Sciences.

Recent Developments: For the year ended Dec 31 2004, net income increased 4.7% to $105,556 thousand from net income of $100,796 thousand a year earlier. Revenues were $883,263 thousand, up 10.5% from $799,622 thousand the year before. Operating income was $137,853 thousand versus an income of $126,644 thousand in the prior year, an increase of 8.9%. Total direct expense was $412,129 thousand versus $369,174 thousand in the prior year, an increase of 11.6%. Total indirect expense was $333,281 thousand versus $303,804 thousand in the prior year, an increase of 9.7%.

Prospects: Co.'s longer-term prospects appear positive. For 2004, Co. experienced revenue growth across all three of its market areas. On Feb 24 2004, Co. announced that it has formed a new Bioscience Division that will focus on life science research and general laboratory applications of Co.'s products and services. The new division combines Co.'s Life Sciences Division and Laboratory Water Division which essentially serves the same customer base. The combination is intended to provide greater organizational clarity, improve sales effectiveness, better serve customers and focus research and development in the laboratory area.

Financial Data

(US$ in Thousands)	12/31/2004	12/31/2003	12/31/2002	12/31/2001	12/31/2000	12/31/1999	12/31/1998	12/31/1997
Earnings Per Share	2.10	2.06	1.73	0.65	2.53	1.42	0.09	(0.89)
Cash Flow Per Share	3.38	2.72	2.23	1.31	2.15	2.35	1.17	1.24
Tang Book Value Per Share	12.24	8.72	5.16	7.60	5.25	2.36	1.37	1.64
Dividends Per Share	...	...	...	0.440	0.440	0.440	0.430	0.390
Dividend Payout %	...	...	...	67.69	17.39	30.99	477.78	...
Income Statement								
Total Revenue	883,263	799,622	704,251	656,898	953,771	771,188	699,307	758,919
EBITDA	182,331	167,105	156,183	131,888	223,247	153,772	79,337	50,098
Depn & Amortn	44,478	40,461	34,957	30,744	46,145	44,291	44,409	40,661
Income Before Taxes	130,479	112,174	103,592	78,399	153,666	82,351	8,544	(18,110)
Income Taxes	24,923	11,378	22,791	14,913	34,472	18,023	(1,320)	20,674
Net Income	105,556	100,796	83,701	31,117	119,194	64,328	4,017	(38,784)
Average Shares	50,201	49,046	48,448	48,060	47,039	45,274	44,289	43,527
Balance Sheet								
Current Assets	540,856	516,362	390,121	311,995	465,483	358,947	304,752	352,408
Total Assets	1,013,819	951,273	786,230	915,767	874,925	792,733	762,440	766,244
Current Liabilities	163,010	222,392	134,429	134,319	234,647	269,783	298,681	304,873
Long-Term Obligations	147,000	216,000	334,000	320,000	300,130	313,107	299,110	286,844
Total Liabilities	374,969	490,232	498,726	521,811	569,557	615,882	625,532	617,250
Stockholders' Equity	638,850	461,041	287,504	393,956	305,368	176,851	136,908	148,994
Shares Outstanding	49,816	48,883	48,412	47,876	46,394	45,194	44,067	43,707
Statistical Record								
Return on Assets %	10.71	11.60	9.84	3.48	14.26	8.27	0.53	N.M.
Return on Equity %	19.14	26.93	24.57	8.90	49.30	41.00	2.81	N.M.
EBITDA Margin %	20.64	20.90	22.18	20.08	23.41	19.94	11.35	6.60
Net Margin %	11.95	12.61	11.89	4.74	12.50	8.34	0.57	N.M.
Asset Turnover	0.90	0.92	0.83	0.73	1.14	0.99	0.91	1.05
Current Ratio	3.32	2.32	2.90	2.32	1.98	1.33	1.02	1.16
Debt to Equity	0.23	0.47	1.16	0.81	0.98	1.77	2.18	1.93
Price Range	56.37-42.50	48.91-30.25	53.68-27.68	58.95-38.17	67.48-32.39	36.59-21.06	33.55-15.64	45.10-30.01
P/E Ratio	26.84-20.24	23.74-14.68	31.03-16.00	90.70-58.72	26.67-12.80	25.77-14.83	372.74-173.78	...
Average Yield %	...	...	...	0.88	0.87	1.48	1.68	1.04

Address: 129 Concord Road, Billerica, MA 01821-3405	**Web Site:** www.millipore.com	**Auditors:** PricewaterhouseCoopers LLP
Telephone: (978) 715-4321	**Officers:** Francis J. Lunger - Chmn., Pres., C.E.O. Donald B. Melson - Contr.	**Investor Contact:** 978-715-1041 **Transfer Agents:** American Stock Transfer & Trust Company, New York,

MILLS CORP

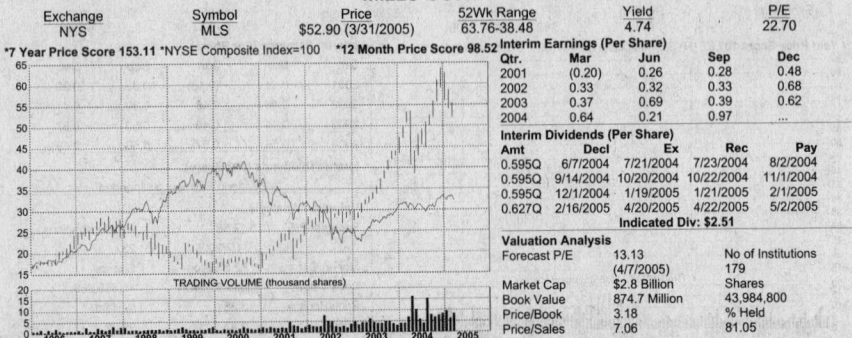

Exchange	Symbol	Price	52Wk Range	Yield	P/E
NYS	MLS	$52.90 (3/31/2005)	63.76-38.48	4.74	22.70

*7 Year Price Score 153.11 ***NYSE Composite Index=100** ***12 Month Price Score 98.52**

Interim Earnings (Per Share)

Qtr.	Mar	Jun	Sep	Dec
2001	(0.20)	0.26	0.28	0.48
2002	0.33	0.32	0.33	0.68
2003	0.37	0.69	0.39	0.62
2004	0.64	0.21	0.97	...

Interim Dividends (Per Share)

Amt	Decl	Ex	Rec	Pay
0.595Q	6/7/2004	7/21/2004	7/23/2004	8/2/2004
0.595Q	9/14/2004	10/20/2004	10/22/2004	11/1/2004
0.595Q	12/1/2004	1/19/2005	1/21/2005	2/1/2005
0.627Q	2/16/2005	4/20/2005	4/22/2005	5/2/2005
			Indicated Div: $2.51	

Valuation Analysis

Forecast P/E	13.13 (4/7/2005)	No of Institutions	179
Market Cap	$2.8 Billion	Shares	43,984,800
Book Value	874.7 Million	% Held	81.05
Price/Book	3.18		
Price/Sales	7.06		

Business Summary: Property, Real Estate & Development (MIC: 8.3 SIC: 798 NAIC: 25930)

The Mills Corporation is a self-managed real estate investment trust that develops, redevelops, leases, acquires, expands, and manages three types of properties. Mills Landmark Centers are retail and entertainment super-regional shopping centers. 21st Century Retail and Entertainment Centers are conventional regional shopping centers anchored by traditional department stores. International Retail and Entertainment Venues can be either super-regional or conventional regional shopping centers outside the U.S. As of Dec 13 2003, Co.'s portfolio consisted of 15 Mills Landmark Centers, ten 21st Century Retail and Entertainment Centers and one International Retail and Entertainment Center.

Recent Developments: For the quarter ended Sep 30 2004, net income increased 151.1% to $63,877 thousand from net income of $25,439 thousand in the year-earlier quarter. Revenues were $100,661 thousand, up 3.8% from $96,978 thousand the year before. Operating income was $32,976 thousand versus income of $37,865 thousand in the prior-year quarter, a decrease of 12.9%. Funds from operations were $58,100 thousand versus $51,900 thousand in the prior-year quarter.

Prospects: On Feb 1 2005, Co. announced that it has entered into an agreement to purchase a portfolio of two regional shopping malls, Southdale Center in suburban Minneapolis, MN, and Southridge Mall in suburban Milwaukee, WI, and related development components from a joint venture comprised of Blackstone Real Estate Advisors affiliates and Polaris Capital. Co. will pay total consideration of approximately $452.0 million before transaction costs. Meanwhile, Co.'s results are benefiting from increases in comparable same-space sales for in-line tenants and higher average initial base rent for in-line store spaces opened versus closed tenants and expiring leases.

Financial Data (US$ in Thousands)	3 Mos	12/31/2003	12/31/2002	12/31/2001	12/31/2000	12/31/1999	12/31/1998	12/31/1997
Earnings Per Share	2.33	2.07	1.66	0.84	1.47	1.17	1.00	0.75
Cash Flow Per Share	3.20	3.95	2.63	3.61	3.36	3.33	3.40	3.73
Tang Book Value Per Share	8.87	8.87	8.14	3.40	2.05	2.59	3.41	4.32
Dividends Per Share	2.260	2.243	2.175	2.115	2.055	1.508	1.950	1.890
Dividend Payout %	96.90	108.33	131.02	251.79	139.80	128.85	195.00	252.00
Income Statement								
Property Income	91,135	371,130	221,041	192,433	185,843	182,080	174,032	163,415
Non-Property Income	3,993	...	...	...	4,868	2,605	3,238	2,561
Total Revenue	95,128	371,130	221,041	192,433	190,711	184,685	177,270	165,976
Depn & Amortn	30,044	103,348	60,906	46,368	42,692	37,680	37,610	36,977
Interest Expense	20,926	76,636	52,168	57,737	56,736	46,808	44,044	41,006
Net Income	41,697	122,312	62,475	21,242	34,420	27,223	23,252	16,411
Average Shares	51,356	45,785	36,355	25,491	23,337	23,923	23,361	21,931
Balance Sheet								
Total Assets	3,507,169	3,294,633	2,155,421	1,329,104	1,125,691	1,039,467	970,362	926,621
Long-Term Obligations	2,223,598	2,119,314	1,298,682	1,023,894	966,505	877,273	782,182	703,713
Total Liabilities	2,408,858	2,310,508	1,403,887	1,100,274	1,045,372	938,462	837,392	758,642
Stockholders' Equity	874,694	854,778	544,273	96,740	47,934	60,027	78,918	99,024
Shares Outstanding	52,538	50,297	43,196	28,462	23,408	23,192	23,131	22,912
Statistical Record								
Return on Assets %	4.66	4.49	3.59	1.73	3.17	2.71	2.45	1.83
Return on Equity %	20.19	17.48	19.49	29.37	63.59	39.19	26.13	22.71
Net Margin %	43.83	32.96	28.26	11.04	18.05	14.74	13.12	9.89
Price Range	53.29-31.20	44.00-27.55	31.00-25.25	26.48-16.38	19.06-15.63	22.38-15.38	27.25-18.63	28.88-22.25
P/E Ratio	22.87-13.39	21.26-13.31	18.67-15.21	31.52-19.49	12.97-10.63	19.12-13.14	27.25-18.63	38.50-29.67
Average Yield %	5.67	6.38	7.67	9.61	11.59	7.96	8.20	7.31

Address: 1300 Wilson Boulevard, Suite 400, Arlington, VA 22209 **Telephone:** (703) 526-5000 **Fax:** (703) 526-5111	**Web Site:** www.millscorp.com **Officers:** Laurence C. Siegel - Chmn., C.E.O. Dietrich von Boetticher - Vice-Chmn.	**Auditors:** Ernst & Young LLP **Investor Contact:** 703-526-5102

MINERALS TECHNOLOGIES, INC.

Exchange	Symbol	Price	52Wk Range	Yield	P/E
NYS	MTX	$65.78 (3/31/2005)	67.67-53.60	0.30	23.33

*7 Year Price Score 108.89 *NYSE Composite Index=100 ***12 Month Price Score 98.23**

Interim Earnings (Per Share)

Qtr.	Mar	Jun	Sep	Dec
2001	0.58	0.52	0.68	0.70
2002	0.66	0.67	0.70	0.59
2003	0.57	0.70	1.18	0.63
2004	0.61	0.73	0.78	0.70

Interim Dividends (Per Share)

Amt	Decl	Ex	Rec	Pay
0.05Q	4/28/2004	5/26/2004	5/28/2004	6/11/2004
0.05Q	7/28/2004	9/1/2004	9/3/2004	9/16/2004
0.05Q	10/27/2004	11/8/2004	11/10/2004	12/16/2004
0.05Q	1/26/2005	3/1/2005	3/3/2005	3/15/2005

Indicated Div: $0.20

Valuation Analysis

Forecast P/E	20.85
	(4/12/2005)
Market Cap	$1.4 Billion
Book Value	799.3 Million
Price/Book	1.69
Price/Sales	1.46
No of Institutions	138
Shares	21,035,100
% Held	N/A

TRADING VOLUME (thousand shares)

Business Summary: Chemicals (MIC: 11.1 SIC: 869 NAIC: 27992)

Minerals Technologies produces a range of specialty mineral, mineral-based and synthetic mineral products and related systems and services. The Specialty Minerals segment produces the synthetic mineral product precipitated calcium carbonate and the processed mineral product quicklime, and mines, processes and sells other natural mineral products, primarily for use in the paper, building materials, paint and coatings, glass, ceramic, polymer, food and pharmaceutical industries. The Refractories segment produces and markets monolithic and shaped refractory materials and specialty products, services and application equipment used primarily by the steel, non-ferrous metal and glass industries.

Recent Developments: For the year ended Dec 31 2004, net income increased 21.4% to $58,563 thousand from net income of $48,220 thousand a year earlier. Revenues were $923,667 thousand, up 13.5% from $813,743 thousand the year before. Operating income was $89,077 thousand versus an income of $77,204 thousand in the prior year, an increase of 15.4%. Total direct expense was $709,032 thousand versus $615,749 thousand in the prior year, an increase of 15.1%. Total indirect expense was $125,558 thousand versus $120,790 thousand in the prior year, an increase of 3.9%.

Prospects: Co. continues to see good growth in the area of precipitated calcium carbonate (PCC) . For instance, Co.'s worldwide PCC sales, which is used mainly in the manufacturing process of the paper industry, increased 11.0% to $484.7 million in 2004. To keep pace with growing demand, Co. dedicated a new facilty in Walsum, Germany for the production of PCC for use in paper coating. The initial annual production capacity at this facility will be 125,000 metric tons of PCC with a future capacity of 500,000 metric tons. Co. is optimistic that in 2005 its PCC programs will continue to grow and Co. will begin to sign contracts for additional satellite plants for use in production.

Financial Data
(US$ in Thousands)

	12/31/2004	12/31/2003	12/31/2002	12/31/2001	12/31/2000	12/31/1999	12/31/1998	12/31/1997
Earnings Per Share	2.82	3.09	2.61	2.48	2.58	2.80	2.50	2.18
Cash Flow Per Share	6.28	4.95	5.83	5.01	4.44	6.09	5.25	5.35
Tang Book Value Per Share	36.26	31.95	26.93	25.89	24.22	18.87	22.42	20.72
Dividends Per Share	0.200	0.100	0.100	0.100	0.100	0.110	0.100	0.100
Dividend Payout %	7.09	3.24	3.83	4.03	3.88	3.93	4.40	4.59
Income Statement								
Total Revenue	923,667	813,743	752,680	684,419	670,917	637,519	609,193	602,335
EBITDA	157,578	143,271	149,314	146,237	144,732	155,158	143,198	130,567
Depn & Amortn	70,467	66,340	68,960	66,518	60,795	58,675	53,084	52,936
Income Before Taxes	84,572	72,344	75,734	72,670	79,772	92,535	86,342	72,188
Income Taxes	24,299	4,116	20,220	21,148	23,735	28,920	27,360	23,104
Net Income	58,563	63,220	53,752	49,793	54,208	62,116	57,224	50,312
Average Shares	20,769	20,431	20,569	20,063	21,004	22,150	22,926	23,113
Balance Sheet								
Current Assets	395,671	340,125	290,965	246,790	215,357	219,947	210,830	226,582
Total Assets	1,154,902	1,035,500	899,877	847,810	799,832	769,131	760,912	741,407
Current Liabilities	152,853	122,035	123,937	160,529	133,527	117,542	97,938	94,218
Long-Term Obligations	94,811	98,159	89,020	88,097	89,857	75,238	88,167	101,571
Total Liabilities	355,589	328,119	305,720	339,991	316,193	284,095	271,749	274,410
Stockholders' Equity	799,313	707,381	594,157	507,819	483,639	485,036	489,163	466,997
Shares Outstanding	20,561	20,491	20,155	19,613	19,966	25,705	21,814	22,540
Statistical Record								
Return on Assets %	5.33	6.53	6.15	6.04	6.89	8.12	7.62	6.91
Return on Equity %	7.75	9.71	9.76	10.04	11.16	12.75	11.97	10.99
EBITDA Margin %	17.06	17.61	19.84	21.37	21.57	24.34	23.51	21.68
Net Margin %	6.34	7.77	7.14	7.28	8.08	9.74	9.39	8.35
Asset Turnover	0.84	0.84	0.86	0.83	0.85	0.83	0.81	0.83
Current Ratio	2.59	2.79	2.35	1.54	1.61	1.87	2.15	2.40
Debt to Equity	0.12	0.14	0.15	0.17	0.19	0.16	0.18	0.22
Price Range	67.67-51.56	60.75-35.45	53.91-33.17	47.66-33.06	53.25-29.38	56.81-37.00	55.25-36.31	46.06-32.13
P/E Ratio	24.00-18.28	19.66-11.47	20.66-12.71	19.22-13.33	20.64-11.39	20.29-13.21	22.10-14.53	21.13-14.74
Average Yield %	0.34	0.21	0.22	0.25	0.24	0.23	0.21	0.25

Address: The Chrysler Building, 405 Lexington Avenue, New York, NY 10174-1901	Web Site: www.mineralstech.com	Auditors: KPMG LLP
Telephone: (212) 878-1800 **Fax:** (212) 878-1801	Officers: Paul R. Saueracker - Chmn., Pres., C.E.O. John A. Sorel - Sr. V.P., Fin., C.F.O., Treas.	Investor Contact: 212-878-1831

MOHAWK INDUSTRIES, INC.

Exchange	Symbol	Price	52Wk Range		Yield	P/E
NYS	MHK	$84.30 (3/31/2005)	93.66-69.41		N/A	15.44

*7 Year Price Score 146.75 *NYSE Composite Index=100 *12 Month Price Score 102.12

Interim Earnings (Per Share)

Qtr.	Mar	Jun	Sep	Dec
2001	0.51	0.88	1.05	1.11
2002	0.77	1.10	1.21	1.26
2003	0.62	1.12	1.36	1.52
2004	0.98	1.29	1.67	1.52

Interim Dividends (Per Share)

No Dividends Paid

Valuation Analysis

Forecast P/E	13.91	No of Institutions	
	(4/7/2005)	249	
Market Cap	$5.6 Billion	Shares	
Book Value	2.7 Billion	59,240,860	
Price/Book	2.11	% Held	
Price/Sales	0.96	88.67	

Business Summary: Textiles (MIC: 4.3 SIC: 273 NAIC: 14110)

Mohawk Industries, through its primary operating subsidiaries, Mohawk Carpet Corp., Aladdin Manufacturing Corp. and Dal-Tile International Inc., produces floorcovering products for residential and commercial applications in the U.S. Co. operates two business segments. The Mohawk segment produces broadloom carpet, rugs, pad, ceramic tile, hardwood, vinyl and laminate through independent floor covering retailers, home centers, mass merchandisers, department stores and commercial dealers and end users. The Dal-Tile segment produces ceramic tile, porcelain tile and stone products through company-operated sales service centers, independent distributors and home centers.

Recent Developments: For the year ended Dec 31 2004, net income increased 18.9% to $368,622 thousand from net income of $310,149 thousand a year earlier. Revenues were $5,880,372 thousand, up 17.6% from $4,999,381 thousand the year before. Operating income was $635,590 thousand versus an income of $542,029 thousand in the prior year, an increase of 17.3%. Total direct expense was $4,259,531 thousand versus $3,605,579 thousand in the prior year, an increase of 18.1%. Total indirect expense was $985,251 thousand versus $851,773 thousand in the prior year, an increase of 15.7%.

Prospects: Co.'s outlook is mixed. On the positive side, Co. believes the economy will continue to expand, resulting in historical growth rates for the flooring industry. However, Co. noted that commodity prices remain uncertain and passing through higher prices to its customers will affect the short-term future. After considering these factors, Co. is forecasting earnings per share for the first quarter ended Mar 31 2005 of between $1.03 and $1.12. Separately, on Feb 4 2005, Co. announced the purchase of Wayn-Tex, Inc., a manufacturer of carpet backing materials. Wayn-Tex operates manufacturing facilities in Waynesboro and Hillsville, VA.

Financial Data
(US$ in Thousands)

	12/31/2004	12/31/2003	12/31/2002	12/31/2001	12/31/2000	12/31/1999	12/31/1998	12/31/1997
Earnings Per Share	5.46	4.62	4.39	3.55	3.00	2.61	1.86	1.30
Cash Flow Per Share	3.63	4.67	8.62	6.32	4.02	2.87	2.81	3.11
Tang Book Value Per Share	14.48	9.07	8.42	15.93	12.28	10.21	8.73	6.78
Income Statement								
Total Revenue	5,880,372	5,005,053	4,522,336	3,445,945	3,255,846	3,083,264	2,639,200	1,901,352
EBITDA	752,392	650,624	614,543	405,370	388,019	397,828	279,575	198,191
Depn & Amortn	121,611	106,615	101,942	84,167	82,346	105,297	67,897	59,288
Income Before Taxes	577,389	488,434	443,629	291,416	267,629	259,899	182,388	112,446
Income Taxes	208,767	178,285	159,140	102,824	105,030	102,660	74,776	44,416
Net Income	368,622	310,149	284,489	188,592	162,599	157,239	107,612	68,030
Average Shares	67,557	67,121	64,861	53,141	54,255	60,349	57,984	52,403
Balance Sheet								
Current Assets	1,783,325	1,533,218	1,298,579	1,031,222	1,024,114	934,410	806,907	573,269
Total Assets	4,403,118	4,163,575	3,596,743	1,768,485	1,792,641	1,682,873	1,331,406	960,955
Current Liabilities	814,402	886,735	616,710	581,861	596,922	374,353	387,690	263,120
Long-Term Obligations	700,000	763,618	793,000	150,067	365,437	562,104	321,792	257,238
Total Liabilities	1,736,781	1,865,774	1,613,864	819,934	1,038,281	990,327	744,697	555,040
Stockholders' Equity	2,666,337	2,297,801	1,982,879	948,551	754,360	692,546	586,709	405,915
Shares Outstanding	66,759	66,535	66,365	52,693	52,300	56,705	57,383	52,167
Statistical Record								
Return on Assets %	8.58	7.99	10.60	10.59	9.33	10.43	9.39	7.10
Return on Equity %	14.81	14.49	19.41	22.15	22.41	24.58	21.68	18.41
EBITDA Margin %	12.79	13.00	13.59	11.76	11.92	12.90	10.59	10.42
Net Margin %	6.27	6.20	6.29	5.47	4.99	5.10	4.08	3.58
Asset Turnover	1.37	1.29	1.69	1.94	1.87	2.05	2.30	1.98
Current Ratio	2.19	1.73	2.11	1.77	1.72	2.50	2.08	2.18
Debt to Equity	0.26	0.33	0.40	0.16	0.48	0.81	0.55	0.63
Price Range	91.57-69.41	75.38-44.26	69.80-42.86	55.01-27.25	29.00-19.19	42.06-19.38	42.06-20.50	21.94-12.92
P/E Ratio	16.77-12.71	16.32-9.58	15.90-9.76	15.50-7.68	9.67-6.40	16.12-7.42	22.61-11.02	16.88-9.94

Address: P.O. Box 12069, 160 S. Industrial Boulevard, Calhoun, GA 30701 **Telephone:** (706) 629 7721 **Fax:** (706) 625 3851	**Web Site:** www.mohawkind.com **Officers:** Jeffrey S. Lorberbaum - Chmn., Pres., C.E.O. Reid Batsel - V.P., Tech.	**Auditors:** Ernst & Young LLP **Investor Contact:** 706-624-2247

MONEYGRAM INTERNATIONAL INC

Exchange	Symbol	Price	52Wk Range	Yield	P/E
NYS	MGI	$18.89 (3/31/2005)	22.75-16.40	0.21	19.08

*7 Year Price Score N/A   *NYSE Composite Index=100   *12 Month Price Score N/A

Interim Earnings (Per Share)
No earnings information available

Interim Dividends (Per Share)

Amt	Decl	Ex	Rec	Pay
0.01Q	8/19/2004	9/14/2004	9/16/2004	10/1/2004
0.01Q	11/18/2004	12/14/2004	12/16/2004	1/3/2005
0.01Q	2/17/2005	3/15/2005	3/17/2005	4/1/2005

Indicated Div: $0.04

Valuation Analysis

Forecast P/E	N/A	No of Institutions
Market Cap	$1.7 Billion	Shares
Book Value	565.2 Million	69,033,224
Price/Book	2.93	% Held
Price/Sales	2.01	77.95

Business Summary: Miscellaneous Business Services (MIC: 12.8 SIC: 389 NAIC: 22320)

MoneyGram International is a global payment services company. Co. offers its products and services to consumers and businesses through its network of agents and its financial institution customers. Co.'s business is conducted through its wholly owned subsidiary, Travelers Express Company, Inc. Co. operates its business in two segments: Global Funds Transfer and Payment Systems. Co.'s Global Funds Transfer provides money transfer services, money orders and bill payment services to consumers. Co.'s Payment Systems segment provides financial institutions with payment processing services, primarily official check outsourcing services and money orders for sale to their customers.

Recent Developments: For the quarter ended Sep 30 2004, net income decreased 1.3% to $24,515 thousand from net income of $24,836 thousand in the year-earlier quarter. Revenues were $216,153 thousand, up 14.9% from $188,048 thousand the year before. Total direct expense was $104,305 thousand versus $97,272 thousand in the prior-year quarter, an increase of 7.2%. Total indirect expense was $77,154 thousand versus $67,264 thousand in the prior-year quarter, an increase of 14.7%.

Prospects: Looking ahead, Co. anticipates full-year 2005 net revenue in the range of $450.0 million to $475.0 million. Portfolio balances are expected to average $6.50 billion for the year, declining slightly from 2004 due to bank consolidation and Co.'s efforts to focus more on fee-based business. In addition, Co. is projecting earnings of between $0.99 and $1.03 per share for the full year 2005. Co. added that net investment margin for 2005 is expected to be in the range of 1.30% to 1.40%. Separately, Co. continues to expand its worldwide network. On Feb 28 2005, Co. announced that it has established service in Laos with Banque pour le Commerce Exterieur Lao and Thai Military Bank.

Financial Data

(US$ in Thousands)	12/31/2004	12/31/2003	12/31/2002
Earnings Per Share	0.99	1.31	0.65
Cash Flow Per Share	5.12	(2.16)	...
Tang Book Value Per Share	1.76	5.14	...
Dividends Per Share	0.020	0.360	0.360
Dividend Payout %	2.02	27.48	55.38
Income Statement			
Total Revenue	826,530	737,223	707,690
EBITDA	118,621	115,465	112,537
Depn & Amortn	29,601	27,294	25,850
Income Before Taxes	89,020	88,171	86,687
Income Taxes	23,891	12,485	11,923
Net Income	86,412	113,902	57,886
Average Shares	87,330	86,619	86,716
Balance Sheet			
Current Assets	1,699,008	1,814,592	...
Total Assets	8,630,735	9,222,154	...
Current Liabilities	7,640,581	7,421,481	...
Long-Term Obligations	150,000	201,351	...
Total Liabilities	8,065,544	8,353,371	...
Stockholders' Equity	565,191	868,783	...
Shares Outstanding	87,754	88,357	...
Statistical Record			
Return on Assets %	0.97	...	...
Return on Equity %	12.02	...	...
EBITDA Margin %	14.35	15.66	15.90
Net Margin %	10.45	15.45	8.18
Asset Turnover	0.09	...	...
Current Ratio	0.22	0.24	...
Debt to Equity	0.27	0.23	...
Price Range	22.75-16.40	...	...
P/E Ratio	22.98-16.57	...	...
Average Yield %	0.10	...	...

Address: 1550 Utica Avenue South, Suite 100, Minneapolis, MN 55416 **Telephone:** (952) 591-3000	**Web Site:** www.moneygram.com **Officers:** Philip W. Milne - Pres., C.E.O. David J. Parrin - V.P., C.F.O.	**Auditors:** Deloitte & Touche LLP

MONSANTO CO. (NEW)

Exchange	Symbol	Price	52Wk Range	Yield	P/E
NYS	MON	$64.50 (3/31/2005)	64.50-31.98	1.05	54.66

*7 Year Price Score N/A   *NYSE Composite Index=100   *12 Month Price Score 126.36

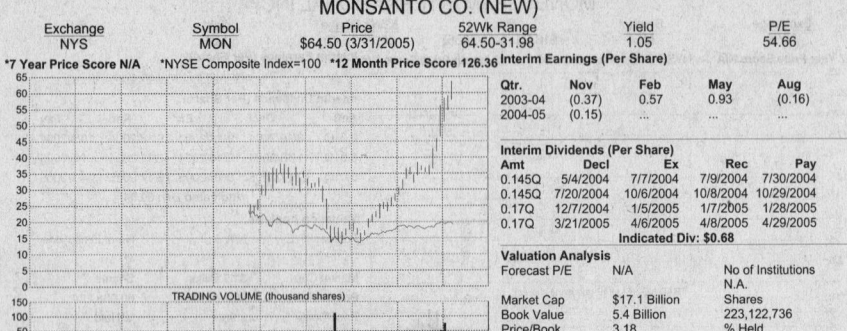

Interim Earnings (Per Share)

Qtr.	Nov	Feb	May	Aug
2003-04	(0.37)	0.57	0.93	(0.16)
2004-05	(0.15)	...	...	...

Interim Dividends (Per Share)

Amt	Decl	Ex	Rec	Pay
0.145Q	5/4/2004	7/7/2004	7/9/2004	7/30/2004
0.145Q	7/20/2004	10/6/2004	10/8/2004	10/29/2004
0.17Q	12/7/2004	1/5/2005	1/7/2005	1/28/2005
0.17Q	3/21/2005	4/6/2005	4/8/2005	4/29/2005

Indicated Div: $0.68

Valuation Analysis

Forecast P/E	N/A	No of Institutions
		N.A.
Market Cap	$17.1 Billion	Shares
Book Value	5.4 Billion	223,122,736
Price/Book	3.18	% Held
Price/Sales	3.11	83.79

Business Summary: Chemicals (MIC: 11.1 SIC: 879 NAIC: 25320)

Monsanto is a provider of agricultural products and integrated solutions for farmers. Co. produces seed brands and develops biotechnology traits that assist farmers in controlling insects and weeds. Co. provides other seed companies with genetic material and biotechnology traits for their seed brands. Co. also makes Roundup herbicide and other herbicides. Co. also provides lawn-and-garden herbicide products for the residential market and animal agricultural products focused on improving dairy cow productivity and swine genetics. Co. manages its business in two segments: Seeds and Genomics, and Agricultural Productivity.

Recent Developments: For the quarter ended Nov 30 2004, loss from continuing operations decreased 63.6% to $126 million from loss of $77 million in the year-earlier quarter. Net loss increased 58.8% to $40 million from net loss of $97 million in the year-earlier quarter. Revenues were $1,098 million, up 6.8% from $1,028 million the year before. Operating income was $97 million versus a loss of $41 million in the prior-year quarter, an increase of 336.6%. Total indirect expense was $403 million versus $509 million in the prior-year quarter, a decrease of 20.8%.

Prospects: Co. recently signed a definitive agreement to acquire Seminis, a global vegetable and fruit seed company, for $1.40 billion in cash and assumed debt, plus a performance-based payment of up to $125.0 million payable by the end of fiscal year 2007. Also, in Feb 2005, Co. signed an agreement to acquire Emergent Genetics, a major cotton seed company, for $300.0 million. Co. now expects fiscal 2005 earnings per share in the range of $0.73 to $0.91 with acquisitions accretive to earnings per share in fiscal 2006. Based on the strong business performance, Co. now expects an increase of cash from operations, projected to be $1.20 billion, compared with $1.05 billion in its previous guidance.

Financial Data

(US$ in Thousands)	3 Mos	08/31/2004	08/31/2003	12/31/2002	12/31/2001	12/31/2000	12/31/1999	12/31/1998
Earnings Per Share	1.18	0.99	(0.09)	(6.45)	1.12	0.58	0.58	(0.48)
Cash Flow Per Share	5.19	4.76	(1.23)	4.22	2.39	2.59	0.19	...
Tang Book Value Per Share	15.24	15.45	14.53	14.46	15.67	14.47	0.99	...
Dividends Per Share	0.550	0.535	0.490	0.480	0.450	...	...	...
Dividend Payout %	46.46	54.04	N.M.	N.M.	40.18	...	...	...
Income Statement								
Total Revenue	1,098,000	5,457,000	3,373,000	4,673,000	5,462,000	5,493,000	5,248,000	4,448,000
EBITDA	(101,000)	921,000	310,000	721,000	1,090,000	1,064,000	1,053,000	402,000
Depn & Amortn	109,000	452,000	302,000	460,000	554,000	546,000	547,000	368,000
Income Before Taxes	(230,000)	402,000	(38,000)	202,000	463,000	334,000	263,000	(60,000)
Income Taxes	(104,000)	131,000	(27,000)	73,000	166,000	159,000	113,000	65,000
Net Income	(40,000)	267,000	(23,000)	(1,693,000)	295,000	149,000	150,000	(125,000)
Average Shares	264,600	269,200	261,700	260,000	258,100	258,543	635,055	...
Balance Sheet								
Current Assets	5,373,000	4,931,000	4,962,000	4,424,000	4,797,000	4,973,000	4,027,000	3,748,000
Total Assets	9,999,000	9,164,000	9,461,000	8,890,000	11,429,000	11,726,000	11,101,000	10,891,000
Current Liabilities	2,404,000	1,894,000	1,944,000	1,810,000	2,377,000	2,757,000	1,704,000	1,869,000
Long-Term Obligations	1,070,000	1,075,000	1,258,000	851,000	893,000	962,000	4,278,000	4,388,000
Total Liabilities	4,613,000	3,906,000	4,305,000	3,710,000	3,946,000	4,385,000	6,456,000	6,766,000
Stockholders' Equity	5,386,000	5,258,000	5,156,000	5,180,000	7,483,000	7,341,000	4,645,000	4,125,000
Shares Outstanding	265,530	264,413	262,681	261,413	258,112	258,043	635,055	...
Statistical Record								
Return on Assets %	3.36	2.86	N.M.	N.M.	2.55	1.30	1.36	...
Return on Equity %	6.16	5.11	N.M.	N.M.	3.98	2.48	3.42	...
EBITDA Margin %	N.M.	16.88	9.19	15.43	19.96	19.37	20.06	9.04
Net Margin %	N.M.	4.89	N.M.	N.M.	5.40	2.71	2.86	N.M.
Asset Turnover	0.57	0.58	0.55	0.46	0.47	0.48	0.48	...
Current Ratio	2.24	2.60	2.55	2.44	2.02	1.80	2.36	2.01
Debt to Equity	0.20	0.20	0.24	0.16	0.12	0.13	0.92	1.06
Price Range	46.02-26.44	38.50-23.24	25.71-14.07	33.80-13.80	38.12-28.20	27.06-21.50	...	...
P/E Ratio	39.00-22.41	38.89-23.47	N.A.	N.A.	34.04-25.18	46.66-37.07	...	...
Average Yield %	1.57	1.70	2.56	2.06	1.34	N.A.	N.A.	N.A.

Address: 800 North Lindbergh Boulevard, St. Louis, MO 63167	Web Site: www.monsanto.com	Auditors: Deloitte & Touche LLP
Telephone: (314) 694-1000	**Officers:** Hugh Grant - Chmn., Pres., C.E.O. Terrell	**Investor Contact:** 314-694-1000
Fax: (314) 694-1057	K. Crews - Exec. V.P., C.F.O.	

MOODY'S CORP.

Exchange	Symbol	Price	52Wk Range	Yield	P/E
NYS	MCO	$80.86 (3/31/2005)	88.50-62.47	0.27	28.98

*7 Year Price Score 158.64 *NYSE Composite Index=100 *12 Month Price Score 105.71

Interim Earnings (Per Share)

Qtr.	Mar	Jun	Sep	Dec
2001	0.60	0.34	0.31	0.37
2002	0.46	0.49	0.43	0.45
2003	0.61	0.66	0.56	0.56
2004	0.68	0.68	0.63	0.79

Interim Dividends (Per Share)

Amt	Decl	Ex	Rec	Pay
0.075Q	10/27/2004	11/17/2004	11/20/2004	12/10/2004
0.075Q	12/14/2004	2/16/2005	2/20/2005	3/10/2005
2-for-1	2/16/2005	5/19/2005	5/4/2005	5/18/2005
0.055Q	2/16/2005	5/25/2005	5/27/2005	6/15/2005

Indicated Div: $0.22

Valuation Analysis

Forecast P/E	25.76	No of Institutions
	(4/7/2005)	400
Market Cap	$12.0 Billion	Shares
Book Value	317.5 Million	132,968,032
Price/Book	37.92	% Held
Price/Sales	8.37	89.18

TRADING VOLUME (thousand shares)

Business Summary: Miscellaneous Business Services (MIC: 12.8 SIC: 323 NAIC: 41618)

Moody's provides credit ratings, research and analysis covering debt instruments and securities in the global capital markets and provides quantitative credit assessment services, credit training services and credit process software to banks and other financial institutions. Moody's Investors Service publishes rating opinions on a broad range of credit obligations issued in domestic and international markets, including various corporate and governmental obligations, structured finance securities and commercial paper programs. It also publishes investor-oriented credit research. Moody's KMV is a provider of credit risk management products for banks and investors in credit-sensitive assets.

Recent Developments: For the year ended Dec 31 2004, net income increased 16.8% to $425,100 thousand from net income of $363,900 thousand a year earlier. Revenues were $1,438,300 thousand, up 15.4% from $1,246,600 thousand the year before. Operating income was $786,400 thousand versus an income of $663,100 thousand in the prior year, an increase of 18.6%. Total indirect expense was $651,900 thousand versus $583,500 thousand in the prior year, an increase of 11.7%.

Prospects: For full-year 2005, Co. is projecting high single-digit percent revenue growth, including the positive impact of currency translation, with diluted earnings per share in the high single-digit percent range. Co. expects the operating margin before the impact of expensing stock-based compensation to be down approximately 100 basis points in 2005 compared with 2004. This reflects slower revenue growth in 2005 than in 2004 and investments Co. is continuing to make in expanding geographically, improving its analytic processes, pursuing ratings transparency and compliance initiatives in its Investors Service business, introducing new products, and improving its technology.

Financial Data

(US$ in Thousands)	12/31/2004	12/31/2003	12/31/2002	12/31/2001	12/31/2000	12/31/1999	12/31/1998	12/31/1997
Earnings Per Share	2.79	2.39	1.83	1.32	0.97	1.56	1.63	0.93
Cash Flow Per Share	3.49	3.15	2.18	1.94	0.42	2.12	2.02	2.86
Tang Book Value Per Share	0.77	...	...	...	...	...	...	...
Dividends Per Share	0.300	0.180	0.180	0.180	0.600	0.740	0.370	0.880
Dividend Payout %	10.75	7.53	9.84	13.64	61.86	47.44	22.70	94.62
Income Statement								
Total Revenue	1,438,300	1,246,600	1,023,300	796,700	602,300	1,971,800	1,934,500	2,154,400
EBITDA	821,600	710,800	563,200	415,400	304,200	577,800	547,100	682,100
Depn & Amortn	34,100	32,600	24,600	17,000	16,600	140,900	141,600	153,900
Income Before Taxes	771,300	656,400	517,400	381,900	284,000	434,900	399,800	476,600
Income Taxes	346,200	292,500	228,500	169,700	125,500	178,900	153,400	165,600
Net Income	425,100	363,900	288,900	212,200	158,500	256,000	280,100	160,400
Average Shares	152,300	152,300	157,500	160,200	163,000	164,284	171,703	172,552
Balance Sheet								
Current Assets	1,022,600	569,000	272,300	371,200	277,600	785,000	764,000	898,300
Total Assets	1,376,000	941,400	630,800	505,400	398,300	1,785,700	1,789,200	2,151,900
Current Liabilities	837,200	432,100	462,000	359,300	253,100	1,414,800	1,352,700	1,561,600
Long-Term Obligations	...	300,000	300,000	300,000	300,000	...	...	...
Total Liabilities	1,058,500	973,500	957,800	809,500	680,800	1,900,400	1,858,500	2,340,200
Stockholders' Equity	317,500	(32,100)	(327,000)	(304,100)	(282,500)	(416,600)	(371,000)	(490,200)
Shares Outstanding	148,912	148,671	148,890	154,407	160,410	160,823	165,054	170,567
Statistical Record								
Return on Assets %	36.59	46.29	50.85	46.96	14.47	14.32	14.21	7.22
Return on Equity %	297.08	...	...	...	...	...	...	...
EBITDA Margin %	57.12	57.02	55.04	52.14	50.51	29.30	28.28	31.66
Net Margin %	29.56	29.19	28.23	26.63	26.32	12.98	14.48	7.45
Asset Turnover	1.24	1.59	1.80	1.76	0.55	1.10	0.98	0.97
Current Ratio	1.22	1.32	0.59	1.03	1.10	0.55	0.56	0.58
Price Range	87.20-59.89	60.56-40.25	51.58-36.65	40.89-26.25	27.56-18.97	29.04-17.74	25.93-16.99	21.27-16.07
P/E Ratio	31.25-21.47	25.34-16.84	28.19-20.03	30.98-19.89	28.41-19.55	18.61-11.37	15.91-10.42	22.88-17.28
Average Yield %	0.43	0.35	0.40	0.56	2.60	3.07	1.68	4.79

Address: 99 Church Street, New York, NY 10007	**Web Site:** www.moodys.com	**Auditors:** PricewaterhouseCoopers LLP
Telephone: (212) 553-0300	**Officers:** John J. Rutherford Jr. - Chmn., C.E.O.	
Fax: (212) 553-4820	Raymond W. McDaniel Jr. - Pres., C.O.O.	

MORGAN STANLEY

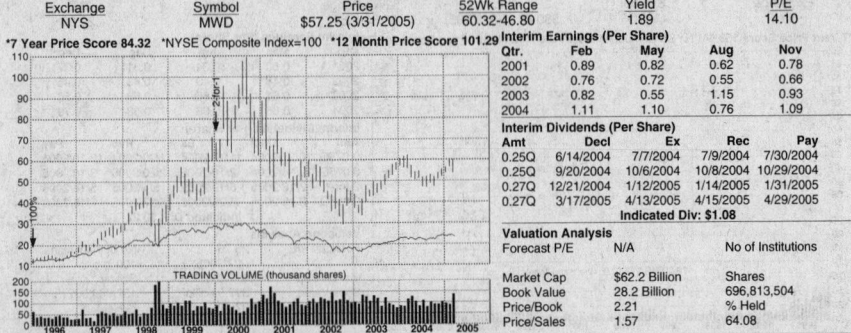

Exchange	Symbol	Price	52Wk Range	Yield	P/E
NYS	MWD	$57.25 (3/31/2005)	60.32-46.80	1.89	14.10

*7 Year Price Score 84.32 ***NYSE Composite Index=100** ***12 Month Price Score 101.29**

Interim Earnings (Per Share)

Qtr.	Feb	May	Aug	Nov
2001	0.89	0.82	0.62	0.78
2002	0.76	0.72	0.55	0.66
2003	0.82	0.55	1.15	0.93
2004	1.11	1.10	0.76	1.09

Interim Dividends (Per Share)

Amt	Decl	Ex	Rec	Pay
0.25Q	6/14/2004	7/7/2004	7/9/2004	7/30/2004
0.25Q	9/20/2004	10/6/2004	10/8/2004	10/29/2004
0.27Q	12/21/2004	1/12/2005	1/14/2005	1/31/2005
0.27Q	3/17/2005	4/13/2005	4/15/2005	4/29/2005

Indicated Div: $1.08

Valuation Analysis

Forecast P/E	N/A	No of Institutions
Market Cap	$62.2 Billion	Shares
Book Value	28.2 Billion	696,813,504
Price/Book	2.21	% Held
Price/Sales	1.57	64.08

Business Summary: Commercial Banking (MIC: 8.1 SIC: 021 NAIC: 22210)

Morgan Stanley is a holding company. Co. is engaged in four businesses. The Institutional Securities business includes securities underwriting and distribution, financial advisory services, sales, trading, financing and market-making activities in equity and fixed income securities, principal investing and aircraft financing activities. The Individual Investor Group provides financial planning and investment advisory services. The Investment Management business provides global asset management products and services for individual and institutional investors. The Credit Services business offers Discover®-branded cards and other consumer finance products and services.

Recent Developments: For the year ended Nov 30 2004, income from continuing operations increased 18.3% to $4,509,000 thousand from income of $3,810,000 thousand a year earlier. Net income increased 18.5% to $4,486,000 thousand from net income of $3,787,000 thousand a year earlier. Net interest income was $18,590,000 thousand, up 18.1% from $15,744,000 thousand the year before. Provision for loan losses was $925,000 thousand versus $1,267,000 thousand in the prior year, a decrease of 27.0%. Non-interest income rose 9.0% to $20,959,000 thousand, while non-interest expense advanced 13.5% to $17,080,000 thousand.

Prospects: On Jan 12 2005, Co. announced that its Discover Financial Services (DFS) business unit has completed the acquisition of PULSE EFT Association, Inc. PULSE is becoming a business unit of DFS and will retain its brand, pricing and operating platform. PULSE and DFS are expected to offer new products later this year that utilize the strengths of both partners. The transaction more than doubles DFS' transaction volume and number of cards in the U.S. marketplace, forming a solid platform for growth and providing a gateway to 4,100 financial institution partners. Separately, Co. results are benefiting from growth across its businesses, particularly in fixed income and Discover.

Financial Data

(US$ in Thousands)	11/30/2004	11/30/2003	11/30/2002	11/30/2001	11/30/2000	11/30/1999	11/30/1998	11/30/1997
Earnings Per Share	4.06	3.45	2.69	3.11	4.73	4.10	2.67	2.08
Cash Flow Per Share	(22.63)	2.19	(4.67)	(22.18)	(2.17)	(26.67)	13.35	(0.54)
Tang Book Value Per Share	23.92	21.53	18.90	18.64	16.91	14.80	11.88	11.00
Dividends Per Share	1.000	0.920	0.920	0.920	0.800	0.480	0.400	0.340
Dividend Payout %	24.63	26.67	34.20	29.58	16.91	11.71	15.01	16.39
Income Statement								
Interest Income	18,590,000	15,744,000	15,866,000	24,127,000	21,234,000	13,755,000	16,436,000	13,583,000
Interest Expense	14,859,000	12,809,000	11,970,000	20,779,000	18,176,000	11,390,000	13,514,000	10,806,000
Net Interest Income	3,731,000	2,935,000	3,896,000	3,348,000	3,058,000	2,365,000	2,922,000	2,777,000
Provision for Losses	925,000	1,267,000	1,336,000	1,052,000	810,000	529,000	1,173,000	1,493,000
Non-Interest Income	20,959,000	19,189,000	16,549,000	19,600,000	24,179,000	20,173,000	14,695,000	13,549,000
Non-Interest Expense	17,080,000	15,090,000	14,389,000	16,212,000	17,936,000	14,281,000	11,744,000	10,559,000
Income Before Taxes	6,685,000	5,767,000	4,720,000	5,684,000	8,526,000	7,728,000	5,385,000	4,274,000
Income Taxes	1,803,000	1,547,000	1,645,000	2,074,000	3,070,000	2,937,000	1,992,000	1,688,000
Net Income	4,486,000	3,787,000	2,988,000	3,521,000	5,456,000	4,791,000	3,276,000	2,586,000
Average Shares	1,105,185	1,099,117	1,109,637	1,121,764	1,145,011	1,159,500	1,212,588	1,218,088
Balance Sheet								
Net Loans & Leases	20,226,000	19,382,000	23,404,000	20,108,000	21,090,000	20,229,000	15,209,000	20,033,000
Total Assets	775,410,000	602,843,000	529,499,000	482,628,000	426,794,000	366,967,000	317,590,000	302,287,000
Total Deposits	13,777,000	12,839,000	13,757,000	12,276,000	11,930,000	10,397,000	8,197,000	8,993,000
Total Liabilities	747,138,000	575,100,000	506,338,000	460,636,000	407,053,000	348,970,000	302,072,000	287,332,000
Stockholders' Equity	28,206,000	24,867,000	21,885,000	20,716,000	19,271,000	17,014,000	14,119,000	13,956,000
Shares Outstanding	1,087,087	1,084,696	1,081,417	1,093,006	1,107,270	1,104,630	1,131,342	1,189,418
Statistical Record								
Return on Assets %	0.65	0.67	0.59	0.77	1.37	1.40	1.06	1.64
Return on Equity %	16.86	16.20	14.03	17.61	29.99	30.78	23.34	29.56
Net Interest Margin %	20.07	18.64	24.56	13.88	14.40	17.19	17.78	20.44
Efficiency Ratio %	43.19	43.20	44.39	37.08	39.50	42.09	37.72	38.92
Loans to Deposits	1.47	1.51	1.70	1.64	1.77	1.95	1.86	2.23
Price Range	62.22-46.80	57.83-33.57	59.64-29.31	89.80-57.60	109.38-59.97	63.63-31.16	48.44-19.22	29.38-16.09
P/E Ratio	15.33-11.53	16.76-9.73	22.17-10.90	28.87-12.10	23.12-12.68	15.52-7.60	18.14-7.20	14.12-7.74
Average Yield %	1.86	2.02	1.98	1.48	1.00	1.02	1.16	1.55

Address: 1585 Broadway, New York, NY 10036	**Web Site:** www.morganstanley.com	**Auditors:** Deloitte & Touche LLP
Telephone: (212) 761-4000	**Officers:** Philip J. Purcell - Chmn., C.E.O. Stephan F. Newhouse - Pres.	**Investor Contact:** 212-762-8131
Fax: (212) 761-0086		**Transfer Agents:** Mellon Investor Services LLC., South Hackensack, NJ

MOTOROLA, INC.

Exchange	Symbol	Price	52Wk Range	Yield	P/E
NYS	MOT	$14.97 (3/31/2005)	18.63-12.70	1.07	23.39

*7 Year Price Score 75.65   *NYSE Composite Index=100   *12 Month Price Score 90.52

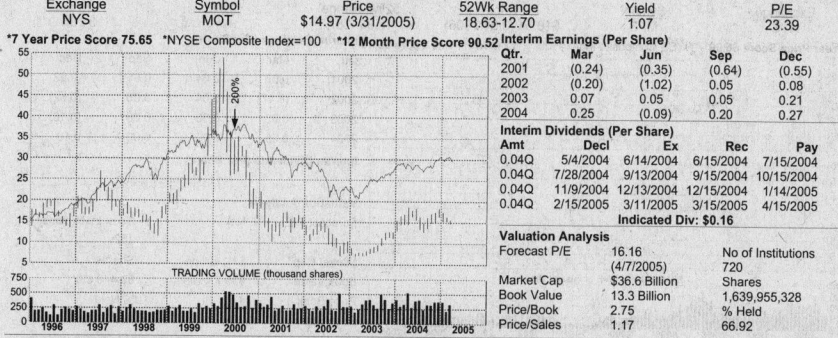

Interim Earnings (Per Share)

Qtr.	Mar	Jun	Sep	Dec
2001	(0.24)	(0.35)	(0.64)	(0.55)
2002	(0.20)	(1.02)	0.05	0.08
2003	0.07	0.05	0.05	0.21
2004	0.25	(0.09)	0.20	0.27

Interim Dividends (Per Share)

Amt	Decl	Ex	Rec	Pay
0.04Q	5/4/2004	6/14/2004	6/15/2004	7/15/2004
0.04Q	7/28/2004	9/13/2004	9/15/2004	10/15/2004
0.04Q	11/9/2004	12/13/2004	12/15/2004	1/14/2005
0.04Q	2/15/2005	3/11/2005	3/15/2005	4/15/2005

Indicated Div: $0.16

Valuation Analysis

Forecast P/E	16.16	No of Institutions
	(4/7/2005)	720
Market Cap	$36.6 Billion	Shares
Book Value	13.3 Billion	1,639,955,328
Price/Book	2.75	% Held
Price/Sales	1.17	66.92

Business Summary: Communications (MIC: 10.1 SIC: 663 NAIC: 34220)

Motorola operates through seven business segments. The Personal Communications segment includes production of digital phones. The Global Telecom Solutions segment manufactures, installs and services wireless and cellular equipment. The Commercial, Government and Industrial Solutions segment produces and services two-way radio, voice and data communications products. The Semiconductor Products segment designs and produces integrated semiconductors. The Broadband Communications segment produces a variety of broadband products. The Integrated Electronic Systems segment produces automotive and industrial electronics systems. The Other Products segment, includes Next Level Communications, Inc.

Recent Developments: For the year ended Dec 31 2004, net income increased 71.6% to $1,532 million from net income of $893 million a year earlier. Revenues were $31,323 million, up 35.3% from $23,155 million the year before. Operating income was $3,132 million versus an income of $1,273 million in the prior year, an increase of 146.0%. Total direct expense was $20,826 million versus $15,588 million in the prior year, an increase of 33.6%. Total indirect expense was $7,365 million versus $6,294 million in the prior year, an increase of 17.0%.

Prospects: On Mar 8 2005, Co. and Comcast Corporation announced that they have entered into a broader strategic relationship that includes an agreement for a multi-year set-top commitment valued at approximately $1.00 billion. Also, Co. and Comcast announced an agreement to form two joint ventures focused on next-generation conditional access technologies. The set-top commitment will extend Co. and Comcast's multi-year agreement for Comcast to purchase set-tops and network equipment. Co. will provide high-definition digital video recorders and standard-definition entry-level models, among others. The joint venture agreements are expected to be completed during the early second quarter of 2005.

Financial Data

(US$ in Thousands)	12/31/2004	12/31/2003	12/31/2002	12/31/2001	12/31/2000	12/31/1999	12/31/1998	12/31/1997
Earnings Per Share	0.64	0.38	(1.09)	(1.78)	0.58	0.41	(0.54)	0.65
Cash Flow Per Share	1.29	1.19	0.59	0.89	(0.53)	1.01	0.57	1.45
Tang Book Value Per Share	4.84	4.74	4.16	5.28	7.47	8.02	6.78	7.41
Dividends Per Share	0.160	0.160	0.160	0.160	0.160	0.160	0.160	0.160
Dividend Payout %	25.00	42.11	N.M.	N.M.	27.59	39.34	N.M.	24.74
Income Statement								
Total Revenue	31,323,000	27,058,000	26,679,000	30,004,000	37,580,000	33,075,000	29,398,000	29,794,000
EBITDA	4,110,000	3,255,000	(982,000)	(2,522,000)	5,001,000	3,675,000	618,000	4,286,000
Depn & Amortn	659,000	1,667,000	2,108,000	2,552,000	2,522,000	2,254,000	2,208,000	2,339,000
Income Before Taxes	3,252,000	1,293,000	(3,446,000)	(5,511,000)	2,231,000	1,283,000	(1,374,000)	1,816,000
Income Taxes	1,061,000	400,000	(961,000)	(1,574,000)	913,000	392,000	(412,000)	636,000
Net Income	1,532,000	893,000	(2,485,000)	(3,937,000)	1,318,000	891,000	(962,000)	1,180,000
Average Shares	2,472,000	2,351,200	2,282,300	2,213,300	2,256,600	2,202,000	1,795,800	1,836,600
Balance Sheet								
Current Assets	21,082,000	17,907,000	17,134,000	17,149,000	19,885,000	17,585,000	13,531,000	13,236,000
Total Assets	30,889,000	32,098,000	31,152,000	33,398,000	42,343,000	40,489,000	28,728,000	27,278,000
Current Liabilities	10,573,000	9,433,000	9,810,000	9,698,000	16,257,000	12,906,000	11,440,000	9,055,000
Long-Term Obligations	4,578,000	6,675,000	7,189,000	8,372,000	4,293,000	3,089,000	2,633,000	2,144,000
Total Liabilities	17,558,000	19,409,000	19,913,000	19,707,000	23,731,000	21,796,000	16,506,000	14,006,000
Stockholders' Equity	13,331,000	12,689,000	11,239,000	13,691,000	18,612,000	18,693,000	12,222,000	13,272,000
Shares Outstanding	2,447,800	2,338,700	2,315,300	2,254,000	2,191,200	2,139,300	1,803,300	1,792,200
Statistical Record								
Return on Assets %	4.85	2.82	N.M.	N.M.	3.17	2.57	N.M.	4.60
Return on Equity %	11.74	7.46	N.M.	N.M.	7.05	5.76	N.M.	9.41
EBITDA Margin %	13.12	12.03	N.M.	N.M.	13.31	11.11	2.10	14.39
Net Margin %	4.89	3.30	N.M.	N.M.	3.51	2.69	N.M.	3.96
Asset Turnover	0.99	0.86	0.83	0.79	0.90	0.96	1.05	1.16
Current Ratio	1.99	1.90	1.75	1.77	1.22	1.36	1.18	1.46
Debt to Equity	0.34	0.53	0.64	0.61	0.23	0.17	0.22	0.16
Price Range	18.63-12.59	12.76-6.93	15.24-6.99	22.20-10.34	54.15-15.74	44.22-18.30	19.47-11.56	26.96-16.24
P/E Ratio	29.11-19.67	33.58-18.25	N.A.	N.A.	93.35-27.13	107.84-44.64	N.A.	41.48-24.99
Average Yield %	1.01	1.75	1.40	1.05	0.50	0.59	0.99	0.80

Address: 1303 E. Algonquin Road, Schaumburg, IL 60196	Web Site: www.motorola.com	Auditors: KPMG LLP
Telephone: (847) 576 5000	**Officers:** Edward J. Zander - Chmn., C.E.O. Mike S. Zafirovski - Pres., C.O.O.	**Investor Contact:** 800-262-8509
Fax: (847) 576 3477		**Transfer Agents:** Mellon Investor Services LLC, Ridgefield Park, NJ

MPS GROUP, INC.

Exchange	Symbol	Price	52Wk Range	Yield	P/E
NYS	MPS	$10.51 (3/31/2005)	12.38-7.87	N/A	31.85

*7 Year Price Score 86.90   *NYSE Composite Index=100   *12 Month Price Score 95.10

Interim Earnings (Per Share)

Qtr.	Mar	Jun	Sep	Dec
2001	0.07	0.04	0.01	(0.03)
2002	(5.47)	0.04	0.05	(0.32)
2003	0.03	0.06	0.06	(0.16)
2004	0.05	0.09	0.09	0.10

Interim Dividends (Per Share)

No Dividends Paid

Valuation Analysis

Forecast P/E	N/A	No of Institutions
		152
Market Cap	$1.1 Billion	Shares
Book Value	835.7 Million	89,478,832
Price/Book	1.30	% Held
Price/Sales	0.76	86.42

Business Summary: Human Resources Services (MIC: 12.6 SIC: 363 NAIC: 61330)

MPS Group is a global provider of business services. The professional services division provides business staffing solutions for accounting and finance, engineering, legal, health care and executive searches through the Badenoch & Clark, Accounting Principals, Special Counsel, Entegee, Soliant Health and Diversified Search brands. The information technology (IT) services division provides IT resource management services and solutions under the Modis brand and software-based human capital management services under the Beeline brand. The IT solutions division is comprised solely of Idea Integration, an e-business consulting and systems integration solutions provider.

Recent Developments: For the year ended Dec 31 2004, net income was $35,420,000 versus net loss of $1,235,000 a year earlier. Revenues were $1,426,842,000, up 30.2% from $1,096,030,000 the year before. Operating income was $52,133,000 versus an income of $35,801,000 in the prior year, an increase of 45.6%. Total direct expense was $1,066,055,000 versus $808,890,000 in the prior year, an increase of 31.8%. Total indirect expense was $308,654,000 versus $251,339,000 in the prior year, an increase of 22.8%.

Prospects: Co.'s Professional Services division is benefiting from strong revenue growth in both North America and Europe. Meanwhile, Co.'s Information Technology division is also benefiting from revenue growth as billable headcount continues to steadily expand. In North America, Co. is seeing improving demand for information technology (IT) staffing services. In addition, Beeline continues to see better sales and delivery activity and has recently introduced a number of workforce optimization modules that should add new resources of revenue in 2005. Co. European IT segment is seeing downward pressure on gross margin, which it intends to counter in 2005 by scaling back certain lower-margin business.

Financial Data (US$ in Thousands)	12/31/2004	12/31/2003	12/31/2002	12/31/2001	12/31/2000	12/31/1999	12/31/1998	12/31/1997
Earnings Per Share	0.33	(0.01)	(5.62)	0.08	1.23	1.00	2.79	0.93
Cash Flow Per Share	0.49	0.69	1.15	1.78	1.99	0.47	0.82	0.36
Tang Book Value Per Share	2.96	2.98	2.64	1.47	1.07	9.00	0.47	N.M.
Income Statement								
Total Revenue	1,426,842	1,096,030	1,154,970	1,500,615	1,827,686	592,455	1,702,113	2,424,826
EBITDA	69,325	53,363	23,016	63,697	110,535	43,481	168,266	222,623
Depn & Amortn	15,755	17,009	21,017	58,292	53,881	13,693	37,105	36,059
Income Before Taxes	53,570	36,354	1,999	5,405	56,654	29,788	117,186	167,575
Income Taxes	18,150	14,519	14,591	3,102	(63,099)	11,191	48,326	65,542
Net Income	35,420	(1,235)	(566,304)	8,343	119,753	97,090	323,831	102,033
Average Shares	106,842	104,518	100,833	98,178	97,539	97,110	116,882	113,109
Balance Sheet								
Current Assets	338,782	303,468	272,561	300,696	372,307	132,145	489,538	521,044
Total Assets	954,604	893,151	897,983	1,543,622	1,653,560	1,490,331	1,571,881	1,479,516
Current Liabilities	106,649	86,589	100,630	95,974	123,919	69,316	473,400	195,656
Long-Term Obligations	...	...	...	101,000	194,000	228,000	15,525	458,870
Total Liabilities	118,941	99,689	116,424	232,811	350,342	307,816	501,771	666,674
Stockholders' Equity	835,663	793,462	781,559	1,310,811	1,303,218	1,182,515	1,070,110	812,842
Shares Outstanding	103,356	102,962	102,241	98,306	96,522	96,043	96,306	103,692
Statistical Record								
Return on Assets %	3.82	N.M.	N.M.	0.52	7.60	6.34	21.23	8.59
Return on Equity %	4.34	N.M.	N.M.	0.64	9.61	8.62	34.40	13.90
EBITDA Margin %	4.86	4.87	1.99	4.24	6.05	7.34	9.89	9.18
Net Margin %	2.48	N.M.	N.M.	0.56	6.55	16.39	19.03	4.21
Asset Turnover	1.54	1.22	0.95	0.94	1.16	0.39	1.12	2.04
Current Ratio	3.18	3.50	2.71	3.13	3.00	1.91	1.03	2.66
Debt to Equity	...	...	...	0.08	0.15	0.19	0.01	0.56
Price Range	12.38-7.87	10.60-4.85	9.79-4.51	8.00-3.70	18.44-3.50	16.75-7.94	37.38-10.75	31.88-16.13
P/E Ratio	37.52-23.85	N.A.	N.A.	100.00-46.25	14.99-2.85	16.75-7.94	13.40-3.85	34.27-17.34

Address: 1 Independent Drive, Jacksonville, FL 32202	Web Site: www.mpsgroup.com	Auditors: PricewaterhouseCoopers LLP
Telephone: (904) 360-2000	Officers: Derek E. Dewan - Chmn. Timothy D. Payne - Pres. C.E.O.	Investor Contact: 904-360-2008
Fax: (904) 360-2521		

MSC INDUSTRIAL DIRECT CO., INC.

Exchange	Symbol	Price	52Wk Range	Yield	P/E
NYS	MSM	$30.56 (3/31/2005)	36.59-27.03	1.57	23.51

*7 Year Price Score 134.99 *NYSE Composite Index=100 *12 Month Price Score 94.34

Interim Earnings (Per Share)

Qtr.	Nov	Feb	May	Aug
2001-02	0.12	0.12	0.16	0.12
2002-03	0.19	0.19	0.19	0.20
2003-04	0.24	0.27	0.34	0.32
2004-05	0.37	...	...	...

Interim Dividends (Per Share)

Amt	Decl	Ex	Rec	Pay
0.08Q	7/1/2004	7/13/2004	7/15/2004	7/26/2004
0.10Q	10/27/2004	11/9/2004	11/12/2004	11/19/2004
0.10Q	1/5/2005	1/19/2005	1/21/2005	1/28/2005
0.12Q	3/22/2005	3/31/2005	4/4/2005	4/11/2005
		Indicated Div: $0.48		

Valuation Analysis

Forecast P/E	18.84	No of Institutions	
	(4/7/2005)	162	
Market Cap	$2.1 Billion	Shares	
Book Value	648.1 Million	47,584,448	
Price/Book	3.25	% Held	
Price/Sales	2.11	99.18	

Business Summary: Machinery Supply Retail (MIC: 12.9 SIC: 084 NAIC: 23830)

MSC Industrial Direct is a direct marketer of a range of industrial products to industrial customers throughout the United States. Co. distributes a line of industrial products intended for maintenance, repair and operations supply requirements. Co. offers over 500,000 stock-keeping units through its master catalogs, weekly, monthly and quarterly specialty and promotional catalogs, newspapers and brochures and the Internet, and services its customers from its branch offices and distribution centers. As of Aug 28 2004, Co. had approximately 90 branch offices and four distribution centers.

Recent Developments: For the quarter ended Nov 27 2004, net income increased 57.7% to $25,987 thousand from net income of $16,476 thousand in the year-earlier quarter. Revenues were $263,328 thousand, up 18.2% from $222,761 thousand the year before. Operating income was $41,897 thousand versus an income of $26,891 thousand in the prior-year quarter, an increase of 55.8%. Total indirect expense was $76,904 thousand versus $73,369 thousand in the prior-year quarter, an increase of 4.8%.

Prospects: Co. is benefiting from solid growth in all of its operating regions, as well as in both its manufacturing and non-manufacturing customer bases. Looking ahead, Co. expects market conditions to remain unchanged in the near-term. Customer order flow should remain solid, although concerns exist about the potential effect of issues such as rising raw material and energy costs and interest rates. Based on existing market conditions, Co. expects to post second-quarter fiscal 2005 earnings of $0.37 to $0.39 per share, provided revenues of $265.0 million to $273.0 million.

Financial Data

(US$ in Thousands)	3 Mos	08/28/2004	08/30/2003	08/31/2002	09/01/2001	08/26/2000	08/28/1999	08/29/1998
Earnings Per Share	1.30	1.17	0.77	0.51	0.58	0.78	0.72	0.69
Cash Flow Per Share	1.21	1.00	1.26	1.23	1.31	0.30	(0.08)	0.69
Tang Book Value Per Share	8.48	8.13	6.80	6.17	5.96	5.25	4.31	3.88
Dividends Per Share	0.340	0.290	0.050	...	...	...	...	...
Dividend Payout %	26.10	24.79	6.49	...	...	...	...	...
Income Statement								
Total Revenue	263,328	955,282	844,663	793,976	869,231	792,874	651,503	583,043
EBITDA	45,057	143,776	98,386	75,181	94,213	107,519	91,414	84,947
Depn & Amortn	3,231	12,714	15,360	15,989	16,880	14,407	9,150	7,782
Income Before Taxes	42,602	133,041	84,413	60,188	73,806	88,117	80,750	78,239
Income Taxes	16,615	51,886	32,321	23,773	33,260	35,191	31,897	30,904
Net Income	25,987	81,155	52,092	36,415	40,546	52,926	48,853	47,335
Average Shares	70,664	69,458	67,912	70,783	69,449	68,203	68,317	68,964
Balance Sheet								
Current Assets	449,688	411,389	432,584	370,892	351,852	375,214	328,043	254,395
Total Assets	768,364	729,387	618,970	562,948	553,908	580,974	514,384	401,702
Current Liabilities	94,527	85,013	78,644	71,632	63,745	78,521	80,795	70,645
Long-Term Obligations	949	997	1,132	1,308	1,517	68,398	69,468	2,430
Total Liabilities	120,228	111,181	108,615	88,269	81,331	159,305	158,757	79,923
Stockholders' Equity	648,136	618,206	510,355	474,679	472,577	421,669	355,627	321,779
Shares Outstanding	68,940	68,303	65,779	66,726	68,618	67,956	66,900	67,825
Statistical Record								
Return on Assets %	12.86	12.10	8.84	6.54	7.03	9.69	10.69	12.89
Return on Equity %	15.35	14.46	10.61	7.71	8.92	13.66	14.46	15.91
EBITDA Margin %	17.11	15.05	11.65	9.47	10.84	13.56	14.03	14.57
Net Margin %	9.87	8.50	6.17	4.59	4.66	6.68	7.50	8.12
Asset Turnover	1.41	1.42	1.43	1.43	1.51	1.45	1.43	1.59
Current Ratio	4.76	4.84	5.50	5.18	5.52	4.78	4.06	3.60
Debt to Equity	N.M.	N.M.	N.M.	N.M.	N.M.	0.16	0.20	0.01
Price Range	36.32-25.00	33.96-20.55	21.78-10.26	23.90-10.51	18.99-12.13	23.06-7.75	26.25-9.44	33.13-18.50
P/E Ratio	27.94-19.23	29.03-17.56	28.29-13.32	46.86-20.61	32.74-20.91	29.57-9.94	36.46-13.11	48.01-26.81
Average Yield %	1.12	1.04	0.30	...	...	...	...	...

Address: 75 Maxess Road, Melville, NY 11747	Web Site: www.mscdirect.com	Auditors: Ernst & Young LLP
Telephone: (516) 812-2000 Fax: (516) 349-7096	Officers: Mitchell Jacobson - Chmn., C.E.O. Charles A. Boehlke - Exec. V.P., C.F.O.	Investor Contact: 516-812-2000

MURPHY OIL CORP.

Exchange	Symbol	Price	52Wk Range	Yield	P/E
NYS	MUR	$98.73 (3/31/2005)	104.70-62.55	0.91	13.15

*7 Year Price Score 161.92 *NYSE Composite Index=100 *12 Month Price Score 113.98

Interim Earnings (Per Share)

Qtr.	Mar	Jun	Sep	Dec
2001	1.08	1.78	0.46	0.32
2002	0.03	0.15	0.41	0.63
2003	0.94	0.86	0.74	0.63
2004	1.05	3.75	1.27	1.44

Interim Dividends (Per Share)

Amt	Decl	Ex	Rec	Pay
0.225Q	8/4/2004	8/12/2004	8/16/2004	9/1/2004
0.225Q	10/5/2004	11/9/2004	11/12/2004	12/1/2004
0.225Q	2/2/2005	2/10/2005	2/14/2005	3/1/2005
0.225Q	4/6/2005	5/9/2005	5/11/2005	6/1/2005

Indicated Div: $0.90

Valuation Analysis

Forecast P/E	16.49	No of Institutions
	(4/7/2005)	273
Market Cap	$9.1 Billion	Shares
Book Value	2.6 Billion	64,404,928
Price/Book	3.43	% Held
Price/Sales	1.09	69.98

Business Summary: Oil and Gas (MIC: 14.2 SIC: 911 NAIC: 24110)

Murphy Oil is a worldwide oil and gas exploration and production company with refining and marketing operations in North America and the U.K. Co.'s exploration and production business explores for and produces crude oil, natural gas and natural gas liquids worldwide. As of Dec 31 2003, Co. operated two refineries in the U.S. and owned a 30.0% interest in a U.K. refinery. Co. markets refined products through a network of retail gasoline stations and branded and unbranded wholesale customers in a 23-state area of the southern and midwestern U.S. As of Dec 31 2003, estimated net proved reserves were: oil, 213.8 million barrels; and natural gas, 449.3 billion cubic feet.

Recent Developments: For the year ended Dec 31 2004, income from continuing operations increased 78.3% to $496,395 thousand from income of $278,410 thousand a year earlier. Net income increased 138.4% to $701,315 thousand from net income of $294,197 thousand a year earlier. Revenues were $8,359,839 thousand, up 61.9% from $5,164,657 thousand the year before. Total direct expense was $6,153,413 thousand versus $3,678,729 thousand in the prior year, an increase of 67.3%. Total indirect expense was $1,367,426 thousand versus $1,091,212 thousand in the prior year, an increase of 25.3%.

Prospects: Co. announced a capital program of approximately $1.07 billion for 2005, comparable to total capital expenditures estimated in 2004. The program for 2005 is expected to approximate projected cash flow levels allowing Co. to enter its main Kikeh development phase in 2005 with extremely low debt levels. Meanwhile, marketing expenditures are expected to increase in 2005 due to a continuation of the aggressive build out of Murphy USA's retail program at Wal-Mart stores, with approximately 150 sites expected to be constructed in 2005, and a modest expansion of its retail network in the UK. Looking ahead, Co. expects first quarter 2005 earnings to range from $0.90 to $1.25 per share.

Financial Data

(US$ in Thousands)	12/31/2004	12/31/2003	12/31/2002	12/31/2001	12/31/2000	12/31/1999	12/31/1998	12/31/1997
Earnings Per Share	7.51	3.17	1.21	3.63	3.28	1.33	(0.16)	1.47
Cash Flow Per Share	11.89	7.10	5.83	7.03	8.28	4.10	3.57	4.48
Tang Book Value Per Share	28.31	20.53	16.82	15.97	13.44	11.75	10.88	12.02
Dividends Per Share	0.850	0.800	0.775	0.750	0.725	0.700	0.700	0.675
Dividend Payout %	11.32	25.24	64.05	20.66	22.10	52.63	N.M.	45.92
Income Statement								
Total Revenue	8,359,839	5,345,238	3,984,327	4,478,509	4,639,165	2,041,198	1,698,848	2,137,767
EBITDA	1,186,878	807,729	503,299	780,410	709,286	414,190	215,356	432,162
Depn & Amortn	347,878	368,051	324,656	255,496	227,615	215,414	213,149	219,891
Income Before Taxes	804,936	419,167	151,675	505,908	465,334	178,502	(8,277)	211,650
Income Taxes	308,541	117,977	54,165	175,005	159,773	64,603	24,586	128,306
Net Income	701,315	294,197	111,508	330,903	296,828	119,707	(14,394)	132,406
Average Shares	93,443	92,742	92,134	91,181	90,479	90,060	89,911	89,920
Balance Sheet								
Current Assets	1,629,363	1,038,855	854,160	598,661	816,937	593,112	437,366	517,752
Total Assets	5,458,243	4,712,647	3,885,775	3,259,099	3,134,353	2,445,508	2,164,419	2,238,319
Current Liabilities	1,204,991	810,326	717,892	560,057	745,227	487,635	380,750	469,419
Long-Term Obligations	613,355	1,090,307	862,808	520,785	524,759	393,164	333,473	205,853
Total Liabilities	2,809,087	2,761,764	2,292,222	1,760,936	1,874,793	1,388,336	1,186,186	1,158,968
Stockholders' Equity	2,649,156	1,950,883	1,593,553	1,498,163	1,259,560	1,057,172	978,233	1,079,351
Shares Outstanding	92,035	91,870	91,689	90,662	90,091	89,995	89,900	89,782
Statistical Record								
Return on Assets %	13.75	6.84	3.12	10.35	10.61	5.19	N.M.	5.91
Return on Equity %	30.41	16.60	7.21	24.00	25.55	11.76	N.M.	12.57
EBITDA Margin %	14.20	15.11	12.63	17.43	15.29	20.29	12.68	20.22
Net Margin %	8.39	5.50	2.80	7.39	6.40	5.86	N.M.	6.19
Asset Turnover	1.64	1.24	1.12	1.40	1.66	0.89	0.77	0.95
Current Ratio	1.35	1.28	1.19	1.07	1.10	1.22	1.15	1.10
Debt to Equity	0.23	0.56	0.54	0.35	0.42	0.37	0.34	0.19
Price Range	86.77-58.08	68.26-38.84	49.66-32.48	43.80-27.81	34.13-24.38	30.09-16.72	27.09-17.63	31.28-21.63
P/E Ratio	11.55-7.73	21.53-12.25	41.05-26.84	12.07-7.66	10.40-7.43	22.63-12.57	N.A.	21.28-14.71
Average Yield %	1.18	1.56	1.82	2.04	2.43	2.92	3.06	2.62

Address: 200 Peach Street, P.O. Box 7000, El Dorado, AR 71731-7000	**Web Site:** www.murphyoilcorp.com	**Auditors:** KPMG LLP
Telephone: (870) 862-6411	**Officers:** William C. Nolan Jr. - Chmn. Claiborne P. Deming - Pres., C.E.O.	**Investor Contact:** 870-864-6315
Fax: (870) 864-3673		

MYERS INDUSTRIES INC.

Exchange	Symbol	Price	52Wk Range	Yield	P/E	Div Achiever
NYS	MYE	$14.11 (3/31/2005)	14.61-10.07	1.42	18.57	28 Years

*7 Year Price Score 97.64   ***NYSE Composite Index=100**   ***12 Month Price Score 103.33**

Interim Earnings (Per Share)

Qtr.	Mar	Jun	Sep	Dec
2001	0.25	0.10	0.05	0.07
2002	0.31	0.20	0.09	0.12
2003	0.22	0.10	0.05	0.13
2004	0.26	0.18	0.11	0.20

Interim Dividends (Per Share)

Amt	Decl	Ex	Rec	Pay
10%	6/28/2004	8/11/2004	8/13/2004	8/31/2004
0.05Q	6/28/2004	9/8/2004	9/10/2004	10/1/2004
0.05Q	9/21/2004	12/8/2004	12/10/2004	1/3/2005
0.05Q	2/17/2005	3/2/2005	3/4/2005	4/1/2005

Indicated Div: $0.20 (Div. Reinv. Plan)

Valuation Analysis

Forecast P/E	15.23	No of Institutions
	(4/13/2005)	104
Market Cap	$488.9 Million	Shares
Book Value	346.0 Million	18,895,372
Price/Book	1.41	% Held
Price/Sales	0.61	54.51

TRADING VOLUME (thousand shares)

Business Summary: Plastics (MIC: 11.7 SIC: 089 NAIC: 26199)

Myers Industries designs, manufactures and markets plastic and rubber products, including plastic material handling containers and storage boxes to rubber OEM parts and tire repair materials. These products are made through a variety of molding processes in 25 facilities throughout North America and Europe. Co. also distributes tools, equipment, and supplies used for tire and wheel service and automotive underbody repair. Co.'s distribution operations are conducted through 40 branches located in major cities throughout the U.S. and in foreign countries through export and businesses in which Co. holds an equity interest.

Recent Developments: For the year ended Dec 31 2004, net income increased 57.5% to $25,709,760 from net income of $16,325,516 a year earlier. Revenues were $803,070,387, up 21.5% from $661,091,504 the year before. Operating income was $50,525,912 versus an income of $34,720,954 in the prior year, an increase of 45.5%. Total direct expense was $564,295,649 versus $460,803,695 in the prior year, an increase of 22.5%. Total indirect expense was $188,248,826 versus $165,566,855 in the prior year, an increase of 13.7%.

Prospects: Co.'s near-term prospects appear promising, supported by higher sales and contributions from the acquisitions of ATP Automotive and Pro Cal. Co. is experiencing stronger sales in most of its markets and expects to benefit from higher selling prices while maintaining its cost reduction initiatives in an attempt to mitigate the impact of large increases in the cost of raw materials. On a segment basis, Co.'s manufacturing segment is benefiting from increased demand from its major markets, including automotive, horticulture, industrial, RV, and heavy truck. Co.'s distribution segment is being driven by stronger sales of equipment items.

Financial Data

(US$ in Thousands)	12/31/2004	12/31/2003	12/31/2002	12/31/2001	12/31/2000	12/31/1999	12/31/1998	12/31/1997
Earnings Per Share	0.76	0.49	0.73	0.47	0.73	0.93	0.86	0.66
Cash Flow Per Share	1.37	1.54	1.99	2.35	2.05	1.71	1.26	1.07
Tang Book Value Per Share	1.73	2.05	1.48	0.82	0.51	0.25	4.86	4.60
Dividends Per Share	0.191	0.182	0.178	0.167	0.151	0.138	0.120	0.104
Dividend Payout %	25.12	37.04	24.50	35.80	20.64	14.78	14.01	15.78
Income Statement								
Total Revenue	803,070	661,092	607,991	607,950	652,660	580,761	392,020	339,626
EBITDA	91,226	71,276	87,884	89,844	106,097	76,748	66,891	51,527
Depn & Amortn	39,175	36,555	35,714	43,905	42,828	7,241	17,518	13,214
Income Before Taxes	38,729	24,647	40,361	27,240	40,910	54,301	48,485	38,066
Income Taxes	13,019	8,321	16,401	12,049	16,909	23,125	19,806	15,727
Net Income	25,710	16,326	23,960	15,191	24,001	31,176	28,679	22,339
Average Shares	33,846	33,138	32,969	32,727	32,811	33,552	33,500	33,804
Balance Sheet								
Current Assets	284,072	207,933	201,140	196,619	219,307	206,991	153,650	107,427
Total Assets	785,603	621,627	602,482	582,166	624,797	600,410	306,708	224,078
Current Liabilities	136,252	94,175	117,369	104,899	115,583	102,244	51,234	39,644
Long-Term Obligations	275,252	211,003	212,223	247,145	284,273	280,104	48,832	4,261
Total Liabilities	439,599	327,102	346,793	364,640	410,894	392,663	104,019	47,401
Stockholders' Equity	346,004	294,524	255,690	217,526	213,903	207,747	202,689	176,677
Shares Outstanding	34,645	33,201	33,078	32,790	32,654	33,254	33,560	33,452
Statistical Record								
Return on Assets %	3.64	2.67	4.05	2.52	3.91	6.87	10.81	10.36
Return on Equity %	8.01	5.93	10.13	7.04	11.35	15.19	15.12	13.17
EBITDA Margin %	11.36	10.78	14.45	14.78	16.26	13.22	17.06	15.17
Net Margin %	3.20	2.47	3.94	2.50	3.68	5.37	7.32	6.58
Asset Turnover	1.14	1.08	1.03	1.01	1.06	1.28	1.48	1.58
Current Ratio	2.08	2.21	1.71	1.87	1.90	2.02	3.00	2.71
Debt to Equity	0.80	0.72	0.83	1.14	1.33	1.35	0.24	0.02
Price Range	13.50-10.06	12.05-8.00	13.16-8.51	10.41-7.60	9.59-6.45	16.39-7.81	15.68-9.08	10.25-7.70
P/E Ratio	17.76-13.24	24.60-16.33	18.03-11.66	22.16-16.18	13.13-8.83	17.63-8.40	18.23-10.56	15.52-11.67
Average Yield %	1.67	1.87	1.66	1.81	1.87	1.18	1.00	1.19

Address: 1293 South Main Street, Akron, OH 44301	Web Site: www.myersind.com	Auditors: Ernst & Young LLP
Telephone: (330) 253-5592	Officers: Stephen E. Myers - Chmn., C.E.O. Milton I. Wiskind - Vice-Chmn., Sec.	Investor Contact: 330-253-5592
Fax: (330) 761-6156		Transfer Agents: National City Bank, Cleveland, Ohio

MYLAN LABORATORIES, INC.

Exchange	Symbol	Price	52Wk Range	Yield	P/E
NYS	MYL	$17.72 (3/31/2005)	24.59-14.69	0.68	20.14

*7 Year Price Score 106.64 ***NYSE Composite Index=100** ***12 Month Price Score 85.88**

Interim Earnings (Per Share)

Qtr.	Jun	Sep	Dec	Mar
2001-02	0.18	0.22	0.27	0.22
2002-03	0.22	0.24	0.25	0.26
2003-04	0.31	0.33	0.31	0.27
2004-05	0.30	0.18	0.13	...

Interim Dividends (Per Share)

Amt	Decl	Ex	Rec	Pay
0.03Q	6/17/2004	6/28/2004	6/30/2004	7/15/2004
0.03Q	9/20/2004	9/28/2004	9/30/2004	10/15/2004
0.03Q	12/20/2004	12/29/2004	12/31/2004	1/14/2005
0.03Q	3/17/2005	3/29/2005	3/31/2005	4/15/2005
		Indicated Div: $0.12		

Valuation Analysis

Forecast P/E	19.46	No of Institutions	
	(4/7/2005)	327	
Market Cap	$4.8 Billion	Shares	
Book Value	1.8 Billion	196,627,360	
Price/Book	2.63	% Held	
Price/Sales	3.77	73.03	

Business Summary: Pharmaceuticals (MIC: 9.1 SIC: 834 NAIC: 25412)

Mylan Laboratories is engaged in the development, licensing, manufacturing, marketing and distribution of generic and branded pharmaceutical products for resale by others. Co.'s generic operations consist of two principal business units, Mylan Pharmaceuticals Inc., Co.'s primary generic pharmaceutical development, manufacturing, marketing and distribution division, and UDL Laboratories, Inc., which packages and markets generic products obtained from Mylan Pharmaceuticals or third parties. Co.'s branded operations are conducted through, Bertek Pharmaceuticals Inc. and Mylan Technologies Inc., and focus on pharmaceutical products that have patent protection.

Recent Developments: For the quarter ended Dec 31 2004, net income decreased 58.9% to $34,770 thousand from net income of $84,618 thousand in the year-earlier quarter. Revenues were $290,972 thousand, down 16.8% from $349,786 thousand the year before. Operating income was $48,982 thousand versus an income of $125,489 thousand in the prior-year quarter, a decrease of 61.0%. Total direct expense was $155,625 thousand versus $150,602 thousand in the prior-year quarter, an increase of 3.3%. Total indirect expense was $86,365 thousand versus $73,695 thousand in the prior-year quarter, an increase of 17.2%.

Prospects: The generic industry continues to be under significant pressure. Specifically, Co. is experiencing increased pricing pressure due to overall market conditions and additional competition on certain products, notably omeprazole and carbidopa/levodopa. This coupled with the impact of authorized generics, the delay in the launch of its fentanyl transdermal system and limited new significant product launches, continues to have an unfavorable effect on results. Meanwhile, Co. revised it diluted earnings per share guidance for fiscal 2005 to $0.75 to $0.80. Separately, Co. and King Pharmaceuticals announced that they have mutually agreed to terminate Co.'s agreement to acquire King.

Financial Data
(US$ in Thousands)

	9 Mos	6 Mos	3 Mos	03/31/2004	03/31/2003	03/31/2002	03/31/2001	03/31/2000
Earnings Per Share	0.88	1.06	1.21	1.21	0.96	0.91	0.13	0.52
Cash Flow Per Share	0.89	1.14	1.28	0.84	1.12	1.23	0.24	0.41
Tang Book Value Per Share	5.90	5.78	5.59	5.30	4.39	3.97	2.97	2.99
Dividends Per Share	0.120	0.120	0.112	0.104	0.080	0.071	0.071	0.071
Dividend Payout %	13.68	11.36	9.30	8.63	8.33	7.84	55.17	13.56
Income Statement								
Total Revenue	936,939	645,967	339,012	1,374,617	1,269,192	1,104,050	846,696	790,145
EBITDA	288,723	224,665	138,144	556,931	466,157	454,434	100,405	278,449
Depn & Amortn	33,426	22,049	10,961	44,323	39,644	46,111	42,392	35,706
Income Before Taxes	255,297	202,616	127,183	512,608	426,513	408,323	58,013	242,743
Income Taxes	89,840	71,929	45,150	177,999	154,160	148,072	20,885	88,497
Net Income	165,457	130,687	82,033	334,609	272,353	260,251	37,128	154,246
Average Shares	273,139	272,930	275,409	276,318	282,330	286,578	285,185	293,004
Balance Sheet								
Current Assets	1,439,690	1,420,052	1,451,857	1,317,841	1,228,211	1,062,082	879,224	686,746
Total Assets	2,028,594	1,993,629	2,018,648	1,875,290	1,745,223	1,616,710	1,465,973	1,341,230
Current Liabilities	169,599	168,043	240,275	173,768	265,771	175,147	291,187	87,770
Long-Term Obligations	18,747	18,760	19,017	...	...	...	...	...
Total Liabilities	213,568	209,574	281,328	215,502	298,891	214,471	333,437	137,508
Stockholders' Equity	1,815,026	1,784,055	1,737,320	1,659,788	1,446,332	1,402,239	1,132,536	1,203,722
Shares Outstanding	269,241	269,103	268,733	268,423	271,760	284,371	281,155	291,114
Statistical Record								
Return on Assets %	12.25	15.25	17.88	18.43	16.20	16.88	2.65	12.07
Return on Equity %	14.06	17.44	20.72	21.49	19.12	20.53	3.18	13.59
EBITDA Margin %	30.82	34.78	40.75	40.52	36.73	41.16	11.86	35.24
Net Margin %	17.66	20.23	24.20	24.34	21.46	23.57	4.39	19.52
Asset Turnover	0.65	0.70	0.74	0.76	0.76	0.72	0.60	0.62
Current Ratio	8.49	8.45	6.04	7.58	4.62	6.06	3.02	7.82
Debt to Equity	0.01	0.01	0.01	...	...	...	...	...
Price Range	25.82-14.69	28.16-14.69	28.16-20.15	28.16-17.45	19.36-11.18	16.85-10.68	14.33-7.56	13.44-7.69
P/E Ratio	29.34-16.69	26.57-13.86	23.27-16.65	23.27-14.42	20.17-11.64	18.52-11.73	110.26-58.12	25.85-14.80
Average Yield %	0.58	0.53	0.47	0.45	0.54	0.50	0.65	0.68

Address: 1500 Corporate Drive, Suite 400, Canonsburg, PA 15317 **Telephone:** (724) 514-1800	**Web Site:** www.mylan.com **Officers:** Milan Puskar - Chmn. Robert J. Coury - Vice-Chmn., C.E.O.	**Auditors:** Deloitte & Touche LLP

NACCO INDUSTRIES INC.

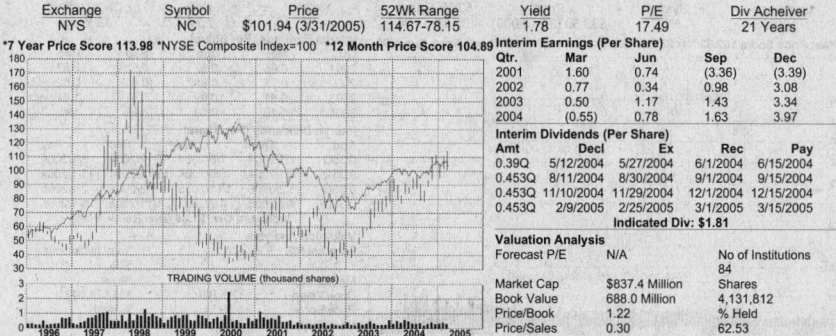

Exchange	Symbol	Price	52Wk Range	Yield	P/E	Div Achiever
NYS	NC	$101.94 (3/31/2005)	114.67-78.15	1.78	17.49	21 Years

*7 Year Price Score 113.98 *NYSE Composite Index=100 ***12 Month Price Score 104.89**

Interim Earnings (Per Share)

Qtr.	Mar	Jun	Sep	Dec
2001	1.60	0.74	(3.36)	(3.39)
2002	0.77	0.34	0.98	3.08
2003	0.50	1.17	1.43	3.34
2004	(0.55)	0.78	1.63	3.97

Interim Dividends (Per Share)

Amt	Decl	Ex	Rec	Pay
0.39Q	5/12/2004	5/27/2004	6/1/2004	6/15/2004
0.453Q	8/11/2004	8/30/2004	9/1/2004	9/15/2004
0.453Q	11/10/2004	11/29/2004	12/1/2004	12/15/2004
0.453Q	2/9/2005	2/25/2005	3/1/2005	3/15/2005

Indicated Div: $1.81

Valuation Analysis

Forecast P/E	N/A		No of Institutions
			84
Market Cap	$837.4 Million		Shares
Book Value	688.0 Million		4,131,812
Price/Book	1.22		% Held
Price/Sales	0.30		62.53

Business Summary: Industrial Machinery and Equipment (MIC: 11.5 SIC: 537 NAIC: 33924)

NACCO Industries is a holding company with three principal businesses. NACCO Materials Handling Group (NMHG) designs, engineers, manufactures, sells, services and leases a full line of lift trucks and replacement parts marketed worldwide under the Hyster™ and Yale™ brand names. NACCO Housewares Group consists of Hamilton Beach/Procter-Silex, Inc., a manufacturer and marketer of small household appliances and commercial products for restaurants, bars and hotels, and The Kitchen Collection, Inc., a national specialty retailer of brand-name kitchenware and electrical appliances. The North American Coal Corporation mines and markets lignite coal primarily as fuel for power generators.

Recent Developments: For the year ended Dec 31 2004, net income decreased 9.3% to $47,900 thousand from net income of $52,800 thousand a year earlier. Revenues were $2,782,600 thousand, up 12.5% from $2,472,600 thousand the year before. Operating income was $88,000 thousand versus an income of $117,200 thousand in the prior year, a decrease of 24.9%. Total direct expense was $2,304,900 thousand versus $2,005,900 thousand in the prior year, an increase of 14.9%. Total indirect expense was $389,700 thousand versus $349,500 thousand in the prior year, an increase of 11.5%.

Prospects: Despite the stronger lift truck markets, Co.'s wholesale material handling segment is working to moderate the effect of increases in material costs, which are largely related to supplier price increases for steel. Price increases implemented in 2004 are expected to help partially offset higher material costs in 2005. Co. is also implementing several program initiatives that should increase near-term costs and inefficiencies. New product development programs are expected to continue at high levels through 2005, as the introduction of new 1 to 8 ton internal combustion engine lift trucks begins in 2005, while its Europe restructuring program is expected to be completed by the end of 2006.

Financial Data

(US$ in Thousands)	12/31/2004	12/31/2003	12/31/2002	12/31/2001	12/31/2000	12/31/1999	12/31/1998	12/31/1997
Earnings Per Share	5.83	6.44	5.17	(4.40)	8.29	6.51	12.53	7.55
Cash Flow Per Share	15.33	15.03	18.20	16.61	16.24	15.84	17.71	25.59
Tang Book Value Per Share	21.01	14.67	5.73	1.98	9.44	11.51	9.52	N.M.
Dividends Per Share	1.675	1.260	0.970	0.930	0.890	0.850	0.810	0.772
Dividend Payout %	28.73	19.57	18.76	N.M.	10.74	13.06	6.46	10.23
Income Statement								
Total Revenue	2,782,600	2,472,600	2,285,000	2,637,900	2,871,300	2,602,800	2,536,200	2,246,900
EBITDA	162,600	184,400	182,800	128,000	213,100	233,600	289,300	212,400
Depn & Amortn	62,900	68,400	70,200	116,500	106,000	103,700	88,700	86,700
Income Before Taxes	52,300	65,000	59,700	(45,400)	60,000	86,600	166,000	89,100
Income Taxes	5,300	15,800	11,300	(9,900)	22,300	31,700	60,700	26,400
Net Income	47,900	52,800	42,400	(36,000)	67,700	53,100	102,300	61,800
Average Shares	8,214	8,204	8,198	8,190	8,167	8,154	8,166	8,189
Balance Sheet								
Current Assets	996,800	812,900	739,500	770,000	815,700	772,200	703,200	599,600
Total Assets	2,038,600	1,839,800	1,780,800	2,161,900	2,193,900	2,013,000	1,898,300	1,729,100
Current Liabilities	672,000	589,800	545,500	874,300	650,200	583,100	548,600	506,500
Long-Term Obligations	407,400	363,200	416,100	519,400	732,700	615,500	569,600	558,200
Total Liabilities	1,350,600	1,202,800	1,221,400	1,632,600	1,587,500	1,450,800	1,380,000	1,304,000
Stockholders' Equity	688,000	637,000	559,400	529,300	606,400	562,200	518,300	425,100
Shares Outstanding	8,214	8,206	8,201	8,195	8,171	9,804	8,120	8,154
Statistical Record								
Return on Assets %	2.46	2.92	2.15	N.M.	3.21	2.72	5.64	3.60
Return on Equity %	7.21	8.83	7.79	N.M.	11.55	9.83	21.69	15.37
EBITDA Margin %	5.84	7.46	8.00	4.85	7.42	8.97	11.41	9.45
Net Margin %	1.72	2.14	1.86	N.M.	2.36	2.04	4.03	2.75
Asset Turnover	1.43	1.37	1.16	1.21	1.36	1.33	1.40	1.31
Current Ratio	1.48	1.38	1.36	0.88	1.25	1.32	1.28	1.18
Debt to Equity	0.59	0.57	0.74	0.98	1.21	1.09	1.10	1.31
Price Range	111.70-77.15	93.77-37.99	75.25-36.65	81.47-42.63	55.56-33.75	96.25-45.13	172.50-78.94	125.88-44.63
P/E Ratio	19.16-13.23	14.56-5.90	14.56-7.09	N.A.	6.70-4.07	14.78-6.93	13.77-6.30	16.67-5.91
Average Yield %	1.86	2.01	1.79	1.47	2.09	1.17	0.69	1.06

Address: 5875 Landerbrook Drive, Mayfield Heights, OH 44124-4017 Telephone: (440) 449-9600 Fax: (440) 449-9607	Web Site: www.naccoind.com Officers: Alfred M. Rankin Jr. - Chmn., Pres., C.E.O. J. C. Butler Jr. - V.P., Corp. Devel., Treas.	Auditors: Ersnt & Young LLP Investor Contact: (440) 449-9676 Transfer Agents: National City Bank, Cleveland, OH

NATIONAL CITY CORP

Exchange	Symbol	Price	52Wk Range	Yield	P/E	Div Acheiver
NYS	NCC	$33.50 (3/31/2005)	39.44-33.00	4.18	7.77	12 Years

*7 Year Price Score 102.83 *NYSE Composite Index=100 *12 Month Price Score 90.29

Interim Earnings (Per Share)

Qtr.	Mar	Jun	Sep	Dec
2001	0.55	0.57	0.58	0.57
2002	0.73	0.63	0.61	0.62
2003	0.81	0.99	0.62	1.01
2004	1.16	0.83	0.86	1.46

Interim Dividends (Per Share)

Amt	Decl	Ex	Rec	Pay
0.35Q	7/1/2004	7/8/2004	7/12/2004	8/1/2004
0.35Q	10/1/2004	10/6/2004	10/11/2004	11/1/2004
0.35Q	1/3/2005	1/11/2005	1/13/2005	2/1/2005
0.35Q	4/1/2005	4/7/2005	4/11/2005	5/1/2005

Indicated Div: $1.40 (Div. Reinv. Plan)

Valuation Analysis

Forecast P/E	N/A	No of Institutions
		500
Market Cap	$21.7 Billion	Shares
Book Value	12.8 Billion	350,574,048
Price/Book	1.69	% Held
Price/Sales	2.05	54.21

Business Summary: Commercial Banking (MIC: 8.1 SIC: 021 NAIC: 22110)

National City is a financial holding company with total assets of $113.93 billion and total deposits of $63.93 billion as of Dec 31 2003. Co. operates through a distribution network in Ohio, Michigan, Pennsylvania, Indiana, Kentucky, and Illinois and conducts selected consumer lending businesses and other financial services nationwide. Co.'s businesses include commercial and retail banking, consumer finance, asset management, mortgage financing and servicing, and payment processing. Operations are primarily conducted through more than 1,100 branch banking offices located within Co.'s six-state footprint and over 330 retail mortgage offices located throughout the United States.

Recent Developments: For the year ended Dec 31 2004, net income increased 31.3% to $2,779,934 thousand from net income of $2,117,064 thousand a year earlier. Net interest income was $4,503,572 thousand, up 3.1% from $4,368,006 thousand the year before. Provision for loan losses was $323,272 thousand versus $638,418 thousand in the prior year, a decrease of 49.4%. Non-interest income rose 4.2% to $3,748,827 thousand, while non-interest expense advanced 11.7% to $4,565,382 thousand.

Prospects: Prospects appear favorable as Co. continues to enjoy solid growth in both its core banking and consumer finance businesses. Also, earnings in Co.'s wholesale banking are up considerably, primarily as a result of reduced credit costs as well as new customer acquisition. For instance, average portfolio loans for the fourth quarter of 2004 rose 27.0% from the previous year, with acquisitions accounting for about half of the growth. Co.'s acquisition and divestiture activity in the past year is consistent with its strategic focus on its core banking business. As a result, Co. should be well positioned to expand its market share in 2005.

Financial Data
(US$ in Thousands)

	12/31/2004	12/31/2003	12/31/2002	12/31/2001	12/31/2000	12/31/1999	12/31/1998	12/31/1997
Earnings Per Share	4.31	3.43	2.59	2.27	2.13	2.22	1.61	1.83
Cash Flow Per Share	7.78	20.92	(10.25)	(19.67)	1.94	3.19	(2.78)	(0.04)
Tang Book Value Per Share	14.36	13.47	11.70	12.15	11.06	9.39	10.69	10.14
Dividends Per Share	1.340	1.250	1.200	1.160	1.140	1.060	0.940	0.835
Dividend Payout %	31.09	36.44	46.33	51.10	53.52	47.75	58.39	45.63
Income Statement								
Interest Income	6,096,907	5,997,822	5,915,920	6,414,752	6,566,583	5,912,609	5,756,677	3,776,140
Interest Expense	1,593,335	1,629,816	1,910,541	2,975,903	3,608,221	2,912,587	2,845,029	1,833,312
Net Interest Income	4,503,572	4,368,006	4,005,379	3,438,849	2,958,362	3,000,022	2,911,648	1,942,828
Provision for Losses	323,272	638,418	681,918	605,295	286,795	249,674	201,400	139,660
Non-Interest Income	4,463,022	3,596,001	2,811,999	2,677,823	2,484,234	2,380,769	2,314,142	1,375,936
Non-Interest Expense	4,565,382	4,088,123	3,729,634	3,344,876	3,183,909	2,982,504	3,377,113	2,010,577
Income Before Taxes	4,077,940	3,237,466	2,405,826	2,166,501	1,971,892	2,148,613	1,647,277	1,168,527
Income Taxes	1,298,006	1,120,402	812,228	778,393	669,515	743,128	576,596	361,094
Net Income	2,779,934	2,117,064	1,593,598	1,388,108	1,302,377	1,405,485	1,070,681	807,433
Average Shares	645,510	616,410	616,174	611,936	612,625	632,452	665,720	441,380
Balance Sheet								
Net Loans & Leases	98,949,373	78,153,524	71,035,824	67,043,315	64,675,857	59,233,441	57,040,923	38,874,720
Total Assets	139,280,377	113,933,460	118,258,415	105,816,700	88,534,609	87,121,499	88,245,632	54,683,521
Total Deposits	85,954,607	63,930,030	65,118,768	63,129,932	55,256,422	50,066,310	58,246,909	36,861,136
Total Liabilities	126,476,848	104,604,789	109,950,403	98,435,477	81,764,788	81,393,766	81,232,724	50,402,170
Stockholders' Equity	12,803,529	9,328,671	8,308,012	7,381,223	6,769,821	5,727,733	7,012,908	4,281,351
Shares Outstanding	646,749	605,996	611,491	607,354	609,188	607,058	652,654	422,196
Statistical Record								
Return on Assets %	2.19	1.82	1.42	1.43	1.48	1.60	1.50	1.53
Return on Equity %	25.05	24.01	20.31	19.62	20.79	22.06	18.96	18.53
Net Interest Margin %	73.87	72.83	67.71	53.61	45.05	50.74	50.58	51.45
Efficiency Ratio %	43.23	42.61	42.73	36.79	35.18	35.96	41.84	39.02
Loans to Deposits	1.15	1.22	1.09	1.06	1.17	1.18	0.98	1.05
Price Range	39.44-32.36	34.58-26.75	33.69-24.68	32.51-24.50	29.38-16.00	37.81-22.13	38.75-28.75	33.50-21.88
P/E Ratio	9.15-7.51	10.08-7.80	13.01-9.53	14.32-10.79	13.79-7.51	17.03-9.97	24.07-17.86	18.31-11.95
Average Yield %	3.71	4.03	4.06	4.06	5.53	3.40	2.79	3.05

Address: 1900 East Ninth Street, Cleveland, OH 44114-3484	**Web Site:** www.nationalcity.com	**Auditors:** Ernst & Young LLP
Telephone: (216) 222-2000	**Officers:** David A. Daberko - Chmn., C.E.O. Jeffrey D. Kelly - Vice-Chmn., C.F.O.	**Investor Contact:** 800-622-4204
Fax: (216) 575-2353		**Transfer Agents:** National City Bank, Corporate Trust Operations, Cleveland,

NATIONAL FUEL GAS CO. (NJ)

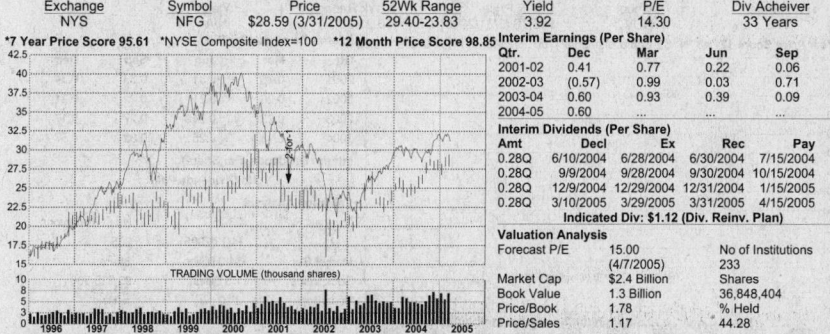

Exchange	Symbol	Price	52Wk Range	Yield	P/E	Div Acheiver
NYS	NFG	$28.59 (3/31/2005)	29.40-23.83	3.92	14.30	33 Years

*7 Year Price Score 95.61   ***NYSE Composite Index=100**   ***12 Month Price Score 98.85**

Interim Earnings (Per Share)

Qtr.	Dec	Mar	Jun	Sep
2001-02	0.41	0.77	0.22	0.06
2002-03	(0.57)	0.99	0.03	0.71
2003-04	0.60	0.93	0.39	0.09
2004-05	0.60	...	...	...

Interim Dividends (Per Share)

Amt	Decl	Ex	Rec	Pay
0.28Q	6/10/2004	6/28/2004	6/30/2004	7/15/2004
0.28Q	9/9/2004	9/28/2004	9/30/2004	10/15/2004
0.28Q	12/9/2004	12/29/2004	12/31/2004	1/15/2005
0.28Q	3/10/2005	3/29/2005	3/31/2005	4/15/2005

Indicated Div: $1.12 (Div. Reinv. Plan)

Valuation Analysis

Forecast P/E	15.00	No of Institutions
	(4/7/2005)	233
Market Cap	$2.4 Billion	Shares
Book Value	1.3 Billion	36,848,404
Price/Book	1.78	% Held
Price/Sales	1.17	44.28

TRADING VOLUME (thousand shares)

Business Summary: Gas Utilities (MIC: 7.4 SIC: 924 NAIC: 21210)

National Fuel Gas is a diversified energy holding company. Through its subsidiaries, Co. operates in six business segments. The Utility segment operations are carried out by National Fuel Gas Distribution Corporation, which sells natural gas to approx. 733,000 customers in western New York and northwestern Pennsylvania. Other business segments include the Exploration and Production segment, the Energy Marketing segment, the International segment, the Pipeline and Storage segment, and the Timber segment. As of Sept 30, 2003, proved developed reserves for crude oil and natural gas were 45,100,000 barrels and 223,500,000,000 cubic ft., respectively.

Recent Developments: For the quarter ended Dec 31 2004, net income increased 2.5% to $50,438 thousand from net income of $49,214 thousand in the year-earlier quarter. Revenues were $544,258 thousand, up 2.2% from $532,513 thousand the year before. Operating income was $99,937 thousand versus an income of $95,817 thousand in the prior-year quarter, an increase of 4.3%. Total direct expense was $379,213 thousand versus $372,016 thousand in the prior-year quarter, an increase of 1.9%. Total indirect expense was $65,108 thousand versus $64,680 thousand in the prior-year quarter, an increase of 0.7%.

Prospects: Co. continues to perform well, with each segment contributing positively to earnings. In addition, Co.'s Exploration and Production segment's initial production volumes from the Sukunka well are encouraging and the discoveries at Vermillion and East Cameron bode well for the future. Meanwhile, commodity pricing allowed Co. to maintain a solid hedge position for future production, and it has taken steps to reduce the volatility associated with the basis differential in its Canadian production. Separately, Co. expects earnings for the second quarter of fiscal 2005 to be in the range of $0.78 to $0.88 per share. Co. expects full-year 2005 earnings of between $1.75 and $1.85 per share.

Financial Data
(US$ in Thousands)

	3 Mos	09/30/2004	09/30/2003	09/30/2002	09/30/2001	09/30/2000	09/30/1999	09/30/1998
Earnings Per Share	2.00	2.01	2.20	1.46	0.82	1.61	1.48	0.30
Cash Flow Per Share	4.81	5.40	4.04	4.33	5.24	3.04	3.52	3.30
Tang Book Value Per Share	15.49	14.49	13.29	12.44	12.63	12.55	12.09	11.38
Dividends Per Share	1.110	1.100	1.060	1.025	0.985	0.945	0.915	0.885
Dividend Payout %	55.51	54.73	48.18	70.21	120.12	58.88	62.03	295.00
Income Statement								
Total Revenue	544,258	2,031,393	2,035,471	1,464,496	2,100,352	1,425,277	1,263,274	1,248,000
EBITDA	149,312	541,384	617,064	484,692	370,750	437,506	386,527	226,835
Depn & Amortn	46,940	189,538	195,226	180,668	174,914	142,170	129,690	118,880
Income Before Taxes	81,410	261,256	316,782	118,412	66,841	128,591	116,653	34,247
Income Taxes	30,035	92,737	128,161	72,034	37,106	77,068	64,829	24,024
Net Income	50,438	166,586	178,944	117,682	65,499	127,207	115,037	23,188
Average Shares	84,638	82,900	81,357	80,534	80,361	79,166	78,084	77,406
Balance Sheet								
Net PPE	3,038,048	3,006,764	2,999,087	2,844,745	2,780,713	2,683,391	2,353,894	2,248,137
Total Assets	3,885,612	3,711,798	3,727,915	3,401,309	3,445,566	3,236,888	2,842,586	2,684,459
Long-Term Obligations	1,130,290	1,133,317	1,147,779	1,145,341	1,046,694	953,622	822,743	692,669
Total Liabilities	2,545,727	2,458,097	2,590,525	2,394,451	2,442,911	2,249,451	1,903,293	1,794,374
Stockholders' Equity	1,339,885	1,253,701	1,137,390	1,006,858	1,002,655	987,437	939,293	875,555
Shares Outstanding	83,214	82,990	81,438	80,264	79,406	78,659	77,674	76,938
Statistical Record								
Return on Assets %	4.32	4.47	5.02	3.44	1.96	4.17	4.16	0.94
Return on Equity %	13.26	13.90	16.69	11.71	6.58	13.17	12.68	2.59
EBITDA Margin %	27.43	26.65	30.32	33.10	17.65	30.70	30.60	18.18
Net Margin %	9.27	8.20	8.79	8.04	3.12	8.93	9.11	1.86
PPE Turnover	0.67	0.67	0.70	0.52	0.77	0.56	0.55	0.61
Asset Turnover	0.53	0.54	0.57	0.43	0.63	0.47	0.46	0.50
Debt to Equity	0.84	0.90	1.01	1.14	1.04	0.97	0.88	0.79
Price Range	28.85-23.83	28.33-21.86	27.17-18.33	25.37-15.97	32.06-22.12	28.98-19.84	24.94-18.94	24.41-19.97
P/E Ratio	14.43-11.91	14.09-10.88	12.35-8.33	17.38-10.94	39.10-26.98	18.00-12.33	16.85-12.80	81.35-66.56
Average Yield %	4.24	4.41	4.73	4.54	3.68	3.92	4.01	3.93

Address: 6363 Main Street, Williamsville, NY 14221	**Web Site:** www.nationalfuelgas.com	**Auditors:** PricewaterhouseCoopers LLP
Telephone: (716) 857-7000	**Officers:** Philip C. Ackerman - Chmn., Pres., C.E.O. Ronald J. Tanski - Treas.	**Investor Contact:** 716-857-6987
Fax: (716) 541-7841		**Transfer Agents:** The Bank of New York, New York, NY

NATIONAL OILWELL VARCO INC

Exchange	Symbol	Price	52Wk Range	Yield	P/E
NYS	NOV	$46.70 (3/31/2005)	50.21-25.76	N/A	36.77

*7 Year Price Score 121.48 *NYSE Composite Index=100 *12 Month Price Score 120.98

Interim Earnings (Per Share)

Qtr.	Mar	Jun	Sep	Dec
2001	0.26	0.31	0.36	0.34
2002	0.26	0.21	0.22	0.21
2003	0.23	0.24	0.27	0.17
2004	0.13	0.25	0.32	0.57

Interim Dividends (Per Share)

No Dividends Paid

Valuation Analysis

Forecast P/E	23.76	No of Institutions
	(4/13/2005)	235
Market Cap	$4.0 Billion	Shares
Book Value	1.3 Billion	93,328,360
Price/Book	3.10	% Held
Price/Sales	1.73	N/A

Business Summary: Machinery Supply Retail (MIC: 12.9 SIC: 084 NAIC: 23830)

National-Oilwell Varco designs, manufactures and sells systems, components, and products used in oil and gas drilling and production. Co. also distributes products and provides services to the exploration and production segment of the oil and gas industry. Co.'s Products and Technology segment designs and manufactures complete land drilling and workover rigs, as well as drilling related systems on offshore rigs. Co.'s Distribution Services segment provides maintenance, repair and operating supplies and spare parts to drill site and production locations throughout North America and to offshore contractors worldwide.

Recent Developments: For the year ended Dec 31 2004, net income increased 43.5% to $110,200 thousand from net income of $76,800 thousand a year earlier. Revenues were $2,318,100 thousand, up 15.6% from $2,004,900 thousand the year before. Operating income was $168,600 thousand versus an income of $159,000 thousand in the prior year, an increase of 6.0%. Total direct expense was $1,821,700 thousand versus $1,540,700 thousand in the prior year, an increase of 18.2%. Total indirect expense was $327,800 thousand versus $305,200 thousand in the prior year, an increase of 7.4%.

Prospects: On Mar 11 2005, Co. completed its acquisition of Varco International, Inc. Co. will issue 0.8363 shares of common stock for each share of Varco common, resulting in a combined company with about 170.0 million shares. Effective Mar 14 2005, Co. changed its name to National Oilwell Varco, Inc. The transaction should be accretive to earnings and cash flow per share in 2005. Co. expects approximately $40.0 million to $50.0 million in annualized pre-tax cost savings and operating synergies to arise from overlapping production facility closures, IT infrastructure rationalization, sales and marketing expense reduction, and corporate overhead eliminations that should be achieved by the end of 2005.

Financial Data

(US$ in Thousands)	12/31/2004	12/31/2003	12/31/2002	12/31/2001	12/31/2000	12/31/1999	12/31/1998	12/31/1997
Earnings Per Share	1.27	0.90	0.89	1.27	0.16	0.03	1.30	0.98
Cash Flow Per Share	1.93	0.37	1.28	(0.44)	0.33	1.45	0.71	(0.02)
Tang Book Value Per Share	6.59	4.98	4.34	6.37	5.44	3.79	4.31	4.91
Income Statement								
Total Revenue	2,318,100	2,004,920	1,521,946	1,747,455	1,149,920	745,215	1,172,013	1,005,572
EBITDA	172,000	153,516	134,875	205,115	59,163	27,025	127,467	95,702
Depn & Amortn	44,000	39,182	25,048	38,873	35,034	23,244	19,179	14,744
Income Before Taxes	131,500	116,651	112,465	168,017	27,037	4,518	109,313	82,482
Income Taxes	19,200	33,685	39,396	63,954	13,901	2,998	40,386	31,201
Net Income	110,200	76,821	73,069	104,063	13,136	1,520	68,927	50,658
Average Shares	86,500	84,985	81,709	81,733	80,760	58,528	52,962	51,956
Balance Sheet								
Current Assets	1,537,400	1,246,400	1,115,068	908,566	743,103	478,376	557,761	463,598
Total Assets	2,598,700	2,242,736	1,968,662	1,471,696	1,278,894	782,311	817,993	567,511
Current Liabilities	800,200	452,215	346,216	277,309	262,782	176,210	211,351	211,461
Long-Term Obligations	350,000	593,980	594,637	300,000	222,477	196,007	205,637	61,565
Total Liabilities	1,284,500	1,136,559	1,025,694	604,156	511,688	387,236	431,190	289,823
Stockholders' Equity	1,296,400	1,090,429	933,364	867,540	767,206	395,075	386,803	277,688
Shares Outstanding	85,995	85,124	81,014	80,902	80,508	58,223	55,996	51,656
Statistical Record								
Return on Assets %	4.54	3.65	4.25	7.57	1.27	0.19	9.95	12.14
Return on Equity %	9.21	7.59	8.11	12.73	2.25	0.39	20.75	26.20
EBITDA Margin %	7.42	7.66	8.86	11.74	5.14	3.63	10.88	9.52
Net Margin %	4.75	3.83	4.80	5.96	1.14	0.20	5.88	5.04
Asset Turnover	0.95	0.95	0.88	1.27	1.11	0.93	1.69	2.41
Current Ratio	1.92	2.76	3.22	3.28	2.83	2.71	2.64	2.19
Debt to Equity	0.27	0.54	0.64	0.35	0.29	0.50	0.53	0.22
Price Range	36.99-21.77	24.78-17.86	28.38-15.48	40.50-12.91	39.19-14.25	18.19-8.75	39.75-7.75	42.44-14.50
P/E Ratio	29.13-17.14	27.53-19.84	31.89-17.39	31.89-10.17	244.92-89.06	606.25-291.67	30.58-5.96	43.30-14.80

Address: 10000 Richmond Avenue, Houston, TX 77042-4200
Telephone: (713) 346-7500
Fax: (713) 960-5212

Web Site: www.natoil.com
Officers: Merrill A. Miller Jr. - Chmn., Pres., C.E.O. Steven W. Krablin - Sr. V.P., C.F.O.

Auditors: ERNST & YOUNG LLP
Investor Contact: 713-346-7500
Transfer Agents: American Stock Transfer and Trust Company, New York

NATIONAL SEMICONDUCTOR CORP.

Exchange	Symbol	Price	52Wk Range	Yield	P/E
NYS	NSM	$20.61 (3/31/2005)	24.27-12.00	0.39	20.21

*7 Year Price Score 105.93 *NYSE Composite Index=100 ***12 Month Price Score 100.24**

Interim Earnings (Per Share)

Qtr.	Aug	Nov	Feb	May
2001-02	(0.16)	(0.13)	(0.11)	0.05
2002-03	0.01	0.01	(0.10)	(0.01)
2003-04	0.07	0.17	0.24	0.25
2004-05	0.31	0.24	...	...

Interim Dividends (Per Share)

Amt	Decl	Ex	Rec	Pay
100%	4/19/2004	5/14/2004	4/29/2004	5/13/2004
0.02Q	10/1/2004	12/13/2004	12/15/2004	1/5/2005
0.02Q	3/10/2005	3/17/2005	3/21/2005	4/11/2005

Indicated Div: $0.08

Valuation Analysis

Forecast P/E	21.26 (4/7/2005)	No of Institutions 303
Market Cap	$7.3 Billion	Shares
Book Value	1.9 Billion	288,142,016
Price/Book	3.94	% Held
Price/Sales	3.57	81.10

Business Summary: IT & Technology (MIC: 10.2 SIC: 674 NAIC: 34413)

National Semiconductor designs, develops, manufactures and markets a range of semiconductor products, most of which are analog and mixed-signal integrated circuits, serving both broad based markets such as the industrial, communications, computing, consumer and automotive markets, and more narrowly defined markets such as wireless handsets, LCD monitors, personal computers and HDTVs. Co.'s analog and mixed-signal devices include: operational and audio amplifiers; power monitors, converters and regulators; analog to digital converters; communication interface circuits; radio frequency integrated circuits; flat panel display drivers and signal processors.

Recent Developments: For the quarter ended Nov 28 2004, net income increased 36.8% to $90,000 thousand from net income of $65,800 thousand in the year-earlier quarter. Revenues were $448,900 thousand, down 5.2% from $473,500 thousand the year before. Operating income was $100,600 thousand versus an income of $74,300 thousand in the prior-year quarter, an increase of 35.4%. Total indirect expense was $126,400 thousand versus $162,700 thousand in the prior-year quarter, a decrease of 22.3%.

Prospects: On Jan 6 2005, Co. initiated a global program to reduce expenses, streamline manufacturing operations in line with the current utilization of its factories, and adjust factory levels required to support its ongoing higher value-added analog business model. These actions will affect approximately 550 people, most of whom work in Co.'s manufacturing plants in the U.S., Europe and Asia. Co.'s wafer fabrication percentage rates have declined to the mid-60s due to significant inventory reductions in the distribution channel and lower-than-expected demand. Furthermore, as Co. de-emphasizes its lower margin and commodity businesses, more capacity becomes available for higher margin analog products.

Financial Data

(US$ in Thousands)	6 Mos	3 Mos	05/30/2004	05/25/2003	05/26/2002	05/27/2001	05/28/2000	05/30/1999
Earnings Per Share	1.02	0.95	0.73	(0.09)	(0.34)	0.65	1.62	(3.02)
Cash Flow Per Share	1.51	1.58	1.30	0.61	0.28	1.39	1.15	0.68
Tang Book Value Per Share	4.74	4.61	4.21	4.17	4.46	4.69	4.63	2.66
Income Statement								
Total Revenue	996,900	548,000	1,983,100	1,672,500	1,494,800	2,112,600	2,139,900	1,956,800
EBITDA	344,200	195,400	533,200	191,100	85,700	498,400	891,000	(677,600)
Depn & Amortn	98,400	49,000	209,900	228,500	230,400	243,300	263,800	405,600
Income Before Taxes	251,900	149,000	333,700	(23,300)	(123,400)	307,100	642,500	(1,085,400)
Income Taxes	44,200	31,300	49,000	10,000	(1,500)	61,400	14,900	(75,500)
Net Income	207,700	117,700	282,800	(33,300)	(121,900)	245,700	620,800	(1,009,900)
Average Shares	374,200	381,700	388,500	363,600	355,000	376,800	383,400	334,200
Balance Sheet								
Current Assets	1,305,100	1,341,800	1,245,800	1,281,200	1,073,100	1,275,000	1,467,600	989,200
Total Assets	2,330,200	2,390,000	2,280,400	2,244,600	2,288,800	2,362,300	2,382,200	2,044,300
Current Liabilities	309,200	398,900	461,300	367,400	403,800	471,800	627,700	665,000
Long-Term Obligations	22,100	21,900	...	19,900	20,400	26,200	48,600	416,300
Total Liabilities	472,100	565,300	599,900	538,600	507,700	594,400	738,900	1,143,500
Stockholders' Equity	1,858,100	1,824,700	1,680,500	1,706,000	1,781,100	1,767,900	1,643,300	900,800
Shares Outstanding	355,305	358,136	357,611	367,144	360,723	347,614	355,122	338,106
Statistical Record								
Return on Assets %	17.67	15.74	12.30	N.M.	N.M.	10.39	28.13	N.M.
Return on Equity %	23.03	20.47	16.43	N.M.	N.M.	14.45	48.94	N.M.
EBITDA Margin %	34.53	35.66	26.89	11.43	5.73	23.59	41.64	N.M.
Net Margin %	20.83	21.48	14.26	N.M.	N.M.	11.63	29.01	N.M.
Asset Turnover	0.93	0.89	0.86	0.74	0.64	0.89	0.97	0.76
Current Ratio	4.22	3.36	2.70	3.49	2.66	2.70	2.34	1.49
Debt to Equity	0.01	0.01	...	0.01	0.01	0.01	0.03	0.46
Price Range	24.27-12.00	24.27-13.48	24.27-9.79	16.30-5.25	18.23-10.32	36.13-9.00	42.50-9.28	11.00-4.00
P/E Ratio	23.79-11.76	25.55-14.19	33.25-13.41	N.A.	N.A.	55.58-13.85	26.23-5.73	N.A.

Address: 2900 Semiconductor Drive, Santa Clara, CA 95052-8090	Web Site: www.national.com	Auditors: KPMG LLP
Telephone: (408) 721-5000	**Officers:** Brian L. Halla - Chmn., Pres., C.E.O. Kamal K. Aggarwal - Exec. V.P., Central Tech., Manufacturing Group	**Investor Contact:** 408-721-5800
Fax: (408) 739-9803		**Transfer Agents:** EquiServe Trust Company, N.A., Providence, RI

NATIONWIDE FINANCIAL SERVICES INC.

Exchange	Symbol	Price	52Wk Range	Yield	P/E
NYS	NFS	$35.90 (3/31/2005)	39.00-32.33	2.12	11.89

*7 Year Price Score 82.85   *NYSE Composite Index=100   *12 Month Price Score 95.28

Interim Earnings (Per Share)

Qtr.	Mar	Jun	Sep	Dec
2001	0.83	0.88	1.03	0.46
2002	0.82	0.63	(1.18)	0.72
2003	0.47	0.63	0.82	0.68
2004	0.78	0.68	0.89	...

Interim Dividends (Per Share)

Amt	Decl	Ex	Rec	Pay
0.18Q	6/29/2004	7/1/2004	7/6/2004	7/15/2004
0.18Q	8/4/2004	9/29/2004	10/1/2004	10/15/2004
0.18Q	12/8/2004	12/30/2004	1/3/2005	1/17/2005
0.19Q	2/23/2005	3/30/2005	4/1/2005	4/15/2005

Indicated Div: $0.76

Valuation Analysis

Forecast P/E	10.25 (4/7/2005)	No of Institutions 171
Market Cap	$5.5 Billion	Shares 36,846,732
Book Value	5.1 Billion	% Held 64.38
Price/Book	1.06	
Price/Sales	1.34	

Business Summary: Insurance (MIC: 8.2 SIC: 311 NAIC: 24113)

Nationwide Financial Services is the holding company for Nationwide Life Insurance and other companies that comprise the domestic life insurance and retirement savings operations of the Nationwide group of companies. Co. develops and sells a diverse range of products including individual annuities, private and public pension plans, life insurance and mutual funds as well as investment management and administrative services. Co's life insurance segment is composed of a wide range of variable universal life insurance, whole life insurance, term life insurance and corporate-owned life insurance products.

Recent Developments: For the quarter ended Sep 30 2004, net income increased 8.6% to $136,400 million from net income of $125,600 million in the year-earlier quarter. Revenues were $1,063,300 million, up 3.1% from $1,031,500 million the year before. Net premiums earned were $102,100 million versus $105,300 million in the prior-year quarter, a decrease of 3.0%. Net investment income rose 3.1% to $582,700 million from $565,300 million a year ago.

Prospects: Results are benefiting from increased sales of retirement plans through Nationwide Retirement Solutions, The 401(k) Company and Nationwide Financial Network, along with increased corporate-owned life insurance sales through TBG Financial, partially offset by lower sales of individual annuities. Separately, on Mar 1 2005, Co. announced that it has completed its acquisition of Dallas, TX-based RIA Services, Inc., a provider of technology products used by sponsors of defined contribution plans to provide their plan participants professional money management services. Looking ahead, Co. expects operating return on average equity to range from 11.0% to 11.5% for the full-year 2005.

Financial Data
(US$ in Thousands)

	9 Mos	6 Mos	3 Mos	12/31/2003	12/31/2002	12/31/2001	12/31/2000	12/31/1999
Earnings Per Share	3.02	2.95	2.90	2.61	1.09	3.20	3.38	2.96
Cash Flow Per Share	13.19	12.06	14.55	9.19	11.19	9.75	10.44	10.42
Tang Book Value Per Share	30.92	28.98	30.74	29.07	26.25	26.73	23.29	19.35
Dividends Per Share	0.670	0.440	0.570	0.520	0.510	0.480	0.560	0.380
Dividend Payout %	22.17	14.91	19.63	19.92	46.79	15.00	16.57	12.84
Income Statement								
Premium Income	298,200	196,100	96,700	1,553,000	1,330,700	1,270,200	1,332,200	1,116,400
Total Revenue	3,088,200	2,024,900	1,027,000	3,935,400	3,287,800	3,179,000	3,170,300	2,803,300
Benefits & Claims	469,900	310,200	152,300	669,200	438,300	321,500	286,100	252,800
Income Before Taxes	486,600	301,100	165,300	517,800	133,500	562,700	623,900	572,800
Income Taxes	123,000	73,900	42,300	119,400	(7,300)	142,800	189,000	191,500
Net Income	360,200	223,800	119,600	397,800	144,200	412,800	434,900	381,300
Average Shares	152,900	152,900	152,900	152,300	132,600	129,200	128,900	128,600
Balance Sheet								
Total Assets	112,556,800	112,562,000	113,330,600	111,027,300	95,560,300	91,960,900	93,178,600	93,054,000
Total Liabilities	107,419,600	107,719,500	108,199,400	106,151,900	90,817,000	88,217,600	89,881,100	90,266,900
Stockholders' Equity	5,137,200	4,842,500	5,131,200	4,875,400	4,443,300	3,443,300	2,997,500	2,487,100
Shares Outstanding	152,100	152,100	152,000	151,900	151,800	128,800	128,700	128,500
Statistical Record								
Return on Assets %	0.41	0.42	0.42	0.39	0.15	0.45	0.47	0.45
Return on Equity %	9.24	9.33	9.19	8.54	3.66	12.82	15.82	15.45
Loss Ratio %	157.58	158.18	157.50	43.09	32.94	25.31	21.48	22.64
Net Margin %	11.66	11.05	11.65	10.11	4.39	12.99	13.72	13.60
Price Range	38.56-31.34	38.56-29.00	38.56-24.37	34.50-21.70	45.35-22.10	47.19-33.74	50.38-20.31	53.94-27.13
P/E Ratio	12.77-10.38	13.07-9.83	13.30-8.40	13.22-8.31	41.61-20.28	14.75-10.54	14.90-6.01	18.22-9.16
Average Yield %	1.92	1.30	1.77	1.74	1.43	1.17	1.64	0.93

Address: One Nationwide Plaza, Columbus, OH 43215 **Telephone:** (614) 249-7111 **Fax:** (614) 249-9071	**Web Site:** www.nationwidefinancial.com **Officers:** Arden L. Shisler - Chmn. Mark R. Thresher - Pres., C.O.O.	**Auditors:** KPMG LLP **Investor Contact:** 888-NYSE-NFS

NAVISTAR INTERNATIONAL CORP.

Exchange	Symbol	Price	52Wk Range	Yield	P/E
NYS	NAV	$36.40 (3/31/2005)	49.80-32.86	N/A	11.37

*7 Year Price Score 95.72 ***NYSE Composite Index=100** ***12 Month Price Score 93.40**

Interim Earnings (Per Share)

Qtr.	Jan	Apr	Jul	Oct
2000-01	(0.58)	0.05	0.03	0.12
2001-02	(0.93)	(0.07)	(0.27)	(7.61)
2002-03	(1.49)	(0.21)	0.25	1.14
2003-04	(0.34)	0.54	0.73	2.01

Interim Dividends (Per Share)

No Dividends Paid

Valuation Analysis

Forecast P/E	7.58	No of Institutions	
	(4/7/2005)	201	
Market Cap	$2.5 Billion	Shares	
Book Value	531.0 Million	71,998,912	
Price/Book	4.80	% Held	
Price/Sales	0.26	N/A	

Business Summary: Automotive (MIC: 15.1 SIC: 711 NAIC: 36120)

Navistar International is a holding company whose principal operating subsidiary is International Truck and Engine Corp. Co.'s truck segment engages in the manufacture and marketing of class 5 through 8 trucks, including school buses, and operates primarily in the U.S., Canada, Mexico and other selected export markets. Co.'s engine segment engages in the design and manufacture of mid-range diesel engines and primarily operates in the U.S. and Brazil. The financial operations of Co. provide wholesale, retail and lease financing for trucks sold by International and its dealers. Product lines include International® brand trucks, diesel engines and IC® brand school buses.

Recent Developments: For the year ended Oct 31 2004, net income was $247 million versus net loss of $21 million a year earlier. Revenues were $9,724 million, up 28.2% from $7,585 million the year before. Total direct expense was $8,159 million versus $6,370 million in the prior year, an increase of 28.1%. Total indirect expense was $1,105 million versus $1,095 million in the prior year, an increase of 0.9%.

Prospects: Co. has made considerable progress in improving its cost structure, while laying the foundation for stronger growth. Going forward, Co. is looking to drive beyond its traditional markets with new ideas for growth. Also, Co. will look to take advantage of its integrated products, its market presence as a supplier of engines and its extensive parts and service business to drive growth. Based on existing market conditions, Co. believes earnings in the first quarter of 2005 are expected to be in the range between $0.20 to $0.25 per diluted common share and will reflect the traditional holiday shutdown at Co.'s manufacturing plants.

Financial Data

(US$ in Thousands)	10/31/2004	10/31/2003	10/31/2002	10/31/2001	10/31/2000	10/31/1999	10/31/1998	10/31/1997
Earnings Per Share	3.20	(0.27)	(8.88)	(0.39)	2.58	8.20	4.11	1.65
Cash Flow Per Share	2.48	(0.74)	(1.23)	3.70	11.27	...	5.22	5.24
Tang Book Value Per Share	7.53	4.45	4.08	18.91	22.05	20.36	8.55	7.79
Income Statement								
Total Revenue	9,724,000	7,340,000	6,784,000	6,722,000	8,451,000	8,647,000	7,885,000	6,371,000
EBITDA	567,000	146,000	(549,000)	170,000	423,000	765,000	569,000	362,000
Depn & Amortn	256,000	191,000	220,000	217,000	199,000	174,000	159,000	120,000
Income Before Taxes	311,000	(45,000)	(769,000)	(47,000)	224,000	591,000	410,000	242,000
Income Taxes	64,000	(31,000)	(293,000)	(24,000)	65,000	47,000	111,000	92,000
Net Income	247,000	(18,000)	(536,000)	(23,000)	159,000	544,000	299,000	150,000
Average Shares	80,100	68,000	60,300	59,500	61,500	66,400	70,000	73,600
Balance Sheet								
Current Assets	3,167,000	2,210,000	2,608,000	2,736,000	2,467,000	2,842,000	3,715,000	3,203,000
Total Assets	7,592,000	6,900,000	6,943,000	7,067,000	6,945,000	6,928,000	6,178,000	5,516,000
Current Liabilities	3,250,000	2,204,000	2,399,000	2,273,000	2,409,000	2,502,000	1,273,000	1,100,000
Long-Term Obligations	2,045,000	2,396,000	2,398,000	2,468,000	2,148,000	2,075,000	2,122,000	1,316,000
Total Liabilities	7,061,000	6,590,000	6,692,000	5,940,000	5,631,000	5,637,000	5,409,000	4,496,000
Stockholders' Equity	531,000	310,000	251,000	1,127,000	1,314,000	1,291,000	769,000	1,020,000
Shares Outstanding	70,000	68,800	60,500	59,400	59,400	63,200	66,200	72,400
Statistical Record								
Return on Assets %	3.40	N.M.	N.M.	N.M.	2.29	7.86	5.11	2.77
Return on Equity %	58.58	N.M.	N.M.	N.M.	12.17	42.14	33.43	15.50
EBITDA Margin %	5.83	1.99	N.M.	2.53	5.01	8.85	7.22	5.68
Net Margin %	2.54	N.M.	N.M.	N.M.	1.88	6.29	3.79	2.35
Asset Turnover	1.34	1.06	0.97	0.96	1.22	1.25	1.35	1.18
Current Ratio	0.97	1.00	1.09	1.20	1.02	1.14	2.92	2.91
Debt to Equity	3.85	7.73	9.55	2.19	1.63	1.61	2.76	1.29
Price Range	52.75-32.86	44.77-20.88	46.99-15.35	37.05-18.81	47.13-29.94	55.88-21.44	35.31-17.63	29.44-9.13
P/E Ratio	16.48-10.27	N.A.	N.A.	N.A.	18.27-11.60	6.81-2.61	8.59-4.29	17.84-5.53

Address: 4201 Winfield Road, P.O.Box 1488, Warrenville, IL 60555	Web Site: www.internationaldelivers.com	Auditors: Deloitte & Touche LLP
Telephone: (630) 753-5000	**Officers:** John R. Horne - Chmn. Robert C. Lannert -	**Investor Contact:** 630-753-2143
Fax: (630) 753-3982	Vice-Chmn., C.F.O.	

NCR CORP. (NEW)

Exchange	Symbol	Price	52Wk Range	Yield	P/E
NYS	NCR	$33.74 (3/31/2005)	39.38-21.13	N/A	22.34

*7 Year Price Score 121.97 ***NYSE Composite Index=100** ***12 Month Price Score 120.73**

Interim Earnings (Per Share)

Qtr.	Mar	Jun	Sep	Dec
2001	0.59	0.17	(0.04)	0.36
2002	0.02	0.13	0.21	0.28
2003	(0.14)	(0.07)	0.10	0.42
2004	(0.03)	0.64	0.23	0.67

Interim Dividends (Per Share)

Amt	Decl	Ex	Rec	Pay
2-for-1	...	1/24/2005	12/31/2004	1/21/2005

Valuation Analysis

Forecast P/E	25.85	No of Institutions
	(4/7/2005)	277
Market Cap	$6.3 Billion	Shares
Book Value	2.1 Billion	155,173,040
Price/Book	3.02	% Held
Price/Sales	1.05	82.98

Business Summary: Office Equipment Supplies (MIC: 11.12 SIC: 578 NAIC: 18210)

NCR provides consulting services, value-added software customer support services, consumable and media products, and hardware. Co. operates in seven reportable segments: data warehousing, financial self service, retail store automation, customer services, Systemedia, payment and imaging and other. Co. provides specific solutions for the retail and financial industries, and through the Data Warehousing and Customer Services businesses, Co. provides solutions for the telecommunications, transportation, insurance, utilities and electronic commerce industries, as well as consumer goods manufacturers and government entities.

Recent Developments: For the year ended Dec 31 2004, net income increased 391.4% to $285.0 million compared with $58.0 million a year earlier. Revenues were $5.98 billion, up 6.9% from $5.60 billion the year before. The improvement in revenues were led by double-digit growth in three core product segments. Total gross margin grew 5.3% to $1.62 billion, or 27.0% as a percentage of total revenue, compared with $1.53 billion, or 27.4%, the year before. Operating income jumped 79.2% to $233.0 million versus $130.0 million in the prior year. Other income amounted to $16.0 million in 2004 compared with other expense of $58.0 million in 2003.

Prospects: For the first quarter, Co. expects 2.0% to 3.0% revenue growth. On a pre-stock-split basis, earnings per share in the seasonally weak first quarter are expected to be $0.04 to $0.10. Separately, Co. remains focused on making continued improvements to its operating model, including its actions to restructure its customer services business and stimulate revenue growth. Co.'s improving operating model generates more free cash flow. Assuming 3.0% to 4.0% revenue growth in 2005, Co. is further increasing its guidance for 2005 earnings per share. On a post-stock-split basis, this revised guidance range equates to $1.20 to $1.25 per share.

Financial Data (US$ in Thousands)	12/31/2004	12/31/2003	12/31/2002	12/31/2001	12/31/2000	12/31/1999	12/31/1998	12/31/1997
Earnings Per Share	1.51	0.30	(1.11)	1.09	0.91	1.68	0.60	0.04
Cash Flow Per Share	2.32	2.32	1.26	0.75	0.90	3.11	(0.28)	1.22
Tang Book Value Per Share	10.51	9.35	6.30	8.06	6.44	7.91	6.80	6.08
Income Statement								
Total Revenue	5,984,000	5,598,000	5,585,000	5,917,000	5,959,000	6,196,000	6,505,000	6,589,000
EBITDA	539,000	404,000	468,000	555,000	618,000	579,000	589,000	373,000
Depn & Amortn	275,000	315,000	328,000	423,000	361,000	358,000	364,000	383,000
Income Before Taxes	251,000	72,000	131,000	124,000	275,000	235,000	212,000	27,000
Income Taxes	(39,000)	14,000	3,000	(97,000)	97,000	(102,000)	90,000	20,000
Net Income	290,000	58,000	(220,000)	217,000	178,000	337,000	122,000	7,000
Average Shares	191,500	191,800	199,800	199,200	196,000	201,200	204,200	204,000
Balance Sheet								
Current Assets	2,633,000	2,422,000	2,186,000	1,963,000	2,234,000	2,541,000	2,632,000	3,271,000
Total Assets	5,554,000	5,480,000	4,672,000	4,855,000	5,106,000	4,895,000	4,892,000	5,293,000
Current Liabilities	1,724,000	1,579,000	1,417,000	1,518,000	1,836,000	1,662,000	1,700,000	1,964,000
Long-Term Obligations	307,000	307,000	306,000	10,000	11,000	40,000	33,000	35,000
Total Liabilities	3,468,000	3,605,000	3,347,000	2,828,000	3,348,000	3,286,000	3,445,000	3,940,000
Stockholders' Equity	2,086,000	1,875,000	1,325,000	2,027,000	1,758,000	1,596,000	1,447,000	1,353,000
Shares Outstanding	186,600	189,400	194,000	194,800	190,400	187,200	197,400	206,400
Statistical Record								
Return on Assets %	5.24	1.14	N.M.	4.36	3.55	6.89	2.40	0.13
Return on Equity %	14.60	3.63	N.M.	11.47	10.59	22.15	8.71	0.51
EBITDA Margin %	9.01	7.22	8.38	9.38	10.37	9.34	9.05	5.66
Net Margin %	4.85	1.04	N.M.	3.67	2.99	5.44	1.88	0.11
Asset Turnover	1.08	1.10	1.17	1.19	1.19	1.27	1.28	1.25
Current Ratio	1.53	1.53	1.54	1.29	1.22	1.53	1.55	1.67
Debt to Equity	0.15	0.16	0.23	N.M.	0.01	0.03	0.02	0.03
Price Range	35.08-19.40	19.64-8.61	22.72-9.46	24.98-14.48	26.50-16.59	26.66-13.38	20.88-11.88	19.94-12.97
P/E Ratio	23.23-12.85	65.45-28.68	N.A.	22.92-13.28	29.12-18.23	15.87-7.96	34.79-19.79	498.44-324.22

Address: 1700 South Patterson Blvd., Dayton, OH 45479 **Telephone:** (937) 445-5000 **Fax:** (937) 445-5541	**Web Site:** www.ncr.com **Officers:** Lars Nyberg - Chmn. Mark V. Hurd - Pres., C.E.O.	**Auditors:** PricewaterhouseCoopers LLP **Investor Contact:** 937-445-4700

NEIMAN-MARCUS GROUP, INC.

Exchange	Symbol	Price	52Wk Range	Yield	P/E
NYS	NMG A	$91.51 (3/31/2005)	91.51-48.00	0.66	20.11

*7 Year Price Score 143.42 *NYSE Composite Index=100 *12 Month Price Score 116.32

Interim Earnings (Per Share)

Qtr.	Oct	Jan	Apr	Jul
2001-02	0.48	0.51	0.98	0.11
2002-03	0.59	0.68	0.87	0.15
2003-04	1.16	1.21	1.40	0.41
2004-05	1.30	1.43	...	...

Interim Dividends (Per Share)

Amt	Decl	Ex	Rec	Pay
0.13Q	6/22/2004	7/28/2004	7/30/2004	8/13/2004
0.13Q	9/21/2004	10/27/2004	10/29/2004	11/12/2004
0.15Q	1/14/2005	1/26/2005	1/28/2005	2/11/2005
0.15Q	4/5/2005	4/27/2005	4/29/2005	5/13/2005

Indicated Div: $0.60

Valuation Analysis

Forecast P/E	18.54	No of Institutions
	(4/7/2005)	199
Market Cap	$4.5 Billion	Shares
Book Value	1.5 Billion	32,487,520
Price/Book	2.97	% Held
Price/Sales	1.21	N/A

Business Summary: Retail - General (MIC: 5.2 SIC: 311 NAIC: 52111)

The Neiman Marcus Group operates specialty retail stores, consisting of 35 Neiman Marcus stores and two Bergdorf Goodman stores as of July 31 2004. Neiman Marcus stores offer women's and men's apparel, fashion accessories, shoes, cosmetics, furs, precious and fashion jewelry, decorative home accessories, fine china, crystal and silver, epicurean gifts, children's apparel and gift items. Bergdorf Goodman stores primarily sell high-end women's apparel and unique fashion accessories. Additionally, Neiman Marcus Direct, Co.'s upscale direct marketing operation, conducts catalogue and online sales through four brands, including Neiman Marcus, Horchow, Chef's Catalogue and Bergdorf Goodman.

Recent Developments: For the quarter ended Jan 29 2005, net income increased 19.3% to $70,587 thousand from net income of $59,171 thousand in the year-earlier quarter. Revenues were $1,129,225 thousand, up 7.7% from $1,048,367 thousand the year before. Operating income was $119,660 thousand versus an income of $90,001 thousand in the prior-year quarter, an increase of 33.0%. Total direct expense was $761,989 thousand versus $718,986 thousand in the prior-year quarter, an increase of 6.0%. Total indirect expense was $247,576 thousand versus $239,380 thousand in the prior-year quarter, an increase of 3.4%.

Prospects: For 2005, Co. is projecting capital expenditures to be approximately $170.0 million to $180.0 million primarily for new store construction, store renovations and upgrades to information systems. Co. is currently remodeling its stores in Newport Beach, Los Angeles and San Francisco, CA and Houston, TX. Co. expects to complete the expansion and renovation of the Newport Beach and Los Angeles stores in the spring of fiscal 2005 and the San Francisco and Houston stores in the spring of fiscal 2006. Also, Co. expects to open its San Antonio, TX and Boca Raton stores in the first quarter of fiscal 2006.

Financial Data

(US$ in Thousands)	6 Mos	3 Mos	07/31/2004	08/02/2003	08/03/2002	07/28/2001	07/29/2000	07/31/1999
Earnings Per Share	4.55	4.33	4.19	2.29	2.08	2.26	2.75	1.90
Cash Flow Per Share	(0.11)	(5.71)	(4.02)	3.57	4.40	2.81	5.28	2.45
Tang Book Value Per Share	30.84	29.53	28.66	24.03	19.55	17.19	14.69	11.68
Dividends Per Share	0.540	0.520	0.390	...	...	...	...	...
Dividend Payout %	11.86	12.00	9.31	...	...	...	...	...
Income Statement								
Total Revenue	2,037,161	907,936	3,545,559	3,098,124	2,948,332	3,015,534	2,854,629	2,553,421
EBITDA	280,771	132,990	439,037	301,086	259,759	272,637	317,232	245,335
Depn & Amortn	51,196	23,075	93,801	78,976	82,109	79,009	68,878	64,921
Income Before Taxes	221,560	105,878	329,313	205,840	162,244	178,440	222,979	155,442
Income Taxes	85,301	40,975	120,932	79,248	61,653	67,807	84,732	60,622
Net Income	134,703	64,116	204,832	109,303	99,574	107,484	134,011	93,510
Average Shares	49,454	49,133	48,873	47,795	47,835	47,586	48,721	49,237
Balance Sheet								
Current Assets	1,842,720	1,853,298	1,706,166	1,246,121	1,127,626	1,063,329	1,069,338	825,166
Total Assets	2,755,193	2,687,488	2,545,750	2,034,430	1,907,546	1,785,870	1,762,057	1,502,188
Current Liabilities	796,581	869,776	727,678	530,409	518,458	497,560	492,306	380,180
Long-Term Obligations	249,768	249,762	324,757	249,733	249,710	249,686	329,663	274,640
Total Liabilities	1,233,918	1,235,007	1,164,890	888,376	845,641	836,490	927,433	761,522
Stockholders' Equity	1,509,611	1,441,007	1,370,562	1,137,848	1,055,313	942,740	825,742	736,181
Shares Outstanding	48,943	48,794	47,815	47,356	47,971	47,708	47,473	49,039
Statistical Record								
Return on Assets %	8.97	8.79	8.97	5.56	5.30	6.08	8.23	6.38
Return on Equity %	16.21	16.16	16.38	10.00	9.81	12.19	17.21	13.46
EBITDA Margin %	13.78	14.65	12.38	9.72	8.81	9.04	11.11	9.61
Net Margin %	6.61	7.06	5.78	3.53	3.38	3.56	4.69	3.66
Asset Turnover	1.48	1.50	1.55	1.58	1.57	1.70	1.75	1.74
Current Ratio	2.31	2.13	2.34	2.35	2.17	2.14	2.17	2.17
Debt to Equity	0.17	0.17	0.24	0.22	0.24	0.26	0.40	0.37
Price Range	72.82-48.00	60.83-46.74	59.18-38.90	40.30-24.95	39.55-23.76	40.18-29.21	33.19-20.00	33.50-16.06
P/E Ratio	16.00-10.55	14.05-10.79	14.12-9.28	17.60-10.90	19.01-11.42	17.78-12.92	12.07-7.27	17.63-8.45
Average Yield %	0.93	0.96	0.77	...	...	...	...	...

Address: One Marcus Square, 1618 Main Street, Dallas, TX 75201	**Web Site:** www.neimanmarcusgroup.com	**Auditors:** Deloitte & Touche LLP
Telephone: (214) 741-6911	**Officers:** Richard A. Smith - Chmn. Robert A. Smith - Vice Chmn.	**Investor Contact:** 214-743-7625
Fax: (214) 741-6857		

NEW PLAN EXCEL REALTY TRUST, INC.

Exchange	Symbol	Price	52Wk Range	Yield	P/E
NYS	NXL	$25.11 (3/31/2005)	27.87-21.32	6.57	22.83

*7 Year Price Score 108.96 *NYSE Composite Index=100 *12 Month Price Score 96.11

Interim Earnings (Per Share)

Qtr.	Mar	Jun	Sep	Dec
2001	0.25	0.25	0.20	0.24
2002	0.18	0.26	0.33	0.36
2003	0.31	0.27	0.27	0.24
2004	0.32	0.27	0.23	0.28

Interim Dividends (Per Share)

Amt	Decl	Ex	Rec	Pay
0.412Q	5/6/2004	6/29/2004	7/1/2004	7/15/2004
0.412Q	7/29/2004	9/29/2004	10/1/2004	10/15/2004
0.412Q	10/28/2004	12/30/2004	1/3/2005	1/18/2005
0.412Q	2/24/2005	3/30/2005	4/1/2005	4/15/2005

Indicated Div: $1.65

Valuation Analysis

Forecast P/E	11.75	No of Institutions
	(4/7/2005)	219
Market Cap	$2.6 Billion	Shares
Book Value	1.6 Billion	46,284,220
Price/Book	1.57	% Held
Price/Sales	5.21	44.93

Business Summary: Property, Real Estate & Development (MIC: 8.3 SIC: 798 NAIC: 25930)

New Plan Excel Realty Trust is a self-administered and self-managed equity real estate investment trust that focuses on owning and managing community and neighborhood shopping centers. As of Dec 31 2003, Co.'s national real estate portfolio consisted of 379 properties in 35 states. Properties included 352 community and neighborhood shopping centers, primarily grocery or name-brand discount chain anchored, with approximately 49.5 million square feet (sq. ft.) of gross leasable space, and 27 related retail real estate assets, with about 2.2 million sq. ft. of gross leasable space. Co. also owned interests in another 22 shopping centers with about 3.9 million sq. ft. of gross leasable space.

Recent Developments: For the year ended Dec 31 2004, income from continuing operations increased 5.8% to $132,655 thousand from income of $125,373 thousand a year earlier. Net income increased 3.8% to $133,940 thousand from net income of $129,021 thousand a year earlier. Revenues were $495,537 thousand, up 5.3% from $470,668 thousand the year before. Operating income was $228,546 thousand versus an income of $219,236 thousand in the prior year, an increase of 4.2%.

Prospects: Co. continues to strengthen its portfolio of properties through acquisitions, dispositions and development. For instance, during 2004, Co. acquired, including through co-investments with its joint venture partners, an aggregate of 18 shopping centers, the remaining 50% interests in two shopping centers in which Co. owned the other 50% interests, and two land parcels for an aggregate purchase price of approximately $434.5 million. The shopping centers totaled approximately 3.5 million square feet of gross leasable area and the land parcels totaled approximately 24 acres.

Financial Data
(US$ in Thousands)

	12/31/2004	12/31/2003	12/31/2002	12/31/2001	12/31/2000	12/31/1999	12/31/1998	12/31/1997
Earnings Per Share	1.10	1.08	1.13	0.94	1.14	1.42	0.62	1.97
Cash Flow Per Share	2.18	2.03	2.41	2.14	2.04	1.87	0.67	2.69
Tang Book Value Per Share	15.64	16.16	16.23	17.09	17.81	18.41	19.18	23.93
Dividends Per Share	1.650	1.650	1.650	1.650	2.060	1.625	1.733	1.633
Dividend Payout %	150.00	152.78	146.02	175.53	180.70	114.44	279.57	82.91
Income Statement								
Property Income	396,123	378,660	316,988	277,383	411,263	414,481	150,411	72,941
Non-Property Income	99,414	101,222	75,411	61,026	12,123	23,546	5,510	32,517
Total Revenue	495,537	479,882	392,399	338,409	423,386	438,027	155,921	105,458
Depn & Amortn	92,837	77,091	73,733	66,710	64,381	59,365	21,366	12,690
Interest Expense	106,054	101,632	92,953	78,779	92,915	81,412	27,168	23,991
Net Income	133,940	129,021	122,062	105,162	123,081	149,513	55,805	48,962
Average Shares	103,345	100,269	95,662	88,799	88,951	90,440	79,396	20,708
Balance Sheet								
Total Assets	3,831,742	3,554,645	3,515,279	2,622,866	2,894,431	2,953,141	2,894,546	1,076,197
Long-Term Obligations	1,996,319	1,776,004	1,742,342	978,854	1,214,976	1,220,451	1,105,271	514,408
Total Liabilities	2,160,797	1,930,637	1,902,996	1,107,361	1,314,912	1,316,522	1,158,321	531,695
Stockholders' Equity	1,640,161	1,586,143	1,572,849	1,493,238	1,555,610	1,611,519	1,695,574	502,516
Shares Outstanding	102,845	97,980	96,916	87,352	87,320	87,555	88,384	20,999
Statistical Record								
Return on Assets %	3.62	3.65	3.98	3.81	4.20	5.11	2.81	5.99
Return on Equity %	8.28	8.17	7.96	6.90	7.75	9.04	5.08	12.01
Net Margin %	27.03	26.89	31.11	31.08	29.07	34.13	35.79	46.43
Price Range	27.87-21.32	25.61-18.21	21.00-16.62	19.48-13.31	17.31-11.94	22.44-15.13	25.63-17.92	23.34-16.64
P/E Ratio	25.34-19.38	23.71-16.86	18.58-14.71	20.72-14.16	15.19-10.47	15.80-10.65	41.34-28.90	11.85-8.44
Average Yield %	6.59	7.62	8.60	9.87	14.47	8.65	7.69	8.26

Address: 1120 Avenue of the Americas, New York, NY 10036 **Telephone:** (212) 869-3000 **Fax:** (212) 869-3989	**Web Site:** www.newplanexcel.com **Officers:** William Newman - Chmn. Scott MacDonald - Pres., C.O.O.	**Auditors:** PricewaterhouseCoopers LLP

NEW YORK COMMUNITY BANCORP INC.

Exchange	Symbol	Price	52Wk Range	Yield	P/E
NYS	NYB	$18.16 (3/31/2005)	34.28-17.39	5.51	13.65

*7 Year Price Score 127.48 ***NYSE Composite Index=100** ***12 Month Price Score 82.28**

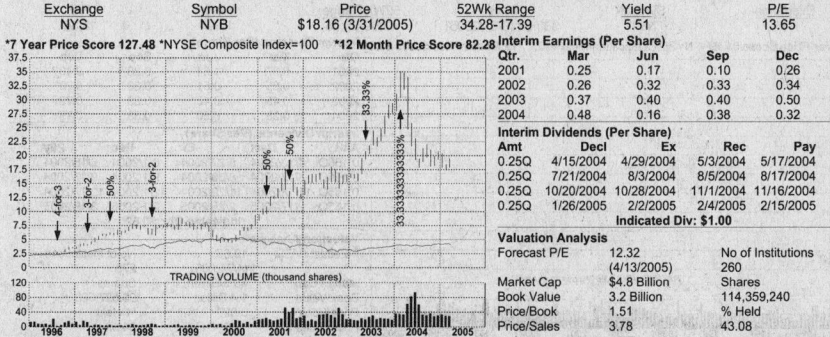

Interim Earnings (Per Share)

Qtr.	Mar	Jun	Sep	Dec
2001	0.25	0.17	0.10	0.26
2002	0.26	0.32	0.33	0.34
2003	0.37	0.40	0.40	0.50
2004	0.48	0.16	0.38	0.32

Interim Dividends (Per Share)

Amt	Decl	Ex	Rec	Pay
0.25Q	4/15/2004	4/29/2004	5/3/2004	5/17/2004
0.25Q	7/21/2004	8/3/2004	8/5/2004	8/17/2004
0.25Q	10/20/2004	10/28/2004	11/1/2004	11/16/2004
0.25Q	1/26/2005	2/2/2005	2/4/2005	2/15/2005
	Indicated Div: $1.00			

Valuation Analysis

Forecast P/E	12.32 (4/13/2005)	No of Institutions 260
Market Cap	$4.8 Billion	Shares 114,359,240
Book Value	3.2 Billion	% Held 43.08
Price/Book	1.51	
Price/Sales	3.78	

Business Summary: Finance Intermediaries & Services (MIC: 8.7 SIC: 163 NAIC: 22310)

New York Community Bancorp is a bank holding company for New York Community Bank. As of Dec 31 2003, Co. operated through a network of 140 banking offices in the five boroughs of New York City, and Nassau, Suffolk, and Westchester counties in New York, and Essex, Union, and Hudson counties in New Jersey. Co. operates through seven divisions: Queens County Savings Bank, Roslyn Savings Bank, Richmond County Savings Bank, Roosevelt Savings Bank, CFS Bank, First Savings Bank of New Jersey and Ironbound Bank. Co. is a significant producer of multi-family mortgage loans in New York City. As of Dec 31 2003, total assets were $23.44 billion and total deposits were $10.33 billion.

Recent Developments: For the year ended Dec 31 2004, net income increased 9.8% to $355,086 thousand from net income of $323,371 thousand a year earlier. Net interest income was $781,257 thousand, up 54.7% from $504,975 thousand the year before. Non-interest loss was $44,217 thousand versus non-interest income of $163,987 thousand, while non-interest expense advanced 14.3% to $193,632 thousand.

Prospects: Co. is benefiting from actions take in 2004 to strengthen its balance sheet. In 2005, Co. expects to maintain the strength of its tangible capital and to further grow loans and deposits, the latter increase reflecting enhancements to customer service and the expansion of the customer base. In 2005, Co. will feature several initiatives designed to broaden its service model to include its larger lending relationships, small business owners, and an array of card and Internet services. Meanwhile, Co. expects that its reduction of its securities portfolio will continue in the coming quarters with securities redemptions and sales continuing to represent a source of loan production funding.

Financial Data

(US$ in Thousands)	12/31/2004	12/31/2003	12/31/2002	12/31/2001	12/31/2000	12/31/1999	12/31/1998	12/31/1997
Earnings Per Share	1.33	1.65	1.25	0.75	0.32	0.42	0.34	0.27
Cash Flow Per Share	1.28	(7.12)	0.49	(3.12)	(1.36)	0.18	0.55	0.43
Tang Book Value Per Share	4.33	3.32	3.45	1.72	1.63	1.63	1.76	1.91
Dividends Per Share	0.960	0.658	0.428	0.303	0.250	0.250	0.167	0.102
Dividend Payout %	72.18	39.89	34.23	40.13	79.36	60.06	49.74	38.18
Income Statement								
Interest Income	1,172,159	749,160	599,507	423,304	174,832	143,123	134,277	117,734
Interest Expense	390,902	244,185	226,251	217,488	101,751	74,220	65,755	55,336
Net Interest Income	781,257	504,975	373,256	205,816	73,081	68,903	68,522	62,398
Provision for Losses	...	...	...	...	...	(2,400)	...	...
Non-Interest Income	(44,217)	98,135	84,834	90,615	21,645	2,523	2,554	2,305
Non-Interest Expense	193,632	169,373	133,062	112,757	49,330	21,390	25,953	27,084
Income Before Taxes	531,968	492,682	336,014	175,246	44,902	52,436	45,123	37,619
Income Taxes	176,882	169,311	106,784	70,779	20,425	20,772	18,179	14,355
Net Income	355,086	323,371	229,230	104,467	24,477	31,664	26,944	23,264
Average Shares	266,837	196,303	183,221	138,760	78,124	75,757	80,722	87,290
Balance Sheet								
Net Loans & Leases	13,317,987	10,422,078	5,443,572	5,361,187	3,616,386	1,601,079	1,486,519	1,395,003
Total Assets	24,037,826	23,441,337	11,313,092	9,202,635	4,710,785	1,906,835	1,746,882	1,603,269
Total Deposits	10,402,117	10,329,106	5,256,042	5,450,602	3,257,194	1,076,018	1,102,285	1,069,161
Total Liabilities	20,851,412	20,572,680	9,989,580	8,219,501	4,403,375	1,769,694	1,597,476	1,432,754
Stockholders' Equity	3,186,414	2,868,657	1,323,512	983,134	307,410	137,141	149,406	170,515
Shares Outstanding	265,190	256,649	187,843	181,053	115,884	84,038	85,001	89,475
Statistical Record								
Return on Assets %	1.49	1.86	2.23	1.50	0.74	1.73	1.61	1.57
Return on Equity %	11.70	15.43	19.88	16.19	10.98	22.10	16.84	12.18
Net Interest Margin %	66.65	67.41	62.26	48.62	41.80	48.14	51.03	53.00
Efficiency Ratio %	15.19	19.99	19.44	21.94	25.11	14.69	18.97	22.56
Loans to Deposits	1.28	1.01	1.04	0.98	1.11	1.49	1.35	1.30
Price Range	35.12-17.88	29.45-15.43	17.99-12.86	17.64-8.42	9.38-4.44	8.92-6.44	7.85-5.72	6.75-3.37
P/E Ratio	26.41-13.44	17.85-9.35	14.39-10.29	23.52-11.23	29.30-13.87	21.24-15.33	23.10-16.82	25.00-12.48
Average Yield %	4.03	3.05	2.70	2.41	4.24	3.34	2.39	2.02

Address: 615 Merrick Avenue, Westbury, NY 11590 **Telephone:** (516) 683 4100 **Fax:** (516) 683 8385	**Web Site:** www.myNYCB.com **Officers:** Michael F. Manzulli - Chmn. Joseph R. Ficalora - Pres. C.E.O.	**Auditors:** KPMG LLP **Investor Contact:** 718-359-6401 x275

NEW YORK TIMES CO.

Exchange	Symbol	Price	52Wk Range	Yield	P/E
NYS	NYT	$36.58 (3/31/2005)	47.09-35.56	1.69	18.66

*7 Year Price Score 85.79   *NYSE Composite Index=100   *12 Month Price Score 83.59

TRADING VOLUME (thousand shares)

Interim Earnings (Per Share)

Qtr.	Mar	Jun	Sep	Dec
2001	0.37	1.64	0.28	0.49
2002	0.35	0.51	0.38	0.70
2003	0.45	0.47	0.33	0.73
2004	0.38	0.50	0.33	0.75

Interim Dividends (Per Share)

Amt	Decl	Ex	Rec	Pay
0.155Q	4/13/2004	5/27/2004	6/1/2004	6/18/2004
0.155Q	6/17/2004	8/30/2004	9/1/2004	9/17/2004
0.155Q	11/18/2004	11/29/2004	12/1/2004	12/17/2004
0.155Q	2/17/2005	2/25/2005	3/1/2005	3/18/2005
		Indicated Div: $0.62		

Valuation Analysis

Forecast P/E	19.65	No of Institutions	
	(4/7/2005)	278	
Market Cap	$5.3 Billion	Shares	
Book Value	1.4 Billion	93,527,520	
Price/Book	3.82	% Held	
Price/Sales	1.62	64.52	

Business Summary: Media (MIC: 13.1 SIC: 711 NAIC: 11110)

New York Times is a diversified media company. The Newspaper segment includes The New York Times, The Boston Globe, The International Herald Tribune, the Worcester Telegram & Gazette, 15 regional newspapers, newspaper distributors, and related businesses. The Broadcasting segment is made up of eight television stations and two New York City radio stations. The New York Times Digital consists of NYTimes.com, Boston.com and the licensing of electronic databases through its Digital Archive Distribution business. Co.'s equity interests include a Canadian newsprint company and a partnership in a supercalendered paper mill in Maine.

Recent Developments: For the year ended Dec 26 2004, net income decreased 3.3% to $292,557 thousand from net income of $302,655 thousand a year earlier. Revenues were $3,303,642 thousand, up 2.4% from $3,227,200 thousand the year before. Operating income was $509,953 thousand versus an income of $539,550 thousand in the prior year, a decrease of 5.5%. Total direct expense was $1,475,548 thousand versus $1,428,795 thousand in the prior year, an increase of 3.3%. Total indirect expense was $1,318,141 thousand versus $1,258,855 thousand in the prior year, an increase of 4.7%.

Prospects: On Feb 17 2005, Co. announced that it had reached an agreement to acquire About, Inc., a on-line consumer information provider, from PRIMEDIA Inc. in an all-cash transaction valued at approximately $410.0 million. The acquisition is subject to customary regulatory approvals and is expected to be completed late this quarter or early in the second quarter of fiscal 2005. About, Inc., through its Web site About.com, reaches an audience of 22.0 million visitors each month. Its network of nearly 500 experts, create web sites on topics from personal finance to consumer electronics to history and geography. Going forward, Co. expects strong revenue and profit growth from the acquisition.

Financial Data

(US$ in Thousands)	12/26/2004	12/28/2003	12/29/2002	12/30/2001	12/31/2000	12/26/1999	12/27/1998	12/28/1997
Earnings Per Share	1.96	1.98	1.94	2.78	2.32	1.73	1.45	1.33
Cash Flow Per Share	3.02	3.11	1.81	3.01	3.45	3.43	2.64	2.35
Tang Book Value Per Share	N.M.	N.M.	N.M.	N.M.	N.M.	0.83	1.12	1.81
Dividends Per Share	0.610	0.570	0.530	0.490	0.450	0.410	0.370	0.320
Dividend Payout %	31.12	28.79	27.32	17.63	19.40	23.70	25.52	24.06
Income Statement								
Total Revenue	3,303,642	3,227,200	3,079,007	3,015,958	3,489,455	3,130,629	2,936,705	2,866,418
EBITDA	665,193	692,351	690,169	581,061	965,157	786,675	737,090	653,377
Depn & Amortn	146,788	147,747	153,347	194,008	227,973	197,493	188,237	173,897
Income Before Taxes	476,645	499,847	491,387	339,854	673,086	538,464	505,520	437,365
Income Taxes	183,499	197,762	191,640	137,632	275,550	228,287	218,890	175,064
Net Income	292,557	302,655	299,747	444,672	397,536	310,177	278,914	262,301
Average Shares	149,357	152,840	154,805	160,081	171,597	179,244	192,846	197,150
Balance Sheet								
Current Assets	613,893	603,311	563,056	559,890	610,766	614,908	512,817	615,835
Total Assets	3,949,857	3,804,739	3,633,842	3,438,684	3,606,679	3,495,802	3,465,109	3,639,018
Current Liabilities	1,119,749	760,364	735,736	860,876	877,370	673,514	624,856	697,487
Long-Term Obligations	471,474	646,909	728,789	598,703	636,866	598,327	597,818	535,428
Total Liabilities	2,414,695	2,321,086	2,364,535	2,289,031	2,325,516	2,047,144	1,933,639	1,910,956
Stockholders' Equity	1,400,542	1,392,242	1,269,307	1,149,653	1,281,163	1,448,658	1,531,470	1,728,062
Shares Outstanding	146,105	149,878	152,216	151,456	162,373	173,818	181,613	193,258
Statistical Record								
Return on Assets %	7.57	8.16	8.50	12.66	11.01	8.94	7.87	7.33
Return on Equity %	21.01	22.81	24.85	36.69	28.65	20.87	17.16	15.69
EBITDA Margin %	20.14	21.45	22.42	19.27	27.66	25.13	25.10	22.79
Net Margin %	8.86	9.38	9.74	14.74	11.39	9.91	9.50	9.15
Asset Turnover	0.85	0.87	0.87	0.86	0.97	0.90	0.83	0.80
Current Ratio	0.55	0.79	0.77	0.65	0.70	0.91	0.82	0.88
Debt to Equity	0.34	0.46	0.57	0.52	0.50	0.41	0.39	0.31
Price Range	49.13-38.72	48.84-42.87	52.79-39.98	47.60-37.42	49.19-33.19	48.75-26.94	40.50-21.00	33.19-18.31
P/E Ratio	25.07-19.76	24.67-21.65	27.21-20.61	17.12-13.46	21.20-14.30	28.18-15.57	27.93-14.48	24.95-13.77
Average Yield %	1.40	1.25	1.13	1.15	1.11	1.12	1.13	1.31

Address: 229 West 43rd Street, New York, NY 10036
Telephone: (212) 556-1234
Fax: (212) 556-4647

Web Site: www.nytco.com
Officers: Arthur Sulzberger Jr. - Chmn. Michael Golden - Vice-Chmn.

Auditors: Deloitte & Touche LLP
Investor Contact: 212-556-1981

NEWELL RUBBERMAID, INC.

Exchange	Symbol	Price	52Wk Range	Yield	P/E
NYS	NWL	$21.94 (3/31/2005)	24.89-19.11	3.83	N/A

*7 Year Price Score 63.36 ***NYSE Composite Index=100** ***12 Month Price Score 91.67**

Interim Earnings (Per Share)

Qtr.	Mar	Jun	Sep	Dec
2001	0.14	0.27	0.31	0.26
2002	(1.73)	0.33	0.29	0.36
2003	0.06	0.27	0.27	(0.77)
2004	(0.27)	0.22	(0.83)	0.46

Interim Dividends (Per Share)

Amt	Decl	Ex	Rec	Pay
0.21Q	5/13/2004	5/26/2004	5/28/2004	6/16/2004
0.21Q	8/5/2004	8/12/2004	8/16/2004	9/3/2004
0.21Q	11/4/2004	11/12/2004	11/16/2004	12/3/2004
0.21Q	2/11/2005	2/17/2005	2/22/2005	3/11/2005

Indicated Div: $0.84

Valuation Analysis

Forecast P/E	15.19	No of Institutions	
	(4/7/2005)	378	
Market Cap	$6.0 Billion	Shares	
Book Value	1.8 Billion	229,254,496	
Price/Book	3.41	% Held	
Price/Sales	0.89	83.43	

Business Summary: Plastics (MIC: 11.7 SIC: 089 NAIC: 26199)

Newell Rubbermaid manufactures name-brand consumer products. Co.'s offerings consist of name-brand consumer products in five business segments. The Cleaning & Organization segment produces organization, storage, food storage, cleaning and refuse products. The Office Products segment produces Ballpoint/roller ball pens, markers, highlighters, pencils, office products and art supplies. The Home Fashions segment produces drapery houseware, window treatments and frames. The Tools & Hardware segment produces hand tools, power tool accessories, manual paint applicators, cabinet hardware and propane torches. Other products include cookware, glassware, hair care and infant and juvenile products.

Recent Developments: For the year ended Dec 31 2004, net loss was $116,100 thousand versus net loss of $46,600 thousand a year earlier. Revenues were $6,748,400 thousand, down 2.2% from $6,899,000 thousand the year before. Operating income was $194,600 thousand versus an income of $497,200 thousand in the prior year, a decrease of 60.9%. Total direct expense was $4,857,900 thousand versus $4,961,800 thousand in the prior year, a decrease of 2.1%. Total indirect expense was $1,695,900 thousand versus $1,440,000 thousand in the prior year, an increase of 17.8%.

Prospects: For full-year 2005, Co. expects internal sales growth to be flat, and overall sales movement to be in the range of a decline of 1.0% to an addition of 1.0%. This range reflects Co.'s strategic decision to exit approximately $200.0 million of lower-margin product lines. Co. expects diluted earnings per share from continuing operations for the full-year 2005 to be in the range of $1.38 to $1.48, excluding a non-cash loss of approximately $75.0 to $95.0 million related to Co.'s intended sale of its European Curver business. For the first quarter 2005, Co. expects internal sales to decline 1.0% to 3.0% and diluted earnings per share from continuing operations to range from $0.24 to $0.28.

Financial Data

(US$ in Thousands)	12/31/2004	12/31/2003	12/31/2002	12/31/2001	12/31/2000	12/31/1999	12/31/1998	12/31/1997
Earnings Per Share	(0.42)	(0.17)	(0.76)	0.99	1.57	0.34	2.38	1.82
Cash Flow Per Share	2.40	2.82	3.25	3.25	2.32	1.97	1.86	2.43
Tang Book Value Per Share	N.M.	N.M.	N.M.	0.44	0.97	2.38	1.57	2.20
Dividends Per Share	0.840	0.840	0.840	0.840	0.840	0.800	0.720	0.640
Dividend Payout %	N.M.	N.M.	N.M.	84.85	53.50	235.29	30.25	35.16
Income Statement								
Total Revenue	6,748,400	7,750,000	7,453,900	6,909,319	6,934,747	6,413,074	3,720,040	3,234,261
EBITDA	454,700	432,600	859,800	882,093	1,108,096	602,691	892,769	684,363
Depn & Amortn	249,100	278,200	280,700	328,775	292,576	271,731	147,526	129,943
Income Before Taxes	86,300	20,100	468,500	415,865	685,487	230,939	684,846	480,799
Income Taxes	105,400	66,700	157,000	151,230	263,912	135,502	288,690	190,397
Net Income	(116,100)	(46,600)	(203,400)	264,635	421,575	95,437	396,156	290,402
Average Shares	274,400	274,100	268,000	267,048	278,365	281,806	173,041	160,214
Balance Sheet								
Current Assets	3,012,400	3,000,200	3,080,000	2,850,652	2,896,652	2,738,569	1,591,075	1,381,620
Total Assets	6,665,900	7,480,700	7,388,900	7,266,122	7,261,825	6,724,088	4,327,912	3,943,812
Current Liabilities	1,871,300	2,022,000	2,614,400	2,533,852	1,550,826	1,629,883	821,456	664,025
Long-Term Obligations	2,424,300	2,868,600	1,856,600	1,365,001	2,314,774	1,455,779	866,211	783,980
Total Liabilities	4,901,700	5,464,400	5,325,400	4,832,746	4,813,184	4,027,082	2,415,905	2,131,046
Stockholders' Equity	1,764,200	2,016,300	2,063,500	2,433,376	2,448,641	2,697,006	1,912,007	1,714,294
Shares Outstanding	274,400	274,400	267,400	266,800	266,600	281,900	162,700	159,200
Statistical Record								
Return on Assets %	N.M.	N.M.	N.M.	3.64	6.01	1.73	9.58	8.36
Return on Equity %	N.M.	N.M.	N.M.	10.84	16.34	4.14	21.85	18.12
EBITDA Margin %	6.74	5.58	11.53	12.77	15.98	9.40	24.00	21.16
Net Margin %	N.M.	N.M.	N.M.	3.83	6.08	1.49	10.65	8.98
Asset Turnover	0.95	1.04	1.02	0.95	0.99	1.16	0.90	0.93
Current Ratio	1.61	1.48	1.18	1.13	1.87	1.68	1.94	2.08
Debt to Equity	1.37	1.42	0.90	0.56	0.95	0.54	0.45	0.46
Price Range	26.16-19.11	31.41-21.00	35.99-26.50	29.21-21.20	31.25-18.69	52.00-26.25	54.44-37.81	43.25-30.38
P/E Ratio	N/A	N/A	N/A	29.51-21.41	19.90-11.90	152.94-77.21	22.87-15.89	23.76-16.69
Average Yield %	3.68	3.20	2.64	3.30	3.40	1.99	1.56	1.68

Address: 10 B Glenlake Parkway, St. 600, Atlanta, GA 30328
Telephone: (770) 670-2232

Web Site: www.newellrubbermaid.com
Officers: William D. Marohn - Chmn. Joseph Galli Jr. - Pres., C.E.O.

Auditors: Ernst & Young LLP
Investor Contact: 815-381-8150

NEWFIELD EXPLORATION CO.

Exchange	Symbol	Price	52Wk Range	Yield	P/E
NYS	NFX	$74.26 (3/31/2005)	76.30-47.28	N/A	14.12

*7 Year Price Score 137.86 ***NYSE Composite Index=100** ***12 Month Price Score 111.59**

Interim Earnings (Per Share)

Qtr.	Mar	Jun	Sep	Dec
2001	1.22	1.18	0.91	(0.76)
2002	0.37	0.36	0.21	0.68
2003	1.17	0.82	0.88	0.71
2004	1.38	1.18	1.27	1.44

Interim Dividends (Per Share)

No Dividends Paid

Valuation Analysis

Forecast P/E	11.22	No of Institutions	
	(4/7/2005)	290	
Market Cap	$4.6 Billion	Shares	
Book Value	2.0 Billion	54,399,064	
Price/Book	2.30	% Held	
Price/Sales	3.43	86.21	

Business Summary: Oil and Gas (MIC: 14.2 SIC: 311 NAIC: 11111)

Newfield Exploration is engaged in the exploration, development and acquisition of crude oil and natural gas properties. Co.'s areas of operation include the Gulf of Mexico, the U.S. onshore Gulf Coast, the Anadarko and Arkoma Basins, China's Bohai Bay and the North Sea. As of Dec 31 2004, Co. had proved reserves of 1.8 Tcfe. Of those reserves: 70% were natural gas; 75% were proved developed; 28% were located in the Gulf of Mexico; 70% were located onshore in the U.S.; and 2% were located internationally. Co. has extensive experience in the Gulf of Mexico and it is where Co. continues to invest the portion of Co.'s capital program.

Recent Developments: For the year ended Dec 31 2004, net income increased 56.4% to $312,100 thousand from net income of $199,500 thousand a year earlier. Revenues were $1,352,700 thousand, up 33.0% from $1,017,000 thousand the year before. Operating income was $551,000 thousand versus an income of $382,800 thousand in the prior year, an increase of 43.9%. Total direct expense was $194,300 thousand versus $157,400 thousand in the prior year, an increase of 23.4%. Total indirect expense was $607,400 thousand versus $476,800 thousand in the prior year, an increase of 27.4%.

Prospects: Co. increased its production volumes 10.0% in 2004 and raised its 2005 production guidance to between 262.00 billion cubic feet equivalent (bcfe) to 272.00 bcfe, representing an increase of about 8.0% to 12.0% over 2004 production. Meanwhile, Co. added 725 bcfe of proved reserved in 2004. Separately, Co. signed ventures to drill two ultra-deep exploration wells in its Treasure Project, located on the Gulf of Mexico shelf, and began drilling the first well, Blackbeard West, on Feb 9 2005. Looking ahead to 2005, Co. plans to fabricate a production facility for its first successful discovery in the North Sea with first production expected in late 2006.

Financial Data

(US$ in Thousands)	12/31/2004	12/31/2003	12/31/2002	12/31/2001	12/31/2000	12/31/1999	12/31/1998	12/31/1997
Earnings Per Share	5.26	3.57	1.61	2.56	2.93	0.81	(1.55)	1.07
Cash Flow Per Share	17.06	12.32	8.95	11.35	7.45	4.49	3.93	...
Tang Book Value Per Share	31.27	24.04	19.51	16.10	12.19	8.99	8.01	8.12
Income Statement								
Total Revenue	1,352,700	1,016,986	661,750	749,405	526,642	281,967	195,685	199,399
EBITDA	1,002,200	768,180	439,875	488,902	403,067	214,231	43,315	158,567
Depn & Amortn	471,400	394,701	303,274	282,567	191,182	152,644	123,147	94,000
Income Before Taxes	498,900	331,619	110,885	191,360	204,689	52,015	(88,376)	62,421
Income Taxes	186,800	120,713	37,038	67,612	69,980	18,811	(30,677)	21,818
Net Income	312,100	199,489	73,847	118,954	132,349	33,204	(57,699)	40,603
Average Shares	59,300	56,744	49,589	48,893	47,227	42,293	37,311	38,017
Balance Sheet								
Current Assets	391,600	238,916	238,827	230,604	179,149	125,929	45,269	64,766
Total Assets	4,327,500	2,733,089	2,315,753	1,663,371	1,023,250	781,561	629,311	553,621
Current Liabilities	474,000	300,218	295,807	165,031	141,060	90,727	54,075	64,394
Long-Term Obligations	992,400	643,459	709,615	428,631	133,711	124,679	208,650	129,623
Total Liabilities	2,310,600	1,364,511	1,162,317	809,643	360,045	262,793	305,363	261,573
Stockholders' Equity	2,016,900	1,368,578	1,009,231	709,978	519,455	375,018	323,948	292,048
Shares Outstanding	62,418	56,255	51,730	44,101	42,607	41,734	40,429	35,976
Statistical Record								
Return on Assets %	8.82	7.90	3.71	8.86	14.63	4.71	N.M.	7.33
Return on Equity %	18.39	16.78	8.59	19.35	29.51	9.50	N.M.	13.90
EBITDA Margin %	74.09	75.53	66.47	65.24	76.54	75.98	22.14	79.52
Net Margin %	23.07	19.62	11.16	15.87	25.13	11.78	N.M.	20.36
Asset Turnover	0.38	0.40	0.33	0.56	0.58	0.40	0.33	36.02
Current Ratio	0.83	0.80	0.81	1.40	1.27	1.39	0.84	1.01
Debt to Equity	0.49	0.47	0.70	0.60	0.26	0.33	0.64	0.44
Price Range	64.55-44.49	45.20-31.63	39.15-28.20	45.81-26.85	48.44-24.63	35.00-15.50	26.50-15.69	32.31-17.63
P/E Ratio	12.27-8.46	12.66-8.86	24.32-17.52	17.90-10.49	16.53-8.40	43.21-19.14	N/A	30.20-16.47

Address: 363 North Sam Houston Parkway East, Suite 2020, Houston, TX 77060
Telephone: (281) 847-6000
Fax: (281) 405-4242

Web Site: www.newfld.com
Officers: David A. Trice - Chmn., Pres., C.E.O. David F. Schaible - Exec. V.P., Opers., Acquisitions

Auditors: PricewaterhouseCoopers LLP
Transfer Agents: JPMorgan Chase Manhattan Bank

NEWMONT MINING CORP. (HOLDING CO.)

Exchange	Symbol	Price	52Wk Range	Yield	P/E
NYS	NEM	$42.25 (3/31/2005)	49.65-35.41	0.95	42.68

7 Year Price Score 133.09 *NYSE Composite Index=100* **12 Month Price Score 94.49**

TRADING VOLUME (thousand shares)

Interim Earnings (Per Share)

Qtr.	Mar	Jun	Sep	Dec
2001	(0.20)	(0.17)	0.11	0.10
2002	(0.04)	0.16	0.06	0.17
2003	0.29	0.22	0.28	0.36
2004	0.20	0.08	0.29	0.42

Interim Dividends (Per Share)

Amt	Decl	Ex	Rec	Pay
0.075Q	4/28/2004	5/28/2004	6/2/2004	6/23/2004
0.075Q	7/28/2004	9/1/2004	9/3/2004	9/22/2004
0.10Q	10/27/2004	11/29/2004	12/1/2004	12/21/2004
0.10Q	2/2/2005	3/1/2005	3/3/2005	3/24/2005

Indicated Div: $0.40

Valuation Analysis

Forecast P/E	N/A	No of Institutions 438
Market Cap	$18.8 Billion	Shares
Book Value	7.9 Billion	294,755,808
Price/Book	2.37	% Held
Price/Sales	4.16	71.89

Business Summary: Precious Metals (MIC: 14.1 SIC: 041 NAIC: 12221)

Newmont Mining is engaged in the production of gold, the exploration for gold and the acquisition and development of gold properties. Co. produces gold from mines in Nevada and California, and, outside of the United States, from operations in Australia, Peru, Indonesia, Canada, Uzbekistan, Turkey, Bolivia, New Zealand and Mexico. Co. also produces copper concentrates from a copper/gold deposit at a location in Indonesia. As of Dec 31 2003, Co. had gold reserves of 91.3 million equity ounces and an aggregate land position of approximately 60,000 square miles (155,840 square kilometers).

Recent Developments: For the year ended Dec 31 2004, net income decreased 6.8% to $443,327 thousand from net income of $475,667 thousand a year earlier. Revenues were $4,524,185 thousand, up 43.3% from $3,157,756 thousand the year before. Total direct expense was $2,303,230 thousand versus $1,700,262 thousand in the prior year, an increase of 35.5%. Total indirect expense was $1,130,227 thousand versus $894,777 thousand in the prior year, an increase of 26.3%.

Prospects: For full-year 2005, Co. expects decreased equity gold sales due to the assumed sale of its Ovacik unit in the first quarter of 2005. Also, Co. expects increased cash costs due to lower ore grades processed and slightly lower than expected recovery rates, as well as assumed ongoing U.S. dollar weakness and higher consumable costs. Guidance for exploration, research and development expenditures for fiscal 2005 is between $170.0 million and $200.0 million on a consolidated basis, reflecting continued optimization of feasibility studies at Minas Conga in Peru, and ongoing exploration and advanced study efforts at Ahafo and Akyem in Ghana, as well as Elang and Martabe in Indonesia.

Financial Data

(US$ in Thousands)	12/31/2004	12/31/2003	12/31/2002	12/31/2001	12/31/2000	12/31/1999	12/31/1998	12/31/1997
Earnings Per Share	0.99	1.15	0.41	(0.16)	(0.11)	0.15	(2.47)	0.44
Cash Flow Per Share	3.50	1.43	1.81	1.95	3.02	2.40	2.35	1.82
Tang Book Value Per Share	11.02	6.52	2.44	7.49	8.58	8.66	8.61	10.17
Dividends Per Share	0.300	0.170	0.090	0.120	0.120	0.12	0.120	0.390
Dividend Payout %	30.30	14.78	21.95	N.M.	N.M.	80.00	N.M.	88.64
Income Statement								
Total Revenue	4,524,185	3,214,059	2,745,007	1,664,101	1,566,673	1,431,588	1,474,913	1,627,992
EBITDA	1,873,864	1,541,949	759,119	305,916	519,387	418,705	(120,184)	452,934
Depn & Amortn	700,615	527,984	542,793	349,144	415,349	296,367	341,701	321,019
Income Before Taxes	1,099,005	925,386	216,326	(43,228)	104,038	122,338	(461,885)	131,915
Income Taxes	275,882	206,950	19,900	(52,817)	11,310	14,400	(180,876)	(7,900)
Net Income	443,327	475,667	158,061	(23,279)	(18,947)	24,793	(393,383)	68,377
Average Shares	446,511	413,723	372,975	195,059	168,386	167,800	159,010	156,347
Balance Sheet								
Current Assets	2,721,149	2,360,468	1,113,256	709,460	511,902	534,053	513,080	641,370
Total Assets	12,770,688	11,050,173	10,154,518	4,062,405	3,510,704	3,383,382	3,186,754	3,613,982
Current Liabilities	1,101,005	834,020	693,463	485,811	290,668	273,873	212,343	394,531
Long-Term Obligations	1,311,260	886,633	1,701,282	1,089,718	976,446	1,014,193	1,201,131	1,179,410
Total Liabilities	4,057,968	3,318,720	4,380,712	2,330,878	1,856,262	1,805,377	1,654,413	1,854,625
Stockholders' Equity	7,937,660	7,384,935	5,419,248	1,480,048	1,466,388	1,451,648	1,439,533	1,591,087
Shares Outstanding	445,599	454,495	401,991	196,150	170,943	167,658	167,191	156,493
Statistical Record								
Return on Assets %	3.71	4.49	2.22	N.M.	N.M.	0.75	N.M.	2.40
Return on Equity %	5.77	7.43	4.58	N.M.	N.M.	1.72	N.M.	5.23
EBITDA Margin %	41.42	47.98	27.65	18.38	33.15	29.25	N.M.	27.82
Net Margin %	9.80	14.80	5.76	N.M.	N.M.	1.73	N.M.	4.20
Asset Turnover	0.38	0.30	0.39	0.44	0.45	0.44	0.43	0.57
Current Ratio	2.47	2.83	1.61	1.46	1.76	1.95	2.42	1.63
Debt to Equity	0.17	0.12	0.31	0.74	0.67	0.70	0.83	0.74
Price Range	49.75-35.41	50.00-24.37	32.00-18.70	24.83-14.09	27.75-13.00	29.75-16.44	34.63-13.69	47.50-27.00
P/E Ratio	50.25-35.77	43.48-21.19	78.05-45.61	N/A	N/A	198.33-109.58	N/A	107.95-61.36
Average Yield %	0.70	0.49	0.34	0.62	0.60	0.52	0.49	1.01

Address: 1700 Lincoln Street, Denver, CO 80203	**Web Site:** www.newmont.com	**Auditors:** PricewaterhouseCoopers LLP
Telephone: (303) 863-7414	**Officers:** Wayne W. Murdy - Chmn., C.E.O. Pierre Lassonde - Pres.	**Investor Contact:** 800-810-6463
Fax: (303) 837-5837		

NICOR INC.

Exchange	Symbol	Price	52Wk Range	Yield	P/E	Div Acheiver
NYS	GAS	$37.09 (3/31/2005)	39.65-32.22	5.01	21.82	17 Years

*7 Year Price Score 83.65   *NYSE Composite Index=100   *12 Month Price Score 96.75

Interim Earnings (Per Share)

Qtr.	Mar	Jun	Sep	Dec
2001	0.85	0.59	0.73	1.00
2002	0.90	0.46	0.68	0.95
2003	1.04	0.54	0.01	0.79
2004	0.44	0.44	(0.26)	1.08

Interim Dividends (Per Share)

Amt	Decl	Ex	Rec	Pay
0.465Q	6/18/2004	6/28/2004	6/30/2004	8/1/2004
0.465Q	7/15/2004	9/28/2004	9/30/2004	11/1/2004
0.465Q	11/18/2004	12/29/2004	12/31/2004	2/1/2005
0.465Q	3/17/2005	3/29/2005	3/31/2005	5/1/2005

Indicated Div: $1.86 (Div. Reinv. Plan)

Valuation Analysis

Forecast P/E	17.80 (4/7/2005)	No of Institutions 205
Market Cap	$1.6 Billion	Shares 27,907,982
Book Value	749.1 Million	% Held
Price/Book	2.18	63.26
Price/Sales	0.60	

TRADING VOLUME (thousand shares)

Business Summary: Gas Utilities (MIC: 7.4 SIC: 924 NAIC: 21210)

NICOR is engaged in the purchase, storage, distribution, transportation, sale, and gathering of natural gas. Co.'s natural gas unit, Northern Illinois Gas, is the largest gas distribution company in Illinois and one of the biggest in the nation. As of Dec 31 2003, Northern Illinois served more than 2.0 million customers in the northern third of the state, generally outside of Chicago. Co. also owns Tropical Shipping Co., a transporter of containerized freight in the Bahamas and Caribbean. Co.'s shipments consist primarily of southbound cargo such as food, building materials and other necessities for developers, manufacturers and residents, as well as tourist-related shipments.

Recent Developments: For the year ended Dec 31 2004, net income decreased 28.7% to $75,100 thousand from net income of $105,300 thousand a year earlier. Revenues were $2,739,700 thousand, up 2.9% from $2,662,700 thousand the year before. Operating income was $2,602,000 thousand versus an income of $2,473,300 thousand in the prior year, an increase of 5.2%. Total direct expense was $1,929,900 thousand versus $1,895,000 thousand in the prior year, an increase of 1.8%. Total indirect expense was $672,100 thousand versus $578,300 thousand in the prior year, an increase of 16.2%.

Prospects: On Feb 28 2005, Co. announced its 2005 annual diluted earnings per common share estimate to be in the range of $1.90 to $2.10. Co.'s noted that its annual earnings guidance for 2005 versus 2004, the latter of which would have been $2.22 per per share when adjusted for a litigation charge, is based on lower projected operating results from its gas distribution segment, due mainly to higher operating and maintenance expenses and depreciation and lower anticipated property sale gains, and higher interest expense, offset in part by projected improved operating results in its shipping segment in 2005. Co. estimates other energy-related businesses earnings will be consistent with levels in 2004.

Financial Data

(US$ in Thousands)	12/31/2004	12/31/2003	12/31/2002	12/31/2001	12/31/2000	12/31/1999	12/31/1998	12/31/1997
Earnings Per Share	1.70	2.38	2.88	3.17	1.00	2.62	2.42	2.61
Cash Flow Per Share	7.18	(0.29)	6.08	10.89	4.97	4.35	7.69	4.33
Tang Book Value Per Share	16.99	17.13	16.55	16.39	15.56	16.80	15.97	15.43
Dividends Per Share	1.860	1.860	1.840	1.760	1.660	1.560	1.480	1.400
Dividend Payout %	109.41	78.15	63.89	55.52	166.00	59.54	61.16	53.64
Income Statement								
Total Revenue	2,739,700	2,662,700	1,897,400	2,544,100	2,298,100	1,615,200	1,465,100	1,992,600
EBITDA	310,800	366,500	379,100	410,800	254,000	375,500	360,600	374,300
Depn & Amortn	166,600	161,700	155,000	148,800	144,300	140,300	136,500	131,200
Income Before Taxes	105,300	169,400	185,600	217,100	61,100	190,100	177,500	196,900
Income Taxes	30,200	59,600	57,600	73,400	14,400	65,700	61,100	69,000
Net Income	75,100	105,300	128,000	143,700	46,700	124,400	116,400	127,900
Average Shares	44,300	44,200	44,300	45,200	46,300	47,400	48,100	48,900
Balance Sheet								
Net PPE	2,549,800	2,484,200	1,796,800	1,768,600	1,729,600	1,735,200	1,731,800	1,735,800
Total Assets	3,975,200	3,797,200	2,899,400	2,574,800	2,885,400	2,451,800	2,364,600	2,394,600
Long-Term Obligations	495,300	495,100	396,200	446,400	347,100	436,100	557,300	550,200
Total Liabilities	3,226,100	3,042,600	2,171,000	1,847,200	2,177,600	1,664,100	1,605,600	1,650,500
Stockholders' Equity	749,100	754,600	728,400	727,600	707,800	787,700	759,000	744,100
Shares Outstanding	44,102	44,040	44,011	44,397	45,491	46,890	47,514	48,217
Statistical Record								
Return on Assets %	1.93	3.14	4.68	5.26	1.75	5.17	4.89	5.29
Return on Equity %	9.96	14.20	17.58	20.02	6.23	16.09	15.49	17.36
EBITDA Margin %	11.34	13.76	19.98	16.15	11.05	23.25	24.61	18.78
Net Margin %	2.74	3.95	6.75	5.65	2.03	7.70	7.94	6.42
PPE Turnover	1.09	1.24	1.06	1.45	1.32	0.93	0.85	1.14
Asset Turnover	0.70	0.80	0.69	0.93	0.86	0.67	0.62	0.82
Debt to Equity	0.66	0.66	0.54	0.61	0.49	0.55	0.73	0.74
Price Range	39.65-32.22	39.10-23.85	48.96-22.75	41.66-34.12	43.56-29.81	42.88-31.31	44.00-37.25	42.56-31.25
P/E Ratio	23.32-18.95	16.43-10.02	17.00-7.90	13.14-10.76	43.56-29.81	16.36-11.95	18.18-15.39	16.31-11.97
Average Yield %	5.28	5.58	4.89	4.58	4.75	4.16	3.64	3.87

Address: 1844 Ferry Road, Naperville, IL 60563-9600	**Web Site:** www.nicor.com	**Auditors:** DELOITTE & TOUCHE LLP
Telephone: (630) 305-9500	**Officers:** Thomas L. Fisher - Chmn., C.E.O. Russ M. Strobel - Pres.	**Transfer Agents:** ComputerShare Investor Services, Chicago, IL
Fax: (630) 983-9328		

NIKE, INC.

Exchange	Symbol	Price	52Wk Range	Yield	P/E
NYS	NKE	$83.31 (3/31/2005)	91.70-66.05	1.20	20.62

*7 Year Price Score 125.63 ***NYSE Composite Index=100** ***12 Month Price Score 99.98**

Interim Earnings (Per Share)

Qtr.	Aug	Nov	Feb	May
2001-02	0.73	0.48	0.46	0.77
2002-03	(0.18)	0.57	0.47	0.92
2003-04	0.98	0.66	0.74	1.13
2004-05	1.21	0.97	...	...

Interim Dividends (Per Share)

Amt	Decl	Ex	Rec	Pay
0.20Q	5/10/2004	6/10/2004	6/14/2004	7/5/2004
0.20Q	8/9/2004	9/9/2004	9/13/2004	10/4/2004
0.25Q	11/22/2004	12/9/2004	12/13/2004	1/3/2005
0.25Q	2/22/2005	3/10/2005	3/14/2005	4/4/2005
		Indicated Div: $1.00		

Valuation Analysis

Forecast P/E	16.62	No of Institutions	
	(4/7/2005)	440	
Market Cap	$22.0 Billion	Shares	
Book Value	5.3 Billion	159,207,824	
Price/Book	4.12	% Held	
Price/Sales	1.68	85.37	

Business Summary: Rubber Products (MIC: 11.6 SIC: 021 NAIC: 16211)

Nike is involved in the design, development and worldwide marketing of footwear, apparel, equipment, and accessory products. Co.'s athletic footwear products are designed for specific athletic use, although some of its products are worn for casual or leisure purposes. Running, basketball, children's, cross-training and women's shoes are some of Co.'s top-selling product categories. Co.'s apparel products cover a wide variety of athletically inspired lifestyle and outdoor activities. As of May 31 2004, Co. sold its products to about 28,000 retail accounts in the U.S. and through a mix of independent distributors, licensees and subsidiaries in over 120 countries.

Recent Developments: For the second quarter ended Nov 30 2004, net income advanced 46.2% to $261.9 million from $179.1 million in the corresponding prior-year quarter. Revenues increased 11.0% to $3.15 billion from $2.84 billion a year earlier. The increased revenues reflected strong growth in Co.'s international regions, as well as growth from its U.S. region. Gross profit climbed 15.7% to $1.39 billion from $1.20 billion the year before, driven by higher footwear in-line pricing margins in the U.S., lower third-party royalties driven by the expiration of the NBA license agreement and a lower level of closeout sales as a percentage of total sales.

Prospects: Co.'s outlook appears favorable, reflecting recent strong top line growth and improved pre-tax income from across its geographic divisions. Additionally, Co. reported worldwide futures orders for athletic footwear and apparel, scheduled for delivery from Mar 2005 through Jul 2005, totaled $5.20 billion, 9.6% higher than such orders reported for the same period last year. Co. noted that about one point of this growth was due to changes in currency exchange rates. By region, futures orders for the U.S. were advanced 9.0%; Europe increased 7.0%; Asia Pacific grew 14.0%; and the Americas climbed 22.0%.

Financial Data

(US$ in Thousands)	6 Mos	3 Mos	05/31/2004	05/31/2003	05/31/2002	05/31/2001	05/31/2000	05/31/1999
Earnings Per Share	4.04	3.73	3.51	1.77	2.44	2.16	2.07	1.57
Cash Flow Per Share	5.69	5.81	5.74	3.47	4.04	2.43	2.75	3.39
Tang Book Value Per Share	18.17	17.06	16.27	14.44	12.78	11.53	10.11	10.30
Dividends Per Share	0.800	0.740	0.680	0.520	0.480	0.480	0.480	0.480
Dividend Payout %	19.79	19.82	19.37	29.38	19.67	22.22	23.19	30.57
Income Statement								
Total Revenue	6,710,100	3,561,800	12,253,100	10,697,000	9,893,000	9,488,800	8,995,100	8,776,900
EBITDA	1,026,300	563,900	1,739,100	1,408,800	1,304,100	1,193,100	1,170,700	1,007,800
Depn & Amortn	117,800	58,400	264,100	242,900	239,200	213,000	206,500	217,600
Income Before Taxes	908,500	505,500	1,450,000	1,123,000	1,017,300	921,400	919,200	746,100
Income Taxes	319,800	178,700	504,400	382,900	349,000	331,700	340,100	294,700
Net Income	588,700	326,800	945,600	474,000	663,300	589,700	579,100	451,400
Average Shares	271,100	269,800	269,700	267,600	272,200	273,300	279,400	288,300
Balance Sheet								
Current Assets	6,050,700	5,621,100	5,512,000	4,679,900	4,157,700	3,625,300	3,596,400	3,264,900
Total Assets	8,558,300	8,052,900	7,891,600	6,713,900	6,443,000	5,819,600	5,856,900	5,247,700
Current Liabilities	2,003,200	1,907,900	2,009,000	2,015,200	1,836,200	1,786,700	2,140,000	1,446,900
Long-Term Obligations	699,000	692,400	682,400	551,600	625,900	435,900	470,300	386,100
Total Liabilities	3,216,000	3,030,800	3,109,900	2,723,200	2,604,000	2,325,100	2,720,900	1,913,100
Stockholders' Equity	5,342,300	5,022,100	4,781,700	3,990,700	3,839,000	3,494,500	3,136,000	3,334,600
Shares Outstanding	264,100	262,500	263,100	263,600	266,100	268,600	269,600	282,300
Statistical Record								
Return on Assets %	13.70	13.39	12.91	7.21	10.82	10.10	10.40	8.48
Return on Equity %	22.49	21.85	21.50	12.11	18.09	17.79	17.85	13.69
EBITDA Margin %	15.29	15.83	14.19	13.17	13.18	12.57	13.01	11.48
Net Margin %	8.77	9.18	7.72	4.43	6.70	6.21	6.44	5.14
Asset Turnover	1.64	1.69	1.67	1.63	1.61	1.63	1.62	1.65
Current Ratio	3.02	2.95	2.74	2.32	2.26	2.03	1.68	2.26
Debt to Equity	0.13	0.14	0.14	0.14	0.16	0.12	0.15	0.12
Price Range	86.43-64.06	78.08-55.39	78.08-49.70	56.76-39.32	63.99-40.81	59.44-35.19	64.13-26.56	65.50-31.75
P/E Ratio	21.39-15.86	20.93-14.85	22.25-14.16	32.07-22.21	26.23-16.73	27.52-16.29	30.98-12.83	41.72-20.22
Average Yield %	1.08	1.07	1.05	1.10	0.92	1.10	1.01	1.02

Address: One Bowerman Drive, Beaverton, OR 97005-6453 **Telephone:** (503) 671-6453 **Fax:** (503) 671-6300	**Web Site:** www.nikebiz.com **Officers:** Philip H. Knight - Chmn. William D. Perez - Pres., C.E.O.	**Auditors:** PricewaterhouseCoopers LLP

99 CENTS ONLY STORES

Exchange	Symbol	Price	52Wk Range	Yield	P/E
NYS	NDN	$13.17 (3/31/2005)	24.80-12.17	N/A	29.93

*7 Year Price Score 66.80 *NYSE Composite Index=100 *12 Month Price Score 88.91

Interim Earnings (Per Share)

Qtr.	Mar	Jun	Sep	Dec
2001	0.14	0.16	0.16	0.23
2002	0.18	0.19	0.19	0.27
2003	0.20	0.21	0.17	0.20
2004	0.13	0.04	0.07	...

Interim Dividends (Per Share)

Amt	Decl	Ex	Rec	Pay
4-for-3	1/19/2000	2/9/2000	1/28/2000	2/8/2000
3-for-2	2/28/2001	3/21/2001	3/14/2001	3/20/2001
4-for-3	3/12/2002	4/4/2002	3/25/2002	4/3/2002

Valuation Analysis

Forecast P/E	47.22	No of Institutions
	(12/29/2003)	144
Market Cap	$915.2 Million	Shares
Book Value	469.4 Million	46,571,576
Price/Book	1.95	% Held
Price/Sales	N/A	67.00

Business Summary: Retail - General (MIC: 5.2 SIC: 331 NAIC: 52990)

99 Cents Only Stores is a deep-discount retailer of primarily name-brand, consumable general merchandise. Co.'s stores offer a wide assortment of regularly available consumer goods and a broad range of first-quality, close-out merchandise. As of Mar 12 2004, Co. operated 194 retail stores with 150 in California, 10 in Nevada, 15 in Arizona and 19 in Texas. These stores have an average size of approximately 21,500 square feet. Co. also sells merchandise through its Bargain Wholesale division at prices generally below normal wholesale levels to retailers, distributors and exporters.

Recent Developments: For the quarter ended Sep 30 2004, net income decreased 61.0% to $4,716 thousand from $12,102 thousand in the year-earlier quarter. Revenues were $238,945 thousand, up 13.0% from $211,536 thousand the year before. Operating income was $6,521 thousand versus an income of $18,123 thousand in the prior-year quarter, a decrease of 64.0%. Total direct expense was $147,865 thousand versus $128,659 thousand in the prior-year quarter, an increase of 14.9%. Total indirect expense was $84,559 thousand versus $64,754 thousand in the prior-year quarter, an increase of 30.6%.

Prospects: Sales are being negatively affected by economic, competitive and executional issues. Accordingly, Co. is in the process of addressing a number of executional issues it has identified in the stores and across the supply chain. Meanwhile, Co. remains encouraged about its overall store model, and believes that its stores in the Texas market will see steady sales growth in the coming year following increased customer awareness through effective marketing and a broad selection of consumables. While the sales for stores in Texas open for a full year are approximately half of Co.'s average, they are generating positive cash flow. Looking ahead, Co. expects to open 25 stores for full-year 2005.

Financial Data

(US$ in Thousands)	9 Mos	6 Mos	3 Mos	12/31/2003	12/31/2002	12/31/2001	12/31/2000	12/31/1999
Earnings Per Share	0.44	0.54	0.71	0.78	0.83	0.69	0.55	0.33
Cash Flow Per Share	0.52	0.04	0.14	1.11	1.03	0.98	0.23	0.39
Tang Book Value Per Share	6.75	6.78	6.93	6.80	5.64	4.60	3.71	2.96
Income Statement								
Total Revenue	706,261	467,316	230,050	862,460	713,942	578,269	451,947	359,958
EBITDA	49,117	34,877	21,115	112,505	109,652	87,744	68,931	61,373
Depn & Amortn	24,524	15,321	7,453	23,643	17,711	12,354	8,666	5,927
Income Before Taxes	27,251	19,494	15,258	91,842	95,348	79,881	63,522	56,505
Income Taxes	10,669	7,629	5,973	35,313	36,374	31,438	24,664	22,367
Net Income	16,582	11,865	9,285	56,529	58,974	48,443	37,808	21,971
Average Shares	69,746	71,828	72,717	72,412	71,181	70,009	68,945	67,969
Balance Sheet								
Current Assets	278,408	252,254	274,397	275,127	244,872	223,119	188,389	122,368
Total Assets	574,309	540,874	561,154	553,238	439,910	352,158	277,285	224,015
Current Liabilities	98,204	58,619	55,065	57,225	38,386	28,817	21,610	16,731
Long-Term Obligations	1,518	1,530	1,542	1,553	1,597	1,637	...	6,442
Total Liabilities	104,902	65,175	61,406	63,352	43,295	32,515	23,752	28,475
Stockholders' Equity	469,407	475,699	499,748	489,886	396,615	319,643	253,533	195,540
Shares Outstanding	69,493	70,116	72,086	72,032	70,369	69,506	68,407	65,975
Statistical Record								
Return on Assets %	11.55	8.77	6.68	11.38	14.89	15.39	13.64	10.41
Return on Equity %	14.13	9.97	7.43	12.75	16.47	16.90	14.91	12.21
EBITDA Margin %	6.95	7.46	9.18	13.04	15.36	15.17	15.25	17.05
Net Margin %	2.35	2.54	4.04	6.55	8.26	8.38	8.37	6.10
Asset Turnover	1.66	1.75	1.64	1.74	1.80	1.84	1.63	1.71
Current Ratio	2.83	4.30	4.98	4.81	6.38	7.74	8.72	7.31
Debt to Equity	N.M.	N.M.	N.M.	N.M.	N.M.	0.01	...	0.03
Price Range	33.79-12.17	36.02-14.10	36.02-23.43	36.02-20.83	32.60-20.31	29.85-13.34	27.66-10.25	19.55-9.42
P/E Ratio	76.80-27.66	66.70-26.11	50.73-33.00	46.18-26.71	39.28-24.47	43.26-19.34	50.28-18.64	59.23-28.55

Address: 4000 Union Pacific Avenue, City of Commerce, CA 90023 **Telephone:** (323) 980-8145 **Fax:** (323) 980-8160	**Web Site:** www.99only.com **Officers:** David Gold - Chmn., C.E.O. Howard Gold - Sr. V.P., Distrib.	**Auditors:** PricewaterhouseCoopers, LLP **Investor Contact:** 323-980-8145

NISOURCE INC. (HOLDING CO.)

Exchange	Symbol	Price	52Wk Range	Yield	P/E
NYS	NI	$22.79 (3/31/2005)	23.14-19.77	4.04	13.90

7 Year Price Score 80.16 *NYSE Composite Index=100 *12 Month Price Score 98.56

Interim Earnings (Per Share)

Qtr.	Mar	Jun	Sep	Dec
2001	0.90	(0.04)	(0.10)	0.26
2002	1.16	0.12	0.11	0.36
2003	0.99	(1.23)	0.06	0.54
2004	0.81	0.13	0.11	0.59

Interim Dividends (Per Share)

Amt	Decl	Ex	Rec	Pay
0.23Q	5/11/2004	7/28/2004	7/30/2004	8/20/2004
0.23Q	8/24/2004	10/27/2004	10/29/2004	11/19/2004
0.23Q	1/6/2005	1/27/2005	1/31/2005	2/18/2005
0.23Q	3/23/2005	4/27/2005	4/29/2005	5/20/2005

Indicated Div: $0.92

Valuation Analysis

Forecast P/E	15.41	No of Institutions	
	(4/7/2005)	335	
Market Cap	$6.2 Billion	Shares	
Book Value	4.8 Billion	198,707,888	
Price/Book	1.29	% Held	
Price/Sales	0.93	73.26	

Business Summary: Electricity (MIC: 7.1 SIC: 931 NAIC: 21121)

NiSource is an energy holding company that provides natural gas, electricity and other products and services to approximately 3.7 million customers from the Gulf Coast through the Midwest to New England as of Dec 31 2003. Co.'s principal subsidiaries include Columbia Energy Resources, Inc., a natural gas distribution, transmission, and storage holding company; Northern Indiana Public Service Company, a gas and electric company providing service to customers in northern Indiana; and Bay State Gas Company, a natural gas distribution company serving customers in New England.

Recent Developments: For the year ended Dec 31 2004, income from continuing operations increased 1.1% to $430,200 thousand from income of $425,700 thousand a year earlier. Net income increased 412.1% to $436,300 thousand from net income of $85,200 thousand a year earlier. Revenues were $6,666,200 thousand, up 6.7% from $6,246,600 thousand the year before. Operating income was $1,072,000 thousand versus an income of $1,116,300 thousand in the prior year, a decrease of 4.0%. Total direct expense was $4,822,200 thousand versus $4,372,200 thousand in the prior year, an increase of 10.3%. Total indirect expense was $772,000 thousand versus $758,100 thousand in the prior year, an increase of 1.8%.

Prospects: Co.'s future prospects appear favorable. Improving economic conditions and continued customer growth are contributing to increased throughput in Co.'s natural gas business and increased electric sales to industrial customers. Meanwhile, results should benefit from Co.'s efforts to renegotiate long-term contracts with its largest customers. In addition, Co. is making notable progress with several major transmission, storage and access expansion initiatives. On Mar 3 2005, Co.'s Columbia Gas Transmission unit announced an open season for a potential expansion of its existing natural gas pipeline system to enable Appalachian producers to transport additional gas supplies to market.

Financial Data

(US$ in Thousands)	12/31/2004	12/31/2003	12/31/2002	12/31/2001	12/31/2000	12/31/1999	12/31/1998	12/31/1997
Earnings Per Share	1.64	0.33	1.75	1.03	1.15	1.27	1.59	1.53
Cash Flow Per Share	3.87	1.82	5.56	5.08	(0.05)	3.64	4.01	3.46
Tang Book Value Per Share	2.14	0.70	1.65	N.M.	N.M.	9.87	9.23	8.10
Dividends Per Share	0.920	1.100	1.160	1.160	1.080	1.035	0.975	0.915
Dividend Payout %	56.10	333.33	66.29	112.62	93.91	81.50	61.32	59.80
Income Statement								
Total Revenue	6,666,200	6,246,600	6,492,300	9,458,700	6,030,700	3,144,576	2,932,778	2,586,541
EBITDA	1,596,900	1,625,700	1,759,700	1,664,700	955,900	876,509	680,026	744,122
Depn & Amortn	531,300	515,900	574,000	671,700	374,200	311,404	256,474	249,804
Income Before Taxes	671,100	659,900	659,600	395,300	277,200	250,862	294,748	295,874
Income Taxes	240,900	234,200	233,900	183,200	130,100	90,448	100,862	105,025
Net Income	436,300	85,200	372,500	216,200	156,900	160,414	193,886	190,849
Average Shares	265,500	261,600	212,800	209,800	135,811	125,339	121,335	123,849
Balance Sheet								
Net PPE	9,384,700	9,304,900	10,068,000	9,554,700	9,546,700	5,230,418	3,748,669	3,752,154
Total Assets	16,988,000	16,623,800	16,896,900	17,374,100	19,696,800	6,835,229	4,986,503	4,937,033
Long-Term Obligations	4,835,900	5,993,400	5,018,000	5,780,600	5,802,700	1,975,184	1,667,965	1,667,925
Total Liabilities	12,119,800	12,126,800	12,292,100	13,471,100	15,803,900	4,997,084	3,694,747	3,527,784
Stockholders' Equity	4,787,100	4,415,900	4,174,900	3,469,400	3,415,200	1,353,504	1,149,708	1,264,788
Shares Outstanding	270,625	262,630	248,860	205,553	205,553	124,139	117,531	147,784
Statistical Record								
Return on Assets %	2.59	0.51	2.17	1.17	1.18	2.71	3.91	4.14
Return on Equity %	9.46	1.98	9.75	6.28	6.56	12.82	16.06	16.14
EBITDA Margin %	23.96	26.03	27.10	17.60	15.85	27.87	23.19	28.77
Net Margin %	6.54	1.36	5.74	2.29	2.60	5.10	6.61	7.38
PPE Turnover	0.71	0.64	0.66	0.99	0.81	0.70	0.78	0.73
Asset Turnover	0.40	0.37	0.38	0.51	0.45	0.53	0.59	0.56
Debt to Equity	1.01	1.36	1.20	1.67	1.70	1.46	1.45	1.32
Price Range	22.78-19.77	21.94-16.46	24.93-14.70	32.18-19.40	31.50-12.88	30.50-16.56	33.63-24.72	24.81-19.06
P/E Ratio	13.89-12.05	66.48-49.88	14.25-8.40	31.24-18.83	27.39-11.20	24.02-13.04	21.15-15.55	16.22-12.46
Average Yield %	4.35	5.65	5.66	4.39	5.23	4.16	3.47	4.39

Address: 801 East 86th Avenue, Merrillville, IN 46410 **Telephone:** (219) 647-5990 **Fax:** (219) 647-6085	Web Site: www.nisource.com **Officers:** Gary L. Neale - Chmn., C.E.O. Robert C. Skaggs Jr. - Pres.	**Auditors:** Deloitte & Touche LLP **Investor Contact:** 219-647-5200

NOBLE CORP.

Exchange	Symbol	Price	52Wk Range	Yield	P/E
NYS	NE	$56.21 (3/31/2005)	58.34-33.95	N/A	44.97

*7 Year Price Score 112.39 *NYSE Composite Index=100 *12 Month Price Score 116.96

Interim Earnings (Per Share)

Qtr.	Mar	Jun	Sep	Dec
1999	0.12	0.21	0.19	0.13
2000	0.19	0.32	0.33	0.38
2001	0.40	0.50	0.58	0.48
2002	0.39	0.43	0.37	0.39

Interim Dividends (Per Share)

No Dividends Paid

Valuation Analysis

Forecast P/E	52.22	No of Institutions
	(4/7/2005)	N/A
Market Cap	$7.4 Billion	Shares
Book Value	2.2 Billion	N/A
Price/Book	3.41	% Held
Price/Sales	7.53	N/A

Business Summary: Oil and Gas (MIC: 14.2 SIC: 381 NAIC: 13111)

Noble is a provider of diversified services for the oil and gas industry. Co. performs contract drilling services with its fleet of 57 offshore drilling units located in key markets worldwide. This fleet consists of 13 semisubmersibles, three drillships, 38 jackup rigs and three submersibles. Approximately 75.0% of Co.'s fleet is deployed in international waters, primarily in the Middle East, Mexico, the North Sea, Brazil, West Africa, India and the Mediterranean Sea. Co. also provides labor contract drilling services, well site and project management services, and engineering services.

Recent Developments: For the year ended Dec 31 2004, net income decreased 12.3% to $146.1 million compared with $166.4 million in the previous year. The decrease in results was largely due to lower average dayrates on Co.'s deepwater assets in the U.S. Gulf of Mexico capable of drilling in water depths of 6,000 or greater, partially offset by higher utilization on international jackups, primarily in West Africa and the Middle East. Operating revenues climbed 7.9% to $1.07 billion from $987.4 million a year earlier. Operating income declined 15.4% to $187.2 million from $221.1 million in 2003.

Prospects: Co. is benefiting from the expansion of its premium fleet of offshore drilling rigs to 60, with the addition of three 300 foot independent leg cantilever jackups financed with net cash provided by operating activities. One unit is under a long-term contract, while a second unit is slated to commence a long-term contract in the first quarter of 2005. Meanwhile, Co. is upgrading the third jackup rig, which will substantially increase in operating capabilities and will cost approximately $30.0 million. As markets continue to tighten, the availability of premium drilling assets is becoming a concern for the industry as exploration and production plans are being developed for 2006 and 2007.

Financial Data

(US$ in Thousands)	12/31/2003	12/31/2002	12/31/2001	12/31/2000	12/31/1999	12/31/1998	12/31/1997	12/31/1996
Earnings Per Share	1.25	1.57	1.96	1.22	0.64	1.23	1.93	0.66
Cash Flow Per Share	2.77	3.37	3.39	2.32	1.92	2.01	1.55	1.25
Tang Book Value Per Share	16.48	15.10	13.47	11.80	10.60	10.00	8.77	7.01
Income Statement								
Total Revenue	987,380	986,356	1,002,329	882,600	705,903	788,241	713,195	514,253
EBITDA	409,865	440,416	539,246	391,672	237,787	301,120	461,073	166,467
Depn & Amortn	182,590	154,469	141,502	110,787	88,981	71,691	77,922	52,159
Income Before Taxes	186,984	243,325	349,992	226,307	125,486	230,919	379,613	101,959
Income Taxes	20,568	33,822	86,082	60,753	30,184	68,887	115,731	22,662
Net Income	166,416	209,503	262,922	165,554	84,469	162,032	257,197	78,637
Average Shares	133,007	133,452	134,174	135,461	132,597	132,269	133,455	110,252
Balance Sheet								
Current Assets	421,959	465,643	494,049	379,132	290,625	438,209	265,015	388,477
Total Assets	3,189,633	3,065,714	2,750,740	2,595,531	2,432,324	2,178,632	1,505,811	1,367,407
Current Liabilities	244,023	280,660	207,549	205,428	233,336	349,489	152,890	151,500
Long-Term Obligations	541,907	589,562	550,131	650,291	730,893	460,842	138,139	239,506
Total Liabilities	1,011,208	1,076,504	972,421	1,018,812	1,034,282	868,159	356,757	442,158
Stockholders' Equity	2,178,425	1,989,210	1,778,319	1,576,719	1,398,042	1,310,473	1,149,054	925,249
Shares Outstanding	132,194	131,743	132,015	133,591	131,882	131,101	130,988	131,980
Statistical Record								
Return on Assets %	5.32	7.20	9.84	6.57	3.66	8.80	17.90	7.44
Return on Equity %	7.99	11.12	15.67	11.10	6.24	13.18	24.80	10.83
EBITDA Margin %	41.51	44.65	53.80	44.38	33.69	38.20	64.65	32.37
Net Margin %	16.85	21.24	26.23	18.76	11.97	20.56	36.06	15.29
Asset Turnover	0.32	0.34	0.37	0.35	0.31	0.43	0.50	0.49
Current Ratio	1.73	1.66	2.38	1.85	1.25	1.25	1.73	2.56
Debt to Equity	0.25	0.30	0.31	0.41	0.52	0.35	0.12	0.26
Price Range	37.39-30.72	45.79-28.15	53.20-21.80	52.56-27.88	32.88-12.06	33.88-11.00	38.00-16.00	21.38-8.44
P/E Ratio	29.91-24.58	29.17-17.93	27.14-11.12	43.08-22.85	51.37-18.85	27.54-8.94	19.69-8.29	32.39-12.78

Address: 13135 South Dairy Ashford, Suite 800, Sugar Land, TX 77478 **Telephone:** (281) 276-6100 **Fax:** (281) 491-2091	**Web Site:** www.noblecorp.com **Officers:** James C. Day - Chmn., C.E.O. Mark A. Jackson - Sr. V.P., C.O.O.	**Auditors:** PricewaterhouseCoopers LLP

NOBLE ENERGY, INC.

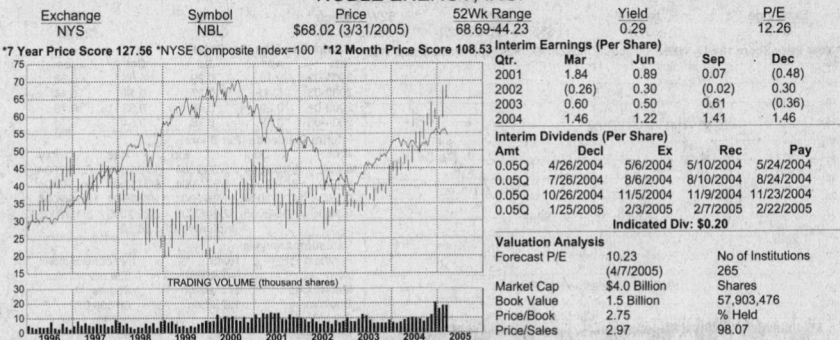

Exchange	Symbol	Price	52Wk Range	Yield	P/E
NYS	NBL	$68.02 (3/31/2005)	68.69-44.23	0.29	12.26

*7 Year Price Score 127.56 *NYSE Composite Index=100 *12 Month Price Score 108.53

Interim Earnings (Per Share)

Qtr.	Mar	Jun	Sep	Dec
2001	1.84	0.89	0.07	(0.48)
2002	(0.26)	0.30	(0.02)	0.30
2003	0.60	0.50	0.61	(0.36)
2004	1.46	1.22	1.41	1.46

Interim Dividends (Per Share)

Amt	Decl	Ex	Rec	Pay
0.05Q	4/26/2004	5/6/2004	5/10/2004	5/24/2004
0.05Q	7/26/2004	8/6/2004	8/10/2004	8/24/2004
0.05Q	10/26/2004	11/5/2004	11/9/2004	11/23/2004
0.05Q	1/25/2005	2/3/2005	2/7/2005	2/22/2005

Indicated Div: $0.20

Valuation Analysis

Forecast P/E	10.23	No of Institutions
	(4/7/2005)	265
Market Cap	$4.0 Billion	Shares
Book Value	1.5 Billion	57,903,476
Price/Book	2.75	% Held
Price/Sales	2.97	98.07

Business Summary: Oil and Gas (MIC: 14.2 SIC: 311 NAIC: 11111)

Noble Energy is engaged in the exploration, production and marketing of crude oil and natural gas. Co.'s domestic areas consist of: offshore in the Gulf of Mexico and California; the Gulf Coast Region, which includes Louisiana, New Mexico and Texas; the Mid-Continent Region, which includes Oklahoma and Kansas; and the Rocky Mountain Region, including Colorado, Montana, North Dakota, Wyoming and California. Co.'s international operations include Argentina, China, Ecuador, Equatorial Guinea, the Mediterranean Sea (Israel), and the North Sea. As of Dec 31 2003, proved reserves were: natural gas and casinghead gas, 1.60 trillion cubic feet; crude oil and condensate, 201.5 million barrels.

Recent Developments: For the year ended Dec 31 2004, income from continuing operations increased 249.1% to $313,850 thousand from income of $89,892 thousand a year earlier. Net income increased 321.5% to $328,710 thousand from net income of $77,992 thousand a year earlier. Revenues were $1,351,176 thousand, up 34.3% from $1,005,950 thousand the year before. Total direct expense was $290,757 thousand versus $270,475 thousand in the prior year, an increase of 7.5%. Total indirect expense was $621,185 thousand versus $700,713 thousand in the prior year, a decrease of 11.3%.

Prospects: On Dec 16 2004, Co. agreed to acquire Patina Oil & Gas Corp. for about $2.76 billion, plus assumed debt. Denver, CO- based Patina owns oil and gas fields mainly in Colorado, Texas, Oklahoma and New Mexico, and had 2003 revenue of $406.7 million. Co. believes the deal should raise its reserves and production by more than 50.0%. For fiscal year 2005, Co. expects production growth of 10.0%. Terms of the deal, scheduled to be completed by April 2005, call for Co. to pay approximately $1.10 billion in cash and 27.0 million of its shares and assume an undisclosed amount of debt.

Financial Data

(US$ in Thousands)	12/31/2004	12/31/2003	12/31/2002	12/31/2001	12/31/2000	12/31/1999	12/31/1998	12/31/1997
Earnings Per Share	5.55	1.36	0.31	2.33	3.38	0.86	(2.88)	1.73
Cash Flow Per Share	12.12	10.58	8.82	11.24	10.16	5.68	5.69	7.83
Tang Book Value Per Share	24.74	18.77	17.60	17.72	15.15	11.98	11.27	14.29
Dividends Per Share	0.200	0.170	0.160	0.160	0.160	0.160	0.160	0.160
Dividend Payout %	3.60	12.50	51.61	6.87	4.73	18.60	N.M.	9.25
Income Statement								
Total Revenue	1,351,176	1,010,986	1,443,728	1,572,263	1,393,591	909,842	911,616	1,116,623
EBITDA	921,305	567,786	405,306	551,790	578,000	384,832	118,194	512,954
Depn & Amortn	357,037	379,170	314,998	301,229	246,875	264,160	321,144	308,500
Income Before Taxes	516,041	141,639	42,599	224,610	299,483	77,631	(246,708)	157,685
Income Taxes	202,191	51,747	24,947	91,035	107,886	28,170	(82,683)	58,407
Net Income	328,710	77,992	17,652	133,575	191,597	49,461	(164,025)	99,278
Average Shares	59,226	57,539	57,763	57,303	56,755	57,349	56,955	57,421
Balance Sheet								
Current Assets	734,302	478,387	310,374	351,571	271,261	147,914	188,289	258,634
Total Assets	3,443,171	2,842,649	2,730,015	2,479,848	1,879,280	1,450,351	1,686,080	1,875,484
Current Liabilities	665,004	654,718	471,754	380,585	325,417	184,471	139,166	217,020
Long-Term Obligations	880,256	776,021	977,116	837,177	525,494	445,319	745,143	644,967
Total Liabilities	1,983,183	1,769,076	1,720,629	1,469,650	1,029,598	766,742	1,044,000	1,062,495
Stockholders' Equity	1,459,988	1,073,573	1,009,386	1,010,198	849,682	683,609	642,080	812,989
Shares Outstanding	59,022	57,194	57,362	57,005	56,090	57,045	56,981	56,899
Statistical Record								
Return on Assets %	10.43	2.80	0.68	6.13	11.48	3.15	N.M.	5.18
Return on Equity %	25.88	7.49	1.75	14.36	24.92	7.46	N.M.	12.95
EBITDA Margin %	68.19	56.16	28.07	35.10	41.48	42.30	12.97	45.94
Net Margin %	24.33	7.71	1.22	8.50	13.75	5.44	N.M.	8.89
Asset Turnover	0.43	0.36	0.55	0.72	0.83	0.58	0.51	0.58
Current Ratio	1.10	0.73	0.66	0.92	0.83	0.80	1.35	1.19
Debt to Equity	0.60	0.72	0.97	0.83	0.62	0.65	1.16	0.79
Price Range	63.95-42.74	45.80-32.58	40.45-27.51	50.35-27.78	47.69-19.38	33.75-19.69	44.50-22.50	49.88-32.56
P/E Ratio	11.52-7.70	33.68-23.96	130.48-88.74	21.61-11.92	14.11-5.73	39.24-22.89	N/A	28.83-18.82
Average Yield %	0.39	0.46	0.45	0.42	0.47	0.47	0.47	0.39

Address: 100 Glenborough Drive, Suite 100, Houston, TX 77067	Web Site: www.nobleenergyinc.com	Auditors: KPMG LLP
Telephone: (281) 872-3100	Officers: Charles D. Davidson - Chmn., Pres., C.E.O.	Investor Contact: 281-872-3100
Fax: (281) 872-3111	Susan M. Cunningham - Sr. V.P., Explor.	Transfer Agents: Wachovia Bank N.A., Charlotte, NC

NORDSTROM, INC.

Exchange	Symbol	Price	52Wk Range	Yield	P/E
NYS	JWN	$55.38 (3/31/2005)	55.38-35.44	0.94	21.98

*7 Year Price Score 134.17 *NYSE Composite Index=100 *12 Month Price Score 112.11

Interim Earnings (Per Share)

Qtr.	Apr	Jul	Oct	Jan
2001-02	0.18	0.29	0.08	0.38
2002-03	(0.18)	0.27	0.14	0.44
2003-04	0.20	0.48	0.33	0.75
2004-05	0.48	0.75	0.54	...

Interim Dividends (Per Share)

Amt	Decl	Ex	Rec	Pay
0.11Q	5/18/2004	5/26/2004	5/28/2004	6/15/2004
0.13Q	8/19/2004	8/27/2004	8/31/2004	9/15/2004
0.13Q	11/17/2004	11/26/2004	11/30/2004	12/15/2004
0.13Q	2/15/2005	2/24/2005	2/28/2005	3/15/2005

Indicated Div: $0.52

Valuation Analysis

Forecast P/E	16.45	No of Institutions
	(4/7/2005)	320
Market Cap	$7.7 Billion	Shares
Book Value	1.9 Billion	88,899,072
Price/Book	4.14	% Held
Price/Sales	1.11	63.46

Business Summary: Retail - Apparel and Accessory Stores (MIC: 5.8 SIC: 651 NAIC: 48140)

Nordstrom operated a total of 148 stores as of Jan 31 2004, including large specialty stores selling a wide selection of apparel, shoes and accessories for women, men and children. Included in the total number of stores are 49 Nordstrom Racks, which purchase merchandise directly from manufacturers and also serve as outlets for clearance merchandise from Co.'s large specialty stores. The remaining stores include 92 full-line stores, five Faconnable boutiques, one free-standing shoe store and one clearance store. In addition, Co. operates 31 Faconnable boutiques throughout Europe. Co. also sells merchandise on-line, through its Nordstrom Direct subsidiary, and through its direct-mail catalogs.

Recent Developments: For the quarter ended Oct 30 2004, net income increased 71.2% to $77,828 thousand from net income of $45,469 thousand in the year-earlier quarter. Revenues were $1,542,075 thousand, up 9.4% from $1,409,109 thousand the year before. Operating income was $91,398 thousand versus an income of $58,674 thousand in the prior-year quarter, an increase of 55.8%. Total direct expense was $984,908 thousand versus $911,429 thousand in the prior-year quarter, an increase of 8.1%. Total indirect expense was $465,769 thousand versus $439,006 thousand in the prior-year quarter, an increase of 6.1%.

Prospects: Co. is benefiting from its continued focus on improving operating efficiency through expense management. For instance, Co. recently saw a 160 basis point reduction in selling, general, and administrative expenses on a percent to sales basis for the fourth-quarter of 2004 due in part to its cost control initiatives. Separately, Co. plans to open one full-line store at Phipps Plaza in Atlanta, GA and relocate a Rack store in Portland, OR during the first quarter of 2005. Looking ahead, Co. anticipates diluted earnings to range from $3.25 to $3.35 per share for fiscal year 2005, a 16.0% to 20.0% increase over the prior year.

Financial Data

(US$ in Thousands)	9 Mos	6 Mos	3 Mos	01/31/2004	01/31/2003	01/31/2002	01/31/2001	01/31/2000
Earnings Per Share	2.52	2.32	2.04	1.76	0.66	0.93	0.78	1.46
Cash Flow Per Share	4.00	3.70	3.99	4.20	2.06	3.09	1.37	2.74
Tang Book Value Per Share	12.40	12.27	11.41	10.79	9.09	8.75	8.12	8.96
Dividends Per Share	0.460	0.430	0.420	0.410	0.380	0.360	0.350	0.320
Dividend Payout %	18.23	18.57	20.57	23.30	57.58	38.71	44.87	21.92
Income Statement								
Total Revenue	5,031,045	3,488,970	1,535,490	6,491,673	5,975,076	5,634,130	5,528,537	5,124,223
EBITDA	646,605	453,213	205,562	712,064	489,297	488,707	421,666	569,784
Depn & Amortn	171,539	114,545	56,251	222,971	211,752	209,181	191,950	187,331
Income Before Taxes	410,806	287,893	112,627	398,141	195,624	204,488	167,018	332,057
Income Taxes	157,336	112,251	43,900	155,300	92,041	79,800	65,100	129,500
Net Income	253,470	175,642	68,727	242,841	90,224	124,688	101,918	202,557
Average Shares	143,149	143,497	141,975	137,739	135,724	134,339	131,113	138,424
Balance Sheet								
Current Assets	2,734,412	2,797,562	2,336,356	2,455,430	2,072,618	2,054,598	1,812,982	1,564,648
Total Assets	4,721,959	4,783,344	4,325,074	4,465,688	4,096,376	4,048,779	3,608,503	3,062,081
Current Liabilities	1,385,983	1,436,685	1,024,801	1,049,549	870,091	947,738	950,568	866,509
Long-Term Obligations	932,384	927,227	1,024,283	1,227,410	1,341,826	1,351,044	1,099,710	746,791
Total Liabilities	2,851,561	2,911,904	2,593,444	2,831,679	2,724,319	2,734,291	2,378,935	1,876,467
Stockholders' Equity	1,870,398	1,871,440	1,731,630	1,634,009	1,372,057	1,314,488	1,229,568	1,185,614
Shares Outstanding	139,933	141,436	139,816	138,376	135,444	134,468	133,797	132,279
Statistical Record								
Return on Assets %	7.88	7.11	6.70	5.67	2.22	3.26	3.05	6.56
Return on Equity %	21.25	19.65	18.23	16.16	6.72	9.80	8.42	16.19
EBITDA Margin %	12.85	12.99	13.39	10.97	8.19	8.67	7.63	11.12
Net Margin %	5.04	5.03	4.48	3.74	1.51	2.21	1.84	3.95
Asset Turnover	1.53	1.49	1.58	1.52	1.47	1.47	1.65	1.66
Current Ratio	1.97	1.95	2.28	2.34	2.38	2.17	1.91	1.81
Debt to Equity	0.50	0.50	0.59	0.75	0.98	1.03	0.89	0.63
Price Range	45.40-29.86	45.40-21.03	40.65-15.86	40.36-15.86	26.37-15.49	25.30-14.10	33.75-14.31	44.19-21.69
P/E Ratio	18.02-11.85	19.57-9.06	19.93-7.77	22.93-9.01	39.95-23.47	27.20-15.16	43.27-18.35	30.27-14.85
Average Yield %	1.20	1.24	1.43	1.71	1.77	1.94	1.66	1.01

Address: 1617 Sixth Avenue, Suite 500, Seattle, WA 98101-1742	**Web Site:** www.nordstrom.com	**Auditors:** DELOITTE & TOUCHE LLP
Telephone: (206) 628-2111	**Officers:** Bruce A. Nordstrom - Chmn. Blake W. Nordstrom - Pres.	**Investor Contact:** 206-373-4034
Fax: (206) 628-1795		

NORFOLK SOUTHERN CORP.

Exchange	Symbol	Price	52Wk Range	Yield	P/E
NYS	NSC	$37.05 (3/31/2005)	38.38-21.54	1.19	16.04

*7 Year Price Score 111.67 *NYSE Composite Index=100 *12 Month Price Score 111.43

Interim Earnings (Per Share)

Qtr.	Mar	Jun	Sep	Dec
2001	0.19	0.28	0.20	0.30
2002	0.22	0.31	0.32	0.33
2003	0.54	0.35	0.35	0.13
2004	0.40	0.54	0.72	0.65

Interim Dividends (Per Share)

Amt	Decl	Ex	Rec	Pay
0.08Q	4/26/2004	5/5/2004	5/7/2004	6/10/2004
0.10Q	7/27/2004	8/4/2004	8/6/2004	9/10/2004
0.10Q	10/25/2004	11/3/2004	11/5/2004	12/10/2004
0.11Q	1/25/2005	2/2/2005	2/4/2005	3/10/2005

Indicated Div: $0.44

Valuation Analysis

Forecast P/E	14.51	No of Institutions
	(4/7/2005)	508
Market Cap	$14.8 Billion	Shares
Book Value	8.0 Billion	273,567,264
Price/Book	1.86	% Held
Price/Sales	2.03	68.34

Business Summary: Rail Transport (MIC: 15.5 SIC: 011 NAIC: 82111)

Norfolk Southern is a holding company engaged principally in the transportation of freight by rail. Operations are conducted through its wholly-owned subsidiary, Norfolk Southern Railway Company. As of Dec 31 2003, Co. operated approximately 21,500 miles of track in 22 states, the District of Columbia and the Province of Ontario, Canada. Co.'s rail freight largely consists of raw materials, intermediate products and finished goods classified in the following groups: coal; intermodal; automotive; chemicals; metals/construction; agricultural/consumer products/government; and paper/clay/forest products.

Recent Developments: For the year ended Dec 31 2004, net income increased 72.5% to $923 million from net income of $535 million a year earlier. Revenues were $7,312 million, up 13.0% from $6,468 million the year before. Operating income was $1,702 million versus an income of $1,064 million in the prior year, an increase of 60.0%. Total direct expense was $2,589 million versus $2,435 million in the prior year, an increase of 6.3%. Total indirect expense was $3,021 million versus $2,969 million in the prior year, an increase of 1.8%.

Prospects: Co.'s top line should continue to benefit from contributions from all of its major business sectors, which is being supported by stronger demand for its services. However, Co. noted that it expects the first quarter 2005 to reflect expenses in the range of $30.0 million to $40.0 million, pretax, relating to the Jan 6 2005 derailment at Graniteville, SC. The amount includes Co.'s self-insurance retention under its insurance policies, as well as other uninsured costs. Separately, on Feb 2 2005, Co. and Motiva Enterprises announced the opening of a new high-capacity ethanol terminal located at Motiva's petroleum distribution terminal in Sewaren, NJ.

Financial Data
(US$ in Thousands)

	12/31/2004	12/31/2003	12/31/2002	12/31/2001	12/31/2000	12/31/1999	12/31/1998	12/31/1997
Earnings Per Share	2.31	1.37	1.18	0.97	0.45	0.63	1.93	1.90
Cash Flow Per Share	4.20	2.70	2.07	1.70	3.49	1.40	2.35	3.05
Tang Book Value Per Share	19.95	17.83	16.71	15.78	15.16	15.50	15.61	14.44
Dividends Per Share	0.360	0.300	0.260	0.240	0.800	0.800	0.800	0.800
Dividend Payout %	15.58	21.90	22.03	24.74	177.78	126.98	41.45	42.11
Income Statement								
Total Revenue	7,312,000	6,468,000	6,270,000	6,170,000	6,159,000	5,195,000	4,221,000	4,223,000
EBITDA	2,387,000	1,611,000	1,753,000	1,633,000	1,318,000	1,371,000	1,811,000	1,815,000
Depn & Amortn	609,000	528,000	529,000	527,000	517,000	489,000	450,000	432,000
Income Before Taxes	1,302,000	586,000	706,000	553,000	250,000	351,000	845,000	998,000
Income Taxes	387,000	175,000	246,000	191,000	78,000	112,000	215,000	299,000
Net Income	923,000	535,000	460,000	375,000	172,000	239,000	734,000	721,000
Average Shares	399,300	392,000	390,000	386,000	383,000	382,000	381,000	380,000
Balance Sheet								
Total Assets	24,750,000	20,596,000	19,956,000	19,418,000	18,976,000	19,250,000	18,180,000	17,350,000
Long-Term Obligations	6,863,000	6,800,000	7,006,000	7,027,000	7,339,000	7,556,000	7,483,000	7,398,000
Total Liabilities	16,760,000	13,620,000	13,456,000	13,328,000	13,152,000	13,318,000	12,259,000	11,905,000
Stockholders' Equity	7,990,000	6,976,000	6,500,000	6,090,000	5,824,000	5,932,000	5,921,000	5,445,000
Shares Outstanding	400,438	391,153	388,985	385,832	384,058	382,681	379,404	377,155
Statistical Record								
Return on Assets %	4.06	2.64	2.34	1.95	0.90	1.28	4.13	5.01
Return on Equity %	12.30	7.94	7.31	6.30	2.92	4.03	12.92	13.84
EBITDA Margin %	32.64	24.91	27.96	26.47	21.40	26.39	42.90	42.98
Net Margin %	12.62	8.27	7.34	6.08	2.79	4.60	17.39	17.07
Asset Turnover	0.32	0.32	0.32	0.32	0.32	0.28	0.24	0.29
Price Range	36.50-20.54	24.33-17.70	26.60-18.05	23.87-13.69	21.75-12.00	36.19-19.75	40.38-27.63	37.88-28.42
P/E Ratio	15.80-8.89	17.76-12.92	22.54-15.30	24.61-14.11	48.33-26.67	57.44-31.35	20.92-14.31	19.93-14.96
Average Yield %	1.34	1.20	1.12	1.31	4.98	2.88	2.50	2.49

Address: Three Commercial Place, Norfolk, VA 23510-2191 Telephone: (757) 629-2600 Fax: (757) 629-2345	Web Site: www.nscorp.com Officers: David R. Goode - Chmn., C.E.O. Henry C. Wolf - Vice-Chmn., C.F.O.	Auditors: KPMG LLP Transfer Agents: The Bank of New York, New York, NY

NORTH FORK BANCORPORATION, INC. (MATTITUCK, N.Y.)

Exchange	Symbol	Price	52Wk Range	Yield	P/E	Div Acheiver
NYS	NFB	$27.74 (3/31/2005)	30.54-23.57	3.17	14.99	10 Years

*7 Year Price Score 119.53 *NYSE Composite Index=100 ***12 Month Price Score 97.44**

Interim Earnings (Per Share)
Qtr.	Mar	Jun	Sep	Dec
2001	0.33	0.33	0.35	0.37
2002	0.41	0.43	0.44	0.45
2003	0.45	0.41	0.42	0.45
2004	0.45	0.45	0.47	0.48

Interim Dividends (Per Share)
Amt	Decl	Ex	Rec	Pay
0.22Q	9/28/2004	10/27/2004	10/29/2004	11/15/2004
3-for-2	9/28/2004	11/16/2004	10/29/2004	11/15/2004
0.22Q	12/14/2004	1/26/2005	1/28/2005	2/15/2005
0.22Q	3/22/2005	4/27/2005	4/29/2005	5/16/2005
		Indicated Div: $0.88		

Valuation Analysis
Forecast P/E	11.81	No of Institutions	
(4/7/2005)		440	
Market Cap	$13.1 Billion	Shares	
Book Value	8.9 Billion		282,815,744
Price/Book	1.48	% Held	
Price/Sales	7.18		59.50

Business Summary: Commercial Banking (MIC: 8.1 SIC: 022 NAIC: 22110)

North Fork Bancorporation is a bank holding company with assets of $20.96 billion as of Dec 31 2003. Co. operates through its primary subsidiary North Fork Bank and its investment management and broker/dealer subsidiaries, Compass Investment Services and Amivest, providing a variety of banking and financial services to middle market and small business organizations, local governmental units, and retail customers. As of Dec 31 2003, North Fork Bank owned 73 branch office facilities and leased 102 branch office facilities. Co.'s other bank subsidiary, Superior Savings of New England, is headquartered in an owned facility in Connecticut and operates a branch in a leased facility in New York.

Recent Developments: For the year ended Dec 31 2004, net income increased 39.5% to $552,996 thousand from net income of $396,365 thousand a year earlier. Net interest income was $1,175,221 thousand, up 44.1% from $815,514 thousand the year before. Provision for loan losses was $27,189 thousand versus $26,250 thousand in the prior year, an increase of 3.6%. Non-interest income rose 59.5% to $248,503 thousand, while non-interest expense advanced 60.7% to $555,802 thousand.

Prospects: Co.'s outlook is bright. For instance, loans held-for-investment at Dec 31 2004 was $30.45 billion, up substantially from the $12.34 billion at the end of 2003. Total interest earning assets amounted to $50.17 billion, more than double the $25.06 billion recorded in the third quarter of 2004. Meanwhile, virtually all of GreenPoint's operating systems will have been converted by mid-February 2005. All major system conversion testing has been completed and Co. anticipates no customer service disruptions. Co. added that it is on track to realize cost savings from the GreenPoint acquisition in excess of $100.0 million in 2005.

Financial Data
(US$ in Thousands)	12/31/2004	12/31/2003	12/31/2002	12/31/2001	12/31/2000	12/31/1999	12/31/1998	12/31/1997
Earnings Per Share	1.85	1.73	1.72	1.37	0.93	1.08	0.79	0.80
Cash Flow Per Share	(0.66)	1.72	2.17	1.77	1.04	0.80	1.18	0.92
Tang Book Value Per Share	5.49	4.61	4.58	4.13	3.59	2.80	3.53	3.38
Dividends Per Share	0.820	0.720	0.653	0.540	0.480	0.383	0.417	0.244
Dividend Payout %	44.32	41.54	37.98	39.51	51.80	35.49	52.97	30.56
Income Statement								
Interest Income	1,578,152	1,110,260	1,189,338	1,109,880	1,072,600	817,746	753,100	484,521
Interest Expense	402,931	294,746	347,560	423,361	480,608	368,440	328,456	206,170
Net Interest Income	1,175,221	815,514	841,778	686,519	591,992	449,306	424,644	278,351
Provision for Losses	27,189	26,250	25,000	17,750	17,000	6,000	15,500	6,000
Non-Interest Income	248,503	155,811	124,139	108,895	102,513	73,017	64,318	41,624
Non-Interest Expense	555,802	345,870	305,186	271,582	301,534	177,294	230,381	122,736
Income Before Taxes	840,733	599,205	635,731	506,082	375,971	339,029	243,081	191,239
Income Taxes	287,737	202,840	218,838	174,598	141,206	118,660	75,106	71,929
Net Income	552,996	396,365	416,893	331,484	234,765	220,369	167,975	119,310
Average Shares	299,219	228,774	242,473	242,072	252,795	203,797	212,647	149,388
Balance Sheet								
Net Loans & Leases	30,242,237	12,222,540	11,254,144	10,295,890	9,305,060	6,548,535	5,642,534	3,644,322
Total Assets	60,667,055	20,961,641	21,413,101	17,232,103	14,840,962	12,108,116	10,679,556	6,829,432
Total Deposits	34,812,428	15,116,115	13,192,530	11,303,306	9,169,195	6,544,750	6,427,622	4,637,191
Total Liabilities	51,785,976	19,483,152	19,899,048	15,550,731	13,382,705	11,290,092	9,649,017	6,028,342
Stockholders' Equity	8,881,079	1,478,489	1,514,053	1,437,008	1,213,918	618,710	831,250	601,826
Shares Outstanding	472,842	228,782	238,135	244,333	241,246	192,662	211,608	149,388
Statistical Record								
Return on Assets %	1.35	1.87	2.16	2.07	1.74	1.93	1.92	1.90
Return on Equity %	10.65	26.49	28.25	25.01	25.55	30.40	23.44	22.52
Net Interest Margin %	74.47	73.45	70.78	61.86	55.19	54.94	56.39	57.45
Efficiency Ratio %	30.43	27.32	23.23	22.28	25.66	19.90	28.18	23.33
Loans to Deposits	0.87	0.81	0.85	0.91	1.01	1.00	0.88	0.79
Price Range	30.54-23.57	27.21-19.13	28.21-21.15	22.32-15.33	16.63-9.67	15.96-11.42	18.22-10.88	15.00-7.58
P/E Ratio	16.51-12.74	15.73-11.06	16.40-12.30	16.29-11.19	17.88-10.39	14.78-10.57	23.07-13.77	18.75-9.48
Average Yield %	2.99	3.14	2.66	2.87	4.05	2.75	2.73	2.29

Address: 275 Broadhollow Road, Melville, NY 11747	Web Site: www.northforkbank.com	Auditors: KPMG LLP
Telephone: (631) 844-1004 **Fax:** (631) 694-1536	**Officers:** John A. Kanas - Chmn., Pres., C.E.O. John Bohlsen - Vice-Chmn.	**Investor Contact:** 631-501-4618

NORTHEAST UTILITIES

Exchange	Symbol	Price	52Wk Range	Yield	P/E
NYS	NU	$19.27 (3/31/2005)	20.03-17.30	3.37	21.18

*7 Year Price Score 88.23   *NYSE Composite Index=100   *12 Month Price Score 93.86

Interim Earnings (Per Share)

Qtr.	Mar	Jun	Sep	Dec
2001	0.78	0.35	0.26	0.38
2002	0.14	0.22	0.38	0.44
2003	0.47	0.21	0.31	(0.08)
2004	0.53	0.18	0.30	(0.10)

Interim Dividends (Per Share)

Amt	Decl	Ex	Rec	Pay
0.15Q	4/14/2004	5/27/2004	6/1/2004	6/30/2004
0.163Q	5/11/2004	8/30/2004	9/1/2004	9/30/2004
0.163Q	10/12/2004	11/29/2004	12/1/2004	12/30/2004
0.163Q	1/31/2005	2/25/2005	3/1/2005	3/31/2005

Indicated Div: $0.65

Valuation Analysis

Forecast P/E	16.84	No of Institutions	
	(4/7/2005)	168	
Market Cap	$2.5 Billion	Shares	
Book Value	2.3 Billion	87,883,808	
Price/Book	1.08	% Held	
Price/Sales	0.37	68.45	

TRADING VOLUME (thousand shares)

Business Summary: Electricity (MIC: 7.1 SIC: 911 NAIC: 21122)

Northeast Utilities is the parent company of Northeast Utilities System, which furnishes franchised retail electric service to over 1.8 million customers in 420 cities in Connecticut, New Hampshire and western Massachusetts through Co.'s subsidiaries: Connecticut Light and Power, Public Service of New Hampshire and Western Massachusetts Electric. The system also furnishes retail natural gas service in Connecticut through Yankee Gas Services for about 192,000 residential, commercial and industrial customers. NU Enterprises owns several energy and related businesses, including Northeast Generation, Northeast Generation Services, Select Energy Services, Mode 1 Communications, and Holyoke Water.

Recent Developments: For the year ended Dec 31 2004, net income increased 0.2% to $116,588 thousand from net income of $116,411 thousand a year earlier. Revenues were $6,686,699 thousand, up 10.2% from $6,069,156 thousand the year before. Operating income was $412,952 thousand versus an income of $424,236 thousand in the prior year, a decrease of 2.7%. Total direct expense was $5,503,538 thousand versus $4,862,883 thousand in the prior year, an increase of 13.2%. Total indirect expense was $770,209 thousand versus $782,037 thousand in the prior year, a decrease of 1.5%.

Prospects: Co. is pleased with its operating performance, supported by stronger results at its regulated utilities. Co.'s utilities earned a combined $155.6 million, or $1.21 per share, in 2004, compared with $132.5 million, or $1.05 per share, in 2003. Meanwhile, Co. believes that its regulated companies will earn between $1.22 per share and $1.30 per share in 2005 and parent and other costs, primarily interest expense, will total between $0.08 and $0.13 per share. The utility business range reflects earnings of between $0.96 and $1.00 per share in the regulated distribution and generation business and between $0.26 and $0.30 per share in the transmission business.

Financial Data
(US$ in Thousands)

	12/31/2004	12/31/2003	12/31/2002	12/31/2001	12/31/2000	12/31/1999	12/31/1998	12/31/1997
Earnings Per Share	0.91	0.91	1.18	1.79	(0.20)	0.26	(1.12)	(1.05)
Cash Flow Per Share	4.02	4.51	4.74	2.78	4.07	4.67	5.08	2.91
Tang Book Value Per Share	15.17	15.04	14.62	13.79	13.17	15.91	15.63	16.34
Dividends Per Share	0.625	0.575	0.525	0.450	0.400	0.100	...	0.250
Dividend Payout %	68.68	63.19	44.49	25.14	N.M.	38.46	...	N.M.
Income Statement								
Total Revenue	6,686,699	6,069,156	5,216,321	6,873,826	5,876,620	4,471,251	3,767,714	3,834,806
EBITDA	655,872	1,017,040	1,205,296	1,910,851	1,219,287	1,504,632	1,012,598	793,002
Depn & Amortn	228,455	584,109	694,813	1,184,050	485,334	953,282	616,380	481,615
Income Before Taxes	173,903	186,573	239,972	447,143	219,457	56,971	(120,313)	(105,422)
Income Taxes	51,756	59,862	82,304	173,952	(68,306)	(82,272)	(76,393)	(10,702)
Net Income	116,588	116,411	152,109	243,510	(28,586)	34,216	(146,753)	(135,708)
Average Shares	128,396	127,240	129,341	135,917	141,967	131,415	130,550	129,568
Balance Sheet								
Net PPE	5,864,161	5,429,916	4,728,369	3,822,139	3,547,215	3,947,434	6,170,881	6,463,158
Total Assets	11,655,834	11,308,884	10,267,617	10,241,409	10,217,149	9,688,052	10,387,381	10,414,412
Long-Term Obligations	2,789,974	2,481,331	2,287,144	2,292,556	2,029,593	2,372,341	3,282,138	3,645,659
Total Liabilities	9,242,923	8,928,564	7,940,896	8,007,569	7,815,132	7,405,717	8,115,386	8,120,544
Stockholders' Equity	2,296,711	2,264,120	2,326,721	2,233,840	2,218,583	2,083,311	2,047,372	2,127,241
Shares Outstanding	129,034	127,695	127,562	130,132	143,820	130,954	130,955	130,183
Statistical Record								
Return on Assets %	1.01	1.08	1.48	2.38	N.M.	0.34	N.M.	N.M.
Return on Equity %	5.10	5.07	6.67	10.94	N.M.	1.66	N.M.	N.M.
EBITDA Margin %	9.81	16.76	23.11	27.80	20.75	33.65	26.88	20.68
Net Margin %	1.74	1.92	2.92	3.54	(0.49)	0.77	(3.90)	(3.54)
PPE Turnover	1.18	1.19	1.22	1.87	1.56	0.88	0.60	0.58
Asset Turnover	0.58	0.56	0.51	0.67	0.59	0.45	0.36	0.36
Debt to Equity	1.21	1.10	0.98	1.03	0.91	1.14	1.60	1.71
Price Range	20.17-17.30	20.17-13.38	20.57-13.20	23.75-16.80	24.25-18.25	21.81-13.75	17.06-11.81	14.13-7.75
P/E Ratio	22.16-19.01	22.16-14.70	17.43-11.19	13.27-9.39	N/A	83.89-52.88	N/A	N/A
Average Yield %	3.31	3.48	3.02	2.33	1.87	0.57	...	2.38

Address: P.O. Box 270, Hartford, CT 01641-0270	Web Site: www.nu.com	Auditors: Deloitte & Touche LLP
Telephone: (413) 785-5871	Officers: Charles W. Shivery - Chmn., Pres., C.E.O. John P. Stack - V.P., Acctg., Contr.	Investor Contact: 800-286-5000

NORTHROP GRUMMAN CORP

Exchange	Symbol	Price	52Wk Range	Yield	P/E
NYS	NOC	$53.98 (3/31/2005)	57.75-48.73	1.93	18.18

*7 Year Price Score 101.90 *NYSE Composite Index=100 *12 Month Price Score 94.37

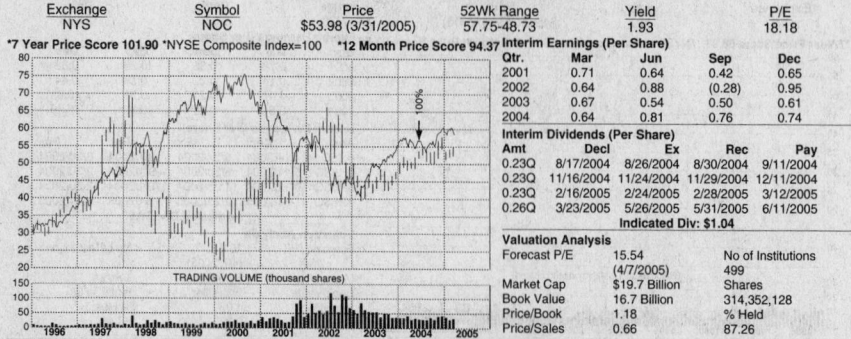

Interim Earnings (Per Share)

Qtr.	Mar	Jun	Sep	Dec
2001	0.71	0.64	0.42	0.65
2002	0.64	0.88	(0.28)	0.95
2003	0.67	0.54	0.50	0.61
2004	0.64	0.81	0.76	0.74

Interim Dividends (Per Share)

Amt	Decl	Ex	Rec	Pay
0.23Q	8/17/2004	8/26/2004	8/30/2004	9/11/2004
0.23Q	11/16/2004	11/24/2004	11/29/2004	12/11/2004
0.23Q	2/16/2005	2/24/2005	2/28/2005	3/12/2005
0.26Q	3/23/2005	5/26/2005	5/31/2005	6/11/2005

Indicated Div: $1.04

Valuation Analysis

Forecast P/E	15.54	No of Institutions
	(4/7/2005)	499
Market Cap	$19.7 Billion	Shares
Book Value	16.7 Billion	314,352,128
Price/Book	1.18	% Held
Price/Sales	0.66	87.26

Business Summary: Instruments and Related Products (MIC: 11.15 SIC: 812 NAIC: 36411)

Northrop Grumman is a technology company operating in seven sectors. Electronic Systems designs and develops a wide variety of defense electronics and systems; Information Technology provides advanced information technologies, systems and services; Integrated Systems designs and produces airborne early warning and electronic warfare and surveillance; Ships is engaged in the building of major surface ships primarily for the U.S. Navy; Newport News designs and builds nuclear-powered aircraft carriers and submarines; Mission Systems is an integrator of complex systems for government and military clients; and Space Technology designs spacecraft systems and subsystems and electronic systems.

Recent Developments: For the year ended Dec 31 2004, income from continuing operations increased 44.2% to $1,093,000 thousand from income of $758,000 thousand a year earlier. Net income increased 25.2% to $1,084,000 thousand from net income of $866,000 thousand a year earlier. Revenues were $29,853,000 thousand, up 13.1% from $26,396,000 thousand the year before. Operating income was $2,006,000 thousand versus an income of $1,468,000 thousand in the prior year, an increase of 36.6%. Total direct expense was $25,135,000 thousand versus $22,535,000 thousand in the prior year, an increase of 11.5%. Total indirect expense was $2,712,000 thousand versus $2,393,000 thousand in the prior year, an increase of 13.3%.

Prospects: On Feb 18 2005, Co. announced that it has entered into a definitive agreement to acquire privately held Integic Corporation, an information technology provider specializing in enterprise health and business process management solutions. The acquisition is expected to be completed in March or April 2005, subject to customary regulatory approvals. Co. anticipates the transaction will be neutral in 2005 and accretive in 2006 to earnings per share from continuing operations. For 2005, Co. is targeting sales of between $31.00 billion and $31.50 billion, along with earnings per share from continuing operations in the range of $3.45 to $3.60.

Financial Data

(US$ in Thousands)	12/31/2004	12/31/2003	12/31/2002	12/31/2001	12/31/2000	12/31/1999	12/31/1998	12/31/1997
Earnings Per Share	2.97	2.32	0.17	2.40	4.29	3.35	1.40	2.99
Cash Flow Per Share	5.37	2.18	7.31	4.84	7.13	8.71	1.78	5.47
Dividends Per Share	0.890	0.800	0.800	0.600	0.800	0.800	0.800	0.800
Dividend Payout %	29.97	34.48	470.59	25.00	18.65	23.92	57.35	26.76
Income Statement								
Total Revenue	29,853,000	26,206,000	17,206,000	13,558,000	7,618,000	8,995,000	8,902,000	9,153,000
EBITDA	2,740,000	2,220,000	1,887,000	1,649,000	1,479,000	1,358,000	933,000	1,298,000
Depn & Amortn	734,000	682,000	496,000	645,000	381,000	389,000	393,000	418,000
Income Before Taxes	1,615,000	1,131,000	1,009,000	699,000	975,000	762,000	312,000	651,000
Income Taxes	522,000	323,000	312,000	272,000	350,000	279,000	118,000	244,000
Net Income	1,084,000	866,000	64,000	427,000	608,000	467,000	194,000	407,000
Average Shares	365,000	368,360	234,860	170,520	141,760	139,400	139,020	136,080
Balance Sheet								
Current Assets	6,907,000	5,745,000	15,835,000	4,589,000	2,526,000	2,793,000	3,033,000	2,936,000
Total Assets	33,361,000	33,009,000	42,266,000	20,886,000	9,622,000	9,285,000	9,536,000	9,677,000
Current Liabilities	6,223,000	6,361,000	11,373,000	5,132,000	2,688,000	2,464,000	2,367,000	2,715,000
Long-Term Obligations	5,116,000	5,410,000	9,398,000	5,033,000	1,605,000	2,000,000	2,562,000	2,500,000
Total Liabilities	16,661,000	17,224,000	27,944,000	13,495,000	5,703,000	6,028,000	6,686,000	7,054,000
Stockholders' Equity	16,700,000	15,785,000	14,322,000	7,391,000	3,919,000	3,257,000	2,850,000	2,623,000
Shares Outstanding	364,430	362,216	365,204	217,112	144,116	139,438	137,673	134,556
Statistical Record								
Return on Assets %	3.26	2.30	0.20	2.80	6.41	4.96	2.02	4.26
Return on Equity %	6.66	5.75	0.59	7.55	16.90	15.29	7.09	17.13
EBITDA Margin %	9.18	8.47	10.97	12.16	19.41	15.10	10.48	14.18
Net Margin %	3.63	3.30	0.37	3.15	7.98	5.19	2.18	4.45
Asset Turnover	0.90	0.70	0.54	0.89	0.80	0.96	0.93	0.96
Current Ratio	1.11	0.90	1.39	0.89	0.94	1.13	1.28	1.08
Debt to Equity	0.31	0.34	0.66	0.68	0.41	0.61	0.90	0.95
Price Range	57.75-47.34	50.22-39.50	66.25-43.73	54.48-38.50	46.25-21.78	37.84-24.50	69.50-29.81	63.16-35.88
P/E Ratio	19.44-15.94	21.64-17.03	389.71-257.24	22.70-16.04	10.78-5.08	11.30-7.31	49.64-21.29	21.12-12.00
Average Yield %	1.72	1.79	1.44	1.33	2.29	2.53	1.68	1.65

Address: 1840 Century Park East, Los Angeles, CA 90067-2199	Web Site: www.northropgrumman.com	Auditors: Deloitte & Touche LLP
Telephone: (310) 553-6262	**Officers:** Ronald D. Sugar - Chmn., Pres., C.E.O., C.O.O. J. Michael Hateley - Corp. V.P., Chief Human Res., Admin. Officer	**Investor Contact:** 310-553-6262
Fax: (310) 201-3023		

NSTAR

Exchange	Symbol	Price	52Wk Range	Yield	P/E
NYS	NST	$54.30 (3/31/2005)	58.25-45.40	4.27	15.47

*7 Year Price Score N/A   ***NYSE Composite Index=100**   ***12 Month Price Score 102.89**

TRADING VOLUME (thousand shares)

Interim Earnings (Per Share)

Qtr.	Mar	Jun	Sep	Dec
2001	(2.52)	0.68	1.26	0.52
2002	0.65	0.10	1.37	0.91
2003	0.79	0.73	1.19	0.68
2004	0.93	0.70	1.18	0.70

Interim Dividends (Per Share)

Amt	Decl	Ex	Rec	Pay
0.555Q	6/29/2004	7/7/2004	7/9/2004	8/2/2004
0.555Q	9/23/2004	10/6/2004	10/8/2004	11/1/2004
0.58Q	12/16/2004	1/6/2005	1/10/2005	2/1/2005
0.58Q	3/24/2005	4/6/2005	4/8/2005	5/2/2005

Indicated Div: $2.32

Valuation Analysis

Forecast P/E	14.89	No of Institutions	
	(4/7/2005)	194	
Market Cap	$2.9 Billion	Shares	
Book Value	1.4 Billion	21,909,364	
Price/Book	2.01	% Held	
Price/Sales	0.98	41.08	

Business Summary: Electricity (MIC: 7.1 SIC: 911 NAIC: 21122)

NSTAR is a holding company engaged through its subsidiaries in the energy delivery business serving approximately 1.4 million customers in Massachusetts, including approximately 1.1 million electric distribution customers in 81 communities and approximately 300,000 natural gas customers in 51 communities as of Dec 31 2004. Co.'s retail utility subsidiaries are Boston Edison Company, Commonwealth Electric Company, Cambridge Electric Light Company and NSTAR Gas Company. Co.'s wholesale electric subsidiary is Canal Electric Company. Co.'s non-utility operations include district energy operations, telecommunications operations and a liquefied natural gas service company.

Recent Developments: For the year ended Dec 31 2004, net income increased 3.8% to $188,481 thousand from net income of $181,574 thousand a year earlier. Revenues were $2,954,332 thousand, up 1.5% from $2,911,711 thousand the year before. Operating income was $338,328 thousand versus an income of $332,511 thousand in the prior year, an increase of 1.7%. Total direct expense was $2,082,467 thousand versus $2,058,221 thousand in the prior year, an increase of 1.2%. Total indirect expense was $533,537 thousand versus $520,979 thousand in the prior year, an increase of 2.4%.

Prospects: Co. has provided diluted earnings per share guidance for 2005 of between $3.60 to $3.75. Co. anticipates that modest improvement in economic conditions and normal weather will result in unit sales growth of electricity of 2% to 3%, and unit sales growth of natural gas of between 5.0% and 6.0%. Co. also expects capital expenditures for 2005 of $398.0 million, including about $110.0 million for its recently approved 345kV transmission line into Boston. On Jan 13 2005, the Massachusetts Energy Facilities Siting Board gave final approval to Co.'s request to build a new, 18-mile underground transmission line. Construction of this 345kV transmission line is expected to begin in the spring of 2005.

Financial Data

(US$ in Thousands)	12/31/2004	12/31/2003	12/31/2002	12/31/2001	12/31/2000	12/31/1999	12/31/1998	12/31/1997
Earnings Per Share	3.51	3.40	3.03	(0.05)	3.18	2.76	2.75	2.71
Cash Flow Per Share	8.21	7.95	11.06	6.13	3.11	3.61	5.52	7.40
Tang Book Value Per Share	19.03	17.39	15.99	15.07	16.34	18.22	22.29	...
Dividends Per Share	2.220	2.160	2.120	2.060	2.000	0.485	...	...
Dividend Payout %	63.25	63.53	69.97	N.M.	62.89	17.57	...	...
Income Statement								
Total Revenue	2,954,332	2,914,131	2,719,067	3,191,836	2,699,506	1,851,427	1,622,515	1,778,531
Depn & Amortn	246,363	16,800	239,800	230,949	225,459	212,880	229,668	223,529
Income Taxes	119,670	124,855	111,061	113,412	123,467	87,821	97,798	93,709
Net Income	188,481	181,574	163,667	3,201	180,962	146,463	141,046	144,642
Average Shares	53,646	53,339	53,297	53,216	55,045	50,921	48,149	48,562
Balance Sheet								
Net PPE	3,579,978	3,376,656	2,977,538	2,731,391	2,629,420	2,665,889	1,857,191	...
Total Assets	7,117,229	6,320,660	6,123,275	5,328,191	5,569,514	5,482,888	3,204,036	...
Long-Term Obligations	2,101,402	1,982,531	2,091,355	1,891,803	2,024,561	1,633,402	955,563	...
Total Liabilities	5,633,347	4,916,068	4,780,970	4,022,595	4,184,289	3,846,962	2,059,098	...
Stockholders' Equity	1,440,882	1,361,592	1,299,305	1,262,596	1,342,225	1,543,647	1,051,898	...
Shares Outstanding	53,275	53,032	53,032	53,032	53,032	58,059	47,184	...
Statistical Record								
Return on Assets %	2.80	2.92	2.86	0.06	3.27	3.37	4.40	...
Return on Equity %	13.41	13.65	12.78	0.25	12.51	11.29	13.41	...
Net Margin %	6.38	6.23	6.02	0.10	6.70	7.91	8.69	8.13
PPE Turnover	0.85	0.92	0.95	1.19	1.02	0.82	0.87	...
Asset Turnover	0.44	0.47	0.47	0.59	0.49	0.43	0.51	...
Debt to Equity	1.46	1.46	1.61	1.50	1.51	1.06	0.91	...
Price Range	54.38-45.40	48.68-39.01	48.00-34.81	45.17-35.44	45.06-37.13	43.19-36.81	...	...
P/E Ratio	15.49-12.93	14.32-11.47	15.84-11.49	N/A	14.17-11.67	15.65-13.34	...	...
Average Yield %	4.53	4.84	4.93	4.98	4.84	1.21	...	...

Address: 800 Boylston Street, Boston, MA 02199-8003	**Web Site:** www.nstaronline.com	**Auditors:** PricewaterhouseCoopers LLP
Telephone: (617) 424-2000	**Officers:** Thomas J. May - Chmn., Pres., C.E.O.	**Investor Contact:** 617-424-2562
Fax: (617) 424-4032	James J. Judge - Sr. V.P., C.F.O., Treas.	

NUCOR CORP.

Exchange	Symbol	Price	52Wk Range	Yield	P/E	Div Acheiver
NYS	NUE	$57.56 (3/31/2005)	63.83-28.63	1.04	8.20	32 Years

*7 Year Price Score 142.78 *NYSE Composite Index=100 *12 Month Price Score 124.22

Interim Earnings (Per Share)

Qtr.	Mar	Jun	Sep	Dec
2001	0.21	0.96	0.13	0.17
2002	0.13	0.38	0.25	0.28
2003	0.12	0.06	0.10	0.13
2004	0.71	1.59	2.59	2.12

Interim Dividends (Per Share)

Amt	Decl	Ex	Rec	Pay
0.13Q	9/9/2004	9/28/2004	9/30/2004	11/11/2004
0.13Q	12/7/2004	12/29/2004	12/31/2004	2/11/2005
0.15Q	2/24/2005	3/29/2005	3/31/2005	5/11/2005
0.25Q	2/24/2005	3/29/2005	3/31/2005	5/11/2005

Indicated Div: $0.60 (Div. Reinv. Plan)

Valuation Analysis

Forecast P/E	7.44 (4/7/2005)	No of Institutions	363
Market Cap	$9.2 Billion	Shares	142,589,440
Book Value	3.5 Billion	% Held	89.25
Price/Book	2.66		
Price/Sales	0.81		

Business Summary: Metal Works (MIC: 11.3 SIC: 312 NAIC: 31111)

Nucor is engaged in the manufacture and sale of steel and steel products. Co.'s principal products from the steel mills segment are hot- and cold-rolled steel, while the steel products segment produces steel joists and joist girders, steel deck, cold finished steel, steel fasteners, metal building systems and light gauge steel framing. Steel joists and hoist girders, and steel deck are sold to general contractors and fabricators domestically. Cold finished steel and steel fasteners are sold primarily to distributors and manufacturers, and hot-rolled steel and cold-rolled steel are sold primarily to steel services centers, fabricators and manufacturers in the U.S.

Recent Developments: For the year ended Dec 31 2004, net income increased 1686.3% to $1,121,485,000 from net income of $62,781,000 a year earlier. Revenues were $11,376,828,000, up 81.6% from $6,265,823,000 the year before. Total direct expense was $9,128,872,000 versus $5,996,547,000 in the prior year, an increase of 52.2%. Total indirect expense was $415,030,000 versus $165,369,000 in the prior year, an increase of 151.0%.

Prospects: Co. is experiencing higher earnings primarily due to higher average selling prices and increased margins, accompanied by the successful integration of the coiled plate mill in Tuscaloosa, AL and the cold rolling mill in Decatur, AL. Co. is benefiting from higher sales prices and increases in total tons of steel shipped to outside customers. Meanwhile, Co. announced the commercial viability of its Castrip® technology and is determining a second location for a Castrip operation in the U.S. Co. also plans to establish at least one joint venture overseas in 2005 to use the Castrip technology. Separately, Co. agreed to purchase the assets of Fort Howard Steel, Inc.'s operations in Oak Creek, WI.

Financial Data
(US$ in Thousands)

	12/31/2004	12/31/2003	12/31/2002	12/31/2001	12/31/2000	12/31/1999	12/31/1998	12/31/1997
Earnings Per Share	7.02	0.40	1.03	0.72	1.90	1.40	1.50	1.68
Cash Flow Per Share	6.48	3.16	3.18	3.19	5.01	3.47	3.65	3.29
Tang Book Value Per Share	21.67	14.90	14.86	14.16	13.73	12.96	11.86	10.66
Dividends Per Share	0.470	0.400	0.380	0.340	0.300	0.260	0.240	0.200
Dividend Payout %	6.70	100.00	36.71	46.90	15.79	18.57	16.00	11.94
Income Statement								
Total Revenue	11,376,828	6,265,823	4,801,777	4,139,249	4,586,146	4,009,346	4,151,232	4,184,498
EBITDA	2,136,933	455,616	551,440	469,449	736,857	630,731	664,595	678,911
Depn & Amortn	383,305	364,112	307,101	289,063	259,365	256,637	253,119	218,764
Income Before Taxes	1,731,276	66,877	230,053	173,861	478,308	379,189	415,309	460,182
Income Taxes	609,791	4,096	67,973	60,900	167,400	134,600	151,600	165,700
Net Income	1,121,485	62,781	162,080	112,961	310,908	244,589	263,709	294,482
Average Shares	159,754	156,833	156,499	155,566	163,554	174,574	175,756	175,844
Balance Sheet								
Current Assets	3,174,948	1,620,560	1,424,139	1,373,666	1,381,447	1,538,509	1,129,467	1,125,508
Total Assets	6,133,207	4,492,353	4,381,001	3,759,348	3,721,788	3,729,848	3,226,546	2,984,383
Current Liabilities	1,065,790	629,595	591,536	484,159	558,068	531,031	486,897	524,454
Long-Term Obligations	923,550	903,550	878,550	460,450	460,450	390,450	215,450	167,950
Total Liabilities	2,677,222	2,150,275	2,058,012	1,557,888	1,590,836	1,467,600	1,153,994	1,107,957
Stockholders' Equity	3,455,985	2,342,078	2,322,989	2,201,460	2,130,952	2,262,248	2,072,552	1,876,426
Shares Outstanding	159,512	157,180	156,360	155,415	155,165	174,494	174,705	175,993
Statistical Record								
Return on Assets %	21.05	1.42	3.98	3.02	8.32	7.03	8.49	10.51
Return on Equity %	38.58	2.69	7.16	5.21	14.12	11.28	13.36	16.90
EBITDA Margin %	18.78	7.27	11.48	11.34	16.07	15.73	16.01	16.22
Net Margin %	9.86	1.00	3.38	2.73	6.78	6.10	6.35	7.04
Asset Turnover	2.14	1.41	1.18	1.11	1.23	1.15	1.34	1.49
Current Ratio	2.98	2.57	2.41	2.84	2.48	2.90	2.32	2.15
Debt to Equity	0.27	0.39	0.38	0.21	0.22	0.17	0.10	0.09
Price Range	55.08-26.67	28.95-17.99	34.58-18.95	28.00-17.25	27.97-15.00	30.31-20.88	30.03-17.97	31.16-22.63
P/E Ratio	7.85-3.80	72.38-44.97	33.57-18.40	38.89-23.96	14.72-7.89	21.65-14.91	20.02-11.98	18.55-13.47
Average Yield %	1.24	1.71	1.41	1.48	1.47	1.06	1.02	0.75

Address: 2100 Rexford Road, Charlotte, NC 28211 **Telephone:** (704) 366 7000 **Fax:** (704) 362 4208	**Web Site:** www.nucor.com **Officers:** Peter C. Browning - Chmn. Daniel R. DiMicco - Vice-Chmn., Pres., C.E.O.	**Auditors:** PricewaterhouseCoopers LLP **Investor Contact:** 704-366-7000 **Transfer Agents:** American Stock Transfer & Trust Company, New York,

NUVEEN INVESTMENTS INC

Exchange	Symbol	Price	52Wk Range	Yield	P/E	Div Acheiver
NYS	JNC	$34.32 (3/31/2005)	42.21-23.89	2.10	21.06	12 Years

*7 Year Price Score 129.01   *NYSE Composite Index=100   *12 Month Price Score 115.03

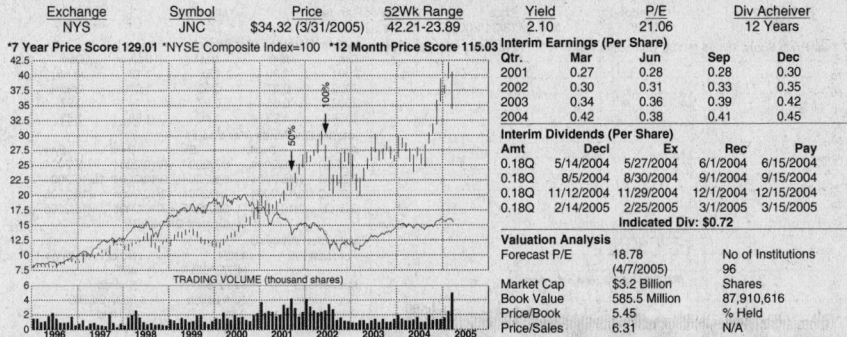

Interim Earnings (Per Share)

Qtr.	Mar	Jun	Sep	Dec
2001	0.27	0.28	0.28	0.30
2002	0.30	0.31	0.33	0.35
2003	0.34	0.36	0.39	0.42
2004	0.42	0.38	0.41	0.45

Interim Dividends (Per Share)

Amt	Decl	Ex	Rec	Pay
0.18Q	5/14/2004	5/27/2004	6/1/2004	6/15/2004
0.18Q	8/5/2004	8/30/2004	9/1/2004	9/15/2004
0.18Q	11/12/2004	11/29/2004	12/1/2004	12/15/2004
0.18Q	2/14/2005	2/25/2005	3/1/2005	3/15/2005

Indicated Div: $0.72

Valuation Analysis

Forecast P/E	18.78	No of Institutions
	(4/7/2005)	96
Market Cap	$3.2 Billion	Shares
Book Value	585.5 Million	87,910,616
Price/Book	5.45	% Held
Price/Sales	6.31	N/A

Business Summary: Finance Intermediaries & Services (MIC: 8.7 SIC: 211 NAIC: 23110)

Nuveen Investments is engaged in asset management and related research, as well as the development, marketing and distribution of investment products and services primarily targeted at affluent, high net-worth individuals and institutional markets. As of Dec 31 2003, total assets under management was approximately $95.36 billion. Co. distributes closed-end exchange-traded funds, mutual funds and defined portfolios through unaffiliated intermediary firms, including broker/dealers, commercial banks, affiliates of insurance providers, financial planners, accountants, consultants and investment advisors. The St. Paul Companies, Inc. owned about 79.0% of Co.'s common stock as of Mar 15 2004.

Recent Developments: For the year ended Dec 31 2004, net income increased 15.9% to $156,408 thousand from net income of $135,005 thousand a year earlier. Revenues were $505,637 thousand, up 11.9% from $452,028 thousand the year before. Total operating expenses increased 12.0% to $252,762 thousand from $225,702 thousand the previous year. Non-operating expenses were $368 thousand versus $5,171 thousand the prior year.

Prospects: Co. is enjoying solid growth in sales, net flows and earnings, driven in large part by the stability and quality of its assets as well as Co.'s success in expanding its investment and distribution capabilities and diversity of its product offerings. Co. continues to focus on product innovation, where it raised more than $700.0 million in the fourth quarter of 2004 with its first closed-end exchange-traded fund. Also, Co. is pleased with the quality and diversity of its current asset base, as equity-based portfolios are approaching 40.0% of its total assets under management.

Financial Data

(US$ in Thousands)	12/31/2004	12/31/2003	12/31/2002	12/31/2001	12/31/2000	12/31/1999	12/31/1998	12/31/1997
Earnings Per Share	1.63	1.50	1.29	1.13	1.05	0.95	0.81	0.71
Cash Flow Per Share	2.19	2.26	2.34	2.20	1.27	1.39	1.37	1.69
Tang Book Value Per Share	N.M.	N.M.	N.M.	0.01	2.07	1.58	1.07	0.67
Dividends Per Share	0.690	0.560	0.500	0.467	0.407	0.377	0.327	0.293
Dividend Payout %	42.33	37.33	38.76	41.30	38.85	39.65	40.33	41.31
Income Statement								
Total Revenue	505,637	452,028	396,447	371,103	358,393	338,760	307,535	268,927
Income Before Taxes	252,507	235,288	206,860	189,554	177,366	161,011	137,737	122,170
Income Taxes	96,099	91,292	80,675	74,856	70,700	63,701	54,092	47,990
Net Income	156,408	143,996	126,185	114,698	106,666	97,310	83,645	74,180
Average Shares	96,121	95,944	98,042	101,688	101,979	102,429	103,281	104,706
Balance Sheet								
Total Assets	1,071,593	954,393	841,042	696,611	576,039	540,965	467,961	492,232
Total Liabilities	483,513	486,212	452,216	284,721	128,138	149,903	118,853	174,112
Stockholders' Equity	585,478	463,953	385,763	406,265	402,901	346,062	304,108	273,120
Shares Outstanding	92,905	92,506	92,726	95,142	93,941	93,189	94,068	95,347
Statistical Record								
Return on Assets %	15.40	16.04	16.41	18.03	19.05	19.29	17.42	17.51
Return on Equity %	29.73	33.89	31.86	28.35	28.41	29.93	28.98	27.22
Price Range	39.47-23.89	30.30-19.99	30.79-20.18	26.86-16.83	19.17-11.19	14.46-11.50	13.83-10.52	12.58-8.79
P/E Ratio	24.21-14.66	20.20-13.33	23.86-15.64	23.77-14.90	18.25-10.65	15.22-12.11	17.08-12.99	17.72-12.38
Average Yield %	2.37	2.18	1.93	2.26	2.86	2.88	2.70	2.79

Address: 333 West Wacker Drive, Chicago, IL 60606 Telephone: (312) 917-7700	Web Site: www.nuveen.com Officers: Timothy R. Schwertfeger - Chmn., C.E.O. John P. Amboian - Pres.	Auditors: KPMG LLP Transfer Agents: The Bank of New York, New York, NY

OCCIDENTAL PETROLEUM CORP

Exchange	Symbol	Price	52Wk Range	Yield	P/E
NYS	OXY	$71.17 (3/31/2005)	74.02-44.08	1.74	11.12

*7 Year Price Score 155.56 ***NYSE Composite Index=100** ***12 Month Price Score 115.75**

Interim Earnings (Per Share)

Qtr.	Mar	Jun	Sep	Dec
2001	1.30	1.26	1.18	(0.66)
2002	0.07	0.63	1.06	0.85
2003	0.85	0.97	1.14	0.97
2004	1.23	1.46	1.88	1.83

Interim Dividends (Per Share)

Amt	Decl	Ex	Rec	Pay
0.275Q	4/29/2004	6/8/2004	6/10/2004	7/15/2004
0.275Q	7/15/2004	9/8/2004	9/10/2004	10/15/2004
0.275Q	10/14/2004	12/8/2004	12/10/2004	1/15/2005
0.31Q	2/10/2005	3/8/2005	3/10/2005	4/15/2005

Indicated Div: $1.24

Valuation Analysis

Forecast P/E	11.24 (4/7/2005)	No of Institutions 466
Market Cap	$28.2 Billion	Shares 309,190,560
Book Value	10.6 Billion	% Held
Price/Book	2.68	77.84
Price/Sales	2.45	

Business Summary: Oil and Gas (MIC: 14.2 SIC: 311 NAIC: 11111)

Occidental Petroleum's principal businesses constitute two industry segments. The oil and gas segment explores for, develops, produces and markets crude oil and natural gas. The chemicals segment manufactures and markets basic chemicals, vinyls, and performance chemicals. Co.'s domestic oil and gas operations are located in California, Kansas, Oklahoma, Texas, New Mexico, and the Gulf of Mexico. International operations are located in Colombia, Ecuador, Oman, Pakistan, Qatar, Russia, United Arab Emirates and Yemen. Net proved developed and undeveloped reserves at Dec 31 2003 were as follows: oil, 1.99 billion barrels, and gas, 2.59 trillion cubic feet.

Recent Developments: For the year ended Dec 31 2004, income from continuing operations increased 62.8% to $2,606,000 thousand from income of $1,601,000 thousand a year earlier. Net income increased 68.2% to $2,568,000 thousand from net income of $1,527,000 thousand a year earlier. Revenues were $11,513,000 thousand, up 23.0% from $9,361,000 thousand the year before. Total direct expense was $4,509,000 thousand versus $3,897,000 thousand in the prior year, an increase of 15.7%. Total indirect expense was $2,589,000 thousand versus $2,229,000 thousand in the prior year, an increase of 16.2%.

Prospects: Strong earnings growth in the Oil and Gas segment is being driven by higher worldwide crude oil and natural gas prices, while results in the Chemicals segment are benefiting from higher sales prices in all major products. Meanwhile, on Jan 31 2005, Co. announced that it was awarded interests in nine exploration blocks in Libya. Co. will be the operator and will hold a 90.0% interest in five of the blocks, as well as a 35.0% interest in four offshore blocks. Separately, on Jan 5 2005, Co. announced that it will exit the vinyl specialty resins business by closing its Pottstown, PA manufacturing facility.

Financial Data

(US$ in Thousands)	12/31/2004	12/31/2003	12/31/2002	12/31/2001	12/31/2000	12/31/1999	12/31/1998	12/31/1997
Earnings Per Share	6.40	3.93	2.61	3.09	4.26	1.24	0.99	(1.43)
Cash Flow Per Share	9.78	8.01	5.58	7.12	6.49	2.94	0.23	4.18
Tang Book Value Per Share	26.59	20.49	16.72	15.03	12.90	9.58	8.97	5.16
Dividends Per Share	1.100	1.040	1.000	1.000	1.000	1.000	1.000	1.000
Dividend Payout %	17.19	26.46	38.31	32.36	23.47	80.65	101.01	N.M.
Income Statement								
Total Revenue	11,513,000	9,447,000	7,491,000	14,126,000	14,543,000	8,551,000	7,381,000	8,101,000
EBITDA	5,477,000	4,076,000	2,942,000	2,725,000	3,919,000	2,016,000	1,545,000	1,361,000
Depn & Amortn	1,322,000	1,183,000	1,019,000	976,000	908,000	817,000	857,000	833,000
Income Before Taxes	4,155,000	2,893,000	1,923,000	1,749,000	3,011,000	1,199,000	688,000	528,000
Income Taxes	1,708,000	1,227,000	422,000	563,000	1,442,000	631,000	363,000	311,000
Net Income	2,568,000	1,527,000	989,000	1,154,000	1,570,000	448,000	363,000	(390,000)
Average Shares	401,100	388,600	379,500	374,200	369,200	355,500	350,601	335,000
Balance Sheet								
Current Assets	4,431,000	2,474,000	1,873,000	1,483,000	2,067,000	1,688,000	2,795,000	1,916,000
Total Assets	21,391,000	18,168,000	16,548,000	17,850,000	19,414,000	14,125,000	15,252,000	15,282,000
Current Liabilities	3,423,000	2,526,000	2,235,000	1,890,000	2,740,000	1,967,000	2,931,000	1,870,000
Long-Term Obligations	3,345,000	3,993,000	3,997,000	4,065,000	5,185,000	4,368,000	5,367,000	4,925,000
Total Liabilities	10,841,000	10,239,000	10,230,000	12,216,000	14,640,000	10,602,000	11,889,000	10,996,000
Stockholders' Equity	10,550,000	7,929,000	6,318,000	5,634,000	4,774,000	3,523,000	3,363,000	4,286,000
Shares Outstanding	396,727	387,047	377,860	374,775	369,984	367,916	347,722	341,000
Statistical Record								
Return on Assets %	12.95	8.80	5.75	6.19	9.34	3.05	2.38	N.M.
Return on Equity %	27.72	21.44	16.55	22.18	37.74	13.01	9.49	N.M.
EBITDA Margin %	47.57	43.15	39.27	19.29	26.95	23.58	20.93	16.80
Net Margin %	22.31	16.16	13.20	8.17	10.80	5.24	4.92	N.M.
Asset Turnover	0.58	0.54	0.44	0.76	0.86	0.58	0.48	0.49
Current Ratio	1.29	0.98	0.84	0.78	0.75	0.86	0.95	1.02
Debt to Equity	0.32	0.50	0.63	0.72	1.09	1.24	1.60	1.15
Price Range	60.31-42.04	42.63-27.28	30.67-23.46	31.08-21.90	25.50-15.75	24.19-14.75	30.00-16.88	30.31-21.88
P/E Ratio	9.42-6.57	10.85-6.94	11.75-8.99	10.06-7.09	5.99-3.70	19.51-11.90	30.30-17.05	N/A
Average Yield %	2.20	3.14	3.56	3.83	4.76	4.98	4.13	3.91

Address: 10889 Wilshire Boulevard, Los Angeles, CA 90024-4201	Web Site: www.oxy.com	Auditors: KPMG LLP
Telephone: (310) 208 8800	Officers: Ray R. Irani - Chmn., C.E.O. Dale R. Laurence - Pres.	Investor Contact: 212-603-8111
Fax: (310) 443 6690		

ODYSSEY RE HOLDINGS CORP.

Exchange	Symbol	Price	52Wk Range	Yield	P/E
NYS	ORH	$25.04 (3/31/2005)	27.54-20.50	0.50	9.24

*7 Year Price Score N/A ***NYSE Composite Index=100** ***12 Month Price Score 98.20**

Interim Earnings (Per Share)

Qtr.	Mar	Jun	Sep	Dec
2001	0.90	0.42	(0.65)	(0.12)
2002	0.86	0.50	1.35	0.48
2003	0.72	1.73	0.65	0.73
2004	0.90	0.91	0.28	0.62

Interim Dividends (Per Share)

Amt	Decl	Ex	Rec	Pay
0.031Q	5/18/2004	6/14/2004	6/16/2004	6/30/2004
0.031Q	8/23/2004	9/14/2004	9/16/2004	9/30/2004
0.031Q	11/18/2004	12/13/2004	12/15/2004	12/29/2004
0.031Q	2/18/2005	3/15/2005	3/17/2005	3/31/2005

Indicated Div: $0.13

Valuation Analysis

Forecast P/E	10.54	No of Institutions
	(4/13/2005)	95
Market Cap	$1.6 Billion	Shares
Book Value	1.6 Billion	17,393,006
Price/Book	1.02	% Held
Price/Sales	0.62	26.86

Business Summary: Insurance (MIC: 8.2 SIC: 321 NAIC: 24130)

Odyssey Re Holdings is a reinsurance holding company. Through its subsidiaries, Co. is engaged in the provision of a full range of property and casualty products on a worldwide basis. Co. offers a broad range of treaty and facultative reinsurance to property and casualty insurers and reinsurers. Co. also writes specialty and non-traditional lines of reinsurance, including professional liability, marine and aerospace. In addition, Co. provides underwriting for medical malpractice and hospital professional liability insurance through a Healthcare unit in Napa, CA. As of Dec 31, 2003, Co. operated through 17 offices in the U.S., London, Paris, Singapore and Latin America.

Recent Developments: For the year ended Dec 31 2004, net income decreased 25.0% to $186,899 thousand from net income of $249,225 thousand a year earlier. Revenues were $2,609,234 thousand, up 13.3% from $2,301,950 thousand the year before. Net premiums earned were $2,331,067 thousand versus $1,965,093 thousand in the prior year, an increase of 18.6%.For the year ended Dec 31 2004, net income decreased 25.0% to $186,899 thousand from net income of $249,225 thousand a year earlier. Revenues were $2,609,234 thousand, up 13.3% from $2,301,950 thousand the year before. Net premiums earned were $2,331,067 thousand versus $1,965,093 thousand in the prior year, an increase of 18.6%.

Prospects: Despite the negative impact of much higher catastrophe losses associated with hurricanes in the U.S. and Caribbean during the second half of 2004, Co. is pleased with its continued strong operating performance, which it attributes to strategic efforts over the past few years to diversify geographically and by product line. Looking ahead, Co.'s prospects appear mostly positive, reflecting improved premium rates and terms and conditions in the marketplace, as well as Co.'s focus on underwriting better-quality business. Positive momentum should also be driven by improvements in Co.'s business-mix diversification, as well as its geographic expansion.

Financial Data
(US$ in Thousands)

	12/31/2004	12/31/2003	12/31/2002	12/31/2001	12/31/2000	12/31/1999	12/31/1998
Earnings Per Share	2.71	3.83	3.20	(0.14)	2.63	3.18	4.10
Cash Flow Per Share	9.35	8.71	3.31	(0.87)	(5.42)	(6.24)	(0.44)
Tang Book Value Per Share	24.48	21.39	16.25	12.60	45.89	38.63	...
Dividends Per Share	0.125	0.106	0.100	0.025	...	...	...
Dividend Payout %	4.61	2.77	3.13	N.M.	...	...	...
Income Statement							
Premium Income	2,331,067	1,965,093	1,432,642	900,537	681,831	508,408	216,566
Total Revenue	2,609,234	2,301,950	1,691,466	1,029,205	835,874	645,946	339,983
Benefits & Claims	1,629,564	1,325,765	987,195	725,767	503,464	383,883	166,052
Income Before Taxes	278,750	378,294	258,066	(15,619)	80,586	79,560	100,592
Income Taxes	91,851	129,069	86,751	(7,658)	25,795	23,526	32,127
Net Income	186,899	249,225	208,177	(7,961)	54,791	56,034	68,465
Average Shares	69,993	65,110	65,129	57,018	20	17	16
Balance Sheet							
Total Assets	7,705,775	6,460,056	5,304,960	4,648,291	4,254,103	4,079,726	...
Total Liabilities	6,120,275	5,069,821	4,248,877	3,827,419	3,296,228	3,273,390	...
Stockholders' Equity	1,585,500	1,390,235	1,056,083	820,872	957,875	806,336	...
Shares Outstanding	64,754	64,996	65,003	65,142	20	20	16
Statistical Record							
Return on Assets %	2.63	4.24	4.18	N.M.	1.31	1.37	...
Return on Equity %	12.53	20.38	22.18	N.M.	6.19	6.95	...
Loss Ratio %	69.91	67.47	68.91	80.59	73.84	75.51	76.68
Net Margin %	7.16	10.83	12.31	(0.77)	6.55	8.67	20.14
Price Range	27.54-20.50	23.01-15.65	19.83-13.02	18.18-11.29	...	...	...
P/E Ratio	10.16-7.56	6.01-4.09	6.20-4.07	N/A	...	...	...
Average Yield %	0.52	0.53	0.59	0.16	...	...	...

Address: 140 Broadway, 39th Floor, New York, NY 10005 **Telephone:** (212) 978-4700	**Web Site:** www.odysseyre.com **Officers:** V. Prem Watsa - Chmn. James F. Dowd - Vice-Chmn.	**Auditors:** PricewaterhouseCoopers LLP **Investor Contact:** 203-940-8610

OFFICE DEPOT, INC.

Exchange	Symbol	Price	52Wk Range	Yield	P/E
NYS	ODP	$22.18 (3/31/2005)	22.85-14.12	N/A	20.92

*7 Year Price Score 98.33 *NYSE Composite Index=100 *12 Month Price Score 106.42

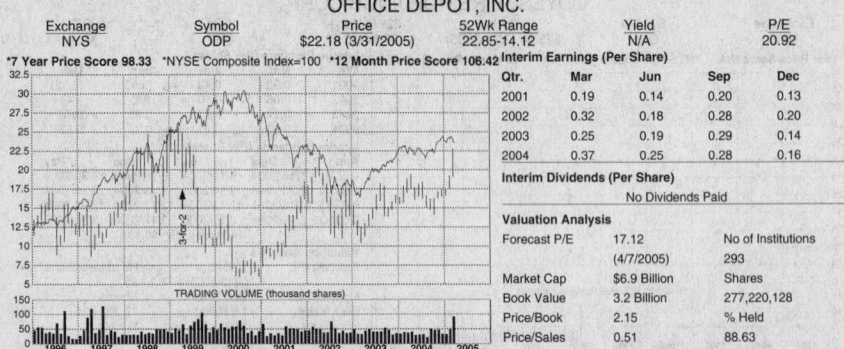

Interim Earnings (Per Share)

Qtr.	Mar	Jun	Sep	Dec
2001	0.19	0.14	0.20	0.13
2002	0.32	0.18	0.28	0.20
2003	0.25	0.19	0.29	0.14
2004	0.37	0.25	0.28	0.16

Interim Dividends (Per Share)

No Dividends Paid

Valuation Analysis

Forecast P/E	17.12	No of Institutions
	(4/7/2005)	293
Market Cap	$6.9 Billion	Shares
Book Value	3.2 Billion	277,220,128
Price/Book	2.15	% Held
Price/Sales	0.51	88.63

Business Summary: Retail - Miscellaneous (MIC: 5.11 SIC: 044 NAIC: 53998)

Office Depot operated 900 office supply stores in the U.S. and Canada as of Dec 27 2003. Co.'s stores, which utilize a warehouse format, stock a wide selection of general office supplies, computers and accessories, and office furniture. Co. also operates a national business-to-business delivery network supported by 22 delivery centers, more than 60 local sales offices and thirteen regional call centers. Co. sells products and services in 21 countries outside the U.S. and Canada, including 40 stores in France, 18 in Japan and six in Spain that are owned and operated by Co. In addition, Co. operates 135 stores under joint venture and licensing agreements in eight foreign countries.

Recent Developments: For the year ended Dec 25 2004, net income increased 22.7% to $335,504 thousand from net income of $273,515 thousand a year earlier. Revenues were $13,564,699 thousand, up 9.8% from $12,358,566 thousand the year before. Operating income was $529,977 thousand versus an income of $465,985 thousand in the prior year, an increase of 13.7%. Total direct expense was $9,308,560 thousand versus $8,483,820 thousand in the prior year, an increase of 9.7%. Total indirect expense was $3,726,162 thousand versus $3,408,761 thousand in the prior year, an increase of 9.3%.

Prospects: International earnings are improving, but the sales contributions from the Guilbert acquisition remain short of Co.'s expectations. Accordingly, Co. is taking steps to improve its cost structure in Europe and to focus on driving sales in the Guilbert business. Meanwhile, Co.'s efforts to improve the profitability of its North America retail operations and grow market share in its North American delivery businesses are beginning to gain momentum. Separately, Co. intends to restate its financial statements for the fiscal years ended in Dec 2002 and 2003. The restatement will have an impact of approximately $0.01 per share for each of such years.

Financial Data

(US$ in Thousands)	12/25/2004	12/27/2003	12/28/2002	12/29/2001	12/30/2000	12/25/1999	12/26/1998	12/27/1997
Earnings Per Share	1.06	0.88	0.98	0.66	0.16	0.69	0.61	0.65
Cash Flow Per Share	2.08	2.11	2.29	2.51	1.01	1.04	1.80	1.64
Tang Book Value Per Share	6.96	5.77	6.61	5.28	4.66	5.06	4.86	4.82
Income Statement								
Total Revenue	13,564,699	12,358,566	11,356,633	11,154,081	11,569,696	10,263,280	8,997,738	6,717,514
EBITDA	769,999	731,749	707,638	544,808	320,568	578,412	526,714	376,870
Depn & Amortn	267,700	246,100	200,747	199,434	205,710	168,553	140,940	97,030
Income Before Taxes	461,233	445,040	479,205	314,130	92,459	413,887	388,727	263,414
Income Taxes	125,729	143,016	167,722	113,087	43,127	156,249	155,531	103,738
Net Income	335,504	276,295	310,708	201,043	49,332	257,638	233,196	159,676
Average Shares	315,625	313,688	322,200	316,424	311,231	393,657	402,319	239,514
Balance Sheet								
Current Assets	3,916,171	3,576,728	3,209,715	2,806,190	2,699,089	2,631,052	2,780,435	2,020,587
Total Assets	6,767,351	6,145,242	4,765,812	4,331,643	4,196,334	4,276,183	4,113,041	2,981,089
Current Liabilities	2,618,357	2,277,253	1,992,009	2,101,514	1,908,337	1,944,045	1,531,001	1,137,782
Long-Term Obligations	583,680	829,302	411,970	317,552	598,499	321,099	470,711	447,020
Total Liabilities	3,544,303	3,351,155	2,468,700	2,483,205	2,595,083	2,368,463	2,084,162	1,652,184
Stockholders' Equity	3,223,048	2,794,087	2,297,112	1,848,438	1,601,251	1,907,720	2,028,879	1,328,905
Shares Outstanding	312,301	310,193	308,515	303,095	296,497	329,442	370,572	237,454
Statistical Record								
Return on Assets %	5.21	5.08	6.85	4.73	1.15	6.16	6.59	5.60
Return on Equity %	11.18	10.88	15.03	11.69	2.77	13.13	13.93	12.89
EBITDA Margin %	5.68	5.92	6.23	4.88	2.77	5.64	5.85	5.61
Net Margin %	2.47	2.24	2.74	1.80	0.43	2.51	2.59	2.38
Asset Turnover	2.11	2.27	2.50	2.62	2.69	2.45	2.54	2.35
Current Ratio	1.50	1.57	1.61	1.34	1.41	1.35	1.82	1.78
Debt to Equity	0.18	0.30	0.18	0.17	0.37	0.17	0.23	0.34
Price Range	19.45-14.12	18.24-10.38	21.74-10.98	18.52-7.31	14.19-6.06	25.67-9.13	24.79-11.42	15.75-8.67
P/E Ratio	18.35-13.32	20.73-11.80	22.18-11.20	28.06-11.08	88.67-37.89	37.20-13.22	40.64-18.72	24.23-13.33

Address: 2200 Old Germantown Road, Delray Beach, FL 33445 **Telephone:** (561) 438-4800 **Fax:** (561) 265-4406	**Web Site:** www.officedepot.com **Officers:** M. Bruce Nelson - Chmn., C.E.O. Charles E. Brown - Exec. V.P., C.F.O.	**Auditors:** Deloitte & Touche LLP **Investor Contact:** 561-438-4930

OGE ENERGY CORP.

Exchange	Symbol	Price	52Wk Range	Yield	P/E
NYS	OGE	$26.95 (3/31/2005)	27.39-23.08	4.94	15.58

*7 Year Price Score 96.37   *NYSE Composite Index=100   *12 Month Price Score 96.42

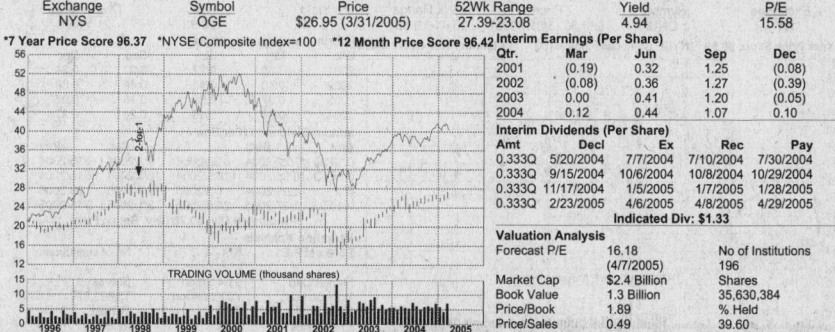

Interim Earnings (Per Share)

Qtr.	Mar	Jun	Sep	Dec
2001	(0.19)	0.32	1.25	(0.08)
2002	(0.08)	0.36	1.27	(0.39)
2003	0.00	0.41	1.20	(0.05)
2004	0.12	0.44	1.07	0.10

Interim Dividends (Per Share)

Amt	Decl	Ex	Rec	Pay
0.333Q	5/20/2004	7/7/2004	7/10/2004	7/30/2004
0.333Q	9/15/2004	10/6/2004	10/8/2004	10/29/2004
0.333Q	11/17/2004	1/5/2005	1/7/2005	1/28/2005
0.333Q	2/23/2005	4/6/2005	4/8/2005	4/29/2005
		Indicated Div: $1.33		

Valuation Analysis

Forecast P/E	16.18	No of Institutions	
	(4/7/2005)	196	
Market Cap	$2.4 Billion	Shares	
Book Value	1.3 Billion	35,630,384	
Price/Book	1.89	% Held	
Price/Sales	0.49	39.60	

Business Summary: Gas Utilities (MIC: 7.4 SIC: 922 NAIC: 86210)

OGE Energy is an energy and energy services provider that conducts its operations through two business segments. The Electric Utility segment generates, transmits, distributes and sells electric energy in Oklahoma and western Arkansas. The operations of the electric utility segment are conducted through Oklahoma Gas and Electric Company (OG&E), which had 725,470 retail customers in Oklahoma and western Arkansas, as of Dec 31 2003. The Natural Gas Pipeline segment, whose assets are located primarily in the major gas producing basins of Oklahoma, is conducted through Enogex Inc. and its subsidiaries. Enogex also owns a controlling interest in and operates the Ozark Gas Transmission System.

Recent Developments: For the year ended Dec 31 2004, income from continuing operations increased 12.8% to $153,000 thousand from income of $135,600 thousand a year earlier. Net income increased 18.3% to $153,500 thousand from net income of $129,800 thousand a year earlier. Revenues were $4,926,600 thousand, up 30.4% from $3,779,000 thousand the year before. Operating income was $317,500 thousand versus an income of $306,900 thousand in the prior year, an increase of 3.5%. Total direct expense was $7,925,400 thousand versus $4,899,300 thousand in the prior year, an increase of 61.8%. Total indirect expense was $646,400 thousand versus $626,100 thousand in the prior year, an increase of 3.2%.

Prospects: Results are benefiting from an improved performance at Enogex, reflecting higher commodity prices and improved profit margins from more favorable contractual terms in the natural gas gathering and processing business. Going forward, Co. expects earnings for 2005 in the range of $1.50 to $1.60 per share. This guidance includes a utility earnings range between $1.17 and $1.22 per share, with a 1.0% to 2.0% growth in margins, normal weather, recovery of Enogex gas transportation and storage costs, and regulatory lag in recovering costs of the McClain plant acquisition. The earnings guidance also includes Enogex earnings of $0.43 to $0.48 per share, with a conservative commodity price outlook.

Financial Data

(US$ in Thousands)	12/31/2004	12/31/2003	12/31/2002	12/31/2001	12/31/2000	12/31/1999	12/31/1998	12/31/1997
Earnings Per Share	1.73	1.58	1.16	1.29	1.89	1.94	2.04	1.62
Cash Flow Per Share	4.07	4.42	3.43	6.90	2.71	2.88	3.62	3.66
Tang Book Value Per Share	13.86	13.29	11.99	12.74	13.66	13.09	12.91	11.58
Dividends Per Share	1.330	1.330	1.330	1.330	1.330	1.330	1.330	0.998
Dividend Payout %	76.88	84.18	114.66	103.10	70.37	68.56	65.20	61.57
Income Statement								
Total Revenue	4,926,600	3,779,000	3,023,900	3,182,363	3,298,727	2,172,434	1,617,737	1,472,307
EBITDA	502,700	482,900	417,200	457,213	528,560	506,523	366,723	384,787
Depn & Amortn	178,600	176,900	182,500	181,224	176,144	165,041	149,818	142,632
Income Before Taxes	233,200	209,300	125,600	153,154	223,540	241,203	284,816	217,302
Income Taxes	80,200	73,700	44,600	52,583	76,505	89,944	118,944	84,752
Net Income	153,500	129,800	90,800	100,571	147,035	151,259	165,872	132,550
Average Shares	88,500	82,100	78,200	77,929	77,688	77,916	80,787	80,746
Balance Sheet								
Net PPE	3,581,000	3,309,500	3,204,300	3,263,748	3,219,464	3,241,987	2,526,550	2,353,851
Total Assets	4,870,300	4,584,700	4,127,200	3,996,592	4,319,630	3,921,334	2,983,929	2,765,865
Long-Term Obligations	1,424,100	1,436,100	1,501,900	1,526,303	1,648,523	1,140,532	935,583	841,924
Total Liabilities	3,584,700	3,383,100	3,143,300	2,956,023	3,255,322	2,901,955	1,940,547	1,731,639
Stockholders' Equity	1,285,600	1,201,600	983,900	1,040,569	1,064,308	1,019,379	1,043,382	984,960
Shares Outstanding	90,000	87,400	78,500	77,991	77,921	77,863	80,797	80,772
Statistical Record								
Return on Assets %	3.24	2.98	2.24	2.42	3.56	4.38	5.77	5.11
Return on Equity %	12.31	11.88	8.97	9.56	14.07	14.67	16.36	14.52
EBITDA Margin %	10.20	12.78	13.80	14.37	16.02	23.32	22.67	26.13
Net Margin %	3.12	3.43	3.00	3.16	4.46	6.96	10.25	9.00
PPE Turnover	1.43	1.16	0.94	0.98	1.02	0.75	0.66	0.67
Asset Turnover	1.04	0.87	0.74	0.77	0.80	0.63	0.56	0.57
Debt to Equity	1.11	1.20	1.53	1.47	1.55	1.12	0.90	0.85
Price Range	26.79-23.08	24.30-16.51	24.02-14.04	24.13-20.73	24.75-16.56	29.00-18.69	29.63-25.75	27.34-20.38
P/E Ratio	15.49-13.34	15.38-10.45	20.71-12.10	18.70-16.07	13.10-8.76	14.95-9.63	14.52-12.62	16.88-12.58
Average Yield %	5.29	6.50	6.59	5.95	6.62	5.64	4.88	4.44

Address: 321 North Harvey, PO Box 321, Oklahoma City, OK 73101-0321 **Telephone:** (405) 553-3000	**Web Site:** www.oge.com **Officers:** Steven E. Moore - Chmn., Pres., C.E.O. Peter B. Delaney - Exec. V.P., C.O.O.	**Auditors:** Ernst & Young LLP

OLD NATIONAL BANCORP (EVANSVILLE, IN)

Exchange	Symbol	Price	52Wk Range	Yield	P/E	Div Acheiver
NYS	ONB	$20.30 (3/31/2005)	25.41-19.83	3.74	20.93	21 Years

*7 Year Price Score 88.69 ***NYSE Composite Index=100** ***12 Month Price Score 84.59**

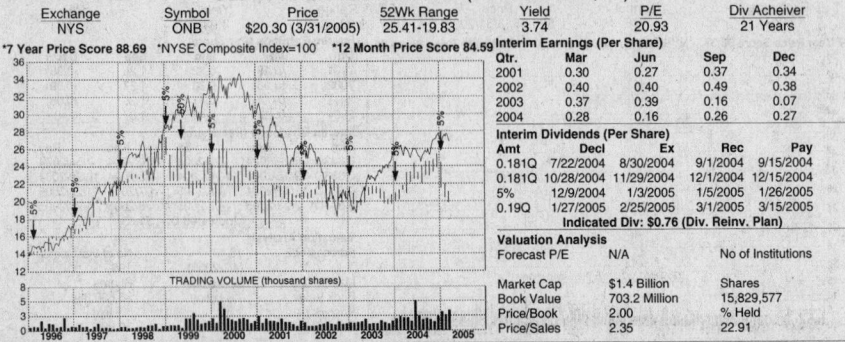

Interim Earnings (Per Share)

Qtr.	Mar	Jun	Sep	Dec
2001	0.30	0.27	0.37	0.34
2002	0.40	0.40	0.49	0.38
2003	0.37	0.39	0.16	0.07
2004	0.28	0.16	0.26	0.27

Interim Dividends (Per Share)

Amt	Decl	Ex	Rec	Pay
0.181Q	7/22/2004	8/30/2004	9/1/2004	9/15/2004
0.181Q	10/28/2004	11/29/2004	12/1/2004	12/15/2004
5%	12/9/2004	1/3/2005	1/5/2005	1/26/2005
0.19Q	1/27/2005	2/25/2005	3/1/2005	3/15/2005

Indicated Div: $0.76 (Div. Reinv. Plan)

Valuation Analysis

Forecast P/E	N/A	No of Institutions
Market Cap	$1.4 Billion	Shares
Book Value	703.2 Million	15,829,577
Price/Book	2.00	% Held
Price/Sales	2.35	22.91

Business Summary: Commercial Banking (MIC: 8.1 SIC: 021 NAIC: 22110)

Old National Bancorp, with total assets of $9.35 billion as of Dec 31 2003, is a financial holding company headquartered in Evansville, IN with banking activity in Indiana, Illinois, Kentucky, Tennessee, and Ohio. As of Dec 31 2003, Co. operated over 120 banking offices serving customers in both urban and rural markets. Co.'s banking centers provide a wide range of financial services, such as commercial, real estate, and consumer loans; lease financing; checking, savings, time deposits; and letters of credit. Co.'s non-bank affiliates provide additional financial or support services incidental to its operations, including issuance and reinsurance of credit life services.

Recent Developments: For the year ended Dec 31 2004, net income decreased 4.0% to $67,571 thousand from net income of $70,413 thousand a year earlier. Net interest income was $250,807 thousand, down 7.8% from $272,007 thousand the year before. Provision for loan losses was $22,400 thousand versus $85,000 thousand in the prior year, a decrease of 73.6%. Non-interest income fell 5.2% to $182,163 thousand, while non-interest expense advanced 12.1% to $335,927 thousand.

Prospects: Co. has successfully strengthened its risk profile, and will continue to diligently monitor the strength of its overall credit quality. In addition, Co. is pleased with the significant strengthening of its internal structure and processes designed to ensure that its day-to-day operations are in compliance with regulatory requirements aimed at bank secrecy, money laundering and other operational safeguards. These internal improvements, along with the implementation of ASCEND ideas and the newly reorganized management team, should allow Co. to shift its focus from operational issues to building long-term earnings value.

Financial Data
(US$ in Thousands)

	12/31/2004	12/31/2003	12/31/2002	12/31/2001	12/31/2000	12/31/1999	12/31/1998	12/31/1997
Earnings Per Share	0.97	1.00	1.67	1.29	0.85	1.38	1.04	1.00
Cash Flow Per Share	1.27	2.91	0.99	1.48	1.44	1.67	1.37	1.07
Tang Book Value Per Share	7.48	7.58	8.40	9.03	8.54	8.16	8.58	8.65
Dividends Per Share	0.724	0.689	0.622	0.559	0.533	0.495	0.436	0.415
Dividend Payout %	74.62	68.93	37.27	43.46	62.87	35.89	41.92	41.33
Income Statement								
Interest Income	417,198	469,748	547,383	629,707	638,275	488,923	437,909	429,446
Interest Expense	166,391	197,741	257,954	338,408	368,404	250,536	223,059	210,208
Net Interest Income	250,807	272,007	289,429	291,299	269,871	238,387	214,850	219,238
Provision for Losses	22,400	85,000	33,500	28,700	29,803	11,489	11,420	26,965
Non-Interest Income	182,163	192,149	154,497	112,967	101,713	67,508	54,557	47,090
Non-Interest Expense	329,692	285,040	257,845	254,812	265,537	185,564	158,125	154,364
Income Before Taxes	74,643	79,440	152,581	120,754	76,244	108,842	99,862	84,999
Income Taxes	7,072	9,027	34,649	27,710	14,548	26,148	28,144	24,339
Net Income	67,571	70,413	117,932	93,044	61,696	86,795	61,864	60,660
Average Shares	70,024	70,173	70,673	72,037	73,173	63,654	60,730	61,823
Balance Sheet								
Net Loans & Leases	4,879,093	5,465,546	5,681,893	6,058,613	6,274,480	4,780,888	4,112,804	3,683,969
Total Assets	8,898,304	9,353,896	9,612,556	9,080,473	8,767,748	6,982,932	6,165,968	5,688,215
Total Deposits	6,414,263	6,493,092	6,439,280	6,616,440	6,583,906	5,071,298	4,443,472	4,298,730
Total Liabilities	8,195,096	8,638,406	8,871,846	8,441,238	8,141,407	6,490,188	5,671,388	5,211,012
Stockholders' Equity	703,208	715,490	740,710	639,235	626,341	492,744	494,580	477,203
Shares Outstanding	69,287	69,903	70,401	70,816	73,308	60,354	57,662	55,192
Statistical Record								
Return on Assets %	0.74	0.74	1.26	1.04	0.78	1.32	1.04	1.10
Return on Equity %	9.50	9.67	17.09	14.70	11.00	17.58	12.73	12.97
Net Interest Margin %	60.12	57.90	52.88	46.26	42.28	48.76	49.06	51.05
Efficiency Ratio %	55.01	43.06	36.74	34.31	35.88	33.35	32.11	32.39
Loans to Deposits	0.76	0.84	0.88	0.92	0.95	0.94	0.93	0.86
Price Range	25.41-20.02	21.73-19.22	22.89-19.70	23.51-16.92	27.23-18.46	27.42-20.71	27.72-21.32	22.45-16.36
P/E Ratio	26.20-20.64	21.73-19.22	13.71-11.80	18.22-13.12	32.03-21.72	19.87-15.01	26.65-20.50	22.45-16.36
Average Yield %	3.19	3.35	2.93	2.71	2.34	2.12	1.87	2.19

Address: 1 Main Street, Evansville, IN 47708 Telephone: (812) 464-1294 Fax: (812) 464-1567	Web Site: www.oldnational.com Officers: Larry E. Dunigan - Chmn. Robert G. Jones - Pres., C.E.O.	Auditors: PricewaterhouseCoopers LLP Investor Contact: 812-464-1366 Transfer Agents: Old National Bancorp, Evansville, IN

OLD REPUBLIC INTERNATIONAL CORP.

Exchange	Symbol	Price	52Wk Range	Yield	P/E	Div Acheiver
NYS	ORI	$23.29 (3/31/2005)	25.79-21.37	2.23	9.87	23 Years

*7 Year Price Score 112.47 *NYSE Composite Index=100   *12 Month Price Score 93.33

Interim Earnings (Per Share)

Qtr.	Mar	Jun	Sep	Dec
2001	0.47	0.51	0.46	0.49
2002	0.53	0.59	0.53	0.51
2003	0.57	0.67	0.65	0.62
2004	0.57	0.65	0.59	0.55

Interim Dividends (Per Share)

Amt	Decl	Ex	Rec	Pay
0.113Q	2/25/2004	3/3/2004	3/5/2004	3/15/2004
0.13Q	5/14/2004	6/2/2004	6/4/2004	6/15/2004
0.13Q	8/12/2004	9/1/2004	9/3/2004	9/15/2004
0.13Q	12/2/2004	12/8/2004	12/10/2004	12/15/2004

Indicated Div: $0.52 (Div. Reinv. Plan)

Valuation Analysis

Forecast P/E	8.92	No of Institutions
	(4/12/2005)	257
Market Cap	$4.3 Billion	Shares
Book Value	3.9 Billion	132,655,872
Price/Book	1.12	% Held
Price/Sales	1.24	72.64

TRADING VOLUME (thousand shares)

Business Summary: Insurance (MIC: 8.2 SIC: 351 NAIC: 24130)

Old Republic International is an insurance holding company. Through its general insurance group, Co. assumes risks and provides related risk management and marketing services pertaining to a large variety of property and liability commercial insurance coverages. Through its mortgage guaranty group, Co. protects mortgage lenders and investors from default related losses on residential mortgage loans. Through its title insurance group, Co. issues policies to real estate purchasers and investors. Co.'s life insurance group markets and writes consumer credit life and disability insurance primarily through automobile dealers.

Recent Developments: For the year ended Dec 31 2004, net income decreased 5.4% to $435,000 thousand from net income of $459,800 thousand a year earlier. Revenues were $3,491,600 thousand, up 6.3% from $3,285,800 thousand the year before. Net premiums earned were $2,804,800 thousand versus $2,582,100 thousand in the prior year, an increase of 8.6%. Net investment income totaled $290,800 thousand, up 4.2% compared with $279,200 thousand the previous year.

Prospects: Co. is benefiting from continuing growth of its General Insurance premiums and greater than average realized investment gains. Over the past year, net investment income has reflected a gradual increase principally due to Co.'s rising invested asset base. In combination, these factors are driving higher revenues. Earned premiums in the General Insurance group are rising as a result of positive pricing and the risk selection changes previously effected, as well as additional business being produced in a fairly stable underwriting environment. In Co.'s Mortgage Guaranty group, net premiums earned are being adversely affected by lower origination volumes and greater reinsurance cessions.

Financial Data

(US$ in Thousands)	12/31/2004	12/31/2003	12/31/2002	12/31/2001	12/31/2000	12/31/1999	12/31/1998	12/31/1997
Earnings Per Share	2.36	2.51	2.15	1.92	1.65	1.17	1.55	1.40
Cash Flow Per Share	4.53	4.16	3.71	2.95	1.92	1.42	1.62	1.93
Tang Book Value Per Share	20.85	19.26	17.00	15.19	13.38	9.35	11.51	10.39
Dividends Per Share	0.503	1.113	0.420	0.393	0.367	0.327	0.258	0.222
Dividend Payout %	21.31	44.36	19.50	20.49	22.27	28.00	16.60	15.87
Income Statement								
Premium Income	2,804,800	2,582,100	2,135,400	1,786,800	1,550,300	1,567,200	1,568,100	1,464,600
Total Revenue	3,491,600	3,285,800	2,756,400	2,373,400	2,070,600	2,102,100	2,171,700	1,962,800
Benefits & Claims	1,305,600	1,097,600	975,300	861,000	760,300	829,900	781,700	787,900
Income Before Taxes	650,900	680,000	560,900	503,900	426,400	317,000	466,700	426,700
Income Taxes	215,900	219,900	167,700	159,700	131,000	92,900	145,900	129,200
Net Income	435,000	459,800	392,900	346,900	297,500	226,800	323,700	298,100
Average Shares	184,607	183,302	182,323	180,491	180,295	194,680	208,725	212,652
Balance Sheet								
Total Assets	10,570,800	9,712,300	8,715,400	7,920,200	7,281,400	6,938,400	7,019,700	6,923,400
Total Liabilities	6,705,100	6,158,600	5,559,500	5,136,100	4,842,000	4,739,200	4,714,200	4,770,200
Stockholders' Equity	3,865,600	3,553,600	3,155,800	2,783,700	2,438,700	2,198,400	2,304,200	2,152,100
Shares Outstanding	185,429	184,471	185,687	183,253	182,167	235,018	200,104	207,105
Statistical Record								
Return on Assets %	4.28	4.99	4.72	4.56	4.17	3.25	4.64	4.39
Return on Equity %	11.69	13.71	13.23	13.29	12.80	10.07	14.53	14.71
Loss Ratio %	46.55	42.51	45.67	48.19	49.04	52.95	49.85	53.80
Net Margin %	12.46	13.99	14.25	14.62	14.37	10.79	14.91	15.19
Price Range	27.19-21.37	25.79-16.53	23.15-16.85	20.04-15.10	21.33-7.17	15.04-8.25	21.25-12.00	17.72-10.94
P/E Ratio	11.52-9.06	10.27-6.58	10.77-7.84	10.44-7.86	12.93-4.34	12.86-7.05	13.71-7.74	12.66-7.82
Average Yield %	2.09	5.17	2.06	2.16	2.86	2.88	1.50	1.57

Address: 307 North Michigan Avenue, Chicago, IL 60601	**Web Site:** www.oldrepublic.com	**Auditors:** PricewaterhouseCoopers LLP
Telephone: (312) 346-8100	**Officers:** Aldo C. Zucaro - Chmn., Pres., C.E.O. Karl W. Mueller - Sr. V.P., C.F.O.	**Transfer Agents:** EquiServe, First Chicago Trust Division, Jersey City, NJ
Fax: (312) 726-0309		

OLIN CORP.

Exchange	Symbol	Price	52Wk Range	Yield	P/E
NYS	OLN	$22.30 (3/31/2005)	25.00-15.50	3.59	27.88

*7 Year Price Score 93.99 ***NYSE Composite Index=100** ***12 Month Price Score 113.14**

Interim Earnings (Per Share)

Qtr.	Mar	Jun	Sep	Dec
2001	0.06	0.15	(0.45)	0.02
2002	(0.26)	(0.15)	(0.02)	(0.22)
2003	(0.67)	0.15	0.10	0.00
2004	0.04	0.15	0.27	0.33

Interim Dividends (Per Share)

Amt	Decl	Ex	Rec	Pay
0.20Q	4/29/2004	5/6/2004	5/10/2004	6/10/2004
0.20Q	7/29/2004	8/6/2004	8/10/2004	9/10/2004
0.20Q	10/28/2004	11/8/2004	11/10/2004	12/10/2004
0.20Q	1/27/2005	2/8/2005	2/10/2005	3/10/2005
		Indicated Div: $0.80		

Valuation Analysis

Forecast P/E	12.18	No of Institutions
	(4/7/2005)	182
Market Cap	$1.6 Billion	Shares
Book Value	356.0 Million	54,336,784
Price/Book	4.42	% Held
Price/Sales	0.79	76.61

Business Summary: Chemicals (MIC: 11.1 SIC: 812 NAIC: 25181)

Olin is a manufacturer concentrated in three business segments: chlor alkali products, metals, and Winchester®. Chlor alkali products include chlorine and caustic soda, sodium hydrosulfite, hydrochloric acid and bleach products. Metals products include copper and copper alloy sheet, strip, foil, rod, welded tube, fabricated parts, metal packages and stainless steel and aluminum strip. The Metals segment also includes a network of metals service centers in the U.S. and Puerto Rico. Winchester® products include sporting ammunition, canister powder, reloading components, small caliber military ammunition, and industrial cartridges.

Recent Developments: For the year ended Dec 31 2004, net income was $55 million versus net loss of $24 million a year earlier. Revenues were $1,997 million, up 28.3% from $1,557 million the year before. Operating income was $77 million versus an income of $12 million in the prior year, an increase of 541.7%. Total direct expense was $1,765 million versus $1,382 million in the prior year, an increase of 27.7%. Total indirect expense was $155 million versus $163 million in the prior year, a decrease of 4.9%.

Prospects: Results are being positively affected by strong sales growth in the Chlor Alkali segment stemming from an increase in chlorine and caustic volumes and higher prices, partially offset by higher electricity and transportation costs. Meanwhile, robust sales in the Metals segment are being fueled primarily by higher copper prices. Increased shipments to the ammunition and coinage segments are being partially offset by reduced shipments to the automotive, electronics, and building products segments. Separately, Co. anticipates first-quarter 2005 earnings of approximately $0.40 per diluted share, reflecting expected further earnings improvement in the Chlor Alkali segment.

Financial Data

(US$ in Thousands)	12/31/2004	12/31/2003	12/31/2002	12/31/2001	12/31/2000	12/31/1999	12/31/1998	12/31/1997
Earnings Per Share	0.80	(0.42)	(0.63)	(0.22)	1.80	0.45	1.63	3.00
Cash Flow Per Share	(2.00)	2.04	0.63	1.74	4.02	0.51	3.78	1.05
Tang Book Value Per Share	3.94	1.63	2.59	6.24	7.48	6.86	17.21	18.01
Dividends Per Share	0.800	0.800	0.800	0.800	0.800	0.900	1.200	1.200
Dividend Payout %	100.00	N.M.	N.M.	N.M.	44.44	200.00	73.62	40.00
Income Statement								
Total Revenue	1,997,000	1,586,000	1,301,000	1,271,000	1,549,000	1,315,000	1,426,000	2,410,000
EBITDA	170,000	106,000	84,000	90,000	226,000	121,000	151,000	334,000
Depn & Amortn	73,000	82,000	88,000	87,000	81,000	80,000	78,000	86,000
Income Before Taxes	79,000	5,000	(27,000)	(13,000)	131,000	27,000	59,000	234,000
Income Taxes	28,000	4,000	4,000	(4,000)	50,000	10,000	21,000	81,000
Net Income	55,000	(24,000)	(31,000)	(9,000)	81,000	21,000	78,000	153,000
Average Shares	68,400	58,300	49,400	43,600	45,000	45,400	47,800	50,800
Balance Sheet								
Current Assets	713,000	681,000	638,000	616,000	528,000	504,000	517,000	936,000
Total Assets	1,618,000	1,445,000	1,424,000	1,219,000	1,123,000	1,063,000	1,577,000	1,946,000
Current Liabilities	322,000	311,000	257,000	335,000	275,000	252,000	292,000	512,000
Long-Term Obligations	261,000	301,000	328,000	329,000	228,000	229,000	230,000	268,000
Total Liabilities	1,262,000	1,269,000	1,193,000	948,000	794,000	754,000	787,000	1,067,000
Stockholders' Equity	356,000	176,000	231,000	271,000	329,000	309,000	790,000	879,000
Shares Outstanding	70,566	59,015	57,622	43,440	43,980	45,061	45,900	48,800
Statistical Record								
Return on Assets %	3.58	N.M.	N.M.	N.M.	7.39	1.59	4.43	7.14
Return on Equity %	20.62	N.M.	N.M.	N.M.	25.32	3.82	9.35	16.77
EBITDA Margin %	8.51	6.68	6.46	7.08	14.59	9.20	10.59	13.86
Net Margin %	2.75	N.M.	N.M.	N.M.	5.23	1.60	5.47	6.35
Asset Turnover	1.30	1.11	0.98	1.09	1.41	1.00	0.81	1.12
Current Ratio	2.21	2.19	2.48	1.84	1.92	2.00	1.77	1.83
Debt to Equity	0.73	1.71	1.42	1.21	0.69	0.74	0.29	0.30
Price Range	22.79-15.50	20.47-15.30	22.15-14.01	22.53-12.21	23.06-14.50	19.81-9.69	30.92-15.92	32.55-22.46
P/E Ratio	28.49-19.38	N/A	N/A	N/A	12.81-8.06	44.03-21.53	18.97-9.76	10.85-7.49
Average Yield %	4.34	4.57	4.61	4.53	4.64	6.38	4.96	4.44

Address: 501 Merritt 7, Norwalk, CT 06856	**Web Site:** www.olin.com	**Auditors:** KPMG LLP
Telephone: (203) 750-3000	**Officers:** Randall W. Larrimore - Chmn. Joseph D. Rupp - Pres., C.E.O.	**Investor Contact:** 203-750-3254
Fax: (203) 750-3205		

OM GROUP, INC.

*7 Year Price Score 70.32   *NYSE Composite Index=100   ***12 Month Price Score 92.59**

Interim Earnings (Per Share)

Qtr.	Mar	Jun	Sep	Dec
2000	0.63	0.76	0.77	0.80
2001	0.81	0.83	0.84	0.62
2002	0.85	0.89	(2.52)	(10.89)
2003	(0.27)	0.15	2.19	...

Interim Dividends (Per Share)

Dividend Payment Suspended

Valuation Analysis

Forecast P/E	0.00	No of Institutions
	(4/7/2005)	156
Market Cap	$862.6 Million	Shares
Book Value	513.8 Million	24,894,720
Price/Book	1.68	% Held
Price/Sales	0.30	87.80

Business Summary: Chemicals (MIC: 11.1 SIC: 819 NAIC: 25188)

OM Group is an international producer and marketer of value-added, metal-based specialty chemicals. Co. supplies customers in 50 countries with more than 3,000 product offerings, primarily organics, inorganics, powders and metals. Co.'s organic, inorganic and powder products serve more than 30 large industries, including automotive, catalysts, coatings, colorants, electronics, fuel cells, jewelry products, liquid detergents, lubricants, plastics, rechargeable batteries, rubber, stainless steel and other specialty chemicals. Co. operates manufacturing facilities in the Americas, Europe, Asia, Africa and Australia.

Recent Developments: For the quarter ended Sep 30 2004, net income was $26.0 million, compared with income of $7.0 million, before income of $74.3 million from discontinued operations, in the corresponding period of the previous year. Net sales advanced 30.8% to $311.9 million from $238.5 million in the year-earlier quarter. Gross profit soared 49.7% to $76.1 million from $50.8 million the year before. Selling, general and administrative expenses decreased 9.1% to $26.7 million from $29.4 million in 2003. Operating income totaled $49.4 million versus $21.4 million in the prior-year period.

Prospects: As fiscal 2005 approaches, Co. is already seeing the fruits from the improvements made to its information systems in the form of streamlining costs, managing inventories and expanding its presence in Asian markets. Meanwhile, Co. is continuing with the restatement process of its 2003 Form 10-K and 2004 Form 10-Qs. Co. is also voluntarily cooperating with the Securities and Exchange Commission's Division of Enforcement regarding the findings of the previously announced investigation by the audit committee of Co.'s directors. This process is not expected to delay the filing of Co.'s restated financial statements.

Financial Data

(US$ in Thousands)	9 Mos	6 Mos	3 Mos	12/31/2002	12/31/2001	12/31/2000	12/31/1999	12/31/1998
Earnings Per Share	(8.82)	(13.53)	(12.79)	(11.69)	3.09	2.95	2.30	2.05
Cash Flow Per Share	4.31	(0.42)	1.80	0.99	2.43	3.39	0.52	(0.05)
Tang Book Value Per Share	11.36	11.68	9.62	9.59	14.76	13.17	11.15	9.09
Dividends Per Share	...	0.140	0.280	0.420	0.520	0.440	0.400	0.360
Dividend Payout %	...	N.M.	N.M.	N.M.	16.83	14.92	17.39	17.56
Income Statement								
Total Revenue	655,149	406,059	1,319,959	4,909,423	2,367,399	887,743	506,955	521,226
EBITDA	55,771	58,377	47,408	(71,596)	232,522	176,668	126,057	112,096
Depn & Amortn	44,730	30,393	19,544	58,943	63,476	39,298	26,864	25,435
Income Before Taxes	(19,140)	7,094	2,954	(204,810)	111,899	99,976	80,293	71,324
Income Taxes	(12,978)	1,542	3,858	(17,844)	27,715	28,476	24,468	22,966
Net Income	57,553	(3,389)	(7,764)	(327,911)	75,640	71,500	55,825	48,358
Average Shares	28,329	28,308	28,303	28,037	24,467	24,251	24,324	23,546
Balance Sheet								
Current Assets	532,121	506,053	1,289,137	1,262,337	1,452,052	611,741	497,024	420,241
Total Assets	1,297,523	2,363,309	2,347,246	2,339,136	2,541,222	1,357,462	1,017,921	870,719
Current Liabilities	243,035	127,542	428,052	414,013	422,722	207,255	124,856	119,567
Long-Term Obligations	400,314	1,145,776	1,167,800	1,187,650	1,300,507	551,079	384,888	309,964
Total Liabilities	783,749	1,842,053	1,875,646	1,869,251	1,971,689	851,332	568,693	466,576
Stockholders' Equity	513,774	521,256	471,600	469,885	569,533	506,130	449,228	404,143
Shares Outstanding	28,354	28,354	28,354	28,354	24,140	23,854	23,794	23,724
Statistical Record								
Return on Assets %	N.M.	N.M.	N.M.	N.M.	3.88	6.00	5.91	6.57
Return on Equity %	N.M.	N.M.	N.M.	N.M.	14.06	14.93	13.08	13.71
EBITDA Margin %	8.51	14.38	3.59	N.M.	9.82	19.90	24.87	21.51
Net Margin %	8.78	N.M.	N.M.	N.M.	3.20	8.05	11.01	9.28
Asset Turnover	1.49	1.60	2.05	2.01	1.21	0.75	0.54	0.71
Current Ratio	2.19	3.97	3.01	3.05	3.44	2.95	3.98	3.51
Debt to Equity	0.78	2.20	2.48	2.53	2.28	1.09	0.86	0.77
Price Range	43.50-4.06	62.75-4.06	73.00-4.06	73.00-4.06	66.19-47.50	56.38-34.13	41.50-27.13	45.94-26.25
P/E Ratio	N/A	N/A	N/A	N/A	21.42-15.37	19.11-11.57	18.04-11.79	22.41-12.80
Average Yield %	...	0.63	0.78	0.85	0.91	1.01	1.13	0.97

Address: 50 Public Square, Suite 3500, Cleveland, OH 44113-2204	**Web Site:** www.omgi.com	**Auditors:** Ernst & Young LLP
Telephone: (216) 781-0083	**Officers:** Frank E. Butler - Chmn., Interim C.E.O.	**Investor Contact:** 216-781-0083
Fax: (216) 781-1502	Michael J. Scott - V.P., Chief Admin. Officer, Sec., Gen. Couns.	

OMNICARE INC.

Exchange	Symbol	Price	52Wk Range	Yield	P/E
NYS	OCR	$35.45 (3/31/2005)	44.43-26.61	0.25	16.34

*7 Year Price Score 114.71 *NYSE Composite Index=100 *12 Month Price Score 92.44

Interim Earnings (Per Share)

Qtr.	Mar	Jun	Sep	Dec
2001	0.19	0.21	0.14	0.25
2002	0.30	0.31	0.31	0.41
2003	0.42	0.44	0.47	0.59
2004	0.61	0.58	0.54	0.45

Interim Dividends (Per Share)

Amt	Decl	Ex	Rec	Pay
0.022Q	5/18/2004	5/27/2004	6/1/2004	6/11/2004
0.022Q	8/5/2004	8/26/2004	8/30/2004	9/13/2004
0.022Q	11/4/2004	11/23/2004	11/26/2004	12/10/2004
0.022Q	2/23/2005	3/7/2005	3/9/2005	3/21/2005
		Indicated Div: $0.09		

Valuation Analysis

Forecast P/E	14.10 (4/7/2005)	No of Institutions	250
Market Cap	$3.7 Billion	Shares	94,662,264
Book Value	1.9 Billion	% Held	90.54
Price/Book	1.92		
Price/Sales	0.90		

Business Summary: Retail - Miscellaneous (MIC: 5.11 SIC: 912 NAIC: 46110)

Omnicare is a provider of pharmaceuticals and related pharmacy services to long-term care institutions such as skilled nursing facilities, assisted living facilities and retirement centers, as well as hospitals and other institutional healthcare facilities. Co. also provides clinical research for the pharmaceutical and biotechnology industries. Co.'s Pharmacy Services segment provides distribution of pharmaceuticals, related pharmacy consulting, data management services and medical supplies to long-term care facilities throughout the United States.

Recent Developments: For the year ended Dec 31 2004, net income increased 21.4% to $236,011 thousand from net income of $194,368 thousand a year earlier. Revenues were $4,119,891 thousand, up 17.7% from $3,499,174 thousand the year before. Operating income was $442,436 thousand versus an income of $387,583 thousand in the prior year, an increase of 14.2%. Total direct expense was $3,089,523 thousand versus $2,601,614 thousand in the prior year, an increase of 18.8%. Total indirect expense was $587,932 thousand versus $509,977 thousand in the prior year, an increase of 15.3%.

Prospects: Looking ahead, Co.'s revenue and earnings growth outlook remains positive based on its solid underlying fundamentals and its proven strategy, combined with its financial strength and flexibility, and the numerous opportunities to leverage its business. There do not appear to be any major reimbursement changes imminent in the long-term care industry that would upset the relatively stable environment of Co.'s customers. Co. continues to monitor the key issues relating to healthcare funding, and currently sees nothing materially adverse about regulations at this time and believes it is well-positioned to add value under the new Medicare Part D benefit.

Financial Data

(US$ in Thousands)	12/31/2004	12/31/2003	12/31/2002	12/31/2001	12/31/2000	12/31/1999	12/31/1998	12/31/1997
Earnings Per Share	2.17	1.93	1.33	0.79	0.53	0.63	0.90	0.69
Cash Flow Per Share	1.63	1.72	1.69	1.64	1.44	1.11	1.00	0.27
Tang Book Value Per Share	N.M.	N.M.	0.91	0.27	N.M.	N.M.	N.M.	0.99
Dividends Per Share	0.090	0.090	0.090	0.090	0.090	0.090	0.080	0.070
Dividend Payout %	4.15	4.66	6.77	11.39	16.98	14.29	8.89	10.14
Income Statement								
Total Revenue	4,119,891	3,499,174	2,632,754	2,159,131	1,971,348	1,861,921	1,517,370	895,702
EBITDA	489,529	435,932	294,491	250,179	206,570	207,201	207,113	128,058
Depn & Amortn	43,909	44,183	34,629	74,070	73,973	69,364	47,636	25,704
Income Before Taxes	375,199	310,449	203,051	119,785	77,523	91,671	135,866	96,790
Income Taxes	139,188	116,081	77,145	45,514	28,706	33,950	55,487	41,085
Net Income	236,011	194,368	125,906	74,271	48,817	57,721	80,379	55,705
Average Shares	112,819	103,243	94,905	93,758	92,012	91,238	89,786	80,303
Balance Sheet								
Current Assets	1,549,779	1,383,088	1,001,558	927,594	817,738	752,345	603,298	471,964
Total Assets	3,899,181	3,395,021	2,427,585	2,290,276	2,210,218	2,167,973	1,903,829	1,289,629
Current Liabilities	467,482	462,760	296,650	269,273	257,009	322,243	233,549	128,110
Long-Term Obligations	1,234,067	1,082,677	720,187	750,669	780,706	736,944	651,556	352,579
Total Liabilities	1,972,073	1,718,997	1,152,523	1,140,493	1,141,795	1,139,593	940,358	515,433
Stockholders' Equity	1,927,108	1,676,024	1,275,062	1,149,783	1,068,423	1,028,380	963,471	774,196
Shares Outstanding	104,496	103,187	94,301	94,671	92,156	91,286	90,265	82,153
Statistical Record								
Return on Assets %	6.45	6.68	5.34	3.30	2.22	2.84	5.03	5.54
Return on Equity %	13.06	13.17	10.38	6.70	4.64	5.80	9.25	7.91
EBITDA Margin %	11.88	12.46	11.19	11.59	10.48	11.13	13.65	14.30
Net Margin %	5.73	5.55	4.78	3.44	2.48	3.10	5.30	6.22
Asset Turnover	1.13	1.20	1.12	0.96	0.90	0.91	0.95	0.89
Current Ratio	3.32	2.99	3.38	3.44	3.18	2.33	2.58	3.68
Debt to Equity	0.64	0.65	0.56	0.65	0.73	0.72	0.68	0.46
Price Range	47.07-26.61	41.68-23.46	28.35-18.41	26.00-17.75	21.94-8.13	36.06-7.00	41.13-26.44	34.31-22.88
P/E Ratio	21.69-12.26	21.60-12.16	21.32-13.84	32.91-22.47	41.39-15.33	57.24-11.11	45.69-29.38	49.73-33.15
Average Yield %	0.24	0.29	0.38	0.42	0.65	0.53	0.23	0.24

| **Address:** 1600 Rivercenter II, 100 East Rivercenter Boulevard, Covington, KY 41011 **Telephone:** (859) 392-3300 | **Web Site:** www.omnicare.com **Officers:** Edward L. Hutton - Chmn. Joel F. Gemunder - Pres., C.E.O. | **Auditors:** PricewaterhouseCoopers LLP **Investor Contact:** 606-392-3331 **Transfer Agents:** EquiServe Trust Company, N.A., Providence, RI |

OMNICOM GROUP, INC.

Exchange	Symbol	Price	52Wk Range	Yield	P/E
NYS	OMC	$88.52 (3/31/2005)	91.07-66.70	1.02	22.81

*7 Year Price Score 90.74   ***NYSE Composite Index=100**   ***12 Month Price Score 103.18**

TRADING VOLUME (thousand shares)

Interim Earnings (Per Share)

Qtr.	Mar	Jun	Sep	Dec
2001	0.52	0.81	0.50	0.87
2002	0.68	1.00	0.68	1.07
2003	0.69	1.02	0.72	1.17
2004	0.72	1.10	0.79	1.28

Interim Dividends (Per Share)

Amt	Decl	Ex	Rec	Pay
0.225Q	5/25/2004	6/4/2004	6/8/2004	7/1/2004
0.225Q	9/14/2004	9/22/2004	9/24/2004	10/7/2004
0.225Q	12/14/2004	12/21/2004	12/24/2004	1/6/2005
0.225Q	2/8/2005	3/8/2005	3/10/2005	4/7/2005
		Indicated Div: $0.90		

Valuation Analysis

Forecast P/E	N/A	No of Institutions
		450
Market Cap	$16.6 Billion	Shares
Book Value	4.1 Billion	152,433,376
Price/Book	4.06	% Held
Price/Sales	1.70	82.50

Business Summary: Advertising, Marketing & PR (MIC: 12.4 SIC: 311 NAIC: 41810)

Omnicom Group is a holding company that owns advertising, marketing and corporate communications companies, which span more than 30 marketing disciplines, 100 countries, 1,500 subsidiary agencies and 5,000 clients. Co.'s agencies provide traditional media advertising services as well as marketing services including customer relationship management, public relations and specialty communications. These services are provided to clients through global, pan-regional and national independent agency brands. These brands include BBDO Worldwide, DDB Worldwide, TBWA Worldwide, and OMD Worldwide.

Recent Developments: For the year ended Dec 31 2004, net income increased 14.7% to $723,500 thousand from net income of $631,000 thousand a year earlier. Revenues were $9,747,200 thousand, up 13.1% from $8,621,400 thousand the year before. Operating income was $1,215,400 thousand versus an income of $1,091,900 thousand in the prior year, an increase of 11.3%. Total indirect expense was $8,531,800 thousand versus $7,529,500 thousand in the prior year, an increase of 13.3%.

Prospects: Co. continues to be please with is operating performance, supported by increased demand for advertising and specialty marketing services. Also, Co. is benefiting from organic revenue growth, which excludes the impact of a weak dollar and recent acquisitions. Meanwhile, Co. should continue to experience this favorable growth as marketers further increase their ad spending globally. Going forward, Co. will continue its efforts to outpace the industry in organic revenue growth, which is considered a key benchmark of strength for the advertising business, as Co. looks to take advantage of an ad recovery.

Financial Data

(US$ in Thousands)	12/31/2004	12/31/2003	12/31/2002	12/31/2001	12/31/2000	12/31/1999	12/31/1998	12/31/1997
Earnings Per Share	3.88	3.59	3.44	2.70	2.73	2.01	1.68	1.37
Cash Flow Per Share	6.91	5.63	5.38	4.24	3.91	5.14	2.84	3.35
Dividends Per Share	0.900	0.800	0.800	0.775	0.700	0.625	0.525	0.450
Dividend Payout %	23.20	22.28	23.26	28.70	25.64	31.09	31.25	32.85
Income Statement								
Total Revenue	9,747,200	8,621,404	7,536,299	6,889,406	6,154,230	5,130,545	4,092,042	3,124,813
EBITDA	1,387,500	1,325,598	1,254,434	1,226,228	1,213,804	919,845	714,598	523,730
Depn & Amortn	172,100	160,923	150,319	258,044	225,670	195,715	154,424	120,184
Income Before Taxes	1,178,800	1,121,849	1,073,623	895,385	911,617	673,708	520,149	381,245
Income Taxes	396,300	380,927	375,637	352,128	369,140	273,247	215,808	156,484
Net Income	723,500	675,883	643,459	503,142	498,795	362,882	285,068	222,415
Average Shares	186,587	188,656	187,602	190,289	189,037	189,884	175,844	169,484
Balance Sheet								
Current Assets	8,095,100	7,285,945	5,637,066	5,233,824	5,366,883	4,712,324	3,981,269	2,988,398
Total Assets	16,002,400	14,499,456	11,819,802	10,617,414	9,891,499	9,017,637	6,910,060	4,965,743
Current Liabilities	8,743,900	7,762,458	6,839,524	6,643,787	6,625,052	6,009,063	4,796,353	3,578,985
Long-Term Obligations	2,358,400	2,536,595	1,944,898	1,340,105	1,245,381	711,632	715,864	341,665
Total Liabilities	11,923,700	11,033,397	9,250,875	8,438,995	8,343,022	7,464,739	5,823,592	4,099,004
Stockholders' Equity	4,078,700	3,466,059	2,568,927	2,178,419	1,548,477	1,552,898	1,086,468	866,739
Shares Outstanding	187,075	190,424	188,401	190,628	184,079	177,487	168,593	162,115
Statistical Record								
Return on Assets %	4.73	5.14	5.74	4.91	5.26	4.56	4.80	4.93
Return on Equity %	19.13	22.40	27.11	27.00	32.08	27.50	29.19	26.68
EBITDA Margin %	14.23	15.38	16.65	17.80	19.72	17.93	17.46	16.76
Net Margin %	7.42	7.84	8.54	7.30	8.10	7.07	6.97	7.12
Asset Turnover	0.64	0.66	0.67	0.67	0.65	0.64	0.69	0.69
Current Ratio	0.93	0.94	0.82	0.79	0.81	0.78	0.83	0.83
Debt to Equity	0.58	0.73	0.76	0.62	0.80	0.46	0.66	0.39
Price Range	88.70-66.70	87.48-48.50	97.21-40.74	97.57-60.01	100.00-70.00	107.44-56.31	58.00-37.88	42.38-22.31
P/E Ratio	22.86-17.19	24.37-13.51	28.26-11.84	36.14-22.23	36.63-25.64	53.45-28.02	34.52-22.54	30.93-16.29
Average Yield %	1.16	1.15	1.11	0.92	0.81	0.83	1.09	1.47

Address: 437 Madison Ave, New York, NY 10022	**Web Site:** www.omnicomgroup.com	**Auditors:** KPMG LLP
Telephone: (212) 415-3600	**Officers:** Bruce Crawford - Chmn. Peter Mead - Vice-Chmn.	**Investor Contact:** 212-415-3393
Fax: (212) 415-3393		

ONEOK INC. (NEW)

Exchange	Symbol	Price	52Wk Range	Yield	P/E
NYS	OKE	$30.82 (3/31/2005)	30.94-19.80	3.24	13.40

*7 Year Price Score 113.38 *NYSE Composite Index=100 *12 Month Price Score 109.57

Interim Earnings (Per Share)

Qtr.	Mar	Jun	Sep	Dec
2001	0.54	0.20	0.16	(0.05)
2002	0.60	0.29	0.17	0.33
2003	0.28	0.23	0.01	0.65
2004	1.04	0.17	0.19	0.92

Interim Dividends (Per Share)

Amt	Decl	Ex	Rec	Pay
0.21Q	4/15/2004	4/28/2004	4/30/2004	5/14/2004
0.23Q	5/20/2004	7/28/2004	7/30/2004	8/16/2004
0.25Q	9/16/2004	10/27/2004	10/29/2004	11/15/2004
0.25Q	1/20/2005	1/27/2005	1/31/2005	2/15/2005

Indicated Div: $1.00

Valuation Analysis

Forecast P/E	N/A
	No of Institutions
	193
Market Cap	$3.2 Billion
Book Value	1.6 Billion	Shares
	82,772,056
Price/Book	2.00	% Held
Price/Sales	0.54	79.43

Business Summary: Gas Utilities (MIC: 7.4 SIC: 923 NAIC: 21210)

Oneok is a diversified energy company. Co.'s Production segment produces natural gas and oil and owns natural gas and oil reserves in Oklahoma and Texas. Co. owns and operates gas processing plants, as well as gathering pipelines in Oklahoma, Kansas and Texas through its Gathering and Processing segment. The Transportation and Storage segment owns and leases natural gas storage facilities and transports gas in Oklahoma, Kansas and Texas. Co.'s Distribution segment provides natural gas distribution services in Oklahoma, Kansas and Texas. The Marketing and Trading segment markets natural gas to wholesale and retail customers and markets electricity to wholesale customers.

Recent Developments: For the year ended Dec 31 2004, net income increased 115.3% to $242,178 thousand from net income of $112,488 thousand a year earlier. Revenues were $5,988,080 thousand, up 99.7% from $2,998,996 thousand the year before. Operating income was $490,010 thousand versus an income of $446,064 thousand in the prior year, an increase of 9.9%. Total direct expense was $5,242,613 thousand versus $2,325,634 thousand in the prior year, an increase of 125.4%. Total indirect expense was $255,457 thousand versus $227,298 thousand in the prior year, an increase of 12.4%.

Prospects: Co. is performing well. Specifically, Co.'s gathering and processing operations are experiencing a significant increase in operating income as a result of favorable commodity pricing, coupled with continued contract restructuring efforts. Results are also benefiting from steady growth in Co.'s production business, primarily related to the acquisition of the Texas oil and gas producing properties in Dec 2003, which produced 9.0 billion cubic feet (Bcf) of natural gas and 121 thousand barrels (MBbls) of oil during 2004. Looking ahead, Co. reaffirmed its 2005 earnings guidance of $2.22 to $2.28 per share, excluding earnings from trading opportunities.

Financial Data

(US$ in Thousands)	12/31/2004	12/31/2003	12/31/2002	12/31/2001	12/31/2000	12/31/1999	08/31/1999	12/31/1998
Earnings Per Share	2.30	1.22	1.39	0.85	1.48	1.04	1.03	1.01
Cash Flow Per Share	2.00	0.05	8.13	1.22	(1.62)	2.31	3.14	2.90
Tang Book Value Per Share	13.26	10.67	20.60	19.19	19.12	18.11	18.11	17.60
Dividends Per Share	0.880	0.675	0.620	0.620	0.620	0.620	0.620	0.605
Dividend Payout %	38.26	55.33	44.60	72.94	41.89	59.33	60.19	59.90
Income Statement								
Total Revenue	5,988,080	2,998,996	2,104,280	6,803,146	6,642,858	2,070,983	1,842,810	1,841,479
EBITDA	683,062	606,904	574,332	514,418	530,587	411,203	389,002	347,166
Depn & Amortn	188,725	160,861	147,843	258,875	143,351	131,195	129,704	117,194
Income Before Taxes	392,145	344,819	258,461	155,950	233,778	173,930	173,413	173,522
Income Taxes	149,967	130,527	102,485	52,234	90,286	67,057	67,056	69,319
Net Income	242,178	112,488	166,624	101,565	145,607	106,873	106,357	104,203
Average Shares	105,461	96,999	100,528	99,671	98,388	102,306	103,142	103,242
Balance Sheet								
Net PPE	3,786,821	3,691,826	3,015,049	3,272,968	3,095,513	2,121,778	2,068,829	1,706,226
Total Assets	7,192,649	6,314,048	5,730,858	5,879,159	7,369,136	3,239,575	3,024,945	2,557,138
Long-Term Obligations	1,630,019	1,978,556	1,620,169	1,620,023	1,473,213	775,074	810,087	336,124
Total Liabilities	5,586,945	5,072,656	4,365,246	4,613,869	6,144,179	2,088,051	1,850,486	1,372,539
Stockholders' Equity	1,605,704	1,241,392	1,365,612	1,265,290	1,224,957	1,151,524	1,174,459	1,184,599
Shares Outstanding	104,106	95,194	60,761	60,002	59,176	59,109	60,338	62,708
Statistical Record								
Return on Assets %	3.58	1.87	2.87	1.53	2.74	3.69	5.72	4.12
Return on Equity %	16.97	8.63	12.67	8.16	12.22	9.15	13.54	9.48
EBITDA Margin %	11.41	20.24	22.29	7.56	7.99	19.86	21.11	18.85
Net Margin %	4.04	3.75	7.92	1.49	2.19	5.16	5.77	5.66
PPE Turnover	1.60	0.89	0.67	2.14	2.54	1.08	1.47	1.08
Asset Turnover	0.88	0.50	0.36	1.03	1.25	0.71	0.99	0.73
Debt to Equity	1.02	1.59	1.19	1.28	1.20	0.67	0.69	0.28
Price Range	28.90-19.80	22.22-16.44	22.77-15.21	24.16-14.42	25.28-10.88	15.75-12.56	18.06-12.38	21.78-14.94
P/E Ratio	12.57-8.61	18.21-13.48	16.38-10.94	28.42-16.96	17.08-7.35	15.14-12.08	17.54-12.01	21.57-14.79
Average Yield %	3.73	3.44	3.21	3.18	3.99	4.29	4.17	3.31

Address: 100 West Fifth Street, Tulsa, OK 74103	Web Site: www.oneok.com	Auditors: KPMG LLP
Telephone: (918) 588-7000	Officers: David L. Kyle - Chmn., Pres., C.E.O. Jim C. Kneale - Exec. V.P., Fin., Admin., C.F.O.	Investor Contact: 918-588-7158
Fax: (918) 588-7273		

OUTBACK STEAKHOUSE, INC.

Exchange	Symbol	Price	52Wk Range	Yield	P/E
NYS	OSI	$45.79 (3/31/2005)	50.55-37.38	1.14	22.78

*7 Year Price Score 113.14 *NYSE Composite Index=100 *12 Month Price Score 99.71

Interim Earnings (Per Share)

Qtr.	Mar	Jun	Sep	Dec
2001	0.49	0.47	0.32	0.42
2002	0.52	0.53	0.46	0.52
2003	0.58	0.60	0.48	0.58
2004	0.62	0.57	0.37	0.46

Interim Dividends (Per Share)

Amt	Decl	Ex	Rec	Pay
0.13Q	4/21/2004	5/19/2004	5/21/2004	6/4/2004
0.13Q	7/21/2004	8/18/2004	8/20/2004	9/3/2004
0.13Q	10/27/2004	11/17/2004	11/19/2004	12/3/2004
0.13Q	1/27/2005	2/16/2005	2/18/2005	3/4/2005
		Indicated Div: $0.52		

Valuation Analysis

Forecast P/E	18.25	No of Institutions
	(4/7/2005)	218
Market Cap	$3.4 Billion	Shares
Book Value	1.1 Billion	59,005,384
Price/Book	3.10	% Held
Price/Sales	1.05	79.97

Business Summary: Hospitality & Tourism (MIC: 5.1 SIC: 812 NAIC: 22110)

Outback Steakhouse, through its subsidiaries and affiliates, develops, franchises and operates 1,175 full-service restaurants as of Dec 31 2004, including 881 Outback Steakhouses, 168 Carrabba's Italian Grills, 31 Fleming's Prime Steakhouse and Wine Bars, 18 Roy's Restaurants, 63 Bonefish Grills, 2 Lee Roy Selmon's, and 10 Cheeseburger in Paradise restaurants in 50 states and 20 countries. Outback Steakhouses feature steaks, prime rib, pork chops, ribs, chicken, seafood and pasta. Carrabba's features a limited menu of Italian dishes. Fleming's features prime cuts of beef, fresh seafood, pork, veal and chicken entrees. Roy's features Euro-Asian cuisine. Lee Roy's features southern cuisine.

Recent Developments: For the year ended Dec 31 2004, net income decreased 6.7% to $156,057 thousand from net income of $167,255 thousand a year earlier. Revenues were $3,201,750 thousand, up 20.1% from $2,665,777 thousand the year before. Operating income was $252,031 thousand versus an income of $258,918 thousand in the prior year, a decrease of 2.7%. Total direct expense was $1,938,520 thousand versus $1,583,885 thousand in the prior year, an increase of 22.4%. Total indirect expense was $1,012,924 thousand versus $828,970 thousand in the prior year, an increase of 22.2%.

Prospects: Co.'s bottom-line results reflect weaker sales at Outback Steakhouse restaurants, a jump in the price of tomatoes resulting from hurricane-related crop damage, nearly $1.2 million in carrying costs for the former Chi-Chi's properties now under development by itself and a $1.6 million contribution to hurricane relief efforts in Florida. Meanwhile, Co. is currently conducting a review of its accounting policies for leases and leasehold improvements, including evaluating the lease term used to calculate straight-line rent expense compared to the useful lives used to depreciate leasehold improvements. The findings could have a slight material affect on Co.'s results for 2004 and prior years.

Financial Data

(US$ in Thousands)	12/31/2004	12/31/2003	12/31/2002	12/31/2001	12/31/2000	12/31/1999	12/31/1998	12/31/1997
Earnings Per Share	2.01	2.17	1.97	1.70	1.78	1.57	1.23	1.27
Cash Flow Per Share	4.34	3.58	4.41	2.99	3.08	2.50	2.43	2.58
Tang Book Value Per Share	12.81	12.52	12.51	11.02	9.53	8.16	6.97	8.26
Dividends Per Share	0.520	0.490	0.120	...	...	...	...	...
Dividend Payout %	25.87	22.58	6.09	...	...	...	...	...
Income Statement								
Total Revenue	3,201,750	2,744,369	2,362,106	2,127,133	1,906,006	1,646,013	1,358,921	1,151,637
EBITDA	344,730	345,274	322,606	272,392	272,494	241,221	190,994	142,502
Depn & Amortn	104,218	84,876	75,691	69,000	58,109	51,390	39,116	44,837
Income Before Taxes	238,232	260,067	248,127	205,828	219,002	191,247	150,721	95,176
Income Taxes	82,175	89,861	87,341	72,451	77,872	66,924	53,506	33,724
Net Income	156,057	170,206	156,364	133,377	141,130	124,323	92,335	61,452
Average Shares	77,604	78,393	79,312	78,349	79,232	79,197	75,228	48,505
Balance Sheet								
Current Assets	218,887	232,610	274,177	206,360	182,047	143,211	122,052	80,251
Total Assets	1,708,031	1,474,787	1,389,575	1,237,748	1,022,535	852,282	705,211	592,780
Current Liabilities	367,190	296,229	239,121	189,760	168,045	130,935	108,811	80,790
Long-Term Obligations	90,243	9,550	14,436	13,830	11,678	1,519	37,475	68,276
Total Liabilities	570,724	388,495	295,111	250,968	198,105	141,613	150,286	153,566
Stockholders' Equity	1,088,402	1,026,270	1,052,976	941,844	807,590	692,965	545,046	434,717
Shares Outstanding	73,767	74,279	75,880	76,913	76,632	77,404	73,962	48,514
Statistical Record								
Return on Assets %	9.78	11.88	11.90	11.80	15.01	15.96	14.23	11.57
Return on Equity %	14.72	16.37	15.68	15.25	18.76	20.08	18.85	15.81
EBITDA Margin %	10.77	12.58	13.66	12.81	14.30	14.65	14.05	12.37
Net Margin %	4.87	6.20	6.62	6.27	7.40	7.55	6.79	5.34
Asset Turnover	2.01	1.92	1.80	1.88	2.03	2.11	2.09	2.17
Current Ratio	0.60	0.79	1.15	1.09	1.08	1.09	1.12	0.99
Debt to Equity	0.08	0.01	0.01	0.01	0.01	N.M.	0.07	0.16
Price Range	50.55-37.38	46.99-30.16	39.63-26.25	34.96-22.06	34.13-22.69	39.56-20.56	27.50-16.00	21.08-12.08
P/E Ratio	25.15-18.60	21.65-13.90	20.12-13.32	20.56-12.98	19.17-12.75	25.20-13.10	22.36-13.01	16.60-9.51
Average Yield %	1.21	1.30	0.36	...	...	...	...	...

Address: 2202 North West Shore Boulevard, Suite 500, Tampa, FL 33607 **Telephone:** (813) 282 1225 **Fax:** (813) 282 1209	**Web Site:** www.outback.com **Officers:** Chris T. Sullivan - Chmn. Robert D. Basham - Co-Chmn.	**Auditors:** PricewaterhouseCoopers LLP **Investor Contact:** 813-282-1225 **Transfer Agents:** Bank of New York, New York, NY

OVERSEAS SHIPHOLDING GROUP, INC.

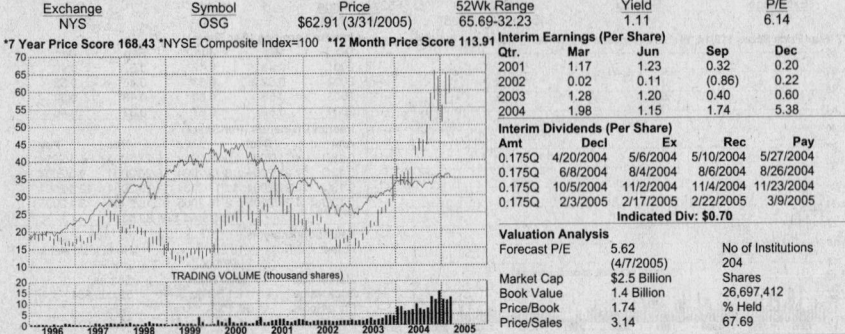

Exchange	Symbol	Price	52Wk Range	Yield	P/E
NYS	OSG	$62.91 (3/31/2005)	65.69-32.23	1.11	6.14

*7 Year Price Score 168.43 *NYSE Composite Index=100 *12 Month Price Score 113.91

Interim Earnings (Per Share)

Qtr.	Mar	Jun	Sep	Dec
2001	1.17	1.23	0.32	0.20
2002	0.02	0.11	(0.86)	0.22
2003	1.28	1.20	0.40	0.60
2004	1.98	1.15	1.74	5.38

Interim Dividends (Per Share)

Amt	Decl	Ex	Rec	Pay
0.175Q	4/20/2004	5/6/2004	5/10/2004	5/27/2004
0.175Q	6/8/2004	8/4/2004	8/6/2004	8/26/2004
0.175Q	10/5/2004	11/2/2004	11/4/2004	11/23/2004
0.175Q	2/3/2005	2/17/2005	2/22/2005	3/9/2005

Indicated Div: $0.70

Valuation Analysis

Forecast P/E	5.62	No of Institutions	
	(4/7/2005)	204	
Market Cap	$2.5 Billion	Shares	26,697,412
Book Value	1.4 Billion	% Held	67.69
Price/Book	1.74		
Price/Sales	3.14		

Business Summary: Shipping (MIC: 15.3 SIC: 412 NAIC: 83111)

Overseas Shipholding Group is an independent bulk shipping company engaged primarily in the ocean transport of crude oil and petroleum products. At Feb 20 2005, Co.'s fleet totaled 100 vessels aggregating 13.4 million deadweight tons (dwt.) Co.'s fleet included 90 vessels that operated in the international market and ten vessels that operated in the U.S. flag market. 97.0% of Co.'s international vessels are double-hulled or double-sided. Adjusted for its participation interest in joint ventures and chartered-in vessels, Co.'s fleet totaled 91.9 vessels aggregating 11.0 million dwt.

Recent Developments: For the year ended Dec 31 2004, net income increased 230.8% to $401,236 thousand from net income of $121,309 thousand a year earlier. Revenues were $789,581 thousand, up 83.1% from $431,136 thousand the year before. Operating income was $463,780 thousand versus an income of $191,107 thousand in the prior year, an increase of 142.7%. Total direct expense was $173,720 thousand versus $110,351 thousand in the prior year, an increase of 57.4%. Total indirect expense was $152,081 thousand versus $129,678 thousand in the prior year, an increase of 17.3%.

Prospects: On Jan 20 2005, Co. announced that it completed the purchase of Stelmar Shipping Ltd., an international provider of petroleum product and crude oil transportation services, for a cash purchase price of $48.00 per share. The acquisition is expected to enhance Co.'s presence in product tanker and Panamax tanker markets and be immediately accretive to earnings. Separately, in Nov 2004, Co. and Qatar Gas Transport Company Limited formed a joint venture that ordered four 216,000 cubic meter Liquified Natural Gas (LNG) Carriers for a total purchase price of $908.0 million. The LNG Carriers will, upon delivery in 2007 and 2008, commence 25-year time charters to Qatar Liquefied Gas Company Limited.

Financial Data

(US$ in Thousands)	12/31/2004	12/31/2003	12/31/2002	12/31/2001	12/31/2000	12/31/1999	12/31/1998	12/31/1997
Earnings Per Share	10.24	3.47	(0.51)	2.92	2.63	0.41	(1.03)	0.52
Cash Flow Per Share	9.49	6.43	0.38	5.32	2.95	1.04	1.53	1.64
Tang Book Value Per Share	36.20	25.54	22.76	23.73	22.07	19.63	17.87	21.19
Dividends Per Share	0.700	0.650	0.600	0.600	0.600	0.600	0.600	0.600
Dividend Payout %	6.84	18.73	N.M.	20.55	22.81	146.34	N.M.	115.38
Income Statement								
Total Revenue	789,581	431,136	266,725	381,018	370,081	253,217	408,784	481,059
EBITDA	645,012	308,265	96,995	255,617	217,529	115,953	97,784	192,090
Depn & Amortn	99,538	83,122	65,166	56,137	37,873	51,181	70,806	77,940
Income Before Taxes	481,014	168,153	(20,864)	154,445	132,186	19,515	(35,222)	31,167
Income Taxes	79,778	46,844	(3,244)	53,004	46,520	6,213	(10,950)	12,150
Net Income	401,236	121,309	(17,620)	101,441	90,391	14,764	(37,920)	19,017
Average Shares	39,176	34,976	34,394	34,696	34,315	35,724	36,794	36,569
Balance Sheet								
Total Assets	2,680,798	2,000,686	2,034,842	1,964,275	1,823,913	1,720,945	1,695,515	2,023,224
Long-Term Obligations	906,183	787,588	985,035	854,929	836,497	827,372	833,893	1,056,306
Total Liabilities	1,254,426	1,083,611	1,250,693	1,150,849	1,073,746	1,056,777	981,481	1,235,994
Stockholders' Equity	1,426,372	917,075	784,149	813,426	750,167	661,058	707,622	779,797
Shares Outstanding	39,399	35,905	34,451	34,277	33,986	33,672	39,591	36,793
Statistical Record								
Return on Assets %	17.09	6.01	N.M.	5.36	5.09	0.86	N.M.	0.94
Return on Equity %	34.15	14.26	N.M.	12.98	12.78	2.16	N.M.	2.46
EBITDA Margin %	81.69	71.50	36.37	67.09	58.78	45.79	23.92	39.93
Net Margin %	50.82	28.14	(6.61)	26.62	24.42	5.83	(9.28)	3.95
Asset Turnover	0.34	0.21	0.13	0.20	0.21	0.15	0.22	0.24
Price Range	65.69-32.23	35.89-15.15	24.75-15.15	37.09-19.90	30.25-13.88	16.81-10.81	22.00-13.25	26.31-16.63
P/E Ratio	6.42-3.15	10.34-4.37	N/A	12.70-6.82	11.50-5.28	41.01-26.37	N/A	50.60-31.97
Average Yield %	1.58	2.91	3.03	2.25	2.60	4.42	3.16	2.88

Address: 511 Fifth Avenue, New York, NY 10017	Web Site: www.osg.com	Auditors: Ernst & Young LLP
Telephone: (212) 953-4100	Officers: Morton Arntzen - Pres., C.E.O. Myles R. Itkin - Sr. V.P., C.F.O., Treas.	
Fax: (212) 536-3776		

OWENS-ILLINOIS, INC.

Exchange	Symbol	Price	52Wk Range	Yield	P/E
NYS	OI	$25.14 (3/31/2005)	26.33-13.56	N/A	17.58

*7 Year Price Score 92.39 *NYSE Composite Index=100 *12 Month Price Score 124.49

TRADING VOLUME (thousand shares)

Interim Earnings (Per Share)

Qtr.	Mar	Jun	Sep	Dec
2001	0.30	1.58	0.44	(0.05)
2002	(4.86)	0.62	0.63	0.31
2003	0.20	0.08	0.16	(7.33)
2004	0.29	0.52	0.42	0.20

Interim Dividends (Per Share)

No Dividends Paid

Valuation Analysis

Forecast P/E	13.04	No of Institutions
	(4/7/2005)	195
Market Cap	$3.8 Billion	Shares
Book Value	1.5 Billion	142,458,192
Price/Book	2.46	% Held
Price/Sales	0.61	93.99

Business Summary: Stone, Clay, Glass, and Concrete Products (MIC: 11.2 SIC: 221 NAIC: 27213)

Owens-Illinois is a manufacturer of glass container and plastics packaging products operating in two product segments. Co.'s principal product lines in the Glass Containers product segment are glass containers for the food and beverage industries. The principal markets and operations for Co.'s glass products are in North America, Europe, South America, and Australia. Co.'s principal product lines in the Plastics Packaging product segment include plastic healthcare containers and closures and prescription products. Major markets for Co.'s plastics packaging products include the United States health care market.

Recent Developments: For the year ended Dec 31 2004, income from continuing operations was $171,500 thousand compared with a loss of $330,100 thousand a year earlier. Net income was $235,500 thousand versus net loss of $990,800 thousand a year earlier. Revenues were $6,263,400 thousand, up 23.6% from $5,065,800 thousand the year before. Total direct expense was $4,918,400 thousand versus $3,967,900 thousand in the prior year, an increase of 24.0%. Total indirect expense was $659,800 thousand versus $1,106,100 thousand in the prior year, a decrease of 40.3%.

Prospects: Co.'s outlook appears satisfactory. Co.'s results in 2005 are expected to be aided by year-over-year unit volume growth, excluding BSN Glasspack, S.A., of approximately 2.0%, as well as improved pricing. Co. also anticipates growth driven by the full year effect of BSN, which was acquired in June 2004. Further, Co. plans to reduce debt by $300.0 million in 2005 as the result of continued strong operating cash flow and the Jan 2005 divestiture of two European glass plants. These positive factors are likely to be somewhat offset by start-up costs for Co.'s new Windsor, CO glass container manufacturing facility, lower pension income, and higher costs for transportation and raw material costs.

Financial Data

(US$ in Thousands)	12/31/2004	12/31/2003	12/31/2002	12/31/2001	12/31/2000	12/31/1999	12/31/1998	12/31/1997
Earnings Per Share	1.43	(6.89)	(3.29)	2.30	(2.00)	1.78	0.62	1.24
Cash Flow Per Share	4.11	2.40	4.11	3.70	2.49	3.66	4.32	3.33
Tang Book Value Per Share	N.M.	N.M.	N.M.	N.M.	N.M.	N.M.	N.M.	0.19
Income Statement								
Total Revenue	6,263,400	6,158,200	5,760,100	6,013,300	5,814,800	5,786,700	5,499,300	4,828,400
EBITDA	685,100	(565,500)	497,300	1,191,000	147,800	1,034,200	665,500	791,700
Depn & Amortn	474,800	525,200	480,700	523,800	539,400	536,400	456,500	339,400
Income Before Taxes	210,300	(1,090,700)	16,600	667,200	(391,600)	497,800	209,000	452,300
Income Taxes	5,900	(125,700)	(18,300)	286,400	(143,900)	185,500	66,700	148,500
Net Income	235,500	(990,800)	(460,200)	356,600	(269,700)	298,300	108,000	167,900
Average Shares	149,679	146,913	146,615	145,660	145,983	155,229	150,943	135,676
Balance Sheet								
Current Assets	2,400,800	2,121,800	1,887,200	1,987,200	2,081,700	2,109,800	2,177,100	1,648,300
Total Assets	10,736,700	9,531,300	9,869,300	10,106,600	10,343,200	10,756,300	11,060,700	6,845,100
Current Liabilities	1,906,500	1,363,400	1,297,400	1,231,500	1,318,000	1,273,100	1,327,100	1,043,800
Long-Term Obligations	5,167,900	5,333,100	5,268,000	5,329,700	5,729,800	5,733,100	5,667,200	3,146,700
Total Liabilities	9,192,400	8,527,900	8,198,500	7,954,800	8,460,200	8,406,400	8,588,700	5,503,200
Stockholders' Equity	1,544,300	1,003,400	1,670,800	2,151,800	1,883,000	2,349,900	2,472,000	1,341,900
Shares Outstanding	150,916	147,853	147,351	146,478	144,954	146,851	155,450	140,526
Statistical Record								
Return on Assets %	2.32	N.M.	N.M.	3.49	N.M.	2.73	1.21	2.59
Return on Equity %	18.44	N.M.	N.M.	17.68	N.M.	12.37	5.66	16.21
EBITDA Margin %	10.94	N.M.	8.63	19.81	2.54	17.87	12.10	16.40
Net Margin %	3.76	N.M.	N.M.	5.93	N.M.	5.15	1.96	3.48
Asset Turnover	0.62	0.63	0.58	0.59	0.55	0.53	0.61	0.75
Current Ratio	1.26	1.56	1.45	1.61	1.58	1.66	1.64	1.58
Debt to Equity	3.35	5.32	3.15	2.48	3.04	2.44	2.29	2.34
Price Range	23.83-10.98	15.50-7.98	19.19-9.98	9.99-3.75	25.06-2.56	33.19-19.50	48.63-24.38	37.94-22.25
P/E Ratio	16.66-7.68	N/A	N/A	4.34-1.63	N/A	18.64-10.96	78.43-39.31	30.59-17.94

Address: One SeaGate, Toledo, OH 43666	**Web Site:** www.o-i.com	**Auditors:** Ernst & Young LLP
Telephone: (419) 247-5000	**Officers:** Steven R. McCracken - Chmn., C.E.O.	**Investor Contact:** 419-247-2400
Fax: (419) 247-2839	Edward C. White - Sr. V.P. Sales, Mktg.	

OWENS & MINOR, INC.

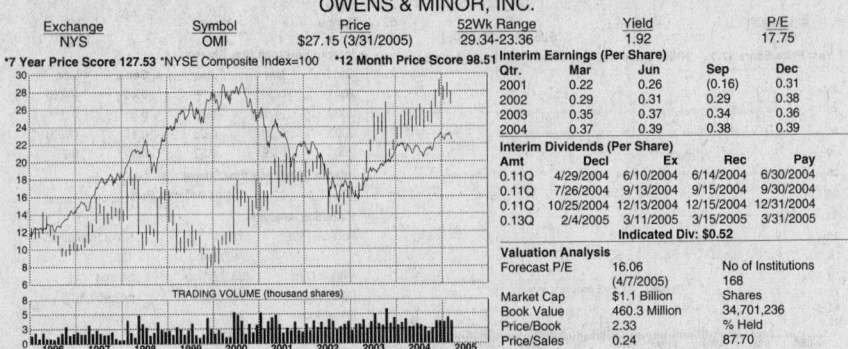

Exchange	Symbol	Price	52Wk Range	Yield	P/E
NYS	OMI	$27.15 (3/31/2005)	29.34-23.36	1.92	17.75

*7 Year Price Score 127.53 *NYSE Composite Index=100 *12 Month Price Score 98.51

Interim Earnings (Per Share)

Qtr.	Mar	Jun	Sep	Dec
2001	0.22	0.26	(0.16)	0.31
2002	0.29	0.31	0.29	0.38
2003	0.35	0.37	0.34	0.36
2004	0.37	0.39	0.38	0.39

Interim Dividends (Per Share)

Amt	Decl	Ex	Rec	Pay
0.11Q	4/29/2004	6/10/2004	6/14/2004	6/30/2004
0.11Q	7/26/2004	9/13/2004	9/15/2004	9/30/2004
0.11Q	10/25/2004	12/13/2004	12/15/2004	12/31/2004
0.13Q	2/4/2005	3/11/2005	3/15/2005	3/31/2005

Indicated Div: $0.52

Valuation Analysis

Forecast P/E	16.06 (4/7/2005)	No of Institutions	168
Market Cap	$1.1 Billion	Shares	34,701,236
Book Value	460.3 Million	% Held	87.70
Price/Book	2.33		
Price/Sales	0.24		

Business Summary: Engineering Services (MIC: 12.1 SIC: 047 NAIC: 23450)

Owens & Minor is a U.S. distributor of medical and surgical supplies and a healthcare supply chain management company, distributing approximately 130,000 finished medical and surgical products produced by nearly 1,000 suppliers to about 4,000 customers from 40 distribution centers nationwide as of Dec 31 2004. Co.'s primary customers are acute care hospitals and integrated healthcare networks, which account for more than 90% of its net sales. Most of Co.'s sales consist of consumable goods such as disposable gloves, dressings, endoscopic products, intravenous products, needles and syringes, sterile procedure trays, surgical products and gowns, urological products and wound closure products.

Recent Developments: For the year ended Dec 31 2004, net income increased 12.8% to $60,500 thousand from net income of $53,641 thousand a year earlier. Revenues were $4,525,105 thousand, up 6.6% from $4,244,067 thousand the year before. Operating income was $110,129 thousand versus an income of $105,711 thousand in the prior year, an increase of 4.2%. Total direct expense was $4,061,806 thousand versus $3,807,665 thousand in the prior year, an increase of 6.7%. Total indirect expense was $353,170 thousand versus $330,691 thousand in the prior year, an increase of 6.8%.

Prospects: For 2005, Co. anticipates it will report revenue growth in the 5.0% to 7.0% range, and diluted earnings per share from $1.71 to $1.73 with stronger comparative earnings growth in the second half of 2005. Co.'s noted that its earnings per share guidance excludes the effect of a new accounting standard calling for the expensing of stock options, which is effective in 2005. Adoption of this standard is expected to reduce the aforementioned annual diluted earnings per share guidance by an estimated $0.03. Separately, on Feb 1 2005, Co. announced that it has acquired Access Diabetic Supply, LLC, a Florida-based distributor of diabetic supplies that posted 2004 revenues of about $32.0 million.

Financial Data
(US$ in Thousands)

	12/31/2004	12/31/2003	12/31/2002	12/31/2001	12/31/2000	12/31/1999	12/31/1998	12/31/1997
Earnings Per Share	1.53	1.42	1.27	0.68	0.94	0.82	0.56	0.60
Cash Flow Per Share	1.50	2.70	(0.42)	0.05	1.32	2.83	1.00	0.25
Tang Book Value Per Share	6.57	5.45	2.15	1.12	0.24	N.M.	0.09	N.M.
Dividends Per Share	0.440	0.350	0.310	0.273	0.248	0.230	0.200	0.180
Dividend Payout %	28.76	24.65	24.41	40.07	26.33	28.05	35.71	30.00
Income Statement								
Total Revenue	4,525,105	4,244,067	3,959,781	3,814,994	3,503,583	3,186,373	3,082,119	3,116,798
EBITDA	124,752	112,475	94,123	87,046	81,675	69,423	53,003	59,595
Depn & Amortn	14,884	15,718	15,926	22,469	21,515	19,365	18,270	17,664
Income Before Taxes	97,610	87,799	78,197	64,577	60,160	50,058	34,733	41,931
Income Taxes	37,110	34,158	30,980	34,474	27,072	22,079	14,588	17,611
Net Income	60,500	53,641	47,267	23,035	33,088	27,979	20,145	24,320
Average Shares	39,668	39,333	40,698	40,387	39,453	39,098	32,591	32,129
Balance Sheet								
Current Assets	864,476	781,375	729,753	679,452	594,291	589,246	504,221	499,264
Total Assets	1,131,833	1,045,748	1,009,477	953,853	867,548	865,000	717,768	712,563
Current Liabilities	430,531	395,632	344,730	367,674	360,654	369,798	268,974	265,475
Long-Term Obligations	207,476	209,499	240,185	203,449	152,872	174,553	150,000	182,550
Total Liabilities	671,577	635,393	612,890	585,610	522,776	550,619	424,642	453,262
Stockholders' Equity	460,256	410,355	271,437	236,243	212,772	182,381	161,126	259,301
Shares Outstanding	39,519	38,979	34,113	33,885	33,180	32,711	32,618	32,213
Statistical Record								
Return on Assets %	5.54	5.22	4.81	2.53	3.81	3.54	2.82	3.49
Return on Equity %	13.86	15.74	18.62	10.26	16.70	16.29	9.58	9.70
EBITDA Margin %	2.76	2.65	2.38	2.28	2.33	2.18	1.72	1.91
Net Margin %	1.34	1.26	1.19	0.60	0.94	0.88	0.65	0.78
Asset Turnover	4.14	4.13	4.03	4.19	4.03	4.03	4.31	4.48
Current Ratio	2.01	1.98	2.12	1.85	1.65	1.59	1.87	1.88
Debt to Equity	0.45	0.51	0.88	0.86	0.72	0.96	0.93	0.70
Price Range	29.34-21.91	26.80-15.86	20.86-13.40	20.96-14.35	18.00-8.31	16.75-7.81	19.50-10.00	16.00-9.88
P/E Ratio	19.18-14.32	18.87-11.17	16.43-10.55	30.82-21.10	19.15-8.84	20.43-9.53	34.82-17.86	26.67-16.46
Average Yield %	1.74	1.70	1.79	1.52	1.84	2.07	1.38	1.40

Address: 4800 Cox Road, Glen Allen, VA 23060 Telephone: (804) 747-9794 Fax: (804) 270-7281	Web Site: www.owens-minor.com Officers: G. Glimer Minor III - Chmn., C.E.O. Craig R. Smith - Pres., C.O.O.	Auditors: KPMG LLP Investor Contact: 804-747-9794

PACIFICARE HEALTH SYSTEMS, INC.

Exchange	Symbol	Price	52Wk Range	Yield	P/E
NMS	PHSY A	$56.92 (3/31/2005)	64.88-29.70	N/A	17.79

*7 Year Price Score 148.46 *NYSE Composite Index=100 *12 Month Price Score 131.68

Interim Earnings (Per Share)

Qtr.	Mar	Jun	Sep	Dec
2001	0.20	0.23	0.25	(0.40)
2002	(12.43)	0.28	0.60	0.57
2003	0.95	0.96	0.86	0.28
2004	0.71	0.80	0.94	0.76

Interim Dividends (Per Share)

No Dividends Paid

Valuation Analysis

Forecast P/E	15.02	No of Institutions
	(4/13/2005)	272
Market Cap	$4.9 Billion	Shares
Book Value	2.2 Billion	82,723,728
Price/Book	2.24	% Held
Price/Sales	0.40	95.45

Business Summary: Insurance (MIC: 8.2 SIC: 324 NAIC: 24114)

Co. offers managed care and other health insurance products to employer groups and Medicare beneficiaries in eight western states and Guam. Co.'s commercial and senior plans include health maintenance organizations (HMOs), preferred provider organizations (PPOs) and Medicare Supplement products. Co. also offers a variety of specialty managed care products and services that employees can purchase as a supplement to basic commercial and senior medical plans or as stand-alone products. These products include pharmacy benefit management (PBM), behavioral health services, group life and health insurance and dental and vision benefit plans.

Recent Developments: For the year ended Dec 31 2004, net income increased 24.9% to $303.2 million compared with $242.7 million a year earlier. Total operating revenue advanced 11.5% to $12.28 billion from $11.01 billion the previous year. Operating income climbed 10.5% to $541.8 million from $490.2 million the year before. Selling, general and administrative expenses amounted to $1.56 billion, or 12.7% of total operating revenue, versus $1.45 billion, or 13.2% of total operating revenue, the year before. Total membership grew to 3.3 million from 3.0 million at Sep 30 2004 and 2.9 million at Dec 31 2003.

Prospects: On Dec 13 2005, Co. announced that is has completed the acquisition of American Medical Security Group, Inc. for a total equity purchase price of approximately $505.0 million. The acquisition will add new proprietary products including health savings accounts and group life products, and will expand Co.'s geographic presence while reducing the portion of its total gross margin that is generated from Medicare Advantage. Meanwhile, Co. estimates full-year 2005 revenue growth of 15.0% over full-year 2004 and net income in the range of $360.0 million to $375.0 million. Also, Co. expects earnings to range from $3.64 to $3.80 per share for 2005.

Financial Data (US$ in Thousands)	12/31/2004	12/31/2003	12/31/2002	12/31/2001	12/31/2000	12/31/1999	12/31/1998	12/31/1997
Earnings Per Share	3.20	3.04	(10.76)	0.28	2.29	3.12	2.25	(0.38)
Cash Flow Per Share	0.33	5.57	3.44	0.58	8.97	6.40	5.20	5.10
Tang Book Value Per Share	7.93	7.63	1.42	N.M.	N.M.	N.M.	N.M.	N.M.
Income Statement								
Total Revenue	12,276,804	11,008,511	11,156,502	11,843,972	11,467,927	9,989,090	9,521,482	8,982,680
EBITDA	615,089	559,060	376,387	279,120	498,285	643,007	567,526	241,537
Depn & Amortn	73,311	68,885	79,520	152,336	130,563	118,097	121,029	116,877
Income Before Taxes	493,737	389,644	221,963	56,502	288,086	481,909	385,574	60,124
Income Taxes	190,583	146,896	82,792	38,371	127,046	203,365	183,147	81,825
Net Income	303,154	242,748	(757,829)	19,006	161,040	278,544	202,427	(21,701)
Average Shares	95,490	79,963	70,474	68,058	70,334	89,434	92,010	81,046
Balance Sheet								
Current Assets	3,281,679	3,031,201	2,628,015	2,588,186	2,708,906	2,344,491	2,033,575	1,990,958
Total Assets	5,226,917	4,619,304	4,251,133	5,096,046	5,323,436	4,884,021	4,630,944	4,867,958
Current Liabilities	1,833,766	2,022,286	2,069,929	2,113,742	2,315,257	1,786,186	1,619,416	1,637,086
Long-Term Obligations	1,051,000	613,000	732,000	794,000	835,000	975,000	650,000	1,010,000
Total Liabilities	3,037,959	2,768,067	2,923,034	3,061,952	3,318,320	2,906,302	2,392,842	2,804,537
Stockholders' Equity	2,188,438	1,851,537	1,328,305	2,033,785	2,003,560	1,977,719	2,238,096	2,062,187
Shares Outstanding	86,072	84,854	72,010	69,074	66,908	74,504	91,232	83,990
Statistical Record								
Return on Assets %	6.14	5.47	N.M.	0.36	3.15	5.85	4.26	N.M.
Return on Equity %	14.97	15.27	N.M.	0.94	8.07	13.21	9.41	N.M.
EBITDA Margin %	5.01	5.08	3.37	2.36	4.35	6.44	5.96	2.69
Net Margin %	2.47	2.21	N.M.	0.16	1.40	2.79	2.13	N.M.
Asset Turnover	2.49	2.48	2.39	2.27	2.24	2.10	2.00	2.79
Current Ratio	1.79	1.50	1.27	1.22	1.17	1.31	1.26	1.22
Debt to Equity	0.48	0.33	0.55	0.39	0.42	0.49	0.29	0.49
Price Range	57.40-28.96	33.85-10.59	16.63-7.38	20.13-5.53	35.94-5.03	46.00-16.25	43.69-23.94	42.50-24.94
P/E Ratio	17.94-9.05	11.13-3.48	N/A	71.88-19.75	15.69-2.20	14.74-5.21	19.42-10.64	N/A

Address: 5995 Plaza Drive, Cypress, CA 90630	Web Site: www.pacificare.com	Auditors: Ernst & Young LLP
Telephone: (714) 952-1121	Officers: Howard G. Phanstiel - Chmn., Pres., C.E.O. Gregory W. Scott - Exec. V.P., C.F.O.	

PACKAGING CORP OF AMERICA

Exchange	Symbol	Price	52Wk Range	Yield	P/E
NYS	PKG	$24.29 (3/31/2005)	25.29-21.17	4.12	37.95

*7 Year Price Score N/A   *NYSE Composite Index=100   *12 Month Price Score 96.86

Interim Earnings (Per Share)

Qtr.	Mar	Jun	Sep	Dec
2001	0.25	0.29	0.27	0.17
2002	0.09	0.11	0.14	0.11
2003	0.07	0.10	(0.31)	0.00
2004	(0.06)	0.13	0.24	0.34

Interim Dividends (Per Share)

Amt	Decl	Ex	Rec	Pay
0.15Q	5/14/2004	6/14/2004	6/15/2004	7/15/2004
0.15Q	9/1/2004	9/13/2004	9/15/2004	10/15/2004
0.15Q	12/8/2004	12/13/2004	12/15/2004	1/18/2005
0.25Q	1/19/2005	3/11/2005	3/15/2005	4/15/2005

Indicated Div: $1.00

Valuation Analysis

Forecast P/E	22.30	No of Institutions
	(4/7/2005)	155
Market Cap	$2.6 Billion	Shares
Book Value	817.6 Million	63,894,544
Price/Book	3.18	% Held
Price/Sales	1.37	59.51

TRADING VOLUME (thousand shares)

1996 1997 1998 1999 2000 2001 2002 2003 2004 2005

Business Summary: Paper Products (MIC: 11.11 SIC: 653 NAIC: 22211)

Packaging Corporation of America is a manufacturer of containerboard and corrugated products. Co.'s converting operations produce various corrugated packaging products, including conventional shipping containers used to protect and transport manufactured goods, multi-color boxes and displays with strong visual appeal that help to merchandise the packaged product in retail locations. In addition, Co. produces meat boxes and wax-coated boxes for the agricultural industry. At Dec 30 2004, Co. operated four paper mills and 66 corrugated product plants in 26 states.

Recent Developments: For the year ended Dec 31 2004, net income was $68,730 thousand versus net loss of $14,358 thousand a year earlier. Revenues were $1,890,085 thousand, up 8.9% from $1,735,534 thousand the year before. Operating income was $140,491 thousand versus an income of $96,856 thousand in the prior year, an increase of 45.1%. Total direct expense was $1,592,371 thousand versus $1,437,667 thousand in the prior year, an increase of 10.8%. Total indirect expense was $151,070 thousand versus $188,694 thousand in the prior year, a decrease of 19.9%.

Prospects: Co. continues to perform well, as its corrugated product volumes per workday grew 6.7% from the year-earlier period. Pricing also continued to improve over the third quarter but was offset by higher wood, energy and transportation costs. Going forward, Co. will be taking its annual mill maintenance outages at its Counce and Valdosta linerboard mills during the first quarter. These outages will result in higher operating costs and less production, negatively impacting earnings. Co. also expects to see seasonally higher energy and wood costs. Accordingly, Co. is projecting first quarter earnings of about $0.12 per share.

Financial Data

(US$ in Thousands)	12/31/2004	12/31/2003	12/31/2002	12/31/2001	12/31/2000	12/31/1999	09/30/1999	04/11/1999
Earnings Per Share	0.64	(0.14)	0.45	0.98	1.33	0.32	0.16	(1.43)
Cash Flow Per Share	2.02	2.34	2.28	2.95	3.22	2.76	2.45	5.87
Tang Book Value Per Share	7.43	7.50	7.58	7.25	6.45	4.39	3.76	...
Dividends Per Share	0.600	0.150	...	...	...	...	...	...
Dividend Payout %	93.75	N.M.						
Income Statement								
Total Revenue	1,890,085	1,735,534	1,735,858	1,789,956	1,921,868	1,262,285	816,538	433,182
EBITDA	292,591	255,678	298,693	395,822	553,050	304,464	185,167	(181,682)
Depn & Amortn	152,100	158,822	153,413	146,367	148,216	112,234	75,952	30,412
Income Before Taxes	110,915	(24,874)	77,614	175,434	287,151	84,636	35,588	(212,315)
Income Taxes	42,185	(10,516)	29,435	67,912	114,190	37,239	14,655	(83,716)
Net Income	68,730	(14,358)	48,179	106,418	161,901	40,500	20,933	(134,926)
Average Shares	107,570	104,628	107,208	108,801	107,518	96,549	92,451	94,600
Balance Sheet								
Current Assets	677,061	567,077	509,554	448,217	403,709	402,927	419,026	...
Total Assets	2,082,774	1,985,126	1,982,551	1,971,780	1,942,112	2,153,208	2,425,839	...
Current Liabilities	335,104	342,977	296,806	191,895	218,548	227,470	216,089	...
Long-Term Obligations	585,724	585,198	629,119	795,163	869,175	1,329,202	1,652,209	...
Total Liabilities	1,265,204	1,187,646	1,186,676	1,201,946	1,254,688	1,633,987	1,971,619	...
Stockholders' Equity	817,570	797,480	795,875	769,834	687,424	416,699	357,720	...
Shares Outstanding	106,993	105,651	104,491	105,567	106,248	94,600	94,600	...
Statistical Record								
Return on Assets %	3.37	N.M.	2.44	5.44	7.89	2.30	1.48	...
Return on Equity %	8.49	N.M.	6.15	14.61	29.25	6.11	4.42	...
EBITDA Margin %	15.48	14.73	17.21	22.11	28.78	24.12	22.68	N.M.
Net Margin %	3.64	N.M.	2.78	5.95	8.42	3.21	2.56	N.M.
Asset Turnover	0.93	0.87	0.88	0.91	0.94	0.72	0.58	...
Current Ratio	2.02	1.65	1.72	2.34	1.85	1.77	1.94	...
Debt to Equity	0.72	0.73	0.79	1.03	1.26	3.19	4.62	...
Price Range	25.00-21.15	21.86-16.45	20.86-16.35	20.50-13.00	16.69-9.56	...	...	...
P/E Ratio	39.06-33.05	N/A	46.36-36.33	20.92-13.27	12.55-7.19	...	...	...
Average Yield %	2.61	0.79	...	...	...	...	...	...

Address: 1900 West Field Court, Lake Forest, IL 60045 **Telephone:** (847) 482-3000 **Fax:** (847) 482-3020	**Web Site:** www.packagingcorp.com **Officers:** Paul T. Stecko - Chmn., C.E.O. William J. Sweeney - Exec. V.P., Corrugated Products	**Auditors:** Ernst & Young LLP **Investor Contact:** 877-454-2509

PACTIV CORP.

Exchange	Symbol	Price	52Wk Range	Yield	P/E
NYS	PTV	$23.35 (3/31/2005)	25.68-21.66	N/A	23.12

*7 Year Price Score N/A   *NYSE Composite Index=100   *12 Month Price Score 90.85

Interim Earnings (Per Share)

Qtr.	Mar	Jun	Sep	Dec
2001	0.20	0.43	0.28	0.28
2002	(0.19)	0.38	0.37	0.36
2003	0.27	0.37	0.16	0.34
2004	0.00	0.33	0.37	0.31

Interim Dividends (Per Share)

No Dividends Paid

Valuation Analysis

Forecast P/E	17.03	No of Institutions
	(4/7/2005)	272
Market Cap	$3.5 Billion	Shares
Book Value	1.1 Billion	125,671,552
Price/Book	3.21	% Held
Price/Sales	1.03	84.37

Business Summary: Paper Products (MIC: 11.11 SIC: 673 NAIC: 22223)

Pactiv is a global supplier of specialty-packaging and consumer products. Co.'s two operating segments are Consumer and Foodservice/Food Packaging, and Protective and Flexible Packaging. Co.'s consumer products include plastic-, aluminum- and paper-based products such as waste bags, food-storage bags and disposable tableware and cookware. Co.'s foodservice/food packaging products include foam, clear plastic, aluminum, pressed-paperboard and molded-fiber packaging for customers in the food distribution channel, including wholesalers, supermarkets and packer processors, which prepare and process food for consumption. Co. operates 80 facilities in 14 countries in 2003.

Recent Developments: For the year ended Dec 31 2004, net income decreased 15.3% to $155,000 thousand from net income of $183,000 thousand a year earlier. Revenues were $3,382,000 thousand, up 7.8% from $3,138,000 thousand the year before. Total direct expense was $2,450,000 thousand versus $2,206,000 thousand in the prior year, an increase of 11.1%. Total indirect expense was $585,000 thousand versus $465,000 thousand in the prior year, an increase of 25.8%.

Prospects: Earnings are being negatively affected by higher raw material prices and increased marketing costs, partially offset by pricing actions taken in 2004 and early 2005, as well as productivity gains. Meanwhile, Co. plans to significantly increase its advertising and promotion program in 2005 in an effort to boost consumer awareness of several new products. Co. is enjoying strong initial consumer response for its recently-introduced Hefty® Serve 'N Store™ disposable tableware products. For full-year 2005, Co. expects sales growth of between 10.0% and 12.0%, along with earnings in the range of $1.30 to $1.40 per share, including non-cash pension income of about $0.20 per share.

Financial Data
(US$ in Thousands)	12/31/2004	12/31/2003	12/31/2002	12/31/2001	12/31/2000	12/31/1999	12/31/1998	12/31/1997
Earnings Per Share	1.01	1.14	0.92	1.20	1.53	(2.05)	0.83	0.52
Cash Flow Per Share	2.42	2.13	2.42	2.34	1.79	(0.19)	3.42	2.38
Tang Book Value Per Share	0.98	0.77	N.M.	4.90	3.79	2.19	...	...
Income Statement								
Total Revenue	3,382,000	3,138,000	2,880,000	2,812,000	3,134,000	2,913,000	2,788,000	2,569,000
Depn & Amortn	169,000	163,000	158,000	177,000	185,000	184,000	175,000	163,000
Income Taxes	90,000	118,000	146,000	118,000	91,000	(47,000)	67,000	75,000
Net Income	155,000	183,000	148,000	193,000	247,000	(344,000)	139,000	89,000
Average Shares	153,763	160,143	160,613	159,527	161,779	167,663	168,835	170,802
Balance Sheet								
Current Assets	1,079,000	982,000	904,000	740,000	900,000	866,000	917,000	924,000
Total Assets	3,741,000	3,706,000	3,412,000	4,060,000	4,341,000	4,588,000	4,798,000	4,618,000
Current Liabilities	984,000	474,000	501,000	459,000	512,000	920,000	1,142,000	744,000
Long-Term Obligations	869,000	1,336,000	1,224,000	1,211,000	1,560,000	1,741,000	1,312,000	1,492,000
Total Liabilities	2,658,000	2,645,000	2,515,000	2,371,000	2,802,000	3,238,000	3,022,000	2,779,000
Stockholders' Equity	1,083,000	1,061,000	897,000	1,689,000	1,539,000	1,350,000	1,776,000	1,839,000
Shares Outstanding	148,711	156,335	158,681	159,431	158,176	168,372	...	...
Statistical Record								
Return on Assets %	4.15	5.14	3.96	4.59	5.52	N.M.	2.95	...
Return on Equity %	14.42	18.69	11.45	11.96	17.05	N.M.	7.69	...
Net Margin %	4.58	5.83	5.14	6.86	7.88	N.M.	4.99	3.46
Asset Turnover	0.91	0.88	0.77	0.67	0.70	0.62	0.59	...
Current Ratio	1.10	2.07	1.80	1.61	1.76	0.94	0.80	1.24
Debt to Equity	0.80	1.26	1.36	0.72	1.01	1.29	0.74	0.81
Price Range	25.68-20.49	23.90-17.92	24.10-15.75	18.10-11.46	13.13-7.63	14.25-9.63	...	...
P/E Ratio	25.43-20.29	20.96-15.72	26.20-17.12	15.08-9.55	8.58-4.98	N/A	...	...

Address: 1900 West Field Court, Lake Forest, IL 60045	Web Site: www.pactiv.com	Auditors: Ernst & Young LLP
Telephone: (847) 482-2000	Officers: Richard L. Wambold - Chmn., Pres., C.E.O.	Investor Contact: 847-482-2429
Fax: (847) 482-4548	Andrew A. Campbell - Sr. V.P., C.F.O.	Transfer Agents: National City Bank, Cleveland, OH

PALL CORP.

Exchange	Symbol	Price	52Wk Range	Yield	P/E
NYS	PLL	$27.12 (3/31/2005)	29.50-22.27	1.47	21.87

*7 Year Price Score 98.74   ***NYSE Composite Index=100**   ***12 Month Price Score 97.57**

Interim Earnings (Per Share)

Qtr.	Oct	Jan	Apr	Jul
2001-02	0.16	0.15	0.21	0.07
2002-03	(0.19)	0.25	0.33	0.44
2003-04	0.19	0.20	0.37	0.44
2004-05	0.17	0.26	...	...

Interim Dividends (Per Share)

Amt	Decl	Ex	Rec	Pay
0.09Q	4/14/2004	4/28/2004	4/30/2004	5/14/2004
0.09Q	7/20/2004	8/2/2004	8/4/2004	8/19/2004
0.09Q	10/14/2004	10/26/2004	10/28/2004	11/12/2004
0.10Q	1/21/2005	2/4/2005	2/8/2005	2/23/2005

Indicated Div: $0.40

Valuation Analysis

Forecast P/E	18.93	No of Institutions	
	(4/7/2005)	271	
Market Cap	$3.4 Billion	Shares	
Book Value	1.1 Billion	103,822,848	
Price/Book	2.95	% Held	
Price/Sales	1.83	83.43	

Business Summary: Industrial Machinery and Equipment (MIC: 11.5 SIC: 569 NAIC: 33411)

Pall manufactures and markets filtration and separation products and systems throughout the world to a diverse group of customers within two principal markets: Life Sciences and Industrial. Co.'s five segments include Medical and BioPharmaceuticals, which comprise the Life Sciences business, and General Industrial, Aerospace and Microelectronics, which comprise the Industrial business. Co.'s proprietary products are used to discover, develop and produce pharmaceuticals, produce safe drinking water, protect hospital patients, remove white blood cells from blood, enhance the quality and efficiency of manufacturing processes, keep equipment running efficiently and protect the environment.

Recent Developments: For the three months ended Oct 31 2004, net earnings slipped 12.0% to $21.7 million versus $24.7 million in the corresponding quarter the previous year. Results for 2004 included restructuring and other non-recurring charges of $5.5 million, while results for 2003 included a restructuring and other non-recurring gain of $3.7 million. Net sales increased 10.8% to $414.7 million from $374.3 million a year earlier. Gross profit totaled $199.9 million, or 48.2% of net sales, up 11.0% compared with $180.1 million, or 48.1% of net sales, the year before.

Prospects: Co. intends to continue to move forward with its cost reduction initiatives. Co. noted that it expects to attain $2.5 million in savings per quarter in fiscal 2005 related to its Indirect Expenditure cost reduction initiatives for items such as freight, office supplies, parcel delivery and travel. The program was implemented in the Western Hemisphere in fiscal 2004 and is expected to be expanded to Europe and Asia this fiscal year. Other cost reduction initiatives focus on Co.'s cost of manufacturing. Consequently, Co. expects to achieve $10.0 million in savings in fiscal 2005 and continuing savings in fiscal 2006 as a result of these efforts.

Financial Data

(US$ in Thousands)	6 Mos	3 Mos	07/31/2004	08/02/2003	08/03/2002	07/28/2001	07/29/2000	07/31/1999
Earnings Per Share	1.24	1.18	1.20	0.83	0.59	0.95	1.18	0.41
Cash Flow Per Share	1.60	1.47	1.53	1.82	1.24	1.65	1.76	0.90
Tang Book Value Per Share	6.65	6.41	6.13	5.10	4.15	6.24	6.13	5.84
Dividends Per Share	0.360	0.360	0.270	0.360	0.520	0.505	0.655	0.635
Dividend Payout %	29.13	30.56	22.50	43.37	88.14	53.16	55.51	154.88
Income Statement								
Total Revenue	884,205	414,732	1,770,747	1,613,635	1,290,820	1,235,423	1,224,101	1,147,066
EBITDA	127,808	57,094	304,716	250,609	188,309	238,453	274,442	146,690
Depn & Amortn	45,030	22,138	86,383	82,935	74,003	71,490	71,961	74,771
Income Before Taxes	70,925	29,249	197,832	143,236	99,975	150,320	188,404	58,904
Income Taxes	17,181	7,550	46,259	40,034	26,741	32,310	41,768	7,397
Net Income	53,744	21,699	151,573	103,202	73,234	118,010	146,636	51,507
Average Shares	125,457	125,009	126,737	124,214	123,532	123,735	124,709	124,755
Balance Sheet								
Current Assets	1,113,456	1,078,243	1,069,815	938,434	915,982	778,988	753,176	744,189
Total Assets	2,234,469	2,160,755	2,140,383	2,016,726	2,027,222	1,548,510	1,507,252	1,488,327
Current Liabilities	399,969	417,020	418,774	421,496	438,171	313,849	437,679	558,279
Long-Term Obligations	543,515	509,673	488,686	489,870	619,705	359,094	223,915	116,815
Total Liabilities	1,091,815	1,080,544	1,085,944	1,082,190	1,207,502	778,468	745,946	757,663
Stockholders' Equity	1,142,654	1,080,211	1,054,439	934,536	819,720	770,042	761,306	730,664
Shares Outstanding	124,448	123,999	124,021	124,682	122,792	122,383	123,118	124,210
Statistical Record								
Return on Assets %	7.19	7.10	7.31	5.12	4.03	7.74	9.82	3.64
Return on Equity %	14.14	14.37	15.28	11.80	9.06	15.45	19.71	6.90
EBITDA Margin %	14.45	13.77	17.21	15.53	14.59	19.30	22.42	12.79
Net Margin %	6.08	5.23	8.56	6.40	5.67	9.55	11.98	4.49
Asset Turnover	0.85	0.86	0.85	0.80	0.71	0.81	0.82	0.81
Current Ratio	2.78	2.59	2.55	2.23	2.09	2.48	1.72	1.33
Debt to Equity	0.48	0.47	0.46	0.52	0.76	0.47	0.29	0.16
Price Range	29.50-22.27	27.78-22.27	27.78-21.82	24.48-15.00	24.90-16.32	26.06-18.19	25.13-17.44	26.44-16.25
P/E Ratio	23.79-17.96	23.54-18.87	23.15-18.18	29.49-18.07	42.20-27.66	27.43-19.14	21.29-14.78	64.48-39.63
Average Yield %	1.44	1.46	1.11	1.92	2.42	2.28	3.07	2.95

Address: 2200 Northern Boulevard, East Hills, NY 11548	Web Site: www.pall.com	Auditors: KPMG LLP
Telephone: (516) 484-5400	Officers: Eric Krasnoff - Chmn., C.E.O. Marcus Wilson - Pres.	Investor Contact: 516-801-9848
Fax: (516) 484-3649		Transfer Agents: EquiServe Trust Company, Providence, RI

PAN PACIFIC RETAIL PROPERTIES, INC.

Exchange	Symbol	Price	52Wk Range	Yield	P/E
NYS	PNP	$56.75 (3/31/2005)	62.70-41.80	4.16	22.52

*7 Year Price Score 148.64 *NYSE Composite Index=100 *12 Month Price Score 101.56

Interim Earnings (Per Share)

Qtr.	Mar	Jun	Sep	Dec
2001	0.45	0.51	0.50	0.50
2002	0.49	0.50	0.60	0.70
2003	0.66	0.69	0.61	0.65
2004	0.59	0.57	0.76	0.60

Interim Dividends (Per Share)

Amt	Decl	Ex	Rec	Pay
0.542Q	5/17/2004	5/26/2004	5/28/2004	6/15/2004
0.542Q	8/4/2004	8/25/2004	8/27/2004	9/15/2004
0.542Q	11/11/2004	11/23/2004	11/26/2004	12/15/2004
0.59Q	2/17/2005	2/23/2005	2/25/2005	3/15/2005

Indicated Div: $2.36

Valuation Analysis

Forecast P/E	14.80	No of Institutions
	(4/7/2005)	150
Market Cap	$2.3 Billion	Shares
Book Value	915.1 Million	34,412,064
Price/Book	2.51	% Held
Price/Sales	7.95	84.71

Business Summary: Property, Real Estate & Development (MIC: 8.3 SIC: 798 NAIC: 25930)

Pan Pacific Retail Properties is a self-administered and self-managed real estate investment trust. Co.'s portfolio consists principally of community and neighborhood shopping centers predominantly located in five key Western U.S. markets. At Dec 31 2004, Co. owned a portfolio comprised of 133 shopping center properties, of which 127 were located in five key Western U.S. markets, including 43 in Northern California, 38 in Southern California, 20 in Oregon, 14 in Washington and 12 in Nevada. The portfolio includes about 21.7 million square feet of retail space, which was 96.8% leased to a diverse mix of 3,388 tenants.

Recent Developments: For the year ended Dec 31 2004, income from continuing operations increased 6.1% to $92,382 thousand from income of $87,075 thousand a year earlier. Net income decreased 2.3% to $101,989 thousand from net income of $104,436 thousand a year earlier. Revenues were $289,436 thousand, up 10.6% from $261,586 thousand the year before.

Prospects: Co. continues to enhance the underlying value of its portfolio through disposing of non-strategic assets and redeploying the proceeds into acquiring dominant, well-established grocery-anchored shopping centers in its core metropolitan markets. During 2004, Co. sold $28.0 million of non-strategic assets and acquired over $160.0 million of shopping centers. Co. also continues to generate strong operating results with its portfolio, including posting a 140 basis point gain in year-over-year occupancy, ending the year at 96.8%. Looking ahead to 2005, Co. expects funds from operations in the range of $0.90 to $0.93 per share for the first quarter and $3.77 to $3.80 per share for the full year.

Financial Data

(US$ in Thousands)	12/31/2004	12/31/2003	12/31/2002	12/31/2001	12/31/2000	12/31/1999	12/31/1998	12/31/1997
Earnings Per Share	2.52	2.61	2.30	1.97	1.48	1.54	1.35	0.49
Cash Flow Per Share	3.38	3.26	2.49	2.48	2.45	2.21	2.02	...
Tang Book Value Per Share	22.58	22.14	19.31	18.98	18.92	17.97	18.10	17.91
Dividends Per Share	2.170	2.030	1.900	1.820	1.540	1.600	1.520	0.575
Dividend Payout %	86.11	77.78	82.61	92.39	104.05	103.90	112.59	117.41
Income Statement								
Property Income	280,544	258,879	186,796	175,611	116,391	98,030	76,941	45,159
Non-Property Income	8,892	5,743	6,197	13,383	4,102	3,032	2,312	1,293
Total Revenue	289,436	264,622	192,993	188,994	120,493	101,062	79,253	46,452
Depn & Amortn	49,843	41,412	31,815	30,277	21,074	18,183	14,995	9,381
Interest Expense	62,619	58,473	45,926	46,196	32,112	23,939	18,295	14,057
Income Before Taxes	...	...	...	...	...	...	...	9,528
Income Taxes	...	...	...	...	...	...	...	19
Net Income	101,989	104,436	77,652	64,222	33,800	32,576	26,634	8,313
Average Shares	41,134	40,707	34,431	33,560	23,168	22,122	19,663	16,866
Balance Sheet								
Total Assets	1,995,444	1,863,348	1,424,240	1,339,618	1,297,690	784,537	705,541	487,220
Long-Term Obligations	1,011,026	897,035	734,218	668,235	626,411	357,290	282,524	170,766
Total Liabilities	1,080,310	971,063	775,605	717,160	690,692	402,671	322,453	186,165
Stockholders' Equity	915,134	892,285	648,635	622,458	606,998	381,866	383,088	301,055
Shares Outstanding	40,530	40,293	33,584	32,789	32,074	21,252	21,162	16,814
Statistical Record								
Return on Assets %	5.27	6.35	5.62	4.87	3.24	4.37	4.47	...
Return on Equity %	11.25	13.56	12.22	10.45	6.82	8.52	7.79	...
Net Margin %	35.24	39.47	40.24	33.98	28.05	32.23	33.61	17.90
Price Range	62.70-41.80	48.43-35.30	36.85-28.13	28.84-21.55	22.75-16.31	20.25-15.13	22.69-17.69	22.00-19.94
P/E Ratio	24.88-16.59	18.56-13.52	16.02-12.23	14.64-10.94	15.37-11.02	13.15-9.82	16.81-13.10	44.90-40.69
Average Yield %	4.20	4.93	5.86	7.33	7.85	8.65	7.34	2.78

Address: 1631 South Melrose Drive, Suite B, Vista, CA 92083 **Telephone:** (760) 727-1002 **Fax:** (760) 727-1430	**Web Site:** www.pprp.com **Officers:** Stuart A. Tanz - Chmn., Pres., C.E.O. Joseph B. Tyson - Exec. V.P., C.F.O., Treas., Sec.	**Auditors:** KPMG LLP **Investor Contact:** 760-727-1002 **Transfer Agents:** Bank of New York

PAR PHARMACEUTICAL COMPANIES INC

Exchange	Symbol	Price	52Wk Range	Yield	P/E
NYS	PRX	$33.44 (3/31/2005)	61.20-32.22	N/A	39.81

*7 Year Price Score 137.70 *NYSE Composite Index=100 ***12 Month Price Score 86.89**

Interim Earnings (Per Share)

Qtr.	Mar	Jun	Sep	Dec
2001	0.05	0.08	0.83	0.71
2002	0.63	0.62	0.59	0.56
2003	0.67	0.68	1.11	1.09
2004	0.85	0.85	(1.03)	0.13

Interim Dividends (Per Share)

No Dividends Paid

Valuation Analysis

Forecast P/E	15.06 (4/7/2005)	No of Institutions 196
Market Cap	$1.1 Billion	Shares
Book Value	413.6 Million	32,804,284
Price/Book	2.74	% Held
Price/Sales	1.64	96.61

Business Summary: Pharmaceuticals (MIC: 9.1 SIC: 834 NAIC: 25412)

Par Pharmaceutical Companies develop, manufacturer and distribute a variety of generic drugs in the United States. In addition, Co. develops and manufactures in small quantities complex synthetic active pharmaceutical ingredients through its subsidiary, FineTech Laboratories, Ltd. based in Haifa, Israel and sells a limited number of mature brand name drugs through an agreement with Bristol-Meyers Squibb. Co. operates primarily through its wholly-owned subsidiary, Par Pharmaceutical, Inc., a manufacturer and distributor of generic drugs. Co. markets its products primarily to wholesalers, retail drug store chains, managed health care providers and drug distributors.

Recent Developments: For the year ended Dec 31 2004, net income decreased 76.1% to $29,246 thousand from net income of $122,533 thousand a year earlier. Revenues were $690,016 thousand, up 4.3% from $661,688 thousand the year before. Operating income was $47,464 thousand versus an income of $201,019 thousand in the prior year, a decrease of 76.4%. Total direct expense was $443,958 thousand versus $378,513 thousand in the prior year, an increase of 17.3%. Total indirect expense was $198,594 thousand versus $82,156 thousand in the prior year, an increase of 141.7%.

Prospects: Although 2004 was a challenging year, Co. has strengthened its position for sustainable growth going forward. In 2004, Co. more than tripled the scale of its research and development organization through the acquisition of Kali Laboratories. As a result, Co. and its partners have filed 32 Abbreviated New Drug Applications and now have more than 50 products awaiting regulatory approval. Co. also has filed its first New Drug Application for the advanced formulation of Megace®, which it expects to introduce as soon as June or July 2005. Meanwhile, Co. expects to introduce at least 20 new products in 2005.

Financial Data

(US$ in Thousands)	12/31/2004	12/31/2003	12/31/2002	12/31/2001	12/31/2000	12/31/1999	12/31/1998	09/30/1998
Earnings Per Share	0.84	3.54	2.40	1.68	(0.03)	(0.06)	(0.23)	(0.45)
Cash Flow Per Share	1.55	3.53	0.98	2.40	(0.09)	(0.31)	(0.08)	(0.24)
Tang Book Value Per Share	8.38	9.76	4.89	4.06	2.03	2.04	2.09	2.32
Income Statement								
Total Revenue	690,016	661,688	381,603	271,035	85,022	80,315	16,775	60,380
EBITDA	60,697	211,055	135,424	79,723	...	659	(6,291)	(6,534)
Depn & Amortn	13,546	10,131	5,775	3,349	2,308	2,370	680	2,712
Income Before Taxes	46,103	200,643	130,253	75,932	...	(1,774)	(6,882)	(9,628)
Income Taxes	16,857	78,110	50,799	22,010	...	...	...	...
Net Income	29,246	122,533	79,454	53,922	(929)	(1,774)	(6,882)	(9,628)
Average Shares	34,873	34,638	33,051	32,189	29,604	29,461	29,318	21,521
Balance Sheet								
Current Assets	493,982	626,975	210,984	175,850	46,800	41,793	39,145	42,179
Total Assets	769,004	762,812	301,457	216,926	89,150	82,686	77,947	82,924
Current Liabilities	154,744	167,173	74,679	72,983	28,288	20,572	14,937	13,055
Long-Term Obligations	200,275	200,211	2,426	1,060	163	1,075	1,102	1,143
Total Liabilities	355,414	367,731	80,667	78,503	29,065	22,347	16,756	14,915
Stockholders' Equity	413,590	395,081	220,790	138,423	60,085	60,339	61,191	68,009
Shares Outstanding	33,915	34,318	32,804	32,035	29,647	29,562	29,322	29,316
Statistical Record								
Return on Assets %	3.81	23.03	30.65	35.23	N.M.	N.M.	N.M.	N.M.
Return on Equity %	7.21	39.79	44.24	54.33	N.M.	N.M.	N.M.	N.M.
EBITDA Margin %	8.80	31.90	35.49	29.41	...	0.82	N.M.	N.M.
Net Margin %	4.24	18.52	20.82	19.89	N.M.	N.M.	N.M.	N.M.
Asset Turnover	0.90	1.24	1.47	1.77	0.99	1.00	0.18	0.78
Current Ratio	3.19	3.75	2.83	2.41	1.65	2.03	2.62	3.23
Debt to Equity	0.48	0.51	0.01	0.01	N.M.	0.02	0.02	0.02
Price Range	66.30-32.22	74.71-29.35	33.80-16.10	41.50-6.63	8.13-4.06	8.69-4.13	4.75-3.25	6.31-1.13
P/E Ratio	78.93-38.36	21.10-8.29	14.08-6.71	24.70-3.94	N/A	N/A	N/A	N/A

Address: One Ram Ridge Road, Spring Valley, NY 10977 **Telephone:** (845) 425-7100 **Fax:** (914) 425-7907	**Web Site:** www.parpharm.com **Officers:** Mark Auerbach - Exec.-Chmn. Scott L. Tarriff - Pres., C.E.O.	**Auditors:** Deloitte & Touche LLP

PARKER HANNIFIN CORP.

Exchange	Symbol	Price	52Wk Range	Yield	P/E	Div Acheiver
NYS	PH	$60.92 (3/31/2005)	77.81-52.58	1.31	13.63	48 Years

*7 Year Price Score 117.52 *NYSE Composite Index=100 *12 Month Price Score 96.58

Interim Earnings (Per Share)

Qtr.	Sep	Dec	Mar	Jun
2001-02	0.52	0.25	0.45	(0.11)
2002-03	0.52	0.32	0.42	0.42
2003-04	0.48	0.47	0.90	1.06
2004-05	1.11	1.41	...	...

Interim Dividends (Per Share)

Amt	Decl	Ex	Rec	Pay
0.19Q	4/22/2004	5/18/2004	5/20/2004	6/4/2004
0.19Q	7/23/2004	8/18/2004	8/20/2004	9/3/2004
0.19Q	10/27/2004	11/16/2004	11/18/2004	12/3/2004
0.20Q	1/27/2005	2/15/2005	2/17/2005	3/4/2005

Indicated Div: $0.80 (Div. Reinv. Plan)

Valuation Analysis

Forecast P/E	11.65	No of Institutions
	(4/7/2005)	347
Market Cap	$7.3 Billion	Shares
Book Value	3.4 Billion	93,310,864
Price/Book	2.16	% Held
Price/Sales	0.94	77.65

Business Summary: Metal Products (MIC: 11.4 SIC: 491 NAIC: 32911)

Parker-Hannifin is a manufacturer of motion-control products, including fluid power systems, electromechanical controls and related components. Co. operates in two main business segments: The Industrial segment includes several business units that manufacture motion-control and fluid power system components for builders and users of various types of manufacturing, packaging, processing, transportation, agricultural, construction, and military vehicles and equipment. The Aerospace segment produces hydraulic, fuel and pneumatic systems and components for domestic commercial, military and general aviation aircraft, as well as naval vessels and land-based weapons systems.

Recent Developments: For the quarter ended Dec 31 2004, income from continuing operations increased 112.8% to $113,853 thousand from income of $53,494 thousand in the year-earlier quarter. Net income increased 206.8% to $171,127 thousand from net income of $55,771 thousand in the year-earlier quarter. Revenues were $1,942,887 thousand, up 21.9% from $1,593,340 thousand the year before. Total direct expense was $1,546,357 thousand versus $1,313,802 thousand in the prior-year quarter, an increase of 17.7%. Total indirect expense was $220,846 thousand versus $183,524 thousand in the prior-year quarter, an increase of 20.3%.

Prospects: Co.'s long-term growth strategy, which includes achieving $10.00 billion in sales with a 20.0% share of the $50.00 billion global motion and control market, consists of 10.0% compounded annual revenue growth, with 5.0% coming from acquisitions and 5.0% organically through global expansion, innovation and increased sales. Subsequently, on Feb 18 2005, Co. announced that it has acquired Markwel Hose Products PVT, Ltd., a manufacturer of braided and spiral hydraulic hose products, with operations in Mumbai and Hyderabad, India. Also, on Feb 14 2005, Co. announced it has acquired Bayside Controls, Inc., a manufacturer of integrated solutions for industrial and precision automation applications.

Financial Data

(US$ in Thousands)	6 Mos	3 Mos	06/30/2004	06/30/2003	06/30/2002	06/30/2001	06/30/2000	06/30/1999
Earnings Per Share	4.47	3.53	2.91	1.68	1.12	2.96	3.31	2.83
Cash Flow Per Share	5.34	5.71	5.61	4.79	5.47	4.66	4.86	4.22
Tang Book Value Per Share	14.30	15.13	14.08	11.45	12.27	13.43	14.94	12.62
Dividends Per Share	0.760	0.760	0.760	0.740	0.720	0.700	0.680	0.640
Dividend Payout %	17.00	21.50	26.12	44.05	64.29	23.65	20.54	22.61
Income Statement								
Total Revenue	3,862,855	1,947,192	7,106,907	6,410,610	6,149,122	5,979,604	5,355,337	4,958,800
EBITDA	510,162	268,593	820,249	638,121	582,118	888,485	827,778	743,437
Depn & Amortn	131,272	63,669	252,785	259,178	281,598	264,527	206,408	202,046
Income Before Taxes	345,285	188,679	494,068	297,382	218,036	533,596	562,187	477,694
Income Taxes	101,000	55,896	148,285	101,110	87,886	189,426	193,955	167,193
Net Income	303,910	132,783	345,783	196,272	130,150	340,792	368,232	310,501
Average Shares	121,122	119,712	119,006	116,894	116,060	115,064	111,224	109,679
Balance Sheet								
Current Assets	2,552,896	2,676,920	2,536,933	2,396,807	2,235,618	2,196,362	2,153,113	1,774,684
Total Assets	6,681,094	6,339,810	6,256,904	5,985,633	5,752,583	5,337,661	4,646,299	3,705,888
Current Liabilities	1,205,878	1,223,041	1,259,741	1,423,727	1,359,837	1,413,129	1,186,303	754,513
Long-Term Obligations	988,828	955,145	953,804	966,332	1,088,883	857,078	701,762	724,757
Total Liabilities	3,293,692	3,223,345	3,274,450	3,464,722	3,169,067	2,808,746	2,336,841	1,852,026
Stockholders' Equity	3,387,402	3,116,465	2,982,454	2,520,911	2,583,516	2,528,915	2,309,458	1,853,862
Shares Outstanding	120,171	119,474	119,483	118,165	118,024	117,309	116,387	111,901
Statistical Record								
Return on Assets %	8.59	6.89	5.63	3.34	2.35	6.83	8.79	8.59
Return on Equity %	17.60	14.77	12.53	7.69	5.09	14.09	17.64	17.56
EBITDA Margin %	13.21	13.79	11.54	9.95	9.47	14.86	15.46	14.99
Net Margin %	7.87	6.82	4.87	3.06	2.12	5.70	6.88	6.26
Asset Turnover	1.24	1.22	1.16	1.09	1.11	1.20	1.28	1.37
Current Ratio	2.12	2.19	2.01	1.68	1.64	1.55	1.81	2.35
Debt to Equity	0.29	0.31	0.32	0.38	0.42	0.34	0.30	0.39
Price Range	77.81-52.58	60.92-44.70	60.92-41.71	48.80-34.65	54.63-31.65	50.03-31.94	52.13-33.94	50.44-27.19
P/E Ratio	17.41-11.76	17.26-12.66	20.93-14.33	29.05-20.63	48.78-28.26	16.90-10.79	15.75-10.25	17.82-9.61
Average Yield %	1.26	1.36	1.43	1.77	1.59	1.72	1.55	1.77

Address: 6035 Parkland Boulevard, Cleveland, OH 44124-4141	**Web Site:** www.phstock.com	**Auditors:** PricewaterhouseCoopers LLP
Telephone: (216) 896-3000	**Officers:** Duane E. Collings - Chmn. Donald E. Washkewicz - Pres., C.E.O.	**Investor Contact:** 216-896-2240
Fax: (216) 383-9414		**Transfer Agents:** National City Bank, Cleveland, Ohio

PAYLESS SHOESOURCE INC. (DE)

Exchange	Symbol	Price	52Wk Range	Yield	P/E
NYS	PSS	$15.79 (3/31/2005)	16.80-9.33	N/A	157.90

*7 Year Price Score 65.07 *NYSE Composite Index=100 *12 Month Price Score 97.24

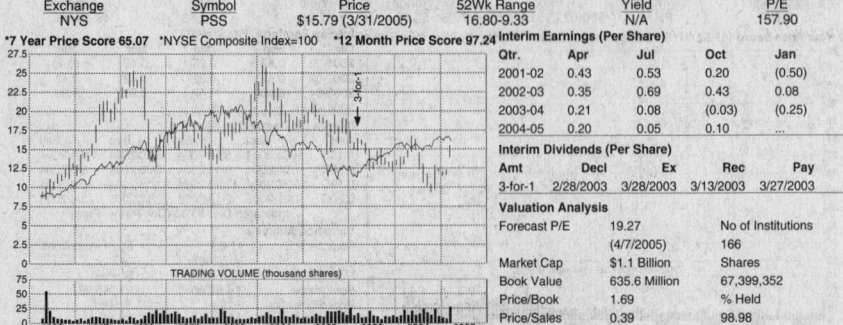

Interim Earnings (Per Share)

Qtr.	Apr	Jul	Oct	Jan
2001-02	0.43	0.53	0.20	(0.50)
2002-03	0.35	0.69	0.43	0.08
2003-04	0.21	0.08	(0.03)	(0.25)
2004-05	0.20	0.05	0.10	...

Interim Dividends (Per Share)

Amt	Decl	Ex	Rec	Pay
3-for-1	2/28/2003	3/28/2003	3/13/2003	3/27/2003

Valuation Analysis

Forecast P/E	19.27
	(4/7/2005)
Market Cap	$1.1 Billion
Book Value	635.6 Million
Price/Book	1.69
Price/Sales	0.39

No of Institutions	
166	
Shares	
67,399,352	
% Held	
98.98	

Business Summary: Retail - Apparel and Accessory Stores (MIC: 5.8 SIC: 661 NAIC: 48210)

Payless ShoeSource is a retailer of family footwear. As of Jan 31 2004, Co. operated a total of 5,042 stores located in 50 states, Canada, Central America, South America, and the Caribbean. Payless ShoeSource® stores, which average about 3,200 square feet, feature footwear for men, women and children, including athletic, casual, dress, sandals, work and fashion boots, slippers and accessories. In addition, Co. operates stores under the Parade® name, that sell women's footwear and accessories. Co. also operates shoe dyeing facilities through its Dyelightssm business.

Recent Developments: For the quarter ended Oct 30 2004, net income was $6,600 thousand versus net loss of $2,200 thousand in the year-earlier quarter. Revenues were $687,300 thousand, down 3.2% from $709,700 thousand the year before. Operating income was $11,700 thousand versus a loss of $900 thousand in the prior-year quarter, an increase of 1400.0%. Total indirect expense was $190,400 thousand versus $190,100 thousand in the prior-year quarter, an increase of 0.2%.

Prospects: Co.'s prospects appear constructive. Although same-store sales decreased 2.3% during the fourth quarter ended Jan 29 2005, gross margin improved to 30.0% of sales versus 25.4% in the fourth quarter 2003. Co. attributed the improvement primarily to fewer markdowns and more favorable initial mark-on, relative to the same period last year. In the fourth quarter of 2004, Co. opened 81 new stores and closed 463, for a net decrease of 382 stores. During fiscal 2004, Co. opened 302 new stores and closed 704, for a net reduction of 402 stores. During fiscal year 2005, Co. intends to open approximately 30 new stores and close approximately 70, for a net reduction of approximately 40 stores.

Financial Data
(US$ in Thousands)

	9 Mos	6 Mos	3 Mos	01/31/2004	02/01/2003	02/02/2002	02/03/2001	01/29/2000
Earnings Per Share	0.10	(0.03)	0.00	...	1.55	0.67	1.67	1.45
Cash Flow Per Share	2.83	2.64	2.98	3.11	1.93	2.33	2.92	2.29
Tang Book Value Per Share	8.91	8.72	8.59	8.51	8.30	7.00	6.22	7.93
Income Statement								
Total Revenue	2,137,200	1,449,900	722,000	2,783,300	2,878,000	2,913,700	2,948,400	2,730,100
EBITDA	106,700	69,900	47,700	99,800	281,200	206,800	330,600	326,000
Depn & Amortn	75,300	50,200	25,800	99,100	103,100	106,900	102,600	99,900
Income Before Taxes	18,200	10,800	17,500	(16,200)	158,900	71,800	203,000	227,000
Income Taxes	4,600	2,500	6,400	(9,100)	58,000	27,600	79,000	90,500
Net Income	24,000	17,500	13,800	(100)	105,800	45,400	120,600	136,500
Average Shares	68,000	68,000	68,000	68,029	68,421	67,776	72,162	94,095
Balance Sheet								
Current Assets	710,000	721,900	683,200	658,900	633,600	536,500	434,700	566,900
Total Assets	1,202,900	1,210,200	1,196,900	1,176,900	1,150,800	1,069,200	1,002,800	1,075,500
Current Liabilities	291,600	310,800	300,200	289,300	341,800	291,200	228,700	197,800
Long-Term Obligations	202,100	204,100	202,600	202,800	140,700	245,100	309,200	126,100
Total Liabilities	567,300	585,700	579,100	569,400	552,600	602,200	592,400	371,700
Stockholders' Equity	635,600	624,500	617,800	607,500	598,200	467,000	410,400	703,800
Shares Outstanding	68,093	68,120	68,050	67,991	67,946	66,758	65,964	88,805
Statistical Record								
Return on Assets %	0.58	N.M.	N.M.	N.M.	9.56	4.39	11.42	13.08
Return on Equity %	1.09	N.M.	N.M.	N.M.	19.92	10.38	21.30	19.46
EBITDA Margin %	4.99	4.82	6.61	3.59	9.77	7.10	11.21	11.94
Net Margin %	1.12	1.21	1.91	N.M.	3.68	1.56	4.09	5.00
Asset Turnover	2.34	2.36	2.39	2.40	2.60	2.82	2.79	2.62
Current Ratio	2.43	2.32	2.28	2.28	1.85	1.84	1.90	2.87
Debt to Equity	0.32	0.33	0.33	0.33	0.24	0.52	0.75	0.18
Price Range	16.80-9.33	16.80-12.00	15.87-12.00	16.48-12.00	21.10-14.25	26.06-17.33	23.90-13.06	19.67-13.63
P/E Ratio	168.00-93.30	...	N.M.	N.M.	13.61-9.19	38.90-25.86	14.31-7.82	13.56-9.40

Address: 3231 South East Sixth Avenue, Topeka, KS 66607-2207
Telephone: (785) 233-5171
Fax: (785) 295-6049

Web Site: www.payless.com
Officers: Steven J. Douglass - Chmn., C.E.O. Duane L. Cantrell - Pres.

Auditors: Deloitte & Touche LLP
Investor Contact: 800-626-3204

PEABODY ENERGY CORP.

Exchange	Symbol	Price	52Wk Range	Yield	P/E
NYS	BTU	$46.36 (3/31/2005)	49.89-21.63	0.65	33.59

*7 Year Price Score N/A *NYSE Composite Index=100 *12 Month Price Score 130.80

Interim Earnings (Per Share)

Qtr.	Mar	Jun	Sep	Dec
2002	0.21	0.23	0.27	0.28
2003	(0.11)	(0.01)	0.20	0.20
2004	0.20	0.32	0.33	0.53

Interim Dividends (Per Share)

Amt	Decl	Ex	Rec	Pay
0.063Q	7/21/2004	8/2/2004	8/4/2004	8/25/2004
0.075Q	10/20/2004	11/1/2004	11/3/2004	11/24/2004
0.075Q	1/25/2005	2/4/2005	2/8/2005	3/1/2005
100%	3/2/2005	3/31/2005	3/16/2005	3/30/2005

Indicated Div: $0.30

Valuation Analysis

Forecast P/E	16.34	No of Institutions
	(4/7/2005)	308
Market Cap	$6.0 Billion	Shares
Book Value	1.7 Billion	57,755,136
Price/Book	3.48	% Held
Price/Sales	1.65	88.41

Business Summary: Coal Mining (MIC: 14.4 SIC: 241 NAIC: 13113)

Peabody Energy is engaged in the mining of coal for sale primarily to electric utilities. Co. owns, through its subsidiaries, majority interests in 32 coal operations located throughout the major U.S. coal producing regions and in Australia. In addition to its mining operations, Co. markets, brokers and trades coal. Co. is also involved in related energy businesses that include the development of mine-mouth coal-fueled generating plants, the management of our vast coal reserve and real estate holdings, coalbed methane production and transportation services.

Recent Developments: For the year ended Dec 31 2004, income from continuing operations increased 329.5% to $178,226 thousand from income of $41,492 thousand a year earlier. Net income increased 459.5% to $175,387 thousand from net income of $31,348 thousand a year earlier. Revenues were $3,631,582 thousand, up 29.0% from $2,815,296 thousand the year before. Operating income was $246,698 thousand versus an income of $144,786 thousand in the prior year, an increase of 70.4%. Total direct expense was $2,969,209 thousand versus $2,335,800 thousand in the prior year, an increase of 27.1%. Total indirect expense was $431,742 thousand versus $341,245 thousand in the prior year, an increase of 26.5%.

Prospects: Against the current backdrop of continuing strength in coal markets, Co. is targeting significantly higher 2005 results year over year. Co. is targeting full-year earnings per share of $4.75 to $5.75 and earnings before interest taxes and amortization of $750.0 million to $850.0 million. The broad range reflects the industry's substantial sensitivity to production and transportation issues, which affect high-margin sales volumes. Co. expects increased pricing and volumes to overcome $35.0 million to $45.0 million in higher energy, steel and explosives costs and $40.0 million to $50.0 million in mostly non-cash increases in health care expenses.

Financial Data
(US$ in Thousands)

	12/31/2004	12/31/2003	12/31/2002	12/31/2001	03/31/2001	03/31/2000	03/31/1999	05/19/1998
Earnings Per Share	1.38	0.28	0.98	(0.10)	1.55	0.41	0.01	...
Cash Flow Per Share	2.28	1.77	2.22	0.65	2.76	4.75	5.82	...
Tang Book Value Per Share	13.31	10.36	10.32	9.95	11.43	9.22	12.56	...
Dividends Per Share	0.263	0.225	0.200	0.100	...	...	...	...
Dividend Payout %	19.02	78.95	20.41	N.M.	...	...	...	...
Income Statement								
Total Revenue	3,631,582	2,829,480	2,717,098	2,026,770	2,669,692	2,710,500	2,094,226	292,408
EBITDA	523,436	333,767	415,869	299,104	573,998	461,930	379,032	34,969
Depn & Amortn	278,489	242,494	242,181	183,573	232,159	268,693	200,311	27,597
Income Before Taxes	153,071	(3,181)	78,804	29,000	152,894	(7,398)	21,143	4,817
Income Taxes	(26,437)	(47,708)	(40,007)	2,465	42,690	(141,522)	9,047	4,341
Net Income	175,387	31,348	105,519	(9,683)	107,060	28,210	10,229	476
Average Shares	127,406	109,671	107,643	101,049	55,049	55,172	53,646	53,646
Balance Sheet								
Current Assets	1,054,602	682,740	549,923	527,454	629,955	632,545	1,832,461	...
Total Assets	6,178,592	5,280,265	5,140,177	5,150,902	5,209,487	5,826,849	7,023,931	...
Current Liabilities	774,144	631,968	631,536	684,303	776,985	720,591	1,345,508	...
Long-Term Obligations	1,405,986	1,173,490	981,696	984,568	1,369,316	2,018,189	2,469,975	...
Total Liabilities	4,452,091	4,146,299	4,021,918	4,068,350	4,536,791	5,277,158	6,504,791	...
Stockholders' Equity	1,724,592	1,132,057	1,081,138	1,035,472	631,238	508,426	495,230	...
Shares Outstanding	129,567	109,293	104,800	104,020	55,221	55,116	39,417	...
Statistical Record								
Return on Assets %	3.05	0.60	2.05	N.M.	1.94	0.44	...	...
Return on Equity %	12.25	2.83	9.97	N.M.	18.79	5.61	...	...
EBITDA Margin %	14.41	11.80	15.31	14.76	21.50	17.04	18.10	11.96
Net Margin %	4.83	1.11	3.88	N.M.	4.01	1.04	0.49	0.16
Asset Turnover	0.63	0.54	0.53	0.21	0.48	0.42	...	...
Current Ratio	1.36	1.08	0.87	0.77	0.81	0.88	1.36	...
Debt to Equity	0.82	1.04	0.91	0.95	2.17	3.97	4.99	...
Price Range	42.01-18.31	21.38-12.32	15.20-9.35	18.98-11.63	...	...	...	...
P/E Ratio	30.44-13.27	76.34-44.02	15.51-9.54	N/A	...	...	...	...
Average Yield %	0.96	1.45	1.53	0.71	...	...	...	...

Address: 701 Market Street, St. Louis, MO 63101	**Web Site:** www.peabodyenergy.com	**Auditors:** Ernst & Young LLP
Telephone: (314) 342-3400	**Officers:** Irl F. Engelhardt - Chmn., C.E.O. Gregory H. Boyce - Pres., C.O.O.	

PENNEY (J.C.) CO.,INC. (HOLDING CO.)

Exchange	Symbol	Price	52Wk Range	Yield	P/E
NYS	JCP	$51.92 (3/31/2005)	51.92-31.60	0.96	N/A

*7 Year Price Score 113.08 *NYSE Composite Index=100 ***12 Month Price Score 109.81**

TRADING VOLUME (thousand shares)

Interim Earnings (Per Share)

Qtr.	Apr	Jul	Oct	Jan
2001-02	0.13	(0.29)	0.09	0.33
2002-03	0.30	(0.05)	0.42	0.69
2003-04	0.20	(0.02)	0.27	(3.58)
2004-05	0.13	(0.02)	0.50	

Interim Dividends (Per Share)

Amt	Decl	Ex	Rec	Pay
0.125Q	5/14/2004	7/7/2004	7/9/2004	8/1/2004
0.125Q	9/17/2004	10/6/2004	10/8/2004	11/1/2004
0.125Q	12/8/2004	1/6/2005	1/10/2005	2/1/2005
0.125Q	3/18/2005	4/6/2005	4/8/2005	5/2/2005

Indicated Div: $0.50

Valuation Analysis

Forecast P/E	N/A	No of Institutions
Market Cap	$13.9 Billion	Shares
Book Value	4.7 Billion	236,364,272
Price/Book	2.92	% Held
Price/Sales	1.81	82.76

Business Summary: Retail - General (MIC: 5.2 SIC: 311 NAIC: 52111)

J.C. Penney is a major retailer, operating 1,020 J.C. Penney department stores in 49 states and Puerto Rico as of Jan 31 2004. In addition, Co. operates 58 Renner department stores in Brazil. Co.'s business consists of providing merchandise and services to consumers through Department stores and Catalog/Internet. Department stores and Catalog/Internet generally serve the same customers and have virtually the same mix of merchandise. In addition, department stores accept returns from sales initiated in department stores, catalog or via the Internet. Co. markets family apparel, jewelry, shoes, accessories and home furnishings.

Recent Developments: For the quarter ended Oct 30 2004, net income increased 86.2% to $149,000 thousand from net income of $80,000 thousand in the year-earlier quarter. Revenues were $4,461,000 thousand, up 3.0% from $4,332,000 thousand the year before. Total indirect expense was $1,475,000 thousand versus $1,458,000 thousand in the prior-year quarter, an increase of 1.2%.

Prospects: For the balance of the first quarter beginning with a strong start in Feb 2005 and full year, comparable store sales are expected to increase low-single digits. Catalog/Internet sales are expected to increase low-to-mid single digits for both the first quarter and full year. Co. currently expects earnings from continuing operations to be in the range of $0.48 to $0.53 per share in the first quarter and $2.89 to $3.01 per share for the full year. Full year earnings guidance reflects the impact of $0.08 per share for charges associated with anticipated open market repurchases of debt. Also included in this guidance is an estimated charge of $0.05 per share related to employee stock options.

Financial Data

(US$ in Thousands)	9 Mos	6 Mos	3 Mos	01/31/2004	01/25/2003	01/26/2002	01/27/2001	01/29/2000
Earnings Per Share	(2.75)	(3.22)	(3.20)	(3.13)	1.37	0.26	(2.81)	1.16
Cash Flow Per Share	3.45	3.87	3.71	2.94	4.99	3.76	5.76	4.87
Tang Book Value Per Share	17.61	18.56	18.65	18.18	11.19	11.46	11.37	14.28
Dividends Per Share	0.500	0.500	0.500	0.500	0.500	...	0.825	...
Dividend Payout %	N.M.	N.M.	N.M.	N.M.	36.50	...	...	...
Income Statement								
Total Revenue	12,351,000	7,890,000	4,033,000	17,786,000	32,347,000	32,004,000	31,846,000	32,510,000
EBITDA	961,000	571,000	324,000	1,211,000	1,639,000	1,306,000	236,000	1,853,000
Depn & Amortn	264,000	173,000	87,000	394,000	667,000	717,000	695,000	710,000
Income Before Taxes	520,000	292,000	180,000	546,000	584,000	203,000	(886,000)	531,000
Income Taxes	181,000	102,000	62,000	182,000	213,000	89,000	(318,000)	195,000
Net Income	191,000	42,000	41,000	(928,000)	405,000	98,000	(705,000)	336,000
Average Shares	309,000	287,000	306,000	297,000	293,000	267,000	262,000	275,000
Balance Sheet								
Current Assets	9,200,000	11,203,000	6,739,000	6,513,000	8,353,000	8,677,000	7,257,000	8,472,000
Total Assets	14,889,000	16,541,000	18,160,000	18,300,000	17,867,000	18,048,000	19,742,000	20,888,000
Current Liabilities	3,905,000	4,848,000	3,563,000	3,754,000	4,159,000	4,499,000	4,235,000	4,465,000
Long-Term Obligations	3,955,000	3,960,000	5,113,000	5,114,000	4,940,000	5,179,000	5,448,000	5,844,000
Total Liabilities	10,146,000	10,939,000	12,562,000	12,875,000	11,497,000	11,919,000	13,483,000	13,660,000
Stockholders' Equity	4,743,000	5,602,000	5,598,000	5,425,000	6,370,000	6,129,000	6,259,000	7,228,000
Shares Outstanding	267,000	284,000	282,000	274,000	269,000	264,000	263,000	261,000
Statistical Record								
Return on Assets %	N.M.	N.M.	N.M.	N.M.	2.26	0.52	N.M.	1.51
Return on Equity %	N.M.	N.M.	N.M.	N.M.	6.50	1.59	N.M.	4.68
EBITDA Margin %	7.78	7.24	8.03	6.81	5.07	4.08	0.74	5.70
Net Margin %	1.55	0.53	1.02	N.M.	1.25	0.31	N.M.	1.03
Asset Turnover	0.46	0.60	0.76	0.97	1.81	1.70	1.57	1.46
Current Ratio	2.36	2.31	1.89	1.73	2.01	1.93	1.71	1.90
Debt to Equity	0.83	0.71	0.91	0.94	0.78	0.84	0.87	0.81
Price Range	40.20-22.96	40.00-17.76	36.24-16.31	27.32-16.31	25.00-14.58	29.10-13.50	19.63-8.75	53.44-17.94
P/E Ratio	N/A	N/A	N/A	N/A	18.25-10.64	111.92-51.92	N/A	46.07-15.46
Average Yield %	1.52	1.74	2.08	2.42	2.42	...	5.75	...

Address: 6501 Legacy Drive, Plano, TX 75024-3698	Web Site: www.jcpenney.net	Auditors: KPMG LLP
Telephone: (972) 431-1000	Officers: Allen I. Questrom - Chmn., C.E.O. Robert	Investor Contact: 214-431-1488
Fax: (972) 591-9322	B. Cavanaugh - Exec. V.P., C.F.O.	

PENTAIR, INC.

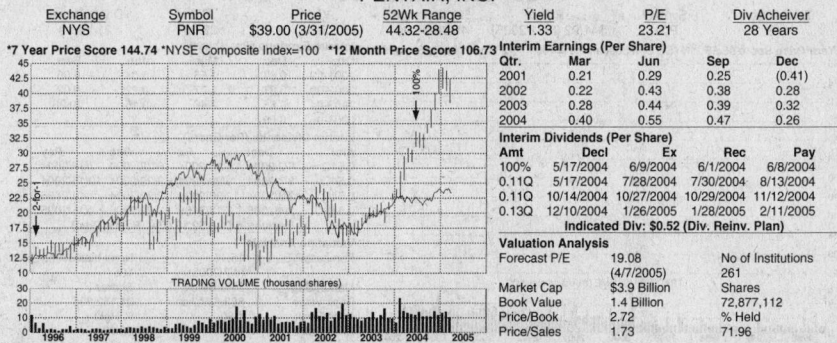

Exchange	Symbol	Price	52Wk Range	Yield	P/E	Div Acheiver
NYS	PNR	$39.00 (3/31/2005)	44.32-28.48	1.33	23.21	28 Years

*7 Year Price Score 144.74 *NYSE Composite Index=100 *12 Month Price Score 106.73

Interim Earnings (Per Share)

Qtr.	Mar	Jun	Sep	Dec
2001	0.21	0.29	0.25	(0.41)
2002	0.22	0.43	0.38	0.28
2003	0.28	0.44	0.39	0.32
2004	0.40	0.55	0.47	0.26

Interim Dividends (Per Share)

Amt	Decl	Ex	Rec	Pay
100%	5/17/2004	6/9/2004	6/1/2004	6/8/2004
0.11Q	5/17/2004	7/28/2004	7/30/2004	8/13/2004
0.11Q	10/14/2004	10/27/2004	10/29/2004	11/12/2004
0.13Q	12/10/2004	1/26/2005	1/28/2005	2/11/2005

Indicated Div: $0.52 (Div. Reinv. Plan)

Valuation Analysis

Forecast P/E	19.08	No of Institutions
	(4/7/2005)	261
Market Cap	$3.9 Billion	Shares
Book Value	1.4 Billion	72,877,112
Price/Book	2.72	% Held
Price/Sales	1.73	71.96

Business Summary: Industrial Machinery and Equipment (MIC: 11.5 SIC: 553 NAIC: 33210)

Pentair is a diversified industrial manufacturer operating through two business segments. Co.'s Water segment manufactures and markets products and systems used in the movement, treatment, storage and enjoyment of water. Co.'s Enclosures segment designs, manufactures and markets standard, modified and custom enclosures that protect sensitive controls and components for markets that include industrial machinery, data communications, networking, telecommunications, test and measurement, automotive, medical, security, defense, and general electronics.

Recent Developments: For the year ended Dec 31 2004, income from continuing operations increased 39.6% to $137,024 thousand from income of $98,150 thousand a year earlier. Net income increased 21.1% to $171,225 thousand from net income of $141,352 thousand a year earlier. Revenues were $2,278,129 thousand, up 38.7% from $1,642,987 thousand the year before. Operating income was $247,242 thousand versus an income of $170,210 thousand in the prior year, an increase of 45.3%. Total direct expense was $1,623,419 thousand versus $1,196,757 thousand in the prior year, an increase of 35.7%. Total indirect expense was $407,468 thousand versus $276,020 thousand in the prior year, an increase of 47.6%.

Prospects: Co.'s outlook appears decent. For the first quarter ended Mar 31 2005, Co. expects earnings per share of between $0.35 and $0.38, and second quarter 2005 earnings per share of $0.61 to $0.65. This guidance reflects the new seasonality of Co.'s business following the Oct 2 2004 sale of its Tools Group and the subsequent increased focus on its Water segment. Co. has also reaffirmed its earnings per share guidance for the full-year 2005 of $1.95 to $2.10. Separately, on Feb 16 2005, Co. announced the formation of a strategic alliance with Ecolab Inc. to deliver water treatment and filtration solutions to the foodservice and hospitality markets through Ecolab's sales-and-service organization.

Financial Data
(US$ in Thousands)

	12/31/2004	12/31/2003	12/31/2002	12/31/2001	12/31/2000	12/31/1999	12/31/1998	12/31/1997
Earnings Per Share	1.68	1.42	1.30	0.34	0.57	1.17	1.23	1.05
Cash Flow Per Share	2.65	2.69	2.75	2.37	1.90	1.67	1.76	1.55
Tang Book Value Per Share	N.M.	N.M.	N.M.	N.M.	N.M.	N.M.	2.35	1.85
Dividends Per Share	0.430	0.410	0.370	0.350	0.330	0.320	0.300	0.270
Dividend Payout %	25.60	28.87	28.35	104.48	57.39	27.47	24.39	25.59
Income Statement								
Total Revenue	2,278,129	2,724,365	2,580,783	2,615,944	2,748,013	2,367,753	1,937,578	1,839,056
EBITDA	301,805	322,483	295,725	259,125	301,058	302,976	261,580	247,951
Depn & Amortn	54,563	62,929	59,733	104,349	99,028	88,645	68,388	67,836
Income Before Taxes	210,032	218,618	192,447	93,288	127,131	166,529	170,944	158,382
Income Taxes	73,008	74,330	62,545	35,772	45,263	63,220	64,104	66,782
Net Income	171,225	141,352	129,902	32,869	55,887	103,309	106,840	91,600
Average Shares	101,706	99,620	99,488	98,594	97,290	88,574	86,298	86,134
Balance Sheet								
Current Assets	825,137	829,451	810,808	835,603	1,091,802	1,150,478	748,569	705,370
Total Assets	3,120,575	2,780,677	2,514,450	2,372,198	2,644,025	2,802,966	1,554,666	1,472,862
Current Liabilities	526,879	497,451	476,092	428,433	648,792	760,947	394,793	392,177
Long-Term Obligations	724,148	732,862	673,911	714,977	781,834	857,296	288,026	294,549
Total Liabilities	1,672,781	1,519,199	1,408,726	1,357,196	1,633,434	1,809,761	845,301	842,300
Stockholders' Equity	1,447,794	1,261,478	1,105,724	1,015,002	1,010,591	993,205	709,365	630,562
Shares Outstanding	100,967	99,005	98,444	98,221	97,423	96,634	77,007	76,370
Statistical Record								
Return on Assets %	5.79	5.34	5.32	1.31	2.05	4.74	7.06	6.63
Return on Equity %	12.61	11.94	12.25	3.25	5.56	12.14	15.95	15.34
EBITDA Margin %	13.25	11.84	11.46	9.91	10.96	12.80	13.50	13.48
Net Margin %	7.52	5.19	5.03	1.26	2.03	4.36	5.51	4.98
Asset Turnover	0.77	1.03	1.06	1.04	1.01	1.09	1.28	1.33
Current Ratio	1.57	1.67	1.70	1.95	1.68	1.51	1.90	1.80
Debt to Equity	0.50	0.58	0.61	0.70	0.77	0.86	0.41	0.47
Price Range	44.03-22.52	23.29-16.40	24.81-14.67	19.64-11.25	22.00-10.50	24.44-15.47	22.88-13.94	19.81-13.75
P/E Ratio	26.21-13.40	16.40-11.55	19.08-11.28	57.76-33.09	38.60-18.42	20.89-13.22	18.60-11.33	18.87-13.10
Average Yield %	1.35	2.09	1.85	2.19	2.00	1.57	1.55	1.59

Address: 1500 Country Road B2 West, Suite 400, St. Paul, MN 55113	**Web Site:** www.pentair.com	**Auditors:** Deloitte & Touche LLP
Telephone: (651) 636-7920	**Officers:** Randall J. Hogan - Chmn., Pres., C.E.O.	**Investor Contact:** 651-639-5278
Fax: (651) 639-5203	Richard J. Cathcart - Vice-Chmn.	**Transfer Agents:** Wells Fargo Bank Minnesota, N.A.

PEOPLES ENERGY CORP.

Exchange	Symbol	Price	52Wk Range	Yield	P/E	Div Achiever
NYS	PGL	$41.92 (3/31/2005)	45.28-38.96	5.20	22.06	21 Years

*7 Year Price Score 95.55   *NYSE Composite Index=100   *12 Month Price Score 94.15

Interim Earnings (Per Share)

Qtr.	Dec	Mar	Jun	Sep
2001-02	0.87	1.55	0.04	0.05
2002-03	0.87	1.77	0.22	0.02
2003-04	0.85	1.46	0.15	(0.28)
2004-05	0.59	...	...	...

Interim Dividends (Per Share)

Amt	Decl	Ex	Rec	Pay
0.54Q	6/2/2004	6/18/2004	6/22/2004	7/15/2004
0.54Q	8/4/2004	9/20/2004	9/22/2004	10/15/2004
0.54Q	12/3/2004	12/20/2004	12/22/2004	1/14/2005
0.545Q	2/4/2005	3/18/2005	3/22/2005	4/15/2005

Indicated Div: $2.18 (Div. Reinv. Plan)

Valuation Analysis

Forecast P/E	15.40	No of Institutions	
	(4/7/2005)	186	
Market Cap	$1.6 Billion	Shares	
Book Value	883.8 Million	21,152,396	
Price/Book	1.80	% Held	
Price/Sales	0.67	55.79	

Business Summary: Gas Utilities (MIC: 7.4 SIC: 924 NAIC: 21210)

Peoples Energy is a holding company. Co.'s regulated utility subsidiaries include The Peoples Gas Light and Coke Company (Peoples Gas) and North Shore Gas Company (North Shore Gas). As of Sep 30 2004, Peoples Gas and North Shore Gas purchased, stored, distributed, sold and transported natural gas to approximately 1.0 million customers through a 6,000-mile distribution system serving Chicago and 54 communities in northeastern Illinois. The customer base includes residential, commercial and industrial sales and transportation accounts. Other businesses of Co. include oil and gas production, power generation, midstream services and retail energy services.

Recent Developments: For the quarter ended Dec 31 2004, net income decreased 28.3% to $22,475 thousand from net income of $31,351 thousand in the year-earlier quarter. Revenues were $737,411 thousand, up 21.9% from $604,884 thousand the year before. Operating income was $46,413 thousand versus an income of $60,152 thousand in the prior-year quarter, a decrease of 22.8%. Total direct expense was $597,217 thousand versus $467,870 thousand in the prior-year quarter, an increase of 27.6%. Total indirect expense was $94,669 thousand versus $76,617 thousand in the prior-year quarter, an increase of 23.6%.

Prospects: Co.'s outlook is tempered by a combination of the recent level of natural gas prices and warmer-than-normal weather that may restrain Gas Distribution segment growth. On the positive side, Co. noted that its Midwest-based diversified businesses are on track to meet expectations, while production volumes from its Oil and Gas segment should grow as its drilling program accelerates over the next nine months. Also, Co. indicated that it may exceed its goals for utility and corporate cost reductions related to its organizational restructuring. Nevertheless, Co. stated that earnings for the fiscal year ended Sep 30 2005 will likely be at the low end of the range of $2.75 to $2.90 per share.

Financial Data
(US$ in Thousands)

	3 Mos	09/30/2004	09/30/2003	09/30/2002	09/30/2001	09/30/2000	09/30/1999	09/30/1998
Earnings Per Share	1.90	2.18	2.87	2.51	2.74	2.44	2.61	2.25
Cash Flow Per Share	5.06	5.41	5.71	9.26	4.79	1.44	5.18	4.50
Tang Book Value Per Share	23.34	23.06	23.11	22.74	22.66	21.86	21.66	20.94
Dividends Per Share	2.160	2.150	2.110	2.070	2.030	1.990	1.950	1.910
Dividend Payout %	113.45	98.62	73.52	82.47	74.09	81.56	74.71	84.89
Income Statement								
Total Revenue	737,411	2,260,199	2,138,394	1,482,534	2,270,218	1,417,533	1,194,381	1,138,057
EBITDA	79,068	293,035	329,330	295,174	315,568	283,615	268,259	...
Depn & Amortn	31,742	125,212	116,773	98,852	95,046	100,935	83,531	77,195
Income Before Taxes	34,816	119,397	163,116	135,392	148,471	129,761	145,217	...
Income Taxes	12,340	37,833	59,182	46,321	51,417	43,346	52,581	145,970
Net Income	22,476	81,564	103,934	89,071	97,020	86,415	92,636	79,423
Average Shares	37,993	37,490	36,193	35,492	35,439	35,413	35,490	35,276
Balance Sheet								
Net PPE	1,903,172	1,904,185	1,838,173	1,773,901	1,753,912	1,645,340	1,519,836	1,446,661
Total Assets	3,320,292	3,094,790	2,928,538	2,723,647	2,994,054	2,501,918	2,100,164	1,904,500
Long-Term Obligations	897,207	897,377	744,345	554,014	644,308	419,663	521,734	516,604
Total Liabilities	2,436,499	2,224,707	2,080,539	1,917,323	2,188,537	1,724,836	1,331,434	1,163,139
Stockholders' Equity	883,793	870,083	847,999	806,324	805,517	777,082	768,730	741,361
Shares Outstanding	37,867	37,733	36,689	35,459	35,544	35,544	35,489	35,402
Statistical Record								
Return on Assets %	2.22	2.70	3.68	3.12	3.53	3.75	4.63	4.26

Address: 130 East Randolph Drive, 24th Floor, Chicago, IL 60601-6207 Telephone: (312) 240-4000 Fax: (312) 240-4220	Web Site: www.peoplesenergy.com Officers: Thomas M. Patrick - Chmn., Pres., C.E.O. William E. Morrow - Exec. V.P., Opers.	Auditors: Deloitte & Touche LLP Investor Contact: 312-240-4730 Transfer Agents: LaSalle Bank, N.A., Chicago, IL

PEPCO HOLDINGS INC.

Exchange	Symbol	Price	52Wk Range	Yield	P/E
NYS	POM	$20.99 (3/31/2005)	22.93-17.04	4.76	14.28

*7 Year Price Score 77.72 *NYSE Composite Index=100 *12 Month Price Score 101.66

TRADING VOLUME (thousand shares)

Interim Earnings (Per Share)

Qtr.	Mar	Jun	Sep	Dec
2002	0.22	...	0.80	0.07
2003	(0.15)	0.25	0.92	(0.37)
2004	0.30	0.53	0.64	0.01

Interim Dividends (Per Share)

Amt	Decl	Ex	Rec	Pay
0.25Q	4/22/2004	6/8/2004	6/10/2004	6/30/2004
0.25Q	7/22/2004	9/8/2004	9/10/2004	9/30/2004
0.25Q	10/28/2004	12/8/2004	12/10/2004	12/31/2004
0.25Q	1/27/2005	3/8/2005	3/10/2005	3/31/2005
			Indicated Div: $1.00	

Valuation Analysis

Forecast P/E	14.03 (4/7/2005)	No of Institutions 227
Market Cap	$4.0 Billion	Shares
Book Value	3.4 Billion	89,743,360
Price/Book	1.17	% Held
Price/Sales	0.55	47.76

Business Summary: Electricity (MIC: 7.1 SIC: 911 NAIC: 21121)

Pepco Holdings is a holding company for Potomac Electric Power and Conectiv. Co. is the largest electricity delivery company in the mid-Atlantic region with a transmission network serving more than 1.8 million customers in a 10,000 square-mile area. Potomac Electric is based in Washington, D.C. and Conectiv is based in Wilmington, DE. Potomac Electric delivers electricity to more than 700,000 customers in Washington, D.C. and the Maryland suburbs. Conectiv is focused on two core energy businesses. Conectiv Power Delivery provides energy to more than one million customers in New Jersey, Delaware, Maryland and Virginia. Conectiv Energy manages a growing portfolio of power plants.

Recent Developments: For the year ended Dec 31 2004, net income increased 127.9% to $258,700 thousand from net income of $113,500 thousand a year earlier. Revenues were $14,443,600 thousand, down 0.7% from $14,542,600 thousand the year before. Operating income was $775,700 thousand versus an income of $616,400 thousand in the prior year, an increase of 25.8%. Total direct expense was $6,137,000 thousand versus $6,392,500 thousand in the prior year, a decrease of 4.0%. Total indirect expense was $309,100 thousand versus $262,400 thousand in the prior year, an increase of 17.8%.

Prospects: Results are benefiting from a significant increase in generation output, as well as higher electric sales and improved commodity margins. Separately, on Jan 6 2005, Co. announced that Pepco Energy Services, Inc. (PES), a wholly-owned subsidiary, has been chosen to implement a Pennsylvania Act 77 energy efficiency and guaranteed savings program for the Ridley School District located in Folsom, PA. As part of the 15-year contract, PES will install new chillers, boilers and windows in nine schools and two administrative buildings. The project also provides occupancy controls, water conservation, lighting upgrades and ongoing training. Construction is expected to be completed by the end of 2005.

Financial Data

(US$ in Thousands)	12/31/2004	12/31/2003	12/31/2002	12/31/2001	12/31/2000
Earnings Per Share	1.47	0.66	1.61	1.50	2.96
Cash Flow Per Share	4.14	3.87	6.14	...	...
Tang Book Value Per Share	10.28	9.13	9.20	17.00	...
Dividends Per Share	1.000	1.000	0.416	...	...
Dividend Payout %	68.03	151.52	25.82	...	...
Income Statement					
Total Revenue	7,221,800	7,271,300	4,324,500	2,400,500	2,989,300
EBITDA	1,246,000	...	...	...	...
Depn & Amortn	440,500	422,100	239,800	170,600	247,600
Income Before Taxes	431,900	...	...	...	...
Income Taxes	173,200	65,900	124,100	83,500	341,200
Net Income	258,700	113,500	210,500	163,400	346,500
Average Shares	176,300	170,700	131,100	108,800	118,300
Balance Sheet					
Net PPE	7,088,000	6,964,900	6,798,000	2,753,400	...
Total Assets	13,349,400	13,434,400	12,861,700	5,285,900	...
Long-Term Obligations	5,072,800	5,372,800	4,832,400	1,722,400	...
Total Liabilities	9,928,200	10,412,900	9,465,200	3,252,900	...
Stockholders' Equity	3,366,300	3,003,300	2,995,800	1,823,200	...
Shares Outstanding	188,327	171,769	169,982	107,221	118,544
Statistical Record					
Return on Assets %	1.93	0.86	...	...	...
Return on Equity %	8.10	3.78	...	...	...
EBITDA Margin %	17.25	...	...	...	...
Net Margin %	3.58	1.56	4.87	6.81	11.59
PPE Turnover	1.02	1.06	...	...	...
Asset Turnover	0.54	0.55	...	...	...
Debt to Equity	1.51	1.79	1.61	0.94	...
Price Range	21.71-17.04	20.56-16.18	23.73-16.22	24.27-20.28	27.31-19.19
P/E Ratio	14.77-11.59	31.15-24.52	14.74-10.07	16.18-13.52	9.23-6.48
Average Yield %	5.05	5.54	1.98	...	...

Address: 701 Ninth Street N.W., Washington, DC 20068 **Telephone:** (202) 872-2000	**Web Site:** www.pepcoholdings.com **Officers:** Dennis R. Wraase - Chmn., Pres., C.E.O. William T. Torgerson - Vice-Chmn., Gen. Couns.	**Auditors:** PricewaterhouseCoopers LLP **Investor Contact:** 202-872-2797

PEPSI BOTTLING GROUP INC

Exchange	Symbol	Price	52Wk Range	Yield	P/E
NYS	PBG	$27.85 (3/31/2005)	31.21-25.80	1.15	16.10

*7 Year Price Score N/A   *NYSE Composite Index=100   *12 Month Price Score 91.60

Interim Earnings (Per Share)

Qtr.	Mar	Jun	Aug	Dec
2001	0.09	0.39	0.51	0.04
2002	0.19	0.47	0.61	1.33
2003	0.12	0.47	0.67	0.26
2004	0.19	0.53	0.73	0.29

Interim Dividends (Per Share)

Amt	Decl	Ex	Rec	Pay
0.05Q	8/10/2004	9/8/2004	9/10/2004	9/30/2004
0.05Q	11/15/2004	12/8/2004	12/10/2004	1/3/2005
0.05Q	2/17/2005	3/9/2005	3/11/2005	3/31/2005
0.08Q	3/24/2005	6/8/2005	6/10/2005	6/30/2005
			Indicated Div: $0.32	

Valuation Analysis

Forecast P/E	N/A	No of Institutions
Market Cap	$6.9 Billion	Shares
Book Value	1.9 Billion	150,631,488
Price/Book	3.56	% Held
Price/Sales	0.64	60.95

Business Summary: Food (MIC: 4.1 SIC: 086 NAIC: 12111)

Pepsi Bottling Group is a manufacturer, seller and distributor of Pepsi-Cola beverages, consisting of bottling operations located in the U.S., Mexico, Canada, Spain, Greece, Russia and Turkey. Pepsi-Cola beverages sold by Co. include Pepsi-Cola, Diet Pepsi, Mountain Dew, Aquafina, Sierra Mist, Lipton Brisk, Diet Mountain Dew, Sobe, Dole and Pepsi Vanilla, and, outside the U.S., Pepsi-Cola, Kas, Aqua Minerale, Manzanita Sol, and Mirinda. Co. has the exclusive right to manufacture, sell and distribute Pepsi-Cola beverages in all or a portion of 41 states and the District of Columbia in the U.S., nine Canadian provinces, Spain, Greece, Russia, Turkey and all or a portion of 21 states in Mexico.

Recent Developments: For the year ended Dec 25 2004, net income increased 9.9% to $457 million from net income of $416 million a year earlier. Revenues were $10,906 million, up 6.2% from $10,265 million the year before. Operating income was $976 million versus an income of $956 million in the prior year, an increase of 2.1%. Total direct expense was $5,656 million versus $5,215 million in the prior year, an increase of 8.5%. Total indirect expense was $4,274 million versus $4,094 million in the prior year, an increase of 4.4%.

Prospects: For full-year 2005, Co. is forecasting worldwide volume in the range of 3.0% to 4.0%, with U.S. and Canada volume in the range of 1.0% to 2.0%. Also, in 2005, Co. expects worldwide selling, delivery and administrative expenses in terms of dollars of between 3.0% and 4.0%. In addition, in 2005, Co. is projecting worldwide operating profit in terms of dollars of between 1.0% and 4.0%. Further, for full-year 2005, Co. is forecasting net interest expense in the range of $244.0 million to $249.0 million. Finally, for full-year 2005, Co. is projecting diluted earnings per share of between $1.78 and $1.87.

Financial Data
(US$ in Thousands)

	12/25/2004	12/27/2003	12/28/2002	12/29/2001	12/30/2000	12/25/1999	12/26/1998	12/27/1997
Earnings Per Share	1.73	1.50	1.46	1.03	0.77	0.46	(1.33)	0.54
Cash Flow Per Share	4.92	4.03	3.61	3.52	2.78	2.80	5.70	5.00
Dividends Per Share	0.160	0.040	0.040	0.040	0.040	0.030	...	...
Dividend Payout %	9.25	2.67	2.74	3.88	5.23	6.52	...	...
Income Statement								
Total Revenue	10,906,000	10,265,000	9,216,000	8,443,000	7,982,000	7,505,000	7,041,000	6,592,000
EBITDA	1,512,000	1,467,000	1,291,000	1,149,000	1,027,000	895,000	501,000	776,000
Depn & Amortn	593,000	568,000	451,000	514,000	471,000	505,000	472,000	439,000
Income Before Taxes	689,000	660,000	649,000	441,000	364,000	188,000	(192,000)	115,000
Income Taxes	232,000	238,000	221,000	136,000	135,000	70,000	(46,000)	56,000
Net Income	457,000	416,000	428,000	305,000	229,000	118,000	(146,000)	59,000
Average Shares	263,000	277,000	293,000	296,000	298,000	256,000	110,000	110,000
Balance Sheet								
Current Assets	2,039,000	3,039,000	1,737,000	1,548,000	1,584,000	1,493,000	1,318,000	1,336,000
Total Assets	10,793,000	11,544,000	10,027,000	7,857,000	7,736,000	7,619,000	7,322,000	7,188,000
Current Liabilities	1,581,000	2,478,000	1,248,000	1,081,000	967,000	947,000	1,025,000	1,147,000
Long-Term Obligations	4,489,000	4,493,000	4,523,000	3,285,000	3,271,000	3,268,000	61,000	96,000
Total Liabilities	8,844,000	9,663,000	8,203,000	6,256,000	6,090,000	6,056,000	7,560,000	7,372,000
Stockholders' Equity	1,949,000	1,881,000	1,824,000	1,601,000	1,646,000	1,563,000	(238,000)	(184,000)
Shares Outstanding	249,000	261,100	281,100	281,100	290,176	298,000	110,000	110,000
Statistical Record								
Return on Assets %	4.10	3.87	4.80	3.92	2.93	1.55	N.M.	0.82
Return on Equity %	23.93	22.52	25.06	18.84	14.04	7.55	N.M.	N.M.
EBITDA Margin %	13.86	14.29	14.01	13.61	12.87	11.93	7.12	11.77
Net Margin %	4.19	4.05	4.64	3.61	2.87	1.57	N.M.	0.90
Asset Turnover	0.98	0.95	1.03	1.09	1.02	0.99	0.97	0.92
Current Ratio	1.29	1.23	1.39	1.43	1.64	1.58	1.29	1.16
Debt to Equity	2.30	2.39	2.48	2.05	1.99	2.09	N.M.	N.M.
Price Range	31.21-24.01	27.53-17.93	34.38-21.70	24.73-16.78	21.13-8.13	12.25-7.91	...	...
P/E Ratio	18.04-13.88	18.35-11.95	23.55-14.86	24.00-16.29	27.44-10.55	26.63-17.19	...	...
Average Yield %	0.57	0.18	0.15	0.19	0.29	0.30	...	...

Address: One Pepsi Way, Somers, NY 10589-2201
Telephone: (914) 767-6000
Fax: (914) 767-1313

Web Site: www.pbg.com
Officers: John T. Cahill - Chmn., C.E.O. Alfred H. Drewes - Sr. V.P., C.F.O.

Auditors: KPMG LLP
Investor Contact: 914-767-7216

PEPSIAMERICAS, INC. (NEW)

Exchange	Symbol	Price	52Wk Range	Yield	P/E
NYS	PAS	$22.66 (3/31/2005)	23.08-18.41	1.50	17.70

*7 Year Price Score 109.76 *NYSE Composite Index=100 *12 Month Price Score 100.84

Interim Earnings (Per Share)

Qtr.	Mar	Jun	Sep	Dec
2001	0.08	0.23	0.21	(0.40)
2002	0.15	0.32	0.33	0.05
2003	0.03	0.37	0.43	0.25
2004	0.14	0.43	0.46	0.25

Interim Dividends (Per Share)

Amt	Decl	Ex	Rec	Pay
0.075Q	4/28/2004	6/14/2004	6/15/2004	7/1/2004
0.075Q	4/28/2004	9/13/2004	9/15/2004	10/1/2004
0.075Q	4/28/2004	12/13/2004	12/15/2004	1/3/2005
0.085Q	2/24/2005	3/11/2005	3/15/2005	4/1/2005

Indicated Div: $0.34

Valuation Analysis

Forecast P/E	N/A	No of Institutions
Market Cap	$3.1 Million	Shares
Book Value	1.6 Billion	53,298,484
Price/Book	0.00	% Held
Price/Sales	0.00	38.24

Business Summary: Food (MIC: 4.1 SIC: 086 NAIC: 12111)

PepsiAmericas manufactures, packages, sells and distributes carbonated and non-carbonated Pepsi-Cola beverages and a variety of other beverages in the United States, Central Europe and the Caribbean. Co.'s three largest brands in terms of volume are Pepsi, Diet Pepsi and Mountain Dew. Co. serves a significant portion of an 18 state region, primarily in the Midwest. Outside the U.S., Co. serves Central European and Caribbean markets including Poland, Hungary, the Czech Republic, Republic of Slovakia, Puerto Rico, Jamaica, the Bahamas, Barbados, and Trinidad and Tobago.

Recent Developments: For the year ended Jan 1 2005, net income increased 15.4% to $181.9 million from net income of $157.6 million a year earlier. Revenues were $3,344.7 million, up 3.3% from $3,236.8 million the year before. Operating income was $339.7 million versus an income of $316.3 million in the prior year, an increase of 7.4%. Total direct expense was $1,922.2 million versus $1,876.6 million in the prior year, an increase of 2.4%. Total indirect expense was $1,082.8 million versus $1,043.9 million in the prior year, an increase of 3.7%.

Prospects: On Jan 10 2005, Co. announced that it has completed its acquisition of Central Investment Corporation, which operates bottling facilities in Southeast Florida and Central Ohio, as well as full-line vending operations in both territories. The acquisition is expected to be accretive to earnings by approximately $0.04 per share in 2005. Co. is continuing to seek similar acquisitions or partnerships in the U.S. and internationally. Looking ahead, Co. is projecting full-year earnings in the range of $1.33 to $1.36 per share. Also, Co. expects worldwide volume to increase between 9.0% and 10.0% during 2005.

Financial Data

(US$ in Thousands)	01/01/2005	01/03/2004	12/28/2002	12/29/2001	12/30/2000	12/31/1999	12/31/1998	12/31/1997
Earnings Per Share	1.28	1.09	0.85	0.12	0.58	(0.07)	0.42	0.04
Cash Flow Per Share	3,343.21	2.05	2.18	2.04	2.35	1.47	1.68	1.50
Tang Book Value Per Share	N.M.	N.M.	N.M.	N.M.	N.M.	N.M.	N.M.	0.76
Dividends Per Share	0.300	0.040	0.040	0.040	0.040	0.030	0.200	0.450
Dividend Payout %	23.44	3.67	4.71	33.33	6.90	N.M.	47.62	1,125.00
Income Statement								
Total Revenue	3,344,700	3,236,800	3,239,800	3,170,700	2,527,600	2,138,200	1,635,000	1,557,500
EBITDA	520,800	480,000	460,400	466,800	391,500	262,100	266,000	186,000
Depn & Amortn	176,400	170,200	163,800	202,100	166,400	126,600	77,700	73,800
Income Before Taxes	282,300	240,200	220,200	173,900	141,100	71,600	152,200	69,900
Income Taxes	100,400	82,600	84,500	83,800	69,600	22,100	69,700	37,900
Net Income	181,900	157,600	129,700	18,900	80,400	(8,800)	43,700	4,100
Average Shares	141	144,100	153,000	156,600	139,500	124,200	102,800	102,900
Balance Sheet								
Current Assets	529,500	560,200	549,900	480,800	477,000	538,000	429,100	560,800
Total Assets	3,529,800	3,580,700	3,562,600	3,419,300	3,335,600	2,864,300	1,569,300	2,029,700
Current Liabilities	521,100	599,500	698,000	652,700	887,000	739,100	233,200	490,000
Long-Term Obligations	1,006,600	1,078,400	1,080,700	1,083,400	860,100	809,000	603,600	604,700
Total Liabilities	1,906,600	2,015,600	2,114,000	1,989,000	1,886,100	1,722,100	1,242,900	1,490,000
Stockholders' Equity	1,623,200	1,565,100	1,448,600	1,430,300	1,449,500	1,142,200	326,400	539,700
Shares Outstanding	138	143,800	147,600	153,600	155,600	139,100	101,000	101,100
Statistical Record								
Return on Assets %	5.13	4.34	3.73	0.56	2.59	N.M.	2.43	0.18
Return on Equity %	11.44	10.29	9.04	1.32	6.20	N.M.	10.09	0.69
EBITDA Margin %	15.57	14.83	14.21	14.72	15.49	12.26	16.27	11.94
Net Margin %	5.44	4.87	4.00	0.60	3.18	N.M.	2.67	0.26
Asset Turnover	0.94	0.89	0.93	0.94	0.82	0.96	0.91	0.70
Current Ratio	1.02	0.93	0.79	0.74	0.54	0.73	1.84	1.14
Debt to Equity	0.62	0.69	0.75	0.76	0.59	0.71	1.85	1.12
Price Range	21.50-16.90	17.25-11.18	15.90-11.66	16.94-12.52	16.38-10.69	25.38-12.81	25.38-15.25	17.26-13.47
P/E Ratio	16.80-13.20	15.83-10.26	18.71-13.72	141.17-104.33	28.23-18.43	N/A	60.42-36.31	431.52-336.70
Average Yield %	1.51	0.29	0.28	0.27	0.31	0.18	1.01	2.93

Address: 4000 Dain Rauscher Plaza, 60 South Sixth Street, Minneapolis, MN 55402 Telephone: (612) 661-3883 Fax: (612) 483-6750	Web Site: www.pepsiamericas.com Officers: Robert C. Pohlad - Chmn., C.E.O. Kenneth E. Keiser - Pres., C.O.O.	Auditors: KPMG LLP Investor Contact: 612-661-3883

PEPSICO INC.

Exchange	Symbol	Price	52Wk Range	Yield	P/E	Div Acheiver
NYS	PEP	$53.03 (3/31/2005)	55.55-47.85	1.73	21.73	33 Years

*7 Year Price Score 102.16 ***NYSE Composite Index=100** ***12 Month Price Score 95.79**

Interim Earnings (Per Share)

Qtr.	Mar	Jun	Aug	Dec
2001	0.34	0.44	0.34	0.37
2002	0.36	0.49	0.54	0.46
2003	0.45	0.58	0.62	0.41
2004	0.46	0.61	0.79	0.58

Interim Dividends (Per Share)

Amt	Decl	Ex	Rec	Pay
0.23Q	5/5/2004	6/9/2004	6/11/2004	6/30/2004
0.23Q	7/23/2004	9/8/2004	9/10/2004	9/30/2004
0.23Q	11/19/2004	12/8/2004	12/10/2004	1/3/2005
0.23Q	1/27/2005	3/9/2005	3/11/2005	3/31/2005

Indicated Div: $0.92 (Div. Reinv. Plan)

Valuation Analysis

Forecast P/E	15.23 (4/7/2005)	No of Institutions 1086
Market Cap	$89.0 Billion	Shares 1,102,368,896
Book Value	13.6 Billion	% Held
Price/Book	6.56	65.69
Price/Sales	3.04	

Business Summary: Food (MIC: 4.1 SIC: 086 NAIC: 12111)

PepsiCo is a global snack and beverage company. Co. manufactures, markets and sells a variety of salty, convenient, sweet and grain-based snacks, carbonated and non-carbonated beverages and foods. Co.'s Frito-Lay North America division's brands include Lay's potato chips, Fritos corn chips, Quaker Chewy granola bars and Rold Gold pretzels. PepsiCo Beverages North America brands include Pepsi, Mountain Dew, Sierra Mist, Mug, SoBe, Gatorade, Tropicana Pure Premium and Propel. PepsiCo International brands include Sabritas in Mexico, Walkers in the UK, and Smith's in Australia. Quaker Foods North America's products include Quaker oatmeal and Cap'n Crunch and Life ready-to-eat cereals.

Recent Developments: For the year ended Dec 25 2004, income from continuing operations increased 17.0% to $4,174,000 thousand from income of $3,568,000 thousand a year earlier. Net income increased 18.0% to $4,212,000 thousand from net income of $3,568,000 thousand a year earlier. Revenues were $29,261,000 thousand, up 8.5% from $26,971,000 thousand the year before. Operating income was $5,259,000 thousand versus an income of $4,781,000 thousand in the prior year, an increase of 10.0%. Total direct expense was $13,406,000 thousand versus $12,379,000 thousand in the prior year, an increase of 8.3%. Total indirect expense was $10,596,000 thousand versus $9,811,000 thousand in the prior year, an increase of 8.0%.

Prospects: Top-line results are being positively affected by continued strong growth in Co.'s international operations, broad-based volume increases, and favorable foreign currency exchange rates. Looking ahead, Co. is projecting full-year 2005 volume and revenue growth in the mid single-digit percentage range, along with operating profit growth of approximately 8.0% across all divisions. In addition, Co. is targeting earnings per share of at least $2.59 for 2005. Separately, Co. plans to reduce its 42.0% stake in Pepsi Bottling Group to 35.0% during 2005.

Financial Data

(US$ in Thousands)	12/25/2004	12/27/2003	12/28/2002	12/29/2001	12/30/2000	12/25/1999	12/26/1998	12/27/1997
Earnings Per Share	2.44	2.05	1.85	1.47	1.48	1.37	1.31	1.36
Cash Flow Per Share	2.99	2.53	2.65	2.39	2.66	2.07	2.18	2.24
Tang Book Value Per Share	4.84	3.82	2.37	2.17	1.91	1.47	N.M.	0.72
Dividends Per Share	0.850	0.630	0.595	0.575	0.555	0.535	0.515	0.490
Dividend Payout %	34.84	30.73	32.16	39.12	37.50	39.05	39.31	36.03
Income Statement								
Total Revenue	29,261,000	26,971,000	25,112,000	26,935,000	20,438,000	20,367,000	22,348,000	20,917,000
EBITDA	6,848,000	6,269,000	6,077,000	5,189,000	4,209,000	4,843,000	3,818,000	3,768,000
Depn & Amortn	1,209,000	1,165,000	1,067,000	1,008,000	854,000	942,000	1,234,000	1,106,000
Income Before Taxes	5,546,000	4,992,000	4,868,000	4,029,000	3,210,000	3,656,000	2,263,000	2,309,000
Income Taxes	1,372,000	1,424,000	1,555,000	1,367,000	1,027,000	1,606,000	270,000	818,000
Net Income	4,212,000	3,568,000	3,313,000	2,662,000	2,183,000	2,050,000	1,993,000	2,142,000
Average Shares	1,729,000	1,739,000	1,789,000	1,807,000	1,475,000	1,496,000	1,519,000	1,570,000
Balance Sheet								
Current Assets	8,639,000	6,930,000	6,413,000	5,853,000	4,604,000	4,173,000	4,362,000	6,251,000
Total Assets	27,987,000	25,327,000	23,474,000	21,695,000	18,339,000	17,551,000	22,660,000	20,101,000
Current Liabilities	6,752,000	6,415,000	6,052,000	4,998,000	3,935,000	3,788,000	7,914,000	4,257,000
Long-Term Obligations	2,397,000	1,702,000	2,187,000	2,651,000	2,346,000	2,812,000	4,028,000	4,946,000
Total Liabilities	14,464,000	13,453,000	14,183,000	13,021,000	11,090,000	10,670,000	16,259,000	13,165,000
Stockholders' Equity	13,572,000	11,896,000	9,298,000	8,648,000	7,249,000	6,881,000	6,401,000	6,936,000
Shares Outstanding	1,679,000	1,705,000	1,722,000	1,756,000	1,446,000	1,455,000	1,471,000	1,502,000
Statistical Record								
Return on Assets %	15.84	14.66	14.71	13.34	11.97	10.22	9.35	9.63
Return on Equity %	33.17	33.76	37.02	33.58	30.40	30.95	29.97	31.68
EBITDA Margin %	23.40	23.24	24.20	19.26	20.59	23.78	17.08	18.01
Net Margin %	14.39	13.23	13.19	9.88	10.68	10.07	8.92	10.24
Asset Turnover	1.10	1.11	1.11	1.35	1.12	1.02	1.05	0.94
Current Ratio	1.28	1.08	1.06	1.17	1.17	1.10	0.55	1.47
Debt to Equity	0.18	0.14	0.24	0.31	0.32	0.41	0.63	0.71
Price Range	55.55-45.39	48.71-37.30	53.12-35.50	50.28-41.26	49.75-30.50	41.81-30.50	44.69-27.88	40.00-26.81
P/E Ratio	22.77-18.60	23.76-18.20	28.71-19.19	34.20-28.07	33.61-20.61	30.52-22.26	34.11-21.28	29.41-19.71
Average Yield %	1.66	1.43	1.29	1.25	1.36	1.46	1.37	1.47

Address: 700 Anderson Hill Road, Purchase, NY 10577-1444	**Web Site:** www.pepsico.com	**Auditors:** KPMG LLP
Telephone: (914) 253-2000	**Officers:** Steven S. Reinemund - Chmn., C.E.O. Indra K. Nooyi - Pres., C.F.O.	**Investor Contact:** 914-253-3035
Fax: (914) 253-2070		**Transfer Agents:** The Bank of New York

PERKINELMER, INC.

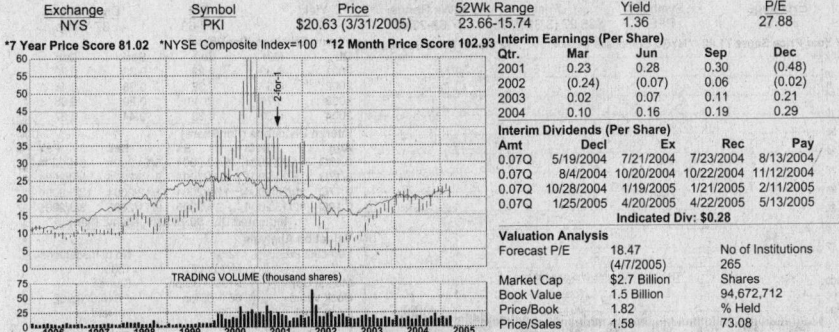

Exchange	Symbol	Price	52Wk Range	Yield	P/E
NYS	PKI	$20.63 (3/31/2005)	23.66-15.74	1.36	27.88

*7 Year Price Score 81.02   *NYSE Composite Index=100   *12 Month Price Score 102.93

Interim Earnings (Per Share)

Qtr.	Mar	Jun	Sep	Dec
2001	0.23	0.28	0.30	(0.48)
2002	(0.24)	(0.07)	0.06	(0.02)
2003	0.02	0.07	0.11	0.21
2004	0.10	0.16	0.19	0.29

Interim Dividends (Per Share)

Amt	Decl	Ex	Rec	Pay
0.07Q	5/19/2004	7/21/2004	7/23/2004	8/13/2004
0.07Q	8/4/2004	10/20/2004	10/22/2004	11/12/2004
0.07Q	10/28/2004	1/19/2005	1/21/2005	2/11/2005
0.07Q	1/25/2005	4/20/2005	4/22/2005	5/13/2005

Indicated Div: $0.28

Valuation Analysis

Forecast P/E	18.47 (4/7/2005)	No of Institutions 265
Market Cap	$2.7 Billion	Shares 94,672,712
Book Value	1.5 Billion	% Held
Price/Book	1.82	73.08
Price/Sales	1.58	

Business Summary: Instruments and Related Products (MIC: 11.15 SIC: 826 NAIC: 41330)

PerkinElmer is a technology company that operates three business units. The Life and Analytical Sciences segment offers drug discovery tools for customers engaged in pharmaceutical, biotechnology and academic laboratory research, and genetic disease screening software, reagents and analysis tools to test for a number of inherited disorders. The Optoelectronics segment provides telecommunications, specialty lighting, sensor and digital imaging to customers in the health sciences, communications and industrial markets. The Fluid Sciences segment provides sealing applications and advanced fluid containment technologies.

Recent Developments: For the year ended Jan 2 2005, income from continuing operations increased 69.6% to $98,252 thousand from income of $57,933 thousand a year earlier. Net income increased 81.4% to $96,043 thousand from net income of $52,959 thousand a year earlier. Revenues were $3,374,462 thousand, up 10.1% from $3,064,100 thousand the year before. Operating income was $177,070 thousand versus an income of $141,841 thousand in the prior year, an increase of 24.8%. Total direct expense was $2,013,356 thousand versus $1,801,516 thousand in the prior year, an increase of 11.8%. Total indirect expense was $503,483 thousand versus $489,451 thousand in the prior year, an increase of 2.9%.

Prospects: For 2005, Co. anticipates substantially higher research and development investments to accelerate innovation. Combined with Co.'s significant cash flow, this provides fuel for its growth investments in key health sciences and industrial technology opportunities. For the first quarter of 2005, Co. projects generally accepted accounting principle (GAAP) earnings per share from continuing operations of between $0.13 and $0.14. Excluding the impact of intangibles amortization, Co. projects earnings per share from continuing operations of between $0.17 and $0.18 for the first quarter of 2005. For full-year 2005, Co. reaffirmed its guidance for GAAP earnings per share of between $0.90 and $0.95.

Financial Data

(US$ in Thousands)	01/02/2005	12/28/2003	12/29/2002	12/30/2001	12/31/2000	01/02/2000	01/03/1999	12/28/1997
Earnings Per Share	0.74	0.41	(1.21)	0.33	0.89	1.66	1.11	0.37
Cash Flow Per Share	1.55	1.33	0.81	1.19	1.49	1.28	0.75	0.38
Tang Book Value Per Share	N.M.	N.M.	N.M.	N.M.	N.M.	N.M.	0.92	2.75
Dividends Per Share	0.280	0.280	0.280	0.280	0.280	0.280	0.280	0.280
Dividend Payout %	37.84	68.29	N.M.	84.85	31.64	16.92	25.23	75.68
Income Statement								
Total Revenue	1,687,231	1,535,222	1,504,981	1,330,054	1,695,267	1,363,129	1,407,896	1,460,805
EBITDA	248,586	211,128	116,496	153,754	269,121	135,904	210,931	109,151
Depn & Amortn	76,281	80,146	96,111	84,259	87,715	66,115	50,379	44,612
Income Before Taxes	136,747	80,884	(8,550)	34,154	144,489	44,870	156,034	54,026
Income Taxes	38,495	25,871	(4,415)	34,774	58,422	16,499	54,032	23,381
Net Income	96,043	52,959	(151,938)	34,505	90,520	154,316	102,002	33,692
Average Shares	129,429	127,741	125,439	103,687	102,278	93,138	91,768	91,796
Balance Sheet								
Current Assets	747,630	766,298	991,343	997,439	893,061	815,094	565,382	488,186
Total Assets	2,575,507	2,607,719	2,836,239	2,919,129	2,260,179	1,714,640	1,184,920	832,103
Current Liabilities	445,967	452,015	697,674	708,210	717,599	852,498	524,908	285,615
Long-Term Obligations	364,874	544,307	614,053	598,125	583,337	114,855	129,835	114,863
Total Liabilities	1,115,422	1,258,669	1,583,895	1,555,572	1,531,790	1,163,864	785,253	503,715
Stockholders' Equity	1,460,085	1,349,050	1,252,344	1,363,557	728,389	550,776	399,667	328,388
Shares Outstanding	129,059	126,909	125,854	124,188	99,548	92,732	89,494	90,666
Statistical Record								
Return on Assets %	3.65	1.95	N.M.	1.34	4.57	10.67	9.95	4.08
Return on Equity %	6.73	4.08	N.M.	3.31	14.19	32.56	27.57	9.74
EBITDA Margin %	14.73	13.75	7.74	11.56	15.87	9.97	14.98	7.47
Net Margin %	5.69	3.45	N.M.	2.59	5.34	11.32	7.24	2.31
Asset Turnover	0.64	0.57	0.52	0.52	0.86	0.94	1.37	1.77
Current Ratio	1.68	1.70	1.42	1.41	1.24	0.96	1.08	1.71
Debt to Equity	0.25	0.40	0.49	0.44	0.80	0.21	0.32	0.35
Price Range	22.89-15.74	18.67-7.41	36.22-4.37	50.03-21.38	59.75-19.53	21.91-12.88	16.84-9.72	12.06-9.13
P/E Ratio	30.93-21.27	45.54-18.07	N/A	151.61-64.77	67.13-21.95	13.20-7.76	15.17-8.76	32.60-24.66
Average Yield %	1.44	2.17	2.15	0.87	0.75	1.68	2.09	2.73

Address: 45 William Street, Wellesley, MA 02481	**Web Site:** www.perkinelmer.com	**Auditors:** Deloitte & Touche LLP
Telephone: (781) 237-5100	**Officers:** Gregory L. Summe - Chmn., Pres., C.E.O. John J. Engel - Exec. V.P.	**Investor Contact:** 781-431-4306
Fax: (781) 431-4255		

PFIZER INC

Exchange	Symbol	Price	52Wk Range	Yield	P/E	Div Achiever
NYS	PFE	$26.27 (3/31/2005)	37.62-23.86	2.89	17.63	37 Years

*7 Year Price Score 71.42 ***NYSE Composite Index=100** ***12 Month Price Score 79.20**

Interim Earnings (Per Share)

Qtr.	Mar	Jun	Sep	Dec
2001	0.30	0.29	0.33	0.30
2002	0.37	0.32	0.38	0.46
2003	0.76	(0.48)	0.29	0.08
2004	0.30	0.38	0.44	0.37

Interim Dividends (Per Share)

Amt	Decl	Ex	Rec	Pay
0.17Q	4/22/2004	5/12/2004	5/14/2004	6/4/2004
0.17Q	6/24/2004	8/11/2004	8/13/2004	9/3/2004
0.17Q	10/28/2004	11/9/2004	11/12/2004	12/3/2004
0.19Q	12/13/2004	2/9/2005	2/11/2005	3/8/2005

Indicated Div: $0.76 (Div. Reinv. Plan)

Valuation Analysis

Forecast P/E	12.57 (4/7/2005)	No of Institutions 1380
Market Cap	$196.3 Billion	Shares 4,648,829,952
Book Value	68.3 Billion	% Held
Price/Book	2.88	62.33
Price/Sales	3.74	

Business Summary: Pharmaceuticals (MIC: 9.1 SIC: 834 NAIC: 25412)

Pfizer is a research-based, global pharmaceutical company that discovers, develops, manufactures and markets medicines for humans and animals as well as consumer healthcare products. The products include Norvasc, for the treatment of hypertension and angina, Zyrtec, an anti-allergy medicine, Viagra, an oral medication for the treatment of erectile dysfunction, Zoloft, a selective serotonin re-uptake inhibitor for the treatment of depression. The animal health segment includes anti-parasitic, anti-infective and anti-inflammatory medicines, and vaccines. The consumer healthcare segment includes Nicorette, for tobacco dependence and Benadryl antihistamine for allergies.

Recent Developments: For the year ended Dec 31 2004, income from continuing operations increased 595.6% to $11,332,000 thousand from income of $1,629,000 thousand a year earlier. Net income increased 190.6% to $11,361,000 thousand from net income of $3,910,000 thousand a year earlier. Revenues were $52,516,000 thousand, up 17.4% from $44,736,000 thousand the year before. Total direct expense was $7,541,000 thousand versus $9,589,000 thousand in the prior year, a decrease of 21.4%. Total indirect expense was $30,215,000 thousand versus $30,892,000 thousand in the prior year, a decrease of 2.2%.

Prospects: Despite a challenging business environment, Co. continues to see good growth in revenues, largely due to continued momentum in sales of Lipitor. Meanwhile, Co. continues to make investments necessary to generate long-term growth. Co. believes that its pipeline of new product candidates is full at all stages, and that it is on target to achieve its goal of submitting 20 New Drug Application filings in the five-year period ending in 2006. This bodes well for Co. as it is facing significant patent expirations in the 2005 to 2007 period that will impact $14.00 billion in revenues.

Financial Data

(US$ in Thousands)	12/31/2004	12/31/2003	12/31/2002	12/31/2001	12/31/2000	12/31/1999	12/31/1998	12/31/1997
Earnings Per Share	1.49	0.54	1.46	1.22	0.59	0.82	0.85	0.57
Cash Flow Per Share	2.16	1.63	1.60	1.49	0.99	0.81	0.77	0.43
Tang Book Value Per Share	1.48	0.85	3.04	2.64	2.26	2.11	2.06	1.71
Dividends Per Share	0.680	0.600	0.520	0.440	0.360	0.307	0.253	0.227
Dividend Payout %	45.64	111.11	35.62	36.07	61.02	37.40	29.80	40.00
Income Statement								
Total Revenue	52,516,000	45,188,000	32,373,000	32,259,000	29,574,000	16,204,000	13,544,000	12,504,000
EBITDA	19,101,000	7,265,000	12,701,000	11,124,000	6,577,000	4,912,000	3,034,000	3,581,000
Depn & Amortn	5,093,000	4,078,000	1,036,000	1,068,000	968,000	542,000	489,000	502,000
Income Before Taxes	14,007,000	3,263,000	11,796,000	10,329,000	5,781,000	4,448,000	2,594,000	3,088,000
Income Taxes	2,665,000	1,621,000	2,609,000	2,561,000	2,049,000	1,244,000	642,000	865,000
Net Income	11,361,000	3,910,000	9,126,000	7,788,000	3,726,000	3,179,000	3,351,000	2,213,000
Average Shares	7,614,001	7,286,001	6,240,999	6,360,999	6,367,999	3,884,000	3,945,000	3,909,000
Balance Sheet								
Current Assets	39,694,000	29,741,000	24,781,000	18,450,000	17,187,000	11,191,000	9,931,000	6,820,000
Total Assets	123,684,000	116,775,000	46,356,000	39,153,000	33,510,000	20,574,000	18,302,000	15,336,000
Current Liabilities	26,458,000	23,657,000	18,555,000	13,640,000	11,981,000	9,185,000	7,192,000	5,305,000
Long-Term Obligations	7,279,000	5,755,000	3,140,000	2,609,000	1,123,000	525,000	527,000	729,000
Total Liabilities	55,406,000	51,398,000	26,406,000	20,860,000	17,434,000	11,687,000	9,492,000	7,403,000
Stockholders' Equity	68,278,000	65,377,000	19,950,000	18,293,000	16,076,000	8,887,000	8,810,000	7,933,000
Shares Outstanding	7,473,001	7,629,001	6,161,999	6,276,999	6,313,999	3,847,000	3,883,000	3,882,000
Statistical Record								
Return on Assets %	9.42	4.79	21.35	21.44	13.74	16.35	19.92	14.75
Return on Equity %	16.95	9.16	47.73	45.32	29.77	35.93	40.03	29.73
EBITDA Margin %	36.37	16.08	39.23	34.48	22.24	30.31	22.40	28.64
Net Margin %	21.63	8.65	28.19	24.14	12.60	19.62	24.74	17.70
Asset Turnover	0.44	0.55	0.76	0.89	1.09	0.83	0.81	0.83
Current Ratio	1.50	1.26	1.34	1.35	1.43	1.22	1.38	1.29
Debt to Equity	0.11	0.09	0.16	0.14	0.07	0.06	0.06	0.09
Price Range	38.85-24.29	36.18-28.56	42.15-25.92	46.13-35.67	49.00-30.00	50.04-31.71	42.04-24.65	25.94-13.65
P/E Ratio	26.07-16.30	67.00-52.89	28.87-17.75	37.81-29.24	83.05-50.85	61.03-38.67	49.46-29.00	45.50-23.94
Average Yield %	2.06	1.88	1.49	1.06	0.87	0.80	0.75	1.21

Address: 235 East 42nd Street, New York, NY 10017-5755	Web Site: www.pfizer.com	Auditors: KPMG LLP
Telephone: (212) 573-2323	Officers: Henry A. McKinnell - Chmn., Pres., C.E.O.	Transfer Agents: EquiServe Trust
Fax: (212) 573-2641	Karen L. Katen - Vice-Chmn., Chief Medical Officer	Company, N.A., Jersey City, NJ

PG&E CORP. (HOLDING CO.)

Exchange	Symbol	Price	52Wk Range	Yield	P/E
NYS	PCG	$34.10 (3/31/2005)	36.00-26.23	N/A	3.23

*7 Year Price Score 111.64 *NYSE Composite Index=100 *12 Month Price Score 105.40

Interim Earnings (Per Share)

Qtr.	Mar	Jun	Sep	Dec
2001	(2.62)	2.07	2.12	1.45
2002	1.71	0.59	1.19	(6.01)
2003	(0.93)	0.56	1.24	0.10
2004	7.21	0.88	0.53	2.02

Interim Dividends (Per Share)

Dividend Payment Suspended

Valuation Analysis

Forecast P/E	N/A	No of Institutions
Market Cap	$14.3 Billion	Shares
Book Value	8.6 Billion	256,362,656
Price/Book	1.65	% Held
Price/Sales	1.29	64.66

Business Summary: Electricity (MIC: 7.1 SIC: 931 NAIC: 21122)

PG&E is an energy-based holding company that conducts its business principally through Pacific Gas and Electric Company (PG&E), a public utility operating throughout all or a part of 46 of California's 58 counties, comprising most of northern and central California. PG&E engages primarily in the businesses of electricity and natural gas distribution, electricity generation, procurement and transmission, and natural gas procurement, transportation and storage. As of Dec 31 2004, PG&E served approximately 4.9 million electricity distribution customers and approximately 4.1 million natural gas distribution customers.

Recent Developments: For the year ended Dec 31 2004, income from continuing operations increased 382.9% to $3,820,000 thousand from income of $791,000 thousand a year earlier. Net income increased 972.4% to $4,504,000 thousand from net income of $420,000 thousand a year earlier. Revenues were $11,080,000 thousand, up 6.2% from $10,435,000 thousand the year before. Operating income was $7,118,000 thousand versus an income of $2,343,000 thousand in the prior year, an increase of 203.8%. Total direct expense was $3,956,000 thousand versus $7,932,000 thousand in the prior year, a decrease of 50.1%. Total indirect expense was $6,000 thousand versus $160,000 thousand in the prior year, a decrease of 96.2%.

Prospects: On Feb 18 2005, Co. reaffirmed its 2005 guidance for earnings from operations in the range of $2.15 to $2.25 per share. Additionally, on Feb 25 2005, Co. provided 2006 guidance for earnings from operations of between $2.30 and $2.40 per share. Co. stated that using the mid-point of its 2005 guidance range as a baseline, it also expects earnings per share from operations to grow on average between 4.0% and 6.0% annually through 2009. Co.'s projections are based on the expectation that it will earn its authorized return on equity of 11.22%, among other assumptions.

Financial Data
(US$ in Thousands)

	12/31/2004	12/31/2003	12/31/2002	12/31/2001	12/31/2000	12/31/1999	12/31/1998	12/31/1997
Earnings Per Share	10.57	1.06	(2.36)	3.02	(9.29)	(0.20)	1.88	1.75
Cash Flow Per Share	5.89	6.50	1.44	14.60	(2.14)	6.21	6.03	6.39
Tang Book Value Per Share	20.62	10.12	8.91	13.22	8.19	19.10	21.08	21.28
Dividends Per Share	...	...	...	...	0.900	1.200	1.200	1.200
Dividend Payout %	...	...	...	...	...	...	63.83	68.57
Income Statement								
Total Revenue	11,080,000	10,435,000	12,495,000	22,959,000	26,232,000	20,820,000	19,942,000	15,400,000
EBITDA	8,517,000	3,556,000	2,531,000	3,766,000	(1,171,000)	2,813,000	3,680,000	3,943,000
Depn & Amortn	1,497,000	1,222,000	1,309,000	1,068,000	3,659,000	1,780,000	1,609,000	2,014,000
Income Before Taxes	6,286,000	1,249,000	(100,000)	1,698,000	(5,352,000)	261,000	1,289,000	1,264,000
Income Taxes	2,466,000	458,000	(43,000)	608,000	(2,028,000)	248,000	570,000	548,000
Net Income	4,504,000	420,000	(874,000)	1,099,000	(3,364,000)	(73,000)	719,000	716,000
Average Shares	426,000	413,000	371,000	363,000	362,000	368,000	383,106	410,000
Balance Sheet								
Net PPE	18,989,000	18,107,000	16,928,000	19,167,000	16,591,000	16,776,000	17,818,000	20,472,000
Total Assets	34,540,000	30,175,000	33,696,000	35,862,000	35,291,000	29,715,000	33,234,000	30,557,000
Long-Term Obligations	7,903,000	4,184,000	5,505,000	8,747,000	6,476,000	8,704,000	9,743,000	10,435,000
Total Liabilities	25,621,000	25,674,000	29,603,000	30,760,000	31,339,000	22,049,000	24,388,000	20,821,000
Stockholders' Equity	8,633,000	4,215,000	3,613,000	4,322,000	3,172,000	6,886,000	8,066,000	9,299,000
Shares Outstanding	418,616	416,520	405,486	326,926	387,193	360,590	382,604	418,000
Statistical Record								
Return on Assets %	13.88	1.32	N.M.	3.09	N.M.	N.M.	2.25	2.53
Return on Equity %	69.92	10.73	N.M.	29.33	N.M.	N.M.	8.28	7.93
EBITDA Margin %	76.87	34.08	20.26	16.40	N.M.	13.51	18.45	25.60
Net Margin %	40.65	4.02	(6.99)	4.79	(12.82)	(0.35)	3.61	4.65
PPE Turnover	0.60	0.60	0.69	1.28	1.57	1.20	1.04	0.78
Asset Turnover	0.34	0.33	0.36	0.65	0.80	0.66	0.63	0.54
Debt to Equity	0.92	0.99	1.52	2.02	2.04	1.26	1.21	1.12
Price Range	34.15-26.23	27.93-12.00	23.68-8.19	19.95-6.90	31.64-18.25	33.94-20.44	35.00-29.38	30.56-21.00
P/E Ratio	3.23-2.48	26.35-11.32	N/A	6.61-2.28	N/A	N/A	18.62-15.63	17.46-12.00
Average Yield %	...	...	...	...	3.61	...	3.81	4.96

Address: One Market, Spear Tower, Suite 2400, San Francisco, CA 94105	Web Site: www.pgecorp.com	Auditors: Deloitte & Touche LLP
Telephone: (415) 267-7000	Officers: Robert D. Glynn Jr. - Chmn. Peter A. Darbee - Pres., C.E.O.	Investor Contact: 415-267-7080
		Transfer Agents: ChaseMellon Shareholder Services LLC, South

PHELPS DODGE CORP.

Exchange	Symbol	Price	52Wk Range	Yield	P/E
NYS	PD	$101.73 (3/31/2005)	108.47-60.60	0.98	9.62

*7 Year Price Score 138.70 *NYSE Composite Index=100 *12 Month Price Score 109.02

Interim Earnings (Per Share)

Qtr.	Mar	Jun	Sep	Dec
2001	0.18	(1.41)	(1.28)	(0.99)
2002	(0.35)	(0.48)	(0.67)	(2.61)
2003	(0.21)	(0.21)	(0.04)	1.37
2004	1.90	2.30	2.95	3.43

Interim Dividends (Per Share)

Amt	Decl	Ex	Rec	Pay
0.25Q	6/2/2004	8/11/2004	8/13/2004	9/3/2004
0.25Q	10/6/2004	11/9/2004	11/12/2004	12/3/2004
0.25Q	2/2/2005	2/11/2005	2/15/2005	3/4/2005
0.25Q	4/6/2005	5/12/2005	5/16/2005	6/3/2005
		Indicated Div: $1.00		

Valuation Analysis

Forecast P/E	8.13	No of Institutions	
	(4/7/2005)	366	
Market Cap	$9.8 Billion	Shares	89,049,104
Book Value	4.3 Billion	% Held	
Price/Book	2.25	92.13	
Price/Sales	1.38		

TRADING VOLUME (thousand shares)

Business Summary: Metal Works (MIC: 11.3 SIC: 331 NAIC: 31411)

Phelps Dodge is among the world's largest producers of copper and molybdenum. Using copper from its own production and purchased from others, Co.'s Phelps Dodge Mining Company (PD Mining) subsidiary produces continuous cast copper rod, the basic feed for the electrical wire and cable industry. In 2003, PD Mining produced 1.1 million equity tons of copper. Phelps Dodge Industries (PDI) is comprised of a group of companies that manufacture engineered products principally for the transportation, energy and telecommunications and specialty chemical sectors. PDI includes Co.'s carbon black operations and its U.S. and international wire and cable and specialty conductor operations.

Recent Developments: For the year ended Dec 31 2004, net income increased 1003.7% to $1,046,300 thousand from net income of $94,800 thousand a year earlier. Revenues were $7,089,300 thousand, up 71.1% from $4,142,700 thousand the year before. Operating income was $1,503,600 thousand versus an income of $197,600 thousand in the prior year, an increase of 660.9%. Total direct expense was $4,781,800 thousand versus $3,285,100 thousand in the prior year, an increase of 45.6%. Total indirect expense was $803,900 thousand versus $660,000 thousand in the prior year, an increase of 21.8%.

Prospects: Strong prices of both copper and molybdenum as well as Co.'s aggressive focus on reducing costs and its operational strength are contributing to its higher earnings. Moreover, the market outlook for Co.'s major products remains positive. In addition, Co.'s current cash flow position is strong. For instance, for the quarter ended Dec 31 2004, cash flow from operating activities was $614.1 million, jumped 172.6% from the year before. Separately, Co. is exploring strategic alternatives for Phelps Dodge Industries, which may include potential subsidiary sales, selective asset sales, restructurings, joint ventures and mergers, or, alternatively, retention and selective growth.

Financial Data

(US$ in Thousands)	12/31/2004	12/31/2003	12/31/2002	12/31/2001	12/31/2000	12/31/1999	12/31/1998	12/31/1997
Earnings Per Share	10.58	0.91	(4.13)	(3.50)	0.37	(4.19)	3.26	6.63
Cash Flow Per Share	18.43	5.30	4.14	3.86	6.50	3.32	6.50	12.51
Tang Book Value Per Share	44.13	29.03	30.61	32.58	37.49	39.46	40.78	39.68
Dividends Per Share	0.500	...	...	0.750	2.000	2.000	2.000	2.000
Dividend Payout %	4.73	...	...	N.M.	540.54	N.M.	61.35	30.17
Income Statement								
Total Revenue	7,089,300	4,142,700	3,722,000	4,002,400	4,525,100	3,114,400	3,063,400	3,914,300
EBITDA	2,000,400	622,800	187,700	400,900	705,900	4,700	701,300	928,100
Depn & Amortn	507,100	422,600	410,200	465,300	464,200	329,100	293,300	283,700
Income Before Taxes	1,388,500	71,400	(393,700)	(262,700)	53,700	(426,700)	337,000	581,900
Income Taxes	142,300	48,300	(110,200)	5,900	19,200	(165,200)	134,000	180,400
Net Income	1,046,300	94,800	(338,100)	(275,000)	29,000	(254,300)	190,900	408,500
Average Shares	98,900	89,400	84,100	78,500	78,800	61,600	58,500	61,600
Balance Sheet								
Current Assets	2,661,700	1,790,000	1,428,200	1,504,200	1,507,600	1,693,400	980,000	1,051,100
Total Assets	8,594,100	7,272,900	7,029,000	7,618,800	7,830,800	8,229,000	5,036,500	4,965,200
Current Liabilities	1,168,000	1,015,300	784,100	1,014,200	1,417,900	1,418,300	651,100	701,100
Long-Term Obligations	972,200	1,703,900	1,948,400	2,522,000	1,963,000	2,172,500	836,400	857,100
Total Liabilities	3,695,900	4,138,900	4,150,100	4,852,200	4,634,100	4,855,900	2,355,800	2,341,500
Stockholders' Equity	4,343,100	3,063,800	2,813,600	2,707,200	3,105,000	3,276,800	2,587,400	2,510,400
Shares Outstanding	95,900	91,000	88,900	78,700	78,700	78,700	57,900	58,634
Statistical Record								
Return on Assets %	13.15	1.33	N.M.	N.M.	0.36	N.M.	3.82	8.35
Return on Equity %	28.17	3.23	N.M.	N.M.	0.91	N.M.	7.49	15.51
EBITDA Margin %	28.22	15.03	5.04	10.02	15.60	0.15	22.89	23.71
Net Margin %	14.76	2.29	N.M.	N.M.	0.64	N.M.	6.23	10.44
Asset Turnover	0.89	0.58	0.51	0.52	0.56	0.47	0.61	0.80
Current Ratio	2.28	1.76	1.82	1.48	1.06	1.19	1.51	1.50
Debt to Equity	0.22	0.56	0.69	0.93	0.63	0.66	0.32	0.34
Price Range	101.55-60.60	79.40-30.66	42.32-23.09	54.69-26.56	71.88-36.72	69.94-42.50	71.56-44.75	89.25-60.13
P/E Ratio	9.60-5.73	87.25-33.69	N/A	N/A 194.26-99.24	N/A	21.95-13.73	13.46-9.07
Average Yield %	0.62	...	...	1.88	4.20	3.57	3.40	2.62

Address: 1 North Central Avenue, Phoenix, AZ 85004-2306 **Telephone:** (602) 366-8100 **Fax:** (602) 366-8100	**Web Site:** www.phelpsdodge.com **Officers:** J. Steven Whisler - Chmn., C.E.O. Timothy R. Snider - Pres., C.O.O.	**Auditors:** PricewaterhouseCoopers LLP **Investor Contact:** 602-234-8100

PIEDMONT NATURAL GAS CO., INC.

Exchange	Symbol	Price	52Wk Range	Yield	P/E	Div Acheiver
NYS	PNY	$23.04 (3/31/2005)	24.05-19.30	3.99	19.69	25 Years

*7 Year Price Score 106.84 *NYSE Composite Index=100 *12 Month Price Score 98.67

Interim Earnings (Per Share)

Qtr.	Jan	Apr	Jul	Oct
2001-02	0.63	0.64	(0.14)	(0.18)
2002-03	0.87	0.47	(0.14)	(0.07)
2003-04	1.09	0.54	(0.11)	(0.19)
2004-05	0.93	...	...	...

Interim Dividends (Per Share)

Amt	Decl	Ex	Rec	Pay
0.215Q	8/27/2004	9/22/2004	9/24/2004	10/15/2004
100%	8/27/2004	11/1/2004	10/11/2004	10/29/2004
0.215Q	12/10/2004	12/20/2004	12/22/2004	1/14/2005
0.23Q	3/4/2005	3/22/2005	3/24/2005	4/15/2005

Indicated Div: $0.92 (Div. Reinv. Plan)

Valuation Analysis

Forecast P/E	18.37	No of Institutions
	(4/7/2005)	165
Market Cap	$1.8 Billion	Shares
Book Value	910.2 Million	30,295,228
Price/Book	1.94	% Held
Price/Sales	1.11	39.51

Business Summary: Gas Utilities (MIC: 7.4 SIC: 924 NAIC: 21210)

Piedmont Natural Gas is an energy services company primarily engaged in the distribution of natural gas to 960,000 residential, commercial and industrial customers in portions of North Carolina, South Carolina and Tennessee, including 60,000 customers served by municipalities who are our wholesale customers. Co.'s subsidiaries are invested in joint venture, energy-related businesses, including unregulated retail natural gas marketing, interstate natural gas storage, intrastate natural gas transportation and regulated natural gas distribution. Co. also sells residential and commercial gas appliances in Tennessee.

Recent Developments: For the quarter ended Jan 31 2005, net income decreased 4.5% to $71,277 thousand from net income of $74,622 thousand in the year-earlier quarter. Revenues were $680,556 thousand, up 10.0% from $618,785 thousand the year before. Operating income was $78,919 thousand versus an income of $77,349 thousand in the prior-year quarter, an increase of 2.0%. Total direct expense was $477,936 thousand versus $422,305 thousand in the prior-year quarter, an increase of 13.2%. Total indirect expense was $123,701 thousand versus $119,131 thousand in the prior-year quarter, an increase of 3.8%.

Prospects: Earnings are benefiting from solid margin growth. For instance, margins for the quarter ended Jan 31 2005 increased 3.0% to $202.6 million compared with $196.5 million for the year before. Separately, for fiscal 2005, Co. reaffirmed its earnings guidance of $1.23 to $1.30 per diluted share. The 2005 earnings guidance assumes normal weather for the remainder of the year, a stable economy and wholesale natural gas prices in the range of prices that prevailed during fiscal year 2004. No general rate case activity is expected that would impact 2005 earnings in any of Co.'s jurisdictions.

Financial Data
(US$ in Thousands)

	3 Mos	10/31/2004	10/31/2003	10/31/2002	10/31/2001	10/31/2000	10/31/1999	10/31/1998
Earnings Per Share	1.17	1.27	1.11	0.94	1.01	1.00	0.93	0.98
Cash Flow Per Share	0.94	2.07	1.49	1.66	2.49	0.86	0.51	2.02
Tang Book Value Per Share	11.23	10.52	8.61	8.91	8.63	8.26	7.86	7.45
Dividends Per Share	0.860	0.853	0.823	0.792	0.760	0.720	0.680	0.640
Dividend Payout %	73.57	67.13	74.10	83.86	75.25	71.64	73.12	65.31
Income Statement								
Total Revenue	680,556	1,529,739	1,220,822	832,028	1,107,856	830,377	686,470	765,277
Depn & Amortn	22,064	86,786	63,611	57,837	52,511	51,532	47,359	45,555
Income Taxes	46,576	63,147	8,524	9,010	7,300	...	...	...
Net Income	71,277	95,188	74,362	62,217	65,485	64,031	58,207	60,313
Average Shares	76,925	74,797	67,006	65,874	64,840	63,558	62,484	61,434
Balance Sheet								
Net PPE	1,856,230	1,850,796	1,813,414	1,159,601	1,115,862	1,071,983	1,046,975	990,640
Total Assets	2,576,278	2,335,877	2,296,406	1,445,088	1,393,658	1,445,003	1,288,657	1,162,844
Long-Term Obligations	660,000	660,000	460,000	462,000	509,000	451,000	423,000	371,000
Total Liabilities	1,666,095	1,480,979	1,666,211	855,492	833,279	917,631	796,910	704,576
Stockholders' Equity	910,183	854,898	630,195	589,596	560,379	527,372	491,747	458,268
Shares Outstanding	76,757	76,670	67,310	66,180	64,926	63,828	62,589	61,476
Statistical Record								
Return on Assets %	3.64	4.10	3.97	4.38	4.61	4.67	4.75	5.34
Return on Equity %	10.26	12.78	12.19	10.82	12.04	12.53	12.25	13.74
Net Margin %	10.47	6.22	6.09	7.48	5.91	7.71	8.48	7.88
PPE Turnover	0.86	0.83	0.82	0.73	1.01	0.78	0.67	0.79
Asset Turnover	0.63	0.66	0.65	0.59	0.78	0.61	0.56	0.68
Debt to Equity	0.73	0.77	0.73	0.78	0.91	0.86	0.86	0.81
Price Range	23.92-19.30	22.84-19.30	20.38-16.45	18.98-14.18	19.69-14.72	16.50-11.88	18.00-14.44	18.22-13.59
P/E Ratio	20.44-16.50	17.98-15.20	18.36-14.82	20.19-15.09	19.49-14.57	16.50-11.88	19.35-15.52	18.59-13.87
Average Yield %	3.98	4.06	4.44	4.56	4.51	5.01	4.14	4.00

Address: 1915 Rexford Road, Charlotte, NC 28211
Telephone: (704) 364-3120
Fax: (704) 365-8515

Web Site: www.piedmontng.com
Officers: Thomas E. Skains - Chmn., Pres., C.E.O.
David J. Dzuricky - Sr. V.P., C.F.O.

Auditors: Deloitte & Touche LLP
Investor Contact: 704-731-4438
Transfer Agents: American Stock Transfer & Trust Company, New York,

PIER 1 IMPORTS INC.

Exchange	Symbol	Price	52Wk Range	Yield	P/E	Div Acheiver
NYS	PIR	$18.23 (3/31/2005)	23.70-15.43	2.19	18.23	13 Years

*7 Year Price Score 107.50 *NYSE Composite Index=100 *12 Month Price Score 92.04

Interim Earnings (Per Share)

Qtr.	May	Aug	Nov	Feb
2001-02	0.13	0.14	0.26	0.51
2002-03	0.23	0.23	0.33	0.57
2003-04	0.21	0.20	0.35	0.53
2004-05	0.13	0.12	0.22	...

Interim Dividends (Per Share)

Amt	Decl	Ex	Rec	Pay
0.10Q	6/25/2004	8/2/2004	8/4/2004	8/18/2004
0.10Q	9/30/2004	11/1/2004	11/3/2004	11/17/2004
0.10Q	12/9/2004	1/31/2005	2/2/2005	2/16/2005
0.10Q	3/31/2005	5/2/2005	5/4/2005	5/18/2005

Indicated Div: $0.40 (Div. Reinv. Plan)

Valuation Analysis

Forecast P/E	18.65	No of Institutions	
	(4/7/2005)	189	
Market Cap	$1.6 Billion	Shares	
Book Value	659.4 Million	72,227,352	
Price/Book	2.38	% Held	
Price/Sales	0.81	83.64	

Business Summary: Retail - Furniture & Home Furnishings (MIC: 5.9 SIC: 712 NAIC: 42110)

Pier 1 Imports is a retailer of decorative home furnishings, furniture, dining and kitchen goods, bath and bedding accessories and other specialty items for the home. As of Feb 28 2004, Co. operated 1,015 Pier 1 Imports® stores in the U.S. and 68 stores in Canada, and also supported eight franchised stores in the U.S. In addition, Co. operated 29 stores located in the U.K. under the name The Pier® and 40 Cargokids® stores located in the U.S. Co. also supplies merchandise, and licenses the Pier 1 Imports name to Sears Mexico and Sears Puerto Rico, which sells Pier 1 merchandise in a store within a store format in 20 Sears Mexico stores and in seven Sears Puerto Rico stores.

Recent Developments: For the quarter ended Nov 27 2004, net income decreased 39.5% to $19,475 thousand from net income of $32,194 thousand in the year-earlier quarter. Revenues were $487,729 thousand, up 1.1% from $482,444 thousand the year before. Operating income was $30,792 thousand versus an income of $50,961 thousand in the prior-year quarter, a decrease of 39.6%. Total indirect expense was $160,286 thousand versus $157,137 thousand in the prior-year quarter, an increase of 2.0%.

Prospects: Sales are disappointing with customer traffic and average ticket in comparable stores both down in the range of mid- to high-single digits during Feb 2005. Co. believes that the lack of national television advertising, some inclement weather and transitional store layouts with lean inventories are contributing to the sales declines. Throughout the month of Feb, stores continued to transition the sell-through of clearance merchandise as well as position newly arriving merchandise assortments in preparation for Co.'s new national advertising campaign that will be launched at the end of Mar 2005.

Financial Data

(US$ in Thousands)	9 Mos	6 Mos	3 Mos	02/28/2004	03/01/2003	03/02/2002	03/03/2001	02/26/2000
Earnings Per Share	1.00	1.13	1.21	1.29	1.36	1.04	0.97	0.75
Cash Flow Per Share	1.98	1.78	1.85	2.00	1.90	2.59	1.12	1.25
Tang Book Value Per Share	7.65	7.53	7.67	7.74	7.10	6.27	5.53	4.70
Dividends Per Share	0.380	0.360	0.340	0.300	0.210	0.160	0.150	0.120
Dividend Payout %	37.85	31.80	28.05	23.26	15.44	15.38	15.46	16.00
Income Statement								
Total Revenue	1,372,027	884,298	432,027	1,868,243	1,754,867	1,548,556	1,411,498	1,231,095
EBITDA	121,617	71,569	36,409	253,614	254,133	204,118	196,554	165,503
Depn & Amortn	54,625	35,753	17,399	64,606	46,432	42,821	43,184	39,973
Income Before Taxes	66,194	35,267	18,658	187,316	205,374	158,997	150,240	118,612
Income Taxes	24,536	13,084	6,921	69,315	75,988	58,788	55,590	43,887
Net Income	41,658	22,183	11,737	118,001	129,386	100,209	94,650	74,725
Average Shares	87,845	89,027	90,517	91,624	95,305	96,185	97,952	103,297
Balance Sheet								
Current Assets	637,957	620,728	642,421	698,151	663,601	605,153	477,066	415,280
Total Assets	1,023,157	1,000,719	1,008,319	1,052,173	967,487	862,672	735,710	670,710
Current Liabilities	269,246	259,349	243,871	279,888	243,589	208,396	144,110	175,966
Long-Term Obligations	19,000	19,000	19,000	19,000	25,000	25,356	25,000	25,000
Total Liabilities	363,721	352,254	334,760	368,542	323,551	277,016	203,831	230,047
Stockholders' Equity	659,436	648,465	673,559	683,631	643,936	585,656	531,879	440,663
Shares Outstanding	86,167	86,163	87,762	88,306	90,734	93,417	96,160	93,830
Statistical Record								
Return on Assets %	8.87	10.56	11.41	11.72	14.18	12.57	13.24	11.31
Return on Equity %	13.66	16.03	16.85	17.83	21.10	17.98	19.15	17.74
EBITDA Margin %	8.86	8.09	8.43	13.58	14.48	13.18	13.93	13.44
Net Margin %	3.04	2.51	2.72	6.32	7.37	6.47	6.71	6.07
Asset Turnover	1.90	1.98	1.96	1.86	1.92	1.94	1.97	1.86
Current Ratio	2.37	2.39	2.63	2.49	2.72	2.90	3.31	2.36
Debt to Equity	0.03	0.03	0.03	0.03	0.04	0.04	0.05	0.06
Price Range	26.19-15.43	26.19-15.43	26.19-17.52	26.19-14.85	23.95-15.20	20.24-8.13	14.00-7.88	12.25-5.38
P/E Ratio	26.19-15.43	23.18-13.65	21.64-14.48	20.30-11.51	17.61-11.18	19.46-7.82	14.43-8.12	16.33-7.17
Average Yield %	1.91	1.73	1.58	1.46	1.08	1.20	1.36	1.52

Address: 301 Commerce Street, Suite 600, Fort Worth, TX 76102 **Telephone:** (817) 252-8000 **Fax:** (817) 334-0191	**Web Site:** www.pier1.com **Officers:** Marvin J. Girouard - Chmn., C.E.O. Charles H. Turner - Exec. V.P., Fin., C.F.O., Treas.	**Auditors:** Ernst & Young LLP **Investor Contact:** 817-252-7835 **Transfer Agents:** Mellon Investor Services, Ridgefield Park, NJ

PINNACLE WEST CAPITAL CORP.

Exchange	Symbol	Price	52Wk Range	Yield	P/E	Div Achiever
NYS	PNW	$42.51 (3/31/2005)	45.41-36.85	4.47	15.98	11 Years

*7 Year Price Score 90.47   *NYSE Composite Index=100   *12 Month Price Score 94.08

Interim Earnings (Per Share)

Qtr.	Mar	Jun	Sep	Dec
2001	0.70	0.79	1.77	0.43
2002	0.63	0.89	1.19	(1.37)
2003	0.28	0.61	1.20	0.54
2004	0.33	0.78	1.15	0.37

Interim Dividends (Per Share)

Amt	Decl	Ex	Rec	Pay
0.45Q	7/16/2004	7/29/2004	8/2/2004	9/1/2004
0.475Q	10/20/2004	10/28/2004	11/1/2004	12/1/2004
0.475Q	1/19/2005	1/28/2005	2/1/2005	3/1/2005
0.475Q	3/23/2005	4/28/2005	5/2/2005	6/1/2005

Indicated Div: $1.90 (Div. Reinv. Plan)

Valuation Analysis

Forecast P/E	14.34	No of Institutions	
	(4/7/2005)	239	
Market Cap	$3.9 Billion	Shares	
Book Value	3.0 Billion	68,748,152	
Price/Book	1.32	% Held	
Price/Sales	1.35	74.66	

TRADING VOLUME (thousand shares)

Business Summary: Electricity (MIC: 7.1 SIC: 911 NAIC: 21121)

Pinnacle West Capital is a holding company whose principal asset is Arizona Public Service (APS). APS is an electric utility that provides retail and wholesale electric service to substantially all of the state of Arizona, with the major exceptions of the Tucson metropolitan area and about one-half of the Phoenix metropolitan area. Through its marketing and trading operation, APS also generates, sells and delivers wholesale electricity. Co.'s other major subsidiaries are Pinnacle West Energy, which owns and operates generating plants; APS Energy Services, which provides commodity-related energy services; and SunCor, which is engaged in real estate development activities.

Recent Developments: For the year ended Dec 31 2004, income from continuing operations increased 4.2% to $235,218 thousand from income of $225,803 thousand a year earlier. Net income increased 1.1% to $243,195 thousand from net income of $240,579 thousand a year earlier. Revenues were $2,899,725 thousand, up 5.1% from $2,759,494 thousand the year before. Operating income was $506,259 thousand versus an income of $473,942 thousand in the prior year, an increase of 6.8%. Total direct expense was $1,870,145 thousand versus $1,740,142 thousand in the prior year, an increase of 7.5%. Total indirect expense was $523,321 thousand versus $545,410 thousand in the prior year, a decrease of 4.0%.

Prospects: Co.'s operating results reflect the adverse impact of milder weather in its operating territory and rising costs necessary to meet Arizona's growing energy needs. Co. noted that its customer growth of 4.0% in 2004 is three times the national average. However, gains being achieved through higher retail sales volumes are being mitigated by the increase in costs related to new electricity generating units placed into service in mid-2003 and mid-2004, an increase in customer service and other operating costs, and higher fuel and purchased power prices. Looking ahead, Co.'s priority for 2005 will center around the positive resolution of its pending rate case.

Financial Data

(US$ in Thousands)	12/31/2004	12/31/2003	12/31/2002	12/31/2001	12/31/2000	12/31/1999	12/31/1998	12/31/1997
Earnings Per Share	2.66	2.63	1.76	3.68	3.56	1.97	2.85	2.74
Cash Flow Per Share	9.19	9.88	10.26	6.74	8.23	7.50	7.15	7.46
Tang Book Value Per Share	32.14	31.00	18.99	29.46	28.09	26.00	25.50	23.90
Dividends Per Share	1.825	1.725	1.625	1.525	1.425	1.325	1.225	1.125
Dividend Payout %	68.61	65.59	92.33	41.44	40.03	67.26	42.98	41.06
Income Statement								
Total Revenue	2,899,725	2,817,852	2,637,279	4,551,373	3,690,175	2,423,353	2,130,586	1,995,026
EBITDA	962,819	959,530	953,567	1,125,127	1,100,278	1,005,493	970,569	951,085
Depn & Amortn	431,551	466,900	456,071	456,265	424,493	416,939	412,535	401,813
Income Before Taxes	364,075	336,136	353,253	540,902	526,184	437,837	407,485	386,137
Income Taxes	128,857	105,560	138,100	213,535	223,852	168,065	164,593	150,281
Net Income	243,195	240,579	149,408	312,166	302,332	167,887	242,892	235,856
Average Shares	91,532	91,405	84,964	84,930	84,935	85,008	85,345	86,023
Balance Sheet								
Net PPE	7,535,487	7,480,090	6,479,398	5,907,315	5,133,193	4,778,515	4,730,563	4,677,568
Total Assets	9,896,747	9,536,378	8,425,806	7,981,748	7,149,151	6,608,506	6,824,546	6,850,417
Long-Term Obligations	2,584,985	2,897,725	2,881,695	2,673,078	1,955,083	2,206,052	2,048,961	2,244,248
Total Liabilities	6,946,551	6,706,599	5,739,653	5,482,425	4,766,437	4,402,773	4,661,195	4,822,981
Stockholders' Equity	2,950,196	2,829,779	1,732,900	2,499,323	2,382,714	2,205,733	2,163,351	2,027,436
Shares Outstanding	91,793	91,287	91,255	84,824	84,824	84,824	84,824	84,825
Statistical Record								
Return on Assets %	2.50	2.68	1.82	4.13	4.38	2.50	3.55	3.41
Return on Equity %	8.39	10.55	7.06	12.79	13.14	7.69	11.59	11.80
EBITDA Margin %	33.20	34.05	36.16	24.72	29.82	41.49	45.55	47.67
Net Margin %	8.39	8.54	5.67	6.86	8.19	6.93	11.40	11.82
PPE Turnover	0.39	0.40	0.43	0.82	0.74	0.51	0.45	0.43
Asset Turnover	0.30	0.31	0.32	0.60	0.53	0.36	0.31	0.29
Debt to Equity	0.88	1.02	1.66	1.07	0.82	1.00	0.95	1.11
Price Range	45.41-36.85	40.24-29.07	46.16-22.49	50.37-38.10	51.88-25.94	42.88-30.44	48.88-39.75	42.50-27.88
P/E Ratio	17.07-13.85	15.30-11.05	26.23-12.78	13.69-10.35	14.57-7.29	21.76-15.45	17.15-13.95	15.51-10.17
Average Yield %	4.48	4.90	4.46	3.45	3.77	3.49	2.82	3.46

Address: 400 North Fifth Street, P.O. Box 53999, Phoenix, AZ 85072-3999 **Telephone:** (602) 250-1000 **Fax:** (602) 379-2625	**Web Site:** www.pinnaclewest.com **Officers:** William J. Post - Chmn., C.E.O. Jack E. Davis - Pres., C.O.O	**Auditors:** Deloitte & Touche LLP **Investor Contact:** 602-250-5668 **Transfer Agents:** Pinnacle West Capital Corporation, Phoenix, AZ

PIONEER NATURAL RESOURCES CO

Exchange	Symbol	Price	52Wk Range	Yield	P/E
NYS	PXD	$42.72 (3/31/2005)	44.75-29.70	0.47	17.37

*7 Year Price Score 145.08 ***NYSE Composite Index=100** ***12 Month Price Score 110.53**

Interim Earnings (Per Share)

Qtr.	Mar	Jun	Sep	Dec
2001	0.68	0.28	0.25	(0.21)
2002	(0.02)	0.10	(0.01)	0.16
2003	0.71	0.65	1.62	0.47
2004	0.50	0.58	0.67	0.71

Interim Dividends (Per Share)

Amt	Decl	Ex	Rec	Pay
0.05S	7/14/1998	8/13/1998	8/17/1998	9/15/1998
0.10S	2/16/2004	3/25/2004	3/29/2004	4/13/2004
0.10S	8/24/2004	9/27/2004	9/29/2004	10/15/2004
0.10S	2/17/2005	3/29/2005	3/31/2005	4/15/2005

Indicated Div: $0.20

Valuation Analysis

Forecast P/E	16.35
	(4/12/2005)
Market Cap	$6.2 Billion
Book Value	2.8 Billion
Price/Book	2.18
Price/Sales	3.35

No of Institutions	289
Shares	115,458,904
% Held	80.36

Business Summary: Oil and Gas (MIC: 14.2 SIC: 311 NAIC: 11111)

Pioneer Natural Resources is an oil and gas exploration and production company with ownership interests in oil and gas properties located in the United States, Argentina, Canada, Equatorial Guinea, Gabon, South Africa, Gabon and Tunisia. Co.'s asset base is anchored by the Spraberry oil field located in West Texas, the Hugoton gas field located in Southwest Kansas and the West Panhandle gas field located in the Texas Panhandle. As of Dec 31 2004, Co.'s proved reserves were as follows: oil and natural gas liquids, 408.8 million barrels; and gas, 3.68 trillion cubic feet.

Recent Developments: For the year ended Dec 31 2004, net income decreased 23.8% to $312,854 thousand from net income of $410,592 thousand a year earlier. Revenues were $1,846,776 thousand, up 43.4% from $1,287,419 thousand the year before. Total direct expense was $345,504 thousand versus $254,750 thousand in the prior year, an increase of 35.6%. Total indirect expense was $911,112 thousand versus $598,521 thousand in the prior year, an increase of 52.2%.

Prospects: Looking ahead, Co. expects to continue to add production from its core properties as it steps up its development drilling program in 2005. For the first quarter of 2005, production is expected to average 175,000 to 190,000 barrels oil equivalent per day (BOEPD), excluding field fuel. First quarter production costs (including production and ad valorem taxes) are expected to average $6.00 to $6.50 per BOE. Co. added that production costs are expected to decline in the second quarter of 2005 as lower-cost volumes resume from the deepwater Gulf of Mexico and workovers return to more normal levels. For the full-year, Co. expects production of 70.0 million to 74.0 million barrels oil equivalent.

Financial Data

(US$ in Thousands)	12/31/2004	12/31/2003	12/31/2002	12/31/2001	12/31/2000	12/31/1999	12/31/1998	12/31/1997
Earnings Per Share	2.46	3.46	0.23	1.00	1.53	(0.22)	(7.46)	(17.14)
Cash Flow Per Share	8.80	6.52	2.95	4.83	4.32	2.54	3.14	4.39
Tang Book Value Per Share	17.37	14.75	11.73	12.37	9.19	7.72	7.87	15.33
Dividends Per Share	0.200	...	...	...	...	...	0.100	0.050
Dividend Payout %	8.13	...	...	...	...	...	...	...
Income Statement								
Total Revenue	1,846,776	1,312,195	717,434	876,481	912,697	710,135	721,499	546,029
EBITDA	1,133,085	725,618	386,993	477,243	535,389	383,331	(229,233)	(1,087,578)
Depn & Amortn	550,485	303,454	237,056	237,520	214,938	236,047	337,308	212,435
Income Before Taxes	479,213	330,776	54,122	107,765	158,499	(23,060)	(730,826)	(1,377,563)
Income Taxes	166,359	(64,403)	5,063	4,016	(6,000)	(600)	15,600	(500,300)
Net Income	312,854	410,592	26,713	99,996	152,181	(22,460)	(746,426)	(890,671)
Average Shares	127,488	118,513	114,288	99,714	99,378	100,307	100,055	56,054
Balance Sheet								
Current Assets	312,199	205,115	147,093	255,643	191,391	183,136	201,988	308,188
Total Assets	6,647,241	3,951,572	3,455,116	3,271,053	2,954,435	2,929,473	3,481,314	3,946,590
Current Liabilities	544,459	429,752	274,592	228,209	216,514	196,813	526,832	261,552
Long-Term Obligations	2,385,950	1,555,461	1,668,536	1,577,304	1,578,776	1,745,108	1,868,744	1,943,718
Total Liabilities	3,815,461	2,191,800	2,080,219	1,985,664	2,049,530	2,154,859	2,692,237	2,397,745
Stockholders' Equity	2,831,780	1,759,772	1,374,897	1,285,389	904,905	774,614	789,077	1,548,845
Shares Outstanding	144,831	119,287	117,252	103,936	98,415	100,339	100,296	101,037
Statistical Record								
Return on Assets %	5.89	11.09	0.79	3.21	5.16	N.M.	N.M.	N.M.
Return on Equity %	13.59	26.20	2.01	9.13	18.07	N.M.	N.M.	N.M.
EBITDA Margin %	61.35	55.30	53.94	54.45	58.66	53.98	N.M.	N.M.
Net Margin %	16.94	31.29	3.72	11.41	16.67	N.M.	N.M.	N.M.
Asset Turnover	0.35	0.35	0.21	0.28	0.31	0.22	0.19	0.21
Current Ratio	0.57	0.48	0.54	1.12	0.88	0.93	0.38	1.18
Debt to Equity	0.84	0.88	1.21	1.23	1.74	2.25	2.37	1.25
Price Range	36.92-29.70	32.75-22.82	27.11-16.11	23.00-12.76	20.19-6.88	13.19-5.13	29.00-7.94	44.06-26.06
P/E Ratio	15.01-12.07	9.47-6.60	117.87-70.04	23.00-12.76	13.19-4.49	N/A	N/A	N/A
Average Yield %	0.60	...	...	...	...	...	0.52	0.14

Address: 5205 N. O'Connor Blvd., Suite 900, Irving, TX 75039 **Telephone:** (972) 444-9001 **Fax:** (972) 969-3587	**Web Site:** www.pioneernrc.com **Officers:** Scott D. Sheffield - Chmn., Pres., C.E.O., Asst. Sec. Richard P. Dealy - Exec. V.P., C.F.O.	**Auditors:** Ernst & Young LLP **Investor Contact:** 972-444-9001

PITNEY BOWES, INC.

Exchange	Symbol	Price	52Wk Range	Yield	P/E	Div Acheiver
NYS	PBI	$45.12 (3/31/2005)	47.30-41.05	2.75	22.01	21 Years

*7 Year Price Score 87.57 *NYSE Composite Index=100 *12 Month Price Score 96.64

Interim Earnings (Per Share)

Qtr.	Mar	Jun	Sep	Dec
2001	0.42	0.71	0.47	0.37
2002	0.53	0.59	0.61	0.24
2003	0.48	0.50	0.50	0.62
2004	0.54	0.58	0.58	0.35

Interim Dividends (Per Share)

Amt	Decl	Ex	Rec	Pay
0.305Q	4/12/2004	5/19/2004	5/21/2004	6/12/2004
0.305Q	7/12/2004	8/18/2004	8/20/2004	9/12/2004
0.305Q	11/8/2004	11/17/2004	11/19/2004	12/12/2004
0.31Q	2/2/2005	2/16/2005	2/18/2005	3/12/2005

Indicated Div: $1.24 (Div. Reinv. Plan)

Valuation Analysis

Forecast P/E	17.27	No of Institutions
	(4/7/2005)	452
Market Cap	$10.4 Billion	Shares
Book Value	1.3 Billion	176,595,264
Price/Book	8.06	% Held
Price/Sales	2.10	76.50

Business Summary: Office Equipment Supplies (MIC: 11.12 SIC: 579 NAIC: 23420)

Pitney Bowes provides integrated mail and document management solutions for organizations of all sizes. Global Mailstream Solutions includes the sale, rental, and financing of postage meters, mailing machines, address hygiene software, manifest systems, letter and parcel scales, mail openers, mailroom furniture, folders, table-top inserters, and postal payment solutions. Global Enterprise Solutions includes facilities management, through Pitney Bowes Management Services, and sales, service and financing of high-speed, software-enabled production mail systems, through Document Messaging Technologies. Capital Services provides large-ticket financing programs for a broad range of products.

Recent Developments: For the year ended Dec 31 2004, net income decreased 3.5% to $480,526 thousand from net income of $498,117 thousand a year earlier. Revenues were $4,957,440 thousand, up 8.3% from $4,576,853 thousand the year before. Total direct expense was $2,241,080 thousand versus $2,026,483 thousand in the prior year, an increase of 10.6%. Total indirect expense was $1,828,500 thousand versus $1,664,455 thousand in the prior year, an increase of 9.9%.

Prospects: In December 2004, Co. announced a plan to pursue a sponsored spin-off of its Capital Services external financing business. The firm would consist of most of the Capital Services assets, including those related to Imagistics International Inc. The decision to move forward with the spin-off will be contingent upon reaching agreement on terms with an investor, prevailing market conditions, regulatory review and the receipt of a favorable ruling from the Internal Revenue Service. Separately, in 2005, Co. expects revenue growth in the range of 9.0% to 11.0% for the first quarter and 7.0% to 9.0% for the full year.

Financial Data
(US$ in Thousands)

	12/31/2004	12/31/2003	12/31/2002	12/31/2001	12/31/2000	12/31/1999	12/31/1998	12/31/1997
Earnings Per Share	2.05	2.11	1.97	1.97	2.41	2.34	2.06	1.80
Cash Flow Per Share	4.08	3.64	2.10	4.22	3.39	3.67	2.79	2.44
Tang Book Value Per Share	N.M.	N.M.	0.10	1.05	4.34	5.28	5.26	5.96
Dividends Per Share	1.220	1.200	1.180	1.160	1.140	1.020	0.900	0.800
Dividend Payout %	59.51	56.87	59.90	58.88	47.30	43.59	43.69	44.44
Income Statement								
Total Revenue	4,957,440	4,576,853	4,409,758	4,122,474	3,880,868	4,432,608	4,220,517	4,100,464
EBITDA	1,170,394	1,164,632	1,047,899	1,268,006	1,316,382	1,576,001	1,374,743	1,303,919
Depn & Amortn	302,200	278,600	249,330	317,449	321,157	412,104	361,333	300,086
Income Before Taxes	699,448	721,091	619,445	766,384	802,848	984,572	864,177	803,098
Income Taxes	218,922	226,244	181,739	252,064	239,723	325,413	296,236	277,071
Net Income	480,526	498,117	475,750	488,343	622,546	636,212	576,394	526,027
Average Shares	234,133	236,165	241,483	247,615	258,602	272,006	279,656	292,517
Balance Sheet								
Current Assets	2,693,086	2,513,175	2,552,625	2,556,608	2,626,708	3,342,574	2,508,963	2,463,515
Total Assets	9,820,580	8,891,388	8,732,314	8,318,471	7,901,266	8,222,672	7,661,039	7,893,389
Current Liabilities	3,294,477	2,646,969	3,350,309	3,083,042	2,881,577	2,872,764	2,721,812	3,373,233
Long-Term Obligations	2,798,894	2,840,943	2,316,844	2,419,150	1,881,947	1,997,856	1,712,937	1,068,395
Total Liabilities	8,220,499	7,494,026	7,568,987	7,117,116	6,306,291	6,287,062	5,702,940	5,720,812
Stockholders' Equity	1,290,081	1,087,362	853,327	891,355	1,284,975	1,625,610	1,648,002	1,872,577
Shares Outstanding	230,318	232,288	235,373	242,028	248,800	264,694	270,378	279,674
Statistical Record								
Return on Assets %	5.12	5.65	5.58	6.02	7.70	8.01	7.41	6.56
Return on Equity %	40.31	51.33	54.54	44.88	42.66	38.87	32.74	25.59
EBITDA Margin %	23.61	25.45	23.76	30.76	33.92	35.55	32.57	31.80
Net Margin %	9.69	10.88	10.79	11.85	16.04	14.35	13.66	12.83
Asset Turnover	0.53	0.52	0.52	0.51	0.48	0.56	0.54	0.51
Current Ratio	0.82	0.95	0.76	0.83	0.91	1.16	0.92	0.73
Debt to Equity	2.17	2.61	2.72	2.71	1.46	1.23	1.04	0.57
Price Range	46.88-39.23	42.44-29.90	43.92-28.80	43.33-31.78	52.45-24.89	69.41-40.74	64.47-41.96	44.13-26.53
P/E Ratio	22.87-19.14	20.11-14.17	22.29-14.62	21.99-16.13	21.77-10.33	29.66-17.41	31.30-20.37	24.52-14.74
Average Yield %	2.83	3.26	3.11	3.09	3.01	1.73	1.80	2.29

Address: 1 Elmcroft Road, Stamford, CT 06926-0700	Web Site: www.pb.com	Auditors: PricewaterhouseCoopers LLP
Telephone: (203) 356-5000	Officers: Michael J. Critelli - Chmn., C.E.O. Murray D. Martin - Pres., C.O.O.	Transfer Agents: First Chicago Trust Company of New York, Jersey City, NJ
Fax: (203) 351-7336		

PLAINS ALL AMERICAN PIPELINE, L.P.

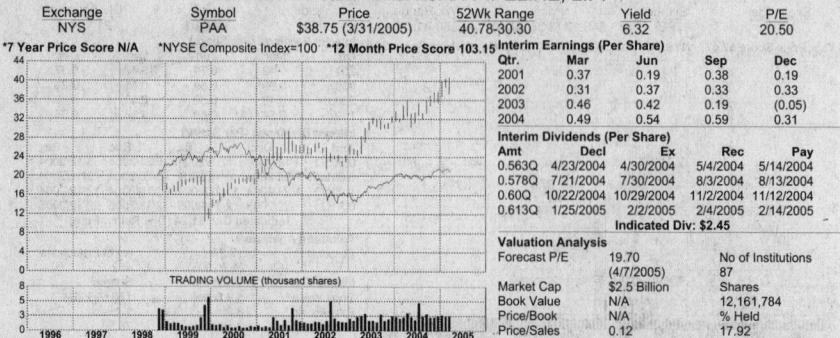

Exchange	Symbol	Price	52Wk Range	Yield	P/E
NYS	PAA	$38.75 (3/31/2005)	40.78-30.30	6.32	20.50

*7 Year Price Score N/A   *NYSE Composite Index=100   *12 Month Price Score 103.15

Interim Earnings (Per Share)

Qtr.	Mar	Jun	Sep	Dec
2001	0.37	0.19	0.38	0.19
2002	0.31	0.37	0.33	0.33
2003	0.46	0.42	0.19	(0.05)
2004	0.49	0.54	0.59	0.31

Interim Dividends (Per Share)

Amt	Decl	Ex	Rec	Pay
0.563Q	4/23/2004	4/30/2004	5/4/2004	5/14/2004
0.578Q	7/21/2004	7/30/2004	8/3/2004	8/13/2004
0.60Q	10/22/2004	10/29/2004	11/2/2004	11/12/2004
0.613Q	1/25/2005	2/2/2005	2/4/2005	2/14/2005

Indicated Div: $2.45

Valuation Analysis

Forecast P/E	19.70	No of Institutions	
	(4/7/2005)	87	
Market Cap	$2.5 Billion	Shares	
Book Value	N/A	12,161,784	
Price/Book	N/A	% Held	
Price/Sales	0.12	17.92	

TRADING VOLUME (thousand shares)

Business Summary: Oil and Gas (MIC: 14.2 SIC: 619 NAIC: 86990)

Plains All American Pipeline is engaged in interstate and intrastate crude oil transportation, and crude oil gathering, marketing, terminalling and storage, as well as the marketing and storage of liquefied petroleum gas and other petroleum products, primarily in Texas, California, Oklahoma, Louisiana and the Canadian Provinces of Alberta and Saskatchewan. As of Dec 31 2003, Co. owned and operated approximately 7,000 miles of gathering and mainline crude oil pipelines located throughout the U.S. and Canada, and approximately 24.0 million barrels of above-ground crude oil terminalling and storage facilities, including tankage associated with its pipeline systems

Recent Developments: For the year ended Dec 31 2004, net income increased 118.7% to $130,006 thousand from net income of $59,448 thousand a year earlier. Revenues were $20,975,470 thousand, up 66.6% from $12,589,849 thousand the year before. Operating income was $180,023 thousand versus an income of $98,204 thousand in the prior year, an increase of 83.3%. Total direct expense was $20,644,038 thousand versus $12,372,440 thousand in the prior year, an increase of 66.9%. Total indirect expense was $151,409 thousand versus $119,205 thousand in the prior year, an increase of 27.0%.

Prospects: On Feb 2 2005, Co. announced that it is proceeding with the Phase V expansion of its Cushing Terminal Facility. Under the Phase V expansion, Co. will construct approximately 1.1 million barrels of additional tankage at its crude oil storage and terminal facility located in Cushing, OK. The Phase V project will expand the total capacity of the facility to approximately 7.4 million barrels and, including site preparation and additional manifold modifications, is expected to cost approximately $13.0 million. The new tankage should become operational during the fourth quarter of 2005.

Financial Data

(US$ in Thousands)	12/31/2004	12/31/2003	12/31/2002	12/31/2001	12/31/2000	12/31/1999	12/31/1998	11/22/1998
Earnings Per Share	1.89	1.00	1.34	1.13	2.64	(3.21)	0.14	0.40
Cash Flow Per Share	1.64	1.30	3.82	(0.80)	(0.97)	(3.36)	0.28	1.41
Dividends Per Share	2.303	2.188	2.112	1.950	1.825	1.587	...	...
Dividend Payout %	121.83	218.75	157.65	172.57	69.13	N.M.	...	...
Income Statement								
Total Revenue	20,975,470	12,589,849	8,384,223	6,868,215	6,641,187	4,701,921	176,445	953,244
EBITDA	...	...	...	...	145,863	(63,332)	6,740	27,027
Depn & Amortn	67	46,800	34,068	24,307	24,523	17,344	1,192	4,179
Income Before Taxes	...	...	...	...	92,649	(101,815)	4,177	11,588
Income Taxes	...	...	...	...	...	...	...	4,563
Net Income	130,006	59,448	65,292	44,179	77,502	(103,360)	4,177	7,025
Average Shares	63,277	53,400	45,546	37,528	34,386	31,633	30,089	17,004
Balance Sheet								
Current Assets	1,101,202	732,974	602,935	558,082	397,904	739,000	166,851	...
Total Assets	3,160,411	2,095,631	1,666,575	1,261,251	885,801	1,223,037	610,208	...
Current Liabilities	1,113,717	801,919	637,249	505,160	350,793	637,461	157,520	...
Long-Term Obligations	949,024	518,991	509,736	351,677	320,000	373,450	175,000	...
Total Liabilities	2,090,207	1,348,904	1,154,965	858,454	671,802	1,030,064	332,565	...
Shares Outstanding	64,047	58,331	49,577	43,252	34,386	34,386	31,396	...
Statistical Record								
Return on Assets %	4.93	3.16	4.46	4.12	7.33	N.M.	1.10	...
EBITDA Margin %	...	...	...	...	2.20	N.M.	3.82	2.84
Net Margin %	0.62	0.47	0.78	0.64	1.17	N.M.	2.37	0.74
Asset Turnover	7.96	6.69	5.73	6.40	6.28	5.13	0.46	...
Current Ratio	0.99	0.91	0.95	1.10	1.13	1.16	1.06	...
Price Range	37.75-30.30	32.53-24.24	27.10-21.35	29.50-19.50	20.00-13.00	20.19-10.38	20.06-16.75	20.00-20.00
P/E Ratio	19.97-16.03	32.53-24.24	20.22-15.93	26.11-17.26	7.58-4.92	N/A	143.30-119.64	50.00-50.00
Average Yield %	6.81	7.55	8.53	7.90	10.42	8.94	...	...

Address: 333 Clay Street, Suite 1600, Houston, TX 77002
Telephone: (713) 646-4100
Fax: (713) 646-4572

Web Site: www.paalp.com
Officers: Greg L. Armstrong - Chmn., C.E.O. Harry N. Pefanis - Pres., C.O.O.

Auditors: PricewaterhouseCoopers LLP
Investor Contact: 713-646-4491

PLAINS EXPLORATION & PRODUCTION CO. L.P.

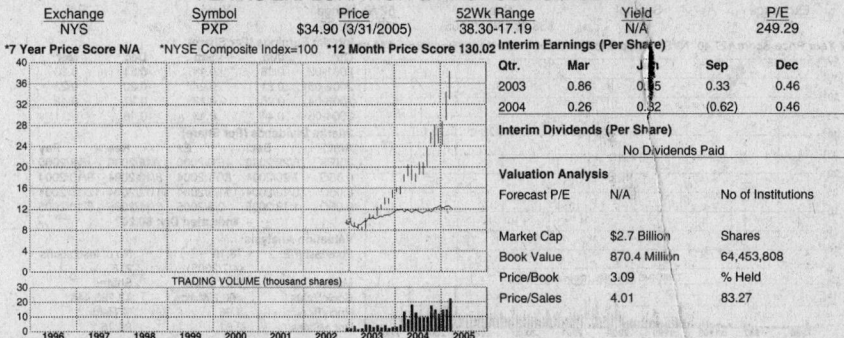

Exchange	Symbol	Price	52Wk Range	Yield	P/E
NYS	PXP	$34.90 (3/31/2005)	38.30-17.19	N/A	249.29

*7 Year Price Score N/A   *NYSE Composite Index=100   *12 Month Price Score 130.02

Interim Earnings (Per Share)

Qtr.	Mar	Jun	Sep	Dec
2003	0.86	0.95	0.33	0.46
2004	0.26	0.32	(0.62)	0.46

Interim Dividends (Per Share)

No Dividends Paid

Valuation Analysis

Forecast P/E	N/A	No of Institutions	
Market Cap	$2.7 Billion	Shares	
Book Value	870.4 Million	64,453,808	
Price/Book	3.09	% Held	
Price/Sales	4.01	83.27	

TRADING VOLUME (thousand shares)

1996 1997 1998 1999 2000 2001 2002 2003 2004 2005

Business Summary: Oil and Gas (MIC: 14.2 SIC: 311 NAIC: 11111)

Plains Exploration & Production is an independent oil and gas company primarily engaged in the upstream activities of acquiring, exploiting, developing and producing oil and gas in the U.S. Co.'s core areas of operation are in the Los Angeles and San Joaquin Basins in California; the Santa Maria Basin offshore California; the Gulf Coast Basin onshore and offshore Louisiana; and the East Texas Basin in east Texas and north Louisiana. Co. had estimated total proved reserves of 419.3 million barrels of oil equivalent as of Dec 31 2004, of which 84.0% was comprised of oil and 68.0% was proved developed.

Recent Developments: For the year ended Dec 31 2004, net income decreased 85.1% to $8,840 thousand from net income of $59,411 thousand a year earlier. Revenues were $671,706 thousand, up 120.9% from $304,090 thousand the year before. Operating income was $208,599 thousand versus an income of $103,629 thousand in the prior year, an increase of 101.3%. Total indirect expense was $463,107 thousand versus $200,461 thousand in the prior year, an increase of 131.0%.

Prospects: Co. outlook is encouraging, reflecting additional exploration opportunities Co. has in its pipeline. Recently, Co. began its multi-year drilling programs in the Inglewood field testing the deeper Sentous and Moynier zones and in the Rocky Point structure offshore California. Co. also increased drilling activity in several of its fields in the San Joaquin Valley and expects to nearly triple that activity in 2005. Co. augmented this activity by agreeing to acquire several California oil and gas properties for $119.0 million. Co. estimates the proved reserves are about 17.4 MMBOE, with additional unproven resource potential. The acquisition should be completed in the second quarter of 2005.

Financial Data

(US$ in Thousands)	12/31/2004	12/31/2003	12/31/2002	12/31/2001	12/31/2000	12/31/1999
Earnings Per Share	0.14	1.78	1.08	2.20	1.19	0.79
Cash Flow Per Share	5.70	3.55	3.26	...	...	...
Tang Book Value Per Share	9.08	5.14	7.18	...	...	...
Income Statement						
Total Revenue	671,706	304,090	188,563	204,139	142,451	107,485
EBITDA	187,302	156,801	92,705	130,597	80,258	52,678
Depn & Amortn	147,985	52,484	30,359	24,105	18,859	13,329
Income Before Taxes	2,023	80,539	42,969	89,081	45,514	24,437
Income Taxes	(6,817)	33,452	16,732	34,388	16,765	5,332
Net Income	8,840	59,411	26,237	53,171	28,749	19,105
Average Shares	64,014	33,469	24,201	...	...	...
Balance Sheet						
Current Assets	258,167	60,325	38,739	42,811	37,452	...
Total Assets	2,633,245	1,184,112	550,880	516,755	401,035	...
Current Liabilities	426,395	155,086	86,175	41,879	44,313	...
Long-Term Obligations	635,468	487,906	233,166	236,183	226,529	...
Total Liabilities	1,762,870	829,856	377,060	336,668	290,003	...
Stockholders' Equity	870,375	354,256	173,820	180,087	111,032	...
Shares Outstanding	77,100	40,299	24,224	...	...	...
Statistical Record						
Return on Assets %	0.46	6.85	4.91	11.59	...	...
Return on Equity %	1.44	22.50	14.83	36.53	...	...
EBITDA Margin %	27.88	51.56	49.16	63.97	56.34	49.01
Net Margin %	1.32	19.54	13.91	26.05	20.18	17.77
Asset Turnover	0.35	0.35	0.35	0.44	...	...
Current Ratio	0.61	0.39	0.45	1.02	0.85	...
Debt to Equity	0.73	1.38	1.34	1.31	2.04	...
Price Range	28.03-14.87	15.68-8.11	10.00-9.10	...	...	...
P/E Ratio	200.21-106.21	8.81-4.56	9.26-8.43	...	...	...

Address: 700 Milam Street, Suite 3100, Houston, TX 77002
Telephone: (713) 579-6000
Fax: (713) 579-6500

Web Site: www.plainsxp.com
Officers: James C. Flores - Chmn., Pres., C.E.O.
Stephen A. Thorington - Exec. V.P., C.F.O.

Auditors: PricewaterhouseCoopers LLP
Transfer Agents: American Stock Transfer & Trust, New York, NY

PLANTRONICS, INC.

Exchange	Symbol	Price	52Wk Range	Yield	P/E
NYS	PLT	$38.08 (3/31/2005)	47.57-32.95	0.53	20.81

*7 Year Price Score 127.40 *NYSE Composite Index=100 *12 Month Price Score 86.99

Interim Earnings (Per Share)

Qtr.	Jun	Sep	Dec	Mar
2001-02	0.16	0.14	0.21	0.23
2002-03	0.21	0.24	0.20	0.23
2003-04	0.25	0.27	0.37	0.42
2004-05	0.44	0.49	0.48	...

Interim Dividends (Per Share)

Amt	Decl	Ex	Rec	Pay
200%	6/29/2000	8/9/2000	7/18/2000	8/8/2000
0.05Q	7/20/2004	8/11/2004	8/13/2004	9/10/2004
0.05Q	10/19/2004	11/9/2004	11/12/2004	12/10/2004
0.05Q	1/18/2005	2/9/2005	2/11/2005	3/10/2005

Indicated Div: $0.20

Valuation Analysis

Forecast P/E	18.19	No of Institutions	
	(4/7/2005)	218	
Market Cap	$1.9 Billion	Shares	
Book Value	400.2 Million	43,298,440	
Price/Book	4.66	% Held	
Price/Sales	3.51	88.25	

Business Summary: Communications (MIC: 10.1 SIC: 661 NAIC: 34210)

Plantronics designs, manufactures and markets lightweight communications headsets, telephone headset systems, accessories and related services for business and personal use. In addition, Co. manufactures specialty products, such as telephones for the hearing-impaired and headset solutions for the aviation market. Co.'s headsets are communications tools, designed to provide the free use of hands while staying "connected," allowing freedom to move around, and freedom from keyboards. Co.'s headsets are widely used for cell phones, in contact centers, in the office, at home for computer applications such as Voice over Internet Protocol and gaming, as well as other specialty applications.

Recent Developments: For the quarter ended Dec 31 2004, net income increased 38.7% to $24,442 thousand from net income of $17,619 thousand in the year-earlier quarter. Revenues were $150,583 thousand, up 39.9% from $107,622 thousand the year before. Operating income was $31,802 thousand versus an income of $23,758 thousand in the prior-year quarter, an increase of 33.9%. Total direct expense was $75,150 thousand versus $51,381 thousand in the prior-year quarter, an increase of 46.3%. Total indirect expense was $43,631 thousand versus $32,483 thousand in the prior-year quarter, an increase of 34.3%.

Prospects: Co. remains cautiously optimistic about the overall economic environment and demand for its products. For its fourth fiscal quarter ended Mar 31 2005, Co. expects revenues to be in the range of $140.0 million to $145.0 million, and gross margins to increase to 53.0% to 54.0% as a result of a more favorable overall product mix. Earnings per diluted share for the fourth quarter are expected to be $0.45 to $0.49 before an anticipated tax benefit, and $0.49 to $0.55 inclusive of the tax benefit. Separately, Co. intends to launch a U.S. advertising campaign with an expected total cost of about $10.0 million, with the majority of the cost and benefits to affect fiscal year 2006.

Financial Data

(US$ in Thousands)	9 Mos	6 Mos	3 Mos	03/31/2004	03/31/2003	03/31/2002	03/31/2001	03/31/2000
Earnings Per Share	1.83	1.72	1.50	1.31	0.89	0.74	1.38	1.22
Cash Flow Per Share	1.48	1.67	1.84	1.61	1.11	1.62	1.34	1.63
Tang Book Value Per Share	7.91	7.15	6.64	6.02	3.07	2.79	3.54	2.62
Dividends Per Share	0.100	0.050	...	...	...	...	...	...
Dividend Payout %	5.48	2.91	...	...	...	...	...	...
Income Statement								
Total Revenue	412,173	261,590	131,370	416,965	337,508	311,181	401,038	315,012
EBITDA	108,096	70,918	33,797	98,852	68,260	52,664	109,293	99,236
Depn & Amortn	8,840	5,609	2,759	12,353	11,500	9,464	7,034	4,272
Income Before Taxes	99,256	65,309	31,038	86,499	56,760	43,200	102,152	94,878
Income Taxes	27,792	18,287	8,691	24,220	15,284	6,952	28,602	30,361
Net Income	71,464	47,022	22,347	62,279	41,476	36,248	73,550	64,517
Average Shares	51,365	50,638	50,428	47,492	46,584	49,238	53,263	53,019
Balance Sheet								
Current Assets	413,642	372,911	344,099	310,627	153,017	148,569	190,926	135,866
Total Assets	481,695	438,265	408,019	368,252	205,209	201,058	233,272	170,030
Current Liabilities	73,356	73,982	71,486	61,230	49,412	51,900	54,148	57,560
Total Liabilities	81,510	82,103	79,205	68,949	58,279	59,065	60,225	64,654
Stockholders' Equity	400,185	356,162	328,814	299,303	146,930	141,993	173,047	105,376
Shares Outstanding	48,996	48,063	47,606	47,606	43,638	45,858	48,896	40,212
Statistical Record								
Return on Assets %	24.35	25.11	23.28	21.66	20.42	16.69	36.47	41.13
Return on Equity %	30.37	31.88	30.02	27.84	28.71	23.01	52.83	66.06
EBITDA Margin %	26.23	27.11	25.73	23.71	20.22	16.92	27.25	31.50
Net Margin %	17.34	17.98	17.01	14.94	12.29	11.65	18.34	20.48
Asset Turnover	1.41	1.44	1.45	1.45	1.66	1.43	1.99	2.01
Current Ratio	5.64	5.04	4.81	5.07	3.10	2.86	3.53	2.36
Price Range	47.57-32.65	43.38-23.87	43.38-21.67	43.38-14.61	23.64-12.78	27.35-16.30	55.13-16.97	31.06-14.83
P/E Ratio	25.99-17.84	25.22-13.88	28.92-14.45	33.11-11.15	26.56-14.36	36.96-22.03	39.95-12.30	25.46-12.16
Average Yield %	0.25	0.14	...	...	...	...	...	...

Address: 345 Encinal Street, Santa Cruz, CA 95060-1802	Web Site: www.plantronics.com	Auditors: PricewaterhouseCoopers LLP
Telephone: (831) 426-5858	**Officers:** Marvin Tseu - Chmn. S. Kenneth Kannappan - Pres., C.E.O.	**Investor Contact:** 831-458-7533
Fax: (831) 426-6098		

PLUM CREEK TIMBER CO., INC.

Exchange	Symbol	Price	52Wk Range	Yield	P/E
NYS	PCL	$35.70 (3/31/2005)	39.32-28.50	4.26	18.12

*7 Year Price Score 105.69 *NYSE Composite Index=100 *12 Month Price Score 100.20

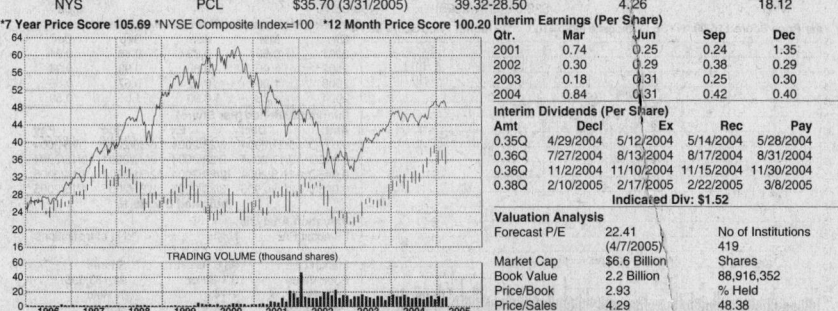

Interim Earnings (Per Share)

Qtr.	Mar	Jun	Sep	Dec
2001	0.74	0.25	0.24	1.35
2002	0.30	0.29	0.38	0.29
2003	0.18	0.31	0.25	0.30
2004	0.84	0.31	0.42	0.40

Interim Dividends (Per Share)

Amt	Decl	Ex	Rec	Pay
0.35Q	4/29/2004	5/12/2004	5/14/2004	5/28/2004
0.36Q	7/27/2004	8/13/2004	8/17/2004	8/31/2004
0.36Q	11/2/2004	11/10/2004	11/15/2004	11/30/2004
0.38Q	2/10/2005	2/17/2005	2/22/2005	3/8/2005

Indicated Div: $1.52

Valuation Analysis

Forecast P/E	22.41	No of Institutions	
	(4/7/2005)	419	
Market Cap	$6.6 Billion	Shares	
Book Value	2.2 Billion	88,916,352	
Price/Book	2.93	% Held	
Price/Sales	4.29	48.38	

Business Summary: Property, Real Estate & Development (MIC: 8.3 SIC: 798 NAIC: 25930)

Plum Creek Timber is a land and timber owner with 8.1 million acres of timberlands located in 21 states and 10 wood product manufacturing facilities in the northwest in 2003. Co.'s two timberland business segments are the Northern Resources segment and the Southern Resources segment. In addition, Co.'s Other segment includes its natural resource businesses that focus on opportunities resulting from its extensive property ownership. The Real Estate and the Manufactured Products segments, are partially conducted through Co.'s taxable real estate investment trust subsidiaries, and refer to its sale and management of higher and better use timberlands, and manufacturing facilities, respectively.

Recent Developments: For the year ended Dec 31 2004, income from continuing operations increased 76.6% to $339,000 thousand from income of $192,000 thousand a year earlier. Net income increased 88.5% to $362,000 thousand from net income of $192,000 thousand a year earlier. Revenues were $1,528,000 thousand, up 27.8% from $1,196,000 thousand the year before. Operating income was $477,000 thousand versus an income of $303,000 thousand in the prior year, an increase of 57.4%.

Prospects: Lumber, plywood, and oriented strand board customers are working to build their log decks in anticipation of a strong first half of 2005. Co. is experiencing good pulpwood demand from pulp and paper mills in all regions. Log prices in several Southern markets are improving modestly. Timber markets in both the Northern and Southern segments are expected to hold at current levels or increase modestly throughout the first half of 2005. During 2005, Co. expects to harvest between 18.5 and 19.5 million tons of timber. Co. expects first quarter 2005 earnings to be between $0.47 and $0.52 per share with full year earnings in the range of $1.45 and $1.65 per share.

Financial Data

(US$ in Thousands)	12/31/2004	12/31/2003	12/31/2002	12/31/2001	12/31/2000	12/31/1999	12/31/1998	12/31/1997
Earnings Per Share	1.97	1.04	1.26	2.58	1.91	1.94	0.90	1.72
Cash Flow Per Share	3.26	2.01	1.99	1.72	2.15	2.47	3.54	4.10
Tang Book Value Per Share	12.19	11.57	12.02	12.22	7.39	7.77	...	...
Dividends Per Share	1.420	1.400	1.490	2.850	2.280	1.140	...	...
Dividend Payout %	72.08	134.62	118.25	110.47	119.37	58.76	...	...
Income Statement								
Total Revenue	1,528,000	1,196,000	1,137,000	598,000	209,054	460,620	699,370	725,571
EBITDA	591,000	410,000	443,000	305,000	212,197	203,968	204,820	241,270
Depn & Amortn	114,000	107,000	105,000	55,000	38,910	59,689	69,287	70,243
Income Before Taxes	366,000	186,000	235,000	196,000	131,254	82,805	75,953	111,776
Income Taxes	27,000	(6,000)	2,000	(142,000)	...	(13,105)	517	80
Net Income	362,000	192,000	233,000	338,000	131,962	125,601	75,436	111,696
Average Shares	184,100	183,900	185,400	130,700	69,213	55,819	...	...
Balance Sheet								
Current Assets	499,000	405,000	378,000	306,000	194,635	133,316	210,463	232,254
Total Assets	4,378,000	4,387,000	4,289,000	4,122,000	1,250,068	1,250,756	1,438,243	1,300,897
Current Liabilities	184,000	168,000	155,000	149,000	179,705	74,204	80,876	73,992
Long-Term Obligations	1,853,000	2,031,000	1,839,000	1,667,000	559,798	642,950	942,608	745,000
Total Liabilities	2,138,000	2,268,000	2,067,000	1,875,000	743,400	717,709	1,032,828	830,560
Stockholders' Equity	2,240,000	2,119,000	2,222,000	2,247,000	506,668	533,047	...	...
Shares Outstanding	183,700	183,100	184,861	183,825	68,572	68,572	46,323	46,323
Statistical Record								
Return on Assets %	8.24	4.43	5.54	12.58	10.52	9.34	5.51	8.47
Return on Equity %	16.56	8.85	10.43	24.55	25.30	...	...	...
EBITDA Margin %	38.68	34.28	38.96	51.00	101.50	44.28	29.29	33.25
Net Margin %	23.69	16.05	20.49	56.52	63.09	27.27	10.79	15.39
Asset Turnover	0.35	0.28	0.27	0.22	0.17	0.34	0.51	0.55
Current Ratio	2.71	2.41	2.44	2.05	1.08	1.80	2.60	3.14
Debt to Equity	0.83	0.96	0.83	0.74	1.10	1.21	...	...
Price Range	39.32-28.50	30.54-21.15	31.80-19.11	29.99-23.35	29.50-22.06	32.13-23.81	34.88-24.50	35.88-26.00
P/E Ratio	19.96-14.47	29.37-20.34	25.24-15.17	11.62-9.05	15.45-11.55	16.56-12.27	38.75-27.22	20.86-15.12
Average Yield %	4.31	5.56	5.44	10.57	9.22	4.11	...	...

Address: 999 Third Avenue, Suite 4300, Seattle, WA 98104-4096 **Telephone:** (206) 467-3600 **Fax:** (206) 467-3795	**Web Site:** www.plumcreek.com **Officers:** David D. Leland - Chmn. Rick R. Holley - Pres., C.E.O.	**Auditors:** Ernst & Young LLP **Investor Contact:** 800-858-5347

PMI GROUP, INC. (THE)

Exchange	Symbol	Price	52Wk Range	Yield	P/E
NYS	PMI	$38.01 (3/31/2005)	44.63-36.70	0.47	9.82

*7 Year Price Score 116.00 *NYSE Composite Index=100 *12 Month Price Score 89.74

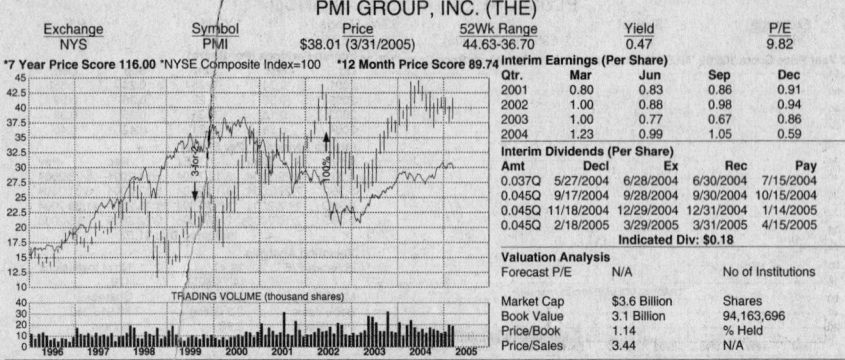

Interim Earnings (Per Share)

Qtr.	Mar	Jun	Sep	Dec
2001	0.80	0.83	0.86	0.91
2002	1.00	0.88	0.98	0.94
2003	1.00	0.77	0.67	0.86
2004	1.23	0.99	1.05	0.59

Interim Dividends (Per Share)

Amt	Decl	Ex	Rec	Pay
0.037Q	5/27/2004	6/28/2004	6/30/2004	7/15/2004
0.045Q	9/17/2004	9/28/2004	9/30/2004	10/15/2004
0.045Q	11/18/2004	12/29/2004	12/31/2004	1/14/2005
0.045Q	2/18/2005	3/29/2005	3/31/2005	4/15/2005
		Indicated Div: $0.18		

Valuation Analysis

Forecast P/E	N/A		No of Institutions
Market Cap	$3.6 Billion		Shares
Book Value	3.1 Billion		94,163,696
Price/Book	1.14		% Held
Price/Sales	3.44		N/A

Business Summary: Insurance (MIC: 8.2 SIC: 351 NAIC: 24130)

PMI Group is an international provider of credit enhancement products and lender services that promote homeownership and facilitate mortgage transactions in the capital markets. Co. conducts its residential mortgage insurance business through PMI Mortgage Insurance, Residential Guaranty, Residential Insurance, TPG Insurance, PMI Mortgage Guaranty, TPG Segregated Portfolio, and PMI Mortgage Insurance. Co. also conducts title insurance business through its subsidiary American Pioneer Title Insurance. In addition, Co. owns PMI Mortgage Services, which is engaged in contract underwriting. Co. has operations in Australia, New Zealand, Europe and Hong Kong.

Recent Developments: For the year ended Dec 31 2004, income from continuing operations increased 33.6% to $366,532 thousand from income of $274,398 thousand a year earlier. Net income increased 33.4% to $399,333 thousand from net income of $299,433 thousand a year earlier. Revenues were $1,038,236 thousand, up 16.4% from $891,721 thousand the year before. Net premiums earned were $770,399 thousand versus $696,928 thousand in the prior year, an increase of 10.5%.

Prospects: For the full year ended Dec 31 2005, Co. expects high single digit to low double digit percentage net income growth in both its U.S. and International mortgage insurance businesses, excluding the effects of currency fluctuations. Co. also expects total incurred losses for its U.S. Mortgage Insurance operations of between $250.0 million and $275.0 million. Additionally, Co. expects net income growth for its Financial Guaranty business segment in the mid-teens percent range. Lastly, Co. anticipates consolidated investment portfolio pre-tax yield for 2005 between 4.5% and 5.0%.

Financial Data

(US$ in Thousands)	12/31/2004	12/31/2003	12/31/2002	12/31/2001	12/31/2000	12/31/1999	12/31/1998	12/31/1997
Earnings Per Share	3.87	3.29	3.79	3.39	2.89	2.26	2.01	1.74
Cash Flow Per Share	4.08	6.19	4.71	3.39	2.50	3.51	1.89	1.86
Tang Book Value Per Share	33.37	29.26	24.39	20.04	16.92	13.62	12.08	10.90
Dividends Per Share	0.165	0.125	0.095	0.080	0.080	0.073	0.067	0.067
Dividend Payout %	4.26	3.80	2.51	2.36	2.77	3.24	3.31	3.82
Income Statement								
Premium Income	770,399	696,928	904,510	754,771	634,362	558,623	491,226	453,948
Total Revenue	1,038,236	891,721	1,121,362	936,963	762,572	670,124	620,909	564,647
Benefits & Claims	237,282	209,088	167,263	118,048	103,079	112,682	135,716	152,257
Income Before Taxes	478,991	393,122	470,790	446,966	373,866	290,086	266,948	242,867
Income Taxes	112,459	118,814	131,745	134,949	113,654	85,620	76,588	67,558
Net Income	399,333	299,433	346,217	307,212	260,212	204,466	190,360	175,309
Average Shares	105,231	91,045	91,380	90,667	90,037	90,488	94,599	100,530
Balance Sheet								
Total Assets	5,145,967	4,794,289	3,517,049	2,989,952	2,392,657	2,100,762	1,777,870	1,686,603
Total Liabilities	2,008,212	2,010,260	1,274,716	1,154,764	794,337	784,419	581,315	526,417
Stockholders' Equity	3,137,755	2,784,029	2,193,833	1,786,688	1,499,211	1,217,268	1,097,515	1,061,180
Shares Outstanding	94,025	95,161	89,943	89,162	88,619	89,403	90,837	97,383
Statistical Record								
Return on Assets %	8.01	7.21	10.64	11.41	11.55	10.54	10.99	10.97
Return on Equity %	13.45	12.03	17.40	18.70	19.11	17.67	17.64	17.12
Loss Ratio %	30.80	30.00	18.49	15.64	16.25	20.17	27.63	33.54
Net Margin %	38.46	33.58	30.87	32.79	34.12	30.51	30.66	31.05
Price Range	44.63-36.15	38.59-24.20	43.92-24.96	36.63-24.44	36.94-16.75	27.44-13.71	28.02-11.54	24.29-15.92
P/E Ratio	11.53-9.34	11.73-7.36	11.59-6.59	10.80-7.21	12.78-5.80	12.14-6.07	13.94-5.74	13.96-9.15
Average Yield %	0.41	0.40	0.27	0.26	0.29	0.37	0.31	0.35

Address: 3003 Oak Road, Walnut Creek, CA 94597-2098 **Telephone:** (925) 658-7878	**Web Site:** www.pmigroup.com **Officers:** W. Roger Haughton - Chmn., C.E.O. L. Stephen Smith - Pres., C.O.O.	**Auditors:** Ernst & Young LLP **Investor Contact:** 888-641-4764

PNC FINANCIAL SERVICES GROUP (THE)

Exchange	Symbol	Price	52Wk Range	Yield	P/E
NYS	PNC	$51.48 (3/31/2005)	57.44-49.42	3.89	12.23

*7 Year Price Score 85.20   *NYSE Composite Index=100   *12 Month Price Score 91.93

Interim Earnings (Per Share)

Qtr.	Mar	Jun	Sep	Dec
2001	1.01	1.00	1.02	(1.77)
2002	1.11	1.12	1.00	0.92
2003	0.92	0.65	1.00	0.98
2004	1.15	1.07	0.91	1.08

Interim Dividends (Per Share)

Amt	Decl	Ex	Rec	Pay
0.50Q	7/6/2004	7/12/2004	7/14/2004	7/24/2004
0.50Q	10/7/2004	10/13/2004	10/15/2004	10/24/2004
0.50Q	1/6/2005	1/12/2005	1/14/2005	1/24/2005
0.50Q	4/6/2005	4/12/2005	4/14/2005	4/24/2005
		Indicated Div: $2.00		

Valuation Analysis

Forecast P/E	12.11	No of Institutions
	(4/7/2005)	479
Market Cap	$14.6 Billion	Shares
Book Value	7.5 Billion	173,201,440
Price/Book	1.95	% Held
Price/Sales	2.31	61.21

Business Summary: Commercial Banking (MIC: 8.1 SIC: 021 NAIC: 22110)

The PNC Financial Services Group is one of the largest diversified financial services companies in the nation with $68.2 billion in total assets as of Dec 31 2003. Co. operates seven major businesses engaged in regional community banking, corporate banking, real estate finance, asset-based lending, wealth management, asset management and global fund services. Co. provides products and services nationally and in Co.'s primary geographic markets in Pennsylvania, New Jersey, Delaware, Ohio and Kentucky. As of Dec 31 2003, assets under management totaled $354.0 billion.

Recent Developments: For the year ended Dec 31 2004, net income increased 19.6% to $1,197,000 thousand from net income of $1,001,000 thousand a year earlier. Net interest income was $1,969,000 thousand, down 1.4% from $1,996,000 thousand the year before. Provision for loan losses was $52,000 thousand versus $177,000 thousand in the prior year, a decrease of 70.6%. Non-interest income rose 6.5% to $3,496,000 thousand, while non-interest expense advanced 7.5% to $3,735,000 thousand.

Prospects: Co.'s outlook is positive, reflecting strong momentum in its loan and deposit balances. Overall asset quality should also remain strong due to Co.'s revised lending practices. Separately, on Feb 10 2005, Co. announced that, as a result of renewed negotiations, it has amended and restated the agreement to acquire Riggs National Corp. Under the terms of the amended agreement, Co. will acquire Riggs for $20.00 per common share, or about $652.0 million. The acquisition remains subject to customary closing conditions, including regulatory approvals and the approval of Riggs shareholders. Co. added that either party may terminate the agreement after May 31 2005 if the transaction has not closed.

Financial Data

(US$ in Thousands)	12/31/2004	12/31/2003	12/31/2002	12/31/2001	12/31/2000	12/31/1999	12/31/1998	12/31/1997
Earnings Per Share	4.21	3.55	4.15	1.26	4.31	4.15	3.60	3.28
Cash Flow Per Share	1.55	5.96	9.37	4.41	10.48	6.26	(0.95)	(0.13)
Tang Book Value Per Share	14.55	14.22	14.78	12.19	14.42	6.20	11.49	12.47
Dividends Per Share	2.000	1.940	1.920	1.920	1.830	1.680	1.580	1.500
Dividend Payout %	47.51	54.65	46.27	152.38	42.46	40.48	43.89	45.73
Income Statement								
Interest Income	2,752,000	2,712,000	3,172,000	4,137,000	4,732,000	4,921,000	5,313,000	5,051,000
Interest Expense	783,000	716,000	975,000	1,875,000	2,568,000	2,488,000	2,740,000	2,556,000
Net Interest Income	1,969,000	1,996,000	2,197,000	2,262,000	2,164,000	2,433,000	2,573,000	2,495,000
Provision for Losses	52,000	177,000	309,000	903,000	136,000	163,000	225,000	70,000
Non-Interest Income	3,563,000	3,257,000	3,197,000	2,543,000	2,891,000	2,745,000	2,302,000	1,775,000
Non-Interest Expense	3,735,000	3,476,000	3,227,000	3,338,000	3,071,000	3,124,000	2,940,000	2,582,000
Income Before Taxes	1,745,000	1,600,000	1,858,000	564,000	1,848,000	1,891,000	1,710,000	1,618,000
Income Taxes	538,000	539,000	621,000	187,000	634,000	627,000	595,000	566,000
Net Income	1,197,000	1,001,000	1,184,000	377,000	1,279,000	1,264,000	1,115,000	1,052,000
Average Shares	284,000	281,000	285,000	290,000	292,800	300,000	305,100	316,200
Balance Sheet								
Net Loans & Leases	42,888,000	33,448,000	34,777,000	37,344,000	49,926,000	49,372,000	56,897,000	53,273,000
Total Assets	79,723,000	68,168,000	66,377,000	69,568,000	69,844,000	75,413,000	77,207,000	75,120,000
Total Deposits	53,269,000	45,241,000	44,982,000	47,304,000	47,664,000	46,668,000	47,496,000	47,649,000
Total Liabilities	71,746,000	61,061,000	58,400,000	62,727,000	62,340,000	68,619,000	70,316,000	69,086,000
Stockholders' Equity	7,473,000	6,645,000	6,859,000	5,823,000	6,656,000	5,946,000	6,043,000	5,384,000
Shares Outstanding	283,000	277,000	285,000	283,000	290,000	293,000	303,700	300,430
Statistical Record								
Return on Assets %	1.61	1.49	1.74	0.54	1.76	1.66	1.46	1.42
Return on Equity %	16.91	14.83	18.67	6.04	20.24	21.09	19.52	18.70
Net Interest Margin %	71.55	73.60	69.26	54.68	45.73	49.44	48.43	49.40
Efficiency Ratio %	59.14	58.23	50.67	49.97	40.29	40.75	38.61	37.83
Loans to Deposits	0.81	0.74	0.77	0.79	1.05	1.06	1.20	1.12
Price Range	58.70-49.42	55.03-41.90	62.63-36.00	75.15-52.42	75.00-36.63	62.00-43.00	64.88-40.25	58.13-36.88
P/E Ratio	13.94-11.74	15.50-11.80	15.09-8.67	59.64-41.60	17.40-8.50	14.94-10.36	18.02-11.18	17.72-11.24
Average Yield %	3.69	4.06	3.87	2.99	3.44	3.10	2.94	3.34

Address: One PNC Plaza, 249 Fifth Avenue, Pittsburgh, PA 15222-2707	Web Site: www.pnc.com	Auditors: Ernst & Young LLP
Telephone: (412) 762-2000	**Officers:** James E. Rohr - Chmn., C.E.O. William S. Demchak - Vice-Chmn., C.F.O.	**Investor Contact:** 412-762-8257
Fax: (412) 762-5798		**Transfer Agents:** Computershare Investor Services, LLC, Chicago, IL

PNM RESOURCES INC

*7 Year Price Score 118.13 *NYSE Composite Index=100 *12 Month Price Score 107.47

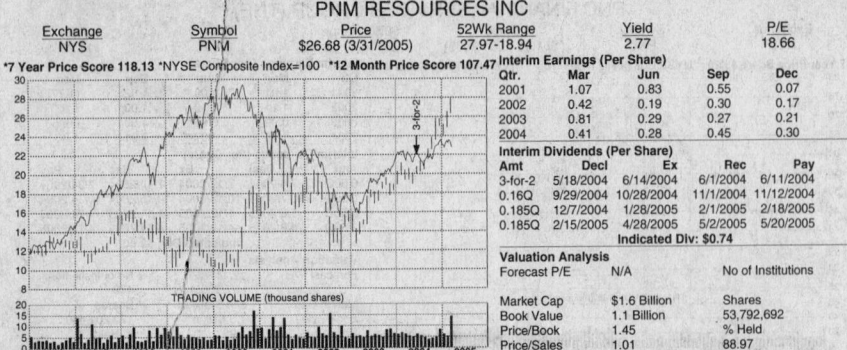

Interim Earnings (Per Share)

Qtr.	Mar	Jun	Sep	Dec
2001	1.07	0.83	0.55	0.07
2002	0.42	0.19	0.30	0.17
2003	0.81	0.29	0.27	0.21
2004	0.41	0.28	0.45	0.30

Interim Dividends (Per Share)

Amt	Decl	Ex	Rec	Pay
3-for-2	5/18/2004	6/14/2004	6/1/2004	6/11/2004
0.16Q	9/29/2004	10/28/2004	11/1/2004	11/12/2004
0.185Q	12/7/2004	1/28/2005	2/1/2005	2/18/2005
0.185Q	2/15/2005	4/28/2005	5/2/2005	5/20/2005

Indicated Div: $0.74

Valuation Analysis

Forecast P/E	N/A	No of Institutions
Market Cap	$1.6 Billion	Shares
Book Value	1.1 Billion	53,792,692
Price/Book	1.45	% Held
Price/Sales	1.01	88.97

TRADING VOLUME (thousand shares)

Business Summary: Electricity (MIC: 7.1 SIC: 719 NAIC: 51112)

PNM Resources is a holding company. Through its subsidiaries, Co. is engaged in the generation, transmission, distribution, sale and marketing of electricity, and in the transmission, distribution and sale of natural gas within the State of New Mexico. As of Dec. 31, 2004, Co. had 412,092 electric customers, consisting of 367,491 residential, 43,425 commercial, 290 industrial, 818 other ultimate and 68 sales for resale customers; 468,572 gas customers, consisting of 430,578 residential, 34,993 commercial, 47 industrial, 2,931 other and 23 transportation customers; and 68 wholesale customers.

Recent Developments: For the twelve months ended Dec 31 2004, net earnings were $87.7 million compared with earnings of $58.6 million a year earlier. Results for 2003 excluded an accounting change gain of $36.6 million. Co. noted that earnings were influenced by a 3.3% increase in retail electric loan growth, results of the previous year's refinancing efforts and the gas delivery rate increase, which went into full effect in Apr 2004. Total operating revenues increased 10.2% to $1.60 billion from $1.46 billion the previous year. Operating income declined 4.8% to $112.9 million versus $118.6 million the year before.

Prospects: Results are being positively affected by increased natural gas consumption, retail electric load growth and the natural gas delivery rate increase. Meanwhile, on Feb 28 2005, Co. announced that it has reached an agreement with New Mexico parties related to its proposed $1.02 billion acquisition of TNP Enterprises. The agreement, if approved by the New Mexico Public Regulation Commission, would provide for cost savings to be passed on to New Mexico customers. The acquisition is expected to be completed by June 2005. Separately, Co. is forecasting full-year 2005 earnings, not including the pending acquisition of TNP Enterprises, of between $1.40 and $1.55 per share.

Financial Data

(US$ in Thousands)	12/31/2004	12/31/2003	12/31/2002	12/31/2001	12/31/2000	12/31/1999	12/31/1998	12/31/1997
Earnings Per Share	1.43	1.58	1.07	2.51	1.69	1.34	1.30	1.27
Cash Flow Per Share	3.89	3.84	1.66	5.54	4.03	3.48	3.37	3.40
Tang Book Value Per Share	18.19	17.84	16.60	17.25	15.76	14.53	13.75	12.84
Dividends Per Share	0.633	0.607	0.573	0.533	0.533	0.533	0.513	0.420
Dividend Payout %	44.29	38.40	53.42	21.22	31.62	39.80	39.49	32.98
Income Statement								
Total Revenue	1,604,792	1,455,714	1,168,996	2,352,098	1,611,274	1,157,543	1,092,445	1,135,267
Depn & Amortn	131,625	144,854	115,415	106,768	103,829	103,891	98,154	94,924
Income Taxes	13,185	(183)	12,144	(7,706)	20,382	17,298	14,985	8,384
Net Income	87,686	95,173	64,272	150,433	100,946	83,155	82,682	80,995
Average Shares	61,340	60,205	59,164	59,596	59,565	61,654	63,108	62,986
Balance Sheet								
Net PPE	2,326,023	2,195,890	1,868,924	1,782,741	1,620,972	1,586,821	1,598,634	1,577,652
Total Assets	3,487,635	3,378,629	3,026,907	2,934,638	2,894,233	2,723,268	2,576,788	2,313,732
Long-Term Obligations	987,823	987,210	980,092	953,884	953,823	988,489	1,008,614	713,995
Total Liabilities	2,376,527	2,288,525	2,040,058	1,909,814	1,956,806	1,823,377	1,702,385	1,496,528
Stockholders' Equity	1,111,108	1,090,104	986,849	1,024,824	937,427	899,891	874,403	817,204
Shares Outstanding	60,464	60,388	58,677	58,676	58,676	61,055	62,661	62,661
Statistical Record								
Return on Assets %	2.55	2.97	2.16	5.16	3.58	3.14	3.38	3.56
Return on Equity %	7.95	9.16	6.39	15.33	10.96	9.37	9.78	10.22
Net Margin %	5.46	6.54	5.50	6.40	6.26	7.18	7.57	7.13
PPE Turnover	0.71	0.72	0.64	1.38	1.00	0.73	0.69	0.72
Asset Turnover	0.47	0.45	0.39	0.81	0.57	0.44	0.45	0.50
Debt to Equity	0.89	0.91	0.99	0.93	1.02	1.10	1.15	0.87
Price Range	25.88-18.73	19.64-12.74	20.44-11.91	25.13-15.63	18.79-9.88	14.17-10.25	16.33-11.67	15.79-10.75
P/E Ratio	18.10-13.10	12.43-8.06	19.10-11.13	10.01-6.23	11.12-5.84	10.57-7.65	12.56-8.97	12.43-8.46
Average Yield %	2.96	3.59	3.55	2.78	4.08	4.04		3.36

Address: Alvarado Square, Albuquerque, NM 87158	**Web Site:** www.pnm.com	**Auditors:** Deloitte & Touche LLP
Telephone: (505) 241-2700	**Officers:** Jeff E. Sterba - Chmn., Pres., C.E.O. J. R. Loyack - Sr. V.P., C.F.O.	**Transfer Agents:** PNM Shareholder Records Departement, Albuquerque, NM
Fax: (505) 241-2359		

POGO PRODUCING CO.

Exchange	Symbol	Price	52Wk Range	Yield	P/E
NYS	PPP	$49.24 (3/31/2005)	52.11-41.45	0.51	12.13

*7 Year Price Score 131.43 *NYSE Composite Index=100 *12 Month Price Score 95.12

Interim Earnings (Per Share)
Qtr.	Mar	Jun	Sep	Dec
2001	0.80	0.53	0.28	0.05
2002	0.17	0.48	0.51	0.60
2003	1.37	1.24	1.07	0.75
2004	1.12	1.01	1.35	0.59

Interim Dividends (Per Share)
Amt	Decl	Ex	Rec	Pay
0.05Q	4/27/2004	5/12/2004	5/14/2004	5/28/2004
0.05Q	7/20/2004	7/28/2004	8/1/2004	8/15/2004
0.063Q	10/19/2004	11/3/2004	11/5/2004	11/19/2004
0.063Q	1/21/2005	2/9/2005	2/11/2005	2/25/2005

Indicated Div: $0.25

Valuation Analysis
Forecast P/E	10.67	No of Institutions
	(4/7/2005)	215
Market Cap	$3.2 Billion	Shares
Book Value	1.7 Billion	55,952,392
Price/Book	1.84	% Held
Price/Sales	2.40	87.97

Business Summary: Oil and Gas (MIC: 14.2 SIC: 311 NAIC: 11111)

Pogo Producing is engaged in oil and gas exploration, development, acquisition and production activities on its properties located offshore in the Gulf of Mexico, onshore in areas of Texas, New Mexico, Wyoming and Louisiana, and internationally, primarily in the Gulf of Thailand, New Zealand and in Hungary. As of Dec. 31 2004, Co. had interests in 91 lease blocks offshore Louisiana and Texas, 705,000 gross acres onshore in the U.S., 588,000 gross acres offshore in the Kingdom of Thailand, 778,000 gross acres in Hungary and 1,044,000 gross acres in New Zealand.

Recent Developments: For the year ended Dec 31 2004, net income decreased 10.0% to $261,754 thousand from net income of $290,941 thousand a year earlier. Revenues were $1,322,979 thousand, up 13.9% from $1,161,996 thousand the year before. Operating income was $524,479 thousand versus an income of $547,729 thousand in the prior year, a decrease of 4.2%. Total direct expense was $144,473 thousand versus $123,098 thousand in the prior year, an increase of 17.4%. Total indirect expense was $654,027 thousand versus $491,169 thousand in the prior year, an increase of 33.2%.

Prospects: In light of spiking drilling and service costs, up one-third to one-half since 2003, Co. announced it would delay the drilling of all discretionary 2005 development wells, a total of some 210 gross wells, until 2006. That postponement should result in savings of $280.0 million in 2005. That capital will be redirected toward accelerated exploration drilling, domestic acquisitions and balance sheet improvements. In addition, Co. announced it is seeking the possible sale or swap of its license holdings in Thailand and Hungary. If these operations are sold for cash, Co. will seek to reinvest the proceeds in attractive domestic properties.

Financial Data
(US$ in Thousands)	12/31/2004	12/31/2003	12/31/2002	12/31/2001	12/31/2000	12/31/1999	12/31/1998	12/31/1997
Earnings Per Share	4.06	4.54	1.77	1.62	1.95	0.55	(1.14)	1.06
Cash Flow Per Share	11.54	11.91	8.05	7.21	5.89	1.71	1.87	4.51
Tang Book Value Per Share	26.78	22.80	17.67	15.37	8.81	6.67	6.22	4.36
Dividends Per Share	0.212	0.200	0.120	0.120	0.120	0.120	0.120	0.120
Dividend Payout %	5.23	4.41	6.78	7.41	6.15	21.82	N.M.	11.32
Income Statement								
Total Revenue	1,322,979	1,161,996	751,441	605,500	497,991	275,116	202,803	286,300
EBITDA	874,083	869,026	524,277	375,967	297,655	152,916	54,649	173,622
Depn & Amortn	365,089	325,820	287,809	206,609	131,151	104,266	110,916	103,157
Income Before Taxes	496,403	515,229	204,811	149,567	155,992	31,717	(70,849)	55,207
Income Taxes	234,649	220,122	97,780	61,613	66,969	9,583	(27,751)	18,091
Net Income	261,754	290,941	107,031	87,954	87,255	22,134	(43,098)	37,116
Average Shares	64,393	64,612	64,321	60,822	50,155	40,390	37,902	38,064
Balance Sheet								
Current Assets	445,410	354,355	287,656	279,850	214,672	99,389	85,367	119,271
Total Assets	3,481,109	2,762,036	2,491,593	2,426,408	1,083,522	948,193	862,396	676,617
Current Liabilities	280,019	183,584	149,685	158,151	106,429	95,229	107,479	110,172
Long-Term Obligations	755,000	487,261	722,903	794,990	365,000	375,000	434,947	348,179
Total Liabilities	1,753,214	1,308,383	1,413,809	1,456,437	580,338	534,930	612,736	530,511
Stockholders' Equity	1,727,895	1,453,653	1,077,784	824,885	358,271	268,512	249,660	146,106
Shares Outstanding	64,525	63,757	61,006	53,675	40,644	40,264	40,121	33,537
Statistical Record								
Return on Assets %	8.36	11.08	4.35	5.01	8.57	2.44	N.M.	6.42
Return on Equity %	16.41	22.99	11.25	14.87	27.77	8.54	N.M.	29.30
EBITDA Margin %	66.07	74.79	69.77	62.09	59.77	55.58	26.95	60.64
Net Margin %	19.79	25.04	14.24	14.53	17.52	8.05	N.M.	12.96
Asset Turnover	0.42	0.44	0.31	0.35	0.49	0.30	0.26	0.50
Current Ratio	1.59	1.93	1.92	1.77	2.02	1.04	0.79	1.08
Debt to Equity	0.44	0.34	0.67	0.96	1.02	1.40	1.74	2.38
Price Range	50.97-39.66	49.50-34.29	38.75-23.00	34.00-20.85	32.63-18.56	23.25-9.06	34.69-10.13	48.88-27.75
P/E Ratio	12.55-9.77	10.90-7.55	21.89-12.99	20.99-12.87	16.73-9.52	42.27-16.48	N/A	46.11-26.18
Average Yield %	0.46	0.48	0.38	0.45	0.49	0.70	0.54	0.31

Address: 5 Greenway Plaza, P.O. Box 2504, Houston, TX 77252-2504 **Telephone:** (713) 297-5000 **Fax:** (713) 297-5100	**Web Site:** www.pogoproducing.com **Officers:** Paul G. Van Wagenen - Chmn., Pres., C.E.O. Stephen R. Brunner - Exec. V.P., Oper.	**Auditors:** PricewaterhouseCoopers LLP **Transfer Agents:** Computershare Investor Services, LLC

POLARIS INDUSTRIES INC.

Exchange	Symbol	Price	52Wk Range	Yield	P/E
NYS	PII	$70.23 (3/31/2005)	73.85-41.39	1.59	30.27

*7 Year Price Score 166.08 *NYSE Composite Index=100 *12 Month Price Score 117.70

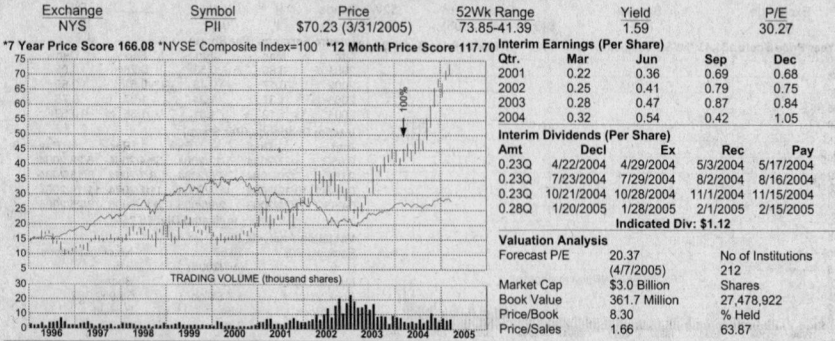

Interim Earnings (Per Share)

Qtr.	Mar	Jun	Sep	Dec
2001	0.22	0.36	0.69	0.68
2002	0.25	0.41	0.79	0.75
2003	0.28	0.47	0.87	0.84
2004	0.32	0.54	0.42	1.05

Interim Dividends (Per Share)

Amt	Decl	Ex	Rec	Pay
0.23Q	4/22/2004	4/29/2004	5/3/2004	5/17/2004
0.23Q	7/23/2004	7/29/2004	8/2/2004	8/16/2004
0.23Q	10/21/2004	10/28/2004	11/1/2004	11/15/2004
0.28Q	1/20/2005	1/28/2005	2/1/2005	2/15/2005

Indicated Div: $1.12

Valuation Analysis

Forecast P/E	20.37	No of Institutions	
	(4/7/2005)	212	
Market Cap	$3.0 Billion	Shares	
Book Value	361.7 Million	27,478,922	
Price/Book	8.30	% Held	
Price/Sales	1.66	63.87	

Business Summary: Automotive (MIC: 15.1 SIC: 799 NAIC: 36999)

Polaris Industries designs, engineers and manufactures snowmobiles, all-terrain vehicles (ATVs), motorcycles and personal watercraft, and markets them, together with related replacement parts, garments and accessories, through dealers and distributors in the U.S., Canada and Europe, and on the Internet. Co.'s full line of snowmobiles range from youth to economy to top performance and competition models. Co.'s line of ATVs include sport and four-wheel drive utility models. Co. has a six-wheel off-road utility vehicle and the Polaris RANGER™. Co. also manufactures a V-twin cruiser motorcycle, the Victory V92C. The Polaris Professional Series is a line of heavy duty Workmobiles™.

Recent Developments: For the year ended Dec 31 2004, net income decreased 5.8% to $104,504 thousand from net income of $110,929 thousand a year earlier. Revenues were $1,805,241 thousand, up 14.6% from $1,575,938 thousand the year before. Operating income was $211,637 thousand versus an income of $179,898 thousand in the prior year, an increase of 17.6%. Total direct expense was $1,348,943 thousand versus $1,189,475 thousand in the prior year, an increase of 13.4%. Total indirect expense was $244,661 thousand versus $206,565 thousand in the prior year, an increase of 18.4%.

Prospects: In 2005, Co. is looking to continue the momentum it generated in 2004 with even more new product introductions, a continued drive in technology development with the opening of its new research and development center in Wyoming, MN, and aggressive cost controls to help offset the higher commodity and transportation costs. Moreover, Co. intends to expand and improve in areas such as International, Victory motorcycles and its dealer network. For full-year 2005, Co. expects sales growth of 7.0% to 10.0% and earnings from continuing operations in the range of $3.28 to $3.42 per diluted share.

Financial Data
(US$ in Thousands)

	12/31/2004	12/31/2003	12/31/2002	12/31/2001	12/31/2000	12/31/1999	12/31/1998	12/31/1997
Earnings Per Share	2.32	2.46	2.19	1.94	1.75	1.53	0.59	1.23
Cash Flow Per Share	5.82	3.63	4.32	4.12	2.28	2.51	2.34	1.91
Tang Book Value Per Share	7.88	6.81	5.67	5.21	3.89	3.02	2.57	2.80
Dividends Per Share	0.920	0.620	0.560	0.500	0.440	0.400	0.360	0.320
Dividend Payout %	39.66	25.20	25.51	25.77	25.14	26.06	60.50	26.12
Income Statement								
Total Revenue	1,805,241	1,629,456	1,535,925	1,512,042	1,425,678	1,321,076	1,175,520	1,048,296
EBITDA	265,649	221,584	214,095	199,364	183,087	161,901	87,513	138,159
Depn & Amortn	59,339	54,780	57,527	52,550	46,997	39,281	36,192	33,168
Income Before Taxes	204,199	164,339	154,171	139,563	128,386	118,335	48,362	102,162
Income Taxes	67,386	53,410	50,579	48,149	45,577	42,009	17,347	36,779
Net Income	104,504	110,929	103,592	91,414	82,809	76,326	31,015	65,383
Average Shares	45,035	45,056	47,232	47,134	47,332	49,800	51,972	53,478
Balance Sheet								
Current Assets	465,655	387,716	343,659	305,317	240,912	214,714	183,840	217,458
Total Assets	792,925	671,352	608,646	565,163	490,186	442,027	378,697	384,746
Current Liabilities	405,193	330,478	313,513	308,337	238,384	233,800	204,964	191,111
Long-Term Obligations	18,000	18,008	18,027	18,043	47,068	40,000	20,500	24,400
Total Liabilities	431,193	351,974	331,540	326,380	285,452	273,800	225,464	215,511
Stockholders' Equity	361,732	319,378	277,106	238,783	204,734	168,227	153,233	169,235
Shares Outstanding	42,741	43,362	44,600	45,854	47,084	48,452	50,710	52,028
Statistical Record								
Return on Assets %	14.23	17.33	17.65	17.32	17.72	18.60	8.13	16.99
Return on Equity %	30.60	37.19	40.16	41.22	44.28	47.49	19.24	38.63
EBITDA Margin %	14.72	13.60	13.94	13.19	12.84	12.26	7.44	13.18
Net Margin %	5.79	6.81	6.74	6.05	5.81	5.78	2.64	6.24
Asset Turnover	2.46	2.55	2.62	2.87	3.05	3.22	3.08	2.72
Current Ratio	1.15	1.17	1.10	0.99	1.01	0.92	0.90	1.14
Debt to Equity	0.05	0.06	0.07	0.08	0.23	0.24	0.13	0.14
Price Range	68.93-40.00	45.40-22.18	38.00-26.94	29.05-18.50	20.53-12.97	22.81-13.50	19.59-12.38	16.63-11.13
P/E Ratio	29.71-17.24	18.45-9.02	17.35-12.30	14.97-9.53	11.73-7.41	14.91-8.82	33.21-20.97	13.52-9.04
Average Yield %	1.85	1.85	1.73	2.16	2.70	2.19	2.13	2.26

Address: 2100 Highway 55, Medina, MN 55340 Telephone: (763) 542-0500 Fax: (763) 542-0599	Web Site: www.polarisindustries.com Officers: Gregory R. Palen - Chmn. Thomas C. Tiller - Pres., C.E.O.	Auditors: Ernst & Young LLP Investor Contact: 763-513-3477

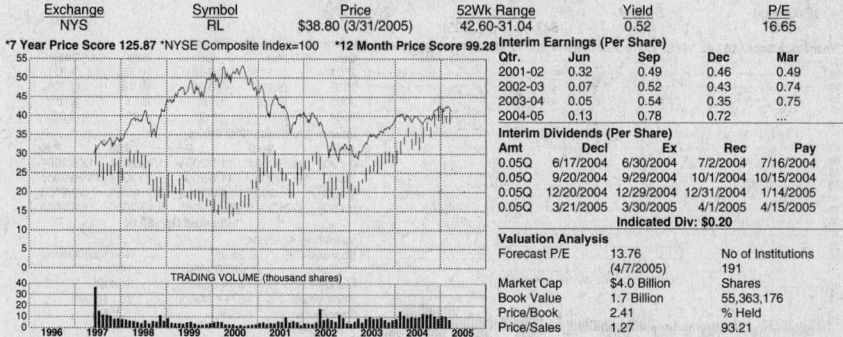

POLO RALPH LAUREN CORP.

Exchange	Symbol	Price	52Wk Range	Yield	P/E
NYS	RL	$38.80 (3/31/2005)	42.60-31.04	0.52	16.65

*7 Year Price Score 125.87 *NYSE Composite Index=100 *12 Month Price Score 99.28

Interim Earnings (Per Share)

Qtr.	Jun	Sep	Dec	Mar
2001-02	0.32	0.49	0.46	0.49
2002-03	0.07	0.52	0.43	0.74
2003-04	0.05	0.54	0.35	0.75
2004-05	0.13	0.78	0.72	...

Interim Dividends (Per Share)

Amt	Decl	Ex	Rec	Pay
0.05Q	6/17/2004	6/30/2004	7/2/2004	7/16/2004
0.05Q	9/20/2004	9/29/2004	10/1/2004	10/15/2004
0.05Q	12/20/2004	12/29/2004	12/31/2004	1/14/2005
0.05Q	3/21/2005	3/30/2005	4/1/2005	4/15/2005

Indicated Div: $0.20

Valuation Analysis

Forecast P/E	13.76 (4/7/2005)	No of Institutions	191
Market Cap	$4.0 Billion	Shares	55,363,176
Book Value	1.7 Billion	% Held	93.21
Price/Book	2.41		
Price/Sales	1.27		

Business Summary: Apparel (MIC: 4.4 SIC: 329 NAIC: 15211)

Polo Ralph Lauren designs, markets and distributes premium lifestyle products in four categories: apparel, home, accessories and fragrance. Apparel products include menswear, womenswear and children's clothing. Brand names include Polo by Ralph Lauren, Ralph Lauren Purple Label, Ralph Lauren, RALPH, Lauren, Polo Jeans Co., RL and Chaps, among others. The Ralph Lauren Home Collection offers products for the home, including bedding and bath products, interior decor, furniture and tabletop and gift items. Accessories include footwear, eyewear, jewelry and leather goods. Fragrance products are sold under Co.'s Polo, Lauren, Romance, Safari and Polo Sport brands, among others.

Recent Developments: For the quarter ended Jan 1 2005, net income increased 111.7% to $74,842 thousand from net income of $35,358 thousand in the year-earlier quarter. Revenues were $887,993 thousand, up 37.6% from $645,365 thousand the year before. Operating income was $114,834 thousand versus an income of $60,458 thousand in the prior-year quarter, an increase of 89.9%. Total direct expense was $449,960 thousand versus $312,363 thousand in the prior-year quarter, an increase of 44.1%. Total indirect expense was $323,199 thousand versus $272,544 thousand in the prior-year quarter, an increase of 18.6%.

Prospects: Co. is benefiting from its efforts to re-ignite its brands with new products and new markets. From the re-launch of Co.'s Lauren business to the completed consolidation of Co.'s European operations, all are supporting Co.'s goal of long-term growth on a global basis. Going forward, Co. will continue to focus on expense and capital spending, improving inventory management and increasing efficiencies generated by its ongoing infrastructure initiatives in hopes of strengthening the balance sheet. Co.'s initial outlook for fiscal 2006 is for mid-single-digit percent consolidated revenue growth. In addition, Co. expects earnings to be in the range of $2.75 to $2.85 per share.

Financial Data

(US$ in Thousands)	9 Mos	6 Mos	3 Mos	04/03/2004	03/29/2003	03/30/2002	03/31/2001	04/01/2000
Earnings Per Share	2.33	1.99	1.73	1.69	1.76	1.75	0.61	1.45
Cash Flow Per Share	3.80	3.02	2.96	2.09	2.74	3.02	1.04	2.46
Tang Book Value Per Share	10.11	9.25	8.38	10.56	8.93	7.38	5.76	5.07
Dividends Per Share	0.200	0.200	0.200	0.200	...	...	...	...
Dividend Payout %	8.57	10.07	11.53	11.83	...	...	...	...
Income Statement								
Total Revenue	2,364,423	1,476,430	592,750	2,649,654	2,439,340	2,363,707	2,225,774	1,955,528
EBITDA	335,787	193,685	42,845	355,121	366,533	378,951	201,666	330,191
Depn & Amortn	73,342	46,474	22,451	83,189	78,645	83,919	78,599	66,280
Income Before Taxes	256,774	143,536	18,764	261,932	274,386	275,999	97,954	248,886
Income Taxes	91,342	51,143	6,849	95,055	100,151	103,499	38,692	101,422
Net Income	168,652	93,810	13,403	170,954	174,235	172,500	59,262	143,497
Average Shares	104,325	103,571	102,802	100,960	99,263	98,522	97,446	98,926
Balance Sheet								
Current Assets	1,264,124	1,112,082	954,734	1,271,319	1,166,007	1,008,057	901,721	852,891
Total Assets	2,590,048	2,399,571	2,216,351	2,270,241	2,038,822	1,749,497	1,626,093	1,620,562
Current Liabilities	529,259	488,011	415,786	501,130	500,347	391,771	439,577	406,228
Long-Term Obligations	307,981	280,948	278,983	277,345	248,494	285,414	296,988	342,707
Total Liabilities	936,841	859,206	771,597	848,168	830,055	751,302	816,784	848,125
Stockholders' Equity	1,653,207	1,540,365	1,444,754	1,422,073	1,208,767	998,195	809,309	772,437
Shares Outstanding	102,601	101,842	101,115	100,632	98,722	98,227	97,177	97,529
Statistical Record								
Return on Assets %	10.19	9.17	8.39	7.81	9.22	10.25	3.66	10.56
Return on Equity %	16.34	14.47	13.20	12.79	15.83	19.14	7.51	20.11
EBITDA Margin %	14.20	13.12	7.23	13.40	15.03	16.03	9.06	16.89
Net Margin %	7.13	6.35	2.26	6.45	7.14	7.30	2.66	7.34
Asset Turnover	1.33	1.31	1.30	1.21	1.29	1.40	1.37	1.44
Current Ratio	2.39	2.28	2.30	2.54	2.33	2.57	2.05	2.10
Debt to Equity	0.19	0.18	0.19	0.20	0.21	0.29	0.37	0.44
Price Range	42.60-27.48	38.45-27.48	36.95-25.06	35.13-22.41	30.64-16.57	30.98-18.41	30.45-13.25	24.63-14.13
P/E Ratio	18.28-11.79	19.32-13.81	21.36-14.49	20.79-13.26	17.41-9.41	17.70-10.52	49.92-21.72	16.98-9.74
Average Yield %	0.57	0.62	0.65	0.71	...	...	...	...

Address: 650 Madison Avenue, New York, NY 10022
Telephone: (212) 318-7000
Fax: (212) 888-5780

Web Site: www.polo.com
Officers: Ralph Lauren - Chmn., C.E.O. F. Lance Isham - Vice-Chmn.

Auditors: Deloitte & Touche LLP
Investor Contact: 212-813-7862

POTLATCH CORP.

Exchange	Symbol	Price	52Wk Range	Yield	P/E
NYS	PCH	$47.07 (3/31/2005)	51.90-34.77	1.27	5.12

*7 Year Price Score 107.42 *NYSE Composite Index=100 *12 Month Price Score 100.28

Interim Earnings (Per Share)

Qtr.	Mar	Jun	Sep	Dec
2001	(1.11)	(0.35)	(0.23)	(1.12)
2002	(5.90)	(0.70)	(0.43)	(1.20)
2003	(0.33)	0.23	0.77	1.10
2004	0.74	1.68	7.05	(0.32)

Interim Dividends (Per Share)

Amt	Decl	Ex	Rec	Pay
0.15Q	9/20/2004	11/9/2004	11/12/2004	12/6/2004
2.50Q	10/25/2004	11/8/2004	11/10/2004	11/29/2004
0.15Q	1/11/2005	2/9/2005	2/11/2005	3/7/2005
0.15Q	2/24/2005	5/11/2005	5/13/2005	6/6/2005
		Indicated Div: $0.60		

Valuation Analysis

Forecast P/E	35.05	No of Institutions	
	(4/7/2005)	147	
Market Cap	$1.4 Billion	Shares	
Book Value	671.4 Million	20,568,000	
Price/Book	2.03	% Held	
Price/Sales	1.01	71.03	

Business Summary: Paper Products (MIC: 11.11 SIC: 621 NAIC: 22121)

Potlatch is a vertically integrated and diversified forest products company that owns and manages approximately 1.5 million acres of timberlands and operates 15 manufacturing facilities. Co. timberlands and all of its manufacturing facilities are located within the continental United States, primarily in Arkansas, Idaho and Minnesota, at Dec 31 2003. Co. is engaged principally in growing and harvesting timber and converting wood fiber into two broad product lines: commodity and specialty wood products; and bleached pulp products. Co.'s business is organized into four operating segments: Resource, Wood Products, Pulp and Paperboard, and Consumer Products.

Recent Developments: For the year ended Dec 31 2004, income from continuing operations was $15,330 thousand compared with a loss of $3,842 thousand a year earlier. Net income increased 434.7% to $271,249 thousand from net income of $50,727 thousand a year earlier. Revenues were $1,351,472 thousand, up 13.3% from $1,192,437 thousand the year before. Operating income was $92,729 thousand versus an income of $21,340 thousand in the prior year, an increase of 334.5%. Total indirect expense was $1,258,743 thousand versus $1,171,097 thousand in the prior year, an increase of 7.5%.

Prospects: Co.'s outlook is generally positive. For instance, lumber markets remain relatively firm, with selling prices for lumber and particleboard higher versus the fourth quarter of 2003. However, lumber shipments are being hampered by downtime at Co.'s Prescott sawmill due to log shortages caused by wet conditions. Pulp and Paperboard market conditions remain encouraging due to increased shipments and higher prices. In addition, production rate gains at Co.'s Lewiston, ID facility are contributing positively to its bottom line. Meanwhile, although markets for consumer tissue products remain competitive, net selling prices are improving due to the addition of Co.'s new ultra towel product.

Financial Data

(US$ in Thousands)	12/31/2004	12/31/2003	12/31/2002	12/31/2001	12/31/2000	12/31/1999	12/31/1998	12/31/1997
Earnings Per Share	9.19	1.77	(8.23)	(2.81)	(1.16)	1.41	1.28	1.24
Cash Flow Per Share	(0.78)	6.32	(2.43)	3.01	3.28	7.06	7.50	5.35
Tang Book Value Per Share	23.22	16.33	15.07	24.98	28.69	31.79	32.19	32.82
Dividends Per Share	3.100	0.600	0.600	1.170	1.740	1.740	1.740	1.710
Dividend Payout %	33.73	33.90	N.M.	N.M.	N.M.	123.40	135.94	137.90
Income Statement								
Total Revenue	1,351,472	1,506,634	1,286,217	1,751,996	1,808,770	1,676,838	1,565,878	1,568,870
EBITDA	67,543	114,637	(25,554)	(54,972)	4,989	111,486	107,919	100,759
Income Before Taxes	25,297	80,555	(83,497)	(130,238)	(54,449)	66,044	58,175	54,635
Income Taxes	9,967	27,334	(32,564)	(50,793)	(21,235)	25,097	20,943	18,576
Net Income	271,249	50,727	(234,381)	(79,445)	(33,214)	40,947	37,232	36,059
Average Shares	29,514	28,718	28,461	28,281	28,522	28,967	29,019	28,985
Balance Sheet								
Current Assets	407,370	330,619	347,764	511,668	483,839	416,502	407,855	403,777
Total Assets	1,594,672	1,597,377	1,616,326	2,487,146	2,542,445	2,446,500	2,377,306	2,365,136
Current Liabilities	152,305	169,817	245,071	356,452	439,099	364,746	310,299	297,556
Long-Term Obligations	335,415	618,278	622,645	1,017,522	801,549	701,798	712,113	722,080
Total Liabilities	923,283	1,126,526	1,185,535	1,779,842	1,729,209	1,525,461	1,446,400	1,413,544
Stockholders' Equity	671,389	470,851	430,791	707,304	813,236	921,039	930,906	951,592
Shares Outstanding	28,919	28,840	28,578	28,311	28,346	28,972	28,918	28,994
Statistical Record								
Return on Assets %	16.95	3.16	N.M.	N.M.	N.M.	1.67	1.57	1.56
Return on Equity %	47.36	11.25	N.M.	N.M.	N.M.	4.45	4.00	3.78
EBITDA Margin %	5.00	7.61	N.M.	N.M.	0.28	6.65	6.89	6.42
Net Margin %	20.07	3.37	N.M.	N.M.	N.M.	2.44	2.38	2.30
Asset Turnover	0.84	0.94	0.63	0.70	0.72	0.68	0.66	0.68
Current Ratio	2.67	1.95	1.42	1.44	1.10	1.14	1.31	1.36
Debt to Equity	0.50	1.31	1.45	1.44	0.99	0.76	0.76	0.76
Price Range	51.90-34.77	35.95-18.75	36.13-23.88	36.22-24.90	44.63-28.94	45.38-32.75	47.94-31.25	52.75-39.38
P/E Ratio	5.65-3.78	20.31-10.59	...	...	...	32.18-23.23	37.45-24.41	42.54-31.75
Average Yield %	7.37	2.27	1.98	3.73	4.83	4.36	4.31	3.77

Address: 601 West Riverside Avenue, Suite 1100, Spokane, WA 99201 **Telephone:** (509) 835-1500	**Web Site:** www.potlatchcorp.com **Officers:** L. Pendleton Siegel - Chmn., C.E.O. Richard L. Paulson - Pres., C.O.O.	**Auditors:** KMPG LLP **Investor Contact:** 509-835-1500

PPG INDUSTRIES, INC.

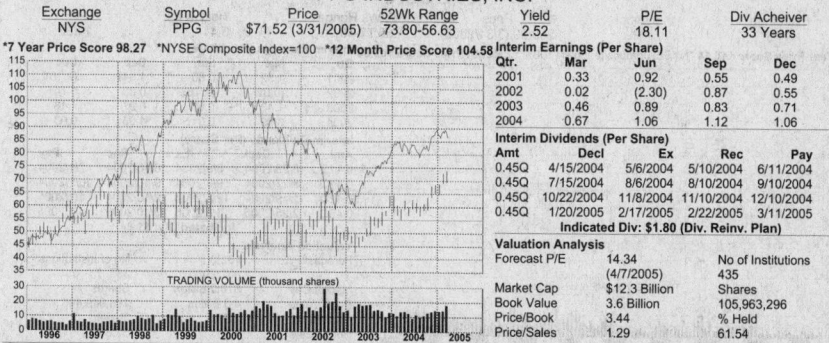

Exchange	Symbol	Price	52Wk Range	Yield	P/E	Div Acheiver
NYS	PPG	$71.52 (3/31/2005)	73.80-56.63	2.52	18.11	33 Years

*7 Year Price Score 98.27   *NYSE Composite Index=100   *12 Month Price Score 104.58

Interim Earnings (Per Share)

Qtr.	Mar	Jun	Sep	Dec
2001	0.33	0.92	0.55	0.49
2002	0.02	(2.30)	0.87	0.55
2003	0.46	0.89	0.83	0.71
2004	0.67	1.06	1.12	1.06

Interim Dividends (Per Share)

Amt	Decl	Ex	Rec	Pay
0.45Q	4/15/2004	5/6/2004	5/10/2004	6/11/2004
0.45Q	7/15/2004	8/6/2004	8/10/2004	9/10/2004
0.45Q	10/22/2004	11/8/2004	11/10/2004	12/10/2004
0.45Q	1/20/2005	2/17/2005	2/22/2005	3/11/2005

Indicated Div: $1.80 (Div. Reinv. Plan)

Valuation Analysis

Forecast P/E	14.34	No of Institutions
	(4/7/2005)	435
Market Cap	$12.3 Billion	Shares
Book Value	3.6 Billion	105,963,296
Price/Book	3.44	% Held
Price/Sales	1.29	61.54

Business Summary: Chemicals (MIC: 11.1 SIC: 851 NAIC: 25510)

PPG Industries is comprised of three basic business segments: coatings, glass and chemicals. Within these business segments, Co. has focused resources on industrial, aerospace, packaging, architectural, automotive original and refinish coatings; flat glass, automotive original and replacement glass, and continuous-strand fiber glass; and chlor-alkali and specialty chemicals. The coatings businesses operate production facilities around the world. Co.'s principal glass production facilities are in North America and Europe. The chemicals businesses operate production facilities around the world including five plants in the United States and one each in Canada and Mexico.

Recent Developments: For the year ended Dec 31 2004, net income increased 38.3% to $683,000 thousand from net income of $494,000 thousand a year earlier. Revenues were $9,513,000 thousand, up 8.6% from $8,756,000 thousand the year before. Total direct expense was $5,999,000 thousand versus $5,521,000 thousand in the prior year, an increase of 8.7%. Total indirect expense was $2,492,000 thousand versus $2,388,000 thousand in the prior year, an increase of 4.4%.

Prospects: Co.'s prospects appear moderately positive, reflecting expectations of favorable global economic conditions that should lead to continued sales growth in 2005. However, Co.'s outlook is somewhat tempered by cost issues that include pensions, other postretirement benefits, natural gas and raw materials. Co. noted that while it has consistently focused on reducing its costs, it continues to be challenged by higher costs for employee benefits, particularly pensions and medical. Meanwhile, Co. plans to address the issue of rising raw material costs by seeking alternate supply sources, reformulating its products, improving its production processes and yields and raising its selling prices.

Financial Data

(US$ in Thousands)	12/31/2004	12/31/2003	12/31/2002	12/31/2001	12/31/2000	12/31/1999	12/31/1998	12/31/1997
Earnings Per Share	3.95	2.89	(0.41)	2.29	3.57	3.23	4.48	3.94
Cash Flow Per Share	5.91	6.61	5.16	6.30	5.04	5.19	5.27	5.55
Tang Book Value Per Share	10.81	7.37	3.48	9.12	8.61	8.30	13.17	21.29
Dividends Per Share	1.790	1.730	1.700	1.680	1.600	1.520	1.420	1.330
Dividend Payout %	45.32	59.86	N.M.	73.36	44.82	47.06	31.70	33.76
Income Statement								
Total Revenue	9,513,000	8,756,000	8,067,000	8,169,000	8,629,000	7,995,000	7,510,000	7,379,000
EBITDA	1,529,000	1,334,000	489,000	1,267,000	1,629,000	1,517,000	1,775,000	1,645,000
Depn & Amortn	388,000	394,000	398,000	447,000	447,000	419,000	383,000	373,000
Income Before Taxes	1,063,000	843,000	(28,000)	666,000	1,017,000	973,000	1,294,000	1,175,000
Income Taxes	322,000	293,000	(7,000)	247,000	369,000	377,000	466,000	435,000
Net Income	683,000	494,000	(69,000)	387,000	620,000	568,000	801,000	714,000
Average Shares	173,000	170,900	169,900	168,300	172,300	175,500	178,700	181,500
Balance Sheet								
Current Assets	4,054,000	3,537,000	2,945,000	2,703,000	3,093,000	3,062,000	2,660,000	2,584,000
Total Assets	8,932,000	8,424,000	7,863,000	8,452,000	9,125,000	8,914,000	7,387,000	6,868,000
Current Liabilities	2,221,000	2,139,000	1,920,000	1,955,000	2,543,000	2,384,000	1,912,000	1,662,000
Long-Term Obligations	1,184,000	1,339,000	1,699,000	1,699,000	1,810,000	1,836,000	1,081,000	1,257,000
Total Liabilities	5,264,000	5,376,000	5,582,000	5,250,000	5,900,000	5,710,000	4,420,000	4,277,000
Stockholders' Equity	3,572,000	2,911,000	2,150,000	3,080,000	3,097,000	3,106,000	2,880,000	2,509,000
Shares Outstanding	172,001	170,926	169,442	168,713	168,222	173,988	175,000	117,826
Statistical Record								
Return on Assets %	7.85	6.07	N.M.	4.40	6.86	6.97	10.84	10.40
Return on Equity %	21.01	19.52	N.M.	12.53	19.94	18.98	27.82	28.46
EBITDA Margin %	16.07	15.24	6.06	15.51	18.88	18.97	23.64	22.29
Net Margin %	7.18	5.64	N.M.	4.74	7.19	7.10	10.67	9.68
Asset Turnover	1.09	1.08	0.99	0.93	0.95	0.98	1.02	1.07
Current Ratio	1.83	1.65	1.53	1.38	1.22	1.28	1.39	1.55
Debt to Equity	0.33	0.46	0.79	0.55	0.58	0.59	0.38	0.50
Price Range	68.55-55.18	64.42-42.64	62.44-41.41	59.54-40.71	64.38-36.13	69.69-48.06	76.31-50.50	67.19-49.00
P/E Ratio	17.35-13.97	22.29-14.75	N/A	26.00-17.78	18.03-10.12	21.58-14.88	17.03-11.27	17.05-12.44
Average Yield %	2.94	3.31	3.24	3.27	3.39	2.57	2.27	2.29

Address: One PPG Place, Pittsburgh, PA 15272	**Web Site:** www.ppg.com	**Auditors:** Deloitte & Touche LLP
Telephone: (412) 434-3131	**Officers:** Raymond W. LeBoeuf - Chmn., C.E.O.	**Investor Contact:** 412-434-3318
Fax: (412) 434-2571	Charles E. Bunch - Pres., C.O.O.	**Transfer Agents:** Mellon Investor Services LLC, Ridgefield Park, NJ

PPL CORP

Exchange	Symbol	Price	52Wk Range	Yield	P/E
NYS	PPL	$53.99 (3/31/2005)	55.77-40.00	3.41	14.32

*7 Year Price Score 116.14 *NYSE Composite Index=100 *12 Month Price Score 103.08

TRADING VOLUME (thousand shares)

Interim Earnings (Per Share)
Qtr.	Mar	Jun	Sep	Dec
2001	1.52	0.80	1.04	(2.15)
2002	(0.02)	(0.18)	0.80	0.74
2003	1.43	0.67	0.97	1.18
2004	0.99	0.81	1.03	0.93

Interim Dividends (Per Share)
Amt	Decl	Ex	Rec	Pay
0.41Q	5/28/2004	6/8/2004	6/10/2004	7/1/2004
0.41Q	8/27/2004	9/8/2004	9/10/2004	10/1/2004
0.41Q	11/19/2004	12/8/2004	12/10/2004	1/1/2005
0.46Q	2/25/2005	3/8/2005	3/10/2005	4/1/2005

Indicated Div: $1.84

Valuation Analysis
Forecast P/E	13.20	No of Institutions
	(4/7/2005)	337
Market Cap	$10.2 Billion	Shares
Book Value	4.3 Billion	108,949,448
Price/Book	2.38	% Held
Price/Sales	1.76	57.63

Business Summary: Electricity (MIC: 7.1 SIC: 911 NAIC: 21122)

PPL is an energy and utility holding company. Through its subsidiaries, Co. generates electricity from power plants in the northeastern and western U.S.; markets wholesale or retail energy primarily in the northeastern and western portions of the U.S.; delivers electricity to nearly 5.0 million customers in Pennsylvania, the U.K. and Latin America; and provides energy services for businesses in the mid-Atlantic and northeastern U.S. Co.'s significant subsidiaries include PPL Energy Supply, PPL Electric, PPL Gas Utilities, PPL Global, PPL EnergyPlus, and PPL Generation.

Recent Developments: For the year ended Dec 31 2004, income from continuing operations decreased 2.6% to $700,000 thousand from income of $719,000 thousand a year earlier. Net income decreased 4.9% to $698,000 thousand from net income of $734,000 thousand a year earlier. Revenues were $5,812,000 thousand, up 3.9% from $5,596,000 thousand the year before. Operating income was $1,387,000 thousand versus an income of $1,340,000 thousand in the prior year, an increase of 3.5%. Total direct expense was $3,609,000 thousand versus $3,500,000 thousand in the prior year, an increase of 3.1%. Total indirect expense was $816,000 thousand versus $756,000 thousand in the prior year, an increase of 7.9%.

Prospects: On Feb 2 2005, Co. reaffirmed its full-year 2005 forecast of $3.80 to $4.20 in earnings per share from ongoing operations. Co. projects that 55.0% to 60.0% of its total earnings from ongoing operations in 2005 will come from its supply business segment and that 20.0% to 25.0% of earnings in 2005 will come from each of its international delivery and Pennsylvania delivery business segments. The 2005 forecast assumes, among other things, a combined 7.1% rise in distribution rates and transmission charges for its Pennsylvania electricity delivery business, beginning Jan 1 2005; modest load growth in its Pennsylvania electricity delivery business; and flat energy margins for its supply business.

Financial Data
(US$ in Thousands)	12/31/2004	12/31/2003	12/31/2002	12/31/2001	12/31/2000	12/31/1999	12/31/1998	12/31/1997
Earnings Per Share	3.77	4.24	1.36	1.22	3.44	2.84	(3.46)	1.80
Cash Flow Per Share	7.78	7.75	5.22	6.22	5.98	4.23	3.87	4.71
Tang Book Value Per Share	15.00	11.06	9.32	12.67	13.87	11.23	11.37	16.82
Dividends Per Share	1.640	1.540	1.440	1.060	1.060	1.000	1.335	1.670
Dividend Payout %	43.50	36.32	105.88	86.89	30.81	35.21	N.M.	92.78
Income Statement								
Total Revenue	5,812,000	5,587,000	5,429,000	5,725,000	5,683,000	4,590,000	3,786,000	3,049,000
EBITDA	2,043,000	2,024,000	1,760,000	1,345,000	1,569,000	1,181,000	1,289,000	578,000
Depn & Amortn	654,000	624,000	487,000	478,000	382,000	212,000	396,000	445,000
Income Before Taxes	905,000	925,000	713,000	480,000	811,000	692,000	663,000	...
Income Taxes	195,000	170,000	210,000	261,000	294,000	174,000	259,000	238,000
Net Income	698,000	734,000	275,000	231,000	524,000	458,000	(544,000)	296,000
Average Shares	184,993	173,392	152,809	146,614	144,781	152,287	164,651	165,000
Balance Sheet								
Net PPE	11,209,000	10,446,000	9,566,000	6,135,000	5,948,000	5,644,000	4,480,000	6,820,000
Total Assets	17,761,000	17,123,000	15,569,000	12,574,000	12,360,000	11,174,000	9,607,000	9,485,000
Long-Term Obligations	6,881,000	8,145,000	5,901,000	5,081,000	4,467,000	3,756,000	3,092,000	2,698,000
Total Liabilities	13,471,000	13,813,000	13,263,000	10,635,000	10,251,000	9,464,000	7,720,000	6,579,000
Stockholders' Equity	4,290,000	3,310,000	2,306,000	1,939,000	2,109,000	1,710,000	1,887,000	2,906,000
Shares Outstanding	189,122	177,362	167,451	146,581	145,041	143,697	157,412	167,000
Statistical Record								
Return on Assets %	3.99	4.49	1.95	1.85	4.44	4.41	N.M.	3.10
Return on Equity %	18.32	26.14	12.96	11.41	27.37	25.47	N.M.	9.68
EBITDA Margin %	35.15	36.23	32.42	23.49	27.61	25.73	34.05	...
Net Margin %	12.01	13.14	5.07	4.03	9.22	9.98	(14.37)	9.71
PPE Turnover	0.54	0.56	0.69	0.95	0.98	0.91	0.67	0.44
Asset Turnover	0.33	0.34	0.39	0.46	0.48	0.44	0.40	0.32
Debt to Equity	1.60	2.46	2.56	2.62	2.12	2.20	1.64	0.93
Price Range	53.77-40.00	44.00-32.27	39.61-26.70	62.22-31.19	45.81-18.50	31.75-20.38	28.94-20.94	24.19-19.00
P/E Ratio	14.26-10.61	10.38-7.61	29.12-19.63	51.00-25.57	13.32-5.38	11.18-7.17	N/A	13.44-10.56
Average Yield %	3.52	3.95	4.25	2.40	3.63	3.69	5.51	7.78

Address: Two North Ninth Street, Allentown, PA 18101-1179	**Web Site:** www.pplweb.com	**Auditors:** PricewaterhouseCoopers LLP
Telephone: (610) 774-5151	**Officers:** William F. Hecht - Chmn., Pres., C.E.O.	**Investor Contact:** 800-345-3085
Fax: (610) 774-5106	John R. Biggar - Exec. V.P., C.F.O.	**Transfer Agents:** Wells Fargo Bank, N.A., South St. Paul, MN

PRAXAIR, INC.

Exchange	Symbol	Price	52Wk Range	Yield	P/E	Div Acheiver
NYS	PX	$47.86 (3/31/2005)	48.31-34.93	1.50	22.79	12 Years

*7 Year Price Score 130.07 *NYSE Composite Index=100 *12 Month Price Score 102.48

Interim Earnings (Per Share)

Qtr.	Mar	Jun	Sep	Dec
2001	0.38	0.39	0.19	0.36
2002	0.39	0.46	0.40	0.42
2003	0.40	0.46	0.46	0.47
2004	0.49	0.53	0.53	0.54

Interim Dividends (Per Share)

Amt	Decl	Ex	Rec	Pay
0.15Q	4/28/2004	6/3/2004	6/7/2004	6/15/2004
0.15Q	7/27/2004	9/2/2004	9/7/2004	9/15/2004
0.15Q	10/26/2004	12/3/2004	12/7/2004	12/15/2004
0.18Q	1/25/2005	3/3/2005	3/7/2005	3/15/2005

Indicated Div: $0.72 (Div. Reinv. Plan)

Valuation Analysis

Forecast P/E	19.90 (4/6/2005)	No of Institutions 493
Market Cap	$15.5 Billion	Shares
Book Value	3.6 Billion	258,983,680
Price/Book	4.29	% Held
Price/Sales	2.35	80.33

Business Summary: Chemicals (MIC: 11.1 SIC: 813 NAIC: 25120)

Praxair is one of the largest global suppliers of industrial gases, particularly in North and South America, and has a growing business in Asia and southern Europe. Co.'s primary products are atmospheric gases (oxygen, nitrogen, argon, and rare gases) and process gases (carbon dioxide, helium, hydrogen, electronics gases, and acetylene). Co. also designs, engineers, and builds equipment that produces industrial gases for internal use and external sales. Co.'s surface technology segment supplies wear-resistant and high-temperature corrosion-resistant metallic and ceramic coatings and powders. Co. serves approximately 25 diverse industries.

Recent Developments: For the year ended Dec 31 2004, net income increased 19.1% to $697,000 thousand from net income of $585,000 thousand a year earlier. Revenues were $6,594,000 thousand, up 17.5% from $5,613,000 thousand the year before. Operating income was $1,103,000 thousand versus an income of $922,000 thousand in the prior year, an increase of 19.6%. Total direct expense was $3,987,000 thousand versus $3,328,000 thousand in the prior year, an increase of 19.8%. Total indirect expense was $2,111,000 thousand versus $1,891,000 thousand in the prior year, an increase of 11.6%.

Prospects: Co. is targeting first-quarter 2005 earnings per share in the range of $0.56 to $0.58. Looking ahead, Co. is projecting full-year 2005 sales and operating profit growth of between 11.0% and 15.0% year over year, along with diluted earnings in the range of $2.33 to $2.45 per share. Continued strong operating results in 2005 are expected to be driven by Co.'s growing hydrogen business, a record pipeline of new contracts and projects under construction, and increased price realization. Separately, on Dec 3 2004, Co. announced that it has completed its acquisition of certain industrial gas assets and related businesses in Germany from Air Liquide S.A. for approximately $650.0 million.

Financial Data
(US$ in Thousands)

	12/31/2004	12/31/2003	12/31/2002	12/31/2001	12/31/2000	12/31/1999	12/31/1998	12/31/1997
Earnings Per Share	2.10	1.77	1.24	1.31	1.13	1.33	1.30	1.23
Cash Flow Per Share	3.80	3.48	3.07	3.16	2.82	2.99	2.95	2.38
Tang Book Value Per Share	6.08	6.00	4.02	4.00	3.95	3.70	3.36	2.89
Dividends Per Share	0.600	0.458	0.380	0.340	0.310	0.280	0.250	0.220
Dividend Payout %	28.57	25.85	30.65	25.86	27.56	21.05	19.23	17.89
Income Statement								
Total Revenue	6,594,000	5,613,000	5,128,000	5,158,000	5,043,000	4,639,000	4,833,000	4,735,000
EBITDA	1,681,000	1,439,000	1,406,000	1,299,000	1,178,000	1,276,000	1,323,000	1,282,000
Depn & Amortn	578,000	517,000	483,000	499,000	471,000	445,000	467,000	444,000
Income Before Taxes	948,000	771,000	717,000	576,000	483,000	627,000	596,000	622,000
Income Taxes	232,000	174,000	158,000	135,000	103,000	152,000	127,000	151,000
Net Income	697,000	585,000	409,000	430,000	363,000	431,000	425,000	405,000
Average Shares	331,403	330,991	329,490	327,014	322,184	324,444	326,712	328,106
Balance Sheet								
Current Assets	1,744,000	1,449,000	1,286,000	1,276,000	1,361,000	1,335,000	1,394,000	1,497,000
Total Assets	9,878,000	8,305,000	7,401,000	7,715,000	7,762,000	7,722,000	8,096,000	7,810,000
Current Liabilities	1,875,000	1,117,000	1,100,000	1,194,000	1,439,000	1,725,000	1,289,000	1,366,000
Long-Term Obligations	2,876,000	2,661,000	2,510,000	2,725,000	2,641,000	2,111,000	2,895,000	2,874,000
Total Liabilities	6,045,000	5,022,000	4,897,000	5,077,000	5,247,000	4,998,000	5,202,000	5,092,000
Stockholders' Equity	3,608,000	3,088,000	2,340,000	2,477,000	2,357,000	2,290,000	2,332,000	2,122,000
Shares Outstanding	323,620	326,085	324,536	324,285	318,758	318,095	315,142	314,746
Statistical Record								
Return on Assets %	7.65	7.45	5.41	5.56	4.68	5.45	5.34	5.28
Return on Equity %	20.76	21.55	16.98	17.79	15.58	18.65	19.08	20.02
EBITDA Margin %	25.49	25.64	27.42	25.18	23.36	27.51	27.37	27.07
Net Margin %	10.57	10.42	7.98	8.34	7.20	9.29	8.79	8.55
Asset Turnover	0.72	0.71	0.68	0.67	0.65	0.59	0.61	0.62
Current Ratio	0.93	1.30	1.17	1.07	0.95	0.77	1.08	1.10
Debt to Equity	0.80	0.86	1.07	1.10	1.12	0.92	1.24	1.35
Price Range	45.97-34.70	38.20-25.33	30.30-22.81	27.64-18.65	27.25-15.84	29.06-16.16	26.78-15.63	28.78-20.47
P/E Ratio	21.89-16.52	21.58-14.31	24.43-18.39	21.10-14.24	24.12-14.02	21.85-12.15	20.60-12.02	23.40-16.64
Average Yield %	1.52	1.48	1.37	1.44	1.54	1.26	1.15	0.89

Address: 39 Old Ridgebury Rd., Danbury, CT 06810-5113	Web Site: www.praxair.com	Auditors: PricewaterhouseCoopers LLP
Telephone: (203) 837-2000	Officers: Dennis H. Reilley - Chmn., Pres., C.E.O. Stephen F. Angel - Exec. V.P.	Investor Contact: 203-837-2210
Fax: (203) 837-2450		Transfer Agents: Registrar and Transfer Company, Cranford, NJ

PRECISION CASTPARTS CORP.

Exchange	Symbol	Price	52Wk Range	Yield	P/E
NYS	PCP	$77.01 (3/31/2005)	78.39-42.14	0.16	N/A

*7 Year Price Score 156.80 *NYSE Composite Index=100 *12 Month Price Score 117.07

Interim Earnings (Per Share)

Qtr.	Jun	Sep	Dec	Mar
2001-02	0.77	0.23	(1.15)	0.94
2002-03	0.78	0.50	0.69	0.39
2003-04	0.64	0.27	0.49	0.65
2004-05	0.81	(2.76)	0.93	...

Interim Dividends (Per Share)

Amt	Decl	Ex	Rec	Pay
0.03Q	6/5/2002	6/5/2002	6/7/2002	7/1/2002
0.03Q	8/14/2002	9/4/2002	9/6/2002	9/30/2002
0.03Q	11/12/2002	12/4/2002	12/6/2002	1/2/2003
0.03Q	2/12/2003	3/5/2003	3/7/2003	3/31/2003

Indicated Div: $0.12

Valuation Analysis

Forecast P/E	17.80	No of Institutions	
	(4/7/2005)	243	
Market Cap	$5.1 Billion	Shares	
Book Value	1.7 Billion	56,534,296	
Price/Book	2.97	% Held	
Price/Sales	1.79	85.57	

Business Summary: Metal Works (MIC: 11.3 SIC: 324 NAIC: 31512)

Precision Castparts is a global manufacturer of metal components and products. In addition, Co. serves the fluid management, metalworking tools and machines, pulp and paper, advanced metalforming technologies, airframe and military components, and other metal products markets. Investment Cast Products include the PCC Structurals, PCC Airfoils and Wyman-Gordon Castings businesses. Forged Products comprises all of the forging businesses of Wyman-Gordon. Fluid Management Products is Co.'s PCC Flow Technologies operation. The Industrial Products segment includes PCC Specialty Products, Inc., J&L Fiber Services, Inc., Advanced Forming Technology and Reed-Rico.

Recent Developments: For the quarter ended Jan 2 2005, income from continuing operations increased 141.6% to $62,100 thousand from income of $25,700 thousand in the year-earlier quarter. Net income increased 121.9% to $61,700 thousand from net income of $27,800 thousand in the year-earlier quarter. Revenues were $743,900 thousand, up 65.2% from $450,200 thousand the year before. Total direct expense was $575,800 thousand versus $348,600 thousand in the prior-year quarter, an increase of 65.2%. Total indirect expense was $58,800 thousand versus $37,300 thousand in the prior-year quarter, an increase of 57.6%.

Prospects: Going forward, improved economic conditions in the aerospace and power generation markets should lead to increased sales in the Investment Cast Products and Forged Products segments. In addition, continued expansion of Co.'s metal injection molding technology in the automotive sector and strength in the pulp and paper market should contribute to higher sales in the Industrial Products segment. Separately, on Jan 25 2005, Co. agreed to acquire Air Industries Corp., a manufacturer of airframe fasteners, and the assets of Air Tuf Products, Inc. for $194.0 million. Co. expects the transaction to close in the fourth quarter of fiscal 2005.

Financial Data

(US$ in Thousands)	9 Mos	6 Mos	3 Mos	03/28/2004	03/30/2003	03/31/2002	04/01/2001	04/02/2000
Earnings Per Share	(0.41)	(0.81)	2.23	2.05	2.35	0.81	2.45	1.74
Cash Flow Per Share	4.79	3.18	3.03	2.79	4.76	6.03	3.56	3.61
Tang Book Value Per Share	4.12	2.58	2.04	1.24	1.32	N.M.	N.M.	N.M.
Dividends Per Share	0.120	0.120	0.120	0.120	0.120	0.120	0.120	0.120
Dividend Payout %	...	...	5.39	5.85	5.11	14.81	4.90	6.92
Income Statement								
Total Revenue	2,109,500	1,365,600	738,800	2,174,700	2,117,200	2,557,400	2,326,300	1,673,700
EBITDA	372,600	238,300	120,100	352,300	380,000	271,300	392,000	259,900
Depn & Amortn	72,000	47,000	26,500	85,800	80,000	70,100	102,400	74,200
Income Before Taxes	256,900	161,900	78,900	212,400	243,600	135,000	208,600	138,600
Income Taxes	86,100	53,400	26,000	75,800	83,400	92,600	83,700	53,300
Net Income	(67,700)	(129,400)	53,600	117,900	124,300	42,400	124,900	85,300
Average Shares	66,600	66,200	65,800	57,600	53,000	52,300	50,900	49,200
Balance Sheet								
Current Assets	1,414,600	1,293,800	1,262,400	1,187,500	785,900	878,500	863,100	751,900
Total Assets	3,702,200	3,606,300	3,819,900	3,756,200	2,467,200	2,564,900	2,572,900	2,415,700
Current Liabilities	957,900	959,100	945,700	912,800	624,800	727,100	656,700	591,500
Long-Term Obligations	747,100	767,700	803,800	823,000	532,100	697,000	838,500	884,500
Total Liabilities	1,988,700	2,015,900	2,049,600	2,041,600	1,405,500	1,613,100	1,671,100	1,641,800
Stockholders' Equity	1,713,500	1,590,400	1,770,300	1,714,600	1,061,700	951,800	901,800	773,900
Shares Outstanding	66,067	65,150	64,930	64,695	52,758	52,158	51,340	24,643
Statistical Record								
Return on Assets %	N.M.	N.M.	4.36	3.80	4.95	1.66	5.02	4.34
Return on Equity %	N.M.	N.M.	9.54	8.52	12.38	4.59	14.95	11.41
EBITDA Margin %	17.66	17.45	16.26	16.20	17.95	10.61	16.85	15.53
Net Margin %	N.M.	N.M.	7.26	5.42	5.87	1.66	5.37	5.10
Asset Turnover	0.77	0.88	0.77	0.70	0.84	1.00	0.94	0.85
Current Ratio	1.48	1.35	1.33	1.30	1.26	1.21	1.31	1.27
Debt to Equity	0.44	0.48	0.45	0.48	0.50	0.73	0.93	1.14
Price Range	67.45-42.00	60.22-34.90	53.17-30.50	49.18-23.83	37.57-17.20	48.80-18.30	43.00-18.30	23.56-11.75
P/E Ratio	...	...	23.84-13.68	23.99-11.62	15.99-7.32	60.25-22.59	17.55-7.50	13.54-6.75
Average Yield %	0.23	0.25	0.29	0.32	0.45	0.37	0.37	0.72

Address: 4650 S.W. Macadam Avenue, Suite 440, Portland, OR 97239-4252	**Web Site:** www.precast.com	**Auditors:** PricewaterhouseCoopers LLP
Telephone: (503) 417-4800	**Officers:** Mark Donegan - Chmn., Pres., C.E.O.	**Investor Contact:** 503-417-4850
Fax: (503) 417-4817	Gregory M. Delaney - Exec. V.P., Special Projects	**Transfer Agents:** The Bank of New York, New York, NY

PREMCOR INC.

Exchange	Symbol	Price	52Wk Range	Yield	P/E
NYS	PCO	$59.68 (3/31/2005)	59.68-29.71	0.13	10.81

*7 Year Price Score N/A   ***NYSE Composite Index=100**   ***12 Month Price Score 125.48**

Interim Earnings (Per Share)

Qtr.	Mar	Jun	Sep	Dec
2001		----4.49----		
2002	(3.13)	(0.82)	(0.43)	0.92
2003	0.54	0.43	0.76	(0.16)
2004	0.66	1.53	1.55	1.69

Interim Dividends (Per Share)

Amt	Decl	Ex	Rec	Pay
0.02Q	10/27/2004	11/29/2004	12/1/2004	12/15/2004
0.02Q	1/27/2005	2/25/2005	3/1/2005	3/15/2005

Indicated Div: $0.08

Valuation Analysis

Forecast P/E	12.40	No of Institutions
	(4/7/2005)	165
Market Cap	$5.3 Billion	Shares
Book Value	2.1 Billion	68,872,584
Price/Book	2.49	% Held
Price/Sales	0.35	77.20

TRADING VOLUME (thousand shares)

Business Summary: Oil and Gas (MIC: 14.2 SIC: 911 NAIC: 24110)

Premcor is a independent petroleum refiner and supplier of unbranded transportation fuels, heating oil, petrochemical feedstocks, petroleum coke and other petroleum products. As of Dec 31 2004, Co. owned and operated refineries in Port Arthur, TX; Memphis, TN; Lima, OH; and Delaware City, DE; with a combined crude oil volume processing capacity of about 800,000 barrels per day. Co. sells petroleum products in the Midwest, the Gulf Coast, Northeastern and Southeastern U.S. Co. sells its products on an unbranded basis to about 1,200 distributors and chain retailers through its own product distribution system and a third-party owned product distribution system, as well as in the spot market.

Recent Developments: For the year ended Dec 31 2004, income from continuing operations increased 290.5% to $483,500 thousand from income of $123,800 thousand a year earlier. Net income increased 309.9% to $477,900 thousand from net income of $116,600 thousand a year earlier. Revenues were $15,334,800 thousand, up 74.2% from $8,803,900 thousand the year before. Operating income was $904,200 thousand versus an income of $330,400 thousand in the prior year, an increase of 173.7%. Total direct expense was $14,106,600 thousand versus $8,244,100 thousand in the prior year, an increase of 71.1%. Total indirect expense was $324,000 thousand versus $229,400 thousand in the prior year, an increase of 41.2%.

Prospects: Co.'s results have benefited from its ability to capture the wider price differentials between light low-sulfur crude oil and heavy high-sulfur crude oil processed at its Port Arthur and Delaware City refineries. Co. noted that while the basic sweet crude oil refining margins were seasonally good during the fourth quarter of 2004, its results were more affected by the light-heavy crude oil spreads. Co. attributed the favorable operating environment to the combination of worldwide crude oil production becoming heavier and higher-sulfur; increased demand for light low-sulfur crude oil; limited heavy high-sulfur crude oil refining capacity; and tightening environmental standards.

Financial Data

(US$ in Thousands)	12/31/2004	12/31/2003	12/31/2002	12/31/2001	12/31/2000	12/31/1999
Earnings Per Share	5.52	1.58	(2.65)	4.13	2.55	(2.08)
Cash Flow Per Share	12.00	2.51	0.32	13.52	4.31	...
Tang Book Value Per Share	23.50	15.26	12.13	9.26	4.78	...
Dividends Per Share	0.020	...	...	...	...	...
Dividend Payout %	0.36	...	...	...	...	...
Income Statement						
Total Revenue	15,334,800	8,803,900	6,772,800	6,417,500	7,301,700	4,520,500
EBITDA	996,600	418,600	(8,900)	470,500	229,300	79,800
Depn & Amortn	96,000	115,700	99,400	103,500	82,600	70,700
Income Before Taxes	772,300	187,800	(210,100)	227,500	64,500	(82,400)
Income Taxes	288,800	64,000	(81,300)	49,300	(25,800)	(12,000)
Net Income	477,900	116,600	(127,100)	153,000	89,700	(36,400)
Average Shares	86,500	73,600	49,000	34,500	31,500	21,600
Balance Sheet						
Current Assets	2,534,400	1,845,700	885,600	1,061,500	959,800	...
Total Assets	5,689,600	3,715,300	2,323,000	2,509,800	2,469,100	...
Current Liabilities	1,310,100	985,600	564,700	578,900	634,800	...
Long-Term Obligations	1,788,700	1,426,000	909,900	1,391,400	1,514,500	...
Total Liabilities	3,555,200	2,570,100	1,619,000	2,096,100	2,215,000	...
Stockholders' Equity	2,134,400	1,145,200	704,000	294,700	152,100	...
Shares Outstanding	89,213	74,119	58,043	31,822	31,822	25,945
Statistical Record						
Return on Assets %	10.14	3.86	N.M.	6.15	...	...
Return on Equity %	29.06	12.61	N.M.	68.49	...	...
EBITDA Margin %	6.50	4.75	N.M.	7.33	3.14	1.77
Net Margin %	3.12	1.32	N.M.	2.38	1.23	N.M.
Asset Turnover	3.25	2.92	2.80	2.58	...	...
Current Ratio	1.93	1.87	1.57	1.83	1.51	...
Debt to Equity	0.84	1.25	1.29	4.72	9.96	...
Price Range	44.55-25.55	26.00-19.28	28.25-13.40	...	...	...
P/E Ratio	8.07-4.63	16.46-12.20	N/A	...	...	...
Average Yield %	0.06	...	...	...	...	...

Address: 1700 E. Putnam Avenue, Suite 400, Old Greenwich, CT 06870 Telephone: (203) 698-7500	Web Site: www.premcor.com Officers: Thomas D. O'Malley - Chmn. Henry M. Kuchta - Pres., C.O.O.	Auditors: DELOITTE & TOUCHE LLP Investor Contact: 203-698-5669

PRIDE INTERNATIONAL, INC. (DE)

Exchange	Symbol	Price	52Wk Range	Yield	P/E
NYS	PDE	$24.84 (3/31/2005)	26.96-15.12	N/A	N.M.

*7 Year Price Score 98.78   ***NYSE Composite Index=100**   ***12 Month Price Score 119.53**

TRADING VOLUME (thousand shares)

Interim Earnings (Per Share)

Qtr.	Mar	Jun	Sep	Dec
2001	0.16	0.22	0.04	0.05
2002	0.00	(0.03)	(0.04)	0.00
2003	0.03	(0.14)	0.19	(0.28)
2004	(0.05)	0.02	(0.13)	...

Interim Dividends (Per Share)

No Dividends Paid

Valuation Analysis

Forecast P/E	N/A	No of Institutions
Market Cap	$3.4 Billion	Shares
Book Value	1.7 Billion	115,281,824
Price/Book	2.00	% Held
Price/Sales	1.93	84.61

Business Summary: Oil and Gas (MIC: 14.2 SIC: 389 NAIC: 13112)

Pride International is an international provider of contract drilling and related services, operating both offshore and on land. As of Mar 1 2004, Co. operated a global fleet of 327 rigs, including two ultra-deepwater drillships, 11 semisubmersible rigs, 35 jackup rigs, 30 tender-assisted, barge and platform rigs and 249 land-based drilling and workover rigs. Co.'s operations are conducted in more than 30 countries and marine provinces in many of the most active oil and gas basins of the world, including South America, the Gulf of Mexico, the Mediterranean, West and North Africa, the Middle East, Asia Pacific, Russia and Kazahkstan.

Recent Developments: For the year ended Dec 31 2004, income from continuing operations decreased 65.1% to $14,273 thousand from income of $40,865 thousand a year earlier. Net loss was $3,459 thousand versus net loss of $23,122 thousand a year earlier. Revenues were $1,712,200 thousand, up 9.3% from $1,565,806 thousand the year before. Operating income was $248,977 thousand versus an income of $218,409 thousand in the prior year, an increase of 14.0%. Total direct expense was $1,146,760 thousand versus $1,039,798 thousand in the prior year, an increase of 10.3%. Total indirect expense was $316,463 thousand versus $307,599 thousand in the prior year, an increase of 2.9%.

Prospects: Top-line results are being negatively affected by sharply lower equipment sales and reduced service revenue. Also, earnings are being hurt by charges related to Co.'s debt refinancing activities, along with expenses for damage caused by Hurricane Ivan. Accordingly, Co. is selling certain assets in an effort to reduce debt and improve profitability. For instance, in the fourth quarter of 2004, Co. completed the sale of its Pride West Virginia jackup rig for $60.0 million. And also sold its Pride Kentucky and Pride Illinois for $11.0 million. In the first quarter of 2005, one of Co.'s French subsidiaries sold the Energy Explorer IV (Pride Ohio) and received $40 million.

Financial Data
(US$ in Thousands)

	9 Mos	6 Mos	3 Mos	12/31/2003	12/31/2002	12/31/2001	12/31/2000	12/31/1999
Earnings Per Share	(0.44)	(0.12)	(0.28)	(0.18)	(0.07)	0.68	0.01	(0.99)
Cash Flow Per Share	1.47	1.63	1.25	0.86	1.14	1.93	1.35	(0.49)
Tang Book Value Per Share	11.91	12.03	12.00	12.07	12.14	12.29	13.39	13.59
Income Statement								
Total Revenue	1,322,697	879,923	433,565	1,689,720	1,269,774	1,512,895	909,007	619,385
EBITDA	309,194	215,244	96,554	384,968	387,142	481,986	236,127	80,124
Depn & Amortn	198,894	136,318	68,113	259,221	245,320	221,736	140,643	106,709
Income Before Taxes	20,759	19,497	(1,839)	(4,298)	11,355	154,613	16,889	(79,025)
Income Taxes	25,094	13,233	(1,011)	(1,130)	3,407	49,231	5,341	(23,258)
Net Income	(22,393)	(4,243)	(6,765)	(23,933)	(8,947)	91,206	736	(51,883)
Average Shares	135,887	137,435	135,542	134,704	133,305	142,778	67,418	52,526
Balance Sheet								
Current Assets	721,077	749,363	700,109	726,924	669,384	632,140	478,148	397,490
Total Assets	4,261,488	4,326,635	4,308,817	4,378,430	4,324,995	4,205,690	2,676,928	2,388,677
Current Liabilities	470,867	600,679	669,670	643,803	546,845	537,085	387,616	264,819
Long-Term Obligations	1,900,800	1,825,344	1,738,424	1,815,078	1,804,130	1,639,885	1,162,320	1,148,886
Total Liabilities	2,572,803	2,624,518	2,610,256	2,675,651	2,625,290	2,508,584	1,718,832	1,563,408
Stockholders' Equity	1,688,685	1,702,117	1,698,561	1,702,779	1,699,705	1,697,106	958,096	825,269
Shares Outstanding	136,038	135,786	135,786	135,400	134,084	132,847	67,689	60,416
Statistical Record								
Return on Assets %	N.M.	N.M.	N.M.	N.M.	N.M.	2.65	0.03	N.M.
Return on Equity %	N.M.	N.M.	N.M.	N.M.	N.M.	6.87	0.08	N.M.
EBITDA Margin %	23.38	24.46	22.27	22.78	30.49	31.86	25.98	12.94
Net Margin %	N.M.	N.M.	N.M.	N.M.	N.M.	6.03	0.08	N.M.
Asset Turnover	0.41	0.41	0.40	0.39	0.30	0.44	0.36	0.27
Current Ratio	1.53	1.25	1.05	1.13	1.22	1.18	1.23	1.50
Debt to Equity	1.13	1.07	1.02	1.07	1.06	0.97	1.21	1.39
Price Range	20.04-15.12	20.04-15.12	20.04-13.38	19.78-13.00	19.52-11.00	32.65-9.75	29.00-13.50	17.94-5.00
P/E Ratio	N/A	N/A	N/A	N/A	N/A	48.01-14.34	N.M.	N/A

Address: 5847 San Felipe, Suite 3300, Houston, TX 77057	**Web Site:** www.prde.com	**Auditors:** PricewaterhouseCoopers LLP
Telephone: (713) 789-1400	**Officers:** William E. Macaulay - Chmn. Paul A. Bragg - Pres., C.E.O.	**Investor Contact:** 713-789-1400
Fax: (713) 789-1430		

PRINCIPAL FINANCIAL GROUP, INC.

Exchange	Symbol	Price	52Wk Range	Yield	P/E
NYS	PFG	$38.49 (3/31/2005)	41.76-32.22	1.43	14.69

*7 Year Price Score N/A   *NYSE Composite Index=100   ***12 Month Price Score 99.19**

Interim Earnings (Per Share)

Qtr.	Mar	Jun	Sep	Dec
2001		------1.02------		
2002	(0.10)	0.34	(0.45)	0.62
2003	0.47	0.62	0.67	0.53
2004	0.60	0.37	0.95	0.70

Interim Dividends (Per Share)

Amt	Decl	Ex	Rec	Pay
0.25A	10/25/2002	11/6/2002	11/8/2002	12/9/2002
0.45A	10/24/2003	11/5/2003	11/7/2003	12/8/2003
0.55A	10/22/2004	11/9/2004	11/12/2004	12/17/2004

Indicated Div: $0.55

Valuation Analysis

Forecast P/E	14.30	No of Institutions
	(4/7/2005)	270
Market Cap	$11.6 Billion	Shares
Book Value	7.5 Billion	160,766,432
Price/Book	1.53	% Held
Price/Sales	1.39	53.67

Business Summary: Insurance (MIC: 8.2 SIC: 311 NAIC: 24113)

Principal Financial Group is a provider of retirement savings, investment and insurance products and services with $144.90 billion in assets under management, as of Dec 31 2003. Co.'s U.S. and international operations concentrate primarily on asset management and accumulation. In addition, Co. offers a range of individual and group life insurance, group health insurance, individual and group disability insurance and residential mortgage loan origination and servicing. Co.'s businesses are organized into the following operating segments: U.S. Asset Management and Accumulation; International Asset Management and Accumulation; Life and Health Insurance; and Mortgage Banking.

Recent Developments: For the year ended Dec 31 2004, income from continuing operations increased 8.5% to $702,500 thousand from income of $647,300 thousand a year earlier. Net income increased 10.6% to $825,600 thousand from net income of $746,300 thousand a year earlier. Revenues were $8,303,700 thousand, up 4.0% from $7,986,700 thousand the year before. Net premiums earned were $3,710,000 thousand versus $3,630,700 thousand in the prior year, an increase of 2.2%.

Prospects: Co. remains optimistic about the growth opportunities across its businesses, as it looks to leverage its strengths to deliver sustainable, profitable growth in earnings and assets under management. In the coming year, Co. will look to capitalize on the 2004 launch of its Total Retirement Suite and High Deductible Health Plan with Savings Account. Also, Co. will seek to capitalize on the expanded array of retirement income management applications in 2004, as well as its increased advisory role, through education, tools and personalized guidance.

Financial Data
(US$ in Thousands)

	12/31/2004	12/31/2003	12/31/2002	12/31/2001	12/31/2000	12/31/1999	12/31/1998
Earnings Per Share	2.62	2.28	0.41	0.99	...	...	...
Cash Flow Per Share	7.18	11.39	16.64	10.89	...	...	...
Tang Book Value Per Share	23.67	16.03	14.78	10.59	...	...	...
Dividends Per Share	0.550	0.450	0.250	...	...	...	...
Dividend Payout %	20.99	19.74	60.98	...	...	...	...
Income Statement							
Premium Income	3,710,000	3,634,100	3,881,800	4,122,300	3,996,400	3,937,600	3,818,400
Total Revenue	8,303,700	9,404,200	8,822,500	8,817,500	8,884,900	8,701,400	8,196,900
Income Before Taxes	881,600	953,700	665,800	448,500	860,500	1,065,600	735,200
Income Taxes	179,100	225,800	45,900	79,000	240,300	323,500	42,200
Net Income	825,600	746,300	142,300	358,800	620,200	742,100	693,000
Average Shares	314,700	326,800	350,200	362,400			
Balance Sheet							
Total Assets	113,798,100	107,754,400	89,861,300	88,350,500	84,404,900	83,953,200	...
Total Liabilities	106,253,800	100,354,800	83,204,100	81,530,200	78,152,400	78,400,300	...
Stockholders' Equity	7,544,300	7,399,600	6,657,200	6,820,300	6,252,500	5,552,900	...
Shares Outstanding	300,600	320,700	334,400	360,100	...	...	...
Statistical Record							
Return on Assets %	0.74	0.76	0.16	0.42	0.73	...	...
Return on Equity %	11.02	10.62	2.11	5.49	10.48	...	...
Net Margin %	9.94	7.94	1.61	4.07	6.98	8.53	8.45
Price Range	41.21-32.22	34.30-25.83	31.00-22.50	24.08-21.00	...	...	...
P/E Ratio	15.73-12.30	15.04-11.33	75.61-54.88	24.32-21.21	N/A	N/A	N/A
Average Yield %	1.54	1.46	0.91	N/A	N/A	N/A	N/A

Address: 711 High Street, Des Moines, IA 50392 Telephone: (515) 247-5111	Web Site: www.principal.com Officers: J. Barry Griswell - Chmn., Pres., C.E.O. Michael H. Gersie - Exec. V.P., C.F.O.	Auditors: Ernst & Young LLP

PROCTER & GAMBLE CO.

Exchange	Symbol	Price	52Wk Range	Yield	P/E	Div Acheiver
NYS	PG	$53.00 (3/31/2005)	56.73-50.97	1.89	21.20	51 Years

*7 Year Price Score 106.04 *NYSE Composite Index=100 *12 Month Price Score 91.36

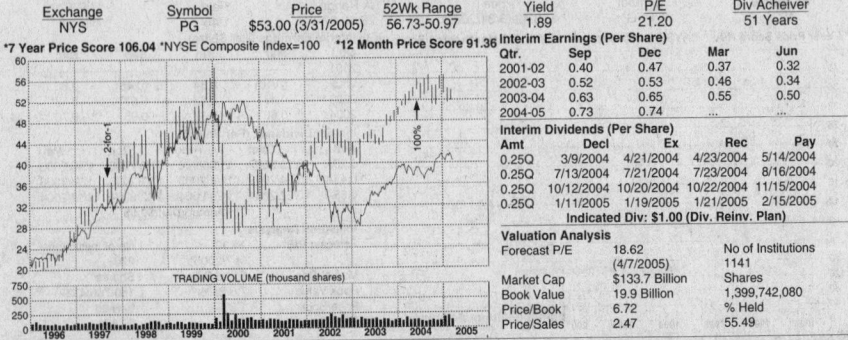

Interim Earnings (Per Share)

Qtr.	Sep	Dec	Mar	Jun
2001-02	0.40	0.47	0.37	0.32
2002-03	0.52	0.53	0.46	0.34
2003-04	0.63	0.65	0.55	0.50
2004-05	0.73	0.74	...	...

Interim Dividends (Per Share)

Amt	Decl	Ex	Rec	Pay
0.25Q	3/9/2004	4/21/2004	4/23/2004	5/14/2004
0.25Q	7/13/2004	7/21/2004	7/23/2004	8/16/2004
0.25Q	10/12/2004	10/20/2004	10/22/2004	11/15/2004
0.25Q	1/11/2005	1/19/2005	1/21/2005	2/15/2005

Indicated Div: $1.00 (Div. Reinv. Plan)

Valuation Analysis

Forecast P/E	18.62 (4/7/2005)	No of Institutions 1141
Market Cap	$133.7 Billion	Shares 1,399,742,080
Book Value	19.9 Billion	% Held
Price/Book	6.72	55.49
Price/Sales	2.47	

Business Summary: Chemicals (MIC: 11.1 SIC: 841 NAIC: 25611)

Procter & Gamble manufactures and markets consumer branded products. Fabric and Home Care includes laundry detergent, fabric conditioners and dish care. Baby and Family Care includes diapers, wipes and bibs. Beauty Care includes hair care/hair color, and cosmetics. Health Care includes oral care, pet health, and pharmaceuticals. Snacks and Beverages includes coffee, snacks and beverages. Co. markets approximately 300 consumer products in more than 160 countries around the world. Co.'s key brands include Tide, Downy, Lenor, Joy, Gain, Ace, Swiffer, Pantene, Olay, Head & Shoulders, Herbal Essences, Max Factor, Pampers, Charmin, Crest, Iams, Eukanuba, Scope, Pringles, and Folgers.

Recent Developments: For the quarter ended Dec 31 2004, net income increased 12.2% to $2,039 million from net income of $1,818 million in the year-earlier quarter. Revenues were $14,452 million, up 9.3% from $13,221 million the year before. Operating income was $3,070 million versus an income of $2,742 million in the prior-year quarter, an increase of 12.0%. Total direct expense was $6,871 million versus $6,324 million in the prior-year quarter, an increase of 8.6%. Total indirect expense was $4,511 million versus $4,155 million in the prior-year quarter, an increase of 8.6%.

Prospects: On Jan 28 2005, Co. agreed to acquire The Gillette Company in a transaction valued at about $57.00 billion. The proposed acquisition is expected to create a stronger brand portfolio, opportunities for innovation and faster sales growth. Co. noted that it expects to achieve revenue and cost synergies of about $14.00 billion to $16.00 billion. In addition, Co. anticipates reductions of about 4.0% of the combined work force of 140,000. As a result, P&G raised its annual sales growth target for 2005 to 5.0% to 7.0%. Also, the combination provides future upside potential to its double-digit annual earnings growth target of 13.0% to 14.0%. The transaction is expected to close in the fall of 2005.

Financial Data

(US$ in Thousands)	6 Mos	3 Mos	06/30/2004	06/30/2003	06/30/2002	06/30/2001	06/30/2000	06/30/1999
Earnings Per Share	2.50	2.41	2.32	1.85	1.54	1.03	1.24	1.29
Cash Flow Per Share	3.70	3.80	3.62	3.35	2.98	2.23	1.78	2.09
Tang Book Value Per Share	N.M.	N.M.	N.M.	0.42	N.M.	0.78	0.68	1.31
Dividends Per Share	0.978	0.955	0.933	0.820	0.760	0.700	0.640	0.570
Dividend Payout %	39.04	39.58	40.19	44.44	49.19	67.63	51.82	44.02
Income Statement								
Total Revenue	28,196,000	13,744,000	51,407,000	43,377,000	40,238,000	39,244,000	39,951,000	38,125,000
EBITDA	7,105,000	3,532,000	11,712,000	9,794,000	8,679,000	7,681,000	8,449,000	8,636,000
Depn & Amortn	928,000	480,000	1,733,000	1,703,000	1,693,000	2,271,000	2,191,000	2,148,000
Income Before Taxes	5,796,000	2,871,000	9,350,000	7,530,000	6,383,000	4,616,000	5,536,000	5,838,000
Income Taxes	1,756,000	870,000	2,869,000	2,344,000	2,031,000	1,694,000	1,994,000	2,075,000
Net Income	4,040,000	2,001,000	6,481,000	5,186,000	4,352,000	2,922,000	3,542,000	3,763,000
Average Shares	2,741,000	2,756,000	2,790,100	2,802,600	2,809,800	2,811,200	2,854,400	2,893,600
Balance Sheet								
Current Assets	20,996,000	18,716,000	17,115,000	15,220,000	12,166,000	10,889,000	10,069,000	11,358,000
Total Assets	63,032,000	59,203,000	57,048,000	43,706,000	40,776,000	34,387,000	34,194,000	32,113,000
Current Liabilities	23,903,000	21,902,000	22,147,000	12,358,000	12,704,000	9,846,000	10,065,000	10,761,000
Long-Term Obligations	13,385,000	13,731,000	12,554,000	11,475,000	11,201,000	9,792,000	8,916,000	6,231,000
Total Liabilities	43,148,000	40,844,000	39,770,000	27,520,000	27,070,000	22,377,000	21,907,000	20,055,000
Stockholders' Equity	19,884,000	18,359,000	17,278,000	16,186,000	13,706,000	12,010,000	12,287,000	12,058,000
Shares Outstanding	2,522,600	2,536,700	2,543,800	2,594,400	2,601,600	2,591,400	2,611,800	2,639,600
Statistical Record								
Return on Assets %	11.85	12.22	12.83	12.28	11.58	8.52	10.65	11.93
Return on Equity %	36.02	37.51	38.63	34.70	33.85	24.05	29.02	30.98
EBITDA Margin %	25.20	25.70	22.78	22.58	21.57	19.57	21.15	22.65
Net Margin %	14.33	14.56	12.61	11.96	10.82	7.45	8.87	9.87
Asset Turnover	0.92	0.96	1.02	1.03	1.07	1.14	1.20	1.21
Current Ratio	0.88	0.85	0.77	1.23	0.96	1.11	1.00	1.06
Debt to Equity	0.67	0.75	0.73	0.71	0.82	0.82	0.73	0.52
Price Range	56.73-49.05	56.73-46.41	55.96-43.35	46.50-37.23	47.20-32.00	38.96-27.08	58.44-26.61	51.09-33.16
P/E Ratio	22.69-19.62	23.54-19.26	24.12-18.69	25.14-20.12	30.65-20.78	37.82-26.29	47.13-21.46	39.60-25.70
Average Yield %	1.83	1.84	1.89	1.87	1.90	2.12	1.48	1.31

Address: One Procter & Gamble Plaza, Cincinnati, OH 45202 Telephone: (513) 983-1100 Fax: (513) 983-2062	Web Site: www.pg.com Officers: Alan G. Lafley - Chmn., Pres., C.E.O. Bruce L. Byrnes - Vice-Chmn.	Auditors: Deloitte & Touche LLP Transfer Agents: The Procter and Gamble Company, Cincinnati, OH

PROGRESS ENERGY, INC.

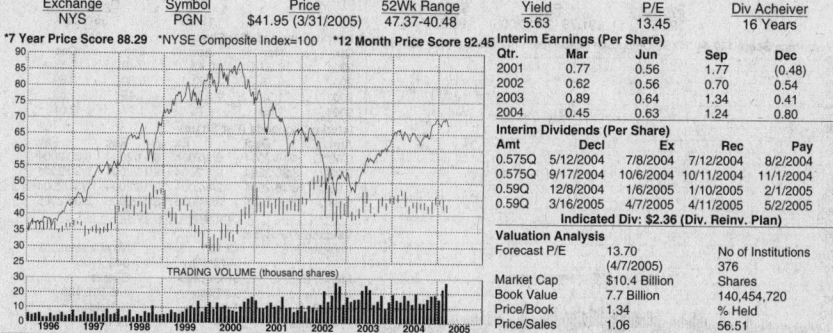

Exchange	Symbol	Price	52Wk Range	Yield	P/E	Div Acheiver
NYS	PGN	$41.95 (3/31/2005)	47.37-40.48	5.63	13.45	16 Years

*7 Year Price Score 88.29 *NYSE Composite Index=100 *12 Month Price Score 92.45

Interim Earnings (Per Share)

Qtr.	Mar	Jun	Sep	Dec
2001	0.77	0.56	1.77	(0.48)
2002	0.62	0.56	0.70	0.54
2003	0.89	0.64	1.34	0.41
2004	0.45	0.63	1.24	0.80

Interim Dividends (Per Share)

Amt	Decl	Ex	Rec	Pay
0.575Q	5/12/2004	7/8/2004	7/12/2004	8/2/2004
0.575Q	9/17/2004	10/6/2004	10/11/2004	11/1/2004
0.59Q	12/8/2004	1/6/2005	1/10/2005	2/1/2005
0.59Q	3/16/2005	4/7/2005	4/11/2005	5/2/2005

Indicated Div: $2.36 (Div. Reinv. Plan)

Valuation Analysis

Forecast P/E	13.70 (4/7/2005)	No of Institutions 376
Market Cap	$10.4 Billion	Shares
Book Value	7.7 Billion	140,454,720
Price/Book	1.34	% Held
Price/Sales	1.06	56.51

Business Summary: Electricity (MIC: 7.1 SIC: 911 NAIC: 21121)

Progress Energy is a utility holding company with over 24,000 megawatts of generating capacity as of Dec 31 2003. Co.'s utility segment includes two major electric utilities, Progress Energy Carolinas and Progress Energy Florida. At Dec 31 2003, Co.'s electric utilities served more than 2.8 million customers in North Carolina, South Carolina and Florida. Co.'s Competitive Commercial Operations segment provides non-regulated electricity generation. The Fuels segment is involved in natural gas drilling and production, coal mining and terminal services and fuel delivery. The Rail Services segment engages in rail and railcar services. Other activities include Co.'s telecommunication services.

Recent Developments: For the year ended Dec 31 2004, income from continuing operations was $753.0 million compared with income of $811.0 million a year earlier. Results excluded income of $6.0 million for 2004 and a loss of $8.0 million for 2003 from discontinued operations. Results for 2003 also excluded an accounting change charge of $21.0 million. Total operating revenues increased 11.8% to $9.77 billion from $8.74 billion the previous year. Electric operating revenues rose 6.1% to $7.15 billion from $6.74 billion in 2003. Diversified business operating revenues advanced 31.0% to $2.62 billion versus $2.00 billion last year. Operating income improved to $1.48 billion, 8.8% higher than the year before.

Prospects: On Dec 8 2004, Co. announced an early-retirement program to be offered to its employees in early 2005. The program will be available to all active, regular full-time employees who are age 50 and older and vested in their retirement plan benefit as of Mar 31 2005. According to Co., approximately 3,500 of its 15,300 employees meet the eligibility requirements of the program. Separately, on Nov 23 2004, Progress Fuels Corp., a wholly owned subsidiary of Co, announced that it has entered into an agreement to sell certain oil and gas interests and related assets in the Fort Worth basin of Texas for a sale price of $255.0 million in cash. Proceeds from the sale will be used to reduce debt.

Financial Data

(US$ in Thousands)	12/31/2004	12/31/2003	12/31/2002	12/31/2001	12/31/2000	12/31/1999	12/31/1998	12/31/1997
Earnings Per Share	3.12	3.28	2.42	2.64	3.03	2.55	2.75	2.66
Cash Flow Per Share	6.62	7.54	7.36	7.06	5.46	5.61	6.39	5.69
Tang Book Value Per Share	14.48	13.78	12.43	10.58	8.60	19.57	19.49	18.63
Dividends Per Share	2.300	2.240	2.180	2.120	1.030	2.015	1.955	1.895
Dividend Payout %	73.72	68.29	90.08	80.30	33.99	79.02	71.09	71.24
Income Statement								
Total Revenue	9,772,000	8,743,000	7,945,120	8,461,459	4,118,873	3,357,615	3,130,045	3,024,089
EBITDA	2,137,000	2,462,000	2,112,404	2,241,745	1,751,386	1,397,927	1,399,790	...
Depn & Amortn	653,000	1,146,000	1,099,128	1,189,171	834,950	588,123	578,348	565,212
Income Before Taxes	851,000	702,000	394,361	389,967	681,135	640,676	656,732	...
Income Taxes	115,000	(109,000)	(157,808)	(151,643)	202,774	258,421	257,494	233,716
Net Income	759,000	782,000	528,386	541,610	478,361	382,255	399,238	388,317
Average Shares	243,100	237,000	218,166	204,683	157,169	148,344	143,941	143,645
Balance Sheet								
Net PPE	16,373,000	16,592,000	12,540,505	11,987,961	11,166,360	7,004,795	6,299,540	6,293,176
Total Assets	25,993,000	26,202,000	21,352,704	20,739,791	20,091,012	9,494,019	8,347,406	8,220,728
Long-Term Obligations	18,772,000	9,934,000	9,747,293	9,483,745	5,890,099	3,028,561	2,614,414	2,415,656
Total Liabilities	27,518,000	18,665,000	14,582,864	14,643,427	14,573,980	6,021,996	5,338,725	5,342,545
Stockholders' Equity	7,726,000	7,537,000	6,769,840	6,096,364	5,517,032	3,472,023	3,008,681	2,878,183
Shares Outstanding	247,000	246,000	237,992	218,725	206,089	159,599	151,338	151,340
Statistical Record								
Return on Assets %	2.90	3.29	2.51	2.65	3.22	4.29	4.82	4.68
Return on Equity %	9.92	10.93	8.21	9.33	10.61	11.80	13.56	13.60
EBITDA Margin %	21.87	28.16	26.59	26.49	42.52	41.63	44.72	...
Net Margin %	7.77	8.94	6.65	6.40	11.61	11.38	12.76	12.84
PPE Turnover	0.59	0.60	0.65	0.73	0.45	0.50	0.50	0.48
Asset Turnover	0.37	0.37	0.38	0.41	0.28	0.38	0.38	0.36
Debt to Equity	2.43	1.32	1.44	1.56	1.07	0.87	0.87	0.84
Price Range	47.78-40.48	47.38-38.32	52.38-33.58	48.44-39.61	49.19-28.56	47.50-29.50	49.06-39.50	42.50-33.00
P/E Ratio	15.31-12.97	14.45-11.68	21.64-13.88	18.35-15.00	16.23-9.43	18.63-11.57	17.84-14.36	15.98-12.41
Average Yield %	5.27	5.29	4.79	4.98	2.88	5.21	4.48	5.26

Address: 410 South Wilmington Street, Raleigh, NC 27601-1748	Web Site: www.progress-energy.com	Auditors: Deloitte & Touche LLP
Telephone: (919) 546 6111	Officers: Robert B. McGehee - Chmn., C.E.O.	Investor Contact: 919-546-7474
Fax: (919) 549 7678	William D. Johnson - Pres., C.O.O.	Transfer Agents: EquiServe Trust Company, N.A., Providence, RI

PROGRESSIVE CORP. (OH)

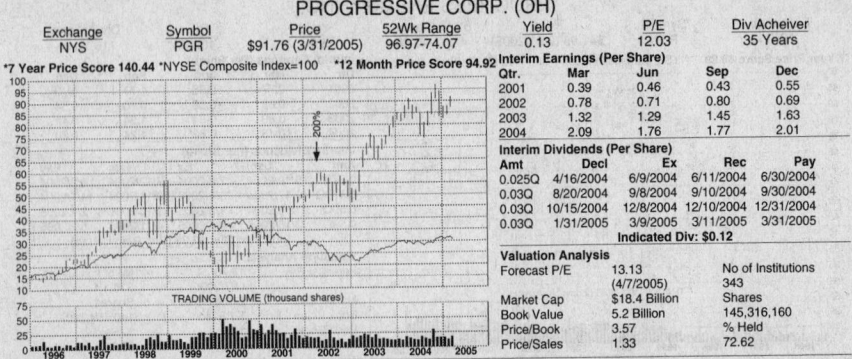

Exchange	Symbol	Price	52Wk Range	Yield	P/E	Div Achiever
NYS	PGR	$91.76 (3/31/2005)	96.97-74.07	0.13	12.03	35 Years

*7 Year Price Score 140.44 *NYSE Composite Index=100 *12 Month Price Score 94.92

Interim Earnings (Per Share)

Qtr.	Mar	Jun	Sep	Dec
2001	0.39	0.46	0.43	0.55
2002	0.78	0.71	0.80	0.69
2003	1.32	1.29	1.45	1.63
2004	2.09	1.76	1.77	2.01

Interim Dividends (Per Share)

Amt	Decl	Ex	Rec	Pay
0.025Q	4/16/2004	6/9/2004	6/11/2004	6/30/2004
0.03Q	8/20/2004	9/8/2004	9/10/2004	9/30/2004
0.03Q	10/15/2004	12/8/2004	12/10/2004	12/31/2004
0.03Q	1/31/2005	3/9/2005	3/11/2005	3/31/2005

Indicated Div: $0.12

Valuation Analysis

Forecast P/E	13.13	No of Institutions
	(4/7/2005)	343
Market Cap	$18.4 Billion	Shares
Book Value	5.2 Billion	145,316,160
Price/Book	3.57	% Held
Price/Sales	1.33	72.62

Business Summary: Insurance (MIC: 8.2 SIC: 331 NAIC: 24126)

Progressive, through its subsidiaries and affiliates, provides personal automobile insurance and other specialty property-casualty insurance and related services throughout the U.S. Co.'s personal lines business units write insurance for private passenger automobiles and recreation vehicles. Co.'s commercial auto business unit writes insurance for automobiles and trucks owned by small businesses. Co.'s other businesses include writing lenders' collateral protection and directors' and officers' liability insurance and providing insurance-related services, primarily processing business for Commercial Auto Insurance Procedures, which are state supervised plans serving the involuntary market.

Recent Developments: For the twelve months ended Dec 31 2004, net income increased 31.3% to $1,648,700 thousand from net income of $1,255,400 thousand a year earlier. Revenues were $13,782,100 thousand, an improvement of 15.9% from $11,892,000 thousand the year before. Net premiums earned were $13,169,900 thousand compared with $11,341,000 thousand in the prior year, an increase of 16.1%.

Prospects: With favorable market conditions continuing, Co. is looking to build on its solid operating momentum from 2004 in the coming year. Key objectives for 2005 include Co.'s focus on creating two top share brands in its personal auto business, which will be the focus of its Agency Business in 2005. Also, Co. will focus on the expansion of its operations and has allocated considerable resources to evaluate its objectives in New Jersey, one of only two states in which Co. does not underwrite personal auto (the other being Massachusetts). Assuming successful promulgation of the proposed ratemaking regulations, Co. expect to make product filings for one or more of its offerings in 2005.

Financial Data
(US$ in Thousands)

	12/31/2004	12/31/2003	12/31/2002	12/31/2001	12/31/2000	12/31/1999	12/31/1998	12/31/1997
Earnings Per Share	7.63	5.69	2.99	1.83	0.21	1.32	2.04	1.77
Cash Flow Per Share	12.47	11.24	8.73	5.58	3.73	3.54	2.84	3.40
Tang Book Value Per Share	25.73	23.25	17.28	14.76	13.01	12.55	11.76	9.85
Dividends Per Share	0.110	0.100	0.097	0.093	0.090	0.087	0.083	0.080
Dividend Payout %	1.44	1.76	3.23	5.11	43.54	6.57	4.09	4.52
Income Statement								
Premium Income	13,169,900	11,341,000	8,883,500	7,161,800	6,348,400	5,683,600	4,948,000	4,189,500
Total Revenue	13,782,100	11,892,000	9,294,400	7,488,200	6,771,000	6,124,200	5,292,400	4,608,200
Benefits & Claims	8,555,000	7,640,400	6,299,100	5,264,100	5,279,400	4,256,400	3,376,300	2,967,500
Income Before Taxes	2,450,800	1,859,700	981,400	587,600	31,800	412,200	661,100	578,500
Income Taxes	802,100	604,300	314,100	176,200	(14,300)	117,000	204,400	178,500
Net Income	1,648,700	1,255,400	667,300	411,400	46,100	295,200	456,700	400,000
Average Shares	216,200	220,500	223,200	225,299	222,900	223,800	224,100	225,900
Balance Sheet								
Total Assets	17,184,300	16,281,500	13,564,400	11,122,400	10,051,600	9,704,700	8,463,100	7,559,600
Total Liabilities	12,028,900	11,250,900	9,796,400	7,871,700	7,181,800	6,951,900	5,906,000	5,423,700
Stockholders' Equity	5,155,400	5,030,600	3,768,000	3,250,700	2,869,800	2,752,800	2,557,100	2,135,900
Shares Outstanding	200,400	216,400	218,000	220,200	220,500	219,300	217,500	216,900
Statistical Record								
Return on Assets %	9.83	8.41	5.41	3.89	0.47	3.25	5.70	5.82
Return on Equity %	32.28	28.54	19.01	13.44	1.64	11.12	19.46	20.98
Loss Ratio %	64.96	67.37	70.91	73.50	83.16	74.89	68.24	70.83
Net Margin %	11.96	10.56	7.18	5.49	0.68	4.82	8.63	8.68
Price Range	96.97-74.07	83.59-46.55	59.49-46.15	50.28-28.00	36.67-16.42	56.92-23.69	56.69-31.98	39.96-20.67
P/E Ratio	12.71-9.71	14.69-8.18	19.90-15.43	27.48-15.30	174.60-78.17	43.12-17.95	27.79-15.68	22.58-11.68
Average Yield %	0.13	0.15	0.18	0.23	0.35	0.22	0.19	0.27

Address: 6300 Wilson Mills Road, Mayfield Village, OH 44143 **Telephone:** (440) 461-5000 **Fax:** (440) 446-7168	**Web Site:** www.progressive.com **Officers:** Peter B. Lewis - Chmn. Glenn M. Renwick - Pres., C.E.O.	**Auditors:** PricewaterhouseCoopers LLP **Investor Contact:** 1-440-446-7165 **Transfer Agents:** Corporate Trust Customer Service, National City Bank,

PROLOGIS

Interim Earnings (Per Share)

Qtr.	Mar	Jun	Sep	Dec
2001	0.25	0.26	0.28	(0.27)
2002	0.31	0.31	0.14	0.44
2003	0.21	0.26	(0.04)	0.73
2004	0.23	0.42	0.42	0.00

Interim Dividends (Per Share)

Amt	Decl	Ex	Rec	Pay
0.365Q	5/3/2004	5/12/2004	5/14/2004	5/28/2004
0.365Q	8/2/2004	8/13/2004	8/17/2004	8/31/2004
0.365Q	11/1/2004	11/12/2004	11/16/2004	11/30/2004
0.37Q	2/1/2005	2/11/2005	2/15/2005	2/28/2005

Indicated Div: $1.48

Valuation Analysis

Forecast P/E	N/A	No of Institutions
Market Cap	$6.9 Billion	Shares
Book Value	3.1 Billion	168,631,952
Price/Book	2.22	% Held
Price/Sales	11.52	90.51

Business Summary: Property, Real Estate & Development (MIC: 8.3 SIC: 531 NAIC: 25930)

Prologis is a real estate investment trust that is a global provider of integrated distribution facilities and services. The Property Operations segment is engaged in long-term ownership, management and leasing of industrial distribution properties. Co. held 1,737 operating properties aggregating 230.4 million square feet in North America, 11 countries in Europe and in Japan, at Dec 31 2003. The Corporate Distribution Facilities Services segment is engaged in the development of distribution properties with the intent to contribute the property to a property fund or to sell the property to a third party.

Recent Developments: For the year ended Dec 31 2004, income from continuing operations decreased 6.3% to $233,542 thousand from income of $249,190 thousand a year earlier. Net income decreased 7.1% to $232,795 thousand from net income of $250,675 thousand a year earlier. Revenues were $598,139 thousand, up 1.5% from $589,373 thousand the year before. Operating income was $366,122 thousand versus an income of $342,314 thousand in the prior year, an increase of 7.0%.

Prospects: Co.'s outlook is enhanced by strengthening global customer demand. Specifically, Co. noted that its business in Asia continues to expand. For example, during the fourth quarter ended Dec 31 2004, Co. started $165.0 million of new developments in Asia and more recently announced two new developments in the Tokyo area totaling $266.0 million. Co. also noted its ProLógis Parc Osaka project, which was completed in the fourth quarter of 2004, is now 80.0% committed. Meanwhile, in China, Co. has began development of two facilities at ProLogis Park Northwest Shanghai and entered into a new joint venture to develop distribution facilities at the planned Yangshan International Deep Water Port.

Financial Data

(US$ in Thousands)	12/31/2004	12/31/2003	12/31/2002	12/31/2001	12/31/2000	12/31/1999	12/31/1998	12/31/1997
Earnings Per Share	1.08	1.16	1.20	0.52	0.96	0.81	0.51	0.04
Cash Flow Per Share	2.63	1.82	2.12	2.01	2.05	1.78	1.96	1.91
Tang Book Value Per Share	14.82	14.35	13.96	12.94	13.53	13.86	12.83	13.14
Dividends Per Share	1.460	1.440	1.420	1.380	1.340	1.300	1.240	1.070
Dividend Payout %	135.19	124.14	118.33	265.38	139.58	160.48	243.12	2,675.00
Income Statement								
Property Income	598,139	674,939	576,252	570,213	558,191	538,504	362,296	296,824
Non-Property Income	...	59,166	98,749	(47,088)	85,330	28,888	10,499	5,670
Total Revenue	598,139	734,105	675,001	523,125	643,521	567,392	372,795	302,494
Depn & Amortn	180,347	170,861	158,042	148,698	156,080	156,887	102,790	78,252
Interest Expense	153,334	155,475	152,958	163,629	172,191	171,691	103,700	52,704
Income Before Taxes	277,104	266,049	277,050	132,869	219,608	183,764	...	...
Income Taxes	43,562	15,374	28,169	4,725	5,130	1,472	...	...
Net Income	232,795	250,675	248,881	128,144	214,478	180,834	111,329	39,749
Average Shares	191,801	187,222	184,869	175,197	164,401	152,739	122,028	100,869
Balance Sheet								
Total Assets	7,097,799	6,369,202	5,923,525	5,603,941	5,946,334	5,848,040	4,330,729	3,033,953
Long-Term Obligations	3,366,285	2,990,669	2,731,978	2,578,340	2,677,736	2,554,808	1,655,745	857,080
Total Liabilities	3,929,033	3,270,757	2,994,571	2,882,303	2,972,333	2,832,232	2,023,066	1,003,912
Stockholders' Equity	3,102,493	3,060,668	2,886,487	2,675,999	2,927,371	2,953,736	2,256,368	1,976,737
Shares Outstanding	185,788	180,182	178,145	175,888	165,287	161,825	123,416	117,364
Statistical Record								
Return on Assets %	3.45	4.08	4.32	2.22	3.63	3.55	3.02	1.45
Return on Equity %	7.53	8.43	8.95	4.57	7.27	6.94	5.26	2.22
Net Margin %	38.92	34.15	36.87	24.50	33.33	31.87	29.86	13.14
Price Range	43.33-28.39	32.26-23.85	26.00-21.03	23.15-19.70	24.50-17.81	22.00-17.06	26.38-20.00	25.50-18.82
P/E Ratio	40.12-26.29	27.81-20.56	21.67-17.53	44.52-37.88	25.52-18.55	27.16-21.06	51.72-39.22	637.50-470.42
Average Yield %	4.21	5.20	5.98	6.47	6.36	6.57	5.27	4.91

Address: 14100 East 35th Place, Aurora, CO 80011	Web Site: www.prologis.com	Auditors: KPMG LLP
Telephone: (303) 375-9292	Officers: K. Dane Brooksher - Chmn. Walter C. Rakowich - Pres., C.O.O.	Investor Contact: 303-576-2622
Fax: (303) 375-8581		Transfer Agents: Equiserve Trust Company N.A.

PROTECTIVE LIFE CORP.

Exchange	Symbol	Price	52Wk Range	Yield	P/E	Div Acheiver
NYS	PL	$39.30 (3/31/2005)	43.33-35.49	1.78	11.91	15 Years

*7 Year Price Score 103.52 ***NYSE Composite Index=100** ***12 Month Price Score 97.00**

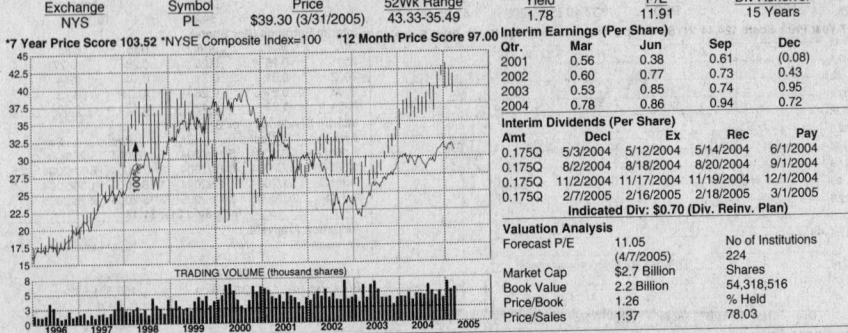

Interim Earnings (Per Share)

Qtr.	Mar	Jun	Sep	Dec
2001	0.56	0.38	0.61	(0.08)
2002	0.60	0.77	0.73	0.43
2003	0.53	0.85	0.74	0.95
2004	0.78	0.86	0.94	0.72

Interim Dividends (Per Share)

Amt	Decl	Ex	Rec	Pay
0.175Q	5/3/2004	5/12/2004	5/14/2004	6/1/2004
0.175Q	8/2/2004	8/18/2004	8/20/2004	9/1/2004
0.175Q	11/2/2004	11/17/2004	11/19/2004	12/1/2004
0.175Q	2/7/2005	2/16/2005	2/18/2005	3/1/2005

Indicated Div: $0.70 (Div. Reinv. Plan)

Valuation Analysis

Forecast P/E	11.05	No of Institutions
	(4/7/2005)	224
Market Cap	$2.7 Billion	Shares
Book Value	2.2 Billion	54,318,516
Price/Book	1.26	% Held
Price/Sales	1.37	78.03

Business Summary: Insurance (MIC: 8.2 SIC: 311 NAIC: 24113)

Protective Life provides financial services through the administration of insurance and investment products. The Life Marketing segment markets premium term and term-like insurance, universal life, variable universal life insurance products. The Acquisitions segment focuses on acquiring, converting, and servicing policies acquired from other companies. The Annuities segment manufactures, sells, and supports fixed and variable annuity products. The Stable Value Products segment markets investment contracts and other retirement plans. The Asset Protection segment markets extended service contracts and credit life and disability insurance.

Recent Developments: For the year ended Dec 31 2004, net income increased 8.1% to $234.6 million from net income of $217.1 million a year earlier. Revenues were $1.99 billion, up 1.6% from $1.96 billion the year before. Total segment operating income increased 23.3% to $363.5 million versus $294.8 million in 2003. Life Marketing segment operating income advanced 4.2% to $165.9 million, Acquisitions operating income declined 8.3% to $87.3 million, Annuities operating income grew 23.1% to $16.5 million, Stable Value Products operating income increased 36.6% to $53.2 million, and Asset Protection operating income decreased 5.5% to $19.1 million.

Prospects: Results are being positively affected by improved performance in the Annuities segment due to significantly higher sales of fixed annuities. Meanwhile, strong earnings growth in the Stable Value Products segment is being fueled by strong spreads and the success of the registered retail note program. Separately, Co. appears to be well positioned to achieve solid earnings growth in 2005 despite the numerous challenges facing the life insurance industry, including low interest rates, a flattening yield curve, tightening spreads, rising reinsurance costs, and regulatory uncertainties. Looking ahead, Co. is targeting full-year 2005 earnings of between $3.35 and $3.65 per share.

Financial Data (US$ in Thousands)	12/31/2004	12/31/2003	12/31/2002	12/31/2001	12/31/2000	12/31/1999	12/31/1998	12/31/1997
Earnings Per Share	3.30	3.07	2.52	1.47	2.32	2.29	2.04	1.78
Cash Flow Per Share	10.60	11.22	12.90	17.02	13.28	5.94	5.92	6.54
Tang Book Value Per Share	30.52	28.33	24.37	19.72	13.38	10.03	11.51	12.30
Dividends Per Share	0.685	0.630	0.590	0.550	0.510	0.470	0.430	0.390
Dividend Payout %	20.76	20.52	23.41	37.41	21.98	20.52	21.08	21.91
Income Statement								
Premium Income	698,652	735,877	783,132	618,669	833,658	761,284	662,795	522,335
Total Revenue	1,988,575	1,957,525	1,920,678	1,614,217	1,733,967	1,533,882	1,366,415	1,147,325
Income Before Taxes	385,201	325,412	267,203	209,596	253,795	255,775	220,724	179,373
Income Taxes	134,820	108,362	88,444	68,538	90,858	92,079	77,845	60,987
Net Income	234,580	217,050	177,355	102,943	153,476	151,327	130,781	111,993
Average Shares	71,064	70,644	70,462	69,950	66,281	66,161	64,088	62,850
Balance Sheet								
Total Assets	27,211,378	24,573,991	21,953,004	19,718,824	15,145,633	12,994,164	11,989,495	10,511,635
Total Liabilities	25,045,051	22,571,847	20,232,302	18,318,680	13,841,575	11,938,941	10,800,301	9,508,438
Stockholders' Equity	2,166,327	2,002,144	1,720,702	1,400,144	1,114,058	865,223	944,194	758,197
Shares Outstanding	69,449	68,991	68,675	68,555	64,557	64,502	64,435	61,642
Statistical Record								
Return on Assets %	0.90	0.93	0.85	0.59	1.09	1.21	1.16	1.19
Return on Equity %	11.22	11.66	11.37	8.19	15.47	16.73	15.36	16.31
Net Margin %	11.80	11.09	9.23	6.38	8.85	9.87	9.57	9.76
Price Range	42.92-33.84	34.22-24.71	33.75-27.20	34.51-25.55	32.25-20.81	40.00-28.50	40.88-28.63	32.63-18.81
P/E Ratio	13.01-10.25	11.15-8.05	13.39-10.79	23.48-17.38	13.90-8.97	17.47-12.45	20.04-14.03	18.33-10.57
Average Yield %	1.81	2.16	1.93	1.82	1.90	1.35	1.24	1.61

Address: 2801 Highway 280 South, Birmingham, AL 35223 Telephone: (205) 268-1000 Fax: (205) 868-3541	Web Site: www.protective.com Officers: John D. Johns - Chmn., Pres., C.E.O. Allen W. Ritchie - Exec. V.P., C.F.O.	Auditors: PricewaterhouseCoopers LLP Investor Contact: 205-268-1000 Transfer Agents: Bank of New York, New York, NY

PROVIDIAN FINANCIAL CORP.

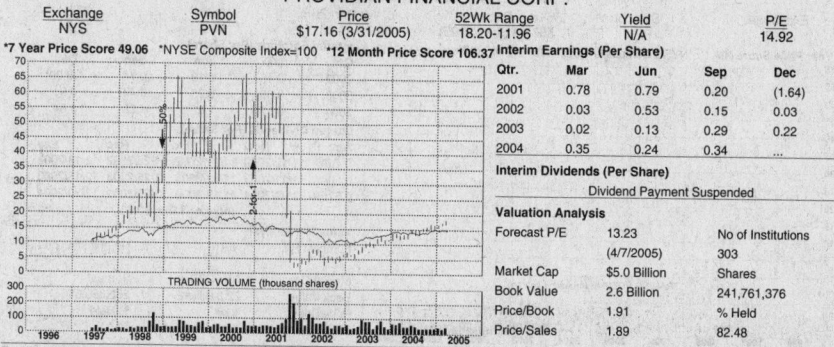

Exchange	Symbol	Price	52Wk Range	Yield	P/E
NYS	PVN	$17.16 (3/31/2005)	18.20-11.96	N/A	14.92

*7 Year Price Score 49.06   *NYSE Composite Index=100   *12 Month Price Score 106.37

Interim Earnings (Per Share)

Qtr.	Mar	Jun	Sep	Dec
2001	0.78	0.79	0.20	(1.64)
2002	0.03	0.53	0.15	0.03
2003	0.02	0.13	0.29	0.22
2004	0.35	0.24	0.34	...

Interim Dividends (Per Share)

Dividend Payment Suspended

Valuation Analysis

Forecast P/E	13.23	No of Institutions
	(4/7/2005)	303
Market Cap	$5.0 Billion	Shares
Book Value	2.6 Billion	241,761,376
Price/Book	1.91	% Held
Price/Sales	1.89	82.48

Business Summary: Credit & Lending (MIC: 8.6 SIC: 153 NAIC: 22210)

Providian Financial provides credit card and deposit products to customers throughout the U.S. Co.'s lending and deposit taking activities are conducted through Providian National Bank. Co.'s primary line of business is its credit card business, which generates consumer loans through Visa and MasterCard credit cards. Co. targets creditworthy customers across the broad middle to prime market segments, with a particular focus on middle market customers. As of Dec 31 2003, Co. had over $6.00 billion in reported receivables, approximately $17.00 billion in managed receivables and approximately 11.0 million customer relationships.

Recent Developments: For the quarter ended Sep 30 2004, net income increased 27.9% to $109,082 thousand from net income of $85,319 thousand in the year-earlier quarter. Net interest income was $144,043 thousand, up 78.1% from $80,877 thousand the year before. Provision for loan losses was $161,351 thousand versus $98,732 thousand in the prior-year quarter, an increase of 63.4%. Non-interest income fell 0.8% to $442,060 thousand, while non-interest expense declined 10.3% to $256,933 thousand.

Prospects: Co.'s outlook is encouraging. During the fourth quarter, Co. added about 470,000 gross new accounts, bringing full year gross new account additions to 2.1 million. Reported net credit losses were $118.9 million, resulting in a reported net credit loss rate of 6.86%, versus 6.99% in the third quarter of 2004. For 2005, Co. is targeting managed loans receivables growth rate in the mid-to-high single digits, with managed net credit losses totaling about $1.80 billion. Separately, on Feb 15 2005, Co. agreed to sell a portfolio of non-core, higher risk credit card loan with a balance of $447.0 million. The sale is expected to have a modestly beneficial impact to earnings in the first quarter.

Financial Data

(US$ in Thousands)	9 Mos	6 Mos	3 Mos	12/31/2003	12/31/2002	12/31/2001	12/31/2000	12/31/1999
Earnings Per Share	1.15	1.10	0.99	0.67	0.75	0.13	2.23	1.89
Cash Flow Per Share	5.96	3.82	2.88	4.43	4.75	5.13	8.61	6.29
Tang Book Value Per Share	8.98	8.56	8.37	8.01	7.39	6.70	7.11	4.72
Dividends Per Share	...	...	...	...	0.090	0.090	0.105	0.100
Dividend Payout %	...	...	...	...	12.00	69.23	4.71	5.29
Income Statement								
Interest Income	752,785	489,368	247,658	1,106,471	1,691,283	2,587,715	2,699,947	1,624,276
Interest Expense	376,089	256,715	133,712	633,790	771,994	934,309	875,174	449,070
Net Interest Income	376,696	232,653	113,946	472,681	919,289	1,653,406	1,824,773	1,175,206
Provision for Losses	432,220	270,869	88,852	622,344	1,291,738	2,014,342	1,515,350	1,099,131
Non-Interest Income	1,269,126	827,066	397,426	1,674,937	2,381,347	2,942,193	3,248,302	2,412,476
Non-Interest Expense	782,032	525,099	266,006	1,201,001	1,808,882	2,347,510	2,471,503	1,571,126
Income Before Taxes	431,570	263,751	156,514	324,273	200,016	233,747	1,086,222	917,425
Income Taxes	151,050	92,313	54,780	128,088	49,006	92,330	434,460	367,153
Net Income	280,520	171,438	101,734	196,185	218,166	38,897	651,762	550,272
Average Shares	333,570	294,248	298,345	290,731	289,042	289,622	294,042	291,094
Balance Sheet								
Net Loans & Leases	6,672,976	6,283,463	5,622,157	5,655,071	5,895,296	9,626,307	12,324,519	10,545,173
Total Assets	13,914,771	13,592,270	13,486,872	14,275,347	16,710,389	19,938,166	18,055,313	14,340,877
Total Deposits	9,062,768	9,001,327	8,963,496	10,101,057	12,708,315	15,318,165	13,113,416	10,538,123
Total Liabilities	11,285,011	11,093,178	11,048,656	11,949,898	14,466,985	17,926,323	15,912,073	12,848,401
Stockholders' Equity	2,629,760	2,499,092	2,438,216	2,325,449	2,139,072	1,907,511	2,032,183	1,332,476
Shares Outstanding	292,950	291,878	291,159	290,447	289,381	284,826	285,911	282,025
Statistical Record								
Return on Assets %	2.37	2.17	1.95	1.27	1.19	0.20	4.01	5.10
Return on Equity %	14.20	13.80	12.81	8.79	10.78	1.97	38.64	51.53
Net Interest Margin %	54.68	49.11	46.01	42.72	54.35	63.89	67.59	72.35
Efficiency Ratio %	36.42	38.59	41.24	43.18	44.42	42.45	41.55	38.92
Loans to Deposits	0.74	0.70	0.63	0.56	0.46	0.63	0.94	1.00
Price Range	15.55-10.30	15.10-9.11	13.73-6.56	13.00-5.25	8.28-2.84	60.91-2.01	66.72-30.06	65.81-35.41
P/E Ratio	13.52-8.96	13.73-8.28	13.87-6.63	19.40-7.84	11.04-3.79	468.54-15.46	29.92-13.48	34.82-18.73
Average Yield %	...	...	...	...	1.65	0.23	0.22	0.21

Address: 201 Mission Street, San Francisco, CA 94105	**Web Site:** www.providian.com	**Auditors:** Ernst & Young LLP
Telephone: (415) 543-0404	**Officers:** Joseph W. Saunders - Chmn., Pres., C.E.O.	**Investor Contact:** 415--278-4977
Fax: (415) 278-6028	Chaomei Chen - Vice-Chmn., Credit & Collections	

PRUDENTIAL FINANCIAL, INC.

Exchange	Symbol	Price	52Wk Range	Yield	P/E
NYS	PRU	$57.40 (3/31/2005)	59.32-41.05	1.09	17.34

*7 Year Price Score N/A *NYSE Composite Index=100 *12 Month Price Score 109.24

TRADING VOLUME (thousand shares)

Interim Earnings (Per Share)

Qtr.	Mar	Jun	Sep	Dec
2002	0.46	0.19	0.70	(0.09)
2003	0.39	0.25	0.44	0.91
2004	0.57	1.02	1.08	0.64

Interim Dividends (Per Share)

Amt	Decl	Ex	Rec	Pay
0.40A	11/12/2002	11/21/2002	11/25/2002	12/18/2002
0.50A	11/11/2003	11/21/2003	11/25/2003	12/18/2003
0.625A	11/9/2004	11/19/2004	11/23/2004	12/20/2004

Indicated Div: $0.63

Valuation Analysis

Forecast P/E	N/A	No of Institutions	
Market Cap	$30.4 Billion	Shares	
Book Value	22.3 Billion	268,889,056	
Price/Book	1.36	% Held	
Price/Sales	1.07	51.31	

Business Summary: Insurance (MIC: 8.2 SIC: 311 NAIC: 24113)

Prudential Financial is a financial services company. Co. offers a range of products and services, including life insurance, property and casualty insurance, mutual funds, annuities, pension and retirement services and administration, asset management, securities brokerage, banking and trust services, real estate brokerage franchises and relocation services. Co.'s Insurance Division is comprised of the Individual Life and Annuities and the Group Insurance segments; its Investment Division is comprised of the Investment Management, Financial Advisory, Retirement and Other Asset Management segments and the International Insurance and Investments Division conducts its international business.

Recent Developments: For the year ended Dec 31 2004, income from continuing operations increased 76.4% to $2,332 million from income of $1,322 million a year earlier. Net income increased 78.5% to $2,256 million from net income of $1,264 million a year earlier. Revenues were $28,348 million, up 1.6% from $27,888 million the year before. Net premiums earned were $12,580 million versus $13,233 million in the prior year, a decrease of 4.9%.

Prospects: Co. is benefiting from its focused efforts to strengthen its core businesses, reduce it cost structure and manage capital more effectively. Also, recent acquisitions have enhanced Co.'s position in the savings and retirement market. Co.'s integration of American Skandia into its annuity business is now complete, and the integration of the retirement business acquired from CIGNA in 2004 is on track. Going forward, Co. expects earnings per share to be in the range of $4.20 to $4.40 for 2005, based on after-tax adjusted operating income in the financial services business.

Financial Data
(US$ in Thousands)

	12/31/2004	12/31/2003	12/31/2002	12/31/2001	12/31/2000	12/31/1999	12/31/1998
Earnings Per Share	3.31	1.98	1.25	...	...	...	...
Cash Flow Per Share	13.64	(1.09)	17.31	...	...	...	...
Tang Book Value Per Share	42.21	39.66	37.94	34.93	...	...	...
Dividends Per Share	0.625	0.500	0.400	...	...	...	...
Dividend Payout %	18.88	25.25	32.00	...	...	...	...
Income Statement							
Premium Income	12,580,000	13,233,000	13,531,000	12,477,000	10,221,000	9,528,000	9,048,000
Total Revenue	28,348,000	27,907,000	26,675,000	27,177,000	26,544,000	26,568,000	27,024,000
Benefits & Claims	12,896,000	13,424,000	13,658,000	12,752,000	10,640,000	10,226,000	9,786,000
Income Before Taxes	3,287,000	1,958,000	64,000	(227,000)	727,000	2,255,000	2,597,000
Income Taxes	955,000	650,000	(192,000)	(57,000)	406,000	1,042,000	970,000
Net Income	2,256,000	1,264,000	194,000	(154,000)	398,000	813,000	1,106,000
Average Shares	531,200	548,363	577,983	...	...	...	...
Balance Sheet							
Total Assets	401,058,000	321,274,000	292,746,000	293,030,000	272,753,000	285,094,000	...
Total Liabilities	378,714,000	299,982,000	270,726,000	271,887,000	252,145,000	265,803,000	...
Stockholders' Equity	22,344,000	21,292,000	21,330,000	20,453,000	20,608,000	19,291,000	...
Shares Outstanding	529,344	536,853	562,227	585,582	...	...	...
Statistical Record							
Return on Assets %	0.62	0.41	0.07	N.M.	0.14	...	...
Return on Equity %	10.31	5.93	0.93	N.M.	1.99	...	...
Loss Ratio %	102.51	101.44	100.94	102.20	104.10	107.33	108.16
Net Margin %	7.96	4.53	0.73	(0.57)	1.50	3.06	4.09
Price Range	55.09-41.05	42.19-27.56	35.75-25.50	33.19-29.30	...	...	...
P/E Ratio	16.64-12.40	21.31-13.92	28.60-20.40	N/A	...	...	...
Average Yield %	1.35	1.44	1.28	N/A	...	...	...

Address: 751 Broad Street, Newark, NJ 07102	Web Site: www.prudential.com	Auditors: PricewaterhouseCoopers LLP
Telephone: (973) 802-6000	Officers: Arthur F. Ryan - Chmn., Pres., C.E.O. Mark B. Grier - Vice-Chmn., Financial Mgmt.	

PUBLIC SERVICE ENTERPRISE GROUP INC.

Exchange	Symbol	Price	52Wk Range	Yield	P/E
NYS	PEG	$54.39 (3/31/2005)	56.09-38.91	4.12	17.83

*7 Year Price Score 96.46 ***NYSE Composite Index=100** ***12 Month Price Score 110.48**

Interim Earnings (Per Share)

Qtr.	Mar	Jun	Sep	Dec
2001	1.25	0.68	0.82	0.94
2002	0.87	(1.28)	0.99	1.17
2003	3.00	0.57	0.92	0.58
2004	1.14	0.52	1.03	0.36

Interim Dividends (Per Share)

Amt	Decl	Ex	Rec	Pay
0.55Q	4/20/2004	6/4/2004	6/8/2004	6/30/2004
0.55Q	7/20/2004	9/7/2004	9/9/2004	9/30/2004
0.55Q	11/16/2004	12/7/2004	12/9/2004	12/31/2004
0.56Q	1/18/2005	3/7/2005	3/9/2005	3/31/2005

Indicated Div: $2.24

Valuation Analysis

Forecast P/E	16.44	No of Institutions
	(4/7/2005)	343
Market Cap	$13.0 Billion	Shares
Book Value	5.8 Billion	135,327,680
Price/Book	2.23	% Held
Price/Sales	1.18	56.78

TRADING VOLUME (thousand shares)

Business Summary: Electricity (MIC: 7.1 SIC: 931 NAIC: 21119)

Public Service Enterprise Group is the holding company of four wholly-owned subsidiaries. Public Service Electric and Gas (PSE&G) supplies electric and gas service in areas of New Jersey in which approximately 5.5 million people reside. PSEG Power is a multi-regional generating and energy trading company established to acquire, own and operate the electric generation-related business of PSE&G. PSEG Energy Holdings is the parent company for Co.'s non-utility businesses, which includes diversified investments, energy-related engineering, consulting and mechanical contracting services, debt financing and real estate investment. PSEG Services provides management and administrative services.

Recent Developments: For the year ended Dec 31 2004, income from continuing operations decreased 15.4% to $721,000 thousand from income of $852,000 thousand a year earlier. Net income decreased 37.4% to $726,000 thousand from net income of $1,160,000 thousand a year earlier. Revenues were $10,996,000 thousand, down 1.3% from $11,139,000 thousand the year before. Operating income was $1,947,000 thousand versus an income of $2,079,000 thousand in the prior year, a decrease of 6.3%. Total direct expense was $8,317,000 thousand versus $8,511,000 thousand in the prior year, a decrease of 2.3%. Total indirect expense was $858,000 thousand versus $663,000 thousand in the prior year, an increase of 29.4%.

Prospects: Co.'s businesses remain fundamentally strong, and Co. expects improved performance at its Salem and Hope Creek facilities in the coming year due to the major maintenance activities completed during 2004 and from the implementation of a nuclear services operating contract with Exelon in January 2005. Going forward, Co. recently announced its outlook for 2005, which included earnings of $3.15 to $3.35 per share. Co.'s earnings expectations for its major businesses are: PSEG Power - $335.0 to $385.0 million; PSE&G - $325.0 to $345.0 million; and Energy Holdings - $135.0 to $155.0 million for the year.

Financial Data

(US$ in Thousands)	12/31/2004	12/31/2003	12/31/2002	12/31/2001	12/31/2000	12/31/1999	12/31/1998	12/31/1997
Earnings Per Share	3.05	5.07	1.17	3.70	3.55	3.29	2.79	2.41
Cash Flow Per Share	6.78	6.34	7.32	6.44	5.27	5.60	6.16	4.72
Tang Book Value Per Share	21.40	20.83	14.78	16.95	19.21	18.46	22.49	22.47
Dividends Per Share	2.200	2.160	2.160	2.160	2.160	2.160	2.160	2.160
Dividend Payout %	72.13	42.60	184.62	58.38	60.85	65.65	77.42	89.63
Income Statement								
Total Revenue	10,996,000	11,116,000	8,390,000	9,815,000	6,848,000	6,497,000	5,931,000	6,370,000
EBITDA	2,806,000	2,767,000	2,107,000	2,462,000	2,320,000	2,404,000	...	...
Depn & Amortn	799,000	616,000	660,000	621,000	492,000	628,000	763,000	690,000
Income Before Taxes	1,167,000	1,316,000	664,000	1,136,000	1,254,000	1,286,000	...	...
Income Taxes	446,000	464,000	248,000	373,000	490,000	563,000	...	...
Net Income	726,000	1,160,000	245,000	770,000	764,000	(81,000)	644,000	560,000
Average Shares	238,286	228,824	208,813	208,226	215,121	219,814	230,974	231,986
Balance Sheet								
Net PPE	13,750,000	12,422,000	11,449,000	10,064,000	7,702,000	7,078,000	10,876,000	11,050,000
Total Assets	29,207,000	28,055,000	25,742,000	25,397,000	20,796,000	19,015,000	17,997,000	17,943,000
Long-Term Obligations	12,925,000	12,945,000	10,991,000	10,301,000	5,297,000	4,575,000	4,813,000	4,925,000
Total Liabilities	23,388,000	22,446,000	20,355,000	20,500,000	15,592,000	13,811,000	11,691,000	12,562,000
Stockholders' Equity	5,819,000	5,609,000	5,387,000	4,897,000	5,204,000	5,204,000	6,306,000	5,381,000
Shares Outstanding	238,099	236,133	225,267	205,839	207,971	216,417	226,643	231,958
Statistical Record								
Return on Assets %	2.53	4.31	0.96	3.33	3.83	3.80	3.58	3.21
Return on Equity %	12.67	21.10	4.76	15.25	14.64	13.89	11.02	10.32
EBITDA Margin %	25.52	24.89	25.11	25.08	33.88	37.00	...	...
Net Margin %	6.60	10.44	2.92	7.85	11.16	(1.25)	10.86	8.79
PPE Turnover	0.84	0.93	0.78	1.10	0.92	0.72	0.54	0.57
Asset Turnover	0.38	0.41	0.33	0.42	0.34	0.35	0.33	0.37
Debt to Equity	2.22	2.31	2.04	2.10	1.02	0.88	0.76	0.92
Price Range	52.39-38.91	44.40-32.10	46.90-21.76	51.41-38.19	49.88-25.88	42.06-32.38	42.19-30.75	31.81-23.13
P/E Ratio	17.18-12.76	8.76-6.33	40.09-18.60	13.89-10.32	14.05-7.29	12.78-9.84	15.12-11.02	13.20-9.60
Average Yield %	5.08	5.46	5.76	4.88	5.89	5.54	6.11	8.22

Address: 80 Park Plaza, Newark, NJ 07102	**Web Site:** www.pseg.com	**Auditors:** Deloitte & Touche LLP
Telephone: (973) 430-7000	**Officers:** E. James Ferland - Chmn., Pres., C.E.O.	**Investor Contact:** 877-773-4111
Fax: (973) 430-5983	Thomas M. O'Flynn - Exec. V.P., C.F.O.	**Transfer Agents:** PSEG Services Corporation, Newark, NJ

PUBLIC STORAGE INC.

Exchange	Symbol	Price	52Wk Range	Yield	P/E
NYS	PSA	$56.94 (3/31/2005)	58.95-40.35	3.16	41.26

*7 Year Price Score 131.05 *NYSE Composite Index=100 *12 Month Price Score 102.71

Interim Earnings (Per Share)

Qtr.	Mar	Jun	Sep	Dec
2001	0.34	0.39	0.41	0.38
2002	0.37	0.30	0.32	0.20
2003	0.27	0.34	0.39	0.30
2004	0.17	0.37	0.38	0.46

Interim Dividends (Per Share)

Amt	Decl	Ex	Rec	Pay
0.45Q	8/5/2003	9/11/2003	9/15/2003	9/30/2003
0.45Q	11/6/2003	12/11/2003	12/15/2003	12/31/2003
0.45Q	5/12/2004	6/14/2004	6/15/2004	6/30/2004
0.45Q	11/4/2004	12/13/2004	12/15/2004	12/31/2004

Indicated Div: $1.80

Valuation Analysis

Forecast P/E	16.92	No of Institutions
	(4/13/2005)	201
Market Cap	$7.3 Billion	Shares
Book Value	4.4 Billion	64,851,988
Price/Book	1.65	% Held
Price/Sales	7.89	50.06

Business Summary: Property, Real Estate & Development (MIC: 8.3 SIC: 798 NAIC: 25930)

Public Storage is a fully integrated, self-administered and self-managed real estate investment trust (REIT) that primarily acquires, develops, owns and operates self-storage facilities. Co.'s self-storage properties are located in 37 states. Co. had interests in 1,464 storage facilities with approximately 89.2 million net rentable square feet and 748,000 rentable units at Dec 31 2004. In addition, Co. has a 44.0% ownership interest in PS Business Parks, Inc., which owns and operates commercial properties containing approximately 18.0 million net rentable square feet of space.

Recent Developments: For the year ended Dec 31 2004, income from continuing operations was $367.4 million compared with income of $333.1 million a year earlier. Results for 2004 included an asset impairment due to casualty loss from hurricanes of $1.3 million and a charge of $10.1 million associated with special distributions and restructuring allocation. Co. attributed higher earnings primarily to improved operations from its same store, acquired and newly developed self-storage facilities, and a decrease in income allocable to minority interests based upon ongoing distributions as a result of its restructuring of $200.0 million of its Series N preferred partnership units. Revenues rose 7.3% to $928.0 million.

Prospects: During the fourth quarter of 2004, Co. opened three conversions of space at former containerized storage facilities at a total cost of $6.9 million, adding 252,000 net rentable square feet of self-storage space. Going forward, Co. has 47 projects that are in construction or are expected to begin construction within the next year, comprised of 10 newly developed self-storage facilities and 754,000 net rentable square feet. Opening dates for these facilities are estimated through the next 24 months. In addition, Co. acquired 43 facilities from third parties, consisting of approximately 3.0 million net rentable square feet, for an aggregate cost of about $251.2 million.

Financial Data (US$ in Thousands)	12/31/2004	12/31/2003	12/31/2002	12/31/2001	12/31/2000	12/31/1999	12/31/1998	12/31/1997
Earnings Per Share	1.38	1.28	1.19	1.51	1.41	1.52	1.30	0.91
Cash Flow Per Share	5.05	4.75	4.79	4.40	3.81	3.64	3.24	2.98
Tang Book Value Per Share	16.69	16.15	17.31	17.77	18.24	17.50	16.65	16.31
Dividends Per Share	1.800	1.800	1.800	1.690	1.480	0.880	0.880	0.880
Dividend Payout %	130.43	140.63	151.26	111.92	104.96	57.89	67.69	96.70
Income Statement								
Total Revenue	927,976	875,071	841,452	834,645	757,310	676,734	582,151	470,844
Depn & Amortn	40,324	199,989	206,712	193,157	170,792	157,440	121,366	102,830
Net Income	366,213	336,653	318,738	324,208	297,088	287,885	227,019	178,649
Average Shares	128,681	126,517	124,571	123,577	131,657	126,669	114,357	98,961
Balance Sheet								
Current Assets	366,255	204,833	103,124	49,347	89,467	55,125	51,225	41,455
Total Assets	5,204,790	4,968,069	4,843,662	4,625,879	4,513,941	4,214,385	3,403,904	3,311,645
Current Liabilities	...	...	...	25,000	...	82,086	...	7,000
Long-Term Obligations	129,519	76,030	115,867	143,552	156,003	167,338	81,426	96,558
Total Liabilities	345,920	322,133	245,194	261,695	256,906	338,685	145,239	174,206
Stockholders' Equity	4,429,967	4,219,799	4,158,969	3,909,583	3,724,117	3,689,100	3,119,340	2,848,960
Shares Outstanding	128,526	133,986	123,991	121,961	130,703	133,697	122,957	105,102
Statistical Record								
Return on Assets %	7.18	6.86	6.73	7.09	6.79	7.56	6.76	6.07
Return on Equity %	8.44	8.04	7.90	8.49	7.99	8.46	7.61	6.93
Net Margin %	39.46	38.47	37.88	38.84	39.23	42.54	39.00	37.94
Asset Turnover	0.18	0.18	0.18	0.18	0.17	0.18	0.17	0.16
Current Ratio	...	...	...	1.97	...	0.67	...	5.92
Debt to Equity	0.03	0.02	0.03	0.04	0.04	0.05	0.03	0.03
Price Range	57.38-40.35	45.75-28.98	39.05-28.96	35.15-24.19	26.88-21.00	29.31-21.13	33.56-23.00	31.00-26.25
P/E Ratio	41.58-29.24	35.74-22.64	32.82-24.34	23.28-16.02	19.06-14.89	19.28-13.90	25.82-17.69	34.07-28.85
Average Yield %	3.70	4.97	5.23	5.68	6.39	3.42	3.10	3.10

Address: 701 Western Avenue, Glendale, CA 91201-2349 Telephone: (818) 244-8080 Fax: (818) 244-0581	Web Site: www.publicstorage.com Officers: B. Wayne Hughes - Chmn. Ronald L. Havner Jr. - Vice-Chmn. C.E.O.	Auditors: Ernst & Young LLP

PUGET ENERGY, INC.

Exchange	Symbol	Price	52Wk Range	Yield	P/E
NYS	PSD	$22.04 (3/31/2005)	24.73-20.54	4.54	40.07

*7 Year Price Score 84.11 *NYSE Composite Index=100 *12 Month Price Score 94.36

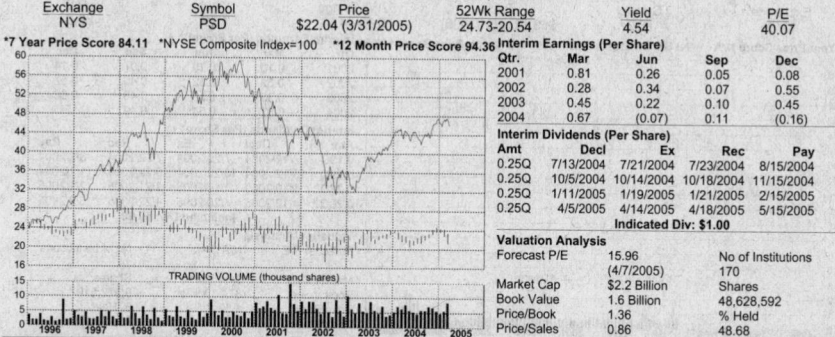

Interim Earnings (Per Share)

Qtr.	Mar	Jun	Sep	Dec
2001	0.81	0.26	0.05	0.08
2002	0.28	0.34	0.07	0.55
2003	0.45	0.22	0.10	0.45
2004	0.67	(0.07)	0.11	(0.16)

Interim Dividends (Per Share)

Amt	Decl	Ex	Rec	Pay
0.25Q	7/13/2004	7/21/2004	7/23/2004	8/15/2004
0.25Q	10/5/2004	10/14/2004	10/18/2004	11/15/2004
0.25Q	1/11/2005	1/19/2005	1/21/2005	2/15/2005
0.25Q	4/5/2005	4/14/2005	4/18/2005	5/15/2005

Indicated Div: $1.00

Valuation Analysis

Forecast P/E	15.96	No of Institutions
	(4/7/2005)	170
Market Cap	$2.2 Billion	Shares
Book Value	1.6 Billion	48,628,592
Price/Book	1.36	% Held
Price/Sales	0.86	48.68

Business Summary: Electricity (MIC: 7.1 SIC: 911 NAIC: 21121)

Puget Energy is an energy services holding company. Through its Puget Sound Energy, Inc. (PSE) subsidiary, Co. provides electric and gas services principally in the Puget Sound region of Washington. As of Dec 31 2004, PSE had about 1.0 million electric customers, consisting of 884,500 residential, 110,500 commercial, 3,900 industrial and 2,300 other customers; and about 672,00 gas customers, consisting of 619,000 residential, 50,200 commercial, 2,700 industrial and 100 transportation customers. Co.'s other subsidiary, InfrastruX, provides contracting services to other gas and electric utilities primarily in the Midwest, Texas, and the south-central and the eastern U.S. regions.

Recent Developments: For the year ended Dec 31 2004, net income increased 5.3% to $126,192 thousand from net income of $119,886 thousand a year earlier. Revenues were $2,198,877 thousand, up 7.7% from $2,041,016 thousand the year before. Operating income was $288,241 thousand versus an income of $297,904 thousand in the prior year, a decrease of 3.2%. Total direct expense was $1,373,216 thousand versus $1,223,771 thousand in the prior year, an increase of 12.2%. Total indirect expense was $537,420 thousand versus $519,341 thousand in the prior year, an increase of 3.5%.

Prospects: On Feb 18 2005, the Washington Commission approved a 3.5% general tariff gas rate case increase and a 4.0% general tariff electric rate case increase. The increases translate to $26.3 million annually for gas customers and $56.6 million for electric customers effective Mar 4 2005. Meanwhile, on Feb 8 2005, Co. announced it would exit the utility construction services sector. Co. intends to sell its interest in InfrastruX through a sale or third party recapitalization and to invest the proceeds in PSE. Separately, Co. is projecting 2005 earnings from continuing operations of between $1.30 and $1.40 per diluted share, and for 2006, a target of between $1.40 and $1.55 per diluted share.

Financial Data
(US$ in Thousands)

	12/31/2004	12/31/2003	12/31/2002	12/31/2001	12/31/2000	12/31/1999	12/31/1998	12/31/1997
Earnings Per Share	0.55	1.22	1.24	1.14	2.16	2.06	1.85	1.28
Cash Flow Per Share	4.58	3.41	8.19	3.45	3.74	3.67	3.72	1.53
Tang Book Value Per Share	15.64	15.17	14.73	14.55	16.61	16.24	16.00	16.06
Dividends Per Share	1.000	1.000	1.210	1.840	1.840	1.840	1.840	1.840
Dividend Payout %	181.82	81.97	97.58	161.40	85.19	89.32	99.46	143.75
Income Statement								
Total Revenue	2,568,813	2,491,523	2,392,322	3,373,991	3,441,672	2,066,630	1,907,340	1,676,902
Depn & Amortn	246,842	236,866	228,743	217,540	196,513	175,710	165,587	161,865
Income Taxes	76,150	73,639	60,582	...	...	...	...	...
Net Income	55,022	121,348	117,883	106,839	193,831	185,567	169,612	123,076
Average Shares	99,911	95,309	88,777	86,445	85,411	84,613	84,768	84,628
Balance Sheet								
Net PPE	4,228,358	4,080,227	3,916,229	3,887,981	3,838,409	3,750,921	3,430,912	3,250,461
Total Assets	5,833,369	5,674,685	5,657,491	5,546,977	5,556,669	5,145,606	4,720,689	4,493,370
Long-Term Obligations	2,492,782	2,249,739	2,149,733	2,127,054	2,170,797	1,783,139	1,474,748	1,411,707
Total Liabilities	4,206,445	4,007,950	4,063,075	4,124,253	4,070,029	3,706,533	3,272,934	3,039,805
Stockholders' Equity	1,622,276	1,655,046	1,583,787	1,422,724	1,486,640	1,439,073	1,447,755	1,453,565
Shares Outstanding	99,868	99,074	93,642	87,023	85,903	84,922	84,561	84,561
Statistical Record								
Return on Assets %	0.95	2.14	2.10	1.92	3.61	3.76	3.68	3.20
Return on Equity %	3.35	7.49	7.84	7.34	13.21	12.86	11.69	8.93
Net Margin %	2.14	4.87	4.93	3.17	5.63	8.98	8.89	7.34
PPE Turnover	0.62	0.62	0.61	0.87	0.90	0.58	0.57	0.61
Asset Turnover	0.45	0.44	0.43	0.61	0.64	0.42	0.41	0.44
Debt to Equity	1.54	1.36	1.36	1.50	1.46	1.24	1.02	0.97
Price Range	24.73-20.54	24.09-18.10	23.41-17.30	27.00-18.80	27.81-19.06	28.00-19.00	30.19-24.56	30.19-23.63
P/E Ratio	44.96-37.35	19.75-14.84	18.88-13.95	23.68-16.49	12.88-8.83	13.59-9.22	16.32-13.28	23.58-18.46
Average Yield %	4.44	4.53	5.73	7.94	7.89	7.80	6.81	7.09

Address: 10885 NE 4th Street, Suite 1200, Bellevue, WA 98004-5591 **Telephone:** (425) 454-6363	**Web Site:** www.pse.com **Officers:** Douglas P. Beighle - Chmn. Stephen P. Reynolds - Pres., C.E.O.	**Auditors:** PricewaterhouseCoopers LLP **Investor Contact:** 425-462-3808

PULITZER, INC.

Exchange	Symbol	Price	52Wk Range	Yield	P/E
NYS	PTZ	$63.73 (3/31/2005)	65.62-44.00	1.26	30.94

*7 Year Price Score N/A *NYSE Composite Index=100 *12 Month Price Score 108.68

Interim Earnings (Per Share)

Qtr.	Mar	Jun	Sep	Dec
2001	0.10	0.19	0.07	0.14
2002	0.32	0.32	0.40	0.57
2003	0.33	0.53	0.43	0.66
2004	0.37	0.54	0.49	...

Interim Dividends (Per Share)

Amt	Decl	Ex	Rec	Pay
0.19Q	7/12/2004	7/20/2004	7/22/2004	8/2/2004
0.19Q	10/12/2004	10/20/2004	10/22/2004	11/1/2004
0.20Q	1/10/2005	1/19/2005	1/21/2005	2/1/2005
0.20Q	4/12/2005	4/20/2005	4/22/2005	5/2/2005
		Indicated Div: $0.80		

Valuation Analysis

Forecast P/E	N/A	No of Institutions
		75
Market Cap	$1.4 Billion	Shares
Book Value	874.3 Million	9,572,510
Price/Book	1.58	% Held
Price/Sales	3.13	43.81

TRADING VOLUME (thousand shares)

1996 1997 1998 1999 2000 2001 2002 2003 2004 2005

Business Summary: Media (MIC: 13.1 SIC: 711 NAIC: 11110)

Pulitzer is a newspaper publishing company with integrated Internet operations in 14 U.S. markets. Co.'s newspaper holdings include two major metropolitan newspapers, the St. Louis Post-Dispatch and The Arizona Daily Star, and other daily newspapers, primarily serving small to mid-size markets in the West and Midwest. Co. also owns the Suburban Journals of Greater St. Louis, a group of 37 weekly papers and various niche publications. Co.'s news media and interactive Web sites include STLtoday.com in St. Louis, MO and azstarnet.com in Tucson, AZ.

Recent Developments: For the year ended Dec 26 2004, Co. reported net income of $44.1 million, up 4.6% from $42.2 million the year before. Total operating revenues rose 5.0% to $443.7 million from $422.7 million in 2003. The increase in revenues was lead by a 5.9% increase to $354.8 million in advertising revenue, an 0.8% increase to $81.3 million in circulation revenue and a 10.6% increase in other revenue. Operating income was $85.1 million, down 2.4% from $87.2 million the year before. Equity in earnings of Tucson newspaper partnership were $18.0 million in 2004 and $16.1 million in 2003.

Prospects: On Jan 30 2004, Co. announced that it has agreed to be acquired by Lee Enterprises for a cash purchase price of $1.46 billion, or $64.00 per share. In the combined company, Co. will represent about 39.0% of the revenue and 34.0% of the daily circulation. Upon completion, Lee will become the fourth largest U.S. newspaper publisher in terms of dailies owned and seventh largest in circulation, growing from 44 to 58 daily newspapers in 23 states, with new total circulation of 1.7 million daily and 2.0 million on Sunday. The transaction is expected to close in the second quarter of calendar 2005.

Financial Data

(US$ in Thousands)	9 Mos	6 Mos	3 Mos	12/31/2003	12/31/2002	12/30/2001	12/31/2000	12/31/1999
Earnings Per Share	2.06	2.01	1.99	1.95	1.62	0.50	1.60	0.07
Cash Flow Per Share	4.12	3.98	4.23	3.77	4.60	3.13	4.60	1.60
Tang Book Value Per Share	1.06	0.83	0.48	0.13	N.M.	N.M.	N.M.	28.42
Dividends Per Share	0.750	0.740	0.730	0.720	0.700	0.680	0.640	0.450
Dividend Payout %	36.32	36.89	36.62	36.92	43.21	136.00	40.00	642.86
Income Statement								
Total Revenue	325,518	215,788	102,735	422,664	415,960	413,506	407,541	391,383
EBITDA	75,116	49,516	21,663	105,092	93,740	78,690	90,507	33,379
Depn & Amortn	15,192	9,896	4,928	19,113	18,714	40,508	33,657	17,091
Income Before Taxes	48,836	32,247	13,200	69,271	58,668	21,146	59,346	41,665
Income Taxes	17,524	11,739	4,884	25,306	22,371	8,021	23,595	18,708
Net Income	30,451	19,851	8,055	42,177	34,699	10,662	34,902	1,508
Average Shares	21,819	21,828	21,855	21,627	21,447	21,364	21,786	22,601
Balance Sheet								
Current Assets	284,752	273,097	266,798	254,730	265,350	272,536	268,193	635,220
Total Assets	1,350,011	1,333,978	1,323,383	1,309,673	1,287,246	1,288,783	1,282,873	978,287
Current Liabilities	51,841	45,368	44,296	40,294	39,802	51,534	49,574	39,690
Long-Term Obligations	306,000	306,000	306,000	306,000	306,000	306,000	306,000	...
Total Liabilities	475,670	467,505	464,870	458,229	472,028	491,546	483,172	164,836
Stockholders' Equity	874,341	866,473	858,513	851,444	815,218	797,237	799,701	813,451
Shares Outstanding	21,613	21,604	21,575	21,515	21,332	21,209	21,152	22,092
Statistical Record								
Return on Assets %	3.37	3.32	3.32	3.25	2.69	0.83	3.08	0.20
Return on Equity %	5.26	5.16	5.17	5.06	4.29	1.34	4.32	0.25
EBITDA Margin %	23.08	22.95	21.09	24.86	22.54	19.03	22.21	8.53
Net Margin %	9.35	9.20	7.84	9.98	8.34	2.58	8.56	0.39
Asset Turnover	0.33	0.33	0.33	0.33	0.32	0.32	0.36	0.51
Current Ratio	5.49	6.02	6.02	6.32	6.67	5.29	5.41	16.00
Debt to Equity	0.35	0.35	0.36	0.36	0.38	0.38	0.38	...
Price Range	56.11-44.00	56.11-45.30	56.11-42.98	54.40-40.93	55.48-41.05	56.91-43.16	47.22-34.00	48.56-36.38
P/E Ratio	27.24-21.36	27.92-22.54	28.20-21.60	27.90-20.99	34.25-25.34	113.82-86.32	29.51-21.25	693.75-519.64
Average Yield %	1.49	1.45	1.44	1.48	1.45	1.36	1.55	1.05

Address: 900 North Tucker Boulevard, St. Louis, MO 63101	Web Site: www.pulitzerinc.com	Auditors: Deloitte & Touche LLP
Telephone: (314) 340-8000	Officers: Michael E. Pulitzer - Chmn. Robert C. Woodworth - Pres., C.E.O.	Investor Contact: 314-340-8402
Fax: (314) 340-3125		

PULTE HOMES, INC.

Exchange	Symbol	Price	52Wk Range	Yield	P/E
NYS	PHM	$73.63 (3/31/2005)	79.64-45.60	0.27	9.71

*7 Year Price Score 193.70 *NYSE Composite Index=100 *12 Month Price Score 116.85

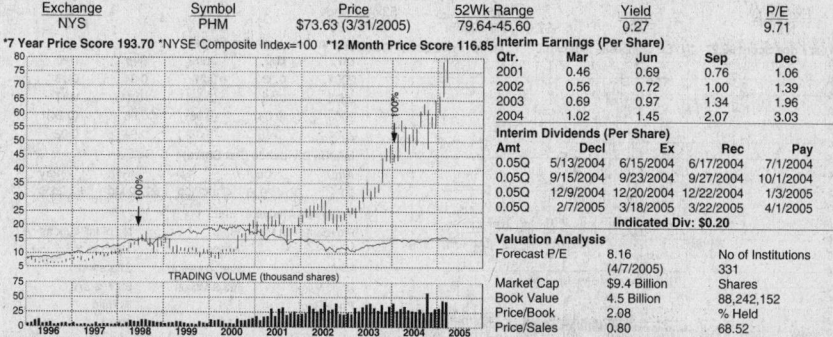

Interim Earnings (Per Share)

Qtr.	Mar	Jun	Sep	Dec
2001	0.46	0.69	0.76	1.06
2002	0.56	0.72	1.00	1.39
2003	0.69	0.97	1.34	1.96
2004	1.02	1.45	2.07	3.03

Interim Dividends (Per Share)

Amt	Decl	Ex	Rec	Pay
0.05Q	5/13/2004	6/15/2004	6/17/2004	7/1/2004
0.05Q	9/15/2004	9/23/2004	9/27/2004	10/1/2004
0.05Q	12/9/2004	12/20/2004	12/22/2004	1/3/2005
0.05Q	2/7/2005	3/18/2005	3/22/2005	4/1/2005

Indicated Div: $0.20

Valuation Analysis

Forecast P/E	8.16 (4/7/2005)	No of Institutions 331
Market Cap	$9.4 Billion	Shares
Book Value	4.5 Billion	88,242,152
Price/Book	2.08	% Held
Price/Sales	0.80	68.52

Business Summary: Building & General Construction (MIC: 3.2 SIC: 531 NAIC: 36115)

Pulte Homes is engaged in the homebuilding and financial services businesses. As of Dec 31 2003, Co.'s domestic homebuilding business operated in 44 markets spanning 27 states and offered homes for sale in 535 communities. Through its Del Webb acquisition, Co. is also a builder of active adult communities for people age 55 and older. Co. has two operating segments: Homebuilding, which includes the domestic, international and active adult markets, and Financial Services, which consists principally of the mortgage banking operations of Pulte Mortgage Corporation.

Recent Developments: For the year ended Dec 31 2004, income from continuing operations increased 61.2% to $998,008 thousand from income of $619,243 thousand a year earlier. Net income increased 57.9% to $986,541 thousand from net income of $624,634 thousand a year earlier. Revenues were $11,711,216 thousand, up 30.0% from $9,011,914 thousand the year before. Total direct expense was $10,078,359 thousand versus $7,973,426 thousand in the prior year, an increase of 26.4%. Total indirect expense was $92,434 thousand versus $78,632 thousand in the prior year, an increase of 17.6%.

Prospects: Prospects appear favorable, given Co.'s strong backlog level, solid housing demand and a robust community pipeline. Looking ahead, Co. is projecting earnings per diluted share from continuing operations to increase at an average annual rate of approximately 20.0% over the next three years. Meanwhile, Co. anticipates full-year 2005 earnings from continuing operations of between $9.00 and $9.50 per diluted share, representing year-over-year growth of 17.0% to 24.0%. Separately, on Jan 7 2005, Co. announced that it has completed the sale of its Argentina operations to Grupo Farallon, S.A. Terms of the transaction were not disclosed.

Financial Data

(US$ in Thousands)	12/31/2004	12/31/2003	12/31/2002	12/31/2001	12/31/2000	12/31/1999	12/31/1998	12/31/1997
Earnings Per Share	7.58	4.97	3.67	3.00	2.23	2.04	1.17	0.60
Cash Flow Per Share	(5.51)	(2.47)	1.34	(4.26)	0.28	0.13	(1.50)	(0.40)
Tang Book Value Per Share	31.90	23.94	18.82	15.27	15.01	12.64	10.67	9.55
Dividends Per Share	0.200	0.110	0.080	0.080	0.080	0.080	0.075	0.060
Dividend Payout %	2.64	2.21	2.18	2.67	3.58	3.93	6.44	10.00
Income Statement								
Total Revenue	11,711,216	9,048,926	7,471,819	5,381,920	4,159,051	3,730,337	2,866,521	2,523,991
EBITDA	1,646,837	1,035,856	728,822	491,787	355,096	286,405	165,814	80,975
Depn & Amortn	46,300	40,200	...	...	...	...	...	...
Income Before Taxes	1,600,537	995,656	728,822	491,787	355,096	286,405	165,814	80,975
Income Taxes	602,529	378,334	284,221	189,362	136,712	108,118	64,666	31,175
Net Income	986,541	624,634	453,645	301,393	188,513	178,165	102,183	52,761
Average Shares	130,117	125,730	123,492	100,646	84,292	87,646	87,768	87,816
Balance Sheet								
Current Assets	7,705,425	5,932,502	4,906,765	3,905,907	2,064,248	1,844,451	1,580,406	1,387,108
Total Assets	10,406,897	8,063,352	6,888,455	5,714,276	2,886,483	2,596,797	2,349,839	2,150,765
Current Liabilities	1,770,061	1,383,833	1,292,100	1,699,742	960,950	920,554	802,025	673,441
Long-Term Obligations	2,861,550	2,150,972	1,913,268	1,737,869	677,602	525,965	570,114	584,313
Total Liabilities	5,884,623	4,615,229	4,128,029	3,437,611	1,638,552	1,503,478	1,428,397	1,337,928
Stockholders' Equity	4,522,274	3,448,123	2,760,426	2,276,665	1,247,931	1,093,319	921,442	812,837
Shares Outstanding	127,874	125,152	122,249	118,498	83,133	86,527	86,334	85,092
Statistical Record								
Return on Assets %	10.65	8.36	7.20	7.01	6.86	7.20	4.54	2.55
Return on Equity %	24.69	20.12	18.01	17.10	16.06	17.69	11.78	6.43
EBITDA Margin %	14.06	11.45	9.75	9.14	8.54	7.68	5.78	3.21
Net Margin %	8.42	6.90	6.07	5.60	4.53	4.78	3.56	2.09
Asset Turnover	1.26	1.21	1.19	1.25	1.51	1.51	1.27	1.22
Current Ratio	4.35	4.29	3.80	2.30	2.15	2.00	1.97	2.06
Debt to Equity	0.63	0.62	0.69	0.76	0.54	0.48	0.62	0.72
Price Range	64.99-42.84	48.98-22.75	29.47-18.30	24.79-13.50	21.88-7.84	15.63-8.50	17.72-10.00	10.56-6.91
P/E Ratio	8.57-5.65	9.86-4.58	8.03-4.99	8.26-4.50	9.81-3.52	7.66-4.17	15.14-8.55	17.60-11.51
Average Yield %	0.38	0.33	0.33	0.42	0.61	0.74	0.57	0.69

Address: 100 Bloomfield Hills Parkway, Suite 300, Bloomfield Hills, MI 48304	**Web Site:** www.pulte.com	**Auditors:** Ernst & Young LLP
	Officers: William J. Pulte - Chmn. Richard J. Dugas Jr. - Pres., C.E.O.	**Investor Contact:** 248-433-4597
Telephone: (248) 647-2750		
Fax: (248) 433-4598		

QUANTA SERVICES, INC.

Exchange	Symbol	Price	52Wk Range	Yield	P/E
NYS	PWR	$7.63 (3/31/2005)	8.40-4.83	N/A	N/A

*7 Year Price Score 36.27   *NYSE Composite Index=100   *12 Month Price Score 106.63

Interim Earnings (Per Share)

Qtr.	Mar	Jun	Sep	Dec
2001	0.38	0.21	0.34	0.18
2002	0.13	(2.26)	(0.11)	0.17
2003	(0.04)	(0.08)	0.05	(0.24)
2004	(0.10)	(0.03)	0.04	0.02

Interim Dividends (Per Share)

Amt	Decl	Ex	Rec	Pay
50%	3/14/2000	4/10/2000	3/27/2000	4/7/2000

Valuation Analysis

Forecast P/E	38.30	No of Institutions
	(4/7/2005)	147
Market Cap	$893.8 Million	Shares
Book Value	663.2 Million	93,782,376
Price/Book	1.35	% Held
Price/Sales	0.55	80.79

Business Summary: Building & General Construction (MIC: 3.2 SIC: 731 NAIC: 38210)

Quanta Services is a provider of specialized contracting services, offering end-to-end network solutions to the electric power, gas, telecommunications and cable television industries. Co.'s services include designing, installing, repairing and maintaining network infrastructure. Co.'s also provides ancillary services, such as inside electrical wiring, intelligent traffic networks, cable and control systems for light rail lines, airports and highways and specialty rock trenching, directional boring and road milling for industrial and commercial customers.

Recent Developments: For the year ended Dec 31 2004, net loss was $9,194 thousand versus net loss of $34,989 thousand a year earlier. Revenues were $1,626,510 thousand, down 1.0% from $1,642,853 thousand the year before. Operating income was $9,854 thousand versus an income of $15,224 thousand in the prior year, a decrease of 35.3%. Total direct expense was $1,445,119 thousand versus $1,442,958 thousand in the prior year, an increase of 0.1%. Total indirect expense was $171,537 thousand versus $184,671 thousand in the prior year, a decrease of 7.1%.

Prospects: Co. enters 2005 with cautious enthusiasm. The Fiber to the Premises initiatives of Co.'s telecommunications customers and increased spending by its utility customers should facilitate its improved performance and provide it with opportunities for growth. In addition, Co. ended 2004 in a strong financial position with more than $265.0 million in cash on its balance sheet, which helps position it financially and operationally to pursue growth opportunities in 2005. Separately, for the first quarter of 2005, Co. expects revenues to range from $345.0 million to $360.0 million, and a loss per share of approximately $0.04 to $0.06.

Financial Data (US$ in Thousands)	12/31/2004	12/31/2003	12/31/2002	12/31/2001	12/31/2000	12/31/1999	12/31/1998	12/31/1997
Earnings Per Share	(0.08)	(0.30)	(7.77)	1.10	1.42	1.00	0.37	0.28
Cash Flow Per Share	1.26	1.06	1.50	2.72	0.77	0.98	0.21	0.56
Tang Book Value Per Share	2.34	2.35	3.05	2.79	2.80	2.41	0.40	0.68
Income Statement								
Total Revenue	1,626,510	1,642,853	1,750,713	2,014,877	1,793,301	925,654	309,209	76,204
EBITDA	77,410	41,753	(97,402)	272,412	282,053	153,285	42,093	8,855
Depn & Amortn	64,988	63,000	60,576	79,374	57,294	35,163	10,600	3,323
Income Before Taxes	(12,645)	(53,069)	(193,844)	156,966	199,051	102,938	26,858	4,313
Income Taxes	(3,451)	(18,080)	(19,710)	71,200	93,328	48,999	11,683	1,786
Net Income	(9,194)	(34,989)	(619,556)	85,766	105,723	53,939	15,175	2,527
Average Shares	114,441	110,906	80,815	78,238	76,583	56,146	41,998	8,892
Balance Sheet								
Current Assets	700,036	676,093	529,497	577,120	602,407	335,063	104,729	16,702
Total Assets	1,459,997	1,466,435	1,364,812	2,042,901	1,874,094	1,159,636	334,958	35,747
Current Liabilities	221,058	199,390	212,141	241,530	252,437	170,923	48,884	14,516
Long-Term Obligations	464,363	500,551	385,667	500,274	491,102	199,658	109,551	7,542
Total Liabilities	796,750	803,303	680,219	836,150	805,138	402,711	164,660	24,537
Stockholders' Equity	663,247	663,132	611,671	1,206,751	1,068,956	756,925	170,298	11,210
Shares Outstanding	117,139	116,567	70,790	60,760	58,166	54,781	48,807	16,418
Statistical Record								
Return on Assets %	N.M.	N.M.	N.M.	4.38	6.95	7.22	8.19	...
Return on Equity %	N.M.	N.M.	N.M.	7.54	11.55	11.63	16.72	...
EBITDA Margin %	4.76	2.54	N.M.	13.52	15.73	16.56	13.61	11.62
Net Margin %	N.M.	N.M.	N.M.	4.26	5.90	5.83	4.91	3.32
Asset Turnover	1.11	1.16	1.03	1.03	1.18	1.24	1.67	...
Current Ratio	3.17	3.39	2.50	2.39	2.39	1.96	2.14	1.15
Debt to Equity	0.70	0.75	0.63	0.41	0.46	0.26	0.64	0.67
Price Range	9.26-4.83	9.78-2.90	18.80-1.82	36.90-10.30	62.06-18.58	29.33-14.00	14.75-7.50	...
P/E Ratio	...	...	...	33.55-9.36	43.71-13.09	29.33-14.00	39.86-20.27	...

Address: 1360 Post Oak Boulevard, Suite 2100, Houston, TX 77056 Telephone: (713) 629-7600 Fax: (713) 629-7676	Web Site: www.quantaservices.com Officers: John R. Colson - C.E.O. Peter T. Dameris - Exec. V.P., C.O.O.	Auditors: PricewaterhouseCoopers LLP Investor Contact: 713-629-7600

QUANTUM CORP.

Exchange	Symbol	Price	52Wk Range	Yield	P/E
NYS	DSS	$2.91 (3/31/2005)	3.88-2.09	N/A	N/A

*7 Year Price Score N/A   ***NYSE Composite Index=100**   ***12 Month Price Score 97.23**

Interim Earnings (Per Share)

Qtr.	Jun	Sep	Dec	Mar
2001-02	0.50	(0.10)	...	(0.14)
2002-03	(0.84)	(0.71)	(0.09)	(0.01)
2003-04	(0.05)	(0.22)	(0.03)	(0.05)
2004-05	(0.06)	(0.03)	0.08	...

Interim Dividends (Per Share)

No Dividends Paid

Valuation Analysis

Forecast P/E	N/A	No of Institutions	
Market Cap	$533.7 Million	Shares	
Book Value	310.8 Million	154,253,472	
Price/Book	1.72	% Held	
Price/Sales	0.70	84.11	

Business Summary: IT & Technology (MIC: 10.2 SIC: 572 NAIC: 34112)

Quantum is engaged in data storage. Co.'s DLTtape™ technology is utilized for backup, recovery, and archiving of business-critical data for the mid-range enterprise. Co. is also engaged in the design, development, manufacture, marketing and selling of tape libraries and autoloaders used to manage, store and transfer data. Co.'s business has two segments: the DLTtape business and the Storage Systems business. The DLTtape business designs, develops, licenses, services, and markets DLTtape and Super DLTtape™ drives, and DLTtape and Super DLTtape media cartridges. The Storage Systems business consists of tape automation systems and service and includes disk-based backup systems.

Recent Developments: For the three months ended Dec 26 2004, net income was $16.3 million compared with a loss from continuing operations of $6.5 million a year earlier. Results for 2004 and 2003 included special charges of $641,000 and $4.6 million, respectively. Total revenue declined 1.9% to $201.4 million from $205.4 million the previous year. Gross margin amounted to $60.1 million, or 29.8% of total revenue, versus $65.1 million, or 31.7% of total revenue, the year before. Income from operations was $4.8 million compared with a loss from operations of $1.5 million in the prior-year quarter.

Prospects: Co. has completed the acquisition of Certance, a supplier of tape drives and data protection solutions. Under the agreement, Co. acquired all of Certance for $60.0 million in cash. Separately, Co. is seeing solid improvements in its revenues and earnings with revenue growth in both storage systems and tape media, and strong sales of its tape drive, tape automation and disk-based product offerings. This recent progress, combined with the acquisition of Certance should is expected to provide a foundation for future growth of Co.'s business in backup, recovery and archive. Going forward, Co. expects leveraging synergies from the acquisition to improve its cost and expense structure.

Financial Data
(US$ in Thousands)

	9 Mos	6 Mos	3 Mos	03/31/2004	03/31/2003	03/31/2002	03/31/2001	03/31/2000
Earnings Per Share	(0.06)	(0.17)	(0.36)	(0.35)	(1.63)	0.27	1.08	0.10
Cash Flow Per Share	0.18	0.12	0.05	(0.01)	0.11	0.25	1.20	2.99
Tang Book Value Per Share	1.19	1.07	1.07	1.11	1.34	1.96	4.60	4.35
Income Statement								
Total Revenue	554,128	352,729	172,684	808,384	870,809	1,087,792	1,405,818	4,727,204
EBITDA	30,064	13,138	5,807	34,841	(61,921)	(9,729)	399,988	248,124
Depn & Amortn	30,535	20,739	10,469	48,181	50,833	76,978	120,695	130,569
Income Before Taxes	(8,777)	(13,152)	(7,439)	(30,957)	(137,173)	(109,801)	261,635	89,170
Income Taxes	(8,730)	3,180	2,750	32,758	(5,085)	(27,331)	94,189	48,326
Net Income	(47)	(16,332)	(10,189)	(62,022)	(264,295)	42,502	160,686	40,844
Average Shares	219,280	180,913	179,713	176,037	162,208	155,169	155,645	165,788
Balance Sheet								
Current Assets	558,302	546,214	545,611	546,544	640,408	724,678	1,360,546	2,013,554
Total Assets	691,951	686,108	696,099	705,558	921,729	1,193,772	1,899,704	2,533,952
Current Liabilities	194,029	205,753	212,448	211,884	253,976	297,135	280,057	854,247
Long-Term Obligations	160,000	160,000	160,000	160,000	287,500	287,500	287,500	325,338
Total Liabilities	381,140	392,880	399,572	399,009	566,567	633,271	603,364	1,234,921
Stockholders' Equity	310,811	293,228	296,527	306,549	355,162	560,501	1,296,340	1,299,031
Shares Outstanding	183,400	182,400	181,900	180,317	175,451	156,967	232,146	241,207
Statistical Record								
Return on Assets %	N.M.	N.M.	N.M.	N.M.	N.M.	2.75	7.25	1.62
Return on Equity %	N.M.	N.M.	N.M.	N.M.	N.M.	4.58	12.38	3.03
EBITDA Margin %	5.43	3.72	3.36	4.31	N.M.	N.M.	28.45	5.25
Net Margin %	N.M.	N.M.	N.M.	N.M.	N.M.	3.91	11.43	0.86
Asset Turnover	1.08	1.08	0.98	0.99	0.82	0.70	0.63	1.88
Current Ratio	2.88	2.65	2.57	2.58	2.52	2.44	4.86	2.36
Debt to Equity	0.51	0.55	0.54	0.52	0.81	0.51	0.22	0.25
Price Range	4.19-2.09	4.19-2.09	4.86-2.47	4.86-2.80	8.10-1.42	12.85-7.35	16.13-9.44	21.44-8.75
P/E Ratio	...	...	...	...	...	47.59-27.22	14.93-8.74	214.38-87.50

Address: 501 Sycamore Drive, Milpitas, CA 95035	Web Site: www.quantum.com	Auditors: Ernst & Young LLP
Telephone: (408) 944-4000	Officers: Richard E. Belluzzo - Chmn., C.E.O. John B. Gannon - Pres., C.O.O.	Investor Contact: 1-877-999-7686
Fax: (408) 894-3218		

QUEBECOR WORLD INC.

Exchange	Symbol	Price	52Wk Range	Yield	P/E
NYS	IQW	$23.56 (3/31/2005)	24.05-16.93	2.38	29.45

*7 Year Price Score 83.21   *NYSE Composite Index=100   *12 Month Price Score 100.71

Interim Earnings (Per Share)

Qtr.	Mar	Jun	Sep	Dec
2001	0.27	0.41	0.46	...
2002	0.28	0.40	0.64	0.45
2003	0.12	(0.51)	0.38	(0.47)
2004	0.20	0.05	0.29	0.25

Interim Dividends (Per Share)

Amt	Decl	Ex	Rec	Pay
0.13Q	5/5/2004	5/12/2004	5/14/2004	6/1/2004
0.13Q	7/28/2004	8/11/2004	8/13/2004	9/1/2004
0.13Q	10/27/2004	11/9/2004	11/12/2004	12/1/2004
0.14Q	2/15/2005	2/22/2005	2/24/2005	3/1/2005
		Indicated Div: $0.56		

Valuation Analysis

Forecast P/E	13.97	No of Institutions	
	(4/13/2005)	50	
Market Cap	$3.1 Billion	Shares	
Book Value	2.6 Billion	46,575,116	
Price/Book	1.20	% Held	
Price/Sales	0.47	54.42	

TRADING VOLUME (thousand shares)

Business Summary: Printing (MIC: 13.4 SIC: 759 NAIC: 23113)

Quebecor World is engaged in commercial print media services. Co.'s product categories include magazines, retail inserts and circulars, books, catalogs, specialty printing and direct mail, directories, digital pre-media, logistics, mail list technologies and other services. As of Dec 31 2004, Co. had approximately 160 printing and related facilities in the United States, Canada, France, the United Kingdom, Spain, Switzerland, Sweden, Finland, Austria, Belgium, Brazil, Chile, Argentina, Peru, Colombia, Mexico and India.

Recent Developments: For the year ended Dec 31 2004, net income increased to $143.7 million compared with a net loss of $31.4 million for the full-year of 2003. Results included an impairment of assets, restructuring and other charges of $122.1 million in 2004 and $98.3 million in 2003. Revenues increase 3.6% to $6.62 billion from $6.39 billion a year earlier. On a geographic basis, North America revenues inched up 1.4% to $5.13 billion, while Europe revenues grew 12.7% to $1.30 billion. Latin America revenues climbed 8.5% to $192.4 million. Operating income increased 66.0% to $361.3 million from $217.6 million in the previous year.

Prospects: Co. is progressing with its restructuring initiatives implemented in 2004 that include the closing and downsizing of certain facilities and the redeployment of equipment within Co.'s platform. In 2005, Co. expects to record $17.8 million in restructuring charges related to the 2004 initiatives. Meanwhile, benefits from these actions are beginning to emerge as Co. is starting to see a turnaround in its operating performance. As Co. goes forward it will continue to focus on cost containment while investing in new technologies to improve performance and enhance its service offerings.

Financial Data

(US$ in Thousands)	12/31/2004	12/31/2003	12/31/2002	12/31/2001	12/31/2000	12/31/1999	12/31/1998	12/31/1997
Earnings Per Share	0.80	(0.50)	1.76	...	...	...	...	...
Cash Flow Per Share	3.67	3.39	3.65	4.05	6.22	...	...	...
Tang Book Value Per Share	N.M.	N.M.	N.M.	N.M.	N.M.	N.M.	5.92	7.27
Dividends Per Share	0.520	0.520	0.490	0.460	0.330	0.280	0.240	0.220
Dividend Payout %	65.00	...	27.84					
Income Statement								
Total Revenue	6,622,100	6,391,500	6,242,000	6,320,100	6,521,077	4,952,537	3,808,155	3,483,199
EBITDA	722,800	591,500	878,800	747,000	1,141,452	579,237	541,288	478,100
Depn & Amortn	361,500	359,400	335,600	399,200	413,920	285,992	239,402	210,729
Income Before Taxes	228,100	10,800	373,000	139,000	496,068	171,068	237,586	201,559
Income Taxes	78,900	39,100	90,900	52,000	137,735	48,161	74,828	69,108
Net Income	143,700	(31,400)	279,300	22,400	295,431	80,056	159,560	130,440
Average Shares	132,600	136,000	145,400	143,000	...	...	...	...
Balance Sheet								
Current Assets	999,100	908,000	967,300	913,200	1,185,274	1,260,977	954,230	958,355
Total Assets	6,244,400	6,213,800	6,205,500	6,149,900	6,484,660	6,756,252	3,842,116	3,475,538
Current Liabilities	1,034,400	1,101,000	1,176,600	1,107,700	1,251,809	1,221,288	710,124	739,046
Long-Term Obligations	1,938,400	1,985,100	1,783,600	2,075,200	2,121,490	2,762,663	1,199,134	973,290
Total Liabilities	3,631,800	3,710,400	3,501,700	3,676,700	4,010,780	4,435,368	2,277,612	2,039,198
Stockholders' Equity	2,612,600	2,503,400	2,703,800	2,473,200	2,473,880	2,320,884	1,564,504	1,436,340
Shares Outstanding	132,591	131,951	141,145	140,184	146,139	159,675	127,790	115,577
Statistical Record								
Return on Assets %	2.30	N.M.	4.52	0.35	4.45	1.51	4.36	4.08
Return on Equity %	5.60	N.M.	10.79	0.91	12.29	4.12	10.63	10.07
EBITDA Margin %	10.91	9.25	14.08	11.82	17.50	11.70	14.21	13.73
Net Margin %	2.17	N.M.	4.47	0.35	4.53	1.62	4.19	3.74
Asset Turnover	1.06	1.03	1.01	1.00	0.98	0.93	1.04	1.09
Current Ratio	0.97	0.82	0.82	0.82	0.95	1.03	1.34	1.30
Debt to Equity	0.74	0.79	0.66	0.84	0.86	1.19	0.77	0.68
Price Range	23.52-16.93	24.30-14.10	29.60-20.30	27.61-19.43	26.25-17.56	24.81-20.81	21.81-15.38	19.81-14.25
P/E Ratio	29.40-21.16	...	16.82-11.53	...	...	...	...	...
Average Yield %	2.52	2.78	1.97	1.93	1.46	1.23	1.31	1.23

Address: 612 Saint Jacques Street, Montreal	Web Site: www.quebecorworld.com	Auditors: KPMG LLP
Telephone: (514) 954-0101	Officers: Pierre Karl Peladeau - Pres., C.E.O. Claude Heile - Exec. V.P., C.F.O.	Investor Contact: 514 877 5118
Fax: (514) 954-9624		Transfer Agents: Computershare Trust of Canada, Canada

QUEST DIAGNOSTICS, INC.

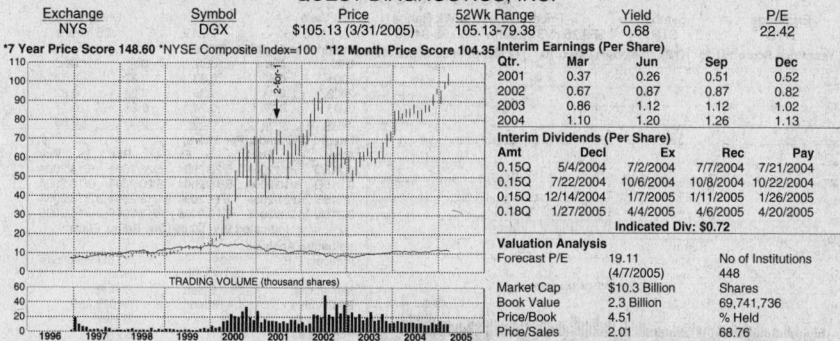

Exchange	Symbol	Price	52Wk Range	Yield	P/E
NYS	DGX	$105.13 (3/31/2005)	105.13-79.38	0.68	22.42

*7 Year Price Score 148.60 *NYSE Composite Index=100 ***12 Month Price Score 104.35**

Interim Earnings (Per Share)

Qtr.	Mar	Jun	Sep	Dec
2001	0.37	0.26	0.51	0.52
2002	0.67	0.87	0.87	0.82
2003	0.86	1.12	1.12	1.02
2004	1.10	1.20	1.26	1.13

Interim Dividends (Per Share)

Amt	Decl	Ex	Rec	Pay
0.15Q	5/4/2004	7/2/2004	7/7/2004	7/21/2004
0.15Q	7/22/2004	10/6/2004	10/8/2004	10/22/2004
0.15Q	12/14/2004	1/7/2005	1/11/2005	1/26/2005
0.18Q	1/27/2005	4/4/2005	4/6/2005	4/20/2005

Indicated Div: $0.72

Valuation Analysis

Forecast P/E	19.11	No of Institutions	
	(4/7/2005)	448	
Market Cap	$10.3 Billion	Shares	69,741,736
Book Value	2.3 Billion	% Held	
Price/Book	4.51		68.76
Price/Sales	2.01		

Business Summary: Diagnostic Services (MIC: 9.5 SIC: 071 NAIC: 41710)

Quest Diagnostics is a provider of diagnostic testing, information and related services. Co. offers patients and physicians access to diagnostic laboratory services through its national network of laboratories and patient service centers. Co. provides interpretive consultation through its medical and scientific staff, with over 300 physicians and Ph.D.'s (Doctorate of Philosophy) across the country. Co. also provides esoteric testing, including gene-based testing and testing for abuse of drugs and provides information technology solutions that can improve practice management and patient care for healthcare organizations and clinicians

Recent Developments: For the year ended Dec 31 2004, net income increased 14.3% to $499,195 thousand from net income of $436,717 thousand a year earlier. Revenues were $5,126,601 thousand, up 8.2% from $4,737,958 thousand the year before. Operating income was $891,217 thousand versus an income of $796,454 thousand in the prior year, an increase of 11.9%. Total direct expense was $2,990,712 thousand versus $2,768,623 thousand in the prior year, an increase of 8.0%. Total indirect expense was $1,244,672 thousand versus $1,172,881 thousand in the prior year, an increase of 6.1%.

Prospects: For full-year 2005, Co. expects revenues to grow between 5.0% and 6.0%. Operating income is expected to be between 18.0% and 19.0% of revenues, cash from operations is expected to approach $800.0 million and capital expenditures are expected to be between $210.0 million and $230.0 million. Moreover, Co. expects full-year earnings per diluted share of between $5.45 and $5.55, an increase of 14.0% to 16.0% compared to 2004 diluted earnings per share of $4.77 before special charges. Estimates for 2005 earnings per diluted share, operating income and cash from operations are before the effect of the accounting change for equity-based compensation, effective July 2005.

Financial Data

(US$ in Thousands)	12/31/2004	12/31/2003	12/31/2002	12/31/2001	12/31/2000	12/31/1999	12/31/1998	12/31/1997
Earnings Per Share	4.69	4.12	3.23	1.66	1.08	(0.05)	0.45	(0.39)
Cash Flow Per Share	7.81	6.41	6.18	5.01	4.12	3.56	2.38	3.02
Tang Book Value Per Share	N.M.	N.M.	N.M.	N.M.	N.M.	N.M.	1.20	0.45
Dividends Per Share	0.600	...	...	...	...	...	...	...
Dividend Payout %	12.79	...	...	...	...	...	...	...
Income Statement								
Total Revenue	5,126,601	4,737,958	4,108,051	3,627,771	3,421,162	2,205,243	1,458,607	1,528,695
EBITDA	1,061,801	951,489	727,441	550,854	448,369	166,669	156,109	98,335
Depn & Amortn	168,726	153,902	131,392	147,727	134,296	90,835	68,845	76,397
Income Before Taxes	835,126	737,798	542,377	332,604	200,981	14,384	53,861	(19,058)
Income Taxes	335,931	301,081	220,223	148,692	96,033	15,658	26,976	3,202
Net Income	499,195	436,717	322,154	162,303	102,052	(3,413)	26,885	(22,260)
Average Shares	107,072	105,932	99,790	97,610	94,300	70,028	60,458	58,400
Balance Sheet								
Current Assets	931,080	995,786	824,443	876,514	980,689	872,661	578,187	571,884
Total Assets	4,203,788	4,301,418	3,324,197	2,930,555	2,864,536	2,878,481	1,360,240	1,400,928
Current Liabilities	1,043,788	723,800	635,977	658,623	954,990	701,244	309,465	295,146
Long-Term Obligations	724,021	1,028,707	796,507	820,337	760,705	1,171,442	413,426	482,161
Total Liabilities	1,915,137	1,906,724	1,555,334	1,594,568	1,833,741	2,016,419	793,310	859,268
Stockholders' Equity	2,288,651	2,394,694	1,768,863	1,335,987	1,030,795	862,062	566,930	541,660
Shares Outstanding	98,110	102,814	97,963	96,024	93,082	88,706	60,054	59,972
Statistical Record								
Return on Assets %	11.71	11.45	10.30	5.60	3.54	N.M.	1.95	N.M.
Return on Equity %	21.26	20.98	20.75	13.72	10.75	N.M.	4.85	N.M.
EBITDA Margin %	20.71	20.08	17.71	15.18	13.11	7.56	10.70	6.43
Net Margin %	9.74	9.22	7.84	4.47	2.98	N.M.	1.84	N.M.
Asset Turnover	1.20	1.24	1.31	1.25	1.19	1.04	1.06	1.09
Current Ratio	0.89	1.38	1.30	1.33	1.03	1.24	1.87	1.94
Debt to Equity	0.32	0.43	0.45	0.61	0.74	1.36	0.73	0.89
Price Range	96.59-72.25	74.12-47.97	94.91-50.71	74.85-39.52	71.53-14.84	15.66-8.91	11.47-7.31	10.28-7.19
P/E Ratio	20.59-15.41	17.99-11.64	29.38-15.70	45.09-23.81	66.23-13.74	...	25.49-16.25	...
Average Yield %	0.70	...	...	...	...	...	...	...

Address: One Malcolm Avenue, Teterboro, NJ 07608 Telephone: (201) 393-5000 Fax: (201) 462-4169	Web Site: www.questdiagnostics.com Officers: Surya N. Mohapatra Ph.D. - Chmn., Pres., C.E.O. Robert A. Hagemann - Sr. V.P., C.F.O.	Auditors: PricewaterhouseCoopers LLP Transfer Agents: Computershare Investor Services, Chicago, IL

QUESTAR CORP.

Exchange	Symbol	Price	52Wk Range	Yield	P/E	Div Acheiver
NYS	STR	$59.25 (3/31/2005)	60.95-34.36	1.45	22.19	25 Years

*7 Year Price Score 141.25 *NYSE Composite Index=100 *12 Month Price Score 112.79

Interim Earnings (Per Share)

Qtr.	Mar	Jun	Sep	Dec
2001	0.80	0.33	0.27	0.52
2002	0.42	0.36	0.28	0.82
2003	0.77	0.24	0.34	0.71
2004	0.89	0.50	0.43	0.85

Interim Dividends (Per Share)

Amt	Decl	Ex	Rec	Pay
0.215Q	5/18/2004	5/26/2004	5/28/2004	6/14/2004
0.215Q	8/10/2004	8/18/2004	8/20/2004	9/13/2004
0.215Q	10/21/2004	11/17/2004	11/19/2004	12/13/2004
0.215Q	2/8/2005	2/16/2005	2/18/2005	3/14/2005

Indicated Div: $0.86 (Div. Reinv. Plan)

Valuation Analysis

Forecast P/E	17.91 (4/7/2005)	No of Institutions	291
Market Cap	$5.0 Billion	Shares	54,025,460
Book Value	1.4 Billion	% Held	63.78
Price/Book	3.48		
Price/Sales	2.63		

Business Summary: Gas Utilities (MIC: 7.4 SIC: 923 NAIC: 21210)

Questar is a natural gas-focused energy company that is involved in a range of natural gas activities through its Market Resources and Regulated Services groups. Market Resources is engaged in gas and oil development and production; cost-of-service gas development; gas gathering and processing; and wholesale gas and hydrocarbon liquids marketing, risk management, and gas storage. Regulated Services, through its two primary subsidiaries, Questar Pipeline Company and Questar Gas Company, conducts interstate gas transmission and storage activities and retail gas distribution services.

Recent Developments: For the year ended Dec 31 2004, net income increased 32.1% to $229,301 thousand from net income of $173,616 thousand a year earlier. Revenues were $1,901,431 thousand, up 30.0% from $1,463,188 thousand the year before. Operating income was $415,587 thousand versus an income of $339,830 thousand in the prior year, an increase of 22.3%. Total direct expense was $1,149,634 thousand versus $826,707 thousand in the prior year, an increase of 39.1%. Total indirect expense was $336,210 thousand versus $296,651 thousand in the prior year, an increase of 13.3%.

Prospects: For fiscal 2005, Co. now expects earnings to range from $3.10 to $3.30 per diluted share. Co.'s previous guidance of $3.25 to $3.45 per diluted share was based on the forward-price curves for natural gas and oil on Oct 18 2004. The reduction is due to the subsequent decline in natural gas and oil prices. The revised guidance is based on natural gas and crude-oil hedges in place on Feb 7 2005, and assumes a 12-month 2005 NYMEX average price for unhedged production of $6.27 per one million British Thermal Units for gas and a NYMEX prompt-month average of $45.71 per barrel for oil. Co.'s guidance also excludes one-time items such as potential gains and losses on the sale of assets.

Financial Data
(US$ in Thousands)

	12/31/2004	12/31/2003	12/31/2002	12/31/2001	12/31/2000	12/31/1999	12/31/1998	12/31/1997
Earnings Per Share	2.67	2.06	1.88	1.94	1.94	1.20	0.93	1.26
Cash Flow Per Share	6.93	5.40	5.68	4.60	3.23	2.60	3.46	2.47
Tang Book Value Per Share	16.06	14.12	12.81	12.14	12.01	11.37	10.62	10.30
Dividends Per Share	0.850	0.780	0.725	0.705	0.685	0.670	0.652	0.620
Dividend Payout %	31.84	37.86	38.56	36.34	35.31	55.83	70.16	49.21
Income Statement								
Total Revenue	1,901,431	1,463,188	1,200,667	1,439,350	1,266,153	924,219	906,256	933,274
EBITDA	587,148	485,609	456,388	405,498	389,723	291,322	234,593	278,914
Depn & Amortn	228,267	203,850	194,369	159,042	147,645	144,704	128,664	128,517
Income Before Taxes	358,881	281,759	262,019	246,456	242,078	146,618	105,929	150,397
Income Taxes	129,580	102,563	91,126	88,270	85,367	47,788	29,030	45,602
Net Income	229,301	173,616	155,596	158,186	156,711	98,830	76,899	104,795
Average Shares	85,722	84,190	82,573	81,658	80,915	82,676	82,817	82,668
Balance Sheet								
Net PPE	2,984,660	2,768,529	2,617,798	2,565,098	1,953,993	1,786,914	1,747,641	1,531,220
Total Assets	3,646,658	3,309,055	3,067,850	3,235,711	2,539,045	2,237,997	2,161,281	1,945,017
Long-Term Obligations	933,195	950,189	1,145,180	997,423	714,537	735,043	615,770	541,986
Total Liabilities	2,207,100	2,047,790	1,929,089	2,154,930	1,547,979	1,312,152	1,283,323	1,099,239
Stockholders' Equity	1,439,558	1,261,265	1,138,761	1,080,781	991,066	925,845	877,958	845,778
Shares Outstanding	84,441	83,233	82,053	81,523	80,818	81,418	82,632	82,142
Statistical Record								
Return on Assets %	6.58	5.45	4.94	5.48	6.54	4.49	3.75	5.57
Return on Equity %	16.93	14.47	14.02	15.27	16.31	10.96	8.92	12.95
EBITDA Margin %	30.88	33.19	38.01	28.17	30.78	31.52	25.89	29.89
Net Margin %	12.06	11.87	12.96	10.99	12.38	10.69	8.49	11.23
PPE Turnover	0.66	0.54	0.46	0.64	0.68	0.52	0.55	0.62
Asset Turnover	0.55	0.46	0.38	0.50	0.53	0.42	0.44	0.50
Debt to Equity	0.65	0.75	1.01	0.92	0.72	0.79	0.70	0.64
Price Range	51.51-34.09	35.35-26.66	29.27-19.40	33.51-18.70	31.50-13.81	19.88-14.94	22.34-16.25	22.31-17.25
P/E Ratio	19.29-12.77	17.16-12.94	15.57-10.32	17.27-9.64	16.24-7.12	16.56-12.45	24.03-17.47	17.71-13.69
Average Yield %	2.10	2.49	2.91	2.73	3.23	3.72	3.29	3.15

Address: 180 East 100 South Street, Salt Lake City, UT 84145-0433 **Telephone:** (801) 324-5000 **Fax:** (801) 324-5483	**Web Site:** www.questar.com **Officers:** Keith O. Rattie - Chmn., Pres., C.E.O. Alan K. Allred - Exec. V.P.	**Auditors:** Ernst & Young LLP **Investor Contact:** 801-324-5497 **Transfer Agents:** U.S. Stock Transfer Corporation, Glendale, CA

QWEST COMMUNICATIONS INTERNATIONAL, INC.

Exchange	Symbol	Price	52Wk Range	Yield	P/E
NYS	Q	$3.70 (3/31/2005)	4.85-2.59	N/A	N/A

*7 Year Price Score 16.71   *NYSE Composite Index=100   *12 Month Price Score 100.12

Interim Earnings (Per Share)

Qtr.	Mar	Jun	Sep	Dec
2001	(0.03)	(1.99)	(0.09)	(0.32)
2002	(0.42)	(10.39)	(0.07)	1.69
2003	(0.42)	(0.04)	1.05	(0.24)
2004	(0.17)	(0.43)	(0.31)	(0.08)

Interim Dividends (Per Share)

Dividend Payment Suspended

Valuation Analysis

Forecast P/E	0.00	No of Institutions
	(4/7/2005)	287
Market Cap	$6.7 Billion	Shares
Book Value	N/A	1,206,848,256
Price/Book	N/A	% Held
Price/Sales	0.49	66.43

TRADING VOLUME (thousand shares)

Business Summary: Communications (MIC: 10.1 SIC: 813 NAIC: 17110)

Qwest Communications International provides local telecommunications and related services, long-distance services and wireless, data and video services within its local service area, which consists of the 14-state region of Arizona, Colorado, Idaho, Iowa, Minnesota, Montana, Nebraska, New Mexico, North Dakota, Oregon, South Dakota, Utah, Washington and Wyoming. Co. also provides long-distance services and broadband data, voice and video communications outside its local service area as well as globally. Co.'s three operating segments include wireline services, wireless services and other services.

Recent Developments: For the year ended Dec 31 2004, net loss was $1,794 million versus net income of $1,512 million a year earlier. Revenues were $13,809 million, down 3.4% from $14,288 million the year before. Operating loss was $288 million versus a loss of $254 million in the prior year. Total direct expense was $5,890 million versus $6,455 million in the prior year, a decrease of 8.8%. Total indirect expense was $8,207 million versus $8,087 million in the prior year, an increase of 1.5%.

Prospects: On Feb 11 2005, Co. transmitted a letter to the Board of Directors of MCI, Inc. in which Co. proposed to acquire MCI. Co. subsequently learned that MCI had agreed to be acquired by Verizon Communications, and, on Feb 17 2005, Co. sent another letter in which it notified MCI of its intention to submit a modified proposal to acquire MCI, notwithstanding MCI's agreement with Verizon, and also noted its expectation that MCI and its advisors will discuss the merits of its proposal and provide it access to due diligence information that Co. believes has been made available to other parties. Co. cannot provide any assurance as to whether it will be successful in its effort to acquire MCI.

Financial Data

(US$ in Thousands)	12/31/2004	12/31/2003	12/31/2002	12/31/2001	12/31/2000	12/31/1999	12/31/1998	12/31/1997
Earnings Per Share	(1.00)	0.87	(22.87)	(2.42)	(0.06)	0.60	(1.51)	0.04
Cash Flow Per Share	1.02	1.25	1.39	2.43	2.89	(0.05)	0.08	(0.10)
Tang Book Value Per Share	...	...	...	1.28	5.37	4.95	1.20	0.92
Dividends Per Share	...	...	...	0.050	0.310	...	...	...
Income Statement								
Total Revenue	13,809,000	14,288,000	15,385,000	19,695,000	16,610,000	3,927,600	2,242,700	696,703
EBITDA	2,948,000	3,092,000	(14,489,000)	2,819,000	4,509,000	1,138,600	(550,800)	51,029
Depn & Amortn	3,123,000	3,167,000	3,847,000	5,335,000	3,342,000	404,100	201,700	20,262
Income Before Taxes	(1,706,000)	(1,832,000)	(20,125,000)	(3,958,000)	126,000	583,500	(849,800)	23,580
Income Taxes	88,000	(519,000)	(2,500,000)	...	207,000	125,000	(5,800)	9,057
Net Income	(1,794,000)	1,512,000	(38,468,000)	(4,023,000)	(81,000)	458,500	(844,000)	14,523
Average Shares	1,801,405	1,738,766	1,682,056	1,661,133	1,272,088	764,300	558,200	388,110
Balance Sheet								
Current Assets	4,218,000	4,416,000	6,420,000	5,757,000	5,376,000	1,785,200	1,439,100	723,942
Total Assets	24,324,000	26,216,000	29,345,000	73,781,000	73,501,000	11,058,100	8,067,600	1,398,105
Current Liabilities	4,286,000	5,548,000	6,895,000	9,989,000	9,893,000	1,238,400	1,237,500	315,422
Long-Term Obligations	16,690,000	15,639,000	19,754,000	20,197,000	15,421,000	2,368,300	2,307,100	630,463
Total Liabilities	26,936,000	27,232,000	32,175,000	37,126,000	32,197,000	4,001,600	3,829,400	1,016,361
Stockholders' Equity	(2,612,000)	(1,016,000)	(2,830,000)	36,655,000	41,304,000	7,001,300	4,238,200	381,744
Shares Outstanding	1,816,386	1,769,896	1,699,115	1,663,546	1,672,218	750,000	694,000	413,340
Statistical Record								
Return on Assets %	N.M.	5.44	N.M.	N.M.	N.M.	4.79	N.M.	1.75
Return on Equity %	...	...	N.M.	N.M.	N.M.	8.16	N.M.	7.43
EBITDA Margin %	21.35	21.64	N.M.	14.31	27.15	28.99	N.M.	7.32
Net Margin %	N.M.	10.58	N.M.	N.M.	N.M.	11.67	N.M.	2.08
Asset Turnover	0.54	0.51	0.30	0.27	0.39	0.41	0.47	0.84
Current Ratio	0.98	0.80	0.93	0.58	0.54	1.44	1.16	2.30
Debt to Equity	...	...	...	0.55	0.37	0.34	0.54	1.65
Price Range	4.90-2.59	6.02-3.10	14.93-1.11	47.50-11.51	64.00-32.38	48.06-25.00	25.03-12.50	16.44-6.81
P/E Ratio	...	6.92-3.56	...	...	...	80.10-41.67	..410.94-170.31	
Average Yield %	...	...	...	0.18	0.67	...	...	...

Address: 1801 California Street, Denver, CO 80202	Web Site: www.qwest.com	Auditors: KPMG LLP
Telephone: (303) 992-1400	Officers: Richard C. Notebaert - Chmn., C.E.O. Oren	
Fax: (303) 291-1724	G. Shaffer - Vice-Chmn., C.F.O.	

RADIAN GROUP, INC.

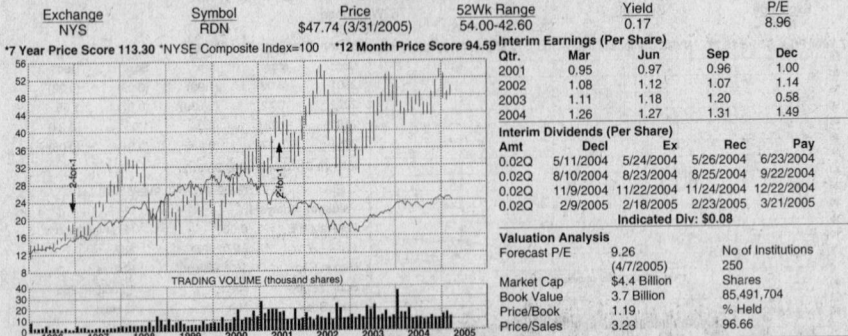

Exchange	Symbol	Price	52Wk Range	Yield	P/E
NYS	RDN	$47.74 (3/31/2005)	54.00-42.60	0.17	8.96

*7 Year Price Score 113.30 *NYSE Composite Index=100 *12 Month Price Score 94.59

Interim Earnings (Per Share)

Qtr.	Mar	Jun	Sep	Dec
2001	0.95	0.97	0.96	1.00
2002	1.08	1.12	1.07	1.14
2003	1.11	1.18	1.20	0.58
2004	1.26	1.27	1.31	1.49

Interim Dividends (Per Share)

Amt	Decl	Ex	Rec	Pay
0.02Q	5/11/2004	5/24/2004	5/26/2004	6/23/2004
0.02Q	8/10/2004	8/23/2004	8/25/2004	9/22/2004
0.02Q	11/9/2004	11/22/2004	11/24/2004	12/22/2004
0.02Q	2/9/2005	2/18/2005	2/23/2005	3/21/2005

Indicated Div: $0.08

Valuation Analysis

Forecast P/E	9.26	No of Institutions
	(4/7/2005)	250
Market Cap	$4.4 Billion	Shares
Book Value	3.7 Billion	85,491,704
Price/Book	1.19	% Held
Price/Sales	3.23	96.66

Business Summary: Insurance (MIC: 8.2 SIC: 351 NAIC: 24130)

Radian Group provides insurance and mortgage services to financial institutions in the U.S. and globally. Co.'s mortgage insurance business provides private mortgage insurance and risk management services to mortgage lending institutions. Co.'s financial guaranty segment provides credit-related insurance coverage, credit default swaps and other financial guaranty contracts. Co.'s mortgage services segment deals primarily with credit-based servicing and securitization of assets in underserved markets such as special assets purchases, servicing and securitization; and mortgage processing, closing and settlement services through the Internet.

Recent Developments: For the year ended Dec 31 2004, net income increased 34.4% to $518,653 thousand from net income of $385,901 thousand a year earlier. Revenues were $1,364,053 thousand, up 6.6% from $1,279,194 thousand the year before. Net premiums earned were $2,058,968 thousand versus $2,016,366 thousand in the prior year, an increase of 2.1%. Net investment income rose 9.8% to $204,349 thousand from $186,163 thousand a year ago.

Prospects: Co.'s near-term prospects appear favorable, reflecting continued growth in earnings and book value. Specifically, Co. achieved net income of $519.0 million for full-year 2004, while book value increased 17.0%. Meanwhile, Co.'s mortgage insurance business should continue to benefit from the low interest rate environment. New primary mortgage insurance written during the fourth quarter was $11.70 billion, consisting of $3.73 billion of structured and $7.97 billion flow mortgage insurance. Separately, Co. announced that it has formed a partnership with Standard Chartered Bank Limited. Through the partnership, Co. will become the provider of mortgage insurance for Standard Chartered.

Financial Data (US$ in Thousands)	12/31/2004	12/31/2003	12/31/2002	12/31/2001	12/31/2000	12/31/1999	12/31/1998	12/31/1997
Earnings Per Share	5.33	4.08	4.41	3.88	3.22	1.92	1.86	1.53
Cash Flow Per Share	3.50	5.72	6.22	5.32	3.71	3.35	2.92	2.08
Tang Book Value Per Share	39.98	34.31	29.43	24.54	17.97	14.17	11.52	9.54
Dividends Per Share	0.081	0.080	0.080	0.075	0.060	0.060	0.060	0.060
Dividend Payout %	1.51	1.96	1.81	1.93	1.86	3.13	3.23	3.92
Income Statement								
Premium Income	1,029,484	1,008,183	847,125	715,880	520,871	472,635	282,152	237,710
Total Revenue	1,364,053	1,363,144	1,152,090	947,201	615,434	552,811	332,966	277,310
Income Before Taxes	725,592	531,479	601,276	505,531	352,470	219,466	125,824	102,493
Income Taxes	206,939	145,578	174,107	145,112	103,532	71,328	34,770	27,526
Net Income	518,653	385,901	427,169	360,419	248,938	148,138	91,054	74,967
Average Shares	97,908	94,643	95,706	91,958	76,298	75,712	47,148	46,832
Balance Sheet								
Total Assets	7,000,820	6,445,767	5,393,405	4,438,626	2,272,811	1,776,712	968,173	704,615
Total Liabilities	3,311,765	3,219,923	2,639,970	2,092,298	870,614	679,456	405,204	234,672
Stockholders' Equity	3,689,055	3,225,844	2,753,435	2,306,328	1,362,197	1,057,256	522,969	429,943
Shares Outstanding	92,280	94,011	93,552	93,982	75,815	74,615	45,412	45,074
Statistical Record								
Return on Assets %	7.69	6.52	8.69	10.74	12.26	10.79	10.89	11.56
Return on Equity %	14.96	12.91	16.88	19.65	20.52	18.75	19.11	19.07
Net Margin %	38.02	28.31	37.08	38.05	40.45	26.80	27.35	27.03
Price Range	54.00-40.95	53.29-30.15	55.20-29.49	43.53-27.19	38.31-17.28	27.78-16.66	34.63-14.00	30.41-16.19
P/E Ratio	10.13-7.68	13.06-7.39	12.52-6.69	11.22-7.01	11.90-5.37	14.47-8.68	18.62-7.53	19.87-10.58
Average Yield %	0.17	0.19	0.18	0.20	0.22	0.26	0.22	0.27

Address: 1601 Market Street, Philadelphia, PA 19103	**Web Site:** www.radiangroupinc.com	**Auditors:** Deloitte & Touche LLP
Telephone: (215) 564 6600	**Officers:** Frank P. Filipps - Chmn., C.E.O. Roy J. Kasmar - Pres., C.O.O.	
Fax: (215) 564 0129		

RADIOSHACK CORP.

Exchange	Symbol	Price	52Wk Range	Yield	P/E
NYS	RSH	$24.50 (3/31/2005)	34.30-24.30	1.02	11.78

*7 Year Price Score 75.49 *NYSE Composite Index=100 *12 Month Price Score 91.01

Interim Earnings (Per Share)

Qtr.	Mar	Jun	Sep	Dec
2001	0.23	0.21	0.23	0.18
2002	0.31	0.28	0.25	0.62
2003	0.33	0.34	0.34	0.76
2004	0.41	0.42	0.43	0.82

Interim Dividends (Per Share)

Amt	Decl	Ex	Rec	Pay
0.055A	7/25/2001	9/27/2001	10/1/2001	10/18/2001
0.22A	10/18/2002	11/26/2002	12/1/2002	12/19/2002
0.25A	10/17/2003	12/4/2003	12/8/2003	12/26/2003
0.25A	9/24/2004	11/29/2004	12/1/2004	12/20/2004
		Indicated Div: $0.25		

Valuation Analysis

Forecast P/E	11.80	No of Institutions
	(4/7/2005)	294
Market Cap	$3.9 Billion	Shares
Book Value	922.1 Million	116,025,656
Price/Book	4.20	% Held
Price/Sales	0.80	73.49

TRADING VOLUME (thousand shares)

Business Summary: Hospitality & Tourism (MIC: 5.1 SIC: 731 NAIC: 43112)

RadioShack is one of America's largest retailers of name-brand and private label consumer electronics and personal computers. As of Dec 31 2003, Co.'s retail operations included more than 7,000 Co.-owned and dealer/franchise RadioShack® stores where dealer/franchise outlets represent approximately 27% of Co.' total retail locations. Co. also designs, installs and maintains cabling systems for the transmission of video, voice and data, primarily for home use, through its wholly-owned subsidiary, AmeriLink Corporation. Private-label brands owned by Co. include Tandy®, Optimus®, Realistic®, DUoFONE, and Archer®.

Recent Developments: For the year ended Dec 31 2004, net income increased 13.0% to $337,200 thousand from net income of $298,500 thousand a year earlier. Revenues were $4,841,200 thousand, up 4.1% from $4,649,300 thousand the year before. Operating income was $558,300 thousand versus an income of $483,700 thousand in the prior year, an increase of 15.4%. Total direct expense was $2,406,700 thousand versus $2,333,600 thousand in the prior year, an increase of 3.1%. Total indirect expense was $1,876,200 thousand versus $1,832,000 thousand in the prior year, an increase of 2.4%.

Prospects: Co. initiated first quarter 2005 earnings per share guidance of $0.39 to $0.41 representing a decline of 5.0% to nil versus first quarter 2004 earnings per share. Looking ahead, for fiscal year 2005, Co. is projecting earnings per share of $2.34 to $2.40. The estimate represents a $0.07 reduction versus previous guidance. In addition, the estimate includes the impact of FAS123R requiring the expensing of stock options. Estimated financial metrics for 2005 include total sales growth of 9.0% to 11.0%, gross margin rate down 20 to 60 basis points, and selling, general and administrative growth of 8.0% to 10.0%.

Financial Data

(US$ in Thousands)	12/31/2004	12/31/2003	12/31/2002	12/31/2001	12/31/2000	12/31/1999	12/31/1998	12/31/1997
Earnings Per Share	2.08	1.77	1.45	0.85	1.84	1.43	0.27	0.81
Cash Flow Per Share	2.18	3.89	3.02	4.22	0.62	2.89	2.06	1.49
Tang Book Value Per Share	5.53	4.07	4.22	3.97	4.37	3.97	3.84	4.68
Dividends Per Share	0.250	0.250	0.220	0.165	0.275	0.205	0.200	0.200
Dividend Payout %	12.02	14.12	15.17	19.41	14.95	14.34	74.07	24.54
Income Statement								
Total Revenue	4,841,200	4,649,300	4,577,200	4,775,700	4,794,700	4,126,200	4,787,900	5,372,200
EBITDA	661,700	587,700	554,000	437,600	737,000	587,500	233,300	434,000
Depn & Amortn	101,400	92,000	94,700	108,300	107,300	90,200	99,000	97,200
Income Before Taxes	542,100	472,800	424,900	291,500	593,600	480,500	99,700	303,900
Income Taxes	204,900	174,300	161,500	124,800	225,600	182,600	38,400	117,000
Net Income	337,200	298,500	263,400	166,700	368,000	297,900	61,300	186,900
Average Shares	162,500	168,900	179,300	191,200	197,700	205,000	211,400	224,400
Balance Sheet								
Current Assets	1,775,100	1,666,600	1,706,900	1,714,300	1,818,200	1,403,300	1,298,600	1,715,500
Total Assets	2,516,700	2,243,900	2,227,900	2,245,100	2,576,500	2,142,000	1,993,600	2,317,500
Current Liabilities	957,400	858,100	828,200	826,400	1,232,400	925,200	879,500	976,400
Long-Term Obligations	506,900	541,300	591,300	565,400	302,900	319,400	235,100	236,100
Total Liabilities	1,594,600	1,474,600	1,499,800	1,467,000	1,596,200	1,290,300	1,142,100	1,258,900
Stockholders' Equity	922,100	769,300	728,100	778,100	880,300	830,700	848,200	1,058,600
Shares Outstanding	158,198	188,184	171,727	176,800	185,764	190,727	194,874	204,618
Statistical Record								
Return on Assets %	14.13	13.35	11.78	6.91	15.56	14.41	2.84	7.63
Return on Equity %	39.76	39.87	34.98	20.10	42.90	35.49	6.43	16.09
EBITDA Margin %	13.67	12.64	12.10	9.16	15.37	14.24	4.87	8.08
Net Margin %	6.97	6.42	5.75	3.49	7.68	7.22	1.28	3.48
Asset Turnover	2.03	2.08	2.05	1.98	2.03	2.00	2.22	2.19
Current Ratio	1.85	1.94	2.06	2.07	1.48	1.52	1.48	1.76
Debt to Equity	0.55	0.70	0.81	0.73	0.34	0.38	0.28	0.22
Price Range	35.41-26.17	32.15-18.74	36.00-17.51	55.19-21.00	69.00-36.63	78.50-20.59	31.28-15.56	22.81-10.19
P/E Ratio	17.02-12.58	18.16-10.59	24.83-12.08	64.93-24.71	37.50-19.90	54.90-14.40	115.86-57.64	28.16-12.58
Average Yield %	0.82	0.98	0.82	0.52	0.53	0.46	0.85	1.33

Address: 100 Throckmorton Street, Suite 1800, Fort Worth, TX 76102 **Telephone:** (817) 415-3700 **Fax:** (817) 878-4887	**Web Site:** www.radioshackcorporation.com **Officers:** Leonard H. Roberts - Chmn., C.E.O. David J. Edmondson - Pres., C.O.O.	**Auditors:** PricewaterhouseCoopers LLP **Investor Contact:** 817-415-3730

RAYMOND JAMES FINANCIAL, INC.

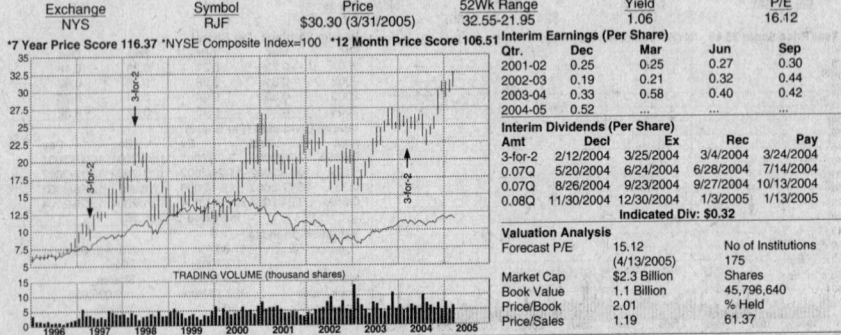

Exchange	Symbol	Price	52Wk Range	Yield	P/E
NYS	RJF	$30.30 (3/31/2005)	32.55-21.95	1.06	16.12

*7 Year Price Score 116.37 *NYSE Composite Index=100 *12 Month Price Score 106.51

Interim Earnings (Per Share)

Qtr.	Dec	Mar	Jun	Sep
2001-02	0.25	0.25	0.27	0.30
2002-03	0.19	0.21	0.32	0.44
2003-04	0.33	0.58	0.40	0.42
2004-05	0.52	...	...	...

Interim Dividends (Per Share)

Amt	Decl	Ex	Rec	Pay
3-for-2	2/12/2004	3/25/2004	3/4/2004	3/24/2004
0.07Q	5/20/2004	6/24/2004	6/28/2004	7/14/2004
0.07Q	8/26/2004	9/23/2004	9/27/2004	10/13/2004
0.08Q	11/30/2004	12/30/2004	1/3/2005	1/13/2005

Indicated Div: $0.32

Valuation Analysis

Forecast P/E	15.12 (4/13/2005)	No of Institutions 175
Market Cap	$2.3 Billion	Shares 45,796,640
Book Value	1.1 Billion	% Held 61.37
Price/Book	2.01	
Price/Sales	1.19	

Business Summary: Finance Intermediaries & Services (MIC: 8.7 SIC: 211 NAIC: 23120)

Raymond James Financial is a holding company, which, through its subsidiaries, is engaged principally in the securities brokerage business, including the underwriting, distribution, trading and brokerage of equity and debt securities and the sale of mutual funds and other investment products. In addition, Co. provides investment management services for retail and institutional clients and banking and trust services for retail clients. Co. operates from the following segments: private client group, capital markets, asset management, RJBank, and other.

Recent Developments: For the three months ended Dec 31 2004, net income increased 62.0% to $39.2 million compared with $24.2 million in the comparable year-earlier period. Total revenues advanced 23.5% to $524.4 million from $424.7 million the previous year. Co.'s improved results were driven by favorable U.S. equities market conditions, which resulted in top line growth and increased profit from across each of its business segments. Total non-interest expenses climbed 15.4% to $432.6 million compared with $374.9 million in the same period the year before, reflecting higher compensation, commissions and benefits expenses.

Prospects: Co. is benefiting from a material increase in net interest income, strong trading profits and solid investment banking, which led to 62.0% growth in Co.'s bottom-line for the first quarter of 2005 versus a year earlier. Although net interest income earnings are in a favorable trend and the investment banking pipeline is still complete with offerings, future results will be likely dependent upon favorable market conditions. While the U.S. economy remains solid and the near-term outlook for corporate earnings appear favorable, a combination of higher inflation and interest rates could undermine future market appreciation.

Financial Data
(US$ in Thousands)

	3 Mos	09/24/2004	09/26/2003	09/27/2002	09/28/2001	09/29/2000	09/24/1999	09/25/1998
Earnings Per Share	1.88	1.72	1.17	1.07	1.32	1.78	1.17	1.24
Cash Flow Per Share	0.92	(2.50)	2.63	0.74	2.53	(1.57)	3.51	6.22
Tang Book Value Per Share	14.23	13.63	11.90	10.68	9.81	8.90	7.39	7.04
Dividends Per Share	0.290	0.330	0.240	0.240	0.240	0.200	0.187	0.160
Dividend Payout %	15.41	19.19	20.51	22.50	18.18	11.24	15.91	12.90
Income Statement								
Total Revenue	524,377	1,829,776	1,497,571	1,515,923	1,657,844	1,698,594	1,232,206	1,082,907
Income Before Taxes	66,394	204,121	138,275	131,516	157,468	204,680	137,519	150,236
Income Taxes	25,562	76,546	51,958	52,213	61,058	79,485	52,429	57,532
Net Income	39,243	127,575	86,317	79,303	96,410	125,195	85,090	92,704
Average Shares	75,334	74,402	73,479	74,443	73,198	70,300	72,673	74,926
Balance Sheet								
Total Assets	7,958,496	7,621,846	6,911,638	6,040,303	6,372,054	6,308,816	5,030,715	3,852,737
Total Liabilities	6,814,256	6,535,260	5,986,903	5,200,667	5,601,178	5,658,298	4,472,229	3,342,839
Stockholders' Equity	1,120,484	1,065,213	924,735	839,636	770,876	650,518	558,486	509,898
Shares Outstanding	74,348	73,560	72,436	72,752	71,992	69,431	70,863	72,402
Statistical Record								
Return on Assets %	1.88	1.76	1.34	1.28	1.52	2.17	1.92	2.61
Return on Equity %	13.46	12.86	9.81	9.88	13.60	20.38	15.97	19.92
Price Range	31.20-21.95	27.47-21.95	25.59-15.47	24.85-15.75	26.75-16.27	21.96-11.21	17.33-11.83	23.46-11.50
P/E Ratio	16.60-11.68	15.97-12.76	21.87-13.22	23.22-14.72	20.27-12.32	12.34-6.30	14.81-10.11	18.92-9.27
Average Yield %	1.13	1.32	1.18	1.15	1.14	1.42	1.33	0.91

Address: 880 Carillon Parkway, St. Petersburg, FL 33716 **Telephone:** (727) 567-1000 **Fax:** (727) 573-8365	**Web Site:** www.raymondjames.com **Officers:** Thomas A. James - Chmn., C.E.O. Francis S. Gobold - Vice-Chmn.	**Auditors:** KPMG LLP **Investor Contact:** 727-573-3800

RAYONIER INC.

Exchange	Symbol	Price	52Wk Range	Yield	P/E
NYS	RYN	$49.53 (3/31/2005)	50.51-38.68	5.01	16.08

*7 Year Price Score 133.82 ***NYSE Composite Index=100** ***12 Month Price Score 98.41**

Interim Earnings (Per Share)

Qtr.	Mar	Jun	Sep	Dec
2001	0.30	0.76	0.15	0.19
2002	0.22	0.38	0.37	0.31
2003	0.19	0.74	0.19	0.03
2004	1.49	0.86	0.47	0.26

Interim Dividends (Per Share)

Amt	Decl	Ex	Rec	Pay
0.56Q	5/21/2004	6/8/2004	6/10/2004	6/30/2004
0.56Q	7/16/2004	9/8/2004	9/10/2004	9/30/2004
0.56Q	10/11/2004	12/8/2004	12/10/2004	12/31/2004
0.62Q	2/18/2005	3/9/2005	3/11/2005	3/31/2005
			Indicated Div: $2.48	

Valuation Analysis

Forecast P/E	24.83	No of Institutions	
	(4/13/2005)	203	
Market Cap	$2.5 Billion	Shares	
Book Value	796.4 Million	32,765,932	
Price/Book	3.11	% Held	
Price/Sales	2.05	65.28	

Business Summary: Wood Products (MIC: 11.9 SIC: 411 NAIC: 13310)

Rayonier, including its subsidiaries, is an international forest products company primarily engaged in activities associated with timberland management, including the sale of timber and real estate and in the production and sale of high value-added performance cellulose fibers. Co. is structured to qualify as a Real Estate Investment Trust (REIT). Co. also manufactures wood products through its lumber manufacturing facilities in the United States and a medium-density fiberboard (MDF) plant in New Zealand. In addition, Co. engages in the trading of logs and wood products.

Recent Developments: For the year ended Dec 31 2004, net income increased to $156.9 million compared with $50.0 million a year earlier. Sales climbed 9.6% to $1.21 billion from $1.10 billion the previous year. Timber and Real Estate segment sales rose 8.9% to $282.0 million, Performance Fibers segment sales grew 9.0% to $582.0 million, Wood Products segment sales advanced 23.2% to $170.0 million, and Other segment sales increased 1.2% to $174.0 million. Operating income rose 65.5% to $169.8 million versus $102.6 million the year before, reflecting improved results from across each of its business segments.

Prospects: As Co. enters 2005, it is experiencing strong demand for all of its products. Co. will continue to capitalize on its tax-efficient real estate investment trust structure by optimizing the use of its consistently strong cash flow to pursue growth opportunities and meet investor objectives. Co. believes that its first quarter 2005 earnings will be above fourth quarter 2004 primarily due to seasonally stronger Northwest timber volume and improved performance fibers and lumber results. However, earnings are expected to be somewhat below first quarter 2004 primarily due to lower sales of highest-and-best use properties.

Financial Data

(US$ in Thousands)	12/31/2004	12/31/2003	12/31/2002	12/31/2001	12/31/2000	12/31/1999	12/31/1998	12/31/1997
Earnings Per Share	3.08	1.16	1.28	1.39	1.88	1.63	1.48	1.98
Cash Flow Per Share	5.94	4.93	6.09	5.91	6.81	5.23	3.72	5.85
Tang Book Value Per Share	15.93	14.51	17.07	17.28	16.73	15.88	15.34	14.91
Dividends Per Share	2.240	1.050	0.960	0.960	0.960	0.860	0.827	0.800
Dividend Payout %	72.73	90.52	75.00	68.90	51.06	52.87	55.86	40.40
Income Statement								
Total Revenue	1,206,996	1,100,852	1,117,431	1,164,913	1,226,878	1,035,871	1,008,566	1,104,228
EBITDA	170,297	104,520	132,230	151,645	194,398	140,313	124,866	146,515
Income Before Taxes	123,448	55,778	69,797	82,562	108,645	98,120	90,154	120,647
Income Taxes	(33,453)	5,806	14,880	24,964	30,458	29,467	26,519	33,328
Net Income	156,901	49,972	54,172	57,598	78,187	68,653	63,635	87,319
Average Shares	51,022	43,093	42,236	41,402	41,554	42,263	42,913	44,145
Balance Sheet								
Current Assets	300,698	244,564	228,845	235,060	270,598	271,606	281,834	310,514
Total Assets	1,933,886	1,838,680	1,887,196	2,025,012	2,162,274	2,280,227	1,600,856	1,595,558
Current Liabilities	242,526	147,286	171,754	152,920	195,767	193,871	172,754	206,538
Long-Term Obligations	610,290	614,935	649,628	842,205	970,415	1,132,930	485,850	421,325
Total Liabilities	1,137,498	1,127,574	1,177,484	1,316,218	1,482,173	1,627,327	961,897	962,876
Stockholders' Equity	796,388	711,106	709,712	708,794	680,101	652,900	638,959	632,682
Shares Outstanding	49,977	49,018	41,579	41,018	40,656	41,110	41,650	42,426
Statistical Record								
Return on Assets %	8.30	2.68	2.77	2.75	3.51	3.54	3.98	5.47
Return on Equity %	20.76	7.03	7.64	8.29	11.70	10.63	10.01	13.90
EBITDA Margin %	14.11	9.49	11.83	13.02	15.84	13.55	12.38	13.27
Net Margin %	13.00	4.54	4.85	4.94	6.37	6.63	6.31	7.91
Asset Turnover	0.64	0.59	0.57	0.56	0.55	0.53	0.63	0.69
Current Ratio	1.24	1.66	1.33	1.54	1.38	1.40	1.63	1.50
Debt to Equity	0.77	0.86	0.92	1.19	1.43	1.74	0.76	0.67
Price Range	49.36-38.68	41.51-22.71	32.95-20.86	28.35-21.00	27.38-18.08	29.28-20.39	28.78-21.20	28.92-19.80
P/E Ratio	16.03-12.56	35.78-19.58	25.74-16.30	20.40-15.11	14.56-9.62	17.96-12.51	19.45-14.33	14.61-10.00
Average Yield %	5.10	3.49	3.52	3.91	4.28	3.46	3.37	3.31

Address: 50 North Laura Street, Jacksonville, FL 32202 **Telephone:** (904) 357-9100	**Web Site:** www.rayonier.com **Officers:** W. Lee Nutter - Chmn., Pres., C.E.O. Paul G. Boynton - Sr. V.P., Performance Fibers	**Auditors:** DELOITTE & TOUCHE LLP

RAYTHEON CO.

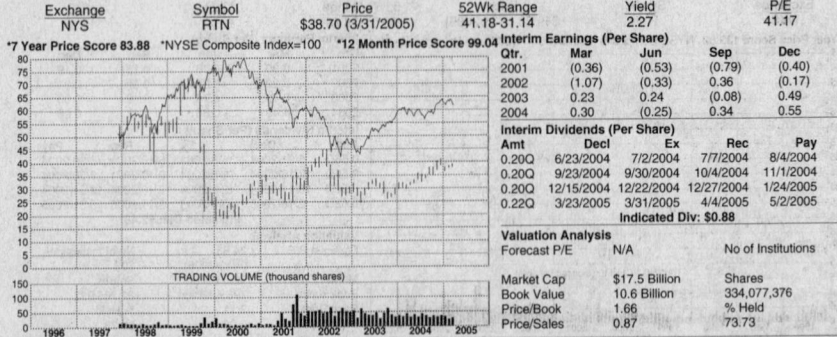

Exchange	Symbol	Price	52Wk Range	Yield	P/E
NYS	RTN	$38.70 (3/31/2005)	41.18-31.14	2.27	41.17

*7 Year Price Score 83.88 *NYSE Composite Index=100 *12 Month Price Score 99.04

Interim Earnings (Per Share)

Qtr.	Mar	Jun	Sep	Dec
2001	(0.36)	(0.53)	(0.79)	(0.40)
2002	(1.07)	(0.33)	0.36	(0.17)
2003	0.23	0.24	(0.08)	0.49
2004	0.30	(0.25)	0.34	0.55

Interim Dividends (Per Share)

Amt	Decl	Ex	Rec	Pay
0.20Q	6/23/2004	7/2/2004	7/7/2004	8/4/2004
0.20Q	9/23/2004	9/30/2004	10/4/2004	11/1/2004
0.20Q	12/15/2004	12/22/2004	12/27/2004	1/24/2005
0.22Q	3/23/2005	3/31/2005	4/4/2005	5/2/2005

Indicated Div: $0.88

Valuation Analysis

Forecast P/E	N/A	No of Institutions
Market Cap	$17.5 Billion	Shares
Book Value	10.6 Billion	334,077,376
Price/Book	1.66	% Held
Price/Sales	0.87	73.73

Business Summary: Instruments and Related Products (MIC: 11.15 SIC: 812 NAIC: 34511)

Raytheon, which operates throughout the U.S., provides products and services in the areas of defense, government and commercial electronics, and business and special mission aircraft. The electronics group designs, manufactures and services electronics devices, equipment and systems for both government and commercial customers. Defense electronics include missiles; radar; sensors and electro-optics; intelligence, surveillance and reconnaissance; and command, control, communication and information systems. The aircraft group markets and supports piston-powered aircraft, jet props and light and medium jets for the world's commercial, regional airlines and military aircraft markets.

Recent Developments: For the year ended Dec 31 2004, income from continuing operations decreased 17.9% to $439,000 thousand from income of $535,000 thousand a year earlier. Net income increased 14.2% to $417,000 thousand from net income of $365,000 thousand a year earlier. Revenues were $20,245,000 thousand, up 11.8% from $18,109,000 thousand the year before. Operating income was $1,388,000 thousand versus an income of $1,316,000 thousand in the prior year, an increase of 5.5%. Total direct expense was $16,933,000 thousand versus $15,000,000 thousand in the prior year, an increase of 12.9%. Total indirect expense was $1,924,000 thousand versus $1,793,000 thousand in the prior year, an increase of 7.3%.

Prospects: Prospects appear favorable as Co. continues to benefit from strength in its government and defense business. For instance, Co.'s government and defense business posted full-year 2004 bookings of $21.90 billion, including fourth-quarter bookings of $4.20 billion and ended the year with a backlog of $3.10 billion in 2004 versus $2.20 billion in 2003. As a result of the positive business outlook, Co. reaffirmed its guidance for 2005 earnings from continuing operations to range from $1.80 to $1.90 per share. This guidance includes higher pension expense attributable to a lower discount rate, partially offset by expected profit improvements in 2005.

Financial Data
(US$ in Thousands)

	12/31/2004	12/31/2003	12/31/2002	12/31/2001	12/31/2000	12/31/1999	12/31/1998	12/31/1997
Earnings Per Share	0.94	0.88	(1.57)	(2.11)	0.41	1.19	2.53	2.18
Cash Flow Per Share	4.71	3.80	2.59	0.37	2.83	(0.94)	2.43	4.03
Dividends Per Share	0.800	0.800	0.800	0.200	1.000	0.800	0.800	0.200
Dividend Payout %	85.11	90.91	...	...	243.90	67.23	31.62	9.17
Income Statement								
Total Revenue	20,245,000	18,109,000	16,760,000	16,867,000	16,895,000	19,841,000	19,530,000	13,673,000
EBITDA	1,386,000	1,642,000	1,908,000	1,506,000	2,307,000	2,265,000	2,939,000	1,606,000
Depn & Amortn	434,000	393,000	364,000	729,000	694,000	724,000	761,000	457,000
Income Before Taxes	579,000	762,000	1,074,000	117,000	877,000	828,000	1,467,000	790,000
Income Taxes	140,000	227,000	319,000	112,000	379,000	371,000	603,000	263,000
Net Income	417,000	365,000	(640,000)	(763,000)	141,000	404,000	864,000	527,000
Average Shares	442,201	415,429	408,031	361,323	341,118	340,784	341,861	242,000
Balance Sheet								
Current Assets	7,124,000	6,585,000	7,190,000	8,362,000	8,013,000	8,931,000	8,637,000	9,233,000
Total Assets	24,153,000	23,668,000	23,946,000	26,636,000	26,777,000	28,110,000	27,939,000	28,598,000
Current Liabilities	5,644,000	3,849,000	5,107,000	5,753,000	4,865,000	7,886,000	6,680,000	11,886,000
Long-Term Obligations	4,637,000	7,376,000	6,280,000	6,875,000	9,054,000	7,298,000	8,163,000	4,406,000
Total Liabilities	13,505,000	14,506,000	15,076,000	15,346,000	15,954,000	17,151,000	17,083,000	18,173,000
Stockholders' Equity	10,551,000	9,162,000	8,870,000	11,290,000	10,823,000	10,959,000	10,856,000	10,425,000
Shares Outstanding	453,096	418,136	408,209	395,432	340,620	338,760	336,798	338,880
Statistical Record								
Return on Assets %	1.74	1.53	N.M.	N.M.	0.51	1.44	3.06	2.65
Return on Equity %	4.22	4.05	N.M.	N.M.	1.29	3.70	8.12	7.02
EBITDA Margin %	6.85	9.07	11.38	8.93	13.65	11.42	15.05	11.75
Net Margin %	2.06	2.02	N.M.	N.M.	0.83	2.04	4.42	3.85
Asset Turnover	0.84	0.76	0.66	0.63	0.61	0.71	0.69	0.69
Current Ratio	1.26	1.71	1.41	1.45	1.65	1.13	1.29	0.78
Debt to Equity	0.44	0.81	0.71	0.61	0.84	0.67	0.75	0.42
Price Range	41.18-29.72	33.71-24.55	45.12-27.04	36.30-24.85	33.19-18.00	73.50-21.63	59.44-40.00	54.75-48.19
P/E Ratio	43.81-31.62	38.31-27.90	...	...	80.95-43.90	61.76-18.17	23.49-15.81	25.11-22.10
Average Yield %	2.34	2.69	2.26	0.66	4.09	1.48	1.49	0.40

Address: 870 Winer Street, Waltham, MA 02451	**Web Site:** www.raytheon.com	**Auditors:** PricewaterhouseCoopers LLP
Telephone: (781) 522-3000	**Officers:** William H. Swanson - Chmn., Pres., C.E.O. Thomas M. Culligan - Exec. V.P., Bus. Devel.	**Investor Contact:** 781-860-2303

READER'S DIGEST ASSOCIATION, INC.

Exchange	Symbol	Price	52Wk Range	Yield	P/E
NYS	RDA	$17.31 (3/31/2005)	17.55-13.09	2.31	75.26

*7 Year Price Score 55.37   *NYSE Composite Index=100   *12 Month Price Score 105.07

Interim Earnings (Per Share)
Qtr.	Sep	Dec	Mar	Jun
2001-02	(0.01)	0.78	0.16	(0.03)
2002-03	(0.05)	0.84	(0.05)	(0.14)
2003-04	(0.14)	0.67	0.02	(0.06)
2004-05	(0.31)	0.58	...	...

Interim Dividends (Per Share)
Amt	Decl	Ex	Rec	Pay
0.05Q	4/19/2004	4/28/2004	4/30/2004	5/13/2004
0.05Q	8/13/2004	8/20/2004	8/24/2004	9/7/2004
0.05Q	10/22/2004	10/29/2004	11/2/2004	11/15/2004
0.10Q	1/21/2005	1/28/2005	2/1/2005	2/15/2005

Indicated Div: $0.40

Valuation Analysis
Forecast P/E	17.51	No of Institutions
	(4/7/2005)	170
Market Cap	$1.7 Billion	Shares
Book Value	501.2 Million	92,237,896
Price/Book	3.44	% Held
Price/Sales	0.72	92.64

Business Summary: Non-Media Publishing (MIC: 13.3 SIC: 731 NAIC: 11130)

Reader's Digest Association is a diversified media company that produces and distributes books, magazines and other products worldwide. Co.'s magazines include its flagship Reader's Digest magazine. As of June 30 2004, Reader's Digest had worldwide circulation of about 19.0 million. Reader's Digest is published in 49 editions and 20 languages. Co. sells these and other products through direct marketing and direct sales channels. Co. conducts its business through three reportable segments: Reader's Digest North America, Consumer Business Services and Reader's Digest International.

Recent Developments: For the quarter ended Dec 31 2004, net income decreased 13.1% to $57,800 thousand from net income of $66,500 thousand in the year-earlier quarter. Revenues were $798,000 thousand, up 0.2% from $796,400 thousand the year before. Operating income was $88,200 thousand versus an income of $113,900 thousand in the prior-year quarter, a decrease of 22.6%. Total direct expense was $308,500 thousand versus $310,100 thousand in the prior-year quarter, a decrease of 0.5%. Total indirect expense was $401,300 thousand versus $372,400 thousand in the prior-year quarter, an increase of 7.8%.

Prospects: On Jan 26 2005, Co. reaffirmed its fiscal 2005 full-year earnings per share guidance of $0.77 to $0.87, not including amortization for deferred magazine promotion costs and special items. Co. cited the recent considerable strength in its core Reader's Digest business, particularly in International. Additionally, Co. has indicated that Books Are Fun has been progressively better since Thanksgiving. Co. expects that its results for the third quarter of 2005 will be down, while results for the fourth quarter 2005 are expected to be significantly higher versus last year due to planned major marketing campaigns and investments in RD International and RD North America.

Financial Data
(US$ in Thousands)	6 Mos	3 Mos	06/30/2004	06/30/2003	06/30/2002	06/30/2001	06/30/2000	06/30/1999
Earnings Per Share	0.23	0.31	0.49	0.60	0.89	1.26	1.61	1.39
Cash Flow Per Share	1.62	1.62	1.79	1.56	1.32	0.16	1.65	2.07
Tang Book Value Per Share	N.M.	N.M.	N.M.	N.M.	N.M.	0.17	0.36	2.01
Dividends Per Share	0.200	0.200	0.200	0.200	0.200	0.200	0.200	0.375
Dividend Payout %	87.04	63.96	40.82	33.33	22.47	15.87	12.42	26.98
Income Statement								
Total Revenue	1,288,000	490,000	2,388,500	2,474,900	2,368,600	2,518,200	2,553,700	2,532,200
EBITDA	70,100	(30,800)	191,200	206,500	190,400	254,500	303,400	248,600
Depn & Amortn	32,400	16,100	75,300	64,700	35,900	56,800	47,500	43,700
Income Before Taxes	37,700	(46,900)	66,100	100,400	140,600	187,800	263,800	211,700
Income Taxes	10,200	(16,600)	16,600	39,100	49,400	55,700	90,000	85,100
Net Income	27,500	(30,300)	49,500	61,300	91,200	132,100	173,800	151,900
Average Shares	99,900	97,300	99,200	99,200	100,600	103,700	107,000	108,000
Balance Sheet								
Current Assets	819,600	807,000	690,300	788,000	863,700	770,600	772,500	1,146,500
Total Assets	2,521,000	2,529,800	2,442,700	2,599,500	2,702,700	1,675,100	1,758,800	1,710,500
Current Liabilities	987,800	1,014,400	892,300	881,200	980,800	859,500	904,400	986,300
Long-Term Obligations	541,800	622,200	637,700	834,700	818,000	...	...	...
Total Liabilities	2,019,800	2,095,000	1,979,600	2,199,200	2,230,800	1,218,900	1,254,500	1,329,000
Stockholders' Equity	501,200	434,800	463,100	400,300	471,900	456,200	504,300	381,500
Shares Outstanding	99,566	99,531	99,058	98,178	99,523	102,649	102,899	141,145
Statistical Record								
Return on Assets %	0.93	1.23	1.96	2.31	4.17	7.69	9.99	9.28
Return on Equity %	5.00	7.78	11.43	14.06	19.65	27.51	39.13	47.46
EBITDA Margin %	5.44	N.M.	8.01	8.34	8.04	10.11	11.88	9.82
Net Margin %	2.14	N.M.	2.07	2.48	3.85	5.25	6.81	6.00
Asset Turnover	0.92	0.91	0.94	0.93	1.08	1.47	1.47	1.55
Current Ratio	0.83	0.80	0.77	0.89	0.88	0.90	0.85	1.16
Debt to Equity	1.08	1.43	1.38	2.09	1.73	...	...	...
Price Range	16.30-13.09	16.30-13.09	16.30-11.94	18.14-9.50	28.64-15.65	41.50-25.83	42.13-26.94	40.94-16.56
P/E Ratio	70.87-56.91	52.58-42.23	33.27-24.37	30.23-15.83	32.18-17.58	32.94-20.50	26.16-16.73	29.45-11.92
Average Yield %	1.39	1.39	1.42	1.40	0.94	0.58	0.61	1.35

Address: Reader's Digest Road, Pleasantville, NY 10570
Telephone: (914) 238-1000
Fax: (914) 238-4559

Web Site: www.rd.com
Officers: Thomas O. Ryder - Chmn., C.E.O. Michael S. Geltzeiler - Sr. V.P., C.F.O.

Auditors: KPMG LLP
Investor Contact: 914 244 5425
Transfer Agents: Mellon Investor Services

REALTY INCOME CORP.

Exchange	Symbol	Price	52Wk Range	Yield	P/E	Div Acheiver
NYS	O	$22.88 (3/31/2005)	26.07-18.13	5.80	19.90	10 Years

*7 Year Price Score 122.82   *NYSE Composite Index=100   *12 Month Price Score 99.23

Interim Earnings (Per Share)

Qtr.	Mar	Jun	Sep	Dec
2001	0.30	0.20	0.25	0.25
2002	0.24	0.24	0.28	0.26
2003	0.23	0.26	0.26	0.34
2004	0.29	0.27	0.28	0.31

Interim Dividends (Per Share)

Amt	Decl	Ex	Rec	Pay
0.11M	12/15/2004	12/30/2004	1/3/2005	1/18/2005
0.11M	1/13/2005	1/28/2005	2/1/2005	2/15/2005
0.11M	2/16/2005	2/25/2005	3/1/2005	3/15/2005
0.111M	3/22/2005	3/30/2005	4/1/2005	4/15/2005
			Indicated Div: $1.33	

Valuation Analysis

Forecast P/E	14.14	No of Institutions	
	(4/7/2005)	111	
Market Cap	$1.8 Billion	Shares	
Book Value	913.7 Million	27,262,490	
Price/Book	1.99	% Held	
Price/Sales	10.34	34.26	

Business Summary: Property, Real Estate & Development (MIC: 8.3 SIC: 798 NAIC: 25930)

Realty Income is a real estate investment trust (REIT) engaged in acquiring and owning freestanding retail properties. As of Dec 31 2003, Co. owned 1,404 retail properties, located in 48 states with approximately 11.3 million square feet of leasable space. Co. is a fully integrated, self-administered real estate company with in-house acquisition, leasing, legal, retail and real estate research, portfolio management and capital markets expertise. Other activities include Crest Net Lease, Inc., Co.'s wholly-owned subsidiary focused on acquiring and subsequently marketing net-leased properties for sale.

Recent Developments: For the year ended Dec 31 2004, income from continuing operations increased 15.8% to $84,098 thousand from income of $72,626 thousand a year earlier. Net income increased 19.6% to $103,397 thousand from net income of $86,435 thousand a year earlier. Revenues were $175,555 thousand, up 20.8% from $145,293 thousand the year before. Funds from Operations (FFO) increased 14.3% to $118,181 thousand compared with $103,366 thousand in 2003. As of Dec 31 2004, Co.'s portfolio occupancy was 97.9%.

Prospects: On Feb 9 2005, Co. announced that it has acquired a property portfolio of 24 stores, for approximately $67.3 million, leased to Rite Aid Corporation. Co. plans to hold approximately $58.0 million in its core portfolio as long-term investments and will place approximately $9.0 million in its Crest Net Lease, Inc. subsidiary for future sales. Meanwhile, Co. is targeting Funds from Operations (FFO) per common share for 2005 of between $1.59 and $1.62, which would equate to an increase of about 6.0% to 8.0% over Co.'s 2004 FFO per share of $1.50. Furthermore, Co. anticipates that Crest Net Lease will contribute between $0.03 and $0.05 per share to Co.'s FFO during 2005.

Financial Data
(US$ in Thousands)

	12/31/2004	12/31/2003	12/31/2002	12/31/2001	12/31/2000	12/31/1999	12/31/1998	12/31/1997
Earnings Per Share	1.15	1.08	1.01	0.99	0.84	0.77	0.78	0.74
Cash Flow Per Share	2.27	1.04	1.84	1.54	1.06	1.35	1.21	1.12
Tang Book Value Per Share	11.31	10.69	10.11	8.46	7.49	7.76	8.02	8.02
Dividends Per Share	1.251	1.184	1.154	1.124	1.184	1.048	0.988	0.948
Dividend Payout %	108.80	110.12	113.67	113.51	140.09	136.04	126.60	128.04
Income Statement								
Property Income	174,446	149,279	137,138	122,061	117,190	104,270	84,876	67,613
Non-Property Income	1,109	6,835	3,842	4,210	1,120	240	256	284
Total Revenue	175,555	156,114	140,980	126,271	118,310	104,510	85,132	67,897
Depn & Amortn	41,765	34,416	31,428	29,426	29,003	25,952	21,935	18,596
Interest Expense	34,132	26,974	23,536	26,466	31,547	24,473	13,723	8,226
Net Income	103,397	86,435	78,667	67,558	54,788	46,241	41,304	34,770
Average Shares	78,598	71,222	67,976	58,562	53,401	53,652	53,276	47,146
Balance Sheet								
Total Assets	1,442,315	1,360,257	1,080,230	1,003,708	934,766	905,404	759,234	577,021
Long-Term Obligations	503,600	506,400	339,700	315,300	404,000	349,200	294,800	132,600
Total Liabilities	528,580	532,491	357,775	331,915	419,197	370,573	309,025	143,706
Stockholders' Equity	913,735	827,766	722,455	671,793	515,569	534,831	450,209	433,315
Shares Outstanding	79,301	75,818	69,749	65,658	53,127	53,644	53,634	51,396
Statistical Record								
Return on Assets %	7.36	7.08	7.55	6.97	5.94	5.56	6.18	6.74
Return on Equity %	11.84	11.15	11.28	11.38	10.40	9.39	9.35	8.61
Net Margin %	58.90	55.37	55.80	53.50	46.31	44.25	48.52	51.21
Price Range	26.07-18.13	20.49-16.53	18.46-14.65	14.99-12.22	12.75-9.63	12.50-10.25	13.63-11.78	13.81-11.50
P/E Ratio	22.67-15.76	18.97-15.31	18.28-14.50	15.14-12.34	15.18-11.46	16.23-13.31	17.47-15.10	18.67-15.54
Average Yield %	5.76	6.22	6.92	8.11	10.43	9.14	7.69	7.39

Address: 220 West Crest Street, Escondido, CA 92025-1707 Telephone: (760) 741-2111 Fax: (760) 741-2235	Web Site: www.realtyincome.com Officers: William E. Clark - Chmn. Thomas A. Lewis - Vice-Chmn., C.E.O.	Auditors: KPMG LLP Transfer Agents: The Bank of New York

RECKSON ASSOCIATES REALTY CORP.

Exchange	Symbol	Price	52Wk Range	Yield	P/E
NYS	RA	$30.70 (3/31/2005)	34.17-23.35	5.53	50.33

*7 Year Price Score 106.49 *NYSE Composite Index=100 *12 Month Price Score 98.25

Interim Earnings (Per Share)

Qtr.	Mar	Jun	Sep	Dec
2001	0.33	0.32	(1.97)	1.22
2002	0.50	0.21	0.25	0.29
2003	0.14	0.12	0.16	3.58
2004	0.26	0.19	0.13	0.04

Interim Dividends (Per Share)

Amt	Decl	Ex	Rec	Pay
0.425Q	6/15/2004	7/2/2004	7/7/2004	7/20/2004
0.425Q	9/16/2004	10/5/2004	10/7/2004	10/20/2004
0.425Q	12/15/2004	12/30/2004	1/3/2005	1/18/2005
0.425Q	3/8/2005	4/1/2005	4/5/2005	4/18/2005
		Indicated Div: $1.70		

Valuation Analysis

Forecast P/E	12.87	No of Institutions
	(4/7/2005)	141
Market Cap	$2.4 Billion	Shares
Book Value	1.2 Billion	76,404,568
Price/Book	1.98	% Held
Price/Sales	4.61	94.34

Business Summary: Property, Real Estate & Development (MIC: 8.3 SIC: 798 NAIC: 25930)

Reckson Associates Realty operates as a fully integrated, self-administered and self-managed real estate investment trust. Co. is engaged in the business of owning, developing, acquiring, constructing, managing and leasing office and industrial properties in the New York City tri-state area. As of Dec 31 2003, Co. owned 89 properties (inclusive of 10 joint venture properties) in the Tri-State Area markets, encompassing approximately 14.7 million rentable square feet, all of which are managed by Co. As of Dec 31 2003, Co. also owned approximately 313 acres of land in 12 separate parcels.

Recent Developments: For the year ended Dec 31 2004, income from continuing operations increased 85.2% to $56,154 thousand from income of $30,313 thousand a year earlier. Net income decreased 56.9% to $70,428 thousand from net income of $163,521 thousand a year earlier. Revenues were $588,677 thousand, up 20.4% from $488,819 thousand the year before. Operating income was $158,702 thousand versus an income of $121,090 thousand in the prior year, an increase of 31.1%.

Prospects: Co.'s near-term outlook appears favorable, supported by increased leasing activity, higher office occupancy, which approximated 94.0% in fiscal 2004, and an improved balance sheet. Also, Co. should benefit from continued investment activity in 2005, which already includes the acquisition of a 150,000 square foot, Class A office building and a 203,000 square foot, Class A office building located in Madison, NJ. After taking into account Co.'s recent equity offering of 4.5 million shares of common stock in the fourth quarter of 2004, Co. is narrowing its fiscal 2005 funds from operations guidance to a range of $2.32 to $2.40 per share from a range of $2.32 to $2.44 per share.

Financial Data
(US$ in Thousands)

	12/31/2004	12/31/2003	12/31/2002	12/31/2001	12/31/2000	12/31/1999	12/31/1998	12/31/1997
Earnings Per Share	0.61	2.54	0.83	(0.92)	1.45	1.17	0.95	1.04
Cash Flow Per Share	2.49	2.77	3.28	3.18	3.17	3.29	2.99	2.16
Tang Book Value Per Share	15.51	17.04	17.10	17.35	20.00	22.05	17.63	11.88
Dividends Per Share	1.698	1.698	1.698	1.660	1.901	1.874	1.325	1.238
Dividend Payout %	278.43	66.85	204.58	...	131.10	160.17	139.47	118.99
Income Statement								
Property Income	514,815	445,781	498,082	497,771	452,077	369,135	252,447	143,759
Non-Property Income	...	24,501	8,010	42,697	57,861	34,018	13,926	9,636
Total Revenue	514,815	470,282	506,092	540,468	509,938	403,153	266,373	153,395
Depn & Amortn	121,285	116,633	112,341	102,931	92,547	74,504	52,957	27,237
Interest Expense	101,872	82,487	88,585	93,072	96,337	74,320	47,795	21,585
Net Income	70,428	163,521	76,368	(36,001)	111,401	103,487	50,386	...
Average Shares	69,235	58,172	60,090	58,405	53,829	47,420	40,010	33,260
Balance Sheet								
Total Assets	3,167,608	2,746,995	2,907,920	2,994,218	2,998,030	2,724,235	1,854,816	1,113,257
Long-Term Obligations	1,542,992	1,390,080	1,506,317	1,472,140	1,394,956	1,281,087	889,313	540,273
Total Liabilities	1,703,638	1,513,136	1,631,675	1,592,811	1,519,150	1,380,689	959,936	572,187
Stockholders' Equity	1,198,861	936,609	942,229	1,045,857	1,112,659	1,116,956	706,064	448,665
Shares Outstanding	77,299	54,956	55,094	60,265	55,635	50,659	40,035	37,770
Statistical Record								
Return on Assets %	2.37	5.78	2.59	N.M.	3.88	4.52	3.40	...
Return on Equity %	6.58	17.41	7.68	N.M.	9.97	11.35	8.73	...
Net Margin %	13.68	34.77	15.09	(6.66)	21.85	(6.04)	(4.69)	...
Price Range	34.17-23.35	24.47-17.94	26.00-20.10	25.88-21.14	26.81-17.69	26.56-18.00	26.44-19.00	28.75-20.44
P/E Ratio	56.02-38.28	5.51-4.04	15.03-11.62	...	8.82-5.82	10.93-7.41	27.83-20.00	27.64-19.65
Average Yield %	6.10	7.99	7.37	7.20	8.53	8.31	5.56	5.15

Address: 225 Broadhollow Road, Melville, NY 11747 Telephone: (631) 694-6900 Fax: (631) 622-6790	Web Site: www.reckson.com Officers: Donald J. Rechler - Chmn. Scott H. Rechler - Pres., C.E.O.	Auditors: Ernst & Young LLP Investor Contact: 631-694-6900

REEBOK INTERNATIONAL, LTD.

Exchange	Symbol	Price	52Wk Range	Yield	P/E
NYS	RBK	$44.30 (3/31/2005)	45.56-31.69	0.68	14.52

*7 Year Price Score 126.95 *NYSE Composite Index=100 *12 Month Price Score 107.42

Interim Earnings (Per Share)

Qtr.	Mar	Jun	Sep	Dec
2001	0.68	0.24	0.66	0.10
2002	0.58	0.39	0.81	0.26
2003	0.63	0.41	0.96	0.44
2004	0.63	0.35	1.36	0.71

Interim Dividends (Per Share)

Amt	Decl	Ex	Rec	Pay
0.15S	7/29/2003	8/15/2003	8/19/2003	9/3/2003
0.15S	2/10/2004	3/3/2004	3/5/2004	3/19/2004
0.15S	7/27/2004	8/17/2004	8/19/2004	9/3/2004
0.15S	2/14/2005	3/2/2005	3/4/2005	3/18/2005
			Indicated Div: $0.30	

Valuation Analysis

Forecast P/E	12.83	No of Institutions	
	(4/7/2005)	224	
Market Cap	$2.6 Billion	Shares	
Book Value	1.2 Billion	51,200,048	
Price/Book	2.15	% Held	
Price/Sales	0.69	85.90	

Business Summary: Rubber Products (MIC: 11.6 SIC: 021 NAIC: 16211)

Reebok International designs and markets sports and fitness products, including footwear and apparel. Co. has four major brand groups. The Reebok Division designs, produces and markets sports, fitness and casual footwear, apparel and accessories under the Reebok® brand. The Reebok® brand also includes Co.'s sports licensing business. Rockport designs, produces and distributes comfort footwear under the Rockport® brand. Ralph Lauren Footwear, a subsidiary of Co., is responsible for footwear and certain apparel sold under the Ralph Lauren® and Polo Sport® brands. The Greg Norman Division produces a range of men's apparel and accessories marketed under the Greg Norman name and logo.

Recent Developments: For the year ended Dec 31 2004, net income increased 22.4% to $192,425 thousand from net income of $157,254 thousand a year earlier. Revenues were $3,785,284 thousand, up 8.6% from $3,485,316 thousand the year before. Total direct expense was $2,287,283 thousand versus $2,147,111 thousand in the prior year, an increase of 6.5%. Total indirect expense was $1,203,654 thousand versus $1,085,841 thousand in the prior year, an increase of 10.8%.

Prospects: Co.'s earnings are benefiting from higher revenues and improving operating margins. Co. has increased its operating margins while at the same time investing in brand building initiatives that it believes are necessary for long-term brand performance. For its Reebok brand, Co. continues to invest in three product and marketing platforms: Performance, Rbk and Classic. Co. plans to expand its successful Rbk product and marketing platform to include a broader range of products, including performance and lifestyle products for men and women. In support of its new product introductions and brand building initiatives, Co. is launching a new global advertising campaign for the Reebok brand.

Financial Data
(US$ in Thousands)

	12/31/2004	12/31/2003	12/31/2002	12/31/2001	12/31/2000	12/31/1999	12/31/1998	12/31/1997
Earnings Per Share	3.05	2.43	1.97	1.66	1.40	0.20	0.42	2.32
Cash Flow Per Share	2.96	2.28	3.77	3.01	3.21	5.02	2.69	2.26
Tang Book Value Per Share	15.20	16.22	13.57	10.90	9.45	8.17	8.05	8.27
Dividends Per Share	0.300	0.150	...	...	...	...	...	...
Dividend Payout %	9.84	6.17	...	...	...	...	...	...
Income Statement								
Total Revenue	3,785,284	3,485,316	3,127,872	2,992,878	2,865,240	2,891,237	3,205,425	3,637,441
EBITDA	318,053	287,195	241,949	210,055	204,132	117,213	134,346	259,064
Depn & Amortn	38,845	35,636	32,033	36,619	46,201	48,643	48,017	47,423
Income Before Taxes	265,796	234,152	195,387	155,806	135,805	28,038	37,030	158,085
Income Taxes	68,491	72,119	60,570	48,300	49,000	10,093	11,925	12,490
Net Income	192,425	157,254	126,458	102,726	80,878	11,045	23,927	135,119
Average Shares	64,122	67,763	68,013	65,495	57,724	56,530	57,029	58,309
Balance Sheet								
Current Assets	1,857,513	1,726,850	1,613,567	1,294,695	1,225,205	1,243,118	1,361,796	1,464,820
Total Assets	2,440,628	1,989,742	1,860,772	1,543,173	1,463,046	1,564,128	1,739,624	1,756,097
Current Liabilities	806,314	565,988	579,920	449,406	488,139	623,903	612,284	577,453
Long-Term Obligations	360,126	353,225	353,329	351,210	345,015	370,302	554,432	639,355
Total Liabilities	1,220,672	956,032	976,202	823,235	855,183	1,035,312	1,215,247	1,248,940
Stockholders' Equity	1,219,956	1,033,710	884,570	719,938	607,863	528,816	524,377	507,157
Shares Outstanding	59,208	59,608	60,224	59,038	57,492	56,269	56,590	53,375
Statistical Record								
Return on Assets %	8.66	8.17	7.43	6.83	5.33	0.67	1.37	7.63
Return on Equity %	17.03	16.40	15.76	15.47	14.19	2.10	4.64	30.42
EBITDA Margin %	8.40	8.24	7.74	7.02	7.12	4.05	4.19	7.12
Net Margin %	5.08	4.51	4.04	3.43	2.82	0.38	0.75	3.71
Asset Turnover	1.70	1.81	1.84	1.99	1.89	1.75	1.83	2.05
Current Ratio	2.30	3.05	2.78	2.88	2.51	1.99	2.22	2.54
Debt to Equity	0.30	0.34	0.40	0.49	0.57	0.70	1.06	1.26
Price Range	44.00-31.69	40.63-28.60	29.83-21.80	34.60-18.95	27.57-7.13	22.63-7.88	33.00-12.63	52.63-28.13
P/E Ratio	14.43-10.39	16.72-11.77	15.14-11.07	20.84-11.42	19.69-5.09	113.13-39.38	78.57-30.06	22.68-12.12
Average Yield %	0.80	0.44	...	...	...	...	...	...

Address: 1895 J.W. Foster Boulevard, Canton, MA 02021	Web Site: www.reebok.com	Auditors: Ernst & Young LLP
Telephone: (781) 401-5000	Officers: Paul B. Fireman - Chmn., C.E.O. Jay M. Margolis - Pres., C.O.O.	Investor Contact: 781-401-7152
Fax: (781) 401-7402		

REGAL ENTERTAINMENT GROUP

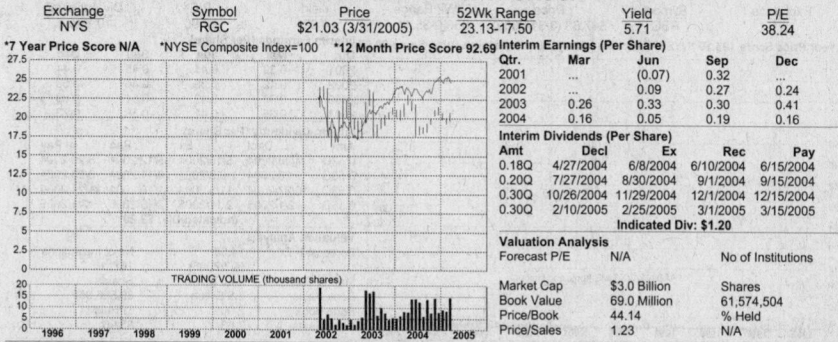

Exchange	Symbol	Price	52Wk Range	Yield	P/E
NYS	RGC	$21.03 (3/31/2005)	23.13-17.50	5.71	38.24

*7 Year Price Score N/A   *NYSE Composite Index=100   *12 Month Price Score 92.69

Interim Earnings (Per Share)

Qtr.	Mar	Jun	Sep	Dec
2001	...	(0.07)	0.32	...
2002	...	0.09	0.27	0.24
2003	0.26	0.33	0.30	0.41
2004	0.16	0.05	0.19	0.16

Interim Dividends (Per Share)

Amt	Decl	Ex	Rec	Pay
0.18Q	4/27/2004	6/8/2004	6/10/2004	6/15/2004
0.20Q	7/27/2004	8/30/2004	9/1/2004	9/15/2004
0.30Q	10/26/2004	11/29/2004	12/1/2004	12/15/2004
0.30Q	2/10/2005	2/25/2005	3/1/2005	3/15/2005

Indicated Div: $1.20

Valuation Analysis

Forecast P/E	N/A	No of Institutions
Market Cap	$3.0 Billion	Shares
Book Value	69.0 Million	61,574,504
Price/Book	44.14	% Held
Price/Sales	1.23	N/A

Business Summary: Movies & Film (MIC: 13.2 SIC: 832 NAIC: 12131)

Regal Entertainment Group is theatre exhibition operator. As of Dec 30 2004, Co.'s theatre circuit in the United States consisted of 6,273 screens in 558 theatres in 40 states. Co. operates its theatre circuit using its Regal Cinemas, United Artists and Edwards brands. Co. primarily operates multi-screen theatres. Co.'s multi-screen theatre complexes typically contain 10 to 18 screens, each with auditoriums ranging from 100 to 500 seats. In addition, many of Co.'s theatres feature amenities such as wall-to-wall screens, digital stereo surround-sound, multi-station concessions stands, computerized ticketing systems, stadium seating, and video game areas adjacent to the theatre lobby.

Recent Developments: For the year ended Dec 30 2004, net income decreased 55.5% to $82,500 thousand from net income of $185,400 thousand a year earlier. Revenues were $2,468,000 thousand, down 0.9% from $2,489,900 thousand the year before. Operating income was $321,100 thousand versus an income of $379,100 thousand in the prior year, a decrease of 15.3%. Total direct expense was $973,400 thousand versus $1,001,800 thousand in the prior year, a decrease of 2.8%. Total indirect expense was $1,173,500 thousand versus $1,109,000 thousand in the prior year, an increase of 5.8%.

Prospects: Co.'s outlook is tempered by its recent lackluster top line results. Nevertheless, Co. remains optimistic regarding the 2005 film slate and is hopeful that the industry will benefit from a year of solid box office performance. Co. cited the film studios' continued efforts to promote and market upcoming 2005 film releases, including releases such as War of the Worlds, King Kong, Star Wars: Episode III, Harry Potter and the Goblet of Fire and Batman Begins. Meanwhile, Co. intends to grow its theatre circuit through selective expansion and through accretive acquisitions. Separately, Co. expects theatre capital expenditures to be in the range of $150.0 million to $165.0 million for fiscal 2005.

Financial Data

(US$ in Thousands)	12/30/2004	01/01/2004	12/26/2002	01/03/2002
Earnings Per Share	0.55	1.30	0.79	...
Cash Flow Per Share	2.71	3.38	3.54	...
Tang Book Value Per Share	N.M.	4.21	7.92	...
Dividends Per Share	5.860	5.650	0.150	...
Dividend Payout %	N.M.	434.62	18.99	...
Income Statement				
Total Revenue	2,468,000	2,489,900	2,140,200	556,900
EBITDA	417,800	542,400	407,400	72,900
Depn & Amortn	180,200	163,800	137,200	42,600
Income Before Taxes	142,000	306,600	208,500	8,500
Income Taxes	59,500	121,200	89,800	3,600
Net Income	82,500	185,400	117,200	4,900
Average Shares	149,220	142,792	112,284	...
Balance Sheet				
Current Assets	321,100	376,600	389,800	132,700
Total Assets	2,542,400	2,471,800	2,310,200	1,122,700
Current Liabilities	644,200	412,800	304,000	196,400
Long-Term Obligations	1,745,600	1,196,100	661,400	423,300
Total Liabilities	2,471,400	1,673,000	1,036,600	656,100
Stockholders' Equity	69,000	794,900	1,270,800	383,000
Shares Outstanding	144,809	141,991	131,736	...
Statistical Record				
Return on Assets %	3.30	7.63	6.98	...
Return on Equity %	19.15	17.66	14.49	...
EBITDA Margin %	16.93	21.78	19.04	13.09
Net Margin %	3.34	7.45	5.48	0.88
Asset Turnover	0.99	1.02	1.27	...
Current Ratio	0.50	0.91	1.28	0.68
Debt to Equity	25.30	1.50	0.52	1.11
Price Range	23.13-17.50	23.73-17.25	24.25-16.20	...
P/E Ratio	42.05-31.82	18.25-13.27	30.70-20.51	...
Average Yield %	29.23	28.59	0.74	...

Address: 9110 East Nichols Avenue, Suite 200, Centennial, CO 80112 Telephone: (303) 792-3600	Web Site: Officers: Michael L. Campbell - Co-Chmn., Co-C.E.O. Kurt C. Hall - Co-Chmn., Co-C.E.O.	Auditors: KPMG LLP Transfer Agents: Wells Fargo Bank Minnesota, National Association

REGENCY CENTERS CORP.

Exchange	Symbol	Price	52Wk Range	Yield	P/E	Div Acheiver
NYS	REG	$47.63 (3/31/2005)	55.40-35.11	4.62	22.90	10 Years

*7 Year Price Score 135.10 *NYSE Composite Index=100 *12 Month Price Score 99.67

Interim Earnings (Per Share)

Qtr.	Mar	Jun	Sep	Dec
2001	0.39	0.41	0.45	0.44
2002	0.42	0.38	0.46	0.58
2003	0.30	0.42	0.51	0.89
2004	0.35	0.41	0.58	0.73

Interim Dividends (Per Share)

Amt	Decl	Ex	Rec	Pay
0.53Q	4/28/2004	5/10/2004	5/12/2004	5/26/2004
0.53Q	7/28/2004	8/9/2004	8/11/2004	8/25/2004
0.53Q	10/27/2004	11/8/2004	11/10/2004	11/24/2004
0.55Q	2/1/2005	2/11/2005	2/15/2005	3/1/2005

Indicated Div: $2.20

Valuation Analysis

Forecast P/E	14.05 (4/7/2005)	No of Institutions 167
Market Cap	$3.0 Billion	Shares 60,526,952
Book Value	1.5 Billion	% Held
Price/Book	2.00	95.96
Price/Sales	7.63	

Business Summary: Property, Real Estate & Development (MIC: 8.3 SIC: 798 NAIC: 25930)

Regency Centers is a self-administered, self-managed real estate investment trust. Co. is a national owner, operator, and developer focused on grocery-anchored, neighborhood retail centers. As of Dec 31 2003, Co. owned 265 retail properties in 22 states, including those held in joint ventures, totaling 30.3 million square feet. Geographically, 19.6% of Co.'s gross leasable area is located in Florida, 19.5% in California, 16.8% in Texas, 6.6% in Georgia, 6.3% in Ohio, and 31.2% spread throughout 17 other states. Co. owns and operates its shopping centers through its operating partnership, Regency Centers, L.P. in which it owns 98.0% of the operating partnership units, as of Dec 31 2003.

Recent Developments: For the year ended Dec 31 2004, income from continuing operations increased 6.7% to $113,309,000 from income of $106,185,000 a year earlier. Net income increased 4.2% to $136,327,000 from net income of $130,789,000 a year earlier. Revenues were $3,919,480,00, up 7.9% from $363,200,000 the year before. Funds from Operations climbed 10.5% to $200,872,985 compared with $181,826,447 in 2003. As of Dec 31 2004, occupancy of Co.'s operating portfolio was 96.1%.

Prospects: Co. and its joint venture partner, Macquarie CountryWide Trust of Australia, agreed to purchase 101 retail centers totaling approximately 13.0 million square feet from CalPERS/First Washington. About 45.0% of the centers are located in metropolitan Washington D.C./Baltimore as well as Northern and Southern California. Separately, Co. and California State Teachers' Retirement System formed a new co-investment partnership to acquire over $200.0 million in neighborhood and community shopping centers, including one of Co.'s stabilized development and three additional properties for $124.5 million and plans to acquire $100.0 million in additional property throughout the country in the next year.

Financial Data

(US$ in Thousands)	12/31/2004	12/31/2003	12/31/2002	12/31/2001	12/31/2000	12/31/1999	12/31/1998	12/31/1997
Earnings Per Share	2.08	2.12	1.84	1.69	1.49	1.61	1.75	1.23
Cash Flow Per Share	2.99	3.84	2.97	3.20	3.14	2.83	2.58	2.47
Tang Book Value Per Share	20.45	19.96	20.34	20.56	20.93	20.41	19.68	19.39
Dividends Per Share	2.120	2.080	2.040	2.000	1.920	1.840	1.760	1.680
Dividend Payout %	101.92	98.11	110.87	118.34	128.86	114.29	100.57	136.59
Income Statement								
Property Income	371,091	359,926	354,183	353,615	331,218	278,960	130,487	89,306
Non-Property Income	20,857	17,695	26,020	34,934	30,365	22,927	12,809	8,481
Total Revenue	391,948	377,621	380,203	388,550	361,583	301,887	143,296	97,787
Depn & Amortn	83,675	76,122	76,016	68,642	60,039	49,168	24,224	17,210
Interest Expense	81,196	86,373	83,620	74,416	71,971	60,067	28,786	19,667
Income Before Taxes	135,613	144,146	117,873	137,417	122,336	107,968	56,239	29,948
Net Income	136,327	130,789	110,525	100,664	87,611	89,846	50,590	27,402
Average Shares	61,481	61,242	60,438	59,274	56,754	55,502	26,898	19,702
Balance Sheet								
Total Assets	3,243,824	3,098,229	3,061,859	3,109,314	3,035,144	2,654,936	1,240,107	826,849
Long-Term Obligations	1,493,090	1,452,777	1,333,524	1,022,721	841,072	764,787	430,495	278,050
Total Liabilities	1,610,743	1,562,530	1,419,280	1,478,812	1,390,795	1,068,805	571,173	291,968
Stockholders' Equity	1,498,717	1,280,978	1,221,720	1,219,051	1,225,415	1,247,249	550,741	513,627
Shares Outstanding	62,808	59,907	59,557	57,601	56,898	59,423	27,988	26,492
Statistical Record								
Return on Assets %	4.29	4.25	3.58	3.28	3.07	4.61	4.90	4.52
Return on Equity %	9.78	10.45	9.06	8.24	7.07	9.99	9.51	7.61
Net Margin %	34.78	34.64	29.07	25.91	24.23	29.76	35.30	28.02
Price Range	55.40-35.11	40.20-30.60	32.40-26.80	27.75-22.94	24.00-18.44	22.94-18.75	27.75-20.50	28.25-24.63
P/E Ratio	26.63-16.88	18.96-14.43	17.61-14.57	16.42-13.57	16.11-12.37	14.25-11.65	15.86-11.71	22.97-20.02
Average Yield %	4.79	5.94	6.84	8.02	8.92	8.94	7.23	6.31

Address: 121 West Forsyth Street, Suite 200, Jacksonville, FL 32202 Telephone: (904) 598 7000 Fax: (904) 634 3428	Web Site: www.regencyrealty.com Officers: Martin E. Stein Jr. - Chmn., C.E.O. Mary Lou Fiala - Pres., C.O.O.	Auditors: KPMG LLP Investor Contact: 904-598-7000

REGIONS FINANCIAL CORP (NEW)

Exchange	Symbol	Price	52Wk Range	Yield	P/E	Div Acheiver
NYS	RF	$32.40 (3/31/2005)	35.79-29.57	4.20	14.79	33 Years

*7 Year Price Score N/A   *NYSE Composite Index=100   *12 Month Price Score N/A

Interim Earnings (Per Share)

Qtr.	Mar	Jun	Sep	Dec
2001	0.57	0.49	0.59	0.60
2002	0.66	0.67	0.70	0.69
2003	0.71	0.73	0.73	0.73
2004	0.75	0.58	0.55	0.31

Interim Dividends (Per Share)

Amt	Decl	Ex	Rec	Pay
0.412Q	4/22/2004	6/15/2004	6/17/2004	7/1/2004
0.333Q	7/16/2004	7/29/2004	8/2/2004	8/16/2004
0.333Q	10/21/2004	10/28/2004	11/1/2004	11/15/2004
0.34Q	1/21/2005	1/28/2005	2/1/2005	2/15/2005
		Indicated Div: $1.36		

TRADING VOLUME (thousand shares)

Valuation Analysis

Forecast P/E	N/A	No of Institutions
		355
Market Cap	$15.1 Billion	Shares
Book Value	10.7 Billion	133,917,616
Price/Book	1.41	% Held
Price/Sales	3.28	28.82

Business Summary: Commercial Banking (MIC: 8.1 SIC: 712 NAIC: 51111)

Regions Financial is a financial holding company which operates primarily within the southeastern United States. Co.'s operations consist of banking, brokerage and investment services, mortgage banking, insurance brokerage, credit life insurance, commercial accounts receivable factoring and specialty financing. At Dec. 31, 2004, Co. had total consolidated assets of approximately $84.1 billion and total consolidated deposits of approximately $58.7 billion. Dec. 31, 2004, Co. operated 1,323 full service banking offices in Alabama, Arkansas, Florida, Georgia, Illinois, Indiana, Iowa, Kentucky, Louisiana, Mississippi, Missouri, North Carolina, South Carolina, Tennessee and Texas.

Recent Developments: For the year ended Dec 31 2004, net income increased 26.4% to $823,765 thousand from net income of $651,841 thousand a year earlier. Net interest income was $2,113,034 thousand, up 43.3% from $1,474,598 thousand the year before. Provision for loan losses was $128,500 thousand versus $121,500 thousand in the prior year, an increase of 5.8%. Non-interest income rose 22.3% to $1,654,354 thousand, while non-interest expense advanced 37.3% to $2,463,306 thousand.

Prospects: Despite a challenging mortgage banking climate and investment spending, Co. is benefiting from improved capital markets business, good core banking results, solid credit quality and incremental merger-related cost savings. Also, Co.'s merger integration remains on target, with the first round of bank branch conversions scheduled for April 2005. In regard to the merger, targeted cost savings are being realized, asset quality continues to be strong, and Co. is achieving net growth in community banking customers, loans and deposits. Looking ahead, Co. remains committed to capitalizing on longer-term growth opportunities through incremental investments.

Financial Data

(US$ in Thousands)	12/31/2004	12/31/2003	12/31/2002	12/31/2001	12/31/2000	12/31/1999	12/31/1998	12/31/1997
Earnings Per Share	2.19	2.90	2.72	2.24	2.38	2.35	1.88	2.15
Cash Flow Per Share	2.90	4.17	1.50	(0.14)	4.31	4.51	(1.38)	1.84
Tang Book Value Per Share	10.73	20.06	18.88	17.54	15.73	13.89	13.61	13.99
Dividends Per Share	.149	1.240	1.160	1.120	1.080	1.000	0.920	0.800
Dividend Payout %	68.04	42.76	42.65	50.00	45.38	42.55	48.94	37.21
Income Statement								
Interest Income	2,955,685	2,219,130	2,536,989	3,055,637	3,234,243	2,854,686	2,597,786	1,653,084
Interest Expense	842,651	744,532	1,039,401	1,630,144	1,845,446	1,428,831	1,272,968	824,203
Net Interest Income	2,113,034	1,474,598	1,497,588	1,425,493	1,388,797	1,425,855	1,324,818	828,881
Provision for Losses	128,500	121,500	127,500	165,402	127,099	113,658	60,505	41,773
Non-Interest Income	1,654,354	1,398,757	1,258,878	981,885	601,210	537,141	474,697	258,553
Non-Interest Expense	2,463,306	1,827,316	1,747,405	1,524,025	1,121,182	1,064,312	1,103,708	600,341
Income Before Taxes	1,175,582	911,572	869,240	717,951	741,726	785,026	635,302	445,320
Income Taxes	351,817	259,731	249,338	209,017	214,203	259,640	213,590	145,628
Net Income	823,765	651,841	619,902	508,934	527,523	525,386	421,712	299,692
Average Shares	373,732	225,118	227,639	227,063	221,989	223,967	223,781	139,421
Balance Sheet								
Net Loans & Leases	56,772,233	31,730,266	30,548,610	30,466,181	30,999,955	27,806,300	24,050,175	16,200,599
Total Assets	84,106,438	48,597,996	47,938,840	45,382,712	43,688,293	42,714,395	36,831,940	23,034,228
Total Deposits	58,667,023	32,732,535	32,926,201	31,548,323	32,022,491	29,989,094	28,350,066	17,750,926
Total Liabilities	73,356,981	44,145,881	43,760,418	41,346,947	40,230,349	39,649,283	33,831,539	21,121,373
Stockholders' Equity	10,749,457	4,452,115	4,178,422	4,035,765	3,457,944	3,065,112	3,000,401	1,912,855
Shares Outstanding	466,241	221,967	221,336	230,081	219,769	220,635	220,454	136,696
Statistical Record								
Return on Assets %	1.24	1.35	1.33	1.14	1.22	1.32	1.41	1.43
Return on Equity %	10.81	15.11	15.09	13.58	16.13	17.32	17.17	17.07
Net Interest Margin %	71.49	66.45	59.03	46.65	42.94	49.95	51.00	50.14
Efficiency Ratio %	53.43	50.51	46.03	37.75	29.23	31.38	35.92	31.40
Loans to Deposits	0.97	0.97	0.93	0.97	0.97	0.93	0.85	0.91
Price Range	35.79-29.57	37.85-30.49	36.13-27.10	32.35-26.34	27.81-18.44	41.44-23.38	45.25-30.25	44.75-25.69
P/E Ratio	16.34-13.50	13.05-10.51	13.28-9.96	14.44-11.76	11.69-7.75	17.63-9.95	24.07-16.09	20.81-11.95
Average Yield %	2.01	3.58	3.45	3.77	4.82	2.89	2.33	2.42

Address: 417 North 20th Street, Birmingham, AL 35203	Web Site: www.regions.com	Auditors: Ernst & Young LLP
Telephone: (205) 944-1300	Officers: Carl E. Jones Jr. - Chmn., C.E.O. Richard D. Horsley - Vice-Chmn., C.O.O.	

REGIS CORP.

Exchange	Symbol	Price	52Wk Range	Yield	P/E
NYS	RGS	$40.93 (3/31/2005)	46.68-38.51	0.39	18.11

*7 Year Price Score 140.76 *NYSE Composite Index=100 *12 Month Price Score 87.74

Interim Earnings (Per Share)

Qtr.	Sep	Dec	Mar	Jun
2001-02	0.36	0.39	0.44	0.45
2002-03	0.44	0.52	0.46	0.50
2003-04	0.55	0.60	0.55	0.59
2004-05	0.55	0.58	...	...

Interim Dividends (Per Share)

Amt	Decl	Ex	Rec	Pay
0.04Q	5/5/2004	5/17/2004	5/19/2004	6/2/2004
0.04Q	8/20/2004	9/1/2004	9/3/2004	9/17/2004
0.04Q	10/29/2004	11/9/2004	11/12/2004	11/26/2004
0.04Q	2/2/2005	2/14/2005	2/16/2005	3/2/2005

Indicated Div: $0.16

Valuation Analysis

Forecast P/E	14.99	No of Institutions
	(4/7/2005)	205
Market Cap	$1.8 Billion	Shares
Book Value	769.9 Million	35,126,536
Price/Book	2.37	% Held
Price/Sales	0.90	78.55

Business Summary: Personal Services (MIC: 5.15 SIC: 231 NAIC: 12112)

Regis is engaged in owning, operating and franchising hair and retail product salons. Co.'s worldwide operations include 10,162 company-owned and franchise salons at June 30, 2004. Co.'s North American operations include 8,148 salons, including 6 beauty career schools and 2,330 franchise salons, operating in North America. Co.'s international operations include 2,014 salons, including four beauty career schools and 1,594 franchise salons, operating throughout Europe, United Kingdom, France, Italy and Spain. Co.'s worldwide operations utilize key hair salon concepts such as: Supercuts, Jean Louis David, Vidal Sassoon, Regis Salons, MasterCuts, Trade Secret, SmartStyle and Cost Cutters.

Recent Developments: For the quarter ended Dec 31 2004, net income decreased 3.2% to $26,764 thousand from net income of $27,662 thousand in the year-earlier quarter. Revenues were $537,332 thousand, up 13.7% from $472,452 thousand the year before. Operating income was $45,045 thousand versus an income of $47,083 thousand in the prior-year quarter, a decrease of 4.3%. Total direct expense was $332,747 thousand versus $287,508 thousand in the prior-year quarter, an increase of 15.7%. Total indirect expense was $159,540 thousand versus $137,861 thousand in the prior-year quarter, an increase of 15.7%.

Prospects: Results are expected to benefit from Co.'s aggressive acquisition activity. During fiscal 2005, Co. expects to have completed the acquisition of approximately 400 company-owned salons, including 122 franchise buybacks, 13 beauty schools and 91 hair restoration centers. In addition, Co. recently made a substantial minority investment in Cool Cuts 4 Kids, a Dallas, TX-based operator of 59 children's salons in seven states. The investment includes an option to purchase this business in three years. Separately, Co. is targeting fiscal 2005 revenue growth of approximately 14.0%, or about $2.20 billion, along with earnings of between $2.35 and $2.47 per diluted share, an increase of 3.0% to 8.0%.

Financial Data

(US$ in Thousands)	6 Mos	3 Mos	06/30/2004	06/30/2003	06/30/2002	06/30/2001	06/30/2000	06/30/1999
Earnings Per Share	2.26	2.28	2.29	1.92	1.63	1.26	1.19	0.76
Cash Flow Per Share	4.53	4.23	4.66	3.46	3.60	2.62	2.10	1.88
Tang Book Value Per Share	N.M.	3.81	3.42	2.89	1.98	2.24	1.73	2.13
Dividends Per Share	0.160	0.150	0.140	0.120	0.120	0.120	0.120	0.100
Dividend Payout %	7.07	6.57	6.11	6.25	7.36	9.52	10.08	13.16
Income Statement								
Total Revenue	1,043,554	506,222	1,923,143	1,684,530	1,454,191	1,311,621	1,142,993	974,872
EBITDA	130,289	63,678	256,869	226,762	193,781	175,284	153,190	108,377
Depn & Amortn	40,337	19,795	74,996	66,767	59,121	64,918	54,117	44,068
Income Before Taxes	80,177	39,575	164,809	138,601	115,650	88,879	83,234	52,733
Income Taxes	27,934	14,096	59,331	51,926	43,596	35,791	33,580	22,387
Net Income	52,243	25,479	105,478	86,675	72,054	53,088	49,654	30,346
Average Shares	46,468	46,293	46,145	45,229	44,172	42,031	41,602	39,740
Balance Sheet								
Current Assets	380,499	331,539	313,442	279,660	256,686	172,647	143,804	113,079
Total Assets	1,680,565	1,313,144	1,271,859	1,112,955	957,190	736,545	628,355	493,624
Current Liabilities	232,514	189,888	201,961	199,065	159,289	111,915	103,044	100,009
Long-Term Obligations	513,295	300,100	282,015	280,634	291,795	256,120	224,618	143,041
Total Liabilities	910,637	595,276	584,298	550,151	512,525	397,004	349,214	257,427
Stockholders' Equity	769,928	717,868	687,561	562,804	444,665	339,501	279,141	236,197
Shares Outstanding	44,661	44,349	44,283	43,527	43,040	41,726	40,702	38,641
Statistical Record								
Return on Assets %	7.31	8.59	8.82	8.37	8.51	7.78	8.83	6.93
Return on Equity %	14.87	16.18	16.83	17.21	18.38	17.16	19.22	14.27
EBITDA Margin %	12.49	12.58	13.36	13.46	13.33	13.36	13.40	11.12
Net Margin %	5.01	5.03	5.48	5.15	4.95	4.05	4.34	3.11
Asset Turnover	1.41	1.60	1.61	1.63	1.72	1.92	2.03	2.23
Current Ratio	1.64	1.75	1.55	1.40	1.61	1.54	1.40	1.13
Debt to Equity	0.67	0.42	0.41	0.50	0.66	0.75	0.80	0.61
Price Range	46.68-38.51	46.00-32.10	46.00-29.05	29.90-21.94	30.49-17.84	20.99-12.50	22.94-10.81	28.44-15.17
P/E Ratio	20.65-17.04	20.18-14.08	20.09-12.69	15.57-11.43	18.71-10.94	16.66-9.92	19.28-9.09	37.42-19.96
Average Yield %	0.37	0.36	0.36	0.45	0.49	0.77	0.71	0.44

Address: 7201 Metro Boulevard, Edina, MN 55439	Web Site: www.regiscorp.com	Auditors: PricewaterhouseCoopers LLP
Telephone: (952) 947-7777	Officers: Paul D. Finkelstein - Chmn., Pres., C.E.O. Myron Kunin - Vice-Chmn.	Investor Contact: 952-947-7777
Fax: (952) 947-7700		Transfer Agents: Wells Fargo Bank Minnesota, N.A., South St. Paul, MN

REINSURANCE GROUP OF AMERICA, INC.

Exchange	Symbol	Price	52Wk Range	Yield	P/E
NYS	RGA	$42.58 (3/31/2005)	48.54-36.90	0.85	12.10

*7 Year Price Score 104.89 *NYSE Composite Index=100 *12 Month Price Score 99.12

Interim Earnings (Per Share)

Qtr.	Mar	Jun	Sep	Dec
2002	0.56	0.56	0.68	0.67
2003	0.66	0.85	0.83	1.02
2004	0.98	1.04	...	...

Interim Dividends (Per Share)

Amt	Decl	Ex	Rec	Pay
0.06Q	4/29/2004	5/6/2004	5/10/2004	6/1/2004
0.06Q	7/27/2004	8/4/2004	8/6/2004	8/27/2004
0.09Q	10/26/2004	11/4/2004	11/8/2004	11/29/2004
0.09Q	1/27/2005	2/3/2005	2/7/2005	2/28/2005

Indicated Div: $0.36

Valuation Analysis

Forecast P/E	10.86	No of Institutions
	(4/7/2005)	124
Market Cap	$2.7 Billion	Shares
Book Value	2.3 Billion	31,162,424
Price/Book	1.17	% Held
Price/Sales	0.66	49.86

Business Summary: Insurance (MIC: 8.2 SIC: 321 NAIC: 24114)

Reinsurance Group of America, through its operating subsidiary companies, is primarily engaged in traditional life, asset-intensive, and financial reinsurance. Approximately 76.3% of Co.'s 2003 net premiums were from its more established operations in the U.S. and Canada. In addition to its North American operations, Co. has subsidiary companies or offices in Australia, Barbados, Hong Kong, India, Ireland, Japan, Mexico, South Africa, South Korea, Spain, Taiwan, and the United Kingdom. As of Dec 31 2003, Co. had $1.25 trillion of life reinsurance in force.

Recent Developments: For the year ended Dec 31 2004, income from continuing operations increased 37.6% to $245,300 thousand from income of $178,319 thousand a year earlier. Net income increased 28.2% to $221,891 thousand from net income of $173,141 thousand a year earlier. Revenues were $4,038,919 thousand, up 26.0% from $3,204,998 thousand the year before. Net premiums earned were $6,694,896 thousand versus $5,286,326 thousand in the prior year, an increase of 26.6%. Net investment income rose 24.7% to $580,528 thousand from $465,579 thousand a year ago.

Prospects: Co.'s success in 2004 was a continuation of the good results that it has seen over the last several years, and Co. enters 2005 on solid footing in terms of its market position and financial strength. Operating results should continue to benefit from solid premium growth and a lower effective tax rate as a result of reduced federal income taxes associated with the favorable resolution of a tax position taken by Co. For 2005, Co. expects consolidated operating earnings per diluted share to be within a range of $3.85 to $4.15 and consolidated net premium growth of 15.0% to 20.0%.

Financial Data
(US$ in Thousands)

	12/31/2004	12/31/2003	12/31/2002	12/31/2001	12/31/2000	12/31/1999	12/31/1998	12/31/1997
Earnings Per Share	3.52	3.36	2.47	0.66	1.56	0.88	1.48	1.42
Cash Flow Per Share	11.44	11.15	3.26	4.89	3.88	6.06	8.30	11.36
Tang Book Value Per Share	36.50	31.33	24.72	20.30	17.51	14.68	16.52	13.21
Dividends Per Share	0.270	0.240	0.240	0.240	0.240	0.220	0.173	0.151
Dividend Payout %	7.67	7.14	9.72	36.36	15.38	25.00	11.71	10.64
Income Statement								
Premium Income	3,347,448	2,643,163	1,980,666	1,661,762	1,404,066	1,315,638	1,016,420	835,460
Total Revenue	4,038,919	3,174,333	2,381,963	1,968,284	1,725,735	1,607,082	1,344,492	1,071,515
Benefits & Claims	2,877,468	2,288,133	1,666,179	1,488,514	1,208,330	1,220,229	951,148	750,103
Income Before Taxes	369,193	271,610	193,978	66,150	175,345	93,072	138,047	84,071
Income Taxes	123,893	93,291	65,515	26,249	69,271	39,059	49,055	28,750
Net Income	221,891	173,141	122,806	33,046	77,669	40,858	62,081	54,619
Average Shares	62,964	51,598	49,648	49,905	49,920	46,246	42,559	38,406
Balance Sheet								
Total Assets	14,048,129	12,113,374	8,892,597	6,894,345	6,061,860	5,123,743	6,318,553	4,673,550
Total Liabilities	11,769,104	10,165,651	7,670,134	5,888,757	5,198,937	4,387,030	5,566,329	4,165,964
Stockholders' Equity	2,279,025	1,947,723	1,222,463	1,005,588	862,923	732,948	748,477	499,321
Shares Outstanding	62,445	62,160	49,456	49,526	49,293	49,940	45,313	37,807
Statistical Record								
Return on Assets %	1.69	1.65	1.56	0.51	1.38	0.71	1.13	1.44
Return on Equity %	10.47	10.92	11.02	3.54	9.71	5.52	9.95	11.81
Loss Ratio %	85.96	86.57	84.12	89.57	86.06	92.75	93.58	89.78
Net Margin %	5.49	5.45	5.16	1.68	4.50	2.54	4.62	5.10
Price Range	48.54-36.90	42.45-24.98	33.56-24.03	41.00-29.56	37.38-16.25	48.71-22.50	46.67-25.58	30.96-19.94
P/E Ratio	13.79-10.48	12.63-7.43	13.59-9.73	62.12-44.79	23.96-10.42	55.35-25.57	31.53-17.29	21.80-14.05
Average Yield %	0.66	0.73	0.82	0.68	0.83	0.60	0.48	0.61

Address: 1370 Timberlake Manor Parkway, Chesterfield, MO 63017	Web Site: www.rgare.com	Auditors: Deloitte & Touche LLP
Telephone: (636) 736-7439	Officers: Stewart G. Nagler - Chmn. A. Greig Woodring - Pres., C.E.O.	Investor Contact: 314-453-7300
Fax: (314) 453-7307		

RELIANT ENERGY INC

Exchange	Symbol	Price	52Wk Range	Yield	P/E
NYS	RRI	$11.38 (3/31/2005)	13.65-7.96	N/A	N/A

*7 Year Price Score N/A   *NYSE Composite Index=100   *12 Month Price Score 106.67

Interim Earnings (Per Share)

Qtr.	Mar	Jun	Sep	Dec
2001	0.34	0.63	0.44	0.58
2002	0.33	0.61	0.20	(2.27)
2003	(1.55)	(0.02)	(3.11)	0.13
2004	(0.13)	(0.24)	1.04	(0.87)

Interim Dividends (Per Share)

No Dividends Paid

Valuation Analysis

Forecast P/E	56.90	No of Institutions
	(4/7/2005)	201
Market Cap	$3.4 Billion	Shares
Book Value	4.4 Billion	226,302,496
Price/Book	0.78	% Held
Price/Sales	0.39	75.34

Business Summary: Electricity (MIC: 7.1 SIC: 911 NAIC: 21122)

Reliant Energy is an electricity and energy supplier to retail and wholesale customers in the U.S. Co. provides a complete suite of energy products and services to more than 1.9 million electricity customers in Texas ranging from residential and small business customers to large commercial, industrial and governmental/institutional customers. Co.'s operations consist primarily of two business segments Retail and Wholesale energy. As of Dec 31, 2004, Co. had approx. 19,000 megawatts of power generation capacity in operation or under contract.

Recent Developments: For the year ended Dec 31 2004, loss from continuing operations was $172,070 thousand compared with a loss of $888,838 thousand a year earlier. Net loss was $29,370 thousand versus net loss of $1,342,117 thousand a year earlier. Revenues were $8,735,538 thousand, down 17.2% from $10,550,811 thousand the year before. Operating income was $156,457 thousand versus a loss of $388,290 thousand in the prior year. Total direct expense was $7,806,098 thousand versus $9,128,515 thousand in the prior year, a decrease of 14.5%. Total indirect expense was $772,983 thousand versus $1,810,586 thousand in the prior year, a decrease of 57.3%.

Prospects: Co. has improved its cash flow position by reducing debt by over $1.00 billion. In addition, Co. accessed the capital markets and refinanced its remaining bank facilities at attractive rates. Also, Co. has made progress toward improving its cost structure and process efficiencies. These actions have helped position Co. to deliver on its goals of reducing costs by $340.0 million by the end of 2006. For full-year 2005, Co. expects free cash flow from continuing operations to be in the range of $275.0 million to $475.0 million. Co. is projecting adjusted earnings before interest, income taxes, depreciation and amortization for full-year 2005 to be between $900.0 million to $1.10 billion.

Financial Data

(US$ in Thousands)	12/31/2004	12/31/2003	12/31/2002	12/31/2001	12/31/2000	12/31/1999	12/31/1998
Earnings Per Share	(0.10)	(4.57)	(1.93)	2.01	1.31	...	...
Cash Flow Per Share	0.97	2.96	2.11	(0.46)	1.35	...	...
Tang Book Value Per Share	11.13	10.76	11.62	16.48	3.57	...	...
Income Statement							
Total Revenue	8,735,538	11,000,319	11,557,998	36,545,739	19,791,922	7,956,052	4,370,756
EBITDA	610,731	77,964	584,527	1,096,893	677,746	73,786	52,295
Depn & Amortn	448,906	418,621	432,618	246,764	193,682	28,583	15,196
Income Before Taxes	(269,000)	(822,075)	(112,107)	825,983	291,113	26,606	38,609
Income Taxes	(96,930)	80,082	214,105	271,594	88,593	2,560	17,477
Net Income	(29,370)	(1,342,117)	(559,812)	557,451	209,965	24,046	21,132
Average Shares	297,527	293,655	289,953	277,473	240,000	...	...
Balance Sheet							
Current Assets	2,629,277	2,689,270	5,071,503	4,745,290	7,162,736	1,622,980	...
Total Assets	12,146,865	13,308,259	17,636,820	12,253,556	13,591,709	5,623,596	...
Current Liabilities	2,070,015	1,998,409	3,925,944	3,586,611	8,574,845	2,246,349	...
Long-Term Obligations	4,577,000	5,709,000	6,045,000	867,712	1,539,235	1,510,274	...
Total Liabilities	7,760,654	8,936,349	11,983,852	6,149,674	11,259,259	4,882,911	...
Stockholders' Equity	4,386,354	4,371,799	5,652,888	6,103,882	2,332,450	740,685	...
Shares Outstanding	299,684	294,591	290,605	299,804	292,000	...	...
Statistical Record							
Return on Assets %	N.M.	N.M.	N.M.	4.31	2.18	...	...
Return on Equity %	N.M.	N.M.	N.M.	13.22	13.63	...	...
EBITDA Margin %	6.99	0.71	5.06	3.00	3.42	0.93	1.20
Net Margin %	N.M.	N.M.	N.M.	1.53	1.06	0.30	0.48
Asset Turnover	0.68	0.71	0.77	2.83	2.05	...	...
Current Ratio	1.27	1.35	1.29	1.32	0.84	0.72	...
Debt to Equity	1.04	1.31	1.07	0.14	0.66	2.04	...
Price Range	13.65-6.73	7.36-3.05	17.11-1.04	36.75-13.55	...	...	...
P/E Ratio	...	...	...	18.28-6.74	...	...	...

Address: 1000 Main Street, Houston, TX 77002	Web Site: www.reliant.com	Auditors: Deloitte & Touche LLP
Telephone: (713) 497-7000	Officers: Joel V. Staff - Chmn., C.E.O. Mark M. Jacobs - Exec. V.P., C.F.O.	

RENAL CARE GROUP INC.

Exchange	Symbol	Price	52Wk Range	Yield	P/E
NYS	RCI	$37.94 (3/31/2005)	40.00-29.93	N/A	21.80

*7 Year Price Score 137.30 *NYSE Composite Index=100 *12 Month Price Score 105.68

Interim Earnings (Per Share)

Qtr.	Mar	Jun	Sep	Dec
2001	0.24	0.25	0.26	0.27
2002	0.28	0.29	0.31	0.33
2003	0.29	0.34	0.35	0.38
2004	0.42	0.42	0.44	0.46

Interim Dividends (Per Share)

Amt	Decl	Ex	Rec	Pay
50%	7/23/1998	8/25/1998	8/7/1998	8/24/1998
3-for-2	4/28/2004	5/25/2004	5/7/2004	5/24/2004

Valuation Analysis

Forecast P/E	18.96	No of Institutions
	(4/7/2005)	205
Market Cap	$2.6 Billion	Shares
Book Value	592.1 Million	57,629,260
Price/Book	4.34	% Held
Price/Sales	1.91	84.97

Business Summary: Diagnostic Services (MIC: 9.5 SIC: 099 NAIC: 21999)

Renal Care Group provides dialysis services to patients with chronic kidney failure, also known as end-stage renal disease (ESRD). Co.'s markets offer home dialysis, either home hemodialysis, peritoneal dialysis or both. Co.'s home dialysis services provide equipment and supplies, training, patient monitoring and follow-up assistance to patients who receive dialysis treatments in their homes. Co. also provides inpatient dialysis services to hospitals in most of Co.'s markets. Co. often refer to these services as acute dialysis services. In Co.'s dialysis facilities, ESRD patients receive dialysis treatments, generally three times a week, in a technologically advanced outpatient setting.

Recent Developments: For the year ended Dec 31 2004, net income increased 19.4% to $121,833 thousand from net income of $102,056 thousand a year earlier. Operating income was $253,847 thousand versus an income of $190,658 thousand in the prior year, an increase of 33.1%. Total direct expense was $893,478 thousand versus $653,307 thousand in the prior year, an increase of 36.8%. Total indirect expense was $197,722 thousand versus $161,354 thousand in the prior year, an increase of 22.5%.

Prospects: Co. reaffirmed its goal of achieving earnings per share growth for full-year 2005 of 15.0%. In addition, Co. expects revenues for full-year 2005 in the range of $1.50 billion to $1.60 billion and earnings per share in the range of $1.95 to $2.05. Capital expenditures for 2005 are expected in the range of $90.0 million to $100.0 million. Co.'s acquisition target for 2005 is projected to be between 1,000 to 1,500 patients. Separately, on Jan 5 2005, Co. acquired the Cape County Dialysis program based in Cape Girardeau, MO. The program provides care to more than 250 patients at four outpatient dialysis facilities.

Financial Data (US$ in Thousands)	12/31/2004	12/31/2003	12/31/2002	12/31/2001	12/31/2000	12/31/1999	12/31/1998	12/31/1997
Earnings Per Share	1.74	1.37	1.21	1.01	0.71	0.69	0.55	0.37
Cash Flow Per Share	2.63	2.57	2.30	1.85	1.30	0.91	0.60	0.36
Tang Book Value Per Share	N.M.	3.83	3.54	3.42	2.41	1.69	0.88	1.01
Income Statement								
Total Revenue	1,345,047	1,005,319	903,387	755,082	622,575	520,607	369,372	214,009
EBITDA	277,027	210,132	190,701	165,513	123,501	110,965	77,336	...
Depn & Amortn	58,349	44,905	40,432	38,945	32,321	26,425	18,418	9,016
Income Before Taxes	198,050	164,598	149,129	123,932	86,165	79,502	55,842	...
Income Taxes	76,217	62,542	56,669	47,331	34,706	31,041	20,631	11,791
Net Income	121,833	102,056	92,460	76,601	51,459	48,461	35,211	19,978
Average Shares	69,892	74,752	76,150	75,649	71,922	69,690	63,975	53,392
Balance Sheet								
Current Assets	373,084	292,104	245,861	213,307	216,337	159,999	109,607	65,805
Total Assets	1,429,585	819,873	740,123	652,257	584,884	482,384	376,845	248,083
Current Liabilities	246,119	169,437	135,380	110,468	100,592	74,390	56,743	41,336
Long-Term Obligations	479,645	2,652	10,161	3,776	58,316	76,102	62,588	15,470
Total Liabilities	837,464	249,028	196,235	142,006	190,762	172,070	147,569	73,324
Stockholders' Equity	592,121	570,845	543,888	510,251	394,122	310,314	229,276	174,759
Shares Outstanding	67,803	70,503	72,289	74,245	70,630	67,146	61,383	56,018
Statistical Record								
Return on Assets %	10.80	13.08	13.28	12.38	9.62	11.28	11.27	10.52
Return on Equity %	20.89	18.31	17.54	16.94	14.57	17.96	17.43	14.90
EBITDA Margin %	20.60	20.90	21.11	21.92	19.84	21.31	20.94	...
Net Margin %	9.06	10.15	10.23	10.14	8.27	9.31	9.53	9.34
Asset Turnover	1.19	1.29	1.30	1.22	1.16	1.21	1.18	1.13
Current Ratio	1.52	1.72	1.82	1.93	2.15	2.15	1.93	1.59
Debt to Equity	0.81	N.M.	0.02	0.01	0.15	0.25	0.27	0.09
Price Range	36.10-27.47	27.75-18.70	23.87-18.48	22.33-15.88	18.83-10.63	22.00-10.00	20.14-12.44	16.11-8.81
P/E Ratio	20.75-15.79	20.25-13.65	19.72-15.27	22.11-15.72	26.53-14.96	31.88-14.49	36.62-22.63	43.54-23.82

Address: 2525 West End Avenue, Suite 600, Nashville, TN 37203 **Telephone:** (615) 345-5500	**Web Site:** www.renalcaregroup.com **Officers:** William P. Johnston - Chmn. Gary A. Brukardt - Pres., C.E.O	**Auditors:** ERNST & YOUNG LLP **Investor Contact:** 615-345-5500

REPUBLIC SERVICES, INC.

Exchange	Symbol	Price	52Wk Range	Yield	P/E
NYS	RSG	$33.48 (3/31/2005)	33.98-26.84	N/A	21.88

*7 Year Price Score N/A   *NYSE Composite Index=100   *12 Month Price Score 99.59

Interim Earnings (Per Share)

Qtr.	Mar	Jun	Sep	Dec
2001	0.29	0.34	0.33	(0.23)
2002	0.32	0.36	0.38	0.37
2003	0.10	0.37	0.28	0.35
2004	0.36	0.39	0.41	0.37

Interim Dividends (Per Share)

Amt	Decl	Ex	Rec	Pay
0.12Q	7/28/2004	4/29/2004	10/1/2004	10/15/2004
0.12Q	11/3/2004	12/30/2004	1/3/2004	1/17/2005
0.12Q	2/8/2005	3/30/2005	4/1/2005	4/15/2005

Valuation Analysis

Forecast P/E	19.88 (4/7/2005)	No of Institutions 246
Market Cap	$5.0 Billion	Shares
Book Value	1.9 Billion	137,016,192
Price/Book	2.69	% Held
Price/Sales	1.86	91.54

Business Summary: Sanitation Services (MIC: 7.3 SIC: 953 NAIC: 62219)

Republic Services provides domestic non-hazardous solid waste collection and disposal services for commercial, industrial, municipal and residential customers through 140 collection companies in 22 states. Co. also owns or operates 96 transfer stations, 58 solid waste landfills and 35 recycling facilities as of Dec 31 2004. Co.'s operations are organized into five regions whose boundaries may change from time to time: Eastern, Central, Southern, Southwestern and Western. Each region is organized into operating areas and each area contains a group of operating locations. Each of Co.'s regions and substantially all its areas provide collection, transfer, recycling and disposal services.

Recent Developments: For the year ended Dec 31 2004, net income increased 34.0% to $237,900 thousand from net income of $177,600 thousand a year earlier. Revenues were $2,708,100 thousand, up 7.6% from $2,517,800 thousand the year before. Operating income was $452,300 thousand versus an income of $412,700 thousand in the prior year, an increase of 9.6%. Total direct expense was $1,714,400 thousand versus $1,605,400 thousand in the prior year, an increase of 6.8%. Total indirect expense was $541,400 thousand versus $499,700 thousand in the prior year, an increase of 8.3%.

Prospects: In 2005, Co. anticipates using free cash flow to repurchase common stock under its $275.0 million repurchase program and to pay a regular quarterly dividend. In addition, Co. remains committed to implementing a broad-based pricing initiative across all lines of service to recover increasing costs. Looking ahead to 2005, Co. anticipates free cash flow of approximately $260.0 million. Co. is targeting internal growth of approximately 4.0% to 4.5%, with 2.5% from price increases and 1.5% to 2.0% from volume growth. Co. expects earnings to range from $1.65 to $1.70 per share. Capital spending for 2005 is expected to be about $300.0 million.

Financial Data

(US$ in Thousands)	12/31/2004	12/31/2003	12/31/2002	12/31/2001	12/31/2000	12/31/1999	12/31/1998	12/31/1997
Earnings Per Share	1.53	1.10	1.44	0.73	1.26	1.14	1.13	...
Cash Flow Per Share	4.35	3.75	3.42	2.68	2.63	1.84	2.00	...
Tang Book Value Per Share	1.86	2.04	1.90	1.20	1.37	1.17	7.41	...
Dividends Per Share	0.360	0.120	...	...	...	...	...	...
Dividend Payout %	23.53	10.91	...	...	...	...	...	...
Income Statement								
Total Revenue	2,708,100	2,517,800	2,365,100	2,257,500	2,103,300	1,838,500	1,369,100	1,127,700
EBITDA	712,900	655,000	658,800	500,400	633,700	550,400	389,700	294,100
Depn & Amortn	259,400	239,100	199,600	215,400	197,400	163,200	106,300	86,100
Income Before Taxes	383,700	347,400	386,500	209,300	356,400	326,500	240,200	182,100
Income Taxes	145,800	132,000	146,900	83,800	135,400	125,700	86,500	65,900
Net Income	237,900	177,600	239,600	125,500	221,000	200,800	153,700	116,200
Average Shares	155,300	162,100	166,700	171,100	175,000	175,700	135,600	...
Balance Sheet								
Current Assets	496,500	556,000	452,300	324,800	405,800	332,000	784,000	175,900
Total Assets	4,464,600	4,554,100	4,209,100	3,856,300	3,561,500	3,288,300	2,812,100	1,348,000
Current Liabilities	446,600	672,000	392,200	386,400	381,800	385,300	783,800	436,100
Long-Term Obligations	1,351,900	1,289,200	1,439,300	1,334,100	1,200,200	1,152,100	557,200	64,300
Total Liabilities	2,592,100	2,649,600	2,328,000	2,100,400	1,886,600	1,785,600	1,513,000	551,200
Stockholders' Equity	1,872,500	1,904,500	1,881,100	1,755,900	1,674,900	1,502,700	1,299,100	750,800
Shares Outstanding	150,581	157,827	163,658	169,644	175,658	175,481	175,412	...
Statistical Record								
Return on Assets %	5.26	4.05	5.94	3.38	6.44	6.58	7.39	9.53
Return on Equity %	12.56	9.38	13.18	7.32	13.87	14.33	15.00	18.66
EBITDA Margin %	26.32	26.01	27.86	22.17	30.13	29.94	28.46	26.08
Net Margin %	8.78	7.05	10.13	5.56	10.51	10.92	11.23	10.30
Asset Turnover	0.60	0.57	0.59	0.61	0.61	0.60	0.66	0.92
Current Ratio	1.11	0.83	1.15	0.84	1.06	0.86	1.00	0.40
Debt to Equity	0.72	0.68	0.77	0.76	0.72	0.77	0.43	0.09
Price Range	33.98-24.83	25.95-18.75	22.11-16.66	20.80-13.75	17.25-10.06	25.38-9.31	27.38-13.75	...
P/E Ratio	22.21-16.23	23.59-17.05	15.35-11.57	28.49-18.84	13.69-7.99	22.26-8.17	24.23-12.17	...
Average Yield %	1.26	0.53	...	...	...	...	...	...

Address: 110 S.E. 6th Street, 28th Floor, Ft. Lauderdale, FL 33301 Telephone: (954) 769-2400	Web Site: Officers: James E. O'Connor - Chmn., C.E.O. Harris W. Hudson - Vice-Chmn.	Auditors: Ernst & Young LLP

RESMED INC.

Exchange	Symbol	Price	52Wk Range	Yield	P/E
NYS	RMD	$56.40 (3/31/2005)	60.50-43.46	N/A	32.05

*7 Year Price Score 125.16 *NYSE Composite Index=100 *12 Month Price Score 105.70

TRADING VOLUME (thousand shares)

Interim Earnings (Per Share)

Qtr.	Sep	Dec	Mar	Jun
2001-02	0.25	0.26	0.31	0.29
2002-03	0.28	0.30	0.35	0.39
2003-04	0.35	0.40	0.43	0.45
2004-05	0.39	...	...	

Interim Dividends (Per Share)

Amt	Decl	Ex	Rec	Pay
2-for-1	2/25/2000	4/3/2000	3/15/2000	3/31/2000

Valuation Analysis

Forecast P/E	24.28	No of Institutions	
	(4/7/2005)	162	
Market Cap	$1.9 Billion	Shares	
Book Value	427.4 Million	25,845,516	
Price/Book	4.50	% Held	
Price/Sales	5.14	75.47	

Business Summary: Medical Instruments & Equipment (MIC: 9.6 SIC: 841 NAIC: 39112)

ResMed is a developer, manufacturer and distributor of medical equipment for treating, diagnosing, and managing sleep disordered breathing, or SDB. SDB includes obstructive sleep apnea, or OSA, and other respiratory discords that occur during sleep. In addition to Co.'s nasal continuous positive airway pressure treatment for OSA, which delivers pressurized air typically through a nasal mask to prevent collapse of the upper airway during sleep, Co. has developed a number of products for SDB. These products include airflow generators, diagnostic products, mask systems, headgear and other accessories.

Recent Developments: For the quarter ended Dec 31 2004, net income increased 23.0% to $17,404 thousand from net income of $14,151 thousand in the year-earlier quarter. Revenues were $103,893 thousand, up 26.2% from $82,292 thousand the year before. Operating income was $25,609 thousand versus an income of $19,393 thousand in the prior-year quarter, an increase of 32.1%. Total direct expense was $35,515 thousand versus $29,868 thousand in the prior-year quarter, an increase of 18.9%. Total indirect expense was $42,769 thousand versus $33,031 thousand in the prior-year quarter, an increase of 29.5%.

Prospects: Co. is pleased with its financial performance through the first half of fiscal 2005, which was led by stronger sales in both its domestic and international markets. Co. attributes its improved domestic performance in part to stronger demand for its Mirage Swift patient interface, while its international operations are enjoying increased demand in all major markets and a stronger Euro. Looking ahead, Co. is focused on growing above the financial results it delivered in the third quarter of last year. As a result, Co. reiterates its expectation for market growth of 15.0% to 20.0% over the next 12 to 18 months.

Financial Data

(US$ in Thousands)	6 Mos	3 Mos	06/30/2004	06/30/2003	06/30/2002	06/30/2001	06/30/2000	06/30/1999
Earnings Per Share	1.76	1.67	1.63	1.33	1.10	0.35	0.69	0.52
Cash Flow Per Share	2.62	2.37	2.27	1.79	1.11	0.95	0.67	0.62
Tang Book Value Per Share	8.85	7.84	7.40	5.41	2.95	1.62	2.84	2.17
Income Statement								
Total Revenue	191,626	87,733	339,338	273,570	204,076	155,156	115,615	88,627
EBITDA	59,935	26,817	104,218	82,259	67,788	36,521	40,303	28,404
Depn & Amortn	12,656	5,826	17,867	12,583	9,972	8,445	6,938	4,606
Income Before Taxes	46,799	20,670	84,668	67,127	54,592	27,314	34,166	24,577
Income Taxes	15,469	6,744	27,384	21,398	17,086	15,684	11,940	8,475
Net Income	31,330	13,926	57,284	45,729	37,506	11,630	22,226	16,102
Average Shares	37,102	35,258	35,125	34,439	34,080	33,484	32,303	31,068
Balance Sheet								
Current Assets	323,246	289,568	277,829	241,905	193,713	177,882	69,172	50,771
Total Assets	624,491	565,104	544,159	459,595	376,191	288,090	115,594	89,889
Current Liabilities	73,302	64,297	60,591	50,583	49,047	33,610	21,622	18,242
Long-Term Obligations	113,250	113,250	113,250	113,250	123,250	150,000	...	...
Total Liabilities	197,092	186,818	182,660	173,162	183,261	187,724	21,622	18,242
Stockholders' Equity	427,399	378,286	361,499	286,433	192,930	100,366	93,972	71,647
Shares Outstanding	34,124	33,858	33,858	33,370	33,108	31,478	30,593	29,616
Statistical Record								
Return on Assets %	10.97	11.18	11.38	10.94	11.29	5.76	21.57	20.84
Return on Equity %	16.33	17.06	17.63	19.08	25.58	11.97	26.77	26.31
EBITDA Margin %	31.28	30.57	30.71	30.07	33.22	23.54	34.86	32.05
Net Margin %	16.35	15.87	16.88	16.72	18.38	7.50	19.22	18.17
Asset Turnover	0.66	0.67	0.67	0.65	0.61	0.77	1.12	1.15
Current Ratio	4.41	4.50	4.59	4.78	3.95	5.29	3.20	2.78
Debt to Equity	0.26	0.30	0.31	0.40	0.64	1.49	...	...
Price Range	51.56-40.69	51.56-38.05	51.56-38.05	41.95-24.89	61.75-24.70	57.68-24.63	39.63-11.81	25.72-9.25
P/E Ratio	29.30-23.12	30.87-22.78	31.63-23.34	31.54-18.71	56.14-22.45	164.80-70.36	57.43-17.12	49.46-17.79

Address: 14040 Danielson St., Poway, CA 92064-6857 Telephone: (858) 746 2400	Web Site: www.resmed.com Officers: Peter C. Farrell - Chmn., Pres., C.E.O. Adrian M. Smith - Sr. V.P., Fin., C.F.O.	Auditors: KPMG LLP

REYNOLDS AMERICAN INC

Exchange	Symbol	Price	52Wk Range	Yield	P/E
NYS	RAI	$80.59 (3/31/2005)	85.60-53.73	4.72	13.06

*7 Year Price Score N/A   *NYSE Composite Index=100   *12 Month Price Score 106.72

Interim Earnings (Per Share)

Qtr.	Mar	Jun	Sep	Dec
2001	0.98	1.26	1.22	0.93
2002	(3.58)	2.29	1.56	(0.65)
2003	0.84	0.83	(41.31)	(1.62)
2004	1.43	...	2.66	0.01

Interim Dividends (Per Share)

Amt	Decl	Ex	Rec	Pay
0.95Q	8/18/2004	9/8/2004	9/10/2004	10/1/2004
0.95Q	11/30/2004	12/8/2004	12/10/2004	1/3/2005
0.95Q	2/2/2005	3/8/2005	3/10/2005	4/1/2005

Indicated Div: $3.80

Valuation Analysis

Forecast P/E	11.22	No of Institutions
	(4/7/2005)	241
Market Cap	$11.9 Billion	Shares
Book Value	6.2 Billion	82,566,072
Price/Book	1.92	% Held
Price/Sales	1.84	56.02

Business Summary: Tobacco Products (MIC: 4.2 SIC: 111 NAIC: 12221)

Reynolds American is the parent company of R.J. Reynolds Tobacco, Santa Fe Natural Tobacco Company, Lane Limited and R.J. Reynolds Global Products. R.J. Reynolds Tobacco manufactures a number of major cigarette brands in the U.S., including Camel, Winston, KOOL, Salem and Doral. Santa Fe Natural Tobacco manufactures Natural American Spirit cigarettes and other tobacco products, and markets them both nationally and internationally. Lane Limited manufactures several roll-your-own, pipe tobacco and little cigar brands, and distributes Dunhill tobacco products. R.J. Reynolds Global Products manufactures American-blend cigarettes and other tobacco products worldwide.

Recent Developments: For the year ended Dec 31 2004, income from continuing operations was $627 million compared with a loss of $3,689 million a year earlier. Net income was $688 million versus net loss of $3,446 million a year earlier. Revenues were $6,437 million, up 22.2% from $5,267 million. Operating income was $882 million versus a loss of $3,841 million in the prior year. Total direct expense was $3,872 million versus $3,218 million in the prior year, an increase of 20.3%. Total indirect expense was $1,683 million versus $5,890 million in the prior year, a decrease of 71.4%.

Prospects: Looking ahead, Co. is targeting full-year 2005 net income in the range of $970.0 million to $1.03 billion, or $6.55 to $6.95 per diluted share, including payments of $2.80 billion for the master settlement agreement between tobacco companies and the states and for buyouts of quotas from tobacco farmers. Meanwhile, Co. anticipates a 6.0% to 8.0% volume decline in 2005 as a result of its new marketing strategy, which is focused on Co.'s higher-priced brands, Camel and Kool. In addition, Co.'s second tier of brands, including Winston, Salem, Doral and Pall Mall, will receive limited marketing support, focused primarily on maintaining brand loyalty among its current customers.

Financial Data
(US$ in Thousands)

	12/31/2004	12/31/2003	12/31/2002	12/31/2001	12/31/2000	12/31/1999	12/31/1998	12/31/1997
Earnings Per Share	6.17	(41.17)	(0.49)	4.39	17.94	21.58	...	...
Cash Flow Per Share	6.63	6.94	5.51	6.45	5.81	8.56	...	...
Dividends Per Share	1.900	3.800	3.730	3.300	3.100	1.550	...	...
Dividend Payout %	30.79	...	...	75.17	17.28	7.18	...	...
Income Statement								
Total Revenue	6,437,000	5,267,000	6,211,000	8,585,000	8,167,000	7,567,000	17,037,000	17,057,000
EBITDA	1,078,000	(3,670,000)	963,000	1,396,000	1,282,000	1,146,000	1,399,000	3,018,000
Depn & Amortn	194,000	166,000	195,000	491,000	485,000	482,000	1,135,000	1,097,000
Income Before Taxes	829,000	(3,918,000)	683,000	892,000	748,000	510,000	(511,000)	1,104,000
Income Taxes	202,000	(229,000)	265,000	448,000	396,000	315,000	19,000	566,000
Net Income	688,000	(3,446,000)	(44,000)	435,000	1,827,000	2,343,000	(516,000)	433,000
Average Shares	111,436	83,679	90,175	98,986	101,857	108,570	...	...
Balance Sheet								
Current Assets	4,624,000	3,331,000	3,992,000	3,856,000	3,871,000	2,468,000	4,427,000	4,621,000
Total Assets	14,428,000	9,677,000	14,651,000	15,050,000	15,554,000	14,377,000	28,863,000	30,657,000
Current Liabilities	4,055,000	2,865,000	3,427,000	2,792,000	2,776,000	3,068,000	4,505,000	3,942,000
Long-Term Obligations	1,595,000	1,671,000	1,755,000	1,631,000	1,674,000	1,653,000	8,655,000	9,456,000
Total Liabilities	8,252,000	6,620,000	7,935,000	7,024,000	7,118,000	7,313,000	18,977,000	19,578,000
Stockholders' Equity	6,176,000	3,057,000	6,716,000	8,026,000	8,436,000	7,064,000	9,886,000	11,079,000
Shares Outstanding	147,364	85,103	86,048	94,235	101,265	106,903	...	...
Statistical Record								
Return on Assets %	5.69	N.M.	N.M.	2.84	12.17	10.84	N.M.	1.40
Return on Equity %	14.86	N.M.	N.M.	5.28	23.51	27.65	N.M.	3.81
EBITDA Margin %	16.75	N.M.	15.50	16.26	15.70	15.14	8.21	17.69
Net Margin %	10.69	N.M.	N.M.	5.07	22.37	30.96	N.M.	2.54
Asset Turnover	0.53	0.43	0.42	0.56	0.54	0.35	0.57	0.55
Current Ratio	1.14	1.16	1.16	1.38	1.39	0.80	0.98	1.17
Debt to Equity	0.26	0.55	0.26	0.20	0.20	0.23	0.88	0.85
Price Range	80.32-53.73	59.56-28.04	71.35-35.10	61.73-45.69	49.13-15.75	33.38-16.00	...	...
P/E Ratio	13.02-8.71	...	...	14.06-10.41	2.74-0.88	1.55-0.74	...	...
Average Yield %	2.88	9.53	6.69	5.92	11.02	5.97	...	...

Address: 401 North Main Street, P.O. Box 2866, Winston-Salem, NC 27102-2866 **Telephone:** (336) 741-5500 **Fax:** (336) 741-5511	**Web Site:** www.rjrholdings.com **Officers:** Andrew J. Schindler - Chmn., C.E.O. Lynn J. Beasley - Pres., C.O.O.	**Auditors:** KPMG LLP **Investor Contact:** 336-741-5165

REYNOLDS & REYNOLDS CO.

Exchange	Symbol	Price	52Wk Range	Yield	P/E
NYS	REY	$27.06 (3/31/2005)	28.28-10.61	1.63	19.90

*7 Year Price Score 135.33 *NYSE Composite Index=100 *12 Month Price Score 125.99

Interim Earnings (Per Share)

Qtr.	Dec	Mar	Jun	Sep
2001-02	0.35	0.39	0.41	0.43
2002-03	0.40	0.42	0.40	0.47
2003-04	0.34	0.38	0.33	0.32
2004-05	0.33	...	...	...

Interim Dividends (Per Share)

Amt	Decl	Ex	Rec	Pay
0.11Q	5/4/2004	5/19/2004	5/21/2004	6/10/2004
0.11Q	8/10/2004	8/17/2004	8/19/2004	9/9/2004
0.11Q	11/9/2004	12/10/2004	12/14/2004	1/7/2005
0.11Q	2/17/2005	3/18/2005	3/22/2005	4/8/2005
			Indicated Div: $0.44	

Valuation Analysis

Forecast P/E	19.48	No of Institutions
	(4/7/2005)	161
Market Cap	$2.1 Billion	Shares
Book Value	471.8 Million	52,516,488
Price/Book	4.47	% Held
Price/Sales	2.17	82.20

Business Summary: Printing (MIC: 13.4 SIC: 761 NAIC: 23116)

Reynolds & Reynolds is a provider of the integrated solutions to automotive retailers. Co.'s software and services solutions include a full range of retail and enterprise management systems. Co. also offers Web and Customer Relationship Management (CRM) solutions; support, training and professional services; documents; data management and integration services; networking; and financial services. Co.operates in four business segments: Software Solutions, Services, Documents and Financial Services.

Recent Developments: For the quarter ended Dec 31 2004, net income decreased 10.4% to $21,354 thousand from net income of $23,822 thousand in the year-earlier quarter. Revenues were $239,322 thousand, down 3.7% from $248,403 thousand the year before. Operating income was $35,604 thousand versus an income of $35,959 thousand in the prior-year quarter, a decrease of 1.0%. Total direct expense was $109,741 thousand versus $109,816 thousand in the prior-year quarter, a decrease of 0.1%. Total indirect expense was $93,977 thousand versus $102,628 thousand in the prior-year quarter, a decrease of 8.4%.

Prospects: Co. anticipates modest top-line growth during the second half of fiscal 2005, fueled by strong demand for Co.'s ERA XT system. As of the end of the first quarter, Co. had taken orders from over 1,000 auto dealerships in the U.S. and Canada for the ERA XT system. Looking ahead, Co. expects earnings per share for the second quarter of fiscal 2005 in the range of $0.32 to $0.36. For full-year fiscal 2005, Co. is projecting earnings in the range of $1.37 to $1.45 per share and revenues to be essentially flat compared to fiscal 2004. Operating margins for fiscal 2005 are expected to be in the mid teens, while net capital expenditures are projected to be approximately $20.0 million.

Financial Data
(US$ in Thousands)

	3 Mos	09/30/2004	09/30/2003	09/30/2002	09/30/2001	09/30/2000	09/30/1999	09/30/1998
Earnings Per Share	1.36	1.37	1.69	1.08	1.33	1.47	1.53	1.27
Cash Flow Per Share	...	2.50	2.20	2.51	2.45	1.65	2.10	2.09
Tang Book Value Per Share	3.94	3.77	3.36	3.52	3.07	4.12	3.88	3.12
Dividends Per Share	0.440	0.440	0.440	0.440	0.440	0.440	0.400	0.360
Dividend Payout %	32.45	32.12	26.04	40.74	33.08	29.93	26.14	28.35
Income Statement								
Total Revenue	239,322	982,241	1,008,245	992,383	1,004,012	924,381	1,563,031	1,485,963
EBITDA	37,559	199,192	231,843	196,621	209,910	189,523	252,828	260,276
Depn & Amortn	...	48,393	36,237	31,395	49,901	38,676	47,344	59,562
Income Before Taxes	36,698	147,869	194,469	164,948	162,524	150,142	199,254	188,023
Income Taxes	15,344	55,226	75,452	49,396	64,590	61,702	82,318	74,467
Net Income	21,354	92,643	119,017	78,989	99,557	116,596	122,721	103,107
Average Shares	65,366	67,815	70,606	73,357	74,919	79,499	80,340	81,146
Balance Sheet								
Current Assets	297,455	276,155	290,413	318,438	286,213	383,546	467,597	372,047
Total Assets	1,071,624	1,060,867	1,124,055	1,137,165	1,142,350	1,217,293	1,262,085	1,157,720
Current Liabilities	151,250	139,345	143,783	157,469	147,862	194,665	211,959	198,208
Long-Term Obligations	289,914	295,643	305,680	324,660	309,317	323,300	383,408	372,102
Total Liabilities	599,873	591,050	666,926	682,139	665,567	718,799	798,650	753,269
Stockholders' Equity	471,751	469,817	457,129	455,026	476,783	498,494	463,435	404,451
Shares Outstanding	77,887	78,126	81,658	84,217	89,593	75,091	96,532	97,757
Statistical Record								
Return on Assets %	8.07	8.46	10.53	6.93	8.44	9.38	10.14	9.12
Return on Equity %	18.98	19.93	26.10	16.95	20.42	24.18	28.28	26.83
EBITDA Margin %	15.69	20.28	22.99	19.81	20.91	20.50	16.18	17.52
Net Margin %	8.92	9.43	11.80	7.96	9.92	12.61	7.85	6.94
Asset Turnover	0.87	0.90	0.89	0.87	0.85	0.74	1.29	1.31
Current Ratio	1.97	1.98	2.02	2.02	1.94	1.97	2.21	1.88
Debt to Equity	0.61	0.63	0.67	0.71	0.65	0.65	0.83	0.92
Price Range	26.51-10.61	25.10-10.61	14.95-9.95	15.78-11.15	12.57-8.47	14.91-8.09	12.56-8.25	11.94-6.31
P/E Ratio	19.49-7.80	18.32-7.74	8.85-5.89	14.61-10.32	9.45-6.37	10.14-5.51	8.21-5.39	9.40-4.97
Average Yield %	2.57	3.03	3.33	3.30	4.16	4.09	3.81	3.79

Address: One Reynolds Way, Dayton, OH 45430	Web Site: www.reyrey.com	Auditors: Deloitte & Touche LLP
Telephone: (937) 485-2000	Officers: Philip A. Odeen - Chmn. Finbarr J. O'Neill - Pres., C.E.O.	Investor Contact: 937-485-1633
Fax: (937) 485-8980		

RITE AID CORP.

*7 Year Price Score 32.70   *NYSE Composite Index=100   *12 Month Price Score 83.04

Interim Earnings (Per Share)

Qtr.	May	Aug	Nov	Feb
2001-02	(0.56)	(0.54)	(0.23)	(0.53)
2002-03	(0.01)	(0.21)	(0.05)	(0.02)
2003-04	(0.08)	(0.04)	0.12	0.09
2004-05	0.10	0.00	(0.01)	...

Interim Dividends (Per Share)

No Dividends Paid

Valuation Analysis

Forecast P/E	26.00	No of Institutions
	(4/7/2005)	160
Market Cap	$2.1 Billion	Shares
Book Value	100.9 Million	168,636,576
Price/Book	20.44	% Held
Price/Sales	0.12	32.39

Business Summary: Retail - Miscellaneous (MIC: 5.11 SIC: 912 NAIC: 46110)

Rite Aid operates the third largest retail drugstore chain in the United States, based on the number of stores. As of Feb 28 2004, Rite Aid Corporation operated approximately 3,400 drugstores in 28 American states and the District of Columbia. The company's stores sell prescription drugs and a wide assortment of general merchandise, which includes prescription health and personal care items, cosmetics, household items, beverages/drinks, convenience foodstuffs, greeting cards, one-hour photo development and seasonal and other convenience produts.

Recent Developments: For the thirteen weeks ended Nov 27 2004, net income totaled $977,000 compared with $73.6 million in the corresponding year-earlier quarter. Results for 2004 included a $20.2 million net charge from debt modifications and retirements. Results also included net charges from sales of assets and investments of $849,000 and $879,000, as well as store closing and impairment charges of $2.6 million and $3.1 million in 2004 and 2003, respectively. Revenues were $4.11 billion, essentially flat versus the previous year. Same-store sales increased 0.2% year over year.

Prospects: Co. continues to focus its initiatives on building long-term value. For instance, Co.'s new store development program is designed to strengthen its market share and competitive positioning. Looking ahead, Co. is targeting full fiscal-2005 sales of between $16.70 billion and $16.80 billion, along with same-store sales growth in the range of 1.2% to 2.1%. Capital expenditure guidance is expected to be $225.0 million to $250.0 million. Finally, net income for fiscal 2005 is expected to be between $49.0 million and $99.0 million or between $0.03 and $0.12 per diluted share.

Financial Data
(US$ in Thousands)

	9 Mos	6 Mos	3 Mos	02/28/2004	03/01/2003	03/02/2002	03/03/2001	02/26/2000
Earnings Per Share	0.18	0.31	0.27	0.11	(0.28)	(1.82)	(5.65)	(4.45)
Cash Flow Per Share	1.26	1.00	0.76	0.44	0.59	0.03	(2.19)	(1.59)
Dividends Per Share	...	...	...	...	...	...	...	0.345
Income Statement								
Total Revenue	12,475,599	8,368,263	4,244,357	16,600,449	15,800,920	15,171,146	14,516,865	14,681,442
EBITDA	270,637	204,039	131,500	612,302	447,709	(95,726)	(326,325)	(94,415)
Depn & Amortn	185,358	125,099	63,118	264,288	285,333	281,047	306,556	500,997
Income Before Taxes	85,279	78,940	68,382	34,516	(167,644)	(772,837)	(1,282,807)	(1,115,748)
Income Taxes	11,139	5,777	5,049	(48,795)	(41,940)	(11,745)	148,957	8
Net Income	74,140	73,163	63,333	83,311	(112,076)	(827,681)	(1,589,224)	(1,143,056)
Average Shares	519,876	533,874	574,091	525,831	515,129	474,028	314,189	259,139
Balance Sheet								
Current Assets	2,896,416	3,433,882	3,501,044	3,377,997	3,243,887	3,289,545	3,616,832	3,805,470
Total Assets	5,677,964	6,283,863	6,360,150	6,246,679	6,133,515	6,479,208	7,913,911	10,807,854
Current Liabilities	1,712,695	1,710,121	1,749,602	1,483,750	1,566,998	1,765,283	1,660,955	2,912,417
Long-Term Obligations	3,028,785	3,625,556	3,668,784	3,867,690	3,758,913	3,847,011	5,857,592	5,388,647
Total Liabilities	5,577,097	6,189,368	6,281,652	6,237,415	6,226,181	6,450,031	8,248,889	10,356,889
Stockholders' Equity	100,867	94,495	78,498	9,264	(112,329)	9,616	(354,435)	431,508
Shares Outstanding	520,602	517,681	517,294	516,496	515,115	515,136	348,055	259,927
Statistical Record								
Return on Assets %	2.23	3.28	2.94	1.35	N.M.	N.M.	N.M.	N.M.
Return on Equity %	644.41	...	...	...	...	...	N.M.	N.M.
EBITDA Margin %	2.17	2.44	3.10	3.69	2.83	N.M.	N.M.	N.M.
Net Margin %	0.59	0.87	1.49	0.50	N.M.	N.M.	N.M.	N.M.
Asset Turnover	2.82	2.70	2.67	2.69	2.51	2.11	1.53	1.39
Current Ratio	1.69	2.01	2.00	2.28	2.07	1.86	2.18	1.31
Debt to Equity	30.03	38.37	46.74	417.50	...	400.06	...	12.49
Price Range	6.40-3.35	6.40-4.38	6.40-3.67	6.40-2.17	4.22-1.75	9.74-2.06	8.19-1.81	41.38-5.38
P/E Ratio	35.56-18.61	20.65-14.13	23.70-13.59	58.18-19.73	...	...	...	...
Average Yield %	...	...	...	...	...	...	...	1.92

Address: 30 Hunter Lane, Camp Hill, PA 17011
Telephone: (717) 761-2633
Fax: (717) 975-5905

Web Site: www.riteaid.com
Officers: Robert G. Miller - Chmn., C.E.O. Mary F. Sammons - Pres., C.O.O.

Auditors: Deloitte & Touche LLP
Investor Contact: 717-975-5750

RLI CORP.

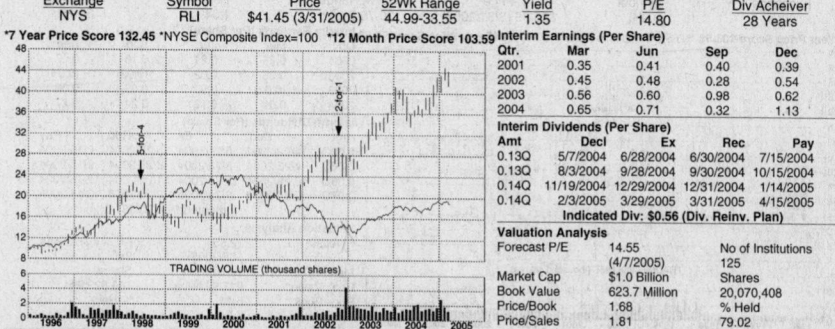

Exchange	Symbol	Price	52Wk Range	Yield	P/E	Div Acheiver
NYS	RLI	$41.45 (3/31/2005)	44.99-33.55	1.35	14.80	28 Years

*7 Year Price Score 132.45 *NYSE Composite Index=100 *12 Month Price Score 103.59

Interim Earnings (Per Share)

Qtr.	Mar	Jun	Sep	Dec
2001	0.35	0.41	0.40	0.39
2002	0.45	0.48	0.28	0.54
2003	0.56	0.60	0.98	0.62
2004	0.65	0.71	0.32	1.13

Interim Dividends (Per Share)

Amt	Decl	Ex	Rec	Pay
0.13Q	5/7/2004	6/28/2004	6/30/2004	7/15/2004
0.13Q	8/3/2004	9/28/2004	9/30/2004	10/15/2004
0.14Q	11/19/2004	12/29/2004	12/31/2004	1/14/2005
0.14Q	2/3/2005	3/29/2005	3/31/2005	4/15/2005

Indicated Div: $0.56 (Div. Reinv. Plan)

Valuation Analysis

Forecast P/E	14.55	No of Institutions
	(4/7/2005)	125
Market Cap	$1.0 Billion	Shares
Book Value	623.7 Million	20,070,408
Price/Book	1.68	% Held
Price/Sales	1.81	79.02

Business Summary: Insurance (MIC: 8.2 SIC: 331 NAIC: 24126)

RLI is a holding company that underwrites selected property and casualty insurance through its insurance subsidiaries. Co.'s property segment includes commercial property consisting of excess surplus lines and specialty insurance such as fire and earthquake in the U.S., and homeowners residential property in Hawaii. The casualty segment consists largely of general liability, commercial transportation, commercial and personal umbrella laibility, executive products, special program business and other specialty coverages. The surety segment specializes in writing small to large commercial and small contract surety products, as well as those for the energy, petrochemical and refining industries.

Recent Developments: For the twelve months ended Dec 31 2004, net income increased 2.4% to $73,036,000 from net income of $71,291,000 a year earlier. Revenues were $5,788,000,00, up 11.3% from $519,886,000 the year before. Net premiums earned were $511,348,000 compared with $463,597,000 in the prior year, an increase of 10.3%. Net investment income advanced 22.5% to $54,087,000 from $44,151,000 the previous year.

Prospects: On Dec 22 2004, Co. announced that its transportation division has launched a new commercial auto insurance unit that will write mono-line commercial auto business with its existing retail independent agents while appointing a limited number of new retail agents in targeted states. The commercial auto unit will target "stand-alone" auto business in specific classes of business, including contractors, public entities, communication related firms, utilities, financial institutions, wholesalers, manufacturers, healthcare, service organizations and other businesses.

Financial Data

(US$ in Thousands)	12/31/2004	12/31/2003	12/31/2002	12/31/2001	12/31/2000	12/31/1999	12/31/1998	12/31/1997
Earnings Per Share	2.80	2.76	1.75	1.55	1.45	1.54	1.33	1.67
Cash Flow Per Share	7.47	7.60	8.12	3.97	2.70	2.88	1.12	2.10
Tang Book Value Per Share	23.60	20.98	17.37	15.36	14.99	13.11	14.12	15.44
Dividends Per Share	0.510	0.400	0.345	0.315	0.295	0.275	0.255	0.236
Dividend Payout %	18.21	14.49	19.71	20.32	20.42	17.86	19.25	14.17
Income Statement								
Premium Income	511,348	463,597	348,065	273,008	231,603	195,274	142,324	141,884
Total Revenue	578,800	519,886	382,153	309,354	263,496	225,756	168,114	169,424
Benefits & Claims	306,131	278,990	203,122	155,876	124,586	96,457	64,728	61,251
Income Before Taxes	100,342	94,278	48,728	41,018	38,293	43,035	37,721	41,522
Income Taxes	27,306	22,987	12,876	10,771	9,600	11,584	9,482	11,351
Net Income	73,036	71,291	35,852	31,047	28,693	31,451	28,239	30,171
Average Shares	26,093	25,846	20,512	20,004	19,890	20,444	21,276	18,742
Balance Sheet								
Total Assets	2,468,775	2,134,364	1,719,327	1,390,970	1,281,323	1,170,363	1,012,685	911,741
Total Liabilities	1,845,114	1,580,230	1,262,772	1,055,538	954,669	877,294	718,726	645,188
Stockholders' Equity	623,661	554,134	456,555	335,432	326,654	293,069	293,959	266,552
Shares Outstanding	25,315	25,165	24,681	19,825	19,607	19,746	20,811	17,268
Statistical Record								
Return on Assets %	3.16	3.70	2.31	2.32	2.33	2.88	2.93	3.43
Return on Equity %	12.37	14.11	9.05	9.38	9.23	10.72	10.08	12.93
Loss Ratio %	59.87	60.18	58.36	57.10	53.79	49.40	45.48	43.17
Net Margin %	12.62	13.71	9.38	10.04	10.89	13.93	16.80	17.81
Price Range	43.20-33.55	38.10-25.40	29.60-22.25	23.00-19.40	22.34-13.25	19.38-13.97	22.65-15.41	20.05-12.20
P/E Ratio	15.43-11.98	13.80-9.20	16.91-12.71	14.84-12.52	15.41-9.14	12.58-9.07	17.03-11.58	12.01-7.31
Average Yield %	1.34	1.28	1.33	1.50	1.66	1.64	1.30	1.57

Address: 9025 North Lindbergh Drive, Peoria, IL 61615-1499	**Web Site:** www.rlicorp.com	**Auditors:** KPMG LLP
Telephone: (309) 692-1000	**Officers:** Jonathan E. Michael - Pres., C.E.O. Joseph E. Dondanville - Sr. V.P., C.F.O.	**Investor Contact:** 309-693-5880
Fax: (309) 692-1068		**Transfer Agents:** Wells Fargo Shareholder Services, St. Paul, MN

ROBERT HALF INTERNATIONAL INC.

Exchange	Symbol	Price	52Wk Range	Yield	P/E
NYS	RHI	$26.96 (3/31/2005)	30.70-23.62	1.04	34.13

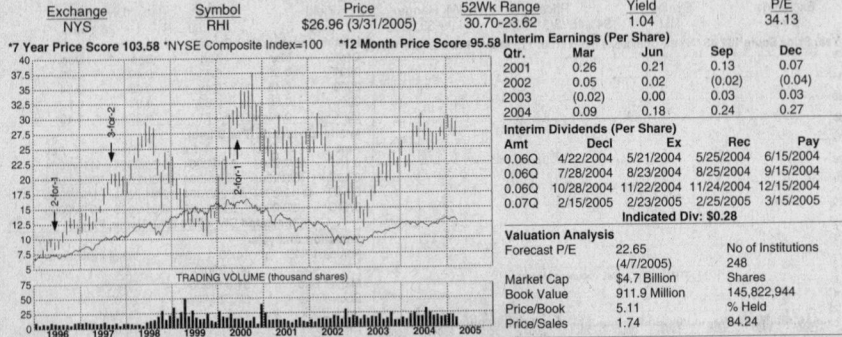

*7 Year Price Score 103.58 *NYSE Composite Index=100 *12 Month Price Score 95.58

Interim Earnings (Per Share)

Qtr.	Mar	Jun	Sep	Dec
2001	0.26	0.21	0.13	0.07
2002	0.05	0.02	(0.02)	(0.04)
2003	(0.02)	0.00	0.03	0.03
2004	0.09	0.18	0.24	0.27

Interim Dividends (Per Share)

Amt	Decl	Ex	Rec	Pay
0.06Q	4/22/2004	5/21/2004	5/25/2004	6/15/2004
0.06Q	7/28/2004	8/23/2004	8/25/2004	9/15/2004
0.06Q	10/28/2004	11/22/2004	11/24/2004	12/15/2004
0.07Q	2/15/2005	2/23/2005	2/25/2005	3/15/2005
		Indicated Div: $0.28		

Valuation Analysis

Forecast P/E	22.65 (4/7/2005)	No of Institutions 248
Market Cap	$4.7 Billion	Shares 145,822,944
Book Value	911.9 Million	% Held 84.24
Price/Book	5.11	
Price/Sales	1.74	

Business Summary: Human Resources Services (MIC: 12.6 SIC: 363 NAIC: 61320)

Robert Half International is a specialized provider of temporary, permanent and project personnel. Co. provides specialized staffing in the fields of accounting and finance, administrative and office support, information technology, legal, advertising, marketing, and Web design on a temporary, full-time and project basis. Co. also provides business and technology risk consulting and internal audit services. Co.'s divisions include Accountemps®, Robert Half® Finance & Accounting, OfficeTeam®, Robert Half® Technology, Robert Half® Management Resources, Robert Half® Legal, The Creative Group®, and Protiviti® .

Recent Developments: For the year ended Dec 31 2004, net income increased 2100.4% to $140,604 thousand from net income of $6,390 thousand a year earlier. Revenues were $2,675,696 thousand, up 35.5% from $1,974,991 thousand the year before. Total direct expense was $1,619,394 thousand versus $1,248,253 thousand in the prior year, an increase of 29.7%. Total indirect expense was $825,407 thousand versus $717,626 thousand in the prior year, an increase of 15.0%.

Prospects: Co. continues to see favorable results being generated in all of its operations. Co. estimates that 17.0% to 20.0% of its consolidated revenue growth relates directly to Sarbanes-Oxley Act compliance work. This broad-based improvement is particularly notable in Co.'s Accountemps and OfficeTeam staffing divisions. Meanwhile, Co. believes there will be ongoing demand for Sarbanes-Oxley related initiatives. This includes remediation efforts to improve controls, annual testing to support ongoing compliance, initial efforts by non accelerated filers, and development of long-term compliance processes and programs.

Financial Data

(US$ in Thousands)	12/31/2004	12/31/2003	12/31/2002	12/31/2001	12/31/2000	12/31/1999	12/31/1998	12/31/1997
Earnings Per Share	0.79	0.04	0.01	0.67	1.00	0.77	0.69	0.50
Cash Flow Per Share	0.95	0.73	0.96	1.58	1.50	0.82	0.85	0.45
Tang Book Value Per Share	4.30	3.65	3.41	3.69	3.13	2.27	1.89	1.32
Dividends Per Share	0.180	...	...	...	...	...	...	...
Dividend Payout %	22.78	...	...	...	...	...	...	...
Income Statement								
Total Revenue	2,675,696	1,974,991	1,904,951	2,452,850	2,699,319	2,081,321	1,793,041	1,302,876
EBITDA	280,008	75,016	71,220	260,881	347,827	267,770	240,224	172,290
Depn & Amortn	49,113	65,904	72,308	73,116	56,639	39,114	24,636	17,652
Income Before Taxes	234,665	11,715	3,497	196,284	301,627	234,697	221,176	158,828
Income Taxes	94,061	5,325	1,329	75,177	115,524	93,256	89,596	65,131
Net Income	140,604	6,390	2,168	121,107	186,103	141,441	131,580	93,697
Average Shares	176,866	173,175	177,791	181,489	186,068	184,588	189,644	187,998
Balance Sheet								
Current Assets	916,316	698,619	643,172	686,006	671,610	490,539	430,406	334,005
Total Assets	1,198,657	979,903	935,671	994,162	971,029	777,188	703,719	561,367
Current Liabilities	280,345	188,899	184,215	176,647	237,156	176,207	152,845	122,095
Long-Term Obligations	2,266	2,343	2,434	2,498	2,577	2,597	3,404	4,530
Total Liabilities	286,787	191,242	190,705	188,466	252,490	201,085	181,249	142,567
Stockholders' Equity	911,870	788,661	744,966	805,696	718,539	576,103	522,470	418,800
Shares Outstanding	172,980	171,775	170,909	174,928	176,050	176,147	182,450	183,292
Statistical Record								
Return on Assets %	12.87	0.67	0.22	12.33	21.23	19.10	20.80	19.17
Return on Equity %	16.49	0.83	0.28	15.89	28.67	25.75	27.96	25.77
EBITDA Margin %	10.46	3.80	3.74	10.64	12.89	12.87	13.40	13.22
Net Margin %	5.25	0.32	0.11	4.94	6.89	6.80	7.34	7.19
Asset Turnover	2.45	2.06	1.97	2.50	3.08	2.81	2.83	2.67
Current Ratio	3.27	3.70	3.49	3.88	2.83	2.78	2.82	2.74
Debt to Equity	N.M.	N.M.	N.M.	N.M.	N.M.	N.M.	0.01	0.01
Price Range	30.70-20.84	24.58-11.74	30.81-12.06	30.47-18.77	37.63-12.69	23.72-10.41	29.50-15.00	21.28-11.21
P/E Ratio	38.86-26.38	614.50-293.50	N.M.	45.48-28.01	37.63-12.69	30.80-13.51	42.75-21.74	42.56-22.42
Average Yield %	0.69	...	...	...	...	...	...	...

Address: 2884 Sand Hill Road, Suite 200, Menlo Park, CA 94025 **Telephone:** (650) 234-6000 **Fax:** (650) 234-6999	**Web Site:** www.rhi.com **Officers:** Harold M. Messmer Jr. - Chmn., Pres., C.E.O. M. Keith Waddell - Vice-Chmn., C.F.O.	**Auditors:** PricewaterhouseCoopers LLP

ROCKWELL COLLINS, INC.

Exchange	Symbol	Price	52Wk Range	Yield	P/E
NYS	COL	$47.59 (3/31/2005)	48.33-29.37	1.01	26.59

*7 Year Price Score N/A   *NYSE Composite Index=100   *12 Month Price Score 115.53

TRADING VOLUME (thousand shares)

Interim Earnings (Per Share)

Qtr.	Dec	Mar	Jun	Sep
2001-02	0.26	0.31	0.33	0.38
2002-03	0.27	0.33	0.43	0.40
2003-04	0.38	0.39	0.42	0.48
2004-05	0.50	...	...	...

Interim Dividends (Per Share)

Amt	Decl	Ex	Rec	Pay
0.09Q	5/3/2004	5/13/2004	5/17/2004	6/7/2004
0.12Q	6/30/2004	8/10/2004	8/12/2004	9/7/2004
0.12Q	11/2/2004	11/10/2004	11/15/2004	12/6/2004
0.12Q	2/2/2005	2/10/2005	2/14/2005	3/7/2005
		Indicated Div: $0.48		

Valuation Analysis

Forecast P/E	22.29 (4/7/2005)	No of Institutions 289
Market Cap	$8.5 Billion	Shares 104,318,432
Book Value	1.2 Billion	% Held 59.09
Price/Book	6.85	
Price/Sales	2.77	

Business Summary: Communications (MIC: 10.1 SIC: 663 NAIC: 34220)

Rockwell Collins is a provider of design, production and support of communications and aviation electronics for commercial and military customers worldwide. While Co.'s products and systems are primarily focused on aviation applications, its Government Systems business also offers products and systems for ground and shipboard applications. Co. also provides services and support to its customers through its network of approx. 60 service centers worldwide, including equipment repair and overhaul, service parts, field service engineering, training, technical information services and aftermarket used equipment sales.

Recent Developments: For the quarter ended Dec 31 2004, net income increased 32.4% to $90 million from net income of $68 million in the year-earlier quarter. Revenues were $763 million, up 21.5% from $628 million the year before. Total direct expense was $545 million versus $455 million in the prior-year quarter, an increase of 19.8%. Total indirect expense was $87 million versus $80 million in the prior-year quarter, an increase of 8.8%.

Prospects: Results are being positively affected by increased demand for Co.'s business jet services and military global positioning systems. Co. expects increasing worldwide travel and continued strong defense spending will boost results in fiscal 2005. Co. is projecting fiscal 2005 sales to be in the range of $3.28 billion to $3.30 billion and earnings per share in the range of $2.00 to $2.10. Government Systems sales are expected to represent approximately 52.0% of total fiscal year 2005 company sales and are projected to increase by 10.0% to 12.0% over fiscal year 2004. Commercial Systems sales are expected to increase in the range of 11.0% to 13.0% year over year, representing 48.0% of 2005 sales.

Financial Data
(US$ in Thousands)

	3 Mos	09/30/2004	09/30/2003	09/30/2002	09/30/2001	09/30/2000	09/30/1999
Earnings Per Share	1.79	1.67	1.43	1.28	0.72	1.35	1.43
Cash Flow Per Share	2.77	2.25	2.09	2.47	1.06	1.49	...
Tang Book Value Per Share	3.87	3.29	2.21	2.93	4.49	...	...
Dividends Per Share	0.420	0.390	0.360	0.360	0.090	...	...
Dividend Payout %	23.52	23.35	25.17	28.13	12.50	...	...
Income Statement							
Total Revenue	763,000	2,930,000	2,542,000	2,492,000	2,820,000	2,510,000	2,438,000
EBITDA	153,000	545,000	474,000	450,000	358,000	498,000	523,000
Depn & Amortn	25,000	109,000	105,000	105,000	131,000	99,000	86,000
Income Before Taxes	129,000	430,000	368,000	341,000	224,000	399,000	437,000
Income Taxes	39,000	129,000	110,000	105,000	85,000	130,000	146,000
Net Income	90,000	301,000	258,000	236,000	139,000	269,000	291,000
Average Shares	180,200	180,000	180,100	184,100	185,500	190,600	195,600
Balance Sheet							
Current Assets	1,672,000	1,663,000	1,427,000	1,438,000	1,639,000	1,311,000	...
Total Assets	2,885,000	2,874,000	2,591,000	2,560,000	2,628,000	2,100,000	...
Current Liabilities	868,000	964,000	901,000	1,043,000	1,135,000	803,000	...
Long-Term Obligations	201,000	201,000	...	...	...	...	...
Total Liabilities	1,648,000	1,741,000	1,758,000	1,573,000	1,518,000	1,192,000	...
Stockholders' Equity	1,237,000	1,133,000	833,000	987,000	1,110,000	908,000	...
Shares Outstanding	178,100	177,000	177,800	181,000	183,600	...	...
Statistical Record							
Return on Assets %	11.52	10.99	10.02	9.10	5.88	...	...
Return on Equity %	30.17	30.54	28.35	22.51	13.78	...	...
EBITDA Margin %	20.05	18.60	18.65	18.06	12.70	19.84	21.45
Net Margin %	11.80	10.27	10.15	9.47	4.93	10.72	11.94
Asset Turnover	1.09	1.07	0.99	0.96	1.19	...	...
Current Ratio	1.93	1.73	1.58	1.38	1.44	1.63	...
Debt to Equity	0.16	0.18	...	...	...	...	...
Price Range	40.87-29.36	37.14-25.25	27.67-17.34	27.55-13.50	26.90-12.95	...	...
P/E Ratio	22.83-16.40	22.24-15.12	19.35-12.13	21.52-10.55	37.36-17.99	...	...
Average Yield %	1.23	1.25	1.60	1.67	0.45	...	...

Address: 400 Collins Road N.E., Cedar Rapids, IA 52498 **Telephone:** (319) 295-1000	**Web Site:** www.rockwellcollins.com **Officers:** Clayton M. Jones - Chmn., Pres., C.E.O. Robert M. Chiusano - Exec. V.P., C.O.O., Commercial Systems	**Auditors:** Deloitte & Touche LLP **Investor Contact:** 319-295-7575

ROCKWELL AUTOMATION, INC.

Exchange	Symbol	Price	52Wk Range	Yield	P/E
NYS	ROK	$56.64 (3/31/2005)	62.30-31.61	1.59	22.13

*7 Year Price Score 163.14 *NYSE Composite Index=100 *12 Month Price Score 128.55

Interim Earnings (Per Share)

Qtr.	Dec	Mar	Jun	Sep
2001-02	(0.03)	0.33	0.47	0.26
2002-03	0.22	0.26	0.67	0.36
2003-04	0.32	0.41	0.66	0.78
2004-05	0.71	...	...	...

Interim Dividends (Per Share)

Amt	Decl	Ex	Rec	Pay
0.165Q	6/2/2004	8/12/2004	8/16/2004	9/7/2004
0.165Q	11/3/2004	11/10/2004	11/15/2004	12/6/2004
0.165Q	2/2/2005	2/10/2005	2/14/2005	3/7/2005
0.225Q	4/6/2005	5/12/2005	5/16/2005	6/6/2005
		Indicated Div: $0.90		

Valuation Analysis

Forecast P/E	21.22
	(4/13/2005)
Market Cap	$10.4 Billion
Book Value	2.0 Billion
Price/Book	5.32
Price/Sales	2.28

No of Institutions	366
Shares	110,936,672
% Held	60.23

Business Summary: Instruments and Related Products (MIC: 11.15 SIC: 829 NAIC: 35314)

Rockwell Automation is a global provider of industrial automation power, control and information products and services. Co. is organized based upon specific products and services and has two operating segments: Control Systems and Power Systems. Control Systems is divided into three units: the Components and Packaged Applications Group, the Automation Control and Information Group and Global Manufacturing Solutions. Co.'s Control Systems segment supplies industrial automation products, systems, software and services focused on helping customers control and improve manufacturing processes. Power Systems is divided into two units: Dodge mechanical and Reliance electrical.

Recent Developments: For the quarter ended Dec 31 2004, income from continuing operations was $122.1 million compared with income of $57.1 million a year earlier. Total sales increased 19.7% to $1.18 billion from $990.3 million the previous year. Co. noted that currency translation accounted for 3.0% of total sales growth. Control Systems segment sales grew 18.9% to $985.5 million, while Power Systems segment sales climbed 23.5% to $199.4 million from $161.5 million in the corresponding year-ago period. Total segment operating earnings advanced 94.9% to $213.6 million versus $109.6 million the year before.

Prospects: Co. is benefiting from the continued transformation of its business model and will look to continue supporting the growth if its advanced technology products and services with a lower investment base and a leaner cost structure. Based upon current economic conditions and business outlook, Co. expects revenue to increase sequentially in each of the remaining quarters of 2005 by 1.0% to 2.0%, resulting in full year 2005 organic revenue growth of approximately 10.0%. Fiscal year 2005 diluted earnings from continuing operations is expected to range from $2.55 to $2.65 per share.

Financial Data
(US$ in Thousands)

	3 Mos	09/30/2004	09/30/2003	09/30/2002	09/30/2001	09/30/2000	09/30/1999	09/30/1998
Earnings Per Share	2.56	2.17	1.51	0.64	1.65	3.35	2.90	(2.16)
Cash Flow Per Share	3.00	3.21	2.35	2.57	1.83	4.92	4.93	3.65
Tang Book Value Per Share	4.41	3.95	2.40	2.61	2.22	6.90	5.76	8.85
Dividends Per Share	0.660	0.660	0.660	0.660	0.930	1.020	1.020	1.020
Dividend Payout %	25.83	30.41	43.71	103.13	56.36	30.45	35.17	...
Income Statement								
Total Revenue	1,184,900	4,411,100	4,104,000	3,909,000	4,323,000	7,220,000	7,151,000	6,840,000
EBITDA	225,800	660,900	543,000	500,000	523,000	1,385,000	1,311,000	389,000
Depn & Amortn	46,200	186,700	198,000	206,000	272,000	369,000	337,000	306,000
Income Before Taxes	179,600	438,100	299,000	233,000	168,000	943,000	890,000	25,000
Income Taxes	57,500	84,000	17,000	7,000	43,000	307,000	308,000	134,000
Net Income	133,400	414,900	286,000	121,000	305,000	636,000	562,000	(427,000)
Average Shares	189,100	191,100	190,100	188,800	185,300	189,900	193,600	197,900
Balance Sheet								
Current Assets	2,066,000	2,026,100	1,736,000	1,775,000	1,697,000	3,206,000	3,582,000	4,096,000
Total Assets	4,276,100	4,201,200	3,986,000	4,024,000	4,074,000	6,390,000	6,704,000	7,170,000
Current Liabilities	845,200	863,600	820,000	966,000	867,000	1,820,000	2,108,000	1,983,000
Long-Term Obligations	754,500	757,700	764,000	767,000	922,000	924,000	911,000	908,000
Total Liabilities	2,316,400	2,340,200	2,399,000	2,415,000	2,474,000	3,721,000	4,067,000	3,925,000
Stockholders' Equity	1,959,700	1,861,000	1,587,000	1,609,000	1,600,000	2,669,000	2,637,000	3,245,000
Shares Outstanding	184,200	183,800	185,600	185,800	183,700	183,500	216,400	216,400
Statistical Record								
Return on Assets %	11.67	10.11	7.14	2.99	5.83	9.69	8.10	N.M.
Return on Equity %	26.85	24.00	17.90	7.54	14.29	23.91	19.11	N.M.
EBITDA Margin %	19.06	14.98	13.23	12.79	12.10	19.18	18.33	5.69
Net Margin %	11.26	9.41	6.97	3.10	7.06	8.81	7.86	N.M.
Asset Turnover	1.10	1.07	1.02	0.97	0.83	1.10	1.03	0.90
Current Ratio	2.44	2.35	2.12	1.84	1.96	1.76	1.70	2.07
Debt to Equity	0.39	0.41	0.48	0.48	0.58	0.35	0.35	0.28
Price Range	49.55-28.57	39.69-26.25	28.55-15.02	22.66-13.40	18.63-11.47	20.72-10.78	24.48-10.35	19.27-10.84
P/E Ratio	19.36-11.16	18.29-12.10	18.91-9.95	35.41-20.94	11.29-6.95	6.19-3.22	8.44-3.57	...
Average Yield %	1.78	1.94	2.95	3.58	5.79	6.28	5.47	6.36

Address: 777 East Wisconsin Avenue, Suite 1400, Milwaukee, WI 53202 Telephone: (414) 212-5200 Fax: (414) 212-5212	Web Site: www.rockwellautomation.com Officers: Don H. Davis Jr. - Chmn. Keith D. Nosbusch - Pres., C.E.O.	Auditors: Deloitte & Touche LLP Investor Contact: 414-212-5210 Transfer Agents: Mellon Investor Services LLC, South Hackensack, NJ

ROHM & HAAS CO.

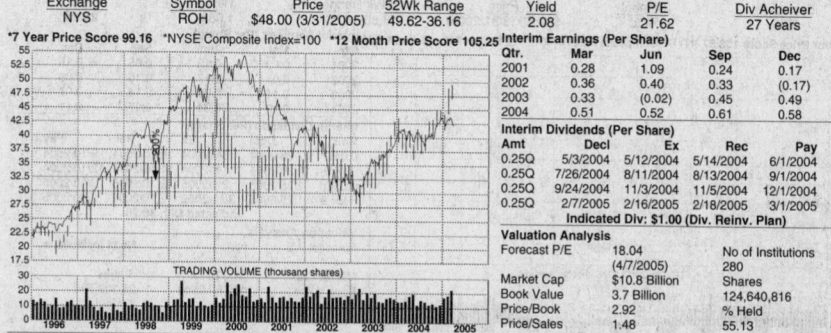

Exchange	Symbol	Price	52Wk Range	Yield	P/E	Div Acheiver
NYS	ROH	$48.00 (3/31/2005)	49.62-36.16	2.08	21.62	27 Years

*7 Year Price Score 99.16   *NYSE Composite Index=100   *12 Month Price Score 105.25

Interim Earnings (Per Share)

Qtr.	Mar	Jun	Sep	Dec
2001	0.28	1.09	0.24	0.17
2002	0.36	0.40	0.33	(0.17)
2003	0.33	(0.02)	0.45	0.49
2004	0.51	0.52	0.61	0.58

Interim Dividends (Per Share)

Amt	Decl	Ex	Rec	Pay
0.25Q	5/3/2004	5/12/2004	5/14/2004	6/1/2004
0.25Q	7/26/2004	8/11/2004	8/13/2004	9/1/2004
0.25Q	9/24/2004	11/3/2004	11/5/2004	12/1/2004
0.25Q	2/7/2005	2/16/2005	2/18/2005	3/1/2005

Indicated Div: $1.00 (Div. Reinv. Plan)

Valuation Analysis

Forecast P/E	18.04	No of Institutions
	(4/7/2005)	280
Market Cap	$10.8 Billion	Shares
Book Value	3.7 Billion	124,640,816
Price/Book	2.92	% Held
Price/Sales	1.48	55.13

Business Summary: Chemicals (MIC: 11.1 SIC: 821 NAIC: 25211)

Rohm & Haas is a global specialty materials company that operates through six reportable segments: coatings, adhesives and sealants, electronic materials, performance chemicals, salt and monomers. Coatings is Co.'s largest segment in terms of sales, and is comprised of three businesses including architectural functional coatings, powder coatings and automotive coatings. Co. operates over 100 manufacturing and 30 research facilities in 27 countries, and serves several industries, including construction and building, electronics, household products and personal care, packaging, food and retail, and automotive.

Recent Developments: For the year ended Dec 31 2004, income from continuing operations increased 72.2% to $496,000 thousand from income of $288,000 thousand a year earlier. Net income increased 77.5% to $497,000 thousand from net income of $280,000 thousand a year earlier. Revenues were $7,300,000 thousand, up 13.7% from $6,421,000 thousand the year before. Total direct expense was $5,170,000 thousand versus $4,506,000 thousand in the prior year, an increase of 14.7%. Total indirect expense was $1,338,000 thousand versus $1,392,000 thousand in the prior year, a decrease of 3.9%.

Prospects: Top-line growth is being fueled by higher selling prices, increased volume and favorable foreign currency exchange rates. Meanwhile, raw materials and energy costs will likely continue to increase throughout 2005, driven by high oil and natural gas prices. Co. plans to continue to increase selling prices to help offset these cost increases. Looking ahead, Co. is targeting full-year 2005 sales growth of between 9.0% and 11.0%, or about $8.00 billion, gross margins in the range of 29.0% to 30.0%, and earnings of between $2.50 and $2.75 per share. In addition, Co. is forecasting capital expenditures of approximately $375.0 million in 2005.

Financial Data

(US$ in Thousands)	12/31/2004	12/31/2003	12/31/2002	12/31/2001	12/31/2000	12/31/1999	12/31/1998	12/31/1997
Earnings Per Share	2.22	1.26	(2.57)	1.79	1.61	1.27	2.45	2.13
Cash Flow Per Share	3.95	4.51	4.41	3.17	3.50	4.24	3.88	4.26
Tang Book Value Per Share	1.37	0.13	N.M.	N.M.	N.M.	N.M.	9.06	8.51
Dividends Per Share	0.970	0.860	0.820	0.800	0.780	0.740	0.693	0.633
Dividend Payout %	43.69	68.25	...	44.69	48.45	58.27	28.30	29.73
Income Statement								
Total Revenue	7,300,000	6,421,000	5,727,000	5,666,000	6,879,000	5,339,000	3,720,000	3,999,000
EBITDA	1,319,000	1,014,000	903,000	672,000	1,428,000	1,061,000	992,000	917,000
Depn & Amortn	481,000	478,000	457,000	562,000	613,000	451,000	271,000	273,000
Income Before Taxes	714,000	415,000	320,000	(64,000)	581,000	464,000	700,000	611,000
Income Taxes	207,000	127,000	102,000	6,000	227,000	215,000	247,000	201,000
Net Income	497,000	280,000	(570,000)	395,000	354,000	249,000	440,000	410,000
Average Shares	224,200	222,400	221,900	220,200	220,500	218,981	179,700	192,300
Balance Sheet								
Current Assets	3,247,000	2,527,000	2,543,000	2,421,000	2,781,000	2,497,000	1,287,000	1,397,000
Total Assets	10,095,000	9,445,000	9,706,000	10,350,000	11,267,000	11,256,000	3,648,000	3,900,000
Current Liabilities	1,740,000	1,797,000	1,621,000	1,624,000	2,194,000	2,510,000	875,000	850,000
Long-Term Obligations	2,563,000	2,468,000	2,872,000	2,720,000	3,225,000	3,122,000	409,000	509,000
Total Liabilities	6,294,000	6,075,000	6,576,000	6,517,000	7,591,000	7,762,000	2,068,000	2,025,000
Stockholders' Equity	3,697,000	3,357,000	3,119,000	3,815,000	3,653,000	3,475,000	1,561,000	1,797,000
Shares Outstanding	225,260	222,453	221,131	220,427	219,937	218,981	154,000	182,700
Statistical Record								
Return on Assets %	5.07	2.92	N.M.	3.65	3.13	3.34	11.66	10.47
Return on Equity %	14.05	8.65	N.M.	10.58	9.91	9.89	26.21	23.26
EBITDA Margin %	18.07	15.79	15.77	11.86	20.76	19.87	26.67	22.93
Net Margin %	6.81	4.36	N.M.	6.97	5.15	4.66	11.83	10.25
Asset Turnover	0.75	0.67	0.57	0.52	0.61	0.72	0.99	1.02
Current Ratio	1.87	1.41	1.57	1.49	1.27	0.99	1.47	1.64
Debt to Equity	0.69	0.74	0.92	0.71	0.88	0.90	0.26	0.28
Price Range	45.17-36.16	42.92-26.67	42.27-30.55	38.27-26.12	47.88-26.00	49.13-28.75	38.54-26.75	33.23-23.83
P/E Ratio	20.35-16.29	34.06-21.17	...	21.38-14.59	29.74-16.15	38.68-22.64	15.73-10.92	15.60-11.19
Average Yield %	2.39	2.53	2.25	2.35	2.26	1.96	2.10	2.15

Address: 100 Independence Mall West, Philadelphia, PA 19106-2399
Telephone: (215) 592-3000
Fax: (215) 592-3377

Web Site: www.rohmhaas.com
Officers: Rajiv L. Gupta - Chmn., C.E.O. Jacques M. Croisetiere - V.P., C.F.O.

Auditors: PricewaterhouseCoopers LLP
Investor Contact: 215 592-3052
Transfer Agents: EquiServe Trust Company, N.A., Providence, RI

ROLLINS, INC.

Exchange	Symbol	Price	52Wk Range	Yield	P/E
NYS	ROL	$18.60 (3/31/2005)	18.60-14.33	1.08	25.14

*7 Year Price Score 136.67 *NYSE Composite Index=100 *12 Month Price Score 97.08

Interim Earnings (Per Share)

Qtr.	Mar	Jun	Sep	Dec
2001	0.03	0.13	0.06	0.15
2002	0.07	0.17	0.10	0.06
2003	0.11	0.20	0.14	0.07
2004	0.13	0.34	0.17	0.11

Interim Dividends (Per Share)

Amt	Decl	Ex	Rec	Pay
0.04Q	7/28/2004	8/6/2004	8/10/2004	9/10/2004
0.04Q	10/26/2004	11/8/2004	11/10/2004	12/10/2004
0.05Q	1/25/2005	2/8/2005	2/10/2005	3/10/2005
3-for-2	1/25/2005	3/11/2005	2/10/2005	3/10/2005

Indicated Div: $0.20

Valuation Analysis

Forecast P/E	N/A	No of Institutions
Market Cap	$1.3 Billion	Shares
Book Value	167.5 Million	25,303,616
Price/Book	7.60	% Held
Price/Sales	1.70	36.94

Business Summary: Miscellaneous Business Services (MIC: 12.8 SIC: 342 NAIC: 61710)

Rollins is a national service company providing pest and termite control services to both residential and commercial customers in North America. Services are performed through a contract that specifies the pricing arrangement with the customer. Co.'s Orkin, Inc. subsidiary provides customized pest and termite control services from over 400 locations to approximately 1.6 million customers, as of Dec 31 2003. Orkin serves customers in the U.S., Canada and Mexico, providing pest control services and protection against termite damage, rodents and insects to homes and businesses, including hotels, food service establishments, food manufacturers, retailers and transportation companies.

Recent Developments: For the year ended Dec 31 2004, net income increased 45.6% to $52,055 thousand from net income of $35,761 thousand a year earlier. Revenues were $750,884 thousand, up 10.9% from $677,013 thousand the year before. Total direct expense was $395,334 thousand versus $362,422 thousand in the prior year, an increase of 9.1%. Total indirect expense was $281,927 thousand versus $256,693 thousand in the prior year, an increase of 9.8%.

Prospects: Co.'s efforts to expand its residential and commercial services are helping increase customer and employee retention levels, as well as attract new customers. Going forward, Co. will continue to focus on implementing sales and productivity initiatives, and other programs expected to generate operating efficiencies and improve customer service. Separately, while growth in lead generation and service improvements are driving residential business growth, Co. is taking steps to fuel commercial business growth through market share expansion. These initiatives should begin to positively effect results in fiscal 2005.

Financial Data
(US$ in Thousands)

	12/31/2004	12/31/2003	12/31/2002	12/31/2001	12/31/2000	12/31/1999	12/31/1998	12/31/1997
Earnings Per Share	0.74	0.51	0.40	0.37	0.21	0.16	0.14	0.03
Cash Flow Per Share	1.05	0.92	0.80	0.65	0.25	0.18	(0.01)	0.11
Tang Book Value Per Share	N.M.	0.53	N.M.	N.M.	N.M.	N.M.	0.87	2.13
Dividends Per Share	0.160	0.133	0.089	0.089	0.089	0.089	0.222	0.267
Dividend Payout %	21.62	25.97	22.22	23.81	41.67	55.56	158.73	999.99
Income Statement								
Total Revenue	750,884	677,013	665,425	652,286	649,558	586,639	549,136	538,639
EBITDA	121,746	80,209	65,361	47,618	33,824	24,965	14,058	(160,620)
Depn & Amortn	23,034	20,179	21,635	20,292	18,421	13,433	8,934	8,382
Income Before Taxes	98,712	60,030	43,726	27,326	15,403	11,532	5,124	(169,002)
Income Taxes	40,453	24,269	16,616	10,384	5,853	4,382	1,947	(64,221)
Net Income	52,055	35,761	27,110	16,942	9,550	7,150	6,587	1,497
Average Shares	70,167	69,309	68,113	45,399	45,069	45,498	48,004	51,049
Balance Sheet								
Current Assets	146,805	170,371	126,222	100,483	88,969	107,749	199,108	301,618
Total Assets	418,780	349,904	317,407	296,559	298,819	312,940	327,265	432,680
Current Liabilities	187,980	145,022	129,862	108,536	110,806	111,441	115,093	130,718
Long-Term Obligations	...	...	...	...	...	256	2,450	6,090	9,239
Total Liabilities	251,231	211,130	226,717	211,061	220,220	241,150	247,030	287,036
Stockholders' Equity	167,549	138,774	90,690	85,498	78,599	71,790	80,235	145,644
Shares Outstanding	68,504	67,735	67,199	45,104	45,054	44,822	45,733	49,918
Statistical Record								
Return on Assets %	13.51	10.72	8.83	5.69	3.11	2.23	1.73	0.40
Return on Equity %	33.89	31.17	30.77	20.65	12.67	9.41	5.83	0.89
EBITDA Margin %	16.21	11.85	9.82	7.30	5.21	4.26	2.56	N.M.
Net Margin %	6.93	5.28	4.07	2.60	1.47	1.22	1.20	0.28
Asset Turnover	1.95	2.03	2.17	2.19	2.12	1.83	1.45	1.45
Current Ratio	0.78	1.17	0.97	0.93	0.80	0.97	1.73	2.31
Debt to Equity	...	...	...	...	N.M.	0.03	0.08	0.06
Price Range	18.07-14.33	16.33-11.14	12.33-8.13	9.36-6.67	9.72-5.06	7.86-6.64	9.47-6.83	10.69-8.33
P/E Ratio	24.41-19.36	32.01-21.84	30.82-20.33	25.29-18.03	46.30-24.07	49.13-41.49	67.66-48.81	356.48-277.78
Average Yield %	0.98	0.99	0.96	1.07	1.29	1.23	2.60	2.96

Address: 2170 Piedmont Road, N.E., Atlanta, GA 30324	Web Site:	Auditors: Grant Thornton LLP
Telephone: (404) 888 2000	Officers: R. Randall Rollins - Chmn. Gary W. Rollins - Pres., C.E.O., C.O.O.	Investor Contact: 404-888-2000
Fax: (404) 888 2670		

ROPER INDUSTRIES, INC

Exchange	Symbol	Price	52Wk Range	Yield	P/E	Div Acheiver
NYS	ROP	$65.50 (3/31/2005)	67.55-47.45	0.65	26.41	12 Years

*7 Year Price Score 128.27 *NYSE Composite Index=100 *12 Month Price Score 103.27

Interim Earnings (Per Share)

Qtr.	Jan	Apr	Jul	Oct
2002-03	0.26	0.46	0.53	...
2004	0.49	0.63	0.73	0.64

Interim Dividends (Per Share)

Amt	Decl	Ex	Rec	Pay
0.096Q	5/24/2004	7/14/2004	7/16/2004	7/30/2004
0.096Q	8/17/2004	10/13/2004	10/15/2004	10/29/2004
0.106Q	11/18/2004	1/12/2005	1/14/2005	1/31/2005
0.106Q	3/3/2005	4/13/2005	4/15/2005	4/29/2005

Indicated Div: $0.42

Valuation Analysis

Forecast P/E	19.85	No of Institutions
	(4/7/2005)	217
Market Cap	$2.8 Billion	Shares
Book Value	1.1 Billion	38,919,948
Price/Book	2.49	% Held
Price/Sales	2.86	91.62

TRADING VOLUME (thousand shares)

Business Summary: Industrial Machinery and Equipment (MIC: 11.5 SIC: 561 NAIC: 33911)

Roper Industries is a diversified industrial company. The Instrumentation segment provides equipment and consumables for material analysis, fluid properties testing and industrial leak testing. The industrial technology segment produces industrial pumps, flow measurement and metering equipment, and water meter and automatic meter reading products and systems. The Energy Systems and Controls segment produces control systems, machinery vibration and other non-destructive inspection and measurement products. The Scientific and Industrial Imaging segment produces high-performance digital imaging products and software and handheld computers and software.

Recent Developments: For the year ended Dec 31 2004, net income increased 107.5% to $93,852 thousand from net income of $45,239 thousand a year earlier. Revenues were $969,764 thousand, up 47.5% from $657,356 thousand the year before. Operating income was $171,302 thousand versus an income of $108,100 thousand in the prior year, an increase of 58.5%. Total direct expense was $484,719 thousand versus $311,218 thousand in the prior year, an increase of 55.7%. Total indirect expense was $313,743 thousand versus $238,038 thousand in the prior year, an increase of 31.8%.

Prospects: Co. appears poised to continue its strong performance in 2005. Co. noted that about 75.0% of its end markets are now in attractive RFID, energy, water and research markets with lower cyclical risk. Additionally, Co. is integrating TransCore with a focus on extending its technologies into targeted growth markets, such as automatic meter reading and security applications. In 2005, Co. expects earnings before interest, taxes, depreciation and amortization of at least $314.0 million. Co. also forecasts over $225.0 million of cash flow from operating activities. Net sales are expected to exceed $1.37 billion, while adjusted diluted earnings per share are expected to be between $3.10 and $3.30.

Financial Data

(US$ in Thousands)	12/31/2004	12/31/2003	12/31/2002	10/31/2002	10/31/2001	10/31/2000	10/31/1999	10/31/1998
Earnings Per Share	2.48	1.41	0.03	1.26	1.77	1.58	1.53	1.24
Cash Flow Per Share	4.42	2.26	0.20	2.79	3.33	2.21	1.75	2.46
Tang Book Value Per Share	N.M.	N.M.	N.M.	N.M.	N.M.	N.M.	0.56	N.M.
Dividends Per Share	0.385	0.350	0.330	0.330	0.300	0.280	0.260	0.240
Dividend Payout %	15.52	24.82	N.M.	26.19	16.95	17.72	16.99	19.35
Income Statement								
Total Revenue	969,764	657,356	83,885	627,030	586,506	503,813	407,256	389,170
EBITDA	199,262	98,442	7,367	129,368	129,811	111,712	95,504	81,906
Depn & Amortn	36,699	15,768	2,620	15,176	27,455	22,298	15,966	14,434
Income Before Taxes	133,716	66,290	1,769	95,686	86,439	75,931	72,284	59,616
Income Taxes	39,864	18,229	529	29,663	30,600	26,653	24,938	20,300
Net Income	93,852	45,239	853	40,053	55,839	49,278	24,938	20,300
Average Shares	37,832	31,992	31,854	31,815	31,493	31,182	30,992	31,717
Balance Sheet								
Current Assets	556,160	381,192	247,565	247,622	233,053	213,955	161,819	139,852
Total Assets	2,366,404	1,514,995	824,966	828,973	762,122	596,902	420,163	381,533
Current Liabilities	253,550	161,497	121,344	130,237	103,880	84,492	72,243	57,578
Long-Term Obligations	855,364	630,186	308,684	311,590	323,830	234,603	109,659	120,307
Total Liabilities	1,252,318	859,214	443,985	452,961	438,616	326,711	188,195	184,500
Stockholders' Equity	1,114,086	655,781	380,981	376,012	323,506	270,191	231,968	197,033
Shares Outstanding	42,416	36,042	31,370	31,363	30,879	30,599	30,282	30,343
Statistical Record								
Return on Assets %	4.82	3.87	0.09	5.03	8.22	9.66	11.81	11.06
Return on Equity %	10.58	8.73	0.21	11.45	18.81	19.57	22.07	20.97
EBITDA Margin %	20.55	14.98	8.78	20.63	22.13	22.17	23.45	21.05
Net Margin %	9.68	6.88	1.02	6.39	9.52	9.78	11.63	10.10
Asset Turnover	0.50	0.56	0.09	0.79	0.86	0.99	1.02	1.09
Current Ratio	2.19	2.36	2.04	1.90	2.24	2.53	2.24	2.43
Debt to Equity	0.77	0.96	0.81	0.83	1.00	0.87	0.47	0.61
Price Range	63.31-45.27	51.58-26.75	43.15-36.46	51.80-27.36	45.50-30.06	38.31-25.00	38.38-15.94	33.88-13.88
P/E Ratio	25.53-18.25	36.58-18.97	N.M.	41.11-21.71	25.71-16.98	24.25-15.82	25.08-10.42	27.32-11.19
Average Yield %	0.71	0.75	0.74	0.80	0.79	0.86	0.93	0.93

Address: 2160 Satellite Boulevard, Suite 200, Duluth, GA 30097 **Telephone:** (770) 495-5100 **Fax:** (770) 495-5150	**Web Site:** www.roperind.com **Officers:** Brian D. Jellison - Chmn., Pres., C.E.O. Shanler D. Cronk - V.P., Sec., Couns.	**Auditors:** PricewaterhouseCoopers LLP **Transfer Agents:** Wachovia Bank, N.A., Charlotte, NC

ROWAN COS., INC.

Exchange	Symbol	Price	52Wk Range	Yield	P/E
NYS	RDC	$29.93 (3/31/2005)	32.92-20.62	N/A	N/A

*7 Year Price Score 99.93 ***NYSE Composite Index=100** ***12 Month Price Score 111.98**

TRADING VOLUME (thousand shares)

Interim Earnings (Per Share)

Qtr.	Mar	Jun	Sep	Dec
2001	0.33	0.36	0.22	(0.10)
2002	0.92	(0.09)	0.11	(0.03)
2003	(0.18)	(0.07)	0.12	0.05
2004	(0.11)	(0.02)	0.09	0.02

Interim Dividends (Per Share)

No Dividends Paid

Valuation Analysis

Forecast P/E	23.51	No of Institutions
	(4/7/2005)	222
Market Cap	$3.2 Billion	Shares
Book Value	1.4 Billion	95,764,144
Price/Book	2.28	% Held
Price/Sales	4.54	88.66

Business Summary: Oil and Gas (MIC: 14.2 SIC: 381 NAIC: 13111)

Rowan Companies is a provider of international and domestic contract drilling and aviation services. As of Dec 31 2003, Co.'s contract drilling operations were conducted through its 23 self-elevating mobile offshore drilling platforms (jack-up rigs), one mobile offshore floating platform and 18 land drilling rigs. Other operations include LeTourneau, Inc., which operates a mini-steel mill, a manufacturing facility, and a drilling products group that designs and builds mobile offshore jack-up drilling rigs. Also, Era Aviation, Inc. provides charter and contract helicopter and fixed-wing aircraft services principally in Alaska, the coastal areas of Louisiana and Texas, and the western U.S.

Recent Developments: For the year ended Dec 31 2004, net loss was $1,273 thousand versus net loss of $7,774 thousand a year earlier. Revenues were $708,501 thousand, up 26.9% from $558,455 thousand the year before. Operating income was $56,677 thousand versus an income of $8,230 thousand in the prior year, an increase of 588.7%. Total direct expense was $533,275 thousand versus $444,768 thousand in the prior year, an increase of 19.9%. Total indirect expense was $118,549 thousand versus $105,457 thousand in the prior year, an increase of 12.4%.

Prospects: Results are being positively affected by improved results in Co.'s drilling business reflecting increased offshore rig utilization and higher average Gulf of Mexico day rates. Favorable drilling results are expected to continue in 2005 if oil and natural gas prices remain stable. Meanwhile, prospects for Co.'s manufacturing operations remain solid, reflecting high backlog levels at the end of 2004. Strong commodity prices will likely continue to generate demand for Co.'s front-end loaders. Separately, on Dec. 31 2004, Co. completed the sale of its wholly-owned subsidiary, Era Aviation, Inc., to SEACOR Holdings Inc. for approximately $118.1 million in cash.

Financial Data (US$ in Thousands)	12/31/2004	12/31/2003	12/31/2002	12/31/2001	12/31/2000	12/31/1999	12/31/1998	12/31/1997
Earnings Per Share	(0.01)	(0.08)	0.90	0.80	0.74	(0.12)	1.43	1.65
Cash Flow Per Share	1.11	0.51	1.26	2.99	1.12	0.46	2.89	2.39
Tang Book Value Per Share	13.12	12.08	12.09	11.84	11.17	8.69	8.77	7.53
Dividends Per Share	...	...	0.250	...	...	...	...	...
Dividend Payout %	...	...	27.78	...	...	...	...	...
Income Statement								
Total Revenue	708,501	679,088	617,258	731,064	645,959	460,562	706,350	695,252
EBITDA	152,743	89,660	222,727	193,394	...	43,899	234,237	228,220
Depn & Amortn	95,650	86,851	78,091	68,499	56,114	51,501	46,505	43,880
Income Before Taxes	42,785	(11,952)	132,819	120,207	...	(14,536)	193,701	173,288
Income Taxes	16,414	(4,178)	46,541	43,209	40,650	(4,870)	69,241	16,863
Net Income	(1,273)	(7,774)	86,278	76,998	70,213	(9,666)	124,460	146,659
Average Shares	107,133	93,820	95,392	95,811	94,637	83,176	87,289	89,223
Balance Sheet								
Current Assets	814,693	444,224	469,902	506,682	483,357	325,075	365,652	412,378
Total Assets	2,492,286	2,190,809	2,054,504	1,938,955	1,678,426	1,356,067	1,249,108	1,122,135
Current Liabilities	234,800	150,365	115,975	201,494	104,354	202,283	79,593	81,526
Long-Term Obligations	574,350	569,067	512,844	438,484	372,212	296,677	310,250	256,150
Total Liabilities	1,083,402	1,053,979	922,727	830,868	625,669	632,343	519,112	469,037
Stockholders' Equity	1,408,884	1,136,830	1,131,777	1,108,087	1,052,757	723,724	729,996	653,098
Shares Outstanding	107,408	94,110	93,606	93,567	94,234	83,302	83,246	86,704
Statistical Record								
Return on Assets %	N.M.	N.M.	4.32	4.26	4.62	N.M.	10.50	14.51
Return on Equity %	N.M.	N.M.	7.70	7.13	7.88	N.M.	18.00	25.52
EBITDA Margin %	21.56	13.20	36.08	26.45	...	9.53	33.16	32.83
Net Margin %	N.M.	N.M.	13.98	10.53	10.87	N.M.	17.62	21.09
Asset Turnover	0.30	0.32	0.31	0.40	0.42	0.35	0.60	0.69
Current Ratio	3.47	2.95	4.05	2.51	4.63	1.61	4.59	5.06
Debt to Equity	0.41	0.50	0.45	0.40	0.35	0.41	0.43	0.39
Price Range	27.05-20.62	26.38-17.93	26.84-16.11	33.42-11.75	33.63-19.44	21.69-8.56	31.44-9.19	43.69-17.63
P/E Ratio	...	...	29.82-17.90	41.78-14.69	45.44-26.27	...	21.98-6.42	26.48-10.68
Average Yield %	...	...	1.19	...	...	...	...	...

Address: 2800 Post Oak Blvd., Suite 5450, Houston, TX 77056-6127 **Telephone:** (713) 621-7800 **Fax:** (713) 960-7660	Web Site: www.rowancompanies.com **Officers:** D. F. McNease - Chmn., Pres., C.E.O. C. R. Palmer - Chmn. Emeritus	Auditors: Deloitte & Touche LLP **Investor Contact:** 713.9075575

RPM INTERNATIONAL INC

Exchange	Symbol	Price	52Wk Range	Yield	P/E	Div Acheiver
NYS	RPM	$18.28 (3/31/2005)	19.83-13.50	3.28	17.25	31 Years

*7 Year Price Score 107.42 *NYSE Composite Index=100   *12 Month Price Score 102.83

Interim Earnings (Per Share)

Qtr.	Aug	Nov	Feb	May
2001-02	0.36	0.24	0.03	0.34
2002-03	0.38	0.26	0.04	(0.38)
2003-04	0.41	0.30	0.05	0.46
2004-05	0.47	0.08	...	...

Interim Dividends (Per Share)

Amt	Decl	Ex	Rec	Pay
0.14Q	7/2/2004	7/8/2004	7/12/2004	7/30/2004
0.15Q	10/8/2004	10/14/2004	10/18/2004	10/29/2004
0.15Q	1/3/2005	1/12/2005	1/14/2005	1/31/2005
0.15Q	4/1/2005	4/13/2005	4/15/2005	4/29/2005

Indicated Div: $0.60 (Div. Reinv. Plan)

Valuation Analysis

Forecast P/E	12.43	No of Institutions
	(4/7/2005)	225
Market Cap	$2.1 Billion	Shares
Book Value	1.1 Billion	65,368,236
Price/Book	2.02	% Held
Price/Sales	0.88	55.78

TRADING VOLUME (thousand shares)

Business Summary: Chemicals (MIC: 11.1 SIC: 851 NAIC: 25510)

RPM International manufactures and markets specialty paints, protective coatings and roofing systems, sealants and adhesives, focusing on the maintenance and improvement needs of both the industrial and consumer markets. Co.'s family of products includes those marketed under brand names such as CARBOLINE, DAP, DAY-GLO, FLECTO, RUST-OLEUM, STONHARD, TREMCO and ZINSSER. As of May 31, 2004, Co. marketed its products in over 140 countries and territories and operated manufacturing facilities in 74 locations in the U.S., Argentina, Belgium, Brazil, Canada, China, Colombia, Germany, Italy, Mexico, New Zealand, The Netherlands, Poland, South Africa, the United Arab Emirates and the United Kingdom.

Recent Developments: For the three months ended Nov 30 2004, net income decreased 74.1% to $9,112 thousand from net income of $35,223 thousand in the year-earlier quarter. Results for 2004 included an asbestos charge of $47,000 thousand. Revenues were $623,469 thousand, up 7.2% from $581,541 thousand the year before. Gross profit amounted to $270,688 thousand, or 43.4% of net sales, compared with $323,966 thousand, or 44.3% of net sales, the previous year. Total indirect expense was $249,034 thousand versus $196,255 thousand in the prior-year quarter, an increase of 26.9%.

Prospects: Results are benefiting from strong sales growth in the industrial segment, partially offset by slower growth in the consumer segment. Meanwhile, Co. will continue to implement price increases in an effort to offset higher raw material costs, which are hampering gross margins, particularly in the consumer segment. Separately, results should benefit from Co.'s strategy of complementing its organic growth with strategic acquisitions both in North America and in Europe. Looking ahead, Co. continues to anticipate high single-digit growth in revenues, and earnings growth of between 10.0% and 12.0% during fiscal 2005.

Financial Data

(US$ in Thousands)	6 Mos	3 Mos	05/31/2004	05/31/2003	05/31/2002	05/31/2001	05/31/2000	05/31/1999
Earnings Per Share	1.06	1.28	1.22	0.30	0.97	0.62	0.38	0.86
Cash Flow Per Share	1.60	1.44	1.32	1.39	1.83	0.73	0.95	1.08
Tang Book Value Per Share	0.96	0.71	0.38	N.M.	0.01	N.M.	N.M.	0.77
Dividends Per Share	0.570	0.560	0.550	0.515	0.500	0.498	0.485	0.465
Dividend Payout %	53.80	43.86	45.08	171.67	51.55	80.24	127.63	54.01
Income Statement								
Total Revenue	1,284,982	661,513	2,341,572	2,083,489	1,986,126	2,007,762	1,954,131	1,712,154
EBITDA	146,835	108,720	307,201	131,205	249,458	246,021	201,280	253,310
Depn & Amortn	32,736	16,275	60,640	56,640	54,870	79,331	77,726	60,932
Income Before Taxes	97,214	84,475	217,616	47,853	154,124	101,487	71,761	159,597
Income Taxes	33,616	29,989	75,730	12,526	52,570	38,526	30,769	65,051
Net Income	63,598	54,486	141,886	35,327	101,554	62,961	40,992	94,546
Average Shares	118,284	117,078	116,710	115,986	105,131	102,212	107,384	111,376
Balance Sheet								
Current Assets	1,157,348	1,011,211	994,617	928,094	801,314	819,420	785,092	705,419
Total Assets	2,539,000	2,369,008	2,353,119	2,247,211	2,036,403	2,078,490	2,099,203	1,737,236
Current Liabilities	445,566	689,713	477,493	427,650	364,714	375,768	376,202	302,549
Long-Term Obligations	837,926	490,284	718,929	724,846	707,921	955,399	959,330	582,109
Total Liabilities	1,480,799	1,350,717	1,377,827	1,370,203	1,178,297	1,438,780	1,453,479	994,360
Stockholders' Equity	1,058,201	1,018,291	975,292	877,008	858,106	639,710	645,724	742,876
Shares Outstanding	117,146	116,271	116,122	115,496	114,696	102,211	103,134	109,443
Statistical Record								
Return on Assets %	5.10	6.44	6.15	1.65	4.94	3.01	2.13	5.53
Return on Equity %	12.23	15.45	15.28	4.07	13.56	9.80	5.89	14.44
EBITDA Margin %	11.43	16.44	13.12	6.30	12.56	12.25	10.30	14.79
Net Margin %	4.95	8.24	6.06	1.70	5.11	3.14	2.10	5.52
Asset Turnover	1.02	1.05	1.02	0.97	0.97	0.96	1.02	1.00
Current Ratio	2.60	1.47	2.08	2.17	2.20	2.18	2.09	2.33
Debt to Equity	0.79	0.48	0.74	0.83	0.82	1.49	1.49	0.78
Price Range	18.83-13.50	17.10-13.06	17.10-12.55	16.06-9.20	17.61-8.05	10.63-7.75	15.00-9.56	17.50-12.81
P/E Ratio	17.76-12.74	13.36-10.20	14.02-10.29	53.53-30.67	18.15-8.30	17.14-12.50	39.47-25.16	20.35-14.90
Average Yield %	3.57	3.70	3.73	3.88	3.84	5.37	4.13	3.11

Address: P.O. Box 777, 2628 Pearl Road, Medina, OH 44258	**Web Site:** www.rpminc.com	**Auditors:** Ciulla, Smith & Dale, LLP
Telephone: (330) 273-5090	**Officers:** Thomas C. Sullivan - Chmn. Frank C. Sullivan - Pres., C.E.O.	**Investor Contact:** 330-273-8820
Fax: (330) 225-8743		**Transfer Agents:** National City Bank, Cleveland, OH

RUBY TUESDAY, INC.

Exchange	Symbol	Price	52Wk Range	Yield	P/E
NYS	RI	$24.29 (3/31/2005)	33.00-23.35	0.19	15.09

*7 Year Price Score 132.05 ***NYSE Composite Index=100** ***12 Month Price Score 85.12**

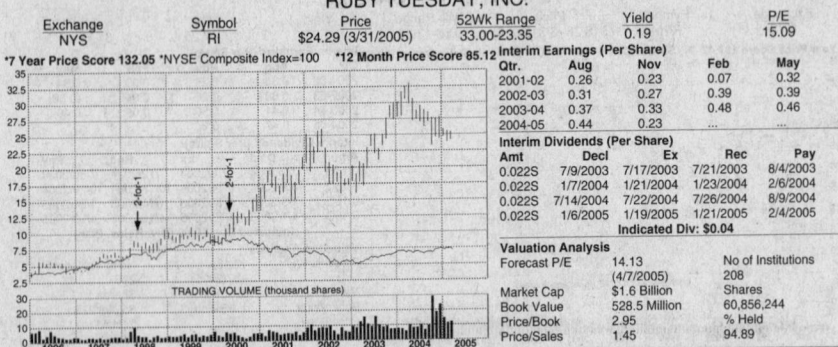

Interim Earnings (Per Share)

Qtr.	Aug	Nov	Feb	May
2001-02	0.26	0.23	0.07	0.32
2002-03	0.31	0.27	0.39	0.39
2003-04	0.37	0.33	0.48	0.46
2004-05	0.44	0.23	...	...

Interim Dividends (Per Share)

Amt	Decl	Ex	Rec	Pay
0.022S	7/9/2003	7/17/2003	7/21/2003	8/4/2003
0.022S	1/7/2004	1/21/2004	1/23/2004	2/6/2004
0.022S	7/14/2004	7/22/2004	7/26/2004	8/9/2004
0.022S	1/6/2005	1/19/2005	1/21/2005	2/4/2005

Indicated Div: $0.04

Valuation Analysis

Forecast P/E	14.13	No of Institutions	
	(4/7/2005)	208	
Market Cap	$1.6 Billion	Shares	
Book Value	528.5 Million	60,856,244	
Price/Book	2.95	% Held	
Price/Sales	1.45	94.89	

Business Summary: Hospitality & Tourism (MIC: 5.1 SIC: 812 NAIC: 22110)

Ruby Tuesday owned and operated 484 full-service, casual restaurants under the name Ruby Tuesday®, as of June 1 2004. The restaurants are located primarily in the southeast, northeast, mid-Atlantic and midwest regions of the United States. Co. also has locations in the Asian Pacific Region, India, Kuwait, Puerto Rico, Iceland, Canada, Mexico, Eastern Europe, and Central and South America. Ruby Tuesday® restaurants offer a variety of entrees and sandwiches in the price range of $6.49 to $16.99. In addition, Co. franchised 216 domestic and 36 international Ruby Tuesday® restaurants as of June 1 2004.

Recent Developments: For the quarter ended Nov 30 2004, net income decreased 31.4% to $15,115 thousand from net income of $22,042 thousand in the year-earlier quarter. Revenues were $258,218 thousand, up 5.4% from $245,004 thousand the year before. Total indirect expense was $167,369 thousand versus $147,609 thousand in the prior-year quarter, an increase of 13.4%.

Prospects: Co. is focused on improving sales as it is challenged with overlapping its previous ValPak coupon strategy over the next couple of quarters. Based on Co.'s plans to invest an additional $3.0 million to $4.0 million in advertising during fiscal 2005 and taking into consideration the estimated $0.07 impact on earnings in fiscal 2005 resulting from the one-time cumulative entry to adjust its accounting for leases and subleases, Co. expects fiscal 2005 diluted earnings per share (EPS) of approximately $1.53 with third quarter diluted EPS in the $0.38 to $0.41 range and fourth quarter diluted EPS in the $0.42 to $0.47 range.

Financial Data
(US$ in Thousands)

	6 Mos	3 Mos	06/01/2004	06/03/2003	06/04/2002	06/05/2001	06/04/2000	06/06/1999
Earnings Per Share	1.61	1.71	1.64	1.36	0.88	0.91	0.57	0.54
Cash Flow Per Share	2.90	3.01	3.12	2.31	2.29	1.21	1.64	1.33
Tang Book Value Per Share	8.05	8.09	7.92	6.31	5.09	4.37	3.59	3.17
Dividends Per Share	0.045	0.045	0.045	0.045	0.045	0.045	0.045	0.045
Dividend Payout %	2.79	2.63	2.74	3.31	5.11	4.95	7.89	8.33
Income Statement								
Total Revenue	525,741	267,523	1,041,359	913,784	833,181	789,634	797,495	722,338
EBITDA	99,034	60,239	229,376	184,112	116,229	123,695	106,749	100,187
Depn & Amortn	30,711	14,671	54,834	46,100	33,924	34,957	42,563	40,117
Income Before Taxes	68,323	45,568	170,816	135,710	88,146	92,274	62,771	57,208
Income Taxes	23,954	16,314	60,807	47,226	29,870	33,035	26,231	20,694
Net Income	44,369	29,254	110,009	88,484	58,218	59,239	36,540	36,514
Average Shares	65,636	66,526	67,076	65,093	65,912	65,088	64,576	67,528
Balance Sheet								
Current Assets	54,049	47,153	59,679	50,463	88,876	64,420	94,455	52,210
Total Assets	991,662	924,072	918,533	805,067	520,327	445,667	439,212	430,815
Current Liabilities	82,323	92,983	90,542	80,554	93,283	88,433	151,796	84,158
Long-Term Obligations	239,264	164,883	168,087	207,064	7,626	15,212	636	76,767
Total Liabilities	463,164	391,665	391,749	390,539	185,921	161,396	209,388	209,014
Stockholders' Equity	528,498	532,407	526,784	414,528	334,406	284,271	229,824	221,801
Shares Outstanding	64,106	64,837	65,549	64,404	64,188	63,211	61,719	64,034
Statistical Record								
Return on Assets %	11.55	12.98	12.80	13.39	12.09	13.35	8.42	8.69
Return on Equity %	21.43	23.51	23.44	23.69	18.87	22.98	16.23	16.83
EBITDA Margin %	18.84	22.52	22.03	20.15	13.95	15.66	13.39	13.87
Net Margin %	8.44	10.94	10.56	9.68	6.99	7.50	4.58	5.05
Asset Turnover	1.15	1.20	1.21	1.38	1.73	1.78	1.84	1.72
Current Ratio	0.66	0.51	0.66	0.63	0.95	0.73	0.62	0.62
Debt to Equity	0.45	0.31	0.32	0.50	0.02	0.05	N.M.	0.35
Price Range	33.00-23.35	33.00-23.36	33.00-21.10	24.21-15.99	25.96-15.06	19.80-10.75	11.50-8.09	10.63-6.97
P/E Ratio	20.50-14.50	19.30-13.66	20.12-12.87	17.80-11.76	29.50-17.11	21.76-11.81	20.18-14.20	19.68-12.91
Average Yield %	0.16	0.16	0.17	0.24	0.22	0.30	0.47	0.51

Address: 150 West Church Avenue, Maryville, TN 37801
Telephone: (865) 379-5700
Fax: (865) 379-6817

Web Site: www.rubytuesday.com
Officers: Samuel E. Beall III - Chmn., Pres., C.E.O. R. D. McClenagan - Pres.

Auditors: KPMG LLP

RUDDICK CORP.

Exchange	Symbol	Price	52Wk Range	Yield	P/E
NYS	RDK	$23.15 (3/31/2005)	24.20-18.76	1.90	16.42

*7 Year Price Score 108.98 ***NYSE Composite Index=100** ***12 Month Price Score 102.09**

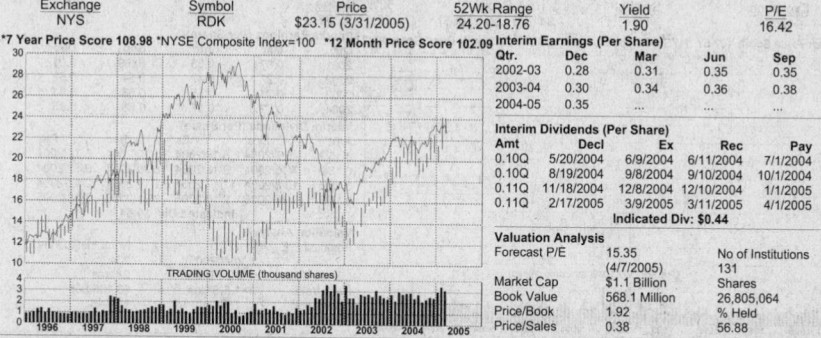

Interim Earnings (Per Share)

Qtr.	Dec	Mar	Jun	Sep
2002-03	0.28	0.31	0.35	0.35
2003-04	0.30	0.34	0.36	0.38
2004-05	0.35	...	...	...

Interim Dividends (Per Share)

Amt	Decl	Ex	Rec	Pay
0.10Q	5/20/2004	6/9/2004	6/11/2004	7/1/2004
0.10Q	8/19/2004	9/8/2004	9/10/2004	10/1/2004
0.11Q	11/18/2004	12/8/2004	12/10/2004	1/1/2005
0.11Q	2/17/2005	3/9/2005	3/11/2005	4/1/2005

Indicated Div: $0.44

Valuation Analysis

Forecast P/E	15.35	No of Institutions
	(4/7/2005)	131
Market Cap	$1.1 Billion	Shares
Book Value	568.1 Million	26,805,064
Price/Book	1.92	% Held
Price/Sales	0.38	56.88

Business Summary: Retail - Food & Beverage (MIC: 5.3 SIC: 411 NAIC: 45110)

Ruddick is a holding company that operates through two wholly-owned subsidiaries, Harris Teeter, Inc. ("Harris Teeter") and American & Efird, Inc. ("A&E"). As of Oct 3 2004, Harris Teeter operated a regional chain of 138 supermarkets in six southeastern states, including North Carolina, South Carolina, Virginia, Georgia, Tennessee, and Florida. A&E is a manufacturer and distributor of sewing thread, produced from natural and synthetic fibers, for worldwide industrial and consumer markets. A&E's customers include manufacturers of apparel, automotive materials, home furnishings, medical supplies, and footwear.

Recent Developments: For the quarter ended Jan 2 2005, net income increased 20.7% to $16,629 thousand from net income of $13,782 thousand in the year-earlier quarter. Revenues were $726,892 thousand, up 5.0% from $692,365 thousand the year before. Operating income was $29,402 thousand versus an income of $25,104 thousand in the prior-year quarter, an increase of 17.1%. Total direct expense was $517,711 thousand versus $496,333 thousand in the prior-year quarter, an increase of 4.3%. Total indirect expense was $179,779 thousand versus $170,928 thousand in the prior-year quarter, an increase of 5.2%.

Prospects: On Mar 2 2005, Co. announced that its sewing thread subsidiary, American & Efird, Inc., has signed an agreement to purchase certain assets of the thread and specialty yarn business of Ludlow Textiles Company, Inc. Meanwhile, results at Harris Teeter are benefiting from comparable-store sales growth and additional sales from recently opened stores. Co. anticipates opening ten new stores and remodeling 16 existing locations, including five store remodels during the first quarter. Co. remains cautious in its expectations for fiscal 2005 due to the intense competition in the retail grocery segment and the continued challenging business conditions in the textile and apparel segment.

Financial Data

(US$ in Thousands)	3 Mos	10/03/2004	09/28/2003	09/29/2002	09/30/2001	10/01/2000	10/03/1999	09/27/1998
Earnings Per Share	1.41	1.38	1.29	1.12	(0.02)	1.10	1.08	1.00
Cash Flow Per Share	2.98	2.87	3.25	3.10	3.74	2.21	1.83	2.65
Tang Book Value Per Share	11.76	11.46	10.44	9.85	9.61	10.23	9.55	8.82
Dividends Per Share	0.410	0.400	0.360	0.360	0.360	0.360	0.330	0.320
Dividend Payout %	29.13	28.99	27.91	32.14	...	32.73	30.56	32.00
Income Statement								
Total Revenue	726,892	2,868,597	2,724,739	2,644,198	2,743,290	2,682,833	2,624,774	2,487,370
EBITDA	48,273	189,246	180,297	168,588	125,230	176,896	166,699	152,851
Depn & Amortn	18,963	77,415	77,237	75,788	80,271	77,016	70,624	66,184
Income Before Taxes	26,574	101,164	92,092	81,592	31,013	84,393	81,389	70,694
Income Taxes	9,945	36,505	32,210	29,609	31,740	33,391	30,675	23,922
Net Income	16,629	64,659	59,882	51,983	(727)	51,002	50,714	46,772
Average Shares	47,369	46,851	46,463	46,577	46,276	46,349	46,746	46,964
Balance Sheet								
Current Assets	453,077	445,886	440,869	425,714	341,251	363,244	358,874	332,753
Total Assets	1,123,406	1,111,992	1,067,203	1,038,947	939,988	1,021,018	970,114	931,618
Current Liabilities	247,104	257,915	279,248	259,596	228,979	230,361	238,868	245,420
Long-Term Obligations	157,389	157,639	157,499	185,165	156,437	224,996	198,532	191,360
Total Liabilities	555,271	562,282	571,938	581,259	494,635	548,013	526,431	520,893
Stockholders' Equity	568,135	549,710	495,265	457,688	445,353	473,005	443,683	410,725
Shares Outstanding	47,093	46,730	46,223	46,454	46,319	46,220	46,451	46,554
Statistical Record								
Return on Assets %	6.04	5.84	5.70	5.27	N.M.	5.14	5.25	5.16
Return on Equity %	12.37	12.18	12.60	11.54	N.M.	11.16	11.68	11.86
EBITDA Margin %	6.64	6.60	6.62	6.38	4.56	6.59	6.35	6.15
Net Margin %	2.29	2.25	2.20	1.97	N.M.	1.90	1.93	1.88
Asset Turnover	2.60	2.59	2.59	2.68	2.81	2.70	2.72	2.75
Current Ratio	1.83	1.73	1.58	1.64	1.49	1.58	1.50	1.36
Debt to Equity	0.28	0.29	0.32	0.40	0.35	0.48	0.45	0.47
Price Range	22.52-17.84	22.45-15.54	17.15-11.98	17.81-14.90	16.95-10.44	18.06-10.63	23.00-15.81	20.88-15.13
P/E Ratio	15.97-12.65	16.27-11.26	13.29-9.29	15.90-13.30	...	16.42-9.66	21.30-14.64	20.88-15.13
Average Yield %	2.02	2.09	2.47	2.21	2.61	2.66	1.79	1.81

Address: 301 S. Tryon St., Suite 1800, Charlotte, NC 28202 **Telephone:** (704) 372-5404 **Fax:** (704) 372-6409	**Web Site:** www.ruddickcorp.com **Officers:** Alan T. Dickson - Chmn. Thomas W. Dickson - Pres., C.E.O.	**Auditors:** KPMG LLP **Investor Contact:** 704-372-5404

RYDER SYSTEM, INC.

Exchange	Symbol	Price	52Wk Range	Yield	P/E
NYS	R	$41.70 (3/31/2005)	55.11-35.34	1.53	12.71

*7 Year Price Score 137.57 *NYSE Composite Index=100 *12 Month Price Score 92.27

Interim Earnings (Per Share)

Qtr.	Mar	Jun	Sep	Dec
2001	0.07	0.33	(0.09)	0.01
2002	0.27	0.47	0.54	0.52
2003	0.31	0.55	0.58	0.61
2004	0.53	0.97	0.83	0.95

Interim Dividends (Per Share)

Amt	Decl	Ex	Rec	Pay
0.15Q	5/7/2004	5/18/2004	5/20/2004	6/18/2004
0.15Q	7/15/2004	8/18/2004	8/20/2004	9/17/2004
0.15Q	10/8/2004	11/17/2004	11/19/2004	12/17/2004
0.16Q	2/10/2005	2/16/2005	2/21/2005	3/18/2005
		Indicated Div: $0.64		

Valuation Analysis

Forecast P/E	12.70	No of Institutions
	(4/7/2005)	234
Market Cap	$2.7 Billion	Shares
Book Value	1.5 Billion	63,136,508
Price/Book	1.78	% Held
Price/Sales	0.52	98.51

Business Summary: Road Transport (MIC: 15.2 SIC: 789 NAIC: 88999)

Ryder System is engaged in the transportation and supply chain management. Co.'s business is divided into three business segments. Fleet Management Solutions provides leasing, commercial rental and programmed maintenance of commercial trucks, tractors and trailers to customers in the U.S., Canada and the U.K. Supply Chain Solutions provides supply chain consulting and lead logistics management solutions throughout North America and in Latin America, Europe and Asia. Dedicated Contract Carriage provides vehicles and drivers as part of a dedicated transportation solution in North America. As of Dec 31 2003, Co. and its subsidiaries held a fleet of 160,200 vehicles.

Recent Developments: For the year ended Dec 31 2004, net income increased 64.0% to $215,609 thousand from net income of $131,436 thousand a year earlier. Revenues were $5,150,278 thousand, up 7.2% from $4,802,294 thousand the year before. Total direct expense was $2,305,703 thousand versus $2,039,156 thousand in the prior year, an increase of 13.1%. Total indirect expense was $2,422,093 thousand versus $2,466,652 thousand in the prior year, a decrease of 1.8%.

Prospects: Co. is reaffirming its first quarter earnings per share forecast of $0.55 to $0.58, and its full-year 2005 forecast range of $3.20 to $3.30 per share. As Co.'s organization works to grow all business segments in 2005, it remains committed to improving its cost of delivering products and services, building on its financial strength, further leveraging its operating model, and aggressively competing for profitable business. Building on the financial and operational improvements Co. has made through the past few years, its growth plan is now about improved, consistent execution of the basic sales, business retention and expansion activities.

Financial Data

(US$ in Thousands)	12/31/2004	12/31/2003	12/31/2002	12/31/2001	12/31/2000	12/31/1999	12/31/1998	12/31/1997
Earnings Per Share	3.28	2.06	1.50	0.31	1.49	6.11	2.16	2.25
Cash Flow Per Share	13.70	12.75	10.28	5.14	17.00	3.94	13.15	8.01
Tang Book Value Per Share	20.65	18.09	17.75	20.24	20.86	20.29	15.37	14.39
Dividends Per Share	0.600	0.600	0.600	0.600	0.600	0.600	0.600	0.600
Dividend Payout %	18.29	29.13	40.00	193.55	40.27	9.82	27.78	26.67
Income Statement								
Total Revenue	5,150,278	4,802,294	4,776,265	5,006,123	5,336,792	4,952,204	5,188,724	4,893,905
EBITDA	1,038,150	837,055	728,374	576,191	721,677	684,259	861,237	856,231
Depn & Amortn	707,028	624,580	552,491	545,485	580,356	566,765	604,281	592,279
Income Before Taxes	331,122	212,475	175,883	30,706	141,321	117,494	256,956	263,952
Income Taxes	115,513	76,916	63,318	12,028	52,289	44,577	97,885	103,714
Net Income	215,609	131,436	93,666	18,678	89,032	419,678	159,071	175,685
Average Shares	65,671	63,871	62,587	60,665	59,759	68,732	73,645	78,192
Balance Sheet								
Current Assets	1,227,669	1,107,100	1,024,171	982,493	928,276	1,209,391	1,109,699	1,091,985
Total Assets	5,637,933	5,278,603	4,766,982	4,923,611	5,474,923	5,770,450	5,708,601	5,509,060
Current Liabilities	1,454,856	1,074,077	862,076	1,013,926	1,302,304	1,449,512	1,362,664	1,089,509
Long-Term Obligations	1,393,666	1,449,489	1,389,099	1,391,597	1,604,242	1,819,136	2,099,697	2,267,554
Total Liabilities	4,127,745	3,934,218	3,658,767	3,692,942	4,222,215	4,565,545	4,612,987	4,448,352
Stockholders' Equity	1,510,188	1,344,385	1,108,215	1,230,669	1,252,708	1,204,905	1,095,614	1,060,708
Shares Outstanding	64,310	64,487	62,440	60,809	60,044	59,395	71,280	73,692
Statistical Record								
Return on Assets %	3.94	2.62	1.93	0.36	1.58	7.31	2.84	3.15
Return on Equity %	15.06	10.72	8.01	1.50	7.23	36.49	14.75	16.22
EBITDA Margin %	20.16	17.43	15.25	11.51	13.52	13.82	16.60	17.50
Net Margin %	4.19	2.74	1.96	0.37	1.67	8.47	3.07	3.59
Asset Turnover	0.94	0.96	0.99	0.96	0.95	0.86	0.93	0.88
Current Ratio	0.84	1.03	1.19	0.97	0.71	0.83	0.81	1.00
Debt to Equity	0.92	1.08	1.25	1.13	1.28	1.51	1.92	2.14
Price Range	55.11-33.67	34.30-20.14	30.84-21.29	23.19-16.19	25.13-15.31	28.38-19.06	40.56-20.00	37.06-27.25
P/E Ratio	16.80-10.27	16.65-9.78	20.56-14.19	74.81-52.22	16.86-10.28	4.64-3.12	18.78-9.26	16.47-12.11
Average Yield %	1.42	2.25	2.31	3.00	3.02	2.46	1.96	1.80

Address: 3600 N.W. 82nd Avenue,	Web Site: www.ryder.com	Auditors: KPMG LLP
Miami, FL 33166	Officers: Gregory T. Swieton - Chmn., Pres., C.E.O.	Investor Contact: 305-500-4210
Telephone: (305) 500-3726	Tracy A. Leinbach - Exec. V.P., C.F.O.	
Fax: (305) 500-4129		

RYLAND GROUP, INC.

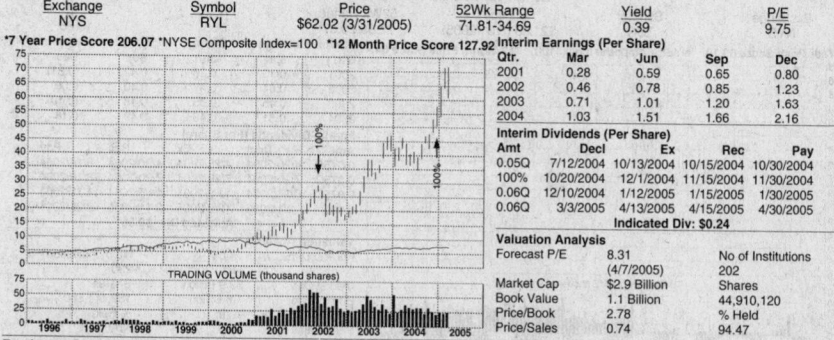

Exchange	Symbol	Price	52Wk Range	Yield	P/E
NYS	RYL	$62.02 (3/31/2005)	71.81-34.69	0.39	9.75

*7 Year Price Score 206.07 *NYSE Composite Index=100 ***12 Month Price Score 127.92**

Interim Earnings (Per Share)

Qtr.	Mar	Jun	Sep	Dec
2001	0.28	0.59	0.65	0.80
2002	0.46	0.78	0.85	1.23
2003	0.71	1.01	1.20	1.63
2004	1.03	1.51	1.66	2.16

Interim Dividends (Per Share)

Amt	Decl	Ex	Rec	Pay
0.05Q	7/12/2004	10/13/2004	10/15/2004	10/30/2004
100%	10/20/2004	12/1/2004	11/15/2004	11/30/2004
0.06Q	12/10/2004	1/12/2005	1/15/2005	1/30/2005
0.06Q	3/3/2005	4/13/2005	4/15/2005	4/30/2005

Indicated Div: $0.24

Valuation Analysis

Forecast P/E	8.31	No of Institutions
	(4/7/2005)	202
Market Cap	$2.9 Billion	Shares
Book Value	1.1 Billion	44,910,120
Price/Book	2.78	% Held
Price/Sales	0.74	94.47

Business Summary: Building & General Construction (MIC: 3.2 SIC: 531 NAIC: 36115)

Ryland Group is a national homebuilder and mortgage-related financial services firm. Co. builds homes in 27 markets across the country. As of Dec 31 2004, Co.'s average closing price was $251,000. Co.'s homebuilding segment specializes in the sale and construction of single-family attached and detached housing. The financial services segment, whose business is conducted through Co. and its subsidiaries, complements Co.'s homebuilding activities by providing various mortgage-related products and services for retail customers, including loan origination, title and escrow services, and by conducting investment activities.

Recent Developments: For the year ended Dec 31 2004, net income increased 32.6% to $320,545 thousand from net income of $241,692 thousand a year earlier. Revenues were $3,951,821 thousand, up 14.7% from $3,444,129 thousand the year before. Total direct expense was $2,964,087 thousand versus $2,615,975 thousand in the prior year, an increase of 13.3%. Total indirect expense was $438,470 thousand versus $389,903 thousand in the prior year, an increase of 12.5%.

Prospects: Co. is benefiting from strong growth in its average closing price. In addition, Co. is experiencing solid growth in its backlog, strong house closings, and growth in new orders. Co.'s backlog at Dec 31 2004 was approximately $2.10 billion, up 43.6% from the previous year. Further, Co.'s unit backlog at year end of 2004 was 7,620 contracts compared with 5,841 contracts, a rise of 30.5%. Also, Co. is being boosted by strong margin growth, which is due to sales prices rising at a greater rate than costs and an increase in the percentage of closings from higher-margin markets. Co. anticipates that diluted earnings per share will exceed $7.25 for the fiscal year ending Dec 31 2005.

Financial Data
(US$ in Thousands)

	12/31/2004	12/31/2003	12/31/2002	12/31/2001	12/31/2000	12/31/1999	12/31/1998	12/31/1997
Earnings Per Share	6.36	4.55	3.32	2.31	1.48	1.08	0.65	0.33
Cash Flow Per Share	(1.64)	2.87	1.65	3.25	2.11	1.01	2.39	1.44
Tang Book Value Per Share	21.94	16.61	13.10	10.30	8.18	6.58	5.39	4.77
Dividends Per Share	0.200	0.040	0.040	0.040	0.040	0.040	0.040	0.095
Dividend Payout %	3.14	0.88	1.20	1.73	2.70	3.72	6.20	28.79
Income Statement								
Total Revenue	3,951,821	3,444,129	2,877,213	2,741,784	2,331,645	2,009,266	1,765,488	1,649,806
EBITDA	586,556	432,653	342,010	262,648	163,329	137,346	100,744	67,866
Depn & Amortn	38,519	36,436	32,670	37,068	28,489	28,010	25,586	31,396
Income Before Taxes	521,212	396,217	309,340	225,580	134,840	109,336	75,158	36,470
Income Taxes	200,667	154,525	123,736	89,104	52,588	42,641	31,566	14,588
Net Income	320,545	241,692	185,604	132,093	82,252	66,695	40,266	21,882
Average Shares	50,378	53,044	55,918	57,022	55,573	62,021	62,413	61,620
Balance Sheet								
Current Assets	2,112,521	1,713,356	1,369,457	1,197,699	1,030,606	892,607	691,546	590,962
Total Assets	2,424,970	2,007,590	1,657,751	1,510,869	1,361,341	1,248,323	1,215,398	1,283,409
Current Liabilities	701,419	415,761	367,031	346,613	360,112	372,802	412,901	475,340
Long-Term Obligations	558,942	540,500	490,500	490,500	471,250	415,339	396,132	447,086
Total Liabilities	1,260,361	1,126,397	977,672	948,007	907,712	861,786	869,115	978,286
Stockholders' Equity	1,056,834	824,542	680,079	562,862	453,629	386,537	346,283	305,123
Shares Outstanding	47,348	48,552	50,520	52,867	52,995	55,403	59,007	58,087
Statistical Record								
Return on Assets %	14.42	13.19	11.72	9.20	6.29	5.41	3.22	1.67
Return on Equity %	33.98	32.13	29.87	25.99	19.53	18.20	12.36	7.11
EBITDA Margin %	14.84	12.56	11.89	9.58	7.00	6.84	5.71	4.11
Net Margin %	8.11	7.02	6.45	4.82	3.53	3.32	2.28	1.33
Asset Turnover	1.78	1.88	1.82	1.91	1.78	1.63	1.41	1.26
Current Ratio	3.01	4.12	3.73	3.46	2.86	2.39	1.67	1.24
Debt to Equity	0.53	0.66	0.72	0.87	1.04	1.07	1.14	1.47
Price Range	57.63-34.69	47.07-16.68	28.98-15.81	18.60-8.95	10.39-3.81	7.61-4.98	7.45-4.88	6.22-2.84
P/E Ratio	9.06-5.45	10.35-3.66	8.73-4.76	8.05-3.87	7.02-2.58	7.05-4.62	11.47-7.50	18.84-8.62
Average Yield %	0.47	0.12	0.19	0.32	0.65	0.64	0.65	2.45

Address: 24025 Park Sorrento, Suite 400, Calabasas, CA 91302	Web Site: www.ryland.com	Auditors: ERNST & YOUNG LLP
Telephone: (818) 223-7500	Officers: R. Chad Dreier - Chmn., Pres., C.E.O.	
Fax: (818) 223-7667	Kipling W. Scott - Exec. V.P.	

SABRE HOLDINGS CORP.

Exchange	Symbol	Price	52Wk Range	Yield	P/E
NYS	TSG	$21.88 (3/31/2005)	27.99-20.07	1.65	15.86

*7 Year Price Score 59.10   *NYSE Composite Index=100   *12 Month Price Score 84.47

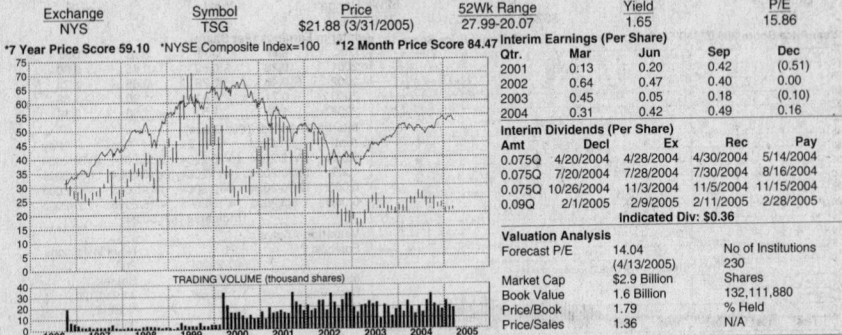

Interim Earnings (Per Share)

Qtr.	Mar	Jun	Sep	Dec
2001	0.13	0.20	0.42	(0.51)
2002	0.64	0.47	0.40	0.00
2003	0.45	0.05	0.18	(0.10)
2004	0.31	0.42	0.49	0.16

Interim Dividends (Per Share)

Amt	Decl	Ex	Rec	Pay
0.075Q	4/20/2004	4/28/2004	4/30/2004	5/14/2004
0.075Q	7/20/2004	7/28/2004	7/30/2004	8/16/2004
0.075Q	10/26/2004	11/3/2004	11/5/2004	11/15/2004
0.09Q	2/1/2005	2/9/2005	2/11/2005	2/28/2005

Indicated Div: $0.36

Valuation Analysis

Forecast P/E	14.04	No of Institutions
	(4/13/2005)	230
Market Cap	$2.9 Billion	Shares
Book Value	1.6 Billion	132,111,880
Price/Book	1.79	% Held
Price/Sales	1.36	N/A

Business Summary: IT & Technology (MIC: 10.2 SIC: 374 NAIC: 18210)

SABRE Holdings offers travel commerce, markets travel offerings and provides distribution and technology applications for the travel industry. Through Co.'s Sabre® global distribution system, subscribers can access information and book reservations for airline trips, hotel stays, car rentals, cruises and tour packages. Sabre Travel Network markets and distributes travel-related products and services through the travel agency channel. Co. engages in consumer and business-direct travel marketing and distribution through its Travelocity™ business. Lastly, Sabre Airline Solutions™ provides technology and services, including development and consulting, to airlines and other travel providers.

Recent Developments: For the year ended Dec 31 2004, net income increased 128.6% to $190,419 thousand from net income of $83,301 thousand a year earlier. Revenues were $2,130,971 thousand, up 4.2% from $2,045,163 thousand the year before. Operating income was $258,730 thousand versus an income of $166,230 thousand in the prior year, an increase of 55.6%. Total direct expense was $1,240,180 thousand versus $1,269,129 thousand in the prior year, a decrease of 2.3%. Total indirect expense was $632,061 thousand versus $609,804 thousand in the prior year, an increase of 3.6%.

Prospects: Co. is experiencing significant earnings growth, which is being driven by the profitability turnaround at Travelocity, ongoing cost reductions and strong travel demand. Going forward, Co. plans to drive operational discipline in support of its strategy to optimize its core distribution business and extend into the higher-margin retail business. As a result of planned investments for 2005, Co. anticipates entering 2006 well-positioned for significant growth. For full-year 2005, Co. expects accelerated revenue growth approaching 10.0% and earnings ranging from $1.41 to $1.51 per share.

Financial Data

(US$ in Thousands)	12/31/2004	12/31/2003	12/31/2002	12/31/2001	12/31/2000	12/31/1999	12/31/1998	12/31/1997
Earnings Per Share	1.38	0.58	1.50	0.24	1.11	2.54	1.78	1.53
Cash Flow Per Share	2.66	1.84	2.13	3.10	2.40	3.82	3.47	2.89
Tang Book Value Per Share	4.80	5.60	5.51	2.84	N.M.	9.72	7.35	5.79
Dividends Per Share	0.300	0.210	...	...	5.203	...	...	...
Dividend Payout %	21.74	36.21	...	...	468.74	...	...	...
Income Statement								
Total Revenue	2,130,971	2,045,163	2,056,466	2,103,090	2,617,375	2,434,619	2,306,387	1,783,547
EBITDA	389,769	260,977	451,515	439,516	628,675	768,267	612,913	500,536
Depn & Amortn	121,000	126,000	117,000	389,000	346,000	258,000	248,000	185,175
Income Before Taxes	257,061	127,377	339,068	34,010	267,237	527,945	371,454	323,649
Income Taxes	66,642	44,076	124,924	80,963	123,185	196,038	139,513	123,796
Net Income	190,419	83,301	214,144	31,227	144,052	331,907	231,941	199,853
Average Shares	137,931	143,407	142,559	132,317	129,841	130,655	130,521	130,988
Balance Sheet								
Current Assets	1,279,960	1,368,311	1,311,643	1,092,238	692,968	976,424	944,404	874,162
Total Assets	3,017,977	2,956,153	2,756,531	2,376,017	2,650,354	1,951,211	1,926,817	1,523,958
Current Liabilities	608,292	503,395	499,914	564,456	1,266,388	525,113	400,810	316,520
Long-Term Obligations	600,423	588,125	435,765	400,375	149,000	...	317,873	317,873
Total Liabilities	1,391,496	1,276,045	1,114,953	1,334,241	1,859,337	689,166	973,074	766,670
Stockholders' Equity	1,626,481	1,680,108	1,641,578	1,041,776	791,017	1,262,045	953,743	757,288
Shares Outstanding	132,942	141,330	142,684	133,143	130,007	129,796	129,813	130,854
Statistical Record								
Return on Assets %	6.36	2.92	8.34	1.24	6.24	17.12	13.44	14.22
Return on Equity %	11.49	5.02	15.96	3.41	13.99	29.96	27.11	30.12
EBITDA Margin %	18.29	12.76	21.96	20.90	24.02	31.56	26.57	28.06
Net Margin %	8.94	4.07	10.41	1.48	5.50	13.63	10.06	11.21
Asset Turnover	0.71	0.72	0.80	0.84	1.13	1.26	1.34	1.27
Current Ratio	2.10	2.72	2.62	1.94	0.55	1.86	2.36	2.76
Debt to Equity	0.37	0.35	0.27	0.38	0.19	...	0.33	0.42
Price Range	27.99-20.30	27.15-15.00	49.16-14.95	54.64-22.50	51.81-23.13	70.63-38.56	44.50-24.81	36.63-23.63
P/E Ratio	20.28-14.71	46.81-25.86	32.77-9.97	227.67-93.75	46.68-20.83	27.81-15.18	25.00-13.94	23.94-15.44
Average Yield %	1.28	1.00	...	...	15.03	...	...	...

Address: 3150 Sabre Drive, Southlake, TX 76092	Web Site: www.sabre-holdings.com	Auditors: Ernst & Young LLP
Telephone: (682) 605-1000	Officers: Paul C. Ely Jr. - Chmn. Michael S. Gilliland - Pres., C.E.O.	Investor Contact: 817-358-1700

SAFEWAY INC.

Interim Earnings (Per Share)

Qtr.	Mar	Jun	Aug	Dec
2001	0.55	0.59	0.60	0.69
2002	(0.74)	0.63	0.60	(2.21)
2003	0.36	0.36	0.45	(1.56)
2004	0.10	0.35	0.35	0.45

Interim Dividends (Per Share)

No Dividends Paid

Valuation Analysis

Forecast P/E	12.93	No of Institutions
	(4/7/2005)	305
Market Cap	$8.3 Billion	Shares
Book Value	4.3 Billion	399,150,656
Price/Book	1.93	% Held
Price/Sales	0.23	89.14

Business Summary: Retail - Food & Beverage (MIC: 5.3 SIC: 411 NAIC: 45110)

Safeway operated 1,817 stores, as of Mar 1 2004, in the United States and Canada that offer a wide selection of both food and general merchandise. U.S. retail operations are located in California, Oregon, Washington, Alaska, Colorado, Arizona, Texas, and the Mid-Atlantic region. Canadian retail operations are located principally in British Columbia, Alberta and Manitoba/Saskatchewan. As of Mar 1 2004, Co. held a 49% interest in Casa Ley, S.A. de C.V., which operates 102 stores in western Mexico, and a 52.5% interest in GroceryWorks Holdings, Inc., an Internet grocer.

Recent Developments: For the year ended Jan 1 2005, net income was $560,200 thousand versus net loss of $169,800 thousand a year earlier. Revenues were $35,822,900 thousand, up 0.3% from $35,727,200 thousand the year before. Operating income was $1,172,800 thousand versus an income of $573,900 thousand in the prior year, an increase of 104.4%. Total direct expense was $25,227,600 thousand versus $25,003,000 thousand in the prior year, an increase of 0.9%. Total indirect expense was $9,422,500 thousand versus $10,150,300 thousand in the prior year, a decrease of 7.2%.

Prospects: Co. confirms its 2005 guidance of $1.41 to $1.51 per diluted share, which includes an estimated stock option expense of $0.09 per diluted share. In addition, Co. expects to generate free cash flow of $500.0 million to $700.0 million in 2005 compared to $1.16 billion in 2004. The decline in free cash flow in 2005 compared with 2004 is attributable to reduced working capital improvements and increased capital expenditures. In 2005, Co. expects to spend approximately $1.40 billion in cash capital expenditures and open approximately 30 to 35 new lifestyle stores and complete approximately 275 to 285 lifestyle remodels.

Financial Data
(US$ in Thousands)

	01/01/2005	01/03/2004	12/28/2002	12/29/2001	12/30/2000	01/01/2000	01/02/1999	01/03/1998
Earnings Per Share	1.25	(0.38)	(1.75)	2.44	2.13	1.88	1.59	1.12
Cash Flow Per Share	5.01	3.58	4.16	4.45	3.83	2.99	2.60	2.60
Tang Book Value Per Share	4.24	2.79	1.77	1.67	1.35	N.M.	N.M.	0.68
Income Statement								
Total Revenue	35,822,900	35,552,700	32,399,200	34,301,000	31,976,900	28,859,900	24,484,200	22,483,800
EBITDA	2,107,500	1,455,100	2,509,100	3,487,600	3,161,400	2,736,600	2,164,900	1,775,000
Depn & Amortn	902,400	871,600	820,300	945,700	837,700	700,400	533,000	457,500
Income Before Taxes	793,900	141,100	1,320,200	2,095,000	1,866,500	1,674,000	1,396,900	1,076,300
Income Taxes	233,700	310,900	751,700	841,100	774,600	703,100	590,200	454,800
Net Income	560,200	(169,800)	(828,100)	1,253,900	1,091,900	970,900	806,700	557,400
Average Shares	449,100	441,900	473,800	513,200	511,600	515,400	508,800	497,700
Balance Sheet								
Current Assets	3,597,700	3,507,700	4,259,100	3,311,800	3,223,500	3,052,100	2,319,900	2,029,700
Total Assets	15,377,400	15,096,700	16,047,300	17,462,600	15,965,300	14,900,300	11,389,600	8,493,900
Current Liabilities	3,792,100	3,464,300	3,936,300	3,882,600	3,779,500	3,582,600	2,893,600	2,538,600
Long-Term Obligations	6,123,700	7,072,300	7,521,500	6,712,300	5,822,100	6,357,400	4,650,600	3,040,900
Total Liabilities	11,070,500	11,452,400	12,419,800	11,573,000	10,575,500	10,814,500	8,307,500	6,344,900
Stockholders' Equity	4,306,900	3,644,300	3,627,500	5,889,600	5,389,800	4,085,800	3,082,100	2,149,000
Shares Outstanding	447,700	444,200	441,000	488,100	504,100	493,600	550,900	476,200
Statistical Record								
Return on Assets %	3.69	N.M.	N.M.	7.52	7.09	7.41	8.14	7.81
Return on Equity %	14.13	N.M.	N.M.	22.29	23.11	27.16	30.93	32.88
EBITDA Margin %	5.88	4.09	7.74	10.17	9.89	9.48	8.84	7.89
Net Margin %	1.56	N.M.	N.M.	3.66	3.41	3.36	3.29	2.48
Asset Turnover	2.36	2.25	1.94	2.06	2.08	2.20	2.47	3.15
Current Ratio	0.95	1.01	1.08	0.85	0.85	0.85	0.80	0.80
Debt to Equity	1.42	1.94	2.07	1.14	1.08	1.08	1.51	1.42
Price Range	25.40-17.34	25.80-16.45	46.09-19.08	60.44-38.50	62.50-31.50	60.81-29.63	61.06-30.91	31.63-21.44
P/E Ratio	20.32-13.87	...	...	24.77-15.78	29.34-14.79	32.35-15.76	38.40-19.44	28.24-19.14

ST. JOE CO. (THE)

Exchange	Symbol	Price	52Wk Range	Yield	P/E
NYS	JOE	$67.30 (3/31/2005)	75.65-35.75	0.83	57.52

*7 Year Price Score 158.02 *NYSE Composite Index=100 *12 Month Price Score 128.95

Interim Earnings (Per Share)

Qtr.	Mar	Jun	Sep	Dec
2001	0.13	0.29	0.19	0.22
2002	0.90	0.40	0.15	0.69
2003	0.18	0.13	0.30	0.37
2004	0.17	0.30	0.34	0.36

Interim Dividends (Per Share)

Amt	Decl	Ex	Rec	Pay
0.12Q	5/18/2004	6/14/2004	6/15/2004	6/30/2004
0.14Q	8/16/2004	9/13/2004	9/15/2004	9/30/2004
0.14Q	11/30/2004	12/13/2004	12/15/2004	12/31/2004
0.14Q	3/2/2005	3/11/2005	3/15/2005	3/31/2005

Indicated Div: $0.56

Valuation Analysis

Forecast P/E	43.61	No of Institutions	
	(4/7/2005)	222	
Market Cap	$5.1 Billion	Shares	
Book Value	495.4 Million	49,188,112	
Price/Book	10.31	% Held	
Price/Sales	5.37	64.66	

Business Summary: Paper Products (MIC: 11.11 SIC: 631 NAIC: 22130)

St. Joe is a real estate operating concern primarily engaged in community residential, commercial, hospitality and leisure resort development, along with residential and commercial real estate services and land sales. Co. also has significant interests in timber and owns Apalachicola Northern Railroad, a short-line railroad operating between Port St. Joe and Chattahoochee, FL. The majority of Co.'s real estate operations are principally in Florida. Co.'s forestry operations are in both Florida and Georgia. Co. conducts business in the following operating segments: community residential development, commercial real estate, land sales, forestry, transportation and other.

Recent Developments: For the year ended Dec 31 2004, income from continuing operations increased 13.2% to $85,083 thousand from income of $75,151 thousand a year earlier. Net income increased 18.7% to $90,100 thousand from net income of $75,915 thousand a year earlier. Revenues were $951,503 thousand, up 26.7% from $750,826 thousand the year before. Operating income was $144,553 thousand versus an income of $126,981 thousand in the prior year, an increase of 13.8%.

Prospects: The first quarter is traditionally Co.'s slowest quarter of the year. Co. expects the first quarter of 2005 to be in line with its performance in the first quarter of 2004. Meanwhile, Co. is projecting full-year 2005 earnings, excluding gains from conservation land sales, to be in the range of $1.35 to $1.50 per share. Co. believes its major segments will produce strong results in 2005 as it brings a broad array of real estate products to market. Co. is well positioned in Florida, a state with one of the nation's strongest economies, where it has significant demographic and geographic advantages.

Financial Data
(US$ in Thousands)

	12/31/2004	12/31/2003	12/31/2002	12/31/2001	12/31/2000	12/31/1999	12/31/1998	12/31/1997
Earnings Per Share	1.17	0.98	2.14	0.83	1.15	1.40	0.31	0.38
Cash Flow Per Share	1.80	1.67	0.47	0.69	(0.07)	0.41	0.64	0.83
Tang Book Value Per Share	5.22	5.27	5.59	4.71	5.14	9.28	8.52	9.89
Dividends Per Share	0.520	0.320	0.080	0.080	0.080	0.020	0.080	3.740
Dividend Payout %	44.44	32.65	3.74	9.64	6.96	1.43	25.81	984.21
Income Statement								
Total Revenue	951,503	760,630	646,352	868,411	880,830	750,412	392,181	346,252
EBITDA	...	...	282,887	160,758	231,105	170,211	120,322	99,651
Depn & Amortn	36,838	31,504	23,845	29,619	51,783	49,368	38,893	32,527
Income Before Taxes	...	...	242,064	113,074	166,920	120,843	81,429	94,374
Income Taxes	53,258	42,626	89,561	42,345	56,643	23,961	36,180	40,520
Net Income	90,100	75,915	174,363	70,205	100,323	124,357	28,838	35,453
Average Shares	76,908	77,825	81,340	84,288	86,867	88,552	92,285	93,074
Balance Sheet								
Current Assets	184,629	133,095	122,987	92,412	140,946	197,484	167,324	302,392
Total Assets	1,403,629	1,275,730	1,169,887	1,340,559	1,115,021	1,821,627	1,604,269	1,546,641
Current Liabilities	212,341	165,867	151,215	108,503	114,443	131,588	93,411	50,662
Long-Term Obligations	421,110	382,176	320,915	498,015	263,807	115,974	9,947	...
Total Liabilities	897,825	780,227	689,794	822,486	545,937	880,773	720,972	639,837
Stockholders' Equity	495,411	487,315	480,093	518,073	569,084	940,854	883,297	906,804
Shares Outstanding	75,893	76,030	76,004	79,509	83,926	86,431	89,154	91,698
Statistical Record								
Return on Assets %	6.71	6.21	13.89	5.72	6.81	7.26	1.83	2.11
Return on Equity %	18.29	15.69	34.94	12.92	13.25	13.63	3.22	3.37
EBITDA Margin %	...	...	43.77	18.51	26.24	22.68	30.68	28.78
Net Margin %	9.47	9.98	26.98	8.08	11.39	16.57	7.35	10.24
Asset Turnover	0.71	0.62	0.51	0.71	0.60	0.44	0.25	0.21
Current Ratio	0.87	0.80	0.81	0.85	1.23	1.50	1.79	5.97
Debt to Equity	0.85	0.78	0.67	0.96	0.46	0.12	0.01	...
Price Range	64.20-35.75	37.97-26.33	33.65-25.09	29.55-21.07	22.00-15.81	19.28-14.14	25.10-12.94	26.27-14.42
P/E Ratio	54.87-30.56	38.74-26.87	15.72-11.72	35.60-25.39	19.13-13.75	13.77-10.10	80.98-41.73	69.14-37.95
Average Yield %	1.18	1.03	0.27	0.32	0.41	0.12	0.42	19.23

Address: 245 Riverside Avenue, Suite 500, Jacksonville, FL 32202 Telephone: (904) 301-4200 Fax: (904) 396-4042	Web Site: www.joe.com Officers: Peter S. Rummell - Chmn., C.E.O. Kevin M. Twomey - Pres., C.F.O., C.O.O.	Auditors: KPMG LLP Investor Contact: 904-301-4347 Transfer Agents: Wachovia Bank, Charlotte, NC

ST. JUDE MEDICAL, INC.

Exchange	Symbol	Price	52Wk Range	Yield	P/E
NYS	STJ	$36.00 (3/31/2005)	42.55-31.48	N/A	32.73

*7 Year Price Score 171.49 ***NYSE Composite Index=100** ***12 Month Price Score 96.19**

Price chart with TRADING VOLUME (thousand shares), years 1996–2005

Interim Earnings (Per Share)

Qtr.	Mar	Jun	Sep	Dec
2001	0.13	0.12	0.09	0.14
2002	0.17	0.19	0.20	0.20
2003	0.22	0.22	0.23	0.26
2004	0.26	0.27	0.25	0.33

Interim Dividends (Per Share)

Amt	Decl	Ex	Rec	Pay
100%	5/16/2002	7/1/2002	6/10/2002	6/28/2002
100%	10/11/2004	11/23/2004	11/1/2004	11/22/2004

Valuation Analysis

Forecast P/E	26.17	No of Institutions	
	(4/7/2005)	375	
Market Cap	$12.9 Billion	Shares	
Book Value	2.3 Billion	290,061,440	
Price/Book	5.53	% Held	
Price/Sales	5.63	80.37	

Business Summary: Medical Instruments & Equipment (MIC: 9.6 SIC: 845 NAIC: 34510)

St. Jude Medical develops, manufactures and distributes cardiovascular medical devices for the global cardiac rhythm management (CRM), cardiac surgery (CS) and cardiology and vascular access (C/VA) markets. Co.'s principal products in each of these markets are bradycardia pacemaker systems, tachycardia implantable cardioverter defibrillator (ICD) systems and electrophysiology (EP) catheters in CRM; mechanical and tissue heart valves and valve repair products in CS; and vascular closure devices, angiography catheters, guidewires and hemostasis introducers in C/VA. The main markets for Co.'s products are the U.S., Western Europe and Japan.

Recent Developments: For the year ended Dec 31 2004, net income increased 21.7% to $409,934 thousand from net income of $336,779 thousand a year earlier. Revenues were $2,294,173 thousand, up 18.7% from $1,932,514 thousand the year before. Operating income was $535,958 thousand versus an income of $455,945 thousand in the prior year, an increase of 17.5%. Total direct expense was $1,358,100 thousand versus $1,206,182 thousand in the prior year, an increase of 12.6%. Total indirect expense was $1,079,165 thousand versus $873,478 thousand in the prior year, an increase of 23.5%.

Prospects: On Feb 15 2005, Co. announced it has signed a definitive agreement to acquire the business of Velocimed, a privately-owned company located in Maple Grove, MN. Velocimed develops and manufactures specialty interventional cardiology devices. Under the terms of the agreement, Co. will acquire Velocimed's business for a cash purchase price of $82.5 million, less an estimated $8.5 million of cash at Velocimed upon closing, plus additional contingent payments tied to revenues in excess of minimum future targets, and a milestone payment upon FDA approval of the Premier™ patent foramen ovale closure system. Co. anticipates this acquisition will close in the second quarter of 2005.

Financial Data
(US$ in Thousands)

	12/31/2004	12/31/2003	12/31/2002	12/31/2001	12/31/2000	12/31/1999	12/31/1998	12/31/1997
Earnings Per Share	1.10	0.92	0.76	0.48	0.38	0.07	0.38	0.14
Cash Flow Per Share	1.70	1.34	1.18	0.90	0.60	0.76	0.32	(0.06)
Tang Book Value Per Share	4.27	3.01	3.26	2.28	1.49	1.02	1.44	2.68
Income Statement								
Total Revenue	2,294,173	1,932,514	1,589,929	1,347,356	1,178,806	1,114,549	1,015,994	994,396
EBITDA	617,703	532,035	444,551	327,583	295,587	178,084	254,583	162,306
Depn & Amortn	85,794	76,683	74,920	90,299	92,349	85,702	68,853	66,061
Income Before Taxes	537,192	458,637	373,358	227,978	177,309	67,004	185,730	88,236
Income Taxes	127,258	119,246	97,073	55,386	48,215	42,777	56,648	33,530
Net Income	409,934	339,391	276,285	172,592	129,094	24,227	129,082	53,140
Average Shares	370,992	370,754	366,004	357,536	343,268	338,940	344,580	368,208
Balance Sheet								
Current Assets	1,863,217	1,492,337	1,114,317	797,546	704,642	690,299	682,464	743,282
Total Assets	3,230,747	2,556,094	1,951,379	1,628,727	1,532,716	1,554,038	1,384,612	1,458,616
Current Liabilities	605,393	510,315	374,652	321,854	297,367	282,522	203,397	251,594
Long-Term Obligations	234,865	351,813	...	123,128	294,500	477,495	374,995	220,000
Total Liabilities	896,819	951,847	374,652	444,982	591,867	760,017	578,392	471,594
Stockholders' Equity	2,333,928	1,604,247	1,576,727	1,183,745	940,849	794,021	806,220	987,022
Shares Outstanding	358,760	346,028	356,056	348,837	341,345	335,122	336,700	367,644
Statistical Record								
Return on Assets %	14.13	15.06	15.43	10.92	8.34	1.65	9.08	3.85
Return on Equity %	20.76	21.34	20.02	16.25	14.84	3.03	14.40	5.83
EBITDA Margin %	26.92	27.53	27.96	24.31	25.08	15.98	25.06	16.32
Net Margin %	17.87	17.56	17.38	12.81	10.95	2.17	12.70	5.34
Asset Turnover	0.79	0.86	0.89	0.85	0.76	0.76	0.71	0.72
Current Ratio	3.08	2.92	2.97	2.48	2.37	2.44	3.36	2.95
Debt to Equity	0.10	0.22	...	0.10	0.31	0.60	0.47	0.22
Price Range	42.55-29.94	31.68-19.84	21.38-15.54	19.42-11.75	15.36-5.98	9.91-5.86	9.86-4.88	10.72-6.77
P/E Ratio	38.68-27.22	34.43-21.57	28.13-20.45	40.46-24.48	40.42-15.75	141.52-83.71	25.95-12.83	76.56-48.33

Address: One Lillehei Plaza, St. Paul, MN 55117	**Web Site:** www.sjm.com	**Auditors:** Ernst & Young LLP
Telephone: (651) 483-2000	**Officers:** Terry L. Shepherd - Chmn., C.E.O. Daniel J. Starks - Pres., C.O.O.	**Investor Contact:** 1-800-552-7664
Fax: (651) 766-3045		

SAKS, INC.

Exchange	Symbol	Price	52Wk Range	Yield	P/E
NYS	SKS	$18.05 (3/31/2005)	18.05-11.81	N/A	53.09

*7 Year Price Score 76.24 *NYSE Composite Index=100 *12 Month Price Score 103.74

Interim Earnings (Per Share)

Qtr.	Apr	Jul	Oct	Jan
2001-02	0.18	(0.41)	(0.15)	...
2002-03	(0.17)	(0.14)	0.01	0.47
2003-04	0.10	(0.18)	0.09	0.57
2004-05	0.15	(0.20)	(0.18)	...

Interim Dividends (Per Share)

Amt	Decl	Ex	Rec	Pay
2.00U	3/15/2004	4/28/2004	4/30/2004	5/17/2004

Valuation Analysis

Forecast P/E	25.75	No of Institutions	
	(4/7/2005)	173	
Market Cap	$2.5 Billion	Shares	
Book Value	2.0 Billion	100,616,168	
Price/Book	1.29	% Held	
Price/Sales	0.40	72.01	

TRADING VOLUME (thousand shares)

Business Summary: Retail - General (MIC: 5.2 SIC: 311 NAIC: 52111)

Saks operates in two business segments. The Saks Department Store Group segment includes 243 stores in 24 states as of Mar 31 2004 operating under the names Younkers, Parisian, Herberger's, Carson Pirie Scott, McRae's, Proffitt's, Bergner's and Boston Store. These stores are principally anchor stores in malls that sell fashion apparel, shoes, accessories, jewelry, cosmetics, and decorative home furnishings, as well as furniture in selected locations. Co. also operates mall-based specialty stores under the Club Libby Lu name. The Saks Fifth Avenue Enterprises segment includes 62 Saks Fifth Avenue stores in 24 states and 54 Off 5th Saks Fifth Avenue Outlet stores in 23 states.

Recent Developments: For the quarter ended Oct 30 2004, net loss was $24,815 thousand versus net income of $12,353 thousand in the year-earlier quarter. Revenues were $1,481,645 thousand, up 1.0% from $1,467,147 thousand the year before. Operating loss was $13,788 thousand versus an income of $27,801 thousand in the prior-year quarter, a decrease of 149.6%. Total indirect expense was $594,151 thousand versus $542,848 thousand in the prior-year quarter, an increase of 9.5%.

Prospects: Co. believes that low single digit comparable store sales growth at Saks Department Store Group and mid-single digit comparable store sales growth at Saks Fifth Avenue Enterprises are reasonable assumptions for 2005. Co. also anticipates modest improvement in the gross margin rate mainly driven by improved inventory control and systems investments. Capital spending for 2005 is expected to be $250.0 million to $300.0 million. Separately, Co. plans to open one new 124,000 square foot Parisian store in 2005, located in Collierville, TN. Co. also has preliminary plans to renovate several Saks Fifth Avenue stores in 2005 that may include Atlanta, Phoenix, Bala Cynwyd, Greenwich, and Boca Raton.

Financial Data (US$ in Thousands)	9 Mos	6 Mos	3 Mos	01/31/2004	02/01/2003	02/02/2002	02/03/2001	01/29/2000
Earnings Per Share	0.34	0.61	0.63	0.58	0.17	...	0.53	1.30
Cash Flow Per Share	1.34	1.55	1.29	3.34	1.94	2.64	3.37	1.46
Tang Book Value Per Share	11.68	11.93	12.17	14.08	13.46	13.27	12.56	11.40
Dividends Per Share	2.000	2.000	2.000	...	...	...	...	...
Dividend Payout %	586.53	328.94	316.91	...	...	...	...	...
Income Statement								
Total Revenue	4,372,195	2,890,550	1,540,193	6,055,055	5,911,122	6,070,568	6,581,236	6,423,819
EBITDA	192.978	148,728	114,229	440,942	450,059	325,225	479,693	635,123
Depn & Amortn	165,425	107,490	53,578	221,350	216,022	219,773	214,099	178,775
Income Before Taxes	(51,858)	(10,890)	34,685	109,879	109,985	(25,587)	115,599	317,380
Income Taxes	(20,129)	(3,976)	12,659	27,052	40,148	(9,851)	40,383	118,476
Net Income	(31,729)	(6,914)	22,026	82,827	24,244	322	75,216	189,643
Average Shares	138,249	141,591	146,496	142,921	146,707	141,988	142,718	146,056
Balance Sheet								
Current Assets	2,174,244	1,948,115	2,362,750	2,043,163	1,918,525	1,769,929	1,916,238	1,894,658
Total Assets	4,775,997	4,537,781	4,975,703	4,654,869	4,579,356	4,595,521	5,050,611	5,098,952
Current Liabilities	1,154,243	904,937	1,317,142	966,410	794,692	786,778	830,282	783,862
Long-Term Obligations	1,428,095	1,349,762	1,348,282	1,125,637	1,327,381	1,356,580	1,801,657	1,966,820
Total Liabilities	2,823,610	2,503,528	2,913,849	2,332,701	2,312,084	2,324,084	2,756,782	2,890,609
Stockholders' Equity	1,952,387	2,034,253	2,061,854	2,322,168	2,267,272	2,271,437	2,293,829	2,208,343
Shares Outstanding	139,397	143,273	142,739	141,835	144,960	143,989	141,897	143,043
Statistical Record								
Return on Assets %	1.03	1.90	1.86	1.80	0.53	0.01	1.46	3.70
Return on Equity %	2.42	4.11	4.18	3.62	1.07	0.01	3.29	9.02
EBITDA Margin %	4.41	5.15	7.42	7.28	7.61	5.36	7.29	9.89
Net Margin %	N.M.	N.M.	1.43	1.37	0.41	0.01	1.14	2.95
Asset Turnover	1.31	1.39	1.28	1.32	1.29	1.26	1.28	1.25
Current Ratio	1.88	2.15	1.79	2.11	2.41	2.25	2.31	2.42
Debt to Equity	0.73	0.66	0.65	0.48	0.59	0.60	0.79	0.89
Price Range	17.85-11.81	17.85-10.69	17.85-8.64	17.27-6.91	15.48-8.75	13.80-5.00	14.94-7.81	38.00-13.69
P/E Ratio	52.50-34.74	29.26-17.52	28.33-13.71	29.78-11.91	91.06-51.47	...	28.18-14.74	29.23-10.53
Average Yield %	13.66	13.63	14.79	...	...	...	...	...

Address: 750 Lakeshore Parkway, Birmingham, AL 35211 **Telephone:** (205) 940-4000 **Fax:** (205) 940-4987	**Web Site:** www.saksincorporated.com **Officers:** R. Brad Martin - Chmn., C.E.O. Stephen I. Sardove - Vice-Chmn., C.O.O.	**Auditors:** PricewaterhouseCoopers LLP **Investor Contact:** 865-981-6243

SARA LEE CORP.

Exchange	Symbol	Price	52Wk Range	Yield	P/E	Div Acheiver
NYS	SLE	$22.16 (3/31/2005)	24.95-20.92	3.56	12.81	28 Years

*7 Year Price Score 89.11 ***NYSE Composite Index=100** ***12 Month Price Score 91.28**

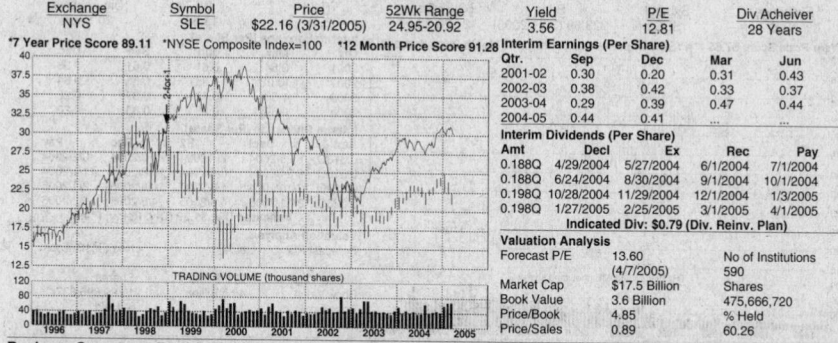

Interim Earnings (Per Share)

Qtr.	Sep	Dec	Mar	Jun
2001-02	0.30	0.20	0.31	0.43
2002-03	0.38	0.42	0.33	0.37
2003-04	0.29	0.39	0.47	0.44
2004-05	0.44	0.41	...	...

Interim Dividends (Per Share)

Amt	Decl	Ex	Rec	Pay
0.188Q	4/29/2004	5/27/2004	6/1/2004	7/1/2004
0.188Q	6/24/2004	8/30/2004	9/1/2004	10/1/2004
0.198Q	10/28/2004	11/29/2004	12/1/2004	1/3/2005
0.198Q	1/27/2005	2/25/2005	3/1/2005	4/1/2005

Indicated Div: $0.79 (Div. Reinv. Plan)

Valuation Analysis

Forecast P/E	13.60
	(4/7/2005)
Market Cap	$17.5 Billion
Book Value	3.6 Billion
Price/Book	4.85
Price/Sales	0.89

No of Institutions	
Shares	590
	475,666,720
% Held	60.26

Business Summary: Food (MIC: 4.1 SIC: 013 NAIC: 11613)

Sara Lee is a global manufacturer and marketer of brand-name products for consumers throughout the world. As of July 3 2004, Co. has operations in 58 countries and markets products in nearly 200 nations. Co. has five reportable segments: Sara Lee Meats, Sara Lee Bakery, Beverage, Household Products and Branded Apparel. Co.'s products and services include fresh and frozen baked goods, processed meats, coffee and tea, beverage systems, intimate apparel, underwear, sportswear, legwear and other apparel, and personal, household and shoe care products.

Recent Developments: For the quarter ended Jan 1 2005, net income increased 4.5% to $326 million from net income of $312 million in the year-earlier quarter. Revenues were $5,199 million, up 3.6% from $5,017 million the year before. Total direct expense was $3,287 million versus $3,070 million in the prior-year quarter, an increase of 7.1%. Total indirect expense was $1,495 million versus $1,523 million in the prior-year quarter, a decrease of 1.8%.

Prospects: On Feb 10 2005, Co. announced a comprehensive transformation plan designed to dramatically improve its performance and better position it for long-term growth. Co. has built its transformation plan upon three pillars: organizing its business operations around consumers, customers and geographic markets; focusing its portfolio; and increasing operational efficiency to fund growth. The plan will not affect Co.'s earnings guidance for the remainder of fiscal 2005. Co. reiterated that it expects diluted earnings per share for the third quarter of fiscal 2005 to fall within a range of $0.29 to $0.34, while fiscal 2005 diluted earnings per share should be in a range of $1.46 to $1.56.

Financial Data

(US$ in Thousands)	6 Mos	3 Mos	07/03/2004	06/28/2003	06/29/2002	06/30/2001	07/01/2000	07/03/1999
Earnings Per Share	1.73	1.71	1.59	1.50	1.23	2.65	1.34	1.26
Cash Flow Per Share	2.29	2.21	2.55	2.34	2.22	1.83	1.76	1.75
Dividends Per Share	0.760	0.750	0.563	0.615	0.595	0.570	0.530	0.490
Dividend Payout %	43.96	43.75	35.38	41.00	48.37	21.51	39.55	38.89
Income Statement								
Total Revenue	10,060,000	4,861,000	19,566,000	18,291,000	17,628,000	17,747,000	17,511,000	20,012,000
EBITDA	1,288,000	671,000	2,457,000	2,356,000	1,975,000	2,630,000	2,345,000	2,365,000
Depn & Amortn	380,000	190,000	734,000	674,000	582,000	599,000	602,000	553,000
Income Before Taxes	822,000	441,000	1,542,000	1,484,000	1,185,000	1,851,000	1,567,000	1,671,000
Income Taxes	144,000	89,000	270,000	263,000	175,000	248,000	409,000	480,000
Net Income	678,000	352,000	1,272,000	1,221,000	1,010,000	2,266,000	1,222,000	1,191,000
Average Shares	795,000	795,000	798,000	812,000	818,000	854,000	912,000	944,000
Balance Sheet								
Current Assets	6,138,000	5,439,000	5,746,000	5,953,000	4,986,000	5,083,000	5,974,000	4,987,000
Total Assets	15,488,000	14,550,000	14,883,000	15,084,000	13,753,000	10,167,000	11,611,000	10,521,000
Current Liabilities	4,912,000	5,044,000	5,423,000	5,199,000	5,463,000	4,958,000	6,759,000	5,953,000
Long-Term Obligations	4,487,000	4,136,000	4,171,000	5,157,000	4,326,000	2,640,000	2,248,000	1,892,000
Total Liabilities	11,878,000	11,528,000	11,935,000	13,032,000	12,011,000	9,045,000	10,377,000	9,255,000
Stockholders' Equity	3,610,000	3,022,000	2,948,000	2,052,000	1,742,000	1,122,000	1,234,000	1,266,000
Shares Outstanding	789,329	784,813	793,924	777,347	784,720	781,964	846,331	883,783
Statistical Record								
Return on Assets %	9.10	9.55	8.35	8.49	8.47	20.87	11.07	10.89
Return on Equity %	46.64	55.16	50.06	64.54	70.72	192.89	98.03	76.04
EBITDA Margin %	12.80	13.80	12.56	12.88	11.20	14.82	13.39	11.82
Net Margin %	6.74	7.24	6.50	6.68	5.73	12.77	6.98	5.95
Asset Turnover	1.29	1.35	1.28	1.27	1.48	1.63	1.59	1.83
Current Ratio	1.25	1.08	1.06	1.15	0.91	1.03	0.88	0.84
Debt to Equity	1.24	1.37	1.41	2.51	2.48	2.35	1.82	1.49
Price Range	24.49-20.31	23.44-18.68	23.44-18.36	23.75-16.50	23.04-19.04	25.19-18.44	27.06-13.63	30.69-21.50
P/E Ratio	14.16-11.74	13.71-10.92	14.74-11.55	15.83-11.00	18.73-15.48	9.50-6.96	20.20-10.17	24.36-17.06
Average Yield %	3.37	3.34	2.69	3.08	2.81	2.75	2.59	1.86

Address: Three First National Plaza, Suite 4600, Chicago, IL 60602-4260	Web Site: www.saralee.com	Auditors: PricewaterhouseCoopers LLP
Telephone: (312) 726-2600	Officers: C. Steven McMillan - Chmn. Brenda C. Barnes - Pres., C.E.O., C.O.O.	Investor Contact: 312-558-4947
Fax: (312) 558-4913		Transfer Agents: Sara Lee Corporation, Chicago, IL

SBC COMMUNICATIONS, INC.

Exchange	Symbol	Price	52Wk Range	Yield	P/E	Div Achiever
NYS	SBC	$23.69 (3/31/2005)	27.20-23.00	5.45	13.38	20 Years

*7 Year Price Score 57.65 *NYSE Composite Index=100 *12 Month Price Score 89.55

Interim Earnings (Per Share)

Qtr.	Mar	Jun	Sep	Dec
2001	0.54	0.61	0.61	0.36
2002	(0.02)	0.55	0.53	0.64
2003	1.50	0.42	0.37	0.28
2004	0.59	0.35	0.63	0.20

Interim Dividends (Per Share)

Amt	Decl	Ex	Rec	Pay
0.313Q	6/25/2004	7/7/2004	7/10/2004	8/2/2004
0.313Q	9/24/2004	10/6/2004	10/8/2004	11/1/2004
0.323Q	12/10/2004	1/6/2005	1/10/2005	2/1/2005
0.323Q	3/11/2005	4/6/2005	4/8/2005	5/2/2005

Indicated Div: $1.29 (Div. Reinv. Plan)

Valuation Analysis

Forecast P/E	N/A		No of Institutions
Market Cap	$78.2 Billion	Shares	
Book Value	40.5 Billion		1,799,896,832
Price/Book	1.93	% Held	
Price/Sales	1.92		54.49

Business Summary: Communications (MIC: 10.1 SIC: 813 NAIC: 51112)

SBC Communications is a global provider of telecommunications services. Co.'s products and services include local exchange services, wireless communications, long-distance services, internet services, telecommunications equipment, and directory advertising and publishing. Co.'s principal wireline subsidiaries provide telecommunications services in thirteen states: Arkansas, California, Connecticut, Illinois, Indiana, Kansas, Michigan, Missouri, Nevada, Ohio, Oklahoma, Texas, and Wisconsin. As of Dec 31 2003, Co. had 54.7 million network access lines in service and maintained a 60.0% equity interest in Cingular Wireless, which serves more than 24.0 million wireless customers.

Recent Developments: For the year ended Dec 31 2004, income from continuing operations decreased 15.0% to $4,979,000 thousand from income of $5,859,000 thousand a year earlier. Net income decreased 30.8% to $5,887,000 thousand from net income of $8,505,000 thousand a year earlier. Revenues were $40,787,000 thousand, up 0.7% from $40,498,000 thousand the year before. Operating income was $5,901,000 thousand versus an income of $6,284,000 thousand in the prior year, a decrease of 6.1%. Total direct expense was $17,383,000 thousand versus $16,739,000 thousand in the prior year, an increase of 3.8%. Total indirect expense was $17,503,000 thousand versus $17,475,000 thousand in the prior year, an increase of 0.2%.

Prospects: On Jan 31 2005, Co. announced an agreement to acquire AT&T. The transaction combines AT&T's global systems capabilities, business and government customers, and Internet protocol-based business with Co.'s local exchange, broadband and wireless applications. Under terms of the agreement, shareholders of AT&T are slated to receive total consideration currently valued at approx. $16.00 billion, consisting of 0.77942 shares of Co.'s common stock for each common share of AT&T. In addition, AT&T will pay its shareholders a special dividend of $1.30 per share. The acquisition, if approved, is expected to close by the first half of 2006.

Financial Data

(US$ in Thousands)	12/31/2004	12/31/2003	12/31/2002	12/31/2001	12/31/2000	12/31/1999	12/31/1998	12/31/1997
Earnings Per Share	1.77	2.56	1.69	2.13	2.32	2.36	2.03	0.80
Cash Flow Per Share	3.30	4.07	4.57	4.40	4.20	4.86	4.28	3.81
Tang Book Value Per Share	11.78	11.08	9.51	8.62	7.38	5.87	4.95	3.61
Dividends Per Share	1.250	1.367	1.066	1.023	1.005	0.965	0.925	0.886
Dividend Payout %	70.62	53.42	63.09	48.00	43.32	40.89	45.57	110.78
Income Statement								
Total Revenue	40,787,000	40,843,000	43,138,000	45,908,000	51,476,000	49,489,000	28,777,000	24,856,000
EBITDA	15,228,000	17,385,000	19,826,000	21,307,000	23,878,000	20,751,000	12,472,000	8,125,000
Depn & Amortn	7,532,000	7,846,000	8,548,000	9,033,000	9,677,000	8,468,000	5,105,000	4,841,000
Income Before Taxes	7,165,000	8,901,000	10,457,000	11,357,000	12,888,000	10,853,000	6,374,000	2,337,000
Income Taxes	2,186,000	2,930,000	2,984,000	4,097,000	4,921,000	4,280,000	2,306,000	863,000
Net Income	5,887,000	8,505,000	5,653,000	7,242,000	7,967,000	8,159,000	4,023,000	1,474,000
Average Shares	3,322,000	3,329,000	3,348,000	3,396,000	3,433,000	3,458,000	1,984,000	1,844,000
Balance Sheet								
Net PPE	50,046,000	52,128,000	48,490,000	49,827,000	47,195,000	46,571,000	29,920,000	27,339,000
Total Assets	108,844,000	100,166,000	95,057,000	96,322,000	98,651,000	83,215,000	45,066,000	42,132,000
Long-Term Obligations	21,231,000	16,060,000	18,536,000	17,133,000	15,492,000	17,475,000	11,612,000	12,019,000
Total Liabilities	68,340,000	61,918,000	61,858,000	63,831,000	68,188,000	56,489,000	32,286,000	32,240,000
Stockholders' Equity	40,504,000	38,248,000	33,199,000	32,491,000	30,463,000	26,726,000	12,780,000	9,892,000
Shares Outstanding	3,300,912	3,305,236	3,318,000	3,354,216	3,386,709	3,395,272	1,959,000	1,837,000
Statistical Record								
Return on Assets %	5.62	8.71	5.91	7.43	8.74	12.72	9.23	4.50
Return on Equity %	14.91	23.81	17.21	23.01	27.79	41.31	35.49	17.62
EBITDA Margin %	37.34	42.57	45.96	46.41	46.39	41.93	43.34	32.69
Net Margin %	14.43	20.82	13.10	15.78	15.48	16.49	13.98	5.93
PPE Turnover	0.80	0.81	0.88	0.95	1.09	1.29	1.01	1.20
Asset Turnover	0.39	0.42	0.45	0.47	0.56	0.77	0.66	0.76
Debt to Equity	0.52	0.42	0.56	0.53	0.51	0.65	0.91	1.22
Price Range	27.59-23.00	31.19-19.34	40.17-20.10	52.38-37.38	58.50-35.44	59.19-44.25	54.13-35.78	38.00-24.94
P/E Ratio	15.59-12.99	12.18-7.55	23.77-11.89	24.59-17.55	25.22-15.27	25.08-18.75	26.66-17.63	47.50-31.17
Average Yield %	4.95	5.77	3.48	2.37	2.19	1.84	2.21	2.99

Address: 175 E. Houston, San Antonio, TX 78205-2233 Telephone: (210) 821 4105 Fax: (210) 351 3553	Web Site: www.sbc.com Officers: Edward E. Whitacre Jr. - Chmn., C.E.O. William M. Daley - Pres.	Auditors: Ernst & Young LLP Investor Contact: 210-351-3990 Transfer Agents: EquiServe Trust Company, N.A., Jersey City, NJ

SCANA CORP

Exchange	Symbol	Price	52Wk Range	Yield	P/E
NYS	SCG	$38.22 (3/31/2005)	40.00-33.09	4.08	16.62

*7 Year Price Score 106.12 *NYSE Composite Index=100 *12 Month Price Score 96.39

TRADING VOLUME (thousand shares)

Interim Earnings (Per Share)

Qtr.	Mar	Jun	Sep	Dec
2001	0.75	3.67	0.61	0.12
2002	(0.68)	0.38	0.74	(1.78)
2003	0.75	0.67	0.76	0.36
2004	0.91	0.54	0.48	0.37

Interim Dividends (Per Share)

Amt	Decl	Ex	Rec	Pay
0.365Q	4/29/2004	6/8/2004	6/10/2004	7/1/2004
0.365Q	7/29/2004	9/8/2004	9/10/2004	10/1/2004
0.365Q	10/29/2004	12/8/2004	12/10/2004	1/1/2005
0.39Q	2/17/2005	3/8/2005	3/10/2005	4/1/2005
		Indicated Div: $1.56		

Valuation Analysis

Forecast P/E	N/A		No of Institutions
Market Cap	$4.3 Billion		Shares
Book Value	2.6 Billion		48,755,056
Price/Book	1.69		% Held
Price/Sales	1.11		43.69

Business Summary: Electricity (MIC: 7.1 SIC: 931 NAIC: 21121)

SCANA is a public utility holding company. Through its wholly owned subsidiaries, Co. is engaged mainly in the generation and sale of electricity to wholesale and retail customers in South Carolina and in the purchase, sale and transportation of natural gas to wholesale and retail customers in South Carolina, North Carolina and Georgia. Co. is also engaged in other energy-related businesses and provides fiber optic communications in South Carolina. Regulated utilities include South Carolina Electric & Gas Company; South Carolina Fuel Company, Inc.; South Carolina Generating Company, Inc.; South Carolina Pipeline Corp.; Public Service Company of North Carolina, Inc.; and SCG Pipeline, Inc.

Recent Developments: For the year ended Dec 31 2004, net income decreased 8.9% to $257,000 thousand from net income of $282,000 thousand a year earlier. Revenues were $3,885,000 thousand, up 13.7% from $3,416,000 thousand the year before. Operating income was $596,000 thousand versus an income of $551,000 thousand in the prior year, an increase of 8.2%. Total direct expense was $2,879,000 thousand versus $2,488,000 thousand in the prior year, an increase of 15.7%. Total indirect expense was $410,000 thousand versus $377,000 thousand in the prior year, an increase of 8.8%.

Prospects: On Dec 30 2004, Co. sold its investment in Knology, Inc., substantially completing its strategy to monetize its remaining telecommunications investments. The transaction follows Co.'s Dec 2004 sale of its ITC DeltaCom investment. Co. indicated that after-tax cash proceeds of approximately $122.0 million from the sale of these investments will be used to repay outstanding debt. Separately, for 2005, Co. estimates that earnings will be in the range of $2.65 to $2.85 per share. Co. noted that this guidance assumes normal weather in its electric and natural gas service areas and excludes any potential gains or losses from litigation or sales of certain assets.

Financial Data

(US$ in Thousands)	12/31/2004	12/31/2003	12/31/2002	12/31/2001	12/31/2000	12/31/1999	12/31/1998	12/31/1997
Earnings Per Share	2.30	2.54	(1.34)	5.15	2.40	1.73	2.12	2.06
Cash Flow Per Share	5.35	5.05	4.66	4.74	3.73	2.16	4.43	3.85
Tang Book Value Per Share	21.71	20.82	19.64	20.95	19.40	20.27	16.86	16.68
Dividends Per Share	1.460	1.380	1.300	1.200	1.150	...	...	...
Dividend Payout %	63.48	54.33	...	23.30	47.92	...	...	...
Income Statement								
Total Revenue	3,885,000	3,416,000	2,954,000	3,451,000	3,433,000	1,650,000	1,632,000	1,523,000
EBITDA	1,413,000	1,476,000	781,000	2,426,000	1,301,000	713,000	761,000	777,000
Depn & Amortn	296,000	270,000	253,000	252,000	243,000	195,000	172,000	195,000
Income Before Taxes	915,000	1,006,000	329,000	1,951,000	833,000	376,000	466,000	461,000
Income Taxes	123,000	135,000	36,000	305,000	141,000			
Net Income	257,000	282,000	(142,000)	539,000	250,000	179,000	223,000	221,000
Average Shares	111,600	110,800	106,000	104,700	104,500	103,600	105,300	107,100
Balance Sheet								
Net PPE	6,866,000	6,513,000	5,569,000	5,356,000	5,028,000	3,851,000	3,787,000	3,648,000
Total Assets	8,996,000	8,456,000	7,754,000	7,822,000	7,420,000	6,011,000	5,281,000	4,932,000
Long-Term Obligations	3,186,000	3,225,000	2,834,000	2,646,000	2,850,000	1,563,000	1,623,000	1,566,000
Total Liabilities	6,439,000	6,044,000	5,421,000	5,472,000	5,232,000	3,756,000	3,379,000	2,988,000
Stockholders' Equity	2,557,000	2,412,000	2,283,000	2,300,000	2,138,000	2,205,000	1,852,000	1,894,000
Shares Outstanding	112,909	110,735	110,831	104,728	104,729	103,572	103,573	107,200
Statistical Record								
Return on Assets %	2.94	3.48	N.M.	7.07	3.71	3.17	4.37	4.56
Return on Equity %	10.32	12.01	N.M.	24.29	11.48	8.82	11.91	12.27
EBITDA Margin %	36.37	43.21	26.44	70.30	37.90	43.21	46.63	51.02
Net Margin %	6.62	8.26	(4.81)	15.62	7.28	10.85	13.66	14.51
PPE Turnover	0.58	0.57	0.54	0.66	0.77	0.43	0.44	0.42
Asset Turnover	0.44	0.42	0.38	0.45	0.51	0.29	0.32	0.31
Debt to Equity	1.25	1.34	1.24	1.15	1.33	0.71	0.88	0.83
Price Range	39.62-33.09	35.52-28.21	31.98-24.25	29.25-24.57	30.89-22.56	32.25-21.31	37.25-28.00	29.94-23.63
P/E Ratio	17.23-14.39	13.98-11.11	...	5.68-4.77	12.87-9.40	18.64-12.32	17.57-13.21	14.53-11.47
Average Yield %	4.03	4.23	4.49	4.43	4.33			

Address: 1426 Main Street, Columbia, SC 29201-2845	Web Site: www.scana.com	Auditors: Deloitte & Touche LLP
Telephone: (803) 217-9000	Officers: William B. Timmerman - Chmn., C.E.O. H. Thomas Arthur II - Sr. V.P., Gen. Couns., Asst. Sec., Pres., C.O.O., SEMI	Investor Contact: 803-217-9240
Fax: (803) 343-2389		

SCHERING-PLOUGH CORP.

*7 Year Price Score 46.32   *NYSE Composite Index=100   *12 Month Price Score 95.20

Interim Earnings (Per Share)

Qtr.	Mar	Jun	Sep	Dec
2001	0.38	0.43	0.41	0.10
2002	0.41	0.43	0.29	0.22
2003	0.12	0.12	(0.18)	(0.12)
2004	(0.05)	(0.04)	0.01	(0.59)

Interim Dividends (Per Share)

Amt	Decl	Ex	Rec	Pay
0.055Q	4/27/2004	5/5/2004	5/7/2004	5/28/2004
0.055Q	6/21/2004	8/4/2004	8/6/2004	8/31/2004
0.055Q	9/28/2004	11/3/2004	11/5/2004	11/30/2004
0.055Q	1/25/2005	2/2/2005	2/4/2005	2/28/2005

Indicated Div: $0.22

Valuation Analysis

Forecast P/E	84.09	No of Institutions
	(4/7/2005)	653
Market Cap	$26.8 Billion	Shares
Book Value	7.6 Billion	1,116,639,488
Price/Book	3.54	% Held
Price/Sales	3.24	75.71

Business Summary: Pharmaceuticals (MIC: 9.1 SIC: 834 NAIC: 25412)

Schering-Plough and its subsidiaries are engaged in the discovery, development, manufacturing and marketing of pharmaceutical products worldwide. Co. operates primarily in the prescription pharmaceutical marketplace. Co. has three reportable segments Prescription Pharmaceuticals, Consumer Health Care and Animal Health. The Prescription Pharmaceuticals segment discovers, develops, manufactures and markets human ethical pharmaceutical products. The Consumer Health Care segment develops, manufactures and markets over-the-counter, foot care and sun care products. The Animal Health segment discovers, develops, manufactures and markets animal health products.

Recent Developments: For the year ended Dec 31 2004, net loss was $947,000 thousand versus net loss of $92,000 thousand a year earlier. Revenues were $8,272,000 thousand, down 0.7% from $8,334,000 thousand the year before. Total direct expense was $3,070,000 thousand versus $2,833,000 thousand in the prior year, an increase of 8.4%. Total indirect expense was $5,418,000 thousand versus $4,943,000 thousand in the prior year, an increase of 9.6%.

Prospects: Looking ahead, Co. should continue to benefit from solid top-line growth, which is being driven in part by the success of its cholesterol franchise as Co.'s sales in this area are annualizing at more than $1.00 billion with the launch of Vytorin in 2004. Co. believes its success in the cholesterol market remains pivotal to the turnaround in its operating performance. Meanwhile, Co. continue to focus on driving bottom-line growth through strategic investments, cost controls and market expansion. Separately, Co. announced that it has completed the acquisition of most of NeoGenesis Pharmaceuticals' assets. Financial terms of the transaction were not disclosed.

Financial Data

(US$ in Thousands)	12/31/2004	12/31/2003	12/31/2002	12/31/2001	12/31/2000	12/31/1999	12/31/1998	12/31/1997
Earnings Per Share	(0.67)	(0.06)	1.35	1.32	1.64	1.42	1.18	0.97
Cash Flow Per Share	(0.10)	0.41	1.35	1.72	1.71	1.29	1.38	1.26
Tang Book Value Per Share	3.75	4.57	5.10	4.41	3.75	3.11	2.33	1.60
Dividends Per Share	0.220	0.565	0.670	0.620	0.545	0.485	0.425	0.368
Dividend Payout %	...	...	49.63	46.97	33.23	34.15	36.02	37.95
Income Statement								
Total Revenue	8,272,000	8,334,000	10,180,000	9,802,000	9,815,000	9,176,000	8,077,000	6,778,000
EBITDA	373,000	395,000	2,888,000	2,843,000	3,487,000	3,059,000	2,564,000	2,113,000
Depn & Amortn	453,000	417,000	372,000	320,000	299,000	264,000	238,000	200,000
Income Before Taxes	(168,000)	(46,000)	2,563,000	2,523,000	3,188,000	2,795,000	2,326,000	1,913,000
Income Taxes	779,000	46,000	589,000	580,000	765,000	685,000	570,000	469,000
Net Income	(947,000)	(92,000)	1,974,000	1,943,000	2,423,000	2,110,000	1,756,000	1,444,000
Average Shares	1,472,000	1,469,000	1,470,000	1,470,000	1,476,000	1,486,000	1,488,000	1,480,000
Balance Sheet								
Current Assets	10,003,000	9,147,000	8,272,000	6,519,000	5,720,000	4,909,000	3,958,000	2,920,000
Total Assets	15,911,000	15,102,000	14,136,000	12,174,000	10,805,000	9,375,000	7,840,000	6,507,000
Current Liabilities	5,208,000	4,609,000	4,729,000	3,917,000	3,645,000	3,209,000	3,032,000	2,891,000
Long-Term Obligations	2,392,000	2,410,000	...	...	...	...	...	46,000
Total Liabilities	8,355,000	7,765,000	5,994,000	5,049,000	4,686,000	4,210,000	3,838,000	3,686,000
Stockholders' Equity	7,556,000	7,337,000	8,142,000	7,125,000	6,119,000	5,165,000	4,002,000	2,821,000
Shares Outstanding	1,475,000	1,471,000	1,468,000	1,465,000	1,463,000	1,472,000	1,472,000	1,466,000
Statistical Record								
Return on Assets %	N.M.	N.M.	15.01	16.91	23.95	24.51	24.48	24.26
Return on Equity %	N.M.	N.M.	25.86	29.34	42.83	46.03	51.47	59.17
EBITDA Margin %	4.51	4.74	28.37	29.00	35.53	33.34	31.74	31.17
Net Margin %	N.M.	N.M.	19.39	19.82	24.69	22.99	21.74	21.30
Asset Turnover	0.53	0.57	0.77	0.85	0.97	1.07	1.13	1.14
Current Ratio	1.92	1.98	1.75	1.66	1.57	1.53	1.31	1.01
Debt to Equity	0.32	0.33	...	...	...	...	...	0.02
Price Range	21.12-15.96	23.68-14.52	36.00-17.30	54.25-32.65	59.13-30.50	60.75-40.75	57.50-30.84	31.72-16.19
P/E Ratio	...	...	26.67-12.81	41.10-24.73	36.05-18.60	42.78-28.70	48.73-26.14	32.70-16.69
Average Yield %	1.23	3.24	2.57	1.57	1.21	0.95	0.94	1.55

Address: 2000 Galloping Hill Road, Kenilworth, NJ 07033-0530 **Telephone:** (908) 298-4000 **Fax:** (908) 822-7048	**Web Site:** www.schering-plough.com **Officers:** Fred Hassan - Chmn., Pres., C.E.O. Robert J. Bertolini CPA - Exec. V.P., C.F.O.	**Auditors:** Deloitte & Touche LLP

SCHLUMBERGER LTD. (NETHERLANDS ANTILLES)

Exchange	Symbol	Price	52Wk Range	Yield	P/E
NYS	SLB	$70.48 (3/31/2005)	78.00-55.46	1.19	34.55

*7 Year Price Score 94.69 ***NYSE Composite Index=100** ***12 Month Price Score 104.62**

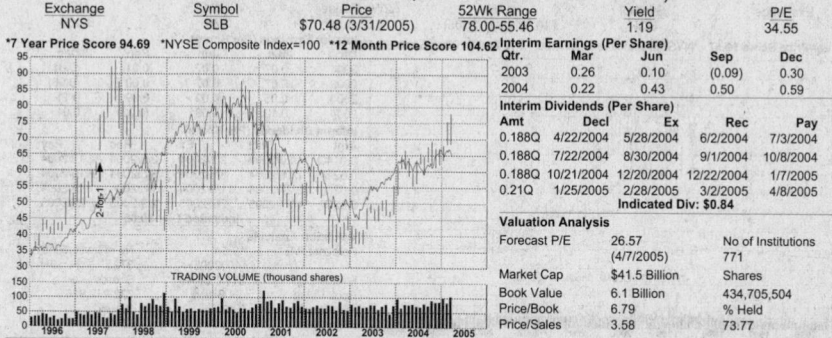

Interim Earnings (Per Share)

Qtr.	Mar	Jun	Sep	Dec
2003	0.26	0.10	(0.09)	0.30
2004	0.22	0.43	0.50	0.59

Interim Dividends (Per Share)

Amt	Decl	Ex	Rec	Pay
0.188Q	4/22/2004	5/28/2004	6/2/2004	7/3/2004
0.188Q	7/22/2004	8/30/2004	9/1/2004	10/8/2004
0.188Q	10/21/2004	12/20/2004	12/22/2004	1/7/2005
0.21Q	1/25/2005	2/28/2005	3/2/2005	4/8/2005

Indicated Div: $0.84

Valuation Analysis

Forecast P/E	26.57
	(4/7/2005)
Market Cap	$41.5 Billion
Book Value	6.1 Billion
Price/Book	6.79
Price/Sales	3.58

No of Institutions	771
Shares	434,705,504
% Held	73.77

Business Summary: Oil and Gas (MIC: 14.2 SIC: 389 NAIC: 13112)

Schlumberger is engaged in the oilfield services company, supplying technology, project management, and information solutions that optimize performance in the oil and gas industry through two segments. Schlumberger Oilfield Services is an international provider of technology, project management and information solutions to the petroleum industry. Schlumberger Oilfield Services manages its business through 27 Oilfield Services GeoMarket regions, which are grouped into geographic areas. WesternGeco provides worldwide reservoir imaging, monitoring, and development seismic services, with the seismic crews and data processing centers in the industry, as well as a multiclient seismic library.

Recent Developments: For the year ended Dec 31 2004, income from continuing operations increased 154.7% to $1,014,052 thousand from income of $398,169 thousand a year earlier. Net income increased 219.5% to $1,223,870 thousand from net income of $383,002 thousand a year earlier. Revenues were $11,608,863 thousand, up 14.0% from $10,183,708 thousand the year before. Total direct expense was $9,041,972 thousand versus $8,428,631 thousand in the prior year, an increase of 7.3%. Total indirect expense was $967,006 thousand versus $963,517 thousand in the prior year, an increase of 0.4%.

Prospects: Co.'s results are benefiting from record levels of oilfield services revenue as activity is increasing in almost all regions, particularly in the Geomarkets in India; Malaysia, Brunei and the Philippines; Canada; East Africa and the Eastern Mediterranean; and Arabia. Co. is also seeing pricing increases in North America, particularly in Canada and U.S. Land. In addition, contract awards and renewals in the Eastern Hemisphere are generally executing at improving pricing levels. WesternGeco's results are being driven by further uptake of Q-Technology and increased multi-client library sales. Increasing exploration budgets and new field development plans should drive growth going forward.

Financial Data

(US$ in Thousands)	12/31/2004	12/31/2003	12/31/2002	12/31/2001	12/31/2000	12/31/1999	12/31/1998	12/31/1997
Earnings Per Share	2.04	0.66	(4.01)	0.91	1.27	0.65	1.81	2.52
Cash Flow Per Share	3.12	3.62	3.78	2.73	...	...	...	...
Tang Book Value Per Share	5.06	3.74	1.40	2.27	11.73	11.29	12.48	11.10
Dividends Per Share	0.750	0.750	0.750	0.750	0.750	0.750	0.750	0.750
Dividend Payout %	36.76	113.64	...	82.42	59.06	115.38	41.44	29.76
Income Statement								
Total Revenue	11,609,165	14,059,097	13,612,730	13,988,064	10,034,717	8,751,705	11,997,309	10,754,413
EBITDA	2,635,368	2,138,594	(685,233)	3,022,305	960,681	470,106	1,322,873	...
Depn & Amortn	1,307,931	1,570,851	1,545,053	1,896,119	...	...	...	...
Income Before Taxes	1,327,437	567,743	(2,230,286)	1,126,186	960,681	470,106	1,322,873	...
Income Taxes	276,949	209,386	279,122	575,424	228,248	140,772	308,674	372,650
Net Income	1,223,870	383,002	(2,319,995)	522,217	734,596	366,694	1,014,199	1,295,697
Average Shares	612,872	586,491	578,588	580,214	580,076	563,789	561,855	514,345
Balance Sheet								
Current Assets	7,059,749	10,369,121	7,185,440	7,704,890	7,493,211	8,605,968	8,805,224	6,071,220
Total Assets	16,000,777	20,041,326	19,435,195	22,326,367	17,172,731	15,081,192	16,077,929	12,096,731
Current Liabilities	4,701,200	6,794,730	6,450,918	6,217,785	3,990,905	3,474,488	3,918,668	3,629,898
Long-Term Obligations	3,944,180	6,097,418	6,028,549	6,215,709	3,573,047	3,183,174	3,285,444	1,069,056
Total Liabilities	9,467,602	13,761,707	13,275,530	13,310,987	8,877,515	7,360,164	7,958,854	5,401,807
Stockholders' Equity	6,116,737	5,881,289	5,606,138	8,378,481	8,295,216	7,721,028	8,119,075	6,694,924
Shares Outstanding	589,258	585,948	582,173	575,890	572,724	565,931	546,134	498,036
Statistical Record								
Return on Assets %	6.77	1.94	N.M.	2.64	4.54	2.35	7.20	11.56
Return on Equity %	20.35	6.67	N.M.	6.26	9.15	4.63	13.69	21.03
EBITDA Margin %	22.70	15.21	N.M.	21.61	9.57	5.37	11.03	...
Net Margin %	10.54	2.72	N.M.	3.73	7.32	4.19	8.45	12.05
Asset Turnover	0.64	0.71	0.65	0.71	0.62	0.56	0.85	0.96
Current Ratio	1.50	1.53	1.11	1.24	1.88	2.48	2.25	1.67
Debt to Equity	0.64	1.04	1.08	0.74	0.43	0.41	0.40	0.16
Price Range	69.26-52.69	55.67-36.07	61.50-34.27	81.75-41.94	87.88-54.06	70.31-46.38	85.56-41.25	94.19-49.25
P/E Ratio	33.95-25.83	84.35-54.65	...	89.84-46.09	69.19-42.57	108.17-71.35	47.27-22.79	37.38-19.54
Average Yield %	1.20	1.66	1.56	1.30	1.00	1.27	1.17	1.10

Address: Parkstraat 83, The Hague	**Web Site:** www.slb.com	**Auditors:** PricewaterhouseCoopers LLP
Telephone: (212) 350-9400	**Officers:** Andrew Gould - Chmn., C.E.O. Jean-Marc Perraud - Exec. V.P., C.F.O.	

SCHWAB (CHARLES) CORP.

Exchange	Symbol	Price	52Wk Range	Yield	P/E
NYS	SCH	$10.51 (3/31/2005)	12.03-8.30	0.76	50.05

*7 Year Price Score 50.57 ***NYSE Composite Index=100** ***12 Month Price Score 98.57**

Interim Earnings (Per Share)

Qtr.	Mar	Jun	Sep	Dec
2001	0.07	0.07	0.01	(0.01)
2002	0.07	0.07	0.00	(0.06)
2003	0.05	0.09	0.09	0.11
2004	0.12	0.08	(0.03)	0.04

Interim Dividends (Per Share)

Amt	Decl	Ex	Rec	Pay
0.014Q	1/20/2004	2/3/2004	2/5/2004	2/19/2004
0.02Q	7/19/2004	8/3/2004	8/5/2004	8/19/2004
0.02Q	10/27/2004	11/3/2004	11/5/2004	11/19/2004
0.02Q	1/27/2005	2/7/2005	2/9/2005	2/23/2005

Indicated Div: $0.08

Valuation Analysis

Forecast P/E	19.94	No of Institutions	
	(4/7/2005)	372	
Market Cap	$14.0 Billion	Shares	
Book Value	4.4 Billion	732,242,816	
Price/Book	3.19	% Held	
Price/Sales	3.12	55.49	

Business Summary: Finance Intermediaries & Services (MIC: 8.7 SIC: 211 NAIC: 23120)

Charles Schwab, through its subsidiaries, engages in securities brokerage, banking, and related financial services. As of Dec 31 2003, Co. had $967.00 billion in client assets. Co.'s principal subsidiary, Charles Schwab & Co., is a securities broker-dealer with 339 domestic branch offices in 48 states, as well as branches in the Commonwealth of Puerto Rico. U.S. Trust is a wealth management firm that also provides fiduciary services and private banking services. Other subsidiaries include Charles Schwab Investment Management, the investment advisor for Co.'s proprietary mutual funds, and Schwab Capital Markets, a market maker in Nasdaq and other securities providing trade execution services.

Recent Developments: For the year ended Dec 31 2004, income from continuing operations decreased 13.0% to $414,000 thousand from income of $476,000 thousand a year earlier. Net income decreased 39.4% to $286,000 thousand from net income of $472,000 thousand a year earlier. Revenues were $4,202,000 thousand, up 7.9% from $3,896,000 thousand the year before.

Prospects: Co. has seen extensive change over the last six months, as it has refocused on its core strategy of meeting the needs of individual investors and the independent advisors who serve them, exited the capital markets business, and launched a firm-wide cost reduction initiative. Throughout all of these corporate actions, however, Co. has remained focused on building stronger relationships with its clients by reducing commission rates and enhancing services. As a result, Co. is set to enter fiscal 2005 as a leaner, more focused organization that can continue to rely on a strong balance sheet with $4.40 billion of stockholders' equity.

Financial Data
(US$ in Thousands)

	12/31/2004	12/31/2003	12/31/2002	12/31/2001	12/31/2000	12/31/1999	12/31/1998	12/31/1997
Earnings Per Share	0.21	0.35	0.08	0.14	0.51	0.47	0.28	0.22
Cash Flow Per Share	0.66	0.01	0.12	(0.43)	1.20	0.97	0.60	0.23
Tang Book Value Per Share	2.57	2.56	2.53	2.58	2.69	1.81	1.15	0.90
Dividends Per Share	0.074	0.050	0.044	0.044	0.041	0.037	0.036	0.031
Dividend Payout %	35.24	14.29	55.00	31.43	7.97	8.00	12.71	14.14
Income Statement								
Total Revenue	4,479,000	4,328,000	4,480,000	4,353,000	5,787,651	3,944,822	2,736,221	2,298,750
Income Before Taxes	645,000	710,000	168,000	135,000	1,231,473	971,239	576,544	447,247
Income Taxes	231,000	238,000	71,000	57,000	513,336	382,362	228,082	176,970
Net Income	286,000	472,000	109,000	199,000	718,137	588,877	348,462	270,277
Average Shares	1,365,000	1,364,000	1,375,000	1,399,000	1,403,763	1,264,635	1,234,515	1,226,589
Balance Sheet								
Total Assets	47,133,000	45,866,000	39,705,000	40,464,000	38,153,969	29,299,061	22,264,390	16,481,707
Total Liabilities	42,747,000	41,405,000	35,694,000	36,301,000	33,924,257	27,025,126	20,835,768	15,336,590
Stockholders' Equity	4,386,000	4,461,000	4,011,000	4,163,000	4,229,712	2,273,935	1,428,622	1,145,117
Shares Outstanding	1,330,656	1,357,638	1,344,795	1,368,562	1,385,625	1,233,373	1,205,649	1,204,599
Statistical Record								
Return on Assets %	0.61	1.10	0.27	0.51	2.12	2.28	1.80	1.79
Return on Equity %	6.45	11.14	2.67	4.74	22.02	31.81	27.08	27.03
Price Range	13.76-8.30	13.98-6.56	18.09-7.26	32.88-8.94	43.33-23.54	50.17-18.08	21.21-6.58	9.65-4.54
P/E Ratio	65.52-39.52	39.94-18.74	226.13-90.75	234.82-63.86	84.97-46.16	106.74-38.48	75.74-23.51	43.88-20.62
Average Yield %	0.71	0.48	0.38	0.26	0.13	0.13	0.39	0.48

Address: 101 Montgomery Street, San Francisco, CA 94104 **Telephone:** (415) 627-7000 **Fax:** (415) 627-8894	**Web Site:** www.schwab.com **Officers:** Charles R. Schwab - Chmn., C.E.O. John Philip Coghlan - Vice-Chmn., Pres., Individual Investors Group	**Auditors:** Deloitte & Touche LLP **Investor Contact:** 415-636-9869 **Transfer Agents:** Wells Fargo Bank.Minnesota, NA

SCIENTIFIC-ATLANTA INC.

Exchange	Symbol	Price	52Wk Range	Yield	P/E
NYS	SFA	$28.22 (3/31/2005)	36.06-25.08	0.14	18.32

*7 Year Price Score 89.31   *NYSE Composite Index=100   *12 Month Price Score 92.35

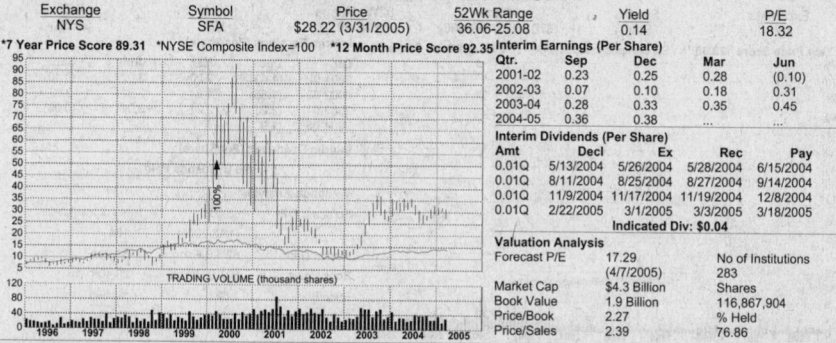

Interim Earnings (Per Share)

Qtr.	Sep	Dec	Mar	Jun
2001-02	0.23	0.25	0.28	(0.10)
2002-03	0.07	0.10	0.18	0.31
2003-04	0.28	0.33	0.35	0.45
2004-05	0.36	0.38	...	...

Interim Dividends (Per Share)

Amt	Decl	Ex	Rec	Pay
0.01Q	5/13/2004	5/26/2004	5/28/2004	6/15/2004
0.01Q	8/11/2004	8/25/2004	8/27/2004	9/14/2004
0.01Q	11/9/2004	11/17/2004	11/19/2004	12/8/2004
0.01Q	2/22/2005	3/1/2005	3/3/2005	3/18/2005

Indicated Div: $0.04

Valuation Analysis

Forecast P/E	17.29	No of Institutions	
	(4/7/2005)	283	
Market Cap	$4.3 Billion	Shares	
Book Value	1.9 Billion	116,867,904	
Price/Book	2.27	% Held	
Price/Sales	2.39	76.86	

Business Summary: Communications (MIC: 10.1 SIC: 663 NAIC: 34220)

Scientific-Atlanta is engaged in the provision of broadband transmission networks, digital interactive subscriber systems and worldwide customer service and support for the cable television industry. Co. is a producer of a variety of broadband products which deliver entertainment, information and communications from content originators to end-users. This content is delivered via hybrid fiber coax networks and, in some cases, all-fiber networks comprised of equipment and software that reside at the programmer's facility, at the operator's headend, in the outside transmission plant (whether underground or above ground), and in the homes of consumers.

Recent Developments: For the quarter ended Dec 31 2004, net income increased 14.8% to $58,693 thousand from net income of $51,131 thousand in the year-earlier quarter. Revenues were $441,672 thousand, up 6.0% from $416,566 thousand the year before. Total direct expense was $277,951 thousand versus $259,204 thousand in the prior-year quarter, an increase of 7.2%. Total indirect expense was $85,766 thousand versus $84,586 thousand in the prior-year quarter, an increase of 1.4%.

Prospects: Co. is benefiting from a mix shift toward higher-end products as consumers increase their adoption rates of high-definition television and digital video recorders. For instance, Co. sold 449,000 digital video recorders (DVRs) during the first half of fiscal 2005, an increase of 72.0% from the year before and 13.0% sequentially. Also, Co. is experiencing favorable growth in sales of subscriber products largely due to the mix shift toward higher-end digital set-top products and higher sales of cable modems, partially offset by lower set-top unit volumes and a reduction in set-top selling prices for all modems.

Financial Data

(US$ in Thousands)	6 Mos	3 Mos	07/02/2004	06/27/2003	06/28/2002	06/29/2001	06/30/2000	07/02/1999
Earnings Per Share	1.54	1.49	1.41	0.65	0.66	1.99	0.94	0.65
Cash Flow Per Share	2.21	2.11	2.09	2.38	2.29	1.61	1.41	0.30
Tang Book Value Per Share	10.69	10.39	9.98	8.00	7.61	8.70	7.58	4.72
Dividends Per Share	0.040	0.040	0.040	0.040	0.040	0.040	0.035	0.030
Dividend Payout %	2.59	2.68	2.84	6.15	6.06	2.01	3.72	4.62
Income Statement								
Total Revenue	894,346	452,674	1,708,004	1,450,353	1,671,117	2,512,016	1,715,410	1,243,473
EBITDA	168,009	84,483	350,118	201,618	196,915	540,276	254,218	184,389
Depn & Amortn	...	...	57,792	71,385	59,946	66,342	50,707	46,075
Income Before Taxes	168,009	84,483	308,333	152,098	158,435	510,402	222,583	146,205
Income Taxes	53,438	28,605	90,332	51,753	54,051	176,728	66,775	43,862
Net Income	114,571	55,878	218,001	100,345	104,384	333,674	155,808	102,343
Average Shares	154,510	155,436	154,849	153,495	158,420	167,688	164,895	157,130
Balance Sheet								
Current Assets	1,712,345	1,727,219	1,707,712	1,323,616	1,317,484	1,548,734	1,150,634	831,461
Total Assets	2,321,571	2,328,646	2,269,627	1,918,629	1,914,627	2,002,828	1,779,460	1,062,274
Current Liabilities	252,875	295,496	305,702	273,609	341,573	394,123	380,163	267,811
Long-Term Obligations	7,772	7,427	7,698	8,567	8,600	...	102	370
Total Liabilities	427,921	465,476	466,270	437,388	477,836	493,889	564,500	324,108
Stockholders' Equity	1,893,650	1,863,170	1,803,357	1,481,241	1,436,791	1,508,939	1,214,960	738,166
Shares Outstanding	151,994	153,544	153,377	149,441	156,630	164,039	159,319	154,694
Statistical Record								
Return on Assets %	10.84	10.77	10.24	5.25	5.34	17.69	11.00	10.06
Return on Equity %	13.51	13.46	13.06	6.90	7.11	24.57	16.00	14.70
EBITDA Margin %	18.79	18.66	20.50	13.90	11.78	21.51	14.82	14.83
Net Margin %	12.81	12.34	12.76	6.92	6.25	13.28	9.08	8.23
Asset Turnover	0.81	0.82	0.80	0.76	0.86	1.33	1.21	1.22
Current Ratio	6.77	5.85	5.59	4.84	3.86	3.93	3.03	3.10
Debt to Equity	N.M.	N.M.	N.M.	N.M.	0.01	0.01	N.M.	N.M.
Price Range	36.06-25.08	36.80-25.08	37.02-23.57	24.89-11.01	44.45-15.82	93.38-30.00	76.50-16.97	19.66-6.34
P/E Ratio	23.42-16.29	24.70-16.83	26.26-16.72	38.29-16.94	67.35-23.97	46.92-15.08	81.38-18.05	30.25-9.75
Average Yield %	0.13	0.13	0.13	0.28	0.17	0.07	0.09	0.23

Address: 5030 Sugarloaf Parkway, Lawrenceville, GA 30044	**Web Site:** www.scientificatlanta.com	**Auditors:** ERNST & YOUNG LLP
Telephone: (770) 236-5000	**Officers:** James F. McDonald - Chmn., Pres., C.E.O.	**Investor Contact:** 770-903-4608
Fax: (770) 903-4775	H. Allen Ecker - Exec. V.P.	

SCOTTS MIRACLE-GRO CO (THE)

Exchange	Symbol	Price	52Wk Range	Yield	P/E
NYS	SMG	$70.23 (3/31/2005)	73.65-56.02	N/A	25.63

*7 Year Price Score 122.30 ***NYSE Composite Index=100** ***12 Month Price Score 98.52**

Interim Earnings (Per Share)

Qtr.	Dec	Mar	Jun	Sep
2001-02	(1.63)	2.20	3.02	(0.40)
2002-03	(1.55)	1.94	2.81	0.03
2003-04	(2.21)	2.21	3.01	(0.06)
2004-05	(1.90)	...	...	...

Interim Dividends (Per Share)

No Dividends Paid

Valuation Analysis

Forecast P/E	15.56	No of Institutions
	(4/13/2005)	184
Market Cap	$2.3 Billion	Shares
Book Value	827.9 Million	20,106,716
Price/Book	2.82	% Held
Price/Sales	1.21	60.44

Business Summary: Chemicals (MIC: 11.1 SIC: 879 NAIC: 25320)

The Scotts Company is engaged in the manufacture, marketing and sale of lawn and garden care products. Co.'s brands include Scotts®, Turf Builder®, Miracle-Gro® and Ortho®. Co. is also Monsanto's exclusive agent for the marketing and distribution of consumer Roundup® non-selective herbicide within the U.S. and other contractually specified countries. Co. operates in three principle business segments: the North America segment, which manufactures and markets products in the U.S. Canada, Latin America and South America; the International segment; and the Scotts LawnService® segment, which provides lawn and tree and shrub fertilization, insect control and other related services in the U.S.

Recent Developments: For the quarter ended Jan 1 2005, loss from continuing operations was $62,500 thousand compared with a loss of $70,700 thousand in the year-earlier quarter. Net loss increased was $62,700 thousand versus a net loss of $70,700 thousand in the year-earlier quarter. Revenues were $243,200 thousand, up 34.7% from $180,600 thousand the year before. Operating loss was $90,500 thousand versus a loss of $59,000 thousand in the prior-year quarter. Total direct expense was $182,100 thousand versus $139,800 thousand in the prior-year quarter, an increase of 30.3%. Total indirect expense was $151,800 thousand versus $101,600 thousand in the prior-year quarter, an increase of 49.4%.

Prospects: Co. is enjoying a strong start to fiscal 2005, led by better than anticipated sales and operating profits in all of its business segments. Also, Co. is benefiting from margin growth, largely due to the positive impact of recently acquired Smith & Hawkins, which typically enjoys higher gross margin than Co.'s other businesses. The strong start, coupled with the combination of new products, trade programs and continued consumer interest in gardening, provides Co. with increased confidence that it can achieve its goal of delivering 10.0% to 12.0% adjusted net income growth for 2005.

Financial Data
(US$ in Thousands)

	3 Mos	09/30/2004	09/30/2003	09/30/2002	09/30/2001	09/30/2000	09/30/1999	09/30/1998
Earnings Per Share	2.74	3.03	3.23	2.61	0.51	2.25	2.08	1.20
Cash Flow Per Share	8.95	6.61	7.06	7.66	2.31	6.13	4.27	3.80
Tang Book Value Per Share	N.M.	0.78	N.M.	N.M.	N.M.	N.M.	N.M.	N.M.
Income Statement								
Total Revenue	242,400	2,037,900	1,910,100	1,760,600	1,747,700	1,764,300	1,648,300	1,113,000
EBITDA	(74,600)	261,700	281,400	279,300	176,700	264,500	250,500	128,600
Depn & Amortn	15,900	54,400	48,900	40,100	60,300	54,300	54,400	34,500
Income Before Taxes	(100,900)	158,500	163,300	162,900	28,700	116,300	117,000	61,900
Income Taxes	(38,400)	58,000	59,500	61,900	13,200	43,200	47,900	24,900
Net Income	(62,700)	100,900	103,800	82,500	15,500	73,100	63,200	36,300
Average Shares	33,000	33,300	32,100	31,700	30,400	29,600	30,500	30,300
Balance Sheet								
Current Assets	855,800	830,300	810,200	730,100	694,200	643,900	641,700	367,200
Total Assets	2,131,100	2,047,800	2,027,900	1,901,400	1,843,000	1,761,400	1,769,600	1,035,200
Current Liabilities	451,700	433,600	445,800	451,800	445,100	409,800	366,900	231,900
Long-Term Obligations	727,200	608,500	702,200	731,200	816,500	813,400	893,600	359,200
Total Liabilities	1,303,200	1,173,200	1,299,700	1,307,500	1,336,800	1,283,500	1,326,300	631,300
Stockholders' Equity	827,900	874,600	728,200	593,900	506,200	477,900	443,300	403,900
Shares Outstanding	33,200	32,800	32,000	30,100	28,700	27,900	18,400	18,300
Statistical Record								
Return on Assets %	4.43	4.94	5.28	4.41	0.86	4.13	4.51	3.98
Return on Equity %	12.28	12.56	15.70	15.00	3.15	15.83	14.92	9.15
EBITDA Margin %	N.M.	12.84	14.73	15.86	10.11	14.99	15.20	11.55
Net Margin %	N.M.	4.95	5.43	4.69	0.89	4.14	3.83	3.26
Asset Turnover	0.93	1.00	0.97	0.94	0.97	1.00	1.18	1.22
Current Ratio	1.89	1.91	1.82	1.62	1.56	1.57	1.75	1.58
Debt to Equity	0.88	0.70	0.96	1.23	1.61	1.70	2.02	0.89
Price Range	73.65-56.02	68.55-54.70	57.70-41.69	50.35-34.45	47.10-28.88	42.00-29.44	47.63-26.63	41.38-26.25
P/E Ratio	26.88-20.45	22.62-18.05	17.86-12.91	19.29-13.20	92.35-56.62	18.67-13.08	22.90-12.80	34.48-21.88

Address: 14111 Scottslawn Rd., Marysville, OH 43041	Web Site: www.scotts.com	Auditors: PricewaterhouseCoopers LLP
Telephone: (937) 644-0011	Officers: James Hagedorn - Chmn., Pres., C.E.O. Michael P. Kelty - Vice-Chmn., Exec. V.P.	Investor Contact: 614-719-5500
Fax: (937) 644-7614		

SCRIPPS (E.W.) CO. (NEW) (OH)

Exchange	Symbol	Price	52Wk Range	Yield	P/E
NYS	SSP	$48.75 (3/31/2005)	54.28-45.40	0.82	26.49

*7 Year Price Score 123.19 ***NYSE Composite Index=100** ***12 Month Price Score 88.80**

Interim Earnings (Per Share)
Qtr.	Mar	Jun	Sep	Dec
2001	0.41	0.25	0.14	0.06
2002	0.25	0.17	0.28	0.47
2003	0.33	0.40	0.32	0.62
2004	0.43	0.53	0.34	0.55

Interim Dividends (Per Share)
Amt	Decl	Ex	Rec	Pay
0.10Q	7/29/2004	8/27/2004	8/31/2004	9/10/2004
100%	7/29/2004	9/13/2004	8/31/2004	9/10/2004
0.10Q	10/28/2004	11/26/2004	11/30/2004	12/10/2004
0.10Q	2/10/2005	2/24/2005	2/28/2005	3/10/2005

Indicated Div: $0.40

Valuation Analysis
Forecast P/E	N/A	No of Institutions
Market Cap	$8.0 Billion	Shares
Book Value	2.1 Billion	86,032,952
Price/Book	3.80	% Held
Price/Sales	3.67	67.96

Business Summary: Media (MIC: 13.1 SIC: 711 NAIC: 11110)

Scripps (E.W.) is a diverse media company with four business segments: newspaper publishing, cable and satellite television programming services, broadcast television and television retailing. Co. also operates United Media, which is the worldwide licensing and syndication home of the Peanuts and Dilbert comic strips. Co. has four national television networks that are distributed by cable and satellite television, including Home & Garden Television, Food Network, Fine Living and Do It Yourself. Co. has a 12.0% interest in FOX Sports Net South and its broadcast television segment includes 10 television stations. Co. has 21 daily newspapers in the U.S.

Recent Developments: For the year ended Dec 31 2004, net income increased 12.2% to $303,811 thousand from net income of $270,815 thousand a year earlier. Revenues were $2,167,503 thousand, up 15.6% from $1,874,845 thousand the year before. Operating income was $465,724 thousand versus an income of $365,330 thousand in the prior year, an increase of 27.5%. Total direct expense was $1,085,025 thousand versus $921,633 thousand in the prior year, an increase of 17.7%. Total indirect expense was $616,754 thousand versus $587,876 thousand in the prior year, an increase of 4.9%.

Prospects: Based on advance advertising sales, Co. anticipates first quarter 2005 advertising revenue for Scripps Networks will be up about 25.0% year over year. Newspaper advertising revenues are expected to be up low single digits over the prior year in the first quarter. At Co.'s broadcast television stations, advertising revenues are expected to be up about 2.0% to 4.0% in the first quarter, excluding political. Co.'s continuing investment in the Shop at Home Network is expected to reduce first quarter segment profit by about $5.0 million. Tribune Company, which owns 31.0% of the Food Network, minority interest is expected to be between $9.0 million and $11.0 million in the first quarter.

Financial Data
(US$ in Thousands)	12/31/2004	12/31/2003	12/31/2002	12/31/2001	12/31/2000	12/31/1999	12/31/1998	12/31/1997
Earnings Per Share	1.84	1.66	1.17	0.86	1.03	0.93	0.81	0.96
Cash Flow Per Share	2.37	2.04	1.34	1.31	1.63	1.24	1.46	1.22
Tang Book Value Per Share	0.72	1.21	N.M.	N.M.	N.M.	N.M.	N.M.	N.M.
Dividends Per Share	0.388	0.300	0.300	0.300	0.280	0.280	0.270	0.260
Dividend Payout %	21.06	18.07	25.64	34.68	27.18	30.11	33.33	26.94
Income Statement								
Total Revenue	2,167,503	1,874,845	1,618,909	1,437,131	1,719,359	1,571,292	1,454,555	1,241,957
EBITDA	642,535	522,742	399,991	379,706	437,101	404,526	380,115	376,450
Depn & Amortn	69,004	68,087	62,768	99,127	109,165	103,851	103,845	77,606
Income Before Taxes	542,653	423,062	308,922	241,382	276,002	255,456	229,162	280,301
Income Taxes	195,773	137,974	115,619	99,622	108,090	104,073	93,075	117,510
Net Income	303,811	270,815	188,297	137,963	163,453	146,933	131,214	157,702
Average Shares	164,917	162,938	161,238	159,940	158,322	157,902	161,842	163,290
Balance Sheet								
Current Assets	643,298	562,437	500,011	450,658	523,985	477,284	407,333	379,114
Total Assets	3,424,849	3,009,402	2,870,337	2,643,760	2,572,866	2,520,204	2,345,112	2,280,833
Current Liabilities	375,346	330,959	426,073	905,511	532,976	577,269	532,491	429,960
Long-Term Obligations	532,686	509,117	649,801	109,966	501,781	501,847	501,834	601,852
Total Liabilities	1,328,728	1,186,871	1,354,872	1,291,860	1,295,056	1,355,929	1,276,380	1,231,871
Stockholders' Equity	2,096,121	1,822,531	1,515,465	1,351,900	1,277,810	1,164,275	1,068,732	1,048,962
Shares Outstanding	163,190	161,936	160,074	158,401	157,477	156,284	157,088	161,260
Statistical Record								
Return on Assets %	9.42	9.21	6.83	5.29	6.40	6.04	5.67	8.41
Return on Equity %	15.46	16.23	13.13	10.49	13.35	13.16	12.39	15.82
EBITDA Margin %	29.64	27.88	24.71	26.42	25.42	25.74	26.13	30.31
Net Margin %	14.02	14.44	11.63	9.60	9.51	9.35	9.02	12.70
Asset Turnover	0.67	0.64	0.59	0.55	0.67	0.65	0.63	0.66
Current Ratio	1.71	1.70	1.17	0.50	0.98	0.83	0.76	0.88
Debt to Equity	0.25	0.28	0.43	0.08	0.39	0.43	0.47	0.57
Price Range	54.28-45.40	47.42-37.56	43.63-32.88	35.63-28.23	31.44-21.25	26.38-20.47	29.19-19.50	24.25-16.13
P/E Ratio	29.50-24.67	28.57-22.62	37.29-28.10	41.44-32.83	30.52-20.63	28.36-22.01	36.03-24.07	25.26-16.80
Average Yield %	0.78	0.70	0.80	0.93	1.12	1.19	1.07	1.32

Address: 312 Walnut Street, Cincinnati, OH 45202	Web Site: www.scripps.com	Auditors: Deloitte & Touche LLP
Telephone: (513) 977-3000	Officers: William R. Burleigh - Chmn. Kenneth W. Lowe - Pres., C.E.O.	Investor Contact: 513-977-3826
Fax: (513) 977-3721		

713

SEALED AIR CORP.

Exchange	Symbol	Price	52Wk Range	Yield	P/E
NYS	SEE	$51.94 (3/31/2005)	53.70-44.28	N/A	23.08

*7 Year Price Score 94.43 ***NYSE Composite Index=100** ***12 Month Price Score 96.49**

Interim Earnings (Per Share)

Qtr.	Mar	Jun	Sep	Dec
2001	0.25	0.30	0.37	0.30
2002	0.56	0.61	0.62	(6.09)
2003	0.52	0.56	0.41	0.50
2004	0.64	0.66	0.69	0.27

Interim Dividends (Per Share)

No Dividends Paid

Valuation Analysis

Forecast P/E	N/A	No of Institutions	
Market Cap	$4.3 Billion	Shares	
Book Value	1.3 Billion	72,140,560	
Price/Book	3.26	% Held	
Price/Sales	1.14	86.33	

Business Summary: Plastics (MIC: 11.7 SIC: 081 NAIC: 26140)

Sealed Air is a holding company. Through its subsidiaries, Co. manufactures and sells a wide range of food, protective and specialty packaging products. Co. operates through two wholly-owned subsidiaries, Cryovac, Inc. and Sealed Air Corporation (US). The Food Packaging segment and Protective and Specialty Packaging segment comprise Co.'s operations. Co.'s food packaging products include its flexible materials and related systems marketed primarily under the Cryovac® trademark for packaging a broad range of perishable foods and Co.'s rigid packaging and absorbent pads. Co.'s protective and specialty packaging products provide cushioning, surface protection and void fill.

Recent Developments: For the year ended Dec 30 2004, net income decreased 10.3% to $215,600 thousand from net income of $240,400 a year earlier. Revenues were $3,798,100 thousand, up 7.5% from $3,531,900 thousand the year before. Operating income was $503,000 thousand versus an income of $540,900 thousand in the prior year, a decrease of 7.0%. Total direct expense was $2,636,000 thousand versus $2,419,100 thousand in the prior year, an increase of 9.0%. Total indirect expense was $659,100 thousand versus $571,900 thousand in the prior year, an increase of 15.2%.

Prospects: Results continue reflect the strength of Co.'s business and its ability to surpass through a challenging raw material cost environment. Co. continues to see strong performance in its global protective packaging business, complemented by solid growth in its international food packaging business. Going forward, Co. plans to use its strong cash flow to invest in the growth of its business and to consider both debt reduction and common stock repurchases. Co. expects that its enhanced supply chain capabilities will enable it to further leverage its global economies of scale and improve its cost structure.

Financial Data

(US$ in Thousands)	12/30/2004	12/31/2003	12/31/2002	12/31/2001	12/31/2000	12/31/1999	12/31/1998	12/31/1997
Earnings Per Share	2.25	2.00	(4.30)	1.22	1.93	1.68	0.02	1.88
Cash Flow Per Share	5.18	5.55	3.86	6.91	3.93	5.15	5.64	2.54
Tang Book Value Per Share	N.M.	N.M.	N.M.	N.M.	N.M.	N.M.	N.M.	4.80
Income Statement								
Total Revenue	3,798,100	3,531,900	3,204,256	3,067,482	3,067,714	2,839,636	2,506,756	842,833
EBITDA	659,300	684,800	(160,919)	595,027	697,901	677,347	448,530	184,520
Depn & Amortn	182,700	173,600	165,699	221,177	219,959	223,568	195,954	45,778
Income Before Taxes	322,900	376,900	(391,933)	297,452	413,429	395,653	198,947	133,488
Income Taxes	107,300	136,500	(82,864)	140,755	188,110	184,192	125,940	53,567
Net Income	215,600	240,400	(309,069)	156,697	225,319	211,461	73,007	79,921
Average Shares	99,360	93,690	84,290	83,900	87,951	84,128	73,273	...
Balance Sheet								
Current Assets	1,611,200	1,427,800	1,056,258	776,352	877,080	803,224	844,614	250,765
Total Assets	4,855,000	4,704,100	4,260,766	3,907,909	4,048,098	3,855,233	4,039,930	498,360
Current Liabilities	1,303,800	1,190,400	1,152,754	626,980	674,568	582,094	534,990	163,610
Long-Term Obligations	2,088,000	2,259,800	868,030	788,111	944,453	665,116	996,526	48,506
Total Liabilities	3,521,500	3,580,500	2,120,801	1,691,603	1,902,596	1,542,541	1,811,792	241,077
Stockholders' Equity	1,333,500	1,123,600	812,960	850,152	753,129	551,030	437,045	257,283
Shares Outstanding	83,624	85,085	84,040	83,776	83,646	83,599	83,311	42,624
Statistical Record								
Return on Assets %	4.51	5.36	N.M.	3.94	5.69	5.36	3.22	16.56
Return on Equity %	17.55	24.83	N.M.	19.55	34.46	42.80	21.03	36.01
EBITDA Margin %	17.36	19.39	N.M.	19.40	22.75	23.85	17.89	21.89
Net Margin %	5.68	6.81	N.M.	5.11	7.34	7.45	2.91	9.48
Asset Turnover	0.79	0.79	0.78	0.77	0.77	0.72	1.10	1.75
Current Ratio	1.24	1.20	0.92	1.24	1.30	1.38	1.58	1.53
Debt to Equity	1.57	2.01	1.07	0.93	1.25	1.21	2.28	0.19
Price Range	54.55-44.28	54.47-35.42	48.13-13.15	46.90-30.81	60.75-26.75	67.75-45.00	69.50-27.88	62.69-39.88
P/E Ratio	24.24-19.68	27.23-17.71	...	38.44-25.26	31.48-13.86	40.33-26.79	N.M.	33.34-21.21

Address: Park 80 East, Saddle Brook, NJ 07663-5291	Web Site: www.sealedair.com	Auditors: KPMG LLP
Telephone: (201) 791-7600	Officers: William V. Hickey - Pres., C.E.O. David H. Kelsey - Sr. V.P., C.F.O.	
Fax: (201) 703-4205		

SEMPRA ENERGY

Exchange	Symbol	Price	52Wk Range	Yield	P/E
NYS	SRE	$39.84 (3/31/2005)	42.18-31.08	2.91	10.40

*7 Year Price Score N/A   *NYSE Composite Index=100   *12 Month Price Score 103.56

Interim Earnings (Per Share)

Qtr.	Mar	Jun	Sep	Dec
2001	0.88	0.66	0.46	0.52
2002	0.71	0.71	0.73	0.72
2003	0.42	0.55	1.00	1.05
2004	0.85	0.52	0.98	1.47

Interim Dividends (Per Share)

Amt	Decl	Ex	Rec	Pay
0.25Q	6/8/2004	6/21/2004	6/23/2004	7/15/2004
0.25Q	9/14/2004	9/27/2004	9/29/2004	10/15/2004
0.25Q	12/3/2004	12/20/2004	12/22/2004	1/15/2005
0.29Q	2/22/2005	3/22/2005	3/24/2005	4/15/2005

Indicated Div: $1.16

Valuation Analysis

Forecast P/E	12.42	No of Institutions
	(4/7/2005)	318
Market Cap	$9.3 Billion	Shares
Book Value	4.9 Billion	133,941,592
Price/Book	1.92	% Held
Price/Sales	0.99	56.85

Business Summary: Electricity (MIC: 7.1 SIC: 932 NAIC: 21210)

Sempra Energy is an energy services holding company that provides a range of electric and natural gas products and services. Co.'s primary subsidiaries are San Diego Gas & Electric and Southern California Gas Company, two utilities providing service through 1.3 million electric meters and 6.3 million gas meters, as of Dec 31 2004, and Sempra Global, which holds Co.'s non-regulated energy-related operations. Sempra Global's operations include wholesale energy trading, competitive power operations, developing regasification terminals for liquid natural gas, and engaging in energy infrastructure projects in North and South America.

Recent Developments: For the year ended Dec 31 2004, net income increased 37.9% to $895,000 thousand from net income of $649,000 thousand a year earlier. Revenues were $9,410,000 thousand, up 19.3% from $7,887,000 thousand the year before. Operating income was $1,272,000 thousand versus an income of $939,000 thousand in the prior year, an increase of 35.5%. Total direct expense was $4,910,000 thousand versus $3,816,000 thousand in the prior year, an increase of 28.7%. Total indirect expense was $3,228,000 thousand versus $3,132,000 thousand in the prior year, an increase of 3.1%.

Prospects: On Mar 8 2005, Co. updated its earnings outlook by providing earnings per share guidance for 2006 of $3.20 to $3.40 and, for 2009, a target of $3.70 to $4.20. Co. expects 2005 earnings per share of $3.10 to $3.30. Separately, Sempra LNG, a unit of Co., announced that it has entered into an Heads of Agreement with Eni S.p.A. for about one-third of the capacity of Sempra LNG's Cameron LNG receipt terminal under development near Lake Charles, LA. With this and other agreements being negotiated, Sempra LNG expects the terminal's 1.50 billion cubic feet per day of capacity to be fully contracted by mid-year, so that construction can begin. The facility is scheduled to be operational in 2008.

Financial Data

(US$ in Thousands)	12/31/2004	12/31/2003	12/31/2002	12/31/2001	12/31/2000	12/31/1999	12/31/1998	12/31/1997
Earnings Per Share	3.83	3.03	2.87	2.52	2.06	1.66	1.24	1.82
Cash Flow Per Share	4.15	5.29	6.69	3.60	4.23	5.01	5.61	3.87
Tang Book Value Per Share	20.77	17.17	13.79	13.17	12.35	12.58	12.14	12.54
Dividends Per Share	1.000	1.000	1.000	1.000	1.000	1.560	0.780	1.270
Dividend Payout %	26.11	33.00	34.84	39.68	48.54	93.98	62.90	69.78
Income Statement								
Total Revenue	9,410,000	7,887,000	6,020,000	8,029,000	7,143,000	5,435,000	5,525,000	5,127,000
EBITDA	1,987,000	1,561,000	1,611,000	1,633,000	1,548,000	1,378,000	1,568,000	1,543,000
Depn & Amortn	621,000	615,000	596,000	579,000	563,000	576,000	929,000	604,000
Income Before Taxes	1,113,000	742,000	721,000	731,000	699,000	573,000	432,000	733,000
Income Taxes	193,000	47,000	146,000	213,000	270,000	179,000	138,000	301,000
Net Income	895,000	649,000	591,000	518,000	429,000	394,000	294,000	432,000
Average Shares	233,852	214,482	206,062	205,338	208,345	237,553	237,000	237,000
Balance Sheet								
Net PPE	11,086,000	10,474,000	6,832,000	6,217,000	5,726,000	5,394,000	5,441,000	6,119,000
Total Assets	23,643,000	22,009,000	17,757,000	15,156,000	15,612,000	11,270,000	10,456,000	10,751,000
Long-Term Obligations	4,192,000	3,841,000	4,083,000	3,436,000	3,268,000	2,902,000	2,795,000	3,175,000
Total Liabilities	18,778,000	18,119,000	14,932,000	12,464,000	13,118,000	8,284,000	7,543,000	7,792,000
Stockholders' Equity	4,865,000	3,890,000	2,825,000	2,692,000	2,494,000	2,986,000	2,913,000	2,959,000
Shares Outstanding	234,175	226,598	204,912	204,475	201,927	237,408	240,000	236,000
Statistical Record								
Return on Assets %	3.91	3.26	3.59	3.37	3.18	3.63	2.77	4.21
Return on Equity %	20.39	19.33	21.42	19.98	15.61	13.36	10.01	14.67
EBITDA Margin %	21.12	19.79	26.76	20.34	21.67	25.35	28.38	30.10
Net Margin %	9.51	8.23	9.82	6.45	6.01	7.25	5.32	8.43
PPE Turnover	0.87	0.91	0.92	1.34	1.28	1.00	0.96	0.82
Asset Turnover	0.41	0.40	0.37	0.52	0.53	0.50	0.52	0.50
Debt to Equity	0.86	0.99	1.45	1.28	1.31	0.97	0.96	1.07
Price Range	37.80-29.74	30.67-22.50	26.01-16.00	28.39-18.19	24.50-16.63	26.00-17.31	29.19-24.06	...
P/E Ratio	9.87-7.77	10.12-7.43	9.06-5.57	11.27-7.22	11.89-8.07	15.66-10.43	23.54-19.41	...
Average Yield %	2.95	3.70	4.38	4.07	5.18	7.34	3.00	...

Address: 101 Ash Street, San Diego, CA 92101-3017
Telephone: (619) 696-2034
Fax: (619) 696-2374

Web Site: www.sempra.com
Officers: Stephen L. Baum - Chmn., Pres., C.E.O. M. Javade Chaudhri - Exec. V.P., Gen. Couns.

Auditors: Deloitte & Touche LLP
Transfer Agents: EquiServe Trust Company, N.A., Providence, RI

SENSIENT TECHNOLOGIES CORP.

Exchange	Symbol	Price	52Wk Range	Yield	P/E
NYS	SXT	$21.56 (3/31/2005)	24.19-18.56	2.78	13.65

*7 Year Price Score 86.58 ***NYSE Composite Index=100** ***12 Month Price Score 95.64**

Interim Earnings (Per Share)

Qtr.	Mar	Jun	Sep	Dec
2001	0.39	0.38	0.35	0.42
2002	0.36	0.44	0.42	0.47
2003	0.43	0.46	0.44	0.40
2004	0.32	0.39	0.46	0.41

Interim Dividends (Per Share)

Amt	Decl	Ex	Rec	Pay
0.15Q	4/22/2004	5/6/2004	5/10/2004	6/1/2004
0.15Q	7/15/2004	8/5/2004	8/9/2004	9/1/2004
0.15Q	10/14/2004	11/4/2004	11/8/2004	12/1/2004
0.15Q	1/20/2005	2/7/2005	2/9/2005	3/1/2005

Indicated Div: $0.60

Valuation Analysis

Forecast P/E	13.01 (4/7/2005)	No of Institutions	159
Market Cap	$1.0 Billion	Shares	44,350,376
Book Value	658.7 Million	% Held	94.14
Price/Book	1.54		
Price/Sales	0.97		

Business Summary: Food (MIC: 4.1 SIC: 087 NAIC: 11930)

Sensient Technologies is a manufacturer and marketer of colors, flavors and fragrances. It employs advanced technologies at facilities around the world to develop specialty chemicals for inkjet inks, display imaging systems and other applications. Co's customers include major international manufacturers representing some of the world's best-known brands. Co's principal products include: flavors, flavor enhancers & bio-nutrients, fragrances & aroma chemicals, dehydrated vegetables & other food ingredients, natural & synthetic food colors, cosmetic & pharmaceutical additives, inkjet inks, technical colors and specialty dyes & pigments and chemicals for laser printing & flat screen display.

Recent Developments: For the year ended Dec 31 2004, net income decreased 9.2% to $73,918 thousand from net income of $81,432 thousand a year earlier. Revenues were $1,047,133 thousand, up 6.1% from $987,209 thousand the year before. Operating income was $129,156 thousand versus an income of $137,484 thousand in the prior year, a decrease of 6.1%. Total direct expense was $724,596 thousand versus $677,414 thousand in the prior year, an increase of 8.4%. Total indirect expense was $183,381 thousand versus $172,311 thousand in the prior year, an increase of 6.4%.

Prospects: Revenues are benefiting from improvement across the company. Co.'s Flavors & Fragrances group is being positively affected by growth in sales of traditional flavors in the North American market. In addition, revenue from Co.'s Color group is benefiting from continuing sales growth for cosmetic and pharmaceutical colors. Meanwhile, Co. recently began seeing improvement in food and beverage color sales as well as higher sales from inkjet inks related to a supply agreement with an original equipment manufacturer. Co. expects its business to continue to strengthen in 2005 and is on track to achieve its cash flow and debt reduction objectives. For 2005, Co. expects earnings of $1.65 per share.

Financial Data
(US$ in Thousands)

	12/31/2004	12/31/2003	12/31/2002	12/31/2001	12/31/2000	12/31/1999	09/30/1999	09/30/1998
Earnings Per Share	1.58	1.73	1.69	1.54	1.26	0.37	1.57	1.40
Cash Flow Per Share	2.69	1.21	1.99	1.25	1.87	(0.08)	2.03	1.84
Tang Book Value Per Share	4.00	2.86	2.16	2.65	2.54	3.32	3.04	3.69
Dividends Per Share	0.600	0.600	0.537	0.530	0.530	0.530	0.530	0.530
Dividend Payout %	37.97	34.68	31.80	34.42	42.06	143.24	33.76	37.86
Income Statement								
Total Revenue	1,047,133	987,408	939,886	816,947	809,163	198,693	920,192	856,772
EBITDA	175,399	180,582	187,785	167,780	157,747	27,907	194,027	173,094
Depn & Amortn	46,243	43,098	41,290	46,290	45,554	...	48,917	44,232
Income Before Taxes	97,891	108,344	116,972	89,959	78,028	20,758	119,076	107,677
Income Taxes	23,973	26,912	36,282	24,996	21,681	6,634	38,938	35,033
Net Income	73,918	81,432	80,690	73,602	62,043	18,497	80,138	72,644
Average Shares	46,877	47,041	47,788	47,926	49,166	50,462	51,109	51,837
Balance Sheet								
Current Assets	536,244	536,730	475,578	415,222	491,398	405,673	404,570	357,755
Total Assets	1,488,578	1,453,528	1,289,971	1,104,820	1,164,248	1,131,713	1,142,708	991,226
Current Liabilities	255,225	282,420	209,330	192,188	252,132	237,715	241,693	209,820
Long-Term Obligations	525,153	525,924	511,707	423,137	417,141	380,378	385,397	291,588
Total Liabilities	829,880	873,410	790,613	674,000	747,190	700,841	711,126	585,581
Stockholders' Equity	658,698	580,118	499,358	430,816	417,058	430,872	431,582	405,645
Shares Outstanding	47,067	46,724	47,208	47,409	48,551	48,192	50,340	51,157
Statistical Record								
Return on Assets %	5.01	5.94	6.74	6.49	5.39	1.39	7.51	7.73
Return on Equity %	11.90	15.09	17.35	17.36	14.59	3.53	19.14	18.48
EBITDA Margin %	16.75	18.29	19.98	20.54	19.50	14.05	21.09	20.20
Net Margin %	7.06	8.25	8.59	9.01	7.67	9.31	8.71	8.48
Asset Turnover	0.71	0.72	0.78	0.72	0.70	0.15	0.86	0.91
Current Ratio	2.10	1.90	2.27	2.16	1.95	1.71	1.67	1.71
Debt to Equity	0.80	0.91	1.02	0.98	1.00	0.88	0.89	0.72
Price Range	24.19-18.15	24.18-18.00	25.85-18.07	23.81-15.60	23.06-16.06	22.94-18.63	27.44-20.06	25.31-19.28
P/E Ratio	15.31-11.49	13.98-10.40	15.30-10.69	15.46-10.13	18.30-12.75	61.99-50.34	17.48-12.78	18.08-13.77
Average Yield %	2.88	2.85	2.41	2.64	2.73	2.63	2.37	2.37

Address: 777 East Wisconsin Avenue, Milwaukee, WI 53202-5304 Telephone: (414) 271-6755 Fax: (414) 347-4795	Web Site: www.sensient-tech.com Officers: Kenneth P. Manning - Chmn., Pres., C.E.O. Richard Carney - V.P., Admin.	Auditors: Deloitte & Touche LLP Transfer Agents: Wells Fargo Bank Minnesota N.A.

SEQUA CORP.

Exchange	Symbol	Price	52Wk Range	Yield	P/E
NYS	SQA A	$51.85 (3/31/2005)	62.02-45.35	N/A	31.62

*7 Year Price Score 92.40   *NYSE Composite Index=100   *12 Month Price Score 96.25

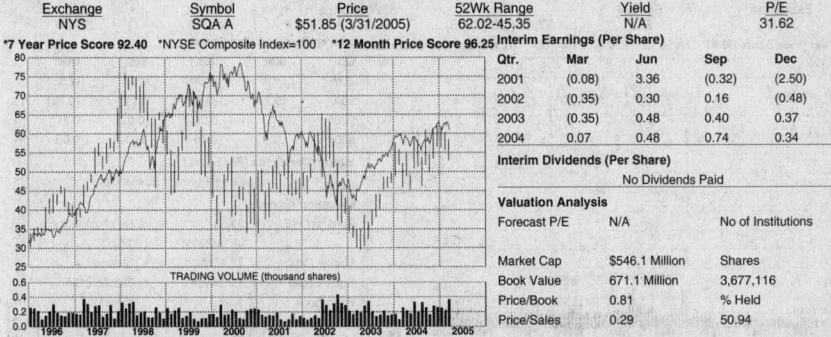

Interim Earnings (Per Share)

Qtr.	Mar	Jun	Sep	Dec
2001	(0.08)	3.36	(0.32)	(2.50)
2002	(0.35)	0.30	0.16	(0.48)
2003	(0.35)	0.48	0.40	0.37
2004	0.07	0.48	0.74	0.34

Interim Dividends (Per Share)

No Dividends Paid

Valuation Analysis

Forecast P/E	N/A	No of Institutions
Market Cap	$546.1 Million	Shares
Book Value	671.1 Million	3,677,116
Price/Book	0.81	% Held
Price/Sales	0.29	50.94

Business Summary: Aviation (MIC: 1.1 SIC: 724 NAIC: 36412)

Sequa is a diversified industrial company that produces a broad range of products through operating units in five business segments: Aerospace consists of Co's largest operating unit, Chromalloy Gas Turbine, which repairs and manufactures components for jet aircraft engines; Propulsion consists of Atlantic Research, a supplier of solid rocket fuel propulsion systems; Metal Coating consists of Precoat Metals, which applies protective and decorative coatings to continuous steel and aluminum coil; Specialty Chemicals consists solely of Warwick International, which is a producer and supplier of TAED, a bleach activator for laundry and dishwasher products; and Other Products.

Recent Developments: For the year ended Dec 31 2004, income from continuing operations was $12,670 thousand compared with a loss of $845 thousand a year earlier. Net income increased 68.1% to $19,227 thousand from net income of $11,438 thousand a year earlier. Revenues were $1,864,063 thousand, up 20.5% from $1,547,284 thousand the year before. Operating income was $79,873 thousand versus an income of $47,823 thousand in the prior year, an increase of 67.0%. Total direct expense was $1,532,012 thousand versus $1,295,668 thousand in the prior year, an increase of 18.2%. Total indirect expense was $252,178 thousand versus $203,793 thousand in the prior year, an increase of 23.7%.

Prospects: Co.'s prospects appear constructive, reflecting recent top line increases from across its business segments, with the exception of Metal Coating. Operating earnings gains for the quarter ended Dec 31 2004 were also broad based. Co. attributed the improved results to several factors, including improvement in the commercial aerospace aftermarket and the effect of sales added at Co.'s aerospace unit through new engine component repair contracts with major airlines; the benefit of higher volumes and improved efficiencies at the automotive operations; the favorable effect of translating foreign currency results into US dollars; and the ongoing contribution of initiatives to enhance productivity.

Financial Data

(US$ in Thousands)	12/31/2004	12/31/2003	12/31/2002	12/31/2001	12/31/2000	12/31/1999	12/31/1998	12/31/1997
Earnings Per Share	1.64	0.90	(11.39)	0.58	2.12	1.93	5.87	1.66
Cash Flow Per Share	1.15	(5.39)	7.67	8.48	4.07	0.50	4.61	10.09
Tang Book Value Per Share	49.45	42.34	30.48	33.25	35.02	32.14	32.51	28.79
Income Statement								
Total Revenue	1,864,063	1,665,461	1,688,498	1,755,775	1,773,138	1,699,529	1,802,393	1,595,125
EBITDA	171,610	148,640	151,013	122,832	183,073	189,560	244,446	173,269
Depn & Amortn	89,566	79,452	84,313	98,560	88,617	87,156	89,321	85,815
Income Before Taxes	12,270	1,665	5,082	(35,651)	42,047	49,399	107,997	41,827
Income Taxes	(400)	(3,200)	(4,100)	(7,700)	18,000	21,600	44,100	22,200
Net Income	19,227	11,438	(116,542)	8,049	24,047	22,067	63,897	19,627
Average Shares	10,519	10,437	10,415	10,384	10,374	10,371	10,894	10,014
Balance Sheet								
Current Assets	1,062,728	1,016,487	859,143	843,950	723,334	680,259	715,868	695,843
Total Assets	1,962,753	1,892,824	1,795,585	1,835,782	1,731,064	1,671,698	1,624,147	1,591,675
Current Liabilities	386,377	368,335	378,034	349,194	337,363	300,703	337,939	366,728
Long-Term Obligations	798,105	798,166	704,335	707,986	590,607	569,917	500,685	508,735
Total Liabilities	1,291,692	1,294,733	1,295,736	1,191,320	1,061,257	1,002,801	958,695	997,281
Stockholders' Equity	671,061	598,091	499,849	644,462	669,807	668,897	665,452	594,394
Shares Outstanding	10,532	10,438	10,431	10,388	10,376	11,008	11,000	10,005
Statistical Record								
Return on Assets %	0.99	0.62	N.M.	0.45	1.41	1.34	3.97	1.25
Return on Equity %	3.02	2.08	N.M.	1.22	3.58	3.31	10.14	3.31
EBITDA Margin %	9.21	8.92	8.94	7.00	10.32	11.15	13.56	10.86
Net Margin %	1.03	0.69	N.M.	0.46	1.36	1.30	3.55	1.23
Asset Turnover	0.96	0.90	0.93	0.98	1.04	1.03	1.12	1.02
Current Ratio	2.75	2.76	2.27	2.42	2.14	2.26	2.12	1.90
Debt to Equity	1.19	1.33	1.41	1.10	0.88	0.85	0.75	0.86
Price Range	62.02-45.35	49.75-29.56	65.39-36.73	53.80-33.88	53.94-30.56	72.75-44.00	75.56-45.88	66.94-36.25
P/E Ratio	37.82-27.65	55.28-32.84	...	92.76-58.41	25.44-14.42	37.69-22.80	12.87-7.82	40.32-21.84

Address: 200 Park Avenue, New York, NY 10166
Telephone: (212) 986-5500
Fax: (212) 370-1969

Web Site: www.sequa.com
Officers: Norman E. Alexander - Chmn., C.E.O. John J. Quicke - Pres., C.O.O.

Auditors: Ernst & Young LLP
Investor Contact: 212-986-5500

SERVICE CORP. INTERNATIONAL

Exchange	Symbol	Price	52Wk Range	Yield	P/E
NYS	SCI	$7.48 (3/31/2005)	7.83-5.90	N/A	22.67

*7 Year Price Score 60.07 *NYSE Composite Index=100 *12 Month Price Score 98.38

Interim Earnings (Per Share)

Qtr.	Mar	Jun	Sep	Dec
2001	0.01	(0.04)	0.02	(2.08)
2002	(0.24)	(0.49)	0.01	(0.02)
2003	0.13	0.05	(0.02)	0.11
2004	0.09	0.15	0.04	0.05

Interim Dividends (Per Share)

Dividend Payment Suspended

Valuation Analysis

Forecast P/E	23.56	No of Institutions
	(4/13/2005)	173
Market Cap	$2.4 Billion	Shares
Book Value	1.9 Billion	205,165,168
Price/Book	1.29	% Held
Price/Sales	1.20	62.11

Business Summary: Personal Services (MIC: 5.15 SIC: 261 NAIC: 12220)

Service Corporation International is a provider of funeral and cemetery services. Co.'s funeral service locations (FSLs) provide services for funerals, including the use of funeral facilities, motor vehicles and preparation and embalming services. FSLs sell caskets, coffins, burial vaults, cremation receptacles, flowers, burial garments and other products and services. Co.'s cemeteries sell interment rights and merchandise such as stone and bronze memorials and cremation memorialization products. Cemeteries perform interment services and maintain cemetery grounds. Certain cemeteries operate crematoria. At Dec 31 2003, Co. operated 2,225 FSLs, 417 cemeteries and 183 crematoria.

Recent Developments: For the twelve months ended Dec 31 2004, income from continuing operations amounted to $117.0 million, up 41.7% compared with income from continuing operations of $82.6 million in the previous year. Results included net gains and impairment on dispositions of $25.6 million and $49.4 million in 2004 and 2003, respectively, as well as a loss of $16.8 million in 2004 and a gain of $1.3 million in 2003 from early extinguishment of debt. Revenues were $1.86 billion, down 20.1% from $2.33 billion the year before. Gross profit was $334.5 million, or 18.0% of revenues, versus $362.0 million, or 15.5% of revenues, in the prior year.

Prospects: Co. expects to generate cash flows in the next several years above its operating and financing needs. As of Sep 30 2004, Co. had less than $140.0 million in debt maturing during the remainder of 2004 and 2005. Co. believes that this financial flexibility, coupled with its liquidity allows it to consider investments or capital structure related transactions that will enhance operating performance. Co. will continue to evaluate internal opportunities such as construction of new funeral homes and development of high-end cemetery inventory. Co. expects to make acquisitions, if such acquisitions are available at reasonable market prices.

Financial Data
(US$ in Thousands)

	9 Mos	6 Mos	3 Mos	12/31/2003	12/31/2002	12/31/2001	12/31/2000	12/31/1999
Earnings Per Share	0.39	0.33	0.23	0.28	(0.79)	(2.10)	(4.93)	(0.12)
Cash Flow Per Share	0.75	0.85	0.92	1.25	1.20	1.34	1.35	1.59
Tang Book Value Per Share	2.19	2.12	1.46	0.83	0.40	0.08	N.M.	3.75
Dividends Per Share	...	...	...	...	...	...	...	0.360
Income Statement								
Total Revenue	1,421,526	1,018,174	589,618	2,341,651	2,272,423	2,510,343	2,564,730	3,321,813
EBITDA	344,827	217,282	142,064	418,817	149,077	(129,865)	(59,894)	395,854
Depn & Amortn	103,607	71,200	35,790	161,058	128,546	193,937	175,536	195,349
Income Before Taxes	95,673	79,302	72,339	114,333	(140,963)	(535,428)	(516,978)	(37,690)
Income Taxes	(4,468)	(8,547)	(4,241)	29,251	(39,740)	61,199	(91,455)	(3,393)
Net Income	87,455	74,879	28,519	85,082	(231,880)	(597,796)	(1,343,251)	(32,412)
Average Shares	340,215	312,725	353,088	300,790	294,533	285,127	272,544	273,792
Balance Sheet								
Current Assets	701,175	708,862	848,809	673,324	754,899	829,953	907,299	996,151
Total Assets	8,308,168	8,438,759	8,777,428	11,202,669	10,723,785	11,579,937	12,898,469	14,601,601
Current Liabilities	445,286	479,473	754,861	668,947	464,283	710,602	684,280	1,057,865
Long-Term Obligations	1,235,691	1,238,792	1,319,373	1,528,883	1,884,508	2,313,973	3,114,515	3,636,067
Total Liabilities	5,756,235	5,888,097	6,492,490	9,675,711	9,420,014	10,147,076	10,922,648	11,106,328
Stockholders' Equity	1,876,793	1,876,458	1,612,952	1,526,958	1,303,771	1,432,861	1,975,821	3,495,273
Shares Outstanding	324,687	337,368	304,208	302,039	297,010	292,153	272,507	272,064
Statistical Record								
Return on Assets %	1.27	1.07	0.73	0.78	N.M.	N.M.	N.M.	N.M.
Return on Equity %	7.32	6.28	4.77	6.01	N.M.	N.M.	N.M.	N.M.
EBITDA Margin %	24.26	21.34	24.09	17.89	6.56	N.M.	N.M.	11.92
Net Margin %	6.15	7.35	4.84	3.63	N.M.	N.M.	N.M.	N.M.
Asset Turnover	0.21	0.23	0.24	0.21	0.20	0.21	0.19	0.24
Current Ratio	1.57	1.48	1.12	1.01	1.63	1.17	1.33	0.94
Debt to Equity	0.66	0.66	0.82	1.00	1.45	1.61	1.58	1.04
Price Range	7.69-4.45	7.69-3.75	7.64-2.67	5.58-2.67	5.50-2.25	7.90-1.56	7.00-1.69	38.50-6.44
P/E Ratio	19.72-11.41	23.30-11.36	33.22-11.61	19.93-9.54	...	...	...	...
Average Yield %	...	...	...	...	...	...	...	2.31

Address: 1929 Allen Parkway, Houston, TX 77019 Telephone: (713) 522-5141	Web Site: www.sci-corp.com Officers: Robert L. Waltrip - Chmn. Thomas L. Ryan - Pres., C.E.O.	Auditors: PricewaterhouseCoopers LLP

SERVICEMASTER CO. (THE)

Exchange	Symbol	Price	52Wk Range	Yield	P/E	Div Achiever
NYS	SVM	$13.50 (3/31/2005)	13.87-11.25	3.26	12.16	34 Years

*7 Year Price Score 80.67 ***NYSE Composite Index=100** ***12 Month Price Score 99.08**

Interim Earnings (Per Share)

Qtr.	Mar	Jun	Sep	Dec
2001	0.10	0.17	0.15	0.09
2002	0.10	0.17	0.19	0.23
2003	0.02	0.22	(1.08)	0.08
2004	0.04	0.24	0.23	0.61

Interim Dividends (Per Share)

Amt	Decl	Ex	Rec	Pay
0.105Q	3/8/2004	4/6/2004	4/9/2004	4/30/2004
0.11Q	4/30/2004	7/7/2004	7/9/2004	7/30/2004
0.11Q	11/1/2004	11/8/2004	11/11/2004	11/30/2004
0.11Q	2/1/2005	2/10/2005	2/14/2005	2/28/2005

Indicated Div: $0.44

Valuation Analysis

Forecast P/E	20.81	No of Institutions
	(4/7/2005)	247
Market Cap	$3.9 Billion	Shares
Book Value	991.5 Million	170,867,200
Price/Book	3.96	% Held
Price/Sales	1.04	58.51

TRADING VOLUME (thousand shares)

Business Summary: Accounting & Management Consulting Services (MIC: 12.2 SIC: 741 NAIC: 61110)

ServiceMaster provides outsourcing services to residential and commercial customers. The TruGreen segment provides lawn care services and landscape maintenance services. The Terminix segment includes domestic termite and pest control services. The American Residential Services and American Mechanical Services (ARS/AMS) segment provides plumbing, drain cleaning, heating, ventilation, air conditioning and electrical services. The American Home Shield segment offers warranty contracts on home systems and appliances and home inspection services. The Other Operations segment includes ServiceMaster Clean, Merry Maids and Furniture Medic franchise operations.

Recent Developments: For the year ended Dec 31 2004, income from continuing operations was $324,057 thousand compared with a loss of $221,975 thousand a year earlier. Net income was $331,227 thousand versus net loss of $224,687 thousand a year earlier. Revenues were $3,758,568 thousand, up 5.3% from $3,568,586 thousand the year before. Operating income was $336,556 thousand versus a loss of $166,243 thousand in the prior year. Total direct expense was $2,525,029 thousand versus $2,430,523 thousand in the prior year, an increase of 3.9%. Total indirect expense was $896,983 thousand versus $1,304,306 thousand in the prior year, a decrease of 31.2%.

Prospects: During the first quarter of 2005, Co. is focusing on taking steps to improve its customer service to help boost its customer retention rates and is making increased investments in its sales force to attract new customers. In addition, Co. plans to implement new marketing programs that could boost sales and contribute to earnings growth in subsequent quarters of the year. Looking ahead, Co. expects revenue growth for full-year 2005 to be in the mid-to-high single digit range with earnings per share growing at a somewhat faster rate than revenues.

Financial Data

(US$ in Thousands)	12/31/2004	12/31/2003	12/31/2002	12/31/2001	12/31/2000	12/31/1999	12/31/1998	12/31/1997
Earnings Per Share	1.11	(0.76)	0.52	0.51	0.57	0.55	0.64	0.55
Cash Flow Per Share	1.29	0.96	1.27	1.22	1.32	0.83	1.40	1.30
Dividends Per Share	0.430	0.420	0.410	0.400	0.380	0.360	0.330	0.31
Dividend Payout %	38.74	...	78.85	78.43	66.67	65.45	51.56	56.36
Income Statement								
Total Revenue	3,758,568	3,568,586	3,589,089	3,601,429	5,970,615	5,703,535	4,724,119	3,961,502
EBITDA	399,396	(103,521)	398,519	50,621	612,829	543,592	516,328	443,788
Depn & Amortn	55,596	55,861	57,434	126,937	157,691	138,444	104,605	93,062
Income Before Taxes	283,092	(224,637)	263,566	(201,373)	318,307	296,193	318,778	274,279
Income Taxes	(40,965)	(2,662)	93,468	(29,594)	133,319	122,630	128,786	(54,797)
Net Income	331,227	(224,687)	156,994	155,033	173,827	173,563	189,992	329,076
Average Shares	303,568	295,610	314,112	311,408	305,518	314,406	298,887	299,640
Balance Sheet								
Current Assets	978,752	890,774	919,174	1,150,658	984,759	959,238	670,202	594,084
Total Assets	3,140,202	2,956,426	3,414,938	3,674,739	3,967,668	3,870,215	2,914,851	2,475,224
Current Liabilities	1,027,927	818,240	839,064	814,401	833,414	845,804	753,697	558,177
Long-Term Obligations	781,841	785,490	804,340	1,105,518	1,756,757	1,697,582	1,076,167	1,247,845
Total Liabilities	2,048,667	2,039,600	2,095,929	2,351,101	2,806,080	2,664,499	1,958,365	1,950,786
Stockholders' Equity	991,535	816,517	1,218,700	1,220,961	1,161,588	1,205,716	956,486	524,438
Shares Outstanding	290,524	293,981	299,221	300,531	298,474	307,530	298,030	279,943
Statistical Record								
Return on Assets %	10.84	N.M.	4.43	4.06	4.42	5.12	7.05	15.23
Return on Equity %	36.54	N.M.	12.87	13.01	14.65	16.05	25.66	49.81
EBITDA Margin %	10.63	N.M.	11.10	1.41	10.26	9.53	10.93	11.20
Net Margin %	8.81	N.M.	4.37	4.30	2.91	3.04	4.02	8.31
Asset Turnover	1.23	1.12	1.01	0.94	1.52	1.68	1.75	1.83
Current Ratio	0.95	1.09	1.10	1.41	1.18	1.13	0.89	1.06
Debt to Equity	0.79	0.96	0.66	0.91	1.51	1.41	1.13	2.38
Price Range	13.87-10.71	11.97-9.05	15.49-9.11	14.10-10.05	14.75-8.75	22.06-10.13	25.38-17.33	19.50-11.06
P/E Ratio	12.50-9.65	...	29.79-17.52	27.65-19.71	25.88-15.35	40.11-18.41	39.65-27.08	35.45-20.10
Average Yield %	3.57	4.06	3.29	3.46	3.43	2.14	1.61	2.03

Address: 3250 Lacey Road, Suite 600, Downers Grove, IL 60515-1700 **Telephone:** (630) 663-2000 **Fax:** (630) 271-2710	**Web Site:** www.servicemaster.com **Officers:** Johnathan P. Ward - Chmn. , C.E.O. Ernest J. Mrozek - Pres., C.O.O.	**Auditors:** Deloitte & Touche LLP **Investor Contact:** 630-271-1300 **Transfer Agents:** Computershare Investor Services, Chicago, IL

SHAW GROUP INC.

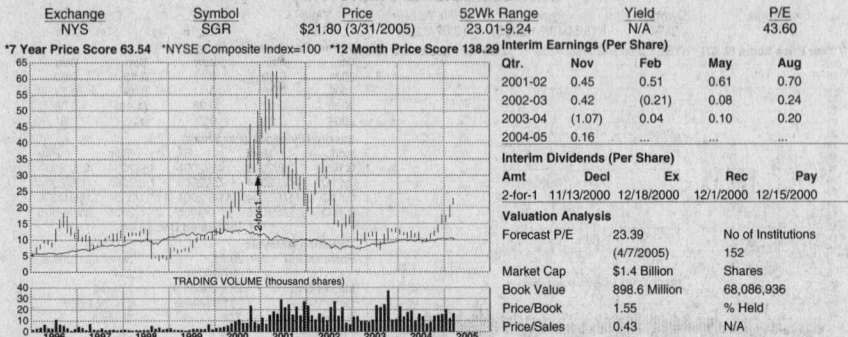

Exchange	Symbol	Price	52Wk Range	Yield	P/E
NYS	SGR	$21.80 (3/31/2005)	23.01-9.24	N/A	43.60

*7 Year Price Score 63.54 ***NYSE Composite Index=100** ***12 Month Price Score 138.29**

Interim Earnings (Per Share)

Qtr.	Nov	Feb	May	Aug
2001-02	0.45	0.51	0.61	0.70
2002-03	0.42	(0.21)	0.08	0.24
2003-04	(1.07)	0.04	0.10	0.20
2004-05	0.16	...	...	...

Interim Dividends (Per Share)

Amt	Decl	Ex	Rec	Pay
2-for-1	11/13/2000	12/18/2000	12/1/2000	12/15/2000

Valuation Analysis

Forecast P/E	23.39	No of Institutions	
	(4/7/2005)	152	
Market Cap	$1.4 Billion	Shares	
Book Value	898.6 Million	68,086,936	
Price/Book	1.55	% Held	
Price/Sales	0.43	N/A	

Business Summary: Metal Products (MIC: 11.4 SIC: 498 NAIC: 32996)

Shaw Group is engaged in providing comprehensive services to the environmental and infrastructure, power and process industries. Co. provides services to the environmental, infrastructure and homeland security markets, including consulting, engineering, construction, remediation and facilities management services to governmental and commercial customers. Co. is also a vertically-integrated provider of engineering, procurement, pipe fabrication, construction and maintenance services to the power and process industries. Co. has three segments: Environmental and Infrastructure segment, Engineering, Construction & Maintenance segment, and Fabrication, Manufacturing and Distribution segment.

Recent Developments: For the quarter ended Nov 30 2004, income$10,780,000 versus loss of $49,451,000 in the year-earlier quarter. Net income was $10,013,000 from net loss of $49,592,000 in the year-earlier quarter. Revenues were $828,137,000 , up 28.0% from $646,940,000 the year before. Operating income was $27,783,000 versus a loss of $60,676,000 in the prior-year quarter, an increase of 145.8%. Total indirect expense was $48,605,000 versus $72,287,000 in the prior-year quarter, a decrease of 32.8%.

Prospects: Co. is encouraged by the improving markets it is seeing in the energy and process industries. Also, Co.'s environmental and infrastructure segment remains strong, as Co. continues to aggressively pursue market opportunities, particularly in rapid response services. Looking ahead, Co. should be well positioned to continue to expand and diversify its business. Co. recently replaced its engineering, construction and maintenance division with two new divisional segments: the energy and chemicals division and a separate maintenance division. Co. believes these organizational refinements will improve overall operational capabilities and enhance sales and marketing efforts.

Financial Data

(US$ in Thousands)	3 Mos	08/31/2004	08/31/2003	08/31/2002	08/31/2001	08/31/2000	08/31/1999	08/31/1998
Earnings Per Share	0.50	(0.53)	0.54	2.26	1.46	0.96	0.73	0.75
Cash Flow Per Share	0.98	(0.43)	(5.33)	7.72	0.28	(2.76)	1.09	(0.13)
Tang Book Value Per Share	5.89	5.68	3.99	4.73	5.60	2.68	6.05	5.17
Income Statement								
Total Revenue	828,137	3,076,945	3,306,762	3,170,696	1,538,932	762,655	494,014	501,638
EBITDA	30,499	53,354	114,554	200,199	152,083	70,359	47,995	42,056
Depn & Amortn	5,445	51,867	52,327	37,677	45,255	16,808	13,271	10,280
Income Before Taxes	16,358	(35,224)	35,590	151,012	99,894	45,548	26,075	23,305
Income Taxes	5,730	(11,624)	11,745	54,348	38,366	16,359	8,635	7,033
Net Income	10,013	(30,975)	20,866	98,367	60,997	29,510	18,121	19,177
Average Shares	63,273	58,005	38,355	48,238	41,828	30,771	24,710	25,663
Balance Sheet								
Current Assets	1,166,035	1,137,783	1,113,561	1,450,354	1,096,041	790,706	252,070	250,994
Total Assets	2,057,272	2,029,936	1,986,115	2,304,200	1,701,854	1,335,083	407,062	389,844
Current Liabilities	866,893	853,737	1,028,115	1,072,470	574,997	682,049	138,095	120,539
Long-Term Obligations	260,774	261,173	251,745	522,147	512,867	254,965	87,841	91,715
Total Liabilities	1,158,648	1,145,165	1,323,825	1,611,943	1,103,461	957,808	232,823	219,149
Stockholders' Equity	898,624	884,771	662,290	692,257	598,393	377,275	174,239	170,695
Shares Outstanding	64,080	63,769	37,790	40,841	41,012	35,402	23,472	26,559
Statistical Record								
Return on Assets %	1.45	N.M.	0.97	4.91	4.02	3.38	4.55	5.88
Return on Equity %	3.30	N.M.	3.08	15.24	12.50	10.67	10.51	12.43
EBITDA Margin %	3.68	1.73	3.46	6.31	9.88	9.23	9.72	8.38
Net Margin %	1.21	N.M.	0.63	3.10	3.96	3.87	3.67	3.82
Asset Turnover	1.64	1.53	1.54	1.58	1.01	0.87	1.24	1.54
Current Ratio	1.35	1.33	1.08	1.35	1.91	1.16	1.83	2.08
Debt to Equity	0.29	0.30	0.38	0.75	0.86	0.68	0.50	0.54
Price Range	14.73-9.24	13.85-8.75	18.65-6.97	35.50-14.80	62.37-24.59	27.84-9.94	10.69-3.41	13.69-4.03
P/E Ratio	29.46-18.48	...	34.54-12.91	15.71-6.55	42.72-16.84	29.00-10.35	14.64-4.67	18.25-5.38

Address: 4171 Essen Lane, Baton Rouge, LA 70809 **Telephone:** (225) 932-2500 **Fax:** (225) 296-1199	**Web Site:** www.shawgrp.com **Officers:** J. M. Bernhard Jr. - Chmn., C.E.O. T. A. Barfield - Pres., C.O.O.	**Auditors:** Ernst & Young LLP **Investor Contact:** 225-932-2500 **Transfer Agents:** Wachovia Bank, N.A., Charlotte, North Carolina

SHERWIN-WILLIAMS CO.

Exchange	Symbol	Price	52Wk Range	Yield	P/E	Div Achiever
NYS	SHW	$43.99 (3/31/2005)	46.29-36.06	1.86	16.17	25 Years

*7 Year Price Score 124.65 *NYSE Composite Index=100* ***12 Month Price Score 99.62**

Interim Earnings (Per Share)

Qtr.	Mar	Jun	Sep	Dec
2001	0.23	0.58	0.58	0.30
2002	(0.98)	0.70	0.73	0.38
2003	0.21	0.75	0.82	0.49
2004	0.35	0.87	0.92	0.58

Interim Dividends (Per Share)

Amt	Decl	Ex	Rec	Pay
0.17Q	4/28/2004	5/26/2004	5/28/2004	6/11/2004
0.17Q	7/21/2004	8/18/2004	8/20/2004	9/3/2004
0.17Q	10/20/2004	11/9/2004	11/12/2004	11/26/2004
0.205Q	2/2/2005	2/24/2005	2/28/2005	3/14/2005

Indicated Div: $0.82 (Div. Reinv. Plan)

Valuation Analysis

Forecast P/E	13.98	No of Institutions
	(4/7/2005)	340
Market Cap	$6.2 Billion	Shares
Book Value	1.6 Billion	95,738,952
Price/Book	3.76	% Held
Price/Sales	1.01	68.16

Business Summary: Chemicals (MIC: 11.1 SIC: 851 NAIC: 25510)

Sherwin-Williams manufactures, distributes and sells coatings and related products. The Paint Stores' division consists of Co.-operated specialty paint stores in the U.S., Canada, the Virgin Islands, Puerto Rico and Mexico. The Consumer segment manufactures and distributes a variety of paints, coatings and related products to third party customers and the Paint stores segment. Automotive Finishes manufactures and distributes motor vehicle finish products in North and South America, the Caribbean Islands and Europe. International Coatings licenses, and distributes a variety of paints, coatings and related products worldwide. Co.'s brands include Sherwin-Williams®, Dutch Boy®, and Krylon®.

Recent Developments: For the year ended Dec 31 2004, net income increased 18.4% to $393,254 thousand from net income of $332,058 thousand a year earlier. Revenues were $6,113,789 thousand, up 13.1% from $5,407,764 thousand the year before. Total direct expense was $3,412,378 thousand versus $2,952,469 thousand in the prior year, an increase of 15.6%. Total indirect expense was $2,068,936 thousand versus $1,881,664 thousand in the prior year, an increase of 10.0%.

Prospects: Co. continues to be encouraged by the strong sales in its Paint Stores Segment in all three paint categories - architectural, industrial maintenance and product finishes. Co. anticipates that first quarter 2005 net sales will increase in the low double digits versus the first quarter of 2004, partially due to the recently completed acquisitions. Co. estimates diluted net income per common share in the first quarter will be in the range of $0.48 to $0.53 per share compared to $0.35 per share earned in the first quarter of 2004. For the full year 2005, Co. expects diluted net income per common share will be in the range of $3.00 to $3.10 per share compared to $2.72 per share earned in 2004.

Financial Data
(US$ in Thousands)

	12/31/2004	12/31/2003	12/31/2002	12/31/2001	12/31/2000	12/31/1999	12/31/1998	12/31/1997
Earnings Per Share	2.72	2.26	0.84	1.68	0.10	1.80	1.57	1.50
Cash Flow Per Share	3.86	3.86	3.72	3.61	2.84	2.89	2.78	2.55
Tang Book Value Per Share	1.90	2.95	3.77	2.59	3.18	2.32	1.76	0.70
Dividends Per Share	0.680	0.620	0.600	0.580	0.540	0.480	0.450	0.403
Dividend Payout %	25.00	27.43	71.43	34.52	540.00	26.67	28.66	26.83
Income Statement								
Total Revenue	6,113,789	5,407,764	5,184,788	5,066,005	5,211,624	5,003,837	4,934,430	4,881,103
EBITDA	745,785	678,232	653,298	627,174	361,638	704,936	659,962	647,316
Depn & Amortn	125,642	116,564	115,659	148,098	156,206	153,650	147,888	139,202
Income Before Taxes	580,195	522,926	497,164	424,449	143,406	490,118	440,103	427,277
Income Taxes	185,662	190,868	186,463	161,291	127,380	186,258	167,239	166,663
Net Income	393,254	332,058	127,565	263,158	16,026	303,860	272,864	260,614
Average Shares	144,735	147,005	152,435	156,893	162,695	169,026	173,536	174,032
Balance Sheet								
Current Assets	1,781,928	1,715,144	1,505,993	1,506,945	1,551,539	1,597,377	1,547,290	1,532,253
Total Assets	4,274,151	3,682,608	3,432,312	3,627,925	3,750,670	4,052,090	4,065,462	4,035,801
Current Liabilities	1,520,137	1,154,170	1,083,496	1,141,353	1,115,243	1,189,862	1,111,973	1,115,663
Long-Term Obligations	488,239	502,992	506,682	503,517	623,587	624,365	730,283	843,919
Total Liabilities	2,626,905	2,223,751	2,090,422	2,140,161	2,278,806	2,353,558	2,349,522	2,443,621
Stockholders' Equity	1,647,246	1,458,857	1,341,890	1,487,764	1,471,864	1,698,532	1,715,940	1,592,180
Shares Outstanding	140,777	143,406	148,910	153,978	159,558	165,664	171,033	172,907
Statistical Record								
Return on Assets %	9.86	9.33	3.61	7.13	0.41	7.49	6.74	7.41
Return on Equity %	25.25	23.71	9.02	17.78	1.01	17.80	16.50	17.41
EBITDA Margin %	12.20	12.54	12.60	12.38	6.94	14.09	13.37	13.26
Net Margin %	6.43	6.14	2.46	5.19	0.31	6.07	5.53	5.34
Asset Turnover	1.53	1.52	1.47	1.37	1.33	1.23	1.22	1.39
Current Ratio	1.17	1.49	1.39	1.32	1.39	1.34	1.39	1.37
Debt to Equity	0.30	0.34	0.38	0.34	0.42	0.37	0.43	0.53
Price Range	45.48-33.06	34.74-24.82	33.00-22.06	28.02-20.31	27.00-17.44	32.44-19.00	37.50-30.06	32.69-24.88
P/E Ratio	16.72-12.15	15.37-10.98	39.29-26.26	16.68-12.09	270.00-174.38	18.02-10.56	23.89-12.78	21.79-16.58
Average Yield %	1.72	2.12	2.14	2.42	2.45	1.87	1.51	1.38

Address: 101 Prospect Avenue, N.W., Cleveland, OH 44115-1075	**Web Site:** www.sherwin.com	**Auditors:** Ernst & Young LLP
Telephone: (216) 566-2000	**Officers:** Christopher M. Connor - Chmn., C.E.O. Joseph M. Scaminace - Pres., C.O.O.	**Investor Contact:** 216-566-2000
Fax: (216) 566-3310		**Transfer Agents:** The Bank of New York, New York, NY

SHURGARD STORAGE CENTERS, INC. (WA)

Exchange	Symbol	Price	52Wk Range	Yield	P/E	Div Acheiver
NYSE	SHU	$40.98 (3/31/2005)	44.76-33.15	5.37	57.72	10 Years

*7 Year Price Score 111.17 *NYSE Composite Index=100 *12 Month Price Score 97.69

Interim Earnings (Per Share)

Qtr.	Mar	Jun	Sep	Dec
2001	0.25	0.38	0.25	0.15
2002	0.27	0.43	0.42	0.38
2003	0.30	0.21	0.28	(0.18)
2004	(0.05)	0.38	0.32	0.07

Interim Dividends (Per Share)

Amt	Decl	Ex	Rec	Pay
0.55Q	5/2/2004	5/11/2004	5/13/2004	5/25/2004
0.55Q	7/23/2004	8/4/2004	8/6/2004	8/20/2004
0.55Q	11/5/2004	11/10/2004	11/15/2004	11/24/2004
0.55Q	2/15/2005	2/25/2005	3/1/2005	3/10/2005
		Indicated Div: $2.20		

Valuation Analysis

Forecast P/E	25.91	No of Institutions	
	(4/7/2005)	139	
Market Cap	$1.9 Billion	Shares	
Book Value	906.2 Million	31,542,656	
Price/Book	2.11	% Held	
Price/Sales	4.49	67.85	

Business Summary: Property, Real Estate & Development (MIC: 8.3 SIC: 798 NAIC: 25930)

Shurgard Storage Centers is an equity real estate investment trust that develops, acquires, invests in, operates and manages self storage centers and related operations located in markets throughout the U.S. and in Western Europe. Co. leases self-storage space to tenants primarily on a month-to-month basis. Co. also provide ancillary services at storage centers consisting primarily of truck rentals and sales of storage products. As of Dec 31 2004, Co. operated a network of 633 storage centers containing approximately 40.0 million net rentable square feet. Co. operates in Europe through its Shurgard Self Storage, SCA subsidiary, which is 87.2% owned.

Recent Developments: For the year ended Dec 31 2004, net income increased 20.3% to $45,295 thousand from net income of $37,638 thousand a year earlier. Revenues were $425,661 thousand, up 42.3% from $299,234 thousand the year before. Storage center operations revenue of $420,560 thousand in 2004 increased $128,203 thousand, or 43.9%, compared with 2003 due mainly to the consolidation of Shurgard Europe, which contributed $101,500 thousand of revenue. Domestic storage center operations revenue increased approximately $26,100 thousand, or 9.0%, compared with 2003 as a result of an increase in the number of storage centers, higher occupancy and increases in rates. Operating income rose 0.2% to $85,232 thousand.

Prospects: Co. is encouraged by the results of both its U.S. and European stores. In particular, the solid growth in its same store revenues and net operating income (NOI). Co. sees a trend of continuing revenue growth in both its U.S. and European store portfolios and projects same-store NOI to grow by 3.0% to 4.0% in the U.S. and by 12.0% to 15.0% in Europe in 2005. Co. also expects to develop about 20 new stores in Europe and five to ten new stores in the U.S. during 2005. For 2005, Co. projects funds from operations will be in the range of $2.25 to $2.40 per share, and expects earnings ranging from $0.39 to $0.54 per share.

Financial Data

(US$ in Thousands)	12/31/2004	12/31/2003	12/31/2002	12/31/2001	12/31/2000	12/31/1999	12/31/1998	12/31/1997
Earnings Per Share	0.71	0.62	1.50	0.64	1.47	1.44	1.39	1.40
Cash Flow Per Share	2.61	3.05	3.69	3.80	2.78	3.05	2.76	2.79
Tang Book Value Per Share	16.10	17.47	16.21	15.90	18.28	18.72	19.27	19.69
Dividends Per Share	2.190	2.150	2.110	2.070	2.030	1.990	1.950	1.910
Dividend Payout %	308.45	346.77	140.67	323.44	138.10	138.19	140.29	136.43
Income Statement								
Total Revenue	425,661	302,314	264,113	232,590	195,867	173,154	159,254	140,434
EBITDA	183,347	141,282	150,406	133,486				
Depn & Amortn	87,001	50,851	52,787	62,110	40,893	36,858	33,645	28,243
Income Before Taxes	13,470	39,249	65,594	34,814	...	...	...	...
Income Taxes	72	1,611	(314)	(1,545)	...	...	...	...
Net Income	45,295	37,638	67,632	34,914	52,632	50,673	44,734	42,311
Average Shares	46,626	41,209	35,401	31,086	29,761	29,130	28,724	28,000
Balance Sheet								
Current Assets	57,458	69,798	62,077	7,797	16,174	18,811	16,338	14,276
Total Assets	2,932,884	2,067,091	1,420,176	1,238,805	1,239,157	1,153,226	1,153,907	955,488
Long-Term Obligations	1,684,502	974,246	560,362	423,093	495,354	434,349	426,137	296,971
Total Liabilities	1,857,454	1,091,731	666,681	516,105	529,748	468,661	467,338	326,026
Stockholders' Equity	906,198	954,420	738,121	716,325	640,565	643,802	651,810	610,787
Shares Outstanding	46,624	45,747	35,934	33,778	29,774	29,248	28,831	28,586
Statistical Record								
Return on Assets %	1.81	2.16	5.09	2.82	4.39	4.39	4.24	4.81
Return on Equity %	4.86	4.45	9.30	5.15	8.17	7.82	7.09	7.63
EBITDA Margin %	43.07	46.73	56.95	57.39	...	...	...	...
Net Margin %	10.64	12.45	25.61	15.01	26.87	29.26	28.09	30.13
Asset Turnover	0.17	0.17	0.20	0.19	0.16	0.15	0.15	0.16
Debt to Equity	1.86	1.02	0.76	0.59	0.77	0.67	0.65	0.49
Price Range	44.76-33.15	38.95-28.48	37.15-28.86	32.25-24.56	26.19-22.00	27.63-20.94	29.56-24.38	29.94-26.00
P/E Ratio	63.04-46.69	62.82-45.94	24.77-19.24	50.39-38.38	17.81-14.97	19.18-14.54	21.27-17.54	21.38-18.57
Average Yield %	5.69	6.41	6.44	7.26	8.64	7.90	7.14	6.81

Address: 1155 Valley Street, Suite 400, Seattle, WA 98109	Web Site: www.shurgard.com	Auditors: PricewaterhouseCoopers LLP
Telephone: (206) 624 8100	Officers: Charles K. Barbo - Chmn., C.E.O. David K. Grant - Pres., C.O.O., Interim C.F.O.	
Fax: (206) 624 1645		

SIERRA PACIFIC RESOURCES

Exchange	Symbol	Price	52Wk Range	Yield	P/E
NYS	SRP	$10.75 (3/31/2005)	11.09-6.57	N/A	67.19

*7 Year Price Score 54.56 *NYSE Composite Index=100 *12 Month Price Score 107.97

Interim Earnings (Per Share)

Qtr.	Mar	Jun	Sep	Dec
2001	(1.06)	0.69	0.89	0.03
2002	(2.98)	(0.41)	0.78	(0.39)
2003	(0.15)	(1.48)	0.28	(0.32)
2004	(0.38)	(0.38)	0.50	0.15

Interim Dividends (Per Share)

Dividend Payment Suspended

Valuation Analysis

Forecast P/E	19.45	No of Institutions	
	(4/13/2005)	170	
Market Cap	$1.3 Billion	Shares	
Book Value	1.5 Billion	132,222,808	
Price/Book	0.84	% Held	
Price/Sales	0.45	N/A	

Business Summary: Electricity (MIC: 7.1 SIC: 931 NAIC: 21121)

Sierra Pacific Resources is a holding company whose principal subsidiaries are Sierra Pacific Power Company (SPPC) and Nevada Power Company (NPC). As of Dec 31 2003, SPPC provided electricity to about 334,000 customers in western, central and northeastern Nevada, including the cities of Reno, Sparks, Carson City, and Elko, and a portion of eastern California, including the Lake Tahoe area. SPPC also provided natural gas service to about 129,000 customers in Reno and Sparks, Nevada. As of Dec 31 2003, NPC provided electric services to about 702,771 customers in Las Vegas, North Las Vegas, Henderson, Searchlight, Laughlin, and adjoining areas, including Nellis Air Force Base.

Recent Developments: For the year ended Dec 31 2004, Co. reported income of $35.6 million, before a $3.2 million loss from discontinued operations, compared with a loss of $104.2 million, before a $32.5 million loss from discontinued operations, in the previous year. Results for 2003 included a $46.1 million unrealized loss on a derivative instrument. Operating revenues increased 1.3% to $2.82 billion from $2.79 billion the year before. Electric revenues grew 1.6% to $2.67 billion from $2.62 billion a year earlier, while gas revenues slipped 4.8% to $153.8 million from $161.6 million in 2003. Operating income was $271.5 million in the prior year.

Prospects: Continuing strong customer growth at both of Co.'s utilities, Nevada Power Company and Sierra Pacific Power Company are driving increased earnings. Earnings are also benefiting from the effects of the general rate case decisions by the Public Utilities Commission of Nevada, and a favorable court decision in the Enron lawsuit resulting in the reversal of interest charges. Nevada Power's revenues are being driven by increases in the number of residential, commercial and industrial customers. Sierra Pacific Power is also benefiting from overall growth in retail electric customers as well as increases in the number of residential and commercial natural gas customers.

Financial Data

(US$ in Thousands)	12/31/2004	12/31/2003	12/31/2002	12/31/2001	12/31/2000	12/31/1999	12/31/1998	12/31/1997
Earnings Per Share	0.16	(1.21)	(3.01)	0.65	(0.51)	0.83	2.49	2.40
Cash Flow Per Share	1.81	2.32	4.49	(11.94)	2.36	3.37	4.69	4.76
Tang Book Value Per Share	12.56	9.60	9.95	13.61	13.25	14.66	21.72	20.49
Dividends Per Share	...	...	0.200	0.650	1.000	0.500	1.285	1.225
Dividend Payout %	...	...	...	100.00	...	60.24	51.61	51.04
Income Statement								
Total Revenue	2,823,839	2,789,158	2,991,703	4,588,730	2,334,254	1,309,131	741,841	663,243
Depn & Amortn	474,307	457,955	368,437	(1,043,302)	167,566	114,984	73,612	68,668
Income Taxes	20,631	(57,337)	(164,440)	(1,230)	(31,022)	26,086	41,815	38,667
Net Income	32,471	(136,629)	(303,621)	56,733	(39,780)	51,750	77,321	74,445
Average Shares	183,400	115,774	102,126	87,542	78,435	62,577	30,955	30,880
Balance Sheet								
Net PPE	4,926,926	4,642,650	4,308,696	4,109,235	3,981,134	4,073,529	1,677,042	1,600,815
Total Assets	7,528,467	7,063,758	6,896,244	8,181,314	5,639,484	5,247,686	2,041,396	1,935,880
Long-Term Obligations	4,081,281	3,579,674	3,062,883	3,376,105	2,133,679	1,556,327	616,754	627,224
Total Liabilities	5,979,851	5,578,364	5,519,078	6,435,978	4,229,772	3,720,257	1,294,849	1,229,371
Stockholders' Equity	1,498,616	1,435,394	1,327,166	1,702,322	1,359,712	1,477,129	673,432	633,394
Shares Outstanding	117,469	117,236	102,177	102,111	78,475	78,428	31,009	30,915
Statistical Record								
Return on Assets %	0.44	N.M.	N.M.	0.82	N.M.	1.42	3.89	...
Return on Equity %	2.21	N.M.	N.M.	3.71	N.M.	4.81	11.83	...
Net Margin %	1.15	(4.90)	(10.15)	1.24	(1.70)	3.95	10.42	11.22
PPE Turnover	0.59	0.62	0.71	1.13	0.58	0.46	0.45	...
Asset Turnover	0.39	0.40	0.40	0.66	0.43	0.36	0.37	...
Debt to Equity	2.72	2.49	2.31	1.98	1.57	1.05	0.92	0.99
Price Range	10.54-6.57	7.37-2.92	16.73-4.88	17.02-10.80	19.25-12.25	26.88-17.00	26.88-22.44	27.25-19.50
P/E Ratio	65.88-41.06	...	...	26.18-16.62	...	32.38-20.48	10.79-9.01	11.35-8.13
Average Yield %	...	...	2.24	4.36	6.50	2.21	5.15	5.77

Address: 6100 Neil Road, Reno, NV 89511	Web Site: www.sierrapacificresources.com	Auditors: DELOITTE & TOUCHE LLP
Telephone: (775) 834-4011	Officers: Walter M. Higgins - Chmn., Pres., C.E.O.	Investor Contact: 775-834-5646
Fax: (775) 834-3614	Michael W. Yackira CPA - Exec. V.P., C.F.O.	

SIMON PROPERTY GROUP, INC.

Exchange	Symbol	Price	52Wk Range	Yield	P/E
NYS	SPG	$60.58 (3/31/2005)	65.35-45.11	4.62	42.07

*7 Year Price Score 139.41 *NYSE Composite Index=100* ***12 Month Price Score 102.14**

Interim Earnings (Per Share)

Qtr.	Mar	Jun	Sep	Dec
2001	0.18	0.21	0.21	0.25
2002	0.17	0.96	0.32	0.52
2003	0.29	0.26	0.22	0.87
2004	0.24	0.34	0.36	0.50

Interim Dividends (Per Share)

Amt	Decl	Ex	Rec	Pay
0.65Q	7/28/2004	8/13/2004	8/17/2004	8/31/2004
0.41Q	10/4/2004	10/15/2004	10/13/2004	11/30/2004
0.24Q	10/27/2004	11/15/2004	11/17/2004	11/30/2004
0.70Q	2/10/2005	2/16/2005	2/21/2005	2/28/2005

Indicated Div: $2.80

Valuation Analysis

Forecast P/E	12.50	No of Institutions
	(4/7/2005)	373
Market Cap	$13.3 Billion	Shares
Book Value	4.6 Billion	192,861,968
Price/Book	2.87	% Held
Price/Sales	5.05	86.43

Business Summary: Property, Real Estate & Development (MIC: 8.3 SIC: 798 NAIC: 25930)

Simon Property Group is a self-administered and self-managed real estate investment trust company. Co. is engaged in the ownership, operation, management, leasing, acquisition, expansion and development of real estate properties, primarily regional malls and community shopping centers. As of Dec 31 2003, Co.'s North America portfolio consisted of 175 regional malls, 67 community shopping centers, and four office and mixed-use properties in 37 states and Canada. In addition, Co. also own interests in three parcels of land held for future development. Co. also has ownership interests in 47 European assets located in France, Italy, Poland and Portugal.

Recent Developments: For the year ended Dec 31 2004, income from continuing operations increased 0.3% to $450,405 thousand from income of $449,078 thousand a year earlier. Net income decreased 7.0% to $342,993 thousand from net income of $368,715 thousand a year earlier. Revenues were $2,641,751 thousand, up 14.8% from $2,300,214 thousand the year before. Operating income was $1,053,599 thousand versus an income of $971,962 thousand in the prior year, an increase of 8.4%.

Prospects: Co. continues to strengthen its portfolio of properties through strategic acquisitions and property development. For instance, Co. recently acquired a mall in Puerto Rico and a lifestyle center in Austin, TX, completed two significant expansion projects, opened two new shopping centers, and at year-end has six new development projects under construction. Looking ahead, Co. will seek to build on the acquisition of Chelsea Property Group, adding in the Premium Outlet® business that will serve as a new growth platform to its business. Co. expects diluted earnings to range from $1.34 to $1.46 per share for 2005.

Financial Data (US$ in Thousands)	12/31/2004	12/31/2003	12/31/2002	12/31/2001	12/31/2000	12/31/1999	12/31/1998	12/31/1997
Earnings Per Share	1.44	1.65	1.99	0.85	1.11	0.97	1.05	1.08
Cash Flow Per Share	5.19	5.02	4.91	4.66	4.08	3.66	4.33	3.71
Tang Book Value Per Share	16.25	14.71	14.10	13.23	14.23	15.95	15.70	11.11
Dividends Per Share	2.600	2.400	2.175	2.080	2.020	2.020	1.548	2.007
Dividend Payout %	180.56	145.45	109.30	244.71	181.98	208.25	147.42	185.88
Income Statement								
Property Income	2,411,416	2,098,252	2,044,799	1,926,192	1,887,124	1,790,854	1,329,390	1,002,578
Non-Property Income	230,335	215,401	141,003	122,643	125,613	104,117	75,682	51,589
Total Revenue	2,641,751	2,313,653	2,185,802	2,048,835	2,012,737	1,894,971	1,405,072	1,054,167
Depn & Amortn	611,090	518,560	491,306	464,892	430,329	393,650	278,246	208,539
Interest Expense	662,090	602,510	602,972	607,625	637,173	579,848	420,282	287,823
Net Income	342,993	368,715	422,588	199,149	228,911	203,015	166,941	137,237
Average Shares	208,857	190,298	181,500	173,027	172,994	172,226	126,879	100,304
Balance Sheet								
Total Assets	22,070,019	15,684,721	14,904,502	13,810,954	13,911,407	14,199,318	13,269,129	7,662,667
Long-Term Obligations	14,586,393	10,266,388	9,546,081	8,841,378	8,728,582	8,768,841	7,972,381	5,077,990
Total Liabilities	16,049,369	11,228,824	10,412,992	9,625,172	9,458,153	9,493,975	8,526,012	5,411,368
Stockholders' Equity	4,642,606	3,338,627	3,467,733	3,214,691	3,054,012	3,237,545	3,394,142	1,556,862
Shares Outstanding	220,306	201,977	185,539	173,802	174,040	166,460	166,775	109,639
Statistical Record								
Return on Assets %	1.81	2.41	2.94	1.44	1.62	1.48	1.60	2.02
Return on Equity %	8.57	10.83	12.65	6.35	7.26	6.12	6.74	9.59
Net Margin %	12.98	15.94	19.33	9.72	11.37	10.71	11.88	13.02
Price Range	65.35-45.11	47.93-31.79	36.84-29.31	30.90-24.31	26.88-21.69	30.13-20.94	34.50-26.19	34.25-28.13
P/E Ratio	45.38-31.33	29.05-19.27	18.51-14.73	36.35-28.60	24.21-19.54	31.06-21.59	32.86-24.94	31.71-26.04
Average Yield %	4.79	5.97	6.52	7.59	8.43	7.83	4.96	6.46

Address: National City Center, 115 West Washington Sreet, Suite 15 East, Indianapolis, IN 46204 **Telephone:** (317) 636-1600 **Fax:** (317) 685-7336	**Web Site:** www.simon.com **Officers:** Melvin Simon - Co-Chmn. Herbert Simon - Co-Chmn.	**Auditors:** Ernst & Young LLP **Investor Contact:** 317-685-7330

SIMPSON MANUFACTURING CO., INC. (DE)

Exchange	Symbol	Price	52Wk Range	Yield	P/E
NYS	SSD	$30.90 (3/31/2005)	37.79-23.85	0.65	18.50

*7 Year Price Score 160.72 ***NYSE Composite Index=100** ***12 Month Price Score 104.79**

Interim Earnings (Per Share)

Qtr.	Mar	Jun	Sep	Dec
2001	0.18	0.26	0.25	0.14
2002	0.20	0.30	0.34	0.21
2003	0.22	0.35	0.37	0.27
2004	0.36	0.45	0.50	0.36

Interim Dividends (Per Share)

Amt	Decl	Ex	Rec	Pay
0.05Q	7/20/2004	10/4/2004	10/6/2004	10/26/2004
100%	9/4/2004	11/19/2004	11/1/2004	11/18/2004
0.05Q	9/24/2004	1/4/2005	1/6/2005	1/25/2005
0.05Q	1/25/2005	4/4/2005	4/6/2005	4/26/2005
		Indicated Div: $0.20		

Valuation Analysis

Forecast P/E	15.23	No of Institutions	
	(4/12/2005)	130	
Market Cap	$1.5 Billion	Shares	
Book Value	462.9 Million	29,164,768	
Price/Book	3.20	% Held	
Price/Sales	2.12	61.17	

Business Summary: Metal Products (MIC: 11.4 SIC: 429 NAIC: 32510)

Simpson Manufacturing through its subsidiary, Simpson Strong-Tie, designs, engineers and manufactures wood-to-wood, wood-to-concrete and wood-to-masonry connectors and pre-fabricated shearwalls. Also, Simpson Strong-Tie offers a full line of adhesives, mechanical anchors and powder actuated tools for concrete, masonry and steel. Co.'s subsidiary, Simpson Dura-Vent Company, designs, engineers and manufactures venting systems for gas, wood, oil and pellet burning appliances. Co. markets its products to the residential construction, light industrial and commercial construction, remodeling and do-it-yourself markets.

Recent Developments: For the year ended Dec 31 2004, net income increased 34.6% to $81,508,343 from net income of $60,562,224 a year earlier. Revenues were $698,053,226, up 27.3% from $548,181,933 the year before. Operating income was $131,216,836 versus an income of $98,072,932 in the prior year, an increase of 33.8%. Total direct expense was $417,417,175 versus $329,902,422 in the prior year, an increase of 26.5%. Total indirect expense was $149,419,215 versus $120,206,579 in the prior year, an increase of 24.3%.

Prospects: Co. is benefiting from continued strong sales growth across its Simpson Strong-Tie and Simpson Dura-Vent subsidiaries. However, margins have slipped a bit in recent weeks due largely to continued high steel costs. To avoid the rising pressure of higher steel costs, Co. has implemented two price increases in 2004, and a third price increase in January of 2005. Separately, on Oct 15 2004, Co. completed the acquisition of the assets of Quik Drive, U.S.A., Inc. and Quik Drive Canada, Inc. and 100% of the equity of Quik Drive Australia Pty. Limited for $30.0 million in cash and $5.0 million in stock. Quik Drive manufactures collated fasteners and fastener delivery systems.

Financial Data

(US$ in Thousands)	12/31/2004	12/31/2003	12/31/2002	12/31/2001	12/31/2000	12/31/1999	12/31/1998	12/31/1997
Earnings Per Share	1.67	1.21	1.04	0.82	0.78	0.79	0.65	0.54
Cash Flow Per Share	0.47	1.45	1.03	1.51	0.64	0.76	0.75	0.46
Tang Book Value Per Share	8.73	7.76	7.11	5.92	5.09	4.38	3.48	2.80
Dividends Per Share	0.150	...	...	...	...	...	...	...
Dividend Payout %	8.98	...	...	...	...	...	...	...
Income Statement								
Total Revenue	698,053	548,182	465,474	415,863	369,088	328,440	279,081	246,074
EBITDA	149,662	113,721	100,106	81,466	72,873	73,413	59,488	50,036
Depn & Amortn	18,445	15,648	14,023	15,650	13,136	10,862	8,258	6,712
Income Before Taxes	131,602	99,072	87,068	67,403	62,747	64,220	52,170	43,753
Income Taxes	50,094	38,510	35,134	27,620	25,639	25,753	21,028	17,767
Net Income	81,508	60,562	51,934	40,518	38,354	38,467	31,142	25,986
Average Shares	48,918	49,990	49,615	49,263	49,179	48,935	48,192	47,863
Balance Sheet								
Current Assets	347,111	323,350	280,014	229,969	200,642	175,750	132,864	104,288
Total Assets	545,137	460,249	396,401	329,612	279,480	247,254	191,600	150,765
Current Liabilities	78,400	54,767	41,737	35,708	32,724	33,693	27,221	20,991
Long-Term Obligations	2,397	5,178	5,480	5,687	2,069	2,415	2,565	...
Total Liabilities	82,212	59,945	47,217	41,495	35,134	36,665	30,317	21,814
Stockholders' Equity	462,925	400,304	349,184	288,117	243,591	210,589	161,282	128,951
Shares Outstanding	47,929	48,510	49,130	48,670	47,866	48,075	46,317	46,068
Statistical Record								
Return on Assets %	16.17	14.14	14.31	13.30	14.52	17.53	18.19	19.02
Return on Equity %	18.83	16.16	16.30	15.24	16.84	20.69	21.46	22.47
EBITDA Margin %	21.44	20.75	21.51	19.59	19.74	22.35	21.32	20.33
Net Margin %	11.68	11.05	11.16	9.74	10.39	11.71	11.16	10.56
Asset Turnover	1.38	1.28	1.28	1.37	1.40	1.50	1.63	1.80
Current Ratio	4.43	5.90	6.71	6.44	6.13	5.22	4.88	4.97
Debt to Equity	0.01	0.01	0.02	0.02	0.01	0.01	0.02	...
Price Range	35.61-22.38	26.27-15.43	18.15-12.66	15.13-11.75	13.25-9.72	13.59-8.22	10.63-6.48	10.47-5.44
P/E Ratio	21.32-13.40	21.71-12.75	17.45-12.18	18.45-14.33	16.99-12.46	17.21-10.40	16.35-9.98	19.39-10.07
Average Yield %	0.53	...	...	...	...	...	...	...

Address: 4120 Dublin Boulevard, Suite 400, Dublin, CA 94568
Telephone: (925) 560-9000
Fax: (925) 833-1496

Web Site: www.simpsonmfg.com
Officers: Barclay Simpson - Chmn. Thomas J. Fitzmyers - Pres., C.E.O.

Auditors: PricewaterhouseCoopers LLP
Investor Contact: 925-560-9097

SIX FLAGS INC

Exchange	Symbol	Price	52Wk Range	Yield	P/E
NYS	PKS	$4.12 (3/31/2005)	8.28-3.49	N/A	N/A

*7 Year Price Score 29.19   *NYSE Composite Index=100   *12 Month Price Score 73.26

Interim Earnings (Per Share)

Qtr.	Mar	Jun	Sep	Dec
2001	(1.76)	0.08	1.39	(1.06)
2002	(1.23)	(0.12)	1.31	(0.82)
2003	(1.25)	(0.19)	1.32	(0.91)
2004	(4.41)	(0.13)	0.53	(1.23)

Interim Dividends (Per Share)

No Dividends Paid

Valuation Analysis

Forecast P/E	0.00		No of Institutions
	(4/7/2005)		127
Market Cap	$383.3 Million		Shares
Book Value	826.1 Million		74,557,776
Price/Book	0.46		% Held
Price/Sales	0.37		80.08

TRADING VOLUME (thousand shares)

Business Summary: Sporting & Recreational (MIC: 13.5 SIC: 996 NAIC: 13110)

Six Flags is engaged in the theme park business. Co. operated 39 parks and had annual attendance of approximately 42.8 million at Dec 31 2003. These parks include 15 of the 50 most highly attended theme parks in North America. Co.'s parks are located in geographically diverse markets across North America and Europe. These theme parks offer a complete family-oriented entertainment experience. Co.'s theme parks generally offer a broad selection of state-of-the-art and traditional thrill rides, water attractions, themed areas, concerts and shows, restaurants, game venues and merchandise outlets.

Recent Developments: For the year ended Dec 31 2004, loss from continuing operations was $2.14 compared with a loss of $0.9 a year earlier. Net loss was $464,809,000 versus net loss of $61,713,000 a year earlier. Revenues were $10,376,920,00, down 1.0% from $1,048,643,000 the year before. Operating income was $149,573,000 versus an income of $188,723,000 in the prior year, a decrease of 20.7%. Total direct expense was $533,061,000 versus $508,257,000 in the prior year, an increase of 4.9%. Total indirect expense was $355,058,000 versus $351,663,000 in the prior year, an increase of 1.0%.

Prospects: Co. is pacing in line with its targets for season pass sales and hard ticket group bookings so far in 2005. Co. is projecting attendance growth in 2005 to be driven by its plan for capital additions to its parks. That plan encompasses new attractions in 13 of its 18 domestic theme parks and three of its water parks, and a children's area in its Montreal park. Co. has also added a major new roller coaster in its park in Mexico City which is already in operation and is generating a strong market reaction. Co.'s largest initiatives are concentrated in its major markets, and are expected to drive significant attendance and revenue growth in 2005.

Financial Data

(US$ in Thousands)	12/31/2004	12/31/2003	12/31/2002	12/31/2001	12/31/2000	12/31/1999	12/31/1998	12/31/1997
Earnings Per Share	(5.23)	(0.90)	(1.38)	(0.95)	(0.96)	(0.69)	0.25	0.38
Cash Flow Per Share	0.36	1.85	2.21	2.05	2.23	2.54	1.79	1.31
Tang Book Value Per Share	N.M.	0.63	2.30	2.52	4.23	4.54	4.55	7.36
Income Statement								
Total Revenue	1,037,692	1,236,669	1,037,933	1,045,964	1,006,981	926,984	813,627	193,904
EBITDA	205,856	314,624	358,696	375,796	366,992	335,690	307,385	63,199
Depn & Amortn	159,539	194,931	160,801	209,170	188,562	161,019	115,192	21,710
Income Before Taxes	(145,264)	(94,846)	(30,171)	(56,768)	(46,337)	5,230	76,344	23,714
Income Taxes	31,984	(33,133)	(4,062)	(7,195)	5,622	24,460	40,716	9,615
Net Income	(464,809)	(61,713)	(105,698)	(58,102)	(51,959)	(30,526)	34,840	14,099
Average Shares	93,036	92,617	92,511	89,221	78,735	77,656	68,518	36,876
Balance Sheet								
Current Assets	290,598	538,633	217,046	155,734	160,965	248,152	689,040	101,057
Total Assets	3,642,227	4,674,716	4,245,158	4,246,142	4,191,339	4,161,572	4,052,465	611,321
Current Liabilities	294,548	512,874	174,016	154,789	143,584	159,302	357,198	33,779
Long-Term Obligations	2,125,121	2,359,844	2,293,732	2,222,442	2,319,912	2,202,933	1,862,687	216,231
Total Liabilities	2,816,162	3,312,666	2,885,466	2,799,520	2,646,352	2,545,956	2,425,900	287,572
Stockholders' Equity	826,065	1,362,050	1,359,692	1,446,622	1,544,987	1,615,616	1,626,565	323,749
Shares Outstanding	93,041	92,616	92,616	92,417	80,068	78,350	76,488	37,746
Statistical Record								
Return on Assets %	N.M.	N.M.	N.M.	N.M.	N.M.	N.M.	1.49	3.08
Return on Equity %	N.M.	N.M.	N.M.	N.M.	N.M.	N.M.	3.57	6.45
EBITDA Margin %	19.84	25.44	34.56	35.93	36.44	36.21	37.78	32.59
Net Margin %	N.M.	N.M.	N.M.	N.M.	N.M.	N.M.	4.28	7.27
Asset Turnover	0.25	0.28	0.24	0.25	0.24	0.23	0.35	0.42
Current Ratio	0.99	1.05	1.25	1.01	1.12	1.56	1.93	2.99
Debt to Equity	2.57	1.73	1.69	1.54	1.50	1.36	1.15	0.67
Price Range	8.29-3.49	9.00-4.40	18.30-3.28	23.25-11.35	28.88-13.50	40.25-24.50	33.31-15.31	21.69-12.94
P/E Ratio	...	...	...	...	...	...	133.25-61.25	57.07-34.05

Address: 11501 Northeast Expressway, Oklahoma City, OK 73131 **Telephone:** (405) 475-2500	**Web Site:** www.sixflags.com **Officers:** Kieran E. Burke - Chmn., C.E.O. Gary Story - Pres., C.O.O.	**Auditors:** KPMG LLP **Investor Contact:** 212-682-6300

SLM CORP.

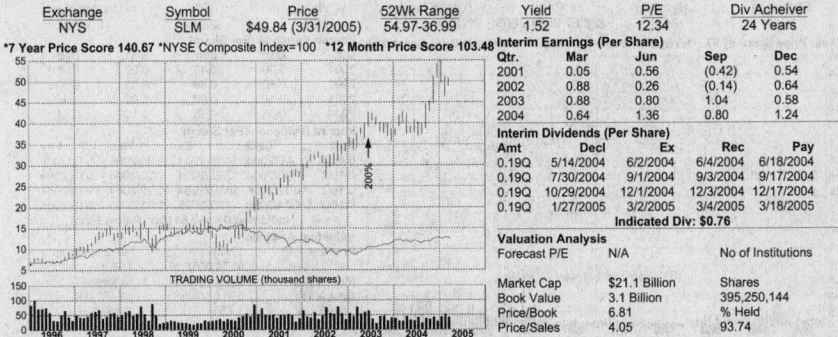

Exchange	Symbol	Price	52Wk Range	Yield	P/E	Div Acheiver
NYS	SLM	$49.84 (3/31/2005)	54.97-36.99	1.52	12.34	24 Years

*7 Year Price Score 140.67 *NYSE Composite Index=100 *12 Month Price Score 103.48

Interim Earnings (Per Share)

Qtr.	Mar	Jun	Sep	Dec
2001	0.05	0.56	(0.42)	0.54
2002	0.88	0.26	(0.14)	0.64
2003	0.88	0.80	1.04	0.58
2004	0.64	1.36	0.80	1.24

Interim Dividends (Per Share)

Amt	Decl	Ex	Rec	Pay
0.19Q	5/14/2004	6/2/2004	6/4/2004	6/18/2004
0.19Q	7/30/2004	9/1/2004	9/3/2004	9/17/2004
0.19Q	10/29/2004	12/1/2004	12/3/2004	12/17/2004
0.19Q	1/27/2005	3/2/2005	3/4/2005	3/18/2005

Indicated Div: $0.76

Valuation Analysis

Forecast P/E	N/A	No of Institutions
Market Cap	$21.1 Billion	Shares
Book Value	3.1 Billion	395,250,144
Price/Book	6.81	% Held
Price/Sales	4.05	93.74

TRADING VOLUME (thousand shares)

Business Summary: Credit & Lending (MIC: 8.6 SIC: 141 NAIC: 22291)

SLM is a provider of education funding, managing nearly $89.00 billion in student loans for more than seven million borrowers. Co. primarily provides federally guaranteed student loans originated under the Federal Family Education Loan Program, and offers comprehensive information and resources to help guide students, parents and guidance professionals through the financial aid process. Through its subsidiaries and divisions, Co. also provides an array of consumer credit loans, including those for lifelong learning and K-12 education, and business and technical outsourcing services for colleges and universities.

Recent Developments: For the year ended Dec 31 2004, net income increased 24.8% to $1,913,270 thousand from net income of $1,533,560 thousand a year earlier. Net interest income was $1,299,299 thousand, down 2.0% from $1,326,369 thousand the year before. Provision for loan losses was $111,066 thousand versus $147,480 thousand in the prior year, a decrease of 24.7%. Non-interest income rose 69.8% to $1,923,561 thousand, while non-interest expense advanced 40.3% to $1,115,780 thousand.

Prospects: On Dec 14 2004, Co. announced that it has completed the purchase of Student Loan Finance Association (SLFA) from the Education Assistance Foundation. The transaction includes SLFA's $1.70 billion loan portfolio and an origination franchise that generates student loans primarily in Washington, Idaho and Oregon. Terms of the transaction were not disclosed. Separately, Co. announced that it has concluded its privatization process by defeasing the remaining debt obligations of its government-sponsored enterprise subsidiary, the Student Loan Marketing Association (SLMA), and by dissolving SLMA's federal charter.

Financial Data

(US$ in Thousands)	12/31/2004	12/31/2003	12/31/2002	12/31/2001	12/31/2000	12/31/1999	12/31/1998	12/31/1997
Earnings Per Share	4.04	3.29	1.64	0.76	0.92	1.02	0.98	0.93
Cash Flow Per Share	(0.73)	1.49	1.65	1.76	1.55	0.70	0.25	0.10
Tang Book Value Per Share	4.42	4.18	2.72	3.23	2.54	1.43	1.33	1.22
Dividends Per Share	0.740	0.593	0.283	0.242	0.220	0.200	0.190	0.170
Dividend Payout %	18.32	18.03	17.24	31.80	23.91	19.61	19.39	18.28
Income Statement								
Interest Income	2,732,995	2,348,275	2,211,761	2,997,531	3,478,659	2,808,575	2,587,649	3,283,834
Interest Expense	1,433,696	1,021,906	1,202,620	2,124,115	2,836,871	2,114,785	1,924,997	2,526,156
Net Interest Income	1,299,299	1,326,369	1,009,141	873,416	641,788	693,790	662,652	757,678
Provision for Losses	111,066	147,480	116,624	65,991	32,119	34,358	28,619	...
Non-Interest Income	2,484,532	1,811,951	1,020,654	517,617	687,632	450,790	476,967	500,872
Non-Interest Expense	1,115,780	807,871	689,772	707,654	585,710	358,570	360,869	493,767
Income Before Taxes	2,556,985	2,182,969	1,223,399	617,388	711,591	751,652	750,131	764,783
Income Taxes	642,689	779,380	431,403	223,322	235,880	240,127	237,973	242,921
Net Income	1,913,270	1,533,560	791,996	383,996	465,017	500,831	501,464	507,895
Average Shares	475,787	463,335	474,519	490,200	493,065	489,474	510,198	548,823
Balance Sheet								
Net Loans & Leases	67,028,795	51,078,136	43,541,720	42,769,017	39,485,817	35,879,327	31,005,649	32,764,280
Total Assets	84,093,526	64,610,651	53,175,005	52,873,959	48,791,788	44,024,784	37,210,009	39,908,797
Total Liabilities	80,919,549	61,980,605	51,177,055	51,201,497	47,162,569	42,969,987	36,342,500	39,020,342
Stockholders' Equity	3,102,304	2,630,046	1,997,950	1,672,462	1,415,336	840,914	653,626	674,572
Shares Outstanding	423,632	447,678	457,740	466,485	492,434	472,729	492,381	550,899
Statistical Record								
Return on Assets %	2.57	2.60	1.49	0.76	1.00	1.23	1.30	1.16
Return on Equity %	66.57	66.27	43.16	24.87	41.11	67.02	75.51	67.34
Net Interest Margin %	47.54	56.48	45.63	29.14	18.45	24.70	25.61	23.07
Efficiency Ratio %	21.39	19.42	21.34	20.13	14.06	11.00	11.78	13.05
Price Range	54.24-36.99	42.64-33.85	35.63-26.38	29.13-19.38	22.67-9.44	17.88-13.38	17.00-9.33	15.60-8.56
P/E Ratio	13.43-9.16	12.96-10.29	21.73-16.09	38.33-25.49	24.64-10.26	17.52-13.11	17.35-9.52	16.77-9.20
Average Yield %	1.76	1.55	0.90	0.96	1.37	1.28	1.44	1.41

Address: 11600 Sallie Mae Drive, Reston, VA 20193 Telephone: (703) 810-3000 Fax: (703) 810-5074	Web Site: www.salliemae.com Officers: Edward A. Fox - Chmn. Thomas J. Fitzpatrick - Pres., C.O.O.	Auditors: PricewaterhouseCoopers LLP Investor Contact: 703-810-7751 Transfer Agents: The Bank of New York, New York, NY

SMITH (A.O.) CORP

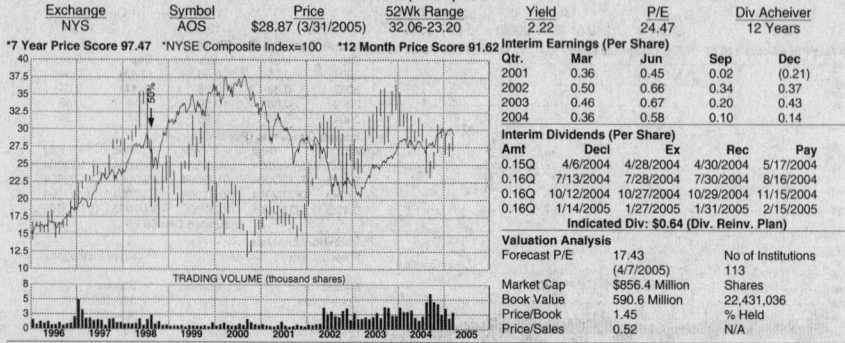

Exchange	Symbol	Price	52Wk Range	Yield	P/E	Div Acheiver
NYS	AOS	$28.87 (3/31/2005)	32.06-23.20	2.22	24.47	12 Years

*7 Year Price Score 97.47   *NYSE Composite Index=100   *12 Month Price Score 91.62

Interim Earnings (Per Share)

Qtr.	Mar	Jun	Sep	Dec
2001	0.36	0.45	0.02	(0.21)
2002	0.50	0.66	0.34	0.37
2003	0.46	0.67	0.20	0.43
2004	0.36	0.58	0.10	0.14

Interim Dividends (Per Share)

Amt	Decl	Ex	Rec	Pay
0.15Q	4/6/2004	4/28/2004	4/30/2004	5/17/2004
0.16Q	7/13/2004	7/28/2004	7/30/2004	8/16/2004
0.16Q	10/12/2004	10/27/2004	10/29/2004	11/15/2004
0.16Q	1/14/2005	1/27/2005	1/31/2005	2/15/2005

Indicated Div: $0.64 (Div. Reinv. Plan)

Valuation Analysis

Forecast P/E	17.43 (4/7/2005)	No of Institutions 113
Market Cap	$856.4 Million	Shares 22,431,036
Book Value	590.6 Million	% Held
Price/Book	1.45	N/A
Price/Sales	0.52	

Business Summary: Electrical (MIC: 11.14 SIC: 621 NAIC: 35312)

A.O. Smith is a manufacturer of electric motors and water heating equipment serving residential, commercial and industrial end markets primarily in the United States. The Electric Products segment manufactures hermetic motors, fractional horsepower alternating current and direct current motors, and integral horsepower motors. The Water Systems segment manufactures and markets a line of residential gas and electric water heaters, standard and specialty commercial water heating equipment, high-efficiency copper-tube boilers, and water systems tanks. Co. operates manufacturing facilities in the United States, Canada, Mexico, England, Ireland, Hungary, the Netherlands and China.

Recent Developments: For the year ended Dec 31 2004, net income decreased 32.2% to $35,400 thousand from net income of $52,200 thousand a year earlier. Revenues were $1,653,100 thousand, up 8.0% from $1,530,700 thousand the year before. Total direct expense was $1,355,100 thousand versus $1,232,000 thousand in the prior year, an increase of 10.0%. Total indirect expense was $235,800 thousand versus $206,200 thousand in the prior year, an increase of 14.4%.

Prospects: Co. has made considerable progress in improving manufacturing inefficiencies at its Water Systems business, which should lead to improved profitability in the coming year. Nevertheless, Co. continues to face a number of challenges, including unprecedented cost increases, principally for steel, which is placing added pressure on its operating margins. Also, Co. is seeing considerable increases in freight costs. Accordingly, Co. has implemented significant price increases in both of its businesses to help mitigate the impact to its bottom-line. The latest of the price increases was made effective at the beginning of 2005.

Financial Data

(US$ in Thousands)	12/31/2004	12/31/2003	12/31/2002	12/31/2001	12/31/2000	12/31/1999	12/31/1998	12/31/1997
Earnings Per Share	1.18	1.76	1.86	0.61	1.26	1.78	1.84	5.46
Cash Flow Per Share	2.29	0.87	4.16	2.11	3.27	2.06	3.29	2.90
Tang Book Value Per Share	9.35	9.07	6.95	6.30	8.64	7.69	10.93	10.69
Dividends Per Share	0.620	0.580	0.540	0.520	0.500	0.480	0.467	0.453
Dividend Payout %	52.54	32.95	29.03	85.25	39.68	26.97	25.36	8.30
Income Statement								
Total Revenue	1,653,100	1,530,700	1,469,100	1,151,156	1,247,945	1,039,281	917,569	832,937
EBITDA	114,900	141,200	141,678	84,345	130,704	125,836	107,195	86,669
Depn & Amortn	53,900	50,000	49,362	45,441	43,514	37,315	31,173	26,286
Income Before Taxes	47,500	79,000	78,390	22,486	65,088	77,092	72,963	61,656
Income Taxes	12,100	26,800	27,045	7,984	23,432	26,822	25,283	21,359
Net Income	35,400	52,200	51,345	14,502	29,753	42,422	44,491	153,830
Average Shares	29,912	29,710	27,649	23,914	23,691	23,787	24,184	28,191
Balance Sheet								
Current Assets	585,000	547,700	488,251	477,574	406,099	388,627	287,389	365,728
Total Assets	1,312,800	1,279,900	1,224,857	1,293,923	1,059,176	1,063,986	767,432	716,516
Current Liabilities	245,200	338,600	261,978	255,950	170,431	168,440	132,157	127,882
Long-Term Obligations	272,500	170,100	239,084	390,385	316,372	351,251	131,203	100,972
Total Liabilities	722,200	703,700	713,805	842,045	610,781	632,902	366,339	316,811
Stockholders' Equity	590,600	576,200	511,052	451,878	448,395	431,084	401,093	399,705
Shares Outstanding	29,665	29,246	29,039	23,786	23,549	23,394	23,252	32,550
Statistical Record								
Return on Assets %	2.72	4.17	4.08	1.23	2.80	4.63	6.00	19.21
Return on Equity %	6.05	9.60	10.66	3.22	6.75	10.20	11.11	37.32
EBITDA Margin %	6.95	9.22	9.64	7.33	10.47	12.11	11.68	10.41
Net Margin %	2.14	3.41	3.49	1.26	2.38	4.08	4.85	18.47
Asset Turnover	1.27	1.22	1.17	0.98	1.17	1.13	1.24	1.04
Current Ratio	2.39	1.62	1.87	1.87	2.38	2.31	2.17	2.86
Debt to Equity	0.46	0.30	0.47	0.86	0.71	0.81	0.33	0.25
Price Range	35.49-23.20	36.50-23.80	32.10-19.15	20.00-14.68	22.63-11.75	31.94-19.00	35.88-15.94	28.58-19.33
P/E Ratio	30.08-19.66	20.74-13.52	17.26-10.30	32.79-24.07	17.96-9.33	17.94-10.67	19.50-8.66	5.24-3.54
Average Yield %	2.13	1.91	2.02	2.96	2.83	1.95	1.71	1.85

Address: P.O. Box 245008, Milwaukee, WI 53224-9508 **Telephone:** (414) 359-4000 **Fax:** (414) 359-4180	**Web Site:** www.aosmith.com **Officers:** Robert J. O'Toole - Chmn., C.E.O. Paul W. Jones - Pres., C.O.O.	**Auditors:** Ernst & Young LLP **Investor Contact:** 414-359-4009 **Transfer Agents:** Wells Fargo Bank Minnesota, N.A., St. Paul, MN

SMITH INTERNATIONAL, INC.

Exchange	Symbol	Price	52Wk Range	Yield	P/E
NYS	SII	$62.73 (3/31/2005)	65.53-48.05	0.77	35.24

*7 Year Price Score 144.65 *NYSE Composite Index=100 *12 Month Price Score 102.13

Interim Earnings (Per Share)

Qtr.	Mar	Jun	Sep	Dec
2001	0.34	0.37	0.42	0.39
2002	0.29	0.27	0.20	0.18
2003	0.21	0.30	0.35	0.38
2004	0.44	0.27	0.51	0.57

Interim Dividends (Per Share)

Amt	Decl	Ex	Rec	Pay
100%	6/6/2002	7/9/2002	6/20/2002	7/8/2002
0.12Q	2/2/2005	3/11/2005	3/15/2005	4/15/2005
		Indicated Div: $0.48		

Valuation Analysis

Forecast P/E	23.98	No of Institutions
	(4/7/2005)	270
Market Cap	$6.3 Billion	Shares
Book Value	1.4 Billion	92,724,024
Price/Book	4.53	% Held
Price/Sales	1.43	87.37

Business Summary: Chemicals (MIC: 11.1 SIC: 899 NAIC: 25998)

Smith International is a worldwide supplier of products and services to the oil and gas exploration and production industry, the petrochemical industry and other industrial markets. Co. provides a range of products and engineering services, including drilling and completion fluid systems, solids-control equipment, waste-management services, production chemicals, three-cone and diamond drill bits, turbines, fishing services, drilling tools, underreamers, casing exit and multilateral systems, packers and liner hangers. Co. also offers supply-chain management solutions through a North American branch network that supplies pipe, valves, fittings, mill, safety and other maintenance products.

Recent Developments: For the year ended Dec 31 2004, net income increased 47.8% to $182,451 thousand from net income of $123,480 thousand a year earlier. Revenues were $4,419,015 thousand, up 22.9% from $3,594,828 thousand the year before. Operating income was $438,764 thousand versus an income of $328,747 thousand in the prior year, an increase of 33.5%. Total direct expense was $3,067,076 thousand versus $2,518,897 thousand in the prior year, an increase of 21.8%. Total indirect expense was $913,175 thousand versus $747,184 thousand in the prior year, an increase of 22.2%.

Prospects: Co.'s results are benefiting from increased demand from the oil and gas exploration and production customers as a result of the prolonged favorable pricing environment for energy commodities. Co.'s revenues are benefiting from increasing activity levels and new contract awards, higher diamond bit rental volumes, demand for recent product introductions, including the Flex-Flo™ design series of three-cone bits, and improved product pricing. Revenues are also benefiting from higher tubular sales volumes, increased North American drilling and completion activity and more project business in the petrochemical market. For the first quarter of 2005, Co. expects earnings of $0.60 to $0.62 per share.

Financial Data

(US$ in Thousands)	12/31/2004	12/31/2003	12/31/2002	12/31/2001	12/31/2000	12/31/1999	12/31/1998	12/31/1997
Earnings Per Share	1.78	1.23	0.93	1.51	0.72	0.57	0.35	1.27
Cash Flow Per Share	1.79	1.43	3.27	2.07	0.58	0.71	1.29	0.54
Tang Book Value Per Share	6.12	5.43	4.47	3.79	3.65	3.79	3.58	3.28
Income Statement								
Total Revenue	4,419,015	3,594,828	3,170,080	3,551,209	2,761,014	1,806,153	2,118,715	1,563,144
EBITDA	544,764	430,456	345,475	464,405	279,714	225,569	195,625	264,195
Depn & Amortn	106,000	101,709	89,327	92,895	80,688	76,037	70,316	46,704
Income Before Taxes	401,302	289,756	217,799	329,046	164,131	110,759	81,938	192,518
Income Taxes	129,721	93,334	66,632	106,397	54,998	47,865	26,279	50,650
Net Income	182,451	123,480	93,189	152,145	72,800	56,724	34,069	102,351
Average Shares	102,569	100,903	100,091	100,448	100,604	98,380	96,682	80,366
Balance Sheet								
Current Assets	2,019,632	1,679,796	1,426,914	1,523,031	1,310,003	1,054,780	997,155	850,971
Total Assets	3,506,778	3,097,047	2,749,545	2,735,828	2,295,287	1,894,575	1,758,988	1,396,033
Current Liabilities	887,357	630,924	595,096	666,004	642,804	457,318	693,300	372,927
Long-Term Obligations	387,798	488,548	441,967	538,842	374,716	346,647	368,823	306,279
Total Liabilities	2,105,967	1,861,271	1,686,010	1,786,669	1,477,806	1,174,355	1,124,954	926,576
Stockholders' Equity	1,400,811	1,235,776	1,063,535	949,159	817,481	720,220	634,034	469,457
Shares Outstanding	101,075	100,336	99,162	98,804	99,526	97,860	96,274	79,320
Statistical Record								
Return on Assets %	5.51	4.22	3.40	6.05	3.47	3.11	2.16	8.29
Return on Equity %	13.80	10.74	9.26	17.22	9.44	8.38	6.17	24.43
EBITDA Margin %	12.33	11.97	10.90	13.08	10.13	12.49	9.23	16.90
Net Margin %	4.13	3.43	2.94	4.28	2.64	3.14	1.61	6.55
Asset Turnover	1.33	1.23	1.16	1.41	1.31	0.99	1.34	1.27
Current Ratio	2.28	2.66	2.40	2.29	2.04	2.31	1.44	2.28
Debt to Equity	0.28	0.40	0.42	0.57	0.46	0.48	0.58	0.65
Price Range	62.50-40.27	42.52-29.85	38.07-23.35	41.95-16.72	43.75-23.19	25.66-12.16	31.78-8.88	43.09-19.31
P/E Ratio	35.11-22.62	34.57-24.27	40.94-25.11	27.78-11.07	60.76-32.20	45.01-21.33	90.80-25.36	33.93-15.21

Address: 411 North Sam Houston Parkway, Suite 600, Houston, TX 77060 **Telephone:** (281) 443-3370 **Fax:** (281) 233-5199	**Web Site:** www.smith.com **Officers:** Douglas L. Rock - Chmn., Pres., C.E.O., C.O.O. Loren K. Carroll - Exec. V.P.	**Auditors:** Deloitte & Touche LLP **Investor Contact:** 800-877-6424

SMITHFIELD FOODS, INC.

Exchange	Symbol	Price	52Wk Range	Yield	P/E
NYS	SFD	$31.55 (3/31/2005)	34.39-23.55	N/A	10.62

*7 Year Price Score 131.16 *NYSE Composite Index=100 *12 Month Price Score 106.32

Interim Earnings (Per Share)

Qtr.	Jul	Oct	Jan	Apr
2001-02	0.53	0.56	0.48	0.21
2002-03	0.11	0.04	0.05	0.05
2003-04	0.20	0.33	0.41	1.09
2004-05	0.49	0.52	0.87	...

Interim Dividends (Per Share)

Amt	Decl	Ex	Rec	Pay
100%	8/29/2001	9/17/2001	9/6/2001	9/14/2001

Valuation Analysis

Forecast P/E	11.28	No of Institutions	
	(4/7/2005)	214	
Market Cap	$3.5 Billion	Shares	
Book Value	1.8 Billion	65,623,008	
Price/Book	1.93	% Held	
Price/Sales	0.32	58.96	

Business Summary: Food (MIC: 4.1 SIC: 011 NAIC: 11611)

Smithfield Foods is a major hog producer and pork processor. Co.'s Pork segment produces a variety of fresh pork and processed meat products in the U.S. and markets them nationwide and to numerous foreign markets, including Canada, Japan and Mexico. The Beef segment primarily produces boxed beef and ground beef (both chub and case-ready) and markets these products in large portions of the U.S. The Hog Production Group operates numerous hog production facilities with approximately 843,000 sows producing about 14.5 million market hogs annually. The Other segment includes Co.'s international meat processing operations and Co.'s turkey production and processing operations in the U.S.

Recent Developments: For the quarter ended Jan 30 2005, net income increased 111.5% to $97,500 thousand from net income of $46,100 thousand in the year-earlier quarter. Revenues were $3,060,100 thousand, up 13.2% from $2,703,700 thousand the year before. Total direct expense was $2,706,300 thousand versus $2,435,500 thousand in the prior-year quarter, an increase of 11.1%. Total indirect expense was $170,000 thousand versus $170,600 thousand in the prior-year quarter, a decrease of 0.4%.

Prospects: Co.'s strong earnings are due to the continuing success of its vertically integrated pork operations, which are enabling it to improve profitability despite increasing livestock costs. Co.'s hog production operations are benefiting from substantial increases in live hog market prices. Despite the sharply higher livestock prices, fresh pork margins remain solid reflecting strong export and domestic pork demand. Meanwhile, Co.'s beef segment earnings are being pressured by weak demand, closed export markets, tight cattle supplies and high cattle costs. Separately, Co. signed an agreement to form a 50/50 standalone joint venture cattle feeding business with ContiBeef LLC.

Financial Data
(US$ in Thousands)

	9 Mos	6 Mos	3 Mos	05/02/2004	04/27/2003	04/28/2002	04/29/2001	04/30/2000
Earnings Per Share	2.97	2.48	2.30	2.03	0.24	1.78	2.03	0.76
Cash Flow Per Share	1.34	1.86	2.11	2.77	0.76	2.77	2.02	1.29
Tang Book Value Per Share	10.88	10.25	9.83	10.07	7.27	8.29	13.44	5.33
Income Statement								
Total Revenue	8,430,900	5,370,800	2,651,700	9,267,000	7,904,500	7,356,119	5,899,927	5,150,469
EBITDA	466,400	266,400	130,700	543,200	305,900	560,173	586,342	310,895
Depn & Amortn	148,300	96,000	47,500	175,100	172,700	148,068	140,050	118,964
Income Before Taxes	318,100	170,400	83,200	246,800	39,200	317,779	357,318	119,987
Income Taxes	107,300	57,100	28,300	84,100	12,900	120,893	133,805	44,875
Net Income	210,800	113,300	54,900	227,100	26,300	196,886	223,513	75,112
Average Shares	112,300	112,100	112,300	111,700	109,800	110,419	110,146	98,772
Balance Sheet								
Current Assets	2,517,400	2,366,600	2,101,000	2,023,600	1,650,500	1,520,356	1,263,695	1,232,726
Total Assets	5,639,400	5,313,500	4,919,300	4,813,700	4,210,600	3,877,998	3,250,888	3,129,613
Current Liabilities	1,169,500	1,046,000	947,200	967,000	817,500	721,930	628,282	622,869
Long-Term Obligations	2,127,800	2,055,800	1,842,400	1,696,800	1,599,100	1,387,147	1,146,223	1,187,770
Total Liabilities	3,795,600	3,606,000	3,296,100	3,183,300	2,898,600	2,497,135	2,149,361	2,193,935
Stockholders' Equity	1,816,300	1,686,300	1,609,500	1,617,200	1,299,200	1,362,774	1,053,132	902,909
Shares Outstanding	111,259	110,993	110,983	110,978	109,460	110,284	52,502	109,410
Statistical Record								
Return on Assets %	6.20	5.40	5.55	4.95	0.65	5.54	7.03	3.07
Return on Equity %	20.46	18.14	17.52	15.32	1.98	16.34	22.92	10.42
EBITDA Margin %	5.53	4.96	4.93	5.86	3.87	7.62	9.94	6.04
Net Margin %	2.50	2.11	2.07	2.45	0.33	2.68	3.79	1.46
Asset Turnover	2.03	2.02	2.11	2.02	1.96	2.07	1.85	2.11
Current Ratio	2.15	2.26	2.22	2.09	2.02	2.11	2.01	1.98
Debt to Equity	1.17	1.22	1.14	1.05	1.23	1.02	1.09	1.32
Price Range	30.76-23.01	30.21-20.30	30.21-19.14	27.95-19.14	21.32-14.80	26.50-17.00	18.93-10.25	16.84-7.44
P/E Ratio	10.36-7.75	12.18-8.19	13.13-8.32	13.77-9.43	88.83-61.67	14.89-9.55	9.32-5.05	22.16-9.79

Address: 200 Commerce Street, Smithfield, VA 23430 **Telephone:** (757) 365-3000 **Fax:** (757) 365-3017	**Web Site:** www.smithfieldfoods.com **Officers:** Joseph W. Luter III - Chmn., C.E.O. C. Larry Pope - Pres., C.O.O.	**Auditors:** Ernst & Young LLP **Investor Contact:** 212-758-2100

SMUCKER (J.M.) CO.

Exchange	Symbol	Price	52Wk Range	Yield	P/E
NYS	SJM	$50.30 (3/31/2005)	53.38-41.28	1.99	21.87

*7 Year Price Score 127.04 ***NYSE Composite Index=100** ***12 Month Price Score 97.22**

Interim Earnings (Per Share)
Qtr.	Jul	Oct	Jan	Apr
2001-02	0.34	0.32	0.32	0.33
2002-03	0.39	0.58	0.56	0.46
2003-04	0.51	0.64	0.62	0.44
2004-05	0.60	0.65	0.61	...

Interim Dividends (Per Share)
Amt	Decl	Ex	Rec	Pay
0.25Q	4/13/2004	5/14/2004	5/18/2004	6/1/2004
0.25Q	7/19/2004	8/16/2004	8/18/2004	9/1/2004
0.25Q	10/28/2004	11/15/2004	11/17/2004	12/1/2004
0.25Q	1/20/2005	2/10/2005	2/14/2005	3/1/2005

Indicated Div: $1.00

Valuation Analysis
Forecast P/E	17.20	No of Institutions
	(4/7/2005)	277
Market Cap	$2.9 Billion	Shares
Book Value	1.7 Billion	30,277,898
Price/Book	1.75	% Held
Price/Sales	1.56	51.83

Business Summary: Food (MIC: 4.1 SIC: 033 NAIC: 11421)

J.M. Smucker manufactures and markets branded food products primarily in the U.S. Co.'s operations outside the U.S. are principally in Canada although products are exported to other countries as well. The principal products of Co. are peanut butter, shortening and oils, fruit spreads, fruit and vegetable juices, beverages, dessert toppings, syrups, frozen sandwiches, flour and scratch baking ingredients, dessert and baking mixes, ready-to-spread frostings, potato mixes, dry breakfast mixes, syrups, and pickles and condiments. Well-recognized brand names include: Smucker's, Simply Jif, Crisco, Dickinson's, Magic Shell, Goober, Martha White, Hungry Jack, Idaho Spuds, Pet, and Farmhouse.

Recent Developments:
For the quarter ended Jan 31 2005, income from continuing operations increased 14.2% to $35,524 thousand from income of $31,120 thousand in the year-earlier quarter. Net income increased 15.3% to $36,108 thousand from net income of $31,318 thousand in the year-earlier quarter. Revenues were $550,234 thousand, up 60.1% from $343,788 thousand. Operating income was $59,745 thousand versus an income of $49,496 thousand in the prior-year quarter, an increase of 20.7%. Total direct expense was $376,036 thousand with $217,262 thousand in the prior-year quarter, an increase of 73.1%. Total indirect expense was $114,453 thousand with $77,030 thousand in the prior-year quarter, an increase of 48.6%.

Prospects:
Co. confirmed its objective to increase its 2005 diluted earnings per share from continuing operations by its long-term growth goal of 8.0%. This equates to an earnings growth rate of approximately 23.0% in 2005 due to an increase of approximately 8.0 million shares outstanding from the June 2004 acquisition of International Multifoods Corporation. Co.'s total merger and integration costs related to the Multifoods transaction at $20.0 million. Approximately $15.0 million of these costs will be incurred in fiscal year 2005 and the remainder is expected to be incurred in fiscal year 2006. Earnings for 2005 are expected to include approximately $10.0 to $12.0 million in restructuring costs.

Financial Data
(US$ in Thousands)	9 Mos	6 Mos	3 Mos	04/30/2004	04/30/2003	04/30/2002	04/30/2001	04/30/2000
Earnings Per Share	2.30	2.30	2.29	2.21	2.02	1.31	1.26	0.97
Cash Flow Per Share	2.53	1.75	1.78	2.52	3.51	2.90	3.67	1.24
Tang Book Value Per Share	4.72	2.73	1.99	7.10	5.58	9.86	8.75	9.83
Dividends Per Share	0.980	0.960	0.940	0.920	0.600	0.680	0.677	0.645
Dividend Payout %	42.70	41.68	40.99	41.63	29.70	51.91	53.78	66.30
Income Statement								
Total Revenue	1,552,423	1,002,189	415,816	1,417,011	1,311,744	687,148	651,242	632,486
EBITDA	215,970	140,948	57,942	221,672	199,854	85,781	81,750	68,134
Depn & Amortn	39,030	24,636	10,891	39,858	37,751	28,557	26,921	26,198
Income Before Taxes	163,010	107,492	43,335	178,819	155,390	50,198	49,960	41,531
Income Taxes	59,336	39,342	15,861	67,469	59,048	19,347	18,301	15,174
Net Income	106,961	70,853	32,848	111,350	96,342	30,851	30,667	26,357
Average Shares	58,743	58,815	54,513	50,395	47,764	23,493	24,249	27,171
Balance Sheet								
Current Assets	587,577	620,854	573,700	425,258	466,660	279,813	229,066	229,132
Total Assets	2,631,080	2,856,620	2,763,640	1,684,125	1,615,407	524,892	470,469	475,384
Current Liabilities	381,483	458,841	408,030	174,883	167,274	80,431	67,103	68,189
Long-Term Obligations	432,300	433,040	451,149	135,000	135,000	135,000	135,000	75,000
Total Liabilities	952,506	1,177,589	1,140,029	473,432	491,236	244,748	223,358	161,911
Stockholders' Equity	1,678,574	1,679,031	1,623,611	1,210,693	1,124,171	280,144	247,111	313,473
Shares Outstanding	58,254	58,451	58,360	50,174	49,767	23,504	23,021	26,770
Statistical Record								
Return on Assets %	5.98	5.49	5.36	6.73	9.00	6.20	6.48	5.78
Return on Equity %	8.97	8.70	8.55	9.51	13.72	11.70	10.94	8.24
EBITDA Margin %	13.91	14.06	13.93	15.64	15.24	12.48	12.55	10.77
Net Margin %	6.89	7.07	7.90	7.86	7.34	4.49	4.71	4.17
Asset Turnover	0.87	0.74	0.67	0.86	1.23	1.38	1.38	1.39
Current Ratio	1.54	1.35	1.41	2.43	2.79	3.48	3.41	3.36
Debt to Equity	0.26	0.26	0.28	0.11	0.12	0.48	0.55	0.24
Price Range	53.38-41.28	53.38-41.28	53.38-37.83	53.38-35.95	41.75-29.55	37.73-24.31	29.00-16.00	25.75-15.00
P/E Ratio	23.21-17.95	23.21-17.95	23.31-16.52	24.15-16.27	20.67-14.63	28.80-18.56	23.02-12.70	26.55-15.46
Average Yield %	2.07	2.04	2.04	2.09	1.66	2.22	2.99	3.17

Address: Strawberry Lane, Orrville, OH 44667	Web Site: www.smuckers.com	Auditors: Ernst & Young LLP
Telephone: (330) 682-3000	Officers: Timothy P. Smucker - Chmn., Co-C.E.O. Richard K. Smucker - Pres., Co-C.E.O.	Investor Contact: 330-684-3838
Fax: (330) 682-3370		Transfer Agents: Computershare Investor Services, LLC, Chicago, IL

SNAP-ON, INC.

Exchange	Symbol	Price	52Wk Range	Yield	P/E
NYS	SNA	$31.79 (3/31/2005)	35.20-27.26	3.15	22.71

*7 Year Price Score 91.29 ***NYSE Composite Index=100** ***12 Month Price Score 95.66**

Interim Earnings (Per Share)
Qtr.	Mar	Jun	Sep	Dec
2001	0.46	0.15	0.01	(0.29)
2002	0.42	0.50	0.33	0.56
2003	0.37	0.38	0.30	0.30
2004	0.22	0.38	0.39	0.41

Interim Dividends (Per Share)
Amt	Decl	Ex	Rec	Pay
0.25Q	4/23/2004	5/18/2004	5/20/2004	6/10/2004
0.25Q	6/25/2004	8/18/2004	8/20/2004	9/10/2004
0.25Q	10/22/2004	11/17/2004	11/19/2004	12/10/2004
0.25Q	2/3/2005	2/15/2005	2/17/2005	3/10/2005

Indicated Div: $1.00

Valuation Analysis
Forecast P/E	19.42	No of Institutions
	(4/7/2005)	212
Market Cap	$2.0 Billion	Shares
Book Value	1.1 Billion	48,293,128
Price/Book	1.78	% Held
Price/Sales	0.82	83.58

Business Summary: Instruments and Related Products (MIC: 11.15 SIC: 825 NAIC: 34515)

Snap-on is a global manufacturer and marketer of tool, diagnostic and equipment solutions for professional tool and equipment users. Product lines include a broad range of hand and power tools, tool storage, saws and cutting tools, pruning tools, vehicle service diagnostics equipment, vehicle service equipment, including wheel service, safety testing and collision repair equipment, vehicle service information, business management systems, equipment repair services, and other tool and equipment solutions. Products are sold through Co.'s franchised dealer van, company-direct, distributor and Internet sales channels.

Recent Developments: For the year ended Jan 1 2005, net income increased 3.8% to $81,700 thousand from net income of $78,700 thousand a year earlier. Revenues were $2,407,200 thousand, up 7.8% from $2,233,200 thousand the year before. Operating income was $142,300 thousand versus an income of $150,100 thousand in the prior year, a decrease of 5.2%. Total direct expense was $1,319,800 thousand versus $1,268,500 thousand in the prior year, an increase of 4.0%. Total indirect expense was $945,100 thousand versus $858,400 thousand in the prior year, an increase of 10.1%.

Prospects: In 2005, Co. expects to focus efforts on improving customer service levels, particularly those relating to production issues in its U.S. hand-tool plants, reducing complexities and associated costs throughout its organization, strengthening and growing its U.S. dealer van franchise system, delivering continued improvements in its global Commercial and Industrial businesses, and enhancing its marketplace position for diagnostics and information products. The costs associated with these actions are expected to be incurred in the first-quarter 2005 results with charges of $10.0 million to $12.0 million and full-year 2005 with restructuring costs totaling $20.0 million to $25.0 million.

Financial Data
(US$ in Thousands)	01/01/2005	01/03/2004	12/28/2002	12/29/2001	12/30/2000	01/01/2000	01/02/1999	01/03/1998
Earnings Per Share	1.40	1.35	1.81	0.33	2.53	2.16	(0.08)	2.44
Cash Flow Per Share	2.54	2.99	3.86	2.84	3.27	4.04	1.27	3.15
Tang Book Value Per Share	9.67	8.29	6.27	6.01	6.95	12.65	11.61	14.74
Dividends Per Share	1.000	1.000	0.970	0.960	0.940	0.900	0.860	0.820
Dividend Payout %	71.43	74.07	53.59	290.91	37.15	41.67	...	33.61
Income Statement								
Total Revenue	2,407,200	2,233,200	2,109,100	2,095,700	2,175,700	1,945,621	1,772,637	1,672,215
EBITDA	204,400	201,400	241,600	151,100	299,500	280,662	77,078	294,707
Depn & Amortn	61,000	60,300	51,700	68,000	66,200	55,367	44,984	38,377
Income Before Taxes	120,400	116,700	161,200	47,600	192,600	197,937	10,840	238,676
Income Taxes	38,700	38,000	58,000	26,100	69,500	70,710	15,619	88,310
Net Income	81,700	78,700	106,000	19,000	148,500	127,227	(4,779)	150,366
Average Shares	58,300	58,400	58,500	58,100	58,600	58,877	59,220	61,686
Balance Sheet								
Current Assets	1,192,600	1,131,700	1,051,000	1,139,400	1,186,400	1,206,341	1,079,832	1,021,709
Total Assets	2,290,100	2,138,500	1,994,100	1,974,300	2,050,400	2,149,822	1,674,920	1,641,357
Current Liabilities	674,200	567,200	552,500	549,400	538,000	452,749	458,053	352,530
Long-Term Obligations	203,200	303,000	304,300	445,500	473,000	607,476	246,644	151,016
Total Liabilities	1,179,400	1,127,600	1,163,700	1,198,500	1,206,400	1,324,561	912,653	749,220
Stockholders' Equity	1,110,700	1,010,900	830,400	775,800	844,000	825,261	762,267	892,137
Shares Outstanding	62,030	63,181	63,571	63,923	60,346	65,224	65,669	60,516
Statistical Record								
Return on Assets %	3.70	3.75	5.36	0.95	7.09	6.67	N.M.	9.36
Return on Equity %	7.72	8.41	13.24	2.35	17.84	16.07	N.M.	17.20
EBITDA Margin %	8.49	9.02	11.46	7.21	13.77	14.43	4.35	17.62
Net Margin %	3.39	3.52	5.03	0.91	6.83	6.54	N.M.	8.99
Asset Turnover	1.09	1.06	1.07	1.04	1.04	1.02	1.07	1.04
Current Ratio	1.77	2.00	1.90	2.07	2.21	2.66	2.36	2.90
Debt to Equity	0.18	0.30	0.37	0.57	0.56	0.74	0.32	0.17
Price Range	34.36-27.26	32.34-22.90	34.96-21.50	34.21-21.65	31.94-21.19	37.38-26.56	46.25-26.19	46.13-35.75
P/E Ratio	24.54-19.47	23.96-16.96	19.31-11.88	103.67-65.61	12.62-8.37	17.30-12.30	...	18.90-14.65
Average Yield %	3.12	3.52	3.29	3.42	3.56	2.77	2.28	2.00

Address: 10801 Corporate Drive, Pleasant Prairie, WI 53158-1603	**Web Site:** www.snapon.com	**Auditors:** Deloitte & Touche LLP
Telephone: (262) 656-5200	**Officers:** Dale F. Elliot - Chmn., Pres., C.E.O. Martin M. Ellen - Sr. V.P., Fin., C.F.O.	**Investor Contact:** 262-656-6488
Fax: (262) 656-5577		

SOLECTRON CORP.

Exchange	Symbol	Price	52Wk Range	Yield	P/E
NYS	SLR	$3.47 (3/31/2005)	6.56-3.39	N/A	347.00

*7 Year Price Score 26.68   *NYSE Composite Index=100   *12 Month Price Score 80.17

TRADING VOLUME (thousand shares)

Interim Earnings (Per Share)

Qtr.	Nov	Feb	May	Aug
2001-02	(0.08)	(0.15)	(0.35)	(3.38)
2002-03	(0.09)	(0.13)	(3.74)	(0.21)
2003-04	(0.14)	(0.08)	0.02	0.01
2004-05	0.06	...	...	...

Interim Dividends (Per Share)

Amt	Decl	Ex	Rec	Pay
2-for-1	1/13/1999	2/25/1999	2/10/1999	2/24/1999
100%	1/13/2000	3/9/2000	2/23/2000	3/8/2000

Valuation Analysis

Forecast P/E	19.56	No of Institutions
	(4/7/2005)	290
Market Cap	$3.4 Billion	Shares
Book Value	2.5 Billion	837,915,712
Price/Book	1.34	% Held
Price/Sales	0.29	86.29

Business Summary: Electrical (MIC: 11.14 SIC: 672 NAIC: 34412)

Solectron provides electronics supply chain services to original equipment manufacturers worldwide. Co. provides services to clients related to product development, manufacturing and post-production requirements. Co.'s services include: collaborative design support and design for manufacturability; new product introduction engineering services; supply chain design and sourcing; prototyping; product testing; product manufacturing; materials purchasing and supply base management; product fulfillment services, including packaging, distribution and installation; product repair and warranty service; and end-consumer technical support and customer relationship management services.

Recent Developments: For the quarter ended Nov 30 2004, income$46,900 thousand versus loss of $52,200 thousand in the year-earlier quarter. Net income was $55,900 thousand from net loss of $119,800 thousand in the year-earlier quarter. Revenues were $2,690,600 thousand, down 0.2% from $2,696,800 thousand the year before. Operating income was $59,100 thousand versus of $14,200 thousand in the prior-year quarter, an increase of 516.2%. Total direct expense was $2,534,400 thousand versus $2,569,300 thousand in the prior-year quarter, a decrease of 1.4%. Total indirect expense was $97,100 thousand versus $141,700 thousand in the prior-year quarter, a decrease of 31.5%.

Prospects: On Feb 17 2005, Co. announced that it had expanded its enclosures and sheet metal facility in Milpitas, CA. The expansion is a part of Co.'s strategy to offer systems-integration applications and showcase its commitment to interact and collaborate with customers in the most critical development stages, improving their time-to-market capabilities. Co. believes this expansion will leverage new opportunities across all sites. Further, Co. stated that it is prepared for high growth in this area and is working closely with its local and global customers to ensure that anticipated demand is met.

Financial Data

(US$ in Thousands)	3 Mos	08/31/2004	08/31/2003	08/31/2002	08/31/2001	08/31/2000	08/31/1999	08/31/1998
Earnings Per Share	0.01	(0.19)	(4.18)	(3.98)	(0.19)	0.80	0.56	0.41
Cash Flow Per Share	0.31	(0.01)	0.37	2.73	0.98	(0.57)	0.08	0.32
Tang Book Value Per Share	2.45	2.33	1.48	3.16	4.81	6.28	5.15	2.51
Income Statement								
Total Revenue	2,690,600	11,638,300	11,014,000	12,276,200	18,692,300	14,137,500	8,391,400	5,288,294
EBITDA	112,100	153,600	(1,996,300)	(2,889,200)	584,000	1,008,100	640,000	423,189
Depn & Amortn	50,000	276,300	348,500	514,300	682,600	303,900	201,100	124,200
Income Before Taxes	51,600	(252,100)	(2,523,900)	(3,577,500)	(157,700)	739,500	432,300	298,983
Income Taxes	4,700	(300)	581,000	(467,300)	(34,200)	238,800	138,400	100,159
Net Income	55,900	(168,900)	(3,462,000)	(3,110,200)	(123,500)	497,200	293,900	198,824
Average Shares	967,400	873,900	827,700	780,900	641,800	623,500	527,000	506,268
Balance Sheet								
Current Assets	4,699,900	4,666,400	4,953,800	6,660,000	8,704,100	8,628,200	3,994,100	1,887,558
Total Assets	5,805,300	5,817,000	6,529,500	11,014,000	12,930,400	10,375,600	4,834,700	2,410,568
Current Liabilities	2,003,500	2,159,100	3,234,900	3,005,200	2,689,300	3,216,800	1,113,200	840,834
Long-Term Obligations	1,215,400	1,221,400	1,817,600	3,183,900	5,027,500	3,319,500	922,600	385,519
Total Liabilities	3,295,900	3,438,200	5,107,500	6,241,300	7,779,700	6,573,500	2,041,600	1,229,242
Stockholders' Equity	2,509,400	2,378,800	1,422,000	4,772,700	5,150,700	3,802,100	2,793,100	1,181,326
Shares Outstanding	971,062	963,600	832,600	824,800	658,200	605,000	542,800	470,668
Statistical Record								
Return on Assets %	0.12	N.M.	N.M.	N.M.	N.M.	6.52	8.11	9.33
Return on Equity %	0.39	N.M.	N.M.	N.M.	N.M.	15.04	14.79	18.93
EBITDA Margin %	4.17	1.32	N.M.	N.M.	3.12	7.13	7.63	8.00
Net Margin %	2.08	N.M.	N.M.	N.M.	N.M.	3.52	3.50	3.76
Asset Turnover	1.86	1.88	1.26	1.03	1.60	1.85	2.32	2.48
Current Ratio	2.35	2.16	1.53	2.22	3.24	2.68	3.59	2.24
Debt to Equity	0.48	0.51	1.28	0.67	0.98	0.87	0.33	0.33
Price Range	7.92-4.50	7.92-4.50	5.93-1.42	16.25-3.12	52.00-13.60	48.25-30.25	39.13-9.86	13.25-7.44
P/E Ratio	792.00-450.00	...	...	...	...	60.31-37.81	69.87-17.61	32.32-18.14

Address: 847 Gibraltar Drive, Milpitas, CA 95035	**Web Site:** www.solectron.com	**Auditors:** KPMG LLP
Telephone: (408) 957-8500	**Officers:** Michael R. Cannon - Pres., C.E.O. Craig London - Exec. V.P., Strategy, Marketing, Services	**Investor Contact:** 408-956-6542
Fax: (408) 956-6077		

SONIC AUTOMOTIVE, INC.

Exchange	Symbol	Price	52Wk Range	Yield	P/E
NYS	SAH	$22.71 (3/31/2005)	26.10-18.40	2.11	10.51

*7 Year Price Score 114.33 *NYSE Composite Index=100 *12 Month Price Score 94.99

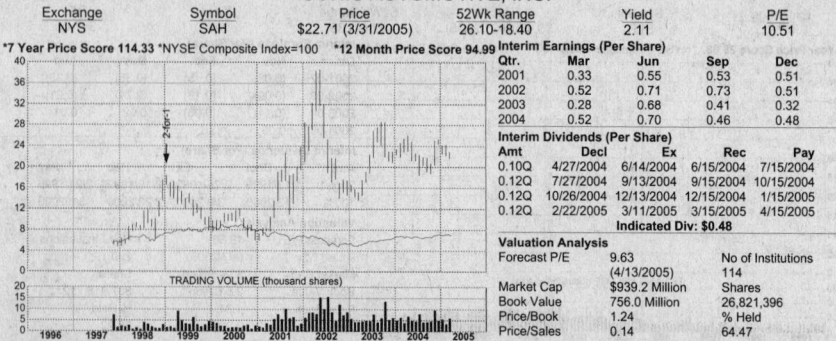

Interim Earnings (Per Share)

Qtr.	Mar	Jun	Sep	Dec
2001	0.33	0.55	0.53	0.51
2002	0.52	0.71	0.73	0.51
2003	0.28	0.68	0.41	0.32
2004	0.52	0.70	0.46	0.48

Interim Dividends (Per Share)

Amt	Decl	Ex	Rec	Pay
0.10Q	4/27/2004	6/14/2004	6/15/2004	7/15/2004
0.12Q	7/27/2004	9/13/2004	9/15/2004	10/15/2004
0.12Q	10/26/2004	12/13/2004	12/15/2004	1/15/2005
0.12Q	2/22/2005	3/11/2005	3/15/2005	4/15/2005

Indicated Div: $0.48

Valuation Analysis

Forecast P/E	9.63	No of Institutions	
	(4/13/2005)	114	
Market Cap	$939.2 Million	Shares	
Book Value	756.0 Million	26,821,396	
Price/Book	1.24	% Held	
Price/Sales	0.14	64.47	

Business Summary: Retail - Automotive (MIC: 5.7 SIC: 511 NAIC: 41110)

Sonic Automotive, an automotive retailer in the United States, operated 192 dealership franchises and 40 collision repair centers in 15 states as of Mar 1 2005. Co.'s franchises provide services including sales of both new and used cars and light trucks, replacement parts and vehicle maintenance, warranty, paint and repair services. Co. also offers extended warranty contracts, financing, insurance, vehicle protection products and other aftermarket products for its customers. Co.'s growth strategy is focused on metropolitan markets, predominantly in the Southeast, Southwest, Midwest and California. As of Mar 1 2005, Co. had a dealership portfolio of 38 American, European and Asian brands.

Recent Developments: For the year ended Dec 31 2004, income totaled $95.7 million, before a $9.4 million loss from discontinued operations, compared with income of $87.3 million, before a $10.1 million loss from discontinued operations and a $5.6 million accounting change charge, a year earlier. Total revenues grew 6.4% to $7.39 billion from $6.95 billion the year before. Gross profit was $1.14 billion, or 15.4% of total revenues, versus $1.06 billion, or 15.3% of total revenues, the previous year. Operating income rose 5.9% to $222.2 million from $209.8 million in the prior year.

Prospects: Earnings reflect a stronger than anticipated retail environment and improved operating efficiencies. Co. continues to focus on improving operating execution and performance. Consistent inventory management is reducing its new vehicle days supply. Co. is also seeing a reduction in its selling, general and administrative expense rate and is targeting a 100 basis point decline to 78.0% in 2005. Looking ahead to 2005, Co. estimates overall same-store sales growth in the 2.0% to 3.0% range. Co. plans on adding targeted acquisitions in the $400.0 million to $700.0 million range in annualized revenue. Co. expects earnings from continuing operations to range from $2.35 to $2.45 per share in 2005.

Financial Data

(US$ in Thousands)	9 Mos	6 Mos	3 Mos	12/31/2003	12/31/2002	12/31/2001	12/31/2000	12/31/1999
Earnings Per Share	2.00	1.95	1.92	1.69	2.47	1.91	1.69	1.27
Cash Flow Per Share	4.14	2.02	2.64	3.37	3.33	3.61	2.49	1.45
Dividends Per Share	0.420	0.400	0.300	0.200	...	...	...	...
Dividend Payout %	21.04	20.56	15.60	11.83	...	...	...	...
Income Statement								
Total Revenue	5,553,012	3,580,885	1,703,793	7,034,215	7,071,015	6,337,358	6,052,476	3,350,823
EBITDA	179,088	122,066	53,743	206,219	248,347	227,204	231,938	128,795
Depn & Amortn	12,772	8,321	3,902	13,341	9,759	25,790	22,714	11,699
Income Before Taxes	120,631	84,092	35,551	134,045	175,330	130,044	119,872	72,974
Income Taxes	44,513	30,795	13,171	46,210	66,821	50,715	45,700	28,325
Net Income	71,458	52,178	22,185	71,560	106,564	79,329	74,172	44,649
Average Shares	42,164	42,557	42,599	42,421	43,158	41,609	43,826	35,248
Balance Sheet								
Current Assets	1,449,008	1,646,227	1,566,528	1,554,197	1,301,627	956,296	1,037,403	835,567
Total Assets	2,784,443	2,881,775	2,740,646	2,686,229	2,375,308	1,805,926	1,789,248	1,501,102
Current Liabilities	1,179,302	1,312,540	1,230,151	1,196,929	1,038,384	737,253	818,321	657,910
Long-Term Obligations	747,808	721,737	698,656	694,898	637,545	511,877	485,212	417,283
Total Liabilities	2,028,410	2,137,008	2,025,714	1,987,896	1,738,130	1,288,665	1,338,326	1,098,529
Stockholders' Equity	756,033	744,767	714,932	698,333	637,178	517,261	450,922	402,573
Shares Outstanding	41,355	41,504	41,221	41,221	41,140	40,549	41,965	40,601
Statistical Record								
Return on Assets %	3.27	3.12	3.19	2.83	5.10	4.41	4.50	4.30
Return on Equity %	11.82	11.79	12.05	10.72	18.46	16.39	17.33	16.38
EBITDA Margin %	3.23	3.41	3.15	2.93	3.51	3.59	3.83	3.84
Net Margin %	1.29	1.46	1.30	1.02	1.51	1.25	1.23	1.33
Asset Turnover	2.66	2.61	2.74	2.78	3.38	3.53	3.67	3.23
Current Ratio	1.23	1.25	1.27	1.30	1.25	1.30	1.27	1.27
Debt to Equity	0.99	0.97	0.98	1.00	1.00	0.99	1.08	1.04
Price Range	28.64-18.40	28.65-20.80	28.65-14.59	28.65-13.65	38.60-14.05	23.86-6.00	12.13-6.00	18.44-7.88
P/E Ratio	14.32-9.20	14.69-10.67	14.92-7.60	16.95-8.08	15.63-5.69	12.49-3.14	7.17-3.55	14.52-6.20
Average Yield %	1.86	1.67	1.32	0.97	...	...	...	...

Address: 5401 East Independence Boulevard, P.O. Box 18747, Charlotte, NC 28212	Web Site: www.sonicautomotive.com	Auditors: Deloitte & Touche LLP
Telephone: (704) 566-2400	**Officers:** O. Bruton Smith - Chmn., C.E.O. B. Scott Smith - Vice-Chmn., Chief Strategic Officer	**Investor Contact:** 888-766-4218
Fax: (704) 536-5116		

SONOCO PRODUCTS CO.

Exchange	Symbol	Price	52Wk Range	Yield	P/E	Div Acheiver
NYS	SON	$28.85 (3/31/2005)	30.07-23.93	3.05	18.86	21 Years

*7 Year Price Score 92.52   ***NYSE Composite Index=100**   ***12 Month Price Score 99.92**

Interim Earnings (Per Share)

Qtr.	Mar	Jun	Sep	Dec
2001	0.05	0.18	0.45	0.29
2002	0.35	0.39	0.30	0.36
2003	0.30	0.24	0.14	0.75
2004	0.38	0.35	0.42	0.35

Interim Dividends (Per Share)

Amt	Decl	Ex	Rec	Pay
0.22Q	4/21/2004	5/19/2004	5/21/2004	6/10/2004
0.22Q	7/21/2004	8/18/2004	8/20/2004	9/10/2004
0.22Q	10/18/2004	11/17/2004	11/19/2004	12/10/2004
0.22Q	2/2/2005	2/16/2005	2/18/2005	3/10/2005
	Indicated Div: $0.88 (Div. Reinv. Plan)			

Valuation Analysis

Forecast P/E	15.46	No of Institutions
	(4/7/2005)	213
Market Cap	$2.9 Billion	Shares
Book Value	1.2 Billion	53,462,472
Price/Book	2.47	% Held
Price/Sales	0.90	54.01

Business Summary: Paper Products (MIC: 11.11 SIC: 631 NAIC: 22130)

Sonoco Products is a manufacturer of industrial and consumer packaging products and provider of packaging services, with 295 locations in 32 countries as of Dec 31 2003. Each of Co.'s operating units has its own sales staff and maintains direct sales relationships with its customers. The industrial packaging segment includes engineered carriers, paper, molded & extruded plastics, wire & cable reels, and protective packaging. The consumer packaging segment includes rigid packaging, closures, printed flexible packaging, packaging services & folding cartons, glass covers & coasters, and artwork management.

Recent Developments: For the year ended Dec 31 2004, net income increased 8.8% to $151,229 thousand from net income of $138,949 thousand a year earlier. Revenues were $3,155,433 thousand, up 14.4% from $2,758,326 thousand the year before. Operating income was $239,405 thousand versus an income of $158,544 thousand in the prior year, an increase of 51.0%. Total direct expense was $2,580,643 thousand versus $2,259,887 thousand in the prior year, an increase of 14.2%. Total indirect expense was $335,385 thousand versus $339,895 thousand in the prior year, a decrease of 1.3%.

Prospects: Earnings are being positively affected by higher volumes, including the effect of acquisitions, and productivity leading to improved margins. Also, Co. is benefiting from cost reduction initiatives, and a reduced debt to capital ratio. In fiscal 2005, Co. will remain focused on paying down debt and maintaining its credit rating. Co. expects cash flow from operations to average approximately $300.0 million annually over the next several years. Additionally, Co. is targeting first quarter fiscal 2005 earnings of $0.36 to $0.39 per share and full-year 2005 earnings per diluted share of $1.75 to $1.79.

Financial Data

(US$ in Thousands)	12/31/2004	12/31/2003	12/31/2002	12/31/2001	12/31/2000	12/31/1999	12/31/1998	12/31/1997
Earnings Per Share	1.53	1.43	1.39	0.96	1.66	1.83	1.73	...
Cash Flow Per Share	2.57	3.43	2.82	3.82	3.62	2.36	2.22	3.27
Tang Book Value Per Share	5.00	6.48	5.26	4.64	5.94	6.37	6.40	7.35
Dividends Per Share	0.870	0.840	0.830	0.800	0.790	0.750	0.704	0.641
Dividend Payout %	56.86	58.74	59.71	83.33	47.59	40.98	40.67	...
Income Statement								
Total Revenue	3,155,433	2,758,326	2,812,150	2,606,276	2,711,493	2,546,734	2,557,917	2,847,831
EBITDA	403,333	312,082	410,296	382,772	477,221	482,558	534,130	269,466
Depn & Amortn	163,928	153,538	159,256	158,574	150,816	145,846	145,669	153,524
Income Before Taxes	197,342	108,333	198,493	175,781	270,595	289,560	339,598	63,719
Income Taxes	58,858	37,698	70,614	82,958	111,999	108,585	153,989	60,111
Net Income	151,229	138,949	135,316	91,609	166,298	187,805	180,243	2,617
Average Shares	98,947	97,129	97,178	95,807	99,900	102,780	104,275	97,591
Balance Sheet								
Current Assets	922,112	755,265	663,267	665,169	695,793	723,081	661,416	873,040
Total Assets	3,041,319	2,520,633	2,390,094	2,352,197	2,212,611	2,297,020	2,082,983	2,176,865
Current Liabilities	639,886	679,594	600,027	460,270	437,080	416,631	436,069	434,144
Long-Term Obligations	813,207	473,220	699,346	885,961	812,085	819,540	686,826	696,669
Total Liabilities	1,888,440	1,506,473	1,522,669	1,548,075	1,411,140	1,395,800	1,261,391	1,328,046
Stockholders' Equity	1,152,879	1,014,160	867,425	804,122	801,471	901,220	821,592	848,819
Shares Outstanding	98,793	97,217	96,640	95,713	95,006	101,448	101,683	95,834
Statistical Record								
Return on Assets %	5.42	5.66	5.71	4.01	7.36	8.58	8.46	0.11
Return on Equity %	13.92	14.77	16.19	11.41	19.48	21.80	21.58	0.30
EBITDA Margin %	12.78	11.31	14.59	14.69	17.60	18.95	20.88	9.46
Net Margin %	4.79	5.04	4.81	3.51	6.13	7.37	7.05	0.09
Asset Turnover	1.13	1.12	1.19	1.14	1.20	1.16	1.20	1.25
Current Ratio	1.44	1.11	1.11	1.45	1.59	1.74	1.52	2.01
Debt to Equity	0.71	0.47	0.81	1.10	1.01	0.91	0.84	0.82
Price Range	29.70-22.86	24.73-19.47	29.70-19.81	26.58-19.69	23.00-16.88	29.94-21.06	38.92-22.44	32.16-22.61
P/E Ratio	19.41-14.94	17.29-13.62	21.37-14.25	27.69-20.51	13.86-10.17	16.36-11.51	22.50-12.97	N.M.
Average Yield %	3.39	3.78	3.25	3.36	3.97	2.95	2.25	2.31

Address: One North Second Street, Hartsville, SC 29550-3305 Telephone: (843) 383-7000 Fax: (843) 383-7008	Web Site: www.sonoco.com Officers: Charles W. Coker - Chmn. Harris E. DeLoach Jr. - Pres., C.E.O.	Auditors: PricewaterhouseCoopers LLP Investor Contact: 843-383-7524 Transfer Agents: EquiServe Trust Company, NA Providence, RI

SOTHEBY'S HOLDINGS, INC.

Exchange	Symbol	Price	52Wk Range	Yield	P/E
NYS	BID	$16.96 (3/31/2005)	18.90-12.84	N/A	12.29

*7 Year Price Score 74.42   *NYSE Composite Index=100   *12 Month Price Score 99.27

Interim Earnings (Per Share)

Qtr.	Mar	Jun	Sep	Dec
2001	(0.38)	0.23	(0.54)	(0.01)
2002	(0.38)	0.29	(0.70)	(0.11)
2003	(0.45)	0.23	(0.45)	0.32
2004	0.59	0.68	(0.46)	0.57

Interim Dividends (Per Share)

Dividend Payment Suspended

Valuation Analysis

Forecast P/E	25.16	No of Institutions
	(4/7/2005)	143
Market Cap	$1.1 Billion	Shares
Book Value	235.9 Million	45,581,044
Price/Book	4.58	% Held
Price/Sales	2.18	98.84

Business Summary: Miscellaneous Business Services (MIC: 12.8 SIC: 389 NAIC: 53920)

Sotheby's Holdings is an auctioneer of fine arts, antiques and collectibles. Co. operates in 34 countries, with principal salesrooms in New York and London. Co. offers property through its worldwide Auction segment in approximately 70 collecting categories, including, fine art, antiques and decorative art, jewelry and collectibles. This segment also is engaged in related activities including purchase and resale of art and collectibles, the brokering of item purchases and sales through private treaty. In addition, Co. conducts art-related financing activities through its Finance segment and, to a lesser extent, is engaged in real estate brokerage activities outside the U.S.

Recent Developments: For the year ended Dec 31 2004, net income was $86,679 thousand versus net loss of $20,656 thousand a year earlier. Revenues were $496,720 thousand, up 56.5% from $317,344 thousand the year before. Operating income was $126,662 thousand versus a loss of $7,426 thousand in the prior year. Total direct expense was $55,526 thousand versus $45,631 thousand in the prior year, an increase of 21.7%. Total indirect expense was $314,532 thousand versus $279,139 thousand in the prior year, an increase of 12.7%.

Prospects: Co.'s earnings are benefiting from a significant increase in auction sales. This increase has been partially offset by lower auction commission margins as a sizeable portion of the increase in auction sales is coming from high-end works of art for which commission margins are traditionally lower due to the competition for such objects. Co.'s ability to attract extraordinary paintings and objects for sale, coupled with a strong art market is resulting in broad-based strength across a number of categories and geographic locations. Co. is encouraged by this strength going into 2005 as well as by the level of consignments for the 2005 spring season.

Financial Data

(US$ in Thousands)	12/31/2004	12/31/2003	12/31/2002	12/31/2001	12/31/2000	12/31/1999	12/31/1998	12/31/1997
Earnings Per Share	1.38	(0.34)	(0.89)	(0.69)	(3.22)	0.56	0.79	0.72
Cash Flow Per Share	2.35	(0.74)	(0.28)	(0.34)	(0.73)	(0.05)	1.63	0.47
Tang Book Value Per Share	3.48	1.85	2.02	2.75	2.81	6.00	4.92	4.05
Dividends Per Share	...	...	...	...	...	0.400	0.400	0.400
Dividend Payout %	...	...	...	...	...	71.43	50.63	55.56
Income Statement								
Total Revenue	496,720	319,599	345,095	336,163	397,788	442,585	447,052	381,792
EBITDA	150,753	18,102	(27,009)	(24,415)	(213,901)	70,818	93,450	78,485
Depn & Amortn	23,830	25,344	24,278	25,456	23,891	17,452	12,652	11,057
Income Before Taxes	96,653	(37,576)	(71,461)	(71,546)	(250,127)	52,150	73,813	64,457
Income Taxes	35,000	(11,093)	(16,706)	(29,850)	(60,433)	19,296	28,788	23,849
Net Income	86,679	(20,656)	(54,755)	(41,696)	(189,694)	32,854	45,025	40,608
Average Shares	61,900	61,600	61,500	60,700	58,900	59,100	57,300	56,300
Balance Sheet								
Current Assets	832,297	480,011	457,868	511,324	726,568	736,247	569,042	593,657
Total Assets	1,225,346	901,470	875,705	864,111	1,074,158	1,073,512	770,010	860,241
Current Liabilities	619,937	387,888	447,929	475,202	687,053	576,787	442,201	471,935
Long-Term Obligations	99,617	271,708	199,466	99,398	99,334	100,000	...	117,000
Total Liabilities	989,427	774,062	735,337	678,241	886,104	696,468	455,923	601,973
Stockholders' Equity	235,919	127,408	140,368	185,870	188,054	377,044	314,087	258,268
Shares Outstanding	63,774	61,573	61,305	61,305	58,842	58,844	57,160	55,728
Statistical Record								
Return on Assets %	8.13	N.M.	N.M.	N.M.	N.M.	3.56	5.52	5.36
Return on Equity %	47.58	N.M.	N.M.	N.M.	N.M.	9.51	15.73	15.87
EBITDA Margin %	30.35	5.66	N.M.	N.M.	N.M.	16.00	20.90	20.56
Net Margin %	17.45	N.M.	N.M.	N.M.	N.M.	7.42	10.07	10.64
Asset Turnover	0.47	0.36	0.40	0.35	0.37	0.48	0.55	0.50
Current Ratio	1.34	1.24	1.02	1.08	1.06	1.28	1.29	1.26
Debt to Equity	0.42	2.13	1.42	0.53	0.53	0.27	...	0.45
Price Range	18.90-12.21	14.10-6.49	17.00-6.57	27.31-10.76	30.00-14.75	46.75-25.06	38.00-15.50	21.00-14.88
P/E Ratio	13.70-8.85	...	...	...	...	83.48-44.75	48.10-19.62	29.17-20.66
Average Yield %	...	...	...	...	...	1.22	1.84	2.29

Address: 38500 Woodward Avenue, Suite 100, Bloomfield Hills, MI 48304	Web Site: www.sothebys.com	Auditors: Deloitte & Touche LLP
Telephone: (248) 646-2400	Officers: Michael I. Sovern - Chmn. Max M. Fisher - Vice-Chmn.	Investor Contact: 800-700-6321

SOUTHERN COMPANY (THE)

Exchange	Symbol	Price	52Wk Range	Yield	P/E
NYS	SO	$31.83 (3/31/2005)	34.08-27.86	4.49	15.45

*7 Year Price Score 114.58 ***NYSE Composite Index=100** ***12 Month Price Score 97.48**

Interim Earnings (Per Share)

Qtr.	Mar	Jun	Sep	Dec
2001	0.47	0.39	0.79	0.16
2002	0.32	0.46	0.83	0.23
2003	0.41	0.59	0.84	0.17
2004	0.45	0.47	0.87	0.27

Interim Dividends (Per Share)

Amt	Decl	Ex	Rec	Pay
0.35Q	4/19/2004	4/29/2004	5/3/2004	6/5/2004
0.357Q	7/19/2004	7/29/2004	8/2/2004	9/4/2004
0.357Q	10/18/2004	10/28/2004	11/1/2004	12/6/2004
0.357Q	1/13/2005	2/3/2005	2/7/2005	3/5/2005

Indicated Div: $1.43

Valuation Analysis

Forecast P/E	N/A	No of Institutions
Market Cap	$23.6 Billion	Shares
Book Value	10.8 Billion	289,910,816
Price/Book	2.18	% Held
Price/Sales	1.98	39.19

TRADING VOLUME (thousand shares)

Business Summary: Electricity (MIC: 7.1 SIC: 911 NAIC: 21119)

The Southern Company is an energy company with more than 4.0 million customers and nearly 39,000 megawatts of electric generating capacity in the Southeast as of Dec 31 2003. Co. is one of the largest producers of electricity in the U.S. Co.'s electric segment consists of the following electric utilities in the Southeast: Alabama Power, Georgia Power, Gulf Power, Mississippi Power and Savannah Electric, as well as Southern Power, a wholesale generator of electricity. Co.'s other segment includes the operations of Southern LINC, Southern Company Gas LLC, Southern Nuclear, Southern Company Services, Southern Management Development, Southern Telecom and Southern Company Holdings.

Recent Developments: For the year ended Dec 31 2004, net income increased 3.9% to $1,532,000 thousand from net income of $1,474,000 thousand a year earlier. Revenues were $11,902,000 thousand, up 6.4% from $11,186,000 thousand the year before, Operating income was $2,827,000 thousand versus an income of $2,805,000 thousand in the prior year, an increase of 0.8%. Total direct expense was $7,493,000 thousand versus $6,768,000 thousand in the prior year, an increase of 10.7%. Total indirect expense was $1,582,000 thousand versus $1,613,000 thousand in the prior year, a decrease of 1.9%.

Prospects: For full-year 2005, Co. is forecasting earnings to range from $2.04 to $2.09 per share, consistent with its goal of achieving 5.0% growth in profit. Longer-term, Co. expects funds from operations from 2005 to 2007 to be $9.40 billion and capital expenditures to be $7.90 billion. Additionally, Co. anticipates earnings from its wholesale generation business of at least $300.0 million by 2007. Also, Co. projects average long-term demand growth in its service territory to be 2.0% and average long-term customer growth is projected to be 1.5% per year for its regulated retail business.

Financial Data

(US$ in Thousands)	12/31/2004	12/31/2003	12/31/2002	12/31/2001	12/31/2000	12/31/1999	12/31/1998	12/31/1997
Earnings Per Share	2.06	2.02	1.85	1.82	2.01	1.86	1.40	1.42
Cash Flow Per Share	3.63	4.22	4.00	3.46	4.30	3.98	3.94	3.83
Tang Book Value Per Share	13.86	13.13	12.15	11.42	15.67	6.68	9.44	9.19
Dividends Per Share	1.415	1.385	1.355	1.340	1.340	1.340	1.340	1.300
Dividend Payout %	68.69	68.56	73.24	73.63	66.67	72.04	95.71	91.55
Income Statement								
Total Revenue	11,902,000	11,251,000	10,549,000	10,155,000	10,066,000	11,585,000	11,403,000	12,611,000
EBITDA	3,910,000	3,740,000	3,474,000	3,565,000	3,527,000	4,419,000	...	...
Depn & Amortn	1,178,000	1,163,000	1,158,000	1,358,000	1,337,000	1,522,000	1,773,000	1,592,000
Income Before Taxes	2,119,000	2,086,000	1,846,000	1,677,000	1,582,000	2,002,000	...	...
Income Taxes	587,000	612,000	528,000	558,000	588,000	726,000	(8,000)	114,000
Net Income	1,532,000	1,474,000	1,318,000	1,262,000	1,313,000	1,276,000	977,000	972,000
Average Shares	743,000	732,000	714,000	694,000	654,194	685,000	697,000	685,000
Balance Sheet								
Net PPE	28,361,000	27,534,000	24,642,000	23,084,000	21,622,000	24,544,000	24,124,000	23,652,000
Total Assets	36,962,000	35,045,000	31,799,000	29,824,000	31,362,000	38,396,000	36,192,000	35,271,000
Long-Term Obligations	12,449,000	10,164,000	8,658,000	8,297,000	7,843,000	11,747,000	10,472,000	10,274,000
Total Liabilities	26,123,000	24,974,000	22,791,000	21,472,000	20,304,000	28,823,000	26,026,000	25,131,000
Stockholders' Equity	10,839,000	10,071,000	9,008,000	8,352,000	11,058,000	9,573,000	10,166,000	10,140,000
Shares Outstanding	741,800	734,800	716,900	699,000	682,000	666,000	693,000	693,000
Statistical Record								
Return on Assets %	4.24	4.41	4.28	4.13	3.75	3.42	2.73	2.97
Return on Equity %	14.61	15.45	15.18	13.00	12.69	12.93	9.62	9.56
EBITDA Margin %	32.85	33.24	32.93	35.11	35.04	38.14	...	...
Net Margin %	12.87	13.10	12.49	12.43	13.04	11.01	8.57	7.71
PPE Turnover	0.42	0.43	0.44	0.45	0.43	0.48	0.48	0.54
Asset Turnover	0.33	0.34	0.34	0.33	0.29	0.31	0.32	0.38
Debt to Equity	1.15	1.01	0.96	0.99	0.71	1.23	1.03	1.01
Price Range	33.92-27.86	31.81-27.71	30.85-23.89	25.87-16.63	20.75-12.52	17.85-13.44	19.11-14.65	15.83-12.18
P/E Ratio	16.47-13.52	15.75-13.72	16.68-12.91	14.21-9.14	10.32-6.23	9.60-7.22	13.65-10.47	11.15-8.58
Average Yield %	4.68	4.74	5.01	6.03	8.29	8.41	8.09	9.64

Address: 270 Peachtree St., N.W., Atlanta, GA 30303
Telephone: (404) 506 5000
Fax: (404) 506 0455

Web Site: www.southerncompany.com
Officers: H. Allen Franklin - Chmn., C.E.O. David M. Ratcliffe - Pres.

Auditors: Deloitte & Touche LLP
Investor Contact: 404-506-5195

SOUTHERN PERU COPPER CORP.

Exchange	Symbol	Price	52Wk Range	Yield	P/E
NYS	PCU	$55.46 (3/31/2005)	64.20-26.53	6.08	7.43

*7 Year Price Score 191.28 *NYSE Composite Index=100 *12 Month Price Score 120.16

Interim Earnings (Per Share)

Qtr.	Mar	Jun	Sep	Dec
2001	0.20	0.10	0.14	0.15
2002	0.08	0.34	0.18	0.19
2003	0.23	0.27	0.45	0.54
2004	1.09	1.51	1.65	3.21

Interim Dividends (Per Share)

Amt	Decl	Ex	Rec	Pay
0.27Q	2/3/2004	2/19/2004	2/23/2004	3/9/2004
0.542Q	4/29/2004	5/17/2004	5/19/2004	6/4/2004
0.755Q	7/23/2004	8/11/2004	8/13/2004	9/1/2004
0.825Q	10/22/2004	11/8/2004	11/10/2004	11/22/2004
		Indicated Div: $3.37		

Valuation Analysis

Forecast P/E	8.83	No of Institutions	
	(4/7/2005)	122	
Market Cap	$4.4 Billion	Shares	12,654,662
Book Value	1.7 Billion	% Held	
Price/Book	2.58		89.64
Price/Sales	2.59		

Business Summary: Non-Precious Metals (MIC: 14.3 SIC: 021 NAIC: 12234)

Southern Peru Copper is an integrated producer of copper, operating mining, smelting and refining facilities in the southern part of Peru. The copper operations of Co. involve mining, milling and flotation of copper ore to produce copper concentrates, the smelting of copper concentrates to produce blister copper and the refining of blister copper to produce copper cathodes. Co. also produces refined copper using the solvent extraction/electrowinning technology ("SX/EW"). Silver, molybdenum and small amounts of other metals are contained in copper ore as by-products.

Recent Developments: For the year ended Dec 31 2004, net income increased 400.5% to $596,773 thousand from net income of $119,231 thousand a year earlier. Revenues were $3,431,838 thousand, up 114.9% from $1,596,812 thousand the year before. Operating income was $927,099 thousand versus an income of $216,834 thousand in the prior year, an increase of 327.6%. Total direct expense was $672,171 thousand versus $468,453 thousand in the prior year, an increase of 43.5%. Total indirect expense was $116,649 thousand versus $113,119 thousand in the prior year, an increase of 3.1%.

Prospects: Co.'s outlook is encouraging. The Ilo smelter modernization project is moving ahead on schedule and Co. expects it to be completed by the end of 2006. Additionally, Co.'s leaching dump, crushing and conveying project at the Toquepala mine is also progressing on schedule. Co. expects this project to be completed in mid-2005 with projected annual operating cost saving of $25.0 million. Meanwhile, the acquisition of the mining assets of Grupo Mexico is moving forward, with an expected completion date in the first quarter. Looking ahead, Co. anticipates a reduction in the volume of copper produced of about 8.0% for 2005, reflecting a decline in ore grade at its Cuajone Mine.

Financial Data

(US$ in Thousands)	12/31/2004	12/31/2003	12/31/2002	12/31/2001	12/31/2000	12/31/1999	12/31/1998	12/31/1997
Earnings Per Share	7.46	1.49	0.76	0.58	1.16	0.37	0.68	2.32
Cash Flow Per Share	8.94	2.39	1.77	2.48	2.29	1.13	2.27	3.46
Tang Book Value Per Share	20.18	15.08	15.52	15.12	14.90	14.07	79.47	13.71
Dividends Per Share	2.392	0.567	0.359	0.360	0.340	0.152	0.510	1.260
Dividend Payout %	32.06	38.04	47.21	62.05	29.31	41.08	75.00	54.31
Income Statement								
Total Revenue	1,715,919	798,406	664,650	657,521	711,057	584,546	627,916	814,156
EBITDA	998,944	290,280	188,397	170,281	229,334	123,413	140,676	291,080
Depn & Amortn	77,753	73,579	67,840	76,285	77,447	74,237	60,859	46,736
Income Before Taxes	916,737	206,899	109,947	71,548	139,534	39,135	80,592	245,705
Income Taxes	315,237	84,969	39,999	22,142	44,648	9,740	25,567	55,610
Net Income	596,773	119,231	60,555	46,551	92,917	29,405	54,564	185,658
Average Shares	80,016	80,017	80,009	80,004	80,003	79,892	79,893	80,197
Balance Sheet								
Current Assets	1,013,553	475,951	310,872	426,645	441,847	269,141	410,062	561,590
Total Assets	2,597,130	1,930,752	1,752,246	1,821,417	1,770,558	1,545,453	1,525,837	1,543,325
Current Liabilities	461,447	187,197	100,794	220,953	132,380	111,157	97,016	85,114
Long-Term Obligations	256,700	289,000	299,000	273,100	322,900	199,200	220,500	234,200
Total Liabilities	864,947	607,436	503,195	597,941	564,438	405,540	400,914	426,302
Stockholders' Equity	1,720,899	1,315,403	1,241,375	1,209,455	1,191,655	1,125,938	1,108,592	1,097,638
Shares Outstanding	80,017	80,013	80,008	80,003	80,000	80,019	13,950	80,058
Statistical Record								
Return on Assets %	26.29	6.47	3.39	2.59	5.59	1.91	3.56	13.15
Return on Equity %	39.20	9.33	4.94	3.88	8.00	2.63	4.95	17.58
EBITDA Margin %	58.22	36.36	28.35	25.90	32.25	21.11	22.40	35.75
Net Margin %	34.78	14.93	9.11	7.08	13.07	5.03	8.69	22.80
Asset Turnover	0.76	0.43	0.37	0.37	0.43	0.38	0.41	0.58
Current Ratio	2.20	2.54	3.08	1.93	3.34	2.42	4.23	6.60
Debt to Equity	0.15	0.22	0.24	0.23	0.27	0.18	0.20	0.21
Price Range	54.10-26.53	48.85-14.40	15.54-10.82	15.10-8.80	16.44-11.00	18.06-8.44	16.69-8.75	21.13-12.75
P/E Ratio	7.25-3.56	32.79-9.66	20.45-14.24	26.03-15.17	14.17-9.48	48.82-22.80	24.54-12.87	9.11-5.50
Average Yield %	5.83	2.69	2.64	2.90	2.55	1.14	4.04	7.25

Address: 2575 East Camelback Rd., Phoenix, AZ 85016	Web Site: www.southerperu.com	Auditors: PricewaterhouseCoopers LLP
Telephone: (602) 977-6595	**Officers:** German Larrea Mota-Velasco - Chmn. Oscar Gonzalez Rocha - Pres., C.E.O.	**Investor Contact:** 800-223-2064 **Transfer Agents:** The Bank of New York, New York, NY

SOUTHWEST AIRLINES CO

Exchange	Symbol	Price	52Wk Range	Yield	P/E
NYS	LUV	$14.24 (3/31/2005)	17.00-13.31	0.13	37.47

*7 Year Price Score 86.67   *NYSE Composite Index=100   *12 Month Price Score 89.42

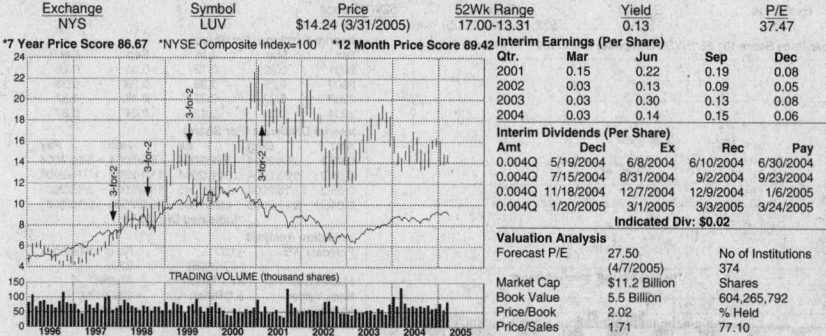

Interim Earnings (Per Share)

Qtr.	Mar	Jun	Sep	Dec
2001	0.15	0.22	0.19	0.08
2002	0.03	0.13	0.09	0.05
2003	0.03	0.30	0.13	0.08
2004	0.03	0.14	0.15	0.06

Interim Dividends (Per Share)

Amt	Decl	Ex	Rec	Pay
0.004Q	5/19/2004	6/8/2004	6/10/2004	6/30/2004
0.004Q	7/15/2004	8/31/2004	9/2/2004	9/23/2004
0.004Q	11/18/2004	12/7/2004	12/9/2004	1/6/2005
0.004Q	1/20/2005	3/1/2005	3/3/2005	3/24/2005

Indicated Div: $0.02

Valuation Analysis

Forecast P/E	27.50	No of Institutions
	(4/7/2005)	374
Market Cap	$11.2 Billion	Shares
Book Value	5.5 Billion	604,265,792
Price/Book	2.02	% Held
Price/Sales	1.71	77.10

Business Summary: Aviation (MIC: 1.1 SIC: 512 NAIC: 81111)

Southwest Airlines is a domestic airline that provides point-to-point, low-fare service. Co. engages in short-haul, medium and long-haul routes; including transcontinental service. At Dec 31 2004, Co. operated 417 Boeing 737 aircrafts and provides service to 60 airports in 59 cities in 31 states throughout the United States.

Recent Developments: For the year ended Dec 31 2004, net income decreased 29.2% to $313,000 thousand from net income of $442,000 thousand a year earlier. Revenues were $6,530,000 thousand, up 10.0% from $5,937,000 thousand the year before. Operating income was $554,000 thousand versus an income of $483,000 thousand in the prior year, an increase of 14.7%. Total direct expense was $2,045,000 thousand versus $1,815,000 thousand in the prior year, an increase of 12.7%. Total indirect expense was $3,931,000 thousand versus $3,639,000 thousand in the prior year, an increase of 8.0%.

Prospects: The airline industry revenue environment continues to be a challenge due to the glut of airline seats, which has placed pressures on both capacity and pricing. Accordingly, Co.expects revenue challenges experienced in 2004 to continue into the coming year. However, Co.'s first-quarter 2005 results should benefit from the timing of the Easter holiday. Meanwhile, Co. continues to be well positioned for growth and currently plan to add 29 net aircraft in 2005. During the fourth quarter of 2004, Co. exercised three Boeing 737-700 options for 2006 delivery, bringing its 2006 firm orders and options to 26 and 8, respectively.

Financial Data
(US$ in Thousands)

	12/31/2004	12/31/2003	12/31/2002	12/31/2001	12/31/2000	12/31/1999	12/31/1998	12/31/1997
Earnings Per Share	0.38	0.54	0.30	0.63	0.76	0.59	0.55	0.41
Cash Flow Per Share	1.47	1.71	0.67	1.95	1.73	1.33	1.18	0.83
Tang Book Value Per Share	7.04	6.40	5.69	5.23	4.56	4.21	3.21	2.69
Dividends Per Share	0.018	0.018	0.018	0.018	0.015	0.014	0.013	0.010
Dividend Payout %	4.74	3.33	6.00	2.86	1.93	2.42	2.30	2.36
Income Statement								
Total Revenue	6,530,000	5,937,000	5,521,771	5,555,174	5,649,560	4,735,587	4,163,980	3,816,821
EBITDA	984,000	1,159,000	832,455	1,180,120	1,322,056	1,033,731	937,441	724,709
Depn & Amortn	467,000	417,000	387,434	345,772	302,426	262,437	232,724	200,694
Income Before Taxes	489,000	708,000	392,682	827,659	1,017,364	773,611	705,112	516,956
Income Taxes	176,000	266,000	151,713	316,512	392,140	299,233	271,681	199,184
Net Income	313,000	442,000	240,969	511,147	603,093	474,378	433,431	317,772
Average Shares	815,000	822,000	809,420	807,115	796,317	803,890	794,623	767,674
Balance Sheet								
Total Assets	11,337,000	9,878,000	8,953,750	8,997,141	6,669,572	5,652,113	4,715,996	4,246,160
Long-Term Obligations	1,700,000	1,332,000	1,552,781	1,327,158	760,992	871,717	623,309	628,106
Total Liabilities	5,813,000	4,826,000	4,532,133	4,983,088	3,218,252	2,816,325	2,318,078	2,237,142
Stockholders' Equity	5,524,000	5,052,000	4,421,617	4,014,053	3,451,320	2,835,788	2,397,918	2,009,018
Shares Outstanding	784,982	789,390	776,663	766,774	756,243	674,139	747,681	746,573
Statistical Record								
Return on Assets %	2.94	4.69	2.68	6.53	9.76	9.15	9.67	7.97
Return on Equity %	5.90	9.33	5.71	13.69	19.13	18.13	19.67	17.38
EBITDA Margin %	15.07	19.52	15.08	21.24	23.40	21.83	22.51	18.99
Net Margin %	4.79	7.44	4.36	9.20	10.68	10.02	10.41	8.33
Asset Turnover	0.61	0.63	0.62	0.71	0.91	0.91	0.93	0.96
Price Range	17.00-13.21	19.54-12.04	21.99-11.60	23.27-12.83	22.67-10.08	15.61-9.75	10.28-7.11	7.61-4.20
P/E Ratio	44.74-34.76	36.19-22.30	73.30-38.67	36.93-20.37	29.83-13.27	26.46-16.53	18.69-12.93	18.56-10.24
Average Yield %	0.12	0.11	0.11	0.10	0.10	0.11	0.14	0.18

Address: P.O. Box 36611, Dallas, TX 75235-1611
Telephone: (214) 792-4000
Fax: (214) 792-5015

Web Site: www.southwest.com
Officers: Herbert D. Kelleher - Chmn. Gary C. Kelly - Vice-Chmn., C.E.O.

Auditors: ERNST & YOUNG LLP
Transfer Agents: Continental Stock Transfer & Trust Co., New York, NY

SOVEREIGN BANCORP, INC.

Exchange	Symbol	Price	52Wk Range	Yield	P/E
NYS	SOV	$22.16 (3/31/2005)	23.73-19.51	0.72	16.29

*7 Year Price Score 131.66 ***NYSE Composite Index=100** ***12 Month Price Score 97.38**

Interim Earnings (Per Share)

Qtr.	Mar	Jun	Sep	Dec
2001	0.02	0.12	0.03	0.28
2002	0.25	0.33	0.33	0.33
2003	0.27	0.37	0.37	0.37
2004	0.33	0.42	0.24	0.37

Interim Dividends (Per Share)

Amt	Decl	Ex	Rec	Pay
0.03Q	6/24/2004	7/29/2004	8/2/2004	8/16/2004
0.03Q	9/23/2004	10/28/2004	11/1/2004	11/15/2004
0.03Q	12/16/2004	1/18/2005	1/20/2005	2/15/2005
0.04Q	3/17/2005	4/28/2005	5/2/2005	5/16/2005

Indicated Div: $0.16

Valuation Analysis

Forecast P/E	11.77	No of Institutions
	(4/7/2005)	373
Market Cap	$7.7 Billion	Shares
Book Value	5.0 Billion	232,914,016
Price/Book	1.55	% Held
Price/Sales	2.86	62.24

Business Summary: Other Depository Banking (MIC: 8.5 SIC: 035 NAIC: 22120)

Sovereign Bancorp, the parent company for Sovereign Bank, is a $43.51 billion financial institution with approximately 535 community banking offices, approximately 950 ATMs and about 8,300 team members in Pennsylvania, New Jersey, Connecticut, New Hampshire, New York, Rhode Island, Delaware and Massachusetts. Co.'s primary business consists of attracting deposits from its network of community banking offices, and originating small business and middle market commercial and loans, residential mortgage loans, home equity lines of credit, and auto and consumer loans in the communities it serves. Co. also purchases portfolios of residential mortgage loans and other consumer loans.

Recent Developments: For the year ended Dec 31 2004, net income increased 12.9% to $453,552 thousand from net income of $401,851 thousand a year earlier. Net interest income was $1,404,817 thousand, up 16.5% from $1,205,628 thousand the year before. Provision for loan losses was $127,000 thousand versus $161,957 thousand in the prior year, a decrease of 21.6%. Non-interest income fell 7.5% to $482,298 thousand, while non-interest expense advanced 12.2% to $944,417 thousand.

Prospects: On Jan 21 2005, Co. completed its acquisition of Waypoint Financial Corp., which has added 66 full-service banking offices in south-central Pennsylvania and northern Maryland with approximately $3.80 billion in assets and $2.80 billion in deposits. Meanwhile, results are being positively affected by commercial and consumer loan growth, higher fee income, and Co.'s cost-control efforts. Looking ahead, Co. is projecting full-year 2005 operating earnings of at least $2.10 per share, excluding one-time charges of between $0.04 and $0.06 per share related to the Waypoint acquisition and after-tax non-cash charges of about $0.17 per share.

Financial Data

(US$ in Thousands)	12/31/2004	12/31/2003	12/31/2002	12/31/2001	12/31/2000	12/31/1999	12/31/1998	12/31/1997
Earnings Per Share	1.36	1.38	1.23	0.45	(0.13)	1.01	0.85	0.63
Cash Flow Per Share	1.83	4.99	0.12	(1.13)	(0.83)	(0.13)	(0.10)	0.63
Tang Book Value Per Share	7.47	6.62	5.27	3.40	2.14	6.03	4.87	5.05
Dividends Per Share	0.115	0.100	0.100	0.100	0.100	0.095	0.077	0.067
Dividend Payout %	8.46	7.25	8.13	22.22	...	9.41	9.02	10.58
Income Statement								
Interest Income	2,224,144	1,929,751	2,059,540	2,222,475	2,269,735	1,607,329	1,355,371	960,728
Interest Expense	819,327	724,123	899,924	1,168,193	1,414,924	992,673	861,759	619,879
Net Interest Income	1,404,817	1,205,628	1,159,616	1,054,282	854,811	614,656	493,612	340,849
Provision for Losses	127,000	161,957	146,500	97,100	56,500	30,000	27,961	37,199
Non-Interest Income	482,298	522,223	432,526	426,066	108,561	130,342	105,638	38,480
Non-Interest Expense	1,015,296	938,344	900,381	922,669	830,431	430,896	348,359	204,311
Income Before Taxes	581,222	554,899	466,555	149,945	(106,232)	268,614	211,206	130,016
Income Taxes	127,670	153,048	124,570	26,575	(65,215)	89,315	74,751	52,376
Net Income	453,552	401,851	341,985	116,821	(30,242)	179,299	136,455	77,640
Average Shares	350,296	290,477	279,039	256,895	225,881	178,167	161,211	122,947
Balance Sheet								
Net Loans & Leases	36,222,363	25,820,765	22,828,575	20,134,917	21,655,889	14,093,554	11,152,038	9,832,629
Total Assets	54,471,313	43,505,329	39,524,193	35,474,838	33,457,797	26,607,112	21,913,873	14,336,283
Total Deposits	32,555,518	27,344,008	26,784,980	23,297,574	24,498,917	11,719,646	12,322,716	7,889,921
Total Liabilities	49,279,035	40,042,787	36,162,918	32,664,557	31,050,698	24,469,271	20,580,755	13,460,564
Stockholders' Equity	4,988,372	3,260,406	2,764,318	2,202,481	1,948,884	1,821,495	1,204,068	778,247
Shares Outstanding	349,061	296,661	264,966	252,277	231,067	230,274	159,727	112,133
Statistical Record								
Return on Assets %	0.92	0.97	0.91	0.34	N.M.	0.74	0.75	0.65
Return on Equity %	10.97	13.34	13.77	5.63	N.M.	11.85	13.77	12.38
Net Interest Margin %	63.16	62.48	56.30	47.44	37.66	38.24	36.42	35.48
Efficiency Ratio %	37.51	38.27	36.13	34.84	34.92	24.80	23.84	20.45
Loans to Deposits	1.11	0.94	0.85	0.86	0.88	1.20	0.90	1.25
Price Range	24.51-19.51	24.99-12.72	15.57-11.31	13.22-7.66	9.88-6.44	17.50-7.19	22.19-9.00	18.02-9.11
P/E Ratio	18.02-14.35	18.11-9.22	12.66-9.20	29.38-17.01	...	17.33-7.12	26.10-10.59	28.60-14.47
Average Yield %	0.53	0.58	0.72	0.97	1.31	0.84	0.48	0.53

Address: 1500 Market Street, Philadelphia, PA 19103 **Telephone:** (215) 557-4630 **Fax:** (610) 320-8448	**Web Site:** www.sovereignbank.com **Officers:** Jay S. Sidhu - Chmn., Pres., C.E.O. Lawrence M. Thompson Jr. - Vice-Chmn., Chief Admin. Officer	**Auditors:** Ernst & Young LLP **Investor Contact:** 610-320-8496

SPRINT CORP

Exchange	Symbol	Price	52Wk Range	Yield	P/E
NYS	FON	$22.75 (3/31/2005)	25.10-16.95	2.20	N/A

*7 Year Price Score 62.33 ***NYSE Composite Index=100** ***12 Month Price Score 105.73**

Interim Earnings (Per Share)

Qtr.	Mar	Jun	Sep	Dec
2001	(0.04)	0.06	(0.11)	(1.35)
2002	0.17	(0.06)	0.58	0.08
2003	1.88	0.02	(0.55)	0.08
2004	0.15	0.16	(1.32)	0.31

Interim Dividends (Per Share)

Amt	Decl	Ex	Rec	Pay
0.125Q	4/20/2004	6/7/2004	6/9/2004	6/30/2004
0.125Q	8/10/2004	9/7/2004	9/9/2004	9/30/2004
0.125Q	10/11/2004	12/7/2004	12/9/2004	12/30/2004
0.125Q	2/8/2005	3/8/2005	3/10/2005	3/31/2005

Indicated Div: $0.50

Valuation Analysis

Forecast P/E	N/A	No of Institutions
Market Cap	$33.6 Billion	Shares
Book Value	13.5 Billion	1,179,690,752
Price/Book	2.48	% Held
Price/Sales	1.22	80.20

Business Summary: Communications (MIC: 10.1 SIC: 813 NAIC: 17110)

Sprint is a global communications company, providing long-distance, local service, and wireless communications. Co.'s global markets division provides a range of communications services targeted to domestic business and residential customers, multinational corporations and other communications companies. The local division consists mainly of regulated local phone companies serving approximately 7.9 million access lines in 18 states, as of Dec 31 2003. The PCS Group includes Co.'s wireless personal communications service (PCS) operations. The PCS Group, combined with Co.'s wholesale and affiliate partners, served more than 20.0 million customers at the end of 2003.

Recent Developments: For the year ended Dec 31 2004, net loss was $1,012,000 thousand versus net income of $1,290,000 thousand a year earlier. Revenues were $27,428,000 thousand, up 4.7% from $26,197,000 thousand the year before. Operating loss was $303,000 thousand versus an income of $1,007,000 thousand in the prior year. Total direct expense was $12,656,000 thousand versus $11,658,000 thousand in the prior year, an increase of 8.6%. Total indirect expense was $15,075,000 thousand versus $13,532,000 thousand in the prior year, an increase of 11.4%.

Prospects: On Feb 14 2005, Co. announced an agreement under which Global Signal Inc. will have exclusive rights to lease or operate more than 6,600 communications towers from Co. for 32 years. Co. expects to receive $1.20 billion in cash at the time of closing. Under the terms of the agreement, Global Signal has the option to purchase the towers at the end of the lease term for about $2.30 billion. Co. has committed to sublease space on the towers for at least 10 years at an initial rate of $1,400 per month, per tower. For 2005, Co. expects low single-digit revenue growth and capital spending of between $4.00 and $4.20 billion.

Financial Data
(US$ in Thousands)

	12/31/2004	12/31/2003	12/31/2002	12/31/2001	12/31/2000	12/31/1999	12/31/1998	12/31/1997
Earnings Per Share	(0.71)	1.43	0.78	(1.44)	0.26	0.50	0.46	1.09
Cash Flow Per Share	4.58	3.39	3.25	2.50	2.33	2.27	4.85	3.93
Tang Value Per Share	3.85	2.79	1.68	1.85	2.63	2.10	5.23	10.49
Dividends Per Share	0.500	0.500	0.500	0.500	0.500	0.500	0.500	0.502
Dividend Payout %	...	34.97	64.10	...	192.31	100.00	109.89	46.10
Income Statement								
Total Revenue	27,428,000	26,197,000	26,634,000	26,071,000	23,613,000	19,928,000	17,134,300	14,873,900
EBITDA	4,365,000	5,756,000	6,747,000	3,754,000	4,432,000	3,440,000	3,606,600	3,496,500
Depn & Amortn	4,720,000	5,005,000	4,912,000	4,599,000	4,144,000	3,652,000	2,036,000	1,726,300
Income Before Taxes	(1,603,000)	(623,000)	429,000	(2,026,000)	(702,000)	(1,072,000)	842,400	1,583,000
Income Taxes	(591,000)	(256,000)	(39,000)	(624,000)	(126,000)	(327,000)	391,900	630,500
Net Income	(1,012,000)	1,215,000	630,000	(1,401,000)	93,000	(935,000)	414,500	952,500
Average Shares	1,443,400	1,931,900	1,909,100	1,876,500	1,858,900	877,200	861,600	873,000
Balance Sheet								
Net PPE	22,628,000	27,276,000	28,745,000	28,977,000	25,316,000	21,969,000	18,983,000	11,494,100
Total Assets	41,321,000	42,850,000	45,293,000	45,793,000	42,601,000	39,250,000	33,231,100	18,184,800
Long-Term Obligations	15,916,000	16,841,000	18,405,000	16,501,000	17,514,000	15,685,000	11,942,400	3,748,600
Total Liabilities	27,553,000	29,379,000	32,444,000	32,921,000	28,638,000	25,690,000	20,782,800	9,148,100
Stockholders' Equity	13,521,000	13,224,000	12,294,000	12,616,000	13,963,000	13,560,000	12,448,300	9,025,200
Shares Outstanding	1,474,800	1,939,700	1,938,000	1,918,600	1,817,300	1,784,600	861,600	860,000
Statistical Record								
Return on Assets %	N.M.	2.76	1.38	N.M.	0.23	N.M.	1.61	5.42
Return on Equity %	N.M.	9.52	5.06	N.M.	0.67	N.M.	3.86	10.86
EBITDA Margin %	15.91	21.97	25.33	14.40	18.77	17.26	21.05	23.51
Net Margin %	(3.69)	4.64	2.37	(5.37)	0.39	(4.69)	2.42	6.40
PPE Turnover	1.10	0.94	0.92	0.96	1.00	0.97	1.12	1.35
Asset Turnover	0.65	0.59	0.58	0.59	0.58	0.55	0.67	0.85
Debt to Equity	1.18	1.27	1.50	1.31	1.25	1.16	0.96	0.42
Price Range	25.10-16.33	16.72-10.68	20.08-7.05	28.19-18.98	67.31-20.00	75.50-37.19	42.53-24.86	26.71-17.22
P/E Ratio	...	11.69-7.47	25.74-9.04	...	258.89-76.92	151.00-74.38	92.46-54.04	24.51-15.80
Average Yield %	2.59	3.56	2.27	1.10	0.93	1.57	2.35	

Address: P.O. Box 7997, Shawnee Mission, KS 66207-0997	**Web Site:** www.sprint.com	**Auditors:** Ernst & Young LLP
Telephone: (913) 624-3000	**Officers:** Gary D. Forsee - Chmn., C.E.O. Len J. Lauer - Pres., C.O.O.	**Investor Contact:** 913-624-2541
Fax: (913) 624-3496		

SPX CORP.

Exchange	Symbol	Price	52Wk Range	Yield	P/E
NYS	SPW	$43.28 (3/31/2005)	49.24-33.30	2.31	N/A

*7 Year Price Score 75.55 *NYSE Composite Index=100 *12 Month Price Score 97.80

TRADING VOLUME (thousand shares)

Interim Earnings (Per Share)

Qtr.	Mar	Jun	Sep	Dec
2001	0.57	0.19	0.72	3.17
2002	(1.00)	0.69	0.91	0.94
2003	0.11	0.69	0.98	1.29
2004	0.49	0.72	0.03	(1.47)

Interim Dividends (Per Share)

Amt	Decl	Ex	Rec	Pay
0.25Q	5/26/2004	6/8/2004	6/10/2004	7/1/2004
0.25Q	8/25/2004	9/8/2004	9/10/2004	10/1/2004
0.25Q	11/17/2004	12/8/2004	12/10/2004	1/1/2005
0.25Q	3/24/2005	4/6/2005	4/8/2005	4/22/2005

Indicated Div: $1.00

Valuation Analysis

Forecast P/E	16.99 (4/14/2005)	No of Institutions	238
Market Cap	$3.2 Billion	Shares	77,680,072
Book Value	2.1 Billion	% Held	N/A
Price/Book	1.51		
Price/Sales	0.73		

Business Summary: Industrial Machinery and Equipment (MIC: 11.5 SIC: 541 NAIC: 33512)

SPX is a holding company. Co.'s segments include Industrial Products and Services, Flow Technology, Technical Products and Systems, Cooling Technologies and Services and Service Solutions. Co. products include networking and switching products, fire detection and building life-safety products, broadcast antennas and towers, life science products and services, transformers, compaction equipment, high-integrity castings, dock products and systems, cooling towers, air filtration products, valves, back-flow protection and fluid-handling devices, and metering and mixing products. Co. also provides specialty service tools, diagnostic systems, service equipment and technical information services.

Recent Developments: For the year ended Dec 31 2004, loss from continuing operations was $114,700 thousand compared with a income of $141,600 thousand a year earlier. Net loss was $17,100 thousand versus net income of $236,000 thousand a year earlier. Revenues were $4,372,000 thousand, up 14.6% from $3,815,700 thousand the year before. Operating loss was $9,100 thousand versus an income of $349,600 thousand in the prior year. Total direct expense was $3,233,200 thousand versus $2,739,500 thousand in the prior year, an increase of 18.0%. Total indirect expense was $1,147,900 thousand versus $726,600 thousand in the prior year, an increase of 58.0%.

Prospects: Co. recently completed the sale of its Cofimco axial fan business, its BOMAG compaction equipment business and its municipal water and wastewater valve business for $28.0 million, $446.0 million and $29.8 million, respectively. In addition, Co. has announced an agreement to sell its Kendro laboratory and life sciences products business to Thermo Electron Corp. for $833.5 million in cash. The Kendro sale will substantially complete Co.'s divestiture strategy undertaken in 2004. The combined net proceeds of this strategy, expected to be complete in the first half of 2005, are approximately $2.00 billion. Proceeds will be used primarily to reduce existing debt by about 70.0%.

Financial Data

(US$ in Thousands)	12/31/2004	12/31/2003	12/31/2002	12/31/2001	12/31/2000	12/31/1999	12/31/1998	12/31/1997
Earnings Per Share	(0.23)	3.04	1.54	4.67	5.97	3.27	(1.94)	(1.08)
Cash Flow Per Share	2.41	8.15	5.39	13.56	5.54	6.88	2.08	(1.25)
Dividends Per Share	1.000	...	...	...	...	...	...	0.050
Income Statement								
Total Revenue	4,372,000	5,081,500	5,045,800	4,114,300	2,678,900	2,712,300	1,825,400	922,316
EBITDA	76,800	735,700	762,000	608,600	541,500	517,800	69,600	56,812
Depn & Amortn	95,100	121,900	139,100	160,900	110,900	105,400	69,400	24,977
Income Before Taxes	(172,300)	416,200	453,200	314,000	335,600	294,800	(44,900)	17,869
Income Taxes	(31,600)	151,600	177,200	141,000	137,300	187,300	(3,200)	21,287
Net Income	(17,100)	236,000	127,400	173,000	189,500	101,500	(41,700)	(13,748)
Average Shares	74,271	77,684	82,959	37,060	31,751	31,055	21,546	12,754
Balance Sheet								
Current Assets	3,870,800	2,661,700	2,573,100	2,429,100	1,062,900	976,500	975,700	383,545
Total Assets	7,588,500	7,625,000	7,091,500	7,080,100	3,164,600	2,846,000	2,968,300	583,807
Current Liabilities	1,814,100	1,530,300	1,620,100	1,532,800	637,100	754,900	679,400	286,554
Long-Term Obligations	2,414,300	2,530,200	2,414,600	2,450,800	1,295,600	1,017,000	1,466,500	202,490
Total Liabilities	5,456,800	5,555,400	5,387,400	5,339,800	2,528,200	2,293,700	2,577,800	625,391
Stockholders' Equity	2,127,800	2,067,200	1,692,400	1,715,300	608,200	552,300	390,500	(43,348)
Shares Outstanding	74,242	74,315	80,626	40,393	30,322	31,168	30,075	12,530
Statistical Record								
Return on Assets %	N.M.	3.21	1.80	3.38	6.29	3.49	N.M.	N.M.
Return on Equity %	N.M.	12.55	7.48	14.89	32.57	21.53	N.M.	N.M.
EBITDA Margin %	1.76	14.48	15.10	14.79	20.21	19.09	3.81	6.16
Net Margin %	N.M.	4.64	2.52	4.20	7.07	3.74	N.M.	N.M.
Asset Turnover	0.57	0.69	0.71	0.80	0.89	0.93	1.03	1.54
Current Ratio	2.13	1.74	1.59	1.58	1.67	1.29	1.44	1.34
Debt to Equity	1.13	1.22	1.43	1.43	2.13	1.84	3.76	...
Price Range	61.66-33.30	59.00-30.83	74.75-36.50	68.45-38.50	89.86-37.00	47.00-24.38	39.53-18.47	35.16-18.94
P/E Ratio	N/A	19.41-10.14	48.54-23.70	14.66-8.24	15.05-6.20	14.37-7.45	N/A	N/A
Average Yield %	2.29	...	...	...	...	...	...	0.18

Address: 13515 Ballantyne Corporate Place, Charlotte, NC 28277	Web Site: www.spx.com	Auditors: Deloitte & Touche LLP
Telephone: (704) 752-4400 Fax: (704) 752-7415	Officers: Charles E. Johnson II - Chmn. Christopher J. Kearney - Pres., C.E.O.	Investor Contact: (231) 724-5194

STANCORP FINANCIAL GROUP INC

Exchange	Symbol	Price	52Wk Range	Yield	P/E
NYS	SFG	$84.78 (3/31/2005)	89.08-59.85	1.18	12.29

*7 Year Price Score N/A   *NYSE Composite Index=100   *12 Month Price Score 108.89

Interim Earnings (Per Share)

Qtr.	Mar	Jun	Sep	Dec
2001	0.83	0.84	0.84	0.93
2002	0.99	0.66	0.93	1.15
2003	1.10	1.27	1.45	1.51
2004	1.48	1.82	1.82	1.79

Interim Dividends (Per Share)

Amt	Decl	Ex	Rec	Pay
0.08A	11/5/2001	11/14/2001	11/16/2001	12/7/2001
0.40A	11/4/2002	11/13/2002	11/15/2002	12/6/2002
0.70A	11/3/2003	11/12/2003	11/14/2003	12/5/2003
1.00A	11/8/2004	11/17/2004	11/19/2004	12/3/2004

Indicated Div: $1.00

Valuation Analysis

Forecast P/E	12.77	No of Institutions
	(4/7/2005)	179
Market Cap	$2.4 Billion	Shares
Book Value	1.4 Billion	18,720,740
Price/Book	1.72	% Held
Price/Sales	1.12	65.83

Business Summary: Insurance (MIC: 8.2 SIC: 311 NAIC: 24113)

Stancorp Financial Group, through its subsidiaries, Standard Insurance Company (SIC); The Standard Life Insurance Company of New York; StanCorp Mortgage Investors; and StanCorp Investment Advisers, is a provider of employee benefits products and services. SIC underwrites group and individual disability and annuity products, and life and dental insurance for groups. The Standard Life Insurance Company of New York provides short-term and long-term disability insurance products. StanCorp Mortgage Investors is engaged in originating and servicing small commercial mortgage loans. StanCorp Investment Advisers provides performance analysis, fund selection support and model portfolios.

Recent Developments: For the year ended Dec 31 2004, net income increased 27.6% to $199,400,000 from net income of $156,300,000 a year earlier. Revenues were $21,497,000,00, up 4.0% from $2,066,800,000 the year before. Net premiums earned were $1,678,700,000 versus $1,609,300,000 in the prior year, an increase of 4.3%. Net investment income rose 2.9% to $464,100,000 from $451,100,000 a year ago.

Prospects: Co.'s results are benefiting from strong sales across all of its lines of business. Co. is being positively affected by favorable claims experience in its Employee Benefits segment. In addition, Co.'s Retirement Plans segment and its individual annuities business continue to produce strong growth in deposits and assets under management. Co.'s premium growth reflects improved sales and strong customer retention. For 2005, Co. expects net income to be in the range of $6.65 to $6.85 per diluted share, before net capital gains and losses, reflecting a growth rate below its long-term objective of 12.0% to 15.0%.

Financial Data
(US$ in Thousands)

	12/31/2004	12/31/2003	12/31/2002	12/31/2001	12/31/2000	12/31/1999	12/31/1998	12/31/1997
Earnings Per Share	6.90	5.33	3.73	3.44	2.95	2.37	...	...
Cash Flow Per Share	14.12	11.64	12.92	8.66	22.96	8.41	...	...
Tang Book Value Per Share	49.26	44.69	39.49	32.69	29.29	25.68	60.29	...
Dividends Per Share	1.000	0.700	0.400	0.300	0.270	0.120	...	...
Dividend Payout %	14.49	13.13	10.72	8.72	9.15	5.06	...	...
Income Statement								
Premium Income	1,678,700	1,609,300	1,383,300	1,231,700	1,102,000	914,400	890,940	1,085,024
Total Revenue	2,149,700	2,066,800	1,750,300	1,585,400	1,462,700	1,234,500	1,232,552	1,391,188
Benefits & Claims	1,291,200	1,297,800	1,117,100	1,017,000	929,500	756,000	760,910	598,788
Income Before Taxes	292,000	239,800	172,000	164,500	141,100	123,400	108,573	59,369
Income Taxes	92,600	83,500	61,000	58,500	46,400	39,000	32,975	20,660
Net Income	199,400	156,300	111,000	106,000	94,700	79,900	69,496	40,859
Average Shares	28,919	29,334	29,772	30,835	32,125	33,674	...	...
Balance Sheet								
Total Assets	11,212,000	9,981,700	8,742,700	7,277,000	6,859,600	5,857,100	5,278,846	4,524,596
Total Liabilities	9,810,900	8,672,200	7,590,100	6,303,300	5,935,200	5,017,200	4,439,564	4,222,437
Stockholders' Equity	1,401,100	1,309,500	1,152,600	973,700	924,400	839,900	839,282	302,159
Shares Outstanding	28,444	29,300	29,185	29,783	31,565	32,706	13,920	...
Statistical Record								
Return on Assets %	1.88	1.67	1.39	1.50	1.49	1.43	1.42	0.95
Return on Equity %	14.67	12.70	10.44	11.17	10.71	9.52	12.18	14.40
Loss Ratio %	76.92	80.64	80.76	82.57	84.35	82.68	85.41	55.19
Net Margin %	9.28	7.56	6.34	6.69	6.47	6.47	5.64	2.94
Price Range	83.17-59.85	63.48-46.61	61.10-46.41	48.40-37.00	49.13-23.75	30.00-21.25	...	...
P/E Ratio	12.05-8.67	11.91-8.74	16.38-12.44	14.07-10.76	16.65-8.05	12.66-8.97	...	...
Average Yield %	1.45	1.28	0.74	0.68	0.81	0.49	...	...

Address: 1100 SW Sixth Avenue, Portland, OR 97204 **Telephone:** (503) 321-7000	**Web Site:** www.stancorpfinancial.com **Officers:** Eric E. Parsons - Chmn., Pres., C.E.O. Cindy J. McPike - Sr. V.P., C.F.O.	**Auditors:** Deloitte & Touche LLP **Investor Contact:** 503-321-7529

STANLEY WORKS (THE)

Exchange	Symbol	Price	52Wk Range	Yield	P/E	Div Acheiver
NYS	SWK	$45.27 (3/31/2005)	48.99-40.27	2.47	10.38	37 Years

*7 Year Price Score 109.08 *NYSE Composite Index=100 *12 Month Price Score 96.85

Interim Earnings (Per Share)

Qtr.	Mar	Jun	Sep	Dec
2001	0.54	0.58	0.62	0.07
2002	0.56	0.72	0.62	0.20
2003	0.22	0.14	0.51	0.41
2004	1.84	0.73	0.76	1.04

Interim Dividends (Per Share)

Amt	Decl	Ex	Rec	Pay
0.26Q	4/23/2004	6/2/2004	6/4/2004	6/29/2004
0.28Q	7/22/2004	9/1/2004	9/3/2004	9/28/2004
0.28Q	10/14/2004	11/24/2004	11/29/2004	12/21/2004
0.28Q	2/23/2005	3/7/2005	3/9/2005	3/29/2005

Indicated Div: $1.12 (Div. Reinv. Plan)

Valuation Analysis

Forecast P/E	14.03	No of Institutions	
	(4/7/2005)	282	
Market Cap	$3.7 Billion	Shares	
Book Value	1.2 Billion	60,506,324	
Price/Book	3.05	% Held	
Price/Sales	1.23	73.24	

Business Summary: Metal Products (MIC: 11.4 SIC: 423 NAIC: 32212)

Stanley Works is a worldwide producer of tools and door products for professional, industrial and consumer use. The Tools segment manufactures and markets carpenters', mechanics', pneumatic and hydraulic tools as well as tool sets. The Doors segment manufactures and markets automatic doors as well as closet doors and systems, home decor, door locking systems, commercial and consumer hardware, security access control systems and patient monitoring devices. A substantial portion of Co.'s products are sold through home centers and mass merchant distribution channels in the U.S.

Recent Developments: For the year ended Jan 1 2005, income from continuing operations increased 164.2% to $240,200 thousand from income of $90,900 thousand a year earlier. Net income increased 240.0% to $366,900 thousand from net income of $107,900 thousand a year earlier. Revenues were $3,043,400 thousand, up 20.3% from $2,530,600 thousand the year before. Total direct expense was $1,931,100 thousand versus $1,673,000 thousand in the prior year, an increase of 15.4%. Total indirect expense was $702,000 thousand versus $667,700 thousand in the prior year, an increase of 5.1%.

Prospects: Co. continues to benefit from strong demand from home center and mass merchant customers. Also, industrial tool sales continue to benefit from favorable market conditions, improved execution in several businesses and higher pricing. Meanwhile, Co. expects earnings from continuing operations to range from $3.15 to $3.30 per fully diluted share for full year 2005. In addition, free cash flow is expected to exceed net income in 2005. Separately, on Jan 4 2005, Co. announced that it completed the acquisition of Security Group, Inc., which is comprised of two companies called Sargent & Greenleaf, Inc. and Safemasters for approximately $56.0 million.

Financial Data

(US$ in Thousands)	01/01/2005	01/03/2004	12/28/2002	12/29/2001	12/30/2000	01/01/2000	01/02/1999	01/03/1998
Earnings Per Share	4.36	1.27	2.10	1.81	2.22	1.67	1.53	(0.47)
Cash Flow Per Share	4.54	5.43	3.31	2.59	2.71	2.49	0.63	2.65
Tang Book Value Per Share	5.32	2.65	5.05	7.04	6.58	6.19	5.32	5.67
Dividends Per Share	1.080	1.030	0.990	0.940	0.900	0.870	0.830	0.770
Dividend Payout %	24.77	81.10	47.14	51.93	40.54	52.10	54.25	...
Income Statement								
Total Revenue	3,043,400	2,678,100	2,593,000	2,624,400	2,748,900	2,751,800	2,729,100	2,669,500
EBITDA	458,500	247,800	368,200	345,200	404,100	344,300	318,200	70,400
Depn & Amortn	95,000	86,530	71,200	82,900	83,300	85,600	79,700	72,400
Income Before Taxes	329,100	133,000	272,500	236,700	293,700	230,800	215,400	(18,600)
Income Taxes	88,900	36,300	87,500	78,400	99,300	80,800	77,600	23,300
Net Income	366,900	107,900	185,000	158,300	194,400	150,000	137,800	(41,900)
Average Shares	84,243	84,839	88,246	87,467	87,667	89,886	90,193	89,469
Balance Sheet								
Current Assets	1,371,900	1,200,700	1,190,400	1,141,400	1,094,300	1,091,000	1,086,400	1,005,300
Total Assets	2,850,600	2,423,800	2,418,200	2,055,700	1,884,800	1,890,600	1,932,900	1,758,700
Current Liabilities	818,800	753,500	680,900	825,500	707,300	693,000	702,100	622,700
Long-Term Obligations	481,800	534,500	564,300	196,800	248,700	290,000	344,800	283,700
Total Liabilities	1,629,300	1,565,200	1,434,400	1,223,400	1,148,300	1,155,200	1,263,500	1,150,900
Stockholders' Equity	1,221,300	858,600	983,800	832,300	736,500	735,400	669,400	607,800
Shares Outstanding	82,407	81,276	86,835	84,658	85,188	88,945	88,772	88,788
Statistical Record								
Return on Assets %	13.95	4.38	8.29	8.06	10.33	7.87	7.49	N.M.
Return on Equity %	35.38	11.52	20.43	20.24	26.49	21.41	21.64	N.M.
EBITDA Margin %	15.07	9.25	14.20	13.15	14.70	12.51	11.66	2.64
Net Margin %	12.06	4.03	7.13	6.03	7.07	5.45	5.05	N.M.
Asset Turnover	1.16	1.09	1.16	1.34	1.46	1.44	1.48	1.54
Current Ratio	1.68	1.59	1.75	1.38	1.55	1.57	1.55	1.61
Debt to Equity	0.39	0.62	0.57	0.24	0.34	0.39	0.52	0.47
Price Range	48.99-36.50	37.87-21.00	51.98-28.38	46.60-28.50	31.19-19.25	33.94-22.13	56.38-24.50	47.19-31.75
P/E Ratio	11.24-8.37	29.82-16.54	24.75-13.51	25.75-15.75	14.05-8.67	20.32-13.25	36.85-16.01	...
Average Yield %	2.53	3.57	2.48	2.46	3.45	3.08	2.01	1.87

Address: 1000 Stanley Drive, New Britain, CT 06053 **Telephone:** (860) 225-5111 **Fax:** (860) 827-3895	**Web Site:** www.stanleyworks.com **Officers:** John F. Lundgren - Chmn., C.E.O. James M. Loree - Exec. V.P., C.F.O.	**Auditors:** Ernst & Young LLP **Investor Contact:** 860-827-3833 **Transfer Agents:** EquiServe Limited Partnership, Boston, MA

STARWOOD HOTELS & RESORTS WORLDWIDE INC

Exchange	Symbol	Price	52Wk Range	Yield	P/E
NYS	HOT	$60.03 (3/31/2005)	60.80-38.61	1.40	32.63

*7 Year Price Score 124.41 ***NYSE Composite Index=100** ***12 Month Price Score 111.99**

TRADING VOLUME (thousand shares)

Interim Earnings (Per Share)

Qtr.	Mar	Jun	Sep	Dec
2001	0.30	0.52	0.14	(0.26)
2002	0.16	0.87	0.26	0.44
2003	(0.58)	1.41	0.23	0.42
2004	0.16	0.72	0.50	0.46

Interim Dividends (Per Share)

Amt	Decl	Ex	Rec	Pay
0.20A	12/20/2001	12/27/2001	12/31/2001	1/21/2002
0.84A	12/18/2002	12/27/2002	12/31/2002	1/21/2003
0.84A	12/19/2003	12/29/2003	12/31/2003	1/21/2004
0.84A	12/16/2004	12/29/2004	12/31/2004	1/21/2005

Indicated Div: $0.84

Valuation Analysis

Forecast P/E	29.61	No of Institutions	
	(4/7/2005)	323	
Market Cap	$12.5 Billion	Shares	
Book Value	4.8 Billion	195,957,152	
Price/Book	2.62	% Held	
Price/Sales	2.33	92.23	

Business Summary: Hospitality & Tourism (MIC: 5.1 SIC: 011 NAIC: 21110)

Starwood Hotels & Resorts Worldwide is a hotel and leisure company that operates directly and through its subsidiary, ITT Sheraton Corporation. The hotel segment offers luxury and upscale full-service hotels under the following brand names: Sheraton®, Westin®, The Luxury Collection®, St. Regis®, W® brands and Four Points® by Sheraton. The vacation ownership segment includes the development, ownership and operation of vacation ownership resorts, marketing and selling vacation ownership interests and providing financing for customers who purchase those interests.

Recent Developments: For the year ended Dec 31 2004, income from continuing operations increased 251.4% to $369,000 thousand from income of $105,000 thousand a year earlier. Net income increased 27.8% to $395,000 thousand from net income of $309,000 thousand a year earlier. Revenues were $5,368,000 thousand, up 15.9% from $4,630,000 thousand the year before. Operating income was $653,000 thousand versus an income of $427,000 thousand in the prior year, an increase of 52.9%. Total direct expense was $4,715,000 thousand versus $4,203,000 thousand in the prior year, an increase of 12.2%. Total indirect expense was $1,708,000 thousand versus $1,471,000 thousand in the prior year, an increase of 16.1%.

Prospects: Assuming revenue per available room at same-store owned hotels in North America rise 8.0% to 10.0% versus the full year 2004, Co. foresees full year 2005 revenues, including other revenues from managed and franchised properties, of about $5.90 billion. Full year net income would be expected to be about $440.0 million, or $2.00 per share versus 2004 earnings per share from continuing operations before special items of $1.62. Full year capital expenditures (excluding timeshare inventory) are projected to be about $600.0 million, including $300.0 million for maintenance, renovation and technology, and about $100.0 million for the completion of the St. Regis San Francisco multi-use project.

Financial Data

(US$ in Thousands)	12/31/2004	12/31/2003	12/31/2002	12/31/2001	12/31/2000	12/31/1999	12/31/1998	12/31/1997
Earnings Per Share	1.84	1.50	1.73	0.70	1.97	(3.96)	4.65	(0.20)
Cash Flow Per Share	2.78	3.80	3.51	3.79	4.35	2.42	(2.05)	(0.43)
Tang Book Value Per Share	10.75	9.11	7.15	2.35	4.99	4.32	...	0.76
Dividends Per Share	0.840	0.840	0.840	0.800	0.690	0.600	...	...
Dividend Payout %	45.65	56.00	48.55	114.29	35.03	...	...	...
Income Statement								
Total Revenue	5,368,000	4,630,000	4,659,000	3,967,000	4,345,000	3,862,000	4,700,000	913,688
EBITDA	1,094,000	694,000	1,079,000	1,084,000	1,511,000	1,518,000	656,000	...
Depn & Amortn	428,000	423,000	489,000	526,000	481,000	492,000	447,000	25,295
Income Before Taxes	412,000	(11,000)	252,000	200,000	610,000	533,000	(380,000)	...
Income Taxes	43,000	(113,000)	4,000	46,000	201,000	1,076,000	(109,000)	...
Net Income	395,000	309,000	355,000	145,000	403,000	(741,000)	860,000	(9,223)
Average Shares	215,000	207,000	205,000	206,000	205,000	189,000	185,000	48,663
Balance Sheet								
Current Assets	1,683,000	1,245,000	950,000	897,000	1,048,000	1,176,000	1,038,000	86,128
Total Assets	12,298,000	11,894,000	12,259,000	12,461,000	12,660,000	12,923,000	11,214,000	558,651
Current Liabilities	2,128,000	1,644,000	2,199,000	1,587,000	1,805,000	2,303,000	2,041,000	448,454
Long-Term Obligations	3,823,000	4,393,000	4,449,000	5,227,000	4,957,000	4,643,000	9,957,000	...
Total Liabilities	7,483,000	7,509,000	8,172,000	8,622,000	8,644,000	8,850,000	14,230,000	508,483
Stockholders' Equity	4,788,000	4,326,000	3,997,000	3,756,000	3,851,000	3,690,000	(3,025,000)	38,997
Shares Outstanding	208,730	201,812	199,579	395,437	194,485	189,271	175,574	51,346
Statistical Record								
Return on Assets %	3.26	2.56	2.87	1.15	3.14	N.M.	14.61	N.M.
Return on Equity %	8.64	7.43	9.16	3.81	10.66	N.M.	...	N.M.
EBITDA Margin %	20.38	14.99	23.16	27.33	34.78	39.31	13.96	...
Net Margin %	7.36	6.67	7.62	3.66	9.28	N.M.	18.30	N.M.
Asset Turnover	0.44	0.38	0.38	0.32	0.34	0.32	0.80	0.98
Current Ratio	0.79	0.76	0.43	0.57	0.58	0.51	0.51	0.19
Debt to Equity	0.80	1.02	1.11	1.39	1.29	1.26	...	...
Price Range	59.46-34.90	37.15-21.94	39.69-19.61	40.77-17.75	36.50-19.75	37.00-19.63	57.88-19.50	60.38-34.25
P/E Ratio	32.32-18.97	24.77-14.63	22.94-11.34	58.24-25.36	18.53-10.03	...	12.45-4.19	...
Average Yield %	1.92	2.83	2.81	2.45	2.35	2.21	...	...

Address: 1111 Westchester Avenue, White Plains, NY 10604
Telephone: (914) 640-8100
Fax: (914) 640-8310

Web Site: www.starwood.com
Officers: Barry S. Sternlicht - Chmn., C.E.O. Robert F. Cotter - Pres., C.O.O.

Auditors: Ernst & Young LLP

STATE STREET CORP.

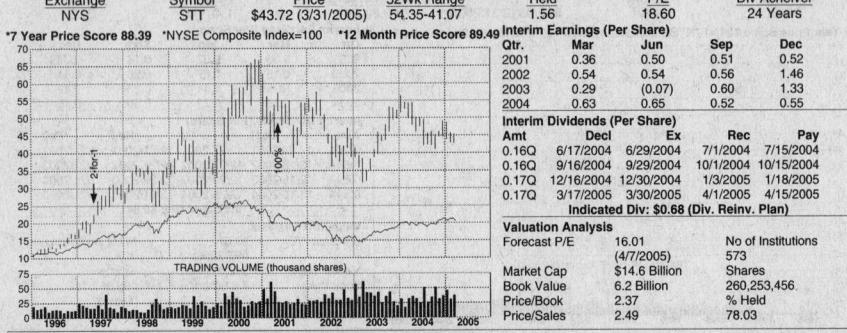

Exchange	Symbol	Price	52Wk Range	Yield	P/E	Div Acheiver
NYS	STT	$43.72 (3/31/2005)	54.35-41.07	1.56	18.60	24 Years

*7 Year Price Score 88.39   *NYSE Composite Index=100   *12 Month Price Score 89.49

Interim Earnings (Per Share)

Qtr.	Mar	Jun	Sep	Dec
2001	0.36	0.50	0.51	0.52
2002	0.54	0.54	0.56	1.46
2003	0.29	(0.07)	0.60	1.33
2004	0.63	0.65	0.52	0.55

Interim Dividends (Per Share)

Amt	Decl	Ex	Rec	Pay
0.16Q	6/17/2004	6/29/2004	7/1/2004	7/15/2004
0.16Q	9/16/2004	9/29/2004	10/1/2004	10/15/2004
0.17Q	12/16/2004	12/30/2004	1/3/2005	1/18/2005
0.17Q	3/17/2005	3/30/2005	4/1/2005	4/15/2005

Indicated Div: $0.68 (Div. Reinv. Plan)

Valuation Analysis

Forecast P/E	16.01	No of Institutions
	(4/7/2005)	573
Market Cap	$14.6 Billion	Shares
Book Value	6.2 Billion	260,253,456
Price/Book	2.37	% Held
Price/Sales	2.49	78.03

Business Summary: Commercial Banking (MIC: 8.1 SIC: 022 NAIC: 22110)

State Street is a bank holding company, with $87.53 billion in assets as of Dec 31 2003, that conducts business worldwide principally through its subsidiary, State Street Bank and Trust Company. Co. has two lines of business: investment servicing and investment management. Investment Servicing includes primarily accounting, custody and other services for large pools of assets. Investment management offers index and active equity strategies, short-term investment funds and fixed income products. As of Dec 31 2003, Co. had $1.10 trillion in assets under management.

Recent Developments: For the year ended Dec 31 2004, net income increased 10.5% to $798.0 million from net income of $722.0 million a year earlier. Total fee revenue increased 13.8% to $4.05 billion from $3.56 billion the previous year, reflecting gains from across its operating units. Servicing fees rose 16.1% to $2.26 billion, management fees grew 16.9% to $623.0 million, securities lending revenue increased 5.7% to $259.0 million, foreign exchange trading revenue rose 7.4% to $420.0 million, brokerage fees climbed 27.0% to $155.0 million, and processing fees and other revenue increased 4.1% to $328.0 million. Net interest revenue amounted to $859.0 million, 6.0% higher than last year.

Prospects: Overall, Co. continues to face a slow growth business environment, although it is seeing solid gains in both Europe and the Asia Pacific, fueled in part by the expanded presence gained from the GSS acquisition and increased customer demand in those regions. Going forward, Co. will continue to balance its objectives for growth with delivering consistency in operating earnings per share. For 2005, Co. estimates operating earnings per share growth of 10.0% to 15.0%, operating revenue growth of 8.0% to 12.0%, and an operating return on equity of 14.0% to 17.0%. Co. expects to deliver at the lower end of these ranges based on the present business environment.

Financial Data

(US$ in Thousands)	12/31/2004	12/31/2003	12/31/2002	12/31/2001	12/31/2000	12/31/1999	12/31/1998	12/31/1997
Earnings Per Share	2.35	2.15	3.10	1.90	1.81	1.89	1.33	1.16
Cash Flow Per Share	1.24	4.57	3.10	1.44	1.98	0.61	2.64	0.78
Tang Book Value Per Share	12.49	11.65	12.92	11.88	10.09	8.31	7.19	5.97
Dividends Per Share	0.640	0.560	0.480	0.405	0.425	0.300	0.260	0.220
Dividend Payout %	27.23	26.05	15.48	21.32	23.42	15.87	19.55	18.97
Income Statement								
Interest Income	1,787,000	1,539,000	1,974,000	2,855,000	3,256,000	2,437,000	2,237,000	1,755,000
Interest Expense	928,000	729,000	995,000	1,830,000	2,362,000	1,656,000	1,492,000	1,114,000
Net Interest Income	859,000	810,000	979,000	1,025,000	894,000	781,000	745,000	641,000
Provision for Losses	(18,000)	...	4,000	10,000	9,000	14,000	17,000	16,000
Non-Interest Income	4,074,000	3,924,000	3,421,000	2,782,000	2,665,000	3,707,000	3,021,000	1,673,000
Non-Interest Expense	3,759,000	3,622,000	2,841,000	2,867,000	2,644,000	2,336,000	2,068,000	1,734,000
Income Before Taxes	1,192,000	1,112,000	1,555,000	930,000	906,000	968,000	657,000	564,000
Income Taxes	394,000	390,000	540,000	302,000	311,000	349,000	221,000	184,000
Net Income	798,000	722,000	1,015,000	628,000	595,000	619,000	436,000	380,000
Average Shares	339,605	335,326	327,477	330,492	328,088	327,502	327,854	327,578
Balance Sheet								
Net Loans & Leases	4,611,000	4,960,000	4,113,000	5,283,000	5,216,000	4,245,000	6,225,000	5,479,000
Total Assets	94,040,000	87,534,000	85,794,000	69,896,000	69,298,000	60,896,000	47,082,000	37,975,000
Total Deposits	55,129,000	47,516,000	45,468,000	38,559,000	37,937,000	34,145,000	27,539,000	24,878,000
Total Liabilities	87,881,000	81,787,000	81,007,000	66,051,000	66,036,000	58,244,000	44,771,000	35,980,000
Stockholders' Equity	6,159,000	5,747,000	4,787,000	3,845,000	3,262,000	2,652,000	2,311,000	1,995,000
Shares Outstanding	333,645	334,474	324,927	323,670	323,422	319,180	321,390	334,446
Statistical Record								
Return on Assets %	0.88	0.83	1.30	0.90	0.91	1.15	1.03	1.09
Return on Equity %	13.37	13.71	23.52	17.67	20.07	24.94	20.25	20.16
Net Interest Margin %	48.07	52.63	49.59	35.90	27.46	32.05	33.30	36.52
Efficiency Ratio %	64.14	66.30	52.66	50.86	44.65	38.02	39.33	50.58
Loans to Deposits	0.08	0.10	0.09	0.14	0.14	0.12	0.23	0.22
Price Range	56.45-41.07	53.18-31.63	57.59-32.38	62.75-38.66	66.93-31.69	47.63-27.94	36.66-24.75	31.13-15.75
P/E Ratio	24.02-17.48	24.73-14.71	18.58-10.45	33.03-20.35	36.98-17.51	25.20-14.78	27.56-18.61	26.83-13.58
Average Yield %	1.33	1.32	1.04	0.80	0.81	0.80	0.81	0.92

Address: 225 Franklin Street, Boston, MA 02110	Web Site: www.statestreet.com	Auditors: Ernst & Young LLP
Telephone: (617) 786-3000	Officers: Ronald E. Logue - Chmn., C.E.O. John R. Towers - Vice Chmn.	Investor Contact: 617-664-3477
Fax: (617) 985-8055		Transfer Agents: EquiServe Trust Company, N.A., Providence, RI

STATION CASINOS, INC.

Exchange	Symbol	Price	52Wk Range	Yield	P/E
NYS	STN	$67.55 (3/31/2005)	69.47-41.40	1.24	67.55

*7 Year Price Score 210.96 *NYSE Composite Index=100 *12 Month Price Score 114.15

TRADING VOLUME (thousand shares)

Interim Earnings (Per Share)

Qtr.	Mar	Jun	Sep	Dec
2001	0.11	0.06	0.08	0.07
2002	0.22	0.13	0.09	0.08
2003	0.21	0.33	0.32	(0.14)
2004	(0.48)	0.43	0.43	0.57

Interim Dividends (Per Share)

Amt	Decl	Ex	Rec	Pay
0.175Q	7/13/2004	8/11/2004	8/13/2004	9/3/2004
0.21Q	10/18/2004	11/9/2004	11/12/2004	12/3/2004
0.21Q	1/24/2005	2/9/2005	2/11/2005	3/4/2005
0.21Q	4/4/2005	5/11/2005	5/13/2005	6/3/2005
			Indicated Div: $0.84	

Valuation Analysis

Forecast P/E	27.52	No of Institutions
	(4/7/2005)	189
Market Cap	$4.5 Billion	Shares
Book Value	488.9 Million	48,621,960
Price/Book	9.27	% Held
Price/Sales	4.59	71.99

Business Summary: Sporting & Recreational (MIC: 13.5 SIC: 993 NAIC: 13290)

Station Casinos is a gaming and entertainment company. Co. owns and operates eight major hotel/casino properties and five smaller casino properties in the Las Vegas metropolitan area. Co. owns and operates Palace Station Hotel & Casino, Boulder Station Hotel & Casino, Texas Station Gambling Hall & Hotel, Sunset Station Hotel & Casino, Santa Fe Station Hotel & Casino, Fiesta Rancho Casino Hotel, Fiesta Henderson Casino Hotel, Wild Wild West Gambling Hall & Hotel, Wildfire Casino, Magic Star Casino, and Gold Rush Casino. Co. owns a 50.0% interest in Green Valley Ranch Station Casino and Barley's Casino and Brewing Company.

Recent Developments: For the year ended Dec 31 2004, net income increased 49.6% to $66,350 thousand from net income of $44,343 thousand a year earlier. Revenues were $986,742 thousand, up 15.0% from $858,089 thousand the year before. Operating income was $257,055 thousand versus an income of $141,071 thousand in the prior year, an increase of 82.2%. Total direct expense was $412,237 thousand versus $388,018 thousand in the prior year, an increase of 6.2%. Total indirect expense was $317,450 thousand versus $329,000 thousand in the prior year, a decrease of 3.5%.

Prospects: Co.'s outlook remains strong, driven by continued growth in the Las Vegas, NV economy. Co. expects its first-quarter earnings before interest, taxes, depreciation and amortization (EBITDA) of about $107.0 million to $113.0 million, excluding development expense and other items. Net income is expected in the range of $0.56 to $0.62. This guidance assumes revenue growth of 9.0% to 13.0% in Las Vegas, excluding Green Valley Ranch Station. For 2005, Co. expects EBITDA of about $425.0 million to $440.0 million, excluding items, with earnings between $2.22 and $2.35 per share. This guidance assumes revenue growth for 2005 of 6.0% to 10.0% in Las Vegas, excluding Green Valley Ranch Station Casino.

Financial Data

(US$ in Thousands)	12/31/2004	12/31/2003	12/31/2002	12/31/2001	12/31/2000	12/31/1999	12/31/1998	03/31/1998
Earnings Per Share	1.00	0.72	0.30	0.32	1.48	(0.76)	(0.27)	(0.19)
Cash Flow Per Share	4.05	3.37	2.25	2.00	2.70	2.95	0.83	1.98
Tang Book Value Per Share	4.96	3.15	1.78	1.04	2.88	3.47	3.14	3.46
Dividends Per Share	0.685	0.250	...	...	...	...	...	...
Dividend Payout %	68.50	34.72	...	...	...	...	...	...
Income Statement								
Total Revenue	986,742	858,089	792,865	839,361	991,678	942,469	642,214	769,610
EBITDA	275,265	239,777	229,582	216,488	308,572	110,718	114,327	148,563
Depn & Amortn	88,752	76,300	76,865	75,952	66,325	73,323	57,229	73,857
Income Before Taxes	105,229	68,177	49,756	43,195	148,149	(47,223)	(9,864)	(4,120)
Income Taxes	38,879	23,834	18,508	15,550	54,098	(14,929)	(871)	(966)
Net Income	66,350	44,343	17,932	19,369	93,505	(42,947)	(12,097)	(5,196)
Average Shares	66,264	61,850	60,730	60,037	63,116	58,692	52,968	52,963
Balance Sheet								
Current Assets	119,521	134,464	102,509	113,033	313,034	120,204	305,936	87,491
Total Assets	2,045,584	1,745,972	1,598,347	1,656,122	1,440,428	1,276,273	1,533,931	1,300,216
Current Liabilities	176,510	142,316	88,799	108,806	124,742	117,689	124,855	197,509
Long-Term Obligations	1,321,296	1,168,935	1,165,600	1,236,758	983,941	933,833	946,308	802,295
Total Liabilities	1,556,663	1,406,033	1,327,669	1,407,218	1,151,541	1,059,472	1,264,170	1,013,329
Stockholders' Equity	488,921	339,939	270,678	248,904	288,887	216,801	269,761	286,887
Shares Outstanding	67,112	60,790	57,958	57,361	60,369	62,515	52,968	52,966
Statistical Record								
Return on Assets %	3.49	2.65	1.10	1.25	6.86	N.M.	N.M.	N.M.
Return on Equity %	15.97	14.52	6.90	7.20	36.88	N.M.	N.M.	N.M.
EBITDA Margin %	27.90	27.94	28.96	25.79	31.12	11.75	17.80	19.30
Net Margin %	6.72	5.17	2.26	2.31	9.43	N.M.	N.M.	N.M.
Asset Turnover	0.52	0.51	0.49	0.54	0.73	0.67	0.26	0.61
Current Ratio	0.68	0.94	1.15	1.04	2.51	1.02	2.45	0.44
Debt to Equity	2.70	3.44	4.31	4.97	3.41	4.31	3.51	2.80
Price Range	58.84-30.21	33.22-16.80	19.00-10.80	17.41-7.69	19.67-11.96	17.79-5.33	10.33-2.73	10.42-4.42
P/E Ratio	58.84-30.21	46.14-23.33	63.33-36.00	54.41-24.03	13.29-8.08	...	...	...
Average Yield %	1.50	0.99	...	...	...	...	...	...

Address: 2411 West Sahara Avenue, Las Vegas, NV 89102 Telephone: (702) 367-2411 Fax: (702) 367-2424	Web Site: www.stationcasinos.com Officers: Frank J. Fertitta III - Chmn., C.E.O. Lorenzo J. Fertitta - Vice-Chmn., Pres.	Auditors: Ernst & Young LLP Transfer Agents: Wells Fargo Shareowner Services, South Saint Paul, MN

STEELCASE, INC.

Exchange	Symbol	Price	52Wk Range	Yield	P/E
NYS	SCS	$13.80 (3/31/2005)	14.65-11.40	1.74	N/A

*7 Year Price Score 78.49 *NYSE Composite Index=100 *12 Month Price Score 97.22

Interim Earnings (Per Share)

Qtr.	May	Aug	Nov	Feb
2001-02	0.16	0.04	0.03	(0.23)
2002-03	(1.26)	(0.05)	(0.21)	(0.28)
2003-04	(0.09)	0.12	(0.06)	(0.13)
2004-05	(0.04)	0.05	0.07	...

Interim Dividends (Per Share)

Amt	Decl	Ex	Rec	Pay
0.06Q	6/24/2004	6/29/2004	7/1/2004	7/15/2004
0.06Q	10/7/2004	10/12/2004	10/14/2004	10/21/2004
0.06Q	12/16/2004	12/29/2004	1/1/2005	1/18/2005
0.06Q	3/25/2005	4/4/2005	4/6/2005	4/15/2005

Indicated Div: $0.24

Valuation Analysis

Forecast P/E	43.94	No of Institutions	
	(4/7/2005)	110	
Market Cap	$2.0 Billion	Shares	50,891,200
Book Value	1.2 Billion	% Held	34.27
Price/Book	1.69		
Price/Sales	0.82		

Business Summary: Chemicals (MIC: 11.1 SIC: 522 NAIC: 37214)

Steelcase is a designer and manufacturer of office furniture. As of Feb 27 2004, Co. operated manufacturing facilities in over 35 locations and distributed products through a network of independent dealers in more than 900 locations. Co.'s offerings in North America include architecture, furniture and technology products, under the Steelcase and Turnstone brands. The Steelcase Design Partnership includes the following companies and their brands: Brayton International, The Designtex Group, Office Details Inc., Metropolitan Furniture Corporation and Vecta. The International segment includes all sales and manufacturing operations of the Steelcase and Werndl brands outside the U.S. and Canada.

Recent Developments: For the quarter ended Nov 26 2004, net income was $10,100 thousand versus net loss of $9,500 thousand in the year-earlier quarter. Revenues were $674,100 thousand, up 9.7% from $614,500 thousand the year before. Operating income was $6,200 thousand versus a loss of $6,000 thousand in the prior-year quarter, an increase of 203.3%. Total direct expense was $485,800 thousand versus $447,800 thousand in the prior-year quarter, an increase of 8.5%. Total indirect expense was $182,100 thousand versus $172,700 thousand in the prior-year quarter, an increase of 5.4%.

Prospects: Incoming orders increased in the third quarter across all business segments. It is typical for orders to slow down during the fourth quarter, particularly in North America and there are some signs of that pattern developing in early December. However, given a strong backlog going into the fourth quarter, Co. expects significant year-over-year revenue growth. Co. expects to report fourth quarter revenue approximately 20.0% higher than the prior year. Co. expects earnings to approximate breakeven, including anticipated restructuring charges of $3.0 million to $6.0 million after-tax in the fourth quarter. Co. expects to be profitable for the year.

Financial Data

(US$ in Thousands)	9 Mos	6 Mos	3 Mos	02/27/2004	02/28/2003	02/22/2002	02/23/2001	02/25/2000
Earnings Per Share	(0.05)	(0.18)	(0.11)	(0.16)	(1.80)	0.01	1.29	1.21
Cash Flow Per Share	0.46	0.70	0.73	0.60	0.28	2.01	1.41	2.01
Tang Book Value Per Share	6.18	6.05	6.02	6.13	6.43	6.89	8.34	7.54
Dividends Per Share	0.240	0.240	0.240	0.240	0.240	0.390	0.440	0.440
Dividend Payout %	...	...	...	...	...	N.M.	34.11	36.36
Income Statement								
Total Revenue	1,922,800	1,248,700	597,700	2,345,600	2,586,900	3,089,500	3,885,800	3,316,100
EBITDA	113,900	73,000	26,500	64,800	114,900	183,300	475,900	437,500
Depn & Amortn	95,800	63,900	32,100	141,400	157,000	172,400	162,500	141,800
Income Before Taxes	6,000	800	(9,600)	(92,000)	(59,200)	(1,300)	303,700	296,400
Income Taxes	(4,700)	200	(2,900)	(50,600)	(22,200)	(1,500)	110,900	115,500
Net Income	11,700	1,600	(5,700)	(23,200)	(266,100)	1,000	193,700	184,200
Average Shares	148,200	148,100	148,000	148,000	147,700	147,700	149,800	152,880
Balance Sheet								
Current Assets	998,100	957,000	897,000	942,000	814,100	882,000	1,205,700	1,127,300
Total Assets	2,356,100	2,318,300	2,285,500	2,350,400	2,342,200	2,967,500	3,157,000	3,037,600
Current Liabilities	605,400	581,300	508,600	543,300	502,500	673,100	885,900	927,200
Long-Term Obligations	258,600	265,700	315,300	319,600	294,200	433,600	327,500	257,800
Total Liabilities	1,145,800	1,126,800	1,096,800	1,145,100	1,087,100	1,412,000	1,520,500	1,475,400
Stockholders' Equity	1,210,300	1,191,500	1,188,700	1,205,300	1,255,100	1,555,500	1,636,500	1,562,200
Shares Outstanding	148,517	148,308	148,258	147,979	147,612	147,291	147,585	151,158
Statistical Record								
Return on Assets %	N.M.	N.M.	N.M.	N.M.	N.M.	0.03	6.27	7.08
Return on Equity %	N.M.	N.M.	N.M.	N.M.	N.M.	0.06	12.14	12.06
EBITDA Margin %	5.92	5.85	4.43	2.76	4.44	5.93	12.25	13.19
Net Margin %	0.61	0.13	N.M.	N.M.	N.M.	0.03	4.98	5.55
Asset Turnover	1.07	1.05	1.05	1.00	0.96	1.01	1.26	1.27
Current Ratio	1.65	1.65	1.76	1.73	1.62	1.31	1.36	1.22
Debt to Equity	0.21	0.22	0.27	0.27	0.23	0.28	0.20	0.17
Price Range	14.65-11.40	14.50-11.23	14.50-9.99	14.50-8.64	17.65-8.55	15.81-11.35	18.13-10.38	20.44-10.38
P/E Ratio	...	...	...	...	...	N.M.	14.05-8.04	16.89-8.57
Average Yield %	1.80	1.86	1.91	2.05	1.87	2.91	3.00	2.96

Address: 901 44th Street SE, Grand Rapids, MI 49508	**Web Site:** www.steelcase.com	**Auditors:** BDO Seidman, LLP
Telephone: (616) 247-2710	**Officers:** Robert C. Pew III - Chmn. James P. Hackett - Pres., C.E.O.	**Investor Contact:** 616-247-2200
Fax: (616) 475-2270		

STERIS CORP.

Exchange	Symbol	Price	52Wk Range	Yield	P/E
NYS	STE	$25.25 (3/31/2005)	27.44-19.97	N/A	19.57

*7 Year Price Score 95.69   *NYSE Composite Index=100   *12 Month Price Score 100.36

Interim Earnings (Per Share)

Qtr.	Jun	Sep	Dec	Mar
2001-02	0.06	0.13	0.20	0.26
2002-03	0.18	0.26	0.30	0.37
2003-04	0.23	0.29	0.38	0.42
2004-05	0.25	0.27	0.35	...

Interim Dividends (Per Share)

No Dividends Paid

Valuation Analysis

Forecast P/E	16.69	No of Institutions
	(4/7/2005)	179
Market Cap	$1.7 Billion	Shares
Book Value	731.0 Million	57,691,256
Price/Book	2.39	% Held
Price/Sales	1.59	83.26

Business Summary: Medical Instruments & Equipment (MIC: 9.6 SIC: 842 NAIC: 39113)

STERIS is a worldwide provider of infection prevention, contamination prevention, microbial control, and surgical and critical care support products and services for healthcare, scientific, research, industrial, and government customers. Co.'s customer support facilities are located in major global market centers with production operations in the U.S., Canada, Germany, Finland, Sweden, and Australia. Co. provides low temperature sterilization, high temperature sterilization, washing and decontamination systems, surgical tables, surgical and examination lights, operating room storage cabinets, warming cabinets, scrub sinks, and associated consumables and services.

Recent Developments: For the quarter ended Dec 31 2004, net income decreased 9.7% to $24,457 thousand from net income of $27,093 thousand in the year-earlier quarter. Revenues were $284,389 thousand, up 3.7% from $274,286 thousand the year before. Operating income was $39,912 thousand versus an income of $37,826 thousand in the prior-year quarter, an increase of 5.5%. Total direct expense was $164,827 thousand versus $159,189 thousand in the prior-year quarter, an increase of 3.5%. Total indirect expense was $79,650 thousand versus $77,271 thousand in the prior-year quarter, an increase of 3.1%.

Prospects: On Jan 7 2005, Co. announced that it has acquired all five medical device sterilization locations of Cosmed Group, a privately-held contract sterilization services provider with corporate offices in Jamestown, RI, for $73.0 million. For the year ending Dec 31 2003, Cosmed's revenues were $21.0 million for these locations. Separately, for the fourth quarter of fiscal 2005, Co. currently anticipates revenue growth of 5.0% to 6.0% and earnings in the range of $0.41 to $0.43 per diluted share. Co. currently expects fiscal 2005 revenue growth of 2.0% to 3.0% and earnings to be in the range of $1.28 to $1.30 per diluted share.

Financial Data

(US$ in Thousands)	9 Mos	6 Mos	3 Mos	03/31/2004	03/31/2003	03/31/2002	03/31/2001	03/31/2000
Earnings Per Share	1.29	1.32	1.34	1.33	1.12	0.65	0.02	0.15
Cash Flow Per Share	2.23	2.27	2.25	1.77	1.92	2.05	1.51	1.05
Tang Book Value Per Share	6.46	6.08	6.40	6.43	5.41	4.27	3.44	3.21
Income Statement								
Total Revenue	804,032	519,643	254,797	1,087,012	972,087	866,697	800,087	760,626
EBITDA	136,287	83,204	39,717	189,039	172,284	127,497	70,745	72,750
Depn & Amortn	37,493	24,322	11,702	48,683	46,515	46,884	46,571	39,672
Income Before Taxes	96,774	57,496	27,314	138,084	124,118	73,337	5,757	16,912
Income Taxes	35,807	20,986	9,697	43,841	44,682	27,135	4,440	6,427
Net Income	60,967	36,510	17,617	94,243	79,436	46,202	1,317	10,485
Average Shares	69,838	69,744	70,442	70,742	70,870	70,607	68,981	68,567
Balance Sheet								
Current Assets	443,254	405,887	450,640	462,678	354,432	316,644	340,199	389,119
Total Assets	1,118,756	1,068,939	1,056,455	1,069,810	894,992	841,572	844,980	903,574
Current Liabilities	185,816	167,038	183,829	190,428	191,051	170,110	154,185	155,902
Long-Term Obligations	103,432	106,771	104,587	109,090	59,704	115,228	205,825	268,700
Total Liabilities	387,708	369,627	383,594	389,111	325,462	354,427	420,596	482,480
Stockholders' Equity	731,048	699,312	672,861	680,699	569,530	487,145	424,384	421,094
Shares Outstanding	69,176	69,117	69,038	69,946	69,741	69,466	68,665	67,517
Statistical Record								
Return on Assets %	8.59	9.23	9.43	9.57	9.15	5.48	0.15	1.18
Return on Equity %	13.26	14.35	15.19	15.03	15.04	10.14	0.31	2.44
EBITDA Margin %	16.95	16.01	15.59	17.39	17.72	14.71	8.84	9.56
Net Margin %	7.58	7.03	6.91	8.67	8.17	5.33	0.16	1.38
Asset Turnover	1.04	1.07	1.07	1.10	1.12	1.03	0.92	0.86
Current Ratio	2.39	2.43	2.45	2.43	1.86	1.86	2.21	2.50
Debt to Equity	0.14	0.15	0.16	0.16	0.10	0.24	0.48	0.64
Price Range	27.44-19.97	27.44-19.99	27.44-19.99	27.21-19.99	27.00-16.30	23.73-12.30	19.05-8.06	27.94-9.50
P/E Ratio	21.27-15.48	20.79-15.14	20.48-14.92	20.46-15.03	24.11-14.55	36.51-18.92	952.50-403.13	186.25-63.33

Address: 5960 Heisley Road, Mentor, OH 44060-1834	Web Site: www.steris.com	Auditors: Ernst & Young LLP
Telephone: (440) 354-2600	Officers: Jerry E. Robertson - Chmn. Les C. Vinney - Pres., C.E.O.	
Fax: (440) 639-4457		

STERLING BANCORP (N.Y.)

Exchange	Symbol	Price	52Wk Range	Yield	P/E	Div Acheiver
NYS	STL	$24.27 (3/31/2005)	28.44-20.97	3.13	17.72	10 Years

*7 Year Price Score 138.52 *NYSE Composite Index=100 *12 Month Price Score 96.78

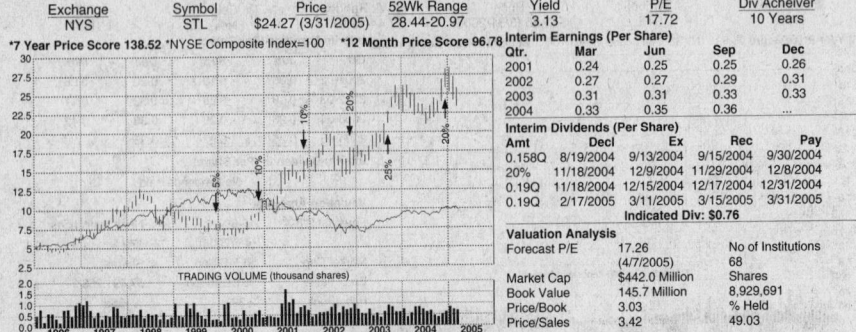

Interim Earnings (Per Share)

Qtr.	Mar	Jun	Sep	Dec
2001	0.24	0.25	0.25	0.26
2002	0.27	0.27	0.29	0.31
2003	0.31	0.31	0.33	0.33
2004	0.33	0.35	0.36	...

Interim Dividends (Per Share)

Amt	Decl	Ex	Rec	Pay
0.158Q	8/19/2004	9/13/2004	9/15/2004	9/30/2004
20%	11/18/2004	12/9/2004	11/29/2004	12/8/2004
0.19Q	11/18/2004	12/15/2004	12/17/2004	12/31/2004
0.19Q	2/17/2005	3/11/2005	3/15/2005	3/31/2005

Indicated Div: $0.76

Valuation Analysis

Forecast P/E	17.26	No of Institutions	
	(4/7/2005)	68	
Market Cap	$442.0 Million	Shares	
Book Value	145.7 Million	8,929,691	
Price/Book	3.03	% Held	
Price/Sales	3.42	49.03	

Business Summary: Commercial Banking (MIC: 8.1 SIC: 021 NAIC: 22110)

Sterling Bancorp is a financial holding company with assets of $1.76 billion and deposits of $8.89 billion as of Dec 31 2003. Co. offers a broad array of banking and financial services products such as business and consumer loans, commercial and residential mortgage lending and brokerage, asset-based financing, factoring/accounts receivable management services, trade financing, equipment leasing, deposit services, trust and estate administration and investment management services. Co. has operations in the metropolitan New York area, North Carolina and many mid-Atlantic states, and conducts business throughout the U.S.

Recent Developments: For the year ended Dec 31 2004, net income increased 2.9% to $24.6 million compared with $23.9 million a year earlier. Net interest income advanced 5.7% to $78.2 million from $74.0 million the previous year. Provision for loan losses amounted to $10.0 million versus $8.7 million the year before. Total noninterest income climbed 6.2% to $34.7 million from $32.7 million in 2003. Total noninterest expenses increased to $65.6 million, 10.7% higher than the year before.

Prospects: Co. is pleased with its continued solid growth trend. In fiscal 2004, Co. achieved an 11.0% increase in net income, a 9.0% increase in loans and a 12.2% increase in demand deposits, when compared to fiscal 2003 results. Co. believes these strong results are due to its continued focus on its core business. Going forward, Co. plans to invest in its franchise business, including expanding its presence in the New York region. Accordingly, Co. is planning the opening of a branch office at 42 Broadway, New York, in early 2005 to enhance its presence in this growing market.

Financial Data

(US$ in Thousands)	9 Mos	6 Mos	3 Mos	12/31/2003	12/31/2002	12/31/2001	12/31/2000	12/31/1999
Earnings Per Share	1.37	1.34	1.30	1.27	1.14	1.00	0.88	0.75
Cash Flow Per Share	4.40	3.30	1.76	2.40	1.12	(0.22)	1.95	2.12
Tang Book Value Per Share	6.84	6.48	6.87	6.68	5.97	5.78	5.19	4.48
Dividends Per Share	0.633	0.633	0.602	0.570	0.427	0.342	0.274	0.222
Dividend Payout %	46.18	47.33	46.23	44.71	37.43	34.24	31.14	29.44
Income Statement								
Interest Income	71,899	47,087	23,589	91,582	94,197	95,865	97,125	79,787
Interest Expense	14,108	9,058	4,539	17,591	19,447	26,816	34,242	26,325
Net Interest Income	57,791	38,029	19,050	73,992	74,750	69,050	62,883	53,462
Provision for Losses	7,236	4,897	2,427	8,740	10,771	7,401	6,563	5,584
Non-Interest Income	26,124	16,949	8,170	32,556	29,256	24,123	22,373	17,944
Non-Interest Expense	47,073	30,757	14,694	58,910	59,157	53,696	50,280	41,583
Income Before Taxes	29,607	19,324	10,099	38,897	34,078	32,076	28,413	24,240
Income Taxes	9,689	6,143	3,639	14,693	12,300	12,689	11,854	9,676
Net Income	19,918	13,180	6,461	24,204	21,778	19,388	16,559	14,564
Average Shares	19,040	19,241	19,261	18,909	19,037	19,304	18,715	19,273
Balance Sheet								
Net Loans & Leases	952,471	888,108	838,245	886,097	777,766	794,649	738,213	677,979
Total Assets	1,809,879	1,798,619	1,735,366	1,758,746	1,561,122	1,482,871	1,270,749	1,218,887
Total Deposits	1,299,370	1,255,787	1,223,297	1,211,741	1,047,093	984,924	866,282	862,520
Total Liabilities	1,664,133	1,659,367	1,586,992	1,615,560	1,406,341	1,354,394	1,153,733	1,113,647
Stockholders' Equity	145,746	139,252	148,374	143,185	129,780	128,477	117,016	105,240
Shares Outstanding	18,212	18,210	18,529	17,925	17,794	18,161	17,998	18,219
Statistical Record								
Return on Assets %	1.51	1.52	1.50	1.46	1.43	1.41	1.33	1.29
Return on Equity %	18.30	18.55	17.62	17.73	16.87	15.79	14.86	14.04
Net Interest Margin %	79.65	80.81	80.76	80.79	79.35	72.03	64.74	67.01
Efficiency Ratio %	48.00	49.77	46.27	47.46	47.92	44.75	42.08	42.55
Loans to Deposits	0.73	0.71	0.69	0.73	0.74	0.81	0.85	0.79
Price Range	26.17-20.97	26.17-18.43	26.17-16.27	26.13-16.15	19.83-14.19	16.69-9.97	11.05-6.54	9.98-7.13
P/E Ratio	19.10-15.30	19.53-13.75	20.13-12.52	20.58-12.71	17.40-12.45	16.69-9.97	12.55-7.43	13.30-9.51
Average Yield %	2.69	2.75	2.77	2.85	2.53	2.59	3.45	2.63

Address: 650 Fifth Avenue, New York, NY 10019-6108 **Telephone:** (212) 757-3300 **Fax:** (212) 421-6053	**Web Site:** www.sterlingbancorp.com **Officers:** Louis J. Cappelli - Chmn., C.E.O. John C. Millman - Pres.	**Auditors:** KPMG LLP **Investor Contact:** 212-757-3000

STORAGE TECHNOLOGY CORP.

Exchange	Symbol	Price	52Wk Range	Yield	P/E
NYS	STK	$30.80 (3/31/2005)	33.92-23.14	N/A	17.91

*7 Year Price Score 108.38 *NYSE Composite Index=100 *12 Month Price Score 105.28

Interim Earnings (Per Share)

Qtr.	Mar	Jun	Sep	Dec
2001	(0.03)	0.12	0.17	0.38
2002	0.06	0.18	0.22	0.56
2003	0.15	0.27	0.28	0.65
2004	0.21	0.32	0.39	0.81

Interim Dividends (Per Share)

No Dividends Paid

Valuation Analysis

Forecast P/E	15.91	No of Institutions
	(4/7/2005)	205
Market Cap	$3.3 Billion	Shares
Book Value	1.4 Billion	99,771,488
Price/Book	2.29	% Held
Price/Sales	1.49	91.55

Business Summary: IT & Technology (MIC: 10.2 SIC: 572 NAIC: 34112)

Storage Technology designs, develops, manufactures, and markets a range of information storage products and provides maintenance and consulting services. Co. is organized into two business segments: storage products and storage services. Co.'s storage product offerings include tape, disk and network products. The storage services segment is divided into two categories: maintenance services and consulting services. Co. provides maintenance services for both Co.'s products and third-party products, while the storage consulting services segment primarily supports sales of Co.'s hardware and software products, particularly for Virtual Storage Manager® and its storage networking products.

Recent Developments: For the year ended Dec 31 2004, net income increased 28.3% to $191,023 thousand from net income of $148,912 thousand a year earlier. Revenues were $2,224,000 thousand, up 1.9% from $2,182,560 thousand the year before. Operating income was $221,927 thousand versus an income of $193,112 thousand in the prior year, an increase of 14.9%. Total direct expense was $1,170,419 thousand versus $1,186,551 thousand in the prior year, a decrease of 1.4%. Total indirect expense was $831,654 thousand versus $802,897 thousand in the prior year, an increase of 3.6%.

Prospects: Co. is benefiting from solid growth in its storage services revenue and earnings. Also, Co. is benefiting from solid margin growth. For instance, at Dec 31 2004, Co.'s storage products margin increased 50.0%, up from 48% the previous year, and service margins grew 44.0% up from 43.0% at Dec 26 2003. Meanwhile, Co.'s Information Lifecycle Management strategy is resonating with customers as they struggle with increasing storage demands and stagnant budgets. Also, Co. will continue to move into new markets with new storage offerings to exploit its opportunities. In 2005, Co. will maintain its disciplined approach to capital management that it has built over the last few years.

Financial Data

(US$ in Thousands)	12/31/2004	12/26/2003	12/27/2002	12/28/2001	12/29/2000	12/31/1999	12/25/1998	12/26/1997
Earnings Per Share	1.72	1.35	1.02	0.64	(0.02)	(0.75)	1.86	1.90
Cash Flow Per Share	3.47	3.38	3.44	2.59	3.35	1.24	0.85	3.72
Tang Book Value Per Share	13.42	12.28	10.86	9.87	9.11	9.13	9.97	10.39
Income Statement								
Total Revenue	2,224,000	2,182,560	2,039,615	2,045,322	2,060,204	2,368,231	2,258,222	2,144,656
EBITDA	300,412	281,002	228,689	205,478	107,018	14,271	404,089	369,813
Depn & Amortn	78,485	87,890	90,533	107,026	103,001	111,507	91,284	79,052
Income Before Taxes	236,921	201,912	146,331	101,807	(2,741)	(116,450)	319,748	316,117
Income Taxes	45,898	53,000	36,300	34,600	(959)	(41,900)	121,500	84,300
Net Income	191,023	148,912	110,031	67,207	(1,782)	(74,550)	198,248	231,817
Average Shares	111,243	110,648	107,437	104,929	100,859	99,900	106,497	122,514
Balance Sheet								
Current Assets	1,952,485	1,805,170	1,464,239	1,254,526	1,173,442	1,228,086	1,364,439	1,269,611
Total Assets	2,407,841	2,305,246	1,976,140	1,758,883	1,653,558	1,735,475	1,842,944	1,740,017
Current Liabilities	955,027	932,658	808,016	714,540	702,840	787,323	826,108	608,405
Long-Term Obligations	11,006	11,150	10,361	9,523	12,083	28,953	17,260	19,109
Total Liabilities	966,033	943,808	818,377	724,063	714,923	816,276	843,368	627,514
Stockholders' Equity	1,441,808	1,361,438	1,157,763	1,034,820	938,635	919,199	999,576	1,112,503
Shares Outstanding	107,427	110,835	106,611	104,832	103,058	100,711	100,221	107,089
Statistical Record								
Return on Assets %	7.97	6.98	5.91	3.95	N.M.	N.M.	11.10	12.83
Return on Equity %	13.41	11.85	10.06	6.83	N.M.	N.M.	18.82	20.27
EBITDA Margin %	13.51	12.87	11.21	10.05	5.19	0.60	17.89	17.24
Net Margin %	8.59	6.82	5.39	3.29	N.M.	N.M.	8.78	10.81
Asset Turnover	0.93	1.02	1.10	1.20	1.22	1.30	1.26	1.19
Current Ratio	2.04	1.94	1.81	1.76	1.67	1.56	1.65	2.09
Debt to Equity	0.01	0.01	0.01	0.01	0.01	0.03	0.02	0.02
Price Range	31.62-23.14	27.90-20.00	24.84-10.13	22.75-9.00	18.44-9.00	40.00-14.63	50.19-21.63	33.19-17.00
P/E Ratio	18.38-13.45	20.67-14.81	24.35-9.93	35.55-14.06	...	...	26.98-11.63	17.47-8.95

Address: One StorageTek Drive,	Web Site: www.storagetek.com	Auditors: PricewaterhouseCoopers LLP
Louisville, CO 80028-4309	Officers: Patrick J. Martin - Chmn., Pres., C.E.O.	Investor Contact: 303-673-5020
Telephone: (303) 673-5151	Robert S. Kocol - V.P., C.F.O.	Transfer Agents: American Stock
Fax: (303) 673-5019		Transfer & Trust Co., New York, NY

STRYKER CORP.

Exchange	Symbol	Price	52Wk Range	Yield	P/E	Div Acheiver
NYS	SYK	$44.61 (3/31/2005)	57.33-41.75	0.13	39.13	12 Years

*7 Year Price Score 149.63 *NYSE Composite Index=100   *12 Month Price Score 94.80

Business Summary: Medical Instruments & Equipment (MIC: 9.6 SIC: 841 NAIC: 39112)

Stryker develops, manufactures and markets specialty surgical and medical products. Operations are divided into two reportable business segments: Orthopaedic Implants and MedSurg Equipment. The Orthopaedic Implants segment includes orthopaedic reconstructive (hip, knee and shoulder), trauma and spinal implants, bone cement and the bone growth factor osteogenic protein-1. The MedSurg Equipment segment includes powered surgical instruments, endoscopic products, hospital beds and stretchers and micro implant and surgical navigation systems. Co. also provides outpatient physical and occupational rehabilitative services in the U.S.

Recent Developments: For the year ended Dec 31 2004, net income increased 2.7% to $465,700 thousand from net income of $453,500 thousand a year earlier. Revenues were $4,262,300 thousand, up 17.6% from $3,625,300 thousand the year before. Operating income was $720,400 thousand versus an income of $671,300 thousand in the prior year, an increase of 7.3%. Total direct expense was $1,510,100 thousand versus $1,312,400 thousand in the prior year, an increase of 15.1%. Total indirect expense was $2,031,800 thousand versus $1,641,600 thousand in the prior year, an increase of 23.8%.

Prospects: Going forward, Co. should continue to perform well, supported by strong demand for its reconstructive (hip, knee and shoulder), trauma, spine and micro implant systems, the bone growth factor osteogenic protein-1 (OP-1) and bone cement. Co.'s recently acquired SpineCore business should allow Co. access to that company's artificial spine technology. Co. expects the commercialization of SpineCore's products to occur 2008. Co. expects development of products in 2008. Meanwhile, Co. should benefit from steady demand for its MedSurg Equipment, particularly its powered surgical instruments, endoscopic products, patient handling and emergency medical equipment and surgical navigation systems.

Financial Data

(US$ in Thousands)	12/31/2004	12/31/2003	12/31/2002	12/31/2001	12/31/2000	12/31/1999	12/31/1998	12/31/1997
Earnings Per Share	1.14	1.12	0.85	0.66	0.55	0.05	0.10	0.32
Cash Flow Per Share	1.47	1.63	1.28	1.19	0.85	0.73	0.40	0.24
Tang Book Value Per Share	4.44	2.98	1.42	0.65	0.04	N.M.	N.M.	1.47
Dividends Per Share	0.090	0.070	0.060	0.050	0.040	0.033	0.030	0.028
Dividend Payout %	7.89	6.28	7.06	7.58	7.27	65.00	30.00	8.59
Income Statement								
Total Revenue	4,262,300	3,625,300	3,011,600	2,602,300	2,289,400	2,103,700	1,103,208	980,135
EBITDA	874,300	817,700	604,400	509,700	471,500	186,300	97,556	227,714
Depn & Amortn	150,500	142,600	57,400	36,100	40,000	33,900	37,596	33,264
Income Before Taxes	717,000	652,500	506,700	405,700	334,900	29,800	59,960	194,450
Income Taxes	251,300	199,000	161,100	133,900	113,900	10,400	20,390	70,000
Net Income	465,700	453,500	345,600	267,000	221,000	19,400	39,570	125,320
Average Shares	410,300	406,800	407,600	406,000	402,200	397,200	392,520	392,528
Balance Sheet								
Current Assets	2,142,600	1,397,600	1,151,300	993,100	997,000	1,110,400	1,311,843	756,608
Total Assets	4,083,800	3,159,100	2,815,500	2,423,600	2,430,800	2,580,500	2,885,852	985,075
Current Liabilities	1,113,500	850,500	707,500	533,400	617,400	669,600	699,455	303,011
Long-Term Obligations	700	18,800	491,000	720,900	876,500	1,181,100	1,487,971	4,449
Total Liabilities	1,331,800	1,004,300	1,317,300	1,367,400	1,575,900	1,909,000	2,233,777	372,300
Stockholders' Equity	2,752,000	2,154,800	1,498,200	1,056,200	854,900	671,500	652,075	612,775
Shares Outstanding	402,500	399,400	396,200	393,400	391,800	388,800	386,160	384,236
Statistical Record								
Return on Assets %	12.82	15.18	13.19	11.00	8.80	0.71	2.04	12.67
Return on Equity %	18.93	24.83	27.06	27.94	28.88	2.93	6.26	21.93
EBITDA Margin %	20.51	22.56	20.07	19.59	20.59	8.86	8.84	23.23
Net Margin %	10.93	12.51	11.48	10.26	9.65	0.92	3.59	12.79
Asset Turnover	1.17	1.21	1.15	1.07	0.91	0.77	0.57	0.99
Current Ratio	1.92	1.64	1.63	1.86	1.61	1.66	1.88	2.50
Debt to Equity	N.M.	0.01	0.33	0.68	1.03	1.76	2.28	0.01
Price Range	57.33-41.75	42.51-30.12	33.62-22.72	30.75-22.06	27.00-12.75	17.92-11.19	13.77-7.86	11.16-6.20
P/E Ratio	50.29-36.62	37.95-26.89	39.55-26.73	46.60-33.42	49.09-23.18	358.44-223.75	137.66-78.59	34.86-19.38
Average Yield %	0.19	0.19	0.21	0.19	0.20	0.23	0.29	0.31

Address: 2725 Fairfield Road, Kalamazoo, MI 49002	**Web Site:** www.stryker.com	**Auditors:** Ernst & Young LLP
Telephone: (269) 385-2600	**Officers:** John W. Brown - Chmn. Stephen P. MacMillan - Pres., C.E.O.	**Investor Contact:** 616-385-2600
Fax: (269) 385-1062		**Transfer Agents:** National City Bank, Cleveland, OH

STUDENT LOAN CORP. (THE)

Exchange	Symbol	Price	52Wk Range	Yield	P/E
NYS	STU	$209.01 (3/31/2005)	210.01-130.31	2.07	14.67

*7 Year Price Score 159.92 *NYSE Composite Index=100 *12 Month Price Score 117.26

Interim Earnings (Per Share)

Qtr.	Mar	Jun	Sep	Dec
2001	1.11	1.95	1.54	2.17
2002	2.48	2.11	2.03	2.15
2003	3.08	2.31	2.58	2.65
2004	3.64	3.48	3.48	...

Interim Dividends (Per Share)

Amt	Decl	Ex	Rec	Pay
0.90Q	4/15/2004	5/12/2004	5/14/2004	6/1/2004
0.90Q	7/15/2004	8/11/2004	8/13/2004	9/1/2004
0.90Q	10/14/2004	11/10/2004	11/15/2004	12/1/2004
1.08Q	1/24/2005	2/11/2005	2/15/2005	3/1/2005
		Indicated Div: $4.32		

Valuation Analysis

Forecast P/E	N/A	No of Institutions
Market Cap	$4.2 Billion	Shares
Book Value	1.1 Billion	19,285,160
Price/Book	3.64	% Held
Price/Sales	4.26	96.43

Business Summary: Credit & Lending (MIC: 8.6 SIC: 111 NAIC: 22298)

The Student Loan Corp. originates, manages and services federally insured student loans through a trust agreement with Citibank, N.A., an indirect wholly-owned subsidiary of Citigroup Inc. Co. is one of the nation's largest originators and holders of student loans guaranteed under the Federal Family Education Loan Program (FFEL), and authorized by the U.S. Department of Education. Co. is eligible to make the following types of FFEL Program loans: subsidized Federal Stafford, unsubsidized Federal Stafford, Federal Parent Loans to Undergraduate Students and Federal Consolidation Loans. Co. also holds student loans not insured under the Federal Higher Education Act of 1965, such as CitiAssist.

Recent Developments: For the year ended Dec 31 2004, net income increased 34.3% to $284,956 thousand from net income of $212,204 thousand a year earlier. Provision for loan losses was $7,989 thousand versus $10,358 thousand in the prior year, a decrease of 22.9%. Non-interest income rose 115.6% to $41,478 thousand, while non-interest expense advanced 16.0% to $132,262 thousand.

Prospects: Co.'s results are being fueled by a combination of solid portfolio growth and improved net interest margins. For 2004, Co.'s student loan assets totaled $24.90 billion, growing $1.70 billion from the 2003 year-end balance. Combined Federal Family Education Loan Program (FFELP) Stafford and PLUS disbursements and new CitiAssist loan commitments for 2004 totaled $4.50 billion, up approximately 16.0% from a year earlier. Also, Co. is experiencing reduced provisions for loan losses, due primarily to lower estimates of future risk-sharing liabilities. Also, Co.'s return on equity for fiscal 2004 improved to 27.3%, up 2.4% from 24.9% in 2003.

Financial Data

(US$ in Thousands)	12/31/2004	12/31/2003	12/31/2002	12/31/2001	12/31/2000	12/31/1999	12/31/1998	12/31/1997
Earnings Per Share	14.25	10.61	8.77	6.77	5.24	4.47	3.67	2.58
Cash Flow Per Share	21.30	17.63	12.37	19.74	7.41	(1.72)	5.98	1.49
Tang Book Value Per Share	57.35	46.57	38.25	32.59	28.61	25.76	23.23	20.16
Dividends Per Share	3.600	3.080	2.800	2.800	2.400	1.950	0.600	0.540
Dividend Payout %	25.26	29.03	31.93	41.36	45.80	43.62	16.35	20.93
Income Statement								
Interest Income	939,187	833,593	974,590	1,151,632	1,093,728	719,949	646,558	588,480
Interest Expense	378,191	379,078	581,242	835,115	835,465	494,167	454,227	412,541
Net Interest Income	560,996	454,515	393,348	316,517	258,263	225,782	192,331	175,939
Provision for Losses	7,989	9,277	11,214	7,324	5,587	4,487	3,882	3,310
Non-Interest Income	41,478	19,237	22,367	10,599	6,365	3,794	2,323	3,292
Non-Interest Expense	132,262	115,051	108,879	91,804	79,600	71,763	65,618	88,607
Income Before Taxes	462,223	349,424	295,622	227,988	179,441	153,326	125,154	87,314
Income Taxes	177,267	137,220	120,131	92,627	74,560	63,868	51,745	35,644
Net Income	284,956	212,204	175,491	135,361	104,881	89,458	73,409	51,670
Average Shares	20,000	20,000	20,000	20,000	20,000	20,000	20,000	...
Balance Sheet								
Net Loans & Leases	24,883,549	23,221,754	20,530,382	18,233,382	15,771,419	10,861,212	8,633,973	7,623,143
Total Assets	25,452,841	23,705,143	21,005,604	18,717,096	16,243,231	11,196,468	8,903,142	7,873,112
Total Liabilities	24,305,934	22,773,819	20,240,568	18,065,394	15,670,969	10,681,336	8,438,611	7,469,990
Stockholders' Equity	1,146,907	931,324	765,036	651,702	572,262	515,132	464,531	403,122
Shares Outstanding	20,000	20,000	20,000	20,000	20,000	20,000	20,000	20,000
Statistical Record								
Return on Assets %	1.16	0.47	0.88	0.77	0.38	0.89	0.88	0.66
Return on Equity %	27.35	12.51	24.77	22.12	9.65	18.26	16.92	12.82
Net Interest Margin %	59.73	54.52	40.36	27.48	23.61	31.36	29.75	29.90
Efficiency Ratio %	13.49	13.49	10.92	7.90	7.24	9.92	10.11	14.97
Price Range	186.69-130.31	146.00-90.91	101.15-74.90	83.20-52.50	56.00-37.19	50.38-37.38	51.06-40.00	53.94-35.75
P/E Ratio	13.10-9.14	13.76-8.57	11.53-8.54	12.29-7.75	10.69-7.10	11.27-8.36	13.91-10.90	20.91-13.86
Average Yield %	2.40	2.64	3.08	4.01	5.28	4.46	1.28	1.27

Address: 750 Washington Blvd., Stamford, CT 06901
Telephone: (203) 975-6237
Fax: (203) 975-6299

Web Site: www.studentloan.com
Officers: Bill Beckmann - Chmn. Sue F. Roberts - Pres.

Auditors: KPMG LLP
Investor Contact: 203-975-6292
Transfer Agents: Citibank Stockholder Services, Providence, RI

SUN COMMUNITIES, INC.

Exchange	Symbol	Price	52Wk Range	Yield	P/E	Div Acheiver
NYS	SUI	$35.80 (3/31/2005)	42.82-34.00	7.04	N/A	10 Years

*7 Year Price Score 91.21   *NYSE Composite Index=100   *12 Month Price Score 88.51

Interim Earnings (Per Share)

Qtr.	Mar	Jun	Sep	Dec
2001	0.64	0.48	0.45	0.38
2002	0.46	0.39	0.32	(0.42)
2003	0.35	0.25	0.34	0.34
2004	0.30	(2.57)	0.03	0.05

Interim Dividends (Per Share)

Amt	Decl	Ex	Rec	Pay
0.61Q	7/1/2004	7/8/2004	7/12/2004	7/22/2004
0.61Q	10/1/2004	10/7/2004	10/12/2004	10/20/2004
0.61Q	1/3/2005	1/10/2005	1/12/2005	1/21/2005
0.63Q	3/22/2005	4/7/2005	4/11/2005	4/21/2005
		Indicated Div: $2.52		

Valuation Analysis

Forecast P/E	12.77	No of Institutions	
	(4/7/2005)	99	
Market Cap	$659.6 Million	Shares	14,601,413
Book Value	211.7 Million	% Held	
Price/Book	3.11	79.26	
Price/Sales	3.28		

Business Summary: Property, Real Estate & Development (MIC: 8.3 SIC: 798 NAIC: 25930)

Sun Communities is a real estate investment trust. Co. owns, operates, develops and finances manufactured housing communities concentrated in the midwestern and southeastern U.S. As of Dec 31 2003, Co. owned and operated a portfolio of 127 properties located in 17 states, including 115 manufactured housing communities, five recreational vehicle communities, and seven properties containing both manufactured housing and recreational vehicle sites. As of Dec 31 2003, Co.'s properties contained an aggregate of 43,875 developed sites comprised of 38,797 developed manufactured home sites and 5,078 recreational vehicle sites and an additional 6,756 manufactured home sites suitable for development.

Recent Developments: For the year ended Dec 31 2004, net loss was $40,468 thousand versus income from continuing operations of $13,742 thousand a year earlier. Results for 2004 included a charge of $51,643 thousand associated with extinguishment of debt, deferred financing costs related to extinguished debt of $5,557 thousand, and costs of $600,000 related to Florida storm damage. Results for 2003 included an impairment charge of $4,932 thousand. Revenues were $200,853 thousand, up 4.4% from $192,452 thousand the year before. Revenues for 2004 included a gain of $5,879 thousand on the sale of land.

Prospects: Through Feb 19 2005, Co. added 61 net leased sites, which represent five weeks of positive performance after losses of 42 net sites in the first two weeks of the year. This leasing rate, if maintained, will result in 445 net leased sites, which is the plan for 2005. For the first fifty days of 2005, Co. has averaged leasing gains and losses of 7.8 and 6.6 per day, respectively. Looking ahead, Co. is anticipating a gradual recovery in new homes sales beginning in 2005. Also, Co. expects occupancy in its portfolio of manufactured housing communities will increase.

Financial Data

(US$ in Thousands)	12/31/2004	12/31/2003	12/31/2002	12/31/2001	12/31/2000	12/31/1999	12/31/1998	12/31/1997
Earnings Per Share	(2.21)	1.29	0.76	1.94	1.91	1.68	1.53	1.37
Cash Flow Per Share	3.15	3.48	2.90	3.82	3.27	3.58	3.12	2.50
Tang Book Value Per Share	11.49	17.20	17.67	18.56	19.19	19.38	19.72	19.70
Dividends Per Share	2.440	2.410	2.290	2.180	2.100	1.530	2.430	1.865
Dividend Payout %	...	186.82	301.32	112.37	109.95	91.07	158.82	136.13
Income Statement								
Property Income	167,835	159,115	151,612	139,022	132,440	125,424	114,346	93,188
Non-Property Income	33,018	30,023	10,684	14,532	14,105	8,992	6,242	3,053
Total Revenue	200,853	189,138	162,296	153,554	146,545	134,416	120,588	96,241
Depn & Amortn	51,670	46,302	39,756	34,581	943	29,416	25,642	20,668
Interest Expense	48,243	36,680	32,375	31,016	29,651	26,751	24,245	14,534
Income Before Taxes	(41,394)	25,362	23,118	47,246	46,304	37,435	32,054	27,927
Net Income	(40,468)	23,714	13,592	33,910	33,294	29,089	26,096	22,255
Average Shares	18,318	18,345	17,781	17,440	17,390	17,343	17,031	16,268
Balance Sheet								
Total Assets	1,403,167	1,221,574	1,163,976	994,449	966,628	911,083	821,439	690,914
Long-Term Obligations	1,078,442	674,328	604,373	402,198	452,508	358,473	339,164	247,264
Total Liabilities	1,110,378	798,161	691,954	521,810	489,651	432,391	389,852	281,882
Stockholders' Equity	211,746	326,610	319,532	329,641	336,034	338,358	340,364	326,780
Shares Outstanding	18,424	18,990	18,079	17,763	17,509	17,459	17,256	16,587
Statistical Record								
Return on Assets %	N.M.	1.99	1.26	3.46	3.54	3.36	3.45	3.49
Return on Equity %	N.M.	7.34	4.19	10.19	9.85	8.57	7.82	7.09
Net Margin %	(20.15)	12.54	8.37	22.08	22.72	21.64	21.64	23.12
Price Range	42.82-34.00	40.85-33.20	42.12-32.60	38.55-30.99	35.63-27.38	37.00-29.88	36.25-30.50	37.88-30.50
P/E Ratio	...	31.67-25.74	55.42-42.89	19.87-15.97	18.65-14.33	22.02-17.78	23.69-19.93	27.65-22.26
Average Yield %	6.31	6.36	6.00	6.26	6.68	4.56	7.18	5.47

Address: 27777 Franklin Road, Suite 200, Southfield, MI 48034	**Web Site:** www.suncommunities.com	**Auditors:** Grant Thornton LLP
Telephone: (248) 208-2500	**Officers:** Gary A. Shiffman - Chmn., Pres., C.E.O.	**Investor Contact:** 248-932-3100
Fax: (248) 932-4070	Jeffrey P. Jorissen - Sr. V.P., C.F.O., Treas., Sec.	

SUNGARD DATA SYSTEMS INC.

Exchange	Symbol	Price	52Wk Range	Yield	P/E
NYS	SDS	$34.50 (3/31/2005)	34.50-22.54	N/A	22.40

*7 Year Price Score 100.17 *NYSE Composite Index=100 *12 Month Price Score 99.25

Interim Earnings (Per Share)

Qtr.	Mar	Jun	Sep	Dec
2001	0.20	0.22	0.22	0.22
2002	0.24	0.28	0.27	0.33
2003	0.26	0.31	0.31	0.38
2004	0.29	0.35	0.52	0.38

Interim Dividends (Per Share)

Amt	Decl	Ex	Rec	Pay
2-for-1	5/14/2001	6/19/2001	5/25/2001	6/18/2001

Valuation Analysis

Forecast P/E	22.19	No of Institutions
	(4/7/2005)	442
Market Cap	$9.9 Billion	Shares
Book Value	3.3 Billion	231,065,776
Price/Book	3.06	% Held
Price/Sales	2.80	80.06

Business Summary: IT & Technology (MIC: 10.2 SIC: 374 NAIC: 18210)

SunGard Data Systems is engaged in integrated software and processing solutions for financial services. Co. serves more than 20,000 clients in over 50 countries, including the world's 50 largest financial services institutions. Co. offers integrated, Web-enabled services and software for the management, trading, processing and accounting of financial assets and offers high-availability infrastructure, outsourcing and hosting for on-line and other operations. Co.'s products and services generally are delivered and supported through individual business units that offer product-specific development and customer support.

Recent Developments: For the year ended Dec 31 2004, net income increased 22.5% to $453,641 thousand from net income of $370,310 thousand a year earlier. Revenues were $3,555,871 thousand, up 20.3% from $2,955,252 thousand the year before. Operating income was $703,384 thousand versus an income of $623,609 thousand in the prior year, an increase of 12.8%. Total direct expense was $1,607,614 thousand versus $1,291,925 thousand in the prior year, an increase of 24.4%. Total indirect expense was $1,244,873 thousand versus $1,039,718 thousand in the prior year, an increase of 19.7%.

Prospects: On Oct 4 2004, Co. announced that it plans to spin off its availability services business to stockholders through a tax-free distribution of shares. The spin-off is expected to be completed during the second quarter of 2005. Going forward, Co.'s outlook for 2005 diluted net income per share is in the range of $1.51 to $1.57 per share, representing growth of between 8.0% and 12.0%. Co. expects growth in internal revenue in both its Software & Processing business and its Availability Services business to be in the low to middle single digits for the full-year 2005.

Financial Data

(US$ in Thousands)	12/31/2004	12/31/2003	12/31/2002	12/31/2001	12/31/2000	12/31/1999	12/31/1998	12/31/1997
Earnings Per Share	1.54	1.27	1.12	0.86	0.79	0.44	0.55	0.44
Cash Flow Per Share	2.71	2.26	2.77	1.72	1.23	1.04	1.09	0.87
Tang Book Value Per Share	1.80	2.75	2.85	2.74	3.73	3.46	2.52	1.14
Income Statement								
Total Revenue	3,555,871	2,955,252	2,593,237	1,928,673	1,660,708	1,444,501	1,159,748	862,151
EBITDA	1,118,479	932,135	816,024	563,152	481,324	297,960	310,642	228,808
Depn & Amortn	337,029	311,406	268,061	175,832	146,062	122,045	107,796	94,763
Income Before Taxes	761,136	615,124	543,297	410,472	356,766	190,456	208,228	133,704
Income Taxes	307,495	244,814	217,656	164,417	143,794	117,306	89,295	56,158
Net Income	453,641	370,310	325,641	246,055	212,972	83,820	118,933	77,546
Average Shares	294,891	292,067	289,654	285,112	271,404	260,390	216,146	178,670
Balance Sheet								
Current Assets	1,794,486	1,363,292	1,135,016	1,118,204	911,742	786,807	584,316	310,079
Total Assets	5,194,641	4,000,107	3,281,596	2,898,158	1,845,185	1,564,762	1,075,321	786,334
Current Liabilities	1,376,125	1,047,385	871,233	748,828	394,770	348,478	311,614	224,523
Long-Term Obligations	509,046	186,854	187,964	355,474	7,939	5,517	2,816	2,765
Total Liabilities	1,943,005	1,234,239	1,059,197	1,104,302	402,709	353,995	314,430	227,288
Stockholders' Equity	3,251,636	2,765,868	2,222,399	1,793,856	1,442,476	1,210,767	760,891	559,046
Shares Outstanding	288,328	288,536	283,738	280,772	266,658	257,010	211,424	177,724
Statistical Record								
Return on Assets %	9.84	10.17	10.54	10.37	12.46	6.35	12.78	10.58
Return on Equity %	15.04	14.85	16.22	15.21	16.01	8.50	18.02	15.15
EBITDA Margin %	31.45	31.54	31.47	29.20	28.98	20.63	26.79	26.54
Net Margin %	12.76	12.53	12.56	12.76	12.82	5.80	10.26	8.99
Asset Turnover	0.77	0.81	0.84	0.81	0.97	1.09	1.25	1.18
Current Ratio	1.30	1.30	1.30	1.49	2.31	2.26	1.88	1.38
Debt to Equity	0.16	0.07	0.08	0.20	0.01	N.M.	N.M.	N.M.
Price Range	31.49-22.54	29.32-17.74	34.89-14.88	32.20-20.53	26.00-11.88	20.75-8.63	19.97-10.88	15.44-9.56
P/E Ratio	20.45-14.64	23.09-13.97	31.15-13.29	37.44-23.87	32.91-15.03	47.16-19.60	36.31-19.77	35.09-21.73

Address: 1285 Drummers Lane, Wayne, PA 19087 **Telephone:** (610) 341-8700 **Fax:** (610) 341-8739	**Web Site:** www.sungard.com **Officers:** James L. Mann - Chmn. Till M. Guldimann - Vice-Chmn.	**Auditors:** PricewaterhouseCoopers LLP **Investor Contact:** 610-341-8709

SUNOCO, INC.

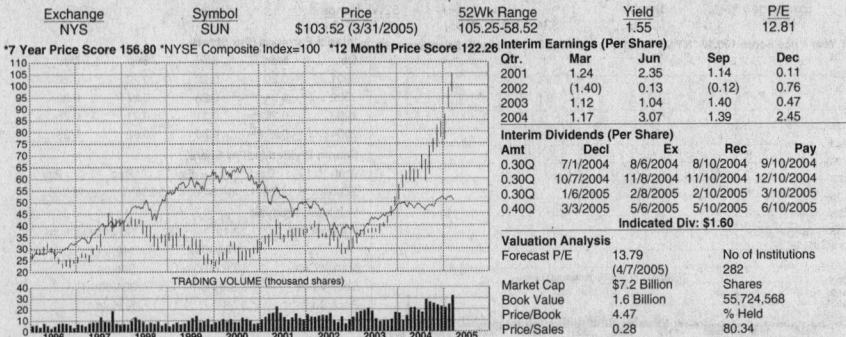

Exchange	Symbol	Price	52Wk Range	Yield	P/E
NYS	SUN	$103.52 (3/31/2005)	105.25-58.52	1.55	12.81

*7 Year Price Score 156.80 *NYSE Composite Index=100 *12 Month Price Score 122.26

Interim Earnings (Per Share)

Qtr.	Mar	Jun	Sep	Dec
2001	1.24	2.35	1.14	0.11
2002	(1.40)	0.13	(0.12)	0.76
2003	1.12	1.04	1.40	0.47
2004	1.17	3.07	1.39	2.45

Interim Dividends (Per Share)

Amt	Decl	Ex	Rec	Pay
0.30Q	7/1/2004	8/6/2004	8/10/2004	9/10/2004
0.30Q	10/7/2004	11/8/2004	11/10/2004	12/10/2004
0.30Q	1/6/2005	2/8/2005	2/10/2005	3/10/2005
0.40Q	3/3/2005	5/6/2005	5/10/2005	6/10/2005

Indicated Div: $1.60

Valuation Analysis

Forecast P/E	13.79	No of Institutions
	(4/7/2005)	282
Market Cap	$7.2 Billion	Shares
Book Value	1.6 Billion	55,724,568
Price/Book	4.47	% Held
Price/Sales	0.28	80.34

TRADING VOLUME (thousand shares)

Business Summary: Oil and Gas (MIC: 14.2 SIC: 911 NAIC: 24110)

Sunoco is principally a petroleum refiner and marketer and chemicals manufacturer with interests in logistics and cokemaking. Co.'s petroleum refining and marketing operations include the manufacturing and marketing of a full range of petroleum products, including fuels, lubricants and some petrochemicals. Co.'s chemical operations comprise the manufacturing, distribution and marketing of commodity and intermediate petrochemicals. The petroleum refining and marketing, chemicals and logistics operations are conducted mainly in the eastern half of the United States. As of Dec 31 2003, Co. operated five refineries and a network of 4,528 retail outlets in 25 states.

Recent Developments: For the year ended Dec 31 2004, net income increased 93.9% to $605 million from net income of $312 million a year earlier. Revenues were $25,508 million, up 41.6% from $18,016 million the year before. Total direct expense was $20,734 million versus $14,154 million in the prior year, an increase of 46.5%. Total indirect expense was $3,682 million versus $3,253 million in the prior year, an increase of 13.2%.

Prospects: In 2005, Co. expects to invest $846.0 million in capital expenditures. Further, Co. specifically plans to invest about $587.0 million in refining and supply, about $130.0 million in retail marketing, approximately $74.0 million in chemicals, about $30.0 million in logistics, and approximately $25.0 million in coke. Subsequent to releasing its fourth quarter earnings on Jan 20 2005, Co. was informed by its independent auditors that the major public accounting firms were reevaluating the accounting by many companies for certain insurance policies issued through an energy industry mutual insurance consortium. Co. expects its 10-K filing to reflect the subsequent revised accounting treatment.

Financial Data

(US$ in Thousands)	12/31/2004	12/31/2003	12/31/2002	12/31/2001	12/31/2000	12/31/1999	12/31/1998	12/31/1997
Earnings Per Share	8.08	4.03	(0.62)	4.85	4.82	1.07	2.95	2.70
Cash Flow Per Share	23.51	12.95	7.18	9.63	8.92	5.53	4.18	6.25
Tang Book Value Per Share	23.18	20.64	18.24	21.74	20.06	16.77	16.82	10.41
Dividends Per Share	1.150	1.025	1.000	1.000	1.000	1.000	1.000	1.000
Dividend Payout %	14.23	25.43	...	20.62	20.75	93.46	33.90	37.04
Income Statement								
Total Revenue	25,508,000	17,929,000	14,384,000	14,143,000	14,300,000	10,068,000	8,583,000	10,531,000
EBITDA	1,501,000	969,000	364,000	1,011,000	972,000	508,000	717,000	715,000
Depn & Amortn	409,000	363,000	329,000	321,000	298,000	276,000	257,000	259,000
Income Before Taxes	995,000	495,000	(73,000)	587,000	596,000	150,000	389,000	385,000
Income Taxes	390,000	183,000	(26,000)	189,000	185,000	53,000	109,000	122,000
Net Income	605,000	312,000	(47,000)	398,000	422,000	97,000	280,000	263,000
Average Shares	74,900	77,500	76,200	82,000	87,500	91,000	95,000	97,400
Balance Sheet								
Current Assets	2,551,000	2,068,000	1,898,000	1,510,000	1,683,000	1,456,000	1,180,000	1,248,000
Total Assets	8,079,000	6,922,000	6,441,000	5,932,000	5,426,000	5,196,000	4,849,000	4,667,000
Current Liabilities	3,022,000	2,170,000	1,776,000	1,778,000	1,646,000	1,766,000	1,384,000	1,464,000
Long-Term Obligations	1,379,000	1,350,000	1,453,000	1,142,000	933,000	878,000	823,000	824,000
Total Liabilities	6,472,000	5,366,000	5,047,000	4,290,000	3,724,000	3,690,000	3,335,000	3,205,000
Stockholders' Equity	1,607,000	1,556,000	1,394,000	1,642,000	1,702,000	1,506,000	1,514,000	1,462,000
Shares Outstanding	69,327	75,380	76,439	75,529	84,832	89,800	90,000	71,000
Statistical Record								
Return on Assets %	8.04	4.67	N.M.	7.01	7.92	1.93	5.88	5.43
Return on Equity %	38.15	21.15	N.M.	23.80	26.24	6.42	18.82	18.14
EBITDA Margin %	5.88	5.40	2.53	7.15	6.80	5.05	8.35	6.79
Net Margin %	2.37	1.74	N.M.	2.81	2.95	0.96	3.26	2.50
Asset Turnover	3.39	2.68	2.33	2.49	2.69	2.00	1.80	2.17
Current Ratio	0.84	0.95	1.07	0.85	1.02	0.82	0.85	0.85
Debt to Equity	0.86	0.87	1.04	0.70	0.55	0.58	0.54	0.56
Price Range	84.39-50.79	52.20-29.99	41.89-27.31	42.50-29.38	33.88-22.31	39.00-23.06	43.81-29.50	45.63-24.00
P/E Ratio	10.44-6.29	12.95-7.44	...	8.76-6.06	7.03-4.63	36.45-21.55	14.85-10.00	16.90-8.89
Average Yield %	1.75	2.62	2.81	2.81	3.57	3.23	2.66	2.99

Address: Ten Penn Center, 1801 Market Street, Philadelphia, PA 19103-1699 **Telephone:** (215) 977-3000 **Fax:** (215) 977-3409	**Web Site:** www.Sunocoinc.com **Officers:** John G. Drosdick - Chmn., Pres., C.E.O. Thomas W. Hofmann - Sr. V.P., C.F.O.	**Auditors:** ERNST & YOUNG LLP **Investor Contact:** 215-977-6082

SUNTRUST BANKS, INC.

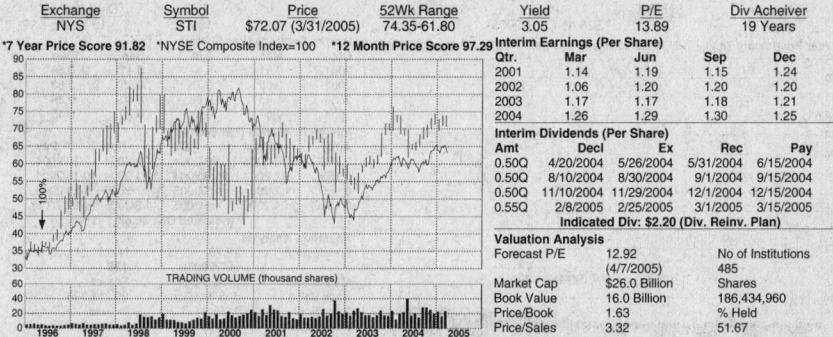

Exchange	Symbol	Price	52Wk Range	Yield	P/E	Div Acheiver
NYS	STI	$72.07 (3/31/2005)	74.35-61.80	3.05	13.89	19 Years

*7 Year Price Score 91.82   *NYSE Composite Index=100   *12 Month Price Score 97.29

Interim Earnings (Per Share)

Qtr.	Mar	Jun	Sep	Dec
2001	1.14	1.19	1.15	1.24
2002	1.06	1.20	1.20	1.20
2003	1.17	1.17	1.18	1.21
2004	1.26	1.29	1.30	1.25

Interim Dividends (Per Share)

Amt	Decl	Ex	Rec	Pay
0.50Q	4/20/2004	5/26/2004	5/31/2004	6/15/2004
0.50Q	8/10/2004	8/30/2004	9/1/2004	9/15/2004
0.50Q	11/10/2004	11/29/2004	12/1/2004	12/15/2004
0.55Q	2/8/2005	2/25/2005	3/1/2005	3/15/2005

Indicated Div: $2.20 (Div. Reinv. Plan)

Valuation Analysis

Forecast P/E	12.92	No of Institutions
	(4/7/2005)	485
Market Cap	$26.0 Billion	Shares
Book Value	16.0 Billion	186,434,960
Price/Book	1.63	% Held
Price/Sales	3.32	51.67

Business Summary: Commercial Banking (MIC: 8.1 SIC: 021 NAIC: 22110)

SunTrust Banks, through its primary subsidiary, SunTrust Bank, provides deposit, credit, trust and investment services to a broad range of retail, business and institutional clients. Other subsidiaries provide mortgage banking, credit-related insurance, asset management, brokerage and capital market services. Co. operates 1,201 traditional and in-store branches and 2,225 ATMs located in Florida, Georgia, Maryland, Tennessee, Virginia and the District of Columbia. In addition, Co. provides customers with a full range of technology-based banking channels including Internet, personal computer and telephone banking. At Dec 31 2003, Co. had total assets of $125.39 billion.

Recent Developments: For the year ended Dec 31 2004, net income increased 18.1% to $1,572,901 thousand from net income of $1,332,297 thousand a year earlier. Net interest income was $3,685,155 thousand, up 11.0% from $3,320,303 thousand the year before. Provision for loan losses was $135,537 thousand versus $313,550 thousand in the prior year, a decrease of 56.8%. Non-interest income rose 13.1% to $2,604,446 thousand, while non-interest expense advanced 14.6% to $3,879,334 thousand.

Prospects: Results are benefiting from a continuation of positive trends from earlier in 2004, notably robust revenue growth, solid credit quality and more effective cost control. In addition, Co. is benefiting from contributions from its acquisition of National Commerce Financial Corporation, which has lead to improvements in net interest margin. Moreover, Co. is experiencing favorable loan growth, with the consumer segments particularly robust, while still sluggish demand in the large corporate segment is partially offsetting strong growth in the rest of the commercial portfolio.

Financial Data

(US$ in Thousands)	12/31/2004	12/31/2003	12/31/2002	12/31/2001	12/31/2000	12/31/1999	12/31/1998	12/31/1997
Earnings Per Share	5.19	4.73	4.66	4.72	4.30	4.13	3.04	3.13
Cash Flow Per Share	3.77	14.85	(5.54)	(4.49)	1.72	11.23	(2.86)	(3.34)
Tang Book Value Per Share	22.50	28.43	26.56	26.67	25.07	23.24	22.99	23.38
Dividends Per Share	2.000	1.800	1.720	1.600	1.480	1.380	1.000	0.925
Dividend Payout %	38.54	38.05	36.91	33.90	34.42	33.41	32.89	29.55
Income Statement								
Interest Income	5,218,382	4,768,842	5,135,197	6,279,574	6,845,419	5,960,208	5,675,900	3,650,739
Interest Expense	1,533,227	1,448,539	1,891,488	3,026,974	3,736,981	2,814,752	2,746,779	1,756,373
Net Interest Income	3,685,155	3,320,303	3,243,709	3,252,600	3,108,438	3,145,456	2,929,121	1,894,366
Provision for Losses	135,537	313,550	469,792	275,165	133,974	170,437	214,602	117,043
Non-Interest Income	2,604,446	2,303,001	2,391,675	2,155,823	1,773,625	1,660,031	1,716,173	934,238
Non-Interest Expense	3,898,837	3,400,616	3,342,268	3,113,538	2,828,533	2,939,393	2,932,386	1,685,595
Income Before Taxes	2,257,026	1,909,138	1,823,324	2,019,720	1,919,556	1,695,657	1,498,306	1,025,966
Income Taxes	684,125	576,841	491,515	650,501	625,456	571,705	527,289	358,713
Net Income	1,572,901	1,332,297	1,331,809	1,375,531	1,294,100	1,326,600	971,017	667,253
Average Shares	303,309	281,434	286,052	291,584	300,956	317,079	319,711	213,480
Balance Sheet								
Net Loans & Leases	100,376,148	79,790,399	72,237,821	68,092,163	71,365,273	65,131,508	60,596,089	39,383,675
Total Assets	158,869,784	125,393,153	117,322,523	104,740,644	103,496,380	95,389,968	93,169,932	57,982,736
Total Deposits	103,361,251	81,189,519	79,706,628	67,536,422	69,533,337	60,100,529	59,033,283	38,197,528
Total Liabilities	142,882,885	115,661,987	108,553,027	96,381,076	95,257,172	87,763,106	84,991,288	52,783,354
Stockholders' Equity	15,986,899	9,731,166	8,769,496	8,359,568	8,239,208	7,626,862	8,178,644	5,199,382
Shares Outstanding	360,840	281,923	270,843	283,040	296,266	293,543	321,124	209,909
Statistical Record								
Return on Assets %	1.10	1.10	1.20	1.32	1.30	1.41	1.28	1.21
Return on Equity %	12.20	14.40	15.55	16.57	16.27	16.79	14.52	13.24
Net Interest Margin %	70.62	69.62	63.17	51.80	45.41	52.77	51.61	51.89
Efficiency Ratio %	49.84	48.09	44.40	36.91	32.82	38.57	39.67	36.76
Loans to Deposits	0.97	0.98	0.91	1.01	1.03	1.08	1.03	1.03
Price Range	76.41-61.80	71.55-51.56	70.00-51.79	71.81-58.10	68.81-42.56	79.81-62.25	87.44-54.94	74.94-44.50
P/E Ratio	14.72-11.91	15.13-10.90	15.02-11.11	15.21-12.31	16.00-9.90	19.33-15.07	28.76-18.07	23.94-14.22
Average Yield %	2.90	2.96	2.71	2.48	2.80	2.01	1.38	1.57

Address: 303 Peachtree Street, NE, Atlanta, GA 30308	Web Site: www.suntrust.com	Auditors: PricewaterhouseCoopers LLP
Telephone: (404) 588-7711	**Officers:** L. Phillip Humann - Chmn., Pres., C.E.O.	**Investor Contact:** 404-658-4879
Fax: (404) 827-6173	James M. Wells III - Vice-Chmn., Pres., C.O.O.	**Transfer Agents:** SunTrust Bank Atlanta, Atlanta, GA

SUPERIOR INDUSTRIES INTERNATIONAL, INC.

Exchange	Symbol	Price	52Wk Range	Yield	P/E	Div Acheiver
NYS	SUP	$26.41 (3/31/2005)	36.48-24.59	2.35	15.81	19 Years

*7 Year Price Score 75.28 *NYSE Composite Index=100 *12 Month Price Score 80.66

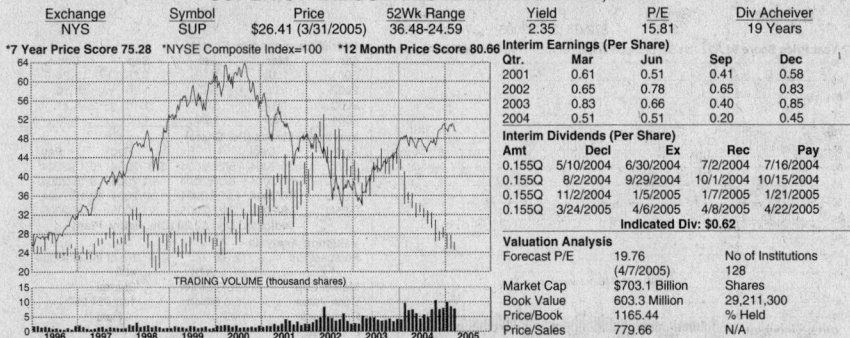

Interim Earnings (Per Share)

Qtr.	Mar	Jun	Sep	Dec
2001	0.61	0.51	0.41	0.58
2002	0.65	0.78	0.65	0.83
2003	0.83	0.66	0.40	0.85
2004	0.51	0.51	0.20	0.45

Interim Dividends (Per Share)

Amt	Decl	Ex	Rec	Pay
0.155Q	5/10/2004	6/30/2004	7/2/2004	7/16/2004
0.155Q	8/2/2004	9/29/2004	10/1/2004	10/15/2004
0.155Q	11/2/2004	1/5/2005	1/7/2005	1/21/2005
0.155Q	3/24/2005	4/6/2005	4/8/2005	4/22/2005

Indicated Div: $0.62

Valuation Analysis

Forecast P/E	19.76	No of Institutions	
	(4/7/2005)	128	
Market Cap	$703.1 Billion	Shares	
Book Value	603.3 Million		29,211,300
Price/Book	1165.44	% Held	
Price/Sales	779.66	N/A	

Business Summary: Automotive (MIC: 15.1 SIC: 714 NAIC: 36399)

Superior Industries International designs and manufactures automotive parts and accessories for original equipment manufacturers (OEMs). Co. supplies cast and forged aluminum wheels to automobile and light truck manufacturers, with wheel manufacturing facilities in the U.S., Mexico and Hungary. The OEM cast aluminum road wheels, Co.'s primary product, are sold to General Motors and Ford, which together accounted for 85.0% of 2003 sales, as well as to DaimlerChrysler, Audi, BMW, Isuzu, Jaguar, Land Rover, Mazda, MG Rover, Mitsubishi, Nissan, Subaru, Toyota and Volkswagen. Co. also manufactures aluminum suspension and underbody components.

Recent Developments: For the year ended Dec 31 2004, net income decreased 39.4% to $44,655,000 from net income of $73,720,000 a year earlier. Revenues were $9,017,550,00, up 7.3% from $840,349,000 the year before. Operating income was $56,340,000 versus an income of $100,889,000 in the prior year, a decrease of 44.2%. Total direct expense was $819,639,000 versus $716,558,000 in the prior year, an increase of 14.4%. Total indirect expense was $25,776,000 versus $22,902,000 in the prior year, an increase of 12.5%.

Prospects: Bottom-line results are being hampered by pricing pressures stemming from the emergence of China and other low-cost developing countries as important centers for the manufacture of automotive components and finished products. Pricing issues will likely continue to hurt profitability in 2005, as well as sluggish auto production expected for the first quarter of 2005. Meanwhile, Co. is implementing new automation, employee training, and best-practices programs in an effort to reduce costs. Separately, during 2004 Co. broke ground on a new facility in Mexico that will manufacture the increasingly popular large-diameter cast aluminum wheels. The facility is expected to be completed in 2006.

Financial Data
(US$ in Thousands)

	12/31/2004	12/31/2003	12/31/2002	12/31/2001	12/31/2000	12/31/1999	12/31/1998	12/31/1997
Earnings Per Share	1.67	2.73	2.91	2.10	3.04	2.62	1.88	1.96
Cash Flow Per Share	0.00	2.87	3.64	2.29	3.67	3.23	2.88	2.66
Tang Book Value Per Share	0.02	22.12	19.96	17.30	15.45	13.35	11.42	10.30
Dividends Per Share	0.585	0.525	0.470	0.420	0.380	0.340	0.300	0.260
Dividend Payout %	35.03	19.23	16.15	20.00	12.50	12.98	15.96	13.27
Income Statement								
Total Revenue	901,755	840,349	782,599	643,395	644,899	571,782	539,431	549,131
EBITDA	102,618	144,265	149,470	108,529	142,107	131,590	103,212	110,955
Depn & Amortn	39,281	33,577	32,605	28,388	26,920	28,523	26,698	26,917
Income Before Taxes	66,109	113,415	120,384	84,189	122,510	108,518	80,801	86,208
Income Taxes	21,454	39,695	42,134	28,835	42,573	37,710	28,482	30,819
Net Income	44,655	73,720	78,250	55,354	79,937	70,808	52,319	55,389
Average Shares	26,809,000	27,033	26,907	26,361	26,255	27,056	27,818	28,221
Balance Sheet								
Current Assets	368,976	388,510	368,941	280,271	245,579	263,740	235,886	199,846
Total Assets	744,528	703,205	645,796	540,838	491,664	460,468	427,430	382,679
Current Liabilities	87,343	83,621	97,123	71,137	75,022	86,847	91,111	65,415
Long-Term Obligations	...	...	...	...	...	340	673	1,344
Total Liabilities	141,264	110,999	115,365	104,277	104,900	120,645	130,258	111,640
Stockholders' Equity	603,264	592,206	530,431	448,741	399,319	353,086	312,034	287,416
Shares Outstanding	26,621,191	26,768	26,573	25,932	25,840	26,454	27,312	27,902
Statistical Record								
Return on Assets %	6.15	10.93	13.19	10.72	16.75	15.95	12.92	14.96
Return on Equity %	7.45	13.13	15.98	13.05	21.19	21.29	17.46	20.57
EBITDA Margin %	11.38	17.17	19.10	16.87	22.04	23.01	19.13	20.21
Net Margin %	4.95	8.77	10.00	8.60	12.40	12.38	9.70	10.09
Asset Turnover	1.24	1.25	1.32	1.25	1.35	1.29	1.33	1.48
Current Ratio	4.22	4.65	3.80	3.94	3.27	3.04	2.59	3.06
Price Range	43.67-26.36	45.91-33.89	53.12-36.20	44.62-29.40	35.31-23.50	29.00-22.81	33.50-20.19	29.38-22.50
P/E Ratio	26.15-15.78	16.82-12.41	18.25-12.44	21.25-14.00	11.62-7.73	11.07-8.71	17.82-10.74	14.99-11.48
Average Yield %	1.78	1.27	1.06	1.13	1.28	1.29	1.10	1.01

Address: 7800 Woodley Avenue, Van Nuys, CA 91406 Telephone: (818) 781-4973 Fax: (818) 780-3500	Web Site: www.supind.com Officers: Louis L. Borick - Chmn., C.E.O. Steven J. Borick - Pres., C.O.O.	Auditors: PricewaterhouseCoopers LLP Transfer Agents: Registrar and Transfer Company, Cranford, NJ

SUPERVALU INC.

Exchange	Symbol	Price	52Wk Range	Yield	P/E	Div Achiever
NYS	SVU	$33.35 (3/31/2005)	34.88-25.95	1.83	12.00	32 Years

*7 Year Price Score 117.07 *NYSE Composite Index=100 *12 Month Price Score 98.90

Interim Earnings (Per Share)

Qtr.	Jun	Aug	Nov	Feb
2001-02	0.45	0.39	0.44	0.25
2002-03	0.57	0.44	0.43	0.47
2003-04	0.55	0.46	0.36	0.69
2004-05	1.09	0.57	0.48	...

Interim Dividends (Per Share)

Amt	Decl	Ex	Rec	Pay
0.153Q	8/11/2004	8/30/2004	9/1/2004	9/15/2004
0.153Q	10/6/2004	11/29/2004	12/1/2004	12/15/2004
0.153Q	2/9/2005	2/25/2005	3/1/2005	3/15/2005
0.153Q	4/6/2005	5/27/2005	6/1/2005	6/15/2005

Indicated Div: $0.61 (Div. Reinv. Plan)

Valuation Analysis

Forecast P/E	13.07	No of Institutions
	(4/7/2005)	284
Market Cap	$4.5 Billion	Shares
Book Value	2.4 Billion	118,557,232
Price/Book	1.85	% Held
Price/Sales	0.23	87.75

Business Summary: Retail - Food & Beverage (MIC: 5.3 SIC: 141 NAIC: 24410)

Supervalu is a major food retailer and distributor to independently-owned retail food stores. As of Feb 28 2004, Co. operated 1,225 Save-A-Lot extreme value stores, including 821 licensed Save-A-Lot locations, 280 Co.-owned stores and 124 Deals-Nothing Over a Dollar general merchandise stores; 258 regional supermarkets under the Cub Foods, Shop 'n Save, Shoppers Food Warehouse, bigg's, Farm Fresh, Scott's Foods, and Hornbacher's banners. Additionally, Co. is the primary supplier to approximately 2,500 retail grocery stores, as well as Co.'s 258 regional supermarkets, while serving as a secondary supplier to about 660 stores.

Recent Developments: For the quarter ended Dec 4 2004, net income increased 33.6% to $64,943 thousand from net income of $48,616 thousand in the year-earlier quarter. Revenues were $4,555,122 thousand, down 3.9% from $4,738,983 thousand the year before. Operating income was $126,539 thousand versus an income of $127,442 thousand in the prior-year quarter, a decrease of 0.7%. Total indirect expense was $533,658 thousand versus $518,188 thousand in the prior-year quarter, an increase of 3.0%.

Prospects: On Feb 7 2005, Co. announced that it has completed its acquisition of Total Logistics, Inc., a national provider of integrated third-party logistics services and manufacturer of refrigeration systems, for approximately $234.0 million, including assumed debt of about $69.0 million. Co. anticipates the acquisition will be slightly accretive to fiscal 2006 earnings. Meanwhile, Co. is targeting fiscal 2005 earnings of between $2.75 and $2.80 per share, which includes a $0.50 diluted earnings per share effect from the net after-tax gain on the sale of its minority interest in WinCo that occurred in the first quarter of fiscal 2005.

Financial Data

(US$ in Thousands)	9 Mos	6 Mos	3 Mos	02/28/2004	02/22/2003	02/23/2002	02/24/2001	02/26/2000
Earnings Per Share	2.78	2.68	2.57	2.07	1.91	1.53	0.62	1.87
Cash Flow Per Share	5.23	6.10	6.10	6.11	4.30	5.93	4.94	2.65
Tang Book Value Per Share	6.44	6.07	5.95	4.84	3.24	2.90	1.64	1.58
Dividends Per Share	0.595	0.588	0.580	0.578	0.565	0.555	0.545	0.403
Dividend Payout %	21.37	21.89	22.59	27.90	29.58	36.27	87.90	21.52
Income Statement								
Total Revenue	14,952,734	10,397,612	5,910,649	20,209,679	19,160,368	20,908,522	23,194,279	20,339,079
EBITDA	788,071	591,847	373,314	902,987	866,999	857,227	688,971	859,908
Depn & Amortn	232,657	162,972	92,994	301,589	297,056	340,750	343,779	277,062
Income Before Taxes	465,772	362,688	238,028	454,880	408,004	343,703	154,357	447,454
Income Taxes	172,882	134,741	88,617	174,742	150,962	138,168	72,392	204,513
Net Income	292,890	227,947	149,411	280,138	257,042	205,535	81,965	242,941
Average Shares	136,240	137,070	137,559	135,418	134,877	133,978	132,829	130,090
Balance Sheet								
Current Assets	2,154,635	2,125,823	2,032,286	2,037,092	1,647,366	1,604,027	2,091,676	2,177,639
Total Assets	6,166,053	6,148,653	6,074,781	6,152,938	5,896,245	5,824,782	6,407,172	6,495,353
Current Liabilities	1,691,268	1,736,926	1,696,831	1,871,972	1,525,307	1,701,489	2,341,170	2,509,620
Long-Term Obligations	1,596,078	1,597,689	1,611,935	1,633,721	2,019,658	1,875,873	2,008,474	1,953,741
Total Liabilities	3,741,778	3,777,317	3,708,165	3,943,364	3,887,005	3,908,089	4,613,677	4,673,874
Stockholders' Equity	2,424,275	2,371,336	2,366,616	2,209,574	2,009,240	1,916,693	1,793,495	1,821,479
Shares Outstanding	134,653	134,207	135,968	134,760	133,688	132,889	132,374	134,662
Statistical Record								
Return on Assets %	6.22	6.00	5.82	4.57	4.40	3.37	1.27	4.53
Return on Equity %	16.74	16.45	15.86	13.07	13.13	11.11	4.55	15.58
EBITDA Margin %	5.27	5.69	6.32	4.47	4.52	4.10	2.97	4.23
Net Margin %	1.96	2.19	2.53	1.39	1.34	0.98	0.35	1.19
Asset Turnover	3.20	3.23	3.30	3.30	3.28	3.43	3.61	3.79
Current Ratio	1.27	1.22	1.20	1.09	1.08	0.94	0.89	0.87
Debt to Equity	0.66	0.67	0.68	0.74	1.01	0.98	1.12	1.07
Price Range	32.51-25.38	32.36-23.86	32.36-21.32	29.43-12.60	30.50-14.32	24.68-12.80	22.50-11.75	26.13-16.19
P/E Ratio	11.69-9.13	12.07-8.90	12.59-8.30	14.22-6.09	15.97-7.50	16.13-8.37	36.29-18.95	13.97-8.66
Average Yield %	2.04	2.09	2.16	2.55	2.63	2.91	3.25	1.88

Address: 11840 Valley View Road, Eden Prairie, MN 55344 **Telephone:** (952) 828-4000 **Fax:** (952) 828-8998	**Web Site:** www.supervalu.com **Officers:** Jeffrey Noddle - Chmn., Pres., C.E.O. Pamela K. Knous - Exec. V.P., C.F.O.	**Auditors:** KPMG LLP **Investor Contact:** 952-828-4000 **Transfer Agents:** Wells Fargo Shareowner Services, St. Paul, MN

SYBASE, INC.

Exchange	Symbol	Price	52Wk Range	Yield	P/E
NYS	SY	$18.46 (3/31/2005)	20.99-12.80	N/A	26.75

*7 Year Price Score 95.27 *NYSE Composite Index=100 *12 Month Price Score 104.43

Interim Earnings (Per Share)

Qtr.	Mar	Jun	Sep	Dec
2001	0.16	(0.42)	(0.07)	0.07
2002	(1.14)	0.20	0.12	(0.11)
2003	0.13	0.15	0.23	0.38
2004	0.13	0.13	0.19	0.25

Interim Dividends (Per Share)

No Dividends Paid

Valuation Analysis

Forecast P/E	16.93	No of Institutions	
	(4/7/2005)	190	
Market Cap	$1.8 Billion	Shares	
Book Value	756.6 Million	81,752,488	
Price/Book	2.33	% Held	
Price/Sales	2.24	85.95	

Business Summary: IT & Technology (MIC: 10.2 SIC: 372 NAIC: 11210)

Sybase is an enterprise software company that delivers the Unwired Enterprise through data management and mobile infrastructure, integration and application development solutions. Co. offers a range of relational database management system servers, application development tools and connectivity software and complements this portfolio by providing consulting and integration services required to support enterprise-wide on-line applications. Co.'s business is organized into five operating divisions: Enterprise Solutions, e-Business, iAnywhere Solutions, Business Intelligence, and Financial Fusion. iAnywhere Solutions and Financial Fusion are wholly-owned subsidiaries.

Recent Developments: For the year ended Dec 31 2004, net income decreased 22.1% to $67,950 thousand from net income of $87,266 thousand a year earlier. Revenues were $788,536 thousand, up 1.3% from $778,062 thousand the year before. Operating income was $89,392 thousand versus an income of $104,329 thousand in the prior year, a decrease of 14.3%. Total direct expense was $222,643 thousand versus $223,377 thousand in the prior year, a decrease of 0.3%. Total indirect expense was $476,501 thousand versus $450,356 thousand in the prior year, an increase of 5.8%.

Prospects: Co.'s results are benefiting from increased license revenues reflecting increased activity with several financial institutions in 2004. Co. took actions to strengthen and enhance its traditional products in 2004. Increased demand for mobility and data management applications, plus strength in its partner channels is helping Co. generate license and total revenue growth. While Co. expects the market for its core database products to remain challenging, it is encouraged by the sales and interest generated by several products that recently became generally available, including its real-time database ASE 12.5.2 and Mirror Activator™.

Financial Data

(US$ in Thousands)	12/31/2004	12/31/2003	12/31/2002	12/31/2001	12/31/2000	12/31/1999	12/31/1998	12/31/1997
Earnings Per Share	0.69	0.89	(0.95)	(0.27)	0.78	0.74	(1.15)	(0.70)
Cash Flow Per Share	1.84	2.13	1.65	0.98	1.95	2.09	1.09	0.94
Tang Book Value Per Share	4.33	5.10	3.49	2.91	3.53	3.41	2.78	3.42
Income Statement								
Total Revenue	788,536	778,062	829,861	926,086	960,458	871,633	867,469	903,937
EBITDA	123,597	143,766	99,435	79,685	165,959	177,181	18,656	54,799
Depn & Amortn	33,539	36,900	39,900	95,659	76,230	90,009	107,798	104,739
Income Before Taxes	100,966	118,095	71,209	978	107,586	100,798	(79,065)	(40,756)
Income Taxes	33,016	30,829	33,428	26,500	35,461	38,303	14,063	14,668
Net Income	67,950	87,266	(94,669)	(25,522)	72,125	62,495	(93,128)	(55,424)
Average Shares	98,001	97,582	99,584	94,592	92,150	84,156	80,893	78,794
Balance Sheet								
Current Assets	668,882	644,482	504,619	514,378	574,113	522,655	477,700	475,661
Total Assets	1,183,522	1,151,356	992,749	1,133,242	915,040	737,335	696,604	781,625
Current Liabilities	378,645	389,728	396,705	405,807	416,627	395,426	393,521	408,151
Total Liabilities	426,966	409,887	412,375	416,723	424,288	401,225	395,532	410,110
Stockholders' Equity	756,556	741,469	580,374	716,519	490,752	336,110	301,072	371,515
Shares Outstanding	95,518	98,525	94,660	98,725	87,656	80,920	81,169	79,998
Statistical Record								
Return on Assets %	5.80	8.14	N.M.	N.M.	8.71	8.72	N.M.	N.M.
Return on Equity %	9.05	13.20	N.M.	N.M.	17.40	19.62	N.M.	N.M.
EBITDA Margin %	15.67	18.48	11.98	8.60	17.28	20.33	2.15	6.06
Net Margin %	8.62	11.22	N.M.	N.M.	7.51	7.17	N.M.	N.M.
Asset Turnover	0.67	0.73	0.78	0.90	1.16	1.22	1.17	1.18
Current Ratio	1.77	1.65	1.27	1.27	1.38	1.32	1.21	1.17
Price Range	22.66-12.80	22.10-11.49	19.00-9.35	25.88-8.58	29.75-16.50	18.50-5.53	13.31-4.53	23.50-12.00
P/E Ratio	32.84-18.55	24.83-12.91	...	...	38.14-21.15	25.00-7.47	...	...

Address: One Sybase Drive, Dublin, CA 94568-7902	Web Site: www.sybase.com	Auditors: Ernst & Young LLP
Telephone: (925) 236 5000	Officers: John S. Chen - Chmn., Pres., C.E.O. Thomas Volk - Exec. V.P., Worldwide Field Organization	Investor Contact: 510-922-3500
Fax: (925) 236 4468		Transfer Agents: American Stock Transfer and Trust Co.

SYMBOL TECHNOLOGIES, INC.

Exchange	Symbol	Price	52Wk Range	Yield	P/E
NYS	SBL	$14.49 (3/31/2005)	18.88-11.70	0.14	43.91

*7 Year Price Score 74.60 *NYSE Composite Index=100 ***12 Month Price Score 107.38**

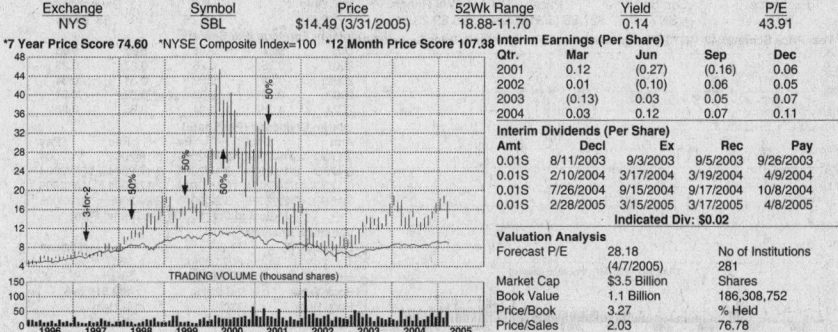

Interim Earnings (Per Share)

Qtr.	Mar	Jun	Sep	Dec
2001	0.12	(0.27)	(0.16)	0.06
2002	0.01	(0.10)	0.06	0.05
2003	(0.13)	0.03	0.05	0.07
2004	0.03	0.12	0.07	0.11

Interim Dividends (Per Share)

Amt	Decl	Ex	Rec	Pay
0.01S	8/11/2003	9/3/2003	9/5/2003	9/26/2003
0.01S	2/10/2004	3/17/2004	3/19/2004	4/9/2004
0.01S	7/26/2004	9/15/2004	9/17/2004	10/8/2004
0.01S	2/28/2005	3/15/2005	3/17/2005	4/8/2005

Indicated Div: $0.02

Valuation Analysis

Forecast P/E	28.18	No of Institutions
	(4/7/2005)	281
Market Cap	$3.5 Billion	Shares
Book Value	1.1 Billion	186,308,752
Price/Book	3.27	% Held
Price/Sales	2.03	76.78

Business Summary: Office Equipment Supplies (MIC: 11.12 SIC: 577 NAIC: 34119)

Symbol Technologies is a provider of secure mobile information systems that integrate application-specific hand-held computers with wireless networks for data, voice and bar code data capture. Co. has two reportable business segments. The Product segment is a designer, manufacturer and marketer of mobile computing, automatic data capture, and wireless network systems. The Services segment global services organization is Global Systems & Services. Under the SymbolCaresm umbrella, it offers Co.'s customers an array of services ranging from "high-touch" consulting and project management to equipment repair and support.

Recent Developments: For the year ended Dec 31 2004, net income increased 2384.0% to $81,847 thousand from net income of $3,295 thousand a year earlier. Revenues were $1,732,123 thousand, up 13.2% from $1,530,278 thousand the year before. Operating income was $140,360 thousand versus an income of $7,521 thousand in the prior year, an increase of 1766.2%. Total direct expense was $923,085 thousand versus $855,029 thousand in the prior year, an increase of 8.0%. Total indirect expense was $668,678 thousand versus $667,728 thousand in the prior year, an increase of 0.1%.

Prospects: Co. expects that first-quarter 2005 revenue will be approximately $465.0 million bolstered by the strength of the fourth-quarter 2004 results. Earnings per share for the first quarter of 2005 are expected to be $0.10 to $0.11. This range does not include the impact, if any, of Co.'s eventual issuing of shares to class action plaintiffs from a settlement approved in Oct 2004. Co. currently has accrued $86.6 million relating to this settlement. However, the accounting requires Co. to mark-to-market the appreciation in the value of shares to be issued above a pre-determined price in the settlement of $16.41 per share through a non-cash charge to earnings.

Financial Data

(US$ in Thousands)	12/31/2004	12/31/2003	12/31/2002	12/31/2001	12/31/2000	12/31/1999	12/31/1998	12/31/1997
Earnings Per Share	0.33	0.01	(0.25)	(0.24)	(0.33)	0.55	0.44	0.34
Cash Flow Per Share	0.92	1.01	0.77	0.12	(0.24)	0.78	0.22	0.54
Tang Book Value Per Share	2.19	2.53	2.38	3.20	3.49	2.23	1.87	1.57
Dividends Per Share	0.020	0.020	0.020	0.017	0.013	0.013	0.010	0.008
Dividend Payout %	6.06	200.00	...	...	...	2.30	2.24	2.33
Income Statement								
Total Revenue	1,732,123	1,530,278	1,401,617	1,452,697	1,449,490	1,139,290	977,901	774,345
EBITDA	218,091	80,309	1,176	32,715	14,745	243,129	197,357	158,291
Depn & Amortn	77,797	68,787	69,337	95,129	82,083	66,184	55,156	45,277
Income Before Taxes	123,769	3,901	(82,640)	(80,389)	(79,558)	171,124	138,751	109,738
Income Taxes	41,922	606	(24,865)	(25,669)	(10,592)	54,760	45,787	39,506
Net Income	81,847	3,295	(57,775)	(53,907)	(68,966)	116,364	92,964	70,232
Average Shares	246,166	236,449	229,593	227,392	206,443	212,357	210,721	206,671
Balance Sheet								
Current Assets	742,767	734,031	690,291	1,000,208	1,078,252	584,201	479,604	399,952
Total Assets	1,930,369	1,646,518	1,572,195	1,892,674	2,093,199	1,047,944	838,399	679,190
Current Liabilities	606,782	536,223	474,100	339,733	458,038	232,588	184,287	158,106
Long-Term Obligations	176,087	99,012	135,614	310,220	308,057	99,623	64,596	40,301
Total Liabilities	857,850	725,920	684,456	711,885	891,503	407,484	307,471	220,774
Stockholders' Equity	1,072,519	920,598	887,739	1,180,789	1,201,696	640,460	530,928	453,742
Shares Outstanding	242,273	230,767	230,627	228,781	224,136	199,512	198,301	198,247
Statistical Record								
Return on Assets %	4.56	0.20	N.M.	N.M.	N.M.	12.34	12.25	10.86
Return on Equity %	8.19	0.36	N.M.	N.M.	N.M.	19.87	18.88	16.46
EBITDA Margin %	12.59	5.25	0.08	2.25	1.02	21.34	20.18	20.44
Net Margin %	4.73	0.22	N.M.	N.M.	N.M.	10.21	9.51	9.07
Asset Turnover	0.97	0.95	0.81	0.73	0.92	1.21	1.29	1.20
Current Ratio	1.22	1.37	1.46	2.94	2.35	2.51	2.60	2.53
Debt to Equity	0.16	0.11	0.15	0.26	0.26	0.16	0.12	0.09
Price Range	18.90-11.70	17.23-8.05	17.14-4.99	34.47-9.70	45.47-18.63	28.25-11.83	18.94-7.37	8.84-5.76
P/E Ratio	57.27-35.45	N.M.	...	...	...	51.36-21.52	43.06-16.75	26.00-16.95
Average Yield %	0.14	0.16	0.21	0.08	0.04	0.07	0.08	0.11

Address: One Symbol Plaza, Holtsville, NY 11742-1300	**Web Site:** www.symbol.com	**Auditors:** Ernst & Young LLP
Telephone: (631) 738 2400	**Officers:** Salvatore Iannuzzi - Chmn. William R. Nuti - Pres., C.E.O., C.O.O.	**Investor Contact:** 631-738-5050
Fax: (631) 738 5990		

SYNOVUS FINANCIAL CORP.

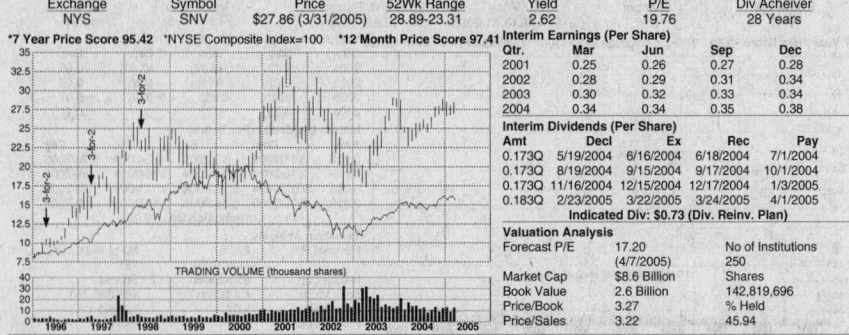

Exchange	Symbol	Price	52Wk Range	Yield	P/E	Div Acheiver
NYS	SNV	$27.86 (3/31/2005)	28.89-23.31	2.62	19.76	28 Years

*7 Year Price Score 95.42 *NYSE Composite Index=100 *12 Month Price Score 97.41

Interim Earnings (Per Share)

Qtr.	Mar	Jun	Sep	Dec
2001	0.25	0.26	0.27	0.28
2002	0.28	0.29	0.31	0.34
2003	0.30	0.32	0.33	0.34
2004	0.34	0.34	0.35	0.38

Interim Dividends (Per Share)

Amt	Decl	Ex	Rec	Pay
0.173Q	5/19/2004	6/16/2004	6/18/2004	7/1/2004
0.173Q	8/19/2004	9/15/2004	9/17/2004	10/1/2004
0.173Q	11/16/2004	12/15/2004	12/17/2004	1/3/2005
0.183Q	2/23/2005	3/22/2005	3/24/2005	4/1/2005
		Indicated Div: $0.73 (Div. Reinv. Plan)		

Valuation Analysis

Forecast P/E	17.20	No of Institutions
	(4/7/2005)	250
Market Cap	$8.6 Billion	Shares
Book Value	2.6 Billion	142,819,696
Price/Book	3.27	% Held
Price/Sales	3.22	45.94

Business Summary: Commercial Banking (MIC: 8.1 SIC: 021 NAIC: 22110)

Synovus Financial, with assets of $21.63 billion as of Dec 31 2003, is a registered bank holding company. Co. provides financial services including commercial and retail banking, financial management, insurance, mortgage and leasing services through affiliate banks and other offices in Georgia, Alabama, South Carolina, Florida and Tennessee. Co. also owns 81.0% of Total System Services, Inc.® (TSYS), which provides electronic payment processing services including consumer, debit, commercial, retail and stored value card processing and related services, as well as student loan processing.

Recent Developments: For the year ended Dec 31 2004, net income increased 12.4% to $437,033 thousand from net income of $388,925 thousand a year earlier. Net interest income was $860,679 thousand, up 12.8% from $763,064 thousand the year before. Provision for loan losses was $75,319 thousand versus $71,777 thousand in the prior year, an increase of 4.9%. Non-interest income rose 11.3% to $1,520,936 thousand, while non-interest expense advanced 11.6% to $1,617,090 thousand.

Prospects: Co.'s results are being fueled by its Synovus Financial Services segment, which is benefiting from improving credit quality, strong loan growth and margin expansion. For 2005, Co. indicated that it will focus on growing deposits, managing loan growth, quality and mix, maintaining the margin, expanding fee income and continuing to refine its processes to improve efficiencies. Based on these assumptions, Co. expects 12.0% to 15.0% earnings per share growth, or earnings of between $1.58 and $1.62 for 2005. Co. noted that this expectation includes the effect of stock option expense beginning in Jul 2005 and expense for new restricted stock awards beginning in the first quarter of 2005.

Financial Data

(US$ in Thousands)	12/31/2004	12/31/2003	12/31/2002	12/31/2001	12/31/2000	12/31/1999	12/31/1998	12/31/1997
Earnings Per Share	1.41	1.28	1.21	1.05	0.92	0.80	0.70	0.62
Cash Flow Per Share	2.60	2.40	2.43	0.61	1.60	1.62	0.60	0.98
Tang Book Value Per Share	7.04	6.50	6.40	5.75	4.98	4.35	3.96	3.44
Dividends Per Share	0.693	0.660	0.590	0.510	0.440	0.360	0.293	0.240
Dividend Payout %	49.16	51.56	48.76	48.57	47.83	45.00	41.89	38.71
Income Statement								
Interest Income	1,159,020	1,061,492	1,055,040	1,130,888	1,097,805	888,007	769,248	725,673
Interest Expense	298,341	298,428	337,536	501,097	535,473	374,713	328,722	313,284
Net Interest Income	860,679	763,064	717,504	629,791	562,332	513,294	440,526	412,389
Provision for Losses	75,319	71,777	65,327	51,673	44,341	34,007	26,660	32,296
Non-Interest Income	1,521,011	1,369,329	1,234,822	937,697	833,513	739,765	561,973	489,246
Non-Interest Expense	1,588,366	1,422,143	1,299,470	1,005,963	923,274	856,549	673,648	601,293
Income Before Taxes	689,281	611,501	563,880	489,993	411,735	349,315	291,632	258,903
Income Taxes	252,248	222,576	198,533	178,377	149,178	124,008	104,524	93,667
Net Income	437,033	388,925	365,347	311,616	262,557	225,307	187,108	165,236
Average Shares	310,330	304,928	301,197	295,850	286,882	283,355	269,151	265,665
Balance Sheet								
Net Loans & Leases	19,214,651	16,238,855	14,264,068	12,247,148	10,604,020	8,940,681	7,301,170	6,506,822
Total Assets	25,050,178	21,632,629	19,036,246	16,657,947	14,908,092	12,547,001	10,498,009	9,260,331
Total Deposits	18,577,468	15,941,609	13,928,834	12,146,198	11,161,710	9,440,087	8,542,798	7,707,927
Total Liabilities	22,241,605	19,245,752	16,878,294	14,864,363	13,410,031	11,256,047	9,375,315	8,314,034
Stockholders' Equity	2,641,289	2,245,039	2,040,853	1,694,946	1,417,171	1,226,669	1,070,601	903,656
Shares Outstanding	309,974	302,090	300,397	294,673	284,642	282,014	270,218	262,808
Statistical Record								
Return on Assets %	1.87	1.91	2.05	1.97	1.91	1.96	1.89	1.85
Return on Equity %	17.84	18.15	19.56	20.03	19.81	19.62	18.95	19.58
Net Interest Margin %	74.26	71.89	68.01	55.69	51.22	57.80	57.27	56.83
Efficiency Ratio %	59.27	58.50	56.75	48.63	47.81	52.62	50.60	49.49
Loans to Deposits	1.03	1.02	1.02	1.01	0.95	0.95	0.85	0.84
Price Range	28.92-22.67	29.04-17.31	31.74-16.81	34.45-23.02	27.19-14.50	25.00-17.50	25.83-18.06	22.21-13.11
P/E Ratio	20.51-16.08	22.69-13.52	26.23-13.89	32.81-21.92	29.55-15.76	31.25-21.88	36.90-25.80	35.82-21.15
Average Yield %	2.69	2.87	2.40	1.82	2.25	1.72	1.30	1.42

Address: 901 Front Avenue, P.O. Box 120, Columbus, GA 31902 **Telephone:** (706) 649-2401 **Fax:** (706) 641-6555	**Web Site:** www.synovus.com **Officers:** James D. Yancey - Chmn., Pres., C.O.O. Richard E. Anthony - Pres.	**Auditors:** KPMG LLP **Investor Contact:** 706-649-5220 **Transfer Agents:** State Street Bank and Trust Company, Boston, MA

SYSCO CORP.

Exchange	Symbol	Price	52Wk Range	Yield	P/E	Div Acheiver
NYS	SYY	$35.80 (3/31/2005)	39.37-29.89	1.68	25.39	28 Years

*7 Year Price Score 118.66 ***NYSE Composite Index=100** ***12 Month Price Score 92.16**

Interim Earnings (Per Share)

Qtr.	Sep	Dec	Mar	Jun
2001-02	0.24	0.24	0.23	0.31
2002-03	0.28	0.28	0.26	0.37
2003-04	0.32	0.34	0.30	0.42
2004-05	0.35	0.36	...	...

Interim Dividends (Per Share)

Amt	Decl	Ex	Rec	Pay
0.13Q	5/14/2004	6/30/2004	7/2/2004	7/23/2004
0.13Q	9/3/2004	9/29/2004	10/1/2004	10/22/2004
0.15Q	11/12/2004	1/5/2005	1/7/2005	1/28/2005
0.15Q	2/18/2005	3/30/2005	4/1/2005	4/22/2005

Indicated Div: $0.60 (Div. Reinv. Plan)

Valuation Analysis

Forecast P/E	21.26	No of Institutions
	(4/7/2005)	717
Market Cap	$22.8 Billion	Shares
Book Value	2.8 Billion	409,808,928
Price/Book	8.01	% Held
Price/Sales	0.77	64.34

Business Summary: Retail - Food & Beverage (MIC: 5.3 SIC: 141 NAIC: 24410)

Sysco is engaged in the marketing and distribution of food and related products to the foodservice or "food-prepared-away-from-home" industry. These services are performed for approximately 400,000 customers from 150 distribution facilities located throughout U.S. and Canada. Broadline segment distributes a full line of food products and non-food products to both traditional and chain restaurant customers. SYGMA segment distributes a full line of food products and non-food products to certain chain restaurant customer locations. "Other" segment includes Co.'s specialty produce, custom-cut meat, Asian cuisine foodservice and lodging industry products segments.

Recent Developments: For the 13 week period ended Jan 1 2005, net income increased 4.8% to $232,643 thousand from net income of $221,981 thousand in the year-earlier quarter. Revenues were $7,331,257 thousand, up 4.2% from $7,036,520 thousand the year before. Co. noted that acquisitions contributed 0.7% to sales growth and inflation, as measured by product cost increases, was 3.8% in the period. Total direct expense was $5,933,515 thousand compared with $5,669,399 thousand in the prior-year quarter, an increase of 4.7%.

Prospects: On Jan 24 2005, Co. agreed to acquire Piranha Produce Inc., a full-line fresh fruit and vegetable foodservice distributor throughout northern and central California, and has also acquired Nashville Tomato Inc., a regional tomato packager in the Southern U.S. Meanwhile, on Feb 14 2005, Co.'s Northeast Redistribution Center began distributing products to its broadline company near Boston, MA. By October 2005, all 14 companies will be receiving scheduled products from the Northeast Redistribution Center. Co. added that it anticipates a negative earnings impact of between $0.03 and $0.04 for fiscal 2005 associated with the start-up of the facility.

Financial Data

(US$ in Thousands)	6 Mos	3 Mos	07/03/2004	06/28/2003	06/29/2002	06/30/2001	07/01/2000	07/03/1999
Earnings Per Share	1.41	1.39	1.37	1.18	1.01	0.88	0.67	0.54
Cash Flow Per Share	1.82	1.74	1.82	2.12	1.64	1.44	1.08	0.86
Tang Book Value Per Share	2.49	2.42	2.11	1.68	1.85	2.07	1.90	1.71
Dividends Per Share	0.390	0.520	0.500	0.400	0.320	0.260	0.170	0.195
Dividend Payout %	27.66	37.48	36.50	33.90	31.68	29.55	25.56	36.11
Income Statement								
Total Revenue	14,863,182	7,531,925	29,335,403	26,140,337	23,350,504	21,784,497	19,303,268	17,422,815
EBITDA	928,361	457,616	1,828,619	1,605,763	1,442,018	1,286,671	1,029,101	871,731
Depn & Amortn	150,294	74,065	283,595	273,142	278,251	248,240	220,661	205,005
Income Before Taxes	742,602	365,852	1,475,144	1,260,387	1,100,870	966,655	737,608	593,887
Income Taxes	284,045	139,938	567,930	482,099	421,083	369,746	283,979	231,616
Net Income	458,557	225,914	907,214	778,288	679,787	596,909	445,588	362,271
Average Shares	652,993	650,779	661,919	661,535	673,445	667,949	669,555	673,594
Balance Sheet								
Current Assets	3,931,578	4,012,781	3,851,411	3,629,534	3,185,289	2,984,882	2,733,215	2,408,767
Total Assets	8,100,887	8,105,806	7,847,632	6,936,521	5,989,753	5,468,521	4,813,955	4,096,582
Current Liabilities	3,169,956	3,170,343	3,126,634	2,701,129	2,239,357	2,089,895	1,782,935	1,427,540
Long-Term Obligations	1,101,852	1,082,345	1,231,493	1,249,467	1,176,307	961,421	1,023,642	997,717
Total Liabilities	5,257,663	5,343,900	5,283,126	4,738,990	3,857,234	3,321,001	3,052,387	2,669,386
Stockholders' Equity	2,843,224	2,761,906	2,564,506	2,197,531	2,132,519	2,147,520	1,761,568	1,427,196
Shares Outstanding	636,545	636,535	636,535	643,657	653,540	665,137	662,969	659,344
Statistical Record								
Return on Assets %	11.97	11.88	12.07	12.08	11.90	11.64	10.03	9.05
Return on Equity %	35.40	35.77	37.49	36.05	31.85	30.62	28.02	25.60
EBITDA Margin %	6.25	6.08	6.23	6.14	6.18	5.91	5.33	5.00
Net Margin %	3.09	3.00	3.09	2.98	2.91	2.74	2.31	2.08
Asset Turnover	3.84	3.82	3.90	4.06	4.09	4.25	4.34	4.35
Current Ratio	1.24	1.27	1.23	1.34	1.42	1.43	1.53	1.69
Debt to Equity	0.39	0.39	0.48	0.57	0.55	0.45	0.58	0.70
Price Range	40.90-29.89	40.90-29.92	40.90-28.75	32.34-21.81	30.15-22.22	30.03-19.59	21.69-13.63	15.75-10.09
P/E Ratio	29.01-21.20	29.42-21.53	29.85-20.99	27.41-18.48	29.85-22.00	34.13-22.27	32.37-20.34	29.17-18.69
Average Yield %	1.09	1.45	1.41	1.39	1.17	1.02	0.95	1.45

Address: 1390 Enclave Parkway, Houston, TX 77077-2099
Telephone: (281) 584-1390
Fax: (281) 584-2880

Web Site: www.sysco.com
Officers: Richard J. Schnieders - Chmn., C.E.O.
Thomas E. Lankford - Pres., C.O.O.

Auditors: Ernst & Young LLP
Investor Contact: 281-584-1458
Transfer Agents: EquiServe Trust Company, N.A., Providence, RI

TALBOTS, INC.

Exchange	Symbol	Price	52Wk Range	Yield	P/E	Div Achiever
NYS	TLB	$31.98 (3/31/2005)	39.81-24.79	1.38	17.67	10 Years

*7 Year Price Score 92.45   *NYSE Composite Index=100   *12 Month Price Score 90.98

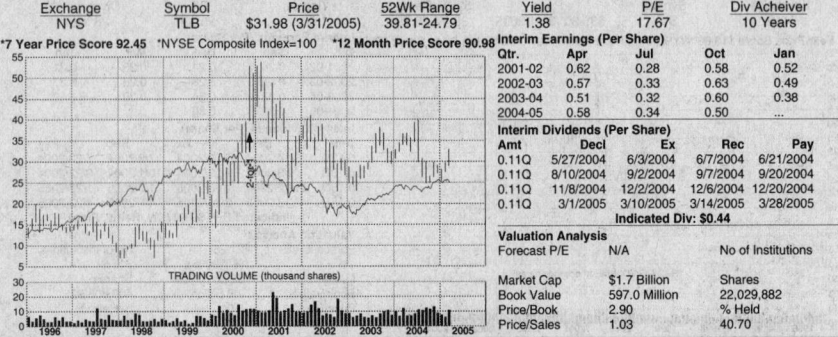

Interim Earnings (Per Share)

Qtr.	Apr	Jul	Oct	Jan
2001-02	0.62	0.28	0.58	0.52
2002-03	0.57	0.33	0.63	0.49
2003-04	0.51	0.32	0.60	0.38
2004-05	0.58	0.34	0.50	...

Interim Dividends (Per Share)

Amt	Decl	Ex	Rec	Pay
0.11Q	5/27/2004	6/3/2004	6/7/2004	6/21/2004
0.11Q	8/10/2004	9/2/2004	9/7/2004	9/20/2004
0.11Q	11/8/2004	12/2/2004	12/6/2004	12/20/2004
0.11Q	3/1/2005	3/10/2005	3/14/2005	3/28/2005

Indicated Div: $0.44

Valuation Analysis

Forecast P/E	N/A
	No of Institutions
Market Cap	$1.7 Billion
	Shares
Book Value	597.0 Million
	22,029,882
Price/Book	2.90
	% Held
Price/Sales	1.03
	40.70

TRADING VOLUME (thousand shares)

Business Summary: Retail - Apparel and Accessory Stores (MIC: 5.8 SIC: 621 NAIC: 48120)

Talbots is a specialty retailer and cataloger of women's, children's and men's classic apparel, accessories and shoes. Talbots offers sportswear, casual wear, dresses, coats, sweaters, accessories and shoes, consisting exclusively of Co.'s own branded merchandise in misses and petites female sizes. Talbots Kids offers clothing and accessories for infants, toddlers, boys and girls. As of Jan 31, 2004, Co. operated 977 stores in U.S., Canada and U.K. This included 492 Talbots Misses stores, 266 Talbots Petites stores, 41 Talbots Accessories and Shoes stores, 68 Talbots Kids stores, 79 Talbots Woman stores, six Talbots Mens stores, one Talbots Collection store and 24 Talbots Outlet stores.

Recent Developments: For the quarter ended Oct 30 2004, net income decreased 20.7% to $27,606 from net income of $34,794 in the year-earlier quarter. Revenues were $421,170 , up 3.2% from $408,148 the year before. Operating income was $37,608 versus an income of $56,119 in the prior-year quarter, a decrease of 33.0%. Total indirect expense was $122,443 versus $118,055 in the prior-year quarter, an increase of 3.7%.

Prospects: Co. reported a 13.4% increase in Jan 2005 comparable store sales resulting in a better than expected performance. Co. believes this result was driven by the strength of its selling markdowns, and a healthy increase in regular price sales of Co.'s early spring/transitional merchandise in the last week of the period. Also, sales for the fifty-two weeks ended Jan 29 2005 increased 7.0% compared to the same period 2004, with a 7.0% increase in retail store sales compared to same period 2004. Going forward, Co. has narrowed its Feb 2005 fourth quarter earnings guidance to $0.28 and $0.29 per share, from a previous outlook of $0.27 and $0.31 per share.

Financial Data

(US$ in Thousands)	9 Mos	6 Mos	3 Mos	01/31/2004	02/01/2003	02/02/2002	02/03/2001	01/29/2000
Earnings Per Share	1.81	1.90	1.89	1.81	2.01	2.00	1.80	1.85
Cash Flow Per Share	2.88	3.44	3.72	3.75	3.80	2.60	2.21	2.96
Tang Book Value Per Share	8.97	9.11	9.11	8.91	7.93	7.56	6.90	10.10
Dividends Per Share	0.420	0.410	0.400	0.390	0.350	0.310	0.270	0.230
Dividend Payout %	23.25	21.54	21.21	21.55	17.41	15.50	15.00	12.43
Income Statement								
Total Revenue	1,249,539	828,369	418,984	1,624,339	1,595,325	1,612,513	1,594,996	1,290,923
EBITDA	174,237	116,454	70,298	237,097	255,180	263,477	237,420	144,945
Depn & Amortn	56,888	36,713	16,590	67,509	59,113	53,461	45,830	43,377
Income Before Taxes	116,046	79,050	53,346	167,493	193,214	204,841	187,321	95,057
Income Taxes	35,683	26,293	20,005	62,810	72,455	77,840	72,119	36,597
Net Income	80,363	52,757	33,341	104,683	120,759	127,001	115,202	58,460
Average Shares	55,364	57,034	57,876	57,901	60,191	63,439	63,995	31,684
Balance Sheet								
Current Assets	560,509	539,578	527,749	496,154	435,898	432,769	506,405	369,786
Total Assets	1,026,094	1,003,351	991,564	958,392	871,925	831,064	858,596	693,904
Current Liabilities	241,345	188,782	180,758	166,142	147,941	130,292	188,040	143,931
Long-Term Obligations	100,000	100,000	100,000	100,000	100,000	100,000	100,000	100,000
Total Liabilities	429,129	381,877	364,489	342,266	304,249	263,188	307,825	262,572
Stockholders' Equity	596,965	621,474	627,075	616,126	567,676	567,876	550,771	431,332
Shares Outstanding	54,121	55,975	56,577	56,675	57,505	60,382	63,106	30,942
Statistical Record								
Return on Assets %	10.35	11.56	11.52	11.47	14.22	15.07	14.60	8.68
Return on Equity %	17.17	18.38	18.25	17.73	21.33	22.77	23.08	14.07
EBITDA Margin %	13.94	14.06	16.78	14.60	16.00	16.34	14.89	11.23
Net Margin %	6.43	6.37	7.96	6.44	7.57	7.88	7.22	4.53
Asset Turnover	1.70	1.76	1.75	1.78	1.88	1.91	2.02	1.92
Current Ratio	2.32	2.86	2.92	2.99	2.95	3.32	2.69	2.57
Debt to Equity	0.17	0.16	0.16	0.16	0.18	0.18	0.18	0.23
Price Range	39.81-24.79	39.81-29.35	38.15-26.01	38.15-23.02	41.02-22.90	53.75-22.33	53.50-14.13	26.38-11.81
P/E Ratio	21.99-13.70	20.95-15.45	20.19-13.76	21.08-12.72	20.41-11.39	26.88-11.16	29.72-7.85	14.26-6.39
Average Yield %	1.31	1.21	1.23	1.28	1.09	0.81	0.83	1.26

Address: One Talbots Drive, Hingham, MA 02043-1586 **Telephone:** (781) 749-7600 **Fax:** (781) 741-4369	**Web Site:** www.talbots.com **Officers:** Arnold B. Zetcher - Chmn., Pres., C.E.O. Harold B. Bosworth - Exec. V.P., Chief Merchandise Off.	**Auditors:** Deloitte & Touche LLP **Investor Contact:** 781-741-7775

TANGER FACTORY OUTLET CENTERS, INC.

Exchange	Symbol	Price	52Wk Range	Yield	P/E	Div Acheiver
NYS	SKT	$22.00 (3/31/2005)	26.48-17.68	5.86	84.62	11 Years

*7 Year Price Score 132.30 *NYSE Composite Index=100 *12 Month Price Score 98.70

Interim Earnings (Per Share)

Qtr.	Mar	Jun	Sep	Dec
2001	0.02	0.06	0.09	0.17
2002	0.06	0.10	0.11	0.27
2003	0.10	0.10	0.17	0.23
2004	0.04	0.14	(0.07)	0.16

Interim Dividends (Per Share)

Amt	Decl	Ex	Rec	Pay
0.313Q	10/14/2004	10/27/2004	10/29/2004	11/15/2004
100%	11/29/2004	12/29/2004	12/17/2004	12/28/2004
0.313Q	1/13/2005	1/27/2005	1/31/2005	2/15/2005
0.323Q	3/1/2005	4/27/2005	4/29/2005	5/16/2005

Indicated Div: $1.29 (Div. Reinv. Plan)

Valuation Analysis

Forecast P/E	11.13	No of Institutions
	(4/7/2005)	105
Market Cap	$603.7 Million	Shares
Book Value	161.1 Million	16,759,218
Price/Book	3.75	% Held
Price/Sales	3.10	61.07

Business Summary: Property, Real Estate & Development (MIC: 8.3 SIC: 798 NAIC: 25930)

Tanger Factory Outlet Centers is a fully-integrated, self-administered and self-managed real estate investment trust, focusing exclusively on developing, acquiring, owning, operating and managing factory outlet centers. As of Dec 31 2003, Co. had ownership interests in or management responsibilities for 40 centers with a total gross leasable area of approximately 9.3 million square feet. These centers were approximately 96.0% occupied, contained over 2,000 stores and represented over 400 store brands. Co.'s factory outlet centers and other assets are held by, and all of its operations are conducted by, Tanger Properties Limited Partnership.

Recent Developments: For the year ended Dec 31 2004, income from continuing operations decreased 34.0% to $7,608 thousand from income of $11,532 thousand a year earlier. Net income decreased 45.2% to $7,046 thousand from net income of $12,849 thousand a year earlier. Revenues were $194,553 thousand, up 64.8% from $118,059 thousand the year before. Operating income was $70,528 thousand versus an income of $41,309 thousand in the prior year, an increase of 70.7%.

Prospects: Looking ahead, Co. is projecting full-year 2005 diluted earnings per share of between $0.56 and $0.60, along with funds from operations in the range of $1.93 to $1.97 per diluted share. Meanwhile, as part of its long-term strategy to dispose of non-core assets and to upgrade its portfolio, on Feb 24 2005, Co. completed the sale of its 141,051 square foot outlet center located in Seymour, IN for a total cash sales price of $2.1 million. Separately, Co. continues its pre-development and leasing of four previously announced sites located in Pittsburgh, PA; Deer Park, NY; Charleston, SC; and Wisconsin Dells, WI, with expected deliveries during 2006 and 2007.

Financial Data (US$ in Thousands)	12/31/2004	12/31/2003	12/31/2002	12/31/2001	12/31/2000	12/31/1999	12/31/1998	12/31/1997
Earnings Per Share	0.26	0.58	0.54	0.34	0.16	0.87	0.62	0.77
Cash Flow Per Share	3.13	2.23	2.35	2.82	2.42	2.75	2.27	2.79
Tang Book Value Per Share	5.87	6.46	5.00	4.82	5.74	6.84	7.22	8.70
Dividends Per Share	1.245	1.229	1.224	1.219	1.214	1.208	1.175	1.085
Dividend Payout %	478.85	210.04	226.62	363.81	783.06	138.79	189.52	140.91
Income Statement								
Property Income	135,222	84,229	79,313	78,089	74,710	72,321	69,274	59,444
Non-Property Income	59,331	37,743	33,854	32,979	34,111	31,695	28,492	25,827
Total Revenue	194,553	121,972	113,167	111,068	108,821	104,016	97,766	85,271
Depn & Amortn	50,947	30,852	30,198	29,881	27,482	25,829	23,230	19,533
Interest Expense	35,117	26,486	28,460	30,134	27,565	24,239	22,028	16,835
Net Income	7,046	12,849	11,007	7,112	4,312	15,588	11,827	12,827
Average Shares	27,261	20,566	17,028	15,896	15,844	15,744	16,018	14,280
Balance Sheet								
Total Assets	936,378	987,437	477,675	476,272	487,408	490,069	471,795	416,014
Long-Term Obligations	488,007	540,319	345,005	358,195	346,843	329,647	302,485	229,050
Total Liabilities	516,951	562,689	363,410	378,395	369,434	349,015	322,432	255,489
Stockholders' Equity	161,133	167,418	90,635	76,371	90,877	107,764	114,039	136,649
Shares Outstanding	27,443	25,921	18,122	15,859	15,837	15,753	15,795	15,708
Statistical Record								
Return on Assets %	0.73	1.75	2.31	1.48	0.88	3.24	2.66	3.43
Return on Equity %	4.28	9.96	13.18	8.50	4.33	14.06	9.44	10.37
Net Margin %	3.62	10.53	9.73	6.40	3.96	14.99	12.10	15.04
Price Range	26.48-17.68	21.18-14.43	15.60-10.43	11.66-9.90	12.44-9.25	13.22-9.41	15.88-9.47	15.47-12.00
P/E Ratio	101.87-67.98	36.52-24.87	28.89-19.31	34.28-29.13	77.73-57.81	15.19-10.81	25.60-15.27	20.09-15.58
Average Yield %	5.77	7.16	9.02	11.27	11.19	10.49	8.15	7.87

Address: 3200 Northline Avenue, Suite 360, Greensboro, NC 27408 **Telephone:** (336) 292-3010 **Fax:** (336) 852-2096	**Web Site:** www.tangeroutlet.com **Officers:** Stanley K. Tanger - Chmn., C.E.O. Steven B. Tanger - Pres., C.O.O.	**Auditors:** PricewaterhouseCoopers LLP **Investor Contact:** 336-292-3010 **Transfer Agents:** EquiServe Trust Company NA, Providence, RI

TARGET CORP

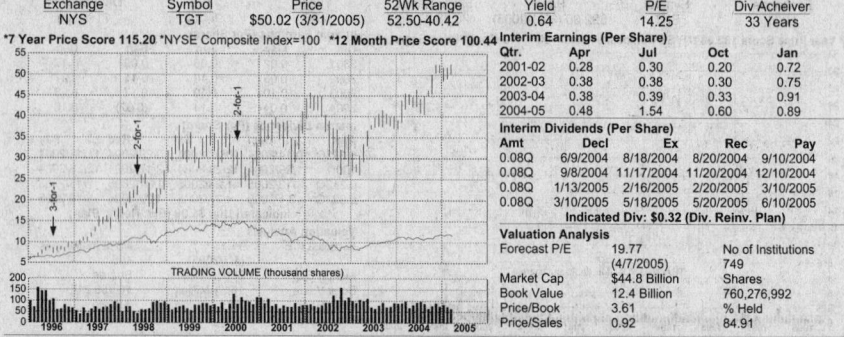

Interim Earnings (Per Share)

Qtr.	Apr	Jul	Oct	Jan
2001-02	0.28	0.30	0.20	0.72
2002-03	0.38	0.38	0.30	0.75
2003-04	0.38	0.39	0.33	0.91
2004-05	0.48	1.54	0.60	0.89

Interim Dividends (Per Share)

Amt	Decl	Ex	Rec	Pay
0.08Q	6/9/2004	8/18/2004	8/20/2004	9/10/2004
0.08Q	9/8/2004	11/17/2004	11/20/2004	12/10/2004
0.08Q	1/13/2005	2/16/2005	2/20/2005	3/10/2005
0.08Q	3/10/2005	5/18/2005	5/20/2005	6/10/2005

Indicated Div: $0.32 (Div. Reinv. Plan)

Valuation Analysis

Forecast P/E	19.77	No of Institutions	
	(4/7/2005)	749	
Market Cap	$44.8 Billion	Shares	760,276,992
Book Value	12.4 Billion	% Held	84.91
Price/Book	3.61		
Price/Sales	0.92		

Business Summary: Retail - General (MIC: 5.2 SIC: 331 NAIC: 52990)

Target is a diversified general merchandise retailer. As of May 13 2004, Co. operated 1,577 stores in 47 states, including 1,249 Target stores, 266 Mervyn's stores and 62 Marshall Field's stores. Target is a national discount store chain offering low prices with stores selling hardlines and fashion softgoods; Mervyn's is a moderate-priced department store chain specializing in active and casual apparel and home softlines. Marshall Field's (including stores formerly named Dayton's and Hudson's) is a full-service, full-line department store chain offering moderate to better merchandise.

Recent Developments: For the twelve months ended Jan 29 2005, earnings from continuing operations increased 16.4% to $1.89 billion from $1.62 billion a year earlier. Total revenues climbed 11.5% to $46.84 billion from $42.03 billion the previous year. Co. attributed the higher revenues to a 5.3% increase in comparable store sales combined with the contribution from new store expansion and its credit card operations. Gross margin amounted to $14.24 billion, or 31.2% of sales, versus $12.54 billion, or 30.6% of sales, the year before. Co. attributed the improved gross margin rate primarily to an increase in markup.

Prospects: Co. is benefiting from solid revenue growth, due in part to improved comparable-store sales, combined with contributions from new store expansion and its credit card operations. Separately, Co. completed the sale of Mervyn's retail subsidiary, including 257 stores and four distribution centers, to an investment group comprised of Sun Capital, Cerberus Capital Management, and Lubert-Adler and Klaff Partners, and all of Mervyn's credit card receivables to GE Consumer Finance, a unit of GE Capital, for a total price of approximately $1.65 billion.

Financial Data
(US$ in Thousands)

	9 Mos	6 Mos	3 Mos	01/31/2004	02/01/2003	02/02/2002	02/03/2001	01/29/2000
Earnings Per Share	3.53	3.26	2.11	2.01	1.81	1.50	1.38	1.23
Cash Flow Per Share	4.14	4.63	4.48	3.48	1.76	2.22	2.07	2.56
Tang Book Value Per Share	13.85	13.69	12.55	12.14	10.38	8.68	7.15	6.43
Dividends Per Share	0.290	0.280	0.270	0.260	0.240	0.220	0.210	0.200
Dividend Payout %	8.21	8.58	12.77	12.94	13.26	14.67	15.22	16.33
Income Statement								
Total Revenue	31,645,000	20,736,000	11,587,000	48,163,000	43,917,000	39,888,000	36,903,000	33,702,000
EBITDA	3,137,000	2,169,000	1,193,000	4,839,000	4,476,000	3,759,000	3,418,000	3,183,000
Depn & Amortn	915,000	591,000	345,000	1,320,000	1,212,000	1,079,000	940,000	854,000
Income Before Taxes	1,759,000	1,228,000	704,000	2,960,000	2,676,000	2,216,000	2,053,000	1,936,000
Income Taxes	665,000	464,000	266,000	1,119,000	1,022,000	842,000	789,000	751,000
Net Income	2,391,000	1,854,000	438,000	1,841,000	1,654,000	1,368,000	1,264,000	1,144,000
Average Shares	902,100	918,000	920,500	917,100	914,000	909,800	913,000	931,400
Balance Sheet								
Current Assets	13,777,000	13,038,000	12,375,000	12,928,000	11,935,000	9,648,000	7,304,000	6,483,000
Total Assets	31,786,000	31,295,000	31,123,000	31,392,000	28,603,000	24,154,000	19,490,000	17,143,000
Current Liabilities	8,485,000	7,952,000	8,235,000	8,314,000	7,523,000	7,054,000	6,301,000	5,850,000
Long-Term Obligations	9,082,000	9,057,000	9,586,000	10,217,000	10,186,000	8,088,000	5,634,000	4,521,000
Total Liabilities	19,388,000	18,929,000	19,660,000	20,327,000	19,160,000	16,294,000	12,971,000	11,281,000
Stockholders' Equity	12,398,000	12,366,000	11,463,000	11,065,000	9,443,000	7,860,000	6,519,000	5,862,000
Shares Outstanding	895,425	903,334	913,400	911,808	909,802	905,165	911,682	911,682
Statistical Record								
Return on Assets %	10.21	9.82	6.41	6.15	6.29	6.29	6.79	6.99
Return on Equity %	28.47	26.70	18.22	18.00	19.17	19.08	20.09	20.53
EBITDA Margin %	9.91	10.46	10.30	10.05	10.19	9.42	9.26	9.44
Net Margin %	7.56	8.94	3.78	3.82	3.77	3.43	3.43	3.39
Asset Turnover	1.54	1.61	1.64	1.61	1.67	1.83	1.98	2.06
Current Ratio	1.62	1.64	1.50	1.55	1.59	1.37	1.16	1.11
Debt to Equity	0.73	0.73	0.84	0.92	1.08	1.03	0.86	0.77
Price Range	50.02-37.05	46.43-37.05	45.63-32.90	41.54-26.06	45.72-26.15	44.41-26.68	38.59-22.75	37.88-27.63
P/E Ratio	14.17-10.50	14.24-11.37	21.63-15.59	20.67-12.97	25.26-14.45	29.61-17.79	27.97-16.49	30.79-22.46
Average Yield %	0.68	0.68	0.68	0.72	0.66	0.60	0.69	0.62

Address: 1000 Nicollet Mall, Minneapolis, MN 55403 Telephone: (612) 304 6073 Fax: (612) 370 5502	Web Site: www.targetcorp.com Officers: Robert J. Ulrich - Chmn., C.E.O. Gerald L. Storch - Vice-Chmn.	Auditors: Ernst & Young LLP Investor Contact: 612-370-6736 Transfer Agents: EquiServe, Jersey City, NJ

TCF FINANCIAL CORP.

Exchange	Symbol	Price	52Wk Range	Yield	P/E	Div Acheiver
NYS	TCB	$27.15 (3/31/2005)	32.53-24.40	3.13	14.60	13 Years

*7 Year Price Score 123.80 *NYSE Composite Index=100 *12 Month Price Score 88.65

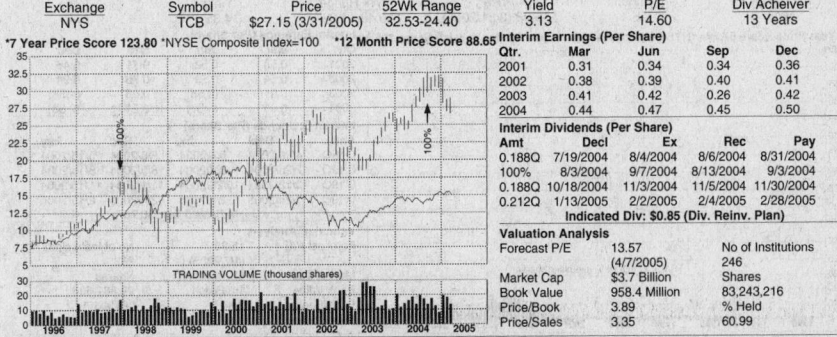

Interim Earnings (Per Share)

Qtr.	Mar	Jun	Sep	Dec
2001	0.31	0.34	0.34	0.36
2002	0.38	0.39	0.40	0.41
2003	0.41	0.42	0.26	0.42
2004	0.44	0.47	0.45	0.50

Interim Dividends (Per Share)

Amt	Decl	Ex	Rec	Pay
0.188Q	7/19/2004	8/4/2004	8/6/2004	8/31/2004
100%	8/3/2004	9/7/2004	8/13/2004	9/3/2004
0.188Q	10/18/2004	11/3/2004	11/5/2004	11/30/2004
0.212Q	1/13/2005	2/2/2005	2/4/2005	2/28/2005

Indicated Div: $0.85 (Div. Reinv. Plan)

Valuation Analysis

Forecast P/E	13.57	No of Institutions
	(4/7/2005)	246
Market Cap	$3.7 Billion	Shares
Book Value	958.4 Million	83,243,216
Price/Book	3.89	% Held
Price/Sales	3.35	60.99

Business Summary: Commercial Banking (MIC: 8.1 SIC: 021 NAIC: 22110)

TCF Financial, with $11.32 billion in assets as of Dec 31 2003, is the holding company for two national banks. As of Dec 31 2003, Co. operated more than 400 banking offices, including 240 full-service supermarket branches, in Illinois, Indiana, Michigan, Minnesota, Wisconsin and Colorado. Co.'s primary focus is lower- and middle-income customers and small- to medium-sized businesses in its markets. Co.'s branches are typically open 12 hours a day, seven days a week and on holidays. Co.'s products include commercial, consumer and residential mortgage loans and deposit and equipment finance, discount brokerage and investment and insurance sales products.

Recent Developments: For the year ended Dec 31 2004, net income increased 18.1% to $254,993 thousand from net income of $215,878 thousand a year earlier. Net interest income was $491,891 thousand, up 2.2% from $481,145 thousand the year before. Provision for loan losses was $10,947 thousand versus $12,532 thousand in the prior year, a decrease of 12.6%. Non-interest income rose 17.0% to $490,466 thousand, while non-interest expense advanced 4.8% to $584,252 thousand.

Prospects: Co.'s earnings reflect the growth of its core businesses through the opening of new branches and new products offerings. During the fourth quarter, Co. opened 12 new branches, comprised of eight traditional branches and four supermarket branches bringing the total number of new branch openings in 2004 to 30 branches. In 2005, Co. plans to open 29 new branches, consisting of 24 traditional branches and five supermarket branches. Separately, growing checking accounts is an important part of Co.'s long-term strategies and it ended 2004 with an increase of 91,331 checking accounts, or 6.0% growth in 2004.

Financial Data

(US$ in Thousands)	12/31/2004	12/31/2003	12/31/2002	12/31/2001	12/31/2000	12/31/1999	12/31/1998	12/31/1997
Earnings Per Share	1.86	1.52	1.58	1.35	1.18	1.00	0.88	0.84
Cash Flow Per Share	3.23	3.10	2.21	0.96	1.28	2.43	1.11	(0.05)
Tang Book Value Per Share	5.50	5.09	5.15	4.95	4.64	3.89	3.87	3.97
Dividends Per Share	0.750	0.650	0.575	0.500	0.412	0.362	0.306	0.234
Dividend Payout %	40.32	42.62	36.51	37.04	35.11	36.25	34.80	27.74
Income Statement								
Interest Income	622,809	641,519	733,363	826,609	826,681	752,101	748,894	682,614
Interest Expense	130,918	160,374	234,138	345,387	388,145	327,888	323,160	289,018
Net Interest Income	491,891	481,145	499,225	481,222	438,536	424,213	425,734	393,596
Provision for Losses	10,947	12,532	22,006	20,878	14,772	16,923	23,280	17,795
Non-Interest Income	490,466	463,624	416,880	351,625	312,384	288,909	256,174	194,440
Non-Interest Expense	586,934	560,109	538,369	501,996	462,528	452,798	428,700	361,562
Income Before Taxes	384,476	327,783	357,692	329,834	302,838	273,091	265,249	240,907
Income Taxes	129,483	111,905	124,761	122,512	116,593	107,052	109,070	95,846
Net Income	254,993	215,878	232,931	207,322	186,245	166,039	156,179	145,061
Average Shares	137,174	141,540	147,881	153,685	158,777	166,142	177,832	172,268
Balance Sheet								
Net Loans & Leases	9,306,779	8,271,159	8,044,120	8,169,174	8,480,030	7,839,988	7,061,165	6,986,605
Total Assets	12,340,567	11,319,015	12,202,069	11,358,715	11,197,462	10,661,716	10,164,594	9,744,660
Total Deposits	7,962,195	7,611,749	7,709,988	7,098,958	6,891,824	6,584,835	6,715,146	6,907,310
Total Liabilities	11,382,149	10,398,157	11,225,049	10,441,682	10,287,242	9,852,734	9,319,092	8,790,980
Stockholders' Equity	958,418	920,858	977,020	917,033	910,220	808,982	845,502	953,680
Shares Outstanding	137,186	140,952	147,711	153,863	160,578	163,882	171,138	185,644
Statistical Record								
Return on Assets %	2.15	1.84	1.98	1.84	1.70	1.59	1.57	1.72
Return on Equity %	27.06	22.75	24.60	22.69	21.61	20.07	17.36	19.30
Net Interest Margin %	78.98	75.00	68.07	58.22	53.05	56.40	56.85	57.66
Efficiency Ratio %	52.72	50.68	46.80	42.61	40.61	43.50	42.65	41.22
Loans to Deposits	1.17	1.09	1.04	1.15	1.23	1.19	1.05	1.01
Price Range	32.53-24.15	26.78-18.52	27.20-17.61	25.35-16.85	22.66-9.31	15.13-11.00	18.38-8.28	17.06-9.66
P/E Ratio	17.49-12.98	17.62-12.19	17.21-11.14	18.78-12.48	19.20-7.89	15.13-11.00	20.88-9.41	20.31-11.50
Average Yield %	2.65	2.91	2.43	2.36	2.78	2.67	2.14	1.86

Address: 200 Lake Street East, Mail Code EX0-03-A, Wayzata, MN 55391-1693
Telephone: (612) 661-6500
Fax: (612) 332-1753

Web Site: www.tcfexpress.com
Officers: William A. Cooper - Chmn., C.E.O. Lynn A. Nagorske - Pres., C.O.O.

Auditors: KPMG LLP
Investor Contact: 952-745-2755
Transfer Agents: EquiServe Trust Company, N.A., Providence, RI

TECO ENERGY INC.

Exchange	Symbol	Price	52Wk Range	Yield	P/E
NYS	TE	$15.68 (3/31/2005)	16.46-11.38	4.85	N/A

*7 Year Price Score 57.38   *NYSE Composite Index=100   *12 Month Price Score 105.80

Interim Earnings (Per Share)

Qtr.	Mar	Jun	Sep	Dec
2001	0.53	0.52	0.71	0.46
2002	0.54	0.59	0.76	0.24
2003	0.01	(0.58)	0.08	(4.58)
2004	0.01	(0.57)	0.21	(2.53)

Interim Dividends (Per Share)

Amt	Decl	Ex	Rec	Pay
0.19Q	4/28/2004	5/4/2004	5/6/2004	5/15/2004
0.19Q	7/28/2004	8/3/2004	8/5/2004	8/15/2004
0.19Q	10/22/2004	10/28/2004	11/1/2004	11/15/2004
0.19Q	1/26/2005	2/2/2005	2/4/2005	2/15/2005

Indicated Div: $0.76

Valuation Analysis

Forecast P/E	15.98	No of Institutions	
	(4/7/2005)	269	
Market Cap	$3.1 Billion	Shares	
Book Value	1.3 Billion		99,382,696
Price/Book	2.44	% Held	
Price/Sales	1.17		48.04

Business Summary: Electricity (MIC: 7.1 SIC: 911 NAIC: 21122)

TECO Energy is a utility holding company. Tampa Electric Company, consisting of Co.'s regulated operations, provides retail electric service to more than 612,000 customers in West Central Florida with a net system generating capability of 4,278 megawatts. Co. also provides gas to over 299,000 customers through its Peoples Gas System division, which is engaged in the purchase distribution and marketing of natural gas for residential industrial and electric power generation customers in Florida. Co.'s unregulated operations engage in coal-mining activities, transports coal and other dry-bulk commodities, has interests in independent power projects; and operates other energy-related businesses.

Recent Developments: For the year ended Dec 31 2004, net loss was $552,000 thousand versus net loss of $909,400 thousand a year earlier. Revenues were $2,669,100 thousand, up 2.7% from $2,598,300 thousand the year before. Operating loss was $457,100 thousand versus an income of $139,300 thousand in the prior year. Total direct expense was $1,939,400 thousand versus $1,777,000 thousand in the prior year, an increase of 9.1%. Total indirect expense was $1,186,800 thousand versus $682,000 thousand in the prior year, an increase of 74.0%.

Prospects: Results are being positively affected by solid customer and energy sales growth at its Florida utilities, while Co.'s transportation operations are beginning to benefit from operational and market improvements. Looking ahead, Co. is projecting full-year 2005 earnings from continuing operations of between $0.95 and $1.05 per share. Meanwhile, Tampa Electric's 2005 results are expected to be driven by continued 2.5% customer growth with energy sales growth slightly above that, while Peoples Gas anticipates customer growth of more than 4.0% in 2005. Separately, results at TECO Coal are expected to improve in 2005 due to sharply higher coal prices and strong earnings from its synfuel facilities.

Financial Data
(US$ in Thousands)

	12/31/2004	12/31/2003	12/31/2002	12/31/2001	12/31/2000	12/31/1999	12/31/1998	12/31/1997
Earnings Per Share	(2.87)	(5.05)	2.15	2.24	1.97	1.42	1.57	1.54
Cash Flow Per Share	0.72	1.83	4.28	3.81	3.02	2.91	3.72	2.68
Tang Book Value Per Share	6.13	8.55	13.75	12.94	11.93	11.19	11.42	11.04
Dividends Per Share	0.760	0.925	1.410	1.370	1.330	1.285	1.225	1.165
Dividend Payout %	...	...	65.58	61.16	67.51	90.49	78.03	75.65
Income Statement								
Total Revenue	2,669,100	2,740,000	2,675,800	2,648,600	2,295,100	1,983,000	1,958,100	1,862,300
EBITDA	(137,600)	508,700	753,500	782,100	713,700	652,900	621,800	643,200
Depn & Amortn	289,800	386,700	317,300	307,700	277,400	241,300	236,100	231,300
Income Before Taxes	(749,000)	(198,700)	259,800	293,600	269,400	287,900	281,400	306,100
Income Taxes	(265,100)	(135,200)	(38,400)	(10,100)	18,500	87,000	81,000	94,700
Net Income	(552,000)	(909,400)	330,100	303,700	250,900	186,100	206,500	201,900
Average Shares	192,600	179,900	153,300	135,400	126,300	131,200	131,700	131,200
Balance Sheet								
Net PPE	4,657,900	5,679,000	5,464,000	4,838,300	3,970,100	3,627,800	3,307,600	3,236,500
Total Assets	9,476,500	10,462,300	8,637,800	6,722,100	5,676,200	4,690,100	4,179,300	3,960,400
Long-Term Obligations	3,880,000	4,392,600	3,324,300	1,842,500	1,374,600	1,207,800	1,279,600	1,080,200
Total Liabilities	8,192,600	8,784,600	6,026,100	4,750,500	4,169,300	3,272,300	2,671,500	2,515,700
Stockholders' Equity	1,283,900	1,677,700	2,611,700	1,971,600	1,506,900	1,417,800	1,507,800	1,444,700
Shares Outstanding	199,700	187,800	175,800	139,600	126,300	126,700	132,000	130,900
Statistical Record								
Return on Assets %	N.M.	N.M.	4.30	4.90	4.83	4.20	5.07	5.37
Return on Equity %	N.M.	N.M.	14.40	17.46	17.11	12.72	13.99	14.81
EBITDA Margin %	N.M.	18.57	28.16	29.53	31.10	32.92	31.76	34.54
Net Margin %	(20.68)	(33.19)	12.34	11.47	10.93	9.38	10.55	10.84
PPE Turnover	0.52	0.49	0.52	0.60	0.60	0.57	0.60	0.60
Asset Turnover	0.27	0.29	0.35	0.43	0.44	0.45	0.48	0.50
Debt to Equity	3.02	2.62	1.27	0.93	0.91	0.85	0.85	0.75
Price Range	15.42-11.38	16.94-9.88	28.72-10.49	32.62-24.94	32.94-17.38	28.19-18.38	30.44-25.06	28.13-23.44
P/E Ratio	...	...	13.36-4.88	14.56-11.13	16.72-8.82	19.85-12.94	19.39-15.96	18.26-15.22
Average Yield %	5.54	7.38	6.59	4.76	5.70	5.93	4.53	4.70

Address: 702 N. Franklin Street, Tampa, FL 33602	Web Site: www.tecoenergy.com	Auditors: PricewaterhouseCoopers LLP
Telephone: (813) 228-1111	Officers: Sherrill W. Hudson - Chmn., C.E.O. John B. Ramil - Pres., C.O.O.	Investor Contact: 813-228-1111
Fax: (813) 228-1670		

TEKTRONIX, INC.

Exchange	Symbol	Price	52Wk Range	Yield	P/E
NYS	TEK	$24.53 (3/31/2005)	34.94-24.53	0.98	20.27

*7 Year Price Score 113.33 *NYSE Composite Index=100 *12 Month Price Score 85.47

Interim Earnings (Per Share)

Qtr.	Aug	Nov	Feb	May
2001-02	0.09	0.09	0.11	0.07
2002-03	0.22	0.05	(0.02)	0.54
2003-04	0.12	0.42	0.50	0.31
2004-05	0.43	(0.03)	...	...

Interim Dividends (Per Share)

Amt	Decl	Ex	Rec	Pay
0.04Q	6/24/2004	7/7/2004	7/9/2004	7/26/2004
0.06Q	9/23/2004	10/6/2004	10/8/2004	10/25/2004
0.06Q	12/16/2004	1/5/2005	1/7/2005	1/24/2005
0.06Q	3/17/2005	4/6/2005	4/8/2005	4/25/2005
		Indicated Div: $0.24		

Valuation Analysis

Forecast P/E	14.73		No of Institutions
	(4/7/2005)		224
Market Cap	$2.2 Billion		Shares
Book Value	1.1 Billion		75,790,696
Price/Book	2.01		% Held
Price/Sales	2.15		84.80

Business Summary: Instruments and Related Products (MIC: 11.15 SIC: 825 NAIC: 34515)

Tektronix manufactures, markets and services test, measurement and monitoring solutions to customers in industries, including computing, communications, semiconductors, broadcast, education, government, military/aerospace, research, automotive and consumer electronics. Co. enables its customers to design, manufacture, deploy, monitor and service next-generation global communications networks, computing, advanced and pervasive technologies. Co.'s products includes: oscilloscopes; logic analyzers; signal sources; communication test equipment, including mobile protocol test, wireless field test and spectrum analysis equipment; video test equipment, support services and accessories.

Recent Developments: For the quarter ended Nov 27 2004, net loss was $2,834 thousand versus net income of $36,487 thousand in the year-earlier quarter. Revenues were $266,828 thousand, up 22.4% from $217,921 thousand the year before. Operating income was $6,883 thousand versus an income of $46,052 thousand in the prior-year quarter, a decrease of 85.1%. Total indirect expense was $153,440 thousand versus $75,785 thousand in the prior-year quarter, an increase of 102.5%.

Prospects: The integration of Inet Technologies, acquired on Sep 30 2004, is on track. In addition, Co. is growing its core business with the recent introduction of the TPS2000 digital storage oscilloscope with an industrial power application, marking its entrance into the industrial power market. Also, Co. continues its investment in its adjacent product categories with the recent introduction of the RSA3408A, an advancement in real-time spectrum analysis. For the third fiscal quarter of 2005, including Inet, Co. expects net sales to be $250.0 million to $260.0 million and earnings per share from continuing operations of $0.26 to $0.30, excluding one-time items and acquisition-related costs.

Financial Data

(US$ in Thousands)	6 Mos	3 Mos	05/29/2004	05/31/2003	05/25/2002	05/26/2001	05/27/2000	05/29/1999
Earnings Per Share	1.21	1.66	1.35	0.29	0.35	1.46	3.63	(0.54)
Cash Flow Per Share	1.58	1.11	1.58	0.88	0.93	1.46	(0.68)	(0.09)
Tang Book Value Per Share	7.42	9.32	9.36	8.24	9.48	10.41	9.93	6.09
Dividends Per Share	0.180	0.160	0.120	...	...	...	0.180	0.240
Dividend Payout %	14.82	9.63	8.89				4.97	
Income Statement								
Total Revenue	517,293	250,465	920,620	791,048	843,329	1,235,275	1,120,555	1,861,490
EBITDA	70,335	53,393	177,751	45,727	63,490	224,908	56,525	15,267
Depn & Amortn	17,804	6,678	29,796	33,545	40,960	44,819	44,124	74,792
Income Before Taxes	61,479	52,094	167,312	33,305	46,849	220,188	19,581	(75,237)
Income Taxes	27,592	15,628	49,087	(1,843)	16,397	80,079	6,855	(24,076)
Net Income	33,574	36,408	116,095	25,329	32,689	140,109	349,038	(51,161)
Average Shares	87,020	85,211	86,038	87,367	92,263	96,103	96,270	95,400
Balance Sheet								
Current Assets	595,987	528,768	545,030	588,304	747,156	933,644	1,112,057	719,658
Total Assets	1,536,926	1,226,144	1,330,703	1,391,302	1,384,189	1,522,097	1,534,637	1,359,365
Current Liabilities	269,580	208,114	248,507	236,732	273,383	315,949	330,224	497,046
Long-Term Obligations	...	...	496	55,002	57,302	127,840	150,369	150,722
Total Liabilities	449,595	375,807	460,123	612,076	457,033	508,752	557,043	737,803
Stockholders' Equity	1,087,331	850,337	870,580	779,226	927,156	1,013,345	977,594	621,562
Shares Outstanding	89,304	82,449	84,179	84,844	90,509	92,077	95,084	93,818
Statistical Record								
Return on Assets %	7.24	11.39	8.55	1.80	2.26	9.19	24.19	N.M.
Return on Equity %	10.81	17.63	14.11	2.92	3.38	14.11	43.77	N.M.
EBITDA Margin %	13.60	21.32	19.31	5.78	7.53	18.21	5.04	0.82
Net Margin %	6.49	14.54	12.61	3.20	3.88	11.34	31.15	N.M.
Asset Turnover	0.71	0.78	0.68	0.56	0.58	0.81	0.78	1.37
Current Ratio	2.21	2.54	2.19	2.49	2.73	2.96	3.37	1.45
Debt to Equity	...	...	N.M.	0.07	0.06	0.13	0.15	0.24
Price Range	34.94-26.49	34.94-23.11	34.49-20.10	21.08-14.70	27.23-17.02	43.00-23.69	34.88-11.19	19.13-6.91
P/E Ratio	28.88-21.89	21.05-13.92	25.55-14.89	72.69-50.69	77.80-48.63	29.45-16.22	9.61-3.08	...
Average Yield %	0.58	0.55	0.44	...	...	...	0.90	1.92

Address: 14200 S.W. Karl Braun Drive, Beaverton, OR 97077	**Web Site:** www.tektronix.com	**Auditors:** Deloitte & Touche LLP
Telephone: (503) 627-7111	**Officers:** Richard H. Wills - Chmn., Pres., C.E.O. Colin L. Slade - Sr. V.P., C.F.O.	**Investor Contact:** 503-627-7727
Fax: (503) 685-4104		**Transfer Agents:** Mellon Investor Services LLC, South Hackensack, NJ

TELEFLEX INCORPORATED

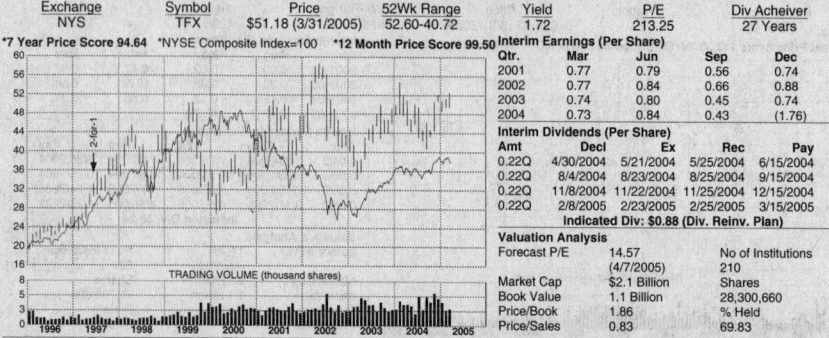

Exchange	Symbol	Price	52Wk Range	Yield	P/E	Div Acheiver
NYS	TFX	$51.18 (3/31/2005)	52.60-40.72	1.72	213.25	27 Years

*7 Year Price Score 94.64   ***NYSE Composite Index=100**   ***12 Month Price Score 99.50**

Interim Earnings (Per Share)

Qtr.	Mar	Jun	Sep	Dec
2001	0.77	0.79	0.56	0.74
2002	0.77	0.84	0.66	0.88
2003	0.74	0.80	0.45	0.74
2004	0.73	0.84	0.43	(1.76)

Interim Dividends (Per Share)

Amt	Decl	Ex	Rec	Pay
0.22Q	4/30/2004	5/21/2004	5/25/2004	6/15/2004
0.22Q	8/4/2004	8/23/2004	8/25/2004	9/15/2004
0.22Q	11/8/2004	11/22/2004	11/25/2004	12/15/2004
0.22Q	2/8/2005	2/23/2005	2/25/2005	3/15/2005

Indicated Div: $0.88 (Div. Reinv. Plan)

Valuation Analysis

Forecast P/E	14.57 (4/7/2005)	No of Institutions	210
Market Cap	$2.1 Billion	Shares	28,300,660
Book Value	1.1 Billion	% Held	69.83
Price/Book	1.86		
Price/Sales	0.83		

Business Summary: Medical Instruments & Equipment (MIC: 9.6 SIC: 841 NAIC: 39112)

Teleflex operates in three segments. Commercial Products designs and manufactures proprietary mechanical and electrical/electronic controls for the automotive market; mechanical, electrical and hydraulic controls, and electronics for the marine market; and proprietary products for fluid transfer and industrial applications. Medical Products manufactures and distributes a broad range of invasive disposable and reusable devices for selected medical care markets. Aerospace Products designs and manufactures cargo handling systems and containers for aviation, and provide surface treatments, repair services and manufactured components for the aerospace and turbine engine markets.

Recent Developments: For the year ended Dec 26 2004, income from continuing operations decreased 42.2% to $68,334 thousand from income of $118,202 thousand a year earlier. Net income decreased 91.3% to $9,517 thousand from net income of $109,103 thousand a year earlier. Revenues were $2,485,378 thousand, up 15.4% from $2,152,855 thousand the year before. Operating income was $139,486 thousand versus an income of $204,185 thousand in the prior year, a decrease of 31.7%. Total direct expense was $1,786,577 thousand versus $1,558,782 thousand in the prior year, an increase of 14.6%. Total indirect expense was $559,315 thousand versus $389,888 thousand in the prior year, an increase of 43.5%.

Prospects: For 2005, operating margins are expected to be positively affected by cost benefits stemming from Co.'s ongoing restructuring and divestiture program, accretion from the 2004 acquisition of HudsonRCI, and the positive impact of portfolio changes in 2004. Operating margins are expected to improve to double-digit levels by the end of 2005. Meanwhile, top-line results should benefit from strength in industrial markets, partially offset by a forecasted decline in revenues for the Tier 1 automotive businesses. Looking forward, Co. is targeting full-year 2005 earnings of between $2.80 and $3.00 per diluted share, including one-time charges related to the restructuring and divestiture program.

Financial Data

(US$ in Thousands)	12/26/2004	12/28/2003	12/29/2002	12/30/2001	12/31/2000	12/26/1999	12/27/1998	12/28/1997
Earnings Per Share	0.24	2.73	3.15	2.86	2.83	2.47	2.15	1.86
Cash Flow Per Share	6.35	5.70	5.12	4.87	4.88	3.55	3.53	2.20
Tang Book Value Per Share	14.49	19.42	16.61	19.99	18.01	15.85	14.21	12.49
Dividends Per Share	0.860	0.780	0.710	0.660	0.580	0.505	0.445	0.388
Dividend Payout %	358.33	28.57	22.54	23.08	20.49	20.45	20.70	20.83
Income Statement								
Total Revenue	2,485,378	2,282,435	2,076,229	1,905,004	1,764,482	1,601,069	1,437,578	1,145,773
EBITDA	253,619	282,180	267,605	252,096	235,631	210,145	184,865	154,345
Depn & Amortn	114,133	104,352	95,117	92,401	77,417	67,389	60,105	47,940
Income Before Taxes	102,368	151,491	172,488	159,695	158,214	142,756	124,760	106,405
Income Taxes	14,351	42,388	47,222	47,384	48,990	47,536	42,210	36,333
Net Income	9,517	109,103	125,266	112,311	109,224	95,220	82,550	70,072
Average Shares	40,495	39,942	39,786	39,280	38,633	38,525	38,425	37,661
Balance Sheet								
Current Assets	1,148,442	1,006,187	837,895	747,477	662,038	604,940	616,942	566,477
Total Assets	2,634,436	2,110,613	1,813,384	1,635,020	1,401,288	1,263,444	1,215,917	1,079,165
Current Liabilities	535,247	612,671	498,483	495,426	383,872	329,412	311,439	294,907
Long-Term Obligations	685,912	229,882	240,123	228,180	220,557	246,191	275,581	237,562
Total Liabilities	1,459,225	1,048,311	901,103	856,877	710,866	660,880	681,467	615,412
Stockholders' Equity	1,109,733	1,062,302	912,281	778,143	690,422	602,564	534,450	463,753
Shares Outstanding	40,424	39,795	39,398	38,932	38,344	38,018	37,615	37,118
Statistical Record								
Return on Assets %	0.40	5.58	7.29	7.42	8.07	7.70	7.21	7.25
Return on Equity %	0.88	11.08	14.86	15.34	16.62	16.80	16.59	16.10
EBITDA Margin %	10.20	12.36	12.89	13.23	13.35	13.13	12.86	13.47
Net Margin %	0.38	4.78	6.03	5.90	6.19	5.95	5.74	6.12
Asset Turnover	1.05	1.17	1.21	1.26	1.30	1.30	1.26	1.19
Current Ratio	2.15	1.64	1.68	1.51	1.72	1.84	1.98	1.92
Debt to Equity	0.62	0.22	0.26	0.29	0.32	0.41	0.52	0.51
Price Range	54.82-40.72	49.95-34.24	58.57-40.92	50.98-35.71	44.69-26.94	50.38-29.69	45.50-30.00	39.38-23.38
P/E Ratio	228.42-169.67	18.30-12.54	18.59-12.99	17.83-12.49	15.79-9.52	20.39-12.02	21.16-13.95	21.17-12.57
Average Yield %	1.82	1.83	1.44	1.49	1.67	1.24	1.14	1.24

Address: 630 West Germantown Pike, Suite 450, Plymouth Meeting, PA 19462	Web Site: www.teleflex.com	Auditors: PricewaterhouseCoopers LLP
Telephone: (610) 834-6301	Officers: Lennox K. Black - Chmn. John J. Sickler - Vice-Chmn.	Investor Contact: 610-834-6362
Fax: (610) 834-8228		Transfer Agents: American Stock Transfer & Trust Company, New York,

TEMPLE-INLAND INC.

Exchange	Symbol	Price	52Wk Range	Yield	P/E
NYS	TIN	$36.27 (3/31/2005)	42.00-28.75	2.48	24.85

*7 Year Price Score 103.48 *NYSE Composite Index=100 *12 Month Price Score 105.58

Interim Earnings (Per Share)

Qtr.	Mar	Jun	Sep	Dec
2001	0.10	0.29	0.45	0.27
2002	0.04	0.14	0.14	0.18
2003	(0.16)	1.44	(0.03)	(0.36)
2004	0.12	0.50	0.36	0.48

Interim Dividends (Per Share)

Amt	Decl	Ex	Rec	Pay
0.18Q	11/5/2004	11/29/2004	12/1/2004	12/15/2004
0.50Q	11/5/2004	11/29/2004	12/1/2004	12/15/2004
0.225Q	2/4/2005	2/25/2005	3/1/2005	3/15/2005
100%	2/4/2005	4/4/2005	3/1/2005	4/1/2005
		Indicated Div: $0.90		

Valuation Analysis

Forecast P/E	16.49	No of Institutions
	(4/7/2005)	266
Market Cap	$4.5 Billion	Shares
Book Value	2.1 Billion	45,353,396
Price/Book	2.13	% Held
Price/Sales	0.94	79.26

Business Summary: Paper Products (MIC: 11.11 SIC: 653 NAIC: 51112)

Temple-Inland is a holding company. Through its subsidiaries, Co. operates three business segments: corrugated packaging, forest products and financial services. Corrugated packaging is a vertically integrated corrugated packaging operation that consisted of five linerboard mills, one corrugating medium mill and 79 converting and other facilities as of Jan 3 2004. Forest products manages forest resources of approximately two million acres of timberland in Texas, Louisiana, Georgia, and Alabama, and manufactures building products. Financial services provides financial services in consumer and commercial banking, mortgage banking, real estate development and insurance brokerage.

Recent Developments: For the year ended Jan 1 2005, income from continuing operations increased 67.0% to $162,000 thousand from income of $97,000 thousand a year earlier. Net income increased 71.9% to $165,000 thousand from net income of $96,000 thousand a year earlier. Revenues were $4,750,000 thousand, up 2.1% from $4,653,000 thousand the year before. Operating income was $358,000 thousand versus an income of $46,000 thousand in the prior year, an increase of 678.3%. Total direct expense was $4,392,000 thousand versus $4,607,000 thousand in the prior year, a decrease of 4.7%.

Prospects: Co. is continuing to focus on improving asset utilization in its box plant system. The benefits of the latest closures within the system will be realized during 2005, and annual savings of $60.0 million from converting facility closures should be achieved by the end of 2005. In addition, Co.'s Project TIP consolidation and supply chain initiatives are on target to produce annualized savings of $75.0 million by the end of 2005. Meanwhile, Co.'s forest products business is benefiting from land sales, low cost operations and improved market conditions for its products. Separately, Co.'s financial services business has completed the sale of its third-party mortgage servicing portfolio.

Financial Data
(US$ in Thousands)

	01/01/2005	01/03/2004	12/28/2002	12/29/2001	12/31/2000	01/01/2000	01/02/1999	12/31/1997
Earnings Per Share	1.46	0.89	0.51	1.11	1.92	0.89	0.57	0.45
Cash Flow Per Share	4.14	8.16	2.52	(1.78)	4.71	5.68	3.08	3.12
Tang Book Value Per Share	13.88	14.51	14.42	17.32	18.64	17.78	17.97	18.16
Dividends Per Share	1.220	0.680	0.640	0.640	0.640	0.640	0.640	0.640
Dividend Payout %	83.56	76.84	125.49	57.66	33.42	71.91	111.30	142.22
Income Statement								
Total Revenue	4,750,000	4,653,000	4,518,000	4,172,000	4,286,000	3,682,000	3,740,000	3,625,000
EBITDA	670,000	390,000	551,000	530,000	677,000	666,000	602,000	502,000
Depn & Amortn	312,000	352,000	311,000	255,000	253,000	265,000	372,000	297,000
Income Before Taxes	233,000	(97,000)	107,000	177,000	320,000	306,000	124,000	95,000
Income Taxes	71,000	(194,000)	42,000	66,000	125,000	115,000	57,000	44,000
Net Income	165,000	96,000	53,000	109,000	195,000	99,000	64,000	51,000
Average Shares	112,400	108,400	104,800	98,600	101,800	111,600	111,800	112,400
Balance Sheet								
Current Assets	6,160,000	7,729,000	6,986,000	4,510,000	4,163,000	3,382,000	869,000	804,000
Total Assets	20,119,000	21,143,000	21,760,000	18,687,000	18,142,000	16,186,000	15,990,000	14,364,000
Current Liabilities	9,751,000	10,025,000	12,110,000	10,137,000	10,423,000	9,027,000	7,338,000	9,330,000
Long-Term Obligations	6,408,000	6,842,000	5,450,000	4,988,000	4,460,000	3,868,000	5,014,000	1,605,000
Total Liabilities	18,027,000	19,175,000	19,811,000	16,791,000	16,309,000	14,259,000	13,992,000	12,319,000
Stockholders' Equity	2,092,000	1,968,000	1,949,000	1,896,000	1,833,000	1,927,000	1,998,000	2,045,000
Shares Outstanding	122,779	109,194	107,612	98,718	98,348	108,400	111,200	112,600
Statistical Record								
Return on Assets %	0.80	0.44	0.26	0.60	1.14	0.62	0.42	0.37
Return on Equity %	8.15	4.82	2.66	5.88	10.37	5.06	3.15	2.49
EBITDA Margin %	14.11	8.38	12.20	12.70	15.80	18.09	16.10	13.85
Net Margin %	3.47	2.06	1.17	2.61	4.55	2.69	1.71	1.41
Asset Turnover	0.23	0.21	0.22	0.23	0.25	0.23	0.25	0.26
Current Ratio	0.63	0.77	0.58	0.44	0.40	0.37	0.12	0.09
Debt to Equity	3.06	3.48	2.80	2.63	2.43	2.01	2.51	0.78
Price Range	34.99-28.75	31.34-18.70	29.90-16.50	31.02-20.81	33.47-17.47	38.13-26.97	33.25-21.38	34.34-24.94
P/E Ratio	23.97-19.69	35.21-21.01	58.62-32.36	27.95-18.75	17.43-9.10	42.84-30.30	58.33-37.50	76.32-55.42
Average Yield %	3.81	2.86	2.50	2.45	2.69	1.99	2.33	2.18

Address: 1300 South MoPac Expressway, Austin, TX 78746 **Telephone:** (512) 434-5800	**Web Site:** www.templeinland.com **Officers:** Kenneth M. Jastrow II - Chmn., C.E.O. M. Richard Warner - Pres.	**Auditors:** ERNST & YOUNG LLP **Investor Contact:** 409-829-1378 **Transfer Agents:** EquiServe Trust Company, N.A., Providence, RI

TENET HEALTHCARE CORP.

Exchange	Symbol	Price	52Wk Range	Yield	P/E
NYS	THC	$11.53 (3/31/2005)	13.41-9.90	N/A	N/A

*7 Year Price Score 43.59 *NYSE Composite Index=100 *12 Month Price Score 90.07

TRADING VOLUME (thousand shares)

Interim Earnings (Per Share)

Qtr.	Mar	Jun	Feb	Dec
2003	(0.04)	(0.42)	(0.66)	(2.05)
2004	(0.26)	(0.91)	(0.15)	(4.33)

Interim Dividends (Per Share)

Amt	Decl	Ex	Rec	Pay
0.007U	3/6/2000	3/13/2000	3/15/2000	3/24/2000
3-for-2	5/22/2002	7/1/2002	6/12/2002	6/28/2002

Valuation Analysis

Forecast P/E	0.00	No of Institutions	
	(4/7/2005)	252	
Market Cap	$5.4 Billion	Shares	
Book Value	1.7 Billion	427,196,544	
Price/Book	3.11	% Held	
Price/Sales	0.54	91.22	

Business Summary: Hospitals & Health Care (MIC: 9.3 SIC: 062 NAIC: 22110)

Tenet Healthcare operates in the provision of health care, primarily through the operation of general acute care hospitals. As of Dec 31 2003, Co. owned and operated 101 acute care hospitals with 25,116 licensed beds in 15 states. Co.'s related health care facilities included a small number of rehabilitation hospitals, specialty hospitals, long-term-care facilities, a psychiatric facility and medical office buildings located on the same campus as, or nearby, its general hospitals, physician practices and various ancillary health care businesses, including outpatient surgery centers, home health care agencies, occupational and rural health care clinics and health maintenance organizations.

Recent Developments: For the year ended Dec 31 2004, loss from continuing operations was $1,797 million compared with a loss of $1,044 million a year earlier. Net loss was $2,640 million versus net loss of $1,477 million a year earlier. Revenues were $9,919 million, down 2.2% from $10,146 million the year before. Operating loss was $1,313 million versus a loss of $984 million in the prior year. Total indirect expense was $11,232 million versus $11,130 million in the prior year, an increase of 0.9%.

Prospects: For the first two months of 2005, same-hospital admissions were flat compared to the same period a year ago, which is encouraging compared to recent trends. Co. is implementing operational initiatives that are intended to increase admissions growth beyond recent levels. Based on current financial objectives, Co. anticipates that net operating revenues in fiscal 2005, will be flat to slightly higher from $9.90 billion in fiscal 2004. Also in fiscal 2005, Co. expects to achieve market level managed care price increases in the mid-to-high single digits with individual renegotiated commercial contracts. Co.'s cost-cutting initiatives in fiscal 2004 are expected to slow growth of costs.

Financial Data

(US$ in Thousands)	12/31/2004	12/31/2003	12/31/2002	05/31/2002	05/31/2001	05/31/2000	05/31/1999	05/31/1998
Earnings Per Share	(5.66)	(3.17)	0.93	1.56	1.31	0.64	0.53	0.56
Cash Flow Per Share	(0.18)	1.80	1.46	4.73	3.79	1.85	1.25	0.88
Tang Book Value Per Share	1.63	4.85	4.81	4.39	3.44	1.57	1.01	0.31
Dividends Per Share	...	...	...	...	...	0.007	...	...
Dividend Payout %	...	...	...	...	...	1.04	...	...
Income Statement								
Total Revenue	9,919,000	13,212,000	8,743,000	13,913,000	12,053,000	11,414,000	10,880,000	9,895,000
EBITDA	(892,000)	(1,074,000)	1,207,000	2,692,000	2,152,000	1,630,000	1,515,000	1,571,000
Depn & Amortn	388,000	471,000	302,000	604,000	554,000	533,000	556,000	460,000
Income Before Taxes	(1,613,000)	(1,841,000)	758,000	1,761,000	1,142,000	618,000	474,000	647,000
Income Taxes	184,000	(437,000)	299,000	736,000	464,000	278,000	225,000	269,000
Net Income	(2,640,000)	(1,477,000)	459,000	785,000	643,000	302,000	249,000	261,000
Average Shares	466,226	465,927	493,530	502,899	490,728	472,377	470,079	468,000
Balance Sheet								
Current Assets	3,992,000	4,248,000	3,792,000	3,394,000	3,226,000	3,594,000	3,962,000	2,890,000
Total Assets	10,078,000	12,298,000	13,780,000	13,814,000	12,995,000	13,161,000	13,771,000	12,833,000
Current Liabilities	2,130,000	2,394,000	2,381,000	2,584,000	2,166,000	1,912,000	2,022,000	1,767,000
Long-Term Obligations	4,395,000	4,039,000	3,872,000	3,919,000	4,202,000	5,668,000	6,391,000	5,829,000
Total Liabilities	8,346,000	7,937,000	8,057,000	8,195,000	7,916,000	9,095,000	9,901,000	9,275,000
Stockholders' Equity	1,732,000	4,361,000	5,723,000	5,619,000	5,079,000	4,066,000	3,870,000	3,558,000
Shares Outstanding	467,236	464,786	473,738	488,541	488,201	470,190	466,536	463,500
Statistical Record								
Return on Assets %	N.M.	N.M.	2.16	5.86	4.92	2.24	1.87	2.13
Return on Equity %	N.M.	N.M.	5.36	14.68	14.06	7.59	6.70	7.70
EBITDA Margin %	N.M.	N.M.	13.81	19.35	17.85	14.28	13.92	15.88
Net Margin %	N.M.	N.M.	5.25	5.64	5.33	2.65	2.29	2.64
Asset Turnover	0.88	1.01	0.41	1.04	0.92	0.85	0.82	0.81
Current Ratio	1.87	1.77	1.59	1.31	1.49	1.88	1.96	1.64
Debt to Equity	2.54	0.93	0.68	0.70	0.83	1.39	1.65	1.64
Price Range	18.20-9.81	18.98-11.45	52.20-14.00	49.85-30.28	31.32-16.79	18.42-10.50	23.33-11.63	27.21-17.33
P/E Ratio	...	...	56.13-15.05	31.96-19.41	23.91-12.82	28.78-16.41	44.03-21.93	48.59-30.95
Average Yield %	...	...	...	...	...	0.05	...	...

Address: 3820 State Street, Santa Barbara, CA 93105 Telephone: (805) 563-7000 Fax: (888) 896-9016	Web Site: www.tenethealth.com Officers: Jeffrey C. Barbakow - Chmn., C.E.O. Barry P. Schochet - Vice-Chmn.	Auditors: KPMG LLP Investor Contact: 805-563-7188 Transfer Agents: Bank of New York, NY

TENNANT CO.

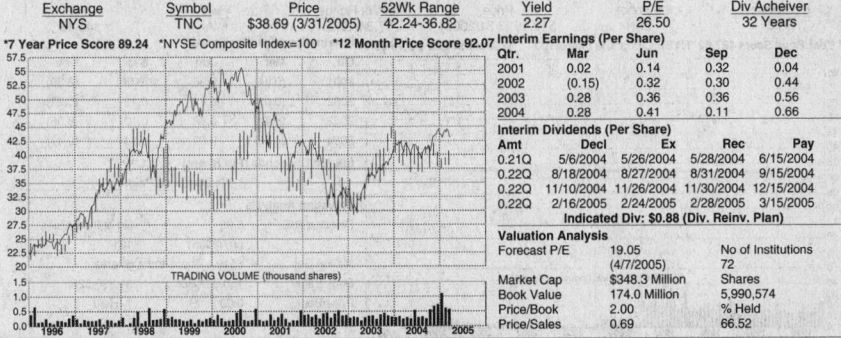

Exchange	Symbol	Price	52Wk Range	Yield	P/E	Div Acheiver
NYS	TNC	$38.69 (3/31/2005)	42.24-36.82	2.27	26.50	32 Years

*7 Year Price Score 89.24 *NYSE Composite Index=100 *12 Month Price Score 92.07

Interim Earnings (Per Share)

Qtr.	Mar	Jun	Sep	Dec
2001	0.02	0.14	0.32	0.04
2002	(0.15)	0.32	0.30	0.44
2003	0.28	0.36	0.36	0.56
2004	0.28	0.41	0.11	0.66

Interim Dividends (Per Share)

Amt	Decl	Ex	Rec	Pay
0.21Q	5/6/2004	5/26/2004	5/28/2004	6/15/2004
0.22Q	8/18/2004	8/27/2004	8/31/2004	9/15/2004
0.22Q	11/10/2004	11/26/2004	11/30/2004	12/15/2004
0.22Q	2/16/2005	2/24/2005	2/28/2005	3/15/2005
		Indicated Div: $0.88 (Div. Reinv. Plan)		

Valuation Analysis

Forecast P/E	19.05	No of Institutions	
	(4/7/2005)	72	
Market Cap	$348.3 Million	Shares	
Book Value	174.0 Million	5,990,574	
Price/Book	2.00	% Held	
Price/Sales	0.69	66.52	

Business Summary: Purpose Machinery (MIC: 11.13 SIC: 589 NAIC: 33319)

Tennant designs, manufactures and markets cleaning products. Co.'s floor maintenance equipment, outdoor cleaning equipment, coatings and related products are used to clean factories, office buildings, parking lots and streets, airports, hospitals, schools, warehouses and shopping centers, among others. Customers include the building service contract cleaners to whom organizations outsource facilities maintenance, as well as user corporations, healthcare facilities, schools and federal, state and local governments that handle facilities maintenance themselves. Co. sells its products through its direct sales and service organization and through a network of authorized distributors worldwide.

Recent Developments: For the year ended Dec 31 2004, net income decreased 5.5% to $13,380 thousand from net income of $14,155 thousand a year earlier. Revenues were $507,785 thousand, up 11.9% from $453,962 thousand the year before. Operating income was $21,307 thousand versus an income of $22,675 thousand in the prior year, a decrease of 6.0%. Total direct expense was $305,277 thousand versus $272,285 thousand in the prior year, an increase of 12.1%. Total indirect expense was $181,201 thousand versus $159,002 thousand in the prior year, an increase of 14.0%.

Prospects: Top-line growth is being driven by strong demand for newly-introduced products, improved market coverage, the 2004 acquisition of Walter-Broadley, and favorable foreign currency exchange rates. However, operating profitability is being hampered by higher costs for steel and petroleum-related materials and higher accruals for performance-based compensation. Meanwhile, cost-reduction initiatives implemented in the third quarter of 2004 are expected to generate annual pre-tax cost savings of between $2.0 million and $3.0 million in 2005 and between $4.0 million and $5.0 million in 2006 and beyond. Co. is targeting full-year 2005 earnings in the range of $1.80 to $2.10 per share.

Financial Data

(US$ in Thousands)	12/31/2004	12/31/2003	12/31/2002	12/31/2001	12/31/2000	12/31/1999	12/31/1998	12/31/1997
Earnings Per Share	1.46	1.56	0.91	0.52	3.09	2.15	2.67	2.41
Cash Flow Per Share	4.07	3.40	2.14	3.76	4.27	4.21	4.53	4.21
Tang Book Value Per Share	16.55	16.43	15.19	15.18	15.16	13.06	12.68	12.12
Dividends Per Share	0.860	0.840	0.820	0.800	0.780	0.760	0.740	0.720
Dividend Payout %	58.90	53.85	90.11	153.85	25.24	35.35	27.72	29.88
Income Statement								
Total Revenue	507,785	453,962	424,183	422,970	454,044	429,407	389,388	372,428
EBITDA	34,019	35,754	31,335	31,916	61,628	50,350	55,163	52,420
Depn & Amortn	12,972	13,879	16,947	18,507	18,391	18,667	17,550	17,468
Income Before Taxes	21,379	22,483	14,898	13,749	44,044	30,586	39,092	37,630
Income Taxes	7,999	8,328	6,633	8,945	15,794	10,893	13,767	13,425
Net Income	13,380	14,155	8,265	4,804	28,250	19,693	25,325	24,205
Average Shares	9,150	9,064	9,048	9,203	9,135	9,140	9,500	10,032
Balance Sheet								
Current Assets	188,631	176,370	162,901	152,387	171,628	165,093	150,868	143,105
Total Assets	285,792	258,873	256,237	246,619	263,285	257,533	239,098	233,870
Current Liabilities	81,853	59,507	70,349	55,648	67,255	74,999	60,809	57,149
Long-Term Obligations	1,029	6,295	5,000	10,000	10,000	16,003	23,038	20,678
Total Liabilities	111,758	93,257	102,092	92,291	108,337	121,618	107,831	99,784
Stockholders' Equity	174,034	165,616	154,145	154,328	154,948	135,915	131,267	134,086
Shares Outstanding	9,003	8,994	8,981	9,036	9,052	8,989	9,123	9,699
Statistical Record								
Return on Assets %	4.90	5.50	3.29	1.88	10.82	7.93	10.71	10.69
Return on Equity %	7.86	8.85	5.36	3.11	19.37	14.74	19.09	18.41
EBITDA Margin %	6.70	7.88	7.39	7.55	13.57	11.73	14.17	14.08
Net Margin %	2.63	3.12	1.95	1.14	6.22	4.59	6.50	6.50
Asset Turnover	1.86	1.76	1.69	1.66	1.74	1.73	1.65	1.64
Current Ratio	2.30	2.96	2.32	2.74	2.55	2.20	2.48	2.50
Debt to Equity	0.01	0.04	0.03	0.06	0.06	0.12	0.18	0.15
Price Range	44.20-36.82	44.99-29.28	44.00-26.62	48.88-32.90	52.31-30.13	42.00-32.00	44.81-33.00	39.50-26.25
P/E Ratio	30.27-25.22	28.84-18.77	48.35-29.25	93.99-63.27	16.93-9.75	19.53-14.88	16.78-12.36	16.39-10.89
Average Yield %	2.15	2.30	2.24	2.01	2.06	2.18	1.88	2.22

Address: 701 North Lilac Drive, P.O. Box 1452, Minneapolis, MN 55440 Telephone: (763) 540-1208 Fax: (612) 513-2142	Web Site: www.tennantco.com Officers: Janet M. Dolan - Pres., C.E.O. Eric A. Blanchard - V.P., Gen. Couns., Sec.	Auditors: KPMG LLP Investor Contact: 763-540-1553 Transfer Agents: Wells Fargo Bank Minnesota, N.A., St. Paul, MN

TENNECO AUTOMOTIVE, INC.

Exchange	Symbol	Price	52Wk Range	Yield	P/E
NYS	TEN	$12.46 (3/31/2005)	17.34-10.21	N/A	40.19

*7 Year Price Score 127.62 *NYSE Composite Index=100 *12 Month Price Score 99.11

Interim Earnings (Per Share)

Qtr.	Mar	Jun	Sep	Dec
2001	(0.84)	0.06	(0.06)	(2.60)
2002	(0.05)	0.45	0.13	(5.27)
2003	0.02	0.58	0.10	(0.05)
2004	(0.05)	0.69	0.14	(0.47)

Interim Dividends (Per Share)

No Dividends Paid

Valuation Analysis

Forecast P/E	8.95	No of Institutions
	(4/7/2005)	131
Market Cap	$518.1 Thousand	Shares
Book Value	150.0 Million	31,396,528
Price/Book	0.00	% Held
Price/Sales	0.00	72.35

Business Summary: Automotive (MIC: 15.1 SIC: 714 NAIC: 22221)

Tenneco Automotive is a producer of automotive emission control and ride control systems and products. Co. serves both original equipment manufacturers (OEMs) and replacement markets worldwide. Co.'s brands include Monroe®, Rancho®, Clevite®Elastomers, and Fric Rot™ ride control products and Walker®, Fonos™, and Gillet™ emission control products. As an automotive parts supplier, Co. designs, engineers, manufactures, markets and sells individual component parts for vehicles as well as groups of components that are combined as modules or systems within vehicles. These parts, modules and systems are sold globally to most leading OEMs and throughout all aftermarket distribution channels.

Recent Developments: For the year ended Dec 31 2004, net income decreased 51.9% to $13 million from net income of $27 million a year earlier. Revenues were $4,213 million, up 11.9% from $3,766 million the year before. Operating income was $171 million versus an income of $176 million in the prior year, a decrease of 2.8%. Total direct expense was $3,371 million versus $2,994 million in the prior year, an increase of 12.6%. Total indirect expense was $670 million versus $594 million in the prior year, an increase of 12.8%.

Prospects: In 2005, Co. plans to continue to aggressively manage costs, adjust its businesses to the market and grow revenues by expanding in new markets and winning new business with its advanced technology offerings. Co.'s goals include maintaining selling and general administrative expenses at less than 11.0% of sales; achieving a ratio of net debt to earnings before income taxes, depreciation and amortization of a multiple of 2.8; and generating at least $300.0 million in new business annually. Co. expects that vehicle mix will continue to be a key revenue driver in 2005 and it will benefit from its strong position on better-selling platforms.

Financial Data
(US$ in Thousands)

	12/31/2004	12/31/2003	12/31/2002	12/31/2001	12/31/2000	12/31/1999	12/31/1998	12/31/1997
Earnings Per Share	0.31	0.65	(4.74)	(3.43)	(1.20)	(12.64)	7.55	9.20
Cash Flow Per Share	4,802.08	6.95	4.72	3.73	6.72	(7.59)	15.83	...
Tang Book Value Per Share	N.M.	N.M.	...	N.M.	N.M.	N.M.	25.75	27.97
Dividends Per Share	...	...	...	...	0.200	4.500	6.000	6.000
Dividend Payout %	...	...	...	...	...	...	79.47	65.22
Income Statement								
Total Revenue	4,213,000	3,766,000	3,459,000	3,364,000	3,549,000	3,292,000	7,605,000	7,318,000
EBITDA	...	339,000	313,000	245,000	271,000	292,000	1,089,000	1,129,000
Depn & Amortn	177,000	163,000	144,000	153,000	151,000	144,000	448,000	365,000
Income Before Taxes	...	27,000	28,000	(78,000)	(66,000)	42,000	401,000	548,000
Income Taxes	(25,000)	(6,000)	(7,000)	51,000	(27,000)	82,000	116,000	163,000
Net Income	13,000	27,000	(187,000)	(130,000)	(42,000)	(423,000)	255,000	315,000
Average Shares	44	41,767	41,667	38,001	34,906	33,656	33,800	34,200
Balance Sheet								
Current Assets	1,278,000	1,105,000	966,000	941,000	1,109,000	1,201,000	2,157,000	2,115,000
Total Assets	3,110,000	2,795,000	2,504,000	2,681,000	2,886,000	2,943,000	8,791,000	8,332,000
Current Liabilities	1,047,000	893,000	1,016,000	876,000	809,000	663,000	2,387,000	1,661,000
Long-Term Obligations	1,401,000	1,410,000	1,217,000	1,324,000	1,435,000	1,578,000	2,360,000	2,633,000
Total Liabilities	2,960,000	2,737,000	2,598,000	2,607,000	2,556,000	2,521,000	6,287,000	5,804,000
Stockholders' Equity	150,000	58,000	(94,000)	74,000	330,000	422,000	2,504,000	2,528,000
Shares Outstanding	41	40,872	40,052	40,060	36,498	33,672	34,600	34,000
Statistical Record								
Return on Assets %	0.44	1.02	N.M.	N.M.	N.M.	N.M.	2.98	...
Return on Equity %	12.47	...	N.M.	N.M.	N.M.	N.M.	10.14	...
EBITDA Margin %	...	9.00	9.05	7.28	7.64	8.87	14.32	15.43
Net Margin %	0.31	0.72	N.M.	N.M.	N.M.	N.M.	3.35	4.30
Asset Turnover	1.42	1.42	1.33	1.21	1.21	0.56	0.89	...
Current Ratio	1.22	1.24	0.95	1.07	1.37	1.81	0.90	1.27
Debt to Equity	9.34	24.31	...	17.89	4.35	3.74	0.94	1.04
Price Range	17.34-6.69	7.34-2.06	8.16-1.95	5.45-1.35	10.88-2.63	21.83-7.06	27.58-17.80	30.18-22.30
P/E Ratio	55.94-21.58	11.29-3.17	...	...	...	...	3.65-2.36	3.28-2.42
Average Yield %	...	...	...	...	2.98	33.18	27.17	23.38

Address: 500 North Field Drive, Lake Forest, IL 60045 **Telephone:** (847) 482-5000 **Fax:** (847) 482-5940	**Web Site:** www.tenneco-automotive.com **Officers:** Mark P. Frissora - Chmn., Pres., C.E.O. Timothy R. Donovan - Exec. V.P., Gen. Couns., Man. Dir.-Int'l	**Auditors:** Deloitte & Touche LLP **Investor Contact:** 847-482-5042

TEPPCO PARTNERS, L.P.

Exchange	Symbol	Price	52Wk Range	Yield	P/E	Div Acheiver
NYS	TPP	$42.00 (3/31/2005)	45.29-34.79	6.31	26.09	12 Years

*7 Year Price Score 112.88 *NYSE Composite Index=100 *12 Month Price Score 99.21

Interim Earnings (Per Share)

Qtr.	Mar	Jun	Sep	Dec
2001	0.55	0.89	0.35	0.39
2002	0.46	0.39	0.48	0.47
2003	0.43	0.43	0.36	0.31
2004	0.46	0.43	0.29	0.43

Interim Dividends (Per Share)

Amt	Decl	Ex	Rec	Pay
0.662Q	4/16/2004	4/28/2004	4/30/2004	5/7/2004
0.662Q	7/16/2004	7/28/2004	7/30/2004	8/6/2004
0.662Q	10/15/2004	10/27/2004	10/29/2004	11/5/2004
0.662Q	1/14/2005	1/27/2005	1/31/2005	2/7/2005

Indicated Div: $2.65

Valuation Analysis

Forecast P/E	23.14	No of Institutions
	(4/7/2005)	133
Market Cap	$2.6 Billion	Shares
Book Value	N/A	11,798,229
Price/Book	N/A	% Held
Price/Sales	0.44	18.73

Business Summary: Oil and Gas (MIC: 14.2 SIC: 613 NAIC: 86910)

TEPPCO Partners operates through three segments. The downstream segment includes transportation and storage of refined products, liquefied petroleum gases and petrochemicals. The upstream segment includes gathering, transportation, marketing and storage of crude oil, and distribution of lubrication oils and specialty chemicals. The midstream segment includes natural gas gathering services, fractionation of natural gas liquids (NGLs) and transportation of NGLs. Texas Eastern Products Pipeline Co., a subsidiary of Duke Energy Field Services (DEFS), serves as the general partner of TPP. Certain assets of the midstream segment are managed and operated by DEFS under an agreement with Co.

Recent Developments: For the year ended Dec 31 2004, net income increased 13.2% to $142,381 thousand from net income of $125,769 thousand a year earlier. Revenues were $5,958,192 thousand, up 40.0% from $4,255,832 thousand the year before. Operating income was $187,133 thousand versus an income of $192,408 thousand in the prior year, a decrease of 2.7%. Total indirect expense was $5,771,059 thousand versus $4,063,424 thousand in the prior year, an increase of 42.0%.

Prospects: Co.'s upstream segment is realizing the benefits from the completion of the integration of the Genesis assets into Co.'s South Texas system and enjoyed substantially increased volumes on Seaway Crude Pipeline. Meanwhile, the Jonah Gas Gathering System continued its strong performance, with throughput exceeding 1.00 billion cubic feet per day (Bcf/day) for the fourth quarter quarter. For 2005, Co. expects earnings before interest, taxes, depreciation and amortization (EBITDA) to be in the range of $365.0 million to $395.0 million, and earnings per unit in the range of $1.80 to $2.15 per unit. Co. noted it anticipates total capital expenditures for 2005 will be about $230.0 million.

Financial Data
(US$ in Thousands)

	12/31/2004	12/31/2003	12/31/2002	12/31/2001	12/31/2000	12/31/1999	12/31/1998	12/31/1997
Earnings Per Share	1.61	1.52	1.79	2.18	1.89	1.91	(0.60)	1.95
Cash Flow Per Share	4.21	4.00	4.77	4.31	3.21	3.13	3.14	2.88
Dividends Per Share	2.638	2.500	2.350	2.150	2.000	1.850	1.750	1.550
Dividend Payout %	163.82	164.47	131.28	98.62	105.82	96.86	...	79.49
Income Statement								
Total Revenue	5,958,192	4,255,832	3,242,163	3,556,413	3,087,941	1,934,883	429,638	222,093
Depn & Amortn	112,900	100,700	86,032	45,899	35,163	32,656	26,938	23,772
Net Income	142,381	125,769	117,862	109,131	77,376	72,120	(19,426)	61,300
Average Shares	62,999	59,765	49,202	39,258	33,594	45,058	74,933	...
Balance Sheet								
Net PPE	1,703,702	1,619,163	1,587,824	1,180,461	949,705	720,919	671,611	567,681
Total Assets	3,197,705	2,940,992	2,770,642	2,065,348	1,622,810	1,041,373	914,969	673,909
Long-Term Obligations	1,480,226	1,339,650	1,377,692	730,472	835,784	455,753	427,722	309,512
Total Liabilities	2,176,257	1,831,671	1,878,800	1,522,167	1,307,753	811,606	687,783	370,942
Shares Outstanding	62,998	62,998	53,809	40,500	32,700	29,000	29,000	29,000
Statistical Record								
Return on Assets %	4.63	4.40	4.87	5.92	5.79	7.37	N.M.	9.11
Net Margin %	2.39	2.96	3.64	3.07	2.51	3.73	(4.52)	27.60
PPE Turnover	3.58	2.65	2.34	3.34	3.69	2.78	0.69	0.39
Asset Turnover	1.94	1.49	1.34	1.93	2.31	1.98	0.54	0.33
Price Range	42.16-34.79	41.15-27.75	33.00-26.10	35.90-24.75	26.63-19.31	27.94-18.00	30.50-24.25	27.88-20.13
P/E Ratio	26.19-21.61	27.07-18.26	18.44-14.58	16.47-11.35	14.09-10.22	14.63-9.42	...	14.29-10.32
Average Yield %	6.73	7.26	7.80	7.32	8.72	7.79	6.35	6.56

Address: 2929 Allen Parkway, P.O. Box 2521, Houston, TX 77252-2521 **Telephone:** (713) 759 3636 **Fax:** (713) 759 3957	**Web Site:** www.teppco.com **Officers:** Jim W. Mogg - Chmn. Barry R. Pearl - Pres., C.E.O., C.O.O.	**Auditors:** KPMG LLP **Investor Contact:** 800-659-0059 **Transfer Agents:** ChaseMellon Shareholder Services, L.L.C., Ridgefield

TERADYNE, INC.

Exchange	Symbol	Price	52Wk Range	Yield	P/E
NYS	TER	$14.60 (3/31/2005)	25.73-12.71	N/A	17.38

*7 Year Price Score 50.36   *NYSE Composite Index=100   *12 Month Price Score 81.03

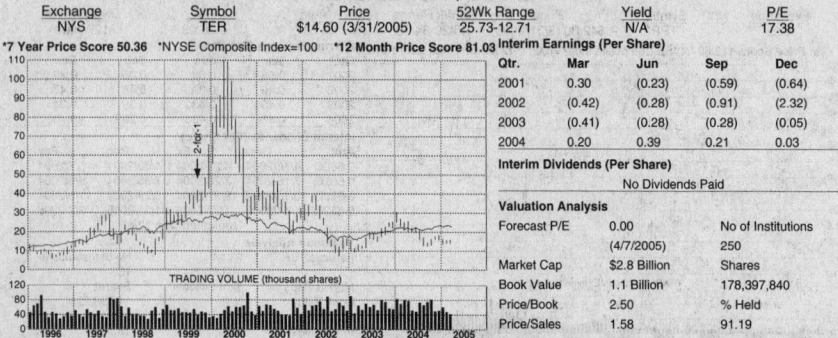

Interim Earnings (Per Share)

Qtr.	Mar	Jun	Sep	Dec
2001	0.30	(0.23)	(0.59)	(0.64)
2002	(0.42)	(0.28)	(0.91)	(2.32)
2003	(0.41)	(0.28)	(0.28)	(0.05)
2004	0.20	0.39	0.21	0.03

Interim Dividends (Per Share)

No Dividends Paid

Valuation Analysis

Forecast P/E	0.00	No of Institutions
	(4/7/2005)	250
Market Cap	$2.8 Billion	Shares
Book Value	1.1 Billion	178,397,840
Price/Book	2.50	% Held
Price/Sales	1.58	91.19

Business Summary: Instruments and Related Products (MIC: 11.15 SIC: 825 NAIC: 34515)

Teradyne is a supplier of automatic test equipment, a provider of high-performance interconnection systems and an emerging provider of electronic manufacturing services. Co.'s customers include major semiconductor, electronics, automotive and network systems companies. Co.'s products include semiconductor test systems, circuit board test and inspection systems, diagnostic solutions, broadband test systems, connection systems (high-bandwidth backplane assemblies and associated connectors used in electronic systems) and electronic manufacturing services of assemblies.

Recent Developments: For the year ended Dec 31 2004, net income was $165,237 thousand versus net loss of $193,993 thousand a year earlier. Revenues were $1,791,880 thousand, up 32.5% from $1,352,867 thousand the year before. Operating income was $188,803 thousand versus a loss of $176,449 thousand in the prior year. Total direct expense was $1,068,007 thousand versus $953,968 thousand in the prior year, an increase of 12.0%. Total indirect expense was $536,800 thousand versus $575,349 thousand in the prior year, a decrease of 6.7%.

Prospects: Co. noted that customer demand remains tentative. In addition, Co.'s competitive position in the System On a Chip test market has strengthened, and it is aggressively funding its FLEX research and development program. Concurrently, Co. is reducing costs across a number of areas in the organization. Separately, for the first quarter of 2005, Co. is projecting sales to be in between $290.0 million and $310.0 million, with a loss per share of between $0.24 and $0.31. This guidance includes pre-tax restructuring and other charges of $13.0 million and a $2.5 million tax provision for foreign and state taxes.

Financial Data

(US$ in Thousands)	12/31/2004	12/31/2003	12/31/2002	12/31/2001	12/31/2000	12/31/1999	12/31/1998	12/31/1997
Earnings Per Share	0.84	(1.03)	(3.93)	(1.15)	2.51	1.07	0.59	0.74
Cash Flow Per Share	1.31	0.18	(0.02)	(0.45)	2.71	2.16	1.42	0.08
Tang Book Value Per Share	5.24	4.33	4.80	8.44	9.89	6.77	6.13	5.62
Income Statement								
Total Revenue	1,791,880	1,352,867	1,222,236	1,440,581	3,043,946	1,790,912	1,489,151	1,266,274
EBITDA	313,518	(27,634)	(397,004)	(206,137)	812,627	344,584	210,238	234,452
Depn & Amortn	122,179	151,689	159,111	138,668	101,862	86,386	76,304	59,151
Income Before Taxes	187,974	(186,193)	(560,945)	(326,153)	739,648	273,849	145,882	193,345
Income Taxes	22,737	7,800	157,524	(123,938)	221,894	82,155	43,765	65,737
Net Income	165,237	(193,993)	(718,469)	(202,215)	453,616	191,694	102,117	127,608
Average Shares	197,432	187,845	182,861	175,828	181,011	178,550	171,930	172,638
Balance Sheet								
Current Assets	805,826	769,277	809,273	1,207,022	1,377,834	907,687	759,540	727,083
Total Assets	1,922,562	1,785,362	1,894,677	2,542,391	2,355,868	1,568,213	1,312,814	1,251,674
Current Liabilities	276,558	280,815	279,365	296,131	619,288	392,326	255,690	277,973
Long-Term Obligations	398,932	407,658	450,561	451,682	8,352	8,948	13,200	13,141
Total Liabilities	788,998	835,792	866,204	778,007	648,897	415,181	286,444	314,543
Stockholders' Equity	1,133,564	949,570	1,028,473	1,764,384	1,706,971	1,153,032	1,026,370	937,131
Shares Outstanding	194,253	191,973	183,196	181,119	172,559	170,319	167,488	166,606
Statistical Record								
Return on Assets %	8.89	N.M.	N.M.	N.M.	23.06	13.31	7.96	10.87
Return on Equity %	15.82	N.M.	N.M.	N.M.	31.63	17.59	10.40	14.34
EBITDA Margin %	17.50	N.M.	N.M.	N.M.	26.70	19.24	14.12	18.52
Net Margin %	9.22	N.M.	N.M.	N.M.	14.90	10.70	6.86	10.08
Asset Turnover	0.96	0.74	0.55	0.59	1.55	1.24	1.16	1.08
Current Ratio	2.91	2.74	2.90	4.08	2.22	2.31	2.97	2.62
Debt to Equity	0.35	0.43	0.44	0.26	N.M.	0.01	0.01	0.01
Price Range	30.69-12.71	25.60-9.58	39.49-7.22	47.19-19.00	110.00-24.31	66.00-21.06	23.59-7.81	29.38-12.00
P/E Ratio	36.54-15.13	...	...	...	43.82-9.69	61.68-19.68	39.99-13.24	39.70-16.22

Address: 321 Harrison Avenue, Boston, MA 02118 **Telephone:** (617) 482-2700 **Fax:** (617) 422-2910	**Web Site:** www.teradyne.com **Officers:** George W. Chamillard - Chmn., C.E.O. Michael A. Bradley - Pres.	**Auditors:** PricewaterhouseCoopers LLP **Investor Contact:** 617-422-2425

TEREX CORP.

Exchange	Symbol	Price	52Wk Range	Yield	P/E
NYS	TEX	$43.30 (3/31/2005)	48.67-28.13	N/A	25.03

*7 Year Price Score 142.37 ***NYSE Composite Index=100** ***12 Month Price Score 104.48**

TRADING VOLUME (thousand shares)

Interim Earnings (Per Share)

Qtr.	Mar	Jun	Sep	Dec
2001	0.37	0.43	(0.41)	0.04
2002	0.44	0.12	0.22	(0.87)
2003	0.26	(1.02)	0.29	(0.07)
2004	0.34	1.17	...	...

Interim Dividends (Per Share)

No Dividends Paid

Valuation Analysis

Forecast P/E	17.30	No of Institutions
	(4/7/2005)	195
Market Cap	$2.1 Billion	Shares
Book Value	932.0 Million	43,096,928
Price/Book	2.29	% Held
Price/Sales	0.49	87.24

Business Summary: Industrial Machinery and Equipment (MIC: 11.5 SIC: 537 NAIC: 33924)

Terex is a diversified global manufacturer of a wide range of equipment for use in various industries including the construction, infrastructure, quarrying, recycling, surface mining, shipping, transportation, refining, utility and maintenance industries. Co. operates in five business segments: Terex Construction, Terex Cranes, Terex Aerial Work Platforms, Terex Mining, and Terex Roadbuilding, Utility Products and Other. Co.'s products are manufactured at plants in the U.S., Canada, Europe, Australia, Asia and South America, and are sold primarily through a worldwide distribution network.

Recent Developments: For the third quarter ended Sep 30 2004, net income surged 108.7% to $31.1 million from $14.9 million in the corresponding prior-year quarter. Net sales advanced 38.1% to $1.25 billion compared with $906.3 million a year earlier, reflecting growth in the Roadbuilding, Utility Products, and other segments. Net sales were driven substantially by the acquisition of Tatra and the American Truck Company and growth in the concrete mixing truck business. Gross profit climbed 29.5% to $172.9 million from $133.5 million the year before. Income from operations increased 33.6% to $59.3 million from $44.4 million in the previous year.

Prospects: In 2004, Co. saw a sharp increase in demand for its products. However, its expected margin improvement was substantially offset by higher costs of materials and components, primarily steel. Looking ahead, Co. will continue to strive to grow revenues; but it will focus on margin improvement. For full-year 2005, Co. expects total revenue to be between $5.40 billion and $5.60 billion, with earnings ranging from $3.40 to $3.60 per share. Separately, on Dec 31 2004, Co. completed the acquisition of the Reedrill division of Metso Corp. Reedrill is a manufacturer of surface drilling equipment for use in the mining, construction and utility business.

Financial Data

(US$ in Thousands)	6 Mos	3 Mos	12/31/2003	12/31/2002	12/31/2001	12/31/2000	12/31/1999	12/31/1998
Earnings Per Share	1.73	(0.45)	(0.53)	(3.07)	0.44	3.41	6.75	1.54
Cash Flow Per Share	5.46	4.16	8.05	1.63	(0.20)	7.35	0.21	(0.94)
Tang Book Value Per Share	6.41	5.48	5.60	3.09	N.M.	N.M.	N.M.	N.M.
Income Statement								
Total Revenue	2,380,200	1,043,800	3,897,100	2,797,400	1,812,500	2,068,700	1,856,600	1,233,200
EBITDA	178,600	64,200	133,400	109,400	147,700	298,900	210,700	139,500
Depn & Amortn	37,100	18,300	70,400	45,000	40,300	41,500	32,200	18,400
Income Before Taxes	98,000	24,400	(35,300)	(25,800)	24,600	159,600	98,400	74,500
Income Taxes	21,900	7,400	(9,800)	(8,300)	7,900	55,700	(74,500)	1,700
Net Income	76,100	17,000	(25,500)	(132,500)	12,800	95,100	172,900	34,500
Average Shares	50,700	50,600	47,700	43,200	28,900	27,900	25,600	22,400
Balance Sheet								
Current Assets	2,371,000	2,292,800	2,194,000	2,221,100	1,383,000	1,242,400	1,315,300	771,600
Total Assets	3,866,500	3,820,400	3,723,800	3,625,700	2,387,000	1,983,700	2,177,500	1,151,200
Current Liabilities	1,321,900	1,240,300	1,159,400	1,106,200	627,100	575,600	579,500	425,400
Long-Term Obligations	1,187,100	1,279,400	1,274,800	1,487,100	1,020,700	882,000	1,098,800	586,600
Total Liabilities	2,934,500	2,937,800	2,847,100	2,856,500	1,791,600	1,532,200	1,744,700	1,053,100
Stockholders' Equity	932,000	882,600	876,700	769,200	595,400	451,500	432,800	98,100
Shares Outstanding	49,300	50,300	48,800	47,400	36,400	26,800	27,500	20,800
Statistical Record								
Return on Assets %	2.34	N.M.	N.M.	N.M.	0.59	4.56	10.39	3.97
Return on Equity %	10.17	N.M.	N.M.	N.M.	2.45	21.45	65.13	43.75
EBITDA Margin %	7.50	6.15	3.42	3.91	8.15	14.45	11.35	11.31
Net Margin %	3.20	1.63	N.M.	N.M.	0.71	4.60	9.31	2.80
Asset Turnover	1.18	1.08	1.06	0.93	0.83	0.99	1.12	1.42
Current Ratio	1.79	1.85	1.89	2.01	2.21	2.16	2.27	1.81
Debt to Equity	1.27	1.45	1.45	1.93	1.71	1.95	2.54	5.98
Price Range	38.80-17.63	37.77-12.36	29.47-9.70	26.71-10.49	24.25-15.56	28.63-11.63	35.38-22.25	31.31-14.00
P/E Ratio	22.43-10.19	...	...	...	55.11-35.37	8.39-3.41	5.24-3.30	20.33-9.09

Address: 500 Post Road East, Suite 320, Westport, CT 06880 Telephone: (203) 222-7170 Fax: (203) 222-7976	Web Site: www.terex.com Officers: Ronald M. DeFeo - Chmn., C.E.O. Phillip C. Widman - Sr. V.P., C.F.O.	Auditors: PricewaterhouseCoopers LLP

TEXAS INSTRUMENTS INC.

Exchange	Symbol	Price	52Wk Range	Yield	P/E
NYS	TXN	$25.49 (3/31/2005)	30.94-18.40	0.39	24.28

*7 Year Price Score 65.20   ***NYSE Composite Index=100**   ***12 Month Price Score 99.77**

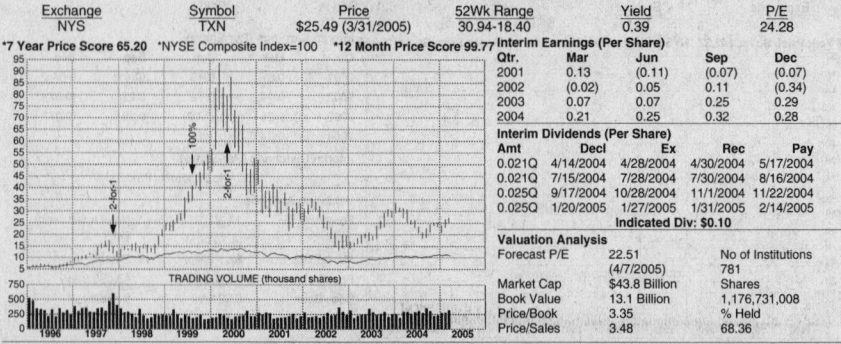

Interim Earnings (Per Share)

Qtr.	Mar	Jun	Sep	Dec
2001	0.13	(0.11)	(0.07)	(0.07)
2002	(0.02)	0.05	0.11	(0.34)
2003	0.07	0.07	0.25	0.29
2004	0.21	0.25	0.32	0.28

Interim Dividends (Per Share)

Amt	Decl	Ex	Rec	Pay
0.021Q	4/14/2004	4/28/2004	4/30/2004	5/17/2004
0.021Q	7/15/2004	7/28/2004	7/30/2004	8/16/2004
0.025Q	9/17/2004	10/28/2004	11/1/2004	11/22/2004
0.025Q	1/20/2005	1/27/2005	1/31/2005	2/14/2005

Indicated Div: $0.10

Valuation Analysis

Forecast P/E	22.51	No of Institutions	
	(4/7/2005)	781	
Market Cap	$43.8 Billion	Shares	
Book Value	13.1 Billion	1,176,731,008	
Price/Book	3.35	% Held	
Price/Sales	3.48	68.36	

Business Summary: IT & Technology (MIC: 10.2 SIC: 674 NAIC: 34413)

Texas Instruments manufactures, markets and sells high-technology components and systems primarily for industrial and consumer markets. The Semiconductor segment designs, manufactures and sells analog semiconductors and digital signal processors used in a wide range of electronic systems. This segment also produces Digital Light Processing™ products for use in projectors and high-definition televisions. The Sensors and Controls segment designs and manufactures sensors, electrical and electronic controls, and radio frequency identification (RFID) systems. The Educational and Productivity Solution segment supplies graphing handheld calculators, as well as business and scientific calculators.

Recent Developments: For the year ended Dec 31 2004, net income increased 55.3% to $1,861,000 thousand from net income of $1,198,000 thousand a year earlier. Revenues were $12,580,000 thousand, up 27.9% from $9,834,000 thousand the year before. Operating income was $2,207,000 thousand versus an income of $965,000 thousand in the prior year, an increase of 128.7%. Total direct expense was $6,954,000 thousand versus $5,872,000 thousand in the prior year, an increase of 18.4%. Total indirect expense was $3,419,000 thousand versus $2,997,000 thousand in the prior year, an increase of 14.1%.

Prospects: Revenues are benefiting from increases in Co.'s Semiconductor segment, primarily due to strong growth in products sold into the wireless market and higher sales of proprietary Digital Light Processing™ (DLP™) products, due to strong demand for projectors and high-definition televisions. Co. believes its distributors made good progress in reducing their inventories in the second half of 2004. Co. is encouraged by the momentum of its products and the overall health of its markets, and it intends to be well-positioned for a resumption in growth. For the first quarter of 2005, Co. expects revenue ranging from $2.90 billion to $3.14 billion and earnings in the range of $0.22 to $0.26 per share.

Financial Data

(US$ in Thousands)	12/31/2004	12/31/2003	12/31/2002	12/31/2001	12/31/2000	12/31/1999	12/31/1998	12/31/1997
Earnings Per Share	1.05	0.68	(0.20)	(0.12)	1.71	0.84	0.26	1.14
Cash Flow Per Share	1.81	1.24	1.15	1.05	1.27	1.26	0.80	1.20
Tang Book Value Per Share	6.95	6.35	5.73	6.42	6.16	5.07	4.17	3.80
Dividends Per Share	0.089	0.085	0.085	0.085	0.085	0.085	0.064	0.085
Dividend Payout %	8.45	12.50	...	...	4.97	10.12	25.00	7.49
Income Statement								
Total Revenue	12,580,000	9,834,000	8,383,000	8,201,000	11,875,000	9,468,000	8,460,000	9,750,000
EBITDA	3,855,000	2,708,000	1,279,000	1,279,000	5,733,000	2,972,000	1,670,000	1,770,000
Depn & Amortn	1,549,000	1,528,000	1,689,000	1,828,000	1,376,000	1,055,000	1,144,000	1,109,000
Income Before Taxes	2,421,000	1,250,000	(346,000)	(426,000)	4,578,000	2,019,000	617,000	713,000
Income Taxes	560,000	52,000	(2,000)	(225,000)	1,491,000	613,000	210,000	411,000
Net Income	1,861,000	1,198,000	(344,000)	(201,000)	3,058,000	1,406,000	407,000	1,805,000
Average Shares	1,768,000	1,766,400	1,733,343	1,734,506	1,791,630	1,673,520	1,604,000	1,590,908
Balance Sheet								
Current Assets	10,190,000	7,709,000	6,126,000	5,775,000	8,115,000	6,055,000	4,846,000	6,103,000
Total Assets	16,299,000	15,510,000	14,679,000	15,779,000	17,720,000	15,028,000	11,250,000	10,849,000
Current Liabilities	1,925,000	2,200,000	1,934,000	1,580,000	2,813,000	2,628,000	2,196,000	2,496,000
Long-Term Obligations	368,000	395,000	833,000	1,211,000	1,216,000	1,097,000	1,027,000	1,286,000
Total Liabilities	3,236,000	3,646,000	3,945,000	3,900,000	5,132,000	5,773,000	4,723,000	4,935,000
Stockholders' Equity	13,063,000	11,864,000	10,734,000	11,879,000	12,588,000	9,255,000	6,527,000	5,914,000
Shares Outstanding	1,718,115	1,732,337	1,730,588	1,733,933	1,732,052	1,625,782	1,564,000	1,557,996
Statistical Record								
Return on Assets %	11.67	7.94	N.M.	N.M.	18.62	10.70	3.68	17.86
Return on Equity %	14.89	10.60	N.M.	N.M.	27.92	17.82	6.54	36.06
EBITDA Margin %	30.64	27.54	15.26	15.60	48.28	31.39	19.74	18.15
Net Margin %	14.79	12.18	N.M.	N.M.	25.75	14.85	4.81	18.51
Asset Turnover	0.79	0.65	0.55	0.49	0.72	0.72	0.77	0.96
Current Ratio	5.29	3.50	3.17	3.66	2.88	2.30	2.21	2.45
Debt to Equity	0.03	0.03	0.08	0.10	0.10	0.12	0.16	0.22
Price Range	33.65-18.40	30.92-14.15	35.71-13.23	52.06-21.73	93.81-36.88	54.24-21.41	22.27-10.41	17.63-7.81
P/E Ratio	32.05-17.52	45.47-20.81	...	...	54.86-21.56	64.57-25.48	85.64-40.02	15.46-6.85
Average Yield %	0.35	0.40	0.35	0.25	0.13	0.24	0.43	0.70

Address: 12500 TI Boulevard, P.O. Box 660199, Dallas, TX 75266-0199 **Telephone:** (972) 995-3773 **Fax:** (972) 995-4360	Web Site: www.ti.com **Officers:** Thomas J. Engibous - Chmn. Richard K. Templeton - Pres., C.E.O.	Auditors: Ernst & Young LLP **Investor Contact:** 972-995-3773

TEXTRON INC.

Exchange	Symbol	Price	52Wk Range	Yield	P/E
NYS	TXT	$74.62 (3/31/2005)	80.05-52.45	1.88	28.59

*7 Year Price Score 97.37   ***NYSE Composite Index=100**   ***12 Month Price Score 107.88**

Interim Earnings (Per Share)

Qtr.	Mar	Jun	Sep	Dec
2001	0.79	0.88	(2.34)	1.81
2002	0.40	0.74	0.51	0.93
2003	0.48	0.46	0.34	0.60
2004	0.26	0.71	0.73	0.90

Interim Dividends (Per Share)

Amt	Decl	Ex	Rec	Pay
0.325Q	4/28/2004	6/9/2004	6/11/2004	7/1/2004
0.325Q	7/28/2004	9/8/2004	9/10/2004	10/1/2004
0.35Q	10/21/2004	12/8/2004	12/10/2004	1/3/2005
0.35Q	2/23/2005	3/9/2005	3/11/2005	4/1/2005

Indicated Div: $1.40

Valuation Analysis

Forecast P/E	19.00	No of Institutions	
	(4/13/2005)	348	
Market Cap	$10.1 Billion	Shares	
Book Value	3.7 Billion	91,107,872	
Price/Book	2.77	% Held	
Price/Sales	0.99	67.41	

TRADING VOLUME (thousand shares)

Business Summary: Aviation (MIC: 1.1 SIC: 721 NAIC: 36411)

Textron is a global, multi-industry company with manufacturing facilities in 40 countries as of Jan 3 2004. Co. operates in five business segments: Bell, which is comprised of Bell Helicopter and Textron Systems Aircraft; Cessna, which is comprised of Cessna Aircraft, a major manufacturer of general aviation aircraft; Industrial, which includes fluid and power systems, golf, turf-care and specialty products, light construction equipment, and electrical and video tools; Fastening Systems, which includes fasteners, fastening systems, engineered assemblies and installation tools; and Finance, which provides diversified commercial lending.

Recent Developments: For the year ended Jan 1 2005, income from continuing operations advanced 27.7% to $373.0 million compared with $292.0 million in the previous year. Earnings for 2004 and 2003 excluded losses from discontinued operations of $8.0 million and $33.0 million, respectively. Results for 2004 and 2003 included special charges of $131.0 million and $152.0 million, respectively. Results for 2003 also included a gain on the sale of businesses of $15.0 million. Total revenues increased 4.6% to $10.24 billion from $9.79 billion a year earlier. Manufacturing revenues rose 5.2% to $9.70 billion, while finance revenues decreased 4.7% to $545.0 million.

Prospects: First quarter 2005 earnings per share are expected to be between $0.70 and $0.80. For full-year 2005, Co. is projecting revenues will be up approximately 7.0%, with earnings per share of between $3.85 and $4.05. Also, Co. expects full-year 2005 manufacturing cash flow from operations to be between $850.0 million and $950.0 million, resulting in free cash flow of between $500.0 million and $600.0 million. Co.'s full-year guidance includes an assumed, $0.11 per share, after-tax cost to reflect the approximate full-year impact of expensing stock options.

Financial Data
(US$ in Thousands)

	01/01/2005	01/03/2004	12/28/2002	12/29/2001	12/30/2000	01/01/2000	01/02/1999	01/03/1998
Earnings Per Share	2.61	1.89	(0.88)	1.16	1.49	14.48	3.68	3.29
Cash Flow Per Share	6.93	6.14	5.02	6.99	7.13	7.44	5.98	6.34
Tang Book Value Per Share	14.70	14.94	12.92	13.86	11.65	10.60	5.59	8.97
Dividends Per Share	1.325	1.300	1.300	1.300	1.300	1.300	1.140	1.000
Dividend Payout %	50.77	68.78	...	112.07	87.25	8.98	30.98	30.40
Income Statement								
Total Revenue	10,242,000	9,859,000	10,658,000	12,321,000	13,090,000	11,579,000	9,683,000	10,544,000
EBITDA	881,000	757,000	858,000	933,000	1,105,000	1,470,000	1,124,000	1,383,000
Depn & Amortn	353,000	356,000	368,000	514,000	494,000	440,000	361,000	435,000
Income Before Taxes	528,000	401,000	490,000	419,000	611,000	1,030,000	763,000	948,000
Income Taxes	155,000	107,000	100,000	227,000	308,000	381,000	294,000	364,000
Net Income	365,000	259,000	(124,000)	166,000	218,000	2,226,000	608,000	558,000
Average Shares	140,169	137,217	140,252	142,937	146,150	153,754	165,374	170,000
Balance Sheet								
Current Assets	4,168,000	3,592,000	3,887,000	4,017,000	3,914,000	3,735,000	4,355,000	14,346,000
Total Assets	15,875,000	15,090,000	15,505,000	16,052,000	16,370,000	16,393,000	13,721,000	18,610,000
Current Liabilities	2,975,000	2,256,000	2,239,000	3,075,000	3,263,000	3,256,000	3,919,000	1,762,000
Long-Term Obligations	6,141,000	6,118,000	6,526,000	5,959,000	6,136,000	5,630,000	3,709,000	10,496,000
Total Liabilities	12,223,000	11,400,000	11,587,000	11,605,000	11,864,000	11,504,000	10,241,000	14,899,000
Stockholders' Equity	3,652,000	3,690,000	3,406,000	3,934,000	3,994,000	4,377,000	2,997,000	3,228,000
Shares Outstanding	135,373	137,238	136,500	141,251	140,933	147,002	154,742	163,000
Statistical Record								
Return on Assets %	2.36	1.67	N.M.	1.03	1.33	14.82	3.77	2.98
Return on Equity %	9.97	7.18	N.M.	4.20	5.22	60.54	19.59	17.13
EBITDA Margin %	8.60	7.68	8.05	7.57	8.44	12.70	11.61	13.12
Net Margin %	3.56	2.63	N.M.	1.35	1.67	19.22	6.28	5.29
Asset Turnover	0.66	0.63	0.68	0.76	0.80	0.77	0.60	0.56
Current Ratio	1.40	1.59	1.74	1.31	1.20	1.15	1.11	8.14
Debt to Equity	1.68	1.66	1.92	1.51	1.54	1.29	1.24	3.25
Price Range	74.63-50.84	57.70-26.85	53.17-32.49	59.89-31.65	74.94-41.44	97.00-68.44	80.69-54.88	70.06-45.94
P/E Ratio	28.59-19.48	30.53-14.21	...	51.63-27.28	50.29-27.81	6.70-4.73	21.93-14.91	21.30-13.96
Average Yield %	2.18	3.19	3.01	2.63	2.30	1.62	1.60	1.71

Address: 40 Westminster Street, Providence, RI 02903	**Web Site:** www.textron.com	**Auditors:** Ernst & Young LLP
Telephone: (401) 421-2800	**Officers:** Lewis B. Campbell - Chmn., Pres., C.E.O. John D. Butler - Exec. V.P., Admin., Chief Human Res. Officer	**Investor Contact:** 401-421-2800
Fax: (401) 421-2878		

THE ST PAUL TRAVELERS COMPANIES INC

Exchange	Symbol	Price	52Wk Range	Yield	P/E	Div Acheiver
NYS	STA	$36.73 (3/31/2005)	42.99-30.99	2.40	24.01	18 Years

*7 Year Price Score 83.70   *NYSE Composite Index=100   *12 Month Price Score 94.70

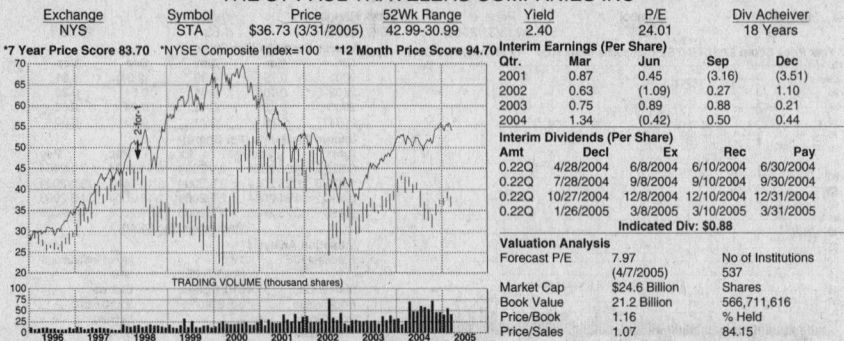

Interim Earnings (Per Share)

Qtr.	Mar	Jun	Sep	Dec
2001	0.87	0.45	(3.16)	(3.51)
2002	0.63	(1.09)	0.27	1.10
2003	0.75	0.89	0.88	0.21
2004	1.34	(0.42)	0.50	0.44

Interim Dividends (Per Share)

Amt	Decl	Ex	Rec	Pay
0.22Q	4/28/2004	6/8/2004	6/10/2004	6/30/2004
0.22Q	7/28/2004	9/8/2004	9/10/2004	9/30/2004
0.22Q	10/27/2004	12/8/2004	12/10/2004	12/31/2004
0.22Q	1/26/2005	3/8/2005	3/10/2005	3/31/2005

Indicated Div: $0.88

Valuation Analysis

Forecast P/E	7.97	No of Institutions
	(4/7/2005)	537
Market Cap	$24.6 Billion	Shares
Book Value	21.2 Billion	566,711,616
Price/Book	1.16	% Held
Price/Sales	1.07	84.15

Business Summary: Insurance (MIC: 8.2 SIC: 331 NAIC: 24130)

The St. Paul Travelers Companies is engaged, through its subsidiaries, in providing commercial property-liability insurance products and services. Under the Travelers brand, Co. is also a major underwriter of homeowners, auto and other insurance products for individuals and families through independent agents. Co. also has a presence in the asset management industry through its 79.0% majority ownership of Nuveen Investments, Inc. As of Apr 1 2004, Co. had total assets of $107.00 billion and a market capitalization of approximately $27.00 billion.

Recent Developments: For the year ended Dec 31 2004, net income decreased 43.7% to $955,000 thousand from net income of $1,696,000 thousand a year earlier. Revenues were $22,934,000 thousand, up 51.5% from $15,139,000 thousand the year before. Net premiums earned were $19,038,000 thousand versus $12,545,000 thousand in the prior year, an increase of 51.8%. Net investment income rose 42.5% to $2,663,000 thousand from $1,869,000 a year earlier. Results included net realized investment losses of $39,000 thousand in 2004 and net realized investment gains of $38,000 thousand in 2003.

Prospects: Co. is seeing improvement in a number of areas of its business, particularly the performance of its personal segment. Moreover, expense savings initiatives are ahead of schedule and Co. is confident that it will achieve its original pre-tax goal of $350.0 million in savings by the end of 2005 and $450.0 million by the end of 2006. Meanwhile, Co. is presently searching for strategic alternatives to divest its 79.0% equity stake in Nuveen Investments, Inc. (Nuveen) and to combine its major insurance pools. Co. believes the divestiture of its equity stake in Nuveen would significantly increase its financial flexibility, operating company capital and tangible net worth.

Financial Data

(US$ in Thousands)	12/31/2004	12/31/2003	12/31/2002	12/31/2001	12/31/2000	12/31/1999	12/31/1998	12/31/1997
Earnings Per Share	1.53	2.72	0.92	(5.22)	4.24	3.41	0.32	3.83
Cash Flow Per Share	8.59	0.58	0.60	4.66	(2.59)	(0.22)	0.29	4.20
Tang Book Value Per Share	20.93	22.26	20.58	21.03	30.54	26.42	25.79	25.09
Dividends Per Share	1.160	1.160	1.160	1.120	1.080	1.040	1.000	0.940
Dividend Payout %	75.82	42.65	126.09	...	25.47	30.50	312.50	24.54
Income Statement								
Premium Income	19,038,000	7,039,000	7,390,000	7,296,000	5,898,000	5,290,000	6,944,575	4,616,456
Total Revenue	22,934,000	8,854,000	8,918,000	8,943,000	8,608,000	7,569,000	9,108,401	6,219,273
Benefits & Claims	15,439,000	5,188,000	5,995,000	7,479,000	4,407,000	4,087,000	5,876,317	3,345,168
Income Before Taxes	1,128,000	836,000	176,000	(1,431,000)	1,453,000	1,017,000	(46,287)	1,018,733
Income Taxes	138,000	137,000	(73,000)	(422,000)	440,000	238,000	(135,635)	245,510
Net Income	955,000	661,000	218,000	(1,088,000)	993,000	834,000	89,348	705,473
Average Shares	628,300	240,000	227,000	212,000	233,000	246,000	238,682	184,522
Balance Sheet								
Total Assets	111,815,000	39,563,000	39,920,000	38,321,000	41,075,000	38,873,000	38,322,708	21,500,657
Total Liabilities	90,614,000	33,338,000	33,285,000	32,314,000	33,511,000	31,976,000	31,183,621	16,666,947
Stockholders' Equity	21,201,000	6,225,000	5,746,000	5,114,000	7,227,000	6,472,000	6,636,387	4,626,710
Shares Outstanding	670,300	228,393	226,798	207,624	218,308	224,830	233,750	167,456
Statistical Record								
Return on Assets %	1.26	1.66	0.56	N.M.	2.48	2.16	0.30	3.34
Return on Equity %	6.95	11.04	4.01	N.M.	14.46	12.72	1.59	16.35
Loss Ratio %	81.10	73.70	81.12	102.51	74.72	77.26	84.62	72.46
Net Margin %	4.16	7.47	2.44	(12.17)	11.54	11.02	0.98	11.34
Price Range	43.35-30.99	39.65-29.33	50.12-24.20	52.12-35.50	56.38-21.75	36.75-25.56	47.09-29.00	42.66-28.94
P/E Ratio	28.33-20.25	14.58-10.78	54.48-26.30	...	13.30-5.13	10.78-7.50	147.19-90.63	11.14-7.56
Average Yield %	3.03	3.30	3.01	2.44	2.73	3.26	2.54	2.53

Address: 385 Washington Street, Saint Paul, MN 55102	**Web Site:** www.stpaul.com	**Auditors:** KPMG LLP
Telephone: (651) 310-7911	**Officers:** Jay S. Fishman - Chmn., Pres., C.E.O. John A. MacColl - Vice-Chmn., Gen. Couns.	**Transfer Agents:** Wells Fargo Bank, Minnesota, N.A., St. Paul, MN
Fax: (651) 310-3386		

THE GAP, INC.

Exchange	Symbol	Price	52Wk Range	Yield	P/E
NYS	GPS	$21.84 (3/31/2005)	25.66-18.65	0.82	18.51

*7 Year Price Score 73.36   *NYSE Composite Index=100   *12 Month Price Score 92.43

Interim Earnings (Per Share)

Qtr.	Apr	Jul	Oct	Jan
2001-02	0.13	0.10	(0.21)	(0.04)
2002-03	0.04	0.06	0.15	0.28
2003-04	0.22	0.22	0.28	0.37
2004-05	0.32	0.21	0.28	...

Interim Dividends (Per Share)

Amt	Decl	Ex	Rec	Pay
0.022Q	7/27/2004	8/25/2004	8/27/2004	9/20/2004
0.022Q	9/28/2004	11/17/2004	11/19/2004	12/13/2004
0.022Q	1/25/2005	2/4/2005	2/8/2005	2/23/2005
0.045Q	3/22/2005	4/1/2005	4/5/2005	4/26/2005

Indicated Div: $0.18

Valuation Analysis

Forecast P/E	N/A	No of Institutions
Market Cap	$19.4 Billion	Shares
Book Value	5.3 Billion	533,035,200
Price/Book	3.66	% Held
Price/Sales	1.19	60.80

Business Summary: Retail - Apparel and Accessory Stores (MIC: 5.8 SIC: 651 NAIC: 48140)

The Gap is a specialty retailer that operates stores selling casual apparel, accessories, and personal care products for men, women, and children under five brand names: Gap, GapKids and babyGap, which offer gender-specific contemporary clothing; Banana Republic, which offers upscale clothing, jewelry, and small leather products; and Old Navy Clothing Co., which offers value-priced merchandise in a warehouse format. As of Jan 31 2004, Co. operated 3,022 stores in the U.S., Canada, the U.K., Japan, France and Germany, including 1,747 Gap stores, 840 Old Navy stores, and 435 Banana Republic stores. All stores are leased and no stores are franchised or operated by others.

Recent Developments: For the quarter ended Oct 30 2004, net income increased 0.8% to $265,000 thousand from net income of $263,000 thousand in the year-earlier quarter. Results for 2004 and 2003 included losses on early retirement of debt of $10,000 thousand and $1,000 thousand, respectively. Revenues were $3,980,000 thousand, up 1.3% from $3,929,000 thousand the year before. Total indirect expense was $1,100,000 thousand versus $1,051,000 thousand in the prior-year quarter, an increase of 4.7%.

Prospects: Co. delivered solid earnings performance in 2004, while mining growth opportunities within its brands, significantly strengthening its balance sheet, retiring debt and completing a $1.00 billion share repurchase program. Going forward, Co. will focus on driving growth opportunities across its brand portfolio and strengthening its operating performance. For fiscal 2005, Co. expects earnings of $1.41 to $1.45 per share and an operating margin of about 13.0%. Capital expenditures for the year are expected to be $625.0 million. Co. expects to open about 175 store locations, weighted toward Old Navy, and close about 135 store locations weighted toward Gap brand.

Financial Data

(US$ in Thousands)	9 Mos	6 Mos	3 Mos	01/31/2004	02/01/2003	02/02/2002	02/03/2001	01/29/2000
Earnings Per Share	1.18	1.18	1.19	1.09	0.54	(0.01)	1.00	1.26
Cash Flow Per Share	2.18	2.31	2.64	2.44	1.42	1.54	1.49	1.74
Tang Book Value Per Share	5.97	5.93	5.68	5.33	4.12	3.48	3.43	2.63
Dividends Per Share	0.089	0.089	0.089	0.089	0.089	0.089	0.089	0.089
Dividend Payout %	7.51	7.51	7.45	8.15	16.44	...	8.88	7.05
Income Statement								
Total Revenue	11,369,000	7,388,000	3,668,000	15,854,000	14,454,709	13,847,873	13,673,460	11,635,398
EBITDA	1,812,000	1,202,000	705,000	2,543,000	1,793,505	1,148,002	2,035,126	2,252,888
Depn & Amortn	454,000	302,000	154,000	664,000	780,876	810,486	590,365	436,184
Income Before Taxes	1,264,000	829,000	511,000	1,683,000	800,875	241,641	1,381,885	1,784,949
Income Taxes	493,000	323,000	199,000	653,000	323,418	249,405	504,388	657,884
Net Income	771,000	506,000	312,000	1,030,000	477,457	(7,764)	877,497	1,127,065
Average Shares	997,620	1,002,743	996,326	988,177	881,477	860,255	879,137	895,029
Balance Sheet								
Current Assets	6,765,000	6,898,000	6,788,000	6,689,000	5,739,725	3,044,550	2,648,050	2,197,790
Total Assets	10,231,000	10,355,000	10,297,000	10,343,000	9,902,004	7,591,326	7,012,908	5,188,756
Current Liabilities	2,417,000	2,367,000	2,261,000	2,492,000	2,726,574	2,056,233	2,799,144	1,752,879
Long-Term Obligations	1,893,000	2,015,000	2,317,000	2,487,000	2,895,794	1,961,397	780,246	784,925
Total Liabilities	4,933,000	4,995,000	5,191,000	5,560,000	6,243,792	4,581,745	4,084,669	2,955,711
Stockholders' Equity	5,298,000	5,360,000	5,106,000	4,783,000	3,658,212	3,009,581	2,928,239	2,233,045
Shares Outstanding	887,572	903,627	899,338	897,202	887,322	865,726	853,996	850,498
Statistical Record								
Return on Assets %	11.07	11.25	11.65	10.20	5.47	N.M.	14.15	24.70
Return on Equity %	23.29	23.80	25.43	24.47	14.36	N.M.	33.45	59.38
EBITDA Margin %	15.94	16.27	19.22	16.04	12.41	8.29	14.88	19.36
Net Margin %	6.78	6.85	8.51	6.50	3.30	N.M.	6.42	9.69
Asset Turnover	1.60	1.62	1.65	1.57	1.46	1.90	2.20	2.55
Current Ratio	2.80	2.91	3.00	2.68	2.11	1.48	0.95	1.25
Debt to Equity	0.36	0.38	0.45	0.52	0.79	0.65	0.27	0.35
Price Range	25.66-18.40	25.66-17.12	23.24-16.00	23.24-12.70	16.89-8.84	34.90-11.40	52.88-18.75	51.63-31.44
P/E Ratio	21.75-15.59	21.75-14.51	19.53-13.45	21.32-11.65	31.28-16.37	...	52.88-18.75	40.97-24.95
Average Yield %	0.42	0.42	0.45	0.49	0.65	0.41	0.27	0.21

Address: Two Folsom St., San Francisco, CA 94105 **Telephone:** (650) 952-4400 **Fax:** (650) 952-4407	**Web Site:** www.gapinc.com **Officers:** Paul S. Pressler - Pres., C.E.O. Byron Pollitt - Exec. V.P., C.F.O.	**Auditors:** Deloitte & Touche LLP **Investor Contact:** 650-874-2053

THERMO ELECTRON CORP.

Exchange	Symbol	Price	52Wk Range	Yield	P/E
NYS	TMO	$25.29 (3/31/2005)	31.00-24.21	N/A	11.65

*7 Year Price Score 117.56 *NYSE Composite Index=100   *12 Month Price Score 89.63

Interim Earnings (Per Share)

Qtr.	Mar	Jun	Sep	Dec
2001	(0.24)	0.14	0.14	(0.03)
2002	0.59	0.38	0.23	0.50
2003	0.22	0.32	0.29	0.37
2004	0.26	0.54	0.65	0.74

Interim Dividends (Per Share)

No Dividends Paid

Valuation Analysis

Forecast P/E	17.00	No of Institutions
	(4/6/2005)	312
Market Cap	$4.1 Billion	Shares
Book Value	2.7 Billion	132,717,536
Price/Book	1.52	% Held
Price/Sales	1.84	82.52

Business Summary: Instruments and Related Products (MIC: 11.15 SIC: 829 NAIC: 34519)

Thermo Electron is a producer of high-tech instruments. Co. operates in two business segments. The Life & Laboratory Sciences segment provides instrument systems and software for use in discovery, research and development and quality assurance in the pharmaceutical, biotechnology and other laboratory markets. The Measurement & Control segment provides analytical tools, on-line process instruments and precision temperature control systems to enable customers to control and optimize manufacturing processes. This segment also offers chemical-, radiation-, and explosive-detection devices.

Recent Developments: For the year ended Dec 31 2004, income from continuing operations increased 24.6% to $218,367 thousand from income of $175,210 thousand a year earlier. Net income increased 80.9% to $361,837 thousand from net income of $200,009 thousand a year earlier. Revenues were $2,205,995 thousand, up 16.1% from $1,899,378 thousand the year before. Operating income was $237,512 thousand versus an income of $187,384 thousand in the prior year, an increase of 26.8%. Total direct expense was $1,191,516 thousand versus $1,019,476 thousand in the prior year, an increase of 16.9%. Total indirect expense was $776,967 thousand versus $692,518 thousand in the prior year, an increase of 12.2%.

Prospects: On Jan 19 2005, Co. agreed to acquire the Kendro Laboratory Products division of SPX Corp. for about $833.5 million. Kendro designs, manufactures, markets and services a wide range of laboratory equipment for sample preparation, processing and storage used primarily in life sciences and drug discovery laboratories as well as in clinical laboratories. Co. expects the acquisition to be slightly dilutive to earnings in 2005 and accretive to earnings in 2006. Separately, Co. remains optimistic about its ability to achieve earnings of $0.29 to $0.31 per share for the first quarter and $1.40 to $1.45 per share for the full year, excluding one-time charges.

Financial Data

(US$ in Thousands)	12/31/2004	12/31/2003	12/28/2002	12/29/2001	12/30/2000	01/01/2000	01/02/1999	01/03/1998
Earnings Per Share	2.17	1.20	1.73	...	(0.22)	(1.13)	1.07	1.41
Cash Flow Per Share	1.62	1.32	0.61	1.05	1.20	2.14	2.03	1.74
Tang Book Value Per Share	6.19	5.00	3.79	3.17	6.34	4.76	2.10	1.92
Income Statement								
Total Revenue	2,205,995	2,097,135	2,086,355	2,188,210	2,280,522	2,471,193	3,867,596	3,558,320
EBITDA	327,318	276,180	337,404	172,481	325,308	204,204	558,538	626,771
Depn & Amortn	66,141	58,544	56,376	98,521	97,486	113,641	162,277	135,738
Income Before Taxes	259,219	218,633	287,986	70,681	184,831	37,486	391,510	488,467
Income Taxes	40,852	45,936	92,987	26,929	112,217	33,073	170,680	174,713
Net Income	361,837	200,009	309,730	(781)	(36,111)	(174,573)	181,901	239,328
Average Shares	167,641	170,730	186,611	183,916	170,519	157,987	178,449	176,082
Balance Sheet								
Current Assets	1,469,654	1,395,256	1,771,559	1,965,210	2,465,529	2,517,207	3,301,329	3,094,198
Total Assets	3,576,725	3,388,969	3,647,062	3,825,070	4,862,977	5,181,842	6,331,645	5,795,869
Current Liabilities	578,728	684,793	1,103,720	1,142,039	728,551	1,066,349	1,138,323	1,092,235
Long-Term Obligations	226,070	229,509	451,341	727,502	1,528,948	1,565,974	2,025,531	1,742,907
Total Liabilities	911,175	1,006,163	1,613,739	1,916,928	2,329,001	3,167,356	4,083,521	3,797,960
Stockholders' Equity	2,665,550	2,382,806	2,033,323	1,908,142	2,533,976	2,014,486	2,248,124	1,997,909
Shares Outstanding	160,549	165,063	162,853	176,357	182,168	165,476	158,493	159,111
Statistical Record								
Return on Assets %	10.36	5.64	8.31	N.M.	N.M.	N.M.	3.01	4.31
Return on Equity %	14.30	8.98	15.76	N.M.	N.M.	N.M.	8.59	12.55
EBITDA Margin %	14.84	13.17	16.17	7.88	14.26	8.26	14.44	17.61
Net Margin %	16.40	9.54	14.85	N.M.	N.M.	N.M.	4.70	6.73
Asset Turnover	0.63	0.59	0.56	0.51	0.46	0.43	0.64	0.64
Current Ratio	2.54	2.04	1.61	1.72	3.38	2.36	2.90	2.83
Debt to Equity	0.08	0.10	0.22	0.38	0.60	0.78	0.90	0.87
Price Range	31.00-24.21	25.37-17.02	24.37-14.50	26.25-15.56	26.76-12.26	17.26-10.92	36.51-11.78	37.85-24.73
P/E Ratio	14.29-11.16	21.14-14.18	14.09-8.38	N.M.	...	...	34.12-11.01	26.85-17.54

Address: 81 Wyman Street, P.O. Box 9046, Waltham, MA 02454-9046
Telephone: (781) 622-1000
Fax: (781) 933-4476

Web Site: www.thermo.com
Officers: Jim P. Manzi - Chmn. Marijn E. Dekkers - Pres., C.E.O.

Auditors: PricewaterhouseCoopers LLP
Investor Contact: 781-622-1111

THOMAS & BETTS CORP.

Exchange	Symbol	Price	52Wk Range	Yield	P/E
NYS	TNB	$32.30 (3/31/2005)	33.58-21.82	N/A	20.57

*7 Year Price Score 87.39   *NYSE Composite Index=100   *12 Month Price Score 107.05

Interim Earnings (Per Share)

Qtr.	Mar	Jun	Sep	Dec
2001	(0.09)	(0.09)	(0.78)	(1.56)
2002	(0.20)	0.01	(0.18)	0.23
2003	0.09	0.12	0.20	0.33
2004	0.27	0.34	0.56	0.40

Interim Dividends (Per Share)

No Dividends Paid

Valuation Analysis

Forecast P/E	18.96		No of Institutions
	(4/7/2005)		206
Market Cap	$1.9 Billion		Shares
Book Value	901.7 Million		55,935,744
Price/Book	2.13		% Held
Price/Sales	1.26		93.89

Business Summary: Electrical (MIC: 11.14 SIC: 678 NAIC: 34417)

Thomas & Betts is a designer and manufacturer of connectors and components for electrical and communication markets. Co. classifies its products into four business segments. The Electrical segment designs, manufactures and markets electrical connectors. The Communications segment designs, manufactures and markets components, subsystems and accessories. The Steel Structures segment designs, manufactures and markets tubular steel transmission and distribution poles and lattice steel transmission towers. The Heating, Ventilation and Air Conditio☐

Recent Developments: For the year ended Dec 31 2004, net income increased 117.8% to $93,255 thousand from net income of $42,813 thousand a year earlier. Revenues were $1,516,292 thousand, up 14.7% from $1,322,297 thousand the year before. Operating income was $144,118 thousand versus an income of $81,595 thousand in the prior year, an increase of 76.6%. Total direct expense was $1,085,150 thousand versus $970,248 thousand in the prior year, an increase of 11.8%. Total indirect expense was $287,024 thousand versus $270,454 thousand in the prior year, an increase of 6.1%.

Prospects: Co. is performing well, as it successfully offset higher commodity costs through disciplined price management and ongoing operational improvements. In addition, Co. experienced strengthening demand for industrial and utility products throughout 2004, which contributed to the improvement in its electrical business. Going forward, Co. expects maintain positive earnings momentum in each of its business segments due to the emerging recovery in industrial and commercial markets. Accordingly, for the full year of 2005, Co. expects to see top-line growth in the mid-single digit range, with earnings in the range of $1.60 to $1.70 per diluted share.

Financial Data
(US$ in Thousands)

	12/31/2004	12/31/2003	12/29/2002	12/30/2001	12/31/2000	01/02/2000	01/03/1999	12/28/1997
Earnings Per Share	1.57	0.73	(0.91)	(2.52)	(0.77)	2.56	1.54	2.81
Cash Flow Per Share	1.09	1.65	1.38	1.83	(4.30)	1.39	1.53	5.31
Tang Book Value Per Share	7.39	4.73	3.21	3.58	6.34	8.33	6.93	8.58
Dividends Per Share	...	0.005	...	0.560	1.120	1.120	1.120	1.120
Dividend Payout %	...	0.68	...	N.M.	N.M.	43.75	72.73	39.86
Income Statement								
Total Revenue	1,516,292	1,322,297	1,345,857	1,497,491	1,756,083	2,522,008	2,230,351	2,114,718
EBITDA	212,574	138,712	83,259	(65,403)	(129,709)	318,778	271,376	371,383
Depn & Amortn	54,136	54,088	50,244	79,736	94,627	98,047	95,333	95,324
Income Before Taxes	127,830	47,745	(2,210)	(187,039)	(272,230)	159,736	124,908	224,436
Income Taxes	34,575	4,932	6,002	(48,162)	(78,847)	11,429	37,407	69,575
Net Income	93,255	42,813	(53,027)	(146,390)	(44,570)	148,307	87,501	154,861
Average Shares	59,357	58,447	58,273	58,116	57,950	57,912	56,990	55,090
Balance Sheet								
Current Assets	778,895	812,279	704,931	770,303	968,561	1,163,935	1,058,402	796,150
Total Assets	1,755,752	1,782,625	1,619,756	1,761,610	2,087,763	2,652,686	2,499,587	2,038,675
Current Liabilities	238,409	364,960	297,159	355,709	419,260	513,445	587,549	439,808
Long-Term Obligations	543,085	551,972	559,982	618,035	669,983	935,731	790,963	502,813
Total Liabilities	854,033	1,051,198	995,620	1,078,325	1,181,853	1,558,554	1,484,482	1,061,294
Stockholders' Equity	901,719	731,427	624,136	683,285	905,910	1,094,132	1,015,105	977,381
Shares Outstanding	59,353	58,475	58,296	58,158	58,148	57,934	56,774	55,006
Statistical Record								
Return on Assets %	5.26	2.50	N.M.	N.M.	N.M.	5.77	3.79	7.45
Return on Equity %	11.39	6.28	N.M.	N.M.	N.M.	14.10	8.64	16.83
EBITDA Margin %	14.02	10.49	6.19	N.M.	N.M.	12.64	12.17	17.56
Net Margin %	6.15	3.24	N.M.	N.M.	N.M.	5.88	3.92	7.32
Asset Turnover	0.85	0.77	0.80	0.78	0.74	0.98	0.97	1.02
Current Ratio	3.27	2.23	2.37	2.17	2.31	2.27	1.80	1.81
Debt to Equity	0.60	0.75	0.90	0.90	0.74	0.86	0.78	0.51
Price Range	32.09-19.72	23.15-13.75	24.48-12.26	23.63-15.50	33.69-13.50	53.44-28.00	64.00-33.69	58.69-41.00
P/E Ratio	20.44-12.56	31.71-18.84	N/A	N/A	N/A	20.87-10.94	41.56-21.88	20.89-14.59
Average Yield %	...	0.03	...	2.81	5.04	2.56	2.34	2.26

Address: 8155 T & B Boulevard, Memphis, TN 38125 **Telephone:** (901) 252-8000 **Fax:** (901) 685-1988	**Web Site:** www.tnb.com **Officers:** T. Kevin Dunnigan - Chmn. Dominic J. Pileggi - Pres., C.E.O., C.O.O.	**Auditors:** KPMG LLP **Investor Contact:** 901-252-8266

THOMSON CORP.

Exchange	Symbol	Price	52Wk Range	Yield	P/E	Div Acheiver
TSX	TOC	C$40.57 (3/31/2005)	47.40-40.10	1.87	26.34	10 Years

*7 Year Price Score 81.59 *NYSE Composite Index=100 *12 Month Price Score 91.27

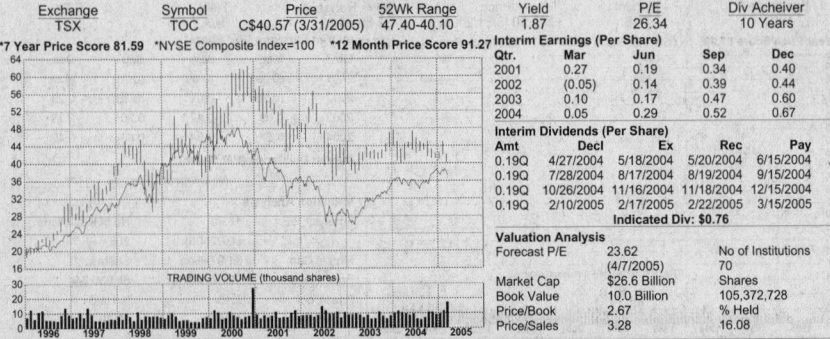

Interim Earnings (Per Share)

Qtr.	Mar	Jun	Sep	Dec
2001	0.27	0.19	0.34	0.40
2002	(0.05)	0.14	0.39	0.44
2003	0.10	0.17	0.47	0.60
2004	0.05	0.29	0.52	0.67

Interim Dividends (Per Share)

Amt	Decl	Ex	Rec	Pay
0.19Q	4/27/2004	5/18/2004	5/20/2004	6/15/2004
0.19Q	7/28/2004	8/17/2004	8/19/2004	9/15/2004
0.19Q	10/26/2004	11/16/2004	11/18/2004	12/15/2004
0.19Q	2/10/2005	2/17/2005	2/22/2005	3/15/2005

Indicated Div: $0.76

Valuation Analysis

Forecast P/E	23.62	No of Institutions	
	(4/7/2005)	70	
Market Cap	$26.6 Billion	Shares	
Book Value	10.0 Billion	105,372,728	
Price/Book	2.67	% Held	
Price/Sales	3.28	16.08	

Business Summary: Information Technologies & Communications (MIC: 10 SIC: 375 NAIC: 18210)

Thomson provides value-added information, software tools and applications to users in the fields of law, tax, accounting, financial services, higher education, reference information, corporate training and assessment, scientific research and healthcare. Co. organizes its operations into four market groups that are structured on the basis of the customers they serve: Thomson Legal & Regulatory, Thomson Learning, Thomson Financial and Thomson Scientific & Healthcare.

Recent Developments: For the year ended Dec 31 2004, income advanced 16.9% to $1.01 billion versus income of $865.0 million the year before. Results for 2004 and 2003 excluded income from discontinued operations of $148.0 million and $32.0 million, respectively. Revenues increased 8.9% to $8.10 billion, primarily due to internal growth, acquisitions, and favorable currency translation. Legal and Regulatory segment revenues rose 8.1% to $3.39 billion. Learnings segment revenues increased 5.9% to $2.17 billion. Financial segment revenues climbed 14.8% to $1.51 billion. Operating profit rose 14.2% to $1.01 billion. Comparisons were made with restated prior-year figures.

Prospects: Looking ahead, for full-year 2005, Co. is projecting revenue growth to be in line with its long-term target of 7.0% to 9.0%, excluding the effects of currency translation. Co. expects full-year 2005 revenue growth to continue to be driven by growth from existing businesses and supplemented by tactical acquisitions. Earnings before, interest, taxes, depreciation and amortization margins are expected to expand slightly in 2005, reflecting continued operating improvements, partially offset by higher pension costs and corporate expenses. Also, Co. expects to continue to generate strong free cash flow in 2005.

Financial Data (US$ in Thousands)	12/31/2004	12/31/2003	12/31/2002	12/31/2001	12/31/2000	12/31/1999	12/31/1998	12/31/1997
Earnings Per Share	1.54	1.34	0.93	1.19	1.96	0.86	2.97	0.91
Cash Flow Per Share	2.75	2.53	2.64	...	...	...	...	...
Dividends Per Share	0.755	1.153	0.705	0.700	0.685	0.657	0.627	0.590
Dividend Payout %	49.03	86.04	75.81	58.82	34.95	76.40	21.11	64.84
Income Statement								
Total Revenue	8,098,000	7,606,000	7,756,000	7,237,000	6,514,000	5,752,000	6,269,000	8,766,000
Depn & Amortn	906,000	873,000	830,000	920,000	743,000	602,000	644,000	667,000
Income Taxes	267,000	156,000	192,000	168,000	(15,000)	105,000	109,000	101,000
Net Income	1,011,000	867,000	615,000	749,000	1,223,000	532,000	1,818,000	550,000
Average Shares	655,927	654,151	641,475	628,239	623,776	618,092	612,000	607,000
Balance Sheet								
Current Assets	2,892,000	3,044,000	3,019,000	2,763,000	2,528,000	2,200,000	2,092,000	2,680,000
Total Assets	19,643,000	18,680,000	18,542,000	18,402,000	15,699,000	12,558,000	12,447,000	13,333,000
Current Liabilities	3,083,000	3,145,000	3,202,000	3,830,000	2,965,000	2,477,000	2,073,000	2,872,000
Long-Term Obligations	4,013,000	3,684,000	3,487,000	3,651,000	2,321,000	1,909,000	2,408,000	4,006,000
Total Liabilities	9,681,000	9,480,000	9,588,000	10,182,000	7,881,000	5,562,000	5,702,000	8,387,000
Stockholders' Equity	9,962,000	9,200,000	8,954,000	8,220,000	7,818,000	6,996,000	6,745,000	4,946,000
Shares Outstanding	655,131	654,579	651,150	630,740	625,764	621,393	616,000	610,000
Statistical Record								
Return on Assets %	5.26	4.66	3.33	4.39	8.63	4.26	14.10	4.15
Return on Equity %	10.52	9.55	7.16	9.34	16.47	7.74	31.10	11.47
Net Margin %	12.48	11.40	7.93	10.35	18.77	9.25	29.00	6.27
Asset Turnover	0.42	0.41	0.42	0.42	0.46	0.46	0.49	0.66
Current Ratio	0.94	0.97	0.94	0.72	0.85	0.89	1.01	0.93
Debt to Equity	0.40	0.40	0.39	0.44	0.30	0.27	0.36	0.81
Price Range	47.74-40.05	47.08-37.59	56.70-36.25	57.85-42.70	62.40-38.00	51.00-35.75	45.60-29.05	39.65-26.60
P/E Ratio	31.00-26.01	35.13-28.05	60.97-38.98	48.61-35.88	31.84-19.39	59.30-41.57	15.35-9.78	43.57-29.23
Average Yield %	1.75	2.76	1.53	1.37	1.31	1.58	1.58	1.84

Address: Suite 2706, Toronto Dominion Bank Tower, P.O. Box 24, Toronto-Dominion Centre, Toronto **Telephone:** (416) 360 8700 **Fax:** (416) 360 8812	Web Site: www.thomson.com **Officers:** Richard J. Harrington - Pres., C.E.O. Robert D. Daleo - Exec. V.P., C.F.O.	**Auditors:** PricewaterhouseCoopers **Transfer Agents:** Computershare Trust Company of Canada, Toronto, Canada

THORNBURG MORTGAGE INC

Exchange	Symbol	Price	52Wk Range	Yield	P/E
NYS	TMA	$28.04 (3/31/2005)	31.28-23.75	9.70	10.01

*7 Year Price Score 140.64 *NYSE Composite Index=100 *12 Month Price Score 94.56

Interim Earnings (Per Share)

Qtr.	Mar	Jun	Sep	Dec
2001	0.42	0.46	0.52	0.69
2002	0.62	0.63	0.67	0.67
2003	0.67	0.67	0.68	0.69
2004	0.70	0.71	0.69	0.71

Interim Dividends (Per Share)

Amt	Decl	Ex	Rec	Pay
0.65Q	4/20/2004	5/3/2004	5/5/2004	5/17/2004
0.66Q	7/19/2004	8/2/2004	8/4/2004	8/17/2004
0.67Q	10/19/2004	11/2/2004	11/4/2004	11/17/2004
0.68Q	12/16/2004	12/29/2004	12/31/2004	1/21/2005

Indicated Div: $2.72

Valuation Analysis

Forecast P/E	9.95	No of Institutions
	(4/12/2005)	155
Market Cap	$2.6 Billion	Shares
Book Value	1.8 Billion	17,649,212
Price/Book	1.44	% Held
Price/Sales	2.72	18.91

Business Summary: Property, Real Estate & Development (MIC: 8.3 SIC: 798 NAIC: 25930)

Thornburg Mortgage is a single-family residential mortgage lender that originates, acquires and retains investments in adjustable-rate mortgage (ARM) assets comprised of ARM securities and ARM loans. Co.'s ARM assets are comprised of ARM securities and loans, which have interest rates that reprice in year or less, and hybrid ARM securities and loans, which have a fixed interest rate for an initial period of three to ten years before converting to traditional ARMs for their remaining terms to maturity. Co. is organized as an externally advised real estate investment trust, managed under a management agreement with Thornburg Advisory Corporation.

Recent Developments: For the year ended Dec 31 2004, net income increased 31.8% to $232.5 million from net income of $176.5 million in the corresponding period a year earlier. Results for 2004 and 2003 included net gains from ARM assets and hedging instruments of $11.6 million and $6.0 million, respectively. Revenues were $930.1 million, up 57.7% compared with $589.6 million the year before. Net interest income advanced 25.8% to $294.3 million from $234.0 million the previous year.

Prospects: Co. continues to deliver solid operating performance despite challenging market conditions. Despite the Federal Reserve's tightening of monetary policy and increased competitive pressures in the mortgage industry, Co. is continuing to produce earnings growth and a solid return on equity. Co. expects additional increases to short-term interest rates and increasing competition in the mortgage market to slow earnings growth in 2005. However, Co.'s loan origination business continues to grow due to demand for its new adjustable-rate mortgage products. As a result, Co. sees strength across all aspects of its business in 2005.

Financial Data

(US$ in Thousands)	12/31/2004	12/31/2003	12/31/2002	12/31/2001	12/31/2000	12/31/1999	12/31/1998	12/31/1997
Earnings Per Share	2.80	2.71	2.59	2.09	1.05	0.88	0.75	1.94
Cash Flow Per Share	3.40	3.30	3.01	3.25	2.27	2.20	3.13	3.99
Tang Book Value Per Share	19.47	16.75	14.54	14.02	11.67	11.40	11.45	14.42
Dividends Per Share	2.660	2.490	2.285	2.000	0.940	0.920	0.905	1.970
Dividend Payout %	95.00	91.88	88.22	95.69	89.52	104.55	120.67	101.55
Income Statement								
Interest Income	930,062	589,615	401,967	278,594	289,973	260,365	287,032	247,721
Interest Expense	635,794	355,662	244,038	199,829	253,343	226,350	255,992	198,657
Net Interest Income	294,268	233,953	157,929	78,765	36,630	34,015	31,040	49,064
Provision for Losses	1,436	3,137	...	653	1,158	2,867	2,032	886
Non-Interest Income	17,264	7,888	1,495	50	287	47	(278)	1,189
Non-Interest Expense	77,057	62,200	39,408	19,500	6,594	5,611	6,035	7,965
Income Before Taxes	233,039	176,504	120,016	58,460	29,145	25,584	22,695	41,402
Income Taxes	475	...	...	...	...	...	...	...
Net Income	232,564	176,504	120,016	58,460	29,165	25,584	22,695	41,402
Average Shares	83,001	65,217	46,350	24,803	21,506	21,490	21,488	18,158
Balance Sheet								
Total Assets	29,189,618	19,118,799	10,512,932	5,803,648	4,190,167	4,375,965	4,344,633	4,691,116
Total Liabilities	27,400,434	17,879,695	9,679,890	5,270,990	3,872,629	4,065,078	4,032,810	4,332,962
Stockholders' Equity	1,789,184	1,239,104	833,042	532,658	317,538	310,887	311,823	358,154
Shares Outstanding	91,904	73,985	52,763	33,305	21,572	21,490	21,490	20,280
Statistical Record								
Return on Assets %	0.96	1.19	1.47	1.17	0.68	0.59	0.50	1.11
Return on Equity %	15.32	17.04	17.58	13.75	9.26	8.22	6.77	14.27
Net Interest Margin %	31.64	39.68	39.29	28.27	12.63	13.06	10.81	19.81
Efficiency Ratio %	8.13	10.41	9.77	7.00	2.27	2.15	2.10	3.20
Price Range	31.28-23.75	27.90-19.70	21.20-17.10	21.03-9.44	9.75-7.06	11.31-7.63	18.06-5.88	24.50-16.31
P/E Ratio	11.17-8.48	10.30-7.27	8.19-6.60	10.06-4.52	9.29-6.73	12.86-8.66	24.08-7.83	12.63-8.41
Average Yield %	9.45	10.35	11.70	13.61	11.11	9.94	7.34	9.44

Address: 150 Washington Avenue, Suite 302, Santa Fe, NM 87501 **Telephone:** (505) 989-1900 **Fax:** (505) 989-8156	**Web Site:** www.thornburgmortgage.com **Officers:** Garrett Thornburg - Chmn., C.E.O. Larry A. Goldstone - Pres., C.O.O.	**Auditors:** PricewaterhouseCoopers LLP **Investor Contact:** 505-989-1900

3M CO

Exchange	Symbol	Price	52Wk Range	Yield	P/E	Div Acheiver
NYS	MMM	$85.69 (3/31/2005)	90.01-75.29	1.96	22.85	46 Years

*7 Year Price Score 121.91 *NYSE Composite Index=100 *12 Month Price Score 95.77

Interim Earnings (Per Share)

Qtr.	Mar	Jun	Sep	Dec
2001	0.56	0.26	0.50	0.48
2002	0.57	0.59	0.69	0.65
2003	0.64	0.78	0.83	0.77
2004	0.90	0.97	0.97	0.91

Interim Dividends (Per Share)

Amt	Decl	Ex	Rec	Pay
0.36Q	5/11/2004	5/19/2004	5/21/2004	6/12/2004
0.36Q	8/9/2004	8/18/2004	8/20/2004	9/12/2004
0.36Q	11/8/2004	11/17/2004	11/19/2004	12/12/2004
0.42Q	2/14/2005	2/23/2005	2/25/2005	3/12/2005

Indicated Div: $1.68 (Div. Reinv. Plan)

Valuation Analysis

Forecast P/E	N/A	No of Institutions	
Market Cap	$66.3 Billion	Shares	
Book Value	10.4 Billion		542,116,096
Price/Book	6.39	% Held	70.18
Price/Sales	3.31		

Business Summary: Chemicals (MIC: 11.1 SIC: 891 NAIC: 25520)

3M is a diversified technology company with positions in health care, industrial, display and graphics, consumer and office, safety, security and protection services, electronics, telecommunications and electrical, and transportation. In the U.S., Co. has 12 sales offices in 10 states and operates 61 manufacturing facilities in 23 states. Internationally, Co. has 185 sales offices, and operates 75 manufacturing and converting facilities in 28 countries. Co.'s brands include icons such as Scotch, Post-it, Scotchgard, Thinsulate, Scotch-Brite, Filtrete, Dyneon and O-Cel-O.

Recent Developments: For the year ended Dec 31 2004, net income increased 24.4% to $2,990 million from net income of $2,403 million a year earlier. Revenues were $20,011 million, up 9.8% from $18,232 million the year before. Operating income was $4,578 million versus an income of $3,713 million in the prior year, an increase of 23.3%. Total direct expense was $9,958 million versus $9,285 million in the prior year, an increase of 7.2%. Total indirect expense was $5,475 million versus $5,234 million in the prior year, an increase of 4.6%.

Prospects: Top-line growth is being driven by higher sales from Co.'s consumer and office, safety and security services, industrial, health care and transportation businesses. Increased demand in these segments is being partially offset by lower sales in Co.'s communications and display and graphics businesses. Co. is targeting first-quarter 2005 earnings in the range of $1.00 to $1.02 per share, and volume growth of between 5.0% and 7.0%. Looking ahead, Co. is projecting full-year 2005 earnings per share in the range of $4.15 to $4.25, including a $0.02 accounting change charge, along with full-year volume growth of between 5.0% and 8.0%.

Financial Data

(US$ in Thousands)	12/31/2004	12/31/2003	12/31/2002	12/31/2001	12/31/2000	12/31/1999	12/31/1998	12/31/1997
Earnings Per Share	3.75	3.02	2.50	1.79	2.23	2.17	1.44	2.53
Cash Flow Per Share	5.47	4.82	3.84	3.90	2.93	3.78	2.95	2.07
Tang Book Value Per Share	9.63	6.62	4.90	6.18	7.17	7.06	7.40	7.32
Dividends Per Share	1.440	1.320	1.240	1.200	1.160	1.120	1.100	1.060
Dividend Payout %	38.40	43.71	49.70	67.04	52.13	51.61	76.39	41.90
Income Statement								
Total Revenue	20,011,000	18,232,000	16,332,000	16,054,000	16,724,000	15,659,000	15,021,000	15,070,000
EBITDA	5,577,000	4,677,000	4,000,000	3,362,000	4,110,000	3,889,000	2,957,000	4,404,000
Depn & Amortn	999,000	964,000	954,000	1,089,000	1,025,000	900,000	866,000	870,000
Income Before Taxes	4,555,000	3,657,000	3,005,000	2,186,000	2,974,000	2,880,000	1,952,000	3,440,000
Income Taxes	1,503,000	1,202,000	966,000	702,000	1,025,000	1,032,000	685,000	1,241,000
Net Income	2,990,000	2,403,000	1,974,000	1,430,000	1,782,000	1,763,000	1,175,000	2,121,000
Average Shares	796,500	795,300	791,000	799,800	799,800	813,000	816,000	838,000
Balance Sheet								
Current Assets	8,720,000	7,720,000	6,059,000	6,296,000	6,379,000	6,066,000	6,318,000	6,168,000
Total Assets	20,708,000	17,600,000	15,329,000	14,606,000	14,522,000	13,896,000	14,153,000	13,238,000
Current Liabilities	6,071,000	5,082,000	4,457,000	4,509,000	4,754,000	3,819,000	4,386,000	3,983,000
Long-Term Obligations	798,000	1,805,000	2,140,000	1,520,000	971,000	1,480,000	1,614,000	1,015,000
Total Liabilities	10,330,000	9,715,000	9,336,000	8,520,000	7,991,000	7,607,000	8,217,000	7,312,000
Stockholders' Equity	10,378,000	7,885,000	5,993,000	6,086,000	6,531,000	6,289,000	5,936,000	5,926,000
Shares Outstanding	773,518	784,117	780,391	782,607	792,170	797,400	802,000	810,000
Statistical Record								
Return on Assets %	15.57	14.60	13.19	9.82	12.51	12.57	8.58	15.95
Return on Equity %	32.65	34.63	32.68	22.67	27.72	28.84	19.81	34.74
EBITDA Margin %	27.87	25.65	24.49	20.94	24.58	24.84	19.69	29.22
Net Margin %	14.94	13.18	12.09	8.91	10.66	11.26	7.82	14.07
Asset Turnover	1.04	1.11	1.09	1.10	1.17	1.12	1.10	1.13
Current Ratio	1.44	1.52	1.36	1.40	1.34	1.59	1.44	1.55
Debt to Equity	0.08	0.23	0.36	0.25	0.15	0.24	0.27	0.17
Price Range	90.01-74.87	85.25-60.51	65.49-51.85	62.75-43.49	60.97-39.50	51.41-34.94	48.72-34.03	51.75-40.50
P/E Ratio	24.00-19.97	28.23-20.03	26.20-20.74	35.06-24.30	27.34-17.71	23.69-16.10	33.83-23.63	20.45-16.01
Average Yield %	1.76	1.92	2.04	2.16	2.52	2.56	2.64	2.32

Address: 3M Center, St. Paul, MN 55144-1000	Web Site: www.3m.com	Auditors: PricewaterhouseCoopers LLP
Telephone: (651) 733-1110	Officers: W. James McNerney Jr. - Chmn., C.E.O.	Investor Contact: 651-733-8206
Fax: (651) 733-9973	Joseph A. Giordano - Exec. V.P., Int'l. Oper.	Transfer Agents: Wells Fargo Shareowner Services, St. Paul, MN

TIDEWATER INC.

Exchange	Symbol	Price	52Wk Range	Yield	P/E
NYS	TDW	$38.86 (3/31/2005)	42.68-25.81	1.54	53.23

*7 Year Price Score 85.47   *NYSE Composite Index=100   *12 Month Price Score 115.17

Interim Earnings (Per Share)

Qtr.	Jun	Sep	Dec	Mar
2001-02	0.69	0.63	0.60	0.49
2002-03	0.41	0.41	0.42	0.33
2003-04	0.32	0.22	0.32	(0.13)
2004-05	0.23	0.29	0.34	...

Interim Dividends (Per Share)

Amt	Decl	Ex	Rec	Pay
0.15Q	4/16/2004	4/22/2004	4/26/2004	5/6/2004
0.15Q	7/15/2004	7/22/2004	7/26/2004	8/5/2004
0.15Q	11/17/2004	11/24/2004	11/29/2004	12/9/2004
0.15Q	1/27/2005	2/3/2005	2/7/2005	2/17/2005

Indicated Div: $0.60

Valuation Analysis

Forecast P/E	18.98	No of Institutions	
	(4/7/2005)	246	
Market Cap	$2.4 Billion	Shares	
Book Value	1.4 Billion	54,988,208	
Price/Book	1.69	% Held	
Price/Sales	3.54	96.08	

Business Summary: Shipping (MIC: 15.3 SIC: 492 NAIC: 83111)

Tidewater provides offshore supply vessels and marine support services to the offshore energy industry. Co., through its fleet of over 575 vessels as of Mar 31 2004, serves most of the world's significant oil and gas exploration and production markets and provides services supporting all phases of offshore exploration, development and production. Co.'s services include: the towing of and anchor-handling of mobile drilling rigs and equipment; transporting supplies and personnel necessary to sustain drilling, workover and production activities; assisting in offshore construction activities; and a variety of specialized services including pipe laying, cable laying and 3-D seismic work.

Recent Developments: For the quarter ended Dec 31 2004, net income increased 7.8% to $19,753 thousand from net income of $18,327 thousand in the year-earlier quarter. Revenues were $187,593 thousand, up 10.7% from $169,407 thousand the year before. Operating income was $29,559 thousand versus an income of $24,917 thousand in the prior-year quarter, an increase of 18.6%. Total indirect expense was $41,202 thousand versus $41,653 thousand in the prior-year quarter, a decrease of 1.1%.

Prospects: Domestic revenues are continuing to be adversely affected by the weak natural gas drilling market in the U.S. Gulf of Mexico. However, prospects for growth in offshore drilling in the Gulf appear to be improving. Exploration and production activity is expected to increase in calendar 2005 due to strong demand for natural gas and crude oil. Meanwhile, Co. international results are benefiting from stable utilization and average day rates and an increase in the number of vessels operating internationally. Strong international results should continue due to attractive crude oil prices as a result of continuing high demand, a tightening inventory and concerns over possible supply interruptions.

Financial Data
(US$ in Thousands)

	9 Mos	6 Mos	3 Mos	03/31/2004	03/31/2003	03/31/2002	03/31/2001	03/31/2000
Earnings Per Share	0.73	0.71	0.64	0.73	1.57	2.41	1.53	1.37
Cash Flow Per Share	2.45	2.14	2.26	2.28	3.58	3.46	2.71	4.22
Tang Book Value Per Share	17.61	17.37	17.19	18.19	18.06	17.02	15.16	12.82
Dividends Per Share	0.600	0.600	0.600	0.600	0.600	0.600	0.600	0.600
Dividend Payout %	82.03	84.92	94.10	82.19	38.22	24.90	39.22	43.80
Income Statement								
Total Revenue	512,537	324,944	158,117	652,630	635,823	729,029	616,679	574,815
EBITDA	145,911	91,565	42,867	156,696	211,275	283,716	208,142	188,496
Depn & Amortn	73,936	48,638	23,925	98,510	83,153	78,132	79,527	82,502
Income Before Taxes	71,975	42,927	18,942	54,503	127,710	204,751	127,420	105,280
Income Taxes	23,032	13,737	6,061	12,841	39,080	68,592	41,277	28,690
Net Income	48,943	29,190	12,881	41,662	88,630	136,159	86,143	76,590
Average Shares	57,268	57,079	56,962	56,688	56,602	56,388	56,267	55,796
Balance Sheet								
Current Assets	229,086	228,603	227,609	224,637	213,492	226,581	288,587	403,693
Total Assets	2,195,664	2,164,020	2,133,558	2,081,790	1,849,578	1,669,370	1,505,492	1,432,336
Current Liabilities	94,271	83,039	85,772	72,052	72,266	73,690	83,587	74,837
Long-Term Obligations	375,000	380,000	365,000	325,000	139,000	54,000	...	...
Total Liabilities	799,362	782,360	762,561	715,680	498,183	383,552	327,152	318,135
Stockholders' Equity	1,396,302	1,381,660	1,370,997	1,366,110	1,351,395	1,285,818	1,178,340	1,114,201
Shares Outstanding	60,633	60,633	60,633	57,032	56,637	56,220	56,036	60,561
Statistical Record								
Return on Assets %	1.97	1.92	1.77	2.11	5.04	8.58	5.86	5.40
Return on Equity %	3.03	2.94	2.66	3.06	6.72	11.05	7.52	7.00
EBITDA Margin %	28.47	28.18	27.11	24.01	33.23	38.92	33.75	32.79
Net Margin %	9.55	8.98	8.15	6.38	13.94	18.68	13.97	13.32
Asset Turnover	0.31	0.31	0.31	0.33	0.36	0.46	0.42	0.41
Current Ratio	2.43	2.75	2.65	3.12	2.95	3.07	3.45	5.39
Debt to Equity	0.27	0.28	0.27	0.24	0.10	0.04	...	...
Price Range	36.25-25.81	33.95-25.81	33.95-25.81	34.09-25.82	45.18-23.54	50.83-24.70	52.15-27.44	36.00-22.94
P/E Ratio	49.66-35.36	47.82-36.35	53.05-40.33	46.70-35.37	28.78-14.99	21.09-10.25	34.08-17.93	26.28-16.74
Average Yield %	1.97	2.04	2.09	2.05	1.88	1.67	1.46	2.02

Address: 601 Poydras Street, Suite 1900, New Orleans, LA 70130
Telephone: (504) 568-1010
Fax: (504) 566-4582

Web Site: www.tdw.com
Officers: Dean E. Taylor - Chmn., Pres., C.E.O. Cliffe F. Laborde - Exec. V.P., Gen. Couns.

Auditors: Ernst & Young LLP
Investor Contact: 504-568-1010

TIFFANY & CO.

Exchange	Symbol	Price	52Wk Range	Yield	P/E
NYS	TIF	$34.52 (3/31/2005)	41.52-27.10	0.70	24.83

*7 Year Price Score 95.84 ***NYSE Composite Index=100** ***12 Month Price Score 88.93**

TRADING VOLUME (thousand shares)

Interim Earnings (Per Share)

Qtr.	Apr	Jul	Oct	Jan
2001-02	0.20	0.24	0.16	0.55
2002-03	0.22	0.22	0.24	0.60
2003-04	0.24	0.28	0.19	0.74
2004-05	0.27	0.25	0.14	...

Interim Dividends (Per Share)

Amt	Decl	Ex	Rec	Pay
0.06Q	5/20/2004	6/17/2004	6/21/2004	7/12/2004
0.06Q	8/19/2004	9/16/2004	9/20/2004	10/11/2004
0.06Q	11/18/2004	12/16/2004	12/20/2004	1/10/2005
0.06Q	2/17/2005	3/17/2005	3/21/2005	4/11/2005

Indicated Div: $0.24

Valuation Analysis

Forecast P/E	22.17	No of Institutions	
	(4/7/2005)	356	
Market Cap	$5.0 Billion	Shares	129,141,912
Book Value	1.5 Billion	% Held	88.76
Price/Book	3.33		
Price/Sales	2.38		

Business Summary: Retail - Miscellaneous (MIC: 5.11 SIC: 944 NAIC: 48310)

Tiffany is a designer, manufacturer, retailer and distributor offering an extensive array of fine jewelry, sterling silverware, china, crystal, timepieces, stationery, and writing instruments. As of Jan 31 2004, Co. operated retail stores worldwide, including 50 stores in the U.S. Co. operates four channels of distribution: U.S. Retail includes retail sales in Co.-operated stores in the U.S.; International Retail includes retail sales through Co.-operated stores outside the U.S, along with business-to-business sales and Internet sales; Direct Marketing includes U.S. business-to-business, catalog and Internet sales; and Specialty Retail includes sales transacted under non-TIFFANY trademarks.

Recent Developments: For the quarter ended Oct 31 2004, net income decreased 25.8% to $20,809 thousand from net income of $28,031 thousand in the year-earlier quarter. Revenues were $461,152 thousand, up 7.2% from $430,123 thousand the year before. Operating income was $38,948 thousand versus an income of $49,215 thousand in the prior-year quarter, a decrease of 20.9%. Total indirect expense was $207,362 thousand versus $188,506 thousand in the prior-year quarter, an increase of 10.0%.

Prospects: Looking ahead, Co. plans to open at least three stores in the U.S. and several internationally in 2005, which in total should increase worldwide retail square footage of company-operated TIFFANY & CO. stores by about 5.0%. Also, Co. intends to continue to introduce new jewelry designs to complement its classics. Overall, Co. expects growth of 8.0% to 10.0% in sales for 2005, with earnings in a range of $1.45 to $1.55 per share. However, Co. expects earnings for the first quarter to be somewhat challenging due to difficult conditions in Japan and higher precious metal and diamond costs. Beyond 2005, Co. expects annual earnings per share growth of at least 12.0% over the following three years.

Financial Data (US$ in Thousands)	9 Mos	6 Mos	3 Mos	01/31/2004	01/31/2003	01/31/2002	01/31/2001	01/31/2000
Earnings Per Share	1.39	1.45	1.48	1.45	1.28	1.15	1.26	0.97
Cash Flow Per Share	0.78	0.89	1.40	1.95	1.52	1.66	0.75	1.61
Tang Book Value Per Share	10.36	10.27	10.18	10.01	8.34	7.15	6.34	5.22
Dividends Per Share	0.220	0.210	0.200	0.190	0.160	0.160	0.150	0.113
Dividend Payout %	15.81	14.50	13.54	13.10	12.50	13.91	11.90	11.54
Income Statement								
Total Revenue	1,394,709	933,557	456,960	2,000,045	1,706,602	1,606,535	1,668,056	1,461,857
EBITDA	237,452	176,812	89,956	448,011	392,774	373,773	380,583	304,639
Depn & Amortn	79,709	52,741	24,944	90,420	78,008	64,627	46,735	41,543
Income Before Taxes	157,743	124,071	65,012	342,685	299,637	289,312	317,641	248,058
Income Taxes	60,010	47,147	24,704	127,168	109,743	115,725	127,057	102,379
Net Income	97,733	76,924	40,308	215,517	189,894	173,587	190,584	145,679
Average Shares	147,750	148,669	149,481	148,472	148,591	150,517	151,816	149,666
Balance Sheet								
Current Assets	1,479,417	1,400,813	1,358,084	1,348,082	1,070,584	954,414	1,004,845	891,661
Total Assets	2,586,114	2,475,610	2,417,549	2,391,088	1,923,586	1,629,868	1,568,340	1,343,562
Current Liabilities	523,502	450,084	404,302	395,159	299,907	341,436	337,198	280,976
Long-Term Obligations	393,194	379,363	382,883	392,991	297,107	179,065	242,157	249,581
Total Liabilities	1,076,219	972,305	922,744	922,888	715,537	592,923	642,857	586,486
Stockholders' Equity	1,509,895	1,503,305	1,494,805	1,468,200	1,208,049	1,036,945	925,483	757,076
Shares Outstanding	145,756	146,371	146,845	146,735	144,865	145,001	145,897	144,952
Statistical Record								
Return on Assets %	8.49	9.35	10.07	9.99	10.69	10.86	13.05	12.14
Return on Equity %	14.49	15.45	16.07	16.11	16.92	17.69	22.59	22.88
EBITDA Margin %	17.03	18.94	19.69	22.40	23.01	23.27	22.82	20.84
Net Margin %	7.01	8.24	8.82	10.78	11.13	10.81	11.43	9.97
Asset Turnover	0.87	0.91	0.94	0.93	0.96	1.00	1.14	1.22
Current Ratio	2.83	3.11	3.36	3.41	3.57	2.80	2.98	3.17
Debt to Equity	0.26	0.25	0.26	0.27	0.25	0.17	0.26	0.33
Price Range	48.72-27.10	48.72-32.49	48.72-27.72	48.72-22.01	40.20-20.41	37.59-20.76	45.38-27.50	44.63-13.28
P/E Ratio	35.05-19.50	33.60-22.41	32.92-18.73	33.60-15.18	31.41-15.95	32.69-18.05	36.01-21.83	46.01-13.69
Average Yield %	0.59	0.53	0.52	0.54	0.54	0.52	0.42	0.42

Address: 727 Fifth Avenue, New York, NY 10022	Web Site: www.tiffany.com	Auditors: PricewaterhouseCoopers LLP
Telephone: (212) 755-8000	Officers: Michael J. Kowalski - Chmn., C.E.O. James E. Quinn - Pres.	Investor Contact: 212-230-5301
Fax: (212) 605-4465		

TIMBERLAND CO. (THE)

Exchange	Symbol	Price	52Wk Range	Yield	P/E
NYS	TBL	$70.93 (3/31/2005)	73.10-52.65	N/A	16.57

*7 Year Price Score 141.04 *NYSE Composite Index=100 *12 Month Price Score 103.55

Interim Earnings (Per Share)

Qtr.	Mar	Jun	Sep	Dec
2001	0.43	0.26	1.22	0.76
2002	0.36	0.13	1.30	0.72
2003	0.53	0.16	1.47	1.08
2004	0.87	0.22	1.92	1.28

Interim Dividends (Per Share)

Amt	Decl	Ex	Rec	Pay
2-for-1	7/28/1999	9/16/1999	8/31/1999	9/15/1999
2-for-1	5/18/2000	7/18/2000	6/30/2000	7/17/2000
2-for-1	3/3/2005	5/3/2005	4/14/2005	5/2/2005

Valuation Analysis

Forecast P/E	15.00	No of Institutions
	(4/7/2005)	200
Market Cap	$2.4 Billion	Shares
Book Value	511.5 Million	26,724,452
Price/Book	4.74	% Held
Price/Sales	1.62	95.42

Business Summary: Leather and Leather Products (MIC: 4.5 SIC: 143 NAIC: 16213)

Timberland designs, develops, engineers, markets and distributes, under the Timberland® and Timberland PRO® brands, premium-quality footwear, apparel and accessories products for men, women and children.Co.'s products are sold primarily through independent retailers, better-grade department stores, athletic stores and other national retailers. In addition, Co.'s products are sold through Timberland® specialty stores, Timberland® factory outlet stores, timberland.com and franchisees in Europe, which are all dedicated exclusively to selling Timberland® products. Co.'s products are sold throughout the United States, Canada, Europe, Asia, Latin America and the Middle East.

Recent Developments: For the year ended Dec 31 2004, net income increased 29.5% to $152,693 thousand from net income of $117,879 thousand a year earlier. Revenues were $1,500,580 thousand, up 11.8% from $1,342,123 thousand the year before. Operating income was $233,863 thousand versus an income of $184,302 thousand in the prior year, an increase of 26.9%. Total direct expense was $761,505 thousand versus $717,666 thousand in the prior year, an increase of 6.1%. Total indirect expense was $505,212 thousand versus $440,155 thousand in the prior year, an increase of 14.8%.

Prospects: Co. has established a Hong Kong procurement company and international treasury center in Switzerland to better align its organizational structure with its expanding global presence. In addition to providing enhanced support to its global sourcing operations and international business, Co. anticipates benefiting from tax savings on foreign earnings, which it estimates will reduce its 2005 tax rate by 1.5 percentage points to 34.0%. Separately, for 2005, Co. is targeting double-digit gains in earnings per share on low to mid single-digit revenue growth, leveraging strategies focused on delivering new products, expanding its global presence and executing its plans.

Financial Data
(US$ in Thousands)

	12/31/2004	12/31/2003	12/31/2002	12/31/2001	12/31/2000	12/31/1999	12/31/1998	12/31/1997
Earnings Per Share	4.28	3.23	2.49	2.65	2.86	1.70	1.26	1.01
Cash Flow Per Share	5.29	5.61	3.70	2.28	3.51	3.15	1.84	2.52
Tang Book Value Per Share	14.39	11.72	9.77	9.00	7.60	6.17	7.05	4.27
Income Statement								
Total Revenue	1,500,580	1,342,123	1,190,896	1,183,623	1,091,478	917,216	862,168	796,458
EBITDA	264,037	207,440	162,156	183,193	211,591	144,363	114,731	102,726
Depn & Amortn	26,604	23,644	22,503	19,904	19,291	24,363	18,199	20,292
Income Before Taxes	236,733	182,757	138,769	161,729	186,652	110,658	86,994	67,601
Income Taxes	84,040	64,878	48,569	54,988	62,528	35,411	27,838	20,280
Net Income	152,693	117,879	95,113	106,741	121,998	75,247	59,156	47,321
Average Shares	35,655	36,475	38,142	40,247	42,647	44,356	47,034	46,950
Balance Sheet								
Current Assets	649,047	539,560	441,783	405,543	381,760	414,641	387,566	342,006
Total Assets	757,510	641,716	538,671	504,612	476,311	493,311	469,467	420,003
Current Liabilities	226,192	196,991	155,756	128,502	145,073	112,355	95,731	99,095
Long-Term Obligations	...	...	...	...	...	100,000	100,000	100,000
Total Liabilities	246,003	213,253	165,886	145,374	159,560	220,943	203,274	205,108
Stockholders' Equity	511,507	428,463	372,785	359,238	316,751	272,368	266,193	214,895
Shares Outstanding	34,181	35,020	36,306	38,334	39,615	41,285	35,040	45,412
Statistical Record								
Return on Assets %	21.77	19.97	18.23	21.76	25.10	15.63	13.30	10.88
Return on Equity %	32.40	29.42	25.99	31.58	41.30	27.94	24.59	24.89
EBITDA Margin %	17.60	15.46	13.62	15.48	19.39	15.74	13.31	12.90
Net Margin %	10.18	8.78	7.99	9.02	11.18	8.20	6.86	5.94
Asset Turnover	2.14	2.27	2.28	2.41	2.25	1.91	1.94	1.83
Current Ratio	2.87	2.74	2.84	3.16	2.63	3.69	4.05	3.45
Debt to Equity	...	...	...	...	...	0.37	0.38	0.47
Price Range	67.13-49.45	58.63-30.68	45.89-27.07	73.25-26.15	69.19-18.50	26.44-10.64	21.72-7.23	20.56-9.44
P/E Ratio	15.68-11.55	18.15-9.50	18.43-10.87	27.64-9.87	24.19-6.47	15.55-6.26	17.24-5.74	20.36-9.34

Address: 200 Domain Drive, Stratham, NH 03885	**Web Site:** www.timberland.com	**Auditors:** Deloitte & Touche LLP
Telephone: (603) 772-9500	**Officers:** Sidney W. Swartz - Chmn. Jeffrey B. Swartz - Pres., C.E.O.	**Investor Contact:** 603-773-1212
Fax: (603) 773-1640		

TIME WARNER INC

Exchange	Symbol	Price	52Wk Range	Yield	P/E
NYS	TWX	$17.55 (3/31/2005)	19.55-15.60	N/A	24.38

*7 Year Price Score 46.82 ***NYSE Composite Index=100** ***12 Month Price Score 95.90**

Interim Earnings (Per Share)

Qtr.	Mar	Jun	Sep	Dec
2001	(0.31)	(0.17)	(0.22)	(0.41)
2002	(12.25)	0.09	0.01	(10.06)
2003	0.09	0.23	0.12	0.14
2004	0.20	0.17	0.11	0.24

Interim Dividends (Per Share)

No Dividends Paid

Valuation Analysis

Forecast P/E	N/A	No of Institutions
Market Cap	$80.5 Billion	Shares
Book Value	60.8 Billion	3,313,982,464
Price/Book	1.33	% Held
Price/Sales	1.91	73.65

TRADING VOLUME (thousand shares)

Business Summary: Communications (MIC: 10.1 SIC: 375 NAIC: 18111)

Time Warner is a media and entertainment company, whose businesses include interactive services, cable systems, filmed entertainment, television networks, music and publishing. Co.'s business interests are classified into six fundamental areas: America Online, which consists primarily of interactive services; Cable, consisting principally of interests in cable systems; filmed entertainment, which consists of interests in filmed entertainment and television production; networks, which consists of cable television and broadcast network programming; music, consisting of recorded music, music publishing; and publishing, which consists of magazine publishing, book publishing and direct marketing.

Recent Developments: For the year ended Dec 31 2004, net income increased 27.5% to $3,364,000 thousand from net income of $2,639,000 thousand a year earlier. Revenues were $42,089,000 thousand, up 6.4% from $39,563,000 thousand the year before. Operating income was $6,165,000 thousand versus an income of $5,254,000 thousand in the prior year, an increase of 17.3%. Total direct expense was $24,449,000 thousand versus $23,422,000 thousand in the prior year, an increase of 4.4%. Total indirect expense was $11,475,000 thousand versus $10,887,000 thousand in the prior year, an increase of 5.4%.

Prospects: Co.'s outlook appears encouraging. For the quarter ended Dec 31 2004, Co. reported top line gains and improved operating profit from across its operating segments, with the exception of Filmed Entertainment. Notably, for the twelve months ended Dec 31 2004 revenues from Co.'s Cable segment, Time Warner Cable, grew 10.2% to $8.48 billion and operating income climbed 15.2% to $1.76 billion. Co. attributed the improved Cable segment results to a 10.0% increase in subscription revenues and an 11.0% rise in advertising revenues. Positively affecting subscription revenues were gains of 24.0% in high-speed revenues and 25.0% in enhanced digital video service revenues, as well as higher cable rates.

Financial Data
(US$ in Thousands)

	12/31/2004	12/31/2003	12/31/2002	12/31/2001	12/31/2000	06/30/2000	06/30/1999	06/30/1998
Earnings Per Share	0.72	0.57	(22.15)	(1.11)	0.45	0.48	0.30	0.04
Cash Flow Per Share	1.45	1.46	1.58	1.20	0.56	0.79	0.53	0.24
Tang Book Value Per Share	N.M.	N.M.	N.M.	N.M.	2.85	2.66	1.38	0.12
Income Statement								
Total Revenue	42,089,000	39,565,000	40,961,000	38,234,000	7,703,000	6,886,000	4,777,000	2,600,000
EBITDA	9,647,000	9,501,000	(37,056,000)	8,187,000	2,265,000	2,314,000	1,338,000	222,000
Depn & Amortn	3,207,000	3,140,000	5,595,000	11,583,000	381,000	300,000	242,000	130,000
Income Before Taxes	4,907,000	4,517,000	(44,434,000)	(4,775,000)	1,884,000	2,014,000	1,096,000	92,000
Income Taxes	1,698,000	1,371,000	140,000	146,000	732,000	782,000	334,000	...
Net Income	3,364,000	2,639,000	(98,696,000)	(4,921,000)	1,152,000	1,232,000	762,000	92,000
Average Shares	4,694,699	4,623,699	4,521,799	4,429,099	2,595,000	2,603,000	2,554,000	2,072,000
Balance Sheet								
Current Assets	14,639,000	12,268,000	11,155,000	10,274,000	4,671,000	4,428,000	1,979,000	930,000
Total Assets	123,339,000	121,783,000	115,450,000	208,559,000	10,827,000	10,673,000	5,348,000	2,214,000
Current Liabilities	14,624,000	15,518,000	13,395,000	12,972,000	2,328,000	2,395,000	1,725,000	894,000
Long-Term Obligations	20,703,000	23,458,000	27,354,000	22,792,000	1,411,000	1,630,000	348,000	372,000
Total Liabilities	62,568,000	65,745,000	62,633,000	56,488,000	4,049,000	4,512,000	2,315,000	1,616,000
Stockholders' Equity	60,771,000	56,038,000	52,817,000	152,071,000	6,778,000	6,161,000	3,033,000	598,000
Shares Outstanding	4,588,699	4,536,199	4,476,199	4,429,199	2,378,601	2,316,495	2,201,788	1,757,128
Statistical Record								
Return on Assets %	2.74	2.22	N.M.	N.M.	9.45	15.34	20.15	6.01
Return on Equity %	5.74	4.85	N.M.	N.M.	15.58	26.73	41.97	25.34
EBITDA Margin %	22.92	24.01	N.M.	21.41	29.40	33.60	28.01	8.54
Net Margin %	7.99	6.67	N.M.	N.M.	14.96	17.89	15.95	3.54
Asset Turnover	0.34	0.33	0.25	0.35	0.63	0.86	1.26	1.70
Current Ratio	1.00	0.79	0.83	0.79	2.01	1.85	1.15	1.04
Debt to Equity	0.34	0.42	0.52	0.15	0.21	0.26	0.11	0.62
Price Range	19.55-15.60	18.10-10.06	32.68-9.64	56.60-29.25	63.00-34.80	94.00-41.41	83.75-10.24	13.51-3.48
P/E Ratio	27.15-21.67	31.75-17.65	...	...	140.00-77.33	195.83-86.26	279.17-34.14	337.70-86.91

Address: 75 Rockefeller Plaza, New York, NY 10019	Web Site: www.aoltimewarner.com	Auditors: Ernst & Young LLP
Telephone: (212) 484-8000	Officers: Richard D. Parsons - Chmn., C.E.O. Edward I. Adler - Exec. V.P., Corp. Communications	Investor Contact: 212-484-6579
Fax: (212) 489-6183		

TIMKEN CO. (THE)

Exchange	Symbol	Price	52Wk Range	Yield	P/E
NYS	TKR	$27.34 (3/31/2005)	29.26-21.00	2.19	18.35

*7 Year Price Score 108.23 *NYSE Composite Index=100 *12 Month Price Score 101.49

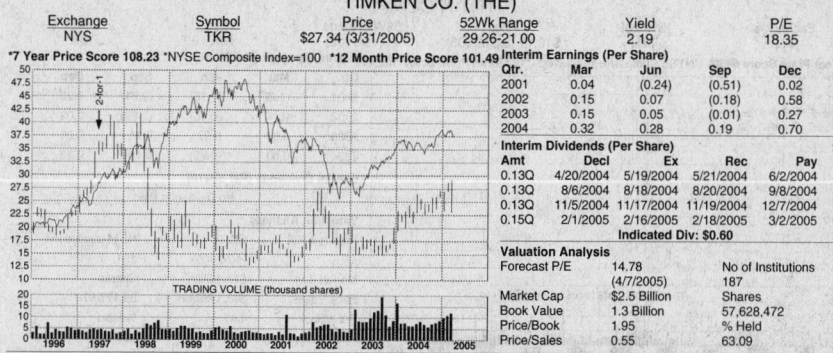

Interim Earnings (Per Share)

Qtr.	Mar	Jun	Sep	Dec
2001	0.04	(0.24)	(0.51)	0.02
2002	0.15	0.07	(0.18)	0.58
2003	0.15	0.05	(0.01)	0.27
2004	0.32	0.28	0.19	0.70

Interim Dividends (Per Share)

Amt	Decl	Ex	Rec	Pay
0.13Q	4/20/2004	5/19/2004	5/21/2004	6/2/2004
0.13Q	8/6/2004	8/18/2004	8/20/2004	9/8/2004
0.13Q	11/5/2004	11/17/2004	11/19/2004	12/7/2004
0.15Q	2/1/2005	2/16/2005	2/18/2005	3/2/2005

Indicated Div: $0.60

Valuation Analysis

Forecast P/E	14.78	No of Institutions	
	(4/7/2005)	187	
Market Cap	$2.5 Billion	Shares	
Book Value	1.3 Billion	57,628,472	
Price/Book	1.95	% Held	
Price/Sales	0.55	63.09	

Business Summary: Industrial Machinery and Equipment (MIC: 11.5 SIC: 562 NAIC: 32991)

Timken is a global manufacturer of engineered antifriction bearings, alloy steels and related products and services. The Automotive and Industrial Groups manufacture and distribute bearings and related products and services. Automotive Group customers include original equipment manufacturers (OEMs) of passenger cars and trucks and their suppliers. Industrial Group customers include both OEMs and distributors for agriculture, construction, mining, energy, mill, machine tooling, aerospace and rail. Steel Group products include different alloys in both solid and tubular sections as well as custom-made steel products for both automotive and industrial applications, including bearings.

Recent Developments: For the year ended Dec 31 2004, net income increased 271.9% to $135,656 thousand from net income of $36,481 thousand a year earlier. Revenues were $4,513,671 thousand, up 19.2% from $3,788,097 thousand the year before. Operating income was $237,228 thousand versus an income of $98,247 thousand in the prior year, an increase of 141.5%. Total direct expense was $3,675,050 thousand versus $3,148,979 thousand in the prior year, an increase of 16.7%. Total indirect expense was $601,357 thousand versus $540,871 thousand in the prior year, an increase of 11.2%.

Prospects: Results are being positively affected by strong steel demand and increased productivity. Co. is targeting first-quarter 2005 earnings in the range of $0.38 to $0.43 per diluted share, reflecting expectations of continued growth in global industrial markets. Looking ahead, Co. is projecting full-year 2005 earnings per diluted share, excluding special items, of between $1.70 and $1.85. Global industrial markets are expected to continue to grow in 2005, supporting strong performance in the Industrial and Steel Groups. Meanwhile, North American light vehicle production is expected to be down slightly in 2005, while medium and heavy truck production is expected to grow but at a lower rate.

Financial Data

(US$ in Thousands)	12/31/2004	12/31/2003	12/31/2002	12/31/2001	12/31/2000	12/31/1999	12/31/1998	12/31/1997
Earnings Per Share	1.49	0.44	0.62	(0.69)	0.76	1.01	1.82	2.69
Cash Flow Per Share	1.54	2.44	3.37	3.00	2.52	4.49	4.69	4.97
Tang Book Value Per Share	9.96	8.07	5.52	8.28	12.75	14.58	14.65	14.20
Dividends Per Share	0.520	0.520	0.520	0.670	0.720	0.720	0.720	0.660
Dividend Payout %	34.90	118.18	83.87	...	94.74	71.29	39.56	24.54
Income Statement								
Total Revenue	4,513,671	3,788,097	2,550,075	2,447,178	2,643,008	2,495,034	2,679,841	2,617,562
EBITDA	458,647	316,931	261,917	156,876	250,087	273,069	351,685	422,455
Depn & Amortn	209,431	208,851	146,535	152,467	151,047	149,949	139,833	134,431
Income Before Taxes	199,779	60,802	85,518	(26,883)	70,597	98,991	185,350	266,592
Income Taxes	64,123	24,321	34,067	14,783	24,709	36,367	70,813	95,173
Net Income	135,656	36,481	38,749	(41,666)	45,888	62,624	114,537	171,419
Average Shares	90,759	83,159	61,635	59,947	60,723	62,025	62,809	63,804
Balance Sheet								
Current Assets	1,733,291	1,377,105	968,292	828,380	898,542	833,526	850,337	855,171
Total Assets	3,938,500	3,689,789	2,748,356	2,533,084	2,564,105	2,441,318	2,450,031	2,326,550
Current Liabilities	1,041,327	1,054,556	634,070	641,156	587,452	557,661	490,423	579,564
Long-Term Obligations	620,634	613,446	350,085	368,151	305,181	327,343	325,086	202,846
Total Liabilities	2,668,652	2,600,162	2,139,270	1,751,349	1,559,423	1,395,337	1,393,950	1,294,474
Stockholders' Equity	1,269,848	1,089,627	609,086	781,735	1,004,682	1,045,981	1,056,081	1,032,076
Shares Outstanding	90,504	89,065	63,411	59,856	59,965	61,196	61,848	62,880
Statistical Record								
Return on Assets %	3.55	1.13	1.47	N.M.	1.83	2.56	4.80	7.80
Return on Equity %	11.47	4.30	5.57	N.M.	4.46	5.96	10.97	17.54
EBITDA Margin %	10.16	8.37	10.27	6.41	9.46	10.94	13.12	16.14
Net Margin %	3.01	0.96	1.52	N.M.	1.74	2.51	4.27	6.55
Asset Turnover	1.18	1.18	0.97	0.96	1.05	1.02	1.12	1.19
Current Ratio	1.66	1.31	1.53	1.29	1.53	1.49	1.73	1.48
Debt to Equity	0.49	0.56	0.57	0.47	0.30	0.31	0.31	0.20
Price Range	27.14-19.49	20.30-14.84	27.35-14.92	18.60-12.49	21.50-12.75	25.13-15.94	41.75-13.69	41.44-22.69
P/E Ratio	18.21-13.08	46.14-33.73	44.11-24.06	...	28.29-16.78	24.88-15.78	22.94-7.52	15.40-8.43
Average Yield %	2.21	3.06	2.61	4.25	4.35	3.83	2.63	2.03

Address: 1835 Dueber Ave., S.W., Canton, OH 44706-2798 **Telephone:** (330) 438-3000 **Fax:** (330) 471-3452	**Web Site:** www.timken.com **Officers:** W. R. Timken Jr. - Chmn., James W. Griffith - Pres., C.E.O.	**Auditors:** ERNST & YOUNG LLP **Investor Contact:** 330-471-3378

TITAN CORP.

Exchange	Symbol	Price	52Wk Range	Yield	P/E
NYS	TTN	$18.16 (3/31/2005)	20.19-11.40	N/A	N/A

*7 Year Price Score 91.43 ***NYSE Composite Index=100** ***12 Month Price Score 102.41**

Interim Earnings (Per Share)

Qtr.	Mar	Jun	Sep	Dec
2001	(1.29)	(0.16)	(0.61)	0.23
2002	(0.47)	(0.16)	(2.89)	0.02
2003	0.09	0.07	0.18	0.01
2004	0.03	(0.79)	0.18	0.13

Interim Dividends (Per Share)

No Dividends Paid

Valuation Analysis

Forecast P/E	18.10	No of Institutions
	(4/7/2005)	151
Market Cap	$1.5 Billion	Shares
Book Value	348.1 Million	68,177,976
Price/Book	4.41	% Held
Price/Sales	0.75	80.31

Business Summary: IT & Technology (MIC: 10.2 SIC: 373 NAIC: 41512)

Titan is a technology developer and system integrator for the U.S. Department of Defense, the U.S. Department of Homeland Security, and intelligence and other key government agencies. Co. provides a range research and development, design, installation, integration, test, logistical support, maintenance and training services. Co. also provides services to government agencies with sophisticated information systems. In addition, Co. develops and produces digital imaging products, sensors, lasers, and electro-optical systems, threat simulation/training systems, intelligence electronic hardware, signal intercept systems and complex military specific systems.

Recent Developments: For the year ended Dec 31 2004, income from continuing operations decreased 56.9% to $13,764 thousand from income of $31,909 thousand a year earlier. Net loss was $38,397 thousand versus net income of $29,097 thousand a year earlier. Revenues were $2,046,525 thousand, up 16.5% from $1,756,206 thousand the year before. Operating income was $70,947 thousand versus an income of $106,462 thousand in the prior year, a decrease of 33.4%. Total direct expense was $1,729,963 thousand versus $1,464,709 thousand in the prior year, an increase of 18.1%. Total indirect expense was $245,615 thousand versus $185,035 thousand in the prior year, an increase of 32.7%.

Prospects: Top-line growth is being driven by contracts related to homeland security/global war on terrorism programs, defense secure communications and intelligence systems, and government enterprise IT systems. Looking ahead, Co. is projecting full-year 2005 revenues in the range of $2.30 billion to $2.38 billion, representing year-over-year growth of between 12.0% and 16.0%, as well as operating margin in the range of 7.9% to 8.5%. In addition, Co. anticipates full-year 2005 net income from continuing operations of between $86.0 million and $95.0 million, or $0.98 to $1.08 per share.

Financial Data

(US$ in Thousands)	12/31/2004	12/31/2003	12/31/2002	12/31/2001	12/31/2000	12/31/1999	12/31/1998	12/31/1997
Earnings Per Share	(0.44)	0.34	(3.58)	(1.76)	(0.44)	0.69	(0.57)	0.25
Cash Flow Per Share	(0.01)	0.94	0.28	(0.48)	(1.50)	0.43	(0.06)	(0.47)
Tang Book Value Per Share	N.M.	N.M.	N.M.	N.M.	N.M.	N.M.	0.31	1.82
Income Statement								
Total Revenue	2,046,525	1,775,007	1,392,160	1,132,052	1,033,213	406,551	303,428	171,186
EBITDA	83,559	105,397	42,373	56,672	59,064	77,577	25,479	19,376
Depn & Amortn	15,916	20,845	21,705	43,091	43,692	9,788	7,126	5,647
Income Before Taxes	30,717	52,304	(10,288)	(21,371)	(20,638)	59,183	11,368	8,688
Income Taxes	16,953	22,353	(2,452)	(347)	(3,985)	21,983	4,155	3,180
Net Income	(38,397)	29,097	(271,461)	(98,614)	(18,728)	31,600	(19,705)	5,165
Average Shares	86,962	83,398	75,988	58,793	52,717	46,032	36,177	21,396
Balance Sheet								
Current Assets	679,488	614,427	611,518	588,330	463,299	199,648	120,947	90,672
Total Assets	1,357,766	1,290,635	1,297,442	1,358,698	959,438	406,196	192,567	138,147
Current Liabilities	354,563	291,591	289,107	261,665	195,523	122,150	56,497	36,762
Long-Term Obligations	553,241	542,238	346,795	322,799	298,890	137,743	70,291	37,310
Total Liabilities	1,009,686	919,226	735,129	627,548	542,022	295,448	141,856	84,795
Stockholders' Equity	348,080	371,409	312,313	481,150	167,416	110,748	50,711	53,352
Shares Outstanding	84,501	81,917	78,098	69,756	53,280	45,395	36,650	17,694
Statistical Record								
Return on Assets %	N.M.	2.25	N.M.	N.M.	N.M.	10.56	N.M.	3.88
Return on Equity %	N.M.	8.51	N.M.	N.M.	N.M.	39.14	N.M.	10.33
EBITDA Margin %	4.08	5.94	3.04	5.01	5.72	19.08	8.40	11.32
Net Margin %	N.M.	1.64	N.M.	N.M.	N.M.	7.77	N.M.	3.02
Asset Turnover	1.54	1.37	1.05	0.98	1.51	1.36	1.83	1.29
Current Ratio	1.92	2.11	2.12	2.25	2.37	1.63	2.14	2.47
Debt to Equity	1.59	1.46	1.11	0.67	1.79	1.24	1.39	0.70
Price Range	21.90-11.40	21.84-7.00	20.04-8.35	23.14-11.25	46.15-9.59	38.01-3.82	6.53-3.16	6.58-2.31
P/E Ratio	...	64.24-20.59	...	...	...	55.09-5.53	...	26.31-9.24

Address: 3033 Science Park Road, San Diego, CA 92121-1199	Web Site: www.titan.com	Auditors: KPMG LLP
Telephone: (858) 552-9500	Officers: Gene W. Ray - Chmn., Pres., C.E.O., C.O.O. Lawrence J. Delaney - Exec. V.P., Opers.	Investor Contact: 858-552-9400
Fax: (858) 552-9645		

TJX COMPANIES, INC.

Exchange	Symbol	Price	52Wk Range	Yield	P/E
NYS	TJX	$24.63 (3/31/2005)	26.35-20.95	0.97	17.35

*7 Year Price Score 120.60 *NYSE Composite Index=100   *12 Month Price Score 95.96

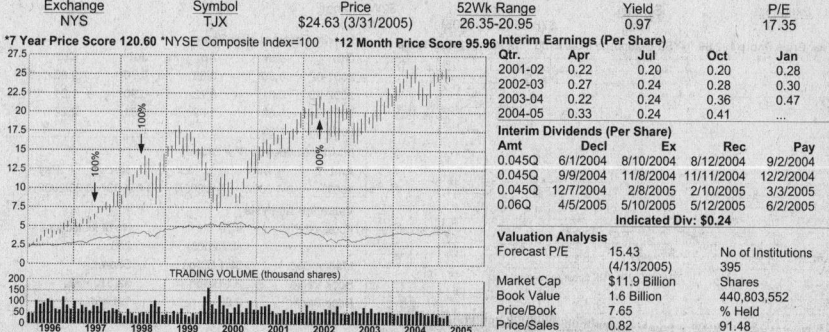

Interim Earnings (Per Share)

Qtr.	Apr	Jul	Oct	Jan
2001-02	0.22	0.20	0.20	0.28
2002-03	0.27	0.24	0.28	0.30
2003-04	0.22	0.24	0.36	0.47
2004-05	0.33	0.24	0.41	...

Interim Dividends (Per Share)

Amt	Decl	Ex	Rec	Pay
0.045Q	6/1/2004	8/10/2004	8/12/2004	9/2/2004
0.045Q	9/9/2004	11/8/2004	11/11/2004	12/2/2004
0.045Q	12/7/2004	2/8/2005	2/10/2005	3/3/2005
0.06Q	4/5/2005	5/10/2005	5/12/2005	6/2/2005
		Indicated Div: $0.24		

Valuation Analysis

Forecast P/E	15.43	No of Institutions
	(4/13/2005)	395
Market Cap	$11.9 Billion	Shares
Book Value	1.6 Billion	440,803,552
Price/Book	7.65	% Held
Price/Sales	0.82	91.48

Business Summary: Retail - Apparel and Accessory Stores (MIC: 5.8 SIC: 651 NAIC: 48140)

TJX Companies is a major off-price retailer of apparel and home fashions in the U.S. and worldwide. As of Jan 31 2004, Co. operated 745 stores, selling brand-name family apparel and accessories, women's shoes, domestic furnishings, jewelry and giftware. Marshalls is an off-price family apparel chain, operating 673 stores. HomeGoods operated 160 off-price home fashion stores in a no-frills environment. T.K. Maxx is an off-price apparel concept operating 147 stores in the United Kingdom and Ireland. A.J. Wright operated 84 off-price family apparel stores. Co. also has 25 HomeSense stores and 160 Winners Apparel Ltd. stores in Canada.

Recent Developments: For the quarter ended Oct 30 2004, net income increased 9.9% to $200,855 thousand from net income of $182,833 thousand in the corresponding prior-year quarter. Revenues were $3,817,350 thousand, up 12.7% from $3,387,452 thousand the year before. Cost of sales, including buying and occupancy costs rose 13.0% to $2,857,105 thousand from $2,528,049 thousand a year earlier. Total indirect expense was $625,987 thousand versus $552,142 thousand in the prior-year quarter, an increase of 13.4%.

Prospects: Results are being positively affected by strong comparable-store sales growth at Co.'s core Marmaxx Group, which includes Marshalls and T.J. Maxx. Looking ahead, results should benefit from expanded selections of jewelry, accessories, and footwear at Marmaxx, as well as the launch of e-commerce web sites for T.J. Maxx and HomeGoods during 2004. Meanwhile, Co. will continue to expand its store base during fiscal 2005. Co. plans to open 161 net new stores during the current fiscal year, representing an 8.0% increase in selling square footage. Co. is targeting first-quarter 2005 earnings in the range of $0.32 to $0.34 per share, and full-year 2005 earnings of between $1.49 and $1.57 per share.

Financial Data

(US$ in Thousands)	9 Mos	6 Mos	3 Mos	01/31/2004	01/25/2003	01/26/2002	01/27/2001	01/29/2000
Earnings Per Share	1.42	1.38	1.38	1.28	1.08	0.90	0.93	0.82
Cash Flow Per Share	2.29	2.15	2.07	1.49	1.71	1.66	0.97	0.92
Tang Book Value Per Share	2.84	2.76	2.83	2.74	2.36	2.14	1.84	1.55
Dividends Per Share	0.160	0.150	0.140	0.135	0.113	0.087	0.077	0.068
Dividend Payout %	11.26	10.90	10.11	10.55	10.42	9.72	8.33	8.23
Income Statement								
Total Revenue	10,584,374	6,767,024	3,352,737	13,327,938	11,981,207	10,708,998	9,579,006	8,795,347
EBITDA	1,027,464	621,709	351,434	1,296,145	1,135,624	1,059,344	1,037,242	1,011,337
Depn & Amortn	211,960	140,463	70,517	227,819	197,900	185,300	172,300	157,400
Income Before Taxes	794,794	467,670	274,334	1,068,326	937,724	874,044	864,942	853,937
Income Taxes	307,585	181,316	106,222	409,961	359,336	333,647	326,876	327,115
Net Income	487,209	286,354	168,112	658,365	578,388	500,397	538,066	521,668
Average Shares	490,015	499,184	504,681	512,874	537,740	556,267	578,392	635,581
Balance Sheet								
Current Assets	3,259,238	2,679,305	2,582,853	2,451,748	2,240,540	2,115,926	1,721,947	1,700,565
Total Assets	5,293,818	4,613,367	4,508,673	4,396,767	3,940,489	3,595,743	2,932,283	2,804,963
Current Liabilities	2,591,658	1,984,614	1,752,543	1,690,520	1,566,345	1,315,010	1,228,759	1,366,368
Long-Term Obligations	598,051	593,504	691,555	692,321	693,764	702,379	319,372	319,367
Total Liabilities	3,743,296	3,080,564	2,923,172	2,844,379	2,531,342	2,255,045	1,713,571	1,685,735
Stockholders' Equity	1,550,522	1,532,803	1,585,501	1,552,388	1,409,147	1,340,698	1,218,712	1,119,228
Shares Outstanding	481,872	488,750	494,931	499,181	520,515	543,075	560,757	599,958
Statistical Record								
Return on Assets %	14.60	15.98	16.51	15.54	15.39	15.37	18.81	18.84
Return on Equity %	47.81	48.23	47.71	43.74	42.18	39.21	46.16	44.71
EBITDA Margin %	9.71	9.19	10.48	9.73	9.48	9.89	10.83	11.50
Net Margin %	4.60	4.23	5.01	4.94	4.83	4.67	5.62	5.93
Asset Turnover	2.96	3.22	3.21	3.15	3.19	3.29	3.35	3.18
Current Ratio	1.26	1.35	1.47	1.45	1.43	1.61	1.40	1.24
Debt to Equity	0.39	0.39	0.44	0.45	0.49	0.52	0.26	0.29
Price Range	26.35-20.65	26.35-18.86	25.71-17.64	23.59-15.93	22.18-16.02	20.31-13.88	15.16-7.06	18.19-8.16
P/E Ratio	18.56-14.54	19.09-13.67	18.63-12.78	18.43-12.45	20.53-14.83	22.56-15.42	16.30-7.59	22.18-9.95
Average Yield %	0.69	0.66	0.65	0.68	0.57	0.52	0.72	0.47

Address: 770 Cochituate Road, Framingham, MA 01701 **Telephone:** (508) 390-1000 **Fax:** (508) 390-2091	**Web Site:** www.tjx.com **Officers:** Bernard Cammarata - Chmn. Edmond J. English - Pres., C.E.O.	**Auditors:** PricewaterhouseCoopers LLP **Investor Contact:** 508-390-2323

TOLL BROTHERS INC.

Exchange	Symbol	Price	52Wk Range	Yield	P/E
NYS	TOL	$78.85 (3/31/2005)	90.00-36.85	N/A	13.74

*7 Year Price Score 192.69 *NYSE Composite Index=100 *12 Month Price Score 144.47

Interim Earnings (Per Share)

Qtr.	Jan	Apr	Jul	Oct
2001-02	0.60	0.69	0.70	0.92
2002-03	0.61	0.72	0.90	1.21
2003-04	0.62	0.89	1.31	2.22
2004-05	1.33	...	...	...

Interim Dividends (Per Share)

Amt	Decl	Ex	Rec	Pay
100%	3/4/2002	4/1/2002	3/14/2002	3/28/2002

Valuation Analysis

Forecast P/E	9.70	No of Institutions
	(4/7/2005)	256
Market Cap	$6.1 Billion	Shares
Book Value	2.1 Billion	52,310,852
Price/Book	2.87	% Held
Price/Sales	1.41	67.49

Business Summary: Building & General Construction (MIC: 3.2 SIC: 531 NAIC: 36115)

Toll Brothers is engaged in the design, build, market and arrange financing for single-family detached and attached homes in residential communities. Co. operates its own land development, architectural, engineering, mortgage, title, security monitoring, landscape, cable T.V., broadband Internet access, lumber distribution, house component assembly and manufacturing operations. Co. also owns and operates golf courses and country clubs associated with several of its communities. At Oct 31, 2004, Co. was operating in 292 communities containing approximately 24,343 home sites.

Recent Developments: For the quarter ended Jan 31 2005, net income increased 120.0% to $110,193 thousand from net income of $50,084 thousand in the year-earlier quarter. Revenues were $999,140 thousand, up 67.1% from $597,912 thousand the year before. Total direct expense was $686,272 thousand versus $427,731 thousand in the prior-year quarter, an increase of 60.4%. Total indirect expense was $107,065 thousand versus $76,653 thousand in the prior-year quarter, an increase of 39.7%.

Prospects: Co.'s near term outlook appears favorable, supported by continued strong market conditions and further improvement in the general economic climate. Consequently, Co. raised its guidance on the number of homes it expects to deliver in the full-year of 2005 as it now expects to deliver between 8,050 and 8,400 homes, an increase from a previous target range of 7,900 to 8,300 homes. Based on the strength of first quarter earnings and the increase in expected deliveries, Co. now believes net income will grow approximately 60.0% in the full-year of 2005 over the year before, compared to its previous guidance of more than 40.0% net income growth in the full-year of 2005.

Financial Data
(US$ in Thousands)

	3 Mos	10/31/2004	10/31/2003	10/31/2002	10/31/2001	10/31/2000	10/31/1999	10/31/1998
Earnings Per Share	5.74	5.04	3.44	2.91	2.76	1.95	1.36	1.11
Cash Flow Per Share	2.58	1.50	(0.65)	(1.34)	(2.07)	(0.23)	(1.65)	(0.64)
Tang Book Value Per Share	27.44	25.66	20.14	16.09	13.12	10.38	8.32	7.12
Income Statement								
Total Revenue	999,140	3,893,093	2,775,241	2,328,972	2,229,605	1,814,362	1,464,115	1,210,816
EBITDA	189,192	762,502	496,473	422,342	405,492	285,663	209,249	175,845
Depn & Amortn	5,201	21,767	12,075	10,495	9,356	8,528	6,594	5,611
Income Before Taxes	183,991	647,432	411,153	347,318	337,889	230,966	162,750	134,293
Income Taxes	73,798	238,321	151,333	127,431	124,216	85,023	59,723	48,474
Net Income	110,193	409,111	259,820	219,887	213,673	145,943	101,566	84,704
Average Shares	83,042	81,165	75,541	75,480	77,366	74,826	74,872	76,720
Balance Sheet								
Current Assets	4,705,533	4,459,123	3,505,600	2,653,398	2,366,381	1,874,243	1,539,766	1,192,006
Total Assets	5,096,974	4,905,578	3,787,391	2,895,365	2,532,200	2,030,254	1,668,062	1,254,468
Current Liabilities	1,628,137	1,257,493	812,458	644,003	562,570	489,073	368,993	275,740
Long-Term Obligations	1,360,206	1,728,098	1,498,305	1,121,853	1,057,047	796,036	682,735	452,972
Total Liabilities	2,988,343	2,985,591	2,310,763	1,765,856	1,619,617	1,285,109	1,051,728	728,712
Stockholders' Equity	2,108,631	1,919,987	1,476,628	1,129,509	912,583	745,145	616,334	525,756
Shares Outstanding	76,847	74,821	73,322	70,217	69,554	71,790	74,070	73,870
Statistical Record								
Return on Assets %	10.50	9.39	7.78	8.10	9.37	7.87	6.95	7.14
Return on Equity %	25.61	24.02	19.94	21.54	25.78	21.38	17.79	18.60
EBITDA Margin %	18.94	19.59	17.89	18.13	18.19	15.74	14.29	14.52
Net Margin %	11.03	10.51	9.36	9.44	9.58	8.04	6.94	7.00
Asset Turnover	0.96	0.89	0.83	0.86	0.98	0.98	1.00	1.02
Current Ratio	2.89	3.55	4.31	4.12	4.21	3.83	4.17	4.32
Debt to Equity	0.65	0.90	1.01	0.99	1.16	1.07	1.11	0.86
Price Range	78.07-36.85	47.80-36.84	36.91-17.75	31.38-15.58	22.00-13.50	17.19-8.06	12.75-7.97	15.63-9.47
P/E Ratio	13.60-6.42	9.48-7.31	10.73-5.16	10.78-5.35	7.97-4.89	8.81-4.13	9.38-5.86	14.08-8.53

Address: 250 Gibraltar Road, Horsham, PA 19044 **Telephone:** (215) 938-8000 **Fax:** (215) 938-8023	**Web Site:** www.tollbrothers.com **Officers:** Robert I. Toll - Chmn., C.E.O. Bruce E. Toll - Vice-Chmn.	**Auditors:** Ernst & Young LLP **Investor Contact:** 215-938-8000 **Transfer Agents:** American Stock Transfer & Trust Co., New York, NY

TOOTSIE ROLL INDUSTRIES INC

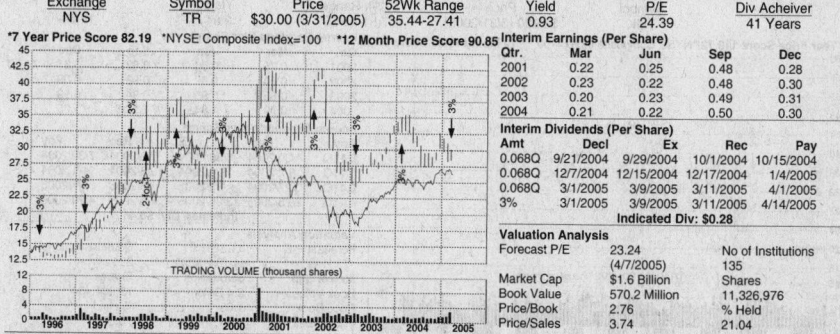

Exchange	Symbol	Price	52Wk Range	Yield	P/E	Div Acheiver
NYS	TR	$30.00 (3/31/2005)	35.44-27.41	0.93	24.39	41 Years

*7 Year Price Score 82.19   *NYSE Composite Index=100   *12 Month Price Score 90.85

Interim Earnings (Per Share)

Qtr.	Mar	Jun	Sep	Dec
2001	0.22	0.25	0.48	0.28
2002	0.23	0.22	0.48	0.30
2003	0.20	0.23	0.49	0.31
2004	0.21	0.22	0.50	0.30

Interim Dividends (Per Share)

Amt	Decl	Ex	Rec	Pay
0.068Q	9/21/2004	9/29/2004	10/1/2004	10/15/2004
0.068Q	12/7/2004	12/15/2004	12/17/2004	1/4/2005
0.068Q	3/1/2005	3/9/2005	3/11/2005	4/1/2005
3%	3/1/2005	3/9/2005	3/11/2005	4/14/2005

Indicated Div: $0.28

Valuation Analysis

Forecast P/E	23.24	No of Institutions	
	(4/7/2005)	135	
Market Cap	$1.6 Billion	Shares	
Book Value	570.2 Million	11,326,976	
Price/Book	2.76	% Held	
Price/Sales	3.74	21.04	

Business Summary: Food (MIC: 4.1 SIC: 064 NAIC: 11340)

Tootsie Roll Industries is primarily engaged in the manufacture and sale of candy products. The majority of Co.'s products are sold under the following registered trademarks: Tootsie Roll, Tootsie Roll Pops, Caramel Apple Pops, Child's Play, Charms, Blow Pop, Blue Razz, Cella's chocolate covered cherries, Mason Dots, Mason Crows, Junior Mints, Charleston Chew, Sugar Daddy, Sugar Babies, Andes and Fluffy Stuff cotton candy. Co. has manufacturing facilities in Illinois, New York, Tennessee, Massachusetts, Wisconsin, Maryland and Mexico. Co.'s principal markets are in the U.S., Canada and Mexico.

Recent Developments: For the year ended Dec 31 2004, net income decreased 1.3% to $64,174 thousand from net income of $65,014 thousand a year earlier. Revenues were $420,110 thousand, up 7.0% from $392,656 thousand the year before. Operating income was $89,904 thousand versus an income of $92,353 thousand in the prior year, a decrease of 2.7%. Total direct expense was $244,501 thousand versus $222,547 thousand in the prior year, an increase of 9.9%. Total indirect expense was $85,705 thousand versus $77,756 thousand in the prior year, an increase of 10.2%.

Prospects: Co.'s recent strong top-line growth is benefiting from internal growth and is being aided by the Concord Confections acquisition, completed Aug 31 2005. For example, at Dec 31 2004, net sales grew 7.0% to $420.1 million from $392.7 million a year earlier. Further, Concord Confections holds a strong market position in the bubble gum category and its products are sold primarily under the Dubble Bubble® brand name. The acquisition of Concord Confections' products reinforces Co.'s commitment to offer solid brands that should contribute to the long-term success of the organization.

Financial Data

(US$ in Thousands)	12/31/2004	12/31/2003	12/31/2002	12/31/2001	12/31/2000	12/31/1999	12/31/1998	12/31/1997
Earnings Per Share	1.23	1.22	1.22	1.23	1.44	1.38	1.33	2.43
Cash Flow Per Share	1.45	1.56	1.30	1.52	1.61	1.40	1.52	2.73
Tang Book Value Per Share	5.78	7.95	7.57	7.31	6.49	6.71	6.08	10.50
Dividends Per Share	0.270	0.262	0.254	0.247	0.233	0.200	0.161	0.125
Dividend Payout %	21.94	21.42	20.92	20.15	16.19	14.51	12.09	5.16
Income Statement								
Total Revenue	420,110	392,656	393,185	423,496	427,054	396,750	388,659	375,594
EBITDA	109,165	107,568	107,798	112,513	124,527	114,820	112,692	102,899
Depn & Amortn	13,565	13,913	12,354	17,926	13,489	10,369	12,807	12,819
Income Before Taxes	94,688	97,947	100,688	100,787	117,808	111,447	106,063	95,361
Income Taxes	30,514	32,933	34,300	35,100	42,071	40,137	38,537	34,679
Net Income	64,174	65,014	66,388	65,687	75,737	71,310	67,526	60,682
Balance Sheet								
Current Assets	192,693	243,705	224,948	246,096	203,211	224,532	228,539	206,961
Total Assets	811,753	665,297	646,080	618,676	562,442	529,416	487,423	436,742
Current Liabilities	82,317	62,887	63,096	57,846	57,446	56,109	53,384	53,606
Long-Term Obligations	93,167	7,500	7,500	7,500	7,500	7,500	7,500	7,500
Total Liabilities	241,574	128,716	119,340	110,215	103,746	98,770	90,966	85,579
Stockholders' Equity	570,179	536,581	526,740	508,461	458,696	430,646	396,457	351,163
Shares Outstanding	52,366	52,706	54,054	53,474	52,011	51,465	50,749	24,822
Statistical Record								
Return on Assets %	8.67	9.92	10.50	11.12	13.84	14.03	14.61	14.65
Return on Equity %	11.57	12.23	12.83	13.58	16.99	17.24	18.06	18.28
EBITDA Margin %	25.98	27.39	27.42	26.57	29.16	28.94	29.00	27.40
Net Margin %	15.28	16.56	16.88	15.51	17.73	17.97	17.37	16.16
Asset Turnover	0.57	0.60	0.62	0.72	0.78	0.78	0.84	0.91
Current Ratio	2.34	3.88	3.57	4.25	3.54	4.00	4.28	3.86
Debt to Equity	0.16	0.01	0.01	0.01	0.02	0.02	0.02	0.02
Price Range	35.45-27.41	33.81-24.26	42.62-26.22	42.80-30.26	40.04-23.53	38.01-24.24	37.30-22.87	24.86-14.04
P/E Ratio	28.82-22.29	27.71-19.88	34.94-21.49	34.79-24.60	27.81-16.34	27.54-17.57	28.04-17.20	10.23-5.78
Average Yield %	0.86	0.93	0.76	0.68	0.78	0.65	0.54	0.67

Address: 7401 South Cicero Avenue, Chicago, IL 60629 **Telephone:** (773) 838 3400 **Fax:** (773) 838 3534	**Web Site:** www.tootsie.com **Officers:** Melvin J. Gordon - Chmn., C.E.O. Ellen R. Gordon - Pres., C.O.O.	**Auditors:** PricewaterhouseCoopers LLP **Transfer Agents:** Mellon Investor Services, LLC, Ridgefield Park, NJ

TORCHMARK CORP.

Exchange	Symbol	Price	52Wk Range	Yield	P/E
NYS	TMK	$52.20 (3/31/2005)	57.51-49.55	0.84	12.46

*7 Year Price Score 119.12 *NYSE Composite Index=100 *12 Month Price Score 92.45

Interim Earnings (Per Share)

Qtr.	Mar	Jun	Sep	Dec
2001	0.76	0.58	0.82	0.67
2002	0.80	0.52	0.98	0.89
2003	0.85	0.95	0.94	0.99
2004	0.99	1.04	1.12	1.05

Interim Dividends (Per Share)

Amt	Decl	Ex	Rec	Pay
0.11Q	4/30/2004	6/30/2004	7/2/2004	7/30/2004
0.11Q	8/2/2004	10/4/2004	10/6/2004	11/1/2004
0.11Q	10/27/2004	1/3/2005	1/5/2005	2/1/2005
0.11Q	2/25/2005	3/30/2005	4/1/2005	4/29/2005

Indicated Div: $0.44

Valuation Analysis

Forecast P/E	11.32	No of Institutions
	(4/13/2005)	295
Market Cap	$5.6 Billion	Shares
Book Value	3.4 Billion	75,004,464
Price/Book	1.65	% Held
Price/Sales	1.83	70.50

Business Summary: Insurance (MIC: 8.2 SIC: 311 NAIC: 24113)

Torchmark is a diversified insurance company that operates through American Income Life Insurance Co., Liberty National Life Insurance Co., Globe Life & Accident Insurance Co., United American Insurance Co. and United Investors Life Insurance Co. Co.'s insurance subsidiaries write a variety of nonparticipating ordinary life insurance products. These include traditional and interest-sensitive whole-life insurance, term life insurance, and other life insurance. Co. also offers supplemental health insurance products classified as Medicare Supplement, cancer and other health policies.

Recent Developments: For the year ended Dec 31 2004, net income increased 9.0% to $468,600 thousand from net income of $430,100 thousand a year earlier. Total revenues were $3,071,500 thousand, up 4.8% from $2,931,000 thousand the year before. Net premiums Climbed 4.0% to $2,471,900 thousand, while net investment income increased 3.5% to $577,000 thousand. Revenues included a net investment gain of $22,200 thousand in 2004 and a net investment loss of $3,300 thousand in 2003. Total policyholder benefits grew 3.5% to $1,645,700 thousand from $1,590,100 thousand a year earlier.

Prospects: Results are being positively affected by continued strength in Co.'s life insurance business. Notably, premium revenue from life insurance increased 6.0% to $352.0 million for the year ended Dec 31 2004 with double-digit premium growth in its Military distribution channel. Also, Co. is experiencing favorable growth in insurance underwriting income, which is the sum of the insurance underwriting margins of the operating segments, plus other income, less insurance administrative expenses. However, Co. will look to improve premium revenue for health insurance, reflecting lower demand for limited benefit supplement health plans to people under age 65.

Financial Data (US$ in Thousands)	12/31/2004	12/31/2003	12/31/2002	12/31/2001	12/31/2000	12/31/1999	12/31/1998	12/31/1997
Earnings Per Share	4.19	3.73	3.18	2.83	2.82	2.04	1.73	2.39
Cash Flow Per Share	6.95	6.45	5.41	5.29	4.15	3.84	2.84	3.51
Tang Book Value Per Share	28.18	25.39	20.91	17.24	14.34	12.05	13.48	10.05
Dividends Per Share	0.440	0.380	0.360	0.360	0.360	0.360	0.430	0.590
Dividend Payout %	10.50	10.19	11.32	12.72	12.77	17.65	24.86	24.69
Income Statement								
Premium Income	2,471,900	2,375,783	2,279,033	2,215,169	2,046,210	1,884,086	1,753,630	1,678,004
Total Revenue	3,071,500	2,930,638	2,737,966	2,707,042	2,515,894	2,226,895	2,157,876	2,282,450
Benefits & Claims	1,645,700	1,590,072	1,524,074	1,454,636	1,339,482	1,236,547	1,150,276	1,108,900
Income Before Taxes	720,800	658,935	584,320	601,429	562,958	402,408	446,991	509,394
Income Taxes	245,100	225,009	197,037	205,967	190,841	134,320	154,338	178,490
Net Income	468,600	430,141	383,433	356,513	362,035	273,956	244,441	337,743
Average Shares	111,907	115,377	120,669	125,860	128,353	141,431	141,351	141,431
Balance Sheet								
Total Assets	14,252,200	13,460,886	12,360,722	12,428,153	12,962,558	12,131,664	11,249,028	10,967,291
Total Liabilities	10,832,400	10,220,787	9,364,842	9,786,469	10,566,803	9,945,003	8,796,241	8,841,356
Stockholders' Equity	3,419,800	3,240,099	2,851,453	2,497,127	2,202,360	1,993,337	2,259,528	1,932,736
Shares Outstanding	107,943	112,714	118,267	122,887	126,389	131,996	136,848	140,040
Statistical Record								
Return on Assets %	3.37	3.33	3.09	2.81	2.88	2.34	2.20	3.25
Return on Equity %	14.03	14.12	14.34	15.17	17.21	12.88	11.66	18.96
Loss Ratio %	66.58	66.93	66.87	65.67	65.46	65.63	65.59	66.08
Net Margin %	15.26	14.68	14.00	13.17	14.39	12.30	11.33	14.80
Price Range	57.51-45.11	45.54-33.32	41.86-31.00	43.05-33.25	40.88-19.00	37.19-24.63	42.90-28.67	36.59-21.66
P/E Ratio	13.73-10.77	12.21-8.93	13.16-9.75	15.21-11.75	14.49-6.74	18.23-12.07	24.80-16.57	15.31-9.06
Average Yield %	0.84	0.96	0.95	0.94	1.32	1.11	1.17	1.98

Address: 2001 3rd Avenue South, Birmingham, AL 35233 **Telephone:** (205) 325-4200 **Fax:** (205) 325-4157	**Web Site:** www.torchmarkcorp.com **Officers:** C. B. Hudson - Chmn., C.E.O. Gary L. Coleman - Exec. V.P., C.F.O.	**Auditors:** Deloitte & Touche LLP **Investor Contact:** 972-569-3627

TOTAL SYSTEM SERVICES, INC.

x

Exchange	Symbol	Price	52Wk Range	Yield	P/E
NYS	TSS	$24.99 (3/31/2005)	26.52-20.96	0.64	32.88

*7 Year Price Score 96.34 ***NYSE Composite Index=100** ***12 Month Price Score 96.92**

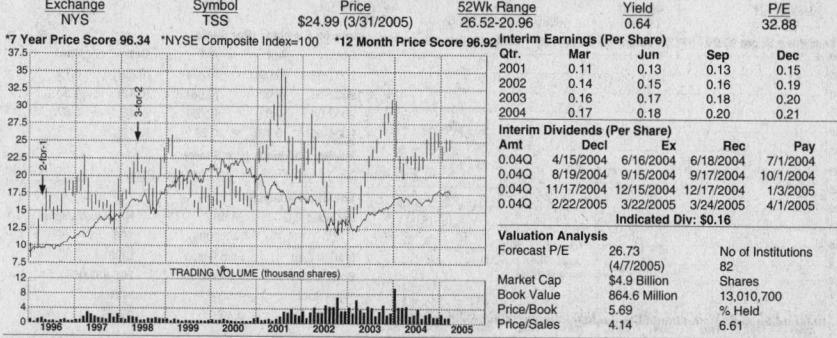

Interim Earnings (Per Share)

Qtr.	Mar	Jun	Sep	Dec
2001	0.11	0.13	0.13	0.15
2002	0.14	0.15	0.16	0.19
2003	0.16	0.17	0.18	0.20
2004	0.17	0.18	0.20	0.21

Interim Dividends (Per Share)

Amt	Decl	Ex	Rec	Pay
0.04Q	4/15/2004	6/16/2004	6/18/2004	7/1/2004
0.04Q	8/19/2004	9/15/2004	9/17/2004	10/1/2004
0.04Q	11/17/2004	12/15/2004	12/17/2004	1/3/2005
0.04Q	2/22/2005	3/22/2005	3/24/2005	4/1/2005

Indicated Div: $0.16

Valuation Analysis

Forecast P/E	26.73	No of Institutions	
	(4/7/2005)	82	
Market Cap	$4.9 Billion	Shares	13,010,700
Book Value	864.6 Million	% Held	
Price/Book	5.69		
Price/Sales	4.14	6.61	

Business Summary: IT & Technology (MIC: 10.2 SIC: 374 NAIC: 18210)

Total System Services is an electronic payment processor of consumer, retail, commercial, government services, stored value and debit cards. Co. provides the electronic link between buyers and sellers with a comprehensive on-line system of data processing services servicing issuing institutions throughout the United States, Canada, Mexico, Honduras, Puerto Rico and Europe. Co. also offers value-added products and services, such as credit evaluation, fraud detection, behavior analysis tools, loyalty programs and bonus rewards. Dec. 31, 2004, Columbus Bank and Trust Company (CB&T), a wholly owned subsidiary of Synovus Financial Corp, 81.1% of Co.'s outstanding share capial.

Recent Developments: For the year ended Dec 31 2004, net income increased 6.8% to $150,558,000 from net income of $140,973,000 a year earlier. Revenues were $9,566,190,00, up 15.5% from $828,301,000 the year before. Operating income was $202,214,000 versus an income of $190,579,000 in the prior year, an increase of 6.1%. Total indirect expense was $988,031,000 versus $862,887,000 in the prior year, an increase of 14.5%.

Prospects: On Mar 2 2005, Co. announced that it has completed its acquisition of Vital Processing Services, LLC, by purchasing the 50.0% equity stake that Visa U.S.A. formerly held. The acquisition of Vital Processing Services, a major processor of merchant accounts in the U.S., is expected to add between $225.0 million and $235.0 million in annual revenue and contribute approximately $0.03 to $0.04 in earnings per share in 2005. Looking ahead, Co. is targeting full-year 2005 revenue growth in the range of 30.0% to 33.0%, along with net income growth of between 19.0% and 22.0%.

Financial Data

(US$ in Thousands)	12/31/2004	12/31/2003	12/31/2002	12/31/2001	12/31/2000	12/31/1999	12/31/1998	12/31/1997
Earnings Per Share	0.76	0.71	0.64	0.53	0.44	0.35	0.28	0.25
Cash Flow Per Share	1.68	1.35	1.00	0.45	0.85	0.69	0.32	0.34
Tang Book Value Per Share	1.97	1.62	1.41	1.31	1.02	0.99	0.86	0.92
Dividends Per Share	0.140	0.077	0.068	0.060	0.048	0.040	0.037	0.030
Dividend Payout %	18.42	10.92	10.55	11.32	10.80	11.43	13.39	12.16
Income Statement								
Total Revenue	1,187,008	1,053,466	955,133	650,408	601,293	533,926	396,194	361,499
EBITDA	310,964	290,037	235,189	210,508	178,272	151,600	116,768	98,382
Depn & Amortn	108,588	98,415	74,504	57,396	51,601	50,183	37,474	29,141
Income Before Taxes	204,291	194,369	163,286	155,793	131,708	103,576	81,787	71,556
Income Taxes	77,210	70,868	57,908	52,891	46,065	34,983	26,956	24,077
Net Income	150,558	140,973	125,805	102,902	85,643	68,593	54,831	47,478
Average Shares	197,236	197,437	197,497	195,604	195,265	195,478	194,669	194,238
Balance Sheet								
Current Assets	448,156	274,363	265,979	206,354	210,955	179,676	119,722	132,406
Total Assets	1,281,943	1,001,236	782,868	652,277	604,393	457,350	348,908	296,858
Current Liabilities	277,903	146,971	113,982	102,553	147,301	103,262	59,250	61,506
Long-Term Obligations	4,508	29,748	67	...	...	160	211	342
Total Liabilities	413,517	265,263	177,918	149,107	192,795	123,057	78,555	75,603
Stockholders' Equity	864,612	732,534	602,206	500,812	409,014	334,292	270,354	221,255
Shares Outstanding	196,849	196,815	197,049	194,778	194,738	194,861	194,043	193,995
Statistical Record								
Return on Assets %	13.15	15.80	17.53	16.38	16.09	17.02	16.98	17.47
Return on Equity %	18.80	21.12	22.81	22.62	22.98	22.69	22.31	23.73
EBITDA Margin %	26.20	27.53	24.62	32.37	29.65	28.39	29.47	27.21
Net Margin %	12.68	13.38	13.17	15.82	14.24	12.85	13.84	13.13
Asset Turnover	1.04	1.18	1.33	1.04	1.13	1.32	1.23	1.33
Current Ratio	1.61	1.87	2.33	2.01	1.43	1.74	2.02	2.15
Debt to Equity	0.01	0.04	N.M.	...	...	N.M.	N.M.	N.M.
Price Range	31.13-19.70	31.13-13.50	29.00-11.67	35.54-19.25	22.38-15.19	25.88-14.25	24.06-14.56	22.92-12.21
P/E Ratio	40.96-25.92	43.85-19.01	45.31-18.23	67.06-36.32	50.85-34.52	73.93-40.71	85.94-52.01	91.67-48.83
Average Yield %	0.60	0.35	0.36	0.24	0.27	0.21	0.19	0.18

Address: 1600 First Avenue, Columbus, GA 31901	Web Site: www.tsys.com	Auditors: KPMG LLP
Telephone: (706) 649-5220	Officers: Richard W. Ussery - Chmn. M. Troy Woods - Pres., C.O.O.	Investor Contact: 706-649-5220
Fax: (706) 649-2456		

TOYS R US INC.

Exchange	Symbol	Price	52Wk Range	Yield	P/E
NYS	TOY	$25.76 (3/31/2005)	26.12-14.08	N/A	36.80

*7 Year Price Score 90.99   *NYSE Composite Index=100   *12 Month Price Score 118.00

Interim Earnings (Per Share)

Qtr.	Apr	Jul	Oct	Jan
2001-02	(0.09)	(0.15)	(0.22)	0.79
2002-03	(0.02)	(0.08)	(0.13)	1.33
2003-04	(0.03)	(0.05)	(0.18)	0.67
2004-05	(0.13)	0.28	(0.12)	...

Interim Dividends (Per Share)

No Dividends Paid

Valuation Analysis

Forecast P/E	24.53	No of Institutions	
	(4/7/2005)	296	
Market Cap	$5.5 Billion	Shares	
Book Value	4.3 Billion	205,482,064	
Price/Book	1.30	% Held	
Price/Sales	0.49	95.55	

Business Summary: Retail - Sporting, Toys & Hobby (MIC: 5.12 SIC: 945 NAIC: 51120)

Toys "R" Us operated 927 toy stores in the U.S. and 574 international toy stores as of Jan 31 2004. These stores sell both children's and adult's toys, sporting goods, electronic and video games, books, infant and juvenile furniture, as well as educational and entertainment computer software for children. In addition, Co. operated 44 Kids "R" Us stores, which sell children's apparel. Co. also operated 198 Babies "R" Us stores, which offer everything for babies from diapers to baby furniture to clothing, and four Geoffrey stores. In addition, Co. sells merchandise through mail order catalogs and the Internet.

Recent Developments: For the quarter ended Oct 30 2004, net loss increased 45.7% to $25,000 thousand from net loss of $46,000 thousand in the year-earlier quarter. Revenues were $2,214,000 thousand, down 1.4% from $2,246,000 thousand the year before. Operating loss was $11,000 thousand versus a loss of $43,000 thousand in the prior-year quarter, an increase of 74.4%. Total indirect expense was $750,000 thousand versus $810,000 thousand in the prior-year quarter, a decrease of 7.4%.

Prospects: On Mar 17 2005, Co. announced that it has concluded its strategic review of its operations and has entered into a definitive agreement to sell the entirety of its worldwide operations, including both its Toys "R" Us and Babies "R" Us businesses, to an investment group consisting of affiliates of Kohlberg Kravis Roberts & Co., Bain Capital Partners LLC, and Vornado Realty Trust. Under the terms of the transaction, the investment group will acquire all the outstanding shares of Co. for $26.75 per share, representing a transaction value of $6.60 billion plus the assumption of about $2.30 billion of debt. The transaction is expected to be completed by July 2005.

Financial Data

(US$ in Thousands)	9 Mos	6 Mos	3 Mos	01/31/2004	02/01/2003	02/02/2002	02/03/2001	01/29/2000
Earnings Per Share	0.70	0.64	0.31	0.41	1.09	0.33	1.88	1.14
Cash Flow Per Share	3.24	3.25	2.80	3.71	2.77	2.56	(0.70)	3.54
Tang Book Value Per Share	18.07	18.14	17.73	18.14	17.33	15.59	15.48	13.82
Income Statement								
Total Revenue	6,294,000	4,080,000	2,058,000	11,566,000	11,305,000	11,019,000	11,332,000	11,862,000
EBITDA	25,000	(47,000)	66,000	628,000	797,000	516,000	1,054,000	809,000
Depn & Amortn	243,000	160,000	81,000	348,000	317,000	308,000	290,000	278,000
Income Before Taxes	(302,000)	(263,000)	(44,000)	138,000	361,000	91,000	637,000	440,000
Income Taxes	(310,000)	(296,000)	(16,000)	50,000	132,000	24,000	233,000	161,000
Net Income	8,000	33,000	(28,000)	88,000	229,000	67,000	404,000	279,000
Average Shares	214,500	217,500	213,800	215,600	209,600	206,000	215,000	245,400
Balance Sheet								
Current Assets	4,227,000	3,553,000	3,737,000	4,684,000	3,560,000	2,631,000	2,907,000	2,873,000
Total Assets	9,718,000	8,942,000	9,140,000	10,218,000	9,397,000	8,076,000	8,003,000	8,353,000
Current Liabilities	2,300,000	1,553,000	1,841,000	2,772,000	2,378,000	2,000,000	2,351,000	2,838,000
Long-Term Obligations	2,293,000	2,268,000	2,253,000	2,349,000	2,139,000	1,816,000	1,567,000	1,230,000
Total Liabilities	5,444,000	4,710,000	4,998,000	5,996,000	5,367,000	4,662,000	4,585,000	4,673,000
Stockholders' Equity	4,274,000	4,232,000	4,142,000	4,222,000	4,030,000	3,414,000	3,418,000	3,680,000
Shares Outstanding	215,057	214,139	213,969	213,600	212,500	196,700	197,500	239,300
Statistical Record								
Return on Assets %	1.49	1.50	0.71	0.90	2.63	0.84	4.86	3.44
Return on Equity %	3.65	3.36	1.63	2.14	6.17	1.97	11.20	7.66
EBITDA Margin %	0.40	N.M.	3.21	5.43	7.05	4.68	9.30	6.82
Net Margin %	0.13	0.81	N.M.	0.76	2.03	0.61	3.57	2.35
Asset Turnover	1.10	1.23	1.21	1.18	1.30	1.37	1.36	1.46
Current Ratio	1.84	2.29	2.03	1.69	1.50	1.32	1.24	1.01
Debt to Equity	0.54	0.54	0.54	0.56	0.53	0.53	0.46	0.33
Price Range	18.08-10.37	17.32-10.37	17.32-10.17	14.80-7.87	20.31-8.70	30.96-17.20	26.63-10.31	24.50-9.88
P/E Ratio	25.83-14.81	27.06-16.20	55.87-32.81	36.10-19.20	18.63-7.98	93.82-52.12	14.16-5.49	21.49-8.66

Address: One Geoffrey Way, Wayne, NJ 07470	**Web Site:** www.toysrusinc.com	**Auditors:** Ernst & Young LLP
Telephone: (973) 617-3500	**Officers:** John H. Eyler Jr. - Chmn., Pres., C.E.O. Richard L. Markee - Vice Chmn.	**Investor Contact:** 201-802-5548

TRANSATLANTIC HOLDINGS, INC.

Exchange	Symbol	Price	52Wk Range	Yield	P/E	Div Acheiver
NYS	TRH	$66.22 (3/31/2005)	73.49-53.80	0.60	17.20	14 Years

*7 Year Price Score 99.42   ***NYSE Composite Index=100**   ***12 Month Price Score 98.40**

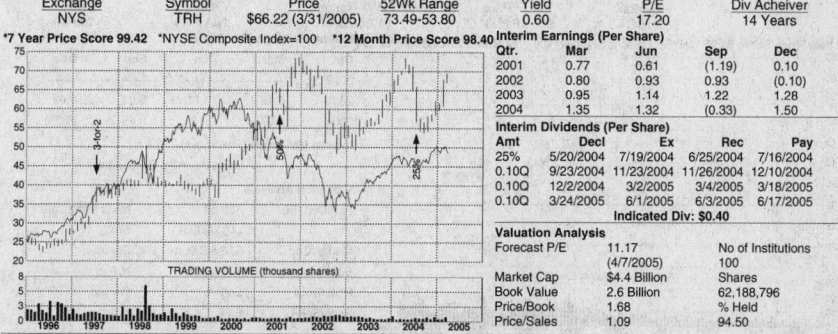

Interim Earnings (Per Share)

Qtr.	Mar	Jun	Sep	Dec
2001	0.77	0.61	(1.19)	0.10
2002	0.80	0.93	0.93	(0.10)
2003	0.95	1.14	1.22	1.28
2004	1.35	1.32	(0.33)	1.50

Interim Dividends (Per Share)

Amt	Decl	Ex	Rec	Pay
25%	5/20/2004	7/19/2004	6/25/2004	7/16/2004
0.10Q	9/23/2004	11/23/2004	11/26/2004	12/10/2004
0.10Q	12/2/2004	3/2/2005	3/4/2005	3/18/2005
0.10Q	3/24/2005	6/1/2005	6/3/2005	6/17/2005

Indicated Div: $0.40

Valuation Analysis

Forecast P/E	11.17		No of Institutions
	(4/7/2005)		100
Market Cap	$4.4 Billion		Shares
Book Value	2.6 Billion		62,188,796
Price/Book	1.68		% Held
Price/Sales	1.09		94.50

Business Summary: Insurance (MIC: 8.2 SIC: 331 NAIC: 24126)

Transatlantic Holdings, through its wholly-owned subsidiaries Transatlantic Reinsurance Company, Trans Re Zurich and Putnam Reinsurance Company, offers reinsurance capacity for a full range of property and casualty products on a treaty and facultative basis, directly and through brokers, to insurance and reinsurance companies, in both the domestic and international markets. Co.'s principal lines of reinsurance include auto liability, other liability, medical malpractice, ocean marine and aviation, accident and health and surety and credit in the casualty lines, along with fire, homeowners multiple peril and auto physical damage in the property lines.

Recent Developments: For the year ended Dec 31 2004, net income decreased 16.2% to $254,584 thousand from net income of $303,644 thousand a year earlier. Revenues were $3,990,057 thousand, up 15.6% from $3,452,140 the year before. Net premiums earned were $3,661,090 thousand versus $3,171,226 thousand in the prior year, an increase of 15.4%. Net investment income rose 13.2% to $306,786 thousand from $270,972 thousand a year ago.

Prospects: Co.'s near-term outlook is somewhat mixed. On the positive side, Co.'s results are benefiting from improved net premiums written, driven by its European operations, where more favorable underwriting opportunities continue to be available. However, Co. indicated that domestically, the pace of improvement remains soft in many sectors and is experiencing greater retention levels. Moreover, given the changing pricing environment and generally greater level of competition in recent quarters, Co. may experience a moderating effect on premium increases. Nevertheless, Co. expects worldwide market conditions to remain generally favorable in 2005 and is optimistic about its future.

Financial Data

(US$ in Thousands)	12/31/2004	12/31/2003	12/31/2002	12/31/2001	12/31/2000	12/31/1999	12/31/1998	12/31/1997
Earnings Per Share	3.85	4.60	2.57	0.29	3.23	2.86	3.79	2.85
Cash Flow Per Share	13.73	14.06	9.15	3.71	(0.23)	2.98	3.50	4.92
Tang Book Value Per Share	39.30	36.24	31.03	28.26	28.47	25.22	24.77	20.93
Dividends Per Share	0.376	0.336	0.314	0.298	0.277	0.251	0.224	0.203
Dividend Payout %	9.77	7.30	12.21	103.33	8.60	8.75	5.92	7.12
Income Statement								
Premium Income	3,661,090	3,171,226	2,369,452	1,790,339	1,631,536	1,484,634	1,380,570	1,259,251
Total Revenue	3,990,057	3,452,140	2,615,527	2,030,182	1,866,021	1,715,373	1,602,570	1,466,897
Benefits & Claims	2,754,560	2,233,447	1,796,352	1,561,529	1,196,896	1,148,817	1,020,888	933,015
Income Before Taxes	276,212	386,674	188,320	(34,107)	267,982	236,097	323,351	234,726
Income Taxes	21,628	83,030	19,002	(52,999)	56,344	48,735	75,828	49,226
Net Income	254,584	303,644	169,318	18,892	211,638	187,362	247,523	185,500
Average Shares	66,189	65,952	65,943	65,920	65,595	65,403	65,371	65,158
Balance Sheet								
Total Assets	10,605,292	8,707,758	7,286,525	6,741,303	5,522,672	5,480,198	5,253,249	4,834,980
Total Liabilities	8,018,163	6,331,171	5,255,758	4,895,293	3,666,307	3,837,681	3,643,110	3,478,321
Stockholders' Equity	2,587,129	2,376,587	2,030,767	1,846,010	1,856,365	1,642,517	1,610,139	1,356,659
Shares Outstanding	65,827	65,585	65,451	65,319	65,200	65,114	65,000	64,805
Statistical Record								
Return on Assets %	2.63	3.80	2.41	0.31	3.84	3.49	4.91	4.03
Return on Equity %	10.23	13.78	8.73	1.02	12.06	11.52	16.69	14.88
Loss Ratio %	75.24	70.43	75.81	87.22	73.36	77.38	73.95	74.09
Net Margin %	6.38	8.80	6.47	0.93	11.34	10.92	15.45	12.65
Price Range	73.49-53.80	64.64-49.18	72.80-48.44	73.60-50.54	56.47-36.77	42.73-36.90	50.33-37.10	40.33-27.24
P/E Ratio	19.09-13.97	14.05-10.69	28.33-18.85	253.79-174.29	17.48-11.38	14.94-12.90	13.28-9.79	14.15-9.56
Average Yield %	0.59	0.59	0.51	0.48	0.61	0.63	0.54	0.59

Address: 80 Pine Street, New York, NY 10005	**Web Site:** www.transre.com	**Auditors:** PricewaterhouseCoopers LLP
Telephone: (212) 770-2000	**Officers:** M. R. Greenberg - Chmn. Robert F. Orlich - Pres., C.E.O.	**Investor Contact:** 212-770-2040
Fax: (212) 785-7230		**Transfer Agents:** American Stock Transfer & Trust Company, New York,

TRANSOCEAN, INC.

Exchange	Symbol	Price	52Wk Range	Yield	P/E
NYS	RIG	$51.46 (3/31/2005)	51.46-25.47	N/A	109.49

*7 Year Price Score 90.05 *NYSE Composite Index=100 *12 Month Price Score 125.94

Interim Earnings (Per Share)

Qtr.	Mar	Jun	Sep	Dec
2002	----------------------7.42----------------------			
2003	0.15	(0.14)	0.03	0.02
2004	0.07	0.15	0.48	(0.23)

Interim Dividends (Per Share)

Dividend Payment Suspended

Valuation Analysis

Forecast P/E	162.69	No of Institutions
	(4/12/2005)	N/A
Market Cap	$16.5 Billion	Shares
Book Value	7.2 Billion	N/A
Price/Book	2.29	% Held
Price/Sales	6.76	N/A

Business Summary: Oil and Gas (MIC: 14.2 SIC: 381 NAIC: 13111)

Transocean is an international provider of offshore contract drilling services for oil and gas wells. At Dec. 31, 2003, Co. owned, had partial ownership interests in or operated 96 mobile offshore and barge drilling units. Co. provides contract drilling services in several market sectors and aggregates these operations into two business segments. Co.'s Transocean Drilling segment is comprised of drillships, semisubmersibles, jackups and other drilling rigs. Co.'s TODCO segment consists of Co.'s interest in TODCO, which conducts jackup, drilling barge, land rig, submersible and other rig operations in the U.S. Gulf of Mexico and inland waters, Mexico, Trinidad and Venezuela.

Recent Developments: For the year ended Dec 31 2004, net income was $152.2 million versus income of $18.4 million, before an accounting change credit of $800,000, in the previous year. Results for 2004 and 2003 included net gains from the sales of assets of $31.9 million and $5.8 million, respectively. Results for 2004 also included a gain from TODCO offerings of $308.8 million. Total operating revenues climbed 7.3% to $2.61 billion from $2.43 billion the year before. Contract drilling revenues rose 3.7% to $2.42 billion from $2.33 billion, while other revenues advanced 86.6% to $197.5 million from $105.8 million in 2003. Operating income jumped 36.7% to $327.9 million from $239.7 million in the prior year.

Prospects: Co. ended 2004 with concentrating its efforts on completing repairs on a jack-up and semisubmersible rig, commencing reactivation efforts on four semisubmersible rigs that had been idle for extended periods and completing the mobilization of three High-Specification Floaters and three Jack-up Rigs between market sectors. For 2005, Co. starts with an improving outlook for all segments of its fleet, particularly among its 13 Fifth-Generation rigs, where capacity constraints are evident for the next 12 to 24 months. However, Co.'s industry will likely experience higher costs in 2005, due to the higher personnel costs required to support the increased level of offshore drilling activity.

Financial Data

(US$ in Thousands)	12/31/2003	12/31/2002	12/31/2001	12/31/2000	12/31/1999	12/31/1998	12/31/1997	12/31/1996
Earnings Per Share	0.06	(11.69)	0.80	0.51	0.53	3.41	1.38	1.09
Cash Flow Per Share	1.64	2.94	1.83	0.94	2.20	4.69	1.62	1.74
Tang Book Value Per Share	15.51	15.42	13.94	14.08	13.53	12.96	9.29	8.39
Dividends Per Share	...	0.060	0.120	0.120	0.090	0.120	0.120	0.120
Dividend Payout %	...	N.M.	15.00	23.53	16.98	3.52	8.70	11.06
Income Statement								
Total Revenue	2,434,300	2,673,900	2,820,100	1,229,513	648,236	1,089,612	891,962	528,903
EBITDA	688,700	(1,795,900)	1,190,700	410,132	159,390	624,454	331,261	169,231
Depn & Amortn	483,900	506,500	625,000	268,910	105,766	116,867	103,017	46,587
Income Before Taxes	21,600	(2,488,800)	360,500	144,416	48,807	487,146	207,245	121,652
Income Taxes	3,000	(123,000)	85,700	36,699	(9,296)	143,730	65,312	43,607
Net Income	19,200	(3,731,900)	252,600	108,548	58,103	343,416	141,933	78,045
Average Shares	321,400	319,100	314,800	211,672	109,636	100,848	102,784	...
Balance Sheet								
Current Assets	1,178,900	1,911,700	1,736,800	448,132	558,866	361,632	307,090	252,246
Total Assets	11,662,600	12,665,100	17,019,800	6,358,764	6,140,170	3,250,943	2,755,088	2,443,214
Current Liabilities	511,100	1,503,900	1,144,400	495,198	528,521	192,421	185,192	231,478
Long-Term Obligations	3,612,300	3,629,900	4,539,600	1,430,266	1,187,578	813,953	728,282	392,322
Total Liabilities	4,470,000	5,523,700	6,109,500	2,354,657	2,230,031	1,272,300	1,133,910	815,505
Stockholders' Equity	7,192,600	7,141,400	10,910,300	4,004,107	3,910,139	1,978,643	1,621,178	1,627,709
Shares Outstanding	319,926	319,219	318,816	210,710	210,119	100,551	99,917	103,046
Statistical Record								
Return on Assets %	0.16	N.M.	2.16	1.73	1.24	11.44	5.46	5.21
Return on Equity %	0.27	N.M.	3.39	2.74	1.97	19.08	8.74	7.82
EBITDA Margin %	28.29	N.M.	42.22	33.36	24.59	57.31	37.14	32.00
Net Margin %	0.79	N.M.	8.96	8.83	8.96	31.52	15.91	14.76
Asset Turnover	0.20	0.18	0.24	0.20	0.14	0.36	0.34	0.35
Current Ratio	2.31	1.27	1.52	0.90	1.06	1.88	1.66	1.09
Debt to Equity	0.50	0.51	0.42	0.36	0.30	0.41	0.45	0.24
Price Range	25.50-18.65	39.26-18.82	57.43-23.98	64.31-29.88	35.75-19.94	59.31-24.00	59.81-27.06	35.00-20.94
P/E Ratio	425.00-310.83	N/A	71.79-29.98	126.10-58.58	67.45-37.62	17.39-7.04	43.34-19.61	32.11-19.21
Average Yield %	...	0.21	0.30	0.25	0.32	0.30	0.31	0.45

Address: 4 Greenway Plaza, Houston, TX 77046	Web Site: www.deepwater.com	Auditors: Ernst & Young LLP
Telephone: (713) 232-7500	Officers: J. Michael Talbert - Chmn. Robert L. Long - Pres., C.E.O.	Investor Contact: 713-232-7551
Fax: (713) 850-3834		

TRIAD HOSPITALS, INC.

Exchange	Symbol	Price	52Wk Range	Yield	P/E
NYS	TRI	$50.10 (3/31/2005)	50.10-30.82	N/A	20.12

*7 Year Price Score N/A   *NYSE Composite Index=100   *12 Month Price Score 114.12

Interim Earnings (Per Share)

Qtr.	Mar	Jun	Sep	Dec
2001	0.22	(0.36)	0.09	0.18
2002	0.55	0.44	0.43	0.48
2003	0.63	0.51	0.14	(0.01)
2004	1.29	(0.07)	0.64	0.63

Interim Dividends (Per Share)

No Dividends Paid

Valuation Analysis

Forecast P/E	18.09	No of Institutions
	(4/7/2005)	264
Market Cap	$3.9 Billion	Shares
Book Value	2.3 Billion	74,807,496
Price/Book	1.67	% Held
Price/Sales	0.88	95.18

Business Summary: Insurance (MIC: 8.2 SIC: 324 NAIC: 25190)

Triad Hospitals is a publicly-owned hospital company that provides health care services through hospitals and ambulatory surgery centers that it owns and operates in small cities primarily in the southern, midwestern and western U.S. As of Feb 23 2004, Co.'s hospital facilities included 56 general acute care hospitals and 16 ambulatory surgery centers located in 18 states with about 8,800 licensed beds. Co. is also a minority investor in three joint ventures that own six general acute care hospitals in Georgia and Nevada. In addition, Co. provides hospital management and advisory services to more than 200 independent community hospitals and health systems throughout the U.S.

Recent Developments: For the year ended Dec 31 2004, income from continuing operations increased 32.1% to $138,000 thousand from income of $104,500 thousand a year earlier. Net income increased 100.6% to $191,000 thousand from net income of $95,200 thousand a year earlier. Revenues were $4,450,200 thousand, up 19.2% from $3,734,400 thousand the year before. Operating income was $208,200 thousand versus an income of $154,500 thousand in the prior year, an increase of 34.8%. Total indirect expense was $4,130,900 thousand versus $3,448,900 thousand in the prior year, an increase of 19.8%.

Prospects: Going forward, Co. expects to achieve diluted earnings from continuing operations of approximately $2.69 to $2.79 per share on revenues of approximately $4.60 to $4.90 billion and same-facility admissions growth of approximately 2.0% to 3.0% for full year 2005. Co.'s diluted earnings per share guidance incorporates an expected provision for doubtful accounts of approximately 9.0% to 9.5% of revenue in 2005. Beyond 2005, Co. expects to achieve annual earnings per share growth in at least the mid-teens percent range and expects to achieve further gradual improvement over time, with occasional fluctuation, in it overall return on invested capital.

Financial Data

(US$ in Thousands)	12/31/2004	12/31/2003	12/31/2002	12/31/2001	12/31/2000	12/31/1999	12/31/1998	12/31/1997
Earnings Per Share	2.49	1.26	1.89	0.05	0.13	(3.12)	(2.90)	(0.66)
Cash Flow Per Share	4.75	4.95	5.00	5.52	2.25	5.07	0.80	3.34
Tang Book Value Per Share	13.02	9.94	8.79	6.03	9.94	11.31	7.59	...
Income Statement								
Total Revenue	4,450,200	3,865,900	3,541,100	2,669,500	1,235,500	1,329,100	1,588,700	1,609,300
EBITDA	409,700	341,400	403,100	218,600	100,500	(22,600)	(15,300)	76,700
Depn & Amortn	186,400	176,400	167,400	170,100	83,200	98,500	109,600	102,900
Income Before Taxes	223,300	165,000	235,700	48,500	17,300	(121,100)	(124,900)	(26,200)
Income Taxes	85,300	65,600	94,200	42,500	12,900	(25,500)	(39,400)	(7,200)
Net Income	191,000	95,200	141,500	2,800	4,400	(95,600)	(87,100)	(19,800)
Average Shares	76,597	75,363	74,996	61,055	34,133	...	30,000	30,000
Balance Sheet								
Current Assets	1,014,300	927,200	844,400	747,300	328,200	353,400	305,900	290,200
Total Assets	4,981,400	4,735,400	4,381,600	4,165,300	1,400,500	1,341,100	1,371,300	1,410,500
Current Liabilities	502,700	507,100	445,200	366,300	136,300	165,800	121,000	139,900
Long-Term Obligations	1,587,300	1,685,000	1,618,900	1,742,900	581,700	537,100	13,400	14,400
Total Liabilities	2,638,100	2,659,100	2,427,100	2,433,800	826,800	781,200	256,900	297,700
Stockholders' Equity	2,343,300	2,076,300	1,954,500	1,731,500	573,700	559,900	500,700	587,800
Shares Outstanding	78,206	75,633	74,937	72,202	34,783	33,943	30,000	...
Statistical Record								
Return on Assets %	3.92	2.09	3.31	0.10	0.32	N.M.	N.M.	...
Return on Equity %	8.62	4.72	7.68	0.24	0.77	N.M.	N.M.	...
EBITDA Margin %	9.21	8.83	11.38	8.19	8.13	N.M.	N.M.	4.77
Net Margin %	4.29	2.46	4.00	0.10	0.36	N.M.	N.M.	N.M.
Asset Turnover	0.91	0.85	0.83	0.96	0.90	0.98	1.14	...
Current Ratio	2.02	1.83	1.90	2.04	2.41	2.13	2.53	2.07
Debt to Equity	0.68	0.81	0.83	1.01	1.01	0.96	0.03	0.02
Price Range	38.00-29.95	34.74-20.53	46.28-28.05	36.70-24.49	34.38-13.44	15.13-9.38	...	...
P/E Ratio	15.26-12.03	27.57-16.29	24.49-14.84	734.00-489.80	264.42-103.37	...	...	...

Address: 5800 Tennyson Parkway, Plano, TX 75024 Telephone: (214) 473-7000	Web Site: www.triadhospitals.com Officers: James D. Shelton - Chmn., Pres., C.E.O. Michael J. Parsons - Exec. V.P., C.O.O.	Auditors: Ernst & Young LLP Investor Contact: 972-789-2259

TRIBUNE CO.

Exchange	Symbol	Price	52Wk Range	Yield	P/E
NYS	TRB	$39.87 (3/31/2005)	51.75-38.63	1.81	23.87

*7 Year Price Score 89.54   *NYSE Composite Index=100   *12 Month Price Score 87.23

Interim Earnings (Per Share)

Qtr.	Mar	Jun	Sep	Dec
2001	0.20	0.21	(0.49)	0.33
2002	(0.33)	0.33	0.71	0.57
2003	0.41	0.67	0.53	1.00
2004	0.35	0.29	0.37	0.66

Interim Dividends (Per Share)

Amt	Decl	Ex	Rec	Pay
0.12Q	5/12/2004	5/25/2004	5/27/2004	6/10/2004
0.12Q	7/28/2004	8/24/2004	8/26/2004	9/9/2004
0.12Q	10/20/2004	11/22/2004	11/24/2004	12/8/2004
0.18Q	2/8/2005	2/22/2005	2/24/2005	3/10/2005
		Indicated Div: $0.72		

Valuation Analysis

Forecast P/E	16.74	No of Institutions	
	(4/7/2005)	394	
Market Cap	$12.6 Billion	Shares	
Book Value	6.8 Billion	152,604,208	
Price/Book	1.85	% Held	
Price/Sales	2.21	48.09	

Business Summary: Media (MIC: 13.1 SIC: 711 NAIC: 11110)

Tribune is a media company operating businesses in broadcasting, publishing and on the Internet. Co. owns and operates 26 major-market television stations and reaches more than 80.0% of U.S. television households. Broadcasting properties include four radio stations, Tribune Entertainment and the Chicago Cubs baseball team. In addition, Co. operates 12 daily newspapers, including The Baltimore Sun, The Los Angeles Times, The Hartford Courant, The Advocate, Chicago Tribune, South Florida Sun-Sentinel, The Morning Call, Greenwich Time, Newsday, Orlando Sentinel, and Daily Press. Co. also distributes entertainment listings and syndicated content, and operates two 24-hour cable news channels.

Recent Developments: For the year ended Dec 26 2004, net income decreased 37.7% to $555,536 thousand from net income of $891,379 thousand a year earlier. Revenues were $5,726,247 thousand, up 2.3% from $5,594,829 thousand the year before. Operating income was $1,218,289 thousand versus an income of $1,360,474 thousand in the prior year, a decrease of 10.5%. Total direct expense was $2,708,394 thousand versus $2,635,538 thousand in the prior year, an increase of 2.8%. Total indirect expense was $1,799,564 thousand versus $1,598,817 thousand in the prior year, an increase of 12.6%.

Prospects: In 2005, Co. is projecting consolidated cash operating expenses to decline due to the absence of the $90.0 million advertising settlement charge and the $41.0 million of position elimination costs. Other consolidated cash operating expenses are expected to be up about 2.0% for 2005 due to higher expenses for retirement and medical plans and newsprint along with a slight increase in broadcast rights expense. Net equity income is projected to be somewhat higher than 2004. Interest expense is expected to be somewhat below 2004 due to the full year impact of the debt refinancing in the second quarter of 2004. Capital expenditures are projected to increase slightly over 2004.

Financial Data
(US$ in Thousands)

	12/26/2004	12/28/2003	12/29/2002	12/30/2001	12/31/2000	12/26/1999	12/27/1998	12/28/1997
Earnings Per Share	1.67	2.61	1.30	0.28	0.70	5.61	1.50	1.41
Cash Flow Per Share	3.34	3.73	2.98	2.53	3.99	2.42	2.26	1.57
Dividends Per Share	0.480	0.440	0.440	0.440	0.400	0.360	0.340	0.320
Dividend Payout %	28.74	16.86	33.85	157.14	57.14	6.42	22.67	22.78
Income Statement								
Total Revenue	5,726,247	5,594,829	5,384,428	5,253,366	4,910,363	3,221,890	2,980,889	2,719,780
EBITDA	1,324,265	1,835,697	1,367,700	956,485	1,175,298	2,727,833	982,996	891,672
Depn & Amortn	233,089	228,386	223,254	441,866	370,627	222,159	195,568	172,513
Income Before Taxes	941,111	1,415,236	939,955	268,951	597,087	2,440,074	705,089	659,000
Income Taxes	367,787	523,857	331,376	157,815	270,351	957,029	290,817	265,375
Net Income	555,536	891,379	442,992	111,136	224,386	1,479,990	414,272	393,625
Average Shares	327,237	336,243	332,466	303,980	299,731	261,819	266,924	245,758
Balance Sheet								
Current Assets	1,452,444	1,605,165	1,524,654	1,363,991	1,491,166	2,084,551	945,129	847,749
Total Assets	14,168,196	14,280,152	14,078,328	14,504,696	14,676,212	8,797,691	5,935,570	4,777,554
Current Liabilities	1,370,460	1,263,881	1,153,976	1,533,192	1,449,224	860,596	828,130	706,220
Long-Term Obligations	2,317,933	2,350,029	3,226,702	3,684,692	4,007,041	2,694,192	1,616,256	1,521,453
Total Liabilities	7,331,352	7,232,698	7,938,228	8,853,528	8,790,296	5,327,793	3,578,953	2,951,550
Stockholders' Equity	6,836,844	7,047,454	6,140,100	5,651,168	5,885,916	3,469,898	2,356,617	1,826,004
Shares Outstanding	317,072	328,297	305,908	298,003	299,517	237,791	238,004	163,734
Statistical Record								
Return on Assets %	3.92	6.30	3.11	0.76	1.88	20.15	7.76	9.31
Return on Equity %	8.02	13.56	7.53	1.93	4.72	50.94	19.86	23.46
EBITDA Margin %	23.13	32.81	25.40	18.21	23.94	84.67	32.98	32.78
Net Margin %	9.70	15.93	8.23	2.12	4.57	45.94	13.90	14.47
Asset Turnover	0.40	0.40	0.38	0.36	0.41	0.44	0.56	0.64
Current Ratio	1.06	1.27	1.32	0.89	1.03	2.42	1.14	1.20
Debt to Equity	0.34	0.33	0.53	0.65	0.68	0.78	0.69	0.83
Price Range	52.84-40.00	50.45-42.17	49.17-35.91	45.35-30.01	55.06-30.81	60.88-30.63	36.97-22.78	30.47-17.88
P/E Ratio	31.64-23.95	19.33-16.16	37.82-27.62	161.96-107.18	78.66-44.02	10.85-5.46	24.65-15.19	21.61-12.68
Average Yield %	1.04	0.93	1.02	1.13	1.03	0.84	1.07	1.34

Address: 435 North Michigan Avenue, Chicago, IL 60611	**Web Site:** www.tribune.com	**Auditors:** PricewaterhouseCoopers LLP
Telephone: (312) 222 9100	**Officers:** Dennis J. FitzSimons - Chmn., Pres., C.E.O. Jerry Agema - Sr. V.P., C.F.O.	**Investor Contact:** 312-222-3787
Fax: (312) 222 4917		

TRINITY INDUSTRIES, INC.

Exchange	Symbol	Price	52Wk Range	Yield	P/E
NYS	TRN	$28.17 (3/31/2005)	35.79-25.35	0.85	N/A

*7 Year Price Score 96.72 ***NYSE Composite Index=100** ***12 Month Price Score 88.12**

Interim Earnings (Per Share)

Qtr.	Mar	Jun	Sep	Dec
2002	(0.19)	(0.13)	0.14	(0.25)
2003	(0.32)	0.08	0.02	(0.03)
2004	(0.25)	0.06	0.00	(0.08)

Interim Dividends (Per Share)

Amt	Decl	Ex	Rec	Pay
0.06Q	5/10/2004	7/13/2004	7/15/2004	7/30/2004
0.06Q	9/9/2004	10/13/2004	10/15/2004	10/29/2004
0.06Q	12/8/2004	1/12/2005	1/14/2005	1/31/2005
0.06Q	3/14/2005	4/13/2005	4/15/2005	4/29/2005

Indicated Div: $0.24

Valuation Analysis

Forecast P/E	30.71	No of Institutions	
	(4/7/2005)	176	
Market Cap	$1.3 Billion	Shares	
Book Value	1.0 Billion	47,510,544	
Price/Book	1.33	% Held	
Price/Sales	0.61	99.38	

Business Summary: Rail Transport (MIC: 15.5 SIC: 743 NAIC: 36510)

Trinity Industries is a diversified industrial growth company providing a variety of products and services for the transportation, industrial, construction, and energy sectors. Trinity principally operates in five business segments: the Trinity Railcar Group; Industrial Products Group; Construction Products Group; Inland Barge Group; and Trinity Railcar Leasing & Management Services Group. Co. manufactures railroad freight cars, principally pressure and non-pressure tank cars, hopper cars, box cars, intermodal cars and gondola cars used for transporting a wide variety of liquids, gases and dry cargo.

Recent Developments: For the year ended Dec 31 2004, net loss was $9,300 thousand versus net loss of $10,000 thousand a year earlier. Revenues were $2,198,100 thousand, up 53.4% from $1,432,800 thousand the year before. Operating income was $14,100 thousand versus an income of $13,400 thousand in the prior year, an increase of 5.2%. Total direct expense was $2,015,800 thousand versus $1,271,800 thousand in the prior year, an increase of 58.5%. Total indirect expense was $168,200 thousand versus $147,600 thousand in the prior year, an increase of 14.0%.

Prospects: Operating results are being adversely affected by the rapid and unexpected increases in prices Co. is paying for steel and other basic materials. Co. expects this trend to continue through the first quarter of 2005 with some residual effects ongoing throughout the year. Meanwhile, Co. is encouraged with its efforts to mitigate the impact through escalation clauses and other arrangements tied to an increasing percentage of its railcar and barge backlogs. These arrangements should enhance Co.'s position against future steel cost increases. In addition, Co. should be well-positioned to benefit as markets continue to improve.

Financial Data

(US$ in Thousands)	12/31/2004	12/31/2003	12/31/2002	12/31/2001	03/31/2001	03/31/2000	03/31/1999	03/31/1998
Earnings Per Share	(0.27)	(0.25)	(0.43)	(0.90)	(1.98)	4.15	4.25	2.36
Cash Flow Per Share	(1.77)	2.52	2.66	2.95	2.42	6.91	4.10	2.81
Tang Book Value Per Share	12.40	11.57	11.60	13.37	23.86	26.37	23.22	20.40
Dividends Per Share	0.240	0.240	0.360	0.720	0.720	0.720	0.680	0.680
Dividend Payout %	...	...	...	...	...	17.35	16.00	28.81
Income Statement								
Total Revenue	2,198,100	1,432,800	1,487,300	1,347,800	1,904,300	2,740,600	2,926,900	2,473,000
EBITDA	104,800	105,500	101,400	44,900	(5,200)	361,600	384,300	258,000
Depn & Amortn	87,200	85,600	90,700	66,200	89,100	80,300	72,000	73,000
Income Before Taxes	(15,100)	(14,300)	(24,400)	(40,500)	(116,300)	262,900	296,400	165,900
Income Taxes	(5,800)	(4,300)	(4,800)	(5,800)	(41,900)	97,400	111,100	62,200
Net Income	(9,300)	(10,000)	(19,600)	(34,700)	(74,400)	165,500	185,300	103,700
Average Shares	46,500	45,600	45,300	38,700	37,500	39,900	43,600	43,900
Balance Sheet								
Current Assets	798,800	502,100	450,600	501,700	611,700	727,300	768,000	736,200
Total Assets	2,210,200	2,007,900	1,942,900	1,952,000	1,825,900	1,738,500	1,684,900	1,573,900
Current Liabilities	511,700	460,200	396,000	424,900	858,000	531,000	547,700	487,600
Long-Term Obligations	518,000	395,200	488,900	476,300	44,000	95,400	120,600	149,600
Total Liabilities	1,139,100	946,300	941,300	942,600	946,900	723,400	725,800	686,400
Stockholders' Equity	1,012,900	1,003,800	1,001,600	1,009,400	879,000	1,015,100	959,100	887,500
Shares Outstanding	47,800	50,900	50,900	44,400	36,842	38,500	41,300	43,500
Statistical Record								
Return on Assets %	N.M.	N.M.	N.M.	N.M.	N.M.	9.64	11.37	7.08
Return on Equity %	N.M.	N.M.	N.M.	N.M.	N.M.	16.72	20.07	12.22
EBITDA Margin %	4.77	7.36	6.82	3.33	N.M.	13.19	13.13	10.43
Net Margin %	N.M.	N.M.	N.M.	N.M.	N.M.	6.04	6.33	4.19
Asset Turnover	1.04	0.73	0.76	0.42	1.07	1.60	1.80	1.69
Current Ratio	1.56	1.09	1.14	1.18	0.71	1.37	1.40	1.51
Debt to Equity	0.51	0.39	0.49	0.47	0.05	0.09	0.13	0.17
Price Range	35.79-25.35	31.76-15.23	27.17-14.93	28.04-17.50	26.63-18.38	37.38-19.88	55.00-28.38	55.00-24.50
P/E Ratio	...	...	...	...	...	9.01-4.79	12.94-6.68	23.31-10.38
Average Yield %	0.79	1.12	1.77	3.07	3.26	2.45	1.74	1.68

Address: 2525 Stemmons Freeway, Dallas, TX 75207-2401
Telephone: (214) 631-4420
Fax: (214) 589-8501

Web Site: www.trin.net
Officers: Timothy R. Wallace - Chmn., Pres., C.E.O. John L. Adams - Exec. V.P.

Auditors: Ernst & Young LLP
Investor Contact: 214-631-4420
Transfer Agents: Wachovia Bank, N.A.

TRIZEC PROPERTIES, INC

Exchange	Symbol	Price	52Wk Range	Yield	P/E
NYS	TRZ	$19.00 (3/31/2005)	19.24-13.75	4.21	30.16

*7 Year Price Score N/A   *NYSE Composite Index=100   *12 Month Price Score 102.56

Interim Earnings (Per Share)

Qtr.	Mar	Jun	Sep	Dec
2002	0.30	0.24	(1.70)	(0.11)
2003	0.39	0.07	0.39	0.47
2004	0.55	(0.91)	0.31	0.67

Interim Dividends (Per Share)

Amt	Decl	Ex	Rec	Pay
0.20Q	6/14/2004	6/28/2004	6/30/2004	7/15/2004
0.20Q	9/14/2004	9/28/2004	9/30/2004	10/15/2004
0.20Q	12/10/2004	12/29/2004	12/31/2004	1/18/2005
0.20Q	3/10/2005	3/29/2005	3/31/2005	4/15/2005

Indicated Div: $0.80

Valuation Analysis

		No of Institutions
Forecast P/E	11.10	153
	(4/13/2005)	Shares
Market Cap	$2.9 Billion	87,054,152
Book Value	2.0 Billion	% Held
Price/Book	1.48	56.59
Price/Sales	4.06	

Business Summary: Property, Real Estate & Development (MIC: 8.3 SIC: 512 NAIC: 31190)

Trizec Properties is a real estate investment trust. Co. owns, develops and manages office buildings and mixed-use properties in the U.S. and Canada. Through its development units, Co. creates retail/entertainment and office projects in North America. As of Dec 31 2003, Co. owned interests in or managed 64 office properties containing approximately 42.5 million square feet, with an ownership interest totaling approximately 39.6 million square feet. Co.'s office properties are concentrated in seven markets in the U.S., which are located in the following metropolitan areas: Atlanta, GA, Chicago, IL, Dallas, TX, Houston, TX, Los Angeles, CA, New York, NY, and Washington, D.C.

Recent Developments: For the year ended Dec 31 2004, income from continuing operations declined 64.9% to $47.4 million compared with $135.1 million, before and accounting change charge of $3.8 million, in the previous year. Earnings for 2004 and 2003 excluded income from discontinued operations of $53.9 million and $72.5 million, respectively. Results for 2004 and 2003 included net non-recurring charges of $38.0 million and $39.9 million, respectively. Total revenues rose 0.9% to $712.1 million from $711.5 million a year earlier. Operating income slipped 0.8% to $177.8 million.

Prospects: Co. believes that office market conditions have generally stabilized, but will not show any substantial improvement in most major markets until at least late 2005. Co. expects its own occupancy levels to remain stable and anticipates rental rates on new and renewal leases to be similar to expiring rates. In addition, Co. is projecting lower termination fee levels in 2005. As a result, for full-year 2005, Co. anticipates funds from operations in the range of $1.60 to $1.70 per diluted share, along with earnings of between $0.53 to $0.61 per diluted share.

Financial Data
(US$ in Thousands)	12/31/2004	12/31/2003	12/31/2002	12/31/2001	12/31/2000	12/31/1999	12/31/1998	12/31/1997
Earnings Per Share	0.63	1.32	(1.26)	(2.81)	1.43	0.59	3.11	...
Cash Flow Per Share	1.90	1.46	1.42	1.73	1.60	1.81	...	...
Tang Book Value Per Share	12.88	13.01	12.52	10.84	14.34	14.01	13.75	8.28
Dividends Per Share	0.800	0.800	0.263	...	...	...	...	...
Dividend Payout %	126.98	60.61						
Income Statement								
Total Revenue	712,137	848,181	947,122	1,099,200	1,176,600	1,188,800	963,500	705,200
Depn & Amortn	175,111	198,497	184,244	193,800	115,100	98,700	73,800	49,100
Income Taxes	4,379	(41,777)		(65,400)	(254,200)			42,600
Net Income	101,313	203,753	(187,917)	(417,900)	222,300	94,000	529,500	84,800
Average Shares	153,109	150,453	149,477	148,600	155,200	170,700	173,700	...
Balance Sheet								
Current Assets	573,953	500,387	367,286	484,400	348,100	263,300	488,500	215,000
Total Assets	4,525,412	5,164,566	5,579,259	7,254,100	7,407,000	8,460,300	7,641,800	4,971,700
Current Liabilities	339,229	321,634	353,016	547,300	646,400	487,700	364,600	246,100
Long-Term Obligations	2,219,282	2,866,975	3,345,238	4,636,200	4,106,900	5,031,000	4,578,200	2,556,500
Total Liabilities	2,558,511	3,188,609	3,698,254	5,635,900	5,282,000	6,235,200	5,542,700	2,840,900
Stockholders' Equity	1,959,353	1,965,470	1,878,265	1,618,420	2,125,000	2,225,100	2,099,100	2,130,800
Shares Outstanding	152,132	151,040	150,029	149,300	148,200	158,800	152,700	257,400
Statistical Record								
Return on Assets %	2.09	3.79	N.M.	N.M.	2.79	1.17	8.40	1.73
Return on Equity %	5.15	10.60	N.M.	N.M.	10.19	4.35	25.04	4.85
Net Margin %	14.23	24.02	N.M.	N.M.	18.89	7.91	54.96	12.02
Asset Turnover	0.15	0.16	0.15	0.15	0.15	0.15	0.15	0.14
Current Ratio	1.69	1.56	1.04	0.89	0.54	0.54	1.34	0.87
Debt to Equity	1.13	1.46	1.78	2.87	1.93	2.26	2.18	1.20
Price Range	18.92-13.75	15.61-8.20	17.20-8.80	...	...	...	...	...
P/E Ratio	30.03-21.83	11.83-6.21	...	...	...	...	...	...
Average Yield %	4.94	7.08	2.05	...	...	...	...	...

Address: 233 South Wacker Drive, 46th Floor, Chicago, IL 60606 Telephone: (312) 798-6000	Web Site: www.trz.com Officers: Peter Munk - Chmn. Timothy H. Callahan - Pres., C.E.O.	Auditors: PricewaterhouseCoopers LLP Investor Contact: 212-382-9300

TUPPERWARE CORP.

Exchange	Symbol	Price	52Wk Range	Yield	P/E
NYS	TUP	$20.36 (3/31/2005)	21.32-16.06	4.32	13.76

*7 Year Price Score 82.69   *NYSE Composite Index=100   *12 Month Price Score 102.79

Interim Earnings (Per Share)

Qtr.	Mar	Jun	Sep	Dec
2001	0.30	0.47	(0.21)	0.48
2002	0.27	0.54	0.14	0.59
2003	0.11	0.24	...	0.47
2004	0.25	0.40	0.22	0.61

Interim Dividends (Per Share)

Amt	Decl	Ex	Rec	Pay
0.22Q	5/12/2004	6/14/2004	6/15/2004	7/1/2004
0.22Q	8/27/2004	9/13/2004	9/15/2004	10/1/2004
0.22Q	11/17/2004	12/6/2004	12/8/2004	1/4/2005
0.22Q	2/18/2005	3/9/2005	3/11/2005	4/4/2005

Indicated Div: $0.88

Valuation Analysis

Forecast P/E	14.01	No of Institutions
	(4/7/2005)	182
Market Cap	$1.2 Billion	Shares
Book Value	290.9 Million	43,869,940
Price/Book	4.12	% Held
Price/Sales	0.98	73.89

Business Summary: Chemicals (MIC: 11.1 SIC: 089 NAIC: 26199)

Tupperware is a worldwide direct-selling consumer products company engaged in the manufacture and sale of food storage, preparation and serving items and beauty and personal care products. The core of Co.'s product line consists of food storage, serving and preparation products. Co. also has a line of kitchen gadgets, children's educational toys, microwave products and gifts. Co.'s premium beauty and skin care products are sold through its BeautiControl brand in North America, Latin America and the Asia Pacific. Co. also has a health and nutritional supplements line.

Recent Developments: For the year ended Dec 25 2004, net income increased 81.4% to $86,900 thousand from net income of $47,900 thousand a year earlier. Revenues were $1,224,300 thousand, up 2.5% from $1,194,000 thousand the year before. Operating income was $116,200 thousand versus an income of $86,300 thousand in the prior year, an increase of 34.6%. Total direct expense was $425,400 thousand versus $422,700 thousand in the prior year, an increase of 0.6%. Total indirect expense was $689,700 thousand versus $691,800 thousand in the prior year, a decrease of 0.3%.

Prospects: Co.'s results are benefiting from the progress on its strategic growth initiatives, which it expects to bring top-line growth in the long term. Meanwhile, Co.'s operating margin is benefiting from higher return on sales. Going forward, Co. expects sales to increase in all segments, except Tupperware North America, with the strongest growth expected in BeautiControl North America. In 2005, the segment profit return on sales in Europe is expected to remain above 20.0%, although it should decline from 2004 due to higher resin costs and promotional and strategic investment. Looking ahead to full-year 2005, Co. expects earnings of $1.45 to $1.55 per diluted share.

Financial Data

(US$ in Thousands)	12/25/2004	12/27/2003	12/28/2002	12/29/2001	12/30/2000	12/25/1999	12/26/1998	12/27/1997
Earnings Per Share	1.48	0.82	1.54	1.04	1.29	1.37	1.18	1.32
Cash Flow Per Share	2.08	1.81	2.21	1.88	1.47	1.97	2.03	2.65
Tang Book Value Per Share	3.99	2.94	2.08	1.21	1.14	2.52	2.36	3.43
Dividends Per Share	0.880	0.880	0.880	0.880	0.880	0.880	0.880	0.880
Dividend Payout %	59.46	107.32	57.14	84.62	68.22	64.23	74.58	66.67
Income Statement								
Total Revenue	1,224,300	1,174,800	1,155,100	1,114,400	1,073,100	1,063,800	1,082,800	1,229,300
EBITDA	165,800	123,000	190,200	153,800	174,200	179,800	178,200	194,700
Depn & Amortn	50,800	52,600	48,800	49,900	52,100	55,600	64,000	66,100
Income Before Taxes	102,000	56,600	117,400	82,200	101,100	103,300	91,500	110,800
Income Taxes	15,100	8,700	27,300	20,700	26,200	24,300	22,400	28,800
Net Income	86,900	47,900	90,100	61,500	74,900	79,000	69,100	82,000
Average Shares	58,800	58,440	58,716	58,900	58,000	57,900	58,700	61,827
Balance Sheet								
Current Assets	466,000	411,400	360,100	366,100	372,400	370,500	385,600	403,100
Total Assets	983,200	889,900	830,600	845,700	849,400	796,100	823,400	847,200
Current Liabilities	292,100	274,200	283,000	352,300	275,800	309,200	290,100	299,800
Long-Term Obligations	246,500	263,500	265,100	276,100	358,100	248,500	300,100	236,700
Total Liabilities	692,300	661,700	653,100	719,100	725,500	650,800	687,600	633,000
Stockholders' Equity	290,900	228,200	177,500	126,600	123,900	145,300	135,800	214,200
Shares Outstanding	58,825	58,516	58,360	58,134	57,884	57,665	57,614	62,367
Statistical Record								
Return on Assets %	9.30	5.58	10.78	7.28	8.96	9.78	8.30	9.01
Return on Equity %	33.57	23.68	59.42	49.24	54.75	56.36	39.59	31.64
EBITDA Margin %	13.54	10.47	16.47	13.80	16.23	16.90	16.46	15.84
Net Margin %	7.10	4.08	7.80	5.52	6.98	7.43	6.38	6.67
Asset Turnover	1.31	1.37	1.38	1.32	1.28	1.32	1.30	1.35
Current Ratio	1.60	1.50	1.27	1.04	1.35	1.20	1.33	1.34
Debt to Equity	0.85	1.15	1.49	2.18	2.89	1.71	2.21	1.11
Price Range	20.27-16.06	17.03-12.18	24.73-14.85	25.14-17.81	23.88-14.63	25.50-15.19	28.63-11.75	54.38-22.69
P/E Ratio	13.70-10.85	20.77-14.85	16.06-9.64	24.17-17.12	18.51-11.34	18.61-11.09	24.26-9.96	41.19-17.19
Average Yield %	4.89	5.90	4.46	3.97	4.76	4.32	3.78	2.50

Address: 14901 South Orange Blossom Trail, Orlando, FL 32837	Web Site: www.tupperware.com	Auditors: PricewaterhouseCoopers LLP
Telephone: (407) 826-5050	**Officers:** E. V. Goings - Chmn., C.E.O. Lillian D. Garcia - Sr. V.P., Human Res.	**Investor Contact:** 407-826-4522
Fax: (407) 826-8849		

TXU CORP

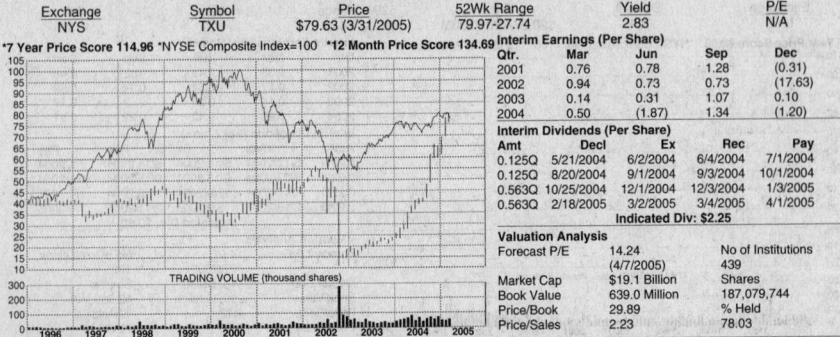

Exchange	Symbol	Price	52Wk Range	Yield	P/E
NYS	TXU	$79.63 (3/31/2005)	79.97-27.74	2.83	N/A

*7 Year Price Score 114.96 ***NYSE Composite Index=100** ***12 Month Price Score 134.69**

Interim Earnings (Per Share)

Qtr.	Mar	Jun	Sep	Dec
2001	0.76	0.78	1.28	(0.31)
2002	0.94	0.73	0.73	(17.63)
2003	0.14	0.31	1.07	0.10
2004	0.50	(1.87)	1.34	(1.20)

Interim Dividends (Per Share)

Amt	Decl	Ex	Rec	Pay
0.125Q	5/21/2004	6/2/2004	6/4/2004	7/1/2004
0.125Q	8/20/2004	9/1/2004	9/3/2004	10/1/2004
0.563Q	10/25/2004	12/1/2004	12/3/2004	1/3/2005
0.563Q	2/18/2005	3/2/2005	3/4/2005	4/1/2005

Indicated Div: $2.25

Valuation Analysis

Forecast P/E	14.24	No of Institutions	
	(4/7/2005)	439	
Market Cap	$19.1 Billion	Shares	
Book Value	639.0 Million	187,079,744	
Price/Book	29.89	% Held	
Price/Sales	2.23	78.03	

TRADING VOLUME (thousand shares)

Business Summary: Electricity (MIC: 7.1 SIC: 911 NAIC: 21122)

TXU is a holding company. Through its subsidiaries, Co. is a global energy services company that engages in electricity generation, wholesale energy trading, retail energy marketing, energy delivery, other energy-related services and, through a joint venture, telecommunications services. Co. delivers or sells energy to approximately 5 million residential, commercial and industrial customers primarily in the United States, Europe and Australia. Co. owns or leases over 20,400 megawatts of power generation and sold 128 terawatt hours of electricity and 206 billion cubic feet of natural gas in 2003.

Recent Developments: For the year ended Dec 31 2004, income from continuing operations decreased 85.7% to $81,000 thousand from income of $566,000 thousand a year earlier. Net income decreased 16.7% to $485,000 thousand from net income of $582,000 thousand a year earlier. Revenues were $8,548,000 thousand, up 8.5% from $7,876,000 thousand the year before. Total direct expense was $5,276,000 thousand versus $5,029,000 thousand in the prior year, an increase of 4.9%. Total indirect expense was $2,547,000 thousand versus $1,348,000 thousand in the prior year, an increase of 88.9%.

Prospects: Co. affirmed its outlook for 2005 operational earnings of $5.65 to $5.85 per share of common stock. In addition, Co. affirmed its preliminary outlook for 2006 operational earnings in a range of 16.0% to 20.0% improvement relative to the $5.75 midpoint of the 2005 outlook. Also, in 2005, Co. expects cash flows to improve substantially as a result of improved earnings and operational improvements. Separately, in 2006, much of the identified improvement potential is driven by having only one unit of the nuclear plant refueled in 2006 versus two units in 2005 and the roll-off on the income statement of the impact of a previously implemented change in hedging strategy.

Financial Data

(US$ in Thousands)	12/31/2004	12/31/2003	12/31/2002	12/31/2001	12/31/2000	12/31/1999	12/31/1998	12/31/1997
Earnings Per Share	(1.29)	1.62	(15.23)	2.52	3.43	3.53	2.79	2.85
Cash Flow Per Share	5.84	8.69	4.82	8.77	6.38	7.80	7.57	7.18
Tang Book Value Per Share	N.M.	11.70	9.87	1.54	1.35	2.96	5.02	22.10
Dividends Per Share	0.938	0.500	1.925	2.400	2.400	2.325	2.225	2.125
Dividend Payout %	...	30.86	...	95.24	69.97	65.86	79.75	74.56
Income Statement								
Total Revenue	8,548,000	11,008,000	10,034,000	27,927,000	22,009,000	17,118,000	14,736,000	7,945,608
EBITDA	949,000	2,010,000	...	3,456,000	3,999,000	4,194,000	3,758,000	2,630,005
Depn & Amortn	826,000	959,000	949,000	1,418,000	1,419,000	1,448,000	1,340,000	838,606
Income Before Taxes	123,000	1,051,000	...	807,000	1,253,000	1,434,000	1,266,000	1,037,352
Income Taxes	42,000	314,000	94,000	(24,000)	337,000	449,000	526,000	376,898
Net Income	485,000	582,000	(4,210,000)	677,000	916,000	985,000	740,000	660,454
Average Shares	300,000	379,000	278,000	259,000	264,000	279,000	265,000	230,958
Balance Sheet								
Net PPE	16,676,000	20,920,000	19,642,000	22,480,000	23,301,000	23,640,000	22,867,000	18,571,030
Total Assets	23,241,000	31,686,000	30,891,000	42,275,000	44,990,000	40,741,000	39,514,000	24,874,129
Long-Term Obligations	12,412,000	12,870,000	11,700,000	16,173,000	15,281,000	16,325,000	15,133,000	8,759,379
Total Liabilities	22,564,000	25,008,000	25,614,000	34,108,000	36,813,000	32,196,000	31,057,000	17,706,273
Stockholders' Equity	639,000	5,919,000	5,066,000	7,956,000	7,856,000	8,334,000	8,246,000	6,843,062
Shares Outstanding	239,852	323,883	321,974	265,140	258,108	276,406	282,333	245,238
Statistical Record								
Return on Assets %	1.76	1.86	N.M.	1.55	2.13	2.45	2.30	2.86
Return on Equity %	14.75	10.60	N.M.	8.56	11.28	11.88	9.81	10.26
EBITDA Margin %	11.10	18.26	...	12.38	18.17	24.50	25.50	33.10
Net Margin %	5.67	5.29	(41.96)	2.42	4.16	5.75	5.02	8.31
PPE Turnover	0.45	0.54	0.48	1.22	0.94	0.74	0.71	0.44
Asset Turnover	0.31	0.35	0.27	0.64	0.51	0.43	0.46	0.34
Debt to Equity	19.42	2.17	2.31	2.03	1.95	1.96	1.84	1.28
Price Range	66.05-23.40	23.73-15.20	56.40-10.88	49.88-35.94	44.75-26.63	46.69-33.31	47.75-38.38	41.75-31.75
P/E Ratio	...	14.65-9.38	...	19.79-14.26	13.05-7.76	13.23-9.44	17.11-13.75	14.65-11.14
Average Yield %	2.31	2.44	4.70	5.38	6.90	5.71	5.27	5.80

Address: Energy Plaza, 1601 Bryan Street, Dallas, TX 75201-3411 Telephone: (214) 812-4600 Fax: (214) 812-4651	Web Site: www.txucorp.com Officers: Erle Nye - Chmn. C. John Wilder - Pres., C.E.O.	Auditors: Deloitte & Touche LLP Investor Contact: 214-812-4641 Transfer Agents: TXU Shareholder Services, Dallas, TX

TYCO INTERNATIONAL LTD.

Exchange	Symbol	Price	52Wk Range	Yield	P/E
NYS	TYC	$33.80 (3/31/2005)	36.37-27.39	1.18	24.14

*7 Year Price Score 78.67   *NYSE Composite Index=100   *12 Month Price Score 99.68

Interim Earnings (Per Share)

Qtr.	Mar	Jun	Sep	Dec
2001-02	0.73	(0.96)	(0.04)	(1.27)
2002-03	0.32	(0.23)	0.27	0.16
2003-04	0.34	0.37	0.43	0.27
2004-05	0.33	...	...	...

Interim Dividends (Per Share)

Amt	Decl	Ex	Rec	Pay
0.013Q	5/12/2004	6/29/2004	7/1/2004	8/2/2004
0.013Q	8/6/2004	9/29/2004	10/1/2004	11/1/2004
0.10Q	12/9/2004	12/30/2004	1/3/2005	2/1/2005
0.10Q	3/10/2005	3/30/2005	4/1/2005	5/2/2005

Indicated Div: $0.40

Valuation Analysis

Forecast P/E	16.88	No of Institutions	
	(4/7/2005)	781	
Market Cap	$67.9 Billion	Shares	
Book Value	30.3 Billion	1,674,474,752	
Price/Book	2.24	% Held	
Price/Sales	1.69	83.17	

Business Summary: Miscellaneous Business Services (MIC: 12.8 SIC: 382 NAIC: 61621)

Co, through its subsidiaries, designs, manufactures, installs, monitors and services electronic security and fire protection systems; designs, manufactures and distributes electrical and electronic components; designs, manufactures and distributes medical devices and supplies, imaging agents, pharmaceuticals and adult incontinence and infant care products; designs, manufactures, distributes and services engineered products, including industrial valves and controls as well as steel tubular goods, and provides environmental and other industrial consulting services; and designs, manufactures and distributes plastic products, adhesives and films.

Recent Developments: For the quarter ended Dec 31 2004, income from continuing operations advanced 2.8% to $741.0 million, before a loss of $32.0 million from discontinued operations, compared with income of $721.0 million, before a loss of $2.0 million from discontinued operations, in the corresponding 2003 period. Results for 2004 and 2003 included restructuring, impairment and other charges of $8.0 million and $28.0 million, respectively. Results for 2004 also included losses and impairments on divestitures of $15.0 million. Net revenue increased 4.1% to $10.1 million from $9.7 million a year earlier, reflecting revenue growth in all five of Co.'s segments. Operating income climbed 12.7% to $37.0 million.

Prospects: For the second quarter of 2005, Co. expects to achieve earnings per share (EPS) from continuing operations of $0.45 to $0.47. Co. continues to expect full-year EPS from continuing operations of $1.88 to $1.98. This EPS outlook excludes charges related to divestitures or early retirement of debt. Co. continues to expect full-year cash from operating activities of approximately $7.00 billion and free cash flow in excess of $4.50 billion. Both cash flow measures are before any voluntary pension contributions. Co.'s prior free cash flow guidance of more than $5.00 billion was reduced by approximately $525.0 million to reflect additional dividend payments planned for fiscal 2005.

Financial Data

(US$ in Thousands)	09/30/2004	09/30/2003	09/30/2002	09/30/2001	09/30/2000	09/30/1999	09/30/1998	09/30/1997
Earnings Per Share	1.35	0.49	(4.73)	2.17	2.64	0.59	0.72	(1.61)
Cash Flow Per Share	2.68	2.69	3.60	3.69	...	...	1.44	...
Dividends Per Share	0.050	0.050	0.050	0.09	0.050	0.050	0.050	0.025
Dividend Payout %	3.70	10.20	N.M.	25.60	1.89	8.47	6.94	N.M.
Income Statement								
Total Revenue	40,153,000	36,801,300	35,643,700	36,388,500	28,931,900	22,496,500	19,061,700	7,588,200
Income Taxes	1,140,000	764,500	257,700	1,479,900	1,926,000	620,200	534,200	187,000
Net Income	2,879,000	979,600	(9,411,700)	3,970,600	4,519,900	985,300	1,166,200	(835,100)
Average Shares	2,216,000	2,002,700	1,988,500	1,831,600	1,713,200	1,641,300	1,624,700	519,500
Balance Sheet								
Current Assets	18,545,000	17,239,500	19,764,600	46,447,500	12,815,700	11,162,800	8,954,900	4,108,800
Total Assets	63,667,000	63,545,000	66,414,400	111,287,300	40,404,300	32,361,600	23,440,700	10,447,000
Current Liabilities	11,152,000	10,572,300	19,632,100	33,619,000	11,678,900	9,179,000	7,006,200	3,991,800
Total Liabilities	33,307,000	37,062,700	41,581,000	78,988,500	23,027,600	20,029,000	13,538,900	7,017,600
Stockholders' Equity	30,292,000	26,369,000	24,790,600	31,737,400	17,033,200	12,332,600	9,901,800	3,429,400
Shares Outstanding	2,009,867	1,998,189	1,995,699	1,935,464	1,684,511	1,690,175	1,620,463	536,357
Statistical Record								
Return on Assets %	4.51	1.51	N.M.	5.24	12.39	3.53	6.88	N.M.
Return on Equity %	10.13	3.83	N.M.	16.28	30.70	8.86	17.50	N.M.
Net Margin %	7.17	2.66	N.M.	10.91	15.62	4.38	6.12	N.M.
Asset Turnover	0.63	0.57	0.40	0.48	0.79	0.81	1.12	1.54
Price Range	33.14-20.43	21.90-11.50	59.76-8.25	62.80-40.80	58.50-28.25	52.69-22.34	34.28-18.09	21.25-10.78
P/E Ratio	24.55-15.13	44.69-23.47	N/A	28.94-18.80	22.16-10.70	89.30-37.87	47.61-25.13	N/A
Average Yield%	0.19	0.30	0.15	0.09	0.11	0.14	0.13	0.15

Address: Second Floor, 90 Pitts Bay Road, Pembroke, HM 08, Bermuda **Telephone:** (441) 292 8674 **Fax:** (441) 295-9647	**Web Site:** www.tyco.com **Officers:** Edward D. Breen - Chmn., C.E.O. David J. FitzPatrick - Exec. V.P., C.F.O.	**Auditors:** PricewaterhouseCoopers LLP **Investor Contact:** 603-778-9700

TYSON FOODS, INC.

Exchange	Symbol	Price	52Wk Range	Yield	P/E
NYS	TSN	$16.68 (3/31/2005)	21.06-14.12	0.96	15.30

*7 Year Price Score 103.40 ***NYSE Composite Index=100** ***12 Month Price Score 89.29**

TRADING VOLUME (thousand shares)

Interim Earnings (Per Share)

Qtr.	Dec	Mar	Jun	Sep
2002-03	0.11	0.20	0.23	0.42
2003-04	0.16	0.33	0.45	0.19
Qtr.	Dec			
2004-05	0.14	...	...	...

Interim Dividends (Per Share)

Amt	Decl	Ex	Rec	Pay
0.04Q	4/30/2004	8/30/2004	9/1/2004	9/15/2004
0.04Q	7/23/2004	11/29/2004	12/1/2004	12/15/2004
0.04Q	11/19/2004	2/25/2005	3/1/2005	3/15/2005
0.04Q	2/7/2005	5/27/2005	6/1/2005	6/15/2005

Indicated Div: $0.16

Valuation Analysis

Forecast P/E	14.34	No of Institutions	
	(4/7/2005)	234	
Market Cap	$5.9 Billion	Shares	
Book Value	4.3 Billion	162,017,296	
Price/Book	1.36	% Held	
Price/Sales	0.23	64.43	

Business Summary: Food (MIC: 4.1 SIC: 015 NAIC: 11615)

Tyson Foods and its subsidiaries, produce, distribute, and market chicken, beef, pork, prepared foods, and related allied products. Co. operates an integrated poultry production process. Co. is also a breeding stock provider. Co. invests in breeding stock research and development which allows it to breed into its flocks the characteristics found to be most desirable. Co.'s integrated operations consist of breeding and raising chickens, as well as the processing, further-processing, and marketing of these food products and related allied products, including animal and pet food ingredients. Co. operates in five business segments: Chicken, Beef, Pork, Prepared Foods and Other.

Recent Developments: For the quarter ended Jan 1 2005, net income decreased 15.8% to $48 million from net income of $57 million in the year-earlier quarter. Revenues were $6,452 million, down 0.8% from $6,505 million the year before. Operating income was $129 million versus an income of $161 million in the prior-year quarter, a decrease of 19.9%. Total direct expense was $6,089 million versus $6,111 million in the prior-year quarter, a decrease of 0.4%. Total indirect expense was $234 million versus $233 million in the prior-year quarter, an increase of 0.4%.

Prospects: Co.'s operating results are being adversely affected by continued restrictions for beef, as well as a lack of cattle supplies, and a tougher pricing environment for pork. However, these negative factors are being partially offset by improved performance from its chicken operations, strong cash flow from operations, and a reduction of debt by $292.0 million. Looking ahead, Co. expects conditions to remain challenging during the first half of fiscal year, with considerable improvement anticipated in the second half of the year. Moreover, Co. estimates diluted earnings to range from $1.05 to $1.30 per share for fiscal 2005.

Financial Data

(US$ in Thousands)	3 Mos	10/02/2004	09/27/2003	09/28/2002	09/29/2001	09/30/2000	10/02/1999	10/03/1998
Earnings Per Share	1.09	1.13	0.96	1.08	0.40	0.67	1.00	0.11
Cash Flow Per Share	3.12	2.66	2.38	3.38	2.32	2.62	2.38	2.15
Tang Book Value Per Share	4.62	4.49	3.17	2.92	1.71	5.50	5.10	4.05
Dividends Per Share	0.160	0.160	0.160	0.160	0.160	0.160	0.115	0.100
Dividend Payout %	14.70	14.16	16.67	14.81	40.00	23.88	11.50	90.91
Income Statement								
Total Revenue	6,452,000	26,441,000	24,549,000	23,367,000	10,751,000	7,158,000	7,362,900	7,414,100
EBITDA	260,000	1,376,000	1,254,000	1,365,000	644,000	643,000	786,100	486,500
Depn & Amortn	126,000	466,000	435,000	467,000	335,000	294,000	291,100	276,400
Income Before Taxes	76,000	635,000	523,000	593,000	165,000	234,000	371,000	71,000
Income Taxes	28,000	232,000	186,000	210,000	58,000	83,000	129,400	45,900
Net Income	48,000	403,000	337,000	383,000	88,000	151,000	230,100	25,100
Average Shares	356,000	357,000	352,000	355,000	222,000	226,000	231,000	227,900
Balance Sheet								
Current Assets	3,361,000	3,532,000	3,371,000	3,144,000	3,290,000	1,576,000	1,726,900	1,765,100
Total Assets	10,344,000	10,464,000	10,486,000	10,372,000	10,632,000	4,854,000	5,082,700	5,242,500
Current Liabilities	2,440,000	2,293,000	2,475,000	2,093,000	2,416,000	886,000	987,000	831,000
Long-Term Obligations	2,706,000	3,024,000	3,114,000	3,733,000	4,016,000	1,357,000	1,515,200	1,966,600
Total Liabilities	6,002,000	6,172,000	6,532,000	6,710,000	7,278,000	2,679,000	2,954,700	3,272,100
Stockholders' Equity	4,342,000	4,292,000	3,954,000	3,662,000	3,354,000	2,175,000	2,128,000	1,970,400
Shares Outstanding	354,000	353,000	353,000	353,000	349,000	225,000	228,600	230,800
Statistical Record								
Return on Assets %	3.72	3.79	3.24	3.66	1.14	3.05	4.47	0.51
Return on Equity %	9.24	9.62	8.87	10.95	3.19	7.04	11.26	1.37
EBITDA Margin %	4.03	5.20	5.11	5.84	5.99	8.98	10.68	6.56
Net Margin %	0.74	1.52	1.37	1.64	0.82	2.11	3.13	0.34
Asset Turnover	2.50	2.48	2.36	2.23	1.39	1.44	1.43	1.51
Current Ratio	1.38	1.54	1.36	1.50	1.36	1.78	1.75	2.12
Debt to Equity	0.62	0.70	0.79	1.02	1.20	0.62	0.71	1.00
Price Range	21.06-12.99	21.06-12.59	14.42-7.28	15.56-8.75	14.38-8.35	18.00-8.56	25.38-15.00	24.44-16.50
P/E Ratio	19.32-11.92	18.64-11.14	15.02-7.58	14.41-8.10	35.94-20.88	26.87-12.78	25.38-15.00	222.18-150.00
Average Yield %	0.91	0.95	1.52	1.30	1.36	1.32	0.56	0.49

Address: 2210 West Oaklawn Drive, Springdale, AR 72762-6999	Web Site: www.tysonfoodsinc.com	Auditors: Ernst & Young LLP
Telephone: (479) 290-4000	Officers: John Tyson - Chmn., C.E.O. Richard L. Bond - Pres., C.O.O.	Transfer Agents: EquiServe, Trust Co., N.A. Providence RI
Fax: (479) 290-7984		

UGI CORP.

Exchange	Symbol	Price	52Wk Range	Yield	P/E	Div Acheiver
NYS	UGI	$45.42 (3/31/2005)	46.98-29.89	2.75	15.19	17 Years

*7 Year Price Score 142.01 *NYSE Composite Index=100 *12 Month Price Score 112.18

Interim Earnings (Per Share)

Qtr.	Dec	Mar	Jun	Sep
2001-02	0.58	1.28	0.09	(0.15)
2002-03	0.86	1.62	(0.05)	(0.14)
2003-04	0.88	1.48	0.16	(0.12)
2004-05	1.49	...	...	...

Interim Dividends (Per Share)

Amt	Decl	Ex	Rec	Pay
0.313Q	4/27/2004	5/26/2004	5/28/2004	7/1/2004
0.313Q	7/27/2004	8/27/2004	8/31/2004	10/1/2004
0.313Q	10/26/2004	11/26/2004	11/30/2004	1/1/2005
0.313Q	1/26/2005	2/24/2005	2/28/2005	4/1/2005

Indicated Div: $1.25 (Div. Reinv. Plan)

Valuation Analysis

Forecast P/E	15.15	No of Institutions	
	(4/7/2005)	195	
Market Cap	$2.3 Billion	Shares	
Book Value	919.0 Million	33,891,528	
Price/Book	2.55	% Held	
Price/Sales	0.55	65.74	

Business Summary: Gas Utilities (MIC: 7.4 SIC: 924 NAIC: 21210)

UGI is a holding company that distributes and markets energy products and related services through its subsidiaries and joint venture affiliates. Co. is a domestic and international distributor of propane and butane, ("LPG"); a provider of natural gas and electric service through regulated local distribution utilities; a generator of electricity through its ownership interests in electric generation facilities; a regional marketer of energy commodities; and a provider of heating and cooling services. Co.'s subsidiaries operate principally in the following five business segments: AmeriGas Propane; International Propane; Gas Utility; Electric Utility; and, Energy Services.

Recent Developments: For the quarter ended Dec 31 2004, net income increased 101.5% to $78,200 thousand from net income of $38,800 thousand in the year-earlier quarter. Revenues were $1,363,100 thousand, up 52.5% from $893,700 thousand the year before. Operating income was $175,000 thousand versus an income of $108,300 thousand in the prior-year quarter, an increase of 61.6%. Total direct expense was $913,300 thousand versus $596,900 thousand in the prior-year quarter, an increase of 53.0%. Total indirect expense was $298,400 thousand versus $193,900 thousand in the prior-year quarter, an increase of 53.9%.

Prospects: Results are being positively affected by the significant contribution to earnings by Antargaz, which was acquired by Co. in 2004 through the purchase of the remaining 80.5% ownership interests in AGZ Holding. The acquisition of Antargaz is expected to drive long-term earnings growth and boost cash flows from the energy distribution and marketing businesses. Meanwhile, Co. is enjoying top-line growth across all of its operating units, despite unfavorable weather conditions that have hampered results across its service territories. Results are expected to benefit from a return to more normal weather patterns.

Financial Data

(US$ in Thousands)	3 Mos	09/30/2004	09/30/2003	09/30/2002	09/30/2001	09/30/2000	09/30/1999	09/30/1998
Earnings Per Share	2.99	2.31	2.29	1.80	1.37	1.09	1.16	0.81
Cash Flow Per Share	4.83	5.43	5.90	5.99	4.99	3.24	2.96	...
Dividends Per Share	1.222	1.195	1.130	1.083	1.050	1.017	0.980	0.967
Dividend Payout %	40.84	51.73	49.34	60.19	76.46	92.99	84.48	118.85
Income Statement								
Total Revenue	1,363,100	3,784,700	3,026,100	2,213,700	2,468,100	1,761,700	1,383,600	1,439,700
EBITDA	191,300	426,100	373,000	326,600	309,000	282,400	274,800	249,100
Depn & Amortn	37,600	131,000	103,000	93,500	105,200	97,500	89,700	87,800
Income Before Taxes	120,200	176,000	160,800	124,000	99,000	86,400	100,500	76,900
Income Taxes	42,000	64,400	60,700	46,900	45,400	40,100	43,200	34,400
Net Income	78,200	111,600	98,900	75,500	56,500	44,700	55,700	40,300
Average Shares	52,600	48,341	43,236	41,907	41,059	40,882	48,024	49,684
Balance Sheet								
Net PPE	1,843,000	1,781,900	1,336,800	1,271,900	1,268,000	1,073,200	1,084,100	999,000
Total Assets	4,680,500	4,235,400	2,781,700	2,614,400	2,550,200	2,278,800	2,135,900	2,074,600
Long-Term Obligations	1,561,900	1,547,300	1,158,500	1,127,000	1,196,900	1,029,700	989,600	890,800
Total Liabilities	3,591,700	3,222,900	2,077,300	2,001,100	2,028,400	1,834,500	1,656,800	1,451,000
Stockholders' Equity	919,000	834,100	569,800	317,300	255,600	247,200	249,200	367,100
Shares Outstanding	51,550	51,211	42,699	41,551	40,944	40,490	40,905	49,234
Statistical Record								
Return on Assets %	3.90	3.17	3.67	2.92	2.34	2.02	2.65	1.94
Return on Equity %	19.67	15.86	22.30	26.36	22.47	17.96	18.08	10.98
EBITDA Margin %	14.03	11.26	12.33	14.75	12.52	16.03	19.86	17.30
Net Margin %	5.74	2.95	3.27	3.41	2.29	2.54	4.03	2.80
PPE Turnover	2.65	2.42	2.32	1.74	2.11	1.63	1.33	1.44
Asset Turnover	1.10	1.08	1.12	0.86	1.02	0.80	0.66	0.69
Debt to Equity	1.70	1.86	2.03	3.55	4.68	4.17	3.97	2.43
Price Range	41.12-29.89	37.26-28.93	34.90-23.47	24.43-17.73	19.39-14.46	16.17-12.17	16.79-10.63	19.88-13.88
P/E Ratio	13.75-10.00	16.13-12.52	15.24-10.25	13.57-9.85	14.16-10.55	14.83-11.16	14.48-9.16	24.54-17.13
Average Yield %	3.55	3.68	3.92	5.26	6.24	7.06	6.89	5.49

Address: 460 North Gulph Road, King of Prussia, PA 19406 **Telephone:** (610) 337-1000 **Fax:** (610) 992-3259	**Web Site:** www.ugicorp.com **Officers:** Lon R. Greenberg - Chmn., Pres., C.E.O. Anthony J. Mendicino - Sr. V.P., Fin., C.F.O.	**Auditors:** PricewaterhouseCoopers LLP **Investor Contact:** 610-337-1000 **Transfer Agents:** Mellon Investor Services LLC, Ridgefield Park, NJ

UNION PACIFIC CORP.

Exchange	Symbol	Price	52Wk Range	Yield	P/E
NYS	UNP	$69.70 (3/31/2005)	69.84-55.09	1.72	30.30

*7 Year Price Score 95.53 ***NYSE Composite Index=100** ***12 Month Price Score 98.19**

TRADING VOLUME (thousand shares)

Interim Earnings (Per Share)

Qtr.	Mar	Jun	Sep	Dec
2001	0.72	0.95	1.04	1.06
2002	0.86	1.15	1.63	1.41
2003	1.67	1.10	1.21	2.10
2004	0.63	0.60	0.77	0.30

Interim Dividends (Per Share)

Amt	Decl	Ex	Rec	Pay
0.30Q	5/28/2004	6/7/2004	6/9/2004	7/1/2004
0.30Q	7/29/2004	9/3/2004	9/8/2004	10/1/2004
0.30Q	11/18/2004	12/6/2004	12/8/2004	1/3/2005
0.30Q	2/24/2005	3/7/2005	3/9/2005	4/1/2005

Indicated Div: $1.20

Valuation Analysis

Forecast P/E	21.56	No of Institutions	
	(4/7/2005)	508	
Market Cap	$18.2 Billion	Shares	
Book Value	12.7 Billion	210,881,664	
Price/Book	1.43	% Held	
Price/Sales	1.49	80.80	

Business Summary: Rail Transport (MIC: 15.5 SIC: 011 NAIC: 82111)

Union Pacific is engaged primarily in rail transportation. Union Pacific Railroad operates over 33,000 route miles linking the Pacific Coast and Gulf Coast ports with the Midwest and eastern U.S. gateways and providing several north/south corridors to key Mexican gateways. Co. serves the western two-thirds of the U.S. and maintains coordinated schedules with other rail carriers for the handling of freight to and from the Atlantic Coast, the Pacific Coast, the Southeast, the Southwest, Canada and Mexico. Major categories of freight are: agricultural products, automotive, chemicals, energy, industrial products and intermodal.

Recent Developments: For the year ended Dec 31 2004, net income decreased 61.9% to $604,000 thousand from net income of $1,585,000 thousand a year earlier. Revenues were $12,215,000 thousand, up 5.7% from $11,551,000 thousand the year before. Operating income was $1,295,000 thousand versus an income of $2,133,000 thousand in the prior year, a decrease of 39.3%. Total direct expense was $7,845,000 thousand versus $6,868,000 thousand in the prior year, an increase of 14.2%. Total indirect expense was $3,075,000 thousand versus $2,550,000 thousand in the prior year, an increase of 20.6%.

Prospects: Co. remains focused on resolving the operational issues that have limited profitability. In early 2005, Co. began implementing a series of initiatives focused on improving network efficiencies and increasing productivity. Co. expects these initiatives to be fully implemented by the end of June 2005. Meanwhile, for the first quarter of 2005, Co. is projecting a year-over-year revenue increase of between 4.0% and 6.0%, and earnings in the range of $0.25 to $0.35 per share. Looking ahead, Co. anticipates full-year 2005 volume growth of between 1.0% and 2.0%, along with revenue growth in the range of 5.0% to 7.0%.

Financial Data

(US$ in Thousands)	12/31/2004	12/31/2003	12/31/2002	12/31/2001	12/31/2000	12/31/1999	12/31/1998	12/31/1997
Earnings Per Share	2.30	6.04	5.05	3.77	3.34	3.22	(2.57)	1.74
Cash Flow Per Share	8.61	9.52	8.93	8.03	7.92	7.58	2.30	6.50
Tang Book Value Per Share	48.58	47.85	41.99	38.26	35.09	32.29	29.93	30.79
Dividends Per Share	1.200	0.990	0.830	0.800	0.800	0.800	0.800	1.720
Dividend Payout %	52.17	16.39	16.44	21.22	23.95	24.84	N.M.	98.85
Income Statement								
Total Revenue	12,215,000	11,551,000	12,491,000	11,973,000	11,878,000	11,273,000	10,553,000	11,079,000
EBITDA	2,484,000	3,270,000	3,855,000	3,408,000	3,173,000	3,018,000	1,088,000	2,324,000
Depn & Amortn	1,111,000	1,067,000	1,206,000	1,174,000	1,140,000	1,083,000	1,070,000	1,043,000
Income Before Taxes	856,000	1,637,000	2,016,000	1,533,000	1,310,000	1,202,000	(696,000)	676,000
Income Taxes	252,000	581,000	675,000	567,000	468,000	419,000	(63,000)	244,000
Net Income	604,000	1,585,000	1,341,000	966,000	842,000	810,000	(633,000)	432,000
Average Shares	262,200	268,000	276,800	271,900	269,450	269,800	246,000	248,000
Balance Sheet								
Total Assets	34,589,000	33,460,000	32,764,000	31,551,000	30,499,000	29,888,000	29,374,000	28,764,000
Long-Term Obligations	7,981,000	7,822,000	7,428,000	7,886,000	8,144,000	8,426,000	8,511,000	8,285,000
Total Liabilities	21,934,000	21,106,000	22,113,000	21,976,000	21,837,000	21,887,000	21,981,000	20,539,000
Stockholders' Equity	12,655,000	12,354,000	10,651,000	9,575,000	8,662,000	8,001,000	7,393,000	8,225,000
Shares Outstanding	260,519	258,160	253,659	250,290	246,820	247,783	247,000	247,000
Statistical Record								
Return on Assets %	1.77	4.79	4.17	3.11	2.78	2.73	N.M.	1.52
Return on Equity %	4.82	13.78	13.26	10.59	10.08	10.52	N.M.	5.25
EBITDA Margin %	20.34	28.31	30.86	28.46	26.71	26.77	10.31	20.98
Net Margin %	4.94	13.72	10.74	8.07	7.09	7.19	(6.00)	3.90
Asset Turnover	0.36	0.35	0.39	0.39	0.39	0.38	0.36	0.39
Price Range	69.48-55.09	69.49-51.34	65.05-54.75	60.60-44.77	52.63-35.06	67.00-40.63	63.38-37.63	72.44-56.75
P/E Ratio	30.21-23.95	11.50-8.50	12.88-10.84	16.07-11.88	15.76-10.50	20.81-12.62	N/A	41.63-32.61
Average Yield %	1.98	1.65	1.39	1.49	1.90	1.52	1.63	2.69

Address: 1400 Douglas Street, Omaha, NE 68179 Telephone: (402) 544-5000	Web Site: www.up.com Officers: Richard K. Davidson - Chmn., Pres., C.E.O. Robert M. Knight Jr. - Exec. V.P., C.F.O.	Auditors: Deloitte & Touche LLP Investor Contact: 215-861-3200

UNIONBANCAL CORP.

Exchange	Symbol	Price	52Wk Range	Yield	P/E
NYS	UB	$61.25 (3/31/2005)	64.78-49.51	2.35	12.58

*7 Year Price Score 126.52 *NYSE Composite Index=100 *12 Month Price Score 97.40

Interim Earnings (Per Share)

Qtr.	Mar	Jun	Sep	Dec
2001	0.67	0.74	0.79	0.84
2002	0.73	0.81	0.88	0.95
2003	0.89	0.96	1.02	1.03
2004	1.05	1.54	1.09	1.19

Interim Dividends (Per Share)

Amt	Decl	Ex	Rec	Pay
0.36Q	4/28/2004	6/2/2004	6/4/2004	7/2/2004
0.36Q	7/28/2004	9/1/2004	9/3/2004	10/1/2004
0.36Q	10/27/2004	12/8/2004	12/10/2004	1/7/2005
0.36Q	1/26/2005	3/2/2005	3/4/2005	4/1/2005

Indicated Div: $1.44

Valuation Analysis

Forecast P/E	N/A	No of Institutions
		152
Market Cap	$9.1 Billion	Shares
Book Value	4.3 Billion	136,271,360
Price/Book	2.12	% Held
Price/Sales	3.21	91.80

Business Summary: Commercial Banking (MIC: 8.1 SIC: 021 NAIC: 22110)

UnionBanCal is a commercial bank holding company based in San Francisco with consolidated assets of $42.50 billion at Dec 31 2003. Co.'s primary subsidiary, Union Bank of California, is the third largest commercial bank in California, based on total assets and total deposits. Union Bank of California has 28 banking offices in California, 4 banking offices in Oregon and Washington, and 21 international facilities. Co. provides a wide range of financial services to consumers, small business, middle-market companies and major corporations, primarily in California, Oregon, and Washington, but also nationally and internationally.

Recent Developments: For the year ended Dec 31 2004, net income increased 24.8% to $732,534 thousand from net income of $587,139 thousand a year earlier. Net interest income was $1,645,223 thousand, up 4.9% from $1,569,066 thousand the year before. Provision for loan losses was $35,000 thousand versus $75,000 thousand in the prior year, a decrease of 146.7%. Non-interest income rose 24.6% to $989,305 thousand, while non-interest expense advanced 8.2% to $1,524,182 thousand.

Prospects: Going forward, results should benefit from Co.'s improvement in its strategic positioning with the recent completion of two bank acquisitions, a retirement plan services acquisition and the sale of its merchant card business. Looking ahead, for the first quarter of 2005 and fiscal 2005, Co. is projecting diluted earnings per share to be in the range of $1.07 to $1.12 and $4.57 to $4.77, respectively. These estimates exclude the effect of expensing employee stock options and assume provisions for credit losses of negative $10.0 million for the first quarter of 2005, and $10.0 million for full-year 2005.

Financial Data

(US$ in Thousands)	12/31/2004	12/31/2003	12/31/2002	12/31/2001	12/31/2000	12/31/1999	12/31/1998	12/31/1997
Earnings Per Share	4.87	3.90	3.38	3.04	2.72	2.64	2.65	2.30
Cash Flow Per Share	5.12	3.22	6.79	6.90	3.70	2.60	3.42	4.38
Tang Book Value Per Share	25.48	23.77	23.68	22.66	20.17	18.18	17.45	16.26
Dividends Per Share	1.390	1.210	1.090	1.000	1.000	0.820	0.610	0.513
Dividend Payout %	28.54	31.03	32.25	32.89	36.76	31.06	23.02	22.32
Income Statement								
Interest Income	1,844,902	1,769,663	1,855,972	2,195,311	2,501,080	2,161,907	2,085,179	2,033,461
Interest Expense	199,679	200,597	294,003	671,269	916,640	746,074	766,956	801,779
Net Interest Income	1,645,223	1,569,066	1,561,969	1,524,042	1,584,440	1,415,833	1,318,223	1,231,682
Provision for Losses	(35,000)	75,000	175,000	285,000	440,000	65,000	45,000	...
Non-Interest Income	989,305	794,253	735,976	716,404	647,180	586,759	533,531	463,001
Non-Interest Expense	1,524,182	1,408,353	1,347,666	1,240,174	1,130,185	1,281,973	1,135,218	1,044,665
Income Before Taxes	1,145,346	879,966	775,279	715,272	661,435	655,619	671,536	650,018
Income Taxes	412,812	292,827	247,376	233,844	221,535	213,888	205,075	238,722
Net Income	732,534	587,139	527,903	481,428	439,900	441,731	466,461	411,296
Average Shares	150,303	150,645	156,415	158,623	161,989	167,149	175,737	165,018
Balance Sheet								
Net Loans & Leases	30,309,800	25,401,783	25,828,893	24,359,521	25,396,496	25,442,580	23,836,783	22,129,566
Total Assets	48,098,021	42,498,467	40,169,773	36,039,089	35,162,475	33,684,776	32,276,316	30,585,265
Total Deposits	40,175,836	35,532,283	32,840,815	28,556,199	27,283,183	26,256,607	24,507,879	23,296,374
Total Liabilities	43,805,777	38,758,031	36,411,584	32,492,847	31,950,910	30,697,308	29,218,072	27,905,966
Stockholders' Equity	4,292,244	3,740,436	3,758,189	3,546,242	3,211,565	2,987,468	3,058,244	2,679,299
Shares Outstanding	148,359	145,758	150,702	156,483	159,234	164,282	175,260	164,748
Statistical Record								
Return on Assets %	1.61	1.42	1.39	1.35	1.27	1.34	1.48	1.38
Return on Equity %	18.19	15.66	14.45	14.25	14.15	14.61	16.26	15.90
Net Interest Margin %	89.18	88.66	84.16	69.42	63.35	65.49	63.22	60.57
Efficiency Ratio %	53.78	54.93	51.99	42.59	35.90	46.64	43.35	41.85
Loans to Deposits	0.75	0.71	0.79	0.85	0.93	0.97	0.97	0.95
Price Range	64.78-49.51	58.45-37.77	49.60-34.98	39.14-24.81	39.44-18.38	46.13-30.19	37.42-23.96	35.83-17.25
P/E Ratio	13.30-10.17	14.99-9.68	14.67-10.35	12.88-8.16	14.50-6.76	17.47-11.43	14.12-9.04	15.58-7.50
Average Yield %	2.43	2.64	2.55	3.10	3.84	2.21	1.95	2.13

Address: 400 California Street, San Francisco, CA 94104 **Telephone:** (415) 765-2969 **Fax:** (415) 765-2950	**Web Site:** www.uboc.com **Officers:** Tetsuo Shimura - Chmn. Takaharu Saegusa - Dep. Chmn.	**Auditors:** Deloitte & Touche LLP **Investor Contact:** 415-765-2969

UNISYS CORP.

Exchange	Symbol	Price	52Wk Range	Yield	P/E
NYS	UIS	$7.06 (3/31/2005)	14.75-6.67	N/A	64.18

*7 Year Price Score 52.19   ***NYSE Composite Index=100**   ***12 Month Price Score 64.71**

Interim Earnings (Per Share)

Qtr.	Mar	Jun	Sep	Dec
2001	0.22	0.04	0.07	(0.53)
2002	0.10	0.13	0.18	0.28
2003	0.12	0.16	0.17	0.34
2004	0.09	0.06	0.07	(0.11)

Interim Dividends (Per Share)

No Dividends Paid

Valuation Analysis

Forecast P/E	38.39	No of Institutions	
	(4/7/2005)	250	
Market Cap	$2.4 Billion	Shares	
Book Value	1.5 Billion	233,871,744	
Price/Book	1.58	% Held	
Price/Sales	0.41	69.34	

TRADING VOLUME (thousand shares)

Business Summary: IT & Technology (MIC: 10.2 SIC: 571 NAIC: 34111)

Unisys is a worldwide information technology services and solutions company. Co. has two business segments: Services and Technology. The Services segment consists of systems integration and consulting; outsourcing; enterprise-wide security solutions and core maintenance. In the Technology segment, Co. develops servers and related products that operate in transaction-intensive, mission-critical environments. Offerings include enterprise-class servers based on Co.'s Cellular MultiProcessing architecture; operating system software and middleware to power high-end servers; and specialized technologies such as payment systems, chip testing and third-party products.

Recent Developments: For the year ended Dec 31 2004, net income decreased 85.1% to $38,600 thousand from net income of $258,700 thousand a year earlier. Revenues were $5,820,700 thousand, down 1.5% from $5,911,200 thousand the year before. Operating loss was $34,800 thousand versus an income of $427,700 thousand in the prior year. Total direct expense was $4,458,300 thousand versus $4,196,200 thousand in the prior year, an increase of 6.2%. Total indirect expense was $1,397,200 thousand versus $1,287,300 thousand in the prior year, an increase of 8.5%.

Prospects: Co.'s near-term outlook appears lackluster, hurt by a write-off of its outsourcing operations and a revenue decline. Going forward, for the first quarter 2005, Co. expects outsourcing contracts and weak sales of large enterprise servers to continue to adversely affect operating performance. Accordingly, Co. expects first quarter 2005 results to come in at breakeven level to a slight loss. Additionally, for fiscal 2005, Co. expects to report earnings of $0.50 to $0.60 per share, excluding the impact of pension accounting and stock-option expensing.

Financial Data

(US$ in Thousands)	12/31/2004	12/31/2003	12/31/2002	12/31/2001	12/31/2000	12/31/1999	12/31/1998	12/31/1997
Earnings Per Share	0.11	0.78	0.69	(0.21)	0.71	1.59	1.06	(5.30)
Cash Flow Per Share	1.40	1.61	1.00	0.64	1.34	1.80	2.58	2.11
Tang Book Value Per Share	2.90	2.67	1.18	5.20	5.99	5.42	N.M.	4.82
Income Statement								
Total Revenue	5,820,700	5,911,200	5,607,400	6,018,100	6,885,000	7,544,600	7,208,400	6,636,000
EBITDA	387,000	792,700	697,100	325,700	729,800	1,163,300	1,042,800	691,300
Depn & Amortn	394,000	342,600	297,800	302,200	271,000	265,200	266,400	1,216,900
Income Before Taxes	(76,000)	380,500	332,800	(46,500)	379,000	770,300	604,700	(758,800)
Income Taxes	(114,600)	121,800	109,800	3,400	134,200	247,500	217,700	94,800
Net Income	38,600	258,700	223,000	(67,100)	225,000	510,700	387,000	(853,600)
Average Shares	338,217	332,948	323,526	318,207	316,651	298,820	266,944	182,016
Balance Sheet								
Current Assets	2,417,600	2,258,000	1,946,000	2,204,100	2,587,000	2,845,700	2,816,700	2,886,500
Total Assets	5,620,900	5,474,600	4,981,400	5,769,100	5,717,700	5,889,700	5,577,700	5,591,300
Current Liabilities	2,022,800	2,053,500	2,184,500	2,323,100	2,685,800	2,618,500	2,582,500	2,577,400
Long-Term Obligations	898,400	1,048,300	748,000	745,000	536,300	950,200	1,105,200	1,438,300
Total Liabilities	4,114,400	4,079,400	4,125,400	3,656,400	3,531,600	3,936,400	4,060,700	4,385,400
Stockholders' Equity	1,506,500	1,395,200	856,000	2,112,700	2,186,100	1,953,300	1,517,000	1,205,900
Shares Outstanding	337,298	331,780	326,202	320,493	315,439	312,500	256,608	250,200
Statistical Record								
Return on Assets %	0.69	4.95	4.15	N.M.	3.87	8.91	6.93	N.M.
Return on Equity %	2.65	22.98	15.02	N.M.	10.84	29.43	28.43	N.M.
EBITDA Margin %	6.65	13.41	12.43	5.41	10.60	15.42	14.47	10.42
Net Margin %	0.66	4.38	3.98	N.M.	3.27	6.77	5.37	N.M.
Asset Turnover	1.05	1.13	1.04	1.05	1.18	1.32	1.29	1.06
Current Ratio	1.20	1.10	0.89	0.95	0.96	1.09	1.09	1.12
Debt to Equity	0.60	0.75	0.87	0.35	0.25	0.49	0.73	1.19
Price Range	15.69-9.55	16.70-8.47	13.67-6.08	18.91-8.00	35.06-9.38	49.31-21.75	35.19-13.69	16.00-5.88
P/E Ratio	142.64-86.82	21.41-10.86	19.81-8.81	N/A	49.38-13.20	31.01-13.68	33.20-12.91	N/A

Address: Unisys Way, Blue Bell, PA 19424	**Web Site:** www.unisys.com	**Auditors:** Ernst & Young LLP
Telephone: (215) 986-4011	**Officers:** Lawrence A. Weinbach - Chmn., Pres., C.E.O. Jack A. Blaine - Exec. V.P., Pres., Worldwide Sales & Services	**Investor Contact:** 215-986-6999
Fax: (215) 986-6850		

UNITED AUTO GROUP INC.

Exchange	Symbol	Price	52Wk Range	Yield	P/E
NYS	UAG	$27.83 (3/31/2005)	32.29-23.10	1.58	11.36

*7 Year Price Score 140.12 *NYSE Composite Index=100 *12 Month Price Score 95.02

Interim Earnings (Per Share)

Qtr.	Mar	Jun	Sep	Dec
2001	0.21	0.40	0.38	0.31
2002	0.40	0.56	0.53	0.01
2003	0.34	0.58	0.61	0.48
2004	0.48	0.71	0.70	0.56

Interim Dividends (Per Share)

Amt	Decl	Ex	Rec	Pay
0.10Q	4/29/2004	5/6/2004	5/10/2004	6/1/2004
0.10Q	7/23/2004	8/5/2004	8/9/2004	9/1/2004
0.11Q	10/26/2004	11/8/2004	11/10/2004	12/1/2004
0.11Q	2/3/2005	2/8/2005	2/10/2005	3/1/2005

Indicated Div: $0.44

Valuation Analysis

Forecast P/E	11.98 (4/7/2005)	No of Institutions 101
Market Cap	$1.3 Billion	Shares 35,375,192
Book Value	1.1 Billion	% Held
Price/Book	1.20	76.02
Price/Sales	0.13	

Business Summary: Retail - Automotive (MIC: 5.7 SIC: 511 NAIC: 41110)

United Auto Group is the second largest automotive retailer in the U.S as measured by total revenue. As of Mar 31 2004, Co. owned and operated 137 franchises in the U.S. and 83 franchises internationally, primarily in the U.K. Co. offers a full range of vehicle brands with the majority of its combined sales generated by foreign brands such as Toyota, Honda, BMW, Lexus and Mercedes. In addition to selling new and used vehicles, Co. generates sales at each of its dealerships through maintenance and repair services and the sale of higher margin products, such as third-party finance and insurance products and extended-service contracts and replacement and aftermarket automotive products.

Recent Developments: For the year ended Dec 31 2004, income from continuing operations increased 30.2% to $112,551 thousand from income of $86,423 thousand a year earlier. Net income increased 34.7% to $111,687 thousand from net income of $82,929 thousand a year earlier. Revenues were $9,886,211 thousand, up 17.8% from $8,389,185 thousand the year before. Operating income was $263,705 thousand versus an income of $232,143 thousand in the prior year, an increase of 13.6%. Total direct expense was $8,436,153 thousand versus $7,171,332 thousand in the prior year, an increase of 17.6%. Total indirect expense was $1,186,353 thousand versus $985,710 thousand in the prior year, an increase of 20.4%.

Prospects: Co.'s results are being positively affected by strong same-store revenue growth for parts revenue, driven by increases in units in operation and capacity increases at many locations. Same-store revenues are also increasing in new and used vehicle sales and finance and insurance revenues. In 2005, Co. expects the overall retail market to remain competitive. With its brand mix and service capacity expansion, Co. estimates same-store growth to be about 3.0% to 5.0% in 2005. Co. also expects between $300.0 million and $500.0 million of revenues from selective acquisitions. Earnings for 2005 are expected to be in the range of $2.32 to $2.39 per share.

Financial Data (US$ in Thousands)	12/31/2004	12/31/2003	12/31/2002	12/31/2001	12/31/2000	12/31/1999	12/31/1998	12/31/1997
Earnings Per Share	2.45	2.00	1.51	1.31	1.02	1.04	(0.04)	(0.54)
Cash Flow Per Share	4.25	4.43	2.19	3.13	2.30	1.86	2.70	(0.09)
Dividends Per Share	0.410	0.100	...	...	...	...	...	...
Dividend Payout %	16.73	5.00	...	...	...	...	...	...
Income Statement								
Total Revenue	9,886,211	8,671,485	7,434,866	6,220,663	4,883,989	4,022,517	3,343,147	2,089,763
EBITDA	320,148	264,904	202,284	191,480	162,427	125,997	73,120	9,252
Depn & Amortn	44,974	33,078	22,304	33,625	24,174	19,131	16,464	9,680
Income Before Taxes	182,478	145,452	105,796	80,635	61,070	48,846	25,194	(15,513)
Income Taxes	67,880	57,456	42,617	35,075	26,558	21,414	11,554	(5,511)
Net Income	111,687	82,929	62,241	44,745	30,031	27,488	(797)	(10,140)
Average Shares	45,613	41,434	41,161	34,196	29,415	26,526	20,932	18,607
Balance Sheet								
Current Assets	1,764,136	1,588,665	1,328,748	921,516	951,616	679,332	590,713	531,779
Total Assets	3,532,801	3,137,181	2,690,314	1,946,576	1,762,695	1,279,337	1,184,194	975,662
Current Liabilities	1,691,708	1,497,304	1,199,475	786,278	858,562	582,290	505,529	426,632
Long-Term Obligations	574,970	643,343	651,256	551,840	377,721	218,535	288,265	239,166
Total Liabilities	2,457,766	2,308,769	1,985,872	1,430,893	1,301,025	848,472	842,544	674,718
Stockholders' Equity	1,075,035	828,412	704,442	515,683	461,670	430,865	341,650	300,557
Shares Outstanding	46,483	41,722	40,598	19,719	18,556	21,321	19,690	18,293
Statistical Record								
Return on Assets %	3.34	2.85	2.68	2.41	1.97	2.23	N.M.	N.M.
Return on Equity %	11.70	10.82	10.20	9.16	6.71	7.12	N.M.	N.M.
EBITDA Margin %	3.24	3.05	2.72	3.08	3.33	3.13	2.19	0.44
Net Margin %	1.13	0.96	0.84	0.72	0.61	0.68	N.M.	N.M.
Asset Turnover	2.96	2.98	3.21	3.35	3.20	3.27	3.10	2.79
Current Ratio	1.04	1.06	1.11	1.17	1.11	1.17	1.17	1.25
Debt to Equity	0.53	0.78	0.92	1.07	0.82	0.51	0.84	0.80
Price Range	32.29-23.10	31.31-9.88	31.13-11.41	26.20-6.63	10.38-6.13	13.19-5.81	26.31-8.88	31.38-14.00
P/E Ratio	13.18-9.43	15.65-4.94	20.62-7.56	20.00-5.06	10.17-6.00	12.68-5.59	N/A	N/A
Average Yield %	1.46	0.50	N/A	N/A	N/A	N/A	N/A	N/A

Address: 2555 Telegraph Road, Bloomfield Hills, MI 48302-0954 Telephone: (248) 648-2500	Web Site: Officers: Roger S. Penske - Chmn., C.E.O. Samuel X. DiFeo - Pres., C.O.O.	Auditors: Deloitte & Touche LLP Investor Contact: 313-592-5266

UNITED DEFENSE INDUSTRIES INC

Exchange	Symbol	Price	52Wk Range	Yield	P/E
NYS	UDI	$73.42 (3/31/2005)	73.52-31.79	N/A	23.31

*7 Year Price Score N/A   *NYSE Composite Index=100   *12 Month Price Score 128.82

Interim Earnings (Per Share)

Qtr.	Mar	Jun	Sep	Dec
2001	0.12	0.37	(0.42)	0.13
2002	0.36	0.52	0.85	0.82
2003	0.73	0.68	0.71	0.54
2004	0.78	0.77	0.99	0.61

Interim Dividends (Per Share)

No Dividends Paid

Valuation Analysis

Forecast P/E	N/A	No of Institutions
		148
Market Cap	$3.7 Billion	Shares
Book Value	226.1 Million	47,207,744
Price/Book	16.43	% Held
Price/Sales	1.62	92.95

TRADING VOLUME (thousand shares)

1996 1997 1998 1999 2000 2001 2002 2003 2004 2005

Business Summary: Defense (MIC: 1.2 SIC: 795 NAIC: 36992)

United Defense Industries is engaged in the design, development, and production of combat vehicles, artillery systems, naval guns, and missile launchers used by the U.S. Department of Defense and allied militaries throughout the world. Co. is organized into two separate product and service lines which are each considered separate reportable segments: Defense Systems and Ship Repair and Maintenance. Co.'s Defense Systems program portfolio consists of a mix of weapons system development, production, upgrade, and life cycle support programs. Co.'s Ship Repair and Maintenance business segment consists of ship repair, maintenance, and modernization service programs.

Recent Developments: For the year ended Dec 31 2003, net income increased 4.5% to $140,648 thousand from net income of $134,576 thousand a year earlier. Revenues were $2,052,591 thousand, up 19.0% from $1,725,346 thousand the year before. Operating income was $219,610 thousand versus an income of $166,251 thousand in the prior year, an increase of 32.1%. Total direct expense was $1,639,706 thousand versus $1,388,616 thousand in the prior year, an increase of 18.1%. Total indirect expense was $193,275 thousand versus $170,479 thousand in the prior year, an increase of 13.4%.

Prospects: On Mar 7 2005, Co. announced that it has entered into a definitive agreement to be acquired by BAE Systems North America Inc., the U.S. subsidiary of BAE Systems plc, for approximately $4.20 billion in cash, including the assumption of Co.'s $217.7 million of net debt at Dec 31 2004. The transaction is expected to be completed during the second quarter of 2005, subject to shareholder and regulatory approvals. Meanwhile, results are benefiting from higher intelligent munitions development and production work at Co.'s Swedish subsidiary, along with initial deliveries of surrogate training vehicles and increased recovery vehicle kit deliveries to Egypt.

Financial Data

(US$ in Thousands)	12/31/2004	12/31/2003	12/31/2002	12/31/2001	12/31/2000	12/31/1999	12/31/1998
Earnings Per Share	3.15	2.66	2.55	0.20	...	...	...
Cash Flow Per Share	4.55	4.31	3.49	2.19	...	...	...
Income Statement							
Total Revenue	2,292,355	2,052,591	1,725,346	1,318,538	1,183,886	1,213,526	1,217,555
EBITDA	332,727	282,518	216,004	138,823	148,522	177,338	111,961
Depn & Amortn	39,855	43,150	35,879	73,196	96,444	135,845	177,959
Income Before Taxes	271,116	215,249	151,435	42,922	26,965	4,478	(116,757)
Income Taxes	105,003	74,601	15,159	5,900	6,000	2,937	3,250
Net Income	166,113	140,648	134,576	8,776	21,645	1,541	(120,007)
Average Shares	52,790	52,943	52,797	43,204	...	...	...
Balance Sheet							
Current Assets	869,204	864,876	739,051	551,495	495,383	410,329	...
Total Assets	1,601,574	1,591,164	1,453,970	912,292	918,094	873,998	...
Current Liabilities	772,735	789,092	765,983	606,158	555,765	482,130	...
Long-Term Obligations	472,904	524,946	576,989	422,593	246,491	326,757	...
Total Liabilities	1,375,458	1,464,083	1,483,675	1,078,658	872,199	849,637	...
Stockholders' Equity	226,116	127,081	(29,705)	(166,366)	45,895	24,361	...
Shares Outstanding	50,611	51,695	50,915	40,582	18,036	18,042	...
Statistical Record							
Return on Assets %	10.38	9.24	9.26	9.62	2.41	0.18	...
Return on Equity %	93.81	288.88	N.M.	N.M.	61.45	6.33	...
EBITDA Margin %	14.51	13.76	12.52	10.53	12.55	14.61	9.20
Net Margin %	7.25	6.85	7.80	0.67	1.83	0.13	N.M.
Asset Turnover	1.43	1.35	1.19	1.45	1.32	1.39	...
Current Ratio	1.12	1.10	0.96	0.91	0.89	0.85	...
Debt to Equity	2.09	4.13	N.M.	N.M.	5.37	13.41	...
Price Range	48.94-29.00	33.90-20.23	28.94-19.09	21.70-19.27	...	...	...
P/E Ratio	15.54-9.21	12.74-7.61	11.35-7.49	108.50-96.35	...	...	...

Address: 1525 Wilson Boulevard, Suite 700, Arlington, VA 22209-2411 **Telephone:** (703) 312-6100	**Web Site:** www.uniteddefense.com **Officers:** William E. Conway Jr. - Chmn. Thomas W. Rabaut - Pres., C.E.O.	**Auditors:** Ernst & Young LLP

UNITED DOMINION REALTY TRUST, INC.

*7 Year Price Score 122.99 *NYSE Composite Index=100 *12 Month Price Score 97.88

Interim Earnings (Per Share)

Qtr.	Mar	Jun	Sep	Dec
2001	(0.03)	0.20	0.07	0.04
2002	(0.08)	0.19	0.13	0.00
2003	0.06	0.02	0.01	0.12
2004	0.07	0.17	0.17	0.16

Interim Dividends (Per Share)

Amt	Decl	Ex	Rec	Pay
0.292Q	5/11/2004	7/14/2004	7/16/2004	8/2/2004
0.292Q	9/24/2004	10/13/2004	10/15/2004	11/1/2004
0.292Q	12/9/2004	1/12/2005	1/14/2005	1/31/2005
0.30Q	3/17/2005	4/13/2005	4/15/2005	5/2/2005

Indicated Div: $1.20 (Div. Reinv. Plan)

Valuation Analysis

Forecast P/E	12.94 (4/7/2005)	No of Institutions	219
Market Cap	$2.8 Billion	Shares	91,060,864
Book Value	1.2 Billion	% Held	66.46
Price/Book	2.38		
Price/Sales	4.69		

TRADING VOLUME (thousand shares)

Business Summary: Property, Real Estate & Development (MIC: 8.3 SIC: 798 NAIC: 25930)

United Dominion Realty Trust is a self-administered real estate investment trust that owns, develops, acquires, renovates, and manages middle-market apartment communities nationwide. At Dec 31 2003, Co.'s apartment portfolio included 264 communities located in 55 markets, with a total of 76,244 completed apartment homes. In addition, Co. had three apartment communities under development. Co. focuses on the broad middle-market segment of the apartment that generally consists of young professionals, blue-collar families, single parent households, older singles, immigrants, non-related parties and families renting while waiting to purchase a home.

Recent Developments: For the year ended Dec 31 2004, income from continuing operations decreased 4.6% to $31,821 thousand from income of $33,349 thousand a year earlier. The decline in earnings was mostly attributed to a $17.2 million increase in depreciation and amortization expense, and a $6.6 million increase in interest expense. Results excluded income from discontinued operations of $65.3 million in 2004 and $37.1 million in2003. Results included a hurricane related expense of $5.5 million in 2004 and an impairment loss on investments of $1.4 million in 2003. Rental income advanced 11.3% to $604.3 million from $542.9 million a year earlier. Non-property income was $2.6 million versus $1.1 million in 2003.

Prospects: During the fourth quarter ended Dec 31 2004, Co. acquired 11 communities with 3,761 apartment homes for a total purchase price of $529.0 million. Also during the fourth quarter of 2004, Co. announced community sales totaling $112.0 million. Co. further noted that it is under contract to sell 11 communities in Houston, Anaheim and Phoenix consisting of 2,623 units for $169.0 million. As a results of these transactions, Co. expects approximately 50.0% of its projected 2005 net operating income to emanate from California, Florida and the Metro D.C. area. Consequently, Co.'s full-year 2005 guidance for diluted funds for operation (FFO) is $1.57 to $1.70 per share.

Financial Data
(US$ in Thousands)

	12/31/2004	12/31/2003	12/31/2002	12/31/2001	12/31/2000	12/31/1999	12/31/1998	12/31/1997
Earnings Per Share	0.56	0.21	0.24	0.27	0.41	0.54	0.49	0.60
Cash Flow Per Share	1.96	2.05	2.14	2.24	2.17	1.84	1.53	1.58
Tang Book Value Per Share	7.43	7.28	6.48	7.10	7.91	8.59	9.11	9.01
Dividends Per Share	1.163	1.133	1.103	1.077	1.067	1.058	1.040	0.757
Dividend Payout %	207.59	539.29	459.38	399.07	260.37	195.83	212.24	126.25
Income Statement								
Property Income	604,270	603,367	594,314	618,590	616,825	618,749	478,718	386,672
Non-Property Income	2,608	1,068	1,806	4,593	5,326	1,942	3,382	1,123
Total Revenue	606,878	604,435	596,120	623,183	622,151	620,691	482,100	387,795
Depn & Amortn	191,294	172,785	168,584	156,292	159,912	131,336	105,294	80,478
Interest Expense	124,087	117,185	130,956	144,379	156,040	153,748	106,238	79,004
Net Income	97,152	70,404	53,229	61,828	76,615	93,622	72,332	70,149
Average Shares	129,080	115,648	106,952	101,037	103,208	103,639	100,062	87,339
Balance Sheet								
Total Assets	4,332,001	3,543,643	3,276,136	3,348,091	3,453,957	3,688,317	3,762,940	2,313,725
Long-Term Obligations	2,879,982	2,132,037	2,057,640	2,064,197	1,992,330	2,127,305	2,117,749	1,156,226
Total Liabilities	3,052,957	2,286,001	2,205,649	2,229,701	2,146,739	2,283,938	2,273,377	1,240,675
Stockholders' Equity	1,195,451	1,163,436	1,001,271	1,042,725	1,218,892	1,310,212	1,374,121	1,058,357
Shares Outstanding	136,429	127,295	106,605	103,133	102,219	102,740	103,639	89,168
Statistical Record								
Return on Assets %	2.46	2.06	1.61	1.82	2.14	2.51	2.38	3.28
Return on Equity %	8.21	6.50	5.21	5.47	6.04	6.98	5.95	7.35
Net Margin %	16.01	11.65	8.93	9.92	12.31	15.08	15.00	18.09
Price Range	24.80-17.52	19.37-15.22	16.70-13.95	14.72-10.75	11.75-9.44	11.94-9.25	14.75-10.06	15.88-13.50
P/E Ratio	44.29-31.29	92.24-72.48	69.58-58.13	54.52-39.81	28.66-23.02	22.11-17.13	30.10-20.54	26.46-22.50
Average Yield %	5.80	6.53	7.18	8.10	10.22	9.86	8.11	5.18

Address: 400 East Cary St., Richmond, VA 23219 Telephone: (720) 283-6120	Web Site: Officers: Robert C. Larson - Chmn. James D. Klingbeil - Vice-Chmn.	Auditors: Ernst & Young LLP Transfer Agents: ChaseMellon Shareholder Services, LLC, Pittsburgh, PA

UNITED PARCEL SERVICE, INC.

Exchange	Symbol	Price	52Wk Range	Yield	P/E
NYS	UPS	$72.74 (3/31/2005)	87.53-68.96	1.81	24.83

*7 Year Price Score N/A   *NYSE Composite Index=100   *12 Month Price Score 93.02

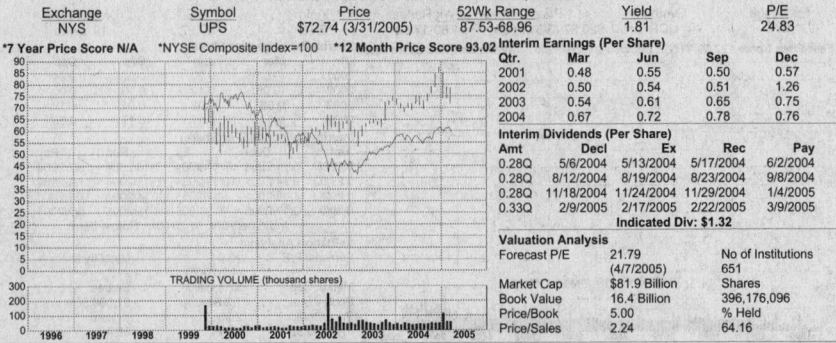

Interim Earnings (Per Share)

Qtr.	Mar	Jun	Sep	Dec
2001	0.48	0.55	0.50	0.57
2002	0.50	0.54	0.51	1.26
2003	0.54	0.61	0.65	0.75
2004	0.67	0.72	0.78	0.76

Interim Dividends (Per Share)

Amt	Decl	Ex	Rec	Pay
0.28Q	5/6/2004	5/13/2004	5/17/2004	6/2/2004
0.28Q	8/12/2004	8/19/2004	8/23/2004	9/8/2004
0.28Q	11/18/2004	11/24/2004	11/29/2004	1/4/2005
0.33Q	2/9/2005	2/17/2005	2/22/2005	3/9/2005
		Indicated Div: $1.32		

Valuation Analysis

Forecast P/E	21.79	No of Institutions	
	(4/7/2005)	651	
Market Cap	$81.9 Billion	Shares	
Book Value	16.4 Billion	396,176,096	
Price/Book	5.00	% Held	
Price/Sales	2.24	64.16	

Business Summary: Road Transport (MIC: 15.2 SIC: 215 NAIC: 92110)

United Parcel Service provides the time-definite delivery service of packages and documents for 1.8 million shipping customers per day throughout the United States and in over 200 other countries and territories. As of Dec 31 2003, Co. operated a ground fleet of more than 88,000 vehicles and almost 600 airplanes. In addition, Co. provides logistics services, including integrated supply chain management, for major companies worldwide. Co. is also an industry provider in the delivery of goods purchased over the Internet. For the year ended Dec 31 2003, the UPS airline delivered 3.44 billion packages, or an average 13.6 million packages per day.

Recent Developments: For the year ended Dec 31 2004, net income increased 15.0% to $3,333 million from net income of $2,898 million a year earlier. Revenues were $36,582 million, up 9.2% from $33,485 million the year before. Operating income was $4,989 million versus an income of $4,445 million in the prior year, an increase of 12.2%. Total direct expense was $4,480 million versus $3,833 million in the prior year, an increase of 16.9%. Total indirect expense was $27,113 million versus $25,207 million in the prior year, an increase of 7.6%.

Prospects: Co. is anticipating solid growth in 2005. In particular, Co.'s international segment should continue its performance with strong export volume growth. U.S. domestic volume should grow 2.0% to 3.0% for the year with improving operating margins. Furthermore, UPS Supply Chain Solutions should add more than $1.00 billion in revenue as a result of the acquisition of Menlo Worldwide Forwarding, which should be slightly accretive to earnings this year. Moreover, Co. expects total earnings per share for 2005 will grow 13.0% to 17.0% over the adjusted $2.90 reported for 2004 and will continue to generate substantial positive cash flow.

Financial Data

(US$ in Thousands)	12/31/2004	12/31/2003	12/31/2002	12/31/2001	12/31/2000	12/31/1999	12/31/1998	12/31/1997
Earnings Per Share	2.93	2.55	2.81	2.10	2.50	0.77	1.57	0.81
Cash Flow Per Share	4.71	4.12	5.02	3.46	2.37	1.98	2.62	4.78
Tang Book Value Per Share	12.84	12.05	11.10	9.15	8.58	10.50	6.42	5.42
Dividends Per Share	1.120	0.920	0.760	0.760	0.680	0.300	...	...
Dividend Payout %	38.23	36.08	27.05	36.19	27.20	38.96	...	...
Income Statement								
Total Revenue	36,582,000	33,485,000	31,272,000	30,646,000	29,771,000	27,052,000	24,788,000	22,458,000
EBITDA	6,614,000	6,040,000	6,646,000	5,517,000	6,212,000	3,455,000	4,241,000	2,803,000
Depn & Amortn	1,543,000	1,549,000	1,464,000	1,396,000	1,173,000	1,139,000	1,112,000	1,063,000
Income Before Taxes	4,922,000	4,370,000	5,009,000	3,937,000	4,834,000	2,088,000	2,902,000	1,553,000
Income Taxes	1,589,000	1,472,000	1,755,000	1,512,000	1,900,000	1,205,000	1,161,000	644,000
Net Income	3,333,000	2,898,000	3,182,000	2,399,000	2,934,000	883,000	1,741,000	909,000
Average Shares	1,137,000	1,138,000	1,134,000	1,144,000	1,175,000	1,141,000	1,108,000	1,116,000
Balance Sheet								
Total Assets	33,026,000	28,909,000	26,357,000	24,636,000	21,662,000	23,043,000	17,067,000	15,912,000
Long-Term Obligations	3,261,000	3,149,000	3,495,000	4,648,000	2,981,000	1,912,000	2,191,000	2,583,000
Total Liabilities	16,642,000	14,057,000	13,902,000	14,388,000	11,927,000	10,569,000	9,894,000	9,825,000
Stockholders' Equity	16,384,000	14,852,000	12,455,000	10,248,000	9,735,000	12,474,000	7,173,000	6,087,000
Shares Outstanding	1,126,000	1,127,000	1,122,000	1,120,508	1,134,693	1,187,484	1,118,000	1,124,000
Statistical Record								
Return on Assets %	10.73	10.49	12.48	10.36	13.09	4.40	10.56	5.71
Return on Equity %	21.28	21.23	28.03	24.01	26.35	8.99	26.26	14.93
EBITDA Margin %	18.08	18.04	21.25	18.00	20.87	12.77	17.11	12.48
Net Margin %	9.11	8.65	10.18	7.83	9.86	3.26	7.02	4.05
Asset Turnover	1.18	1.21	1.23	1.32	1.33	1.35	1.50	1.41
Price Range	87.53-67.98	74.81-53.18	67.00-54.46	61.90-47.95	69.06-50.63	75.00-63.13	...	...
P/E Ratio	29.87-23.20	29.34-20.85	23.84-19.38	29.48-22.83	27.63-20.25	97.40-81.98	...	...
Average Yield %	1.51	1.44	1.24	1.35	1.15	0.45	...	...

Address: 55 Glenlake Parkway, NE, Atlanta, GA 30328	Web Site: www.ups.com	Auditors: DELOITTE & TOUCHE LLP
Telephone: (404) 828-6000	Officers: Michael L. Eskew - Chmn., C.E.O. D. Scott Davis - Sr. V.P., C.F.O., Treas.	Investor Contact: 404-828-6977
Fax: (404) 828-6562		

UNITED RENTALS, INC.

Exchange	Symbol	Price	52Wk Range	Yield	P/E
NYS	URI	$20.21 (3/31/2005)	21.55-14.30	N/A	N/A

*7 Year Price Score 74.98 *NYSE Composite Index=100 *12 Month Price Score 102.28

Interim Earnings (Per Share)

Qtr.	Mar	Jun	Sep	Dec
2001	0.04	0.14	0.63	0.34
2002	(2.88)	0.51	0.43	(3.31)
2003	(0.11)	0.25	0.34	(3.85)
2004	(1.38)	0.36	(0.83)	...

Interim Dividends (Per Share)

No Dividends Paid

Valuation Analysis

Forecast P/E	17.01	No of Institutions
	(4/7/2005)	161
Market Cap	$1.6 Billion	Shares
Book Value	1.0 Billion	64,102,792
Price/Book	1.49	% Held
Price/Sales	0.54	82.35

Business Summary: General Construction Supplies & Services (MIC: 3.3 SIC: 359 NAIC: 32412)

United Rentals, through its subsidiaries, is an equipment rental company. Co. offers for rent over 600 types of equipment through its network of over 730 rental locations in the U.S., Canada and Mexico. Co.'s customers include construction and industrial companies, manufacturers, utilities, municipalities, and homeowners. Co.'s fleet of rental equipment, which includes over 500,000 units, consists of general construction and industrial equipment, aerial work platforms, general tools and light equipment, and trench safety equipment. Also, Co. sells used rental equipment, acts a dealer for new equipment and sells related merchandise and contractor supplies, parts and service.

Recent Developments: For the quarter ended Sep 30 2004, Co. reported a net loss of $64,381 thousand versus net income of $31,884 thousand in the year-earlier quarter. Revenues were $849,718 thousand, up 5.5% from $805,134 thousand the year before. Operating loss was $5,873 thousand versus an operating income of $113,406 thousand in the prior-year quarter. Total direct expense was $572,100 thousand versus $546,575 thousand in the prior-year quarter, an increase of 4.7%. Total indirect expense was $144,185 thousand versus $145,153 thousand in the prior-year quarter, a decrease of 0.7%.

Prospects: Despite ongoing weakness in its traffic control division, Co. is optimistic about its prospects for 2005 due in large part to continuing good growth in its general rentals business. Co.'s 2005 outlook is for total revenues of $3.40 billion, and assumes 11.0% revenue growth in the general rentals segment, partially offset by a continued decline in its traffic control segment. Growth in general rentals is expected to be driven by continuing rate initiatives, targeted for at least a 5.0% increase in rental rates, the expansion of Co.'s rental fleet, the planned opening of 30 to 35 new locations and increased contractor supplies revenues.

Financial Data

(US$ in Thousands)	3 Mos	12/31/2003	12/31/2002	12/31/2001	12/31/2000	12/31/1999	12/31/1998	12/31/1997
Earnings Per Share	(4.64)	(3.35)	(5.25)	1.18	1.89	1.53	0.18	...
Cash Flow Per Share	5.97	4.45	6.83	9.66	7.19	5.91	3.26	0.04
Tang Book Value Per Share	N.M.	N.M.	N.M.	N.M.	N.M.	N.M.	N.M.	4.49
Income Statement								
Total Revenue	644,713	2,867,236	2,820,989	2,886,605	2,918,861	2,233,628	1,220,282	10,633
EBITDA	(36,057)	311,132	490,870	870,015	944,707	725,143	354,765	1,809
Depn & Amortn	91,958	428,325	396,293	433,902	414,432	343,508	212,311	1,301
Income Before Taxes	(177,584)	(326,521)	(101,384)	214,550	301,496	241,807	78,297	54
Income Taxes	(70,981)	(67,940)	8,102	91,977	125,121	99,141	43,499	21
Net Income	(106,603)	(258,581)	(397,825)	111,256	176,375	142,666	13,461	34
Average Shares	77,285	96,145	96,730	94,387	99,253	93,035	73,075	26,496
Balance Sheet								
Current Assets	815,996	2,874,506	2,554,193	2,443,762	2,474,686	2,329,459	1,527,087	116,304
Total Assets	4,819,297	4,722,141	4,690,557	5,061,516	5,123,933	4,497,738	2,634,663	169,110
Current Liabilities	239,994	377,576	207,038	204,773	260,155	242,946	121,940	5,698
Long-Term Obligations	3,227,739	3,038,638	2,512,798	2,459,522	2,675,367	2,266,148	1,314,574	1,074
Total Liabilities	3,772,804	3,581,266	3,132,502	3,136,006	3,277,990	2,800,252	1,608,433	11,380
Stockholders' Equity	1,046,493	1,140,875	1,331,505	1,625,510	1,545,943	1,397,486	726,230	157,730
Shares Outstanding	77,349	77,150	76,657	73,361	71,065	72,051	68,427	23,899
Statistical Record								
Return on Assets %	N.M.	N.M.	N.M.	2.18	3.66	4.00	0.96	0.02
Return on Equity %	N.M.	N.M.	N.M.	7.02	11.95	13.44	3.05	0.02
EBITDA Margin %	N.M.	10.85	17.40	30.14	32.37	32.46	29.07	17.01
Net Margin %	N.M.	N.M.	N.M.	3.85	6.04	6.39	1.10	0.32
Asset Turnover	0.61	0.61	0.58	0.57	0.61	0.63	0.87	0.63
Current Ratio	3.40	7.61	12.34	11.93	9.51	9.59	12.52	20.41
Debt to Equity	3.08	2.66	1.89	1.51	1.73	1.62	1.81	0.01
Price Range	23.20-9.37	19.85-8.29	30.54-6.04	26.25-13.19	24.31-12.00	35.25-14.69	48.00-12.44	19.31-15.00
P/E Ratio	N/A	N/A	N/A	22.25-11.18	12.86-6.35	23.04-9.60	266.67-69.10	...

Address: Five Greenwich Office Park,	Web Site: www.unitedrentals.com	Auditors: Ernst & Young LLP
Greenwich, CT 06830	Officers: Bradley S. Jacobs - Chmn. Wayland R.	Investor Contact: 203-622-3131
Telephone: (203) 622-3131	Hicks - C.E.O.	
Fax: (203) 622-6080		

UNITED STATES STEEL CORP.

Exchange	Symbol	Price	52Wk Range	Yield	P/E
NYS	X	$50.85 (3/31/2005)	63.12-25.78	0.63	6.00

*7 Year Price Score 146.15 *NYSE Composite Index=100 *12 Month Price Score 126.58

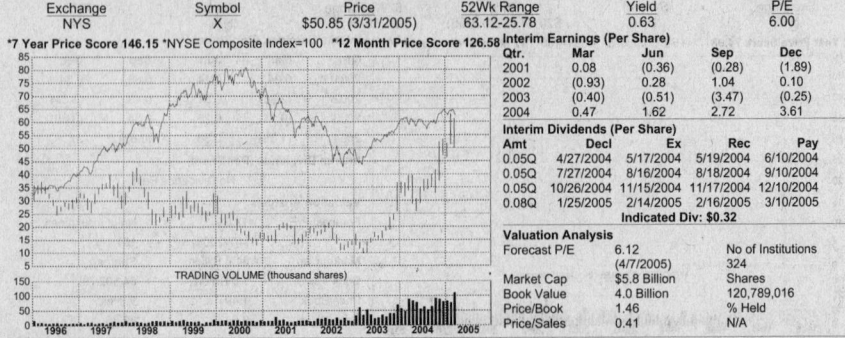

Interim Earnings (Per Share)

Qtr.	Mar	Jun	Sep	Dec
2001	0.08	(0.36)	(0.28)	(1.89)
2002	(0.93)	0.28	1.04	0.10
2003	(0.40)	(0.51)	(3.47)	(0.25)
2004	0.47	1.62	2.72	3.61

Interim Dividends (Per Share)

Amt	Decl	Ex	Rec	Pay
0.05Q	4/27/2004	5/17/2004	5/19/2004	6/10/2004
0.05Q	7/27/2004	8/16/2004	8/18/2004	9/10/2004
0.05Q	10/26/2004	11/15/2004	11/17/2004	12/10/2004
0.08Q	1/25/2005	2/14/2005	2/16/2005	3/10/2005
		Indicated Div: $0.32		

Valuation Analysis

Forecast P/E	6.12	No of Institutions	
	(4/7/2005)	324	
Market Cap	$5.8 Billion	Shares	
Book Value	4.0 Billion	120,789,016	
Price/Book	1.46	% Held	
Price/Sales	0.41	N/A	

Business Summary: Oil and Gas (MIC: 14.2 SIC: 911 NAIC: 24110)

United States Steel is an integrated steel producer with major production operations in the U.S. and Central Europe. Co. has domestic annual raw steel production capability of 19.4 million tons and Central European annual raw steel production capability of 7.4 million tons. Also, Co. is engaged in the production of iron-bearing taconite pellets in the U.S. and coke in both the U.S. and Central Europe; transportation services, railroad and barge operations; real estate operations and engineering and consulting services. Co.'s five reportable operating segments include Flat-rolled Products, U. S. Steel Europe, Tubular Products, Real Estate and Straightline.

Recent Developments: For the year ended Dec 31 2004, net income was $1,091 million versus net loss of $463 million a year earlier. Revenues were $14,108 million, up 49.2% from $9,458 million the year before. Operating income was $1,580 million versus a loss of $730 million in the prior year. Total direct expense was $11,407 million versus $8,469 million in the prior year, an increase of 34.7%. Total indirect expense was $1,121 million versus $1,719 million in the prior year, a decrease of 34.8%.

Prospects: On Feb 22 2005, Co. announced that it will build a new hot dip galvanizing facility at its steelmaking operation in Slovakia, USSK, for $160.0 million with start-up expected in early 2007. With an annual capability of about 350,000 metric tons, the facility will serve the growing demand for coated steels in the Central European automotive and construction industries. Separately, capital expenditures for 2005 are expected to total approximately $755.0 million, reflecting domestic spending of approximately $475.0 million and European spending of approximately $280.0 million. Domestic expenditures include the rebuild of the Gary No. 13 blast furnace, scheduled for the third quarter.

Financial Data

(US$ in Thousands)	12/31/2004	12/31/2003	12/31/2002	12/31/2001	12/31/2000	12/31/1999	12/31/1998	12/31/1997
Earnings Per Share	8.48	(4.64)	0.62	(2.45)	(0.33)	0.40	3.92	4.88
Cash Flow Per Share	12.48	5.59	2.86	7.50	(7.06)	(0.91)	4.28	...
Tang Book Value Per Share	32.60	3.76	15.74	28.09	21.60	23.23	24.02	20.45
Dividends Per Share	0.200	0.200	0.200	0.100	1.000	1.000	1.000	1.000
Dividend Payout %	2.36	N.M.	32.26	N.M.	N.M.	250.00	25.51	20.49
Income Statement								
Total Revenue	14,108,000	9,458,000	7,054,000	6,375,000	6,132,000	5,314,000	6,283,000	6,941,000
EBITDA	1,975,000	(357,000)	482,000	(30,000)	441,000	418,000	849,000	1,035,000
Depn & Amortn	382,000	363,000	350,000	344,000	360,000	304,000	283,000	303,000
Income Before Taxes	1,461,000	(860,000)	13,000	(546,000)	(1,000)	76,000	537,000	686,000
Income Taxes	351,000	(454,000)	(48,000)	(328,000)	20,000	25,000	173,000	234,000
Net Income	1,091,000	(463,000)	61,000	(218,000)	(21,000)	44,000	364,000	452,000
Average Shares	128,643	103,179	97,428	89,200	88,613	88,396	87,000	94,000
Balance Sheet								
Current Assets	4,243,000	3,107,000	2,440,000	2,073,000	2,717,000	1,981,000	1,275,000	1,531,000
Total Assets	10,956,000	7,838,000	7,977,000	8,337,000	8,711,000	7,525,000	6,693,000	6,694,000
Current Liabilities	2,531,000	2,130,000	1,372,000	1,259,000	1,391,000	1,266,000	1,016,000	1,334,000
Long-Term Obligations	1,363,000	1,890,000	1,408,000	1,434,000	2,236,000	902,000	464,000	456,000
Total Liabilities	6,958,000	6,745,000	5,950,000	5,831,000	6,792,000	5,469,000	4,600,000	4,912,000
Stockholders' Equity	3,970,000	1,093,000	2,027,000	2,506,000	1,919,000	2,056,000	2,093,000	1,782,000
Shares Outstanding	114,003	103,663	102,485	89,197	88,767	88,392	87,000	87,000
Statistical Record								
Return on Assets %	11.58	N.M.	0.75	N.M.	N.M.	0.62	5.44	6.75
Return on Equity %	42.98	N.M.	2.69	N.M.	N.M.	2.12	18.79	25.36
EBITDA Margin %	14.00	N.M.	6.83	N.M.	7.19	7.87	13.51	14.91
Net Margin %	7.73	N.M.	0.86	N.M.	N.M.	0.83	5.79	6.51
Asset Turnover	1.50	1.20	0.86	0.75	0.75	0.75	0.94	1.04
Current Ratio	1.68	1.46	1.78	1.65	1.95	1.56	1.25	1.15
Debt to Equity	0.34	1.73	0.69	0.57	1.17	0.44	0.22	0.26
Price Range	53.43-25.78	36.83-9.83	21.71-10.92	21.74-13.36	33.00-12.94	33.88-22.19	42.75-20.75	40.06-25.50
P/E Ratio	6.30-3.04	N/A	35.02-17.61	N/A	N/A	84.69-55.47	10.91-5.29	8.21-5.23
Average Yield %	0.54	1.15	1.23	0.58	4.94	3.73	3.31	3.06

Address: 600 Grant Street, Pittsburgh, PA 15219-2800	**Web Site:** www.ussteel.com	**Auditors:** PricewaterhouseCoopers LLP
Telephone: (412) 433-1121	**Officers:** Thomas J. Usher - Chmn. Dan D. Sandman - Vice-Chmn., Chief Legal & Admin. Officer, Sec., Gen.	**Investor Contact:** 412-433-1139
Fax: (412) 433-4818	Couns.	

UNITEDHEALTH GROUP INC

Exchange	Symbol	Price	52Wk Range	Yield	P/E
NYS	UNH	$95.38 (3/31/2005)	95.71-60.08	0.03	24.21

*7 Year Price Score 174.30 *NYSE Composite Index=100 ***12 Month Price Score 114.25**

Interim Earnings (Per Share)

Qtr.	Mar	Jun	Sep	Dec
2001	0.32	0.34	0.35	0.38
2002	0.46	0.51	0.56	0.60
2003	0.65	0.71	0.77	0.83
2004	0.88	0.93	1.04	1.09

Interim Dividends (Per Share)

Amt	Decl	Ex	Rec	Pay
0.015A	2/14/2002	3/27/2002	4/1/2002	4/17/2002
0.015A	2/12/2003	3/28/2003	4/1/2003	4/17/2003
100%	5/8/2003	6/19/2003	6/2/2003	6/18/2003
0.03A	2/2/2005	3/30/2005	4/1/2005	4/18/2005

Indicated Div: $0.03

Valuation Analysis

Forecast P/E	20.37	No of Institutions	
	(4/7/2005)	640	
Market Cap	$61.3 Billion	Shares	
Book Value	10.7 Billion	562,032,640	
Price/Book	5.72	% Held	
Price/Sales	1.65	87.62	

TRADING VOLUME (thousand shares)

Business Summary: Insurance (MIC: 8.2 SIC: 324 NAIC: 24114)

UnitedHealth Group is a diversified health and well-being company. Co.'s Uniprise segment delivers health care and well-being services nationwide to large national employers, individual consumers and other health care organizations. Co.'s Health Care Services segment includes its UnitedHealthcare, Ovations and AmeriChoice businesses. Co.'s Specialized Care Services companies offer specialty health and wellness and ancillary benefits, services and resources to specific customer markets nationwide. Ingenix offers database and data management services, software products, publications, consulting services, outsourced services and pharmaceutical services on a nationwide and international basis.

Recent Developments: For the year ended Dec 31 2004, net income increased 41.8% to $2,587,000 thousand from net income of $1,825,000 thousand a year earlier. Revenues were $37,218,000 thousand, up 29.1% from $28,823,000 thousand the year before. Net premiums earned were $33,495,000 thousand versus $25,448,000 thousand in the prior year, an increase of 31.6%.

Prospects: Co.'s outlook appears constructive. Excluding account-based products like flexible spending vehicles, Co. expects to serve a total of about 1.3 million people through its offerings by the end of the first quarter of 2005, including 880,000 using new consumer directed account-based health benefits products. Co. also stated that new products should provide 3.0 million current customers with better access for non-covered services. Co. noted that it expects further expansion of these programs, and in the number of people they serve, during 2005 and 2006. Thus, Co. now expects 2005 earnings per share to range from $4.75 to $4.80, an increase of $0.05 per share over its previous guidance.

Financial Data

(US$ in Thousands)	12/31/2004	12/31/2003	12/31/2002	12/31/2001	12/31/2000	12/31/1999	12/31/1998	12/31/1997
Earnings Per Share	3.94	2.96	2.13	1.40	1.10	0.80	(0.28)	0.56
Cash Flow Per Share	6.59	5.10	3.99	2.95	2.34	1.71	1.40	0.91
Tang Book Value Per Share	0.07	2.47	1.57	1.76	1.67	1.81	2.23	3.18
Dividends Per Share	0.030	0.015	0.015	0.015	0.007	0.007	0.007	0.007
Dividend Payout %	0.76	0.51	0.71	1.08	0.68	0.94	N.M.	1.33
Income Statement								
Total Revenue	37,218,000	28,823,000	25,020,000	23,454,000	21,122,000	19,562,000	17,355,000	11,794,000
EBITDA	4,475,000	3,234,000	2,441,000	1,831,000	1,474,000	1,176,000	143,000	888,000
Depn & Amortn	374,000	299,000	255,000	265,000	247,000	233,000	185,000	146,000
Income Before Taxes	3,973,000	2,840,000	2,096,000	1,472,000	1,155,000	894,000	(46,000)	742,000
Income Taxes	1,386,000	1,015,000	744,000	559,000	419,000	326,000	120,000	282,000
Net Income	2,587,000	1,825,000	1,352,000	913,000	736,000	568,000	(166,000)	460,000
Average Shares	656,000	617,000	636,200	653,600	673,000	710,000	764,000	764,000
Balance Sheet								
Current Assets	8,241,000	6,120,000	5,174,000	4,946,000	4,405,000	4,568,000	4,280,000	2,193,000
Total Assets	27,879,000	17,634,000	14,164,000	12,486,000	11,053,000	10,273,000	9,701,000	7,623,000
Current Liabilities	11,329,000	8,768,000	8,379,000	7,491,000	6,570,000	5,892,000	5,342,000	2,570,000
Long-Term Obligations	3,350,000	1,750,000	950,000	900,000	650,000	400,000	249,000	...
Total Liabilities	17,162,000	12,506,000	9,736,000	8,595,000	7,365,000	6,410,000	5,663,000	3,089,000
Stockholders' Equity	10,717,000	5,128,000	4,428,000	3,891,000	3,688,000	3,863,000	4,038,000	4,534,000
Shares Outstanding	643,000	583,000	598,916	617,252	634,470	669,880	735,720	764,444
Statistical Record								
Return on Assets %	11.34	11.48	10.15	7.76	6.88	5.69	N.M.	6.29
Return on Equity %	32.56	38.20	32.50	24.09	19.44	14.38	N.M.	11.01
EBITDA Margin %	12.02	11.22	9.76	7.81	6.98	6.01	0.82	7.53
Net Margin %	6.95	6.33	5.40	3.89	3.48	2.90	N.M.	3.90
Asset Turnover	1.63	1.81	1.88	1.99	1.98	1.96	2.00	1.61
Current Ratio	0.73	0.70	0.62	0.66	0.67	0.78	0.80	0.85
Debt to Equity	0.31	0.34	0.21	0.23	0.18	0.10	0.06	...
Price Range	88.03-56.20	58.19-39.88	50.19-34.06	36.09-25.78	31.25-11.91	17.44-10.03	18.19-7.83	15.00-10.77
P/E Ratio	22.34-14.26	19.66-13.47	23.56-15.99	25.78-18.42	28.41-10.82	21.80-12.54	N/A	26.79-19.22
Average Yield %	0.04	0.03	0.04	0.05	0.04	0.05	0.06	0.06

Address: 9900 Bren Road East,	Web Site: www.unitedhealthgroup.com	Auditors: Deloitte & Touche LLP
Minnetonka, MN 55343	Officers: William W. McGuire M.D. - Chmn., C.E.O.	Investor Contact: 612-936-1300
Telephone: (952) 936-1300	Stephen J. Hemsley - Pres., C.O.O.	
Fax: (952) 936-0044		

UNIVISION COMMUNICATIONS INC.

Exchange	Symbol	Price	52Wk Range	Yield	P/E
NYS	UVN	$27.69 (3/31/2005)	36.72-25.99	N/A	38.46

*7 Year Price Score 79.07   ***NYSE Composite Index=100**   ***12 Month Price Score 84.12**

Interim Earnings (Per Share)

Qtr.	Mar	Jun	Sep	Dec
2001	0.03	0.12	0.03	0.05
2002	0.03	0.09	0.08	0.14
2003	0.05	0.16	0.16	0.18
2004	0.09	0.24	0.21	0.19

Interim Dividends (Per Share)

Amt	Decl	Ex	Rec	Pay
2-for-1	12/4/1997	1/13/1998	12/17/1997	1/12/1998
100%	7/18/2000	8/14/2000	7/28/2000	8/11/2000

Valuation Analysis

Forecast P/E	32.15	No of Institutions	
	(4/7/2005)	312	
Market Cap	$9.0 Billion	Shares	
Book Value	5.4 Billion	239,215,040	
Price/Book	1.66	% Held	
Price/Sales	5.01	93.47	

Business Summary: Media (MIC: 13.1 SIC: 833 NAIC: 17510)

Univision Communications is a major Spanish-language media company. Co.'s operations include: Univision Network, a Spanish-language broadcast television network reaching 98.0% of U.S. Hispanic households as of Dec 31 2003; TeleFutura Network, a 24-hour general-interest Spanish-language broadcast television network reaching 79.0% of U.S. Hispanic households; Univision Television Group, which owns and operates 23 Univision Network television stations and 1 non-Univision television station; TeleFutura Television Group, which owns and operates 29 television stations; Univision Music Group, which includes the Univision Music label, Fonovisa Records label, Fonomusic and America Musical Publishing.

Recent Developments: For the year ended Dec 31 2004, net income increased 64.6% to $255,883 thousand from net income of $155,427 thousand a year earlier. Revenues were $1,786,935 thousand, up 36.3% from $1,311,015 thousand the year before. Operating income was $493,255 thousand versus an income of $348,696 thousand in the prior year, an increase of 41.5%. Total direct expense was $663,457 thousand versus $513,741 thousand in the prior year, an increase of 29.1%. Total indirect expense was $630,223 thousand versus $448,578 thousand in the prior year, an increase of 40.5%.

Prospects: Co. is pleased with its operating performance, and based on the momentum of its television and radio ratings, believes that it is poised for solid growth in 2005 and beyond. For the first quarter of 2005, Co. expects net revenues to increase in the high teen percentages. Moreover, operating income before depreciation and amortization is expected to increase in the high teen percentages, with depreciation and amortization expense expected to be approximate $25.0 million. This outlook includes the positive impact of variable interest entities, which are expected to add about $27.0 million in revenues. Diluted earnings per share should be in the range of $0.10 and $0.11 for the first quarter.

Financial Data

(US$ in Thousands)	12/31/2004	12/31/2003	12/31/2002	12/31/2001	12/31/2000	12/31/1999	12/31/1998	12/31/1997
Earnings Per Share	0.72	0.55	0.34	0.22	0.57	0.34	0.04	0.71
Cash Flow Per Share	1.31	1.30	0.69	1.04	1.15	0.79	0.53	0.62
Tang Book Value Per Share	N.M.	N.M.	N.M.	N.M.	0.89	N.M.	N.M.	N.M.
Income Statement								
Total Revenue	1,786,935	1,311,015	1,091,293	887,870	863,459	693,090	577,053	459,741
EBITDA	591,370	425,322	322,102	260,229	324,588	268,004	153,897	165,741
Depn & Amortn	101,382	89,355	82,991	86,696	68,126	64,024	66,115	60,270
Income Before Taxes	420,457	260,813	148,032	117,582	225,004	175,080	50,275	63,694
Income Taxes	164,574	105,386	61,504	62,865	108,081	91,536	40,348	(19,465)
Net Income	255,883	155,427	86,528	52,411	116,923	80,933	9,927	83,159
Average Shares	353,019	283,838	256,337	239,817	238,963	236,236	232,418	232,690
Balance Sheet								
Current Assets	664,684	520,566	384,958	596,093	249,872	177,910	153,991	138,754
Total Assets	8,227,126	7,642,917	3,402,396	3,163,544	1,448,305	974,457	938,329	967,755
Current Liabilities	291,515	288,633	223,222	269,680	362,961	141,901	152,891	144,029
Long-Term Obligations	1,227,680	1,368,346	1,432,233	1,662,018	377,689	303,138	377,435	460,830
Total Liabilities	2,580,028	2,539,940	1,844,308	1,980,764	746,973	451,589	534,591	609,406
Stockholders' Equity	5,387,704	5,102,977	1,558,088	813,280	695,272	513,778	394,648	346,229
Shares Outstanding	323,331	322,227	228,112	209,461	206,064	203,354	180,904	170,598
Statistical Record								
Return on Assets %	3.22	2.81	2.64	2.27	9.63	8.46	1.04	8.98
Return on Equity %	4.86	4.67	7.30	6.95	19.29	17.82	2.68	27.34
EBITDA Margin %	33.09	32.44	29.52	29.31	37.59	38.67	26.67	36.05
Net Margin %	14.32	11.86	7.93	5.90	13.54	11.68	1.72	18.09
Asset Turnover	0.22	0.24	0.33	0.39	0.71	0.72	0.61	0.50
Current Ratio	2.28	1.80	1.72	2.21	0.69	1.25	1.01	0.96
Debt to Equity	0.23	0.27	0.92	2.04	0.54	0.59	0.96	1.33
Price Range	39.93-27.73	39.72-22.25	46.71-19.97	50.81-18.53	62.13-26.00	51.09-17.63	20.81-10.53	17.45-7.94
P/E Ratio	55.46-38.51	72.22-40.45	137.38-58.74	230.97-84.23	108.99-45.61	150.28-51.84	520.31-263.28	24.58-11.18

Address: 1999 Avenue of the Stars, Suite 3050, Los Angeles, CA 90067	Web Site: www.univision.net	Auditors: Ernst & Young LLP
Telephone: (310) 556-7676	Officers: A. Jerrold Perenchio - Chmn., C.E.O. Robert V. Cahill - Vice-Chmn., Sec.	
Fax: (310) 556-3568		

U.S. BANCORP (DE)

Exchange	Symbol	Price	52Wk Range	Yield	P/E
NYS	USB	$28.82 (3/31/2005)	31.53-25.13	4.16	13.22

*7 Year Price Score 103.20 *NYSE Composite Index=100   *12 Month Price Score 95.44

Interim Earnings (Per Share)

Qtr.	Mar	Jun	Sep	Dec
2001	0.21	0.29	0.02	0.36
2002	0.39	0.43	0.45	0.44
2003	0.47	0.49	0.51	0.46
2004	0.52	0.54	0.56	0.56

Interim Dividends (Per Share)

Amt	Decl	Ex	Rec	Pay
0.24Q	6/15/2004	6/28/2004	6/30/2004	7/15/2004
0.24Q	9/15/2004	9/28/2004	9/30/2004	10/15/2004
0.30Q	12/21/2004	12/29/2004	12/31/2004	1/17/2005
0.30Q	3/16/2005	3/29/2005	3/31/2005	4/15/2005

Indicated Div: $1.20

Valuation Analysis

Forecast P/E	N/A	No of Institutions
		655
Market Cap	$53.5 Billion	Shares
Book Value	19.5 Billion	1,035,688,512
Price/Book	2.74	% Held
Price/Sales	3.64	55.75

Business Summary: Commercial Banking (MIC: 8.1 SIC: 021 NAIC: 22110)

U.S. Bancorp is a financial holding company and parent company of U.S. Bank, which served 13.1 million customers and operated 2,370 branch offices and 4,620 ATMs in 24 states as of Dec 31 2004. Co. provides an array of banking, brokerage, insurance, investment, mortgage, trust and payment services products to consumers, businesses, governments and institutions. Major lines of business provided by Co. through U.S. Bank and other subsidiaries include Wholesale Banking; Payment Services; Private Client, Trust & Asset Management; and Consumer Banking. As of Dec 31 2004, Co. had total assets of $195.10 billion.

Recent Developments: For the year ended Dec 31 2004, net income increased 11.6% to $4,166,800 thousand from net income of $3,732,600 thousand a year earlier. Net interest income was $7,111,300 thousand, down 1.1% from $7,189,300 thousand the year before. Provision for loan losses was $669,600 thousand versus $1,254,000 thousand in the prior year, a decrease of 46.6%. Non-interest income rose 3.9% to $5,519,200 thousand, while non-interest expense advanced 3.4% to $5,784,500 thousand.

Prospects: Co.'s outlook appears favorable, reflecting positive fee revenue trends, strengthening commercial loan growth and solid asset quality. For example, for the fourth quarter ended Dec 31 2004, fee revenue increased 12.3% over the fourth quarter of 2003, driven by Co.'s Payment Services and Consumer Banking business units. Additionally, Co. noted that compared with the third quarter of 2004, average commercial loans for the fourth quarter ended Dec 31 2004 grew at an annualized rate of 9.0%. Meanwhile, the ratio of nonperforming assets to loans and other real estate improved to 0.59% at Dec 31 2004 compared with 0.65% at Sep 30 2004 and 0.97% at Dec 31 2003.

Financial Data
(US$ in Thousands)

	12/31/2004	12/31/2003	12/31/2002	12/31/2001	12/31/2000	12/31/1999	12/31/1998	12/31/1997
Earnings Per Share	2.18	1.93	1.71	0.88	2.13	2.06	1.78	1.11
Cash Flow Per Share	2.76	4.51	1.98	1.13	3.46	3.69	1.87	2.03
Tang Book Value Per Share	5.87	5.77	4.93	4.64	7.11	6.07	5.50	5.96
Dividends Per Share	1.020	0.855	0.780	0.750	0.860	0.780	0.700	0.62
Dividend Payout %	46.79	44.30	45.61	85.23	40.38	37.86	39.33	55.86
Income Statement								
Interest Income	9,186,500	9,258,000	9,553,700	11,083,600	6,707,100	5,676,700	5,407,400	5,293,600
Interest Expense	2,075,200	2,068,700	2,714,000	4,674,800	3,235,800	2,416,000	2,346,800	2,245,500
Net Interest Income	7,111,300	7,189,300	6,839,700	6,408,800	3,471,300	3,260,700	3,060,600	3,048,100
Provision for Losses	669,600	1,254,000	1,349,000	2,528,800	670,000	531,000	379,000	460,300
Non-Interest Income	5,519,200	5,313,000	5,868,600	5,359,400	3,258,400	2,758,700	2,256,600	1,615,200
Non-Interest Expense	5,784,500	5,596,900	6,256,600	6,605,200	3,598,400	3,126,900	2,844,300	2,812,300
Income Before Taxes	6,176,400	5,651,400	5,102,700	2,634,200	2,461,300	2,361,500	2,093,900	1,390,700
Income Taxes	2,009,600	1,941,300	1,776,300	927,700	869,300	855,000	766,500	552,200
Net Income	4,166,800	3,732,600	3,289,100	1,706,500	1,592,000	1,506,500	1,327,400	838,500
Average Shares	1,912,900	1,936,200	1,926,100	1,939,500	747,900	732,990	744,178	742,914
Balance Sheet								
Net Loans & Leases	124,235,000	115,866,000	113,829,000	111,948,000	68,024,000	61,890,000	58,121,000	53,699,000
Total Assets	195,104,000	189,286,000	180,027,000	171,390,000	87,336,000	81,530,000	76,438,000	71,295,000
Total Deposits	120,741,000	119,052,000	115,534,000	105,219,000	53,257,000	51,530,000	50,034,000	49,027,000
Total Liabilities	175,565,000	170,044,000	161,926,000	154,929,000	78,696,000	73,892,000	70,468,000	65,405,000
Stockholders' Equity	19,539,000	19,242,000	18,101,000	16,461,000	8,640,000	7,638,000	5,970,000	5,890,000
Shares Outstanding	1,857,622	1,922,920	1,916,956	1,951,709	752,059	753,330	725,762	739,932
Statistical Record								
Return on Assets %	2.16	2.02	1.87	1.32	1.88	1.91	1.80	1.56
Return on Equity %	21.43	19.99	19.03	13.60	19.51	22.14	22.38	18.75
Net Interest Margin %	77.41	77.66	71.59	57.82	51.76	57.44	56.60	57.58
Efficiency Ratio %	39.34	38.41	40.57	40.17	36.11	37.07	37.11	40.71
Loans to Deposits	1.03	0.97	0.99	1.06	1.28	1.20	1.16	1.10
Price Range	31.53-25.13	29.35-18.71	24.10-16.02	25.25-16.57	27.35-15.40	34.06-19.96	30.55-17.45	19.05-9.84
P/E Ratio	14.46-11.53	15.21-9.69	14.09-9.37	28.70-18.83	12.84-7.23	16.54-9.69	17.16-9.80	17.17-8.87
Average Yield %	3.60	3.64	3.75	3.48	4.02	2.89	2.92	4.29

Address: 800 Nicollet Mall, Minneapolis, MN 55402-4302	**Web Site:** www.usbank.com	**Auditors:** Ernst & Young LLP
Telephone: (612) 973 1111	**Officers:** Jerry A. Grundhofer - Chmn., Pres., C.E.O.	**Investor Contact:** 612-303-0786
Fax: (612) 370 4352	David M. Moffett - Vice-Chmn., C.F.O.	

UNITED TECHNOLOGIES CORP.

Exchange	Symbol	Price	52Wk Range	Yield	P/E	Div Acheiver
NYS	UTX	$101.66 (3/31/2005)	105.52-81.50	1.73	18.42	11 Years

*7 Year Price Score 116.45 *NYSE Composite Index=100 *12 Month Price Score 100.10

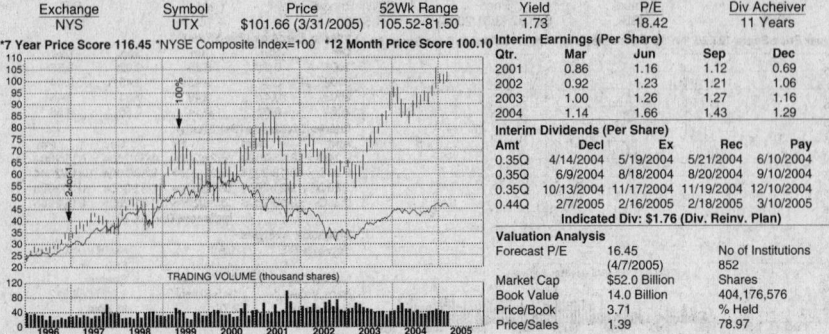

Interim Earnings (Per Share)

Qtr.	Mar	Jun	Sep	Dec
2001	0.86	1.16	1.12	0.69
2002	0.92	1.23	1.21	1.06
2003	1.00	1.26	1.27	1.16
2004	1.14	1.66	1.43	1.29

Interim Dividends (Per Share)

Amt	Decl	Ex	Rec	Pay
0.35Q	4/14/2004	5/19/2004	5/21/2004	6/10/2004
0.35Q	6/9/2004	8/18/2004	8/20/2004	9/10/2004
0.35Q	10/13/2004	11/17/2004	11/19/2004	12/10/2004
0.44Q	2/7/2005	2/16/2005	2/18/2005	3/10/2005
	Indicated Div: $1.76 (Div. Reinv. Plan)			

Valuation Analysis

Forecast P/E	16.45	No of Institutions
	(4/7/2005)	852
Market Cap	$52.0 Billion	Shares
Book Value	14.0 Billion	404,176,576
Price/Book	3.71	% Held
Price/Sales	1.39	78.97

Business Summary: Aviation (MIC: 1.1 SIC: 724 NAIC: 36412)

United Technologies provides technology products and services to the building systems and aerospace industries worldwide. Co.'s operating units include businesses with operations throughout the world. Co. conducts its business through six principal segments: Otis, Carrier, Chubb, Pratt & Whitney, Hamilton Sundstrand and Sikorsky. The segments are based on the management structure of the businesses and the grouping of similar operating companies, where each management organization has general operating autonomy over a range of products and services. Through these segments Co. produces aircraft engines, HVAC products, and other products. Co. also designs and produces fuel cells.

Recent Developments: For the year ended Dec 31 2004, net income increased 18.1% to $2,788 million from net income of $2,361 million a year earlier. Revenues were $37,445 million, up 20.7% from $31,034 million the year before. Operating income was $4,470 million versus an income of $3,845 million in the prior year, an increase of 16.3%. Total direct expense was $27,221 million versus $22,508 million in the prior year, an increase of 20.9%. Total indirect expense was $5,754 million versus $4,681 million in the prior year, an increase of 22.9%.

Prospects: Co.'s results are benefiting from increasing revenues reflecting organic growth, the addition of the Linde commercial refrigeration business and the continuing benefit of foreign exchange. Organic revenue growth reflects good conditions and favorable market share trends in many of Co.'s markets worldwide. Cost reductions continue to offset higher research and development, higher commodity costs, pension and healthcare expense headwinds and the roll-in effects of lower margin rates in the Chubb and Linde businesses. For 2005, Co. expects earnings per share growth of 10.0% to 15.0% and cash flow after capital expenditures again in the range of net income.

Financial Data

(US$ in Thousands)	12/31/2004	12/31/2003	12/31/2002	12/31/2001	12/31/2000	12/31/1999	12/31/1998	12/31/1997
Earnings Per Share	5.52	4.69	4.42	3.83	3.55	3.01	2.52	2.11
Cash Flow Per Share	7.43	6.07	6.04	6.14	5.58	4.96	5.50	4.55
Tang Book Value Per Share	3.68	4.63	2.93	3.32	1.89	3.11	5.84	6.75
Dividends Per Share	1.400	1.135	0.980	0.900	0.825	0.760	0.695	0.620
Dividend Payout %	25.36	24.20	22.17	23.50	23.24	25.25	27.52	29.45
Income Statement								
Total Revenue	37,445,000	31,034,000	28,212,000	27,897,000	26,583,000	24,127,000	25,715,000	24,713,000
EBITDA	5,448,000	4,644,000	4,384,000	4,138,000	3,999,000	2,361,000	3,021,000	2,807,000
Depn & Amortn	978,000	799,000	727,000	905,000	859,000	844,000	854,000	848,000
Income Before Taxes	4,107,000	3,470,000	3,276,000	2,807,000	2,758,000	1,257,000	1,963,000	1,764,000
Income Taxes	1,085,000	941,000	887,000	755,000	853,000	325,000	623,000	573,000
Net Income	2,788,000	2,361,000	2,236,000	1,938,000	1,808,000	1,531,000	1,255,000	1,072,000
Average Shares	505,419	502,900	505,579	505,400	508,010	506,700	494,000	508,000
Balance Sheet								
Current Assets	15,522,000	12,364,000	11,751,000	11,263,000	10,662,000	10,627,000	9,355,000	9,248,000
Total Assets	40,035,000	34,648,000	29,090,000	26,969,000	25,364,000	24,366,000	18,375,000	16,719,000
Current Liabilities	12,947,000	10,295,000	7,903,000	8,371,000	9,344,000	9,215,000	7,735,000	7,311,000
Long-Term Obligations	4,231,000	4,257,000	4,632,000	4,237,000	3,476,000	3,086,000	1,575,000	1,275,000
Total Liabilities	26,027,000	22,941,000	20,735,000	18,600,000	17,702,000	17,249,000	13,997,000	12,646,000
Stockholders' Equity	14,008,000	11,707,000	8,355,000	8,369,000	7,662,000	7,117,000	4,378,000	4,073,000
Shares Outstanding	511,098	514,062	469,620	472,159	470,306	474,546	450,000	458,000
Statistical Record								
Return on Assets %	7.45	7.41	7.98	7.41	7.25	7.16	7.15	6.41
Return on Equity %	21.62	23.54	26.74	24.18	24.40	26.64	29.70	25.59
EBITDA Margin %	14.55	14.96	15.54	14.83	15.04	9.79	11.75	11.36
Net Margin %	7.45	7.61	7.93	6.95	6.80	6.35	4.88	4.34
Asset Turnover	1.00	0.97	1.01	1.07	1.07	1.13	1.47	1.48
Current Ratio	1.20	1.20	1.49	1.35	1.14	1.15	1.21	1.26
Debt to Equity	0.30	0.36	0.55	0.51	0.45	0.43	0.36	0.31
Price Range	105.52-81.50	95.54-54.15	77.25-49.19	87.21-41.64	79.75-48.06	74.69-52.31	55.88-34.25	43.63-32.81
P/E Ratio	19.12-14.76	20.37-11.55	17.48-11.13	22.77-10.87	22.46-13.54	24.81-17.38	22.17-13.59	20.68-15.55
Average Yield %	1.52	1.56	1.50	1.29	1.33	1.21	1.54	1.61

Address: One Financial Plaza, Hartford, CT 06103	Web Site: www.utc.com	Auditors: PricewaterhouseCoopers LLP
Telephone: (860) 728-7000	Officers: George David - Chmn., Pres., C.E.O.	Transfer Agents: EquiServe Trust
Fax: (860) 728-7028	William H. Trachsel - Sr. V.P., Gen. Couns	Company, N.A. of Providence, RI

UNITRIN, INC.

Exchange	Symbol	Price	52Wk Range	Yield	P/E
NYS	UTR	$45.40 (3/31/2005)	49.87-37.13	3.74	13.05

*7 Year Price Score 106.98 *NYSE Composite Index=100   *12 Month Price Score 98.73

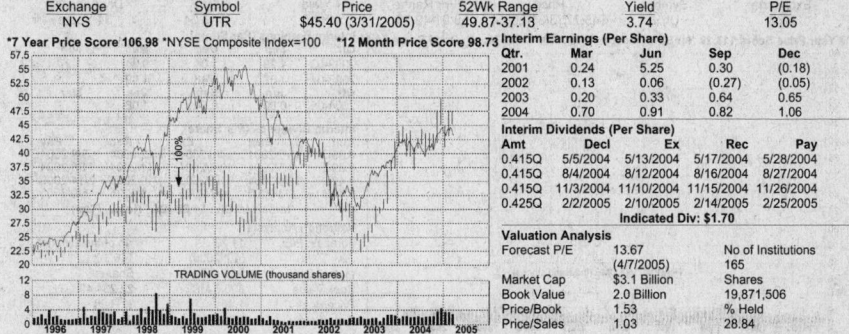

Interim Earnings (Per Share)

Qtr.	Mar	Jun	Sep	Dec
2001	0.24	5.25	0.30	(0.18)
2002	0.13	0.06	(0.27)	(0.05)
2003	0.20	0.33	0.64	0.65
2004	0.70	0.91	0.82	1.06

Interim Dividends (Per Share)

Amt	Decl	Ex	Rec	Pay
0.415Q	5/5/2004	5/13/2004	5/17/2004	5/28/2004
0.415Q	8/4/2004	8/12/2004	8/16/2004	8/27/2004
0.415Q	11/3/2004	11/10/2004	11/15/2004	11/26/2004
0.425Q	2/2/2005	2/10/2005	2/14/2005	2/25/2005
		Indicated Div: $1.70		

Valuation Analysis

Forecast P/E	13.67	No of Institutions	
	(4/7/2005)	165	
Market Cap	$3.1 Billion	Shares	
Book Value	2.0 Billion	19,871,506	
Price/Book	1.53	% Held	
Price/Sales	1.03	28.84	

Business Summary: Insurance (MIC: 8.2 SIC: 331 NAIC: 24126)

Unitrin provides property and casualty insurance, life and health insurance and consumer finance services. Co. conducts its operations through six operating segments: Multi Lines Insurance, Specialty Lines Insurance, Kemper Auto and Home, Unitrin Direct, Life and Health Insurance and Consumer Finance. Co.'s property and casualty businesses provide automobile, homeowners, commercial multi-peril, motorcycle, boat and watercraft, fire, casualty, workers compensation, and other types of property and casualty insurance. Co. also provides life and health insurance through employee and independent agents. In addition, Co.'s Fireside Bank is engaged in the consumer finance business.

Recent Developments: For the year ended Dec 31 2004, net income increased 94.3% to $240,200 thousand from net income of $123,600 thousand a year earlier. Revenues were $3,040,800 thousand, up 3.3% from $2,943,800 thousand the year before. Net premiums earned were $2,485,200 thousand versus $2,457,200 thousand in the prior year, an increase of 1.1%.

Prospects: Results are benefiting from actions Co. has taken over the past two years to improve profitability. These actions include the implementation of rate increases, diversification and the re-underwriting of select books of business. Going forward, Co. intends to combine the personal lines insurance operations of its Multi Lines Insurance segment with the operations of its Kemper Auto and Home segment in 2005. Co. expects that the combination will help it achieve greater economies of scale, reduce expenses and provide more options for its independent agents. Co. additional pre-tax expenses in the range between $8.0 million to $11.0 million over the next 24 months associated with this transition.

Financial Data (US$ in Thousands)	12/31/2004	12/31/2003	12/31/2002	12/31/2001	12/31/2000	12/31/1999	12/31/1998	12/31/1997
Earnings Per Share	3.48	1.82	(0.12)	5.60	1.32	2.74	6.51	1.55
Cash Flow Per Share	4.35	8.66	5.85	2.84	1.14	0.16	1.76	2.05
Tang Book Value Per Share	24.61	21.75	21.56	23.27	19.93	18.98	20.06	17.24
Dividends Per Share	1.660	1.660	1.660	1.600	1.500	1.400	1.300	1.200
Dividend Payout %	47.70	91.21	N.M.	28.57	113.64	51.09	19.97	77.17
Income Statement								
Premium Income	2,485,200	2,457,200	1,878,000	1,568,000	1,447,900	1,373,300	1,228,300	1,222,000
Total Revenue	3,040,800	2,943,800	2,298,200	2,533,800	1,953,200	1,813,600	2,085,900	1,530,100
Income Before Taxes	335,500	158,900	(24,600)	542,500	152,200	237,000	687,100	139,800
Income Taxes	98,900	34,100	(18,300)	190,300	54,400	77,900	238,600	47,100
Net Income	240,200	123,600	(8,200)	380,900	91,000	201,000	510,800	117,900
Average Shares	68,900	67,700	67,700	67,900	68,800	73,100	78,200	75,200
Balance Sheet								
Total Assets	8,790,300	8,536,800	7,705,600	7,133,700	6,164,800	5,934,800	5,909,900	4,920,700
Total Liabilities	6,751,600	6,717,900	5,903,200	5,216,900	4,463,600	4,217,800	4,087,500	3,387,700
Stockholders' Equity	2,038,700	1,818,900	1,802,400	1,916,800	1,701,200	1,717,000	1,822,400	1,533,000
Shares Outstanding	68,828	67,778	67,596	67,547	67,648	70,993	76,000	75,170
Statistical Record								
Return on Assets %	2.76	1.52	N.M.	5.73	1.50	3.39	9.43	2.41
Return on Equity %	12.42	6.83	N.M.	21.06	5.31	11.36	30.45	7.83
Net Margin %	7.90	4.20	(0.36)	15.03	4.66	11.08	24.49	7.71
Price Range	49.87-37.13	42.20-22.29	42.40-28.00	40.19-31.88	38.16-25.89	38.97-28.50	34.09-26.00	31.47-22.63
P/E Ratio	14.33-10.67	23.19-12.25	N/A	7.18-5.69	28.91-19.61	14.22-10.40	5.24-3.99	20.30-14.60
Average Yield %	3.88	5.64	4.69	4.48	4.88	4.18	4.16	4.43

Address: One East Wacker Drive, Chicago, IL 60601 Telephone: (312) 661 4600 Fax: (312) 661 4690	Web Site: www.unitrin.com Officers: Richard C. Vie - Chmn., C.E.O. Donald G. Southwell - Pres., C.O.O.	Auditors: Deloitte & Touche LLP Investor Contact: 312-661-4930

UNIVERSAL CORP.

Exchange	Symbol	Price	52Wk Range	Yield	P/E	Div Acheiver
NYS	UVV	$45.77 (3/31/2005)	53.01-42.25	3.67	13.04	34 Years

*7 Year Price Score 113.10 *NYSE Composite Index=100 *12 Month Price Score 94.13

Interim Earnings (Per Share)

Qtr.	Sep	Dec	Mar	Jun
2002-03	1.09	1.04	0.94	1.27
2003-04	1.37	1.48	1.09	...
Qtr.	Jun	Sep	Dec	Mar
2004-05	0.80	0.54	1.08	...

Interim Dividends (Per Share)

Amt	Decl	Ex	Rec	Pay
0.39Q	5/6/2004	7/8/2004	7/12/2004	8/9/2004
0.39Q	8/5/2004	10/6/2004	10/11/2004	11/8/2004
0.42Q	11/4/2004	1/6/2005	1/10/2005	2/14/2005
0.42Q	2/3/2005	4/7/2005	4/11/2005	5/9/2005

Indicated Div: $1.68 (Div. Reinv. Plan)

Valuation Analysis

Forecast P/E	11.23	No of Institutions
	(4/7/2005)	146
Market Cap	$1.2 Billion	Shares
Book Value	800.6 Million	22,234,496
Price/Book	1.46	% Held
Price/Sales	N/A	86.78

Business Summary: Trusts & Holding Entities (MIC: 8.9 SIC: 719 NAIC: 51112)

Universal is a holding company. Through its primary subsidiaries, Co. is a major independent leaf tobacco merchant and has operations in agri-products and the distribution of lumber and building products. Co.'s tobacco business includes the selecting, buying, shipping, processing, packing, storing, and financing of leaf tobacco for sale to manufacturers of tobacco products. Co.'s agri-products business involves selecting, buying and processing a number of products, including tea, rubber, sunflower seeds, nuts, dried fruit, and canned and frozen foods. Co. is also engaged in lumber and building products distribution and processing in the Netherlands and other countries in Europe.

Recent Developments: For the quarter ended Dec 31 2004, net income increased 0.2% to $27,907 thousand from net income of $27,841 thousand in the year-earlier quarter. Revenues were $852,346 thousand, up 24.7% from $683,540 thousand the year before. Operating income was $51,986 thousand versus an income of $55,475 thousand in the prior-year quarter, a decrease of 6.3%. Total direct expense was $705,758 thousand versus $541,318 thousand in the prior-year quarter, an increase of 30.4%. Total indirect expense was $94,602 thousand versus $86,747 thousand in the prior-year quarter, an increase of 9.1%.

Prospects: Co.'s results are being negatively affected by the changes in the monetary system in Zimbabwe, the effects of the change in its fiscal year end last year, the value-added tax provision in Brazil, and pricing pressures caused by larger crops and competitive pricing, particularly in South America and Africa. Meanwhile, Co.'s agri-products segment is benefiting from the acquisition of a controlling interest in nuts and dried fruits trading company, as well as higher volumes in rubber and canned meats. Meanwhile, Co.'s lumber and building products operations continue to perform well. Looking ahead, the larger tobacco crops may lead to certain market imbalances in fiscal 2006.

Financial Data

(US$ in Thousands)	9 Mos	6 Mos	3 Mos	03/31/2004	06/30/2003	06/30/2002	06/30/2001	06/30/2000
Earnings Per Share	3.51	2.43	3.37	3.94	4.34	4.00	4.08	3.77
Cash Flow Per Share	0.60	(4.57)	(2.69)	(1.39)	(1.76)	6.41	5.85	5.87
Tang Book Value Per Share	25.85	25.01	24.79	24.57	19.56	17.64	15.77	13.04
Dividends Per Share	1.560	1.530	1.500	1.470	1.400	1.320	1.260	1.220
Dividend Payout %	44.44	62.96	44.51	37.31	32.26	33.00	30.88	32.36
Income Statement								
Total Revenue	2,449,658	1,597,312	737,141	2,271,152	2,636,776	2,500,078	3,017,579	3,401,969
EBITDA	207,386	126,708	60,567	246,537	271,758	273,805	305,370	298,478
Depn & Amortn	54,554	34,779	16,433	48,867	53,504	54,987	56,399	52,022
Income Before Taxes	110,348	65,166	31,526	162,638	172,984	170,987	187,395	189,587
Income Taxes	49,259	31,303	12,453	59,329	53,094	59,821	66,336	68,221
Net Income	62,247	34,340	20,479	99,636	110,594	106,662	112,669	113,805
Average Shares	25,723	25,677	25,688	25,277	25,499	26,680	27,645	30,205
Balance Sheet								
Current Assets	1,759,433	1,846,530	1,795,725	1,526,669	1,374,997	1,105,037	1,132,646	1,088,150
Total Assets	2,789,673	2,842,616	2,748,326	2,482,773	2,243,074	1,844,415	1,782,373	1,748,100
Current Liabilities	982,613	993,307	1,012,608	739,110	824,281	673,431	581,765	883,234
Long-Term Obligations	741,519	851,735	769,348	770,296	614,994	435,592	515,349	223,262
Total Liabilities	1,957,033	2,034,694	1,949,355	1,722,940	1,622,796	1,256,420	1,230,244	1,250,325
Stockholders' Equity	800,611	774,693	766,699	759,833	620,278	587,995	552,129	497,779
Shares Outstanding	25,621	25,533	25,532	25,446	24,920	26,224	27,184	28,146
Statistical Record								
Return on Assets %	4.00	4.16	2.98	5.60	5.41	5.88	6.38	6.36
Return on Equity %	13.94	7.16	10.68	19.16	18.31	18.71	21.46	21.89
EBITDA Margin %	8.47	7.93	8.22	10.86	10.31	10.95	10.12	8.77
Net Margin %	2.54	2.15	2.78	4.39	4.19	4.27	3.73	3.35
Asset Turnover	1.22	1.21	1.07	1.28	1.29	1.38	1.71	1.90
Current Ratio	1.79	1.86	1.77	2.07	1.67	1.64	1.95	1.23
Debt to Equity	0.93	1.10	1.00	1.01	0.99	0.74	0.93	0.45
Price Range	53.01-42.25	53.01-40.78	53.01-40.78	52.32-40.78	43.01-31.81	43.05-31.74	41.30-20.63	31.00-13.56
P/E Ratio	15.10-12.04	21.81-16.78	15.73-12.10	13.28-10.35	9.91-7.33	10.76-7.93	10.12-5.06	8.22-3.60

Address: 1501 North Hamilton Street,	Web Site: www.universalcorp.com	Auditors: Ernst & Young LLP
Richmond, VA 23230	Officers: Allen B. King - Chmn., Pres., C.E.O.,	Investor Contact: 804-359-9311
Telephone: (804) 359 9311	C.O.O. Hartwell H. Roper - V.P., C.F.O.	Transfer Agents: Wells Fargo Bank
Fax: (804) 254 3594		Minnesota, N.A., St. Paul, MN

UNIVERSAL HEALTH REALTY INCOME TRUST

Exchange	Symbol	Price	52Wk Range	Yield	P/E	Div Acheiver
NYS	UHT	$28.25 (3/31/2005)	34.50-24.82	7.12	14.13	17 Years

*7 Year Price Score 110.03 *NYSE Composite Index=100 ***12 Month Price Score 93.73**

Interim Earnings (Per Share)
Qtr.	Mar	Jun	Sep	Dec
2001	0.46	0.44	0.42	0.43
2002	0.53	0.44	0.43	0.43
2003	0.48	0.45	0.45	0.68
2004	0.43	0.54	0.47	0.56

Interim Dividends (Per Share)
Amt	Decl	Ex	Rec	Pay
0.50Q	6/3/2004	6/14/2004	6/16/2004	6/30/2004
0.50Q	9/1/2004	9/13/2004	9/15/2004	9/30/2004
0.505Q	12/1/2004	12/14/2004	12/16/2004	12/31/2004
0.505Q	3/1/2005	3/14/2005	3/16/2005	3/31/2005
	Indicated Div: $2.01 (Div. Reinv. Plan)			

Valuation Analysis
Forecast P/E	N/A	No of Institutions 74
Market Cap	$332.1 Million	Shares
Book Value	154.1 Million	4,268,792
Price/Book	2.16	% Held
Price/Sales	10.45	36.31

Business Summary: Property, Real Estate & Development (MIC: 8.3 SIC: 798 NAIC: 25930)

Universal Health Realty Income Trust is an organized Maryland real estate investment trust (REIT). As of Dec 31 2003, Co. had investments in 44 facilities located in 15 states consisting of investments in healthcare and human service related facilities including acute care hospitals, behavioral healthcare facilities, rehabilitation hospitals, sub-acute care facilities, surgery centers, pre-school and childcare centers and medical office buildings. Six of Co.'s hospital facilities and three medical office buildings are leased to subsidiaries of Universal Health Services, Inc. (UHS). As of Dec 31 2003, UHS owned 6.6% of Co.'s outstanding shares.

Recent Developments: For the year ended Dec 31 2004, income from continuing operations decreased 7.3% to $21,712,000 from income of $23,433,000 a year earlier. Net income decreased 3.1% to $23,671,000 from net income of $24,425,000 a year earlier. Results for 2004 included property write-down from hurricane damage of $1,863,000, offset by a recovery of $1,863,000 property damage from UHS. Revenues were $31,777,000, up 17.5% from $27,052,000 the year before.

Prospects: Co. is experiencing higher revenues due to an increase in base rentals from Universal Health Services, Inc.'s facilities likely due to lease renewals at a higher annual base rental rate. Also, Co.'s revenues are being positively effected by higher base rental and tenant reimbursements reflecting a decrease in the vacancy rate. Meanwhile, Co.'s hospital facilities continue to experience an increase in outpatient revenue, which is primarily the result of advances in medical technologies and pharmaceutical improvements, that allow more services to be provided on an outpatient basis.

Financial Data
(US$ in Thousands)	12/31/2004	12/31/2003	12/31/2002	12/31/2001	12/31/2000	12/31/1999	12/31/1998	12/31/1997
Earnings Per Share	2.00	2.07	1.84	1.74	1.81	1.56	1.76	1.56
Cash Flow Per Share	2.29	2.48	2.25	2.17	2.22	2.19	2.08	1.98
Tang Book Value Per Share	13.10	12.97	12.73	12.85	11.05	11.09	11.32	11.47
Dividends Per Share	2.000	1.960	1.920	1.875	1.840	1.810	1.755	1.705
Dividend Payout %	100.00	94.69	104.35	107.76	101.66	116.03	99.72	109.29
Income Statement								
Property Income	31,777	28,313	28,429	27,574	27,315	23,584	23,123	22,180
Non-Property Income	...	...	...	...	...	281	111	584
Total Revenue	31,777	28,313	28,429	27,574	27,315	23,865	23,234	22,764
Depn & Amortn	5,312	4,536	4,431	4,401	4,461	3,919	4,003	3,899
Interest Expense	3,357	2,497	2,403	3,896	6,114	4,004	3,490	2,943
Net Income	23,671	24,425	21,623	18,349	16,256	13,972	14,337	13,967
Average Shares	11,813	11,779	11,750	10,536	9,003	8,977	8,974	8,967
Balance Sheet								
Total Assets	204,583	194,291	185,117	187,904	183,658	178,821	169,406	146,755
Long-Term Obligations	46,210	...	...	1,446	1,359	1,289	1,216	1,147
Total Liabilities	50,291	42,093	36,255	37,870	84,401	79,146	68,058	44,063
Stockholders' Equity	154,053	152,198	148,862	150,034	99,257	99,675	101,348	102,692
Shares Outstanding	11,755	11,736	11,698	11,678	8,980	8,990	8,955	8,954
Statistical Record								
Return on Assets %	11.84	12.88	11.59	9.88	8.94	8.02	9.07	9.46
Return on Equity %	15.42	16.23	14.47	14.72	16.30	13.90	14.05	13.52
Net Margin %	74.49	86.27	76.06	66.54	59.51	58.55	61.71	61.36
Price Range	34.50-24.82	30.55-25.30	28.50-22.69	25.70-18.94	19.88-14.31	20.50-14.63	22.50-18.06	22.38-18.50
P/E Ratio	17.25-12.41	14.76-12.22	15.49-12.33	14.77-10.88	10.98-7.91	13.14-9.38	12.78-10.26	14.34-11.86
Average Yield %	6.66	7.19	7.59	8.48	10.90	9.70	8.75	8.46

Address: Universal Corporate Center, 367 South Gulph Road, King of Prussia, PA 19406-0958 Telephone: (610) 265 0688 Fax: (610) 768 3336	Web Site: www.uhrit.com Officers: Alan B. Miller - Chmn., Pres., C.E.O. Charles F. Boyle - V.P., C.F.O., Contr.	Auditors: KPMG LLP Transfer Agents: EquiServe Trust Company, N.A., Providence, RI

UNIVERSAL HEALTH SERVICES, INC.

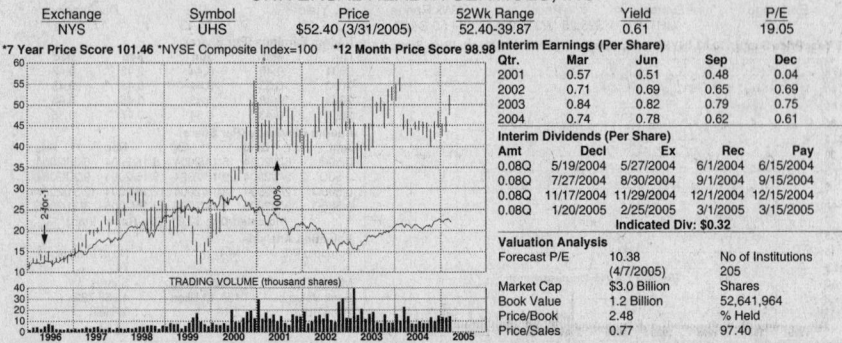

Exchange	Symbol	Price	52Wk Range	Yield	P/E
NYS	UHS	$52.40 (3/31/2005)	52.40-39.87	0.61	19.05

*7 Year Price Score 101.46 *NYSE Composite Index=100   *12 Month Price Score 98.98

Interim Earnings (Per Share)

Qtr.	Mar	Jun	Sep	Dec
2001	0.57	0.51	0.48	0.04
2002	0.71	0.69	0.65	0.69
2003	0.84	0.82	0.79	0.75
2004	0.74	0.78	0.62	0.61

Interim Dividends (Per Share)

Amt	Decl	Ex	Rec	Pay
0.08Q	5/19/2004	5/27/2004	6/1/2004	6/15/2004
0.08Q	7/27/2004	8/30/2004	9/1/2004	9/15/2004
0.08Q	11/17/2004	11/29/2004	12/1/2004	12/15/2004
0.08Q	1/20/2005	2/25/2005	3/1/2005	3/15/2005
		Indicated Div: $0.32		

Valuation Analysis

Forecast P/E	10.38	No of Institutions
	(4/7/2005)	205
Market Cap	$3.0 Billion	Shares
Book Value	1.2 Billion	52,641,964
Price/Book	2.48	% Held
Price/Sales	0.77	97.40

Business Summary: Hospitals & Health Care (MIC: 9.3 SIC: 062 NAIC: 22110)

Universal Health Services is engaged in the ownership and operation of acute care hospitals, behavioral health centers, ambulatory surgery centers, radiation oncology centers and women's centers. As of Dec 31 2003, Co. operated 62 hospitals, consisting of 25 selected acute care hospitals, and 37 selected behavioral health centers in Arkansas, California, Delaware, the District of Columbia, Florida, Georgia, Illinois, Indiana, Kentucky, Louisiana, Massachusetts, Michigan, Mississippi, Missouri, Nevada, New Jersey, Oklahoma, Pennsylvania, Puerto Rico, South Carolina, Tennessee, Texas, Utah and Washington.

Recent Developments: For the year ended Dec 31 2004, income from continuing operations decreased 11.5% to $170,006 thousand from income of $192,079 thousand a year earlier. Net income decreased 14.9% to $169,492 thousand from net income of $199,269 thousand a year earlier. Revenues were $3,938,320 thousand, up 16.1% from $3,391,506 thousand the year before. Operating income of $334,764 thousand versus an income of $366,416 thousand in the prior year, a decrease of 8.6%. Total direct expense was $1,607,103 thousand versus $1,355,047 thousand in the prior year, an increase of 18.6%. Total indirect expense was $1,770,506 thousand versus $1,480,525 thousand in the prior year, an increase of 19.6%.

Prospects: On Feb 7 2005, Co. announced that it has signed a definitive agreement to sell two acute care facilities in Puerto Rico: Hospital San Pablo, a 430-bed acute care hospital in Bayamon, and Hospital San Pablo del Este, a 180-bed acute care hospital in Fajardo. The two facilities will be sold to a local hospital operator in Puerto Rico, Centro Medico and HIMA San Pablo Properties. The sale proceeds will be approximately $120.0 million, excluding net working capital. The sale is subject to customary regulatory approvals and is expected to close by Mar 31 2005. Separately, for full-year 2005, Co. expects earnings from continuing operations of between $2.85 and $2.95.

Financial Data

(US$ in Thousands)	12/31/2004	12/31/2003	12/31/2002	12/31/2001	12/31/2000	12/31/1999	12/31/1998	12/31/1997
Earnings Per Share	2.75	3.20	2.74	1.60	3.01	2.43	2.39	2.03
Cash Flow Per Share	6.80	6.53	5.55	5.21	6.04	5.59	4.67	5.37
Tang Book Value Per Share	10.42	11.17	8.59	7.27	13.36	11.93	10.80	11.62
Dividends Per Share	0.320	0.080	...	...	...	...	...	...
Dividend Payout %	11.64	2.50	...	...	...	...	...	...
Income Statement								
Total Revenue	3,938,320	3,643,566	3,258,898	2,840,491	2,242,444	2,042,380	1,874,487	1,442,677
EBITDA	470,621	500,398	401,865	285,420	258,917	231,116	228,454	186,609
Depn & Amortn	156,073	144,466	124,794	127,523	112,809	108,333	105,442	80,686
Income Before Taxes	271,143	317,699	277,071	157,897	146,108	122,783	123,012	105,923
Income Taxes	101,137	118,430	101,710	57,147	52,746	45,008	43,454	38,647
Net Income	169,492	199,269	175,361	99,742	93,362	77,775	79,558	67,276
Average Shares	64,865	65,089	67,075	67,220	32,410	31,990	33,293	33,098
Balance Sheet								
Current Assets	808,925	645,791	606,576	548,262	476,455	403,249	319,615	230,022
Total Assets	3,022,843	2,772,730	2,323,229	2,114,584	1,742,377	1,497,973	1,448,095	1,085,349
Current Liabilities	469,656	395,753	370,413	322,716	248,840	217,200	170,053	160,456
Long-Term Obligations	852,229	868,566	680,514	718,830	548,064	419,203	418,188	272,466
Total Liabilities	1,802,257	1,681,808	1,405,770	1,306,684	1,025,803	856,362	821,088	558,742
Stockholders' Equity	1,220,586	1,090,922	917,459	807,900	716,574	641,611	627,007	526,607
Shares Outstanding	57,750	58,072	59,041	59,879	29,915	30,652	32,195	32,421
Statistical Record								
Return on Assets %	5.83	7.82	7.90	5.17	5.75	5.28	6.28	6.56
Return on Equity %	14.62	19.84	20.33	13.09	13.71	12.26	13.79	13.74
EBITDA Margin %	11.95	13.73	12.33	10.05	11.55	11.32	12.19	12.93
Net Margin %	4.30	5.47	5.38	3.51	4.16	3.81	4.24	4.66
Asset Turnover	1.36	1.43	1.47	1.47	1.38	1.39	1.48	1.41
Current Ratio	1.72	1.63	1.64	1.70	1.91	1.86	1.88	1.43
Debt to Equity	0.70	0.80	0.74	0.89	0.76	0.65	0.67	0.52
Price Range	56.51-39.87	54.30-34.77	56.20-37.80	52.60-37.81	55.88-18.00	27.44-11.84	29.81-19.38	25.19-13.94
P/E Ratio	20.55-14.50	16.97-10.87	20.51-13.80	32.88-23.63	18.56-5.98	11.29-4.87	12.47-8.11	12.41-6.87
Average Yield %	0.70	0.18	...	...	...	...	...	...

Address: Universal Corporate Center, 367 South Gulph Road, King Of Prussia, PA 19406 Telephone: (610) 768-3300 Fax: (610) 768-3336	Web Site: www.uhsinc.com Officers: Alan B. Miller - Chmn., Pres., C.E.O. Steve G. Filton - Sr. V.P., C.F.O., Sec.	Auditors: KPMG LLP Investor Contact: 610-768-3300

UNOCAL CORP.

Exchange	Symbol	Price	52Wk Range	Yield	P/E
NYS	UCL	$61.69 (3/31/2005)	62.89-34.26	1.30	13.77

*7 Year Price Score 102.93 *NYSE Composite Index=100 *12 Month Price Score 119.91

Interim Earnings (Per Share)

Qtr.	Mar	Jun	Sep	Dec
2001	1.18	0.99	0.42	(0.09)
2002	0.09	0.46	0.41	0.38
2003	0.52	0.68	0.58	0.68
2004	1.00	1.25	1.23	1.00

Interim Dividends (Per Share)

Amt	Decl	Ex	Rec	Pay
0.20Q	5/24/2004	7/8/2004	7/12/2004	8/12/2004
0.20Q	7/28/2004	10/7/2004	10/12/2004	11/12/2004
0.20Q	12/3/2004	1/7/2005	1/11/2005	2/11/2005
0.20Q	2/8/2005	4/7/2005	4/11/2005	5/11/2005
			Indicated Div: $0.80	

Valuation Analysis

Forecast P/E	12.66	No of Institutions
	(4/7/2005)	376
Market Cap	$16.2 Billion	Shares
Book Value	5.2 Billion	227,555,408
Price/Book	3.11	% Held
Price/Sales	1.98	84.10

Business Summary: Oil and Gas (MIC: 14.2 SIC: 311 NAIC: 11111)

Unocal is an independent oil and gas exploration and production company, with principal operations in North America and Asia. Co.'s oil and gas exploration, development and production activities are carried out by its North America operations in the U.S., Canada and by its international operations in about a dozen countries around the world. Co. is also a producer of geothermal energy and a provider of electrical power in Asia. Also, Co. has ownership in proprietary and common carrier pipelines, natural gas storage facilities and markets and trades hydrocarbon commodities.

Recent Developments: For the year ended Dec 31 2004, income from continuing operations increased 64.0% to $1,145 million from income of $698 million a year earlier. Net income increased 87.9% to $1,208 million from net income of $643 million a year earlier. Revenues were $8,204 million, up 26.0% from $6,512 million the year before. Total direct expense was $4,637 million versus $3,462 million in the prior year, an increase of 33.9%. Total indirect expense was $1,718 million versus $1,798 million in the prior year, a decrease of 4.4%.

Prospects: Results are benefiting from higher worldwide crude oil and natural gas prices and increased international production, partially offset by lower North American natural gas and liquids production and higher dry hole costs. Looking ahead, Co. is projecting first-quarter 2005 earnings in the range of $1.20 to $1.35 per diluted share. This guidance assumes average NYMEX benchmark prices of $46.70 per barrel of crude oil and $6.25 per million British thermal units for North American natural gas for the period, as well as pre-tax dry hole costs of between $30.0 million and $40.0 million. Also, Co. expects production for full-year 2005 to exceed 425,000 barrels of oil equivalent per day.

Financial Data
(US$ in Thousands)

	12/31/2004	12/31/2003	12/31/2002	12/31/2001	12/31/2000	12/31/1999	12/31/1998	12/31/1997
Earnings Per Share	4.48	2.46	1.34	2.50	3.08	0.56	0.54	2.31
Cash Flow Per Share	9.69	7.53	6.36	8.67	6.85	4.24	4.16	4.57
Tang Book Value Per Share	19.31	14.88	12.31	12.80	11.19	9.42	9.14	9.52
Dividends Per Share	0.800	0.800	0.800	0.800	0.800	0.800	0.800	0.800
Dividend Payout %	17.86	32.52	59.70	32.00	25.97	142.86	148.15	34.63
Income Statement								
Total Revenue	8,204,000	6,539,000	5,297,000	6,752,000	9,202,000	6,057,000	5,479,000	6,064,000
EBITDA	2,887,000	2,337,000	1,687,000	2,154,000	2,207,000	1,083,000	1,172,000	1,733,000
Depn & Amortn	1,058,000	1,096,000	1,071,000	1,062,000	971,000	833,000	867,000	962,000
Income Before Taxes	1,829,000	1,241,000	616,000	1,092,000	1,236,000	250,000	305,000	771,000
Income Taxes	673,000	522,000	280,000	452,000	497,000	121,000	175,000	102,000
Net Income	1,208,000	643,000	331,000	615,000	760,000	137,000	130,000	581,000
Average Shares	275,000	273,000	248,000	257,000	256,000	255,000	242,000	262,000
Balance Sheet								
Current Assets	2,930,000	1,991,000	1,375,000	1,295,000	1,802,000	1,631,000	1,388,000	1,501,000
Total Assets	13,101,000	11,798,000	10,760,000	10,425,000	10,010,000	8,967,000	7,952,000	7,530,000
Current Liabilities	2,581,000	2,085,000	1,632,000	1,422,000	1,845,000	1,559,000	1,376,000	1,160,000
Long-Term Obligations	2,571,000	2,635,000	3,002,000	2,897,000	2,392,000	2,853,000	2,558,000	2,169,000
Total Liabilities	7,884,000	7,267,000	6,940,000	6,779,000	6,769,000	6,261,000	5,228,000	4,694,000
Stockholders' Equity	5,217,000	4,009,000	3,298,000	3,124,000	2,719,000	2,184,000	2,202,000	2,314,000
Shares Outstanding	263,190	260,594	257,980	243,998	243,044	231,818	241,000	243,000
Statistical Record								
Return on Assets %	9.68	5.70	3.12	6.02	7.99	1.62	1.68	6.98
Return on Equity %	26.12	17.60	10.31	21.05	30.92	6.25	5.76	25.32
EBITDA Margin %	35.19	35.74	31.85	31.90	23.98	17.88	21.39	28.58
Net Margin %	14.72	9.83	6.25	9.11	8.26	2.26	2.37	9.58
Asset Turnover	0.66	0.58	0.50	0.66	0.97	0.72	0.71	0.73
Current Ratio	1.14	0.95	0.84	0.91	0.98	1.05	1.01	1.29
Debt to Equity	0.49	0.66	0.91	0.93	0.88	1.31	1.16	0.94
Price Range	46.13-34.26	36.86-25.21	39.63-26.79	39.97-29.96	39.94-25.75	44.38-27.50	41.75-28.81	45.13-36.25
P/E Ratio	10.30-7.65	14.98-10.25	29.57-19.99	15.99-11.98	12.97-8.36	79.24-49.11	77.31-53.36	19.53-15.69
Average Yield %	2.06	2.69	2.36	2.29	2.42	2.18	2.24	1.98

Address: 2141 Rosecrans Avenue, Suite 4000, El Segundo, CA 90245	**Web Site:** www.unocal.com	**Auditors:** PricewaterhouseCoopers LLP
	Officers: Charles R. Williamson - Chmn., C.E.O. John W. Creighton Jr. - Vice-Chmn.	**Investor Contact:** 310-726-7665
Telephone: (310) 726-7600		**Transfer Agents:** Mellon Investor Services, L.L.C., Ridgefield Park, NJ

UNUMPROVIDENT CORP.

Exchange	Symbol	Price	52Wk Range	Yield	P/E
NYS	UNM	$17.02 (3/31/2005)	18.14-12.19	1.76	N/A

*7 Year Price Score 49.30   ***NYSE Composite Index=100**   ***12 Month Price Score 101.98**

Interim Earnings (Per Share)

Qtr.	Mar	Jun	Sep	Dec
2001	0.75	0.60	0.52	0.51
2002	0.30	0.40	0.45	0.53
2003	(1.02)	0.36	0.36	(1.25)
2004	(1.91)	0.02	0.55	0.45

Interim Dividends (Per Share)

Amt	Decl	Ex	Rec	Pay
0.075Q	4/15/2004	4/22/2004	4/26/2004	5/21/2004
0.075Q	7/12/2004	7/22/2004	7/26/2004	8/20/2004
0.075Q	10/12/2004	10/21/2004	10/25/2004	11/19/2004
0.075Q	1/10/2005	1/27/2005	1/31/2005	2/18/2005
		Indicated Div: $0.30		

Valuation Analysis

Forecast P/E	9.36	No of Institutions	
	(4/7/2005)	303	
Market Cap	$5.0 Billion	Shares	
Book Value	7.2 Billion	308,949,760	
Price/Book	0.70	% Held	
Price/Sales	0.48	N/A	

Business Summary: Insurance (MIC: 8.2 SIC: 321 NAIC: 24114)

UnumProvident is a holding company for a group of insurance companies that collectively operate throughout North America, the U.K., Japan and elsewhere around the world. Co.'s principal operating subsidiaries are Unum Life Insurance Company of America, Provident Life and Accident Insurance Company, The Paul Revere Life Insurance Company, and Colonial Life & Accident Insurance Company. The Co. is the largest provider of group and individual disability insurance in North America and the U.K. Co. also provides a complementary portfolio of life insurance products, including long-term care insurance, life insurance, employer- and employee-paid group benefits, and related services.

Recent Developments: For the year ended Dec 31 2004, loss from continuing operations was $192,200 thousand compared with a loss of $264,600 thousand a year earlier. Net loss was $253,000 thousand versus net loss of $386,400 thousand a year earlier. Revenues were $10,464,900 thousand, up 4.7% from $9,991,600 thousand the year before. Net premiums earned were $7,839,600 thousand versus $7,615,700 thousand in the prior year, an increase of 2.9%.

Prospects: Co.'s outlook appears satisfactory. Co. noted that submitted incidence in its group long-term income protection line was lower in the fourth quarter of 2004 than last year as well as the prior quarter, but claim recovery experience was generally lower. Co. also reported improved earnings in its U. K. subsidiary, Unum Limited, and its group short-term income protection line of business. Meanwhile, Co. indicated that the recent decline in sales activity from its income protection line was mainly due to its disciplined pricing strategy and the competitive market environment. For 2005, Co. intends to again focus its efforts on re-pricing portions of its business to further improve profitability.

Financial Data
(US$ in Thousands)

	12/31/2004	12/31/2003	12/31/2002	12/31/2001	12/31/2000	12/31/1999	12/31/1998	12/31/1997
Earnings Per Share	(0.86)	(1.40)	1.65	2.38	2.33	(0.77)	2.57	2.59
Cash Flow Per Share	2.52	4.87	7.38	7.32	5.02	6.55	5.86	3.37
Tang Book Value Per Share	23.45	22.94	25.57	21.74	20.29	17.79	19.74	17.61
Dividends Per Share	0.300	0.373	0.590	0.590	0.590	0.590	0.585	0.565
Dividend Payout %	N.M.	N.M.	35.76	24.79	25.32	N.M.	22.76	21.81
Income Statement								
Premium Income	7,839,600	7,615,700	7,453,100	7,078,200	7,057,000	6,843,200	3,841,700	3,188,700
Total Revenue	10,464,900	9,991,600	9,613,000	9,394,800	9,432,300	9,329,600	4,641,400	4,076,700
Benefits & Claims	7,248,400	7,868,100	6,582,400	6,234,300	6,407,500	6,787,600	2,886,200	2,395,300
Income Before Taxes	(259,500)	(435,200)	610,900	825,100	865,600	(165,500)	517,400	536,400
Income Taxes	(67,300)	(170,600)	202,600	243,000	301,400	17,400	154,000	166,100
Net Income	(253,000)	(386,400)	401,200	579,200	564,200	(182,900)	363,400	370,300
Average Shares	295,224	276,132	243,070	243,608	242,061	239,080	141,400	142,923
Balance Sheet								
Total Assets	50,832,300	49,718,300	45,259,500	42,442,700	40,363,900	38,447,500	15,182,900	13,200,300
Total Liabilities	43,608,200	42,447,300	38,116,300	36,202,800	34,488,400	33,165,300	12,445,200	10,765,500
Stockholders' Equity	7,224,100	7,271,000	6,843,200	5,939,900	5,575,500	4,982,200	2,737,700	2,434,800
Shares Outstanding	296,545	296,143	241,587	242,218	241,134	240,338	138,709	138,272
Statistical Record								
Return on Assets %	N.M.	N.M.	0.91	1.40	1.43	N.M.	2.56	2.58
Return on Equity %	N.M.	N.M.	6.28	10.06	10.66	N.M.	14.05	15.76
Loss Ratio %	92.46	103.31	88.32	88.08	90.80	99.19	75.13	75.12
Net Margin %	N.M.	N.M.	4.17	6.17	5.98	N.M.	7.83	9.08
Price Range	18.14-12.19	19.40-5.97	29.45-16.58	33.75-22.43	32.06-12.06	61.88-26.94	59.94-42.13	54.38-33.81
P/E Ratio	N/A	N/A	17.85-10.05	14.18-9.42	13.76-5.18	N/A	23.32-16.39	20.99-13.06
Average Yield %	1.97	2.70	2.50	2.12	2.65	1.32	1.12	1.32

Address: 1 Fountain Square, Chattanooga, TN 37402	**Web Site:** www.unum.com	**Auditors:** Ernst & Young LLP
Telephone: (423) 755-1011	**Officers:** C. William Pollard - Co-Chmn. Lawrence R.	**Investor Contact:** 207-770-4330
Fax: (423) 755-3962	Pugh - Co-Chmn.	

USG CORP.

Exchange	Symbol	Price	52Wk Range	Yield	P/E
NYS	USG	$33.16 (3/31/2005)	40.72-12.60	N/A	4.57

*7 Year Price Score 79.62 *NYSE Composite Index=100 *12 Month Price Score 124.61

Interim Earnings (Per Share)

Qtr.	Mar	Jun	Sep	Dec
2001	0.25	(0.29)	0.61	(0.21)
2002	0.60	1.11	1.03	0.49
2003	0.13	0.73	0.89	1.07
2004	1.33	1.86	2.10	1.98

Interim Dividends (Per Share)

Dividend Payment Suspended

Valuation Analysis

Forecast P/E	7.61	No of Institutions
	(4/7/2005)	164
Market Cap	$1.4 Billion	Shares
Book Value	1.0 Billion	41,306,560
Price/Book	1.40	% Held
Price/Sales	0.32	95.37

Business Summary: Stone, Clay, Glass, and Concrete Products (MIC: 11.2 SIC: 275 NAIC: 27420)

USG is a holding company. Through its subsidiaries, Co. is a manufacturer and distributor of building materials, producing a range of products for use in new residential, new nonresidential, and repair and remodel construction as well as products used in certain industrial processes. Co.'s North American Gypsum operating segment manufactures and markets gypsum and related products in the United States, Canada and Mexico. Co.'s Worldwide Ceilings segment manufactures and markets interior systems products worldwide. Co.'s Building Products Distribution segment consists of L&W Supply, a U.S. specialty building products distribution business.

Recent Developments: For the year ended Dec 31 2004, net income increased 155.7% to $312 million from net income of $122 million a year earlier. Revenues were $4,509 million, up 23.0% from $3,666 million the year before. Operating income was $508 million versus an income of $210 million in the prior year, an increase of 141.9%. Total direct expense was $3,672 million versus $3,121 million in the prior year, an increase of 17.7%. Total indirect expense was $329 million versus $335 million in the prior year, a decrease of 1.8%.

Prospects: On Feb 2 2005, Co. announced that its United States Gypsum Company subsidiary will invest $132.0 million to rebuild and modernize its SHEETROCK® Brand Gypsum Panels manufacturing plant in Norfolk, VA. The modernization project is scheduled to be completed by the end of 2006. Looking ahead, Co. cautioned that a decline in housing starts and higher interest rates could reduce the level of demand from both the new housing and residential remodeling markets. Co. also noted that while office vacancy rates remain at relatively high levels, the commercial construction market is showing signs of improvement. Meanwhile, Co. expects costs of energy, raw materials and employee benefits to remain high.

Financial Data

(US$ in Thousands)	12/31/2004	12/31/2003	12/31/2002	12/31/2001	12/31/2000	12/31/1999	12/31/1998	12/31/1997
Earnings Per Share	7.26	2.82	1.00	0.36	(5.62)	8.39	6.61	3.03
Cash Flow Per Share	9.92	5.78	10.28	5.46	7.90	12.70	7.63	7.22
Tang Book Value Per Share	22.65	15.10	12.37	11.30	10.69	17.74	10.57	3.13
Dividends Per Share	...	...	...	0.025	0.600	0.450	0.11	...
Dividend Payout %	...	...	...	6.94	N.M.	5.36	1.66	...
Income Statement								
Total Revenue	4,509,000	3,666,000	3,468,000	3,296,000	3,781,000	3,600,000	3,130,000	2,874,000
EBITDA	628,000	331,000	366,000	187,000	(277,000)	818,000	663,000	574,000
Depn & Amortn	120,000	112,000	106,000	107,000	96,000	91,000	81,000	197,000
Income Before Taxes	509,000	217,000	256,000	52,000	(420,000)	684,000	534,000	320,000
Income Taxes	197,000	79,000	117,000	36,000	(161,000)	263,000	202,000	172,000
Net Income	312,000	122,000	43,000	16,000	(259,000)	421,000	332,000	148,000
Average Shares	43,025	43,076	43,282	43,435	45,972	50,216	50,000	49,000
Balance Sheet								
Current Assets	1,790,000	1,498,000	1,393,000	1,197,000	876,000	873,000	797,000	640,000
Total Assets	4,278,000	3,799,000	3,617,000	3,464,000	3,214,000	2,773,000	2,357,000	1,926,000
Current Liabilities	570,000	414,000	438,000	321,000	896,000	491,000	429,000	376,000
Long-Term Obligations	...	1,000	2,000	2,000	564,000	577,000	561,000	610,000
Total Liabilities	3,254,000	3,110,000	3,082,000	2,973,000	2,750,000	1,906,000	1,839,000	1,779,000
Stockholders' Equity	1,024,000	689,000	535,000	491,000	464,000	867,000	518,000	147,000
Shares Outstanding	43,309	43,049	43,238	43,457	43,401	48,860	49,000	47,000
Statistical Record								
Return on Assets %	7.70	3.29	1.21	0.48	N.M.	16.41	15.50	7.91
Return on Equity %	36.33	19.93	8.38	3.35	N.M.	60.79	99.85	238.71
EBITDA Margin %	13.93	9.03	10.55	5.67	N.M.	22.72	21.18	19.97
Net Margin %	6.92	3.33	1.24	0.49	N.M.	11.69	10.61	5.15
Asset Turnover	1.11	0.99	0.98	0.99	1.26	1.40	1.46	1.54
Current Ratio	3.14	3.62	3.18	3.73	0.98	1.78	1.86	1.70
Debt to Equity	...	N.M.	N.M.	N.M.	1.22	0.67	1.08	4.15
Price Range	40.72-12.60	23.20-4.03	8.71-3.43	23.88-3.65	47.13-13.75	64.31-42.50	57.69-36.50	51.50-29.88
P/E Ratio	5.61-1.74	8.23-1.43	8.71-3.43	66.32-10.14	N/A	7.67-5.07	8.73-5.52	17.00-9.86
Average Yield %	...	...	...	0.26	1.92	0.87	0.23	...

Address: 125 South Franklin Street, Chicago, IL 60606-4678	**Web Site:** www.usgcorp.com	**Auditors:** Deloitte & Touche LLP
Telephone: (312) 606-4000	**Officers:** William C. Foote - Chmn., Pres., C.E.O.	**Investor Contact:** 312-606-4125
Fax: (312) 606-4093	Richard H. Fleming - Exec. V.P., C.F.O.	

UST, INC.

Exchange	Symbol	Price	52Wk Range	Yield	P/E
NYS	UST	$51.70 (3/31/2005)	56.48-35.64	4.26	16.21

*7 Year Price Score 116.11 ***NYSE Composite Index=100** ***12 Month Price Score 116.02**

TRADING VOLUME (thousand shares)

Interim Earnings (Per Share)

Qtr.	Mar	Jun	Sep	Dec
2001	0.66	0.74	0.75	0.82
2002	0.61	0.80	0.77	(3.78)
2003	0.66	0.77	0.75	(0.27)
2004	0.73	0.89	0.80	0.77

Interim Dividends (Per Share)

Amt	Decl	Ex	Rec	Pay
0.52Q	5/4/2004	6/14/2004	6/15/2004	6/30/2004
0.52Q	7/29/2004	9/10/2004	9/14/2004	9/30/2004
0.52Q	10/28/2004	12/13/2004	12/15/2004	12/31/2004
0.55Q	2/17/2005	3/11/2005	3/15/2005	3/31/2005

Indicated Div: $2.20

Valuation Analysis

Forecast P/E	15.46	No of Institutions	
	(4/7/2005)	302	
Market Cap	$8.5 Billion	Shares	
Book Value	9.6 Million	130,739,664	
Price/Book	889.72	% Held	
Price/Sales	4.63	79.09	

Business Summary: Tobacco Products (MIC: 4.2 SIC: 131 NAIC: 12229)

UST is a holding company. Primary subsidiaries are U.S. Smokeless Tobacco Company and International Wine & Spirits Ltd. U.S. Smokeless Tobacco Company produces eight moist tobacco brands and three dry brands, including Copenhagen, Skoal, Rooster, Bruton, CC and Red Seal. International Wine & Spirits Ltd. is a producer of premium varietal, table and sparkling wines under the labels Chateau Ste. Michelle, Columbia Crest, Domaine Ste. Michelle, Villa Mt. Eden and Conn Creek. Other consumer products marketed by UST subsidiaries include Don Tomas, Don Tomas Dominican Selection, Astral and Helix premium cigars.

Recent Developments: For the year ended Dec 31 2004, net income increased 66.5% to $530,837 thousand from net income of $318,789 thousand a year earlier. Revenues were $1,838,238 thousand, up 6.1% from $1,731,862 thousand the year before. Operating income was $912,609 thousand versus an income of $596,635 thousand in the prior year, an increase of 53.0%. Total direct expense was $412,641 thousand versus $384,487 thousand in the prior year, an increase of 7.3%. Total indirect expense was $512,988 thousand versus $750,740 thousand in the prior year, a decrease of 31.7%.

Prospects: Co. is benefiting from its strategy to accelerate growth in its moist smokeless tobacco category by attracting adult smokers at a faster rate. The success of this strategy, coupled with ongoing emphasis on product innovation, provides Co. with confidence that it will experienced continued solid results in this category in 2005. Meanwhile, Co.'s wine segment continues to yield results above expectations, led by increased distribution and new product offerings. As a result, Co. announced its diluted earnings per share estimate for full-year 2005 will be in a range of $3.30 to $3.40.

Financial Data

(US$ in Thousands)	12/31/2004	12/31/2003	12/31/2002	12/31/2001	12/31/2000	12/31/1999	12/31/1998	12/31/1997
Earnings Per Share	3.19	1.90	(1.61)	2.97	2.70	2.68	2.44	2.37
Cash Flow Per Share	3.40	(4.26)	4.72	3.45	3.34	2.64	2.51	2.24
Tang Book Value Per Share	0.03	N.M.	N.M.	2.86	1.32	0.96	2.25	2.37
Dividends Per Share	2.080	2.000	1.920	1.840	1.760	1.680	1.620	1.620
Dividend Payout %	65.20	105.26	N.M.	61.95	65.19	62.69	66.39	68.35
Income Statement								
Total Revenue	1,838,238	1,742,629	1,682,877	1,670,315	1,547,644	1,512,331	1,423,246	1,401,718
EBITDA	960,256	633,160	(348,570)	876,224	792,326	813,491	766,191	734,348
Depn & Amortn	47,647	41,583	49,653	43,196	39,603	37,013	31,726	30,491
Income Before Taxes	837,590	514,675	(444,363)	799,268	718,435	762,943	734,465	703,857
Income Taxes	299,538	195,886	(172,894)	307,666	276,549	293,650	279,186	264,719
Net Income	530,837	318,789	(271,469)	491,602	441,886	469,293	455,279	439,138
Average Shares	166,622	167,376	168,786	165,682	163,506	175,114	186,880	185,602
Balance Sheet								
Current Assets	1,173,133	1,247,966	2,291,267	891,959	691,405	580,024	507,213	441,844
Total Assets	1,659,483	1,726,494	2,765,275	2,011,702	1,646,399	1,015,648	913,319	826,714
Current Liabilities	618,873	521,093	1,462,442	222,462	169,572	261,327	197,316	166,519
Long-Term Obligations	840,000	1,140,000	1,140,000	862,575	869,175	411,000	100,000	100,000
Total Liabilities	1,649,918	1,841,681	2,812,265	1,430,640	1,375,827	814,844	445,026	388,783
Stockholders' Equity	9,565	(115,187)	(46,990)	581,062	270,572	200,804	468,293	437,931
Shares Outstanding	164,606	165,491	168,019	203,420	204,743	208,936	208,095	184,789
Statistical Record								
Return on Assets %	31.27	14.19	N.M.	26.88	33.11	48.66	52.33	53.75
Return on Equity %	N.M.	N.M.	N.M.	115.45	186.98	140.28	100.48	121.99
EBITDA Margin %	52.24	36.33	N.M.	52.46	51.20	53.79	53.83	52.39
Net Margin %	28.88	18.29	N.M.	29.43	28.55	31.03	31.99	31.33
Asset Turnover	1.08	0.78	0.70	0.91	1.16	1.57	1.64	1.72
Current Ratio	1.90	2.39	1.57	4.01	4.08	2.22	2.57	2.65
Debt to Equity	87.82	N.M.	N.M.	1.48	3.21	2.05	0.21	0.23
Price Range	48.90-34.53	37.72-27.42	41.06-25.36	35.90-24.81	28.69-14.00	34.88-24.19	36.94-24.88	36.94-25.75
P/E Ratio	15.33-10.82	19.85-14.43	N/A	12.09-8.35	10.63-5.19	13.01-9.03	15.14-10.19	15.59-10.86
Average Yield %	5.36	6.06	5.64	6.02	8.81	5.73	5.26	5.41

Address: 100 West Putnam Avenue, Greenwich, CT 06830	**Web Site:** www.ustinc.com	**Auditors:** Ernst & Young LLP
Telephone: (203) 661 1100	**Officers:** Vincent A. Gierer Jr. - Chmn., Pres., C.E.O.	**Investor Contact:** 800-730-4001
Fax: (203) 661 1129	Robert T. D'Alessandro - Sr. V.P., C.F.O.	

VALASSIS COMMUNICATIONS, INC.

Exchange	Symbol	Price	52Wk Range	Yield	P/E
NYS	VCI	$34.96 (3/31/2005)	37.72-27.59	N/A	18.11

7 Year Price Score 86.01 *NYSE Composite Index=100 *12 Month Price Score 104.35

Interim Earnings (Per Share)

Qtr.	Mar	Jun	Sep	Dec
2001	0.60	0.62	0.43	0.52
2002	0.60	0.62	0.61	(0.06)
2003	0.50	0.53	0.51	0.44
2004	0.47	0.51	0.43	0.52

Interim Dividends (Per Share)

No Dividends Paid

Valuation Analysis

Forecast P/E	18.31	No of Institutions	
	(4/7/2005)	145	
Market Cap	$1.8 Billion	Shares	
Book Value	140.5 Million	53,870,520	
Price/Book	12.74	% Held	
Price/Sales	1.71	N/A	

Business Summary: Advertising, Marketing & PR (MIC: 12.4 SIC: 319 NAIC: 41870)

Valassis Communications provides a wide range of marketing services to consumer packaged goods manufacturers, retailers, technology companies and other customers with operations in the U.S., Europe, Mexico and Canada. Co. generates most of its revenues by printing and publishing cents-off coupons and other consumer purchase incentives primarily for packaged goods manufacturers. Co. also prints and publishes refund offers, premiums, sweepstakes and contests distributed to households throughout the U.S. Co. operates printing and manufacturing facilities in Michigan, North Carolina, Kansas and Mexico.

Recent Developments: For the year ended Dec 31 2004, net income decreased 2.9% to $100,747 thousand from net income of $103,708 thousand a year earlier. Revenues were $1,044,069 thousand, up 13.9% from $916,520 thousand the year before. Operating income was $159,067 thousand versus an income of $176,138 thousand in the prior year, a decrease of 9.7%. Total direct expense was $748,075 thousand versus $619,927 thousand in the prior year, an increase of 20.7%. Total indirect expense was $136,998 thousand versus $120,455 thousand in the prior year, an increase of 13.7%.

Prospects: Co. is pleased with its operating performance, particularly its achievement of surpassing the milestone of $1.00 billion in revenue in 2004 by diversifying its product portfolio, broadening its customer base and executing effective integrated services for its customers. Also, Co. has been able to improve margins by maintaining a lower-cost producer status. Co. expects this positive momentum to continue into 2005. For full-year 2005, Co. expects revenue to be up by a percentage in the mid-single digits, with earnings per share range from $1.80 and $2.00.

Financial Data
(US$ in Thousands)	12/31/2004	12/31/2003	12/31/2002	12/31/2001	12/31/2000	12/31/1999	12/31/1998	12/31/1997
Earnings Per Share	1.93	1.98	1.77	2.17	2.27	1.97	1.19	1.13
Cash Flow Per Share	1.48	2.36	3.65	2.52	2.09	2.59	1.50	1.37
Tang Book Value Per Share	0.11	N.M.	N.M.	N.M.	N.M.	N.M.	N.M.	N.M.
Income Statement								
Total Revenue	1,044,069	916,520	853,019	849,529	863,121	794,566	741,383	675,496
EBITDA	183,688	190,840	161,905	201,424	213,419	201,553	152,353	130,585
Depn & Amortn	15,521	14,873	12,708	13,735	11,302	12,903	15,844	15,555
Income Before Taxes	156,805	162,833	149,197	187,689	202,117	188,650	136,509	115,030
Income Taxes	56,058	59,125	53,943	68,545	76,418	67,516	52,223	45,100
Net Income	100,747	103,708	95,254	117,859	125,699	114,201	70,688	69,930
Average Shares	52,214	52,269	53,752	54,406	55,478	58,084	59,308	61,962
Balance Sheet								
Current Assets	501,183	456,623	241,976	183,547	167,659	142,311	143,059	151,087
Total Assets	737,965	692,754	386,079	363,025	325,717	247,205	232,014	240,885
Current Liabilities	315,395	349,175	161,794	173,067	171,050	169,564	158,566	148,453
Long-Term Obligations	273,703	259,819	257,280	252,383	325,490	291,354	340,461	367,075
Total Liabilities	597,459	616,695	419,366	428,709	498,221	462,789	500,538	517,852
Stockholders' Equity	140,506	76,059	(33,287)	(65,684)	(172,504)	(215,584)	(268,524)	(276,967)
Shares Outstanding	51,191	52,072	51,995	53,698	53,562	56,128	57,589	59,274
Statistical Record								
Return on Assets %	14.04	19.23	25.43	34.22	43.76	47.66	29.90	27.18
Return on Equity %	92.79	484.93	N.M.	N.M.	N.M.	N.M.	N.M.	N.M.
EBITDA Margin %	17.59	20.82	18.98	23.71	24.73	25.37	20.55	19.33
Net Margin %	9.65	11.32	11.17	13.87	14.56	14.37	9.53	10.35
Asset Turnover	1.46	1.70	2.28	2.47	3.00	3.32	3.14	2.63
Current Ratio	1.59	1.31	1.50	1.06	0.98	0.84	0.90	1.02
Debt to Equity	1.95	3.42	N.M.	N.M.	N.M.	N.M.	N.M.	N.M.
Price Range	35.77-27.59	30.57-21.71	41.00-25.26	37.25-28.30	42.31-21.69	45.69-29.79	34.42-19.88	24.67-12.17
P/E Ratio	18.53-14.30	15.44-10.96	23.16-14.27	17.17-13.04	18.64-9.55	23.19-15.12	28.92-16.70	21.83-10.77

Address: 19975 Victor Parkway, Livonia, MI 48152
Telephone: (734) 591-3000
Fax: (734) 591-4994

Web Site: www.valassis.com
Officers: Alan F. Schultz - Chmn., Pres., C.E.O.
Robert L. Recchia - Exec. V.P., C.F.O.

Auditors: Deloitte & Touche LLP
Investor Contact: 734-591-7374

VALEANT PHARMACEUTICALS INTERNATIONAL

Exchange	Symbol	Price	52Wk Range	Yield	P/E
NYS	VRX	$22.52 (3/31/2005)	27.09-17.06	1.38	N/A

*7 Year Price Score 80.84   *NYSE Composite Index=100   **12 Month Price Score 97.68

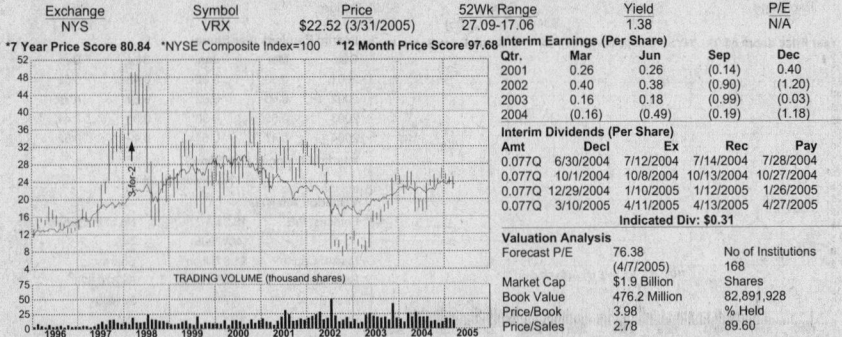

Interim Earnings (Per Share)

Qtr.	Mar	Jun	Sep	Dec
2001	0.26	0.26	(0.14)	0.40
2002	0.40	0.38	(0.90)	(1.20)
2003	0.16	0.18	(0.99)	(0.03)
2004	(0.16)	(0.49)	(0.19)	(1.18)

Interim Dividends (Per Share)

Amt	Decl	Ex	Rec	Pay
0.077Q	6/30/2004	7/12/2004	7/14/2004	7/28/2004
0.077Q	10/1/2004	10/8/2004	10/13/2004	10/27/2004
0.077Q	12/29/2004	1/10/2005	1/12/2005	1/26/2005
0.077Q	3/10/2005	4/11/2005	4/13/2005	4/27/2005

Indicated Div: $0.31

Valuation Analysis

Forecast P/E	76.38	No of Institutions
	(4/7/2005)	168
Market Cap	$1.9 Billion	Shares
Book Value	476.2 Million	82,891,928
Price/Book	3.98	% Held
Price/Sales	2.78	89.60

TRADING VOLUME (thousand shares)

Business Summary: Pharmaceuticals (MIC: 9.1 SIC: 834 NAIC: 25412)

Valeant Pharmaceutical is a global, research-based specialty pharmaceutical company that discovers, develops, manufactures and markets a broad range of products sold in 128 global markets. Co.'s products encompass a broad range of therapeutic areas, with a primary focus upon its three targeted areas: infectious disease, neurology and dermatology. Co.'s research and new product development initiatives focus on innovative treatments for infectious diseases and cancer. Through its wholly-owned subsidiary, Ribapharm, Co. conducts research and new product development, and generates royalty revenues from the sale of ribavirin.

Recent Developments: For the year ended Dec 31 2004, loss from continuing operations was $136,253 thousand compared with a loss of $64,986 thousand a year earlier. Net loss was $169,797 thousand versus net loss of $55,640 thousand a year earlier. Revenues were $682,520 thousand, down 0.5% from $685,953 thousand the year before. Operating income was $4,161 thousand versus an income of $21,573 thousand in the prior year, a decrease of 80.7%. Total direct expense was $200,313 thousand versus $184,669 thousand in the prior year, an increase of 8.5%. Total indirect expense was $478,046 thousand versus $479,711 thousand in the prior year, a decrease of 0.3%.

Prospects: On Mar 1 2005, Co. announced that it has completed its acquisition of Xcel Pharmaceuticals for approximately $280.0 million. The transaction will help boost Co.'s North American business and enhance its neurology franchise through the acquisition of key products and a specialized neurology sales organization. In addition, the acquisition adds several marketed neurology products that include Diastat, a treatment of acute repetitive epileptic seizures outside of a hospital setting, and Migranal, a nasal spray used for the treatment of acute migraine headaches. The acquisition also adds Retigabine, a new Phase 3 candidate in clinical development for the treatment of epilepsy, to Co.'s pipeline.

Financial Data
(US$ in Thousands)

	12/31/2004	12/31/2003	12/31/2002	12/31/2001	12/31/2000	12/31/1999	12/31/1998	12/31/1997
Earnings Per Share	(2.02)	(0.67)	(1.61)	0.77	1.10	1.45	(4.78)	1.69
Cash Flow Per Share	0.21	2.26	0.27	1.70	2.28	1.12	0.13	0.17
Tang Book Value Per Share	0.28	2.05	3.80	4.46	3.99	2.88	1.60	7.98
Dividends Per Share	0.310	0.310	0.308	0.297	0.287	0.270	0.233	0.211
Dividend Payout %	N.M.	N.M.	N.M.	38.64	26.14	18.62	N.M.	12.50
Income Statement								
Total Revenue	682,520	685,953	737,074	858,104	800,304	747,412	838,064	752,202
EBITDA	71,548	78,304	270,392	261,531	241,908	252,536	(318,973)	141,261
Depn & Amortn	87,138	64,807	56,242	71,025	64,540	65,502	51,096	28,753
Income Before Taxes	(52,423)	(13,760)	176,938	144,357	129,554	139,985	(395,081)	105,571
Income Taxes	83,597	39,463	74,963	58,600	37,683	28,996	1,983	(27,736)
Net Income	(169,797)	(55,640)	(134,834)	64,134	90,180	118,626	(352,074)	113,924
Average Shares	83,887	83,602	83,988	83,166	82,264	82,089	73,637	69,650
Balance Sheet								
Current Assets	770,667	1,142,152	576,573	772,929	565,416	564,730	440,748	786,751
Total Assets	1,521,875	1,976,937	1,488,549	1,754,365	1,477,072	1,472,261	1,356,396	1,491,745
Current Liabilities	192,205	166,784	179,503	161,480	158,777	140,622	203,754	201,145
Long-Term Obligations	793,139	1,119,802	481,548	734,933	510,781	596,961	510,808	315,088
Total Liabilities	1,013,596	1,356,878	736,791	943,648	719,878	788,689	770,232	695,417
Stockholders' Equity	476,223	605,361	703,690	810,717	757,194	683,572	586,164	796,328
Shares Outstanding	84,219	83,185	84,066	81,689	80,197	78,950	76,411	71,432
Statistical Record								
Return on Assets %	N.M.	N.M.	N.M.	3.97	6.10	8.39	N.M.	10.04
Return on Equity %	N.M.	N.M.	N.M.	8.18	12.48	18.69	N.M.	20.50
EBITDA Margin %	10.48	11.42	36.68	30.48	30.23	33.79	N.M.	18.78
Net Margin %	N.M.	N.M.	N.M.	7.47	11.27	15.87	N.M.	15.15
Asset Turnover	0.39	0.40	0.45	0.53	0.54	0.53	0.59	0.66
Current Ratio	4.01	6.85	3.21	4.79	3.56	4.02	2.16	3.91
Debt to Equity	1.67	1.85	0.68	0.91	0.67	0.87	0.87	0.40
Price Range	27.09-17.06	25.50-7.87	33.50-6.88	34.26-21.60	40.19-19.75	35.00-16.75	51.13-14.13	36.83-13.08
P/E Ratio	N/A	N/A	N/A	44.49-28.05	36.53-17.95	24.14-11.55	N/A	21.79-7.74
Average Yield %	1.37	2.04	1.57	1.07	1.01	1.06	0.71	0.96

Address: 3300 Hyland Avenue, Costa Mesa, CA 92626	Web Site: www.icnpharm.com	Auditors: PricewaterhouseCoopers LLP
Telephone: (714) 545-0100	Officers: Robert W. O'Leary - Chmn. Timothy C. Tyson - Pres., C.E.O.	Transfer Agents: American Stock Transfer and Trust Corporation, Brooklyn, NY
Fax: (714) 641-7215		

VALERO ENERGY CORP.

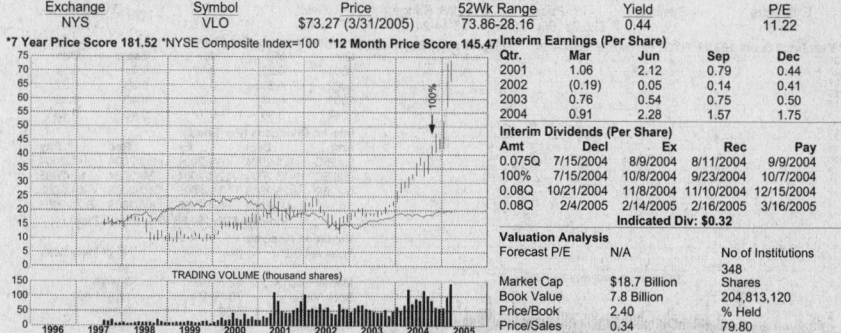

Exchange	Symbol	Price	52Wk Range	Yield	P/E
NYS	VLO	$73.27 (3/31/2005)	73.86-28.16	0.44	11.22

*7 Year Price Score 181.52 *NYSE Composite Index=100 *12 Month Price Score 145.47

Interim Earnings (Per Share)

Qtr.	Mar	Jun	Sep	Dec
2001	1.06	2.12	0.79	0.44
2002	(0.19)	0.05	0.14	0.41
2003	0.76	0.54	0.75	0.50
2004	0.91	2.28	1.57	1.75

Interim Dividends (Per Share)

Amt	Decl	Ex	Rec	Pay
0.075Q	7/15/2004	8/9/2004	8/11/2004	9/9/2004
100%	7/15/2004	10/8/2004	9/23/2004	10/7/2004
0.08Q	10/21/2004	11/8/2004	11/10/2004	12/15/2004
0.08Q	2/4/2005	2/14/2005	2/16/2005	3/16/2005

Indicated Div: $0.32

Valuation Analysis

Forecast P/E	N/A	No of Institutions
		348
Market Cap	$18.7 Billion	Shares
Book Value	7.8 Billion	204,813,120
Price/Book	2.40	% Held
Price/Sales	0.34	79.80

Business Summary: Oil and Gas (MIC: 14.2 SIC: 911 NAIC: 24110)

Valero Energy is an independent refining and marketing company that owned and operated 14 refineries as of Dec 31 2003. The 14 refineries are as follows: six in Texas, two each in California and Louisiana, and one each in Colorado, New Jersey, Oklahoma and Quebec, Canada with a combined throughput capacity of approximately 2.1 million barrels per day. Co. markets refined products through an extensive bulk and rack marketing network and a network of more than 4,500 retail and wholesale branded outlets in the U.S. and eastern Canada under various brand names including primarily Diamond Shamrock®, Shamrock®, Ultramar®, Valero® and Beacon®.

Recent Developments: For the year ended Dec 31 2004, net income increased 190.2% to $1,803,800 thousand from net income of $621,500 thousand a year earlier. Revenues were $54,618,600 thousand, up 43.9% from $37,968,600 thousand the year before. Operating income was $2,979,200 thousand versus an income of $1,222,000 thousand in the prior year, an increase of 143.8%. Total direct expense was $47,797,300 thousand versus $33,587,100 thousand in the prior year, an increase of 42.3%. Total indirect expense was $3,842,100 thousand versus $3,159,500 thousand in the prior year, an increase of 21.6%.

Prospects: Co. is beginning 2005 with wide sour crude discounts and it expects them to continue throughout 2005. In the first quarter, the discount for Mars sour crude oil has averaged more than $7.00 per barrel while the Maya discount has averaged $16.75 per barrel. With regard to refined product fundamentals, distillate margins are at strong levels. With solid fundamentals in place for 2005, Co. believes that its earnings in 2005 should be in excess of its earnings in 2004, even if average refined product margins are lower than 2004. In addition to Co.'s sour crude leverage, it will also have the Aruba refinery for the full first quarter, and incremental earnings from its strategic capital projects.

Financial Data

(US$ in Thousands)	12/31/2004	12/31/2003	12/31/2002	12/31/2001	12/31/2000	12/31/1999	12/31/1998	12/31/1997
Earnings Per Share	6.53	2.54	0.41	4.42	2.80	0.13	(0.42)	0.87
Cash Flow Per Share	11.56	7.63	1.29	7.45	5.12	3.88	1.48	2.14
Tang Book Value Per Share	19.09	11.69	6.47	7.80	12.55	9.67	9.70	10.32
Dividends Per Share	0.290	0.210	0.200	0.170	0.160	0.160	0.160	0.080
Dividend Payout %	4.44	8.25	48.19	3.85	5.71	128.00	N.M.	9.20
Income Statement								
Total Revenue	54,618,600	37,968,600	26,976,200	14,988,339	14,671,087	7,961,168	5,539,346	5,756,220
EBITDA	3,588,200	1,758,400	884,700	1,235,715	777,521	214,639	75,937	310,439
Depn & Amortn	618,400	510,500	449,300	252,354	173,056	139,023	126,549	92,427
Income Before Taxes	2,710,100	986,600	149,700	894,853	528,220	20,187	(83,091)	175,557
Income Taxes	906,300	365,100	58,200	331,300	189,100	5,900	(35,800)	63,789
Net Income	1,803,800	621,500	91,500	563,553	339,120	14,287	(47,291)	96,096
Average Shares	276,100	244,000	220,220	127,606	121,050	113,516	112,156	110,258
Balance Sheet								
Current Assets	5,264,400	3,817,300	3,536,400	4,113,144	1,285,067	828,858	639,710	789,025
Total Assets	19,391,600	15,664,200	14,465,200	14,377,096	4,307,704	2,979,272	2,725,664	2,493,043
Current Liabilities	4,533,500	3,064,300	3,006,700	4,730,246	1,038,992	718,982	497,744	597,284
Long-Term Obligations	3,945,500	4,299,700	4,494,100	2,805,247	1,042,417	785,472	822,335	430,183
Total Liabilities	11,593,600	9,929,000	10,156,900	10,174,533	2,780,649	1,894,503	1,640,377	1,334,202
Stockholders' Equity	7,798,000	5,735,200	4,308,300	4,202,563	1,527,055	1,084,769	1,085,287	1,158,841
Shares Outstanding	255,475	240,532	214,274	208,394	121,676	112,133	111,873	112,272
Statistical Record								
Return on Assets %	10.26	4.13	0.63	6.03	9.28	0.50	N.M.	3.41
Return on Equity %	26.58	12.38	2.15	19.67	25.90	1.32	N.M.	8.56
EBITDA Margin %	6.57	4.63	3.28	8.24	5.30	2.70	1.37	5.39
Net Margin %	3.30	1.64	0.34	3.76	2.31	0.18	N.M.	1.67
Asset Turnover	3.11	2.52	1.87	1.60	4.02	2.79	2.12	2.04
Current Ratio	1.16	1.25	1.18	0.87	1.24	1.15	1.29	1.32
Debt to Equity	0.51	0.75	1.04	0.67	0.68	0.72	0.76	0.37
Price Range	47.63-23.01	23.40-16.55	24.76-11.73	25.93-16.38	19.19-9.47	12.50-8.38	18.22-8.94	17.44-16.34
P/E Ratio	7.29-3.52	9.21-6.52	60.39-28.61	5.87-3.70	6.85-3.38	96.15-64.42	N/A	20.04-16.34
Average Yield %	0.83	1.08	1.05	0.89	1.08	1.55	1.16	0.50

Address: One Valero Place, San Antonio, TX 78212-0500	Web Site: www.valero.com	Auditors: KPMG LLP
Telephone: (210) 370-2000	Officers: William E. Greehey - Chmn., C.E.O.	Investor Contact: 800-531-7911
Fax: (210) 246-2646	Gregory C. King - Pres.	

VALLEY NATIONAL BANCORP

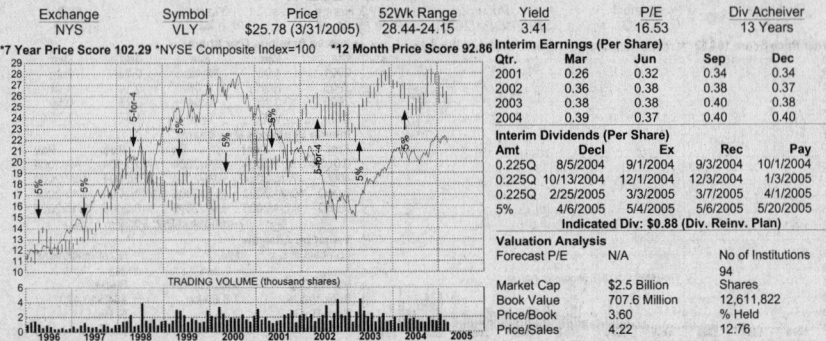

Exchange	Symbol	Price	52Wk Range	Yield	P/E	Div Acheiver
NYS	VLY	$25.78 (3/31/2005)	28.44-24.15	3.41	16.53	13 Years

*7 Year Price Score 102.29 *NYSE Composite Index=100 *12 Month Price Score 92.86

Interim Earnings (Per Share)

Qtr.	Mar	Jun	Sep	Dec
2001	0.26	0.32	0.34	0.34
2002	0.36	0.38	0.38	0.37
2003	0.38	0.38	0.40	0.38
2004	0.39	0.37	0.40	0.40

Interim Dividends (Per Share)

Amt	Decl	Ex	Rec	Pay
0.225Q	8/5/2004	9/1/2004	9/3/2004	10/1/2004
0.225Q	10/13/2004	12/1/2004	12/3/2004	1/3/2005
0.225Q	2/25/2005	3/3/2005	3/7/2005	4/1/2005
5%	4/6/2005	5/4/2005	5/6/2005	5/20/2005

Indicated Div: $0.88 (Div. Reinv. Plan)

Valuation Analysis

Forecast P/E	N/A	No of Institutions
		94
Market Cap	$2.5 Billion	Shares
Book Value	707.6 Million	12,611,822
Price/Book	3.60	% Held
Price/Sales	4.22	12.76

Business Summary: Commercial Banking (MIC: 8.1 SIC: 021 NAIC: 22110)

Valley National Bancorp, with $9.88 billion in assets as of Dec 31 2003, is a bank holding company. Co.'s principal subsidiary is Valley National Bank (VNB). VNB is a national banking association, which provides a full range of commercial and retail banking services through 129 branch offices located in 83 communities serving 11 counties throughout northern New Jersey and Manhattan. These services include the acceptance of demand, savings and time deposits; extension of consumer, real estate, small business administration and other commercial credits; title insurance; investment services; and full personal and corporate trust, as well as pension and fiduciary services.

Recent Developments: For the year ended Dec 31 2004, net income increased 0.6% to $154,398 thousand from net income of $153,415 thousand a year earlier. Net interest income was $372,319 thousand, up 6.8% from $348,576 thousand the year before. Provision for loan losses was $8,003 thousand versus $7,345 thousand in the prior year, an increase of 9.0%. Non-interest income increased to $220,049 thousand, while non-interest expense advanced 1.7% to $220,049 thousand.

Prospects: On Dec 2 2004, Co. announced that it has entered into an agreement to acquire Shrewsbury Bancorp in a transaction valued at approximately $136.0 million. Shrewsbury is the holding company for Shrewsbury State Bank, a commercial bank with approximately $425.0 million in assets. The announced acquisition of Shrewsbury, coupled with the earlier announced acquistion of NorCrown, are anticipated to close before mid-year 2005. Both acquisitions are expected to be accretive within one year and expand Co.'s market presence. Separately, Co. expects to open between seven to 10 de novo branches during 2005, the first of which opened Jan 3 2005 in South Orange, NJ.

Financial Data

(US$ in Thousands)	12/31/2004	12/31/2003	12/31/2002	12/31/2001	12/31/2000	12/31/1999	12/31/1998	12/31/1997
Earnings Per Share	1.56	1.54	1.50	1.26	1.21	1.20	1.15	1.32
Cash Flow Per Share	1.63	2.26	1.11	1.52	1.33	2.43	3.64	2.52
Tang Book Value Per Share	6.69	6.09	6.33	6.44	6.27	6.73	6.62	7.39
Dividends Per Share	0.889	0.847	0.805	0.757	0.710	0.670	0.608	0.533
Dividend Payout %	57.01	54.89	53.76	60.27	58.72	56.05	52.79	40.50
Income Statement								
Interest Income	518,926	497,498	517,419	553,486	460,853	427,535	389,656	368,318
Interest Expense	146,607	148,922	157,723	218,653	202,756	169,177	160,104	155,977
Net Interest Income	372,319	348,576	359,696	334,833	258,097	258,358	229,552	212,341
Provision for Losses	8,003	7,345	13,644	15,706	6,130	9,120	12,370	12,250
Non-Interest Income	84,328	108,197	81,238	68,476	50,883	47,252	43,073	42,315
Non-Interest Expense	220,049	216,278	207,994	188,248	141,013	137,946	134,757	123,228
Income Before Taxes	228,595	233,150	219,296	199,355	161,837	158,544	125,498	119,178
Income Taxes	74,197	79,735	64,680	64,151	55,064	52,220	28,150	34,186
Net Income	154,398	153,415	154,616	135,204	106,773	106,324	97,348	84,992
Average Shares	99,178	99,223	103,274	107,547	88,426	88,711	84,488	64,677
Balance Sheet								
Net Loans & Leases	6,868,616	6,107,759	5,698,401	5,268,004	4,607,679	4,499,632	3,927,982	(46,372)
Total Assets	10,763,391	9,880,740	9,134,674	8,583,765	6,425,837	6,360,394	5,541,207	5,090,655
Total Deposits	7,518,739	7,162,968	6,683,387	6,306,974	5,123,717	5,051,255	4,674,689	4,402,954
Total Liabilities	10,055,793	9,227,951	8,302,936	7,705,390	5,880,763	5,806,894	4,985,420	4,615,296
Stockholders' Equity	707,598	652,789	631,738	678,375	545,074	553,500	555,787	475,359
Shares Outstanding	98,855	98,605	99,802	105,381	86,876	82,264	83,970	64,361
Statistical Record								
Return on Assets %	1.49	1.61	1.75	1.80	1.67	1.79	1.83	1.74
Return on Equity %	22.64	23.89	23.60	22.10	19.39	19.17	18.88	19.50
Net Interest Margin %	71.75	70.07	69.52	60.50	56.00	60.43	58.91	57.65
Efficiency Ratio %	36.48	35.71	34.74	30.27	27.56	29.05	31.14	30.01
Loans to Deposits	0.91	0.85	0.85	0.84	0.90	0.89	0.84	...
Price Range	28.44-24.15	28.54-21.77	26.25-22.18	23.91-17.72	23.15-14.23	19.29-15.51	22.25-15.75	20.18-12.12
P/E Ratio	18.23-15.48	18.53-14.14	17.50-14.78	18.98-14.06	19.13-11.76	16.08-12.93	19.35-13.69	15.29-9.18
Average Yield %	3.39	3.31	3.25	3.68	3.98	3.87	3.21	3.66

Address: 1455 Valley Road, Wayne, NJ 07470	**Web Site:** www.valleynationalbank.com	**Auditors:** Ernst & Young LLP
Telephone: (973) 305-8800	**Officers:** Gerald H. Lipkin - Chmn., Pres., C.E.O.	**Investor Contact:** 973-305-8800
Fax: (973) 305-1605	Peter Crocitto - Exec. V.P.	**Transfer Agents:** American Stock Transfer & Trust Company

VALSPAR CORP.

Exchange	Symbol	Price	52Wk Range	Yield	P/E	Div Acheiver
NYS	VAL	$46.54 (3/31/2005)	51.35-44.87	1.72	18.04	26 Years

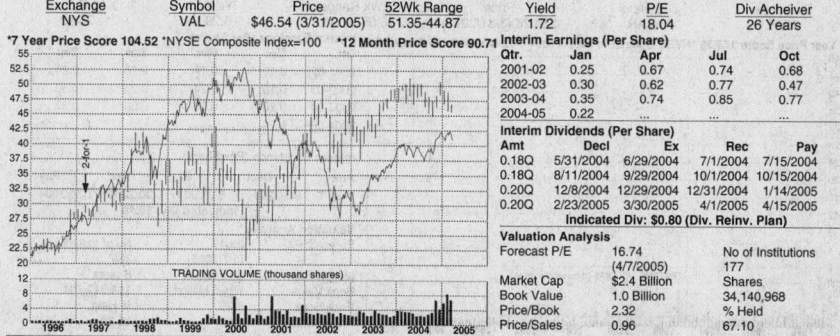

*7 Year Price Score 104.52 *NYSE Composite Index=100 *12 Month Price Score 90.71

Interim Earnings (Per Share)

Qtr.	Jan	Apr	Jul	Oct
2001-02	0.25	0.67	0.74	0.68
2002-03	0.30	0.62	0.77	0.47
2003-04	0.35	0.74	0.85	0.77
2004-05	0.22	...	...	...

Interim Dividends (Per Share)

Amt	Decl	Ex	Rec	Pay
0.18Q	5/31/2004	6/29/2004	7/1/2004	7/15/2004
0.18Q	8/11/2004	9/29/2004	10/1/2004	10/15/2004
0.20Q	12/8/2004	12/29/2004	12/31/2004	1/14/2005
0.20Q	2/23/2005	3/30/2005	4/1/2005	4/15/2005

Indicated Div: $0.80 (Div. Reinv. Plan)

Valuation Analysis

Forecast P/E	16.74 (4/7/2005)	No of Institutions 177
Market Cap	$2.4 Billion	Shares 34,140,968
Book Value	1.0 Billion	% Held
Price/Book	2.32	67.10
Price/Sales	0.96	

Business Summary: Chemicals (MIC: 11.1 SIC: 851 NAIC: 25510)

Valspar is a global paint and coatings manufacturer. The Paints segment includes interior and exterior decorative paints, primers, varnishes and specialty decorative products, such as enamels, aerosols and faux finishes for the do-it-yourself and professional markets, as well as automotive refinish and high performance floor coatings. In the Coatings segment, the Industrial coatings product line includes decorative and protective coatings for wood, metal, plastic and glass. The Packaging coatings product line includes coatings and inks for rigid packaging containers. Other products include specialty polymers and colorants,as well as composites and furniture protection plans.

Recent Developments: For the quarter ended Jan 28 2005, net income dropped 36.4% to $11.7 million compared with $18.4 million in the equivalent 2003 quarter, primarily reflecting a sharp increase in the cost of raw materials used in the manufacture of coatings due to issues of availability and unprecedented increases in the price of raw material feedstocks. Net sales grew 11.1% to $557.1 million from $501.6 million the year before. Sales benefited primarily from the strength in all of Co.'s businesses and the contribution of recent acquisitions. Gross profit declined 2.3% to $152.8 million versus $156.4 million a year earlier. Operating income decreased 23.7% to $30.7 million from $40.3 million in 2003.

Prospects: Co. is encouraged by its revenue growth, which reflects continuing sales strength in all of its businesses. However, the effects of higher raw material costs is adversely affecting Co.'s profit margins. While these trends are expected to continue, Co. believes additional pricing actions should begin to restore its margins to acceptable levels. Effective Mar 1 2005, Co. raised its prices on all industrial powder products by 15.0% and on all liquid and electrocoat products between 5.0% and 15.0%. This is in response to the rapid run-up in the cost of raw materials used in the manufacture of industrial coatings due to issues of availability and increases in the price of raw material feedstocks.

Financial Data

(US$ in Thousands)	3 Mos	10/29/2004	10/31/2003	10/25/2002	10/26/2001	10/27/2000	10/29/1999	10/30/1998
Earnings Per Share	2.58	2.71	2.17	2.34	1.10	2.00	1.87	1.63
Cash Flow Per Share	4.09	4.81	4.88	4.33	4.30	2.19	2.95	2.63
Tang Book Value Per Share	N.M.	N.M.	N.M.	N.M.	N.M.	5.39	4.07	5.42
Dividends Per Share	0.740	0.720	0.600	0.560	0.540	0.520	0.460	0.420
Dividend Payout %	28.64	26.57	27.65	23.93	49.09	26.00	24.60	25.77
Income Statement								
Total Revenue	557,144	2,440,692	2,247,926	2,126,853	1,920,970	1,483,320	1,387,677	1,155,134
EBITDA	44,840	330,473	282,939	298,402	236,759	208,973	193,975	160,237
Depn & Amortn	15,739	60,537	55,622	51,143	73,050	45,238	39,800	30,742
Income Before Taxes	18,569	228,537	181,474	198,548	91,150	141,746	135,086	118,788
Income Taxes	6,871	85,701	68,960	78,427	39,650	55,280	52,944	46,658
Net Income	11,698	142,836	112,514	120,121	51,500	86,466	82,142	72,130
Average Shares	52,632	52,709	51,924	51,370	46,657	43,195	43,835	44,319
Balance Sheet								
Current Assets	846,983	802,315	738,831	701,788	661,494	533,864	514,928	426,069
Total Assets	2,695,201	2,634,258	2,496,524	2,419,552	2,226,070	1,125,030	1,110,720	801,680
Current Liabilities	823,991	718,211	531,063	503,895	475,067	334,288	374,712	267,984
Long-Term Obligations	465,246	549,073	749,199	885,819	1,006,217	300,300	298,874	164,768
Total Liabilities	1,658,445	1,633,895	1,627,207	1,682,299	1,571,505	687,459	716,964	461,492
Stockholders' Equity	1,036,756	1,000,363	869,317	737,253	654,565	437,571	393,756	340,188
Shares Outstanding	51,661	51,304	50,730	50,104	49,481	42,481	42,983	43,418
Statistical Record								
Return on Assets %	5.18	5.58	4.50	5.19	3.08	7.76	8.61	10.21
Return on Equity %	14.10	15.32	13.78	17.31	9.46	20.86	22.45	22.77
EBITDA Margin %	8.05	13.54	12.59	14.03	12.32	14.09	13.98	13.87
Net Margin %	2.10	5.85	5.01	5.65	2.68	5.83	5.92	6.24
Asset Turnover	0.95	0.95	0.90	0.92	1.15	1.33	1.46	1.63
Current Ratio	1.03	1.12	1.39	1.39	1.39	1.60	1.37	1.59
Debt to Equity	0.45	0.55	0.86	1.20	1.54	0.69	0.76	0.48
Price Range	51.35-44.87	51.35-44.87	47.95-37.69	49.91-33.21	37.49-25.45	43.06-20.60	39.56-28.06	42.00-26.31
P/E Ratio	19.90-17.39	18.95-16.56	22.10-17.37	21.33-14.19	34.08-23.14	21.53-10.30	21.16-15.01	25.77-16.14
Average Yield %	1.53	1.48	1.37	1.33	1.69	1.55	1.33	1.20

Address: 1101 Third Street South, Minneapolis, MN 55415 **Telephone:** (612) 332-7371 **Fax:** (612) 375-7723	**Web Site:** www.valspar.com **Officers:** Richard M. Rompala - Chmn. William L. Mansfield - Pres., C.E.O.	**Auditors:** Ernst & Young LLP **Transfer Agents:** Mellon Investor Services LLC, Ridgefield Park, NJ

VARIAN MEDICAL SYSTEMS, INC.

Exchange	Symbol	Price	52Wk Range	Yield	P/E
NYS	VAR	$34.28 (3/31/2005)	46.06-31.38	0.29	26.99

*7 Year Price Score 173.36 *NYSE Composite Index=100 *12 Month Price Score 87.97

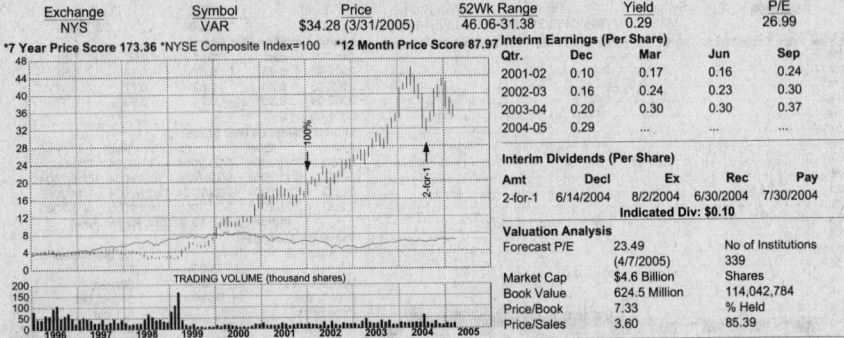

Interim Earnings (Per Share)

Qtr.	Dec	Mar	Jun	Sep
2001-02	0.10	0.17	0.16	0.24
2002-03	0.16	0.24	0.23	0.30
2003-04	0.20	0.30	0.30	0.37
2004-05	0.29	...	...	...

Interim Dividends (Per Share)

Amt	Decl	Ex	Rec	Pay
2-for-1	6/14/2004	8/2/2004	6/30/2004	7/30/2004

Indicated Div: $0.10

Valuation Analysis

Forecast P/E	23.49 (4/7/2005)	No of Institutions	339
Market Cap	$4.6 Billion	Shares	114,042,784
Book Value	624.5 Million	% Held	85.39
Price/Book	7.33		
Price/Sales	3.60		

Business Summary: Industrial Machinery and Equipment (MIC: 11.5 SIC: 845 NAIC: 33319)

Varian Medical Systems is engaged in the design and production of equipment and software for treating cancer with radiation therapy, as well as X-ray tubes for original equipment manufacturers, or OEMs, replacement X-ray tubes and imaging subsystems. In addition, Co. also develops software products and devices designed to enhance the productivity and quality of its equipment, devices manufactured by other companies and the general delivery of health care services. Co.'s products can be classified as Oncology Systems, X-ray Products, including X-ray tubes and imaging subsystems, and BrachyTherapy and other technologies developed by Co.'s Ginzton Technology Center.

Recent Developments: For the quarter ended Dec 31 2004, net income increased 37.6% to $40,309 thousand from net income of $29,286 thousand in the year-earlier quarter. Revenues were $298,956 thousand, up 12.0% from $266,965 thousand the year before. Operating income was $60,626 thousand versus an income of $44,633 thousand in the prior-year quarter, an increase of 35.8%. Total direct expense was $173,772 thousand versus $160,256 thousand in the prior-year quarter, an increase of 8.4%. Total indirect expense was $64,558 thousand versus $62,076 thousand in the prior-year quarter, an increase of 4.0%.

Prospects: Co.'s results are benefiting from strong net order growth in the international market and in its emerging product lines for flat panel imaging, brachytherapy, and image-guided radiation therapy (IGRT) despite declining North American Oncology Systems' orders. For fiscal 2005, Co. expects total revenues to increase about 13.0% to 14.0% and earnings per diluted share to rise approximately 22.0%. In January 2005, Co. announced its acquisition of Sigma Micro Informatique Conseil for about $13.0 million in cash. The acquisition enables Co. to provide French-speaking and other international clinics and hospitals with information management technology.

Financial Data
(US$ in Thousands)

	3 Mos	10/01/2004	09/26/2003	09/27/2002	09/28/2001	09/29/2000	10/01/1999	10/02/1998
Earnings Per Share	1.27	1.18	0.92	0.67	0.40	0.41	(0.20)	0.61
Cash Flow Per Share	1.63	1.69	1.55	1.16	0.90	0.68	(0.28)	1.08
Tang Book Value Per Share	3.83	3.74	3.71	3.04	2.93	2.13	1.51	4.69
Dividends Per Share	...	...	...	...	...	...	0.025	0.098
Dividend Payout %	...	...	...	...	...	...	N.M.	16.05
Income Statement								
Total Revenue	298,956	1,235,523	1,041,557	873,092	773,643	689,700	590,440	1,422,125
EBITDA	67,134	281,124	218,664	164,826	125,015	106,824	61,709	157,820
Depn & Amortn	6,508	25,123	20,314	19,849	20,124	19,121	37,398	42,663
Income Before Taxes	61,079	257,303	201,368	146,259	107,040	84,875	18,239	112,740
Income Taxes	20,770	90,060	70,480	52,650	39,070	31,826	10,021	38,900
Net Income	40,309	167,243	130,888	93,609	54,250	53,049	(24,238)	73,840
Average Shares	139,938	142,215	142,152	140,478	136,912	124,416	122,108	121,676
Balance Sheet								
Current Assets	895,828	885,136	805,524	651,359	619,503	450,588	382,246	839,781
Total Assets	1,193,262	1,170,192	1,053,487	910,277	759,199	602,550	539,183	1,218,295
Current Liabilities	470,635	461,339	409,416	358,083	285,354	249,896	269,802	504,889
Long-Term Obligations	55,733	53,250	58,500	58,500	58,500	58,500	58,500	111,090
Total Liabilities	568,723	556,478	489,811	437,474	364,803	332,191	354,192	660,750
Stockholders' Equity	624,539	613,714	563,676	472,803	394,396	270,359	184,991	557,545
Shares Outstanding	133,543	134,045	135,942	135,580	134,720	127,076	122,252	118,972
Statistical Record								
Return on Assets %	15.73	14.80	13.37	11.24	7.99	9.32	N.M.	6.26
Return on Equity %	29.68	27.95	25.33	21.65	16.37	23.36	N.M.	13.43
EBITDA Margin %	22.46	22.75	20.99	18.88	16.16	15.49	10.45	11.10
Net Margin %	13.48	13.54	12.57	10.72	7.01	7.69	N.M.	5.19
Asset Turnover	1.12	1.09	1.06	1.05	1.14	1.21	0.67	1.20
Current Ratio	1.90	1.92	1.97	1.82	2.17	1.80	1.42	1.66
Debt to Equity	0.09	0.09	0.10	0.12	0.15	0.22	0.32	0.20
Price Range	46.06-31.38	46.06-28.25	31.15-21.00	23.45-15.04	19.20-10.64	12.20-5.05	6.31-2.38	5.01-2.39
P/E Ratio	36.27-24.71	39.04-23.94	33.86-22.83	35.00-22.44	47.99-26.60	29.76-12.31	N/A	8.21-3.91
Average Yield %	...	...	...	...	...	...	0.63	2.67

Address: 3100 Hansen Way, Palo Alto, CA 94304-1030	Web Site: www.varian.com	Auditors: PricewaterhouseCoopers LLP
Telephone: (650) 493-4000	Officers: Richard M. Levy - Chmn., Pres., C.E.O. Timothy E. Guertin - Exec. V.P., C.O.O.	Investor Contact: 650-424-5855 Transfer Agents: First Chicago Trust Company of New York, Jersey City, NJ
Fax: (650) 493-0307		

VECTREN CORP

Exchange	Symbol	Price	52Wk Range	Yield	P/E	Div Acheiver
NYS	VVC	$26.64 (3/31/2005)	27.86-22.90	4.43	18.76	29 Years

*7 Year Price Score 96.93 ***NYSE Composite Index=100** ***12 Month Price Score 98.23**

Interim Earnings (Per Share)

Qtr.	Mar	Jun	Sep	Dec
2001	0.67	(0.26)	0.07	0.48
2002	0.67	0.21	0.21	0.59
2003	0.82	0.06	0.10	0.60
2004	0.72	0.04	0.13	0.53

Interim Dividends (Per Share)

Amt	Decl	Ex	Rec	Pay
0.285Q	4/28/2004	5/12/2004	5/14/2004	6/1/2004
0.285Q	7/28/2004	8/11/2004	8/13/2004	9/1/2004
0.295Q	10/28/2004	11/10/2004	11/15/2004	12/1/2004
0.295Q	1/26/2005	2/11/2005	2/15/2005	3/1/2005

Indicated Div: $1.18 (Div. Reinv. Plan)

Valuation Analysis

Forecast P/E	14.97
	(4/7/2005)
Market Cap	$2.0 Billion
Book Value	1.1 Billion
Price/Book	1.85
Price/Sales	1.20

No of Institutions	179
Shares	29,756,494
% Held	39.11

Business Summary: Electricity (MIC: 7.1 SIC: 932 NAIC: 21210)

Vectren is an energy and applied technology holding company. At Dec 31 2003, Co. supplied natural gas service to 972,230 Indiana and Ohio customers, including 887,891 residential, 80,292 commercial, and 4,047 industrial and other customers. In addition, at Dec 31 2003, Co. supplied electric service to 135,098 Indiana customers, including 117,868 residential, 17,054 commercial, and 176 industrial and other customers. Co. is also involved in nonregulated activities in four primary business areas: Energy Marketing and Services, Coal Mining, Utility Infrastructure Services, and Broadband.

Recent Developments: For the year ended Dec 31 2004, net income decreased 3.0% to $107,900 thousand from net income of $111,200 thousand a year earlier. Revenues were $1,689,800 thousand, up 6.4% from $1,587,700 thousand the year before. Operating income was $202,700 thousand versus an income of $199,400 thousand in the prior year, an increase of 1.7%. Total direct expense was $1,038,800 thousand versus $968,900 thousand in the prior year, an increase of 7.2%. Total indirect expense was $448,300 thousand versus $419,400 thousand in the prior year, an increase of 6.9%.

Prospects: During 2004, Co. made progress in implementing its regulatory initiatives, which are expected to provide the opportunity for significantly improved earnings from regulated operations in 2005. In addition, Co. implemented new base rates in it Indiana gas territories in 2004 and expects to implement new rates for its Ohio service area late in the first quarter of 2005. Looking ahead, Co. is targeting full-year 2005 earnings in the range of $1.70 to $1.90 per share. This projection is based on several factors, including normal weather conditions, continued growth from Co.'s complementary nonregulated businesses, and securing rate relief at Vectren Energy Delivery of Ohio.

Financial Data

(US$ in Thousands)	12/31/2004	12/31/2003	12/31/2002	12/31/2001	12/31/2000	12/31/1999	12/31/1998
Earnings Per Share	1.42	1.57	1.68	0.95	1.17	1.48	1.40
Cash Flow Per Share	3.18	2.51	4.32	2.75	0.66	2.43	2.80
Tang Book Value Per Share	11.70	11.46	9.83	9.68	8.69	11.58	...
Dividends Per Share	1.150	1.110	1.070	1.030	0.740	0.940	0.900
Dividend Payout %	80.99	70.70	63.69	108.42	63.25	63.51	64.29
Income Statement							
Total Revenue	1,689,800	1,587,700	1,804,300	2,170,000	1,648,690	1,068,417	997,706
EBITDA	357,200	344,200	341,100	293,700	270,070	267,236	251,209
Depn & Amortn	140,100	128,700	119,600	123,700	105,661	86,998	81,558
Income Before Taxes	147,000	149,000	153,400	87,400	107,276	137,376	129,350
Income Taxes	39,000	37,700	38,900	18,600	34,232	45,708	42,328
Net Income	107,900	111,200	114,000	63,600	72,040	90,748	86,600
Average Shares	75,900	70,800	67,900	66,900	61,380	61,430	61,578
Balance Sheet							
Net PPE	2,385,400	2,226,000	1,876,100	1,776,700	1,659,238	1,400,807	...
Total Assets	3,586,900	3,353,400	2,926,500	2,856,800	2,909,187	1,980,467	...
Long-Term Obligations	1,016,600	1,072,800	954,200	1,014,000	631,954	486,726	...
Total Liabilities	2,492,000	2,281,500	2,056,300	2,007,700	2,160,538	1,251,428	...
Stockholders' Equity	1,094,800	1,071,700	869,500	848,600	731,684	709,757	...
Shares Outstanding	75,900	75,600	67,900	67,700	61,419	61,305	...
Statistical Record							
Return on Assets %	3.10	3.54	3.94	2.21	2.94	4.58	...
Return on Equity %	9.93	11.45	13.27	8.05	9.97	12.78	...
EBITDA Margin %	21.14	21.68	18.90	13.53	16.38	25.01	25.18
Net Margin %	6.39	7.00	6.32	2.93	4.37	8.49	8.68
PPE Turnover	0.73	0.77	0.99	1.26	1.07	0.76	...
Asset Turnover	0.49	0.51	0.62	0.75	0.67	0.54	...
Debt to Equity	0.93	1.00	1.10	1.19	0.86	0.69	...
Price Range	27.08-22.90	26.00-20.01	25.87-18.69	24.19-19.90	26.50-15.13	24.63-17.75	26.38-19.88
P/E Ratio	19.07-16.13	16.56-12.75	15.40-11.13	25.46-20.95	22.65-12.93	16.64-11.99	18.84-14.20
Average Yield %	4.61	4.81	4.49	4.70	3.79	4.54	3.99

Address: 20 N.W. Fourth Street,	Web Site: www.vectren.com	Auditors: Deloitte & Touche LLP
Evansville, IN 47708	Officers: Niel C. Ellerbrook - Chmn., Pres., C.E.O.	Investor Contact: 800-227-8625
Telephone: (812) 491-4000	Jerome A. Benkert Jr. - Exec. V.P., C.F.O.	Transfer Agents: National City Bank,
Fax: (812) 491-4149		Cleveland, OH

VERIZON COMMUNICATIONS INC

Exchange	Symbol	Price	52Wk Range	Yield	P/E
NYS	VZ	$35.50 (3/31/2005)	42.22-34.13	4.56	12.72

*7 Year Price Score 70.16 ***NYSE Composite Index=100** ***12 Month Price Score 87.52**

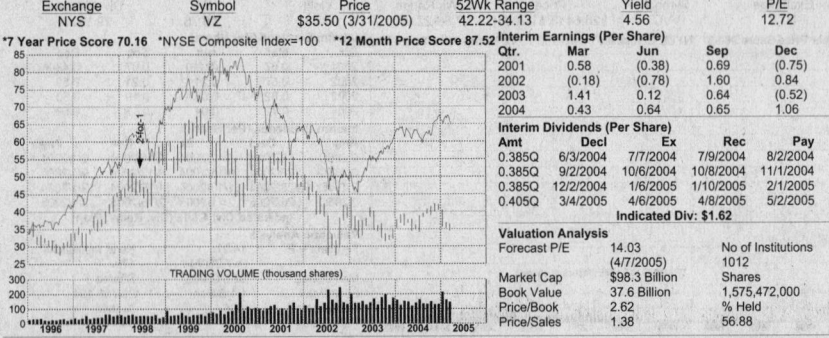

Interim Earnings (Per Share)

Qtr.	Mar	Jun	Sep	Dec
2001	0.58	(0.38)	0.69	(0.75)
2002	(0.18)	(0.78)	1.60	0.84
2003	1.41	0.12	0.64	(0.52)
2004	0.43	0.64	0.65	1.06

Interim Dividends (Per Share)

Amt	Decl	Ex	Rec	Pay
0.385Q	6/3/2004	7/7/2004	7/9/2004	8/2/2004
0.385Q	9/2/2004	10/6/2004	10/8/2004	11/1/2004
0.385Q	12/2/2004	1/6/2005	1/10/2005	2/1/2005
0.405Q	3/4/2005	4/6/2005	4/8/2005	5/2/2005

Indicated Div: $1.62

Valuation Analysis

Forecast P/E	14.03 (4/7/2005)	No of Institutions 1012
Market Cap	$98.3 Billion	Shares 1,575,472,000
Book Value	37.6 Billion	% Held
Price/Book	2.62	56.88
Price/Sales	1.38	

Business Summary: Communications (MIC: 10.1 SIC: 813 NAIC: 17110)

Verizon Communications is a provider of communications services. Verizon is a major provider of wireline and wireless communications in the United States, with 140.3 million access line equivalents and 37.5 million wireless customers. Verizon is the third largest long distance carrier for U.S. consumers, with 16.6 million long distance lines, and Co. is also the largest directory publisher in the world, as measured by directory titles and circulation. Verizon's international presence extends primarily to the Americas, as well as investments in Europe.

Recent Developments: For the year ended Dec 31 2004, income from continuing operations increased 109.9% to $7,261,000 thousand from income of $3,460,000 thousand a year earlier. Net income increased 154.5% to $7,831,000 thousand from net income of $3,077,000 thousand a year earlier. Revenues were $71,283,000 thousand, up 5.7% from $67,468,000 thousand the year before. Operating income was $13,117,000 thousand versus an income of $7,407,000 thousand in the prior year, an increase of 77.1%. Total direct expense was $23,168,000 thousand versus $21,701,000 thousand in the prior year, an increase of 6.8%. Total indirect expense was $34,998,000 thousand versus $38,360,000 thousand the prior year, a decrease of 8.8%.

Prospects: In 2004, Co. changed its growth profile by divesting non-strategic assets, by extending its market position in wireless, and by gaining momentum in the broadband, long-distance and enterprise markets. Meanwhile, Co.'s wireline business has maintained stable margins, and its information services and international businesses have continued to contribute significant revenue, income and cash flow. Going forward, Co. is diversifying and investing in growth areas to provide customers with continuous service enhancements and product innovations. Separately, On Feb 14 2005, Co.announced that it has agreed to acquire MCI, Inc. for $4.80 billion in equity and $488.0 million in cash.

Financial Data

(US$ in Thousands)	12/31/2004	12/31/2003	12/31/2002	12/31/2001	12/31/2000	12/31/1999	12/31/1998	12/31/1997
Earnings Per Share	2.79	1.11	1.49	0.14	4.31	2.65	1.86	1.56
Cash Flow Per Share	7.86	8.16	8.10	7.30	5.82	6.86	6.48	5.71
Tang Book Value Per Share	N.M.	N.M.	N.M.	N.M.	N.M.	10.23	8.39	8.11
Dividends Per Share	1.155	1.540	1.540	1.540	1.540	1.540	1.540	1.485
Dividend Payout %	41.40	138.74	103.36	N.M.	35.73	58.11	82.80	94.89
Income Statement								
Total Revenue	71,283,000	67,752,000	67,625,000	67,190,000	64,707,000	33,174,000	31,565,900	30,193,900
EBITDA	26,290,000	21,079,000	22,862,000	19,792,000	33,570,000	14,098,000	12,084,300	10,968,200
Depn & Amortn	13,910,000	13,617,000	13,423,000	13,657,000	12,261,000	6,070,000	5,750,000	5,754,100
Income Before Taxes	10,112,000	4,761,000	6,202,000	2,766,000	17,819,000	6,765,000	4,998,900	3,984,100
Income Taxes	2,851,000	1,252,000	1,618,000	2,176,000	7,009,000	2,557,000	2,008,100	1,529,200
Net Income	7,831,000	3,077,000	4,079,000	389,000	11,797,000	4,202,000	2,965,300	2,454,900
Average Shares	2,831,000	2,789,000	2,745,000	2,730,000	2,737,000	1,583,000	1,578,300	1,571,000
Balance Sheet								
Current Assets	19,479,000	18,293,000	20,921,000	23,187,000	22,121,000	10,596,000	9,082,300	9,000,800
Total Assets	165,958,000	165,968,000	167,468,000	170,795,000	164,735,000	62,614,000	55,143,900	53,964,100
Current Liabilities	23,129,000	26,570,000	27,047,000	38,020,000	34,236,000	13,467,000	10,531,200	13,664,200
Long-Term Obligations	35,674,000	39,413,000	44,791,000	45,657,000	42,491,000	18,463,000	17,646,400	13,265,200
Total Liabilities	128,398,000	132,502,000	134,852,000	138,256,000	130,157,000	46,734,000	42,118,500	41,175,000
Stockholders' Equity	37,560,000	33,466,000	32,616,000	32,539,000	34,578,000	15,880,000	13,025,400	12,789,100
Shares Outstanding	2,769,652	2,767,760	2,743,027	2,716,478	2,702,436	1,552,677	1,553,300	1,576,052
Statistical Record								
Return on Assets %	4.71	1.85	2.41	0.23	10.35	7.14	5.44	6.23
Return on Equity %	21.99	9.31	12.52	1.16	46.63	29.07	22.97	24.29
EBITDA Margin %	36.88	31.11	33.81	29.46	51.88	42.50	38.28	36.33
Net Margin %	10.99	4.54	6.03	0.58	18.23	12.67	9.39	8.13
Asset Turnover	0.43	0.41	0.40	0.40	0.57	0.56	0.58	0.77
Current Ratio	0.84	0.69	0.77	0.61	0.65	0.79	0.86	0.66
Debt to Equity	0.95	1.18	1.37	1.40	1.23	1.16	1.35	1.04
Price Range	42.22-34.13	44.07-31.50	50.61-27.43	57.16-46.00	65.19-40.38	69.50-51.00	59.75-41.13	45.50-28.81
P/E Ratio	15.13-12.23	39.70-28.38	33.97-18.41	408.29-328.57	15.12-9.37	26.23-19.25	32.12-22.11	29.17-18.47
Average Yield %	3.02	4.31	3.90	2.96	2.90	2.55	3.19	4.03

Address: 1095 Avenue of the Americas, New York, NY 10036	**Web Site:** www.verizon.com	**Auditors:** Ernst & Young LLP
Telephone: (212) 395-2121	**Officers:** Ivan G. Seidenberg - Chmn., Pres., C.E.O.	**Investor Contact:** 212-395-1525
Fax: (212) 921-2917	Lawrence T. Babbio Jr. - Vice-Chmn., Pres.	

VF CORP.

Exchange	Symbol	Price	52Wk Range	Yield	P/E	Div Acheiver
NYS	VFC	$59.14 (3/31/2005)	60.46-43.90	1.83	14.05	32 Years

*7 Year Price Score 110.88 *NYSE Composite Index=100 *12 Month Price Score 104.76

Interim Earnings (Per Share)

Qtr.	Mar	Jun	Sep	Dec
2001	0.67	0.60	0.90	(0.98)
2002	(4.11)	0.79	1.15	0.67
2003	0.83	0.68	1.14	0.96
2004	0.93	0.80	1.38	1.10

Interim Dividends (Per Share)

Amt	Decl	Ex	Rec	Pay
0.26Q	4/27/2004	6/9/2004	6/11/2004	6/21/2004
0.26Q	7/21/2004	9/8/2004	9/10/2004	9/20/2004
0.27Q	10/21/2004	12/8/2004	12/10/2004	12/20/2004
0.27Q	2/8/2005	3/9/2005	3/11/2005	3/21/2005

Indicated Div: $1.08 (Div. Reinv. Plan)

Valuation Analysis

Forecast P/E	12.84 (4/7/2005)	No of Institutions 286
Market Cap	$6.6 Billion	Shares 98,224,088
Book Value	2.5 Billion	% Held 87.43
Price/Book	2.62	
Price/Sales	1.09	

Business Summary: Apparel (MIC: 4.4 SIC: 329 NAIC: 15228)

VF designs, manufactures and markets branded jeanswear, sportswear, intimate apparel, occupational apparel, knitwear, outdoor apparel and equipment, and other apparel. Co. manages its business through over 25 marketing units that support specific brands. Marketing units with similar products have been grouped together into four reportable segments: consumer apparel, occupational apparel, outdoor apparel and equipment, and all other. Co.'s principal brands include: Lee®, Rustler®, Wrangler®, Riders®, Vanity Fair®, Vassarette®, Bestform®, Lily of France®, Lee Sport®, Healthtex®, JanSport®, Eastpak®, Red Kap®, Nautica® and The North Face®.

Recent Developments: For the year ended Jan 1 2005, net income increased 19.3% to $474,702 thousand from net income of $397,933 thousand a year earlier. Revenues were $6,054,536 thousand, up 16.3% from $5,207,459 thousand the year before. Operating income was $777,788 thousand versus an income of $644,889 thousand in the prior year, an increase of 20.6%. Total direct expense was $3,644,255 thousand versus $3,262,375 thousand in the prior year, an increase of 11.7%. Total indirect expense was $1,676,769 thousand versus $1,331,814 thousand in the prior year, an increase of 25.9%.

Prospects: Co. is achieving growth across all of its businesses, jeanswear, outdoor, intimates, imagewear and sportswear. Co. is benefiting from a powerful combination of strong category-driven businesses that are highly profitable and generate healthy cash flow, plus the addition of new lifestyle brands, including Vans®, Napapijri® and Kipling®. Co.'s new long-term annual sales growth target is now 8.0%. Co. is planning for 6.0% to 8.0% sales growth in 2005, before any additional acquisitions. For 2005, Co. expects earnings per share growth of at least 8.0% and believes cash flow from operations will be approximately $550.0 million.

Financial Data

(US$ in Thousands)	01/01/2005	01/03/2004	01/04/2003	12/29/2001	12/30/2000	01/01/2000	01/02/1999	01/03/1998
Earnings Per Share	4.21	3.61	(1.38)	1.19	2.21	2.99	3.10	2.70
Cash Flow Per Share	6.66	5.06	5.82	6.18	3.90	3.58	3.59	3.63
Tang Book Value Per Share	6.57	8.61	10.91	9.97	12.56	10.08	9.33	8.68
Dividends Per Share	1.050	1.010	0.970	0.930	0.890	0.850	0.810	0.770
Dividend Payout %	24.94	27.98	N.M.	78.15	40.27	28.43	26.13	28.52
Income Statement								
Total Revenue	6,054,536	5,207,459	5,083,523	5,518,805	5,747,879	5,551,616	5,478,807	5,222,246
EBITDA	907,324	756,437	733,054	518,289	685,987	825,498	848,854	768,009
Depn & Amortn	126,268	108,019	107,398	168,972	173,422	167,432	161,385	156,252
Income Before Taxes	712,120	598,506	561,728	262,801	431,533	595,576	631,598	585,880
Income Taxes	237,418	200,573	197,300	124,971	164,417	229,334	243,292	234,938
Net Income	474,702	397,933	(154,543)	137,830	260,334	366,242	388,306	350,942
Average Shares	112,730	110,323	112,336	114,764	117,218	122,258	124,995	129,720
Balance Sheet								
Current Assets	2,378,568	2,208,531	2,074,540	2,031,420	2,110,096	1,877,416	1,848,152	1,601,466
Total Assets	5,004,278	4,245,552	3,503,151	4,103,016	4,358,156	4,026,514	3,836,666	3,322,782
Current Liabilities	1,372,214	871,857	874,844	813,833	1,006,200	1,113,473	1,033,006	765,908
Long-Term Obligations	556,629	956,383	602,287	904,035	905,036	517,834	521,657	516,226
Total Liabilities	2,464,984	2,264,258	1,808,401	1,944,589	2,117,860	1,811,152	1,716,014	1,399,672
Stockholders' Equity	2,513,241	1,951,307	1,657,848	2,112,796	2,191,813	2,163,818	2,066,308	1,866,769
Shares Outstanding	111,388	108,170	108,525	109,998	86,807	116,204	119,466	121,225
Statistical Record								
Return on Assets %	10.29	10.30	N.M.	3.27	6.23	9.34	10.88	10.39
Return on Equity %	21.32	22.11	N.M.	6.42	11.99	17.36	19.80	18.33
EBITDA Margin %	14.99	14.53	14.42	9.39	11.93	14.87	15.49	14.71
Net Margin %	7.84	7.64	N.M.	2.50	4.53	6.60	7.09	6.72
Asset Turnover	1.31	1.35	1.32	1.31	1.37	1.42	1.53	1.55
Current Ratio	1.73	2.53	2.37	2.50	2.10	1.69	1.79	2.09
Debt to Equity	0.22	0.49	0.36	0.43	0.41	0.24	0.25	0.28
Price Range	55.38-42.36	44.05-32.85	45.33-32.09	41.99-28.61	36.56-22.00	54.25-28.00	53.81-34.00	47.88-32.63
P/E Ratio	13.15-10.06	12.20-9.10	N/A	35.29-24.04	16.54-9.95	18.14-9.36	17.36-10.97	17.73-12.08
Average Yield %	2.17	2.64	2.43	2.56	3.38	2.13	1.73	1.90

Address: 105 Corporate Center Boulevard, Greensboro, NC 27408 Telephone: (336) 424 6000 Fax: (336) 547 7634	Web Site: www.vfc.com Officers: Mackey J. McDonald - Chmn., Pres., C.E.O. Robert K. Shearer - V.P., Fin., C.F.O.	Auditors: PricewaterhouseCoopers LLP Transfer Agents: EquiServe Trust Company, Jersey City, NJ

VIACOM INC

Exchange	Symbol	Price	52Wk Range	Yield	P/E
NYS	VIA	$35.04 (3/31/2005)	41.15-32.65	0.80	N/A

*7 Year Price Score 71.98 ***NYSE Composite Index=100** ***12 Month Price Score 92.50**

Interim Earnings (Per Share)

Qtr.	Mar	Jun	Sep	Dec
2001	0.00	0.01	(0.11)	(0.02)
2002	(0.63)	0.31	0.36	0.37
2003	0.25	0.37	0.40	(0.22)
2004	0.41	0.43	(0.28)	(10.75)

Interim Dividends (Per Share)

Amt	Decl	Ex	Rec	Pay
0.06Q	5/19/2004	5/27/2004	6/1/2004	7/1/2004
0.06Q	7/21/2004	8/27/2004	8/31/2004	10/1/2004
0.07Q	10/28/2004	11/26/2004	11/30/2004	1/1/2005
0.07Q	1/26/2005	2/24/2005	2/28/2005	4/1/2005

Indicated Div: $0.28

Valuation Analysis

Forecast P/E	N/A	No of Institutions
		167
Market Cap	$57.7 Billion	Shares
Book Value	42.0 Billion	25,104,450
Price/Book	1.37	% Held
Price/Sales	2.56	19.09

Business Summary: Movies & Film (MIC: 13.2 SIC: 812 NAIC: 12110)

Viacom is a diversified worldwide entertainment company with operations in five reportable segments: Cable Networks (MTV Networks, including MTV, VH1, Nickelodeon/Nick at Nite, TV Land, Spike TV, CMT and Comedy Central; BET; Showtime Networks Inc), Television (CBS and UPN Television Networks and stations; television production and syndication), Radio (185 stations through Infinity Radio), Outdoor (outdoor advertising properties), and Entertainment (Paramount Pictures, Simon & Schuster, Famous Players, Paramount Parks and Famous Music Publishing).

Recent Developments: For the year ended Dec 31 2004, loss from continuing operations was $15,059,500 thousand compared with an income of $2,237,800 thousand a year earlier. Net loss was $17,462,200 thousand versus net income of $1,416,900 thousand a year earlier. Revenues were $22,525,900 thousand, up 8.2% from $20,827,600 thousand the year before. Operating loss was $12,969,000 thousand versus an income of $4,473,600 thousand in the prior year. Total direct expense was $30,542,900 thousand versus $11,879,800 thousand in the prior year, an increase of 157.1%. Total indirect expense was $4,952,000 thousand versus $4,474,200 thousand in the prior year, an increase of 10.7%.

Prospects: Co.'s outlook is tempered by the recent lackluster performance from its Radio segment, which has been negatively affected by weakness in the local advertising market as well as higher contractual talent and increased advertising and promotion expenditures. Looking ahead to 2005, Co. expects to deliver mid single-digit growth in revenues and operating income and high single-digit growth in earnings per share. Co. noted that its business outlook is based on 2004 revenues of $22.5 billion, operating income of $5.1 billion and diluted earnings per share of $1.54, which exclude charges and tax benefits. The 2005 guidance does not include the effect of expensing stock options.

Financial Data

(US$ in Thousands)	12/31/2004	12/31/2003	12/31/2002	12/31/2001	12/31/2000	12/31/1999	12/31/1998	12/31/1997
Earnings Per Share	(10.19)	0.80	0.41	(0.13)	(0.67)	0.45	(0.21)	1.03
Cash Flow Per Share	2.12	2.01	1.78	2.03	1.89	0.42	1.22	0.48
Dividends Per Share	0.250	0.120	...	...	...	...	...	...
Dividend Payout %	N.M.	15.00	...	...	...	...	...	...
Income Statement								
Total Revenue	22,525,900	26,585,300	24,605,700	23,222,800	20,043,700	12,858,800	12,096,100	13,206,100
EBITDA	(12,151,500)	4,622,200	5,512,300	2,668,700	2,207,200	1,842,000	1,240,700	2,574,700
Depn & Amortn	809,900	999,800	945,600	953,800	877,500	576,900	504,400	589,000
Income Before Taxes	(13,655,000)	2,861,200	3,734,200	782,800	560,600	843,900	137,300	1,222,700
Income Taxes	1,378,600	1,599,000	1,448,900	922,500	729,400	411,400	138,700	689,600
Net Income	(17,462,200)	1,416,900	725,700	(223,500)	(816,100)	334,000	(122,400)	793,600
Average Shares	1,714,400	1,760,700	1,774,800	1,731,600	1,225,300	709,500	708,700	708,600
Balance Sheet								
Current Assets	7,493,500	7,736,300	7,166,800	7,206,400	7,832,400	5,198,400	5,064,500	5,713,500
Total Assets	68,002,300	89,848,500	89,754,200	90,809,900	82,646,100	24,486,400	23,613,100	28,288,700
Current Liabilities	6,879,500	7,584,800	7,341,100	7,561,700	7,758,200	4,399,700	5,632,600	5,052,500
Long-Term Obligations	9,649,200	9,683,200	10,205,200	10,823,700	12,473,800	5,697,700	3,813,400	7,423,000
Total Liabilities	25,978,000	26,643,500	27,266,400	28,093,100	34,679,200	13,354,400	11,563,500	14,905,100
Stockholders' Equity	42,024,300	63,205,000	62,487,800	62,716,800	47,966,900	11,132,000	12,049,600	13,383,600
Shares Outstanding	1,645,300	1,734,600	1,746,600	1,756,500	1,495,900	697,800	695,000	695,800
Statistical Record								
Return on Assets %	N.M.	1.58	0.80	N.M.	N.M.	1.39	N.M.	2.78
Return on Equity %	N.M.	2.25	1.16	N.M.	N.M.	2.88	N.M.	6.11
EBITDA Margin %	N.M.	17.39	22.40	11.49	11.01	14.32	10.26	19.50
Net Margin %	N.M.	5.33	2.95	N.M.	N.M.	2.60	N.M.	6.01
Asset Turnover	0.28	0.30	0.27	0.27	0.37	0.53	0.47	0.46
Current Ratio	1.09	1.02	0.98	0.95	1.01	1.18	0.90	1.13
Debt to Equity	0.23	0.15	0.16	0.17	0.26	0.51	0.32	0.55
Price Range	44.61-32.65	47.45-33.62	51.49-32.13	59.58-29.78	74.63-44.94	60.44-36.09	36.78-20.00	20.84-12.75
P/E Ratio	N/A	59.31-42.02	125.59-78.37	N/A	N/A	134.31-80.21	N/A	20.24-12.38
Average Yield %	0.67	0.29	...	...	...	...	...	...

Address: 1515 Broadway, New York, NY 10036
Telephone: (212) 258-6000

Web Site: www.viacom.com
Officers: Sumner M. Redstone - Chmn., C.E.O. Tom Freston - Co-Pres., Co-C.O.O.

Auditors: PricewaterhouseCoopers LLP

VIAD CORP.

Exchange	Symbol	Price	52Wk Range	Yield	P/E
NYS	VVI	$26.90 (3/31/2005)	28.80-21.50	0.59	N/A

*7 Year Price Score 88.92 ***NYSE Composite Index=100** ***12 Month Price Score 102.51**

Interim Earnings (Per Share)

Qtr.	Mar	Jun	Sep	Dec
2001	1.12	0.80	(0.76)	1.16
2002	1.48	1.44	1.64	0.60
2003	1.00	1.88	1.16	1.20
2004	1.88	0.42	(3.14)	(0.21)

Interim Dividends (Per Share)

Amt	Decl	Ex	Rec	Pay
0.04Q	8/13/2004	9/1/2004	9/3/2004	10/1/2004
0.04Q	12/2/2004	12/15/2004	12/17/2004	1/3/2005
0.04Q	2/23/2005	3/21/2005	3/23/2005	4/1/2005

Indicated Div: $0.16

Valuation Analysis

Forecast P/E	22.28	No of Institutions
	(4/7/2005)	123
Market Cap	$595.6 Million	Shares
Book Value	346.5 Million	18,471,436
Price/Book	1.72	% Held
Price/Sales	0.76	82.79

TRADING VOLUME (thousand shares)

Business Summary: Miscellaneous Business Services (MIC: 12.8 SIC: 389 NAIC: 61920)

Viad is comprised of operating companies and a division which constitute a diversified services business. Most of Co.'s services are provided to businesses for use by their customers. Co. provides services that address the needs of trade show organizers and exhibitors, as well as travel and recreation services in the United States and Canada. Co.'s services are classified into three reportable business segments, namely (1) GES Exposition Services, Inc. ("GES"), (2) Exhibitgroup/Giltspur, a division of Viad Corp ("Exhibitgroup"), and (3) Travel and Recreation Services provided by the Brewster Transport Company Limited and Glacier Park, Inc.

Recent Developments: For the year ended Dec 31 2004, loss from continuing operations was $58,329 thousand compared with a income of $21,091 thousand a year earlier. Net loss was $56,002 thousand versus net income of $21,091 thousand a year earlier. Revenues were $785,657 thousand, up 2.0% from $770,468 thousand the year before. Total direct expense was $732,276 thousand versus $719,252 thousand in the prior year, an increase of 1.8%. Total indirect expense was $89,939 thousand versus $-5,015 thousand in the prior year, an increase of 1893.4%.

Prospects: Looking ahead, Co. is not expecting a significant improvement in the tradeshow industry. However, Co. is optimistic that the modest growth in tradeshows experienced in 2004 will continue. Co. expects exhibiting companies to remain focused on ways to reduce their tradeshow costs, including using lighter-weight exhibits and refurbishing existing exhibits rather than building new ones. In this environment, much of Co.'s expected year-over-year improvement is dependent upon cost control and capitalizing on new business opportunities at both GES and Exhibitgroup. Meanwhile, Co.'s Travel and Recreation Services segment appears back on track following a substantial rebound in 2004.

Financial Data

(US$ in Thousands)	12/31/2004	12/31/2003	12/31/2002	12/31/2001	12/31/2000	12/31/1999	12/31/1998	12/31/1997
Earnings Per Share	(2.58)	5.24	3.44	2.32	6.32	14.36	6.08	3.76
Cash Flow Per Share	1.64	(8.02)	47.04	93.17	23.08	29.69	38.86	25.31
Tang Book Value Per Share	7.10	7.46	5.32	4.34	5.02	3.37	N.M.	N.M.
Dividends Per Share	0.080	1.440	1.440	1.440	1.440	1.400	1.280	1.280
Dividend Payout %	N.M.	27.48	41.86	62.07	22.78	9.75	21.05	34.04
Income Statement								
Total Revenue	785,657	1,572,093	1,646,984	1,659,390	1,726,808	1,581,169	2,542,135	2,417,470
EBITDA	(28,556)	254,421	224,918	141,778	267,061	253,462	344,402	266,100
Depn & Amortn	23,385	88,851	51,483	69,096	68,600	62,979	85,896	78,501
Income Before Taxes	(52,983)	156,793	154,167	46,746	173,158	163,595	217,688	138,947
Income Taxes	5,346	44,435	40,334	(4,388)	28,666	35,036	67,048	41,153
Net Income	(56,002)	113,902	76,094	51,134	144,492	347,513	150,640	89,336
Average Shares	21,741	21,654	21,679	21,580	22,731	24,099	24,591	23,446
Balance Sheet								
Current Assets	238,482	2,146,102	2,391,342	1,855,376	1,551,006	922,161	843,391	925,830
Total Assets	658,432	9,222,155	9,690,528	8,364,059	6,300,231	5,210,871	4,802,772	3,730,313
Current Liabilities	166,698	7,815,814	8,343,800	6,957,018	4,938,980	3,921,196	3,396,448	2,636,002
Long-Term Obligations	16,998	230,232	257,662	354,147	377,306	342,603	531,348	377,849
Total Liabilities	311,927	8,372,318	8,989,416	7,644,386	5,537,075	4,502,226	4,156,891	3,201,152
Stockholders' Equity	346,505	849,837	701,112	719,673	763,156	708,645	645,881	529,161
Shares Outstanding	22,140	22,089	22,025	22,233	24,934	23,560	24,848	24,805
Statistical Record								
Return on Assets %	N.M.	1.20	0.84	0.70	2.50	6.94	3.53	2.49
Return on Equity %	N.M.	14.69	10.71	6.90	19.58	51.31	25.64	18.58
EBITDA Margin %	N.M.	16.18	13.66	8.54	15.47	16.03	13.55	11.01
Net Margin %	N.M.	7.25	4.62	3.08	8.37	21.98	5.93	3.70
Asset Turnover	0.16	0.17	0.18	0.23	0.30	0.32	0.60	0.67
Current Ratio	1.43	0.27	0.29	0.27	0.31	0.24	0.25	0.35
Debt to Equity	0.05	0.27	0.37	0.49	0.49	0.48	0.82	0.71
Price Range	28.80-21.50	24.70-17.80	29.01-16.53	25.63-17.13	28.30-19.04	31.56-22.78	28.83-17.74	19.22-14.12
P/E Ratio	N/A	4.71-3.40	8.43-4.80	11.05-7.39	4.48-3.01	2.20-1.59	4.74-2.92	5.11-3.76
Average Yield %	0.34	6.74	6.26	6.43	5.99	5.11	5.39	7.60

Address: 1850 North Central Avenue, Suite 800, Phoenix, AZ 85004-4545 **Telephone:** (602) 207-4000 **Fax:** (602) 207-5900	**Web Site:** www.viad.com **Officers:** Robert H. Bohannon - Pres., C.E.O. G. Michael Latta - V.P., Contr.	**Auditors:** Deloitte & Touche LLP **Investor Contact:** 602-207-1040 **Transfer Agents:** Wells Fargo Shareowner Services, South St. Paul,

VISHAY INTERTECHNOLOGY, INC.

Exchange	Symbol	Price	52Wk Range	Yield	P/E
NYS	VSH	$12.43 (3/31/2005)	22.70-11.57	N/A	46.04

*7 Year Price Score 71.35   ***NYSE Composite Index=100**   ***12 Month Price Score 80.04**

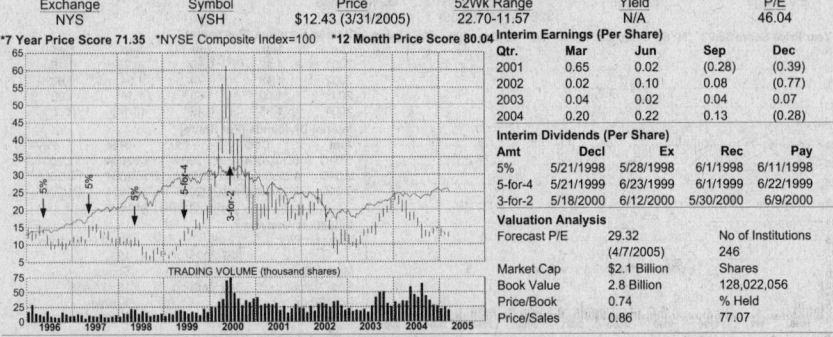

Interim Earnings (Per Share)

Qtr.	Mar	Jun	Sep	Dec
2001	0.65	0.02	(0.28)	(0.39)
2002	0.02	0.10	0.08	(0.77)
2003	0.04	0.02	0.04	0.07
2004	0.20	0.22	0.13	(0.28)

Interim Dividends (Per Share)

Amt	Decl	Ex	Rec	Pay
5%	5/21/1998	5/28/1998	6/1/1998	6/11/1998
5-for-4	5/21/1999	6/23/1999	6/1/1999	6/22/1999
3-for-2	5/18/2000	6/12/2000	5/30/2000	6/9/2000

Valuation Analysis

Forecast P/E	29.32	No of Institutions	
	(4/7/2005)	246	
Market Cap	$2.1 Billion	Shares	
Book Value	2.8 Billion	128,022,056	
Price/Book	0.74	% Held	
Price/Sales	0.86	77.07	

Business Summary: Electrical (MIC: 11.14 SIC: 676 NAIC: 34415)

Vishay Intertechnology is an international manufacturer and supplier of passive and active electronic components, including resistors, capacitors, inductors, strain gages, load cells, force measurement sensors, displacement sensors, photoelastic sensors, power MOSFETS, power conversion and motor control integrated circuits, transistors, diodes and optoelectronic components. Electronic components manufactured by Co. are used in virtually all types of electronic products, including those in the computer, telecommunications, military/aerospace, instrument, automotive, medical, and consumer electronics industries.

Recent Developments: For the year ended Dec 31 2004, net income increased 66.5% to $44,696 thousand from net income of $26,842 thousand a year earlier. Revenues were $2,413,576 thousand, up 11.2% from $2,170,597 thousand the year before. Operating income was $92,491 thousand versus an income of $59,367 thousand in the prior year, an increase of 55.8%. Total direct expense was $1,858,693 thousand versus $1,701,659 thousand in the prior year, an increase of 9.2%. Total indirect expense was $462,392 thousand versus $409,571 thousand in the prior year, an increase of 12.9%.

Prospects: Co.'s financial position appears strong and Co. is confident in its future prospects. Accordingly, Co. expects sales in the first quarter of 2005 to be in the range of $540.0 million to $560.0 million. In addition to the expected annual savings of $23.0 million due to restructuring actions incurred in 2004, Co. is implementing an aggressive program to reduce its fixed costs by $50.0 million in 2005. Consequently, Co. expects gross margin for the first quarter of 2005 to improve sequentially as a result of the above mentioned restructuring. Separately, Co. expects the acquisition of SI Technologies, Inc. to be finalized in the first half of 2005.

Financial Data
(US$ in Thousands)

	12/31/2004	12/31/2003	12/31/2002	12/31/2001	12/31/2000	12/31/1999	12/31/1998	12/31/1997
Earnings Per Share	0.27	0.17	(0.58)	...	3.77	0.65	0.06	0.42
Cash Flow Per Share	1.42	1.60	2.30	1.14	4.00	1.89	1.34	1.39
Tang Book Value Per Share	7.29	5.74	5.51	7.57	11.15	4.83	4.49	5.31
Income Statement								
Total Revenue	2,413,576	2,170,597	1,822,813	1,655,346	2,465,066	1,760,091	1,572,745	1,125,219
EBITDA	295,751	270,764	101,512	172,274	843,504	326,214	214,738	186,835
Depn & Amortn	200,184	193,735	180,748	160,415	137,754	138,207	126,864	80,547
Income Before Taxes	70,017	46,426	(100,045)	10,103	690,225	134,711	38,836	87,469
Income Taxes	13,729	11,528	(16,900)	5,695	148,186	36,940	30,624	34,167
Net Income	44,696	26,842	(92,614)	513	517,864	83,237	8,212	53,302
Average Shares	165,938	160,443	159,413	142,514	137,463	128,232	126,796	126,903
Balance Sheet								
Current Assets	1,682,420	1,637,253	1,473,693	1,574,627	1,474,874	926,749	956,571	645,971
Total Assets	4,638,590	4,572,513	4,315,159	3,951,523	2,783,658	2,323,781	2,462,744	1,719,648
Current Liabilities	517,738	587,361	576,237	478,593	417,674	345,199	316,788	190,837
Long-Term Obligations	752,145	836,606	706,316	605,031	140,467	656,943	814,838	347,463
Total Liabilities	1,865,255	2,058,479	1,956,372	1,584,978	949,803	1,310,189	1,460,225	760,000
Stockholders' Equity	2,773,335	2,514,034	2,358,787	2,366,545	1,833,855	1,013,592	1,002,519	959,648
Shares Outstanding	166,102	160,050	159,680	159,291	137,926	127,023	126,879	126,759
Statistical Record								
Return on Assets %	0.97	0.60	N.M.	0.02	20.22	3.48	0.39	3.25
Return on Equity %	1.69	1.10	N.M.	0.02	36.27	8.26	0.84	5.60
EBITDA Margin %	12.25	12.47	5.57	10.41	34.22	18.53	13.65	16.60
Net Margin %	1.85	1.24	N.M.	0.03	21.01	4.73	0.52	4.74
Asset Turnover	0.52	0.49	0.44	0.49	0.96	0.74	0.75	0.69
Current Ratio	3.25	2.79	2.56	3.29	3.53	2.68	3.02	3.38
Debt to Equity	0.27	0.33	0.30	0.26	0.08	0.65	0.81	0.36
Price Range	24.88-11.57	22.90-8.90	26.00-7.03	27.75-14.44	61.17-14.00	21.08-5.97	12.27-5.23	16.03-9.56
P/E Ratio	92.15-42.85	134.71-52.35	N/A	N/A	16.22-3.71	32.44-9.18	204.44-87.22	38.17-22.75

Address: 63 Lincoln Highway, Malvern, PA 19355-2143 Telephone: (610) 644 1300 Fax: (610) 296 0657	Web Site: www.vishay.com Officers: Felix Zandman - Chmn., Chief Tech. Officer, Chief Bus. Devel. Officer Marc Zandman - Vice-Chmn.	Auditors: Ernst & Young LLP Investor Contact: 610-644-1300

VISTEON CORP.

Exchange	Symbol	Price	52Wk Range	Yield	P/E
NYS	VC	$5.71 (3/31/2005)	12.15-5.67	N/A	N/A

*7 Year Price Score N/A   *NYSE Composite Index=100   *12 Month Price Score 69.42

Interim Earnings (Per Share)

Qtr.	Mar	Jun	Sep	Dec
2001	0.24	(0.31)	(0.74)	(0.11)
2002	(2.63)	0.56	(0.40)	(0.27)
2003	(0.12)	(1.33)	(1.34)	(6.87)
2004	0.23	0.24	(10.86)	(1.59)

Interim Dividends (Per Share)

Dividend Payment Suspended.

Valuation Analysis

Forecast P/E	N/A	No of Institutions
	(4/7/2005)	206
Market Cap	$742.3 Million	Shares
Book Value	407.0 Million	120,070,976
Price/Book	1.82	% Held
Price/Sales	0.04	93.31

Business Summary: Automotive (MIC: 15.1 SIC: 714 NAIC: 36399)

Visteon is a major full-service supplier of automotive systems, modules and components to global vehicle manufacturers and the automotive aftermarket. The Automotive Operations segment provides climate control, interior, exterior, powertrain, chassis and electronic products for vehicles. The Glass Operations segment produces glass products for Ford Motor Company and aftermarket customers and float glass for commercial architecture. As of Apr 22 2004, Co. operated a system of more than 200 technical, manufacturing, sales and service facilities located in 25 countries.

Recent Developments: For the year ended Dec 31 2004, net loss was $1,499 million versus net loss of $1,207 million a year earlier. Revenues were $18,657 million, up 5.6% from $17,660 million the year before. Operating loss was $448 million versus a loss of $1,166 million in the prior year. Total direct expense was $18,111 million versus $17,818 million in the prior year, an increase of 1.6%. Total indirect expense was $994 million versus $1,008 million in the prior year, a decrease of 1.4%.

Prospects: Co. has implemented cost and headcount reductions in the U.S., but material surcharges and lower North American Ford production is significantly pressuring results. On Mar 10 2004, Co. announced a financial agreement with Ford Motor Company that should improve Co.'s operating results and cash flow. Under the agreement, Ford agreed to reduced wage reimbursements from Co. for hourly Ford-UAW employees assigned to its facilities; accelerate payment terms to Co.; and pay for capital expenditures at certain of Co.'s plants in North America. Meanwhile, Co. is continuing to explore strategic and structural changes to its business in the U.S. that involve its legacy business and Ford.

Financial Data

(US$ in Thousands)	12/31/2004	12/31/2003	12/31/2002	12/31/2001	12/31/2000	12/31/1999	12/31/1998	12/31/1997
Earnings Per Share	(11.96)	(9.65)	(2.75)	(0.91)	2.08	5.65	5.41	3.93
Cash Flow Per Share	3.33	2.94	8.97	3.33	(4.04)	19.09	10.58	...
Tang Book Value Per Share	3.13	14.40	22.73	25.12	26.76	10.86	...	...
Dividends Per Share	0.240	0.240	0.240	0.240	0.120	...	...	...
Dividend Payout %	N.M.	N.M.	N.M.	N.M.	5.77	...	...	...
Income Statement								
Total Revenue	18,657,000	17,660,000	18,395,000	17,843,000	19,467,000	19,366,000	17,762,000	17,220,000
EBITDA	271,000	(399,000)	594,000	573,000	1,173,000	1,887,000	1,725,000	1,470,000
Depn & Amortn	685,000	674,000	631,000	666,000	676,000	651,000	565,000	590,000
Income Before Taxes	(499,000)	(1,150,000)	(117,000)	(169,000)	439,000	1,172,000	1,116,000	815,000
Income Taxes	965,000	34,000	(58,000)	(72,000)	143,000	422,000	416,000	305,000
Net Income	(1,499,000)	(1,213,000)	(352,000)	(118,000)	270,000	735,000	703,000	511,000
Average Shares	125,300	125,800	127,700	131,000	130,000	130,000	130,000	130,000
Balance Sheet								
Current Assets	4,444,000	4,410,000	4,737,000	4,753,000	5,005,000	5,196,000	3,191,000	...
Total Assets	10,309,000	10,964,000	11,170,000	11,078,000	11,325,000	12,449,000	9,373,000	...
Current Liabilities	3,843,000	3,572,000	3,466,000	3,435,000	3,804,000	5,475,000	3,164,000	...
Long-Term Obligations	1,513,000	1,467,000	1,298,000	1,293,000	1,397,000	1,358,000	816,000	...
Total Liabilities	9,902,000	9,106,000	8,192,000	7,787,000	7,820,000	10,950,000	7,718,000	...
Stockholders' Equity	407,000	1,858,000	2,978,000	3,291,000	3,505,000	1,499,000	1,655,000	...
Shares Outstanding	130,000	129,000	131,000	131,000	131,000	138,000	...	...
Statistical Record								
Return on Assets %	N.M.	N.M.	N.M.	N.M.	2.27	6.74	7.50	...
Return on Equity %	N.M.	N.M.	N.M.	N.M.	10.76	46.61	42.48	...
EBITDA Margin %	1.45	N.M.	3.23	3.21	6.03	9.74	9.71	8.54
Net Margin %	N.M.	N.M.	N.M.	N.M.	1.39	3.80	3.96	2.97
Asset Turnover	1.75	1.60	1.65	1.59	1.63	1.77	1.90	...
Current Ratio	1.16	1.23	1.37	1.38	1.32	0.95	1.01	...
Debt to Equity	3.72	0.79	0.44	0.39	0.40	0.91	0.49	...
Price Range	12.35-6.61	10.43-5.60	16.55-6.57	21.32-10.99	19.25-9.81	...	...	...
P/E Ratio	N/A	N/A	N/A	N/A	9.25-4.72	...	...	...
Average Yield %	2.46	3.50	2.00	1.54	0.81	...	...	...

Address: 17000 Rotunda Drive, Dearborn, MI 48120	Web Site: www.visteon.com	Auditors: PricewaterhouseCoopers LLP
Telephone: (313) 755-3699	Officers: Peter J. Pestillo - Chmn. Michael F.	
Fax: (313) 755-2776	Johnston - Pres., C.E.O.	

VISX, INC.

Interim Earnings (Per Share)

Qtr.	Mar	Jun	Sep	Dec
2001	0.21	(0.19)	0.08	0.08
2002	0.12	0.11	0.08	(0.02)
2003	0.11	0.08	0.10	0.18
2004	0.23	0.19	0.22	0.12

Interim Dividends (Per Share)

No Dividends Paid

Valuation Analysis

Forecast P/E	24.26	No of Institutions
	(4/7/2005)	157
Market Cap	$1.2 Billion	Shares
Book Value	178.7 Million	36,548,268
Price/Book	6.55	% Held
Price/Sales	7.06	73.03

Business Summary: Medical Instruments & Equipment (MIC: 9.6 SIC: 845 NAIC: 34510)

VISX is engaged in the design and development of proprietary technologies and systems for laser vision correction. Co.'s products require FDA approval in the U.S. and comparable regulatory agency approvals in other countries. Approvals in the U.S. and key markets for laser vision correction cover most types of refractive vision disorders including: Nearsightedness; Farsightedness; and Astigmatism. Co.'s CustomVue procedure is also available for all of these refractive vision disorders in certain international markets. Co. generates the majority of its revenues and cash through licensing fees charged for performing laser vision correction procedures using the VISX STAR™ Excimer Laser System.

Recent Developments: For the year ended Dec 31 2004, net income increased 65.3% to $38,442 thousand from net income of $23,251 thousand a year earlier. Revenues were $165,858 thousand, up 15.3% from $143,905 thousand the year before. Operating income was $59,552 thousand versus an income of $34,605 thousand in the prior year, an increase of 72.1%. Total direct expense was $42,386 thousand versus $52,070 thousand in the prior year, a decrease of 18.6%. Total indirect expense was $63,920 thousand versus $57,230 thousand in the prior year, an increase of 11.7%.

Prospects: Co. has agreed to be acquired by Advanced Medical Optics, Inc. (AMO), a global provider of opthalmic surgical devices and eye care products. Under the terms of the agreement, Co.'s stockholders will receive 0.552 shares of AMO stock and $3.50 in cash for each share of Co.'s common stock held. Upon completion of the transaction, Co.'s stockholders will own approximately 41.5% of AMO. AMO's strength in international markets and broad product portfolio, together with Co.'s refractive surgery business and strong market position in the U.S., is expected to enable the combined company to achieve accelerated growth worldwide. The acquisition is expected to close in the second quarter of 2005.

Financial Data

(US$ in Thousands)	12/31/2004	12/31/2003	12/31/2002	12/31/2001	12/31/2000	12/31/1999	12/31/1998	12/31/1997
Earnings Per Share	0.76	0.46	0.29	0.19	0.55	1.35	0.39	0.22
Cash Flow Per Share	1.00	0.54	0.76	0.11	0.99	0.94	0.23	0.27
Tang Book Value Per Share	3.58	2.58	3.02	3.23	4.42	4.88	2.26	1.79
Income Statement								
Total Revenue	165,858	143,905	139,926	169,566	200,248	271,252	133,750	68,631
EBITDA	62,652	43,332	23,190	10,968	47,651	145,230	26,303	12,874
Depn & Amortn	3,100	8,727	4,320	3,617	3,515	3,132	2,083	1,854
Income Before Taxes	61,587	38,057	24,481	18,031	58,216	152,946	29,756	16,019
Income Taxes	23,145	14,806	9,139	7,122	22,995	61,178	4,166	1,922
Net Income	38,442	23,251	15,342	10,909	35,221	91,768	25,590	14,097
Average Shares	50,869	50,937	53,816	58,081	63,778	68,119	65,398	63,272
Balance Sheet								
Current Assets	206,466	141,977	183,753	203,582	298,397	349,474	166,638	123,933
Total Assets	222,823	163,963	200,592	219,925	321,507	362,721	176,619	130,352
Current Liabilities	44,167	38,164	45,402	43,647	52,735	45,928	37,630	20,053
Total Liabilities	44,167	38,164	45,402	43,647	52,735	45,928	37,630	20,053
Stockholders' Equity	178,656	125,799	155,190	176,278	268,772	316,793	138,989	110,299
Shares Outstanding	49,923	48,694	51,337	54,553	60,756	64,888	61,598	61,448
Statistical Record								
Return on Assets %	19.82	12.76	7.30	4.03	10.27	34.03	16.67	11.28
Return on Equity %	25.18	16.55	9.26	4.90	12.00	40.27	20.53	13.45
EBITDA Margin %	37.77	30.11	16.57	6.47	23.80	53.54	19.67	18.76
Net Margin %	23.18	16.16	10.96	6.43	17.59	33.83	19.13	20.54
Asset Turnover	0.86	0.79	0.67	0.63	0.58	1.01	0.87	0.55
Current Ratio	4.67	3.72	4.05	4.66	5.66	7.61	4.43	6.18
Price Range	26.85-15.60	25.77-7.93	17.80-7.18	23.80-10.25	53.50-9.31	103.75-21.86	21.86-4.88	7.38-4.59
P/E Ratio	35.33-20.53	56.02-17.24	61.38-24.76	125.26-53.95	97.27-16.93	76.85-16.19	56.05-12.50	33.52-20.88

VORNADO REALTY TRUST

Exchange	Symbol	Price	52Wk Range	Yield	P/E
NYS	VNO	$69.27 (3/31/2005)	76.40-48.09	4.39	15.92

*7 Year Price Score 129.11 *NYSE Composite Index=100 *12 Month Price Score 102.76

Interim Earnings (Per Share)

Qtr.	Mar	Jun	Sep	Dec
2001	0.52	0.64	0.74	0.57
2002	0.40	0.57	0.52	0.42
2003	0.77	0.71	0.60	1.71
2004	0.59	1.21	0.79	1.76

Interim Dividends (Per Share)

Amt	Decl	Ex	Rec	Pay
0.16Q	11/7/2004	12/16/2003	12/18/2003	12/29/2003
0.76Q	1/26/2005	2/3/2005	2/7/2005	2/15/2005
0.05Q	1/26/2005	2/3/2005	2/7/2005	2/15/2005
0.76Q	2/25/2005	5/3/2005	5/5/2005	5/13/2005

Indicated Div: $3.04

Valuation Analysis

Forecast P/E	14.30	No of Institutions
	(4/7/2005)	259
Market Cap	$8.8 Billion	Shares
Book Value	4.0 Billion	89,421,056
Price/Book	2.20	% Held
Price/Sales	5.17	69.96

Business Summary: Property, Real Estate & Development (MIC: 8.3 SIC: 798 NAIC: 25930)

Vornado Realty Trust is a fully integrated real estate investment trust. Co. operates in five business segments: Office, Retail, Merchandise Mart, Temperature Controlled Logistics and other investments. As of Dec 31 2003, the office segment was comprised of all or portions of 83 office properties in New York City, and in the Washington D.C. and Northern Virginia area totaling approximately 27.3 million square feet. Also, The retail properties segment consists of 60 shopping centers totaling approximately 12.9 million square feet in six states and Puerto Rico as of Dec 31 2003. The Merchandise Mart Properties contain approximately 8.6 million square feet.

Recent Developments: For the year ended Dec 31 2004, income from continuing operations increased 80.9% to $514,320 thousand from income of $284,315 thousand a year earlier. Net income increased 28.7% to $592,917 thousand from net income of $460,703 thousand a year earlier. Revenues were $1,707,262 thousand, up 14.0% from $1,497,983 thousand the year before. Operating income was $637,865 thousand versus an income of $580,897 thousand in the prior year, an increase of 9.8%.

Prospects: On Nov 4 2004, Co. announced that AmeriCold Realty Trust, a joint venture owned 60.0% by Co. and 40.0% by Crescent Real Estate Equities Company, purchased AmeriCold's tenant, AmeriCold Logistics, LLC for $47.7 million in cash. The sale is expected to result in a gain for Co. of approximately $20.0 million. In addition, Co. and Crescent Operating Inc. announced that they had entered into definitive agreements to collectively sell 20.7% of the newly combined AmeriCold common shares to The Yucaipa Companies for $145.0 million. Co. and Crescent, after the completion of the transaction, will own 47.6% and 31.7% of AmeriCold, respectively.

Financial Data
(US$ in Thousands)

	12/31/2004	12/31/2003	12/31/2002	12/31/2001	12/31/2000	12/31/1999	12/31/1998	12/31/1997
Earnings Per Share	4.35	3.80	1.91	2.47	2.20	1.94	1.59	0.79
Cash Flow Per Share	5.29	4.71	4.72	4.35	2.81	2.06	2.35	2.10
Tang Book Value Per Share	26.95	23.90	21.74	21.22	18.40	18.26	17.63	14.33
Dividends Per Share	3.050	2.910	2.660	2.629	1.970	1.807	1.640	1.360
Dividend Payout %	70.11	76.58	139.27	106.44	89.55	93.14	103.14	172.15
Income Statement								
Property Income	1,344,812	1,261,042	1,248,903	841,999	695,078	590,814	425,496	168,321
Non-Property Income	362,450	242,013	186,167	143,774	131,454	106,144	84,364	40,810
Total Revenue	1,707,262	1,503,055	1,435,070	985,773	826,532	696,958	509,860	209,131
Depn & Amortn	239,252	210,864	220,692	123,862	99,846	83,585	59,227	47,377
Net Income	592,917	460,703	232,903	263,738	233,991	202,519	152,854	61,023
Average Shares	133,135	116,651	109,669	92,072	88,692	93,302	82,656	57,217
Balance Sheet								
Total Assets	11,580,517	9,518,928	9,018,179	6,777,343	6,370,314	5,479,218	4,425,779	2,524,089
Long-Term Obligations	4,936,633	4,064,385	4,071,320	2,477,173	2,656,897	2,048,804	2,051,000	956,654
Total Liabilities	5,619,905	4,520,069	4,353,465	2,727,313	2,835,435	2,201,819	2,209,800	1,031,760
Stockholders' Equity	4,012,741	3,077,573	2,627,356	2,570,372	2,078,720	2,055,368	1,782,678	1,313,762
Shares Outstanding	127,478	118,247	108,629	99,035	86,803	86,335	85,076	72,165
Statistical Record								
Return on Assets %	5.60	4.97	2.95	4.01	3.94	4.09	4.40	3.95
Return on Equity %	16.68	16.15	8.96	11.35	11.29	10.55	9.87	7.68
Net Margin %	34.73	30.65	16.23	26.75	28.31	29.06	29.98	29.18
Price Range	76.40-48.09	55.66-33.30	47.10-34.41	41.65-34.56	40.75-29.88	39.50-30.06	49.16-26.93	46.38-25.26
P/E Ratio	17.56-11.06	14.65-8.76	24.66-18.02	16.86-13.99	18.52-13.58	20.36-15.50	30.92-16.94	58.71-31.98
Average Yield %	5.04	6.66	6.44	6.89	5.57	5.23	4.34	3.88

Address: 888 Seventh Avenue, New York, NY 10019	Web Site: www.vno.com	Auditors: Deloitte & Touche LLP
Telephone: (212) 894-7000	Officers: Steven Roth - Chmn., C.E.O. Michael D. Fascitelli - Pres.	
Fax: (212) 587-0600		

VULCAN MATERIALS CO.

Exchange	Symbol	Price	52Wk Range	Yield	P/E	Div Acheiver
NYS	VMC	$56.83 (3/31/2005)	59.65-42.35	2.04	20.52	12 Years

*7 Year Price Score 98.89 ***NYSE Composite Index=100** ***12 Month Price Score 106.22**

Interim Earnings (Per Share)

Qtr.	Mar	Jun	Sep	Dec
2001	0.06	0.78	0.90	0.44
2002	0.11	0.64	0.75	0.36
2003	(0.17)	0.55	0.96	0.56
2004	0.14	0.85	0.96	0.82

Interim Dividends (Per Share)

Amt	Decl	Ex	Rec	Pay
0.26Q	5/14/2004	5/26/2004	5/28/2004	6/10/2004
0.26Q	7/9/2004	8/24/2004	8/26/2004	9/10/2004
0.26Q	10/8/2004	11/22/2004	11/24/2004	12/10/2004
0.29Q	2/11/2005	2/23/2005	2/25/2005	3/10/2005

Indicated Div: $1.16 (Div. Reinv. Plan)

Valuation Analysis

Forecast P/E	18.77	No of Institutions	
	(4/7/2005)	257	
Market Cap	$5.8 Billion	Shares	
Book Value	2.0 Billion	75,940,112	
Price/Book	2.90	% Held	
Price/Sales	2.38	73.79	

Business Summary: Earth & Rock Mining (MIC: 14.5 SIC: 422 NAIC: 12312)

Vulcan Materials and its subsidiaries are engaged in the production, distribution and sale of construction materials and industrial and specialty chemicals, including chloralkali. Co.'s construction materials business consists of the production and sale of construction aggregates and other construction materials and related services. Construction aggregates include crushed stone, sand and gravel, rock asphalt, recrushed concrete, and are employed in virtually all types of construction, including highway construction and maintenance. Other Construction Materials products and services include asphalt mix and related products and ready-mixed concrete.

Recent Developments: For the year ended Dec 31 2004, income from continuing operations increased 10.0% to $261,213 thousand from income of $237,513 thousand a year earlier. Net income increased 47.4% to $287,385 thousand from net income of $194,952 thousand a year earlier. Revenues were $2,454,335 thousand, up 6.3% from $2,309,642 thousand the year before. Total direct expense was $1,871,662 thousand versus $1,753,895 thousand in the prior year, an increase of 6.7%. Total indirect expense was $180,740 thousand versus $177,429 thousand in the prior year, an increase of 1.9%.

Prospects: Co. sees 2005 as another solid year for aggregates demand. Construction spending should continue to benefit from economic growth. Residential construction activity should remain strong. Modest recovery in private nonresidential construction should continue. Highway construction should benefit from improving state and local tax receipts. As a result, demand for Co.'s aggregates should increase 2.0% to 4.0% versus 2004 shipments. Co. expects to continue to achieve price improvements. Healthcare costs and unit costs for diesel and liquid asphalt are projected to be higher. Therefore, Co. expects earnings from continuing operations to be in the range of $2.80 to $3.10 per diluted share for 2005.

Financial Data
(US$ in Thousands)

	12/31/2004	12/31/2003	12/31/2002	12/31/2001	12/31/2000	12/31/1999	12/31/1998	12/31/1997
Earnings Per Share	2.77	1.90	1.66	2.17	2.16	2.35	2.50	2.03
Cash Flow Per Share	5.65	5.10	4.54	5.03	4.13	3.99	3.60	3.41
Tang Book Value Per Share	13.77	12.01	11.04	10.02	9.00	8.63	11.47	9.81
Dividends Per Share	1.040	0.980	0.940	0.900	0.840	0.780	0.693	0.627
Dividend Payout %	37.55	51.58	56.63	41.47	38.89	33.19	27.73	30.82
Income Statement								
Total Revenue	2,454,335	2,892,186	2,796,577	3,019,990	2,491,744	2,355,778	1,776,434	1,678,581
EBITDA	643,898	638,108	576,805	659,098	588,012	602,915	512,764	424,849
Depn & Amortn	233,651	277,091	267,676	278,209	232,365	207,108	137,792	120,624
Income Before Taxes	375,566	311,425	257,660	324,053	312,238	351,561	374,844	300,501
Income Taxes	114,353	87,971	67,247	101,373	92,345	111,868	118,936	91,356
Net Income	287,385	194,952	169,876	222,680	219,893	239,693	255,908	209,145
Average Shares	103,664	102,710	102,515	102,497	102,012	102,190	102,177	102,849
Balance Sheet								
Current Assets	1,417,959	1,050,242	789,688	729,952	694,504	624,724	576,381	487,132
Total Assets	3,665,133	3,636,860	3,448,221	3,398,224	3,228,574	2,839,493	1,658,611	1,449,246
Current Liabilities	426,689	542,952	297,709	344,495	572,231	386,642	211,462	207,697
Long-Term Obligations	604,522	607,654	857,757	906,299	685,361	698,862	76,533	81,931
Total Liabilities	1,651,158	1,742,037	1,658,577	1,793,950	1,757,078	1,515,840	504,911	457,749
Stockholders' Equity	2,013,975	1,802,836	1,696,986	1,604,274	1,471,496	1,323,653	1,153,700	991,497
Shares Outstanding	102,659	101,811	101,557	101,320	101,043	100,734	100,596	101,061
Statistical Record								
Return on Assets %	7.85	5.50	4.96	6.72	7.23	10.66	16.47	15.10
Return on Equity %	15.02	11.14	10.29	14.48	15.69	19.35	23.86	22.31
EBITDA Margin %	26.24	22.06	20.63	21.82	23.60	25.59	28.86	25.31
Net Margin %	11.71	6.74	6.07	7.37	8.82	10.17	14.41	12.46
Asset Turnover	0.67	0.82	0.82	0.91	0.82	1.05	1.14	1.21
Current Ratio	3.32	1.93	2.65	2.12	1.21	1.62	2.73	2.35
Debt to Equity	0.30	0.34	0.51	0.56	0.47	0.53	0.07	0.08
Price Range	54.95-42.35	48.25-29.06	49.55-32.37	55.10-38.15	48.50-36.69	50.50-34.88	44.06-31.63	34.44-18.46
P/E Ratio	19.84-15.29	25.39-15.29	29.85-19.50	25.39-17.58	22.45-16.98	21.49-14.84	17.63-12.65	16.96-9.09
Average Yield %	2.16	2.56	2.23	1.91	1.95	1.81	1.86	2.41

Address: 1200 Urban Center Drive, Birmingham, AL 35242	**Web Site:** www.vulcanmaterials.com	**Auditors:** Deloitte & Touche LLP
Telephone: (205) 298-3000	**Officers:** Donald M. James - Chmn., C.E.O. Mark E. Tomkins - Sr. V.P., C.F.O., Treas.	**Investor Contact:** 205-298-3220
Fax: (205) 298-2963		**Transfer Agents:** The Bank of New York, New York, NY

WACHOVIA CORP

Exchange	Symbol	Price	52Wk Range	Yield	P/E
NYS	WB	$50.91 (3/31/2005)	56.01-43.56	3.61	13.36

*7 Year Price Score 101.44 *NYSE Composite Index=100 *12 Month Price Score 100.82

Interim Earnings (Per Share)

Qtr.	Mar	Jun	Sep	Dec
2001	0.59	0.65	(0.31)	0.60
2002	0.66	0.63	0.67	0.65
2003	0.76	0.77	0.83	0.83
2004	0.94	0.95	0.96	0.96

Interim Dividends (Per Share)

Amt	Decl	Ex	Rec	Pay
0.40Q	4/20/2004	5/26/2004	5/28/2004	6/15/2004
0.40Q	8/17/2004	8/27/2004	8/31/2004	9/15/2004
0.46Q	10/18/2004	11/26/2004	11/30/2004	12/15/2004
0.46Q	2/15/2005	2/24/2005	2/28/2005	3/15/2005

Indicated Div: $1.84

Valuation Analysis

Forecast P/E	N/A	No of Institutions
		692
Market Cap	$80.8 Billion	Shares
Book Value	47.3 Billion	858,241,856
Price/Book	1.71	% Held
Price/Sales	2.88	54.11

Business Summary: Commercial Banking (MIC: 8.1 SIC: 021 NAIC: 22110)

Wachovia, with assets of $400.87 billion as of Dec 31 2003, is a provider of financial services to retail, brokerage and corporate customers throughout the East Coast and the U.S. Co. operates full-service banking offices in 11 East Coast states and Washington, D.C., and offers full-service brokerage with 700 offices in 48 states and global services through 32 international offices. Co. operated 3,360 financial centers and 4,408 automatic teller machines, as of Dec 31 2003. On-line banking and brokerage products and services are available through wachovia.com.

Recent Developments: For the year ended Dec 31 2004, net income increased 22.3% to $5,214 million from net income of $4,264 million a year earlier. Net interest income was $11,961 million, up 12.8% from $10,607 million the year before. Provision for loan losses was $257 million versus $586 million in the prior year, a decrease of 56.1%. Non-interest income rose 13.7% to $10,779 million, while non-interest expense advanced 10.6% to $14,850 million.

Prospects: Co. believes it is well positioned for the future, with the integration of its nationwide retail brokerage business largely complete and the acquisition of SouthTrust Corporation finalized on Nov 1 2004. With solid earnings in the fourth quarter and full-year of 2004, Co. enters 2005 with good momentum and is looking forward to delivering more products and services across the fast-growing southeast portion of the U.S. Separately, on Feb 7 2005, Co. announced plans to combine its Equity Capital Markets and Equity Linked Products units into a newly formed Equity Division.

Financial Data
(US$ in Thousands)

	12/31/2004	12/31/2003	12/31/2002	12/31/2001	12/31/2000	12/31/1999	12/31/1998	12/31/1997
Earnings Per Share	3.81	3.18	2.60	1.45	0.07	3.33	2.95	2.99
Cash Flow Per Share	(5.82)	(4.35)	0.37	6.65	8.12	(0.12)	4.55	3.83
Tang Book Value Per Share	15.25	15.27	14.48	11.50	11.92	11.22	12.36	14.71
Dividends Per Share	1.660	1.250	1.000	0.240	1.920	1.880	1.580	1.220
Dividend Payout %	43.57	39.31	38.46	16.55	N.A.	56.46	53.56	40.80
Income Statement								
Interest Income	17,288,000	15,080,000	15,586,000	16,100,000	17,534,000	15,151,000	14,988,000	10,933,000
Interest Expense	5,327,000	4,473,000	5,763,000	8,325,000	10,097,000	7,699,000	7,711,000	5,190,000
Net Interest Income	11,961,000	10,607,000	9,823,000	7,775,000	7,437,000	7,452,000	7,277,000	5,743,000
Provision for Losses	257,000	586,000	1,479,000	1,947,000	1,736,000	692,000	691,000	840,000
Non-Interest Income	10,779,000	9,394,000	8,005,000	6,296,000	6,712,000	6,933,000	6,555,000	3,396,000
Non-Interest Expense	14,666,000	13,192,000	11,682,000	9,831,000	11,710,000	8,862,000	9,176,000	5,589,000
Income Before Taxes	7,633,000	6,080,000	4,667,000	2,293,000	703,000	4,831,000	3,965,000	2,710,000
Income Taxes	2,419,000	1,833,000	1,088,000	674,000	565,000	1,608,000	1,074,000	814,000
Net Income	5,214,000	4,264,000	3,579,000	1,619,000	92,000	3,223,000	2,891,000	1,896,000
Average Shares	1,370,000	1,340,000	1,369,000	1,105,000	974,172	966,863	980,000	634,000
Balance Sheet								
Net Loans & Leases	221,083,000	163,067,000	160,299,000	160,806,000	122,038,000	133,809,000	133,557,000	95,661,000
Total Assets	493,324,000	401,032,000	341,839,000	330,452,000	254,170,000	253,024,000	237,363,000	157,274,000
Total Deposits	295,053,000	221,225,000	191,518,000	187,453,000	142,668,000	141,047,000	142,467,000	102,889,000
Total Liabilities	443,189,000	366,094,000	309,761,000	301,997,000	238,823,000	236,315,000	220,190,000	144,251,000
Stockholders' Equity	47,317,000	32,428,000	32,078,000	28,455,000	15,347,000	16,709,000	17,173,000	12,032,000
Shares Outstanding	1,588,000	1,312,000	1,357,000	1,362,000	980,000	988,000	982,000	636,000
Statistical Record								
Return on Assets %	1.16	1.15	1.06	0.55	0.04	1.31	1.47	1.28
Return on Equity %	13.04	13.22	11.82	7.39	0.57	19.02	19.80	17.21
Net Interest Margin %	69.19	70.34	63.02	48.29	42.41	49.18	48.55	52.53
Efficiency Ratio %	52.25	53.90	49.52	43.90	48.30	40.13	42.59	39.00
Loans to Deposits	0.75	0.74	0.84	0.86	0.86	0.95	0.94	0.93
Price Range	54.52-43.56	46.59-32.72	39.50-28.75	36.38-27.81	38.88-24.00	65.06-32.44	65.69-44.69	52.88-36.69
P/E Ratio	14.31-11.43	14.65-10.29	15.19-11.06	25.09-19.18	555.36-342.86	19.54-9.74	22.27-15.15	17.68-12.27
Average Yield %	3.50	3.08	2.84	0.75	6.29	4.06	2.81	2.65

Address: One Wachovia Center, Charlotte, NC 28288-0013	**Web Site:** www.wachovia.com	**Auditors:** KPMG LLP
Telephone: (704) 374-6565	**Officers:** G. Kennedy Thompson - Chmn., Pres., C.E.O. Robert P. Kelly - Sr. Exec. V.P., C.F.O.	**Investor Contact:** 704-374-2137
Fax: (704) 374-4609		

WADDELL & REED FINANCIAL, INC.

Exchange	Symbol	Price	52Wk Range	Yield	P/E
NYS	WDR	$19.74 (3/31/2005)	25.01-19.01	3.04	15.79

*7 Year Price Score 81.93   ***NYSE Composite Index=100**   ***12 Month Price Score 88.98**

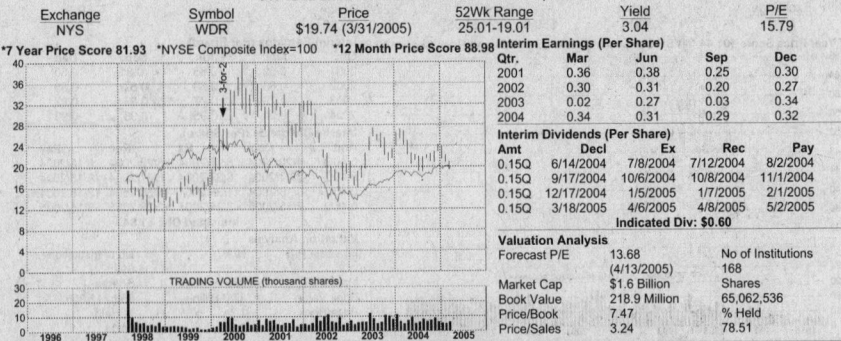

Interim Earnings (Per Share)

Qtr.	Mar	Jun	Sep	Dec
2001	0.36	0.38	0.25	0.30
2002	0.30	0.31	0.20	0.27
2003	0.02	0.27	0.03	0.34
2004	0.34	0.31	0.29	0.32

Interim Dividends (Per Share)

Amt	Decl	Ex	Rec	Pay
0.15Q	6/14/2004	7/8/2004	7/12/2004	8/2/2004
0.15Q	9/17/2004	10/6/2004	10/8/2004	11/1/2004
0.15Q	12/17/2004	1/5/2005	1/7/2005	2/1/2005
0.15Q	3/18/2005	4/6/2005	4/8/2005	5/2/2005

Indicated Div: $0.60

Valuation Analysis

Forecast P/E	13.68	No of Institutions	
	(4/13/2005)	168	
Market Cap	$1.6 Billion	Shares	
Book Value	218.9 Million	65,062,536	
Price/Book	7.47	% Held	
Price/Sales	3.24	78.51	

Business Summary: Finance Intermediaries & Services (MIC: 8.7 SIC: 211 NAIC: 23120)

Waddell & Reed Financial, with assets under management of $36.60 billion as of Dec 31 2003, is the holding company of Waddell & Reed, Waddell & Reed Investment Management, and Waddell & Reed Services. Waddell & Reed is a registered broker-dealer and registered investment advisor that acts as the national distributor and underwriter for shares of Co.'s mutual funds and the distributor of insurance products issued primarily by Nationwide Life Insurance. Waddell & Reed Investment Management is a registered investment advisor that provides investment management and advisory services to Co.'s mutual funds and institutions. Waddell & Reed Services provides transfer agency and accounting services.

Recent Developments: For the year ended Dec 31 2004, net income increased 88.3% to $102.2 million from net income of $54.3 million a year earlier. Results for 2003 included a pre-tax special charge of $59.1 million. Total operating revenues were $504.1 million, up 11.7% from $451.2 million the year before. Investment management fees advanced 17.8% to $240.3 million from $203.9 million the previous year. Underwriting and distribution fees rose 6.1% to $187.3 million from $176.6 million in 2003, while shareholder service fees grew 8.3% to $76.5 million from $70.7 million the prior year.

Prospects: Prospects are encouraging as Co. is seeing marked improvement in both sales and advisor productivity. With regard to Co.'s wholesale channel, demand for Co.'s mutual funds in its non-proprietary products continues to accelerate. For instance, gross and net sales during the fourth quarter of 2004 were $460.0 million, and represent a compound annual growth rate of 67.0% since the re-launch of Co.'s non-proprietary sales efforts in July of 2003. Co. is also experiencing an improvement in its overall management fees rate due to a mix shift between advisors, Ivy and W&R Target Funds that occurred when Co. acquired the Securian assets into the IVY and W&R Target Funds in the second half of 2003.

Financial Data (US$ in Thousands)	12/31/2004	12/31/2003	12/31/2002	12/31/2001	12/31/2000	12/31/1999	12/31/1998	12/31/1997
Earnings Per Share	1.25	0.66	1.07	1.28	1.60	0.89	0.85	0.73
Cash Flow Per Share	1.42	1.21	1.26	1.76	2.08	1.21	0.88	0.65
Tang Book Value Per Share	N.M.	N.M.	N.M.	N.M.	N.M.	0.15	1.18	N.M.
Dividends Per Share	0.600	0.548	0.486	0.354	0.354	0.353	0.265	...
Dividend Payout %	48.00	83.00	45.44	27.63	22.10	39.55	31.30	...
Income Statement								
Total Revenue	504,077	451,182	439,125	482,562	520,702	356,657	287,289	241,772
Income Before Taxes	158,210	84,934	132,598	171,120	227,946	132,025	135,498	115,147
Income Taxes	56,045	30,669	45,173	63,953	88,941	50,258	51,763	44,855
Net Income	102,165	54,265	87,425	107,167	139,005	81,767	83,735	70,292
Average Shares	81,924	82,590	81,874	83,423	86,895	91,548	99,268	96,000
Balance Sheet								
Total Assets	619,907	565,804	560,492	433,105	422,186	335,073	327,179	446,964
Total Liabilities	401,030	390,399	411,187	319,307	280,576	208,730	120,043	676,855
Stockholders' Equity	218,877	175,405	149,305	113,798	141,610	126,343	207,136	(229,891)
Shares Outstanding	82,798	82,048	80,637	80,204	83,410	86,450	94,227	63,450
Statistical Record								
Return on Assets %	17.19	9.64	17.60	25.06	36.61	24.69	21.63	16.04
Return on Equity %	51.68	33.42	66.46	83.92	103.47	49.04	40.43	N.M.
Price Range	27.21-19.01	27.41-16.01	32.69-15.43	36.01-24.03	40.00-16.63	18.63-12.54	18.08-11.08	N.M.
P/E Ratio	21.77-15.21	41.53-24.26	30.55-14.42	28.13-18.77	25.00-10.39	20.93-14.09	21.27-13.04	N.M.
Average Yield %	2.64	2.48	2.07	1.17	1.22	2.27	1.79	N.M.

Address: 6300 Lamar Avenue, Overland Park, KS 66202
Telephone: (913) 236 2000
Fax: (913) 236 2017

Web Site: www.waddell.com
Officers: Keith A. Tucker - Chmn., C.E.O. Henry J. Herrmann - Pres., Chief Investment Officer

Auditors: KPMG LLP
Investor Contact: 913-236-1880
Transfer Agents: Equiserve Trust Company NA

WAL-MART STORES, INC.

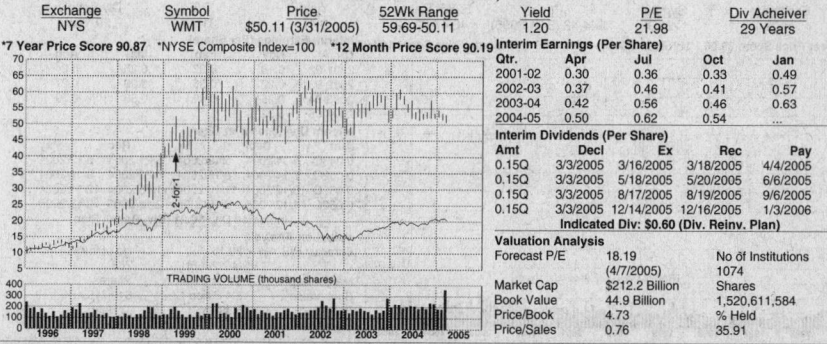

Exchange	Symbol	Price	52Wk Range	Yield	P/E	Div Acheiver
NYS	WMT	$50.11 (3/31/2005)	59.69-50.11	1.20	21.98	29 Years

*7 Year Price Score 90.87   *NYSE Composite Index=100   *12 Month Price Score 90.19

Interim Earnings (Per Share)

Qtr.	Apr	Jul	Oct	Jan
2001-02	0.30	0.36	0.33	0.49
2002-03	0.37	0.46	0.41	0.57
2003-04	0.42	0.56	0.46	0.63
2004-05	0.50	0.62	0.54	...

Interim Dividends (Per Share)

Amt	Decl	Ex	Rec	Pay
0.15Q	3/3/2005	3/16/2005	3/18/2005	4/4/2005
0.15Q	3/3/2005	5/18/2005	5/20/2005	6/6/2005
0.15Q	3/3/2005	8/17/2005	8/19/2005	9/6/2005
0.15Q	3/3/2005	12/14/2005	12/16/2005	1/3/2006

Indicated Div: $0.60 (Div. Reinv. Plan)

Valuation Analysis

Forecast P/E	18.19	No of Institutions
	(4/7/2005)	1074
Market Cap	$212.2 Billion	Shares
Book Value	44.9 Billion	1,520,611,584
Price/Book	4.73	% Held
Price/Sales	0.76	35.91

Business Summary: Retail - General (MIC: 5.2 SIC: 331 NAIC: 52990)

Wal-Mart Stores operated 1,478 discount department stores, 1,471 Supercenters, 538 Sam's Clubs and 64 Neighborhood Markets in the U.S. as of Jan 31 2004. Co. also operated 623 Wal-Mart stores in Mexico, 267 in the U.K., 235 in Canada, 92 in Germany, 53 in Puerto Rico, 25 in Brazil, 15 in South Korea, and eleven in Argentina. Co. also operated 34 stores in China under joint venture agreements. Co.'s supercenters combine food, general merchandise, and services including pharmacy, dry cleaning, portrait studios, photo finishing, hair salons, and optical shops. In addition, Co. owns a 37.8% interest in Seiyu, Ltd., which operates over 400 stores throughout Japan.

Recent Developments: For the quarter ended Oct 31 2004, net income increased 12.7% to $2,286,000 thousand from net income of $2,028,000 thousand in the year-earlier quarter. Revenues were $69,261,000 thousand, up 9.9% from $63,035,000 thousand the year before. Operating income was $3,784,000 thousand versus an operating income of $3,399,000 thousand in the prior-year quarter, an increase of 11.3%. Total indirect expense was $12,910,000 thousand versus $11,344,000 thousand in the prior-year quarter, an increase of 13.8%.

Prospects: Results are being positively affected by strong sales growth stemming from Co.'s aggressive store expansion program. During fiscal 2005, Co. opened 389 new stores. In addition, results are benefiting from Co.'s efforts to lower its cost of sales through improved global sourcing initiatives, partially offset by higher healthcare and labor expenses, as well as fuel costs. Co. is targeting first-quarter earnings in a range of $0.56 to $0.58 per share. Looking ahead, Co. is projecting earnings per share of between $2.70 and $2.72 during the current fiscal year, along with same-store sales growth at the lower end of the 3.0% to 5.0% range.

Financial Data

(US$ in Thousands)	9 Mos	6 Mos	3 Mos	01/31/2004	01/31/2003	01/31/2002	01/31/2001	01/31/2000
Earnings Per Share	2.28	2.21	2.14	2.07	1.81	1.49	1.40	1.20
Cash Flow Per Share	3.69	3.41	3.30	3.67	2.83	2.30	2.15	1.84
Tang Book Value Per Share	8.19	7.78	7.55	7.83	6.78	5.95	4.99	3.69
Dividends Per Share	0.480	0.440	0.400	0.360	0.300	0.280	0.240	0.200
Dividend Payout %	21.02	19.95	18.66	17.39	16.57	18.79	17.14	16.67
Income Statement								
Total Revenue	205,170,000	135,909,000	65,443,000	258,681,000	246,525,000	219,812,000	193,295,000	166,809,000
EBITDA	14,954,000	10,076,000	4,642,000	18,877,000	17,076,000	15,367,000	14,358,000	12,480,000
Depn & Amortn	3,161,000	2,068,000	1,037,000	3,852,000	3,432,000	3,290,000	2,868,000	2,375,000
Income Before Taxes	11,104,000	7,561,000	3,397,000	14,193,000	12,719,000	10,751,000	10,116,000	9,083,000
Income Taxes	3,853,000	2,646,000	1,189,000	5,118,000	4,487,000	3,897,000	3,692,000	3,338,000
Net Income	7,103,000	4,817,000	2,166,000	9,054,000	8,039,000	6,671,000	6,295,000	5,377,000
Average Shares	4,249,000	4,272,000	4,301,999	4,372,999	4,445,999	4,480,999	4,483,999	4,473,999
Balance Sheet								
Current Assets	40,977,000	35,616,000	34,753,000	34,421,000	30,483,000	28,246,000	26,555,000	24,356,000
Total Assets	118,089,000	110,059,000	107,580,000	104,912,000	94,685,000	83,451,000	78,130,000	70,349,000
Current Liabilities	47,016,000	43,007,000	41,066,000	37,418,000	32,617,000	27,282,000	28,949,000	25,803,000
Long-Term Obligations	22,147,000	20,144,000	20,500,000	20,099,000	19,608,000	18,732,000	15,655,000	16,674,000
Total Liabilities	73,203,000	66,915,000	65,196,000	61,289,000	55,348,000	48,349,000	46,787,000	44,515,000
Stockholders' Equity	44,886,000	43,144,000	42,384,000	43,623,000	39,337,000	35,102,000	31,343,000	25,834,000
Shares Outstanding	4,234,867	4,242,513	4,269,433	4,310,999	4,394,999	4,452,999	4,469,999	4,456,999
Statistical Record								
Return on Assets %	8.79	9.14	9.15	9.07	9.03	8.26	8.46	8.94
Return on Equity %	22.50	22.26	22.60	21.83	21.60	20.08	21.96	22.91
EBITDA Margin %	7.29	7.41	7.09	7.30	6.93	6.99	7.43	7.48
Net Margin %	3.46	3.54	3.31	3.50	3.26	3.03	3.26	3.22
Asset Turnover	2.51	2.62	2.61	2.59	2.77	2.72	2.60	2.77
Current Ratio	0.87	0.83	0.85	0.92	0.93	1.04	0.92	0.94
Debt to Equity	0.49	0.47	0.48	0.46	0.50	0.53	0.50	0.65
Price Range	61.05-50.74	61.05-50.74	61.05-50.74	60.08-46.74	63.75-44.60	59.98-44.00	63.56-43.25	69.44-40.19
P/E Ratio	26.78-22.25	27.62-22.96	28.53-23.71	29.02-22.58	35.22-24.64	40.26-29.53	45.40-30.89	57.86-33.49
Average Yield %	0.87	0.78	0.71	0.66	0.55	0.53	0.45	0.40

Address: 702 S.W. Eighth Street, Bentonville, AR 72716 **Telephone:** (479) 273-4000 **Fax:** (479) 273-1986	**Web Site:** www.wal-mart.com **Officers:** S. Robson Walton - Chmn. H. Lee Scott Jr. - Pres., C.E.O.	**Auditors:** Ernst & Young LLP **Transfer Agents:** EquiServe Trust Company, N.A., Providence, RI

WALGREEN CO.

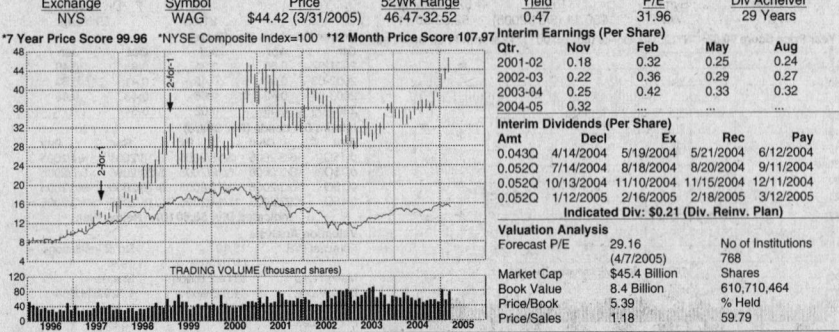

Exchange	Symbol	Price	52Wk Range	Yield	P/E	Div Acheiver
NYS	WAG	$44.42 (3/31/2005)	46.47-32.52	0.47	31.96	29 Years

*7 Year Price Score 99.96   ***NYSE Composite Index=100**   ***12 Month Price Score 107.97**

Interim Earnings (Per Share)

Qtr.	Nov	Feb	May	Aug
2001-02	0.18	0.32	0.25	0.24
2002-03	0.22	0.36	0.29	0.27
2003-04	0.25	0.42	0.33	0.32
2004-05	0.32	...	...	...

Interim Dividends (Per Share)

Amt	Decl	Ex	Rec	Pay
0.043Q	4/14/2004	5/19/2004	5/21/2004	6/12/2004
0.052Q	7/14/2004	8/18/2004	8/20/2004	9/11/2004
0.052Q	10/13/2004	11/10/2004	11/15/2004	12/11/2004
0.052Q	1/12/2005	2/16/2005	2/18/2005	3/12/2005

Indicated Div: $0.21 (Div. Reinv. Plan)

Valuation Analysis

Forecast P/E	29.16	No of Institutions
	(4/7/2005)	768
Market Cap	$45.4 Billion	Shares
Book Value	8.4 Billion	610,710,464
Price/Book	5.39	% Held
Price/Sales	1.18	59.79

TRADING VOLUME (thousand shares)

Business Summary: Retail - Miscellaneous (MIC: 5.11 SIC: 912 NAIC: 46110)

Walgreen is engaged in the operation of retail drugstores. Co.'s drugstores are engaged in the retail sale of prescription and non-prescription drugs and carry additional product lines such as general merchandise, cosmetics, toiletries, household items, food and beverages. Customer prescription purchases can be made at the drugstores as well as through the mail, by telephone and on the Internet. The total number of stores at Aug 31 2004 was 4,579 stores located in 44 states and Puerto Rico. In addition, Co. operates three mail service facilities.

Recent Developments: For the quarter ended Nov 30 2004, net income advanced 30.5% to $332,700 thousand from net income of $254,900 thousand in the year-earlier quarter. Revenues were $9,889,100 thousand, up 13.4% from $8,720,800 thousand the year before. Gross profit margins as a percent of total sales were 27.4% compared with 26.4% in 2003. Total indirect expense climbed 16.6% to $2,210,300 thousand versus $1,895,100 thousand in the prior-year quarter. Selling, occupancy and adminstration expenses were 22.4% of sales from 21.7% a year ago. The increase, as a percent to sales, was principally caused by higher store salaries and costs associated with Co.'s ongoing conversion to digital photo labs from analog.

Prospects: Co. is performing well, supported by solid prescription and general merchandise sales, as well as significantly higher gross profit margins due to better purchasing terms, digital photofinishing and growth in generic drug sales. However, Co. is incurring significant costs associated with its conversion to digital labs. Nevertheless, Co. believes this conversion will be a worthwhile investment as a strong customer reception to its push on digital photo processing is leading early sales strength and improved customer satisfaction. Going forward, Co. plans to open about 450 new stores during fiscal 2005, for a net increase after closings and relocations of about 365 stores.

Financial Data
(US$ in Thousands)

	3 Mos	08/31/2004	08/31/2003	08/31/2002	08/31/2001	08/31/2000	08/31/1999	08/31/1998
Earnings Per Share	1.39	1.32	1.14	0.99	0.86	0.76	0.62	0.51
Cash Flow Per Share	1.55	1.61	1.46	1.44	0.71	0.96	0.62	0.58
Tang Book Value Per Share	8.24	8.04	7.02	6.08	5.11	4.19	3.47	2.86
Dividends Per Share	0.191	0.182	0.156	0.145	0.140	0.135	0.130	0.125
Dividend Payout %	13.80	13.78	13.65	14.65	16.28	17.76	20.97	24.51
Income Statement								
Total Revenue	9,889,100	37,508,200	32,505,400	28,681,100	24,623,000	21,206,900	17,838,800	15,307,000
EBITDA	512,600	2,562,100	2,224,000	1,937,700	1,689,600	1,487,700	1,225,500	1,061,000
Depn & Amortn	...	403,100	346,100	307,300	269,200	230,100	210,100	189,000
Income Before Taxes	517,700	2,176,300	1,888,700	1,637,300	1,422,700	1,263,300	1,027,300	877,000
Income Taxes	185,000	816,100	713,000	618,100	537,100	486,400	403,200	340,000
Net Income	332,700	1,360,200	1,175,700	1,019,200	885,600	776,900	624,100	511,000
Average Shares	1,029,400	1,031,798	1,031,580	1,032,270	1,028,946	1,019,888	1,014,281	1,005,692
Balance Sheet								
Current Assets	8,385,100	7,764,400	6,358,100	5,166,500	4,393,900	3,550,100	3,221,700	2,623,000
Total Assets	14,149,700	13,342,100	11,405,900	9,878,800	8,833,800	7,103,700	5,906,700	4,902,000
Current Liabilities	4,645,000	4,077,900	3,420,500	2,955,200	3,011,600	2,303,700	1,923,800	1,580,000
Total Liabilities	5,731,600	5,114,100	4,210,200	3,648,600	3,626,600	2,869,700	2,422,400	2,053,000
Stockholders' Equity	8,418,100	8,228,000	7,195,700	6,230,200	5,207,200	4,234,000	3,484,300	2,849,000
Shares Outstanding	1,021,119	1,023,292	1,024,908	1,024,908	1,019,425	1,010,818	1,004,022	996,488
Statistical Record								
Return on Assets %	10.92	10.96	11.05	10.89	11.11	11.91	11.55	11.22
Return on Equity %	18.15	17.59	17.51	17.82	18.76	20.08	19.71	19.57
EBITDA Margin %	5.18	6.83	6.84	6.76	6.86	7.02	6.87	6.93
Net Margin %	3.36	3.63	3.62	3.55	3.60	3.66	3.50	3.34
Asset Turnover	2.94	3.02	3.05	3.07	3.09	3.25	3.30	3.36
Current Ratio	1.81	1.90	1.86	1.75	1.46	1.54	1.67	1.66
Price Range	39.48-32.45	37.74-30.57	35.96-27.35	40.24-30.98	45.63-31.43	36.00-22.75	32.88-19.19	24.47-12.81
P/E Ratio	28.40-23.35	28.59-23.16	31.54-23.99	40.65-31.29	53.05-36.55	47.37-29.93	53.02-30.95	47.98-25.12
Average Yield %	0.54	0.52	0.52	0.40	0.35	0.48	0.49	0.71

Address: 200 Wilmot Road, Deerfield, IL 60015 Telephone: (847) 940-2500	Web Site: www.walgreens.com Officers: David W. Bernauer - Chmn., C.E.O. Jeffrey A. Rein - Pres., C.O.O.	Auditors: Deloitte & Touche LLP Investor Contact: 847-914-2972 Transfer Agents: Computershare Investor Services, Chicago, IL

WASHINGTON MUTUAL INC.

Exchange	Symbol	Price	52Wk Range	Yield	P/E	Div Acheiver
NYS	WM	$39.50 (3/31/2005)	44.25-37.63	4.66	12.12	15 Years

*7 Year Price Score 106.62 ***NYSE Composite Index=100** ***12 Month Price Score 94.64**

Interim Earnings (Per Share)

Qtr.	Mar	Jun	Sep	Dec
2001	0.77	0.91	0.94	0.96
2002	0.98	1.01	1.01	1.04
2003	1.07	1.10	1.11	0.94
2004	1.18	0.55	0.76	0.76

Interim Dividends (Per Share)

Amt	Decl	Ex	Rec	Pay
0.43Q	4/19/2004	4/28/2004	4/30/2004	5/14/2004
0.44Q	7/21/2004	7/28/2004	7/30/2004	8/13/2004
0.45Q	10/20/2004	10/27/2004	10/29/2004	11/15/2004
0.46Q	1/19/2005	1/27/2005	1/31/2005	2/15/2005

Indicated Div: $1.84 (Div. Reinv. Plan)

Valuation Analysis

Forecast P/E	10.92	No of Institutions
	(4/7/2005)	680
Market Cap	$34.5 Billion	Shares
Book Value	21.2 Billion	634,416,512
Price/Book	1.63	% Held
Price/Sales	2.16	72.15

Business Summary: Other Depository Banking (MIC: 8.5 SIC: 036 NAIC: 22120)

Washington Mutual is a holding company for both banking and nonbanking subsidiaries. Co.'s primary banking subsidiaries are Washington Mutual Bank, FA, Washington Mutual Bank and Washington Mutual Bank fsb. These organizations provide consumer banking, mortgage lending, commercial banking, consumer finance and financial services. Co. operates in two segments: consumer group, which offers products and services to consumers and manages activities and operations affecting consumers; and commercial group, which offers a full array of commercial banking products and services. As of Dec 31 2003, Co. and its subsidiaries had assets of $275.18 billion and operated more than 2,400 offices nationwide.

Recent Developments: For the year ended Dec 31 2004, net income decreased 25.8% to $2,878,000 thousand from net income of $3,880,000 thousand a year earlier. Net interest income was $7,116,000 thousand, down 6.7% from $7,629,000 thousand the year before. Provision for loan losses was $209,000 thousand versus $42,000 thousand in the prior year, an increase of 397.6%. Non-interest income fell 21.8% to $7,133,000 thousand, while non-interest expense advanced 1.7% to $7,535,000 thousand.

Prospects: Results are being negatively affected by reduced mortgage refinancing activity versus the prior year, due to rising interest rates, and lower securities gains. In addition, bottom-line results are being hampered by increased costs related to Co.'s aggressive branch expansion program. During 2005, Co. anticipates opening 250 new retail banking branches, primarily in existing markets. Meanwhile, Co. plans to remodel approximately 200 existing stores during 2005 in markets such as Washington, Oregon, California, Texas, New York, New Jersey and Florida.

Financial Data
(US$ in Thousands)	12/31/2004	12/31/2003	12/31/2002	12/31/2001	12/31/2000	12/31/1999	12/31/1998	12/31/1997
Earnings Per Share	3.26	4.21	4.05	3.59	2.36	2.11	1.71	0.83
Cash Flow Per Share	(22.78)	13.84	0.03	(12.68)	3.76	6.13	8.17	0.34
Tang Book Value Per Share	10.21	7.88	9.03	6.29	9.96	8.41	8.85	7.97
Dividends Per Share	1.740	1.400	1.060	0.897	0.760	0.653	0.547	0.471
Dividend Payout %	53.37	33.25	26.17	24.98	32.20	31.01	32.03	56.99
Income Statement								
Interest Income	11,350,000	12,163,000	14,247,000	15,065,000	13,783,000	12,062,198	11,221,468	6,810,964
Interest Expense	4,234,000	4,534,000	5,906,000	8,189,000	9,472,000	7,610,408	6,929,743	4,154,491
Net Interest Income	7,116,000	7,629,000	8,341,000	6,876,000	4,311,000	4,451,790	4,291,725	2,656,473
Provision for Losses	209,000	42,000	595,000	575,000	185,000	167,076	161,968	207,139
Non-Interest Income	4,612,000	5,850,000	4,790,000	2,627,000	1,984,000	1,508,997	1,577,019	750,892
Non-Interest Expense	7,535,000	7,408,000	6,382,000	4,617,000	3,126,000	2,909,551	3,337,319	2,299,100
Income Before Taxes	3,984,000	6,029,000	6,154,000	4,311,000	2,984,000	2,884,160	2,369,457	901,126
Income Taxes	1,505,000	2,236,000	2,258,000	1,579,000	1,085,000	1,067,096	882,525	419,348
Net Income	2,878,000	3,880,000	3,896,000	3,114,000	1,899,000	1,817,064	1,486,932	481,778
Average Shares	884,050	921,757	960,152	864,700	804,694	861,829	867,843	555,851
Balance Sheet								
Net Loans & Leases	205,770,000	174,394,000	145,875,000	131,587,000	118,612,000	113,497,225	108,370,906	67,140,157
Total Assets	307,918,000	275,178,000	268,298,000	242,506,000	194,716,000	186,513,630	165,493,281	96,981,099
Total Deposits	173,658,000	153,181,000	155,516,000	107,182,000	79,574,000	81,129,768	85,492,141	50,986,017
Total Liabilities	286,692,000	255,436,000	248,164,000	228,341,000	184,550,000	177,460,951	156,148,881	91,672,028
Stockholders' Equity	21,226,000	19,742,000	20,134,000	14,063,000	10,166,000	9,052,679	9,344,400	5,309,071
Shares Outstanding	874,261	880,985	944,046	873,089	809,783	857,383	890,112	579,510
Statistical Record								
Return on Assets %	0.98	1.43	1.53	1.42	0.99	1.03	1.13	0.68
Return on Equity %	14.01	19.46	22.79	25.70	19.71	19.75	20.29	12.50
Net Interest Margin %	62.70	62.72	58.55	45.64	31.28	36.91	38.25	39.00
Efficiency Ratio %	47.21	41.13	33.52	26.10	19.83	21.44	26.08	30.40
Loans to Deposits	1.18	1.14	0.94	1.23	1.49	1.40	1.27	1.32
Price Range	45.28-37.63	46.55-32.98	39.45-28.41	42.69-28.56	37.25-14.54	30.17-16.75	33.94-19.00	32.17-19.00
P/E Ratio	13.89-11.54	11.06-7.83	9.74-7.01	11.89-7.96	15.78-6.16	14.30-7.94	19.85-11.11	38.76-22.89
Average Yield %	4.27	3.57	3.00	2.55	3.50	2.74	1.98	1.79

Address: 1201 Third Avenue, Seattle, WA 98101	**Web Site:** www.wamu.com	**Auditors:** DELOITTE & TOUCHE LLP
Telephone: (206) 461-2000	**Officers:** Kerry K. Killinger - Chmn., Pres., C.E.O.	**Investor Contact:** 206-461-3186
Fax: (206) 554-2778	William A. Longbrake - Vice-Chmn.	**Transfer Agents:** Mellon Investor Services, L.L.C., Ridgefield Park, NJ

WASHINGTON POST CO.

Exchange	Symbol	Price	52Wk Range	Yield	P/E
NYS	WPO	$894.00 (3/31/2005)	996.74-845.50	0.83	25.85

*7 Year Price Score 121.99 *NYSE Composite Index=100 *12 Month Price Score 91.79

Interim Earnings (Per Share)

Qtr.	Mar	Jun	Sep	Dec
2001	20.90	1.50	0.14	1.53
2002	2.44	5.34	4.99	9.84
2003	7.59	6.32	2.06	9.15
2004	6.15	8.82	8.57	11.05

Interim Dividends (Per Share)

Amt	Decl	Ex	Rec	Pay
1.75Q	6/24/2004	7/21/2004	7/23/2004	8/6/2004
1.75Q	9/9/2004	10/20/2004	10/22/2004	11/5/2004
1.85Q	1/20/2005	1/27/2005	1/31/2005	2/4/2005
1.85Q	2/24/2005	4/27/2005	4/29/2005	5/13/2005

Indicated Div: $7.40

Valuation Analysis

Forecast P/E	23.11	No of Institutions
	(4/7/2005)	246
Market Cap	$8.6 Billion	Shares
Book Value	2.4 Billion	6,036,256
Price/Book	3.55	% Held
Price/Sales	2.59	76.74

TRADING VOLUME (thousand shares)

Business Summary: Media (MIC: 13.1 SIC: 711 NAIC: 11110)

The Washington Post is a diversified media and education company. Co.'s media properties include The Washington Post, The Gazette Newspapers, The Herald and Newsweek. Co.'s cable television business includes subscribers in Detroit, MI; Houston, TX; Miami and Orlando, FL; San Antonio, TX; Jacksonville, FL; and cable systems in midwestern, western and southern U.S. Co. also owns Kaplan, Inc., a provider of educational and career services; Washingtonpost.Newsweek Interactive, a provider of electronic information services; and PostNewsweek Tech Media Group, which produces technology publications and trade shows primarily for government technology managers and contractors.

Recent Developments: For the year ended Jan 2 2005, net income increased 38.0% to $332,732 thousand from net income of $241,088 thousand a year earlier. Revenues were $3,300,104 thousand, up 16.2% from $2,838,911 thousand the year before. Operating income was $563,006 thousand versus an income of $363,820 thousand in the prior year, an increase of 54.7%. Total direct expense was $1,717,059 thousand versus $1,549,262 thousand in the prior year, an increase of 10.8%. Total indirect expense was $1,020,039 thousand versus $925,829 thousand in the prior year, an increase of 10.2%.

Prospects: Co. is experiencing strong top-line growth in all of its operating segments. Specifically, Co.'s newspaper publishing division is benefiting from higher print and on-line advertising revenue. Also, education division revenues are being driven by growth primarily in the higher education division and the professional training schools that are part of supplemental education. Co.'s television broadcasting division is enjoying favorable results from incremental advertising at Co.'s NBC affiliates. Separately, on Jan 14 2005, Co. announced that it completed the acquisition of Slate, the on-line magazine, from Microsoft Corporation. Terms of the transaction were not disclosed.

Financial Data

(US$ in Thousands)	01/02/2005	12/28/2003	12/29/2002	12/30/2001	12/31/2000	01/02/2000	01/03/1999	12/28/1997
Earnings Per Share	34.59	25.12	21.34	24.06	14.32	22.30	41.10	26.15
Cash Flow Per Share	57.79	35.53	52.49	36.87	39.13	28.21	21.76	30.08
Tang Book Value Per Share	92.76	64.70	61.18	50.32	50.03	51.03	69.84	42.64
Dividends Per Share	7.000	5.800	5.600	5.600	5.400	5.200	5.000	4.800
Dividend Payout %	20.24	23.09	26.24	23.28	37.71	23.32	12.17	18.36
Income Statement								
Total Revenue	3,300,104	2,838,911	2,584,203	2,416,673	2,412,150	2,215,571	2,110,360	1,956,253
EBITDA	753,480	584,687	559,718	652,245	464,216	563,872	817,597	565,892
Depn & Amortn	184,638	175,248	172,563	217,233	180,582	162,798	139,137	105,037
Income Before Taxes	542,432	382,588	353,668	387,539	229,870	375,385	668,059	463,074
Income Taxes	209,700	141,500	137,300	157,900	93,400	149,600	250,800	181,500
Net Income	332,732	241,088	204,268	229,639	136,470	225,785	417,259	281,574
Average Shares	9,591	9,554	9,522	9,499	9,459	10,082	10,129	10,733
Balance Sheet								
Current Assets	754,367	495,836	382,955	396,857	405,067	476,159	404,878	308,492
Total Assets	4,316,641	3,901,558	3,583,894	3,559,098	3,200,743	2,986,944	2,729,661	2,077,317
Current Liabilities	688,161	711,873	736,112	434,090	408,797	822,548	389,079	608,756
Long-Term Obligations	425,889	422,471	405,547	883,078	873,267	397,620	395,000	...
Total Liabilities	1,891,892	1,814,077	1,733,685	1,862,481	1,706,588	1,607,281	1,129,685	881,296
Stockholders' Equity	2,412,482	2,074,941	1,837,293	1,683,485	1,481,007	1,367,790	1,588,103	1,184,074
Shares Outstanding	9,576	9,541	9,510	9,494	9,460	9,439	10,093	11,828
Statistical Record								
Return on Assets %	7.97	6.46	5.74	6.81	4.42	7.92	17.08	14.30
Return on Equity %	14.59	12.36	11.64	14.55	9.61	15.32	29.62	22.53
EBITDA Margin %	22.83	20.60	21.66	26.99	19.24	25.45	38.74	28.93
Net Margin %	10.08	8.49	7.90	9.50	5.66	10.19	19.77	14.39
Asset Turnover	0.79	0.76	0.73	0.72	0.78	0.78	0.86	0.99
Current Ratio	1.10	0.70	0.52	0.91	0.99	0.58	1.04	0.51
Debt to Equity	0.18	0.20	0.22	0.52	0.59	0.29	0.25	...
Price Range	996.74-790.22	814.78-657.40	738.50-518.00	632.76-491.65	620.75-472.65	591.00-490.13	602.00-465.88	489.63-326.25
P/E Ratio	28.82-22.85	32.44-26.17	34.61-24.27	26.30-20.43	43.35-32.96	26.50-21.98	14.65-11.34	18.72-12.48
Average Yield %	0.77	0.81	0.89	0.99	1.05	0.95	0.95	1.20

Address: 1150 15th Street N.W., Washington, DC 20071
Telephone: (202) 334-6000
Fax: (202) 334-1031

Web Site: www.washpostco.com
Officers: Donald E. Graham - Chmn., C.E.O. Diana M. Daniels - V.P., Gen. Couns., Sec.

Auditors: PricewaterhouseCoopers LLP
Investor Contact: 202-334-6000

WASHINGTON REAL ESTATE INVESTMENT TRUST

Exchange	Symbol	Price	52Wk Range	Yield	P/E	Div Acheiver
NYS	WRE	$28.75 (3/31/2005)	34.43-25.80	5.46	26.38	43 Years

*7 Year Price Score 111.65 *NYSE Composite Index=100 *12 Month Price Score 90.99

Interim Earnings (Per Share)

Qtr.	Mar	Jun	Sep	Dec
2001	0.30	0.33	0.43	0.32
2002	0.42	0.30	0.30	0.31
2003	0.28	0.29	0.28	0.28
2004	0.27	0.26	0.26	0.30

Interim Dividends (Per Share)

Amt	Decl	Ex	Rec	Pay
0.393Q	5/5/2004	6/14/2004	6/16/2004	6/30/2004
0.393Q	8/4/2004	9/14/2004	9/16/2004	9/30/2004
0.393Q	11/17/2004	12/14/2004	12/16/2004	12/30/2004
0.393Q	2/17/2005	3/15/2005	3/17/2005	3/31/2005

Indicated Div: $1.57 (Div. Reinv. Plan)

Valuation Analysis

Forecast P/E	13.91	No of Institutions	
	(4/13/2005)	144	
Market Cap	$1.2 Billion	Shares	
Book Value	366.0 Million	16,413,984	
Price/Book	3.30	% Held	
Price/Sales	7.00	39.08	

Business Summary: Property, Real Estate & Development (MIC: 8.3 SIC: 798 NAIC: 25930)

Washington Real Estate Investment Trust is a self-administered qualified equity real estate investment trust. Co.'s business consists of the ownership and operation of income-producing real estate properties principally in the Greater Washington, D.C.-Baltimore, MD area. Upon the purchase of a property, Co. begins a program of improving the real estate to increase the value and to improve the operations, with the goals of generating higher rental income and reducing expenses. As of Mar 12 2004, Co. owned a diversified portfolio of 67 properties consisting of 11 retail centers, 29 office buildings, nine multifamily buildings and 18 industrial/flex properties.

Recent Developments: For the year ended Dec 31 2004, income from continuing operations increased 0.2% to $40,865,000 from income of $40,792,000 a year earlier. Net income increased 1.5% to $45,564,000 from net income of $44,887,000 a year earlier. Revenues were $172,394,000, up 11.6% from $154,418,000 the year before. Property operating expenses climbed 13.8% to $37,298 thousand from $32,771 thousand a year earlier. Other operating expenses advanced 16.2% to $80,135 thousand versus $68,937 thousand the year before. Total net operating income increased 10.4% to $120,673 thousand, largely reflecting Co.'s acquisition of six office buildings, which added 1,176 thousand square feet of net rentable space.

Prospects: Co. continues to reduce its exposure to the general office market through selected asset dispositions and an increased focus on the acquisition of medical office buildings in conjunction with acquiring industrial/flex, retail and multi-family properties. On Dec 27 2004, Co. acquired a portfolio of five office buildings within Dulles Business Park in Chantilly, VA for $46.0 million. The portfolio consists of 264,657 rentable square feet and 994 surface parking spaces. The property is 98.9% leased and is projected to achieve a first-year unleveraged yield of 7.5%. On Feb 2 2005, Co. sold three office buildings located in Tysons Corner, VA, for $67.5 million, resulting in a gain of $33.0 million.

Financial Data

(US$ in Thousands)	12/31/2004	12/31/2003	12/31/2002	12/31/2001	12/31/2000	12/31/1999	12/31/1998	12/31/1997
Earnings Per Share	1.09	1.13	1.32	1.38	1.26	1.24	1.15	0.90
Cash Flow Per Share	1.91	1.94	1.80	1.98	1.73	1.47	1.50	1.27
Tang Book Value Per Share	8.71	9.10	8.33	8.33	7.24	7.20	7.11	7.07
Dividends Per Share	1.550	1.470	1.390	1.310	1.230	1.158	1.110	1.070
Dividend Payout %	142.20	130.09	105.30	94.93	97.62	93.35	96.52	118.89
Income Statement								
Property Income	172,067	163,405	152,929	148,424	134,732	118,975	103,597	79,429
Non-Property Income	327	414	680	...	...	...	...	...
Total Revenue	172,394	163,819	153,609	148,424	134,732	118,975	103,597	79,429
Depn & Amortn	41,961	35,755	29,212	26,954	22,723	19,590	15,399	10,911
Interest Expense	34,500	30,040	27,849	27,071	25,531	22,271	17,106	9,691
Net Income	45,564	44,887	51,836	52,353	45,139	44,301	41,064	30,136
Average Shares	41,863	39,600	39,281	37,951	35,872	35,700	35,700	33,400
Balance Sheet								
Total Assets	1,012,393	927,129	755,997	707,935	632,047	608,480	558,707	468,571
Long-Term Obligations	493,429	517,182	351,951	359,726	351,260	297,038	238,912	107,461
Total Liabilities	644,755	546,780	428,266	382,717	371,833	349,769	303,447	216,483
Stockholders' Equity	366,009	378,748	326,177	323,607	258,656	257,189	253,733	252,088
Shares Outstanding	42,000	41,607	39,168	38,829	35,740	35,721	35,692	35,678
Statistical Record								
Return on Assets %	4.69	5.33	7.08	7.81	7.26	7.59	7.99	7.66
Return on Equity %	12.20	12.74	15.95	17.98	17.45	17.34	16.24	13.46
Net Margin %	26.43	27.40	33.75	35.27	33.50	37.24	39.64	37.94
Price Range	34.43-25.80	31.04-24.10	30.15-21.96	25.45-21.27	25.00-14.31	18.63-14.00	18.63-15.56	19.38-15.88
P/E Ratio	31.59-23.67	27.47-21.33	22.84-16.64	18.44-15.41	19.84-11.36	15.02-11.29	16.20-13.53	21.53-17.64
Average Yield %	5.16	5.33	5.31	5.59	6.89	7.11	6.53	6.25

Address: 6110 Executive Boulevard, Rockville, MD 20852-3927	Web Site: www.writ.com	Auditors: Ernst & Young LLP
Telephone: (301) 984-9400	Officers: Edmund B. Cronin Jr. - Chmn., Pres., C.E.O. George F. McKenzie - Exec. V.P., Real Estate	Transfer Agents: EquiServe Trust Company N.A., Providence, RI
Fax: (301) 984-9610		

WASTE MANAGEMENT, INC. (DE)

Exchange	Symbol	Price	52Wk Range	Yield	P/E
NYS	WMI	$28.85 (3/31/2005)	31.10-26.17	2.77	17.92

*7 Year Price Score 84.68 ***NYSE Composite Index=100** ***12 Month Price Score 95.30**

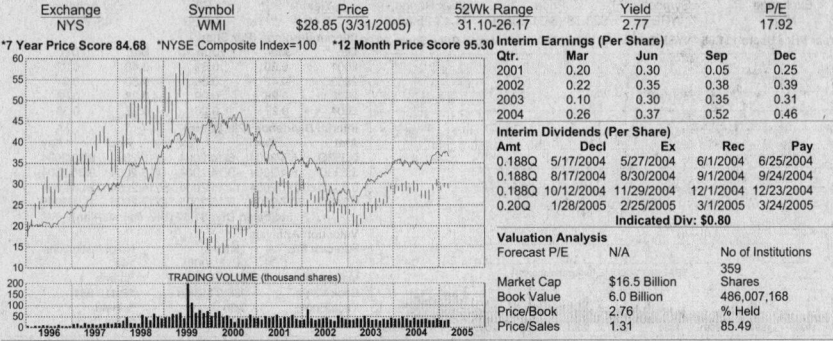

Interim Earnings (Per Share)

Qtr.	Mar	Jun	Sep	Dec
2001	0.20	0.30	0.05	0.25
2002	0.22	0.35	0.38	0.39
2003	0.10	0.30	0.35	0.31
2004	0.26	0.37	0.52	0.46

Interim Dividends (Per Share)

Amt	Decl	Ex	Rec	Pay
0.188Q	5/17/2004	5/27/2004	6/1/2004	6/25/2004
0.188Q	8/17/2004	8/30/2004	9/1/2004	9/24/2004
0.188Q	10/12/2004	11/29/2004	12/1/2004	12/23/2004
0.20Q	1/28/2005	2/25/2005	3/1/2005	3/24/2005

Indicated Div: $0.80

Valuation Analysis

Forecast P/E	N/A	No of Institutions
		359
Market Cap	$16.5 Billion	Shares
Book Value	6.0 Billion	486,007,168
Price/Book	2.76	% Held
Price/Sales	1.31	85.49

Business Summary: Sanitation Services (MIC: 7.3 SIC: 953 NAIC: 62211)

Waste Management is a holding company. Through its subsidiaries, Co. provides comprehensive waste management services to its customers throughout North America. Co. provides solid waste collection, transfer, recycling and resource recovery services, and disposal services. In addition, Co. is a developer, operator and owner of waste-to-energy facilities in the U.S. Co.'s customers include commercial, industrial, municipal and residential customers, other waste management companies, electric utilities and governmental entities. Co. owned or operated 284 solid waste and five hazardous waste landfills at Dec 31 2004.

Recent Developments: For the year ended Dec 31 2004, net income increased 49.0% to $939,000 thousand from net income of $630,000 thousand a year earlier. Revenues were $12,516,000 thousand, up 7.5% from $11,648,000 thousand the year before. Operating income was $1,699,000 thousand versus an income of $1,540,000 thousand in the prior year, an increase of 10.3%. Total direct expense was $8,228,000 thousand versus $7,591,000 thousand in the prior year, an increase of 8.4%. Total indirect expense was $2,589,000 thousand versus $2,517,000 thousand in the prior year, an increase of 2.9%.

Prospects: For fiscal 2005, Co. is projecting total revenue of approximately $13.00 billion. Internal revenue growth on base business is expected to be 2.7%, with the majority of growth from higher yield, and based on an expectation of a favorable pricing environment. Co. is projecting diluted earnings per share near the lower end of the current analyst range $1.56 to $1.80. For fiscal 2005, Co. expects net cash provided by operating activities to be in the range of $2.25 billion to $2.35 billion. Co. is projecting free cash flow in the range of $1.10 billion to $1.20 billion for fiscal 2005. Capital expenditures are expected to be in the range of $1.25 billion to $1.35 billion in fiscal 2005.

Financial Data
(US$ in Thousands)

	12/31/2004	12/31/2003	12/31/2002	12/31/2001	12/31/2000	12/31/1999	12/31/1998	12/31/1997
Earnings Per Share	1.61	1.06	1.33	0.80	(0.16)	(0.65)	(1.32)	1.23
Cash Flow Per Share	3.84	3.27	3.51	3.76	3.41	2.76	2.57	2.17
Tang Book Value Per Share	0.91	0.24	0.21	0.43	N.M.	N.M.	N.M.	4.51
Dividends Per Share	0.750	0.010	0.010	0.010	0.010	0.010	0.010	...
Dividend Payout %	46.58	0.94	0.75	1.25	N.M.	N.M.	N.M.	...
Income Statement								
Total Revenue	12,516,000	11,574,000	11,142,000	11,322,000	12,492,000	13,126,920	12,703,469	2,613,768
EBITDA	2,899,000	2,815,000	2,910,000	2,662,000	2,467,000	2,182,591	1,453,461	863,135
Depn & Amortn	1,336,000	1,265,000	1,222,000	1,371,000	1,429,000	1,614,165	1,498,712	303,241
Income Before Taxes	1,178,000	1,123,000	1,247,000	787,000	321,000	(162,732)	(699,879)	463,267
Income Taxes	247,000	404,000	424,000	284,000	418,000	232,319	66,923	189,944
Net Income	939,000	630,000	822,000	503,000	(97,000)	(397,564)	(770,702)	267,030
Average Shares	581,100	592,500	617,500	630,800	621,257	612,932	584,301	233,371
Balance Sheet								
Current Assets	2,819,000	2,588,000	2,700,000	3,124,000	2,457,000	6,220,545	3,881,397	655,386
Total Assets	20,905,000	20,656,000	19,631,000	19,490,000	18,565,000	22,681,424	22,715,198	6,622,845
Current Liabilities	3,205,000	3,332,000	3,173,000	3,721,000	2,937,000	7,489,455	4,293,666	568,650
Long-Term Obligations	8,182,000	7,997,000	8,062,000	7,709,000	8,372,000	8,399,346	11,114,201	2,724,443
Total Liabilities	14,652,000	14,843,000	14,304,000	14,085,000	13,749,000	18,271,138	18,230,626	3,993,869
Stockholders' Equity	5,971,000	5,563,000	5,308,000	5,392,000	4,801,000	4,402,612	4,372,496	2,628,976
Shares Outstanding	570,212	576,118	594,600	628,017	622,650	627,209	608,244	217,782
Statistical Record								
Return on Assets %	4.51	3.13	4.20	2.64	N.M.	N.M.	N.M.	5.65
Return on Equity %	16.24	11.59	15.36	9.87	N.M.	N.M.	N.M.	14.11
EBITDA Margin %	23.16	24.32	26.12	23.51	19.75	16.63	11.44	33.02
Net Margin %	7.50	5.44	7.38	4.44	N.M.	N.M.	N.M.	10.22
Asset Turnover	0.60	0.57	0.57	0.60	0.60	0.58	0.87	0.55
Current Ratio	0.88	0.78	0.85	0.84	0.84	0.83	0.90	1.15
Debt to Equity	1.37	1.44	1.52	1.43	1.74	1.91	2.54	1.04
Price Range	31.10-26.17	29.60-19.72	31.91-20.87	32.38-23.01	27.94-13.06	59.00-14.38	57.75-34.75	43.88-29.75
P/E Ratio	19.32-16.25	27.92-18.60	23.99-15.69	40.48-28.76	N/A	N/A	N/A	35.67-24.19
Average Yield %	2.61	0.04	0.04	0.04	0.05	0.03	0.02	...

Address: 1001 Fannin Street, Suite 4000, Houston, TX 77002	**Web Site:** www.wmx.com	**Auditors:** Ernst & Young LLP
Telephone: (713) 512-6200	**Officers:** A. Maurice Myers - Chmn., Pres., C.E.O.	**Investor Contact:** 713-512-6548
Fax: (713) 512-6299	David P. Steiner - Exec. V.P., C.F.O.	

WATERS CORP.

Exchange	Symbol	Price	52Wk Range	Yield	P/E
NYS	WAT	$35.79 (3/31/2005)	51.11-35.79	N/A	19.66

*7 Year Price Score 107.20 *NYSE Composite Index=100 *12 Month Price Score 96.41

Interim Earnings (Per Share)

Qtr.	Mar	Jun	Sep	Dec
2001	0.28	0.29	0.28	(0.01)
2002	0.26	0.28	0.29	0.30
2003	0.26	0.33	0.29	0.47
2004	0.33	0.49	0.42	0.58

Interim Dividends (Per Share)

Amt	Decl	Ex	Rec	Pay
100%	2/26/1999	6/11/1999	5/27/1999	6/10/1999
100%	7/13/2000	8/28/2000	8/4/2000	8/25/2000

Valuation Analysis

Forecast P/E	18.14	No of Institutions	
	(4/13/2005)	330	
Market Cap	$4.3 Billion	Shares	
Book Value	678.7 Million	103,975,312	
Price/Book	6.32	% Held	
Price/Sales	3.88	88.24	

Business Summary: Instruments and Related Products (MIC: 11.15 SIC: 826 NAIC: 34516)

Waters is a manufacturer, designer, and seller of analytical instruments. Co.'s Waters Division provides high performance liquid chromatography and mass spectrometry instrument systems and associated service and support products, including chromatography columns and other consumable products. Co.'s TA Instruments Division designs, manufactures, services and sells thermal analysis and rheology instruments. Co. is also a developer and supplier of software based products, which interface with Co.'s instruments. Co.'s products are used in the pharmaceutical, life science, biochemical, industrial, academic and government markets.

Recent Developments: For the year ended Dec 31 2004, net income increased 31.1% to $224,053 thousand from net income of $170,891 thousand a year earlier. Revenues were $1,104,536 thousand, up 15.3% from $958,205 thousand the year before. Operating income was $284,858 thousand versus an income of $219,172 thousand in the prior year, an increase of 30.0%. Total direct expense was $454,807 thousand versus $397,848 thousand in the prior year, an increase of 14.3%. Total indirect expense was $364,871 thousand versus $331,123 thousand in the prior year, an increase of 10.2%.

Prospects: Co.'s results are being fueled by solid top line growth and strengthening gross margins. For example, for the three months ended Dec 31 2004, net sales climbed 17.8% to $324.2 million and gross margin improved to 59.9% from 58.9% a year earlier. Co. attributed its recent top line growth to broad-based customer demand and successful new product launches. For instance, Co.'s Waters division benefited from sales of new products including ACQUITY UPLC™ and the QTof Premier™, while its TA Instruments division experienced continued robust customer demand. Accordingly, Co. is optimistic regarding its prospects for 2005.

Financial Data

(US$ in Thousands)	12/31/2004	12/31/2003	12/31/2002	12/31/2001	12/31/2000	12/31/1999	12/31/1998	12/31/1997
Earnings Per Share	1.82	1.34	1.09	0.83	1.06	0.92	0.57	(0.08)
Cash Flow Per Share	2.16	1.27	1.68	1.45	1.37	1.22	0.92	0.83
Tang Book Value Per Share	3.05	2.67	3.42	3.19	2.21	0.98	N.M.	N.M.
Income Statement								
Total Revenue	1,104,536	958,205	889,967	859,208	795,071	704,400	618,813	465,470
EBITDA	325,770	252,770	227,608	176,412	235,284	206,193	148,313	42,282
Depn & Amortn	41,926	33,848	37,194	33,951	24,457	29,684	28,488	21,095
Income Before Taxes	285,671	223,686	195,411	147,426	210,962	167,561	101,547	7,467
Income Taxes	61,618	52,795	43,193	32,883	54,849	45,243	27,148	15,755
Net Income	224,053	170,891	147,712	114,543	145,342	122,318	74,399	(8,288)
Average Shares	123,069	127,579	135,762	137,509	136,743	132,632	129,284	116,508
Balance Sheet								
Current Assets	973,884	715,399	636,456	522,744	343,796	247,330	251,624	216,499
Total Assets	1,460,426	1,130,861	1,010,947	886,911	692,345	584,437	577,701	552,059
Current Liabilities	492,990	378,521	320,215	281,006	220,533	197,841	185,573	170,656
Long-Term Obligations	250,000	125,000	...	...	...	81,105	218,250	305,340
Total Liabilities	781,740	540,384	345,637	305,166	240,564	292,275	427,582	489,762
Stockholders' Equity	678,686	590,477	665,310	581,745	451,781	292,162	150,119	62,297
Shares Outstanding	119,835	120,691	128,104	130,918	129,811	124,518	121,188	118,332
Statistical Record								
Return on Assets %	17.25	15.96	15.57	14.51	22.70	21.05	13.17	N.M.
Return on Equity %	35.21	27.22	23.69	22.17	38.97	55.31	70.05	N.M.
EBITDA Margin %	29.49	26.38	25.57	20.53	29.59	29.27	23.97	9.08
Net Margin %	20.28	17.83	16.60	13.33	18.28	17.36	12.02	N.M.
Asset Turnover	0.85	0.89	0.94	1.09	1.24	1.21	1.10	1.01
Current Ratio	1.98	1.89	1.99	1.86	1.56	1.25	1.36	1.27
Debt to Equity	0.37	0.21	...	...	...	0.28	1.45	4.90
Price Range	48.88-33.12	33.20-20.10	38.89-17.97	78.88-22.65	90.38-22.00	33.50-19.03	21.81-9.14	11.73-5.84
P/E Ratio	26.86-18.20	24.78-15.00	35.68-16.49	95.03-27.29	85.26-20.75	36.41-20.69	38.27-16.04	...

Address: 34 Maple Street, Milford, MA 01757	Web Site: www.waters.com	Auditors: PricewaterhouseCoopers LLP
Telephone: (508) 478-2000	Officers: Douglas A. Berthiaume - Chmn., Pres., C.E.O. John R. Nelson - Exec.V.P., Chief Tech. Officer	Investor Contact: 508-482-2349
Fax: (508) 872-1990		Transfer Agents: EquiServe Trust Company, N.A., Kansas City, MO

WATSON PHARMACEUTICALS, INC.

Exchange	Symbol	Price	52Wk Range	Yield	P/E
NYS	WPI	$30.73 (3/31/2005)	43.46-24.70	N/A	24.20

*7 Year Price Score 65.12   *NYSE Composite Index=100   *12 Month Price Score 93.48

Interim Earnings (Per Share)

Qtr.	Mar	Jun	Sep	Dec
2001	0.58	0.61	(0.55)	0.42
2002	0.30	0.56	0.38	0.40
2003	0.44	0.47	0.47	0.48
2004	0.42	0.32	0.13	0.40

Interim Dividends (Per Share)

No Dividends Paid

Valuation Analysis

Forecast P/E	22.86	No of Institutions
	(4/7/2005)	271
Market Cap	$3.4 Billion	Shares
Book Value	2.2 Billion	88,717,952
Price/Book	1.50	% Held
Price/Sales	2.06	80.64

Business Summary: Pharmaceuticals (MIC: 9.1 SIC: 834 NAIC: 25412)

Watson Pharmaceuticals is engaged in the development, production, marketing and distribution of branded and off-patent pharmaceutical products. Co.'s products include therapeutic and preventive agents generally sold by prescription or over-the-counter for the treatment of human diseases and disorders. Co.'s branded pharmaceutical business operates primarily in four specialty areas: Women's Health, General Products, Urology and Nephrology. Co. is also engaged in the development, manufacture and sale of off-patent or generic pharmaceutical products.

Recent Developments: For the year ended Dec 31 2004, net income decreased 25.4% to $151,333 thousand from net income of $202,864 thousand a year earlier. Revenues were $1,640,551 thousand, up 12.5% from $1,457,722 thousand the year before. Operating income was $265,940 thousand versus an income of $338,913 thousand in the prior year, a decrease of 21.5%. Total direct expense was $820,794 thousand versus $624,651 thousand in the prior year, an increase of 31.4%. Total indirect expense was $553,817 thousand versus $494,158 thousand in the prior year, an increase of 12.1%.

Prospects: Overall results continue to benefit from solid revenue growth and cash flow. Co. enters full-year 2005 fundamentally stronger, with both a sharper focus and renewed commitment to future growth, as its continues to make significant investment in its research and development to ensure a strong pipeline of products for both its generic and brand businesses. Meanwhile, Co.'s research and development investment for 2005 is expected to be approximately 8.0% of expected total net revenue, due primarily to an increase in clinical study costs associated with its product pipeline. Moreover, Co. expects diluted earnings to range from $1.33 to $1.43 per share for full-year 2005.

Financial Data

(US$ in Thousands)	12/31/2004	12/31/2003	12/31/2002	12/31/2001	12/31/2000	12/31/1999	12/31/1998	12/31/1997
Earnings Per Share	1.27	1.86	1.64	1.07	1.52	1.83	1.32	1.01
Cash Flow Per Share	2.82	2.44	2.89	1.89	(0.40)	1.29	1.32	1.12
Tang Book Value Per Share	7.97	5.54	4.33	3.79	N.M.	5.00	3.08	3.14
Income Statement								
Total Revenue	1,640,551	1,457,722	1,223,198	1,160,676	811,524	689,232	556,148	338,264
EBITDA	350,258	438,766	387,747	327,989	451,095	327,673	237,456	159,192
Depn & Amortn	106,666	100,352	86,576	101,225	71,409	44,008	31,317	14,594
Income Before Taxes	236,878	318,112	279,090	198,952	355,402	272,544	199,076	144,598
Income Taxes	85,545	115,248	103,294	82,591	184,678	93,663	78,247	54,414
Net Income	151,333	202,864	175,796	116,361	157,495	178,881	120,829	90,184
Average Shares	124,727	108,927	107,367	108,340	103,575	97,780	91,593	89,325
Balance Sheet								
Current Assets	1,370,186	1,323,489	920,781	889,738	831,345	434,711	293,255	246,765
Total Assets	3,243,683	3,282,600	2,663,464	2,528,334	2,579,898	1,438,750	1,070,043	754,981
Current Liabilities	255,629	338,685	375,465	245,125	280,440	129,186	94,781	99,840
Long-Term Obligations	587,653	722,535	331,877	415,703	483,272	149,503	149,872	2,385
Total Liabilities	1,000,534	1,225,254	865,180	856,284	1,031,929	383,798	319,165	189,112
Stockholders' Equity	2,243,149	2,057,346	1,798,284	1,672,050	1,547,969	1,054,552	750,478	565,010
Shares Outstanding	109,719	108,330	106,878	106,458	105,600	96,133	89,508	87,882
Statistical Record								
Return on Assets %	4.62	6.82	6.77	4.56	7.82	14.26	13.24	15.36
Return on Equity %	7.02	10.52	10.13	7.23	12.07	19.82	18.37	19.03
EBITDA Margin %	21.35	30.10	31.70	28.26	55.59	47.54	42.70	47.06
Net Margin %	9.22	13.92	14.37	10.03	19.41	25.95	21.73	26.66
Asset Turnover	0.50	0.49	0.47	0.45	0.40	0.55	0.61	0.58
Current Ratio	5.36	3.91	2.45	3.63	2.96	3.37	3.09	2.47
Debt to Equity	0.26	0.35	0.18	0.25	0.31	0.14	0.20	N.M.
Price Range	49.11-24.70	48.80-27.02	32.81-18.62	65.85-27.88	69.72-33.88	62.88-27.31	62.88-30.75	33.63-16.31
P/E Ratio	38.67-19.45	26.24-14.53	20.01-11.35	61.54-26.06	45.87-22.29	34.36-14.92	47.63-23.30	33.29-16.15

Address: 311 Bonnie Circle, Corona, CA 92880-2882	Web Site: www.watsonpharm.com	Auditors: PricewaterhouseCoopers LLP
Telephone: (909) 493-5300	Officers: Allen Chao Ph.D. - Chmn., C.E.O. Joseph C. Papa - Pres., C.O.O.	
Fax: (909) 270-1096		

WEATHERFORD INTERNATIONAL, LTD.

Exchange	Symbol	Price	52Wk Range	Yield	P/E
NYS	WFT	$57.94 (3/31/2005)	61.10-39.93	N/A	25.19

*7 Year Price Score 114.49 ***NYSE Composite Index=100** ***12 Month Price Score 108.84**

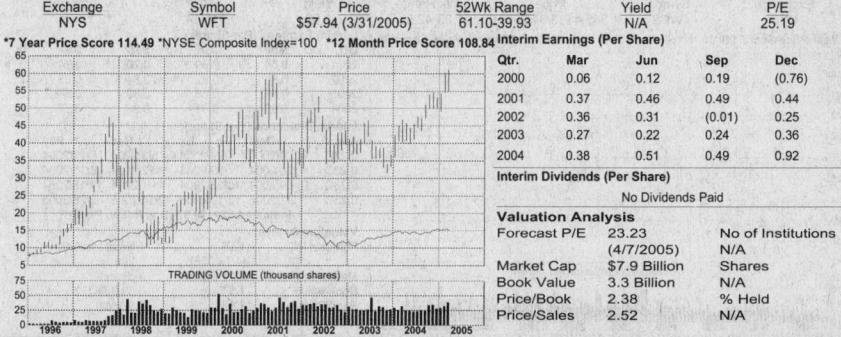

Interim Earnings (Per Share)

Qtr.	Mar	Jun	Sep	Dec
2000	0.06	0.12	0.19	(0.76)
2001	0.37	0.46	0.49	0.44
2002	0.36	0.31	(0.01)	0.25
2003	0.27	0.22	0.24	0.36
2004	0.38	0.51	0.49	0.92

Interim Dividends (Per Share)

No Dividends Paid

Valuation Analysis

Forecast P/E	23.23	No of Institutions
	(4/7/2005)	N/A
Market Cap	$7.9 Billion	Shares
Book Value	3.3 Billion	N/A
Price/Book	2.38	% Held
Price/Sales	2.52	N/A

Business Summary: Oil and Gas (MIC: 14.2 SIC: 533 NAIC: 33132)

Weatherford International provides equipment and services used for drilling, completion and production of oil and natural gas wells. Co. conducts its operations through two principal operating divisions. The Drilling Services division provides drilling methods, well construction, drilling tools and intervention services. The Production Systems division provides completion systems, artificial lift systems and production optimization. As of Dec 31 2003, Co. had operations in approximately 100 countries and had approximately 500 service and sales locations worldwide.

Recent Developments: For the year ended Dec 31 2004, income from continuing operations increased 129.1% to $337,299 thousand from income of $147,243 thousand a year earlier. Net income increased 130.3% to $330,146 thousand from net income of $143,352 thousand a year earlier. Revenues were $3,131,774 thousand, up 22.2% from $2,562,034 thousand the year before. Operating income was $415,747 thousand versus an income of $286,217 thousand in the prior year, an increase of 45.3%. Total direct expense was $2,158,752 thousand versus $1,799,518 thousand in the prior year, an increase of 20.0%. Total indirect expense was $579,680 thousand versus $491,246 thousand in the prior year, an increase of 18.0%.

Prospects: Co.'s Drilling Services segment is benefiting from strong growth in the Middle East and higher activity levels in Canada, partially offset by a seasonal decline in the North sea. Separately, Co.'s Products Systems segment is growing from contributions from its North American revenues. For instance, sequentially, North American revenues at Dec 31 2004 increased $34.0 million, led by a 22.0% growth in Canada. International markets grew by 8.0%, led by strong growth in the Middle East sequentially. On a product line basis, production optimization improved 39.0%, artificial lift systems improved 31.0% and completions systems improved 18.0% over 2003 levels.

Financial Data

(US$ in Thousands)	12/31/2004	12/31/2003	12/31/2002	12/31/2001	12/31/2000	12/31/1999	12/31/1998	12/31/1997
Earnings Per Share	2.30	1.09	(0.05)	1.76	(0.39)	(0.20)	0.66	1.58
Cash Flow Per Share	3.75	2.26	2.25	2.18	1.21	0.62	1.32	(0.29)
Tang Book Value Per Share	9.90	6.21	1.80	3.85	2.61	7.78	7.01	2.63
Income Statement								
Total Revenue	3,131,774	2,591,408	2,328,930	2,328,715	1,814,261	1,240,200	2,010,654	892,264
EBITDA	746,363	518,452	303,820	633,495	325,906	236,767	321,648	179,742
Depn & Amortn	255,900	249,013	230,773	223,519	206,634	166,658	170,732	33,653
Income Before Taxes	430,747	194,617	(9,835)	338,587	71,275	28,384	99,388	128,654
Income Taxes	92,672	50,601	(4,356)	123,048	109,450	8,477	34,551	44,959
Net Income	330,146	143,352	(6,030)	214,651	(42,350)	(20,875)	64,837	74,685
Average Shares	148,684	131,761	120,058	133,255	109,457	102,889	97,757	47,367
Balance Sheet								
Current Assets	1,943,178	1,436,024	1,259,239	1,231,333	1,241,587	869,149	1,082,392	631,025
Total Assets	5,543,482	5,000,212	4,494,989	4,296,362	3,461,579	3,513,789	2,831,715	1,366,066
Current Liabilities	660,006	782,342	877,477	759,597	462,716	666,080	556,841	314,165
Long-Term Obligations	1,404,431	1,379,611	1,513,907	1,499,794	1,132,676	629,103	632,163	445,698
Total Liabilities	2,230,093	2,292,144	2,520,493	2,458,122	2,123,121	1,680,391	1,337,835	838,833
Stockholders' Equity	3,313,389	2,708,068	1,974,496	1,838,240	1,338,458	1,833,398	1,493,880	527,233
Shares Outstanding	136,235	131,314	120,629	118,325	109,960	108,242	97,404	47,190
Statistical Record								
Return on Assets %	6.25	3.02	N.M.	5.53	N.M.	N.M.	3.09	6.73
Return on Equity %	10.94	6.12	N.M.	13.51	N.M.	N.M.	6.42	15.22
EBITDA Margin %	23.83	20.01	13.05	27.20	17.96	19.09	16.00	20.14
Net Margin %	10.54	5.53	N.M.	9.22	N.M.	N.M.	3.22	8.37
Asset Turnover	0.59	0.55	0.53	0.60	0.52	0.39	0.96	0.80
Current Ratio	2.94	1.84	1.44	1.62	2.68	1.30	1.94	2.01
Debt to Equity	0.42	0.51	0.77	0.82	0.85	0.34	0.42	0.85
Price Range	54.75-36.00	46.54-31.47	53.33-32.72	59.69-23.77	49.63-23.85	27.68-11.30	38.60-10.17	47.53-16.13
P/E Ratio	23.80-15.65	42.70-28.87	...	33.91-13.51	...	...	58.49-15.41	30.08-10.21

Address: 515 Post Oak Boulevard, Suite 600, Houston, TX 77027-3415
Telephone: (713) 693-4000
Fax: (713) 297-8488

Web Site: www.weatherford.com
Officers: Bernard J. Duroc-Danner - Pres., C.E.O. E. Lee Colley - Sr. V.P., Pres., Completion & Production Systems

Auditors: Ernst & Young LLP
Investor Contact: 713-693-4000

WEBSTER FINANCIAL CORP (WATERBURY, CONN)

Exchange	Symbol	Price	52Wk Range	Yield	P/E	Div Acheiver
NYS	WBS	$45.41 (3/31/2005)	51.33-42.56	2.03	15.14	12 Years

*7 Year Price Score 119.10   *NYSE Composite Index=100   *12 Month Price Score 88.14

Interim Earnings (Per Share)

Qtr.	Mar	Jun	Sep	Dec
2001	0.54	0.69	0.70	0.74
2002	0.80	0.82	0.84	0.85
2003	0.86	0.88	0.89	0.84
2004	0.90	0.91	0.92	0.27

Interim Dividends (Per Share)

Amt	Decl	Ex	Rec	Pay
0.23Q	4/20/2004	4/29/2004	5/3/2004	5/17/2004
0.23Q	7/20/2004	7/29/2004	8/2/2004	8/16/2004
0.23Q	10/19/2004	10/28/2004	11/1/2004	11/15/2004
0.23Q	2/1/2005	2/10/2005	2/14/2005	2/28/2005

Indicated Div: $0.92 (Div. Reinv. Plan)

Valuation Analysis

Forecast P/E	12.57 (4/7/2005)	No of Institutions	206
Market Cap	$2.4 Billion	Shares	33,339,172
Book Value	1.5 Billion	% Held	62.00
Price/Book	1.58		
Price/Sales	2.56		

Business Summary: Other Depository Banking (MIC: 8.5 SIC: 035 NAIC: 22120)

Webster Financial is a holding company with $14.57 billion in assets as of Dec 31 2003. Through its subsidiaries, Co. is engaged in providing financial services to individuals, families and businesses, primarily in Connecticut and equipment financing, asset-based lending, mortgage origination and financial advisory services to public and private companies throughout the U.S. Co. provides business and consumer banking, mortgage origination and lending, trust and investment services and insurance services through 119 banking and other offices, 233 ATMs and its Internet website.

Recent Developments: For the year ended Dec 31 2004, net income decreased 5.8% to $153,833 thousand from net income of $163,248 thousand a year earlier. Net interest income was $347,555 thousand, up 15.0% from $302,208 thousand the year before. Provision for loan losses was $18,000 thousand versus $25,000 thousand in the prior year, a decrease of 28.0%. Non-interest income fell 5.5% to $219,707 thousand, while non-interest expense advanced 18.3% to $447,137 thousand.

Prospects: In the near-term, operating results should reflect costs associated with Co.'s balance sheet de-leveraging program. However, the balance sheet restructuring should strengthen Co.'s capital position and improve its ability to respond to rising interest rates by moving to a modestly asset sensitive position. Meanwhile, Co. is looking to enhance its competitive position in its markets served through the growth of its core franchise and additions to its products and service. As Co. continues to grow loans and deposits, it will be specifically focused on increasing its net interest margin.

Financial Data

(US$ in Thousands)	12/31/2004	12/31/2003	12/31/2002	12/31/2001	12/31/2000	12/31/1999	12/31/1998	12/31/1997
Earnings Per Share	3.00	3.52	3.16	2.68	2.55	2.10	1.83	1.22
Cash Flow Per Share	7.08	10.93	(1.76)	0.23	4.63	3.76	1.70	1.20
Tang Book Value Per Share	15.85	17.76	16.18	13.97	11.53	10.98	12.77	12.20
Dividends Per Share	0.900	0.820	0.740	0.670	0.620	0.470	0.430	0.390
Dividend Payout %	30.00	23.30	23.42	25.00	24.31	22.38	23.50	31.97
Income Statement								
Interest Income	732,108	658,718	692,034	757,235	738,911	645,792	622,453	445,848
Interest Expense	263,947	245,199	286,306	389,756	412,395	342,279	377,018	253,923
Net Interest Income	468,161	413,519	405,728	367,479	326,516	303,513	245,435	191,925
Provision for Losses	18,000	25,000	29,000	14,400	11,800	9,000	6,800	15,835
Non-Interest Income	219,707	232,483	185,572	162,098	128,821	92,630	74,163	35,990
Non-Interest Expense	447,137	377,982	328,323	308,932	267,130	244,461	197,789	158,547
Income Before Taxes	222,731	243,020	233,977	206,245	176,407	142,682	115,009	53,533
Income Taxes	68,898	79,772	73,965	69,430	58,116	47,332	44,544	19,735
Net Income	153,833	163,248	152,732	133,188	118,291	95,350	70,465	33,798
Average Shares	51,352	46,362	48,392	42,742	46,427	45,393	38,571	27,656
Balance Sheet								
Net Loans & Leases	11,562,663	9,091,135	7,795,835	6,869,911	6,819,209	6,022,236	4,993,509	3,824,602
Total Assets	17,020,597	14,568,690	13,468,004	11,857,382	11,249,508	9,931,744	9,033,917	7,019,621
Total Deposits	10,571,288	8,372,135	7,606,122	7,066,471	6,941,522	6,191,091	5,651,273	4,365,756
Total Liabilities	15,467,046	13,406,218	12,301,714	10,691,338	10,159,557	9,096,500	8,279,461	6,487,858
Stockholders' Equity	1,543,974	1,152,895	1,035,458	1,006,467	890,374	635,667	554,879	382,186
Shares Outstanding	53,628	46,276	45,625	49,149	48,939	45,243	37,327	27,306
Statistical Record								
Return on Assets %	0.97	1.16	1.21	1.15	1.11	1.01	0.88	0.62
Return on Equity %	11.38	14.92	14.96	14.04	15.46	16.02	15.04	11.49
Net Interest Margin %	63.95	62.78	58.63	48.53	44.19	47.00	39.43	43.05
Efficiency Ratio %	46.98	42.41	37.41	33.60	30.78	33.11	28.39	32.90
Loans to Deposits	1.09	1.09	1.02	0.97	0.98	0.97	0.88	0.88
Price Range	51.65-42.56	46.50-33.93	39.96-30.65	37.06-26.44	29.63-20.13	32.00-21.88	36.25-18.55	33.38-17.56
P/E Ratio	17.22-14.19	13.21-9.64	12.65-9.70	13.83-9.86	11.62-7.89	15.24-10.42	19.81-10.31	27.36-14.40
Average Yield %	1.87	2.11	2.09	2.15	2.68	1.70	1.45	1.62

Address: Webster Plaza, Waterbury, CT 06702	**Web Site:** www.websteronline.com	**Auditors:** KPMG LLP
Telephone: (203) 578-2476	**Officers:** James C. Smith - Chmn., C.E.O. William T. Bromage - Pres., C.O.O.	**Investor Contact:** 203-578-2318
Fax: (203) 755-5539		**Transfer Agents:** American Stock Transfer & Trust Co, New York, NY

WEIGHT WATCHERS INTERNATIONAL, INC.

Exchange	Symbol	Price	52Wk Range	Yield	P/E
NYS	WTW	$42.98 (3/31/2005)	47.33-32.57	N/A	25.13

*7 Year Price Score N/A   *NYSE Composite Index=100   *12 Month Price Score 102.34

Interim Earnings (Per Share)

Qtr.	Mar	Jun	Sep	Dec
2001	0.45	0.43	0.68	(1.41)
2002	0.34	0.38	0.34	0.26
2003	0.37	0.49	0.10	0.35
2004	0.34	0.49	0.47	0.41

Interim Dividends (Per Share)

No Dividends Paid

Valuation Analysis

Forecast P/E	N/A	No of Institutions
Market Cap	$4.8 Billion	Shares
Book Value	196.4 Million	43,111,164
Price/Book	24.50	% Held
Price/Sales	4.70	41.99

Business Summary: Personal Services (MIC: 5.15 SIC: 299 NAIC: 12191)

Weight Watchers International is a global branded consumer company and a provider of weight-loss services, operating in 30 countries around the world. Co.'s programs are designed to help people lose weight and maintain their weight loss. At the core of Co.'s business are weekly meetings, which promote weight loss through education and group support in conjunction with a flexible, healthy diet and exercise method. Co. conducts its business through company-owned and franchise operations, with company-owned operations accounting for approximately 74.0% of total worldwide attendance in 2003.

Recent Developments: For the year ended Jan 1 2005, net income increased 27.2% to $183,084 thousand from net income of $143,941 thousand a year earlier. Revenues were $1,024,919 thousand, up 8.6% from $943,932 thousand the year before. Operating income was $305,885 thousand versus an income of $316,069 thousand in the prior year, a decrease of 3.2%. Total direct expense was $468,312 thousand versus $440,398 thousand in the prior year, an increase of 6.3%. Total indirect expense was $231,912 thousand versus $187,465 thousand in the prior year, an increase of 23.7%.

Prospects: Co. is encouraged with the recent performance of its North American company-owned operations, which is benefiting from improved organic attendance trends. Co. believes that this improvement in performance will continue as 2005 progresses and its North American company-owned operations will re-emerge as a solid growth engine for the company. Meanwhile, Co. expects earnings to range between $1.85 and $1.95 per fully-diluted share in 2005, excluding the impact of FIN 46R and expense related to stock-based compensation required beginning in the second half of 2005 under FASB 123R.

Financial Data (US$ in Thousands)	01/01/2005	01/03/2004	12/28/2002	12/29/2001	12/30/2000	04/29/2000	04/24/1999	04/25/1998
Earnings Per Share	1.71	1.31	1.31	1.31	0.13	0.20	0.17	...
Cash Flow Per Share	2.42	2.15	1.56	1.12	0.15	0.27	0.21	...
Tang Book Value Per Share	N.M.	N.M.	N.M.	...	...	...	0.35	...
Income Statement								
Total Revenue	1,024,919	943,932	809,644	623,870	273,175	399,574	364,608	297,245
EBITDA	316,549	273,069	283,885	196,848	66,037	108,393	88,253	48,484
Depn & Amortn	10,243	7,142	6,051	15,340	7,889	10,398	9,586	8,775
Income Before Taxes	289,547	232,229	235,535	126,971	21,023	66,916	85,835	44,585
Income Taxes	94,522	88,288	91,807	(23,198)	5,857	28,323	36,360	19,969
Net Income	183,084	143,941	143,694	147,187	15,019	37,759	47,982	23,771
Average Shares	106,985	109,724	109,663	110,975	112,171	182,206	276,430	...
Balance Sheet								
Current Assets	125,816	114,625	145,438	83,879	93,440	77,493	186,754	...
Total Assets	816,186	769,688	609,903	482,848	346,217	334,207	371,434	...
Current Liabilities	152,622	134,170	123,381	108,010	83,241	78,451	95,554	...
Long-Term Obligations	466,125	454,320	436,319	458,320	456,530	460,510	15,500	...
Total Liabilities	619,747	588,500	563,355	570,369	542,999	542,448	122,486	...
Stockholders' Equity	196,439	181,188	46,548	(113,517)	(222,778)	(234,116)	248,948	...
Shares Outstanding	111,988	106,349	106,277	105,500	111,988	111,988	276,430	...
Statistical Record								
Return on Assets %	23.15	20.53	26.37	35.60	2.48	10.53	...	...
Return on Equity %	97.23	124.37	...	...	68.01	500.92	...	...
EBITDA Margin %	30.89	28.93	35.06	31.55	24.17	27.13	24.20	16.31
Net Margin %	17.86	15.25	17.75	23.59	5.50	9.45	13.16	8.00
Asset Turnover	1.30	1.35	1.49	1.51	0.45	1.11	...	...
Current Ratio	0.82	0.85	1.18	0.78	1.12	0.99	1.95	...
Debt to Equity	2.37	2.51	9.37	...	...	...	0.06	...
Price Range	44.24-32.57	48.10-35.34	49.61-31.95	35.28-29.50	...	...	...	...
P/E Ratio	25.87-19.05	36.72-26.98	37.87-24.39	26.93-22.52	...	...	...	...

Address: 175 Crossways Park West, Woodbury, NY 11797-2055 **Telephone:** (516) 390-1400 **Fax:** (516) 390-1334	**Web Site:** www.WeightWatchers.com **Officers:** Raymond Debbane - Chmn. Linda Huett - Pres., C.E.O.	**Auditors:** PricewaterhouseCoopers LLP **Investor Contact:** 516-390-1400

WEINGARTEN REALTY INVESTORS

Exchange	Symbol	Price	52Wk Range	Yield	P/E	Div Acheiver
NYS	WRI	$34.51 (3/31/2005)	40.90-27.55	5.10	22.41	16 Years

*7 Year Price Score 125.73 *NYSE Composite Index=100 *12 Month Price Score 98.12

Interim Earnings (Per Share)

Qtr.	Mar	Jun	Sep	Dec
2001	0.30	0.29	0.31	0.33
2002	0.31	0.34	0.43	0.34
2003	0.32	0.27	0.36	0.29
2004	0.32	0.42	0.33	0.47

Interim Dividends (Per Share)

Amt	Decl	Ex	Rec	Pay
0.415Q	2/23/2004	3/3/2004	3/5/2004	3/15/2004
0.415Q	7/26/2004	9/1/2004	9/3/2004	9/15/2004
0.415Q	10/25/2004	12/1/2004	12/3/2004	12/15/2004
0.44Q	2/24/2005	3/3/2005	3/7/2005	3/15/2005

Indicated Div: $1.76 (Div. Reinv. Plan)

Valuation Analysis

Forecast P/E	12.55	No of Institutions
	(4/7/2005)	226
Market Cap	$3.1 Billion	Shares
Book Value	1.1 Billion	41,025,288
Price/Book	2.80	% Held
Price/Sales	6.12	46.13

Business Summary: Property, Real Estate & Development (MIC: 8.3 SIC: 798 NAIC: 25930)

Weingarten Realty Investors is a self-administered and self-managed real estate investment trust that acquires, develops and manages real estate, primarily anchored neighborhood and community shopping centers and, to a lesser extent, industrial properties. As of Dec 31 2003, Co. owned or operated under long-term leases interests in 327 developed income-producing real estate projects. Co. owned 266 shopping centers located in the Houston metropolitan area and in other parts of Texas and in California, Louisiana, Arizona, Nevada, Arkansas, New Mexico, Oklahoma, Tennessee, Kansas, Colorado, Missouri, Illinois, Florida, North Carolina, Utah, Georgia, Mississippi and Maine.

Recent Developments: For the year ended Dec 31 2004, income from continuing operations increased 7.2% to $114,497 thousand from income of $106,849 thousand a year earlier. Net income increased 21.6% to $141,381 thousand from net income of $116,280 thousand a year earlier. Revenues were $502,291 thousand, up 21.8% from $412,486 thousand the year before. Operating income was $112,318 thousand versus an income of $104,115 thousand in the prior year, an increase of 7.9%.

Prospects: Going forward, given its list of well-known, successful anchor supermarkets and discount retailers, coupled with its prime locations and well-managed centers, Co. appears poised for further growth. Co. noted that its occupancy levels have remained above 90.0%, and with current levels of leasing activity and other factors, Co. anticipates that occupancy will remain strong throughout 2005. For 2005, Co. expects investing about $500.0 million in acquisitions, $50.0 million in new development, and an estimated $100.0 million in expected property dispositions. Full-year funds from operations are expected to be between $2.68 and $2.75 per share.

Financial Data
(US$ in Thousands)

	12/31/2004	12/31/2003	12/31/2002	12/31/2001	12/31/2000	12/31/1999	12/31/1998	12/31/1997
Earnings Per Share	1.54	1.24	1.43	1.23	0.97	1.27	0.90	0.91
Cash Flow Per Share	2.44	2.08	2.16	2.03	2.20	1.97	1.62	...
Tang Book Value Per Share	12.30	10.03	11.95	11.92	10.39	10.75	8.88	6.50
Dividends Per Share	1.660	1.560	1.480	1.404	1.333	1.262	1.191	1.138
Dividend Payout %	107.79	125.81	103.26	114.49	136.99	99.65	132.02	124.88
Income Statement								
Property Income	492,036	410,490	359,044	309,457	264,552	225,244	194,624	169,041
Non-Property Income	10,255	8,670	6,366	5,435	8,822	5,012	3,501	5,471
Total Revenue	502,291	419,160	365,410	314,892	273,374	230,469	198,467	174,512
Depn & Amortn	117,053	94,455	79,344	68,316	58,518	49,612	41,946	38,635
Interest Expense	115,506	88,871	65,863	54,473	45,545	33,186	33,654	22,110
Income Before Taxes	...	...	...	...	...	...	...	54,966
Net Income	141,381	116,280	131,867	108,542	79,001	96,130	60,365	54,966
Average Shares	89,511	81,574	80,040	72,553	60,594	60,502	60,455	60,234
Balance Sheet								
Total Assets	3,470,318	2,923,794	2,423,889	2,095,747	1,646,011	1,309,396	1,107,043	946,793
Long-Term Obligations	2,105,948	1,810,706	1,330,369	1,070,835	869,627	594,185	516,366	507,366
Total Liabilities	2,300,428	2,052,427	1,435,493	1,170,789	943,451	663,494	573,864	556,807
Stockholders' Equity	1,095,960	821,563	933,413	921,072	629,867	645,902	533,179	389,986
Shares Outstanding	89,066	81,888	78,114	77,280	60,572	60,063	60,014	59,985
Statistical Record								
Return on Assets %	4.41	4.35	5.84	5.80	5.33	7.96	5.88	...
Return on Equity %	14.71	13.25	14.22	14.00	12.35	16.31	13.08	...
Net Margin %	28.15	27.74	36.09	34.47	28.90	41.71	30.42	31.50
Price Range	40.90-27.55	30.70-23.80	25.76-20.57	22.40-17.80	19.89-15.42	20.28-16.61	20.61-16.25	20.11-17.39
P/E Ratio	26.56-17.89	24.76-19.19	18.01-14.38	18.21-14.48	20.50-15.89	15.97-13.08	22.90-18.06	22.10-19.11
Average Yield %	5.03	5.59	6.26	6.99	7.47	7.06	6.25	6.05

Address: 2600 Citadel Plaza Drive, P.O. Box 924133, Houston, TX 77292-4133
Telephone: (713) 866-6000
Fax: (713) 866-6049

Web Site: www.weingarten.com
Officers: Stanford Alexander - Chmn. Martin Debrovner - Vice-Chmn.

Auditors: Deloitte & Touche LLP
Investor Contact: 713-866-6050
Transfer Agents: Mellon Investor Services, LLC, Ridgefield Park, NJ

WELLCHOICE INC

Exchange	Symbol	Price	52Wk Range	Yield	P/E
NYS	WC	$53.31 (3/31/2005)	54.20-34.61	N/A	18.13

*7 Year Price Score N/A *NYSE Composite Index=100 *12 Month Price Score 111.90

Interim Earnings (Per Share)

Qtr.	Mar	Jun	Sep	Dec
2003	0.57	0.59	0.62	0.63
2004	0.71	0.78	0.74	0.71

Interim Dividends (Per Share)

No Dividends Paid

Valuation Analysis

Forecast P/E	N/A	No of Institutions N/A
Market Cap	$4.5 Billion	Shares
Book Value	1.7 Billion	23,870,476
Price/Book	2.66	% Held
Price/Sales	0.77	28.40

TRADING VOLUME (thousand shares)

1996 1997 1998 1999 2000 2001 2002 2003 2004 2005

Business Summary: Insurance (MIC: 8.2 SIC: 321 NAIC: 24114)

Wellchoice is a health insurance company in the state of New York. Co. offers a portfolio of managed care products and traditional indemnity products. Co. has the exclusive right to use the Blue Cross and Blue Shield names and marks throughout the New York City metropolitan area and one or both of these names and marks in selected counties in upstate New York. As of Dec 31 2004, Co. served about 5.0 million members through its service area. Co.'s managed care product offerings include health maintenance organizations, or HMOs; preferred provider organizations, or PPOs; exclusive provider organizations, or EPOS, point of service, or POS, products; and dental-only coverage.

Recent Developments: For the year ended Dec 31 2004, net income increased 22.4% to $246.2 million from net income of $201.1 million in the corresponding period a year earlier. Total revenue amounted to $5.83 billion, up 8.3% compared with $5.38 billion the year before. Net premiums earned totaled $5.25 billion versus $4.88 billion in the prior year, an increase of 7.8%. Administrative service fees climbed 12.7% to $502.2 million from $445.8 million the previous year, while net investment income rose 10.3% to $69.5 million from $63.0 million in 2003.

Prospects: Co.'s outlook is encouraging, reflecting strong growth in its core managed care products and ongoing administrative efficiencies. Co. also launched its new consumer directed product, Empire Total Blue, effective January 2005. It was well received by the market and as of January, Co. had enrolled more than 42,000 members in this plan. Looking ahead, Co. expects full-year 2005 earnings to be in the range of $3.35 to $3.41 per share, excluding stock compensation charges. With respect to national account membership, Co. anticipates improved performance in the profitable middle market. Accordingly, Co. is targeting core commercial managed care membership growth in a range of 7.5% to 8.5%.

Financial Data
(US$ in Thousands)

	12/31/2004	12/31/2003	12/31/2002	12/31/2001	12/31/2000	12/31/1999
Earnings Per Share	2.94	2.41	4.51	...	...	...
Cash Flow Per Share	4.05	3.53	2.19	...	...	...
Tang Book Value Per Share	20.02	17.12	14.81	10.08	...	...
Income Statement						
Premium Income	5,254,617	4,875,380	4,628,035	4,246,168	3,876,927	3,362,269
Total Revenue	5,826,983	5,382,555	5,105,660	4,631,206	4,233,684	3,664,880
Income Before Taxes	387,374	343,622	309,768	147,565	120,487	129,303
Income Taxes	141,199	142,496	(67,847)	135	(74,540)	9,139
Net Income	246,175	201,126	376,559	130,978	190,380	120,164
Average Shares	83,848	83,518	83,490	...	...	...
Balance Sheet						
Total Assets	3,390,099	3,042,993	2,777,455	2,449,587	2,252,483	...
Total Liabilities	1,707,774	1,610,636	1,541,193	1,620,342	1,577,805	...
Stockholders' Equity	1,682,325	1,432,357	1,236,262	829,245	674,678	...
Shares Outstanding	84,047	83,676	83,490	82,300	...	...
Statistical Record						
Return on Assets %	7.63	6.91	14.41	5.57	...	...
Return on Equity %	15.76	15.07	36.46	17.42	...	...
Net Margin %	4.22	3.74	7.38	2.83	4.50	3.28
Price Range	53.40-34.50	36.25-18.30	27.43-22.92	...	...	...
P/E Ratio	18.16-11.73	15.04-7.59	6.08-5.08	...	...	...

Address: 11 West 42nd Street, New York, NY 10036
Telephone: (212) 476-7800
Fax: (212) 476-1281

Web Site: www.wellchoice.com
Officers: John F. McGillicuddy - Chmn. Michael A. Stocker M.D. - Pres., C.E.O.

Auditors: Ernst & Young LLP
Investor Contact: 212-476-7011

WELLS FARGO & CO. (NEW)

Exchange	Symbol	Price	52Wk Range	Yield	P/E	Div Acheiver
NYS	WFC	$59.80 (3/31/2005)	63.25-54.79	3.21	14.62	17 Years

*7 Year Price Score 107.61 ***NYSE Composite Index=100** ***12 Month Price Score 94.42**

Interim Earnings (Per Share)

Qtr.	Mar	Jun	Sep	Dec
2001	0.67	(0.05)	0.67	0.68
2002	0.64	0.82	0.84	0.86
2003	0.88	0.90	0.92	0.95
2004	1.03	1.00	1.02	1.04

Interim Dividends (Per Share)

Amt	Decl	Ex	Rec	Pay
0.45Q	4/27/2004	5/5/2004	5/7/2004	6/1/2004
0.48Q	7/27/2004	8/4/2004	8/6/2004	9/1/2004
0.48Q	10/25/2004	11/3/2004	11/5/2004	12/1/2004
0.48Q	1/25/2005	2/2/2005	2/4/2005	3/1/2005

Indicated Div: $1.92 (Div. Reinv. Plan)

Valuation Analysis

Forecast P/E	N/A	No of Institutions	
Market Cap	$101.3 Billion	Shares	1,133,717,504
Book Value	37.9 Billion	% Held	66.86
Price/Book	2.68		
Price/Sales	2.99		

Business Summary: Commercial Banking (MIC: 8.1 SIC: 021 NAIC: 22110)

Wells Fargo is the fifth largest bank holding company in the U.S., based on total assets of $387.80 billion as of Dec 31 2003. Through its subsidiaries, Co. engages in banking and a variety of related financial services businesses. Retail, commercial and corporate banking services are provided through banking stores in 23 states. Other financial services are engaged in various businesses, principally wholesale banking, mortgage banking, consumer finance, equipment leasing, agricultural finance, commercial finance, securities brokerage and investment banking, insurance agency services, computer services, trust services, mortgage-backed securities servicing and venture capital investment.

Recent Developments: For the year ended Dec 31 2004, net income increased 13.1% to $7,014,000 thousand from net income of $6,202,000 thousand a year earlier. Net interest income was $17,150,000 thousand, up 7.1% from $16,007,000 thousand the year before. Provision for loan losses was $1,717,000 thousand versus $1,722,000 thousand in the prior year, a decrease of 0.3%. Non-interest income rose 4.3% to $12,909,000 thousand, while non-interest expense advanced 2.2% to $17,573,000 thousand.

Prospects: Co. is performing well. Revenue growth was broad based, with particularly strong growth in consumer lending, deposits, small business banking, credit and debit cards, consumer finance, market-sensitive revenues and mortgage banking. Balance sheet repositioning actions taken during 2004 designed to improve earning asset yields and to reduce long-term debt costs appear to be working. Meanwhile, as a result of stronger sales, customer cross-sell reached a record high of 4.6 products per consumer, up from about 3.0 in 1998. Co. hopes to broaden its reach even more in the months ahead with the recent acquisition of mutual fund provider Strong Financial Corp.

Financial Data

(US$ in Thousands)	12/31/2004	12/31/2003	12/31/2002	12/31/2001	12/31/2000	12/31/1999	12/31/1998	12/31/1997
Earnings Per Share	4.09	3.65	3.16	1.97	2.33	2.23	1.17	1.75
Cash Flow Per Share	11.84	18.56	(8.22)	(6.57)	0.52	8.17	(3.18)	(3.18)
Tang Book Value Per Share	10.86	9.56	8.90	6.02	5.84	5.11	4.84	5.25
Dividends Per Share	1.860	1.500	1.100	1.000	0.900	0.785	0.700	0.615
Dividend Payout %	45.48	41.10	34.81	50.76	38.63	35.20	59.83	35.14
Income Statement								
Interest Income	20,967,000	19,418,000	18,832,000	19,201,000	18,725,000	14,375,000	14,055,000	6,697,400
Interest Expense	3,817,000	3,411,000	3,977,000	6,741,000	7,860,000	5,020,000	5,065,000	2,664,000
Net Interest Income	17,150,000	16,007,000	14,855,000	12,460,000	10,865,000	9,355,000	8,990,000	4,033,400
Provision for Losses	1,717,000	1,722,000	1,733,000	1,780,000	1,329,000	1,045,000	1,545,000	524,700
Non-Interest Income	12,909,000	12,382,000	9,641,000	7,690,000	8,843,000	7,420,000	6,427,000	2,962,300
Non-Interest Expense	17,573,000	17,190,000	13,857,000	12,912,000	11,888,000	9,798,000	10,254,000	4,421,300
Income Before Taxes	10,769,000	9,477,000	8,854,000	5,479,000	6,549,000	5,948,000	3,293,000	2,049,700
Income Taxes	3,755,000	3,275,000	3,144,000	2,056,000	2,523,000	2,201,000	1,343,000	698,700
Net Income	7,014,000	6,202,000	5,434,000	3,423,000	4,026,000	3,747,000	1,950,000	1,351,000
Average Shares	1,713,400	1,697,500	1,718,000	1,726,900	1,718,400	1,665,200	1,641,800	750,059
Balance Sheet								
Net Loans & Leases	283,824,000	249,182,000	192,772,000	168,738,000	157,405,000	116,294,000	104,860,000	41,287,700
Total Assets	427,849,000	387,798,000	349,259,000	307,569,000	272,426,000	218,102,000	202,475,000	88,540,200
Total Deposits	274,858,000	247,527,000	216,916,000	187,266,000	169,559,000	132,708,000	136,788,000	55,457,100
Total Liabilities	389,983,000	353,329,000	279,040,903	280,355,000	245,938,000	195,971,000	181,716,000	81,518,000
Stockholders' Equity	37,866,000	34,469,000	30,358,000	27,214,000	26,488,000	22,131,000	20,759,000	7,022,200
Shares Outstanding	1,694,591	1,698,109	1,685,906	1,695,494	1,714,645	1,626,849	1,644,057	758,619
Statistical Record								
Return on Assets %	1.72	1.68	1.65	1.18	1.64	1.78	1.34	1.60
Return on Equity %	19.34	19.13	18.88	12.75	16.52	17.47	14.04	20.65
Net Interest Margin %	81.80	82.43	78.88	64.89	58.02	65.08	63.96	60.22
Efficiency Ratio %	51.87	54.06	48.67	48.02	43.12	44.96	50.06	45.77
Loans to Deposits	1.03	1.01	0.89	0.90	0.93	0.88	0.77	0.74
Price Range	63.25-54.79	58.94-44.15	53.21-42.63	53.94-38.85	55.75-31.00	49.06-32.75	43.44-29.75	38.88-21.63
P/E Ratio	15.46-13.40	16.15-12.10	16.84-13.49	27.38-19.72	23.93-13.30	22.00-14.69	37.13-25.43	22.21-12.36
Average Yield %	3.18	2.97	2.26	2.17	2.11	1.93	1.86	2.14

Address: 420 Montgomery Street, San Francisco, CA 94104	Web Site: www.wellsfargo.com	Auditors: KPMG LLP
Telephone: (800) 333-0343	Officers: Richard M. Kovacevich - Chmn., Pres.,	Investor Contact: 415-396-0523
Fax: (651) 450-4033	C.E.O. Howard I. Atkins - Exec. V.P., C.F.O.	Transfer Agents: Wells Fargo Shareowners Services, St. Paul, MN

WENDY'S INTERNATIONAL, INC.

Exchange	Symbol	Price	52Wk Range	Yield	P/E
NYS	WEN	$39.04 (3/31/2005)	41.98-31.80	1.38	17.43

*7 Year Price Score 110.16 *NYSE Composite Index=100 *12 Month Price Score 98.72

Interim Earnings (Per Share)

Qtr.	Mar	Jun	Sep	Dec
2001	0.33	0.47	0.44	0.41
2002	0.39	0.54	0.52	0.44
2003	0.38	0.53	0.58	0.56
2004	0.45	0.62	0.60	...

Interim Dividends (Per Share)

Amt	Decl	Ex	Rec	Pay
0.12Q	4/22/2004	4/29/2004	5/3/2004	5/17/2004
0.12Q	7/22/2004	7/29/2004	8/2/2004	8/16/2004
0.12Q	10/21/2004	10/28/2004	11/1/2004	11/15/2004
0.135Q	2/7/2005	2/15/2005	2/17/2005	3/4/2005
		Indicated Div: $0.54		

Valuation Analysis

Forecast P/E	18.75	No of Institutions	
	(4/13/2005)	290	
Market Cap	$4.4 Billion	Shares	
Book Value	1.9 Billion	86,289,280	
Price/Book	2.36	% Held	
Price/Sales	1.26	75.71	

TRADING VOLUME (thousand shares)

Business Summary: Hospitality & Tourism (MIC: 5.1 SIC: 812 NAIC: 22211)

Wendy's International operates a system of distinctive quick-service and fast-casual restaurants with $9.29 billion in systemwide sales during 2003. As of Dec 28 2003, Co. owned and franchised a total of 6,481 Wendy's Old Fashioned Hamburgers® restaurants, 2,527 Tim Hortons restaurants and 283 Baja Fresh Mexican Grill restaurants. Wendy's menu includes hamburgers, chicken sandwiches, hot stuffed baked potatoes, pita sandwiches and desserts. The Super Value Menu offers several products each priced at $0.99. Tim Hortons restaurants sell coffee and baked goods primarily in Canada as well as in the U.S.

Recent Developments: For the quarter ended Jan 2 2005, net income fell 78.0% to $52,035 thousand from net income of $235,999 thousand in the previous year. Revenues were $3,635,438 thousand, up 15.4% from $3,148,912 thousand the year before. Operating income was $226,604 thousand versus income of $418,442 thousand in the prior year, a decrease of 45.9%. Total direct expense was $2,738,075 thousand versus $2,303,977 thousand in the prior year, an increase of 18.8%. Total indirect expense was $678,364 thousand versus $426,493 thousand in the prior year, an increase of 59.0%.

Prospects: Going forward, Co. expects earnings in 2005 to get a boost from new menu options, such as fruit and to allow customers to forego french fries in favor of salads, chili, or a baked potato in combination meals at its Wendy's restaurants. New menu items, including a Mediterranean Chicken Salad and a Mozzarella Cheeseburger, are also expected to contribute to improved earnings. Meanwhile, Co. plans to continue expanding its franchises, forecasting 510 to 560 new restaurants during the year, an increase of about 4.0% to 5.0% from 2004. As a result, Co. is confident it can achieve full year revenue growth of 8.0% to 9.0% in 2005, with earnings per share between $2.17 and $2.23.

Financial Data
(US$ in Thousands)

	9 Mos	6 Mos	3 Mos	12/28/2003	12/29/2002	12/30/2001	12/31/2000	01/02/2000
Earnings Per Share	2.24	2.22	2.12	2.05	1.89	1.65	1.44	1.32
Cash Flow Per Share	4.74	4.38	4.08	3.79	3.98	2.73	2.65	2.39
Tang Book Value Per Share	13.07	12.24	12.10	12.15	9.84	9.40	9.48	8.60
Dividends Per Share	0.420	0.360	0.300	0.240	0.240	0.240	0.240	0.240
Dividend Payout %	18.78	16.25	14.12	11.71	12.70	14.55	16.67	18.18
Income Statement								
Total Revenue	2,657,683	1,743,655	834,753	3,148,912	2,730,261	2,391,197	2,236,946	2,072,244
EBITDA	472,581	306,474	138,536	586,286	488,672	430,618	384,928	371,655
Depn & Amortn	135,933	89,302	44,824	167,844	142,773	123,238	113,491	102,969
Income Before Taxes	304,682	195,864	83,078	377,598	345,899	307,380	271,437	268,686
Income Taxes	111,209	71,490	30,323	141,599	127,118	113,731	101,789	102,101
Net Income	193,473	124,374	52,755	235,999	218,781	193,649	169,648	166,585
Average Shares	115,151	115,724	116,606	115,021	116,558	121,144	122,483	131,039
Balance Sheet								
Current Assets	462,475	421,157	429,213	462,665	330,819	266,353	319,099	349,835
Total Assets	3,257,494	3,119,748	3,117,497	3,164,013	2,667,361	2,076,041	1,957,716	1,883,597
Current Liabilities	508,625	479,256	484,232	528,473	360,075	296,687	296,416	284,209
Long-Term Obligations	691,100	688,685	692,694	692,632	681,679	451,246	248,384	249,019
Total Liabilities	1,375,805	1,335,973	1,363,694	1,405,407	1,218,756	1,046,264	831,573	818,158
Stockholders' Equity	1,881,689	1,783,775	1,753,803	1,758,606	1,448,605	1,029,779	1,126,143	1,065,439
Shares Outstanding	113,693	113,515	113,868	114,697	114,692	105,175	114,210	118,230
Statistical Record								
Return on Assets %	8.38	8.67	8.50	8.12	9.25	9.63	8.86	8.98
Return on Equity %	14.72	15.23	15.18	14.76	17.70	18.01	15.52	15.66
EBITDA Margin %	17.78	17.58	16.60	18.62	17.90	18.01	17.21	17.93
Net Margin %	7.28	7.13	6.32	7.49	8.01	8.10	7.58	8.04
Asset Turnover	1.14	1.16	1.14	1.08	1.15	1.19	1.17	1.12
Current Ratio	0.91	0.88	0.89	0.88	0.92	0.90	1.08	1.23
Debt to Equity	0.37	0.39	0.39	0.39	0.47	0.44	0.22	0.23
Price Range	42.40-31.48	42.40-27.70	42.40-26.80	40.45-24.28	41.35-26.45	30.18-20.35	27.00-14.13	31.44-20.06
P/E Ratio	18.93-14.05	19.10-12.48	20.00-12.64	19.73-11.84	21.88-13.99	18.29-12.33	18.75-9.81	23.82-15.20
Average Yield %	1.12	0.99	0.88	0.78	0.71	0.93	1.19	0.92

Address: P.O. Box 256, 4288 West Dublin-Granville Road, Dublin, OH 43017-0256	Web Site: www.wendys.com	Auditors: PricewaterhouseCoopers LLP
Telephone: (614) 764-3100	**Officers:** John T. Schuessler - Chmn., Pres., C.E.O. Kerrii B. Anderson - Exec. V.P., C.F.O.	**Investor Contact:** 614-764-3019
Fax: (614) 764-3330		

WESCO INTERNATIONAL, INC.

Exchange	Symbol	Price	52Wk Range	Yield	P/E
NYS	WCC	$28.00 (3/31/2005)	36.62-14.30	N/A	19.05

*7 Year Price Score N/A *NYSE Composite Index=100 *12 Month Price Score 128.99

Interim Earnings (Per Share)

Qtr.	Mar	Jun	Sep	Dec
2001	0.07	0.16	0.11	0.09
2002	0.08	0.12	0.19	0.10
2003	0.10	0.16	0.18	0.21
2004	0.23	0.44	0.43	0.37

Interim Dividends (Per Share)

No Dividends Paid

Valuation Analysis

Forecast P/E	15.65	No of Institutions
	(4/7/2005)	137
Market Cap	$1.2 Billion	Shares
Book Value	353.6 Million	28,192,772
Price/Book	3.33	% Held
Price/Sales	0.31	60.34

Business Summary: Engineering Services (MIC: 12.1 SIC: 063 NAIC: 44190)

Wesco International is a major distributor of electrical construction products and electrical and industrial maintenance, repair and operating (MRO) supplies, and is the nation's largest provider of integrated supply services. As of Dec 31 2003, Co. operated approximately 350 branch locations and five distribution centers in the United States, Canada, Puerto Rico, Mexico, Guam, the United Kingdom, Nigeria and Singapore. Co. maintains relationships with over 24,000 suppliers, and serves more than 100,000 customers worldwide. Major markets include commercial and industrial firms, contractors, government agencies, educational institutions, telecommunications businesses and utilities.

Recent Developments: For the year ended Dec 31 2004, net income increased 116.4% to $64,932 thousand from net income of $30,006 thousand a year earlier. Revenues were $3,741,253 thousand, up 13.8% from $3,286,766 thousand the year before. Operating income was $149,446 thousand versus an income of $86,045 thousand in the prior year, an increase of 73.7%. Total direct expense was $3,029,132 thousand versus $2,676,701 thousand in the prior year, an increase of 13.2%. Total indirect expense was $562,675 thousand versus $524,020 thousand in the prior year, an increase of 7.4%.

Prospects: Prospects appear favorable as the economy continues to show strength on a broad basis, and the recovery in the industrial markets throughout 2004 has had a positive impact of Co.'s operating performance. Co is now seeing strengthening in the commercial construction market, particularly the small-and medium-sized projects. Looking ahead, Co. believes the economic fundamentals are favorable for larger-sized projects to materialize during 2005, and fully believes that it is well positioned to participate in this market segment as it begins to recover.

Financial Data

(US$ in Thousands)	12/31/2004	12/31/2003	12/31/2002	12/31/2001	12/31/2000	12/31/1999	12/31/1998	12/31/1997
Earnings Per Share	1.47	0.65	0.49	0.43	0.70	0.53	(0.17)	0.55
Cash Flow Per Share	0.52	0.80	0.45	3.59	1.03	1.54	6.15	...
Tang Book Value Per Share	N.M.	N.M.	N.M.	N.M.	N.M.	N.M.	...	2.14
Income Statement								
Total Revenue	3,741,253	3,286,766	3,325,780	3,658,033	3,881,096	3,420,113	3,025,439	2,594,819
EBITDA	158,946	104,681	89,667	110,648	126,094	126,949	61,985	91,805
Depn & Amortn	18,657	23,273	20,712	32,140	25,601	21,503	16,081	11,749
Income Before Taxes	99,498	39,091	25,970	33,368	56,713	58,478	783	59,947
Income Taxes	34,566	9,085	2,847	13,143	23,275	23,333	8,519	23,710
Net Income	64,932	30,006	23,123	20,225	33,438	24,658	(7,736)	36,237
Average Shares	44,109	46,349	46,820	46,901	47,746	47,524	45,052	66,679
Balance Sheet								
Current Assets	854,916	656,288	577,057	718,035	764,225	653,801	582,071	696,838
Total Assets	1,356,855	1,161,205	1,015,118	1,157,958	1,170,033	1,028,793	950,522	870,860
Current Liabilities	564,245	479,710	398,475	529,479	523,842	454,785	466,467	360,535
Long-Term Obligations	386,173	420,042	412,196	446,436	482,740	422,539	579,238	294,275
Total Liabilities	1,003,302	993,517	845,830	1,013,307	1,045,046	911,488	1,071,577	677,347
Stockholders' Equity	353,553	167,688	169,288	144,651	124,987	117,305	(142,561)	184,535
Shares Outstanding	42,076	40,938	45,103	44,890	44,769	47,944	25,210	53,944
Statistical Record								
Return on Assets %	5.14	2.76	2.13	1.74	3.03	2.49	N.M.	...
Return on Equity %	24.85	17.81	14.73	15.00	27.53	...	N.M.	...
EBITDA Margin %	4.25	3.18	2.70	3.02	3.25	3.71	2.05	3.54
Net Margin %	1.74	0.91	0.70	0.55	0.86	0.72	N.M.	1.40
Asset Turnover	2.96	3.02	3.06	3.14	3.52	3.46	3.32	...
Current Ratio	1.52	1.37	1.45	1.36	1.46	1.44	1.25	1.93
Debt to Equity	1.09	2.50	2.43	3.09	3.86	3.60	...	1.59
Price Range	29.94-8.85	9.13-3.44	7.40-3.14	11.00-4.05	10.69-6.63	22.88-6.38	...	...
P/E Ratio	20.37-6.02	14.05-5.29	15.10-6.41	25.58-9.42	15.27-9.46	43.16-12.03	...	...

Address: Suite 700, 225 West Station Square Drive, Pittsburgh, PA 15219-1122 **Telephone:** (412) 454-2200 **Fax:** (412) 454-2595	**Web Site:** www.wescodist.com **Officers:** Roy W. Haley - Chmn., C.E.O. Stephen A. Van Oss - Sr. V.P., C.F.O., Chief Admin. Officer	**Auditors:** PricewaterhouseCoopers LLP

WEST PHARMACEUTICAL SERVICES, INC.

Exchange	Symbol	Price	52Wk Range	Yield	P/E	Div Acheiver
NYS	WST	$23.90 (3/31/2005)	26.96-18.31	1.84	37.94	12 Years

*7 Year Price Score 123.61 *NYSE Composite Index=100 *12 Month Price Score 107.77

Interim Earnings (Per Share)

Qtr.	Mar	Jun	Sep	Dec
2001	0.19	0.11	0.20	(0.68)
2002	0.21	0.19	0.13	0.12
2003	0.13	0.24	0.14	0.58
2004	0.23	0.25	0.14	0.01

Interim Dividends (Per Share)

Amt	Decl	Ex	Rec	Pay
100%	8/24/2004	9/30/2004	9/15/2004	9/29/2004
0.11Q	8/24/2004	10/18/2004	10/20/2004	11/3/2004
0.11Q	12/14/2004	1/14/2005	1/19/2005	2/2/2005
0.11Q	3/7/2005	4/18/2005	4/20/2005	5/4/2005
Indicated Div: $0.44 (Div. Reinv. Plan)				

Valuation Analysis

Forecast P/E	17.05	No of Institutions	
	(4/7/2005)	99	
Market Cap	$733.9 Million	Shares	
Book Value	301.1 Million	22,966,500	
Price/Book	2.44	% Held	
Price/Sales	1.36	74.12	

Business Summary: Rubber Products (MIC: 11.6 SIC: 069 NAIC: 26299)

West Pharmaceutical Services provides closure systems and components, primarily for use with parenterally administered drugs, and conducts research and development of proprietary drug formulation and delivery technology for nasal and targeted oral delivery of drugs. Operations are divided into two segments. The pharmaceutical systems segment designs, manufactures and sells stoppers, closures, medical device components and assemblies made from elastomers, metals and plastics and provides contract laboratory services for testing drug packaging. The drug delivery systems segment identifies and develops products using Co.'s proprietary drug delivery technology.

Recent Developments: For the year ended Dec 31 2004, income from continuing operations decreased 21.9% to $33,500 thousand from income of $42,900 thousand a year earlier. Net income decreased 39.2% to $19,400 thousand from net income of $31,900 thousand a year earlier. Revenues were $541,600 thousand, up 12.0% from $483,400 thousand the year before. Operating income was $48,200 thousand versus an income of $72,000 thousand in the prior year, a decrease of 33.1%. Total direct expense was $385,700 thousand versus $330,000 thousand in the prior year, an increase of 16.9%. Total indirect expense was $107,600 thousand versus $81,700 thousand in the prior year, an increase of 31.7%.

Prospects: Co. is progressing with the disposition of its Drug Delivery Division, which is comprised of a drug delivery technology development business and a clinical services business. The sale of the drug delivery business was announced in Dec 2004 and completed in Feb 2005. Presently, the clinical services business is being operated pending disposition, which Co. plans to complete in 2005. Accordingly, Co. intends to continue to focus its technical and financial resources on opportunities in pharmaceutical and medical device components and delivery systems. Co. estimates diluted earnings from continuing operations for 2005 to be between $1.37 and $1.47 per share.

Financial Data

(US$ in Thousands)	12/31/2004	12/31/2003	12/31/2002	12/31/2001	12/31/2000	12/31/1999	12/31/1998	12/31/1997
Earnings Per Share	0.63	1.10	0.64	(0.18)	0.06	1.28	0.20	1.34
Cash Flow Per Share	2.70	2.38	1.58	1.08	1.68	2.33	2.16	2.05
Tang Book Value Per Share	8.38	7.15	5.42	5.03	5.32	5.62	5.62	6.82
Dividends Per Share	0.425	0.405	0.385	0.365	0.345	0.325	0.305	0.285
Dividend Payout %	67.46	36.99	60.16	...	627.27	25.29	152.50	21.27
Income Statement								
Total Revenue	541,600	490,700	419,700	396,900	430,100	469,100	449,700	452,500
EBITDA	81,500	87,500	59,700	73,300	52,200	102,600	67,300	94,900
Depn & Amortn	33,300	33,000	33,000	32,000	37,000	35,700	32,300	31,900
Income Before Taxes	41,200	47,000	17,200	27,800	2,100	56,500	27,800	57,400
Income Taxes	11,100	16,700	4,100	8,600	1,500	18,400	21,200	13,300
Net Income	19,400	31,900	18,400	(5,200)	1,600	38,700	6,700	44,400
Average Shares	30,842	29,092	28,868	28,696	28,818	30,096	33,008	33,144
Balance Sheet								
Current Assets	226,500	216,700	161,300	158,500	173,100	184,700	159,700	170,700
Total Assets	658,700	623,600	536,800	511,300	557,400	551,800	505,600	477,900
Current Liabilities	116,500	118,900	87,700	75,300	79,300	104,000	104,200	58,000
Long-Term Obligations	150,800	167,000	159,200	184,300	195,800	141,500	105,000	87,400
Total Liabilities	357,600	366,000	335,300	334,500	352,600	320,600	275,500	200,200
Stockholders' Equity	301,100	257,600	201,500	176,800	204,800	231,200	230,100	277,700
Shares Outstanding	30,709	29,264	28,960	28,688	28,620	29,328	30,052	33,136
Statistical Record								
Return on Assets %	3.02	5.50	3.51	N.M.	0.29	7.32	1.36	9.30
Return on Equity %	6.93	13.90	9.73	N.M.	0.73	16.78	2.64	16.76
EBITDA Margin %	15.05	17.83	14.22	18.47	12.14	21.87	14.97	20.97
Net Margin %	3.58	6.50	4.38	N.M.	0.37	8.25	1.49	9.81
Asset Turnover	0.84	0.85	0.80	0.74	0.77	0.89	0.91	0.95
Current Ratio	1.94	1.82	1.84	2.10	2.18	1.78	1.53	2.94
Debt to Equity	0.50	0.65	0.79	1.04	0.96	0.61	0.46	0.31
Price Range	25.03-16.55	17.80-8.50	16.05-8.28	14.03-11.45	15.84-9.94	20.13-15.44	17.84-12.91	17.47-13.56
P/E Ratio	39.73-26.26	16.18-7.73	25.07-12.93	...264.06-165.63		15.72-12.06	89.22-64.53	13.04-10.12

Address: 101 Gordon Drive, P.O. Box 645, Lionville, PA 19341-0645 Telephone: (610) 594-2900 Fax: (610) 594-3000	Web Site: www.westpharma.com Officers: Donald E. Morel Jr. - Chmn., Pres., C.E.O. William J. Federici - V.P., C.F.O.	Auditors: PricewaterhouseCoopers LLP Investor Contact: 610-594-3346 Transfer Agents: American Stock Transfer and Trust Company, New York,

WESTAR ENERGY INC

Exchange	Symbol	Price	52Wk Range	Yield	P/E
NYS	WR	$21.64 (3/31/2005)	23.75-18.45	4.25	10.16

*7 Year Price Score 85.14 *NYSE Composite Index=100 *12 Month Price Score 99.85

TRADING VOLUME (thousand shares)

Interim Earnings (Per Share)

Qtr.	Mar	Jun	Sep	Dec
2001	0.06	(0.43)	0.50	(0.44)
2002	(9.41)	0.18	0.60	(1.35)
2003	1.71	0.38	(1.11)	0.19
2004	0.21	0.16	0.69	1.05

Interim Dividends (Per Share)

Amt	Decl	Ex	Rec	Pay
0.19Q	4/28/2004	6/7/2004	6/9/2004	7/1/2004
0.19Q	8/25/2004	9/7/2004	9/9/2004	10/1/2004
0.23Q	11/23/2004	12/7/2004	12/9/2004	1/3/2005
0.23Q	2/23/2005	3/7/2005	3/9/2005	4/1/2005

Indicated Div: $0.92

Valuation Analysis

Forecast P/E	N/A	No of Institutions	
Market Cap	$1.9 Billion	Shares	56,346,864
Book Value	1.4 Billion	% Held	65.22
Price/Book	1.32		
Price/Sales	1.27		

Business Summary: Electricity (MIC: 7.1 SIC: 931 NAIC: 21121)

Westar Energy supplies electric utilities in Kansas. Co. provides electric generation, transmission and distribution services to residential, commercial, and industrial customers in Kansas. Co. provides these services in central and northeastern Kansas, including the Topeka, Lawrence, Manhattan, Salina and Hutchinson metropolitan areas at retail to approximately 352,000 customers. Co.'s subsidiary, Kansas Gas and Electric Company, provides these services in south-central and southeastern Kansas, including the Wichita metropolitan area at retail to approximately 301,000 customers.

Recent Developments: For the year ended Dec 31 2004, income from continuing operations decreased 38.6% to $100,080 thousand from income of $162,915 thousand a year earlier. Net income increased 110.4% to $178,870 thousand from net income of $85,010 thousand a year earlier. Revenues were $1,464,489 thousand, up 0.2% from $1,461,143 thousand the year before. Operating income was $289,891 thousand versus an income of $371,398 thousand in the prior year, a decrease of 21.9%. Total direct expense was $419,788 thousand versus $390,312 thousand in the prior year, an increase of 7.6%. Total indirect expense was $754,810 thousand versus $699,433 thousand in the prior year, an increase of 7.9%.

Prospects: Co.'s outlook is improving. During the fourth quarter, retail sales increased $3.5 million versus the year-earlier period, due primarily to a 2.2% increase in sales volumes. Market-based wholesale sales also grew $8.5 million due largely to an increase in the average price per megawatt hour sold. Meanwhile, during 2004, Co. reduced debt by $533.4 million and through the sale of its interest in Protection One eliminated an additional $305.2 million of debt from its balance sheet. Going forward, Co. is targeting full-year 2005 earnings from continuing operations in the range of $1.50 to $1.60 per share, excluding special items.

Financial Data

(US$ in Thousands)	12/31/2004	12/31/2003	12/31/2002	12/31/2001	12/31/2000	12/31/1999	12/31/1998	12/31/1997
Earnings Per Share	2.13	1.15	(11.06)	(0.31)	1.96	0.17	0.67	7.51
Cash Flow Per Share	4.26	1.60	5.20	3.18	4.14	5.56	6.10	(1.32)
Tang Book Value Per Share	16.13	13.98	12.79	13.15	13.28	11.47	11.38	17.73
Dividends Per Share	0.800	0.760	1.200	1.200	1.435	2.140	2.140	2.100
Dividend Payout %	37.56	66.09	...	...	73.21	1,258.82	319.40	27.96
Income Statement								
Total Revenue	1,464,489	1,461,143	1,771,118	2,186,262	2,368,476	2,036,158	2,034,054	2,151,765
EBITDA	455,293	630,941	236,475	526,437	841,220	656,636	567,515	1,322,689
Depn & Amortn	179,619	161,902	290,839	401,814	414,541	395,179	280,673	256,725
Income Before Taxes	133,523	244,683	(323,647)	(143,601)	137,111	(32,647)	60,722	872,739
Income Taxes	33,443	81,768	(157,605)	(80,875)	46,061	(33,364)	14,557	378,645
Net Income	178,870	85,010	(793,001)	(20,876)	136,481	12,459	47,756	494,094
Average Shares	82,941	73,354	71,731	70,649	68,962	...	...	...
Balance Sheet								
Net PPE	3,910,987	3,909,500	3,995,371	4,042,852	3,993,438	3,889,444	3,795,143	3,786,528
Total Assets	5,085,711	5,734,505	6,443,099	7,513,065	7,767,208	8,008,206	7,951,428	6,976,960
Long-Term Obligations	1,639,901	2,069,132	3,058,323	2,978,382	3,237,849	2,883,066	3,063,064	2,181,835
Total Liabilities	3,676,389	4,697,745	5,464,977	5,669,004	5,835,788	6,107,882	5,988,587	4,887,895
Stockholders' Equity	1,409,322	1,036,760	978,122	1,844,061	1,931,420	1,900,324	1,962,841	2,089,065
Shares Outstanding	86,029	72,636	71,506	71,107	70,082	67,401	65,909	65,410
Statistical Record								
Return on Assets %	3.30	1.40	N.M.	N.M.	1.73	0.16	0.64	7.25
Return on Equity %	14.59	8.44	N.M.	N.M.	7.10	0.65	2.36	26.43
EBITDA Margin %	31.09	43.18	13.35	24.08	35.52	32.25	27.90	61.47
Net Margin %	12.21	5.82	(44.77)	(0.95)	5.76	0.61	2.35	22.96
PPE Turnover	0.37	0.37	0.44	0.54	0.60	0.53	0.54	0.53
Asset Turnover	0.27	0.24	0.25	0.29	0.30	0.26	0.27	0.32
Debt to Equity	1.16	2.00	3.13	1.62	1.68	1.52	1.56	1.04
Price Range	22.87-18.25	20.39-9.88	17.96-8.50	25.65-15.68	25.75-14.94	33.50-16.94	43.88-33.00	43.00-29.75
P/E Ratio	10.74-8.57	17.73-8.59	...	...	13.14-7.62	197.06-99.63	65.49-49.25	5.73-3.96
Average Yield %	3.92	4.79	8.58	5.81	7.83	8.41	5.46	6.28

Address: 818 Kansas Avenue, Topeka, KS 66612	Web Site: www.wr.com	Auditors: DELOITTE & TOUCHE LLP
Telephone: (785) 575-6300	Officers: Charles Q. Chandler IV - Chmn. James S. Haines Jr. - Pres., C.E.O.	Investor Contact: 785-575-8227
Fax: (785) 575-6596		

WESTERN DIGITAL CORP.

Exchange	Symbol	Price	52Wk Range	Yield	P/E
NYS	WDC	$12.75 (3/31/2005)	12.75-6.52	N/A	17.00

*7 Year Price Score 101.79 *NYSE Composite Index=100 ***12 Month Price Score 114.54**

Interim Earnings (Per Share)

Qtr.	Sep	Dec	Mar	Jun
2001-02	0.11	0.07	0.10	0.07
2002-03	0.11	0.36	0.26	0.15
2003-04	0.02	0.32	0.22	0.14
2004-05	0.14	0.26	...	...

Interim Dividends (Per Share)

No Dividends Paid

Valuation Analysis

Forecast P/E	11.21	No of Institutions	
	(4/7/2005)	196	
Market Cap	$2.6 Billion	Shares	
Book Value	568.3 Million	135,465,680	
Price/Book	4.65	% Held	
Price/Sales	0.82	64.91	

Business Summary: IT & Technology (MIC: 10.2 SIC: 572 NAIC: 34112)

Western Digital designs, develops, manufactures and markets hard disk drives. A hard drive is a device that stores data on one or more rotating magnetic disks to allow fast access to non-volatile data for computing needs. Co.'s hard drives are used in desktop personal computers, enterprise servers, network attached storage devices, video game consoles, personal/digital video recorders, satellite and cable set-top boxes, and as external storage devices. Co.'s hard drive products include 3.5-inch form factor drives with capacities ranging from 8 gigabytes ("GB") to 250 GB, rotation speeds of 5400, 7200 and 10,000 revolutions per minute.

Recent Developments: For the quarter ended Dec 31 2004, net income decreased 18.6% to $56,000 thousand from net income of $68,800 thousand in the year-earlier quarter. Revenues were $954,900 thousand, up 14.4% from $834,800 thousand the year before. Operating income was $56,600 thousand versus an income of $71,300 thousand in the prior-year quarter, a decrease of 20.6%. Total direct expense was $804,700 thousand versus $693,000 thousand in the prior-year quarter, an increase of 16.1%. Total indirect expense was $93,600 thousand versus $70,500 thousand in the prior-year quarter, an increase of 32.8%.

Prospects: Co.'s outlook is solid, supported by a strong demand in the desktop personal computer and personal and digital video recorder markets. Co. noted that it shipped about 1.6 million drives during the most recent quarter, an increase of over 200.0% from the year-earlier period. In addition, Co. expanded its product coverage, adding that it shipped in volume its 2.5-inch WD Scorpio™ drives for mobile computing applications and shipped its new 320 GB WD Caviar® hard drive for the high-capacity markets. Meanwhile, Co. entered the miniature hard drive market with a family of 1-inch drives that enable a variety of devices, including MP3 players and, in the future, multi-function mobile phones.

Financial Data

(US$ in Thousands)	6 Mos	3 Mos	07/02/2004	06/27/2003	06/28/2002	06/29/2001	06/30/2000	07/03/1999
Earnings Per Share	0.75	0.80	0.70	0.89	0.34	(0.59)	(1.53)	(5.51)
Cash Flow Per Share	1.79	1.44	0.91	1.44	0.44	(0.42)	(1.25)	(1.53)
Tang Book Value Per Share	2.74	2.43	2.37	1.61	0.54	0.04		
Income Statement								
Total Revenue	1,778,500	823,600	3,046,700	2,718,500	2,151,152	1,953,392	1,957,580	2,767,206
EBITDA	147,600	59,400	254,500	235,000	101,981	(33,518)	(286,070)	(345,726)
Depn & Amortn	61,500	29,000	101,700	50,400	45,794	51,905	78,452	131,066
Income Before Taxes	88,600	31,200	155,200	188,400	52,095	(87,092)	(374,415)	(492,690)
Income Taxes	2,200	800	3,900	7,600	(1,140)	...	(19,500)	...
Net Income	86,400	30,400	151,300	182,100	65,428	(98,863)	(188,016)	(492,690)
Average Shares	213,600	212,600	216,700	205,500	193,708	168,715	122,624	89,478
Balance Sheet								
Current Assets	1,018,800	967,600	857,300	744,100	527,509	385,709	451,395	688,347
Total Assets	1,368,700	1,295,000	1,159,200	866,200	636,680	507,652	615,574	1,022,402
Current Liabilities	726,200	715,700	586,900	505,700	492,676	340,344	445,066	626,618
Long-Term Obligations	42,700	47,700	52,700	...	...	112,491	225,496	534,144
Total Liabilities	800,400	787,500	671,600	538,800	533,818	500,849	725,408	1,176,192
Stockholders' Equity	568,300	507,500	487,600	327,400	102,862	6,803	(109,834)	(153,790)
Shares Outstanding	207,200	208,800	206,100	202,900	192,143	186,380	153,335	90,611
Statistical Record								
Return on Assets %	12.94	14.99	14.70	24.30	11.47	N.M.	N.M.	N.M.
Return on Equity %	32.63	40.42	36.53	84.88	119.65	...	...	N.M.
EBITDA Margin %	8.30	7.21	8.35	8.64	4.74	N.M.	N.M.	N.M.
Net Margin %	4.86	3.69	4.97	6.70	3.04	N.M.	N.M.	N.M.
Asset Turnover	2.60	2.70	2.96	3.63	3.77	3.49	2.40	2.21
Current Ratio	1.40	1.35	1.46	1.47	1.07	1.13	1.01	1.10
Debt to Equity	0.08	0.09	0.11	...	...	16.54	...	...
Price Range	13.25-6.52	14.83-6.52	14.83-7.89	12.82-3.05	7.50-2.05	6.63-2.25	8.75-2.81	20.38-6.25
P/E Ratio	17.67-8.69	18.54-8.15	21.19-11.27	14.40-3.43	22.06-6.03	...	...	...

Address: 20511 Lake Forest Drive, Lake Forest, CA 92630	**Web Site:** www.westerndigital.com	**Auditors:** KPMG LLP
Telephone: (949) 672 7000	**Officers:** Matthew H. Massengill - Chmn., C.E.O.	
Fax: (949) 932 5612	Arif Shakeel - Pres., C.O.O.	

WESTERN GAS RESOURCES, INC.

Exchange	Symbol	Price	52Wk Range	Yield	P/E
NYS	WGR	$34.45 (3/31/2005)	37.90-25.06	0.58	21.40

*7 Year Price Score 166.71 *NYSE Composite Index=100 *12 Month Price Score 106.43

Interim Earnings (Per Share)

Qtr.	Mar	Jun	Sep	Dec
2001	0.54	0.39	0.18	0.13
2002	0.09	0.17	0.17	0.19
2003	0.32	0.28	0.28	0.26
2004	0.40	0.19	0.47	0.55

Interim Dividends (Per Share)

Amt	Decl	Ex	Rec	Pay
100%	5/24/2004	6/21/2004	6/4/2004	6/18/2004
0.05Q	9/2/2004	9/28/2004	9/30/2004	11/12/2004
0.05Q	12/1/2004	12/29/2004	12/31/2004	2/14/2005
0.05Q	3/1/2005	3/29/2005	3/31/2005	5/13/2005

Indicated Div: $0.20

Valuation Analysis

Forecast P/E	N/A		No of Institutions	
Market Cap	$2.6 Billion		Shares	50,942,940
Book Value	682.0 Million		% Held	68.67
Price/Book	3.74			
Price/Sales	0.83			

TRADING VOLUME (thousand shares)

Business Summary: Gas Utilities (MIC: 7.4 SIC: 922 NAIC: 86210)

Western Gas Resources explores for, develops and produces, gathers, processes and treats, transports and markets natural gas and natural gas liquids. In Co.'s upstream operations, it explores for, develops and produces natural gas reserves primarily in the Rocky Mountain region. In Co.'s midstream operations, which are comprised of three segments, Co. designs, constructs, owns and operates natural gas gathering, processing and treating facilities. Also, Co. owns and operates regulated transportation facilities and offers marketing services. Co.'s midstream operations are conducted in major gas-producing basins in the Rocky Mountain, Mid-Continent and West Texas regions of U.S.

Recent Developments: For the year ended Dec 31 2004, net income increased 41.6% to $119,215 thousand from net income of $84,219 thousand a year earlier. Revenues were $3,069,713 thousand, up 6.8% from $2,874,010 thousand the year before. Total direct expense was $2,636,667 thousand versus $2,544,785 thousand in the prior year, an increase of 3.6%. Total indirect expense was $236,052 thousand versus $166,574 thousand in the prior year, an increase of 41.7%.

Prospects: For fiscal year 2005, Co.'s total net equivalent natural gas production is expected to increase approximately10.0% to15.0% from fiscal 2004 levels with the majority of the increase to occur in the second half of the year. Natural gas production from the Powder River Basin coal bed methane development is expected to average approximately 109.0 to 112.0 million cubic feet per day (MMcfd) net in 2005. Natural gas production volumes from activities in the Greater Green River Basin are expected to average approximate 45.0 to 48.0 million cubic feet equivalent per day (MMcfed) net in fiscal 2005. Natural gas production from other areas is expected to average 13 to 15 MMcfed net in fiscal 2005.

Financial Data
(US$ in Thousands)

	12/31/2004	12/31/2003	12/31/2002	12/31/2001	12/31/2000	12/31/1999	12/31/1998	12/31/1997
Earnings Per Share	1.61	1.13	0.61	1.24	0.69	(0.43)	(1.21)	(0.14)
Cash Flow Per Share	2.88	3.75	1.99	2.35	1.80	1.48	(0.55)	1.79
Tang Book Value Per Share	9.21	8.24	7.30	7.24	6.05	5.43	5.98	7.27
Dividends Per Share	0.175	0.100	0.100	0.100	0.100	0.100	0.100	0.100
Dividend Payout %	10.87	8.85	16.26	8.06	14.39	...	...	...
Income Statement								
Total Revenue	3,069,713	2,874,010	2,489,698	3,354,952	3,281,988	1,910,724	2,133,566	2,385,260
EBITDA	278,804	218,442	157,708	216,288	149,303	25,797	(46,277)	61,468
Depn & Amortn	95,536	73,906	77,005	64,162	57,919	50,981	59,346	59,248
Income Before Taxes	183,268	144,536	80,703	152,126	91,384	(25,184)	(105,623)	2,220
Income Taxes	68,767	53,593	30,114	56,489	33,562	(9,167)	(38,418)	733
Net Income	119,215	84,219	50,589	95,637	56,108	(17,124)	(67,205)	1,487
Average Shares	73,494	74,694	67,215	74,044	65,669	64,301	64,294	64,276
Balance Sheet								
Net PPE	1,225,909	996,761	866,646	848,307	747,734	692,317	846,487	956,723
Total Assets	1,840,112	1,460,524	1,302,144	1,267,942	1,431,422	1,049,486	1,219,377	1,348,276
Long-Term Obligations	382,000	339,000	359,933	366,667	358,700	378,250	504,881	441,357
Total Liabilities	1,158,084	898,015	819,076	794,590	1,039,888	699,743	834,161	880,164
Stockholders' Equity	682,028	562,509	483,068	473,352	391,534	349,743	385,216	468,112
Shares Outstanding	74,028	68,221	66,105	65,327	64,672	64,323	64,296	64,292
Statistical Record								
Return on Assets %	7.20	6.10	3.94	7.09	4.51	N.M.	N.M.	0.11
Return on Equity %	19.11	16.11	10.58	22.12	15.10	N.M.	N.M.	0.31
EBITDA Margin %	9.08	7.60	6.33	6.45	4.55	1.35	N.M.	2.58
Net Margin %	3.88	2.93	2.03	2.85	1.71	(0.90)	(3.15)	0.06
PPE Turnover	2.75	3.08	2.90	4.20	4.55	2.48	2.37	2.62
Asset Turnover	1.85	2.08	1.94	2.49	2.64	1.68	1.66	1.76
Debt to Equity	0.56	0.60	0.75	0.77	0.92	1.08	1.31	0.94
Price Range	34.93-22.88	23.75-15.91	19.86-13.67	21.50-12.44	17.22-5.44	9.88-2.06	11.06-2.66	12.78-7.63
P/E Ratio	21.70-14.21	21.02-14.08	32.56-22.41	17.33-10.03	24.95-7.88	...	...	...
Average Yield %	0.62	0.52	0.58	0.63	1.00	1.62	1.47	1.02

Address: 1099 18th Street, Suite 1200, Denver, CO 80202	Web Site: www.westerngas.com	Auditors: PricewaterhouseCoopers LLP
Telephone: (303) 452 5603	Officers: James A. Senty - Chmn. Walter L. Stonehocker - Vice-Chmn.	Investor Contact: 800-933-5603 Ext.20(
Fax: (303) 252 6150		

WESTWOOD ONE, INC.

Exchange	Symbol	Price	52Wk Range	Yield	P/E
NYS	WON	$20.35 (3/31/2005)	32.40-19.21	N/A	20.98

*7 Year Price Score 79.17   *NYSE Composite Index=100   *12 Month Price Score 85.74

Interim Earnings (Per Share)

Qtr.	Mar	Jun	Sep	Dec
2001	0.04	0.11	0.09	0.14
2002	0.16	0.28	0.25	0.32
2003	0.16	0.23	0.27	0.31
2004	0.18	0.26	0.24	0.31

Interim Dividends (Per Share)

Amt	Decl	Ex	Rec	Pay
2-for-1	1/27/2000	3/23/2000	3/8/2000	3/22/2000

Valuation Analysis

Forecast P/E	18.45	No of Institutions	
	(4/7/2005)	159	
Market Cap	$1.9 Billion	Shares	
Book Value	784.5 Million	74,516,984	
Price/Book	2.46	% Held	
Price/Sales	3.43	78.97	

Business Summary: Communications (MIC: 10.1 SIC: 899 NAIC: 12191)

Westwood One supplies radio and television stations with information services and programming. Co. is a domestic outsource provider of traffic reporting services, and a radio network that produces and distributes national news, sports, talk, music and special event programs, in addition to local news, sports, weather, video news and other information. Co. derives substantially all of its revenues from the sales of ten second, 30 second and 60 second commercial airtime to advertisers. Co. receives the commercial airtime it sells to advertisers from radio and television affiliates in exchange for its programming. Co. is managed by Infinity Broadcasting Corporation.

Recent Developments: For the year ended Dec 31 2004, net income decreased 4.5% to $95,490 thousand from net income of $100,039 thousand a year earlier. Revenues were $562,246 thousand, up 4.3% from $539,226 thousand the year before. Operating income was $165,577 thousand versus an income of $170,025 thousand in the prior year, a decrease of 2.6%. Total direct expense was $369,634 thousand versus $350,582 thousand in the prior year, an increase of 5.4%. Total indirect expense was $27,035 thousand versus $18,619 thousand in the prior year, an increase of 45.2%.

Prospects: Top-line results are being positively affected by an increase in net revenues from both local/regional and national commercial advertisements. However, operating profitability is being negatively affected by incremental amortization expenses, increased programming and distribution, as well as higher professional fees and corporate governance related expenses. Looking ahead, Co. anticipates full-year 2005 revenue growth in the low to mid single-digit range, along with operating income growth, before depreciation and amortization, in the mid single digit range.

Financial Data
(US$ in Thousands)

	12/31/2004	12/31/2003	12/31/2002	12/31/2001	12/31/2000	12/31/1999	12/31/1998	12/31/1997
Earnings Per Share	0.97	0.97	1.00	0.38	0.36	0.30	0.20	0.37
Cash Flow Per Share	1.31	1.07	1.39	1.35	1.41	0.75	0.71	0.32
Income Statement								
Total Revenue	562,246	539,226	550,751	515,940	553,693	358,305	259,310	240,790
EBITDA	177,059	180,238	188,739	165,075	166,257	91,621	52,195	49,270
Depn & Amortn	10,534	10,161	9,732	67,611	62,104	30,214	18,409	13,031
Income Before Taxes	154,614	159,945	172,052	88,759	93,368	49,257	23,446	27,726
Income Taxes	59,124	59,906	62,937	45,564	51,085	25,370	10,400	2,230
Net Income	95,490	100,039	109,115	43,195	42,283	23,887	13,046	25,496
Average Shares	98,454	103,625	109,101	112,265	115,864	78,930	66,868	69,302
Balance Sheet								
Current Assets	174,346	165,495	153,628	138,482	153,881	169,259	85,663	77,933
Total Assets	1,246,279	1,262,034	1,266,312	1,207,972	1,285,556	1,334,888	345,279	335,850
Current Liabilities	81,341	79,873	90,086	105,515	138,202	128,005	78,552	65,753
Long-Term Obligations	359,439	300,366	232,135	152,000	168,000	158,000	170,000	115,000
Total Liabilities	461,786	426,084	363,272	292,601	335,664	315,113	268,061	211,172
Stockholders' Equity	784,493	835,950	903,040	915,371	949,892	1,019,775	77,218	124,678
Shares Outstanding	94,645	99,760	104,692	107,565	130,003	127,897	57,333	63,438
Statistical Record								
Return on Assets %	7.59	7.91	8.82	3.46	3.22	2.84	3.83	8.37
Return on Equity %	11.75	11.51	12.00	4.63	4.28	4.35	12.92	24.11
EBITDA Margin %	31.49	33.43	34.27	31.99	30.03	25.57	20.13	20.46
Net Margin %	16.98	18.55	19.81	8.37	7.64	6.67	5.03	10.59
Asset Turnover	0.45	0.43	0.45	0.41	0.42	0.43	0.76	0.79
Current Ratio	2.14	2.07	1.71	1.31	1.11	1.32	1.09	1.19
Debt to Equity	0.46	0.36	0.26	0.17	0.18	0.15	2.20	0.92
Price Range	34.66-19.21	39.15-29.30	40.20-25.66	36.85-18.31	39.81-14.25	38.00-11.59	18.56-7.88	18.56-8.31
P/E Ratio	35.73-19.80	40.36-30.21	40.20-25.66	96.97-48.19	110.59-39.58	126.67-38.65	92.81-39.38	50.17-22.47

Address: 40 West 57th Street, 5th Floor, New York, NY 10019 Telephone: (212) 641-2000 Fax: (212) 840-4052	Web Site: www.westwoodone.com Officers: Norman J. Pattiz - Chmn. Shane Coppola - Pres., C.E.O.	Auditors: PricewaterhouseCoopers LLP

WEYERHAEUSER CO.

Exchange	Symbol	Price	52Wk Range	Yield	P/E
NYS	WY	$68.50 (3/31/2005)	69.39-56.04	2.34	12.62

*7 Year Price Score 97.69 *NYSE Composite Index=100 *12 Month Price Score 97.49

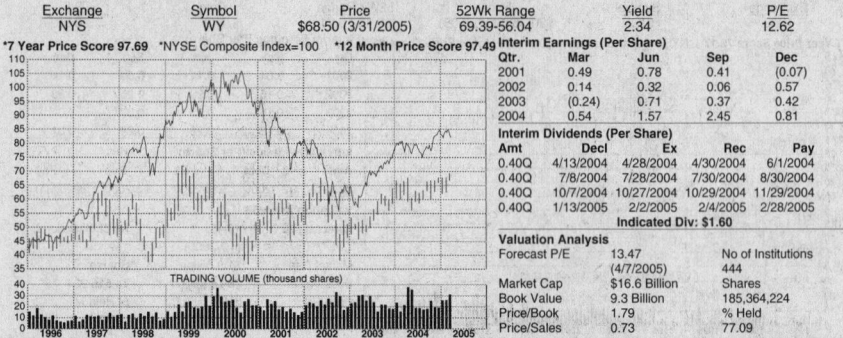

Interim Earnings (Per Share)

Qtr.	Mar	Jun	Sep	Dec
2001	0.49	0.78	0.41	(0.07)
2002	0.14	0.32	0.06	0.57
2003	(0.24)	0.71	0.37	0.42
2004	0.54	1.57	2.45	0.81

Interim Dividends (Per Share)

Amt	Decl	Ex	Rec	Pay
0.40Q	4/13/2004	4/28/2004	4/30/2004	6/1/2004
0.40Q	7/8/2004	7/28/2004	7/30/2004	8/30/2004
0.40Q	10/7/2004	10/27/2004	10/29/2004	11/29/2004
0.40Q	1/13/2005	2/2/2005	2/4/2005	2/28/2005

Indicated Div: $1.60

Valuation Analysis

Forecast P/E	13.47	No of Institutions	
	(4/7/2005)	444	
Market Cap	$16.6 Billion	Shares	
Book Value	9.3 Billion	185,364,224	
Price/Book	1.79	% Held	
Price/Sales	0.73	77.09	

TRADING VOLUME (thousand shares)

Business Summary: General Construction Supplies & Services (MIC: 3.3 SIC: 031 NAIC: 23310)

Weyerhaeuser is engaged in the growing and harvesting of timber; the manufacture, distribution and sale of forest products; and real estate development and construction. The Timberlands segment manages Co.-owned and leased commercial forestlands. The Wood Products segment produces a full-line of wood products. The Pulp and Paper segment manufactures and sells pulp, coated and uncoated paper, and liquid packaging board. The Containerboard, Packaging and Recycling segment sells containerboard and packaging products and operates an extensive wastepaper recycling system. The Real Estate and Related Assets segment develops single-family housing and residential lots for sale.

Recent Developments: For the year ended Dec 26 2004, net income increased 363.2% to $1,283 million from net income of $277 million a year earlier. Revenues were $22,665 million, up 14.0% from $19,873 million the year before. Operating income was $2,653 million versus an income of $1,168 million in the prior year, an increase of 127.1%. Total direct expense was $17,012 million versus $15,594 million in the prior year, an increase of 9.1%. Total indirect expense was $3,258 million versus $3,355 million in the prior year, a decrease of 2.9%.

Prospects: Results reflect increased single-family home closings, and higher sales prices and margins. However, in the fourth quarter, some of Co.'s businesses experienced higher than expected costs due to weather-related transportation disruptions and shortages. Going forward, Co. warned that these costs could hurt its first-quarter results, especially if recent storms lead to a slowdown in housing construction. Separately, on Feb 18 2005, Co. agreed to sell its B.C. Coastal Group assets to Brascan Corp. for about $970.0 million, plus working capital. This sale will allow Co. to focus on its core North American softwood lumber business, while strengthening its balance sheet.

Financial Data
(US$ in Thousands)

	12/26/2004	12/28/2003	12/29/2002	12/30/2001	12/31/2000	12/26/1999	12/27/1998	12/28/1997
Earnings Per Share	5.43	1.25	1.09	1.61	3.72	2.55	1.47	1.71
Cash Flow Per Share	9.37	8.21	6.85	5.10	6.24	7.32	5.66	5.27
Tang Book Value Per Share	24.79	17.40	15.78	25.47	25.92	27.17	22.74	23.30
Dividends Per Share	1.600	1.600	1.600	1.600	1.600	1.600	1.600	1.600
Dividend Payout %	29.47	128.00	146.79	99.38	43.01	62.75	108.84	93.57
Income Statement								
Total Revenue	22,665,000	19,873,000	18,521,000	14,545,000	15,980,000	12,262,000	10,766,000	11,210,000
EBITDA	4,096,000	2,550,000	2,367,000	1,736,000	2,533,000	1,887,000	1,352,000	1,464,000
Depn & Amortn	1,322,000	1,318,000	1,225,000	876,000	859,000	640,000	616,000	628,000
Income Before Taxes	1,945,000	436,000	371,000	516,000	1,323,000	970,000	463,000	539,000
Income Taxes	662,000	148,000	130,000	162,000	483,000	354,000	169,000	197,000
Net Income	1,283,000	277,000	241,000	354,000	840,000	527,000	294,000	342,000
Average Shares	236,546	222,000	221,456	219,957	225,608	206,626	199,250	199,869
Balance Sheet								
Current Assets	5,446,000	4,052,000	3,895,000	3,063,000	3,296,000	4,546,000	2,177,000	2,316,000
Total Assets	29,954,000	28,109,000	28,219,000	18,293,000	18,195,000	18,339,000	12,834,000	13,075,000
Current Liabilities	3,149,000	2,525,000	2,994,000	1,863,000	2,704,000	2,934,000	1,499,000	1,384,000
Long-Term Obligations	10,146,000	12,397,000	12,784,000	6,073,000	5,114,000	5,129,000	4,662,000	4,743,000
Total Liabilities	20,699,000	21,000,000	21,596,000	11,598,000	11,363,000	11,166,000	8,308,000	8,426,000
Stockholders' Equity	9,255,000	7,109,000	6,623,000	6,695,000	6,832,000	7,173,000	4,526,000	4,649,000
Shares Outstanding	242,471	222,493	221,253	219,863	219,213	234,849	199,009	199,486
Statistical Record								
Return on Assets %	4.43	0.99	1.04	1.95	4.52	3.39	2.28	2.57
Return on Equity %	15.72	4.05	3.63	5.25	11.80	9.03	6.43	7.41
EBITDA Margin %	18.07	12.83	12.78	11.94	15.85	15.39	12.56	13.06
Net Margin %	5.66	1.39	1.30	2.43	5.26	4.30	2.73	3.05
Asset Turnover	0.78	0.71	0.80	0.80	0.86	0.79	0.83	0.84
Current Ratio	1.73	1.60	1.30	1.64	1.22	1.55	1.45	1.67
Debt to Equity	1.10	1.74	1.93	0.91	0.75	0.72	1.03	1.02
Price Range	67.86-56.04	63.01-45.80	67.83-38.04	62.05-45.70	74.13-36.69	72.13-49.88	61.81-37.44	63.13-42.88
P/E Ratio	12.50-10.32	50.41-36.64	62.23-34.90	38.54-28.39	19.93-9.86	28.28-19.56	42.05-25.47	36.92-25.07
Average Yield %	2.53	2.96	2.86	2.98	3.20	2.81	3.29	3.10

Address:	Web Site:	Auditors:
Address: 33663 Weyerhaeuser Way South, Federal Way, WA 98063-9777	**Web Site:** www.weyerhaeuser.com	**Auditors:** KPMG LLP
Telephone: (253) 924-2345	**Officers:** Steven R. Rogel - Chmn., Pres., C.E.O. Richard J. Taggart - Exec. V.P., C.F.O.	**Investor Contact:** 253-924-2058
Fax: (253) 924-3332		

WGL HOLDINGS, INC.

Exchange	Symbol	Price	52Wk Range	Yield	P/E	Div Acheiver
NYS	WGL	$30.96 (3/31/2005)	31.71-26.78	4.30	15.40	28 Years

*7 Year Price Score 93.60 ***NYSE Composite Index=100** ***12 Month Price Score 98.19**

Interim Earnings (Per Share)

Qtr.	Dec	Mar	Jun	Sep
2001-02	0.62	0.94	(0.29)	(0.47)
2002-03	1.06	1.66	(0.05)	(0.37)
2003-04	0.81	1.60	(0.08)	(0.37)
2004-05	0.88	...	...	...

Interim Dividends (Per Share)

Amt	Decl	Ex	Rec	Pay
0.325Q	6/30/2004	7/7/2004	7/9/2004	8/1/2004
0.325Q	9/29/2004	10/6/2004	10/8/2004	11/1/2004
0.325Q	12/17/2004	1/6/2005	1/10/2005	2/1/2005
0.333Q	2/23/2005	4/6/2005	4/8/2005	5/1/2005

Indicated Div: $1.33 (Div. Reinv. Plan)

Valuation Analysis

Forecast P/E	16.17	No of Institutions
	(4/7/2005)	167
Market Cap	$1.5 Billion	Shares
Book Value	881.3 Million	24,768,524
Price/Book	1.71	% Held
Price/Sales	0.71	50.87

TRADING VOLUME (thousand shares)

Business Summary: Gas Utilities (MIC: 7.4 SIC: 924 NAIC: 21210)

WGL Holdings is a holding company. Through its subsidiaries, Co. sells and delivers natural gas and provides energy-related products and services to customers in the metropolitan Washington, D.C., Maryland and Virginia areas and beyond. Co. has three operating segments: regulated utility; retail energy marketing and heating, ventilating and air conditioning (HVAC). As of Sept 30 2004, Co. had approximately 1.02 million connected customer meters.

Recent Developments: For the quarter ended Dec 31 2004, net income increased 9.1% to $43,132 thousand from net income of $39,543 thousand in the year-earlier quarter. Revenues were $163,245 thousand, up 0.3% from $162,767 thousand the year before. Operating income was $51,957 thousand versus an income of $47,725 thousand in the prior-year quarter, an increase of 8.9%. Total direct expense was $306,805 thousand versus $279,191 thousand in the prior-year quarter, an increase of 9.9%. Total indirect expense was $261,754 thousand versus $253,714 thousand in the prior-year quarter, an increase of 3.2%.

Prospects: Results are benefiting from continued customer growth and Co.'s success in implementing new utility rates. Going forward, Co. appears poised to deliver sold results in fiscal year 2005 as it capitalizes on the growth of its region and opportunities to operate more efficiently. Accordingly, Co. raised its earnings estimate for the full fiscal year 2005 to a range of $1.83 to $1.93 per share, up from its previous guidance of $1.79 to $1.89 per share. This estimate includes an increase in projected earnings from its unregulated businesses to a range of $0.09 to $0.13 per share. For the second quarter of 2005, Co. expects earnings in the range of $1.40 to $1.46 per share.

Financial Data
(US$ in Thousands)

	3 Mos	09/30/2004	09/30/2003	09/30/2002	09/30/2001	09/30/2000	09/30/1999	09/30/1998
Earnings Per Share	2.01	1.98	2.30	0.80	1.75	1.79	1.47	1.54
Cash Flow Per Share	4.10	4.97	2.96	4.23	1.70	1.90	3.32	2.79
Tang Book Value Per Share	18.10	17.54	16.83	15.78	16.24	15.31	14.72	13.83
Dividends Per Share	1.295	1.290	1.275	1.265	1.250	1.230	1.210	1.190
Dividend Payout %	64.35	65.15	55.43	158.13	71.43	68.72	82.31	77.27
Income Statement								
Total Revenue	408,951	2,089,603	2,064,248	1,569,969	1,933,024	1,247,954	1,112,214	1,040,618
Depn & Amortn	22,798	95,348	88,375	77,021	72,362	68,908	65,193	59,357
Income Taxes	35,333	60,638	68,801	30,427	59,372	49,263	42,519	38,006
Net Income	43,132	(1,320)	113,662	40,441	83,765	84,574	68,768	68,629
Average Shares	48,936	48,847	48,756	48,563	47,120	46,473	45,984	43,691
Balance Sheet								
Net PPE	1,922,247	1,915,551	1,874,923	1,606,843	1,519,747	1,460,280	1,402,742	1,319,501
Total Assets	2,769,911	2,504,908	2,436,052	2,113,664	2,081,113	1,939,840	1,766,724	1,682,433
Long-Term Obligations	573,721	590,164	636,650	667,951	584,370	559,576	506,084	428,641
Total Liabilities	1,860,394	1,623,311	1,589,661	1,319,088	1,264,687	1,200,172	1,054,270	1,046,254
Stockholders' Equity	881,344	881,597	846,391	794,576	816,426	739,669	712,454	636,179
Shares Outstanding	48,692	48,652	48,611	48,564	48,542	46,469	46,473	43,955
Statistical Record								
Return on Assets %	0.01	N.M.	5.00	1.93	4.17	4.55	3.99	4.24
Return on Equity %	0.03	N.M.	13.85	5.02	10.77	11.62	10.20	10.95
Net Margin %	10.55	(0.06)	5.51	2.58	4.33	6.78	6.18	6.60
PPE Turnover	1.11	1.10	1.19	1.00	1.30	0.87	0.82	0.82
Asset Turnover	0.78	0.84	0.91	0.75	0.96	0.67	0.64	0.64
Debt to Equity	0.65	0.67	0.75	0.84	0.72	0.76	0.71	0.67
Price Range	31.22-26.78	30.28-26.27	28.64-22.38	29.45-20.16	31.44-25.19	29.25-22.63	28.50-21.63	30.94-23.44
P/E Ratio	15.53-13.32	15.29-13.27	12.45-9.73	36.81-25.20	17.96-14.39	16.34-12.64	19.39-14.71	20.09-15.22
Average Yield %	4.50	4.58	4.97	4.82	4.55	4.72	4.76	4.50

Address: 101 Constitution Avenue, N.W., Washington, DC 20080 **Telephone:** (703) 750-2000	**Web Site:** www.wglholdings.com **Officers:** James H. DeGraffenreidt Jr. - Chmn., C.E.O. Terry D. McCallister - Pres., C.O.O.	**Auditors:** Deloitte & Touche LLP **Transfer Agents:** The Bank of New York, New York, NY

WHIRLPOOL CORP.

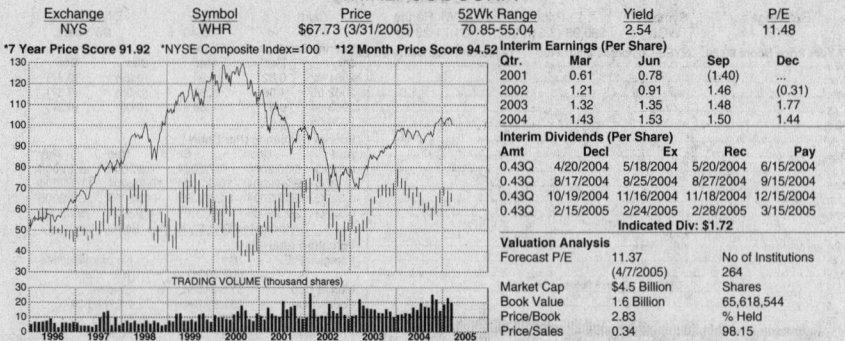

Exchange	Symbol	Price	52Wk Range	Yield	P/E
NYS	WHR	$67.73 (3/31/2005)	70.85-55.04	2.54	11.48

*7 Year Price Score 91.92 *NYSE Composite Index=100 *12 Month Price Score 94.52

Interim Earnings (Per Share)

Qtr.	Mar	Jun	Sep	Dec
2001	0.61	0.78	(1.40)	...
2002	1.21	0.91	1.46	(0.31)
2003	1.32	1.35	1.48	1.77
2004	1.43	1.53	1.50	1.44

Interim Dividends (Per Share)

Amt	Decl	Ex	Rec	Pay
0.43Q	4/20/2004	5/18/2004	5/20/2004	6/15/2004
0.43Q	8/17/2004	8/25/2004	8/27/2004	9/15/2004
0.43Q	10/19/2004	11/16/2004	11/18/2004	12/15/2004
0.43Q	2/15/2005	2/24/2005	2/28/2005	3/15/2005

Indicated Div: $1.72

Valuation Analysis

Forecast P/E	11.37	No of Institutions
	(4/7/2005)	264
Market Cap	$4.5 Billion	Shares
Book Value	1.6 Billion	65,618,544
Price/Book	2.83	% Held
Price/Sales	0.34	98.15

Business Summary: Electrical (MIC: 11.14 SIC: 639 NAIC: 35228)

Whirlpool and its consolidated subsidiaries manufacture and market a full line of major home appliances and other related products. The principal products include home laundry appliances, home refrigeration, home cooking appliances, home dishwashers, room air-conditioning equipment and small household appliances. As of Dec 31 2003, Co. owned nearly 50 manufacturing and technology research centers worldwide in more than 170 countries. Co. markets Whirlpool, KitchenAid, Brastemp, Bauknecht, Consul and other major brand names. Co. is also the principal supplier to Sears, Roebuck and Co. of many products marketed under the Kenmore brand name.

Recent Developments: For the year ended Dec 31 2004, net income decreased 1.9% to $406,000 thousand from net income of $414,000 thousand a year earlier. Revenues were $13,220,000 thousand, up 8.6% from $12,176,000 thousand the year before. Operating income was $758,000 thousand versus an income of $830,000 thousand in the prior year, a decrease of 8.7%. Total direct expense was $10,358,000 thousand versus $9,423,000 thousand in the prior year, an increase of 9.9%. Total indirect expense was $2,104,000 thousand versus $1,923,000 thousand in the prior year, an increase of 9.4%.

Prospects: Looking ahead, Co. will likely face a difficult material cost environment during 2005. Accordingly, Co. announced that it was taking specific actions to offset higher levels of material and oil related cost increases. As expected, these costs accelerated in late 2004 and Co. now estimates that its material cost base will increase an additional 7.0% to 8.0% during 2005. To address this challenging environment, Co. implemented global price increases of approximately 5.0% to 10.0%, effective Jan 2005, in most of its key markets around the world. Also, Co. has initiated actions to improve productivity, leverage its operating platform and reduce non-product investment spending.

Financial Data

(US$ in Thousands)	12/31/2004	12/31/2003	12/31/2002	12/31/2001	12/31/2000	12/31/1999	12/31/1998	12/31/1997
Earnings Per Share	5.90	5.91	(5.68)	0.31	5.20	4.56	4.25	(0.20)
Cash Flow Per Share	11.75	10.83	11.96	15.35	6.32	10.65	10.07	7.94
Tang Book Value Per Share	19.85	15.23	5.82	11.10	13.91	14.40	14.00	11.36
Dividends Per Share	1.720	1.360	1.360	1.360	1.360	1.360	1.360	1.360
Dividend Payout %	29.15	23.01	...	438.71	26.15	29.82	32.00	...
Income Statement								
Total Revenue	13,220,000	12,176,000	11,016,000	10,343,000	10,325,000	10,511,000	10,323,000	8,617,000
EBITDA	1,189,000	1,216,000	1,043,000	651,000	1,157,000	1,097,000	1,262,000	330,000
Depn & Amortn	445,000	427,000	405,000	396,000	400,000	417,000	438,000	333,000
Income Before Taxes	616,000	652,000	495,000	93,000	577,000	514,000	564,000	(171,000)
Income Taxes	209,000	228,000	193,000	43,000	200,000	197,000	209,000	(9,000)
Net Income	406,000	414,000	(394,000)	21,000	367,000	347,000	325,000	(15,000)
Average Shares	68,900	70,100	69,300	68,000	70,600	75,200	75,800	74,700
Balance Sheet								
Current Assets	4,514,000	3,865,000	3,327,000	3,311,000	3,237,000	3,177,000	3,882,000	4,281,000
Total Assets	8,181,000	7,361,000	6,631,000	6,967,000	6,902,000	6,826,000	7,935,000	8,270,000
Current Liabilities	3,985,000	3,589,000	3,505,000	3,082,000	3,303,000	2,892,000	3,267,000	3,676,000
Long-Term Obligations	1,160,000	1,134,000	1,092,000	1,295,000	795,000	714,000	1,087,000	1,074,000
Total Liabilities	6,507,000	5,997,000	5,814,000	5,382,000	5,071,000	4,543,000	5,320,000	5,726,000
Stockholders' Equity	1,606,000	1,301,000	739,000	1,458,000	1,684,000	1,867,000	2,001,000	1,771,000
Shares Outstanding	67,000	69,000	68,000	68,000	66,265	74,463	76,089	75,262
Statistical Record								
Return on Assets %	5.21	5.92	N.M.	0.30	5.33	4.70	4.01	N.M.
Return on Equity %	27.86	40.59	N.M.	1.34	20.61	17.94	17.23	N.M.
EBITDA Margin %	8.99	9.99	9.47	6.29	11.21	10.44	12.23	3.83
Net Margin %	3.07	3.40	N.M.	0.20	3.55	3.30	3.15	N.M.
Asset Turnover	1.70	1.74	1.62	1.49	1.50	1.42	1.27	1.06
Current Ratio	1.13	1.08	0.95	1.07	0.98	1.10	1.19	1.16
Debt to Equity	0.72	0.87	1.48	0.89	0.47	0.38	0.54	0.61
Price Range	79.38-55.04	72.67-42.91	79.66-40.60	73.54-47.25	67.25-34.81	77.25-41.00	74.75-44.00	69.31-45.25
P/E Ratio	13.45-9.33	12.30-7.26	...237.23-152.42	12.93-6.69	16.94-8.99	17.59-10.35	...
Average Yield %	2.61	2.23	2.19	2.27	2.72	2.27	2.27	2.55

Address: 2000 M-63, Benton Harbor, MI 49022-2692	Web Site: www.whirlpoolcorp.com	Auditors: Ernst & Young LLP
Telephone: (269) 923-5000	Officers: Jeff M. Fettig - Chmn., Pres., C.E.O.	Investor Contact: 616-923-3189
Fax: (269) 923-3978	Michael D. Thieneman - Exec. V.P., Chief Tech. Officer	

WILEY (JOHN) & SONS INC.

Exchange	Symbol	Price	52Wk Range	Yield	P/E	Div Achiever
NYS	JW A	$35.25 (3/31/2005)	36.11-29.27	0.85	25.00	11 Years

*7 Year Price Score 123.19 *NYSE Composite Index=100 ***12 Month Price Score 99.43**

Interim Earnings (Per Share)

Qtr.	Jul	Oct	Jan	Apr
2001-02	0.31	0.28	0.34	(0.02)
2002-03	0.32	0.55	0.39	0.13
2003-04	0.35	0.41	0.51	0.14
2004-05	0.32	0.42	0.53	...

Interim Dividends (Per Share)

Amt	Decl	Ex	Rec	Pay
0.075Q	6/17/2004	7/1/2004	7/6/2004	7/19/2004
0.075Q	9/15/2004	9/29/2004	10/1/2004	10/18/2004
0.075Q	12/16/2004	12/23/2004	12/28/2004	1/17/2005
0.075Q	3/9/2005	3/31/2005	4/4/2005	4/15/2005
		Indicated Div: $0.30		

Valuation Analysis

Forecast P/E	22.51	No of Institutions
	(4/7/2005)	125
Market Cap	$2.1 Billion	Shares
Book Value	453.8 Million	32,602,788
Price/Book	4.64	% Held
Price/Sales	2.19	66.89

Business Summary: Non-Media Publishing (MIC: 13.3 SIC: 731 NAIC: 11130)

John Wiley & Sons is a publisher of print and electronic products, providing must-have content and services to customers worldwide. Core businesses include professional and consumer books and subscription services; scientific, technical, and medical journals, encyclopedias, books, and online products and services; and educational materials. Co. has publishing, marketing, and distribution centers in the United States, Canada, Europe, Asia, and Australia. In addition, Co. imports, adapts, markets and distributes books from other publishers. Co. also develops and markets computer software and electronic databases for educational use and professional research and training.

Recent Developments: For the quarter ended Jan 31 2005, net income increased 4.6% to $32,791 thousand from net income of $31,344 thousand in the year-earlier quarter. Revenues were $258,428 thousand, up 6.6% from $242,357 thousand the year before. Operating income was $50,425 thousand versus an income of $43,850 thousand in the prior-year quarter, an increase of 15.0%. Total direct expense was $85,708 thousand versus $81,979 thousand in the prior-year quarter, an increase of 4.5%. Total indirect expense was $122,295 thousand versus $116,528 thousand in the prior-year quarter, an increase of 4.9%.

Prospects: Co. continues to anticipate revenue and earnings growth in the mid-to-high single digits for its fiscal year ended Apr 30 2005, due in part to recent strength from its global Scientific, Technical and Medical business. Meanwhile, during the quarter ended Oct 31 2004, Co. signed a licensing deal with Acadient for the creation of a CPA exam review online course. Co. also reached an agreement to be Agora Publishing's financial book publisher, and entered into a brand licensing agreement with American Media Inc. to publish For Dummies-branded micro magazines that will be sold at cash register display racks at mass merchandisers, drug and grocery chain outlets in North America.

Financial Data

(US$ in Thousands)	9 Mos	6 Mos	3 Mos	04/30/2004	04/30/2003	04/30/2002	04/30/2001	04/30/2000
Earnings Per Share	1.41	1.38	1.38	1.41	1.38	0.91	0.93	0.81
Cash Flow Per Share	3.65	3.78	3.59	3.43	2.75	2.31	2.17	2.13
Dividends Per Share	0.290	0.280	0.270	0.260	0.200	0.180	0.160	0.142
Dividend Payout %	20.59	20.22	19.63	18.44	14.49	19.78	17.20	17.59
Income Statement								
Total Revenue	732,417	473,989	226,939	922,962	853,971	734,396	613,790	594,815
EBITDA	177,675	107,603	47,925	169,784	153,563	122,267	129,550	119,290
Depn & Amortn	56,349	36,702	18,335	39,515	33,040	33,669	31,298	28,269
Income Before Taxes	116,605	68,154	29,590	125,110	112,559	81,118	90,227	82,631
Income Taxes	37,471	21,811	9,706	36,270	25,284	23,802	31,309	30,243
Net Income	79,134	46,343	19,884	88,840	87,275	57,316	58,918	52,388
Average Shares	60,513	62,548	62,851	63,226	63,086	63,094	63,300	64,825
Balance Sheet								
Current Assets	413,789	267,776	298,132	324,006	283,844	275,259	189,535	177,111
Total Assets	1,108,349	957,275	989,193	1,014,582	955,972	896,145	588,002	569,337
Current Liabilities	358,667	226,637	265,836	306,365	323,265	320,393	246,761	254,050
Long-Term Obligations	200,000	200,000	200,000	200,000	200,000	235,000	65,000	95,000
Total Liabilities	654,532	522,601	559,860	599,518	611,968	619,495	367,979	396,599
Stockholders' Equity	453,817	434,674	429,333	415,064	344,004	276,650	220,023	172,738
Shares Outstanding	59,699	61,118	61,474	61,694	61,630	61,701	60,734	60,712
Statistical Record								
Return on Assets %	8.27	9.05	8.99	8.99	9.42	7.72	10.18	9.52
Return on Equity %	20.22	20.96	21.60	23.34	28.12	23.08	30.00	31.20
EBITDA Margin %	24.26	22.70	21.12	18.40	17.98	16.65	21.11	20.05
Net Margin %	10.80	9.78	8.76	9.63	10.22	7.80	9.60	8.81
Asset Turnover	0.89	0.98	0.96	0.93	0.92	0.99	1.06	1.08
Current Ratio	1.15	1.18	1.12	1.06	0.88	0.86	0.77	0.70
Debt to Equity	0.44	0.46	0.47	0.48	0.58	0.85	0.30	0.55
Price Range	35.25-26.28	33.05-24.24	32.77-24.24	31.58-24.07	27.30-19.61	27.46-18.65	25.69-17.56	22.75-13.88
P/E Ratio	25.00-18.64	23.95-17.57	23.75-17.57	22.40-17.07	19.78-14.21	30.18-20.49	27.62-18.88	28.09-17.13
Average Yield %	0.92	0.95	0.96	0.97	0.87	0.80	0.77	0.82

Address: 111 River Street, Hoboken, NJ 07030-5774	**Web Site:** www.wiley.com	**Auditors:** KPMG LLP
Telephone: (201) 748-6000	**Officers:** Peter Booth Wiley - Chmn. William J. Pesce - Pres., C.E.O.	**Investor Contact:** 201-748-6000
Fax: (201) 748-6088		**Transfer Agents:** Registrar and Transfer Company

WILLIAMS COS INC (THE)

Exchange	Symbol	Price	52Wk Range	Yield	P/E
NYS	WMB	$18.81 (3/31/2005)	19.29-9.57	1.06	60.68

*7 Year Price Score 51.14 *NYSE Composite Index=100 *12 Month Price Score 123.99

Interim Earnings (Per Share)

Qtr.	Mar	Jun	Sep	Dec
2001	0.41	0.69	0.44	(2.49)
2002	0.07	(0.68)	(0.58)	(0.43)
2003	(1.59)	0.46	0.20	(0.12)
2004	0.02	(0.03)	0.19	0.14

Interim Dividends (Per Share)

Amt	Decl	Ex	Rec	Pay
0.01Q	5/20/2004	6/9/2004	6/11/2004	6/28/2004
0.01Q	7/16/2004	8/25/2004	8/27/2004	9/13/2004
0.05Q	11/17/2004	12/8/2004	12/10/2004	12/27/2004
0.05Q	1/28/2005	3/9/2005	3/11/2005	3/28/2005

Indicated Div: $0.20

Valuation Analysis

Forecast P/E	22.18
	(4/7/2005)
Market Cap	$10.5 Billion
Book Value	5.0 Billion
Price/Book	2.12
Price/Sales	0.84

No of Institutions	410
Shares	358,484,416
% Held	62.89

TRADING VOLUME (thousand shares)

Business Summary: Gas Utilities (MIC: 7.4 SIC: 922 NAIC: 86210)

Williams Companies is an energy company that primarily discovers, produces, gathers, processes and transports natural gas. Co.'s operations serve the Northwest, California, Rocky Mountains, Gulf Coast and Eastern Seaboard markets. Co.'s ongoing business segments include Gas Pipeline, Exploration and Production, Midstream Gas and Liquids and Energy Marketing and Trading. As of Dec 31 2003, approximately 98.6% of Exploration and Production's domestic reserves were natural gas. As of Dec 31 2003, Co. had 2.8 trillion cubic feet of proved natural gas reserves.

Recent Developments: For the year ended Dec 31 2004, income from continuing operations was $93,200 thousand compared with a loss of $57,500 thousand a year earlier. Net income was $163,700 thousand versus net loss of $492,200 thousand a year earlier. Revenues were $12,461,300 thousand, down 25.2% from $16,651,000 thousand the year before. Operating income was $1,285,900 thousand versus an income of $1,159,700 thousand in the prior year, an increase of 10.9%. Total direct expense was $10,751,700 thousand versus $15,004,300 thousand in the prior year, a decrease of 28.3%. Total indirect expense was $423,500 thousand versus $487,000 thousand in the prior year, a decrease of 13.0%.

Prospects: On Mar 3 2005, Co. announced it is gauging market interest for an expansion of its Northwest Pipeline system that would provide additional natural gas transportation capacity from supply basins in the Rockies to markets in the western United States served by Northwest. Additionally, Co. believes that with the growth in Rockies gas production, there is a need for additional pipeline capacity to bring new supplies to the market. Based on the level of interest, Co. will determine the cost, facilities, final capacity and rates for the expansion project. Subject to sufficient market support and approval, it is anticipated that service could be available in Nov 2007.

Financial Data

(US$ in Thousands)	12/31/2004	12/31/2003	12/31/2002	12/31/2001	12/31/2000	12/31/1999	12/31/1998	12/31/1997
Earnings Per Share	0.31	(1.01)	(1.63)	(0.95)	1.17	0.50	0.28	0.80
Cash Flow Per Share	2.80	1.49	(1.05)	3.59	1.21	3.41	1.44	2.86
Tang Book Value Per Share	7.06	5.96	7.15	9.43	13.26	11.59	8.34	9.50
Dividends Per Share	0.080	0.040	0.420	0.680	0.600	0.600	0.600	0.540
Dividend Payout %	25.81	...	...	...	51.28	120.00	214.29	67.50
Income Statement								
Total Revenue	12,461,300	16,834,100	5,608,400	11,034,700	10,398,000	8,593,100	7,658,300	4,409,600
EBITDA	1,735,200	2,138,600	1,514,200	3,010,100	3,052,600	1,663,200	1,387,800	1,416,600
Depn & Amortn	678,000	843,900	886,000	797,700	831,900	742,000	646,300	499,500
Income Before Taxes	224,500	51,600	(696,500)	1,465,600	1,427,200	323,000	257,000	528,500
Income Taxes	131,300	36,400	(195,000)	630,200	554,000	161,200	110,400	178,000
Net Income	163,700	(492,200)	(754,700)	(477,700)	524,300	221,400	127,500	271,400
Average Shares	535,611	518,137	516,793	500,567	449,320	441,512	431,816	337,539
Balance Sheet								
Current Assets	6,043,600	8,795,000	12,886,100	12,938,000	15,476,700	6,516,600	3,532,100	2,255,900
Total Assets	23,993,000	27,021,800	34,988,500	38,906,200	40,197,000	25,288,500	18,647,300	13,879,000
Current Liabilities	5,145,900	6,270,100	11,308,500	13,494,500	16,803,500	5,772,200	4,439,200	3,027,400
Long-Term Obligations	7,711,900	11,039,800	11,896,400	9,500,700	10,342,400	9,235,300	6,366,400	4,565,300
Total Liabilities	19,037,100	22,919,700	29,939,500	32,862,200	34,305,000	19,703,300	14,389,900	10,307,300
Stockholders' Equity	4,955,900	4,102,100	5,049,000	6,044,000	5,892,000	5,585,200	4,257,400	3,571,700
Shares Outstanding	558,000	518,200	516,700	515,500	444,300	444,500	428,300	315,307
Statistical Record								
Return on Assets %	0.64	N.M.	N.M.	N.M.	1.60	1.01	0.78	2.06
Return on Equity %	3.60	N.M.	N.M.	N.M.	9.11	4.50	3.26	7.76
EBITDA Margin %	13.92	12.70	27.00	27.28	29.36	19.36	18.12	32.13
Net Margin %	1.31	N.M.	N.M.	N.M.	5.04	2.58	1.66	6.15
Asset Turnover	0.49	0.54	0.15	0.28	0.32	0.39	0.47	0.34
Current Ratio	1.17	1.40	1.14	0.96	0.92	1.13	0.80	0.75
Debt to Equity	1.56	2.69	2.36	1.57	1.76	1.65	1.50	1.28
Price Range	17.10-8.75	10.62-2.60	25.97-0.88	43.45-22.10	44.69-27.83	48.77-25.76	33.79-21.11	26.16-16.70
P/E Ratio	55.16-28.23	...	...	...	38.20-23.78	97.53-51.52	120.69-75.40	32.70-20.87
Average Yield %	0.67	0.56	4.03	2.01	1.59	1.66	2.17	2.57

Address: One Williams Center, Tulsa, OK 74172
Telephone: (918) 573-2000
Fax: (918) 588-2334

Web Site: www.williams.com
Officers: Steven J. Malcolm - Chmn., Pres., C.E.O. Donald R. Chappel - Sr. V.P., C.F.O.

Auditors: ERNST & YOUNG LLP
Investor Contact: 800-600-3782

WILLIAMS-SONOMA, INC.

Exchange	Symbol	Price	52Wk Range	Yield	P/E
NYS	WSM	$36.75 (3/31/2005)	41.21-28.79	N/A	24.34

*7 Year Price Score 131.45 *NYSE Composite Index=100   ***12 Month Price Score 95.16**

Interim Earnings (Per Share)

Qtr.	Apr	Jul	Oct	Jan
2001-02	0.01	0.01	0.04	0.60
2002-03	0.13	0.12	0.13	0.67
2003-04	0.11	0.15	0.20	0.86
2004-05	0.18	0.23	0.24	...

Interim Dividends (Per Share)

Amt	Decl	Ex	Rec	Pay
2-for-1	4/17/2002	5/10/2002	4/29/2002	5/9/2002

Valuation Analysis

Forecast P/E	19.54 (4/7/2005)	No of Institutions 255
Market Cap	$4.3 Billion	Shares 88,228,464
Book Value	905.4 Million	% Held
Price/Book	4.75	75.37
Price/Sales	1.40	

Business Summary: Retail - Furniture & Home Furnishings (MIC: 5.9 SIC: 719 NAIC: 42299)

Williams-Sonoma is a specialty retailer of products for the home. As of Feb 1 2004, Co. operated 512 retail stores including 237 Williams-Sonoma, 174 Pottery Barn, 78 Pottery Barn Kids, eight Hold Everything, one West Elm and 14 outlet stores. Williams-Sonoma stores offer a selection of culinary and serving equipment, along with a variety of foods including gourmet coffees and pasta sauces. Pottery Barn stores feature an assortment of items in casual home furnishings, flatware and table accessories from around the world, while Hold Everything stores provide products for household storage needs. Co. also sells merchandise through eight mail-order catalogs and three e-commerce web sites.

Recent Developments: For the quarter ended Oct 31 2004, net income increased 19.2% to $28,467 thousand from net income of $23,876 thousand in the year-earlier quarter. Revenues were $722,761 thousand, up 14.2% from $632,824 thousand the year before. Total indirect expense was $235,018 thousand versus $210,065 thousand in the prior-year quarter, an increase of 11.9%.

Prospects: Co. is optimistic about its outlook for 2005. In its retail channel, Co. expects a high-single digit increase in retail leased square footage. In its direct-to-customer channel, Co. is expecting strong growth in all of its emerging brands, including PBteen, West Elm, Hold Everything, and its newest catalog, Williams-Sonoma Home. Additionally, Co. will be continuing to invest in increased catalog circulation, electronic direct marketing, and online marketing in all of its brands. Accordingly, Co. is projecting a low double-digit to mid-teen percentage increase in net revenues for 2005, with a mid-teen to high-teen percentage increase in diluted earnings per share.

Financial Data

(US$ in Thousands)	9 Mos	6 Mos	3 Mos	02/01/2004	02/02/2003	02/03/2002	01/28/2001	01/30/2000
Earnings Per Share	1.51	1.47	1.39	1.32	1.04	0.65	0.50	0.58
Cash Flow Per Share	2.63	2.57	2.50	1.82	2.70	1.79	1.63	0.95
Tang Book Value Per Share	7.74	7.40	7.12	6.95	5.63	4.65	3.83	3.40
Income Statement								
Total Revenue	2,053,291	1,330,531	640,910	2,754,368	2,360,830	2,086,662	1,829,483	1,383,993
EBITDA	191,132	122,981	56,453	335,058	285,014	199,845	151,047	149,678
Depn & Amortn	65,203	43,249	21,649	80,271	82,712	71,871	51,531	36,512
Income Before Taxes	125,590	79,447	34,668	255,638	202,282	122,106	92,329	110,721
Income Taxes	48,104	30,428	13,278	98,427	77,879	47,010	35,547	42,621
Net Income	77,486	49,019	21,390	157,211	124,403	75,096	56,782	68,100
Average Shares	119,862	119,229	119,155	119,016	119,550	115,440	114,920	117,224
Balance Sheet								
Current Assets	766,995	686,840	631,100	687,889	625,384	417,239	392,909	409,880
Total Assets	1,617,995	1,500,493	1,421,141	1,470,735	1,264,455	994,903	891,928	738,942
Current Liabilities	478,040	406,729	366,955	442,884	424,828	297,179	311,286	215,787
Long-Term Obligations	19,935	27,046	27,858	28,389	18,071	24,625	23,189	34,726
Total Liabilities	712,563	637,719	594,312	666,144	620,477	462,372	464,470	355,633
Stockholders' Equity	905,432	862,774	826,829	804,591	643,978	532,531	427,458	383,309
Shares Outstanding	117,037	116,517	116,064	115,827	114,317	114,486	111,605	112,757
Statistical Record								
Return on Assets %	12.03	12.68	12.68	11.53	11.04	7.83	6.98	10.38
Return on Equity %	21.96	22.37	22.01	21.77	21.21	15.39	14.05	19.93
EBITDA Margin %	9.31	9.24	8.81	12.16	12.07	9.58	8.26	10.81
Net Margin %	3.77	3.68	3.34	5.71	5.27	3.60	3.10	4.92
Asset Turnover	2.05	2.15	2.20	2.02	2.10	2.18	2.25	2.11
Current Ratio	1.60	1.69	1.72	1.55	1.47	1.40	1.26	1.90
Debt to Equity	0.02	0.03	0.03	0.04	0.03	0.05	0.05	0.09
Price Range	38.33-28.79	37.15-26.93	37.15-25.71	37.15-20.37	32.80-19.96	23.00-10.87	22.38-8.09	29.59-12.81
P/E Ratio	25.38-19.07	25.27-18.32	26.73-18.50	28.14-15.43	31.54-19.19	35.38-16.72	44.75-16.19	51.02-22.09

Address: 3250 Van Ness Avenue, San Francisco, CA 94109	Web Site: www.williams-sonoma.com	Auditors: Deloitte & Touche LLP
Telephone: (415) 421-7900	Officers: W. Howard Lester - Chmn. Edward A. Mueller - C.E.O.	Investor Contact: 415-616-7856
Fax: (415) 434-0881		

WILMINGTON TRUST CORP. (DE)

Exchange	Symbol	Price	52Wk Range	Yield	P/E	Div Acheiver
NYS	WL	$35.10 (3/31/2005)	38.04-33.52	3.25	16.79	23 Years

*7 Year Price Score 101.45 *NYSE Composite Index=100 *12 Month Price Score 90.98

TRADING VOLUME (thousand shares)

Interim Earnings (Per Share)

Qtr.	Mar	Jun	Sep	Dec
2001	0.47	0.47	0.47	0.48
2002	0.48	0.52	0.52	0.49
2003	0.44	0.49	0.52	0.57
2004	0.53	0.54	0.50	0.52

Interim Dividends (Per Share)

Amt	Decl	Ex	Rec	Pay
0.27Q	1/16/2004	1/29/2004	2/2/2004	2/16/2004
0.285Q	4/16/2004	4/29/2004	5/3/2004	5/17/2004
0.285Q	10/22/2004	10/28/2004	11/1/2004	11/15/2004
0.285Q	1/21/2005	1/28/2005	2/1/2005	2/15/2005

Indicated Div: $1.14 (Div. Reinv. Plan)

Valuation Analysis

Forecast P/E	15.72 (4/7/2005)	No of Institutions 222
Market Cap	$2.4 Billion	Shares
Book Value	905.3 Million	28,170,064
Price/Book	2.61	% Held
Price/Sales	3.51	41.79

Business Summary: Commercial Banking (MIC: 8.1 SIC: 022 NAIC: 22110)

Wilmington Trust, with assets of $8.82 billion as of Dec 31 2003, is a financial services holding company with offices in California, Delaware, Florida, Georgia, Maryland, Nevada, New York, Pennsylvania, Tennessee, the Cayman and Channel Islands, Dublin, London, and Milan. Co. provides wealth management and specialized corporate services to clients throughout the United States and in more than 50 other countries, and commercial banking services throughout the Delaware Valley region. In addition, Co. is authorized to do business in Luxembourg and the Netherlands.

Recent Developments: For the year ended Dec 31 2004, net income increased 5.6% to $141,900 thousand from net income of $134,400 thousand a year earlier. Net interest income was $294,400 thousand, up 6.2% from $277,100 thousand the year before. Provision for loan losses was $15,600 thousand versus $21,600 thousand in the prior year, a decrease of 27.8%. Non-interest income rose 10.5% to $756,100 thousand, while non-interest expense advanced 10.3% to $688,000 thousand.

Prospects: Looking ahead, Co.'s balance sheet remains asset sensitive and should benefit from increases in short-term interest rates. For the first quarter of fiscal 2005, Co. expects loan growth to be in the range of 6.0% to 7.0%, and net interest margin to continue to improve and exceed 3.60%. Additionally, Co. expects wealth advisory services will be on par with the fourth quarter of 2004, which totaled $64.3 million, up 7.5% from the previous year. However, Co. anticipates revenue from affiliate money managers will be lower in the first quarter than it was during the fourth quarter. Total expenses should be between $90.0 million and $92.0 million.

Financial Data

(US$ in Thousands)	12/31/2004	12/31/2003	12/31/2002	12/31/2001	12/31/2000	12/31/1999	12/31/1998	12/31/1997
Earnings Per Share	2.09	2.02	2.01	1.90	1.85	1.61	1.67	1.54
Cash Flow Per Share	2.97	2.99	2.66	4.14	2.28	2.54	2.12	1.98
Tang Book Value Per Share	7.78	8.08	7.31	7.25	6.48	5.17	6.07	7.51
Dividends Per Share	1.125	1.065	1.005	0.945	0.885	0.825	0.765	0.705
Dividend Payout %	53.83	52.72	50.00	49.74	47.84	51.40	45.81	45.78
Income Statement								
Interest Income	386,500	368,800	392,871	468,798	530,454	462,176	456,939	430,639
Interest Expense	92,100	91,700	116,341	209,985	275,315	216,263	219,242	200,623
Net Interest Income	294,400	277,100	276,530	258,813	255,139	245,913	237,697	230,016
Provision for Losses	15,600	21,600	22,013	19,850	21,900	17,500	20,000	21,500
Non-Interest Income	286,700	264,200	262,159	228,003	216,210	191,453	183,917	157,542
Non-Interest Expense	344,000	312,000	309,892	276,917	264,682	258,204	230,066	207,671
Income Before Taxes	221,500	207,700	206,784	190,049	184,767	161,662	171,548	158,387
Income Taxes	78,700	72,200	73,002	66,009	63,828	54,365	57,223	52,343
Net Income	141,900	134,400	133,157	125,170	120,939	107,297	114,325	106,044
Average Shares	67,755	66,536	66,301	65,942	65,360	66,766	68,550	68,932
Balance Sheet								
Net Loans & Leases	6,673,300	6,135,400	5,939,947	5,407,175	5,111,670	4,743,154	4,247,727	3,930,130
Total Assets	9,510,200	8,820,200	8,131,275	7,518,462	7,321,616	7,201,944	6,300,565	6,122,351
Total Deposits	6,871,900	6,577,200	6,337,093	5,590,785	5,286,016	5,369,484	4,536,763	4,169,030
Total Liabilities	8,604,800	8,019,200	7,390,041	6,835,932	6,729,716	6,703,713	5,754,356	5,619,344
Stockholders' Equity	905,300	800,800	741,269	682,530	591,900	498,231	546,209	503,007
Shares Outstanding	67,405	66,063	65,627	65,400	64,786	64,705	66,658	66,956
Statistical Record								
Return on Assets %	1.54	1.59	1.70	1.69	1.66	1.59	1.84	1.81
Return on Equity %	16.59	17.43	18.70	19.64	22.13	20.55	21.79	21.92
Net Interest Margin %	76.17	75.14	70.39	55.21	48.10	53.21	52.02	53.41
Efficiency Ratio %	51.10	49.29	47.31	39.74	35.45	39.50	35.90	35.31
Loans to Deposits	0.97	0.93	0.94	0.97	0.97	0.88	0.94	0.94
Price Range	38.30-33.95	36.21-26.35	34.58-25.30	33.42-25.65	31.56-20.75	31.25-23.00	34.00-23.25	32.88-19.69
P/E Ratio	18.33-16.24	17.93-13.04	17.20-12.59	17.59-13.50	17.06-11.22	19.41-14.29	20.36-13.92	21.35-12.78
Average Yield %	3.11	3.47	3.22	3.14	3.58	2.97	2.60	2.86

Address: Rodney Square North, 1100 North Market Street, Wilmington, DE 19890-0001 **Telephone:** (302) 651-1000 **Fax:** (302) 651-8010	**Web Site:** www.wilmingtontrust.com **Officers:** Ted T. Cecala - Chmn., C.E.O. Robert V. A. Harra Jr. - Pres., C.O.O., Treas.	**Auditors:** KPMG LLP **Investor Contact:** 302-651-8069 **Transfer Agents:** National Bank Trust Company, Montreal, Quebec

WINN-DIXIE STORES, INC.

Exchange	Symbol	Price	52Wk Range	Yield	P/E
NBB	WNDX Q	$0.93 (3/31/2005)	8.20-0.60	N/A	N/A

*7 Year Price Score 20.31   *NYSE Composite Index=100   *12 Month Price Score 32.06

Interim Earnings (Per Share)

Qtr.	Sep	Dec	Mar	Jun
2001-02	0.16	0.30	0.31	(0.15)
2002-03	0.25	0.65	0.36	0.44
2003-04	0.01	(0.57)	...	(0.16)
2004-05	(1.09)	(2.84)	...	...

Interim Dividends (Per Share)

Amt	Decl	Ex	Rec	Pay
0.05Q	4/21/2003	4/29/2003	5/1/2003	5/15/2003
0.05Q	7/21/2003	7/30/2003	8/1/2003	8/15/2003
0.05Q	10/20/2003	10/30/2003	11/3/2003	11/17/2003
0.05Q	1/20/2004	1/29/2004	2/2/2004	2/17/2004

Valuation Analysis

Forecast P/E	0.00	No of Institutions	
	(4/7/2005)	151	
Market Cap	$132.2 Million	Shares	
Book Value	364.8 Million	69,042,544	
Price/Book	0.36	% Held	
Price/Sales	0.01	48.57	

Business Summary: Retail - Food & Beverage (MIC: 5.3 SIC: 411 NAIC: 45110)

Winn-Dixie Stores and its subsidiaries is a food and drug retailer operating in 12 states in the southeastern United States and the Bahama Islands. Co. operates primarily under the "Winn-Dixie" and "Winn-Dixie Marketplace" banners. Co. operates grocery warehouse stores under the "SaveRite" banner and most of its Bahama stores under the "City Markets" banner. As of June 30, 2004, Co. operated 1,049 retail stores, 32 fuel centers and 59 liquor stores. In support of its retail operations, Co. operates 14 warehouse distribution centers and 15 manufacturing plants.

Recent Developments: For the quarter ended Jan 12 2005, loss from continuing operations decreased 398.0% to $327,402 thousand from loss of $65,744 thousand in the year-earlier quarter. Net loss decreased 402.5% to $399,701 thousand from net loss of $79,540 thousand in the year-earlier quarter. Revenues were $3,075,633 thousand, down 4.7% from $3,228,118 thousand the year before. Operating loss was $68,603 thousand versus a loss of $99,616 thousand in the prior-year quarter, a decrease of 31.1%. Total direct expense was $2,264,446 thousand versus $2,408,848 thousand in the prior-year quarter, a decrease of 6.0%. Total indirect expense was $879,790 thousand versus $918,886 thousand in the prior-year quarter, a decrease of 4.3%.

Prospects: On Feb 22 2005, Co. announced that it filed for protection under Chapter 11 of the U.S. Bankruptcy Code in order to address the financial and operational challenges that have hampered its performance. Co. will use the reorganization process to take additional action to improve its operations and strengthen its business. As a part of the process, Co. will implement new sales and merchandising initiatives to help customer service and drive sales growth across its chain. In addition, Co. will implement further asset rationalization, additional asset sales and expense reduction plans to enhance productivity and take better advantage of its asset base.

Financial Data

(US$ in Thousands)	6 Mos	3 Mos	06/30/2004	06/25/2003	06/26/2002	06/27/2001	06/28/2000	06/30/1999
Earnings Per Share	...	...	(0.71)	1.70	0.62	0.32	(1.57)	1.23
Cash Flow Per Share	0.03	1.30	1.28	2.75	2.69	1.76	5.12	2.89
Tang Book Value Per Share	2.57	5.40	5.85	6.68	5.15	4.83	6.03	9.50
Dividends Per Share	0.050	0.100	0.150	0.200	0.355	1.020	1.020	1.020
Dividend Payout %	...	...	...	11.76	57.26	318.75	...	82.93
Income Statement								
Total Revenue	5,412,242	2,336,609	10,632,850	12,168,383	12,334,353	12,903,373	13,697,547	14,136,503
EBITDA	(169,877)	(147,433)	95,407	527,406	541,526	310,044	1,341	618,542
Depn & Amortn	81,225	35,066	168,534	166,385	175,520	183,559	256,671	292,414
Income Before Taxes	(269,141)	(189,773)	(87,504)	320,579	308,167	73,642	(302,411)	296,480
Income Taxes	181,814	(66,220)	(36,709)	81,349	118,644	28,331	(73,516)	114,145
Net Income	(552,778)	(153,077)	(100,404)	239,230	86,866	45,311	(228,895)	182,335
Average Shares	140,748	140,724	140,664	140,826	140,617	140,399	145,445	148,680
Balance Sheet								
Current Assets	1,200,966	1,333,619	1,350,798	1,473,454	1,638,306	1,599,201	1,471,922	1,797,990
Total Assets	2,235,557	2,564,810	2,618,891	2,790,431	2,937,578	3,041,670	2,747,093	3,149,147
Current Liabilities	865,594	958,755	938,866	1,018,730	1,109,904	1,149,907	1,421,553	1,547,324
Long-Term Obligations	464,539	313,509	314,171	332,111	565,399	726,367	32,239	38,493
Total Liabilities	1,870,785	1,798,526	1,701,546	1,761,927	2,125,194	2,270,016	1,879,258	1,738,068
Stockholders' Equity	364,772	766,284	917,345	1,028,504	812,384	771,654	867,835	1,411,079
Shares Outstanding	142,168	142,020	142,028	140,818	140,592	140,466	140,830	148,577
Statistical Record								
Return on Assets %	N.M.	N.M.	N.M.	8.38	2.91	1.57	N.M.	5.77
Return on Equity %	N.M.	N.M.	N.M.	26.06	11.00	5.54	N.M.	12.91
EBITDA Margin %	N.M.	N.M.	0.90	4.33	4.39	2.40	0.01	4.38
Net Margin %	N.M.	N.M.	N.M.	1.97	0.70	0.35	N.M.	1.29
Asset Turnover	3.91	3.79	3.87	4.26	4.14	4.47	4.66	4.47
Current Ratio	1.39	1.39	1.44	1.45	1.48	1.39	1.04	1.16
Debt to Equity	1.27	0.41	0.34	0.32	0.70	0.94	0.04	0.03
Price Range	9.59-3.09	10.25-3.77	12.74-5.81	17.83-11.51	26.13-10.50	33.03-13.56	41.63-14.25	52.19-30.44
P/E Ratio	...	...	...	10.49-6.77	42.15-16.94	103.22-42.38	...	42.43-24.75
Average Yield %	0.86	1.37	1.75	1.39	2.13	4.84	4.10	2.57

Address: 5050 Edgewood Court, Jacksonville, FL 32254-3699 **Telephone:** (904) 783-5000 **Fax:** (904) 783-5548	**Web Site:** www.winn-dixie.com **Officers:** H. Jay Skelton - Chmn. Peter L. Lynch - Pres., C.E.O.	**Auditors:** KPMG LLP

WISCONSIN ENERGY CORP.

Exchange	Symbol	Price	52Wk Range	Yield	P/E
NYS	WEC	$35.50 (3/31/2005)	36.04-29.65	2.48	13.81

*7 Year Price Score 107.28 *NYSE Composite Index=100 *12 Month Price Score 99.53

Interim Earnings (Per Share)

Qtr.	Mar	Jun	Sep	Dec
2001	0.74	0.39	0.41	0.32
2002	(0.04)	0.39	0.45	0.64
2003	0.79	0.42	0.26	0.60
2004	0.76	0.32	0.71	0.78

Interim Dividends (Per Share)

Amt	Decl	Ex	Rec	Pay
0.21Q	2/4/2004	5/12/2004	5/14/2004	6/1/2004
0.21Q	8/4/2004	8/11/2004	8/13/2004	9/1/2004
0.21Q	11/2/2004	11/9/2004	11/12/2004	12/1/2004
0.22Q	1/20/2005	2/9/2005	2/11/2005	3/1/2005

Indicated Div: $0.88

Valuation Analysis

Forecast P/E	15.10	No of Institutions	
	(4/7/2005)	256	
Market Cap	$4.2 Billion	Shares	
Book Value	2.5 Billion	70,011,256	
Price/Book	1.65	% Held	
Price/Sales	1.21	59.85	

Business Summary: Electricity (MIC: 7.1 SIC: 931 NAIC: 21121)

Wisconsin Energy is a diversified holding company with subsidiaries primarily in a utility energy segment and a non-utility energy segment. Co.'s utility energy segment, consisting of Wisconsin Electric Power Company and Wisconsin Gas Company and Edison Sault Electric Company, is engaged primarily in the business of generating electricity and distributing electricity and natural gas in Wisconsin and the Upper Peninsula of Michigan. Co.'s non-utility energy segment primarily consists of W.E. Power, LLC, which engages in engineering, construction and development of electric power generating facilities for long term lease to Wisconsin Electric and other utilities, and Wisvest Corporation.

Recent Developments: For the year ended Dec 31 2004, income from continuing operations decreased 39.0% to $122,200 thousand from income of $200,400 thousand a year earlier. Net income increased 25.4% to $306,400 thousand from net income of $244,300 thousand a year earlier. Revenues were $3,431,100 thousand, up 3.7% from $3,308,300 thousand the year before. Operating income was $379,800 thousand versus an income of $482,200 thousand in the prior year, a decrease of 21.2%. Total direct expense was $2,486,500 thousand versus $2,368,300 thousand in the prior year, an increase of 5.0%. Total indirect expense was $564,800 thousand versus $457,800 thousand in the prior year, an increase of 23.4%.

Prospects: Co. is enthusiastic regarding the progress it has made executing its Power the Future plan and reducing debt. Also, Co. is experiencing higher results due to customer growth, slightly colder weather and the absence of a nuclear refueling outage. Meanwhile, Co. is benefiting from the sale of non-core assets, the strength of its balance sheet, and improved operating and financial performance. Accordingly, Co. will continue to place emphasis on improving its operating efficiencies. Moreover, construction of the first of two 545 megawatt generating units at its Port Washington site was more than 75.0% complete at year end 2004.

Financial Data

(US$ in Thousands)	12/31/2004	12/31/2003	12/31/2002	12/31/2001	12/31/2000	12/31/1999	12/31/1998	12/31/1997
Earnings Per Share	2.57	2.06	1.44	1.86	1.27	1.79	1.65	0.54
Cash Flow Per Share	5.07	5.33	6.16	4.75	3.81	2.79	4.02	3.49
Tang Book Value Per Share	17.53	12.86	11.26	10.60	10.03	16.89	16.46	16.51
Dividends Per Share	0.830	0.800	0.800	0.800	1.370	1.560	1.555	1.535
Dividend Payout %	32.30	38.83	55.56	43.01	107.87	87.15	94.24	284.26
Income Statement								
Total Revenue	3,431,100	4,054,300	3,736,200	3,928,500	3,354,700	2,272,639	1,979,986	1,789,602
EBITDA	780,100	992,000	870,300	982,200	889,900	...	...	...
Depn & Amortn	384,200	408,700	389,100	409,800	400,200	322,649	288,893	273,552
Income Before Taxes	202,500	379,400	272,700	358,900	280,100	...	...	...
Income Taxes	80,300	135,100	105,700	150,400	125,900	111,147	92,166	31,005
Net Income	306,400	244,300	167,000	219,000	154,200	208,989	188,132	60,716
Average Shares	119,100	118,400	116,300	117,900	121,200	117,019	114,315	112,570
Balance Sheet								
Net PPE	5,903,100	5,926,100	4,398,800	4,188,000	4,152,400	3,846,578	3,238,385	3,184,979
Total Assets	9,565,400	10,025,700	8,364,900	8,328,700	8,406,100	6,233,120	5,361,757	5,037,684
Long-Term Obligations	3,239,500	3,574,300	3,030,500	3,237,300	2,732,700	2,134,636	1,749,024	1,532,405
Total Liabilities	7,042,600	7,636,700	6,195,100	6,242,200	6,358,900	4,194,926	3,428,202	3,144,302
Stockholders' Equity	2,522,800	2,389,000	2,169,800	2,086,500	2,047,200	2,038,194	1,933,555	1,893,382
Shares Outstanding	116,985	118,425	116,027	115,420	118,645	118,904	115,607	112,866
Statistical Record								
Return on Assets %	3.12	2.66	2.00	2.62	2.10	3.60	3.62	1.23
Return on Equity %	12.44	10.72	7.85	10.60	7.53	10.52	9.83	3.14
EBITDA Margin %	22.74	24.47	23.29	25.00	26.53	...	...	...
Net Margin %	8.93	6.03	4.47	5.57	4.60	9.20	9.50	3.39
PPE Turnover	0.58	0.79	0.87	0.94	0.84	0.64	0.62	0.57
Asset Turnover	0.35	0.44	0.45	0.47	0.46	0.39	0.38	0.36
Debt to Equity	1.28	1.50	1.40	1.55	1.33	1.05	0.90	0.81
Price Range	34.49-29.65	33.46-22.67	26.36-20.75	24.37-19.44	23.00-16.81	31.44-19.25	33.63-27.06	29.06-23.25
P/E Ratio	13.42-11.54	16.24-11.00	18.31-14.41	13.10-10.45	18.11-13.24	17.56-10.75	20.38-16.40	53.82-43.06
Average Yield %	2.56	2.85	3.30	3.61	6.81	6.25	5.23	6.01

Address: 231 West Michigan Street,	Web Site: www.wisconsinenergy.com	Auditors: DELOITTE & TOUCHE LLP
Milwaukee, WI 53201	Officers: Gale E. Klappa - Chmn., Pres., C.E.O.	Investor Contact: 414-221-2592
Telephone: (414) 221-2345	Richard R. Grigg - Exec. V.P.	
Fax: (414) 221-2172		

WOLVERINE WORLD WIDE, INC.

Exchange	Symbol	Price	52Wk Range	Yield	P/E	Div Acheiver
NYS	WWW	$21.43 (3/31/2005)	23.35-14.40	1.21	19.66	11 Years

*7 Year Price Score 140.91 *NYSE Composite Index=100 *12 Month Price Score 109.83

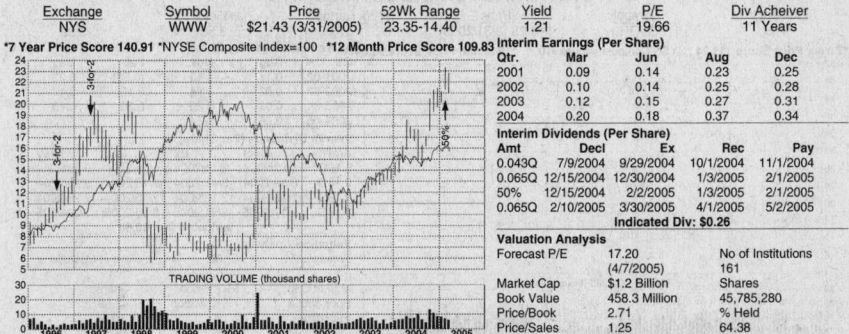

Interim Earnings (Per Share)

Qtr.	Mar	Jun	Aug	Dec
2001	0.09	0.14	0.23	0.25
2002	0.10	0.14	0.25	0.28
2003	0.12	0.15	0.27	0.31
2004	0.20	0.18	0.37	0.34

Interim Dividends (Per Share)

Amt	Decl	Ex	Rec	Pay
0.043Q	7/9/2004	9/29/2004	10/1/2004	11/1/2004
0.065Q	12/15/2004	12/30/2004	1/3/2005	2/1/2005
50%	12/15/2004	2/2/2005	1/3/2005	2/1/2005
0.065Q	2/10/2005	3/30/2005	4/1/2005	5/2/2005

Indicated Div: $0.26

Valuation Analysis

Forecast P/E	17.20	No of Institutions
	(4/7/2005)	161
Market Cap	$1.2 Billion	Shares
Book Value	458.3 Million	45,785,280
Price/Book	2.71	% Held
Price/Sales	1.25	64.38

Business Summary: Leather and Leather Products (MIC: 4.5 SIC: 149 NAIC: 16219)

Wolverine World Wide is a designer, manufacturer and marketer of a broad line of casual shoes, rugged outdoor and work footwear, and constructed slippers and moccasins. The products are marketed throughout the world under brand names including Bates®, CAT®, Coleman®, Harley-Davidson®, Hush Puppies®, HyTest®, Merrell®, Sebago®, Stanley® and Wolverine®. Co.'s footwear is distributed domestically through 64 Co.-owned retail stores and to numerous accounts including department stores, footwear chains, catalogs, specialty retailers, mass merchants and Internet retailers as of Jan 3 2004. Co.'s products are distributed worldwide in over 140 markets through licensees and distributors.

Recent Developments: For the year ended Jan 1 2005, net income increased 27.5% to $65,938 thousand from net income of $51,716 thousand a year earlier. Revenues were $991,909 thousand, up 11.6% from $888,926 thousand the year before. Total direct expense was $617,774 thousand versus $562,338 thousand in the prior year, an increase of 9.9%. Total indirect expense was $274,125 thousand versus $246,652 thousand in the prior year, an increase of 11.1%.

Prospects: Co. has increased its previously stated full-year 2005 estimates of revenue by $5.0 million to a range of $1.04 billion to $1.06 billion and raised its earnings per share estimates by approximately $0.01 per share to a range of $1.19 to $1.24. Co. noted that these estimates are in line with its long-term financial objectives of growing revenue in the mid to upper single-digit range and generating double-digit earnings per share growth. Co. stated that these estimates do not include the effect of accounting changes which require the expensing of stock options and do not reflect any effect from the potential repatriation of foreign earnings under the American Jobs Creation Act of 2004.

Financial Data

(US$ in Thousands)	01/01/2005	01/03/2004	12/28/2002	12/29/2001	12/30/2000	01/01/2000	01/02/1999	01/03/1998
Earnings Per Share	1.09	0.85	0.77	0.71	0.17	0.52	0.65	0.64
Cash Flow Per Share	1.86	1.71	1.47	0.87	1.14	0.77	(0.07)	(0.00)
Tang Book Value Per Share	7.16	6.56	5.59	5.76	5.18	5.10	4.59	4.13
Dividends Per Share	0.195	0.147	0.117	0.107	0.113	0.080	0.073	0.058
Dividend Payout %	17.89	17.32	15.22	14.95	65.38	15.38	11.34	9.04
Income Statement								
Total Revenue	991,909	888,926	827,106	720,066	701,291	665,576	669,329	665,125
EBITDA	116,141	93,095	88,514	86,168	32,710	64,427	74,844	70,232
Depn & Amortn	19,071	17,947	16,860	17,621	17,695	14,881	13,036	9,151
Income Before Taxes	97,070	75,148	71,654	68,547	15,015	49,546	61,808	61,081
Income Taxes	30,879	23,262	23,599	23,307	4,325	17,166	20,157	19,542
Net Income	65,938	51,716	47,912	45,240	10,690	32,380	41,651	41,539
Average Shares	60,474	61,081	62,689	63,673	62,692	62,229	64,428	65,196
Balance Sheet								
Current Assets	430,855	386,636	363,345	374,802	325,086	349,301	340,978	303,861
Total Assets	639,521	578,881	531,994	543,678	494,568	534,395	521,478	449,663
Current Liabilities	110,251	85,766	80,177	74,521	54,004	48,539	51,268	64,895
Long-Term Obligations	32,169	43,903	57,885	75,818	87,878	134,831	157,089	89,847
Total Liabilities	180,714	148,473	162,754	169,526	157,330	202,290	221,158	167,233
Stockholders' Equity	458,291	430,094	369,097	374,152	337,238	332,105	300,320	282,430
Shares Outstanding	57,898	59,179	59,955	62,333	62,329	61,950	61,147	63,829
Statistical Record								
Return on Assets %	10.85	9.16	8.93	8.74	2.08	6.15	8.60	10.07
Return on Equity %	14.89	12.73	12.93	12.75	3.20	10.27	14.33	15.67
EBITDA Margin %	11.71	10.47	10.70	11.97	4.66	9.68	11.18	10.56
Net Margin %	6.65	5.82	5.79	6.28	1.52	4.86	6.22	6.25
Asset Turnover	1.63	1.57	1.54	1.39	1.37	1.26	1.38	1.61
Current Ratio	3.91	4.51	4.53	5.03	6.02	7.20	6.65	4.68
Debt to Equity	0.07	0.10	0.16	0.20	0.26	0.41	0.52	0.32
Price Range	21.48-13.57	14.19-9.59	12.83-8.60	12.80-8.37	11.04-5.75	9.33-6.00	20.33-5.63	20.25-12.89
P/E Ratio	19.71-12.45	16.69-11.29	16.66-11.17	18.03-11.79	64.95-33.82	17.95-11.54	31.28-8.65	31.64-20.14
Average Yield %	1.14	1.19	1.08	1.00	1.55	1.07	0.56	0.36

Address: 9341 Courtland Drive, Rockford, MI 49351	Web Site: www.wolverineworldwide.com	Auditors: Ernst & Young LLP
Telephone: (616) 866 5500	Officers: Geoffrey B. Bloom - Chmn. Timothy J. O'Donovan - Pres., C.E.O.	Investor Contact: 616-866-5589
Fax: (616) 866 0257		Transfer Agents: Computershare Investor Services, Chicago, IL

WORTHINGTON INDUSTRIES, INC.

Exchange	Symbol	Price	52Wk Range	Yield	P/E
NYS	WOR	$19.28 (3/31/2005)	22.71-17.00	3.53	9.99

*7 Year Price Score 115.24 *NYSE Composite Index=100 *12 Month Price Score 94.84

Interim Earnings (Per Share)

Qtr.	Aug	Nov	Feb	May
2001-02	0.17	0.13	(0.53)	0.32
2002-03	0.32	0.24	0.13	0.18
2003-04	0.07	0.20	0.28	0.45
2004-05	0.66	0.54	...	...

Interim Dividends (Per Share)

Amt	Decl	Ex	Rec	Pay
0.16Q	5/22/2004	6/14/2004	6/15/2004	6/29/2004
0.16Q	8/19/2004	9/13/2004	9/15/2004	9/29/2004
0.16Q	11/18/2004	12/13/2004	12/15/2004	12/29/2004
0.17Q	2/17/2005	3/11/2005	3/15/2005	3/29/2005

Indicated Div: $0.68

Valuation Analysis

Forecast P/E	12.80 (4/7/2005)	No of Institutions 204
Market Cap	$1.7 Billion	Shares 42,601,632
Book Value	777.2 Million	% Held 48.50
Price/Book	2.18	
Price/Sales	0.59	

TRADING VOLUME (thousand shares)

Business Summary: Metal Works (MIC: 11.3 SIC: 316 NAIC: 31221)

Worthington Industries is a diversified metal processing company, focused on value-added steel processing and manufactured metal products such as metal framing, pressure cylinders, automotive part stampings and, through joint ventures, metal ceiling grid systems and laser welded blanks. As of May 31 2004, Co. operates 44 manufacturing facilities worldwide and holds equity positions in eight joint ventures, which operate an additional 17 manufacturing facilities worldwide. Co. operates in three business segments: Processed Steel Products, Metal Framing and Pressure Cylinders.

Recent Developments: For the quarter ended Nov 30 2004, net income increased 182.1% to $47,623 thousand from net income of $16,883 thousand in the year-earlier quarter. Revenues were $745,168 thousand, up 38.0% from $540,078 thousand the year before. Operating income was $68,388 thousand versus an income of $21,999 thousand in the prior-year quarter, an increase of 210.9%. Total indirect expense was $56,130 thousand versus $45,243 thousand in the prior-year quarter, an increase of 24.1%.

Prospects: Co. continues to perform well despite ongoing weakness in two of its key market segments, automotive and commercial construction. In Co.'s process steels segment, net sales reflect a sharp increase in selling prices, partially offset by lower sales volumes, which are being adversely affected by the sale of the Decatur cold rolling assets in August 2004 and lower automotive production. In the metal framing segment, sales are benefiting from higher prices as well, while volumes are lower as customers are faced with higher inventories and delayed construction projects due to increased costs.

Financial Data

(US$ in Thousands)	6 Mos	3 Mos	05/31/2004	05/31/2003	05/31/2002	05/31/2001	05/31/2000	05/31/1999
Earnings Per Share	1.93	1.59	1.00	0.87	0.08	0.42	1.06	0.59
Cash Flow Per Share	0.75	0.15	0.92	2.11	1.58	3.76	1.57	1.12
Tang Book Value Per Share	6.93	6.98	6.48	6.04	6.21	6.67	6.92	6.74
Dividends Per Share	0.640	0.640	0.640	0.640	0.640	0.640	0.600	0.560
Dividend Payout %	33.21	40.31	64.00	73.56	800.00	152.38	56.60	94.92
Income Statement								
Total Revenue	1,514,508	769,340	2,379,104	2,219,891	1,744,961	1,826,100	1,962,606	1,763,072
EBITDA	204,804	113,101	216,964	212,583	101,867	160,039	261,418	254,367
Depn & Amortn	28,507	14,059	67,302	69,419	68,887	70,582	70,997	78,490
Income Before Taxes	164,923	93,320	127,464	118,398	10,240	56,008	150,642	132,751
Income Taxes	59,441	35,461	40,712	43,215	3,738	20,443	56,491	49,118
Net Income	105,482	57,859	86,752	75,183	6,502	35,565	94,151	54,912
Average Shares	88,665	88,112	86,950	86,537	85,929	85,623	88,598	93,106
Balance Sheet								
Current Assets	814,652	847,697	833,110	506,246	490,340	449,719	624,229	624,255
Total Assets	1,712,523	1,667,934	1,643,139	1,478,069	1,457,314	1,475,862	1,673,873	1,686,951
Current Liabilities	458,093	459,692	475,060	318,171	339,351	306,619	433,270	427,725
Long-Term Obligations	287,961	287,915	288,422	289,689	289,250	309,208	362,190	365,802
Total Liabilities	935,325	938,419	962,764	841,775	851,058	826,197	1,000,519	997,302
Stockholders' Equity	777,198	729,515	680,374	636,294	606,256	649,665	673,354	689,649
Shares Outstanding	87,838	87,585	86,855	85,948	85,512	85,375	85,754	89,949
Statistical Record								
Return on Assets %	10.60	8.91	5.54	5.12	0.44	2.26	5.59	3.11
Return on Equity %	23.95	20.42	13.14	12.10	1.04	5.38	13.78	7.47
EBITDA Margin %	13.52	14.70	9.12	9.58	5.84	8.76	13.32	14.43
Net Margin %	6.96	7.52	3.65	3.39	0.37	1.95	4.80	3.11
Asset Turnover	1.79	1.70	1.52	1.51	1.19	1.16	1.16	1.00
Current Ratio	1.78	1.84	1.75	1.59	1.44	1.47	1.44	1.46
Debt to Equity	0.37	0.39	0.42	0.46	0.48	0.48	0.54	0.53
Price Range	22.71-14.59	20.59-12.47	19.37-12.47	19.88-11.93	16.20-10.30	12.85-6.44	17.63-11.38	17.56-11.25
P/E Ratio	11.77-7.56	12.95-7.84	19.37-12.47	22.85-13.71	202.50-128.75	30.60-15.33	16.63-10.73	29.77-19.07
Average Yield %	3.38	3.72	4.04	4.01	4.55	6.38	4.18	4.18

Address: 200 Old Wilson Bridge Road, Columbus, OH 43085 **Telephone:** (614) 438-3210 **Fax:** (614) 438-3256	**Web Site:** www.worthingtonindustries.com **Officers:** John P. McConnell - Chmn., C.E.O. John S. Christie - Pres., C.O.O.	**Auditors:** KPMG LLP

WPS RESOURCES CORP.

Exchange	Symbol	Price	52Wk Range	Yield	P/E	Div Acheiver
NYS	WPS	$52.92 (3/31/2005)	54.64-43.52	4.20	14.23	46 Years

*7 Year Price Score 111.97 *NYSE Composite Index=100 ***12 Month Price Score 102.11**

Interim Earnings (Per Share)

Qtr.	Mar	Jun	Sep	Dec
2001	0.89	0.41	0.76	0.70
2002	0.89	0.68	0.95	0.90
2003	1.02	0.08	1.04	0.71
2004	1.14	0.12	0.93	1.53

Interim Dividends (Per Share)

Amt	Decl	Ex	Rec	Pay
0.545Q	4/1/2004	5/26/2004	5/28/2004	6/19/2004
0.555Q	7/8/2004	8/27/2004	8/31/2004	9/20/2004
0.555Q	10/14/2004	11/26/2004	11/30/2004	12/20/2004
0.555Q	2/10/2005	2/24/2005	2/28/2005	3/19/2005
	Indicated Div: $2.22 (Div. Reinv. Plan)			

Valuation Analysis

Forecast P/E	14.27	No of Institutions	
	(4/7/2005)	172	
Market Cap	$2.0 Billion	Shares	
Book Value	1.1 Billion	11,722,600	
Price/Book	1.74	% Held	
Price/Sales	0.41	31.47	

Business Summary: Electricity (MIC: 7.1 SIC: 931 NAIC: 21121)

WPS Resources operates as a holding company with both regulated utility and non-regulated business units serving an 11,000 square mile service territory in northeastern Wisconsin and an adjacent portion of the Upper Peninsula of Michigan. Co.'s principal wholly-owned subsidiaries are: Wisconsin Public Service Corporation (WPSC), a regulated electric and gas utility in Wisconsin and Michigan; Upper Peninsula Power Company, a regulated electric utility in Michigan; and WPS Energy Service, Inc. and WPS Power Development, Inc., both non-regulated subsidiaries. As of Dec 31 2003, WPSC served 414,295 electric retail and 300,859 gas retail customers.

Recent Developments: For the year ended Dec 31 2004, net income increased 46.0% to $142,800 thousand from net income of $97,800 thousand a year earlier. Revenues were $4,890,600 thousand, up 13.2% from $4,321,300 thousand the year before. Operating income was $189,300 thousand versus an income of $130,700 thousand in the prior year, an increase of 44.8%. Total direct expense was $4,548,200 thousand versus $4,008,400 thousand in the prior year, an increase of 13.5%. Total indirect expense was $153,100 thousand versus $182,200 thousand in the prior year, a decrease of 16.0%.

Prospects: For 2005, Co. will focus its efforts toward regulated growth. Co. stated that its long-term basic earnings per share growth rate target for income from continuing operations remains at 6.0% to 8.0% on an average annualized basis. Co.'s 2005 basic earnings per share guidance for income from continuing operations is between $3.90 and $4.15, assuming normal weather, availability of its generation units, and completion of its planned land sales. Co. noted that this guidance does not take into consideration the potential sale of the Kewaunee Nuclear Power Plant. On Nov 19 2004, the Public Service Commission of Wisconsin rejected Co.'s application to sell Kewaunee to Dominion Resources.

Financial Data

(US$ in Thousands)	12/31/2004	12/31/2003	12/31/2002	12/31/2001	12/31/2000	12/31/1999	12/31/1998	12/31/1997
Earnings Per Share	3.72	2.85	3.42	2.74	2.53	2.24	1.76	2.25
Cash Flow Per Share	6.48	1.89	6.12	5.07	5.31	4.31	4.14	5.99
Tang Book Value Per Share	28.97	27.39	24.43	22.73	20.21	19.97	19.48	20.00
Dividends Per Share	2.200	2.160	2.120	2.080	2.040	2.000	1.960	1.920
Dividend Payout %	59.14	75.79	61.99	75.91	80.63	89.29	111.36	85.33
Income Statement								
Total Revenue	4,890,600	4,321,300	2,674,900	2,675,500	1,951,574	1,098,540	1,063,736	878,340
EBITDA	230,900	186,700	344,000	243,400	146,635	140,134	117,491	126,394
Depn & Amortn	44,700	42,400	148,600	102,100	19,746	14,949	16,257	14,665
Income Before Taxes	186,200	144,300	137,300	85,500	76,109	92,417	72,597	85,326
Income Taxes	30,000	33,700	24,800	4,800	6,005	29,741	23,445	29,270
Net Income	142,800	97,800	112,500	80,700	70,104	59,565	49,763	56,853
Average Shares	37,600	33,200	31,700	28,300	26,463	26,644	26,511	...
Balance Sheet								
Net PPE	2,002,600	1,828,700	1,610,200	1,463,600	1,198,324	1,150,902	1,010,158	886,360
Total Assets	4,445,600	4,292,300	3,207,900	2,870,000	2,816,142	1,816,548	1,510,387	1,299,602
Long-Term Obligations	865,700	871,900	824,400	727,800	587,017	510,917	343,037	304,008
Total Liabilities	3,302,700	3,238,000	2,324,000	2,053,000	2,099,242	1,105,470	891,997	770,579
Stockholders' Equity	1,142,900	1,054,300	833,900	767,000	593,945	587,493	568,390	529,023
Shares Outstanding	37,682	36,621	32,040	31,496	26,851	26,851	26,551	23,897
Statistical Record								
Return on Assets %	3.26	2.61	3.70	2.84	3.02	3.58	3.54	4.32
Return on Equity %	12.96	10.36	14.05	11.86	11.84	10.31	9.07	10.85
EBITDA Margin %	4.72	4.32	12.86	9.10	7.51	12.76	11.05	14.39
Net Margin %	2.92	2.26	4.21	3.02	3.59	5.42	4.68	6.47
PPE Turnover	2.55	2.51	1.74	2.01	1.66	1.02	1.12	0.99
Asset Turnover	1.12	1.15	0.88	0.94	0.84	0.66	0.76	0.67
Debt to Equity	0.76	0.83	0.99	0.95	0.99	0.87	0.60	0.57
Price Range	50.32-43.52	46.77-37.12	42.45-31.52	36.55-31.82	38.69-22.81	35.50-24.63	37.25-30.25	34.19-23.50
P/E Ratio	13.53-11.70	16.41-13.02	12.41-9.22	13.34-11.61	15.29-9.02	15.85-10.99	21.16-17.19	15.19-10.44
Average Yield %	4.68	5.27	5.55	6.08	6.89	6.74	5.88	6.89

Address: 700 North Adams Street, P.O. Box 19001, Green Bay, WI 54307-9001 **Telephone:** (920) 433-4901 **Fax:** (920) 433-1526	Web Site: www.wpsr.com **Officers:** Larry L. Weyers - Chmn., Pres., C.E.O. Thomas P. Meinz - Sr. V.P., Public Affairs	Auditors: Deloitte & Touche LLP **Investor Contact:** 920-433-1857 **Transfer Agents:** American Stock Transfer & Trust Company, New York,

WRIGLEY (WILLIAM) JR. CO.

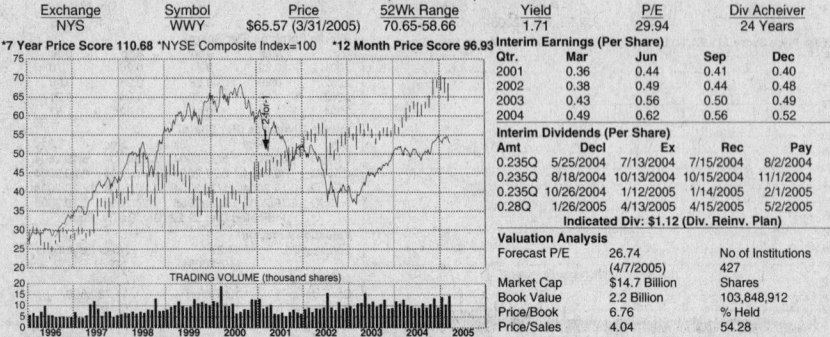

Exchange	Symbol	Price	52Wk Range	Yield	P/E	Div Acheiver
NYS	WWY	$65.57 (3/31/2005)	70.65-58.66	1.71	29.94	24 Years

*7 Year Price Score 110.68 *NYSE Composite Index=100 *12 Month Price Score 96.93

Interim Earnings (Per Share)

Qtr.	Mar	Jun	Sep	Dec
2001	0.36	0.44	0.41	0.40
2002	0.38	0.49	0.44	0.48
2003	0.43	0.56	0.50	0.49
2004	0.49	0.62	0.56	0.52

Interim Dividends (Per Share)

Amt	Decl	Ex	Rec	Pay
0.235Q	5/25/2004	7/13/2004	7/15/2004	8/2/2004
0.235Q	8/18/2004	10/13/2004	10/15/2004	11/1/2004
0.235Q	10/26/2004	1/12/2005	1/14/2005	2/1/2005
0.28Q	1/26/2005	4/13/2005	4/15/2005	5/2/2005

Indicated Div: $1.12 (Div. Reinv. Plan)

Valuation Analysis

Forecast P/E	26.74	No of Institutions
	(4/7/2005)	427
Market Cap	$14.7 Billion	Shares
Book Value	2.2 Billion	103,848,912
Price/Book	6.76	% Held
Price/Sales	4.04	54.28

TRADING VOLUME (thousand shares)

Business Summary: Food (MIC: 4.1 SIC: 067 NAIC: 11340)

William Wrigley Jr. is a manufacturer and marketer of chewing gum and other confectionery products, both in the United States and abroad. Two domestic wholly-owned associated companies, L.A. Dreyfus Company and Northwestern Flavors, LLC, manufacture products, gum base and mint oil, respectively, other than chewing gum or confectionery products. As of Dec 31 2004, Co.'s brands were sold in over 180 countries and territories. Brand names include, among numerous others, Doublemint®, Eclipse®, Extra®, Orbit®, Wrigley's Spearmint®, Winterfresh®, Airwaves®, Alpine®, Big Red®, Cool Air®, Excel®, Freedent®, Juicy Fruit®, Hubba Bubba®, and P.K.®

Recent Developments: For the year ended Dec 31 2004, net income increased 10.6% to $492,954 thousand from net income of $445,894 thousand a year earlier. Revenues were $3,648,592 thousand, up 18.9% from $3,069,088 thousand the year before. Operating income was $720,219 thousand versus an income of $649,362 thousand in the prior year, an increase of 10.9%. Total direct expense was $1,609,978 thousand versus $1,317,416 thousand in the prior year, an increase of 22.2%. Total indirect expense was $1,318,395 thousand versus $1,102,310 thousand in the prior year, an increase of 19.6%.

Prospects: On Nov 15 2004, Co. announced that it has entered into an agreement to purchase certain confectionery assets of Kraft Foods for $1.48 billion. The transaction includes such brands as Life Savers, Creme Savers®, and Altoids as well as a number of local or regional brands and production facilities in the United States and Europe. Co. anticipates that the transaction, including one-time costs, will be slightly dilutive to earnings in the first full year of combined operations and accretive thereafter. Subject to customary closing conditions, including certain regulatory clearances, Co. expects that the transaction will be completed by mid-2005.

Financial Data

(US$ in Thousands)	12/31/2004	12/31/2003	12/31/2002	12/31/2001	12/31/2000	12/31/1999	12/31/1998	12/31/1997
Earnings Per Share	2.19	1.98	1.78	1.61	1.45	1.33	1.31	1.17
Cash Flow Per Share	3.22	2.87	1.66	1.73	1.97	1.55	1.40	1.27
Tang Book Value Per Share	8.76	8.10	6.77	5.67	4.87	4.97	4.98	4.25
Dividends Per Share	0.925	0.865	0.805	0.745	0.700	0.665	0.650	0.585
Dividend Payout %	42.24	43.69	45.22	46.27	48.28	50.00	49.43	50.00
Income Statement								
Total Revenue	3,648,592	3,069,088	2,746,318	2,429,646	2,145,706	2,079,238	2,023,355	1,954,174
EBITDA	864,245	771,581	668,989	595,692	537,192	506,364	497,268	445,637
Depn & Amortn	143,749	120,040	85,568	68,326	57,880	61,225	55,774	50,439
Income Before Taxes	720,496	651,541	583,421	527,366	479,312	444,430	440,879	394,240
Income Taxes	227,542	205,647	181,896	164,380	150,370	136,247	136,378	122,614
Net Income	492,954	445,894	401,525	362,986	328,942	308,183	304,501	271,626
Average Shares	225,473	224,963	225,145	225,349	227,036	231,722	231,928	231,928
Balance Sheet								
Current Assets	1,505,910	1,290,591	1,006,292	913,843	828,715	803,746	843,172	797,673
Total Assets	3,166,703	2,520,410	2,108,296	1,765,648	1,574,740	1,547,745	1,520,855	1,343,126
Current Liabilities	717,970	464,794	386,087	332,324	288,210	251,825	218,626	225,816
Total Liabilities	988,019	699,589	585,720	489,451	441,843	408,970	363,823	357,747
Stockholders' Equity	2,178,684	1,820,821	1,522,576	1,276,197	1,132,897	1,138,775	1,157,032	985,379
Shares Outstanding	224,771	224,860	225,056	224,950	232,442	228,992	232,220	231,938
Statistical Record								
Return on Assets %	17.29	19.27	20.73	21.73	21.01	20.09	21.26	21.08
Return on Equity %	24.58	26.67	28.69	30.13	28.88	26.85	28.43	28.85
EBITDA Margin %	23.69	25.14	24.36	24.52	25.04	24.35	24.58	22.80
Net Margin %	13.51	14.53	14.62	14.94	15.33	14.82	15.05	13.90
Asset Turnover	1.28	1.33	1.42	1.45	1.37	1.36	1.41	1.52
Current Ratio	2.10	2.78	2.61	2.75	2.88	3.19	3.86	3.53
Price Range	69.73-55.23	58.11-51.18	58.35-44.52	52.92-43.34	47.91-30.31	50.00-33.66	51.66-36.56	40.81-27.63
P/E Ratio	31.84-25.22	29.35-25.85	32.78-25.01	32.87-26.92	33.04-20.91	37.59-25.31	39.43-27.91	34.88-23.61
Average Yield %	1.49	1.56	1.51	1.54	1.80	1.58	1.53	1.74

Address: 410 North Michigan Avenue, Chicago, IL 60611	**Web Site:** www.wrigley.com	**Auditors:** Ernst & Young LLP
Telephone: (312) 644-2121	**Officers:** William Wrigley Jr. - Chmn., Pres., C.E.O. Dushan Petrovich - Sr. V.P., Chief Admin. Officer	**Investor Contact:** 1-800-874-0474
Fax: (312) 645-4083		**Transfer Agents:** EquiServe Trust Company, N.A., Providence, RI

WYETH

Exchange	Symbol	Price	52Wk Range	Yield	P/E
NYS	WYE	$42.18 (3/31/2005)	44.99-33.80	2.18	46.35

*7 Year Price Score 67.28 ***NYSE Composite Index=100** ***12 Month Price Score 96.70**

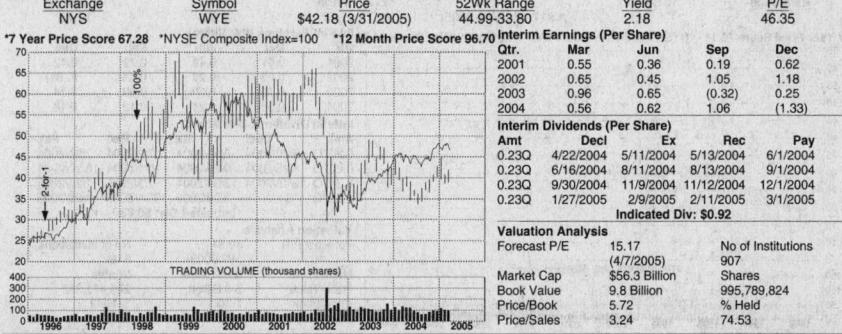

Interim Earnings (Per Share)

Qtr.	Mar	Jun	Sep	Dec
2001	0.55	0.36	0.19	0.62
2002	0.65	0.45	1.05	1.18
2003	0.96	0.65	(0.32)	0.25
2004	0.56	0.62	1.06	(1.33)

Interim Dividends (Per Share)

Amt	Decl	Ex	Rec	Pay
0.23Q	4/22/2004	5/11/2004	5/13/2004	6/1/2004
0.23Q	6/16/2004	8/11/2004	8/13/2004	9/1/2004
0.23Q	9/30/2004	11/9/2004	11/12/2004	12/1/2004
0.23Q	1/27/2005	2/9/2005	2/11/2005	3/1/2005
		Indicated Div: $0.92		

Valuation Analysis

Forecast P/E	15.17	No of Institutions	
	(4/7/2005)	907	
Market Cap	$56.3 Billion	Shares	995,789,824
Book Value	9.8 Billion	% Held	
Price/Book	5.72	74.53	
Price/Sales	3.24		

Business Summary: Pharmaceuticals (MIC: 9.1 SIC: 834 NAIC: 25412)

Wyeth engages in the discovery, development, manufacturing and marketing of products in three primary businesses: Wyeth Pharmaceuticals, Wyeth Consumer Healthcare and Fort Dodge Animal Health. Pharmaceuticals include branded human ethical pharmaceuticals, biologicals and nutritionals. Principal products include women's health care products, neuroscience therapies, cardiovascular products, nutritionals, astroenterology drugs, anti-infectives, vaccines, oncology therapies, musculoskeletal therapies, hemophilia treatments and immunological products. Consumer Healthcare includes over-the-counter health care products. Animal Health includes animal biological and pharmaceutical products.

Recent Developments: For the year ended Dec 31 2004, net income decreased 39.8% to $1,233,997 thousand from net income of $2,051,192 thousand a year earlier. Revenues were $17,358,028 thousand, up 9.5% from $15,850,632 thousand the year before. Total direct expense was $4,947,269 thousand versus $4,590,148 thousand in the prior year, an increase of 7.8%. Total indirect expense was $8,260,401 thousand versus $7,561,707 thousand in the prior year, an increase of 9.2%.

Prospects: Co. is pleased with its continued strong product performance, driven higher sales of Effexor® XR, Enbrel®, Prevnar®, Zosyn®, and Rapamune®, and believes that 2005 will be a year of solid growth in both net revenue and earnings. For 2005, Co. expects to see an increase of more than $350.0 million in research and development spending to support its late-stage pipeline. Also, Co. is excited about the anticipated approval of its Grange Castle, Ireland site for the production of Enbrel®. For full year, Co. expects net revenue to grow 5.0% to 9.0% and gross margin to be approximately 70.0% to 72.0% of sales.

Financial Data

(US$ in Thousands)	12/31/2004	12/31/2003	12/31/2002	12/31/2001	12/31/2000	12/31/1999	12/31/1998	12/31/1997
Earnings Per Share	0.91	1.54	3.33	1.72	(1.81)	(0.94)	1.85	1.56
Cash Flow Per Share	2.15	2.19	0.14	(3.38)	0.42	1.67	1.15	1.31
Tang Book Value Per Share	4.33	4.01	3.22	0.17	N.M.	N.M.	1.23	N.M.
Dividends Per Share	0.920	0.920	0.920	0.920	0.920	0.905	0.870	0.830
Dividend Payout %	101.10	59.74	27.63	53.49	...	...	47.03	53.21
Income Statement								
Total Revenue	17,358,028	15,850,632	14,584,035	14,128,514	13,262,754	13,550,176	13,462,687	14,196,026
EBITDA	602,825	3,002,635	6,783,997	3,622,834	(508,429)	(1,029,421)	4,457,272	3,887,428
Depn & Amortn	622,367	537,883	484,700	607,729	535,049	682,339	664,655	702,025
Income Before Taxes	(129,847)	2,361,612	6,097,245	2,868,747	(1,101,040)	(1,925,626)	3,585,460	2,814,707
Income Taxes	(1,363,844)	310,420	1,650,040	583,453	(200,000)	(698,505)	1,111,122	771,584
Net Income	1,233,997	2,051,192	4,447,205	2,285,294	(2,370,687)	(1,227,121)	2,474,338	2,043,123
Average Shares	1,354,489	1,335,910	1,334,127	1,330,809	1,306,474	1,308,876	1,336,641	1,312,975
Balance Sheet								
Current Assets	14,438,029	14,962,242	11,595,852	9,766,753	10,180,811	9,738,108	7,955,632	7,361,326
Total Assets	33,629,704	31,031,922	25,994,949	22,967,922	21,092,466	23,906,277	21,079,068	20,825,111
Current Liabilities	8,535,542	8,429,510	5,475,659	7,257,181	9,742,059	7,110,223	4,210,721	4,327,018
Long-Term Obligations	7,792,311	8,076,429	7,546,041	7,357,277	2,394,790	3,668,643	3,859,163	5,031,861
Total Liabilities	23,781,801	21,737,541	17,839,037	18,895,349	18,274,373	17,691,530	11,243,053	12,649,859
Stockholders' Equity	9,847,903	9,294,381	8,155,912	4,072,573	2,818,093	6,214,747	9,614,796	8,175,252
Shares Outstanding	1,335,091	1,332,451	1,326,055	1,320,570	1,311,774	1,303,916	1,312,399	1,300,754
Statistical Record								
Return on Assets %	3.81	7.19	18.17	10.37	N.M.	N.M.	11.81	9.82
Return on Equity %	12.86	23.51	72.74	66.33	N.M.	N.M.	27.82	26.99
EBITDA Margin %	3.47	18.94	46.52	25.64	N.M.	N.M.	33.11	27.38
Net Margin %	7.11	12.94	30.49	16.18	N.M.	N.M.	18.38	14.39
Asset Turnover	0.54	0.56	0.60	0.64	0.59	0.60	0.64	0.68
Current Ratio	1.69	1.77	2.12	1.35	1.05	1.37	1.89	1.70
Debt to Equity	0.79	0.87	0.93	1.81	0.85	0.59	0.40	0.62
Price Range	44.65-33.80	49.16-33.57	66.21-29.75	63.65-53.10	64.50-39.25	69.75-38.00	58.31-38.25	42.44-28.63
P/E Ratio	49.07-37.14	31.92-21.80	19.88-8.93	37.01-30.87	...	...	31.52-20.68	27.20-18.35
Average Yield %	2.38	2.20	1.87	1.57	1.69	1.69	1.77	2.34

Address: Five Giralda Farms, Madison, NJ 07940-0874	**Web Site:** www.wyeth.com	**Auditors:** PricewaterhouseCoopers LLP
Telephone: (973) 660-5000	**Officers:** Robert Essner - Chmn., Pres., C.E.O.	**Investor Contact:** 973-660-5706
Fax: (973) 660-5012	Kenneth J. Martin - Exec. V.P., C.F.O.	**Transfer Agents:** The Bank of New York, New York, NY

XCEL ENERGY, INC.

Exchange	Symbol	Price	52Wk Range	Yield	P/E
NYS	XEL	$17.18 (3/31/2005)	18.73-15.67	4.83	19.75

*7 Year Price Score 70.11   ***NYSE Composite Index=100**   ***12 Month Price Score 94.08**

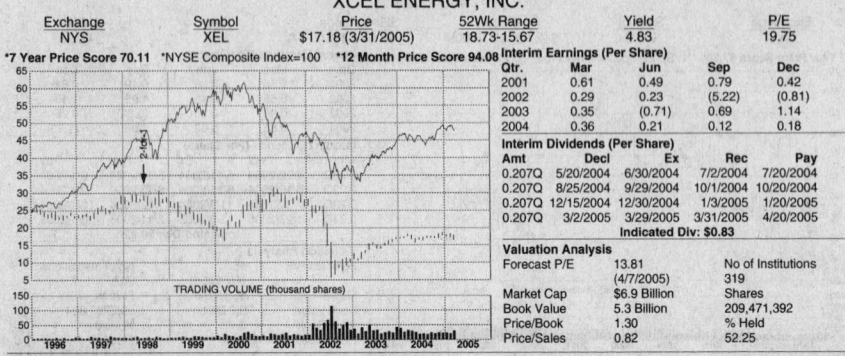

Interim Earnings (Per Share)

Qtr.	Mar	Jun	Sep	Dec
2001	0.61	0.49	0.79	0.42
2002	0.29	0.23	(5.22)	(0.81)
2003	0.35	(0.71)	0.69	1.14
2004	0.36	0.21	0.12	0.18

Interim Dividends (Per Share)

Amt	Decl	Ex	Rec	Pay
0.207Q	5/20/2004	6/30/2004	7/2/2004	7/20/2004
0.207Q	8/25/2004	9/29/2004	10/1/2004	10/20/2004
0.207Q	12/15/2004	12/30/2004	1/3/2005	1/20/2005
0.207Q	3/2/2005	3/29/2005	3/31/2005	4/20/2005

Indicated Div: $0.83

Valuation Analysis

Forecast P/E	13.81	No of Institutions	
	(4/7/2005)	319	
Market Cap	$6.9 Billion	Shares	209,471,392
Book Value	5.3 Billion	% Held	
Price/Book	1.30		52.25
Price/Sales	0.82		

Business Summary: Electricity (MIC: 7.1 SIC: 931 NAIC: 21121)

Xcel Energy is engaged principally in the generation, purchase, transmission, distribution and sale of electricity and in the purchase, transportation, distribution and sale of natural gas. Co.'s directly owned utility subsidiaries comprise its regulated utility operations and they serve electric and natural gas customers in 11 states, as well as provide an interstate natural gas pipeline. Co.'s non-regulated subsidiaries in continuing operations provide the following products and services: engineering, construction and design, broadband telecommunications services, energy management solutions, and investments in rental housing projects that qualify for low-income housing tax credits.

Recent Developments: For the year ended Dec 31 2004, income from continuing operations increased 0.2% to $526,929 thousand from income of $525,840 thousand a year earlier. Net income decreased 42.8% to $355,961 thousand from net income of $622,392 thousand a year earlier. Revenues were $8,345,259 thousand, up 6.2% from $7,859,005 thousand the year before. Operating income was $1,073,216 thousand versus an income of $1,113,013 thousand in the prior year, a decrease of 3.6%. Total direct expense was $6,218,915 thousand versus $5,680,083 thousand in the prior year, an increase of 9.5%. Total indirect expense was $1,053,128 thousand versus $1,065,909 thousand in the prior year, a decrease of 1.2%.

Prospects: Results are being favorably affected by electric sales growth, short-term wholesale markets, and lower depreciation, partially offset by higher legal settlement costs and certain regulatory accruals. Meanwhile, Co. is moving forward with a number of initiatives to grow its business and build long-term earnings value. For instance, Co. initiated the refurbishment of its King Plant as part of its Minnesota Metro Emissions Reduction Plan, received approval from the Colorado Public Utilities Commission to build the 750-megawatt Comanche 3 unit and replaced its Prairie Island Unit 1 steam generators.

Financial Data

(US$ in Thousands)	12/31/2004	12/31/2003	12/31/2002	12/31/2001	12/31/2000	12/31/1999	12/31/1998	12/31/1997
Earnings Per Share	0.87	1.50	(5.82)	2.30	1.54	1.43	1.84	1.61
Cash Flow Per Share	2.04	3.46	4.49	4.62	4.16	4.44	4.66	4.91
Tang Book Value Per Share	12.99	12.95	11.44	17.91	16.32	15.97	15.62	15.27
Dividends Per Share	0.810	0.750	1.125	1.500	1.844	1.445	1.425	1.403
Dividend Payout %	93.10	50.00	...	65.22	119.75	101.05	77.45	87.11
Income Statement								
Total Revenue	8,345,259	7,937,516	9,524,372	15,028,204	11,591,796	2,869,011	2,819,174	2,733,746
EBITDA	1,896,236	1,898,112	(408,656)	2,950,925	2,366,034	...	...	...
Depn & Amortn	772,651	817,434	1,063,897	974,616	858,076	473,863	423,213	398,943
Income Before Taxes	686,515	668,662	(2,306,426)	1,193,910	850,653	...	...	...
Income Taxes	159,586	158,642	(627,985)	336,723	304,865	(61,011)	(40,588)	(48,145)
Net Income	355,961	622,392	(2,217,991)	794,966	526,828	224,336	282,373	237,320
Average Shares	423,334	418,912	382,051	343,742	338,111	153,443	150,743	140,870
Balance Sheet								
Net PPE	14,095,955	13,667,116	18,815,794	21,165,117	15,272,914	4,451,451	4,395,234	4,361,320
Total Assets	20,304,843	20,205,380	27,257,842	28,735,062	21,768,843	9,767,731	7,396,297	7,144,066
Long-Term Obligations	6,493,020	6,518,853	6,550,248	12,117,516	7,583,441	3,453,364	1,851,146	1,878,875
Total Liabilities	14,996,945	14,933,960	22,487,538	22,435,265	16,101,739	7,104,861	4,809,711	4,571,998
Stockholders' Equity	5,307,898	5,271,420	4,770,304	6,299,797	5,667,104	2,662,870	2,586,586	2,572,068
Shares Outstanding	400,461	398,964	398,714	345,801	340,834	153,040	152,696	149,236
Statistical Record								
Return on Assets %	1.75	2.62	N.M.	3.15	3.33	2.61	3.88	3.44
Return on Equity %	6.71	12.40	N.M.	13.29	12.61	8.55	10.95	9.59
EBITDA Margin %	22.72	23.91	N.M.	19.64	20.41	...	...	...
Net Margin %	4.27	7.84	(23.29)	5.29	4.54	7.82	10.02	8.68
PPE Turnover	0.60	0.49	0.48	0.82	1.17	0.65	0.64	0.63
Asset Turnover	0.41	0.33	0.34	0.60	0.73	0.33	0.39	0.40
Debt to Equity	1.22	1.24	1.37	1.92	1.34	1.30	0.72	0.73
Price Range	18.73-15.67	17.34-10.59	28.34-5.66	31.64-24.56	29.75-16.25	27.75-19.50	30.63-25.88	29.38-22.25
P/E Ratio	21.53-18.01	11.56-7.06	...	13.76-10.68	19.32-10.55	19.41-13.64	16.64-14.06	18.25-13.82
Average Yield %	4.67	5.27	6.57	5.32	8.05	6.09	5.10	5.66

Address: 800 Nicollet Mall, Minneapolis, MN 55402
Telephone: (612) 330-5500
Fax: (612) 330-5688

Web Site: www.xcelenergy.com
Officers: Wayne H. Brunetti - Chmn., C.E.O. Richard C. Kelly - Pres., C.O.O.

Auditors: Deloitte & Touche LLP
Investor Contact: 612-215-4559

XEROX CORP

Exchange	Symbol	Price	52Wk Range	Yield	P/E
NYS	XRX	$15.15 (3/31/2005)	17.12-12.66	N/A	17.62

*7 Year Price Score 58.87 *NYSE Composite Index=100 *12 Month Price Score 96.86

Interim Earnings (Per Share)

Qtr.	Mar	Jun	Sep	Dec
2001	0.25	(0.40)	(0.29)	0.31
2002	(0.06)	0.12	0.05	(0.09)
2003	(0.01)	0.09	0.11	0.25
2004	0.25	0.21	0.17	0.23

Interim Dividends (Per Share)

Dividend Payment Suspended

Valuation Analysis

Forecast P/E	16.43	No of Institutions	
	(4/7/2005)	379	
Market Cap	$14.5 Billion	Shares	
Book Value	7.1 Billion	780,898,560	
Price/Book	2.03	% Held	
Price/Sales	0.92	81.57	

Business Summary: Consumer Accessories (MIC: 4.6 SIC: 861 NAIC: 33315)

Xerox is engaged in the developing, manufacturing, marketing and servicing of document equipment, software, solutions and services. Co. is also engaged in computer laser printing, which combines computer, laser, communications and xerographic technologies. Co. distributes its products in the Western Hemisphere through divisions and wholly-owned subsidiaries, and in Europe, Africa, the Middle East, India and parts of Asia through Xerox Limited. In the Pacific Rim, Australia and New Zealand, Co.'s products are distributed by Fuji Xerox Co. Ltd., an unconsolidated joint venture owned 75.0% by Fuji Photo Film Co., Ltd. and 25.0% by Xerox Limited, as of Dec 31 2003.

Recent Developments: For the year ended Dec 31 2004, income from continuing operations increased 115.6% to $776,000 thousand from income of $360,000 thousand a year earlier. Net income increased 138.6% to $859,000 thousand from net income of $360,000 thousand a year earlier. Revenues were $15,722,000 thousand, up 0.1% from $15,701,000 thousand the year before. Total direct expense was $8,994,000 thousand versus $8,747,000 thousand in the prior year, an increase of 2.8%. Total indirect expense was $5,467,000 thousand versus $6,068,000 thousand in the prior year, a decrease of 9.9%.

Prospects: Co.'s near-term prospects appear favorable, reflecting increase sales, higher demand for document services and improved operating efficiency. Also, Co. is benefiting from 40 new products announced in 2004, the accelerated growth of Xerox Global Services, designed to help customers streamline work processes, and growing demand for its Xerox iGen3® digital color production press, DocuColor® systems and Phaser® solid ink printers. Going forward, Co. will look to strengthen its operations through its focus on reducing costs and debt and generating significant operating cash flow. For the first quarter of 2005, Co. expects earnings to range from $0.17 to $0.20 per share.

Financial Data

(US$ in Thousands)	12/31/2004	12/31/2003	12/31/2002	12/31/2001	12/31/2000	12/31/1999	12/31/1998	12/31/1997
Earnings Per Share	0.86	0.36	0.02	(0.12)	(0.44)	1.96	0.52	2.02
Cash Flow Per Share	2.09	2.44	2.57	2.22	(0.99)	1.84	(1.77)	0.72
Tang Book Value Per Share	4.29	1.57	N.M.	N.M.	N.M.	4.34	4.19	4.37
Dividends Per Share	...	...	...	0.050	0.650	0.800	0.720	0.640
Dividend Payout %	...	...	...	...	...	40.82	138.46	31.68
Income Statement								
Total Revenue	15,722,000	15,701,000	15,849,000	17,008,000	18,701,000	19,228,000	19,449,000	18,166,000
EBITDA	1,518,000	1,041,000	1,037,000	1,518,000	564,000	2,971,000	1,584,000	2,880,000
Depn & Amortn	553,000	605,000	785,000	1,153,000	948,000	935,000	821,000	739,000
Income Before Taxes	965,000	436,000	252,000	365,000	(384,000)	2,036,000	763,000	2,141,000
Income Taxes	340,000	134,000	60,000	485,000	(109,000)	631,000	207,000	728,000
Net Income	859,000	360,000	91,000	(71,000)	(257,000)	1,424,000	395,000	1,452,000
Average Shares	1,046,947	828,387	807,444	704,181	667,581	737,400	675,000	722,000
Balance Sheet								
Current Assets	10,928,000	10,335,000	11,019,000	12,600,000	13,022,000	11,985,000	12,475,000	10,766,000
Total Assets	24,884,000	24,591,000	25,458,000	27,689,000	29,475,000	28,814,000	30,024,000	27,732,000
Current Liabilities	6,300,000	7,569,000	7,787,000	10,260,000	6,268,000	7,950,000	8,507,000	7,692,000
Long-Term Obligations	7,050,000	6,930,000	9,794,000	10,128,000	15,404,000	11,044,000	11,003,000	8,946,000
Total Liabilities	17,751,000	19,912,000	21,283,000	23,639,000	24,745,000	22,818,000	24,224,000	21,879,000
Stockholders' Equity	7,133,000	4,679,000	2,401,000	2,290,000	3,919,000	5,281,000	5,174,000	4,929,000
Shares Outstanding	955,997	793,884	738,273	722,314	665,156	665,156	657,000	652,000
Statistical Record								
Return on Assets %	3.46	1.44	0.34	N.M.	N.M.	4.84	1.37	5.32
Return on Equity %	14.50	10.17	3.88	N.M.	N.M.	27.24	7.82	31.58
EBITDA Margin %	9.66	6.63	6.54	8.93	3.02	15.45	8.14	15.85
Net Margin %	5.46	2.29	0.57	N.M.	N.M.	7.41	2.03	7.99
Asset Turnover	0.63	0.63	0.60	0.60	0.64	0.65	0.67	0.67
Current Ratio	1.73	1.37	1.42	1.23	2.08	1.51	1.47	1.40
Debt to Equity	0.99	1.48	4.08	4.42	3.93	2.09	2.13	1.81
Price Range	17.12-12.66	13.80-8.05	11.45-4.30	11.35-4.95	29.75-4.44	63.69-19.88	60.44-34.19	43.66-26.13
P/E Ratio	19.91-14.72	38.33-22.36	572.50-215.00	...	...	32.49-10.14	116.23-65.75	21.61-12.93
Average Yield %	...	...	...	0.63	3.55	1.68	1.47	1.83

Address: 800 Long Ridge Road, Stamford, CT 06904 **Telephone:** (203) 968-3000 **Fax:** (203) 968-4566	**Web Site:** www.xerox.com **Officers:** Anne M. Mulcahy - Chmn., C.E.O. Carlos Pascual - Exec. V.P., Pres., Developing Markets Oper.	**Auditors:** PricewaterhouseCoopers LLP **Investor Contact:** 800-828-6396

XL CAPITAL LTD.

Exchange	Symbol	Price	52Wk Range	Yield	P/E
NYS	XL	$72.37 (3/31/2005)	79.56-67.62	2.76	8.90

*7 Year Price Score 88.02   ***NYSE Composite Index=100**   ***12 Month Price Score 93.53**

TRADING VOLUME (thousand shares)

Interim Earnings (Per Share)

Qtr.	Mar	Jun	Sep	Dec
2003	1.74	2.51	0.71	(2.29)
2004	3.26	2.62	0.16	2.09

Interim Dividends (Per Share)

Amt	Decl	Ex	Rec	Pay
0.49Q	4/30/2004	6/3/2004	6/7/2004	6/30/2004
0.49Q	7/28/2004	9/1/2004	9/6/2004	9/30/2004
0.49Q	10/29/2004	12/2/2004	12/6/2004	12/31/2004
0.50Q	1/14/2005	3/8/2005	3/10/2005	3/31/2005

Indicated Div: $2.00

Valuation Analysis

Forecast P/E	7.35 (4/7/2005)	No of Institutions N/A
Market Cap	$10.1 Billion	Shares
Book Value	7.7 Billion	N/A
Price/Book	1.30	% Held
Price/Sales	1.00	N/A

Business Summary: Insurance (MIC: 8.2 SIC: 351 NAIC: 24126)

XL Capital is a holding company organized under the laws of the Cayman Islands. Co. provides commercial property and casualty insurance products. Products are divided into two categories: risk management products and specialty lines products. Risk management products include umbrella liability, product recall, U.S. workers' compensation, property catastrophe and primary master property and liability coverages. Specialty lines products include professional liability insurance, environmental liability insurance, political risk insurance, aviation and satellite insurance, marine and offshore energy insurance, surety, specie, equine, and other insurance coverages including program business.

Recent Developments: For the year ended Dec 31 2004, net income more than doubled to $1.17 billion compared with $412.0 million in the previous year. Results for 2004 and 2003 included net realized gains on investments were $246.5 million versus $120.2 million, respectively. Total revenues advanced 25.3% to $10.03 billion from $8.00 billion the year before. Net premiums earned increased 22.8% to $8.39 billion from $6.83 billion a year earlier. Revenues included net realized and unrealized gains of $324.6 million in 2004 and $92.7 million in 2003. Net investment income jumped 27.6% to $995.0 million from $779.6 million in the prior year.

Prospects: Outside of the adverse impact of catastrophe-related losses of $550.0 million incurred in 2004, Co.'s underlying business fundamentals remain strong. Co. noted that it is seeing healthy year-over-year increases in net invested assets, cash flow from operations, net investment income and book value per ordinary share. Moreover, Co. is benefiting from the introduction of several strategic initiatives over the last twelve months, including the launch of both its global whole account commercial property program and its primary Directors and Officers liability product in Europe, and the start-up of its U.S. primary casualty operations.

Financial Data

(US$ in Thousands)	12/31/2004	12/31/2003	12/31/2002	12/31/2001	12/31/2000	12/31/1999	11/30/1998	11/30/1997
Earnings Per Share	8.13	2.69	2.88	(4.55)	4.03	3.62	6.20	7.84
Cash Flow Per Share	31.62	25.06	22.39	11.35	2.10	...	...	...
Income Statement								
Premium Income	8,549,533	6,969,150	5,989,810	3,475,522	...	...	...	...
Total Revenue	10,028,460	8,017,008	6,578,049	4,056,759	2,717,459	2,510,987	1,217,648	1,159,026
Income Before Taxes	1,112,169	457,071	457,565	(758,636)	451,089	431,159	593,852	682,016
Income Taxes	84,526	30,049	22,647	(189,914)	(56,356)	(39,570)	5,363	5,085
Net Income	1,166,613	411,979	405,571	(576,135)	506,352	470,509	587,663	676,961
Average Shares	138,582	138,187	137,388	126,676	125,697	130,304	94,785	86,314
Balance Sheet								
Total Assets	49,014,632	40,764,215	35,647,369	27,963,075	16,941,952	15,090,912	10,108,650	6,088,462
Total Liabilities	41,275,937	33,827,300	29,077,780	22,525,891	11,368,284	9,513,834	5,290,770	3,609,332
Stockholders' Equity	7,738,695	6,936,915	6,569,589	5,437,184	5,573,668	5,577,078	4,817,880	2,479,130
Shares Outstanding	138,932	137,343	136,063	134,734	125,020	127,807	111,803	84,407
Statistical Record								
Return on Assets %	2.59	1.08	1.28	N.M.	3.15	3.44	7.26	...
Return on Equity %	15.86	6.10	6.76	N.M.	9.06	8.34	16.11	...
Net Margin %	11.63	5.14	6.17	(14.20)	18.63	18.74	48.26	58.41
Price Range	81.54-67.62	88.00-64.57	97.38-61.00	96.12-62.00	88.56-39.56	75.19-42.19	83.25-59.06	64.00-36.50
P/E Ratio	10.03-8.32	32.71-24.00	33.81-21.18	...	21.98-9.82	20.77-11.65	13.43-9.53	8.16-4.66

Address: XL House, One Bermudiana Road, Hamilton **Telephone:** (441) 292 8515 **Fax:** (441)-292-5280	**Web Site:** www.xlcapital.com **Officers:** Brian M. O'Hara - Pres., C.E.O. Fiona E. Luck - Exec. V.P., Global Head, Corp. Serv., Asst. Sec.	**Auditors:** PricewaterhouseCoopers LLP

XTO ENERGY, INC.

Exchange	Symbol	Price	52Wk Range	Yield	P/E
NYS	XTO	$32.84 (3/31/2005)	34.25-18.56	0.61	21.75

*7 Year Price Score 221.67 *NYSE Composite Index=100 *12 Month Price Score 121.59

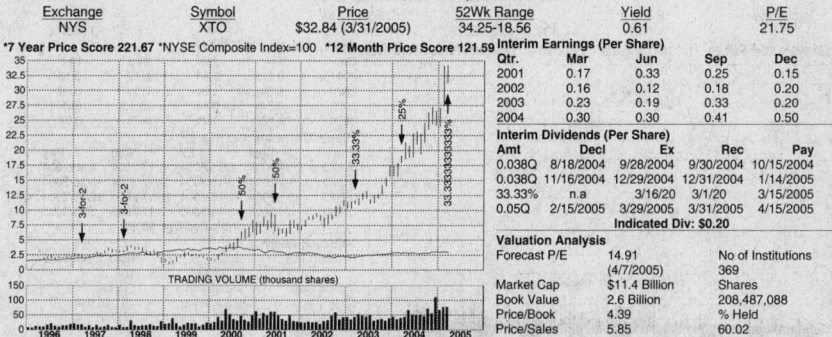

Interim Earnings (Per Share)

Qtr.	Mar	Jun	Sep	Dec
2001	0.17	0.33	0.25	0.15
2002	0.16	0.12	0.18	0.20
2003	0.23	0.19	0.33	0.20
2004	0.30	0.30	0.41	0.50

Interim Dividends (Per Share)

Amt	Decl	Ex	Rec	Pay
0.038Q	8/18/2004	9/28/2004	9/30/2004	10/15/2004
0.038Q	11/16/2004	12/29/2004	12/31/2004	1/14/2005
33.33%	n.a	3/16/20	3/1/20	3/15/2005
0.05Q	2/15/2005	3/29/2005	3/31/2005	4/15/2005

Indicated Div: $0.20

Valuation Analysis

Forecast P/E	14.91	No of Institutions
	(4/7/2005)	369
Market Cap	$11.4 Billion	Shares
Book Value	2.6 Billion	208,487,088
Price/Book	4.39	% Held
Price/Sales	5.85	60.02

Business Summary: Oil and Gas (MIC: 14.2 SIC: 311 NAIC: 11111)

XTO Energy Inc. is engaged in the acquisition, development, exploitation and exploration of producing oil and gas properties, and in the production, processing, marketing and transportation of oil and natural gas. Co.'s proved reserves are concentrated in the following areas: the Eastern Region, located in East Texas and North Louisiana; the San Juan and Raton Basins of northern New Mexico and southern Colorado; the Arkoma Basin of Arkansas and Oklahoma; the Hugoton Field of Oklahoma and Kansas; the Anadarko Basin of Oklahoma; the Green River Basin of Wyoming; the Permian Basin of West Texas and southeastern New Mexico; and the Middle Ground Shoal Field of Alaska's Cook Inlet.

Recent Developments: For the year ended Dec 31 2004, net income increased 76.2% to $507,882 thousand from net income of $288,279 thousand a year earlier. Revenues were $1,947,601 thousand, up 63.7% from $1,189,555 thousand the year before. Operating income was $919,281 thousand versus an income of $501,664 thousand in the prior year, an increase of 83.2%. Total direct expense was $245,892 thousand versus $164,864 thousand in the prior year, an increase of 49.1%. Total indirect expense was $782,428 thousand versus $523,027 thousand in the prior year, an increase of 49.6%.

Prospects: With improved production and cash flow, Co. enters 2005 with a promising outlook for the year. Expanded drilling activity and producing property acquisitions are contributing to Co.'s production growth. For instance, gas production for the 2004 was a solid 835.0 million cubic feet per day (Mmcfpd), up 25.0% from 2003 daily production of 668.0 Mmcfpd. Oil production averaged a record 22,696 barrels per day, a 75.0% increase from 2003 production of 12,943 barrels per day, and natural gas liquids production rose 16.0% to 7,484 barrels per day. Going forward, Co. expects to grow production to a range of 21.0% to 23.0% in 2005.

Financial Data

(US$ in Thousands)	12/31/2004	12/31/2003	12/31/2002	12/31/2001	12/31/2000	12/31/1999	12/31/1998	12/31/1997
Earnings Per Share	1.51	0.95	0.66	0.90	0.46	0.19	(0.33)	0.12
Cash Flow Per Share	3.65	2.65	1.77	1.99	1.59	0.57	(0.21)	0.49
Tang Book Value Per Share	7.49	4.69	3.22	2.99	1.82	1.02	0.67	0.72
Dividends Per Share	0.090	0.024	0.018	0.017	0.010	0.008	0.032	0.029
Dividend Payout %	5.96	2.52	2.73	1.83	2.15	4.21	...	24.86
Income Statement								
Total Revenue	1,947,601	1,189,555	810,163	838,748	600,851	341,295	249,486	200,672
EBITDA	1,326,030	792,285	544,413	665,280	385,153	247,183	(74,123)	60,245
Depn & Amortn	406,749	284,006	204,109	154,322	129,807	112,364	83,560	47,721
Income Before Taxes	825,620	444,510	286,749	455,351	176,432	70,605	(105,570)	39,201
Income Taxes	317,738	158,000	100,690	161,952	59,380	23,965	(35,851)	13,517
Net Income	507,882	288,279	186,059	248,816	116,993	46,743	(69,719)	25,684
Average Shares	335,681	303,751	281,086	276,939	252,347	246,923	218,779	201,704
Balance Sheet								
Current Assets	436,965	261,163	244,790	239,367	193,437	113,492	137,578	52,162
Total Assets	6,110,372	3,611,134	2,648,193	2,132,327	1,591,904	1,477,081	1,207,594	788,455
Current Liabilities	500,966	320,557	285,896	201,843	218,751	74,218	99,588	54,893
Long-Term Obligations	2,042,732	1,252,000	1,118,170	856,000	769,000	991,100	921,000	539,000
Total Liabilities	3,510,999	2,145,492	1,740,407	1,311,277	1,094,537	1,199,264	1,030,143	618,212
Stockholders' Equity	2,599,373	1,465,642	907,786	821,050	497,367	277,817	177,451	170,243
Shares Outstanding	347,178	312,335	282,170	275,043	258,512	244,439	223,629	197,245
Statistical Record								
Return on Assets %	10.42	9.21	7.78	13.36	7.60	3.48	N.M.	3.92
Return on Equity %	24.92	24.29	21.52	37.74	30.10	20.53	N.M.	16.42
EBITDA Margin %	68.09	66.60	67.20	79.32	64.10	72.43	N.M.	30.02
Net Margin %	26.08	24.23	22.97	29.67	19.47	13.70	N.M.	12.80
Asset Turnover	0.40	0.38	0.34	0.45	0.39	0.25	0.25	0.31
Current Ratio	0.87	0.81	0.86	1.19	0.88	1.53	1.38	0.95
Debt to Equity	0.79	0.85	1.23	1.04	1.55	3.57	5.19	3.17
Price Range	27.26-15.61	17.49-10.33	11.71-6.63	9.57-5.53	8.42-1.51	2.95-0.97	4.14-1.14	3.74-1.97
P/E Ratio	18.05-10.34	18.41-10.87	17.74-10.04	10.64-6.15	18.31-3.29	15.53-5.09	...	31.20-16.39
Average Yield %	0.43	0.19	0.20	0.23	0.24	0.39	1.03	1.08

Address: 810 Houston Street, Fort Worth, TX 76102	Web Site: www.xtoenergy.com	Auditors: KPMG LLP
Telephone: (817) 870-2800	**Officers:** Bob R. Simpson - Chmn., C.E.O. Steffen E. Palko - Vice-Chmn., Pres.	
Fax: (817) 870-1671		

YORK INTERNATIONAL CORP.

Exchange	Symbol	Price	52Wk Range	Yield	P/E
NYS	YRK	$39.18 (3/31/2005)	42.95-29.99	2.04	19.99

*7 Year Price Score 94.00   *NYSE Composite Index=100   *12 Month Price Score 99.24

Interim Earnings (Per Share)

Qtr.	Mar	Jun	Sep	Dec
2001	(0.23)	0.84	0.42	0.13
2002	(0.38)	1.21	0.65	0.54
2003	(0.34)	0.48	(0.13)	(0.10)
2004	(0.10)	0.91	0.75	0.37

Interim Dividends (Per Share)

Amt	Decl	Ex	Rec	Pay
0.20Q	6/4/2004	6/15/2004	6/17/2004	6/30/2004
0.20Q	9/3/2004	9/15/2004	9/17/2004	9/30/2004
0.20Q	12/1/2004	12/15/2004	12/17/2004	12/31/2004
0.20Q	3/4/2005	3/15/2005	3/17/2005	3/31/2005

Indicated Div: $0.80

Valuation Analysis

Forecast P/E	15.32	No of Institutions	
	(4/7/2005)	168	
Market Cap	$1.6 Billion	Shares	
Book Value	878.9 Million	43,076,044	
Price/Book	1.86	% Held	
Price/Sales	0.36	N/A	

Business Summary: Purpose Machinery (MIC: 11.13 SIC: 585 NAIC: 33415)

York International is a full-line, global provider of heating, ventilating, air conditioning, and refrigeration (HVAC&R) products and services. The Global Applied business is comprised of three geographic regions: the Americas, Europe, Middle East, Africa, and Asia. Global Applied service businesses sell replacement parts, replacement equipment, and controls, and deliver various services and service solutions. Unitary Products Group produces heating and air conditioning solutions designed for use in residential and light commercial applications and distributes proprietary and non-proprietary parts to the aftermarket. Bristol Compressors manufactures reciprocating and scroll compressors.

Recent Developments: For the year ended Dec 31 2004, net income was $81,579 thousand versus net loss of $3,998 thousand a year earlier. Revenues were $9,020,286 thousand, up 10.6% from $8,152,108 thousand the year before. Operating income was $128,181 thousand versus an income of $56,021 thousand in the prior year, an increase of 128.8%. Total direct expense was $7,358,652 thousand versus $6,585,608 thousand in the prior year, an increase of 11.7%. Total indirect expense was $702,636 thousand versus $727,229 thousand in the prior year, a decrease of 3.4%.

Prospects: For 2005, Co. expects stable to improving markets, with the exception of Europe. Co. is seeing lower levels of quoting activity in Europe as a result of deteriorating macroeconomic indicators in this region. Co. anticipates strong growth in China and the Middle East and modest growth in the Americas. Co. anticipates material cost increases of approximately $100.0 million in 2005. A majority of the incremental material cost increases in 2005 will be seen in the first half of the year. These factors resulted in an expected first quarter loss in the range of $0.25 to $0.35 per share. Co. reiterated its full-year guidance to achieve earnings in the range of $2.60 to $2.90 per share.

Financial Data (US$ in Thousands)	12/31/2004	12/31/2003	12/31/2002	12/31/2001	12/31/2000	12/31/1999	12/31/1998	12/31/1997
Earnings Per Share	1.96	(0.10)	(2.47)	1.17	2.78	1.91	3.36	1.10
Cash Flow Per Share	3.13	4.07	6.65	6.54	3.25	1.84	5.77	3.61
Tang Book Value Per Share	7.10	5.16	3.68	2.24	1.44	N.M.	9.84	7.44
Dividends Per Share	0.800	0.600	0.600	0.600	0.600	0.600	0.480	0.480
Dividend Payout %	40.82	...	...	51.28	21.58	31.41	14.29	43.64
Income Statement								
Total Revenue	4,510,143	4,076,054	3,843,373	3,930,677	3,883,207	3,866,615	3,289,201	3,193,657
EBITDA	216,337	135,559	220,311	190,794	294,114	267,522	303,674	188,098
Depn & Amortn	79,587	73,956	64,935	86,679	91,558	88,290	74,844	68,754
Income Before Taxes	94,977	14,068	106,891	36,965	120,969	118,082	187,303	78,468
Income Taxes	13,398	2,653	25,715	(9,024)	14,362	41,303	50,810	31,075
Net Income	81,579	(3,998)	(98,260)	45,989	106,607	75,882	136,493	47,393
Average Shares	41,623	40,206	39,770	39,147	38,281	39,832	40,622	43,040
Balance Sheet								
Current Assets	1,606,642	1,330,795	1,275,247	1,250,469	1,457,809	1,490,369	1,310,533	1,221,620
Total Assets	3,010,415	2,673,135	2,506,122	2,572,509	2,774,211	2,874,539	2,106,538	1,996,298
Current Liabilities	1,204,832	968,301	838,659	777,639	918,008	1,005,135	789,479	686,497
Long-Term Obligations	545,468	582,027	618,224	724,378	831,354	854,494	362,724	452,344
Total Liabilities	2,131,552	1,896,735	1,823,308	1,833,075	2,025,235	2,142,609	1,375,739	1,350,013
Stockholders' Equity	878,863	776,400	682,814	739,434	748,976	731,930	730,799	646,285
Shares Outstanding	41,771	40,828	39,651	39,222	38,372	38,362	39,995	40,628
Statistical Record								
Return on Assets %	2.86	N.M.	N.M.	1.72	3.76	3.05	6.65	2.33
Return on Equity %	9.83	N.M.	N.M.	6.18	14.36	10.38	19.82	6.64
EBITDA Margin %	4.80	3.33	5.73	4.85	7.57	6.92	9.23	5.89
Net Margin %	1.81	N.M.	N.M.	1.17	2.75	1.96	4.15	1.48
Asset Turnover	1.58	1.57	1.51	1.47	1.37	1.55	1.60	1.57
Current Ratio	1.33	1.37	1.52	1.61	1.59	1.48	1.66	1.78
Debt to Equity	0.62	0.75	0.91	0.98	1.11	1.17	0.50	0.70
Price Range	42.95-29.99	40.74-18.82	38.70-21.94	39.37-26.94	30.69-18.13	46.25-21.19	52.50-28.00	55.88-38.63
P/E Ratio	21.91-15.30	...	...	33.65-23.03	11.04-6.52	24.21-11.09	15.63-8.33	50.80-35.11
Average Yield %	2.20	2.09	1.87	1.84	2.42	1.68	1.16	1.04

Address: 631 South Richland Avenue, York, PA 17403 Telephone: (717) 771-7890 Fax: (717) 771-7381	Web Site: www.york.com Officers: C. David Myers - Pres., C.E.O. Iain A. Campbell - V.P., Pres., York Americas	Auditors: KPMG LLP Investor Contact: 717-771-6183

YUM! BRANDS, INC.

Exchange	Symbol	Price	52Wk Range	Yield	P/E
NYS	YUM	$51.81 (3/31/2005)	53.19-35.72	0.77	21.41

*7 Year Price Score 138.30 *NYSE Composite Index=100 ***12 Month Price Score 108.53**

Interim Earnings (Per Share)

Qtr.	Mar	Jun	Aug	Dec
2001	0.29	0.38	0.41	0.54
2002	0.40	0.45	0.47	0.56
2003	0.39	0.40	0.53	0.70
2004	0.47	0.58	0.61	0.76

Interim Dividends (Per Share)

Amt	Decl	Ex	Rec	Pay
0.10Q	5/20/2004	7/14/2004	7/16/2004	8/6/2004
0.10Q	9/24/2004	10/13/2004	10/15/2004	11/5/2004
0.10Q	1/4/2005	1/12/2005	1/14/2005	2/4/2005
0.10Q	3/17/2005	4/13/2005	4/15/2005	5/6/2005
			Indicated Div: $0.40	

Valuation Analysis

Forecast P/E	19.58	No of Institutions	
	(4/7/2005)	421	
Market Cap	$15.0 Billion	Shares	
Book Value	1.6 Billion	228,592,144	
Price/Book	9.42	% Held	
Price/Sales	1.67	78.45	

Business Summary: Hospitality & Tourism (MIC: 5.1 SIC: 812 NAIC: 22211)

Yum! Brands operates and franchises KFC, Pizza Hut, Taco Bell, Long John Silver's and A&W All-American Food restaurants. Each of Co.'s operating restaurant divisions is engaged in the operation, development, franchising and licensing of a system of both traditional and non-traditional quick-service-restaurant units. Non-traditional units include express units and kiosks, which have a more limited menu and operate in non-traditional locations like airports, gas and convenience stores and colleges. Co. owned, franchised and licensed nearly 33,000 restaurants in more than 100 countries and territories at Dec 25 2004.

Recent Developments: For the year ended Dec 25 2004, net income increased 19.9% to $740 million from net income of $617 million a year earlier. Revenues were $9,011 million, up 7.5% from $8,380 million the year before. Operating income was $1,155 million versus an income of $1,059 million in the prior year, an increase of 9.1%. Total direct expense was $6,833 million versus $6,337 million in the prior year, an increase of 7.8%. Total indirect expense was $1,023 million versus $986 million in the prior year, an increase of 3.8%.

Prospects: Co. is experiencing strong revenue and earnings growth fueled by continuing profitable international expansion including dynamic growth in China, combined with another strong performance from Taco Bell in the U.S. Co. expects earnings per share to grow at least 10.0% each year with the continued execution of its four key strategies: building dominant restaurant brands in China, driving profitable international expansion, improving restaurant operations and multibranding category-leading brands. For full-year 2005, Co. expects earnings to be approximately $2.60 per share before special items.

Financial Data
(US$ in Thousands)

	12/25/2004	12/27/2003	12/28/2002	12/29/2001	12/30/2000	12/25/1999	12/26/1998	12/27/1997
Earnings Per Share	2.42	2.02	1.88	1.62	1.39	1.96	1.42	(0.36)
Cash Flow Per Share	3.90	3.60	3.69	2.84	1.64	1.85	2.21	...
Tang Book Value Per Share	2.40	0.83	N.M.	N.M.	...	...	...	...
Dividends Per Share	0.200	...	...	...	...	...	...	...
Dividend Payout %	8.26	...	...	...	...	...	...	...
Income Statement								
Total Revenue	9,011,000	8,380,000	7,757,000	6,953,000	7,093,000	7,822,000	8,468,000	9,681,000
EBITDA	1,603,000	1,460,000	1,400,000	1,245,000	1,214,000	1,626,000	1,445,000	777,000
Depn & Amortn	448,000	401,000	370,000	354,000	354,000	386,000	417,000	536,000
Income Before Taxes	1,026,000	886,000	858,000	733,000	684,000	1,038,000	756,000	(35,000)
Income Taxes	286,000	268,000	275,000	241,000	271,000	411,000	311,000	76,000
Net Income	740,000	617,000	583,000	492,000	413,000	627,000	445,000	(111,000)
Average Shares	305,000	306,000	310,000	304,000	298,000	320,000	312,000	...
Balance Sheet								
Current Assets	747,000	806,000	730,000	547,000	688,000	486,000	625,000	683,000
Total Assets	5,696,000	5,620,000	5,400,000	4,388,000	4,149,000	3,961,000	4,531,000	5,098,000
Current Liabilities	1,376,000	1,461,000	1,520,000	1,805,000	1,216,000	1,298,000	1,473,000	1,579,000
Long-Term Obligations	1,731,000	2,056,000	2,299,000	1,552,000	2,397,000	2,391,000	3,436,000	4,551,000
Total Liabilities	4,101,000	4,500,000	4,806,000	4,284,000	4,471,000	4,521,000	5,694,000	6,718,000
Stockholders' Equity	1,595,000	1,120,000	594,000	104,000	(322,000)	(560,000)	(1,163,000)	(1,620,000)
Shares Outstanding	290,000	292,000	294,000	292,000	294,000	302,000	306,000	304,000
Statistical Record								
Return on Assets %	13.11	11.23	11.95	11.56	10.02	14.81	9.27	...
Return on Equity %	54.66	72.19	167.51	...	...	...	...	...
EBITDA Margin %	17.79	17.42	18.05	17.91	17.12	20.79	17.06	8.03
Net Margin %	8.21	7.36	7.52	7.08	5.82	8.02	5.26	N.M.
Asset Turnover	1.60	1.53	1.59	1.63	1.72	1.85	1.76	...
Current Ratio	0.54	0.55	0.48	0.30	0.57	0.37	0.42	0.43
Debt to Equity	1.09	1.84	3.87	14.92	...	...	...	...
Price Range	46.95-32.56	35.13-22.06	32.89-21.31	26.54-15.97	19.31-11.88	36.75-17.88	24.75-12.97	17.66-14.16
P/E Ratio	19.40-13.45	17.39-10.92	17.49-11.34	16.38-9.86	13.89-8.54	18.75-9.12	17.43-9.13	...
Average Yield %	0.51	...	...	...	...	...	...	...

Address: 1441 Gardiner Lane, Louisville, KY 40213 **Telephone:** (502) 874-8300 **Fax:** (502) 454-2410	**Web Site:** www.yum.com **Officers:** David C. Novak - Chmn., Pres., C.E.O. Christian L. Campbell - Sr. V.P., Sec., Gen. Couns., Chief Franchise Policy Officer	**Auditors:** KPMG LLP **Investor Contact:** 502-874-2543

ZENITH NATIONAL INSURANCE CORP.

Exchange	Symbol	Price	52Wk Range	Yield	P/E
NYS	ZNT	$51.86 (3/31/2005)	51.86-37.40	2.55	10.23

*7 Year Price Score 135.60 ***NYSE Composite Index=100** ***12 Month Price Score 101.48**

TRADING VOLUME (thousand shares)

Interim Earnings (Per Share)

Qtr.	Mar	Jun	Sep	Dec
2001	(0.01)	0.16	(1.10)	(0.41)
2002	0.15	0.34	0.46	(0.41)
2003	0.62	0.97	0.85	0.93
2004	1.09	1.06	1.09	1.83

Interim Dividends (Per Share)

Amt	Decl	Ex	Rec	Pay
0.28Q	5/26/2004	7/28/2004	7/30/2004	8/13/2004
0.28Q	9/2/2004	10/27/2004	10/29/2004	11/12/2004
0.28Q	12/2/2004	1/27/2005	1/31/2005	2/14/2005
0.33Q	2/10/2005	4/27/2005	4/29/2005	5/13/2005
			Indicated Div: $1.32	

Valuation Analysis

Forecast P/E	N/A	No of Institutions
		110
Market Cap	$1.0 Billion	Shares
Book Value	502.1 Million	15,518,960
Price/Book	2.00	% Held
Price/Sales	0.96	79.11

Business Summary: Insurance (MIC: 8.2 SIC: 331 NAIC: 24126)

Zenith National Insurance is a holding company that owns, directly or indirectly, 100.0% of the outstanding stock of Zenith Insurance Company; ZNAT Insurance Company; Zenith Star Insurance Company; Zenith of Nevada, Inc.; and Zenith National Insurance Capital Trust I. Through its subsidiaries Co. is engaged in the property-casualty insurance business. Workers' compensation is Co.'s main insurance activity, supplemented by a smaller-assumed reinsurance operation. In addition, Co. maintains a portfolio of investments, principally in fixed-maturity securities, funded by the cash flows from its insurance operations and capital.

Recent Developments: For the year ended Dec 31 2004, income from continuing operations increased 78.8% to $117,714 thousand from income of $65,846 thousand a year earlier. Net income increased 77.6% to $119,000 thousand from net income of $67,000 thousand a year earlier. Revenues were $1,044,880 thousand, up 23.0% from $849,335 thousand the year before. Net premiums earned were $944,425 thousand versus $773,799 thousand in the prior year, an increase of 22.1%. Net investment income rose 10.3% to $61,876 thousand from $56,103 thousand a year ago.

Prospects: Co. premium growth reflects the interaction of an increase in the number of policies and a change in net rates, experience modifications and payrolls. Co. estimates that the majority of the growth in premiums is due to rate changes and the balance is from its growth in payroll and policies. At year-end 2004, there were 43,400 policies in-force, up 4.6% from the prior year. Co. offers guaranteed cost, deductible, dividend and retro plans. Co.'s rates in California are expected to be lower in 2005 due to recently enacted reform legislation and favorable inflation trends, but at amounts still sufficient to cover the estimated loss cost trends and to provide a reasonable underwriting profit.

Financial Data
(US$ in Thousands)

	12/31/2004	12/31/2003	12/31/2002	12/31/2001	12/31/2000	12/31/1999	12/31/1998	12/31/1997
Earnings Per Share	5.07	3.38	0.54	(1.35)	(2.72)	3.15	1.11	1.57
Cash Flow Per Share	18.01	15.09	7.66	4.81	(2.73)	(3.01)	(2.77)	1.52
Tang Book Value Per Share	24.84	19.16	15.77	15.15	16.47	19.32	18.73	19.66
Dividends Per Share	1.090	1.000	1.000	1.000	1.000	1.000	1.000	1.000
Dividend Payout %	21.50	29.59	185.19	N.M.	N.M.	31.75	90.09	63.69
Income Statement								
Premium Income	944,425	773,799	557,055	476,876	338,752	369,403	529,855	488,721
Total Revenue	1,044,880	849,335	602,235	622,046	459,569	492,108	636,779	600,480
Benefits & Claims	628,763	537,922	442,051	432,290	336,962	360,172	382,890	348,165
Income Before Taxes	173,546	96,664	(1,261)	(35,539)	(72,309)	83,067	28,835	43,478
Income Taxes	57,213	33,664	(914)	(11,739)	(24,516)	28,967	9,735	15,378
Net Income	119,000	67,000	10,200	(23,800)	(46,800)	54,100	19,100	28,100
Average Shares	24,464	20,183	18,895	17,765	17,269	17,172	17,158	17,886
Balance Sheet								
Total Assets	2,414,655	2,023,704	1,615,113	1,540,059	1,472,190	1,573,786	1,818,726	1,252,156
Total Liabilities	1,912,508	1,640,458	1,298,089	1,171,779	1,096,796	1,145,830	1,398,433	890,290
Stockholders' Equity	502,147	383,246	317,024	302,611	309,776	354,559	346,952	361,866
Shares Outstanding	19,371	18,910	18,768	18,553	17,443	17,150	17,148	17,819
Statistical Record								
Return on Assets %	5.35	3.68	0.65	N.M.	N.M.	3.19	1.24	2.25
Return on Equity %	26.81	19.14	3.29	N.M.	N.M.	15.42	5.39	8.04
Loss Ratio %	66.58	69.52	79.36	90.65	99.47	97.50	72.26	71.24
Net Margin %	11.39	7.89	1.69	(3.83)	(10.18)	10.99	3.00	4.68
Price Range	51.05-32.10	32.65-19.33	32.24-23.30	30.30-23.10	29.44-18.94	26.69-19.31	30.44-22.94	28.69-24.88
P/E Ratio	10.07-6.33	9.66-5.72	59.70-43.15	N/A	N/A	8.47-6.13	27.42-20.66	18.27-15.84
Average Yield %	2.55	3.77	3.55	3.66	4.37	4.38	3.72	3.72

Address: 21255 Califa Street, Woodland Hills, CA 91367-5021 **Telephone:** (818) 713-1000 **Fax:** (818) 713-0177	**Web Site:** www.thezenith.com **Officers:** Stanley R. Zax - Chmn., Pres. Jack D. Miller - Exec. V.P.	**Auditors:** PricewaterhouseCoopers LLP **Investor Contact:** 818-713-1000 **Transfer Agents:** Mellon Investor Services LLC

ZIMMER HOLDINGS, INC.

Exchange	Symbol	Price	52Wk Range	Yield	P/E
NYS	ZMH	$77.81 (3/31/2005)	89.15-67.90	N/A	35.53

*7 Year Price Score N/A   ***NYSE Composite Index=100**   ***12 Month Price Score 97.26**

Interim Earnings (Per Share)

Qtr.	Mar	Jun	Sep	Dec
2001	...	0.22	0.14	0.22
2002	0.28	0.34	0.33	0.36
2003	0.68	0.45	0.43	0.09
2004	0.40	0.47	0.52	0.81

Interim Dividends (Per Share)

No Dividends Paid

Valuation Analysis

Forecast P/E	26.43		No of Institutions
	(4/7/2005)		672
Market Cap	$19.1 Billion		Shares
Book Value	3.9 Billion		183,062,512
Price/Book	4.85		% Held
Price/Sales	6.41		74.21

Business Summary: Medical Instruments & Equipment (MIC: 9.6 SIC: 842 NAIC: 39113)

Zimmer Holdings designs, develops, manufactures and markets reconstructive orthopaedic implants, including joint and dental, spinal implants, and trauma products. Joint reconstructive implants restore function in joints such as knees. Dental reconstructive implants restore function and aesthetics in patients that have lost teeth. Trauma products are devices used primarily to reattach or stabilize damaged bone and tissue to support the body's natural healing process. Also, Co. manufactures and markets related orthopaedic surgical products and a limited array of sports medicine products. Co. has operations in over 24 countries.

Recent Developments: For the year ended Dec 31 2004, net income increased 56.5% to $541,800 thousand from net income of $346,300 thousand a year earlier. Revenues were $2,980,900 thousand, up 56.8% from $1,901,000 thousand the year before. Operating income was $763,200 thousand versus an income of $450,700 thousand in the prior year, an increase of 69.3%. Total direct expense was $779,900 thousand versus $516,200 thousand in the prior year, an increase of 51.1%. Total indirect expense was $1,437,800 thousand versus $934,100 thousand in the prior year, an increase of 53.9%.

Prospects: Co. expects the combination with Centerpulse to deliver a minimum of 10.0% sales growth in 2005 with sales in a range of $3.33 billion and $3.35 billion. Also, Co. expects to report earnings per share in the first half of 2005 in the range of $1.32 to $1.33, and adjusted earnings per share to be in a range of $1.40 to $1.41, with approximately $0.66 to $0.67 in the first quarter and approximately $0.74 in the second quarter. Additionally, Co. expects reported earnings per share in the second half of 2005 to be in a range of $1.44 to $1.45, and adjusted earnings per share estimates for full-year 2005 in a range of $2.89 to $2.91.

Financial Data

(US$ in Thousands)	12/31/2004	12/31/2003	12/31/2002	12/31/2001	12/31/2000	12/31/1999	12/31/1998
Earnings Per Share	2.19	1.64	1.31	0.77	0.91	...	...
Cash Flow Per Share	3.52	2.38	1.13	0.89	1.20	...	...
Tang Book Value Per Share	2.52	0.38	1.88	0.41	0.08	...	...
Income Statement							
Total Revenue	2,980,900	1,901,000	1,372,400	1,178,600	1,041,000	939,000	861,000
EBITDA	944,500	554,000	426,200	271,700	291,000	253,000	237,000
Depn & Amortn	181,300	103,300	25,300	23,400	23,000	22,000	26,000
Income Before Taxes	731,500	437,500	388,900	240,900	268,000	231,000	211,000
Income Taxes	189,600	146,800	131,100	91,100	92,000	81,000	66,000
Net Income	541,800	346,300	257,800	149,800	176,000	150,000	145,000
Average Shares	247,800	211,200	196,800	194,300	193,600	...	...
Balance Sheet							
Current Assets	1,560,900	1,338,700	612,400	508,600	419,000	430,000	...
Total Assets	5,695,500	5,156,000	858,900	745,000	597,000	606,000	...
Current Liabilities	701,000	645,300	400,800	373,100	336,000	215,000	...
Long-Term Obligations	624,000	1,007,800	...	213,900	...	...	...
Total Liabilities	1,745,900	2,005,700	492,600	666,300	336,000	215,000	...
Stockholders' Equity	3,942,500	3,143,300	366,300	78,700	261,000	391,000	...
Shares Outstanding	245,500	242,400	195,200	193,900	3,200,000	...	...
Statistical Record							
Return on Assets %	9.96	11.51	32.15	22.32	29.18	...	...
Return on Equity %	15.25	19.73	115.87	88.20	53.84	...	...
EBITDA Margin %	31.69	29.14	31.06	23.05	27.95	26.94	27.53
Net Margin %	18.18	18.22	18.78	12.71	16.91	15.97	16.84
Asset Turnover	0.55	0.63	1.71	1.76	1.73	...	...
Current Ratio	2.23	2.07	1.53	1.36	1.25	2.00	...
Debt to Equity	0.16	0.32	...	2.72	...	...	...
Price Range	89.15-67.90	71.17-38.16	42.60-29.37	32.85-25.02	...	...	...
P/E Ratio	40.71-31.00	43.40-23.27	32.52-22.42	42.66-32.49	...	...	...

Address: 345 East Main Street, Warsaw, IN 46580 Telephone: (574) 267-6131 Fax: (574) 372-4988	Web Site: www.zimmer.com Officers: J. Raymond Elliott - Chmn., Pres., C.E.O. David C. Dvorak - Exec. V.P., Corp. Services, Sec., Chief Couns.	Auditors: PricewaterhouseCoopers LLP Transfer Agents: Bank of New York, New York, NY

CONDENSED

STATISTICAL

TABULATION

The tab section consists of statistical highlights for all U.S. companies listed on the New York Stock Exchange.

Statistics for companies whose fiscal year ends prior to June 30 are listed under the prior calendar year. Statistics for companies whose fiscal year ends June 30 or after are listed under the current calendar year. Dividends and price ranges are on a calendar year basis.

Because of editorial constraints a column for fourth quarter results was not included. At fiscal year-end, full fiscal year per share earnings are listed and quarterly figures are eliminated. Quarterly per share earnings are inserted as the company reports in the current fiscal year.

NOTE: Figures listed under "Earnings Per Share" for investment companies are net asset value per share.

For abbreviations, see the blue section of the Handbook.

SYMBOL	COMPANY	NATURE OF BUSINESS	FISCAL YEAR-END	TOTAL REV. $MILL	NET INCOME $MILL	TOTAL ASSETS $MILL	NET STK EQUITY $MILL	NO. OF INST.	INST. HOLDINGS (SHARES)
BDF	1838 Bond-Debenture Trading F	Investment company	3/31/04	5.6	4.9	104.7	104.6	13	304235
TW	21st Century Insurance Group	Property & casualty insurance	12/31/03	1246.5	53.6	1715.6	679.1	51	64305340
MMM	3M Co (United States)	Conglomerate	12/31/03	18232.0	6060.0	16679.0	7885.0	960	281361495
KDE	4 Kids Entertainment Inc. (U	Services	12/31/03	102.1	14.8	173.4	160.5	83	8617524
CFD	40/86 Strategic Income Fund	Investment company	6/30/03	8.2	6.6	73.2	69.8	—	—
SE	7-Eleven Inc.	Grocery chain	12/31/03	10881.7	228.4	2873.4	340.0	66	9086243
NDN	99 Cents Only Stores	Discount & variety stores	12/31/03	862.5	56.5	531.2	489.9	148	39793548
RNT	Aaron Rents, Inc. (United St	Furniture & fixtures	12/31/03	766.8	36.4	555.0	320.2	93	14092356
ABB	ABB Ltd		12/31/03	—	—	—	—	7	721146
SXA	Abbey National Plc (United Ki	Financial services	12/31/03	—	—	—	—	4	319350
ABT	Abbott Laboratories	Medical & dental equipment	12/31/03	19680.6	6487.6	24961.0	13072.3	1079	979957364
ANF	Abercrombie & Fitch Co.	Specialty stores	1/31/04	1707.8	205.1	1185.0	871.3	320	89867307
ABY	Abitibi Consolidated Inc.	Paper	12/31/03	—	—	—	—	104	237948935
ABM	ABM Industries, Inc.	Maint. & security services	10/31/03	2262.5	36.4	702.3	444.0	127	31459272
ABN	ABN AMRO Holding N.V.		12/31/03	—	—	—	—	85	48696996
AKR	Acadia Realty Trust	Real estate investment trust	12/31/03	69.4	18.6	388.2	169.7	52	15190027
AOF	ACM Govt. Opportunity Fd, Inc	Investment company	7/31/03	10.5	8.5	165.4	108.3	12	4474520
ACG	ACM Income Fund, Inc.	Investment company	12/31/03	203.8	172.8	2860.0	1904.9	54	2191537
ADF	ACM Managed Dollar Income Fd	Investment company	9/30/03	20.9	18.3	254.7	173.2	10	27445
AMF	ACM Managed Income Fund, Inc.	Investment company	8/31/03	—	—	—	—	14	255376
AMU	ACM Municipal Securities Inco	Investment company	10/31/03	12.8	10.7	212.6	122.3	7	33215
ATN	Action Performance Cos., Inc	Recreation	9/30/03	370.6	24.2	374.8	261.6	120	18720589
ATU	Actuant Corp.	Engineering & construction	8/31/03	585.4	50.4	260.2	d11.6	97	10211349
AYI	Acuity Brands, Inc.		8/31/03	2049.3	47.8	1288.2	408.3	122	27144920
ADX	Adams Express Co.	Investment company	12/31/03	20.7	15.6	1344.2	1218.9	57	3325537
ASF	Administaff, Inc.	Services	12/31/03	891.7	65.5	348.1	122.6	105	23719030
PVD	Administradora de Fondos de P	Finance	12/31/03	—	—	—	—	15	1471389
AAP	Advance Auto Parts Inc (Unit		1/3/04	3493.7	135.7	1931.4	631.2	147	27874164
AVO	Advanced Medical Optics Inc (		12/31/03	601.5	27.6	461.3	93.2	135	22784617
AMD	Advanced Micro Devices, Inc.	Electronic components	12/28/03	3519.2	d288.4	6484.8	2438.3	261	195034383
AD	ADVO, Inc.		9/27/03	1163.1	53.4	325.3	89.9	118	18111973
AEG	AEGON N.V. (Netherlands)	Insurance	12/31/03	—	—	—	—	172	31514213
ARO	Aeropostale Inc		1/31/04	734.9	54.3	307.0	185.7	80	16140380
AES	AES Corp. (United States)	Electric power	12/31/03	8415.0	975.0	29810.0	645.0	305	382702862
AET	Aetna Inc. (New)	Insurance	12/31/03	17976.4	933.8	40746.5	7924.0	349	137028680
ACS	Affiliated Computer Services	Computer services	6/30/03	3787.2	306.8	3471.4	2429.2	413	119160324
AMG	Affiliated Managers Group Inc	Financial services	12/31/03	495.0	60.5	1463.4	614.8	204	25302657
ARC	Affordable Residential Commun	Real estate investment trust	12/31/03	170.2	d34.4	1045.5	265.3	—	—
AFL	AFLAC Inc.	Insurance	12/31/03	11447.0	1259.0	48471.0	4153.0	553	282099914
AG	AGCO Corp.		12/31/03	3495.3	172.7	2647.8	906.1	193	68866071
AGR A	Agere Systems Inc.	Comp. components & periphs.	9/30/03	1839.0	d696.0	2388.0	511.0	275	630656541
A	Agilent Technologies, Inc.	Electrical equipment	10/31/03	816.0	d7755.0	5941.0	2824.0	456	294557799
ATG	AGL Resources Inc.	Natural gas distributor	12/31/03	983.7	135.7	3331.5	945.3	210	35061161
AEM	Agnico-Eagle Mines Ltd.	Mining & processing	12/31/03	—	—	—	—	105	47433137
ADC	Agree Realty Corp.	Real estate investment trust	12/31/03	27.5	11.5	189.7	96.2	13	306098
AGU	Agrium Inc. (Canada)	Fertilizer	12/31/03	—	—	—	—	99	74230356
APD	Air Products & Chemicals, Inc	Specialty chemicals	9/30/03	6297.3	1024.5	9014.5	3782.5	463	186862742
ARG	Airgas Inc.	Specialty chemicals	3/31/04	p1895.0	p1895.0	—	—	197	48407979
ANS	AirNet Systems, Inc.		12/31/03	149.2	2.8	134.3	84.3	22	6767331
AAI	Airtran Holdings, Inc.		12/31/03	918.0	100.5	781.4	302.2	95	34318844
AKS	AK Steel Holding Corp	Steel producer	12/31/03	4041.7	d1633.3	4999.7	d52.8	155	75105634
ALF	Alabama Power Co.	Electric power	12/31/03	3960.2	491.5	11062.0	3873.2	—	—
ALG	Alamo Group, Inc.	Machinery & equipment	12/31/03	279.1	21.0	153.1	144.1	33	5570906
ALK	Alaska Air Group, Inc.		12/31/03	2444.8	13.5	3259.2	674.2	127	23867199
AIN	Albany International Corp (N	Paper	12/31/03	869.0	54.1	1253.0	668.7	147	25065011
ALB	Albemarle Corp.	Chemicals	12/31/03	1102.1	162.2	1170.9	636.2	174	19945927
ACV	Alberto-Culver Co.	Cosmetics & toiletries	9/30/03	2891.4	413.6	1902.4	1062.1	244	25408860
ABS	Albertson's Inc.	Grocery chain	1/29/04	35436.0	556.0	15394.0	5381.0	401	253601103
AL	Alcan Inc. (Canada)	Industrial	12/31/03	—	—	—	—	186	181847732
ALA	Alcatel (France)	Telecommunications	12/31/03	—	—	—	—	127	111775613
AA	Alcoa, Inc.	Metal products	12/31/03	21504.0	2561.0	29735.0	12075.0	636	674706387
ALX	Alexander's Inc.	Real estate	12/31/03	87.2	30.0	921.0	50.9	40	1560595
ARE	Alexandria Real Estate Equiti	Real estate investment trust	12/31/03	160.6	62.7	1272.6	507.1	131	16669509
Y	Alleghany Corp. (New)	Property & casualty insurance	12/31/03	1018.2	162.4	3563.5	1562.8	109	4512279
AYE	Allegheny Energy, Inc.	Electric power	12/31/03	2472.4	d334.2	8432.8	1515.9	256	70229775
ATI	Allegheny Technologies, Inc.	Conglomerate	12/31/03	1937.4	d593.5	1849.9	174.7	179	35493244
AGN	Allergan, Inc	Medical & dental equipment	12/31/03	1771.4	d82.0	1667.7	718.6	372	117433302
ALE	ALLETE Inc.	Electric power	12/31/03	1618.8	143.1	3044.3	1460.2	—	—
AMO	Alliance All-Market Advantage	Investment company	9/30/03	0.3	d0.8	51.9	49.8	5	39260
AKP	Alliance California Municipal	Investment company	10/31/03	11.1	9.8	204.4	123.2	3	110593
AC	Alliance Capital Management	Financial services	12/31/03	100.4	78.6	1166.1	—	187	12467133
ADS	Alliance Data Systems Corp.	Computer services	12/31/03	1049.1	130.4	1631.7	702.3	89	17632324
AGI	Alliance Gaming Corp. (United	Gaming	6/30/03	407.6	40.4	337.5	91.6	146	36585150
AIQ	Alliance Imaging, Inc.	Medical & dental equipment	12/31/03	415.3	d31.6	625.1	d70.8	46	9795336
AFB	Alliance National Municipal I	Investment company	10/31/03	27.2	24.3	503.0	307.6	9	118233
AYN	Alliance New York Municipal I	Investment company	10/31/03	6.0	5.2	114.7	69.5	1	26500
AWG	Alliance World Dollar Govt Fd	Investment company	10/31/03	11.4	9.3	120.2	116.0	17	310685
LNT	Alliant Energy Corp.	Electric power	12/31/03	3128.2	159.6	7374.6	2615.1	189	24928721
ATK	Alliant Techsystems Inc.	Defense systems & equip.	3/31/04	2366.2	283.0	2200.5	564.2	252	33956142
AZ	Allianz AG Holding	Insurance brokerage	12/31/03	—	—	—	—	30	4392871
ALD	Allied Capital Corp. (New)	Investment company	12/31/03	329.2	192.0	3019.9	1914.6	197	41865795
AED	Allied Domecq PLC (United Kin		8/31/03	—	—	—	—	24	767917
AW	Allied Waste Industries, Inc.	Pollution control	12/31/03	5247.7	111.2	13642.1	2517.7	235	158284172
AFC	Allmerica Financial Corp.	Insurance	12/31/03	3263.6	115.6	25112.5	2220.2	150	34821045
ALM	Allmerica Securities Trust	Investment company	12/31/03	4.8	4.2	94.1	91.5	13	727353
ALL	Allstate Corp. (The)	Insurance	12/31/03	32149.0	6783.0	134142.0	20565.0	620	463510839
AT	ALLTEL Corp. (United States)	Telecommunications	12/31/03	7979.9	953.5	16661.1	7022.2	580	186114168
ALO	Alpharma, Inc.	Drugs	12/31/03	1297.3	22.5	2327.8	1135.1	175	38185659
MO	Altria Group Inc	Tobacco	12/31/03	81832.0	24166.0	96175.0	25077.0	844	1265286134
AWC	Alumina Ltd	Mining & processing	12/31/03	4.8	236.9	1799.1	1323.8	15	1060569
ACH	Aluminum Corp of China Ltd.	Metal products	12/31/03	—	—	—	—	9	1116558
AMB	AMB Property Corp.	Real estate investment trust	12/31/03	615.0	82.6	5420.7	1666.9	198	65722001
ABK	Ambac Financial Group, Inc.	Finance	12/31/03	1272.2	628.1	16747.3	4254.6	399	101629513
ACO	AMCOL International Corp.	Mining & processing	12/31/03	364.0	49.2	239.0	184.9	55	11658634
AHC	Amerada Hess Corp.	Oil	12/31/03	14480.0	1588.0	12441.0	5340.0	315	67740438
AEE	Ameren Corp.	Electric power	12/31/03	4593.0	455.0	13820.0	4354.0	331	74604988

1st	2nd	3rd	2004	2003	2002	P/E RATIO	Div 2004	Div 2003	Div 2002	AV. YLD. %	AMOUNT	PAYABLE	PRICE RANGE 2004
—	—	—	—	21.32	21.50	—	1.25	1.36	1.40	6.8	0.2875Q	5/4/05	20.20 - 16.71
0.23	—	—	—	0.63	d0.14	—	0.10	0.08	0.24	0.7	0.04Q	3/30/05	15.24 - 11.94
0.90	—	—	—	3.02	2.50	—	1.44	1.32	1.24	1.8	0.42Q	3/12/05	90.05 - 71.28
0.22	—	—	—	1.05	0.51	—	—	—	—		2-for-1	9/13/99	30.00 - 11.80
—	—	—	—	10.20	7.81	—	0.88	0.94	0.97	8.6	0.075M	4/8/05	11.36 - 9.00
0.09	—	—	—	0.76	0.48	—	—	—	—				24.20 - 6.96
0.13	—	—	—	0.78	0.83	—					4-for-3	4/3/02	29.88 - 12.10
0.38	—	—	—	1.10	0.86	—	0.04	0.02	0.02	0.2	0.013Q	4/1/05	33.90 - 17.75
—	—	—	—	—	—	—		1.21			12/16/03		6.73 - 2.12
—	—	—	—	—	—	—	1.81	1.81	1.89	7.0		5/16/05	26.51 - 24.95
0.52	—	—	—	1.75	1.78	—	1.02	0.97	0.91	2.5	0.275Q	5/15/05	47.60 - 35.62
0.31	—	—	—	2.06	1.94	—	0.50	—	—	1.4	0.125Q	3/22/05	47.42 - 23.40
—	—	—	—	—	—	—	0.13	0.25	0.40	1.9	0.025Q	3/1/05	8.45 - 5.05
0.14	0.14	—	—	0.73	0.92	—	0.40	0.38	0.36	2.2	0.105Q	5/2/05	22.49 - 13.14
—	—	—	—	—	—	—	1.20	1.01	0.86	5.8	0.64S	6/1/05	26.77 - 14.65
0.10	—	—	—	0.29	0.42	—	0.64	0.56	0.51	5.3	0.1725Q	4/15/05	16.49 - 7.82
—	—	—	—	8.46	7.95	—	0.65	0.72	0.72	7.7	0.0425M	4/22/05	9.43 - 7.55
—	—	—	—	8.39	7.91	—	0.78	0.87	0.96	9.8	0.06M	4/22/05	8.89 - 7.11
—	—	—	—	7.68	5.58	—	0.77	0.81	0.83	9.9	0.0565M	4/22/05	8.60 - 6.80
—	—	—	—	—	4.06	—	0.38	0.51	0.51	8.9	0.0195M	4/22/05	4.99 - 3.60
d0.09	0.07	—	—	11.05	10.85	—	0.86	0.87	0.87	7.4	0.058M	4/22/05	12.72 - 10.26
0.01	0.35	—	—	1.33	2.46	—	0.20	0.16	0.03	1.4	0.05Q	1/5/05	19.27 - 8.37
0.30	0.22	—	—	1.18	0.60	—	—	—	—		100%	10/21/03	53.43 - 31.41
—	—	—	—	1.15	1.26	—	0.60	0.60	0.60	2.6	0.15Q	5/2/05	32.24 - 13.25
—	—	—	—	14.36	12.12	—	0.90	0.78	0.76	7.5	0.04Q	3/1/05	13.99 - 10.05
0.33	—	—	—	0.55	d0.15	—	—	—	—		0.07Q	4/1/05	18.45 - 5.00
—	—	—	—	—	—	—	1.29	1.11	1.04	5.0	0.47632S	11/1/04	29.72 - 22.30
0.68	—	—	—	1.68	1.04	—					100%	1/2/04	44.41 - 33.02
0.15	—	—	—	0.35	—	—							43.69 - 11.55
0.12	—	—	—	d0.79	d3.81	—					2-for-1	8/21/00	24.95 - 5.24
0.37	0.38	—	—	1.64	1.38	—	0.44	0.17	—	1.4	0.11Q	2/4/05	36.74 - 26.50
—	—	—	—	—	—	—	0.49	0.23	0.74	4.2		5/17/05	16.23 - 7.26
0.11	—	—	—	0.93	0.55	—					50%	4/26/04	37.80 - 9.91
0.12	—	—	—	0.56	d4.81	—					2-for-1	6/1/00	13.71 - 3.32
2.03	—	—	—	5.91	2.57	—	0.02	0.02	0.02	0.0	100%	3/1/05	127.56 - 42.12
0.62	1.80	0.72	—	2.20	1.76	—					100%	2/22/02	61.23 - 44.26
0.57	—	—	—	1.85	1.65	—					3-for-2	3/29/04	88.33 - 41.57
d1.20	—	—	—	d2.21	d2.89	—	0.77	—	—	4.9	0.3125Q	4/15/05	19.25 - 12.40
0.61	—	—	—	1.52	1.55	—	0.38	0.30	0.23	1.0	0.11Q	3/1/05	42.60 - 30.10
0.33	—	—	—	0.98	d0.81	—					0.01Q	3/1/01	23.13 - 16.10
d0.02	—	—	—	d0.22	d1.11	—							4.14 - 1.60
0.14	0.21	—	—	d3.78	d2.20	—							37.60 - 13.15
1.00	—	—	—	2.13	1.82	—	1.15	1.11	1.08	4.1	0.31Q	3/1/05	33.65 - 22.15
—	—	—	—	—	—	—	0.03	0.03	0.02	0.2	0.03A	3/15/05	16.73 - 10.02
0.45	—	—	—	1.79	1.97	—	1.94	1.91	1.84	7.7	0.49Q	4/14/05	33.24 - 17.59
—	—	—	—	—	—	—	0.11	0.11	0.11	0.7	0.055S	1/13/05	18.75 - 10.74
0.58	0.62	—	—	1.79	2.36	—	1.04	0.88	0.82	2.1	0.32Q	5/9/05	59.18 - 38.76
—	—	—	—	—	p0.94	—	0.18	0.12	—	0.8	0.045Q	3/31/05	27.19 - 16.75
0.03	—	—	—	0.28	0.33	—							6.15 - 2.08
0.05	—	—	—	1.21	0.15	—					2-for-1	11/21/95	14.30 - 5.95
d0.15	—	—	—	d5.48	d4.42	—					0.0625Q	5/30/01	15.96 - 1.91
—	—	—	—	—	—	—	0.68	—	—	3.0		4/15/05	25.24 - 20.00
0.23	—	—	—	0.82	0.65	—	0.24	0.24	0.24	1.2	0.06Q	5/4/05	27.49 - 11.25
d1.59	—	—	—	0.51	d2.53	—					0.05Q	11/5/92	33.67 - 15.66
0.10	—	—	—	1.61	1.68	—	0.29	0.23	0.20	1.0	0.08Q	4/5/05	35.46 - 22.14
0.32	—	—	—	1.76	1.73	—	0.58	0.56	0.53	1.8	0.15Q	4/1/05	40.65 - 24.35
0.02	0.44	—	—	1.80	1.55	—	0.40	0.28	0.24	0.8	0.115Q	2/18/05	65.32 - 41.10
0.15	—	—	—	1.51	2.17	—	0.76	0.76	0.76	3.3	0.19Q	5/10/05	26.64 - 18.83
—	—	—	—	—	—	—	0.60	0.60	0.60	1.5	0.15Q	3/21/05	52.65 - 27.90
—	—	—	—	—	—	—	—	—	0.12		0.1206U	5/13/02	18.32 - 6.89
0.40	—	—	—	1.20	0.58	—	0.60	0.60	0.60	2.0	0.15Q	2/25/05	39.20 - 19.38
d4.60	—	—	—	d3.79	2.66	—							230.05 - 63.85
0.70	—	—	—	2.52	2.26	—	2.44	2.12	1.96	4.2	0.66Q	4/15/05	75.24 - 41.35
8.08	—	—	—	21.29	7.16	—					2%	4/22/05	300.77 - 161.18
0.25	—	—	—	d2.64	d4.00	—	—	—	1.29		0.43Q	9/30/02	20.20 - 5.99
d0.63	—	—	—	d3.87	d0.82	—	0.24	0.24	0.66	1.8	0.06Q	3/29/05	23.48 - 2.90
0.61	—	—	—	d0.40	0.49	—	0.36	0.36	0.36	0.5	0.10Q	3/10/05	92.61 - 60.67
0.63	—	—	—	1.72	1.46	—	0.30	—	—	0.9	0.30Q	3/1/05	37.46 - 26.47
—	—	—	—	13.69	13.65	—	1.42	1.32	1.95	9.4	0.347Q	4/8/05	16.30 - 12.25
—	—	—	—	14.46	—	—	0.96	0.92	0.68	7.1	0.08M	4/22/05	14.75 - 12.30
0.58	—	—	—	1.01	2.11	—	1.19	1.97	2.30	3.4	0.82Q	2/17/05	42.30 - 28.20
0.39	—	—	—	0.84	0.35	—							48.54 - 16.60
p0.56	0.28	0.24	—	0.81	1.34	—	—	—	—		2-for-1	4/8/02	34.16 - 8.83
0.09	—	—	—	d0.66	0.72	—							11.75 - 3.14
—	—	—	—	15.02	14.81	—	1.00	0.96	0.72	7.3	0.083M	4/22/05	14.91 - 12.50
—	—	—	—	14.40	14.67	—	0.92	0.92	0.69	6.8	0.0765M	4/22/05	14.76 - 12.10
—	—	—	—	13.05	9.98	—	0.90	1.05	1.08	7.6	0.069M	4/22/05	14.09 - 9.77
0.31	—	—	—	1.57	0.84	—	1.01	1.00	2.00	4.5	0.2625Q	2/15/05	28.80 - 15.76
—	—	—	—	4.14	3.27	—					3-for-2	6/10/02	67.82 - 47.90
—	—	—	—	—	—	—	0.14	1.14	0.11	1.5		5/2/05	14.26 - 4.95
—	—	—	—	—	—	—	2.28	2.31	2.20	8.9	0.57Q	3/31/05	31.12 - 19.98
—	—	—	—	—	—	—	1.06	0.87	—	3.5	0.72815S	2/9/05	40.29 - 19.42
d0.01	—	—	—	d2.36	0.76	—							14.44 - 7.50
1.29	—	—	—	1.63	d3.18	—					0.25A	11/20/01	38.32 - 13.18
—	—	—	—	10.64	10.57	—	0.55	0.56	0.58	5.9	0.135Q	3/31/05	9.92 - 8.70
1.34	—	—	—	3.83	1.60	—	1.08	0.90	0.82	2.6	0.32Q	4/1/05	51.99 - 31.63
0.61	—	—	—	3.05	2.96	—	1.48	1.40	1.36	2.8	0.38Q	4/3/05	60.62 - 43.42
d0.06	—	—	—	0.43	d1.96	—	0.18	0.18	0.18	1.0	0.045Q	4/29/05	24.00 - 12.34
1.07	—	—	—	4.52	5.21	—	2.77	2.60	2.38	6.0	0.73Q	4/11/05	61.87 - 29.96
—	—	—	—	0.21	0.16	—	0.58	0.57	0.39	3.7	0.2296U	4/11/05	21.16 - 9.89
—	—	—	—	—	—	—	1.15	0.54	0.21	2.1	1.2265A	7/11/05	92.12 - 16.16
0.19	—	—	—	0.85	1.02	—	1.69	1.65	1.23	4.9	0.44Q	4/15/05	41.35 - 27.30
1.55	—	—	—	5.74	3.97	—	0.47	0.42	0.38	0.7	0.125Q	3/2/05	84.62 - 48.85
0.16	—	—	—	0.67	0.43	—	0.28	0.14	0.08	1.8	0.09Q	3/9/05	25.05 - 5.67
2.77	—	—	—	5.17	d2.48	—	1.20	1.20	1.20	1.7	0.30Q	3/31/05	93.89 - 44.26
0.55	—	—	—	3.14	2.60	—	2.54	2.54	2.54	5.7	0.635Q	3/31/05	50.36 - 38.99

SYMBOL	COMPANY	NATURE OF BUSINESS	FISCAL YEAR-END	TOTAL REV. $MILL	NET INCOME $MILL	TOTAL ASSETS $MILL	NET STK EQUITY $MILL	NO. OF INST.	INST. HOLDINGS (SHARES)
AMX	America Movil, S.A. de C.V.	Telecommunications	12/31/03	—	—	—	—	201	248234203
AWA	America West Holding Corp.		12/31/03	2254.5	57.4	1626.9	138.5	32	14095127
AXL	American Axle & Mfg Hldg In		12/31/03	3682.7	504.2	2400.5	1017.4	156	26855082
AEP	American Electric Power Co.,	Electric power	12/31/03	14545.0	522.0	36093.0	7874.0	416	235186175
AEL	American Equity Investment Li	Finance	12/31/03	452.1	25.4	8926.0	263.7	—	—
AXP	American Express Co. (United	Financial services	12/31/03	25866.0	3000.0	175001.0	15323.0	977	960317910
AFR	American Financial Realty Tru		12/31/03	p135.6	p142.1	—	—	—	—
AM	American Greetings Corp.	Printing & engraving	2/29/04	2008.9	500.8	2413.1	1267.5	221	83762785
AHM	American Home Mortgage Inves	Real estate investment trust	12/31/03	432.1	87.4	2270.2	398.0	—	—
AIG	American International Group	Insurance	12/31/03	81303.0	23173.0	678346.0	71253.0	1266	1582295942
PLB	American Italian Pasta, Co.	Food processing	10/3/03	438.8	56.2	469.8	343.5	170	21977388
ANL	American Land Lease, Inc.	Real estate investment trust	12/31/03	64.9	11.7	247.1	94.8	23	1152395
XAA	American Municipal Incm Port	Investment company	1/31/04	6.9	5.9	133.7	90.1	4	28365
ACP	American Real Estate Partners	Real estate	12/31/03	283.8	75.4	1489.9	—	19	40774506
ARL	American Realty Investors, I	Real estate	12/31/03	267.2	d10.5	1240.2	75.7	11	92502
ACR	American Retirement Corp.	Hospitals & nursing homes	12/31/03	368.1	12.6	715.0	0.8	16	4190542
SLA	American Select Portfolio, In	Investment company	11/30/03	12.9	11.2	191.9	143.0	16	1430593
ASD	American Standard Cos Inc DE	Machinery & equipment	12/31/03	8567.6	954.4	5614.5	1004.4	277	57656984
AWR	American States Water Co. (U	Water company	12/31/03	212.7	11.9	757.5	212.5	103	5511870
ASP	American Strategic Income Por	Investment company	11/30/03	4.5	3.8	69.3	53.6	11	821386
AMT	American Tower Corp.	Communications electronics	12/31/03	715.1	d524.3	4627.8	1711.5	172	155046587
ACF	AmeriCredit Corp.	Industrial	6/30/03	981.3	21.2	8036.3	1875.5	173	150659287
APU	AmeriGas Partners, L.P. (Uni	Oil producer	12/31/03	p1644.0	p1644.0	—	—	49	1027220
AGP	Amerigroup Corp		12/31/03	1622.2	67.3	771.7	461.7	134	20209103
ABC	AmerisourceBergen Corp. (Uni	Drugs	9/30/03	49657.3	476.0	12040.1	4005.3	394	93734886
AFG	Amern Financial Grp Inc Hldg	Property & casualty insurance	12/31/03	3359.6	321.2	20197.3	2076.2	142	29571700
AMN	Ameron International Corp.		11/30/03	—	d570.6	443.6	256.1	60	2576540
AMH	AmerUs Group Co.	Life Insurance	12/31/03	1680.0	183.9	21458.9	1409.8	163	20545082
AME	Ametek, Inc. (New)	Machinery & equipment	12/31/03	1091.6	217.9	1214.8	529.1	180	24374701
AML	Amli Residential Properties	Real estate investment trust	12/31/03	100.6	d48.7	945.3	384.0	95	8310904
AHS	AMN Healthcare Services, Inc		12/31/03	714.2	37.8	295.6	116.1	102	23721952
AP	Ampco-Pittsburgh Corp.	Metal products	12/31/03	180.2	7.2	234.1	144.5	53	5188289
APH	Amphenol Corp. (New)	Electronic components	12/31/03	1239.5	262.4	1181.4	323.4	127	21245681
AMR	AMR Corp. (DE)		12/31/03	17440.0	d1228.0	28496.0	46.0	160	119033808
ASO	AmSouth Bancorporation (Unit	Banking - South	12/31/03	2942.2	626.1	45615.5	3229.7	346	133144217
APC	Anadarko Petroleum Corp	Oil	12/31/03	5122.0	3571.0	19324.0	8599.0	642	194699829
ADI	Analog Devices, Inc.	Electronic components	11/1/03	2047.3	298.3	3663.1	3288.1	460	291223351
AGL	Angelica Corp. (United State		1/31/04	374.3	246.0	235.8	146.7	88	6507074
AU	AngloGold Ashanti Ltd	Mining & processing	12/31/03	—	—	—	—	109	22569867
BUD	Anheuser-Busch Cos., Inc.		12/31/03	14146.7	2075.9	14689.5	2711.7	799	494795434
AXE	Anixter International Inc. (	Electrical equipment	1/3/04	p2625.2	p2625.2	—	—	142	23946818
ANN	Ann Taylor Stores Corp.	Specialty stores	1/31/04	1587.7	100.9	1151.9	830.6	200	43160738
NLY	Annaly Mortgage Management In	Real estate investment trust	12/31/03	378.3	196.3	12990.3	1149.2	148	28620096
ANT	Anteon International Corp. (	Computer services	12/31/03	1042.5	94.8	459.0	174.5	95	17708500
WLP	Anthem, Inc.	Insurance	12/31/03	16771.4	3898.6	12625.8	5999.9	—	—
AHR	Anthracite Capital, Inc.	Real estate investment trust	12/31/03	163.8	d8.6	2398.8	417.4	94	20411271
ANH	Anworth Mortgage Asset Corp.	Real estate investment trust	12/31/03	103.6	50.2	4285.2	479.3	69	8958690
AOC	Aon Corp.	Insurance	12/31/03	9810.0	8896.0	27027.0	4498.0	330	244756145
APA	Apache Corp.	Oil	12/31/03	4190.3	3017.5	12410.9	6532.8	577	130365518
AIV	Apartment Investment & Manage	Real estate investment trust	12/31/03	1516.3	99.5	9986.8	2860.7	229	97623144
APX	Apex Municipal Fund, Inc.	Investment company	6/30/03	13.0	11.4	176.3	176.1	14	104062
ABI	Applera Corp - Applied Biosy		6/30/03	1682.9	199.6	2126.7	1338.2	301	191570623
APN	Applica Inc	'Wholesaler, distributor'	12/31/03	640.6	40.6	393.2	237.6	81	13621091
AIT	Applied Indl Technologies In	Services	6/30/03	1464.4	19.8	527.5	307.9	95	12564064
AHG	Apria Healthcare Group Inc.	Hospitals & nursing homes	12/31/03	1380.9	282.8	990.2	365.9	200	50598602
ATR	AptarGroup Inc.	Containers	12/31/03	1114.7	201.9	1137.6	783.1	183	31042804
WTR	Aqua America Inc	Water company	12/31/03	367.2	70.8	1973.3	659.0	—	—
ILA	Aquila Inc (New) (DE) (United	Electric power	12/31/03	1674.0	d842.9	6733.2	1359.3	170	71308483
ARA	Aracruz Celulose S.A.	Paper	12/31/03	—	—	—	—	94	29824226
RMK	Aramark Corp. (New)		10/3/03	9447.8	9201.8	4410.7	1039.0	123	67963650
ARB	Arbitron Inc.	Computers	12/31/03	273.6	131.0	67.8	d18.1	152	27737597
ARJ	Arch Chemicals Inc (United S	Chemicals	12/31/03	1009.1	37.7	949.4	337.7	107	17318754
ACI	Arch Coal, Inc.	Coal	12/31/03	42.4	d1415.1	2090.2	688.0	173	48471659
ADM	Archer Daniels Midland Co.	Food -grain & agriculture	6/30/03	30708.0	451.1	17182.9	7069.2	374	410625150
ASN	Archstone Smith Trust	Real estate investment trust	12/31/03	900.4	148.3	8817.9	4144.7	240	142753652
ARI	Arden Realty, Inc.	Real estate investment trust	12/31/03	413.5	64.1	2580.4	1210.3	136	58323234
AGY	Argosy Gaming Co.	Gaming	12/31/03	959.5	51.7	1357.6	303.2	136	25353424
AH	Armor Holdings, Inc.	Defense systems & equip.	12/31/03	365.2	17.0	585.6	295.4	99	22592305
ARW	Arrow Electronics, Inc.	Consumer electronics	12/31/03	8679.3	130.5	5333.0	1505.3	216	92413818
ARM	ArvinMeritor, Inc.		9/30/03	p7788.0	p7784.0	—	—	189	42355681
ABG	Asbury Automotive Group, Inc		12/31/03	683.0	d4073.7	1212.1	433.7	45	3804994
AHT	Ashford Hospitality Trust In	Real estate investment trust	12/31/03	18.3	2.4	266.0	172.3	—	—
ASH	Ashland, Inc.	Oil producer	9/30/03	7865.0	232.0	6446.0	2253.0	232	49155614
APB	Asia Pacific Fund, Inc.	Investment company	3/31/04	3.6	1.0	154.9	154.1	23	525707
GRR	Asia Tigers Fund, Inc. (The)	Investment company	10/31/03	2.4	0.6	92.3	91.5	28	4926101
AEC	Associated Estates Realty Cor	Real estate investment trust	12/31/03	157.3	d4.8	699.8	121.4	48	3517539
AIZ	Assurant Inc	Insurance	12/31/03	7066.2	185.7	23728.3	2632.1	—	—
AF	Astoria Financial Corp. (Unit	Banking - Northeast	12/31/03	1176.9	228.3	22457.7	1396.5	241	60030695
AZN	AstraZeneca Plc (United Kingd	Chemicals	12/31/03	—	—	—	—	144	90766457
T	AT&T Corp	Telecommunications	12/31/03	34529.0	4553.0	47838.0	13956.0	546	495993503
APL	Atlas Pipeline Partners LP	Natural gas	12/31/03	15.7	11.3	47.8	—	9	124015
ATO	Atmos Energy Corp.	Natural gas	9/30/03	2799.9	79.5	2518.5	857.5	139	16505070
ATW	Atwood Oceanics, Inc. (Unite	Oil service & equipment	9/30/03	144.8	d10.1	317.7	263.5	110	11290467
AUO	AU Optronics Corp.	Electronic components	12/31/03	—	—	18095.5	157051.8	92654.5	25	6277445
ANZ	Australia and New Zealand Ban		9/30/03	4311.0	2962.0	195591.0	13770.0	30	23860562
ALV	Autoliv Inc. (United States)		12/31/03	5300.8	665.4	4894.3	2402.0	133	29167897
ADP	Automatic Data Processing In	Computer services	6/30/03	7147.0	2663.3	19833.7	5371.5	799	426603497
AN	AutoNation, Inc.	Pollution control	12/31/03	19381.1	506.1	8493.4	3949.7	225	199713560
AZO	AutoZone, Inc.		8/30/03	5457.1	517.6	3509.3	373.8	376	89365746
AVB	AvalonBay Communities, Inc.	Real estate investment trust	12/31/03	609.7	100.5	4858.5	2311.3	219	57691510
AV	Avaya Inc		9/30/03	1833.0	d2588.0	3642.0	200.0	287	199253128
AVY	Avery Dennison Corp.	Office equipment & supplies	12/27/03	4762.6	242.8	4105.3	1318.7	437	77909236
AVL	Aviall, Inc.		12/31/03	1013.3	20.7	671.0	300.1	78	12617604
AVA	Avista Corp.	Electric power	12/31/03	1123.4	148.1	3661.5	751.3	121	22516346
AVP	Avon Products, Inc.	Cosmetics & toiletries	12/31/03	6876.0	1658.3	2910.7	371.3	467	201050215
AVX	AVX Corp.	Electronic components	3/31/04	1136.6	d211.0	1518.7	1386.5	117	43563948

T4

EARNINGS PER SHARE QUARTERLY 1st	2nd	3rd	2004	ANNUAL 2003	2002	P/E RATIO	DIVIDENDS PER SHARE 2004	2003	2002	AV. YLD. %	DIV. DECLARED AMOUNT	PAYABLE	PRICE RANGE 2004
0.02				1.29	d5.33	—	0.21	0.10	0.09	0.6	0.05323U	3/31/05	52.48 - 13.37
						—							13.37 - 1.85
0.66				3.70	3.38	—	0.45	—		1.4	0.15Q	3/28/05	42.10 - 21.04
0.74				1.35	0.06	—	1.40	1.65	2.40	4.9	0.35Q	3/10/05	35.53 - 21.78
0.25				1.21	0.80	—	0.02	0.01		0.2	0.02A	12/20/04	13.15 - 8.79
0.66				2.31	2.01	—	0.42	0.36	0.32	0.9	0.12Q	5/10/05	57.05 - 33.23
pd0.06						—	1.01	0.25		6.5	0.27Q	4/18/05	18.62 - 12.60
				1.40	1.63	—	0.06			0.3	0.08Q	5/5/05	27.92 - 13.10
0.70				4.07	2.65	—	2.32			8.3	0.71Q	4/27/05	34.50 - 21.10
1.08				3.53	2.10	—	0.28	0.22	0.18	0.4	0.125Q	6/17/05	76.97 - 49.29
0.44	0.41			2.31	2.21	—	0.56	—		1.9	0.1875Q	3/8/05	41.90 - 18.69
0.33				1.27	0.87	—	1.00	1.00	1.00	5.4	0.25Q	2/28/05	22.60 - 14.47
				15.66	15.13	—	0.94	0.94	0.90	6.6	0.078M	4/27/05	15.45 - 13.03
0.94				1.01	1.12	—							29.23 - 10.35
d1.29				d3.24	d5.49	—							11.25 - 6.99
d0.23				d0.84	d5.08	—							12.25 - 1.72
				13.41	13.48	—	1.04	1.06	1.20	8.0	0.07M	4/27/05	14.25 - 1.60
0.38				1.83	1.68	—					0.15Q	3/25/05	115.41 - 34.45
0.08				0.78	1.34	—	0.89	0.88	0.87	3.7	0.225Q	3/1/05	26.80 - 20.92
				12.67	12.61	—	0.87	0.87	1.00	7.1	0.065M	4/27/05	13.60 - 10.80
d0.19				d1.17	d1.61	—							18.75 - 4.69
0.21	0.30	0.40		0.15	3.87	—					100%	9/30/98	24.98 - 1.99
p1.99					p1.42	—	2.20	2.20	2.20	8.1	0.55Q	2/18/05	30.50 - 24.01
0.72				2.95	2.19	—					100%	1/18/05	76.74 - 25.69
0.94	1.23			3.89	3.16	—	0.10	0.10	0.10	0.2	0.025Q	3/7/05	64.02 - 49.74
1.00				4.51	1.81	—	0.50	0.50	0.50	1.9	0.125Q	4/25/05	32.58 - 19.83
d0.34				3.67	3.48	—	0.80	0.76	0.64	2.5	0.20Q	2/15/05	40.25 - 24.98
0.74				4.05	1.56	—	0.40	0.40	0.40	1.1	0.40A	12/15/04	45.96 - 24.54
0.36				1.30	1.25	—	0.24	0.12	0.12	0.6	0.06Q	3/31/05	51.76 - 23.05
0.13				0.52	0.79	—	1.92	1.92	1.92	7.2	0.48Q	2/22/05	33.11 - 20.20
0.15				0.95	1.12	—							21.56 - 9.10
0.12				0.27	0.53	—	0.40	0.40	0.40	3.1	0.10Q	4/29/05	14.68 - 10.75
0.40				1.18	0.93	—					0.03Q	4/6/05	69.30 - 27.90
d1.03				d7.76	d16.22	—					0.00U	3/15/05	17.65 - 2.10
0.45				1.77	1.68	—	0.96	0.92	0.88	4.1	0.25Q	4/1/05	26.91 - 19.88
1.55				4.91	3.21	—	0.56	0.44	0.33	1.0	0.18Q	3/23/05	71.55 - 41.52
0.30	0.39			0.78	0.28	—	0.22	0.04		0.6	0.06Q	3/16/05	52.35 - 23.93
0.27				1.03	1.25	—	0.44	0.40	0.32	2.2	0.11Q	4/1/05	27.77 - 16.79
						—	0.75	1.33	1.13	2.0	0.3037S	3/7/05	48.25 - 28.22
0.67				2.48	2.20	—	0.93	0.83	0.75	1.8	0.245Q	3/9/05	54.62 - 46.50
0.37					p1.13	—	1.50	—		4.9	1.50U	3/31/04	39.00 - 22.31
0.43				1.42	1.15	—					3-for-2	5/26/04	47.15 - 18.61
0.52				1.94	2.67	—	1.95	2.16	2.59	10.5	0.45Q	4/27/05	21.22 - 15.94
0.36				0.98	0.85	—							43.16 - 22.45
2.08				5.45	4.51	—							125.57 - 101.00
0.20				d0.34	1.04	—	1.12	1.33	1.40	9.8	0.28Q	5/2/05	13.10 - 9.70
0.41				1.52	1.80	—	1.31	1.73	2.05	10.8	0.27Q	5/17/05	14.28 - 10.04
0.60				2.08	1.64	—	0.60	0.60	0.82	2.5	0.15Q	2/16/05	29.40 - 18.17
1.06				3.35	1.80	—	0.26	0.21	0.19	0.4	0.08Q	5/23/05	84.86 - 38.36
d0.15				d0.25	0.94	—	2.40	3.06	3.28	7.2	0.60Q	4/28/05	39.25 - 27.50
				8.99	9.24	—	0.57	0.57	0.56	6.8	0.048M	4/28/05	9.06 - 7.93
d0.19				0.95	0.78	—	0.17	0.17	0.17	0.8	0.0425Q	7/1/05	24.44 - 15.83
	p0.25	p0.22		0.63	0.21	—		0.00			0.00001Q	4/1/03	14.30 - 3.60
0.25	0.26	0.54		1.03	0.76	—	0.35	0.32	0.32	1.1	0.12Q	2/28/05	45.38 - 16.39
0.55				2.15	2.08	—							34.21 - 22.03
0.57				2.16	1.82	—	0.44	0.26	0.24	1.1	0.15Q	2/24/05	54.89 - 28.68
0.17				0.79	0.78	—	0.49	0.46	0.43	2.3	0.13Q	3/1/05	24.64 - 18.90
d0.43				d1.80	d10.65	—			0.77		0.175Q	9/12/02	4.86 - 1.44
						—	1.86	1.07	0.73	6.3	0.08998U	1/19/05	39.61 - 19.35
0.35	0.24			1.34	1.34	—	0.21	0.05		0.8	0.055Q	3/11/05	29.35 - 20.99
0.57				1.63	1.42	—	0.10				0.10Q	4/1/05	45.25 - 31.17
0.13				0.67	0.35	—	0.80	0.80	0.80	3.4	0.20Q	3/24/05	30.83 - 16.52
1.14				0.26	d0.05	—	0.30	0.23	0.23	1.1	0.08Q	3/15/05	38.99 - 17.26
0.23	0.34	0.35		0.70	0.78	—	0.30	0.24	0.22	1.8	0.085Q	3/10/05	22.55 - 10.80
0.21				0.41	1.34	—	2.72	1.71	1.70	8.9	0.4325Q	2/28/05	39.00 - 21.96
0.18				0.72	1.07	—	2.02	2.02	2.00	6.9	0.505Q	4/20/05	37.82 - 21.06
0.13				1.76	2.43	—							46.97 - 16.01
0.42				0.59	0.69	—							49.40 - 10.00
0.27				0.25	0.12	—					2-for-1	10/15/97	29.10 - 11.87
0.28	0.59				p2.06	—	0.40	0.40	0.40	2.0	0.10Q	3/14/05	26.24 - 13.99
0.33				0.61	1.20	—							19.70 - 7.35
0.02				d0.07		—	0.30			3.1	0.16Q	4/15/05	11.09 - 8.61
0.56	d0.16			1.37	1.83	—	1.10	1.10	1.10	2.5	0.275Q	3/15/05	60.17 - 27.74
				14.90	9.10	—	0.18	—		1.6	0.15A	1/14/05	14.89 - 8.10
				10.62	7.65	—	0.07			0.8	0.07A	1/9/04	11.64 - 6.21
d0.14				d0.85	d0.69	—	0.68	0.68	1.00	8.5	0.17Q	5/2/05	10.50 - 5.50
0.73				1.70	2.38	—	0.21	—		0.8	0.08Q	6/7/05	31.29 - 23.40
0.71				2.49	2.85	—	0.67	0.57	0.51	2.0	50%	3/1/05	42.55 - 23.23
						—	0.83	0.72	0.70	2.0	0.645S	3/21/05	51.10 - 32.12
0.38				2.36	1.26	—	0.95	0.80		5.3	0.2375Q	5/2/05	22.10 - 13.59
0.49				2.17	1.54	—	2.57	2.30	2.18	7.6	0.75Q	5/13/05	42.50 - 25.30
0.57	1.12			1.71	1.45	—	1.22	1.21	1.18	5.0	0.31Q	3/10/05	27.59 - 21.26
d0.14	0.03			d0.92	2.02	—					2-for-1	11/19/97	53.98 - 23.98
				3.61	1.58	—	0.25	0.11		1.5	5%	7/19/04	28.25 - 4.95
				1.48	1.47	—	3.71	5.58	2.39	5.7	2.0576S	12/27/04	81.00 - 50.08
0.80				2.81	1.84	—	0.77	0.54	0.44	2.2	0.30Q	6/2/05	48.80 - 19.97
0.32	0.38	0.50		1.68	1.75	—	0.56	0.48	0.46	1.4	0.155Q	4/1/05	47.30 - 30.79
0.32				1.76	1.19	—					0.00U	6/30/00	19.33 - 11.90
1.35	1.04	1.68		5.34	4.00	—					100%	4/20/94	92.35 - 65.71
0.30				1.30	1.49	—	2.80	2.80	2.74	5.0	0.71Q	4/15/05	75.93 - 36.71
0.07	d0.22			d0.23	d2.44	—							19.00 - 2.04
0.52				2.43	2.59	—	1.49	1.45	1.35	2.6	0.38Q	3/16/05	66.60 - 50.20
0.30				d0.29	0.88	—					0.10Q	1/2/96	24.00 - 6.70
0.26				1.02	0.67	—	0.52	0.49	0.48	3.5	0.135Q	3/15/05	19.43 - 10.21
0.31				1.39	1.11	—	0.56	0.42	0.40	0.9	0.165Q	3/1/05	89.52 - 36.10
				d0.62	d0.07	—	0.15	0.15	0.15	1.1	0.0375Q	2/25/05	19.12 - 8.80

SYMBOL	COMPANY	NATURE OF BUSINESS	FISCAL YEAR-END	TOTAL REV. $MILL	NET INCOME $MILL	TOTAL ASSETS $MILL	NET STK EQUITY $MILL	NO. OF INST.	INST. HOLDINGS (SHARES)
AXA	AXA (France)	Insurance	12/31/03	—	—	—	—	125	32833043
AZR	Aztar Corp.	Gaming	1/1/04	813.1	140.2	1201.3	534.6	123	30943207
AZZ	AZZ incorporated	Services	2/29/04	136.2	4.3	108.7	69.3	18	2468233
BZ	Bairnco Corp.	Plastics & plastic products	12/31/03	152.7	6.5	115.2	51.4	12	2459426
BHI	Baker Hughes Inc.	Oil service & equipment	12/31/03	5292.8	508.3	6275.5	3350.4	408	295049968
BEZ	Baldor Electric Co.	Electrical equipment	1/3/04	563.4	24.8	445.6	261.5	117	16586101
BLL	Ball Corp	Containers	12/31/03	4977.0	549.6	3889.0	807.8	258	45191385
BFT	Bally Total Fitness Hldg Cor	Recreation	12/31/03	953.5	d24.1	1013.4	d158.3	105	28597712
BBV	Banco Bilbao Vizcaya Argenta	—	12/31/03	—	—	—	—	77	64238714
ITU	Banco Itau Holding Financeir	—	12/31/03	—	—	—	—	5	2157471
BXS	BancorpSouth Inc.	Banking - South	12/31/03	717.0	131.1	10305.0	868.9	92	12304520
BDG	Bandag, Inc. (United States)	Tires and/or rubber goods	12/31/03	828.2	144.1	660.5	477.1	109	5514436
BAC	Bank of America Corp. (United	Banking - South	12/31/03	48065.0	10810.0	711919.0	47980.0	1024	881323003
IKJ	Bank of America Corp. (United	Banking - South	12/31/03	48065.0	10810.0	711919.0	47980.0	3	84750
IKL	Bank of America Corp. (United	Banking - South	12/31/03	48065.0	10810.0	711919.0	47980.0	—	—
BOH	Bank of Hawaii Corp (DE) (Un	Banking - West	12/31/03	641.2	135.2	9461.6	793.1	175	39520532
BMO	Bank of Montreal (Canada)	—	10/31/03	—	—	—	—	74	122573702
BK	Bank of New York Co., Inc.	Banking - Northeast	12/31/03	6336.0	3015.0	92397.0	8428.0	633	475425742
BNS	Bank of Nova Scotia (Toronto,	—	10/31/03	—	—	—	—	65	155478197
BBX	BankAtlantic Bancorp, Inc.	Savings & loan	12/31/03	543.6	38.6	4831.5	413.5	118	30729779
BN	Banta Corp.	Printing & engraving	1/3/04	1418.5	142.6	847.0	513.4	165	19689799
BCS	Barclays PLC	—	12/31/03	—	—	—	—	77	28127333
BCR	Bard (C.R.), Inc.	Medical & dental equipment	12/31/03	1433.1	391.7	1613.8	1045.7	320	45548185
BKS	Barnes & Noble Inc	Specialty stores	1/31/04	5951.0	151.9	3507.3	1259.7	205	42696411
B	Barnes Group Inc.	—	12/31/03	890.8	71.4	734.7	321.7	86	8700913
BRL	Barr Pharmaceuticals Inc	Drugs	6/30/03	902.9	167.6	1180.9	868.0	289	47462942
ABX	Barrick Gold Corp.	Mining & processing	12/31/03	—	—	—	—	253	278014119
BF	BASF AG (Germany)	Chemicals	12/31/03	—	—	—	—	61	18815147
BOL	Bausch & Lomb, Inc.	Photo & optical	12/27/03	2019.5	323.4	2890.7	1203.4	241	52020975
BAX	Baxter International Inc. (Un	Medical & dental equipment	12/31/03	8916.0	2409.0	12451.0	3323.0	660	449734547
BVC	Bay View Capital Corp. (DE)	Savings & loan	12/31/03	15.0	4.9	225.8	155.8	—	—
BAY	Bayer AG (Germany)	—	12/31/03	—	—	—	—	51	8186616
BBT	BB&T Corp. (Lumberton, NC) (	Financial services	12/31/03	6243.9	1064.9	90466.6	9934.7	395	128614396
BFR	BBVA Banco Frances S.A. (Arg	—	12/31/03	—	—	—	—	17	3513679
BCE	BCE Inc.	Telecommunications	12/31/03	—	—	—	—	146	326984514
BSC	Bear Stearns Cos., Inc. (The)	Securities brokerage	11/30/03	7395.4	1260.2	210218.0	7470.1	371	66490609
BE	Bearingpoint Inc	—	12/31/03	1554.4	1134.7	2028.2	1131.7	153	121820948
BZH	Beazer Homes USA, Inc. (Unit	Home-building	9/30/03	3177.4	172.7	2086.5	993.7	140	12799289
BEC	Beckman Coulter, Inc.	Medical & dental equipment	12/31/03	2192.5	448.6	2418.5	893.7	273	51379628
BDX	Becton, Dickinson & Co.	Medical & dental equipment	9/30/03	4527.9	1256.8	5467.2	2897.0	473	214376429
BED	Bedford Property Investors In	Real estate investment trust	12/31/03	108.0	33.4	773.6	303.9	93	8686806
BDC	Belden, Inc.	Electrical equipment	12/31/03	826.5	d156.9	585.0	274.4	—	—
BLS	Bellsouth Corp.	Telecommunications	12/31/03	22635.0	3589.0	49039.0	19712.0	853	965264945
BLC	Belo Corp.	Publishing	12/31/03	1436.0	128.5	3438.1	1563.8	225	69694826
BMS	Bemis, Inc. (United States)	—	12/31/03	2635.0	386.4	2292.9	1138.7	270	33946016
BHE	Benchmark Electronics, Inc	Communications electronics	12/31/03	1839.8	141.3	1038.0	664.3	196	27523215
BNT	Bentley Pharmaceuticals Inc	Drugs	12/31/03	64.7	6.1	99.5	76.2	35	5764533
BER	Berkley (W. R.) Corp. (Unite	Property & casualty insurance	12/31/03	3630.1	1124.4	9334.7	1682.6	190	46391719
BRK A	Berkshire Hathaway Inc. (Unit	Property & casualty insurance	12/31/03	63859.0	8151.0	180559.0	77596.0	400	237629
BRY	Berry Petroleum, Co.	Oil	12/31/03	180.9	43.9	332.1	195.7	61	9133490
BBY	Best Buy Co., Inc. (United S	Specialty stores	2/28/04	24547.0	800.0	8352.0	3422.0	500	217525389
BEV	Beverly Enterprises, Inc.	Hospitals & nursing homes	12/31/03	1997.0	23.5	1346.4	238.2	96	65928889
BRG	BG Group Plc (United Kingdom	Industrial	12/31/03	—	—	—	—	35	6985173
BHP	BHP Billiton Ltd. (Australia)	Mining & processing	6/30/03	16713.0	1860.0	28877.0	12761.0	105	28119525
BLI	Big Lots, Inc.	Specialty stores	1/31/04	4174.4	90.9	1679.1	1116.1	205	111511038
BVF	Biovail Corp (Canada)	Drugs	12/31/03	—	—	—	—	225	75911529
BSG	Bisys Group, Inc. (The) (Uni	Services	6/30/03	958.4	123.9	1299.9	785.1	230	107632560
BJS	BJ Services Co. (United Stat	Oil service & equipment	9/30/03	2142.9	463.5	2771.2	1650.6	348	157251686
BJ	BJ's Wholesale Club, Inc. (	Discount & variety stores	1/31/04	6724.2	113.7	1625.5	852.2	229	61039306
BKF	BKF Capital Group Inc	Investment company	12/31/03	102.7	d8.4	160.3	92.1	45	4092700
BDK	Black & Decker Corp.	Hardware & tools	12/31/03	4482.7	709.7	3835.7	846.5	324	63893905
BKH	Black Hills Corp.	Electric power	12/31/03	1250.1	130.4	2062.8	709.7	166	12288486
BAT	BlackRock Advantage Term Trus	Investment company	12/31/03	9.5	7.9	139.7	108.4	12	1302467
BFC	BlackRock CA Insd Mun 2008 T	Investment company	12/31/03	11.8	9.9	284.0	178.9	8	232184
BJZ	Blackrock California Municip	Investment company	12/31/03	7.7	6.7	151.1	95.0	1	50000
BDV	BlackRock Dividend Achievers	Investment company	12/15/03	—	d0.0	0.1	0.1	—	—
BKF	BlackRock Florida Insred Mu	Investment company	12/31/03	9.2	7.7	227.4	143.1	10	178728
BIE	Blackrock Florida Municipal	Investment company	8/31/03	4.3	3.8	79.1	48.0	1	10000
BFO	BlackRock Florida Municipal 2	Investment company	12/31/03	0.9	0.7	133.3	80.7	—	—
BNA	BlackRock Income Opportunity	Investment company	10/31/03	34.2	28.9	572.6	411.0	25	11222200
BKT	BlackRock Income Trust Inc.	Investment company	10/31/03	—	—	264.1	—	31	1091534
BMT	BlackRock Insured Mun Term T	Investment company	12/31/03	21.7	18.7	467.4	295.0	20	949706
BRM	BlackRock Insured Muni 2008	Investment company	12/31/03	33.7	29.0	744.4	472.8	20	1645368
BMN	BlackRock Mun Target Term Tr	Investment company	12/31/03	33.1	28.2	798.1	498.3	30	1903461
BPK	Blackrock Municipal 2018 Ter	Investment company	12/31/03	21.5	19.3	386.0	247.0	5	39306
BKK	Blackrock Municipal 2020 Term	Investment company	12/31/03	3.6	3.0	473.3	293.6	—	—
BBK	Blackrock Municipal Bond Tru	Investment company	8/31/03	14.2	12.9	234.7	143.0	2	15750
BLN	BlackRock New York Insred Mu	Investment company	12/31/03	13.3	11.3	302.6	192.8	10	75867
BLH	Blackrock New York Municipal	Investment company	12/31/03	4.4	3.8	88.1	56.4	1	9800
BQH	Blackrock New York Municipal	Investment company	8/31/03	3.5	3.0	62.7	38.2	2	91800
BPP	Blackrock Preferred Opportun	Investment company	8/31/03	37.3	31.5	705.2	468.2	6	59700
BSD	Blackrock Strategic Mun Trus	Investment company	12/31/03	9.9	8.9	178.0	115.2	8	36925
BLK	BlackRock, Inc.		12/31/03	598.2	262.7	967.2	713.3	91	14268537
HRB	Block (H. & R.), Inc.	Services	4/30/04	p4205.6	p4199.2	—	—	463	140477409
BBI	Blockbuster, Inc.		FISCAL	5911.7	793.0	4701.1	3249.3	114	39577782
BLT	Blount International Inc (Ne	Engineering & construction	12/31/03	559.1	d33.7	400.4	d397.3	25	27665395
BLU	Blue Chip Value Fund, Inc.	Investment company	12/31/03	1.9	0.4	154.0	150.1	17	238341
BXG	Bluegreen Corp. (United Stat	Real estate	12/31/03	438.5	25.8	505.3	186.9	23	3145362
BTH	Blyth, Inc. (United States)		1/31/04	1505.6	223.2	1088.1	589.0	153	28634553
BMC	BMC Software, Inc.	Computer services	3/31/04	1418.7	153.3	2337.2	1215.2	338	181178083
BOX	BOC Group Plc (UK)	Conglomerate	9/30/03	—	—	—	—	23	3587849
BA	Boeing Co.		12/31/03	50485.0	3486.0	48122.0	8139.0	682	505660352
OMX	Boise Cascade Corp.	Paper	12/31/03	8245.1	195.2	6451.8	2323.6	—	—
BBA	Bombay Co., Inc. (The)	Furniture & fixtures	1/31/04	596.4	26.2	253.2	191.4	67	18477203
BGP	Borders Group, Inc.	Specialty stores	1/25/04	3731.0	329.5	1870.3	1153.0	184	71636447
BWA	Borg Warner Inc		12/31/03	3069.2	431.6	2677.7	1260.4	221	23239225

T6

| EARNINGS PER SHARE | | | | | | P/E RATIO | DIVIDENDS PER SHARE | | | AV. YLD. % | DIV. DECLARED | | PRICE RANGE |
| QUARTERLY | | | ANNUAL | | | | | | | | | | 2004 |
1st	2nd	3rd	2004	2003	2002		2004	2003	2002	%	AMOUNT	PAYABLE	
0.10	—	—	—	1.66	1.51	—	0.38	0.38	0.43	2.1	0.6722A	5/19/05	24.94 - 11.79
—	—	—	—	0.79	1.63	—							35.35 - 11.83
—	—	—	—	0.36	0.19	—					0.16A	4/27/01	17.30 - 8.40
0.17	—	—	—	0.36	0.19	—	0.20	0.20	0.20	2.4	0.06Q	4/1/05	11.90 - 4.98
0.29	—	—	—	0.54	0.66	—	0.46	0.46	0.46	1.3	0.115Q	2/18/05	45.30 - 28.00
0.22	—	—	—	0.74	0.69	—	0.56	0.52	0.52	2.3	0.15Q	3/31/05	28.75 - 19.14
0.82	—	—	—	4.02	2.77	—	0.35	0.24	0.18	0.6	0.10Q	3/15/05	75.18 - 35.04
pd0.42	—	—	—	d1.91	0.11	—							8.04 - 2.95
—	—	—	—	—	—	—	0.42	0.33	0.30	3.2	0.1554Q	4/21/05	17.85 - 8.32
—	—	—	—	—	—	—	1.52	0.73	—	3.11	0.0265M	5/12/05	75.92 - 21.91
0.35	—	—	—	1.68	1.39	—	0.72	0.64	0.60	3.3	0.19Q	4/1/05	25.25 - 18.40
0.20	—	—	—	3.11	2.52	—	1.30	1.28	1.26	3.2	0.33Q	4/20/05	51.05 - 30.32
1.83	—	—	—	7.13	5.91	—	1.70	1.44	1.22	2.6	0.45Q	3/25/05	89.28 - 42.94
1.83	—	—	—	7.13	5.91	—	1.63	1.56	—	6.2	0.40625Q	4/15/05	26.14 - 26.01
1.83	—	—	—	7.13	5.91	—	1.38	0.31	—	5.5	0.34375Q	4/15/05	24.87 - 24.80
0.69	—	—	—	2.21	1.70	—	1.23	0.87	0.73	3.0	0.33Q	3/14/05	51.10 - 30.46
—	—	—	—	—	—	—	1.59	1.34	1.20	4.2	0.46Q	5/30/05	49.23 - 27.31
0.47	—	—	—	1.52	1.24	—	0.79	0.76	0.76	2.9	0.20Q	5/5/05	34.85 - 20.50
—	—	—	—	—	—	—	1.35	0.84	0.72	3.4	0.32Q	4/27/05	56.67 - 23.75
0.26	—	—	—	0.62	0.67	—	0.13	0.13	0.12	0.9	0.035Q	4/16/05	20.12 - 9.07
0.54	—	—	—	1.81	1.71	—	0.68	0.66	0.64	1.8	0.17Q	5/2/05	47.50 - 28.49
—	—	—	—	—	—	—	1.56	1.23	1.03	4.5	1.175S	4/29/05	45.99 - 23.01
0.68	—	—	—	1.60	1.47	—	0.47	0.45	0.43	0.6	0.12Q	2/4/05	111.71 - 51.15
0.17	—	—	—	2.07	1.39	—	—	—	—	—	0.00U	11/12/04	37.58 - 17.40
0.40	—	—	—	1.49	1.42	—	0.80	0.80	0.80	3.0	0.20Q	3/10/05	33.57 - 19.05
0.37	0.33	0.33	—	1.62	2.08	—					50%	3/15/04	80.99 - 46.09
—	—	—	—	—	—	—	0.22	0.22	0.22	1.1	0.11S	12/15/04	25.52 - 14.95
—	—	—	—	—	—	—	1.32	1.25	0.92	2.4	1.7926A	5/9/05	72.46 - 36.58
0.43	—	—	—	2.36	1.34	—	0.52	0.52	0.78	1.0	0.13Q	4/1/05	69.00 - 30.80
0.31	—	—	—	1.52	1.67	—	0.58	0.58	0.58	2.2	0.582A	1/5/05	34.75 - 18.64
d0.02	—	—	—	d0.01	—	—	4.75	—	—	27.0	2.25U	12/31/04	20.00 - 15.21
—	—	—	—	—	—	—	0.47	0.80	0.64	2.0		5/12/05	34.27 - 13.42
0.60	—	—	—	2.07	2.70	—	1.34	1.22	1.10	3.6	0.35Q	5/2/05	43.25 - 31.43
—	—	—	—	—	—	—	0.43	—	—	6.1	0.4299U	11/4/04	10.15 - 4.05
—	—	—	—	—	—	—	1.20	1.20	1.20	5.6	0.33Q	1/15/06	24.64 - 18.32
2.57	—	—	—	8.52	6.47	—	0.85	0.74	0.62	1.0	0.25Q	4/29/05	109.82 - 62.05
0.01	—	—	—	d0.86	0.22	—							11.30 - 6.37
3.41	—	—	—	12.78	10.74	—	0.13	0.03	—	0.1	200%	3/22/05	148.30 - 57.55
0.54	—	—	—	3.21	2.08	—	0.48	0.40	0.35	1.0	0.14Q	6/2/05	68.07 - 32.21
0.48	0.62	—	—	2.07	1.79	—	0.60	0.40	0.39	0.4	0.18Q	3/31/05	58.17 - 32.80
0.29	—	—	—	1.65	1.91	—	2.04	2.01	1.94	7.1	0.51Q	4/15/05	32.10 - 25.36
0.10	—	—	—	d2.41	d0.64	—	0.05	—	—	0.2	0.05Q	9/10/01	24.48 - 18.75
0.63	—	—	—	1.94	1.44	—	1.04	0.87	0.78	3.9	0.27Q	5/2/05	31.00 - 21.67
0.19	—	—	—	1.11	1.15	—	0.38	0.34	0.30	1.6	0.10Q	6/3/05	29.75 - 18.00
0.40	—	—	—	1.37	1.54	—	0.64	0.56	0.52	1.7	0.18Q	3/1/05	52.23 - 24.63
0.36	—	—	—	1.39	1.01	—	—	—	—	—	3-for-2	11/13/03	40.45 - 23.65
0.04	—	—	—	0.28	0.08	—							14.50 - 8.02
1.33	—	—	—	3.87	2.21	—	0.19	0.18	0.17	0.5	50%	4/8/05	47.40 - 26.26
1008.00	—	—	—	5309.00	2795.00	—					—	—	9570000 -1000000
0.55	—	—	—	1.56	1.37	—	0.52	0.47	0.40	1.6	0.12Q	3/29/05	50.58 - 15.00
—	—	—	—	2.44	1.91	—	0.41	0.30	—	0.9	0.11Q	5/11/05	62.20 - 26.09
0.18	—	—	—	0.22	d0.31	—							9.41 - 1.91
—	—	—	—	—	—	—	0.32	0.25	0.23	1.2	0.19552S	5/20/05	35.40 - 19.26
—	—	—	—	0.30	0.27	—	0.36	0.31	0.27	2.1	0.27S	3/23/05	24.38 - 10.55
p0.06	—	—	—	0.78	0.66	—					0.01U	9/10/01	15.61 - 11.05
—	—	—	—	—	—	—					2-for-1	10/13/00	26.01 - 14.32
0.04	0.17	0.16	—	0.92	0.94	—					100%	2/22/02	18.75 - 12.13
0.38	0.45	—	—	1.17	1.04	—	0.08	—	—	0.2	0.08Q	4/15/05	54.62 - 30.57
0.23	—	—	—	1.50	2.05	—					100%	3/2/99	32.00 - 11.30
—	—	—	—	—	—	—	0.33	—	—	1.2	0.925Q	4/29/05	38.26 - 16.25
0.93	—	—	—	3.68	2.84	—	0.84	0.57	0.48	1.3	0.28Q	3/25/05	89.64 - 34.86
0.30	—	—	—	1.84	2.33	—	1.24	1.20	1.16	4.4	0.32Q	3/1/05	32.49 - 23.63
—	—	—	—	11.40	12.01	—	1.00	0.70	0.63	9.1	0.05M	4/29/05	11.54 - 10.32
—	—	—	—	17.19	17.34	—	0.80	1.23	0.89	4.9		5/2/05	17.45 - 15.37
—	—	—	—	14.77	14.59	—	0.74	0.74	0.74	5.4	0.06125M	5/2/05	14.53 - 12.79
—	—	—	—	12.46	—	—	0.90	—	—	6.5	0.225Q	3/31/05	15.27 - 12.28
—	—	—	—	16.43	16.41	—	0.82	1.15	0.79	5.2	0.0625M	5/2/05	16.80 - 15.00
—	—	—	—	14.52	—	—	0.93	1.00	0.46	6.7		5/2/05	15.20 - 12.71
—	—	—	—	14.50	—	—	0.90	0.07	—	6.3	0.0675M	5/2/05	15.57 - 12.95
—	—	—	—	11.93	11.83	—	0.84	1.07	0.75	7.8	0.07M	4/29/05	11.64 - 9.96
—	—	—	—	—	8.13	—	0.61	1.01	0.58	8.5		4/29/05	8.02 - 6.33
—	—	—	—	11.40	11.29	—	0.61	0.71	0.69	5.5		5/2/05	11.80 - 10.40
—	—	—	—	17.38	17.62	—	0.94	1.18	0.87	5.6	0.06625M	5/2/05	17.85 - 15.83
—	—	—	—	10.97	11.16	—	0.51	0.65	0.73	4.6	0.04M	5/2/05	11.85 - 10.30
—	—	—	—	15.53	14.66	—	0.78	0.78	0.78	5.4	0.065M	5/2/05	15.22 - 13.50
—	—	—	—	14.51	—	—	0.94	0.08	—	6.5		5/2/05	15.75 - 13.27
—	—	—	—	14.12	—	—	1.04	1.07	0.51	7.3		5/2/05	15.38 - 13.03
—	—	—	—	17.13	17.09	—	0.87	1.01	0.77	5.3	0.0625M	5/2/05	17.41 - 15.45
—	—	—	—	15.53	15.11	—	0.74	0.74	0.74	5.1	0.06125M	5/2/05	15.20 - 13.49
—	—	—	—	14.15	—	—	0.93	0.98	0.46	6.7		5/2/05	14.95 - 12.54
—	—	—	—	25.58	—	—	2.07	1.90	—	8.9		4/29/05	25.59 - 20.90
0.84	—	—	—	15.91	15.01	—	0.96	0.92	0.88	6.7		5/2/05	15.61 - 12.95
—	—	—	—	2.36	2.04	—	1.00	0.40	—	1.7	0.30Q	3/23/05	78.24 - 41.60
—	—	—	—	—	p3.15	—	0.82	0.74	0.66	1.7	0.22Q	4/1/05	60.94 - 37.89
0.62	—	—	—	d5.44	1.04	—	5.08	0.08	0.08	39.3	0.02Q	3/28/01	19.37 - 6.50
0.21	—	—	—	d1.09	d0.15	—							18.50 - 4.43
—	—	—	—	5.58	4.85	—	0.55	0.49	0.61	9.7	0.14Q	4/29/05	6.92 - 4.37
0.17	—	—	—	0.94	0.58	—					5%	3/28/96	20.15 - 3.46
0.38	—	—	—	1.88	1.93	—	0.36	0.28	0.22	1.2	0.21S	5/13/05	36.00 - 24.85
—	—	—	—	d0.12	0.20	—					2-for-1	5/15/98	21.87 - 13.31
—	—	—	—	—	—	—	1.41	1.26	1.13	4.5	0.59717S	2/8/05	38.80 - 23.82
0.77	—	—	—	0.89	2.87	—	0.77	0.68	0.68	1.9	0.25Q	3/4/05	55.48 - 25.06
0.66	—	—	—	0.07	d0.03	—	0.60	0.60	0.60	1.9	0.15Q	4/15/05	32.83 - 28.96
d0.16	—	—	—	0.28	0.22	—					3-for-2	12/31/93	8.40 - 4.47
0.04	—	—	—	1.57	1.36	—	0.32	—	—	1.6	0.09Q	4/27/05	25.52 - 14.20
0.91	—	—	—	3.20	2.79	—	0.63	0.36	0.30	0.9	0.14Q	2/15/05	98.64 - 38.39

SYMBOL	COMPANY	NATURE OF BUSINESS	FISCAL YEAR-END	TOTAL REV. $MILL	NET INCOME $MILL	TOTAL ASSETS $MILL	NET STK EQUITY $MILL	NO. OF INST.	INST. HOLDINGS (SHARES)
SAM	Boston Beer Co., Inc	—	12/27/03	207.9	25.2	82.0	62.5	75	5319042
BXP	Boston Properties, Inc.	Real estate investment trust	12/31/03	1309.6	335.3	8551.1	2400.2	255	83760998
BSX	Boston Scientific Corp. (Uni	Medical & dental equipment	12/31/03	3476.0	1169.0	5532.0	2911.0	452	243727263
BOW	Bowater Inc. (United States)	Paper	12/31/03	2721.1	d76.5	5615.8	1612.7	195	56117590
BNE	Bowne & Co., Inc.	Printing & engraving	12/31/03	1064.8	d17.6	714.6	348.7	102	26106251
BYD	Boyd Gaming Corp.	—	12/31/03	154.9	d425.8	1539.6	441.3	119	20324729
FOB	Boyds Collection Ltd (The)	—	12/31/03	113.0	10.9	180.3	138.0	37	11438336
BOY	Boykin Lodging Co (United Sta	Real estate investment trust	12/31/03	269.2	5.5	519.3	231.5	71	7381053
BP	BP p.l.c. (United Kingdom)	Oil	12/31/03	—	—	—	—	912	537344151
BPT	BP Prudhoe Bay Royalty Trust	Oil producer	12/31/03	56.0	54.8	15.0	14.7	37	1099821
BDY	Bradley Pharmaceuticals, Inc	Drugs	12/31/03	74.7	16.8	203.4	152.9	60	5418206
BRC	Brady Corp.	—	7/31/03	554.9	53.9	449.5	339.0	90	16562950
BDN	Brandywine Realty Trust	Real estate investment trust	12/31/03	305.7	74.5	1550.8	771.0	141	27381901
BNN	Brascan Corp	Financial services	12/31/03	—	—	—	—	69	60166357
BRP	Brasil Telecom Participacoes	Telecommunications	12/31/03	—	—	—	—	28	73109832
BTM	Brasil Telecom S.A. (Brazil)	Telecommunications	12/31/03	—	—	—	—	1	32800
BAK	Braskem S A	Specialty chemicals	12/31/03	—	—	—	—	1	1947
BZF	Brazil Fund, Inc.	Investment company	6/30/03	12.0	8.2	293.4	292.6	23	7263478
BZL	Brazilian Equity Fund, Inc.	Investment company	5/31/04	1.7	1.1	42.1	40.5	5	2650795
BRE	BRE Properties, Inc. (United	Real estate investment trust	12/31/03	275.1	69.1	1932.0	960.5	152	28479555
BGG	Briggs & Stratton Corp.	Machinery & equipment	6/30/03	p1657.6	p1657.6	—	—	182	18145131
BCO	Brinks Co (The)	Coal	12/31/03	3998.6	90.4	2271.9	495.6	4	1193395
BRW	Bristol West Holdings Inc	Property & casualty insurance	12/31/03	353.1	50.9	777.9	138.7	—	—
BMY	Bristol-Myers Squibb Co.	Drugs	12/31/03	20894.0	7999.0	27395.0	9786.0	1104	1216131427
BAB	British Airways Plc	—	3/31/04	—	—	—	—	41	6602541
BSY	British Sky Broadcasting Gr	Broadcasting	6/30/03	—	—	—	—	31	3493369
BHS	Brookfield Homes Corp	Engineering & construction	12/31/03	1023.3	88.2	1013.4	382.3	49	10826557
BPO	Brookfield Properties Corp. (	Real estate	12/31/03	—	—	—	—	84	56411030
BRO	Brown & Brown, Inc.	Insurance	12/31/03	551.0	110.3	834.3	498.0	193	41567275
BWS	Brown Shoe Co., Inc. (United	Shoe manufacturing	1/31/04	1832.1	46.9	602.7	355.1	131	12690482
BFA	Brown-Forman Corp.	Distilling	4/30/04	p2577.0	p2577.0	—	—	53	15504331
BRT	BRT Realty Trust	Real estate investment trust	9/30/03	14.8	13.7	139.0	125.9	12	186978
BC	Brunswick Corp.	Recreation	12/31/03	4128.7	361.3	3198.9	1323.0	241	75882314
BW	Brush Engineered Materials I	Metal products	12/31/03	401.0	d25.9	334.2	153.6	67	10516562
BPL	Buckeye Partners, L.P.	Oil	12/31/03	272.9	45.1	935.4	—	96	2718873
BKI	Buckeye Technologies Inc.	Paper	6/30/03	641.1	d24.5	1073.6	261.9	85	23916434
BKE	Buckle, Inc. (The)	—	1/31/04	422.8	48.8	337.9	297.6	40	5185658
BNL	Bunzl Plc (United Kingdom)	Paper	12/31/03	—	—	—	—	6	151872
BNI	Burlington Northern Santa Fe	Railroads	12/31/03	9413.0	777.0	26521.0	8495.0	418	284072113
BR	Burlington Resources Inc.	Oil producer	12/31/03	4311.0	2830.0	12884.0	5521.0	504	168624486
CHP	C&D Technologies Inc.	Electrical equipment	1/31/04	324.8	14.9	385.9	269.5	128	23569505
CVC	Cablevision Systems Corp. (Ne	—	12/31/03	4186.1	d272.4	10894.5	d1989.8	251	200566614
CBT	Cabot Corp.	Specialty chemicals	9/30/03	1795.0	169.0	2263.0	1079.0	190	39944003
COG	Cabot Oil & Gas Corp.	Oil	12/31/03	509.4	53.1	1012.0	365.2	144	27762505
CAI	CACI International, Inc.	Computer services	6/30/03	843.1	44.7	517.6	421.5	195	24119561
CSG	Cadbury Schweppes PLC	Soft drinks	12/28/03	—	—	—	—	104	22809688
CDN	Cadence Design Systems, Inc.	Comp. components & periphs.	1/3/04	456.0	d598.5	2579.4	1572.3	250	217673435
CZR	Caesars Entertainment Inc	Gaming	12/31/03	4455.0	111.0	9542.0	3058.0	—	—
CCC	Calgon Carbon Corp.	Chemicals	12/31/03	278.3	4.5	302.2	161.9	73	27140141
CWT	California Water Service Grou	Water company	12/31/03	277.1	60.4	851.1	248.0	71	2797079
ELY	Callaway Golf Co. (DE)	Recreation	12/31/03	814.0	178.9	735.9	589.4	193	62710011
CPE	Callon Petroleum Co. (DE)	Oil	12/31/03	73.7	d13.5	440.9	133.3	27	4799775
CPN	Calpine Corp. (United States	Electric power	12/31/03	8919.5	219.4	26155.2	4621.3	343	224544207
CBM	Cambrex Corp	Specialty chemicals	12/31/03	410.6	38.4	673.3	396.6	130	22380669
CPT	Camden Property Trust	Real estate investment trust	12/31/03	416.5	45.7	2625.6	784.9	142	29009900
CCJ	Cameco Corp. (Canada)	Mining & processing	12/31/03	—	—	—	—	41	26760199
CPB	Campbell Soup Co.	Food processing	8/3/03	6678.0	1550.0	6103.0	387.0	324	144175770
BCM	Canadian Imperial Bank of Co	—	10/31/03	—	—	—	—	64	92331706
CNI	Canadian National Railway Co	Railroads	12/31/03	—	—	—	—	170	115957620
CNQ	Canadian Natural Resources L	Natural gas	12/31/03	—	—	—	—	90	53395765
CP	Canadian Pacific Railway Ltd	Railroads	12/31/03	—	—	—	—	115	53714663
CAJ	Canon, Inc. (Japan)	Office equipment & supplies	12/31/03	—	—	—	—	136	18661982
CMN	Cantel Medical Corp (United	Medical & dental equipment	7/31/03	129.3	20.1	109.8	70.2	50	3216408
CWG	CanWest Global Communication	Broadcasting	8/31/03	—	—	—	—	8	374408
COF	Capital One Financial Corp. (	Financial services	12/31/03	9783.6	1150.9	45943.9	6051.8	424	191281556
CSU	Capital Senior Living Corp.	Hospitals & nursing homes	12/31/03	66.3	17.5	421.3	124.4	8	3235368
CT	Capital Trust, Inc. (MD)	Real estate	12/31/03	47.8	16.4	358.3	96.0	17	2901339
CSE	CapitalSource Inc	Finance	12/31/03	225.8	131.1	1829.1	867.1	—	—
CBC	Capitol Bancorp Ltd. (United	Banking - Northeast	12/31/03	184.5	23.4	2737.1	218.9	51	1450696
CRR	Carbo Ceramics Inc.	Mining & processing	12/31/03	169.9	29.6	235.1	200.1	86	9816582
CAH	Cardinal Health, Inc. (United	Drugs	6/30/03	56737.0	9707.4	18457.1	7758.1	790	345078604
CMX	Caremark Rx, Inc.	Hospitals & nursing homes	12/31/03	9067.3	290.8	2228.0	640.6	346	212697669
CSL	Carlisle Cos., Inc.	Conglomerate	12/31/03	2108.2	88.9	1242.9	631.9	170	18504187
KMX	Carmax Inc.	—	2/29/04	4597.7	116.5	1032.6	680.8	194	93613460
CCL	Carnival Corp.	Recreation	11/30/03	6718.0	1194.0	24101.0	13793.0	56	119458835
CRS	Carpenter Tech. Corp.	Steel producer	6/30/03	871.1	d10.9	1373.1	474.6	113	12602146
CRE	CarrAmerica Realty Corp. (Uni	Real estate investment trust	12/31/03	491.9	78.4	2592.5	907.6	173	46276964
CSV	Carriage Services, Inc.	Services	12/31/03	150.8	17.5	678.5	105.9	24	6595686
CRI	Carter's Inc	—	1/3/04	703.8	23.3	537.0	272.5	—	—
CAE	Cascade Corp.	Machinery & equipment	1/31/04	297.8	46.9	277.5	183.7	70	6423835
CGC	Cascade Natural Gas Corp (Uni	Natural gas distributor	9/30/03	302.8	9.1	371.5	112.6	89	4873165
CSH	Cash America Intl., Inc.	Finance	12/31/03	437.7	76.2	397.1	276.5	104	17553377
CDX	Catellus Development Corp (Ne	Real estate	12/31/03	511.9	228.3	2464.4	709.7	—	—
CAT	Caterpillar Inc	Machinery & equipment	12/31/03	22763.0	2576.0	36465.0	6078.0	583	249420375
CTR	Cato Corp. (New)	—	1/31/04	747.3	31.4	338.1	194.1	100	16165769
CBL	CBL & Associates Properties,	Real estate investment trust	12/31/03	667.5	169.8	4264.3	837.3	166	24291043
CDI	CDI Corp.	Services	12/31/03	1060.3	860.3	392.6	297.4	103	8834862
CEC	CEC Entertainment, Inc.	Restaurants	12/28/03	654.6	69.3	580.4	392.5	150	25846460
FUN	Cedar Fair, L.P.	—	12/31/03	510.0	85.9	781.6	—	110	9414760
CDR	Cedar Shopping Centers Inc	Real estate investment trust	12/31/03	26.5	d18.2	341.3	151.1	—	—
CRA	Celera Genomics Group	—	6/30/03	88.3	d81.9	1122.1	1002.2	153	4351398
CLS	Celestica, Inc.	Electronic components	12/31/03	—	—	—	—	166	93160547
CD	Cendant Corp.	Services	12/31/03	18192.0	5075.0	37507.0	10186.0	535	817243298
CNC	Centene Corp	Services	12/31/03	769.7	121.6	359.0	220.1	91	12295510
CNP	Centerpoint Energy, Inc.	Electric power	12/31/03	9760.1	420.0	20118.7	1760.6	269	138331894
CNT	CenterPoint Properties Trust	Real estate	12/31/03	161.4	40.6	1205.5	482.5	128	21314301

T8

1st	2nd	3rd	2004	2003	2002	P/E RATIO	2004	2003	2002	AV. YLD. %	AMOUNT	PAYABLE	PRICE RANGE 2004
0.09	—	—	—	0.70	0.52	—	—	—	—	—	—	—	27.95 - 12.56
0.61	—	—	—	2.94	4.40	—	2.56	2.48	2.38	5.1	0.65Q	4/29/05	64.90 - 35.90
0.23	—	—	—	0.56	0.45	—	—	—	—	—	100%	11/5/03	45.93 - 31.25
d0.57	—	—	—	d3.52	d2.50	—	0.80	0.80	0.80	1.9	0.20Q	4/1/05	48.00 - 34.15
0.09	—	—	—	d0.27	0.01	—	0.22	0.22	0.22	1.6	0.055Q	2/18/05	17.99 - 9.80
0.20	—	—	—	0.62	0.73	—	0.32	0.15	—	1.2	0.085Q	3/1/05	42.50 - 12.51
0.05	—	—	—	0.18	0.53	—	—	—	—	—	—	—	4.60 - 2.21
d0.31	—	—	—	d0.40	d0.09	—	—	0.36	0.18	—	0.18Q	5/1/03	9.86 - 7.00
—	—	—	—	—	—	—	1.66	1.53	1.41	3.3	0.51Q	3/14/05	62.04 - 38.11
—	—	—	—	2.56	1.51	—	3.82	2.56	1.51	11.7	—	4/19/05	50.50 - 14.73
0.35	—	—	—	1.35	0.67	—	—	—	—	—	—	—	30.00 - 11.25
0.44	0.34	p0.68	—	1.79	2.37	—	0.42	0.41	0.39	0.9	0.11Q	5/2/05	64.40 - 26.56
0.33	—	—	—	1.09	1.02	—	1.76	1.76	1.76	6.9	0.44Q	4/15/05	30.82 - 20.00
—	—	—	—	—	—	—	0.63	0.68	0.67	2.1	0.15Q	5/31/05	40.54 - 19.72
—	—	—	—	—	—	—	0.91	0.47	1.06	2.6	—	1/26/05	46.33 - 24.56
—	—	—	—	—	—	—	0.20	0.87	0.39	1.4	—	1/26/05	19.88 - 8.46
—	—	—	—	—	—	—	—	—	0.36	—	0.7095U	1/3/05	51.00 - 2.30
—	—	—	—	17.91	15.43	—	0.63	0.27	0.72	2.8	0.78A	1/12/05	34.89 - 10.71
—	—	—	—	7.25	3.85	—	0.15	0.03	—	2.4	0.16A	1/7/05	9.37 - 3.34
0.27	—	—	—	0.97	1.56	—	1.95	1.95	1.95	5.4	0.50Q	3/31/05	42.54 - 29.45
p0.18	0.87	p2.88	—	—	p3.49	—	0.67	0.65	0.64	1.1	0.17Q	4/1/05	89.00 - 36.41
0.32	—	—	—	0.34	1.30	—	0.10	0.10	0.10	0.4	0.025Q	3/1/05	39.91 - 12.75
0.48	—	—	—	1.32	0.48	—	0.15	—	—	0.8	0.05Q	3/10/05	23.10 - 15.22
0.49	—	—	—	1.59	1.05	—	1.12	1.12	1.12	4.3	0.28Q	5/2/05	31.00 - 21.13
—	—	—	—	—	—	—	—	—	—	—	1.8214S	8/7/01	62.50 - 16.25
—	—	—	—	—	—	—	0.43	—	—	0.9	0.298U	4/29/05	59.24 - 33.22
0.31	—	—	—	2.75	1.35	—	9.16	0.16	—	37.4	0.08S	12/31/04	38.50 - 10.52
—	—	—	—	—	—	—	0.41	0.33	0.27	1.5	0.18Q	6/30/05	38.33 - 18.21
0.53	—	—	—	1.60	1.22	—	0.29	0.24	0.20	0.8	0.08Q	2/16/05	46.75 - 28.82
0.45	—	—	—	2.52	2.52	—	0.40	0.40	0.40	1.2	0.10Q	4/1/05	41.95 - 24.18
—	—	—	—	—	p1.81	—	0.85	0.75	0.70	1.2	0.245Q	4/1/05	97.00 - 44.20
0.43	0.42	—	—	1.80	1.68	—	1.79	1.30	1.04	8.3	0.48Q	4/1/05	29.35 - 13.59
0.50	—	—	—	1.47	1.14	—	0.60	0.50	0.50	1.7	0.60A	12/15/04	49.81 - 18.90
0.22	—	—	—	d0.80	d2.15	—	—	—	—	—	0.12Q	7/6/01	23.07 - 5.07
0.69	—	—	—	1.05	2.64	—	2.64	2.54	2.50	6.5	0.6875Q	2/28/05	45.30 - 35.60
d0.07	0.27	d0.74	—	d0.67	d0.42	—	—	—	—	—	100%	2/17/98	13.30 - 4.65
0.27	—	—	—	1.56	1.47	—	0.42	0.10	—	1.2	0.12Q	4/27/05	31.97 - 16.60
—	—	—	—	—	—	—	1.09	0.92	0.78	2.9	0.8827S	7/11/05	45.04 - 29.02
0.52	—	—	—	2.09	2.00	—	0.62	0.51	0.48	1.7	0.17Q	4/1/05	49.20 - 24.90
0.89	—	—	—	3.15	1.13	—	0.31	0.28	0.28	0.6	0.085Q	4/8/05	69.80 - 31.70
0.08	—	—	—	0.58	0.74	—	0.07	0.04	0.07	0.4	0.01375Q	4/6/05	21.32 - 11.98
d0.39	—	—	—	d0.99	d1.91	—	—	—	—	—	0.001	3/29/01	27.58 - 16.16
0.43	0.53	—	—	1.08	1.48	—	0.61	0.56	0.52	1.9	0.16Q	3/11/05	40.81 - 21.90
0.58	—	—	—	0.87	0.50	—	0.11	0.11	0.11	0.3	50%	3/31/05	48.89 - 23.51
0.44	0.48	0.53	—	1.52	1.24	—	—	—	—	—	100%	12/6/01	69.18 - 33.05
—	—	—	—	—	—	—	0.88	0.77	0.66	3.0	0.6612S	6/6/05	37.99 - 20.15
d0.03	—	—	—	d0.07	0.27	—	—	—	—	—	2-for-1	11/14/97	19.48 - 9.92
0.20	—	—	—	0.18	0.51	—	—	—	—	—	—	—	20.20 - 11.13
d0.01	—	—	—	0.11	0.11	—	0.12	0.12	0.12	1.6	0.03Q	3/9/05	9.69 - 4.90
0.08	—	—	—	1.21	1.25	—	1.13	1.13	1.12	3.6	0.285Q	2/18/05	37.88 - 24.35
0.59	—	—	—	0.68	1.03	—	0.28	0.28	0.28	1.9	0.07Q	4/7/05	20.00 - 9.28
0.12	—	—	—	d1.42	d0.22	—	—	—	—	—	—	—	14.72 - 3.91
d0.23	—	—	—	0.28	0.14	—	—	—	—	—	2-for-1	11/14/00	6.42 - 2.25
0.31	—	—	—	0.01	1.37	—	0.12	0.12	0.12	0.5	0.03Q	2/18/05	28.74 - 17.40
0.22	—	—	—	0.71	1.00	—	2.54	2.54	2.52	6.2	0.21872Q	4/15/05	51.00 - 31.50
—	—	—	—	—	—	—	0.20	0.19	0.17	0.3	0.06Q	4/15/05	105.60 - 24.13
0.51	0.57	0.34	—	1.52	1.28	—	0.64	0.63	0.63	2.5	0.17Q	5/2/05	30.52 - 20.74
—	—	—	—	—	—	—	2.20	1.64	1.60	4.8	0.65Q	4/28/05	62.59 - 28.66
—	—	—	—	—	—	—	0.78	0.67	0.57	1.5	0.25Q	3/31/05	64.45 - 36.51
—	—	—	—	—	—	—	0.19	0.14	0.12	0.4	2-for-1	5/27/05	60.12 - 29.72
—	—	—	—	—	—	—	0.52	0.51	0.51	1.9	0.1325Q	4/25/05	34.50 - 20.00
—	—	—	—	—	—	—	0.52	0.24	0.18	1.2	0.34604U	4/7/05	54.39 - 35.09
0.18	0.26	0.30	—	0.80	0.74	—	—	—	—	—	50%	1/12/05	38.19 - 12.77
—	—	—	—	—	—	—	—	—	—	—	0.15S	4/16/01	11.03 - 4.03
1.84	—	—	—	4.92	3.93	—	0.11	0.11	0.11	0.2	—	2/22/05	84.45 - 30.01
d0.09	—	—	—	0.25	0.24	—	—	—	—	—	—	—	7.28 - 2.71
0.46	—	—	—	2.23	d1.62	—	1.80	0.90	—	6.9	0.55Q	4/15/05	34.56 - 17.76
0.20	—	—	—	1.01	0.42	—	—	—	—	—	—	—	25.98 - 17.00
0.30	—	—	—	1.77	1.57	—	0.65	0.51	0.44	2.3	0.17Q	3/1/05	36.00 - 20.90
0.60	—	—	—	1.88	1.28	—	0.44	0.38	0.36	0.8	0.12Q	2/15/05	77.80 - 31.95
0.74	0.87	0.98	—	3.12	2.45	—	0.12	0.11	0.10	0.2	0.03Q	4/15/05	76.54 - 36.25
0.29	—	—	—	1.10	3.15	—	—	—	—	—	—	—	39.95 - 17.46
0.76	—	—	—	2.88	2.37	—	0.90	0.87	0.85	1.7	0.23Q	3/1/05	67.31 - 40.49
p0.33	—	—	—	1.10	0.91	—	—	—	—	—	—	—	37.00 - 14.57
p0.25	—	—	—	1.66	1.73	—	0.53	0.33	—	1.2	0.15Q	3/11/05	58.74 - 27.59
—	0.31	0.39	—	d0.56	d0.35	—	0.35	0.33	1.07	1.0	0.10Q	3/3/05	61.91 - 10.15
0.20	—	—	—	0.64	1.04	—	2.00	2.00	2.00	6.9	0.50Q	2/28/05	34.34 - 24.01
0.17	—	—	—	0.37	1.16	—	—	—	—	—	—	—	5.50 - 3.13
0.35	—	—	—	0.92	0.82	—	—	—	—	—	—	—	35.59 - 24.65
0.65	—	—	—	1.49	1.45	—	0.44	0.30	0.10	1.6	0.12Q	4/14/05	42.00 - 14.18
0.71	0.76	—	—	0.82	0.97	—	0.96	0.96	0.96	4.6	0.24Q	5/13/05	23.05 - 19.04
0.39	—	—	—	1.13	0.75	—	0.37	0.07	0.05	1.9	0.025Q	2/23/05	30.45 - 8.92
0.29	—	—	—	2.23	0.97	—	1.08	—	—	4.0	0.27Q	4/15/05	32.20 - 21.25
1.16	—	—	—	3.13	2.30	—	1.56	1.42	1.40	2.2	0.41Q	2/19/05	98.72 - 43.98
0.81	—	—	—	1.33	1.77	—	0.67	0.62	0.57	2.9	0.175Q	3/28/05	29.45 - 17.00
0.96	—	—	—	3.84	2.58	—	2.90	2.62	2.21	5.0	0.8125Q	4/15/05	77.13 - 38.45
0.25	—	—	—	1.14	0.21	—	2.40	2.18	—	9.5	0.11Q	3/30/05	34.99 - 15.74
0.82	—	—	—	1.75	1.64	—	—	—	—	—	50%	3/15/04	58.19 - 25.31
d0.59	—	—	—	1.67	1.39	—	1.79	1.74	1.65	6.1	0.46Q	5/16/05	36.00 - 22.80
0.08	—	—	—	d7.09	d1.41	—	0.84	—	—	6.6	0.225Q	2/22/05	14.45 - 10.95
pd0.23	pd0.19	pd0.30	—	d1.15	d3.21	—	—	—	—	—	100%	2/18/00	11.18 - 10.87
—	—	—	—	—	—	—	—	—	—	—	100%	12/21/99	21.75 - 11.43
0.42	—	—	—	1.41	1.04	—	0.32	—	—	1.8	0.09Q	3/15/05	25.19 - 11.08
0.47	—	—	—	1.73	1.47	—	—	—	—	—	100%	12/17/04	59.50 - 17.00
0.24	—	—	—	1.37	1.29	—	0.40	0.40	0.16	4.7	0.10Q	3/31/05	12.32 - 4.65
0.53	—	—	—	1.18	1.41	—	1.56	1.22	1.16	2.6	0.4275Q	4/25/05	83.34 - 37.25

SYMBOL	COMPANY	NATURE OF BUSINESS	FISCAL YEAR-END	TOTAL REV. $MILL	NET INCOME $MILL	TOTAL ASSETS $MILL	NET STK EQUITY $MILL	NO. OF INST.	INST. HOLDINGS (SHARES)
CTX	Centex Corp.	Home-building	3/31/04	10363.4	882.7	16068.6	3050.2	328	53672937
CPF	Central Pacific Financial Co	Banking - West	12/31/03	124.3	33.9	2170.3	194.6	3	67700
CPC	Central Parking Corp. (Unite	Services	9/30/03	1136.3	78.8	827.9	416.5	106	18107802
CV	Central Vermont Pub Svc Corp	Electric power	12/31/03	306.0	18.4	505.1	228.3	75	4872130
CTL	CenturyTel, Inc. (United Stat	Telecommunications	12/31/03	2380.7	344.7	7895.9	3478.5	358	116773234
CVO	Cenveo Inc	Paper	12/31/03	1671.7	15.8	1034.1	68.0	—	—
CEN	Ceridian Corp. (New)	Services	12/31/03	1253.2	318.9	4981.8	1271.9	191	137628375
CEY	Certegy, Inc. (United States	Financial services	12/31/03	—	d40.2	733.4	261.1	224	50163566
GIB	CGI Group, Inc.	Telecommunications	9/30/03	—	—	—	—	41	76449131
CHG	CH Energy Group, Inc.	Electric power	12/31/03	806.7	44.0	1292.3	506.5	122	6791773
CHB	Champion Enterprises, Inc	Mobile homes	1/3/04	1140.7	d172.0	453.4	15.0	89	52468474
CRL	Charles River Lab. Intl Inc.	—	12/27/03	613.7	422.3	768.7	464.6	210	45640970
CWF	Chartwell Dividend & Income F	Investment company	11/30/03	—	9.6	191.7	139.1	10	131749
CKP	Checkpoint Systems Inc	Electronic components	12/28/03	723.3	79.9	742.7	327.6	115	23877952
CHE	Chemed Corp (New)	Specialty chemicals	12/31/03	308.9	55.3	272.4	192.7	—	—
CSK	Chesapeake Corp.	Paper	12/31/03	p899.3	p899.3	—	—	106	9132345
CHK	Chesapeake Energy Corp.	Oil producer	12/31/03	1717.4	334.3	4426.1	1732.8	260	151050680
CPK	Chesapeake Utilities Corp.	Natural gas distributor	12/31/03	162.3	10.1	217.9	72.9	34	780559
CVX	ChevronTexaco Corp.	Oil	12/31/03	—	7426.0	81280.0	36295.0	1124	630495420
CME	Chicago Mercantile Exchange H	Finance	12/31/03	536.0	122.1	4823.9	563.0	70	5234649
CHS	Chico's FAS, Inc. (United S	Specialty stores	1/31/04	768.5	100.2	465.5	374.8	268	82438966
CH	Chile Fund, Inc.	Investment company	12/31/03	2.7	0.9	151.5	146.8	24	4514901
SNP	China Petroleum & Chemical C	Oil	12/31/03	—	—	—	—	27	8975056
CHA	China Telecom Corp Ltd	Telecommunications	12/31/03	—	—	—	—	31	9732804
CHU	China Unicom Ltd.	Telecommunications	12/31/03	67636.3	4217.1	149837.9	69615.5	29	3834938
CHZ	Chittenden Corp (VT)	Banking - Northeast	12/31/03	368.5	74.8	5900.6	580.0	126	18440127
CHH	Choice Hotels Intl Inc (New)	Motel/hotel lodging	12/31/03	386.1	184.3	252.4	d118.2	92	14088014
CPS	ChoicePoint, Inc.	Insurance brokerage	12/31/03	795.7	108.1	1021.3	790.5	251	67519834
CBK	Christopher & Banks Corp.	—	2/28/04	p390.7	p390.7	—	—	117	21880247
CB	Chubb Corp.	Property & casualty insurance	12/31/03	11394.0	808.8	38360.6	8522.0	479	144869835
CHT	Chunghwa Telecom Co Ltd (Tai	Telecommunications	12/31/03	—	—	—	—	—	—
CHD	Church & Dwight Co., Inc.	Soaps & cleansers	12/31/03	1056.9	197.9	1109.3	438.5	163	24922726
CBR	CIBER, Inc.	Computer services	12/31/03	692.0	54.4	535.4	304.6	115	36902902
CI	CIGNA Corp.	Insurance	12/31/03	18808.0	620.0	90953.0	4519.0	371	115814360
IIS	Cigna Investment Securities (	Investment company	12/31/03	4.4	3.5	92.2	90.7	13	554650
XEC	Cimarex Energy Co	Oil	12/31/03	454.2	110.6	758.9	534.7	258	50070070
CBB	Cincinnati Bell Inc (New)	Telecommunications	12/31/03	1557.8	1169.4	1427.9	d679.4	—	—
CIN	Cinergy Corp (United States)	Electric power	12/31/03	4415.9	434.4	13904.2	3700.7	334	113282036
CIR	Circor International Inc	Oil service & equipment	12/31/03	359.5	43.5	406.9	275.2	66	9675817
CIT	CIT Group Inc. (DE)	Financial services	12/31/03	3729.5	572.3	46342.8	5394.2	193	207009792
CDL	Citadel Broadcasting Corp (U	Broadcasting	12/31/03	371.5	d79.5	—	1232.4	—	—
C	Citigroup Inc	Financial services	12/31/03	94713.0	17853.0	—	98014.0	1331	d978925589
CZN	Citizens Communications Co	Telecommunications	12/31/03	2444.9	128.3	7689.1	1415.2	262	218987844
CIA	Citizens, Inc. (Austin, TX)	Life Insurance	12/31/03	95.1	3.1	390.1	127.0	31	2542481
CYN	City National Corp. (Beverly	Banking - West	12/31/03	753.0	186.7	13018.2	1219.3	215	28879113
CKR	CKE Restaurants, Inc. (Unite	Restaurants	1/26/04	1413.4	62.0	708.0	146.2	72	17044280
CLE	Claire's Stores, Inc. (United	—	1/31/04	1132.8	289.5	726.9	632.5	205	38012387
CLC	Clarcor Inc.	—	11/30/03	741.4	140.6	503.1	370.4	166	18754210
CLK	Clark Inc	Life Insurance	12/31/03	325.9	170.5	660.2	258.5	—	—
CCU	Clear Channel Communications	Broadcasting	12/31/03	8930.9	1145.6	27357.2	15553.9	572	461145050
CNL	Cleco Corp. (New)	Electric power	12/31/03	874.6	d34.9	2159.4	501.5	157	26570878
CLF	Cleveland-Cliffs, Inc.	Mining & processing	12/31/03	857.7	d26.2	817.7	228.1	90	8729683
CLX	Clorox Co.	Soaps & cleansers	6/30/03	4144.0	514.0	3446.0	1215.0	442	115801911
CMS	CMS Energy Corp (United State	Electric power	12/31/03	5513.0	443.0	13153.0	1890.0	234	80355610
CNA	CNA Financial Corp.	Property & casualty insurance	12/31/03	11716.0	d1433.0	68223.0	8952.0	121	220306256
SUR	CNA Surety Corp.	Property & casualty insurance	12/31/03	332.6	d14.2	1169.1	410.1	71	40584230
CNF	CNF, Inc.	Trucking lines	12/31/03	5104.3	92.0	2611.3	818.8	186	44296791
CEO	Cnooc Ltd. (Hong Kong)	Oil	12/31/03	—	—	—	—	51	7206716
COA	Coachmen Industries, Inc	Mobile homes	12/31/03	711.4	40.7	271.5	211.2	71	12397739
KO	Coca-Cola Co (The) (United St	Soft drinks	12/31/03	21044.0	9842.0	26983.0	14090.0	1043	1404902381
CCE	Coca-Cola Enterprises, Inc.	Soft drinks	12/31/03	17330.0	676.0	23801.0	4365.0	279	156157229
KOF	Coca-Cola FEMSA, S.A. de C.V	Soft drinks	12/31/03	—	—	—	—	94	18950956
CCH	Coca-Cola Hellenic Bottling	Soft drinks	12/31/03	—	—	—	—	1	70000
CDE	Coeur d'Alene Mines Corp (Ida	Mining & processing	12/31/03	109.7	d64.7	258.3	196.3	57	10508168
RLF	Cohen & Steers Advantage Inc	Investment company	12/31/03	32.5	28.6	772.4	484.8	20	939637
RNP	Cohen & Steers Reit and Prefe	Investment company	12/31/03	40.2	33.2	1970.7	1287.2	—	—
RFI	Cohen & Steers Total Return	Investment company	12/31/03	6.7	5.4	157.3	157.1	17	398119
KCP	Cole (Kenneth) Productions,	—	12/31/03	468.4	32.6	247.7	196.3	94	11355659
CM	Coles Myer Ltd. (Australia)	Discount & variety stores	7/27/03	27208.8	429.5	5953.7	3776.4	7	452798
CL	Colgate-Palmolive Co.	Soaps & cleansers	12/31/03	9903.4	3463.2	6850.4	887.1	797	368800753
CKC	Collins & Aikman Corp. (New)	Textiles	12/31/03	3983.7	d79.5	2728.5	440.3	54	15643607
CNB	Colonial Bancgroup Inc.	Banking - South	12/31/03	908.3	155.0	16273.3	1178.3	178	48885747
CLP	Colonial Properties Trust (AL	Real estate investment trust	12/31/03	334.2	63.7	1969.5	601.7	133	11460162
CCZ	Comcast Holdings Corp	—	12/31/03	7719.0	570.0	40402.0	18904.0	3	33168237
CMA	Comerica, Inc.	Banking - Midwest	12/31/03	3299.0	661.0	52592.0	5110.0	377	107012352
FIX	Comfort Systems USA, Inc.	Services	12/31/03	785.0	d1.0	332.6	200.7	51	13465086
CBH	Commerce Bancorp, Inc. (NJ)	Banking - Northeast	12/31/03	1248.1	194.3	22712.2	1277.3	259	52088552
CGI	Commerce Group, Inc. (MA) (U	Property & casualty insurance	12/31/03	1640.8	160.9	3164.2	912.2	84	7541953
CFB	Commercial Federal Corp.	Savings & loan	12/31/03	797.4	89.0	12188.9	755.4	141	31399305
CMC	Commercial Metals Co.	Metal products	8/31/03	2875.9	18.9	1260.4	506.9	110	17174011
NNN	Commercial Net Lease Realty,	Real estate investment trust	12/31/03	102.7	62.8	1180.5	730.8	98	12042896
CTV	Commscope, Inc.	Communications electronics	12/31/03	573.3	d70.6	716.5	455.7	146	44294828
CBU	Community Bank System, Inc.	Banking - Northeast	12/31/03	226.1	40.4	3855.4	404.8	87	4562995
CYH	Community Health Sys Inc	Hospitals & nursing homes	12/31/03	2834.6	408.0	3265.2	1350.6	153	56568689
GGY	Compagnie Generale de Geophy	Oil service & equipment	12/31/03	—	—	—	—	3	563741
CBD	Companhia Brasileira de Distr	Grocery chain	12/31/03	—	—	—	—	43	15270015
ABV C	Companhia de Bebidas das Amer	—	12/31/03	—	—	—	—	5	604121
ELP	Companhia Paranaense De Energ	Electric power	12/31/03	—	—	—	—	17	19402840
VNT	Compania Anonima Nacional Te	Telecommunications	12/31/03	—	—	—	—	65	34632329
CU	COMPANIA CERVECERIAS UNIDAS	—	12/31/03	—	—	—	—	21	2589712
CTC	Compania de Telecom de Chile	Telecommunications	12/31/03	—	—	—	—	63	39290851
CMP	Compass Minerals Internation	Mining & processing	12/31/03	600.6	27.2	659.0	d144.1	—	—
CA	Computer Associates Internati	Computer services	3/31/04	3092.0	d106.0	9469.0	4718.0	368	356769938
CSC	Computer Sciences Corp.	Computer services	4/2/04	14767.6	1266.3	11469.8	5503.7	410	150425489
CTG	Computer Task Group, Inc.	Computer services	12/31/03	252.3	5.6	96.4	56.1	50	10568508
CIX	CompX International, Inc.	Hardware & tools	12/31/03	207.5	3.5	208.8	154.4	40	4012674

T10

EARNINGS PER SHARE — QUARTERLY / ANNUAL						P/E RATIO	DIVIDENDS PER SHARE			AV. YLD. %	DIV. DECLARED		PRICE RANGE 2004
1st	2nd	3rd	2004	2003	2002		2004	2003	2002		AMOUNT	PAYABLE	
—	—	—	—	6.01	4.42	—	0.19	0.08	0.08	0.2	0.04Q	3/23/05	116.80 - 39.95
0.48	—	—	—	2.07	2.04	—	0.80	0.59	0.38	2.7	0.16Q	3/18/05	36.74 - 22.80
0.27	0.10	—	—	d0.17	1.19	—	0.06	0.06	0.06	0.4	0.015Q	4/14/05	21.70 - 9.61
d0.18	—	—	—	1.41	1.53	—	0.92	0.88	0.88	4.5	0.23Q	5/13/05	24.08 - 16.85
0.58	—	—	—	2.38	1.33	—	0.23	0.22	0.21	0.7	0.06Q	3/18/05	35.54 - 26.22
d0.35	—	—	—	0.08	d1.33	—	—	—	—	—	2-for-1	6/10/98	3.70 - 2.40
0.16	—	—	—	0.83	0.62	—	—	—	—	—	—		22.57 - 13.80
0.32	—	—	—	1.42	1.32	—	0.20	0.05	—	0.6	0.05Q	4/15/05	39.73 - 24.06
—	—	—	—	—	—	—	—	—	—	—	2-for-1	1/14/00	6.99 - 4.69
1.45	—	—	—	2.77	2.53	—	2.16	2.16	2.16	4.8	0.54Q	5/2/05	49.58 - 41.18
d0.23	—	—	—	d1.52	d5.22	—	—	—	—	—	2-for-1	5/31/96	11.65 - 6.36
0.36	—	—	—	1.64	1.42	—	—	—	—	—	—		49.04 - 25.52
—	—	—	—	8.52	7.47	—	1.00	1.00	1.10	11.0	0.0833M	4/29/05	10.72 - 7.51
0.15	—	—	—	0.84	0.75	—	—	—	—	—	0.005U	4/8/97	22.40 - 9.31
d0.65	—	—	—	d0.35	d0.82	—	0.24	0.24	0.22	0.4	100%	5/11/05	68.30 - 42.51
0.04	—	—	—	—	p1.74	—	0.88	0.88	0.88	4.1	0.22Q	5/13/05	27.81 - 15.19
0.38	—	—	—	1.20	0.17	—	0.16	0.13	0.03	1.2	0.045Q	4/15/05	18.31 - 7.86
0.99	—	—	—	1.76	1.03	—	1.11	1.10	1.10	4.8	0.28Q	4/5/05	27.55 - 18.80
2.37	—	—	—	7.14	1.07	—	1.93	1.43	1.40	2.6	0.40Q	3/10/05	100.25 - 47.15
1.35	—	—	—	3.60	3.13	—	1.04	0.63	—	0.8	0.46Q	3/28/05	42.50
p0.40	—	—	—	1.14	0.78	—	—	—	—	—	2-for-1	2/22/05	47.60 - 18.07
—	—	—	—	14.48	8.39	—	0.74	0.09	0.21	6.3	0.40S	1/7/05	16.35 - 7.10
—	—	—	—	—	—	—	1.21	1.09	1.21	3.8		10/12/04	45.00 - 18.23
—	—	—	—	—	—	—	0.83	0.11	—	2.6	0.8334U	6/30/05	45.17 - 17.95
—	—	—	—	0.34	0.37	—	0.12	0.12	—	1.3	0.1208U	6/17/05	13.30 - 5.37
0.47	—	—	—	2.07	1.96	—	0.69	0.64	0.63	2.2	0.18Q	2/11/05	37.80 - 25.80
0.30	—	—	—	1.96	1.52	—	0.82	—	—	2.0	0.225Q	4/22/05	60.00 - 21.07
0.37	—	—	—	1.21	1.28	—	—	—	—	—	33%	6/6/02	46.49 - 33.69
—	—	—	—	—	p0.97	—	0.16	0.04	—	1.0	0.04Q	4/5/05	22.82 - 9.55
1.88	—	—	—	4.46	1.29	—	1.53	1.43	1.39	2.5	0.43Q	4/5/05	77.46 - 44.32
—	—	—	—	—	—	—	1.05	0.93	—	0.6	1.0538U	8/9/04	21.34 - 13.79
0.70	—	—	—	1.92	1.60	—	0.21	0.21	0.20	0.6	0.06Q	3/1/05	47.93 - 26.85
0.10	—	—	—	0.31	0.22	—	—	—	—	—	2-for-1	3/31/98	11.41 - 4.76
1.54	—	—	—	4.41	d2.83	—	0.71	1.32	1.31	1.1	0.025Q	4/11/05	82.80 - 42.97
—	—	—	—	18.93	18.74	—	1.08	0.93	1.12	6.6	0.22Q	3/10/05	17.60 - 15.20
0.70	—	—	—	2.18	1.31	—	—	—	—	—	—		41.45 - 18.68
0.03	—	—	—	5.02	d11.18	—	—	—	—	—	—		6.01 - 3.14
0.57	—	—	—	2.43	2.34	—	1.88	1.84	1.80	5.1	0.48Q	2/15/05	42.63 - 31.70
0.27	—	—	—	1.14	1.00	—	0.15	0.15	0.15	0.8	0.0375Q	3/18/05	24.27 - 13.59
0.88	—	—	—	2.66	0.67	—	0.52	0.48	0.12	1.7	0.13Q	2/28/05	44.17 - 16.86
d0.23	—	—	—	d0.83	d0.93	—	—	—	—	—	—		22.40 - 12.25
1.01	—	—	—	3.42	2.59	—	1.60	1.10	0.70	3.7	0.44Q	2/25/05	52.84 - 33.34
0.15	—	—	—	0.42	d2.93	—	2.50	—	—	20.3	0.25Q	3/31/05	14.80 - 9.79
0.01	—	—	—	0.09	0.13	—	—	—	—	—	7%	12/31/04	10.00 - 6.05
1.00	—	—	—	3.72	3.56	—	1.28	0.97	0.78	2.3	0.36Q	2/15/05	70.99 - 41.17
—	—	—	—	d0.77	0.44	—	—	—	—	—	0.04S	5/4/00	14.77 - 3.53
0.28	—	—	—	1.17	0.80	—	0.30	0.11	0.08	1.3	0.10Q	3/24/05	27.41 - 18.11
0.45	—	—	—	2.15	1.85	—	0.25	0.25	0.24	0.6	2-for-1	4/29/05	54.96 - 32.50
0.23	—	—	—	0.68	1.02	—	—	—	—	—	0.06Q	4/1/05	21.00 - 11.95
0.19	—	—	—	1.85	1.18	—	0.43	0.10	—	1.1	0.125Q	4/15/05	47.55 - 29.96
0.27	—	—	—	d0.79	1.47	—	0.90	0.90	0.90	5.5	0.225Q	2/15/05	20.75 - 11.69
d0.16	—	—	—	d3.40	d6.58	—	0.10	—	—	0.2	0.10Q	3/1/05	108.10 - 15.10
0.60	0.52	0.59	—	2.33	1.37	—	1.08	0.98	0.86	2.2	0.28Q	5/13/05	59.45 - 38.22
0.06	—	—	—	d0.30	d2.99	—	—	—	1.09	—	0.18Q	11/22/02	10.65 - 4.41
d0.55	—	—	—	d6.58	1.10	—	—	—	—	—	3-for-1	6/1/98	30.45 - 21.49
0.15	—	—	—	d0.33	0.67	—	—	—	0.45	—	0.15Q	10/7/02	13.96 - 7.20
0.45	—	—	—	1.57	1.96	—	0.40	0.40	0.40	1.0	0.10Q	3/15/05	50.96 - 25.38
—	—	—	—	—	—	—	1.79	1.60	0.67	4.2	1.026S	5/12/05	58.95 - 25.91
p0.04	—	—	—	0.48	0.62	—	0.24	0.24	0.22	1.5	0.06Q	3/29/05	20.15 - 10.90
0.46	—	—	—	1.77	1.60	—	1.00	0.88	0.80	2.2	0.28Q	4/1/05	53.50 - 38.30
0.22	—	—	—	1.46	1.07	—	0.16	0.16	0.16	0.7	0.04Q	4/1/05	28.99 - 17.05
—	—	—	—	—	—	—	0.24	—	0.41	1.1	0.244U	5/24/04	27.30 - 17.14
—	—	—	—	—	—	—	0.24	2.63	—	1.2	0.2414U	7/1/04	28.19 - 13.65
d0.01	—	—	—	d0.39	d1.04	—	—	—	—	—	0.15A	4/19/96	7.69 - 1.32
—	—	—	—	18.78	13.71	—	1.49	1.48	1.38	8.2	0.15M	6/30/05	22.33 - 14.26
—	—	—	—	26.68	—	—	2.19	0.85	—	9.2	0.195M	6/30/05	27.39 - 20.35
—	—	—	—	16.99	13.52	—	1.15	1.02	0.99	6.7	0.11M	6/30/05	19.98 - 14.16
0.36	—	—	—	1.59	1.27	—	0.52	0.16	—	1.8	0.16Q	3/25/05	37.39 - 19.49
—	—	—	—	0.33	0.27	—	1.68	1.41	1.13	4.3		5/16/05	50.65 - 27.65
0.59	—	—	—	2.46	2.19	—	0.96	0.90	0.72	1.9	0.29Q	5/13/05	59.00 - 42.89
d0.28	—	—	—	d0.71	d1.15	—	—	—	—	—	—		7.06 - 2.56
0.31	—	—	—	1.20	1.17	—	0.58	0.56	0.52	3.4	0.1525Q	2/11/05	22.70 - 11.25
0.24	—	—	—	0.97	2.39	—	2.68	2.66	2.64	7.2	0.675Q	2/7/05	42.79 - 32.02
—	—	—	—	—	—	—	1.43	1.43	1.43	4.5	0.4826Q	4/15/05	41.08 - 22.70
0.92	—	—	—	3.75	3.40	—	2.06	1.98	1.88	4.1	0.55Q	4/1/05	63.80 - 37.88
0.03	—	—	—	d0.05	0.14	—	—	—	—	—	—		7.95 - 1.97
0.75	—	—	—	2.61	2.04	—	0.38	0.33	0.30	0.7	0.11Q	4/15/05	67.64 - 37.10
1.56	—	—	—	4.99	1.42	—	1.31	1.27	1.23	2.7	0.33Q	3/11/05	62.68 - 34.02
0.43	—	—	—	2.02	2.37	—	0.52	0.38	0.34	2.0	0.135Q	4/7/05	30.38 - 21.20
0.44	0.71	—	—	0.66	1.43	—	0.18	0.16	0.15	0.5	0.06Q	4/15/05	52.80 - 13.95
0.28	—	—	—	1.08	1.04	—	1.29	1.28	1.27	7.1	0.325Q	2/15/05	21.25 - 14.85
d0.27	—	—	—	d1.19	d1.10	—	—	—	—	—	—		22.65 - 7.50
0.38	—	—	—	1.50	1.47	—	0.66	0.59	0.55	1.9	0.18Q	4/11/05	50.77 - 18.86
0.39	—	—	—	1.30	1.05	—	—	—	—	—	—		30.87 - 18.75
—	—	—	—	—	—	—	0.16	0.18	0.19	0.8	0.1617U	7/8/04	12.41 - 2.80
—	—	—	—	—	—	—	0.39	0.83	0.29	1.7	0.2819U	3/7/05	28.27 - 12.49
—	—	—	—	—	—	—	0.04	—	0.11	1.2	0.1182U	4/26/05	35.30 - 12.03
—	—	—	—	—	—	—							4.97 - 2.24
—	—	—	—	—	—	—	3.70	1.68	2.09	22.2	1.6483U	4/28/05	24.34 - 8.98
—	—	—	—	—	—	—	0.46	3.00	0.32	2.2	0.34787S	5/6/05	25.80 - 15.65
—	—	—	—	—	—	—	3.32	0.10	0.01	25.2		11/10/04	17.09 - 9.33
0.94	—	—	—	1.01	0.23	—	0.94	—	—	4.9	0.275Q	3/15/05	24.40 - 14.00
—	—	—	—	d0.06	d0.46	—	0.08	0.08	0.08	0.4	0.04S	1/5/05	31.71 - 13.35
—	—	—	—	2.75	2.54	—	—	—	—	—	0.00166U	4/13/98	58.00 - 30.60
0.05	—	—	—	0.16	0.08	—	—	—	—	—	0.05A	5/26/00	6.55 - 1.93
0.10	—	—	—	0.08	0.04	—	0.13	0.13	0.50	1.1	0.125Q	3/24/05	17.61 - 5.03

SYMBOL	COMPANY	NATURE OF BUSINESS	FISCAL YEAR-END	TOTAL REV. $MILL	NET INCOME $MILL	TOTAL ASSETS $MILL	NET STK. EQUITY $MILL	NO. OF INST.	INST. HOLDINGS (SHARES)
CRK	Comstock Resources, Inc.	Oil	12/31/03	235.1	60.3	675.0	289.7	92	15660381
COP	Conocophillips (United States	Natural gas distributor	12/31/03		12930.0	75377.0	34366.0	771	529353388
CNX	Consol Energy Inc (United Sta	Coal	12/31/03	2222.5	d9.0	3663.3	290.6	112	16852331
ED	Consolidated Edison, Inc.	Electric power	12/31/03	9827.0	536.0	20903.0	6439.0	367	84558696
CGX	Consolidated Graphics, Inc.	Printing & engraving	3/31/04	708.1	71.9	486.6	245.6	98	8042260
STZ	Constellation Brands Inc	Distilling	2/29/04	3552.4	564.8	5374.2	2377.6	279	67489463
STZ B	Constellation Brands Inc	Distilling	2/29/04	3552.4	564.8	5374.2	2377.6	6	42748
CEG	Constellation Energy Group I	Electric power	12/31/03	9703.0	475.7	15158.5	4140.5	318	105843378
CAL	Continental Airlines Inc (Uni		12/31/03	8870.0	38.0	10649.0	792.0	126	58103704
CVG	Convergys Corp.	Computer services	12/31/03	2288.8	171.6	1743.0	1143.5	292	98874860
CAM	Cooper Cameron Corp.	Machinery & equipment	12/31/03	1634.3	135.8	2135.4	1136.7	221	51402428
COO	Cooper Companies, Inc.	Medical & dental equipment	10/31/03	411.8	159.3	636.9	422.0	197	35994618
CTB	Cooper Tire & Rubber Co.	Tires and/or rubber goods	12/31/03	3514.4	199.0	2866.1	1030.4	214	48033022
CPO	Corn Products International	Food -grain & agriculture	12/31/03	2102.0	212.0	2210.0	911.0	180	27251166
CRN	Cornell Companies Inc	Services	12/31/03	271.6	30.8	442.9	166.2	47	10812403
GLW	Corning, Inc. (United States)	Conglomerate	12/31/03	3090.0	d569.0	10514.0	5464.0	511	698237576
OFC	Corporate Office Properties T	Real estate investment trust	12/31/03	174.4	28.5	1332.1	450.4	98	14591431
CPV	Correctional Properties Trus	Real estate investment trust	12/31/03	32.4	15.8	270.8	212.7	43	2767210
CXW	Corrections Corporation of Am	Real estate investment trust	12/31/03	1036.7	183.0	1884.2	775.5	85	12375620
CGA	Corus Group Plc (UK)	Metal products	1/3/04					34	17453331
COT	Cott Corp. (Quebec)	Soft drinks	1/3/04	1417.8	77.4	908.8	345.1	77	23572595
CFC	Countrywide Financial Corp	Financial services	12/31/03	9967.1	2372.9	97949.8	8084.7	403	120348793
CUZ	Cousins Properties Inc. (Unit	Real estate investment trust	12/31/03	189.6	170.8	1140.4	578.8	127	19184228
CVD	Covance Inc.	Services	12/31/03	974.2	826.6	703.4	542.0	246	52766958
CVH	Coventry Health Care Inc.	Insurance	12/31/03	4535.1	250.1	1907.8	929.0	212	45465864
CXR	Cox Radio Inc.	Telecommunications	12/31/03	425.9	82.9	2277.0	1181.7	144	36096682
CPY	CPI Corp.	Photo & optical	2/7/04	301.7	1.2	167.2	51.8	57	5918799
CR	Crane Co.	Machinery & equipment	12/31/03	1636.0	255.5	1718.6	786.3	195	35732811
CRD B	Crawford & Co.	Finance	12/31/03	732.9	24.3	493.8	172.6	50	17030657
CIK	Credit Suisse Asset Mgmt Inc	Investment company	12/31/03	20.0	18.4	220.3	219.9	22	441861
CSR	Credit Suisse Group (Switzer	Financial services	12/31/03					35	8393169
CEI	Crescent Real Estate Equities	Real estate investment trust	12/31/03	949.2	71.9	4318.5	1221.8	174	56732804
CGW	Cristalerias de Chile S.A. (	Plastics & plastic products	12/31/03					5	780169
CK	Crompton Corp	Specialty chemicals	12/31/03	2185.0	d195.7	2529.2	302.7	157	92043901
CRT	Cross Timbers Royalty Trust	Oil	12/31/03	12.9	12.7	25.7	24.7	27	647231
CCI	Crown Castle International Co	Telecommunications	12/31/03	930.3	d301.4	6737.6	1984.4	136	150417527
CCK	Crown Holdings Inc	Containers	12/31/03	6630.0	87.0	6581.0	140.0	178	121573430
CRY	CryoLife, Inc.	Medical & dental equipment	12/31/03	31.3	d36.6	73.9	48.3	68	7445740
CAO	CSK Auto Corp.		2/1/04	1578.1	10.8	1153.5	331.6	95	33831871
CSS	CSS Industries, Inc.	Paper	3/31/04	539.3	29.9	370.4	249.2	52	3772865
CSX	CSX Corp.	Railroads	12/31/03	p7793.0	p7850.0			361	152734947
CFR	Cullen/Frost Bankers, Inc.	Electronic components	12/31/03	463.0	18.8	462.0	294.2	112	24435889
CMI	Cummins, Inc.	Banking - Southwest	12/31/03	584.3	130.5	9672.1	770.0	175	33244258
CW	Curtiss-Wright Corp.	Defense systems & equip.	12/31/03	6296.0	122.0	4792.0	949.0	199	34317766
CVS	CVS Corp. (DE)	Specialty stores	1/3/04	746.1	143.1	973.7	478.9	108	4755759
CY	Cypress Semiconductor Corp.	Electronic components	12/28/03	26588.0	847.3	10543.1	6021.8	571	336629346
CYT	Cytec Industries, Inc.	Chemicals	12/31/03	836.8	d7.8	1506.5	569.2	226	87566162
				1471.8	267.1	1963.0	755.4	201	32522816
DCN	Dana Corp.		12/31/03	8067.0	254.0	9310.0	2050.0	246	100636119
DHR	Danaher Corp.		12/31/03	5293.9	536.8	6363.4	3646.7	440	111017252
DAB	Dave & Busters, Inc.	Restaurants	2/1/04	362.8	36.0	290.6	182.9	52	4890483
DVA	Davita Inc.	Hospitals & nursing homes	12/31/03	2016.4	371.1	782.6	306.9	155	57897317
DF	Dean Foods Co. (New) (United	Food processing	12/31/03	9184.6	673.0	4988.7	2542.8	306	79521291
DE	Deere & Co.		10/31/03	15534.2	642.1	24332.1	4002.1	431	189800394
DPH	Delphi Corp. (United States)		12/31/03	28096.0	d198.0	18946.0	3839.0	381	417663652
DFG	Delphi Financial Group, Inc.	Insurance	12/31/03	918.2	98.9	4177.5	798.4	135	14753715
DLP	Delta & Pine Land Co.		8/31/03	281.3	43.2	431.6	217.1	143	32010601
DAL	Delta Air Lines, Inc. (DE)		12/31/03	13303.0	d773.0	26356.0	d659.0	251	104414220
DNT	Delta Air Lines, Inc. (DE)		12/31/03	13303.0	d773.0	26356.0	d659.0	4	29852
DEL	Deltic Timber Corp. (United		12/31/03	134.9	18.0	311.5	170.2	75	7310496
DLX	Deluxe Corp.	Printing & engraving	12/31/03	1242.1	192.5	540.9	d298.1	260	40590619
DNR	Denbury Resources, Inc. (DE)	Oil	12/31/03	333.0	69.1	933.4	421.2	118	23535693
DFS	Department 56, Inc.	'Wholesaler, distributor'	1/3/04	191.7	16.4	142.3	114.3	92	10423835
DDR	Developers Diversified Realt	Real estate, investment trust	12/31/03	476.1	167.2	3941.2	1614.1	188	59801666
DVN	Devon Energy Corp. (New)	Natural gas	12/31/03	1460.0	443.0	25618.0	11056.0	449	130992402
DV	DEVRY Inc. (DE)		6/30/03	679.6	139.5	675.4	415.7	194	54812544
DEO	Diageo Plc	Food processing	6/30/03					169	37281212
DP	Diagnostic Products Corp.	Medical & dental equipment	12/31/03	381.4	185.2	487.6	403.0	130	17165823
DO	Diamond Offshore Drilling In	Oil service & equipment	12/31/03	680.9	d73.8	3096.5	1680.5	176	125913176
DKS	Dick's Sporting Goods, Inc (U	Specialty stores	1/3/04	1470.8	59.3	470.2	243.0	62	8853903
DBD	Diebold, Inc.	Office equipment & supplies	12/31/03	2109.7	920.1	1622.4	1148.2	311	51597739
DDS	Dillard's Inc. (United Stat	Department stores	1/31/04	7863.7	9.3	5953.6	2237.1	215	64512697
DMN	DiMon, Inc.	Tobacco	3/31/04	835.3	d68.7	1041.2	414.9	93	25432602
DTV	DIRECTV Group Inc (The)	Services	12/31/03	10121.2	d628.8	16757.5	9631.1		
DIS	Disney (Walt) Co. (The)		9/30/03	27061.0	3592.0	49988.0	23791.0	930	1275402420
DJO	dj Orthopedics, Inc. (United		12/31/03	197.9	12.1	320.5	117.3	34	13460480
DNP	DNP Select Income Fund Inc (U	Investment company	12/31/03	190.1	159.6	2896.2	1738.3	95	4428553
DG	Dollar General Corp. (TN)	Discount & variety stores	1/30/04	6872.0	311.0	2560.0	1581.3	289	212580464
DTG	Dollar Thrifty Automotive Gr		12/31/03	1227.9	19.8	3137.5	533.5	105	23088864
DOM	Dominion Res Black Warrior T	Natural gas	12/31/03	20.8	20.8	44.8	44.7	18	363666
D	Dominion Resources Inc (New)	Electric power	12/31/03	12078.0	2495.0	39673.0	10538.0	530	171467014
DTC	Domtar Inc.	Paper	12/31/03					48	79023738
DCI	Donaldson Co., Inc.	Pollution control	7/31/03	1218.3	95.3	726.2	447.4	202	27013878
RHD	Donnelley (R.H.) Corp.		12/31/03	256.4	d2.0	1176.3	d56.2	152	28156087
RRD	Donnelley (R.R.) & Son	Printing & engraving	12/31/03	4787.2	176.5	3188.9	983.2	319	85388516
DRL	Doral Financial Corp.	Financial services	12/31/03	864.3	321.3	10392.0	1592.4	184	43943221
DOV	Dover Corp. (United States)	Machinery & equipment	12/31/03	4413.3	657.1	4958.7	2742.7	378	159743749
DDE	Dover Downs Gaming & Entertai	Gaming	12/31/03	13.8	d15.0	149.5	95.0	54	7056579
DVD	Dover Motorsports, Inc.		12/31/03	d9.0	d7.0	244.9	137.4	54	9206589
DOW	Dow Chemical Co.	Chemicals	12/31/03	32632.0	3485.0	38482.0	10666.0	658	607590042
DJ	Dow Jones & Co., Inc	Publishing	12/31/03	1548.5	391.5	671.4	129.9	249	55948842
DSL	Downey Financial Corp. (DE)	Banking - West	12/31/03	613.4	133.6	11646.0	917.0	135	13275548
DPL	DPL, Inc.	Electric power	12/31/03	p1191.0	p1191.0			217	41493373
DW	Drew Industries, Inc.		12/31/03	353.1	19.4	129.1	93.7	34	4943001
LEO	Dreyfus Strategic Municipals	Investment company	9/30/03	50.3	42.7	842.4	549.7	35	1808665
DRQ	Dril-Quip, Inc.	Oil service & equipment	12/31/03	219.5	21.9	278.2	199.6	66	6169816

T12

| EARNINGS PER SHARE QUARTERLY | | | | ANNUAL | | P/E RATIO | DIVIDENDS PER SHARE | | | AV. YLD. | DIV. DECLARED | | PRICE RANGE |
1st	2nd	3rd	2004	2003	2002		2004	2003	2002	%	AMOUNT	PAYABLE	2004
—	—	—	—	1.51	0.37	—	—	—	—	—	—	—	24.45 - 9.93
2.31	—	—	—	6.70	1.47	—	0.89	0.81	0.74	1.3	100%	6/1/05	91.21 - 48.19
1.26	—	—	—	d0.15	0.15	—	0.56	0.56	0.84	1.9	0.14Q	2/25/05	43.90 - 15.48
0.68	—	—	—	2.36	3.13	—	2.26	2.24	2.22	5.5	0.57Q	3/15/05	45.59 - 37.23
—	—	—	—	1.44	d0.96	—	—	—	—	—	2-for-1	1/10/97	47.90 - 16.81
—	—	—	—	2.06	2.19	—	—	—	—	—	2-for-1	5/13/05	47.82 - 22.70
—	—	—	—	2.06	2.19	—	—	—	—	—	2-for-1	5/13/05	33.39 - 33.39
0.66	—	—	—	2.85	3.20	—	1.11	1.02	0.84	3.1	0.335Q	4/1/05	44.90 - 26.22
d1.88	—	—	—	0.58	d7.02	—	—	—	—	—	2-for-1	7/16/96	18.52 - 5.10
0.22	—	—	—	1.15	0.88	—	—	—	—	—	—	—	19.96 - 12.30
0.31	—	—	—	1.04	1.10	—	—	—	—	—	2-for-1	6/12/97	56.74 - 40.34
0.55	0.64	—	—	2.13	1.57	—	0.06	0.06	0.05	0.1	0.03S	1/5/05	75.75 - 25.61
0.32	—	—	—	1.00	1.51	—	0.42	0.42	0.42	2.3	0.105Q	3/31/05	13.20 - 12.20
0.70	—	—	—	2.11	1.77	—	0.24	0.20	0.20	0.6	0.07Q	4/25/05	55.84 - 29.16
0.05	—	—	—	0.30	0.55	—	—	—	—	—	—	—	15.46 - 7.05
0.04	—	—	—	d0.18	d1.85	—	—	—	—	—	0.06Q	6/29/01	13.89 - 4.08
0.14	—	—	—	0.19	0.52	—	0.96	0.89	0.85	4.4	0.255Q	4/15/05	29.37 - 14.03
0.41	—	—	—	1.50	1.40	—	1.80	1.72	1.60	6.8	0.45Q	3/30/05	32.41 - 20.64
0.36	—	—	—	3.46	2.75	—	—	—	—	—	—	—	41.15 - 29.00
—	—	—	—	—	—	—	—	—	—	—	0.1452U	10/23/00	10.84 - 0.99
0.21	—	—	—	1.09	0.83	—	—	—	—	—	0.025Q	6/30/98	32.99 - 16.95
2.22	—	—	—	8.31	3.25	—	0.47	0.15	0.12	0.7	0.14Q	3/3/05	97.24 - 30.36
0.20	—	—	—	2.79	1.00	—	8.63	3.55	1.48	27.0	0.37Q	2/22/05	39.67 - 24.15
0.34	—	—	—	1.21	1.03	—	—	—	—	—	—	—	41.49 - 17.73
0.82	—	—	—	2.75	1.59	—	—	—	—	—	50%	1/30/04	67.60 - 27.75
0.11	—	—	—	0.66	0.60	—	—	—	—	—	3-for-1	5/19/00	25.18 - 13.83
d1.09	—	—	—	0.15	0.94	—	0.64	0.60	0.56	3.7	0.16Q	2/28/05	22.26 - 12.06
0.37	—	—	—	1.75	0.28	—	0.40	0.40	0.40	1.6	0.10Q	3/10/05	34.40 - 16.12
0.05	—	—	—	0.16	0.50	—	0.24	0.24	0.40	3.9	0.06Q	2/25/05	8.30 - 4.00
—	—	—	—	4.41	3.91	—	0.42	0.45	0.70	9.6	0.035M	4/15/05	4.85 - 3.90
—	—	—	—	—	—	—	0.38	0.05	1.36	1.3	1.2831U	6/9/05	42.71 - 17.38
d0.18	—	—	—	0.12	0.64	—	1.50	1.50	1.50	8.9	0.375Q	2/15/05	19.36 - 14.18
—	—	—	—	—	—	—	0.30	0.45	0.43	1.2	0.3157U	4/19/05	30.00 - 18.25
0.53	—	—	—	d1.05	0.13	—	0.20	0.20	0.20	2.5	0.05Q	2/25/05	11.80 - 4.05
0.51	—	—	—	2.12	1.47	—	2.41	2.16	1.40	8.0	—	4/14/05	41.75 - 18.85
d0.34	—	—	—	d2.08	d1.16	—	—	—	—	—	—	—	17.55 - 3.88
d0.11	—	—	—	d0.19	d1.33	—	—	—	—	—	—	—	14.20 - 5.30
d0.32	—	—	—	d1.64	d1.43	—	—	—	—	—	3-for-2	12/27/00	8.48 - 4.43
0.28	—	—	—	0.23	0.63	—	—	—	—	—	—	—	20.08 - 8.76
—	—	—	—	2.42	2.09	—	0.38	0.29	—	1.3	0.10Q	3/15/05	36.98 - 21.59
0.14	—	—	—	—	p0.88	—	0.40	0.40	0.40	1.2	0.10Q	3/15/05	40.46 - 26.86
0.07	—	—	—	0.36	d0.54	—	0.12	0.12	0.12	1.1	0.03Q	4/29/05	15.85 - 6.10
0.62	—	—	—	2.48	2.33	—	1.04	0.94	0.88	2.6	0.265Q	3/15/05	49.20 - 30.38
p0.76	—	—	—	1.36	2.06	—	1.20	1.20	1.20	2.2	0.30Q	6/1/05	84.67 - 23.97
0.74	—	—	—	2.50	2.17	—	0.36	0.32	0.30	0.7	0.09Q	4/22/05	60.25 - 43.95
0.59	—	—	—	2.06	1.75	—	0.27	0.23	0.23	0.8	0.0725Q	5/2/05	46.94 - 22.62
0.16	—	—	—	d0.04	d2.02	—	—	—	—	—	100%	10/31/95	24.08 - 5.25
0.78	—	—	—	2.27	1.96	—	0.40	—	—	—	0.10Q	2/25/05	51.93 - 27.85
0.33	—	—	—	1.17	0.39	—	0.48	0.09	0.04	3.2	0.12Q	3/15/05	23.20 - 7.06
0.45	—	—	—	1.69	1.40	—	0.05	0.05	0.04	0.1	0.015Q	4/29/05	44.64 -
0.25	—	—	—	0.80	0.40	—	—	—	—	—	50%	9/15/97	20.39 - 8.14
0.51	—	—	—	1.66	1.52	—	—	—	—	—	3-for-2	6/15/04	51.98 - 26.02
0.43	—	—	—	2.27	1.77	—	—	—	—	—	3-for-2	6/9/03	38.00 - 25.88
0.68	1.88	—	—	2.64	1.33	—	1.06	0.88	0.88	1.4	0.31Q	5/2/05	74.93 - 39.26
0.10	—	—	—	d0.10	0.61	—	0.28	0.28	0.28	3.0	0.03Q	5/2/05	11.78 - 6.83
0.94	—	—	—	3.09	1.91	—	0.32	0.28	0.19	0.8	0.09Q	3/9/05	35.99 -
d0.19	0.24	—	—	0.70	0.76	—	0.48	0.32	0.20	2.0	0.12Q	6/14/05	27.70 - 19.75
d3.12	—	—	—	d6.40	d10.44	—	—	0.05	0.10	—	0.025Q	6/1/03	13.20 - 2.75
d3.12	—	—	—	d6.40	d10.44	—	2.03	2.03	2.03	33.4	—	4/1/05	6.20 - 5.95
0.11	—	—	—	0.73	1.33	—	0.25	0.25	0.25	0.7	0.0625Q	3/15/05	46.64 - 23.90
0.94	—	—	—	3.49	3.36	—	1.48	1.48	1.48	3.6	0.40Q	3/7/05	45.09 - 36.20
0.40	—	—	—	0.97	0.86	—	—	—	—	—	—	—	29.30 - 10.60
d0.11	—	—	—	1.24	2.42	—	—	—	—	—	—	—	17.34 - 9.82
0.50	—	—	—	2.28	1.14	—	1.89	1.61	1.51	5.5	0.54Q	4/4/05	45.85 - 22.42
2.00	—	—	—	8.00	0.32	—	0.20	0.10	0.10	0.4	0.075Q	3/31/05	76.27 - 37.21
0.15	0.22	0.23	—	0.87	0.95	—	—	—	—	—	100%	6/19/98	32.24 - 13.05
—	—	—	—	—	—	—	2.02	1.67	1.44	4.1	0.8513S	4/12/05	58.05 - 39.34
0.52	—	—	—	2.08	1.60	—	0.25	0.24	0.24	0.6	0.07Q	2/15/05	56.51 - 33.91
d0.08	—	—	—	d0.37	0.47	—	0.25	0.44	0.50	0.9	0.0625Q	3/1/05	40.47 - 17.84
0.21	—	—	—	1.05	0.94	—	—	—	—	—	2-for-1	4/5/04	61.20 - 19.00
0.40	—	—	—	2.40	1.83	—	0.74	0.68	0.66	1.6	0.205Q	3/11/05	56.45 - 33.94
0.64	—	—	—	0.11	1.60	—	0.16	0.16	0.16	0.8	0.04Q	5/2/05	27.50 - 12.92
—	—	—	—	d0.73	0.58	—	0.30	0.30	0.22	4.7	0.075Q	3/23/05	7.72 - 5.04
0.13	—	—	—	d0.21	—	—	—	—	—	—	—	—	18.68 - 14.70
0.33	0.26	—	—	0.65	0.60	—	0.21	0.21	—	0.9	0.24A	1/6/05	28.41 - 17.02
0.19	—	—	—	0.64	d0.85	—	—	—	—	—	—	—	27.60 - 3.91
—	—	—	—	7.94	7.37	—	0.79	0.78	0.81	7.4	0.065M	6/10/05	11.95 - 9.60
p0.20	—	—	—	0.89	0.79	—	0.15	0.14	0.10	0.9	0.04Q	4/14/05	23.19 - 10.39
0.11	—	—	—	0.78	1.88	—	—	—	—	—	—	—	30.31 - 16.41
0.57	—	—	—	2.53	2.37	—	2.98	2.53	2.37	9.8	—	3/11/05	38.80 - 22.21
1.36	—	—	—	2.98	4.82	—	2.60	2.58	2.58	4.2	0.67Q	3/20/05	68.50 - 53.90
—	—	—	—	—	—	—	0.24	0.19	0.14	2.1	0.06Q	4/1/05	13.25 - 9.85
0.28	0.28	0.33	—	1.05	0.95	—	0.22	0.18	0.17	0.5	0.06Q	3/11/05	59.31 - 25.05
0.54	—	—	—	d3.53	1.40	—	—	—	—	—	0.175Q	12/10/98	59.35 - 29.68
d0.35	—	—	—	1.54	1.24	—	1.04	1.02	0.98	3.9	0.26Q	6/1/05	35.37 - 18.26
0.86	—	—	—	2.72	1.89	—	0.60	0.40	0.28	1.5	0.18Q	3/4/05	49.35 - 29.10
0.41	—	—	—	1.40	1.04	—	0.62	0.57	0.54	1.8	0.16Q	3/15/05	44.13 - 24.22
0.17	—	—	—	0.65	0.80	—	0.23	0.20	0.13	2.2	0.06Q	3/10/05	13.10 - 8.02
d0.08	—	—	—	d0.56	0.04	—	0.04	0.04	0.10	0.9	0.01Q	3/10/05	6.08 - 3.18
0.50	—	—	—	1.88	d0.44	—	1.34	1.34	1.34	3.4	0.335Q	4/29/05	51.34 - 27.30
0.22	—	—	—	2.08	2.40	—	1.00	1.00	1.00	2.3	0.25Q	3/1/05	52.74 - 35.44
0.32	—	—	—	3.64	3.99	—	0.40	0.36	0.36	0.8	0.10Q	2/25/05	59.98 - 39.41
—	—	—	—	—	p0.72	—	0.96	0.94	0.94	5.1	0.24Q	3/1/05	25.39 - 12.01
0.57	—	—	—	1.88	1.57	—	—	—	—	—	100%	3/21/97	41.50 - 15.10
—	—	—	—	9.14	9.37	—	0.62	0.72	0.69	6.9	0.046M	4/27/05	10.25 - 7.80
0.15	—	—	—	0.52	0.50	—	—	—	—	—	—	—	25.45 - 13.67

SYMBOL	COMPANY	NATURE OF BUSINESS	FISCAL YEAR-END	TOTAL REV. $MILL	NET INCOME $MILL	TOTAL ASSETS $MILL	NET STK EQUITY $MILL	NO. OF INST.	INST. HOLDINGS (SHARES)
DRS	DRS Technologies Inc	Electronic components	3/31/04	p1001.0	p1001.0			159	21313117
DST	DST Systems Inc. (DE)	Computer services	12/31/03	2416.3	761.9	3103.6	683.7	226	54726498
DTE	DTE Energy Co.	Electric power	12/31/03	7041.0	480.0	19388.0	5287.0	335	85772961
DD	Du Pont (E.I.) de Nemours & C	Conglomerate	12/31/03	27730.0	1159.0	34456.0	9781.0	883	572279035
DCO	Ducommun Inc.	Electronic components	12/31/03	225.9	16.2	193.4	137.8	56	7003564
DUC	Duff & Phelps Utility & Corpo	Investment company	12/31/03	31.1	24.6	512.7	369.6	30	270665
DUK	Duke Energy Corp.	Electric power	12/31/03	22529.0	d2717.0	56203.0	13748.0	654	533673086
DRE	Duke Realty Corp. (United Sta	Real estate investment trust	12/31/03	1049.8	207.0	5210.2	2666.7	267	75085449
DNB	Dun & Bradstreet Corp (DE) (	Financial services	12/31/03	1386.4	467.6	1402.6	318.8	274	64851011
DQE	Duquesne Light Holdings Inc	Electric power	12/31/03	902.8	93.2	2510.9	575.4	—	—
DY	Dycom Industries, Inc.	Electrical equipment	7/26/03	618.2	87.2	518.3	450.3	134	38188653
DYN	Dynegy Inc (New)	Natural gas distributor	12/31/03	5787.0	d780.0	13207.0	2045.0	238	111589922
DX	Dynex Capital, Inc.	Real estate investment trust	12/31/03	152.2	d12.5	1865.2	149.8	11	363303
ET	E* Trade Financial Corp	Securities brokerage	12/31/03	2008.4	770.9	25969.9	1918.3	213	203052637
EON	E.ON AG (Germany)	Electrical equipment	12/31/03					61	14867137
EXP	Eagle Materials Inc	Cement & gypsum	3/31/04	502.6	66.9	693.0	439.0	—	—
NGT	Eastern Amern Nat Gas Tr	Natural gas	12/31/03	13.2	10.9	37.4	34.9	13	99591
EGP	EastGroup Properties, Inc.	Real estate investment trust	12/31/03	108.4	25.3	676.7	366.9	103	7273016
EMN	Eastman Chemical Co.	Plastics & plastic products	12/31/03	5800.0	d740.0	5524.0	1043.0	284	58532371
EK	Eastman Kodak Co.	Photo & optical	12/31/03	13317.0	410.0	11983.0	3264.0	459	225112268
ETN	Eaton Corp.	—	12/31/03	8061.0	894.0	8223.0	3117.0	348	53123371
EV	Eaton Vance Corp	Financial services	10/31/03	523.1	106.1	658.7	416.3	179	36129354
EVF	Eaton Vance Senior Income Tr	Investment company	6/30/03	29.1	20.5	535.0	306.4	22	1089838
ECL	Ecolab, Inc.	Soaps & cleansers	12/31/03	3761.8	837.9	3162.7	1295.4	361	74345702
EIX	Edison International	Electric power	12/31/03	12135.0	1771.0	34962.0	5383.0	301	204122811
EDO	EDO Corp. (United States)	Defense systems & equip.	12/31/03	460.7	13.4	491.4	190.3	111	15562238
AGE	Edwards (A.G.), Inc.	Securities brokerage	2/29/04	2498.9	159.5	3787.6	1778.3	229	42924346
EW	Edwards Lifesciences Corp	Medical & dental equipment	12/31/03	860.1	68.8	1062.2	635.1	223	48679161
EFD	eFunds Corporation	Financial services	12/31/03	532.1	68.8	512.3	401.7	134	36077547
EE	El Paso Electric Company	Electric power	12/31/03	664.4	20.6	1595.9	499.8	122	44747410
EDS	Electronic Data Systems Corp.	Services	12/31/03	21476.0	d641.0	16262.0	5714.0	524	404919696
ELK	Elkcorp	Engineering & construction	6/30/03	506.1	24.1	442.1	196.5	87	14343967
AKO A	Embotelladora Andina S.A.	Soft drinks	12/31/03					17	7891776
ERJ	Embraer-Empresa Brasileira de	—	12/31/03					6	1291133
EMT	Embratel Participacoes SA (Br	Telecommunications	12/31/03					—	—
EMC	EMC Corp. (MA)	Comp. components & periphs.	12/31/03	6236.8	1226.7	12927.9	10824.7	843	1320738223
EME	EMCOR Group, Inc.	Electronic components	12/31/03	4534.6	62.5	1655.8	521.4	162	14864922
EMR	Emerson Electric Co.	Electrical equipment	9/30/03	13958.0	2427.0	15153.0	6460.0	814	296876647
EDE	Empire District Electric Co.	Electric power	12/31/03	325.5	29.4	1008.8	378.8	69	6243695
EOC	Empresa Nacional de Electric	Electric power	12/31/03					33	7992741
EEQ	Enbridge Energy Management L	Natural gas	12/31/03	35.1	22.8	358.0	348.5	46	4790280
EEP	Enbridge Energy Partners, L.	Transportation	12/31/03	3172.3	111.7	3231.8		46	58266660
ENB	Enbridge Inc	Oil producer	12/31/03					46	58266660
ECA	EnCana Corp. (Canada)	Natural gas	12/31/03					211	203084870
EAC	Encore Acquisition Co.	Oil	12/31/03	220.1	71.5	628.4	359.0	55	17391853
ELE	Endesa S.A. (Spain)	Electric power	12/31/03					85	39215660
EN	ENEL S.p.A. (Italy)	Electric power	12/31/03					11	5274139
EGN	Energen Corp.	Natural gas distributor	12/31/03	842.2	110.3	1774.5	729.6	192	21511099
ENR	Energizer Holdings, Inc. (Un	Consumer electronics	9/30/03	2232.5	407.7	2252.9	808.0	234	56400135
EAS	Energy East Corp.	Electric power	12/31/03	4593.8	207.4	10415.5	2572.3	225	71160110
EPL	Energy Partners Ltd.	Natural gas	12/31/03	230.2	57.7	499.7	261.5	52	4276370
ETP	Energy Transfer Partners L P	Services	8/31/03	571.5	31.1	738.8		—	—
ENI	Enersis S.A. (Chile)	Electric power	12/31/03					19	3183840
ENC	Enesco Group, Inc.	Specialty stores	12/31/03	249.1	31.6	202.5	147.2	55	8079440
EC	Engelhard Corp.	Mining & processing	12/31/03	3714.5	537.1	2852.7	1285.4	273	113500902
E	ENI S.p.A.	Oil	12/31/03					117	18341494
EBF	Ennis Business Forms	Office equipment & supplies	2/29/04	259.4	18.0	132.3	110.6	62	8291666
ENO	Enodis Plc (United Kingdom)	—	9/27/03					1	39050
NPO	EnPro Industries Inc	—	12/31/03	730.1	86.7	987.3	436.6	64	10726151
ESV	ENSCO International Inc. (Un	Oil	12/31/03	790.8	278.5	3160.1	2081.1	310	125610212
ETS	Enterasys Networks, Inc.	Comp. components & periphs.	1/3/04	414.5	d208.7	347.4	180.1	147	123980629
ETM	Entercom Communications Corp	Broadcasting	12/31/03	401.1	88.2	1326.4	1031.6	196	36469159
EHB	Entergy Arkansas, Inc. (Unite	Electric power	12/31/03	1589.7	126.0	4858.5	1394.8	1	8000
ETR	Entergy Corp.	Electric power	12/31/03	9194.9	813.4	28554.2	8703.7	376	171166169
EHL	Entergy Louisiana, Inc. (Unit	Electric power	12/31/03	2165.6	146.2	4451.5	1068.5	2	18400
EMO	Entergy Mississippi, Inc. (Un	Electric power	12/31/03	1035.4	67.1	1858.4	564.5	1	367000
EPD	Enterprise Prods Partners LP	Natural gas	12/31/03	5346.4	104.5	4511.4	1706.0	79	9278885
EPR	Entertainment Properties Trus	Real estate investment trust	12/31/03	91.2	41.5	945.9	422.8	96	9436172
EVC	Entravision Communications Co	Broadcasting	12/31/03	238.0	d6.6	1535.3	1046.0	100	44571666
ENZ	Enzo Biochem, Inc.	—	7/31/03	52.8	27.4	114.3	109.4	92	7718253
EOG	EOG Resources, Inc.	Natural gas	12/31/03	1744.7	1191.6	4466.6	2223.4	316	107581710
EFX	Equifax, Inc.	Services	12/31/03	1225.4	461.6	1510.3	371.5	319	97569663
EQT	Equitable Resources, Inc.	Natural gas	12/31/03	1047.3	173.6	2802.3	965.3	242	44097480
ENN	Equity Inns Inc.	Real estate investment trust	12/31/03	230.1	d2.9	674.3	356.4	85	18430021
EOP	Equity Office Properties Trus	Real estate investment trust	12/31/03	3195.6	549.1	23855.0	10059.9	445	287009096
EQY	Equity One, Inc.	Real estate investment trust	12/31/03	190.0	69.6	1515.4	830.6	87	8912994
EQR	Equity Residential (United St	Real estate investment trust	12/31/03	1823.3	250.4	11456.9	5015.4	371	211959122
EQS	Equus II, Inc.	Investment company	12/31/03	2.9	3.4	127.9	71.5	10	757672
ESE	ESCO Technologies, Inc.	Defense systems & equip.	9/30/03	396.7	26.7	375.9	275.4	135	10785092
ESS	Essex Property Trust, Inc.	Real estate investment trust	12/31/03	234.4	45.1	1635.5	589.7	133	17302470
ESL	Esterline Technologies Corp	Meas. & control instruments	10/31/03	562.5	29.7	797.9	393.9	119	17141998
ETH	Ethan Allen Interiors, Inc.	Furniture & fixtures	6/30/03	907.3	212.4	702.3	537.7	201	33577122
NEU	Ethyl Corp. (United States)	Chemicals	12/31/03	756.3	50.0	622.5	199.7	—	—
EF	Europe Fund Inc.	Investment company	12/31/03	1.9	0.7	111.4	110.4	24	1542040
EXC	Exelon Corp. (United States)	Electric power	12/31/03	15812.0	793.0	37891.0	8503.0	454	203012003
XJT	Expressjet Holdings Inc. (Un	—	12/31/03	1311.4	108.5	384.4	d10.3	91	26303984
EXE	Extendicare Inc. (Canada)	Hospitals & nursing homes	12/31/03					13	5454292
XOM	Exxon Mobil Corp.	Oil	12/31/03		20960.0	158385.0	90940.0	1334	d869299780
FNB	F.N.B. Corp (PA)	Banking - Mid-Atlantic	12/31/03	553.9	60.0	8308.3	606.9	98	12415635
FDS	FactSet Research Systems Inc	Computer services	8/31/03	222.3	51.4	246.3	212.2	166	29745250
FIC	Fair Isaac Corp	Services	9/30/03	629.3	107.2	1463.6	849.5	232	46312842
FA	Fairchild Corp. (The)	—	6/30/03	77.5	d86.1	390.5	137.8	24	8434641
FCS	Fairchild Semiconductor Intl	Electronic components	12/28/03	1395.8	d190.0	2214.2	1147.7	211	102525429
FFH	Fairfax Financial Holdings, L	Insurance	12/31/03					41	3431287
FDO	Family Dollar Stores	Discount & variety stores	8/31/03	p4750.2	p4750.2			331	137512857
FNM	Fannie Mae (United States)	Finance	12/31/03	53768.0	7720.0		22373.0	1022	879714632

| EARNINGS PER SHARE | | | | | | P/E | DIVIDENDS | | | AV. | DIV. DECLARED | | PRICE RANGE |
| QUARTERLY | | | | ANNUAL | | RATIO | PER SHARE | | | YLD. | | | 2004 |
1st	2nd	3rd	2004	2003	2002		2004	2003	2002	%	AMOUNT	PAYABLE	
—	—	—	—	—	p1.58	—	—	—	—	—	—	—	45.79 - 22.59
0.60	—	—	—	2.77	1.72	—	—	—	—	—	100%	10/19/00	52.53 - 27.20
1.13	—	—	—	2.85	3.83	—	2.06	2.06	2.06	5.1	0.515Q	4/15/05	45.43 - 35.71
0.66	—	—	—	0.99	1.84	—	1.40	1.40	1.40	3.3	0.35Q	3/14/05	49.39 - 36.67
0.22	—	—	—	1.63	0.99	—	—	—	—	—	3-for-2	6/10/98	25.65 - 10.20
—	—	—	—	13.85	13.03	—	1.02	1.02	1.02	7.4	0.085M	4/29/05	15.49 - 12.15
0.07	—	—	—	d2.43	1.22	—	1.10	1.10	1.10	5.5	0.275Q	3/16/05	26.16 - 13.51
0.21	—	—	—	1.08	1.15	—	1.85	1.83	1.81	6.1	0.465Q	2/28/05	36.00 - 25.05
0.66	—	—	—	2.30	1.87	—	—	—	—	—	—	—	60.80 - 35.35
0.28	—	—	—	1.22	0.40	—	1.00	1.00	1.51	5.5	0.25Q	4/1/05	20.50 - 15.70
0.29	0.34	0.23	—	0.36	d0.80	—	—	—	—	—	3-for-2	2/16/00	36.09 - 10.33
0.12	—	—	—	1.30	d6.24	—	—	—	0.15	—	0.075Q	6/17/02	6.09 - 1.87
d0.60	—	—	—	d1.31	d2.25	—	—	—	—	—	2-for-1	5/21/99	7.83 - 4.63
0.23	—	—	—	0.55	0.30	—	—	—	—	—	3-for-1	3/28/05	15.39 - 4.20
—	—	—	—	—	—	—	0.62	0.52	0.39	0.9	3-for-1	3/28/05	91.34 - 41.41
—	—	—	—	3.57	3.11	—	6.95	0.20	0.20	9.9	0.30Q	4/20/05	86.76 - 53.30
0.43	—	—	—	1.86	1.32	—	1.81	1.78	1.26	7.7	0.6169Q	3/15/05	27.79 - 19.00
0.21	—	—	—	0.69	0.84	—	1.92	1.90	1.88	5.9	0.485Q	3/31/05	35.70 - 29.62
d0.07	—	—	—	d3.54	1.02	—	1.76	1.76	1.76	4.0	0.44Q	4/1/05	58.17 - 28.99
0.06	—	—	—	0.83	2.72	—	0.50	1.15	1.80	1.8	0.25S	12/14/04	34.52 - 20.50
0.85	—	—	—	2.56	1.96	—	1.08	0.92	0.88	1.2	0.31Q	2/25/05	124.25 - 52.80
0.44	0.50	—	—	1.51	1.70	—	0.28	0.20	0.15	0.7	0.08Q	2/14/05	52.39 - 25.54
—	—	—	—	8.50	8.42	—	0.43	0.49	0.55	4.8	0.039M	4/18/05	10.04 - 7.86
0.25	—	—	—	1.06	0.81	—	0.32	0.29	0.27	1.1	0.0875Q	4/15/05	35.59 - 24.53
0.30	—	—	—	2.37	3.46	—	0.80	—	—	3.6	0.25Q	4/30/05	32.52 - 12.33
0.22	—	—	—	0.76	0.81	—	0.12	0.12	0.12	0.5	0.03Q	4/8/05	32.42 - 16.10
—	—	—	—	1.97	1.46	—	0.64	0.64	0.64	1.8	0.16Q	4/1/05	43.65 - 25.90
d1.04	—	—	—	1.29	0.91	—	—	—	—	—	—	—	42.30 - 25.51
0.19	—	—	—	0.61	0.53	—	—	—	—	—	—	—	24.40 - 6.17
0.06	—	—	—	0.42	0.61	—	—	—	—	—	—	—	19.12 - 10.30
d0.07	—	—	—	d0.53	2.06	—	0.40	0.60	0.60	2.0	0.05Q	3/10/05	25.07 - 15.50
0.46	0.35	0.31	—	1.23	0.77	—	0.20	0.20	0.20	0.8	0.05Q	2/25/05	34.85 - 16.06
—	—	—	—	—	—	—	0.33	0.47	0.52	3.5	—	5/11/05	12.55 - 6.45
—	—	—	—	—	—	—	0.91	0.34	0.74	3.8	0.19242U	4/22/05	37.00 - 10.31
—	—	—	—	—	—	—	0.69	—	—	5.3	0.6899U	2/17/04	17.46 - 8.76
0.06	—	—	—	0.22	d0.05	—	—	—	—	—	0.00U	2/7/01	15.80 - 7.23
0.37	—	—	—	1.33	4.07	—	—	—	—	—	—	—	47.38 - 34.06
0.58	0.75	—	—	2.41	2.52	—	1.61	1.58	1.55	2.8	0.415Q	3/10/05	70.88 - 45.35
0.06	—	—	—	1.29	1.19	—	1.28	1.28	1.28	6.2	0.32Q	3/15/05	23.48 - 17.55
—	—	—	—	—	—	—	0.09	—	0.03	0.7	—	4/20/04	18.66 - 7.02
0.38	—	—	—	2.35	1.05	—	—	—	—	—	0.00Q	2/14/05	49.75 - 39.75
0.50	—	—	—	1.93	1.76	—	3.70	3.70	3.60	7.9	0.925Q	2/14/05	51.95 - 41.35
—	—	—	—	—	—	—	0.92	0.83	0.76	2.4	0.50Q	3/1/05	49.99 - 27.74
—	—	—	—	—	—	—	0.40	0.40	0.40	0.9	0.10Q	3/31/05	57.42 - 31.41
0.55	—	—	—	2.07	1.25	—	—	—	—	—	—	—	36.88 - 17.24
—	—	—	—	—	—	—	0.74	0.64	0.24	4.1	—	1/10/05	23.60 - 12.05
—	—	—	—	—	—	—	3.19	1.50	1.30	8.2	—	12/3/04	49.63 - 28.20
1.65	—	—	—	3.09	2.09	—	0.76	0.73	0.71	1.7	0.20Q	3/1/05	60.07 - 30.37
1.32	0.63	—	—	1.93	2.01	—	—	—	—	—	—	—	50.00 - 24.40
0.82	—	—	—	1.42	1.44	—	1.06	1.00	0.96	4.7	0.275Q	5/15/05	27.08 - 17.80
0.20	—	—	—	0.87	d0.44	—	—	—	—	—	—	—	20.90 - 9.88
d0.09	2.38	—	—	1.79	0.25	—	1.46	1.28	1.27	3.1	0.4625Q	4/14/05	59.50 - 34.50
—	—	—	—	—	—	—	—	0.12	—	—	—	3/30/05	8.63 - 3.89
d0.31	—	—	—	1.20	1.47	—	—	—	—	—	0.28Q	4/1/04	14.09 - 6.05
0.40	—	—	—	1.86	1.31	—	0.44	0.41	0.40	1.6	0.12Q	3/31/05	32.72 - 20.71
—	—	—	—	—	—	—	3.30	3.13	2.69	3.4	4.30335A	6/30/05	126.97 - 66.77
—	—	—	—	1.08	0.93	—	0.62	0.62	0.62	3.7	0.155Q	5/2/05	22.23 - 11.10
—	—	—	—	—	—	—	—	—	1.18	—	1.175U	4/22/02	7.26 - 2.20
0.54	—	—	—	1.61	d0.62	—	—	—	—	—	—	—	30.15 - 3.98
0.14	—	—	—	0.71	0.42	—	0.10	0.10	0.10	0.3	0.025Q	3/31/05	34.15 - 24.95
d0.16	—	—	—	d0.56	d0.57	—	—	—	—	—	0.00U	8/6/01	5.34 - 1.19
0.23	—	—	—	1.39	1.12	—	—	—	—	—	—	—	53.60 - 30.25
—	—	—	—	—	—	—	1.50	1.45	—	6.1	0.375Q	5/2/05	27.20 - 21.67
0.88	—	—	—	3.42	2.64	—	1.89	1.60	1.34	3.3	0.54Q	3/1/05	68.67 - 44.45
—	—	—	—	—	—	—	1.90	1.90	0.97	7.3	0.475Q	4/1/05	27.94 - 24.44
—	—	—	—	—	—	—	1.81	1.86	—	6.8	—	3/1/05	27.59 - 25.60
0.23	—	—	—	0.41	0.50	—	1.51	1.44	1.33	6.7	0.40Q	2/14/05	25.99 - 19.00
0.49	—	—	—	1.77	1.64	—	2.19	1.98	1.87	6.4	0.625Q	4/15/05	45.19 - 23.50
d0.09	—	—	—	d0.16	d0.18	—	—	—	—	—	—	—	11.55 - 5.40
d0.01	d0.05	d0.02	—	0.13	0.23	—	—	—	—	—	5%	11/15/04	20.95 - 11.70
0.83	—	—	—	3.66	0.65	—	0.11	0.09	0.08	0.2	0.04Q	4/29/05	76.50 - 37.38
0.38	—	—	—	1.31	1.38	—	0.11	0.08	0.08	0.5	0.03Q	3/15/05	28.46 - 19.18
1.10	—	—	—	2.74	2.36	—	1.44	0.97	0.67	3.0	0.38Q	3/1/05	61.18 - 36.30
d0.09	—	—	—	d0.48	—	—	0.52	0.52	0.38	6.0	0.15Q	5/2/05	11.84 - 5.45
0.23	—	—	—	1.26	1.75	—	2.00	2.00	2.00	7.4	0.50Q	4/15/05	30.39 - 23.90
0.26	—	—	—	0.95	0.88	—	1.13	1.10	1.08	6.1	0.29Q	3/31/05	23.88 - 13.08
0.12	—	—	—	0.43	1.18	—	1.73	1.73	1.73	5.7	0.4325Q	4/8/05	36.75 - 24.07
10.54	—	—	—	10.81	12.35	—	0.72	—	—	9.3	0.57A	1/17/05	8.71 - 6.76
0.50	0.57	—	—	2.04	1.67	—	—	—	—	—	—	—	78.95 - 32.80
0.26	—	—	—	1.70	2.38	—	3.15	3.11	3.01	4.6	0.81Q	4/15/05	85.42 - 50.48
0.09	0.43	—	—	1.41	1.49	—	—	—	—	—	2-for-1	4/20/98	36.62 - 15.90
0.50	0.64	0.61	—	1.95	2.06	—	3.45	0.29	0.20	9.1	0.15Q	4/25/05	46.65 - 29.07
0.34	—	—	—	1.22	0.57	—	—	—	—	—	—	—	22.98 - 17.98
—	—	—	—	10.97	8.07	—	0.77	0.58	0.84	8.3	0.7749A	12/31/04	12.14 - 6.60
0.56	—	—	—	1.21	2.58	—	1.26	0.96	0.88	2.5	0.40Q	3/10/05	69.79 - 30.92
0.53	—	—	—	1.80	1.38	—	—	—	—	—	—	—	15.66 - 8.00
—	—	—	—	—	—	—	—	—	—	—	0.05Q	5/16/05	14.00 - 1.85
0.83	—	—	—	3.15	1.61	—	1.06	0.98	0.92	2.5	0.27Q	3/10/05	52.05 - 34.02
0.34	—	—	—	1.25	1.34	—	0.92	0.93	0.81	4.4	0.23Q	3/15/05	22.91 - 18.80
0.39	0.43	—	—	1.48	1.17	—	0.18	0.15	0.13	0.4	0.05Q	3/21/05	59.25 - 25.59
0.39	0.42	—	—	1.41	0.32	—	0.07	0.05	0.05	0.2	0.02Q	3/9/05	62.30 - 23.90
d0.26	d0.59	—	—	d3.42	d0.41	—	—	—	—	—	0.00U	4/14/04	5.63 - 2.98
0.10	—	—	—	d0.69	d0.02	—	—	—	—	—	—	—	28.50 - 10.46
—	—	—	—	—	—	—	1.40	1.50	1.00	1.2	1.40A	1/28/05	187.20 - 50.95
0.37	0.47	—	—	—	p1.43	—	0.33	0.29	0.26	1.0	0.095Q	4/15/05	39.66 - 25.09
1.90	—	—	—	7.72	4.53	—	2.08	1.68	1.32	2.9	0.26Q	2/25/05	80.82 - 62.95

T15

SYMBOL	COMPANY	NATURE OF BUSINESS	FISCAL YEAR-END	TOTAL REV. $MILL	NET INCOME $MILL	TOTAL ASSETS $MILL	NET STK EQUITY $MILL	NO. OF INST.	INST. HOLDINGS (SHARES)
FFG	FBL Financial Group, Inc.	Life Insurance	12/31/03	641.5	65.9	7949.1	747.8	62	7646015
FJC	Fedders Corp.	Appliances & utensils	8/31/03	421.7	8.8	392.9	74.9	52	7039472
AGM A	Federal Agricultural Mortgag	Finance	12/31/03	54.8	33.3	4299.6	213.3	7	97411
FRT	Federal Realty Investment Tru	Real estate investment trust	12/31/03	357.9	73.0	2143.4	691.4	153	28818927
FSS	Federal Signal Corp.	—	12/31/03	1206.8	84.2	1204.5	440.6	166	30897086
FD	Federated Department Stores,	Department stores	1/31/04	15264.0	693.0	12832.0	5940.0	364	174999852
FII	Federated Investors Inc (PA)	Financial services	12/31/03	823.2	204.6	874.6	395.9	185	45093253
FCH	FelCor Lodging Trust, Inc.	Real estate investment trust	12/31/03	1199.9	d131.6	3590.9	1296.3	133	32895325
FGP	Ferrellgas Partners, L.P.	Natural gas	7/31/03	1221.6	87.5	934.7	—	43	1218201
FOE	Ferro Corp.	Specialty chemicals	12/31/03	1622.4	41.6	1558.7	525.9	138	33497291
FNF	Fidelity National Financial,	Insurance brokerage	12/31/03	7715.2	2685.1	6664.6	3873.4	280	70212976
FIF	Financial Federal Corp. (Unit	—	7/31/03	130.2	30.1	1426.1	316.4	103	16821118
FAC	First Acceptance Corp	Real estate investment trust	6/30/03	1.3	d1.9	58.1	58.1	—	—
FAF	First American Corp (The)	Insurance	12/31/03	6213.7	2180.1	4446.7	1879.5	201	49406543
FBP	First Bancorp (PR)	Banking - South	12/31/03	655.4	152.3	12667.9	1089.6	101	13505297
FCF	First Commonwealth Fin (PA)	Banking - Mid-Atlantic	12/31/03	292.2	52.7	5189.2	430.9	68	10224837
FDC	First Data Corp	Financial services	12/31/03	8400.2	1394.0	24094.7	4047.3	769	662912005
FF	First Financial Fund, Inc.	Investment company	3/31/04	7.9	3.4	460.1	438.6	20	2606578
FHN	First Horizon National Corp	Banking - South	12/31/03	2693.4	473.3	24506.7	1890.3	—	—
FR	First Industrial Realty Trust	Real estate investment trust	12/31/03	341.4	52.6	2452.1	889.2	177	22111086
ISL	First Israel Fund, Inc.	Finance	9/30/03	0.1	d0.9	52.9	52.6	16	1426003
FMD	First Marblehead Corp	Finance	6/30/03	91.4	47.6	87.1	52.4	—	—
FRC	First Republic Bank (CA)	Savings & loan	12/31/03	p250.0	p250.0	—	—	96	10278122
FUR	First Union Real Estate Inves	Real estate investment trust	12/31/03	16.6	1.0	146.8	96.7	29	18968022
FE	FirstEnergy Corp.	Electric power	12/31/03	12307.0	422.0	32909.9	8289.3	349	185867671
FED	Firstfed Financial Corp. (DE	Savings & loan	12/31/03	252.6	64.5	4825.0	436.6	126	13096048
FSH	Fisher Scientific Intl, Inc.	Property & casualty insurance	12/31/03	3564.4	174.5	2782.1	575.4	190	48604861
FLA	Fla. East Coast Industries	Railroads	12/31/03	339.0	41.4	1008.4	558.1	79	12144719
FBC	Flagstar Bancorp, Inc. (Unit	Banking - Midwest	12/31/03	968.9	334.3	10570.2	654.7	130	14020880
FBC	Flaherty & Crumrine/Claymore	Investment company	11/30/03	68.7	60.1	1607.1	1058.5	—	—
FRA	Floating Rate Income Strategi	Investment company	10/15/03	—	—	—	0.5	0.1	—
FRK	Florida Rock Industries	—	9/30/03	746.1	92.8	785.1	574.4	127	15106541
FLO	Flowers Foods, Inc. (United	Food processing	1/3/04	1453.0	52.8	787.9	577.7	113	17869838
FLS	Flowserve Corp.	Machinery & equipment	12/31/03	2404.4	126.7	2774.9	820.7	166	50858527
FLR	Fluor Corp. (New)	—	12/31/03	8805.7	595.3	2833.4	1081.5	248	64522156
FMC	FMC Corp.	Chemicals	12/31/03	1921.4	77.8	2605.6	588.3	162	27568660
FTI	FMC Technologies, Inc.	—	12/31/03	2.3	0.2	1.4	0.4	195	53250882
FMX	Fomento Economico Mexicano S	Conglomerate	12/31/03	—	—	—	—	92	35876586
FL	Foot Locker, Inc.	Discount & variety stores	1/31/04	4779.0	534.0	2544.0	1375.0	197	130103250
F	Ford Motor Co. (DE)	—	12/31/03	—	890.0	297371.0	11651.0	559	604710528
FCZ	Ford Motor Credit Co (United	Finance	12/31/03	7601.0	1869.0	174620.0	12474.0	3	154600
FCJ	Ford Motor Credit Co (United	Finance	12/31/03	7601.0	1869.0	174620.0	12474.0	3	416800
FCE A	Forest City Enterprises, Inc.	Engineering & construction	1/31/04	1021.6	39.0	5838.8	748.9	84	25315449
FRX	Forest Laboratories, Inc.	Drugs	3/31/04	2680.3	1672.7	3593.3	3255.9	508	306137977
FST	Forest Oil Corp. (United Stat	Oil	12/31/03	657.2	126.5	2153.0	1185.8	174	35177808
FO	Fortune Brands Inc (United St	—	12/31/03	6214.5	1483.1	7128.5	2719.5	459	92390746
FPL	FPL Group, Inc.	Electric power	12/31/03	9630.0	893.0	24534.0	6972.0	513	115998329
FTE	France Telecom S.A.	Telecommunications	12/31/03	—	—	—	—	36	3310083
FC	Franklin Covey Co.	Services	8/31/03	307.2	d45.3	259.7	185.8	17	4879288
FMI	Franklin Multi-Income Trust	Investment company	3/31/04	4.1	2.6	64.2	49.3	6	168250
BEN	Franklin Resources, Inc.	Financial services	9/30/03	2624.4	502.8	6649.7	4310.1	325	95780988
FCX	Freeport-McMoRan Copper & Gol	Mining & processing	12/31/03	2212.2	277.5	4495.1	776.0	302	132026318
FMT	Fremont General Corp.	Property & casualty insurance	12/31/03	903.7	212.0	9521.9	664.7	104	35907946
FMS	Fresenius Medical Care AG (Ge	Medical & dental equipment	12/31/03	5527.5	331.2	7503.3	3243.7	49	8076920
FBR	Friedman Billings Ramsey Gro	Financial services	12/31/03	628.5	201.4	11327.4	1554.3	45	27090040
FTO	Frontier Oil Corp.	Oil	12/31/03	2170.5	3.2	642.3	169.3	117	20538576
FCN	FTI Consulting Inc.	Services	12/31/03	375.7	64.8	539.3	455.2	187	28633106
FUL	Fuller (H.B.) Co.	Specialty chemicals	11/30/03	p1287.0	p1287.0	—	—	139	19298659
FBN	Furniture Brands Internationa	Furniture & fixtures	12/31/03	2367.7	94.6	1248.9	966.9	196	50476871
GBL	Gabelli Asset Management, Inc	Banking - Northeast	12/31/03	207.4	49.8	736.5	378.3	58	5502937
GCV	Gabelli Convertible and Incom	Investment company	12/31/03	5.4	3.1	152.9	101.7	14	1649102
GDV	Gabelli Dividend & Income Tru	Investment company	12/31/03	1.8	d0.0	1493.7	1451.7	—	—
GAB	Gabelli Equity Trust Inc. (Th	Investment company	12/31/03	21.0	1.8	1527.1	1094.5	51	1653263
GGT	Gabelli Global Multimedia Tru	Investment company	12/31/03	1.8	d0.9	201.0	150.2	24	1835511
GUT	Gabelli Utility Trust	Investment company	12/31/03	3.9	1.7	214.6	156.5	24	201489
GBP	Gables Residential Trust	Real estate investment trust	12/31/03	237.3	30.9	1609.9	582.5	119	17942013
AJG	Gallagher (Arthur J.) & Co.	Financial services	12/31/03	1263.8	339.5	2883.4	619.1	239	64261786
GLH	Gallaher Group Plc (UK)	Tobacco	12/31/03	—	—	—	—	20	12297333
GME	Gamestop Corp. (United State	Computer services	1/31/04	1578.8	63.5	898.9	594.0	88	17545776
GCI	Gannett Co., Inc.	Broadcasting	12/28/03	6711.1	1211.2	14706.2	8423.0	687	216627389
GDI	Gardner Denver, Inc.	Machinery & equipment	12/31/03	439.5	20.6	424.4	265.9	84	12208748
IT	Gartner, Inc.	Services	12/31/03	858.4	59.2	601.7	375.7	111	41056080
GTW	Gateway Inc	Comp. components & periphs.	12/31/03	3402.4	d514.8	1846.0	722.0	219	138619026
GMT	GATX Corp.	Equip. & vehicle leasing	12/31/03	1242.7	187.9	6080.6	888.9	195	47071404
GET	Gaylord Entertainment Co New	Broadcasting	12/31/03	448.8	d22.0	2470.4	904.5	58	17571004
GY	GenCorp Inc. (United States)	Defense systems & equip.	11/30/03	1192.0	39.0	1795.0	428.0	110	33500175
DNA	Genentech, Inc.	—	12/31/03	678.8	d2124.5	8361.7	6520.3	372	168556595
GAM	General American Investors Co	Investment company	12/31/03	12.0	0.9	1213.1	1186.3	37	1752284
BGC	General Cable Corp. (DE) (New	Electronic components	12/31/03	1538.4	d4.8	1001.1	240.1	61	27094472
GD	General Dynamics Corp.	Defense systems & equip.	12/31/03	16617.0	1055.0	14888.0	5921.0	576	126487106
GEC	General Electric Capital Corp	—	12/31/03	52916.0	7232.0	503887.0	43700.0	11	196725
GED	General Electric Capital Corp	—	12/31/03	52916.0	7232.0	503887.0	43700.0	8	132350
GE	General Electric Co. (United	Electrical equipment	12/31/03	61833.0	—	647271.0	79180.0	1395	844046535
GGP	General Growth Properties, In	Real estate investment trust	12/31/03	1270.7	259.5	9582.9	1670.4	251	57650240
GMA	General Motors Acceptance Cor	Financial services	12/31/03	22628.0	2793.0	286402.0	20236.0	1	5050
GM	General Motors Corp	—	12/31/03	—	6223.0	448507.0	25268.0	579	390974739
GCO	Genesco Inc. (United States)	Shoe manufacturing	1/31/04	837.4	29.6	420.9	215.6	122	20691786
GWR	Genesee & Wyoming Inc.	Railroads	12/31/03	244.8	103.6	494.8	267.1	85	10978051
GPC	Genuine Parts Co.	—	12/31/03	8449.3	353.6	3409.9	2312.3	352	128606979
GGI	Geo Group Inc	Services	12/28/03	617.5	164.2	505.5	87.0	—	—
GGC	Georgia Gulf Corp.	Chemicals	12/31/03	1444.5	12.5	855.0	136.4	140	23558713
GPJ	Georgia Power Co.	Electric power	12/31/03	4913.5	635.6	14249.8	4540.2	—	—
GPW	Georgia Power Co.	Electric power	12/31/03	4913.5	635.6	14249.8	4540.2	—	—
GPU	Georgia Power Co.	Electric power	12/31/03	4913.5	635.6	14249.8	4540.2	—	—
GP	Georgia-Pacific Corp.	Forest products	1/3/04	20255.0	1426.0	23888.0	5394.0	311	186684629
GNA	Gerdau Ameristeel Corp	Steel producer	12/31/03	—	—	—	—	—	112874

T16

| EARNINGS PER SHARE — QUARTERLY | | | | ANNUAL | | P/E RATIO | DIVIDENDS PER SHARE | | | AV. YLD. % | DIV. DECLARED | | PRICE RANGE 2004 |
1st	2nd	3rd	2004	2003	2002		2004	2003	2002		AMOUNT	PAYABLE	
0.45				2.23	1.64	—	0.40	0.40	0.40	1.6	0.105Q	3/31/05	29.72 - 19.59
d0.20				0.27	0.25	—	0.12	0.12	0.09	2.2	0.03Q	3/1/05	8.23 - 2.70
0.64				2.08	1.69	—	0.10			0.5	0.10Q	3/31/05	23.00 - 16.70
0.28				1.15	0.60	—	1.97	1.94	1.92	4.9	0.505Q	4/15/05	52.95 - 28.04
0.05				0.79	1.01	—	0.40	0.80	0.80	2.3	0.06Q	4/4/05	20.29 - 14.20
0.52				3.71	3.21	—	0.52	0.25	—	1.2	0.135Q	4/1/05	58.16 - 25.50
0.46				1.71	1.74	—	0.41	0.30	0.22	1.4	0.125Q	2/28/05	33.79 - 25.32
d0.47				d5.52	d3.78	—		0.15	0.50	—	0.15Q	1/31/03	14.95 - 6.23
d0.54	p1.65	p0.63		1.33	1.34	—	2.00	2.00	2.00	8.9	0.50Q	3/15/05	25.83 - 19.29
0.33				0.38	0.81	—	0.58	0.58	0.58	2.5	0.145Q	6/10/05	27.50 - 18.47
0.88				5.63	3.91	—	0.79	0.63	0.29	2.2	10.00Q	3/28/05	45.68 - 26.26
0.39	0.42	0.44		1.67	1.99	—				—	0.10Q	4/29/05	39.72 - 19.10
0.04	d0.04	0.10		d0.09	0.02	—			0.01	—	0.006U	6/28/02	9.08 - 5.83
0.62				5.22	2.92	—	0.60	0.45	0.31	2.1	0.18Q	4/15/05	35.36 - 22.77
0.73				2.98	2.01	—	0.48	0.44	0.45	1.1	0.14Q	3/31/05	65.49 - 24.75
0.22				0.90	0.74	—	0.64	0.62	0.60	4.6	0.165Q	4/15/05	15.90 - 11.65
0.61				1.86	1.61	—	0.08	0.08	0.06	0.2	0.06Q	4/11/05	46.80 - 34.40
—				19.24	14.40	—	5.10	2.75	2.96	27.0	0.38A	12/30/04	24.20 - 13.62
0.92				3.62	2.89	—	1.60	1.20	1.00	3.6	0.43Q	4/1/05	46.95 - 40.85
0.02				0.49	1.01	—	2.74	2.74	2.72	7.9	0.695Q	4/18/05	42.23 - 27.15
—				d0.22	d0.17	—		0.35	0.17	—	0.351A	6/20/03	15.77 - 7.48
d0.06	0.58	d0.06		0.51	0.20	—				—			59.56 - 22.09
p0.56					p1.70	—	0.35	0.17	—	0.9	50%	3/15/05	53.85 - 21.20
d0.02				d0.26	d0.20	—			0.20	—	0.10Q	7/31/02	4.29 - 1.54
0.53				1.39	2.33	—	1.50	1.50	1.50	4.1	0.4125Q	6/1/05	43.41 - 29.50
0.86				3.70	3.15	—				—	2-for-1	7/30/98	54.30 - 28.91
0.51				1.29	1.67	—				—	5-for-1	4/1/98	63.00 - 27.96
0.16				1.12	1.37	—	0.19	1.65	0.10	0.5	0.05Q	3/18/05	46.83 - 23.44
0.57				3.99	1.79	—	1.00	0.50	0.11	5.0	0.25Q	3/31/05	28.10 - 11.54
—				25.74	—	—	2.23	2.45	—	9.0	0.155M	4/29/05	27.95 - 21.70
—				19.10	—	—	0.91			4.8		4/29/05	19.98 - 18.33
0.73	0.56			1.73	1.59	—	1.70	0.37	0.25	3.5	0.20Q	4/1/05	64.90 - 33.42
0.38				1.15	0.13	—	0.47	0.33	0.03	2.0	0.125Q	3/11/05	32.17 - 15.67
p0.19				0.96	1.16	—				—	0.14Q	12/3/99	27.91 - 11.65
0.57				2.23	2.13	—	0.64	0.64	0.64	1.5	0.16Q	4/1/05	55.19 - 28.23
0.20				1.12	2.01	—				—	0.00U	12/31/01	50.50 - 15.53
0.20				1.13	0.96	—				—			34.50 - 18.82
—						—	0.47	0.39	0.70	1.1	0.4676A	6/11/04	53.28 - 32.25
0.31				1.40	1.10	—	0.24	0.12	—	1.3	0.075Q	4/29/05	27.42 - 10.10
0.95				0.50	0.15	—	0.40	0.40	0.40	3.2	0.10Q	6/1/05	17.34 - 7.52
—				—	—	—	1.84	1.84	1.86	7.6	0.46Q	4/15/05	26.60 - 21.81
—				—	—	—	1.90	1.90	1.45	7.2	0.475Q	3/1/05	26.80 - 26.12
0.13				0.77	0.87	—	0.38	0.30	0.22	0.8	0.10Q	6/15/05	58.59 - 32.29
—				1.95	1.66	—				—	2-for-1	1/8/03	78.00 - 36.20
0.36				1.79	0.51	—				—			34.12 - 20.78
0.92				3.86	3.41	—	1.26	1.14	1.02	2.0	0.33Q	3/1/05	80.50 - 42.87
0.77				5.02	4.01	—	1.30	1.20	1.16	2.0	2-for-1	3/15/05	76.10 - 56.01
—				—	—	—	0.29	2.74	0.84	1.1	0.2948U	5/17/04	33.57 - 22.00
d0.27	d0.10		—	d2.69	d5.29	—				—	0.035M	4/15/05	3.02 - 0.71
—				8.42	6.40	—	0.42	0.42	0.65	5.9			8.05 - 6.10
0.67	0.68		—	1.97	1.65	—	0.34	0.30	0.28	0.7	0.10Q	4/15/05	71.45 - 32.67
d0.10			—	1.07	0.89	—	1.10	0.27	—	3.6	0.25Q	5/1/05	44.90 - 17.02
p1.12			—	2.98	1.40	—	0.22	0.14	0.10	1.2	0.07Q	4/29/05	31.00 - 4.71
—				3.49	3.12	—	0.33	0.29	0.21	1.6	0.32735A	6/7/04	27.28 - 14.17
0.54			—	1.63	1.08	—	1.48	1.02	—	8.0	0.34Q	4/29/05	28.60 - 8.44
d0.14			—	0.12	0.04	—	0.21	0.20	0.20	1.0	0.06Q	4/11/05	26.93 - 14.80
0.27			—	1.54	1.02	—				—	50%	6/4/03	24.14 - 14.60
0.16			—		p1.35	—	0.46	0.45	0.44	1.7	0.115Q	2/25/05	30.34 - 22.02
0.58			—	1.68	2.11	—	0.53	0.13	—	2.0	0.15Q	2/28/05	35.09 - 18.21
p0.52			—	1.65	1.76	—	1.16	0.02	—	3.0	0.02Q	3/28/05	50.50 - 27.55
—			—	8.90	8.44	—	0.80	0.80	0.75	7.7	0.20Q	3/24/05	11.90 - 8.77
—			—	19.26		—	1.20		—	9.7	0.10M	6/24/05	20.13 - 15.63
—			—	7.98	6.28	—	0.80	0.69	0.95	9.8	0.18Q	3/24/05	9.40 - 6.88
—			—	10.56	7.67	—			0.49	—	0.12Q	3/24/05	10.78 - 6.09
—			—	6.83	6.27	—	0.72	0.72	0.72	8.0	0.06M	6/24/05	10.00 - 8.00
0.10			—	0.58	1.69	—	2.41	2.41	2.41	7.7		6/30/05	37.35 - 25.03
0.41			—	1.57	1.41	—	0.93	0.69	0.58	3.2	0.28Q	4/15/05	34.25 - 24.47
—						—	2.17	1.87	1.56	4.4	1.6442S	5/31/05	62.19 - 35.52
—			—	1.06	0.87	—				—			23.51 - 8.50
1.00			—	4.46	4.31	—	1.02	0.97	0.93	1.3	0.27Q	4/1/05	91.00 - 70.43
0.39			—	1.27	1.22	—				—	3-for-2	12/29/97	37.95 - 17.75
—			—	0.26	d0.18	—				—			13.30 - 6.95
d0.51			—	d1.62	d0.95	—				—	2-for-1	9/7/99	6.92 - 2.18
0.46			—	1.56	0.59	—	0.80	1.28	1.28	3.6	0.20Q	3/31/05	30.27 - 14.48
d0.49			—	d0.97	0.38	—				—	0.20Q	12/28/05	42.52 - 17.67
d0.43		pd0.43	—	0.50	0.69	—	0.06	0.12	0.12	0.5	0.03Q	5/28/04	18.75 - 6.25
0.17			—	0.57	0.06	—				—	100%	5/12/04	136.40 - 35.01
—				33.11	26.48	—	1.01	0.54	0.62	3.7	0.002A	3/10/05	31.74 - 22.94
d0.09			—	d0.16	d0.55	—			0.15	—	0.05Q	8/23/02	14.10 - 3.70
1.34			—	5.00	5.18	—	1.40	1.26	1.18	1.7	0.40Q	5/6/05	109.98 - 55.07
—				—	—	—	1.52	1.52	—	5.8	0.38125Q	2/15/05	26.16 - 26.08
—				—	—	—	1.47	1.10	—	6.2		2/22/05	26.27 - 21.17
0.32			—	1.55	1.51	—	0.80	0.76	0.72	2.6	0.22Q	4/25/05	37.72 - 23.14
0.27			—	1.20	0.99	—	1.26	1.02	0.89	4.1	0.36Q	4/29/05	36.90 - 24.35
—						—	1.82	1.82	1.82	7.4	0.45625Q	3/9/05	26.32 - 22.97
2.25			—	5.03	3.35	—	2.00	2.00	2.00	4.5	0.50Q	3/10/05	55.55 - 33.62
0.26			—	1.33	1.47	—				—			31.39 - 13.65
0.35			—	1.07	0.99	—				—	50%	3/15/04	37.75 - 15.30
0.57			—	2.03	2.10	—	1.19	1.18	1.15	3.3	0.3125Q	4/1/05	44.32 - 28.80
0.22			—	2.86	1.01	—				—	2-for-1	6/3/96	26.75 - 17.02
0.57			—	0.38	0.97	—	0.32	0.32	0.32	0.8	0.08Q	4/8/05	58.75 - 19.04
—				—	—	—	1.47			5.8	0.375Q	4/15/05	25.68 - 25.10
—				—	—	—	1.05			4.6		4/15/05	25.26 - 20.40
—				—	—	—	0.35			1.4	0.375Q	5/16/05	26.45 - 25.20
0.55			—	0.90	d0.80	—	0.50	0.50	0.50	1.9	0.175Q	2/24/05	38.60 - 13.90
—				—	—	—				—	0.02Q	3/4/05	7.32 - 4.42

SYMBOL	COMPANY	NATURE OF BUSINESS	FISCAL YEAR-END	TOTAL REV. $MILL	NET INCOME $MILL	TOTAL ASSETS $MILL	NET STK EQUITY $MILL	NO. OF INST.	INST. HOLDINGS (SHARES)
GGB	Gerdau S.A. (Brazil)	Steel producer	12/31/03	—	—	—	—	32	5375565
GER	Germany Fund, Inc.	Investment company	12/31/03	2.0	0.3	130.7	130.4	19	1852979
GYI	Getty Images, Inc. (United St	Services	12/31/03	523.2	170.2	1207.2	835.8	180	41410064
GTY	Getty Realty Corp. (New)	Real estate	12/31/03	68.3	41.5	272.0	228.0	70	6745112
GI	Giant Industries, Inc.	Oil	12/31/03	1808.3	12.3	692.3	139.4	15	2489962
GIL	Gildan Activewear Inc	—	10/5/03	—	—	—	—	26	10988822
G	Gillette Co., (The)	Cosmetics & toiletries	12/31/03	9252.0	3339.0	8977.0	2224.0	760	728969589
GLT	Glatfelter	Printing & engraving	12/31/03	543.2	40.4	942.3	371.4	124	31279673
GSK	GlaxoSmithKline Plc (UK)	Drugs	12/31/03	—	—	—	—	417	148928707
GLB	Glenborough Realty Trust, Inc	Real estate investment trust	12/31/03	185.8	14.9	1313.8	591.8	129	16874750
GRT	Glimcher Realty Trust	Real estate investment trust	12/31/03	316.9	54.1	1837.4	441.9	108	17921576
GEG	Global Power Equipment Group	Machinery & equipment	12/27/03	263.8	51.7	266.0	154.4	58	24320572
GFI	Gold Fields Ltd. (New)	Mining & processing	6/30/03	—	—	—	—	106	41144354
GG	Goldcorp Inc (New) (Canada)	Mining & processing	12/31/03	—	—	—	—	120	76939001
GDW	Golden West Financial	Savings & loan	12/31/03	3841.7	1106.1	79534.0	5947.3	368	105809193
GS	Goldman Sachs Group, Inc.	Industrial	11/28/03	23623.0	3005.0	399843.0	21632.0	562	282215903
GR	Goodrich Corp.	Chemicals	12/31/03	4382.9	107.7	5674.3	1193.5	281	86875956
GDP	Goodrich Petroleum Corp. (Hol	Oil	12/31/03	32.7	9.2	87.6	48.1	15	529862
GT	Goodyear Tire & Rubber Co.	Tires and/or rubber goods	12/31/03	15119.0	d1195.7	11472.8	d13.1	239	94553410
GOT	Gottschalks, Inc. (United St	Department stores	1/31/04	667.8	2.8	245.2	108.3	10	1294655
GPP	Government Properties Trust	Real estate investment trust	12/31/03	3.0	0.1	39.6	7.8	—	—
GPX	GP Strategies Corp.	Conglomerate	12/31/03	168.7	d7.0	182.0	92.8	18	7359499
GRA	Grace (W.R.) Co. (DE) (New)	Specialty chemicals	12/31/03	1997.2	117.3	2829.4	d183.6	71	27355599
GGG	Graco Inc.	Machinery & equipment	12/26/03	535.1	251.1	341.9	169.8	152	35885989
GTI	Graftech International Ltd (U	Metal products	12/31/03	712.0	d45.0	936.0	d128.0	83	52416279
GWW	Grainger (W.W.) Inc.	Hardware & tools	12/31/03	4667.0	227.0	2491.2	1845.1	354	61231668
GVA	Granite Construction Inc.	Engineering & construction	12/31/03	1844.5	214.1	988.9	504.9	134	23498083
GRP	Grant Prideco Inc	—	12/31/03	838.5	89.3	1247.7	606.1	206	96368750
GPK	Graphic Packaging Corp (DE)	—	12/31/03	1683.3	d165.6	3166.0	572.5	—	—
GTN	Gray Television Inc (United S	Broadcasting	12/31/03	295.4	14.0	939.2	362.8	83	37456897
GFR	Great American Financial Res	Finance	12/31/03	920.6	119.3	9945.1	942.5	36	39749732
GAP	Great Atlantic & Pacific Tea	Grocery chain	2/28/04	10812.5	d454.4	2654.3	385.8	81	14242531
GAJ	Great Atlantic & Pacific Tea	Grocery chain	2/28/04	10812.5	d454.4	2654.3	385.8	1	500
GLK	Great Lakes Chemical Corp.	Chemicals	12/31/03	1464.6	d122.9	1672.2	743.5	196	45220242
GNI	Great Northern Iron Ore Prop	Mining & processing	12/31/03	12.2	10.0	17.4	14.7	12	17102
GXP	Great Plains Energy, Inc.	Electric power	12/31/03	2149.5	153.6	3702.2	1033.2	203	21895061
GCH	Greater China Fund, Inc (The)	Investment company	12/31/03	6.6	3.4	248.1	208.7	24	4588675
GMP	Green Mountain Power Corp	Electric power	12/31/03	280.5	10.3	324.1	99.9	51	1645670
GBX	Greenbrier Cos., Inc. (The)	Railroads	8/31/03	435.0	4.4	479.2	111.1	24	2929934
GHL	Greenhill & Co Inc	Financial services	12/31/03	126.7	55.0	60.6	32.3	—	—
GPT	GreenPoint Financial Corp.	Banking - Northeast	12/31/03	1731.0	471.0	22985.0	1839.0	259	59937102
GEF	Greif Inc	Containers	10/31/03	1916.4	4.7	1493.5	629.0	60	8224181
GFF	Griffon Corp.	Conglomerate	9/30/03	1254.7	126.1	674.1	284.1	125	26144434
GPI	Group 1 Automotive, Inc.	—	12/31/03	4518.6	76.1	994.6	518.1	112	14085815
DA	Groupe Danone (France)	Food wholesalers	12/31/03	—	—	—	—	49	5423985
TV	Grupo Televisa, S.A. de C.V.	Broadcasting	12/31/03	—	—	—	—	127	70869039
GTK	GTECH Holdings Corp.	Gaming	2/28/04	1051.3	474.0	1559.1	562.3	214	54533563
GES	GUESS ?, Inc. (United States	—	12/31/03	636.6	20.1	362.8	182.8	34	6037449
GDT	Guidant Corp.	Medical & dental equipment	12/31/03	3698.8	974.4	4420.5	2713.3	507	252313866
GUI	Gulf Power Co.	Electric power	12/31/03	877.7	69.2	1771.4	565.6	—	—
GUQ	Gulf Power Co.	Electric power	12/31/03	877.7	69.2	1771.4	565.6	—	—
HQH	H & Q Healthcare Investors	Investment company	9/30/03	1.0	d3.2	291.5	286.8	35	1390783
HAE	Haemonetics Corp.	—	4/3/04	364.2	75.1	407.4	279.7	101	24288694
HAL	Halliburton Co. (Holding Co.	Oil service & equipment	12/31/03	16271.0	14870.0	14959.0	2547.0	486	313771234
HKF	Hancock Fabrics, Inc. (Unite	Specialty stores	2/1/04	443.6	17.4	240.8	131.6	90	13243282
HDL	Handleman Co.	'Wholesaler, distributor'	5/1/04	p1216.0	p1216.0	—	—	97	20672145
HGR	Hanger Orthopedic Group, Inc	Medical & dental equipment	12/31/03	547.9	16.2	713.0	182.7	90	15120173
HC	Hanover Compressor Co. (Hldg	Machinery & equipment	12/31/03	1095.3	d173.3	2801.4	753.5	171	54274012
HAN	Hanson Plc New	—	12/31/03	—	—	—	—	—	—
JH	Harland (John H.) Co.	Printing & engraving	12/31/03	786.7	56.0	567.0	255.4	144	21633138
HDI	Harley-Davidson, Inc.	—	12/31/03	4903.7	760.9	4764.6	2957.7	535	207787497
HAR	Harman International Inds In	Electronic components	6/30/03	2228.5	105.5	1720.7	672.9	235	31955586
HMY	Harmony Gold Mining Co. Ltd.	Mining & processing	6/30/03	—	—	—	—	89	26584850
HET	Harrah's Entertainment, Inc.	Gaming	12/31/03	4322.7	318.0	5435.3	1738.4	283	97061597
HSC	Harsco Corp.	Metal products	12/31/03	2118.5	1194.6	2092.0	777.0	171	20974698
HHS	Harte-Hanks, Inc. (United St	—	12/31/03	944.6	87.4	759.1	555.6	179	44952744
HIG	Hartford Financial Services G	Property & casualty insurance	12/31/03	18733.0	d91.0	225853.0	11639.0	445	213182841
HMX	Hartmarx Corp.	—	11/30/03	563.7	23.9	370.7	192.5	28	9898955
HNR	Harvest Natural Resources Inc	Oil	12/31/03	106.1	43.0	562.5	199.7	74	16365366
HAS	Hasbro, Inc. (United States)	—	12/28/03	3138.7	667.5	2978.3	1405.2	277	147400887
HVT	Haverty Furniture Cos., Inc.	Specialty stores	12/31/03	751.0	26.3	420.0	252.7	89	12146027
HE	Hawaiian Electric Ind.Inc.	Electric power	12/31/03	1781.3	118.0	9201.2	1089.0	194	11272572
HCA	HCA, Inc.	Hospitals & nursing homes	12/31/03	21808.0	3539.0	19838.0	6209.0	518	403665028
HCC	HCC Insurance Holdings, Inc.	Insurance brokerage	12/31/03	942.0	106.9	4864.3	1046.9	192	60552563
HW	Headwaters Inc	Mining & processing	9/30/03	387.6	36.6	364.6	140.2	106	17166175
HCP	Health Care Property Investor	Real estate investment trust	12/31/03	400.2	179.8	2838.0	1440.6	225	25505950
HCN	Health Care REIT, Inc.	Real estate investment trust	12/31/03	201.0	87.2	2182.7	1149.7	132	15009854
HMA	Health Management Associates,	Hospitals & nursing homes	9/30/03	2560.6	283.4	2979.5	1637.1	349	220778299
HNT	Health Net, Inc.	Services	12/31/03	11064.7	1235.6	3371.2	1294.2	230	109187299
HR	Healthcare Realty Trust, Inc	Real estate investment trust	12/31/03	192.0	80.3	1371.7	902.3	174	20610525
HTV	Hearst-Argyle Television Inc	Broadcasting	12/31/03	686.8	113.3	3774.1	1672.4	123	18917781
HL	Hecla Mining Co. (United Stat	Mining & processing	12/31/03	—	d120.9	270.9	171.4	87	28617252
HEI	Heico Corp. (New) (United St	—	10/31/03	176.5	12.2	295.8	221.5	36	3623503
HNZ	Heinz (H.J.) Co. (United Stat	Food processing	4/28/04	p8414.5	p8439.9	—	—	548	221630503
HP	Helmerich & Payne, Inc.	Oil service & equipment	9/30/03	515.3	92.8	1406.2	917.3	223	39146690
HPC	Hercules, Inc.	Chemicals	12/31/03	1846.0	169.0	2678.0	66.0	199	83517735
HTG	Heritage Property Investment	—	12/31/03	301.0	37.0	1984.5	958.5	95	22216320
HSY	Hershey Foods Corp.	—	12/31/03	4172.6	1197.8	3391.2	1279.9	409	55696934
HEW	Hewitt Associates Inc (Unite	—	9/30/03	2031.3	102.3	1386.5	690.1	73	13316540
HPQ	Hewlett-Packard Co. (DE) (Uni	Computers	10/31/03	72596.0	14921.0	69638.0	37746.0	959	1863055080
HXL	Hexcel Corp. (New)	Metal products	12/31/03	896.9	d11.1	720.8	d93.4	41	10667425
HIB	Hibernia Corp.	Banking - South	12/31/03	1260.4	258.3	18526.1	1777.5	241	79700964
HIH	Highland Hospitality Corp	Real estate investment trust	12/31/03	0.7	d2.7	379.5	355.3	—	—
HIW	Highwoods Properties, Inc.	Real estate investment trust	12/31/03	422.1	48.6	3271.8	1491.0	160	30948292
HRH	Hilb Rogal & Hobbs Co	Life Insurance	12/31/03	563.6	75.0	884.2	433.5	172	30142311
HB	Hillenbrand Industries, Inc.	Conglomerate	9/30/03	2042.0	464.0	5203.0	1159.0	215	29055573

EARNINGS PER SHARE QUARTERLY 1st	2nd	3rd	2004	ANNUAL 2003	2002	P/E RATIO	DIVIDENDS PER SHARE 2004	2003	2002	AV. YLD. %	DIV. DECLARED AMOUNT	PAYABLE	PRICE RANGE 2004
—	—	—	—	8.38	5.25	—	0.57	0.24	0.14	3.6	50%	4/18/05	24.65 - 7.04
—	—	—	—	—	—	—	0.03	—	0.01	0.4	0.025S	12/31/04	8.23 - 3.97
0.43	—	—	—	1.11	0.39	—	—	—	—	—	—	—	70.30 - 27.46
0.37	—	—	—	1.49	1.44	—	1.70	1.66	1.65	7.0	0.435Q	4/14/05	30.10 - 18.35
0.50	—	—	—	1.40	d1.40	—	—	—	—	—	0.05Q	9/30/98	28.98 - 3.18
—	—	—	—	—	—	—	—	—	—	—	100%	2/27/01	34.40 - 24.87
0.37	—	—	—	1.34	1.14	—	0.65	0.65	0.65	1.7	0.1625Q	6/3/05	45.62 - 29.90
0.83	—	—	—	0.30	0.86	—	0.36	0.61	0.70	2.8	0.09Q	5/1/05	15.49 - 9.95
—	—	—	—	—	—	—	1.54	1.17	1.14	3.7	0.44438Q	4/7/05	47.53 - 35.05
0.03	—	—	—	d0.10	0.49	—	1.40	1.64	1.72	7.4	0.35Q	4/15/05	22.57 - 15.46
d0.06	—	—	—	0.42	0.21	—	1.92	1.92	1.92	8.3	0.4808Q	4/15/05	28.83 - 17.53
0.02	—	—	—	0.43	1.14	—	—	—	—	—	—	—	11.58 - 4.65
—	—	—	—	—	—	—	0.12	0.32	0.27	1.0	0.0511S	3/10/05	15.19 - 9.13
—	—	—	—	—	—	—	0.28	0.15	0.11	2.1	0.015M	4/26/05	16.45 - 10.18
1.93	—	—	—	7.14	6.12	—	0.18	0.18	0.15	0.2	0.06Q	3/10/05	121.95 - 59.67
2.50	—	—	—	5.87	4.03	—	1.00	0.74	0.48	1.1	0.25Q	5/26/05	110.88 - 68.08
0.25	—	—	—	0.33	1.57	—	0.80	0.80	0.95	3.3	0.20Q	4/1/05	33.90 - 14.06
0.10	—	—	—	0.19	d0.03	—	—	—	—	—	—	—	16.99 - 3.69
—	—	—	—	d4.58	d6.62	—	—	—	0.48	—	0.12Q	12/16/02	15.01 - 4.00
d0.16	—	—	—	0.21	d0.94	—	—	—	—	—	—	—	9.15 - 1.08
d0.20	—	—	—	d0.46	d0.24	—	0.45	—	—	4.0	0.15Q	4/15/05	14.03 - 8.70
0.01	—	—	—	d0.48	d0.34	—	—	—	—	—	0.00U	11/24/04	8.95 - 4.72
0.24	—	—	—	d0.84	0.34	—	—	—	—	—	—	—	15.40 - 1.48
0.32	—	—	—	1.23	1.05	—	1.87	0.22	0.20	5.3	0.13Q	5/4/05	14.10 - 26.62
—	—	—	—	d0.38	d0.28	—	—	—	—	—	—	—	15.85 - 2.85
0.69	—	—	—	2.46	2.50	—	0.79	0.73	0.72	1.4	0.20Q	3/1/05	66.99 - 42.90
d0.23	—	—	—	1.48	1.21	—	0.40	0.38	0.32	1.9	0.10Q	4/15/05	27.90 - 15.20
0.09	—	—	—	0.04	0.12	—	—	—	—	—	—	—	22.31 - 10.40
d0.06	—	—	—	d0.56	—	—	—	—	—	—	—	—	8.81 - 3.69
0.09	—	—	—	0.21	0.32	—	0.12	0.08	0.08	1.0	0.03Q	3/31/05	16.22 - 9.00
0.41	—	—	—	1.13	0.79	—	0.10	0.10	0.10	0.6	0.10A	12/17/04	17.75 - 13.11
—	—	—	—	d5.49	d5.34	—	—	—	—	—	0.10Q	11/3/00	10.50 - 4.31
—	—	—	—	d5.49	d5.34	—	2.34	2.34	2.34	11.0	0.10Q	5/2/05	21.47 - 21.00
d0.08	—	—	—	d0.67	0.94	—	0.38	0.36	0.33	1.5	0.10Q	4/29/05	29.83 - 20.40
1.94	—	—	—	6.65	5.11	—	7.50	6.30	5.50	7.7	2.20Q	4/29/05	127.75 - 67.70
0.42	—	—	—	2.20	2.04	—	1.66	1.66	1.66	5.7	0.415Q	3/21/05	35.69 - 22.45
—	—	—	—	16.57	10.06	—	0.55	0.26	0.04	3.8	0.1013A	12/30/04	20.25 - 8.59
0.72	—	—	—	2.01	1.96	—	0.88	0.76	0.60	3.6	0.25Q	3/31/05	29.14 - 19.51
0.21	0.15	—	—	0.30	d0.30	—	0.12	—	—	0.5	0.06Q	5/4/05	36.99 - 6.95
0.23	—	—	—	—	—	—	0.16	—	—	0.7	0.10Q	3/15/05	30.35 - 18.40
0.94	—	—	—	3.78	3.69	—	0.90	1.02	0.67	2.4	0.30Q	8/16/04	47.30 - 28.46
d0.30	0.75	—	—	0.41	2.74	—	0.60	0.56	0.56	1.6	0.16Q	4/1/05	56.92 - 17.98
0.41	0.27	—	—	1.28	0.97	—	—	—	—	—	10%	9/4/01	27.22 - 12.90
0.45	—	—	—	3.26	2.80	—	—	—	—	—	—	—	38.73 - 21.40
—	—	—	—	—	—	—	0.29	0.26	0.19	1.1	2-for-1	6/22/04	55.77 - 15.30
—	—	—	—	—	—	—	2.10	0.36	—	4.8	2.10405U	5/28/04	62.77 - 24.18
—	—	—	—	2.84	2.43	—	0.43	0.17	—	1.0	0.085Q	4/29/05	64.93 - 19.79
0.02	—	—	—	0.17	d0.26	—	—	—	—	—	—	—	19.58 - 3.55
0.48	—	—	—	1.36	2.00	—	0.40	0.24	—	0.7	0.10Q	3/15/05	74.05 - 33.62
—	—	—	—	—	—	—	1.44	0.36	—	6.0	—	—	26.80 - 21.25
—	—	—	—	—	—	—	0.69	—	—	2.8	—	4/1/05	24.89 - 24.36
—	—	—	—	19.63	18.16	—	1.55	0.61	1.53	8.7	0.37Q	3/30/05	21.59 - 13.96
—	—	—	—	1.19	1.13	—	—	—	—	—	2-for-1	1/8/93	37.25 - 17.73
0.17	—	—	—	0.78	d0.80	—	0.50	0.50	0.50	1.7	0.125Q	3/24/05	41.69 - 18.76
0.04	—	—	—	0.94	1.06	—	0.46	0.38	0.28	3.6	0.06Q	4/15/05	17.45 - 7.84
—	—	—	—	—	p1.06	—	0.28	0.07	—	1.5	0.08Q	4/8/05	26.47 - 11.95
0.16	—	—	—	0.39	0.99	—	—	—	—	—	—	—	19.25 - 4.15
d0.11	—	—	—	d1.34	d0.94	—	—	—	—	—	2-for-1	6/13/00	14.65 - 6.50
—	—	—	—	—	—	—	1.53	1.29	1.05	4.0	0.125Q	5/13/05	43.37 - 33.40
0.46	—	—	—	1.97	1.73	—	0.45	0.35	0.30	1.5	0.125Q	2/25/05	36.41 - 22.05
0.68	—	—	—	2.50	1.90	—	0.41	0.20	0.14	0.8	0.0125Q	3/25/05	63.75 - 39.59
0.29	0.60	0.63	—	1.55	0.85	—	0.05	0.05	0.05	0.1	0.0125Q	2/23/05	130.82 - 58.57
—	—	—	—	—	—	—	0.10	0.35	0.43	0.8	0.0447S	9/16/04	17.80 - 9.05
0.73	—	—	—	2.64	2.86	—	1.26	0.60	—	2.5	0.33Q	2/23/05	67.25 - 32.84
0.41	—	—	—	2.12	2.17	—	1.10	1.05	1.00	2.6	0.30Q	5/16/05	56.24 - 28.68
0.21	—	—	—	0.97	0.96	—	0.16	0.12	0.10	0.7	0.05Q	3/15/05	26.90 - 18.00
2.01	—	—	—	d0.33	3.97	—	1.12	1.08	1.04	2.1	0.29Q	4/1/05	69.57 - 35.29
0.06	—	—	—	0.25	0.10	—	—	—	—	—	0.15Q	11/15/91	8.66 - 2.01
0.20	—	—	—	0.74	2.78	—	—	—	—	—	2-for-1	2/26/91	18.50 - 4.86
0.03	—	—	—	0.98	0.43	—	0.21	0.12	0.12	1.2	0.09Q	5/16/05	23.33 - 12.00
0.27	—	—	—	1.08	1.10	—	0.25	0.23	0.22	1.4	0.0625Q	3/28/05	23.98 - 10.75
0.40	—	—	—	1.57	1.62	—	1.55	1.24	1.24	3.9	0.31Q	3/10/05	53.75 - 24.89
0.69	—	—	—	2.61	1.59	—	0.41	0.08	0.08	1.0	0.15Q	6/1/05	46.60 - 32.04
0.68	—	—	—	1.66	1.68	—	0.31	0.27	0.25	1.1	0.085Q	4/15/05	34.75 - 24.10
0.35	0.55	—	—	1.30	0.94	—	—	—	—	—	2-for-1	1/22/96	34.96 - 14.02
0.23	—	—	—	0.94	0.96	—	1.67	1.66	1.63	4.3	0.42Q	2/18/05	56.90 - 20.25
0.36	—	—	—	1.44	1.47	—	2.38	2.34	2.34	7.2	0.60Q	2/22/05	40.88 - 25.76
0.29	0.37	—	—	1.13	0.97	—	0.10	0.08	0.02	0.5	0.04Q	3/7/05	25.55 - 17.06
0.13	—	—	—	2.73	1.89	—	—	—	—	—	—	—	33.57 - 21.60
0.42	—	—	—	1.66	1.55	—	2.55	2.47	2.39	7.5	0.65Q	3/3/05	44.03 - 24.42
0.19	—	—	—	1.00	1.15	—	0.24	—	—	1.0	0.07Q	4/15/05	29.25 - 20.69
d0.04	—	—	—	d0.17	d0.15	—	—	—	—	—	0.05Q	12/21/90	9.25 - 3.29
0.13	0.16	—	—	0.50	0.62	—	0.05	0.05	0.05	0.3	0.025S	1/16/05	23.41 - 7.42
—	—	—	—	—	p1.57	—	1.11	1.22	1.62	3.2	0.285Q	4/10/05	39.41 - 29.20
0.11	0.12	—	—	0.35	1.07	—	0.33	0.32	0.31	1.1	0.0825Q	6/1/05	34.25 - 23.93
0.24	—	—	—	0.69	d0.45	—	—	—	—	—	0.08Q	9/29/04	15.25 - 8.03
0.23	—	—	—	0.87	0.19	—	2.10	2.10	0.89	7.2	0.525Q	4/15/05	34.00 - 24.11
0.41	—	—	—	1.76	1.47	—	1.03	0.72	0.63	1.5	0.22Q	3/15/05	90.37 - 45.03
0.30	0.31	—	—	0.97	d0.27	—	—	—	—	—	—	—	35.80 - 22.85
0.30	0.29	—	—	0.83	0.37	—	0.32	0.32	0.32	1.5	0.08Q	4/7/05	26.16 - 15.55
0.09	—	—	—	d0.54	d0.35	—	—	—	—	—	—	—	17.92 - 2.88
0.42	—	—	—	1.64	1.56	—	0.76	0.63	0.57	3.2	0.20Q	2/22/05	30.00 - 16.96
0.01	—	—	—	d0.07	—	—	0.22	—	—	2.0	0.14Q	4/15/05	12.53 - 9.91
d0.11	—	—	—	d0.13	0.75	—	1.70	1.86	2.34	7.0	0.425Q	3/4/05	28.00 - 20.25
0.67	—	—	—	2.06	1.89	—	0.41	0.37	0.36	1.2	0.105Q	3/31/05	38.92 - 29.53
0.89	0.85	—	—	2.93	d0.16	—	1.09	1.02	1.02	1.8	0.28Q	3/31/05	72.92 - 47.37

SYMBOL	COMPANY	NATURE OF BUSINESS	FISCAL YEAR-END	TOTAL REV. $MILL	NET INCOME $MILL	TOTAL ASSETS $MILL	NET STK EQUITY $MILL	NO. OF INST.	INST. HOLDINGS (SHARES)
HLT	Hilton Hotels Corp.	Motel/hotel lodging	12/31/03	3819.0	164.0	8031.0	2239.0	274	268870975
HNI	HNI Corp	Furniture & fixtures	1/3/04	1755.7	98.1	931.6	709.9	—	—
HOC	Holly Corp.	Oil	12/31/03	1403.2	46.1	708.9	268.6	82	11423372
HD	Home Depot, Inc.	Specialty stores	2/1/04	64816.0	12379.0	32737.0	22407.0	1118	1388398686
HME	Home Properties Inc	Real estate investment trust	12/31/03	434.5	61.2	2513.3	741.3	128	22206184
HON	Honeywell International, Inc	Conglomerate	12/31/03	23103.0	2984.0	28716.0	10729.0	676	634283995
HMN	Horace Mann Educators Corp.	Property & casualty insurance	12/31/03	853.7	19.0	4908.6	466.1	113	40561726
HRL	Hormel Foods Corp.	Meat packing & processing	10/25/03	4200.3	310.4	2375.1	1252.7	185	35825168
DHI	Horton (D.R.) Inc.	Home-building	9/30/03	8728.1	724.3	7279.4	3031.3	257	114032753
HPT	Hospitality Properties Trust	Real estate investment trust	12/31/03	552.8	255.0	2560.6	1645.5	209	22621306
HMT	Host Marriott Corp (New)	Motel/hotel lodging	12/31/03	3448.0	d225.0	8592.0	2136.0	212	191402886
HTB	Household Finance Corp.	Financial services	12/31/03	9658.8	3665.9	102959.9	13727.5	—	—
THX	Houston Exploration Co.	Natural gas	12/31/03	492.8	153.4	1257.1	735.5	117	11635780
HOV	Hovnanian Enterprises, Inc.	Real estate	10/31/03	3201.9	323.4	2165.7	819.7	140	15412053
HRP	HRPT Properties Trust (United	Real estate investment trust	12/31/03	500.7	133.8	3601.2	2011.7	172	48695536
HNP	Huaneng Power International	Electric power	12/31/03	—	—	—	—	44	3474672
HUB A	Hubbell Inc.	Electrical equipment	12/31/03	1770.7	270.6	1499.4	829.7	38	6595369
HU	Hudson United Bancorp	Banking - Mid-Atlantic	12/31/03	527.2	112.3	8100.7	458.2	182	21597254
HUG	Hughes Supply, Inc.	'Wholesaler, distributor'	1/30/04	3253.4	57.7	1842.0	1012.0	135	19499967
HGT	Hugoton Royalty Trust (TX)	Natural gas	12/31/03	80.7	80.4	199.0	193.2	49	6425018
HUM	Humana Inc.	Hospitals & nursing homes	12/31/03	12226.3	10108.4	4741.2	1835.9	268	109884876
HBP	Huttig Building Products, In		12/31/03	909.3	3.3	89.5	72.2	32	5071840
HYC	Hypercom Corp	Computer services	12/31/03	231.5	12.0	262.5	204.3	56	17953959
HTO	Hyperion 2005 Invt Grade Oppo	Investment company	12/31/03	10.4	8.0	251.5	166.3	11	1497093
HTR	Hyperion Tot Return Fund Inc	Investment company	11/30/03	30.6	25.0	452.2	285.1	17	219127
IDA	Idacorp, Inc. (United States	Electric power	12/31/03	823.0	46.6	3101.7	864.3	159	12108644
IEX	IDEX Corp.	Hardware & tools	12/31/03	797.9	160.5	896.7	604.6	135	30947111
IDT C	IDT Corp.	Telecommunications	7/31/03	1834.5	d75.6	1480.2	897.5	102	13835510
IHP	IHOP Corp. (New) (United Sta	Restaurants	12/31/03	404.8	100.4	843.0	382.4	100	19679019
IKN	Ikon Office Solutions, Inc.	Paper	9/30/03	4322.7	934.0	6129.2	1635.5	174	98508466
ITW	Illinois Tool Works, Inc.	Plastics & plastic products	12/31/03	10035.6	2616.3	10722.3	7874.3	632	235706334
IGI	Imagistics International, In	Machinery & equipment	12/31/03	622.2	56.4	436.7	267.4	123	12456415
IMN	Imation Corp.	Comp. components & periphs.	12/31/03	1163.5	202.9	1130.6	820.3	219	29605892
MOS	IMC Global, Inc.	Fertilizer	12/31/03	2190.6	d34.3	3531.9	526.6	—	—
ARS	IMCO Recycling, Inc.	Metal products	12/31/03	892.0	5.0	523.5	127.5	—	—
IMH	IMPAC Mortgage Holdings, Inc	Real estate investment trust	12/31/03	417.8	127.2	10674.7	508.5	94	12122738
ICI	Imperial Chemical Industries	Chemicals	12/31/03	—	—	—	—	58	18711991
ITY	Imperial Tobacco Group Plc	Tobacco	9/30/03	—	—	—	—	48	21580014
RX	IMS Health, Inc.	Services	12/31/03	1381.8	463.6	1522.4	211.5	407	211351357
NWG	INCO Ltd.	Mining & processing	12/31/03	—	—	—	—	12	4289238
IHC	Independence Holding Co	Insurance	12/31/03	187.9	18.6	898.3	168.9	29	836910
IFN	India Fund, Inc. (The) (Unite	Investment company	12/31/03	9.9	2.9	560.4	556.8	38	13491459
IJD	Indiana Michigan Power Co (Un	Electric power	12/31/03	1595.6	89.5	3893.1	1086.1	1	4000
NDE	IndyMac Bancorp Inc	Real estate investment trust	12/31/03	992.7	171.3	13240.2	1017.4	166	45746986
IFX	Infineon Technologies AG	Electronic components	9/30/03	—	—	—	—	32	11146479
PPR	ING Prime Rate Trust (United	Investment company	2/29/04	88.2	64.9	1692.5	1010.3	39	3164806
IM	Ingram Micro Inc.	Comp. components & periphs.	12/31/03	22613.0	265.0	5474.2	1872.9	143	81882073
KPA	Innkeepers USA Trust	Real estate investment trust	12/31/03	81.4	d9.8	705.9	403.9	104	24330011
IO	Input/Output, Inc.		12/31/03	150.0	d6.4	238.4	132.6	92	39548005
IFF	Int'l. Flavors & Fragrances	Cosmetics & toiletries	12/31/03	1901.5	424.5	2183.4	829.1	298	66605807
IES	Integrated Electrical Svcs	Electrical equipment	9/30/03	1448.6	20.4	726.2	267.6	67	21154486
IDC	Interactive Data Corp.	Securities brokerage	12/31/03	442.7	330.3	833.8	762.5	86	24950158
IHG	Intercontinental Hotels Grou	Conglomerate	9/30/03	—	—	—	—	—	—
IAL	International Aluminum Corp.		6/30/03	192.5	4.4	133.2	109.5	17	786880
IBM	International Business Machin	Computers	12/31/03	89131.0	7613.0	104457.0	27864.0	1256	960401635
IGT	International Game Technolog	Gaming	9/30/03	2128.1	988.4	4103.1	1687.5	379	73842669
IP	International Paper Co.	Paper	12/31/03	25179.0	599.0	35525.0	8237.0	563	403647302
IPR	International Power Plc (Uni	Electrical equipment	12/31/03	—	—	—	—	8	806799
IRF	International Rectifier Corp	Electrical equipment	6/30/03	—	d1080.3	1791.7	1012.2	238	48828143
ISG	International Steel Group In	Steel producer	12/31/03	4070.0	d23.5	1994.1	949.2	—	—
IPG	Interpublic Group of Cos., In		12/31/03	5863.4	d797.1	11708.1	2605.9	408	367010452
IHR	Interstate Hotels & Resorts	Motel/hotel lodging	12/31/03	1027.0	66.5	231.9	118.7	26	4528551
ITP	Intertape Polymer Group Inc.	Plastics & plastic products	12/31/03	—	—	—	—	37	19737486
ISH	Intl Shipholding Corp.	Freight transportation	12/31/03	257.8	21.1	376.1	121.4	19	2444678
IDR	Intrawest Corp.	Recreation	6/30/03	—	—	—	—	54	20288343
IVC	Invacare Corp.	Medical & dental equipment	12/31/03	1247.2	177.8	1041.1	613.2	132	24226002
PPM	Investment Grade Municipal In	Investment company	9/30/03	12.3	9.9	249.2	248.9	12	60245
ITG	Investment Technology Group	Securities brokerage	12/31/03	334.0	42.0	602.5	353.2	171	39166107
IOM	Iomega Corp. (United States)	Comp. components & periphs.	12/31/03	391.3	d51.5	258.7	137.9	120	24221241
IRM	Iron Mountain Inc (PA) (New)	Services	12/31/03	1501.3	241.6	3578.8	1066.1	162	59911154
IRS	IRSA Inversiones y Representa	Real estate	6/30/03	—	—	—	—	22	6213576
IFC	Irwin Financial Corp. (IN)	Banking - Midwest	12/31/03	700.3	72.8	4988.4	432.3	112	11878283
SFI	iStar Financial Inc	Real estate investment trust	12/31/03	606.5	334.4	5834.0	2415.2	196	51054733
ESI	ITT Educational Services, In		12/31/03	522.9	338.9	232.9	146.1	182	42967005
ITT	ITT Industries Inc.	Electronic components	12/31/03	5626.6	921.6	5302.3	1847.7	344	66240435
IVN	Ivanhoe Mines Ltd (Canada)	Mining & processing	12/31/03	—	—	—	—	3	3503970
JPM	J.P. Morgan Chase & Co. (Unit		12/31/03	44363.0	7389.0	770912.0	46154.0	978	1328697534
JBL	Jabil Circuit, Inc.	Computer services	8/31/03	4729.5	95.2	3244.7	1588.5	318	132842747
JBX	Jack in the Box, Inc. (Unite	Restaurants	9/28/03	2058.3	73.6	1203.1	497.5	126	28895655
JEC	Jacobs Engineering Group, In	Engineering & construction	9/30/03	4615.6	4314.7	1414.5	842.1	258	43709953
JJZ	Jacuzzi Brands Inc		9/30/03	p1193.0	p1193.0	—	—	—	—
JNS	Janus Capital Group Inc	Financial services	12/31/03	994.7	943.4	4332.2	2661.2	298	179369726
JAH	Jarden Corp.	Metal products	12/31/03	587.4	34.8	759.7	249.9	103	13104203
JEF	Jefferies Group, Inc. (New)	Finance	12/31/03	926.7	84.1	10992.3	838.4	147	15120998
JP	Jefferson-Pilot Corp.	Insurance	12/31/03	3573.0	641.0	32696.0	3806.0	375	75022235
JFC	JF China Region Fund Inc	Investment company	12/31/03	1.1	d0.1	64.2	63.9	—	—
JLG	JLG Industries, Inc.	Machinery & equipment	7/31/03	759.8	14.2	938.0	249.5	108	27923858
JAS	Jo-Ann Stores, Inc. (United	Specialty stores	1/31/04	1734.1	41.0	629.5	346.2	—	—
JHI	John Hancock Investors Trust	Investment company	12/31/03	12.5	11.0	261.2	174.6	16	569504
PDF	John Hancock Patriot Prm Dv	Investment company	9/30/03	12.9	10.5	202.4	202.1	18	141281
JNJ	Johnson & Johnson	Medical & dental equipment	12/28/03	41862.0	7197.0	48263.0	26869.0	1392	1851388985
JCI	Johnson Controls Inc (United	Services	9/30/03	22646.0	682.9	13127.3	4261.3	425	62464925
JNY	Jones Apparel Group, Inc.		12/31/03	4375.3	855.6	4187.7	2537.8	356	118645051
JLL	Jones Lang LaSalle Inc. (Uni	Real estate	12/31/03	949.8	80.4	788.6	431.0	76	21970776
JRN	Journal Communications Inc	Publishing	12/31/03	p798.3	p798.3	—	—	—	—
JRC	Journal Register Co.	Newspapers	12/28/03	406.0	72.0	562.8	72.3	108	35079189

T20

1st	2nd	3rd	2004	2003	2002	P/E RATIO	Div 2004	Div 2003	Div 2002	AV. YLD. %	AMOUNT	PAYABLE	PRICE RANGE 2004
0.10				0.43	0.53	—	0.08	0.08	0.08	0.5	0.02Q	3/18/05	22.95 - 10.99
0.38	—	—	—	1.68	1.55	—	0.56	0.52	0.50	1.4	0.155Q	3/1/05	43.34 - 36.87
0.87	—	—	—	2.88	2.01	—	0.27	0.22	0.21	0.9	0.08Q	4/4/05	41.25 - 19.85
0.49	—	—	—	1.88	1.56	—	0.33	0.26	0.21	1.0	0.10Q	3/24/05	44.30 - 20.90
0.15	—	—	—	0.92	0.78	—	2.49	2.45	2.41	6.6	0.63Q	2/28/05	43.96 - 31.75
0.34	—	—	—	1.56	d0.27	—	0.75	0.75	0.75	2.5	0.20625Q	3/10/05	38.46 - 21.36
0.51	—	—	—	0.44	0.28	—	0.42	0.42	0.42	2.6	0.105Q	3/30/05	19.30 - 13.12
0.37	0.38	—	—	1.33	1.35	—	0.45	0.42	0.39	1.7	0.13Q	5/15/05	31.94 - 21.01
0.78	0.80	—	—	2.73	1.91	—	0.24	0.14	0.11	0.8		3/16/05	41.85 - 18.31
0.36	—	—	—	3.57	2.15	—	2.88	2.88	2.86	7.6	0.72Q	5/19/05	47.35 - 28.81
d0.12	—	—	—	d0.92	d0.24	—	0.05	—	—	0.4	0.08Q	4/15/05	17.40 - 6.92
	—	—	—			—	1.72	1.29	—	6.4		5/2/05	27.30 - 26.74
1.25	—	—	—	4.29	2.28	—	—	—	—	—			61.80 - 27.00
0.87	1.06	—	—	3.92	2.15	—	—	—	—	—	100%	3/26/04	91.95 - 29.01
0.22	—	—	—	0.50	0.64	—	0.82	0.80	0.80	7.7	0.21Q	5/23/05	12.99 - 8.25
	—	—	—	—		—	2.42	0.82	0.72	4.3	1.2082U	7/11/05	86.01 - 27.05
0.56	—	—	—	1.91	1.81	—	1.32	1.32	1.32	3.4	0.33Q	4/11/05	48.50 - 28.85
0.69	—	—	—	2.50	2.72	—	1.36	1.18	1.10	3.7	0.37Q	3/1/05	41.74 - 30.80
0.97	—	—	—	2.46	2.45	—	0.24	0.20	0.17	0.6	0.09Q	5/13/05	63.70 - 23.20
0.47	—	—	—	2.01	0.74	—	2.01	1.95	0.70	9.3		4/14/05	29.95 - 13.07
0.41	—	—	—	1.41	0.85	—	—	—	—	—			31.00 - 9.60
0.14	—	—	—	0.17	0.05	—	—	—	—	—			10.52 - 2.04
d0.04	—	—	—	0.08	d0.50	—	—	—	—	—			8.50 - 2.92
	—	—	—	9.79	9.84	—	0.16	0.38	0.54	1.7	0.001M	4/28/05	9.86 - 9.37
	—	—	—	9.29	9.24	—	0.90	0.90	0.90	9.4	0.075M	4/28/05	10.65 - 8.48
0.51	—	—	—	1.22	1.63	—	1.20	1.70	1.86	4.4	0.30Q	5/31/05	32.95 - 21.74
0.35	—	—	—	1.25	1.11	—	0.43	0.37	0.37	1.1	0.12Q	4/29/05	48.60 - 27.72
d0.17	0.20	d0.84	—	d0.22	d2.08	—	—	—	—	—	0.00U	5/23/05	23.00 - 12.80
0.50	—	—	—	1.70	1.92	—	1.00	0.75	—	3.1	0.25Q	5/23/05	43.40 - 21.29
0.18	0.19	—	—	0.75	0.99	—	0.16	0.16	0.16	1.6	0.04Q	3/10/05	25.37 - 7.01
0.93	—	—	—	3.37	3.02	—	1.00	0.93	0.89	1.3	0.28Q	4/18/05	96.62 - 58.15
0.34	—	—	—	1.19	0.86	—	—	—	—	—			45.50 - 18.62
0.60	—	—	—	2.25	2.05	—	0.38	0.24	—	1.1	0.10Q	3/30/05	42.72 - 28.46
0.06	—	—	—	d0.37	d0.12	—	—	—	—	—			18.58 - 14.80
0.18	—	—	—	0.33	0.47	—	—	—	—	—	0.06Q	12/29/04	17.40 - 14.00
0.76	—	—	—	2.46	1.84	—	2.90	2.53	1.72	14.6	0.75Q	4/15/05	27.91 - 11.94
	—	—	—			—	0.49	0.46	0.75	3.9		4/22/05	18.91 - 6.00
	—	—	—			—	1.66	1.11	6.13	3.8	1.32664S	2/25/05	56.46 - 31.41
0.34	—	—	—	0.56	0.93	—	0.08	0.08	0.08	0.4	0.02Q	3/31/05	26.80 - 15.00
	—	—	—			—				—			20.90 - 4.40
	—	—	—	2.35	1.98	—	0.05	0.03	0.03	0.2	0.025S	1/21/05	38.63 - 16.60
	—	—	—	23.76	12.72	—	0.13	0.09	0.07	0.6	1.52A	1/14/05	31.75 - 9.63
	—	—	—			—	1.50	1.66	—	6.3	0.375Q	3/31/05	26.59 - 21.31
0.70	—	—	—	3.01	2.41	—	1.21	0.55	—	4.2	0.36Q	3/10/05	38.10 - 19.10
	—	—	—			—				—	0.4304U	4/17/01	16.12 - 6.47
	—	—	—	7.34	6.73	—	0.43	0.42	0.46	5.7	0.037M	4/22/05	8.46 - 6.41
0.24	—	—	—	0.98	0.04	—	—	—	—	—			20.97 - 10.40
d0.17	—	—	—	d0.50	d0.23	—	0.15	0.30	0.25	1.4	0.06Q	4/26/05	14.43 - 6.50
d0.01	—	—	—	d0.45	d2.37	—	—	—	—	—	2-for-1	1/9/96	11.22 - 3.11
0.59	—	—	—	1.83	1.84	—	0.67	0.62	0.60	1.8	0.175Q	4/7/05	43.20 - 30.15
0.16	0.14	—	—	0.52	0.25	—	—	—	—	—			11.58 - 2.22
0.19	—	—	—	0.76	0.65	—	—	—	—	—	0.2948U	1/16/01	22.17 - 13.26
	—	—	—			—				—	0.1926U	6/13/05	13.05 - 12.25
0.36	0.37	0.20	—	1.04	0.24	—	1.20	1.20	1.20	4.5	0.30Q	4/11/05	35.00 - 18.15
0.95	—	—	—	4.34	3.07	—	0.70	0.63	0.59	0.8	0.18Q	3/10/05	100.41 - 77.95
0.33	0.32	—	—	1.07	0.80	—	0.32	0.28	—	1.0	0.12Q	3/29/05	47.10 - 19.65
0.14	—	—	—	0.66	0.61	—	1.00	1.00	1.00	2.5	0.25Q	3/15/05	45.01 - 33.80
	—	—	—			—	2.74	—	—	12.3	0.4817U	7/18/05	31.00 - 13.50
0.25	0.25	0.39	—	d1.40	0.75	—	—	—	—	—	2-for-1	12/22/95	54.97 - 19.67
0.68	—	—	—	d1.26	0.99	—	—	—	—	—			43.50 - 25.45
d0.05	—	—	—	d1.43	0.26	—	—	—	0.38	—	0.095Q	12/16/02	17.31 - 9.30
d0.12	—	—	—	d0.21	d2.86	—	—	—	—	—			6.20 - 3.96
	—	—	—			—	—	—	—	—	0.16A	6/8/00	13.34 - 3.90
0.48	—	—	—	0.90	d0.03	—	—	—	—	—	0.0625Q	6/15/01	17.10 - 6.15
	—	—	—			—	0.16	0.16	0.16	1.0	0.08S	1/26/05	23.02 - 10.44
0.44	—	—	—	2.25	2.05	—	0.05	0.05	0.05	0.1	0.0125Q	4/15/05	52.32 - 30.34
	—	—	—	16.31	16.46	—	1.01	1.45	1.13	7.0	0.0625M	4/29/05	15.74 - 12.82
0.19	—	—	—	0.89	1.51	—	—	—	—	—	3-for-2	12/7/01	20.22 - 11.91
d0.09	—	—	—	d0.37	0.68	—	—	5.00	—	—	5.00U	10/1/03	7.10 - 3.77
0.26	—	—	—	0.98	0.78	—	—	—	—	—	50%	6/30/04	46.35 - 28.80
	—	—	—			—				—		12/23/02	11.62 - 6.50
0.67	—	—	—	2.45	1.87	—	0.32	0.28	0.27	1.2	0.10Q	3/25/05	36.17 - 17.87
d0.50	—	—	—	2.36	1.93	—	2.79	2.65	2.52	7.6	0.7325Q	4/29/05	45.82 - 27.99
0.19	—	—	—	1.27	0.94	—	—	—	—	—	100%	6/5/02	60.75 - 26.95
0.93	—	—	—	4.15	4.06	—	0.67	0.63	0.60	1.0	0.18Q	4/1/05	86.72 - 53.41
	—	—	—			—				—			8.44 - 3.69
0.92	—	—	—	3.24	0.80	—	1.36	1.36	1.36	4.1	0.34Q	4/30/05	43.84 - 22.68
0.20	0.19	—	—	0.21	0.17	—	—	—	—	—	100%	3/30/00	32.40 - 15.61
0.43	0.53	—	—	1.99	2.07	—	—	—	—	—			38.99 - 16.10
0.59	0.61	—	—	2.27	1.98	—	—	—	—	—	100%	4/1/02	48.18 - 36.86
0.05	0.08	—	—	—	p0.14	—	—	—	—	—	0.05Q	1/22/01	9.99 - 5.29
d0.08	—	—	—	4.17	0.38	—	0.04	0.04	0.05	0.3	0.04A	7/30/04	17.90 - 11.39
0.27	—	—	—	1.35	1.68	—	—	—	—	—	3-for-2	11/26/03	44.21 - 26.00
0.51	—	—	—	1.42	1.14	—	0.36	0.21	0.10	1.2	0.12Q	3/15/05	43.20 - 28.10
0.90	—	—	—	3.44	3.04	—	1.47	1.29	1.18	3.1	0.4175Q	6/5/05	56.10 - 37.70
	—	—	—	13.93	7.47	—	—	—	—	—	0.04A	12/30/99	19.50 - 9.74
0.01	0.05	p0.20	—	0.33	0.30	—	0.02	0.02	0.02	0.2	0.005Q	3/31/05	20.26 - 4.70
0.30	—	—	—	1.86	2.33	—	—	—	—	—			30.49 - 19.86
	—	—	—	21.55	21.21	—	1.66	2.01	1.22	8.0	0.39Q	3/31/05	22.85 - 18.60
	—	—	—	8.82	8.30	—	0.65	0.72	0.65	7.1	0.0465M	4/29/05	10.29 - 8.00
0.83	—	—	—	2.40	2.16	—	1.09	0.92	0.79	1.9	0.285Q	3/8/05	64.23 - 49.55
0.86	0.82	—	—	3.60	3.17	—	1.13	0.72	0.66	2.0	0.25Q	3/31/05	63.98 - 49.57
0.73	—	—	—	2.48	2.46	—	0.36	0.16	—	1.1	0.10Q	3/11/05	39.82 - 27.43
d0.20	—	—	—	1.12	0.81	—	—	—	—	—			38.46 - 13.66
p0.20	—	—	—		p2.46	—	0.26	0.07	—	1.5	0.065Q	3/4/05	20.35 - 15.48
0.24	—	—	—	1.72	1.16	—	—	—	—	—			22.10 - 15.17

SYMBOL	COMPANY	NATURE OF BUSINESS	FISCAL YEAR-END	TOTAL REV. $MILL	NET INCOME $MILL	TOTAL ASSETS $MILL	NET STK EQUITY $MILL	NO. OF INST.	INST. HOLDINGS (SHARES)
KTO	K2 Inc.	—	12/31/03	718.5	90.8	871.9	434.0	103	15875067
KAI	Kadant Inc	Machinery & equipment	1/3/04	203.5	30.9	271.7	211.8	93	10655654
KPP	Kaneb Pipeline Partners, L.P	Oil	12/31/03	570.4	83.9	1264.7	—	52	1248629
KSL	Kaneb Services, LLC	Oil service & equipment	12/31/03	865.8	61.8	1184.5	77.7	38	2737434
KT	Katy Industries, Inc. (Unite	Machinery & equipment	12/31/03	436.4	d40.9	223.0	102.3	13	2890269
KDN	Kaydon Corp.	Engineering & construction	12/31/03	294.1	85.7	580.2	280.5	130	23135048
KBH	KB HOME	Home-building	11/30/03	5850.6	957.1	4235.9	1592.9	264	38046258
KCS	KCS Energy, Inc.	Oil	12/31/03	164.8	77.9	314.0	98.0	27	9929525
KEA	Keane, Inc.	Computer services	12/31/03	805.0	29.2	744.3	458.1	151	37785730
KEI	Keithley Instruments, Inc.	Meas. & control instruments	9/30/03	106.7	d7.7	109.1	84.8	77	7831802
K	Kellogg Co	Food processing	12/27/03	8811.5	1956.6	9637.1	1443.2	409	333966582
KWD	Kellwood Co.	—	1/31/04	2346.5	183.1	1289.7	643.4	168	22489607
KEM	KEMET Corp.	Electronic components	3/31/04	433.9	d219.9	914.4	684.5	164	64406281
KMT	Kennametal, Inc.	Metal products	6/30/03	1759.0	52.4	1501.4	721.6	159	31305048
KMG	Kerr-McGee Corp.	Oil	12/31/03	4185.0	254.0	9598.0	2636.0	369	83810085
KEY	KeyCorp (New)	Banking - Midwest	12/31/03	5730.0	903.0	84487.0	6969.0	437	222276452
KSE	KeySpan Corp.	Natural gas distributor	12/31/03	6915.2	424.2	14626.8	3745.5	342	72339346
KRC	Kilroy Realty Corp.	Real estate investment trust	12/31/03	227.8	66.4	1277.6	489.9	118	23843465
KMB	Kimberly-Clark Corp.	Paper	12/31/03	14348.0	1694.0	16779.0	6629.0	834	360807114
KIM	Kimco Realty Corp.	Real estate investment trust	12/31/03	479.7	272.4	4603.9	2135.8	221	58100335
KMP	Kinder Morgan Energy Partner	Natural gas distributor	12/31/03	6624.3	843.3	8626.5	—	239	29253734
KMR	Kinder Morgan Management, LL	Oil service & equipment	12/31/03	94.8	58.8	1506.3	1425.6	102	31402334
KMI	Kinder Morgan, Inc. (KS)	Natural gas	12/31/03	1097.9	453.4	10036.7	2666.1	307	69014245
KND	Kindred Healthcare Inc	Hospitals & nursing homes	12/31/03	3284.0	49.5	1342.0	597.6	60	10007669
KCI	Kinetic Concepts Inc (New)	Equip. & vehicle leasing	12/31/03	763.8	106.1	108.8	d507.3	—	—
KG	King Pharmaceuticals, Inc.	Drugs	12/31/03	1521.4	105.9	3123.8	2042.2	329	173264360
KGC	Kinross Gold Corp.	Mining & processing	12/31/03	—	—	—	—	—	—
KEX	Kirby Corp.	Freight transportation	12/31/03	613.5	40.9	829.4	372.1	110	15281225
KNX	Knight Transportation Inc.	Freight transportation	12/31/03	340.1	35.5	306.4	239.9	132	22980030
KRI	Knight-Ridder, Inc.	Newspapers	12/28/03	2946.0	296.0	3971.7	1489.2	321	67093810
CRO	Koger Equity, Inc.	Real estate investment trust	12/31/03	146.4	27.8	848.2	403.0	—	—
KSS	Kohl's Corp. (United States	Department stores	1/31/04	10282.1	634.7	6646.1	4191.3	540	281116104
AHO	Koninklijke Ahold NV	Grocery chain	12/28/03	—	—	—	—	78	47787602
PHG	Koninklijke Philips Electron	Communications electronics	12/31/03	—	—	—	—	199	115284713
KB	Kookmin Bank (New) (South Ko	—	12/31/03	—	—	—	—	117	29363773
KEF	Korea Equity Fund, Inc.	Investment company	10/31/03	0.7	d0.2	45.4	45.2	10	3656712
KF	Korea Fund, Inc. (The) (Unit	Investment company	6/30/03	19.5	8.6	880.3	878.6	44	20618465
KFY	Korn/Ferry International (DE	Services	4/30/04	p350.7	p350.7	—	—	86	20004517
KFT	Kraft Foods, Inc.	Food processing	12/31/03	31010.0	3826.0	57242.0	28530.0	444	201923634
KRT	Kramont Realty Trust	Real estate investment trust	12/31/03	112.9	26.9	810.7	313.8	60	7574456
KKD	Krispy Kreme Doughnuts Inc (	—	2/1/04	665.6	94.0	553.5	452.2	172	34209917
KR	Kroger Co.	Grocery chain	1/31/04	53791.0	315.0	19246.0	4011.0	504	531411330
KRO	Kronos Worldwide Inc	Chemicals	12/31/03	1008.2	196.3	1293.9	331.4	—	—
KV B	KV Pharmaceutical Co.	Drugs	3/31/04	283.9	44.1	528.4	257.7	29	2194590
LLL	L-3 Communications Hldgs Inc	Defense systems & equip.	12/31/03	5061.6	711.6	6250.3	2574.5	419	93056654
LQI	La Quinta Corp. (United State	Real estate investment trust	12/31/03	513.0	d23.5	2803.9	1416.5	121	81217644
LZB	La-Z-Boy Inc.	Furniture & fixtures	4/24/04	—	d1996.3	1004.5	522.3	154	28584244
LRW	Labor Ready, Inc.	Services	1/2/04	891.2	670.0	363.0	154.1	111	32790146
LH	Laboratory Corp. of America	Medical & dental equipment	12/31/03	2939.4	861.4	2817.9	1861.2	303	131593007
LAB	LaBranche & Co., Inc.	Securities brokerage	12/31/03	306.0	d179.4	1959.6	773.0	149	33505684
LG	Laclede Group Inc	Natural gas distributor	9/30/03	1050.3	34.6	1156.4	299.1	95	4534764
LAF	Lafarge North America, Inc.	Cement & gypsum	12/31/03	3318.9	568.1	4541.5	2807.1	132	26591012
LR	Lafarge S.A. (France)	Cement & gypsum	12/31/03	—	—	—	—	28	2556429
LI	Laidlaw International Inc	—	8/31/03	997.1	d9.9	3203.8	1290.3	—	—
LMS	Lamson & Sessions Co.	Plastics & plastic products	1/3/04	343.8	3.7	197.7	38.5	23	6923300
LFL	Lan Chile, S.A. (Chile)	—	12/31/03	—	—	—	—	5	1200585
LFG	Landamerica Finl Group Inc	Insurance brokerage	12/31/03	3406.0	1703.8	2717.5	1044.5	142	15075857
LDR	Landauer, Inc.	Services	9/30/03	64.8	15.0	47.6	38.4	77	6260254
LNY	Landry's Restaurants, Inc.	Restaurants	12/31/03	1105.8	429.5	980.8	604.6	143	20223114
LHO	LaSalle Hotel Properties (Uni	Real estate investment trust	12/31/03	202.0	10.3	707.9	436.9	86	14612699
LAQ	Latin America Equity Fund In	Investment company	12/31/03	3.3	2.2	113.4	112.2	19	2589227
LDF	Latin American Discovery Fund	Investment company	12/31/03	4.7	2.9	164.0	157.1	18	5061381
EL	Lauder (Estee) Cos., Inc. (Th	Cosmetics & toiletries	6/30/03	5117.6	319.8	2880.0	1423.6	270	89435191
LJF	Leapfrog Enterprises Inc (Uni	—	12/31/03	680.0	188.0	535.0	415.1	127	21984407
LEA	Lear Corp.	—	12/31/03	15746.7	914.9	8177.6	2257.5	256	64816834
LEE	Lee Enterprises, Inc.	Newspapers	9/30/03	656.7	135.8	1213.4	802.2	163	28061922
LM	Legg Mason, Inc.	Securities brokerage	3/31/04	p2004.3	p2011.4	—	—	249	47122290
LEG	Leggett & Platt, Inc.	Furniture & fixtures	12/31/03	4388.2	521.0	3769.5	2114.0	277	117648191
LEH	Lehman Brothers Holdings Inc	Securities brokerage	11/30/03	17287.0	1699.0	312061.0	13174.0	466	152353771
LEN	Lennar Corp.	Home-building	11/30/03	8907.6	751.4	6775.4	3263.8	304	56656133
LEN B	Lennar Corp.	Home-building	11/30/03	8907.6	751.4	6775.4	3263.8	—	—
LII	Lennox International Inc	—	12/31/03	p3087.3	p3087.3	—	—	131	28982781
LUK	Leucadia National Corp.	Conglomerate	12/31/03	556.4	84.4	3797.8	2134.2	157	23699312
LEV	Levitt Corp (Fla)	Real estate	12/31/03	285.5	26.8	392.7	125.5	—	—
LXP	Lexington Corporate Propertie	Real estate investment trust	12/31/03	179.4	101.4	1314.4	579.8	88	6890613
LXK	Lexmark International, Inc.	Office equipment & supplies	12/31/03	4754.7	1032.7	3302.5	1643.0	416	118900207
LBY	Libbey Inc.	Industrial	12/31/03	518.6	63.3	537.0	139.9	92	12271918
USA	Liberty All-Star Equity Fund	Investment company	12/31/03	11.1	1.0	1171.8	1152.9	38	1005361
ASG	Liberty All-Star Growth Fd.	Investment company	12/31/03	0.5	d1.2	165.8	162.9	16	269546
LC	Liberty Corp.	Broadcasting	12/31/03	200.3	25.6	662.0	521.8	91	10571127
L	Liberty Media Corp. (New)	—	12/31/03	4028.0	d1222.0	51239.0	28842.0	658	1832095286
LRY	Liberty Property Trust (Unit	Real estate investment trust	12/31/03	p625.0	p637.9	—	—	215	61547942
LLY	Lilly (Eli) & Co.	Drugs	12/31/03	12582.5	2560.8	21678.1	9764.8	849	755414404
LTD	Limited Brands Inc. (United	Specialty stores	1/31/04	8934.0	1883.0	7654.0	5266.0	345	382761499
TVL	LIN TV Corp (United States)	Broadcasting	12/31/03	349.5	d171.2	1922.4	762.1	97	23457599
LNC	Lincoln National Corp. (ID)	Insurance	12/31/03	5283.9	767.2	106392.6	5811.6	389	126622772
LND	Lincoln National Incm Fd Inc	Investment company	12/31/03	9.3	7.6	141.3	98.1	16	269774
LNV	Lincoln Natl Conv Secs Fd Inc	Investment company	12/31/03	3.7	2.6	87.1	87.1	14	743685
LNN	Lindsay Manufacturing Co.	—	8/31/03	163.4	23.2	131.2	104.3	90	8836598
LIN	Linens'n Things, Inc.	Textiles	1/3/04	2395.3	74.8	1335.3	761.7	195	44615328
LAD	Lithia Motors, Inc.	—	12/31/03	2513.5	35.6	643.2	358.9	68	11522571
LIZ	Liz Claiborne, Inc. (United	—	1/3/04	4241.1	298.0	2474.1	1578.0	331	94072765
LRT	LL&E Royalty Trust Co.	Real estate investment trust	12/31/03	8.5	7.9	1.9	1.9	13	211579
LYG	Lloyds TSB Group Plc (UK)	—	12/31/03	—	—	—	—	53	8411285
LMT	Lockheed Martin Corp.	Defense systems & equip.	12/31/03	31824.0	1053.0	26175.0	6756.0	533	441458477
LTR	Loews Corp.	Conglomerate	12/31/03	16461.0	1298.5	77600.9	11054.3	316	106711463

T22

EARNINGS PER SHARE — QUARTERLY				ANNUAL		P/E RATIO	DIVIDENDS PER SHARE			AV. YLD. %	DIV. DECLARED		PRICE RANGE 2004
1st	2nd	3rd	2004	2003	2002		2004	2003	2002		AMOUNT	PAYABLE	
0.27	—	—	—	0.44	0.67	—				—	0.11Q	4/1/99	18.83 - 7.72
0.19	—	—	—	0.85	0.45	—				—			23.49 - 13.90
0.65	—	—	—	2.74	2.96	—	3.39	3.25	3.12	7.0	0.855Q	5/13/05	61.40 - 35.67
0.50	—	—	—	2.84	4.02	—	1.94	1.76	1.60	6.2	0.495Q	5/13/05	45.32 - 18.85
d0.67	—	—	—	d3.06	d7.47	—				—	0.075Q	1/29/01	6.50 - 2.73
0.32	—	—	—	1.18	0.85	—	0.48	0.48	0.48	1.8	0.12Q	4/4/05	33.96 - 18.00
1.75	—	—	—	8.80	7.15	—	0.50	0.15	0.15	0.7	0.1875Q	5/26/05	106.80 - 44.71
0.39	—	—	—	1.63	0.14	—				—	0.02Q	2/25/99	15.08 - 2.53
0.09	—	—	—	0.44	0.11	—				—	2-for-1	8/29/97	18.20 - 8.01
0.07	0.16	—	—	d0.27	0.20	—	0.15	0.15	0.15	0.7	0.0375Q	3/31/05	24.85 - 19.05
0.53	—	—	—	1.92	1.75	—	1.01	1.01	1.01	2.7	0.2525Q	3/15/05	45.32 - 29.57
0.90	—	—	—	2.68	1.69	—	0.64	0.64	0.64	1.9	0.16Q	4/1/05	43.74 - 23.73
—	—	—	—	d1.30	d0.65	—				—	2-for-1	6/1/00	16.70 - 7.44
0.24	0.30	0.66	—	0.51	1.22	—	0.68	0.68	0.68	1.7	0.17Q	2/23/05	52.69 - 28.13
1.41	—	—	—	2.48	d6.09	—	1.80	1.80	1.80	3.5	0.45Q	4/1/05	63.24 - 40.61
0.59	—	—	—	2.12	2.27	—	1.24	1.22	1.20	4.4	0.325Q	3/15/05	34.30 - 22.56
1.53	—	—	—	2.62	2.75	—	1.78	1.78	1.78	4.9	0.455Q	5/1/05	41.34 - 31.97
0.26	—	—	—	1.65	0.16	—	1.98	1.98	1.96	6.0	0.51Q	4/15/05	43.97 - 21.85
0.91	—	—	—	3.33	3.24	—	1.54	1.32	1.18	2.7	0.45Q	4/4/05	69.00 - 45.49
0.64	—	—	—	2.07	2.19	—	2.28	2.16	2.08	5.0	0.61Q	4/15/05	59.28 - 31.40
0.52	—	—	—	1.98	1.96	—	2.81	2.58	2.36	6.6	0.74Q	2/14/05	49.11 - 35.95
0.32	—	—	—	1.24	1.23	—	—	—	1.14	—	0.00Q	2/14/05	44.06 - 31.92
1.02	—	—	—	3.08	2.50	—	2.25	1.10	0.30	3.8	0.70Q	2/14/05	73.82 - 45.00
0.38	—	—	—	1.41	0.93	—				—	2-for-1	5/27/04	59.90 - 11.31
d1.19	—	—	—	0.93	1.93	—				—			78.37 - 37.75
d0.01	—	—	—	0.44	0.74	—				—	4-for-3	7/19/01	20.56 - 10.05
—	—	—	—			—				—			7.74 - 6.76
0.36	—	—	—	1.67	1.13	—				—	0.10A	9/5/89	36.43 - 30.19
0.24	—	—	—	0.93	0.73	—	0.02	—	—	0.1	0.02Q	4/18/05	30.22 - 18.07
0.70	—	—	—	3.63	3.33	—	1.33	1.18	1.02	1.9	0.345Q	2/28/05	80.00 - 58.50
0.12	—	—	—	0.69	0.77	—	1.40	1.40	3.14	6.1	0.35Q	4/24/00	25.18 - 20.96
0.33	—	—	—	1.72	1.87	—				—	100%	4/24/00	54.10 - 39.59
—	—	—	—			—	—	0.68	0.52	—	0.6799S	12/17/03	9.19 - 3.34
—	—	—	—			—	0.44	0.39	0.32	1.8	0.5144U	4/11/05	33.38 - 15.59
—	—	—	—			—	—	0.67	0.06	—	0.6654A	4/3/03	44.20 - 23.00
—	—	—	—	5.38	4.28	—				—	0.02	12/29/95	5.98 - 3.22
—	—	—	—	17.62	20.20	—	0.30	0.85	0.12	1.7	0.45A	1/12/05	24.25 - 11.59
—	—	—	—		pd0.63	—				—			21.86 - 6.00
0.33	—	—	—	2.01	1.96	—	0.74	0.63	0.54	2.3	0.205Q	4/4/05	36.06 - 27.81
d0.55	—	—	—	0.48	0.55	—	1.30	1.30	1.30	6.8	0.325Q	1/21/05	23.65 - 14.40
0.16	—	—	—	0.92	0.56	—				—	100%	6/14/01	39.94 - 9.37
—	—	—	—	0.42	1.56	—				—	2-for-1	6/28/99	19.67 - 13.15
0.20	—	—	—	1.79	1.35	—	1.00	—	—	3.1	0.25Q	3/25/05	48.84 - 16.00
—	—	—	—	0.90	0.55	—				—	3-for-2	9/29/03	24.99 - 18.12
0.67	—	—	—	2.71	2.29	—	0.40	—	—	0.7	0.125Q	3/15/05	77.26 - 36.12
d0.07	—	—	—	d0.55	d1.74	—				—	0.5625Q	10/1/01	9.26 - 3.05
—	—	—	—	0.05	1.67	—	0.43	0.40	0.39	2.4	0.11Q	3/10/05	23.58 - 12.75
0.02	—	—	—	0.41	0.28	—				—	3-for-2	7/12/99	17.02 - 5.40
0.61	—	—	—	2.22	1.77	—	—	—	—	—	2-for-1	5/10/02	50.03 - 26.75
0.11	—	—	—	d3.08	1.34	—	—	0.24	—	—	0.08Q	8/14/03	21.77 - 6.96
0.87	1.12	—	—	1.82	1.18	—	1.35	1.34	1.34	4.9	0.345Q	4/1/05	32.50 - 22.75
d0.96	—	—	—	2.93	3.64	—	0.84	0.70	0.60	2.1	0.22Q	3/1/05	52.00 - 28.28
—	—	—	—			—	0.52	1.35	0.42	2.7	0.52355A	7/14/04	24.41 - 14.30
0.22	0.01	—	—	d0.10	3.05	—	—	—	—	—			21.77 - 11.96
0.09	—	—	—	0.27	0.36	—	—	—	—	2.5	0.05U	12/10/85	10.53 - 3.11
—	—	—	—			—	0.48	0.50	0.01	2.5	0.3498U	1/13/05	33.00 - 5.30
1.11	—	—	—	10.31	8.04	—	0.50	0.34	0.24	1.1	0.15Q	3/15/05	57.73 - 35.51
0.45	0.54	—	—	1.69	1.83	—	1.60	1.50	1.40	3.8	0.425Q	4/8/05	50.30 - 34.63
0.40	—	—	—	1.62	1.54	—	0.18	0.10	0.10	0.7	0.05Q	4/25/05	33.74 - 16.40
d0.27	—	—	—	d0.38	d0.31	—	0.89	0.98	0.24	4.0	0.08M	4/15/05	32.70 - 11.95
—	—	—	—	17.74	11.55	—	0.14	0.21	0.48	0.9	0.46A	1/7/05	21.64 - 9.03
—	—	—	—	14.71	9.33	—	0.27	0.15	0.16	2.1	0.254A	1/7/05	18.50 - 7.28
0.33	0.54	0.43	—	1.26	0.78	—	0.70	0.20	0.15	1.8	0.40A	12/28/04	49.30 - 28.05
d0.20	—	—	—	1.20	0.86	—				—			32.24 - 11.50
1.30	—	—	—	5.55	4.65	—	1.00	—	—	1.9	0.25Q	3/14/05	69.20 - 35.35
0.55	0.36	—	—	1.75	1.83	—	0.72	0.68	0.68	1.8	0.18Q	4/1/05	48.99 - 31.52
—	—	—	—		p2.78	—	0.45	0.32	0.27	0.6	0.15Q	4/4/05	96.17 - 48.74
0.32	—	—	—	1.05	1.17	—	0.57	0.53	0.49	2.3	0.15Q	4/15/05	30.68 - 18.28
2.21	p2.01	—	—	6.35	3.47	—	0.64	0.48	0.36	0.9	0.20Q	2/22/05	89.72 - 54.53
0.84	—	—	—	4.65	3.86	—	0.51	0.14	0.03	0.8	0.1375Q	5/16/05	95.60 - 40.30
0.84	—	—	—	4.65	3.86	—	0.51	0.14		1.2	0.1375Q	5/16/05	45.34 - 44.00
—	—	—	—		p1.00	—	0.38	0.38	0.38	2.3	0.10Q	4/8/05	20.50 - 12.81
d0.17	—	—	—	1.37	2.72	—	0.38	0.17	0.17	0.7	50%	12/31/04	70.50 - 33.62
0.87	—	—	—	1.77	1.30	—	0.04	—	—	0.2	0.02Q	2/15/05	31.46 - 16.25
0.20	—	—	—	0.80	1.10	—	1.40	1.34	1.32	7.1	0.36Q	2/14/05	23.28 - 16.15
0.91	—	—	—	3.34	2.79	—	—	—	—	—	100%	6/10/99	96.85 - 60.54
0.04	—	—	—	2.11	1.82	—	0.40	0.40	0.30	1.7	0.10Q	3/3/05	26.80 - 16.80
—	—	—	—	9.13	7.14	—	0.89	0.75	0.94	10.4	0.22Q	3/21/05	10.40 - 6.65
—	—	—	—	6.51	5.44	—	0.64	0.56	0.72	10.1	0.15Q	3/21/05	7.70 - 4.99
0.24	—	—	—	1.24	1.68	—	4.99	0.94	0.88	11.1	0.25Q	4/4/05	51.76 - 38.55
—	—	—	—	d0.44	d1.34	—	—	—	—	—	0.00U	6/7/04	12.43 - 8.33
0.43	—	—	—		p1.92	—	2.42	2.41	2.37	6.4	0.61Q	4/15/05	45.51 - 29.99
0.37	—	—	—	2.37	2.50	—	1.42	1.34	1.24	2.2	0.38Q	3/10/05	76.95 - 50.35
0.19	—	—	—	1.36	0.95	—	0.48	0.40	0.30	2.4	0.15Q	3/15/05	27.75 - 11.88
d0.04	—	—	—	d1.81	d0.33	—				—			26.60 - 17.41
0.86	—	—	—	4.27	0.49	—	1.40	1.34	1.28	3.6	0.365Q	5/1/05	49.94 - 28.00
—	—	—	—	13.41	12.99	—	1.98	1.26	1.34	14.5	0.155Q	4/29/05	15.25 - 12.10
—	—	—	—		12.56	—	0.85	0.92	0.86	6.4	0.17Q	3/14/05	14.28 - 12.13
0.09	0.29	—	—	1.08	0.90	—	0.21	0.17	0.14	0.9	0.055Q	2/28/05	29.51 - 18.55
—	—	—	—	1.67	1.60	—				—	2-for-1	5/7/98	36.40 - 20.32
0.40	—	—	—	1.92	1.84	—	0.30	0.14	—	1.4	0.08Q	3/14/05	30.79 - 12.30
0.62	—	—	—	2.55	2.16	—	0.23	0.23	0.23	0.6	0.05625Q	3/15/05	42.47 - 28.20
0.17	—	—	—	0.41	0.11	—	0.54	0.42	0.11	11.4		4/15/05	7.00 - 2.41
—	—	—	—			—	2.44	2.21	2.03	8.4		5/16/05	37.03 - 20.80
0.65	—	—	—	2.34	1.18	—	0.91	0.58	0.44	1.7	0.25Q	3/31/05	61.76 - 43.10
0.05	—	—	—	d4.21		—	0.60	0.60	0.60	1.1	0.15Q	3/14/05	71.00 - 39.84

SYMBOL	COMPANY	NATURE OF BUSINESS	FISCAL YEAR-END	TOTAL REV. $MILL	NET INCOME $MILL	TOTAL ASSETS $MILL	NET STK. EQUITY $MILL	NO. OF INST.	INST. HOLDINGS (SHARES)
LSS	Lone Star Technologies, Inc.	Industrial	12/31/03	534.1	d68.2	548.3	278.1	124	25110122
LDG	Longs Drug Stores Corp. (Uni	Drug stores	1/29/04	4526.5	29.8	1392.1	713.9	137	22649728
LFB	Longview Fibre Co.	Forest products	10/31/03	773.3	5.4	1255.4	432.3	129	28399663
LPX	Louisiana-Pacific Corp.	Forest products	12/31/03	2300.2	299.7	3156.6	1310.9	228	73272286
LOW	Lowe's Cos., Inc.	Specialty stores	1/30/04	30838.0	1990.0	18633.0	10309.0	775	603955079
LSI	LSI Logic Corp.	Electronic components	12/31/03	1693.1	d592.9	3447.9	2042.5	331	192307486
LTC	LTC Properties, Inc.	Real estate investment trust	12/31/03	63.4	21.9	574.9	368.8	40	2605953
LZ	Lubrizol Corp. (United State	Chemicals	12/31/03	2052.1	242.4	1870.6	953.3	215	39906907
LUB	Luby's, Inc. (United States)	Restaurants	8/27/03	318.5	22.9	181.3	131.9	48	8775096
LU	Lucent Technologies Inc.	Telecommunications	9/30/03	8470.0	d315.0	15765.0	d4239.0	631	1473273066
LUM	Luminent Mortgage Capital Inc	Real estate investment trust	12/31/03	14.8	2.8	2179.3	282.5	—	—
LDL	Lydall, Inc.	Textiles	12/31/03	271.4	21.1	216.7	143.3	79	12601772
WLS	Lyon (William) Homes	Real estate	12/31/03	897.8	122.5	790.5	252.0	31	3803713
LYO	Lyondell Chemical Co	Specialty chemicals	12/31/03	3801.0	d783.0	7161.0	1156.0	187	112382740
MFW	M & F Worldwide Corp.	—	12/31/03	95.7	55.7	379.1	304.7	35	5879135
MTB	M & T Bank Corp	Banking - Northeast	12/31/03	2957.7	573.9	49826.1	5717.2	262	53410413
MDC	M.D.C. Holdings, Inc.	Home-building	12/31/03	2920.1	212.2	1890.6	1015.9	145	17753583
MHO	M/I Homes Inc	Home-building	12/31/03	1069.6	141.4	720.4	402.4	74	8522272
TUC	Mac-Gray Corp.	Services	12/31/03	149.7	13.6	105.2	68.7	7	1185036
MRD	MacDermid, Inc.	Specialty chemicals	12/31/03	619.9	53.4	693.9	236.7	129	21492344
MAC	Macerich Co. (The)	Real estate investment trust	12/31/03	486.6	115.5	4145.6	953.5	159	53843120
CLI	Mack Cali Realty Corp	Real estate investment trust	12/31/03	586.2	139.7	3749.6	1541.5	204	48700318
MAD	Madeco S.A. (Chile)	Copper	12/31/03	—	—	—	—	—	—
MMP	Magellan Midstream Partners	—	12/31/03	482.5	147.3	1194.6	—	—	—
MGA	Magna International Inc.	—	12/31/03	15345.0	589.0	9448.0	4930.0	148	47082718
MAG	MagneTek, Inc.	Electrical equipment	6/30/03	201.8	d34.8	280.7	79.7	70	18185389
MHR	Magnum Hunter Resources, Inc	Oil	12/31/03	325.0	47.8	1043.6	389.7	92	29566830
MPG	Maguire Properties Inc	Real estate	12/31/03	137.4	d10.5	1775.2	343.4	—	—
MF	Malaysia Fund, Inc.	Investment company	12/31/03	1.5	0.6	57.0	55.8	14	1922590
MHY	Managed High Income Portfoli	Investment company	2/29/04	30.2	26.4	328.5	325.1	28	3183844
MBG	Mandalay Resort Group	Gaming	1/31/04	2491.1	629.9	4283.4	1030.3	186	50015558
MTW	Manitowoc Co., Inc.	—	12/31/03	1593.2	41.1	1300.1	298.4	131	18413163
HCR	Manor Care, Inc. (New)	Hospitals & nursing homes	12/31/03	3029.4	276.6	2286.5	975.1	242	82027764
MAN	Manpower Inc. (WI)	Services	12/31/03	12184.5	10185.4	4153.3	1310.3	248	75032828
ELS	Manufactured Home Communitie	Real estate investment trust	12/31/03	269.5	25.5	1473.9	5.8	—	—
MFC	Manulife Financial Corp.	Financial services	12/31/03	—	—	—	—	157	135346597
MRO	Marathon Oil Corp.	Oil	12/31/03	41234.0	1012.0	19010.0	6075.0	424	246312688
HZO	MarineMax, Inc.	Specialty stores	9/30/03	607.5	19.7	329.2	166.1	40	6851720
TUG	Maritrans, Inc.	Freight transportation	12/31/03	138.2	27.3	191.4	85.2	26	3669717
MKL	Markel Corp (Holding Co) (Un	Insurance brokerage	12/31/03	2091.9	305.1	8152.4	1112.4	138	6788393
MAR	Marriott International, Inc.	Motel/hotel lodging	1/2/04	9014.0	476.0	7765.0	3838.0	298	150192586
MMC	Marsh & McLennan Cos., Inc.	Insurance brokerage	12/31/03	11588.0	3973.0	15053.0	5451.0	686	357744839
MI	Marshall & Ilsley Corp. (Uni	Banking - Midwest	12/31/03	2745.7	544.1	31921.6	3328.7	292	88236631
MSO	Martha Stewart Living Omnime	—	12/31/03	245.8	52.6	309.1	236.7	68	9624394
MLM	Martin Marietta Materials, In	—	12/31/03	1711.5	101.1	2253.4	1129.8	187	47469703
MVL	Marvel Enterprises, Inc. (Uni	—	12/31/03	347.6	151.6	673.9	469.4	115	28224925
MAS	Masco Corp.	Furniture & fixtures	12/31/03	10936.0	1884.0	11864.0	5456.0	394	381410971
MYS	Masisa S.A. (Chile)	—	12/31/03	—	—	—	—	9	924806
MEE	Massey Energy Co.	Engineering & construction	12/31/03	1553.4	d27.3	2376.7	759.0	171	68782499
MCI	Massmutual Corporate Inv. In	Investment company	12/31/03	18.1	12.8	223.4	193.8	20	343518
MPV	MassMutual Participation Inv	Investment company	12/31/03	10.1	7.7	111.1	94.4	11	789630
MTZ	MasTec Inc. (FL)	Water company	12/31/03	p873.9	p873.9	—	—	78	16932466
MSC	Material Sciences Corp.	Steel producer	2/29/04	243.2	d14.0	203.5	111.0	72	10988421
MAT	Mattel Inc	—	12/31/03	4960.1	1278.5	4378.6	2216.2	448	355062073
MVK	Maverick Tube Corp.	Steel producer	12/31/03	884.3	58.7	617.1	384.8	173	36384163
MMS	Maximus Inc.	Services	9/30/03	558.3	35.3	415.0	333.3	121	20881450
MXO	Maxtor Corp.(New)	Comp. components & periphs.	12/27/03	4086.4	100.5	2378.3	720.5	180	233828833
MAY	May Department Stores Co	Department stores	1/31/04	13343.0	467.0	11678.0	4191.0	403	241559375
MYG	Maytag Corp.	Appliances & utensils	1/3/04	4791.9	114.4	2754.0	65.8	278	44565256
MBI	MBIA, Inc.	Insurance brokerage	12/31/03	1688.9	1962.2	29830.1	6259.0	447	130978292
KRB	MBNA Corp.	Banking - Mid-Atlantic	12/31/03	11684.4	2338.1	59113.4	11113.0	648	883237787
MNI	McClatchy Co. (The)	Newspapers	12/28/03	1099.4	144.2	1816.9	1216.0	130	16868941
MKC V	McCormick & Co., Inc.	Food processing	11/30/03	2269.6	469.2	1969.4	755.2	10	156481
MKC	McCormick & Co., Inc.	Food processing	11/30/03	2269.6	469.2	1969.4	755.2	286	91810398
MDR	McDermott International, Inc	Machinery & equipment	12/31/03	2335.4	d102.2	1030.6	d363.2	147	38428155
MCD	McDonald's Corp.	Restaurants	12/31/03	17140.5	4126.7	25525.1	11981.9	754	848923562
MHP	McGraw-Hill Cos., Inc.	Publishing	12/31/03	4827.9	1818.1	4677.6	2557.1	522	136532351
MCK	McKesson Corp. (New)	'Wholesaler, distributor'	3/31/04	69506.1	646.5	15697.2	5165.3	413	225873283
MMR	McMoran Exploration Co	Oil	12/31/03	16.1	d22.1	155.8	d84.6	52	6397842
MDZ	MDS Inc. (Canada)	Medical & dental equipment	10/31/03	—	—	—	—	35	50183189
MDU	MDU Resources Group, Inc.	Natural gas distributor	12/31/03	2352.2	182.9	3380.6	1450.6	203	26172878
MIG	Meadowbrook Insurance Group	Insurance brokerage	12/31/03	210.8	10.1	692.3	155.1	30	14478512
MWV	MeadWestvaco Corp. (United S	Paper	12/31/03	7553.0	d31.0	12122.0	4768.0	316	142074177
MHS	Medco Health Solutions, Inc.	Drugs	12/27/03	34264.5	615.5	10263.0	5080.0	—	—
MEG	Media General, Inc.	Telecommunications	12/28/03	837.4	59.0	2058.3	1158.4	167	16482490
MRN	Medical Staffing Network Hol	Services	12/28/03	513.0	407.0	184.3	151.3	51	9875952
MRX	Medicis Pharmaceutical Corp.	Drugs	6/30/03	247.5	51.3	934.6	458.7	224	31078004
MDT	Medtronic, Inc. (United Stat	Medical & dental equipment	4/30/04	p9087.2	p9087.2	—	—	1004	829788418
MEL	Mellon Financial Corp.	Banking - Mid-Atlantic	12/31/03	4550.0	677.0	33831.0	3702.0	499	302371083
WFR	MEMC Electronic Materials, In	Comp. components & periphs.	12/31/03	781.1	268.4	631.6	193.6	73	15373932
MW	Men's Wearhouse, Inc. (The)	—	1/31/04	1392.7	50.0	836.2	493.5	130	29196771
MNT	Mentor Corp. (MN)	Medical & dental equipment	3/31/04	422.2	54.8	404.9	198.3	147	38109153
MRK	Merck & Co., Inc.	Drugs	12/31/03	22485.9	6589.6	39852.3	15576.4	1335	1335962051
MCY	Mercury General Corp.	Property & casualty insurance	12/31/03	2265.5	184.3	3119.8	1255.5	121	23444665
MDP	Meredith Corp.	Publishing	6/30/03	1080.1	91.1	1178.1	500.8	232	33404920
TMR	Meridian Resource Corp. (The	Natural gas	12/31/03	137.5	26.8	433.4	184.3	53	9146391
MHX	Meristar Hospitality Corp (U	Real estate investment trust	12/31/03	843.8	23.2	2471.5	653.6	106	34047761
MTH	Meritage Corp (United States	Real estate	12/31/03	1471.0	148.3	891.6	411.9	88	8341522
MER	Merrill Lynch & Co Inc	Securities brokerage	12/26/03	27745.0	3988.0	494518.0	27651.0	652	618213071
MTR	Mesa Royalty Trust	Oil	12/31/03	9.3	9.3	11.7	9.5	10	1106164
MSB	Mesabi Trust	—	1/31/04	7.3	6.8	5.4	1.4	18	1045377
MCC	Mestek Inc. (United States)	—	1/31/04	366.5	34.4	209.6	95.5	32	1972491
MPR	Met-Pro Corp.	Pollution control	1/31/04	75.1	14.2	81.1	60.3	24	2152081
MET	Metlife Inc	Insurance brokerage	12/31/03	35789.0	4015.0	326841.0	21149.0	394	300253471
MXT	Metris Cos., Inc.	—	12/31/03	595.5	d147.7	1392.4	909.2	94	43894058
MX	Metso Oy (Finland)	—	12/31/03	—	—	—	—	8	1012275

| EARNINGS PER SHARE | | | | | | P/E RATIO | DIVIDENDS PER SHARE | | | AV. YLD. % | DIV. DECLARED | | PRICE RANGE |
| QUARTERLY | | | | ANNUAL | | | | | | | | | 2004 |
1st	2nd	3rd	2004	2003	2002		2004	2003	2002		AMOUNT	PAYABLE	
0.28	—	—	—	d2.40	d2.52	—							40.00 - 13.99
0.25	—	—	—	0.79	0.82	—	0.56	0.56	0.56	2.7	0.14Q	4/11/05	28.10 - 13.81
d0.18	0.12	—	—	0.10	0.10	—	0.05	0.04	0.03	0.4	0.02Q	4/8/05	18.44 - 6.05
1.03	—	—	—	2.67	d0.21	—	0.30	—	—	1.7	0.10Q	3/1/05	28.31 - 7.30
0.57	—	—	—	2.32	1.85	—	0.14	0.11	0.08	0.3	0.04Q	4/29/05	60.54 - 34.18
0.02	—	—	—	d0.82	d0.79	—	—	—	—	—	2-for-1	2/16/00	11.48 - 4.01
0.05	—	—	—	0.22	0.17	—	1.13	0.65	0.40	8.5	0.30Q	3/31/05	20.23 - 6.20
0.72	—	—	—	1.75	2.44	—	1.04	1.04	1.04	3.1	0.26Q	3/10/05	37.37 - 28.93
d0.11	d0.09	p0.02	—	d0.11	d0.43	—	—	—	—	—	0.10Q	9/25/00	8.08 - 1.32
0.07	0.02	—	—	d0.29	d3.51	—	—	—	—	—	0.00Q	5/31/02	4.91 - 1.47
p0.43	—	—	—	0.27	—	—	1.73	0.50	—	13.4	0.36Q	5/20/05	15.35 - 10.50
0.06	—	—	—	0.52	0.72	—	—	—	—	—	2-for-1	6/21/95	12.01 - 8.75
1.55	—	—	—	7.27	4.73	—	—	—	—	—	—	—	93.75 - 21.95
d0.08	—	—	—	d1.84	d0.99	—	0.90	0.90	0.90	4.3	0.225Q	3/15/05	29.59 - 11.91
0.27	—	—	—	1.18	0.71	—	—	—	—	—	—	—	15.00 - 6.58
1.30	—	—	—	4.95	5.07	—	1.60	1.20	1.05	1.7	0.40Q	3/31/05	108.75 - 78.58
1.79	—	—	—	6.36	4.98	—	0.43	0.29	0.20	0.7	0.15Q	2/24/05	87.24 - 34.13
1.35	—	—	—	5.51	4.30	—	0.10	0.10	0.10	0.2	0.025Q	4/21/05	55.41 - 25.90
0.14	—	—	—	0.32	0.30	—	—	—	—	—	—	—	8.10 - 3.15
0.42	—	—	—	1.59	0.29	—	0.15	0.09	0.08	0.5	0.06Q	4/1/05	39.73 - 20.45
0.31	—	—	—	1.74	1.16	—	2.48	2.32	2.22	5.3	0.65Q	3/8/05	64.66 - 29.70
0.44	—	—	—	2.37	2.43	—	2.52	2.52	2.49	6.7	0.63Q	4/18/05	47.01 - 28.50
													11.00 - 3.95
0.87	—	—	—	3.31	3.67	—	1.72	1.53	1.29	3.3	2-for-1	4/12/05	59.45 - 44.20
—	—	—	—	5.91	5.82	—	1.48	1.36	1.36	2.2	0.38Q	3/23/05	85.20 - 52.28
d0.15	d0.15	0.01	—	d1.48	0.06	—	—	—	—	—	—	—	8.35 - 2.16
0.28	—	—	—	0.37	0.26	—	—	—	—	—	0.00U	5/13/05	13.82 - 5.43
0.14	—	—	—	d0.74	—	—	1.60	0.42	—	6.8	0.40Q	4/30/05	27.96 - 19.25
—	—	—	—	5.76	4.63	—	0.11	0.15	0.09	2.0	0.0638A	1/7/05	7.25 - 3.60
—	—	—	—	7.12	6.30	—	0.59	0.65	0.69	9.1	0.043M	5/27/05	7.28 - 5.79
1.30	—	—	—	2.31	1.68	—	0.81	0.48	—	1.7	0.27Q	8/2/04	70.50 - 25.24
0.25	—	—	—	0.69	1.56	—	0.28	0.28	0.28	1.0	0.07Q	3/14/05	39.28 - 16.81
0.46	—	—	—	1.31	1.33	—	0.56	0.25	—	2.0	0.15Q	2/28/05	37.25 - 18.33
0.45	—	—	—	1.74	1.46	—	0.30	0.20	0.20	0.7	0.20S	12/15/04	50.77 - 29.88
0.21	—	—	—	0.78	1.54	—	8.04	1.96	1.87	22.6	0.025Q	4/8/05	36.52 - 34.58
—	—	—	—	—	—	—	0.94	0.78	0.60	2.7	0.26Q	3/19/05	46.93 - 23.15
0.83	—	—	—	3.26	1.72	—	1.03	0.96	0.92	3.2	0.28Q	3/10/05	42.60 - 20.90
0.14	0.34	—	—	1.26	1.10	—	—	—	—	—	—	—	32.02 - 9.02
0.21	—	—	—	2.22	1.10	—	0.44	0.44	0.42	2.8	0.11Q	3/16/05	19.10 - 11.93
4.29	—	—	—	12.52	7.65	—	—	—	—	—	—	—	365.00 - 203.40
0.47	—	—	—	1.94	1.74	—	0.32	0.29	0.27	0.7	0.085Q	4/28/05	63.86 - 30.22
0.83	—	—	—	2.81	2.45	—	1.30	1.18	1.09	3.6	0.17Q	5/13/05	49.48 - 22.90
0.65	—	—	—	2.38	2.16	—	0.81	0.70	0.55	2.3	0.21Q	3/11/05	44.60 - 25.56
d0.41	—	—	—	d0.04	0.27	—	—	—	—	—	—	—	33.49 - 7.35
d0.14	—	—	—	2.06	2.00	—	0.76	0.69	0.58	1.9	0.20Q	3/31/05	53.91 - 27.58
0.27	—	—	—	1.34	d0.71	—	—	—	—	—	3-for-2	3/26/04	35.72 - 11.08
0.52	—	—	—	1.51	1.33	—	0.66	0.58	0.55	2.4	0.20Q	5/9/05	37.01 - 18.19
—	—	—	—	—	—	—	0.09	0.11	0.23	0.7	0.0879A	5/24/04	19.40 - 6.20
d0.03	—	—	—	d0.43	d0.44	—	0.16	0.16	0.16	0.7	0.04Q	4/12/05	36.94 - 8.10
—	—	—	—	21.84	19.40	—	2.18	1.44	1.73	8.9	0.46Q	1/14/05	29.50 - 19.67
—	—	—	—	9.84	8.78	—	1.10	0.80	0.90	9.6	0.24Q	1/14/05	13.60 - 9.30
—	—	—	—	—	pd2.15	—	—	—	—	—	3-for-2	6/19/00	16.48 - 1.51
—	—	—	—	d1.00	0.14	—	—	0.01	—	—	0.01U	5/16/03	18.16 - 8.05
0.02	—	—	—	1.22	1.03	—	0.45	0.40	0.05	2.5	0.45A	12/17/04	19.79 - 15.94
0.72	—	—	—	0.55	0.08	—	—	—	—	—	2-for-1	8/21/97	32.24 - 15.34
0.42	—	—	—	1.66	1.73	—	—	—	—	—	0.10Q	2/28/05	41.24 - 21.22
0.04	—	—	—	0.40	d1.09	—	—	—	—	—	—	—	12.60 - 2.81
0.24	—	—	—	1.41	1.76	—	0.97	0.96	0.95	3.5	0.245Q	6/15/05	36.48 - 19.62
0.49	—	—	—	1.45	2.44	—	0.72	0.72	0.72	3.0	0.18Q	5/16/05	31.99 - 15.30
1.42	—	—	—	5.61	3.98	—	0.92	0.77	0.66	1.7	0.28Q	4/15/05	67.34 - 38.13
0.40	—	—	—	1.79	1.34	—	0.46	0.33	0.26	2.1	0.14Q	4/1/05	29.05 - 13.85
p0.62	—	—	—	3.10	2.84	—	0.48	0.43	0.40	0.8	0.13Q	4/1/05	74.38 - 53.59
0.27	—	—	—	1.40	1.26	—	0.56	0.46	0.42	2.0	0.16Q	4/15/05	34.50 - 22.25
0.27	—	—	—	1.40	1.26	—	0.56	0.46	0.42	1.7	0.16Q	4/15/05	35.11 - 30.42
pd0.17	—	—	—	d1.59	d12.71	—	—	—	—	—	0.05Q	7/1/00	18.49 - 2.90
0.40	—	—	—	1.18	0.77	—	0.55	0.40	0.23	2.4	0.55A	12/1/04	32.96 - 13.61
0.39	—	—	—	3.58	2.96	—	1.20	1.08	1.02	1.6	0.33Q	3/10/05	92.11 - 55.59
—	—	—	—	2.19	1.90	—	0.24	0.24	0.24	0.8	0.06Q	4/1/05	35.08 - 22.61
d0.68	—	—	—	d2.62	0.93	—	—	—	—	—	—	—	19.45 - 5.88
0.20	—	—	—	1.62	1.38	—	0.08	0.10	0.09	0.6	0.0325Q	4/1/05	17.35 - 12.50
0.11	—	—	—	0.35	0.08	—	0.69	0.65	0.62	2.8	0.18Q	4/1/05	27.70 - 21.85
—	—	—	—	—	—	—	—	—	—	—	0.03Q	10/5/01	5.86 - 2.26
d0.01	—	—	—	d0.01	d0.01	—	0.92	0.92	0.92	3.2	0.23Q	3/1/05	34.34 - 22.78
0.38	—	—	—	1.57	1.34	—	—	—	—	—	—	—	41.90 - 24.67
0.38	—	—	—	2.52	2.30	—	0.80	0.76	0.72	1.3	0.21Q	3/15/05	72.48 - 49.24
d0.02	—	—	—	0.18	0.62	—	—	—	—	—	—	—	12.31 - 5.21
d0.50	0.23	0.33	—	0.91	0.80	—	0.13	0.05	—	0.2	0.03Q	4/29/05	78.40 - 32.85
—	—	—	—	—	p1.30	—	0.31	0.27	0.24	0.6	0.08375Q	4/29/05	53.60 - 44.70
0.57	—	—	—	1.57	1.52	—	0.70	0.57	0.49	2.5	0.18Q	2/15/05	34.11 - 21.26
0.16	—	—	—	0.53	d0.17	—	—	—	—	—	—	—	13.28 - 7.33
0.41	—	—	—	1.27	1.04	—	—	—	—	—	50%	6/19/98	34.51 - 14.01
—	—	—	—	1.15	1.15	—	0.62	0.21	0.06	2.3	0.17Q	4/21/05	36.50 - 17.12
0.73	—	—	—	2.92	3.14	—	1.49	1.45	1.41	4.0	0.38Q	4/1/05	49.33 - 25.60
1.26	—	—	—	3.38	1.21	—	1.48	1.32	1.20	3.1	0.43Q	3/31/05	60.26 - 36.21
0.39	0.39	0.65	—	1.78	1.79	—	0.48	0.38	0.36	1.0	0.14Q	3/15/05	55.51 - 38.18
p0.08	—	—	—	0.13	d1.05	—	—	—	—	—	0.32U	3/5/86	9.02 - 1.10
d0.42	—	—	—	d5.00	d2.83	—	—	—	0.04	—	0.01Q	10/31/02	8.57 - 1.99
1.92	—	—	—	6.84	5.31	—	—	—	—	—	100%	1/7/05	114.33 - 31.60
1.22	—	—	—	4.05	2.63	—	0.64	0.64	0.64	1.3	0.16Q	2/28/05	64.85 - 34.08
1.16	—	—	—	4.97	2.58	—	4.65	4.52	2.49	8.1	—	4/29/05	71.25 - 44.25
0.06	—	—	—	0.52	0.36	—	0.77	0.38	0.25	8.0	0.33Q	5/20/05	14.82 - 4.49
d0.04	—	—	—	d4.95	d0.12	—	—	—	—	—	0.15Q	9/4/79	20.30 - 17.10
0.10	—	—	—	0.76	0.71	—	0.29	0.30	0.26	1.9	0.0775Q	6/8/05	18.00 - 12.65
0.87	—	—	—	2.57	1.58	—	0.46	0.23	0.21	1.4	0.46A	12/13/04	41.27 - 26.17
0.47	—	—	—	d3.27	d1.20	—	—	—	0.04	—	0.01Q	12/31/02	13.35 - 1.50
—	—	—	—	—	—	—	0.20	0.56	0.45	1.6	0.3924A	4/25/05	16.49 - 9.12

SYMBOL	COMPANY	NATURE OF BUSINESS	FISCAL YEAR-END	TOTAL REV. $MILL	NET INCOME $MILL	TOTAL ASSETS $MILL	NET STK EQUITY $MILL	NO. OF INST.	INST. HOLDINGS (SHARES)
MTD	Mettler-Toledo International	Meas. & control instruments	12/31/03	1304.4	420.8	1225.2	654.0	143	38699736
MXE	Mexico Equity & Income Fd In	Investment company	7/31/03	0.6	0.0	25.7	25.1	7	268438
MXF	Mexico Fund Inc.	Investment company	10/31/03	5.0	0.4	270.2	269.8	32	1697771
MFA	MFA Mortgage Investments Inc	Real estate investment trust	12/31/03	120.4	57.8	4564.9	485.0	76	23319104
MMT	MFS Multimarket Income Trust	Investment company	10/31/03	37.0	31.8	568.2	563.8	42	6869037
MTG	MGIC Investment Corp.	Finance	12/31/03	1685.4	493.9	5917.4	3796.9	356	106972117
MGG	MGM Mirage	Motel/hotel lodging	12/31/03	2307.6	d495.0	9957.6	2533.8	177	70191609
MIM	MI Developments Inc	—	12/31/03	p814.0	p814.0	—	—	—	—
MIK	Michaels Stores, Inc. (Unite	Specialty stores	1/31/04	3091.3	185.9	1714.8	1167.3	240	57106406
MFI	MicroFinancial, Inc.	Finance	12/31/03	91.6	d15.7	156.4	71.3	19	3523695
MU	Micron Technology Inc.	Electronic components	8/28/03	3091.3	d1273.2	7018.6	4971.0	352	481858322
MAA	Mid-America Apartment Communi	Real estate investment trust	12/31/03	240.9	22.6	1406.5	361.3	98	5266276
MDS	Midas, Inc.	—	1/3/04	311.0	d83.0	272.6	36.1	71	8203930
MWY	Midway Games Inc. (United Sta	—	12/31/03	92.5	d115.2	125.4	47.9	102	22982016
MEH	Midwest Air Group Inc	—	12/31/03	383.9	d13.3	376.1	124.3	53	7208711
MZ	Milacron, Inc.	Machine tools	12/31/03	739.7	d296.3	599.2	d33.9	96	23613168
MLR	Miller Industries Inc. (TN)	—	12/31/03	192.0	d11.9	65.5	28.0	15	2244597
MIL	Millipore Corp	Medical & dental equipment	12/31/03	799.6	213.0	824.8	461.0	248	47701970
MLS	Mills Corp	Real estate	12/31/03	371.1	180.5	3067.6	854.8	154	23708021
MSA	Mine Safety Appliances Co	—	12/31/03	698.2	48.9	569.1	307.9	54	4336617
MTX	Minerals Technologies, Inc.	Metal products	12/31/03	813.7	147.6	1005.5	707.4	148	20379561
MPJ	Mississippi Power Co.	Electric power	12/31/03	869.9	75.5	1412.2	564.3	—	—
NUT	ML Macadamia Orchards, L.P.	Food -grain & agriculture	12/31/03	15.4	1.2	59.2	—	8	353796
MOD	Modine Manufacturing Co	—	3/31/04	1199.8	98.1	926.3	586.5	109	18075131
MHK	Mohawk Industries, Inc. (Uni	Floor coverings	12/31/03	5005.1	310.1	3917.8	2297.8	241	57204306
MOH	Molina Healthcare, Inc. (Uni	Services	12/31/03	793.5	42.5	344.6	221.3	—	—
MNC	Monaco Coach Corp. (United S	—	1/3/04	1168.3	22.2	474.8	286.2	126	22697041
MON	Monsanto Co. (New)	—	8/31/03	3373.0	d54.0	9444.0	5156.0	367	210442198
MTS	Montgomery Str Incme Secs Inc	Investment company	12/31/03	12.5	11.2	249.1	203.9	16	319592
MCO	Moody's Corp.	Services	12/31/03	1246.6	363.9	600.7	d32.1	405	129484033
MOG A	Moog, Inc.	—	9/27/03	755.5	42.7	816.6	424.1	105	10124995
MWD	Morgan Stanley	Securities brokerage	11/30/03	34933.0	3941.0	602843.0	24867.0	730	701766859
RBT	Morgan Stanley	Securities brokerage	11/30/03	34933.0	3941.0	602843.0	24867.0	—	—
RNE	Morgan Stanley Eastern Europ	Investment company	12/31/03	1.7	d0.2	125.2	106.2	13	1459787
MSD	Morgan Stanley Emerging Marke	Investment company	12/31/03	19.6	17.0	241.6	225.8	28	2289882
MSF	Morgan Stanley Emerging Marke	Investment company	12/31/03	6.1	2.5	287.2	282.1	30	7083261
MGB	Morgan Stanley Global Opportu	Investment company	12/31/03	3.2	2.6	39.5	33.1	6	44166
MSY	Morgan Stanley High Yield Fu	Investment company	12/31/03	9.0	7.9	109.4	81.4	16	343706
IIF	Morgan Stanley India Investme	Investment company	12/31/03	6.4	2.6	370.8	367.0	34	4820301
MOT	Motorola, Inc.	Communications electronics	12/31/03	27058.0	2086.0	29982.0	12689.0	738	1367791164
MOV	Movado Group, Inc.	Jewelry	1/31/04	330.2	22.8	391.0	274.7	55	7721173
MPS	MPS Group, Inc. (United Stat	Services	12/31/03	1096.0	256.2	893.2	793.5	146	87521101
APF	MS Asia-Pac Fd Inc (New)	Investment company	12/31/03	6.3	1.8	444.0	439.8	46	12241727
MSM	MSC Industrial Direct Co. In	Machinery & equipment	8/31/03	844.7	52.1	603.9	510.4	109	32604043
MLI	Mueller Industries, Inc.	Metal products	12/27/03	999.1	95.7	1029.6	814.9	141	25205725
MUI	Muni Intermediate Duration Fu	Investment company	7/17/03	—	—	0.7	0.1	—	—
MNE	Muni New York Intermediate Du	Investment company	7/17/03	—	—	0.2	0.1	—	—
MHF	Municipal High Income Fund,	Investment company	10/31/03	13.2	11.9	166.4	165.8	15	204975
MMA	Municipal Mortgage & Equity	Financial services	12/31/03	172.0	66.1	2224.8	641.8	45	854814
MEN	Munienhanced Fund, Inc.	Investment company	1/31/04	27.2	23.8	498.7	497.5	17	270622
MFL	Muniholdings FL Insured Fd	Investment company	8/31/03	49.7	43.3	931.2	566.0	14	484645
MUH	Muniholdings Fund II, Inc.	Investment company	7/31/03	14.7	12.8	236.5	149.3	10	153400
MUR	Murphy Oil Corp.	Oil	12/31/03	5345.2	720.4	4460.3	1950.9	261	66075139
MVC	MVC Capital	Investment company	10/31/03	2.9	d4.5	137.9	137.0	19	3606775
MYE	Myers Industries Inc.	—	12/31/03	661.1	109.2	522.7	294.5	89	15548982
MYK	Mykrolis Corp.	—	12/31/03	185.9	d11.2	269.8	223.0	119	36252123
MYL	Mylan Laboratories, Inc. (Un	Drugs	3/31/04	1374.6	426.8	1817.3	1659.8	384	123776068
NC	Nacco Industries Inc.	Conglomerate	12/31/03	2472.6	114.8	1796.9	679.3	67	3723851
NTE	Nam Tai Electronics, Inc.	Consumer electronics	—	—	—	—	—	37	4317867
NSH	Nashua Corp. (MA)	Office equipment & supplies	12/31/03	289.8	20.9	164.4	73.9	21	3570601
NTG	Natco Group Inc	Oil service & equipment	12/31/03	281.5	1.0	216.3	92.5	39	7638800
NAU	National Australia Bank Ltd.	—	9/30/03	14459.0	3955.0	375992.0	27211.0	21	5948440
NCC	National City Corp (United St	Banking - Midwest	12/31/03	9593.8	2117.1	113057.7	9328.7	493	307315412
NFP	National Financial Partners	Financial services	12/31/03	479.6	47.9	671.6	465.3	—	—
NFG	National Fuel Gas Co. (NJ)	Natural gas distributor	9/30/03	2035.5	187.8	3727.9	1137.4	201	36489525
NHI	National Health Investors, In	Real estate investment trust	12/31/03	162.5	46.8	613.6	398.9	74	7308660
NPK	National Presto Inds., Inc.	Appliances & utensils	12/31/03	133.8	17.3	279.0	246.3	65	3202677
NVH	National R.V. Holdings, Inc.	—	12/31/03	342.0	d0.5	117.9	88.0	29	7732493
NOV	National-Oilwell Inc.	Oil service & equipment	12/31/03	2004.9	193.5	2108.5	1090.4	232	73844888
NFS	Nationwide Financial Svcs In	Life Insurance	12/31/03	3935.4	398.4	111027.3	4875.4	173	27366199
NHP	Nationwide Health Properties	Real estate investment trust	12/31/03	161.7	56.0	1384.6	602.4	138	27877892
NRP	Natural Resources Partners L	Coal	12/31/03	85.5	46.7	503.9	—	23	645327
NCI	Navigant Consulting, Inc.	Services	12/31/03	317.8	284.2	213.5	188.8	75	27828589
NAV	Navistar International Corp.	—	10/31/03	307.0	d6795.0	5703.0	310.0	206	75636854
NTY	NBTY Inc.	Drugs	9/30/03	1192.5	81.6	1204.4	514.8	189	43308256
NCS	NCI Building Systems, Inc. (	—	11/1/03	898.1	22.8	708.2	331.8	72	13542111
NCR	NCR Corp. (New)	Computer services	12/31/03	5598.0	2394.0	5480.0	1875.0	266	71410877
NMG B	Neiman-Marcus Group, Inc.	Specialty stores	8/2/03	3098.1	124.1	1999.5	1137.8	56	11850728
NMG A	Neiman-Marcus Group, Inc.	Specialty stores	8/2/03	3098.1	124.1	1999.5	1137.8	146	30115603
NNI	Nelnet Inc	Financial services	12/31/03	492.8	27.1	11931.5	305.5	—	—
NWK	Network Equipment Technologi	Telecommunications	3/26/04	18.9	d98.8	164.6	123.7	78	18806461
MFE	Networks Associates, Inc. (U	Computer services	12/31/03	936.3	345.9	1726.5	888.1	—	—
HYB	New America High Income Fd	Investment company	12/31/03	23.9	21.5	343.9	334.7	22	705943
NEW	New Century Financial Corp.	Financial services	12/31/03	976.0	320.1	5623.0	542.0	—	—
NJR	New Jersey Resources Corp (U	Natural gas distributor	9/30/03	2544.4	65.4	1567.7	418.9	136	12581747
NXL	New Plan Excel Realty Trust,	Real estate investment trust	12/31/03	479.9	156.0	3246.1	1586.1	205	34203584
NYB	New York Community Bancorp I	Banking - Northeast	12/31/03	847.3	369.8	23441.3	2868.7	248	56603516
NYT	New York Times Co.	Newspapers	12/31/03	p3227.2	p3227.2	—	—	360	91370642
NCT	Newcastle Investment Corp (Ne	Real estate investment trust	12/31/03	169.2	62.4	3498.2	539.4	36	5187991
NWL	Newell Rubbermaid, Inc.	Hardware & tools	12/31/03	7750.0	198.4	7108.9	2016.3	442	221826988
NFX	Newfield Exploration Co.	Oil	12/31/03	1017.0	604.2	2427.8	1395.0	222	41484062
NEM	Newmont Mining Corp. (Holding	Mining & processing	12/31/03	3214.1	1565.9	10507.1	7384.9	414	255196880
NR	Newpark Resources, Inc.	Oil service & equipment	12/31/03	373.2	247.1	501.8	314.0	120	67525405
NWS A	News Corp. Ltd. (The)	Newspapers	6/30/03	29913.0	1808.0	67747.0	38721.0	—	—
NXY	Nexen Inc.	Oil producer	12/31/03	—	—	—	—	45	80979541
GAS	Nicor, Inc.	Oil service & equipment	12/31/03	2662.7	109.8	3797.2	754.6	247	21571048

T26

1st	2nd	3rd	2004	2003	2002	P/E RATIO	2004	2003	2002	AV. YLD. %	AMOUNT	PAYABLE	2004 High	2004 Low
0.41	—	—	—	2.11	2.21	—	—	—	—	—	—	—	52.30	29.79
—	—	—	—	10.15	8.74	—	—	0.02	—	—	—	12/10/03	17.50	7.13
—	—	—	—	17.36	15.46	—	0.31	1.79	2.79	1.9	0.0406A	1/14/05	22.37	10.71
0.32	—	—	—	1.07	1.35	—	0.99	1.16	1.20	10.7	0.18Q	4/29/05	10.80	7.66
—	—	—	—	6.76	6.32	—	0.39	0.40	0.42	6.5	0.032M	4/29/05	6.56	5.50
1.31	—	—	—	4.99	6.04	—	0.23	0.11	0.10	0.4	0.075Q	3/1/05	78.95	39.27
0.66	—	—	—	1.56	1.83	—	—	—	—	—	100%	5/18/05	73.50	25.62
p0.36	—	—	—	—	—	—	0.36	—	—	1.4	0.09Q	4/15/05	30.45	21.62
—	—	—	—	2.54	2.09	—	0.31	0.10	—	0.7	0.07Q	4/29/05	61.35	23.50
d0.36	—	—	—	1.20	d1.72	—	—	—	0.20	—	0.05Q	5/13/05	4.99	0.71
—	d0.04	—	—	d2.11	d1.51	—	—	—	—	—	100%	5/11/00	18.25	7.99
0.07	—	—	—	d0.07	d0.03	—	2.34	2.34	2.34	7.2	0.585Q	4/29/05	41.74	23.31
d0.16	—	—	—	d4.93	d2.25	—	—	—	—	—	0.08A	4/11/01	20.60	7.30
d0.27	—	—	—	d2.43	d1.61	—	—	—	—	—	—	—	12.97	2.15
d0.39	—	—	—	d0.85	d0.72	—	—	—	—	—	50%	5/27/98	4.90	1.29
d0.47	—	—	—	d5.49	d0.56	—	—	0.02	0.04	—	0.01Q	6/12/03	4.48	1.86
0.10	—	—	—	0.22	0.38	—	—	—	—	—	—	—	11.48	2.99
0.55	—	—	—	2.06	1.67	—	—	—	0.11	—	0.00Q	2/27/02	57.20	32.31
0.64	—	—	—	2.06	1.68	—	2.35	2.24	2.17	5.1	0.6275Q	5/2/05	63.76	28.00
0.43	—	—	—	1.31	0.85	—	0.37	1.72	0.22	0.6	0.10Q	3/10/05	95.75	21.37
0.61	—	—	—	3.26	2.61	—	0.20	0.10	0.10	0.4	0.05Q	3/15/05	68.18	38.07
—	—	—	—	—	—	—	1.41	0.71	—	5.9	—	5/2/05	26.64	20.80
d0.01	—	—	—	0.01	d0.06	—	0.18	0.18	0.20	3.9	0.05Q	5/12/05	6.00	3.24
—	—	—	—	1.19	1.02	—	0.60	0.54	0.50	2.5	0.1625Q	3/3/05	33.99	14.99
0.98	—	—	—	4.62	4.39	—	—	—	—	—	3-for-2	12/4/97	92.44	47.94
0.43	—	—	—	1.88	1.48	—	—	—	—	—	—	—	49.45	23.25
0.40	—	—	—	0.75	1.51	—	0.20	—	—	1.0	0.06Q	3/15/05	31.25	10.36
d0.29	0.58	—	—	d0.04	0.49	—	0.55	0.50	0.48	1.5	0.17Q	4/29/05	56.44	16.40
—	—	—	—	19.64	19.43	—	1.23	1.29	1.33	6.8	0.29Q	4/29/05	19.56	16.46
0.68	—	—	—	2.39	1.83	—	0.15	0.09	0.09	0.2	0.055Q	6/15/05	87.72	41.88
0.48	p0.53	—	—	1.84	1.67	—	—	—	—	—	3-for-2	4/1/05	57.47	30.60
1.11	—	—	—	3.45	2.69	—	1.00	0.92	0.92	2.1	0.27Q	4/29/05	48.92	18.11
1.11	—	—	—	3.45	2.69	—	—	—	—	—	—	—	10.85	9.55
—	—	—	—	29.46	20.40	—	7.12	0.61	—	27.4	2.597A	1/7/05	35.27	16.72
—	—	—	—	10.24	10.08	—	0.81	0.63	0.73	9.2	0.18Q	4/15/05	10.10	7.51
—	—	—	—	15.67	10.08	—	0.19	0.01	—	1.5	0.0679A	1/7/05	17.87	7.89
—	—	—	—	7.91	6.32	—	0.52	0.55	0.76	6.3	0.135Q	4/15/05	10.40	6.20
—	—	—	—	6.96	5.46	—	0.59	0.48	0.82	9.5	0.045M	4/15/05	6.84	5.62
—	—	—	—	22.95	11.98	—	0.20	0.02	0.21	1.0	0.0714S	1/7/05	31.84	9.05
0.25	—	—	—	0.38	d1.09	—	0.16	0.16	0.16	1.1	0.04Q	4/15/05	20.87	7.91
0.06	—	—	—	1.84	1.65	—	0.15	0.09	0.06	0.7	0.05Q	4/29/05	32.50	12.99
0.05	—	—	—	0.21	d0.12	—	—	—	—	—	3-for-1	3/27/96	12.55	4.91
—	—	—	—	12.29	8.57	—	0.10	0.01	—	1.0	0.0938U	1/7/05	12.98	7.00
0.24	0.27	—	—	0.77	0.51	—	0.34	0.10	—	1.3	0.12Q	4/11/05	37.00	15.99
0.49	—	—	—	1.19	1.92	—	6.90	—	—	19.9	0.10Q	3/15/05	44.75	24.62
—	—	—	—	14.32	—	—	1.05	0.29	—	7.7	0.072M	4/28/05	14.90	12.45
—	—	—	—	14.32	—	—	0.72	0.24	—	5.2	0.06M	4/28/05	15.07	12.52
—	—	—	—	7.92	8.16	—	0.53	0.56	0.57	7.0	0.039M	5/27/05	8.10	6.96
0.02	—	—	—	1.61	1.13	—	1.84	1.79	1.75	7.6	0.4725Q	2/11/05	27.40	21.25
—	—	—	—	11.83	11.65	—	0.73	0.72	0.69	6.8	0.061M	4/28/05	11.54	9.83
—	—	—	—	15.04	15.41	—	1.03	0.96	0.95	7.2	0.083M	4/28/05	15.61	12.80
—	—	—	—	13.46	13.51	—	1.04	1.00	0.88	7.7	0.087M	4/28/05	14.85	12.25
0.86	—	—	—	3.25	1.06	—	0.85	0.80	0.78	1.3	0.225Q	6/1/05	87.38	41.65
8.76	8.85	—	—	8.48	11.84	—	0.12	—	0.04	1.4	0.12A	10/29/04	9.75	7.92
0.29	—	—	—	0.54	0.80	—	0.19	0.18	0.18	1.5	0.05Q	4/1/05	14.89	9.50
0.16	—	—	—	d0.20	d0.80	—	—	—	—	—	—	—	17.98	6.74
d0.55	—	—	—	1.21	0.96	—	0.12	0.10	0.07	0.6	0.03Q	4/15/05	25.99	14.24
—	—	—	—	6.07	6.05	—	1.67	1.26	0.97	2.2	0.4525Q	3/15/05	113.03	40.50
—	—	—	—	—	—	—	0.41	0.97	0.44	1.9	0.33Q	1/21/06	34.24	8.39
0.15	—	—	—	0.02	0.39	—	—	—	—	—	0.01Q	5/12/00	11.65	7.95
d0.03	—	—	—	d0.06	0.24	—	—	—	—	—	—	—	9.25	5.65
—	—	—	—	2.44	2.02	—	1.97	1.97	1.97	5.4	—	3/31/05	40.70	32.50
1.16	—	—	—	3.43	2.59	—	1.34	1.25	1.20	4.0	0.35Q	5/1/05	39.66	27.62
0.19	—	—	—	0.74	0.40	—	0.40	—	—	1.3	0.12Q	4/7/05	39.44	23.40
0.60	0.93	—	—	2.31	1.46	—	1.10	1.06	1.02	4.5	0.28Q	4/15/05	29.06	19.54
0.49	—	—	—	1.56	0.89	—	1.77	1.55	1.50	7.8	0.45Q	5/10/05	30.83	14.68
0.22	—	—	—	2.27	1.27	—	1.17	0.92	0.92	3.2	0.92A	3/11/05	46.70	26.15
0.06	—	—	—	d0.84	d2.19	—	—	—	—	—	3-for-2	7/24/98	18.55	3.90
0.13	—	—	—	0.90	0.89	—	—	—	—	—	2-for-1	11/18/97	37.38	18.06
0.78	—	—	—	2.61	1.06	—	0.67	0.52	0.50	2.1	0.19Q	4/15/05	39.04	24.30
0.20	—	—	—	0.87	0.75	—	1.48	1.57	1.84	8.1	0.37Q	3/4/05	23.87	12.85
0.47	—	—	—	1.59	0.28	—	2.38	2.01	—	5.9	0.6625Q	2/14/05	57.98	22.05
0.16	—	—	—	0.40	0.21	—	—	—	—	—	3-for-2	4/1/98	27.06	5.30
d0.34	0.54	—	—	d0.21	d7.88	—	—	—	—	—	0.01U	11/15/01	52.95	23.63
0.34	0.60	—	—	1.19	1.41	—	—	—	—	—	200%	4/3/98	39.60	15.49
0.29	0.39	—	—	1.20	1.72	—	—	—	—	—	2-for-1	7/22/98	39.45	15.51
d0.05	—	—	—	0.61	1.27	—	—	—	—	—	2-for-1	1/21/05	70.60	18.34
1.16	1.21	1.40	—	2.60	2.08	—	0.52	—	—	1.0	0.15Q	5/13/05	52.02	51.60
1.16	1.21	1.40	—	2.60	2.08	—	0.52	—	—	1.0	0.15Q	5/13/05	73.40	27.08
0.17	—	—	—	0.60	1.08	—	—	—	—	—	—	—	27.00	16.76
—	—	—	—	d0.02	d0.39	—	—	—	—	—	—	—	14.89	6.01
0.32	—	—	—	0.36	0.80	—	—	—	—	—	3-for-2	5/29/98	33.55	15.79
—	—	—	—	2.19	2.61	—	0.21	0.21	0.30	10.3	0.0175M	4/29/05	2.32	1.75
2.06	—	—	—	6.56	4.62	—	—	—	—	—	1.55Q	4/29/05	66.95	51.30
0.87	1.82	—	—	2.38	2.09	—	1.30	1.24	1.20	3.4	0.34Q	4/1/05	44.55	31.81
0.30	—	—	—	1.07	0.06	—	1.65	1.65	1.65	7.1	0.4125Q	4/15/05	27.87	18.69
0.48	—	—	—	1.65	1.25	—	1.03	0.66	0.43	3.3	0.25Q	2/15/05	44.81	17.60
0.38	—	—	—	—	p1.98	—	0.61	0.57	0.53	1.4	0.155Q	3/18/05	49.23	38.47
0.59	—	—	—	2.05	1.65	—	2.30	1.84	—	9.2	0.625Q	4/27/05	33.89	15.95
0.12	—	—	—	d0.17	1.16	—	0.84	0.84	0.84	3.7	0.21Q	3/11/05	26.41	19.05
1.38	—	—	—	3.77	1.61	—	—	—	—	—	2-for-1	12/30/96	65.83	33.07
0.20	—	—	—	1.23	0.39	—	0.30	0.17	0.09	0.8	0.10Q	3/24/05	49.98	26.15
0.02	—	—	—	0.01	0.01	—	—	—	—	—	2-for-1	11/26/97	6.80	4.00
p0.28	p0.27	p0.32	—	0.34	d2.43	—	0.20	0.17	0.14	1.1	0.05B	4/20/05	18.75	17.02
—	—	—	—	—	—	—	0.20	0.15	0.15	0.6	2-for-1	5/17/05	46.50	19.90
0.44	—	—	—	2.48	2.88	—	1.86	1.85	1.82	5.6	0.465Q	5/1/05	38.80	27.32

SYMBOL	COMPANY	NATURE OF BUSINESS	FISCAL YEAR-END	TOTAL REV. $MILL	NET INCOME $MILL	TOTAL ASSETS $MILL	NET STK EQUITY $MILL	NO. OF INST.	INST. HOLDINGS (SHARES)
NI	NiSource Inc. (Holding Co.)	Electric power	12/31/03	6246.6	425.7	16567.0	4415.9	359	186563092
NL	NL Industries, Inc.	Chemicals	12/31/03	1008.2	63.7	1143.5	200.9	68	4249860
NBL	Noble Energy, Inc. (United S	Oil producer	12/31/03	1011.0	231.5	2262.1	1073.6	231	49144248
NOK	Nokia Corp.	Telecommunications	12/31/03	—	—	—	—	683	844232468
NRD	Noranda Inc.	Mining & processing	12/31/03	—	—	—	—	39	16157003
JWN	Nordstrom, Inc.	Specialty stores	1/31/04	6491.7	242.8	4465.7	1634.0	233	76957346
NSC	Norfolk Southern Corp.	Freight transportation	12/31/03	6468.0	411.0	20596.0	6976.0	433	264779430
NHY	Norsk Hydro ASA (Norway)	—	12/31/03	—	—	—	—	63	11700322
NTL	Nortel Inversora S.A. (Argent	Telecommunications	12/31/03	—	—	—	—	2	543919
NT	Nortel Networks Corp (Holding	Telecommunications	12/31/03	p9807.0	p9807.0	—	—	385	1683292479
NRT	North European Oil Royalty T	Real estate investment trust	10/31/03	18.2	17.4	4.1	0.0	31	720230
NFB	North Fork Bancorp, Inc (NY)	Banking - Northeast	12/31/03	1266.1	396.4	20961.6	1478.5	380	88524031
NU	Northeast Utilities	Electric power	12/31/03	6069.2	126.7	11039.2	2264.1	182	85304452
NBP	Northern Border Partners L.P	Natural gas	12/31/03	555.9	d92.0	2362.1	—	109	4287246
NOC	Northrop Grumman Corp	—	12/31/03	7856.0	—	30523.0	15785.0	506	144084862
NWN	Northwest Natural Gas Co. (U	Natural gas distributor	12/31/03	611.3	46.0	1567.4	506.3	126	10420787
NCX	Nova Chemicals Corp.	Chemicals	12/31/03	—	—	—	—	67	43088165
NVS	Novartis AG Basel (Switzerla	Drugs	12/31/03	—	—	—	—	234	72431215
NFI	NovaStar Financial, Inc.	Financial services	12/31/03	170.4	139.8	1400.0	300.2	64	6344450
NVO	Novo-Nordisk A/S	Drugs	12/31/03	—	—	—	—	58	6173321
NRG	NRG Energy Inc (New)	Electric power	12/31/03	152.1	35.2	8754.3	2437.3	—	—
NSS	NS Group, Inc. (United State	Steel producer	12/31/03	259.0	d17.3	133.2	88.6	47	12711041
NST	Nstar	Electric power	12/31/03	2914.1	181.6	6320.7	1361.6	207	22430048
NUS	NU Skin Enterprises, Inc.	Cosmetics & toiletries	12/31/03	986.5	465.5	609.1	290.2	104	25725537
NUE	Nucor Corp.	Steel producer	12/31/03	6265.8	62.8	4401.2	2342.1	330	58567163
NCA	Nuveen California Municipal	Investment company	8/31/03	14.2	12.5	251.0	250.7	14	152173
JDD	Nuveen Diversified Dividend a	Investment company	12/31/03	4.2	3.6	431.4	304.4	—	—
NAD	Nuveen Dividend Advantage Mu	Investment company	10/31/03	48.3	43.0	891.8	595.3	18	357725
NQF	Nuveen FL Inv. Qual. Mun Fd.	Investment company	6/30/03	21.2	18.1	400.1	261.9	12	262533
NUF	Nuveen Fla Qual Inc Munic Fd	Investment company	6/30/03	18.1	15.4	351.0	224.3	11	218871
NIO	Nuveen Ins Mun Opportunity F	Investment company	10/31/03	101.1	86.2	1975.6	1288.1	49	917068
NPX	Nuveen Insd Prem Incm Mun Fd	Investment company	10/31/03	41.9	35.7	800.7	531.0	29	457181
NQI	Nuveen Insd Quality Mun Fd	Investment company	10/31/03	49.0	41.8	917.0	598.1	31	570060
NFL	Nuveen Insured Florida Premiu	Investment company	6/30/03	17.6	14.9	361.2	237.5	15	282083
JNC	Nuveen Investments Inc	Securities brokerage	12/31/03	452.0	151.7	923.7	464.0	97	13046264
NQM	Nuveen Invt Quality Mun Fd	Investment company	10/31/03	46.5	39.7	861.3	559.6	26	504499
NMA	Nuveen Mun Advantage Fd Inc	Investment company	10/31/03	56.7	48.7	1029.9	671.1	30	566089
NMO	Nuveen Mun Mkt Opp Fd Inc	Investment company	10/31/03	55.6	47.1	1068.8	688.0	31	507082
NAN	Nuveen New York Dividend Adva	Investment company	9/30/03	10.9	9.9	213.0	143.9	7	51900
NQJ	Nuveen NJ Inv. Qual. Mun. Fd.	Investment company	6/30/03	25.0	21.2	489.6	317.0	14	388778
NNY	Nuveen NY Mun Value Fd Inc	Investment company	9/30/03	7.9	6.6	150.5	150.4	15	314929
NPP	Nuveen Perfomance Plus Mun F	Investment company	10/31/03	74.9	64.0	1405.6	925.5	41	917613
JQC	Nuveen Preferred & Convertib	Investment company	7/31/03	6.5	5.4	2070.2	1950.6	—	—
NIF	Nuveen Premier Ins Mun Inc F	Investment company	10/31/03	24.1	20.4	465.3	303.9	16	153000
NPF	Nuveen Premier Mun Inc Fund	Investment company	10/31/03	25.1	21.3	479.6	304.0	15	501558
NPI	Nuveen Premium Incm Mun Fd	Investment company	10/31/03	78.5	66.9	1487.3	948.3	33	851953
NPM	Nuveen Premium Incm Mun Fd 2	Investment company	10/31/03	51.8	44.3	990.3	619.9	29	1037621
NPT	Nuveen Premium Incm Mun Fd 4	Investment company	10/31/03	48.2	40.3	907.9	568.8	37	718047
NQU	Nuveen Quality Income Mun Fd	Investment company	10/31/03	67.5	57.7	1269.8	815.3	33	1073475
JTP	Nuveen Quality Preferred Inc	Investment company	7/31/03	100.9	83.7	1356.7	1347.7	19	401637
JPS	Nuveen Quality Preferred Inc	Investment company	7/31/03	144.0	120.9	2592.5	2589.8	23	622953
JHP	Nuveen Quality Preferred Inc	Investment company	7/31/03	19.1	15.9	507.1	505.5	3	48841
NQS	Nuveen Select Quality Mun Fd	Investment company	10/31/03	43.0	36.5	799.0	519.4	26	516706
NSL	Nuveen Senior Income Fund	Investment company	7/30/03	22.3	18.1	382.8	279.2	9	986437
NYM	NYMAGIC, Inc.	Insurance	12/31/03	120.8	36.5	875.1	244.3	29	2971828
OO	Oakley, Inc.	Photo & optical	12/31/03	521.5	155.9	404.6	326.6	88	20781655
OXY	Occidental Petroleum Corp	Specialty chemicals	12/31/03	9447.0	1658.0	18168.0	7929.0	419	291385747
OII	Oceaneering Intl, Inc.	Oil service & equipment	12/31/03	639.2	29.3	585.1	359.4	137	19640056
OTL	Octel Corp.	Chemicals	12/31/03	462.2	131.8	739.2	430.2	65	9150076
OCN	Ocwen Financial Corp.	Banking - South	12/31/03	201.6	4.8	1240.1	317.3	55	21177011
ORH	Odyssey Re Holdings Corp. (Un	Property & casualty insurance	12/31/03	2301.9	249.2	6460.1	1390.2	91	20304785
ODP	Office Depot, Inc.	Specialty stores	12/27/03	12358.6	1097.9	6045.1	2794.1	363	251865499
OLG	Offshore Logistics, Inc. (Uni	—	3/31/04	567.6	167.3	1044.9	446.1	129	18255999
OGE	OGE Energy Corp.	Electric power	12/31/03	3779.0	135.6	4584.7	1201.6	186	26143498
OIS	Oil States International, In	—	12/31/03	723.7	103.1	508.2	455.1	104	21791024
ODC	Oil-Dri Corp. of America	Pollution control	7/31/03	173.0	3.1	118.4	69.0	16	2867670
ONB	Old National Bancorp (Evansv	Banking - Midwest	12/31/03	661.9	70.4	9353.9	715.5	79	6883342
ORI	Old Republic International Co	Insurance	12/31/03	3285.7	460.1	9711.6	3553.5	284	87250728
OLN	Olin Corp.	Chemicals	12/31/03	—	d1580.0	1390.0	176.0	171	43293748
OHI	Omega Healthcare Investors, I	Real estate investment trust	12/31/03	86.3	29.3	725.1	436.2	45	2463167
OME	Omega Protein Corp.	—	12/31/03	117.9	5.8	176.8	145.2	28	5769457
OCR	Omnicare Inc.	Drugs	12/31/03	3499.2	194.4	3372.6	1676.0	240	89037283
OMC	Omnicom Group, Inc.	—	12/31/03	8621.4	1797.7	14499.5	3466.1	507	153198317
OMN	Omnova Solutions, Inc.	Chemicals	11/30/03	682.6	d8.8	438.9	67.7	79	23457697
OLP	One Liberty Properties, Inc.	Real estate investment trust	12/31/03	19.8	10.7	259.1	146.0	22	1749378
OKE	Oneok Inc. (New)	Natural gas	12/31/03	2999.0	214.3	6314.0	1241.4	203	55405186
ORB	Orbital Sciences Corp.	—	12/31/03	581.5	24.1	389.9	166.9	100	31467922
OS	Oregon Steel Mills, Inc.	Steel producer	12/31/03	723.3	d227.4	653.3	198.2	58	18308930
OFG	Oriental Financial Group, Inc	—	6/30/03	190.7	51.3	3039.5	201.7	57	3305720
OCA	Orthodontic Centers of Amer	Services	12/31/03	375.4	107.5	643.4	492.7	—	—
OSK	Oshkosh Truck Corp.	Transportation	9/30/03	1926.0	75.6	1054.0	518.9	176	12396443
OSI	Outback Steakhouse, Inc.	Restaurants	12/31/03	2744.4	170.2	1474.8	1026.3	257	55990595
OSG	Overseas Shipholding Grp Inc	Freight transportation	12/31/03	431.1	328.3	1991.7	917.1	95	16018455
OMI	Owens & Minor, Inc.	Medical & dental equipment	12/31/03	4244.1	53.6	1045.7	410.4	151	30358970
OI	Owens-Illinois, Inc.	Plastics & plastic products	12/31/03	6158.2	d2081.5	9413.9	1003.4	145	103919111
PAI	Pacific Amer. Income Shs. Inc	Investment company	12/31/03	10.1	8.7	166.9	155.1	16	360366
PPX	Pacific Energy Partners L.P.	Natural gas distributor	12/31/03	135.8	40.4	571.0	—	17	378512
PHS	Pacificare Health Systems In	Services	12/31/03	11008.5	242.7	4123.1	1851.5	184	33463889
PKG	Packaging Corp of America	Containers	12/31/03	1735.5	d14.4	1816.6	797.5	145	59255208
PTV	Pactiv Corp.	Plastics & plastic products	12/31/03	3138.0	206.0	4568.0	2002.0	326	129155108
PLL	Pall Corp.	Pollution control	8/2/03	1613.6	91.2	1991.7	934.5	296	98648947
PNP	Pan Pacific Retail Propertie	Real estate investment trust	12/31/03	264.6	101.6	1809.1	892.3	146	32549446
PRX	Par Pharmaceutical Companies	Drugs	12/31/03	661.7	122.5	762.8	395.1	—	—
PTC	Par Technology Corp.	Computer services	12/31/03	79.5	d57.4	73.7	55.2	8	762945
PKE	Park Electrochemical Corp.	Electronic components	2/29/04	194.2	d3.2	285.8	243.9	101	14479515
PKD	Parker Drilling Co. (United S	Oil service & equipment	12/31/03	313.8	d67.6	841.2	192.8	109	35587360

T28

| EARNINGS PER SHARE | | | | | | P/E | DIVIDENDS PER SHARE | | | AV. YLD. | DIV. DECLARED | | PRICE RANGE |
| QUARTERLY | | | ANNUAL | | | RATIO | | | | % | | | 2004 |
1st	2nd	3rd	2004	2003	2002		2004	2003	2002		AMOUNT	PAYABLE	
0.82	—	—	—	1.63	2.00	—	0.92	1.10	1.16	4.6	0.23Q	5/20/05	22.82 - 16.94
0.08	—	—	—	1.33	0.76	—	—	0.80	3.30	—	0.00Q	3/29/05	23.17 - 9.65
1.29	—	—	—	1.56	0.31	—	0.20	0.17	0.16	0.4	0.05Q	2/22/05	64.60 - 33.20
—	—	—	—	—	—	—	0.36	0.30	0.24	2.1	—	4/29/05	23.52 - 10.89
—	—	—	—	—	—	—	0.48	0.64	0.80	3.5	0.12Q	3/15/05	18.87 - 8.43
0.48	—	—	—	1.76	0.66	—	0.48	0.41	0.38	1.5	0.13Q	3/15/05	47.32 - 16.20
0.40	—	—	—	1.05	1.18	—	0.36	0.30	0.26	1.3	0.11Q	3/10/05	36.69 - 18.56
—	—	—	—	—	—	—	1.39	1.32	1.04	2.3	2.72165A	4/29/05	83.62 - 37.99
—	—	—	—	—	—	—	—	—	—	—	0.0139U	5/11/01	7.94 - 1.69
—	—	—	—	—	pd0.93	—	—	—	—	—	0.01875Q	6/29/01	8.49 - 2.08
0.46	—	—	—	1.95	1.89	—	1.59	1.95	1.89	6.8	0.54Q	2/23/05	25.99 - 20.59
0.68	—	—	—	2.60	2.58	—	0.82	0.72	0.65	2.2	0.22Q	5/16/05	45.75 - 27.20
0.53	—	—	—	0.95	1.18	—	0.63	0.57	0.53	3.7	0.1625Q	3/31/05	20.27 - 13.92
0.73	—	—	—	d2.16	2.44	—	3.20	3.20	3.20	7.5	0.80Q	2/14/05	49.54 - 35.70
1.25	—	—	—	4.32	5.72	—	0.89	0.80	0.80	1.2	0.26Q	6/11/05	105.00 - 49.54
1.24	—	—	—	1.76	1.62	—	1.30	1.27	1.26	4.4	0.325Q	5/13/05	34.13 - 24.50
—	—	—	—	—	—	—	0.40	0.40	0.40	1.2	0.10Q	8/15/05	47.72 - 17.95
—	—	—	—	—	—	—	0.78	0.71	0.46	1.8	0.88322U	4/6/05	50.77 - 36.58
1.17	—	—	—	4.91	2.25	—	5.35	4.59	1.58	10.8	1.25Q	1/14/05	70.29 - 28.75
—	—	—	—	—	—	—	0.52	0.38	0.28	1.3	0.61725A	3/22/05	55.28 - 27.45
0.28	—	—	—	0.10	—	—	—	—	—	—	—	—	36.18 - 18.85
0.24	—	—	—	d0.83	d1.90	—	—	—	—	—	0.03Q	3/27/92	29.94 - 6.72
0.93	—	—	—	3.40	3.03	—	2.22	2.16	2.12	4.7	0.58Q	5/2/05	54.45 - 40.02
0.20	—	—	—	0.85	0.78	—	0.32	0.28	0.24	1.7	0.09Q	3/23/05	28.15 - 9.00
1.43	—	—	—	0.80	2.07	—	0.57	0.40	0.37	0.8	0.25Q	5/11/05	99.25 - 37.72
—	—	—	—	9.93	10.27	—	0.56	0.57	0.53	5.9	0.0385M	5/2/05	10.00 - 8.72
—	—	—	—	15.13	—	—	1.23	0.20	—	8.5	0.1025M	5/2/05	16.50 - 12.45
—	—	—	—	15.17	14.94	—	1.03	1.00	0.95	6.9	0.0825M	5/2/05	16.46 - 13.25
—	—	—	—	15.87	15.19	—	1.01	1.19	1.07	6.6	0.0775M	5/2/05	17.40 - 13.41
—	—	—	—	15.75	15.23	—	0.99	1.14	1.16	6.6	0.076M	5/2/05	17.15 - 13.05
—	—	—	—	15.89	15.83	—	1.00	1.00	1.06	6.7	0.078M	5/2/05	16.77 - 13.32
—	—	—	—	14.24	14.17	—	0.88	0.86	0.83	6.4	0.07M	5/2/05	15.18 - 12.04
—	—	—	—	15.72	15.87	—	1.07	1.06	1.05	7.0	0.0815M	5/2/05	17.07 - 13.75
—	—	—	—	16.57	15.66	—	1.07	1.05	0.91	6.9	0.077M	5/2/05	17.50 - 13.71
0.42	—	—	—	1.50	1.29	—	0.69	0.56	0.50	2.2	0.18Q	3/15/05	39.50 - 22.27
—	—	—	—	15.65	15.63	—	1.11	1.00	0.98	7.6	0.081M	5/2/05	16.12 - 13.02
—	—	—	—	15.62	15.41	—	1.05	1.04	1.03	7.0	0.083M	5/2/05	16.42 - 13.42
—	—	—	—	15.11	14.60	—	0.95	0.95	0.92	6.8	0.076M	5/2/05	15.39 - 12.53
—	—	—	—	15.66	—	—	0.99	0.97	0.87	6.5	0.0825M	5/2/05	16.75 - 13.52
—	—	—	—	15.65	15.07	—	1.07	1.14	0.98	7.1	0.077M	5/2/05	16.82 - 13.50
—	—	—	—	9.95	10.16	—	0.43	0.46	0.48	4.7	0.0355M	5/2/05	9.55 - 8.49
—	—	—	—	15.45	15.38	—	0.99	0.96	0.93	6.8	0.078M	5/2/05	15.94 - 13.01
—	—	—	—	13.83	14.32	—	1.19	0.49	—	8.9	0.093M	5/2/05	15.20 - 11.50
—	—	—	—	15.69	15.59	—	1.06	1.00	0.99	7.0	0.0785M	5/2/05	16.89 - 13.41
—	—	—	—	15.13	15.23	—	1.11	0.99	1.05	7.8	0.074M	5/2/05	15.79 - 12.85
—	—	—	—	14.87	14.87	—	0.96	0.96	0.92	6.9	0.077M	5/2/05	15.49 - 12.46
—	—	—	—	15.09	15.27	—	1.08	0.98	1.07	7.6	0.0785M	5/2/05	15.55 - 12.75
—	—	—	—	13.15	13.46	—	0.85	0.87	0.85	7.2	0.068M	5/2/05	13.85 - 11.10
—	—	—	—	15.04	14.70	—	0.97	0.96	0.96	6.9	0.0775M	5/2/05	15.47 - 12.63
—	—	—	—	14.10	14.32	—	1.23	1.26	0.52	8.7	0.097M	5/2/05	16.23 - 12.09
—	—	—	—	14.97	14.32	—	1.45	1.36	0.21	10.0	0.099M	5/2/05	16.66 - 12.37
—	—	—	—	14.38	14.32	—	1.29	1.26	—	9.2	0.10M	5/2/05	15.77 - 13.01
—	—	—	—	15.33	15.00	—	1.00	1.06	0.94	6.9	0.08M	5/2/05	15.77 - 13.01
—	—	—	—	7.84	7.38	—	0.53	0.52	0.58	6.0	0.051M	5/2/05	10.20 - 7.51
0.28	—	—	—	1.74	3.08	—	0.24	0.18	—	1.0	0.06Q	4/6/05	28.85 - 18.46
0.06	—	—	—	0.56	0.59	—	0.15	0.14	—	1.2	0.15A	10/29/04	16.18 - 7.99
1.23	—	—	—	4.11	3.07	—	1.08	1.03	1.00	2.4	0.31Q	4/15/05	60.75 - 29.21
0.19	—	—	—	1.20	1.63	—	—	—	—	—	—	—	39.06 - 21.85
0.64	—	—	—	4.29	4.15	—	0.12	0.05	0.05	0.5	0.07S	4/1/05	32.00 - 13.35
0.10	—	—	—	0.07	d1.26	—	—	—	—	—	2-for-1	11/20/97	12.44 - 2.89
0.90	—	—	—	3.83	3.20	—	0.13	0.11	0.10	0.6	0.03125Q	3/31/05	27.80 - 17.03
0.37	—	—	—	0.96	0.98	—	—	—	—	—	3-for-2	4/1/99	19.50 - 11.74
—	—	—	—	2.29	1.77	—	—	—	—	—	0.12Q	12/15/83	38.39 - 18.05
0.11	—	—	—	1.65	1.04	—	1.33	1.33	1.33	6.0	0.3325Q	4/29/05	26.95 - 17.09
0.32	—	—	—	0.90	0.81	—	—	—	—	—	—	—	21.10 - 11.25
0.30	0.29	0.30	—	0.54	d0.19	—	0.41	0.37	0.36	2.9	0.11Q	6/10/05	18.50 - 9.50
0.29	—	—	—	1.05	1.75	—	0.72	0.69	0.62	3.0	0.19Q	3/15/05	26.75 - 20.88
0.57	—	—	—	2.51	2.15	—	0.50	1.11	0.42	2.1	0.13Q	3/15/05	27.55 - 21.13
0.04	—	—	—	0.02	d0.63	—	0.80	0.80	0.80	4.2	0.20Q	3/10/05	22.99 - 15.20
d1.29	—	—	—	0.08	d1.00	—	0.72	0.15	—	9.4	0.20Q	2/15/05	12.95 - 2.30
0.02	—	—	—	0.22	0.48	—	—	—	—	—	—	—	10.90 - 3.87
0.61	—	—	—	1.93	1.33	—	0.09	0.09	0.09	0.2	0.0225Q	3/21/05	47.80 - 25.05
0.72	—	—	—	3.59	3.44	—	0.88	0.80	0.80	1.2	0.225Q	4/7/05	88.82 - 52.98
d0.14	—	—	—	d2.10	0.18	—	—	—	—	—	0.05Q	5/31/01	6.79 - 2.95
0.23	—	—	—	1.18	1.04	—	0.99	1.65	1.29	5.0	0.33Q	4/1/05	24.05 - 15.87
1.04	—	—	—	2.13	1.30	—	0.88	0.68	0.62	3.8	0.25Q	2/15/05	28.99 - 17.15
0.18	—	—	—	0.35	0.31	—	—	—	—	—	—	—	13.99 - 5.17
0.28	—	—	—	d4.77	0.51	—	—	—	—	—	0.02Q	8/31/00	21.77 - 2.35
0.63	0.70	0.71	—	2.41	1.82	—	0.51	0.46	0.39	1.8	0.14Q	4/15/05	32.50 - 24.70
0.14	—	—	—	0.97	1.13	—	—	—	—	—	2-for-1	9/5/96	6.75 - 3.75
0.83	0.62	—	—	2.16	1.73	—	0.29	0.20	0.17	0.6	0.0875Q	2/14/05	69.05 - 27.72
0.62	—	—	—	2.17	2.03	—	0.52	0.49	0.12	1.3	0.13Q	3/4/05	50.55 - 32.20
1.98	—	—	—	3.47	d0.51	—	0.70	0.65	0.60	1.7	0.175Q	3/9/05	65.99 - 15.94
0.37	—	—	—	1.42	1.26	—	0.44	0.35	0.31	1.9	0.13Q	3/31/05	34.39 - 16.15
0.29	—	—	—	d6.89	d0.08	—	—	—	—	—	—	—	23.89 - 8.89
—	—	—	—	16.52	15.12	—	1.45	0.98	1.00	9.8	0.115Q	3/15/05	15.99 - 13.56
0.31	—	—	—	1.09	0.55	—	1.95	1.88	0.34	7.8	0.50Q	2/14/05	30.39 - 19.71
0.71	—	—	—	3.04	1.98	—	—	—	—	—	100%	1/20/04	69.50 - 21.60
d0.06	—	—	—	d0.14	0.45	—	0.60	—	—	2.9	0.25Q	4/15/05	25.02 - 16.77
—	—	—	—	1.21	1.37	—	—	—	—	—	—	—	25.73 - 19.55
0.19	0.20	—	—	0.83	0.59	—	0.36	0.36	0.44	1.6	0.10Q	2/23/05	29.80 - 15.51
0.59	—	—	—	2.23	1.94	—	2.17	2.03	1.90	4.4	0.59Q	3/15/05	62.72 - 36.60
0.85	—	—	—	3.54	2.40	—	—	—	—	—	—	—	43.75 - 32.10
0.09	—	—	—	0.32	0.32	—	—	—	—	—	—	—	12.35 - 4.89
—	—	—	—	1.50	d2.58	—	1.24	0.24	0.24	5.4	0.08Q	5/10/05	30.70 - 15.14
d0.09	—	—	—	d0.55	d0.44	—	—	—	—	—	0.01Q	2/17/87	4.49 - 1.96

SYMBOL	COMPANY	NATURE OF BUSINESS	FISCAL YEAR-END	TOTAL REV. $MILL	NET INCOME $MILL	TOTAL ASSETS $MILL	NET STK EQUITY $MILL	NO. OF INST.	INST. HOLDINGS (SHARES)
PH	Parker Hannifin Corp.	Electronic components	6/30/03	6410.6	196.3	5548.5	2520.9	299	88675546
PKY	Parkway Properties Inc. (Unit	Real estate	12/31/03	146.1	47.4	685.4	408.0	92	6327861
POG	Patina Oil & Gas Corp.	Oil	12/31/03	406.7	112.5	780.3	330.5	183	22910939
PXR	Paxar Corp. (New)	Printing & engraving	12/31/03	712.0	14.6	674.7	377.3	125	28648903
PSS	Payless Shoesource Inc. (DE)	Department stores	1/31/04	2783.3	1.2	1176.9	607.5	177	58159544
BTU	Peabody Energy Corp. (United	Coal	12/31/03	2829.5	38.3	4524.1	1132.1	150	48138466
PSO	Pearson Plc (United Kingdom)	Publishing	12/31/03	—	—	—	—	65	14026430
PDX	Pediatrix Medical Group Inc	Services	12/31/03	551.2	84.3	650.8	572.4	146	21467803
PNN A	Penn Engineering & Manufactur	Electronic components	12/31/03	190.7	37.2	231.0	191.6	13	1787412
PNN	Penn Engineering & Manufactur	Electronic components	12/31/03	190.7	37.2	231.0	191.6	44	11061393
PTA	Penn Treaty American Corp	Life insurance	12/31/03	364.1	45.8	1145.5	150.7	21	3006113
PVA	Penn Virginia Corp.	Oil	12/31/03	181.3	52.1	607.0	211.6	83	6753875
PVR	Penn Virginia Resource Partn	Coal	12/31/03	55.6	32.5	255.2	—	35	1308205
JCP	Penney (J.C.) Co.,Inc. (Hold	Department stores	1/31/04	17786.0	364.0	14606.0	5425.0	372	246218303
PEI	Pennsylvania Real Estate Inve	Real estate investment trust	12/31/03	183.4	48.5	2685.5	1023.6	78	4402456
PNR	Pentair, Inc.	Machine tools	12/31/03	2724.4	362.9	2559.3	1261.5	212	35688122
PGL	Peoples Energy Corp.	Natural gas distributor	9/30/03	2138.4	103.9	2928.5	848.0	223	16151178
PBY	Pep Boys-Manny, Moe & Jack (		1/31/04	2134.3	d11.4	1655.4	615.6	148	34634061
POM	Pepco Holdings Inc. (United	Electric power	12/31/03	7271.3	132.7	13358.2	3003.3	244	60098597
PBG	Pepsi Bottling Group Inc (Un	Soft drinks	12/27/03	10265.0	1082.0	10990.0	1881.0	306	155558331
PAS	PepsiAmericas, Inc. (New)	Conglomerate	12/31/03	3236.8	397.8	3610.1	1594.5	153	58289236
PEP	Pepsico Inc.	Soft drinks	12/27/03	26971.0	3691.0	22687.0	11896.0	1123	1130193889
PCR	Perini Corp.	Real estate	12/31/03	1374.1	83.8	565.4	126.6	18	12000559
PKI	PerkinElmer, Inc.	Electronic components	12/28/03	1300.5	d102.3	2538.7	1349.0	256	90971743
PBT	Permian Basin Royalty Trust	Oil	12/31/03	32.6	32.1	4.9	2.0	14	4167649
PER	Perot Systems Corp.	Computer services	12/31/03	1460.8	134.2	996.0	712.8	95	39478391
PCZ	Petro-Canada (Canada)	Oil producer	12/31/03	—	—	—	—	76	84668410
PZE	Petrobras Energia Participaci	Oil	12/31/03	—	—	—	—		
PKZ	PetroKazakhstan Inc	Oil	12/31/03	—	—	—	—		
PEO	Petroleum & Resources Corp.	Investment company	12/31/03	11.6	8.1	548.1	522.9	27	3192254
PV	Pfeiffer Vacuum Technology A		12/31/03	—	—	—	—	4	106798
PFB	PFF Bancorp Inc.	Banking - West	3/31/04	205.4	48.9	3677.7	316.4	72	7851156
PFE	Pfizer Inc (United States)	Drugs	12/31/03	45188.0	11012.0	115022.0	65377.0	1449	d412057101
PCG	PG&E Corp. (Holding Co.)	Electric power	12/31/03	10435.0	791.0	26954.0	4215.0	315	239268474
PD	Phelps Dodge Corp.	Copper	12/31/03	4142.7	83.2	7049.5	3063.8	276	80720466
PVH	Phillips-Van Heusen Corp. (U		2/1/04	1582.0	37.6	1439.3	296.2	107	20011543
PNX	Phoenix Companies, Inc. (The)	Insurance	12/31/03	2614.4	d4.1	27559.2	1947.8	152	54722333
PNY	Piedmont Natural Gas Co., Inc	Natural gas distributor	10/31/03	1220.8	74.4	2050.5	630.2	155	9510422
PIR	Pier 1 Imports, Inc.	Specialty stores	2/28/04	1868.2	118.0	1052.2	683.6	269	74001332
PPC	Pilgrim's Pride Corp.	Meat packing & processing	9/27/03	2619.3	56.0	1257.5	446.7	42	7911647
PCM	PIMCO Coml Mtg Secs Tr Inc	Investment company	12/31/03	14.7	12.5	212.4	139.9	16	394471
RCS	PIMCO Strategic Global Govern	Investment company	1/31/04	31.6	27.4	917.5	407.1	28	2262182
PNK	Pinnacle Entertainment Inc		12/31/03	531.5	82.5	957.1	200.9	86	14608993
PNW	Pinnacle West Capital Corp.	Electric power	12/31/03	2817.9	230.6	9536.4	2829.8	243	74865713
PHT	Pioneer High Income Trust (U	Investment company	3/31/04	51.2	47.3	604.3	433.6	13	496165
MUO	Pioneer Interest Shares	Investment company	12/31/03	5.9	5.1	96.7	93.0	20	667953
MAV	Pioneer Municipal High Income	Investment company	3/31/04	11.5	10.1	487.5	327.5		
MHI	Pioneer Municipal High Income	Investment company	7/11/03	—	d0.1	0.8	0.1		
PXD	Pioneer Natural Resources Co	Oil	12/31/03	1312.2	786.9	3357.7	1759.8	250	91964417
PJC	Piper Jaffray Companies	Securities brokerage	12/31/03	786.7	29.9	2186.1	669.8		
PBI	Pitney Bowes, Inc. (United St	Office equipment & supplies	12/31/03	4576.9	1387.1	8388.0	1087.4	508	179716463
PDG	Placer Dome Inc. (Canada)	Mining & processing	12/31/03	—	—	—	—	171	156909209
PAA	Plains All American Pipeline	Oil producer	12/31/03	12589.8	132.5	1973.4	—	75	8270673
PXP	Plains Exploration & Product	Oil	12/31/03	304.1	70.4	939.3	354.3	80	15479915
PLT	Plantronics, Inc.	Communications electronics	3/31/04	417.0	62.3	342.0	299.3	181	42416121
PLA A	Playboy Enterprises, Inc.	Publishing	12/31/03	315.8	d7.6	364.1	106.6	13	763720
PYX	Playtex Products, Inc.	Cosmetics & toiletries	12/27/03	657.7	47.1	963.1	27.8	97	37290263
PCL	Plum Creek Timber Co., Inc.	Forest products	12/31/03	1196.0	192.0	3749.0	2119.0	378	79662795
PMI	PMI Group, Inc. (The) (United	Insurance brokerage	12/31/03	891.7	274.3	4750.1	2784.0	266	83431884
PNC	PNC Financial Services Group	Banking - Mid-Atlantic	12/31/03	5969.0	1029.0	68168.0	6645.0	494	173276501
PNM	PNM Resources, Inc. (Holding	Electric power	12/31/03	1455.7	217.3	3332.2	1090.1	172	33776739
PPP	Pogo Producing Co.	Oil	12/31/03	1162.0	1014.8	2694.8	1457.2	212	53666365
PII	Polaris Industries Inc.	Recreation	12/31/03	1629.5	179.1	519.5	319.4	206	17875350
RL	Polo Ralph Lauren Corp.		3/28/04	2649.7	432.9	2223.4	1422.1	160	37865192
POL	PolyOne Corp.	Plastics & plastic products	12/31/03	1964.5	d95.3	1777.7	366.8	128	80040420
POP	Pope & Talbot, Inc.	Forest products	12/31/03	612.7	d65.3	534.0	146.5	99	11512563
PKX	POSCO (South Korea)	Steel producer	12/31/03	—	—	—	—	118	59564976
PPS	Post Properties, Inc.	Real estate investment trust	12/31/03	290.4	d4.9	2143.4	796.5	149	23090844
POT	Potash Corp. of Saskatchewan	Mining & processing	12/31/03	—	—	—	—	120	34647669
PCH	Potlatch Corp.	Forest products	12/31/03	1506.6	53.2	1588.4	504.3	122	15680074
PPG	PPG Industries, Inc.	Chemicals	12/31/03	8756.0	559.0	7415.0	2913.0	436	97852153
PPL	PPL Corp	Electric power	12/31/03	5587.0	748.0	17002.0	3310.0	332	87021721
PX	Praxair, Inc.	Specialty chemicals	12/31/03	5613.0	1748.0	8142.0	3088.0	438	132022410
PPD	Pre-Paid Legal Services, Inc	Services	12/31/03	361.3	76.6	107.2	29.6	102	16811680
PCP	Precision Castparts	Metal products	3/28/04	2174.7	359.6	3641.0	1743.6	222	40800679
PDS	Precision Drilling Corp.	Oil service & equipment	12/31/03	—	—	—	—	129	26393249
PSW	Preferred & Corporate Income	Investment company	7/17/03	—	—	0.5	0.1		
PCO	Premcor Inc. (United States)	Oil service & equipment	12/31/03	8803.9	190.9	3629.7	1145.2	119	42914690
PP	Prentiss Properties Trust (U	Real estate investment trust	12/31/03	356.4	54.1	2080.5	912.2	139	32870180
PR	Price Communications Corp	Telecommunications	12/31/03	32.5	17.6	1245.7	642.0	103	28227394
PDE	Pride International, Inc. (DE	Oil service & equipment	12/31/03	1689.7	92.2	4022.9	1702.8	217	114102938
PGE	Prime Group Realty Trust	Real estate investment trust	12/31/03	197.4	d28.6	948.8	263.3	34	8493753
PRM	Primedia, Inc.	Publishing	12/31/03	1345.6	d91.8	1389.6	d1013.3	91	63052708
PFG	Principal Financial Group, I	Insurance	12/31/03	9404.2	727.9	107139.4	7399.6	304	160040344
PRA	ProAssurance Corp.	Property & casualty insurance	12/31/03	709.6	38.7	2879.4	546.3	-102	16208829
PG	Procter & Gamble Co. (United	Soaps & cleansers	6/30/03	43377.0	5186.0	43706.0	16186.0	1138	730345282
PGN	Progress Energy, Inc.	Electric power	12/31/03	8743.0	811.0	26202.0	7537.0	407	134492423
PGR	Progressive Corp. (OH)	Property & casualty insurance	12/31/03	11892.0	1255.4	16281.5	5030.6	349	156978223
PLD	Prologis	Real estate investment trust	12/31/03	734.1	316.6	6369.2	3060.7	245	156376057
PQE	ProQuest Co. (United States)	Comp. components & periphs.	1/3/04	469.7	133.6	654.9	187.4	99	29371323
CNN	Prospect Street Income Share	Investment company	12/31/03	6.8	5.9	95.4	63.5	8	239773
PL	Protective Life Corp.	Life Insurance	12/31/03	1957.5	217.1	24574.0	2002.1	241	52081851
PFV	Provident Financial Group Inc	Banking - Midwest	12/31/03	1602.8	97.9	17017.5	899.1	—	—
PFS	Provident Financial Services		12/31/03	208.3	18.7	4399.2	931.4	80	22447332
PVN	Providian Financial Corp.	Financial services	12/31/03	2781.4	196.2	14275.3	2325.4	323	194639125
PRV	Province Healthcare Co. (Uni	Hospitals & nursing homes	12/31/03	762.0	115.4	1006.4	446.9	147	48684641

| EARNINGS PER SHARE | | | | | | P/E RATIO | DIVIDENDS PER SHARE | | | AV. YLD. % | DIV. DECLARED | | PRICE RANGE |
| QUARTERLY | | | ANNUAL | | | | | | | | | | |
1st	2nd	3rd	2004	2003	2002		2004	2003	2002		AMOUNT	PAYABLE	2004
0.48	0.47	0.90	—	1.68	1.12	—	0.76	0.76	0.72	1.3	0.20Q	3/4/05	78.42 - 38.74
0.37	—	—	—	2.79	1.84	—	2.60	2.60	2.56	6.1	0.65Q	3/30/05	51.30 - 34.10
0.59	—	—	—	1.32	0.84	—	0.21	0.12	0.08	0.5	0.06Q	3/31/05	53.57 - 24.62
0.22	—	—	—	0.37	1.00	—	—	—	—	—	5-for-4	9/9/97	24.19 - 10.33
0.20	—	—	—	—	1.55	—	—	—	—	—	3-for-1	3/27/03	17.70 - 9.20
0.40	—	—	—	0.76	1.96	—	0.26	0.22	0.20	0.5	100%	3/30/05	86.80 - 25.55
—	—	—	—	—	—	—	0.44	0.38	0.34	4.3	0.3011S	5/16/05	12.51 - 7.72
0.85	—	—	—	3.43	2.58	—	—	—	—	—	2-for-1	2/26/99	72.03 - 25.14
0.33	—	—	—	0.28	0.23	—	0.26	0.24	0.30	1.8	0.07Q	1/17/05	17.30 - 11.00
0.33	—	—	—	0.28	0.23	—	0.26	0.24	0.30	1.5	0.07Q	1/17/05	19.35 - 16.42
0.32	—	—	—	d0.64	d1.31	—	—	—	—	—	3-for-2	5/15/95	2.27 - 1.37
1.11	—	—	—	1.50	0.66	—	0.45	0.45	0.45	0.9	0.1125Q	3/17/05	69.00 - 33.02
0.44	—	—	—	1.25	1.57	—	2.12	2.06	1.84	5.5	0.62Q	5/13/05	54.30 - 23.00
0.38	—	—	—	1.21	1.25	—	0.50	0.50	0.38	1.7	0.125Q	5/2/05	41.82 - 16.85
0.11	—	—	—	1.33	1.21	—	2.16	2.07	2.04	6.2	0.54Q	3/15/05	43.70 - 25.70
0.40	—	—	—	1.45	1.30	—	0.43	0.41	0.37	0.9	0.0025Q	2/11/05	63.13 - 29.75
0.85	1.46	—	—	2.87	2.51	—	2.15	2.11	2.07	5.6	0.545Q	4/15/05	46.03 - 35.77
0.27	—	—	—	d0.22	0.82	—	0.27	0.27	0.27	1.5	0.0675Q	4/25/05	29.37 - 7.60
0.30	—	—	—	0.63	1.61	—	1.00	1.00	0.42	5.2	0.25Q	3/31/05	21.71 - 16.94
0.19	—	—	—	1.52	1.46	—	0.12	0.04	0.04	0.5	0.08Q	6/30/05	31.40 - 17.93
0.14	—	—	—	1.09	0.89	—	0.22	0.04	0.04	1.3	0.085Q	4/1/05	21.67 - 11.76
0.46	—	—	—	2.05	1.85	—	0.78	0.62	0.59	1.7	0.23Q	3/31/05	55.24 - 38.32
0.44	—	—	—	2.10	0.91	—	—	—	—	—	0.20Q	12/18/90	19.99 - 3.90
0.10	—	—	—	0.43	d0.03	—	0.28	0.28	0.28	1.8	0.07Q	5/13/05	23.26 - 7.80
0.19	—	—	—	0.69	0.50	—	0.90	0.68	0.49	8.5	0.08586M	4/14/05	15.29 - 5.84
0.16	—	—	—	0.45	0.68	—	—	—	—	—	—	—	17.00 - 10.01
—	—	—	—	—	—	—	0.55	0.40	0.40	1.2	0.15Q	4/1/05	57.30 - 33.00
—	—	—	—	—	—	—	—	—	—	—	—	5/2/01	14.32 - 8.35
—	—	—	—	—	—	—	0.45	—	—	1.6	0.20Q	5/2/05	42.62 - 12.47
—	—	—	—	24.06	20.98	—	1.32	1.19	1.11	5.6	0.05Q	3/1/05	27.80 - 18.95
—	—	—	—	—	—	—	0.66	0.51	0.42	2.1	0.6645A	6/24/04	43.50 - 19.00
—	—	—	—	2.45	2.02	—	0.53	0.31	0.16	1.5	0.15Q	3/24/05	47.18 - 22.78
0.30	—	—	—	0.22	1.47	—	0.68	0.60	0.52	2.2	0.19Q	3/8/05	38.87 - 23.52
7.21	—	—	—	1.96	d0.15	—	—	—	—	—	0.30Q	4/15/05	34.46 - 12.75
1.90	—	—	—	0.06	d3.54	—	0.50	—	—	0.8	0.25Q	6/3/05	101.55 - 31.19
d0.12	—	—	—	0.18	1.08	—	0.15	0.15	0.15	0.7	0.0375Q	3/31/05	29.95 - 11.85
0.16	—	—	—	d0.04	d1.18	—	0.16	0.16	0.16	1.5	0.16A	7/12/04	14.53 - 7.24
2.18	1.08	—	—	2.22	1.89	—	0.85	0.82	0.79	2.5	0.23Q	4/15/05	46.06 - 22.75
—	—	—	—	1.29	1.36	—	0.38	0.28	0.19	1.9	0.10Q	5/18/05	25.09 - 15.36
0.20	0.50	—	—	1.36	0.35	—	0.06	0.06	0.06	0.3	0.015Q	3/31/05	35.00 - 7.52
—	—	—	—	12.53	12.80	—	1.13	1.41	1.35	8.3	0.09375M	4/14/05	15.10 - 11.90
—	—	—	—	11.41	11.33	—	0.91	1.01	0.89	8.2	0.074M	4/14/05	12.97 - 9.30
0.04	—	—	—	d1.09	d0.50	—	—	—	—	—	25%	4/15/05	20.50 - 3.97
0.33	—	—	—	2.52	2.53	—	1.82	1.73	1.63	4.8	0.475Q	6/1/05	45.84 - 30.54
—	—	—	—	16.20	13.43	—	1.78	1.65	0.96	11.2	0.1375M	4/29/05	17.57 - 14.25
—	—	—	—	12.58	12.22	—	0.72	0.68	0.81	6.5	0.17Q	3/31/05	11.78 - 10.51
—	—	—	—	14.51	—	—	1.21	0.09	—	8.6	0.08375M	4/29/05	15.13 - 12.90
—	—	—	—	14.32	—	—	1.17	0.36	—	8.2	0.08M	5/2/05	15.45 - 13.07
0.50	—	—	—	3.33	0.43	—	0.20	—	—	0.7	0.10S	4/15/05	37.50 - 23.92
0.71	—	—	—	1.35	0.01	—	—	—	—	—	—	—	59.59 - 37.15
0.54	—	—	—	2.10	1.81	—	1.22	1.20	1.18	3.1	0.31Q	6/12/05	46.97 - 31.04
—	—	—	—	—	—	—	0.10	0.10	0.10	0.6	0.05S	4/11/05	22.79 - 9.80
0.49	—	—	—	1.00	1.34	—	2.30	2.19	2.11	7.3	0.6125Q	2/14/05	37.99 - 24.80
0.26	—	—	—	1.41	1.08	—	—	—	—	—	—	—	28.40 - 8.25
—	—	—	—	1.31	0.89	—	0.10	—	—	0.3	0.05Q	3/10/05	47.93 - 14.23
0.06	—	—	—	d0.31	d0.67	—	—	—	—	—	—	—	14.49 - 7.60
0.14	—	—	—	0.30	1.04	—	—	—	—	—	—	—	8.69 - 5.47
0.84	—	—	—	1.04	1.26	—	1.42	1.40	1.49	4.7	0.38Q	3/8/05	39.45 - 21.59
0.88	—	—	—	3.01	3.71	—	0.16	0.11	0.09	0.4	0.045Q	4/15/05	44.81 - 25.55
1.15	—	—	—	3.65	4.20	—	2.00	1.94	1.92	3.9	0.50Q	4/24/05	59.18 - 42.38
0.41	—	—	—	1.58	1.07	—	0.63	0.61	0.57	2.4	0.185Q	5/20/05	31.82 - 20.09
1.12	—	—	—	4.60	1.77	—	0.21	0.20	0.12	0.5	0.0625Q	2/25/05	51.34 - 35.50
0.32	—	—	—	2.46	2.19	—	0.92	0.62	0.56	1.4	0.28Q	2/15/05	91.47 - 41.06
—	—	—	—	1.69	1.76	—	0.20	0.10	—	0.6	0.05Q	4/15/05	42.83 - 20.19
d0.02	—	—	—	d1.05	d0.07	—	—	—	0.25	—	0.0625Q	12/16/02	9.69 - 3.52
d0.21	—	—	—	d1.59	d1.34	—	0.32	0.32	0.60	2.0	0.08Q	3/3/05	20.93 - 10.49
—	—	—	—	—	—	—	1.16	0.68	0.40	3.4	1.3461S	3/14/05	48.49 - 19.70
pd0.02	—	—	—	d0.83	0.80	—	1.80	2.13	3.12	6.1	0.45Q	4/15/05	35.70 - 23.36
—	—	—	—	—	—	—	0.53	0.50	0.50	0.7	0.15Q	5/13/05	103.00 - 50.00
0.74	—	—	—	1.85	d8.23	—	3.10	0.60	0.90	8.6	0.15Q	6/6/05	52.31 - 19.43
0.67	—	—	—	2.92	0.36	—	1.79	1.73	1.70	3.1	0.45Q	3/11/05	68.79 - 45.08
0.99	—	—	—	4.15	2.35	—	1.61	1.52	1.35	3.6	0.46Q	4/1/05	54.15 - 35.00
0.49	—	—	—	1.77	1.67	—	0.60	0.59	0.38	1.5	0.18Q	3/15/05	46.25 - 34.60
0.63	—	—	—	2.27	1.82	—	—	—	—	—	0.30Q	5/16/05	40.36 - 17.15
—	—	—	—	2.35	3.01	—	0.09	0.15	0.12	0.2	0.03Q	4/4/05	68.38 - 23.60
—	—	—	—	—	—	—	—	—	—	—	2-for-1	5/26/05	66.19 - 33.37
—	—	—	—	23.88	—	—	2.00	0.67	—	9.0	—	4/29/05	24.50 - 20.12
0.66	—	—	—	1.68	d2.65	—	0.02	—	—	0.1	0.02Q	3/15/05	44.73 - 20.95
0.30	—	—	—	1.37	1.52	—	2.24	2.24	2.19	6.8	0.56Q	4/8/05	39.25 - 26.21
0.10	—	—	—	0.37	7.94	—	—	—	—	—	5%	5/24/04	18.70 - 11.96
d0.05	—	—	—	0.18	d0.06	—	—	—	—	—	—	—	20.58 - 13.49
d0.31	—	—	—	d2.35	d1.32	—	—	—	—	—	0.3375Q	10/26/01	6.90 - 4.99
d0.12	—	—	—	d0.51	d1.47	—	—	—	—	—	—	—	4.06 - 1.64
0.62	—	—	—	2.23	1.77	—	0.55	0.45	0.25	1.6	0.55A	12/17/04	24.16 - 27.14
0.54	—	—	—	1.33	0.39	—	—	—	—	—	5%	2/15/00	40.58 - 22.10
1.26	1.30	1.09	—	3.69	3.09	—	0.98	0.86	0.79	1.2	0.28Q	5/16/05	108.85 - 50.60
0.45	—	—	—	3.40	2.53	—	2.30	2.24	2.18	5.3	0.59Q	5/2/05	47.95 - 38.90
2.09	—	—	—	5.69	2.99	—	0.11	0.10	0.10	0.2	0.03Q	3/31/05	96.66 - 48.34
0.19	—	—	—	1.16	1.20	—	1.46	1.44	1.42	4.3	0.37Q	2/28/05	43.33 - 24.78
0.40	—	—	—	1.75	1.59	—	—	—	—	—	—	—	32.53 - 15.91
—	—	—	—	6.49	5.90	—	0.57	0.62	0.68	9.4	0.1175Q	4/15/05	6.65 - 5.36
0.92	—	—	—	3.07	2.54	—	0.68	0.63	0.59	2.0	0.175Q	3/1/05	43.17 - 26.75
0.51	—	—	—	1.92	1.88	—	2.09	2.09	0.51	7.9	0.52344Q	4/15/05	27.95 - 24.89
0.19	—	—	—	0.31	—	—	0.24	0.14	—	1.4	0.07Q	2/28/05	19.71 - 15.25
0.35	—	—	—	0.67	0.52	—	—	—	—	—	0.03Q	9/17/01	16.85 - 6.10
0.24	—	—	—	0.86	0.73	—	—	—	—	—	50%	4/30/02	22.74 - 6.60

SYMBOL	COMPANY	NATURE OF BUSINESS	FISCAL YEAR-END	TOTAL REV. $MILL	NET INCOME $MILL	TOTAL ASSETS $MILL	NET STK EQUITY $MILL	NO. OF INST.	INST. HOLDINGS (SHARES)
PRU	Prudential Financial, Inc.	Life Insurance	12/31/03	27907.0	8910.0	320247.0	21292.0	403	227075458
PUK	Prudential Plc (United Kingd	Insurance brokerage	12/31/03	—	—	—	—	23	4775904
POH	Public Service Company of Ok	Electric power	12/31/03	1102.8	53.9	1912.8	488.3	2	76450
PEG	Public Service Enterprise Gr	Electric power	12/31/03	11116.0	852.0	28055.0	5609.0	378	110245276
PSA	Public Storage, Inc.	Real estate investment trust	12/31/03	875.1	350.9	4968.1	4219.8	215	55371596
PSD	Puget Energy, Inc. (Holding	Electric power	12/31/03	2491.5	121.5	5674.7	1655.0	201	35569055
PTZ	Pulitzer, Inc.	Newspapers	12/31/03	342.0	d38.5	1279.1	851.4	91	8908456
PHM	Pulte Homes, Inc.	Home-building	12/31/03	9048.9	617.3	8063.4	3448.1	268	46350802
PCF	Putnam High Income Bond Fund	Investment company	8/31/03	9.1	8.0	108.3	106.9	20	198220
PIM	Putnam Master Interm Incm Tr	Investment company	9/30/03	53.9	48.0	797.0	700.7	36	2003774
KWR	Quaker Chemical Corp.	Specialty chemicals	12/31/03	340.2	39.0	247.4	112.4	70	4847177
NX	Quanex Corp. (United States)	Steel producer	10/31/03	1031.2	42.9	665.9	445.2	133	13707113
PWR	Quanta Services, Inc.	Electrical equipment	12/31/03	1642.9	d35.0	1304.8	663.1	123	39320162
IQW	Quebecor World Inc. (Canada)	Printing & engraving	12/31/03	—	—	—	—	43	43708763
DGX	Quest Diagnostics, Inc.	Services	12/31/03	4738.0	3261.7	4182.7	2394.7	409	77499113
STR	Questar Corp.	Natural gas	12/31/03	1463.2	179.2	3238.9	1261.3	266	52753029
KWK	Quicksilver Resources, Inc.	Oil producer	12/31/03	140.9	26.7	651.8	241.8	79	9939278
ZQK	Quiksilver, Inc.		10/31/03	975.0	58.5	626.1	446.5	173	22663545
LQ	Quinenco S.A. (Chile)	Telecommunications	12/31/03	—	—	—	—	16	7215426
Q	Qwest Communications Intl In	Telecommunications	12/31/03	14288.0	d1313.0	24923.0	d1016.0	383	1007619172
RGF	R&G Financial Corp.	—	12/31/03	602.0	223.9	8191.2	750.4	105	10958343
RDN	Radian Group, Inc.	Insurance	12/31/03	1363.1	385.9	6445.8	3225.8	272	93324762
RSH	RadioShack Corp.	Specialty stores	12/31/03	4649.3	801.8	2173.9	769.3	265	123699156
RRA	RailAmerica, Inc.	Railroads	12/31/03	358.4	67.1	1035.1	371.8	84	25275787
RAS	RAIT Investment Trust (Unite	Real estate investment trust	12/31/03	78.6	47.2	534.6	363.4	72	8951197
RAH	Ralcorp Holdings, Inc. (New)	Food processing	9/30/03	1303.6	d7.2	794.2	412.7	152	22052646
RPT	Ramco-Gershenson Properties	Real estate investment trust	12/31/03	108.4	18.5	752.0	295.7	65	7796277
RRC	Range Resources Corp	Oil	12/31/03	249.2	55.3	464.5	274.1	84	35404371
RJF	Raymond James Financial, Inc	Financial services	9/26/03	1452.0	86.3	6911.4	924.7	161	28900483
RYN	Rayonier Inc.	Forest products	12/31/03	1100.9	50.3	1838.7	711.1	173	23118356
ROV	Rayovac Corp. (United States	Electronic components	9/30/03	922.1	107.8	1539.9	202.0	137	30476271
RAY	Raytech Corp.	Metal products	12/28/03	205.9	d105.5	199.6	75.9	32	3435339
RTN	Raytheon Co.	Electronic components	12/31/03	18109.0	535.0	22858.0	9162.0	498	282871052
RDA	Reader's Digest Association	Publishing	6/30/03	2474.9	161.7	2184.7	400.3	190	73950821
O	Realty Income Corp.	Real estate investment trust	12/31/03	156.1	79.2	1360.3	827.8	99	6292776
OUI	Realty Income Corp.	Real estate investment trust	12/31/03	156.1	79.2	1360.3	827.8	1	900
RA	Reckson Associates Realty Co	Real estate investment trust	12/31/03	470.3	44.9	2578.0	936.6	146	45382236
RWT	Redwood Trust Inc. (United S	Real estate investment trust	12/31/03	339.6	132.4	17626.8	553.3	95	9327762
RBK	Reebok International, Ltd.	Shoe manufacturing	12/31/03	3485.3	391.4	1741.2	1033.7	258	45708033
RUK	Reed Elsevier Plc (New) (Unit	Publishing	12/31/03	—	—	—	—	36	7485839
RGC	Regal Entertainment Group (U	Motion pictures/theaters	1/1/04	2489.9	247.5	2406.7	794.9	117	30566455
RBC	Regal-Beloit Corp.	Machine tools	12/31/03	619.1	26.1	543.4	398.7	115	18556321
REG	Regency Centers Corp.	Real estate investment trust	12/31/03	377.6	135.5	2903.2	1281.0	118	54016430
RGS	Regis Corp.	Cosmetics & toiletries	6/30/03	67.7	d761.6	1063.7	562.8	197	34867533
RHB	RehabCare Group Inc.	Hospitals & nursing homes	12/31/03	539.3	d12.4	229.9	178.0	111	16066651
RGA	Reinsurance Group of America,	Insurance	12/31/03	3174.3	178.3	12014.7	1947.7	103	27224874
RS	Reliance Steel & Aluminum Co	Metal products	12/31/03	1885.8	34.0	1369.4	647.6	93	18760993
RRI	Reliant Energy Inc (New)	Electric power	12/31/03	11000.3	d1724.6	12775.9	4413.2	212	143785861
REM	Remington Oil & Gas Corp.	Oil	12/31/03	183.1	42.9	305.6	241.9	117	17620748
RCI	Renal Care Group Inc.	Hospitals & nursing homes	12/31/03	1005.3	225.2	773.8	570.8	196	39880801
RWY	Rent-Way, Inc. (United State	Department stores	9/30/03	491.3	d10.6	444.9	106.8	48	12168355
REP	Repsol YPF, S.A. (Spain)	Oil	12/31/03	—	—	—	—	98	74825794
RSG	Republic Services, Inc.	Pollution control	12/31/03	2517.8	215.4	4459.5	1904.5	254	146900011
RMD	ResMed Inc.	Medical & dental equipment	6/30/03	273.6	112.9	442.1	286.4	132	16518797
RVI	Retail Ventures Inc	Department stores	1/31/04	2594.2	d4.4	712.8	216.8	—	—
REV	Revlon, Inc.	Cosmetics & toiletries	12/31/03	1299.3	d307.1	781.4	d1603.6	40	2852796
RSC	Rex Stores Corp. (United Sta	Consumer electronics	1/31/04	417.4	27.4	274.1	183.9	49	7232058
REY	Reynolds & Reynolds Co.	Office equipment & supplies	9/30/03	1008.2	119.0	1124.1	457.1	214	57713430
RAI	Reynolds (R.J.) Tobacco Hldg	Tobacco	12/31/03	5267.0	d7623.0	9779.0	3542.0	—	—
RHA	Rhodia S.A. (France)	Chemicals	12/31/03	—	—	—	—	3	85051
RTP	Rio Tinto Plc (UK)	Mining & processing	12/31/03	—	—	—	—	90	18543728
RAD	Rite Aid Corp.	Drug stores	2/28/04	16600.4	83.3	6246.7	9.3	190	129950154
RLI	RLI Corp.	Property & casualty insurance	12/31/03	519.9	71.3	2134.4	554.1	133	17045213
RSF	RMK Strategic Income Fund Inc	Investment company	3/31/04	0.5	0.4	329.8	300.5	—	—
RBN	Robbins & Myers, Inc.	Electrical equipment	8/31/03	560.8	14.4	691.8	287.0	86	9338025
RHI	Robert Half International In	Services	12/31/03	1975.0	16.9	979.9	788.7	239	138803439
RKT	Rock-Tenn Co. (United States	Paper	9/30/03	1433.3	29.5	1287.8	422.0	95	12031560
ROK	Rockwell Automation, Inc. (U	Electronics	9/30/03	4104.0	579.0	3957.0	1587.0	329	102842775
COL	Rockwell Collins, Inc.	Communications electronics	9/30/03	2542.0	617.0	2499.0	833.0	309	100129034
RG	Rogers Communications Inc.	Telecommunications	12/31/03	—	—	—	—	50	79204788
ROG	Rogers Corp.		12/28/03	243.3	61.3	314.4	226.9	101	12165002
ROH	Rohm & Haas Co.	Chemicals	12/31/03	6421.0	684.0	9067.0	3357.0	325	177678661
ROL	Rollins, Inc.	Services	12/31/03	677.0	398.2	259.8	138.8	104	15448686
ROP	Roper Industries, Inc (New)	Machinery & equipment	12/31/03	657.4	114.4	1445.9	655.8	167	28922445
RDC	Rowan Cos., Inc.	Oil service & equipment	12/31/03	679.1	5.6	2153.4	1136.8	269	86502040
RSA	Royal & Sun Alliance Insuran	Insurance brokerage	12/31/03	—	—	—	—	16	7688578
RY	Royal Bank of Canada		10/31/03	—	—	—	—	118	197449008
RYG	Royal Group Technologies Ltd	Plastics & plastic products	9/30/03	—	—	—	—	39	24157041
RMT	Royce Micro-Cap Trust, Inc.	Investment	12/31/03	2.0	d1.6	350.9	253.4	19	2871705
RVT	Royce Value Trust Inc.	Investment company	12/31/03	7.9	d2.5	1144.6	850.8	53	3912942
RES	RPC, Inc.	Oil service & equipment	12/31/03	270.5	10.9	223.9	151.1	37	7593685
RTI	RTI International Metals, Inc	Metal products	12/31/03	205.5	12.2	389.9	317.7	90	17470338
RDK	Ruddick Corp.	Grocery chain	9/28/03	2724.7	59.9	1029.2	495.3	136	24637372
RUS	Russ Berrie & Co., Inc.		12/31/03	329.7	83.2	456.6	415.4	103	9776767
RML	Russell Corp.		1/3/04	1186.3	43.0	932.6	514.9	118	19866032
RT	Ryder System, Inc.	Equip. & vehicle leasing	12/31/03	4802.3	348.0	4723.4	1344.4	242	52888457
RYI	Ryerson Tull, Inc. (New)	Steel producer	12/31/03	2189.4	d14.1	1114.4	382.3	86	18495164
RYL	Ryland Group, Inc. (United S		12/31/03	3441.1	266.0	1993.3	824.5	194	24091468
SBR	Sabine Royalty Trust	Oil	12/31/03	38.8	38.8	5.6	4.7	33	744104
TSG	SABRE Holdings Corp. (United	Computer services	12/31/03	2045.2	83.3	2921.4	1680.1	237	134742782
SDA	Sadia S.A. (Brazil)	Food processing	12/31/03	—	—	—	—	1	8733
SFE	Safeguard Scientifics, Inc.	Services	12/31/03	1622.6	77.9	821.8	236.2	97	27768032
SWY	Safeway Inc.	Grocery chain	1/3/04	35552.7	d169.8	14690.7	3644.3	495	347631791
SGA	Saga Communications, Inc.	Broadcasting	12/31/03	121.3	13.9	142.2	107.2	73	17255869
SKS	Saks, Inc. (United States)	Specialty stores	1/31/04	6055.1	87.7	4630.7	2322.2	164	83348920
EFL	Salomon Brothers Emerging Ma	Investment company	2/29/04	5.6	4.4	59.7	57.1	—	—

T32

| | EARNINGS PER SHARE | | | | | P/E | DIVIDENDS PER SHARE | | | AV. YLD. | DIV. DECLARED | | PRICE RANGE |
| QUARTERLY | | | ANNUAL | | | RATIO | | | | % | AMOUNT | PAYABLE | 2004 |
1st	2nd	3rd	2004	2003	2002		2004	2003	2002				
0.72	—	—	—	2.06	1.36	—	0.63	0.50	0.40	1.5	0.625A	12/20/04	55.62 - 29.25
—	—	—	—	—	—	—	1.07	0.73	0.76	7.0	0.4047S	6/2/05	20.46 - 10.05
—	—	—	—	—	—	—	1.50	1.65	—	6.2	0.375Q	3/31/05	26.78 - 21.60
1.14	—	—	—	3.72	1.99	—	2.20	2.16	2.16	5.0	0.56Q	3/31/05	52.64 - 34.63
0.17	—	—	—	1.27	1.28	—	1.80	1.80	1.80	4.1	0.45Q	3/31/05	57.64 - 30.30
0.67	—	—	—	1.22	1.24	—	1.00	1.00	1.21	4.5	0.25Q	5/15/05	24.81 - 19.80
0.37	—	—	—	1.95	1.62	—	0.76	0.72	0.70	1.4	0.20Q	5/2/05	64.90 - 42.64
1.02	—	—	—	4.91	3.60	—	0.20	0.08	0.08	0.4	0.05Q	4/1/05	65.00 - 40.50
—	—	—	—	7.73	6.56	—	0.56	0.56	0.60	7.4	0.0465M	4/1/05	8.20 - 6.81
—	—	—	—	6.99	6.26	—	0.48	0.47	0.54	7.5	0.035M	4/1/05	6.96 - 5.80
0.33	—	—	—	1.52	1.51	—	0.85	0.84	0.83	3.4	0.215Q	4/29/05	30.45 - 19.50
0.39	0.69	—	—	2.62	3.52	—	0.56	0.45	0.43	1.1	0.135Q	3/31/05	70.40 - 28.76
d0.10	—	—	—	d0.30	d2.26	—	—	—	—	—	50%	4/7/00	9.52 - 3.20
—	—	—	—	—	—	—	0.52	0.52	0.49	2.7	0.14Q	3/1/05	23.59 - 14.26
1.10	—	—	—	4.12	3.23	—	0.60	—	—	0.8	0.18Q	4/20/05	96.80 - 52.76
0.89	—	—	—	2.13	2.07	—	0.85	0.78	0.72	2.1	0.215Q	3/14/05	52.12 - 27.50
0.24	—	—	—	0.81	0.68	—	—	—	—	—	100%	6/30/04	51.05 - 20.25
0.16	—	—	—	1.03	0.77	—	—	—	—	—	2-for-1	5/11/05	31.15 - 12.55
—	—	—	—	—	—	—	0.19	—	0.07	2.6	0.0627U	5/21/04	9.98 - 4.53
d0.17	—	—	—	d0.76	d10.48	—	—	—	—	—	0.05A	6/29/01	4.97 - 2.56
0.67	—	—	—	2.25	1.66	—	0.39	0.29	0.22	1.2	0.117Q	3/24/05	45.26 - 22.00
1.26	—	—	—	4.08	4.41	—	0.08	0.08	0.08	0.2	0.02Q	3/21/05	54.94 - 33.38
0.41	—	—	—	1.77	1.45	—	0.25	0.25	0.22	0.9	0.25A	12/20/04	36.21 - 19.64
0.14	—	—	—	0.75	0.16	—	—	—	—	—	—	—	14.73 - 4.88
0.60	—	—	—	2.23	2.48	—	2.40	2.46	2.39	9.4	0.60Q	4/15/05	29.55 - 21.25
0.39	0.54	—	—	0.25	1.77	—	1.00	—	—	3.0	1.00U	10/22/04	42.51 - 24.76
0.24	—	—	—	0.54	0.93	—	1.81	1.68	1.68	6.8	0.4375Q	4/1/05	32.95 - 19.98
0.10	—	—	—	0.53	0.44	—	0.05	—	—	0.4	0.02Q	3/31/05	21.65 - 5.71
0.33	0.58	—	—	1.17	1.07	—	0.27	0.24	0.24	0.9	0.08Q	4/13/05	40.17 - 21.77
1.49	—	—	—	1.16	1.30	—	2.24	1.05	0.96	5.7	0.62Q	3/31/05	49.68 - 28.25
0.63	0.12	—	—	0.48	0.90	—	—	—	—	—	—	—	31.34 - 10.40
0.03	—	—	—	d1.59	d0.07	—	0.16	—	—	6.3	0.05A	3/17/88	3.88 - 1.20
0.24	—	—	—	1.29	1.85	—	0.80	0.80	0.80	2.3	0.22Q	5/2/05	41.79 - 27.05
d0.14	0.67	0.02	—	0.60	0.89	—	0.20	0.20	0.20	1.5	0.10Q	2/15/05	16.07 - 10.21
0.46	—	—	—	1.95	1.86	—	1.24	1.18	1.15	2.9	—	4/15/05	52.15 - 33.88
0.46	—	—	—	1.95	1.86	—	2.06	2.06	2.06	7.2	—	4/15/05	28.50 - 28.46
0.26	—	—	—	0.55	1.71	—	1.70	1.70	1.70	6.4	0.4246Q	4/18/05	34.34 - 18.80
2.49	—	—	—	7.09	3.44	—	8.66	7.46	2.73	18.3	0.70Q	4/21/05	66.25 - 28.20
0.63	—	—	—	2.43	2.04	—	0.30	0.15	—	0.8	0.15S	3/18/05	44.37 - 30.24
—	—	—	—	—	—	—	0.86	0.72	0.63	2.5	0.7323S	5/31/05	39.84 - 29.00
0.16	—	—	—	1.30	0.79	—	5.86	5.65	0.15	28.6	0.30Q	3/15/05	23.30 - 17.73
p0.27	—	—	—	1.00	1.01	—	0.48	0.48	0.48	2.1	0.12Q	4/15/05	29.38 - 15.31
0.34	—	—	—	1.79	1.35	—	2.12	2.08	2.04	4.9	0.55Q	3/1/05	55.40 - 31.68
0.55	0.60	0.55	—	1.92	1.63	—	0.16	0.12	0.12	0.5	0.04Q	3/2/05	46.88 - 23.28
0.31	—	—	—	d0.86	1.38	—	—	—	—	—	100%	6/19/00	29.04 - 13.75
1.00	—	—	—	3.46	2.59	—	0.27	0.24	0.24	0.7	0.09Q	2/28/05	48.65 - 26.28
0.92	—	—	—	1.07	0.95	—	0.25	0.24	0.24	0.9	0.09Q	4/1/05	42.76 - 15.10
—	—	—	—	d3.07	d1.12	—	—	—	—	—	—	—	13.92 - 3.56
0.39	—	—	—	1.53	0.42	—	—	—	—	—	—	—	29.35 - 15.67
0.42	—	—	—	1.37	1.21	—	—	—	—	—	3-for-2	5/24/04	52.29 - 28.90
0.17	0.24	—	—	d0.53	d1.26	—	—	—	—	—	3-for-2	8/18/95	10.05 - 3.60
—	—	—	—	—	—	—	0.42	0.29	0.15	2.1	0.2781U	1/21/05	26.26 - 14.02
0.36	—	—	—	1.33	1.44	—	0.30	0.06	—	1.1	0.12Q	4/15/05	33.98 - 19.07
0.35	0.40	0.43	—	1.33	1.10	—	—	—	—	—	2-for-1	3/31/00	51.63 - 31.41
d0.05	—	—	—	d0.13	0.01	—	—	—	—	—	—	—	8.17 - 4.70
d0.63	—	—	—	d2.47	d5.49	—	—	—	—	—	—	—	3.93 - 1.96
0.32	—	—	—	2.17	1.62	—	—	—	—	—	50%	2/11/02	18.63 - 10.14
0.34	0.38	—	—	1.69	1.58	—	0.44	0.44	0.44	1.7	0.11Q	4/8/05	30.00 - 21.11
1.43	—	—	—	d44.08	4.64	—	0.95	—	—	1.3	0.95Q	4/1/05	80.50 - 65.62
—	—	—	—	—	—	—	0.50	0.10	0.09	16.2	—	5/5/04	5.05 - 1.13
—	—	—	—	—	—	●	2.64	2.42	2.74	2.7	1.80S	4/11/05	119.65 - 74.10
—	—	—	—	0.11	d0.31	—	—	—	—	—	0.115Q	10/25/99	6.22 - 2.24
0.65	—	—	—	2.76	1.75	—	0.48	0.38	0.43	1.4	0.14Q	4/15/05	43.70 - 25.93
—	—	—	—	14.31	—	—	1.23	—	—	7.8	0.15M	5/19/05	17.49 - 13.90
0.15	0.02	—	—	1.00	1.15	—	0.22	0.22	0.22	1.2	0.055Q	4/29/05	24.75 - 13.46
0.09	—	—	—	0.04	0.01	—	0.18	—	—	0.8	0.07Q	3/15/05	30.10 - 13.31
0.12	0.09	—	—	0.85	0.77	—	0.35	0.33	0.30	2.2	0.09Q	2/21/05	17.87 - 12.80
0.30	0.41	—	—	1.49	1.20	—	0.66	0.66	0.66	1.9	0.225Q	6/6/05	49.97 - 20.70
0.38	0.39	—	—	1.43	1.28	—	0.42	0.36	0.36	1.4	0.12Q	3/7/05	40.94 - 18.37
—	—	—	—	—	—	—	0.10	0.05	—	0.6	0.05S	1/4/05	26.43 - 9.24
0.72	—	—	—	1.61	1.16	—	—	—	—	—	100%	5/26/00	70.15 - 25.20
0.51	—	—	—	1.30	0.98	—	0.97	0.86	0.82	2.6	0.25Q	3/1/05	45.41 - 28.54
0.19	—	—	—	0.77	0.60	—	0.16	0.15	0.09	0.7	3-for-2	3/10/05	27.45 - 17.52
0.49	—	—	—	1.50	0.04	—	0.39	0.35	0.33	0.8	0.10625Q	4/29/05	27.26 - 19.63
d0.11	—	—	—	d0.08	0.90	—	—	—	0.25	—	0.25U	2/25/05	10.68 - 5.48
—	—	—	—	—	—	—	0.42	1.51	0.83	5.2	—	6/9/05	13.27 - 4.65
—	—	—	—	—	—	—	2.02	1.72	1.52	4.5	0.55Q	5/24/05	53.85 - 36.50
—	—	—	—	13.33	9.39	—	1.33	0.92	0.80	11.4	0.31Q	3/23/05	15.60 - 7.68
—	—	—	—	17.03	13.22	—	1.55	1.30	1.51	9.4	0.40Q	3/23/05	20.80 - 12.20
0.20	—	—	—	0.38	d0.19	—	0.08	0.07	0.07	0.4	3-for-2	3/10/05	28.35 - 9.15
0.13	—	—	—	0.23	0.72	—	—	—	—	—	—	—	22.49 - 9.20
0.30	0.34	—	—	1.29	1.12	—	0.40	0.36	0.36	2.3	0.11Q	4/1/05	22.53 - 12.21
0.02	—	—	—	1.68	2.25	—	8.20	1.12	1.04	29.7	0.10Q	4/21/05	37.24 - 18.05
0.02	—	—	—	1.32	1.45	—	0.16	0.16	0.16	0.9	0.04Q	2/28/05	19.73 - 15.59
0.53	—	—	—	2.12	1.80	—	0.60	0.60	0.60	1.6	0.16Q	3/18/05	55.55 - 20.51
0.46	—	—	—	d0.58	d0.51	—	0.20	0.20	0.20	1.7	0.05Q	5/1/05	17.84 - 6.08
2.06	—	—	—	9.11	6.64	—	0.20	0.04	0.04	0.3	0.06Q	4/30/05	106.48 - 39.64
0.63	—	—	—	2.54	1.82	—	2.79	2.52	1.88	8.8	0.3391M	4/29/05	42.49 - 21.05
0.31	—	—	—	0.58	1.50	—	0.30	0.21	—	1.4	0.09Q	2/28/05	27.98 - 15.91
—	—	—	—	—	—	—	0.67	0.43	0.37	1.7	0.0401U	3/24/05	67.29 - 9.90
d0.04	—	—	—	d0.30	d1.12	—	—	—	—	—	200%	3/17/00	6.25 - 1.28
0.10	—	—	—	d0.38	1.20	—	—	—	—	—	2-for-1	2/25/98	25.45 - 16.62
0.12	—	—	—	0.65	0.66	—	—	—	—	—	5-for-4	6/15/02	20.73 - 16.10
0.15	—	—	—	0.58	0.48	—	2.00	—	—	15.6	2.00U	5/17/04	17.88 - 7.69
—	—	—	—	13.28	11.23	—	0.88	1.08	1.13	7.0	0.073M	5/27/05	14.10 - 11.00

SYMBOL	COMPANY	NATURE OF BUSINESS	FISCAL YEAR-END	TOTAL REV. $MILL	NET INCOME $MILL	TOTAL ASSETS $MILL	NET STK EQUITY $MILL	NO. OF INST.	INST. HOLDINGS (SHARES)
SBF	Salomon Brothers Fund Inc.	Investment company	12/31/03	21.2	13.5	1458.0	1403.6	58	4481422
HIF	Salomon Brothers High Income	Investment company	12/31/03	4.8	4.1	56.4	53.5	6	35782
MNP	Salomon Brothers Municipal P	Investment company	12/31/03	6.6	5.5	129.6	89.4	—	—
SJT	San Juan Basin Royalty Trust	Oil	12/31/03	92.0	90.4	36.9	29.8	65	21448584
SNY	Sanofi-Synthelabo S.A. (Franc	Drugs	12/31/03	—	—	—	—	36	2413444
SFF	Santa Fe Energy Trust	Oil	12/31/03	22.2	21.4	10.1	10.0	20	74955
SBP	Santander Bancorp (Holding C		12/31/03	445.5	39.4	7366.4	480.8	38	2295601
SAP	Sap AG (Germany)	Computer services	12/31/03	—	—	—	—	193	73738871
SSL	Sasol Ltd.	Conglomerate	6/30/03	—	—	—	—	30	19862705
SHS	Sauer-Danfoss Inc.	Machinery & equipment	12/31/03	1126.8	22.0	860.9	397.2	52	6773317
BFS	Saul Centers, Inc.	Real estate investment trust	12/31/03	97.9	25.5	471.6	92.6	67	2811212
SBC	SBC Communications, Inc.	Telecommunications	12/31/03	40843.0	5971.0	100166.0	38248.0	1027	1657824044
SCG	SCANA Corp (New)	Electric power	12/31/03	3416.0	281.9	8319.0	2412.0	250	43980706
SGK	Schawk, Inc.	Printing & engraving	12/31/03	201.0	17.0	154.6	106.4	22	2215590
SHR	Schering A.G. (Germany)	Drugs	12/31/03	—	—	—	—	39	1388306
SGP	Schering-Plough Corp.	Drugs	12/31/03	8334.0	d138.0	15102.0	7337.0	845	1068772294
SLB	Schlumberger Ltd.	Oil service & equipment	12/31/03	14059.1	472.6	20041.3	5881.3	813	412776060
SCH	Schwab (Charles) Corp.	Securities brokerage	12/31/03	4087.0	472.0	45866.0	4461.0	467	693569292
SWM	Schweitzer-Mauduit Intl. Inc	Paper	12/31/03	566.9	58.1	572.7	284.5	121	11520544
SCO	SCOR S.A	Insurance	12/31/03	—	—	—	—	5	17193
SMG	Scotts Co., (The)	Chemicals	9/30/03	1910.1	267.1	1625.5	728.2	197	18887757
SKP	SCPIE Holdings Inc.	Property & casualty insurance	12/31/03	187.0	d12.8	991.3	204.2	40	2869061
SSP	Scripps (E.W.) Co. (New) (OH	Newspapers	12/31/03	1874.8	360.5	2882.2	1820.8	202	29570248
KHI	Scudder High Income Trust	Investment company	11/30/03	23.2	20.3	253.7	182.5	22	766241
KGT	Scudder Intermediate Governm	Investment company	12/31/03	10.2	7.8	252.9	252.1	17	3462235
KMM	Scudder Multi-Market Income T	Investment company	11/30/03	17.5	15.0	233.8	179.2	19	255163
SAF	Scudder New Asia Fund, Inc.	Investment company	12/31/03	2.3	0.3	136.3	135.1	27	2863012
KST	Scudder Strategic Income Trus	Investment company	11/30/03	4.4	3.6	55.7	44.3	4	13634
CKH	SEACOR Holdings Inc (New)	Oil service & equipment	12/31/03	406.2	91.1	1373.3	753.9	111	15696494
SEE	Sealed Air Corp. (New)	Plastics & plastic products	12/31/03	3531.9	617.3	4572.1	1123.6	305	77816430
SRJ	Sears Roebuck Acceptance Corp	Finance	1/3/04	1876.0	248.0	9057.0	3616.0	3	46098
SEM	Select Medical Corp.	Hospitals & nursing homes	12/31/03	1396.8	170.3	992.8	419.2	109	23724256
SEN	SEMCO Energy Inc.	Public utility	12/31/03	545.4	d30.0	951.2	174.4	52	4115382
SRE	Sempra Energy (United States)	Natural gas distributor	12/31/03	7887.0	1437.0	22009.0	3890.0	290	108603751
SNH	Senior Housing Properties Tr	Real estate investment trust	12/31/03	131.1	45.9	1304.1	727.9	105	18987800
SXT	Sensient Technologies Corp.	Food processing	12/31/03	987.4	189.8	1368.6	580.1	195	36851326
SQA A	Sequa Corp.	—	12/31/03	1665.5	6.5	1792.5	598.1	74	3464649
SQA B	Sequa Corp.	—	12/31/03	1665.5	6.5	1792.5	598.1	9	1472853
SCI	Service Corp. International	Services	12/31/03	2341.7	377.5	11069.9	1527.0	156	176994502
SVM	ServiceMaster Co. (The)	Services	12/31/03	3568.6	d222.0	2487.7	816.5	248	156554869
SJR	Shaw Communications Inc	Telecommunications	8/31/03	—	—	—	—	58	107744045
SGR	Shaw Group Inc.	Oil producer	8/31/03	3306.8	56.5	1974.1	662.3	167	29072976
SC	Shell Trans & Trading Co. PL	Oil producer	12/31/03	—	—	—	—	187	37182402
SHW	Sherwin-Williams Co.	Paints & related products	12/31/03	5407.8	855.0	3513.8	1458.9	336	102370881
SKO	Shopko Stores, Inc. (WI) (Un	Department stores	12/31/03	3196.9	39.1	1225.1	590.7	141	31704088
SHU	Shurgard Storage Centers, Inc	Industrial	12/31/03	302.3	37.6	1803.9	954.4	148	16667103
SI	Siemens AG (Germany)	Electrical equipment	9/30/03	—	—	—	—	87	12444768
SIE	Sierra Health Services Inc.	Hospitals & nursing homes	12/31/03	1485.1	219.4	578.0	150.8	124	21920696
SRP	Sierra Pacific Resources (New	Electric power	12/31/03	2789.2	d129.4	7063.8	1435.4	151	87359085
SRC	Sierra Pacific Resources (New	Electric power	12/31/03	2789.2	d129.4	7063.8	1435.4	5	662190
SIG	Signet Group Plc (UK)	Specialty stores	1/31/04	—	—	—	—	14	5522810
SPG	Simon Property Group, Inc.	Real estate investment trust	12/31/03	2313.7	368.2	15356.8	3338.6	339	149212843
SSD	Simpson Manufacturing Co.Inc	Furniture & fixtures	12/31/03	548.2	131.1	432.1	400.3	123	14386667
SIR	Sirva Inc	Trucking lines	12/31/03	2349.9	385.7	1511.2	395.3	—	—
SWW	Sitel Corp.	Services	12/31/03	846.5	547.2	372.8	150.9	54	32235404
PKS	Six Flags Inc	Recreation	12/31/03	1236.7	d61.7	4021.4	1362.0	142	81784470
SIZ	Sizeler Property Investors, I	Real estate investment trust	12/31/03	52.9	7.6	315.9	90.9	39	3537334
SKX	Skechers U S A, Inc	Shoe manufacturing	12/31/03	839.1	216.3	466.5	255.7	86	10261906
SLG	SL Green Realty Corp.	Real estate investment trust	12/31/03	309.0	73.6	2261.8	950.8	163	34080784
SLM	SLM Corp.	Financial services	12/31/03	4160.2	1403.6	58294.0	2603.0	425	140895997
SMF	Smart & Final, Inc.	Grocery chain	12/28/03	1730.1	27.4	572.4	213.6	41	8821362
SNN	Smith & Nephew Plc (UK)	Medical & dental equipment	12/31/03	—	—	—	—	40	3287045
AOS	Smith (A.O.) Corp		12/31/03	1530.7	131.2	1254.5	576.2	137	17692136
SII	Smith International, Inc. (U	Oil service & equipment	12/31/03	3594.8	575.4	2957.3	1235.8	268	94273150
SFD	Smithfield Foods, Inc.	Meat packing & processing	5/2/04	p9267.0	p9267.0	—	—	177	64133802
SNA	Snap-On, Inc.	Hardware & tools	1/3/04	2233.2	195.4	2033.4	1010.9	226	46596620
SQM	Sociedad Quimica y Minera	Chemicals	12/31/03	—	—	—	—	19	1344923
SQM A	Sociedad Quimica y Minera	Chemicals	12/31/03	—	—	—	—	2	68980
SDX	Sodexho Alliance S.A. (Franc	Restaurants	8/31/03	—	—	—	—	4	66344
SLR	Solectron Corp.	Electronic components	8/31/03	11014.0	d5628.8	6388.5	1422.0	377	678598949
SAH	Sonic Automotive, Inc.		12/31/03	7034.2	87.8	1623.3	698.3	109	23779595
SON	Sonoco Products Co.	Paper	12/31/03	2758.3	267.4	2520.6	1014.2	211	47928315
BID	Sotheby's Holdings, Inc.	—	12/31/03	319.6	23.4	876.7	127.4	119	40185849
SOR	Source Capital, Inc.	Investment company	12/31/03	7.2	3.3	521.8	521.2	18	181445
SJI	South Jersey Industries, Inc	Natural gas distributor	12/31/03	696.8	34.6	1102.2	299.7	85	4488521
SO	Southern Co.	Electric power	12/31/03	11251.0	1474.0	33124.0	10071.0	541	263785366
PCU	Southern Peru Copper Corp.	Mining & metals	12/31/03	798.4	120.7	1775.4	1315.4	56	3532516
SUG	Southern Union Co. (New)	Natural gas	6/30/03	1188.5	43.7	4590.9	920.4	122	20289739
LUV	Southwest Airlines Co		12/31/03	5937.0	442.0	9596.0	5052.0	443	582372259
SWX	Southwest Gas Corp.	Natural gas distributor	12/31/03	1231.0	38.5	2608.1	630.5	119	20048023
SWN	Southwestern Energy Co.	Natural gas	12/31/03	p327.4	p326.5	—	—	139	29193762
SOV	Sovereign Bancorp, Inc. (Uni	Savings & loan	12/31/03	2452.0	401.9	43505.3	3260.4	309	182963962
SSS	Sovran Self Storage, Inc. (Un	Real estate investment trust	12/31/03	113.2	38.0	671.0	368.2	72	4032580
SNF	Spain Fund, Inc.	Investment company	11/30/03	1.4	0.1	74.0	72.8	10	33725
SEH	Spartech Corp.	Plastics & plastic products	11/1/03	956.2	87.4	763.7	322.4	97	21645977
SPA	Sparton Corp.	Electronic components	6/30/03	169.9	3.8	105.3	91.2	10	1580154
SP	Specialty Laboratories, Inc.		12/31/03	119.7	d6.4	135.5	120.5	40	7427460
SSI	Spectrasite Inc	Telecommunications	12/31/03	289.7	d0.1	1073.1	669.7	5	388704
TRK	Speedway Motorsports, Inc.	Recreation	12/31/03	404.5	118.4	1035.6	548.1	76	11406864
SFN	Spherion Corp.	Services	12/26/03	2069.5	1562.8	828.0	411.8	106	50737135
SKE	Spinnaker Exploration Co	Natural gas	12/31/03	226.8	40.1	958.0	744.1	159	28305774
SPM	Spirent Plc (United Kingdom)	Electrical equipment	12/31/03	—	—	—	—	3	123583
TSA	Sports Authority Inc (The)	Recreation	1/31/04	1760.5	60.2	1323.8	439.3	—	—
FON	Sprint Corp. (FON Group)	Telecommunications	12/31/03	—	—	—	—	456	709971869
SPW	SPX Corp.	Conglomerate	12/31/03	5081.5	680.8	7191.4	2067.2	281	68997118
SRX	SRA International Inc		6/30/03	450.4	29.7	364.7	283.0	77	8759810

EARNINGS PER SHARE						P/E RATIO	DIVIDENDS PER SHARE			AV. YLD. %	DIV. DECLARED		PRICE RANGE 2004
QUARTERLY				ANNUAL									
1st	2nd	3rd	2004	2003	2002		2004	2003	2002		AMOUNT	PAYABLE	
—	—	—	—	14.04	10.75	—	0.13	0.13	0.18	1.2	0.03Q	3/18/05	13.10 - 8.80
—	—	—	—	10.47	9.02	—,	0.88	0.96	1.00	7.9	0.06M	5/27/05	12.25 - 9.92
—	—	—	—	15.52	15.35	—	0.91	0.84	0.79	6.8	0.07M	5/27/05	14.69 - 12.11
0.44	—	—	—	1.94	0.78	—	2.28	1.88	0.69	9.6	0.29862M	4/14/05	33.69 - 13.95
—	—	—	—	—	—	—	0.52	0.42	—	1.6	0.6794U	7/1/05	40.48 - 25.55
0.72	—	—	—	3.39	1.77	—	3.11	3.39	1.77	10.8	0.92772Q	2/28/05	34.35 - 23.10
0.59	—	—	—	0.76	0.38	—	0.41	0.40	0.37	1.8	0.16Q	4/1/05	32.21 - 13.36
—	—	—	—	—	—	—	0.19	0.14	0.10	0.6	0.186A	5/17/04	45.83 - 18.96
—	—	—	—	—	—	—	0.68	0.59	0.38	4.1	0.3996S	4/21/05	22.00 - 10.70
0.23	—	—	—	0.24	0.29	—	0.31	0.28	0.28	2.1	0.12Q	4/15/05	22.15 - 7.94
0.27	—	—	—	1.15	1.31	—	1.56	1.56	1.56	5.1	0.39Q	4/29/05	39.40 - 22.15
0.59	—	—	—	1.80	2.23	—	1.25	1.37	1.07	5.2	0.3225Q	5/2/05	27.73 - 20.06
0.91	—	—	—	2.54	0.83	—	1.44	1.36	1.28	4.1	0.39Q	4/1/05	39.71 - 29.92
0.16	—	—	—	0.78	0.62	—	0.13	0.13	0.13	0.9	0.0325Q	3/30/05	18.90 - 9.28
—	—	—	—	—	—	—	0.88	0.78	0.58	1.6	1.04937A	4/22/05	75.36 - 37.35
d0.05	—	—	—	d0.06	1.35	—	0.22	0.57	0.67	1.2	0.055Q	2/28/05	21.37 - 15.00
p0.22	—	—	—	0.81	d4.18	—	0.75	0.75	0.75	1.4	0.21Q	4/8/05	69.87 - 37.70
0.12	—	—	—	0.35	0.07	—	0.07	0.05	0.04	0.2	0.02Q	2/23/05	13.91 - 7.22
0.42	—	—	—	2.28	2.14	—	0.60	0.60	0.60	2.1	0.15Q	3/14/05	35.87 - 21.89
—	—	—	—	—	—	—	0.98	—	5.40	54.7	0.9849U	1/9/04	2.37 - 1.23
pd2.21	2.21	—	—	3.23	3.19	—	—	—	—	—	—	—	74.00 - 49.50
0.09	—	—	—	d1.37	d4.12	—	—	0.40	0.40	—	0.10Q	12/31/03	11.00 - 6.24
0.86	—	—	—	3.32	2.34	—	0.49	0.30	0.30	0.6	0.10Q	3/10/05	108.99 - 44.73
—	—	—	—	5.81	4.91	—	0.64	0.64	0.70	9.5	0.053M	4/29/05	7.72 - 5.60
—	—	—	—	7.42	7.55	—	0.30	0.36	0.46	4.6	0.0265M	4/29/05	6.94 - 6.31
—	—	—	—	8.77	7.52	—	0.75	0.76	0.83	8.9	0.065M	4/29/05	9.55 - 7.23
—	—	—	—	15.43	9.42	—	0.02	—	—	0.2	0.022U	4/30/04	15.31 - 7.44
—	—	—	—	12.73	11.10	—	1.08	1.08	1.13	8.8	0.09M	4/29/05	13.85 - 10.61
d0.16	—	—	—	0.63	2.35	—	—	—	—	—	50%	6/15/00	56.37 - 35.00
0.64	—	—	—	2.00	d4.30	—	—	—	—	—	—	—	54.90 - 36.27
—	—	—	—	—	—	—	1.75	1.75	0.53	7.0	0.4375Q	4/15/05	26.99 - 22.95
0.27	—	—	—	0.72	0.45	—	0.09	0.06	—	0.6	0.03Q	9/17/04	19.75 - 10.25
0.44	—	—	—	d1.34	0.48	—	0.15	0.40	0.58	3.0	0.075Q	5/15/04	6.38 - 3.52
1.81	—	—	—	3.24	2.79	—	1.00	1.00	1.00	3.3	0.29Q	4/15/05	37.93 - 23.20
0.21	—	—	—	0.80	0.92	—	1.25	1.24	1.23	7.9	0.32Q	5/20/05	20.34 - 11.19
0.32	—	—	—	1.73	1.69	—	0.60	0.60	0.54	2.8	0.15Q	3/1/05	24.25 - 18.12
d0.02	—	—	—	0.27	0.68	—	—	—	—	—	0.15Q	7/1/93	62.52 - 30.76
d0.02	—	—	—	0.27	0.68	—	—	—	—	—	0.125Q	7/1/93	58.50 - 57.75
0.23	—	—	—	0.28	d0.34	—	—	—	—	—	0.025Q	4/29/05	7.71 - 2.78
0.04	—	—	—	d0.75	0.56	—	0.43	0.42	0.41	3.8	0.11Q	2/28/05	13.87 - 9.05
—	—	—	—	—	—	—	0.17	0.08	0.05	1.2	—	5/31/05	18.88 - 9.28
d1.07	0.04	—	—	0.54	2.26	—	—	—	—	—	2-for-1	12/15/00	17.95 - 8.51
—	—	—	—	—	—	—	1.72	1.48	1.33	4.0	1.2277S	3/21/05	51.70 - 34.73
0.35	—	—	—	2.26	2.04	—	0.68	0.62	0.60	1.9	0.205Q	3/14/05	45.61 - 26.43
d0.08	—	—	—	1.33	1.41	—	—	—	—	—	0.11Q	9/15/96	20.40 - 10.95
—	—	—	—	0.62	1.45	—	2.19	2.15	2.11	5.9	0.55Q	3/10/05	44.98 - 29.39
—	—	—	—	—	—	—	1.09	0.85	0.65	1.7	1.28261U	2/4/05	87.50 - 39.73
0.75	—	—	—	2.70	1.36	—	—	—	—	—	3-for-2	6/8/98	58.55 - 12.09
d0.37	—	—	—	d1.12	d3.00	—	—	—	0.20	—	0.20Q	3/15/02	10.59 - 2.99
d0.37	—	—	—	d1.12	d3.00	—	4.50	4.50	4.49	11.7	1.125Q	2/15/05	38.89 - 38.20
—	—	—	—	—	—	—	0.60	0.35	0.28	1.4	3-for-1	10/18/04	65.75 - 19.14
0.24	—	—	—	1.53	1.93	—	2.60	2.40	2.18	5.3	0.70Q	2/28/05	65.87 - 32.70
0.73	—	—	—	2.42	2.09	—	0.15	—	—	0.3	0.05Q	4/26/05	66.95 - 31.50
0.09	—	—	—	0.27	0.33	—	—	—	—	—	—	—	26.00 - 15.85
0.07	—	—	—	d0.07	0.12	—	—	—	—	—	2-for-1	10/21/96	4.38 - 1.05
d1.35	—	—	—	0.90	d0.52	—	—	—	—	—	2-for-1	8/7/98	8.80 - 3.36
d0.04	—	—	—	0.03	0.19	—	0.66	0.92	0.92	6.8	0.10Q	3/4/05	11.95 - 7.37
0.18	—	—	—	d0.31	1.20	—	—	—	—	—	—	—	15.23 - 5.88
0.40	—	—	—	1.90	2.01	—	2.00	1.86	1.77	4.4	0.54Q	4/15/05	60.59 - 29.45
p0.64	—	—	—	3.01	1.64	—	0.74	0.59	0.28	1.6	0.19Q	3/18/05	54.44 - 35.40
0.21	—	—	—	0.46	0.23	—	—	—	—	—	0.05Q	1/29/99	17.72 - 3.30
—	—	—	—	—	—	—	0.45	0.39	0.35	0.9	0.2969U	5/23/05	58.53 - 40.36
0.36	—	—	—	1.76	1.86	—	0.62	0.58	0.54	2.0	0.16Q	2/15/05	34.28 - 28.57
0.44	—	—	—	1.24	0.93	—	—	—	—	—	0.12Q	4/15/05	62.97 - 31.84
—	—	—	—	—	p0.24	—	—	—	—	—	100%	9/14/01	29.98 - 17.72
0.22	—	—	—	1.35	1.76	—	1.00	1.00	0.97	3.4	0.25Q	3/10/05	34.67 - 24.76
—	—	—	—	—	—	—	0.58	0.50	0.41	1.4	1.1883A	5/4/05	62.97 - 22.30
—	—	—	—	—	—	—	0.58	0.50	0.41	1.7	1.1883A	5/4/05	43.99 - 22.40
—	—	—	—	—	—	—	0.63	0.56	—	2.3	0.7847U	3/30/05	33.05 - 20.80
d0.06	pd0.11	—	—	d3.75	d3.98	—	—	—	—	—	100%	3/8/00	8.20 - 3.02
0.53	—	—	—	2.07	2.51	—	0.42	0.10	—	2.0	0.12Q	4/15/05	26.35 - 14.70
0.38	—	—	—	1.43	1.39	—	0.87	0.84	0.83	3.4	0.22Q	3/10/05	29.73 - 20.75
0.22	—	—	—	d0.43	d0.89	—	—	—	—	—	0.10Q	12/3/99	18.95 - 7.44
—	—	—	—	56.62	41.90	—	4.00	3.50	4.60	7.0	1.00Q	3/15/05	71.54 - 43.00
1.82	—	—	—	2.73	2.43	—	1.64	1.56	1.88	3.9	0.425Q	4/4/05	53.10 - 31.55
0.45	—	—	—	2.02	1.85	—	1.42	1.39	1.35	4.6	0.3575Q	3/5/05	33.96 - 27.44
1.09	—	—	—	1.51	0.86	—	2.39	0.57	0.36	6.8	—	3/1/05	55.89 - 14.60
d0.05	0.47	0.96	—	0.74	0.33	—	—	—	—	—	5%	8/31/04	20.19 - 17.76
0.03	—	—	—	0.54	0.30	—	0.02	0.02	0.01	0.1	0.0045Q	3/24/05	16.85 - 12.07
1.18	—	—	—	1.13	1.32	—	0.82	0.83	0.82	3.6	0.205Q	6/1/05	25.89 - 20.25
0.67	—	—	—	—	p0.55	—	—	—	—	—	0.06Q	5/5/00	55.45 - 11.70
0.33	—	—	—	1.38	1.23	—	0.11	0.10	0.10	0.6	0.04Q	5/16/05	24.70 - 13.58
0.32	—	—	—	1.46	1.64	—	2.41	2.40	2.37	6.8	0.605Q	4/22/05	43.60 - 27.16
—	—	—	—	8.41	6.81	—	0.86	0.63	0.76	8.5	0.265Q	4/8/05	13.79 - 6.52
0.26	0.41	—	—	1.15	1.21	—	0.44	0.50	0.38	1.8	0.12Q	4/15/05	28.31 - 21.36
d0.26	d0.18	0.02	—	1.07	0.34	—	—	—	—	—	5%	12/15/04	10.50 - 7.51
d0.11	—	—	—	d0.29	d0.61	—	—	—	—	—	—	—	17.50 - 7.02
0.15	—	—	—	d0.42	6.66	—	—	—	—	—	2-for-1	8/21/03	59.65 - 12.78
0.57	—	—	—	1.37	1.43	—	0.31	0.30	0.30	1.0	0.31A	11/15/04	39.30 - 21.87
d0.07	—	—	—	d0.18	d4.60	—	—	—	—	—	100%	9/5/97	11.17 - 3.97
0.40	—	—	—	1.18	0.97	—	—	—	—	—	—	—	40.60 - 19.15
—	—	—	—	—	—	—	—	—	0.26	—	0.0838S	11/14/02	6.70 - 0.76
0.15	—	—	—	0.84	1.86	—	—	—	—	—	—	—	44.75 - 19.96
p0.34	—	—	—	—	p1.18	—	0.50	0.50	0.50	2.7	0.125Q	3/31/05	25.57 - 11.51
0.49	—	—	—	3.41	3.33	—	0.75	—	—	1.6	0.25Q	4/22/05	62.25 - 32.46
0.29	0.33	0.37	—	1.25	0.66	—	—	—	—	—	—	—	65.94 - 23.65

SYMBOL	COMPANY	NATURE OF BUSINESS	FISCAL YEAR-END	TOTAL REV. $MILL	NET INCOME $MILL	TOTAL ASSETS $MILL	NET STK EQUITY $MILL	NO. OF INST.	INST. HOLDINGS (SHARES)
JOE	St. Joe Co. (The) (United St	Forest products	12/31/03	760.6	110.4	1202.2	487.3	145	27463990
STJ	St. Jude Medical, Inc. (Unit	Medical & dental equipment	12/31/03	1932.5	798.0	2359.1	1597.4	386	147368357
SM	St. Mary Land & Exploration	Oil	12/31/03	393.9	115.3	693.1	390.7	144	20877003
SFG	Stancorp Financial Group Inc	Insurance	12/31/03	2066.8	156.3	9981.7	1309.5	173	17583486
STW	Standard Commercial Corp.	Tobacco	3/31/04	780.0	74.8	690.5	229.1	68	9515294
SMP	Standard Motor Products	—	12/31/03	678.8	5.9	594.8	226.0	60	6247472
SPF	Standard Pacific Corp. (New)	—	12/31/03	2360.1	204.4	2460.7	1033.2	142	24917592
SR	Standard Register Co.	Office equipment & supplies	12/28/03	916.3	92.8	469.1	248.6	92	13938706
SXI	Standex International Corp.	Industrial	6/30/03	574.5	13.8	388.3	161.9	83	6312127
SWK	Stanley Works (The)	Hardware & tools	1/3/04	2678.1	265.8	2394.6	858.6	249	59025352
SGU	Star Gas Partners, L.P.	Oil	9/30/03	1463.7	62.2	950.9	—	37	789917
SRT	Startek, Inc.	—	12/31/03	—	d37.9	152.1	131.5	80	4682127
HOT	Starwood Hotel&Res Wrldwide	Real estate investment trust	12/31/03	4630.0	94.0	11351.0	4326.0	301	175475625
STT	State Street Corp.	Financial services	12/31/03	5463.0	832.0	87534.0	5747.0	563	255304512
SBZ	State Street Corp.	Financial services	12/31/03	5463.0	832.0	87534.0	5747.0	37	1298773
STN	Station Casinos, Inc.	Gaming	12/31/03	858.1	82.3	1566.1	339.9	145	46217388
STO	Statoil ASA (Norway)	Oil	12/31/03	—	—	—	—	30	6596791
SNS	Steak n Shake Co. (The)	Restaurants	9/24/03	499.1	65.9	414.6	188.6	89	12281911
SCS	Steelcase, Inc. (United Stat	Furniture & fixtures	2/27/04	2345.6	d41.4	2193.0	1205.3	84	32283006
LVB	Steinway Musical Instruments	—	12/31/03	337.2	47.2	421.9	152.6	44	6748042
SCL	Stepan Co.	Chemicals	12/31/03	784.9	10.2	444.8	162.1	43	3082934
STE	Steris Corp.	Medical & dental equipment	3/31/04	1087.0	232.3	1023.7	676.5	242	55375804
STL	Sterling Bancorp (NY)	Banking - Northeast	12/31/03	124.1	24.2	1758.7	143.2	67	5573853
SVC	Stewart & Stevenson Svcs Inc	Oil service & equipment	1/31/04	1175.6	d52.3	599.6	297.5	119	22193768
STC	Stewart Information Services	Finance	12/31/03	2243.3	1148.0	1031.9	621.4	113	13671229
SF	Stifel Financial Corp.	Financial services	12/31/03	221.6	15.0	412.0	100.0	17	2587893
SWC	Stillwater Mining Co.	Metal products	12/31/03	240.2	d322.9	690.6	479.3	104	24417545
STM	STMicroelectronics N.V.	Electronic components	12/31/03	—	—	—	—	154	72394115
SGY	Stone Energy Corp.	Oil producer	12/31/03	508.3	133.2	1185.4	710.3	173	21304742
SRI	Stoneridge Inc.	Electrical equipment	12/31/03	606.7	52.4	567.4	243.4	54	7202563
SEO	Stora Enso AB (Finland)	Paper	12/31/03	—	—	—	—	69	25884782
STK	Storage Technology Corp. (Un	Comp. components & periphs.	12/26/03	2182.6	836.6	2129.1	1361.4	236	95685148
SRR	Stride Rite Corp.	Shoe manufacturing	11/28/03	550.1	25.5	343.8	267.7	114	31856786
SYK	Stryker Corp.	Medical & dental equipment	12/31/03	3625.3	1106.0	3159.1	2154.8	493	136586687
STU	Student Loan Corp. (The)	Finance	12/31/03	852.8	214.3	23547.6	931.3	88	19157014
RGR	Sturm, Ruger& Co., Inc.	Steel producer	12/31/03	147.9	18.2	162.4	142.3	99	8925464
SPH	Suburban Propane Partners LP	Natural gas distributor	9/27/03	771.7	82.8	657.8	—	58	3255205
SZE	Suez S.A. (France)	Engineering & construction	12/31/03	—	—	—	—	21	2287091
SUI	Sun Communities, Inc.	Real estate	12/31/03	189.1	13.7	1122.6	326.6	109	14647543
SU	Suncor Energy, Inc. (Canada)	Oil producer	12/31/03	—	—	—	—	166	230327379
SDS	Sungard Data Systems Inc.	Computer services	12/31/03	2955.3	367.8	3307.1	2765.9	467	236640921
SXL	Sunoco Logistics Partners L.	Oil service & equipment	12/31/03	2674.2	59.4	1115.5	—	24	624390
SUN	Sunoco, Inc.	Natural gas	12/31/03	17929.0	312.0	6857.0	1556.0	274	55709599
SRZ	Sunrise Senior Living Inc	Hospitals & nursing homes	12/31/03	1188.3	62.2	1009.8	490.3	141	18450242
SFO	Sunset Financial Resources I	Real estate investment trust	12/31/03	—	d0.0	0.3	0.0	—	—
STI	Suntrust Banks, Inc.	Banking - South	12/31/03	7071.8	1690.9	123541.1	9731.2	469	136966850
SPN	Superior Energy Services, In	Oil service & equipment	12/31/03	500.6	30.5	832.9	368.1	125	40595596
SUP	Superior Industries Intl.	—	12/31/03	840.3	73.7	680.3	592.2	167	18783728
SVU	Supervalu Inc.	Food wholesalers	2/28/04	20209.7	280.1	5904.2	2209.6	301	106646236
SFY	Swift Energy Co.	Oil	12/31/03	208.9	99.1	850.4	397.4	109	22725833
SWZ	Swiss Helvetia Fund Inc (The	Investment company	12/31/03	3.7	d0.2	373.9	369.0	39	6209314
SY	Sybase, Inc.	Computer services	12/31/03	778.1	457.6	944.5	741.5	212	78780178
SYD	Sybron Dental Specialities	Medical & dental equipment	9/30/03	526.4	147.0	611.7	208.0	141	34931820
SBL	Symbol Technologies, Inc.	Comp. components & periphs.	12/31/03	1530.3	295.2	1519.3	920.6	313	177333957
SYM	Syms Corp.	Discount & variety stores	2/28/04	275.2	d4.7	252.5	223.2	23	5565799
SYT	Syngenta AG (Switzerland)	—	12/31/03	—	—	—	—	64	33541211
SNX	Synnex Corp	Comp. components & periphs.	11/30/03	4126.2	30.0	753.6	252.8	—	—
SNV	Synovus Financial Corp.	Bank	12/31/03	2430.8	388.9	21632.6	2245.0	256	150329687
SYX	Systemax, Inc.	—	12/31/03	1657.8	16.5	445.7	212.6	24	2900732
TWN	Taiwan Fund, Inc.	Investment company	8/31/03	3.6	d0.1	210.5	209.8	21	3824169
TSM	Taiwan Semiconductor Mfg Co	Electronic components	12/31/03	—	55458.7	404152.3	—	255	264322991
TLB	Talbots, Inc. (United States	—	1/31/04	1624.3	272.2	928.9	616.1	141	22514631
TLM	Talisman Energy, Inc.	Oil producer	12/31/03	—	—	—	—	126	70808101
SKT	Tanger Factory Outlet Center	Real estate investment trust	12/31/03	122.0	22.4	964.8	167.4	82	3256452
TGT	Target Corp	Department stores	1/31/04	48163.0	1841.0	31392.0	11065.0	817	781055025
TBC	Tasty Baking Co. (United Sta	Food processing	12/27/03	159.1	d2.4	99.0	42.4	47	3937877
TCO	Taubman Centers, Inc.	Real estate investment trust	12/31/03	388.5	11.5	2187.0	321.5	138	38424412
TCB	TCF Financial Corp.	Savings & loan	12/31/03	1105.1	215.9	11282.0	920.9	262	45300135
CVT	TCW Convertible Securities F	Investment company	12/31/03	12.1	10.0	324.6	278.4	33	1774167
TOA	Technical Olympic USA, Inc.	Home-building	12/31/03	1687.8	83.5	1511.5	536.4	24	2004714
TKP	Technip	Engineering & construction	12/31/03	—	—	—	—	19	2849194
TNL	Technitrol, Inc.	Electrical equipment	12/26/03	509.2	26.8	571.3	448.8	139	27711467
TE	TECO Energy, Inc.	Electric power	12/31/03	2740.0	9.9	10462.3	1677.7	348	75130472
TRC	Tejon Ranch Co.	—	12/31/03	18.7	d2.9	97.5	74.6	42	7089137
TRO	Tele Centro Oeste Celular Pa	Telecommunications	12/31/03	—	—	—	—	7	1185800
TCN	Tele Norte Celular Participac	Telecommunications	12/31/03	—	—	—	—	1	16900
TNE	Tele Norte Leste Participaco	Telecommunications	12/31/03	—	—	—	—	30	13446224
TSD	Tele Sudeste Celular Particip	Telecommunications	12/31/03	—	—	—	—	1	40
TEO	Telecom Argentina SA	Telecommunications	12/31/03	—	—	—	—	49	31479929
NZT	Telecom Corp. of New Zealand	Telecommunications	6/30/03	5191.0	712.0	7755.0	1765.0	59	15033119
TBH	Telecomunicacoes Brasileiras	Telecommunications	12/31/03	—	—	—	—	65	25309387
TFX	Teleflex Incorporated	Engineering & construction	12/28/03	840.7	29.7	428.1	221.0	132	19826009
TFX	Teleflex Inc.	Medical & dental equipment	12/28/03	2282.4	260.6	1911.0	1062.3	233	25955114
TAR	Telefonica de Argentina S.A.	Telecommunications	12/31/03	—	—	—	—	9	206898
TEF	Telefonica, S.A.	Telecommunications	12/31/03	—	—	—	—	184	55945385
TMX	Telefonos de Mexico, S.A. de	Telecommunications	12/31/03	—	—	—	—	260	256373958
TMB	Telemig Celular Participacoe	Telecommunications	12/31/03	—	—	—	—	7	216177
TLS	Telstra Corp., Ltd.	Telecommunications	6/30/03	21616.0	3394.0	35599.0	15422.0	18	21891895
TU	TELUS Corp. (Canada) (New)	Telecommunications	12/31/03	—	—	—	—	40	47094648
TIN	Temple-Inland Inc. (United St	Paper	1/3/04	4653.0	97.0	21143.0	1968.0	275	45397650
TDF	Templeton Dragon Fund, Inc.	Investment company	12/31/03	30.9	22.7	648.5	627.0	43	10599448
EMF	Templeton Emerging Markets F	Investment company	8/31/03	6.0	3.1	191.9	191.1	26	1751449
TEI	Templeton Emerging Markets In	Investment company	8/31/03	50.1	43.6	654.8	591.0	37	1942746
GIM	Templeton Global Income Fund	Investment company	8/31/03	60.6	53.1	1059.9	1058.8	62	6786313
TRF	Templeton Russia and East Eur	Investment company	3/31/04	3.8	0.8	215.6	214.2	13	400325
TPX	Tempur-Pedic International I	Furniture & fixtures	12/31/03	479.1	87.9	579.2	122.7	—	—

| EARNINGS PER SHARE | | | | | | P/E RATIO | DIVIDENDS PER SHARE | | | AV. YLD. % | DIV. DECLARED | | PRICE RANGE |
| QUARTERLY | | | | ANNUAL | | | | | | | | | 2004 |
1st	2nd	3rd	2004	2003	2002		2004	2003	2002		AMOUNT	PAYABLE	
0.17				0.98	2.14	—	0.52	0.32	0.08	1.1	0.14Q	3/31/05	64.75 - 27.20
0.52				1.83	1.51	—					100%	11/22/04	78.83 - 37.16
0.66				2.65	0.97	—	0.05	0.05	0.05	0.1	2-for-1	3/31/05	43.00 - 24.72
1.48				5.33	3.73	—	1.00	0.70	0.40	1.5	1.00A	12/3/04	83.60 - 49.75
				2.28	2.91	—	0.35	0.30	0.22	1.9	0.0875Q	3/15/05	22.22 - 14.60
d0.03				0.01	0.51	—	0.36	0.36	0.36	2.7	0.09Q	3/1/05	16.57 - 10.02
1.21				6.08	3.67	—	0.32	0.32	0.32	0.7	0.08Q	2/24/05	65.23 - 25.25
d0.23				d1.38	1.14	—	0.92	0.92	0.92	6.1	0.23Q	3/4/05	20.00 - 10.14
0.43	0.40	0.37		1.14	1.66	—	0.84	0.84	0.84	3.4	0.21Q	2/25/05	29.95 - 19.05
0.70				1.14	2.10	—	1.08	1.03	0.99	2.9	0.28Q	3/29/05	49.33 - 23.99
0.56	p2.27			0.01	d0.38	—	1.72	2.30	2.30	12.2	0.575Q	8/13/04	25.79 - 2.60
0.46				1.52	1.05	—	1.58	0.73	—	4.8	0.42Q	2/24/05	43.15 - 22.85
0.16				0.51	1.20	—	0.84	0.84	0.20	2.0	0.84A	1/21/05	59.50 - 22.61
0.63				2.15	3.10	—	0.62	0.54	0.46	1.4	0.17Q	4/15/05	56.90 - 31.63
0.63				2.15	3.10	—	13.50	11.03	—	5.4	3.375Q	2/15/05	251.25 - 250.50
d0.48				0.72	0.51	—	0.69	0.25	—	1.8	0.21Q	6/3/05	59.12 - 18.15
						—	0.37	0.37	0.30	3.1	0.43758A	6/10/05	16.00 - 7.66
0.17	0.29			0.77	0.83	—							21.90 - 9.14
				d0.28	d0.24	—	0.24	0.24	0.24	2.0	0.06Q	4/15/05	14.68 - 9.21
0.39				1.09	1.68	—							36.50 - 13.35
0.42				0.45	2.05	—	0.77	0.76	0.74	3.3	0.195Q	3/15/05	25.73 - 21.55
				1.33	1.12	—					2-for-1	8/24/98	27.70 - 19.80
0.40				1.53	1.37	—	0.67	0.57	0.43	2.5	0.19Q	3/31/05	33.40 - 19.71
0.19				d1.83	0.38	—	0.34	0.34	0.34	2.3	0.085Q	5/13/05	20.47 - 9.68
0.61				6.88	5.30	—	0.46	0.46	—	1.3	0.46A	12/20/04	47.49 - 22.02
0.76				1.82	0.34	—			0.05	—	33%	9/15/04	29.74 - 11.65
0.17				d4.76	0.74	—					3-for-2	12/31/98	18.18 - 2.34
						—	0.09	0.06	0.03	0.4	0.09A	6/1/04	29.90 - 16.36
1.33				5.02	2.09	—							51.35 - 33.58
0.40				0.94	1.09	—							17.97 - 9.63
						—	0.55	0.48	0.40	4.3	0.5764A	4/13/05	16.08 - 9.24
0.21				1.35	1.02	—					2-for-1	6/26/98	32.64 - 20.22
0.19				0.64	0.58	—	0.20	0.20	0.20	2.0	0.05Q	3/15/05	12.26 - 7.93
0.33				1.11	0.85	—	0.07	0.06	0.05	0.1	0.09A	1/31/05	102.46 - 40.30
3.64				10.61	8.77	—	3.60	3.08	2.80	2.6	1.08Q	3/1/05	187.27 - 94.30
0.14				0.46	0.31	—	0.60	0.80	0.80	5.4	0.10Q	3/15/05	13.97 - 8.29
0.71	2.51			1.77	2.12	—	2.41	2.23	2.27	7.6	0.6125Q	2/8/05	35.70 - 27.60
						—	0.64	0.61	0.48	3.4		5/12/04	26.84 - 11.60
0.30				0.75	0.74	—	2.44	2.41	2.29	6.4	0.63Q	4/20/05	42.90 - 33.30
						—	0.23	0.19	0.17	0.9	0.06Q	3/24/05	36.15 - 16.45
0.29				1.27	1.12	—					2-for-1	6/18/01	31.65 - 19.44
0.57				2.53	1.86	—	2.32	1.99	1.16	6.8	0.625Q	2/14/05	43.35 - 24.48
1.17				4.03	d0.62	—	1.15	1.02	1.00	2.0	0.40Q	6/10/05	84.51 - 31.32
0.60				2.63	2.33	—							46.49 - 22.38
d0.85				d0.05		—	0.07			0.6	0.18Q	4/21/05	12.95 - 9.34
1.26				0.41	4.66	—	2.00	1.80	1.72	3.1	0.55Q	3/15/05	76.65 - 52.65
0.05				0.41	0.30	—							15.73 - 7.95
0.51				2.73	2.91	—	0.58	0.53	0.47	1.7	0.155Q	4/22/05	43.80 - 25.21
				2.07	1.91	—	0.59	0.57	0.56	2.4	0.1525Q	6/15/05	35.14 - 13.92
0.52				1.24	0.45	—					10%	10/23/97	30.41 - 8.32
				15.31	11.82	—	0.22	1.25	0.09	1.8	0.474S	1/21/05	15.22 - 8.86
0.13				0.89	0.38	—					100%	11/19/93	23.20 - 12.65
0.30	p0.44			1.46	0.90	—							36.07 - 16.12
0.03				0.01	d0.25	—	0.02	0.02	0.02	0.1	0.01S	4/8/05	19.37 - 8.43
				d0.31	d0.58	—					1.00Q	5/12/05	14.01 - 6.43
						—	0.28	0.11	0.08	1.8	0.2763A	7/26/04	21.49 - 9.15
				1.22	1.16	—							24.21 - 13.70
0.34				1.28	1.21	—	0.68	0.64	0.57	2.9	0.1825Q	4/1/05	29.09 - 17.89
0.07				0.16	d0.23	—							8.00 - 1.45
				12.82	11.31	—					0.03044A	1/15/05	14.50 - 7.93
				2.33	1.14	—	0.07			0.8		7/15/04	11.67 - 6.20
0.58				1.81	2.01	—	0.43	0.39	0.35	1.3	0.11Q	3/28/05	39.82 - 24.11
						—	0.30	0.23	0.20	0.7	0.15S	12/31/04	62.28 - 19.61
0.08				1.17	0.80	—	1.25	1.23	1.22	3.1	0.3225Q	5/16/05	53.55 - 25.96
0.48				2.01	1.81	—	0.30	0.26	0.24	0.7	0.08Q	6/10/05	54.14 - 28.21
0.06				d0.29	d0.54	—	0.20	0.20	0.48	2.0	0.05Q	3/1/05	10.79 - 8.99
0.07				d0.13	d0.17	—	1.08	1.04	1.02	4.6	0.285Q	4/20/05	30.55 - 16.36
0.88				3.05	3.15	—	0.75	0.65	0.57	1.6	0.2125Q	2/28/05	64.14 - 28.75
				5.62	4.63	—	0.18	0.26	0.84	3.7	0.101Q	4/15/05	5.48 - 4.36
0.40				1.95	1.60	—	0.04			0.1	25%	3/31/05	33.49 - 20.00
						—	1.28	0.67	0.61	4.1	0.31443A	4/28/05	46.73 - 15.53
0.14				0.30	d0.75	—			0.03		0.0875Q	4/22/05	23.28 - 17.80
0.15				d0.08	1.95	—	0.76	0.93	1.41	5.8	0.19Q	2/15/05	15.49 - 10.63
d0.09				0.20	0.03	—					0.025S	12/10/99	43.21 - 25.15
						—	0.22		0.15		0.1467U	4/1/05	12.49 - 3.45
						—	0.35			3.9	0.3454U	5/13/04	13.25 - 4.66
						—	0.74	0.33	0.35	5.9	1.0242U	5/5/05	18.34 - 6.75
						—	0.20	0.05	0.48	1.8	0.0105U	3/30/05	13.00 - 8.50
						—					0.1799U	5/10/01	12.10 - 3.18
				0.38	d0.10	—	1.66	0.94	0.76	6.1	0.47515U	3/18/05	35.79 - 18.80
						—	1.13	0.54	0.72	4.0	0.8661U	5/12/05	40.37 - 16.90
0.18				0.91	0.77	—							30.90 - 12.55
0.73				2.73	3.15	—	0.86	0.78	0.71	1.9	0.22Q	3/15/05	54.93 - 35.70
						—							13.20 - 5.16
						—	1.37	1.19	—	3.2	0.77148U	11/18/04	56.94 - 28.05
						—	1.18	1.11	1.11	3.5	0.30403Q	3/24/05	38.60 - 29.07
				0.27	0.28	—	0.74	0.42	0.62	2.3	0.7397U	5/13/04	48.35 - 14.65
						—	0.95	0.89	0.60	5.9	0.5467S	5/9/05	19.80 - 12.24
0.24				1.78	1.25	—	0.60	0.60	0.60	3.0	0.20Q	4/1/05	29.27 - 10.63
						—	1.22	0.68	0.64	2.3	100%	4/1/05	70.02 - 37.40
				16.62	9.73	—	0.60	0.19	—	4.1	0.0143S	4/8/05	19.99 - 8.96
				10.82	8.76	—	0.20	0.21	0.16	1.6	0.0606A	1/14/05	17.25 - 7.98
				12.53	11.11	—	1.00	1.06	1.26	8.1	0.25Q	4/4/05	14.10 - 10.55
				8.18	7.29	—	0.63	0.54	0.54	7.2	0.04M	4/29/05	10.05 - 7.25
				39.89	22.11	—	4.68	0.39	0.19	14.1	2.4124A	1/14/05	47.39 - 19.01
0.11				0.39	d0.67	—							21.50 - 11.25

SYMBOL	COMPANY	NATURE OF BUSINESS	FISCAL YEAR-END	TOTAL REV. $MILL	NET INCOME $MILL	TOTAL ASSETS $MILL	NET STK EQUITY $MILL	NO. OF INST.	INST. HOLDINGS (SHARES)
TS	Tenaris SA	Steel producer	12/31/03	—	—	—	—	66	11776105
THC	Tenet Healthcare Corp.	Hospitals & nursing homes	12/31/03	13212.0	319.0	11719.0	4361.0	446	382471836
TNC	Tennant Co.	Machinery & equipment	12/31/03	454.0	14.2	216.6	165.6	65	6820136
TEN	Tenneco Automotive, Inc.	—	12/31/03	3766.0	54.0	2162.0	58.0	82	15093760
TPP	Teppco Partners L.P.	Oil	12/31/03	4255.8	125.8	2941.0	—	117	10455140
TER	Teradyne Inc.	Electrical equipment	12/31/03	1352.9	d380.2	1785.4	949.6	304	181287162
TEX	Terex Corp. (New)	Machinery & equipment	12/31/03	3897.1	d49.9	2613.4	876.7	127	40418746
TRA	Terra Industries, Inc.	Fertilizer	12/31/03	1351.1	d82.0	1120.1	265.1	39	14853545
TNH	Terra Nitrogen Co., L.P.	Fertilizer	12/31/03	405.4	d35.3	196.2	—	8	807238
TSO	Tesoro Petroleum Corp. (Unit	Oil	12/31/03	8845.7	76.1	3577.1	965.4	112	42049992
TTI	Tetra Technologies, Inc. (DE	Industrial	12/31/03	318.7	228.0	290.1	210.8	106	13329183
TXN	Texas Instruments, Inc.	Electronic components	12/31/03	9834.0	2448.0	15510.0	11864.0	858	1171219541
TPL	Texas Pacific Land Trust	Real estate investment trust	12/31/03	10.0	5.3	18.3	14.0	20	258036
TXT	Textron Inc.	—	1/3/04	9859.0	695.0	14531.0	3690.0	355	79856817
TTF	Thai Fund, Inc.	Investment company	12/31/03	2.3	0.9	6.6	5.4	15	407653
GPS	The Gap, Inc.	Specialty stores	1/31/04	15854.0	1030.0	10343.0	4783.0	437	552181361
STA	The St Paul Travelers Compani	Insurance	12/31/03	8854.0	699.0	39265.0	6229.0	405	206910671
TGX	Theragenics Corp.	Medical & dental equipment	12/31/03	35.6	d0.1	152.8	142.3	84	15743240
TMO	Thermo Electron Corp.	Meas. & control instruments	12/31/03	2097.1	391.3	3274.9	2382.8	303	128085748
TNB	Thomas & Betts Corp.	Electrical equipment	12/31/03	1322.3	90.6	1782.6	731.4	182	53349907
TII	Thomas Industries	Conglomerate	12/31/03	408.9	93.0	471.9	383.4	92	12295804
TNM	Thomas Nelson, Inc.	Publishing	3/31/04	222.6	16.3	157.0	103.0	55	6840522
TNM B	Thomas Nelson, Inc.	Publishing	3/31/04	222.6	16.3	157.0	103.0	3	43036
TOC	Thomson Corp.	Publishing	12/31/03	—	—	—	—	51	77904859
THO	Thor Industries, Inc.	—	7/31/03	1571.4	78.6	589.9	414.8	122	15508280
TMA	Thornburg Mortgage Inc	Real estate investment trust	12/31/03	589.6	176.5	18749.5	1239.1	127	12817645
TFS	Three-Five Systems, Inc.	Electronic components	12/31/03	159.0	d53.5	167.2	117.0	77	12727016
TDW	Tidewater, Inc.	Oil service & equipment	3/31/04	26.7	d523.9	2056.8	1366.1	267	47687027
TIF	Tiffany & Co.	Jewelry	1/31/04	2000.0	558.2	2286.7	1454.9	338	140336462
TBL	Timberland Co. (The) (United	Shoe manufacturing	12/31/03	1342.1	201.6	606.2	428.5	186	17811284
TWX	Time Warner Inc (New)	Computer services	12/31/03	39565.0	7663.0	117162.0	56038.0	—	—
TKR	Timken Co. (The)	Steel producer	12/31/03	3788.1	97.3	3260.1	1089.6	188	44865636
TTN	Titan Corp.	Computer services	12/31/03	1775.0	32.2	927.1	371.4	184	55213698
TWI	Titan International Inc (IL)	Tires and/or rubber goods	12/31/03	491.7	d70.3	509.2	112.0	18	11345099
TIE	Titanium Metals Corp.	Metal products	12/31/03	385.3	d24.1	588.0	209.0	19	691166
TJX	TJX Companies, Inc. (New)	—	1/31/04	13327.9	658.4	4273.3	1552.4	425	436177774
TNS	TNS Inc	Services	12/31/03	223.4	118.7	335.0	d37.5	—	—
THE	Todco	Oil service & equipment	12/31/03	227.7	d477.2	708.9	137.7	—	—
TOD	Todd Shipyards Corp.	Defense systems & equip.	3/28/04	147.8	3.8	147.9	71.4	13	1157804
TOL	Toll Brothers Inc. (United St	Home-building	10/31/03	2775.2	259.8	3787.4	1476.6	200	41672790
TKS	Tomkins Plc (United Kingdom)	—	1/3/04	—	—	—	—	16	5432861
TOO	TOO, Inc.	Specialty stores	1/31/04	598.7	28.5	391.5	281.8	148	29142961
TR	Tootsie Roll Industries Inc (	—	12/31/03	392.7	162.4	636.6	536.6	143	12300560
TRU	Torch Energy Royalty Trust	Oil	12/31/03	9.0	8.0	26.5	26.3	6	71800
TMK	Torchmark Corp.	Insurance brokerage	12/31/03	2930.6	755.7	13460.9	3240.1	312	78510969
TTC	Toro Co. (The)	Machinery & equipment	10/31/03	1496.6	201.3	784.2	437.2	162	9511432
TD	Toronto Dominion Bank	—	10/31/03	—	—	—	—	86	171850315
TOT	Total S.A. (New)	Oil	12/31/03	—	—	—	—	214	64859089
TSS	Total System Services, Inc.	Services	12/31/03	1053.5	141.3	957.0	732.5	81	13767355
TCT	Town & Country Trust (The)	Real estate investment trust	12/31/03	118.0	17.0	589.0	39.4	71	4587566
TOY	Toys R Us Inc. (United	Specialty stores	1/31/04	11566.0	88.0	10192.0	4222.0	291	209794057
TCC	Trammell Crow Co.	Real estate	12/31/03	707.8	18.3	546.4	327.6	68	24996479
TAI	Transamerica Income Shares,	Investment company	3/31/04	10.0	9.0	163.8	153.8	15	50929
TRH	Transatlantic Holdings Inc.	Property & casualty insurance	12/31/03	3452.1	303.6	8707.8	2376.6	102	50354381
TRP	Transcanada Corp	Natural gas	12/31/03	—	—	—	—	1	350
TCI	Transcontinental Realty Inve	Real estate investment trust	12/31/03	114.4	d18.6	881.0	220.0	10	7882
RIG	Transocean, Inc. (Cayman Isl	Oil	12/31/03	2434.3	83.7	11376.9	7192.6	480	255089408
TGS	Transportadora de Gas del Sur	Natural gas	12/31/03	—	—	—	—	13	2749636
TPK	Travelers Property Casualty	Property & casualty insurance	12/31/03	15139.2	1696.0	64872.0	11986.7	—	—
TRR	TRC Companies, Inc.	Pollution control	6/30/03	315.6	12.2	249.8	138.8	53	5668147
TG	Tredegar Corp. (United State	Plastics & plastic products	12/31/03	746.5	49.4	732.6	447.8	100	13459015
TWP	Trex Co., Inc.	Plastics & plastic products	12/31/03	191.0	21.0	211.5	130.4	97	5831945
TY	Tri-Continental Corp.	Investment company	12/31/03	35.9	21.6	2352.1	2348.6	83	3851559
TRI	Triad Hospitals, Inc.	Hospitals & nursing homes	12/31/03	3865.9	496.6	4567.0	2076.3	247	68633652
TRY	Triarc Companies, Inc. (Unite	Restaurants	12/31/03	293.6	d30.0	1019.0	287.6	104	12263908
TRB	Tribune Co.	Newspapers	12/31/03	p5594.8	p5594.8	—	—	471	153166140
TRN	Trinity Industries, Inc.	Metal products	12/31/03	1432.8	d24.3	1814.0	1003.8	136	40149463
TPC	Triton PCS Hldgs Inc	Telecommunications	12/31/03	810.1	194.8	1473.8	d320.3	63	46267355
TGI	Triumph Group Inc.	—	3/31/04	608.3	19.4	869.2	515.1	101	14560417
TRZ	Trizec Properties, Inc	Finance	12/31/03	848.2	184.4	5164.6	1965.5	111	88845699
TRW	TRW Automotive Holdings Corp	—	12/31/03	9435.0	d104.0	7943.0	728.0	—	—
TUP	Tupperware Corp.	Plastics & plastic products	12/27/03	1174.8	104.5	862.2	228.2	218	43592970
TXU	TXU Corp (United States)	Electric power	12/31/03	11008.0	737.0	30041.0	5919.0	382	219266234
TYC	Tyco International Ltd. (Ber	Services	9/30/03	—	—	—	—	762	1539822818
TYL	Tyler Technologies, Inc.	Computer services	12/31/03	145.5	26.0	138.4	117.9	57	12993934
TSN	Tyson Foods, Inc.	Meat packing & processing	9/27/03	24549.0	337.0	9648.0	3954.0	235	143363201
USB	U.S. Bancorp (DE)	Banking - Midwest	12/31/03	14571.0	3710.1	189286.0	19242.0	746	962259741
UBH	U.S.B. Holding Co., Inc. (NY	Banking - Northeast	12/31/03	147.3	29.3	2906.5	168.3	37	1398266
UGI	UGI Corp. (New)	Public utility	9/30/03	3026.1	98.9	2781.7	569.8	191	16626984
UCI	UICI	Life insurance	12/31/03	1813.2	87.3	2140.3	587.6	108	19497614
UIL	UIL Holding Corp	Electric power	12/31/03	963.7	29.5	1756.2	492.8	112	5891316
UGP	UltraPar Participacoes S.A. (	Specialty chemicals	12/31/03	—	—	—	—	15	3235299
UBB	Unibanco-Uniao de Bancos Bra	—	12/31/03	—	—	—	—	59	5438815
UNF	UniFirst Corp.	—	8/30/03	596.9	29.3	448.9	335.4	60	6455293
UN	Unilever N.V.	Food processing	12/31/03	—	—	—	—	260	77122768
UL	Unilever Plc (United Kingdom	Food processing	12/31/03	—	—	—	—	103	36557886
UNP	Union Pacific Corp. (United	Railroads	12/31/03	11551.0	999.0	33460.0	12354.0	576	200629223
UB	UnionBanCal Corp.	Banking - West	12/31/03	2563.9	587.1	42498.5	3740.4	157	141163536
UNS	UniSource Energy Corp.	Electric power	12/31/03	969.9	45.3	3092.1	539.7	118	24191023
UIS	Unisys Corp.	Computers	12/31/03	5911.2	639.2	5148.7	1395.2	295	219500560
UNT	Unit Corp.	Oil service & equipment	12/31/03	302.6	58.1	711.1	515.8	133	29323437
UAG	United Auto Group Inc. (Unit	—	12/31/03	8671.5	95.1	1651.5	828.4	89	31469727
UDI	United Defense Industries In	—	12/31/03	2052.6	140.6	1014.2	127.1	109	42429149
UDR	United Dominion Realty Trust	Real estate investment trust	12/31/03	604.4	51.6	3543.6	1163.4	216	57184831
UIC	United Industrial Corp. (Uni	Defense systems & equip.	12/31/03	310.9	15.7	134.6	40.9	60	5983495
UMC	United Microelectronics Corp.	Electronic components	12/31/03	—	—	—	—	112	128478898

EARNINGS PER SHARE QUARTERLY 1st	2nd	3rd	2004	ANNUAL 2003	2002	P/E RATIO	DIVIDENDS PER SHARE 2004	2003	2002	AV. YLD. %	DIV. DECLARED AMOUNT	PAYABLE	PRICE RANGE 2004
—	—	—	—	—	—	—	1.14	0.99	—	3.2	1.144U	6/21/04	51.70 - 19.60
d0.04	—	—	—	d3.01	0.93	—	—	—	—	—	3-for-2	6/28/02	18.73 - 9.15
0.28	—	—	—	1.56	0.91	—	0.86	0.84	0.82	2.3	0.22Q	3/15/05	44.34 - 30.30
d0.05	—	—	—	0.65	0.74	—	—	—	—	—	0.05Q	12/5/00	17.47 - 2.26
0.46	—	—	—	1.52	1.79	—	2.64	2.50	2.35	7.4	0.6625Q	2/7/05	42.35 - 29.28
0.20	—	—	—	d1.03	d3.93	—	—	—	—	—	2-for-1	8/31/99	30.70 - 10.39
0.34	—	—	—	d0.53	d0.41	—	—	—	—	—	0.06A	6/5/91	48.23 - 11.29
0.23	—	—	—	d0.16	d0.48	—	—	—	—	—	0.02Q	6/11/99	9.38 - 1.07
0.64	—	—	—	d1.87	0.33	—	1.75	0.25	0.40	11.5	0.65Q	2/28/05	25.95 - 4.45
0.75	—	—	—	1.17	d1.93	—	—	—	—	—	0.10Q	8/25/86	34.65 - 4.10
0.08	—	—	—	0.84	0.40	—	—	—	—	—	50%	8/21/03	32.57 - 13.41
0.21	—	—	—	0.68	d0.20	—	0.09	0.09	0.09	0.4	0.025Q	2/14/05	33.98 - 15.90
0.53	—	—	—	2.34	2.09	—	2.25	0.75	0.40	2.5	0.55A	3/15/05	138.50 - 43.00
0.26	—	—	—	2.05	2.60	—	1.30	1.30	1.30	2.5	0.35Q	4/1/05	74.91 - 27.46
—	—	—	—	8.93	4.02	—	0.08	0.05	0.01	1.0	0.1246S	1/31/05	11.95 - 4.05
0.32	—	—	—	1.09	0.54	—	0.11	0.07	0.09	0.6	0.045Q	4/26/05	24.56 - 13.04
1.34	—	—	—	2.88	1.06	—	1.45	1.16	1.15	3.9	0.22Q	3/31/05	43.63 - 30.23
—	—	—	—	d0.01	0.19	—	—	—	—	—	2-for-1	4/15/98	6.25 - 3.31
0.26	—	—	—	1.04	1.12	—	—	—	—	—	0.00U	11/15/01	31.40 - 17.60
0.27	—	—	—	0.73	d0.14	—	—	0.01	—	—	0.005Q	11/15/03	32.47 - 14.18
0.60	—	—	—	2.12	2.00	—	0.38	0.36	0.34	1.2	0.095Q	4/1/05	40.06 - 24.75
—	—	—	—	1.09	0.70	—	0.17	0.04	—	0.9	0.05Q	4/18/05	29.09 - 8.51
—	—	—	—	1.09	0.70	—	0.17	0.04	—	0.8	0.05Q	4/18/05	20.75 - 20.75
—	—	—	—	—	—	—	0.76	1.15	0.71	2.4	0.19Q	3/15/05	36.83 - 25.97
0.41	0.30	0.57	—	1.37	0.94	—	0.10	0.04	0.02	0.2	0.03Q	4/1/05	63.20 - 22.00
0.70	—	—	—	2.71	2.59	—	2.62	2.44	2.25	10.2	0.68Q	1/21/05	31.28 - 20.03
d0.31	—	—	—	d1.59	d0.79	—	—	—	—	—	0.00U	9/15/05	7.78 - 1.84
—	—	—	—	0.73	1.57	—	0.60	0.60	0.60	1.9	0.15Q	2/17/05	36.45 - 25.74
0.27	—	—	—	1.45	1.28	—	0.22	0.18	0.16	0.7	0.06Q	4/11/05	44.00 - 23.25
0.87	—	—	—	3.23	2.36	—	—	—	—	—	2-for-1	5/2/05	67.98 - 30.95
0.15	—	—	—	0.68	d10.01	—	—	—	—	—			19.85 - 15.47
0.32	—	—	—	0.44	0.83	—	0.52	0.52	0.52	2.4	0.15Q	3/2/05	27.50 - 15.30
0.04	—	—	—	0.35	d0.11	—	—	—	—	—	0.00U	8/5/02	21.90 - 7.45
0.25	—	—	—	d1.75	d1.73	—	0.02	0.02	0.02	0.2	0.005Q	4/15/05	15.70 - 0.70
d0.52	—	—	—	d4.06	d21.27	—	—	—	—	—	400%	8/26/04	108.50 - 19.05
0.33	—	—	—	1.28	1.08	—	0.17	0.14	0.11	0.8	0.06Q	6/2/05	26.12 - 16.07
0.34	—	—	—	d1.31	d1.38	—	—	—	—	—			23.50 - 17.70
d0.53	—	—	—	d18.28	d43.57	—	—	—	—	—			19.05 - 13.38
—	—	—	—	0.72	0.74	—	0.40	0.30	—	2.6	0.10Q	6/23/05	17.80 - 12.95
0.62	0.89	—	—	3.44	2.91	—	—	—	—	—	100%	3/28/02	68.95 - 19.30
—	—	—	—	—	—	—	0.90	0.80	0.73	5.6	0.5937S	6/6/05	20.63 - 11.52
0.15	—	—	—	0.82	1.38	—	—	—	—	—			26.75 - 13.28
0.22	—	—	—	1.26	1.25	—	0.27	0.26	0.25	0.8	0.07Q	4/1/05	38.88 - 27.48
0.15	—	—	—	0.93	1.00	—	0.67	0.93	1.01	10.3	0.217Q	3/10/05	7.75 - 5.19
1.05	—	—	—	3.73	3.18	—	0.44	0.38	0.36	0.9	0.11Q	4/29/05	57.57 - 35.80
0.36	2.00	—	—	3.12	2.31	—	0.12	0.15	0.12	0.2	100%	4/12/05	82.33 - 31.51
—	—	—	—	—	—	—	1.36	1.16	1.12	4.3	0.40Q	4/30/05	41.69 - 21.31
—	—	—	—	—	—	—	3.73	1.99	1.48	4.3	1.6661A	6/15/05	110.56 - 63.27
0.17	—	—	—	0.71	0.64	—	0.12	0.08	0.07	0.5	0.04Q	4/1/05	31.00 - 14.75
0.12	—	—	—	0.70	1.07	—	1.72	1.72	1.72	7.0	0.43Q	3/10/05	29.21 - 20.10
d0.13	—	—	—	0.41	1.09	—	—	—	—	—	3-for-2	6/29/90	20.77 - 8.08
0.05	—	—	—	0.49	0.38	—	—	—	—	—			18.44 - 7.96
—	—	—	—	—	22.97	—	1.62	1.77	2.12	6.9	0.13M	4/15/05	25.48 - 21.43
1.69	—	—	—	5.75	3.21	—	0.38	0.34	0.31	0.5	0.10Q	6/17/05	93.35 - 53.15
—	—	—	—	—	—	—	1.14	0.54	—	5.4	0.305Q	4/29/05	24.91 - 17.57
d1.25	—	—	—	d3.45	d4.60	—	—	—	—	—	0.18Q	9/29/00	17.23 - 10.99
p0.07	—	—	—	0.06	d7.42	—	—	—	0.06	—	0.03Q	6/13/02	26.21 - 25.65
—	—	—	—	—	—	—	—	—	—	—		8/29/01	5.80 - 1.48
—	—	—	—	1.68	0.23	—	1.13	1.13	0.62	4.8	0.28125Q	4/15/05	25.32 - 21.40
0.20	0.24	0.17	—	0.82	1.14	—	—	—	—	—	3-for-2	3/5/02	23.33 - 11.39
0.06	—	—	—	0.50	0.16	—	0.16	0.16	0.16	1.0	0.04Q	4/1/05	20.39 - 11.32
0.63	—	—	—	1.43	1.16	—	—	—	—	—			54.25 - 31.88
—	—	—	—	19.55	15.72	—	0.23	0.17	0.26	1.5	0.05Q	3/24/05	18.33 - 12.81
0.66	—	—	—	1.32	1.89	—	—	—	—	—			38.09 - 22.01
d0.10	—	—	—	d0.22	d0.48	—	0.26	0.13	—	2.3	0.065Q	3/15/05	13.18 - 9.51
0.35	—	—	—	—	p2.61	—	0.48	0.44	0.44	1.0	0.18Q	3/10/05	53.00 - 39.20
d0.25	—	—	—	d0.25	d0.43	—	0.24	0.24	0.36	0.9	0.06Q	4/29/05	36.10 - 16.21
d0.60	—	—	—	d2.52	d2.08	—	—	—	—	—			7.04 - 1.64
—	—	—	—	1.22	2.36	—	—	—	—	—			41.40 - 22.45
0.55	—	—	—	1.01	d1.26	—	0.80	0.60	0.26	5.8	0.20Q	4/15/05	19.05 - 8.50
0.02	—	—	—	d1.16	—	—	—	—	—	—			25.64 - 16.65
0.25	—	—	—	0.82	1.54	—	0.88	0.88	0.88	5.3	0.22Q	4/4/05	21.00 - 12.47
0.57	—	—	—	2.03	0.55	—	0.50	0.50	2.40	3.5	0.5625Q	4/1/05	67.00 - 15.97
—	—	—	—	—	—	—	0.05	0.05	0.05	0.2	0.10Q	5/2/05	36.42 - 12.86
0.05	—	—	—	0.58	0.12	—	—	—	—	—			11.05 - 3.53
0.16	0.33	—	—	0.96	1.08	—	0.16	0.16	0.16	1.1	0.04Q	6/15/05	21.28 - 7.75
0.52	—	—	—	1.92	1.73	—	0.96	0.81	0.77	3.8	0.30Q	4/15/05	31.65 - 18.98
0.36	—	—	—	1.46	1.35	—	0.43	0.37	0.32	2.0	0.13Q	4/15/05	29.15 - 14.23
p1.48	1.48	—	—	2.29	1.80	—	1.19	1.27	1.08	3.5	0.3125Q	4/1/05	41.40 - 27.60
0.68	—	—	—	1.82	1.05	—	0.25	—	—	1.1	0.25S	3/15/05	36.40 - 9.61
0.39	—	—	—	2.07	3.08	—	2.88	2.88	2.88	6.6	0.72Q	4/1/05	54.65 - 31.99
—	—	—	—	—	—	—	0.57	0.32	0.27	4.3	0.3326S	3/14/05	20.00 - 6.61
—	—	—	—	—	—	—	0.92	0.77	0.86	4.3	0.1816S	5/9/05	31.84 - 11.35
0.49	0.34	—	—	1.52	1.39	—	0.15	0.15	0.15	0.7	0.0375Q	4/4/05	29.95 - 15.45
—	—	—	—	—	—	—	2.17	2.00	1.50	3.4		6/13/05	75.02 - 54.00
—	—	—	—	—	—	—	1.31	1.11	0.90	3.5	0.9547U	6/13/05	43.85 - 32.10
0.63	—	—	—	4.07	5.05	—	1.20	0.92	0.80	1.9	0.30Q	4/1/05	68.95 - 54.80
1.05	—	—	—	3.90	3.38	—	1.34	1.18	1.06	2.6	0.36Q	4/1/05	86.46 - 39.42
0.19	—	—	—	1.31	0.97	—	0.64	0.60	0.50	3.1	0.19Q	3/8/05	24.94 - 16.45
0.09	—	—	—	0.78	0.69	—	—	—	—	—	0.25Q	8/7/90	15.88 - 9.26
0.34	—	—	—	1.12	0.47	—	—	—	—	—			40.63 - 17.86
0.49	—	—	—	2.07	1.50	—	0.41	0.10	—	1.9	0.11Q	4/1/05	32.05 - 11.13
0.78	—	—	—	2.66	2.58	—	—	—	—	—	0.125U	3/1/05	48.95 - 21.48
0.05	—	—	—	0.05	0.21	—	1.16	1.13	1.10	5.8	0.30Q	5/2/05	24.80 - 15.57
0.34	—	—	—	1.10	0.28	—	0.40	0.40	0.30	1.5	0.10Q	3/31/05	41.45 - 12.35
—	—	—	—	—	—	—	—	—	—	—	8%	8/17/04	6.14 - 2.89

SYMBOL	COMPANY	NATURE OF BUSINESS	FISCAL YEAR-END	TOTAL REV. $MILL	NET INCOME $MILL	TOTAL ASSETS $MILL	NET STK EQUITY $MILL	NO. OF INST.	INST. HOLDINGS (SHARES)
UPS	United Parcel Service, Inc.	Freight transportation	12/31/03	33485.0	7277.0	28909.0	14852.0	562	312005927
URI	United Rentals, Inc. (United	Equip. & vehicle leasing	12/31/03	2867.2	d258.6	4630.5	1140.9	160	56062387
X	United States Steel Corp. (N	Steel producer	12/31/03	9458.0	d406.0	7838.0	1093.0	249	89023926
UTX	United Technologies Corp.		12/31/03	31034.0	5831.0	35999.0	13592.0	818	342652829
UNH	UnitedHealth Group Inc	Hospitals & nursing homes	12/31/03	28823.0	1825.0	16790.0	4979.0	557	260596336
UTR	Unitrin, Inc.	Insurance	12/31/03	2943.8	123.6	8536.8	1818.9	144	17057212
UCO	Universal Compression Holding	Equip. & vehicle leasing	3/31/04	688.8	32.6	1887.5	799.2	98	17193654
UVV	Universal Corp.	Tobacco	6/30/03	2636.8	283.6	1879.9	620.3	161	18174032
UHT	Universal Health Rlty. Inc.	Real estate investment trust	12/31/03	28.3	24.4	194.3	152.2	88	3961551
UHS	Universal Health Services In	Hospitals & nursing homes	12/31/03	3643.6	527.1	2772.7	1090.9	246	51497245
UTI	Universal Technical Institut	—	9/30/03	196.5	20.4	62.3	d83.2		
UVN	Univision Communications Inc	Broadcasting	12/31/03	1311.0	155.4	7538.7	5103.0	295	179998292
UCL	Unocal Corp.	Oil producer	12/31/03	6539.0	2211.0	9911.0	4009.0	389	211901162
UNA	Unova, Inc.	Services	12/31/03	1122.6	d9.7	1090.8	430.8	92	48464326
UNM	UNUMProvident Corp.	Life Insurance	12/31/03	9991.6	d264.6	47084.5	6099.8	315	196366364
UPM	UPM - Kymmene Corp. (Finland	Paper	12/31/03					48	7055208
URS	URS Corp. (United States)	Engineering & construction	10/31/03	3186.7	1059.1	2191.5	765.1	101	21380103
UBP	Urstadt Biddle Properties, In	Real estate investment trust	10/31/03	60.4	23.5	392.7	219.7	19	654036
USU	USEC, Inc.	Mining & processing	12/31/03	1460.3	11.8	2053.8	886.2	111	50677347
USG	USG Corp. (United States)	Cement & gypsum	12/31/03	3666.0	355.0	3751.0	689.0	81	20399654
UST	UST, Inc.	Tobacco	12/31/03	1742.6	598.8	1631.8	d115.2	300	124305270
MTN	Vail Resorts Inc.	Recreation	7/31/03	710.4	d8.5	1321.6	496.2	55	19005023
VCI	Valassis Communications, Inc	Printing & engraving	12/31/03	916.5	270.4	692.8	76.1	180	51582766
VRX	Valeant Pharmaceuticals Inte	Drugs	12/31/03	686.0	d78.7	1904.3	605.4		
VLO	Valero Energy Corp. (New)	Natural gas	12/31/03	37968.6	1907.5	14560.6	5735.2	336	92492814
VLI	Valero L.P. (United States)	Oil	12/31/03	181.4	77.1	817.7		39	3549642
VHI	Valhi, Inc. (New)	Conglomerate	12/31/03	1259.7	38.9	2129.5	659.7	45	5263062
VLY	Valley National Bancorp	Banking - Northeast	12/31/03	605.7	153.4	9880.7	652.8	101	11892014
VMI	Valmont Industries, Inc.	Machinery & equipment	12/27/03	837.6	25.9	604.8	265.5	92	8509823
VAL	Valspar Corp.	Paints & related products	10/31/03	2247.9	294.0	2176.1	869.3	202	32098750
VBF	Van Kampen Bond Fund	Investment company	6/30/03	13.9	12.5	228.3	224.7	21	331658
VIT	Van Kampen High Income Trust	Investment company	12/31/03	6.7	5.7	88.2	50.0	8	153393
VLT	Van Kampen High Income Trust	Investment company	12/31/03	5.0	4.2	65.4	64.9	4	123393
VIN	Van Kampen Income Trust	Investment company	12/31/03	5.9	5.0	117.2	99.4	17	522463
VMT	Van Kampen Municipal Income T	Investment company	6/30/03	22.6	19.0	475.6	307.9	23	1173779
VVR	Van Kampen Senior Income Trus	—	7/31/03	114.6	83.7	1949.5	1458.6	48	14283228
VKV	Van Kampen Value Municipal In	Investment company	10/31/03	30.8	25.8	601.2	366.9	21	173705
VAR	Varian Medical Systems, Inc.	Electronic components	9/26/03	133.9	d568.3	1053.5	563.7	299	60129566
VGR	Vector Group Ltd	Tobacco	12/31/03	583.7	d15.6	628.2	d46.5	59	14685755
VVC	Vectren Corp	Natural gas distributor	12/31/03	1587.7	111.2	3353.4	1071.7	187	27054205
VTR	Ventas, Inc.	Hospitals & nursing homes	12/31/03	205.0	109.5	812.9	56.3	141	60445558
VTS	Veritas DGC Inc.	Oil service & equipment	7/31/03	503.0	d32.7	744.9	490.1	136	27859519
VZ	Verizon Communications Inc	Telecommunications	12/31/03	67752.0	3509.0	161135.0	33466.0	1117	1425284485
VTA	Vesta Insurance Group, Inc	Property & casualty insurance	12/31/03	617.7	d37.0	1912.4	111.6	55	15429700
VFC	VF Corp. (United States)	—	1/3/04	5207.5	996.4	3950.1	1951.3	300	96976864
VIA	Viacom Inc	Broadcasting	12/31/03	26585.3	4296.6	89250.6	63205.0	186	34353423
RBV	Viacom Inc	Broadcasting	12/31/03	26585.3	4296.6	89250.6	63205.0	6	115395
VVI	Viad Corp.	Conglomerate	12/31/03	1572.1	1476.9	9182.6	881.4		
VAS	Viasys Healthcare, Inc. (Uni	Medical & dental equipment	1/3/04	394.9	65.0	496.1	431.7	123	23772635
VCO	Vina Concha y Toro S.A.	Distilling	12/31/03					14	552066
VPI	Vintage Petroleum, Inc.	Oil	12/31/03	756.3	d532.1	1302.2	422.5	157	41226584
VSH	Vishay Intertechnology, Inc.	Electrical equipment	12/31/03	2170.6	102.7	4285.0	2514.0	268	110740891
VC	Visteon Corp.		12/31/03	17660.0	d1213.0	10407.0	1858.0	261	78402110
EYE	VISX, Inc.	Industrial	12/31/03	143.9	61.3	162.2	125.8	123	38907875
V	Vivendi Universal (France)	Telecommunications	12/31/03					117	62366108
VOL	Volt Information Sciences, I	Services	11/2/03	1409.9	4.8	538.7	241.9	62	5498333
VNO	Vornado Realty Trust	Real estate investment trust	12/31/03	1503.1	407.2	9342.6	3021.2	235	74808261
VMC	Vulcan Materials.	Conglomerate	12/31/03	2892.2	534.9	3486.9	1802.8	255	70289533
WHI	W Holding Co Inc		12/31/03	p461.9	p461.9	—	—	115	21668584
WHQ	W-H Energy Services Inc.	Oil service & equipment	12/31/03	398.3	50.6	326.7	247.5	112	23099653
WPC	W.P. Carey & Co. LLC	Real estate investment trust	12/31/03	163.4	105.9	906.5	594.8	58	1683932
WNC	Wabash National Corp.		12/31/03	887.9	d19.8	379.0	22.2	91	23264377
WAB	Wabtec Corp.	Railroads	12/31/03	717.9	57.3	603.0	248.3	98	29366351
WB	Wachovia Corp 2nd (New)	Banking - South	12/31/03	24474.0	4247.0	401032.0	32428.0	755	714491854
WDR	Waddell & Reed Financial, In	Investment company	12/31/03	451.2	124.1	543.4	175.4	171	62300177
WMT	Wal-Mart Stores, Inc.	Discount & variety stores	1/31/04	258054.0	104912.0	104912.0	43623.0	1144	1670160788
WAG	Walgreen Co.	Drug stores	8/31/03	32505.4	1175.7	8952.5	7195.7	774	613079538
WLT	Walter Industries, Inc. (Uni		12/31/03	1325.5	17.9	2941.5	276.6	99	29272332
WM	Washington Mutual Inc. (Unite	Financial services	12/31/03	18013.0	3793.0	268883.0	19742.0	770	705281507
WPO	Washington Post Co.	Publishing	12/31/03	p2838.9	p2838.9	—	—	256	5817513
WRE	Washington R.E. Inv. Trust	Real estate investment trust	12/31/03	163.8	50.2	927.1	378.7	130	12246018
WCN	Waste Connections, Inc.	Services	12/31/03	563.5	65.3	1353.4	537.5	198	28768269
WMI	Waste Management, Inc. (DE) (	Pollution control	12/31/03	11574.0	1842.0	19103.0	5563.0	430	489940739
PIK	Water Pik Technologies, Inc.		12/31/03	305.1	48.7	184.0	111.3	55	4748952
WAT	Waters Corp.		12/31/03	958.2	508.2	1086.0	590.5	310	110836714
WPI	Watson Pharmaceuticals, Inc.	Drugs	12/31/03	1457.7	202.9	3138.6	2057.3	323	84684294
WW	Watson Wyatt & Co. Holdings		6/30/03	709.6	50.4	583.5	220.8	106	14328161
WTS	Watts Water Technologies Inc	Meas. & control instruments	12/31/03	705.7	95.3	767.1	436.4	102	16293485
WPP	Wausau-Mosinee Paper Corp. (	Paper	12/31/03	971.4	15.9	830.2	350.3	144	32938730
WCI	WCI Communities Inc (United S		12/31/03	1452.2	105.6	2183.7	758.7	55	18421211
WBS	Webster Financial Corp (Water	Savings & loan	12/31/03	891.2	164.7	14568.7	1152.9	181	28594741
WTW	Weight Watchers Internationa		1/3/04	943.9	423.5	732.4	181.2	180	38907223
WRI	Weingarten Realty Investors	Real estate investment trust	12/31/03	419.2	123.6	2923.8	821.6	189	19936534
WMK	Weis Markets, Inc.	Food wholesalers	12/27/03	2042.5	54.6	722.2	571.0	74	5063857
WC	Wellchoice Inc	Life Insurance	12/31/03	5382.6	201.1	3043.0	1432.4	71	12945307
WLM	Wellman, Inc.	Textiles	12/31/03	1109.3	d234.1	1110.6	465.6	123	26565402
WFC	Wells Fargo & Co. (New)	Banking - Midwest	12/31/03	31800.0	6202.0	387798.0	34469.0	1027	1107055982
WEN	Wendy's International, Inc.	Restaurants	12/28/03	3148.9	874.7	3071.2	1712.5	319	79947631
WCC	Wesco International, Inc.	Electrical equipment	12/31/03	3286.8	69.1	1161.2	167.7	43	11000471
WST	West Pharmaceutical Svcs Inc	Plastics & plastic products	12/31/03	490.7	78.9	556.6	257.6	71	10277379
WR	Westar Energy Inc	Electric power	12/31/03	1461.1	162.9	5063.1	1036.8	163	40772850
WEH	WestCoast Hospitality Corp (	Motel/hotel lodging	12/31/03	184.0	1.2	348.4	152.2	14	5150234
WES	Westcorp, Inc.	Financial services	12/31/03	1355.2	123.6	14615.9	1122.5	61	8581364
WIA	Western Asset / Claymore U S	Investment company	12/31/03	6.1	4.7	630.9	413.2		
WEA	Western Asset Premier Bond Fu	Investment company	12/31/03	16.8	14.8	243.7	169.8	3	486108
WDC	Western Digital Corp. (Unite	Comp. components & periphs.	6/30/03	p2718.5	p2719.8	—	—	211	154225041

| EARNINGS PER SHARE | | | | | | P/E RATIO | DIVIDENDS PER SHARE | | | AV. YLD. % | DIV. DECLARED | | PRICE RANGE |
| QUARTERLY | | | | ANNUAL | | | | | | | | | 2004 |
1st	2nd	3rd	2004	2003	2002		2004	2003	2002		AMOUNT	PAYABLE	
0.67	—	—	—	2.55	2.87	—	1.09	0.86	0.76	1.5	0.33Q	3/9/05	87.70 - 57.00
d1.38	—	—	—	d3.35	d1.45	—							23.35 - 8.63
0.36	—	—	—	d4.09	0.62	—	0.20	0.20	0.20	0.6	0.08Q	3/10/05	54.06 - 9.83
1.14	—	—	—	4.69	4.42	—	1.40	1.14	0.98	1.7	0.44Q	3/10/05	106.28 - 57.78
0.88	—	—	—	2.96	2.13	—	0.03	0.01	0.01	0.0	0.03A	4/18/05	88.76 - 41.45
0.70	—	—	—	1.82	d0.12	—	1.66	1.66	1.66	4.5	0.425Q	2/25/05	49.99 - 23.17
				0.98	1.08	—							37.46 - 17.45
1.37	1.48	—	—	4.34	4.00	—	1.56	1.44	1.36	3.4	0.42Q	5/9/05	53.72 - 36.93
0.43	—	—	—	2.07	1.84	—	2.00	1.96	1.92	6.8	0.505Q	3/31/05	34.50 - 24.15
0.74	—	—	—	3.20	2.74	—	0.32	0.08		0.7	0.08Q	3/15/05	56.95 - 38.67
0.30	0.28	—	—	0.79	0.44	—							48.50 - 24.26
0.09	—	—	—	0.55	0.34	—					100%	8/11/00	39.93 - 24.51
1.00	—	—	—	2.70	1.34	—	0.80	0.80	0.80	2.2	0.20Q	5/11/05	46.38 - 26.31
0.17	—	—	—	d0.19	0.04	—							26.58 - 5.37
d1.93	—	—	—	d0.96	1.68	—	0.30	0.37	0.59	2.1	0.075Q	5/20/05	18.25 - 9.80
						—	0.90	1.61	0.66	5.0	0.9975A	4/19/05	22.80 - 13.25
0.24	0.54	—	—	1.76	2.03	—							32.34 - 8.89
0.40	0.36	—	—	0.73	0.87	—	0.78	0.76	0.74	5.5	0.20Q	4/15/05	15.99 - 12.14
d0.13	—	—	—	0.13	d0.18	—	0.55	0.55	0.55	6.6	0.1375Q	3/15/05	11.14 - 5.50
1.33	—	—	—	3.19	3.22	—					0.025Q	3/21/01	41.60 - 4.16
0.73	—	—	—	1.90	d1.61	—	2.08	2.00	1.92	5.4	0.55Q	3/31/05	48.97 - 27.60
d0.72	d0.19	—	—	d0.24	0.26	—							53.20 - 11.15
0.47	—	—	—	1.98	1.77	—					0.00U	9/15/99	35.91 - 22.78
d0.12	—	—	—	d0.78	1.00	—	0.31	0.31	0.31	1.4	0.0775Q	4/27/05	27.37 - 16.25
1.82	—	—	—	5.09	0.83	—	0.29	0.21	0.20	0.5	0.08Q	3/16/05	81.37 - 34.39
0.80	—	—	—	3.02	2.72	—	3.15	2.90	2.65	6.4	0.80Q	2/14/05	61.75 - 36.70
0.03	—	—	—	0.32	0.01	—	0.24	0.24	0.24	2.0	0.10Q	3/31/05	16.31 - 8.17
0.39	—	—	—	1.54	1.50	—	0.84	0.80	0.75	3.2	5%	5/20/05	29.18 - 23.46
0.22	—	—	—	1.06	1.37	—	0.32	0.31	0.28	1.4	0.08Q	4/15/05	25.97 - 19.32
0.35	0.74	—	—	2.17	2.34	—	0.72	0.60	0.56	1.6	0.20Q	4/15/05	51.51 - 40.93
—	—	—	—	19.78	18.78	—	1.06	1.17	1.28	6.0	0.25Q	3/31/05	18.60 - 16.85
—	—	—	—	3.64	3.03	—	0.36	0.36	0.47	8.8	0.03M	4/29/05	4.68 - 3.48
—	—	—	—	4.57	3.79	—	0.44	0.45	0.62	9.5	0.037M	4/29/05	5.38 - 3.96
—	—	—	—	6.46	6.10	—	0.33	0.37	0.47	5.9	0.0275M	4/29/05	5.97 - 5.26
—	—	—	—	10.73	9.99	—	0.61	0.63	0.53	6.5	0.046M	4/29/05	10.28 - 8.36
—	—	—	—	0.46		—	0.41	0.42	0.46	5.0	0.0396M	4/29/05	9.14 - 7.05
—	—	—	—	15.58	15.63	—	0.97	1.01	0.99	6.9	0.0725Q	4/11/05	15.64 - 12.73
0.41	0.61	—	—	1.84	1.33	—					2-for-1	7/30/04	92.98 - 30.80
0.11	—	—	—	d0.40	d0.87	—	1.54	1.49	1.42	10.5	0.40Q	3/30/05	18.25 - 11.00
0.72	—	—	—	1.57	1.68	—	1.15	1.11	1.07	4.8	0.295Q	3/1/05	27.09 - 20.60
0.28	—	—	—	1.21	0.75	—	1.24	1.04	0.97	6.1	0.36Q	4/5/05	29.48 - 11.35
d0.78	0.42	0.29	—	d1.80	d0.71	—							25.01 - 6.65
0.43	—	—	—	1.27	1.67	—	1.16	1.54	1.54	3.1	0.405Q	5/2/05	42.27 - 22.77
0.42	—	—	—	d2.95	d0.29	—	0.07	0.10	0.10	1.6	0.075Q	8/31/04	7.13 - 2.24
0.93	—	—	—	3.61	3.24	—	1.05	1.01	0.97	2.3	0.27Q	3/21/05	55.61 - 33.85
0.41	—	—	—	0.82	1.24	—	0.24	0.06		0.6	0.07Q	4/1/05	44.88 - 32.56
0.41	—	—	—	0.82	1.24	—	1.81	1.81	1.81	6.8		3/30/05	26.87 - 26.71
0.33	—	—	—	1.29	1.30	—	0.04			0.2	0.04Q	4/1/05	29.33 - 20.45
0.09	—	—	—	0.89	0.74	—							25.25 - 12.68
						—	0.66	0.50	0.42	1.4	0.1307Q	4/11/05	48.15 - 32.55
0.29	—	—	—	d4.04	d1.66	—	0.19	0.17	0.15	1.1	0.05Q	4/5/05	24.50 - 9.50
0.20	—	—	—	0.17	d0.58	—					3-for-2	6/9/00	24.90 - 10.10
0.23	—	—	—	d9.65	d0.68	—	0.24	0.24	0.24	2.6	0.06Q	12/1/04	12.50 - 5.94
0.23	—	—	—	0.46	0.29	—					100%	5/12/99	27.20 - 8.25
						—			0.77		0.685U	5/25/05	32.39 - 13.40
d0.10	0.28	—	—	0.31	d0.26	—					3-for-2	5/27/97	31.99 - 10.26
0.58	—	—	—	2.29	2.18	—	3.05	2.91	2.97	5.5	0.76Q	5/13/05	76.99 - 34.50
0.15	—	—	—	2.18	1.86	—	1.04	0.98	0.94	2.4	0.29Q	3/10/05	55.53 - 30.23
p0.31	—	—	—		p0.73	—	0.14	0.12	0.10	0.7		5/16/05	23.31 - 15.44
0.16	—	—	—	0.69	0.62	—					0.00U	6/6/02	23.40 - 14.06
0.29	—	—	—	1.64	1.28	—	1.75	1.73	1.71	5.8	0.444Q	4/15/05	35.90 - 24.74
0.23	—	—	—	d2.26	d2.43	—					0.045Q	4/4/05	30.91 - 5.30
0.11	—	—	—	0.51	0.40	—	0.04	0.04	0.04	0.2	0.01Q	2/28/05	22.70 - 11.00
0.94	—	—	—	3.17	2.60	—	1.66	1.25	1.00	3.7	0.46Q	3/15/05	55.00 - 34.07
						—	0.60	0.55	0.49	2.7	0.15Q	5/2/05	27.28 - 16.71
0.50	—	—	—	2.03	1.81	—	0.48	0.35	0.29	0.9	0.15Q	1/3/06	61.31 - 47.80
0.25	0.42	—	—	1.4	0.99	—	0.19	0.16	0.15	0.6	0.0525Q	3/12/05	39.38 - 28.14
d0.11	—	—	—	0.08	1.64	—	0.13	0.12	0.12	0.6	0.04Q	3/17/05	34.13 - 8.72
0.73	—	—	—	4.12	4.05	—	1.74	1.40	1.06	4.4	0.46Q	2/15/05	45.47 - 34.45
6.15	—	—	—		p25.12	—	7.00	5.80	5.60	0.8	1.85Q	5/13/05	999.50 - 676.00
0.27	—	—	—	1.13	1.22	—	1.55	1.47	1.39	5.2	0.3925Q	3/31/05	34.48 - 24.89
p0.53	—	—	—	2.17	1.90	—					50%	6/24/04	42.50 - 27.32
0.25	—	—	—	1.21	1.33	—	0.75	0.01	0.01	2.9	0.20Q	3/24/05	31.42 - 19.90
d0.07	—	—	—	0.89	0.85	—							18.08 - 6.53
0.33	—	—	—	1.34	1.12	—					100%	8/25/00	49.80 - 21.16
0.42	—	—	—	1.86	1.64	—					100%	10/29/97	49.19 - 24.50
0.37	0.32	0.42	—	1.51	1.41	—	0.15			0.6	0.075Q	4/15/05	27.50 - 18.90
0.34	—	—	—	1.32	1.21	—	0.28	0.25	0.24	1.2	0.08Q	3/11/05	32.59 - 13.94
0.07	—	—	—	0.31	0.45	—	0.34	0.34	0.34	2.4	0.085Q	2/15/05	19.12 - 9.71
0.30	—	—	—	2.34	2.41	—							29.81 - 8.92
0.90	—	—	—	3.52	3.31	—	0.90	0.82	0.74	2.1	0.23Q	2/28/05	52.15 - 35.12
p0.34	—	—	—	1.31	1.31	—							46.30 - 31.83
0.32	—	—	—	1.16	1.17	—	1.66	1.56	1.48	4.2	0.44Q	3/15/05	51.88 - 26.80
0.60	—	—	—	2.01	2.17	—	2.12	1.10	1.08	6.1	0.28Q	5/13/05	39.90 - 29.05
0.71	—	—	—	2.41	4.51	—							53.55 - 20.30
d0.99	—	—	—	d3.38	0.82	—	0.20	0.36	0.36	2.3	0.05Q	3/15/05	10.88 - 6.38
1.03	—	—	—	3.65	3.32	—	1.86	1.50	1.10	3.4	0.48Q	3/1/05	63.38 - 44.99
0.45	—	—	—	2.05	1.89	—	0.48	0.24	0.24	1.4	0.135Q	3/4/05	42.75 - 25.33
0.23	—	—	—	0.65	0.49	—							30.14 - 3.50
0.46	—	—	—	2.19	0.89	—	0.42	0.41	0.39	1.4	0.11Q	5/4/05	43.33 - 18.98
0.12	—	—	—	2.21	d2.32	—	0.76	0.87	1.20	4.5	0.23Q	4/1/05	22.92 - 11.16
d0.21	—	—	—	d0.10	0.42	—							6.88 - 3.75
0.83	—	—	—	2.85	2.05	—	0.55	0.51	0.47	1.7	0.15Q	5/17/05	46.22 - 18.57
—	—	—	—	14.28		—	0.89	0.13		6.3		4/29/05	15.71 - 12.68
—	—	—	—	15.00	13.57	—	1.31	1.28	0.85	8.8	0.09375M	4/29/05	16.44 - 13.50
0.02	0.32	0.22	—		p0.88	—					2-for-1	6/3/97	13.55 - 6.39

SYMBOL	COMPANY	NATURE OF BUSINESS	FISCAL YEAR-END	TOTAL REV. $MILL	NET INCOME $MILL	TOTAL ASSETS $MILL	NET STK EQUITY $MILL	NO. OF INST.	INST. HOLDINGS (SHARES)
WGR	Western Gas Resources, Inc.	Natural gas distributor	12/31/03	2874.0	90.9	1366.5	562.5	147	19871064
WHG	Westwood Holdings Group, Inc	—	12/31/03	20.1	6.4	26.2	21.9	26	2726845
WON	Westwood One, Inc.	Broadcasting	12/31/03	539.2	107.1	1131.1	836.0	232	77464765
WY	Weyerhaeuser Co. (United Sta	Forest products	12/28/03	19873.0	1839.0	27546.0	7109.0	440	158900911
WGL	WGL Holdings, Inc.	Natural gas distributor	9/30/03	2064.2	113.7	2436.1	846.4	169	22156278
WHR	Whirlpool Corp. (United Stat	Appliances & utensils	12/31/03	12176.0	1066.0	7361.0	1301.0	309	61891382
JWL	Whitehall Jewellers Inc	Jewelry	1/31/04	344.7	d8.7	202.2	105.8	50	10404445
WLL	Whiting Petroleum Corp (New)	Natural gas	12/31/03	167.4	35.0	343.9	259.6	—	
WG	Willbros Group Inc.	Oil service & equipment	12/31/03					49	15068860
WTU	Williams Coal Seam Gas Rty T	Oil	12/31/03	14.8	14.8	14.7	14.6	10	32745
WMB	Williams Cos., Inc (The) (Uni	Conglomerate	12/31/03	16834.1	102.2	26944.1	4102.1	366	273408244
WSM	Williams-Sonoma, Inc. (Unite	Appliances & utensils	2/1/04	2754.4	157.2	1470.7	804.6	261	94730256
WL	Wilmington Trust Corp. (DE)	Banking - Mid-Atlantic	12/31/03	633.0	203.7	8812.2	800.8	210	26249231
GB	Wilson Greatbatch Tech., Inc.	Electronic components	1/2/04	216.4	23.3	423.5	235.3	115	20707157
WBD	Wimm-Bill-Dann Foods OJSC	Food processing	12/31/03	p938.5	p938.5			25	5780458
WRS	Windrose Medical Properties	Finance	12/31/03	17.7	2.1	187.9	102.2	16	2945289
WGO	Winnebago Industries Inc.	Mobile homes	8/31/03	845.2	48.7	377.5	210.6	152	13244599
WXH	Winston Hotels, Inc.	Real estate investment trust	12/31/03	128.8	16.6	387.3	231.9	69	6914948
WEC	Wisconsin Energy Corp.	Electric power	12/31/03	4054.3	289.9	9282.0	2389.0	278	64008333
WMS	WMS Industries Inc.	—	6/30/03	178.7	d8.3	347.9	221.2	92	17520737
WOS	Wolseley PLC (UK)	—	7/31/03					6	96065
WLV	Wolverine Tube, Inc.	Copper	12/31/03	596.3	d91.5	549.4	179.4	62	8653508
WWW	Wolverine World Wide, Inc. (	Shoe manufacturing	1/3/04	888.9	51.7	573.1	430.1	147	31973038
INT	World Fuel Services Corp. (U	Oil service & equipment	12/31/03	2661.8	28.2	348.1	148.4	64	7018971
WPS	WPS Resources Corp.	Electric power	12/31/03	4321.3	110.6	3910.4	1054.3	169	11242611
WWY	Wrigley (William) Jr. Co. (U	—	12/31/03	3069.1	1097.4	2520.4	1820.8	428	93550025
WYE	Wyeth (United States)	Drugs	12/31/03	15850.6	2051.2	30021.2	9294.4	1004	915092326
XNR	Xanser Corp.	Oil service & equipment	12/31/03	135.7	d14.3	95.1	52.5	32	8266964
XEL	Xcel Energy, Inc.	Electric power	12/31/03	7937.5	510.0	20205.4	5271.4	357	177025279
XRX	Xerox Corp	Office equipment & supplies	12/31/03	15701.0	796.0	24340.0	4679.0	345	623094921
XTO	XTO Energy, Inc.	Oil service & equipment	12/31/03	1189.6	394.2	2901.1	1465.6	291	137275298
YCC	Yankee Candle Co., Inc. (The	—	1/3/04	508.6	74.8	273.8	190.3	101	23921471
YRK	York International Corp.	—	12/31/03	4076.1	25.5	2043.9	776.4	176	35207919
YPF	YPF SA (Argentina)	Oil	12/31/03					6	60500
YUM	Yum! Brands, Inc. (United St	Restaurants	12/27/03	8380.0	2491.0	5620.0	1120.0	419	222219601
ZLC	Zale Corp. (New)	Jewelry	7/31/03	2212.2	d40.6	1294.1	652.3	172	28992245
ZAP	Zapata Corp. (NV)	Food processing	12/31/03	181.4	8.4	349.2	182.5	14	665471
ZNT	Zenith National Ins. Corp.	Insurance	12/31/03	849.3	65.8	2023.7	383.2	86	9795545
ZIF	Zenix Income Fund Inc.	Investment company	3/31/04	8.5	7.3	92.8	57.3	5	286676
ZMH	Zimmer Holdings, Inc.	Medical & dental equipment	12/31/03	1901.0	808.3	3996.6	3143.3	586	142860681
ZF	Zweig Fund, Inc.	Investment company	12/31/03	7.4	2.1	436.9	416.7	35	2238960
ZTR	Zweig Total Return Fund, Inc.	Investment company	12/31/03	14.2	8.7	540.5	525.7	34	1141675

T42

| EARNINGS PER SHARE | | | | | | P/E | DIVIDENDS PER SHARE | | | AV. | DIV. DECLARED | | PRICE RANGE |
| QUARTERLY | | | | ANNUAL | | RATIO | | | | YLD. | | | |
1st	2nd	3rd	2004	2003	2002		2004	2003	2002	%	AMOUNT	PAYABLE	2004
0.79	—	—	—	2.26	1.23	—	0.15	0.10	0.10	0.4	0.05Q	5/13/05	56.97 - 26.92
0.21	—	—	—	0.90	0.97	—	0.94	1.17	0.02	5.7	0.08Q	4/1/05	19.70 - 13.03
0.18	—	—	—	0.97	1.00	—	—	—	—	—	2-for-1	3/22/00	34.50 - 19.02
0.54	—	—	—	1.30	1.09	—	1.60	1.60	1.60	2.8	0.40Q	2/28/05	68.05 - 47.83
0.81	1.60	—	—	2.30	0.80	—	1.30	1.28	1.27	4.6	0.3325Q	5/1/05	31.43 - 25.14
1.43	—*	—	—	5.91	3.78	—	1.72	1.36	1.36	2.7	0.43Q	3/15/05	79.48 - 49.03
d0.27	—	—	—	d0.62	0.66	—	—	—	—	—	3-for-2	1/4/00	10.00 - 7.05
0.51	—	—	—	1.18	0.41	—	—	—	—	—	—	—	34.22 - 18.61
—	—	—	—	—	—	—	—	—	—	—	—	—	23.60 - 7.34
0.32	—	—	—	1.44	0.89	—	1.50	1.45	0.89	10.4	—	3/1/05	18.95 - 10.03
0.01	—	—	—	d0.03	1.14	—	0.08	0.04	0.42	0.8	0.05Q	3/28/05	17.17 - 3.24
0.18	—	—	—	1.32	1.04	—	—	—	—	—	2-for-1	5/9/02	40.84 - 21.80
0.53	—	—	—	2.02	2.01	—	1.13	1.06	1.00	3.4	0.285Q	2/15/05	38.80 - 26.91
0.31	—	—	—	1.08	0.68	—	—	—	—	—	—	—	45.15 - 14.41
p0.12	—	—	—	—	—	—	—	—	—	—	—	—	19.98 - 11.90
0.08	—	—	—	0.21	0.01	—	0.88	0.61	—	7.3	0.225Q	3/15/05	14.68 - 9.50
0.51	0.46	—	—	1.29	1.34	—	0.22	0.15	0.10	0.4	0.07Q	7/6/05	75.76 - 25.10
0.01	—	—	—	0.17	d0.28	—	0.60	0.60	0.60	6.5	0.15Q	4/15/05	11.96 - 6.62
0.69	—	—	—	2.06	1.44	—	0.83	0.80	0.80	2.9	0.22Q	3/1/05	34.60 - 22.85
d0.06	d0.01	0.02	—	d0.27	0.30	—	—	—	—	—	—	—	33.85 - 11.61
—	—	—	—	—	—	—	0.89	1.18	0.50	1.7	0.334S	6/10/05	74.00 - 28.00
0.11	—	—	—	d3.18	0.58	—	—	—	—	—	—	—	13.15 - 4.10
0.30	—	—	—	1.27	1.15	—	0.17	0.14	0.12	0.7	0.065Q	5/2/05	32.49 - 14.95
0.52	—	—	—	1.96	0.91	—	0.15	0.15	0.15	0.4	0.0375Q	4/6/05	50.00 - 20.00
1.22	—	—	—	3.24	3.42	—	2.20	2.16	2.12	5.0	0.555Q	3/19/05	50.53 - 37.83
0.49	—	—	—	1.98	1.78	—	0.92	0.86	0.80	1.5	0.28Q	5/2/05	69.98 - 53.63
0.56	—	—	—	1.54	3.33	—	0.92	0.92	0.92	2.4	0.23Q	3/1/05	44.70 - 33.50
—	—	—	—	d0.41	d0.07	—	—	—	—	—	0.00Q	6/29/01	19.98 - 1.53
0.35	—	—	—	1.23	d4.36	—	0.79	0.75	1.31	5.3	0.2075Q	4/20/05	18.77 - 11.02
0.17	—	—	—	0.36	0.10	—	—	—	—	—	0.05Q	4/1/01	17.16 - 8.70
0.40	—	—	—	1.26	0.88	—	0.06	0.02	0.02	0.2	0.05Q	4/15/05	36.88 - 18.26
0.21	—	—	—	1.40	1.17	—	—	—	—	—	0.125S	6/1/05	34.02 - 16.23
d0.10	—	—	—	0.28	2.04	—	0.80	0.60	0.60	2.5	0.20Q	3/31/05	43.10 - 21.00
—	—	—	—	—	—	—	4.69	2.67	1.12	16.2	1.5202U	11/15/04	44.29 - 13.79
0.47	—	—	—	2.02	1.88	—	0.20	—	—	0.6	0.10Q	5/6/05	47.47 - 23.18
d0.17	1.83	0.22	—	d0.63	1.48	—	—	—	—	—	2-for-1	6/8/04	62.38 - 24.64
0.75	—	—	—	0.37	2.70	—	—	—	—	—	8-for-1	4/6/05	63.49 - 35.50
1.09	—	—	—	3.33	0.05	—	1.09	1.00	1.00	3.1	0.33Q	5/13/05	51.29 - 20.01
—	—	—	—	3.14	2.63	—	0.38	0.43	0.46	10.4	0.027M	5/27/05	4.20 - 3.20
0.40	—	—	—	1.38	1.31	—	—	—	—	—	—	—	89.44 - 41.00
—	—	—	—	5.69	5.46	—	0.22	0.50	0.70	4.3	0.149Q	4/26/05	5.58 - 4.67
—	—	—	—	5.69	5.80	—	0.34	0.48	0.621	6.7	0.046M	4/25/05	5.36 - 4.86

T43